Touring Europe

Mont Blanc

Shutterstock/ Roman Mikhailiuk

© The Caravan Club Limited 2021

Published by The Caravan and Motorhome Club Limited

East Grinstead House, East Grinstead

West Sussex RH19 1UA

General Enquiries: 01342 326944

Travel Service Reservations: 01342 316101

Red Pennant Emergency Assistance: 01342 336633

www.camc.com

Editor: Kate Walters
Publishing service provided by Fyooz Ltd
Printed by Stephens & George Ltd, Merthyr Tydfil

Maps and distance charts generated from Collins Bartholomew Digital Database Maps ©Collins Bartholomew Ltd 2021, reproduced by permission of Harper Collins Publishers.

ISBN: 978-1-9993236-5-3

Caravan and Motorhome Club products, including Insurance and Financial Services products, are featured in advertorials throughout this book.

Caravan Cover is provided directly by the Caravan and Motorhome Club.

Red Pennant: This is promotional information only and a sample policy wording including the limitations and exclusions that apply is available upon request. Terms and conditions apply.

Caravan and Motorhome Club is a trading name of The Caravan Club Limited which is authorised and regulated by the Financial Conduct Authority for general insurance and credit activities.

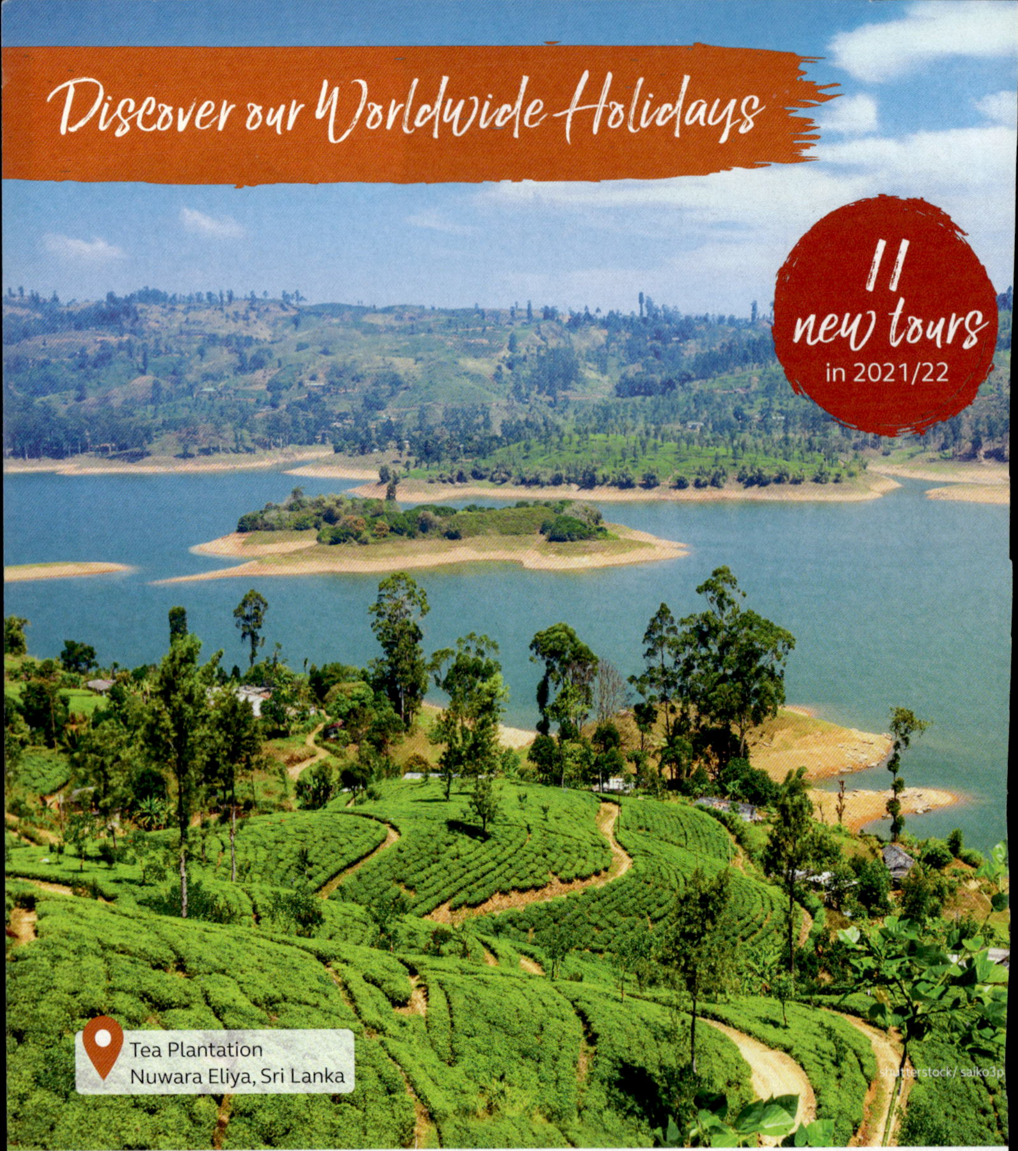

Welcome...

...to another year of touring across Europe!

For those who are familiar with previous versions of this book, you'll know that there are normally three seperate volumes covering France, Spain and Portugal and the rest of Europe. For the first time this year, we've produce a guide that covers the whole of Europe so all the countries you may want to visit are conveniently packaged together.

The Covid pandemic scuppered a lot of people's travel plans in 2020, and into 2021 it is still causing disruption and uncertainty. However as a vaccination program rolls out across Europe and the UK we can be a little bit hopeful that getting away to the continent is once again on the horizon.

At the time of going to press, there are still some potential changes afoot due to Brexit, and remember that countries may well introduce their own entry requirements while we are still seeing cases of Covid. For that reason it's always best to check camc.com/overseas for the most up-to-date travel information when you're planning your overseas trips.

If you manage to fit in a trip overseas in 2021 then we'd love to hear about it. If you can, please spare five minutes to fill in one of the site report forms at the back of this book or visit camc.com/europereport to let us know what you think about the sites you've stayed on this year. Happy touring!

Kate Walters

Kate Walters, Editor

Contents

How to use this guide

Planning your trip

Motoring advice

During your stay

Shutterstock/ Feel good studio

How to Use This Guide

The Handbook

This section at the front of the book is a comprehensive guide to everything you need to know when touring across Europe. You'll find legal requirements, advice and regulations for before you travel, while you're away and for your return to the UK.

Country Introductions

In the Country Introductions you'll find more information, regulations and advice specific to that country. You should read the Country Introduction in conjunction with the Handbook chapters before you set off on your holiday.

Campsite Entries

After the country introduction you will find the campsite entries listed alphabetically under their nearest town or village. Where there are several campsites shown in and around the same town they will be listed in clockwise order from the north.

To find a campsite all you need to do is look for the town or village of where you would like to stay, or use the maps at the back of the book to find a town where sites are listed.

For an explanation of the site entries and a guide to symbols please see the following pages. You'll also find a guide to site entries on the fold out on the rear cover.

Campsite Fees

Campsite entries show high season fees per night for an outfit plus two adults. Prices given may not include electricity or showers, unless indicated. Outside of the main holiday season many sites offer discounts on the prices shown and some sites may also offer a reduction for longer stays.

Campsite fees may vary to the prices stated in the site entries, especially if the site has not been reported on for a few years. You are advised to always check fees when booking, or at least before pitching, as those shown in site entries should be used as a guide only.

Site Maps

Each town and village listed alphabetically in the site entry pages has a map grid reference number, e.g. 3B4. The map grid reference number is shown on each site entry.

The maps can be found at the end of each country section. The reference number will show you where each town or village is located, and the site entry will tell you how far the site is from that town.

Place names are shown on the maps in two colours:

Red where we list a site which is open all year (or for at least eleven months of the year)

Black where we only list seasonal sites which close in winter.

These maps are intended for general campsite location purposes only; a detailed road map is essential for route planning when touring.

The scale of the map means that it isn't possible to show every town or village where a campsite is listed, so some sites in small villages may be listed under a nearby larger town instead.

Satellite Navigation

Most campsite entries now show a GPS (sat nav) reference. There are several different formats of writing co-ordinates, and in this guide we use decimal degrees, for example 48.85661 (latitude north) and 2.35222 (longitude east).

Minus readings, shown as -1.23456, indicate that the longitude is west of the Greenwich meridian. This will only apply to sites in the west of France, most of Spain and all of Portugal as the majority of Europe is east of the Greenwich meridian.

Manufacturers of sat navs all use different formats of co-ordinates so you may need to convert the co-ordinates before using them with your device. There are plenty of online conversion tools which enable you to do this quickly and easily - just type 'co-ordinate converter' into your search engine.

Please be aware if you are using a sat nav device some routes may take you on roads that are narrow and/or are not suitable for caravans or large outfits.

The GPS co-ordinates given in this guide are provided by members and checked wherever possible, however we cannot guarantee their accuracy due to the rural nature of most sites. The Caravan and Motorhome Club cannot accept responsibility for any inaccuracies, errors or omissions or for their effects.

Shutterstock/Dmitry Naumov

Site Report Forms

With the exception of campsites in The Club's Overseas Site Booking Service (SBS) network, The Caravan and Motorhome Club does not inspect sites listed in this guide. Most of the sites listed in Touring Europe are from site reports submitted by users of these guides.

Sites which are not reported on for five years are archived from the guide, so even if you visit a site and find nothing has changed we'd still appreciate an update to make sure that the site isn't archived.

You will find site report forms towards the back of the book, or you can submit them at camc.com/europereport - use the abbreviated site report form if you are reporting no changes, or only minor changes, to a site entry. The full report form should be used for new sites or if sites have changed a lot.

Please submit reports as soon as possible. Information received by mid August will be used wherever possible in the next edition of Touring Europe. Reports received after that date are still very welcome and will appear in the following edition. The editor is unable to respond individually to site reports submitted due to the large quantity that we receive.

Tips for Completing Site Reports

If possible fill in a site report form while a the campsite. Once back at home it can be difficult to remember details of individual sites, especially if you visited several during your trip.

When giving directions to a site, remember to include the direction of travel, e.g. 'from north on D137, turn left onto D794 signposted Combourg' or 'on N83 from Poligny turn right at petrol station in village'. Wherever possible give road numbers, junction numbers and/or kilometre post numbers, where you exit from motorways or main roads. It is also helpful to mention useful landmarks such as bridges, roundabouts, traffic lights or prominent buildings.

We very much appreciate the time and trouble you take submitting reports on campsites that you have visited; without your valuable contributions it would be impossible to update this guide.

Acknowledgements

Thanks go to the AIT/FIA Information Centre (OTA), the Alliance Internationale de Tourisme (AIT), the Fédération International de Camping et de Caravaning (FICC) and to the national clubs and tourist offices of those countries who have assisted with this publication.

Every effort is made to ensure that information provided in this publication is accurate. The Caravan and Motorhome Club Ltd has not checked these details by inspection or other investigation and cannot accept responsibility for the accuracy of these reports as provided by members and non-members, or for errors, omissions or their effects. In addition The Caravan and Motorhome Club Ltd cannot be held accountable for the quality, safety or operation of the sites concerned, or for the fact that conditions, facilities, management or prices may have changed since the last recorded visit. Any recommendations, additional comments or opinions have been contributed by people staying on the site and are not those of The Caravan and Motorhome Club.

The inclusion of advertisements or other inserted material does not imply any form of approval or recognition, nor can The Caravan and Motorhome Club Ltd undertake any responsibility for checking the accuracy of advertising material.

Shutterstock/nnattalli

Explanation of a Campsite Entry

Site map grid reference

Distance and direction of the site from the centre of the listing town in kilometres (or metres), together with the aspect of the site (urban, rural or coastal).

GPS co-ordinates – latitude and longitude in decimal degrees. Minus figures indicate that the site is west of the Greenwich meridian

The town under which the campsite is listed, as shown on the relevant Sites Location Map at the end of each country's site entry pages

Campsite name

Site information shown by symbols, a guide to which can be found on the next page or inside the rear cover. Where further information is available (e.g. a price for dogs or if a toilet block is heated) is shown after the symbol.

Additional site information, including pitch information and electric information. For details of the abbreviations used please see the following pages.

Guide price for 2 adults, an outfit and a pitch in high season.

Opening dates for the site, may give specific dates or the general months of opening. If no dates are present the site will be open all year, as shown by the 12 in the symbols section.

Campsite address.

Site contact details, including telephone number, email address and website address where available.

Directions to the site are shown in bold text.

Comments and opinions of tourers who have visited the site shown in italic text

The year in which the site was last reported on by a visitor. Sites are archived if we don't receive a report for 5 years so please consider sending in a report if you visit a site with an older date shown.

Booking reference for a site the Club's Overseas Travel Service work with, i.e. bookable via the Club.

OSSIACH *D3 (1km SW Rural) 46.66388, 13.97500*
Terrassen Camping Ossiacher See, Ostrich 67, 9570
Ossiach **(04243) 436; martinz@camping.at;**
www.terrassen.camping.at

**Leave A10/E55/E66 at exit for Ossiachersee, turn
L onto B94 twd Feldkirchen & shortly R to Ossiach
Süd. Site on lake shore just S of Ossiach vill.**
Lge, mkd, pt shd, terr, EHU (4-10A) €3; gas; bbq; sw;
red long stay; twin axles; TV; ccard acc; clsd 1200-
1500 LS; games area; horseriding; games rm;
windsurfing; bike hire; fishing; tennis; watersports;
CKE. *"Ideal Carinthian lakes, Hochosterwitz castle
& excursions into Italy; parking adj; cash machine;
beautiful scenery; many activities, excel san facs;
pitches sm and diff for big o'fits; dogs confined to
pitches next to entrance; but site in lovely location."*
€41.00, 1 May-30 Sep, G05.   2019

Guide to symbols

Symbol	Explanation
12	The site is open all year. Some sites may decide to close if they are not busy so call ahead out of season.
(dog)	Dogs are allowed on site, usually at an extra cost (shown if known). Please see the description or member comments for any restrictions.
(toilets)	Toilets available. If followed by (cont) they will be continental style toilets.
WD	Chemical toilet disposal.
(shower)	Showers available.
(baby)	Family bathroom or baby and toddler room on site. Facilities may vary.
(disabled)	Toilet and/or shower facilities available for disabled guests on site. Facilities may vary.
(laundry)	Laundry facilities available. Facilities and costs may vary.
(electric)	Electric hook ups are available. See the description for details of the amperage, costs and any further information.
MSP	Motorhome service point. low level waste discharge point for motor caravans; fresh water tap and rinse facilities should also be available

Symbol	Explanation
(butterfly)	Quiet site - set in a peaceful location although at busy times you may still experience noise from other site users.
(wifi)	Wi-Fi available, usually at an extra cost.
(bar)	Bar on site or nearby if followed by nr.
(restaurant)	Restaurant on site or nearby if followed by nr.
(snack bar)	Snack bar, cafe or takeaway on site.
(shop)	Shop on site or nearby if followed by nr.
(playground)	Playground or play area on site. Age restrictions may apply.
(entertainment)	Entertainment on site - this may either be evening entertainment or organised daytime activities or excursions.
(pool)	Pool on site. Where known the listing will specify if heated (htd), covered (covrd).
(paddling pool)	Paddling pool for younger children on site
(beach)	Beach nearby, followed by the distance and information about the type of beach where known.

Site Description Abbreviations

Each site entry assumes the following unless stated otherwise:

Level ground, open grass pitches, drinking water on site, clean wc unless otherwise stated (own sanitation required if wc not listed), site is suitable for any length of stay within the dates shown.

aspect
   urban – within a city or town, or on its outskirts
   rural – within or on edge of a village or in open countryside
   coastal – within one kilometre of the coast

size of site
   sm – max 50 pitches
   med – 51 to 150 pitches
   lge – 151 to 500 pitches
   v lge – 501+ pitches

pitches
   hdg pitch – hedged pitches
   mkd pitch – marked or numbered pitches
   hdstg – some hard standing or gravel

levels
   sl – sloping site
   pt sl – sloping in parts
   terr – terraced site

shade
   shd – plenty of shade
   pt shd – part shaded
   unshd – no shade

Site Facilities

adv bkg -
   acc - advance booking accepted
   rec – advance booking recommended
   req - advance booking required

beach - symbol followed by:
   1km – distance to beach
   sand beach – sandy beach
   shgl beach – shingle beach

bus/metro/tram
   Public transport within 5km

chem disp
   Dedicated chemical toilet disposal facilities;
   chem disp (wc) – no dedicated point; disposal via wc only

CKE
   Camping Key Europe accepted

CL-type
   Very small, privately-owned, informal and usually basic, farm or country site similar to those in the Caravan and Motorhome Club's network of Certificated Locations

el pnts - symbol followed by
   Mains electric hook-ups available for a fee;
   inc – cost included in site fee quoted
   10A – amperage provided
   conn fee – one-off charge for connection to metered electricity supply
   rev pol – reversed polarity may be present (see Electricity and Gas section

Eng spkn
   English spoken by campsite reception staff

gas
   Supplies of bottled gas available on site or nearby

Mairie
   Town hall (France); will usually make municipal campsite reservations

NH
   Suitable as a night halt

open 1 Apr-15 Oct
   Where no specific dates are given, opening dates are assumed to be inclusive, ie Apr-Oct – beginning April to end October (NB: opening dates may vary from those shown; check before travelling, particularly when travelling out of the main holiday season)

phone
   Public payphone on or adjacent to site

pool - symbol followed by:
   Indoor – indoor pool
   htd – heated pool
   covrd – indoor pool or one with retractable cover

red CCI/CCS
   Reduction in fees on production of a Camping Card International or Camping Card Scandinavia

BBQ
   barbecues allowed (may be restricted to a separate, designated area)

serviced pitch
: Electric hook-ups and mains water inlet and grey water waste outlet to pitch;
: all – to all pitches
: 50% – percentage of pitches

shwrs - symbol followed by:
: inc – cost included in site fee quoted

ssn
: Season;
: high ssn – peak holiday season
: low ssn – out of peak season

50% statics
: Percentage of static caravans/mobile homes/chalets/fixed tents/cabins or long term seasonal pitches on site, including those run by tour operators

sw
: Swimming nearby;
: 1km – nearest swimming
: lake – in lake
: rv – in river

TV
: TV rm – separate TV room (often also a games room)
: TV (pitch) – cable or satellite connections to pitches

Other Abbreviations

AIT	Alliance Internationale de Tourisme
a'bahn	Autobahn
a'pista	Autopista
a'route	Autoroute
a'strada	Autostrada
adj	Adjacent, nearby
alt	Alternative
app	Approach, on approaching
arr	Arrival, arriving
avail	Available
Ave	Avenue
bdge	Bridge
bef	Before
bet	Between
Blvd	Boulevard
C	Century, eg 16thC
c'van	Caravan
CC	Caravan and Motorhome Club
ccard acc	Credit and/or debit cards accepted (check with site for specific details)
cent	Centre or central
clsd	Closed
conn	Connection
cont	Continue or continental (wc)
conv	Convenient
covrd	Covered
dep	Departure
diff	Difficult, with difficulty
dir	Direction
dist	Distance
dual c'way	Dual carriageway
E	East
ent	Entrance/entry to
espec	Especially
ess	Essential
excel	Excellent
facs	Facilities
FIA	Fédération Internationale de l'Automobile
FICC	Fédération Internationale de Camping & de Caravaning
FFCC	Fédération Française de Camping et de Caravaning
FKK/FNF	Naturist federation, ie naturist site
foll	Follow
fr	From
g'ge	Garage

gd	Good
grnd(s)	Ground(s)
hr(s)	Hour(s)
immac	Immaculate
immed	Immediate(ly)
inc	Included/inclusive
indus est	Industrial estate
INF	Naturist federation, ie naturist site
int'l	International
irreg	Irregular
junc	Junction
km	Kilometre
L	Left
LH	Left-hand
LS	Low season
ltd	Limited
mkd	Marked
mkt	Market
mob	Mobile (phone)
m'van	Motor caravan
m'way	Motorway
N	North
narr	Narrow
nr, nrby	Near, nearby
opp	Opposite
o'fits	Outfits
o'look(ing)	Overlook(ing)
o'night	Overnight
o'skts	Outskirts
PO	Post office
poss	Possible, possibly
pt	Part
R	Right
rd	Road or street
rec	Recommend/ed
recep	Reception
red	Reduced, reduction (for)
reg	Regular
req	Required
RH	Right-hand
rlwy	Railway line
rm	Room
rndabt	Roundabout
rte	Route
RV	Recreational vehicle, ie large motor caravan
rv/rvside	River/riverside
S	South

Shutterstock/Kryvoshei.Anell

san facs	Sanitary facilities ie wc, showers, etc
snr citizens	Senior citizens
sep	Separate
sh	Short
sp	Sign post, signposted
sq	Square
ssn	Season
stn	Station
strt	Straight, straight ahead
sw	Swimming
thro	Through
TO	Tourist Office
tour ops	Tour operators
traff lts	Traffic lights
twd	Toward(s)
unrel	Unreliable
vg	Very good
vill	Village
W	West
w/end	Weekend
x-ing	Crossing
x-rds	Cross roads

Documents

Camping Key Europe

Camping Key Europe (CKE) is a useful touring companion. Not only does it serve as ID at campsites, meaning that you don't have to leave your passport at reception, it also entitles you to discounts at over 2200 sites and offers third- party liability insurance. For more information visit www.campingkey.com.

You can purchase the CKE from the Club by calling 01342 336633, or it is provided free with our Red Pennant Emergency Assistance 'Motoring' cover.

Driving Licence

A full driving licence should be carried at all times when driving abroad. You must produce it when asked by the police and other authorities, or you may be liable for a fine and confiscation of your vehicle(s).

If your driving licence is due to expire while you are away it can be renewed up to three months before expiry - contact the DVLA if you need to renew more than three months ahead.

Rules regarding driving with a provisional licences vary across Europe, so you may not be entitled to drive in some EU countries unless you have a full licence.

All EU countries recognise the photocard driving licence introduced in the UK in 1990, subject to the minimum age requirements (normally 18 years for a vehicle with a maximum weight of 3,500 kg carrying no more than 8 people).

Old-style green paper licences or Northern Irish licences issued before 1991 should be updated before travelling as they may not be recognised by local authorities.

If you only have a paper licence or your licence was issues in Gibraltar, Guernsey, Jersey or the Isle of Man you will need to obtain an International Driving Permit, which can be bought at Post Offices for £5.50.

EHIC

The European Health Insurance Card (EHIC) allows any EU citizen access to state medical care when they are travelling in another EU country - although in many circumstances, there are significant limitations to what treatment UK citizens are able to receive.

After January 2021, UK issued European Health Insurance Cards remain valid until their expiry date within the EU but not in Switzerland, Liechtenstein, Norway and Iceland. New EHICs will not be issued for UK travellers but a replacement Global Health Insurance Card (GHIC) is being developed.

Given the limitations of EHIC, we always recommend that you have suitable travel insurance before you go on holiday. Make sure you get travel insurance that covers your health needs. Visit GOV.UK to check what your travel insurance should cover.

It is now even more important to have personal health and accident cover, and breakdown cover for your vehicle, when travelling overseas. The Club's Red Pennant Emergency Assistance covers all these things and is tailored to your personal situation.

Passport

In many EU countries everyone is required to carry photographic ID at all times. Enter next-of-kin details in the back of your passport and keep a separate photocopy. It's also a good idea to leave a photocopy with a relative or friend at home.

You can also take a photo of your passport to keep saved on your phone or in a cloud storage service so it is easily accessed.

The following information applies to British passport holders only. For information on passports issued by other countries you should contact the local embassy.

Applying for a Passport

Each person travelling out of the UK (including babies) must hold a valid passport - it is no longer possible to include children on a parent's passport. A standard British passport is valid for ten years, or 5 years for under 16s.

All newly issued UK passports are now biometric, also known as e-passports, which contain a microchip with information which can be used to authenticate the holder's identity.

Full information and application forms are available from main post offices or from the Identity & Passport Service's website, www.gov.uk where you can complete an online application. Allow at least six weeks for first-time passport applications, for which you may need to attend an interview at your nearest Identity and Passport Service (IPS) regional office. Allow three weeks for a renewal application or replacement of a lost, stolen or damaged passport.

Passport Validity

New rules apply to UK Nationals visiting Europe from January 2021. You must check your passport validity online and renew it if you need to. You can check whether your passport is valid at **gov.uk/checkpassport**.

If your passport will be older than 9 years and 6 months on the date you plan to travel, the official advice is that you should renew it in advance.

According to the Schengen Border Code, on the day of arrival you'll need your passport to both:

- Have at least 6 months' validity remaining
- Be less than 10 years old (even if it has 6 months or more left)

Please note that if you renewed your passport before it expired, extra months may have been added to your current passport expiry date. These extra months on your passport over 10 years may not count towards the 6 months that should be remaining on your passport.

So, if your passport will be older than 9 years and 6 months on the date of travel to the EU you should renew it in advance.

If you do need to renew your passport, we recommend doing this as soon as possible before you intend to travel as it can take up to 3 weeks for your new passport to arrive. It may take longer to issue a first adult passport. Note: these rules do not apply if travelling to the Republic of Ireland and you can continue to use your passport as long as it is valid for the length of your stay).

Burgundy passports, whether with "European Union" on the cover or not, remain valid alongside the new blue passport.

Schengen Agreement

The Schengen Agreement allows people and vehicles to pass freely without border checks from country to country within the Schengen area (26 countries). Where there are no longer any border checks you should still not attempt to cross land borders without a full, valid passport.

It is likely that random identity checks will be made for the foreseeable future in areas surrounding borders.

Shutterstock/ LightField Studios

Regulations for Pets

Some campsites do not accept dogs at all and some have restrictions on the number and breed of dogs allowed. Visit camc.com/overseasadvice for more information and country specific advice.

Pet travel documentation

This information applies to people travelling with their pet cats, ferrets or dogs, including assistance dogs. If you're travelling with any other pets you should check the national rules of the country that you are planning to visit.

From 1 January 2021, a current EU pet passport issued in GB will not be valid for travel to the EU or Northern Ireland (NI).

Before your pet can travel to the EU for the first time after 1 January 2021 you'll need to take these steps to get an Animal Health Certificate (AHC) instead of a pet passport.

- Your pet must be microchipped.
- Your pet must be vaccinated against rabies – your pet must be at least 12 weeks old before it can be vaccinated.
- Wait 21 days after the primary

vaccination before travel.

- Visit your vet to get an AHC for your pet, no more than 10 days before travel.
- As long as you keep your pet's rabies vaccinations up to date, you will not need to get repeat vaccinations for repeat trips to the EU.

Getting an animal health certificate (AHC) for travel

Within 10 days of your travel date, take your pet to an official vet who is permitted to sign and issue AHC's. Take proof of your pet's microchipping date and vaccination history.

Your pet's AHC will be valid for:

- 10 days after the issue date for entry into the EU.
- Onward travel within the EU for 4 months after the date of issue
- Re-entry to GB for 4 months after the date of issue

Arriving in the EU

Travellers with pets will need to enter through a designated Travellers' Point of Entry (TPE) where you may need to present your pet's original AHC along with proof of:

- Your pet's microchip
- Rabies vaccination
- Tapeworm treatment (if required)

The Eurotunnel terminal and all of the ferry ports booked by the Club are designated TPEs.

Repeat trips

Your pet will need a new AHC for each trip. Take your pet to an official vet no more than 10 days before you travel and show proof of your pet's microchipping date and rabies vaccination history. If your pet has an up-to-date vaccination history, it will not need a repeat rabies vaccination before travelling again.

Returning to Great Britain

There are no changes to the current health preparations for pets entering GB from 1 January 2021. Your pet must have one of the following documents when returning to GB from the EU:

- An EU pet passport (issued in the EU, or in GB before 1 January 2021)
- The AHC issued in GB used to travel to the EU – which you can use up to 4 months after it was issued
- A UK pet health certificate (issued outside the UK for travel into GB only)

Dogs should have a tapeworm treatment between 24 and 120 hours before entering Great Britain. This treatment must be approved for use in the country where it is applied and contain praziquantel or an equivalent proven to be effective against tapeworm (Echinococcus Multilocularis).

Your pet will not need this documentation or tapeworm treatment if entering GB directly from Northern Ireland or the Republic of Ireland.

You can travel with up to five pets with an Animal Health Certificate. If there are more than five pets you must either provide proof that they are participating in a competition, exhibition or sporting event or comply with animal health rules which apply to the commercial import of animals into the EU.

For more details please check gov.uk or with your vet.

Travelling with Children

If you are a lone adult travelling with children some countries require evidence of parental responsibility, especially those who have a different surname to them (including lone parents and grandparents). The authorities may want to see a birth certificate, a letter of consent from the child's parent (or other parent) and some evidence as to your responsibility for the child.

For further information on exactly what will be required at immigration contact the Embassy or Consulate of the countries you intend to visit.

Vehicle documents

Caravan Proof of Ownership (CRIS)

In Britain, unlike most other European countries, caravans are not formally registered in the same way as cars. This may not be fully understood by police and other authorities on the Continent. You are strongly advised, therefore, to carry a copy of your Caravan Registration Identification Scheme (CRIS) document.

GB Sticker

You do not need a GB sticker if your number plate includes the GB identifier on its own or with the Union flag. But you will need to display a GB sticker clearly on the rear of your vehicle if your number plate has any of the following:

- A Euro symbol
- A national flag of England, Scotland or Wales
- Numbers and letters only - no flag or identifier

If you're in Spain, Cyprus or Malta, you must display a GB sticker no matter what is on your number plate.

Green card

A Green Card is now required if you are driving abroad (including travel from Northern Ireland into the Republic of Ireland) in your own vehicle. A separate Green Card is required for each vehicle (if you have a multi-car policy for instance) and anything you may be towing such as your caravan or trailer tent or folding camper (unless it is under 750kgs or not braked).

A Green Card for a car or motorhome needs to have Category A ('Car') ticked, a Green Card for a caravan, trailer or trailer tent / folding camper needs to have Category F ('Trailer') ticked.

You must carry a physical copy of your Green Card/s when driving abroad - Green Cards won't be accepted in an electronic format so remember to print out your Green Card or request a physical copy from your insurer before you travel. If you require a physical copy to be sent from your insurer, it is recommended that you contact your insurer six weeks before travelling.

When driving abroad you may be required to show your Green Card/s at the border when entering the EU/EEA or moving between EU/EEA member states, but this will depend on the border authorities of the relevant country. You may also face police checks while driving abroad and will need to present your Green Card/s should you be unfortunate enough to be involved in an accident.

The Government is working on the UK remaining part of the Green Card-free circulation area which continues to be discussed with the EU Commission, so the situation may change. Further information can be found at biba.org.uk

International Driving Permit

If you still have a paper driving licence or have a licence issued in Gibraltar, Guernsey, Jersey or the Isle of Man you may also need an International Driving Permit which can be obtained from the Post Office.

MOT Certificate

Carry your vehicle's MOT certificate (if applicable) as you may need to show it to the authorities if your vehicle is involved in an accident, or in the event of random vehicle checks. If your MOT certificate is due to expire while you are away you should have the vehicle tested before you leave home.

Tax

While driving abroad you still need to have current UK vehicle tax. If your vehicle's tax is due to expire while you are abroad you may apply to re-license the vehicle at a post office, by post, or in person at a DVLA local office, up to two months in advance.

Vehicle Registration Certificate (V5C)

You must always carry your Vehicle Registration Certificate (V5C) and MOT Certificate (if applicable) when taking your vehicle abroad. If yours has been lost, stolen or destroyed call DVLA Customer Enquiries on 0300 790 6802 for more information.

Hired or Borrowed Vehicles

If using a borrowed vehicle you must obtain a letter of authority to use the vehicle from the registered owner. You should also carry the Vehicle Registration Certificate (V5C).

In the case of hired or leased vehicles, including company cars, when you don't possess the V5C, ask the company which owns the vehicle to supply a Vehicle On Hire Certificate, form VE103, which is the only legal substitute for a V5C. The BVRLA, the trade body for the vehicle rental and leasing sector, provide advice on hired or leased vehicles - see www.bvrla.co.uk or call them on 01494 434747 for more information.

If you are caught driving a hired vehicle abroad without this certificate you may be fined and/or the vehicle impounded.

Visas

British Citizens do not need a visa for short trips to the EU of up to 90 days in any 180 day period. You may need a visa or permit to stay for longer and we recommend checking the gov.uk website for more information on how to get a visa or permit. Travel to the Republic of Ireland will not change from 1 January 2021.

Note: Days spent in Croatia will not count towards the visa free 90 day limit.

The European Travel Information and Authorisation System (ETIAS) is the electronic system that the EU is planning to introduce. ETIAS will track individuals entering the area from countries that do not need a visa, much like the ESTA scheme in USA.

The planned launch date is 2022 and UK citizens may need to pay a fee (of around 7 Euros) for this visa exemption.

Shutterstock/mythja

Customs

Caravans and Vehicles

Vehicles and caravans may be temporarily imported into non-EU countries generally for a maximum of six months in any twelve month period, provided they are not hired, sold or otherwise disposed of in that country.

If you intend to stay longer than six months, dispose of a vehicle in another country or leave your vehicle there in storage you should seek advice well before your departure from the UK.

Borrowed Vehicles

If you are borrowing a vehicle from a friend or relative, or loaning yours to someone, you should be aware of the following:

- The total time the vehicle spends abroad must not exceed the limit for temporary importation (generally six months).
- The owner of the caravan must provide the other person with a letter of authority.
- The owner cannot accept a hire fee or reward.
- The number plate on the caravan must match the number plate on the tow car.
- Both drivers' insurers must be informed if a caravan is being towed and any additional premium must be paid.

Currency

You must declare cash of €10,000 (or equivalent in other currencies) or more when travelling between the UK and a non-EU country. The term 'cash' includes cheques, travellers' cheques, bankers' drafts, notes and coins. You don't need to declare cash when travelling within the EU.

For further information contact HMRC Excise & Customs Helpline on 0300 200 3700.

Customs Allowances

If you're travelling to Great Britain from outside the UK, your personal allowances mean you can bring in a certain amount of goods without paying tax or duty.

If you go over your allowances you must declare all your goods and pay tax and duty on all the goods of the same type in that category.

You cannot combine allowances with other people to bring in more than your individual allowance and there are no personal allowances for tobacco or alcohol if you're under 17.

The allowances are:

- 200 cigarettes, or 100 cigarillos, or 50 cigars, or 250g tobacco, or a combination adding up to the same total (e.g. 100 cigarettes and 25 cigars - both 50% of your allowance)
- 18 litres of wine (not sparkling)
- 42 litres of beer
- 4 litres of spirits or 9 litres of fortified wine (e.g. port or sherry), sparking wine or alcoholic drinks up to 22% volume or a combination adding up to the same total (e.g. 2 litres of spirits and 4.5 litres of fortified wine - both 50% of your allowance)
- £390 worth of all other goods including perfume, gifts and souvenirs without having to pay tax and/or duty

For further information contact HMRC National Advice Service on 0300 200 3700.

Medicines

There is no limit to the amount of over the counter medicines you can take abroad. Medicines prescribed by your doctor may contain controlled drugs (e.g. morphine), for which you will need a licence if you're leaving the UK for 3 months or more.

You don't need a licence for less than 3 months' supply or if your medication doesn't contain controlled drugs, but you should carry a letter from your doctor stating your name, a list of your prescribed drugs and dosages. You may have to show this letter when going through customs.

Visit www.gov.uk/travelling-controlled-drugs or call 020 7035 0771 for a list of controlled drugs and to apply for a licence.

Plants and Food

If you're bringing animal and animal products into the UK, then Andorra, the Canary Islands, Channel Islands, Isle of Man, Liechtenstein, Norway, San Marino and Switzerland also count as EU countries. You can bring:

- Meat
- Dairy
- Other animal products, for example, fish, eggs and honey

You can bring in any plants or plant products as long as they're:

- Free from pests and diseases
- For your own use or consumption

When travelling into the EU from 1 January 2021 you cannot take:

- Meat and meat products
- Milk or dairy products, other than powdered infant milk, infant food, special foods and special pet feed needed for medical reasons

This includes for your immediate personal consumption, for example sandwiches containing meat.

For up to date information contact the Department for Environment, Food and Rural Affairs (Defra) on 0345 33 55 77 or +44 20 7238 6951 from outside the UK. You can also visit www.defra.gov.uk to find out more.

Prohibited Goods

The importation of some goods into the UK is restricted or banned. These include:

- Endangered animals or plants including live animals, birds and plants, ivory, skins, coral, hides, shells and goods made from them such as jewellery, shoes, bags and belts.
- Controlled, unlicensed or dangerous drugs.
- Counterfeit or pirated goods such as watches, CDs and clothes; goods bearing a false indication of their place of manufacture or in breach of UK copyright.
- Offensive weapons such as firearms, flick knives, knuckledusters, push daggers, self-defence sprays and stun guns.
- Pornographic material depicting extreme violence or featuring children

This list is not exhaustive; if in doubt contact HMRC on 0300 200 3700 (+44 2920 501 261 from outside the UK) or go through the red Customs channel and ask a Customs officer when returning to the UK.

Insurance and Cover

Shutterstock/Tanasan Sungkaew

Cover for your vehicles

It is important to make sure your outfit is covered whilst you are travelling abroad. Your car or motorhome insurance may already cover you for driving in the EU, but check what you are covered for before you travel. If you are travelling outside the EU or associated countries you'll need to inform your insurer and may have to pay an additional premium.

Make sure your caravan cover includes travel outside of the UK, speak to your provider to check this. You may need to notify them of your dates of travel and may be charged an extra premium. At the time of publication a Green Card is required if you are driving abroad. Please see the Documents section for more information.

The Caravan and Motorhome Club's Car and Motorhome Insurance schemes and Caravan Cover extend to provide cover for travel within the EU free of charge, provided the total period of foreign travel in any one year does not exceed 270 days for Car and Motorhome Insurance and 182 for Caravan Cover. It may be possible to extend this period, although a charge may apply. Should you be delayed beyond these limits notify your cover or insurance provider immediately in order to maintain your cover until you can return to the UK.

If your outfit is damaged during ferry travel (including while loading or unloading) it must be reported to the carrier at the time of the incident. Most policies will cover short sea crossings (up to 65 hours) but check with your insurer before travelling.

For details of our Caravan Cover visit camc.com/caravancover or call 01342 336610 or for Car or Motorhome Insurance call 0345 504 0334.

European Accident Statement

Your car or motorhome insurer may provide you with a European Accident Statement form (EAS), or you may be given one if you are involved in an accident abroad. The EAS is a standard form, available in different languages, which gives all parties involved in an accident the opportunity to agree on the facts. Signing the form doesn't mean that you are accepting liability, just that you agree with what has been stated on the form. Only sign an EAS if you are completely sure that you understand what has been written and always make sure that you take a copy of the completed EAS.

Vehicles Left Behind Abroad

If you are involved in an accident or breakdown abroad which prevents you taking your vehicle home, you must ensure that you are covered if you leave your vehicle overseas while you return home. Also check if you're covered for the cost of recovering it to your home address.

In this event you should remove all items of baggage and personal belongings from your vehicles before leaving them unattended. If this isn't possible then check if you can extend your cover to protect your belongings.

In all circumstances, you must remove any valuables and items liable for customs duty, including wine, beer, spirits and cigarettes.

Legal Costs Abroad

If an accident abroad leads to you being taken to court you may find yourself liable for legal costs – even if you are not found to be at fault. Most UK vehicle insurance policies include cover for legal costs or have the option to add cover for a small additional cost – check if you are covered before you travel.

Holiday Travel Insurance and Motor Breakdown Cover

A standard motor insurance policy won't cover you for all eventualities, for example vehicle breakdown, medical expenses or alternative accommodation, so it's important to also take out adequate travel insurance. Make sure that the travel insurance you take out is suitable for a caravan or motorhome holiday.

Remember to check exemptions and exclusions, especially those relating to pre-existing medical conditions and be sure to declare any pre-existing medical conditions to your insurer.

Shutterstock/Juan Aunion

The Club's Red Pennant Emergency Assistance is designed specifically for touring holidays and provides cover both motoring related incidents and medical emergencies or cancellations.

Visit camc.com/redpennant for full details or call us on 01342 336633.

Holiday Insurance for Pets

If you're taking your pet overseas with you then you'll need to make sure they're covered too. Some holiday insurance policies, including the Club's Red Pennant Emergency Assistance, can be extended to cover pet expenses relating to an incident normally covered under the policy – such as pet repatriation in the event that your vehicle is written off.

However in order to provide cover for pet injury or illness you will need a separate pet insurance policy. Make sure you check with your pet insurance provider that you are covered for fees that are incurred overseas.

Home Insurance

Your home insurer may require advance notification if you are leaving your home unoccupied for 30 days or more. There may be specific requirements, such as turning off mains services (except electricity), draining water down and having somebody check your home periodically. Read your policy documents or speak to your provider.

The Club's Home Insurance policy provides full cover for up to 90 days when you are away from home (for instance when touring) and requires only common sense precautions for longer periods of unoccupancy. Visit camc.com/homeinsurance or call 0345 504 0335 for details.

Personal Belongings

The majority of travellers are able to cover their valuables such as jewellery, watches, cameras, laptops, and bikes under a home insurance policy. This includes the Club's Home Insurance scheme.

Specialist gadget insurance is now commonly available and can provide valuable benefits if you are taking smart phones, tablets, laptops or other gadgets on holiday with you.

Shutterstock/ Alohaflaminggo

Money

Being able to safely access your money while you're away is a necessity for you to enjoy your break. It isn't a good idea to rely on one method of payment, so always have a backup plan. A mixture of a small amount of cash plus one or two electronic means of payment are a good idea.

Traveller's cheques have become less popular in recent years as fewer banks and hotels are willing or able to cash them. There are alternative options which offer the same level of security but are easier to use, such as prepaid credit cards.

Local Currency

It is a good idea to take enough foreign currency for your journey and immediate needs on arrival, don't forget you may need change for tolls or parking on your journey. Currency exchange facilities will be available at ports and on ferries but rates offered may not be as good as you would find elsewhere.

The Post Office, banks, exchange offices and travel agents offer foreign exchange. All should stock Euros but during peak holiday times or if you need a large amount it may be sensible to pre-order your currency. You should also pre-order less common currencies. Shop around and compare commission and exchange rates, together with minimum charges.

Banks and money exchanges in central and eastern Europe won't usually accept Scottish and Northern Irish bank notes and may be reluctant to change any sterling which has been written on or is creased or worn.

Foreign Currency Bank Accounts

Frequent travellers or those who spend long periods abroad may find a Euro bank account useful. Most such accounts impose no currency conversion charges for debit or credit card use and allow fee-free cash withdrawals at ATMs. Some banks may also allow you to spread your account across different currencies, depending on your circumstances. Speak to your bank about the services they offer.

Prepaid Travel Cards

Prepaid travel money cards are issued by various providers including the Post Office, Travelex, Lloyds Bank and American Express.

They are increasingly popular as the PIN protected travel money card offers the security of Traveller's Cheques, with the convenience of paying by card. You load the card with the amount you need before leaving home, and then use cash machines to make withdrawals or use the card to pay for goods and services as you would a credit or debit card. You can top the card up over the telephone or online while you are abroad. However there can be issues with using them with some automated payment systems, such as pay-at-pump petrol stations and toll booths, so you should always have an alternative payment method available.

These cards can be cheaper to use than credit or debit cards for both cash withdrawals and purchases as there are usually no loading or transaction fees to pay. In addition, because they are separate from your bank account, if the card is lost or stolen you bank account will still be secure.

Credit and Debit Cards

Credit and debit cards offer a convenient way of spending abroad. For the use of cards abroad most banks impose a foreign currency conversion charge of up to 3% per transaction. If you use your card to withdraw cash there will be a further commission charge of up to 3% and you will be charged interest (possibly at a higher rate than normal) as soon as you withdraw the money.

There are credit cards available which are specifically designed for spending overseas and will give you the best available rates. However they often have high interest rates so are only economical if you're able to pay them off in full each month.

If you have several cards, take at least two in case you encounter problems. Credit and debit 'Chip and PIN' cards issued by UK banks may not be universally accepted abroad so check that your card will be accepted if using it in restaurants or other situations where you pay after you have received goods or services.

Contact your credit or debit card issuer before you leave home to let them know that you will be travelling abroad. In the battle against card fraud, card issuers frequently query transactions which they regard as unusual or suspicious, causing your card to be declined or temporarily stopped.

You should always carry your card issuer's helpline number with you so that you can contact them if this happens. You will also need this number should you need to report the loss or theft of your card.

Dynamic Currency Conversion

When you pay with a credit or debit card, retailers may offer you the choice of currency for payment, e.g. a euro amount will be converted into sterling and then charged to your card account. This is known as a 'Dynamic Currency Conversion' but the exchange rate used is likely to be worse than the rate offered by your card issuer, so will work out more expensive than paying in the local currency.

Emergency Cash

If an emergency or theft means that you need cash in a hurry, then friends or relatives at home can send you emergency cash via money transfer services. The Post Office, MoneyGram and Western Union all offer services which, allows the transfer of money to over 233,000 money transfer agents around the world. Transfers take approximately ten minutes and charges are levied on a sliding scale.

Shutterstock/vrvalerian

Crossing the Channel

Booking Your Ferry

It's always wise to make reservations as early as possible to get the best prices but especially so if travelling at peak times, such as Easter or school holidays. Each ferry will have limited room for caravans and large vehicles so spaces can fill up quickly and prices tend to increase as the ship fills up. If you need any special assistance request this at the time of booking.

When booking any ferry crossing, make sure you give the correct measurements for your outfit including bikes, roof boxes or anything which may add to the length or height - if you underestimate your vehicle's size you may be turned away or charged an additional fee.

The Club is an agent for most major ferry companies operating services.Call the Club's Travel Service on 01342 316 101 or visit camc. com/ferries to book and save the £10 booking fee that is applied via the Contact Centre.

The table at the end of this section shows ferry routes from the UK to the Continent and Ireland. Some ferry routes may not be operational all year, and during peak periods there may be a limit to the number of caravans or motorhomes accepted. For the most up-to-date information visit camc.com/ferries or call the Club's Travel Services team.

On the Ferry

Arrive at the port with plenty of time before your boarding time. Motorhomes and car/caravan outfits will usually either be the first or last vehicles boarded onto the ferry. Almost all ferries are now 'drive on – drive off' so you won't be required to do any complicated manoeuvres. You may be required to show ferry staff that your gas is switched off before boarding the ferry.

Be careful using the ferry access ramps, as they are often very steep which can mean there is a risk of grounding the tow bar or caravan hitch. Drive slowly and, if your ground clearance is low, consider whether removing your jockey wheel and any stabilising devices would help.

Vehicles are often parked close together on ferries, meaning that if you have towing extension mirrors they could get knocked or damaged by people trying to get past your vehicle. If you leave them attached during the ferry crossing then make sure you check their position on returning to your vehicle.

Channel Tunnel

The Channel Tunnel operator, Eurotunnel, accepts cars, caravans and motorhomes (except those running on LPG) on their service between Folkestone and Calais. You can just turn up and see if there is availability on the day, however prices increase as it gets closer to the departure time so if you know your plans in advance it is best to book as early as possible.

On the Journey

You will be asked to open your roof vents prior to travel and you will also need to apply the caravan brake once you have parked your vehicle on the train. You will not be able to use your caravan until arrival.

Pets

It is possible to transport your pet on a number of ferry routes to the Continent and Ireland, as well as on Eurotunnel services from Folkestone to Calais. Advance booking is essential as restrictions apply to the number of animals allowed on any one crossing. You`ll need to contact an Official Veterinarian one month prior to travel to check the required vaccinations and documentation needed for your pet to travel. Make sure you understand the carrier's terms and conditions for transporting pets.

Brittany Ferries ask for all dogs to be muzzled when out of the vehicle but this varies for other operators so please check at the time of booking. Once on board pets are normally required to remain in their owner's vehicle or in kennels on the car deck and you won't be able to access your vehicle to check on your pet while the ferry is at sea.

On longer crossings you should make arrangements at the on-board information desk for permission to visit your pet in order to check its well-being. You should always make sure that ferry staff know your vehicle has a pet on board.

On some ships operating longer routes, specific `pet friendly` cabins are available and as these are very popular we recommend booking well in advance. Information and advice on the welfare of animals before and during a journey is available on the website of the Department for Environment, Food and Rural Affairs (Defra), www.defra.gov. ukInformation and advice on the welfare of animals before and during a journey is available on the website of the Department for Environment, Food and Rural Affairs (Defra), www.defra.gov.uk.

Gas

UK based ferry companies usually allow up to three gas cylinders per caravan, including the cylinder currently in use, however some may restrict this to a maximum of two cylinders. Some operators may ask you to hand over your gas cylinders to a member of the crew so that they can be safely stored during the crossing. Check that you know the rules of your ferry operator before you travel.

Cylinder valves should be fully closed and covered with a cap, if provided, and should remain closed during the crossing. Cylinders should be fixed securely in or on the caravan in the position specified by the manufacturer.

Gas cylinders must be declared at check-in and the crew may ask to inspect each cylinder for leakage before travel.

The carriage of spare petrol cans, whether full or empty, is not permitted on ferries or through the Channel Tunnel.

LPG Vehicles

Vehicles fully or partially powered by LPG can't be carried through the Channel Tunnel. Gas for domestic use (e.g. heating, lighting or cooking) can be carried, but the maximum limit is 47kg for a single bottle or 50kg in multiple bottles. Tanks must be switched off before boarding and must be less than 80% full; you will be asked to demonstrate this before you travel.

Most ferry companies will accept LPG-powered vehicles but you must let them know at the time of booking. During the crossing the tank must be no more than 75% full and it must be turned off. In the case of vehicles converted to use LPG, some ferry companies also require a certificate showing that the conversion has been carried out by a professional - before you book speak to the ferry company to check their requirements.

Club Sites Near Ports

If you've got a long drive to the ferry port, or want to catch an early ferry then an overnight stop near to the port gives you a relaxing start to your holiday. The following table lists Club sites which are close to ports.

Club Members can book online at camc.com or call 01342 327490. Non-members can book by calling the sites directly on the telephone numbers below when the sites are open.

Please note that Commons Wood, Fairlight Wood, Hunter's Moon and Old Hartley are open to Club members only. Non-members are welcome at all other sites listed below.

Port	Nearest Club Site	Tel No.
Cairnryan	New England Bay	01776 860275
Dover, Folkestone, Channel Tunnel	Bearsted	01622 730018
	Black Horse Farm*	01303 892665
	Daleacres	01303 267679
	Fairlight Wood	01424 812333
Fishguard, Pembroke	Freshwater East	01646 672341
Harwich	Cambridge Cherry Hinton*	01223 244088
	Commons Wood*	01707 260786
Holyhead	Penrhos	01248 852617
Hull	York Beechwood Grange*	01904 424637
	York Rowntree Park*	01904 658997
Newcastle upon Tyne	Old Hartley	0191 237 0256
Newhaven	Brighton*	01273 626546
Plymouth	Plymouth Sound	01752 862325
Poole	Hunter's Moon*	01929 556605
Portsmouth	Rookesbury Park	01329 834085
Rosslare	River Valley	00353 (0)404 41647
Weymouth	Crossways	01305 852032

* Site open all year

Ferry Routes and Operators

Route	Operator	Approximate Crossing Time	Maximum Frequency
France			
Dover – Calais	P & O Ferries	1½ hrs	22 daily
Dover – Calais	DFDS Seaways	1½ hrs	10 daily
Dover – Dunkerque	DFDS Seaways	2 hrs	12 daily
Folkestone – Calais	Eurotunnel	35 mins	3 per hour
Newhaven – Dieppe	DFDS Seaways	4 hrs	2 daily
Plymouth – Roscoff	Brittany Ferries	6 hrs	2 daily
Poole – St Malo (via Channel Islands)*	Condor Ferries	6.5 hrs	1 daily (Apr to Sep)
Portsmouth – Caen	Brittany Ferries	6 / 7 hrs	3 daily (maximum)
Portsmouth – Cherbourg	Brittany Ferries	3 hrs	2 daily (maximum)
Portsmouth – Le Havre	Brittany Ferries	3¼ / 8 hrs	1 daily (minimum)
Portsmouth – St Malo	Brittany Ferries	9 hrs	1 daily
Ireland – Northern			
Cairnryan – Larne	P & O Irish Sea	1 / 2 hrs	7 daily
Liverpool (Birkenhead) – Belfast	Stena Line	8 hrs	2 daily
Cairnryan – Belfast	Stena Line	2 / 3 hrs	7 daily
Ireland – Republic			
Cork – Roscoff*	Brittany Ferries	14 hrs	1 per week
Dublin - Cherbourg	Irish Ferries	19 hrs	1 per week
Fishguard – Rosslare	Stena Line	3½ hrs	2 daily
Holyhead – Dublin	Irish Ferries	2-4 hrs	Max 4 daily
Holyhead – Dublin	Stena Line	2-4 hrs	Max 4 daily
Liverpool – Dublin	P & O Irish Sea	8 hrs	2 daily
Pembroke – Rosslare	Irish Ferries	4 hrs	2 daily
Rosslare – Cherbourg*	Irish Ferries	19½ hrs	3 per week
Rosslare – Cherbourg	Stena Line	19 hrs	3 per week
Rosslare – Roscoff*	Irish Ferries	19½ hrs	4 per week
Netherlands			
Harwich – Hook of Holland	Stena Line	7 hrs	2 daily
Hull – Rotterdam	P & O Ferries	11-12 hrs	1 daily
Newcastle – Ijmuiden (Amsterdam)	DFDS Seaways	15½ hrs	1 daily
Spain			
Portsmouth – Bilbao	Brittany Ferries	24 / 32 hrs	1 - 3 per week
Portsmouth or Plymouth – Santander	Brittany Ferries	20 / 32 hrs	4 per week

*Not bookable through The Club's Travel Service.

Note: Note: Services and routes are subject to change. At time of publication ferry companies are operating reduced and amended sailing schedules because of Covid-19 restrictions.

Shutterstock/ Worton

Motoring Advice

Preparing for Your Journey

The first priority in preparing your outfit for your journey should be to make sure it has a full service. Make sure that you have a fully equipped spares kit, and a spare wheel and tyre for your caravan – it is easier to get hold of them from your local dealer than to have to spend time searching for spares where you don't know the local area.

Club members should carry their UK Sites Directory & Handbook with them, as it contains a section of technical advice which may be useful when travelling.

The Club also has a free advice service covering a wide range of technical topics – download free information leaflets at camc.com/advice or contact the team by calling 01342 336611 or emailing technical@ caravanclub.co.uk.

For advice on issues specific to countries other than the UK, Club members can contact the Travel Service Information Officer, email: travelserviceinfo@caravanclub.co.uk or call 01342 336766.

Weight Limits

From both a legal and a safety point of view, it is essential not to exceed vehicle weight limits. It is advisable to carry documentation confirming your vehicle's maximum permitted laden weight - if your Vehicle Registration Certificate (V5C) does not state this, you will need to produce alternative certification, e.g. from a weighbridge.

If you are pulled over by the police and don't have certification you will be taken to a weighbridge. If your vehicle(s) are then found to be overweight you will be liable to a fine and may have to discard items to lower the weight before you can continue on your journey.

Some Final Checks

Before you start any journey make sure you complete the following checks:

- All car and caravan or motorhome lights are working and sets of spare bulbs are packed
- The coupling is correctly seated on the towball and the breakaway cable is attached
- Windows, vents, hatches and doors are shut
- On-board water systems are drained
- Mirrors are adjusted for maximum visibility
- Corner steadies are fully wound up and the brace is handy for your arrival on site
- Any fires or flames are extinguished and the gas cylinder tap is turned off. Fire extinguishers are fully charged and close at hand

- The over-run brake is working correctly
- The jockey wheel is raised and secured, the handbrake is released

Driving in Europe

Driving abroad for the first time can be a daunting prospect, especially when towing a caravan. Here are a few tips to make the transition easier:

- Remember that Sat Navs may take you on unsuitable roads, so have a map or atlas to hand to help you find an alternative route
- It can be tempting to try and get to your destination as quickly as possible but we recommend travelling a maximum of 250 miles a day when towing
- Share the driving if possible, and on long journeys plan an overnight stop
- Remember that if you need to overtake or pull out around an obstruction you will not be able to see clearly from the driver's seat. If possible, always have a responsible adult in the passenger seat who can advise you when it is clear to pull out. If that is not possible then stay well back to get a better view and pull out slowly
- If traffic builds up behind you, pull over safely and let it pass
- Driving on the right should become second nature after a while, but pay particular attention when turning left, after leaving a rest area, petrol station or site or after a one-way system
- Stop at least every two hours to stretch your legs and take a break

Fuel

Grades of petrol sold on the Continent are comparable to those sold in the UK; 95 octane is frequently known as 'Essence' and 98 octane as 'Super'. Diesel may be called 'Gasoil' and is widely available across Europe. E10 petrol (containing 10% Ethanol) can be found in certain countries in Europe. Most modern cars are E10 compatible, but those which aren't could be damaged by filling up with E10. Check your vehicle handbook or visit www.acea.be and search for 'E10' to find the publication 'Vehicle compatibility with new fuel standards'.

Members of The Caravan and Motorhome Club can check current average fuel prices by country at camc.com/overseasadvice.

Away from major roads and towns it is a good idea not to let your fuel tank run too low as you may have difficulty finding a petrol station, especially at night or on Sundays. Petrol stations offering a 24-hour service may involve an automated process, in some cases only accepting credit cards issued in the country you are in.

Automotive Liquefied Petroleum Gas (LPG)

The increasing popularity of dual-fuelled vehicles means that the availability of LPG – also known as 'autogas' or 'GPL' – has become an important issue for more drivers.

There are different tank-filling openings in use in different countries. Currently there is no common European filling system, and you might find a variety of systems. Most Continental motorway services will have adaptors but these should be used with care – see www.autogas.ltd.uk for more information.

Low Emission Zones

Many cities in countries around Europe have introduced 'Low Emission Zones' (LEZ's) in order to regulate vehicle pollution levels. Some schemes require you to buy a windscreen sticker, pay a fee or register your vehicle before entering the zone. You may also need to provide proof that your vehicle's emissions meet the required standard. Before you travel visit www.lowemissionzones.eu for maps and details of LEZ's across Europe. Also see the Country Introductions later in this guide for country specific information.

Motorhomes Towing Cars

If you are towing a car behind a motorhome, our advice would be to use a trailer with all four wheels of the car off the ground. Although most countries don't have specific laws banning A-frames, there may be laws in place which prohibit motor vehicle towing another motor vehicle.

Priority and Roundabouts

When driving on the Continent it can be difficult to work out which vehicles have priority in different situations. Watch out for road signs which indicate priority and read the Country Introductions later in this guide for country specific information.

Take care at intersections – you should never rely on being given right of way, even if you have priority; especially in small towns and villages where local traffic may take right of way. Always give way to public service and military vehicles and to buses and trams.

In some countries in Europe priority at roundabouts is given to vehicles entering the roundabout (i.e. on the right) unless the road signs say otherwise.

Public Transport

In general in built-up areas be prepared to stop to allow a bus to pull out from a bus stop when the driver is signalling his intention to do so.

Take particular care when school buses have stopped and passengers are getting on and off.

Overtaking trams in motion is normally only allowed on the right, unless on a one way

Shutterstock/ Leonid Andronov

street where you can overtake on the left if there is not enough space on the right. Do not overtake a tram near a tram stop. These may be in the centre of the road. When a tram or bus stops to allow passengers on and off, you should stop to allow them to cross to the pavement. Give way to trams which are turning across your carriageway. Don't park or stop across tram lines; trams cannot steer round obstructions!

Pedestrian Crossings

Stopping to allow pedestrians to cross at zebra crossings is not always common practice on the Continent as it is in the UK. Pedestrians expect to wait until the road is clear before crossing, while motorists behind may be taken by surprise by your stopping. The result may be a rear-end shunt or vehicles overtaking you at the crossing and putting pedestrians at risk.

Traffic Lights

Traffic lights may not be as easily visible as they are in the UK, for instance they may be smaller or suspended across the road with a smaller set on a post at the roadside. You may find that lights change directly from red to green, bypassing amber completely. Flashing amber lights generally indicate that you may proceed with caution if it is safe to do so but you must give way to pedestrians and other vehicles.

A green filter light should be treated with caution as you may still have to give way to pedestrians who have a green light to cross the road. If a light turns red as approached, continental drivers will often speed up to get through the light instead of stopping. Be aware that if you brake sharply because a traffic light has turned red as you approached, the driver behind might not be expecting it.

Shutterstock/Daniel_Kay

Essential Equipment

The equipment that you legally have to carry differs by country. For a full list see the Essential Equipment table at the end of this chapter. Please note equipment requirements and regulations can change frequently. To keep up to date with the latest equipment information visit camc.com/overseasadvice.

Child Restraint Systems

Children under 10 years of age are not permitted to travel in front seats of vehicles, unless there are no rear seats in the vehicle, the rear seats are already occupied with other children, or there are no seat belts in the rear. In these situations a child must not be placed in the front seats in a rear-facing child seat, unless any airbag is deactivated. Children up to 10 must travel in an approved child seat or restraint system, adapted to their size. A baby up to 13kg in weight must be carried in a rear facing baby seat. A child between 9kg and 18kg in weight must be seated in a child seat. A child from 15kg in weight up to the age of 10 can use a booster seat with a seat belt.

Children must not travel in the front of a vehicle if there are rear seats available. If they travel in the front the airbag must be deactivated and again they must use an EU approved restraint system for their size.

Fire Extinguisher

As a safety precaution, an approved fire extinguisher should be carried in all vehicles. This is a legal requirement in several countries in Europe.

Lights

When driving in on the right headlights should be adjusted if they are likely to dazzle other road users. You can do this by applying beam deflectors, or some newer vehicles have a built-in adjustment system. Some high-density discharge (HID), xenon or halogen lights, may need to be taken to a dealer to make the necessary adjustment.

Remember also to adjust headlights according to the load being carried and to compensate for the weight of the caravan on the back of your car. Even if you do not intend to drive at night, it is important to ensure that your headlights are correctly adjusted as you may need to use them in heavy rain, fog or in tunnels. If using tape or a pre-cut adhesive mask remember to remove it on your return home.

All vehicle lights must be in working condition. If your lights are not in working order you may be liable for a fine of up to €450 and confiscation of your vehicle is a possibility in some European countries.

Headlight-Flashing

On the Continent headlight-flashing is used as a warning of approach or as an overtaking signal at night, and not, as is commonly the case in the UK, an indication that you are giving way. Be more cautious with both flashing your headlights and when another driver flashes you. If a driver flashes his headlights they are generally indicating that he has priority and you should give way, contrary to standard practice in the UK.

Hazard Warning Lights

Hazard warning lights should not be used in place of a warning triangle, but should be used in addition to it.

Nationality Plate

You need to display a GB identifier on the rear of your vehicle when travelling in Europe. If your number plate includes GB on its own or GB with the Union flag then you do not need a separate GB sticker, unless you are travelling in Spain in which case a separate GB sticker is also required.

You will need a separate GB sticker displayed on the rear of your vehicle if your number plate has a Euro symbol, a national flag of England, Scotland or Wales or no flag or identifier.

Reflective Jackets/Waistcoats

If you break down outside of a built-up area it is normally a legal requirement that anyone leaving the vehicle must be wearing a reflective jacket or waistcoat. Make sure that your jacket is accessible from inside the car as you will need to put it on before exiting the vehicle. Carry one for each passenger as well as the driver.

Route Planning

It is always a good idea to carry a road atlas or map of the countries you plan to visit, even if you have Satellite Navigation. You can find information on UK roads from Keep Moving – www.keepmoving.co.uk or call 09003 401100. Websites offering a European route mapping service include www.google.co.uk/maps, www.mappy.com or www.viamichelin.com.

Satellite Navigation/GPS

European postcodes don't cover just one street or part of a street in the same way as UK postcodes, they can cover a very large area. GPS co-ordinates and full addresses are given for site entries in this guide wherever possible, so that you can programme your device as accurately as possible.

It is important to remember that sat nav devices don't usually allow for towing or driving a large motorhome and may try to send you down unsuitable roads. Always use your common sense, and if a road looks unsuitable find an alternative route.

Use your sat nav in conjunction with the directions given in the site entries, which have been provided by members who have actually visited. Please note that directions given in site entries have not been checked by the Caravan and Motorhome Club.

In nearly all European countries it is illegal to use car navigation systems which actively search for mobile speed cameras or interfere with police equipment (laser or radar detection).

Car navigation systems which give a warning of fixed speed camera locations are legal in most countries with the exception of France, Germany, and Switzerland where this function must be de-activated.

Seat Belts

The wearing of seat belts is compulsory throughout Europe. On-the-spot fines will be incurred for failure to wear them and, in the event of an accident failure to wear a seat belt may reduce any claim for injury. See the country introductions for specific regulations on both seat belts and car seats.

Spares

Caravan Spares

It will generally be much harder to get hold of spare parts for caravans on the continent, especially for UK manufactured caravans. It is therefore advisable to carry any commonly required spares (such as light bulbs) with you.

Take contact details of your UK dealer or manufacturer with you, as they may be able to assist in getting spares delivered to you in an emergency.

Car Spares

Some car manufacturers produce spares kits; contact your dealer for details. The choice of spares will depend on the vehicle and how long you are away, but the following is a list of basic items which should cover the most common causes of breakdown:

- Radiator top hose
- Fan belt
- Fuses and bulbs
- Windscreen wiper blade
- Length of 12V electrical cable
- Tools, torch and WD40 or equivalent water repellent/ dispersant spray

Spare Wheel

Your local caravan dealer should be able to supply an appropriate spare wheel. If you have any difficulty in obtaining one, the Club's Technical Department can provide Club members with a list of suppliers on request.

Tyre legislation across Europe is more or less consistent and, while the Club has no specific knowledge of laws on the Continent regarding the use of space-saver spare wheels, there should be no problems in using such a wheel provided its use is in accordance with the manufacturer's instructions. Space-saver spare wheels are designed for short journeys to get to a place where it can be repaired and there will usually be restrictions on the distance and speed at which the vehicle should be driven.

Towbar

The vast majority of cars registered after 1 August 1998 are legally required to have a European Type approved towbar (complying with European Directive 94/20) carrying a plate giving its approval number and various technical details, including the maximum noseweight. Your car dealer or specialist towbar fitter will be able to give further advice.

All new motorhomes will need some form of type approval before they can be registered in the UK and as such can only be fitted with a type approved towbar. Older vehicles can continue to be fitted with non-approved towing brackets.

Tyres

Tyre condition has a major effect on the safe handling of your outfit. Caravan tyres must be suitable for the highest speed at which you can legally tow, even if you choose to drive slower.

Most countries require a minimum tread depth of 1.6mm but motoring organisations recommend at least 3mm. If you are planning a long journey, consider if they will still be above the legal minimum by the end of your journey.

Tyre Pressure

Tyre pressure should be checked and adjusted when the tyres are cold; checking warm tyres will result in a higher pressure reading. The correct pressures will be found in your car handbook, but unless it states otherwise to add an extra 4 - 6 pounds per square inch to the rear tyres of a car when towing to improve handling. Make sure you know what pressure your caravan tyres should be. Some require a pressure much higher than that normally used for cars. Check your caravan handbook for details.

Tyre Sizes

It is worth noting that some sizes of radial tyre to fit the 13" wheels commonly used on older UK caravans are virtually impossible to find in stock at retailers abroad, e.g. 175R13C.

After a Puncture

A lot of cars now have a liquid sealant puncture repair kit instead of a spare wheel. These should not be considered a permanent repair, and in some cases have been known to make repair of the tyre impossible. If you need to use a liquid sealant you should get the tyre repaired or replaced as soon as possible.

Following a caravan tyre puncture, especially on a single-axle caravan, it is advisable to have the non-punctured tyre removed from its wheel and checked inside and out for signs of damage resulting from overloading during the deflation of the punctured tyre.

Winter Driving

Snow chains must be fitted to vehicles using snow covered roads in compliance with the relevant road signs. Fines may be imposed for non-compliance. Vehicles fitted with chains must not exceed 50 km/h (31mph).

They are not difficult to fit but it's a good idea to carry sturdy gloves to protect your hands when handling the chains in freezing conditions. Polar Automotive Ltd sells and hires out snow chains, contact them on 01892 519933, www.snowchains.com, or email: polar@snowchains.com.

In Andorra winter tyres are recommended. Snow chains must be used when road conditions necessitate their use and/or when road signs indicate.

Warning Triangles

In almost all European countries it is compulsory to carry a warning triangle which, in the event of vehicle breakdown or accident, must be placed (providing it is safe to do so) on the carriageway at least 30 metres from the vehicle. In some instances it is not compulsory to use the triangle but only when this action would endanger the driver.

A warning triangle should be placed on the road approximately 30 metres (100 metres on motorways) behind the broken down vehicle on the same side of the road. Always assemble the triangle before leaving your vehicle and walk with it so that the red, reflective surface is facing oncoming traffic. If a breakdown occurs round a blind corner, place the triangle in advance of the corner. Hazard warning lights may be used in conjunction with the triangle but they do not replace it.

Essential Equipment Table

The table below shows the essential equipment required for each country. Please note that this information was correct at the time of going to print but is subject to change.

For up to date information on equipment requirements for countries in Europe visit camc.com/overseasadvice.

Country	Warning Triangle	Spare Bulbs	First Aid Kit	Reflective Jacket	Additional Equipment to be Carried/Used
Andorra	Yes (2)	Yes	Rec	Yes	Dipped headlights in poor daytime visibility. Winter tyres recommended; snow chains when road conditions or signs dictate.
Austria	Yes	Rec	Yes	Yes	Winter tyres from 1 Nov to 15 April.*
Belgium	Yes	Rec	Rec	Yes	Dipped headlights in poor daytime visibility.
Croatia	Yes (2 for vehicle with trailer)	Yes	Yes	Yes	Dipped headlights at all times from last Sunday in Oct - last Sunday in Mar. Spare bulbs compulsory if lights are xenon, neon or LED. Snow chains compulsory in winter in certain regions.*
Czech Rep	Yes	Yes	Yes	Yes	Dipped headlights at all times. Replacement fuses. Winter tyres or snow chains from 1 Nov - 31st March.*
Denmark	Yes	Rec	Rec	Rec	Dipped headlights at all times. On motorways use hazard warning lights when queues or danger ahead.
Finland	Yes	Rec	Rec	Yes	Dipped headlights at all times. Winter tyres Dec - Feb.*
France	Yes	Rec	Rec	Yes	Dipped headlights recommended at all times. Legal requirement to carry a breathalyser, but no penalty for non-compliance.
Germany	Rec	Rec	Rec	Rec	Dipped headlights recommended at all times. Winter tyres to be used in winter weather conditions.*
Greece	Yes	Rec	Yes	Rec	Fire extinguisher compulsory. Dipped headlights in towns at night and in poor daytime visibility.

Country	Warning Triangle	Spare Bulbs	First Aid Kit	Reflective Jacket	Additional Equipment to be Carried/Used
Hungary	Yes	Rec	Yes	Yes	Dipped headlights at all times outside built-up areas and in built-up areas at night. Snow chains compulsory on some roads in winter conditions.*
Italy	Yes	Rec	Rec	Yes	Dipped headlights at all times outside built-up areas and in poor visibility. Snow chains from 15 Oct - 15 April.*
Luxembourg	Yes	Rec	Rec	Yes	Dipped headlights at night and daytime in bad weather.
Netherlands	Yes	Rec	Rec	Rec	Dipped headlights at night and in bad weather and recommended during the day.
Norway	Yes	Rec	Rec	Rec	Dipped headlights at all times. Winter tyres compulsory when snow or ice on the roads.*
Poland	Yes	Rec	Rec	Rec	Dipped headlights at all times. Fire extinguisher compulsory.
Portugal	Yes	Rec	Rec	Rec	Dipped headlights in poor daytime visibility, in tunnels and in lanes where traffic flow is reversible.
Slovakia	Yes	Rec	Yes	Yes	Dipped headlights at all times. Winter tyres compulsory when compact snow or ice on the road.*
Slovenia	Yes (2 for vehicle with trailer)	Yes	Rec	Yes	Dipped headlights at all times. Hazard warning lights when reversing. Use winter tyres or carry snow chains 15 Nov - 15 Mar.
Spain	Yes (2 Rec)	Rec	Rec	Yes	Dipped headlights at night, in tunnels and on 'special' roads (roadworks).
Sweden	Yes	Rec	Rec	Rec	Dipped headlights at all times. Winter tyres 1 Dec to 31 March.
Switzerland (inc Liechtenstein)	Yes	Rec	Rec	Rec	Dipped headlights recommended at all times, compulsory in tunnels. Snow chains where indicated by signs.

NOTES:
1) All countries: seat belts (if fitted) must be worn by all passengers.
2) Rec: not compulsory for foreign-registered vehicles, but strongly recommended
3) Headlamp converters, spare bulbs, fire extinguisher, first aid kit and reflective waistcoat are strongly recommended for all countries.
4) In some countries drivers who wear prescription glasses must carry a spare pair.
5) Please check information for any country before you travel. This information is to be used as a guide only and it is your responsibility to make sure you have the correct equipment.

* For more information and regulations on winter driving please see the Country Introduction.

Route Planning - Northern Europe

ICELAND

Seyðisfjörður

N
W — E
S

Motorways
Major roads
Main roads
Ferry routes
Major airports

0   300 km
0   150   miles

Faroe Islands
(Denmark)   Torshavn

ATLANTIC

OCEAN

Shetland Islands

Ålesund

Bergen

Orkney Islands

Stavanger

Inverness

Kristiansand

Aberdeen

Skagerra

Dundee

North

Glasgow   Edinburgh

Sea

UNITED
KINGDOM

Newcastle upon Tyne

Esbjerg

Belfast

Douglas

Galway   IRELAND

Isle of Man
(British Crown
Dependency)   Irish
Sea

Kingston upon Hull

Leeds

DUBLIN   Liverpool

Limerick   Holyhead   Manchester

Crewe

NETHERLANDS   Bremerhaven
Leeuwarden   Groningen

Cork   Rosslare

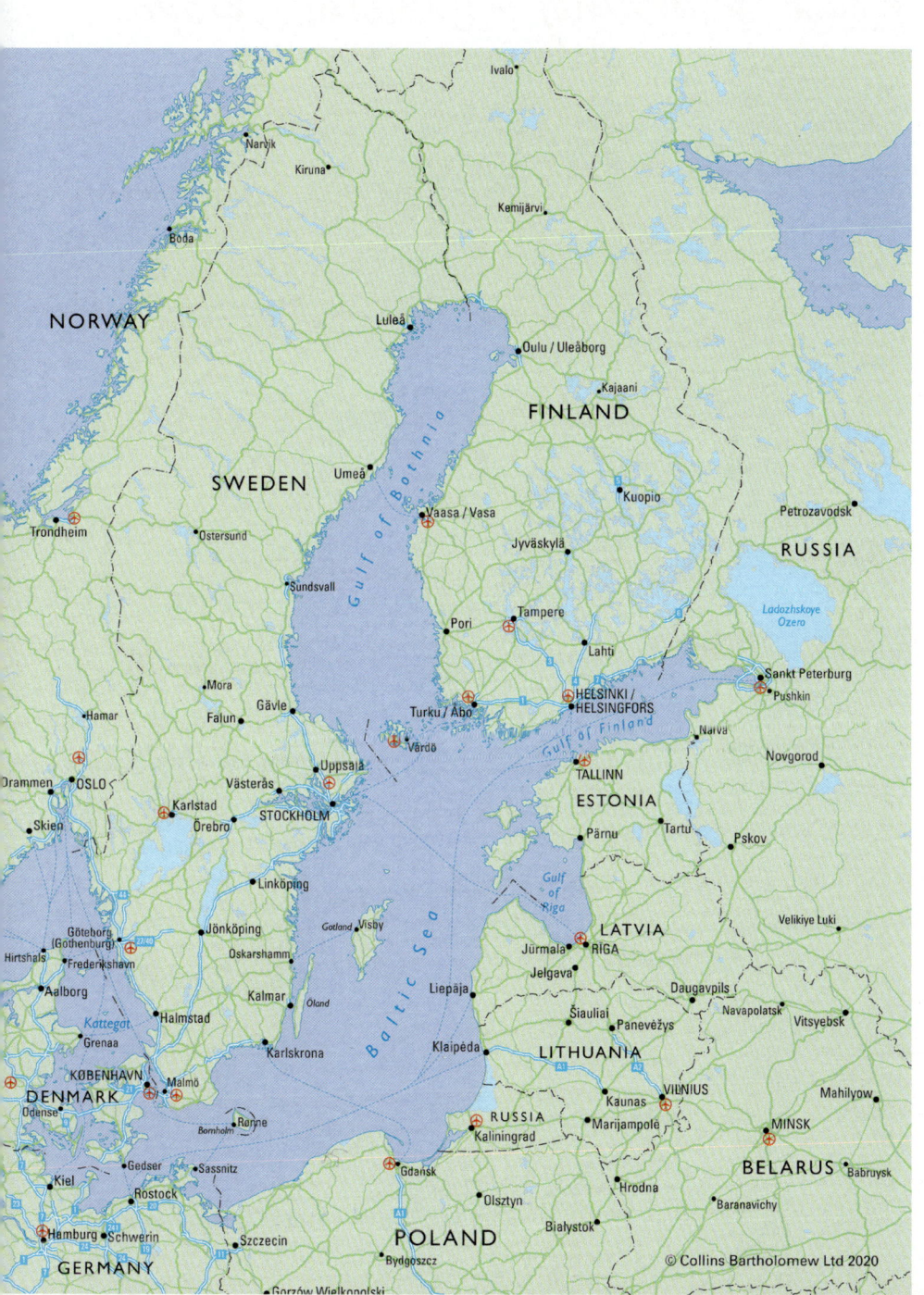

NORWAY

Narvik
Kiruna

Bodø

Kemijärvi

Ivalo

Luleå

Oulu / Uleåborg

FINLAND

SWEDEN
Umeå

Kajaani

Gulf of Bothnia

Vaasa / Vasa

Kuopio

Petrozavodsk

RUSSIA

Trondheim

Östersund

Sundsvall

Jyväskylä

Ladozhskoye
Ozero

Pori

Tampere

Lahti

Mora
Hamar
Falun
Gävle

Turku / Åbo

HELSINKI /
HELSINGFORS

Sankt Peterburg
Pushkin

Drammen
OSLO
Skien

Karlstad
Örebro

Västerås
Uppsala

Vårdö

Gulf of Finland

Narva

Novgorod

STOCKHOLM

TALLINN

ESTONIA

Pärnu
Tartu

Pskov

Velikiye Luki

Linköping

Gulf
of
Riga

Jönköping
Gotland Visby

Baltic Sea

LATVIA

Jūrmala
RIGA

Oskarshamn

Jelgava

Daugavpils

Navapolatsk

Vitsyebsk

Göteborg
(Gothenburg)
Hirtshals
Frederikshavn
Aalborg

Kalmar
Öland

Liepāja

Šiauliai
Panevėžys

Kattegat
Halmstad
Grenaa

Klaipėda

LITHUANIA

Karlskrona

Kaunas
VILNIUS

Mahilyow

KØBENHAVN
Odense
Malmö
DENMARK

Rønne
Bornholm

RUSSIA
Kaliningrad

Marijampolė

MINSK

BELARUS
Babruysk

Kiel
Rostock

Gedser
Sassnitz

Gdańsk

Hrodna

Baranavichy

Hamburg
Schwerin
GERMANY

Szczecin

Olsztyn

POLAND
Bydgoszcz

Białystok

© Collins Bartholomew Ltd 2020

Gorzów Wielkopolski

Route Planning - Central Europe

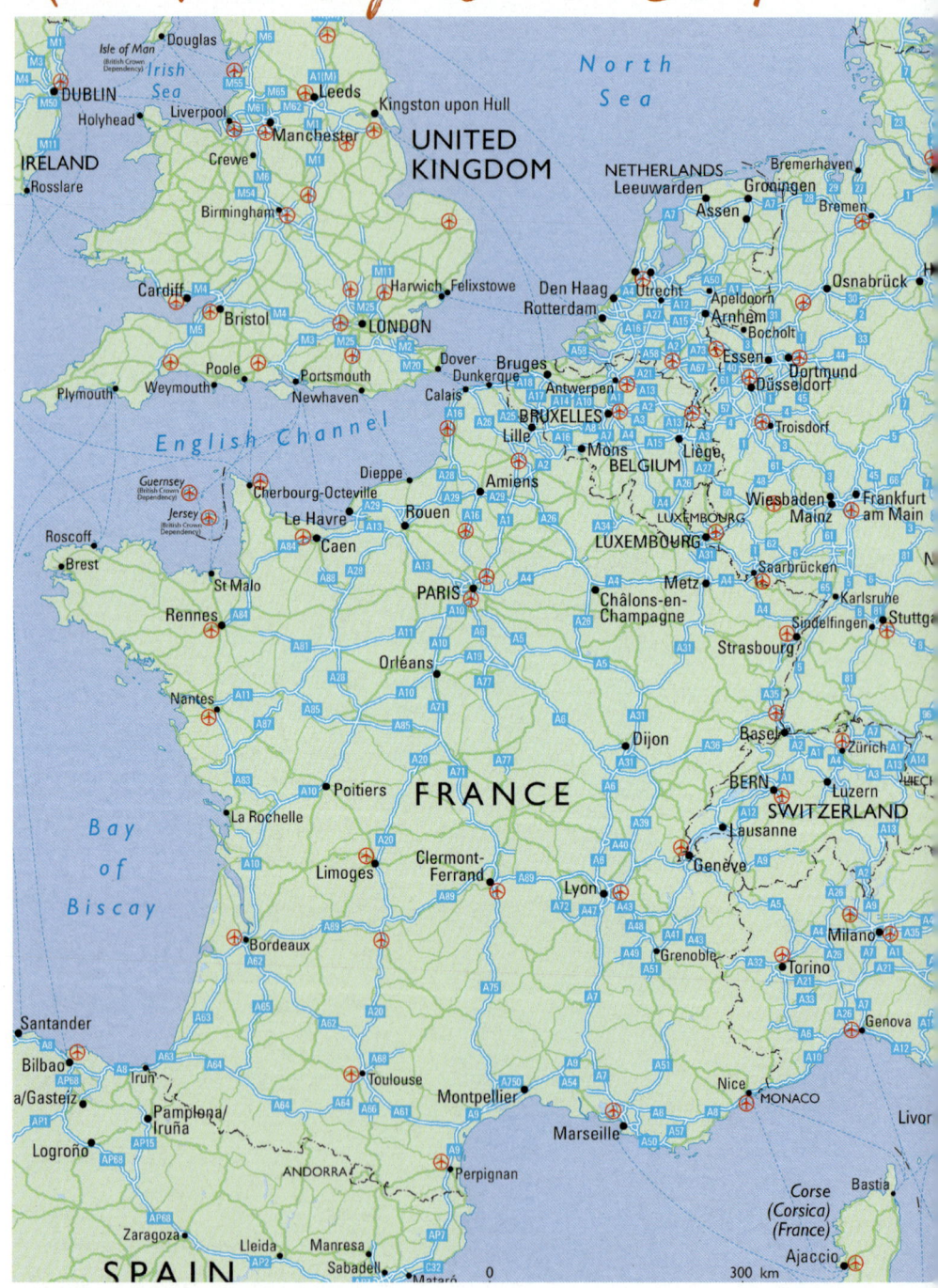

Route Planning - Southern Europe

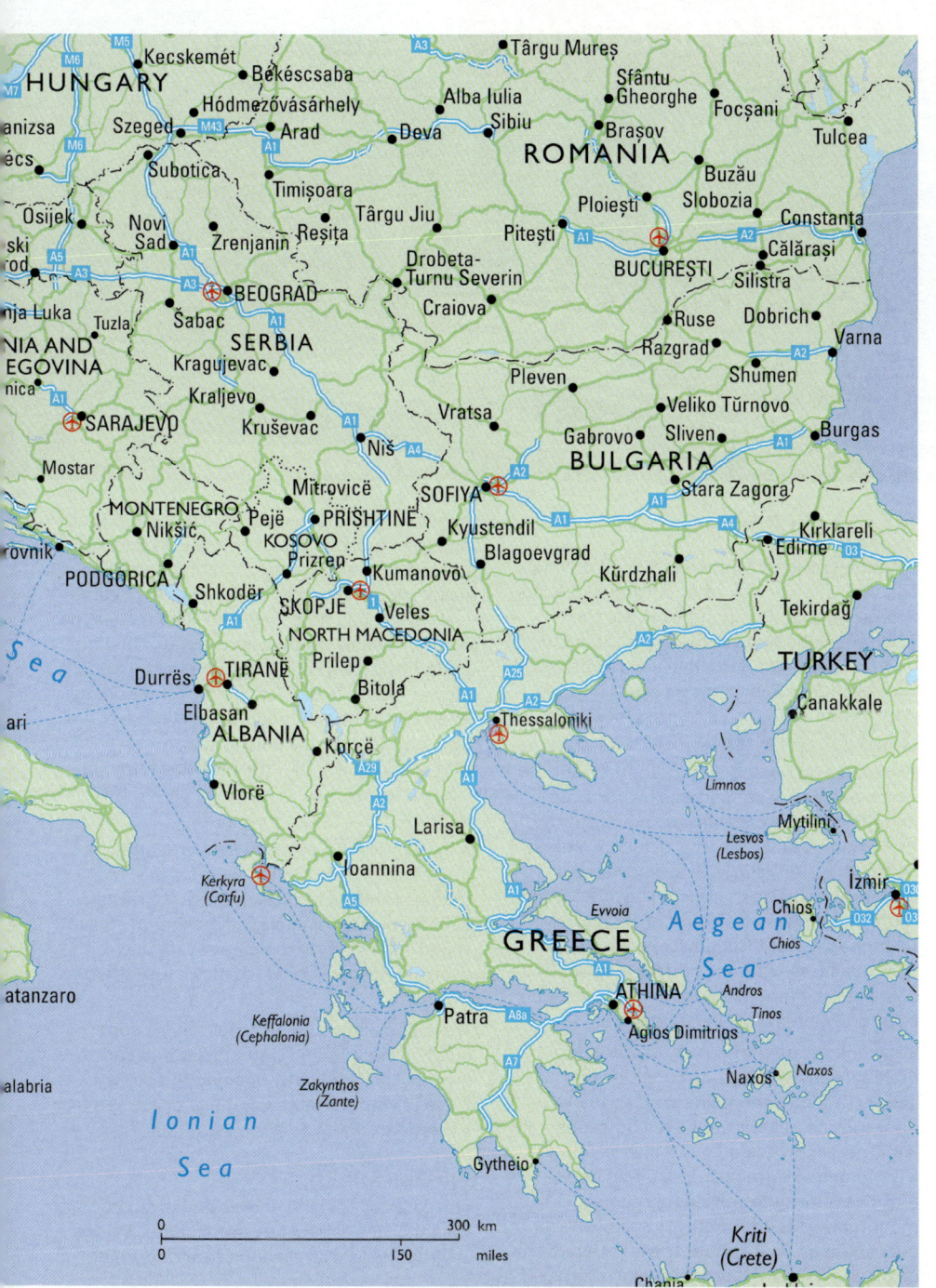

Mountain Roads

Shutterstock/ FooT Too

Mountain Passes

Mountain passes can create difficult driving conditions, especially when towing or driving a large vehicle. You should only use them if you have a good power to weight ratio and in good driving conditions. If in any doubt as to your outfit's suitability or the weather then stick to motorway routes across mountain ranges if possible.

The tables on the following pages show which passes are not suitable for caravans, and those where caravans are not permitted. Motorhomes aren't usually included in these restrictions, but relatively low powered or very large vehicles should find an alternative route. Road signs at the foot of a pass may restrict access or offer advice, especially for heavy vehicles. Warning notices are usually posted at the foot of a pass if it is closed, or if chains or winter tyres must be used.

Caravanners are particularly sensitive to gradients and traffic/road conditions on passes. The maximum gradient is usually on the inside of bends but exercise caution if it is necessary to pull out. Always engage a lower gear before taking a hairpin bend and give priority to vehicles ascending. On mountain roads it is not the gradient which puts strain on your car but the duration of the climb and the loss of power at high altitudes:

approximately 10% at 915 metres (3,000 feet) and even more as you get higher. To minimise the risk of the engine overheating, take high passes in the cool part of the day, don't climb any faster than necessary and keep the engine pulling steadily. To prevent a radiator boiling, pull off the road safely, turn the heater and blower full on and switch off air conditioning. Keep an eye on water and oil levels. Never put cold water into a boiling radiator or it may crack. Check that the radiator is not obstructed by debris sucked up during the journey.

A long descent may result in overheating brakes; select the correct gear for the gradient and avoid excessive use of brakes. Even if you are using engine braking to control speed, caravan brakes may activate due to the overrun mechanism, which may cause them to overheat.

Travelling at altitude can cause a pressure build up in tanks and water pipes. You can prevent this by slightly opening the blade valve of your portable toilet and opening a tap a fraction.

Mountain Pass Information

The dates of opening and closing given in the following tables are approximate. Before attempting late afternoon or early morning journeys across borders, check their opening times as some borders close at night.

Gradients listed are the maximum which may be encountered on the pass and may be steeper at the inside of curves, particularly on older roads.

Gravel surfaces (such as dirt and stone chips) vary considerably; they can be dusty when dry and slippery when wet. Where known to exist, this type of surface has been noted.

In fine weather winter tyres or snow chains will only be required on very high passes, or for short periods in early or late summer. In winter conditions you will probably need to use them at altitudes exceeding 600 metres (approximately 2,000 feet).

Tunnels

Long tunnels are a much more commonly seen feature in Europe than in the UK, especially in mountainous regions. Tolls are usually charged for the use of major tunnels.

Dipped headlights are usually required by law even in well-lit tunnels, so switch them on before you enter. Snow chains, if used, must be removed before entering a tunnel in lay-bys provided for this purpose.

'No overtaking' signs must be strictly observed. Never cross central single or double lines. If overtaking is permitted in twin-tube tunnels, bear in mind that it is very easy to underestimate distances and speed once inside. In order to minimise the effects of exhaust fumes close all car windows and set the ventilator to circulate air, or operate the air conditioning system coupled with the recycled air option.

If you break down, try to reach the next lay-by and call for help from an emergency phone. If you cannot reach a lay-by, place your warning triangle at least 100 metres behind your vehicle. Modern tunnels have video surveillance systems to ensure prompt assistance in an emergency. Some tunnels can extend for miles and a high number of breakdowns are due to running out of fuel so make sure you have enough before entering the tunnel.

Tables and Maps

Much of the information contained in the following tables was originally supplied by The Automobile Association and other motoring and tourist organisations. The Caravan and Motorhome Club haven't checked this information and cannot accept responsibility for the accuracy or for errors or omissions to these tables.

The mountain passes, rail and road tunnels listed in the tables are shown on the following maps. Numbers and letters against each pass or tunnel in the tables correspond with the numbers and letters on the maps.

Converting Gradients

20% = 1 in 5	11% = 1 in 9
16% = 1 in 6	10% = 1 in 8
14% = 1 in 7	8% = 1 in 12
12% = 1 in 8	6% = 1 in 16

Abbreviations

MHV	Maximum height of vehicle
MLV	Maximum length of vehicle
MWV	Maximum width of vehicle
MWR	Minimum width of road
OC	Occasionally closed between dates
UC	Usually closed between dates
UO	Usually open between dates, although a fall of snow may obstruct the road for 24-48 hours.

Major Alpine Mountain Passes

Before using any of these passes, please read the advice at the beginning of this chapter.

Pass / Height In Metres (Feet)	From / To	Max gradient	Conditions and Comments
① **Achenpass** (Austria – Germany) 941 (3087)	Achenwald / Glashütte	4%	UO. Well-engineered road, B181/307. Gradient not too severe.
② **Albula** (Switzerland) 2312 (7585)	Tiefencastel / La Punt	10%	UC Nov-early Jun. MWR 3.5m (11'6") MWV 2.25m (7'6") Inferior alternative to the Julier; fine scenery. Alternative rail tunnel. Not recommended for caravans.
③ **Allos** (France) 2250 (7382)	Colmars / Barcelonette	10%	UC early Nov-early Jun. MWR 4m (13'1") Very winding, narrow, mostly unguarded pass on D908 but not difficult otherwise; passing bays on southern slope; poor surface, MWV 1.8m (5'11"). Not recommended for caravans.
④ **Aprica** (Italy) 1176 (3858)	Tresenda / Edolo	9%	UO. MWR 4m (13'1") Fine scenery; good surface; well-graded on road S39. Narrow in places; watch for protruding rock. Not recommended for caravanners to attempt this pass E or W. Poor road conditions, repairs reduce width drastically.
⑤ **Aravis** (France) 1498 (4915)	La Clusaz / Flumet	9%	OC Dec-Mar. MWR 4m (13'1"). Fine scenery; D909, fairly easy road. Poor surface in parts on Chamonix side. Some single-line traffic.
⑥ **Arlberg** (Austria) 1802 (5912)	Bludenz / Landeck	13%	OC Dec-Apr. MWR 6m (19'8"). Good modern road B197/E60 with several pull-in places. Steeper fr W easing towards summit; heavy traffic. Caravans prohibited. Parallel road tunnel (tolls) available on E60 (poss long queues).
⑦ **Ballon d'Alsace** (France) 1178 (3865)	Giromagny / St Maurice-sur-Moselle	11%	OC Dec-Mar. MWR 4m (13'1") Fairly straightforward ascent/descent; narrow in places; numerous bends. On road D465.
⑧ **Bayard** (France) 1248 (4094)	Chauffayer / Gap	14%	UO. MWR 6m (19'8") Part of the Route Napoléon N85. Fairly easy, steepest on the S side with several hairpin bends. Negotiable by caravans from N-to-S via D1075 (N75) and Col-de-la-Croix Haute, avoiding Gap.
⑨ **Bernina** (Switzerland) 2330 (7644)	Pontresina / Poschiavo	12.50%	OC Dec-Mar. MWR 5m (16'5") MWV 2.25m (7'6") Fine scenery. Good with care on open narrow sections towards summit on S-side; on road no. 29.
⑩ **Bracco** (Italy) 613 (2011)	Riva Trigoso / Borghetto di Vara	14%	UO. MWR 5m (16'5") A two-lane road (P1) more severe than height suggests due to hairpins and volume of traffic; passing difficult. Rec cross early to avoid traffic. Alternative toll m'way A12 available.

Before using any of these passes, please read the advice at the beginning of this chapter.

Pass / Height In Metres (Feet)	From / To	Max gradient	Conditions and Comments
11 **Brenner (Europabrücke)** (Austria – Italy) 1374 (4508)	Innsbruck / *Vipiteno/Sterzing*	14%	UO. MWR 5m (16'8") On road no. 182/12. Parallel toll m'way A13/A22/E45 (6%) suitable for caravans. Heavy traffic may delay at Customs. **Pass road closed to vehicles towing trailers.**
12 **Brouis** (France) 1279 (4196)	Nice / *Col-de-Tende*	12.50%	UO. MWR 5m (16'8") Good surface but many hairpins on D6204 (N204)/S20. Steep gradients on approaches. Height of tunnel at Col-de-Tende at the Italian border is 3.8m (12'4") **Not recommended for caravans.**
13 **Brünig** (Switzerland) 1007 (3340)	Brienzwiler Station / *Giswil*	8.50%	UO. MWR 5m (16'8") MWV 2.5m (8'2") An easy but winding road (no. 4); heavy traffic at weekends; frequent lay-bys. Or-going road improvement (2009) may cause delays – check before travel.
14 **Bussang** (France) 721 (2365)	Thann / *St Maurice-sur-Moselle*	7%	UO. MWR 4m (13'1") A very easy road (N66) over the Vosges; beautiful scenery.
15 **Cabre** (France) 1180 (3871)	Luc-en-Diois / *Aspres-sur-Buëch*	9%	UO. MWR 5.5m (18') An easy pleasant road (D93/D993), winding at Col-de-Cabre.
16 **Campolongo** (Italy) 1875 (6152)	Corvara-in-Badia / *Arabba*	12.50%	OC Dec-Mar. MWR 5m (16'5") A winding but easy ascent on rd P244; long level stretch on summit followed by easy descent. Good surface, fine scenery.
17 **Cayolle** (France) 2326 (7631)	Barcelonnette / *Guillaumes*	10%	UC early Nov-early Jun. MWR 4m (13'1") Narrow, winding road (D902) with hairpin bends; poor surface, broken edges with steep drops. Long stretches of single-track road with passing places. **Caravans prohibited.**
18 **Costalunga (Karer)** (Italy) 1745 (5725)	Bolzano / *Pozza-di-Fassa*	15%	OC Dec-Apr. MWR 5m (16'5") A good well-engineered road (S241) but mostly winding with many blind hairpins. **Caravans prohibited.**
19 **Croix** (Switzerland) 1778 (5833)	Villars-sur-Ollon / *Les Diablerets*	13%	UC Nov-May. MWR 3.5m (11'6") A narrow, winding route but extremely picturesque. **Not recommended for caravans.**
20 **Croix Haute** (France) 1179 (3868)	Monestier-de-Clermont / *Aspres-sur-Buëch*	7%	UO on N75. MWR 5.5m (18') Well-engineered road (D1075/N75); several hairpin bends on N side.
21 **Falzárego** (Italy) 2117 (6945)	Cortina-d'Ampezzo / *Andraz*	8.50%	OC Dec-Apr. MWR 5m (16'5") Well-engineered bitumen surface on road R48; many blind hairpin bends on both sides; used by tour coaches.

Before using any of these passes, please read the advice at the beginning of this chapter.

Pass Height In Metres (Feet)	From To	Max gradient	Conditions and Comments
㉒ Faucille (France) 1323 (4341)	Gex *Morez*	10%	UO. MWR 5m (16'5") Fairly wide, winding road (N5) across the Jura mountains; negotiable by caravans but probably better to follow route via La Cure-St Cergue-Nyon.
㉓ Fern (Austria) 1209 (3967)	Nassereith *Lermoos*	8%	UC. MWR 6m (19'8") Obstructed intermittently during winter. An easy pass on road 179 but slippery when wet; heavy traffic at summer weekends. Connects with Holzleiten Sattel Pass at S end for travel to/from Innsbruck – see below.
㉔ Flexen (Austria) 1784 (5853)	Lech *Rauzalpe (nr Arlberg Pass)*	10%	UC. MWR 5.5m (18') The magnificent 'Flexenstrasse', a well-engineered mountain road (no. 198) with tunnels and galleries. The road from Lech to Warth, N of the pass, is usually closed Nov-Apr due to danger of avalanche. **Not recommended for caravans.**
㉕ Flüela (Switzerland) 2383 (7818)	Davos-Dorf *Susch*	12.50%	OC Nov-May. MWR 5m (16'5") MWV 2.3m (7'6") Easy ascent from Davos on road no. 28; some acute hairpin bends on the E side; bitumen surface.
㉖ Forclaz (Switzerland – France) 1527 (5010)	Martigny *Argentière*	8.50%	UO Forclaz; OC Montets Dec-early Apr. MWR 5m (16'5") MWV 2.5m (8'2") Good road over the pass and to the French border; long, hard climb out of Martigny; narrow and rough over Col-des-Montets on D1506 (N506).
㉗ Foscagno (Italy) 2291 (7516)	Bormio *Livigno*	12.50%	OC Nov-May. MWR 3.3m (10'10") Narrow and winding road (S301) through lonely mountains, generally poor surface. Long winding ascent with many blind bends; not always well-guarded. Descent includes winding rise and fall over the Passo-d'Eira 2,200m (7,218). **Not recommended for caravans.**
㉘ Fugazze (Italy) 1159 (3802)	Rovereto *Valli-del-Pasubio*	14%	UO. MWR 3.5m (11'6") Very winding road (S46) with some narrow sections, particularly on N side. The many blind bends and several hairpin bends call for extra care. **Not recommended for caravans.**
㉙ Furka (Switzerland) 2431 (7976)	Gletsch *Realp*	11%	UC Oct-Jun. MWR 4m (13'1") MWV 2.25m (7'6") Well-graded road (no. 19) with narrow sections (single track in place on E side) and several hairpin bends on both ascent and descent. Fine views of the Rhône Glacier. Beware of coaches and traffic build-up. **Not recommended for caravans.** Alternative rail tunnel available.
㉚ Galibier (France) 2645 (8678)	La Grave *St Michel-de-Maurienne*	12.50%	UC Oct-Jun. MWR 3m (9'10") Mainly wide, well-surfaced road (D902) but unprotected and narrow over summit. From Col-du-Lautaret it rises over the Col-du-Telegraphe then 11 more hairpin bends. Ten hairpin bends on descent then 5km (3.1 miles) narrow and rough; easier in N to S direction. Limited parking at summit. **Not recommended for caravans.** (Single-track tunnel under the Galibier summit, controlled by traffic lights; caravans are not permitted.)
㉛ Gardena (Grödner-Joch) (Italy) 2121 (6959)	Val Gardena *Corvara-in-Badia*	12.50%	OC Dec-Jun. MWR 5m (16'5") A well-engineered road (S243), very winding on descent. Fine views. **Caravans prohibited.**
㉜ Gavia (Italy) 2621 (8599)	Bormio *Ponte-di-Legno*	20%	UC Oct-Jul. MWR 3m (9'10") MWV 1.8m (5'11") Steep, narrow, difficult road (P300) with frequent passing bays; many hairpin bends and gravel surface; not for the faint-hearted; extra care necessary. **Not recommended for caravans.** Long winding ascent on Bormio side.

Before using any of these passes, please read the advice at the beginning of this chapter.

	Pass Height In Metres (Feet)	From To	Max gradient	Conditions and Comments
33	**Gerlos** (Austria) 1628 (5341)	Zell-am-Ziller *Wald im Pinzgau*	9%	UO. MWR 4m (13'1") Hairpin ascent out of Zell to modern toll road (B165); the old, steep, narrow and winding route with passing bays and 14% gradient is not rec but is negotiable with care. Views of Krimml waterfalls. **Caravans prohibited.**
34	**Gorges-du-Verdon** (France) 1032 (3386)	Castellane *Moustiers–Ste Marie*	9%	UO. MWR probably 5m (16'5") On road D952 over Col-d'Ayen and Col-d'Olivier. Moderate gradients but slow, narrow and winding. Poss heavy traffic.
35	**Grand St Bernard** (Switzerland – Italy) 2469 (8100)	Martigny *Aosta*	~1%	UC Oct-Jun. MWR 4m (13'1") MWV 2.5m (8' 2") Modern road to entrance of road tunnel on road no. 21/E27 (UO), then narrow but bitumen surface over summit to border; also good in Italy. Suitable for caravans using tunnel. Pass road feasible but not recommended. See *Road Tunnels* in this section.
36	**Grimsel** (Switzerland) 2164 (7100)	Innertkirchen *Gletsch*	10%	UC mid Oct-late Jun. MWR 5m (16'5") MWV 2.25m (7'6") A fairly easy, modern road (no. 6) with heavy traffic at weekends. A long winding ascent, finally hairpin bends; then a terraced descent with six hairpins (some tight) into the Rhône valley. Good surface; fine scenery.
37	**Grossglockner** (Austria) 2503 (8212)	Bruck-an-der- Grossglocknerstrasse *Heiligenblut*	12.50%	UC late Cct-early May. MWR 5.5m (18') Well-engineered road (no. 107) but many hairpins; heavy traffic; moderate but very long ascent/descent. Negotiable preferably S to N by caravans. Avoid side road to highest point at Edelweissespitze if towing, as road is very steep and narrow. Magnificent scenery. Tolls charged. Road closed from 2200-0500 hrs (summer). Alternative Felbertauern road tunnel between Lienz and Mittersil (toll).
38	**Hahntennjoch** (Austria) 1894 (6250)	Imst *Elmen*	15%	UC Nov-May. A minor pass. **Caravans prohibited.**
39	**Hochtannberg** (Austria) 1679 (5509)	Schröcken *Warth (nr Lech)*	14%	OC Jan-Mar. MWR 4m (13'1") A reconstructed modern road (no. 200). W to E long ascent with many hairpins. Easier E to W. **Not recommended for caravans.**
40	**Holzleiten Sattel** (Austria) 1126 (3694)	Nassereith *Obsteig*	12.50%	(12.5%), UO. MWR 5m (16'5") Road surface good on W side; poor on E. Light traffic; gradients no problem. **Not recommended for caravans.**
41	**Iseran** (France) 2770 (9088)	Bourg-St Maurice *Lanslebourg*	11%	UC mid Cct-late Jun. MWR 4m (13'1") Second highest pass in the Alps on road D902. Well-graced with reasonable bends, average surface. Several unlit tunnels on N approach. **Not recommended for caravans.**

Before using any of these passes, please read the advice at the beginning of this chapter.

	Pass Height in Metres (Feet)	From To	Max gradient	Conditions and Comments
42	**Izoard** (France) 2360 (7743)	Guillestre *Briançon*	12.50%	UC late Oct–mid Jun. MWR 5m (16'5") Fine scenery. Winding, sometimes narrow road (D902) with many hairpin bends; care required at several unlit tunnels near Guillestre. **Not recommended for caravans.**
43	**Jaun** (Switzerland) 1509 (4951)	Bulle *Reidenbach*	14%	UC. MWR 4m (13'1") MWV 2.25m (7'6") A modern but generally narrow road (no. 11); some poor sections on ascent and several hairpin bends on descent.
44	**Julier** (Switzerland) 2284 (7493)	Tiefencastel *Silvaplana*	13%	UO. MWR 4m (13'1") MWV 2.5m (8'2") Well-engineered road (no. 3) approached from Chur via Sils. Fine scenery. Negotiable by caravans, preferably from N to S, but a long haul and many tight hairpins. Alternative rail tunnel from Thusis to Samedan. See *Rail Tunnels* in this section.
45	**Katschberg** (Austria) 1641 (5384)	Spittal-an-der-Drau *St Michael*	20%	UO. MWR 6m (19'8") Good wide road (no. 99) with no hairpins but steep gradients particularly from S. Suitable only light caravans. Parallel Tauern/Katschberg toll motorway A10/E55 and road tunnels.
46	**Klausen** (Switzerland) 1948 (6391)	Altdorf *Linthal*	10%	UC late Oct–early Jun. MWR 5m (16'5") MWV 2.30m (7'6") Narrow and winding in places, but generally easy in spite of a number of sharp bends. **Caravans prohibited** between Unterschächen and Linthal (no. 17).
47	**Larche (della Maddalena)** (France – Italy) 1994 (6542)	La Condamine-Châtelard *Vinadio*	8.50%	OC Dec–Mar. MWR 3.5m (11'6") An easy, well-graded road (D900); long, steady ascent on French side, many hairpins on Italian side (S21). Fine scenery; ample parking at summit.
48	**Lautaret** (France) 2058 (6752)	Le Bourg-d'Oisans *Briançon*	12.50%	OC Dec–Mar. MWR 4m (13'1") Modern, evenly graded but winding road (D1091), and unguarded in places; very fine scenery; suitable for caravans but with care through narrow tunnels.
49	**Leques** (France) 1146 (3760)	Barrême *Castellane*	8%	UO. MWR 4m (13'1") On Route Napoléon (D4085). Light traffic; excellent surface; narrow in places on N ascent. S ascent has many hairpins.
50	**Loibl (Ljubelj)** (Austria – Slovenia) 1067 (3500)	Unterloibl *Kranj*	20%	UO. MWR 6m (19'8") Steep rise and fall over Little Loibl pass (E652) to 1.6km (1 mile) tunnel under summit. **Caravans prohibited**. The old road over the summit is closed to through-traffic.
51	**Lukmanier (Lucomagno)** (Switzerland) 1916 (6286)	Olivone *Disentis*	9%	UC early Nov–late May. MWR 5m (16'5") MWV 2.25m (7'6") Rebuilt, modern road.
52	**Maloja** (Switzerland) 1815 (5955)	Silvaplana *Chiavenna*	9%	UO. MWR 4m (13'1") MWV 2.5m (8'2") Escarpment facing south; fairly easy, but many hairpin bends on descent; negotiable by caravans but possibly difficult on ascent. On road no.3/S37.

Before using any of these passes, please read the advice at the beginning of this chapter.

	Pass / Height In Metres (Feet)	From / To	Max gradient	Conditions and Comments
53	**Mauria** (Italy) 1298 (4258)	Lozzo di Cadore / Ampezzo	7%	UO. MWR 5m (16'5") A well-designed road (S52) with easy, winding ascent and descent.
54	**Mendola** (Italy) 1363 (4472)	Appiano/Eppan / Sarnonico	12.50%	UO. MWR 5m (16'5") A fairly straightforward but winding road (S42), well-guarded, many hairpins. Take care overhanging cliffs if towing. The E side going down to Bolzano is not wide enough for caravans, especially difficult on busy days, not recommended for caravans.
55	**Mont Cenis** (France – Italy) 2083 (6834)	Lanslebourg / Susa	12.50%	UC Nov-May. MWR 5m (16'5") Approach by industrial valley. An easy highway (D1006/S25) with mostly good surface spectacular scenery; long descent into Italy with few stopping places. Alternative Fréjus road tunnel available.
56	**Monte Croce-di-Comélico (Kreuzberg)** (Italy) 1636 (5368)	San Candido / Santo-Stefano-di-Cadore	8.50%	UO. MWR 5m (16'5") A winding road (S52) with moderate gradients, beautiful scenery.
57	**Montgenèvre** (France – Italy) 1850 (6072)	Briançon / Cesana-Torinese	9%	UO. MWR 5m (16'5") Easy, modern road (N94/S24), some tight hairpin bends, good road surface on French side; road widened & tunnels improved on Italian side, in need of some repair but still easy. Much used by lorries; may need to give way to large vehicles on hairpins.
58	**Monte Giovo (Jaufen)** (Italy) 2094 (6870)	Merano / Vipiteno/Sterzing	12.50%	UC Nov-May. MWR 4m (13'1") Many well-engineered hairpin bends on S44; good scenery. **Caravans prohibited.**
	Montets (See Forclaz)			
59	**Morgins** (France – Switzerland) 1369 (4491)	Abondance / Monthey	14%	UO. MWR 4m (13'1") A lesser used route (D22) through pleasant, forested countryside crossing French/Swiss border. **Not recommended for caravans.**
60	**Mosses** (Switzerland) 1445 (4740)	Aigle / Château-d'Oex	8.50%	UO. MWR 4m (13'1") MWV 2.25m (7'6") A modern road (no. 11). Aigle side steeper and narrow in places.
61	**Nassfeld (Pramollo)** (Austria – Italy) 1530 (5020)	Tröpolach / Pontebba	20%	OC Late Nov-Mar. MWR 4m (13'1") The winding descent on road no. 90 into Italy has been improved but not rec for caravans.
62	**Nufenen (Novena) (Switzerland)** 2478 (8130)	Ulrichen / Airolo	10%	UC Mid Oct-mid Jun. MWR 4m (13'1") MWV 2.25m (7'6") The approach roads are narrow, with tight bends, but the road over the pass is good; negotiable with care. Long drag from Ulrichen.
63	**Oberalp** (Switzerland) 2044 (6706)	Andermatt / Disentis	10%	UC Nov-late May. MWR 5m (16'5") MWV 2.3m (7'6") Much improved and widened road (no.19) but narrow in places on E side; many tight hairpin bends, but long level stretch on summit. Alternative rail tunnel during the winter. **Not recommended for caravans.**

Before using any of these passes, please read the advice at the beginning of this chapter.

Pass Height in Metres (Feet)	From To	Max gradient	Conditions and Comments
64 **Ofen (Fuorn)** (Switzerland) 2149 (7051)	Zernez *Santa Maria-im-Münstertal*	12.50%	UO. MWR 4m (13'1") MWV 2.25m (7'6") Good road (no. 28) through Swiss National Park.
65 **Petit St Bernard** (France–Italy) 2188 (7178)	Bourg-St Maurice *Pré-St Didier*	8.50%	UC mid Oct-Jun. MWR 5m (16'5") Outstanding scenery, but poor surface and unguarded broken edges near summit. Easiest from France (D1090); sharp hairpins on climb from Italy (S26). Caravans prohibited.
66 **Pillon** (Switzerland) 1546 (5072)	Le Sépey *Gsteig*	9%	OC Jan-Feb. MWR 4m (13'1") MWV 2.25m (7'6") A comparatively easy modern road.
67 **Plöcken (Monte Croce-Carnico)** (Austria–Italy) 1362 (4468)	Kötschach *Paluzza*	14%	OC Dec-Apr. MWR 5m (16'5") A modern road (no. 110) with long, reconstructed sections; OC to caravans due to heavy traffic on summer weekends; delay likely at the border. Long, slow, twisty pull from S, easier from N.
68 **Pordoi** (Italy) 2239 (7346)	Arabba *Canazei*	10%	OC Dec-Apr. MWR 5m (16'5") An excellent modern road (S48) with numerous blind hairpin bends; fine scenery, used by tour coaches. Long drag when combined with Falzarego pass.
69 **Pötschen** (Austria) 982 (3222)	Bad Ischl *Bad Aussee*	9%	UO. MWR 7m (23') A modern road (no. 145). Good scenery.
70 **Radstädter-Tauern** (Austria) 1738 (5702)	Radstadt *Mauterndorf*	16%	OC Jan-Mar. MWR 5m (16'5") N ascent steep (road no. 99) but not difficult otherwise; but negotiable by light caravans using parallel toll m'way (A10) through tunnel.
71 **Résia (Reschen)** (Italy–Austria) 1504 (4934)	Spondigna *Pfunds*	10%	UO. MWR 6m (19'8") A good, straightforward alternative to the Brenner Pass. Fine views but no stopping places. On road S40/180.
72 **Restefond (La Bonette)** (France) 2802 (9193)	Barcelonnette *St Etienne-de-Tinée*	16%	UC Oct-Jun. MWR 3m (9'10") The highest pass in the Alps. Rebuilt, resurfaced road (D64) with rest area at summit – top loop narrow and unguarded. Winding with hairpin bends. Not recommended for caravans.
73 **Rolle** (Italy) 1970 (6463)	Predazzo *Mezzano*	9%	OC Dec-Mar. MWR 5m (16'5") A well-engineered road (S50) with many hairpin bends on both sides; very beautiful scenery; good surface.
Rombo (See Timmelsjoch)			
74 **St Gotthard (San Gottardo)** (Switzerland) 2108 (6916)	Göschenen *Airolo*	10%	UC mid Oct-early Jun. MWR 6m (19'8") MHV 3.6m (11'9") MWV 2.5m (8'2") Modern, fairly easy two- to three-lane road (A2/E35). Heavy traffic. Alternative road tunnel.

Pass Height In Metres (Feet)	From To	Max gradient	Conditions and Comments
75 San Bernardino (Switzerland) 2066 (6778)	Mesocco Hinterrhein	10%	UC Oct-late Jun. MWR 4m (13'1") MWV 2.25m (7'6") Easy modern road (A13/E43) on N and S approaches to tunnel, narrow and winding over summit via tunnel suitable for caravans.
76 Schlucht (France) 1139 (3737)	Gérardmer Munster	7%	UO. MWR 5m (16'5") An extremely picturesque route (D417) crossing the Vosges mountains, with easy, wide bends on the descent. Good surface.
77 Saeberg (Jezersko) (Austria–Slovenia) 1218 (3996)	Eisenkappel Kranj	12.50%	UO. MWR 5m (16'5") An alternative to the steeper Loibl and Wurzen passes on B82/210; moderate climb with winding, hairpin ascent and descent. Not recommended for caravans.
78 Sella (Italy) 2240 (7349)	Selva Canazei	11%	OC Dec-Jan. MWR 5m (16'5") A well-engineered, winding road; exceptional views of Dolomites. Caravans prohibited.
79 Sestriere (Italy) 2033 (6670)	Cesana-Torinese Pinarolo	10%	UO MWR 6m (19'8") Mostly bitumen surface on road R23. Fairly easy, fine scenery.
80 Silvretta (Bielerhöhe) (Austria) 2032 (6666)	Partenen Galtur	11%	UC late Oct-early Jun. MWR 5m (16'5") Mostly reconstructed road (188); 32 easy hairpin bends on W ascent; E side more straightforward. Tolls charged. Caravans prohibited.
81 Simplon (Switzerland – Italy) 2005 (6578)	Brig Domodóssola	11%	OC Nov-Apr. MWR 7m (23') MWV 2.5m (8'2") An easy, reconstructed, modern road (E62/S33), 21km (13 miles) lo ng, continuous ascent to summit; good views, many stopping places. Surface better on Swiss side. Alternative rail tunnel fr Kandersteg in operation from Easter to September.
82 Splügen (Switzerland – Italy) 2113 (6932)	Splügen Chiavenna	13%	UC Nov-Jun. MWR 3.5m (11'6") MHV 2.8m (9'2") MWV 2.3m (7'6") Mostly narrow, winding road (S36), with extremely tight hairpin bends, not well guarded; care also required at many tunnels/galleries. Not recommended for caravans.
83 Stelvio (Italy) 2757 (9045)	Bormio Spondigna	12.50%	UC Oct-late Jun. MWR 4m (13'1") MLV 10m (32') Third highest pass in Alps on S38; 40-50 acute hairpin bends either side, all well-engineered; good surface, traffic often heavy. Hairpin bends too acute for long vehicles. Not recommended for caravans.
84 Susten (Switzerland) 2224 (7297)	Innertkirchen Wassen	9%	UC Nov-Jun. MWR 6m (19'8") MWV 2.5m (8'2") Scenic, well-guarded road (no. 11); easy gradients and turns; heavy weekend traffic. East side easier than west. Negotiable by caravans (rec small/medium sized only) with care, not for the faint-hearted. Large summit parking area.
85 Tenda (Tende) Italy–France 1321 (4334)	Borgo-San Dalmazzo Tende	9%	UO. MWF 6m (19'8") Well-guarded, modern road (S20/ND6204) with several hairpin bends; road tunnel (height 3.3m) at summit narrow with poor road surface. Less steep on Italian side. Caravans prohibited during winter.

Before using any of these passes, please read the advice at the beginning of this chapter.

	Pass Height in Metres (Feet)	From To	Max gradient	Conditions and Comments
86	**Thurn** (Austria) 1274 (4180)	Kitzbühel *Mittersill*	8.50%	UO. MWR 5m (16'5") MWV 2.5m (8'2") A good road (no. 161) with narrow stretches; N approach rebuilt. Several good parking areas.
87	**Timmelsjoch (Rombo)** (Austria – Italy) 2509 (8232)	Obergurgl *Moso*	14%	UC mid Oct-Jun. MWR 3.5m (11'6") Border closed at night 8pm to 7am. On the pass (road no 186/S44b) caravans are prohibited. (toll charged), as some tunnels on Italian side too narrow for larger vehicles. Easiest N to S.
88	**Tonale** (Italy) 1883 (6178)	Edolo *Dimaro*	10%	UO. MWR 5m (16'5") A relatively easy road (S42); steepest on W; long drag. Fine views.
89	**Tre Croci** (Italy) 1809 (5935)	Cortina-d'Ampezzo *Auronzo-di-Cadore*	11%	OC Dec-Mar. MWR 6m (19'8") An easy pass on road R48; fine scenery.
90	**Turracher Höhe** (Austria) 1763 (5784)	Predlitz *Ebene-Reichenau*	23%	UO. MWR 4m (13'1") Formerly one of the steepest mountain roads (no. 95) in Austria; now improved. Steep, fairly straightforward ascent followed by a very steep descent; good surface and mainly two-lane; fine scenery. Not recommended for caravans.
91	**Umbrail** (Switzerland – Italy) 2501 (8205)	Santa Maria-im-Münstertal *Bormio*	9%	UC Nov-early Jun. MWR 4.3m (14'1") MWV 2.3m (7'6") Highest Swiss pass (road S38); mostly tarmac with some gravel surface. Narrow with 34 hairpin bends. Not recommended for caravans.
92	**Vars** (France) 2109 (6919)	St Paul-sur-Ubaye *Guillestre*	9%	OC Dec-Mar. MWR 5m (16'5") Easy winding ascent and descent on D902 with 14 hairpin bends; good surface.
93	**Wurzen (Koren)** (Austria – Slovenia) 1073 (3520)	Riegersdorf *Kranjska Gora*	20%	UO. MWR 4m (13'1") Steep two-lane road (no. 109), otherwise not particularly difficult; better on Austrian side; heavy traffic summer weekends; delays likely at the border. Caravans prohibited.
94	**Zirler Berg** (Austria) 1009 (3310)	Seefeld *Zirl*	16.50%	UO. MWR 7m (23') South facing escarpment, good, modern road (no. 171). Heavy tourist traffic and long steep descent with one hairpin bend into Inn Valley. Steepest section from hairpin bend down to Zirl. Caravans not permitted northbound and not recommended southbound.

Technical information by courtesy of the Automobile Association. Additional update and amendments supplied by caravanners and tourers who have themselves used the passes and tunnels. The Caravan and Motorhome Club has not checked the information contained in these tables and cannot accept responsibility for their accuracy, or for any errors, omissions, or their effects.

Major Alpine Rail Tunnels

Before using any of these tunnels, please read the advice at the beginning of this chapter.

	Tunnel	Route	Journey Time	General Information and Comments	Contact
A	**Albula** (Switzerland) 5.9 km (3.5 miles)	Chur – St Moritz Thusis to Samedan	80 mins	MHV 2.85m + MWV 1.40m or MHV 2.50m + MWV 2.20 This tunnel no longer operates a car transport service, but there are regular passenger transport services.	Thusis (081) 2884716 Samedan (081) 2885511 www.rhb.ch
B	**Furka** (Switzerland) 15.4 km (9.5 miles)	Andermatt – Brig Realp to Oberwald	15 mins	Hourly all year from 6am to 9pm weekdays; half-hourly weekends. MHV 3.5m Saturdays in February and March are exceptionally busy.	(027) 9277777 www.mgbahn.ch
C	**Oberalp** (Switzerland) 28 km (17.3 miles)	Andermatt – Disentis Andermatt to Sedrun	60 mins	MHV 2.50m 2-6 trains daily when the Oberalp Pass is closed for winter. Advance booking is compulsory.	(027) 9277777 www.mgbahn.ch
D	**Lötschberg** (Switzerland) 14 km (8.7 miles)	Bern – Brig Kandersteg to Goppenstein	15 mins	MHV 2.90m Frequent all year half-hourly service. Journey time 15 minutes. Advance booking unnecessary; extension to Hohtenn operates when Goppenstein-Gampel road is closed.	Kandersteg (0900 553333 www.bls.ch/autoverlad
E	**Simplon** (Switzerland – Italy)	Brig – Domodossola Brig to Iselle	20 mins	10 trains daily, all year.	(0900 300300 http://mct.sbb.ch/mct/ autoverlad
F	**Lötschberg/ Simplon** Switzerland – Italy	Bern – Domodossola Kandersteg to Iselle	75 mins	Limited service Easter to mid-October up to 3 days a week (up to 10 times a day) and at Christmas for vehicles max height 2.50m, motor caravans up to 5,000 kg. Advance booking compulsory.	(0900 553333 www.bls.ch
F	**Tauerbahn** (Austria)	Bad Gastein – Spittal an der Drau Böckstein to Mallnitz	11 mins	East of and parallel to Grossglockner pass. Half-hourly service all year.	(05) 1717 http://autoschleuse.oebb.at
G	**Vereina** (Switzerland) 19.6 km (11.7 miles)	Klosters – Susch Selfranga to Sagliains	18 mins	MLV 12m Half-hourly daytime service all year. Journey time 18 minutes. Restricted capacity for vehicles over 3.30m high during winter w/ends and public holidays. Steep approach to Klosters.	(081) 2883737 www.rhb.ch

NOTES: Information believed to be correct at time of publication. Detailed timetables are available from the appropriate tourist offices. Always check for current information before you travel.

Major Alpine Road Tunnels

Before using any of these tunnels, please read the advice at the beginning of this chapter.

	Tunnel	Route and Height above Sea Level	General Information and Comments
H	**Arlberg** (Austria) 14 km (8.75 miles)	**Langen to St Anton** 1220m (4000')	On B197 parallel and to S of Arlberg Pass which is closed to caravans/trailers. **Motorway vignette required; tolls charged.** www.arlberg.com
I	**Bosruck** (Austria) 5.5 km (3.4 miles)	**Spital am Pyhrn to Selzthal** 742m (2434')	To E of Pyhrn pass; with Gleinalm Tunnel (see below) forms part of A9 a'bahn between Linz & Graz. Max speed 80 km/h (50 mph). Use dipped headlights, no overtaking. Occasional emergency lay-bys with telephones. **Motorway vignette required; tolls charged.**
J	**Felbertauern** (Austria) 5.3 km (3.25 miles)	**Mittersill to Matrei** 1525m (5000')	MWR 7m (23'), tunnel height 4.5m (14'9"). On B109 W of and parallel to Grossglockner pass; downwards gradient of 9% S to N with sharp bend before N exit. Wheel chains may be needed on approach Nov-Apr. **Tolls charged.**
K	**Fréjus** (France – Italy) 12.8 km (8 miles)	**Modane to Bardonecchia** 1220m (4000')	MWR 9m (29'6"), tunnel height 4.3m (14'). Min/max speed 60/70 km/h (37/44 mph). Return tickets valid until midnight on 7th day after day of issue. Season tickets are available. Approach via A43 and D1006; heavy use by freight vehicles. Good surface on approach roads. **Tolls charged.** www.sftrf.fr
L	**Gleinalm** (Austria) 8.3 km (5 miles)	**St Michael to Fiesach (nr Graz)** 817m (2680')	Part of A9 Pyhrn a'bahn. **Motorway vignette required; tolls charged.**
M	**Grand St Bernard** (Switzerland – Italy) 5.8 km (3.6 miles)	**Bourg-St Pierre to St Rhémy (Italy)** 1925m (7570')	MHV 4m (13'1"), MWV 2.55m (8'2.5"), MLV 18m (60'). Min/max speed 40/80 km/h (24/50 mph). On E27. Passport check, Customs & toll offices at entrance; breakdown bays at each end with telephones; return tickets valid one month. Although approaches are covered, wheel chains may be needed in winter. Season tickets are available. **Motorway vignette required; tolls charged.** For 24-hour information tel: (027) 7884400 (Switzerland) or 0165 780902 (Italy), www.letunnel.com
N	**Karawanken** (Austria – Slovenia) 8 km (5 miles)	**Rosenbach to Jesenice** 610m (2000')	On A11. **Motorway vignette required; tolls charged.**
O	**Mont Blanc** (France – Italy) 11.6 km (7.2 miles)	**Chamonix to Courmayeur** 1381m (4530')	MHV 4.7m (15'5"), MWV 6m (19'6") On N205 France, S26 (Italy). Max speed in tunnel 70 km/h (44 mph) – lower limits when exiting; min speed 50 km/h. Leave 150m between vehicles; ensure enough fuel for 30km. Return tickets valid until midnight on 7th day after issue. Season tickets are available. **Tolls charged.** www.tunnelmb.net

Before using any of these tunnels, please read the advice at the beginning of this chapter.

	Tunnel	Route and Height above Sea Level	General Information and Comments
P	**Munt La Schera** (Switzerland – Italy) 3.5 km (2 miles)	**Zernez to Livigno** 1706m (5597')	MHV 3.6m (11'9"), MWV 2.5m (8'2"). Open 24 hours; single lane traffic controlled by traffic lights; roads from Livogno S to the Bernina Pass and Bormio closed Dec-Apr. On N28 (Switzerland). **Tolls charged.** Tel: ((081) 8561888, www.livigno.eu
Q	**St Gotthard** (Switzerland) 16.3 km (10 miles)	**Göschenen to Airolo** 1159m (3800')	Tunnel height 4.5m (14'9"), single carriageway 7.5m (25') wide. Max speed 80 km/h (50 mph). No tolls, but tunnel is part of Swiss motorway network (A2). **Motorway vignette required.** Tunnel closed 8pm to 5am Monday to Friday for periods during June and September. Heavy traffic and delays high season. www.gotthard-strassentunnel.ch
-	**Ste Marie-aux-Mines** 6.8 km (4.25 miles)	**St Dié to Ste-Marie-aux-Mines** 772m (2533')	Re-opened October 2008; the longest road tunnel situated entirely in France. Also known as Maurice Lemaire Tunnel, through the Vosges in north-east France from Lusse on N159 to N59. **Tolls charged.** Alternate route via Col-de-Ste Marie on D459.
R	**San Bernardino** (Switzerland) 6.6 km (4 miles)	**Hinterrhein to San Bernardino** 1644m (5396')	Tunnel height 4.8m (15'9"), width 7m (23'). On A13 motorway. No stopping or overtaking; keep 100m between vehicles; breakdown bays with telephones. Max speed 80 km/h (50 mph). **Motorway vignette required.**
S	**Tauern and Katschberg** (Austria) 6.4 km (4 miles) & 5.4km (3.5 miles)	**Salzburg to Villach** 1340m (4396') & 1110m (3642')	The two major tunnels on the A10, height 4.5m (14'9"), width 7.5m (25'). **Motorway vignette required; tolls charged.**

NOTES: Dipped headlights should be used (unless stated otherwise) when travelling through road tunnels, even when the road appears well lit. In some countries police make spot checks and impose on-the-spot fines. During the winter wheel chains may be required on the approaches to some tunnels. These must not be used in tunnels and lay-bys are available for the removal and refitting of wheel chains. Much of the information contained in the table was originally supplied by The Automobile Association and other motoring and tourist organisations. Updates and amendments are supplied by caravanners and tourers who have themselves used the passes and tunnels.

The Caravan and Motorhome Club has not checked the information contained in these tables and cannot accept responsibility for their accuracy, or for any errors, omissions, or for their effects.

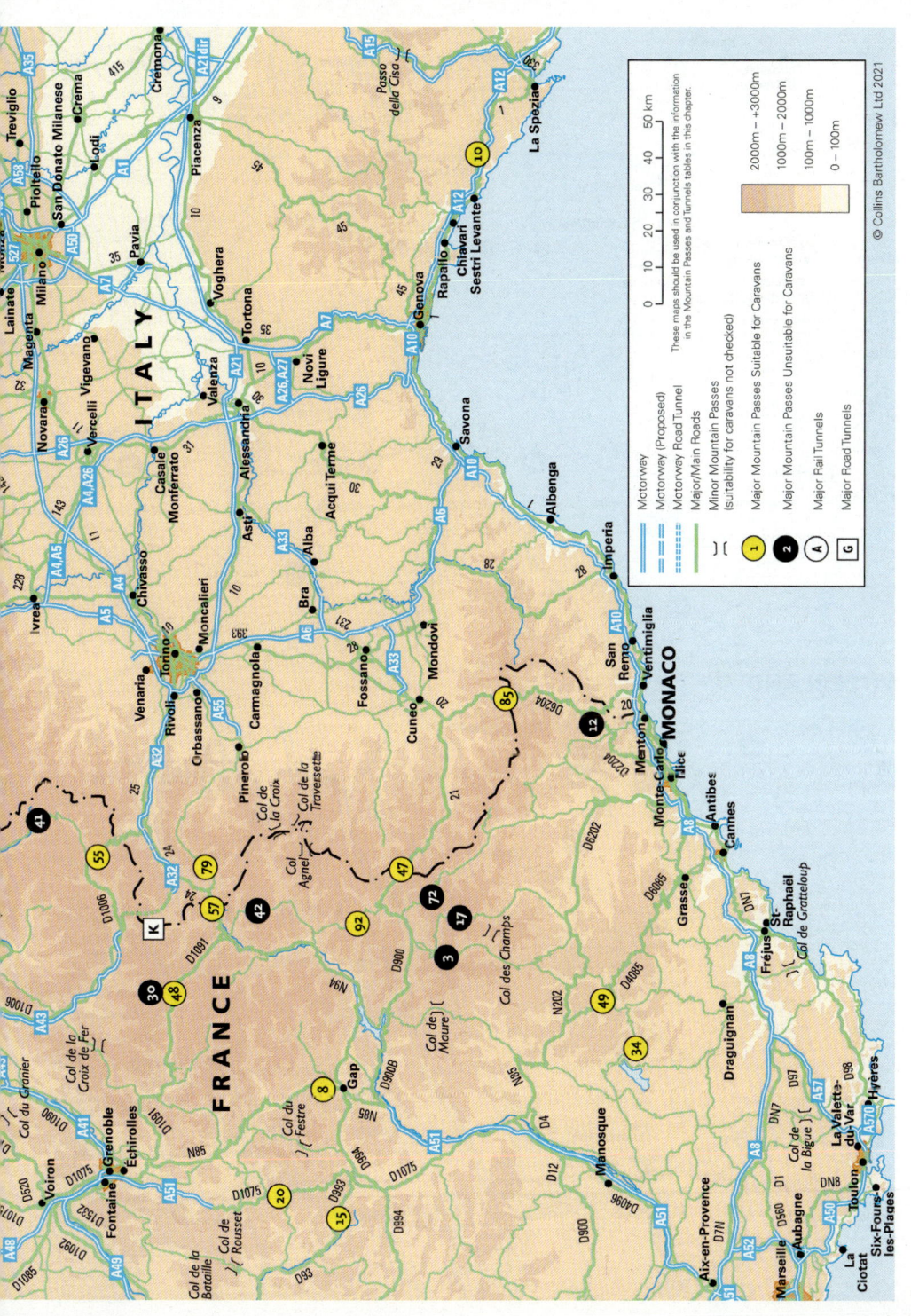

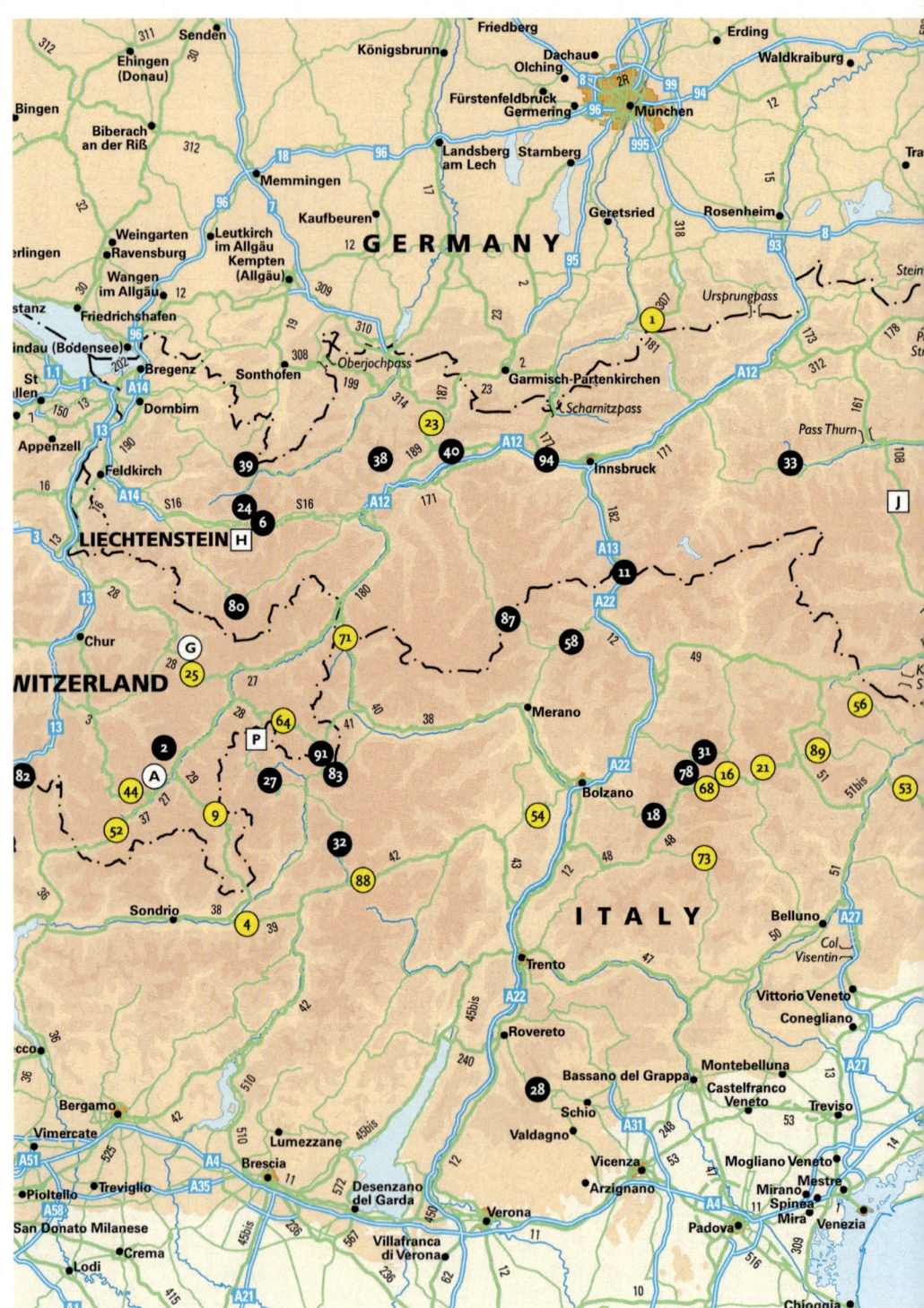

Legend

Motorway	
Motorway (Proposed)	
Motorway Road Tunnel	
Major/Main Roads	
Minor Mountain Passes (suitability for caravans not checked)	
①	Major Mountain Passes Suitable for Caravans
● 2	Major Mountain Passes Unsuitable for Caravans
Ⓐ	Major Rail Tunnels
Ⓖ	Major Road Tunnels

Scale: 0 10 20 30 40 50 km

These maps should be used in conjunction with the information in the Mountain Passes and Tunnels tables in this chapter.

Elevation legend:
- 2000m – +3000m
- 1000m – 2000m
- 100m – 1000m
- 0 – 100m

© Collins Bartholomew Ltd 2021

Major Mountain Passes – Pyrenees and Northern Spain

Before using any of these passes, please read the advice at the beginning of this chapter.

	Pass / Height In Metres (Feet)	From / To	Max Gradient	Conditions and Comments
1	**Aubisque** (France) 1710 (5610)	Eaux Bonnes / Argelés-Gazost	10%	UC mid Oct–Jun. MWR 3.5m (11'6") Very winding; continuous on D918 but easy ascent; descent including Col-d'Aubisque 1709m (5607 feet) and Col-du-Soulor 1450m (4757 feet); 8km (5 miles) of very narrow, rough, unguarded road with steep drop. **Not recommended for caravans.**
2	**Bonaigua** (Spain) 2072 (6797)	Viella (Vielha) / Esterri-d'Aneu	8.5%	UC Nov–Apr. MWR 4.3m (14'1") Twisting, narrow road (C28) with many hairpins and some precipitous drops. **Not recommended for caravans.** Alternative route to Lerida (Lleida) through Viella (Vielha) Tunnel is open all year.
3	**Cabrejas** (Spain) 1167 (3829)	Tarancon / Cuenca	14%	UO. On N400/A40. Sometimes blocked by snow for 24 hours. MWR 5m (16')
4	**Col-d'Haltza and Col-de-Burdincurutcheta** (France) 782 (2565) and 1135 (3724)	St Jean-Pied-de-Port / Larrau	11%	UO. A narrow road (D18/D19) leading to Iraty skiing area. Narrow with some tight hairpin bends; rarely has central white line and stretches are unguarded. Not for the faint-hearted. **Not recommended for caravans.**
5	**Envalira** (France – Andorra) 2407 (7897)	Pas-de-la-Casa / Andorra	12.5%	OC Nov–Apr. MWR 6m (19'8") Good road (N22/CG2) with wide bends on ascent and descent; fine views. MHV 3.5m (11'6") on N approach near l'Hospitalet. Early start rec in summer to avoid border delays. Envalira Tunnel (toll) reduces congestion and avoids highest part of pass.
6	**Escudo** (Spain) 1011 (3317)	Santander / Burgos	17%	UO. MWR probably 5m (16'5") Asphalt surface but many bends and steep gradients. **Not recommended in winter.** On N632; A67/N611 easier route.
7	**Guadarrama** (Spain) 1511 (4957)	Guadarrama / San Rafael	14%	UO. MWR 6m (19'8") On NVI to the NW of Madrid but may be avoided by using AP6 motorway from Villalba to San Rafael or Villacastín (toll).
8	**Ibañeta (Roncevalles)** (France – Spain) 1057 (3468)	St Jean-Pied-de-Port / Pamplona	10%	UO. MWR 4m (13'1") Slow and winding, scenic route on N135.
9	**Manzanal** (Spain) 1221 (4005)	Madrid / La Coruña	7%	UO. Sometimes blocked by snow for 24 hours. On A6.

Before using any of these passes, please read the advice at the beginning of this chapter.

	Pass / Height In Metres (Feet)	From / To	Max Gradient	Conditions and Comments
10	**Navacerrada** (Spain) 1860 (6102)	Madrid / *Segovia*	17%	OC Nov-Mar. On M601/CL601. Sharp hairpins. Possible but **not recommended for caravans.**
11	**Orduna** (Spain) 900 (2953)	Bilbao / *Burgos*	15%	UO. On A625/BU556; sometimes blocked by snow for 24 hours. Avoid by using AP68 motorway.
12	**Pajares** (Spain) 1270 (4167)	Oviedo / *Léon*	16%	UO. On N630; sometimes blocked by snow for 24 hours. **Not recommended for caravans.** Avoid by using AP66 motorway.
13	**Paramo-de-Masa** (Spain) 1050 (3445)	Santander / *Burgos*	8%	UO. On N623; sometimes blocked by snow for 24 hours.
14	**Peyresourde** (France) 1563 (5128)	Arreau / *Bagnères-de-Luchon*	10%	UO. MWR 4m (13'1") D618 somewhat narrow with several hairpin bends, though not difficult. **Not recommended for caravans.**
15	**Picos-de-Europa: Puerto-de-San Glorio, Puerto-de-Pontón, Puerto-de-Pandetrave** (Spain), 1609 (5279)	Unquera / *Riaño* ; Riaño / *Cangas-de-On:s* ; Portilla-de-La-Reina / *Santa Marina-de-Valdeón*	12%	UO. MWR probably 4m (13'1") Desfiladero de la Hermida on N621 good condition. Puerto-de-San-Glorio steep with many hairpin bends. For confident drivers only. Puerto-de-Ponton on N625, height 1280 metres (4200 feet). Best approach fr S as from N is very long uphill pull with many tight turns. Puerto-de-Pandetrave, height 1562 metres (5124 feet) on LE245 not rec when towing as main street of Santa Marina steep & narrow.
16	**Piqueras** (Spain) 1710 (5610)	Logroño / *Soria*	7%	UO. On N111; sometimes blocked by snow for 24 hours.
17	**Port** (France) 1249 (4098)	Tarascon-sur-Ariège / *Massat*	10%	OC Nov-Mar. MWR 4m (13'1") A fairly easy, scenic road (D618), but narrow on some bends.
18	**Portet-d'Aspet** (France) 1069 (3507)	Audressein / *Fronsac*	14%	UO. MWR 3.5m (11'6") Approached from W by the easy Col-des-Ares and Col-de-Buret; well-engineered but narrow road (D618); care needed on hairpin bends. **Not recommended for caravans.**
19	**Pourtalet** (France – Spain) 1792 (5879)	Laruns / *Biescas*	10%	UC late Oct-early Jun. MWR 3.5m (11'6") A fairly easy, unguarded road, but narrow in places. Easier from Spain (A136), steeper in France (D934). **Not recommended for caravans.**

Before using any of these passes, please read the advice at the beginning of this chapter.

Pass Height In Metres (Feet)	From To	Max Gradient	Conditions and Comments
20 **Puymorens** (France) 1915 (6283)	Ax-les-Thermes *Bourg-Madame*	10%	OC Nov-Apr. MWR 5.5m (18') MHV 3.5m (11'6") A generally easy, modern tarmac road (N20). Parallel toll road tunnel available.
21 **Quillane** (France) 1714 (5623)	Axat *Mont-Louis*	8.5%	OC Nov-Mar. MWR 5m (16'5") An easy, straightforward ascent and descent on D118.
22 **Somosierra** (Spain) 1444 (4738)	Madrid *Burgos*	10%	OC Mar-Dec. MWR 7m (23') On A1/E5; may be blocked following snowfalls. Snow-plough swept during winter months but wheel chains compulsory after snowfalls. Well-surfaced dual carriageway, tunnel at summit.
23 **Somport** (France–Spain) 1632 (5354)	Accous *Jaca*	10%	UO. MWR 3.5m (11'6") A favoured, old-established route; not particularly easy and narrow in places with many unguarded bends on French side (N134); excellent road on Spanish side (N330). Use of road tunnel advised – see *Pyrenean Road Tunnels* in this section. NB Visitors advise re-fuelling no later than Sabiñánigo when travelling south to north.
24 **Toses (Tosas)** (Spain) 1800 (5906)	Puigcerda *Ribes-de-Freser*	10%	UO MWR 5m (16'5") A fairly straightforward, but continuously winding, two-lane road (N152) with with a good surface but many sharp bends; some unguarded edges. Difficult in winter.
25 **Tourmalet** (France) 2114 (6936)	Ste Marie-de-Campan *Luz-St Sauveur*	12.5%	UC Oct-mid Jun. MWR 4m (13'1") The highest French Pyrenean route (D918); approaches good, though winding, narrow in places and exacting over summit; sufficiently guarded. Rough surface & uneven edges on west side. Not recommended for caravans.
26 **Urquiola** (Spain) 713 (2340)	Durango (Bilbao) *Vitoria/Gasteiz*	16%	UO. Sometimes closed by snow for 24 hours. On BI623/A623. Not recommended for caravans.

Major Pyrenean Road Tunnels

Before using any of these tunnels, please read the advice at the beginning of this chapter.

	Tunnel	Route and Height Above Sea Level	General Information and Comments
AA	**Bielsa** (France – Spain) 3.2 km (2 miles)	**Aragnouet to Bielsa** 1830m (6000')	Open 24 hours but possibly closed October–Easter. On French side (D173) generally good road surface but narrow with steep hairpin bends and steep gradients near summit. Often no middle white line. Spanish side (A138) has good width and is less steep and winding. Used by heavy vehicles. No tolls.
BB	**Cadi** (Spain) 5 km (3 miles)	**Bellver de Cerdanya to Berga** 1220m (4000')	W of Toses (Tosas) pass on E9/C16; link from La Seo de Urgel to Andorra; excellent approach roads; heavy weekend traffic. Tolls charged.
CC	**Envalira** (France – Spain via Andorra) 2.8 km (1.75 miles)	**Pas de la Casa to El Grau Roig** 2000m (6562')	Tunnel width 8.25m. On N22/CG2 France to Andorra. Tolls charged.
DD	**Puymorens** (France –Spain) 4.8 km (2.9 miles)	**Ax-les-Thermes to Puigcerda** 1515m (4970')	MHV 3.5m (11'6"). Part of Puymorens pass on N20/E9. Tolls charged.
EE	**Somport** (France – Spain) 8.6 km (5.3 miles)	**Urdos to Canfranc** 1116m (3661')	Tunnel height 4.55m (14'9"), width 10.5m (34'). Max speed 90 km/h (56 mph); leave 100m between vehicles. On N134 (France), N330 (Spain). No tolls.
FF	**Vielha (Viella)** (Spain) 5.2 km (3.2 miles)	**Vielha (Viella) to Pont de Suert** 1635m (5390')	Tunnel height 5.3m, width 12m. Max speed 80km/h. 3 lane, well lit, modern tunnel on N230. Gentle gradients on both sides. Good road surface. Narrow on approach from Vielha. No tolls.

Mountain Passes and Tunnels

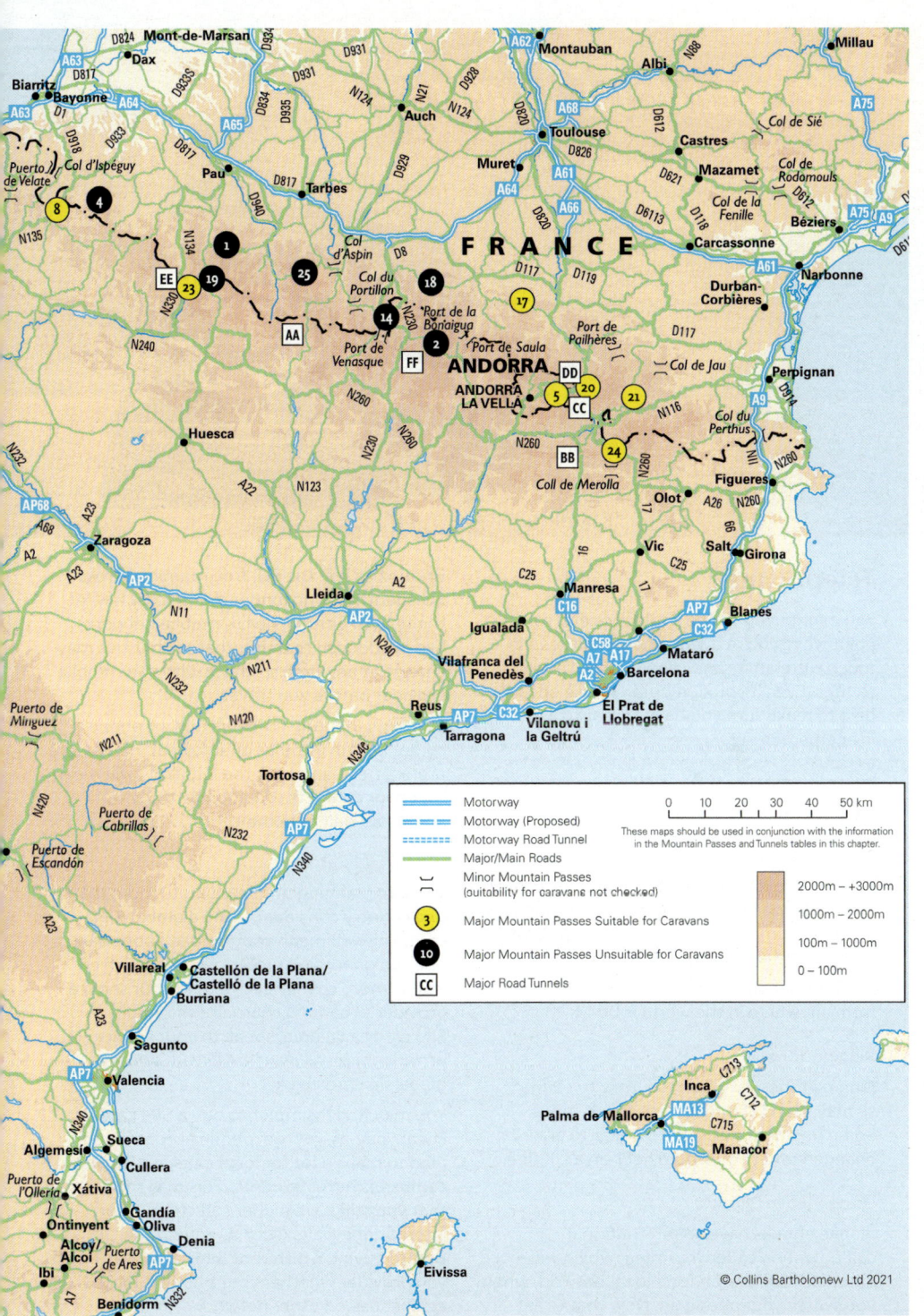

Shutterstock/ BrAt82

Keeping in Touch

Telephones

You might need to use a telephone at some point while you're away, whether to keep in touch with family and friends or call ahead to sites. Even if you don't plan to use one, it's best to make sure you have access to a phone in anemergencies.

International Direct Dial Calls

Each country has a unique dialing code you must use if phoning from outside that country. You can find the international dialing code for any country by visiting www.thephonebook.bt.com. First dial the code then the local number. If the area code starts with a zero this should be omitted.

The international access code to dial the UK from anywhere in the world is 0044.

Ringing Tones

Ringing tones vary from country to country, so may sound very different to UK tones. Some ringing tones sound similar to error or engaged tones you would hear on a UK line.

Using Mobile Phones

Mobile phones have an international calling option called 'roaming' which will automatically search for a local network when you switch your phone on. Now that Great Britain has left the EU, free roaming across EU countries is no longer required by law. At the time of writing, no UK mobile networks had introduced roaming charges but this may change at any time so check with your mobile provider before you travel.

Storing telephone numbers in your phone's contact list in international format (i.e. use the prefix of +44 and omit the initial '0') will mean that your contacts will automatically work abroad as well as in the UK.

Global SIM Cards

If you're planning on travelling to more than one country consider buying a global SIM card. This will mean your mobile phone can operate on foreign mobile networks, which will be more cost effective than your service provider's roaming charges. For details of SIM cards available, speak to your service provider or visit www.0044.co.uk or www.globalsimcard.co.uk.

You may find it simpler to buy a SIM card or cheap 'pay-as-you-go' phone abroad if you plan to make a lot for local calls, e.g. to book campsites or restaurants. This may mean that you still have higher call charges for international calls (such as calling the UK). Before buying a different SIM card, check with you provider whether your phone is locked against use on other networks.

Shutterstock/Andrey Armyagov

Hands-Free

Legislation in Europe forbids the use of mobile or car phones while driving except when using hands-free equipment. In some European countries it is now also illegal to drive while wearing headphones or a headset - including hands-free kits. If you are involved in an accident whilst driving and using a hand-held mobile phone, your insurance company may refuse to honour the claim.

Internet Access

Wi-Fi is available on lots of campsites in Europe, either included in the pitch fee or for an additional charge. Lots of fast food restaurants and coffee chains now offer free Wi-Fi for customers so you can get access for the price of a coffee or bite to eat.

Many people now use their smartphones or a dongle (a device which connects to your laptop to give Internet access using a mobile network) for internet access. Be aware that now that Great Britain has lef tthe EU you may be charged data roaming charges. If you plan on using your smartphone or a dongle abroad speak to your service provider before you leave the UK to make sure you understand the costs or add an overseas data roaming package to your phone contract.

Making Calls from your Laptop

If you download Skype to your laptop you can make free calls to other Skype users anywhere in the world using a Wi-Fi connection. Rates for calls to non-Skype users (landline or mobile phone) are also very competitively-priced.

You'll need a computer with a microphone and speakers, and a webcam is handy too. It is also possible to download Skype to an internet-enabled mobile phone to take advantage of the same low-cost calls – see www.skype.com.

Club Together

If you want to chat to other members either at home or while you're away, you can do so on The Club's online community Club Together. You can ask questions and gather opinions on the forums at camc.com/together.

Radio and Television

The BBC World Service broadcasts radio programmes 24 hours a day worldwide and you can listen on a number of platforms: online, via satellite or cable, DRM digital radio, internet radio or mobile phone. You can find detailed information and programme schedules at www.bbc.co.uk/worldservice.

Whereas analogue television signals were switched off in the UK during 2012, no date has yet been fixed for the switch off of analogue radio signals.

Digital Terrestrial Television

As in the UK, television transmissions in most of Europe have been converted to digital. The UK's high definition transmission technology may be more advanced than any currently implemented or planned in Europe. This means that digital televisions intended for use in the UK might not be able to receive HD terrestrial signals in some countries.

Satellite Television

For English-language TV programmes the only realistic option is satellite, and satellite dishes are a common sight on campsites all over Europe. A satellite dish mounted on the caravan roof or clamped to a pole fixed to the drawbar, or one mounted on a foldable free-standing tripod, will provide good reception and minimal interference. Remember however that obstructions to the south east (such as tall trees or even mountains) or heavy rain, can interrupt the signals. A specialist dealer will be able to advise you on the best way of mounting your dish. You will also need a satellite receiver and ideally a satellite-finding meter.

The main entertainment channels such as BBC1, ITV1 and Channel 4 can be difficult to pick up in mainland Europe as they are now being transmitted by new narrow-beam satellites. A 60cm dish should pick up these channels in most of France, Belgium and the Netherlands but as you travel further afield, you'll need a progressively larger dish. See www.satelliteforcaravans.co.uk (created and operated by a Club member) for the latest changes and developments, and for information on how to set up your equipment.

Shutterstock/ Sunny studio

Medical matters

Before You Travel

You can find country specific medical advice, including any vaccinations you may need, from www.nhs.uk/healthcareabroad, or speak to your GP surgery. For general enquiries about medical care abroad contact NHS England on 0300 311 22 33 or email england.contactus@nhs.uk.

If you have any pre-existing medical conditions you should check with your GP that you are fit to travel. Ask your doctor for a written summary of any medical problems and a list of medications, which is especially imporant for those who use controlled drugs or hypodermic syringes.

Always make sure that you have enough medication for the duration of your holiday and some extra in case your return is delayed. Take details of the generic name of any drugs you use, as brand names may be different abroad, your blood group and details of any allergies (translations may be useful for restaurants).

An emergency dental kit is available from High Street chemists which will allow you temporarily to restore a crown, bridge or filling or to dress a broken tooth until you can get to a dentist.

A good website to check before you travel is www.nathnac.org/travel which gives general health and safety advice, as well as highlighting potential health risks by country.

European Heath Insurance Card

The European Health Insurance Card (EHIC) allows any EU citizen access to state medical care when they are travelling in another EU country - although in many circumstances, there are significant limitations to what treatment UK citizens are able to receive.

After January 2021, UK issued European Health Insurance Cards remain valid until their expiry date within the EU but not in Switzerland, Liechtenstein, Norway and Iceland. New EHICs will not be issued for UK travellers but a replacement Global Health Insurance Card (GHIC) is being developed.

Given the limitations of EHIC, we always recommend that you have suitable travel insurance before you go on holiday. Make sure you get travel insurance that covers your health needs. Visit GOV.UK to check what your travel insurance should cover.

It is now even more important to have personal health and accident cover, and breakdown cover for your vehicle, when travelling overseas.

Travel Insurance

Despite having an EHIC you may incur high medical costs if you fall ill or have an accident. The cost of bringing a person back to the UK in the event of illness or death is never covered by the EHIC.

Separate additional travel insurance adequate for your destination is essential, such as the Club's Red Pennant Emergency Assistance – see camc.com/redpennant.

First Aid

A first aid kit containing at least the basic requirements is an essential item, and in some countries it is compulsory to carry one in your vehicle (see the Essential Equipment Table in the chapter Motoring – Equipment). Kits should contain items such as sterile pads, assorted dressings, bandages and plasters, antiseptic wipes or cream, cotton wool, scissors, eye bath and tweezers. Also make sure you carry something for upset stomachs, painkillers and an antihistamine in case of hay fever or mild allergic reactions.

If you're travelling to remote areas then you may find it useful to carry a good first aid manual. The British Red Cross publishes a comprehensive First Aid Manual in conjunction with St John Ambulance and St Andrew's Ambulance Association.

Accidents and Emergencies

If you are involved in or witness a road accident the police may want to question you about it. If possible take photographs or make sketches of the scene, and write a few notes about what happened as it may be more difficult to remember the details at a later date.

For sports activities such as skiing and mountaineering, travel insurance must include provision for covering the cost of mountain and helicopter rescue. Visitors to the Savoie and Haute-Savoie areas should be aware that an accident or illness may result in a transfer to Switzerland for hospital treatment. There is a reciprocal healthcare agreement for British citizens visiting Switzerland but you will be required to pay the full costs of treatment and afterwards apply for a refund.

Sun Protection

Never under-estimate how ill exposure to the sun can make you. If you are not used to the heat it is very easy to fall victim to heat exhaustion or heat stroke. Avoid sitting in the sun between 11am and 3pm and cover your head if sitting or walking in the sun. Use a high sun protection factor (SPF) and re-apply frequently. Make sure you drink plenty of fluids.

Shutterstock/Rido

Tick-Borne Encephalitis (TBE) and Lyme Disease

Hikers and outdoor sports enthusiasts planning trips to forested, rural areas should be aware of tick-borne encephalitis, which is transmitted by the bite of an infected tick. If you think you may be at risk, seek medical advice on prevention and immunisation before you leave the UK.

There is no vaccine against Lyme disease, an equally serious tick-borne infection, which, if left untreated, can attack the nervous system and joints. You can minimise the risk by using an insect repellent containing DEET, wearing long sleeves and long trousers, and checking for ticks after outdoor activity.

Avoid unpasteurised dairy products in risk areas. See www.tickalert.org or telephone 01943 468010 for more information.

Water and food

Water from mains supplies throughout Europe is generally safe, but may be treated with chemicals which make it taste different to tap water in the UK. If in any doubt, always drink bottled water or boil it before drinking.

Food poisoning is potential anywhere, and a complete change of diet may upset your stomach as well. In hot conditions avoid any food that hasn't been refrigerated or hot food that has been left to cool. Be sensible about the food that you eat – don't eat unpasteurised or undercooked food and if you aren't sure about the freshness of meat or seafood then it is best avoided.

Returning Home

If you become ill on your return home tell your doctor that you have been abroad and which countries you have visited. Even if you have received medical treatment in another country, always consult your doctor if you have been bitten or scratched by an animal while on holiday. If you were given any medicines in another country, it may be illegal to bring them back into the UK. If in doubt, declare them at Customs when you return.

Electricity and Gas

Shutterstock/ sumroeng chinnapan

Electricity

General Advice

The voltage for mains electricity is 230V across the EU, but varying degrees of 'acceptable tolerance' mean you may find variations in the actual voltage. Most appliances sold in the UK are 220-240V so should work correctly. However, some high-powered equipment, such as microwave ovens, may not function well – check your instruction manual for any specific instructions. Appliances marked with 'CE' have been designed to meet the requirements of relevant European directives.

The table below gives an approximate idea of which appliances can be used based on the amperage which is being supplied (although not all appliances should be used at the same time). You can work it out more accurately by making a note of the wattage of each appliance in your caravan. The wattages given are based on appliances designed for use in caravans and motorhomes. Household kettles, for example, have at least a 2000W element. Each caravan circuit will also have a maximum amp rating which should not be exceeded.

Electrical Connections – EN60309-2 (CEE17)

EN60309-2 (formerly known as CEE17) is the European Standard for all newly fitted connectors. Most sites should now have these connectors, however there is no requirement to replace connectors which were installed before this was standardised so you may still

Amps	Wattage (Approx)	Fridge	Battery Charger	Air Conditioning	LCD TV	Water Heater	Kettle (750W)	Heater (1kW)
2	400	✓	✓					
4	900	✓	✓		✓	✓		
6	1300	✓	✓	*	✓	✓	✓	
8	1800	✓	✓	✓**	✓	✓	✓	✓**
10	2300	✓	✓	✓**	✓	✓	✓	✓**
16	3600	✓	✓	✓	✓	✓	✓	✓**

*	Usage possible, depending on wattage of appliance in question
**	Not to be used at the same time as other high-wattage equipment

find some sites where your UK 3 pin connector doesn't fit. For this reason it is a good idea to carry a 2-pin adapter. If you are already on site and find your connector doesn't fit, ask campsite staff to borrow or hire an adaptor. You may still encounter a poor electrical supply on site even with an EN60309-2 connection.

If the campsite does not have a modern EN60309-2 (CEE17) supply, ask to see the electrical protection for the socket outlet. If there is a device marked with IDn = 30mA, then the risk is minimised.

Hooking Up to the Mains

Connection should always be made in the following order:

- Check your outfit isolating switch is at 'off'.
- Uncoil the connecting cable from the drum. A coiled cable with current flowing through it may overheat. Take your cable and insert the connector (female end) into your outfit inlet.
- Insert the plug (male end) into the site outlet socket.
- Switch outfit isolating switch to 'on'.
- Use a polarity tester in one of the 13A sockets in the outfit to check all connections are correctly wired. Never leave it in the socket. Some caravans have these devices built in as standard.

It is recommended that the supply is not used if the polarity is incorrect (see Reversed Polarity).

Warnings:

If you are in any doubt of the safety of the system, if you don't receive electricity once connected or if the supply stops then contact the site staff.

If the fault is found to be with your outfit then call a qualified electrician rather than trying to fix the problem yourself.

To ensure your safety you should never use an electrical system which you can't confirm to be safe. Use a mains tester such as the one shown on the right to test the electrical supply.

Always check that a proper earth connection exists before using the electrics. Please note that these testers may not pick up all

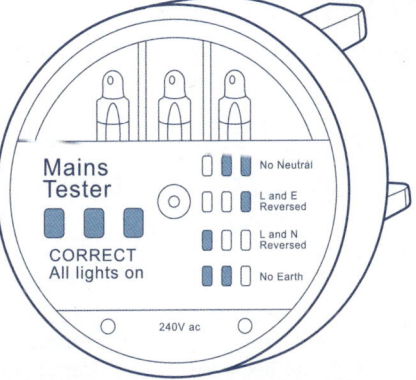

earth faults so if there is any doubt as to the integrity of the earth system do not use the electrical supply.

Disconnection

- Switch your outfit isolating switch to 'off'.
- At the site supply socket withdraw the plug.
- Disconnect the cable from your outfit.

Motorhomes – if leaving your pitch during the day, don't leave your mains cable plugged into the site supply, as this creates a hazard if the exposed live connections in the plug are touched or if the cable is not seen during grass-cutting.

Reversed Polarity

Even if the site connector meets European Standard EN60309-2 (CEE17), British caravanners are still likely to encounter the problem known as reversed polarity. This is where the site supply 'live' line connects to the outfit's 'neutral' and vice versa. You should always check the polarity immediately on connection, using a polarity tester available from caravan accessory shops. If polarity is reversed the caravan mains electricity should not be used. Try using another nearby socket instead. Frequent travellers to the Continent can make up an adaptor themselves, or ask an electrician to make one for you, with the live and neutral wires reversed. Using a reversed polarity socket will probably not affect how an electrical appliance works, however your protection is greatly reduced. For example, a

lamp socket may still be live as you touch it while replacing a blown bulb, even if the light switch is turned off.

Shaver Sockets

Most campsites provide shaver sockets with a voltage of 220V or 110V. Using an incorrect voltage may cause the shaver to become hot or break. The 2-pin adaptor available in the UK may not fit Continental sockets so it is advisable to buy 2-pin adaptors on the Continent. Many modern shavers will work on a range of voltages which make them suitable for travelling abroad. Check you instruction manual to see if this is the case.

Gas

General Advice

Gas usage can be difficult to predict as so many factors, such as temperature and how often you eat out, can affect the amount you need. As a rough guide allow 0.45kg of gas a day for normal summer usage.

With the exception of Campingaz, LPG cylinders normally available in the UK cannot be exchanged abroad. If possible, take enough gas with you and bring back the empty cylinders. Always check how many you can take with you as ferry and tunnel operators may restrict the number of cylinders you are permitted to carry for safety reasons.

The full range of Campingaz cylinders is widely available from large supermarkets and hypermarkets, although at the end of

Site hooking up adaptor

Adaptateur de prise au site (secteur)
Campingplatz-anschluss (netz)

Extension lead to outfit

Câble de rallonge à la caravane
Verlâengerungskabel zum wohnwagen

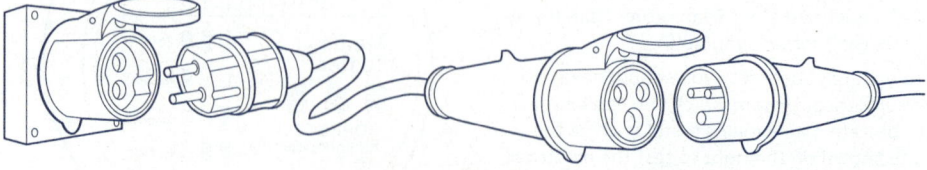

Site outlet
Prise du site
Campingplatz-Steckdose

Mains adaptor
Adaptateur Secteur
Netzanschlußstacker

16A 230V AC

the holiday season stocks may be low. Other popular brands of gas are Primagaz, Butagaz, Totalgaz and Le Cube. A loan deposit is required and if you are buying a cylinder for the first time you may also need to buy the appropriate regulator or adaptor hose.

If you are touring in cold weather conditions use propane gas instead of butane. Many other brands of gas are available in different countries and, as long as you have the correct regulator, adaptor and hose and the cylinders fit in your gas locker these local brands can also be used.

Gas cylinders are now standardised with a pressure of 30mbar for both butane and propane within the EU. On UK-specification caravans and motorhomes (2004 models and later) a 30mbar regulator suited to both propane and butane use is fitted to the bulkhead of the gas locker. This is connected to the cylinder with a connecting hose (and sometimes an adaptor) to suit different brands or types of gas. Older outfits and some foreign-built ones may use a cylinder-mounted regulator, which may need to be changed to suit different brands or types of gas.

Shutterstock/ Adrian Georg Rahl

Warnings:

- Refilling gas cylinders intended to be exchanged is against the law in most countries, however you may still find that some sites and dealers will offer to refill cylinders for you. Never take them up on this service as it can be dangerous; the cylinders haven't been designed for user-refilling and it is possible to over fill them with catastrophic consequences.

- Regular servicing of gas appliances is important as a faulty appliance can emit carbon monoxide, which could prove fatal. Check your vehicle or appliance handbook for service recommendations.

- Never use a hob or oven as a space heater.

The Caravan and Motorhome Club publishes a range of technical leaflets for its members including detailed advice on the use of electricity and gas – you can request copies or see camc.com/advice-and-training.

Safety and security

Shutterstock/ Alena Ozerova

EU countries have good legislation in place to protect your safety wherever possible. However accidents and crime will still occur and taking sensible precautions can help to minimise your risk of being involved.

Beaches, Lakes and Rivers

Check for any warning signs or flags before you swim and ensure that you know what they mean. Check the depth of water before diving and avoid diving or jumping into murky water as submerged objects may not be visible. Familiarise yourself with the location of safety apparatus and/or lifeguards.

Use only the designated areas for swimming, watersports and boating and always use life jackets where appropriate. Watch out for tides, undertows, currents and wind strength and direction before swimming in the sea. This applies in particular when using inflatables, windsurfing equipment, body boards, kayaks or sailing boats. Sudden changes of wave and weather conditions combined with fast tides and currents are particularly dangerous.

Campsite Safety

Once you've settled in, take a walk around the site to familiarise yourself with its layout and locate the nearest safety equipment. Ensure that children know their way around and where your pitch is.

Natural disasters are rare, but always think about what could happen. A combination of heavy rain and a riverside pitch could lead to flash flooding, for example, so make yourself aware of site evacuation procedures.

Be aware of sources of electricity and cabling on and around your pitch – electrical safety might not be up to the same standards as in the UK.

Poison for rodent control is sometimes used on sites or surrounding farmland. Warning notices are not always posted and you are strongly advised to check if staying on a rural site with dogs or children.

Incidents of theft on campsites are rare but when leaving your caravan unattended make sure you lock all doors and shut windows. Conceal valuables from sight and lock up any bicycles.

Children

Watch out for children as you drive around the site and don't exceed walking pace.

Children's play areas are generally unsupervised, so check which are suitable for your children's ages and abilities. Read and respect the displayed rules. Remember it is your responsibility to supervise your children at all times.

Be aware of any campsite rules concerning ball games or use of play equipment, such as roller blades and skateboards. When your children attend organised activities, arrange when and where to meet afterwards. You should never leave children alone inside a caravan.

Fire

Fire prevention is important on sites, as fire can spread quickly between outfits. Certain areas of southern Europe experience severe water shortages in summer months leading to an increased fire risk. This may result in some local authorities imposing restrictions at short notice on the use of barbecues and open flames.

Fires can be a regular occurrence in forested areas, especially along the Mediterranean coast during summer months. They are generally extinguished quickly and efficiently but short term evacuations are sometimes necessary. If visiting forested areas familiarise yourself with local emergency procedures in the event of fire. Never use paraffin or gas heaters inside your caravan. Gas heaters should only be fitted when air is taken from outside the caravan. Don't change your gas cylinder inside the caravan. If you smell gas turn off the cylinder immediately, extinguish all naked flames and seek professional help.

Make sure you know where the fire points and telephones are on site and know the site fire drill. Make sure everyone in your party knows how to call the emergency services.

Where site rules permit the use of barbecues, take the following precautions to prevent fire:

- Never locate a barbecue near trees or hedges.
- Have a bucket of water to hand in case of sparks.
- Only use recommended fire-lighting materials.
- Don't leave a barbecue unattended when lit and dispose of hot ash safely.
- Never take a barbecue into an enclosed area or awning – even when cooling they continue to release carbon monoxide which can lead to fatal poisoning.

Shutterstock/ Andrey Armyagov

Swimming Pools

Familiarize yourself with the pool area before you venture in for a swim - check the pool layout and identify shallow and deep ends and the location of safety equipment. Check the gradient of the pool bottom as pools which shelve off sharply can catch weak or non-swimmers unawares.

Never dive or jump into a pool without knowing the depth – if there is a no diving rule it usually means the pool isn't deep enough for safe diving.

For pools with a supervisor or lifeguard, note any times or dates when the pool is not supervised. Read safety notices and rules posted around the pool.

On the Road

Don't leave valuables on view in cars or caravans, even if they are locked. Make sure items on roof racks or cycle carriers are locked securely.

Near to ports British owned cars have been targeted by thieves, both while parked and on the move, e.g. by flagging drivers down or indicating that a vehicle has a flat tyre. If you stop in such circumstances be wary of anyone offering help, ensure that car keys are not left in the ignition and that vehicle doors are locked while you investigate.

Always keep car doors locked and windows closed when driving in populated areas. Beware of a 'snatch' through open car windows at traffic lights, filling stations or in traffic jams. When driving through towns and cities keep your doors locked. Keep handbags, valuables and documents out of sight.

If flagged down by another motorist for whatever reason, take care that your own car is locked and windows closed while you check outside, even if someone is left inside.

Be particularly careful on long, empty stretches of motorway and when you stop for fuel. Even if the people flagging you down appear to be officials (e.g. wearing yellow reflective jackets or dark, 'uniform-type' clothing) lock your vehicle doors. They may appear to be friendly and helpful, but could be opportunistic thieves. Have a mobile phone to hand and, if necessary, be seen to use it.

Road accidents are a increased risk in some countries where traffic laws may be inadequately enforced, roads may be poorly maintained, road signs and lighting inadequate, and driving standards poor. It's a good idea to keep a fully-charged mobile phone with you in your car with the number of your breakdown organisation saved into it. On your return to the UK there are increasing issues with migrants attempting to stowaway in vehicles, especially if you're travelling through Calais.

The UK government have issued the following instructions to prevent people entering the UK illegally:

- Where possible all vehicle doors and storage compartments should be fitted with locks.

- All locks must be engaged when the vehicle is stationary or unattended.

- Immediately before boarding your ferry or train check that the locks on your vehicle haven't been compromised.

- If you have any reason to suspect someone may have accessed your outfit speak to border control staff or call the police. Do not board the ferry or train or you may be liable for a fine of up to £2000.

Overnight Stops

Overnight stops should always be at campsites and not at motorway service areas, ferry terminal car parks, petrol station forecourts or isolated 'aires de services' on motorways where robberies are occasionally reported. If you decide to use these areas for a rest then take appropriate precautions, for example, shutting all windows, securing locks and making a thorough external check of your vehicle(s) before departing. Safeguard your property, e.g. handbags, while out of the caravan and beware of approaches by strangers.

For a safer place to take a break, there is a wide network of 'Aires de Services' in cities, towns and villages across Europe, many specifically for motorhomes with good security and overnight facilities. They are often less isolated and therefore safer than

the motorway aires. It is rare that you will be the only vehicle staying on such areas, but take sensible precautions and trust your instincts.

Personal Security

Petty crime happens all over the world, including in the UK; however as a tourist you are more vulnerable to it. This shouldn't stop you from exploring new horizons, but there are a few sensible precautions you can take to minimise the risk.

- Leave valuables and jewellery at home. If you do take them, fit a small safe in your caravan or lock them in the boot of your car. Don't leave money or valuables in a car glovebox or on view. Don't leave bags in full view when sitting outside at cafés or restaurants, or leave valuables unattended on the beach.

Shutterstock/ DGLimages

- When walking be security-conscious. Avoid unlit streets at night, walk away from the kerb edge and carry handbags or shoulder bags on the side away from the kerb. The less of a tourist you appear, the less of a target you are.

- Keep a note of your holiday insurance details and emergency telephone numbers in more than one place, in case the bag or vehicle containing them is stolen.

- Beware of pickpockets in crowded areas, at tourist attractions and in cities. Be especially aware when using public transport in cities.

- Be cautious of bogus plain-clothes policemen who may ask to see your foreign currency or credit cards and passport. If approached, decline to show your money or to hand over your passport but ask for credentials and offer instead to go to the nearest police station.

- Laws and punishment vary from country to country so make yourself aware of anything which may affect you before you travel. Be especially careful on laws involving alcohol consumption (such as drinking in public areas), and never buy or use illegal drugs abroad.

- Respect customs regulations - smuggling is a serious offence and can carry heavy penalties. Do not carry parcels or luggage through customs for other people and never cross borders with people you do not know in your vehicle, such as hitchhikers.

The Foreign & Commonwealth Office produces a range of material to advise and inform British citizens travelling abroad - www.gov.uk/foreign-travel-advice has country specific guides.

Money Security

We would rarely walk around at home carrying large amounts of cash, but as you may not have the usual access to bank accounts and credit cards you are more likely to do so on holiday. You are also less likely to have the same degree of security when online banking as you would in your own home.

Take the following precautions to keep your money safe:

- Carry only the minimum amount of cash and don't rely on one person to carry everything. Never carry a wallet in your back pocket. Concealed money belts are the most secure way to carry cash and passports.

- Keep a separate note of bank account and credit/debit card numbers. Carry your credit card issuer/bank's 24-hour UK contact number with you.

- Be careful when using cash machines (ATMs) – try to use a machine in an area with high footfall and don't allow yourself to be distracted. Put your cash away before moving away from the cash machine.

- Always guard your PIN number, both at cash machines and when using your card to pay in shops and restaurants. Never let your card out of your sight while paying.

- If using internet banking do not leave the PC or mobile device unattended and make sure you log out fully at the end of the session.

Shutterstock.Rawpixel.com

Winter Sports

If you are planning a skiing or snowboarding holiday you should research the safety advice for your destination before you travel. A good starting point may be the relevant embassy for the country you're visitng. All safety instructions should be followed meticulously given the dangers of avalanches in some areas.

The Ski Club of Great Britain offer a lot of advice for anyone taking to the mountains, visit their website www.skiclub.co.uk to pick up some useful safety tips and advice on which resorts are suitable for different skill levels.

British Consular Services Abroad

British Embassy and Consular staff offer practical advice, assistance and support to British travellers abroad. They can, for example, issue replacement passports, help Britons who have been the victims of crime, contact relatives and friends in the event of an accident, illness or death, provide information about transferring funds and provide details of local lawyers, doctors and interpreters. But there are limits to their powers and a British Consul cannot, for example, give legal advice, intervene in court proceedings, put up bail, pay for legal or medical bills, or for funerals or the repatriation of bodies, or undertake work more properly done by banks, motoring organisations and travel insurers.

If you are charged with a serious offence, insist on the British Consul being informed. You will be contacted as soon as possible by a Consular Officer who can advise on local procedures, provide access to lawyers and insist that you are treated as well as nationals of the country which is holding you. However, they cannot get you released as a matter of course. British and Irish embassy contact details can be found in the Country Introduction chapters.

Shutterstock/JGA

Campsites

The quantity and variety of sites across Europe means you're sure to find one that suits your needs – from full facilities and entertainment to quiet rural retreats. If you haven't previously toured outside of the UK you may notice some differences, such as pitches being smaller or closer together. In hot climates hard ground may make putting up awnings difficult.

In the high season all campsite facilities are usually open, however bear in mind that toilet and shower facilities may be busy. Out of season some facilities such as shops and swimming pools may be closed and office opening hours may be reduced and the sanitary facilities may be reduced to a few unisex toilet and shower cubicles.

Booking a Campsite

To save the hassle of arriving to a full site try to book in advance, especially in high season. If you don't book ahead arrive no later than 4pm to secure a pitch, after this time sites fill up quickly. Allow time to find another campsite if your first choice is fully booked.

You can often book directly via a campsite's website. Some sites regard a deposit as a booking or admin fee and will not deduct the amount from your final bill.

Overseas Travel Service

The Club's Overseas Travel Service offers members an site booking service on over 250 campsites in Europe. Full details of these sites plus information on ferry special offers and Red Pennant Emergency Assistance can be found in the Club's Venture Abroad brochure – call 01342 327410 to request a copy or visit camc.com/overseas.

Overseas Site Booking Service sites show heir booking code (e.g. G04) at the end of their listing. We can't make reservations for any other campsites in this guide.

Overseas Site Night Vouchers

The Club offers Overseas Site Night Vouchers which can be used at over 300 Club inspected sites in Europe. The vouchers cost £21.95 each (2019 cost) and you'll need one voucher per night to stay on a site in low season and two per night in high season. You'll also be eligible for the Club's special packaged ferry rates when you're buying vouchers. For more information and the view the voucher terms and conditions visit www.camc.com/overseasoffers or call 01342 327 410.

Caravan Storage

Storing your caravan on a site in Europe can be a great way to avoid a long tow and to save on ferry and fuel costs. Before you leave your caravan in storage always check whether your insurance covers this, as many policies don't.

If you aren't covered then look for a specialist policy - Towergate Insurance (tel: 01242 538431 or www.towergateinsurance.co.uk) or Look Insurance (tel: 0333 777 3035 or www.lookinsuranceservices.co.uk) both offer insurance policies for caravans stored abroad.

Facilities and Site Description

All of the site facilities shown in the site listings of this guide have been taken from member reports, as have the comments at the end of each site entry. Please remember that opinions and expectations can differ significantly from one person to the next.

The year of report is shown at the end of each site listing – sites which haven't been reported on for a few years may have had significant changes to their prices, facilities, and opening dates. It is always best to check any specific details you need to know before travelling by contacting the site or looking at their website

Sanitary Facilities

Facilities normally include toilet and shower blocks with shower cubicles, wash basins and razor sockets. In site listings the abbreviation 'wc' indicates that the site has the kind of toilets we are used to in the UK (pedestal style). Some sites have footplate style toilets and, where this is known, you will see the abbreviation 'cont', i.e. continental. European sites do not always provide sink plugs, toilet paper or soap so take them with you.

Waste Disposal

Site entries show (when known) where a campsite has a chemical disposal and/or a motorhome service point, which is assumed to include a waste (grey) water dump station and toilet cassette-emptying point. You may find fewer waste water disposal facilities as on the continent more people use the site sanitary blocks rather than their own facilities.

Chemical disposal points may be fixed at a high level requiring you to lift cassettes in order to empty them. Disposal may simply be down a toilet. Wastemaster-style emptying points are not very common in Europe. Formaldehyde chemical cleaning products are banned in many countries. In Germany the 'Blue Angel' (Blaue Engel) Standard, and in the Netherlands the 'Milieukeur' Standard, indicates that the product has particularly good environmental credentials.

Finding a Campsite

Directions are given for all campsites listed in this guide and most listings also include GPS co-ordinates. Full street addresses are also given where available. The directions have been supplied by member reports and haven't been checked in detail by The Club.

For information about using satellite navigation to find a site see the Motoring Equipment section.

Overnight Stops

Many towns and villages across Europe provide dedicated overnight or short stay areas specifically for motorhomes, usually with security, electricity, water and waste facilities. These are known as 'Aires de Services', 'Stellplatz' or 'Aree di Sosta' and are usually well signposted with a motorhome icon. Facilities and charges for these overnight stopping areas will vary significantly.

Many campsites in popular tourist areas will also have separate overnight areas of hardstanding with facilities often just outside the main campsite area. There are guidebooks available which list just these overnight stops, Vicarious Books publish an English guide to Aires including directions and GPS co-ordinates. Please contact 0131 208 3333 or visit their website www.vicarious-shop.com.

For security reasons you shouldn't spend the night on petrol station service areas, ferry terminal car parks or isolated 'Aires de Repos' or 'Aires de Services' along motorways.

Municipal Campsites

Municipal sites are found in towns and villages all over Europe, in particular in France. Once very basic, many have been improved in recent years and now offer a wider range of facilities. They can usually be booked in advance through the local town hall or tourism office. When approaching a town you may find that municipal sites are not always named and signposts may simply state 'Camping' or show a tent or caravan symbol. Most municipal sites are clean, well-run and very reasonably priced but security may be basic.

These sites may be used by seasonal workers, market traders and travellers in low season and as a result there may be restrictions or very high charges for some types of outfits (such as twin axles) in order to discourage this. If you may be affected check for any restrictions when you book.

Naturist Campsites

Some naturist sites are included in this guide and are shown with the word 'naturist' after their site name. Those marked 'part naturist' have separate areas for naturists. Visitors to naturist sites aged 16 and over usually require an INF card or Naturist Licence - covered by membership of British Naturism (tel 01604 620361, visit www.british-naturism.org.uk or email headoffice@british-naturism.org.uk) or you can apply for a licence on arrival at any recognised naturist site (a passport-size photograph is required).

Opening Dates and times

Opening dates should always be taken with a pinch of salt - including those given in this guide. Sites may close without notice due to refurbishment work, a lack of visitors or bad weather. Outside the high season it is always best to contact campsites in advance, even if the site advertises itself as open all year. Most sites will close their gates or barriers overnight – if you are planning to arrive late or are delayed on your journey you should call ahead to make sure you will be able to gain access to the site. There may be a late arrivals area outside of the barriers where you can pitch overnight. Motorhomers should also consider barrier closing times if leaving site in your vehicle for the evening.

Check out time is usually between 10am and 12 noon – speak to the site staff if you need to leave very early to make sure you can check out on departure. Sites may also close for an extended lunch break, so if you're planning to arrive or check out around lunchtime check that the office will be open.

Pets on Campsites

Dogs are welcome on many sites, although you may have to prove that all of their vaccinations are up to date before they are allowed onto the site. Certain breeds of dogs are banned in some countries and other breeds will need to be muzzled and kept on a lead at all times.

A list of breeds with restrictions by country can be found at camc.com/pets.

Sites usually charge for dogs and may limit the number allowed per pitch. On arrival make yourself aware of site rules regarding dogs, such as keeping them on a lead, muzzling them or not leaving them unattended in your outfit.

In popular tourist areas local regulations may ban dogs from beaches during the summer. Some dogs may find it difficult to cope with changes in climate. Also watch out for diseases transmitted by ticks, caterpillars, mosquitoes or sandflies - dogs from the UK will have no natural resistance. Consult your vet about preventative treatment before you travel.

Visitors to southern Spain and Portugal, parts of central France and northern Italy should be aware of the danger of Pine Processionary Caterpillars from mid-winter to late spring. Dogs should be kept away from pine trees if possible or fitted with a muzzle that prevents the nose and mouth from touching the ground. This will also protect against poisoned bait sometimes used by farmers and hunters.

In the event that your pet is taken ill abroad a campsite should have information about local vets.

Most European countries require dogs to wear a collar identifying their owners at all times. If your dog goes missing, report the matter to the local police and the local branch of that country's animal welfare organisation.

See the Documents section of this book for more information about the Pet Travel Scheme.

Prices and Payment

Prices per night (for an outfit and two adults) are shown in the site entries. If you stay on site after midday you may be charged for an extra day. Many campsites have a minimum amount for credit card transactions, meaning they can't be used to pay for overnight or short stays. Check which payment methods are accepted when you check in.

Sites with automatic barriers may ask for a deposit for a swipe card or fob to operate it.

Extra charges may apply for the use of facilities such as swimming pools, showers or laundry rooms. You may also be charged extra for dogs, Wi-Fi, tents and extra cars.

A tourist tax, eco tax and/or rubbish tax may be imposed by local authorities in some European countries. VAT may also be added to your campsite fees.

Registering on Arrival

Local authority requirements mean you will usually have to produce an identity document on arrival, which will be held by the site until you check out. If you don't want to leave your passport with reception most sites accept a document such as the Camping Key Europe (CKE) or Camping Card International (CCI).

Shutterstock/alicja neumiler

CKE are available for Club members to purchase by calling 01342 336633 or are free to members if you take out the 'motoring' level of cover from the Club's Red Pennant Overseas Holiday Insurance.

General Advice

If you've visiting a new site ask to take a look around the site and facilities before booking in. Riverside pitches can be very scenic but keep an eye on the water level; in periods of heavy rain this may rise rapidly.

Speed limits on campsites are usually restricted to 10 km/h (6 mph). You may be asked to park your car in a separate area away from your caravan, particularly in the high season.

The use of the term 'statics' in the campsite reports in this guide may to any long-term accommodation on site, such as seasonal pitches, chalets, cottages, fixed tents and cabins, as well as static caravans.

Complaints

If you want to make a complaint about a site issue, take it up with site staff or owners at the time in order to give them the opportunity to rectify the problem during your stay.

The Caravan and Motorhome Club has no control or influence over day to day campsite operations or administration of the sites listed in this guide. Therefore we aren't able to intervene in any dispute you should have with a campsite, unless the booking has been made through our Advanced Booking Service - see listings that have a booking code at the end of the entry (e.g. G04).

Campsite Groups

Across Europe there are many campsite groups or chains with sites in various locations.

You will generally find that group sites will be consistent in their format and the quality and variety of facilities they offer. If you liked one site you can be fairly confident that you will like other sites within the same group.

If you're looking for a full facility site, with swimming pools, play areas, bars and restaurants on site you're likely to find these on sites which are part of a group. You might even find organised excursions and activities such as archery on site.

Austria

📍 Innsbruck

Shutterstock/Adisa

Highlights

From bustling, cosmopolitan cities, packed with culture, to stunning mountain vistas that will take your breath away, Austria is a rich and varied country that caters to every taste.

The Alps offer endless appeal for those looking to enjoy an active, outdoor holiday while the picturesque towns and villages that punctuate the landscape are ideal for relaxing and soaking up the local culture. During the summer months walking and hiking are the order of the day, while winter sports are abundant once the weather turns colder.

Austria is an important centre for European culture; in particular music. As the birthplace of many notable composers – Mozart, Strauss and Haydn to name just a few – Austria is a magnet for classical music fans.

When it comes to food, one of Austria's most famous dishes is strudel, and there are many different varieties of flavours and types available. Also make sure to try Wiener Schnitzel, a meat escalop which is breaded and fried, and Tafelspitz, a beef soup served with apple and horseradish.

Major towns and cities

- Vienna – enjoy a slice of sachertorte in this historic capital.
- Innsbruck – an alpine city famous for winter sports, Imperial architechture and Christmas Markets.
- Graz – the old town is filled with sights and is on the UNESCO World Heritage List.
- Salzburg – this fairytale city was the birthplace of Mozart.

Attractions

- Schönbrunn Palace – a Baroque palace in the heart of Vienna.
- Hallstatt – this Alpine village has a fascinating history as well as picturesque views.
- Grossglockner Alpine Road – the highest road in Austria with unparalleled mountain views.
- Innsbruck – a renowned winter sports centre packed with historical sights.

Find out more

www.austria.info
E: info@austria.info Tel: 0043 (0)1 58 86 60

Country Information

Population (approx): 8.7 million

Capital: Vienna

Area: 83,870 sq km

Bordered by: Czech Republic, Germany, Hungary, Italy, Liechtenstein, Slovakia, Slovenia, Switzerland

Terrain: Mountainous in south and west; flat or gently sloping in extreme north and east

Climate: Temperate; cold winters with frequent rain in the lowlands and snow in the mountains; moderate summers, sometimes very hot

Highest Point: Grossglockner 3,798m

Language: German

Local Time: GMT or BST + 1, i.e. 1 hour ahead of the UK all year

Currency: Euros divided into 100 cents; £1 = €1.14, €1 = £0.88 (Feb 2021)

Telephoning: From the UK dial 0043 for Austria and omit the initial zero of the area code of the number you are calling.

Emergency numbers: Police 133; Fire brigade 122; Ambulance 144, or dial 112 for any service (operators speak English).

Public Holidays 2021: Jan 1, 6; Apr 5; May 1, 13, 24; Jun 3; Aug 15; Sep 24 (Salzburg only); Oct 26 (National Day); Nov 1, 15 (Vienna only); Dec 8, 25, 26.

School summer holidays last the whole of July, August and early September

Entry Formalities

British and Irish passport holders may stay for up to 90 days in any 180 day period without a visa. Following Brexit you may be asked to show a return or onward ticket at the border to confirm your length of stay, or to prove that you have enough money for your stay.

Your passport will need to have a minimum of 6 months' validity remaining, and be less than 10 years old (even if it has 6 months or more left).

Visitors arriving at a campsite or hotel must complete a registration form.

Medical Services

Minor matters can be dealt with by staff at pharmacies (apotheke). Pharmacies operate a rota system for out of hours access; when closed a notice is often displayed giving the addresses of the nearest open pharmacies.

Free treatment is available from doctors and hospital outpatient departments as long as the doctor is contracted to the local health insurance office (Gebietskrankenkasse). To be covered for hospital treatment you will need a doctor's referral. In-patient treatment will incur a daily non-refundable charge for the first 28 days.

You will need to present your European Health Insurance Card (EHIC) to receive treatment. Only a limited amount of dental treatment is covered under the state healthcare system. Private medical cover and services like mountain rescue are not covered by the EHIC.

Opening Hours

Banks: Mon-Fri 8am-12.30pm & 1.30pm-3pm (5.30pm Thu), main branches don't close for lunch; closed Sat/Sun. (Hours may vary).

Museums: Mon-Fri 10am-6pm (summer), 9am-4pm (winter); Sat, Sun & public holidays 9am-6pm.

Post Offices: Mon-Fri 8am-12pm & 2pm-6pm; city post offices don't close for lunch; in some towns open Sat 9am-12pm.

Shops: Mon-Fri 8am-6pm; some open until 7.30pm Thu; some close 12pm-2pm for lunch; Sat 8am-5pm; some open Sun and public holidays.

Safety and Security

Most visits to Austria are trouble-free, but visitors should take sensible precautions to avoid becoming a victim of crime at crowded tourist sites and around major railway stations and city centre parks after dark. Pickpockets and muggers operate in and around the city centre of Vienna.

Drivers, especially on the autobahns in Lower Austria, should be wary of bogus plain clothes police officers. In all traffic-related matters police officers will be in uniform and unmarked vehicles will have a flashing sign in the rear window which reads 'Stopp –Polizei – Folgen'. If in any doubt contact the police on the emergency number 133 or 112 and ask for confirmation. The winter sports season lasts from December to March, or the end of May in higher regions. If you plan to ski contact the Austrian National 8.5

British Embassy

JAURESGASSE 12
1030 VIENNA
Tel: +43 (1) 716130
www.ukinaustria.fco.gov.uk/en/

Irish Embassy

ROTENTURMSTRAßE
16-18, 1010 VIENNA
Tel: +43 (0)1 715 4246
www.embassyofireland.at

Documents

Driving Licence

If you hold a UK driving licence which does not bear your photograph you should carry your passport as further proof of identity, or obtain a photocard licence. You may need an International Driving Permit if you have an old style paper licence or a licence issued in Gibraltar, Guernsey, Jersey or the Isle of Man. These can be obtained from the Post Office before you travel.

Money

Cash dispensers (Bankomaten) have instructions in English. Major credit cards are widely accepted in large cities although a number of small hotels, shops and restaurants may refuse. Visa and Mastercard are more readily accepted than American Express and Diner's Club.

Passport

You are advised to carry your passport or photocard licence at all times.

Vehicle(s)

You should carry your vehicle registration certificate (V5C), insurance details and MOT certificate.

Driving

Alcohol

The maximum permitted level of alcohol in the bloodstream is 0.049%, i.e. lower than that permitted in the UK. Penalties for exceeding this are severe. A limit of virtually zero (0.01%) applies to drivers who have held a full driving licence for less than two years.

Breakdown Service

The motoring organisation, ÖAMTC, operates a breakdown service 24 hours a day on all roads.

The emergency number is 120 throughout the country from a land line or mobile phone. Motorists pay a set fee, which is higher at night; towing charges also apply. Payment by credit card is accepted.

Members of AIT and FIA affiliated clubs, such as the Caravan and Motorhome Club, qualify for reduced charges on presentation of a valid Club membership card.

Child Restraint System

Children under 14 years of age and less than 1.5 metres in height must use a suitable child restraint system for their height and weight when travelling in the front and rear of a vehicle. Children under 14 years aren't allowed to travel in two seater sports cars.

Children under 14 years of age but over 1.35 metres are allowed to use a 3-point seat belt without a special child seat, as long as the seat belt does not cut across the child's throat or neck.

Fuel

Most petrol stations are open from 8am to 8pm. Motorway service stations and some petrol stations in larger cities stay open 24 hours. Fuel is normally cheaper at self-service filling stations.

LPG (flüssiggas) is available at a limited number of outlets – a list should be available on www.oeamtc.at.

Lights

Dipped headlights must be used in poor visibility or bad weather. Headlight flashing is used as a warning of approach, not as an indication that a driver is giving way.

Motorways

Orange emergency telephones on motorways are 2 km to 3 km apart. A flashing orange light at the top of telephone posts indicates danger ahead.

Whenever congestion occurs on motorways and dual carriageways drivers are required to create an emergency corridor. Drivers in the left-hand lane must move as far over to the left as possible, and drivers in the central and right-hand lanes must move as far over to the right as possible to provide access for emergency vehicles.

Motorway Tolls (Vehicles under 3,500 kg)

Drivers of vehicles under 3,500 kg using motorways and expressways (A and S roads) must purchase a motorway vignette (sticker). One vignette covers your caravan as well. Vignettes may be purchased at all major border crossings into Austria and from OeAMTC offices, larger petrol stations and post offices in Austria. A two-month vignette is available for a car (with or without a trailer) or a motorhome at a cost of €26.20. Also available are a 10 day vignette at €9 and a one year vignette at €87.30 (2015 tariffs).

Failure to display a vignette incurs a fine of at least €120, plus the cost of the vignette. Credit cards or foreign currency may be used in payment. If you have visited Austria before, make sure you remove your old sticker.

There are special toll sections in Austria which are excluded from the vignette and where the toll needs to be paid at respective toll points. These include A10 Tauern tunnel, A13 Brenner motorway and S16 Alberg tunnel.

Motorway Tolls (Vehicles over 3,500 kg)

Tolls for vehicles over 3,500 kg are calculated according to the number of axles and EURO emissions category and are collected electronically by means of a small box (called the GO-Box) fixed to your vehicle's windscreen. They are available for a one-off handling fee of €5 from around 220 points of sale – mainly petrol stations – along the primary road network in Austria and neighbouring countries, and at all major border crossing points.

You can pre-load a set amount onto your Go box or pay after you have travelled. Tolls are calculated according to the number of axles on a vehicle; those with two axles are charged between €0.156 and €0.211 per kilometre + 20% VAT, according to the vehicle's emissions rating. Visit www.go-maut.at to register for the scheme. Telephone 0043 19551266 or email info@go-maut.at for help before you travel. Operators speak English.

This distance-related toll system does not apply to a car/caravan combination even if its total laden weight is over 3,500 kg, unless the laden weight of the towing vehicle itself exceeds that weight.

Parking

Regulations on the parking of motorhomes and caravans vary according to region, but restrictions apply in areas protected for their natural beauty or landscape and beside lakes. If in doubt, ask the local municipality. You cannot leave a caravan without its towing vehicle in a public place.

A zigzag line marked on the road indicates that parking is prohibited. Blue lines indicate a blue zone (Kurzparkzone) where parking is restricted to a period for up to two hours and you need to purchase a voucher (Parkschein) from a local shop, bank or petrol station.

Most cities have 'Pay and Display' machines, parking meters or parking discs, and in main tourist areas the instructions are in English. Illegally-parked cars may be impounded or clamped. Large areas of Vienna are pedestrianised and parking places are limited. However, there are several underground car parks in Vienna District 1.

Priority

Outside built-up areas, road signs on main roads indicate where traffic has priority or if there are no signs priority is given to traffic from the right.

Buses have priority when leaving a bus stop. Do not overtake school buses with flashing yellow lights which have stopped to let children on and off. Trams have priority even if coming from the left.

In heavy traffic, drivers must not enter an intersection unless their exit is clear, even if they have priority or if the lights are green.

Prohibited Equipment

Dashboard cameras are not allowed.

Roads

Austria has a well developed and engineered network of roads classified as: federal motorways (A roads), expressways (S' roads), provincial (B roads) and local (L roads). There are over 2180km of motorways and expressways.

Road Signs and Markings

Most signs conform to international usage. The following are exceptions:

Diversions

Street lights not on all night

Tram turns at yellow or red

You may be stopped and fined in Austria for using roads that prohibit trailers and caravans. This is indicated by the below sign:

If there is an additional sign which shows a weight limit, then this indicates the maximum gross vehicle weight of the trailer. You can also find these signs with a length limit.

Some other signs that are also in use which you may find useful Include:

Austrian	English Translation
Abblendlicht	Dipped headlights
Alle richtungen	All directions
Bauarbeiten	Roadworks
Durchfahrt verboten	No through traffic
Einbahn	One-way street
Fussgänger	Pedestrians
Beschrankung für halten oder parken	Stopping/parking restricted
Lawinen gefahr	Avalanche danger
Links einbiegen	Turn left
Raststätte	Service area

Austrian	English Translation
Raststätte Rechts einbiegen	Turn right
Strasse gesperrt	Road closed
Überholen verboten	No passing
Umleitung	Detour

Speed Limits

	Open Road (km/h)	Motorway (km/h)
Car Solo	100	130
Car towing caravan/trailer	80	100
Motorhome under 3500kg	100	130
Motorhome 3500-7500kg	70	80

Exceptions

If the total combined weight of a car and caravan outfit or a motorhome exceeds 3,500 kg the speed limit on motorways is reduced to 80 km/h (50 mph) and on other roads outside built-up areas to 70 km/h (43 mph).

On motorways where the speed limit for solo vehicles is 130 km/h (81 mph) overhead message signs may restrict speed to 100 km/h (62 mph). Between 10pm and 5am solo cars are restricted to 110 km/h (68 mph) on the A10 (Tauern), A12 (Inntal), A13 (Brenner) and A14 (Rheintal). There is a general speed limit of 60 km/h (37 mph) on most roads in the Tyrol, unless indicated otherwise. There is a speed limit of 50km/h in build up areas unless otherwise indicated by road signs. A built-up area starts from the road sign indicating that place name as you enter a town or village.

Some sections of the A12 and A13 are limited to 100km/h, day and night.

The minimum speed on motorways, as indicated by a rectangular blue sign depicting a white car, is 60 km/h (37 mph). A number of towns have a general speed limit of 30 km/h (18 mph), except where a higher speed limit is indicated.

Traffic Lights

At traffic lights a flashing green light indicates the approach of the end of the green phase.

An orange light combined with the red light indicates that the green phase is imminent.

Traffic Jams

In recent years traffic has increased on the A1 from Vienna to the German border (the West Autobahn). There are usually queues at the border posts with Czech Republic, Slovakia and Hungary. As a result, traffic has also increased on the ring road around Vienna and on the A4 (Ost Autobahn).

Other bottlenecks occur on the A10 (Salzburg to Villach) before the Tauern and Katschberg tunnels, the A12 (Kufstein to Landeck) before the Perjen tunnel and before Landeck, and the A13 (Innsbruck to Brenner) between Steinach and the Italian border. Busy sections on other roads are the S35/S6 between Kirchdorf or Bruck an der Mur and the A9, the B320/E651 in the Schladming and Gröbming areas, and the B179 Fern Pass.

Violation of Traffic Regulations

Police can impose and collect on-the-spot fines of up to €90 from drivers who violate traffic regulations. For higher fines you will be required to pay a deposit and the remainder within two weeks. An official receipt should be issued. A points system operates which applies to drivers of Austrian and foreign-registered vehicles.

Winter Driving

From 1 November to 15 April vehicles, including those registered abroad, must be fitted with winter tyres marked M&S (mud & snow) on all wheels when there is snow or ice on the road. Snow chains are allowed on roads fully covered by snow or ice, as long as road surfaces will not be damaged by the chains. The maximum recommended speed with snow chains is generally 50 km/h.

Between 15 November to 15 March vehicles weighing over 3500kg are required to have winter tyres on at least one of the driving axles, regardless of the road conditions. They must also carry snow chains, and use them where road signs indicate that they are compulsory.

It is the driver's legal responsibility to carry the required winter equipment; therefore, it is essential to check that it is included in any hire car.

Essential Equipment

First aid kit

All vehicles must carry a first aid kit kept in a strong, dirt-proof box.

Reflective Jackets/Waistcoats

If your vehicle breaks down or you are in an accident you must wear a reflective jacket or waistcoat when getting out of your vehicle (compliant with EU Standard EN471). This includes when setting up a warning triangle. It is also recommended that a passenger who leaves the vehicle, for example, to assist with a repair, should also wear one. Keep the jackets within easy reach inside your vehicle, not in the boot.

Warning Triangle

An EU approved warning triangle must be used if the vehicle breaks down, has a puncture or is involved in an accident.

Touring

Austria is divided into nine federal regions, namely Burgenland, Carinthia (Kärnten), Lower Austria (Niederösterreich), Salzburg, Styria (Steiermark), Tyrol (Tirol), Upper Austria (Oberösterreich), Vienna (Wien) and Voralberg.

A 10-15% service charge is included in restaurant bills, but it is customary to add a further 5% tip if satisfied with the service.

The Vienna Card offers unlimited free public transport and discounts at museums, restaurants, theatres and shops. The Card is valid for three days and is available from hotels, tourist information and public transport offices; see www.wienkarte.at.

A Salzburg Card and an Innsbruck Card are also available – see www.austria.info/uk or contact the Austrian National Tourist Office for more information.

Camping and Caravanning

There are approximately 500 campsites in Austria, around 150 of which are open all year, mostly in or near to ski resorts.

Casual/wild camping is not encouraged and is prohibited in Vienna, in the Tyrol and in forests and nature reserves. Permission to park a caravan should be obtained in advance from the owners of private land, or from the local town hall or police station in the case of common land or state property.

Cycling

There is an extensive network of cycle routes, following dedicated cycle and footpaths, such as the 360 km cycle lane that follows the Danube. Many cities encourage cyclists with designated cycle lanes. A Citybike hire scheme operates in Vienna from more than 60 rental offices situated close to underground/metro stations. See www.citybikewien.at for more information or email kontakt@citybikewien.at. There are eight signposted mountain bike routes between 10 and 42 kilometres long in the Vienna woods.

Cycle helmets are compulsory for children under 12 years, or 15 years in Lower Austria (Niederösterreich).

Bikes may be carried on the roof or rear of a car. When carried at the rear, the width must not extend beyond the width of the vehicle, and the rear lights and number plate must be visible.

Electricity and Gas

Current on campsites varies from 4 - 16 amps. Plugs have two round pins and most campsites have CEE connections. Electricity points tend to be in locked boxes, so you will need to check polarity on arrival before the box is locked. Arrangements also need to be made for the box to be unlocked if making an early departure.

Some sites in Austria make a one-off charge for connection to the electricity supply, which is then metered at a rate per kilowatt hour (kwh) The full range of Campingaz cylinders is widely available.

Public Transport & Local Travel

All major cities have efficient, integrated public transport systems including underground and light rail systems, trams and buses. Two to five people travelling as a group by train can buy an Einfach-Raus-Ticket (ERT), which is good for a day's unlimited travel on all Austrian regional trains – see www.oebb.at (English option) for more information or ask at any station.

In Vienna there are travel concessions on public transport for senior citizens (show your passport as proof of age). Buy a ticket from a tobacconist or from a ticket machine in an underground station. Otherwise single tickets are available from vending machines in the vehicles themselves – have plenty of coins ready. Tickets are also available for periods of 24 and 72 hours. Children under six travel free and children under 15 travel free on Sundays, public holidays and during school holidays.

Car ferry services operate throughout the year on the River Danube, and hydrofoil and hovercraft services transport passengers from Vienna to Bratislava (Slovakia) and to Budapest (Hungary).

ABERSEE *B3* (3km N Rural) *47.74040, 13.40665*
Seecamping Primus, Schwand 39, 5342 Abersee
06227 3228; seecamping.primus@aon.at

B158 fr St Gilgen to Strobl. After 3 km turn L. Camp
is last but one. Med, mkd, pt shd, EHU (10A); sw; twin
axles; bus 1km; Eng spkn; games area; CCI. "*Very
helpful owner; beautiful area nr shipping on lake; ideal
for boating; excel; mountain views.*"
€25.70, 25 Apr-30 Sep.   **2016**

ABERSEE *B3* (3km SE Rural) *47.71336, 13.45138*
Camping Schönblick, Gschwendt 33, 5342 Abersee
(06137) 7042; laimer.schoenblick@aon.at;
www.camping-schoenblick.at

Fr B158 at km 36 dir Schiffstation & site in 1km on L.
Med, mkd, hdstg, pt shd, pt sl, terr, EHU (10A) inc; gas;
sw nr; 40% statics; ccard acc; CKE. "*Beautiful, friendly,
family-run site nr lakeside opp St Wolfgang town; ferry
stn; excel san facs but stretched at busy times; walks &
cycle path fr site; vg site.*" **€26.90, 1 May-15 Oct.**
                                                     2019

ABERSEE *B3* (1.5km NW Rural) *47.73656, 13.43250*
Camping Wolfgangblick, Seestrasse 115, 5342
Abersee (06227) 3475; camping@wolfgangblick.at;
www.wolfgangblick.at

Fr B158 fr St Gilgen, on ent Abersee turn L at km 34
twds lake. Site in 1km foll sp to site. Med, mkd, hdstg,
pt shd, EHU (12A) metered; 50% statics; Eng spkn;
ccard acc. "*Pleasant site; gd, friendly family run site by
lake; helpful owners; beautiful scenery; excel for walking
& cycling; lake adj; on bus rte to Salzburg and local vills;
poss cr, adv bkg advised.*" **€32.50, 1 May-30 Sep.**
                                                     2019

ABERSEE *B3* (2.5km NW Rural) *47.73910, 13.40065*
Camping Birkenstrand Wolfgangsee, Schwand 4, 5342
Abersee (06227) 3029; camp@birkenstrand.at;
www.birkenstrand.at

Fr B158 fr St Gilgen, on ent Abersee turn L at km 32
twds lake. Site on both sides of rd in 1km. 4*, Med,
mkd, unshd, pt sl, EHU (10A) metered; bbq; sw nr;
TV; 20% statics; Eng spkn; adv bkg acc; boat hire; golf
15km; bike hire. "*Excel area for walking, cycling; lovely
situation; immac site; ACSI card acc; new facs (2015).*"
€25.00, 27 Mar-31 Oct.   **2016**

ABERSEE *B3* (3km NW Rural) *47.73945, 13.40245*
Romantik Camping Wolfgangsee Lindenstrand,
Schwand 19, 5342 St Gilgen (06227) 32050;
camping@lindenstrand.at; www.lindenstrand.at

Fr St Gilgen take B158 dir Bad Ischl. In 4km at km
32 foll sp Schwand, site on L on lakeside. Lge, mkd,
hdstg, pt shd, serviced pitches; EHU (10A) metered;
10% statics; phone; bus; Eng spkn; adv bkg acc;
ccard acc; watersports; CKE. "*Lovely site; rec adv
bkg for lakeside pitches; elec conn by staff; lake adj,
no dogs in water; poss req long leads; bus & boat to
local towns & Salzburg; continental plugs high ssn.*"
€23.60, 1 Apr-31 Oct.   **2019**

ASCHACH AN DER DONAU *B3* (16km N Rural)
48.42026, 13.98400 **Camping Kaiserhof,** Kaiserau
1, 4082 Aschach-an-der-Donau (07273) 62210;
kaiserhof@aschach.at; www.pension-kaiserhof.at

Fr town cent foll site sp. Site adj rv & Gasthof
Kaiserhof. Sm, pt shd, EHU; red long stay;
80% statics; Eng spkn; ccard acc; CKE. "*Beautiful
location on Danube.*" **€19.00, 15 Apr-30 Sep.**   **2016**

ATTERSEE *B3* (16km S Rural) *47.80100, 13.48266*
Inselcamping, Unterburgau 37, 4866 Unterach-am-
Attersee (07665) 8311; camping@inselcamp.at;
www.inselcamp.at

Leave A1 at junc 243 St Georgen/Attersee, foll B151
to Unterach fr Attersee vill. Site sp on app to
Unterach. Med, pt shd, EHU (6-16A); gas; sw;
25% statics; Eng spkn; adv bkg acc; CKE. "*Excel site
next to lake with sw; helpful owner; 5 min walk to
attractive town; conv Salzburg & Salzkammergut; lots
to see locally; clsd 1200-1400; gd boat trips; extra for
lakeside pitches - some with boat mooring; vg san facs;
adv bkg for over 6 days.*" **€24.00, 1 May-15 Sep.**
                                                     2018

BAD AUSSEE *C3* (11km E Rural) *47.63783, 13.90365*
Campingplatz Gössl, Gössl 201, 8993 Grundlsee
(03622) 81810; office@campinggoessl.com;
www.campinggoessl.com

Fr B145 toll sp to Grundlsee, then along lake to Gössl
at far end. Ent adj gasthof off mini-rndbt, site on L.
Med, EHU (10A) metered + conn fee; sw nr; bus; adv
bkg acc; fishing. "*Excel walking cent; scenery v beautiful;
boating (no motor boats); local gasthofs vg; daily bus &
ferry services; v clean facs.*" **€17.00, 1 May-31 Oct.**
                                                     2019

BAD GLEICHENBERG *C4 (3km E Rural) 46.87470, 15.93360* **Camping Feriendorf in Thermenland,** Haus Nr 240, 8344 Bairisch-Kölldorf **(03159) 3941;** camping.bk@aon.at; **www.bairisch-koelldorf.at**

 (covrd)

Exit A2 at Gleisdorf Süd onto B68 dir Feldbach. Take B66 dir Bad Gleichenberg & at 2nd rndabt turn L, site sp. 4*, Med, unshd, EHU (16A) metered; gas; bbq; sw; 10% statics; adv bkg acc; bike hire; golf 3km; tennis 600m; games area. **€20.00** 2016

BLUDENZ *C1 (2km N Rural) 47.16990, 9.80788* **Terrassencamping Sonnenberg,** Hinteroferstrasse 12, 6714 Nüziders **(05552) 64035;** sonnencamp@aon.at; **www.camping-sonnenberg.com**

Exit A14/E60 junc 57 onto B190 N, foll sp Nüziders & foll site sp thro Nüziders vill. Med, hdstg, mkd, pt shd, terr, EHU (5-13A) metered over 4kw; red long stay; TV; phone; Eng spkn; adv bkg acc; sep car park. "Friendly, v helpful owners; superb facs; beautiful scenery - extra for Panorama pitches at top of site; excel mountain views; excel walking; lifts to mountains; ltd opening hrs for recep - use phone at bldg on L at main ent; no arr after 2200 hrs but sep o'night area; rec bk in adv in high ssn; gd for m'vans; highly rec; excel site; gd value." **€32.60, 27 Apr-6 Oct.** 2019

BLUDENZ *C1 (3km S Rural) 47.14651, 9.81630* **Auhof Camping,** Aulandweg 5, 6706 Bürs **(05552) 67044;** auhof.buers@aon.at; **www.buers.at**

Exit A14/E60 junc 59 dir Bludenz/Bürs, then Brand. Site sp in 300m at Zimba Park shopping cent on edge of sm indus est. Med, unshd, EHU (4A); gas. "Friendly, tidy, clean site on wkg farm; conv Arlberg Tunnel, m'way, Liechtenstein & mountain resorts; muddy in wet; conv NH for m'way; lovely owners." **€23.00** 2016

BRUCK AN DER GROSSGLOCKNERSTRASSE *C2 (0.9km SW Urban) 47.28386, 12.81736* **Sportcamp Woferlgut,** Krössenbach 40, 5671 Bruck-an-der-Grossglocknerstrasse **(06545) 73030;** info@sportcamp.at; **www.sportcamp.at**

Exit A10 junc 47 dir Bischofshofen, B311 dir Zell-am-See. Take 2nd exit to Bruck, site sp fr by-pass, & foll sps thro town to site. 4*, Lge, pt shd, serviced pitches; EHU (10-16A) €2.20 conn fee & €0.80 per kw; sw nr; red long stay; TV; 80% statics; phone; bus to Zell-am-Zee & glacier; Eng spkn; adv bkg acc; ccard acc; tennis; games rm; sauna. "Extended facs area with R numbered pitches preferable; excel site for sh or long stay; gym & fitness cent; ski cent; farm produce; big pitches; excel mntn walking, local horseriding; helpful recep; tour ops tents & statics; excel for young/teenage families; vg san facs; indoor play area; warm welcome; sm supmkt nrby & plenty of rests & cafes; excel." **€37.80, G06.** 2018

See advertisement

"There aren't many sites open at this time of year"

If you're travelling outside peak season remember to call ahead to check site opening dates – even if the entry says 'open all year'.

BRUCK AN DER MUR *C4 (4km W Urban) 47.40311, 15.22755* **Camping Raddörf'l,** Bruckerstrasse 110, 8600 Oberaich **(03862) 51418;** info@gasthofpichler.at; **www.gasthofpichler.at**

Fr S6 take Oberaich exit 4km W of Bruck. Foll site sp (in opp dir to vill of Oberaich), go under rlwy bdge, turn L at T-junc. Site is 300m on L at Gasthof Pichler, ent thro car park. Sm, pt shd, EHU (10A) inc; CKE. "Gd NH; site (10 o'fits max) in orchard at rear of Gasthof; gd rest; cramped." **€21.00, 1 May-1 Oct.** 2015

DELLACH IM DRAUTAL *D2* (1km S Rural) *46.73085, 13.07846* **Camping Waldbad,** 9772 Dellach-im-Drautal (Kärnten) **(04714) 234-18 or (04714) 288; info@ camping-waldbad.at; www.camping-waldbad.at**

🏕 €2.50 ♿ WC ⚓ ♨ ♿ ⚡ ✉ MSP 🦋 ⛲ 🍴 🛒 🛍 ⚠ ✂

Clearly sp on B100 & in vill of Dellach on S side or Rv Drau. Med, hdg, mkd, pt shd, EHU (6A) inc; gas; 5% statics; adv bkg acc; ccard acc; games rm; games area. *"Peaceful, wooded site; htd pool complex, paddling pool adj; waterslide adj; vg leisure facs adj."* **€31.00, 1 May-30 Sep.**   **2019**

DOBRIACH *D3* (2km S Rural) *46.77020, 13.64788* **Komfort Campingpark Burgstaller,** Seefeldstrasse 16, A-9873 Döbriach (Kärnten) **04246 7774; info@ burgstaller.co.at; www.burgstaller.co.at**

12 🏕 €4.10 ♿ WC ⚓ ♨ ♿ ⚡ ✉ MSP 🦋 ⛲ nr 🍴 nr 🛒 ⚠ ✂ 🚣 (htd)

Fr on A10/E55/E66 take exit Millstätter See. Turn L at traff lts on B98 dir Radenthein. Thro Millstatt & Dellach, turn R into Döbriach, sp Camping See site on L by lake after Döbriach. V lge, hdg, mkd, pt shd, EHU (6-10A) inc; gas; sw; TV; 10% statics; Eng spkn; adv bkg acc; solarium; golf 8km; bike hire; games area; horseriding; boating; sauna; CKE. *"Organised walks & trips to Italy; excel rest; private san facs avail; cinema; some pitches tight; fantastic facs."* **€28.90**   **2019**

DOBRIACH *D3* (2km SW Urban) *46.76811, 13.64809* **Camping Brunner am See,** Glanzerstrasse 108, 9873 Döbriach **(04246) 7189 or 7386; office@camping-brunner.at; www.camping-brunner.at**

12 🏕 €5 ♿ WC ⚓ ♨ ♿ ⚡ 🍴 🛒 ⚠

Fr Salzburg on A10 a'bahn take Seeboden-Millstatt exit bef Spittal. Foll rd 98 N of Millstattersee to camping sp. Med, pt shd, EHU (6A) inc; adv bkg acc; ccard acc; tennis; watersports; CKE. *"Great site with excel, clean san facs; pool 300m; gd size pitches; lakeside location; supmkt nrby & rests in vicinity; superb scenery."* **€34.40**   **2019**

EBEN IM PONGAU *C3* (1.5km S Rural) *47.39932, 13.39566* **See-Camping Eben,** Familie Schneider, Badeseestraße 54, 5531 Eben I Pg **06458 8231 or 0664 450 2000; info@seecamping-eben.at; www.seecamping-eben.at**

12 🏕 €3 ♿ (htd) ⚓ ♨ ♿ ⚡ MSP 🦋 ⛲ 🍴

Head E on A10, take exit 60 - Eben. Turn L onto B99. R onto Badeseestr. Campsite 800m on the L. Med, pt shd, EHU (16A) inc; train 800m; adv bkg acc; games area. *"Helpful owners; saunas; steam rm; lake adj; direct access fr mountains; clean & well organise; gd site."* **€30.00**   **2019**

EHRWALD *C1* (3km SW Rural) *47.38249, 10.90222* **Camping Biberhof,** Schmitte 8, 6633 Biberwier (Tirol) **(05673) 2950; info@biberhof.at; www.biberhof.at**

12 🏕 €1.90 ♿ WC ⚓ ♨ ♿ ⚡ ✉ MSP 🦋 ⛲ 🍴 🛒 ⚠

Fr Reutte, leave B179 sp Lermoos. In Leermoos cent turn R sp Biberwier. At t-junc in Biberwier turn L sp Ehrwald. Site on R in 300mtrs. Med, mkd, hdstg, pt shd, EHU (10A); bbq; twin axles; 80% statics; bus adj; Eng spkn; adv bkg acc; games area. *"Site under power cables; sometimes noisy; trampoline, volleyball, wall climbing, table tennis, walking/cycle rtes adj; mountain views; 3 scenic vill; pool at Lermoos 2km; outstanding san facs; drying rm; beautiful setting; generous pitches; clean san facs; free gd wifi; ideal NH."* **€29.50**   **2018**

EHRWALD *C1* (3km W Rural) *47.40250, 10.88893* **Happy Camp Hofherr,** Garmischerstrasse 21, 6631 Lermoos **(05673) 2980; info@camping-lermoos.com; www.camping-lermoos.com**

12 🏕 ♿ (htd) WC ⚓ ♨ ⚡ ✉ MSP 🦋 ⛲ 🍴 🛒 nr ⚠

On ent Lermoos on B187 fr Ehrwald site located on R. Med, pt shd, pt sl, EHU (16A) metered; gas; TV (pitch); 40% statics; phone; adv bkg acc; ccard acc; site clsd 1 Nov-mid Dec; tennis. *"Ideal for walks/cycling; v picturesque; adj park; ask for guest card for discount on ski lifts etc; ski lift 300m; excel san facs; htd pool 200m; superb rest (clsd Mon & Tue eve); family run site."* **€29.70**   **2019**

EISENSTADT *B4* (16km SE Rural) *47.80132, 16.69185* **Storchencamp Rust,** Ruster Bucht, 7071 Rust-am-Neusiedlersee (Burgenland) **(02685) 595; office@ gmeiner.co.at; www.gmeiner.co.at**

🏕 €4 ♿ WC ⚓ ♿ ⚡ 🦋 ⛲ 🍴 🛒

Fr Eisenstadt take rd to Rust & Mörbisch. In Rust foll sps to site & Zee; lakeside rd to ent. Lge, pt shd, EHU (16A) €3; sw nr; 60% statics; boating. *"Nr Hungarian border; attractive vill with nesting storks."* **€30.00, 1 Apr-31 Oct.**   **2019**

ENGELHARTSZELL *B3* (1km NW Rural) *48.51238, 13.72428* **Camp Municipal an der Donau,** Nibelungenstrasse 113, 4090 Engelhartszell **(0664) 8708787; tourismus@engelhartszell.ooe.gv.at; www.camping-audonau.at**

♿ WC ⚓ ♨ ♿ ⚡ ✉ 🦋 🍴 ⚠

Fr Passau (Germany) exit SE on B130 along Rv Danube. Site on L in approx 28km just bef Engelhartszell adj municipal pool complex. Sm, unshd, EHU (6A) metered; 50% statics; bus nr. *"Excel, clean, friendly site on rvside; pool adj; Danube cycleway passes site."* **€22.60, 15 Apr-15 Oct.**   **2016**

AUSTRIA

FURSTENFELD *C4 (2km NW Rural) 47.05631, 16.06255* **Camping Fürstenfeld,** Campingweg 1, 8280 Fürstenfeld **(03382) 54940; camping.fuerstenfeld@ chello.at; www.camping-fuerstenfeld.at**

Exit A2/E59 sp Fürstenfeld onto B65. Site well sp fr town cent. 4*, Med, pt shd, pt sl, EHU (10A) €2.30 (poss long lead req); 25% statics; phone; golf 5km; waterslide; rv fishing; CKE. *"Pleasant rvside site; ltd facs but clean; conv Hungarian border."*
€21.00, 15 Apr-15 Oct.   2016

GMUND (KARNTEN) *C3 (6km NW Rural) 46.94950, 13.50940* **Terrassencamping Maltatal,** Malta 6, 9854 Malta **(04733) 234; info@maltacamp.at**

Exit A10/E14 onto B99 to Gmünd. Foll sp Malta & after 6km site sp, on R next to filling stn. 5*, Lge, mkd, pt shd, terr, serviced pitches; EHU (10A) inc; bbq; 5% statics; phone; adv bkg acc; tennis; games area; canoeing; sauna; games rm; trout fishing; CKE. *"Gmund & Spittal gd shopping towns; Millstättersee 15km, Grossglocknerstrasse 1hr's drive; magnificant area with rvs, waterfalls, forests & mountains; guided walks; vg rest; children's mini farm; excel site."*
€30.00, 1 Apr-31 Oct.   2019

GNESAU *D3 (1km W Rural) 46.77966, 13.95062* **Camping Hobitsch,** Sonnleiten 24, 9563 Gnesau (Kärnten) **(0676) 6032848; office@camping-hobitsch.at; www.camping-hobitsch.at**

Site sp on B95. Sm, pt shd, EHU €3.50; Eng spkn; tennis; games area. *"Beautiful setting in meadow; excel san facs; adj to cycle path."*
€16.60, 1 May-30 Sep.   2016

GRAN *C1 (1km N Rural) 47.51000, 10.55611* **Comfort-Camp Grän,** Engetalstrasse 13, 6673 Grän (Tirol) **(05675) 6570; info@comfortcamp.at; www.comfortcamp.at**

Leave A7 (Germany) at Oy exit, foll 310 via Wertach, Oberjoch to Gran. Rtes fr Sonthofen or Reutte only suitable for MH's. 4*, Med, mkd, unshd, pt sl, terr, EHU (16A) 0.75 per kWh; gas; bbq; TV; 20% statics; phone; bus; Eng spkn; adv bkg acc; games rm; solarium; CKE. *"Ski-rm facs avail; private bthrms avail extra cost; vg facs; luxurious facs, sauna, massage; beautiful area; cable car nrby; walking/cycle rtes fr site; ACSI site."* €36.00, 10 May-1 Nov & 15 Dec-16 Apr.
                    2018

GRAN *C1 (6km W Rural) 47.50825, 10.49468* **Panoramacamp Alpenwelt,** Kienzerle 3, 6675 Tannheim **(05675) 43070; alpenwelt@tirol.com; www.tannheimertal-camping.com**

Fr N leave A7 junc 137 Oy-Mittelberg onto B310 to Oberjoch, then B199 to Tannheim. Fr S on B198 dir Reutte, turn onto B199 at Weissenbach to Tannheim. 5*, Med, mkd, hdstg, unshd, terr, serviced pitches; EHU (16A) metered; sw nr; TV (pitch); 30% statics; Eng spkn; adv bkg acc; sauna; CKE. *"Excel site & san facs; ski lift 2km; ski bus; gd walking/ cycling area; lovely views; pool 4km; wifi at cafe."*
€36.00, 20 Dec-19 Apr & 1 May-30 Oct.   2017

GRAZ *C4 (7km SW Urban) 47.02447, 15.39719* **Stadt-Camping Central,** Martinhofstrasse 3, 8054 Graz-Strassgang **(0316) 697824 or 0676 3785102 (mob); office@reisemobilstellplatz-graz.at; www.reisemobilstellplatz-graz.at**

Fr A9/E57 exit Graz-Webling, then dir Strassgang onto B70, site sp on R after Billa supmkt & filling stn. Med, mkd, hdstg, pt shd, EHU (6A) inc; gas; bbq; 20% statics; bus to city; tennis. *"Pleasant, conv site; reg bus service fr the nrby main rd (no traff noise); dogs free; pool, paddling pool adj; free ent superb lido (pt naturist); site manager v helpful; mainly MH."*
€30.00, 1 Apr-31 Oct.   2017

GREIFENBURG *D2 (2km E Rural) 46.74744, 13.19448* **Fliergercamp am See,** Seeweg 333, 9761 Greifenburg (Kärnten) **(04712) 8666; info@fliegercamp.at; www.fliegercamp.at**

Leave A10 & J139 onto 100 dir Lienz. Site on L after 15km, mkd & visible fr rd. Med, hdg, mkd, pt shd, EHU (16A) inc; gas; sw nr; twin axles; 20% statics; Eng spkn; ccard acc; games area; CCI. *"Gd cycling; vg site; pool adj; well run."* €24.00   2015

GREIN *B3 (0.7km SW Urban) 48.22476, 14.85428* **Campingplatz Grein,** Donaulände 1, 4360 Grein **07268 21230; office@camping-grein.at; www.camping-grein.at**

Sp fr A1 & B3 on banks of Danube. Med, pt shd, EHU (6-10A) €3; gas; red long stay; 10% statics; canoeing; fishing; CKE. *"Friendly, helpful owner lives on site; recep in café/bar; vg, modern san facs; htd covrd pool 200m; open air pool 500m; lovely scenery; quaint vill; gd walking; excursions; conv Danube cycle rte & Mauthausen Concentration Camp."*
€33.00, 1 Mar-31 Oct.   2019

For a guide to symbols see the fold out on the rear cover

HALL IN TIROL *C2 (6km E Rural) 47.28711, 11.57223*
Schlosscamping Aschach, Hochschwarzweg 2,
6111 Volders **(05224) 52333; info@schlosscamping.
com; www.schlosscamping.com**

🐕 €2.50 � 🚿 🕶 ⊘ MSP ♟ 🍴 ⊕ 🗑 🛒 ⅏ ⚴(htd)

Fr A12 leave at either Hall Mitte & foll sp to Volders,
or leave at Wattens & travel W to Volders (easiest
rte). Site well sp on B171. Narr ent bet lge trees.
Lge, mkd, pt shd, pt sl, EHU (16A) €2.70 (long cable
req some pitches, adaptor lead avail); gas; bbq; red
long stay; TV; phone; bus 250m; Eng spkn; adv bkg
acc; ccard acc; horseriding; tennis; CKE. *"Well-run,
efficient, clean site with vg, modern facs & helpful
management; few water & waste points; grassy pitches;
beautiful setting & views; gd walking/touring; arr early
to ensure pitch; excel."* **€29.00, 1 May-20 Sep.**   2017

HALL IN TIROL *C2 (1km NW Urban) 47.28423,
11.49658* **Schwimmbad-Camping,** Scheidenstein
strasse 26, 6060 Hall-in-Tirol **(05223) 5855550;
h.niedrist@hall.at; www.hall.ag**

🐕 ♟♟♟ 🚿 🕶 ⊘ MSP ♟ ⊕ 🛒 ⅏

Exit A12/E45/E60 at junc 68 at Hall-in-Tirol. Cross
rv strt into town & foll camp sp fr 2nd turn L; site
on B171. Diff ent. 3*, Med, pt shd, EHU (6A) €2.50;
red long stay; 15% statics; bus; red long stay; adv bkg
acc; tennis adj; CKE. *"Well-cared for site; friendly
welcome; vg, modern facs, poss stretched high ssn;
local excursions, walking; pt of sports complex; Hall
pretty, interesting medieval town; mini golf adj;
frequent music festivals; less cr than Innsbruck sites; no
twin axles; htd pool adj; walk to town; conv for m'vans;
NB m'vans only 1 Oct-30 Apr for €7.50 per night."*
€28.00, 1 May 30 Sep.   2015

HALLEIN *B2 (5km NW Rural) 47.70441, 13.06868*
Camping Auwirt, Salzburgerstrasse 42, 5400 Hallein
(06245) 80417; info@auwirt.com; www.auwirt.com

🐕 €2 ♟♟♟ 🚿 🕶 ⅙ ⊘ MSP ♟ 🍴 ⊕ 🗑 ⅏ ⚲

Exit A10/E55 junc 8 onto B150 sp Salzburg Süd, then
B159 twd Hallein. Site on L in 4km. Med, pt shd, EHU
(10A) €3; bus to Salzburg at site ent; Eng spkn; adv bkg
acc; CKE. *"Mountain views; cycle path to Salzburg nr; gd
san facs & rest; conv salt mines at Hallein & scenic drive
to Eagles' Nest; conv for Berchtesgaden; friendly helpful
family owners; flat site; excel."* **€36.00, 26 Mar-8 Oct,
9 Apr-5 Oct & 1 Dec-31 Dec.**   2017

HALLSTATT *C3 (1km S Rural) 47.55296, 13.64786*
Camping Klausner-Höll, Lahnstrasse 201, 4830 Hallstatt
**(06134) 6134 or 8322; camping@hallstatt.net;
camping.hallstatt.net**

🐕 €3 ♟♟♟ 🚿 🕶 ⊘ 🍴 ⊕ nr 🗑 🛒 ⅏

On exit tunnel 500m thro vill, site on R nr lge filling
stn. Med, pt shd, EHU (16A) €1 per person; sw; red
long stay; Eng spkn; ccard acc; boat trips; CKE. *"Excel,
level site; gd, clean san facs; chem disp diff to use; conv
Salzkammergut region, Hallstatt salt mines, ice caves;
pretty town 10 mins walk; family run site; relaxed &
friendly; walks; idyllic quiet setting with mountains
all around; cycle path around lake; pool adj; supmkt
300m."* **€40.00, 15 Apr-15 Oct.**   2019

HIRSCHEGG *C3 (0.5km N Rural) 47.02300, 14.95325*
Campingplatz Hirschegg, Haus No. 53, 8584 Hirschegg
info@camping-hirschegg.at; www.camping-hirschegg.at

12 🐕 €1 ♟♟♟ 🕶 🚿 🕶 ⊘ 🦋 ♟ 🍴 nr ⊕ nr 🛒 nr ⅏ ⚴

Exit A2 junc 224 Modriach N. At T-junc foll sp to
Hirschegg & in cent of vill turn R at petrol stn. Site
in 300m on L by fire stn. Med, mkd, hdg, pt shd, EHU
(10A) €2; sw nr; 30% statics; adv bkg acc. *"Excel,
family-run site."* **€18.00**   2016

IMST *C1 (1.5km S Rural) 47.22861, 10.74305*
Caravanpark Imst-West, Langgasse 62, 6460 Imst
**(05412) 66293; info@imst-west.com;
www.imst-west.com**

12 🐕 €1.80-€2 ♟♟♟ 🕶 🚿 🕶 ⊘ MSP 🦋 🍴 ⊕ nr 🗑 🛒 nr ⅏

Fr A12/E60 exit Imst-Pitztal onto B171 N dir Imst. In
1km at rndabt turn L and sweep R round Billa store.
Immed turn L & L again to site (sp). Med, mkd, pt shd,
pt sl, EHU (6-10A) €3; gas; Eng spkn. *"Gd cent for Tirol,
trips to Germany & en rte for Innsbruck; lovely views;
pool 1.5km; immac new san facs (2015); ski lift 2km;
free ski bus; gd."* **€28.00**   2017

INNSBRUCK *C1 (9.5km SW Rural) 47.23724,
11.33865* **Camping Natterersee,** Natterer See 1,
6161 Natters **(0512) 546732; info@natterersee.com;
www.natterersee.com**

12 🐕 €4.50 ♟♟♟(htd) 🕶 🚿 🕶 ⅙ ⊘ MSP ♟ 🍴 ⊕ 🗑 🛒 ⅏ ⅏ ⚲

App Innsbruck fr E or W on A12 take A13/E45
sp Brenner. Leave at 1st junc sp Innsbruck Süd,
Natters. Foll sp Natters - acute R turns & severe
gradients (care across unguarded level x-ing),
turn sharp R in vill & foll sp to site. Take care
on negotiating ent. Narr rds & app. Fr S on A13
Brennerautobahn exit junc 3 & foll dir Mutters &
Natters. 5*, Med, pt shd, sl, EHU (10A)€3.75; gas;
bbq; sw; TV; bus to Innsbruck; Eng spkn; adv bkg acc;
ccard acc; bike hire; waterslide; games rm; tennis;
clsd 1 Nov-mid Dec; games area; CKE. *"Well-kept
site adj local beauty spot; lakeside pitches gd views
(extra charge); gd, scenic cent for walking & driving
excursions; gd for children; friendly, helpful staff; excel
modern san facs; some sm pitches & narr site rds diff
lge o'fits; fantastic setting; sep car park high ssn; no
dogs Jul/Aug; guided hiking; special shwr for dogs;
excel."* **€42.00, G01.**   2018

INNSBRUCK *C1 (7km W Rural) 47.26339, 11.32629*
Camping Kranebittohof, Kranebitter Allee 216,
6020 Innsbruck-Kranebitten **(0512) 281958; info@
kranebitterhof.at; www.kranebitterhof.at**

12 🐕 ♟♟♟(htd) 🕶 🚿 🕶 ⅙ ⊘ MSP ♟ ⊕ 🛒

Fr W fork L after Zirl bef main rd rv bdge, sp
Innsbruck & foll B171 for 5km. Fr S on A13 fr border
foll dir Bregenz on A12 exit Kranebitten & foll sp
to site. Sharp ent on R. Med, mkd, hdstg, pt shd, pt
sl, terr, EHU (6-10A) inc; red long stay; 20% statics;
bus; Eng spkn; ccard acc; CKE. *"Excel, refurbished site
in lovely situation; vg, modern san facs; some m'way
& airport noise; hiking; friendly, helpful staff; ski lift
5km; site easy to find fr m'way, excel rest on site."*
€25.00   2016

INNSBRUCK *C1* (7.5km W Urban) *47.25307,
11.32661* **Campingplatz Pizzeria Stigger,**
Bahnhofstraße 10, 6176 Völs **(0512) 303533;**
campingvoels@aon.at; www.camping-stigger.at

🈯 ♀♂ WD 🛒 🚿 📵 MSP 🍷 ⑭ 🍴 🐾 nr

Exit A12/E60 at Völs exit & foll site sp. 1*, Sm, pt
shd, EHU inc; bus adj; Eng spkn; ccard acc; CKE. *"Gd;
pool 200m; conv Innsbruck; few lge pitches and quite
expensive."* **€28.00**   **2018**

JENBACH *C2* (6.5km NW Rural) *47.42156, 11.74043*
Camping Karwendel, 6212 Maurach **(05243) 6116;**
info@karwendel-camping.at; www.karwendel-
camping.at

🈯 ♀♂ €3 ♀♂ (htd) WD 🛒 🚿 ♿ ✏ 🦋 ⛺ 🍷 ⑭ 🐾 nr 🏔

Exit A12/E45/E50 junc 39 onto B181. Foll sp Pertisau
& Maurach. In 8km (climbing fr a'route turn L at
Maurach. Foll rd thro vill, turn L at T-junc, then strt
across rndabt twd lake. Site sp past recycling cent.
Med, unshd, EHU (10A) metered; sw nr; TV; 80%
statics; golf 4km; site clsd Nov. *"In open country,
glorious views of lake & mountains; diff access lge
o'fits; site neglected & rundown."* **€36.00**   **2019**

**"That's changed – Should I let
the Club know?"**

If you find something on site that's different
from the site entry, fill in a report and let us
know. See camc.com/europereport.

KALS AM GROßGLOCKNER *C2* (3km N Rural) *47.01912,
12.63680* **National Park Camping,** Berg 22, A9981 Kals
am Großglockner **(043) 4852 67389;** info@nationalpark-
camping-kals.at; www.nationalpark-camping-kals.at

♀♂ (htd) WD 🛒 🚿 ✏ MSP

Fr 108 (Leinz - Millersill) take L26 to Kals am
Großglockner. Site thro vill in abt 2km well sp. Care
needed at 3 way rd junc at end of vill, take ctr rd.
4*, Med, mkd, unshd, terr, EHU 10A; CKE. *"Excel, brand
new purpose built site in Hohe Tauren Nat Park at 1460m;
superb san facs."* **€30.00,** 1 Apr-31 Oct.   **2015**

KITZBUHEL *C2* (3km NW Rural) *47.45906, 12.3619*
Campingplatz Schwarzsee, Reitherstrasse 24, 6370
Kitzbühel **(05356) 62806;** office@bruggerhof-
camping.at; www.bruggerhof-camping.at

🈯 🐕 €5.50 ♀♂ (htd) WD 🛒 🚿 ♿ ✏ MSP 🍷 ⑭ nr 🐾 🏔

Site sp fr Kitzbühel dir Kirchberg-Schwarzsee.
Lge, pt shd, pt sl, EHU (16A) metered; gas; sw nr; TV
(pitch); 80% statics; phone; bus; Eng spkn; adv bkg acc;
ccard acc; sauna; CKE. *"Gd walks, cable cars & chair
lifts; vg, well-maintained site; poss mosquito & vermin
prob; some pitches in statics area; friendly owner;
well equipped with lots of activities; excel saunas
(site naturist in sauna area only); gd for families."*
€50.00   **2019**

KLAGENFURT *D3* (5km W Rural) *46.61826, 14.25641*
Camping Wörthersee, Metnitzstrand 5, 9020
Klagenfurt am wörthersee (Kärnten) **(0463) 287810;**
info@campingfreund.at; www.camping-woerthersee.at

🐕 €4.90 ♀♂ WD 🚿 ♿ 🛒 📵 ✏ 🦋 ⑭ 🐾 🏔 ⚓ 🏊 sand adj

Fr A2/E66 take spur to Klagenfurt-West, exit at
Klagenfurt-Wörthersee. Turn R at traff lts & immed
L at rd fork (traff lts), then foll sp to site. Lge, shd,
EHU (10A) inc; 10% statics; bus; ccard acc; sauna;
bike hire. *"V clean facs; local tax €3.50 per visit."*
€39.40, 1 May-30 Sep.   **2019**

KLOSTERNEUBURG *B4* (0.7km N Rural) *48.31097,
16.32810* **Donaupark Camping Klosterneuburg,**
In der Au, 3402 Klosterneuburg **(02243) 25877;** camp
klosterneuburg@oeamtc.at; www.campingkloster
neuburg.at

🐕 ♀♂ (htd) WD 🚿 ♿ 🛒 📵 ✏ 🦋 🍗 ⑭ nr 🐾 🏔

Fr A22/E59 exit junc 7 onto B14, site sp in cent of
town behind rlwy stn. After passing Klosterneuburg
Abbey on L turn 1st R (sharp turn under rlwy). Site
immed ahead. 4*, Med, mkd, pt shd, EHU (6-12A) €3;
gas; bbq; cooking facs; TV; 5% statics; phone; bus;
train to Vienna; ccard acc; bike hire; boat hire; tennis;
CKE. *"Well-organised, popular site; leisure cent adj; vg
san facs; helpful staff; sm pitches; htd pools adj; conv
Danube cycle path & Vienna; church & monastery worth
visit."* **€36.00,** 13 Mar-5 Nov.   **2017**

KOSSEN *B2* (3km SE Rural) *47.65388, 12.41544*
Eurocamping Wilder Kaiser, Kranebittau 18, 6345
Kössen **(05375) 6444;** info@eurocamp-koessen.com;
www.eurocamp-koessen.com

🈯 🐕 €4-6 ♀♂ (htd) WD 🚿 ♿ 🛒 📵 ✏ MSP 🍗 ⑭ 🐾 🏔 ⚓

Leave A12 at Oberaudorf/Niederndorf junc, head E
on 172 thro Niederndorf & Walchsee to Kössen. Strt
across at rndabt, in 1km turn R sp Hinterburg Lift.
At next junc turn R & site located after 400m.
5*, Lge, mkd, pt shd, serviced pitches; EHU (6A)
metered + conn fee; gas; TV (pitch); 50% statics;
Eng spkn; adv bkg acc; ccard acc; games area; sauna;
tennis; golf 2km; solarium; CKE. *"Lovely site; excel play
area & organised activities; htd pool adj; rafting, hang-
gliding & canoeing 1km; excel."* **€39.90**   **2019**

KOTSCHACH *D2* (1km SW Rural) *46.66946, 12.99153*
Alpencamp, Kötschach 284, 9640 Kötschach-Mauthen
(04715) 429; info@alpencamp.at; www.alpencamp.at

🈯 🐕 €2 ♀♂ (htd) WD 🚿 ♿ 🛒 📵 ✏ 🦋 🍗 ⑭ nr 🐾 🏔
🏊 (covrd, htd)

At junc of rds B110 & B111 in Kötschach turn W
onto B111, foll camp sps to site in 800m on L.
4*, Med, mkd, pt shd, EHU (16A) inc; TV; phone;
Eng spkn; ccard acc; games rm; bike hire; tennis;
waterslide; site clsd 1 Nov-14 Dec; boat hire; tennis
400m; sauna; games area. *"Useful for Plöcken Pass;
cycle tracks on rv bank nrby; vg san facs; friendly,
helpful owner; vg site."* **€19.00**   **2016**

LANDECK *C1* (0.5km W Urban) *47.14263, 10.56147*
Camping Riffler, Bruggfeldstrasse 2, 6500 Landeck
**(05442) 64898; info@camping-riffler.at;
www.camping-riffler.at**

**Exit E60/A12 at Landeck-West, site in 1.5km, 500m
fr cent on L.** Sm, pt shd, EHU (10A) €2.70 (poss rev pol); gas; ccard acc; bike hire; site clsd May; CKE. *"Well-kept, clean, friendly site; sm pitches; dogs free; narr rds; recep open 1800-2000 LS - site yourself & pay later; pool 500m; excel NH."* **€25.00** **2016**

LIENZ *C2* (6km SE Rural) *46.80730, 12.80350* **Camping
Seewiese,** Tristachersee 2, 9900 Tristach **(04852) 69767;
seewiese@hotmail.com; www.campingtirol.com**

**On B100 to Lienz dir Tristach, turn sharp L after rlwy
underpass & rv bdge to by-pass Trisach. Turn R after
4km opp golf course. Steep (11%) climb to site. Sp.**
4*, Med, hdstg, pt shd, sl, EHU (6-16A) €2.70; gas; sw nr; TV; phone; bus high ssn to Tristach; Eng spkn; bike hire; tennis; CKE. *"Fairly secluded, relaxing site; htd pool 5km; mountain views; gd walks; gd san facs; helpful owner."* **€36.00, 15 May-14 Sep.** **2015**

LIENZ *C2* (2km S Rural) *46.81388, 12.76388*
Dolomiten-Camping Amlacherhof, Lake rd 20, 9908
Amlach Lienz **(04852) 62317 or 69917 62317-1
(mob); info@amlacherhof.at; www.amlacherhof.at**

**S fr Lienz on B100, foll sp in 1.5km to Amlach. In vill,
foll site sp.** 4*, Med, hdg, mkd, pt shd, EHU (16A) metered inc; bbq; TV; 5% statics; bus adj; Eng spkn; adv bkg acc; site clsd 1 Nov-15 Dec; games rm; golf 7km; tennis; bike hire. *"Excel touring cent; many mkd walks & cycle rtes; cable cars; ski lifts 3km; attractive, historic town; excel, scenic site; local taxes €5."* **€32.40, 1 Mar-31 Oct.** **2019**

LIEZEN *C3* (11km SW Rural) *47.52061, 14.13080*
Camping Putterersee, Hohenberg 2A, 8943 Aigen
**(03682) 22859; camping.putterersee@aon.at;
www.camping-putterersee.at**

**S on A10 fr Salzburg, exit 63 for E651/B320 twds
Hohenberg. Foll sp.** Med, pt shd, pt sl, EHU (13A); gas; bbq; sw; twin axles; Eng spkn; adv bkg acc; bike hire; boat hire; fishing; games rm; CKE. *"Excel san facs; gd views, walking & cycling; v helpful staff; vg."* **€21.00, 15 Apr-31 Oct.** **2015**

LINZ *B3* (14km SE Rural) *48.23527, 14.37888* **Camping-
Linz am Pichlingersee,** Wienerstrasse 937, 4030 Linz
**(0732) 305314; office@camping-linz.at;
www.camping-linz.at**

**Exit A1/E60 junc 160; take Enns dir; go L on 1st
rndabt; do not go under rndabt thro underpass;
site is sp on R.** Med, mkd, pt shd, EHU (6A) inc; gas; cooking facs; sw nr; red long stay; 40% statics; bus; Eng spkn; adv bkg acc; tennis. *"Excel modern san facs, well-run, family-run site; friendly staff; site clsd 1300-1500; gd walks around lake; monastery at St Florian worth visit; conv NH; gd."* **€26.50, 15 Mar-15 Oct.** **2017**

LUNZ AM SEE *B4* (0.9km E Urban) *47.86194, 15.03638*
Ötscherland Camping, Zellerhofstrasse 23, 3293 Lunz-am-See (07486) 8413; info@oetscherlandcamping.at; www.oetscherlandcamping.at

12 ⛺ €1 ♦♦(htd) ⬜ ⚓ ♨ ∥ MSP 🦋 ⊞ nr ⚓ nr

Fr S on B25 turn R into Lunz-am-See. In 300m turn L, cross rv & take 1st L, site on L on edge of vill. Sm, hdstg, pt shd, EHU (16A) inc; sw nr; 80% statics; Eng spkn. *"Excel walking; immac facs; winter skiing; vg site on Rv Ybbs & Eisenstrasse."* **€19.50**   **2016**

MARBACH AN DER DONAU *B4* (1km W Rural)
48.21309, 15.13828 **Campingplatz Marbacher,** Granz 51, 3671 Marbach-an-der-Donau (07413) 20733; info@marbach-freizeit.at; www.marbach-freizeit.at

⛺ €2 ♦♦(htd) ⬜ ⚓ ♨ ∥ MSP 🦋 ⊞ nr ⚓ nr ⚒

Fr W exit A1 junc 100 at Ybbs onto B25. Cross Rv Danube & turn R onto B3. Site in 7km. Fr E exit A1 junc 90 at Pöchlarn, cross rv & turn L onto B3 to Marbach, site sp. Med, mkd, pt shd, EHU (16A) €1.9; bbq; sw; 5% statics; Eng spkn; adv bkg acc; ccard acc; bike hire; boat hire; tennis 800m; watersports; CKE. *"Beautiful, well-managed site; sm, narr pitches; excel facs & staff; gd rst & bar; gd cycling & watersports; v clean facs; gd NH fr m'way or longer stay for touring."* **€25.40, 1 Apr-31 Oct.**   **2019**

MARIAZELL *B4* (4km NW Rural) *47.79009, 15.28221*
Campingplatz am Erlaufsee, Erlaufseestrasse 3, 8630 St Sebastien-bei-Mariazell (03882) 4937 or (066460) 644400 (mob); gemeinde@st-sebastian.at; www.st-sebastian.at

⛺ €1.90 ♦♦ ⬜ ⚓ ♨ ∥ 🦋 ⊞ nr ⚓ nr

On B20 1km N of Mariazell turn W sp Erlaufsee. Site in 3km on app to lake, turn L thro car park ent to site. Med, pt shd, pt sl, EHU (12A) metered; bus high ssn. *"Cable car in Mariazell; beach nrby; pilgrimage cent; all hot water by token fr owner."* **€16.30, 1 May-15 Sep.**   **2016**

MATREI IN OSTTIROL *C2* (0.5km S Rural) *46.99583, 12.53906* **Camping Edengarten,** Edenweg 15a, 9971 Matrei-in-Osttirol (04875) 5111; info@campingeden garten.at; www.campingedengarten.at

⛺ ♦♦ ⬜ ⚓ ♨ ∥ MSP ☂ ⊞ nr ⚓ ⚓

App fr Lienz on B108 turn L bef long ascent (by-passing Matrei) sp Matrei-in-Osttirol & Camping. App fr N thro Felbertauern tunnel, by-pass town, turn R at end of long descent, sps as above. Med, pt shd, EHU (10A); gas; 10% statics; bus. *"Gd mountain scenery; helpful owner; beautiful views; pool 300m; pretty town; some rd noise during daytime."* **€32.00, 1 Apr-31 Oct.**   **2019**

MATREI IN OSTTIROL *C2* (23km W Rural) *47.01912, 12.63695* **Camping Kals Am Großglockner,** Burg 22, 9981 Kals am Großglockner 04852 67389; info@ nationalpark-camping-kals.at; www.nationalpark-camping-kals.at

⛺ €3.70 ♦♦(htd) ⬜ ⚓ ♨ ⚒ ∥ MSP 🦋 ☂ ⚓

Fr 108 Matrei in Osttirol to Lienz, exit at Huben onto L26 to Kals. 3km after vill foll sp to Dorfertal. National Park campsite on L. Med, unshd, EHU metered; twin axles; Eng spkn; ccard acc; CCI. *"Excel site; ski bus; excel walking & climbing."* **€31.50, 17 May-13 Oct.**   **2019**

MAYRHOFEN *C2* (1km N Rural) *47.17617, 11.86969*
Camping Mayrhofen, Laubichl 125, 6290 Mayrhofen (05285) 6258051; camping@alpenparadies.com; www.alpenparadies.com

⛺ €4.50 ♦♦♦ ⬜ ⚓ ♨ ⚒ ∥ MSP ☂ ⊞ ⚒ ⚓ nr 🏔 ⚓

Site at N end of vill off B169. Lge, hdstg, mkd, pt shd, EHU (10A) metered; gas; 50% statics; adv bkg acc; bike hire; sauna; CKE. *"Modern san facs; diff for lge o'fits, narr rds; some factory noise; gd rest."* **€31.20, 1 Jan-31 Oct & 15 Dec-31 Dec.**   **2019**

MELK *B4* (3km N Urban) *48.24298, 15.34040* **Donau Camping Emmersdorf,** Bundesstrasse 133, 3644 Emmersdorf-an-der-Donau (02752) 71707; office@ emmersdorf.at; www.emmersdorf.at

⛺ ♦♦ ⬜ ⚓ ♨ ⚒ ∥ ⊞ nr ⚓ nr

Fr A1 take Melk exit. Turn R, foll sp Donaubrücke, cross rv bdge. Turn R, site 200m on L, well sp. Sm, hdg, mkd, pt shd, EHU (6A) inc; bbq; phone; ccard acc; games rm; bike hire; tennis; fishing; CKE. *"Liable to close if rv in flood; clean facs; noise fr rd & disco w/end; attractive vill; vg."* **€20.50, 1 May-30 Sep.**   **2019**

MELK *B4* (6km NE Rural) *48.25395, 15.37115*
Campingplatz Stumpfer, 3392 Schönbühel (02752) 8510; office@stumpfer.com; www.stumpfer.com

⛺ ♦♦ ⬜ ⚓ ♨ ∥ ⊞ nr ⚓ nr

Exit A1 junc 80. Foll sp for Melk on B1 as far as junc with B33. Turn onto B33 (S bank of Danube) for 2km to Schönbühel. Site on L adj gasthof, sp. Sm, pt shd, EHU (10-16A) €2.40 or metered; gas; red long stay; Eng spkn; adv bkg acc; ccard acc; CKE. *"On beautiful stretch of Danube; arr early for rvside pitch; abbeys in Melk & Krems worth visit; lower end site unrel in wet; helpful staff; vg facs but poss stretched high ssn; cycle path adj."* **€28.50, 1 Apr-31 Oct.**   **2017**

MELK *B4* (3.6km NW Rural) *48.23347, 15.32888*
Camping Fährhaus Melk, Kolomaniau 3, 3390 Melk (02752) 53291; info@faehrhaus-melk.at; www.faehrhaus-melk.at

♦♦ ⚓ ∥ ☂ ⊞ nr ⚒ ⚓ 🏔

Skirt Melk on B1, immed after abbey at traff lts, turn N on bdge over rv (sp). Site in 700m. Sm, pt shd, EHU (6A) inc; bbq; fishing. *"Basic site but adequate; abbey adj & boating on Danube; NB all sites on banks of Danube liable to close if rv in flood."* **€12.50, 1 Apr-31 Oct.**   **2016**

MICHELDORF IN OBERÖSTERREICH *B3* (4km S Rural) *47.851081, 14.146745* **Schön Camping,** Schön 60, 4563 Micheldorf **(07582) 60917; reservierung@ schoen-menschen.at; schoen-menschen.at**

🏕🕿👫⛺🚿🅿🖃 MP 🦋 ⊕♿♨🛒🚲⚓(indoor)

Fr m'way J28 take rd 138 N dir Micheldorf, foll Schon camping sp (not Schon-Menschen sp) to avoid 3.1m rlwy bdge. Narr country rd. Drive thro complex to camping area at top. Hdstg, pt shd, pt sl, EHU inc; cooking facs; sw nr; phone; bus on rd 138; Eng spkn; adv bkg acc. "*Literally self service, pay in honesty box by facs bldg; part of disabled complex; free minigolf, access to indoor pool; walks witin site and local area; cafe (ltd hrs); vg.*"
€25.50, 1 May-30 Sep. 2019

MILLSTATT *D3* (4km SE Rural) *46.78863, 13.61418* **Camping Neubauer,** Dellach 3, 9872 Millstatt-am-See **(04766) 2532; info@camping-neubauer.at; www.camping-neubauer.at**

🏕🕿€2.50 👫(htd) 🖃⛺🚿♿🅿🖃✗🦋👟🍴⊕nr 🚲🛒⚓🎣

Exit A10/E55 dir Seeboden & Millstatt. Take lakeside rd B98 fr Millstatt to Dellach, R turn & foll sp camping sp. Med, mkd, hdstg, pt shd, terr, EHU (6A) inc; gas; bbq; sw; 10% statics; ccard acc; tennis; golf 6km; bike hire; watersports. "*Gd touring base; easy access to Italy; superb scenery with lakes & mountains; gd walks; excel facs; boat trips nr; gd rest; steep narr rd's to pitches, tractor avail to help; pt shd on lake pitches.*" **€31.70, 1 May-15 Oct.** 2019

MITTERSILL *C2* (1km E Rural) *47.27761, 12.49267* **Camping Schmidl,** Museumstrasse 6, 5730 Mittersill **(06562) 6158**

🏕🕿👫🖃⛺🚿✗🦋🛒nr

Fr Zell-am-See or Kitzbühel, exit to Mittersill, fr town sq foll camping sp past hospital. Sm, pt shd, EHU (15A) inc. "*Friendly & welcoming; useful stop bef Felbertauern tunnel; conv Krimml waterfall & Grossglockner; large CL type with pitches for 10 o'fits; gd for NH.*"
€12.00, 1 May-30 Sep. 2015

MONDSEE *B3* (5km SE Rural) *47.82956, 13.36554* **Austria Camp,** Achort 60, 5310 St Lorenz **(06232) 2927; office@austriacamp.at; austriacamp.at**

🏕🕿€2.90 👫🖃⛺🚿♿🅿🖃✗ MP 🦋🍴⊕🚲🛒⚓🎣

Exit A1/E55/E60 junc 265 onto B154. In 4km at St Lorenz at km 21.4 turn L onto unclassified rd to site in 600m at lakeside. Fr SW via Bad Ischl, at St Gilgen take Mondsee rd; 500m after Plomberg turn R at St Lorenz; Austria Camp sps clear. Med, shd, EHU (6A) €2.90; sw; 45% statics; adv bkg acc; boat launch; sauna; fishing; bike hire; golf nr; tennis; CKE. "*Gd, clean san facs; gd rest; friendly, family-run site; no arrivals bet 1200 & 1500.*" **€30.00, 1 Apr-30 Sep.**
2015

MURAU *C3* (3km W Rural) *47.10791, 14.13883* **Camping Olachgut,** Kaindorf 90, 8861 St Georgen-ob-Murau **(03532) 2162 or 3233; office@olachgut.at; www.olachgut.at**

12 🏕€3 👫🖃⛺🚿♿🅿🖃✗ MP 🦋♨🍴⊕🛒🚲nr ⚓🎣

Site sp on rd B97 bet Murau & St Georgen. Med, pt shd, EHU (16A) inc; gas; sw; 40% statics; adv bkg acc; sauna; horseriding; bike hire; games area. "*Rural site nr rlwy; ski lift 2.5km.*" **€30.00** 2019

MURECK *D4* (0.7km S Rural) *46.70491, 15.77240* **Campingplatz Mureck,** Austrasse 10, 8480 Mureck **(03472) 210512; m.rauch@mureck.steiermark.at; www.mureck.gv.at/tourismus-freizeit/campingplatz**

🏕€3.50 👫🖃⛺🚿♿🅿🖃✗🦋🍴⊕🛒🚲nr ⚓

Fr Graz on A9, turn E at junc 226 onto B69 sp Mureck. NB: Low archway in Mureck. Med, mkd, hdstg, shd, EHU (10A) inc; bbq; red long stay; 30% statics; phone; adv bkg acc; ccard acc; bike hire; fishing; tennis; games area; CKE. "*Off beaten track in pleasant country town; htd pool complex inc waterslide adj; pt of leisure complex; gd, modern san facs.*"
€23.00, 1 May-3 Nov. 2016

NASSEREITH *C1* (2.5km SE Rural) *47.30975, 10.85466* **Camping Rossbach,** Rossbach 325, 6465 Nassereith **(05265) 5154; rainer.ruepp@gmx.at; www.campingrossbach.com**

12 🏕€1.50 👫(htd) 🖃⛺🚿♿🅿🖃✗ MP 🦋🍴⊕🚲🛒⚓🎣🚣(htd) 🏊

On ent vill of Nassereith turn E & foll dir Rossbach/Dormitz, site in 1.5km. Foll sm green sps. Narr app. 4*, Med, mkd, pt shd, EHU (6A); bbq; TV; 5% statics; phone; adv bkg acc; fishing; games rm; CKE. "*Mountain views; friendly welcome; ACSI prices; ski lift 500m; ski bus; pitch in various sep areas; vg san facs.*"
€23.50 2017

NAUDERS *C1* (4km S Rural) *46.85139, 10.50472* **Alpencamping,** Bundestrasse 279, 6543 Nauders **(05473) 87217; info@camping-nauders.at; www.camping-nauders.com**

🏕€2 👫(htd) 🖃⛺🚿♿🅿🖃✗🍴⊕🚲🛒

On W side of B180 just bef Italian border. Sm, hdstg, unshd, EHU €1.90; gas; phone; ccard acc; CKE. "*Conv NH for Reschen pass; gd touring base, excel cycling, walking; excel san facs.*" **€25.00, 1 Jan-16 Apr, 30 Apr-15 Oct, 20 Dec-31 Dec.** 2016

NEUSTIFT IM STUBAITAL *C1* (0.5km NE Rural)
47.10977, 11.30770 **Camping Stubai,** Stubaitalstrasse
94, 6167 Neustift-im-Stubaital **(05226) 2537;
info@campingstubai.at; www.campingstubai.at**

12 🐕 €2.60 ♀♂ (htd) WD ⚓ ♨ 🖥 ╱ MSP 🍽 🛜 nr 🛒 nr ⛺

**S fr Innsbruck on B182 or A13, take B183 dir
Fulpmes & Neustift. Site sp, in vill opp church &
adj Billa supmkt. If app via A13 & Europabrucke,
toll payable on exit junc 10 into Stubaital Valley.**
4*, Med, mkd, pt shd, pt sl, terr, EHU (6A) €2.90;
50% statics; Eng spkn; adv bkg acc; games rm; sauna;
CKE. *"Friendly, family-run site; pitches nr rv poss flood;
recep open 0900-1100 & 1700-1900 - barrier down
but can use farm ent & find space; htd pool 500m;
excel mountain walking & skiing; lovely location."*
€34.00 **2017**

NEUSTIFT IM STUBAITAL *C1* (6km SW Rural)
47.06777, 11.25388 **Camping Edelweiss,** Volderau
29, 6167 Neustift-im-Stubaital **(05226) 3484;
info@camping-edelweiss.at; camping-edelweiss.at**

12 🐕 €3 ♀♂ (htd) WD ⚓ 🖥 ╱ MSP 🦋 🔵 ♨

**Fr B182 or A13 exit junc 10 take B183 to Neustift,
site on R at Volderau vill.** Med, hdstg, unshd, EHU
(4A) €3; gas; 30% statics; phone; bus. *"Excel peaceful
site in scenic valley; vg, modern san facs; haphazard
mix of statics & tourers; winter skiing."* **€18.00** **2019**

OBERNBERG AM INN *B3* (1km SW Rural) *48.31506,
13.32313* **Panorama Camping,** Saltzburgerstrasse 28,
4982 Obernberg-am-Inn **(07758) 30024 or 173 2306
571 (mob); obernberg-panoramacamping@aon.at;
http://obernberg-panoramacamping.jimdo.com**

12 ♀♂ WD ⚓ ╱ 🦋 🔵 nr 🛒 nr

**Exit A8/E56 junc 65 to Obernberg. Then take dir
Braunau, site well sp.** Sm, hdg, pt shd, pt sl, serviced
pitches; EHU (10A) metered or €2 (poss rev pol); Eng
spkn; adv bkg acc; tennis 800m. *"Friendly, excel sm
site; site yourself if office clsd; nr to border; spectacular
views; san facs clean; gd walking, birdwatching; o'night
m'vans area; network of cycle paths around vills on
other side of rv; pool 800m; pleasant walk to town past
rv viewpoint."* **€29.00** **2015**

OETZ *C1* (10km S Rural) *47.13533, 10.9316* **Ötztal
Arena Camp Krismer,** Mühlweg 32, 6441 Umhausen
**(05255) 5390; www.oetztalcamping.com;
www.oetztal-camping.at**

12 🐕 €2.60 ♀♂ WD ⚓ 🖥 ╱ 🦋 🛜 🍽 🔵 🛒 nr ⛺

**Fr A12 exit junc 123 S onto B186 sp Ötztal. S of
Ötztal turn L into Umhausen vill & foll site sp.**
4*, Med, mkd, pt shd, pt sl, EHU (16A) metered (poss
rev pol); gas; bbq; sw; phone; Eng spkn; adv bkg req.
*"Well-run site; immac facs; lots of local info given on
arr; friendly owners; poss diff pitching on sm
pitches; pool 200m; excel cent for Stuibenfal waterfall
(illuminated Wed night high ssn) & Ötztaler Valley; pool
& lake sw 200m; wonderful scenery; gd walking fr site;
narr app rd; very cr in high ssn."* **€29.00** **2018**

OSSIACH *D3* (1km SW Rural) *46.66388, 13.97500*
Terrassen Camping Ossiacher See, Ostriach 67, 9570
Ossiach **(04243) 436; martinz@camping.at;
www.terrassen.camping.at**

🐕 €3 ♀♂ (htd) WD ⚓ 🖥 ♨ ╱ MSP 🦋 🛜 🍽 🔵 ♨ 🛒 ⛺ ╱

**Leave A10/E55/E66 at exit for Ossiachersee, turn
L onto B94 twd Feldkirchen & shortly R to Ossiach
Süd. Site on lake shore just S of Ossiach vill.**
Lge, mkd, pt shd, terr, EHU (4-10A) €3; gas; bbq;
sw; red long stay; twin axles; TV; ccard acc; clsd
1200-1500 LS; games area; horseriding; games rm;
windsurfing; bike hire; fishing; tennis; watersports;
CKE. *"Ideal Carinthian lakes, Hochosterwitz castle
& excursions into Italy; parking adj; cash machine;
beautiful scenery; many activities; excel san facs;
pitches sm and diff for big o'fits; dogs confined to
pitches next to entrance; but site in lovely location."*
€41.00, 1 May-30 Sep, G05. **2019**

POYSDORF *A4* (1km W Urban) *48.66454, 16.61168*
Veltlinerland Camping, Laaerstrasse 106, 2170
Poysdorf **(02552) 20371; veltlinerlandcamping.
poysdorf@gmx.at; www.poysdorf.at**

🐕 WD 🖥 ╱ MSP 🔵 🛜 nr ♨

**Fr rd 7/E461 at traff lts in Poysdorf turn W onto
rd 219 dir Laa an der Thaya. Site sp on R in approx
1km on edge of park.** Sm, mkd, hdstg, unshd, terr,
EHU (6A) €2.20; sw nr; 50% statics; Eng spkn; tennis.
*"Gd, under-used site 1hr N of Vienna; htd wc & shwrs at
park adj (key issued); no other site in area; conv Czech
border."* **€13.00, 1 May-31 Oct.** **2016**

PRUTZ *C1* (0.6km NE Rural) *47.07955, 10.6588*
Aktiv-Camping Prutz, Pontlatzstrasse 22, 6522 Prutz
**(05472) 2648; info@aktiv-camping.at; www.aktiv-
camping.at**

12 🐕 €3 ♀♂ (htd) WD ⚓ ♨ 🖥 ╱ MSP 🍽 🔵 ♨ 🛒 ⛺

**Fr Landeck to Prutz on rd B180 turn R at Shell stn
over rv bdge, site sp.** 4*, Med, hdg, mkd, pt shd, EHU
(16A) inc; gas; sw nr; red long stay; TV; 20% statics;
Eng spkn; adv bkg acc; ccard acc; bike hire; site clsd
Nov; CKE. *"Excel, clean facs; gd views; o'night m'vans
area; pool complex in vill; office clsd 1000-1630 - find
pitch & pay later; walks & cycle rtes; conv NH en rte
Italy & for tax-free shopping in Samnaun, Switzerland;
gd site; cards given for free bus travel."* **€32.00** **2015**

PURBACH AM NEUSIEDLERSEE *B4* (1km SE Rural)
47.90958, 16.70580 **Storchencamp Purbach,**
Türkenhain, 7083 Purbach-am-Neusiedlersee
(Burgenland) **(02683) 5170; office@gmeiner.co.at;
www.gmeiner.co.at**

🐕 €2.90 ♀♂ (htd) WD ⚓ 🖥 ♨ ╱ MSP 🦋 🍽 🔵 🛒 ⛺

**Exit A4/E6 junc 43 onto B50 at Neuseidl-am-See to
Purbach. Site sp in town nr pool complex.** Sm, pt shd,
EHU (6A) €2.30; bbq; 80% statics; bus/train 1km;
Eng spkn; games area. *"Open field for tourers; excel
sw complex adj free with local visitor card; free public
transport & red ent to museums etc; modern facs; conv
NH."* **€17.50, 1 Apr-31 Oct.** **2016**

RATTENBERG *C2 (4.5km N Rural) 47.45670, 11.88084*
Seen-Camping Stadlerhof, Seebühel 15, 6233 Kramsach-am-Reintalersee **(05337) 63371; camping.stadlerhof@chello.at; www.camping-stadlerhof.at**

12 🐕 €4.90 �(htd) 🚿 ♿ ⚒ 🚽 ⚐ 🦋 ⛲ 🍴 ⓤ 🛒 nr ⛰️ 🏊(htd) 🚤

Exit A12/E45/E60 junc 32 Rattenberg dir Kramsach. At rndabt turn R, then immed L & foll sp 'Zu den Seen' & site sp. Site on L at Lake Krumsee. 5*, Lge, mkd, hdstg, pt shd, pt sl, EHU (10A) inc; gas; bbq; sw nr; TV (pitch); 50% statics; phone; adv bkg acc; games rm; bike hire; fishing; tennis; sauna. *"Beautiful, well laid-out site in lovely setting; excel san facs."*
€35.80 2019

RATTENBERG *C2 (4km NE Rural) 47.46198, 11.90708*
Camping Seehof, Moosen 42, 6233 Kramsach-Reintalersee **(05337) 63541; info@camping-seehof.com; www.camping-seehof.com**

12 🐕 €5 �(htd) 🚿 ♿ ⚒ 🚽 ⚐ 🦋 ⛲ 🍴 ⓤ 🛒 ⛰️ 🚤

Exit A12/E45/E60 junc 32 sp Kramsach, foll sp 'Zu den Seen' for 5km. Site immed bef Camping Seeblick-Toni Brantlhof. 5*, Med, mkd, pt shd, EHU (6-13A) €3; bbq; sw; red long stay; TV (pitch); 30% statics; phone; Eng spkn; adv bkg acc; ccard acc; bike hire; gym; solarium; horseriding nr; CKE. *"Friendly staff; gd views fr some pitches; gd, modern san facs; gd rest; Excel site, local walks, excel museum next door; local taxes €2."* **€33.00** 2019

REUTTE *C1 (1km S Rural) 47.47763, 10.72258*
Camping Reutte, Ehrenbergstrasse 53, 6600 Reutte **(05672) 62809 or (06641) 858279 (mob); camping-reutte@aon.at; www.camping-reutte.com**

12 🐕 €2 � 🚿 ⚒ 🚽 ⚐ 🦋 ⓤ 🛒

Foll B179 (Fern pass rd), exit at Reutte Süd. Site sp in 1.5km on L. Med, mkd, hdstg, pt shd, EHU (16A) €2.40; TV (pitch); phone; Eng spkn; adv bkg acc; CKE. *"Conv for Fern Pass; barriers clsd 2100; clean, popular site; excel; ski lift 500m; pool adj; free guest cards for facs & transport."* **€29.70** 2016

RIED IM OBERINNTAL *C1 (0.6km E Rural) 47.05480, 10.65630* **Camping Dreiländereck,** Gartenland 37, 6531 Ried Im Oberinntal **05472 6025; info@tirolcamping.at; www.tirolcamping.at**

12 🐕 €4 �(htd) 🚿 ⚒ 🚽 ⚐ 🦋 ⛲ 🍴 🛒 nr

Fr Landeck take 180 twd Reschenpass. Exit at Ried & foll sp. Sm, unshd, EHU (15A) metered; sw nr; twin axles; TV; bus adj; Eng spkn; adv bkg acc; CCI. *"Wellness cent; conv to vill shops; bike hire; helpful owners; gd clean san facs; adventure sports fac nrby; gd site."* **€40.60** 2019

ST ANTON AM ARLBERG *C1 (2km E Rural) 47.14505, 10.33890* **Camping Arlberg,** Strohsack 235c, 6574 Pettneu-am-Arlberg (Tirol) **(05448) 222660; info@camping-arlberg.at; www.camping-arlberg.at**

🐕 ♿ � 🚿 ♿ ⚒ 🚽 ⚐ 🦋 🍴 ⓤ ⛰️ 🛷(covrd, htd) 🚤

Fr W on S16/E60, thro Arlberg tunnel, then take Pettneu exit after St Anton to N; site sp in 200m. 4*, Lge, hdg, mkd, pt shd, EHU (16A) metered; twin axles; 10% statics; phone; bus; Eng spkn; adv bkg acc; sauna; fishing. *"Mountain views; htd private bathrms & sat TV each pitch; o'night m'vans area; beauty treatments avail; excel site;ski & boot rm; ski bus; ski lift 1km; wellness ctr adj with pool; site fees inc free bus, cable car & sw pool for 1 day."*
€30.00, 1 Jan-30 Apr, 1 Jun-31 Sep & 1 Dec-31 Dec. 2017

ST JOHANN IM PONGAU *C2 (1km S Urban) 47.34141, 13.19793* **Camping Kastenhof,** Kastenhofweg 6, 5600 St Johann-im-Pongau **(06412) 5490; info@kastenhof.at; www.kastenhof.at**

12 🐕 ♿ ♿ 🚿 ⚒ 🚽 ⚐ 🦋 ⓤ nr 🛒 ⛰️ 🚤

Take A10 S fr Salzburg onto B311 for Alpendorf. Go over rv & turn L into Liechtensteinklamm twd St Johann, site on L, sp. 1*, Med, unshd, EHU (15A) metered + €2 conn fee; TV (pitch); 10% statics; bus; adv bkg acc; sauna; CKE. *"Conv Tauern tunnel, Grossglockner Hochalpenstrasse, Zell-am-See; gd clean site."* **€28.00** 2018

ST JOHANN IN TIROL *C2 (12km SE Rural) 47.46845, 12.55440* **Tirol Camp,** Lindau 20, 6391 Fieberbrunn (Tirol) **(05354) 56666; office@tirol-camp.at; www.tirol-camp.at**

🐕 FR ♿ (htd) 🚿 ⚒ 🚽 ⚐ 🦋 ⛲ 🍴 ⓤ 🛒 ⛰️ 🖊️ 🛷(covrd, htd)

Fr St Johann thro vill of Fieberbrunn, site sp at end of vill. Turn R up to Streuböden chair lift, site 200m on L. 4*, Lge, pt shd, terr, EHU (6A) metered; sw; TV; 30% statics; phone; train; adv bkg acc; ccard acc; games area; tennis; waterslide; sauna. *"Superb site & facs; gd base for skiing, gd walking; wellness cent; trips to Innsbruck & Salzburg; noise fr adj farm."*
€38.00, 1 Jan-12 Apr, 11 May-1 Nov & 9 Dec-31 Dec. 2015

ST MICHAEL IM LUNGAU *C3 (0.2km S Rural) 47.09685, 13.63706* **Camping St Michael,** Waaghausgasse 277, 5582 St Michael-im-Lungau **(06477) 8276; camping-st.michael@sgb.at; www.camping-sanktmichael.at**

12 🐕 ♿ ♿ 🚿 ⚒ 🚽 ⚐ 🦋 ⓤ nr 🛒 ⛰️

Exit junc 104 fr A10/E55, site sp at turn into vill, then on L after 200m bef hill. Sm, pt shd, EHU (16A) €3.50 (poss rev pol); gas; adv bkg acc; ccard acc; CKE. *"Delightful site adj vill; excel san facs (shared with adj sports club); ski lift 1km; pool adj; poss full if arr after 6pm, but o'flow area avail."* **€20.00** 2016

ST PETER AM KAMMERSBERG *C3* (3km ESE Rural) *47.17905, 14.21671* **Camping Bella Austria,** Peterdorf 100, 8842 St Peter-am-Kammersberg **(03536) 73902; info@camping-bellaustria.com; www.camping-bell austria.com**

🛖 €2 � 👭 WC ♨ ♿ 🚿 ⊟ ⁄ MSP 🦋 ⁇ 🍸 ⑪ 🍴 🛒 ⚠ ♒ 🏊 (htd)

Fr B96 turn N onto L501 into Katschtal Valley dir Oberdorf, Althofen & St Peter-am-Kammersberg. Site sp. 4*, Lge, hdstg, pt shd, EHU (16A) inc; sw; TV; 70% statics; Eng spkn; adv bkg acc; sauna; games area; bike hire. *"Superb walking area; excel."* €26.00, 12 Apr-28 Sep.   2019

ST PRIMUS *D3* (0.8km N Rural) *46.58569, 14.56598* **Strandcamping Turnersee Breznik,** Unternarrach 21, 9123 St Primus **(04239) 2350; info@breznik.at; www.breznik.at**

🛖 €2.40 👭 (htd) WC ♨ ♿ 🚿 ⊟ ⁄ MSP 🦋 ⁇ 🍸 ⑪ 🍴 🛒 ⚠ ♒

Exit A2 at junc 298 Grafenstein onto B70. After 4km turn R & go thro Tainach, St Kanzian twd St Primus. Site is on W side of Turnersee. 5*, Lge, mkd, pt shd, serviced pitches; EHU (6A) inc; bbq; sw; TV; 30% statics; adv bkg acc; fishing; golf 2km; tennis 500m; games area; bike hire; games rm; CKE. *"Lovely situation; cinema rm; excel site."* €20.40, 16 Apr-2 Oct.   2016

ST VEIT AN DER GLAN *D3* (6km NE Rural) *46.80245, 14.41260* **Camping Wieser,** Bernaich 8, 9313 St Georgen-am-Längsee (Kärnten) **(04212) 3535; info@ campingwieser.com; www.campingwieser.com**

👭 WC ♨ ⊟ ⁄ 🦋 ⁇ 🍸 ⑪ 🛒 nr ⚠

Fr St Veit take B317 NE dir Freisach. After 4km turn R to Bernaich, St Georgen. Site sp on L after 500m. Med, mkd, pt shd, terr, EHU (10A) inc; sw nr; TV; phone; CKE. *"Farm site; pool 5km; friendly owner."* €27.00, 1 May-10 Oct.   2016

ST WOLFGANG IM SALZKAMMERGUT *B3* (1km W Rural) *47.74277, 13.43361* **Seeterrassen Camping Reid,** Ried 18, 5360 St Wolfgang/Salzkammergut **(06138) 3201; camping-ried@aon.at; www.seeterrassen camping-ried.at**

🛖 €4 👭 (htd) WC ♨ ♿ 🚿 ⊟ ⁄ MSP 🍸 ⑪ 🍴 🛒 ⚠

Fr Salzburg take B158 thro St Gilgen dir Bad Ischl. Exit at sp Strobl & foll sp St Wolfgang. Go thro tunnel to avoid town cent, foll rd along lake to site. Sm, pt shd, pt sl, terr, EHU (16A) metered; gas; sw nr; TV; 10% statics; phone; Eng spkn; watersports adj; tennis nr; fishing adj; CKE. *"Mountain rlwy stn nr; lake views; gd touring base; easy walk into town; friendly site; v clean san facs."* €30.20, 16 Apr-31 Oct.   2019

SALZBURG *B2* (3km N Rural) *47.82843, 13.05221* **Panorama Camping Stadtblick,** Rauchenbichlerstrasse 21, 5020 Salzburg **(0662) 450652; info@panorama-camping.at; www.panorama-camping.at**

🛖 €2 (htd) WC ♨ ♿ 🚿 ⁄ MSP ⁇ 🍸 ⑪ 🛒

Fr A1/E55/E60 exit 288 Salzburg Nord/Zentrum & at end of slip rd turn R & sharp R at traff lts, site sp. If coming fr S, foll ring rd to W then N. Med, mkd, hdstg, pt shd, terr, EHU (4A) inc (long lead req some pitches); gas; red long stay; phone; bus to town nrby (tickets fr recep); Eng spkn; adv bkg acc; CKE. *"Conv a'bahn; views of Salzburg; cycle track by rv to town; Salzburg card avail fr recep; sm pitches - rec phone ahead if lge o'fit; v helpful family owners; vg rest; excel, modern san facs; cash only; rec arr early; also open some dates in Dec & Jan; excel; 'Sound of Music' Tour; v conv for Salzburg; gd views; beautiful city; helpful owner."* €37.00, 1 Jan-8 Jan, 20 Mar-5 Nov, 6 Dec-17 Dec.   2017

SALZBURG *B2* (5km SE Urban) *47.78058, 13.08985* **Camping Schloss Aigen,** Weberbartlweg 20, 5026 Salzburg **(0662) 622079; camping.aigen@ elsnet.at; www.campingaigen.com**

🛖 €1 👭 WC ♨ ⁄ 🦋 🍸 ⑪ 🍴 🛒

Fr S leave A10/E55 at junc 8 Salzburg-Süd & take B150 twds Salzburg on Alpenstrasse. Turn R at rndabt dir Glasenbach, then L into Aignerstrasse. 1km S of Aigen stn turn R into Glasenstrasse & foll sps to site. Lge, pt shd, pt sl, EHU (6-16A) €2.50; gas; red long stay; bus to town 700m; adv bkg acc; CKE. *"Friendly, family-run site; washing machine avail; sl pitches v slippery & boggy when wet; excel rest; conv for city; gd walks."* €26.50, 1 May-30 Sep.   2019

> ## "We must tell the Club about that great site we found"
>
> Get your site reports in by mid-August and we'll do our best to get your updates into the next edition.

SCHARNSTEIN *B3* (2.5km NE Rural) *47.91580, 13.97372* **Almcamp Schatzlmühle,** Viechtwang 1A, 4644 Scharnstein 07615 20269; office@almcamp.at; **www.almcamp.at**

🛖 €2 👭 WC ♨ ♿ 🚿 ⊟ ⁄ MSP 🦋 ⁇ 🍸 ⑪ 🛒 ⚠

Fr A1 take exit 207 Vorchtdorf to Pettenbach on the L536. Head twd Scharnstein on 120. Turn R 2km bef vill (dir Viechtwang). Foll sp. Alt take A9, exit 5, dir Scharnstein. Sm, mkd, hdstg, hdg, pt shd, EHU (16A); bbq; twin axles; TV; 10% statics; phone; Eng spkn; adv bkg acc; games area; games rm; CCI. *"Child friendly; family run site; site by rv, scenic location; gd cycling & walking rtes; htd, excel site & san facs."* €28.00, 12 Mar-31 Oct.   2019

SEEFELD IN TIROL *C1* (1.6km NW Rural) *47.33661, 11.17756* **Alpin Camp,** Leutascherstrasse 810, 6100 Seefeld (05212) 4848; info@camp-alpin.at; www.camp-alpin.at

[icons]

Fr N on B177/E533 turn W into Seefeld. Thro main rd, turn R sp Leutasch, site on L in 2km. Apps fr SE & SW via v steep hills/hairpins, prohibited to trailers. 3*, Med, hdstg, pt shd, pt sl, terr, EHU (16A) €2.80 or metered; gas; 10% statics; bus to town; Eng spkn; adv bkg acc; golf 1.5km; site clsd Nov; bike hire. *"Excel site; htd, covrd pool 1.5km; sauna & steambath inc; excel facs; friendly owners; vg walking; delightful setting; ski tows at gate; lovely vill; free bus to town/funicular."* **€42.00** **2018**

SILLIAN *D2* (4km E Rural) *46.74583, 12.46315* **Camping Lienzer Dolomiten,** Tassenbach 191, 9918 Strassen-bei-Sillian (04842) 5228; camping-dolomiten@gmx.at; www.camping-tirol.at

[icons]

B100 fr Sillian dir Lienz, turn R after filling stn, over level x-ing, then immed R; site sp. 3*, Med, mkd, hdstg, unshd, pt sl, EHU (6A) €2; sw; red long stay; 25% statics. *"Informal, peaceful site; clean facs; ski lift 3km; helpful staff; mountain views."* **€28.50** **2016**

SOLDEN *C1* (1km S Rural) *46.95786, 11.01193* **Camping Sölden,** Wohlfahrtsstrasse 22, 6450 Sölden (05254) 26270; info@camping-soelden.com; www.camping-soelden.com

[icons]

Turn L off main rd at cable car terminal. Turn R at rv & foll narr track on rv bank for about 200m, turn R into site. Med, mkd, pt shd, pt sl, terr, serviced pitches; EHU (10A) metered; gas; Eng spkn; adv bkg acc; ccard acc; site clsd mid-Apr to mid-Jun approx; gym; sauna; og-washing facs. *"Excel for touring or climbing in upper Ötz Valley; pitches tight for lge o'fits; superb site; excel san facs."* **€33.00, 1 Jan-12 Apr & 27 Jun-31 Dec.** **2015**

SPITTAL AN DER DRAU *D3* (5.6km NE Urban) *46.81510, 13.52001* **Strandcamping Winkler,** Seepromenade 33, 9871 Seeboden 04 76 28 19 27; http://www.campsite.at/strandcamping-winkler

[icons]

Leave A10 Villach-Salzburg at junc 139 twd Seeboden. Cont along main st across 2 rndabts & turn R down narr rd sp Strandcamping Winkler. Sm, mkd, pt shd, pt sl, EHU (16A); sw nr; twin axles; Eng spkn; adv bkg acc; CCI. *"Cycling & walking rtes rnd beautiful Millstätter; gd site."* **€36.50, 1 May-1 Oct.** **2019**

SULZ IM WIENERWALD *B4* (1km N Rural) *48.10510, 16.13348* **Camping Wienerwald,** Leopoldigasse 2, 2392 Sulz-im-Wienerwald (0)664 4609796; ww-camp@aon.at; www.camping-wienerwald.at

[icons]

Leave A21/E60 at junc 26 dir Sittendorf, Foll sp to site at Sulz (7km fr m'way). Sm, mkd, pt shd, pt sl, EHU (6A) €1.90 (poss long lead req); 10% statics. *"Conv Vienna - 25km; gd walks."* **€17.00, 15 Apr-15 Oct.** **2016**

TELFS *C1* (9km SW Rural) *47.27510, 10.98661* **Camping Eichenwald,** Schiess-Standweg 10, 6422 Stams (05263) 6159; info@camping-eichenwald.at or info@tirol-camping.at; www.tirol-camping.at

[icons]

Exit A12 at exit Stams-Mötz, foll B171 sp Stams. Turn R into vill, site behind monastery nr dry ski jump; steep app. 4*, Med, pt shd, terr, EHU (6A) €2.70; gas; TV; Eng spkn; adv bkg acc; games rm; bike hire; tennis 500m; games area; CKE. *"Beautiful views; friendly owner; private bthrms some pitches; statics (sep area); vg site; gd rest; san facs v clean."* **€31.00** **2018**

> ## "I need an on-site restaurant"
> We do our best to make sure site information is correct, but it is always best to check any must-have facilities are still available or will be open during your visit.

VELDEN AM WORTHERSEE *D3* (8km E Rural) *46.61890, 14.10565* **Camping Weisses Rössl,** Auenstrasse 47, Schiefling-am-See, 9220 Velden-Auen (04274) 2898; office@weisse-roessl-camping.at; www.weisses-roessl-camping.at

[icons]

Fr A2 exit 335 dir Velden. At rndabt bef town fol sp twd Maria Wörth for 9km on S side of Wörthersee. Site on R up hill. Lge, hdstg, pt shd, pt sl, terr, EHU (16A) inc; gas; bbq; sw nr; TV; phone; Eng spkn; CKE. *"Gd."* **€24.50, 1 May-30 Sep.** **2016**

VILLACH *D3* (7km NE Rural) *46.65641, 13.89196* **Camping Bad Ossiacher See,** Seeuferstrasse 109, 9520 Annenheim (04248) 2757; office@camping-ossiachersee.at; www.camping-ossiachersee.at

[icons]

Fr A10/E55/E66 exit sp Villach/Ossiacher See onto B94. Turn R for St Andrä sp Süd Ossiacher See. Site on L in 300m. Lge, pt shd, EHU (10-16A) inc; bbq; sw nr; twin axles; 5% statics; phone; Eng spkn; adv bkg acc; ccard acc; tennis; games area; sailing; waterskiing. *"Well-kept site; barrier clsd 1200-1400; handy NH even when wet; Annenheim cable car; lge level grass pitches; excel."* **€35.60, 7 Apr-26 Oct.** **2017**

AUSTRIA

WAIDHOFEN AN DER THAYA *A4* (1km SE Rural) *48.81113, 15.28839* **Campingplatz Thayapark,** Badgasse, 3830 Waidhofen-an-der Thaya **(02842) 50356 or 0664 5904433 (mob); stadtamt@ waidhofen-thaya.gv.at; www.waidhofen-thaya.at/ Campingplatz_Thayapark**

Site sp fr town cent. Med, pt shd, EHU (10A) €2.30; TV (pitch); 5% statics; CKE. *"Quiet site nr attractive town; pool 300m; recep open 0800-1000 & 1600-1800."* **€14.80, 1 May-30 Sep.** **2016**

WERFEN *C2* (4km S Rural) *47.44501, 13.21165* **Camping Vierthaler,** Reitsam 8, 5452 Pfarrwerfen **(06468) 57570; vierthaler@camping-vierthaler.at; www.camping-vierthaler.at**

Fr A10 exit 43 or 44 sp Werfen/Pfarrwerfen. Turn S onto B159 twd Bischofshofen. After 2km site on L bet rd & rv. 1*, Sm, pt shd, EHU (10-16A) €2; gas; 10% statics; adv bkg rec; ccard acc; rafting; fishing. *"Scenic site; friendly owners; htd pool 2km; Werfen castle & ice caves worth a visit; cycle path; walking; ltd san facs, sometimes stretched."* **€22.00, 15 Apr-30 Sep.** **2018**

WIEN *B4* (9km E Urban) *48.20861, 16.44722* **Aktiv-Camping Neue Donau,** Am Kleehäufel, 1220 Wien-Ost **(01) 2024010; neuedonau@campingwien.at; www.campingwien.at**

Take A21-A23, exit sp Olhafen/Lobau. After x-ing Rv Danube turn R, sp Neue-Donau Sud. In 150m turn L at traff lts after Shell g'ge; site on R. Fr E on A4 turn R onto A23 & take 1st slip rd sp N-Donau after x-ing rv Danube. Lge, unshd, serviced pitches; EHU (16A) €4 (poss rev pol); bus/metro to city 1km; Eng spkn; adv bkg acc; ccard acc; tennis; games area; CKE. *"Conv Vienna; lovely site; excel facs but poss stretched high ssn; poss v cr due bus tours on site; cycle track to city cent (map fr recep); 3 classes of pitch (extra charge for serviced); recep clsd 1200-1430; standard san facs."* **€32.00, 15 Apr-30 Sep.** **2019**

WIEN *B4* (13km W Urban) *48.21396, 16.2505* **Camping Wien-West,** Hüttelbergstrasse 80, 1140 Wien **(01) 9142314; west@campingwien.at; www.campingwien.at**

Fr Linz, after Auhof enter 3 lane 1-way rd. On app to traff lts get into L hand (fast) lane & turn L at traff lts. At next lts (Linzerstrasse) go strt over into Hüttelburgstrasse & site is uphill. Fr Vienna, foll sp A1 Linz on W a'bahn & site sp to R 100m bef double rlwy bdge. After this turn L on rd with tramlines & foll to v narr section, R at traff lts. Lge, mkd, hdstg, pt shd, EHU (16A) €4; 10% statics; bus; Eng spkn; adv bkg acc; ccard acc; CKE. *"Rec arr early; gd bus service to U-Bahn & city cent - tickets fr recep + Vienna Card; clean facs, but poss stretched high ssn & ltd LS; poss travellers; site poss unkempt LS; sm pitches; sep car park; site clsd Feb; well run; well position for Vienna."* **€36.00, 1 Jan-31 Jan & 16 Feb-31 Dec.** **2017**

WORGL *C2* (13km SE Rural) *47.43068, 12.14990* **Camping Reiterhof,** Kelchsauerstrasse 48, 6361 Hopfgarten **(05335) 3512; info@campingreiterhof.at; www.campingreiterhof.at**

Fr Wörgl S on B170, thro Hopfgarten, site sp on R dir Kelchsau. 4*, Med, mkd, pt shd, EHU (10A) €2.80; 45% statics; Eng spkn; adv bkg acc; CKE. *"V friendly, v welcoming, helpful staff; immac san facs; ski lift 2km; excel for families or couples; lge recreation park adj; htd pool 200m; excel walking & cycling area; free ski bus; excel."* **€18.00** **2016**

ZELL AM SEE *C2* (7km N Rural) *47.37740, 12.79583* **Campingplatz Bad Neunbrunnen,** Neunbrunnen 56, 5751 Maishofen **(06542) 68548 or (0664) 3512282 (mob); camping@neunbrunnen.at; www.camping-neunbrunnen.at**

Foll B311 N fr Zell-am-See dir Saalfelden; 500m after Maishofen turn L bef tunnel & foll site sp. Med, mkd, hdstg, unshd, EHU (10A) €2.20; sw; ccard acc; fishing; games rm. *"Vg, scenic site; cycle & walking tracks fr site; winter sports area; vg rest."* **€19.50** **2015**

ZELL AM SEE *C2* (6km SE Rural) *47.30133, 12.8150* **Panorama Camp Zell am See,** Seeuferstrasse 196, 5700 Zell am See **(06542) 56228; info@panorama camp.at; www.panoramacamp.at**

S fr Zell on B311 sp Salzburg (using tunnel). At 3rd rndabt turn L dir Thumersbach, site on L in 1.5km, sp. Med, hdg, pt shd, serviced pitches; EHU (16A) metered + conn fee; red long stay; TV; 30% statics; bus; Eng spkn; adv bkg acc; CKE. *"Conv Salzburg & Krimml falls; clsd 1200-1330; cycle & footpaths round lake adj; helpful owners; excel facs; peaceful site; nicely laid out site with adequate pitches; owners take you to pitch and make elec conn; shop nr; rest nr; pizzas & rolls fr recep; lovely view of mountains; easy access."* **€33.50** **2019**

ZWETTL *A4* (12km E Rural) *48.58956, 15.31805* **Campingplatz Lichtenfels,** Friedersbach 69, 3533 Friedersbach **(02826) 7492 or 0664 5746866 (mob); forstverwaltung@thurnforst.at; www.thurnforst.at**

Fr E on B38 fr Zwettl on app Rastenfeld look for rv bdge & ruins of castle. Site sp on L. Med, pt shd, bbq; sw nr; 40% statics; games area. *"Pretty lake setting; open air concerts in ruins of castle high ssn; friendly owner; v clean facs."* **€15.50, 1 May-10 Oct.** **2016**

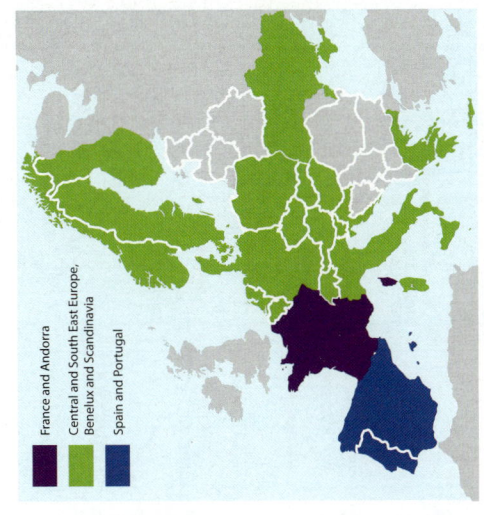

- France and Andorra
- Central and South East Europe, Benelux and Scandinavia
- Spain and Portugal

Landeck to Wien (Vienna) = 550km

	Bludenz	Braunau-am-Inn	Bregenz	Bruck an der Mur	Eisenstadt	Fürstenfeld	Gmünd	Gmunden	Graz	Innsbruck	Judenburg	Kitzbühel	Klagenfurt	Landeck	Leibnitz	Lienz	Liezen	Linz	Mariazell	Radstadt	Reutte	Salzburg	Schärding	Sillian	Spittal an der Drau	St. Pölten	Villach	Wien (Vienna)	Wörgl
Braunau-am-Inn	324																												
Bregenz	59	451																											
Bruck an der Mur	562	263	620																										
Eisenstadt	66	345	722	129																									
Fürstenfeld	658	388	715	123	126																								
Gmünd	552	213	611	246	190	369																							
Gmunden	399	80	455	187	280	311	164																						
Graz	590	322	643	56	174	68	299	243																					
Innsbruck	148	245	204	421	513	510	405	251	444																				
Judenburg	503	239	563	63	195	155	261	164	88	354																			
Kitzbühel	243	138	299	291	403	415	296	143	347	95	260																		
Klagenfurt	487	292	544	161	292	215	340	242	140	340	97	243																	
Landeck	70	323	123	498	596	588	482	330	522	79	432	173	415																
Leibnitz	627	359	685	94	200	357	340	282	39	469	126	386	130	547															
Lienz	337	233	395	301	421	227	391	235	290	190	224	94	149	266	280														
Liezen	464	168	521	97	229	308	187	90	126	315	70	190	150	392	198	229													
Linz	454	113	510	185	231	59	99	68	241	304	189	197	268	383	279	293	115												
Mariazell	585	263	643	63	135	186	184	199	118	438	126	329	223	517	155	363	119	149											
Radstadt	367	134	425	167	331	291	291	142	224	220	136	124	182	297	260	158	67	184	187										
Reutte	110	338	133	511	604	601	494	344	535	90	446	187	432	76	558	280	399	397	529	311									
Salzburg	338	64	395	230	331	353	221	68	285	190	198	82	252	269	322	176	126	123	255	75	281								
Schärding	442	47	501	270	309	379	177	74	309	295	237	186	305	372	355	279	151	79	231	183	384	110							
Sillian	368	264	425	331	452	388	422	269	320	222	254	124	181	297	311	32	260	322	394	189	310	208	311						
Spittal an der Drau	413	216	470	210	342	281	393	237	212	263	150	170	75	344	204	76	163	279	276	95	356	155	266	109					
St. Pölten	559	238	617	141	113	196	117	171	198	410	207	304	302	49[illegible]	236	398	204	125	80	252	503	229	202	430	355				
Villach	449	255	506	189	320	253	368	269	178	303	124	205	38	38[illegible]	168	113	201	297	253	131	392	191	302	142	36	331			
Wien (Vienna)	619	299	678	150	50	171	141	234	198	470	215	363	312	550	221	440	265	186	140	361	561	300	264	469	386	65	349		
Wörgl	127	180	273	325	437	449	330	177	381	66	394	34	277	144	420	128	224	131	363	158	158	110	220	158	204	338	239	397	
Zell am See	299	141	352	239	408	365	299	145	296	150	209	56	211	230	310	91	142	198	261	74	240	84	188	122	106	305	143	366	90

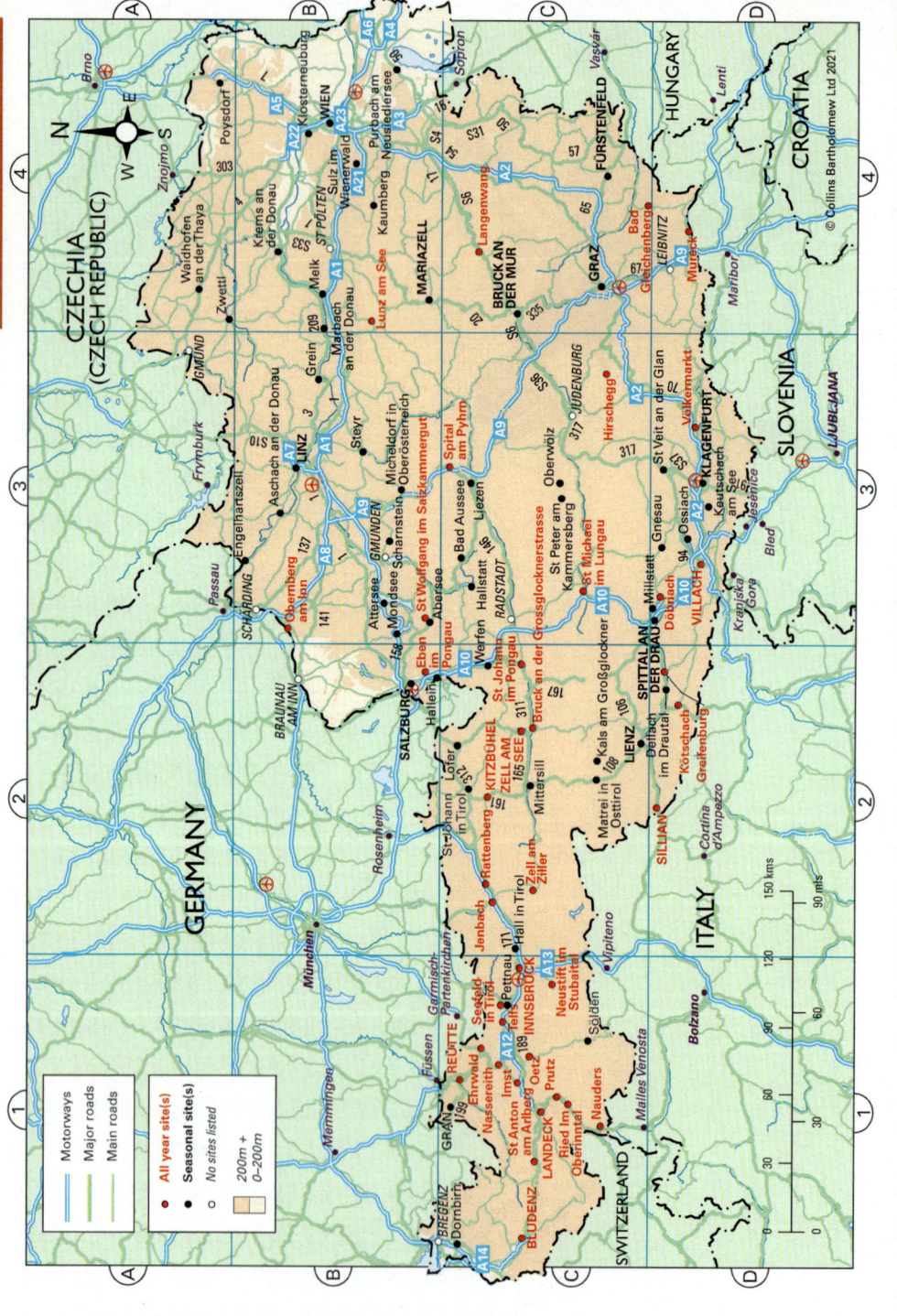

Belgium

📍 Bruge

Shutterstock/SenSeHi

Highlights

Although a country of two halves, with French-speaking Wallonia making up the southern part of the country, and Dutch-speaking Flanders the north, Belgium is very much united when it comes to delicious cuisine, fascinating historic attractions and breathtaking architecture.

With several UNESCO world heritage sites, a diverse landscape and a range of museums and art galleries, you will be spoilt for choice when deciding how best to spend your time in this delightful country.

Most people associate Belgium with chocolate, mussels and beer, but there are other products which share an equal amount of tradition. Lace making has been practiced in Belgium for centuries, Bruges still renowned for the intricate designs and delicacy of its product.

Belgium has also played an important role in the development of comics, and can boast Georges Remi (Hergé), the creator of Tintin, and Pierre Culliford (Peyo) the man behind the smurfs amongst its talented celebrities.

Major towns and cities

- Brussels - this historic city is Belgium's capital.
- Ghent - a city filled with beautiful buildings and important museums.
- Antwerp - Belgium's largest city is filled with stunning landmarks.
- Liège - famous for its folk festivals and for hosting a large annual Christmas Market.

Attractions

- Grand-Place, Brussels - this opulent central square is a UNESCO World Heritage site.
- Gravensteen Castle, Ghent - a magnificent 12th century castle that houses a museum.
- Historic Centre, Bruges - the medieval architecture of the city centre is a must-see.
- Ypres - an ancient town filled with historic monuments, including the Menin Gate.

Find out more

www.visitbelgium.com
E: tourist@visit.brussels T: 0032 (2) 513 89 40

Country Information

Population (approx): 11.5 million
Capital: Brussels (population approx 1 million)
Area: 30,528 sq km
Bordered by: France, Germany, Luxembourg, Netherlands
Terrain: Flat coastal plains in north-west; central rolling hills; rugged Ardennes hills and forest in south-east.
Climate: Mild winters with snow likely in the Ardennes. Cool summers, rain any time of the year; coast can be windy
Coastline: 66km
Highest Point: Signal de Botrange 694m
Languages: Flemish, French, German
Local Time: GMT or BST + 1, i.e. 1 hour ahead of the UK all year
Currency: Euros divided into 100 cents; £1 = €1.14, €1 = £0.88 (Feb 2021)
Emergency numbers: Police 112, Fire Brigade 112, Ambulance 112.
Public Holidays 2020: Jan 1; Apr 4, 5; May 1, 13, 23, 24; Jul 21 (National Day); Aug 15; Nov 1, 11 (Armistice Day); Dec 25.
School summer holidays extend over July and August.

Entry Formalities

British and Irish passport holders may stay in Belgium for up to 90 days in any 180 day period without a visa. Following Brexit you may be asked to show a return or onward ticket at the border to confirm your length of stay, or to prove that you have enough money for your stay.

Your passport will need to have a minimum of 6 months' validity remaining, and be less than 10 years old (even if it has 6 months or more left).

Medical Services

The standard of health care is high. Emergency medical and hospital treatment is available at a reduced cost on production of a European Health Insurance Card (EHIC). Check whether a doctor you wish to see is registered with the national health service (conventionné/geconventioneerd) or offers private healthcare. You will have to pay for services provided but 75% of the cost of treatment and approved medicines will be refunded if you apply to a local Sickness Fund Office with your EHIC.

At night and at weekends at least one local pharmacy will remain open and its address will be displayed in the window of all local pharmacies.

Opening Hours

Banks: Open hours vary from one bank to another, however usual open hours are Mon-Fri 9am-12pm & 2pm-4pm; Sat 9am-12pm (some banks).

Museums: Tue-Sun 10am-5pm; most museums close Monday.

Shops: Mon-Sat 10am-6pm or 8pm (supermarkets); some close 12pm-2pm; most shops closed Sunday.

Safety and Security

Belgium is relatively safe for visitors but you should take the usual sensible precautions to avoid becoming a victim of muggers, bag-snatchers and pickpockets, especially at major railway stations and on the public transport in Antwerp and Brussels.

There have been recent reports of thefts from luggage racks on high-speed trains. Keep your possessions close to you, especially when the train is in a station and could be grabbed.

Belgium shares with the rest of Europe an underlying threat from terrorism. Attacks could be indiscriminate and against civilian and tourist targets. The area around Brussels hosts a number of international institutions (EU, NATO) which are sensitive locations where you should be vigilant.

British Embassy

AVENUE D'AUDERGHEM 10
1040 BRUXELLES
Tel: (02) 2876211
www.ukinbelgium.fco.gov.uk/en/
public.brussels@fco.gov.uk

Irish Embassy

RUE FROISSART - FROISSARTSTRAAT 50
1040 BRUXELLES
Tel: (02) 2823400
www.embassyofireland.be
brusselsembassy@dfa.ie
There is also an Honorary Consulate in Antwerp.

Documents

Money

Major credit cards are widely accepted by shops, hotels, restaurants and petrol stations.

Carry your credit card issuer or bank's 24-hour UK contact numbers in case of loss or theft of your cards. If you have difficulty reporting the theft of your card(s) to your UK bank or credit card company, ask the Belgian group 'Card Stop' to send a fax to your UK company to block your card. Card Stop's telephone number is (070) 344344.

Passport

Belgian law requires everyone to carry some form of identification, for example passport or photocard driving licence, at all times.

Vehicle(s)

You should carry your vehicle registration certificate (V5C), insurance details and MOT certificate (if applicable).

Driving

Accidents

The police must be called after an accident if an unoccupied stationary vehicle is damaged or if people are injured. If it isn't necessary to call the police to the scene of the accident you must still report it at the local police station within 24 hours.

Alcohol

The maximum permitted level of alcohol is 50 milligrams in 100 millilitres of blood, i.e. lower than in the UK (80 milligrams). Penalties for exceeding this limit are severe including suspension of driving licence and a possible jail sentence.

Breakdown Service

The Touring Club Royal de Belgique (TCB) operates a breakdown service 24 hours a day throughout the country, tel (070) 344777. On motorways, use the roadside telephones called 'telestrade' which are controlled by the police and are situated approximately every 2km. Ask for 'Touring Secours' or, when in the north of the country, 'Touring Wegenhulp'. It will be necessary to pay a fee which is variable depending on the time of day.

Child Restraint System

Children under 1.35m must be seated in a child seat or child restraint when travelling in the front or rear seat of a vehicle. If a child seat/restraint is not available, i.e. when two child restraint systems are being used on rear seats and there isn't enough space for a third to be placed, a child must travel in the back of the vehicle using an adult seat belt. If the child is three years or under they must not travel in a vehicle without being seated in a child seat/restraint.

The child restraint must correspond to the child's weight and be of an approved type. A rear facing child restraint must not be used on a front seat with a front air bag unless it is deactivated.

Fuel

Petrol stations on motorways and main roads are open 24 hours and credit cards are generally accepted. Others may close from 8pm to 8am and often all day Sunday.

LPG, also known as GPL, is widely available at many service stations.

Motorways

Belgium has a network of approximately 1,750km of motorways. Although Belgian motorways are toll free for most vehicles, there is a toll for vehicles over 3,500kg.

Service areas usually have a petrol station, restaurant, shop, showers and toilets. Rest areas have picnic facilities. For detailed information see www.autosnelwegen.net.

Some motorways are so heavily used by lorries that the inside lane may become heavily rutted and/or potholed. These parallel ruts are potentially dangerous for caravans travelling at high speed. It is understood that parts of the A2/E314 and A3/E40 are particularly prone to this problem.

Parking

Blue zones indicating limited parking are used to denote where vehicles must display a parking disc on Monday to Saturday, from 9am to 6pm. Discs are available from police stations, petrol stations and some shops. Outside blue zones a parking disc must also be used where the parking sign has a panel showing the disc symbol. Parking areas are also regulated by parking meters and if these exist inside a blue zone parking discs must not be used, except if the parking meter or ticket machine is out of action. Illegally parked vehicles may be towed away or clamped.

Do not park in a street where there is a triangular sign 'Axe Rouge/Ax Rode'.

Pollution

From 1 November to 31 March during levels of high pollution, known as pollution peaks, restrictions are imposed on driving in Brussels. There are different levels of restriction, from reduced speed limits to a total ban on driving, depending on the severity of the pollution. When in place restrictions are announced on local media and an electronic signs around the city. Visit www.brussels.be and search for 'pollution peak' for more information.

Priority

You should take great care to obey the 'priority to the right' rule which is designed to slow traffic in built-up areas. Drivers must give priority to vehicles joining from the right, even if those vehicles have stopped at a road junction or stopped for pedestrians or cyclists, and even if you are on what appears to be a main road. Exemptions to this rule apply on motorways, roundabouts and roads signposted with an orange diamond on a white background.

Trams have priority over other traffic. If a tram or bus stops in the middle of the road to allow passengers on or off, you must stop.

From 2014 a 'Zip Merging' rule has been in place in Belgium. Where a lane is ending or closed, drivers in that lane must continue to where that lane starts to close up before merging into the open lane. Drivers in the lane which remains open must give way in turn to the drivers merging into their lane.

Roads

Roads are generally in good condition and well lit, however, some stretches of motorways have poor surfacing and signs to advise drivers to slow down. Traffic is fast and the accident rate is high, especially at weekends, mainly due to speeding.

Road Signs and Markings

Roads signs and markings conform to international standards. A sign has been introduced prohibiting the use of cruise control. This sign will normally only be encountered on motorways where there is a risk of multiple crashes due to congestion or road works. Where this particular sign shows a weight limit, the prohibition applies to drivers of vehicles with a higher maximum permitted weight.

Destination road signs can be confusing because a town may be signposted either by its French or its Flemish name, according to the predominant language in that particular area.

The most important of these towns are:

Flemish	French
Aalst	Alost
Aken (Aachen)	Aix-la-Chapelle (Germany)
Antwerpen	Anvers
Bergen	Mons
Brugge	Bruges
Brussel	Bruxelles
Doornik	Tournai
Gent	Gand
Geraardsbergen	Grammont
Ieper	Ypres
Kortrijk	Courtrai
Leuven	Louvain
Luik	Liège
Mechelen	Maline
Namen	Namur
Rijsel	Lille (France)
Roeselare	Roulers
Tienen	Tirlemont
Veurne	Furnes

Generally signposts leading to and on motorways show foreign destination place names in the language of the country concerned. e.g. German. Exceptions do occur, particularly on the E40 and E314 where city names may be given in Flemish or French.

Roads with the prefix N are regional roads; those with numbers 1 to 9 radiate from

Brussels. Motorways have the prefix A and have blue and white signs. When route planning through Belgium follow the green European road numbers with the prefix E which may be the only road numbers displayed.

Road signs you may see include the following:

You may pass right or left

Cyclists have priority over turning traffic

Cyclists have priority at junction

Use of Cruise Control prohibited

Speed Limits

	Open Road (km/h)	Motorway (km/h)
Car Solo	90*	120
Car towing caravan/trailer	90*	120
Motorhome under 3500kg	90*	120
Motorhome 3500-7500kg	90*	90

*70 in Flanders

Whilst the general speed limit in built-up areas is 50 km/h (31mph), lower limits of 30 km/h (18 mph) or 20 km/h (12mph) may be imposed and indicated by signs in residential areas, town centres and near schools. Brussels city centre is a 30 km/h (18mph) speed limit zone. The start and finish points of these zones are not always clearly marked. Vehicles over 3,500 kg in weight are restricted to 90 km/h (56mph) outside built-up areas and on motorways.

Traffic Jams

During good weather roads to the coast, the Ardennes and around Brussels and Antwerp are very busy during the weekends.

Other busy routes are the E40 (Brussels to Ostend), the E25 (Liège to Bastogne and Arlon), the E411 (Brussels to Namur and Luxembourg), and the N4 from Bastogne to Arlon around the border town of Martelange caused by motorists queuing for cheap petrol in Luxembourg. Avoid traffic on the E40

by taking the R4 and N49, and on the E411 by taking the N4 Bastogne to Marche-en-Famenne and Namur. These routes are heavily used and consequently the road surface can be poor.

Traffic Lights

A green light (arrow) showing at the same time as a red or amber light means that you can turn in that direction providing you give way to other traffic and pedestrians. An amber light, possibly flashing, in the form of an arrow inclined at an angle of 45 degrees to the left or to the right, shows that the number of traffic lanes will be reduced.

Tunnels

Three road tunnels go under the River Scheldt at Antwerp. In the Liefkenhoeks tunnel on road R2 to the north of the city a toll of €17.60-19.00 (2018) for vehicles over 2.75m in height. Vehicles under 2.75m are charged €4.95-6.00. If you're towing your caravan will be included within this height categorisation. The Kennedy Tunnel on road R1 to the south of the city is toll-free but is heavily congested in both directions for much of the day. The smallest tunnel, the Waasland Tunnel is part of the N59a and is also toll-free.

Violation of Traffic Regulations

The police may impose on-the-spot fines on visitors who infringe traffic regulations such as speeding and parking offences. If you can't pay on the spot your vehicle(s) may be impounded or your driving licence withdrawn. Fines can be paid in cash or with a debit or credit card - make sure you get an official receipt.

In an effort to improve road safety the authorities have increased the number of speed traps throughout the country in the form of cameras and unmarked police vehicles.

Vehicles of 3,500 kg or over are not allowed to use the left lane on roads with more than three lanes except when approaching a fork in a motorway when vehicles have to move to the left or right lane

Essential Equipment

First aid kit

It is not compulsory for foreign registered vehicles to carry a first aid kit, but it is still recommended.

Warning Triangle

An EU approved warning triangle must be used if the vehicle breaks down, has a puncture or is involved in an accident.

Reflective Jacket/Waistcoat

If you have broken down or are in an accident where stopping or parking is prohibited, you must wear a reflective jacket or waistcoat when getting out of your vehicle, or face a €58.00 fine. Anyone leaving the vehicle should also wear one. Keep the jacket(s) to hand in your vehicle, not in the boot.

Touring

Flemish is spoken in the north of Belgium, whilst French is spoken in the south. Brussels is bi-lingual. English is widely spoken.

Prices in restaurants are quoted 'all inclusive' and no additional tipping is necessary. Smoking is severely restricted in public places including restaurants and cafés.

Carrier bags are generally not provided in supermarkets, so take your own.

When visiting Brussels visitors may buy a Brussels Card, valid for 24, 48 or 72 hours, which offers free access to virtually every major museum in the city and unlimited use of public transport, together with discounts at a number of other attractions. The pass is available from the tourist information office in the Hotel de Ville and from many hotels, museums and public transport stations, or visit www.brusselscard.be to buy online.

Camping and Caravanning

There are more than 900 campsites in Belgium, most of which are near the coast or in the Ardennes. Coastal sites tend to consist largely of mobile homes/statics and can be very crowded at the height of the holiday season. A local tourist tax is usually included in the rates charged.

Twin-axle caravans are not permitted on municipal sites in and around Antwerp.

Caravans and vehicles longer than 6 metres are prohibited from Liège city centre.

Casual/wild camping is prohibited in Flanders. Elsewhere permission must first be sought from the landowner or police. Camping is not permitted alongside public highways for more than a 24-hour period, nor is it permitted in lay-bys, in state forests or along the seashore, or within a 100 metre radius of a main water point, or on a site classified for the conservation of monuments.

Cycling

Belgium is well equipped for cyclists, with an extensive network of signposted cycling routes. Cycle lanes are marked on the carriageway by means of a broken double white line or by circular signs depicting a white bicycle on a blue or black background.

Bikes may be carried at the rear of a vehicle as long as its width doesn't extend beyond the width of the vehicle or more than one metre from the rear, and providing the rear lights and number plate remain visible.

Electricity and Gas

The current on most campsites varies from 4 - 16 amps although on some it is as low as 2 amps. Plugs have two round pins. CEE connections are not yet available at all sites.

Use a mains tester to test a connection before hooking up as problems are more common in Belgium than other EU countries. Issues may include reversed polarity, no earth and/or incorrectly alternating current.

The full range of Campingaz cylinders are available.

Public Transport

Anyone under the age of 25 is entitled to free or reduced prices on public transport in Brussels. During periods of severe air pollution public transport in that region is free to all.

Brussels and Antwerp have metro systems and extensive networks of trams and buses. Tram and bus stops are identified by a red and white sign and all stops are request stops; hold out your arm to stop a bus or tram. Tickets, including 10-journey and one-day travel cards, are available from vending machines at metro stations and some bus stops, newsagents, supermarkets and tourist information centres.

The MOBIB Smartcard, similar to an Oyster card, can be purchased and topped up at metro station kiosks, supermarkets and newsagents, and is valid for all STIB public transport in Brussels (including trams, buses and metros).

Belgium has a good train network and most main routes pass through Antwerp, Brussels or Namur. Trains are modern, comfortable and punctual and fares are reasonable. Buy tickets before boarding the train or you may be charged a supplement.

Grand Place, Brussels

AISCHE EN REFAIL *B3* (0.4km E Rural) *50.59977, 4.84335* **Camping du Manoir de Là-Bas,** Route de Gembloux 180, 5310 Aische-en-Refail **(081) 655353; europa-camping.sa@skynet.be; www.camping-manoirdelabas.be**

🐕€3 ♀♀♀ WD ⚓ ♿ 🚿 ⧖ 🅿 MSP 🦋 ☂ Ⓗ 🛒 ♨ 🛒nr ⚠ ✍ 🏊(htd) 🛶

Fr E411/A4 exit junc 12 & foll sps to Aische-en-Refail. Site on o'skts of vill. 2*, Lge, pt shd, pt sl, EHU (6A) inc; gas; bbq; 50% statics; phone; Eng spkn; adv bkg acc; fishing; tennis; games rm; CKE. *"Friendly staff; site little run down; ltd hot water; poor san facs, dated & long way fr pitches; some site rds are narr; recep far side of chateau; gd rest & bar (clsd in Sep); site needs updating (2014); poor; NH only; sm pitches; rec NH only."* **€25.00,** 1 Apr-31 Oct. 2017

ANTWERPEN *A3* (6km NW Urban) *51.23347, 4.39261* **Camping De Molen,** Thonelaan - Jachthavenweg 6, St Annastrand, 2050 Antwerpen **(03) 2198179; info@camping-de-molen.be; www.camping-de-molen.be**

12 ♀♀♀ WD ⚓ ♿ ✍ Ⓗnr 🛒nr

Clockwise on ring rd, take 1st exit after Kennedy tunnel, exit 6. R at traff lts, 3rd L where cannot go strt on (rv on R), site on R in 1km on bank of Rv Schelde. Or on ent Antwerp foll sp Linkeroever, go strt on at 3 traff lts, then turn L & foll camping sp. Fr A14/E17 exit junc 7 & foll sp for Linkeroever Park & Ride until site sp appear, then foll sp. 2*, Med, pt shd, EHU (10A) €2.50 (poss rev pol) - €30 deposit for adaptor/cable; bus nrby; Eng spkn; adv bkg rec. *"Popular site; max 14 nt stay; pedestrian/cycle tunnel to city cent 1km; metro 1km; gd for rollerblading, cycling; friendly, helpful staff; mosquitoes poss a problem; san facs satisfactory; 30 min walk or bus to city cent; site tired."* **€28.00** 2016

ARLON *D3* (2km N Urban) *49.70215, 5.80678* **Camping Officiel Arlon,** 373 Rue de Bastogne, Bonnert, 6700 Arlon **(063) 226582; campingofficiel@skynet.be; www.campingofficielarlon.be**

12 🐕€2 ♀♀♀ WD ⚓ ♿ 🚿 🅿 🛉 ☂ Ⓗ 🛒 ♨ 🛒nr ⚠ 🏊

Fr E411 exit junc 31 onto N82 Arlon for 4km, turn twd Bastogne on N4. Site sp on R. 2*, Med, pt shd, pt sl, EHU (6-10A) €2.40 (check earth); gas; bbq; red long stay; TV; Eng spkn; adv bkg acc; CKE. *"Charming, clean, well laid out, pretty site; levelling blocks/ramps req - supplied by site; c'vans tight-packed when site busy; 5km approx to Luxembourg for cheap petrol; Arlon interesting town; vg NH & longer stay; thoroughly rec for stop over; cash only; 3 hdstgs for m'van; new pool; san facs updated, v clean; busy but organised; gd vet 0.5m."* **€24.50** 2018

ARLON *D3* (7.6km N Rural) *49.74833, 5.78697* **Camping Sud,** 75 Voie de la Liberté, 6717 Attert **(063) 223715; info@campingsudattert.com; www.campingsudattert.com**

🐕€2 ♀♀♀(htd) WD ⚓ 🚿 ✍ ☂ Ⓗ ♨ 🛒 ⚠ 🏊

Off N4 Arlon rd on E side of dual c'way. Sp to site fr N4 (500m). U-turn into site ent. 4*, Med, hdg, mkd, hdstg, pt shd, EHU (5-10A) €2.50 (check earth); bbq; red long stay; phone; bus; Eng spkn; adv bkg acc; CKE. *"Vg, well-organised site; special NH pitches; fishing & walking; peaceful site; v friendly staff; highly rec."* **€25.00,** 1 Apr-15 Oct. 2019

BASTOGNE *C3* (1.6km WNW Urban) *50.00340, 5.69525* **Camping de Renval,** 148 Route de Marche, 6600 Bastogne **(061) 212985; www.campingderenval.be**

🐕€2 ♀♀♀(htd) WD ⚓ 🚿 🅿 ✍ 🦋 ♈ ♨ 🛒nr ⚠ ✍

Fr N leave A26 exit 54, foll Bastogne sp. Fr Marche-en-Famenne dir, exit N4 at N84 for Bastogne; site on L in 150m opp petrol stn. Fr E foll Marche, in 1km site on R opp petrol stn. 3*, Med, hdstg, pt shd, pt sl, terr, EHU (10A) inc (poss rev pol); bbq; 95% statics; ccard acc; site clsd Jan; games area; tennis. *"Take care speed bumps; helpful staff; clean san facs but long walk fr tourers' pitches; gd security; facs ltd LS; gd NH."* **€23.00,** 1 Feb-31 Dec. 2019

BRUGGE *A2* (5km E Urban) *51.20722, 3.26305* **Camping Memling,** Veltemweg 109, 8310 Sint Kruis **(050) 355845; info@camping-memling.be; www.brugescamping.be**

12 🐕€2 ♀♀♀(htd) WD ⚓ 🚿 ✍ MSP 🦋 ♈ Ⓗnr Ⓗnr ♨ 🛒nr

Exit A10 junc 8 Brugge. In 2km turn R onto N397 dir St Michiels & cont 2km to rlwy stn on R. Turn R under rlwy tunnel & at 1st rndbt take dir Maldegem onto ring rd & in a few kms take N9 sp Maldegem & St Kruis. After 3km at traff lts adj MacDonalds, turn R & immed L sp Camping to site on R in 400m past sw pool. Fr Gent exit E40 sp Oostkamp & foll Brugge sp for 7km to N9 as above. 2*, Med, hdstg, hdg, mkd, pt shd, EHU (6A) inc (poss rev pol); red long stay; 13% statics; bus 200m; Eng spkn; adv bkg acc; ccard acc; bike hire; CKE. *"Busy site; friendly, helpful owners; recep open 0800-2200 (all day to 2200 high ssn); arr early high ssn to ensure pitch; conv Zeebrugge ferry (30mins) & allowed to stay to 1500; conv bus svrs every 20 mins to Bruges; htd pool adj; adv bkgs taken but no pitch reserved; m'van pitches sm, rec pay extra for standard pitch; cycle rte or 35 min walk to Bruges; nice site; rec; facs OAY; pitches nr ent barrier get most sun; vg; automated check-in sys with credit card payment only; immac new san facs (2019)."* **€36.00** 2019

BRUGGE *A2* (4km S Urban) *51.19634, 3.22573*
Motorcaravan Park, Off ring rd R30, Buiten Katelijnevest, Brugge

12 🦮 WD ⬆ 🐾nr ⛺

Exit A10 at junc 7 twd Brugge. After going under rlwy bdge, turn R on ring rd immed after marina to dedicated mv parking adj coach parking, nr marina. Med, hdstg, pt shd, EHU (10A) inc. *"M'vans only; in great location - gd view of canal, sh walk to town cent thro park; rec arr early high ssn; washrm nr; if full, take ticket & park in coach park opp; NH only; vg for city ctr; narr spaces; traff noise; bef leaving pay at machine & leave thro coach pk; gd."* **€25.00**   **2018**

BRUGGE *A2* (13km SW Urban) *51.18448, 3.10445*
Recreatiepark Klein Strand, Varsenareweg 29, 8490 Jabbeke (050) 811440; info@kleinstrand.be; www.kleinstrand.be

12 🦮 €2 ⬆⬆ WD ⬆ ♨ 🚻 ⬆ / MSP ♱ ♈ ⬆ 🐾 ⛺ ✎ 🎣

Fr W leave A10/E40 at Jabbeke exit, junc 6; turn R at rndabt & in 100m turn R into narr rd. Foll site to statics car pk on L & park - walk to check-in at recep bef proceeding to tourer site in 400m. Fr E leave A10/E40 at junc 6 (Jabbeke) turn L at 1st rndabt. Drive over m'way twd vill. Turn L at next rndabt & foll site sp into site car pk as above. Out of ssn carry on along rd to recep by lake. 4*, V lge, hdg, mkd, pt shd, EHU (10A) inc; gas; bbq; sw nr; TV; 75% statics; bus to Brugge; Eng spkn; ccard acc; bike hire; fishing; tennis; watersports; games rm; CKE. *"Busy site; vg touring base; lge pitches; no o'fits over 12m; wide range of entmnt & excursions; direct access to lake adj; bus every 20 mins; v welcoming; ACSI acc."* **€33.00, H15.**   **2019**

BRUXELLES *B2* (13km N Rural) *50.93548, 4.38226*
Camping Grimbergen, Veldkantstraat 64, 1850 Grimbergen (0479) 760378 or (02) 2709597; camping-grimbergen@webs.com; camping-grimbergen.webs.com

🦮 €1 ⬆⬆ WD ⬆ ⬆ / ✖ ⬆nr 🐾nr

Fr Ostend on E40/A10 at ringrd turn E & foll sp Leuven/Luik (Liège)/Aachen. Exit junc 7 N sp Antwerpen/Grimbergen N202. At bus stn traff lts turn R twd Vilvoorde N211. Turn L at 2nd traff lts (ignore no L turn - lorries only). Site sp 500m on R. Ent via pool car pk. 3*, Med, hdg, pt shd, pt sl, EHU (10A) €4; phone; bus to city (hourly) 200m; Eng spkn; adv bkg acc; bike hire; CKE. *"Well-run, popular site - rec arr early, gd, clean, modern san facs; helpful staff; sh walk to town; train to Brussels fr next vill; red facs LS; gates clsd 1130-1400 and 2000 onwards; gd rest by bus stop; conv Brussels; excel san facs; rec; pool adj; gd NH."* **€22.00, 1 Apr-25 Oct.**   **2019**

BRUXELLES *B2* (13km E Urban) *50.85720, 4.48506*
RCCC de Belgique, Warandeberg 52, 1970 Wezembeek (02) 7821009; info@campingbrussels.be; www.rcccb.com

🦮 €1 ⬆⬆ WD ⬆ ⬆ / ♱ ⬆nr 🐾nr ⛺

Leave ringrd RO at junc 2 sp Kraainem turning E. In 140m 1st intersection on dual c'way (by pedestrian x-ing) turn L into Wezembeek. Foll orange camping sp taking rd to the R around church. Foll rd to crest of hill. Site on L bet houses. Narr ent, easy to miss. 2*, Med, mkd, hdstg, pt shd, pt sl, terr, EHU (6A) inc (poss rev pol & no earth); 65% statics; Eng spkn; adv bkg acc; ccard acc; CKE. *"Poss diff for lge o'fits due narr site ent, v tight corners, metro nr; gates clsd 1200-1400 & 2200-0800; raised kerbs; updated san facs (2015); gd for metro into Brussels fr Kraainem; welcoming wardens; no Eng spkn; unkept."* **€22.50, 1 Apr-30 Sep.**   **2018**

DE HAAN *A1* (2.6km ENE Coastal) *51.28330, 3.05610*
Camping Ter Duinen, Wenduinesteenweg 143, Vlissegem, 8421 De Haan (050) 413593; lawrence. sansens@scarlet.be; www.campingterduinen.be

🦮 €5.75 ⬆⬆ (htd) WD ⬆ ♨ 🚻 ⬆ / MSP 🦋 ♱ ♈ ⬆ 🐾 ⛺

🌳 shgl 500m

Exit A10/E40 junc 6 Jabbeke onto N377 dir De Haan. Go thro town dir Wenduine, site on R in 4km. 3*, Med, mkd, pt shd, EHU (6A) inc; bbq; sw nr; 85% statics; phone; tram nrby; Eng spkn; adv bkg req; horseriding 1km; fishing 200m; golf 4km; CKE. *"Neat, clean, well-managed site; friendly staff; poss long walk to excel san facs inc novelty wcs!; water complex 1km; htd pool 200m; conv ferries, Bruges; bike hire 200m; excel, hot dish water req tokens, mkt in nrby towns."* **€40.00, 15 Mar-15 Oct.**   **2019**

DE PANNE *A1* (3km S Rural) *51.08288, 2.59094*
Camping Ter Hoeve, Duinhoekstraat 101, 8660 Adinkerke (058) 412376; info@campingterhoeve.be; www.camping-terhoeve.be

12 🦮 €1.50 ⬆⬆ WD ⬆ ⬆ / MSP ♈ ⬆ 🐾 ⛺ 🌳 2km

Leave Calais-Ostend m'way at junc 1 (ignore junc 1a) dir De Panne. Foll rd past theme park (Plopsaland), L at filling stn, site 1km on L. 2*, Lge, hdg, pt shd, EHU (4A) inc (poss no earth); 60% statics; tram 1km; Eng spkn; adv bkg rec; ccard acc. *"Nice pitches; lge grassed area for tourers & hdstg area for late arr/early dep; barrier clsd 2200-0800 - go to visitors' car park on R bef booking in; v busy site high ssn, phone to check opening times LS; conv Dunkerque ferries & Plopsaland park; some daytime noise fr nrby theme park, tram tickets avail at filling stn; coin operated dishwash water; san facs basic; Oct-Mar by appointment only; under new management (2018); elec may lack earth; supermkt close."* **€28.50**   **2019**

DINANT *C3* (2km N Urban) 50.27722, 4.89694
Camping Communal Devant-Bouvignes, 1 Quai de
Camping, 5500 Dinant **(082) 224002; camping.
communal@dinant.be; www.dinant.be**

🔟 🐕 ♀♀ (htd) 🆆🅳 🏕 ♿ ⚡ ∥ 🍴 ♐nr 🏔

Exit E11 junc 20 onto N936; drive to cent of Dinant
(steep descent) to T-junc; turn R onto N92; cont
along rv for 1.5km; site on L after bend. Med, pt shd,
EHU (16A) €3; sw; 50% statics; bus at ent; adv bkg
acc. *"Excel situation on rv bank; dogs free; scruffy san
facs; 25 min walk to interesting town."* **€25.00** 2017

DOCHAMPS *C3* (0.7km ESE Rural) 50.23080, 5.63180
Panorama Campsite Petite Suisse, Al Bounire 27,
6960 Dochamps **(084) 444030; info@petitesuisse.be;
www.petitesuisse.be**

🔟 🐕 €5 ♀♀ (htd) 🆆🅳 🏕 ♿ ⚡ ∥ 🦋 ♉ 🍴 🍷 ⑭ å ♐ 🏔

🏊 (htd) ⛵

Fr E25, take N89 (La Roche) at Samrée turn R onto
N841 headed twrds Dochamp. Turn R into rd sp Al
Bounire and foll sp to site. 4*, Lge, hdstg, mkd, pt shd,
pt sl, terr, EHU (10A) inc; gas; bbq; TV; 50% statics;
phone; adv bkg acc; ccard acc; games area; waterslide;
games rm; tennis; CKE. *"Outstanding facs; beautiful
spot; busy, popular, excel site."* **€35.50** 2017

EEKLO *A2* (7km E Rural) 51.18093, 3.64180 **Camping
Malpertuus,** Tragelstraat 12, 9971 Lembeke
**(09) 3776178; campingmalpertuus@telenet.be;
www.vkt.be**

🔟 🐕 ♀♀ (htd) 🆆🅳 🏕 ♿ ⚡ ∥ 🦋 🍷 ⑭nr å ♐nr

Exit A10/E40 junc 11 onto N44 dir Aalter &
Maldegem. Foll sp Eekloo onto N49 & then foll sp
Lembeke, site sp. Med, pt shd, EHU (4A) €3; gas;
85% statics; phone; bus 300m; Eng spkn; adv bkg acc;
CKE. *"Gd site in lovely area; friendly staff; entmnt/
events at w/end; gd size pitches; gd site; unisex facs."*
€20.00 2018

EUPEN *B4* (3km SW Rural) 50.61457, 6.01686
Camping Hertogenwald, Oestraat 78, 4700 Eupen
**(087) 743222; info@camping-hertogenwald.be;
www.camping-hertogenwald.be**

🔟 🐕 €1.60 ♀♀ (htd) 🆆🅳 🏕 ♿ ⚡ ∥ 🦋 🍷 ⑭ å ♐nr 🏔

Fr German border customs on E40 a'bahn for Liège,
take 2nd exit for Eupen. In Eupen L at 3rd traff lts
& 1st R in 100m. Drive thro Eupen cent, foll sp to
Spa. Camping sp immed at bottom of hill, sharp
hairpin R turn onto N629, site on L in 2km. 3*, Med,
unshd, EHU (6A) inc (long lead req & poss no earth);
90% statics; phone; Eng spkn; games area. *"Sm tourer
area; clean site adj rv & forest; htd covrd pool 3km;
muddy after rain; gd walking & cycling beside rv; conv
Aachen."* **€18.00** 2016

FLORENVILLE *D3* (17km E Rural) 49.68499, 5.52058
Camping Chênefleur, Norulle 16, 6730 Tintigny **(063)
444078; info@chenefleur.be; www.chenefleur.be**

🐕 €4 (htd) 🆆🅳 🏕 ♿ ⚡ 🚿 ∥ 🍴 ♉ 🍷 🍸 ⑭ å ♐ 🏔 🖊

🏊 (htd) ⛵

Fr Liège foll E25 dir Luxembourg. Exit junc 29 sp
Habay-la-Neuve to Etalle, then N83 to Florenville.
Site sp off N83 at E end of Tintigny vill. 4*, Med, pt
shd, EHU (6-8A) inc; gas; Eng spkn; adv bkg acc; ccard
acc; games area; bike hire. *"Orval Abbey, Maginot Line
worth visit; friendly staff; gd, clean site & modern san
facs; well kept site."* **€32.00, 1 Apr-30 Sep.** 2020

GHENT *A2* (14km SW Rural) 51.00508, 3.57228
Camping Groeneveld, Groenevelddreef 14, Bachte-
Maria-Leerne, 9800 Deinze **(09) 3801014; info@
campinggroeneveld.be; www.campinggroeneveld.be**

🐕 €2 ♀♀ (htd) 🆆🅳 🏕 ∥ 🍴 🦋 ♉ 🍷 🍸 ⑭ å ♐nr 🏔 🖊

E or W E40/E10 on Brussels to Ostend m'way
exit junc 13 at sp Gent W/Drongen. Take N466 sp
Dienze. Approx 1km beyond junc with N437, turn L
just after 2nd 70 km/h sp down narr side rd - house
on corner has advert hoarding. Site on L opp flour
mill. Sm sp at turning. Med, hdg, pt shd, EHU (10A)
inc (poss no earth); red long stay; TV; 40% statics;
phone; Eng spkn; adv bkg acc; fishing; CKE. *"Gd
welcome; additional san facs at lower end of site; office
open 1900-2000 LS but staff in van adj san facs, or site
yourself; barrier (€25 deposit for card) clsd until 0800;
do not arr bef 1400; 1km fr Ooidonk 16th Castle; OK
NH; gd site; bus to vill; some pitches tight; cash only."*
€24.00, 1 Apr-4 Oct. 2018

GHENT *A2* (4km W Urban) 51.04638, 3.68083
Camping Blaarmeersen, Zuiderlaan 12, 9000 Gent
**(09) 2668160; blaarmeersen.camping@farys.be;
www.blaarmeersen.be**

🐕 €1.25 ♀♀ (htd) 🆆🅳 🏕 ⚡ ∥ 🍴 🍸 ⑭ å ♐ 🏔

Exit A10/E40 Brussels-Ostend m'way at junc 13 sp
Gent W & Drongen. At T-junc turn onto N466 twd
Gent. In 4km cross canal then turn R to site, sp (3
rings) Sport & Recreatiecentrum Blaarmeersen.
Fr Gent cent foll N34 twd Tielt for 1km past
city boundary & turn L to site; adj lake & De
Ossemeersen nature reserve. NB Due to rd layout,
rec foll camping sp on app to site rather than sat
nav. 4*, Lge, hdg, mkd, pt shd, serviced pitches; EHU
(10A) metered + conn fee €1.25 (poss rev pol); sw nr;
5% statics; phone; bus to Gent; Eng spkn; ccard acc;
tennis; watersports. *"Clean, well-organised, busy site;
beautiful lake with path around; helpful staff; rest gd
value; full sports facs adj; passport req; gd cycle track
fr site; cycle into cent avoiding main rd; gd location
for walks & activities; no dep bef 0815 hrs; poss
travellers LS; pitches muddy when wet; pool adj; some
m'van pitches sm & v shd; excel; best free info pack."*
€31.00, 1 Mar-8 Nov. 2019

GODARVILLE *B2* (12km E Rural) *50.50501, 4.39928*
Camping Trieu du Bois, Rue Picolome, 63 6238 Luttre
(Pont-a-Celles) (Hainaut) Belgique **(071) 845937 or
(0477) 200343; trieudubois@hotmail.com;
www.trieudobois.be**

12 🐕 ♟ WD ♨ ✕ 🐾

Fr J21 Luttre, foll sp twrds Luttre. After 1km at
T-junc turn L. Site on R after 1km. Sm, hdg, pt shd,
EHU (6A) €2; bbq; twin axles; 20% statics; Eng spkn;
adv bkg acc. *"Conv for Waterloo & Brussels; adj canal
path dir fr site; fair."* **€15.00** 2017

GODARVILLE *B2* (2km S Rural) *50.48794, 4.29318*
Camping Domaine Claire-Fontaine, 11 Ave
Clémenceau, 7160 Godarville **(064) 443675; sites.
voiesdeau@hainaut.be**

🐕 ♟ WD ♨ ✕ / ▽ 🍴 🗼 nr ⛱

Exit A15/E42 junc 18 onto N59 to Godarville, site sp.
3*, Lge, unshd, EHU (6A) inc; bbq; sw; 85% statics;
phone; ccard acc; games area; CKE. *"Facs better than
1st impression but avoid san facs nr touring area &
avoid area outside barrier; helpful warden; NH only."*
€22.00, 1 Mar-31 Oct. 2016

HAN SUR LESSE *C3* (0.3km N Urban) *50.12727,
5.18773* **Camping Aire Gîte d'Etape,** Rue du Gîte
d'Etape 10, 5580 Han-sur-Lesse **(084) 377441; gite.
han@gitesdetape.be; www.gitesdetape.be/han**

12 ♟ / MSP ⊕ nr 🗼 nr ✏

Exit A4/E411 junc 23 sp Ave-et-Auffe & Rochefort.
Go over 2 rv bdges then immed L & 1st R. Site on
L. Sm, hdstg, unshd, EHU 10A; games area. *"M'van
only, excel; attendant calls; v conv for show caves."*
€11.00 2018

HAN SUR LESSE *C3* (5km SW Rural) *50.11178,
5.13308* **Camping Le Roptai,** Rue Roptai 34, 5580
Ave-et-Auffe **(084) 388319; info@leroptai.be;
www.leroptai.be**

12 🐕 €1.50 ♟ WD ♨ / MSP ✕ 🍴 🗼 ⛱ 🛶 (htd)

Fr A4 exit 23 & take N94 dir Dinant. At bottom of
hill turn R onto N86. Turn L in vill of Ave, foll sp,
200m to L. 3*, Med, mkd, hdstg, pt shd, pt sl, terr, EHU
(6A) €1.80; gas; TV; 80% statics; Eng spkn; adv bkg
acc; site clsd Jan; CKE. *"Some pitches awkwardly sl;
generally run down & poor facs; ltd facs LS; NH only."*
€23.50 2019

HAN SUR LESSE *C3* (0.2km NW Urban) *50.12632,
5.18478* **Camping Le Pirot,** Rue Joseph Lamotte 3,
5580 Han-sur-Lesse **(084) 377280; han.tourisme@
skynet.be; www.valdelesse.be**

🐕 ♟ / ▽ 🍴 nr ⊕ nr 🗼 nr

Exit A4/E411 junc 23 sp Ave-et-Auffe & Rochefort.
Go over 1st bdge then L immed bef 2nd bdge in Han
cent; sh, steep incline. 1*, Sm, unshd, EHU (10A) inc
(poss rev pol); bus adj; adv bkg acc; ccard acc; CKE.
*"Excel position on raised bank of rv; adj attractions
& rests; interesting town; helpful staff; basic, dated
san facs; conv NH or sh stay in attractive town."*
€20.00, 1 Apr-15 Nov. 2015

HASSELT *B3* (12km NE Rural) *50.99775, 5.42537*
Camping Holsteenbron, Hengelhoefseweg 9,
3520 Zonhoven **011 817140; camping.holsteenbron@
telenet.be; www.holsteenbron.be**

🐕 €1 ♟ (htd) WD ♨ ♨ / ▽ 🍴 ♟ ⛱

Leave A2 junc 29 twd Hasselt; turn L at 1st traff lts
in 1km, foll sp thro houses & woods for 3km. Site is
NE of Zonhoven. Med, hdstg, hdg, mkd, pt shd, EHU
(6A) inc; TV; 30% statics; phone; Eng spkn; games
area; CKE. *"Pleasant, happy site in woodland; gd
touring base; friendly owners."*
€22.00, 1 Apr-13 Nov. 2016

HOTTON *C3* (0.9km NW Urban) *50.27085, 5.43833*
Camping Eau Zone, rue des Fonzays 10, 6990 Hotton
**(084) 477715; campingeauzone@hotmail.be;
www.campingeauzone.be**

🐕 ♟ WD ♨ & / 🔔 🍴 ♟

E411 exit 18 to Marche then N86 to Hotton, over
bdge in Hotton, turn L twds Melreux, foll rv and sp.
Sm, pt shd, EHU (10A); bbq; twin axles; 20% statics;
phone; Eng spkn; adv bkg rec; CKE. *"Site conv for
Hotton caves; public transport 1km; easy walk to town;
gd NH."* **€20.00, 1 Mar-30 Nov.** 2015

"Satellite navigation makes touring much easier"

Remember most sat navs don't know if you're
towing or in a larger vehicle – always use yours
alongside maps and site directions.

HOUTHALEN *B3* (4km E Rural) *51.03222, 5.41613*
Camping De Binnenvaart (formerly Kelchterhoef),
Binnenvaartstraat, 3530 Houthalen-Helchteren **(011)
526720; debinnenvaart@limburgcampings.be;
www.limburgcampings.be**

12 ♟ (htd) WD ♨ ♨ / ▽ 🔔 ♟ 🗼 ⛱ ✏

Exit A2/E314 junc 30 N. In 2km at x-rds turn L, in
2km at rndabt turn R into Binnenvaartstraat, then
foll site sp. 2*, Lge, mkd, pt shd, EHU (16A) inc; sw nr;
TV; 40% statics; Eng spkn; adv bkg acc. *"Press button
at ent for access; friendly welcome; lge serviced
pitches; excel NH or longer."* **€26.00** 2017

KNOKKE HEIST *A2* (1.6km S Urban) *51.33530,
3.28959* **Holiday Village Knokke,** Natiënlaan 70-72,
8300 Knokke-Heist **(050) 601203; info@holiday
knokke.be; www.holidayknokke.be/**

🐕 1st free, 2nd for 2 euros ♟ WD ♨ ♨ / ⊕ nr 🗼 nr ⛱ ♟ 1.5km

On N49/E34 opp Knokke-Heist town boundary sp.
Site ent at side of Texaco g'ge. 2*, Med, unshd, EHU
(6A) €1.90 (poss rev pol); 60% statics; phone; adv bkg
acc; bike hire. *"V clean, tidy site but ltd san facs and
waste disp pnts; may need to manhandle c'van onto
pitch."* **€27.00, Easter-30 Sep.** 2020

KOKSIJDE *A1 (2km W Rural) 51.10287, 2.63066*
Camping Noordduinen, Noordduinen 12, 8670
Koksijde aan Zee **(058) 512546 or 0477 276469 (mob);**
**roos@campingbenelux.be; www.camping
noordduinen.be**

🔢12 🐕 💶€2.50 🏕 ♿ 🚿 ∅ 🦋 ⛲ nr 🏖 sand 3km

Exit A18/E40 junc 1A onto N8. Foll sp Koksijde to
rndabt, strt over into Leopold III Laan, site on L. Do
not use SatNav. Sm, hdg, hdstg, pt shd, EHU €2.50;
80% statics; bus 500m; Eng spkn; adv bkg acc; CKE.
*"Gd site; adj cycle rte to Veurne - attractive, historic
town; san facs now closer to pitches."* **€30.00** 2017

MARCHE EN FAMENNE *C3 (6.5km NW Rural)
50.24911, 5.27978* **Camping Le Relais,** 16 Rue de
Serinchamps, 5377 Hogne **(0475) 423049; info@
campinglerelais.com; www.campinglerelais.com**

🔢12 🐕 🚻 (htd) WD 🏕 ♿ 🚿 ∅ 🌐 🚂 ⛩

Sp fr N4 bet Marche-en-Famenne & Namur.
Fr Namur ent immed R under new bdge. 3*, Med,
unshd, pt sl, EHU (10A) €2.50; TV; 30% statics; adv
bkg acc; CKE. *"V pleasant; lake adj; gd, clean facs but
dated (2015); conv for N4."* **€20.50** 2015

NAMUR *C3 (9km SW Rural) 50.44164, 4.80182*
Camping Les Trieux, 99 Rue Les Tris, 5020 Malonne
**(081) 445583 or 473 810742 (mob); camping.les.
trieux@skynet.be; www.campinglestrieux.be**

🚻 (htd) WD 🏕 🚿 ∅ MSP 🦋 🐕 🚂 ⛩

Fr Namur take N90 sp Charleroi, after 8km take
L fork sp Malonne (camp sp at junc). After 400m
turn L at camp sp & site at top of 1 in 7 (13%) hill,
approx 200m. To miss steep hill, fr Namur take
Dinant (N92) S. In 2km R at camping sp. Take care at
hairpin in 200m. Foll site sps. Located up steep, but
surfaced rd. Med, mkd, pt shd, terr, EHU (10A) €2; TV;
50% statics; phone; Eng spkn; CKE. *"Friendly owners;
pretty site, but steep - take care ent pitch; pitches
diff for lge o'fits; basic san facs but clean; NH only."*
€21.00, 1 Apr-31 Oct. 2015

NEUFCHATEAU *D3 (2.5km SW Rural) 49.83305,
5.41721* **Camping Spineuse,** Rue de Florenville, 6840
Neufchâteau **061 27 73 20; info@camping-spineuse.
be; www.camping-spineuse.be**

🔢12 🐕 💶€1.25 🚻 (htd) WD 🏕 ♿ 🚿 ∅ 🦋 ⛲ 🍴 ⛩ 🌐 🚂 nr ⛩ 🚣

Fr A4/E411 exit junc 26 or junc 27 fr E25 to
Neufchâteau. Take N85 dir Florenville, site is 3rd on
L. Ent easy to miss. 3*, Med, pt shd, EHU (16A) €3;
TV; 30% statics; phone; Eng spkn; ccard acc. *"Pleasant,
pretty site; poss diff lge o'fits if site full; vg san facs;
some flooding after heavy rain."* **€28.50** 2018

NIEUWPOORT *A1 (1.5km NE Rural) 51.13324,
2.76031* **Parking De Zwerver,** Brugsesteenweg 16,
8620 Nieuwpoort **(0474) 669526; de_zwerver@
telenet.be**

🔢12 🚻 ♿ 🚿 🚽 MSP ⛩

Nr Kompass Camping - see dirs under Kompass
Camping. Site behind De Zwerver nursery. Sm, mkd,
hdstg, unshd, bbq. *"M'vans only; coin & note operated
facs; modern & efficient; walking/cycling dist to town
cent & port."* **€0.50** 2016

NIEUWPOORT *A1 (3km E Rural) 51.12960, 2.77220*
Kompascamping Nieuwpoort, Brugsesteenweg 49,
8620 Nieuwpoort **(058) 236037; nieuwpoort@
kompascamping.be; www.kompascamping.be**

🐕 💶€3.20 🚻 (htd) WD 🏕 ♿ 🚿 ∅ 🦋 ⛲ 🍴 🌐 🚂 ⛩ 🖊
🚣 (covrd, htd) 🎣

Exit E40/A18 at junc 3 sp Nieuwpoort; in 500m turn
R at full traff lts; after 1km turn R at traff lts; turn
R at rndabt & immed turn L over 2 sm canal bdgs.
Turn R to Brugsesteenweg, site on L approx 1km.
Fr Ostende on N34 (coast rd) turn L at rndabt after
canal bdge as above. 4*, V lge, hdg, mkd, hdstg, pt
shd, EHU (10A) inc; gas; red long stay; 50% statics;
adv bkg acc; tennis; bike hire; waterslide; golf 10km;
CKE. *"Well-equipped site; helpful staff; boat-launching
facs; sep area for sh stay tourers; sports/games
area adj; very busy w/ends; excel cycle rtes; conv
Dunkerque ferry; excel facs; superb san facs; lge site."*
€44.00, 23 Mar-5 Nov, H19. 2018

NIEUWPOORT *A1 (16km S Rural) 51.02401, 2.84370*
De Ijzerhoeve, Kapellestraat 4, B-8600 Diksmuide
**(51) 439439 or (472) 961220; info@deijzerhoeve.be;
www.deijzerhoeve.be**

🐕 💶€1 🚻 WD 🏕 ♿ ∅ 🚂 nr

Fr Ypres take N369 to Diksmuide. Turn L onto N35,
L again strt after bdge then R onto Kapellestraat.
Site in 1km on R. Sm, unshd, EHU (6A); red long stay;
TV; 50% statics; phone; bus; Eng spkn; adv bkg acc.
"Site conv & cheap; renovation in progress(2017); gd."
€14.00, 1 Apr-31 Oct. 2017

OOSTENDE *A1 (5km NE Coastal) 51.24882, 2.96710*
Camping 17 Duinzicht, Rozenlaan 23, 8450 Bredene
**(059) 323871; info@campingduinzicht.be;
www.campingduinzicht.be**

🔢12 🐕 🚻 (htd) WD 🏕 ♿ 🚿 🚽 MSP 🦋 ⛲ 🍴 nr 🌐 🚂 nr ⛩
🏖 sand 500m

Fr Ostend take dual c'way to Blankenberge on N34.
Turn R sp Bredene, L into Driftweg which becomes
Kappelstraat & turn R into Rozenlaan. Site sp.
Lge, mkd, hdstg, unshd, serviced pitches; EHU (10A)
inc (poss no earth); gas; bbq; 60% statics; phone;
Eng spkn; adv bkg acc; ccard acc; CKE. *"Excel site;
poss long walk to san facs; security barrier; take care
slippery tiles in shwrs; Bredene lovely, sm seaside
town."* **€24.00** 2020

BELGIUM

BELGIUM

OOSTENDE *A1* (6km NE Rural) *51.24366, 2.98002*
Camping T Minnepark, Zandstraat 105, 8450
Bredene-Dorp **(059) 322458; info@minnepark.be;**
www.minnepark.be

12 🐕 €3 👤🕴 WC 🚿 ♨ 🏊 nr 🏧 🏖 sand 2km

Fr Ostend take N34 sp Blankenberge. After tunnel
under rlwy turn R sp Brugge. Cross canal & turn L
at traff lts in 300m. In 2km after water tower, turn
L at X-rds. at Mini rndabt turn R pass Aldi. Site on
L in 1km after Zanpolder (sm yellow sp on L). V
lge, unshd, EHU (16A) €1 (poss rev pol); TV (pitch);
75% statics; Eng spkn; adv bkg rec. *"Lge pitches;
friendly, helpful staff; warm welcome; excel, well-run,
well maintained family run site; excel san facs; conv
ferries, Bruges & coast; lge pitches; conv for exploring
Brugge, Ghent, Ypres & coast."* **€30.00**   **2019**

OPGLABBEEK *B3* (2km SE Rural) *51.02825, 5.59745*
Wilhelm Tell, Hoeverweg 3, 3660 Opglabbeek
(089) 854444; wilhelmtell@limburgcampings.be;
www.wilhelmtell.com

12 🐕 €5 👤🕴 WC 🚿 ♿ ♨ 🚮 🦋 👤 ♨ Ⴒ 🍽 🛗 🏧 🏊 🏧 🪑 ✏

🏊 (covrd, htd) 🛗

Leave A2/E314 at junc 32, take rd N75 then N730 N
sp As. In As take Opglabbeek turn, site sp in 1km.
4*, Med, mkd, pt shd, EHU (10A) inc; gas; bbq; red long
stay; TV; 55% statics; phone; adv bkg acc; golf 10km;
tennis; bike hire; waterslide; CKE. *"Nice site; narr ent;
superb pools, wave machine; site in nature reserve;
helpful staff; san facs dist; bit expensive; not suitable
for lge o'fits."* **€32.00**   **2020**

> ## "There aren't many sites open at this time of year"
>
> If you're travelling outside peak season
> remember to call ahead to check site opening
> dates – even if the entry says 'open all year'.

OTEPPE *B3* (0.5km N Rural) *50.58239, 5.12455*
Camping L'Hirondelle Château, Rue de la Burdinale
76A, 4210 Oteppe **(085) 711131; info@lhirondelle.be;**
www.lhirondelle.be

🐕 €2.50 👤🕴 ♨ 🚿 ♨ 🦋 👤 ♨ 🍽 🛗 🏧 🏊 🏧 🏊

App fr E A15/E42 at exit 8; turn W on N643 for
1.5km; turn at sp on R for Oteppe. In vill 3km pass
church to x-rds & R by police stn: site 150m on L.
Fr W exit A15 at exit 10 onto N80, turn R onto N652
at Burdinne for Oteppe - easier rte. V lge, shd, pt sl,
EHU (6A) inc; gas; bbq; 75% statics; ccard acc; games
area; waterslide; tennis; CKE. *"Site in grnds of chateau;
excel facs for children; touring pitches at top of site
poss diff (steep); gd area for walking, fishing; conv NH;
v quiet LS."* **€29.00, 1 Apr-31 Oct.**   **2019**

PHILIPPEVILLE *C2* (11km NW Rural) *50.23920,
4.45927* **Camping Le Chesle,** 1 rue d'Yves, 5650
Vogenee **(071) 612632; info.camping.chesle@gmail.
com; www.chesle.be**

🐕 👤🕴 WC 🚿 ♿ ♨ 🚮 🦋 👤 ♨ 🏧 🏧

N5 Charleroi-Philippeville, exit Yves Gomezee. After
rlwy, turn R to Vogenee and foll sp. Med, unshd, pt
sl, EHU (16A); bbq; TV; 50% statics; bus 1km; Eng
spkn; adv bkg acc; CKE. *"Pleasant walking rtes fr site,
ask for map; cycling poss, but v hilly; vg; v friendly,
helpful owners."* **€24.60, 1 Feb-15 Dec.**   **2018**

ROCHE EN ARDENNE, LA *C3* (0.8km S Rural)
50.17465, 5.57774 **Camping Le Vieux Moulin,** Rue
Petite Strument 62, 6980 La Roche-en-Ardenne **(084)
411507; info@strument.com; www.strument.com**

🐕 €2 👤🕴 (htd) WC 🚿 ♨ 🦋 👤 ♨ 🍽 🛗 🏊 nr

Off N89 site sp fr La Roche town cent (dir Barrièr-
de-Champlon), site in 800m. Med, hdg, shd, pt sl,
EHU (6A) €2.50 (poss no earth); bbq; 70% statics; Eng
spkn; adv bkg acc; canoeing; fishing; CKE. *"Beautiful
site; gd pitches; poss unclean san facs & dishwashing
(7/09); poss youth groups; poor security; gd walking
(map avail)."* **€14.00, Easter-Nov.**   **2020**

ROCHEFORT *C3* (0.5km E Rural) *50.15947, 5.22609*
Camping Communal Les Roches, 26 Rue du Hableau,
5580 Rochefort **(084) 211900 or (479) 261759 (mob);
campingrochefort@lesroches.be; www.lesroches.be**

🐕 👤🕴 (htd) WC 🚿 ♿ ♨ 🚮 🦋 👤 ♨ 🍽 🛗 nr ♨ nr 🏊 nr 🏧 ✏

Fr Rochefort cent on N86 & turn L at rndabt, then
1st R. Site well sp. 4*, Lge, hdg, mkd, hdstg, unshd,
pt sl, serviced pitches; EHU (16A) metered; bbq; TV;
50% statics; phone; bus 250m; Eng spkn; ccard acc;
games rm; tennis; games area. *"Vg, well-managed,
pleasant, refurbished site; pool high ssn adj; gd walking;
sh walk to charming town; gd, modern clean san facs;
v popular site; rest at w-ends only."*
€27.00, 1 Apr-11 Nov.   **2018**

SINT MARGRIETE *A2* (2.6km NW Rural) *51.2860,
3.5164* **Camping De Soetelaer,** Sint Margrietepolder
2, 9981 Sint Margriete **(09) 3798151; camping.
desoetelaer@telenet.be; www.desoetelaer.be**

👤🕴 WC 🚿 ♨ 🚮 🦋 🏊 nr

Fr E on N49/E34 to Maldegem or fr W on N9 or
N49 turn N onto N251 to Aardenburg (N'lands),
then turn R twd St Kruis (N'lands) - site situated
1.5km strt on fr St Margriete (back in Belgium).
Med, mkd, pt shd, serviced pitches; EHU (6A) inc;
Eng spkn; adv bkg acc; CKE. *"Vg, clean site; excel,
modern san facs; peace & quiet, privacy & space; highly
rec for relaxation; o'fits pitched v close end to end."*
€24.00, Easter-15 Oct.   **2019**

BELGIUM

SOUMAGNE *B3* (3.5km S Rural) *50.61099, 5.73840*
Domaine Provincial de Wégimont, Chaussée de
Wégimont 76, 4630 Soumagne **(04) 2372400;
wegimont@prov-liege.be; www.prov-liege.be/
wegimont**

Exit A3 at junc 37 onto N3 W twd Fléron & Liège. In
500m at traff lts turn L sp Soumagne. In Soumagne
at traff lts form R dir Wégimont, site on top of hill
on R directly after bus stop. Med, hdg, pt shd, pt sl,
EHU (16A) inc poss rev pol; bbq; 70% statics; bus; site
clsd Jan; tennis; games area; CKE. *"Welcoming site in
chateau grnds (public access); pool adj high ssn; clean
facs; conv sh stay/NH nr m'way."* **€13.50** 2016

SPA *C4* (1.6km SE Rural) *50.48559, 5.88385* **Camping
Parc des Sources,** Rue de la Sauvenière 141, 4900 Spa
**(087) 772311; info@parcdessources.be;
www.parcdessources.be**

Bet Spa & Francorchamps on N62, sp on R. Med, mkd,
pt shd, pt sl, EHU (10A) €2.75; gas; 60% statics; phone.
*"Excel facs, modern lndry, beautiful location, nr forest;
friendly & helpful staff."* **€25.00, 25 Mar-31 Oct.** 2016

STEKENE *A2* (4km SW Rural) *51.18366, 4.00730*
Camping Vlasaard, Heirweg 143, 9190 Stekene
**(03) 7798164; info@camping-vlasaard.be; www.
camping-vlasaard.be**

Fr N49 Antwerp-Knokke rd, exit sp Stekene.
In Stekene, take dir Moerbeke, site on L in 4km.
V lge, mkd, unshd, serviced pitches; EHU (16A);
75% statics; Eng spkn; ccard acc; games area.
€18.00, 7 Jan-20 Dec. 2016

TOURINNES LA GOSSE *B3* (0.5km SW Rural) *50.77952,
4.73657* **Camping au Val Tourinnes,** Rue du Grand
Brou 16A, 1320 Tourinnes-la-Grosse **(010) 866642;
campingopassage@gmail.com; www.opassage.be**

Fr N on E40/A3 m'way exit junc 23 onto N25 S dir
Hamme-Mille. In Hamme-Mille turn L at traff lts,
site on R in 2km. Or fr S on E411/A4 exit junc 8 onto
N25 to Hamme-Mille & turn R at traff lts, then as
above. Don't use site name on Sat Nav. 2*, Sm, hdg,
pt shd, EHU (2A) €4, (10A) €8; twin axles; Eng spkn;
adv bkg acc; ccard acc; lake fishing. *"New owners
(2019), will be gd when finished; at present only a few
EHU pitches; some pitches diff to access due to grass
kerbs; vg, modern san facs; access tight for lge o'fits;
airshow 1st w/end July; peaceful, quirky site; fair."*
€20.00 2019

TOURNAI *B2* (2km SE Urban) *50.59967, 3.41349*
Camp Municipal de l'Orient, Jean-Baptiste Moens 8,
7500 Tournai **(069) 222635; campingorient@tournai.be**

Exit E42 junc 32 R onto N7 twd Tournai. L at 1st
traff lts, foll sp Aquapark, L at rndabt, site immed
on L (no sp). 4*, Med, hdg, hdstg, pt shd, serviced
pitches; EHU (10A) inc (poss rev pol/no earth) or
metered; gas; Eng spkn; adv bkg req; CKE. *"Well-kept
site in interesting area & old town; facs stretched high
ssn, but excel site; take care raised kerbs to pitches;
max length of c'van 6.5m due narr site rds & high hdgs;
helpful wardens; lake adj; E side of site quietest; htd,
indoor pool adj; EHU had no earth on a nbr of pitches;
rest, bar & playgrnd at leisure complex adj (50% disc
to campers); handy for Lille and Dunkerque ferries."*
€16.00 2018

"That's changed – Should I let the Club know?"

If you find something on site that's different
from the site entry, fill in a report and let us
know. See camc.com/europereport.

TURNHOUT *A3* (9.6km SW Rural) *51.28253, 4.83750*
Recreatie de Lilse Bergen, Strandweg 6, 2275 Lille-
Gierle **(014) 557901; info@lilsebergen.be;
www.delilsebergen.be**

Exit A21/E34 junc 22 N dir Beerse; at rndabt foll sp
Lilse Bergen. Site in 1.5km. 4*, Lge, mkd, shd, EHU
(10A) inc; bbq; sw; 60% statics; phone; Eng spkn; adv
bkg acc; ccard acc; bike hire; tennis; games area; sep
car park; watersports; CKE. *"Site sep pt of lge leisure
complex; pitches amongst pine trees; modern san facs,
poss stretched high ssn; excel for children/teenagers;
gd."* **€30.00** 2019

VIRTON *D3* (3km NE Rural) *49.57915, 5.54892*
Camping Colline de Rabais, 1 Rue Clos des Horlès,
6760 Virton **(063) 571195; info@collinederabais.be;
www.collinederabais.be**

Take junc 29 fr A4/E411 onto N87, 2km fr Virton
turn into wood at site sp. At end of rd bef lge
building turn R, then 3rd turn R at phone box.
4*, Lge, pt shd, pt sl, terr, EHU (16A) €3.20; sw nr; TV
(pitch); 20% statics; phone; Eng spkn; adv bkg acc;
ccard acc; bike hire; tennis 1km; fishing 1km; CKE.
"Pleasant site; gd facs." **€14.00** 2016

WAASMUNSTER *A2* (2.4km N Rural) *51.12690, 4.08455* **Camping Gerstekot,** Vinkenlaan 30, 9250 Waasmunster **(0323) 7723424; campinggerstekot. be@gmail.com; www.gerstekot.be**

🏠12 � (htd) 🆆🅳 ♨ ⚬ ♿ ♒ ∿ 🅼🆂🅿 ▾ 🍽 📶 🔌 🆁 ⚒

Exit A14/E17 at junc 13 Waasmunster onto N446 S; take 1st L in 100m into Patrijzenlaan & L again into Vinkenlaan, foll camp sp. Med, mkd, pt shd, EHU (16A) inc; bbq; TV; 95% statics; phone; adv bkg acc; ccard acc; games area; games rm; CKE. *"Busy at w/end; water use metered; key req for shwrs; gd."* **€18.00** **2016**

WESTENDE *A1* (0.4km SW Coastal) *51.15728, 2.76561* **Camping Westende,** Westendelaan 341, 8434 Westende **(058) 233254; info@camping westende.be; www.campingwestende.be**

🏠 €2 ♠♦♠ (htd) ♨ ⚬ ♿ ♒ ∿ 🅼🆂🅿 ▾ 🔌 📶 ♒ 🆁 nr ⚒ ⊿ (htd)
⊿ sand 1km

Fr Middelkerke foll N318; just after Westende vill church take dir Nieupoort, site on L in 150m. Lge, mkd, unshd, EHU (10A) inc; gas; 90% statics; phone; bus; Eng spkn; CKE. *"Sm but tidy touring area; friendly owners; beach nrby; tram 1km; excel cycling; gd."* **€34.00, 1 Apr-14 Nov.** **2016**

YPRES/IEPER *B1* (3km E Urban) *50.8467, 2.8994* **Camping Jeugdstadion,** Bolwerkstraat 1, 8900 Leper, Ypres **(057) 217282; info@jeugdstadion.be; www.jeugdstadion.be**

🏠 €1 ♠♦♠ (htd) 🆆🅳 ♨ ∿ 🅼🆂🅿 📶 ⚒ nr ⚒

Fr S ent town cent on N336, after rlwy x-ing turn R at rndabt onto ring rd & L at 2nd rndabt, foll camping sp. Site in 300m on L, sp fr ring rd. If app town cent fr N on N8 fr Veurne take ring rd N37; at rndabt turn L, site in 300m on L, well sp. Fr N38 in Ypres turn off at rndabt sp Industrie/Jeugdstadion, take 2nd L, site at end. NB site open all year for m'vans. 2*, Med, mkd, hdstg, hdg, pt shd, pt sl, EHU (10A) inc (poss rev pol); Eng spkn; adv bkg rec; ccard acc; bike hire. *"Automatic registration/check out avail when office clsd; peaceful, well-refurbished site; conv WW1 battle fields & museums; 10 min walk to Menin Gate for daily Last Post Ceremony; helpful staff; gd, modern san facs; sports park adj; soft grass pitches - ask for one with 'rubber tracks' to avoid sinking; hdstg m'van (OAY with own san facs only) pitches in sep area like an Aire; site poss v full local public hols; pool adj; site not fully enclsd; excel, clean, tidy, well run site; rec; noise fr adj processing plant."* **€20.00, 1 Mar-12 Nov.** **2019**

YPRES/IEPER *B1* (10km SW Rural) *50.78643, 2.82035* **Camping Ypra,** Pingelaarstraat 2, 8956 Kemmel-Heuvelland **(057) 444631; info@camping-ypra.be; www.camping-ypra.be**

🏠 €1.90 ♠♦♠ (htd) 🆆🅳 ♨ ⚬ ∿ ▾ 🍽 🔌 nr ⚒ ⚒

On N38 Poperinge ring rd turn S at rndabt onto N304. Foll sp Kemmel. Site on R in 12km on N edge of Kemmel. 3*, Med, mkd, hdstg, pt shd, pt sl, EHU (16A) inc (poss rev pol); 90% statics; Eng spkn; adv bkg acc; CKE. *"Clean, well-maintained site; gd, modern san facs, but ltd; helpful, friendly staff; access to some pitches poss diff; interesting rest in vill; conv for WW1 battlefields; pitches varied sizes; poss noise fr club hse & bar; gd."* **€25.00, 1 Mar-30 Nov.** **2019**

ZELE *A2* (6.5km SW Rural) *51.05273, 3.97996* **Camping Groenpark,** Gentsesteenweg 337, 9240 Zele **(09) 3679071; Groenpark@scarlet.be; www.campinggroenpark.be**

🏠 ♠♦♠ (htd) 🆆🅳 ♨ ∿ 🅼🆂🅿 ▾ 🍽 nr 🔌 nr 🔌 ⚒ nr ⚒

Fr A14 Ghent/Antwerp, J12 S onto N47. In 10km turn Ronto N445 to Overmeer. Site on L (flags) in 10km. 3*, Sm, mkd, pt shd, EHU (10A) inc; bbq; sw nr; TV; 10% statics; tram; Eng spkn; adv bkg acc; CKE. *"Nr Park & Ride to Ghent; wooded area for tourers; gd; pleasant site; nice walk around lake; sm site in tall pines 50mtrs fr Donkmeer Lake; v pretty; not well maintained; fair."* **€25.00, 31 Mar-1 Oct.** **2018**

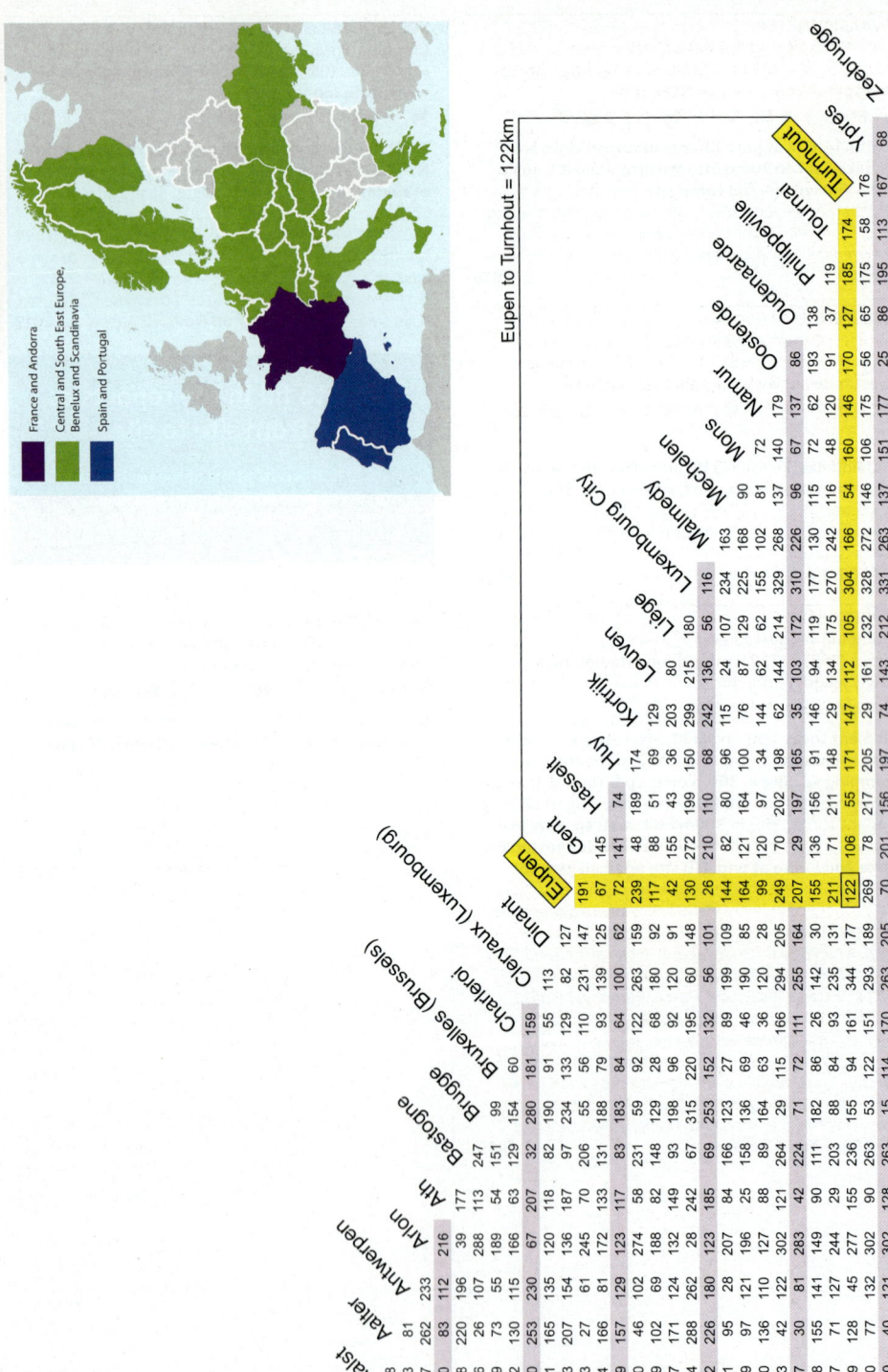

France and Andorra

Central and South East Europe, Benelux and Scandinavia

Spain and Portugal

Eupen to Turnhout = 122km

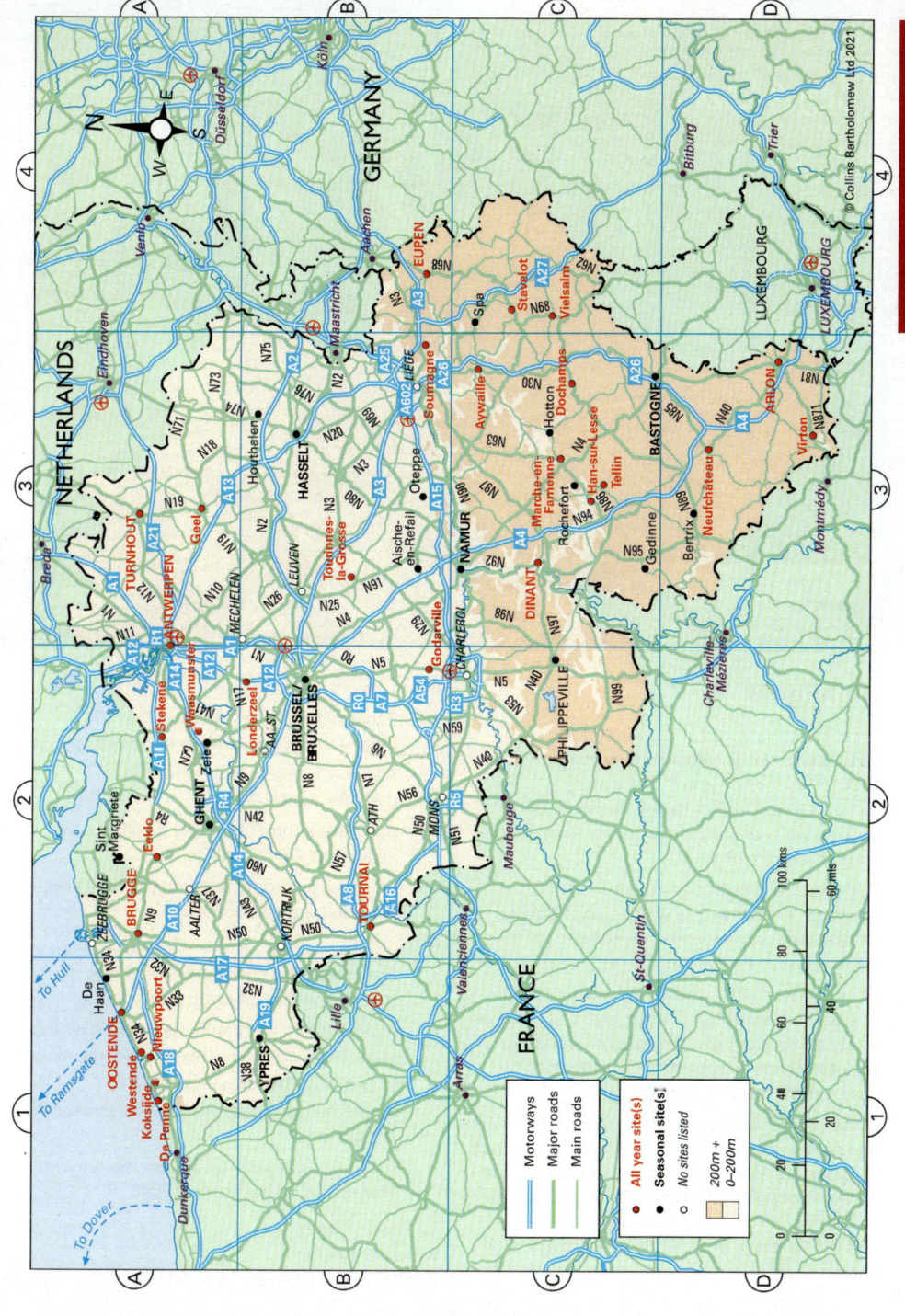

Croatia

Plitvice Lakes

Shutterstock/ Creative Travel Projects

Highlights

Croatia's Adriatic coast is a land of sun, beauty and history. Soaked in culture going back thousands of years, there are so many different sights to see, from the 16th century walls of Dubrovnik to the Roman amphitheatre in Pula.

With countless galleries, museums and churches to discover, as well as an exquisite natural landscape to explore, there truly is something for everyone.

Licitars are brightly decorated biscuits made of sweet honey dough. Often given as a gift at celebrations such as Christmas or weddings, they are an integral part of Croatian identity dating from the 16th century.

Croatia is well known for its carnivals, festivals and celebrations, which take place throughout the year. Some of the most important are the Spring Procession of Queens from Gorjani, the Bell Ringer's Pageant from the Kastav Area and the Festivity of St. Blaise, Dubrovnik's patron saint.

Major towns and cities

- Zagreb – the capital of Croatia has a rich history that dates from Roman times.
- Rijeka – Croatia's principal port city overlooking the Adriatic.
- Split – the centre of the city is built around an ancient Roman palace.
- Osijek – a gastronomic centre, and the best place to try a traditional dish.

Attractions

- Dubrovnik – a wonderfully-preserved medieval walled city with plenty to see.
- Plitvice Lakes - a stunning series of lakes and waterfalls set in an enchanting woodland.
- Pula Arena – this ancient Roman amphitheatre is one of the best preserved in the world.
- Diocletian's Palace – an ancient monument that makes up the heart of Split.

Find out more

www.croatia.hr
E: info@htz.hr T: 0038 5 14 55 64 55

Country Information

Population (approx): 4.2 million

Capital: Zagreb

Area: 56,540 sq km, divided into 20 counties

Bordered by: Bosnia-Herzegovina, Hungary, Serbia, Montenegro and Slovenia

Terrain: Flat plains along border with Hungary; low mountains and highlands near Adriatic coast and islands

Climate: Mediterranean climate along the coast with hot, dry summers and mild, wet winters; continental climate inland with hot summers and cold winters

Coastline: 5,835km (inc 4,058km islands)

Highest Point: Dinara 1,830m

Language: Croatian

Local Time: GMT or BST + 1, i.e. 1 hour ahead of the UK all year

Currency: Kuna (HRK) divided into 100 lipa; £1 = HRK 8.65, HRK 10 = £1.16 (Feb 2021)

Emergency Numbers: Police 192; Fire brigade 193; Ambulance 194. Or dial 112 and specify the service you need.

Public Holidays in 2021: Jan 1, 6; Apr 5; May 1, 30 (National Day); Jun 3, 22; Aug 5 (Thanksgiving Day), 15; Nov 1; Dec 25, 26.

Some Christian Orthodox and Muslim festivals are also celebrated locally. School summer holidays take place from the last week in June to the end of August.

Entry Formalities

British and Irish passport holders may visit Croatia for up to three months without a visa.

Unless staying at official tourist accommodation (hotel or campsite) all visitors are obliged to register at the nearest police station or tourist agency within 24 hours of arrival. Campsites should carry out this function for their guests but make sure you check with them. If you fail to register you may receive a fine or you may have to leave Croatia.

British citizens intending to stay for an extended period should seek advice from the Croatian Embassy.

Medical Services

For minor ailments, first of all consult staff in a pharmacy (ljekarna).

Emergency hospital and medical treatment is available at a reduced cost on production of a valid EHIC. You will be expected to pay a proportion of the cost (normally 20%). Only basic health care facilities are available in outlying areas and islands.

Opening Hours

Banks: Mon-Fri 7am-7pm; Sat 7am-1pm.

Museums: Tue-Sun 10am-5pm; most close Mon and some close Sun afternoons.

Post Offices: Mon-Fri 7am-7pm (2pm in small villages). In major towns or tourist places, post offices on duty are open until 9pm.

Shops: Mon-Fri 8am-8pm; Sat & Sun 8am-2pm.

Safety and Security

The level of street crime is low, but you should be aware of pickpockets in major cities, coastal areas (e.g. pavement cafés) and take sensible precautions when carrying money, credit cards and passports.

Beware of people trying to make you pull over when driving, either by requesting help or indicating that something is wrong with your vehicle. If possible wait until you are in a populated area before pulling over to check.

If you are planning to travel outside the normal tourist resorts you should be aware that there are areas affected by the war, which ended in 1995, where unexploded mines remain. These include Eastern Slavonia, Brodsko-Posavska County, Karlovac County, areas around Zadar County and in more remote areas of the Plitvice Lakes National Park. See the Croatian Mine Action Centre's website at www.hcr.hr/en/protuminUvod.asp for more specific information about mine-affected areas.

Croatia shares with the rest of Europe an underlying threat from terrorism. Attacks could be indiscriminate and against civilian targets, including places frequented by tourists.

British Embassy

UL IVANA LUČIĆA 4
HR-10000 ZAGREB
Tel: (01) 6009100
www.british.embassyzagreb@fco.gov.uk

Irish Honorary Consulate

MIRAMARSKA 23 (EUROCENTER)
10000 ZAGREB
Tel: (01) 6310025
irish.consulate.zg@inet.hr

TRUMBICEVA OBALA 3
21000 SPLIT
Tel: (021) 343715
9csain@cpad.hr

Customs Regulations

Customs Posts

Main border crossings are open 24 hours a day.

Foodstuffs

Up to 10kg of meat and meat products and 10kg of dairy products may be imported from EU countries. If you are entering from outside the EU, you can bring 2kg of meat products as long as they are in sealed packages.

Documents

Driving Licence

Full, valid British driving licence are recognised but if you have an old-style green licence then it is advisable to change it for a photocard licence in order to avoid any local difficulties.

Green Card

While an International Motor Insurance Certificate (Green Card) is not necessary, you should ensure that your vehicle insurance includes cover for Croatia.

If you are driving to or through Bosnia and Herzegovina (for example, along the 20 km strip of coastline at Neum on the Dalmatian coastal highway to Dubrovnik) you should ensure that you have obtained Green Card cover for Bosnia and Herzegovina. For Club members insured under the Club's Motor Insurance schemes full policy cover is available for this 20km strip, however you must ask at the time of taking out or renewing your insurance policy for one that specifically covers Bosnia. If you have difficulties obtaining this cover before departure Club members can contact the Club's Travel Service Information Officer for advice, email travelserviceinfo@caravanclub.co.uk. Alternatively, temporary third-party insurance can be purchased at the country's main border posts, or in Split and other large cities. It is not generally obtainable at the Neum border crossing itself.

As an alternative, you can take the ferry from Ploče to Trpanj on the Pelješac peninsula and avoid the stretch of road in Bosnia and Herzegovina altogether. There are frequent ferries during summer months, but be aware that motorhome drivers are sometimes requested to reverse onto them.

Money

Visitors may exchange money in bureaux de change, banks, post offices, hotels and some travel agencies but you are likely to get the best rates in banks. Exchange slips should be kept in order to convert unspent kuna on leaving the country. Many prices are quoted in both kuna and euros, both are widely accepted.

Most shops and restaurants accept credit cards. There are cash machines in all but the smallest resorts.

The police are warning visitors about a recent increase in the number of forged Croatian banknotes in circulation, especially 200 and 500 kuna notes. Take care when purchasing kuna and use only reliable outlets, such as banks and cash points.

Passport

You must be able to show some form of identification if required by the authorities and, therefore, should carry your passport or photocard driving licence at all times.

Vehicle(s)

Carry your vehicle registration certificate (V5C), insurance details and MOT certificate (if applicable).

Driving

Accidents

Any visible damage to a vehicle entering Croatia must be certified by the authorities at the border and a Certificate of Damage issued, which must be produced when leaving the country. In the event of a minor accident resulting in material damage only, call the police and they will assist with the exchange of information between drivers and will issue a Certificate of Damage to the foreign driver. You should not try to leave the country with a damaged vehicle without this Certificate as you may be accused of a 'hit and run' offence.

Confiscation of passport and a court appearance within 24 hours are standard procedures for motoring accidents where a person is injured.

The Croatian Insurance Bureau in Zagreb can assist with Customs and other formalities following road accidents, tel: (01) 4696600, email: huo@huo.hr or see www.huo.hr.

Alcohol

The general legal limit of alcohol is 50 milligrams in 100 millilitres of blood, i.e. less than the level in the UK (80 milligrams). For drivers of vehicles over 3,500 kg and for drivers under 24 years of age the alcohol limit is zero. The general legal limit also applies to cyclists.

It is prohibited to drive after having taken any medicine whose side-effects may affect the ability to drive a motor vehicle.

Breakdown Service

The Hrvatski Auto-Klub (HAK) operates a breakdown service throughout the country, telephone 987 (or 01987 from a mobile phone) for assistance. On motorways use the roadside emergency phones which are placed at 2km intervals. Towing and breakdown services are available 24 hours a day in and around most major cities and along the coast in summer (6am to midnight in Zagreb).

Child Restraint Systems

Children under the age of 12 are not allowed to travel in the front seats of vehicles, with the exception of children under 2 years of age who can travel in the front if they are placed in a child restraint system adapted to their size. It must be rear-facing and the airbag must be de-activated.

Children up to 5 years old must be placed in a seat adapted to their size on the back seat. Children between the ages of 5 and 12 must travel on the back seat using a 3 point seat belt with a booster seat if necessary for their height.

Fuel

Petrol stations are generally open from 7am to 7 or 8pm, later in summer. Some of those on major stretches of road stay open 24 hours a day. Payment by credit card is widely accepted. LPG (Autogas) is fairly widely available.

Lights

Dipped headlights are compulsory at all times, regardless of weather conditions, from the end of October to the end of March and in reduced visibility at other times of the year. It is compulsory to carry spare bulbs, however this rule does not apply if your vehicle is fitted with xenon, neon, LED or similar lights.

Motorways

There is just over 1250km of motorways, with the major stretches being shown in the table below. Tolls (cestarina) are levied according to vehicle category. Electronic display panels above motorways indicate speed limits, road conditions and lane closures. Information on motorways can be found on www.hac.hr.

Motorway Tolls

Class 1   Vehicle with 2 axles, height up to 1.3m measured from front axle) excluding vans.

Class 2   Vehicle with 2 or more axles, height up to 1.3m (measured from front axle), including car + caravan or trailer, motorhomes and vans.

Class 3   Vehicle with 2 or 3 axles, height over 1.3m (measured from front axle), including van with trailer.

Class 4   Vehicle with 4 or more axles, height over .3m (measured from front axle).

Tolls can be paid in cash or by credit card. Details of toll prices can be found in English at www.hac.hr.

Parking

Lines at the roadside indicate parking restrictions. Traffic wardens patrol roads and impose fines for illegal parking. Vehicles, including those registered outside Croatia, may be immobilised by wheel clamps.

Roads

In general road conditions are good in and around the larger towns. The Adriatic Highway or Jadranksa Magistrala (part of European route E65) runs the whole length of the Adriatic coast and is in good condition, despite being mostly single-carriageway. Minor road surfaces may be uneven and, because of the heat-resisting material used to surface them, may be very slippery when wet. Minor roads are usually unlit at night.

Motorists should take care when overtaking and be aware that other drivers may overtake unexpectedly in slow-moving traffic. The standard of driving is generally fair.

Road Signs and Markings

Road signs and markings conform to international standards. Motorway signs have a green background; national road signs have a blue background.

Speed Limits

	Open Road (km/h)	Motorway (km/h)
Car Solo	90-110	130
Car towing caravan/trailer	80	90
Motorhome under 3500kg	90-110	130
Motorhome 3500-7500kg	80	90

In addition to complying with other speed limits, drivers under the age of 25 must not exceed 80 km/h (50 mph) on the open road, 100 km/h (62 mph) on expressways and 120 km/h (74 mph) on motorways.

Traffic Jams

During the summer, tailbacks may occur at the border posts with Slovenia at Buje on the E751 (road 21), at Bregana on the E70 (A3) and at Donji Macelj on the E59 (A1). During July and August there may be heavy congestion, for example at Rupa/Klenovica and at other tourist centres, and on the E65 north-south Adriatic Highway. This is particularly true on Friday evenings, Saturday mornings, Sunday evenings and holidays.

Queues form at ferry crossings to the main islands. Road and traffic conditions can be viewed on the HAK website (in English), www.hak.hr or tel: (01) 4640800 (English spoken) or (072) 777777 while in Croatia for round-the-clock recorded information.

Violation of Traffic Regulations

The police may impose on-the-spot fines for parking and driving offences. If you are unable to pay the police may confiscate your passport. Motoring law enforcement, especially for speeding offences, is strictly observed.

Winter Driving

It is compulsory to carry snow chains in your vehicle and they must be used if required by the weather conditions (5cm of snow or black ice). The compulsory winter equipment in Croatia consists of a shovel in your vehicle and a set of snow chains on the driving axel.

Essential Equipment

First aid kit

All vehicles, including those registered abroad, must carry a first aid kit.

Reflective Jacket/Waistcoat

It is obligatory to carry a reflective jacket inside your car (not in the boot) and you must wear it if you need to leave your vehicle to attend to a breakdown, e.g. changing a tyre. It is also common sense for any passenger leaving the vehicle to also wear one.

Warning Triangle(s)

All motor vehicles must carry a warning triangle. If you are towing a caravan or trailer you must have two warning triangles.

Touring

There are a number of national parks and nature reserves throughout the country, including the World Heritage site at the Plitvice lakes, the Paklenica mountain massif, and the Kornati archipelago with 140 uninhabited islands, islets and reefs. Dubrovnik, itself a World Heritage site, is one of the world's best-preserved medieval cities, having been extensively restored since recent hostilities.

While Croatia has a long coastline, there are few sandy beaches; instead there are pebbles, shingle and rocks with man-made bathing platforms.

The Croatian National Tourist Board operates 'Croatian Angels', a multi-lingual tourist information and advice service available from the end of March to mid-October, tel: 062 999 999 or 00385 62 999 999 from outside Croatia.

Croatia originated the concept of commercial naturist resorts in Europe and today attracts an estimated 1 million naturist tourists annually. There are approximately 20 official naturist resorts and beaches and numerous other unofficial or naturist-optional 'free' beaches. Smoking is prohibited in restaurants, bars and public places. A service charge is general included in the bill. English is widely spoken.

Camping and Caravanning

There are more than 150 campsites in Croatia including several well-established naturist sites, mainly along the coast. Sites are licensed according to how many people they can accommodate, rather than by the number of vehicles or tents, and are classed according to a grading system of 1 to 4 stars. There are some very large sites catering for up to 10,000 people at any one time but there are also many small sites, mainly in Dalmatia, situated in gardens, orchards and farms.

Many sites open from April to October; few open all year. They are generally well-equipped.

A tourist tax is levied of between HRK 4 and HRK 7 per person per day according to region and time of year.

Casual/wild camping is illegal and is particularly monitored at beaches, harbours and rural car parks. Most campsites have overnight areas for late arrivals and there are a number of rest areas established along main roads for overnight stays or brief stopovers.

Electricity and Gas

Current on campsites ranges from 10 to 16 amps. Plugs have 2 round pins. There may not be CEE connections and a long cable might be required.

Campingaz cylinders are not available, so take a good supply of gas with you.

Public Transport

Rail travel is slow and cab be unreliable. By contrast the bus network offers the cheapest and most extensive means of public transport. Buy bus tickets when you board or from kiosks, which you must validate once on board. Trams operate in Zagreb and you can buy tickets from kiosks.

Coastal towns and cities have regular scheduled passenger and car ferry services. Most ferries are drive-on/drive-off – see www.jadrolinija.hr for schedules and maps.

Car ferries operate from Ancona, Bari, Pescara and Venice in Italy to Dubrovnik, Korèula, Mali Lošinj, Poreè, Pula, Rijecka, Rovinj, Sibenik, Split, Starigrad, Vis and Zadar. Full details from:

VIAMARE LTD
SUITE 108, 582 HONEYPOT LANE
STANMORE
MIDDX HA7 1JS
Tel: 020 8206 3420

Email: ferries@viamare.com
www.viamare.com

BIOGRAD NA MORU *B3* (12km NW Coastal) *44.00532, 15.36748* **Autokamp Filko,** Aleksandar Colic 23207 Sveti Petar Na Moru **02 33 91 177; info@autokamp-filko.hr; www.autokamp-filko.hr**

🏠12 🐕 🕴🕴 📶 🏕 🍽 ➿ 🛝 ⛱ 🍴 🚰 nr 🛝 shgl

On D8 bet Zadar & Biograd Na Moru at Sv Petar NM. 1st camp on the R by sea. Sm, pt shd, 30% statics; Eng spkn. *"Some pitches by water on hdstg with views across to islands; dir access fr rd; ideal LS; gd."* **HRK 170** **2019**

DUBROVNIK *C4* (10km S Coastal) *42.62444, 18.19301* **Autocamp Matkovica,** Srebreno 8, 20207 Dubrovnik **(020) 485867; u.o.matkovica@hotmail.com**

🏠12 🐕 🕴🕴 📶 🏕 🍽 ➿ 🛝 ⛱ 🍴 nr 🚰 nr 🛝 nr 🛝 shgl adj

Fr Dubrovnik S on coast rd. At Kupari foll sp to site behind Camping Porto. 1*, Sm, mkd, shd, EHU (6A) inc; phone; bus 200m; Eng spkn. *"Well-kept site; friendly, helpful owners; cash only; san facs old but clean; water bus to Dubrovnik 1km."* **HRK 135** **2019**

DUBROVNIK *C4* (7km S Coastal) *42.62471, 18.20801* **Autocamp Kate,** Tupina 1, 20207 Mlini **(020) 487006; info@campingkate.com; www.campingkate.com**

🐕 HRK4 🕴🕴 📶 🏕 🍽 ➿ 🛝 ⛱ 🍴 nr 🚰 🛝 shgl 200m

Fr Dubrovnik on rd 8 foll sp Cavtat or Čilipi or airport into vill of Mlini. Fr S past Cavtat into Mlini. Site well sp fr main rd. Sm, hdstg, pt shd, pt sl, terr, EHU (10-16A) inc; bbq; red long stay; phone; bus to Dubrovnik 150m; Eng spkn; adv bkg acc; ĊKE. *"Family-run site in lovely setting; v helpful, hard-working, welcoming owners; vg clean facs; boats fr vill to Dubrovnik; long, steep climb (steps) down to beach."* **HRK 173, 4 Apr-27 Oct.** **2017**

FAZANA *A3* (1km S Coastal) *44.91717, 13.81105* **Camping Bi-Village,** Dragonja 115, 52212 Fažana **(052) 300300; info@bivillage.com; www.bivillage.com**

🐕 HRK37 🕴🕴 (htd) 📶 🏕 🛝 ⛱ 🍴 MSP 🦋 🍽 ➿ 🛝 🎣 🛝 shgl adj

N fr Pula on rd 21/A9/E751 at Vodnjan turn W sp Fažana. Foll sp for site. 4*, V lge, mkd, pt shd, EHU (10A) inc; gas; bbq; 30% statics; phone; bus; Eng spkn; adv bkg acc; ccard acc; bike hire; waterslide; golf 2km; tennis 1km; boat hire; games area; watersports; ĊKE. *"Excel, modern, clean san facs; private bthrms avail; site surrounded by pine trees; some beachside pitches; conv Brijuni Island National Park; excel leisure facs for families; vg cycle paths; no emptying point for Wastermaster; vg; prices vary per ssn."* **HRK 342, 20 Apr-14 Oct.** **2017**

KARLOVAC *B2* (12km SW Rural) *45.41962, 15.48338* **Autocamp Slapić,** Mrežničke Brig, 47250 Duga Resa **(098) 860601; autocamp@inet.hr; www.campslapic.hr**

🐕 HRK20 🕴🕴 📶 🏕 🛝 ⛱ 🍴 🍽 ➿ 🛝 nr 🚰 nr 🛝 nr 🛝

Exit A1/E65 junc 3 for Karlovac; strt over traff lts immed after toll booth sp Split & Rijecka. Take D23 to Duga Resa; turn L by church in Duga Resa; cont over bdge & turn R; foll rd keeping rv on your R; cont thro vill of Mrnžnički Brig in 3km; site sp in another 1km. NB new bdge at Belavici. Site well sp fr Duga Resa. 4*, Sm, mkd, pt shd, EHU (16A) HRK30; bbq; sw nr; phone; train to Zagreb 500m; Eng spkn; adv bkg acc; ccard acc; canoeing; fishing; games area; tennis; bike hire. *"Friendly, pleasant, family-owned site in gd location on rv; lovely area; gd bar/rest; gd clean facs; lge pitches; long hoses req LS; easy drive into Zagreb; excel; new, superb sans block (2014); poss noise fr daytrippers; rds to site narr."* **HRK 220, 1 Apr-31 Oct.** **2019**

KORENICA *B3* (1.5km NW Urban) *44.76527, 15.68833* **Camping Borje,** Vranovaca bb, 53230 Korenica **(053) 751790; info@np-plitvicka-jezera.hr; np-plitvicka-jezera.hr/camp-borje**

🐕 HRK20 🕴🕴 (htd) 📶 🏕 🛝 ⛱ 🍴 MSP 🦋 🍽 ➿ 🛝 🍴 🚰 nr 🛝

Exit A1/A6 at Karlovac & take rd 1/E71 S dir Split. Site on R approx 15km after Plitvička Jezera National Park, well sp. 3*, Med, mkd, pt shd, sl, EHU (10A) inc; bbq; sw nr; twin axles; Eng spkn; adv bkg acc; ccard acc; ĊKE. *"Vg, clean, well-kept, spacious, sl site - levelling poss tricky; gd, modern, immac facs, helpful staff; well run by Plitvicka National Park; excel for visiting the Lakes & waterfalls; free bus runs to park at 1030 and returns at 1730; excel; mountain views."* **HRK 250, 1 Apr-15 Oct.** **2019**

LABIN *A2* (3km SW Rural) *45.08179, 14.10167* **Mini Camping Romantik,** HR-52220 Labin, Kapelica 47b **(911) 396423; mario.braticic@pu.t-com.hr**

🐕 🕴🕴 📶 🛝 ⛱ 🍴 🍽 ➿ 🛝 🏊

Fr Labin on A21/E751, take 5103 twds Koramomacno for 2km. Site sp on this rd. Turn L into sm lane. Foll sp. 3*, Sm, hdstg, mkd, unshd, EHU (10A); bbq; cooking facs; 10% statics; Eng spkn; adv bkg rec; games area. *"Sm family site; 4 mkd and 4 unmkd pitches; v friendly, helpful, lovely family run site; 2km walk to old Labin."* **HRK 164, 24 Apr-15 Oct.** **2016**

MOLUNAT *D4* (0.5km N Coastal) *42.45298, 18.4276*
Autokamp Monika, Molunat 28, 20219 Molunat **(020)**
794557; info@camp-monika.hr

[12] 🐕 HRK8 ♦♦♦ [WD] 🛁 🍴 ⚡ 🚿 🦋 🛈 🍽 ♟ 🛒 ⚓ sand adj

Site well sp in Molunat off Adriatic Highway E65.
Sm, pt shd, terr, EHU (6A) HRK20; bbq; bus; Eng spkn.
*"Gd site close to Montenegro border & in quiet cove;
sea view fr all pitches; owner's wine & olive oil for sale;
beautiful views, v quiet LS; v friendly & helpful owner;
highly rec."* **HRK 135**   **2019**

OMIS *C4* (1.5km W Coastal) *43.44040, 16.67960*
Autocamp Galeb, Vukovarska bb, 21310 Omiš **(021)**
864430; camping@galeb.hr; www.camp.galeb.hr

[12] 🐕 HRK33 ♦♦♦ [WD] 🛁 ♟ ⚡ 🚿 🦋 🛈 🍽 ♟ 🛒 nr ⚓ 🖊

⚓ sand

Site sp on rd 2/E65 fr Split to Dubrovnik.
3*, Lge, mkd, pt shd, serviced pitches; EHU (16A) inc;
gas; bbq (elec, gas); red long stay; 50% statics; bus;
ccard acc; bike hire; games area; tennis; white water
rafting; watersports; CKE. *"Excel, well-maintained site
in gd position; private bthrms avail; extra for waterside
pitch; clean san facs; suitable young children; easy walk
or water taxi to town; v friendly staff; excel new rest,
with set breakfast."* **HRK 281, X02.**   **2018**

OREBIC *C4* (2.6km ENE Coastal) *42.982485,
17.205609* **Camping Lavanda,** Dubravica bb, HR
20250 Orebič **(385) 20454484; info@lavanda-
camping.com; www.lavanda-camping.com**

🐕 🐕 [WD] 🛁 ♟ ⚡ 🚿 🦋 🍴 🍽 ♟ 🛈 ⚓ 🖊 🏊 ⚓

On main rd 1km bef Orebic app fr Trpanj.
4*, Med, hdstg, mkd, pt shd, terr, EHU (16A); bbq; TV;
5% statics; phone; bus adj; Eng spkn; adv bkg acc;
sauna; CKE. *"Brand new site (2018); excel san facs;
dog shwr; ATM; beach for dogs; ferry to island avail;
great views fr almost every pitch; supmkt 500m; petrol
200m; excel."* **HRK 177, 15 Apr-31 Oct.**   **2018**

PAKOSTANE *B3* (4km SE Coastal) *43.88611,
15.53305* **Autocamp Oaza Mira,** Ul. Dr. Franje
Tudmana 2, 23211 Drage **023 635419; info@oaza-
mira.hr; www.oaza-mira.hr**

🐕 4 - 9 euros (depending on low/high season) ♦♦♦ [WD] 🛁 ♟ ⚡ 🚿 🦋 [MSP]

🦋 🍴 🍽 🛈 🛒 ⚓ 🏊 ⚓ adj

**A1 Karlovac-Split past Zadar, exit Biograd dir
Sibenik on coast rd; sp on coastal side of rd; foll sp
site after bay.** Med, hdstg, pt shd, terr, EHU inc; bbq;
Eng spkn; adv bkg acc; games rm; beach volley court;
2 tennis courts; multi-purpose court for basketball/
soccer. *"Excel new lovely site in beautiful location;
generous pitches; rec using ACSI card; 2 beautiful bays
adj to site; highly rec."* **HRK 427, 1 Apr-31 Oct.**
                                                            2020

POREC *A2* (10km N Coastal) *45.29728, 13.59425*
Camping Lanterna, Lanterna 1, 52465 Tar **(052)**
**404 500; lanterna@valamar.com; www.camping-
adriatic.com/camp-lanterna**

🐕 HRK 55 [WD] 🛁 ♟ ⚡ 🚿 🦋 🍴 🍽 ♟ 🛈 ⚓ 🖊 🏊 ⚓

🛒 ⚓ shgl adj

**Site sp 5km S of Novigrad (Istria) & N of Poreč on
Umag-Vrsar coast rd.** 4*, V lge, hdstg, mkd, hdg,
pt shd, pt sl, terr, EHU (10A); gas; bbq; 10% statics;
phone; adv bkg req; ccard acc; bike hire; watersports;
games area; boat launch; tennis; CKE. *"V busy,
well-run site; excel san facs & leisure facs; 2 hydromassage pools; noise fr ships loading across bay; bkg
fee; although many san facs they may be a long walk;
variety of shops; gd sightseeing; extra for seaside/hdg
pitch; vg."* **HRK 355, 12 Apr-10 Oct, X10.**   **2019**

POREC *A2* (8km NW Coastal) *45.25680, 13.58350*
Naturist-Center Ulika (Naturist), 52440 Poreč
(Istra) **(052) 436325; reservations@plavalaguna.hr;**
www.lagunaporec.com

🐕 HRK48 ♦♦♦ 🛁 ⚡ 🚿 🦋 🍴 🛈 ⚓ 🖊 🏊 ⚓ shgl

Site sp on rd fr Poreč to Tar & Novigrad. 4*, V lge,
shd, pt sl, EHU (6A) HRK23; red long stay; 9% statics;
adv bkg acc; ccard acc; watersports; tennis. *"Excel
site; picturesque shore; vg facs, poss far fr some
pitches; lge site, bike useful for getting around."*
HRK 287, 8 Apr-1 Oct.   **2017**

PRIMOSTEN *B4* (2km N Coastal) *43.60646, 15.92085*
Auto Kamp Adriatic, Huljerat BB, 22202 Primošten
(022) 571223; camp-adriatiq@adriatiq.com;
www.autocamp-adriatiq.com

🐕 HRK32 [WD] 🛁 ♟ ⚡ 🚿 [MSP] 🦋 🍴 🍽 🛈 🛒 🖊

⚓ shgl adj

Off Adriatic Highway, rd 8/E65, sp. 3*, V lge, hdstg,
unshd, pt sl, terr, EHU (16A) inc; gas; Eng spkn;
watersports; games area; tennis; boat hire; CKE. *"Gd
sea views; excel san facs; diving cent; some pitches
poss diff to get onto; beautiful views fr beach."*
HRK 190, 7 Apr-31 Oct.   **2016**

PULA *A3* (10km S Coastal) *44.82393, 13.85069*
Camping Indije, Indije 96, 52203, Banjole, Pula 052
573066; info@arenaturist.hr; arenacamps.com
🐕€4 � wc ♨ ⚓ ♿ ⚡ / MSP ♥ ♈ Ⓓ ♨ ♨ ⚐ ✂ ⚓

Fr Pula ring rd, drive twd Premantura. At Banjole,
exit rndbt 1st R and foll site sp. 2*, Lge, mkd, pt shd,
pt sl, terr, EHU (10A); bbq; red long stay; twin axles;
TV; 20% statics; phone; Eng spkn; adv bkg acc; games
area; bike hire; CKE. *"Watersports/diving; mkd walks &
cycle tracks; vg site."* **HRK 222, 21 Apr-25 Sep.**
                                                    2016

PULA *A3* (7km S Coastal) *44.82290, 13.85080*
Camping Peškera, Indije 73 52100 Banjole/Pula (Istra)
**052 573209; info@camp-peskera.com; www.camp-
peskera.com**
🐕 HRK22 � wc ⚓ ♿ / MSP ⚡ ♥ ♈ Ⓓ nr ♨ ⚓ shgl adj

Fr N take A9 to Pula. Cont on m'way twd Premantura.
Exit at Banjole, cont twd Indije. Campsite is 100m
after Indije. 3*, Sm, pt shd, pt sl, EHU; bus 0.5km; Eng
spkn; adv bkg acc; ccard acc; CCI. *"Beautiful situation;
helpful & friendly owners; gd clean san facs; vg."*
HRK 276, 1 Apr-31 Oct.   **2019**

PULA *A3* (8km S Rural) *44.82472, 13.85885* **Camping
Diana,** Castagnes b b, 52100 Banjole **(385) 99 293 1963
or (385) 99 738 0313; kristijan.modrusan@gmail.com;
www.camp-diana.com**
♚♛ wc ⚓ / ⚡ ♥ ♈ ♈ nr ⚐ ⚓ ♨

Fr Pula ring rd foll sp Premantura & Camping Indije.
Site 1km bef Cmp Indije. 3*, Sm, pt shd, pt sl, EHU
(16A) inc; adv bkg acc; tennis; games area. *"Pleasant
site in garden setting; gd range of facs; immac san facs;
welcoming family owners; narr ent poss diff for lge
o'fits."* **HRK 254, 15 May-22 Sep.**   **2016**

PULA *A3* (9km S Coastal) *44.82012, 13.90252*
Autocamp Pomer, Pomer bb, 52100 Pula **052 573746;
acpomer@arenaturist.hr; www.arenacamps.com**
🐕 HRK23 ♚♛ ⚓ ⚡ / ⚡ ♈ Ⓓ ⚐ ⚠ ✂ ♨ shgl adj

Fr N on A9 to Pula, take exit to Pula. At bottom
of hill turn L after filling stn & foll dir Medulin/
Premantura. In Premantura turn L by Consum
supmkt & foll sp to Pomer & site. Med, mkd, shd, terr,
EHU (16A) HRK21 (long lead poss req); bbq; 10%
statics; phone; Eng spkn; adv bkg acc; watersports;
fishing; games area; CKE. *"Clean san facs poss
stretched high ssn; friendly owner; quiet, relaxing site."*
HRK 127, 21 Apr-15 Oct.   **2016**

RAKOVICA *B3* (7km SW Rural) *44.95020, 15.64160*
Camp Korana, Plitvička Jezera, 47246 Drežnik Grad
**(053) 751888; autokamp.korana@np-plitvicka-
jezera.hr; www.np-plitvicka-jezera.hr**
🐕 HRK23 ♚♛ wc ⚓ ♨ ⚓ / MSP ♥ ♈ Ⓓ ♨ ⚓

On A1/E59 2km S of Grabovac, site on L. Site is 5km
N of main ent to Plitvička Nat Park, sp. Lge, hdstg,
pt shd, pt sl, EHU (16A) inc (poss long lead req); own
san req; bbq; 10% statics; Eng spkn; ccard acc; CKE.
*"Lovely site, v busy; poss long way fr facs; gd new san
facs but inadequate for size of site; efficient, friendly
site staff; poss muddy in wet; bus to National Park
(6km) high ssn; gd rest."* **HRK 232, 1 Apr-31 Oct.**
                                                    2018

RIJEKA *A2* (9km W Coastal) *45.35638, 14.34222*
Camping Preluk, Preluk 1, 51000 Rijeka **(051) 662185;
camp.preluk@gmail.com**
🐕 ♚♛ wc ⚓ / ⚡ ♨

On Rijeka to Opatija coast rd. 2*, Sm, shd, EHU
(10A) inc; own san req; 80% statics; bus; Eng spkn.
*"NH only; many statics; facs recently renovated
(2012); bus to town; sm beach on site; gd windsurfing."*
HRK 158, 1 May-30 Sep.   **2020**

RIZVANUSA *B3* (10km W Rural) *44.49580, 15.29165*
Eco Camp Rizvan City, Rizvanuša 1, 53000 Gospić
**053 57 33 33; info@adria-velebitica.hr;
www.camp-rizvancity.com**
🐕 ♚♛ wc ⚓ ♨ ♿ ⚡ / MSP ♥ ♈ ⚐

Fr A1 take exit 12 (Gospic). Head 10km E twd
Karlobag on highway 25. Turn L off main rd into Vill
Rizvanusa. Camp 500m. Sm, pt shd, EHU (16A); bbq;
twin axles; Eng spkn; adv bkg acc; games area. *"Walks,
high rope course; quad & jeep safari; archery; paintball;
zip line; wall climbing; giant swing; bike trails; vg."*
HRK 150, 1 Mar-1 Nov.   **2019**

ROVINJ *A2* (5km N Coastal) *45.10444, 13.62527*
Camping Valdaliso, Monsena b.b, 52210 Rovinj
**(052) 805505; ac-valdaliso@maistra.hr;
www.campingrovinjvrsar.com**
♚♛ (htd) wc ⚓ ♨ ♿ ⚡ / MSP ♥ ♈ ♈ Ⓓ ♨ ♨ ⚐ ✂ ♨ shgl adj

N fr Rovinj dir Valalta for 2km, turn W to coast,
site sp. 3*, Lge, hdg, hdstg, mkd, pt shd, pt sl, EHU
(10A) inc; gas; bbq; TV (pitch); 10% statics; phone;
bus; Eng spkn; adv bkg acc; ccard acc; waterslide; bike
hire; games area; tennis; games rm; CKE. *"Pretty site
in olive trees; use of all amenities in hotel adj; excel
modern san facs; poss waterlogged after heavy rain;
excel; water taxi; facs stretched if site full; pitches
uneven; closing in Sep 2015 for redevelopment."*
HRK 288, 12 Apr-26 Sep.   **2015**

ROVINJ *A2* (7km N Coastal) *45.12287, 13.62970*
Campsite Valalta Naturist (Naturist), Cesta Za
Valaltu-Lim 7, 52210 Rovinj (Istra) **052 804800;**
valalta@valalta.hr; www.valalta.hr

7km NW fr Rovinj. Foll signs to Valalta.
5*, V lge, hdg, mkd, hdstg, pt shd, EHU (16A); bbq;
twin axles; TV; phone; Eng spkn; adv bkg acc; games
area; games rm; waterslide; bike hire. *"Excel site."*
HRK 450, 1 May-1 Oct. 2019

ROVINJ *A2* (0.7km NW Coastal) *45.09472, 13.64527*
Autocamp Porton Biondi, Aleja Porton Biondi 1,
52210 Rovinj **(052) 813557; portonbiondi@web.de;**
www.portonbiondirovinj.com

HRK24 nr shgl nrby

Site sp on ent Rovinj. 3*, Lge, shd, pt sl, terr, EHU inc;
red long stay; adv bkg acc; ccard acc; watersports;
CKE. *"Gd site within walking dist Rovinj old town;
beautiful views; new san facs; sm pitches not suitable
lge o'fits & care needed when ent site; excel rest; 2nd
& subsequent nights at red rate."*
HRK 207, 15 Mar-31 Oct. 2018

ROVINJ *A2* (5km NW Coastal) *45.10909, 13.61974*
Camping Amarin, Monsena bb, 52210 Rovinj **(052)**
802000; ac-amarin@maistra.hr; www.camping
rovinjvrsar.com

HRK47 (htd) shgl adj

Fr town N in dir Valalta, turn L & foll site sp.
3*, V lge, mkd, pt shd, pt sl, EHU (10A) inc; TV;
30% statics; phone; Eng spkn; adv bkg acc; ccard acc;
sports facs; tennis; bike hire; waterslide; CKE. *"Excel
site; clean, well-maintained san facs & pool; gd entmnt;
views of town & islands; lovely situation in pine & olive
trees; water taxi to town; some pitches obstructed by
trees & uneven; wifi hotspots but free."*
HRK 302, 20 Apr-30 Sep. 2018

SELCE *A2* (1.3km SE Coastal) *45.15361, 14.72488*
Autocamp Selce, Jasenová 19, 51266 Selce **(051)**
764038; autokampselce@jadran-crikvenica.hr;
www.jadran-crikvenica.hr

HRK17 shgl adj

Thro Selce town cent, site is 500m SE of town, sp.
2*, Lge, hdstg, pt shd, pt sl, terr, EHU (10A) HRK27;
red long stay; TV; phone; ccard acc; CKE. *"Wooded
site; seaside location; helpful staff; long stay; blocks &
wedges ess; san facs run down & neglected; long lead
rec; door security."* **HRK 247, 1 Apr-15 Oct.** 2019

SENJ *A3* (6km NW Coastal) *45.04403, 14.87817*
Autocamp Sibinj, Sibinj 9, 51252 Klenovica **(051)**
796916; milieijko.tomijanovic@ri.hinet.hr

shgl adj

Fr Novi Vinodolski, take rd S. In approx 12km site sp.
2*, Med, pt shd, sl, terr, EHU (10A). *"Well-run site;
clean facs but in need of modernising; magnificent
views; poss open all yr; noisy rd; NH only."*
HRK 152, 1 May-31 Oct. 2016

SIBENIK *B3* (10km NE Rural) *43.80063, 15.94210*
Camp Krka, Skocici 21, 22221 Lozovac **(022) 778495;**
goran.skocic@si.t-com.hr; www.camp-krka.hr

nr

**Exit A1 at junc 22 Šibenik, turn E at T-junc, thro
tunnel & site in approx 4km. Fr main coast rd at
Sibenik turn N onto rte 33 twd Drniš. After 15km
turn L dir Skradin, site sp on L.** 3*, Med, hdstg, pt
shd, EHU (16A) HRK23 (poss rev pol, check earth);
10% statics; Eng spkn; CKE. *"Pleasant, basic site in
orchard; friendly owner; B&B; gd modern san facs;
conv Krka National Park & Krka gorge; gd; clean
new shwr/wc facs (2014); rest, cheap basic food."*
HRK 151, 1 Apr-30 Oct. 2019

SIBENIK *B3* (4km S Coastal) *43.69925, 15.87942*
Camping Solaris, Hotelsko Naselje Solaris, 22000
Šibenik **(022) 364000; info@solaris.hr;**
www.solaris.hr

(htd) nr

Sp fr E65 Zadar-Split rd, adj hotel complex.
4*, V lge, hdg, mkd, pt shd, serviced pitches; EHU
(6A) inc; bbq; red long stay; TV; bus; ccard acc; bike
hire; waterslide; tennis; sauna; watersports; CKE.
*"Well-situated in olive & pine trees; mv service pnt
nr; some pitches adj marina; excel, modern san facs."*
HRK 225, 15 Apr-31 Oct. 2019

"I need an on-site restaurant"

We do our best to make sure site information
is correct, but it is always best to check any
must-have facilities are still available or will
be open during your visit.

SPLIT *B4* (8km E Coastal) *43.50451, 16.52598*
Camping Stobreč-Split, Sv Lovre 6, 21311 Stobreč
(021) 325426; camping.split@gmail.com;
www.campingsplit.com

12 HRK45 sand

**Fr N foll E65 & m'way thro Split to sp Stobreč. Site
sp R off E65 at traff lts in Stobreč.** 4*, Lge, hdstg,
mkd, shd, pt sl, EHU (16A) inc (long lead poss req); bus
to Split; Eng spkn; games area. *"Superb, well-run site
in lovely setting with views; helpful, welcoming staff;
gd facs; own sandy beach; public footpath thro site; rec
arr early to secure pitch; gd value for money; highly rec;
Diocletian's Palace worth a visit; excel; wellness ctr -
pool, sauna, gym."* **HRK 278** 2017

CROATIA

STARLGRAD PAKLENICA *B3* (1km N Coastal) *44.31340, 15.43579* **Auto-Kamp Plantaža,** Put Plantaza 2, 23244 Starigrad Paklenica **(038) 23 369131; plantaza@hi.t-com.hr; www.pansion-plantaza.com**

🕿 12 ♟ (htd) 🚹 ⚓ ♨ ⚡ 🅿 🦋 ▼ ▼ 🅗 🛖 ⚓

Fr Rijeka foll M2/E27 coast rd until 1 km N of Steligrad. V Steep pull out of site. Sm, mkd, hdstg, shd, terr, EHU 10A; bbq; Eng spkn; CKE. *"Vg site; ACSI; excel new facs; handy for NP; shopping for fresh food v ltd locally."* **HRK 114** **2020**

TUHELJSKE TOPLICE *B2* (0km S Urban) *46.06583, 15.78513* **Camping Terme Tuhelj,** Ljudevita Gaja 4, 49215 Tuhelj **(049) 203000; info@terme-tuhelj.hr; www.terme-tuhelj.hr**

🕿 HKR25 ♟ ⚓ ♨ ⚡ 🅿 🦋 ♈ ▼ 🅗 ⚓ (htd) 🛖

N fr Zagreb on A2 for approx 24km, exit junc 5 Zabok & foll rds 24/301/205 to sp Tuheljske Toplice. Check in at Hotel Toplice. Sm, pt shd, EHU (6A) HRK25; TV; phone; bus; Eng spkn; adv bkg acc; games area; games rm; waterslide. *"Gd, conv Zagreb & gd alt to Zagreb site; thermal spa adj."* **HRK 210, 1 Apr-31 Oct.** **2016**

UMAG *A2* (6km S Coastal) *45.39271, 13.54193* **Autocamp Finida,** Križine br 45A, 52470 Umag **(052) 756296; camp.finida@instraturist.hr; www.istracamping.com**

🕿 HKR25 ♟ ⚓ ♨ ⚡ 🅿 🦋 ▼ 🅗 ⚓ 🛖 shgl adj

Site clearly sp. 4*, Lge, mkd, pt shd, pt sl, EHU (10A) inc; red long stay; TV; 50% statics; phone; bus; Eng spkn; adv bkg acc; ccard acc; bike hire; CKE. *"Gd base for touring Istria; gd, clean, modern facs, lovely site amongst oak trees; friendly staff."* **HRK 125, 23 Apr-30 Sep.** **2016**

ZADAR *B3* (3.5km N Coastal) *44.13408, 15.21115* **Falkensteiner Camping Zadar (formerly Autocamp Borik),** Majstora Radovana 7, 23000 Zadar **(023) 206 555 602; reservations.campingzadar@falkensteiner. com; www.falkensteiner.com**

♟ ⚓ ♨ ⚡ 🅿 ▼ 🅗 ⚓ 🛖 shgl

Exit A2 at Zadar 1/West, cont for approx.19 km. In Zadar, turn R at 2nd x-rds with traff lts and take the bypass (dir Nin, Vir). Cont across 2 x-rds (dir Puntamika). In 70m turn R to Falkensteiner Resort Borik. 3*, V lge, shd, EHU (10A) inc; own san req; phone; bus 450m; Eng spkn; ccard acc; tennis; watersports; CKE. *"Pt of resort complex of 6 hotels; facs poor & some cold water only; poor security; gd sw beach; gd rests nrby; site run down; NH only."* **HRK 229, 1 May-30 Sep.** **2016**

ZAGREB *B2* (12km SW Urban) *45.77389, 15.87778* **Camping Motel Plitvice,** Lučko, 10090 Zagreb **(01) 6530444; motel@motel-plitvice.hr; www.motel-plitvice.hr**

♟ (htd) ⚓ ♨ ⚡ 🅿 ▼ 🅗 ⚓ 🛖

Site at motel attached to Plitvice services on A3/E70. Access only fr m'way travelling fr N, otherwise long m'way detour fr S. Lge, pt shd, EHU (16A) inc; TV; phone; bus to town fr site; ccard acc; tennis; CKE. *"Ask at motel recep (excel Eng) for best way back fr city &/or details minibus to city; Zagreb well worth a visit; site shabby but facs clean & adequate - stretched when site full & in need of update."* **HRK 168, 1 May-30 Sep.** **2016**

ZAGREB *B2* (16km W Rural) *45.80217, 15.82696* **Camp Zagreb,** Jezerska 6, 10437 Rakitje **(01) 3324567; info@campzagreb.com; www.campzagreb.com**

🕿 12 ♟ ♟ ⚓ ♨ ⚡ 🅿 🦋 ♈ ▼ 🅗 ⚓

Exit A3 J2 sp Bestovje. Turn R and cont for approx 3km. At rndabt before x-ing over m'way turn R. Cont for 1km. Site on L. 4*, Med, hdg, mkd, pt shd, EHU (16A); bbq; sw; twin axles; 5% statics; train 1km; Eng spkn; adv bkg acc; games rm; bike hire; CKE. *"Excel site; lake adj; sauna & massage; kayak & bike hire; horse trail; public trans 1.5km; free shuttle to rlw stn into city ctr."* **HRK 256** **2018**

ZAOSTROG *C4* (0.5km SE Coastal) *43.13925, 17.28047* **Camp Viter,** Obala A.K. Miosica 1, 21334 Zaostrog (Dalmatija) **098 704018; info@camp-viter.com; www.camp-viter.com**

🕿 HKR25 ♟ ⚓ ♨ ⚡ 🅿 🦋 ♈ ▼ nr 🅗 nr ⚓ 🛖

Foll Camp Viter signs 600m on R after Zaostrog sp. Sm, hdstg, pt shd, EHU (16A) HRK25; bbq; twin axles; Eng spkn; adv bkg acc; CCI. *"Very helpful, friendly owners; vg."* **HRK 237, 1 Apr-31 Oct.** **2019**

ZATON *B3* (1.5km N Coastal) *44.23434, 15.16605* **Camping Zaton Holiday Resort,** Široka ulica bb, 23232 Zaton **023 280215; camping@zaton.hr; www.zaton.hr**

🕿 HRK65 ♟ (htd) ⚓ ♨ ⚓ ⚡ 🅿 🦋 ♈ ▼ 🅗 ⚓ 🛖 🅿 🛖 sand adj

Site 16km NW of Zadar on Nin rd. Pt of Zaton holiday vill. Wel sp. 3*, V lge, pt shd, EHU (10A) inc; gas; 15% statics; phone; adv bkg acc; ccard acc; games area; boat hire; watersports; tennis; CKE. *"Excel, well-run, busy site; own beach; excel, modern san facs; cont of site is 'vill' with gd value shops & rests; gd for all ages; nr ancient sm town of Nin, in walking dist; conv National Parks; v expensive outside ACSI discount period but has first class facs and nrby town well worth a visit; Croatia's best campsite; superbly laid out & equipped."* **HRK 480, 1 May-30 Sep.** **2019**

BRAC ISLAND

BOL *C4 (0.5km W Urban/Coastal)* *43.26373, 16.64799*
Kamp Kito (formerly Konobo Kito), Braćke Ceste
bb, 21420 Bol **(021) 635551 or 635091; info@
camping-brac.com; www.camping-brac.com**

[icons] 500m

Take ferry fr Makarska to Brač & take rd 113/115 to
Bol (37km). On o'skrts do not turn L into town but
cont twd Zlatni Rat. Pass Studenac sup'mkt on R,
site on L. Sm, pt shd, EHU (16A) HRK20; gas; bbq; TV;
10% statics; Eng spkn; adv bkg acc. *"Excel for beaches
& boating; gd local food in rest; vg, friendly, family-run
site; clean, well-equipped; well worth effort to get
there."* **HRK 141**   **2016**

CRES ISLAND

MARTINSCICA *A3 (1km NW Coastal)* *44.82108,
14.34298* **Camping Slatina,** 51556 Martinščica
**(051) 574127; info@camp-slatina.com;
www.camp-slatina.com**

[icons] HRK23 shgl adj

Fr Cres S on main rd sp Mali Lošinj for 17km. Turn
R sp Martinščica, site in 8km at end of rd. 4*, V lge,
hdg, hdstg, shd, terr, EHU (10A) inc (long lead req);
20% statics; phone; Eng spkn; adv bkg acc; ccard acc;
boat launch. *"Site on steep slope; newest san facs
superb; beautiful island; dog & car washing facs; vg
supmkt; ATM on site."* **HRK 234, 19 Mar-10 Oct.**
                    2016

KRK ISLAND

BASKA *A3 (1.4km SW Coastal)* *44.965613, 14.747772*
Baška Beach Camping Resort, Put Zablaca 40, 51523
Baska **552 465010; camping@valamar.com;
www.camping-adriatic.com**

[icons] HRK29 (htd)

Drive over bdge to islnd of KRK (no chge on
Sun) and take main rd 103 to Krk, then on to the
southern tip of islnd and Baska. Site sp on ent town.
4*, Lge, mkd, pt shd, EHU (16A) inc; bbq; twin axles;
TV; 20% statics; phone; bus adj; Eng spkn; adv bkg
acc; sauna; sports area; bike hire; CKE. *"Excellent, new
san facs (2018); kids club; rest adj; perfect experience
creator; free use of pool & gym at Baska Wellness Ctr;
excel site."* **HRK 396, 19 Apr-6 Oct.**   **2018**

KRK *A3 (4km SE Coastal)* *45.01638, 14.62833*
Autocamp Pila, Šetalište Ivana Brusića 2, 51521
Punat **(051) 854020; pila@hoteli-punat.hr; www.
hoteli-punat.hr**

[icons] HRK32 nr adj

Take coast rd, rte 2 twd Split. At Kraljevica, turn
R onto rd 103 over Krk toll bdge. Foll sp for Krk,
Punat. Site sp at T-junc after Punat Marina & vill.
3*, Lge, pt shd, serviced pitches; EHU (10-16A) inc;
cooking facs; TV; 80% statics; ccard acc; fishing;
watersports; CKE. *"Well-run, big site; clean facs; gd
for families with sm children; boat hire; boat trips;
sm picturesque vill; lots to do; poss cr."*
HRK 347, 12 Apr-18 Oct.   **2019**

NJIVICE *A2 (0.4km N Coastal)* *45.16971, 14.54701*
Kamp Njivice, 51512 Njivice **(051) 846168;
reservation@kampnjivice.hr; www.kampnjivice.com**

[icons] HRK24.50 shgl adj

8km S of Krk Bdge on rd 102 turn R to Njivice. Site
not well sp but foll sp to hotel area N of town cent.
2*, V lge, shd, EHU (6-10A) HRK28; 60% statics;
phone; bus; Eng spkn; ccard acc; CKE. *"Less cr than
other Krk sites; gd facs."* **HRK 173, 1 May-30 Sep.**
                    2016

LOSINJ ISLAND

MALI LOSINJ *A3 (4km NW Coastal)* *44.55555,
14.44166* **Camping Village Poljana,** Privlaka 19,
51550 Mali Lošinj **(051) 231726 or (0365) 520682;
www.campingpoljana.com**

[icons] HRK61 shgl

On main island rd 1km bef vill of Lošinj, sp. Two
ferries a day fr Rijeka take car & c'van on 2hr trip to
island. 3*, V lge, shd, pt sl, terr, EHU (6-16A) inc;
gas; 50% statics; phone; adv bkg acc; ccard acc; bike
hire; tennis; games area; boat hire; watersports;
CKE. *"Site in pine forest; private washrms avail;
sw with dolphins nrby; sep naturist beach."*
HRK 312, 24 Mar-31 Oct.   **2016**

RAB ISLAND

LOPAR *A3 (3km E Coastal)* *44.82345, 14.73735* **Hotel
Village San Marino,** 51281 Lopar **(051) 775133; ac-
sanmarino@imperial.hr; www.rab-camping.com**

[icons] HRK29 sand adj

Fr Rab town N to Lopar, sp ferry. At x-rds turn
R sp San Marino, site sp. 3*, V lge, mkd, hdstg,
shd, terr, EHU (16A) inc; TV; 10% statics; phone;
bus; Eng spkn; adv bkg acc; ccard acc; games area;
tennis; watersports; CKE. *"Superb, family site on
delightful island; pitches on sandy soil in pine woods."*
HRK 187, 1 Apr-30 Sep.   **2016**

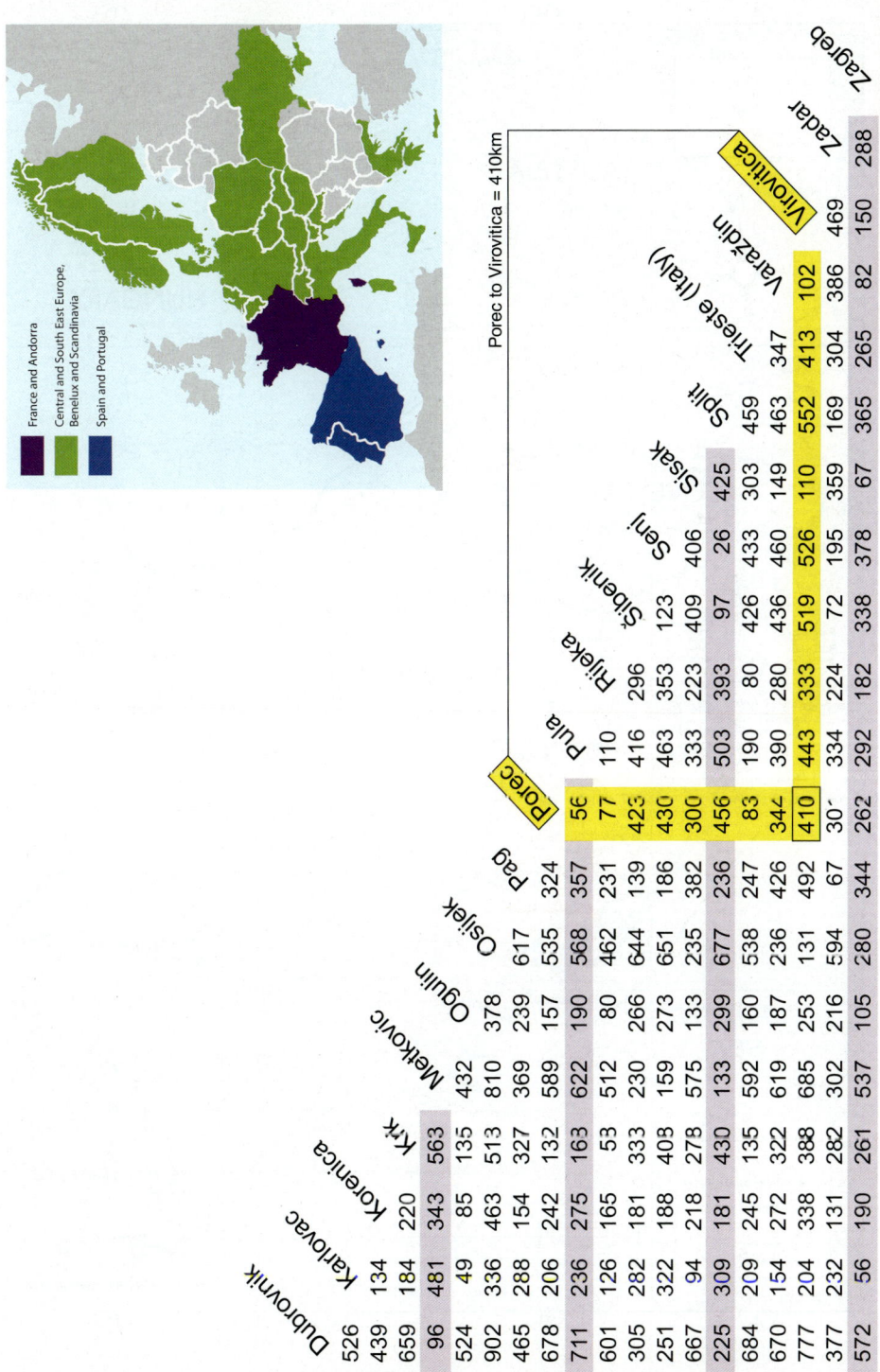

CROATIA

Legend:
- Motorways
- Major roads
- Main roads

- All year site(s)
- Seasonal site(s)
- No sites listed

200m +
0–200m

© Collins Bartholomew Ltd, 2021

Kutná Hora

Shutterstock/ Viliam M

Czech Republic

Highlights

Lying in the heart of Europe, the Czech Republic is renowned for its ornate castles, fantastically preserved medieval buildings, and numerous other cultural sights.

Considered to be one of the most beautiful cities in the world, the capital, Prague, is a wonderful mix of traditional and modern with treasures old and new waiting to be discovered around every corner.

Traditions are important in the Czech Republic, one of which takes places on the 30th of April – Walpurgis Night. Known as pálení čarodějnic (the burning of the witches), this is a night of bonfires and celebrations throughout the country.

The Czech Republic is the home of Bohemian glass or crystal, which is international renowned for its beauty, quality and craftsmanship. They are immensely popular as gifts and souvenirs and are one of the best known Czech exports.

Major towns and cities

- Prague – home to an impressive castle and old town.
- Brno – filled with gorgeous architecture and historic sights.
- Plzeň – famous worldwide for Pilsner beer, created here in 1842.
- Olomouc – a quaint city of cobbled streets and historic buildings.

Attractions

- Wenceslas Square, Prague – bursting with monuments, restaurants and shops.
- Český Krumlov – the old town is a UNESCO site and the castle houses a theatre.
- Kutná Hora – Founded in the 12th century, with many spectacular churches.
- Hrad Karlštejn – this imposing gothic castle is one of the most famous in the country.

Find out more

www.czechtourism.com
E: czechtourism@czechtourism.cz
T:0042 (0)22 1580 111

Country Information

Population (approx): 10.6 million

Capital: Prague

Area: 78,864 sq km

Bordered by: Austria, Germany, Poland, Slovakia

Terrain: Diverse landscape with rolling hills and plains in the west (Bohemia) surrounded by low mountains; higher hills and heavily forested mountains in the east (Moravia)

Climate: Temperate continental with warm, showery summers and cold, cloudy, snowy winters

Highest Point: Snezka 1,602m

Language: Czech

Local Time: GMT or BST + 1, i.e. 1 hour ahead of the UK all year

Currency: Czech crown (CZK) £1 = CZK 29.58, CZK 100 = £3.38 (Feb 2021)

Emergency numbers: Police 158; Fire brigade 150; Ambulance 155 (operators speak English) or 112.

Public Holidays in 2021: Jan 1; Apr 10, 13; May 1, 8 (National Liberation Day); Jul 5, 6; Sep 28 (St Wenceslas), Oct 28 (Independence Day); Nov 17; Dec 24, 25, 26.

School summer holidays are from the beginning of July to the end of August.

Entry Formalities

British and Irish passport holders may stay for up to 90 days in any 180 day period without a visa. Following Brexit you may be asked to show a return or onward ticket at the border to confirm your length of stay, or to prove that you have enough money for your stay.

Your passport will need to have a minimum of 6 months' validity remaining, and be less than 10 years old (even if it has 6 months or more left).

Visitors arriving at a campsite or hotel must complete a registration form.

Medical Services

For minor ailments first consult staff at a pharmacy (lékárna) who can give advice and are sometimes able to sell drugs normally only available on prescription in the UK. Language may be a problem outside Prague; if you need particular drugs or a repeat prescription, take an empty bottle or remaining pills with you. For more serious matters requiring a visit to a doctor go to a medical centre (poliklinika) or hospital (nemocnice).

British nationals may obtain emergency medical and hospital treatment and prescriptions on presentation of a European Health Insurance Card (EHIC). You may have to make a contribution towards costs. Make sure that the doctor or dentist you see is contracted to the public health insurance service, the CMU (most are), otherwise you will have to pay in full for private treatment and for any prescription medicines and the Czech insurance service will not reimburse you. See www.cmu.cz, email info@cmu.cz for advice on healthcare in the Czech Republic.

In parts of the country where few foreign visitors venture, medical staff may not be aware of the rights conferred on you by an EHIC. If you have difficulties contact the British Embassy in Prague.

Outbreaks of hepatitis A occur sporadically, particularly in the Prague and Central Bohemia areas, and immunisation is advised for long-stay visitors to rural areas and those who plan to travel outside tourist areas. Take particular care with food and water hygiene.

Opening Hours

Banks: Mon-Fri 9am-5pm. Some foreign exchange bureaux in Prague are open 24 hours.

Museums: Tue-Sun 10am-6pm; closed Monday

Post Offices: Mon-Fri 8am-6pm, some open on Saturday morning; main post office in Prague (Jindrisska Street 14) is open 2am-12am

Shops: Mon-Fri 9am-6pm, small shops usually close at lunchtime; Sat 9am-1pm; some food shops open on Sundays

Safety and Security

There is a high incidence of petty theft, particularly in major tourist areas in Prague, and pickpocketing is common at popular tourist attractions. Care should be taken around the main railway station and on public transport particularly routes to and from Prague Castle where pickpockets may operate.

Beware of fake plain-clothes police officers asking to see your foreign currency and passport. If approached, don't get out your passport. You can call 158 or 112 to check if they are genuine officers, or offer to go to the nearest police station or find a uniformed officer. No police officer has the right to check your money or its authenticity.

If your passport, wallet or other items are lost or stolen you should report the incident immediately to the nearest police station and obtain a police report. A police station that is used to dealing with foreign travellers is at Jungmannovo Námìstí 9, Praha 1, 24 hour telephone number 974 851 750; nearest metro: Müstek. Any theft of property must be reported in person to the police within 24 hours in order to obtain a crime number.

The Czech Republic shares with the rest of Europe an underlying threat from terrorism. Attacks could be indiscriminate and against civilian targets, including tourist attractions.

British Embassy

THUNOVSKÁ 14
118 00 PRAGUE 1
Tel: 257402111
www.ukinczechrepublic.fco.gov.uk
Email: ukinczechrepublic@fco.gov.uk

Irish Embassy

VELVYSLANECTVÍ IRSKA
TRŽIŠTĚ 13, 118 00 PRAHA 1
Tel: 257011280
www.embassyofireland.cz
Email: pragueembassy@dfa.ie

Documents

Driving Licence

The Czech Republic authorities require foreign drivers to carry a photocard driving licence. If you still have an old-style driving license you should update it to a photocard before you travel, or obtain an International Driving Permit to accompany your old-style licence. The minimum driving age is 18.

Money

The best place to exchange foreign currency is at banks, where commission rates are generally lower. In Prague some foreign exchange bureaux are open 24 hours. Scottish and Northern Irish bank notes will not be changed. Never exchange money with street vendors as notes are often counterfeit.

Credit cards are often accepted in tourist areas. Cash points are widely available but take care using them from a personal security point of view. Many retail outlets accept Euros.

Passport

You must have a valid passport to enter Czech Republic. It is recommended that your passport is valid after your planned departure date in case of an unforeseen emergency, which may prevent you from leaving. British nationals with passports in poor condition have been refused entry so you should ensure that your passport is in an acceptable state.

If you hold a British passport where your nationality is shown as anything other than British Citizen contact the Czech Embassy in London to determine whether you require a visa for entry.

Vehicle(s)

Carry your vehicle registration certificate (V5C), insurance details and MOT certificate (if applicable). If you are not the owner of the vehicle you are advised to carry a letter of authority from the owner permitting you to drive it.

Driving

Accidents

If an accident causes injury or damage in excess of CZK 100,000 it must be reported to the police immediately. You should wait at the scene of the accident until the police arrive and then obtain a police report. If your vehicle is only slightly damaged it is still a good idea to report the accident to the police as they will issue a certificate which will facilitate the exportation of the vehicle.

Alcohol

It is prohibited to drink alcohol before or whilst driving. No degree of alcohol is permitted in the blood and driving under the influence of alcohol is considered a criminal offence. This rule also applies to cyclists and horse riders. Frequent random breath-testing takes places and drivers are likely to be breathalysed after an accident, even a minor one.

Breakdown Service

The motoring organisation ÚAMK provides roadside assistance and towing services 24 hours a day, telephone 1230 or 261104123. Emergency operators speak English. Breakdown assistance is provided for all motorists at a basic cost of approximately CZK 400 for 30 minutes + CZK 24 per kilometre travelled, payable in cash (2015). Extra charges apply at night, at weekends and for towing.

The vehicles used for road assistance are yellow Skodas, bearing the ÚAMK and/or ARC Transistance logos or the words 'Silniční Služba', together with the telephone number of the emergency centre. ÚMAK also uses the services of contracted companies who provide assistance and towing. These vehicles are also marked with the ÚAMK logo and the telephone number of the emergency centre.

Child Restraint System

Children under 1.5m in height must use a suitable child restraint conforming to ECE standard 44/03 or 44/04. If in the front seat, the restraint must be rear facing with any airbag deactivated. If there are no seatbelts fitted children over the age of 3 may travel in the rear of the vehicle without a child restraint.

Fuel

Some petrol stations on main roads, international routes and in main towns are open 24 hours a day. Most accept credit cards.

Diesel pumps are marked 'Nafta'. LPG is called 'Autoplyn' or 'Plyn' and is widely available at many filling stations. A list of these is available from the ÚAMK and a map is available from filling stations, or see www.lpg.cz and click on 'Čerpací stanice'.

Motorways

There are approximately 1240 km of motorways and express roads. New sections of motorways are being built and on some motorways junctions are being renumbered to correspond with kilometre markers.

There is a good network of service areas with petrol stations, restaurants and shops, together with rest areas with picnic facilities. Emergency telephones connected to the motorway police are placed at 2 km intervals.

Emergency corridors are compulsory on motorways and dual carriageways. Drivers must create a corridor at least 3m wide for emergency vehicles whenever congestion occurs. Drivers in the left-hand lane must move as far to the left as possible, and drivers in the central and right-hand lanes move to the right.

Motorway Tolls (vehicles under 3,500kg)

To use motorways and express roads you must purchase a vignette (sticker) which must be displayed on the right hand side of your windscreen. This is available from post offices, ÚAMK branch offices, petrol stations and border posts. Old Vignettes must be removed.

Charges in 2019 are CZK 1,500 for an annual vignette, CZK 440 for one month and CZK 310 for 10 days. For more information please visit www.motorway.cz/stickers.

Motorway Tolls (vehicles over 3,500kg)

Vehicles over 3,500kg will need to purchase an electronic tag to calculate tolls. You can find a full list of distribution points and a toll calculator (tolls vary by time and day of the week) at www.mytocz.com/en.

Parking

Vehicles may only be parked on the right of the road. In a one-way road, parking is also allowed on the left.

Continuous or broken yellow lines indicate parking prohibitions or restrictions. Illegally-parked vehicles may be clamped or towed away.

Prague city centre is divided into parking zones: orange and green zones are limited to two and six hours respectively between 8am and 6pm, and blue zones are for residents only.

Priority

At uncontrolled intersections which are not marked by a priority road sign, priority must be given to vehicles coming from the right. Where there are priority signs, these may easily be missed and care is therefore needed at junctions which, according to recent visitors, may have no road markings.

Trams turning right have priority over traffic moving alongside them on the right. Drivers must slow down and, if necessary, stop to allow buses and trams to merge with normal traffic at the end of a bus lane. On pedestrian crossings pedestrians have right of way, except if the vehicle approaching is a tram.

Roads

Czech drivers are sometimes described as reckless (particularly when overtaking). Speeding is common and the law on the wearing of seat belts is sometimes ignored.

In general roads are in a good condition and well-signposted. Roads are being upgraded and many have new numbers. It is essential, therefore, to have an up-to-date road map or atlas.

Road Signs and Markings

Road signs and markings conform to international standards. Continuous white lines indicate no overtaking, but are often ignored.

The following road signs may be encountered:

Czech	English Translation
Bez poplatků	Free of charge
Choďte vlevo	Pedestrians must walk on the left
Dálkový provoz	By-pass
Nebezpečí smyku	Danger of skidding
Nemocnice	Hospital
Objízdka	Diversion
Pozor děti	Attention children
Průjezd zakázán	Closed to all vehicles
Rozsviť světla	Lights needed
Úsek častých nehod	Accident blackspot
Zákaz zastavení	Stopping prohibited

Speed Limits

	Open Road (km/h)	Motorway (km/h)
Car Solo	90	130
Car towing caravan/trailer	80	80
Motorhome under 3500kg	90	130
Motorhome 3500-7500kg	80	80

Motorhomes over 3,500 kg and cars towing a caravan or trailer are restricted to 80 km/h (50 mph) on motorways and main roads and lower limits in urban areas. Speed limits are strictly enforced and drivers exceeding them may be fined on the spot. Police with radar guns are much in evidence.

The use of radar detectors is prohibited and GPS systems which indicate the position of fixed speed cameras must have that function deactivated.

Traffic Lights

A traffic light signal with a green arrow shows that drivers may turn in that direction. If a yellow walking figure accompanies the signal, pedestrians may cross the road and drivers must give them right of way. A green light lit at the same time as a red or yellow light means that drivers may turn in the direction indicated by the arrow, giving way to other traffic and pedestrians.

An illuminated speed signal indicates the speed at which to travel in order to arrive at the next set of traffic lights when they are green.

Traffic Jams

The volume of traffic has increased considerably in recent years, particularly in and around Prague, including its ring road. Traffic jams may also occur on the E50/D1 (Prague-Mirošovice), the E48/R6 (Prague-Kladno), the E50/D5 (Plzeň-Rozvadov) and on the E50/D1 (Prague-Brno).

Traffic may be heavy at border crossings from Germany, Austria and Slovakia, particularly at weekends, resulting in extended waiting times. Petrol is cheaper than in Germany and you may well find queues at petrol stations near the border. Traffic information can be obtained from the ÚAMK Information Centre: tel 261104333, or www.uamk.cz

Vehicles over 3,500 kg

Vehicles over 3,500 kg are subject to an electronic toll (mýto) and vehicle owners must register with the toll-collection service to obtain an on-board device called a Premid which must be fixed on your windscreen inside the vehicle and for which a deposit is required.

Tolls vary according to, emissions category, weight and distance driven. You must be able to show your vehicle documentation when obtaining the device but if your vehicle registration certificate (V5C) does not give an emissions category, then your vehicle will be classified in category Euro 2 for the purposes of this system. For more information please visit www.premid.cz before you travel.

Violation of Traffic Regulations

The police are authorised to impose and collect on-the-spot fines up to CZK 5,000 and to withdraw a driving licence in the case of a serious offence. An official receipt should be obtained. Efforts are under way to improve enforcement of traffic regulations and a points system has been introduced, together with stricter penalties.

Winter Driving

Winter tyres are compulsory from 1 November to 31 March on all wheels of vehicles up to 3.5 tonnes when there is compacted snow or ice on the road. They are also compulsory whenever the temperature is lower than 4°C and there is a possibility of snow or ice on the road. On roads where there are winter tyres signs (see below), the regulations apply even if the road surface is free of snow and ice, regardless of the weather.

 Sign for winter tyres (if shown with a line through indicates the end of restriction)

Vehicles over 3,500 kg must be fitted with winter tyres on the driving wheels or carry snow chains. A full list of roads where this rule applies can be found on www.uamk.cz.

Essential Equipment

First aid kit

You are required to carry a basic first aid kit in your vehicle.

Lights

Dipped headlights are compulsory at all times, regardless of weather conditions. Bulbs are more likely to fail with constant use and it is recommended that you carry a complete set of spares.

Drivers are required to signal when leaving a roundabout and when overtaking cyclists.

Reflective Jacket/Waistcoat

If your vehicle has broken down, or in the event of an emergency, you must wear a reflective jacket or waistcoat on all roads, carriageways and motorways when getting out of your vehicle. Passengers who leave the vehicle, for example to assist with a repair, should also wear one. Jackets should, therefore, be kept inside your vehicle, and not in the boot. These must be of an EU standard EN471.

Warning Triangles

You must carry a warning triangle, which must be placed at least 100m behind the vehicle on motorways and highways and 50m behind on other roads. Drivers may use Hazard Warning lights in conjunction with the warning triangle.

Touring

It is not necessary to tip in restaurants but if you have received very good service add 10% to the bill or round it up.

Smoking is not permitted in public places (including public transport) and restaurant owners must provide an area for non-smokers.

A Prague Card offers entrance to over 50 tourist attractions and discounts on excursions and activities. It is available from tourist offices, main metro stations, some travel agents and hotels or order online from www.praguecard.com.

German is the most widely spoken foreign language and a basic understanding is particularly helpful in southern Bohemia. However, many young people speak English.

Camping and Caravanning

Campsites are divided into four categories from 1 to 4 stars. Normally campsites are open from May to mid September, although some campsites stay open all year. They usually close at night between 10pm and 6am.

Campsites are generally good value and in recent years many have upgraded their facilities. Privacy in the showers may be a problem due to a shortage of, or lack of, shower curtains and only a communal dressing area.

Some sites have communal kitchen facilities which enable visitors to make great savings on their own gas supply.

Motorhomes are recommended to carry a very long hose with a variety of tap connectors. Refill the onboard tank whenever possible as few sites have easily accessible mains water.

Casual/wild camping is not permitted and fines are imposed for violation of this law, especially in national parks. It is prohibited to sleep in a caravan or motorhome outside a campsite.

Cycling

There are around 2,500km of cycle tracks, known as Greenways, in tourist areas. A long-distance cycle track links Vienna and Prague and there are many tracks linking the Czech Republic to Austria and Poland. Helmets are compulsory for cyclists under the age of 18.

Electricity and Gas

Current on campsites varies between 6 and 16 amps. Plugs have two round pins. A few campsites have CEE connections but not many. Reversed polarity may be encountered.

You may find that Campingaz 907 cylinders are available from large DIY warehouses.

Public Transport

Prague city centre is very congested, so park outside and use buses, trams or the metro which are efficient and cheap. There are guarded Park and Ride facilities at a number of metro stations around Prague.

Public transport tickets must be purchased before travelling and are available from newspaper stands ('Trafika'), tobacconists, convenience stores and from vending machines at stations. Special tourist tickets are available for one or three days. Tickets must be validated before the start of your journey at the yellow machines at metro stations or on board trams and buses, including before boarding the funicular tram at Petřín. Failure to do so may result in an on-the-spot fine.

Take extra care when in the vicinity of tram tracks and make sure you look both ways. Trams cannot stop quickly nor can they avoid you if you are on the track.

As a pedestrian you may be fined if you attempt to cross the road or cross tram tracks within 50 metres of a designated crossing point or traffic lights. You may also be fined if you cross at a pedestrian crossing if the green pedestrian light is not illuminated.

For reasons of safety and economy use major taxi companies wherever possible. If you telephone to order a taxi these companies are usually able to tell you in advance the type, number and colour of the car allocated to you. If you do pick up a taxi in the street always check the per kilometre price before getting in. The price list must be clearly displayed and the driver must provide a receipt if requested.

BEROUN *B2* (10km NE Rural) *50.0115, 14.1505*
Camping Valek, Chrustenice 155, 267 12 Chrustenice
**tel 311 672 147; info@campvalek.cz;
www.campvalek.cz**

CZK80

SW fr Prague on E50; take exit 10 twd Loděnice
then N to Chrustenice. Foll sp. Lge, pt shd, EHU
(10A) CZK100; bbq; red long stay; TV; 10% statics;
phone; Eng spkn; adv bkg acc; tennis; CKE. *"Vg
location; money change on site; entmnt (w/end); excel
rest; metro to Prague at Zličín (secure car park adj)."*
CZK 430, 1 May-30 Sep.   2016

BESINY *C1* (0.5km SW Rural) *49.29533, 13.32086*
Eurocamp Běšiny, Běšiny 150, 339 01 Běšiny
**tel 376 375 011; eurocamp@besiny.cz;
www.eurocamp.besiny.cz**

12 (htd)

Fr E53/rd 27 take rd 171 twd Sušice. Site just
outside vill on L. Med, unshd, EHU (6A) inc; bbq;
cooking facs; 50% statics; adv bkg acc; ccard acc;
games area; tennis; CKE. *"Pleasant setting; nrby vill
drab."* CZK 303   2016

BOSKOVICE *C3* (15km SE Rural) *49.42296, 16.73585*
Camping Relaxa, 679 13 Sloup **tel + 420 704 022
518; camp.relaxa@seznam.cz; www.camprelaxa.cz**

(htd)   nr   nr

Fr Boskovice take dir Valchov; at Ludikov head S &
onto rte 373 to Sloup. Site sp up track on R.
Sm, unshd, pt sl, EHU (6A) inc (poss rev pol); bus 1km;
CKE. *"Conv Moravski Kras karst caves; pool 250m;
immed access walking/cycling trails."*
CZK 400, 1 May-30 Sep.   2020

BRECLAV *D3* (6km NW Rural) *48.78549, 16.82663*
Autocamp Apollo, Charvátská Nová Ves, 691 44
Břeclav **tel 519 340 414; info@atcapollo.cz;
www.atcapollo.cz**

CZK30   nr   nr

Fr Breclav take Lednice rd. Site is 3km S of Lednice
vill. Lge, pt shd, pt sl, EHU CZK30; sw nr; bus; CKE.
*"Fair sh stay; site in beautiful area; excel cycling &
walking; Lednice Castle worth a visit; poss school
parties."* CZK 280, 1 May-30 Sep.   2016

BRNO *C3* (21km W Rural) *49.21182, 16.40745*
Camping Oáza, Náměstí Viléma Mrštíka 10, 66481
Ostrovačice **tel 606 457 448; info@kempoaza.cz;
www.kempoaza.cz**

nr

Leave E65/E50 Prague-Brno at junc 178 for
Ostrovačice. At T-junc in vill turn L, site on R 100m.
Sm, pt shd, pt sl, EHU (10A) inc; CKE. *"Excel CL-type
site, v clean facs; friendly, helpful lady owner; narr,
uneven ent poss diff lge o'fits; poss unrel opening
dates; super."* CZK 365, 1 Apr-31 Oct.   2019

BUDISOV NAD BUDISOVKOU *B4* (0.8km SE Urban)
49.79089, 17.63668 **Autokemp Budišov,** Nábřeží č.
688, 747 87, Budišov nad Budišovkou **tel 736 767 588;
autokemp@budisov.cz; www.autokemp.budisov.cz**

CZK30   nr

Ent town fr E on rd 443; at T junc turn L sp; foll rd
which will take you under rlwy; site on R in 100m.
Sm, unshd, sl, EHU (6A) CZK80; bbq; 50% statics; CKE.
*"Space for 20 vans only, with 4 elec pnts; mini golf
onsite & bike hire avail; valid vaccination card req for
dogs."* CZK 240, 1 May-30 Sep.   2016

CESKE BUDEJOVICE *C2* (22km N Rural) *49.13701,
14.47413* **Camping Kostelec,** Kostelec 8, 373 41
Hluboká nad Vltavou **tel 731 272 098; info@camping
kostelec.nl; www.campingkostelec.nl**

Fr České Budějovice N twd Hluboká nad Vltavou,
then foll unnumbered rd thro forest to Poněšice &
Kostelec for approx 14km. Med, pt shd, pt sl, terr,
EHU (10A) inc; gas; bbq (elec, gas); bus adj; Eng spkn;
adv bkg acc; games rm; fishing; CKE. *"Remote,
peaceful site; gd walking; dogs free; conv Prague, České
Budějovice & Český Krumlov."*
CZK 570, 30 Apr-15 Sep.   2016

CESKY KRUMLOV *C2* (11km NE Rural) *48.83954,
14.37525* **Camping Paradijs,** Rajov 26, 38101
Cesky Krumlov **tel 776 898 022; jakesova.jana@
centrum.cz; www.camping-paradijs.eu**

NE of Cesky Krumlov on rte 39 heading twrds Cesky
Budejovice. Site sp at bottom of hill. Sm, mkd, pt shd,
Eng spkn; adv bkg req; games rm. *"A sm picturesque
rural site beside rv; narr app rd, not suitable for lge
o'fits; clean but ltd san facs; rafting & canoeing avail."*
CZK 483, 1 Apr-15 Oct.   2017

"Satellite navigation makes touring much easier"

Remember most sat navs don't know if you're
towing or in a larger vehicle – always use yours
alongside maps and site directions.

CHEB *B1* (10km W Rural) *50.05258, 12.16572*
Camping Bříza, Bříza 19, 350 02 Briza, Cheb 2
**tel (0420) 773 570 196; campingbriza@gmail.com;
www.camping bohemen.com**

12

Fr W on 303/E48 thro border take the 2nd exit to
Leba, travel back down E48 to Bříza, foll sp to site.
Sm, sw; Eng spkn. *"Excel site; lakeside fishing; boat
trips; cycling."* **CZK 500**   2020

CHOMUTOV *B1* (1km NE Rural) *50.46899, 13.42278*
Autokemp Kamencové Jezero, Tomáše ze Štítného,
430 01 Chomutov **tel (420) 777 187 843; reception@
kamencovejezero.cz; www.kamencovejezero.cz**

👤‍👤 (htd) ♨ ⚡ 🚽 nr 🍽 ♿ nr ⛱

Foll site sps in town, look for camp sp on L bet flats.
Next sp on R bet more flats. Lge, pt shd, sl, EHU; sw;
Eng spkn. *"Site on edge of town with gd bathing facs;
gd site based in N Czech Rep in v interesting area."*
CZK 160, 1 May-30 Sept. **2020**

> ## "There aren't many sites open at this time of year"
>
> If you're travelling outside peak season
> remember to call ahead to check site opening
> dates – even if the entry says 'open all year'.

DOMAZLICE *C1* (11km SE Rural) *49.40314, 13.05763*
Autocamping Hájovna, Na Kobyle 209, 345 06 Kdyně
**tel 379 731 233; automotoklub@kdyne.cz; www.
camphajovna.cz**

🐕 CZK45 👤‍👤 ♨ 🚽 ⚡ 🦋 ♈ ⚡ nr 🍽 ♿ 🏊

In Kdyně going twd Klatovy on rd 22, turn L at end
of town sq; then 1st R twd cobbled rd (for 300m);
site on L in 2km. 3*, Med, hdstg, pt shd, pt sl, EHU
(10A) CZK70 (poss rev pol); TV; 10% statics; phone;
CKE. *"Hořovský Týn & Domažlice interesting towns;
gd walking; friendly owner; ltd level pitches."*
CZK 240, 1 May-30 Sep. **2016**

FRENSTAT *C4* (750km NW Urban) *49.551722,
18.204618* **Autokemp Frenstat Pod Radhostem,**
Dolni 1807, 74401 Frenstat pod Radhostem **tel 556
836 624 or 607 265 107; autokemp@mufrenstat.cz;
www.autokemp-frenstat.cz**

12 🐕 CZK35 👤‍👤 ♨ ♨ ♨ 🚽 ⚡ 🦋 🍽 ⚡ ♿ ♈ 🏊 ♨ (htd) 🏊

Fr S on 58 turn R at Aquapark, site on L in 250m.
Med, hdstg, mkd, hdg, pt shd, EHU (10A) CZK100;
cooking facs; red long stay; 25% statics; 25m; Eng
spkn; adv bkg acc; games area; bike hire. *"Vg site
aimed at families/young people; all rds mkd for cycling;
school parties visit LS; easy walk to town; gd hill walks
& mountain biking area; excel outdoor museum in
Roznov."* **CZK 395** **2018**

FRYDEK MISTEK *B4* (5km SW Rural) *49.66459,
18.31161* **Autokemp Olešná,** Nad Přehradou, 738 02
Frýdek-Místek **tel 558 434 806; olesna@tsfm.cz;
www.autokempolesna.cz**

🐕 CZK25 👤‍👤 ♨ 🚽 ⚡ 🦋 🍽 ♈ 🏊

Nr Tesco on S side of E462/rte 48 on lakeside.
1*, Sm, unshd, sl, EHU (10A); cooking facs; Eng spkn;
fishing. *"Unisex san facs; individual shwr cabins."*
CZK 230, 1 May-30 Sep. **2016**

FRYMBURK *D2* (1km S Rural) *48.65556, 14.17008*
Camping Frymburk, Frymburk 20/55, 382 79
Frymburk **tel 380 735 284 or 733 745 435; info@
campingfrymburk.cz; www.campingfrymburk.cz**

🐕 CZK60 🚻 ♨ 🚽 ⚡ 🦋 ♈ ⚡ nr 🍽 🏊 🏊 ♿

Fr Černa on lake, take rd 163 dir Loucovice to site.
Fr Český Krumlov take Rožmberk nad Vltavou rd,
turn R at Větřni on rd 162 sp Světlik. At Frymburk
turn L to Lipno then site 500m on R on lake
shore. 4*, Med, pt shd, sl, terr, EHU (6A) inc; sw;
TV; 10% statics; adv bkg acc; bike hire; fishing; boat hire;
boating. *"Beautiful lakeside site; modern, clean san
facs; some pitches poss tight for lge o'fits; gd rest
nrby; v friendly, helpful Dutch owners; private san facs
some pitches; gd walking; adv bkg rec bef 1st Apr."*
CZK 764, 29 Apr-25 Sep. **2016**

JICIN *B2* (8km NW Rural) *50.47236, 15.31161*
Chatový tábor Jinolice, Jičín Jinolice, 50601
**tel (0420) 493 591 929; info@kemp-jinolice.cz;
www.kempy-ceskyraj.cz**

🐕 👤‍👤 (htd) ♨ ⚡

Fr Jicin foll rte 35 twrds Turnov. After 6km turn
L to Jinolice and foll sp thro vill. Lge, pt sl, sw; TV;
boating. *"In cent of Bohemian Tourist area; sports;
cycling."* **CZK 355, 1 May-30 Sep.** **2020**

JIHLAVA *C3* (8km S Rural) *49.44732, 15.59911*
Autocamping Pávov, Pávov 90, 586 01 Jihlava **tel
776 293 393; camp@pavov.com; www.pavov.com**

🐕 👤‍👤 ♨ ⚡ ♿ 🍽 🏊 ♿

Fr D1/E50/E65 exit junc 112 sp Jihlava. Foll sp
Pávov & site for 2km. Fr N/S on rte 38, nr a'bahn
pick up sp for Pávov. Recep in adj pension/rest.
2*, Med, mkd, unshd, EHU (6A); sw nr; 30% statics;
fishing; tennis. *"Grand Hotel in Jihlava gd; m'way noise;
friendly rest."* **CZK 135, 1 May-30 Sep.** **2016**

KARLOVY VARY *B1* (5.5km NNE Rural) *50.26450,
12.90013* **Autokamp Sasanka,** Sadov 7, 360 01 Sadov
**tel 353 590 130 or 603 202 051 (mob); campsadov@
seznam.cz**

🐕 CZK50 👤‍👤 ♨ 🚽 ⚡ 🦋 ♈ 🍽 🍽 🏊 nr ♿

Fr Karlovy Vary on rd 13/E442 NE twds Chomutov,
exit to Sadov, site sp. 3*, Med, pt shd, pt sl, EHU
(16A) CZK60 (poss rev pol); red long stay; CKE.
*"Lovely, well-run site; friendly, helpful staff; modern,
clean san facs; picturesque vill of Loket a must; excel
bus service fr vill to Karlovy Vary; take care height
restriction on app to Tesco fr m'way; rec; excel."*
CZK 458, 1 Apr-31 Oct. **2018**

KLATOVY *C1* (19km S Rural) *49.28177, 13.24003*
Camping U dvou Orecha, Splz 13 Strážov na Sumava
34024 **tel (0420) 376 382 421; info@camping-tsjechie.nl; www.camping-tsjechie.nl**

nr

Fr Klatovy twrds Nýrsko on 191, after Janovice turn
L twrds Strážov, after 5.5km in Strážov turn R sp
Desenice. Site sp on L after 2.4km. Sm, pt shd, terr,
EHU 10A; Eng spkn; adv bkg acc; CKE. "*Delightful, vg
CL type site; warm welcome fr friendly, helpful Dutch
owners.*" CZK 545, 1 May-1 Oct.   2018

KUTNA HORA *B2* (3km NE Urban) *49.96416,
15.30250* **Autocamp Transit,** Malín 35, 284 05 Kutná
Hora **tel 327 523 785; egidylada@seznam.cz;
www.transit.zde.cz**

nr nr

Fr N on rd 38 fr Kolín, turn R immed after flyover
onto rd No 2 then turn L twrds town, In 1km turn L
immed bef rlwy bdge. Sm, pt shd, EHU (16A); cooking
facs; TV; phone; bus 800m; Eng spkn; CKE. "*Poss noise
fr nrby rlwy; sw high ssn; family run; Int UNESCO World
Heritage Town; clean, well-kept, with garden area.*"
CZK 390, 1 Apr-30 Sep.   2017

LIPNO NAD VLTAVOU *D2* (3km W Rural) *48.63891,
14.20880* **Autocamp Lipno Modřín,** 382 78 Lipno
nad Vltavou **tel 380 736 272; camp@lipnoservis.cz;
www.campinglipno.cz**

CZK70

Site sp on rd 163 on lakeside. 1*, Lge, mkd, unshd,
EHU (6A) inc; sw; 10% statics; adv bkg acc; games
area; bike hire; tennis; boat hire. "*Pleasant, popular
site; htd pool complex 500m.*"
CZK 660, 1 Apr-30 Sep.   2016

LITOMERICE *A2* (2km SE Urban) *50.53185, 14.13899*
Autocamping Slavoj, Střelecký Ostrov, 412 01
Litoměřice **tel 416 734 481 or 777 687 667 (mob);
kemp.litomerice@post.cz; www.autokemp
litomerice.com**

CZK30 nr

Fr N on rd 15 N of rv make for bdge over Rv Elbe
(Labe) sp Terezín; R down hill immed bef bdge
(cobbled rd), L under rlwy bdge, L again, site 300m
on R bef tennis courts at sports cent beside rv.
Fr S on rd 15 turn L immed after x-ing rv bdge to
cobbled rd. 3*, Sm, pt shd, EHU (8-16A) CZK75;
10% statics; Eng spkn; tennis; CKE. "*Friendly, family-
run site; gd, modern san facs; vg rest; 10 mins walk
town cent; Terezín ghetto & preserved concentration
camp; v friendly.*" CZK 430, 1 May-30 Sep.   2019

LITOMYSL *B3* (1.5km E Urban) *49.86776, 16.32440*
ATC Primátor Camping, Strakovská, 570 01 Litomyšl
**tel 461 612 238 or 732 148 723 (mob); primator@
camplitomysl.cz; www.camplitomysl.cz**

CZK45 nr

Fr S on E442/35 turn R at sp on edge of town, site
on L in 500m. 3*, Sm, hdstg, pt shd, sl, EHU (6A)
CZK60; TV; 80% statics; Eng spkn; CKE. "*Worth visit
to Litomyšl - steep walk; easy (paid) parking in town
sq; pool 300m; sports facs 300m; vg san facs; v sl site;
friendly owner.*" CZK 210, 1 May-30 Sep.   2016

MOHELNICE *B3* (1.5km NW Urban) *49.78308,
16.90808* **Autocamping Morava,** ul Petra Bezruče
13, 789 85 Mohelnice **tel 583 430 129; info@atc-
morava.cz; www.atc-morava.cz**

Fr E keep on D35/E442 to town boundary, turn
R down rd 35. Site sp 300m on R. 3*, Lge, pt shd,
EHU (10A) inc; TV; 20% statics; Eng spkn; bike hire;
tennis; CKE. "*Pleasant, well-run site; v quiet LS;
hourly trains to Olomouc; excel modern san fac.*"
CZK 188, 15 May-15 Oct.   2016

NACHOD *B3* (8km SW Rural) *50.39866, 16.06302*
Autocamping Rozkoš, Masaryka 836, 552 03 Česká
Skalice **tel 491 451 112 or 491 451 108; atc@
atcrozkos.com; www.atcrozkos.com**

12 CZK30

On rd 33/E67 fr Náchod dir Hradec Králové, site
sp 2km bef Česká Skalice on lakeside. V lge, EHU
(16A) CZK70; sw nr; 10% statics; ccard acc; bike
hire; windsurfing school; watersports; sauna. "*Lovely
countryside.*" CZK 290   2016

NOVE STRASECI *B2* (6km NW Rural) *50.17221,
13.83951* **Camping Bucek,** Trtice 170, 271 01 Nové
Strašecí **tel 313 564 212; info@campingbucek.cz;
www.campingbucek.cz**

CZK60 nr (htd)

Site sp fr E48/rd 6, 2km S of Řevničov on lakeside &
approx 40km fr Prague. 4*, Med, mkd, pt shd, pt sl,
EHU (6A) inc; bbq; sw nr; TV; Eng spkn; boating adj.
"*Helpful owner; modern san facs; gd walks in woods.*"
CZK 630, 1 May-3 Sep.   2016

ORLIK NAD VLTAVOU *C2* (5km S Rural) *49.52458,
14.15563* **Camping Velký Vír,** Kožlí 23, 398 07 Oriík
nad Vltavou **tel 382 275 192; obec.kozli@seznam.cz;
www.velkyvir.cz**

CZK30

Fr Milevsko head W on rte 19; turn N to Orlík vill;
foll camp sp 7km N to Velký Vír. Med, unshd, pt sl,
EHU (6A) CZK70; sw nr; 10% statics; adv bkg acc;
tennis; CKE. "*V quiet site by rv; few EHU & may not
work.*" CZK 210, 1 May-30 Sep.   2016

PODEBRADY *B2* (2km SE Rural) *50.13549, 15.13794*
Autocamping Golf, U Nové Vodárny 428, 290 01
Poděbrady **tel 325 612 833; ATCAutokemp@gmail.
com; www.kemp-golf.cz**

🐕 CZK20 � 🚾 ♨ 🔥 ⚘ ☂ ⛱

Fr D11/E67 (Prague/Poděbrady) take Poděbrady
exit N onto rd 32 for 3km; at junc with rte 11/E67
turn W sp Poděbrady (care needed, priority not
obvious); site sp on L on E edge of town; site opp
town name sp 400m down lane; app fr E if poss.
3*, Med, pt shd, EHU (long cable req) CZK80; own
san rec; CKE. *"Conv for touring area; gd supmkt with
parking in town; basic site."*
CZK 260, 1 May-31 Sep. 2016

PRAHA *B2* (6km N Urban) *50.11694, 14.42361*
Camping Sokol Trója, Trojská 171a, 171 00 Praha 7
**tel 233 542 908 or 283 850 486; tj.sokol.troja@
quick.cz or info@camp-sokol-troja.cz; www.camp-
sokol-troja.cz**

12 🐕 CZK50 ♦fltltl ♨ 🔥 ⚘ / ⛱ 🕯 ☂

Fr Pilsen (E50/D5) head into cent to rte D8/E55 sp
Treplice. Foll N to Trója sp. Immed after rv x-ing
take exit under rte 8 & foll camp sp & site on L 100m
past Autocamp Trojská. Fr Dresden on E55/D8 foll
sp to Centrum to Trója exit on R, foll camping sp.
NB: There are 5 sites adj to each other with similar
names. Best app fr Treplice. 2*, Med, hdstg, pt
shd, EHU (10A) CZK100; ccard acc; CKE. *"Easy tram
transport to city; Trója Palace & zoo 1km; v helpful,
friendly owner; bar & rest gd value; noise fr bar; facs
basic & run down (2017); hostel; 10 min walk to shops."*
CZK 520 2018

"That's changed – Should I let the Club know?"

If you find something on site that's different
from the site entry, fill in a report and let us
know. See camc.com/europereport.

PRAHA *B2* (22km E Urban) *50.09833, 14.68472*
Camping Praha Klánovice, V Jehličině 1040
190 14 Praha 9 – Klánovice **tel 00420 774 553 743;
info@campingpraha.cz; www.campingpraha.cz**

🐕 €2 ♦fltltl 🚾 ♨ 🔥 ⚘ / 🅿 🕯 ⚘ ☂ 🍽 ⊕ 🛝 🐎 ☂

Fr Prague ring rd exit at Běchovice onto rd 12
dir Kolin. At Újezd nad Lesy turn L at x-rds twd
Klánovice & in approx 3km turn R into Šlechtitelská,
site on R in approx 1km. 4*, Med, mkd, pt shd, EHU
(16A) €4; gas; bbq; TV; 50% statics; phone; bus to
Prague; Eng spkn; adv bkg acc; ccard acc; games rm;
bike hire; games area; sauna. *"New site 2010; gd public
transport to city; excel site, lge woods for walks &
cycling."* **CZK 688, 1 May-13 Sep.** 2020

PRAHA *B2* (20km S Rural) *49.93277, 14.37294*
Camp Matyáš, U Elektrárny, 252 46 Vrané nad
Vltavou **tel 257 761 228 or 777 016073 (mob);
campmatyas@centrum.cz; www.camp-matyas.com**

🐕 ♦fltltl 🚾 ♨ 🔥 ⚘ 🅿 / 📶 ⚘ 🕯 ☂ ⊕ 🛝 🐎 ⚓ 🌊

Fr Plzen take E50/D5 NE twd Prague.Take E48/
E50 heading approx SE twd R4. Exit onto R4 sp
Strakonice. Exit R4 twd Zbraslav. Enter vill, turn L
in Sq. Foll rd to cross major bdge over Rv Vltava.
After bdge turn immed R. Foll this rd keeping rv
on your R. Camp is on R in 6km. 3*, Med, pt shd,
EHU (10A) CZK120; cooking facs; sw nr; bus, train
nr; Eng spkn; adv bkg acc; fishing adj; CKE. *"In
lovely location; friendly owners; train & tram service to
Prague (1 hr); boat trips on Rv Vltava; superb family
site."* CZK 550, 1 Apr-30 Sep. 2016

PRAHA *B2* (10km SW Urban) *50.05583, 14.41361*
Caravan Camping Praha, Císařská Louka 162,
Smíchov, 150 00 Praha 5 **tel 257 317 555; info@
caravancamping.cz; www.caravancamping.cz**

12 ♦fltltl 🚾 ♨ 🔥 ⚘ / ⊕ 🕯 ☂

Foll dir as for Prague Yacht Club C'van Park. This
site just bef on R, look for lge yellow tower. Sm,
unshd, EHU CZK95; Eng spkn; CKE. *"V helpful gd
staff; busy sh stay site on island; conv for Prague cent
metro - St Wenceslas Sq 15/20mins; no privacy in
shwrs; san fanc modernised & v clean (2015); v busy."*
CZK 600 2015

PRAHA *B2* (10km SW Urban) *50.06233, 14.41331*
Praha Yacht Club Caravan Park, Cisařská Louka
599, Smíchov, 150 00 Praha 5 **tel 257 318 387 or
060 2343701 (mob); caravanpark.cl@gmail.com;
www.volny.cz/convoy**

12 🐕 CZK57 ♦fltltl 🚾 ♨ 🔥 / ⚘ 🕯 nr

Fr E50 access only poss fr S by travelling N on W
side of rv. After complex junc (care needed), turn
sharp R bef Shell petrol stn to Cisařská Island, foll
rd to end. Nr C'van Camping CSK. Diff app fr N due
no L turns on Strakonická. Sm, pt shd, EHU (16A)
CZK95; adv bkg acc; ccard acc; tennis 100m. *"Boats
for hire; launch trips on rv; water taxi fr Prague, book
at site recep; helpful staff; friendly, secure site; san facs
clean & adequate; unmkd pitches; excel location; views
of city; milk etc avail fr Agip petrol stn on Strakonická;
busy site, rec arr early; 5 min to ferry & metro to
Prague."* **CZK 484** 2017

PRAHA *B2* (14km SW Rural) *50.04388, 14.28416*
Camp Drusus, Třebonice 4, 155 00 Praha 5 **tel 235
514 391; drusus@drusus.com; www.drusus.com**

🐕 CZK30 ♦fltltl 🚾 ♨ 🔥 ⚘ / 📶 🕯 ⚘ 🛝 🍽

Fr Plzeň take E50/D5 to exit 1/23 Třebonice,
then E50 dir Brno. Fr Brno exit E50/D5 at junc
19 sp Řeporyje, site in 2km, sp. 1*, Med, pt shd,
sl, EHU (10A) CZK110; gas; cooking facs; red long
stay; TV; 10% statics; bus; Eng spkn; adv bkg acc;
ccard acc; games area; CKE. *"Reg bus service to
Prague nrby, tickets fr site; owner v helpful; vg."*
CZK 617, 1 Apr-15 Oct. 2018

PRAHA *B2* (12km NW Rural) *50.09890, 14.33569*
Camping Džbán, Nad Lávkou 5, Vokovice, 160 00
Praha 6 tel 725 956 457 or 777 327 595; info@camp
dzban.eu; www.campdzban.eu

♿ CZK60 🆗 ⛺ 🚿 ⚕ 🍴 🛒 🏊

Exit 28 off ring rd onto rd 7 Chomutov-Prague; site
approx 4km after airport twd Prague; at traff lts on
brow of hill just bef Esso stn on L turn L; take 2nd L
& strt on for 600m; site adj go-kart racing.
3*, Lge, unshd, pt sl, EHU (10A) CZK90; tram 200m;
Eng spkn; ccard acc; tennis; games area; CKE. *"Tram
direct to Prague (Republic Sq) 25 mins, tickets at
bureau; gd security; long way bet shwrs & wcs; san facs
old but clean; communal male shwrs; narr pitches; new
Metro."* CZK 681, 1 May-30 Sep.   2016

ROZNOV POD RADHOSTEM *C4* (2km NE Rural)
49.46654, 18.16376 **Camping Rožnov,** Radhoštská
940, 756 61 Rožnov pod Radhoštěm tel 731 504 073;
camproznov@seznam.cz; www.camproznov.cz

♿ (htd) 🆗 ⛺ 🚿 ⚕ 🦋 🕙 nr 🛒 🏊 (htd)

On rd 35/E442; on E o'skts of Rožnov on N of rd
200m past ent to Camping Sport, take L fork opp
Benzina petrol stn (site sp obscured by lamp post).
4*, Med, pt shd, EHU (16A) CZK60; 60% statics;
phone; Eng spkn; ccard acc; tennis; CKE. *"Welcoming;
gd cooking & washing facs; pitches v close together;
basic, worn san facs; annexe; nr open-air museum
(clsd Mon); gd walking cent; cycle to town thro park."*
CZK 469, 1 May-31 Oct.   2018

STERNBERK *B3* (2km N Rural) *49.74800, 17.30641*
Autocamping Šternberk, Dolní Žleb, 785 01
Šternberk tel 585 011 300; info@campsternberk.cz;
www.campsternberk.cz

♿ CZK30 🆗 ⛺ 🚿 ⚕ 🦋 🍴 🕙 nr 🛒 🏊

Fr Olomouc take rte 46 to Šternberk. At Šternberk
go thro town cent & foll sp Dalov, site just bef vill
of Dolní Žleb. Or circumnavigate to W on rds 444
& 445, site sp. Med, pt shd, EHU (10A) CZK75 (poss
rev pol); cooking facs; TV; 30% statics; phone; adv bkg
acc; CKE. *"Gd, clean facs even when full; helpful staff."*
CZK 215, 15 May-15 Sep.   2016

STRIBRO *B1* (16km NE Rural) *49.79073, 13.16869*
Transkemp Hracholusky, 330 23 Hracholusky
tel 420 337 914 113 or 420 728 470 650; info@
hracholusky.com; www.hracholusky.com

♿ 🆗 ⛺ 🚿 ⚕ 🕙 🛒 nr 🏊 shgl adj

Fr Ulice bet Stribro & Plzen on rte 5/E50 turn
N, sp Plesnice, & foll vill sp to site in 4km at E
end of lake. Med, unshd, pt sl, EHU inc (adaptor
for hire); sw; 25% statics; Eng spkn; adv bkg acc;
waterskiing; boating. *"Lake steamer trips; gd sh stay/
NH; gd location on lakeside; fair site; facs basic."*
CZK 270, 1 May-31 Dec.   2019

STRMILOV *C2* (2km SE Rural) *49.14956, 15.20890*
Autokemp Komorník, 378 53 Strmilov tel 384 392
468; recepce@autokempkomornik.cz;
www.autokempkomornik.cz

♿ CZK40 🆗 ⛺ 🚿 ♿ 🦋 🍴 🕙 🛒 🏊 ⛰ 🛶 sand adj

Sp fr rd 23 at Strmilov. Lge, pt shd, pt sl, EHU (10A)
CZK75 (long lead rec); bbq; 20% statics; CKE. *"V
pleasant setting by lake; lake adj; clean, modern san
facs; gd rest & bar; conv Telč & Slavonice historic
towns."* CZK 215, 1 Jun-15 Sep.   2016

"I like to fill in the reports as I travel from site to site"

You'll find report forms at the back of this
guide, or you can fill them in online at
camc.com/europereport.

TABOR *C2* (6km E Rural) *49.40985, 14.73157*
Autocamping & Hotel Knížecí Rybník, Měšice 399,
39156 Tábor tel 381 252 546; knizecak@seznam.cz;
www.knizecirybnik.cz

12 ♿ CZK50 🆗 ⛺ 🚿 🍴 🕙 🛒 🏊

On N side of rd 19 fr Tábor to Jihlava, in woods
by lake adj hotel. 3*, Lge, mkd, hdg, pt shd, EHU
(6-10A) CZK60; sw nr; 10% statics; ccard acc; fishing;
tennis; CKE. *"Pleasant, lakeside site; modern san facs."*
CZK 200   2016

TANVALD *A2* (3km W Rural) *50.74205, 15.28269*
Camping Tanvaldská Kotlina (Tanvald Hollow),
Pod Špičákem 650, 46841 Tanvald tel 483 311 928;
kotlina@tanvald.cz; www.tanvald.cz

12 ♿ CZK20 🆗 ⛺ 🚿 ⚕ MSP ⚕ 🕙 ⛰ 🎣

Fr S on rte 10, in cent Tanvald at rndabt turn foll
sp Desnou & Harrachov. In 500m take L fork under
rlwy bdge, then immed turn L & foll rd past hospital.
Turn R bef tennis courts, site in 600m. Sm, pt shd,
EHU CZK30 + metered; bbq; cooking facs; games area.
"Excel; pool in town." CZK 230   2020

TELC *C2* (10km NW Rural) *49.22785, 15.38442* **Camp
Velkopařezitý,** Řásná 10, 58856 Mrákotín tel 567 379
449; campvelkoparezity@tiscali.cz; www.camp
velkoparezity.cz

12 ♿ CZK30 ♿ ⛺ ⚕ 🕙 ⛰ 🛶 1km

Exit Telč on Jihlava rd; turn L in 300m (sp) & foll sp
to site beyond Rásná. Well sp fr Telč. Steep site ent.
Sm, pt shd, pt sl, EHU CZK100; 10% statics. *"Friendly
atmosphere; poor san facs; gd walking & cycling; Telč
wonderful World Heritage site."* CZK 270   2016

TREBON *C2 (1km S Rural) 48.99263, 14.76753*
Autocamp Třeboňsky Ráj, Domanin 285, 37901
Třeboň **tel 384 722 586; info@autocamp-trebon.cz;
www.autocamp-trebon.cz**

🏕 CZK60 ♦♦♦ WD 📶 ⛓ 🍽 ✗ 🦋 ⚲ 🍸 🄗 🛒 🧺 ⚠ ⚓

Exit town by rd 155 sp Borovany heading SW.
Site on L just past lake. Note: site Not accessible
fr other end of this rd. 3*, Med, pt shd, pt sl, EHU (6A)
CZK70 (long cable req & poss rev pol); bbq; cooking
facs; sw; twin axles; TV; 5% statics; phone; bus 2km;
Eng spkn; adv bkg acc; bike hire; games area; games
rm; boat hire; CKE. *"Attractive unspoilt town; helpful
owner; facs stretched when site full; insect repellant
rec; gd cycle paths; gd rest on site; indiv shwrs but
no curtains, changing area opp shwr; gd cycle paths."*
CZK 340, 27 Apr-30 Sep. **2018**

TURNOV *A2 (6km SSE Rural) 50.5580, 15.1867*
Autocamping Sedmihorky, Sedmihorky 72, 51101
Turnov **tel 481 389 162; camp@campsedmihorky.cz;
www.campsedmihorky.cz**

12 🏕 CZK50 ♦♦♦ WD 📶 ⛓ 🍽 ✗ 🦋 🍸 🄗 🛒 🧺 ⚠

Fr rte 35/E442 fr Turnov. Turn SW over rlwy x-ing at
camping sp S of Sedmihorky. 300m along ave take
1st R. 3*, Lge, pt shd, pt sl, EHU (16A) CZK60; sw;
phone; Eng spkn; ccard acc; bike hire; CKE. *"V beautiful
site in National Park, sometimes called Bohemian
Paradise; v busy site high ssn; dep bef 1000 otherwise
charge for extra day; excel site."* **CZK 370** **2018**

UHERSKY BROD *C4 (14km E Urban) 49.04034,
17.79993* **Eurocamping Bojkovice,** Stefánikova 1008,
68771 Bojkovice **tel 420 604 236 631; info@euro
camping.com; www.eurocamping.cz**

🏕 CZK50 ♦♦♦ WD 📶 ⛓ ✗ 🍸 🄗 🛒 🧺 ⚠ ⚓ 🚿

Off E50 at Uherský Brod turn onto rd 495. Find rlwy
stn at Bojkovice on rd 495 at SW end of town. Cross
rlwy at NE (town) end of stn & foll sp round L & R
turns to site. 4*, Med, pt shd, pt sl, terr, EHU (6A) inc;
cooking facs; adv bkg acc; games area. *"Gd walking
area."* **CZK 520, 1 May-30 Sep.** **2020**

VRCHLABI *A3 (1km S Rural) 50.61036, 15.60263*
Holiday Park Liščí Farma, Dolní Branná 350,
54362 Vrchlabí **tel 499 421 473; info@liscifarma.cz;
www.liscifarma.cz**

12 🐕 CZK20 ♦♦♦ (htd) WD ♿ 🍽 ✗ MSP 🦋 🍸 🄗 🛒 nr ⚠
⚓ 🚿

S fr Vrchlabí on rd 295, site sp. 4*, Lge, mkd, pt shd,
EHU (6A) CZK125; cooking facs; TV; adv bkg acc;
ccard acc; games area; bike hire; golf 5km; canoeing;
horseriding 2km; tennis; sauna. *"Private bthrms avail."*
CZK 220 **2016**

ZAMBERK *B3 (1km E Urban) 50.08638, 16.47527*
Autocamping Jan Kulhanek, U koupaliště, 564 01
Žamberk **tel 465 614 755; kemp@orlicko.cz;
www.autocamping.cz**

🏕 CZK50 ♦♦♦ 📶 ⛓ ✗ 🦋 ⚲ 🍸 nr 🄗 nr 🛒 nr

Fr Zamberk cent on rd 11, foll sp. Sm, pt shd, EHU
(16A) CZK70; cooking facs; TV; 50% statics; phone;
bus adj, train 1km; Eng spkn; CKE. *"Site is pt of sports
cent & aqua park with many diff facs inc mini golf,
volleyball & bowling; playgrnd, pool, games area,
games rm at sports cent; site leaflet avail at recep
showing town plans with supmkt & info office; gd site."*
CZK 241, 1 Apr-31 Oct. **2016**

ZNOJMO *C3 (8km N Rural) 48.92018, 16.02588*
Camping Country, 67152 Hluboké Mašůvky **tel 515
255 249; camping-country@cbox.cz;
www.camp-country.com**

🏕 CZK50 ♦♦♦ WD ♿ 🍽 ✗ 🄗 🛒 nr ⚠ 🚿

N fr Znojmo on E59/38 4km; turn E on 408 to
Přímětice; then N on 361 4km to Hluboké Mašůvky.
Sharp turn into site fr S. 4*, Med, pt shd, sl, EHU
(16A) CZK80 (long lead poss req); sw nr; TV;
20% statics; Eng spkn; tennis; bike hire; horseriding;
CKE. *"Gd, clean, well-manicured site; v helpful owner
& family; not easy to find level pitch; excel meals."*
CZK 400, 1 May-30 Oct. **2016**

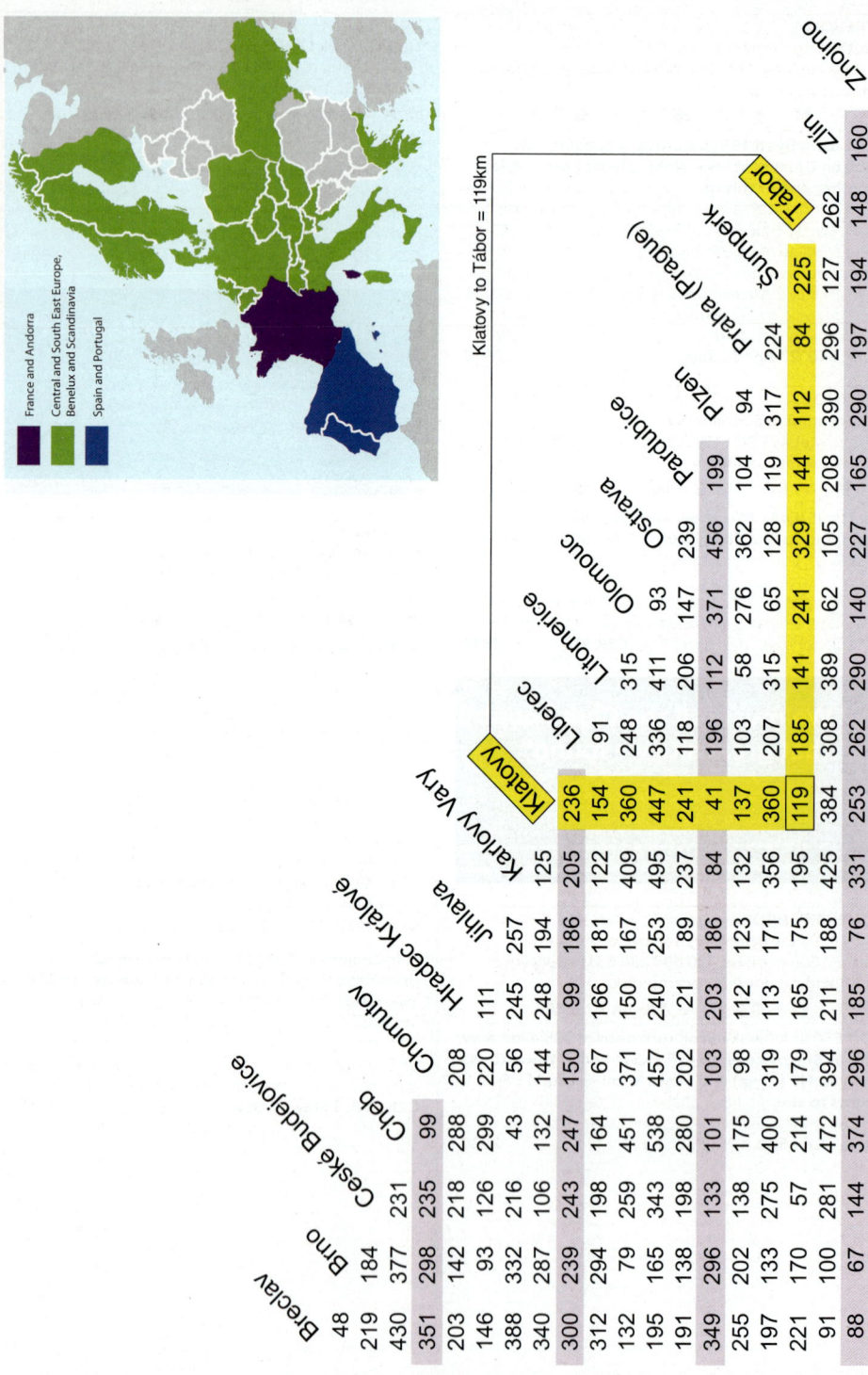

Legend
- France and Andorra
- Central and South East Europe, Benelux and Scandinavia
- Spain and Portugal

Klatovy to Tábor = 119km

Distance chart (kilometres). Each cell gives the distance between the two cities named on its row and column.

From \ To	Brno	České Budějovice	Cheb	Chomutov	Hradec Králové	Jihlava	Karlovy Vary	Klatovy	Liberec	Litoměřice	Olomouc	Ostrava	Pardubice	Plzen	Praha (Prague)	Šumperk	Tábor	Zlín	Znojmo
Břeclav	48	219	430	351	203	146	388	340	300	312	132	195	191	349	255	197	221	91	88
Brno		184	377	298	142	93	332	287	239	294	79	165	138	296	202	133	170	100	67
České Budějovice			231	235	218	126	216	106	243	198	259	343	198	133	138	275	57	281	144
Cheb				99	288	220	43	132	247	164	451	538	280	101	175	400	214	394	472
Chomutov					208	299	56	144	150	67	371	457	202	103	98	319	179	211	296
Hradec Králové						111	245	248	99	181	167	150	21	240	112	203	113	165	185
Jihlava							205	154	237	186	150	247	89	186	132	171	75	188	76
Karlovy Vary								122	205	132	409	495	237	84	125	356	195	425	331
Klatovy									236	154	360	447	241	41	137	360	119	384	253
Liberec										91	248	336	118	196	103	207	185	315	262
Litoměřice											315	411	206	112	58	315	141	411	262
Olomouc												93	147	371	276	65	241	128	140
Ostrava													239	456	362	128	329	119	227
Pardubice														199	104	119	144	208	165
Plzen															94	317	112	390	290
Praha (Prague)																224	84	296	197
Šumperk																	225	127	194
Tábor																		262	148
Zlín																			160

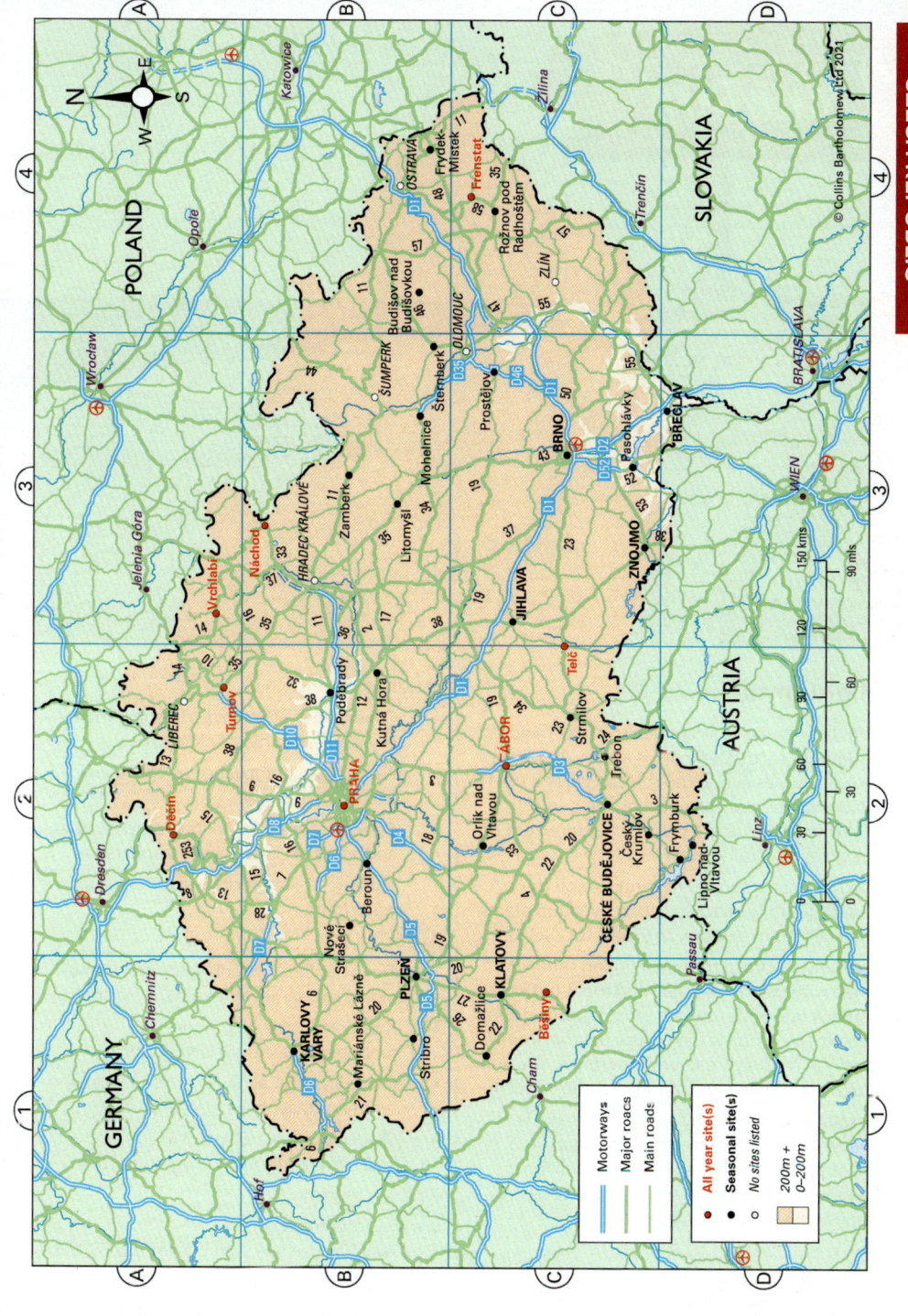

© Collins Bartholomew Ltd 2021

Legend

Motorways
Major roads
Main roads

All year site(s) (red dots)
Seasonal site(s) (black dots)
No sites listed (open circles)

200m +
0–200m

Map labels:

POLAND
GERMANY
SLOVAKIA
AUSTRIA

Katowice
Opole
Wrocław
Jelenia Góra
Dresden
Chemnitz
Hof
Cham
Passau
Linz
WIEN
BRATISLAVA
Trenčín
Žilina
Frenstat
Frýdek Místek
Rožnov pod Radhoštěm
ZLÍN
OSTRAVA
OLOMOUC
ŠUMPERK
Budišov nad Budišovkou
Šternberk
Prostějov
Mohelnice
BRNO
Pasohlávky
BŘECLAV
ZNOJMO
JIHLAVA
Telč
Strmilov
Třeboň
Frymburk
Lipno nad Vltavou
ČESKÉ BUDĚJOVICE
Český Krumlov
KLATOVY
Domažlice
Bešiny
PLZEŇ
Stříbro
Nové Strašecí
Mariánské Lázně
KARLOVY VARY
Beroun
PRAHA
Poděbrady
Kutná Hora
Orlík nad Vltavou
TÁBOR
HRADEC KRÁLOVÉ
Zámberk
Litomyšl
Náchod
Vrchlabí
Turnov
LIBEREC
Děčín

Road numbers (visible):
11, 33, 57, 48, 35, 55, 43, 50, 52, 55, 38, 44, 34, 35, 37, 23, 19, 11, 17, 38, 19, 13, 16, 9, 15, 6, 28, 14, 10, 13, 253, 7, 21, 20, 22, 3, 4, 24, 23, 19, 20, 22, 18, 2, 36, 12

Scale: 0 30 60 90 120 150 kms
       0 30 60 90 mls

161

Denmark

Skagen

Shutterstock/Ioana Catalina E

Highlights

Regularly found high on the list of the happiest nations on earth, Denmark is a friendly country that welcomes everyone. You can enjoy a charming, fairytale atmosphere working together with modern cities at the forefront of design and sustainability.

The landscape, too, is enchanting, and the beautiful sandy beaches, lakes, river and plains are a delight to explore, and ideal for cyclists.

The smørrebrød, a traditional open sandwich made with rye bread, salad and meat or fish, is perhaps one of Denmark's most famous dishes. Equally renowned is the Danish pastry - known locally as Vienna bread or wienerbrød. You'll find these at bakeries throughout the country.

A traditional Scandinavian drink, Akvavit is believed to have originated in Denmark in the 16th century. The spirit takes its distinct flavour from herbs and spices and is often sipped slowly from a small shot glass.

Major towns and cities

- Copenhagen – Denmark's bustling capital city is a perfect mix of old and new.
- Aarhus – this compact city is well known for its musical heritage.
- Odense – one of the country's oldest cities, and home of Hans Christian Anderson.
- Aalborg – a vibrant city with an atmospheric waterfront.

Attractions

- Tivoli Gardens, Copenhagen – one of the oldest amusement parks in the world.
- Kronborg Castle, Helsingør – This renaissance castle is a UNESCO site.
- Frederiksborg Castle, Hillerød – a palatial residence that now houses a museum.
- Skagen Beaches – 60km of white, sandy beaches and stunning, rugged coastline.

Find out more

www.visitdenmark.com
E: contact@visitdenmark.com T: 0045 (0) 32 88 99 00

Country Information

Population (approx): 5.6 million

Capital: Copenhagen

Area: 43,094 sq km (excl Faroe Islands and Greenland)

Bordered by: Germany

Terrain: Mostly fertile lowland, undulating hills, woodland, lakes and moors

Climate: Generally mild, changeable climate without extremes of heat or cold; cold winters but usually not severe; warm, sunny summers; the best time to visit is between May and September

Coastline: 7,400km

Highest Point: Ejer Bavnehøj 173m

Languages: Danish

Local Time: GMT or BST + 1, ie 1 hour ahead of the UK all year

Currency: Krone (DKK) divided into 100 øre; £1 = DKK 8.53, DKK 10 = £1.17 (Feb 2021)

Emergency numbers: Police 112 (114 for non-urgent calls); Fire brigade 112; Ambulance 112 (operators speak English).

Public Holidays 2021: Jan 1; Apr 1, 2, 5, 30; May 13, 23, 24; Jun 5; Dec 25, 26.

School summer holidays extend from end June to mid August.

Entry Formalities

British and Irish passport holders may stay for up to 90 days in any 180 day period without a visa. Following Brexit you may be asked to show a return or onward ticket at the border to confirm your length of stay, or to prove that you have enough money for your stay.

Your passport will need to have a minimum of 6 months' validity remaining, and be less than 10 years old (even if it has 6 months or more left).

Visitors arriving at a campsite or hotel must complete a registration form.

Medical Services

The standard of healthcare is high. Citizens of the UK are entitled to the same emergency medical services as the Danish, including free hospital treatment, on production of a European Health Insurance Card (EHIC). Tourist offices and health offices (kommunes social og sundhedforvaltning) have lists of doctors and dentists who are registered with the public health service. For a consultation with a doctor you may have to pay the full fee but you will be refunded if you apply to a local health office if they are registered with the Danish Public Health Service. Partial refunds may be made for dental costs and approved medicines. Prescriptions are dispensed at pharmacies (apotek).

Opening Hours

Banks: Mon-Fri 10am-4pm (Thu to 6pm). In the Provinces opening hours vary from town to town.

Museums: Tue-Sun 9am/10am-5pm; most close Mon.

Post Offices: Mon-Fri 9am/10am-5pm/6pm, Sat 9am/10am-12pm/2pm or closed all day.

Shops: Mon-Fri 9am-5.30pm (Fri to 7pm); Sat 9am-1pm/2pm; supermarkets open Mon-Fri 9am-7pm & Sat 9am-4pm/5pm; open on first Sunday of the month 10am-5pm. Most shops close on public holidays but you may find some bakers, sandwich shops, confectioners and kiosks open.

Regulations for Pets

Between April and September all dogs must be kept on a lead. This applies not only on campsites but throughout the country in general.

Safety and Security

Denmark has relatively low levels of crime and most visits to the country are trouble-free. The majority of public places are well lit and secure, most people are helpful and often speak good English. Visitors should, however, be aware of pickpocketing or bag-snatching in Copenhagen, particularly around the central station and in the Christiania and Nørrebro areas, as well as in other large cities and tourist attractions. Car break-ins have increased in recent years; never leave valuables in your car.

Denmark shares with the rest of Europe a general threat from terrorism. Attacks could be indiscriminate and against civilian targets in public places, including tourist sites.

British Embassy

KASTELSVEJ 36-40
DK-2100 Copenhagen Ø
Tel: 35 44 52 00
www.ukindenmark.fco.gov.uk/en

There are also Honorary Consulates in Aabenraa, Åarhus, Fredericia and Herning

Irish Embassy

ØSTBANEGADE 21
DK-2100 Copenhagen Ø
Tel: 35 47 32 00
www.embassyofireland.dk

Documents

Money

Some shops and restaurants, particularly in the larger cities, display prices in both krone and euros and many will accept payment in euros.

Major credit cards are widely, but not always, accepted. Credit cards are not normally accepted in supermarkets. Cash machines are widespread. A 5% surcharge is usually applied to credit card transactions. Some banks and/or cash machines may not accept debit cards issued by non-Danish banks.

It is advisable to carry your passport or photocard driving licence if paying with a credit card as you may well be asked for photographic proof of identity. Carry your credit card issuers'/banks' 24-hour UK contact numbers in case of loss or theft of your cards.

Passport

Your passport must be valid for the proposed duration of your stay, however in case of any unforeseen delays it is strongly recommended to have a period of extra validity on your passport.

Vehicle(s)

Carry your vehicle documentation, including vehicle registration certificate (V5C), certificate of insurance and MOT certificate (if applicable). You may be asked to produce your V5C if driving a motorhome over the Great Belt Bridge between Funen and Zealand in order to verify the weight of your vehicle. For more information see the 'Motorways' section of this introduction.

The minimum age you can drive, with a valid driver's licence, is 17.

Driving

Alcohol

The level of alcohol cannot exceed 50 milligrams (0.05%) in 100 millilitres of blood which is lower than in the UK. Drivers caught over this limit will be fined and their driving licence withdrawn. Police carry out random breath tests.

Breakdown Service

24 hours assistance is available from SOS Dansk Autohjaelp (Danish Automobile Assistance) call Tel: 70 10 80 90.

The hourly charge between Monday and Friday is DKK 638 + VAT and an administration charge; higher charges apply at night and at weekends and public holidays. On-the-spot repairs and towing must be paid for in cash.

On motorways use the emergency telephones, situated every 2 km, to call the breakdown service. The telephone number to dial in case of an accident is 112.

Child Restraint System

Children under three years of age must be seated in an approved child restraint system adapted to their size. Children over three years old and under 1.35 metres in height must be seated in an approved child restraint suitable for both their height and weight. If the vehicle is fitted with an active airbag children must not be placed in the front seat in a rear-facing child seat.

Fuel

Some petrol stations in larger towns stay open 24 hours a day and they often have self-service pumps which accept DKK 50, 100 and occasionally DKK 200 notes. Few display instructions in English and it is advisable to fill up during normal opening hours when staff are on hand. Unleaded petrol pumps are marked 'Blyfri Benzine'. Major credit cards are normally accepted.

LPG (Autogas or Bilgas) is available from a handful of BP, OK, Q8, Uno-X, YX, Shell and Statoil service stations – the Danish Tourist Board publishes a list of outlets on its website www.visitdenmark.com

Lights and Indicators

Dipped headlights are compulsory at all times, regardless of weather conditions. Bulbs are more likely to fail with constant use and you are recommended to carry spares.

On motorways drivers must use their hazard warning lights to warn other motorists of sudden queues ahead or other dangers such as accidents.

By law indicators must be used when overtaking or changing lanes on a motorway and when pulling out from a parked position at the kerb.

Low Emission Zones

Low Emission zones are in operation in many large cities. The rules affect all diesel powered vehicles over 3,500kg, which must meet European Emission Standard 4 (EURO 4). All vehicles over 3,500kg must display an Environmental Zone sticker (Eco-label) You can order the Eco-label online from www.applusbilsyn.dk for DKK 93 or visit a car inspection station in Denmark where the Eco-label will cost DKK 165.
Vehicles which do not meet European Emission Standard 4 are not allowed into the Low Emission Zone. A fine of DKK 20,000 (Approximately £1900 in 2015) is payable for non-compliance.

Motorways

There are approximately 1,000 km of motorways, mainly two-lane and relatively uncongested. No tolls are levied except on bridges. Lay-bys with picnic areas and occasionally motorhome service points are situated at 25 km intervals. These often also have toilet facilities. Service areas and petrol stations are situated at 50 km intervals and are generally open from 7am to 10pm.

Parking

Parking prohibitions and limitations are indicated by signs. Hours during which parking is not allowed are displayed in black for weekdays, with brackets for Saturdays and in red for Sundays and public holidays. Parking meters and discs are used and discs are available free of charge from post offices, banks, petrol stations and tourist offices. The centre of Copenhagen is divided into red, green and blue zones and variable hourly charges apply round the clock Monday to Friday

(Saturday to 5pm; Sunday and public holidays free). 'Pay and display' tickets may be bought from machines with cash or a credit card. Cars must be parked on the right-hand side of the road (except in one-way streets). An illegally parked vehicle may be removed by the police.

Priority

At intersections where there are 'give way' or 'stop' signs and/or a transverse line consisting of triangles (shark's teeth) with one point facing towards the driver, drivers must give way to traffic at an intersection. If approaching an intersection of two roads without any signs you must give way to vehicles coming from the right. Give way to cyclists and to buses signalling to pull out. On the Danish islands take care as many people travel by foot, bicycle or on horseback.

Roads

Roads are generally in good condition, well-signposted and largely uncongested and driving standards are fairly high.

Caravanners should beware of strong crosswinds on exposed stretches of road. Distances are short; it is less than 500 km (310 miles) from Copenhagen on the eastern edge of Zealand, to Skagen at the tip of Jutland, and the coast is never more than an hour away.

Road Signs and Markings

Signs directing you onto or along international E-roads are green with white lettering. E-roads, having been integrated into the Danish network, usually have no other national number.

Signs above the carriageway on motorways have white lettering on a blue background. Signs guiding you onto other roads are white with red text and a hexagonal sign with red numbering indicates the number of a motorway exit.

Primary (main roads) connecting large towns and ferry connections have signs with black numbers on a yellow background. Secondary (local) roads connecting small towns and primary routes are indicated by signs with black numbers on a white background. Signs of any colour with a dotted frame refer you to a road further ahead. Road signs themselves may be placed low down and, as a result, may be easy to miss.'Sharks teeth' markings at junctions indicate stop and give way to traffic on the road you are entering.

General roads signs conform to international standards. You may see the following:

Place of interest

Recommended speed limits

Dual Carriage-way ends

The following are some other common signs:

Danish	English Translation
Ensrettet kørsel	One-way street
Fare	Danger
Farligt sving	Dangerous bend
Fodgægerovergang	Pedestrian crossing
Gennemkørsel forbudt	No through road
Hold til hojre	Keep to the right
Hold til venstre	Keep to the left
Omkørsel	Diversion
Parkering forbudt	No parking
Vejen er spærret	Road closed

Speed Limits

	Open Road (km/h)	Motorway (km/h)
Car Solo	80-90	110-130
Car towing caravan/trailer	70	80
Motorhome under 3500kg	80-90	110-130
Motorhome 3500-7500kg	70	70

Vehicles over 3,500 kg are restricted to 70 km/h (44 mph) on the open road and on motorways. It is prohibited to use radar detectors.

Traffic Jams

British drivers will enjoy the relatively low density of traffic. At most, traffic builds up during the evening rush hours around the major cities of Copenhagen, Århus, Aalborg and Odense. During the holiday season traffic jams may be encountered at the Flensburg border crossing into Germany, on the roads to coastal areas, on approach roads to ferry crossings and on routes along the west coast of Jutland.

Toll Bridges

The areas of Falster and Zealand are linked by two road bridges, 1.6 km and 1.7 km in length respectively.

The areas of Funen and Zealand are linked by an 18 km suspension road bridge and rail tunnel known as the Great Belt Link (Storebæltsbroen), connecting the towns of Nyborg and Korsør. The toll road is part of the E20 between Odense and Ringsted and tolls for single journeys on the bridge are shown in Table 1 below (2015 prices subject to change).

Table 1 – Great Belt Bridge

Vehicle(s)	Price
Solo Car up to 6 metres	DKK 240
Car + trailer/caravan	DKK 365
Motorhome (under 3,500 kg) under 6 metres	DKK 240
Motorhome (under 3,500kg) over 6 metres	DKK 365
Motorhome (over 3,500 kg) up to 10 metres	DKK 610
Motorhome (over 3,500 kg) over 10 metres	DKK 965

You may be asked to produce your Vehicle Registration Certificate (V5C) to verify the weight of your vehicle. Day return and weekend return tickets are also available. For more information see www.storebaelt.dk/english.

The 16 km Øresund Bridge links Copenhagen in Denmark with Malmö in Sweden and means that it is possible to drive all the way from mainland Europe to Sweden by motorway. The crossing is via a 7.8 km bridge to the artificial island of Peberholm, and a 4 km tunnel. Tolls for single journeys (payable in cash, including euros, or by credit card) are levied on the Swedish side, and are shown in Table 2 below (2015 prices subject to change).

Table 2 – Øresund Bridge

Vehicle(s)	Price
Solo Car or motorhome up to 6 metres	€50
Car + caravan/trailer or motorhome over 6 metres	€ 100

Speed limits apply, and during periods of high wind the bridge is closed to caravans. Bicycles are not allowed. Information on the Øresund Bridge can be found on www.oeresundsbron.com

On both the Øresund and Storebælts bridges vehicle length is measured electronically and even a slight overhang over six metres, e.g. towbars, projecting loads and loose items, will result in payment of the higher tariff.

Violation of Traffic Regulations

The police are authorised to impose and collect on-the-spot fines for traffic offences. Driving offences committed in Denmark are reported to the UK authorities.

Essential Equipment

Reflective Jacket

It is recommended, though not compulsory, to carry a reflectorised jacket on board the vehicle in the event the driver has to step out of the car in an emergency.

Warning Triangle

An EU approved red warning triangle must be used if the vehicle breaks down, punctures or is involved in an accident.

Touring

The peak holiday season and school holidays are slightly earlier than in the UK and by mid-August some attractions close or operate reduced opening hours.

Service charges are automatically added to restaurant bills although you may round up the bill if service has been good, but it is not expected. Tips for taxi drivers are included in the fare. Smoking is not allowed in enclosed public places, including restaurants and bars. The 3,500 km Marguerite Route, marked by brown signs depicting a flower (see below), takes motorists to the best sights and scenic areas in Denmark.

Tourist
Route

A route map and guide (in English) are available from bookshops, tourist offices and Statoil service stations all over Denmark. Stretches of the route are not suitable for cars towing caravans as some of the roads are narrow and twisting.

The capital and major port, Copenhagen, is situated on the island of Zealand. Grundtvig Cathedral, Amalienborg Palace and the Viking Museum are well worth a visit, as are the famous Tivoli Gardens open from mid April to the third week in September and again for a few days in October and from mid November to the end of December (excluding Christmas). The statue of the Little Mermaid, the character created by Hans Christian Andersen, can be found at the end of the promenade called Langelinie. Copenhagen is easy to explore and from there visitors may travel to the north of Zealand along the 'Danish Riviera' to Hamlet's castle at Kronborg, or west to Roskilde with its Viking Ship Museum and 12th century cathedral.

A Copenhagen Card (CPH Card) offers unlimited use of public transport throughout Greater Copenhagen and North Zealand, free entry to over 60 museums and attractions and discounts at restaurants and other attractions. Cards are valid for 24 or 72 hours and may be purchased from selected tourist offices, travel agents, hotels and railway stations or online from www.visitcopenhagen.com. Two children up to the age of nine are included free of charge on an adult card. The Copenhagen Card is also available to buy via a mobile app.

National Parks in the country include Thy National Park near Thisted along Jutland's north-west coast, Mols Bjerge National Park in eastern Jutland and Wadden Sea National Park in the south-west of the country.

English is widely spoken.

Camping and Caravanning

Denmark has approximately 500 approved, well-equipped, annually inspected campsites.

A green banner flies at each campsite entrance, making it easy to spot. Campsites are graded from 1 to 5 stars, many having excellent facilities including baby-changing areas, private family bathrooms, self-catering cooking facilities and shops. Prices are regulated and there is very little variation.

All except the most basic 1-star sites have water and waste facilities for motorhomes and at least some electric hook-ups. You may find it useful to take your own flat universal sink plug. During the high season it is advisable to book in advance as many Danish holidaymakers take pitches for the whole season for use at weekends and holidays resulting in minimal space for tourers.

A Camping Key Europe (CKE) or Camping Card International (CCI) is required on all campsites.

Approximately 190 campsites have a 'Quick Stop' amenity which provides safe, secure overnight facilities on or adjoining campsites, including the use of sanitary facilities. Quick Stop rates are about two thirds of the regular camping rate but you must arrive after 8pm and leave by 10am next morning. A list of Quick Stop sites may be obtained from local tourist offices or downloaded from DK-Camp www.dk-camp.dk

Wild camping is prohibited on common or State land, in stopping bays and parking sites, in the dunes, or on the beaches, unless there is an organised camp site. Farmers or landowners may allow you to pitch on their land, but you must always seek permission from them is advance.

Cycling

Although not as flat as the Netherlands, Denmark is very cyclist-friendly and many major and minor roads, including those in all major towns, have separate cycle lanes or tracks. They have their own traffic lights and signals. Cyclists often have the right of way and, when driving, you should check cycle lanes before turning left or right.

In Åarhus and Copenhagen city centre bicycles are free to use between mid-April and November - you will need to pay a refundable deposit. Simply look for one of the many bicycle racks around the central area; see www.visitcopenhagen.com for more information.

There are many separate cycle routes, including eleven national routes, which may be long distance, local or circular, mainly on quiet roads and tracks. Local tourist offices can provide information. When planning a route, take the (often strong) prevailing westerly winds into account.

Copenhagen

Shutterstock/Oleksiy Mark

Bicycles may be carried on the roof of a car as well as at the rear. When carried at the rear, the lights and number plate must remain visible.

Electricity and Gas

Current on campsites varies between 6 and 16 amps, a 10 amp supply being the most common. Plugs have 2 round pins. Some sites have CEE17 electric hook-ups or are in the process of converting. If a CEE17 connection is not available site staff will usually provide an adaptor. Visitors report that reversed polarity is common.

Campingaz 904 and 907 butane cylinders are readily available from campsites, or some Statoil service stations and at camping or hardware shops. If travelling on to Norway, Statoil agencies there will exchange Danish propane cylinders.

Public Transport

Public transport is excellent and you can buy a variety of bus, train and metro tickets at station kiosks and at some supermarkets. Children under the age of 12 travel free on buses and metro trains in the Greater Copenhagen area when accompanied by an adult. Tickets must be purchased for dogs and bicycles.

Numerous car ferry connections operate daily between different parts of the country. The ferry is a common mode of transport in Denmark and there may be long queues, especially at weekends in summer. The most important routes connect the bigger islands of Zealand and Funen with Jutland using high-speed vessels on day and night services. Vehicle length and height restrictions apply on routes between Odden (Zealand) and Århus and Æbeltoft (Jutland) and not all sailings transport caravans – check in advance. The Danish Tourist Board can provide general information on car ferry services or contact Scandlines for information on inter-island services including timetables and prices - www.scandlines.dk, email scandlines@scandlines.com or telephone 0045 (0) 33 15 15 15.

International ferry services are particularly busy during July and August and it is advisable to book in advance. Popular routes include Frederikshavn to Gothenburg (Sweden), Helsingør to Helsingborg (Sweden), Copenhagen to Oslo (Norway), and Rødby to Puttgarden in Germany (this route involves a road bridge which is occasionally closed to high-sided vehicles because of high winds). The ferry route from Copenhagen to Hamburg is a good alternative to the busy E45 motorway linking Denmark and Germany.

Frederiksborg Castle

AABENRAA *B3* (2.7km S Coastal) *55.02490, 9.41461*
Fjordlyst Aabenraa City Camping, Sønderskovvej 100, 6200 Aabenraa **tel 45 74 62 26 99; mail@ fjordlyst.dk; www.fjordlyst.dk**

🐕 DKK10 🛉🛉 WD ♨ ᵭ ♿ ⊟ ✎ MSP 🦋 ☂ 🍴 ⬤ 🎠 ⛱ 500m

Fr S take E45 & exit at junc 72 to Aabenraa. Foll Rd 42 then turn L onto Rd 24. Site sp on R. 3*, Med, mkd, pt shd, sl, terr, EHU (16A) DKK35; bbq; twin axles; TV; 10% statics; bus adj; Eng spkn; adv bkg acc; games area; CCI. *"Scenic location with views over the bay; excel facs; friendly, helpful staff; some steep slopes on site rds; vg."* **DKK 225, 19 Mar-23 Sep.**

2016

AALBORG *B1* (3km W Urban) *57.05500, 9.88500*
Strandparken Camping, Skydebanevej 20, 9000 Aalborg **tel 98 12 76 29; info@strandparken.dk; www.strandparken.dk**

🐕 DKK10 🛉🛉 WD ♨ ᵭ ♿ ✎ ⛲ 🍴 ⬤ nr 🎠

Turn L at start of m'way to Svenstrup & Aalborg W, foll A180 (Hobrovej rd) twd town cent. Turn L bef Limfjorden bdge onto Borgergade for 2km, site on R. Fr N turn R after bdge onto Borgergade. 3*, Med, shd, EHU (10A) DKK30 (poss rev pol); cooking facs; TV; 10% statics; phone; bus nr; Eng spkn; adv bkg acc; ccard acc; CKE. *"Gd cent for town & N Jutland; gd security; facs block excel; pool adj; card for elec."* **DKK 248, 24 Marr-11 Sep.**

2016

AALESTRUP *B2* (1km E Rural) *56.69166, 9.49991*
Aalestrup Camping, Aalestrup Campingplads, Parkvænget 2, 9620 Aalestrup **tel 22 79 92 64; pouledb@ofir.dk; www.rosenparken.dk**

🛉🛉 WD ♨ ✎ 🦋 ⬤ 🍴 ⬤ nr 🎠

Fr E45 turn W onto rd 561 to Aalestrup; 500m after junc with rd 13 turn L into Borgergade, cross rlwy line. Site sp. 1*, Med, pt shd, EHU DKK30. *"Free ent beautiful rose garden; gd touring base; friendly staff."* **DKK 125, 1 Mar-1 Nov.**

2016

AARHUS *C2* (8km N Rural) *56.22660, 10.16260*
Åarhus Camping, Randersvej 400, Lisbjerg, 8200 Åarhus Nord **tel 86 23 11 33; info@aarhuscamping.dk; www.aarhuscamping.dk**

12 DKK10 🛉🛉 WD ♨ ᵭ ♿ ⊟ ✎ MSP ⛲ 🍴 ⬤ 🎠 🛝 (htd) 🚲

Exit E45 junc 46 Århus N, then to Ikea rndabt. Then foll sp Lisbjerg & head for smoking factory chimney. Site 400m N of Lisbjerg. 3*, Med, pt shd, pt sl, EHU (16A) metered; gas; bbq; cooking facs; TV; 10% statics; phone; adv bkg acc; golf 10km; games area; CKE. *"Conv Århus; gd, tidy site; modern san facs; conv for bus into Aarhus, helpful owner; elec cards for shwrs."* **DKK 203**

2015

AARHUS *C2* (8km S Coastal) *56.11030, 10.23209*
Blommehaven Camping, Ørneredevej 35, 8270 Højbjerg **tel 86 27 02 07; info@blommehaven.dk; www.blommehaven.dk**

🐕 DKK10 🛉🛉 WD ♨ ᵭ ♿ ⊟ ✎ MSP 🦋 ⬤ 🎠 ⛱ sand adj

Fr S on E45 at junc 50 take rd 501 twd Århus. In 10km this becomes 01 ring rd. Take 2nd R Dalgas Ave, at T-junc turn L & immed R into Strandvejen. Site 3km on L in Marselisborg Forest. 3*, Lge, mkd, hdg, pt shd, terr, EHU DKK35; bbq; cooking facs; TV; 4% statics; phone; bus; Eng spkn; adv bkg acc; Quickstop o'night facs. *"Some pitches sm & bare earth; helpful staff; clean facs; easy reach woods, cliffs & beach; conv for open-air museum."* **DKK 251, 18 Mar-23 Oct.**

2016

AARS *B2* (2km N Rural) *56.81530, 9.50695* **Aars Camping,** Tolstrup Byvej 17, 9600 Aars **tel 98 62 36 03; aarscampingplads@ gmail.com; www.aarscamping.dk**

🐕 (htd) WD ♨ ᵭ ⊟ ✎ MSP 🦋 ⛲ 🍴 ⬤ 🎠

Fr E45 exit junc 33 W to Aars on rd 535. Turn N onto rd 29 (Aggersundvej), site sp. 3*, Med, pt shd, pt sl, EHU (16A) DKK30; gas; bbq; cooking facs; TV; 10% statics; Eng spkn; adv bkg acc; ccard acc; horseriding; tennis; CKE. *"Vg."* **DKK 150, 1 Apr-1 Nov.**

2016

ALBAEK *C1* (9.6km N Coastal) *57.64433, 10.46179*
Bunken Camping, Ålbækvej 288, Bunken Klitplantage, 9982 Ålbæk **tel 98 48 71 80; info@bunkenstrand camping.dk; www.bunkenstrandcamping.dk**

🐕 DKK15 🛉🛉 WD ♨ ᵭ ⊟ ✎ ⬤ 🎠 ⛱ sand 150m

Site in fir plantation E of A10. 3*, V lge, hdg, pt shd, EHU DKK39 (poss rev pol); gas; cooking facs; TV; phone; adv bkg acc; boating; fishing. *"Beautiful site in trees; spacious pitches."* **DKK 215, 3 Apr-18 Oct.**

2016

ASSENS *B3* (12km N Coastal) *55.33400, 9.89002*
Sandager Naes Camping, Strandgårdsvej 12, DK 5610 Assens **tel 45 64 79 11 56; info@sandagernaes.dk; www.sandagernaes.dk**

🐕 🛉🛉 WD ♨ ᵭ ⊟ ✎ ⛲ 🍴 🎠 🎠 ⛱ (htd) ⛱ 0.5km

Fr E20, take exit 57 dir Assens. R at Sandager & foll sp. Med, hdg, mkd, pt shd, pt sl, EHU (13A); bbq; cooking facs; TV; 50% statics; phone; Eng spkn; adv bkg acc; games area; games rm; waterslide; CCI. *"Excel site."* **DKK 330, 23 Mar-15 Sep.**

2019

ASSENS *B3* (1.6km W Urban/Coastal) *55.26569, 9.88390* **Camping Assens Strand,** Næsvej 15, 5610 Assens **tel (45) 63 60 63 62; assens@campone.dk; www.campone.dk/assens**

🐕 DKK25 👬👫 (htd) 🚿 ⚓ ♿ 🚮 ⁄ MSP 🛒 🛖 ⛱ sand adj

Site on beach at neck of land W of town adj marina. 3*, Med, pt shd, EHU (10A) DKK30; gas; TV; 20% statics; phone; adv bkg acc; watersports; fishing. *"Pleasant site on beach."*
DKK 215, Easter-13 Sep. **2016**

BILLUND *B3* (12km SE Rural) *55.68877, 9.26864* **Randbøldal Camping,** Dalen 9, 7183 Randbøl **tel 75 88 35 75; info@randboldalcamping.dk; www.randboldalcamping.dk**

12 🐕 DKK20 👬👫 (htd) 🚿 ⚓ ♿ 🚮 ⁄ MSP 🦋 🛒 🛖

Fr Vejle take Billund rd. After approx 18km take L turn to Randbol & Bindebolle. Foll sp, site located approx 5km on L. 3*, Med, shd, pt sl, EHU (10A) DKK35; cooking facs; sw; TV; 15% statics; phone; Eng spkn; adv bkg acc; ccard acc; fishing nr; waterslide nr. *"Wooded site nr rv & trout hatchery; facs stretched high ssn; conv Legoland & Lion Park."* **DKK 234** **2016**

BOGENSE *C3* (2km SW Urban/Coastal) *55.56144, 10.08530* **Bogense Strand Camping,** Vestre Engvej 11, 5400 Bogense **tel 64 81 35 08; info@ bogensecamp.dk; www.bogensecamp.dk**

🐕 DKK20 👬👫 WD 🚿 ⚓ ♿ 🚮 ⁄ MSP 🦋 🛒 🛖 ⛵ 🛶 ⛱ shgl adj

Fr E20 at junc 57 & take 317 NE to Bogense. At 1st traff lts turn L for harbour, site sp at side of harbour. Lge, pt shd, EHU (12A) DKK35; cooking facs; TV; 10% statics; phone; adv bkg acc; CKE. *"Well-run site; excel facs; interesting sm town 5 mins walk."*
DKK 325, 3 Apr-18 Oct. **2016**

BORRE *D3* (6km SE Rural) *54.97971, 12.52198* **Camping Møns Klint,** Klintevej 544, 4791 Magleby **tel 55 81 20 25; camping@klintholm.dk; www.campingmoensklint.dk**

🐕 👬👫 WD 🚿 ⚓ ⁄ MSP 🦋 🎿 ⛺ (htd) ⛱ shgl 3km

Site nr end of metalled section of rd 287 fr Stege to E of Magleby, site sp. 3*, Lge, pt shd, pt sl, EHU (10A) DKK40; gas; cooking facs; TV; 20% statics; phone; Eng spkn; adv bkg acc; ccard acc; boating; games area; bike hire; tennis; fishing; CKE. *"150m chalk cliffs adj - geological interest; much flora, fauna, fossils; gd walks; friendly staff; excel facs."*
DKK 292, 1 Apr-31 Oct. **2016**

BRAEDSTRUP *B2* (6.3km SSE Rural) *55.93552, 9.65314* **Gudenå Camping Brædstrup,** Bolundvej 4, 8740 Brædstrup **tel 75763070; info@gudenaacamping.dk; www.gudenaacamping.dk**

🐕 DKK10 👬👫 (htd) WD 🚿 ⚓ ♿ 🚮 ⁄ MSP 🦋 🛒 🎡 Ⓣ 🛖 🛶

Fr Silkeborg take rd 52 twds Horsens; site sp R off rd 52 approx 4km fr Braedstrup. 3*, Sm, mkd, unshd, EHU (10A) metered; bbq; TV; 25% statics; adv bkg rec; games rm; CKE. *"Sm, attractive site beside Rv Gudenå; v well run fam site; fishing fr site; excel san facs."*
DKK 223, 29 Apr-27 Sep. **2015**

COPENHAGEN *D3* (13km S Urban) *55.582578, 12.628996* **Copenhagen Camping,** Bachersmindevej 11, DK-2791 Dragør **tel 32 94 20 07; info@ copenhagencamping.dk; copenhagencamping.dk**

12 🐕 👬👫 (htd) WD 🚿 ⚓ 🚮 MSP 🛒 🎿

Exit E20 at junc 18. Lge, hdstg, hdg, unshd, 60% statics; Eng spkn; adv bkg acc; ccard acc; CKE. *"Gd; some airport noise; barrier clsd 2300-0700; of for short stay to visit Copenhagen."* **DKK 220** **2019**

ENGESVANG *B2* (3km N Rural) *56.18736, 9.35627* **Bøllingsø Camping,** Kragelundvej 5, 7442 Engesvang **tel 86 86 51 44; post@bollingso-camping.dk; www.bollingso-camping.dk**

🐕 DKK10 👬👫 (htd) WD 🚿 ⚓ ♿ 🚮 ⁄ 🦋 Ⓣ nr 🎡 🛒 🛖 🛶 🎿

Fr A13 dir Viborg, turn E to N of Engesvang & foll minor rd so Kragelund. Site on L 1km after museum. 3*, Med, mkd, pt shd, pt sl, EHU (16A) DKK30; cooking facs; TV; 2% statics; phone; adv bkg acc; lake fishing 250m; games area; CKE. *"Conv NH for A13; well-kept family site; clean, dated facs; nr Danish lake district."*
DKK 170, 1 Apr-1 Oct. **2016**

ESBJERG *A3* (13km NW Rural/Coastal) *55.54359, 8.33921* **Sjelborg Camping,** Sjelborg Standvej 11, Hjerting, 6710 Esbjerg Vest **tel 75 11 54 32; info@sjelborg.dk; www.sjelborg.dk**

👬👫 WD 🚿 ⚓ ♿ 🚮 ⁄ MSP 🦋 🛒 ⛱ shgl nr

Fr Esbjerg take coast rd N twds Hjerting & Sjelborg. At T-junc, Sjelborg Vej, turn L & in 100m turn R onto Sjelborg Kirkevej (camping sp); in 600m turn L into Sjelborg Strandvej (sp); site on R in 600m. 3*, Lge, mkd, hdg, pt shd, EHU (10A)€4.50; phone; bus to town; adv bkg acc; fishing; golf 5km. *"Excel, well maintained site in a quiet country setting; superb facs & activities all ages; lake adj; spacious on edge of conservation area; mkd walks & bird sanctuary; v welcoming & friendly."* **DKK 190, 11 Apr-20 Sep.**
2015

FAABORG *C3* (8.5km W Coastal) *55.10568, 10.10776* **Bøjden Strandcamping,** Bøjden Landevej 12, 5600 Bøjden **tel 63 60 63 60; info@bojden.dk; www.bojden.dk**

🐕 DKK15 👬👫 (htd) WD 🚿 ⚓ ♿ 🚮 ⁄ MSP Ⓣ 🎡 nr 🛒 🛖 ✏️ 🎿 (htd) 📶 ⛱ sand adj

Rd 8 W fr Fåborg dir Bøjden/Fynshav, site sp nr ferry. 5*, Lge, mkd, hdg, pt shd, pt sl, terr, serviced pitches; EHU (16A) DKK31; cooking facs; TV; 80% statics; Eng spkn; adv bkg acc; ccard acc; games rm; golf 12km; bike hire; sep car park; boat hire. *"Excel family site with activity cent; blue flag beach; sea views fr pitches; interesting area; excel facs."*
DKK 395, 9 Apr-22 Oct. **2017**

FREDERICIA *B3* (12.6km N Coastal) *55.65696, 9.72580* **Morkholt Strand Camping,** Hagenvej 105B, DK-7080 Borkop **tel 75 95 91 22; info@morkholt.dk; morkholt.dk**

12 DKK20 (htd) (htd) adj

Fr Vejle take A28 twrds Fredericia. Exit to Garslev. After Garslev foll sp to Morkholt. Strt on at island. Stay L at junc (camping sp - dead end rd). After 1.5km site on L. 3*, Lge, hdg, mkd, unshd, EHU 6A; bbq (charcoal, elec, gas); cooking facs; twin axles; Eng spkn; adv bkg acc; games area; 2 football pitches; crazy golf; pedal go-karts; 3 bouncy pillows; visitor carpk; sea kayaking courses; CKE. *"Excel."*
DKK 268 **2019**

FREDERIKSHAVN *C1* (2km N Coastal) *57.46415, 10.52778* **Nordstrand Camping A/S (Formerly TopCamp),** Apholmenvej 40, 9900 Frederikshavn **tel 98 42 93 50; info@nordstrand-camping.dk; www.nordstrand-camping.dk**

DKK12 (covrd) 1km

Fr E45/Rd40 foll rd N twd Skagen to outside town boundary (over rlwy bdge), turn R at rndabt into Apholmenvej; site sp. 4*, Lge, mkd, unshd, EHU (10A); gas; red long stay; TV; 10% statics; phone; Eng spkn; adv bkg acc; ccard acc; excursions; CKE. *"Vg NH for ferries; recep open 24hrs peak ssn; well-run, clean site; some pitches sm; cycle track to town."*
DKK 305, 14 Mar-24 Sep. **2017**

GRASTEN *B3* (2km SW Coastal) *54.9007, 9.57121* **Lærkelunden Camping,** Nederbyvej 17-25, Rinkenæs, 6300 Gråsten **tel 74 65 02 50; info@laerkelunden.dk; www.laerkelunden.dk**

(covrd, htd) sand adj

Fr Kruså E on rd 8 twds Gråsten & Sønderborg; on E o'skts of Rinkenæs turn R Nederbyvej (car dealer on corner) & foll sp to site in 400m. 4*, Lge, hdstg, unshd, pt sl, serviced pitches; EHU (10A) DKK30; gas; bbq; cooking facs; TV; 10% statics; phone; Eng spkn; ccard acc; boat launch; sauna; solarium; CKE. *"Gd sailing/surfing; views over Flensburg fjord; coastal footpath; gd cent for S Jutland & N Germany; excel; lovely, well run site."* **DKK 317, 21 Mar-22 Oct.** **2017**

GRENAA *C2* (4km S Coastal) *56.38957, 10.91213* **Grenaa Strand Camping,** Fuglsangsvej 58, 8500 Grenå **tel 86 32 17 18; info@722.dk; www.grenaastrand camping.dk**

DKK30 sand 250m

Fr Grenå harbour foll coast rd due S foll sp. 3*, V lge, unshd, EHU (10A) DKK35; gas; TV; 10% statics; phone; adv bkg acc; solarium. *"Conv for ferries to Sweden; busy site."* **DKK 264, 1 Apr-16 Sep.** **2016**

HADERSLEV *B3* (13.6km S Coastal) *55.15313, 9.49424* **Vikaer Strand Camping,** Dundelum 29, Djernaes, 6100 Haderslev **tel 74 57 54 64; info@vikaercamp.dk; www.vikaercamp.dk**

DKK 12

S on Katsund twd Lille Klingbjerg, turn R onto Lille Klingbjerg, L onto Højgade, R onto Møllepladsen, L to stay on Møllepladsen then take rte 170 to Diernæs Strandvej for 10.9km, then take 1st R onto Ny Erlevvej for 450m, turn L onto Omkørselsvejen/ Rte 170, cont to foll Rte 170 for 8.1km, go thro 1 rndbt, turn L onto Diernæsvej Strandvej for 2.3km foll Diernæs Strandvej to Dundelum, L onto Diernæs Strandvej, R to stay on same rd, R onto Dundelum, L to stay on Dundelum and site on R. Lge, mkd, unshd, pt sl, EHU (10-16A); Eng spkn; CCI. *"Super site, many outlets for children; lovely beach; immac san facs."*
DKK 240, Easter-31 Oct. **2019**

HADERSLEV *B3* (1km W Urban) *55.24431, 9.47701* **Haderslev Camping,** Erlevvej 34, 6100 Haderslev **tel 74 52 13 47; haderslev@danhostel.dk; www.danhostel-haderslev.dk/campingplads**

DKK 10 (htd) nr

Turn of E45 at junc 68 sp Haderslev Cent; turn R onto rd 170. On ent town, cross lake & turn R at traff lts. Site on R at rndabt in 500m. 3*, Med, hdstg, mkd, pt shd, pt sl, EHU (16A) DKK35; bbq; cooking facs; sw nr; TV; 10% statics; phone; bus 1km; Eng spkn; adv bkg acc; ccard acc; games rm; CKE. *"Gd, well-kept site conv E45; all facs to high standard; attractive old town; part of youth hostel complex (2018)."* **DKK 180, 23 Mar-21 Oct.** **2018**

"Satellite navigation makes touring much easier"

Remember most sat navs don't know if you're towing or in a larger vehicle – always use yours alongside maps and site directions.

HANSTHOLM *B1* (4km E Coastal) *57.10913, 8.66731* **Hanstholm Camping,** Hamborgvej 95, 7730 Hanstholm **tel 97 96 51 98; info@hanstholm-camping.de; www.hanstholm-camping.dk**

12 DKK10 (htd) (htd) sand 1km

Ent town fr S on rte 26. At rndabt turn R onto coast rd sp Vigsø. Site on L in about 4km. 3*, Lge, hdg, mkd, pt shd, pt sl, EHU (10A) DKK40; gas; bbq; TV; 30% statics; phone; Eng spkn; adv bkg acc; ccard acc; horseriding; sauna; fishing; CKE. *"Fine view of North Sea coast; nr wildlife area; gd cycling/walking on coast path; excel, busy, well-maintained site; generous pitches; gd rest; excel childrens facs."* **DKK 230** **2016**

HEJLSMINDE *B3* (9km N Coastal) *55.41109, 9.59228*
Gronninghoved Strand Camping, Mosvigvej 21,
6093 Sjolund **tel 75 57 40 45; info@gronninghoved.dk;
www.gronninghoved.dk**

🐴 👫 wc ♨ ⚡ ♿ 🚿 ⊿ MSP ✕ 🦋 🍴 ▱ 🛶 (htd) ⛱ 🌳 shgl 0.2km

Fr E45 at exit 65 take 25 twds Kolding. At lights
turn R onto 170. After 3.4km turn L sp Sjolund.
On entry Sjolund take 1st L sp Gronninghoved.
Take 2nd R in Gronninghoved, then 1st L, foll sp
to site. 4*, Lge, mkd, hdg, pt shd, pt sl, EHU (10A)
DKK37; cooking facs; twin axles; TV; 75% statics;
Eng spkn; adv bkg acc; games area; games rm; CKE.
"Excel site; tennis, mini golf, billards & waterslide."
DKK 270, 18 Mar-15 Sep. 2016

HELSINGOR *D2* (3km NE Urban/Coastal) *56.04393,
12.60433* **Helsingør Camping Grønnehave,**
Strandalleen 2, 3000 Helsingør **tel 49 28 49 50 or
25 31 12 12; campingpladsen@helsingor.dk;
www.helsingorcamping.dk**

12 👫 wc ♨ ⚡ ♿ 🚿 ⊿ MSP 🍴 ▱ 🌳

Site in NE o'skts of town, twd Hornbæk. Site nr
beach o'looking channel to Sweden on E side of
rd. Foll sps on app or in town (beware: sp are sm
& low down). 2*, Med, pt shd, EHU (10A) DKK30;
cooking facs; 25% statics; phone. *"10 min walk to
Hamlet's castle; 20 min walk to town & stn; gd train
service to Copenhagen; max stay 14 days 15 Jun-15
Aug; Baltic ships w/end mid-Aug; v busy/cr high ssn."*
DKK 217 2019

HELSINGOR *D2* (13km SSW Coastal) *55.93949,
12.51643* **Niva Camping,** Sølyst Allé 14, 2290 Nivå
**tel 49 14 52 26; nivaacamping@post8.tele.dk;
www.nivaacamping.dk**

🐴 (htd) 👫 wc ♨ ⚡ ⊿ MSP 🍴 ▱ 🌳 800m

Take coast rd bet Copenhagen & Helsingør. Fr N foll
sp to Nivå, & site 500m fr main rd, sp. Fr S site 2km
after vill. 2*, Lge, mkd, hdstg, pt shd, pt sl, EHU (16A);
bbq; cooking facs; twin axles; TV; 10% statics; Eng
spkn; adv bkg acc; ccard acc; fishing adj; games rm;
CKE. *"Conv Helsingborg ferry, Copenhagen, Kronborg
Castle (Hamlet); excel san facs; vg location; quiet; best
site in Zealand; excel help; upper level pitches quietest
& coolest if hot."* **DKK 240, 31 Mar-30 Sep.** 2019

HELSINGOR *D2* (10km NW Urban) *56.08104,
12.51348* **Skibstrup Camping,** Stormlugen 20, 3140
Ålsgårde **tel 49 70 99 71; info@skibstrup-camping.dk;
www.skibstrup-camping.dk**

🐴 👫 wc ♨ ⚡ ♿ 🚿 ⊿ MSP ✕ 🍴 nr ▱ 🛶 ⛱ 🌳 500m

Fr Helsingør take N coast rd to Ålsgårde; then foll
site sp. 3*, Lge, shd, EHU (10A) DKK35; cooking facs;
TV; 10% statics; phone; adv bkg acc; ccard acc.
*"Pleasant site amongst trees; conv for ferry &
Copenhagen."* **DKK 150, 1 Apr-31 Oct.** 2015

HILLEROD *D2* (1km SW Urban) *55.9246, 12.2941*
Hillerød Camping, Blytækkervej 18, 3400 Hillerød
**tel 48 26 48 54; info@hillerodcamping.dk;
www.hillerodcamping.dk**

🐴 DKK10 👫 wc ♨ ⚡ ♿ 🚿 ⊿ MSP ✕ 🍴 (H) nr ▱ 🌳

Fr Roskilde or Copenhagen on A16 twd Hillerød,
take 1st L at traff lts sp Hillerød & Frederiksborg
Slot Rv233. Site in town cent, not well sp. Med, pt
shd, pt sl, EHU (13A) DKK40 (long lead poss req); gas;
cooking facs; sw nr; TV; phone; bus, train nr; Eng spkn;
adv bkg acc; ccard acc; bike hire; CCI. *"Frederiksborg
castle in town cent; gd base for N Sealand; 30 min
by train to Copenhagen; v helpful, charming owner;
common/dining rm; pleasant, well-run site; excel,
new san facs 2010; no mkd pitch, but owner positions
o'fits carefully; many personal touches - eg courtyard
with herbs, fruit trees, candles & torches; best site;
owner takes pride in environment and quality of facs."*
DKK 250, 4 Apr-20 Sept. 2019

HIRTSHALS *C1* (5km SW Coastal) *57.55507, 9.93254*
Tornby Strand Camping, Strandvejen 13, 9850
Tornby **tel 98 97 78 77; mail@tornbystrand.dk;
www.tornbystrand.dk**

12 🐴 DKK5 wc ♨ ⚡ ♿ 🚿 ⊿ MSP 🦋 ⊿ nr ▱ 🌳 sand 1km

Take rd 55 fr Hjørring twd Hirtshals. In 12km turn L
sp Tornby Strand & Camping, site on L in 200m. 3*,
Lge, pt shd, EHU (16A) DKK30; gas; TV; 75% statics;
phone; Eng spkn; adv bkg acc; CKE. *"Useful for ferries
to Kristiansand, Arendal, Faroe & Iceland; helpful
owner."* **DKK 254** 2016

HIRTSHALS *C1* (1.5km W Urban) *57.58650, 9.94583*
Hirtshals Camping, Kystvejen 6, 9850 Hirtshals
**tel 98 94 25 35; info@hirtshals-camping.dk;
www.dk-camp.dk/hirtshals**

🐴 DKK10 👫 wc ♨ ⚡ ♿ 🚿 ⊿ MSP 🦋 (H) nr ▱ 🌳 200m

Located 16km N of Hjørring. Turn L off rd 14 3km
SW of Hirtshals & site on L. Fr ferry foll sp town
cent, then site sp. 3*, Med, unshd, terr, EHU (10A)
DKK30; sw nr; TV; phone; bike hire; fishing 200m.
*"Open site on cliff top; san facs dated; friendly staff;
conv ferries; on coastal cycle path; late arr area; busy
but efficient; conv for NH."*
DKK 225, 25 Mar-31 Oct. 2016

HJORRING *C1* (14km W Urban) *57.47375, 9.80100*
Lønstrup Camping, Møllebakkevej 20, Lonstrup, 9800
Hjørring **tel 45 21 44 56 37; loenstrupcamping@
mail.dk; www.campingloenstrup.dk**

🐴 10DKK 👫 (htd) wc ♨ ⚡ ♿ 🚿 ⊿ MSP 🦋 🍴 ▱ 🌳 500m

Fr E39 take Exit 3 dir Hjørring for Rte 35 twd Rte 55.
Turn R onto Lonstrupvej. Foll sp to site. Med, mkd,
pt shd, EHU (10A) 35DKK; bbq; cooking facs; twin
axles; 30% statics; bus 200m; Eng spkn; adv bkg
acc; CCI. *"Vg site; friendly, helpful family owned; lge
units may be tight access; close to sm vill & coast."*
DKK 245, 28 Mar-29 Sep. 2019

DENMARK

HOLBAEK D3 (4km E Coastal) 55.71799, 11.76020
FDM Holbæk Fjord Camping, Sofiesminde Allé 1,
4300 Holbæk **tel 59 43 50 64; c-holbaek@fdm.dk**

12 🐕 DKK15 ♦♦(htd) WD ▲ 👶 ⚙ 🖥 🗑 MP 🦋 📶 ⊕ 🎣 🛒 ⛺
⚓(htd) 🏖

Fr Rv21 exit junc 20 (fr N) or junc 18 (fr S) & foll sp
to harbour. Turn R (E) at harbour - Munkholmvej.
Approx 1.5km along Munkholmvej, after traff lts,
turn L into Sofiesminde Allé dir marina. Site on R,
close to marina. 3*, Lge, hdg, mkd, pt shd, EHU (10A)
inc; gas; bbq; cooking facs; TV; 80% statics; phone; adv
bkg acc; ccard acc; sauna; golf nr; games area; bike
hire; games rm; fishing nr; watersports nr. *"Well-run
site in attractive position; helpful staff; pitches poss
tight lge o'fits; whirlpool; spa; clean san facs; no o'fits
over 10m high ssn; gd walks & cycle tracks."* **DKK 328,
H17.** **2015**

"There aren't many sites open at this time of year"

If you're travelling outside peak season
remember to call ahead to check site opening
dates – even if the entry says 'open all year'.

HORSENS B2 (6km W Rural/Coastal) 55.85928,
9.91747 **Husodde Strand Camping,** Husoddevej
85, 8700 Horsens **tel 75 65 70 60; camping@
husodde.dk; www.husodde-camping.dk**

12 🐕 DKK10 ♦♦ WD ▲ 👶 ⚙ 🖥 🗑 MP 🦋 ⊕ nr 🛒 nr ⛺ sand adj

Site sp to R of Horsens-Odder rd (451), foll rd to
fjord, site sp. 3*, Med, mkd, pt shd, pt sl, EHU (10A)
DKK35; bbq; cooking facs; TV; 10% statics; phone; Eng
spkn; fishing adj; CKE. *"Lovely location; lge pitches;
well-maintained, well-managed site; friendly welcome;
pool 3km; cycle tracks."* **DKK 238** **2015**

HVIDE SANDE A2 (7.6km S Coastal) 55.94975,
8.15030 **Nordsø Camping & Badeland,** Tingodden 3,
Årgab, 6960 Hvide Sande **tel 75 52 14 82;
info@dancamps.dk; www.dancamps.dk**

🐕 DKK20 ♦♦(htd) WD ▲ 👶 ⚙ 🖥 🗑 MP 🦋 📶 🍴 ⊕ 🎣 🛒 ⛺ 🛝
🏊(covrd, htd) 🗑 ⛱ sand 200m

Fr E20 take exit 73 onto rd 11 to Varde. Then take rd
181 twd Nymindegab & Hvide Sande. 3*, Lge, hdstg,
unshd, serviced pitches; EHU (10A) DKK30; TV;
10% statics; phone; adv bkg acc; fishing; waterslide;
tennis; sauna. *"Well-maintained facs; extra charge
seaview pitches; private san facs avail; vg."*
DKK 199, 15 Apr-31 Oct. **2016**

JELLING B3 (13km NW Rural) 55.83138, 9.29944
Topcamp Riis & Feriecenter, Østerhovedvej 43, Riis
7323 Give **tel 75 73 14 33; info@riisferiepark.dk;
www.riisferiepark.dk**

🐕 DKK20 ♦♦ WD ▲ 👶 ⚙ 🖥 🗑 🗑 MP 🦋 📶 🍴 ⊕ 🎣 🛒 ⛺ 🛝 🏊(htd) 🗑

Fr S exit E45 at junc 61, turn L & foll rd 28 for approx
8km. Turn R onto rd 441 for 15km, then turn R into
Østerhovedvej for 2km & turn L into site. Or fr N
on E45 exit junc 57, turn R & foll rd for 25km; turn
L & foll 442 for 500m; turn R into Østerhovedvej &
cont for 1.5km; turn R into site. 4*, Med, hdstg, mkd,
hdg, pt shd, serviced pitches; EHU (13A) inc; gas; bbq;
TV; 60% statics; phone; adv bkg acc; ccard acc; sauna;
fishing 3.5km; golf 4km; bike hire; games rm; jacuzzi;
waterslide; CKE. *"Attractive, well laid-out, well-run site
in beautiful countryside; jacuzzi; fitness cent; vg san
facs; no o'fits over 15m high ssn; conv for Legoland,
Safari Park, Center Mobilium museum in Billund, lakes
& E coast; excel; recep 0800-2200; friendly & relaxed;
spacious pitches."* **DKK 430, 19 Mar-25 Sep, H11.**
2019

KARISE D3 (5km S Rural) 55.27086, 12.22281
Lægårdens Camping, Vemmetoftevej 2A, Store
Spjellerup, 4653 Karise **tel 56 71 00 67; info@
laegaardenscamping.dk; www.laegaardens
camping.dk**

12 🐕 DKK10 ♦♦(htd) WD ▲ 🖥 🗑 MP ⊕ nr 🛒 ⛺ 3km

Turn S off rd 209 in Karise, site sp. 2*, Med, mkd, hdg,
pt shd, EHU DKK30; TV; 60% statics; Eng spkn; adv
bkg acc; CKE. **DKK 150** **2016**

"That's changed – Should I let the Club know?"

If you find something on site that's different
from the site entry, fill in a report and let us
know. See camc.com/europereport.

KOBENHAVN D3 (10km N Coastal) 55.74536,
12.58331 **Camping Charlottenlund Fort,** Strandvejen
144B, 2290 Charlottenlund **tel 39 62 36 88;
camping@gentofte.dk; www.campingcopenhagen.dk**

♦♦ WD ▲ 👶 ⚙ 🖥 🗑 MP 🍴 nr ⊕ nr 🛒 nr ⛱ sand

Take København-Helsingør coast rd O2/152, site on
seaside 2km N of Tuborg factory. Sm, mkd, hdstg,
shd, EHU (10A) metered; cooking facs; bus; Eng spkn;
adv bkg rec; ccard acc; CKE. *"Experimentarium Science
Park at Tuborg brewery; in grnds of old moated fort;
conv Copenhagen & Sweden; gd facs but inadequate
high ssn; quiet but noisy during mid-summer festivities;
friendly staff."* **DKK 260, 30 Apr-6 Sep.** **2019**

KOBENHAVN *D3* (9km W Urban) *55.67055, 12.43353* **DCU Absalon Camping,** Korsdalsvej 132, 2610 Rødovre **tel 36 41 06 00; copenhagen@dcu.dk; www.camping-absalon.dk**

🏕12 🐕 DKK23 👥 (htd) 🚿 ⚒ ♿ 🖥 ✗ MSP 📶 ① nr 🎣 🛒 🎡 🛶

Fr E55/E20/E47 exit junc 24 dir København, site on L in 1km, sp. Or fr København foll A156 W for 9km. Sp Rødovre then Brøndbyøster, shortly after this site sp to R at traff lts; ent on L after 100m down side rd, sp. 2*, V lge, hdg, mkd, unshd, pt sl, EHU (10-16A) DKK30 or metered + conn fee; gas; bbq; cooking facs; twin axles; TV; 10% statics; bus/train nr; Eng spkn; adv bkg acc; ccard acc; games area; golf 10km; games rm; CKE. *"Well located nr Brøndbyøster rlwy stn & bus Copenhagen (rail tickets fr recep); some pitches unrel in wet & dusty when dry; vg, modern san facs; office clsd 1200-1400 LS; htd pool 300m; sep area for c'vans & m'vans; helpful staff; cycle rte to city; excel site; v well run; fitness rm; outdoor chess; attrac & boat trips can be booked; muddy when wet."* **DKK 260**   2018

KOLDING *B3* (16km E Coastal) *55.46777, 9.67972* **Gammel Ålbo Camping,** Gammel Aalbovej 30, 6092 Sønder Stenderup **tel 75 57 11 16; camping@ gl-aalbo.dk; www.gl-aalbo.dk**

🏕12 🐕 👥 (htd) 🚿 ⚒ ♿ 🖥 ✗ MSP 🦋 🛒 🎣 shgl adj

Foll rd SE fr Kolding to Agtrup then on to Sønder Bjert & Sønder Stenderup. Foll site sp thro vill twd coast, site at end of rd. 3*, Med, hdg, hdstg, pt shd, terr, EHU (16A) DKK38.50; cooking facs; 10% statics; Eng spkn; fishing; boat hire; CKE. *"Well-kept, relaxing site o'looking Lillebælt; skin-diving; v cr in high ssn."* **DKK 224**   2015

KOLDING *B3* (5km S Urban) *55.46290, 9.47290* **Kolding City Camp,** Vonsildvej 19, 6000 Kolding **tel 75 52 13 88; info@koldingcitycamp.dk; www.koldingcitycamp.dk**

🏕12 🐕 DKK20 👥 (htd) 🚿 ⚒ ♿ 🖥 ✗ MSP 📶 ① nr 🛒 🎡

E45 (Flensbury-Frederikshavn) take exit 65 at Kolding Syd twrds Kolding; at 1st traff lts turn R site 800m on L. 3*, Lge, pt shd, pt sl, EHU (10A) DKK40; gas; bbq; cooking facs; TV; phone; bus to town; Eng spkn; adv bkg acc; ccard acc; fishing 5km; tennis; CKE. *"Friendly & v quiet; conv NH Legoland; htd covrd pool 3km; vg san facs; gd site; level pitches; private san facs avail; full kitchen facs."* **DKK 301**   2019

KORSOR *C3* (10km SE Rural) *55.28991, 11.2649* **Boeslunde Camping,** Rennebjergvej 110, 4242 Boeslunde **tel 58 14 02 08; info@campinggaarden.dk; www.campinggaarden.dk**

🐕 DKK10 👥 🚿 ⚒ ♿ 🖥 ✗ MSP 🦋 🍽 🛒 🎡 🏖 🐕 1.5km

Take rd 265 S out of Korsør & in 8km, bef Boeslunde at camping sp, turn R. Site on L in 2km. 3*, Med, pt shd, pt sl, EHU DKK30 (long lead poss req); gas; TV (pitch); phone; adv bkg acc; CKE. *"Gd size, grassy pitches; well kept; gate barrier."* **DKK 235, 1 Apr-1 Oct.**   2018

MIDDELFART *B3* (11km NE Coastal) *55.51948, 9.85025* **Vejlby Fed Camping,** Rigelvej 1, 5500 Vejlby Fed **tel 64 40 24 20; mail@vejlbyfed.dk; www.vejlbyfed.dk**

🐕 DKK20 👥 🚿 ⚒ ♿ 🖥 ✗ MSP 📶 🍽 🎣 🛒 🎡 🛶 (htd) 🏖 🐕 sand adj

Exit E20 junc 57 or 58. Site sp in Vejlby Fed, NE fr Middelfart dir Bogense, on coast. 4*, Lge, mkd, pt shd, EHU (10A) DKK39; cooking facs; 30% statics; phone; Eng spkn; adv bkg acc; sauna; fishing; tennis; boating; CKE. **DKK 430, 15 Mar-14 Sep.**   2019

MIDDELFART *B3* (5km NW Rural) *55.51694, 9.68225* **Gals Klint Camping,** Galsklintvej 11, 5500 Middelfart **tel 64 41 20 59; mail@galsklint.dk; www.galsklint.dk**

🐕 👥 (htd) 🚿 ⚒ ♿ 🖥 ✗ MSP 🦋 ① 🎣 🛒 🎡 🐕 shgl adj

Fr W on E20 take rd 161. At 2 traff lts turn L & cross Little Belt Bdge. In 300m turn R into Galsklintvej & foll sp. 3*, Lge, hdg, mkd, pt shd, EHU (16A) DKK28; bbq; cooking facs; 10% statics; Eng spkn; adv bkg acc; ccard acc; boat hire; fishing; CKE. *"Site surrounded by forest; gd cycling/walking; vg; well run mod facs shoreside next woodland."* **DKK 208, 18 Mar-3 Oct.**   2016

NYBORG *C3* (4km N Coastal) *55.35853, 10.78660* **Gronnehave Strand,** Regstrupvej 83, 5800 Nyborg **tel 65 36 15 50; info@gronnehave.dk; www.gronnehave.dk**

🐕 👥 (htd) 🚿 ⚒ 🖥 ✗ MSP 🦋 📶 🛒 nr 🎡 🐕 adj

10 mins N on Skaboeshusevej - sp. Fr E20 junc 46 turn N and foll sp. 3*, Med, mkd, unshd, terr, EHU (10A) DKK36; TV; Eng spkn; games area. *"Friendly owner; gd views; bdge to Zeeland; vg."* **DKK 261, 29 Mar-23 Sep.**   2019

NYBORG *C3* (3km SE Coastal) *55.30457, 10.82453* **Nyborg Strandcamping,** Hjejlevej 99, 5800 Nyborg **tel 65 31 02 56; mail@strandcamping.dk; www.strandcamping.dk**

🐕 👥 ✗ 🚿 ⚒ ♿ 🖥 ✗ MSP 📶 ① nr 🎣 🛒 🎡 🐕 sand adj

Exit E20 at junc 44. Turn N, site sp in 1km. 3*, Lge, mkd, pt shd, EHU (10A) metered; gas; TV; 50% statics; phone; Eng spkn; adv bkg acc; fishing; golf 1km; CKE. *"Conv m'way, rlwy & ferry; excel views of bdge; gd facs; gd site; well difined pitches next to beach."* **DKK 256, 13 Apr-21 Sep.**   2019

NYBORG *C3* (13km S Rural) *55.23693, 10.8080* **Tårup Stand Camping,** Lersey Allé 25, Tårup Strand, 5871 Frørup **tel 65 37 11 99; mail@taarupstrandcamping. dk; www.taarupstrandcamping.dk**

🐕 👥 (htd) 🚿 ⚒ ♿ 🖥 ✗ MSP 🦋 🛒 🎡 🐕 shgl

S fr Nyborg take 163 twds Svendborg; after 6.5km turn L sp Tårup. In 2.7km turn L sp Tårup Strand. Site 1.5km on R. 3*, Med, mkd, EHU (6-10A) DKK26; TV; 70% statics; phone; adv bkg acc; ccard acc; games rm; CKE. *"Quiet family site; excel views of bdge; fishing; excel site."* **DKK 222, 4 Apr-21 Sep.**   2019

DENMARK

ODENSE *C3 (5km S Rural) 55.36966, 10.39316* **DCU Camping Odense,** Odensevej 102, 5260 Odense **tel 66 11 47 02; odense@dcu.dk; www.camping-odense.dk**

12 🐕 DKK23 ♂♀(htd) WD ♨ ⚌ ♿ 🖥 🗑 MSP 🦋 📶 nr 🍴 🏛 🛶 ⚽

Exit E20 junc 51 foll sp 'centrum' (Stenlosevej). After rndabt site on L just after 3rd set traff lts. Ent to R of petrol stn. 3*, Lge, mkd, hdg, pt shd, EHU (16A) DKK30; gas; bbq; cooking facs; twin axles; TV; 10% statics; phone; bus; Eng spkn; adv bkg acc; ccard acc; games area; games rm; CKE. *"Hans Christian Andersen's hse; many attractions; excel, friendly, family-run site; busy high ssn & facs stretched; easy bus access to town cent; lovely, easy cycle rte into town cent; excel san fac; pitches tight for larger units; quick stop area for MH; sep c'van & MH areas; pitches muddy when wet; excel."* **DKK 380** **2018**

ODENSE *C3 (11km W Rural) 55.3894, 10.2475* **Campingpladsen Blommenslyst,** Middelfartvej 494, 5491 Blommenslyst **tel 65 96 76 41; info@ blommelyst-camping.dk; www.blommenslyst-camping.dk**

🐕 DKK10 ♂♀(htd) WD ♨ ♿ 🖥 🗑 MSP 🦋 🍴 🏛

Exit E20 onto 161 (junc 53); sp 'Odense/Blommenslyst', site on R after 2km; lge pink Camping sp on side of house. 2*, Sm, shd, pt sl, EHU (4A) DKK30; 10% statics; bus; Eng spkn; adv bkg req; CKE. *"Picturesque setting round sm lake; gd, clean, rustic facs; welcoming owners; frequent bus to town outside site; excel; lovely site."* **DKK 168, 5 Jan-20 Dec.** **2019**

RANDERS *B2 (8km SW Rural) 56.44984, 9.95287* **Randers City Camp,** Hedevej 9, Fladbro, 8920 Randers **tel 45 29 47 36 55; info@randerscitycamp.dk; www.randerscitycamp.dk**

12 🐕 DKK10 ♂♀(htd) WD ♨ ⚌ ♿ 🖥 🗑 MSP 🦋 📶 🍴 🛶 (covrd, htd)

Take exit 40 fr E45 & turn twd Randers. Approx 100m fr m'way turn R at traff lts dir Langå. Site clearly sp in 3km & also sp fr rd 16. 3*, Lge, mkd, pt shd, terr, EHU (10A) DKK35; bbq; cooking facs; twin axles; TV; 50% statics; phone; bus 0.5km; Eng spkn; adv bkg acc; ccard acc; games rm; golf adj; fishing; CKE. *"On heather hills with view of Nørreå valley; rec arr early for pitch with view; golf course; Randers tropical zoo; ideal for walkers, cyclist & runners; fishing; gd."* **DKK 239** **2017**

RIBE *B3 (2km SE Rural) 55.31725, 8.75952* **Parking Storkesøen,** Haulundvej 164, 6760 Ribe **tel 75 41 04 11; info@storkesoen.dk; www.storkesoen.dk**

12 ♂♀ WD ♨ ♿ ⚽

Fr S on rte 11, turn R at 1st rndabt onto rte 24 & R at next rndabt. Site 100m on R, sp fishing. Fr S on rte 24, at 1st rndabt after rlwy turn L, site 200m on R. M'vans only - check in at fishing shop on R. Sm, hdstg, unshd, EHU (5A/16A) inc; own san req; lake fishing. *"Picturesque, quiet site o'looking fishing lakes; walking dist Denmark's oldest city; m'vans & c'vans acc, ideal NH; fishing shop; vg facs."* **DKK 140** **2016**

RIBE *B3 (2.4km NNW Rural) 55.34115, 8.76506* **Ribe Camping,** Farupvej 2, 6760 Ribe **tel 75 41 07 77; info@ribecamping.dk; www.ribecamping.dk**

12 🐕 DKK15 ♂♀(htd) ♨ ⚌ ♿ 🖥 🗑 MSP 🦋 📶 ⚽ 🍴 🏛 🛶 (htd)

Fr S foll A11 by-pass W of Ribe to traff lts N of town; turn W off A11 at traff lts; site 500m on R. Fr N (Esbjerg ferry) to Ribe, turn R at traff lts sp Farup. Site on R, sp. 3*, Lge, pt shd, serviced pitches; EHU (10A) DKK35; gas; cooking facs; TV; 10% statics; phone; adv bkg acc; ccard acc; games rm; Quickstop o'night facs; CKE. *"Ribe oldest town in Denmark; much historical interest; helpful, friendly staff; well-run; excel, modern san facs; conv Esbjerg ferry."* **DKK 271** **2016**

RINGKØBING *A2 (5km E Rural) 56.08856, 8.31659* **Ringkøbing Camping,** Herningvej 105, 6950 Ringkøbing **tel 97 32 04 20; info@ringkobing camping.dk; www.ringkøbingcamping.dk**

🐕 DKK10 ♂♀ ♨ ♿ 🖥 MSP 🦋 🍴 🏖 sand 3km

Take rd 15 fr Ringkøbing dir Herning, site on L. 3*, Med, hdg, mkd, pt shd, EHU (10A) DKK29; gas; TV; phone; adv bkg acc; Quickstop o'night facs. *"Beautiful site in mixed forest; friendly welcome; excel facs; gd walks; 3km to fjord; 14km to sea."* **DKK 226, 1 Apr-30 Sep.** **2016**

ROSKILDE *D3 (4km N Rural) 55.67411, 12.07955* **Roskilde Camping,** Baunehøjvej 7-9, 4000 Veddelev **tel 46 75 79 96; mail@roskildecamping.dk; www.roskildecamping.dk**

♂♀(htd) WD ♨ ⚌ ♿ 🖥 🗑 MSP 🦋 📶 🕐 🍴 🏛 🏖 shgl

Leave rd 21/23 at junc 11 & turn N on rd 6 sp Hillerød. Turn R onto rd 02 (E ring rd); then rejoin 6; (watch for camping sp). At traff lts with camping sp turn L twds city & foll site sp. 3*, Lge, mkd, pt shd, pt sl, EHU (10A) DKK30; own san req; gas; TV; Eng spkn; adv bkg acc; ccard acc; games rm; watersports; CKE. *"Beautiful views over fjord; nr Viking Ship Museum (a must) - easy parking; beautiful Cathedral; excel rest & shop open 0800-2000; bus service to stn, frequent trains to Copenhagen; ltd flat pitches; lovely site; immac, new state of the art san facs block with card for ent (2014); v welcoming & helpful staff."* **DKK 225, 31 Mar-23 Sep.** **2019**

RY *B2 (4km NW Rural) 56.10388, 9.74555* **Birkede Camping,** Lyngvej 14, 8680 Ry **tel 86 89 13 55; info@birkhede.dk; www.birkhede.dk**

🐕 ♂♀ WD ♨ ⚌ ♿ 🖥 🗑 MSP 🦋 📶 🍴 🍴 🏛 🛶 (htd)

Fr S on rd 52 exit onto rd 445 to Ry, then foll sp N on rd dir Laven. Turn R in 1km to site on lakeside. Clearly sp in cent of Ry. 3*, Lge, mkd, pt shd, pt sl, EHU (10A) metered + conn fee; gas; cooking facs; TV; phone; Eng spkn; adv bkg acc; bike hire; golf 10km; fishing; boat hire; games rm; CKE. *"Gd site."* **DKK 260, 11 Apr-21 Sep.** **2019**

RY *B2* (7km NW Rural) *56.12421, 9.71055* **Terrassen Camping,** Himmelbjergvej 9a, 8600 Laven **tel 86 84 13 01; info@terrassen.dk; www.terrassen.dk**

🐕 DKK15 ♂♀ WC ♨ ♿ 🚿 ⚊ / MSP 🦋 ⌖ ⊕ nr 🛒 nr 🏕 ✂ 🏊(htd)

In Silkeborg take Århus rd 15 to Linå. In Linå turn R for Laven. In Laven turn R parallel to lake; site up hill on R in 300m. Sharp turn R into ent. 4*, Lge, pt shd, terr, EHU (10A) DKK32; gas; sw; TV; 15% statics; phone; adv bkg acc; ccard acc; games area; sauna; fishing. *"Excel views of lake & woods; pet zoo; British owner; Jutland's lake district."* **DKK 268, 11 Apr-14 Sep.**
2019

SAEBY *C1* (3km N Coastal) *57.35498, 10.51026* **Hedebo Strandcamping,** Frederikshavnsvej 108, 9300 Sæby **tel 98 46 14 49; info@hedebocamping.dk; www.hedebocamping.dk**

🐕 ♂♀(htd) WC ♨ ♿ 🚿 ⚊ / MSP 🦋 ⌖ Y ⊕ ⊿ 🛒 🏕 🏊(htd) 🛶 adj

Sp on rd 180. 3*, Lge, mkd, hdg, unshd, EHU (10A) DKK40; bbq; cooking facs; 60% statics; phone; bus adj; Eng spkn; adv bkg acc; CKE.
DKK 250, 31 Mar-7 Sep.
2016

SAEBY *C1* (3.7km N Coastal) *57.36000, 10.50861* **Svalereden Camping And Hytteby,** Frederikshavnsvej 112b, 9900 Frederikshavn **tel 98 46 19 37; info@svaleredencamping.dk; svaleredencamping.dk**

12 🐕 ♂♀(htd) ♨ ♿ 🚿 ⚊ / MSP 🦋 ⌖ 🛒 🏕 🛶

Take coastal rte 180, exit 13 and 12. Site bet Frederikshavn & Saeby. 3*, Med, EHU (16A); bbq; twin axles; TV; bus; Eng spkn; adv bkg acc; ccard acc; games area; CKE. *"Conv for Frederikshavn-Gothenburg ferry; outstanding san facs; excel."*
DKK 280
2017

SAKSKOBING *C3* (0.8km W Urban) *54.79840, 11.64070* **Sakskøbing Camping,** Saxes Allé 15, 4990 Sakskøbing **tel 45 54 70 45 66 or 45 54 70 47 57; sax@sport.dk; www.saxcamping.dk**

♂♀ ♨ ♿ ⚊ / 🦋 ⊕ nr 🛒

N fr Rødby exit E47 at Sakskøbing junc 46, turn L twd town: at x-rds turn R. In 300m turn R into Saxes Allé, site sp. 3*, Med, hdg, mkd, pt shd, EHU (6A) DKK30; gas; cooking facs; phone; adv bkg acc; fishing. *"Conv for Rødby-Puttgarden ferry; pool 100m; gd touring base; excel site in pretty area; v welcoming & friendly."* **DKK 194, 15 Mar-28 Sep.**
2019

SILKEBORG *B2* (12km W Rural) *56.14869, 9.39697* **DCU Hesselhus Camping,** Moselundsvej 28, Funder, 8600 Silkeborg **tel 86 86 50 66; hesselhus@dcu.dk; www.camping-hesselhus.dk**

12 🐕 DKK20 ♂♀ WC ♨ ♿ 🚿 ⚊ / MSP 🦋 🛒 🏕 🏊(htd)

Take rd 15 W fr Silkeborg twd Herning; after 6km bear R, sp Funder Kirkeby, foll camping sps for several km to site. 3*, Lge, mkd, pt shd, EHU DKK35; gas; TV; 40% statics; phone; adv bkg acc; CKE. *"Great family site; beautiful natural surroundings; 1 hr fr Legoland; busy at w'ends."* **DKK 144**
2016

SINDAL *C1* (2km W Rural) *57.46785, 10.17851* **Sindal Camping,** Hjørringvej 125, 9870 Sindal **tel 98 93 65 30; info@sindal-camping.dk; www.sindal-camping.dk**

12 🐕 DKK10 ♂♀ WC ♨ ♿ 🚿 ⚊ / MSP 🦋 ⌖ 🛒 🏕 🏊 🛁

On rte 35 due W of Frederikshavn on S side of rd. 3*, Lge, mkd, hdg, pt shd, EHU (16A) metered; gas; bbq; twin axles; red long stay; TV; 50% statics; phone; Eng spkn; adv bkg acc; games area; bike hire; golf 3km; CKE. *"Train & bus v conv; lovely beaches 30 mins; excel modern san facs; helpful owners; hg rec; excel."* **DKK 220**
2017

SKAELSKOR *C3* (1km NW Rural) *55.25648, 11.28461* **Skælskør Nør Camping,** Kildehusvej 1, 4230 Skælskør **tel 58 19 43 84; kildehuset@cafeer.dk; www.campnor.dk**

12 ♂♀ WC ♨ ♿ 🚿 ⚊ / Y ⊕ 🛒 nr 🏕 🛶 shgl 2km

Exit E20 junc 42 sp Korsør. Take rd 265 S sp Skælskør, site on L just bef town, nr Kildehuset Rest. 4*, Med, mkd, unshd, EHU (10A) DKK35; cooking facs; TV; 80% statics; phone; Eng spkn; adv bkg acc; ccard acc; CKE. *"Lovely location by lake in nature reserve; woodland walks; excel facs; helpful owners."* **DKK 221**
2018

SVENDBORG *C3* (7km SE Coastal) *55.0537, 10.6304* **Svendborg Sund Camping (formerly Vindebyøre),** Vindebyørevej 52, Tåsinge, 5700 Svendborg **tel 21 72 09 13 or 62 22 54 25; maria@svendborgsund-camping.dk; www.svendborgsund-camping.dk**

🐕 DKK25 ♂♀(htd) WC ♨ ♿ 🚿 ⚊ / MSP 🦋 ⌖ ⊿ 🛒 🏕 ✂ 🛶 sand

Cross bdge fr Svendborg (dir Spodsbjerg) to island of Tåsinge on rd 9; at traff lts over bdge turn L, then immed 1st L to Vindeby, thro vill, L at sp to site. 3*, Med, pt shd, pt sl, EHU (16A) DKK35; bbq; cooking facs; TV; 10% statics; phone; adv bkg acc; ccard acc; boat hire; bike hire; CKE. *"V helpful owners; swipe card for facs; excel touring base & conv ferries to islands; beautiful views; o'night area; immac, excel site; narr sandy beach; gd size pitches and san facs."* **DKK 250, 3 Apr-27 Sep.**
2019

TARM *A2* (1.5km S Rural) *55.89309, 8.51278* **Tarm Camping,** Vardevej 79, 6880 Tarm **tel 30 12 66 35; tarm.camping@pc.dk; www.tarm-camping.dk**

🐕 ♂♀ WC ♨ ♿ 🚿 ⚊ / MSP 🏕 🏊

Fr rd 11 S of Tarm take exit twds Tarm; immed turn R, site on L in 500m, sp. 3*, Med, mkd, pt shd, EHU (10A) DKK30; gas; cooking facs; 10% statics; phone; Eng spkn; adv bkg acc; CKE. *"Friendly & helpul staff; vg."* **DKK 168, 27 Mar-4 Oct.**
2015

DENMARK

THISTED *B2* (1km SE Coastal) *56.95226, 8.71286*
Thisted Camping, Iversensvej 3, 7700 Thisted
**tel 97 92 16 35; mail@thisted-camping.dk;
www.thisted-camping.dk**

🔢12 ♿ 🚿 WC 🏕 ♨ ⚲ 🗑 ♒ MSP 🦋 ☕ 🍽 🛒 ⚓ 🛶

On side of fjord on o'skts of Thisted, sp fr rd 11.
3*, Med, unshd, pt sl, EHU (16A) DKK30; gas; bbq;
cooking facs; TV; Eng spkn; adv bkg acc; fishing;
games rm; CKE. *"Attractive views fr some pitches; nice,
friendly, helpful, well run site; grnd soft aft heavy rain;
easy walk to town; gd facs."* **DKK 240**   **2016**

THORSMINDE *A2* (0.5km N Coastal) *56.37626,
8.12251* **Thorsminde Camping,** Klitrosevej 4, 6990
Thorsminde **tel 20 45 19 76; mail@thorsminde
camping.dk; www.thorsmindecamping.dk**

♿ WC 🏕 ♨ ⚲ 🗑 ♒ MSP 🦋 🍺 🛒 ⚓ 🛶 (covrd) 🛟 300m

On rd 16/28 to Ulfborg, turn W twd coast & Husby
Klitplantage. Turn N onto rd 181 to Thorsminde, 1st
turn R past shops, site sp. 3*, Lge, unshd, EHU (10A)
DKK30; cooking facs; TV; 10% statics; phone; adv
bkg acc; sauna. *"Pleasant site; helpful staff; excel sea
fishing."* **DKK 200, 8 Apr-23 Oct.**   **2016**

TONDER *B3* (5km W Rural) *54.93746, 8.80008*
Møgeltønder Camping, Sønderstrengvej 2,
Møgeltonder, 6270 Tønder **tel 74 73 84 60; info@
mogeltondercamping.dk; www.mogeltonder
camping.dk**

🔢12 🐕 DKK10 ♿(htd) WC 🏕 ♨ ⚲ 🗑 ♒ MSP 🦋 ☕ 🛒 ⚓ 🛶(htd)

N fr Tønder thro Møgeltønder (avoid cobbled main
rd by taking 2nd turning sp Møgeltønder) site sp
on L in 200m outside vill. 3*, Lge, mkd, pt shd, EHU
(10A) DKK25; bbq; cooking facs; TV; 25% statics;
phone; Eng spkn; adv bkg acc; CKE. *"Gd cycle paths;
beautiful & romantic little vill adj; Ribe worth visit
(43km); friendly owner."* **DKK 234**   **2019**

VEJERS STRAND *A3* (12km S Coastal) *55.54403,
8.13386* **Hvidbjerg Strand Feriepark,** Hvidbjerg
Strandvej 27, 6857 Blåvand **tel 75 27 90 40; info@
hvidbjerg.dk; www.hvidbjerg.dk**

🐕 DKK30 ♿ 🏕 ♨ ⚲ 🗑 ♒ MSP 🦋 🍽 🍺 🛒 ⚓ ✏ 🛶 (covrd, htd) 🛟 sand

Exit rd 11 at Varde on minor rd, sp Blåvand, turn
L at sp to Hvidbjerg Strand 2km; site 1km on L.
5*, V lge, hdg, pt shd, serviced pitches; EHU (6A)
inc; gas; cooking facs; TV; 10% statics; phone; adv
bkg acc; ccard acc; tennis; games area. *"Superb
facs; excel family site; young groups not acc."*
DKK 453, 7 Apr-22 Oct.   **2019**

VEJLE *B3* (2km ENE Urban) *55.7151, 9.5611*
Vejle City Camping, Helligkildevej 5, 7100 Vejle
**tel 75 82 33 35; info@vejlecitycamping.dk;
www.vejlecitycamping.dk**

🐕 DKK5 ♿ WC 🏕 ♨ ⚲ 🗑 ♒ MSP 🦋 🍺 🛒 ⚓ 🛶 sand 2km

Exit E45 m'way at Vejle N. Turn L twd town. In 250m
turn L at camping sp & 'stadion' sp. 3*, Med,
pt sl, EHU (6-10A) DKK30; cooking facs; red long stay;
TV; phone; Eng spkn; adv bkg acc; ccard acc. *"Site adj
woods & deer enclosure; quickstop o'night facs; walk to
town; conv Legoland (26km); lovely well kept site; helpful
friendly staff."* **DKK 255, 19 Mar-25 Sep.**   **2016**

VIBORG *B2* (15km N Rural/Coastal) *56.53452,
9.33117* **Hjarbæk Fjord Camping,** Hulager 2,
Hjarbæk, 8831 Løgstrup **tel 86 64 23 09; info@
hjarbaek.dk; www.hjarbaek.dk**

🔢12 🐕 DKK10 ♿(htd) WC 🏕 ♨ ⚲ 🗑 ♒ MSP 🦋 ☕ 🍽 🛒 ⚓ 🛶 🛟 sand adj

Take A26 (Viborg to Skive) to Løgstrup, turn R (N)
to Hjarbæk, keep R thro vill, site sp. 3*, Lge, mkd, pt
shd, terr, EHU metered; gas; bbq; cooking facs; TV;
3% statics; phone; Eng spkn; adv bkg acc; ccard acc;
lake fishing; CKE. *"Friendly & well-run; gd views; close
to attractive vill & harbour."* **DKK 299**   **2019**

"I like to fill in the reports as I travel from site to site"

You'll find report forms at the back of this
guide, or you can fill them in online at
camc.com/europereport.

VINDERUP *B2* (6.7km ESE Rural) *56.45901, 8.86918*
Sevel Camping, Halallé 6, Sevel, 7830 Vinderup
**tel 97 44 85 50; mail@sevelcamping.dk;
www.sevelcamping.dk**

🔢12 🐕 DKK6 ♿(htd) WC 🏕 ♨ 🗑 ♒ MSP 🦋 🍺 nr ⚓ nr 🛶

Fr Struer on rd 513. In Vinderup L nr church then
R past Vinderup Camping. Site sp on R on edge
of vill. 2*, Sm, hdg, pt shd, pt sl, EHU (16A) DKK30;
cooking facs; 10% statics; Eng spkn; adv bkg acc; ccard
acc; CKE. *"Family-run site; pleasant, helpful owners;
picturesque, historic area."* **DKK 182**   **2016**

VORDINGBORG *D3* (3.6km W Urban/Coastal)
55.00688, 11.87509 **Ore Strand Camping,** Orevej
145, 4760 Vordingborg **tel 55 77 8822; mail@
orestrandcamping.dk; www.orestrandcamping.dk**

♿ WC 🏕 ⚲ 🗑 ♒ MSP 🦋 🛒 ⚓ 🛶 🛟 shgl adj

Fr E55/47 exit junc 41 onto rd 59 to Vordingborg
7km. Rd conts as 153 sp Sakskøbing alongside
rlwy. Turn R at site sp into Ore, site on L. 3*, Med,
pt shd, EHU (6A) inc; cooking facs; phone; Eng spkn;
adv bkg acc; ccard acc. *"Gd touring cent; fine views
if nr water; interesting old town; poss busy san facs."*
DKK 170, 1 Apr - 1. Oct.   **2019**

AERO ISLAND

MARSTAL *C3 (2km S Urban/Coastal) 54.84666, 10.51823* **Marstal Camping,** Eghovedvej 1, 5960 Marstal **tel 63 52 63 69; mail@marstalcamping.dk; www.marstalcamping.dk**

12 ⌂ DKK15 ♻ wc ♿ 🚿 💧 🛒 ⚡ MSP ⊤ nr ⊕ nr 🔥 🏔

Fr Ærøskobing ferry to E end of Ærø Island, thro town of Marstal & turn R at harbour twd sailing club; site adj to club. 3*, Med, mkd, pt shd, EHU (16A) DKK48; bbq; TV; 10% statics; phone; adv bkg acc; ccard acc; CKE. **DKK 160**   **2016**

BORNHOLM ISLAND

GUDHJEM *A1 (2km S Coastal) 55.19566, 14.98602* **Sannes Familiecamping,** Melstedvej 39, 3760 Melsted **tel 56 48 52 11; sannes@familiecamping.dk; www.familiecamping.dk**

♻ ⌂ wc ♿ 🚿 💧 🛒 ⚡ MSP 🦋 ⌗ ⊕ nr 🔥 🏔 🛶 (htd) 🏊 ⌂ sand adj

SW fr Gudhjem on rd 158, in 2km site on L. Pass other sites. NB: Bornholm Is can be reached by ferry fr Sassnitz in Germany or Ystad in Sweden. 4*, Med, mkd, hdstg, pt shd, terr, EHU (6A) DKK30; gas; TV; 10% statics; phone; Eng spkn; adv bkg acc; ccard acc; bike hire; fishing; sauna; fitness rm; CKE. *"Friendly & helpful staff; gd cycle paths in area; bus service fr site."* **DKK 270, 1 Apr-18 Sep.**   **2016**

NEXO *A1 (5.5km S Urban/Coastal) 55.02895, 15.11130* **FDM Camping Balka Strand,** Klynevej 6, Snogebæk, 3730 Nexø **tel 56 48 80 74; c-balka@fdm.dk; www.balka.fdmcamping.dk**

⌂ DKK15 (htd) wc 🚿 💧 🛒 ⚡ MSP 🦋 ⌗ ⊕ nr 🔥 🏔 ⌂ sand 200m

Fr ferry at Rønne on rd 38 to Nexø, foll sp to site N of Snogebæk. 3*, Lge, mkd, pt shd, EHU (6A) DKK49; bbq; cooking facs; TV; 10% statics; adv bkg acc; ccard acc; windsurfing 1km; fishing 500m; games area; bike hire; golf 5km. *"Superb beach; vg touring base Bornholm Is."* **DKK 217, 25 Apr-13 Sep.**   **2016**

RONNE *A1 (1km S Coastal) 55.08978, 14.70565* **Galløkken Camping,** Strandvejen 4, 3700 Rønne **tel 56 95 23 20; info@gallokken.dk; www.gallokken.dk**

⌂ ♻ (htd) wc 🚿 💧 🛒 ⚡ MSP 🦋 ⌗ ⊕ nr 🔥 🏔 ⌂ sand 200m

Fr Rønne cent foll dir airport, site well sp. 3*, Med, mkd, hdg, pt shd, EHU (13A) DKK31; bbq; cooking facs; TV; 10% statics; adv bkg acc; bike hire; games rm; tennis 1km. *"Lovely location; private san facs avail; gd, modern san facs."* **DKK 200, 1 May-31 Aug.**   **2016**

LANGELAND ISLAND

LOHALS *C3 (0.4km W Urban) 55.13383, 10.90578* **Lohals Camping,** Birkevej 11, 5953 Lohals **tel 62 55 14 60; mail@lohalscamping.dk; www.lohalscamping.dk**

12 ⌂ ♻ wc 🚿 💧 🛒 ⚡ MSP 🦋 ⊕ nr 🔥 🏔 🛶 (htd) 🏊 ⌂ sand 1km

On island of Langeland. Cross to Rudkøbing, fr island of Tåsinge, then 28km to N of island (only 1 main rd); site in middle of vill nr ferry to Sjælland Island. 3*, Med, shd, EHU (10A) DKK35; TV; 10% statics; phone; adv bkg acc; tennis; bike hire; fishing; boat hire; games area. *"Conv ferry (Lohals-Korsor) 500m."* **DKK 210**   **2016**

> ## "We must tell the Club about that great site we found"
>
> Get your site reports in by mid-August and we'll do our best to get your updates into the next edition.

ROMO ISLAND

HAVNEBY *A3 (2km N Coastal) 55.09883, 8.54395* **Kommandørgårdens Camping,** Havnebyvej 201, 6792 Rømø **tel 74 75 51 22; info@kommandoergaarden.dk; www.kommandoergaarden.dk**

12 ⌂ DKK20 ♻ (htd) wc 🚿 💧 🛒 ⚡ MSP 🦋 ⊕ ♿ 🔥 🏔 🛶 (htd) 🏊 ⌂ sand 1km

Turn S after exit causeway fr mainland onto rd 175 sp Havneby. Site on L in 8km. 3*, V lge, mkd, pt shd, EHU (10A) DKK35; gas; TV; 30% statics; phone; adv bkg acc; tennis. *"Family-owned site; wellness & beauty cent on site; ferry to German island of Sylt."* **DKK 240**   **2016**

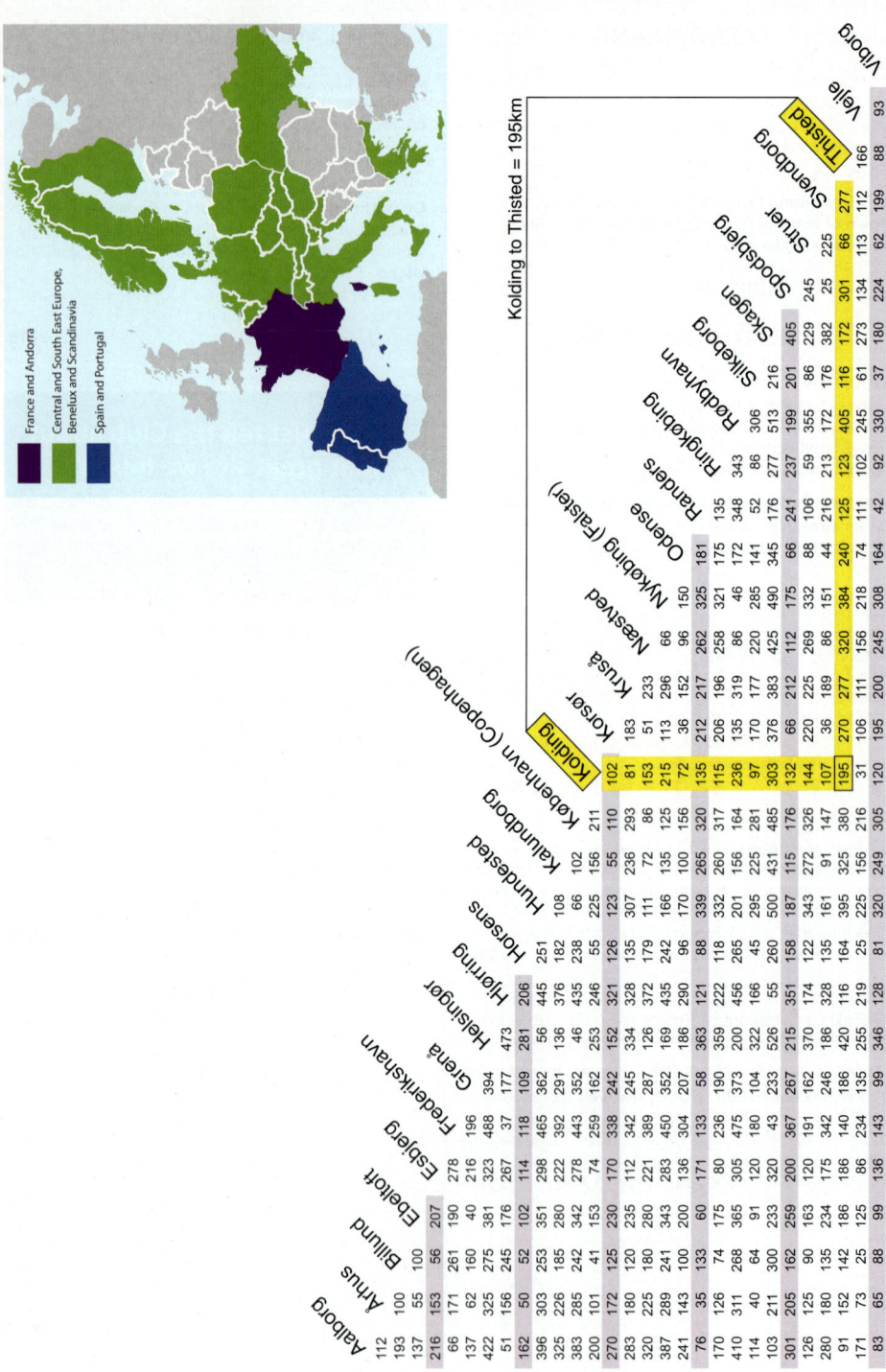

France and Andorra

Central and South East Europe, Benelux and Scandinavia

Spain and Portugal

Kolding to Thisted = 195km

Kuusamo Lake

Highlights

Finland is a country filled with vast forests, crystal clear lakes and a diverse range of flora and fauna. With the Northern Lights visible from Lapland, the outstanding natural world is one of Finland's finest assets, with a vast, pristine wilderness that captures the imagination.

The cities of Finland are not to be missed, with vibrant atmospheres, museums, galleries, delicious restaurants and gorgeous architecture in spades.

Saunas are an important part of life in Finland, and have been for hundreds of years. They are used as a place to relax with friends and family and are generally sociable spaces.

Design and fashion have always been popular in Finland, with one of its most famous companies, Marimekko, a huge contributor to fashion in the 20th century.

Visit Svalbard to witness the unique spectacle of the Midnight Sun. This natural phenomenon occurs each year around the summer solstice.

Major towns and cities

- Helsinki – this capital city is a hub of shopping and architecture.
- Tempere – Finland's cultural home with theatrical, musical and literary traditions.
- Turku – Finland's oldest city and a former European City of Culture.
- Oulu – a quirky city where many technology companies, including Nokia, are based.

Attractions

- Olavinlinna Castle, Savolinna – a medieval stone fortress that houses several exhibitions.
- Lapland– This region is famous for the midnight sun and the Northern Lights.
- Repovesi National Park – a stunning natural area with plenty of walking and hiking trails.
- Temppeliaukio Kirkko, Helsinki – This church is built directly into solid rock.

Find out more

www.visitfinland.com
E: helsinki.tourist.info@hel.fi
T: 0035 (0) 82 95 05 80 00

Country Information

Population (approx): 5.5 million

Capital: Helsinki

Area: 338,145 sq km

Bordered by: Norway, Sweden, Russia

Terrain: Flat, rolling, heavily forested plains interspersed with low hills and over 60,000 lakes; one third lies within the Arctic Circle

Climate: Short, warm summers; long, very cold, dry winters; the best time to visit is between May and September

Coastline: 1,250km (excluding islands)

Highest Point: Haltiatunturi 1,328m

Languages: Finnish, Swedish

Local Time: GMT or BST + 2, ie 2 hours ahead of the UK all year

Currency: Euros divided into 100 cents; £1 = €1.14, €1 = £0.88 (Feb 2021)

Emergency numbers: Police 112; Fire brigade 112; Ambulance 112 (operators speak English)

Public Holidays 2021: Jan 1, 6; Apr 2, 5; May 1, 13; Jun 25,26; Nov 6; Dec 6, 24, 25, 26.

School summer holidays from early June to mid-August.

Border Posts

The main border posts with Sweden are at Tornio, Ylitornio and Kaaresuvanto. Those with Norway are at Kilpisjärvi, Kivilompolo, Karigasniemi, Utsjoki Ohcejohka and Nuorgam. Border posts are open day and night. The Finnish-Russian border can only be crossed by road at certain official points – contact the Finnish Tourist Board for details.

Border guards patrol the area close to the Russian border and it is important, therefore, to carry identification at all times.

Entry Formalities

British and Irish passport holders may stay for up to 90 days in any 180 day period without a visa. Following Brexit you may be asked to show a return or onward ticket at the border to confirm your length of stay, or to prove that you have enough money for your stay.

Your passport will need to have a minimum of 6 months' validity remaining, and be less than 10 years old (even if it has over 6 months left).

Medical Services

The local health system is good and Finland generally has a high level of healthcare. British citizens are entitled to obtain emergency health care at municipal health centres on presentation of a European Health Insurance Card (EHIC). Treatment will either be given free or for a standard fee. Dental care is provided mainly by private practitioners.

There is a non-refundable charge for hospital treatment, whether for inpatient or outpatient visits. Refunds for the cost of private medical treatment may be obtained from Sickness Insurance Department, KELA, (www.kela.fi) up to six months from the date of treatment.

Prescribed drugs can be obtained from pharmacies (apteekki), some of which have late opening hours. Some medicines that are available in stores and supermarkets in other countries, such as aspirin and various ointments, are only available in pharmacies in Finland.

Mosquitoes are abundant and very active during damp summers, particularly in the north of Finland. The use of mosquito repellant and a topical cream to prevent bites becoming infected is highly recommended.

Opening Hours

Banks: Mon-Fri 9.15am-4.15pm.

Museums: Check locally as times vary.

Post Offices: Mon-Fri 9am-5pm. During winter some post offices may stay open until 6pm.

Shops: Mon-Fri 7am/8am/9am-9pm; Sat 7am/8am/9am/10am-6pm; Sun noon-6pm (some supermarkets until 11pm). On the eve of a public holiday some shops close early.

Safety and Security

The crime rate is relatively low in Finland although the tourist season attracts pickpockets in crowded areas. You should take the usual commonsense precautions to safeguard your person and property.

There is a low threat from international terrorism but you should be aware of the global risks of indiscriminate terrorist attacks which could be against civilian targets in public places, including tourist sites.

British Embassy

ITÄINEN PUISTOTIE 17, 00140 HELSINKI
Tel: (09) 22865100 Fax: (09) 22865262
www.ukinfinland.fco.gov.uk
info.helsinki@fco.gov.uk

There are also Honorary Consulates in Åland Islands, Jyväskylä, Kotka, Kuopio, Oulu, Rovaniemi, Tampere, Turku and Vaasa.

Irish Embassy

EROTTAJANKATU 7A, FIN-00130 HELSINKI
Tel: (09) 6824240
www.embassyofireland.fi

Documents

Driving Licence/Vehicle(s)

When driving you should carry your driving licence, vehicle registration certificate (V5C), insurance certificate plus MOT certificate (if applicable).

Money

Currency may be exchanged at banks and at bureaux de change.

Major credit cards are widely accepted and cash machines are widespread.

Carry your credit card issuers'/banks' 24-hour UK contact numbers in case of loss or theft of your cards.

Passport

You should carry your passport at all times.

Driving

Accidents

Accidents must be reported to the police and if a foreign motorist is involved the Finnish Motor Insurers Bureau (Liikennevakuutuskeskus) should also be informed. Their address is Bulevardi 28, FIN-00120 Helsinki, tel (09) 40 450 4700/4750, www.lvk.fi./en. At the site of an accident other road users must be warned by the use of a warning triangle.

Alcohol

The maximum permitted level of alcohol is 50 milligrams in 100 millilitres of blood, i.e. lower than that permitted in the UK (80 milligrams). It is advisable to adopt the 'no drink and drive' rule at all times as anyone exceeding this limit will be arrested immediately and could face a prison sentence. Breath tests and blood tests may be carried out at random.

Breakdown Service

The Automobile & Touring Club of Finland, Autoliitto, has approximately 300 roadside patrols manned by volunteers and these can be called out at weekends and on public holidays. At other times, or if the Autoliitto patrol cannot be reached, contracted partners will provide assistance. For 24-hour assistance telephone (0)200 8080. Charges are made for assistance and towing, plus a call-out fee.

Emergency telephone boxes are installed around Helsinki, Kouvola, Jamsa, and Rovaniemi, and on the roads Kouvola-Lappeenranta-Imatra-Simpele and Rovaniemi-Jaatila. Drivers are connected to the national breakdown service.

Child Restraint System

Children under the height of 1.35m must be seated in a suitable child restraint.

If there is not a child restraint/seat available children of 3 years or older must travel in the rear seat using a seat belt or other safety device attached to the seat. Unless in a taxi a child under the age of 3 must not travel in a vehicle without a child restraint. It is the responsibility of the driver to ensure all children under the age of 15 years old are correctly and safely restrained.

Fuel

Petrol stations are usually open from 7am to 9pm on weekdays and for shorter hours at weekends, although a few stay open 24 hours. Their frequency reduces towards the north, so it is advisable not to let your tank run low. Credit cards are accepted at most manned petrol stations. There are many unmanned stations, which have automatic petrol pumps perated with bank notes or credit cards. It is understood that automatic payment machines at petrol pumps do not accept cards issued outside Finland.

LPG is not available.

Motorways

There are 700km of motorway (moottoritie) in Finland linking Helsinki, Tampere and Turku. No tolls are levied. There are no emergency phones located on motorways. In the case of breakdown on a motorway drivers of all vehicles must use a warning triangle.

Parking

A vehicle that has been illegally or dangerously parked may be removed by the police and the owner fined. Parking fines may be enforced on the spot, the minimum charge being €10. Parking meters operate for between 15 minutes and four hours; the free use of unexpired time is allowed. In some built-up areas you will need a parking disc obtainable from petrol stations or car accessory shops.

| Restriction applies 8-17 hrs (Mon-Fri) | Restriction applies 8-13 hrs (Sat) | Restriction applies 8-14 hrs (Sun) |

In some towns streets are cleaned on a regular basis. Road signs indicate when the cleaning takes place and the street should be kept clear of parked vehicles. Parked vehicles will be removed and drivers fined.

If you have a low emission car you may be entitled to 50% off parking fees in Helsinki. To qualify for this reduction the parking fees must be made by mobile phone and you will need to have obtained a green sticker with the letter 'P' from the Helsinki town authorities, which then needs to be attached to the windscreen. For further information visit www.easypark.fi or www.nextpark.com.

Priority

At intersections, vehicles coming from the right have priority, except when otherwise indicated. The approach to a main road from a minor road is indicated by a sign with a red triangle on a yellow background. When this sign is supplemented by a red octagon with STOP in the centre, vehicles must stop before entering the intersection. Trams and emergency vehicles, even coming from the left, always have priority. Vehicles entering a roundabout must give way to traffic already on the roundabout, i.e. on the left.

Roads

In general there is a good main road system, traffic is light and it is possible to cover long distances quickly, but there are still some gravelled roads in the countryside which have speed restrictions to avoid windscreens being broken by loose stones. During the spring thaw and during the wet season in September, gravelled roads may be in a poor condition. Roadworks take place during the summer months and sections under repair can extend for many miles.

There are large numbers of elk in Finland and they often wander across roads, especially at dawn and dusk. The same applies to reindeer in Lapland. Warning signs showing approximate lengths of danger zones are posted in these areas. If you collide with an elk, deer or reindeer you must notify the police.

The Finnish Transport Agency operates an information service on weather and road conditions, recommended driving routes and roadworks, tel 0295 020 600 or visit www.liikennevirasto.fi.

Road Signs and Markings

Road markings are generally white. Road signs conform to international conventions. Signs for motorway and end of motorway are on a green background while those for main roads are on a blue background. The following signs may also be found:

Finnish	English Translation
Aja hitaasti	Drive slowly
Aluerajoitus	Local speed limit
Kelirikko	Frost damage
Kokeile jarruja	Test your brakes
Kunnossapitotyö	Roadworks (repairs)
Lossi färja	Ferry
Päällystetyötä	Roadworks (resurfacing)
Tulli	Customs
Tie rakenteilla	Roadworks (road under construction)
Varo irtokiviä	Beware of loose stones

Speed Limits

	Open Road (km/h)	Motorway (km/h)
Car Solo	80-100	120
Car towing caravan/trailer	80	80
Motorhome under 3500kg	100	100
Motorhome 3500-7500kg	80	80

On all roads outside built-up areas, other than motorways, differing speed limits between 70 and 100 km/h (44 and 62 mph) apply – except where vehicles are subject to a lower limit – according to the road quality and traffic. Where there is no sign, the basic speed limit is usually 80 km/h (50 mph) on main roads and 70 km/h (44 mph) on secondary roads, whether solo or towing. The road sign which indicates this basic limit bears the word 'Perusnopeus' in Finnish, and 'Grundhastighet' in Swedish.

Reduced speed limits apply from October to March and these are generally 20 km/h (13 mph) lower than the standard limits.

The maximum speed limit for motorhomes up to 3,500kg is 100 km/h (62 mph).

Recommended maximum speed limits are indicated on some roads by square or rectangular signs bearing white figures on a blue background. The maximum speed limit in residential areas is 20 km/h (13 mph).

Slow moving vehicles must let others pass wherever possible, if necessary by moving onto the roadside verge. Maintain a sufficient distance behind a slow moving vehicle to allow an overtaking vehicle to pull in front.

Radar detectors are prohibited.

Violation of Traffic Regulations

The police can impose, but not collect, fines when road users violate traffic regulations. Fines should be paid at banks.

Winter Driving

Winter tyres are compulsory from 1 December to 28 February. Snow chains may be used temporarily when conditions necessitate.

The main arctic road leads from Kemi on the Gulf of Bothnia through Rovaniemi to the Norwegian border. During the winter, all high volume, main roads are kept open including routes to Norway and Sweden. In total between 6,000 and 7,000km of roads are mainly kept free of ice and snow by the use of salt. Other roads will consist of compacted snow. Drivers should expect winter conditions as early as October.

Essential Equipment

Lights

Dipped headlights are compulsory at all times, regardless of weather conditions. Bulbs are more likely to fail with constant use and you are recommended to carry spares.

Reflective Jacket/Waistcoat

Pedestrians must wear reflective devices during the hours of darkness (any type of reflector is acceptable). If you get out of your vehicle you are required to wear one and the standard reflective jacket is probably the best option for driver and passengers.

Warning Triangles

All vehicles must carry a warning triangle and use it when broken down.

Touring

Both Finnish and Swedish are official languages. As a result, many towns and streets have two names, e.g. Helsinki is also known as Helsingfors, and Turku as Åbo. Finnish street names usually end 'katu', while Swedish street names usually end 'gatan' or 'vägen'. Swedish place names are more commonly used in the south and west of the country.

The Helsinki Card offers free entry to several major museums and other attractions, and unlimited travel for 24, 48 or 72 hours on public transport, plus discounts for sightseeing, restaurants, shopping, concert tickets, sports, etc. For more information see www.helsinkicard.fi

The sale of wine and spirits is restricted to Alko shops which are open Monday to Friday until 6pm or 8pm, Saturday until 4pm or 6pm, and closed on Sunday and public holidays. Medium strength beer is also sold in supermarkets and other stores.

A service charge is generally included in most restaurant bills and tips are not expected, but if the service has been good it is customary to round up the bill.

Most lakes are situated in the south east of the country and they form a web of waterways linked by rivers and canals, making this a paradise for those who enjoy fishing, canoeing and hiking. In Lapland the vegetation is sparse, consisting mostly of dwarf birch. Reindeer roam freely so motorists must take special care and observe the warning signs. Rovaniemi is the biggest town in Lapland, just south of the Arctic Circle. It has a special post office and 'Santa Claus Land'.

A number of 'Uniquely Finnish' touring routes have been established including the King's Road along the south coast which takes you through many places of interest including Porvoo, a small town with well-preserved, old, wooden houses, Turku, the former capital, and the famous Imatra waterfall near the southern shore of Lake Saimaa. Swedish influence is evident in this area in local customs, place names and language. These 'Uniquely Finnish' touring routes are marked with brown sign posts; contact the Finnish Tourist Board for more information.

Southern and central Finland are usually snow covered from early December to mid or late April, although in recent years the south coast has had little or no snow. Northern Finland has snow falls from October to May and temperatures can be extremely low. Thanks to the Gulf Stream and low humidity, Finland's winter climate does not feel as cold as temperature readings might indicate but if you plan a visit during the winter you should be prepared for harsh weather conditions.

In the summer many Finnish newspapers have summaries of main news items and weather forecasts in English and radio stations have regular news bulletins in English. English is taught in all schools and is widely spoken.

Camping and Caravanning

There are around 150 campsites in Finland. Campsites are graded from 1 to 5 stars according to facilities available. Most have cabins for hire in addition to tent and caravan pitches, and most have saunas.

At some sites visitors who do not already have one must purchase a Camping Key Europe, which replaced the Camping Card Scandinavia (CCS) in 2012. The Camping Key is valid across Europe and you may purchase it for €16 on arrival at your first campsite or from local tourist offices - for more information visit www.camping.fi

During the peak camping season from June to mid August it is advisable to make advance reservations. Prices at many campsites may double (or treble) over the midsummer holiday long weekend in June and advance booking is essential for this period. Approximately 70 campsites stay open all year.

Casual or wild camping may be allowed for a short period - one or 2 days. For longer periods, permission must be obtained from the landowner. Camping is be prohibited on public beaches and in public recreation areas campers are often directed to special areas, many of which have facilities provided free of charge.

Cycling

Finland is good for cyclists as it is relatively flat. Most towns have a good network of cycle lanes which are indicated by traffic signs. In built up areas pavements are sometimes divided into two sections, one for cyclists and one for pedestrians. It is compulsory to wear a safety helmet.

Electricity and Gas

Current on campsites is usually between 10 and 16 amps. Plugs are round with two pins. Some sites have CEE connections.

Butane gas is not generally available and campsites and service stations do not have facilities for replacing empty foreign gas cylinders. You will need to travel with sufficient supplies to cover your needs while in Finland or purchase propane cylinders locally, plus an adaptor. The Club does not recommend the refilling of cylinders.

The Midnight Sun and Northern Lights

Areas within the Arctic Circle have 24 hours of daylight in the height of summer and no sun in winter for up to two months. There are almost 20 hours of daylight in Helsinki in the summer.

The Northern Lights (Aurora Borealis) may be seen in the arctic sky on clear dark nights, the highest incidence occurring in February/March and September/October in the Kilpisjärvi region of Lapland when the lights are seen on three nights out of four.

The Order of Bluenosed Caravanners

Visitors to the Arctic Circle from anywhere in the world may apply for membership of the Order of Bluenosed Caravanners which will be recognised by the issue of a certificate by the International Caravanning Association (ICA).

For more information contact bluenosed@icacaravanning.org and attach a photograph of yourselves and your outfit under any Arctic Circle signpost, together with the date and country of crossing and the names of those who made the crossing.

This service is free to members of the ICA (annual membership £20); the fee for non-members is £5. Coloured plastic decals for your outfit, indicating membership of the Order, are also available at a cost of £4. Cheques should be payable to the ICA. Visit www.icacaravanning.org for more information.

Public Transport & Local Travel

The public transport infrastructure is of a very high standard and very punctual. You can buy a variety of bus, train, tram and metro tickets at public transport stations, HKL service points, newspaper kiosks and shops all over the country. Single tickets, which are valid for 60 minutes, can be purchased from ticket machines, bus and tram drivers or train conductors. Tourist tickets valid for one, three or five days can also be purchased from kiosks, ticket machines and bus and tram drivers and are valid on all forms of public transport including the Suomenlinna ferry.

Within the Helsinki city area you may hire city bicycles in the summer for a token fee (refundable) from one of 26 Citybike stands.

Vehicle ferries operate all year to Estonia, Germany and Russia and it is now possible to enjoy a visa free ferry trip to St Petersburg for up to 72 hours from Helsinki; see www.visitfinland.com for more information or contact the Finnish Tourist Board.

Internal ferry services (in Finnish 'lossi') transport motor vehicles day and night. Those situated on the principal roads, taking the place of a bridge, are state-run and free of charge. There are regular services on Lake Paijanne, Lake Inari and Lake Pielinen, and during the summer there are daily tours and longer cruises through Finland's lake region. Popular routes are between Hameenlinna and Tampere, Tampere and Virrat, as well as the Saimaa Lake routes. Details are available from the Finnish Tourist Board.

Aurora Borealis over the Artic Circle

Shutterstock/Jamen Percy

HAMINA *C4 (7km SE Coastal) 60.52644, 27.25191*
Hamina Camping, Vilniementie 375, 49400 Hamina
**(40) 1513446; camping.hamina@gmail.com;
hamina-camping.fi**

ቶ⊦ (htd) ⚓ ᴎ ⚏ ⛄ 🦋 ☂ 🍴 🛒 ⛲sand

Fr Hamina take rte 7/E18 dir Vaalimaa E. In 3km
turn R rd 3513 sp Virolahti, site sp. 3*, Med, hdstg,
pt shd, EHU (16A); twin axles; 20% statics; CKE. *"Site
in pine forest; secluded pitches; attractive coastline;
conv for visiting Russia & Kings Rte; sm museum at
Virolahti worth visit; facs poss stretched when site full;
interesting town; site under refurb (2016); helpful staff;
gd."* €26.50, 1 May-18 Sep. 2017

HANKO/HANGO *B4 (4km NE Coastal) 59.85271,
23.01716* **Camping Silversand,** Hopeahietikko, 10960
Hanko Pohjoinen **(019) 248 5500; cornia@cornia.fi;
www.cornia.fi**

ቶ⊦ ⊞ ⚓ & ⛏ ⚏ ᴎ ⚏ ⛲ ☂ ⓝr 🛒 ⛲

Site sp fr rd 25. 3*, Lge, shd, EHU (16A) inc; cooking
facs; TV; 10% statics; Eng spkn; ccard acc; sauna; boat
hire; fishing; games rm; bike hire; CKE. *"Beautiful
location on edge of sea in pine forest."*
€30.60, 25 Apr-30 Sep. 2016

HELSINKI/HELSINGFORS *C4 (14km ENE Urban/
Coastal) 60.20668, 25.12116* **Rastila Municipal
Camping,** Karavaanikatu 4, Vuosaari, 00980 Helsinki
**(09) 31078517; rastilacamping@hel.fi;
www.hel.fi/rastila**

⧆ ቶ⊦ ⚓ & ⛏ ⚏ ᴎ ⚏ 🦋 ⛲ ⓝ 🛒 nr ⛲ ⛲sand 1.2km

E fr Helsinki on rte 170, over Vuosaari bdge; or get
to ring rd 1, turn E dir Vuosaari, site sp. Also sp fr
Silja & other ferry terminals & fr rte 170 to Porvoo.
Also sp on rte 167. Fr N on E75 exit at Ring I then
immed L fork. Foll 101, 170 then sp. 3*, V lge, hdstg,
pt shd, EHU (16A) €4.50; cooking facs; red long stay;
TV; 10% statics; Eng spkn; ccard acc; games rm;
sauna; CKE. *"Conv Helsinki & district; pleasant site; gd
san facs; helpful staff; poss ssn workers but site clean &
tidy; metro nr; weekly rates avail; best place we stayed
at."* €37.00 2016

INARI *B1 (0.5km SE Rural) 68.90233, 27.0370* **Holiday
Village/Lomakylä Inari,** Inarintie 26, 99780 Inari **(016)
671108; info@lomakyla-inari.fi; www.saariselka.fi/
lomakylainari**

⧆ ቶ ⊦ ⊞ ⚓ ⛏ & ⚏ ᴎ ⚏ ⛲ ⓝ 🛒 nr ⛲ ⛲sand adj

Fr S on rte 4/E75, site on R app Inari, clearly sp. Fr N
on E75 500m past town cent, site on L, sp. 3*, Sm,
hdstg, unshd, EHU (16A) inc (long lead poss req) no
earth; bbq; sw nr; twin axles; 40% statics; bus 500m;
Eng spkn; ccard acc; canoe hire; sauna; CKE. *"Gd for
walking; midnight sun cruises on Lake Inari; excel Lapp
museum; motorboat hire; poss boggy in wet; poss low
voltage if site full; some lge pitches suitable RVs & lge
o'fits; clean site; boat/canoe hire; fab Sami ctr in vill."*
€25.00 2017

IVALO *B1 (2km S Rural) 68.64369, 27.52714* **Holiday
Village Näverniemi,** 99800 Ivalo **(016) 677601;
naverniemen@lomakyla.inet.fi; www.narkka.com**

ቶ⊦ ⊞ ⚓ ⛏ ᴎ ⚏ 🦋 ⓝ ⚓ 🛒 ⛲ ⚏

Sp on W side of rte 4/E75. Lge, unshd, EHU (10A)
€2.50; sw nr; TV; adv bkg acc; ccard acc; sauna; CKE.
*"Gd cent for birdwatchers; rvside site; reindeer herds
nr site; insufficient el hook-ups; helpful, friendly owner;
phone ahead early ssn to check open - poss flooding
during spring thaw."* €26.00, 1 Jun-30 Sep. 2016

IVALO *B1 (4km S Rural) 68.62475, 27.54296* **Ivalo
River Camping,** Kerttuojantie 1, 99800 Ivalo **(400)
395046; info@ivalorivercamping.com;
www.ivalorivercamping.com**

ቶ ⊦ቶ⊦ ⚓ ᴎ ⚏ ⛲ ☂ 🛒

At side of Rte4/E75, on R when travelling N. Sp on
Rte 4/E75. Pt of petrol stn & café. Sm, hdstg, pt shd,
pt sl, EHU; cooking facs; 50% statics; Eng spkn; adv
bkg acc; CKE. *"Gd cent for birdwatching; conv NH; only
site open in mid May; gd."* €20.00, May-Sep. 2016

JUUKA *C3 (35km SE Rural) 63.04004, 29.70994* **Koli
Freetime Oy,** Kopravaarantie 27, Juuka **010 322
3040; koli@kolifreetime.fi; www.kolifreetime.fi**

ቶ ⊦ቶ⊦ (htd) ⊞ ⚓ ⛏ ⚏ ᴎ ⚏ 🦋 ⛲ ☂ 🍴 ⚓ ⛲ ⛲sand adj

Site is well sp on rte 6 heading N of Juuka. Turn off
onto gravel rd as indicated for 2km. Sm, pt shd, sl,
EHU (16A) inc; bbq; sw nr; twin axles; TV; 10% statics;
Eng spkn; adv bkg acc; ccard acc; games rm; CKE.
*"Sauna inc; sm site on edge of lake with sw; in forest;
nature walks; 10km fr Koli & nearest supmkt; vg."*
€28.00 2016

JYVASKYLA *C3 (4km N Urban) 62.25536, 25.6983*
Laajis Camping, Laajavuorentie 15, 40740 Jyväskylä
207 436 436; laajis@laajis.fi; www.laajis.fi

⧆ ቶ ⊦ቶ⊦ (htd) ⊞ ⚓ ⛏ & ⚏ ᴎ ⚏ 🦋 ⛲ ⓝ ⚓ 🛒 nr ⚏

Well sp fr N on E75 & E63 fr S, site sp adj youth
hostel. Med, mkd, hdstg, unshd, EHU (16A) inc;
cooking facs; red long stay; TV (pitch); Eng spkn;
sauna; CKE. *"Facs stretched if site full; htd pool 3km;
ski lift/jumps adj; c'vans only."* €29.00 2016

KAMMENNIEMI *B4 (7km NW Rural) 61.65423,
23.77748* **Camping Taulaniemi,** Taulaniementie
357, 34240 Kämmenniemi **(03) 3785753;
taulaniemi@yritys.soon.fi; www.taulaniemi.fi**

ቶ⊦ (htd) ⊞ ⚓ ᴎ ⚏ ⚏ 🦋 ⓝ ⚓ 🛒 ⛲

Fr Tampere take rte 9/E63 dir Jyvaskyla. In 10km
take rte 338 thro Kämmenniemi. Foll sp Taulaniemi
on unmade rd to lakeside site. 3*, Sm, unshd, pt sl,
terr, EHU (16A) €3; cooking facs; TV; adv bkg acc;
boat hire; sauna; CKE. *"Beautiful site."*
€30.50, 1 Jun-31 Sep. 2017

KARIGASNIEMI *B1* (0.9km NW Rural) *69.39975, 25.84278* **Camping Tenorinne,** Ylätenontie 55, 99950 Karigasniemi **040 832 8487; camping@ tenorinne.com; www.tenorinne.com**

N of town cent on rd 970 Karigasniemi to Utsjoki. Sm, pt shd, EHU (16A) €4; TV; 10% statics; ccard acc; sauna; CKE. **€26.00, 5 Jun-20 Sep.** 2016

KILPISJARVI *A1* (4.6km SSE Rural) *69.01413, 20.88235* **Kilpisjärvi Holiday Village,** Käsivarrentie 14188, 99490 Kilpisjärvi **(0400) 396684; www.tundrea.com**

On main rd 21 almost opp g'ge, in middle of vill, sp. Lge, hdstg, unshd, EHU (10A) inc; bbq; cooking facs; bus adj; Eng spkn. *"Gd NH to/fr N Norwegian fjords; access to Saana Fells for gd walking/trekking; winter sports cent."* **€20.00** 2016

KOKKOLA *B3* (2.5km N Coastal) *63.85500, 23.11305* **Kokkola Camping,** Vanhansatamanlahti, 67100 Kokkola **(06) 8314006; info@kokkola-camping.fi; www.kokkola-camping.fi**

Exit A8 at Kokkola onto rte 749. Site on R, sp fr town. Med, pt shd, EHU inc; cooking facs; games area; sauna; CKE. *"Lovely site, no adv bkg; call ahead in winter for pitching instructions."* **€30.00, 1 Jun-31 Aug.** 2016

KUHMO *C3* (3km SE Rural) *64.11898, 29.57771* **Kalevala Caravan Parking,** Vainamoinen 2, 88900 Kuhmo **(086) 557111; kalevalan.kuntoutuskoti@ kalevalankk.fi; www.hyvinvointisampo.fi**

Fr Kajaani on 76 turn R in ctr of town to 912 Kalevala (brown sp). After 1.6km turn L onto 912. Site on R. Obtain key fr Hyvinvoiti Sampo (old peoples home) on R as you enter. Site at bottom of hill. Hdstg, EHU (10A). *"Clean modern san facs; waste water & chem disp in town (ask recep)."* **€10.00** 2016

KUOPIO *C3* (9km SW Rural) *62.86432, 27.64165* **Rauhalahti Holiday Centre,** Kiviniementie, 70700 Kuopio **(017) 473000; sales@visitrauhalahti.fi; www.visitrauhalahti.fi**

Well sp fr rte 5 (E63). Site 1.5km fr E63 dir Levänen, on Lake Kallavesi. 4*, Lge, hdstg, pt shd, pt sl, EHU (16A) inc; gas; cooking facs; sw; TV; adv bkg rec; ccard acc; sauna; boat trips; watersports; CKE. *"Hdstg for cars, grass for van & awning; ltd services Sept-May."* **€35.00** 2016

KUUSAMO *C2* (5km N Rural) *66.00143, 29.16713* **Camping Rantatropiikki,** Kylpyläntie, 93600 Kuusamo/ Petäjälampi **(08) 8596000; myyntipalvelu.tropiikki@ holidayclub.fi**

Three sites in same sm area on rd 5/E63, sp. Med, pt shd, EHU (10A) inc; sw; ccard acc; sauna; tennis; bike hire; CKE. *"Conv falls area; pool in hotel adj; LS site recep at hotel 500m past site ent."* 2016

LAHTI *C4* (5km N Rural) *61.01599, 25.64855* **Camping Mukkula,** Ritaniemenkatu 10, 15240 Lahti **(03) 7535380; tiedustelut@mukkulacamping.fi; www.mukkulacamping.fi**

Fr S on rte 4/E75 foll camping sps fr town cent. 3*, Med, pt shd, EHU (10A) inc; cooking facs; sw; TV; ccard acc; tennis; bike hire; fishing; sauna; CKE. *"Beautiful lakeside views."* 2016

"I need an on-site restaurant"

We do our best to make sure site information is correct, but it is always best to check any must-have facilities are still available or will be open during your visit.

LAHTI *C4* (8km NW Rural) *61.01872, 25.56387* **Camping Messila,** Rantatie 5, 15980 Hollola **3876290; messila@campingmessila.fi; www.campingmessila.fi**

Off A12 onto Messilantie (N), foll rd to lakeshore. Lge, hdg, mkd, hdstg, pt shd, EHU (16A) €5; bbq; sw nr; twin axles; Eng spkn; CKE. *"Gd sized pitches; barrier; v welcoming; well kept; next to marina; golf nr; conv for Lahti; vg."* **€26.00** 2017

LIEKSA *D3* (3km SW Rural) *63.30666, 30.00532* **Timitranniemi Camping,** Timitra, 81720 Lieksa **(04) 51237166; loma@timitra.com; www.timitra.com**

Rte 73, well sp fr town on Lake Pielinen. 3*, Med, pt shd, pt sl, EHU (16A) €4; cooking facs; sw; TV; ccard acc; bike hire; sauna; boat hire; fishing; CKE. *"Pt of recreational complex; Pielinen outdoor museum worth visit."* **€28.00, 20 May-10 Sep.** 2016

MERIKARVIA *B4* (3km SW Coastal) *61.84777, 21.47138* **Mericamping,** Palosaarentie 67, 29900 Merikarvia **(04) 00 719589; info@mericamping.fi; www.mericamping.fi**

Fr E8 foll sp to Merikarvia, site sp 2km W beyond main housing area. Med, mkd, unshd, EHU €5; Eng spkn; ccard acc; CKE. *"Vg site on water's edge; some cottages; friendly, helpful staff."* **€22.00, 1 Jun-31 Aug.** 2016

FINLAND

MUONIO *B1* (3km S Rural) *67.93333, 23.6575*
Harrinivan Lomakeskus, Harrinivantie 35, 99300
Muonio **400 155 110; sales@harriniva.fi;**
www.harriniva.fi

👪(htd) ⬜ 🚿 ♿ 🦋 🍴 🍽 ⑪ 🐕nr 🏧

On E8 5km S of Muonio, well sp on R going S.
Sm, hdstg, pt shd, pt sl, EHU (16A) €4; bbq; twin axles;
Eng spkn; adv bkg acc; ccard acc; rv; CCI. *"Canoe hire
for white water rafting; huskies; san facs stretch in high
ssn; fair."* **€32.00, 1 Jun-30 Sep.** **2019**

NOKIA *B4* (5km S Rural) *61.44798, 23.49247*
Camping Viinikanniemi, Viinikanniemenkatu, 37120
Nokia **(400) 420772; info@viinikanniemi.com;**
www.viinikanniemi.com

12 🐕 👪(htd) ⬜ 🚿 ♨ ♿ 🖿 ♿ 🦋 🍴 🍽 ⑪ 🐕 🏧 ✏

SW fr Tampere on rd 12, site well sp. 4*, Med, mkd,
hdstg, pt shd, pt sl, EHU (16A) €5.90-10; gas; bbq;
sw nr; 10% statics; Eng spkn; adv bkg acc; ccard acc;
fishing; games area; bike hire; boat hire; CKE. *"Excel
site; conv Tampere."* **€21.00** **2016**

NURMES *C3* (4km SE Rural) *63.53274, 29.19889*
Hyvärilä Camping, Lomatie 12, 75500 Nurmes **(013)**
6872500; hyvarila@nurmes.fi; www.hyvarila.com

🐕 👪 ⬜ 🚿 🖿 🦋 🍽 ⑪ 🐕 🏧

On rte 73 to Lieksa, turn R 4km fr rte 6/73 junc.
Well sp on Lake Pielinen. Check in at hotel. 3*, Lge,
unshd, EHU (16A) €5; sw; red long stay; 10% statics;
ccard acc; sauna; games area; tennis; CKE. *"Gd
base for N Karelia; pt of recreational complex."*
€24.00, 1 Jun-15 Sep. **2016**

OULU/ULEABORG *B2* (6km NW Coastal) *65.0317,
25.4159* **Camping Nallikari,** Leiritie 10, Hietasaari,
90500 Oulu/Uleåborg **(08) 55861350; nallikari.
camping@ouka.fi; www.nallikari.fi**

12 👪(htd) ⬜ 🚿 ♿ 🖿 🦋 🍴 🍽 ⑪nr 🐕 🏧 ✏

Off Kemi rd. Sp fr town & rte 4/E75 fr Kemi. (Do not
take Oulu by-pass app fr S). Lge, pt shd, EHU (16A)
€4.50; bbq; cooking facs; sw nr; TV; 20% statics;
ccard acc; sauna; games area; bike hire; CKE. *"Gd
cycling; spa adj; pool adj; excel modern services block."*
€23.00 **2016**

PELLO *B2* (1km NW Rural) *66.78413, 23.94540*
Camping Pello, Nivanpääntie 58, 95700 Pello
**050 3606611; pello.camping@gmail.com;
www.travelpello.fi/palvelu/camping-pello**

👪(htd) ⬜ 🚿 🖿 🦋 ⑪nr 🐕 🏧

Foll site sp fr town cent. Med, hdstg, pt shd, EHU
(16A) inc; 30% statics; Eng spkn; ccard acc; boat hire;
rv fishing adj; sauna. *"Rvside pitches avail - insects!"*
€21.00, 1 Jun-20 Sep. **2016**

PERANKA *C2* (2km E Rural) *65.39583, 29.07094*
Camping Piispansaunat, Selkoskyläntie 19, 89770
Peranka **(040) 5916784 or (0400) 387615;**
piispansaunat@elisanet.fi; piispansaunat@elisanet.fi

🐕 👪 ⬜ 🚿 🖿 🦋 🐕 🏧

Take rte 5/63 N or S; at Peranka turn E on rd 9190
for 2km; site on R in trees. Sm, hdstg, shd, pt sl, EHU
(10A) €4; bbq; cooking facs; sw nr; Eng spkn; fishing;
sauna; CKE. **€25.00, 1 Jun-31 Aug.** **2016**

PORVOO/BORGA *C4* (2km S Rural) *60.3798,
25.66673* **Camping Kokonniemi,** Uddaksentie 17,
06100 Porvoo **(452) 550074; myynti@suncamping.fi**

👪 ⬜ 🚿 🖿 🦋 ⑪nr 🐕 🏧

Fr E on rte 7/E18 m'way ignore 1st exit Porvoo,
site sp fr 2nd exit. 3*, Med, hdstg, sl, EHU (16A)
€5; Eng spkn; ccard acc; sauna; CKE. *"Access to old
town & rv walk; conv Helsinki & ferry; nice welcome;
v clean; ideal NH or longer; Porvoo interesting."*
€33.00, 1 Jun-26 Aug. **2017**

PUNKAHARJU *D4* (9km NW Rural) *61.80032,
29.29088* **Punkaharjun Camping,** Tuunaansaarentie
4, 58540 Punkaharju **29 007 4050; info@punkaharju
resort.fi; www.punkaharjuresort.fi**

12 👪 ⬜ 🚿 🖿 🦋 ⑪ 🐕 🏧

27km SE of Savonlinna on rte 14 to Imatra, sp on R.
4*, Med, pt shd, EHU (16A) €7; sw; TV; ccard acc;
waterslide; fishing; tennis; games area; sauna; CKE.
*"Theme park nrby (closes 15/8); Kerimäki, world's
largest wooden church; Retretti Art Cent adj."*
€24.00 **2016**

RAUMA *B4* (3km NW Coastal) *61.13501, 21.17085*
Poroholma Camping, Poroholmantie 8, 26100 Rauma
**(02)533 5522; info@poroholma.fi;
www.poroholma.fi**

12 🐕 👪 ⬜ 🚿 🖿 🦋 🍴 🐕 🏧 ⛺sand

Enter town fr coast rd (8) or Huittinen (42). Foll
campsite sp around N pt of town to site on coast.
Site well sp. 3*, Lge, shd, pt sl, EHU (16A) €5; ccard
acc; sauna; CKE. *"Attractive, peaceful location on
sm peninsula in yacht marina & jetty for ferry (foot
passengers only) to outlying islands; pool 250m; excel
beach; warm welcome fr helpful staff; clean facs."*
€25.00 **2016**

ROVANIEMI *B2* (7km E Rural) *66.51706, 25.84678*
Camping Napapiirin Saarituvat, Kuusamontie 96,
96900 Saarenkylä **(016) 3560045; reception@
saarituvat.fi; www.saarituvat.fi**

🐕 👪(htd) ⬜ 🚿 🖿 🦋 🍴 ⑪ 🐕 🏧

Fr town cent take rd 81, site on R at side of rd on
lakeside. NB ignore 1st campsite sp after 2km.
Sm, pt shd, terr, EHU (16A) €5.50; bbq; Eng spkn; adv
bkg acc; sauna; CKE. *"Excel; friendly staff; vg base for
Santa Park & Vill."* **€32.50, 20 May-9 Sep.** **2019**

ROVANIEMI *B2* (1km SE Urban) *66.49743, 25.74340*
Ounaskoski Camping, Jäämerentie 1, 96200
Rovaniemi **(016) 345304; ounaskoski-camping@
windowslive.com**

🐕 ♀♂ (htd) 🆗 ⚓ ♿ 🚿 🗑 ⚡ MSP 🦋 📶 🅗 nr 🅿 🔋 🏔 🌊 sand

Exit rte 4 onto rte 78 & cross rv. Over bdge turn S on
rvside along Jäämerentie. Site on R in approx 500m
immed bef old rd & rail bdge, sp. 3*, Med, mkd, hdstg,
unshd, EHU (16A) inc; bbq; cooking facs; sw; twin
axles; TV; 10% statics; bus 500m; Eng spkn; adv bkg
acc; ccard acc; sauna; bike hire; CKE. *"Helpful staff;
excel site beside rv in parkland; gd facs; suitable RVs
& twin axles; 9km fr Arctic Circle; 6km to Santa Park,
'official' home of Santa; Artikum Museum worth visit;
easy walk to town cent; gd flea mkts; excel san facs."*
€38.50, 21 May-24 Sep.   **2017**

SAVONLINNA *C4* (7km W Rural) *61.86216, 28.80513*
Camping Vuohimäki, Vuohimäentie 60, 57600
Savonlinna **(015) 537353 or (045) 2550073;
savonlinna@suncamping.fi; www.suncamping.fi**

🐕 ♀♂ 🆗 ⚓ ♿ 🚿 🗑 ⚡ 🦋 🍽 🅗 🔋 nr 🏔

On rte 14, 4km W of Savonlinna turn L immed after
bdge twd Pihlajaniemi; site sp for approx 4km on R.
4*, Med, EHU (16A) €5; sw; 10% statics; bus; Eng spkn;
adv bkg acc; ccard acc; watersports; sauna; bike hire;
CKE. *"Gd area for touring; lake trips; views over lake; gd
san facs."* **€31.00, 10 Jun-22 Aug.**   **2016**

TORNIO *B2* (3km SE Rural) *65.83211, 24.19953*
Camping Tornio, Matkailijantie, 95420 Tornio **(016)
445945; camping.tornio@co.inet.fi; www.camping
tornio.com**

♀♂ ♿ 🚿 🗑 ⚡ 🦋 🔋 nr 🏔

App Tornio on E4 coast rd fr Kemi sp on L of dual c/
way; turn L at traff lts then immed R. Site well sp.
3*, Lge, pt shd, EHU (16A) €4; cooking facs; TV; ccard
acc; sauna; tennis; bike hire; CKE. *"Poss boggy in wet."*
€28.00, 5 May-30 Sep.   **2016**

TURKU/ABO *B4* (12km SW Rural) *60.42531, 22.10258*
Ruissalo Camping (Part Naturist), Saaronniemi,
20100 Turku **(02) 2625100; ruissalocamping@turku.fi**

12 ♀♂ (htd) 🆗 ⚓ ♿ 🚿 🗑 ⚡ MSP 🦋 📶 🅗 nr 🔋 🏔 🌊 sand adj

Well sp fr m'way & fr Turku docks; recep immed
after sharp bend in a layby. 3*, Med, hdstg, pt shd,
EHU (16A) inc; TV; 10% statics; bus; Eng spkn; ccard
acc; watersports; sauna; games area; CKE. *"Conv for
ferry; modern, clean san facs; sep area for naturists; ltd
EHU some parts."* **€32.00**   **2016**

VAASA/VASA *B3* (3km NW Coastal) *63.1008, 21.57618*
Top Camping Vaasa, Niemeläntie 1, 65170 Vaasa
**(0)20 7961 255; vaasa@topcamping.fi;
www.topcamping.fi/vaasa**

🐕 ♀♂ (htd) 🆗 ⚓ ♿ 🚿 🗑 ⚡ MSP 🦋 🍽 🔋 🏔

Fr town cent foll sp to harbour (Satama), site sp.
3*, Lge, pt shd, EHU (10A) €7; red long stay; TV;
10% statics; ccard acc; sauna; bike hire; CKE.
€29.50, 25 May-10 Aug.   **2016**

VIRRAT *B4* (6km SE Rural) *62.20883, 23.83501*
Camping Lakarin Leirintä, Lakarintie 405, 34800
Virrat **(03) 4758639; lakari@virtainmatkailu.fi;
www.virtainmatkailu.fi**

♀♂ (htd) 🆗 ⚓ 🗑 ⚡ 🦋 🔋 🏔

Fr Virrat on rte 66 twd Ruovesi. Fr Virrat pass info/
park & take 2nd L, then 1st L. Site 1.7km on R
(poor surface), sp. Med, pt shd, pt sl, EHU (16A)
€3.40; sw nr; 50% statics; Eng spkn; sauna;
boating; fishing; CKE. *"Beautiful lakeside pitches."*
€20.00, 1 May-30 Sep.   **2016**

VUOSTIMO *C2* (2km SW Rural) *66.95783, 27.50350*
Camping Kuukiurun, Sodankyläntie, 98360
Vuostimo **(0) 400 199 184; office@kuukiuru.fi;
www.kuukiuru.fi**

12 🐕 ♀♂ 🆗 ⚓ 🗑 ⚡ 🦋 🔋

N fr Kemijarvi on rd 5, site on R of rd leaving
Vuostimo adj rv. Sm, mkd, unshd, pt sl, EHU inc;
TV; 80% statics; fishing; sauna; boat hire. *"Beautiful,
peaceful site; x-country skiing; friendly owners."* **2016**

ALAND ISLANDS

SUND *A4* (12km SE Coastal) *60.21252, 20.23508*
Puttes Camping, Bryggvägen 40, Bomarsund, 22530
Sund **(018) 44040; puttes.camping@aland.net;
www.visitaland.com/puttescamping**

🐕 ♀♂ 🆗 ⚓ ♿ 🚿 🗑 ⚡ MSP 🦋 🍽 🅗 🔋 🌊 shgl adj

N fr Mariehamn on rd 2 for 40+ km, site at
Bomarsund fortress ruins. 3*, Med, pt shd, pt sl, EHU
(10A) inc; bbq; cooking facs; 5% statics; phone; bus
adj; Eng spkn; adv bkg acc; games area; bike hire; CKE.
"Basic, but clean & welcoming; vg."
€12.00, 15 May-11 Sep.   **2016**

VARDO *A4* (4km N Coastal) *60.27073, 20.38819*
Sandösunds Camping, Sandösundsvägen, 22550
Vårdö **(018) 47750; info@sandocamping.aland.fi;
www.sandocamping.aland.fi**

🐕 ♀♂ (htd) 🆗 ⚓ ♿ 🚿 🗑 ⚡ MSP 🦋 🍽 🅗 🔋 🏔 🌊 sand adj

Site sp fr ferry at Hummelvik & fr rd 2. 3*, Med, pt
shd, pt sl, EHU (10A) €4 (long lead poss req); bbq;
cooking facs; 5% statics; phone; Eng spkn; adv bkg acc;
bike hire; kayak hire; games area; CKE. *"Well-run site
in beautiful location; excel facs."*
€14.00, 15 Apr-31 Oct.   **2016**

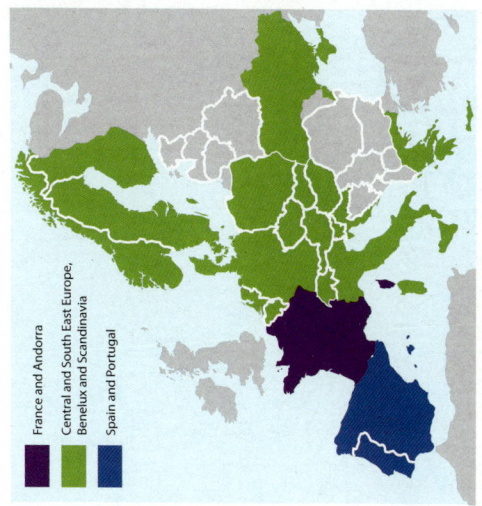

Legend (map):
- France and Andorra
- Central and South East Europe, Benelux and Scandinavia
- Spain and Portugal

Kuusamo to Turku = 848km

Distance chart (km)

Cities (order along the diagonal, top → bottom):
Varkaus, Vaasa, Turku, Tornio, Tampere, Sodankylä, Savonlinna, Rovaniemi, Pori, Oulu, Nurmes, Muonio, Mikkeli, Lappeenranta, Lahti, Kyyjärvi, Kuusamo, Kuhmo, Kuopio, Kouvola, Kokkola, Kemijärvi, Kajaani, Jyväskylä, Joensuu, Ivalo, Hämeenlinna, Helsinki, Hanko, Forssa

Each row below lists the distances (km) from the named city to the cities that follow it in the chart (reading toward Varkaus).

From	Distances to following cities (km)
Forssa	150, 114, 56, 1091, 464, 555, 889, 417, 192, 383, 263, 792, 127, 275, 258, 975, 514, 580, 127, 807, 362, 929, 92, 711, 88, 317, 344
Hanko	129, 195, 1238, 546, 664, 1031, 544, 271, 493, 390, 910, 219, 354, 341, 1121, 624, 723, 257, 941, 449, 1070, 242, 851, 140, 453, 429
Helsinki	100, 1122, 439, 556, 920, 391, 143, 382, 345, 803, 107, 220, 231, 1004, 512, 612, 242, 831, 333, 960, 173, 742, 165, 418, 320
Hämeenlinna	1041, 410, 500, 835, 876, 134, 332, 345, 740, 73, 221, 204, 918, 459, 510, 242, 747, 310, 876, 74, 659, 148, 316, 288
Ivalo	839, 848, 623, 268, 160, 1037, 800, 882, 406, 1062, 957, 325, 720, 1019, 287, 958, 160, 1002, 1144, 827, 875
Joensuu	244, 229, 600, 428, 310, 135, 449, 230, 208, 114, 782, 130, 550, 561, 142, 207, 680, 395, 523, 304, 494, 118
Jyväskylä	313, 646, 241, 192, 170, 145, 437, 220, 330, 208, 718, 272, 339, 332, 207, 332, 680, 152, 309, 282, 250, 125
Kajaani	505, 384, 821, 557, 679, 140, 813, 820, 718, 230, 437, 330, 943, 626, 355, 190, 634, 118
Kemijärvi	432, 264, 356, 680, 411, 310, 82, 99, 356, 162, 717
Kokkola	310, 302, 405, 750, 510, 329, 274, 430, 379, 75
Kouvola	264, 266, 162, 207, 448, 448, 194, 362
Kuopio	335, 415, 310, 177, 593, 444, 722, 353
Kuhmo	585, 137, 294, 424, 345, 434, 370
Kuusamo	503, 704, 682, 579, 420, 339, 212, 725, 192, 578, 248, 702, 315, 848, 530, 496
Kyyjärvi	288, 338, 233, 686, 296, 414, 363, 105, 147, 129
Lahti	147, 129, 901, 414, 508, 551, 774, 730, 232, 904, 128, 637, 217, 364, 363, 502, 191
Lappeenranta	945, 363, 290, 447, 669, 106, 155, 858, 275, 682, 349, 217, 398, 87
Mikkeli	840, 290, 447, 369, 230, 839, 166, 798, 256, 578, 262, 711, 461, 206, 756
Muonio	660, 390, 900, 272, 882, 420, 882, 256, 577, 1027, 461, 206, 756
Nurmes	278, 535, 429, 447, 560, 352, 420, 406, 129, 577, 317, 362
Oulu	510, 221, 447, 131, 493, 115, 640, 138, 489, 317, 362
Pori	730, 471, 862, 710, 115, 640, 194, 540, 390
Rovaniemi	671, 798, 131, 355, 576, 621, 668, 714
Savonlinna	841, 252, 986, 668, 714
Sodankylä	855, 444, 986, 668, 714
Tampere	621, 153, 245, 276
Tornio	764, 448, 494
Turku	346, 428
Vaasa	396

193

France

Mont Saint-Michel

Shutterstock/Neirfy

Highlights

Home to vibrant cities, exceptional cuisine and beatiful landscapes, each region of France offers a unique holiday. Landscapes range from rolling fields to dramatic mountains and beautiful coastlines.

There's also history around every corner, from the Châteaux of the Loire valley to the prehistoric sites of the Dordogne. The beaches also rival the best in the world; the Atlantic coast offers wide sandy expanses perfect for water sports, while the Mediterannean provides glitz and glamour courtesy of Cannes, Nice and St Tropez. The coastline of the North East is dotted with quaint fishing villages and sandy coves.

The cuisine of France is world famous too, from the refined restaurants of Paris to the rich stews and fresh baked bread of the country provinces. Your trip won't be complete without vsiting a Pâtisserie to sample some traditional French pastries. Visiting a vineyard or winery is another highlight, with over 200 wine varieties grown across France.

Major towns and cities

- Paris - the Capital city is brimful with cultural highlights and top-notch cuisine.
- Nice - this coastal gem is known for it's elegance and stunning views.
- Bordeaux - in the heart of the wine growing region, and home to historic architechture.
- Strasbourg - an historic city which offers a mix of French and German cultures.

Attractions

- Eiffel Tower - the symbol of Paris and a must-see if you're in the Capital.
- Palace of Versailles - designed to show off the full glory of the French monarchy.
- Mont Saint-Michel - a dramatic island fortress housing a medieval abbey.
- Rocamadour - this sacred pilgramage site is carved into a limestone cliff.
- Loire Valley Châteaux - the valley is a UNESCO heritage site.

Find out more

www.franceguide.com
E: info.uk@atout-france.fr T: 09068 244123

FRANCE

Country Information

Population (approx): 67 million

Capital: Paris

Area: 549,970 sq km

Bordered by: Andorra, Belgium, Germany, Italy, Luxembourg, Monaco, Spain, Switzerland

Terrain: Mostly flat plains or gently rolling hills in north and west; mountain ranges in south and east

Climate: Temperate climate with regional variations; generally warm summers and cool winters; harsh winters in mountainous areas; hot summers in central and Mediterranean areas

Coastline: 3,427km

Highest Point: Mont Blanc 4,807m

Language: French

Local Time: GMT or BST + 1, i.e. 1 hour ahead of the UK all year

Currency: Euros divided into 100 cents; £1 = €1.14, €1 = £0.88 (Feb 2021)

Telephoning: From the UK dial 0033 for France and omit the initial 0 of the 10-digit number you are calling. Mobile phone numbers start 06. For Monaco the code is 00377.

Emergency Numbers: Police 112; Fire brigade 112; Ambulance 112.

Public Holidays 2021: Jan 1; Apr 5; May 1, 8 (VE Day), 13; 24; Jul 14 (Bastille Day); Aug 15; Nov 1, 11 (Armistice Day); Dec 25.

Entry Formalities

British and Irish passport holders may stay for up to 90 days in any 180 day period without a visa. Following Brexit you may be asked to show a return or onward ticket at the border to confirm your length of stay, or to prove that you have enough money for your stay.

Your passport will need to have a minimum of 6 months' validity remaining, and be less than 10 years old (even if it has over 6 months left).

Visitors arriving at a campsite or hotel must complete a registration form.

Medical Services

In France an EHIC will allow you to claim reimbursement of around 70% of standard doctors' and dentists' fees, and between 35% and 65% of the cost of most prescribed medicines.

For the address of a doctor 'conventionné', i.e. working within the French state healthcare system, ask at a pharmacy. After treatment make sure you are given a signed statement of treatment ('feuille de soins') showing the amount paid as you will need this for a refund.

Pharmacies dispense prescriptions and first aid. Your prescription will be returned to you and you should attach this, together with the stickers (vignettes) attached to the packaging of any medication or drugs, to the 'feuille de soins' in order to obtain a refund.

If you are admitted to hospital make sure you present your EHIC on admission. This will save you from paying any refundable costs up front and ensure that you only pay the patient contribution. You may have to pay a co-payment towards your treatment and if you are an inpatient you will have to pay a daily hospital charge. These charges are not refundable in France but you may be able to seek reimbursement when back in the UK. Applications for refunds should be sent to a local sickness insurance office (Caisse Primaire d'Assurance-Maladie) and you should receive payment at your home address within about two months.

Andorra is not a member of the EU and there are no reciprocal emergency healthcare arrangements with Britain. You will be required to pay the full cost of medical treatment so make sure that you have comprehensive travel insurance which includes cover for travel to non-EU countries.

Opening Hours

Banks – Mon-Fri 9am-noon & 2pm-4pm/5pm/6pm; in Paris Mon-Fri 10am-5pm; some open Sat & close on Mon. Early closing the day before a public holiday.

Museums – 10am-5pm; closed Mon or Tues. In Paris many open late once a week.

Post Offices – Mon-Fri 8am/9am-6pm/7pm; Sat 8am/9am-noon.

Shops: Food shops - Tues-Sat 7am/9am-6.30pm/7.30pm; some food shops i.e. bakers, grocers, etc, are open sun morning. Other shops - Tues-Sat 9am/10am-7.30pm. Shops generally close all or half day on Mon; in small towns shops close for lunch from noon to

2pm. Major Shops - Mon-Sat 9am/10am-7pm. Supermarkets may stay open until 9pm/10pm. Shops in tourist areas may open on Sunday.

Safety and Security

Most visits to France are trouble free but visitors should take the usual commonsense precautions against mugging, pickpocketing and bag snatching, particularly in areas around railway stations, airports in large cities and at Christmas markets. Do not leave valuables unattended.

France shares with the rest of Europe a general threat from terrorism. Attacks could be indiscriminate and against civilian targets in public places, including tourist sites. You should maintain a high level of vigilance at all times.

British Embassy in France

35 RUE DU FAUBOURG ST HONORE
75363 PARIS CEDEX 08 PARIS
Tel: 01 44 51 31 00
www.ukinfrance.fco.gov.uk

There are also Consulates in Bordeaux, Lille, Lyon and Marseilles.

Irish Embassy in France

12 AVENUE FOCH, 75116 PARIS
Tel. 01 44 17 67 00
www.embassyofireland.fr

There are also Irish Consulates-General/ Consulates in Cannes, Cherbourg, Lyon and Monaco.

For Consular help while in Andorra contact the British Consulate-General in Barcelona:

AVDA DIAGNOL 477-13, 08036 BARCELONA
Tel: 00 34 902 109 356
www.ukinspain.fco.gov.uk

Documents

Passport

You legally have to carry some form of photographic identification at all times while in France, however this doesn't need to be your passport.

Money

The major debit and credit cards, including American Express, are widely accepted by shops, hotels, restaurants and petrol stations. However, you may find that credit cards are not as widely accepted in smaller establishments as they are in the UK, including many shops and campsites, due to the high charges imposed on retailers, and debit cards are preferred. Cash machines are widespread and have instructions in English.

You can be arrested for possession of counterfeit currency and the authorities advise against changing money anywhere other than at banks or bureaux de change.

Carry your credit card issuers'/banks' 24-hour UK contact numbers in case of loss or theft.

Vehicle(s)

Carry your valid driving licence, insurance and vehicle documents with you in your vehicle at all times. It is particularly important to carry your vehicle registration document V5C, as you will need it if entering low emission zones.

Driving

Accidents

Drivers involved in an accident or those who commit a traffic offence may be required to take a saliva or urine drugs test as well as a breathalyser test. In the event of an accident where people are injured or if emergency assistance is required, dial 17 (police) or 112 from any phone.

Alcohol

In both France and Andorra the maximum legal level of alcohol is 50 milligrams in 100 millilitres of blood, i.e. less than in the UK (80 milligrams). To ensure you stay under the limit it is best to avoid drinking at all if you plan to drive. For drivers with less than 3 years' experience the limit is 20 milligrams, which effectively means you cannot drink any alcohol at all. The police carry out random breath tests and penalties are severe.

There is a legal requirement to carry a breathalyser, however there is currently no punishment for non-compliance.

Blind spot stickers

From 5 January 2021 all vehicles with a total weight exceeding 3.5 tonnes must have a sticker showing the position of the blind spots.

The stickers:

- Must be visible from the sides and rear of the vehicle, and at a height between 0.90 and 1.50 meters from the ground.

- Can be glued, painted on the bodywork or affixed by riveting or any other means.

- Must not obstruct the visibility of the vehicle's registration plates and various lights and signalling devices as well as the driver's field of vision.

- Foreign vehicles passing through France are also subject to this signing obligation.

There are no specific blind spot stickers for motorhomes or caravans so you can use either of the stickers listed on the link below. There is no official distribution point for the stickers at present, but these can be purchased online at most big retailers.

To view the stickers and more information, visit https://www.securite-routiere.gouv.fr

Breakdown Service

If you break down on a motorway or in a motorway service area you must call the police from one of the orange emergency telephones placed every 2km along motorways. If you are in a service area, ask service station staff to contact the police for you, or dial 112 from a public phone and the police will be able to pinpoint your exact whereabouts. The police will arrange breakdown and towing assistance. No breakdown vehicle will enter a motorway without police authority.

Charges for motorway assistance are fixed by the government. If you have taken out breakdown insurance you should contact your insurance provider once the breakdown service has arrived in order to establish a means of payment. Your insurance provider cannot summon the police on your behalf if you breakdown on a motorway.

Headphones

It is illegal to drive a vehicle or cycle while wearing headphones or headsets. This includes listening to music or using headphones or earpieces to make phone calls. It is not illegal to make or receive phone calls using a hands-free system connected via Bluetooth to the car speaker system, or the speaker function on the phone.

Fuel

Unleaded petrol pumps are marked 'Essence Sans Plomb'. Diesel pumps are marked Gas Oil or Gazole.

Petrol stations may close on Sundays. Credit cards are generally accepted. Some automatic pumps are operated by credit cards and may not accept cards issued outside France. Away from major roads and towns don't let your fuel tank run too low as you may have difficulty finding an open petrol station, especially at night or on Sundays.

Fuel containing 10% bioethanol is on sale at many petrol stations in France alongside the regular Euro 95 unleaded fuel. Pumps are labelled SP95-E10. This fuel can be used in most modern vehicles manufactured since 2000 but if you are in any doubt about using it then regular Euro 95 or 98 Super Plus unleaded fuel is still available at most petrol stations. Check your vehicle handbook or visit www.acea.be for more information.

To find the cheapest fuel in any area log on to www.zagaz.com and simply click on the map of France to find the locations of petrol stations, together with prices charged.

Automotive Liquefied Petroleum Gas (LPG)

LPG (also called Gepel or GPL) is available in petrol stations across France, especially on motorways. However LPG may not be available in more rural areas so fill up at the first opportunity. Maps showing their company's outlets are issued free by most LPG suppliers, e.g. Shell, Elf, etc. A list of locations is available at the website stations. gpl.online.fr. LPG is not available in Andorra.

Low Emission Zones

There are Low Emission Zones operating in cities across France. For details of the rules and areas covered by each zone visit https://urbanaccessregulations.eu before you travel.

Motorhomes Towing Cars

If you are towing a car behind a motorhome, our advice would be to use a trailer with all four wheels of the car off the ground. Although France doesn't have a specific law banning A-frames, they do have a law which prohibits a motor vehicle towing another motor vehicle.

Overtaking and Passing

Crossing a solid single or double centre line is heavily penalised. Outside built-up areas, outfits weighing more than 3,500 kg, or more than 7m in length, are required by law to leave at least 50m between themselves and the vehicle in front. They are only permitted to use the two right-hand lanes on roads with three or more lanes and, where overtaking is difficult, should slow down or stop to allow other smaller vehicles to pass.

Parking

As a general rule, all prohibitions are indicated by road signs or by yellow road markings. Stopping or parking on the left-hand side is prohibited except in one-way streets.

In most cities parking is largely by 'pay and display' machines which take coins and credit or debit cards. Where parking signs show 'Horodateur' or 'Stationnement Payant' you must obtain a ticket from a nearby machine.

In Paris two red routes ('axe rouge') have been created on which stopping and parking are prohibited. Car parks are expensive and the best advice is to use public transport, which is cheap and efficient.

Priority

In built up areas, give way to traffic coming from the right, unless otherwise indicated. Outside built-up areas traffic on all main roads of any importance has right of way, indicated by the following signs:

Priority road   Priority road

On entering towns, the same sign will often have a line through it, warning that vehicles may pull out from a side road on the right and will have priority.

End of priority road

On steep gradients, vehicles travelling downhill give way to vehicles travelling uphill.

Public Transport

In built-up areas you must stop to allow a bus to pull out from a bus stop. Take particular care when school buses have stopped and passengers are getting on and off.

Overtaking trams in motion is normally only allowed on the right, unless on a one way street where you can overtake on the left if there is not enough space on the right. Do not overtake a tram near a tram stop, which can be in the centre of the road. When a tram or bus stops to allow passengers on and off, you should stop to allow them to cross to the pavement. Give way to trams which are turning across your carriageway.

Pedestrian Crossings

Stopping to allow pedestrians to cross at zebra crossings is not always common practice. Pedestrians expect to wait until the road is clear before crossing, and motorists behind may be taken by surprise if you stop to allow people to cross.

Roads

French roads fall into three categories: autoroutes (A) i.e. motorways; national (N) roads; and departmental (D) roads. There are over 10,500 kilometres of motorways, on most of which tolls are levied.

Andorra

Conditions on the road from Toulouse to Andorra, the N20/E9, can quickly become difficult in severe winter weather and you should be prepared for delays. Stick to main roads in Andorra when towing and don't attempt the many unsurfaced roads.

Road Signs and Markings

Directional signposting on major roads is generally good. Signs may be placed on walls pointing across the road they indicate and this may be confusing at first. Generally a sign on the right pointing left means that you go straight ahead. The same sign on the right pointing right means 'turn right' at the first opportunity. The words 'tout droit' mean 'go straight ahead' or 'straight on'.

Road signs on approach to roundabouts and at junctions usually do not show road numbers, just destinations, with numbers displayed once you are on the road itself.

Once you have seen your destination town signposted continue along the road until directed otherwise.

Lines on the carriageway are generally white. A yellow zigzag line indicates a bus stop, blue markings indicate that parking is restricted and yellow lines on the edge of the roadway indicate that stopping and/or parking is prohibited. A solid single or double white line in the centre of the road indicates that overtaking is not permitted. STOP signs mean stop - you must come to a complete halt otherwise you may be liable to a fine if caught.

Whilst road signs conform to international standards, some other commonly used signs you may see include:

French	English translation
Allumez vos feux	Switch on lights
Attention	Caution
Bouchon	Traffic jam
Chausée deformée	Uneven road
Chemin sans issue	No through road
Col	Mountain pass
Créneau de dépassement	2-lane passing zone, dual carriageway
Déviation	Diversion
Fin d'interdiction de stationner	End of parking restrictions
Gravillons	Loose chippings
Itineraire bis	Alternative route
Péage	Toll
Ralentissez	Slow down
Rappel	Continued restriction
Rétrécissement	Narrow lane
Route barrée	Road closed
Sens interdit	No entry
Sens unique	One-way street
Serrez à gauche/droite	Keep left/right
Stationnement interdit	No parking
Tout droit	Straight on
Toutes directions	All directions
Travaux	Road works
Virages	Bends

Andorra

Main roads are prefixed 'CG' (Carretera General) and side roads are prefixed 'CS' (Carretera Secundaria). CG road signs are white on red and CS signs are white on green.

Recently-Qualified Drivers

The minimum age to drive in France is 18 years and this also applies to foreign drivers. Driving without professionally qualified supervision/instruction on a provisional licence is not allowed.

Roundabouts

At roundabouts drivers must give way to traffic already on the roundabout, i.e. on the left, if indicated by a red-bordered triangular sign showing a roundabout symbol with the words 'Vous n'avez pas la priorité' or 'Cédez le passage' underneath.

Traffic on the roundabout has priority

In the absence of these signs traffic entering the roundabout has priority, however it is always very important to be watchful and to take extra care at roundabouts and junctions to avoid accidents.

Traffic Jams

The A6/A7 (the Autoroute du Soleil) from Paris via Lyon to the south are busy motorways prone to traffic jams. Travelling from the north, bottlenecks are often encountered at Auxerre, Chalon-sur-Saône, Lyon, Valence and Orange. An alternative route to the south is the A20, which is largely toll-free, or the toll-free A75 via Clermont-Ferrand.

During periods of congestion on the A6, A7 and A10 Paris-Bordeaux motorways, traffic police close off junctions and divert holiday traffic onto alternative routes or 'Itinéraires Bis' which run parallel to main roads.

Realtime traffic information on traffic conditions on motorways can be found on www.autoroutes.fr

In general, Friday afternoons and Saturday mornings are busiest on roads leading south, and on Saturday and Sunday afternoons roads leading north may well be congested. Many French people stop for lunch and, therefore, between noon and 2pm roads are quieter.

At the start of the school holidays in early July, at the end of July and during the first and last few days of August, roads are particularly busy. Avoid the changeover weekend at the end of July/beginning of August when traffic both north and south bound can be virtually at a standstill. Traffic can also be very heavy around the Christmas/New Year period and on the weekend of any public holiday.

Andorra

There is heavy traffic in Andorra-la-Vella on most days of the year. During the summer holiday period you are likely to encounter queues on the Envalira pass from France on the N22. Traffic is at its worst in the morning from France and in the afternoon and evening from Andorra and you are recommended to use the Envalira Tunnel to avoid some of the congestion and reduce travel time.

Traffic Lights

There is no amber light after the red light in the traffic light sequence.

A flashing amber light indicates caution, slow down, proceed but give way to vehicles coming from the right. A flashing red light indicates no entry; it may also be used to mark level crossings, obstacles, etc.

A yellow arrow at the same time as a red light indicates that drivers may turn in the direction of the arrow, traffic permitting, and providing they give way to pedestrians.

Watch out for traffic lights which may be mounted high above the road and hard to spot.

Violation of Traffic Regulations

Severe fines and penalties are in force for motoring offences and the police are authorised to impose and collect fines on the spot. Violations include minor infringements such as not wearing a seat belt, not carrying a set of spare bulbs or not respecting a STOP sign. More serious infringements such as dangerous overtaking, crossing a continuous central white line and driving at very high speeds, can result in confiscation of your driving licence.

If the offence committed is serious and likely to entail a heavy fine and the suspension of your driving licence or a prison sentence, a motorist who is not resident in France and has no employment there must deposit a guarantee. The police may hold a vehicle until payment is made.

Drivers who are deemed to have deliberately put the lives of others in danger face a maximum fine of €15,000 and a jail sentence. Failure to pay may result in your car being impounded. Your driving licence may also be suspended for up to five years.

By paying fines on the spot (request a receipt) or within three days, motorists can avoid court action and even reduce the fine. Standard fines can now be paid electronically in post offices and newsagents equipped with a dedicated terminal or by visiting www.amendes.gouv.fr.

Motorways

France has 11,500 kilometres of excellent motorways. Tolls are payable on most routes according to distance travelled and category of vehicle(s) and, because motorways are privately financed, prices per km vary in different parts of the country. Emergency telephones connected to the police are located every 2km.

Motorway Service Areas

Stopping is allowed for a few hours at the service areas of motorways, called 'aires', and some have sections specially laid out for caravans. Most have toilet facilities and a water supply but at 'aires' with only basic facilities, water may not be suitable for drinking, indicated by a sign 'eau non potable'. In addition there are 'aires de repos' which have picnic and play areas, whereas 'aires de services' resemble UK motorway service areas with fuel, shop, restaurant and parking facilities for all types of vehicle.

Motorway Tolls

Motorways tolls are common throughout France by a number of different operating companies, although there are numerous stretches, particularly around large cities, where no tolls are levied. Vehicles are classified as follows:

Category 1: (Light Vehicles) Vehicle with overall height under 2m and gross vehicle weight not exceeding 3,500kg. Train with overall height under 2m and gross vehicle weight of towing vehicle not exceeding 3,500kg.

Category 2: (Intermediate Vehicles) Vehicle with overall height from 2m to 3m and gross vehicle weight up to 3,500kg. Train with overall height from 2m to 3m and gross vehicle weight up to 3,500kg.

Category 3: (HGV or bus with two axles) Vehicle with overall height of 3m or more. Vehicle with gross vehicle weight of more than 3,500kg. On the A14 all twin-axle buses are in category 4.

Category 4: (HGV or bus with three or more axles) Vehicle with more than two axles and height of 3m or more, or gross vehicle weight of more than 3,500kg. Train with overall height of 3m or more. Train with towing vehicle having gross vehicle weight of more than 3,500kg.

Motorists driving Category 2 vehicles adapted for the transport of disabled persons pay the toll specified for Category 1 vehicles. Holding a disabled person's Blue Badge does not automatically entitle foreign motorists to pay Category 1 charges, and the decision whether to downgrade from Category 2 to 1 will be made by the person at the toll booth.

To calculate the tolls payable on your planned route see www.viamichelin.com and tick the box marked 'Caravan' (ticking this box will also give the toll for a motorhome) and select the 'Michelin recommended' route. For more detailed information, consult the websites of the individual motorway operating companies, a list of which can be found on www.autoroutes.fr/en/asfa/french-motorway-companies (English option). Alternatively calculate tolls payable on your chosen route on www.autoroutes.fr

Toll payments may be made in cash or by credit card, but be aware that when paying with a credit card you may not be asked for a signature or required to key in a PIN. Pre-paid credit cards, Maestro and Electron are not accepted.

On less frequently-used motorways, toll collection is increasingly by automatic machines equipped with height detectors.

It is simplest to pay with a credit card but there should be a cash/change machine adjacent. There are lanes at nearly all toll plazas specifically for drivers who have a Liber-t toll tag which allows them to pay for tolls directly from their bank account. Club members can benefit from a free Liber-t tag application (normally €10) - visit camc.com/sanef for details.

Speed Limits

Police are strict about speeding - motorists caught driving more than 40 km/h (25mph) over the speed limit face immediate confiscation of their driving licence. Speed limits on motorways (in dry weather) are higher than in the UK – although they are lower on ordinary roads.

Fixed speed cameras are common on both motorways and major roads. The use of mobile speed cameras and radar traps is frequent, even on remote country roads, and may be operated from parked vans or motor bikes, or they may be hand-held. They may also be in use on exit slip roads from motorways or major roads where there is a posted speed limit. Motorway toll booths will also calculate your speed from the distance you have travelled and the time it has taken.

Radar Detectors

Radar detectors, laser detectors or speed camera jammers are illegal in France. If caught carrying one, even if it is not in use, you are liable to both a fine of up to €1,500 and confiscation of the device, and possibly confiscation of your vehicle if you're unable to pay the fine. GPS or sat nav devices which pinpoint the position of fixed speed cameras are also illegal in France. You can still use the device, but you must disable the function which pinpoints speed cameras.

Inside Built-up Areas

The general speed limit is 50 km/h (31 mph) which may be raised to 70 km/h (44 mph) on important through roads, indicated by signs. The beginning of a built-up area is marked by a road sign giving the name of the town or village in blue or black letters on a light background with a red border. The end of the built-up area is indicated by the same sign with a red diagonal line through it. See examples below:

Therefore, when you enter a town or village, even if there is no actual speed limit warning sign, the place name sign itself indicates that you are entering a 50 km/h zone. The end of the 50 km/h zone is indicated by the place name sign crossed out. The word 'rappel' on a speed limit sign is a reminder of that limit.

The speed limit on stretches of motorway in built-up areas is 110 km/h (68 mph), except on the Paris ring road where the limit is 80 km/h (50 mph).

Outside Built-up Areas

General speed limits are as follows:

- On single carriageway roads 90 km/h (56 mph)
- On dual-carriageways separated by a central reservation 110 km/h (68 mph)
- On motorways 130 km/h (81 mph)

These general speed limits also apply to private cars towing a trailer tent or caravan, provided the gross train mass (fully laden weight of the car, plus the cars towing limit) of the vehicle does not exceed 3,500 kg. If the gross train mass of the towing vehicle is over 3,500 kg the speed limits are 90 km/h (56 mph) on motorways, 80-90 km/h (50 mph) on dual carriageways and 80 km/h (50 mph) on single carriageways.

Large motorhomes over 3,500 kg have a speed limit of 110 km/h (68 mph) on motorways, 100 km/h (62 mph) on dual carriageways and 80 km/h (50 mph) on single carriageway roads.

Adverse Weather Conditions

In case of rain or adverse weather conditions, general speed limits are lowered as follows:

- On motorways 110 km/h (68 mph)
- On urban motorways and dual carriageways 100 km/h (62 mph)
- Outside built-up areas 80 km/h (50 mph)

A speed limit of 50 km/h (31 mph) applies on all roads (including motorways) in foggy conditions when visibility is less than 50 metres.

Touring

France is divided administratively into 'régions', each of which consists of several 'départements'. There are 96 départements in total including Corsica, and these are approximately equivalent to our counties.

Paris, the capital and hub of the region known as the Ile-de-France, remains the political, economic, artistic, cultural and tourist centre of France. Visit www.parisinfo.com for a wealth of information on what to see and do in the city. A Paris Pass, valid for 2 to 6 days, entitles you to free entrance (ahead of the queues) to over 60 Paris attractions and free unlimited public transport plus discounts and free offers – see www.parispass.com.

Visitors under the age of 26 are admitted free to permanent collections in national museums; show your passport as proof of age. National museums, including the Louvre, are closed on Tuesday, with the exception of Versailles and the Musée d'Orsay which are closed on Monday. Entrance to national museums is free on the first Sunday of every month.

Restaurants must display priced menus outside and most offer a set menu 'plat du jour' or 'table d'hôte' which usually represents good value. A service charge of 15% is included in restaurant bills but it is also expected to leave a small tip if you have received good service. Smoking is not allowed in bars and restaurants.

France has a large network of well-marked, long-distance footpaths and hiking trails – Les Sentiers de Grande Randonnée – which generally follow ancient tracks. In addition to these 'GR' paths there are also 'PR' paths (Chemins de Petite Randonnée) which are most suited for local hiking. For a list of GR routes see www.gr-infos.com

Camping and Caravanning

There are approximately 10,400 campsites throughout France classified from 1 to 5 stars, including many small farm sites. Higher rated sites often have a wider range of facilities available. All classified sites must display their classification, current charges, capacity and site regulations at the site entrance.

Following incidents in recent years some authorities in southern France have introduced tighter regulations for sites liable to flooding, including limiting opening dates from April/May until August/September in some areas.

Casual/wild camping is prohibited in many state forests, national parks and nature reserves, and in all public or private forests in the départements of Landes and Gironde, along the Mediterranean coast including the Camargue, parts of the Atlantic and Brittany coasts, Versailles and Paris, and along areas of coast that are covered by spring tides.

Cycling

You may hire bicycles at many local tourist offices and from some railway stations.

Recent initiatives to encourage cycling have included the improvement of cycle tracks along rivers and canals and many former gravel tracks have been replaced with tarmac along the Rivers Rhône, Loire and Yonne/Canal de Nivernais. It is understood that similar improvements will take place along the Canal de Bourgogne.

In and around Paris there are 370 kilometres of cycle lanes, and bicycles, known as 'Les Vélibs', are available for hire at very reasonable rates at more than 1,600 self-service stations – roughly one every 300 metres.

The French Tourist Board has information on cycle routes and tours throughout France.

Public Transport

Several large cities have metro or tram systems and all have a bus network. The Paris metro network comprises 16 lines and around 300 stations, and has many connections to the RER (regional suburban rail network) and the SNCF national railway system. Tickets for the metro, also valid on RATP buses, can be bought singly from vending machines at the turnstiles or from ticket offices, but a 'carnet' of 10 tickets is a more economical option. Your ticket is valid for an hour and a half from the time it is validated at the machines, on buses or at metro stations.

For tourists Paris Visite travel passes are available allowing unlimited travel for one to five days across some or all of the travel zones and a range of discounts at attractions. For further information see www.ratp.fr

People aged 60 and over are entitled to a discount of up to 25% when using French railways. Show your passport as proof of age.

Ferries

Car ferry services operate all year across the Gironde estuary between Royan and Le Verdon eliminating a 155km detour. See www.bernezac.com for more details.

Ferry services operate from Marseille, Nice and Toulon to Corsica. For information see www.southernferries.co.uk

Channel Islands

Ferry services operate for cars and passengers between Poole and Portsmouth and St Malo via Jersey and Guernsey. Caravans and motorhomes are permitted to enter Jersey, subject to certain conditions, including pre-booking direct with a registered campsite and the acquisition of a permit. For further information and details of the campsites on Jersey where caravans are permitted, see www.jersey.com or contact The Club's Travel Service Information Officer, email: travelserviceinfo@camc.com

There are three campsites on Guernsey but, for the moment, the authorities in Guernsey do not permit entry to trailer caravans. Motorhomes can only be taken onto the island if they are stored under cover and not used for human habitation. Trailer tents can be taken onto the island without restrictions.

ABBEVILLE *3B3* (14km SE Rural) *50.03416, 1.98383*
Camp Municipal La Peupleraie, 80510 Long **03 22 31 84 27 or 03 22 31 80 21; bacquet.lionel@free.fr; www.long.fr**

🐕 � ⓦ ⏚ ⟲ ⟋ ♈ nr ⓗ nr ⟆ nr ⟏

Exit A16 at junc 21 for D1001 N then turn L at Ailly-le-Haut Clocher onto D32 for Long & foll sp. 2*, Med, mkd, pt shd, EHU (6A) inc (caution - poss rev pol & poss other elec concerns) (long lead req); bbq; red long stay; 90% statics; adv bkg acc; fishing adj; CKE. *"Pretty, busy site beside Rv Somme; gd san facs; gd walking/cycling by rv; site busy 1st week Sep - flea mkt in town; interesting area; old power stn museum; warden lives on site; conv en rte Calais; san facs v clean; quiet peaceful site; highly rec."* **€9.00, 15 Mar-15 Nov.** 2018

ABBEVILLE *3B3* (10km SW Rural) *50.08586, 1.71519*
Camping Le Clos Cacheleux, Rue des Sources, Route de Bouillancourt, 80132 Miannay **03 22 19 17 47; raphael@camping-lecloscacheleux.fr; www.camping-lecloscacheleux.fr**

🐕 €2.10 ♦11 ⓦ ⏚ ⚲ ⟲ ⟆ ⟋ ❀ ♈ ♈ ⓗ ⟏ ⟆ ⟏ ⟍
⟆ (covrd, htd, indoor) ⛳

Fr A28 exit junc 2 onto D925 sp Cambron. In 5km at Miannay turn S onto D86 sp Bouillancourt. Site thro vill of R opp sister site Camping Le Val de Trie which is sp fr A28. 3*, Med, hdg, pt shd, pt sl, EHU (10A) inc (poss long lead req); gas; bbq (charcoal, gas); cooking facs; TV; Eng spkn; adv bkg acc; ccard acc; tennis 3km; games area; games rm; sauna; spa; treatment rooms; library; kids' club; bike rental; CKE. *"Pleasant, peaceful, wooded site; lge pitches, charming, helpful owner; farm animals; fishing pond; all services (inc shop, rest & pool) are on sister site 'Le Val de Trie' on opp side of rd, accessed via steep track 500m fr site ent; no o'fits over18m; htd covrd pool, paddling pool adj; jacuzzi; gd walking, cycling; gd for dogs; san facs in a bad state (2019)."* **€28.60, 1 Mar-15 Oct, P12.** 2019

ABBEVILLE *3B3* (10km SW Rural) *50.08570, 1.71480*
Camping Le Val de Trie, 1 Rue des Sources, Bouillancourt-sous-Miannay, 80870 Moyenneville **03 22 31 48 88; raphael@camping-levaldetrie.fr; www.camping-levaldetrie.fr**

🐕 €2.10 ♦11 (htd) ⓦ ⏚ ⚲ ⟲ ⟆ ⟋ ⓂⓈⓅ ♈ ⟆ ⟏ ⟆ ⟏ ⟍
⟆ (covrd, htd) ⛳

Fr A28 exit junc 2 onto D925 sp Cambron. In 5km at Miannay turn S onto D86 sp Bouillancourt. Site thro vill on L. Site sp fr A28. NB Last pt of app narr with bends. 4*, Med, hdstg, mkd, hdg, shd, pt sl, EHU (6-10A) inc; gas; bbq; red long stay; TV; 1% statics; phone; Eng spkn; adv bkg acc; ccard acc; lake fishing; games rm; CKE. *"Beautiful, well-run site; well- shd; welcoming, helpful, conscientious owner; excel, clean, modern, san facs, ltd LS; gd family site; woodland walks; interesting area; conv Calais; great location for visiting the Somme area."* **€28.00, 1 Apr-29 Sep.** 2019

ABBEVILLE *3B3* (7km NW Rural) *50.14166, 1.76237*
Camping Le Château des Tilleuls, Rue de la Baie, 80132 Port-le-Grand **03 22 24 07 75; contact@ chateaudestilleuls.com; www.chateaudestilleuls.com**

🐕 ♦11 (htd) ⓦ ⏚ ⚲ ⚲ ⟲ ⟆ ⟋ ♈ ♈ ♈ ⓗ ⟆ ⟏ ⟆ (htd)

Fr N on A16 join A28 dir Rouen. At junc 1 take D40 dir St Valery-sur-Somme, site on R in approx 3km. 3*, Med, hdstg, hdg, mkd, pt shd, sl, terr, EHU (10-16A) €4; bbq; red long stay; TV; Eng spkn; adv bkg acc; ccard acc; games rm; bike hire; tennis; CKE. *"Pleasant site; improvements in progress (2011); lge, v sl pitches; find suitable pitch bef booking in; long uphill walk fr recep; unisex san facs; new pitches far fr ent; site being updated; new san facs (2015); well run; v clean; excel."* **€26.50, 1 Mar-30 Dec.** 2015

ABRETS, LES *9B3* (2km E Rural) *45.54065, 5.60834*
Kawan Village Le Coin Tranquille, 6 Chemin des Vignes, 38490 Les Abrets **04 76 32 13 48; contact@ coin-tranquille.com; www.coin-tranquille.com**

🐕 €2 ♦11 ⓦ ⏚ ⚲ ⟲ ⟆ ⟋ ⓂⓈⓅ ♈ ♈ ⓗ ⟆ ⟏ ⟏ ⟍
⟆ (covrd, htd) ⛳

Fr N exit A43 at junc 10 Les Abrets & foll D592 to town cent. At rndbt at monument take D1006 twd Chambéry/Campings; cont for 500m then turn L sp Le Coin Tranquille; cross level x-ing & cont for 500m to site. Fr S on A48 exit junc 10 at Voiron onto D1075 to Les Abrets; turn R at rndabt onto D1006 twd Le Pont-de-Beauvoisin, then as above. 4*, Lge, mkd, hdg, pt shd, EHU (10A) €5; gas; bbq; TV; Eng spkn; adv bkg req; ccard acc; bike hire; archery; games area; games rm; CKE. *"Well-kept, well-run site in gd location; no o'fits over 8m unless bkd in adv; lge narr pitches; busy/noisy site, but some quiet pitches avail; helpful & friendly staff; horseriding 7km; fishing 7km; golf 15km; well-kept, clean san facs, ltd LS; lovely pool; vg activities for children; poss flooding in wet weather; excel."* **€34.00, 1 Apr-31 Oct, M05.** 2019

ABRETS, LES *9B3* (3km S Rural) *45.47079, 5.54688*
Camping Le Calatrin (formerly Municipal), 799 Rue de la Morgerie, 38850 Paladru **04 76 32 37 48; camping.le.calatrin@gmail.com; www.camping-paladru.fr**

🐕 €3.50 ♦11 ⓦ ⏚ ⚲ ⟲ ⟆ ⟋ ⓂⓈⓅ ♈ ♈ ⟆ ⟏ ⟍

S fr Les Abrets on D1075; turn R onto D50 to Paladru; site 1km beyond vill on L, on brow of hill. Or exit A48 junc 9 & foll sp 'Lac de Paladru'; 3km after rndabt junc of D50 & D17, site on R (by another rndabt). 3*, Med, mkd, hdg, shd, terr, EHU (10A) €4 (long lead poss req); gas; bbq; sw nr; red long stay; TV; 30% statics; bus 200m; Eng spkn; adv bkg acc; fishing; games area; watersports; games rm; tennis 500m; bike hire; CKE. *"Attractive site; direct access to lake; lge pitches; welcoming & helpful owners; gd recreational facs; nice walks; excel."* **€17.00, 1 Apr-30 Sep.** 2017

FRANCE

ACCOUS *8G2* (0.5km NW Rural) *42.97717, -0.60592*
Camping Despourrins, Route du Somport, D'Arrechau, 64490 Accous **06 76 45 42 61 or 05 59 34 53 50; info@maison-despourrins.com; www.maison-des pourrins.com**

🐕 ♿ ⛺ ♨ ♿ 🚿 ⊠ 🚰 💧 Ⓣ nr Ⓗ nr 🐾 nr

On N134 rte to & fr Spain via Somport Pass. Site sp on main rd. 2*, Sm, pt shd, EHU (6A) €2.70; bbq; 10% statics; fishing. *"Clean, tidy NH; conv Col de Somport."* **€10.50, 1 Mar-31 Oct.** 2019

AGAY *10F4* (0.7km E Coastal) *43.4328, 6.86868*
Camping Agay Soleil, 1152, Boulevard de la plage RD559, 83530 Agay **04 94 82 00 79; contact@agay-soleil.com; www.agay-soleil.com**

🐕 €2 ♿ (htd) ⊠ ⛺ ♨ ♿ 🚿 ⊠ 💧 MP 🍴 Ⓣ 🍴 🛢 🐾 ⚓ 🏖 sand adj

E fr St Raphaël on D559 site on R after passing Agay dir Cannes. Or (to avoid busy St Raphaël) fr A8 exit junc 38 on D37 & foll sp St Raphaël, then Agay/ Valescure on D100 for approx 8 km; L at rndabt by beach in Agay; site far side of bay immed after watersports club. 3*, Med, mkd, hdstg, pt shd, pt sl, terr, EHU (10A) €5; gas; bbq (elec); train & bus 500m; Eng spkn; adv bkg rec; games area; watersports; CKE. *"Superb location on sea front; excel modern facs; many pitches too sm for awning; extra for beach pitches; dogs not acc high ssn;excel; sm pleasant site; direct access to beach; lge o'fits phone ahead; vg."* **€31.00, 1 Mar-1 Nov.** 2019

AGAY *10F4* (1.5km S Coastal) *43.41995, 6.85696*
Royal Camping, Plage de Camp-Long, 83530 Agay **04 94 82 00 20; contact@royalcamping.net; www.royalcamping.net**

🐕 ♿ ⊠ ⛺ ♨ ♿ 🚿 💧 🍴 Ⓣ nr Ⓗ nr 🐾 ⚓ sand adj

On D559 twd St Raphaël. Turn at sp Tiki Plage & site. Stop in ent rd at recep bef ent site. 3*, Sm, mkd, hdstg, pt shd, EHU (6A) €3.50; gas; 10% statics; phone; bus 200m; Eng spkn; adv bkg acc; CKE. *"Gd walks; lovely site; some pitches adj to beach in sep area; vg."* **€25.00, 10 Feb-4 Nov.** 2018

AGAY *10F4* (1km W Coastal) *43.43376, 6.85245*
Camping des Rives de l'Agay, Ave de Gratadis, 83530 Agay **04 94 82 02 74; reception@lesrivesdelagay.fr; www.lesrivesdelagay.fr**

🐕 €3 ♿ (htd) ⊠ ⛺ ♨ ♿ 🚿 ⊠ 💧 🍴 Ⓗ 🛢 🐾 ✎ 🏊 (htd) 🚮
🏖 sand 500m

Fr Agay take D100 dir Valescure, site in 400m on L. NB Dangerous bend & steep ent. 4*, Med, hdg, mkd, shd, EHU (6A) €3.60; gas; 10% statics; Eng spkn; adv bkg acc; CKE. *"San facs & pool v clean; gd pool with shd; excel site."* **€28.00, 9 Mar-7 Nov.** 2016

AGAY *10F4* (4km NW Rural/Coastal) *43.45408, 6.83254* **Esterel Caravaning,** Ave des Golfs, 83530 Agay/St Raphaël **04 94 82 03 28; contact@esterel-caravaning.fr; www.esterel-caravaning.fr**

🐕 €28 p/w ♿ (htd) WD ⊠ ♨ ♿ 🚿 ⊠ 💧 MP 🍴 Ⓣ Ⓗ 🛢 🐾 ⚓ 🏕 ✎
🏊 (covrd, htd) 🚮 🏖 sand 3km

Fr A8 foll sps for St Raphaël & immed foll sp 'Agay (par l'interieur)/Valescure' into D100/Ave des Golfs, approx 6km long. Pass golf courses & at end of rd turn L at rndabt twds Agay. Site ent immed after a L hand bend. 5*, Lge, hdstg, mkd, hdg, pt shd, pt sl, terr, serviced pitches; EHU (16A) inc; gas; bbq (charcoal, elec, gas); red long stay; twin axles; TV; 50% statics; Eng spkn; adv bkg acc; ccard acc; squash; waterslide; tennis; golf nr; archery; bike hire; games rm; games area; CKE. *"Superbly situated, busy site adj Esterel forest; undergrnd disco; 8 local golf clubs; friendly, helpful staff; gd san facs; gd for families - excel leisure activities; excel rest & shop; now classified as a 5 star site; conv Gorges du Verdon, Massif de l'Estérel, Monaco, Cannes & St Tropez; individual san facs to some pitches (extra charge); min stay 1 week high ssn (Sun to Sun); various pitch prices; ltd lge pitches avail; some pitches v sl & poss diff; ltd facs LS; mkt Wed; excel."* **1 Apr-26 Sep, C21.** 2019

AGDE *10F1* (7km SE Coastal) *43.29645, 3.52255* **Centre Hélio-Marin René Oltra (Naturist),** 1 Rue des Néréides, 34307 Le Cap-d'Agde **04 67 01 06 36 or 04 67 01 06 37; contact@centrenaturiste-oltra.fr; www.centrenaturiste-oltra.fr**

🐕 €3.40 ♿ WD ⊠ ♨ ♿ 🚿 ⊠ 💧 MP 🦋 🍴 Ⓗ 🐾 ⚓ 🏊 sand adj

S fr m'way A9 Agde-Pézenas junc on N312/D612 for 14km to Cap d'Agde turn-off; foll Camping Naturist sp to site on E side of Le Cap-d'Agde. 4*, V lge, mkd, hdg, pt shd, serviced pitches; EHU (6A) inc; 50% statics; bus adj; Eng spkn; adv bkg rec; ccard acc; INF card. *"Naturist area in Cap-d'Agde has all facs; lovely beach; gd size pitches; friendly atmosphere; modern san facs; gd family facs; excel; great location; gd public transport & walking; facs upgraded (2015); v busy but mostly quiet."* **€42.00, 15 Mar-14 Oct.** 2018

AGDE *10F1* (2km SW Rural) *43.29806, 3.45639* **Camping Le Neptune,** 46 Boulevard St Christ, 34300 Agde **04 67 94 23 94; info@campingleneptune.com; www.campingleneptune.com**

🐕 €3 ♿ WD ⊠ ♨ ♿ 🚿 ⊠ 💧 🦋 ♨ 🍴 Ⓗ nr 🐾 🏕 ✎ 🏊
(htd) 🚮 🏖 sand 2km

Fr A9 exit junc 34 onto N312, then E on D612. Foll sp Grau d'Agde after x-ing bdge. Site on D32E on E bank of Rv Hérault on 1-way system. 4*, Lge, mkd, hdg, pt shd, EHU (6-10A) inc; gas; bbq; TV; 40% statics; phone; Eng spkn; adv bkg rec; ccard acc; games area; tennis; CKE. *"Peaceful, pleasant, clean site; helpful owners; dog breed restrictions - check bef travel; modern facs, ltd LS; liable to flood after heavy rain; easy rvside walk/cycle to vill; gd cycleways; rv cruises; boat launch/slipway 500m; v popular site; gd facs; excel."* **€41.00, 1 Apr-30 Sep.** 2018

AGDE *10F1* (3km SW Coastal) *43.29440, 3.45010*
Camping Les Romarins, Le Grau d'Agde, 34300 Agde
**04 67 94 18 59; contact@romarins.com;
www.romarins.com**

🏕 €3.30 ♀♀ wc ♨ ⌂ ♿ 🚿 ⁄ MSP 🦋 ▾ 🍽 💢 ⊕ ⓵ 📶 nr ⚠ ✎
≋ (htd) 🏖 sand 1km

Fr Agde take rd to Grau d'Agde, site at ent to Grau d'Agde adj Rv Hérault. 4*, Med, hdstg, mkd, pt shd, EHU (10A) inc; bbq; twin axles; 25% statics; bus; Eng spkn; adv bkg acc; bike hire; games area; CKE. *"Pleasant town with many bars, rests; shop; helpful owner; excel site; v.busy; small pitches; crowded; gd location; nr rv & cycling to beach."*
€40.00, 30 May-12 Oct. 2019

AGEN *8E3* (8km NW Rural) *44.24368, 0.54290*
Camping Le Moulin de Mellet, Route de Prayssas, 47450 St Hilaire-de-Lusignan **05 53 87 50 89;
moulin.mellet@wanadoo.fr; www.camping-moulin-mellet.com**

🏕 €3.80 ♀♀ wc ♨ ⌂ ♿ 🚿 ⁄ 🦋 ⊕ ⓵ 📶 nr ⚠ ≋

NW fr Agen on N113 twd Bordeaux for 5km. At traff lts just bef Colayrac-St Cirq take D107 N twd Prayssas for 3km. Site on R. 3*, Sm, mkd, shd, EHU (10A) €3.80 (poss rev pol); gas; bbq; phone; Eng spkn; adv bkg acc; games rm; CKE. *"Delightful, well-run site; helpful, friendly new owners; sm children's farm; RVs & twin axles phone ahead; excel; spotless facs; rest & bar open in LS; pretty location; gd for long stay."*
€30.00, 1 Apr-10 Oct. 2019

AGON COUTAINVILLE *1D4* (0.3km NE Urban/Coastal) *49.05105, -1.59112* **Camp Municipal Le Martinet,** Blvd Lebel-Jéhenne, 50230 Agon-Coutainville **02 33 47 05 20; martinetmarais@wanadoo.fr; www.agoncoutainville.fr or www.coutainville.com**

🏕 €3.20 ♀♀ wc ♨ ♿ 🚿 ⁄ MSP 📶 nr ⚠ 🏖 sand 600m

Fr Coutances take D44 to Agon-Coutainville; site sp nr Hippodrome. 2*, Med, hdg, mkd, pt shd, EHU (6A) bbq; 55% statics; bus; Eng spkn; adv bkg acc; ccard acc; CKE. *"V pleasant site; ltd facs LS; horse racecourse adj; vg."* **€18.00, 1 Apr-30 Oct.** 2018

AIGLE, L' *4E2* (14km W Rural) *48.78841, 0.46533*
Camp Municipal des Saints-Pères, 61550 St Evroult-Notre-Dame-du-Bois **06 78 33 04 94 (mob) or 02 33 34 93 12 (Mairie); mairiestevroultnddubois @wanadoo.fr**

🏕 €0.20 ♀♀ wc ♨ ♿ ⁄ MSP ▾ nr ⊕ nr 📶 nr ⚠

Fr L'Aigle on D13, on ent vill site on L by lake. 2*, Sm, hdstg, pt shd, terr, EHU (4-10A) €1.50-2.50; sw nr; watersports; fishing; CKE. *"Pleasant lakeside vill; facs gd & clean with hot water, ltd LS; quiet; walks; on edge of sm vill opp ruins of ancient abbey; friendly, helpful staff, but no Eng spkn."*
€14.00, 1 Apr-30 Sep. 2016

AIGNAN *8E2* (0.6km S Rural) *43.69290, 0.07528*
Camping Le Domaine du Castex, 32290 Aignan
05 62 09 25 13; info@domaine-castex.com; www.gers-vacances.com

12 🏕 €4 ♀♀ wc ♨ ♿ 🚿 ⁄ MSP 🦋 ▾ 🍽 💢 ⊕ ⓵ 📶 nr ⚠ ≋

Fr N on D924/N124 turn S on D20 thro Aignan onto D48; in 500m g'ge on R, immed after turn L; site sp. Fr S on D935 turn E at Monplaisir onto D3/D48 to Aignan; site on R bef vill. 3*, Sm, hdg, mkd, hdstg, pt shd, EHU (10A) €3; bbq; sw nr; TV; 4% statics; phone; Eng spkn; adv bkg acc; ccard acc; tennis adj; games area; CKE. *"Lovely site in grnds of medieval farmhouse; helpful Dutch owners; modern san facs; excel pool & rest; squash adj; gd touring cent for Bastide vills; mkt Mon; phone ahead LS; vg."* **€20.00** 2016

AIGREFEUILLE D'AUNIS *7A1* (2km N Rural) *46.14621, -0.94571* **Camp Municipal de la Garenne,** 47 Avenue de l'Île Madame 17730 PORT DES BARQUES **05 46 84 80 66; camping@ville-portdesbarques.fr; www.camping-municipal-portdesbarques.com/**

🏕 €3 ♀♀ wc ♨ ⌂ ♿ 🚿 ⁄ MSP 🦋 ⁌ ⊕ 📶 nr ⚠ ≋ ⛱

Fr Aigrefeuille-d'Aunis take D112 2.5km N to vill of St Christophe, site sp. 3*, Sm, mkd, hdg, pt shd, EHU (4A) €2.50; sw nr; lake fishing 3km; horseriding; tennis; CKE. *"V clean site in sm vill; unrel opening dates, phone ahead LS."* **€23.00, 1 Apr -31 Oct.** 2020

AIGUES MORTES *10F2* (3.5km W Rural) *43.56300, 4.15910* **Yelloh! Village La Petite Camargue,** 30220 Aigues-Mortes **04 66 53 98 98; info@yellohvillage-petite-camargue.fr; www.yellohvillage-petite-camargue.com or www.yellohvillage.co.uk**

🏕 €6 ♀♀ wc ♨ ⌂ ♿ 🚿 ⁄ MSP 🦋 ⁌ 🍽 💢 ⊕ ⓵ 📶 ✎ ≋ ⛱
🏖 sand 3km

Heading S on N979 turn L onto D62 bef Aigues-Mortes & go over canal bdge twd Montpellier; site on R in 3km; sp. 5*, V lge, mkd, pt shd, EHU (10A) inc; bbq (charcoal, gas); red long stay; TV; 50% statics; Eng spkn; adv bkg acc; ccard acc; games rm; serviced; horseriding; bike hire; tennis; games area; jacuzzi; CKE. *"Lively, busy, well-run, youth-oriented commercial site with many sports facs; no o'fits over 7m; clean san facs, poss stretched high ssn; excel pool complex; bus to beach high ssn; some sm pitches; take care o'head branches; gd cycling; mkt Wed & Sun; some pitches diff to access."* **€44.00, 10 Apr-14 Sep, C04.** 2019

AIGUILLON *7D2* (0.9km NE Rural) *44.30467, 0.34491*
Camp Municipal du Vieux Moulin, Route de Villeneuve, 47190 Aiguillon **05 53 79 60 12; www.ville-aiguillon.eu**

♀♀ wc ♨ ▾ ⁄ ▾ nr ⊕ nr 📶 nr ⚠

On ent town on D813, turn E onto D666 to site on bank of Rv Lot. Clearly sp. Or exit A62 junc 6 at Damazan onto D8 to Aiguillon. 2*, Med, mkd, shd, EHU (10A) inc. *"Gd site adj old mill house by rv; gd san facs; conv A62; NH only."* **€10.00, 1 Jul-31 Aug.** 2019

AIGUILLON SUR MER, L' *7A1* (1km W Coastal) *46.34349, -1.32006* **Camp'Atlantique Bel Air,** 2 Route de Bel Air, 85460 L'Aiguillon-sur-Mer 02 51 20 41 94; belair.camp-atlantique.co.uk

🐕 €3.50 ⛺🏕 🚿 ⬛ 💧 ♿ 🍴 🛒🐕 🎿 🛖 ⚓ 🏇 sand 800m

Fr La Roche-sur-Yon take D747 to La Tranche-sur-Mer via coast rd D46 to La Faute-sur-Mer. Cross bdge to L'Aiguillon-sur-Mer. Site 1km W of town on D44. Sp fr all dir. 4*, Lge, pt shd, EHU (3A) €3.50; bbq; 10% statics; adv bkg acc; waterslide; archery; bike hire. *"Excel, clean, friendly site; pony trekking."* €42.00, 1 Apr-30 Sep. 2015

AINHOA *8F1* (2.5km SW Rural) *43.29143, -1.50394* **Camping Xokoan,** Quartier Dancharia, 64250 Ainhoa 05 59 29 90 26; etchartenea@orange.fr; www.camping-xokoan.com

12 🏕 🚿 ⬛ ♿ 🛒🐕 🍴 🛖 ⚓ MSP 🦋 🍴 🐕 nr 🛖

S fr Ainhoa on D20, site on L in 2km. Narr ent & app. Fr Spain on N121B, pass Frontier site 250m on R. 3*, Sm, mkd, hdstg, pt shd, pt sl, EHU (6A) €3.50; bbq; adv bkg acc; games rm; CKE. *"Conv for N Spain & Pyrenees; gd walks; v interesting & scenic site in grnds of sm hotel; gd."* €17.50 2017

AINHOA *8F1* (0.4km NW Urban) *43.30913, -1.50178* **Aire Naturelle Harazpy (Zaldua),** 64250 Ainhoa 05 59 29 89 38 or 05 59 29 90 26 (LS); etchartenea@orange.fr; www.camping-harazpy.com

🐕 🏇 WD 🏕 ♿ 💧 🛒 MSP 🦋 ⚓

Take D918 E fr St Jean-de-Luz sp Espelette: in approx 20km turn R on D20 sp Ainhoa. App church in Ainhoa turn R thro open car park to rd at rear; site on R in 250m. Site sp. Sm, mkd, pt shd, pt sl, terr, EHU (10A) inc; phone; adv bkg acc; CKE. *"Beautiful location; conv Spanish border; helpful staff; excel walking area."* €17.50, 1 Apr-30 Sep. 2016

AIRE SUR LA LYS *3A3* (2km NE Urban) *50.64390, 2.40630* **Camp Municipal de la Lys,** Bassin des Quatre Faces, Rue de Fort Gassion, 62120 Aire-sur-la-Lys 03 21 95 40 40; camping@ville-airesurlalys.fr; www.ville-airesurlalys.fr

🏇 (htd) WD 🏕 ♿ 🚿

Fr town cent, find main sq & exit to R of town hall. Thro traff lts turn R into narr lane just bef rv bdge dir of Hazebrouck. Site poorly sp. High vehicles beware low bdge at site ent. 2*, Sm, hdstg, mkd, hdg, pt shd, EHU (6A) €2.10; 95% statics. *"Ltd touring pitches; ltd but clean san facs; not suitable lge o'fits; rec for NH only; v welcoming; waterside pitches; vg NH; easy walk to town."* €12.00, 1 Apr-31 Oct. 2016

AIRE SUR L'ADOUR *8E2* (0.7km NE Urban) *43.70259, -0.25792* **Camping Les Ombrages de l'Adour,** Rue des Graviers, 40800 Aire-sur-l'Adour 05 58 71 75 10; hetapsarl@yahoo.fr; www.camping-adour-landes.com

🐕 €1.80 🏇 WD 🏕 ♿ 💧 MSP 🐕 ⚓ ⛵

Turn E on S side of bdge over Rv Adour in town. Site close to bdge & sp, past La Arena off rd to Bourdeaux. 2*, Med, pt shd, EHU (10A) inc; bbq; adv bkg acc; ccard acc; fishing 500m; tennis 500m; games area. *"Vg; htd pool 500m; canoeing 500m; v clean facs but dated."* €19.00, 16 Apr-15 Oct. 2016

AIRE SUR L'ADOUR *8 E2* (14.6km SW Rural) *43.63582, -0.38150* **Camping Municipal de Geaune,** 11 Route de Cledes, Geaune 05 58 44 50 27

🐕 🏇 WD 🏕 ♿ 💧 MSP 🦋 🍴 🐕 nr 🐕 nr

Foll D2 fr Aire sur l'Adour to Geaune. Thro town ctr and L on D111 twrds Cledes. Site on L in 300m. Sm, mkd, pt shd, terr, EHU 6A; bbq (sep area); sw nr; CKE. *"Vg."* €14.00, 1 Apr-31 Oct. 2019

AIRVAULT *4H1* (1km N Rural) *46.83200, -0.14690* **Camping de Courte Vallée,** 8 Rue de Courte Vallée, 79600 Airvault 05 49 64 70 65; info@caravanning france.com; www.caravanningfrance.com

🐕 €1.50 🏇 WD 🏕 ♿ 💧 MSP 🦋 🍴 🍴 ⚓ 🛖 ⛵ (htd)

Fr N, S or W leave D938 sp Parthenay to Thouars rd at La Maucarrière twd Airvault & foll lge sp to site. Site on D121 twd Availles-Thouarsais. NB If app fr NE or E c'vans not permitted thro Airvault - watch carefully for sp R at Gendarmerie. Well sp fr all dirs. 3*, Sm, mkd, hdstg, hdg, pt shd, pt sl, EHU (13A) inc (poss long lead req); gas; bbq; red long stay; twin axles; TV; 8% statics; adv bkg acc; ccard acc; games rm; bike hire; fishing; CKE. *"Peaceful, popular; pleasant, helpful British owners; excel, clean & vg facs, poss stretched high ssn; conv Futuroscope & Puy du Fou theme park; mkt Sat; not as well kept & expensive compared to similar sites; c'van storage; town dissapointing, empty shops; new rest & bar(2018)."* €33.00, 1 Mar-15 Nov, L14. 2018

AIX EN PROVENCE *10F3* (9km E Rural) *43.51771, 5.54128* **FFCC Camping Ste Victoire,** Quartier La Paradou, 13100 Beaurecueil 04 42 66 91 31; camping victoire@orange.fr; www.campingsaintevictoire.com

🐕 €1.10 🏇 (htd) WD 🏕 ♿ 💧 MSP 🦋 🍴 🐕 nr 🛖

Exit A8/E80 junc 32 onto D7n dir Aix, then R onto D58 & foll sp for 3km. 2*, Sm, hdg, mkd, hdstg, shd, EHU (6A)(some rev pol & poss no neutral); red long stay; TV; phone; bus; adv bkg acc; archery; bike hire; CKE. *"Well-run site in attractive hilly, wooded area; friendly, helpful owners; clean, basic, dated & small san facs, ltd LS, but clean; various pitch sizes; lge o'fits poss diff manoeuvring; pool 9km; some pitches too soft for lge o'fits when wet; no twin axles; no lighting at night; gd walking & climbing; lovely location; shady; frequent cheap bus to Aix; narr rds; site can be diff to find."* €21.50, 5 Mar-30 Nov. 2018

FRANCE

AIX EN PROVENCE *10F3* (3km SE Urban) *43.51556, 5.47431* **Airotel Camping Chantecler,** Val-St André, 13100 Aix-en-Provence **04 42 26 12 98; info@camping chantecler.com; www.campingchantecler.com**

Fr town inner ring rd foll sps Nice-Toulon, after 1km look for sp Chantecler to L of dual c'way. Foll camp sp past blocks of flats. Well sp in Val-St André. If on A8 exit at junc 31 sp Val-St André; R at rndabt; R at Rndabt; L at 2nd traff lts onto Ave Andre Magnan; R ar rndabt; site sp. If app fr SE on D7n turn R immed after passing under A8. 4*, Lge, hdstg, hdg, pt shd, sl, terr, EHU (5A) €4.10 (long lead poss req); gas; bbq (elec, gas); red long stay; TV; bus; adv bkg acc; ccard acc; site clsd 1 & 2 Jan; CKE. *"Lovely, well-kept, wooded site; facs ltd LS; some site rds steep - gd power/weight ratio rec; access poss diff some pitches; rec request low level pitch & walk to pitch bef driving to it; ent narr; recep clsd 12.30-13.30; gd pool; conv city; vg touring base; access diff to some pitches, refurb san facs now htd & excel (2014)."* **€28.70** **2019**

AIX EN PROVENCE *10F3* (8.6km SE Urban) *43.51250, 5.47196* **Camping L'Arc-en-Ciel,** Ave Henri Malacrida, Pont des 3 Sautets, 13100 Aix-en-Provence **04 42 26 14 28; camping-arenciel@neuf.fr; www.camping arenciel.com**

Fr E or W exit A8 at junc 31 for D7n dir SE; (turn N for 300m to 1st rndabt where turn R; in 200m at 2nd rndabt turn R again onto D7n dir SE); pass under m'way; site ent immed on R; sp. Take care at ent. NB Access easier if go past site for 1km to rndabt, turn round & app fr S. 4*, Sm, hdg, mkd, shd, terr, EHU (6A) inc; gas; bbq; TV; phone; bus adj; Eng spkn; adv bkg acc; fishng; canoeing; golf 1km; games area; CKE. *"Delightful, well-kept, well-run, great site; friendly, helpful owner; some pitches sm; some steep site rds, tow avail; vg immac facs; superb pool; if recep clsd use intercom in door; gd dog walk adj; bus to Marseille; conv NH nr a'route; highly rec; v secure; easy access to Aix town; bank cards not acc."* **€26.00, 4 Apr-4 Oct.** **2019**

AIX LES BAINS *9B3* (3km W Rural) *45.70005, 5.88666* **Camp Municipal International du Sierroz,** Blvd Robert Barrier, Route du Lac, 73100 Aix-les-Bains **04 79 61 89 89; info@camping-sierroz.com; www.camping-sierroz.com**

Fr Annecy S on D1201, thro Aix-les-Bains, turn R at site sp. Keep to lakeside rd, site on R. Nr Grand Port. 3*, Lge, hdg, mkd, shd, EHU (6A) inc; gas; TV; 5% statics; bus (ask at recep for free pass); adv bkg acc; ccard acc; golf 4km; games area; CKE. *"Pleasant location; lake adj for watersports; lge pitches; poss travellers & v unclean facs LS (June 2010)."* **€23.60, 15 Mar-15 Nov.** **2019**

AIZELLES *3C4* (0.4km NW Rural) *49.49076, 3.80817* **Camping du Moulin (Merlo),** 16 Rue du Moulin, 02820 Aizelles **03 23 22 41 18 or 06 14 20 47 43 (mob); magali.merlo@orange.fr; www.camping-du-moulin.fr**

Fr Laon take D1044 dir Reims; in 13km turn L on D88 to Aizelles; site sp in vill 'Camping à la Ferme'. Fr Reims on A26 exit junc 14 onto D925 then D1044 N. Turn R to Aizelles on D889 past Corbeny. Turn onto Rue du Moulin & site on R in 250m. Camping sp at church says 100m but allow 300m to see ent. Sm, pt shd, pt sl, EHU (10A) inc (poss rev pol, poss long lead req); Eng spkn; ccard acc; fishing 800m; CKE. *"Attractive, well-kept CL-type farm site; v friendly, helpful owners; basic san facs need update; gates clsd 2200-0700; wonderful well maintained site in a sm pretty vil; conv Calais 3 hrs; vg site; conv for Zeebrugge; few statics."* **€16.00, 1 Apr-15 Oct.** **2018**

AIZENAY *2H4* (1.7km SE Rural) *46.73410, -1.58950* **FFCC Camping La Forêt,** 1 Rue de la Clairière, 85190 Aizenay **02 51 34 78 12; info@camping-laforet.com; www.camping-laforet.com**

Exit Aizenay on D948 twd La Roche-sur-Yon. Site 1.5km on L. 3*, Med, hdg, mkd, pt shd, EHU (6A) €2.70; gas; bbq; sw nr; 10% statics; phone; adv bkg acc; ccard acc; tennis; bike hire; CKE. *"Undergoing refurbishment 2013; new bar & ent; v pleasant site; gd size pitches."* **€18.00, Easter-30 Sep.** **2015**

AIZENAY *2H4* (8km NW Rural) *46.75282, -1.68645* **Camping Val de Vie,** Rue du Stade, 85190 Maché **02 51 60 21 02; campingvaldevie@bbox.fr; www.campingvaldevie.fr**

Fr Aizenay on D948 dir Challans. After 5km turn L onto D40 to Maché. Fr vill cent cont twd Apremont. Sm, blue site sp 100m on L. 3*, Med, hdg, mkd, pt shd, pt sl, serviced pitches; EHU (6-10A) €3.50-4; gas; bbq; twin axles; red long stay; 20% statics; Eng spkn; adv bkg acc; fishing; bike hire; tennis adj; boat hire. *"Lovely, peaceful, well-run site in pretty vill; new young owners upgrading facs & rds (2011); warm welcome; clean san facs; steel pegs useful; gd touring base; gd cycling; excel."* **€25.60, 1 Apr-1 Oct.** **2016**

AJACCIO *10H2* (26km N Coastal) *42.04791, 8.74919* **Camping A Marina,** Golfe de la Liscia, 20111 Calcatoggio **95 52 21 84 or 72 83 62 34; fabiani.famille@ wanadoo.fr; www.camping-amarina.com**

Take D81 N fr Ajaccio for 20km; site ent on L 3km fr turn off to Calcatoggio. Foll sp to end of site. Sm, hdg, pt shd, EHU (16A) €4; bbq; 50% statics; Eng spkn; ccard acc; games area. *"Sm garden site adj to beautiful sandy bay; excell san facs, bar; friendly, family run; an oasis; excel."* **€35.00, 1 Apr-31 Oct.** **2015**

ALBAN 8E4 (1km NW Rural) 43.89386, 2.45416
Camp Municipal La Franquèze, 81250 Alban **05 63 55
91 87 or 05 63 55 82 09 (Mairie); mairie.alban
@wanadoo.fr; www.campingtarn.com/fr/camping-
municipal-la-franqueze**

W of Albi on D999 turn L at ent to Alban. Site 300m
on R, sp. 2*, Sm, hdg, pt shd, pt sl, terr, EHU (6A)
€2.10; adv bkg acc; rv fishing; CKE. *"Beautiful area,
conv Tarn Valley; vg; water taps scarce; gd hilltop site
with views."* **€14.00, 1 Jun-30 Sep.**   2019

ALBERT 3B3 (1.5km N Urban) 50.01136, 2.65556
Camp Municipal du Vélodrome, Ave Henri Dunant,
80300 Albert **03 64 62 22 53 or 06 42 58 71 64;
campingalbert@laposte.net; www.camping-albert
.com**

Fr town cent take Rue Godin E adj to Basilica &
foll sp for site. Easiest access fr Bapaume (N) twds
Albert; turn R at camping sp on edge of town.
2*, Med, mkd, pt shd, EHU (4-10A) €2.20-4.40 (rev
pol); red long stay; 40% statics; Eng spkn; adv bkg acc;
fishing adj; CKE. *"Pleasant, well-run, well maintained,
clean site; nr lake; friendly, helpful warden; poss
security prob; conv for Lille, Arras & Amien by train &
for WW1 battlefields etc; poss rlwy noise; facs basic
but rates reasonable; if office close find pitch and
inform warden later; gates clsd fairly early, will need
ent code if late; easy walk into Albert; semi sep aire;
unisex shwrs & wc."* **€19.50, 1 Apr-11 Oct.**   2019

"There aren't many sites open at this time of year"

If you're travelling outside peak season
remember to call ahead to check site opening
dates – even if the entry says 'open all year'.

ALBERT 3B3 (5km NE Rural) 50.04141, 2.66868
International Camping Bellevue, 25 Rue d'Albert,
80300 Authuille **03 22 74 59 29 or 06 71 96 88 78
(mob); camping.bellevue0767@orange.fr;
campingbellevue.pagesperso-orange.fr**

Take D929 Albert to Bapaume rd; in 3km turn L at
La Boiselle, foll sp to Aveluy cont to Authuille. Site
on R in vill cent. 2*, Med, mkd, pt shd, pt sl, EHU (6A)
inc (rev pol); 80% statics; adv bkg acc; rv fishing 500m;
CKE. *"Helpful owner; basic site, well maintained; useful
touring Somme WW1 battlefields; walking dist of
Thiepval Ridge; gd NH; lovely site; excel rest in vill; san
facs old fashioned but clean; church clock chiming thro
night."* **€17.00, 15 Mar-31 Oct.**   2017

ALBERT 3B3 (14km SW Rural) 49.91930, 2.57985
FFCC Camping Les Puits Tournants, 6 Rue du Marais,
80800 Sailly-le-Sec **03 22 76 65 56; camping.puits
tournants@wanadoo.fr; www.camping-les-puits-
tournants.com**

Fr N exit A1 junc 14 onto D929 dir Amiens, at Albert
take D42 S to Sailly-Laurette then turn R onto D233
to Sailly-le-Sec & foll sp. Or fr S exit junc 13 twd
Albert onto D1029. At Lamotte-Warfusée R onto
D42 to Sailly-Laurette, turn L to Sailley-le-Sec.
3*, Med, hdstg, mkd, pt shd, EHU (4A) €3; gas; bbq;
sw; TV; 60% statics; Eng spkn; adv bkg acc; ccard acc;
games area; bike hire; canoe hire; fishing; horseriding
5km; tennis 2km. *"Lovely, pleasant family-run site;
amiable staff; gd clean san facs, need updating; grass
pitches muddy when wet; tight ent, lge o'fits poss
diff; gd pool; walks by rv; excel; picturesque site nr
rv Somme; nice dog walks by rv; facs poss stretched
in HS; new pools & rest under construction (2017)."*
€25.00, 1 Apr-31 Oct.   2017

ALBERTVILLE 9B3 (0.7km NNE Urban) 45.67922,
6.39636 **Camp Municipal Les Adoubes,** Ave du
Camping, 73200 Albertville **04 79 32 06 62 or 06 85
84 02 56; hello@camping-albertville.fr;
www.camping-albertville.fr**

Site is 200m fr town cent; over bdge on banks of
Rv Arly. Med, mkd, pt shd, pt sl, EHU (10A) €3.50;
gas; bbq; twin axles; TV; 5% statics; Eng spkn; adv
bkg acc; ccard acc; CKE. *"Excel site in excel location;
plenty of rm, even high ssn; v helpful staff; site yourself
if recep clsd; well kept; 10% red for CC memb; under
new management; site being upgraded for 2015; rallies
acc."* **€20.50, 1 Jan-30 Oct & 1 Dec-31 Dec.**   2015

ALBI 8E4 (2km NE Urban) 43.93485, 2.16213
**Albirondack Park, Camping Lodge & Spa (formerly
Camping Caussels),** 31 Allée de la Piscine, 81000
Albi **05 63 60 37 06 or 06 84 04 23 13 (mob);
albirondack@orange.fr; www.albirondack.fr**

Fr Albi ring rd/bypass exit sp Lacause/St Juéry (do
not turn twd Millau). Strt over & foll sp Géant-
Casino hypmkt & 'Centre Ville', then foll camping/
piscine sp. 3*, Med, mkd, pt shd, pt sl, EHU (10A)
€5.70; bbq; 10% statics; bus; adv bkg acc; CKE. *"Vg,
popular site in conv position; pitches unlevelled - soft in
wet & some poss diff lge o'fits due trees; gd walk
(40 min) by rv to town cent; Albi Cathedral; spa;
Toulouse Lautrec exhibitions; spa & pool inc; excel
rest; excel clean modern san facs; beware of low lying
wooden & concrete posts; v cramped site; rec arr early."*
€36.50, 20 Jan-10 Nov & 2 Dec-31 Dec.   2018

FRANCE

ALENCON *4E1* (3km SW Rural) *48.42566, 0.07321*
Camp Municipal de Guérame, 65 Rue de Guéramé,
61000 Alençon **02 33 26 34 95; camping.guerame@
orange.fr; www.ville-alencon.fr**

€1.90 (htd) nr nr

Located nr town cent. Fr N on D38 take N12 W
(Carrefour sp). In 5km take D1 L sp Condé-sur-
Sarthe. At rndabt turn L sp Alençon then R immed
after Carrefour supmkt, foll site sp. Site is sp
fr D112 inner ring rd. 2*, Med, hdg, hdstg, pt shd, EHU
(5A) €3.10 (check EHU carefully) (poss long lead req);
bbq; TV; Eng spkn; adv bkg acc; bike hire; horseriding;
rv fishing; tennis; canoeing; CKE. *"Helpful warden;
clean san facs; o'night m'vans area; pool complex
700m; barrier/recep clsd 1800 LS; LS phone ahead to
check site open; some pitches poss flood in heavy rain;
rvside walk to town thro arboretum; peaceful site."*
€15.00, 1 Apr-30 Sep.   **2015**

ALERIA *10H2* (7km N Coastal) *42.16155, 9.55265*
Camping-Village Riva-Bella (Part Naturist), 20270
Aléria **04 95 38 81 10; riva-bella@orange.fr;
www.naturisme-rivabella.com**

12 €3.50

sand adj

Fr Bastia S on N198 for 60km, site sp to L. Poor rd
access (2011). 3*, Med, pt shd, EHU €4.30; red long
stay; TV; 10% statics; adv bkg acc; fishing; games area;
watersports; bike hire; tennis; INF card. *"Site untidy
early ssn (2011); fitness rm; steam rm; sauna; spa
treatments; poss insect problem; naturist site 15 May-
20 Sep, non-naturist rest of year - but always sm end
beach avail for naturists."* **€36.00**   **2016**

"That's changed – Should I let the Club know?"

If you find something on site that's different
from the site entry, fill in a report and let us
know. See camc.com/europereport.

ALET LES BAINS *8G4* (0.3km W Rural) *42.99490,
2.25525* **Camping Val d'Aleth,** Ave Nicolas Pavillon,
11580 Alet-les-Bains **04 68 69 90 40; info@valdaleth.
com; www.valdaleth.com**

12 €1.55 (htd) nr

Fr Limoux S on D118 twd Quillan; in approx 8km
ignore 1st L turn over Aude bdge into vill but take
alt rte for heavy vehicles. Immed after x-ing rv, turn
L in front of casino & ent town fr S; site sp on L.
2*, Sm, hdg, mkd, hdstg, shd, pt sl, EHU (10A) €2.75-4;
gas; bbq (gas); red long stay; 25% statics; phone; Eng
spkn; adv bkg acc; ccard acc; bike hire; CKE. *"Rvside
(no sw) site in attractive, medieval vill; sm pitches (lge
o'fits need to book); friendly, helpful British owner; gd
clean san facs; v few facs in vill; poss unkempt early
ssn; conv Carcassonne & Cathar country - scenic; ACSI
acc."* **€20.00**   **2016**

ALLEGRE LES FUMADES *10E2* (2km NE Rural)
44.2089, 4.25665 **Camping Le Château de Boisson,**
30500 Allègre-les-Fumades **04 66 24 85 61 or 04 66
24 82 21; reception@chateaudeboisson.com; www.
chateaudeboisson.com or www.les-castels.com**

€5 (covrd, htd)

Fr Alès NE on D904, turn R after Les Mages onto
D132, then L onto D16 for Boisson. Fr A7 take exit
19 Pont l'Esprit, turn S on N86 to Bagnols-sur-Cèze
& then D6 W. Bef Vallérargues turn R onto D979
Lussan, then D37 & D16 to Boisson. 4*, Lge, mkd,
hdg, shd, pt sl, EHU (6A) inc; gas; bbq (elec, gas); red
long stay; 80% statics; phone; Eng spkn; adv bkg acc;
ccard acc; games rm; tennis; bike hire. *"Vg, well-run,
peaceful site; no o'fits over 7m high ssn; no dogs 9 Jul-
20 Aug; gd sized pitches, poss some v sm; helpful staff;
excel san facs; excel rest & facs; superb pool complex."*
€39.00, 12 Apr-27 Sep, C34.   **2016**

"I like to fill in the reports as I travel from site to site"

You'll find report forms at the back of this
guide, or you can fill them in online at
camc.com/europereport.

AMBAZAC *7B3* (3km NE Rural) *45.97158, 1.41315*
Camping L'Ecrin Nature, 87240 Ambazac **06 52 92 71
65 or 05 55 56 60 25; contact@campinglecrinature.
com; www.campinglecrinature.com**

(htd)

Fr A20 foll sp to Ambazac; site on D914.
3*, Med, hdg, mkd, pt shd, pt sl, terr, EHU (6A) €3.50;
bbq; 15% statics; Eng spkn; adv bkg acc; ccard acc;
lake fishing. *"Excel waterside site with lovely lake
views, o'looking lake; v friendly new owners, who
cont to improve this eco site; san facs clean; ctr for
mountain biking & walking; much improved site; gd
pool; hg rec; use barrier intercom to contact bureau
on arr (bureau clsd midday-3pm); shgl beach adj (sw
not allowed); excel site; peaceful; use intercom to gain
access."* **€21.00, 10 Apr-3 Oct.**   **2019**

AMBERT *9B1* (1km S Urban) *45.53951, 3.72867*
Camping Les Trois Chênes, Rue de la Chaise-Dieu,
63600 Ambert **04 73 82 34 68; tourisme@
ville-ambert.fr; www.camping-ambert.com**

€1 nr nr

On main rd D906 S twd Le Puy on L bet Leisure Park
& Aquacentre. 3*, Med, hdg, mkd, pt shd, serviced
pitches; EHU (10A) €3.25; 80% statics; adv bkg acc;
waterslide; CKE. *"Excel, well-kept site; gd, clean san
facs; rvside walk to town; htd pool adj; rec arrive bef
noon peak ssn; recep & barrier clsd 1900 LS; steam
museum & working paper mill nr; steam train 1.5km;
vg."* **€21.60, 26 Apr-29 Sep.**   **2019**

AMBIALET *8E4* (0.8km ESE Rural) *43.94181, 2.38686*
Camping La Mise à l'Eau, Fédusse, 81430 Ambialet
**05 63 79 58 29; contact@camping-ambialet.com;
www.camping-ambialet.fr**

🐕 €1.50 👪 ♿ 🚿 ⚡ 🛒 nr ⓗ nr 🏪 🔥 ⛱

Fr Albi E on D999; in 15km, after Villefranche-
d'Albigeois, turn L onto D74 to Ambialet; turn R at
junc; in 100m bear L; site on L. Sharp turn, turning
pnt avail down rd. NB App via D74 as v narr tunnels
on D172/D700 to E & W of Ambialet. Sm, mkd, pt
shd, EHU (6-10A) €2.15; adv bkg acc; kayaking; CKE.
*"Easy walk to pretty vil; bar 500ml; clean facs; excel;
pretty rvside site; no chem disp facs on site, use public
toilet in vill."* **€17.00, 1 May-31 Oct.**   **2016**

AMBOISE *4G2* (1km N Rural) *47.41763, 0.98717*
Camp Municipal L'Ile d'Or, 37400 Amboise **02 47
57 23 37 or 02 47 23 47 38 (Mairie); camping@
ville-amboise.fr; www.camping-amboise.com**

🐕 €1.15 👪 🅦 🚿 ♿ 🛒 ⚡ 🅜 ♈ ⓗ 🏪 nr 🖊

Fr N exit A10 exit junc 18 onto D31/D431 to
Amboise; at turn R onto D751 dir Blois & get in L
lane to cross bdge on D431; site a turning L off
bdge, on lge wooded island in Rv Loire. Fr S exit
A85 junc 11 onto D31 dir Amboise; foll Centre Ville
sp to rv on D431; get in L/H lane to cross bdge (dir
Nazelles); turn R off bdge to site on island.
2*, Lge, mkd, pt shd, EHU (6A) inc (poss rev pol); red
long stay; TV; phone; Eng spkn; adv bkg acc; ccard acc;
fishing; games area; tennis; CKE. *"Lovely, spacious,
secure site in gd location adj Rv Loire & park; well-kept;
lge pitches; htd pool & waterslide 500m (high ssn); nice
rest & bar; easy walk to interesting old town; vg dog
walking; conv Parc Léonardo Da Vinci (last place he
lived) & Château d'Amboise; midsummer week music
festival in adj park - check date; no twin axles; m'van
o'night area open all year, excel stop out of ssn; gd
value; vg; excel san facs, stretched in high ssn; v busy."*
€16.00, 31 Mar-9 Oct.   **2017**

AMBOISE *4G2* (7km NE Rural) *47.44580, 1.04669*
Camping Le Jardin Botanique, 9 bis, Rue de la Rivière,
37530 Limeray **02 47 30 13 50; campingjardin
botanique@wanadoo.fr; www.camping-jardin
botanique.com**

12 🐕 €1.50 👪 (htd) 🅦 🚿 ♿ 🛒 ⚡ 🅜 ♈ ⓗ 🏪 nr 🔥 ⛱

NE fr Amboise on D952 on N side of Rv Loire dir
Blois; in approx 6km turn L for Limeray & then
immed turn L onto Rue de la Rivière; site on L in
500m. NB Rec not to app fr Limeray, narr rds & diff
for lge o'fits. 3*, Med, hdg, mkd, hdstg, pt shd, EHU
(10A) €5 (poss rev pol); gas; bbq; red long stay; TV;
20% statics; Eng spkn; adv bkg acc; bike hire; tennis;
games area; CKE. *"Gd for Loire chateaux; 500m fr rv;
friendly & helpful owner; gd for children; gd gourmet
rest adj; poss muddy when wet; gd cycle rtes; poorly
maintained facs (2014)."* **€20.50**   **2015**

AMBRIERES LES VALLEES *4E1* (2km SW Rural)
48.39121, -0.61680 **Camping Le Parc de Vaux,**
35 Rue des Colverts, 53300 Ambrières-les-Vallées
**02 43 04 90 25; parcdevaux@camp-in-ouest.com;
www.parcdevaux.com**

🐕 €1.80 👪 ♿ 🚿 ⚡ 🛒 🅜 ♈ 🍽 ⓗ 🏪 nr 🔥 🖊 ⛱ (htd)

Fr S on D23 turn R at sp 'Parc de Loisirs de Vaux'.
Site in approx 100m on bank Rv Varenne. Check in
at Office de Tourisme bef site recep.
3*, Med, hdg, mkd, hdstg, pt shd, terr, EHU (10A)
€3.20 (poss long lead req) (poss rev pol); bbq; red long
stay; TV; 40% statics; Eng spkn; adv bkg acc; tennis;
canoe hire; fishing; games area; bike hire; waterslide;
CKE. *"Excel site in beautiful surroundings; lake adj;
helpful recep; nice rvside site adj to leisure pool; vill 20
mins along rv."* **€19.00, 6 Apr-4 Nov.**   **2019**

AMIENS *3C3* (10km N Rural) *49.97240, 2.30150*
FFCC Camping du Château, Rue du Château, 80260
Bertangles **09 51 66 32 60; camping@chateau
bertangles.com; www.chateaubertangles.com**

👪 🅦 🚿 ♿ ⚡ 🦋 🍽 nr

Foll N25 N of Amiens; after 8km turn W on D97
to Bertangles. Well sp in vill. 2*, Sm, hdg, pt shd,
EHU (5A) €3.70 (poss rev pol); red long stay; bus;
CKE. *"Pleasant, peaceful, well-kept site by chateau
wall; busy high ssn, early arr rec (bef 1600); pleasant
welcome; clean, old san facs; ltd recep hrs, pitch
yourself; grnd soft when wet; Amiens attractive city;
gd walks; conv a'routes & NH; excel; gd value; basic
site, needs updating; lovely location; gd dogs walk adj."*
€21.00, 21 Apr-11 Sep.   **2017**

AMIENS *3C3* (5km NW Urban) *49.92091, 2.25883*
Camping Parc des Cygnes, 111 Ave des Cygnes,
80080 Amiens-Longpré **03 22 43 29 28; contact@
amiens-campingdescygnes.com; www.parcdes
cygnes.com**

🐕 €2 (htd) 🅦 🚿 ♿ ⚡ 🛒 🦋 🕊 ♈ 🍽 ⓗ 🏪 nr 🔥

Exit A16 junc 20 twds Amiens onto ring rd Rocade
Nord exit junc 40. At 1st rndabt foll sp Amiens,
Longpré D412; foll sp Parc de Loisirs & site.
4*, Med, mkd, pt shd, EHU (10A) inc on most pitches
(poss long lead req); gas; bbq; twin axles; TV; phone;
bus to city adj; adv bkg rec; ccard acc; fishing nr; bike
hire; games rm; kayaking; CKE. *"Peaceful, well-kept,
secure site in parkland; leisure park adj; lge pitches;
helpful, welcoming staff; gd, clean san facs, ltd LS;
ring bell by recep if office clsd; no o'fits over 11m high
ssn; access to grass pitches off hard areas - m'vans
can keep driving wheels on in wet weather; gd canal-
side cycling/walk to city; Amiens cathedral worth
visit; longer leads req for some pitches; gd; rec; 50% of
pitches have EHU; new
san facs (2019); Veloroute Vallee de la Somme adj."*
€26.00, 1 Apr-14 Oct, P11.   **2019**

FRANCE

ANCENIS *2G4* (5km SW Rural) *47.34400, -1.20693*
Camp Municipal Beauregret, 49530 Drain
02 40 98 20 30 or 02 40 98 20 16 (Mairie); mairie-sg.drain@wanadoo.fr

Fr Ancenis take D763 S for 2km, turn R onto D751 & cont for 3km. Site on R bef vill of Drain on L.
2*, Sm, hdg, pt shd, EHU (10A) inc (poss rev pol); bbq; TV; adv bkg acc; games area. *"Secluded, tranquil site; immac san facs up steps - ltd number; poss not suitable lge o'fits; warden calls am & pm; gd fishing; lake nrby; nice quiet site."* €13.00, 1 May-30 Sep. 2019

ANCENIS *2G4* (1.5km W Rural) *47.36201, -1.18721*
FFCC Camping de l'Ile Mouchet, 44156 Ancenis Cedex
02 40 83 08 43 or 06 62 54 24 73 (mob); camping-ile-mouchet@orange.fr; www.camping-estivance.com

Fr S, exit N249 at Vallet onto D763 to Ancenis; turn L immed after x-ing Rv Loire & foll sp; site on banks of rv. Or fr N, exit A11 junc 20 onto D923 to Ancenis; cont on D923 over rndabt; foll D923 along rv; in 400m, at next rndabt, do not cross rv but cont strt on onto D23; site sp to L in 700m. 3*, Med, mkd, pt shd, EHU (6-10A) €4 (rev pol); gas; TV; 12% statics; Eng spkn; adv bkg acc; ccard acc; waterslide; tennis 50m; games rm; CKE. *"Excel touring base; ltd facs LS; some steps; rvside walks; gd site with modern facs; worth a couple of nights; recep clsd 1200-1430."* €11.00, 2 Apr-23 Oct. 2016

ANDELYS, LES *3D2* (2.5km SW Rural) *49.23582, 1.40016* **Camping de L'Ile des Trois Rois,** 1 rue Gilles Nicolle, 27700 Les Andelys **02 32 54 23 79; camping troisrois@aol.com; www.camping-troisrois.com**

Fr Rouen S on A13, exit junc 18 onto D135 & foll sp Les Andelys. Cross bdge over Rv Seine & turn immed R at rndabt, site on R on rvside. Site sp fr town cent. 3*, Med, hdstg, mkd, hdg, pt shd, EHU (10A) inc; gas; bbq; red long stay; TV; 20% statics; phone; Eng spkn; adv bkg acc; ccard acc; fishing; bike hire; games rm; CKE. *"Well-kept site on Rv Seine; extra lge pitches avail; friendly, helpful staff; gd security; conv Rouen, Evreux, Giverny; bowling alley; view ruins of Château Gaillard; nice place, nice people; excel; refurbished, clean, modern san facs, sw pool, vg bar & rest; easy walk to old town; huge site; gd dog walk adj."* €29.00, 15 Mar-15 Nov. 2019

See advertisement

ANDERNOS LES BAINS *7D1* (5km NW Coastal) *44.77287, -1.14144* **Camping La Cigale,** Route de Lège, 33740 Arès 05 56 60 22 59; contact@camping-lacigale-ares.com; www.camping-lacigale-ares.com

Fr Andernos proceed NW on D3 to Arès. Take Cap-Ferret rd D106. Site on L in 1km. 4*, Sm, mkd, pt shd, EHU (6-10A); gas; bbq; twin axles; 50% statics; bus 1km; Eng spkn; adv bkg rec; games rm. *"Excel family-run site; v clean; gd sized pitches; bike hire adj; cycle rtes; supmkt 2km."* €42.00, 27 Apr-25 Sep. 2017

FRANCE

ANDERNOS LES BAINS *7D1* (5km NW Coastal) *44.77792, -1.14280* **FLOWER Camping La Canadienne,** 82 Rue du Général de Gaulle, 33740 Arès **44.778539, -1.143136; info@lacanadienne.com; www. lacanadienne.com** or **www.flowercampings.com**

🐕 €2.50 ♂♀ ⏚ ♿ 🚿 ⚗ 🦋 Ⓨ 🍴 ⒽⒹ 🛒 ⛺ ✗ 🏊

⛱ sand 2km

N fr town sq at Arès on D3 (Rue du Général de Gaulle) dir Cap Ferret. Site on R after 1km. 4*, Med, shd, EHU (15A) inc; gas; TV; adv bkg rec; bike hire; archery; tennis; windsurfing 1km; fishing 1km; canoe hire; games rm; sailing 1km. **€31.00, 1 Feb-30 Nov.** 2020

ANDUZE *10E1* (1.5km SE Rural) *44.03824, 3.99454* **Camping Le Bel Eté,** 1870 Route de Nîmes, 30140 Anduze **04 66 61 76 04; contact@camping-bel-ete. com; www.camping-bel-ete.com**

🐕 €1.50 ♂♀ 🆆🅳 ⏚ ♿ 🚿 ⚗ 🦋 Ⓗ 🛒 nr 🏊

S fr Alès on D6110; W on D910A to Anduze. In Anduze take D907 SE twds Nîmes. Site on L, 200m after rlwy bdge. 4*, Med, mkd, pt shd, serviced pitches; EHU (6A) €4.50; gas; 10% statics; phone; adv bkg req; ccard acc; CKE. *"Delightful, well-kept site in superb location; vg facs but ltd LS; helpful owner; rv adj; gd base for Cévennes area; Thurs mkt."* **€33.50, 8 May-17 Sep.** 2020

ANDUZE *10E1* (1.4km NW Rural) *44.06430, 3.97694* **Camping Castel Rose,** 30140 Anduze **04 66 61 80 15; castelrose@wanadoo.fr; www.castelrose.com**

🐕 €2 ♂♀ ⚗ ⚗ 🍴 Ⓨ 🍴 Ⓗ 🛒 ⛺ ✗ 🏊

Fr Alès S on D6110 & W on N910A to Anduze. Foll sp Camping L'Arche. 3*, Lge, shd, EHU (6-10A) €3.20-4; gas; TV; Eng spkn; adv bkg rec; fishing; boating. *"Excel site by rv; friendly, helpful owners; attractive countryside; gd cent touring Cévennes."* **€50.00, 12 Apr-22 Sep.** 2019

ANDUZE *10E1* (2km NW Rural) *44.06785, 3.97336* **Camping L'Arche,** Route de Saint Jean du Gard, 30140 Anduze **04 66 61 74 08; contact@camping-arche.fr; www.camping-arche.fr**

🐕 €3.80 ♂♀(htd) 🆆🅳 ⚗ ⏚ ♿ 🚿 ⚗ 🅼🅿 🦋 Ⓨ Ⓗ 🛒 ⛺ ✗

🏊 (covrd, htd)

Fr Alès S on D6110/D910A to Anduze. On D907, sp on R. Access poss dff lge o'fits/m'vans. 3*, Lge, mkd, shd, EHU (10A) €2; gas; bbq; red long stay; TV; 10% statics; Eng spkn; adv bkg acc; waterslide; CKE. *"Well-run site; gd san facs; beautiful area; bamboo gardens worth visit; 24hr security patrols; excel rest; outstanding site; vg value."* **€48.00, 1 Apr-30 Sep.** 2019

ANET *3D2* (1km N Urban) *48.86278, 1.41552* **Camp Municipal Les Trillots,** Chemin des Trillots, 27530 Ezy-sur-Eure **02 37 64 73 21** or **02 37 64 73 48 (Mairie)**

🐕 ♂♀(htd) ⚗ ⏚ ✗ 🦋 Ⓨ 🍴 nr Ⓗ 🛒 nr

N fr Dreux on D928/D143. Site on N side of Rv Eure. Med, pt shd, EHU (4A) inc; bbq; 95% statics. *"Quiet site adj rvside walks; gd san facs; helpful warden; poss not suited to tourers; not rec."* **€13.00, 1 Mar-15 Nov.** 2020

"Satellite navigation makes touring much easier"

Remember most sat navs don't know if you're towing or in a larger vehicle – always use yours alongside maps and site directions.

ANGERS *4G1* (15km SE Rural) *47.44332, -0.40881* **Camping du Port Caroline,** Rue du Pont Caroline, 49800 Brain-sur-l'Authion **02 41 80 42 18; info@ campingduportcaroline.fr; www.campingduport caroline.fr**

🐕 €3 ♂♀(htd) 🆆🅳 ⚗ ⏚ ♿ 🚿 ⚗ 🛒 nr ⛺ ✗ 🏊(htd) 🎣

E fr Angers on D347 turn onto D113, site sp at ent to vill. 3*, Med, hdg, mkd, hdstg, pt shd, EHU (10A) inc; bbq; TV; 5% statics; adv bkg acc; ccard acc; games rm; tennis nr; fishing nr. *"Gd touring base; games area adj; skateboarding; site clsd Feb; lge pitches."* **€15.00, 1 Apr-31 Oct.** 2017

"There aren't many sites open at this time of year"

If you're travelling outside peak season remember to call ahead to check site opening dates – even if the entry says 'open all year'.

ANGERS *4G1* (7km SE Urban) *47.42442, -0.52701* **Slow Camp Loire Vallée (formerly Camping L'Ile du Château),** Ave de la Boire Salée, 49130 Les Ponts-de-Cé **02 85 35 97 47; contact@slow-camp.fr; www.slow-village.fr/loire-vallee**

🐕 €2 ♂♀ 🆆🅳 ⚗ ⏚ ♿ 🚿 ⚗ 🅼🅿 Ⓨ Ⓗ 🛒 ⛺ ✗ 🏊

⛱ sand 500m

Fr Angers take D160 (sp Cholet) to Les Ponts-de-Cé. Foll sp 'Centre Ville' & turn R at rndabt in town opp Hôtel de Ville, & site on R in 200m on banks of Rv Loire. 3*, Med, hdg, shd, EHU (10A) inc (poss rev pol); bbq; TV; 4% statics; phone; Eng spkn; tennis; games rm; golf 5km; waterslide adj; games area; CKE. *"Well-kept, scenic site; excel pool adj; gd touring base for chateaux, vineyards; htd pool adj; gd dog walking; highly rec; v shd, few sunny pitches; v busy area; organised entmnt."* **€24.00, 4 Apr-30 Oct.** 2019

ANGERS *4G1* (6km SW Urban) *47.45387, -0.59463*
Camping du Lac de Maine, Ave du Lac de Maine,
49000 Angers **02 41 73 05 03; camping@lacdemaine.
fr; www.camping-angers.fr**

🐕 €2.30 👫 (htd) WD ♨ ♿ 🚿 🍽 / MSP 🦋 ♒ ♿ 🍴 🍸 🕐 ♨ 🛒nr ⚠️
⛱ (htd) 🏪

W fr Angers on D723, exit at 'Quartier du Lac de
Maine' then foll sp to site & Bouchemaine. After 4
rndabts site on L; sp W of Rv Maine. Fr S on D160 or
A87, turn onto D4 at Les Ponts-de-Cé. In 6km, cross
Rv Maine to Bouchemaine & turn R to Pruniers dir
Angers. Site on R at Pruniers town exit sp.
4*, Med, hdstg, mkd, hdg, pt shd, serviced pitches;
EHU (10A) €4.20 (rev pol); gas; bbq; sw nr; red long
stay; twin axles; TV; 10% statics; phone; bus adj; Eng
spkn; adv bkg rec; ccard acc; boating; fishing; tennis
800m; games area; windsurfing 500m; jacuzzi; bike
hire; CKE. *"Excel, lge, well-run site in leisure park;
pitches narr, some suitable v l'ge o'fits; height barrier
at ent 3.2m; conv Loire chateaux; pay 6 nights, stay
7; hypmkt 2km; facs ltd in LS; solar shwrs; few lights
on site; gd cycling & walking rte; canoeing; gd bus
svrs; excel san facs; v helpful recep; bread avail."*
€30.00, 23 Mar-28 Oct. 2018

ANGOULEME *7B2* (6.7km N Rural) *45.68573, 0.14994*
Camping du Plan d'Eau, 1 rue du Camping, 16710
St Yrieix-sur-Charante **05 45 92 14 64; camping@
grandangouleme.fr; www.camping-angouleme.fr**

🐕 👫 (htd) WD ♨ ♿ 🚿 / MSP 🦋 ♒ 🕐 ♨ ⚠️ ⛱

Fr N or S on N10/E606 turn NW & foll sp St Yrieix-
sur-Charante, 'Plan d'Eau' & 'Nautilis - Centre
Nautique'. Site sp. 3*, Med, hdg, mkd, pt shd, EHU
(10A) €3.50; gas; bbq; sw nr; TV; 10% statics; Eng
spkn; adv bkg acc; ccard acc; games area; watersports.
*"Superb location; gd; rather bare site, notices warn of
poss flooding."* **€16.50, 1 Apr-31 Oct.** 2015

ANGOULEME *7B2* (23km NW Rural) *45.79769,
000.63639* **Camping Marco de Bignac (formerly Les
Sablons),** Chemin de la Résistance, 16170 Bignac
**05 45 21 78 41; info@marcodebignac.com;
www.marcodebignac.com**

🐕 👫 (htd) WD ♨ ♿ 🚿 / MSP 🦋 ♒ 🕐 ⚠️ 🚲 ⛱

Fr N10 approx 14km N Angoulême take exit La
Touche & foll D11 W thro Vars; at Basse turn R onto
D117 & foll sp in Bignac. (Foll sp not Sat Nav due to
new rd layout at Basse). 3*, Med, mkd, pt shd, EHU
(3-6A) €3-4; bbq (charcoal, elec, gas); twin axles; red
long stay; 3% statics; bus adj; Eng spkn; adv bkg acc;
ccard acc; games area; tennis; fishing; watersports;
bike hire; pets corner; CKE. *"Attractive, peaceful,
tidy, lakeside site; worth long drive; scenic area; lge
pitches; welcoming, helpful British owners; clean refurb
san facs; gd rest; pleasant walk round lake; lake adj;
ideal for Angoulême Circuit des Remparts; excel; pets
corner; excel."* **€29.00, 1 Feb-30 Nov.** 2019

ANNECY *9B3* (10km SE Rural) *45.84070, 6.16450*
Camping Le Solitaire du Lac, 615 Route de Sales,
74410 St Jorioz **04 50 68 59 30 or 06 88 58 94 24
(mob); contact@campinglesolitaire.com or
campinglesolitaire@wanadoo.fr; www.campingles
olitaire.com**

🐕 €2.60 👫 WD ♨ ♿ 🚿 / MSP 🦋 ♒ 🍸 🕐 ♨ 🛒 nr ⚠️

Exit Annecy on D1508 twd Albertville. Site sp on N
o'skts of St Jorioz. 3*, Med, mkd, pt shd, EHU (5A)
€3.50; gas; bbq; sw; red long stay; TV; 10% statics;
Eng spkn; adv bkg acc; ccard acc; boat launch; games
area; bike hire; CKE. *"Nice, well-run site in excel
location; water to MH's charge €0.20 per 60l; popular
but quiet; cycle track; sm pitches; clean, modern san
facs; direct access to Lake Annecy; sh walk to public
beach & water bus; cycle path nr; gd touring base;
excel; perfect for boating & cycling; v helpful staff."*
€29.00, 8 Apr-23 Sep. 2017

ANNECY *9B3* (11km SE Rural) *45.82423, 6.18523*
Camping Le Familial, 400 Route de Magnonnet,
74410 Duingt **04 50 68 69 91; contact@annecy-
camping-familial.com; www.annecy-camping-familial
.com**

🐕 €1.70 👫 WD ♨ ♿ 🚿 / 🦋 ♒ ♨ ⚠️

Fr Annecy on D1508 twd Albertville. 5km after
St Jorioz turn R at site sp Entrevernes onto D8, foll
sp past Camping Champs Fleuris. 2*, Sm, mkd, hdstg,
pt shd, pt sl, EHU (6A) €4.30; bbq; twin axles; TV; Eng
spkn; adv bkg rec; ccard acc; games area; CKE. *"Gd
site in scenic area; gd atmosphere; generous pitches;
friendly, helpful owner; communal meals & fondu
evenings; conv lakeside cycle track; mobile homes for
rent, sleeps 6; excel."* **€22.50, 1 Apr-30 Sep.** 2018

ANNECY *9B3* (12km SE Rural) *45.88990, 6.22367*
Camping La Ferme de Ferrières, 74290 Alex **04 50 02
87 09; campingfermedesferrieres@voila.fr;
www.camping-des-ferrieres.com**

🐕 €1 👫 (cont) WD ♨ ♿ 🚿 / ⚠️ 🚲 ⛱ ⚠️

Take D909 on E side of lake out of Annecy twds
Thônes; look out for sp on L after turn off to
Château de Menthon. Site off D909 approx 1km W
of Alex. 2*, Med, pt shd, pt sl, terr, EHU (5A) €2.80;
bbq; phone; Eng spkn; adv bkg acc; ccard acc; games
rm; CKE. *"Spectacular views; peaceful, clean site away
fr crowds; friendly & accommodating owner; high
standard san facs; pitches muddy when wet; gd NH;
basic facs; fair."* **€16.50, 1 Jun-30 Sep.** 2015

ANNECY *9B3* (8km SE Rural) *45.86305, 6.19690*
Camping Le Clos Don Jean, Route du Clos Don Jean,
74290 Menthon-St-Bernard **04 50 60 18 66;
donjean74@orange.fr; www.campingclosdonjean.com**

🐕 €1 👫 WD ♨ 🚿 / MSP 🦋 ♒ 🛒 ⚠️

Fr N site clearly sp fr vill of Menthon. L uphill for
400m. 2*, Med, mkd, pt shd, pt sl, EHU (3-6A) €2.60-
3; gas; sw nr; Eng spkn; Bakery; CKE. *"Excel site in
orchard; clean san facs, ltd LS; fine views chateau &
lake; walk to lake."* **€21.00, 1 Jun-31 Aug.** 2020

FRANCE

ANNECY *9B3* *(1.7km S Rural)* *45.89100, 6.13236*
Camp Municipal Le Belvédère, 8 Route du Semnoz,
74000 Annecy **04 50 45 48 30; camping@
ville-annecy.fr; www.annecy.fr**

🐕 ♿ ⏏ (htd) 🚾 🏕 👍 💧 ⊟ ⁄ 🕯 ⁄ⁱ ⑾ 🍴 🛒 ♨ ⚠

Exit A41 junc 16; initially foll sp 'Albertville' into
town; then foll sp 'Le Lac' and 'Le Semnoz'; site is on
R off Route du Semnoz (Route du Semnoz is A41).
'Le Semnoz is a mountain running S fr Annecy.
3*, Lge, mkd, pt shd, pt sl, terr, EHU (16A) €3.20
(poss rev pol); gas; TV; phone; Eng spkn; adv bkg
rec; ccard acc; fishing; bike hire; excursions; sailing;
CKE. *"Lovely, tidy site in beautiful setting; well lit
at night; sm pitches; staff helpful; san facs OK;
steep footpath to old town; sep statics area; excel;
dogs free; v friendly helpful staff, forest walks."*
€27.00, 25 Mar-16 Oct. **2016**

ANNECY *9B3* *(10km S Rural)* *45.82995, 6.18215*
Village Camping Europa, 1444 Route d'Albertville,
74410 St Jorioz **04 50 68 51 01; info@camping-
europa.com; www.camping-europa.com**

🐕 €3 ♿ 🚾 🏕 👍 💧 ⊟ ⁄ MSP 🦋 🕯 ⁄ 🍸 ⑾ 🛒 ♨ 🎾 nr ⚠ ✏
♒ (htd)

Fr Annecy take D1508 sp Albertville. Site on R 800m
S of St Jorioz dir Albertville. Look for lge yellow sp
on o'skirts of St Jorioz. 4*, Med, hdg, pt shd, serviced
pitches; EHU (6A) €3.80; bbq (elec, gas); red long
stay; twin axles; TV; 20% statics; Eng spkn; adv bkg
acc; ccard acc; bike hire; jacuzzi; boat hire; fishing;
waterslide; games rm; tennis 700m; windsurfing;
CKE. *"Peaceful site; friendly staff; facs stretched high
ssn; vg rest; excel for m'vans; conv Chamonix & Mont
Blanc; variable pitch prices; cycle track adj; some
pitches tight lge o'fits; gd tourist base; excel; no water
points around site, collect fr toilet block; brilliant
pool complex; no hot water in sinks; gd cycling area."*
€40.00, 30 Apr-17 Sep. **2016**

ANNECY *9B3* *(6km S Urban)* *45.85482, 6.14395*
Camping au Coeur du Lac, Les Choseaux, 74320
Sévrier **04 50 52 46 45; info@aucoeurdulac.com;
www.campingaucoeurdulac.com**

🐕 ♿ 🚾 👍 💧 ⊟ ⁄ MSP 🦋 🕯 🛒 ⚠ ✏ ♒

S fr Annecy on D1508 sp Albertville. Pass thro
Sévrier cent. Site on L at lakeside 1km S of Sévrier.
300m after McDonald's. 3*, Med, mkd, hdstg, pt shd,
pt sl, terr, EHU (4A) €3.60, long cable rec; sw; bus
nrby; Eng spkn; adv bkg req; ccard acc; boat hire; bike
hire; CKE. *"Busy, nice site in lovely location; gd views
of lake fr upper terr; tight for lge o'fits - sm, sl pitches;
dogs not acc high ssn; ok san facs; gd access to lake
beach & cycle path; excel, espec LS; v popular site."*
€28.00, 1 Apr-30 Sep. **2016**

ANNECY *9B3* *(6km S Rural)* *45.84333, 6.14175*
Camping Le Panoramic, 22 Chemin des Bernets,
Route de Cessenaz, 74320 Sévrier **04 50 52 43 09;
info@camping-le-panoramic.com; www.camping-le-
panoramic.com**

🐕 €1.60 ♿ (htd) 🚾 👍 💧 ⊟ ⁄ 🦋 🕯 🍸 ⑾ ♨ ⚠ 🏊
♒ 2km

Exit A41 junc 16 Annecy Sud onto D1508 sp
Albertville. Thro Sévrier to rndabt at Cessenaz
(ignore all prior sp to site) & take 1st R onto D10.
In 200m turn R up hill to site in 2km. 3*, Lge, mkd,
pt shd, pt sl, terr, EHU (4-6A) €3.20-4.20 (some rev
pol); sw; TV; Eng spkn; ccard acc; games rm; CKE.
*"Fantastic views fr many pitches; blocks/wedges ess for
sl pitches; excel pool/bar area; rec for families; new san
facs (2012); excel views of lake; v friendly staff; high
rec."* **€31.00, 19 Apr-29 Sep.** **2019**

ANNECY *9B3* *(6.5km S Urban)* *45.84412, 6.15354*
Camping de l'Aloua, 492 Route de Piron, 74320
Sévrier **04 50 52 60 06; camping.aloua@wanadoo.fr;
www.camping-aloua-lac-annecy.com**

🐕 €2 ♿ 🚾 👍 💧 ⊟ ⁄ MSP 🕯 ⑾ 🛒 ♨ ⚠ ✏ ♒ shgl 300m

Foll sp for Albertville D1508 S fr Annecy. Site on
E side, approx 1.4km S of Sevrier vill. Turn L at
Champion supmkt rndabt & foll sp twd lake.
2*, Lge, hdg, mkd, shd, EHU (2-10A) €2.50-4.80;
sw nr; TV; phone; Eng spkn; adv bkg acc; fishing
adj; watersports adj; archery; boating adj; CKE.
*"Gd base for lake (no dir access fr site); cycle track
around lake; night security; poss noisy at night with
youths & some rd noise; basic san facs; pleasant
owners; well run & maintained site; nr lac Annecy,
Carrefour & g'ge; bike track or bus to Annecy; vg."*
€23.00, 18 Apr-19 Sep. **2015**

ANNECY *9B3* *(6.5km S Rural)* *45.84806, 6.15129*
FFCC Camping Les Rives du Lac, 331 Chemin du
Communaux, 74320 Sévrier **04 50 52 40 14;
lesrivesdulac-annecy@ffcc.fr; www.lesrivesdulac-
annecy.com**

🐕 €1.20 ♿ 🚾 🏕 👍 💧 ⊟ ⁄ MSP 🦋 🕯 🛒 nr ⚠ ✏ ♒ shgl

Take D1508 S fr Annecy sp Albertville, thro Sévrier
sp FFCC. Turn L 100m past (S) Lidl supmkt, cross
cycle path & turn R & foll sp FFCC keeping parallel
with cycle path. Site on L in 400m. 3*, Med, mkd, pt
shd, EHU (10A) €4; bbq; sw; bus nr; Eng spkn; adv bkg
acc; sailing; fishing; CKE. *"Beautiful situation; generous
pitches; helpful staff; excel new toilet block; water
bus to Annecy nr; gd touring base; walking; red CC
members (check first); walking, sailing & cycling; cycle
rte adj."* **€32.00, 30 Mar-29 Sep.** **2019**

For a guide to symbols see the fold out on the rear cover

ANNECY *9B3* (9km S Rural) *45.49484, 6.1055*
Camping International du Lac d'Annecy, 1184 Route d'Albertville, 74410 St Jorioz **04 50 68 67 93; contact@camping-lac-annecy.com; www.camping-lac-annecy.com**

🐕 €2.50 ♨♿ ⬛ ♿ ⬛ / ⬛ 🦋 ♈ ♈ ⊕ ⬛ ⬛ ⚠ ⚓ (htd)

Fr Annecy take D1508 sp Albertville. Site on R just after St Jorioz. 4*, Med, hdstg, mkd, hdg, pt shd, EHU (6-10A) €4-5.60; gas; bbq (elec, gas); sw nr; TV; 30% statics; phone; bus 500m; Eng spkn; adv bkg acc; ccard acc; bike hire; games area; Mini Club: Children's entertainment (July and August); CKE. *"Lovely site; gd san facs; excel for touring lake area; site ent tight for med/lge o'fits (2009); vg cycling; gd rest nrby."* **€36.00, 30 April -21 Sep.**   2020

ANNONAY *9C2* (4km N Urban) *45.25799, 4.67426*
Camp Municipal de Vaure, Rue Mathieu Duret, 07100 Annonay **04 75 33 73 73 or 04 75 33 46 54; www.mairie-annonay.fr**

🐕 €1.50 ♨♿ ⬛ ⬛ / 🦋 ♈ ⬛ ⬛ nr ⚓ (covrd, htd) 📶

Sp fr o'skts of town & foll sp St Etienne. Fr St Etienne & NW on D1082 & D820 twd Annonay. For R onto D206 S & foll camping/piscine sp to site. Sm, hdg, mkd, pt shd, EHU (6-10A) €2.50-3.50; 10% statics; tennis; games area. *"Helpful staff; gd; basic facs; site not v secure."* **€10.00, 1 Apr-31 Oct.**   2016

ANTIBES *10E4* (2km N Urban/Coastal) *43.60536, 7.11255* **Camping Caravaning Le Rossignol,** Ave Jean Michard-Pelissier, Juan-les-Pins, 06600 Antibes **04 93 33 56 90; campinglerossignol@wanadoo.fr; www.campingrossignol.com**

🐕 €2.50 ♨♿ ⬛ ♿ ⬛ / ⬛ 🦋 ♈ ♈ ⬛ nr ⚠ ♈ ⚓ (htd) 📶 ♈ shgl 1.2km

Turn W off N7 Antibes-Nice at sp to Hospitalier de la Fontonne then bear L along Chemin des Quatres past hospital & traff lts junc. In 400m turn R at rndabt into Ave Jean Michard Pelissier, site 200m on R. NB Narr ent off busy rd. 3*, Med, hdstg, mkd, hdg, shd, terr, EHU (10A) €5; gas; bbq (elec, gas); red long stay; TV; Eng spkn; adv bkg acc; ccard acc; games area; games rm; tennis 2km; CKE. *"Conv Antibes & surrounding area; peaceful site; sm pitches."* **€32.60, 13 Apr-28 Sep.**   2019

APT *10E3* (8km N Rural) *43.92050, 5.34120*
Domaine des Chenes Blancs, Route de Gargas, 84490 St Saturnin-lès-Apt **04 90 74 09 20 or 06 63 90 37 66; contact@leschenesblancs.com; www.vaucluse-camping.com**

🐕 €4 ♨♿ ⬛ ♿ ⬛ / ⬛ 🦋 ♈ ⊕ ⬛ ⬛ ⚠ ♈ ⚓ (htd) 📶

Fr W on D900 twd Apt, at NW o'skts of Apt turn N on D101, cont approx 2km turn R on D83 into Gargas; thro Gargas & in 4km turn L at camp sp; site on R in 300m. Narr rd. 3*, Lge, hdg, shd, EHU (6A) inc; bbq; TV; Eng spkn; adv bkg rec; ccard acc; lake fishing 5km; games area. *"Well-run, popular site in gd location; pitches amongst oaks poss diff lge o'fits; steel pegs req due stony grnd; friendly staff; vg, modern san facs; nice pool; excel touring base; lots of facs; dated san facs (2015); dusty."* **€32.60, 28 Mar-17 Oct.**   2015

APT *10E3* (0.5km NE Urban) *43.87753, 5.40302*
Camp Municipal Les Cèdres, 63 Impasse de la Fantaisie, 84400 Apt **04 90 74 14 61 or 04 90 74 14 61 (mob); lucie.bouillet@yahoo.fr; www.camping-les-cedres.fr**

🐕 €1 ♨♿ (htd) ⬛ ♿ ⬛ / ⬛ 🦋 ♈ ⬛ ⚠ ♈

In town turn N off D900 onto D22 twd Rustrel, site sp. Site on R in 200m immed after going under old rlwy bdge. 2*, Med, mkd, pt shd, EHU (6-10A) €3.50; gas; cooking facs; adv bkg acc; ccard acc; CKE. *"Excel site in lovely location; sm pitches; pitching poss haphazard LS; friendly staff; clean san facs; some pitches muddy when wet; cycle tracks; conv Luberon vills & ochre mines; phone ahead to check open LS; v lge mkt Sat; gd NH; site in 2 parts; popular; gd touring cent."* **€16.00, 1 Mar-31 Oct.**   2019

ARAMITS *8F1* (0.3km W Rural) *43.12135, -0.73215*
Camping Barétous-Pyrénées, Quartier Ripaude, 64570 Aramits **05 59 34 12 21; contact@camping-pyrenees.com; www.camping-pyrenees.com**

🐕 €2.80 ♨♿ ⬛ ♿ ⬛ / ⬛ 🦋 ♈ ⊕ nr ♈ nr ⚠ ⚓ (htd) 📶

SW fr Oloron-Ste Marie take D919 sp Aramits, Arette. Fr Aramits cont on D919 sp Lanne; site on R; well sp. 4*, Sm, mkd, pt shd, serviced pitches; EHU (10A) €4.90; twin axles; TV; 50% statics; Eng spkn; adv bkg acc; games rm; bike hire; CKE. *"Friendly, helpful owner; well-kept, clean, lovely site but muddy when wet; ltd facs LS; dated but v clean; gd base for Pyrenees; poss unrel opening dates - phone ahead LS; excel bistro 400m; vg."* **€28.00, 1 Apr-17 Oct.**   2015

FRANCE

ARBOIS *6H2* (1.5km E Urban) *46.90331, 5.78691*
Camp Municipal Les Vignes, 5 Rue de la Piscine,
39600 Arbois **03 84 66 14 12 or 03 84 25 26 19;**
campinglesvignes@hotmail.fr; http://alexandrachti
.wix.com/camping-les-vignes

€2.50 [symbols]

Fr N or S, ent town & at rndabt in cent foll camp
sp on D107 dir Mesnay. Site adj stadium & pool.
NB Steep slopes to terr & narr ent unsuitable lge
o'fits. 3*, Med, hdg, mkd, hdstg, pt shd, pt sl, terr,
EHU (10A) inc; gas; twin axles; TV; Eng spkn; adv bkg
acc; ccard acc; tennis; fishing 1km; CKE. *"Beautiful
setting; clean san facs but poss stretched high ssn; site
clsd 2200-0800 LS; ltd facs LS; pitches on lower tier
mostly sl; pleasant sm town, home of Louis Pasteur
a must see; htd pool adj; Roman salt works, grottoes
nr; lge fair 1st w/end in Sep; excel; linear site; shd
pitches at W end furthest fr main facs; poss rallies."*
€25.00, 16 Apr-2 Oct. 2019

ARC EN BARROIS *6F1* (0.5km W Urban) *47.95052,
5.00523* **Camp Municipal Le Vieux Moulin,** 52210
Arc-en-Barrois **03 25 02 51 33 (Mairie);** contact@
arc-en-barrois.fr; www.arc-en-barrois.fr

€2.18 (htd) [symbols] nr [symbols]

Exit A5 junc 24 onto D10 S to Arc-en-Barrois; turn
R onto D3 thro vill; site on L on o'skirts. Or fr D65
turn L onto D6 about 4km S of Châteauvillain; site
on R on D3 at ent to vill, adj rv. 4*, Med, pt shd,
EHU (6A) inc; bbq; TV; tennis adj; CKE. *"Attractive,
peaceful, lovely, well-kept site by sm rv; adj vill sports
field; basic, clean san facs but need update - excel hot
shwrs; warden calls early eve, poss not on Sundays; gd
wildlife; gd facs; beautiful vill; conv NH fr A5 or longer."*
€12.50, 1 May-30 Sep. 2019

> ## "We must tell the Club about that great site we found"
>
> Get your site reports in by mid-August and we'll
> do our best to get your updates into the next
> edition.

ARCACHON *7D1* (0.5km E Coastal) *44.65089,
-1.17381* **Camping Club d'Arcachon,** 5 Allée de la
Galaxie, 33312 Arcachon **05 56 83 24 15;** info@
camping-arcachon.com; www.camping-arcachon.com

€4 (htd) [symbols]

[symbols] sand 1.5km

Exit A63 ont A660 dir Arcachon. Foll sp 'Hôpital
Jean Hameau' & site sp. 4*, Lge, hdstg, mkd, hdg, pt
shd, terr, EHU (10A) €4; gas; bbq; TV; 40% statics;
Eng spkn; adv bkg acc; ccard acc; bike hire; site clsd
mid-Nov to mid-Dec; CKE. *"Vg site in pine trees;
excel touring base; gd facs; access rds narr - poss
diff manoeuvring into pitches; gd network cycle
tracks; private san facs avail; easy walk to town."*
€44.00, 1 Jan-14 Nov, 15 Dec-31 Dec. 2017

ARCACHON *7D1* (9km E Coastal) *44.64400, -1.11167*
Camping de Verdalle, 2 Allée de l'Infante, La Hume,
33470 Gujan-Mestras **05 56 66 12 62;** camping.
verdalle@wanadoo.fr; www.campingdeverdalle.com

€1.50 [symbols] nr [symbols] sand adj

Fr A63 take A660 twd Arcachon. Turn R at rndabt
junc with D652 sp La Hume. In vill at junc with
D650 turn L, then R at rndabt; then 3rd turning
on R after rlwy line. 2*, Med, hdg, pt shd, EHU
(10A) inc; bbq (sep area); phone; bus adj; Eng spkn;
adv bkg acc; ccard acc; CKE. *"Lovely, well-kept site
in excel position in Arcachon bay; friendly, helpful
owner; cycling/walking; conv local attractions; vg."*
€28.00, 1 Apr-3 Oct. 2019

ARCIS SUR AUBE *4E4* (0.5km N Urban) *48.53907,
4.14270* **Camping de l'Ile Cherlieu,** Rue de Châlons,
10700 Arcis-sur-Aube **03 25 37 98 79;** camping-arcis@
hermans.cx

€1.60 [symbols] nr [symbols] nr [symbols] nr [symbols]

Fr A26 junc 21 foll sp to Arcis. Fr town cent take
D677/N77 dir Châlons-en-Champagne. Turn R after
rv bdge, site sp. 3*, Med, mkd, shd, EHU (10-16A)
inc (poss rev pol); bbq; Eng spkn; rv fishing adj; CKE.
*"Pleasant, well-kept site on island surrounded by rv;
friendly, helpful Dutch owners; gd, clean san facs;
popular NH, rec arr early; bar 500m; vg site; quiet by
10pm; muddy in wet weather; gd site, improves each
year; excel facs."* **€22.00, 10 Apr-1 Oct.** 2018

ARCIS SUR AUBE *4E4* (8km S Rural) *48.46696, 4.12633*
FFCC Camping La Barbuise, 10700 St Remy-sous-
Barbuise **03 25 37 50 95 or 03 25 37 41 11;**
www.camping-ffcc.com

[12] [symbols]

Fr Arcis-sur-Aube, take D677 twd Voué; site on L bef
vill of Voué, sp. Fr S exit A26 junc 21 onto D441 W;
then onto D677 S twd Voué & as bef. 1*, Sm, pt shd,
pt sl, EHU (4A) inc (poss rev pol); bbq; phone; adv bkg
acc; CKE. *"Lovely, peaceful, spacious CL-type site; early
arr rec; site yourself, owner calls eves (cash only); easy
access & pitching for lge o'fits; charming owners; san
facs basic but clean; elec heaters not allowed; dogs on
leads only; pool 8km; conv NH off A26 or sh stay; 2 pin
adapter ess; bar high ssn only."* **€9.00** 2019

ARDRES *3A3* (0.5km N Urban) *50.85726, 1.97551*
Camping Ardresien, 64 Rue Basse, 62610 Ardres
03 21 82 82 32

[symbols]

Fr St Omer on D943 to Ardres, strt on at lights in
town onto D231; site 500m on R - easy to o'shoot;
v narr ent, not suitable twin-axles. 1*, Sm, hdg,
pt shd, EHU (16A) inc; 95% statics; CKE. *"Basic
site; friendly staff; walk to lakes at rear of site; ltd
touring pitches; conv Calais & local vet; NH only."*
€15.00, 1 May-30 Sep. 2018

ARDRES *3A3* (10km SE Rural) *50.83865, 1.97612*
Camping St Louis, 223 Rue Leulène, 62610 Autingues
**03 21 35 46 83; camping-saint-louis@sfr.fr;
www.campingstlouis.com**

🛉🐕♿ 🚿 ⚓ ♨ ⚗ 🚻 ⛽ 🍽 🍴 ⑭ 🛒 🖾 ⛺ 🖉

Fr Calais S on D943 to Ardres; fr Ardres take D224 S twd Licques, after 2km turn L on D227; site well sp in 100m. Or fr junc 2 off A26 onto D943 dir Ardres. Turn L just after Total g'ge on R on app to Ardres. Well sp. If app fr S via Boulogne avoid Nabringhen & Licques as narr, steep hill with bends. NB Mkt Thurs am - avoid R turn when leaving site. 3*, Med, hdg, mkd, pt shd, EHU (10A) inc (long lead poss req, poss rev pol); gas; bbq; 70% statics; phone; Eng spkn; adv bkg req; ccard acc; games rm; CKE. *"Peaceful, well-kept, well-run, busy site; conv Dunkerque, Calais ferries; some gd sized pitches; gd welcome & friendly; clean san facs poss stretched high ssn; ltd touring pitches; phone ahead to check avail high ssn; early dep/late arr area; automatic exit barrier; barrier opens 0600 high ssn; gd rest; vg vet in Ardres; vg, conv NH; lovely clean, improved site; newly refurb san facs, excel (2015); well maintained; can be booked thro Pitchup.com."*
€25.00, 1 Apr-18 Oct.   **2018**

ARDRES *3A3* (10km SE Rural) *50.80867, 2.05569*
Hôtel Bal Caravaning, 500 Rue du Vieux Château, 62890 Tournehem-sur-la-Hem **03 21 35 65 90;
contact@hotel-bal.com; www.hotel-bal.com**

🚻 ⚓ ♨ ⚗ 🖾 🍴 🛒 nr ⑭ nr ⛺ 🖉

Fr S on A26 leave at exit 2; turn R onto D217 then R onto D943 dir St Omer. Turn R in Nordausques onto D218 (approx 1km), pass under A26, site is 1km on L - ent thro Bal Parc Hotel gates. Fr N or S on D943, turn R or L in Nordausques, then as above. 3*, Med, mkd, hdg, hdstg, pt shd, pt sl, EHU (10A) inc (poss rev pol); gas; 80% statics; Eng spkn; adv bkg acc; ccard acc; tennis; CKE. *"Tidy area for tourers, but few touring pitches; sports grnd & leisure cent adj; htd wc (in hotel in winter); gd rest & bar; 25km Cité Europe mall; gd NH; ltd facs in LS."* **€20.00, 1 Apr-31 Oct.**   **2016**

ARDRES *3A3* (9km SE Rural) *50.82193, 2.07577*
Camping Le Relax, 318 Route de Gravelines, 62890 Nordausques **03 21 35 63 77; camping.le.relax@
cegetel.net**

🛉🛉 🚻 ⚓ ♨ 🖾 🛒 nr ⛺

Fr N on D943 in vill 25km S of Calais at beginning of vill, turn L at sp. Site 200m on R. Or fr S on A26, leave at junc 2 & take D943 S for 1km into Nordausques, then as above. NB Ent diff, beware low o'hanging roof on recep. 2*, Med, hdg, pt shd, EHU (6A) €2.20 (poss rev pol); 90% statics; adv bkg req; CKE. *"Obliging owner; sm pitches & sharp access, not suitable lge o'fits; basic san facs, poss tired high ssn; conv A26, Calais & war sites; NH only."*
€13.00, 1 Apr-30 Sep.   **2016**

ARGELES GAZOST *8G2* (1km N Rural) *43.01218, -0.09709* **Camping Sunêlia Les Trois Vallées,**
Ave des Pyrénées, 65400 Argelès-Gazost
05 62 90 35 47; 3-vallees@wanadoo.fr; www.l3v.fr

🛉🐕 €2 🛉🛉(htd) 🚻 ⚓ ♨ 🖾 🍴 🍽 🛒 nr ⛺ 🖉 🏊(htd)

S fr Lourdes on D821, turn R at rndabt sp Argelès-Gazost on D821A. Site off next rndabt on R. 4*, Lge, mkd, pt shd, EHU (6A) inc (poss rev pol); TV; 30% statics; adv bkg req; ccard acc; sauna; games area; bike hire; waterslide; games rm; golf 11km. *"Excel touring base; views of Pyrenees; conv Lourdes; interesting area; red facs LS; excel san facs; v helpful staff."* **€46.00, 11 Apr-18 Oct.**   **2015**

ARGELES GAZOST *8G2* (4km NE Rural) *43.01124, -0.07748* **Camping Deth Potz,** 40 route de Silhen, 65400 Boô-Silhen **05 62 90 37 23; contact@
deth-potz.fr; www.deth-potz.fr**

🛉🐕 €1 🛉🛉 🚻 ⚓ ♨ ⚗ 🖾 🖾 🦋 🍴 ⑭ 🛒 🖉 🏊

Fr Lourdes on D821 to Argeles Gazost. At 2nd rndabt foll Luz-St-Sauveur sp for 100m over rv and turn L sp Boo-Silhen. Site on L in 1km. 2*, Med, mkd, pt shd, pt sl, terr, EHU (3-10A) inc; bbq; twin axles; TV; 20% statics; Eng spkn; adv bkg req; games rm; games area; CKE. *"Family run site, o'looking woodland; site has upper (terr) and lower (flat) area; gd for walking, climbing, stunning scenery; vg site; ltd wifi."*
€17.00, 1 Jan-10 Oct & 10 Dec-31 Dec.   **2019**

ARGELES GAZOST *8G2* (7km SE Rural) *42.98120, -0.06535* **Camping Le Viscos,** 16 Route de Préchac, 65400 Beaucens **05 62 97 05 45; domaineviscos@
orange.fr**

🛉🐕 €1 🛉🛉 🚻 ⚓ 🖾 🦋 🛒 nr ⛺

Fr Lourdes S twd Argelès-Gasost on D821. Cont twd Luz & Gavarnie to L of Argelès town, & turn L within 500m, sp Beaucens. Turn R to D13, site 2.5km on L. 2*, Med, shd, pt sl, EHU (2-10A) €2-4.50 (rev pol); gas; bbq; red long stay; adv bkg req; lake fishing 500m; CKE. *"Delightful site; landscaped grnds; excel, clean san facs; pool 4km; gd rests in area."*
€17.50, 1 May-15 Oct.   **2015**

ARGELES GAZOST *8G2* (1km S Rural) *42.98670, -0.08854* **Camping Les Frênes,** 46 Route des Vallées, 65400 Lau-Balagnas **05 62 97 25 12;
campinglesfrenes.fr**

🛉🛉(htd) 🚻 ⚓ ♨ 🖾 🦋 🛒 nr ⛺ 🖉 🏊

Site on R of D821 twd S. 3*, Med, hdg, shd, EHU (10A)€4.40; gas; bbq; red long stay; TV; 10% statics; adv bkg rec; games rm; rv fishing 1km. *"Gd site."*
€18.40, 15 Dec-15 Oct.   **2017**

ARGELES GAZOST *8G2* (2km S Rural) *42.98826, -0.08923* **Kawan Village Le Lavedan,** 44 Route des Vallées, 65400 Lau-Balagnas **05 62 97 18 84; contact@lavedan.com; www.lavedan.com**

€2.50 (htd) nr (covrd, htd)

Fr Lourdes S on D821 dir Argelès-Gazost/Cauterets; 2km after Argelès on D921 site on R after vill of Lau-Balagnas. 4*, Med, mkd, shd, EHU (3A) €3 (poss rev pol, extra for 10A); gas; bbq; TV; 80% statics; phone; Eng spkn; adv bkg acc; ccard acc; games rm; CKE. *"In beautiful valley; friendly, relaxed staff; clean modern san facs; rd noise if pitched adj to rd & poss noise fr entmnt in café; excel cycle rte to Lourdes; vg; quiet pleasant site."* **€37.00, 15 Mar-30 Oct. 2017**

ARGELES GAZOST *8G2* (3km S Rural) *42.9871, -0.1061* **Camping du Lac,** 29 Chemin d'Azun, 65400 Arcizans-Avant **05 62 97 01 88; campinglac@campinglac65.fr; www.campinglac65.fr**

€2.50 nr (htd)

Fr Lourdes S thro Argelès-Gazost on D821 & D921. At 3rd rndabt take exit for St Savin/Arcizans-Avant. Cont thro St Savin vill & foll camp sp; site on L just thro Arcizans-Avant vill. NB: Dir rte to Arcizans-Avant prohibited to c'vans. 4*, Med, hdg, mkd, pt shd, pt sl, EHU (5-10A) €4.30-5; gas; TV; Eng spkn; adv bkg acc; bike hire; games rm; CKE. *"Excel, beautiful, peaceful, scenic & attractive site; mountain views; gd size pitches; clean san facs; gd for touring; excel rest."* **€34.00, 20 May-20 Sep. 2015**

ARGELES GAZOST *8G2* (11km SW Rural) *42.94139, -0.17714* **Camping Pyrénées Natura,** Route du Lac, 65400 Estaing **05 62 97 45 44; info@camping-pyrenees-natura.com; www.camping-pyrenees-natura.com**

€3 (htd)

Fr Lourdes take D821 to Argelès Gazost; fr Argelès foll sp Col d'Aubisque & Val d'Azun onto D918; after approx 7.5km turn L onto D13 to Bun; after Bun cross rv & turn R onto D103 twd Estaing; site in 3km - rd narr. NB Rd fr Col d'Aubisque steep, narr & not suitable c'vans or lge m'vans. 4*, Med, hdg, mkd, pt shd, terr, EHU (3-10A) €2-5 (poss rev pol); gas; bbq; TV; 20% statics; Eng spkn; adv bkg acc; ccard acc; sauna; games area; solarium; games rm; CKE. *"Superb, peaceful, well-kept, scenic site; friendly, helpful owners; clean unisex san facs; vg takeaway; gd for young families; no plastic grnd-sheets allowed; adj National Park; birdwatching area; excel; home cooked food at bar; no o'fits over 7.5m high ssn; pool 4km; vg site, one of the best ever visited."*
€30.00, 18 Apr-10 Oct, D22. 2015

ARGELES SUR MER *10G1* (1km N Coastal) *42.56320, 3.03498* **Camping Les Marsouins,** Ave de la Retirada, 66702 Argelès-sur-Mer **04 68 81 14 81; lesmarsouins@cielavillage.com; www.campsud.com**

€3 (htd) sand 800m

Fr Perpignan take exit 10 fr D914 & foll sp for Argelès until Shell petrol stn on R. Take next L just bef rv into Allée Ferdinand Buisson to T-junc, turn L at next rndabt dir Plage-Nord. Take 2nd R at next rndabt, site on L opp Spanish war memorial. 3*, V lge, mkd, hdg, shd, EHU (5A) inc; gas; bbq (elec, gas); 20% statics; Eng spkn; adv bkg acc; ccard acc; games area; windsurfing 1km; games rm; bike hire; sailing 1km. *"Lovely, well-kept, well-run site; clean san facs; busy rd to beach, but worth it; many sm coves; gd area for cycling; TO on site; excel; gd pool/slides; v conv for town/beach."* **€47.00, 14 Apr-8 Oct. 2017**

"I need an on-site restaurant"

We do our best to make sure site information is correct, but it is always best to check any must-have facilities are still available or will be open during your visit.

ARGELES SUR MER *10G1* (3km NE Coastal) *42.55583, 3.04222* **Camping Les Pins,** Ave du Tech, Zone des Pins, 66700 Argelès-sur-Mer **04 68 81 10 46; camping@les-pins.com; www.les-pins.com**

€4 sand 200m

Exit D914 junc 10, foll sp Pujols & Plage-Nord, site sp. 3*, Lge, mkd, hdg, pt shd, EHU (6A) inc; gas; Eng spkn; adv bkg rec; ccard acc; games area; CCI. *"Cent for beach & town; pleasant, helpful staff; clean, modern san facs; quiet peaceful site; supmkt nrby."*
€48.00, 4 Apr-4 Oct. 2019

ARGELES SUR MER *10G1* (3.5km NE Coastal) *42.57543, 3.0431* **Camping Le Soleil,** Route du Littoral, Plage-Nord, 66700 Argelès-sur-Mer **04 68 81 14 48; camping.lesoleil@wanadoo.fr; www.camping-le-soleil.fr**

sand adj

Exit D914 junc 10 & foll sp Argelès Plage-Nord. Turn L onto D81 to site. Site sp among others. 4*, V lge, mkd, pt shd, EHU (6A) €3.70; gas; TV; 50% statics; phone; Eng spkn; adv bkg req; ccard acc; bike hire; rv fishing adj; horseriding; tennis; games area. *"Lovely views; excel site for partially-sighted & handicapped; rec visit to Collioure; vg."*
€32.50, 16 May-30 Sep. 2016

ARGELES SUR MER *10G1* (4km NE Coastal) *42.57245, 3.04115* **Camping La Marende,** Avenue du Littoral, 66702 Argelès-sur-Mer **04 68 81 03 88; info@marende.com; www.marende.com**

🐕 €2.50 ♂️♀️ �WⅮ � ♿ ⛽ 🚿 / ⓂⓈⓅ 🦋 ⛲ 🍴 ⓗ 🛒 🅿️ 🏊 ⛱️

🏕️ sand adj

Fr Perpignan S on D914 exit junc 10 Argelès-sur-Mer; foll sp Plage Nord; after 2km at rndabt turn L sp St Cyprian; at next rndabt turn R sp Plages Nord & Sud; site on L in 800m. L onto unmade rd. 4*, V lge, mkd, hdg, shd, serviced pitches; EHU (6-10A) inc; gas; bbq (elec, gas); TV; 12% statics; phone; Eng spkn; adv bkg acc; ccard acc; jacuzzi; games area; CKE. "Beautiful site; lge pitches; friendly, helpful family owners; 1st class facs; excel pool; many static tents high ssn; gd area for cycling & walking; aquarobics, scuba diving lessons Jul & Aug; v quiet Sept; shared facs." **€38.00, 29 Apr-24 Sep.** 2016

ARGELES SUR MER *10G1* (2km E Urban/Coastal) *42.55317, 3.04375* **Camping La Chapelle,** Ave du Tech, 66702 Argelès-sur-Mer **04 68 81 28 14; contactlc@camping-la-chapelle.com; www.camping -la-chapelle.com**

🐕 €4 ♂️♀️ ⚖ ♿ ⛽ / 🦋 🍴 nr ⓗ 🅿️ 🏊 � 🏕️ 200m

Fr A9 exit junc 42 onto D900/D914 to Argelès-sur-Mer. At junc 10 cont thro Argelès vill & foll sp Argelès-Plage. In 2.5km turn L at rndabt, bear L at Office de Tourisme, site immed L. 3*, Lge, mkd, hdg, shd, EHU (6A) €6.50; 30% statics; Eng spkn; adv bkg acc; tennis 200m; CKE. "Narr site poss diff lge o'fits; ltd facs LS; gd." **€30.00, 20 Apr-28 Sep, C25.** 2019

ARGELES SUR MER *10G1* (5km SE Coastal) *42.53413, 3.06826* **Camping Les Criques de Porteils,** Corniche de Collioure, 66701 Argelès-sur-Mer **04 68 81 12 73; contactcdp@lescriques.com; www.lescriques.com**

🐕 €4 ♂️♀️ (htd) �Ⓦ ⚖ ♿ ⛽ / 🦋 🍴 ⓗ 🅿️ 🏊 (htd)

🏕️ shgl adj

Fr N on A9/E15 take exit junc 42 onto D914 Argelès-sur-Mer. Fr S exit junc 43 onto D618. In abt 16km R onto D914. At exit 13 leave D914 sp Collioure & foll site sp. Site by Hôtel du Golfe 1.5km fr Collioure. 5*, Lge, mkd, hdg, pt shd, pt sl, terr, EHU (5A) €6; gas; TV; 15% statics; phone; Eng spkn; adv bkg acc; fishing; tennis; games area; games rm; watersports; CKE. "Excel, well-run site; variable size pitches, some uneven - not all suitable for lge o'fits; splendid views fr many terr pitches; steps to beach; scuba diving; clean, modern, well kept san facs; exposed, poss v windy; gd walks; v challenging (30 min) walk to Collioure but stunning; some narr site rds; gd rest; site shop fully stocked." **€58.50, 24 Mar-27 Oct, C16.** 2018

ARGELES SUR MER *10G1* (8km W Urban) *42.52667, 2.93515* **Camp Municipal Le Vivier,** 31 Rue du Stade, 66740 Laroque-des-Albères **04 68 89 00 93 or 04 68 95 49 97; tourisme@laroque-des-albères.fr; www.laroque-des-albères.fr**

🐕 €4 ♂️♀️ Ⓦ ♿ ⛽ / 🛒 🅿️ nr 🏊

D2 fr Argelès-sur-Mer to Laroque-des-Albères; foll sp in cent of vill. Site on rvside. 2*, Lge, mkd, pt shd, pt sl, EHU (6A) €3; bbq; 5% statics; bus 300m; adv bkg acc; CKE. "Peaceful, simple site on edge Pyrenees, pleasant vill; vg." **€24.00, 15 Jun-15 Sep.** 2016

ARGELES SUR MER *10G1* (8km W Rural) *42.52366, 2.94446* **Camping Les Albères,** 66740 Laroque-des-Albères **04 68 89 23 64; contact@camping-des-alberes.com; www.camping-des-alberes.com**

♂️♀️ Ⓦ ⚖ ♿ ⛽ / ⓂⓈⓅ 🍴 ⓗ 🛒 nr 🅿️ 🏊 (covrd, htd)

Fr A9 exit junc 43 onto D618 dir Argelès-sur-Mer/Port Vendres. Turn R onto D50 to Laroque-des-Albères. In vill at T-junc turn L, then turn R at rndabt & foll sp to site on D11. 3*, Med, mkd, pt shd, terr, EHU (6A) €5; bbq (gas); TV; 5% statics; phone; Eng spkn; tennis; games area; CKE. "Attractive, peaceful site under slopes of Pyrenees; friendly owners; gd san facs; gd walking area; excel." **€36.00, 6 Apr-28 Sep.** 2019

ARGENTAN *4E1* (0.5km SE Urban) *48.73991, -0.01668* **Camp Municipal du Parc de la Noé,** 34 Rue de la Noé, 61200 Argentan **02 33 36 05 69; camping@argentan.info; www.argentan.fr**

♂️♀️ (htd) Ⓦ ⚖ ♿ ⛽ / 🦋 🍴 🅿️ nr 🏊

S fr Caen on D958 foll camping sp fr by-pass. At rndabt in town cent foll sp to Alencon (Blvd Carnot). In 300m turn L and foll camping signs. NB. Site ent immed on R on entering Rue de la Noe. 2*, Sm, shd, EHU (12A) inc; TV; 10% statics; adv bkg req; games area; rv. "Superb, clean, tidy site adj town park; excel, clean san facs; gd touring base; lovely town; park adj; lake adj; immac site run by efficient, helpful warden; busy even mid Sept, rec arr early; gates close at 8pm, use adj aire." **€12.00, 2 Apr-1 Oct.** 2018

ARGENTAN *4E1* (3.6km S Rural) *48.71841, -0.01077* **FFCC Aire Naturelle du Val de Baize (Huet des Aunay),** 18 Rue de Mauvaisville, 61200 Argentan **02 33 67 27 11; mhuetdesaunay@orange.fr; www.normandieala ferme.com**

🐕 ♂️♀️ Ⓦ ♿ / ⓂⓈⓅ 🦋 🅿️ nr 🏊

Take D958 fr Argentan twd Sées & Alençon; site clearly sp on D958 - turn R just bef leaving Argentan boundary. Site adj T-junc N of farm buildings. Sm, hdstg, pt shd, EHU (6A); 10% statics; Eng spkn; adv bkg acc; CKE. "Charming, well-kept site; pool 2.5km; B&B; lge pitches in orchard; clean but dated facs, ltd LS; friendly welcome; NH only; ring in advance to check opening dates." **€13.00, Unknown 30 Sep.** 2016

ARGENTAT *7C4* (4km SW Rural) *45.07531, 1.91689*
Camping Sunêlia au Soleil d'Oc, 19400 Monceaux-sur-Dordogne 05 55 28 84 84; info@campingsoleil doc.com; www.campingsoleildoc.com

🐕 €3 ♨♿ ♨ ⚊ ♿ 🛒 🍴 ∅ MSP 🦋 ⚓ 🏊 🌊 🖐

Fr N exit A20 junc 46a dir Tulle, then D1120 to Argentat. Fr Argentat take D12 sp Beaulieu. In 4km in Laygues turn L over bdge x-ing Rv Dordogne, site in 300m. 4*, Med, mkd, hdg, pt shd, terr, EHU (6A) €4.10; gas; bbq; red long stay; TV; 10% statics; phone; Eng spkn; adv bkg acc; ccard acc; canoeing; games area; games rm; bike hire; rv; archery; CKE. *"Ideal family site high ssn & peaceful LS; some pitches on rv bank; ltd water points; gd walking & other activities; many beautiful vills in area; tours arranged."* **€20.70, 16 Apr-30 Oct.** **2016**

ARGENTIERE LA BESSEE, L' *9C3* (5km S Rural) *44.75765, 6.57995* **FFCC Camping Le Verger,** 05310 La Roche-de-Rame 04 92 20 92 23; info@campingleverger.com; www.campingleverger.com

12 ♨ 🐕 ♨ WD ⚊ ∅ MSP 🦋 🍴 nr ⊕ nr 🖐 nr

S fr Briançon on N94; site 500m L of rd bef vill; sp. 3*, Sm, hdg, shd, terr, EHU (3-10A) €3.50; sw nr; TV; 25% statics; phone; Eng spkn; adv bkg acc. *"Grass pitches in orchard; excel, well-maintained facs; beautiful; ideal loc for visiting Ecrins area; fantastic value; hg rec."* **€16.00** **2018**

ARGENTIERE LA BESSEE, L' *9C3* (8km NW Rural) *44.84354, 6.48989* **Camping Indigo Vallouise (formerly Les Chambonnettes),** 05290 Vallouise 04 92 23 30 26 or 06 82 23 65 09 (mob); vallouise@camping-indigo.com; www.camping-indigo.com

🐕 €1.80 ♨♿ (htd) WD ⚊ ♿ 🛒 ∅ MSP 🦋 🍴 ⊕ nr 🖐 nr 🏕

Take N94 Briançon-Gap, on N o'skts of L'Argentière-la-Bessée take D994 W dir Vallouise. In cent of Vallouise turn L over bdge & immed L, site in 200m on rvside. 2*, Med, mkd, pt shd, pt sl, EHU (10A) €5.30; bbq; twin axles; TV; 25% statics; phone; Eng spkn; adv bkg acc; ccard acc; games area; games rm; tennis; CKE. *"Mountain scenery; gd facs; bar 500m; gd cent for walking, skiing, canoeing; pool 3km; white-water rafting at nrby rv; interesting vill; gd."* **€32.00, 25 May-29 Sep, M17.** **2019**

ARGENTON LES VALLEES *4H1* (0.9km N Rural) *46.9877, -0.4504* **Camp Municipal du Lac d'Hautibus,** Rue de la Sablière, 79150 Argenton-les-Vallées 05 49 65 95 08 or 05 49 65 70 22 (Mairie); mairie-argenton-chateau@cegetel.net; www.campings-poitou-charentes.com

♨♿ WD ⚊ ♿ 🛒 ∅ 🦋 🖐 nr 🏕

Fr E or W on D759, site well sp in town, on lakeside. 2*, Med, hdg, pt sl, EHU (6A) €2.50; sw nr; 10% statics; Eng spkn; games rm; tennis 100m; CKE. *"Beautifully-situated, well-kept site; pool 100m; interesting, quiet town; excel."* **€14.00, 1 Apr-30 Sep.** **2016**

ARGENTON SUR CREUSE *7A3* (13km SW Rural) *46.54192, 1.40328* **Camping La Petite Brenne (Naturist),** La Grande Metairie, 36800 Luzeret 02 54 25 05 78; info@lapetitebrenne.com; www.lapetitebrenne.com

♨♿ WD ⚊ ♿ 🛒 ∅ 🍴 ⊕ 🦋 ∅ 🏊 (covrd, htd) 🖐

Fr A20 exit junc 18 sp Luzeret/Prissac; foll D55 to Luzeret vill. After bdge in vill turn L, then next L to site. Med, pt shd, pt sl, EHU (10A) €5 (long leads poss req); bbq; red long stay; twin axles; 10% statics; phone; Eng spkn; adv bkg rec; ccard acc; games rm; sauna; horseriding; games area; CKE. *"Excel family site; friendly Dutch owners; lge pitches; excel san facs; ideal for children; pools excel; gd rest; gd walking in National Park; great facs."* **€32.00, 22 Apr-1 Oct.** **2017**

"Satellite navigation makes touring much easier"

Remember most sat navs don't know if you're towing or in a larger vehicle – always use yours alongside maps and site directions.

ARGENTON SUR CREUSE *7A3* (2km NW Rural) *46.59636, 1.50619* **Camp Municipal Les Chambons,** 37 Rue des Chambons, 36200 Argenton-sur-Creuse 06 47 81 59 35 & 09 66 84 06 01; campingleschambons@gmail.com; www.campingleschambons.fr

12 ♨♿ WD ∅ ♨ 🍴 ⊕ nr 🖐 nr

Fr A20 exit junc 17 onto D937 dir Argenton; turn R at rndabt, then L at mini rndabt nr supmkt sp St Marcel; foll rd downhill over rlwy bdge; then 1st R in 100m. But best app fr N on D927 to avoid traff calming rd humps; at town sp cross rlwy bdge & turn R immed past LH turn for Roman archaeological museum; foll camping sp on narr, busy app rd. 3*, Med, hdstg, mkd, shd, pt sl, EHU (5A) €3.60 (poss long lead req); gas. *"Beautiful, peaceful, well-kept site by rv; helpful warden; v muddy after heavy rain & poss uneven pitches by rv; rvside walk into interesting old town; no need to unhitch so useful for early start; quiet in day, busy in evening as popular NH high ssn; excel."* **€20.00** **2019**

ARGENTON SUR CREUSE *7A3* (6km NW Rural) *46.62965, 1.47882* **Camp Municipal Les Rives de la Bouzanne,** 36800 Le Pont Chrétien-Chabenet 02 54 25 80 53 or 02 54 25 81 40 (Mairie); commune.pontchretien@wanadoo.fr

🐕 €0.50 ♨♿ WD ⚊ ∅ 🦋 🍴 nr 🖐 nr 🏕

Exit A20 junc 17 onto D927; site well sp over rv bdge. Or fr St Gaultier on D927 dir Argenton-sur-Creuse; turn R in Le Pont Chrétien-Chabenet, bef rv bdge, site 50m on L. 2*, Med, pt shd, EHU (6A) inc; bbq; phone; Eng spkn; adv bkg rec; CKE. *"Picturesque, quiet, rvside site; site yourself, warden calls; gd, drained pitches; immac san facs; conv A20; excel NH."* **€13.00, 15 Jun-10 Sep.** **2016**

ARLES *10E2* (8km NE Rural) *43.72336, 4.71861*
Huttopia Fontvieille (formerly Municipal des Pins), Rue Michelet, 13990 Fontvieille **04 90 54 78 69; fontvieille@huttopia.com; www.huttopia.com**

🐕€1.50 👫 ⓦⒹ 🚮 🛁 ♨ 🚿 nr ⛺

Take D570 fr Arles to Avignon, in 2km turn R on D17 to Fontvieille, at far end of vill turn R at rndabt, foll sp. 3*, Med, mkd, hdg, pt shd, pt sl, EHU (6A) €3; red long stay; TV; bus; Eng spkn; adv bkg acc; games area; games rm; CKE. *"Delightful, pleasant quiet site in pines; friendly staff; vg san facs; 15-20 mins walk to lively vill with rests & 2 supmkts; quiet forest walks; tennis in vill; nr Arles; lots of attractions locally; vg."* €35.00, 30 Mar-14 Oct. **2018**

ARLES *10E2* (7km E Rural) *43.64799, 4.70625*
Camping La Bienheureuse, 13280 Raphèle-les-Arles **04 90 98 48 06; contact@labienheureuse.com; www.labienheureuse.com**

🐕€2.50 👫 ⓦⒹ ♨ 🛁 ♿ 🚿 ♨ 🦋 ♈ ⛄ 🍴 🏧 ⛺ 🚴 🛶 🎣

Fr Arles E on D453, site on L 5km after Pont-de-Crau. W fr Salon-de-Provence on A54/N113; exit N113 junc 12 onto N1435 to St Martin-de-Crau; cont past St Martin-de-Crau on N1435; in 2km rd becomes D435 to Raphèle-les-Arles; site on R 900m after Raphèle-les-Arles. 3*, Med, hdg, pt shd, EHU (16A); twin axles; 50% statics; phone; bus adj; Eng spkn; adv bkg acc; horseriding nr; CKE. *"Pleasant site; obliging British owners; 700m to shops/bar in vill; gd facs; gd dog walk along nrby lanes and canal."* €21.00, 1 Mar-31 Oct. **2019**

"There aren't many sites open at this time of year"

If you're travelling outside peak season remember to call ahead to check site opening dates – even if the entry says 'open all year'.

ARLES *10E2* (5km SE Urban) *43.65942, 4.65416*
Camping L'arlesienne, 149 Draille Marseillaise, Pont de Crau, 13631, Arles **04 90 96 02 12; contact@larlesienne.com; www.larlesienne.com**

🐕€1.50 👫 (htd) ⓦⒹ ♨ 🛁 ♨ ⓂⓅ 🍴 ♈ 🚿 nr ⛺ 🚴 🎣

Exit Arles E by D453 sp Pont-de-Crau or junc 7 fr N113 dir Raphèle-les-Arles; 200m after exit vill take 1st exit at rndabt then R at Flor Hotel sp on D83E. Site in 50m on R adj hotel. 3*, Med, pt shd, EHU (6A) €4; TV; 80% statics; bus fr rndabt; Eng spkn; games area. *"Many mosquitoes; red facs LS; v muddy after rain; visit Les Baux citadel early morning bef coach parties arr; no o'fits over 5.5m allowed (but poss not enforced); gd birdwatching; poss no site lighting LS; conv Arles."* €27.00, 1 Apr-1 Nov. **2016**

ARMENTIERES *3A3* (3km E Rural) *50.68774, 2.93279*
Camping L'Image, 140 Rue Brune, 59116 Houplines **03 20 35 69 42 or 06 81 61 56 82 (mob); campimage@wanadoo.fr; www.campingimage.com**

🔟 👫 (htd) ⓦⒹ 🚮 🛁 ♨ ⓂⓅ 🦋 ♈ ♨ ⛺ 🚴

Exit A25 junc 8 sp Armentières, onto D945 N twd Houplines; pass on R Chemin du Pilori in 1.8km; then pass on R Hameau de L'Hépinette in 2.2km; turn R into Rue Brune in 3km; site in 1km on R. Ent not v clearly sp. 3*, Med, hdg, shd, serviced pitches; EHU (6-10A) inc (take care electrics, poss prob 2011); 90% statics; Eng spkn; adv bkg acc; games area; CKE. *"Mainly statics, adv bkg rec; friendly, helpful staff; dated san facs, poss unclean & unkempt (2011); pitches exposed & poss v windy; gd NH prior to ferry."* €28.00 **2017**

ARNAY LE DUC *6H1* (1km E Rural) *47.13388, 4.49835*
Camping L'Etang de Fouché, Rue du 8 Mai 1945, 21230 Arnay-le-Duc **03 80 90 02 23; info@campingfouche.com; www.campingfouche.com**

🐕€2 (htd) ⓦⒹ ♨ 🛁 ♿ 🚿 ♨ 🦋 ♈ 🍴 ⓗ 🏧 ⛺ 🚴 🚤 (htd) 🎣

App by D906 to Arnay (site sp); turn E onto D17, site on R in 2km. 4*, Lge, hdstg, mkd, hdg, pt shd, EHU (6A) €4; bbq; sw nr; TV (pitch); TV; Eng spkn; adv bkg acc; ccard acc; bike hire; waterslide; fishing; tennis; games rm; CKE. *"Excel lakeside site with pleasant views; lge pitches; friendly staff; gd san facs; attractive sm town; gd touring base S Burgundy; gd for young families."* €32.00, 19 Apr-13 Oct. **2019**

ARRAS *3B3* (14km E Rural) *50.27347, 2.94852*
Camping La Paille Haute, 145 Rue de Sailly, 62156 Boiry-Notre-Dame **03 21 48 15 40; lapaillehaute@wanadoo.fr; www.la-paille-haute.com**

🐕 👫 ⓦⒹ ♨ 🛁 ♿ 🚿 ♨ 🦋 ♈ 🍴 ⓗ 🏧 ⛺ 🚴 (htd) 🎣

Fr Calais take A26/A1 twd Paris, exit junc 15 onto D939 twd Cambrai; in 3km take D34 NE to Boiry-Notre-Dame & foll camp sp. Fr D950 Douai-Arras rd, at Fresnes turn S onto D43, foll sp to Boiry in 7km, site well sp in vill. 3*, Med, hdg, hdstg, pt shd, terr, EHU (6A) €4 (poss rev pol); bbq; red long stay; 60% statics; Eng spkn; ccard acc; tennis; games rm; site open w/ends in winter; lake fishing; CKE. *"Popular NH; useful & reliable; pretty site with views; rec arr early; lge pitches; friendly, helpful owner; gd for children; Calais over 1hr; conv WW1 sites & A26; gd reg used site; gd for long stay; peaceful vill; pitches muddy in wet weather; san facs updated and excel; gd dogs walk adj; cycle route, 15km canal side to Arras."* €27.50, 27 Mar-23 Oct. **2019**

ARRENS-MARSOUS *8G2* (0.9km NE Rural) *42.95991, -0.20645* **Camping Mialanne,** 63 route du Val d'Azun, 65400 Arrens-Marous **05 62 92 67 14 or 05 62 37 96 08; mialanne@orange.fr; www.campingmialanne.fr**

🐕 (€0.50) 🛉🛉 �🛆 ♨ 🚿 🗑 MP ⟆ ⟆ Ỵ nr ⊕ nr 🐟 nr ⚠ ♿

Sp on D918 bet Arrens-Marsous, 10km WSW of Argeles-Gazost. (Opp ent of Camping La Heche). 3*, Med, mkd, pt shd, terr, EHU (10A) €3.10; bbq (charcoal, gas); twin axles; phone; bus 300m; Eng spkn; adv bkg acc; ccard acc; games rm; CKE. *"Friendly fam site; htd pool 300m; 300m to vill, conv Arrens & Estaing; san facs extended (2015); vg."* **€17.00, 1 Jun-30 Sep.** 2016

ARROMANCHES LES BAINS *3D1* (3km E Coastal) *49.33963, -0.58188* **Camp Municipal Quintefeuille,** Ave Maurice Schumann, 14960 Asnelles **02 31 22 35 50; campingquintefeuille@wanadoo.fr; www.camping-asnelles.com**

🛉🛉 🔏 ⚓ 🛆 🗑 🚿 ✗ ⟆ Ỵ nr ⊕ nr 🐟 nr ⚠ 🏖 sand 300m

Site sp on D514, but visible fr vill sq in Asnelles. 2*, Med, mkd, unshd, EHU; fishing; tennis; games area. **€14.50, 1 Apr-2 Nov.** 2019

ARROMANCHES LES BAINS *3D1* (0.5km W Urban/ Coastal) *49.33793, -0.62647* **Camp Municipal,** Ave de Verdun, 14117 Arromanches-les-Bains **02 31 22 36 78; camping.arromanches@wanadoo.fr; www.arromanches.com/camping_accueil**

🐕 €1 🛉🛉 ⚓ ✗ 🏖 sand 500m.

App fr Bayeux on D516. Turn R on onto D65 on app to Arromanches to site on L. 2*, Med, pt shd, pt sl, terr, EHU (10A) inc; gas. *"Conv Mulberry Harbour exhibition & invasion beaches; friendly warden; gd san facs; levelling blocks req most pitches; grnd soft when wet; sh stay pitches stony; water access diff for m'vans (2010); town centre nrby; v gd."* **€22.00, 1 Apr-30 Oct.** 2019

ARROU *4F2* (0.9km NW Rural) *48.10189, 1.11556* **Camp Municipal du Pont de Pierre,** 28290 Arrou **02 37 97 02 13 (Mairie); mairie.arrou@ wanadoo.fr; www.loirevalleytourism.com**

🛉🛉 🔏 ⚓ 🛆 🗑 🚿 ✗ ⟆ Ỵ nr ⊕ nr 🐟 nr ⚠ 🏖 sand adj

Take D15 fr Cloyes. Site sp in vill of Arrou. 2*, Med, hdg, mkd, unshd, pt sl, EHU (6-10A) €2-3; bbq; 10% statics; phone; adv bkg acc; horseriding; lake fishing; bike hire; tennis; CKE. *"Lovely, peaceful, well-kept site in park-like setting; lge pitches; excel, clean san facs; gd security; htd pool, paddling pool adj; phone warden (or call at hse) if off & barrier clsd; gd rvside walks/cycle rides; excel value; rec."* **€8.00, 1 May-30 Sep.** 2017

ARTIGAT *8F3* (0.7km NE Urban) *43.13776, 1.44407* **Camping Les Eychecadous,** 09130 Artigat **(033) 05 67 44 51 65; campingartigat@hotmail.fr; www.campingartigat.com/**

12 🐕 🛉🛉 🔏 ⚓ ♨ 🛆 ♿ 🚿 MP ⟆ Ỵ ⊕ 🍽 🐟 🛒 ⚠ ✗ 🏊

Fr Toulouse take A64 S, take exit 28 twrds Capens. Marquefave, St. Sulpice. Turn L onto D10, at rndabt take 2nd exit onto D622, turn L sp Av. Antonin Triqué, cont twrds Lombardi on D622, go thro 1 rndabt, turn R sp Rue de la République/ D622 cont on D622, to Av. Des Pyrénées/D4 cont onto D919 cont thro 3 rndabts then L onto Chemin du Comté then L twrds Les Eychecadous, then R, then L to site. 3*, Sm, mkd, pt shd, EHU (10A); bbq; twin axles; TV; 10% statics; adv bkg acc; CKE. *"Vg site on edge of Lèze; warm welcome; fishing, boating, & horseriding."* **€12.00** 2020

ARZON *2G3* (0.8km NE Coastal) *47.55303, -28.8294* **Camp Municipal Le Tindio,** Kerners, 56640 Arzon **02 97 41 25 59; www.camping-arzon.fr**

🐕 €1.20 🔏 ⚓ 🛆 ♿ 🗑 ✗ MP 🐟 🏖 sand 1km

Fr Vannes or Muzillac on D780 turn R at rndabt on o'skts of Arzon. Site clearly sp. 3*, Lge, pt shd, pt sl, EHU (6-10A) €2.50; 3% statics; adv bkg acc; golf nr. *"Site o'looks Gulf of Morbihan; direct access to sea; excel san facs; gd value; sm boat launching fr site."* **€13.00, 1 Apr-3 Nov.** 2016

ARZON *2G3* (2km NE Coastal) *47.56031, -2.87854* **Camping de Bilouris,** Route de Kerners, 56640 Arzon **02 97 53 70 55; campingbilouris@gmail.com; www.campingdebilouris.com**

🐕 €2.50 🛉🛉 🔏 ⚓ 🛆 🗑 ✗ Ỵ 🏖

Fr Vannes foll D780 for abt 23km. On app Arzon foll sp for site. Sm, hdg, pt shd, pt sl, EHU (6A) €3; bbq; 60% statics; Eng spkn; adv bkg rec. *"Coastal walks, boating & kayaking; miles of off-rd cycling; vg."* **€23.00, 1 Apr-1 Nov.** 2017

ARZON *2G3* (2km W Coastal) *47.54403, -2.90945* **Camp Municipal de Port-Sable,** Port Navalo, 56640 Arzon **02 97 53 71 98; portsable@arzon.fr; www.camping-arzon.fr**

🐕 €1.40 🛉🛉 🔏 ⚓ 🛆 🗑 ✗ MP ♿ 🐟 nr ⚠ 🏖 sand adj

Fr N165/E60 take D780 to Sarzeau, cont to Arzon. Site sp fr last rndabt bef fort. 3*, Med, pt shd, pt sl, EHU (6A) €2.30; gas; Eng spkn; ccard acc; fishing; sailing school. *"Vg, spacious site; beautiful position nr beach with views; gd beach for children; walk into marina; boat excursions; gd facs; gd for m'vans - rests nrby."* **€18.50, 1 Apr-15 Oct.** 2016

ASPET *8G3* (1km SW Rural) *43.00969, 0.79665*
Camp Municipal Le Cagire, 31160 Aspet **05 61
88 51 55; camping.aspet@wanadoo.fr; www.
mairie-aspet.fr/rubrique/afficher/21**

🐕 €0.50 ♟ ⓦⅅ ♨ ♿ 🚿 ➴ 🛈 🍴 nr Ⓗ nr 🅿 nr

Exit A64 at junc 18 St Gaudens & take D5 S. In
14km, site sp on R in vill of Aspet. Sp 'Camping,
Stade.' 2*, Sm, mkd, shd, EHU (6A) €2.50;
30% statics; adv bkg acc; games area; tennis 300m;
CKE. "Pleasant, gd, clean, well kept site nr lively, sm
town; rec arr bef 1800 hrs high ssn; pool 300m; basic
facs; some pitches muddy when wet; some hdstg."
€11.00, 1 Apr-30 Sep. 2015

"That's changed – Should I let the Club know?"

If you find something on site that's different
from the site entry, fill in a report and let us
know. See camc.com/europereport.

ASPRES SUR BUECH *9D3* (6.5km W Rural) *44.53048,
5.68371* **FFCC Aire Naturelle La Source (Pardoe),**
05140 St Pierre-d'Argençon **04 92 58 67 81 or 06 78
32 30 40 (mob); info@lasource-hautesalpes.com;
www.lasource-hautesalpes.com**

🐕 €1.50 ♟ ⓦⅅ ♿ 🚿 ➴ 🛈 🦋 ♀ 🍴 Ⓗ ⚓ 🏕

Fr S on D1075 at Aspres-sur-Buëch turn onto D993
dir Valence to St Pierre-d'Argençon; after 6km site
sp. Fr N on D93, cont onto D993 over Col de Cabre;
site sp on L bef St Pierre-d'Argençon.
Sm, mkd, pt shd, pt sl, FHU (6/10A) €4; bbq; twin axles;
red long stay; phone; Eng spkn; adv bkg acc; ccard acc;
CKE. "Peaceful, well-kept CL-type site in woodland/open
field; friendly, helpful British owners; clean san facs;
takeaway; chambre d'hôte on site; htd pool (4km); highly
rec; ideally located for all mountain sports, walking,
climbing, watersports, gliding, flying & cycling; 3 luxury
Teepees for hire; major improvements planned(2014);
excel." **€18.00, 15 Apr-15 Oct.** 2017

ASSERAC *2G3* (5km NW Coastal) *47.44533, -2.44766*
Camping Le Moulin de l'Eclis, Pont Mahé, 44410
Assérac **02 40 01 76 69; info@camping-leclis.com;
www.camping-leclis.com**

🐕 €3 ♟ ⓦⅅ ♨ ♿ 🚿 ➴ 🛈 MSP 🦋 ♀ 🍴 Ⓗ ⚓ 🅿 🏕 ✎
🏊 (covrd, htd) 🚲 🏖 sand adj

Fr D774 turn N onto D83 to Assérac. Take D82 two
coast to Pont Mahé, site sp. 4*, Lge, mkd, hdg, pt shd,
EHU (6-10A) €3.60-4; bbq (elec, gas); TV; 60% statics;
phone; Eng spkn; adv bkg acc; ccard acc; games area;
bike hire; waterslide; sailing school; watersports. "Excel
family site; conv Guérande; vg touring base; superb new
(2013) san facs." **€41.60, 1 Apr-20 Oct.** 2019

ATTICHY *3C4* (1km SSE Rural) *49.40664, 3.05295*
**Camping De l'Aigrette (Formaly Camp municipal
Fleury),** 22 Rue Fontaine-Aubier, 60350 Attichy
**03 44 42 15 97 or 06 62 83 79 35 (mob); contact@
campingdelaigrette.com; www.campingdela
igrette.com**

🐕 €0.50 ♟ (htd) ⓦⅅ ♨ ♿ 🚿 ➴ 🛈 MSP 🦋 ♀ Ⓗ nr 🅿 nr 🏊

Fr Compiègne E on N31. After 16km turn L at traff
lts sp Attichy & site. Over iron bdge & turn R to
site on lakeside. 3*, Sm, hdg, pt shd, EHU (10A) €2;
bbq; 30% statics; fishing; site clsd 25 Dec - 31 Jan;
CKE. "Attractive, clean site in pleasant vill; many w/end
statics, few touring pitches; helpful wardens live on site;
modern san facs, stretched high ssn; gd security; excel
NH LS; excel site." **€16.00, 1 Mar-30 Nov.** 2015

AUBENAS *9D2* (2km E Rural) *44.61885, 4.43220*
Camping Le Plan d'Eau, Route de Lussas, 07200 St
Privat **04 75 35 44 98; info@campingleplandeau.com;
www.campingleplandeau.fr**

🐕 €2.70 ♟ ⓦⅅ ♨ ♿ 🚿 ➴ 🛈 🦋 ♀ 🍴 Ⓗ ⚓ 🅿 nr 🏕 ✎ 🏊 (htd)

Exit A7 at Montélimar dir Aubenas. Bef Aubenas
turn R at rndabt onto D104 dir St Privat. In approx
1km turn R twd Lussas & foll site sp. Site on R on
rvside. 3*, Med, mkd, pt shd, EHU (8A) €4.20; bbq
(gas); cooking facs; red long stay; TV; 25% statics;
phone; Eng spkn; adv bkg acc; games rm
Animation from July 6 to August 24; CKE.
"Vg, peaceful site; gd san & sports facs."
€43.00, 27 Apr-16 Sep. 2020

"I like to fill in the reports as I travel from site to site"

You'll find report forms at the back of this
guide, or you can fill them in online at
camc.com/europereport.

AUBENAS *9D2* (10km S Rural) *44.53693, 4.41039*
Camping Les Peupliers, 07200 Vogüé **04 75 37 71 47;
girard.jean-jacques@club-internet.fr;
www.campingpeupliers.com**

🐕 €2.30 ♟ ⓦⅅ ♨ ♿ 🚿 ➴ 🛈 MSP ♀ 🍴 Ⓗ ⚓ 🅿 🏕 ✎ 🏊

Fr Aubenas take D104 S twd Alès. In 2km, turn L onto
D579 dir Vogüé/Vallon Pont d'Arc. In 9km, pass L
turn to Vogüé. Immed after x-ing rv, turn R at rndabt.
Site on R in 300m, (2nd site of 3 on rd). 3*, Lge, mkd,
pt shd, EHU (6A) €4.10; gas; bbq; 10% statics; phone;
adv bkg acc; ccard acc; CKE. "Gd touring base; access
to rv for canoeing & fishing; sm shop on site with ltd
stock." **€24.00, 5 Apr-30 Sep.** 2015

FRANCE

AUBERIVES SUR VAREZE *9B2* (8km E Rural)
45.42830, 4.92823 **Kawan Village Camping Le
Bontemps,** 5 Impasse du Bontemps, 38150 Vernioz
**04 66 60 07 00; contact@camping-lebontemps.fr;
www.camping-lebontemps.com**

🏕🐕🚻♿🛁♨🛒🍴☕🍷🔌(H)📶🅿🎱⛱🏖🛶⛲

Take N7 S fr Vienne. At Le Clos turn L onto D37 thro
Cheyssieu & Vernioz, site approx 9km E of Vernioz.
Fr S, on N7 N of vill of Auberives R onto D37, site
on R in 8km. Tight ent - rec swing wide. NB Also sp
Hotel de Plein Air. 4*, Lge, mkd, pt shd, terr, EHU (6A)
inc (poss long lead req); bbq; TV; 30% statics; adv bkg
acc; ccard acc; games rm; tennis; lake fishing; games
area; CKE. *"Attractive, well-kept site; popular NH high
ssn; wildlife sanctuary; helpful staff; no o'fits over 10m
high ssn; excel sports facs; vg NH/long stay; new san
facs (2014)."* €30.00, 13 Apr-29 Sep, M10.   2019

"We must tell the Club about that great site we found"

Get your site reports in by mid-August and we'll
do our best to get your updates into the next
edition.

AUBERIVES SUR VAREZE *9B2* (1.6km S Rural)
45.41284, 4.81358 **Camping des Nations,** 38550
Clonas-sur-Varèze **04 74 84 95 13 or 04 14 42 42 84;
contact@campingdesnations.com; www.camping
desnations.com**

🏕🐕🚻(htd)♿🛁♨🔌(H)nr🛶⛲

Fr Vienne S on N7; site sp on R in 12km. Or fr S exit
A7 junc 12 onto N7 dir Vienne; do not go into Clonas
vill; site on L adj Hotel des Nations.
3*, Med, mkd, hdg, shd, EHU (9A) inc; bbq; adv bkg req;
CKE. *"Pleasant, well-kept, well-laid out site; gd sized
pitches; gd, v clean san facs; site muddy when wet; poss
under-used; ltd facs LS; poss irreg cleaning end of ssn;
useful NH/touring base for Spain & the Med; vg site;
friendly, helpful staff."* €22.00, 1 Mar-31 Oct.   2016

AUBETERRE SUR DRONNE *7C2* (1km SE Rural)
45.26786, 0.17474 **Camping Base de Loisirs
d'Aubeterre Sur Dronne (formerly Municipal),** Route
de Ribérac, 16390 Aubeterre-sur-Dronne **05 45 98 50
33; mairie.aubeterre-sur-dronne@wanadoo.fr; www.
aubeterresurdronne.com/hebergement/camping**

🏕🐕🚻(cont)♿🛁♨🍴☕🔌(H)nr⛱🛶nr🏖

On D2 fr Chalais, take D17 around S end of town.
Turn R over rv & site on R adj sports grnd. 3*, Med, pt
shd, EHU (10A) €2.50; 10% statics; Eng spkn; rv fishing
adj; bike hire; tennis adj; boating adj. *"Excel site; gd for
children; friendly staff; picturesque town; conv touring
Périgord."* €20.00, 1 May-30 Sep.   2019

AUBIGNY SUR NERE *4G3* (1.5km E Rural) *47.48435,
2.45703* **FLOWER Camping des Etangs,** Route de
Sancerre, 18700 Aubigny-sur-Nère **02 48 58 02 37;
camping.aubigny@orange.fr; www.camping-aubigny
.com or www.flowercampings.com**

🏕🐕🚻(htd)🗜♿🛁♨🔌🦋🍴☕nr🍷🏖
🛶(covrd, htd)

D940 fr Gien, turn E in vill of Aubigny onto D923,
foll sp fr vill; site 1km on R by lake, after Camp des
Sports & just bef end of vill sp. Avoid town cent due
congestion. 4*, Med, mkd, hdstg, pt shd, EHU (6-10A)
inc; bbq; TV; 10% statics; phone; Eng spkn; adv bkg
acc; bike hire; fishing; games rm; CKE. *"Vg site with
lake views; pretty medieval vill with historical links to
Scotland; mkt Sat; 2nd w/e July Scottish Son & Lumière
event adj site!"* €26.00, 1 Apr-30 Sep.   2019

AUDIERNE *2F1* (3km SE Coastal) *48.00723, -4.50799*
Camping de Kersiny-Plage, 1 Rue Nominoé, 29780
Plouhinec **02 98 70 82 44; info@kersinyplage.com;
www.kersinyplage.com**

🏕🐕🚻🗜♿🛁♨🦋🍴☕⛱🏖 sand

Fr Audierne on D784 turn R at 2nd traff lts in
Plouhinec, cont for 1km; turn L into Rue Nominoé
(sp diff to see) for 100m. Or fr Quimper on D784 to
Plouhinec, turn L at 1st traff lts & as bef.
2*, Med, hdg, pt shd, terr, EHU (8A) €3; bbq (gas); Eng
spkn; CKE. *"Quiet, peaceful site; beautiful location
& beach; most pitches superb sea views; welcoming,
friendly owner; clean san facs; barrier clsd 2300-0730;
not much in area for children except beach; gd coastal
walks; vg, rec."* €15.00, 14 May-17 Sep.   2016

AULUS LES BAINS *8G3* (0.5km NW Rural) *42.79402,
1.33197* **Camp Municipal Le Coulédous,** 09140 Aulus-
les-Bains **05 61 66 43 56; campinglecouledous@
orange.fr; www.camping-aulus-couledous.com**

12🏕🐕🚻(htd)🗜♿🛁♨🔌📶🦋🍷☕nr🏖

Take D618 fr St Girons. After 13km cross rv; turn
R onto D3 sp Aulus-les-Bains. On app to Oust turn
L onto D32, site approx 17km on R at ent to vill on
rvside. 2*, Med, hdstg, mkd, pt shd, sl, EHU (10A)
€4.50-6.50; 10% statics; Eng spkn; adv bkg acc; site
clsd mid-Nov to mid-Dec; CKE. *"Gd walking & skiing
(16km); sm spa in vill; bar 300m; excel; san facs clean
but tired; church clock chimes thro night."*
€19.00   2017

AUMALE *3C3* (0.5km W Rural) *49.76618, 1.74618*
Camp Municipal Le Grand Mail, Chemin du Grand
Mail, 76390 Aumale **02 35 93 40 50 (Mairie);
communeaumale@wanadoo.fr; www.aumale.com**

🏕🐕🚻🛁♿🛁♨🔌📶🏖nr🏖

Clearly sp in town; long steep climb to ent.
2*, Med, pt shd, EHU (6A) €2.40; bike hire; fishing
1km. *"Gd site; clean, modern san facs; conv
Channel ports; steep slope fr town to site; gd NH."*
€18.00, 1 Apr-30 Sep.   2019

AUNAY SUR ODON *3D1* (0.5km NE Urban) *49.02530, -0.62515* **Camp Municipal La Closerie,** Rue de Caen, 14260 Aunay-sur-Odon **02 31 77 32 46 or 07850 511893; mairieaunaysurodon@orange.fr; www.aunaysurodon.fr**

🐕 €1.55 ♦♦♦ WD ♨ ♿ ✎ MSP 🛒 nr

Exit A84 junc 43 sp Villers-Bocage/Aunay & take D6 twd Aunay. In approx 3km bef Aunay town sp, turn L sp 'Zone Industrielle', in 200m turn R at rndabt. Site on R in 100m nr sports stadium. 2*, Sm, mkd, pt shd, pt sl, EHU €2.80; Eng spkn; games area; CKE. *"Delightful, attractive vill; Sat mkt; vet avail; conv NH for Caen ferry & gd touring base; helpful, welcoming warden."* **€7.50, 6 Jul-31 Aug.** 2017

AUPS *10E3* (0.9km SE Rural) *43.62378, 6.22903* **Camping Les Prés,** 181 Route de Tourtour, 83630 Aups **04 94 70 00 93; lespres.camping@wanadoo.fr; www.campinglespres.com**

♦♦♦ (htd) ♨ ♿ ✎ 🦋 🍴 ⑪ 🛒 nr 🎿

Fr cent of Aups on rd to Tourtour, site on R. Rough rd. 3*, Med, hdg, mkd, pt shd, EHU (10A); gas; TV; 10% statics; adv bkg acc. *"Peaceful, friendly site; recep clsd 1200 to 1500; ent not rec for lge o'fits."* **€27.00, 1 Mar-31 Oct.** 2015

AUPS *10E3* (0.5km W Rural) *43.62455, 6.21760* **International Camping,** Route de Fox-Amphoux, 83630 Aups **04 94 70 06 80; camping-aups@ internationalcamping-aups.com; www.international camping-aups.com**

🐕 €1 ♦♦♦ WD ✎ 🍴 ⑪ 🛒 nr 🎿

Site on L on D60 nr vill cent. 3*, Lge, mkd, hdg, pt shd, EHU (16A) €5.30; 80% statics; Eng spkn; adv bkg rec; ccard acc; tennis; games rm. *"Vg site in beautiful area; lge pitches; gd rest."* **€19.00, 1 Apr-30 Sep.** 2016

AURAY *2F3* (7km S Rural) *47.64402, -2.93774* **FFCC Camping du Parc-Lann,** 52 Rue Thiers, Le Varquez, 56400 Le Bono **02 97 57 93 93 or 07 88 00 79 47; campingduparclann@wanadoo.fr; www.campingduparclann.fr**

🐕 €0.70 ♦♦♦ WD ♨ ♿ ✎ MSP 🛒 nr 🎿

S fr Auray on D101 sp Le Bono. Site well sp in Le Bono. 2*, Med, hdg, mkd, pt shd, EHU (6A) €2.30 (long lead req); bbq; phone; bus; games area; ice; CKE. *"Lovely quiet site in pretty area; gd, clean san facs poss stretched high ssn & ltd LS; pool 5km; warden on site 1800-1900 only LS; gd walking."* **€14.00, 1 May-30 Sep.** 2016

AURAY *2F3* (8km SW Rural) *47.64256, -3.05406* **FFCC Camping de Kergo,** Route de Carnac, 56400 Ploemel **02 97 56 80 66; contact@campingkergo. com; www.campingkergo.com**

🐕 €0.70 ♦♦♦ WD ♨ ♿ ✎ 🛒 nr 🎿 🎿 sand 5km

Fr Auray take D768 SW sp Carnac. After 4km turn NW on D186 twd Ploemel & foll sp. 3*, Med, mkd, pt shd, EHU (6-10A) inc; 10% statics; adv bkg rec; CKE. *"Lovely, peaceful site, lots of trees; gd, clean san facs but dated (2015), ltd LS; welcoming, friendly, helpful owners; gd size pitches; ideal for cycling into Carnac."* **€16.00, 1 May-30 Sep.** 2017

AURAY *2F3* (8km W Rural) *47.66406, -3.09985* **FFCC Camp Municipal Le St Laurent,** Kergonvo, 56400 Ploemel **02 97 56 85 90; contact@camping-saint-laurent.fr; www.camping-saint-laurent.fr**

12 🐕 €1.40 ♦♦♦ (htd) WD ♨ ♿ ✎ MSP 🦋 🍴 ⑪ 🛒 🎿 🎿 (htd) 🎿

Fr Auray on D22 twd Belz/Etel; after 8km turn L on D186 to Ploemel & site on L in 200m. 3*, Med, hdstg, shd, EHU (10A) €4; bbq; 10% statics; adv bkg acc; games area. *"Peaceful site; friendly staff; red facs LS."* **€23.50** 2019

AURILLAC *7C4* (1.4km NE Urban) *44.93551, 2.45596* **Camping De l'Ombrade,** Chemin du Gué Bouliaga, 15000 Aurillac **04 71 48 28 87**

🐕 ♦♦♦ ♨ ♿ ✎ 🦋 🛒 nr 🎿

Take D17 N fr Aurillac twd Puy-Mary; site on banks of Rv Jordanne. Well sp fr town. 3*, Lge, mkd, shd, pt sl, EHU 10A (inc); bbq; TV; games rm. *"Well-managed, spacious site; lge pitches; interesting, lge mkt town; vg; excl new san fac (2014)."* **€17.40, 15 Jun-15 Sep.** 2019

AUTRANS *9C3* (0.5km E Rural) *45.17520, 5.54770* **Kawan Village au Joyeux Réveil,** Le Château, 38880 Autrans **04 76 95 33 44; camping-au-joyeux-reveil@ wanadoo.fr; www.camping-au-joyeux-reveil.fr**

🐕 ♦♦♦ (htd) WD ♨ ♿ ✎ MSP 🦋 ⑪ 🍴 ⑪ nr 🎿 🛒 nr 🎿 🎿 (htd) 🎿

Fr Villard-de-Lans take D531 to Lans-en-Vercors & turn L onto D106 to Autrans. On E side of vill site sp at 1st rndabt. NB App on D531 fr W fr Pont-en-Royans not rec - v narr rd & low tunnels. 4*, Med, mkd, pt shd, pt sl, EHU (2-10A) €2-8; gas; bbq; TV (pitch); TV; 60% statics; phone; bus 300m; Eng spkn; adv bkg acc; ccard acc; golf 20km; games area; tennis 300m; bike hire; rv fishing; waterslide; CKE. *"Site in Vercors National Park with excel views; winter sport facs, 1050m altitude; modern san facs; excel; well run site; friendly staff."* **€44.00, 1 May-30 Sep.** 2019

AUTUN *6H1* (2km N Rural) *46.96478, 4.29381*
Camp de la Porte d'Arroux (formerly Municipal),
Les Chaumottes, 71400 Autun **03 85 52 10 82;**
www.aquadis-loisirs.com

🚶🐕 €1.35 👪 WD 🏊 ♨ ⚷ 🚱 ✉ MSP ⬢ 🍴 Ⓗⓓ🐾🚲 ⛺

Fr Autun foll dir for Saulieu on D980; site on L 500m
after passing thro Roman Arch; only site in Autun.
3*, Sm, hdg, hdstg, pt shd, EHU (10A) €3.30 (poss
rev pol); bbq; sw; twin axles; TV; phone; Eng spkn;
adv bkg acc; ccard acc; bike hire; fishing; canoeing;
games area; CKE. "Lovely, quiet, clean site; busy NH
high ssn; sm pitches, views fr some pitches; friendly,
helpful staff; gd san facs, poss stretched high ssn; no
twin axles; v muddy when wet (tow avail); vg, lively
rest & bar; medieval architecture & Roman walls
around town; m'van Aire de Service nr lake in town;
mkt Wed/Fri; poss overpriced for nature of site."
€21.00, 6 Mar-5 Nov. 2016

> ## "I need an on-site restaurant"
>
> We do our best to make sure site information
> is correct, but it is always best to check any
> must-have facilities are still available or will
> be open during your visit.

AUTUN *6H1* (12km NW Rural) *47.01227, 4.19150*
Camping Les Deux Rivières, Le Pré Bouché, 71400
La Celle-en-Morvan **03 45 74 01 38; info@les2rivieres
.com; www.les2rivieres.com**

🚶🐕 👪 WD 🏊 ♨ ⚷ 🚱 ✉ MSP 🦋 ⬢ ⛺ 🏊 (htd)

Fr Autun take D978 sp to Chateau-Chinon for
approx 12km. Site on R as entering vill. 300m
fr main rd. 3*, Med, mkd, hdg, pt shd, bbq; twin axles;
Eng spkn; adv bkg acc; games area; CKE. "V friendly
Dutch owners; well kept clean site; supmkt in Autun;
excel." **€26.00, 1 May-20 Sep.** 2015

AUXERRE *4F4* (2km SE Urban) *47.78678, 3.58721*
Camp Municipal, 8 Rue de Vaux, 89000 Auxerre
03 86 52 11 15 or 03 86 72 43 00 (Mairie);
camping.mairie@auxerre.com; www.auxerre.com

🚶🐕 👪 WD 🏊 🚱 ✉ MSP 🍴 🚲 ⛺

Exit A6 at Auxerre; at junc N6 ring rd foll sp Vaux &
'Stade'; site sp by Rv Yonne. Or fr N6 (N) take ring
rd, site/stadium sp. Site also well sp fr town cent
as 'L'Arbre Sec'. 3*, Lge, mkd, pt shd, EHU (6A) inc
(long lead poss req); TV; adv bkg acc; fishing 300m;
CKE. "Lovely, peaceful, well-kept site; lge pitches;
friendly staff; gd clean san facs, tight access to sinks;
pool 250m; poss cr & noisy during football ssn; site
poss flooded stormy weather; ltd EHU for site size,
pnts locked & unlocked by warden; no vehicles 2200-
0700; pretty town; popular NH; few water taps."
€13.00, 15 Apr-15 Sep. 2015

AUXERRE *4F4* (10km S Rural) *47.70704, 3.63563*
FFCC Camping Les Ceriselles, Route de Vincelottes,
89290 Vincelles **03 86 42 50 47; www.camping
ceriselles.com**

🚶🐕 2.50 € 👪 (htd) WD 🏊 ♨ ⚷ 🚱 ✉ MSP 🦋 ⬢ 🍴 Ⓗⓓ🐾 nr ⛺
🏊 (covrd, htd)

Leave A6 at Auxerre Sud. Fr Auxerre, take D606 S
twd Avallon. 10km fr Auxerre turn L into Vincelles.
In 400m immed after 'Atac Marche', turn L into
site access rd, sp as Camping Les Ceriselles. Site is
approx 16km fr a'route exit. 4*, Med, mkd, hdstg, pt
shd, EHU (10A) inc (poss rev pol); bbq; red long stay;
TV; 10% statics; phone; Eng spkn; adv bkg acc; ccard
acc; bike hire; CKE. "Excel, busy site by canal, poss full
late Jun; friendly, helpful owner; 1st dog free, max 2; gd
san facs, poss insufficient high ssn & ltd LS; lovely walks
to vill & along canal; cycle track to Auxerre & Clamecy;
highly rec; high ssn overflow area; secure o'night area;
gas adj; v popular." **€21.00, 1 Apr-1 Oct.** 2019

AUXI LE CHATEAU *3B3* (0.5km NW Rural) *50.2341,
2.1058* **Camp Municipal des Peupliers,** 22 Rue du
Cheval, 62390 Auxi-le-Château **03 21 41 10 79**

👪 🏊 ♨ 🚱 ✉ 🍴 nr Ⓗ nr 🐾 nr ⛺

Fr S on D925, turn N onto D933 at Bernaville to
Auxi-le-Château; turn W onto D941; then turn R in
300m into Rue du Cheval; site sp on R in 500m by
football stadium. Or take D928 S fr Hesdin; in 11km
take D119 to Auxi-le-Château.
3*, Med, hdg, unshd, EHU (3-6A) €1.85; 5% statics;
adv bkg acc; fishing; sailing. "Easy walk into town; dir
access to rv; supmkt 300m; excel NH or short stay."
€14.00, 1 Apr-30 Sep. 2018

AUXONNE *6G1* (1km NW Rural) *47.19838, 5.38120*
Camping L'Arquebuse, Route d'Athée, 21130
Auxonne **03 80 31 06 89; camping.arquebuse@
wanadoo.fr; www.campingarquebuse.com**

🚶🐕 €1.80 👪 (htd) WD 🏊 🚱 ✉ MSP ⬢ 🍴 Ⓗⓓ🐾 nr ⛺ 🎣

On D905 Dijon-Geneva, site sp on L bef bdge at ent
to Auxonne. 3*, Med, pt shd, EHU (10A) €3.70 (poss
rev pol); gas; bbq; twin axles; TV; 40% statics; Eng
spkn; adv bkg acc; ccard acc; waterskiing; fishing; clsd
2200-0700; windsurfing; sailing; CKE. "Pleasant rvside
site; friendly staff; san facs tatty & dated; htd pool
adj; poss busy w/ends as NH; interesting town; child
friendly site." **€21.00, 4 Mar-16 Dec.** 2017

AVAILLES LIMOUZINE *7A3* (7km E Rural) *46.12342,
0.65975* **FFCC Camp Municipal Le Parc,** 86460
Availles-Limouzine **05 49 48 51 22; camping.leparc@
wanadoo.fr; www.campingleparc.monsite-orange.fr**

🚶🐕 €2.65 👪 WD 🏊 ♨ 🚱 ✉ MSP ⬢ 🐾 nr ⛺ 🏊

Fr Confolens N on D948 & turn R on D34 to Availles-
Limouzine. Site on Rv Vienne by town bdge.
2*, Med, pt shd, EHU (10A) inc; gas; Eng spkn; adv
bkg acc; CKE. "Attractive, well-run site in beautiful
position; rv views; vg playgrnd; barrier clsd 2200-
0800; poss scruffy LS; vg value; permanent warden."
€16.50, 1 Apr-30 Sep. 2017

AVALLON *4G4* (2km SE Rural) *47.48030, 3.91246*
Camp Municipal Sous Roche, Rue Sous Roche;
89200 Avallon **03 86 34 10 39; campingsousroche@
ville-avallon.fr; www.campingsousroche.com**

App town fr a'route or fr SE on N6. Turn sharp L at
2nd traff lts in town cent, L in 2km at sp Vallée du
Cousin (bef bdge), site 250m on L. If app fr S care
needed when turning R after bdge.
3*, Med, hdstg, pt shd, terr, EHU (10A) inc; bbq; rv
fishing adj; CKE. *"Popular, well-kept site in lovely
location nr rv; friendly, helpful staff; excel immac san
facs; conv Morvan National Park; poss flood warning
after heavy rain; no twin axles or o'fits over 2,500kg;
attractive town; steep walk to town; excel; M'vans max
3,500kg."* **€19.50, 1 Apr-15 Oct.** 2019

AVESNES-SUR-HELPE *3B4* (9km ENE Rural) *50.143096,
4.028659* **Camping Municipal de La Boissellerie,**
rue de la Place 59740, Felleries **06 83 80 87 29 or
03 27 59 03 46; campingdaboisselleriefelleries@
orange.fr; www.felleries.fr**

Fr N2 19km S of Maubeuge. Turn E on D962. At
Sars-Poteries turn S on D80 or D104. Site sp in vill.
Med, pt shd, EHU (6A) €4; bbq (charcoal, elec, gas);
Eng spkn; adv bkg acc. *"Conv N2 N/S or D1043 W/E;
lovely area of wooded hills; Rock Fest 1 w/e per year;
excel."* **€15.40, 15 Apr-30 Sep.** 2019

"Satellite navigation makes touring much easier"

Remember most sat navs don't know if you're
towing or in a larger vehicle – always use yours
alongside maps and site directions.

AVIGNON *10E2* (4km N Rural) *43.97063, 4.79928*
Viva Camp la Laune (formerly Municipal), Chemin
St Honoré, 30400 Villeneuve-lès-Avignon **04 90 25 76
06 or 04 90 25 61 33; campingdelalaune@wanadoo.
fr; www.camping-villeneuvelezavignon.com**

Fr Avignon, take N100 twd Nîmes over rv bdge. At
W end of 2nd pt of rv bdge, turn R onto N980 sp
Villeneuve-lès-Avignon. Site is 3km on R just past
town battlements on L. Adj sports complex. **NB
Do not foll sat nav rote thro Pujaut.** 3*, Med, mkd,
hdstg, hdg, shd, EHU (6A) €3.10 (poss rev pol); bbq;
twin axles; TV; 10% statics; phone; bus; Eng spkn; adv
bkg acc; ccard acc; games area; CKE. *"Lovely, peaceful;
helpful staff; excel security; sports facs adj; gd walks/
cycle rides; htd pool adj; in walking dist of Villeneuve-
lès-Avignon with fort & abbey; gd bus to Avignon;
sports complex adj (free to campers, but ltd acc); vg
local mkt; poss rlwy noise at night; floods in heavy
rain; new owners, site deteriorated; scruffy out of ssn."*
€26.00, 1 Apr-15 Oct. 2016

AVIGNON *10E2* (9km NE Rural) *43.99057, 4.91340*
Camping Avignon Parc (formerly Camping Flory),
385 Route d'Entraigues, 84270 Vedène **04 90 31 00 51**

Fr A7 exit 23 dir Carpentras for 3km then Vedene.
3*, Lge, mkd, pt shd, pt sl, EHU (10A) €4 (poss rev
pol); gas; bbq; twin axles; 15% statics; phone; bus;
Eng spkn; adv bkg acc; games area; games rm; CKE.
*"Conv touring base Vaucluse; uneven pitches & paths;
facs poss stretched high ssn & ltd LS; lovely pool; vg."*
€29.00, 24 May-24 Sep. 2017

AVIGNON *10E2* (8km S Urban) *43.88361, 4.87010*
Camping de la Roquette, 746 Ave Jean Mermoz,
13160 Châteaurenard **04 90 94 46 81; contact@
camping-la-roquette.com; www.camping-la-
roquette.com**

Exit A7/D907 Avignon S to Noves; take D28 to
Châteaurenard 4km; foll sp to site & Piscine
Olympic/Complex Sportiv. 3*, Med, hdg, mkd, pt shd,
serviced pitches; EHU (10A) €4; TV; phone; Eng spkn;
adv bkg rec; ccard acc; tennis; CKE. *"Gd touring cent;
sm pitches; owners friendly, helpful; clean facs; gd
walks."* **€22.00, 1 Apr-31 Oct.** 2019

AVIGNON *10E2* (12km W Rural) *43.95155, 4.66451*
Camping Le Bois des Ecureuils, 947 Chemin De La
Beaume, 30390 Domazan **04 66 57 10 03; infos@
boisdesecureuils.com; www.boisdesecureuils.com**

Exit A9/E15 at Remoulins junc 23 twd Avignon on
N100. Site on R in 6km. Fr S on N7 foll sp for Nîmes
onto N100. Go over 2 lge rndabts, site about 6km
on L at rndabt. 2*, Sm, mkd, hdstg, shd, EHU (6A) inc;
gas; bbq; TV; 5% statics; phone; Eng spkn; adv bkg
rec; CKE. *"Ideal for touring Avignon & Pont du Gard;
friendly owners; clean facs; steel awning pegs ess;
many long-stay residents LS; v shd; tired site; mostly
residential in LS."* **€20.00** 2018

AVIGNON *10E2* (1km NW Urban) *43.95670, 4.80222*
Camping du Pont d'Avignon, 10 Chemin de la
Barthelasse, 84000 Avignon **04 90 80 63 50;
camping.avignon@aquadis-loisirs.com;
www.aquadis-loisirs.com**

Exit A7 junc 23 Avignon Nord dir Avignon Centre
(D225) then Villeneuve-les-Avignon. Go round
wall & under Pont d'Avignon; then cross rv dir
Villeneuve, Ile de la Barthelasse. Turn R onto Ile
de la Barthelasse. 4*, Lge, mkd, hdg, shd, EHU (10A)
inc; gas; bbq; cooking facs; red long stay; TV; phone;
Eng spkn; adv bkg req; ccard acc; games rm; car wash;
games area; tennis; CKE. *"Superb, well-run, busy site;
welcoming, helpful staff; lovely pool; gd sized pitches
but most with high kerbs; poss flooded LS; extra for
c'vans over 5.5m; Avignon festival Jul/Aug; best site
for Avignon - 20 mins walk or free ferry; rec arr early
even LS; san facs ltd but recently refurbished (2014)."*
€39.00, 2 Mar-15 Nov. 2019

FRANCE

AVIGNON *10E2* (1km NW Urban) *43.95216, 4.79946*
FFCC Camping Bagatelle, 25 allée Antoine Pinay - Ile de la Barthelasse, 84000 Avignon **04 90 86 30 39; camping.bagatelle@wanadoo.fr; www.camping bagatelle.com**
12 €2.40 (htd)

Exit D907 at Avignon Nord. After passing end of old bdge bear L, then onto new Daladier bdge & take immed R turn over bdge foll sp to Barthelasse & Villeneuve-lès-Avignon. Caution - do not foll Nîmes sp at more southerly bdge (Pont d'Europe). 3*, Lge, mkd, pt shd, EHU (6-10A) €3.50-4.50; gas; ccard acc; fishing; games area; boating; tennis 2km; CKE. *"Busy site on rv bank; sm pitches; helpful staff; facs dated but clean, ltd LS & poss stretched high ssn; narr site rds, suggest find pitch bef driving in; pool 100m; if recep unmanned, go to bar or supmkt to check in; free ferry to town; site low lying & poss damp; highly rec; ideal location, sh walk into Avignon Cent."* **€30.00** **2016**

AVIGNON *10E2* (5km NW Rural) *43.99573, 4.81843*
Campéole Camping L'Ile des Papes, Quartier l'Islon, 30400 Villeneuve-lès-Avignon **04 90 15 15 90; ile-des-papes@campeole.com; www.campeole.com**
€3.50

Fr A9 exit sp Roquemaure; head S on D980. Site adj to rv 2km NW of city. Fr D907 (A7) exit Avignon Nord, twds Avignon cent & cross bdge twds Villeneuve. Turn off after x-ing rv bef x-ing canal. Site bet rv & canal. 4*, Lge, pt shd, EHU (10A) inc; bbq; cooking facs; red long stay; TV; 35% statics; Eng spkn; adv bkg acc; ccard acc; archery; lake fishing adj; CKE. *"Lovely area; hiking; well-run site; pleasant staff; lge pitches; gd site rest."* **€25.00, 3 Apr-1 Nov.** **2019**

> **"There aren't many sites open at this time of year"**
>
> If you're travelling outside peak season remember to call ahead to check site opening dates – even if the entry says 'open all year'.

AVRANCHES *2E4* (10km W Rural) *48.69663, -1.47434*
FFCC Camping La Pérame, 50530 Genêts
02 33 70 82 49
€0.90

Fr Avranches on N175; in 1km turn L on D911 thro Genêts. Turn R onto D35 immed after passing thro Genêts, site on R in 1km. 2*, Sm, pt shd, EHU (10A) €3 (rev pol); 60% statics; phone; CKE. *"CL-type site in apple orchard nr sm vill; pleasant owner; gd views of Mont-St Michel fr vill; poss ltd & unkempt LS; poss boggy after heavy rain; guided walks to Mont St Michel; rec; farm produce; excel, quiet, simple site; all grass; pricey but special."* **€15.00, 1 May-30 Sep.** **2017**

AXAT *8G4* (2km E Rural) *42.80775, 2.25408*
Camping de la Crémade, 11140 Axat **06 70 07 43 21 or 04 68 74 06 12; campinglacremade@orange.fr; www.campinglacremade.com**
€1 WD

S fr Quillan on D117, cont 1km beyond junc with D118 twd Perpignan. Turn R into site, sp, narr access. Med, hdg, pt shd, pt sl, EHU (6A) €2.50; bbq; 5% statics; Eng spkn; adv bkg acc; games rm; CKE. *"Pleasant, well-maintained site in beautiful location; few level pitches; gd san facs; conv for gorges in Aude Valley."* **€22.00, 1 May-24 Sep.** **2019**

> **"That's changed – Should I let the Club know?"**
>
> If you find something on site that's different from the site entry, fill in a report and let us know. See camc.com/europereport.

AYDAT *9B1* (2km NE Rural) *45.66777, 2.98943*
Camping du Lac d'Aydat, Forêt du Lot, 63970 Aydat
04 73 79 38 09; info@camping-lac-aydat.com; www.camping-lac-aydat.com
€1.50 WD MSP nr

Exit A75 S fr Clermont-Ferrand at junc 5 onto D13 W. Foll sp Lake Aydat. At x-rds at end of Rouillas-Bas, turn L at rndabt & foll site sp. 3*, Med, mkd, hdstg, shd, terr, serviced pitches; EHU (10A) €4; sw nr; 30% statics; phone; adv bkg acc; fishing; CKE. *"On shore of Lake Aydat; gd for m'vans; bar 500m; charming woodland pitches, facs tired."* **€24.00, 1 Apr-30 Sep.** **2020**

AYDAT *9B1* (3km W Rural) *45.66195, 2.94857*
Camping Les Volcans, La Garandie, 63970 Aydat
04 73 79 33 90; campinglesvolcans@akeonet.com; www.campinglesvolcans.com
€2 WD MSP nr (htd)
sand 3km

Fr N exit A75 junc 2 onto D2089 dir Bourboule; in 18km turn S onto D213 to Verneuge; in 1km fork R onto D5 dir Murol; in 1.5km turn R onto D788 sp La Grandie; turn R into vill; turn R again & site on L in 100m. Fr S exit A73 junc 5 onto D213 W; in 16km turn S in Verneuge onto D5; after 1.5km turn W onto D788 sp La Garandie; in vill turn R just after phone box, site on L in 100m. 3*, Sm, mkd, pt shd, pt sl, EHU (6A) €5; sw nr; 2% statics; Eng spkn; adv bkg acc; games area; horseriding 3km; watersports 3km. *"Relaxing site; friendly, helpful new owners improving (2011); lge pitches; no twin axles; excel walking & cycle rtes nr; beautiful area; gd touring base; excel clean & well stocked facs; loads of hot water always on supply."* **€18.00, 6 Apr-2 Nov.** **2019**

AZAY LE FERRON *4H2* (8km N Rural) *46.91949, 1.03679* **Camping Le Cormier,** Route de St Flovier, 36290 Obterre **02 54 39 27 95 or 0844 232 7271 (UK); mike@loireholidays.biz; www.loireholidays.biz**

12 ♂ ♦♦(htd) WD ♣ ▣ ∥ ♥ ♀ ⓗnr ⚓

Fr Azay-le-Ferron N on D14, site on R just N of Obterre. Or fr Loches S on D943 for 3.5km, turn onto D41 to St Flovier then turn L onto D21 sp Obterre. In 1km turn R onto D14, site on L in 4km. Sm, mkd, hdstg, hdg, pt shd, EHU (10A) €4; bbq; twin axles; TV; Eng spkn; adv bkg acc; ice; games area; games rm. *"Friendly, helpful British owners (CC members); dogs free; spacious pitches; gd san facs; excel touring/walking base; nr Brenne National Park; excel birdwatching; vg."* **€20.00** **2019**

AZAY LE RIDEAU *4G1* (0.6km SE Urban) *47.25919, 0.46992* **Camping Le Sabot (formerly Municipal),** Rue du Stade, 37190 Azay-le-Rideau **02 47 45 42 72; campinglesabot@onlycamp.fr; www.onlycamp. fr/en/campsite-in-the-heart-of-the-loire-valley**

♂ ♦♦ WD ♣ ♿ ▣ ∥ MSP ♥ ♀ ⓗnr ▣nr ⚠

Best app is fr D751 by-pass to avoid narr town - ignore Azay-le-Rideau sps until Carrefour rndabt. Strt ahead for 1km, site visible at 2nd rndabt. 3*, V lge, mkd, pt shd, EHU (10A) €4.50 (poss rev pol); bbq; red long stay; TV; phone; Eng spkn; adv bkg rec; ccard acc; games area; fishing; CKE. *"Pleasant, spacious, scenic site by rv (Rv Indre) & chateau; friendly, helpful recep; poss long dist to san facs fr some pitches - cent facs have steps; san facs stretched high ssn, ltd LS; htd pool adj; site prone to flooding; recep open 0800-1200 & 1400-1700; when site clsd m'vans can stay on car park by rv o'night - no facs but well lit (eng al TO); gd loc nr to town and rests; excel."* JN 21/12/2020 Site name changed. **€24.20, 5 Apr-3 Nov.** **2019**

BADEN *2F3* (0.9km SW Rural) *47.61410, -2.92540* **Camping Mané Guernehué,** 52 Rue Mané er Groëz, 56870 Baden **02 97 57 02 06; info@camping-baden. com; www.camping-baden.com or www.yelloh village.co.uk**

♂ €6 ♦♦(htd) WD ♣ ♣ ♿ ▣ ∥ MSP ♥ ♀ ⓗ ▣ ⚠ ✏ ⚓(covrd, htd) ⛱ ☂ sand 3km

Exit N165 sp Arradon/L'Ile aux Moines onto D101 to Baden (10km); in Baden vill turn R at camp sp immed after sharp L-hand bend; in 200m bear R at junc; site on R. Sp at both ends of vill. 4*, Lge, mkd, hdg, pt shd, terr, serviced pitches; EHU (10A) €4.70; bbq; red long stay; TV; 35% statics; phone; Eng spkn; ccard acc; sauna; jacuzzi; games rm; golf 1.5km; waterslide; lazy river; spa treatments; fishing; bike hire; games area; tennis 600m; horse riding school; kids' clubs; gym; mini golf; watersports 3km. *"Mature, pleasant site; fitness rm; gd views; excel san facs; some narr site rds; excel."* **€55.00, 5 Apr-30 Sep, B26.** **2019**

BAERENTHAL *5D3* (2km N Rural) *48.98170, 7.51230* **Camp Municipal Ramstein-Plage,** Rue de Ramstein, 57230 Baerenthal **03 87 06 50 73; camping.ramstein@ wanadoo.fr; www.baerenthal.eu**

♂ €1.90 ♦♦(htd) WD ♣ ♿ ▣ ∥ MSP ♥ ♀ ⓗ ▣ ▣nr ⚠ ✏ ⚓(htd)

Fr N62 turn onto D36 sp Baerenthal, site sp on lakeside. 3*, Lge, hdg, mkd, pt shd, pt sl, EHU (12A) €3.50; sw nr; 80% statics; Eng spkn; adv bkg acc; tennis; games area. *"Attractive location in important ecological area; generous pitches; modern san facs; m'van o'night area; gd walks; birdwatching; conv Maginot Line; excel."* **€22.60, 1 Apr-30 Sep.** **2015**

BAGNERES DE BIGORRE *8F2* (2km SE Rural) *43.05566, 0.16510* **Camping La Pommeraie,** 2 Ave Philadelphe, 65200 Gerde **05 62 91 32 24; campinglapommeraie@gmail.com; www.camping lapommeraie.com**

12 ♂ (€1.30) ♦♦(htd) WD ♣ ♿ ▣ ∥ MSP ♥ ♀ ⓗnr ▣nr ⚠

App fr E, exit A64 junc 14 (Tournay) onto D20/ D938 to Bagnères-de-Bigorre; on ent town turn L at traff lts & foll sp to site. App fr W, exit A64 junc 12 (Tarbes); leave ring rd at junc with D935 & cont to Bagnères-de-Bigorre; foll site sps fr town. 2*, Sm, mkd, hdstg, shd, pt sl, EHU (10A) €4.50; bbq; 10% statics; phone; Eng spkn; adv bkg acc; games rm; CKE. *"Mountain views; htd covrd pool 2km; friendly owners; bike hire in Bagnères; excel walking, mountain biking & touring base; gd, clean, well maintained site; ideal tourist area."* **€9.00** **2017**

BAGNERES DE BIGORRE *8F2* (2km SE Urban) *43.07485, 0.16869* **Camping Les Palomieres,** 20 Route Palomieres, 65200 Bagnères-de-Bigorre **05 62 95 59 79; camping-les-palomieres@ wanadoo.fr; www.camping-les-palomieres.com**

12 ♂ ♦♦ WD ♣ ▣ ∥ ♥ ▣ ⚠

Take D938 fr Bagnères dir Toulouse, after 2km turn R at Haut de la Côte. Site sp. Sm, pt shd, pt sl, EHU (A-6A) €1.50-4.25; sw nr; 50% statics; adv bkg rec. *"Gd views of Pyrenees; simple site; local specialities."* **€8.50** **2018**

BAGNERES DE BIGORRE *8F2* (13km NW Rural) *43.11196, 0.04931* **Aire Naturelle Le Cerf Volant (Dhom),** 7 Cami de la Géline, 65380 Orincles **05 62 42 99 32; lecerfvolant1@yahoo.fr**

♂ ♦♦ WD ♣ ▣ ∥ ⚠

Fr Bagnères-de-Bigorre on D935; turn L onto D937 dir Lourdes; site on L opp D407. Single track app rd for 150m. Sm, pt shd, EHU (15A) €2.30; CKE. *"Farm site - produce sold Jul-Aug; conv Lourdes & touring Pyrenees; gd, clean site; lovely site; quiet."* **€11.00, 15 May-15 Oct.** **2015**

FRANCE

CAMPING DE LA VÉE *
BAGNOLES DE L'ORNE NORMANDIE**

Located between Paris and Brittany, at about 55 miles from the Mont Saint Michel and the landing beaches, in the heart of the Normandy, in green surroundings, with casino, golf, swimming pool, tennis and horseback riding. Come and discover the charm of the countryside and the untouched magic of a 19th century touristic and thermal region.

CAMPING DE LA VÉE *
250 pitches on offer
F-61140 Bagnoles de l'Orne Normandie
Tel : 0033(0) 233 378 745
camping@bagnolesdelorne.com – www.campingbagnolesdelorne.com

BAGNOLES DE L'ORNE *4E1* (1.6km SW Urban) *48.54783, -0.41995* **Camp Municipal de la Vée,** Avenue du President Coty, 61140 Bagnoles-de-l'Orne **02 33 37 87 45; info@campingbagnolesdelorne.com; www.campingbagnolesdelorne.com**

🏕 €1.70 👫(htd) 🛗 ♨ ⚡ 🚿 ♿ 🛒 MSP 🦋 ⛲ 🍽 🏧 🅿 🚮 nr 🚲

Access fr D335 in vill of Bagnoles-Château. Or fr La Ferté-Macé on D916 for 6km sp Couterne. Well sp fr all dirs. 3*, Lge, hdg, mkd, pt shd, pt sl, EHU (10A) €3.50 (poss rev pol); gas; bbq; TV; phone; bus adj; Eng spkn; ccard acc; golf nr; tennis nr; CKE. *"Excel, well-kept, well-run site in vg location; vg, spotless facs; htd pool 1.5km; mini golf nr; easy walk to beautiful thermal spa town & lake; free bus to town cent at site ent; forest walks; archery nrby; gd for dogs; gd value; town bus €1 per day."* **€18.00, 3 Mar-11 Nov.** 2018

See advertisement

"I like to fill in the reports as I travel from site to site"

You'll find report forms at the back of this guide, or you can fill them in online at camc.com/europereport.

BAGNOLS SUR CEZE *10E2* (3km NE Rural) *44.17358, 4.63694* **Camping Les Genêts d'Or,** Chemin de Carmigan, 30200 Bagnols-sur-Cèze **04 66 89 58 67; info@camping.genets-dor.com; www.camping-genets-dor.com**

🏕 👫(htd) 👫 WD 🛗 ♨ ⚡ ♿ 🚿 🦋 ⛲ 🍽 🏧 🅿 🚮 🛝 🚲 (htd) 🏊

N fr Bagnols on N86 over rv bdge, turn R into D360 immed after Total stn. Foll sp to site on rv. 4*, Med, mkd, hdstg, pt shd, pt sl, EHU (6A) €5.50 (poss rev pol); gas; 10% statics; Eng spkn; adv bkg req; ccard acc; games rm; fishing 2km; games area. *"Excel, clean site; welcoming Dutch owners; gd pool; canoeing 2km; no dogs Jul/Aug; wildlife in rv; gd rest; highly rec."* **€33.00, 20 Apr-20 Sep.** 2016

BAIGNES STE RADEGONDE *7B2* (0.5km SW Rural) *45.38187, -0.23862* **FFCC Camp Municipal,** Le Plein, 16360 Baignes-Ste-Radegonde **05 45 78 79 95 or 05 45 78 40 04 (Mairie); point.i@live.fr; www.baignes-sainte-radegonde.fr**

👫 👫 🛗 ⚡ 🚿 ♿ 🦋 🚲 nr

Fr N10 turn W onto D2 to Baignes; site well sp on rvside. 2*, Sm, pt shd, EHU (6A) €3; adv bkg acc; ccard acc; tennis nr; CKE. *"Warden calls pm; excel new san facs (2018); chem disp in vill; attractive sm town nr cycle track; excel."* **€27.00, 1 Apr-31 Oct.** 2018

BAILLEUL *3A3* (3.5km N Rural) *50.76160, 2.74956* **Camping Les Saules (Notteau),** 453 Route du Mont Noir, 59270 Bailleul **03 28 49 13 75; www.ferme-des-saules.com**

🏕 👫 🛗 WD ♨ ⚡ 🦋 🚲 🛝

N fr Lille on A25 exit junc 10 & head N into Bailleul cent; in town cent at traff lts turn R onto D23/N375; after 400m turn L on D23; in 2km just bef Belgian border turn L onto D223. Site on L in 300m. Sm, hdstg, pt shd, EHU (6A) €3.35; bbq; 90% statics; Eng spkn; CKE. *"Farm site; friendly owner; conv Calais, Dunkerque & WW1 sites; lovely, excel site, highly rec well kept and comfortable site; 1st class farm shop; unkempt in LS; 2 pin adapter ess; new san facs (2017)."* **€11.50, 1 Apr-31 Oct.** 2017

BAIN DE BRETAGNE *2F4* (13km W Rural) *47.8200, -1.8299* **Camp Municipal Le Port,** Rue de Camping, 35480 Guipry **02 99 34 72 90 (Mairie) or 02 99 34 28 26**

👫 👫 ♨ ⚡ ♿ 🦋 MSP 🚮 nr 🚲 nr 🛝

W fr Bain-de-Bretagne on D772, cross rv at Messac; cont on D772 sharp L at Leader supmkt into Ave du Port; site sp bef ent Guipry. NB Do not app after dark as rv is at end of app rd. V sharp turn at Leader supmkt into Ave du Camping. 2*, Med, mkd, hdg, pt shd, EHU (10A) €3 (poss long lead req); rv fishing; CKE. *"Excel, pretty site; friendly; warden on duty am & late pm; barrier 1.9m locked at times but phone for help or go to pitch 30; delightful rv walks & cycle paths; cruising & hire boats avail; nr classic cars museum; phone Mairie for warden's number, who calls early PM."* **€10.00, Easter-15 Oct.** 2018

BALAZUC 9D2 (2km E Rural) 44.50778, 4.40333
Camping Le Chamadou, Mas de Chaussy, 07120
Balazuc 08 20 36 61 97 or 07 87 64 34 77 (mob);
infos@camping-le-chamadou.com; www.camping-le-chamadou.com

🐕€2.60 ♦♦(htd) ⬛ ▲ ♨ ♿ ⬛ ✎ 🦋 ⛱ 🍴 ⬛ 🚲 ⛺ 🅿 ⛵ 🏊

Fr Ruoms foll D579 dir Aubenas. After approx 9km
turn R under viaduct, site sp. Keep R up narr rd
to site. App recep on foot fr car pk. 3*, Med, hdg,
hdstg, pt shd, pt sl, EHU (10A) €4.20 (some rev pol);
bbq (elec); TV; 10% statics; phone; Eng spkn; adv bkg
rec; ccard acc; canoe hire; kayak hire; waterslide; CKE.
"Excel, well-run, family site; panoramic views; most
pitches spacious." €24.00, 1 Apr-31 Oct.   2017

BALBIGNY 9B1 (2.7km NW Rural) 45.82558, 4.16196
Camping La Route Bleue, Route D56 du Lac de
Villerest, Pralery, 42510 Balbigny 04 77 27 24 97
or 06 85 52 98 66 (mob); camping.balbigny@
wanadoo.fr; camping-de-la-route-bleue.fr

♦♦ ⬛ ▲ ♨ ♿ ⬛ ✎ ⬛ 🦋 🍴 ⬛ 🚲 ⬛nr ⛺ ⛵ 🏊

Fr N on D1082, take 1st R after a'route (A89/72)
junc N of Balbigny onto D56. Fr S on D1082, turn L
at RH bend on N o'skirts of Balbigny, D56, sp Lac de
Villerest & St Georges-de-Baroille. Well sp.
3*, Med, hdg, mkd, pt shd, pt sl, EHU (10A) (poss long
lead req); bbq; red long stay; adv bkg acc; ccard acc;
fishing; games rm; CKE. "Nice site on rv bank; views
over rv some pitches; helpful, friendly & welcoming
staff; san facs updated (2017); sports complex
adj; ltd EHU; extra for twin axles; conv A72; excel;
lovely area; lge pitches; gd NH; ok long stay; fishing."
€22.00, 15 Mar-31 Oct.   2017

BALLEROY 1D4 (1km NE Rural) 49.18680, -0.82463
Camping Le Clos De Balleroy, Route de Castillon,
14490 Balleroy 02 31 21 41 48; info@camping-leclosdeballeroy.fr; www.camping-leclosde
balleroy.fr

♦♦ ⬛ ▲ ♨ ⬛ ✎ ⬛ 🍴 ⬛ 🏊

Fr N13 junc 37 turn S onto D572. After 6.8km in Le
Tronquay turn L onto D73, sp Castillon. Site on R in
5km bef Balleroy. 3*, Sm, pt shd, EHU (16A); games
area. "Conv for Normandy coast and Bayeux; gd."
€24.00, 15 Mar-15 Nov.   2016

BANON 10E3 (2km S Rural) 44.02607, 5.63088
Camping L'Epi Bleu, Les Gravières, 04150 Banon
04 92 73 30 30 or 06 15 61 68 63 (mob);
campingepibleu@aol.com; www.campingepibleu.com

🐕€4 ♦♦ ⬛ ▲ ♨ ♿ ⬛ ✎ ⬛ 🦋 🍴 ⬛ 🚲 ⬛ ⛺ 🏊 (htd) 🚲

Fr D4100 8km S of Forcalquier turn R onto D5 N
thro St Michel-L'Observatoire & Revest twd Banon
(approx 25km). Turn L on D51 twds Simiane-la-Rotunde. Site on R in 500m immed bef town,
sp at junc. 3*, Med, shd, EHU (10A) €5; bbq; TV;
70% statics; Eng spkn; adv bkg acc; games area; CKE.
"Vg, wooded site; pleasant owners; gd walking & cycling
tours; access to some pitches diff for lge o'fits; san fac
tired but clean (2015); uphill 30m walk to vill with sm
supmkt." €30.00, 4 Apr-30 Sep.   2015

BANYULS SUR MER 10H1 (1.5km SW Rural) 42.47665,
3.11904 **Camp Municipal La Pinède,** Ave Guy Malé,
66650 Banyuls-sur-Mer 04 68 88 32 13; camp.banyuls
@banyuls-sur-mer.com; www.banyuls-sur-mer.com

🐕 ♦♦ ⬛ ▲ ♨ ♿ ⬛ ✎ ⬛ 🦋 ⬛ ⬛nr ⛺ 🌳shgl 1km

On D914 foll sp to Banyuls-sur-Mer; turn R at
camping sp at cent of sea-front by town hall; foll
sp to site. 2*, Lge, hdg, mkd, pt shd, pt sl, terr, EHU
(4-13A) €2-3; Eng spkn; ccard acc; CKE. "Busy, friendly
site; spacious pitches, some with sea view; narr site rds;
vg, clean facs." €17.50, 23 Feb-12 Nov.   2018

BAR LE DUC 6E1 (2km E Urban) 48.77433, 5.17415
FFCC Camp Municipal du Château de Marbeaumont,
Rue du Stade, off Rue de St Mihiel, 55000 Bar-le-Duc
03 29 79 17 33 (TO) or 03 29 79 11 13 (LS);
barleduc.tourisme@wanadoo.fr; www.tourisme-
barleduc.com

♦♦ ⬛ ▲ ♨ ⬛ ✎ ⬛nr

Fr town cent foll Camping sps. Rue de St Mihiel is
pt of D1916 dir Verdun. Fr NW on D994/D694 or
fr SE on N1135, at rndabt turn E onto D1916 sp
Metz, Verdun & St Mihiel. In 200m turn L into Rue du
Stade sp Camping. Site on L in 100m.
1*, Sm, pt shd, EHU (16A) €3 (poss long lead req).
"Barrier clsd 1100-1500; delightful site in grnds of
chateau; friendly & helpful warden; clean, modern san
facs; no twin axles; check gate opening times; lovely
walk into historic town; gd NH; vg site; nice open plan
site." €13.00, 1 May-15 Oct.   2018

BARCARES, LE 10G1 (1km SW Coastal) 42.77462,
3.02207 **Camping L'Europe,** Route de St Laurent,
66420 Le Barcarès 04 68 86 15 36; reception@
europe-camping.com; www.europe-camping.com

12 🐕€8 ♦♦ ⬛ ▲ ♨ ♿ ⬛ ✎ ⬛ 🍴 ⬛ 🚲 ⬛ 🌳

Exit A9 at Perpignan N & take D83 sp Le Barcarès.
After 9km turn R on D81 sp Canet Plage, L on D90
sp Le Barcarès. Site on R. 3*, Lge, mkd, hdg, shd, EHU
(16A) inc; gas; red long stay; 50% statics; Eng spkn;
adv bkg acc; tennis; archery; waterslide; CKE. "Gd
location; tidy pitches, all have individual san facs (tired
early ssn 2010); ltd facs LS; gd cycle rte to beach &
shops; disco; gd winter NH." €21.00   2017

BARCELONNETTE 9D4 (9km W Rural) 44.39686,
6.54605 **Domaine Loisirs de l'Ubaye,** Vallée de
l'Ubaye, 04340 Barcelonnette 04 92 81 01 96;
info@loisirsubaye.com; www.loisirsubaye.com

🐕€3.50 ♦♦ ⬛ ▲ ♨ ♿ ⬛ ✎ ⬛ 🍴 ⬛ 🚲 ⬛ 🌳 ⛵ 🏊(htd)

Site on S side of D900. 4*, Lge, mkd, shd, terr, EHU
(6A) €3.50; gas; red long stay; TV; phone; watersports;
bike hire; CKE. "Magnificent scenery; gd site; friendly."
€29.50, 15 May-15 Oct.   2016

FRANCE

BARFLEUR *1C4* (0.7km NW Urban/Coastal) *49.67564, -1.26645* **Camp Municipal La Blanche Nef,** 12 Chemin de la Masse, 50760 Gatteville-le-Phare **02 33 23 15 40; www.camping-barfleur.fr**

🐕 €2.04 ♟(htd) ⬚ ♨ ♿ 🚿 ⊿ 🦋 ⚲ 🍴 ⌂ nr ⛰ 🏖 sand adj

Foll main rd to harbour; half-way on L side of harbour & turn L at mkd gap in car pk; cross sm side-rd & foll site sp on sea wall; site visible on L in 300m. Site accessible only fr S (Barfleur).
3*, Med, unshd, pt sl, EHU (6-10A); 45% statics; Eng spkn; adv bkg acc; ccard acc; CKE. *"Gd sized pitches; vg facs; lovely site; sea views; gd beach; gd birdwatching, walking, cycling; m'vans all year; walking dist to fishing vill; clean washing facs; bread van at 9am."*
€21.40, 15 Feb-15 Nov. **2018**

BARFLEUR *1C4* (1km NW Coastal) *49.67971, -1.27364* **Camping La Ferme du Bord de Mer,** 43 Route du Val de Saire, 50760 Gatteville-Phare **060 895 2434; camping.gatteville@gmail.com; www.camping-gatteville.fr**

12 🐕 €1.45 ♟ ⬚ ♿ 🚿 ⊿ 🦋 🍴 ⚲ nr ⛰ ✎ 🏖 sand adj

On D901 fr Cherbourg; on o'skts of Barfleur turn L onto D116 for Gatteville-Phare. Site on R in 1km. 2*, Sm, mkd, hdg, pt shd, pt sl, serviced pitches; EHU (3-10A) €3.40-5.30; gas; 25% statics; phone; games rm. *"CL-type site; sheltered beach; coastal path to vill & lighthouse; conv ferries (30 mins); Sep 2002 member reported high-strength poison against rodents in field adj site - no warning notices displayed, beware children or dogs; gd."* **€15.00** **2016**

BARNEVILLE CARTERET *1C4* (3.5km SE Coastal) *49.35952, -1.74879* **Camping du Golf,** Saint Jean de la Rivière, 50270 Barneville-Cartere **02 33 04 78 90; contact@camping-du-golf.fr; www.camping-du-golf.co.uk**

🐕 €4 ♟ ⬚ ♿ 🚿 ⊿ 🦋 🍴 ⚲ nr ⛰ ✎ 🏊(covrd, htd) 🏖 sandy 1km

Fr Barneville-Carteret, turn W on D130, after 1.5km turn L. Site on R after 1.5km. Site well sp fr Barneville-Carteret. 4*, Lge, hdg, mkd, unshd, EHU (6A) inc; gas; twin axles; adv bkg req; ccard acc; games rm; CKE. *"Gd quiet site with clean facs; 18 hole course; horse ridding nrby."*
€37.00, 1 Apr-1 Nov. **2017**

BASTIA *10G2* (5km N Coastal) *42.74039, 9.45982* **Camping Les Orangers,** 4 Chemin de Fiumicellu, 20200 San-Martino-di-Lota, Corsica **06 12 53 73 33; camping.lesorangers@gmail.com; www.camping-lesorangers.com**

♟ ⬚ ⊿ 🦋 ⚲ 🍴 ⚲ nr ⛰ 🏖 shgl adj

Foll main coast rd D80 N 4km fr ferry. Site well sp on L of rd. 1*, Sm, shd, EHU; TV; Eng spkn; CKE. *"Poss run down LS; friendly owners; vg rest; site ent tight for lge o'fits; no m'vans (2011); poss unrel opening dates."*
€19.00, 1 Apr-30 Sep. **2020**

BASTIA *10G2* (11km S Coastal) *42.62922, 9.46835* **Camping San Damiano,** Lido de la Marana, 20620 Biguglia **04 95 33 68 02; san.damiano@wanadoo.fr; www.campingsandamiano.com**

🐕 €0.90 ♟ ⬚ ♿ 🚿 ⊿ ⊕ ⚲ ⛰ 🏊 🏖 sandy adj

S fr Bastia on N193 for 4km. Turn SE onto Lagoon Rd (sp Lido de Marana). Site on L in 7km. 3*, Lge, pt shd, EHU (6A) €3.40; red long stay; 60% statics; Eng spkn; ccard acc; games area; games rm; CKE. *"San facs basic but clean; cycle path; big site, spread out; no water points; rd and aircraft noise."*
€34.00, 1 Apr-31 Oct. **2019**

BAUD *2F3* (7km W Rural) *47.88239, 3.10818* **Camp Municipal de Pont Augan,** Pont Augan, 56150 Baud **02 97 51 04 74; camping.p.augan@live.fr; camping-pontaugan.com**

🐕 ♟(htd) ⬚ ♿ 🚿 ⊿ ⚲ nr ⊕ nr ⚲ ⛰

Fr Baud, W on D6. Site on R on ent vill. 3*, Sm, mkd, hdg, pt shd, EHU (10A) €3; bbq; Eng spkn; adv bkg acc; canoeing adj; fishing adj; games area; bike hire; CKE. *"Peaceful site; barrier & office ltd opening hrs but parking area avail; warden calls morning & teatime; ltd groceries; 4 gites on site; vg."*
€15.00, 1 Apr-30 Sep. **2018**

BAUGE *4G1* (1km E Rural) *47.53889, -0.09637* **Camp Municipal du Pont des Fées,** Chemin du Pont des Fées, 49150 Baugé **02 41 89 14 79 or 02 41 89 18 07 (Mairie); camping@ville-bauge.fr; www.ville-bauge.fr**

♟ ⬚ ⊿ ⚲ 🦋 ⚲ nr

Fr Saumur traveling N D347/D938 turn 1st R in Baugé onto D766. Foll camping sp to site by sm rv; ent bef rv bdge. 2*, Sm, mkd, hdg, pt shd, EHU (4A) €2.70; bbq; phone; adv bkg acc; ccard acc; fishing; tennis 150m. *"Excel countryside; pleasant, well-kept site; pools 150m; obliging wardens; Aldi within walking dist; camping car site adj; excel municipal well kept site."* **€13.50, 15 May-15 Sep.** **2015**

BAULE, LA *2G3* (2km NE Rural) *47.29833, -2.35722* **Airotel Camping La Roseraie,** 20 Ave Jean Sohier, Route du Golf, 44500 La Baule-Escoublac **02 40 60 46 66; camping@laroseraie.com; www.laroseraie.com**

🐕 €5 ♟ ⬚ ♿ 🚿 ⊿ ⚲ 🦋 ⚲ 🍴 ⊕ ⚲ nr ⛰ ✎ 🏊(covrd, htd) 🏖 sand 2km

Take N171 fr St Nazaire to La Baule. In La Baule-Escoublac turn R at x-rds by church, site in 300m on R; sp fr La Baule cent. 4*, Lge, hdstg, mkd, hdg, pt shd, EHU (6-10A) €5.50-€7.50; gas; bbq; red long stay; TV; 80% statics; phone; Eng spkn; adv bkg acc; ccard acc; games rm; waterslide; watersports; tennis; fishing; games area; CKE. *"Gd site & facs; sm pitches; fitness rm; clean unisex san facs; ltd facs LS; easy walk into La Baule-Escoublac; excel beach nrby; vg."*
€40.00, 1 Apr-25 Sep. **2020**

BAUME LES DAMES 6G2 (6km S Rural) 47.32506, 6.36127 **Camping L'Ile**, 1 Rue de Pontarlier, 25110 Pont-les-Moulins 03 81 84 15 23; info@camping delile.fr; www.campingdelile.fr

S fr Baume-les-Dames on D50, site on L on ent Pont-les-Moulins. 1*, Sm, pt shd, EHU (6A) €2.50; gas; red long stay; 10% statics; Eng spkn; adv bkg acc; CKE. "Tidy, basic site in pleasant setting by Rv Cusancin; helpful, friendly owner; bread 100m; bar 500m; pool 6km; clean, basic facs; gd."
€11.50, 1 May-7 Sep. 2016

"We must tell the Club about that great site we found"

Get your site reports in by mid-August and we'll do our best to get your updates into the next edition.

BAYEUX 3D1 (0.5km N Urban) 49.28392, -0.69760 **Camp Municipal des Bords de L'Aure**, Blvd d'Eindhoven, 14400 Bayeux 02 31 92 08 43; campingmunicipal@mairie-bayeux.fr; www.mairie-bayeux.fr

Site sp off Périphérique d'Eindhoven (Bayeux by-pass, D613). Fr W (Cherbourg) exit N13 junc 38, turn L over N13, then R onto D613 thro Vaucelles. At rndabt cont on D613 (3rd exit) Blvd d'Eindhoven. Site on R immed after traff lts, almost opp Briconaute DIY store. Fr E (Caen) on N13 exit junc 36 onto D613 N; foll ring rd across 2 rndabts, 4 traff lts, site on L opp Bayeux town sp. 3*, Lge, hdstg, hdg, pt shd, EHU (6A) inc (poss rev pol); gas; sw nr; red long stay; phone; Eng spkn; adv bkg req; CKE. "Excel, well-kept site; indoor pool adj; avoid perimeter pitches (narr hdstgs & rd noise); no twin axles; office open LS; gd footpath to town along stream; Bayeux festival 1st w/ end July; conv ferries; lge mkt Sat; new, clean san facs & lndry facs (2018)." €22.00, 30 Mar-3 Nov. 2019

BAYEUX 3D1 (18km SE Rural) 49.15722, -0.76018 **Camping Caravaning Escapade**, Rue de l'église, 14490 CAHAGNOLLES 02 31 21 63 59; escapadecamping@orange.fr; www.campingles capade.net

Fr Saint Paul du Varnay take D99 Cahagnolles on the L; foll rd for aprrox 2.5km; turn L & aft church campsite on R. 4*, Med, mkd, pt shd, EHU (10A) €3.90; bbq; adv bkg acc; ccard acc. "Lovely site; well looked after & cared for; clean san facs; friendly owners & staff; recep rm for events; pt of Flower Campings chain." €28.00, 1 Apr-30 Sep. 2019

BAYEUX 3D1 (7km SE Rural) 49.24840, -0.60245 **Camping Le Château de Martragny,** 52 Hameau Saint-Léger, 14740 Martragny 02 31 80 21 40; chateau.martragny@wanadoo.fr; www.chateau-martragny.com or www.chateau-martragny.fr

Fr Caen going NW on N13 dir Bayeux/Cherbourg, leave at Martragny/Carcagny exit. Strt on & take 2nd R (past turn for Martragny/Creully) into site & chateau grnds. Fr Bayeux after leaving N13 (Martragny/Carcagny), go L over bdge to end of rd, turn L then take 2nd R into Chateau grnds. 4*, Lge, mkd, pt shd, pt sl, EHU (15A) €5.50 (long lead poss req, poss rev pol); gas; bbq; TV; Eng spkn; adv bkg acc; ccard acc; games rm; tennis; fishing; horseriding 500m; CKE. "Popular, attractive, 1st class site on lawns of chateau; attractive area; relaxed atmosphere; friendly, helpful staff; new superb, modern san facs (2013); gd rest; no o'fits over 8m; poss muddy when wet; conv cemeteries; D-Day beaches 15km; Sat mkt in Bayeux; conv Caen ferry; excel." €36.00, 2 May-12 Sep, N06. 2019

BAYEUX 3D1 (8km SE Rural) 49.25041, -0.59251 **Camping Le Manoir de l'Abbaye (Godfroy),** 15 Rue de Creully, 14740 Martragny 02 31 80 25 95; yvette.godfroy@libertysurf.fr; http://godfroy.pages perso-orange.fr

Take N13 Bayeux, Caen dual c'way for 7km, fork R sp Martagny. Over dual c'way L at T-junc, then 1st R sp D82 Martragny & Creully site on R 500m. Sharp L steep turn into site. Sm, pt shd, EHU (15A) €4.(poss rev pol); Eng spkn; adv bkg acc; CKE. "Peaceful, relaxing, well-kept site; lovely grnds; helpful, welcoming owners; steps to ltd san facs; meals & wine avail on request; winter storage; conv Ouistreham ferries; highly rec; wc, shwr, kitchen fac's in same rm; v restful; some elec hookups rev polarity." €23.00, 15 Mar-15 Oct. 2019

BAYEUX 3D1 (9km NW Rural) 49.33120, -0.80240 **Camping Reine Mathilde**, 14400 Etréham 02 31 21 76 55; campingreinemathilde@gmail.com; www.camping-normandie-reinemathilde.com

NW fr Bayeux on D6 turn L to Etréham (D100); site 3km (sp). Or W fr Bayeux on N13 for 8km, exist junc 38. At x-rds 1.5km after vill of Tour-en-Bessin turn R on D206 to Etréham & bear L at church. 3*, Med, mkd, hdg, pt shd, EHU (6A) €4.70; TV; 15% statics; phone; Eng spkn; adv bkg acc; fishing 1km; bike hire; CKE. "Well-kept, attractive site; lge, well spaced hdg pitches; mv service pnt nr; app rds quite narr; friendly, helpful warden; gd, clean san facs; conv D-Day beaches etc; excel." €26.70, 30 Mar-30 Sep. 2019

FRANCE

BAYONNE *8F1* (11km NE Rural) *43.52820, -1.39157*
Camping Lou P'tit Poun, 110 Ave du Quartier Neuf,
40390 St Martin-de-Seignanx 05 59 56 55 79;
contact@louptitpoun.com; www.louptitpoun.com

🛉 €5.90 🏕 ⅏ 🚿 ♿ 🛁 ⚡ 🗑 MSP ❓ ⊞ 🛒 nr ⚙ ✎ 🛶 ⛲

Fr Bordeaux exit A63 junc 6 dir Bayonne Nord;
then take D817 dir Pau & St Martin-de-Seignanx;
site sp on R in 7km. 3*, Lge, mkd, hdg, pt shd, terr,
serviced pitches; EHU (10A) inc; gas; bbq (elec, gas);
red long stay; TV; 17% statics; phone; Eng spkn; adv
bkg acc; ccard acc; games area; games rm; tennis;
CKE. *"Charming, spacious, family-run site; gd sized
pitches; friendly staff; gd clean san facs; ltd facs
LS; conv Biarritz, St Jean-de-Luz & a'route; excel."*
€40.00, 9 Jun-15 Sep, A39. **2017**

"I need an on-site restaurant"

We do our best to make sure site information
is correct, but it is always best to check any
must-have facilities are still available or will
be open during your visit.

BAZAS *7D2* (2km SE Rural) *44.43139, -0.20167*
Campsite Le Paradis de Bazas, Route de Casteljaloux,
33430 Bazas 05 56 65 13 17; paradis@franceloc.fr;
www.camping-paradis-bazas.fr

🛉 €3 🛉 WC 🏕 ♿ 🛁 ⚡ 🗑 MSP ❓ 🦋 ❓ 🛒 nr ⚙ 🛶 (htd)

Exit A62 junc 3 onto N524 twd Bazas, then D655.
Cont thro town cent & foll sp Casteljaloux/
Grignols. Site sp on R. 4*, Sm, hdg, mkd, pt shd, pt
sl, EHU (6-16A) €3.25-4.90; gas; red long stay; TV;
6% statics; Eng spkn; adv bkg acc; CKE. *"Pleasant,
relaxed, well-kept site in picturesque location; views
of chateau & town; friendly, helpful staff; san facs
v smart but poss stretched high ssn; pleasant walk/
cycle track to interesting, walled town; vineyards nr."*
€25.00, 1 Apr-29 Sep. **2017**

BEAUGENCY *4F2* (0.8km E Rural) *47.77628, 1.64294*
Camp Municipal du Val de Flux, Route de
Lailly-en-Val, 45190 Beaugency 02 38 44 50 39 or
02 38 44 83 12; camping@ville-beaugency.fr;
www.camping-beaugency.fr

🛉 €2 🛉 (htd) WC 🏕 ♿ 🛁 ⚡ 🗑 🦋 ❓ 🗑 nr ⚙ 🛶 ✎ ⛱ sand

Exit A10 junc 15 onto D2152. In Beaugency turn L at
traff lts nr water tower onto D925 & again over rd
bdge. Site sp on S bank of Rv Loire.
3*, Lge, mkd, pt shd, EHU (10A) inc (rev pol); red
long stay; 10% statics; Eng spkn; ccard acc; fishing;
watersports; CKE. *"Beautiful, welcoming, well-kept site;
views over Loire; helpful, friendly staff; free 1 night site for
m'vans over rv on other side of town; poss unrel opening
dates LS, rec phone ahead; vg location close to town;
coded ent barrier; next to rv and bdge to town; some
rd noise at busy times; facs gd but far away fr pitches;
scruffy & unkempt; town dilapidated; free WiFi around
shop; gd cycling."* €21.40, 1 Apr-20 Sep. **2019**

BEAULIEU SUR DORDOGNE *7C4* (3km N Rural)
45.00911, 1.85059 **Aire Naturelle La Berge
Ombragée (Lissajoux),** Valeyran, 19120 Brivezac
+33 670786563; contact@berge-ombragee.com;
www.berge-ombragee.com

🛉 €0.30 🛉 WC 🏕 ♿ 🛁 ⚡ 🗑 ❓ ❓ 🛒 🛶 ⛺

N fr Beauliew-sur-Dordogne on D940; in 500m
turn R onto D12; site on R in 2km. Office down on
rv bank. NB Front wheel drive tow cars may find
diff on gravel hill leading up fr office. Sm, pt shd,
pt sl, EHU (6A) €3; bbq; sw nr; Canoeing; Volleyball;
Badminton; CKE. *"CL-type site; friendly; canoeing fr
site; gd."*
€22.40, 1 May-15 Sep. **2020**

BEAULIEU SUR DORDOGNE *7C4* (5km N Rural)
45.02167, 1.83960 **Camping la Champagne,**
La Champagne, 19120 Brivezac 06 48 47 23 51;
info@campinglachampagne.com; www.campingla
champagne.com

🛉 €2.50 🐕 🛉 WC 🏕 ♿ 🛁 ⚡ 🗑 MSP ❓ 🦋 ❓ 🛶

Fr Beaulieu-sur-Dordogne take D940, sp Tulle. R onto
D12, sp Argentat. R onto D136. R again after bdge.
Site 600m on R. 2*, Sm, mkd, pt shd, terr, EHU (6A) €3;
bbq; sw nr; twin axles; phone; Eng spkn; adv bkg acc;
CCI. *"Aire Naturella (max 25 vans); fishing; canoeing;
horseriding nr; peaceful, spacious rvside location; Dutch
owners."* €22.00, 1 May-15 Sep. **2019**

"Satellite navigation makes touring much easier"

Remember most sat navs don't know if you're
towing or in a larger vehicle – always use yours
alongside maps and site directions.

BEAULIEU SUR DORDOGNE *7C4* (0.3km E Urban)
44.97950, 1.84040 **Huttopia Beaulieu Sur Dordogne
(formerly Camping des Iles),** Blvd Rodolphe-
de-Turenne, 19120 Beaulieu-sur-Dordogne
05 55 91 02 65; www.huttopia.com

🛉 €2 🛉 (htd) WC 🏕 ♿ 🛁 ⚡ 🗑 ❓ ❓ ⊞ 🛒 nr ⚙ ✎ 🛶

Exit A20 junc 52 ont D158/D38 dir Collonges-la-
Rouge; cont on D38 & turn R onto D940 to Beaulieu-
sur-Dordogne; site sp fr o'skts of town. Or on D940 N
fr Bretenoux, turn R in Beaulieu town sq, site about
200m on island in Rv Dordogne. NB 3m height limit
at ent. 3*, Med, mkd, shd, EHU (10A) inc (poss long lead
req); bbq (gas); red long stay; 15% statics; Eng spkn;
adv bkg rec; games rm; rv; fishing; bike hire; games
area; canoeing. *"Delightful, wooded site; pitches by rv
excel (extra charge); plenty shd; friendly staff; gd clean
san facs, ltd LS; attractive medieval town; gd value;
highly rec."* €30.70, 20 Apr-30 Sep, A21. **2018**

FRANCE

BEAULIEU SUR LOIRE *4G3* (0.3km E Rural) *47.54407, 2.82167* **FFCC Camp Municipal du Canal,** Route de Bonny, 45630 Beaulieu-sur-Loire **02 38 35 89 56 or 02 38 35 32 16 (LS);** renault.campingbeaulieu@orange.fr; www.beaulieu-sur-loire.fr

Exit A77 junc 21 Bonny-sur-Loire, cross rv to Beaulieu-sur-Loire on D296. On E o'skirts of vill on D926, nr canal. 2*, Sm, mkd, hdstg, hdg, pt shd, EHU (10A) €4; Eng spkn; adv bkg acc; CKE. "Well-kept site in pleasant area; direct access to canal; some sm pitches diff lge o'fits; site yourself, warden calls 0800-0900 & 1830-1930; no security; clean modern san facs; gd walking along canal & Rv Loire; boat trips; poss workers' statics LS; mkt Wed; lovely hdg pitches; conv Aqueduct at Briare." **€10.40, 4 Apr-1 Nov.** 2017

BEAUMONT DE LOMAGNE *8E3* (1km E Urban) *43.88406, 0.99800* **Village de Loisirs Le Lomagnol,** Ave du Lac, 82500 Beaumont-de-Lomagne **05 63 26 12 00;** villagedeloisirslelomagnol@wanadoo.fr; www.villagelelomagnol.fr

On SE of D928 at E end of vill. Sp 'Centre de Loisirs, Plan d'Eau'. 3*, Med, mkd, pt shd, EHU (10A) inc (poss long lead req); sw; 25% statics; canoe hire; golf; tennis; jacuzzi; sauna; waterslide; bike hire; fishing. "Gd quality, modern site; interesting old town; mkt Sat; facs tired LS." **€18.00, 1 Apr-30 Oct.** 2016

BEAUMONT DU PERIGORD *7D3* (7km SW Rural) *44.75603, 0.70216* **Centre Naturiste de Vacances Le Couderc (Naturist),** 24440 Naussannes **05 53 22 40 40;** info@lecouderc.com; www.lecouderc.com

Fr D660 al D25 W thro Naussannes & hamlet of Leydou. Just beyond Leydou turn R into site, well sp. 1*, Lge, mkd, pt shd, pt sl, EHU (5A) €4.50; red long stay; 10% statics; adv bkg req; ccard acc; jacuzzi; sauna; bike hire. "Beautiful site with relaxed atmosphere; friendly, helpful Dutch owners; gd san facs; superb pool; naturist walks on site; gd walking/cycling area; Bastide towns nrby; new sauna,steam rm/spa (2015); new camping field, pond cleaned & enlarged; vg entmnt & activity prog for kids & adults." **€41.00, 1 Apr-15 Oct.** 2017

BEAUMONT SUR OISE *3D3* (8km SW Rural) *49.12805, 2.18318* **Parc de Séjour de l'Etang,** 10 Chemin des Belles Vues, 95690 Nesles-la-Vallée **01 34 70 62 89;** campinparis@gmail.com; www.campinparis.com

Fr D927 Méru-Pontoise rd, turn L onto D64 at sp L'Isle Adam. After passing thro Nesles-la-Vallée camp sp on L. 4*, Med, hdg, pt shd, serviced pitches; EHU (3A) inc (rev pol); Eng spkn; lake fishing adj; CKE. "Lovely, peaceful, out-of-the-way setting; spacious pitches; friendly, helpful staff; gd facs; conv day trips to Paris & Versailles; excel." **€22.00, 1 Apr-30 Sep.** 2016

BEAUMONT SUR SARTHE *4F1* (1km E Rural) *48.22382, 0.13651* **FFCC Camp Municipal du Val de Sarthe,** Rue de l'Abreuvoir, 72170 Beaumont-sur-Sarthe **02 43 97 01 93;** camping-beaumontssarthe@orange.fr; www.beaumontsursarthe.com

Fr D338 Alençon-Le Mans, turn sharp L at 2nd set of traff lts in cent of Beaumont & foll site sp twd E of town. Fr Le Mans on A28 exit 21 onto D6, R onto D338 & R at traff lts & foll sp. NB Narr, sloping app thro town rds with blind corners. Narr site access. 3*, Med, hdg, mkd, pt shd, EHU (10A) inc (long cable poss req & poss rev pol); TV; Eng spkn; adv bkg rec; ccard acc; fishing adj; rv boating adj; CKE. "Beautiful, peaceful, well-run rvside site; lge pitches, some by rv; no twin axles & poss no c'vans over 2,000 kg; barrier clsd 2200; easy walk to interesting, pretty town; mkt Tues; rec; nice clean site; pleasant & friendly; well maintained site; recep open 1000-1200, 1600-1900 (May, Jun & Sep), 900-1200, 1500-2000 (Jul & Aug); barrier unattended bet 1200-1400; pool 500m; admission only aft 4pm; popular NH." **€15.50, 1 May-30 Sep.** 2018

"There aren't many sites open at this time of year"

If you're travelling outside peak season remember to call ahead to check site opening dates – even if the entry says 'open all year'.

BEAUNE *6H1* (1km N Urban) *47.03304, 4.83911* **Camp Municipal Les Cent Vignes,** 10 Rue Auguste Dubois, 21200 Beaune **03 80 22 03 91;** campingles centvignes@mairie-beaune.fr; www.beaune.fr

Fr N on A31 & fr S on A6 at junc with m'ways A6/A31 take A6 sp Auxerre-Paris; after 1km leave at junc 24 to join D974 twd Beaune; after approx 1.5km, turn R at 2nd traff lts fr a'route to site (sp) in 200m. If app fr S on D974 site well sp fr inner ring rd & foll sp to Dijon (not a'route sps). Also sp fr Mersault/L'Hôpital x-rds. 4*, Med, hdg, mkd, hdstg, pt shd, EHU (16A) inc (some rev pol); gas; bbq; TV; phone; Eng spkn; ccard acc; bike hire; games area; tennis; CKE. "Popular, well-run site; rec arr early even LS; gd modern san facs; vg rest; most pitches gd size but narr site rds makes access some pitches diff, a mover useful; tight turns & low trees poss diff lge o'fits; twin axles; in walking dist of Beaune; v conv site; hypmkt 2km; superb new san facs 2013; excel site; adv bkg in writing only bef 30 May; pool 800m; many pitches with own service pnts; v busy site." **€30.00, 15 Mar-31 Oct.** 2018

BEAUNE *6H1* (3.5km NE Rural) *47.02668, 4.88294*
Camping Les Bouleaux, 11 Rue Jaune, 21200
Vignoles **03 80 22 26 88**

12 🐕 ♿ ⚹⚹⚹ (htd) 🅦🅞 ☖ & ⚟ 🦋 🐾

Exit A6 at junc 24.1; 500m after toll turn R at
rndabt, in 1.5km turn R sp Dole rndabt. Immed after
x-ing m'way turn L sp Vignoles. L again at next junc
then R & foll camping sp. Site in approx 1.5km in
cent Chevignerot; fr town cent take D973 (E) sp
Dole. In 2km cross a'route & 1st L (N) sp Vignoles.
Well sp. 3*, Sm, hdg, mkd, pt shd, EHU (6A) inc (rev
pol altered on request); adv bkg rec; CKE. *"Attractive,
well-kept, busy site, even in LS; rec arr early high ssn;
some gd sized pitches, most sm; superb clean new san
facs, poss stretched high ssn & ltd LS; poss muddy after
rain - park on rdways; conv NH fr a'route; basic site;
long lead may be req'd; excel site; excel walking in area;
helpful owner."* **€19.00** **2018**

BEAUNE *6H1* (8km SW Rural) *46.98573, 4.76855*
La Grappe d'Or (formally Kawan Village), 2 Route
de Volnay, 21190 Meursault **03 80 21 22 48;**
**info@camping-meursault.com; www.camping-
meursault.com**

🐕 €1.40 ⚹⚹⚹ (htd) 🅦🅞 ☖ & ⚟ ⚟ 🅜🅢🅟 🍴 ⑾ 🎮 🔊 🏛 ⚓

Fr N-S, Exit A6 Junc 24.1 SP Beaune Centre
Hospices, at rndabt foll sp to Chalon sur Saône RN
74, after 7km foll sp to Meursault, turn r, foll sp for
site. 3*, Med, mkd, pt shd, terr, EHU (10A) inc; gas;
sw; phone; Eng spkn; adv bkg req; waterslide; bike
hire; tennis; games area; CKE. *"Lovely family site; busy
high ssn - arr early; all pitches views over vineyards;
friendly, helpful owners; basic facs stretched; ltd water
pnts & poss steep climb fr lower pitches; some pitches
uneven, sm or obstructed by trees - poss diff access
lge o'fits; poss muddy when wet; barrier clsd 2200-
0730; rambling; sh walk to lovely vill; gd cycle paths;
vg; popular site; well run; if full use site at Santenay."*
€26.60, 5 Apr-13 Oct. **2019**

BEAUNE *6H1* (7km NW Rural) *47.06861, 4.8029*
Camping de Savigny-les-Beaune, Route de Bouilland,
21420 Savigny-lès-Beaune **03 80 26 15 06 or 06 83
23 93 37 (mob); contact@camping-savigny-les-
beaune.fr; www.camping-savigny-les-beaune.fr**

🐕 €1.20 ⚹⚹⚹ 🅦🅞 ☖ & ⚟ 🦋 🍴 🎮 🔊 nr ⚓

Fr Beaune ring rd turn N on D974 sp Dijon; in 200m
turn L sp Savigny; in 100m ignore camping sp &
bear R to Savigny (3km); site 1km thro vill on L.
2*, Med, mkd, pt shd, pt sl, EHU (6A) €3.50 (some
rev pol); bbq; adv bkg rec; bike hire; CKE. *"Pleasant,
busy NH in beautiful area; pleasant staff; modern
basic san facs; no twin axles; gd touring base; conv A6,
A31, A36 & Beaune; easy walk to vill; excel quiet site."*
€14.00, 15 Mar-15 Oct. **2016**

BEAUVAIS *3C3* (16km E Rural) *49.40506, 2.25803*
Camping de la Trye, Rue de Trye, 60510 Bresles
**03 44 07 80 95 or 06 10 40 30 29 (mob);
www.camping-de-la-trye.com**

12 🐕 ⚹⚹⚹ 🅦🅞 ☖ & ⚟ 🅜🅢🅟 🍴 🏛 🔊

Exit N31 (Beauvais to Clermont) at Bresles; foll
site sp. Med, hdg, mkd, pt shd, sl, EHU (6A) inc; bbq;
75% statics; adv bkg acc; ccard acc; bike hire; CKE.
*"Helpful Dutch owners; cycle & walking rtes; theme
parks nrby; trampoline; largely a holiday chalet/static
site with ltd no of touring pitches; pony rides; fair NH/
sh stay."* **€20.00** **2016**

BEAUVILLE *7D3* (0.5km SE Rural) *44.27210, 0.88850*
Camping Les Deux Lacs, 47470 Beauville
**05 53 95 45 41; camping-les-2-lacs@wanadoo.fr;
www.les2lacs.info**

🐕 €2.15 ⚹⚹⚹ 🅦🅞 ☖ & ⚟ 🦋 🍴 🏛 ⚓ nr 🏛

Fr D656 S to Beauville, site sp on D122. NB Steep
descent to site - owners help when leaving if
necessary. 3*, Med, hdg, mkd, shd, terr, EHU (6A)
€2.45; sw nr; red long stay; 10% statics; Eng spkn; adv
bkg acc; ccard acc; fishing; games area; watersports;
CKE. *"Peaceful; gd fishing; pleasant walk to vill;
vg; Dutch owners; facs inadequate when site full."*
€28.00, 1 Apr-31 Oct. **2017**

BEAUVOIR SUR MER *2H3* (5km E Rural) *46.92298,
-1.99036* **Camping Le Fief d'Angibaud,** 85230 St
Gervais **02 51 68 43 08; camping.fief.angibaud@
orange.fr; www.campinglefiefangibaud.com**

🐕 €1.50 ⚹⚹⚹ 🅦🅞 ☖ & ⚟ 🦋 🏛 nr ⚓ sand 5km

Fr Beauvoir-sur-Mer E on D948 to St Gervais turn
L after PO/Mairie onto D59 twd Bouin (narr ent
easy to miss); in 2km pass sm chapel; take 2nd rd
on L; site on R after 500m. Sm, mkd, pt shd, EHU
(6-13A) €3.50; bbq; twin axles; red long stay; Eng spkn;
adv bkg rec; golf nr; fishing nr; CKE. *"Excel, simple
site adj farm; lge pitches; pleasant, helpful British
owners; clean san facs but need update (2010); conv
Ile de Noirmoutier; ferry to Ile d'Yeu, coastal resorts;
free parking close to beach (blue flag); gd cycling
area; vg value; gd for rallies; gite on site; bike hire."*
€19.50, 16 Apr-24 Sep. **2016**

BEDOIN *10E2* (0.5km W Rural) *44.12468, 5.17249*
Camp Municipal de la Pinède, Chemin des Sablières,
84410 Bédoin **04 90 65 61 03; campingmunicipal@
bedoin.fr; www.bedoin.fr**

🐕 €1.50 ⚹⚹⚹ (htd) 🅦🅞 ☖ & ⚟ 🅜🅢🅟 🦋 🔊 nr 🏛 ⚓ (htd)

Take D938 S fr Malaucène for 3km, L onto D19 for
9km to Bédoin. Site adj to vill & sp. 2*, Med, hdstg,
mkd, shd, sl, terr, EHU (16A) inc; bus; Eng spkn; adv
bkg acc; ccard acc; CKE. *"Pool clsd Mon; 5 min walk
to vill; mkt Mon; steep terr site; vans towed to pitch if
req; steep climb to some san facs; v clean; v friendly;
excel pool; v popular; MH site adj; easy walk to town."*
€18.50, 15 Mar-31 Oct. **2017**

BELCAIRE *8G4* (4km SW Rural) *42.79207, 1.92477*
Camping Les Sapins, Ternairols, 11340 Camurac
04 68 20 38 11; info@lessapins-camurac.com;
www.lessapins-camurac.com

🕭 €2 ⛺ (htd) ⬚ ♿ ♿ ⚕ 🦋 ♈ 🍴 Ⓗ 🛒 🚲 nr ⛰ 🛶 🚣

Easiest app fr N - at Bélesta on D117 turn S
onto D16/D29/D613 to Belcaire then cont to
Camurac, site 1km SE of vill. Or take D613 fr Ax-
les-Thermes (1st 10km over Col de Chioula diff
climb - gd power/weight ratio). Site sp in vill of
Camurac & visible fr rd. App rd fairly steep for
sh dist. 2*, Med, mkd, pt shd, pt sl, EHU (10A) €3;
bbq (elec, gas); TV; 33% statics; Eng spkn; adv bkg
acc; ccard acc; horseriding; games area; site clsd 1
Nov-15 Dec; CKE. *"Lovely, peaceful site in beautiful
surroundings; welcoming, friendly, helpful Dutch
owners; excel walking; in Cathar region; vg; highly
rec; winter sports; mountain biking; ltd facs LS."*
€24.50, 1 Jan-1 Nov, 15 Dec-31 Dec.   2017

BELCAIRE *8G4* (0.3km W Rural) *42.81598, 1.95098*
Les Chalets Du Lac (formerly Municipal), 4 Chemin
Lac, 11340 Belcaire 04 68 20 39 47; chaletsdulac@
gmail.com; www.camping-pyrenees-cathare.fr

🕭 ⛺ ⛺ ⬚ ♿ ⚕ ♿ / 🦋

Site on D613 bet Ax-les-Thermes & Quillan.
2*, Sm, mkd, shd, pt sl, EHU (10A) €2; sw nr; phone;
tennis nr; horseriding nr; CKE. *"Site by lake; site
yourself, warden calls; gd cent for walking; historic vill
of Montaillou nr; excel; conv for Georges de la Frau."*
€20.30, 1 Jun-15 Sep.   2019

"That's changed – Should I let the Club know?"

If you find something on site that's different
from the site entry, fill in a report and let us
know. See camc.com/europereport.

BELFORT *6G3* (1.8km N Urban) *47.65335, 6.86445*
FFCC Camping de l'Etang des Forges, 11 Rue du
Général Béthouart, 90000 Belfort 03 84 22 54 92;
contact@camping-belfort.com; www.camping-
belfort.com

🕭 €2 ⛺ (htd) ⬚ ♿ ♿ ⚕ / 🅿 🦋 ♈ 🍴 Ⓗ nr 🛒 🚲 nr ⛰ 🚣 🛶

Exit A36 junc 13; go thro cent of Belfort; then foll sp
Offemont on D13, then site sp. Or fr W on N19 site
well sp. 3*, Med, hdg, mkd, pt shd, EHU (6A) €3.50;
bbq; red long stay; twin axles; TV; 5% statics; bus; Eng
spkn; adv bkg acc; ccard acc; fishing adj; watersports
adj; archery; CKE. *"Pleasant, well-kept, basic site; some
lovely pitches; friendly; modern, unisex san facs with
third cont wc, but needs updating (2014); lovely walk
around lake fr site ent; cycle paths; conv for Corbusier's
chapel at Ronchamp."* **€21.00, 7 Apr-30 Sep.**   2016

BELLAC *7A3* (11km SW Rural) *46.05718, 0.97766*
Fonclaire Holidays, 87300 Blond 05 55 60 88 26;
fontclair@neuf.fr; www.fonclaireholidays.com

12 🕭 ⛺ ⬚ ♿ ♿ 🅿 / 🦋 ♈ 🍴 nr Ⓗ nr 🛒 ⛰ 🚣

Fr Bellac take D675 S dir St Junien. Site on L in
approx 7km, 2km bef Mortemart. Sm, hdstg, pt shd,
EHU (6A) €4 (poss long lead req); sw; Eng spkn; adv
bkg acc; Badminton; CKE. *"Lovely & peaceful, spacious
CL-type site in lovely location; welcoming, helpful British
owners; Glamping units on site; gd facs; gd hdstg in wet;
nr Oradour-sur-Glane martyr vill; conv Futuroscope; gd
cycling; gd; v quiet rural location; no night lighting; gd
NH/longer; excel."* **€18.00**   2019

BELLEME *4E2* (1km SW Urban) *48.37420, 0.55370*
Camp Municipal Le Val, Route de Mamers, 61130
Bellême 02 33 25 30 77 or 06 24 70 55 17;
www.campingduperchebellemois.com

🕭 €0.50 ⛺ ⬚ ♿ / 🛒 nr ⛰ 🚣

Fr Mortagne, take D938 S to Bellême; turn R ent
town on D955 Alençon rd; site sp on L half-way
down hill. 2*, Sm, hdg, pt shd, pt sl, EHU (8A) €2.65
(poss long lead req); adv bkg rec; tennis adj; fishing.
*"Pretty, well-kept site; some pitches v sl; warden
visits twice daily; gd san facs; poss long water hoses
req; pitches poss soft when wet; steep walk to town."*
€14.50, 15 Apr-15 Oct.   2019

BELLENTRE *9B4* (2km E Rural) *45.57576, 6.73553*
Camping L'Eden, 73210 Landry 04 79 07 61 81;
info@camping-eden.net; www.camping-eden.net

🕭 €1.50 ⛺ (htd) ⬚ ♿ 🅿 / 🦋 ♈ 🍴 🛒 ⛰ 🚣 (htd)

Fr N90 Moûtiers to Bourg-St Maurice at 20km
turn R sp Landry; site on L after 500m adj Rv
Isère. 4*, Med, mkd, hdstg, hdg, pt shd, EHU (10A)
€4-6; gas; TV; phone; Eng spkn; adv bkg acc; ccard
acc; games rm. *"Gd cent mountain sports; helpful,
friendly owner; red facs LS; ltd site lighting; ski bus;
poss unkempt end of ssn; gd cycle track to town."*
€26.00, 15 Dec-5 May & 25 May-15 Sep.   2016

BELLEY *9B3* (8km E Rural) *45.76860, 5.76985*
Camping Du Lac du Lit du Roi, La Tuilière, 01300
Massignieu-de-Rives 04 79 42 12 03; info@
camping-savoie.com; www.camping-savoie.com

🕭 €4 ⛺ (htd) ⬚ ♿ ♿ 🅿 / 🦋 ♈ 🍴 Ⓗ ⛰ 🚣

Fr D1504 turn E onto D992 to Massignieu-de-Rives,
site sp. Site on NE of lake nr Les Mures.
4*, Med, hdg, mkd, pt shd, terr, EHU (10A) inc (long
lead req); gas; bbq; sw; red long stay; TV; 20% statics;
phone; Eng spkn; adv bkg req; ccard acc; boating;
tennis; bike hire; CKE. *"Superb location; many pitches
on lake with lovely views; some lge pitches, others v
sm; lack of site maintenance (2010); few water pnts
(2009); bkg fee; v friendly site, idyllic location; recep
clsd 1200-1330."* **€28.60, 16 Apr-17 Sep.**   2016

FRANCE

BELMONT SUR RANCE

BELMONT SUR RANCE *8E4* (0.5km W Rural)
43.81777, 2.75108 **Camping Val Fleuri du Rance,**
Route de Lacaune, 12370 Belmont-sur-Rance 05 65
99 04 76 or 06 88 42 28 78 (mob); marjandejong@
wanadoo.fr; www.campinglevalfleuri.com

🏕 €1.50 ♨ 🚾 🛁 ♿ 🖭 🥾 🦋 ♟ ⓗ ♨nr

On D32 on ent vill fr SW; on L side of rd on sh
unmade service rd. NB diff ent/exit to/fr S.
3*, Sm, hdg, mkd, pt shd, EHU (6A) €3.50; gas;
10% statics; Eng spkn; adv bkg acc; rv fishing; tennis;
CKE. "Attractive valley setting; helpful Dutch owners;
attractive sm town; pool 500m; v welcoming."
€20.00, 1 Apr-15 Oct.   2019

BELVES *7D3* (12km SW Rural) *44.75813, 0.90222*
Camping Terme d'Astor (Naturist), 24540,
St Avit-Rivière 05 53 63 24 52; camping@
termedastor.com; www.termedastor.com

🏕 ♨ 🚾 🛁 ♿ 🖭 🥾 🦋 ♟ 🍽 ⓗ 🏊 🔼 🖊 🚣 🏊

Leave D710 at Belvès onto D53; in 4km turn R onto
D26 to Bouillac; pass thro vill; then turn 2nd L. Well
sp. 3*, Med, mkd, shd, pt sl, EHU (6A) €5.20; gas; bbq;
TV; 10% statics; phone; Eng spkn; adv bkg acc; ccard
acc; INF; rafting; games rm; jacuzzi; archery; canoeing
nr; tennis nr; excursions. "Gd cent for Dordogne rv &
chateaux; vg; horseriding nrby; poss low ampage & rev
pol on some pitches." €37.00, 1 May-30 Sep.   2016

BELVES *7D3* (5km SW Rural) *44.75258, 0.98330*
FLOWER Caming Les Nauves, Le Bos-Rouge,
24170 Belvès 05 53 29 12 64; campinglesnauves@
hotmail.com; www.lesnauves.com
or www.flowercampings.com

🏕 €4 ♨ 🚾 🛁 ♿ 🖭 🥾 🅿 🦋 ♟ 🍽 ⓗ 🏊 ♨nr 🔼 🖊 🚣 🏊

On D53 fr Belvès. Site on L just after junc to Larzac.
Avoid Belves cent - use lorry rte dir Monpazier.
3*, Med, hdg, pt shd, pt sl, EHU (6A) inc; bbq; twin axles;
TV; 10% statics; Eng spkn; adv bkg acc; ccard acc; bike
hire; games area; games rm; horseriding; CCI. "Excel
site; gd views fr some pitches; sl site; interesting towns
nrby; sm pool." €28.00, 11 Apr-26 Sep.   2015

BENODET *2F2* (1.5km E Coastal) *47.86670, -4.09080*
Camping Du Letty, Rue du Canvez, 29950 Bénodet
02 98 57 04 69; reception@campingduletty.com;
www.campingduletty.com

🏕 €2.30 ♨ 🚾 🛁 ♿ 🖭 🥾 🦋 ♟ 🍽 🏊 🔼 🖊
🚣 (covrd, htd) 🏊 🏖 sand adj

Fr N ent town on D34, foll sp Fouesnant D44. Le
Letty sp R at rndabt. Fr E on N165 take D44 sp
Fouesnant & foll rd to o'skirts Bénodet. After town
sp, site is sp. 4*, Lge, mkd, hdstg, hdg, pt shd, pt sl,
EHU (10A) €4; gas; bbq (gas); TV; phone; Eng spkn;
adv bkg acc; ccard acc; golf nr; tennis; games area;
kayak hire; sauna; games rm; gym; squash; horseriding
nr; waterslide; CKE. "Excel, well-run, beautifully laid-
out site; clean & well-equipped; lovely beach adj; excel
playgrnd; many activities; aqua park; library; friendly,
helpful staff; highly rec."
€33.00, 11 Jun-5 Sep.   2017

BENODET *2F2* (0.5km SE Coastal) *47.86780, -4.09750*
Camping du Poulquer, 23 rue du Poulquer, 29950
Bénodet 02 98 57 04 19; contact@campingdu
poulquer.com; www.campingdupoulquer.com

🏕 €3.50 ♨ 🚾 🛁 ♿ 🖭 🥾 🦋 ♟ 🍽 ⓗnr 🏊 🔼 🖊
🚣 (covrd, htd) 🏊 🏖 sand adj

Fr N ent town on D34. At rndabt after junc with
D44 strt onto Rue Penfoul. At next rndabt (tourist
info office on R after rndabt) go strt dir La Plage
until reach seafront; turn L at seafront then L at
end of prom at camping sp; site in 100m on R. Fr E
on N165 take D44 sp Fouesnant & foll rd to o'skirts
Bénodet. After town sp, site is sp. 4*, Lge, mkd, hdg,
pt shd, pt sl, EHU (6-10A) €5.50 (long lead poss req,
poss rev pol); bbq; TV; 5% statics; Eng spkn; adv bkg
acc; jacuzzi; games rm; waterslide; golf nr; tennis; CKE.
"Lovely, well-kept, family-run site; bike hire 1km; boat
trips nrby; friendly, helpful owner; aqua park; no o'fits
over 7.5m high ssn; quiet site LS; mkt Mon; rec; vg;
gd cafe/bar & shop; indoor pool open LS; 1st class san
facs." €29.60, 1 May-30 Sep, B16.   2020

BENODET *2F2* (5km W Coastal) *47.86903, -4.12848*
Camping Le Helles, 55 Rue du Petit-Bourg, 29120
Combrit-Ste Marine 02 98 56 31 46; contact@
le-helles.com; www.le-helles.com

🏕 €2.60 ♨ (htd) 🚾 🛁 ♿ 🖭 🥾 🦋 ♟ 🏊 🔼 🖊 🚣 (htd)
🏊 🏖 sand 300m

Exit D44 S dir Ste Marine, site sp. 3*, Med, mkd, pt
shd, pt sl, EHU (6-10A); bbq; 10% statics; Eng spkn; adv
bkg acc; ccard acc; CKE. "Vg site with lge pitches, some
shd; gd, clean modern san facs; friendly, helpful owners;
excel beach within 5 min walk; vg long stay; 2 pools
indoor and out." €14.00, 1 Apr-23 Oct.   2016

BERGERAC *7C3* (2km S Urban) *44.84902, 0.47635*
Camping La Pelouse (formerly Municipal), 8 bis Rue
Jean-Jacques Rousseau, 24100 Bergerac
05 53 57 06 67; campinglapelouse@orange.fr;
www.entreprisefrery.com

🏕 €1.25 ♨ (htd) 🚾 🛁 ♿ 🖭 🥾 🦋 🏊nr 🔼

On S bank of Rv Dordogne 300m W of old bdge opp
town cent. Do not ent town, foll camping sp fr bdge,
ent on R after L turn opp block of flats. Well sp, on
Rv Dordogne. 3*, Med, mkd, pt shd, pt sl, EHU (6A);
gas; Eng spkn; adv bkg acc; rv fishing adj; CKE. "Peaceful,
spacious site on rv bank; friendly warden; san facs ltd LS;
easy walk by rv into attractive old town; no twin axles
& c'vans over 6m; site poss clsd earlier if weather bad;
pitches poss muddy when wet; rec arr bef 1400 high ssn
site has lots of trees so not all pitches in sun; facs updated
2012." €20.00, 1 Apr-31 Oct.   2017

For a guide to symbols see the fold out on the rear cover

BERGERAC *7C3* (14km W Rural) *44.83849, 0.33052*
FFCC Camping Parc Servois, 11 Rue du Bac, 24680
Gardonne 06 84 38 24 33; mfounaud24@orange.fr;
www.parcservois.com

🏕 €0.70 ♦♦ wo ♨ ⚊ ⛵ MsP 🦋 🕀 nr ⚓ nr

Fr D936 Bergerac to Bordeaux, in vill of Gardonne
turn R into sm rd 100m after traff lts; site at end
of rd by rv. Well sp in vill. 1*, Sm, pt shd, EHU (10A)
poss rev pol; Eng spkn; CKE. *"Pretty, CL-type site on
bank of Rv Dordogne; lge pitches; helpful warden; facs
immac but dated & poss stretched when site full; gates
clsd 2200-0800 with pedestrian access; sm mkt Wed &
Sun; excel, well run site."*
€14.00, 30 Apr-30 Sep.   2019

BERGUES *3A3* (0.6km N Urban) *50.97248, 2.43420*
Camping Le Vauban, Blvd Vauban, 59380 Bergues
03 28 68 65 25; cassiopee.tourisme@wanadoo.fr

🏕 €1.05 ♦♦ (cont) wo ♨ ⚊ ⛵ MsP ⚓ 🍽 nr 🕀 nr ⚓ nr 🔺

Exit A16 junc 60 twd Bergues on D916. In 2km turn
L onto D2 dir Coudekerque vill. In 2km turn R at
rndabt onto D72 to Bergues thro Couderkerque vill,
then turn R immed after canal. Site on R as rd bends
to L. 3*, Med, hdg, mkd, pt shd, terr, EHU (6A) inc
(poss rev pol); 60% statics; adv bkg acc; CKE. *"Pleasant
site; sm pitches poss diff lge o'fits; ltd manoeuvring
in site rds; friendly & helpful; gates clsd 2130-0700
& poss clsd 1230-1730; lovely fortified town; conv
Dunkerque & Calais; NH only; san facs updated (2015)."*
€16.00, 1 Apr-31 Oct.   2015

> **"I like to fill in the reports as I
> travel from site to site"**
>
> You'll find report forms at the back of this
> guide, or you can fill them in online at
> camc.com/europereport.

BERNAY *3D2* (2km S Urban) *49.08020, 0.58703*
Camp Municipal, Rue des Canadiens, 27300 Bernay
02 32 43 30 47; camping@bernay27.fr;
www.ville-bernay27.fr

🏕 ♦♦ wo ♨ ⚊ ⛵ MsP 🦋 🕀 🍽 nr 🕀 nr ⚓ nr 🔺

Site sp fr S'most (Alençon) rndabt off Bernay by-
pass D438; twd France Parc Exposition then 1st L
& on R. Well sp. 3*, Sm, mkd, hdg, pt shd, EHU (10A)
€3.65 (poss rev pol); TV; phone; adv bkg acc; CKE.
*"Well-kept site; well set-out pitches, diff sizes; helpful
& friendly staff; gd clean facs, but dated; barrier clsd
2200-0700; excel, conv NH A28; excel, lovely site;
pool 300m; debit card acc; Bernay worth a visit."*
€16.00, 1 May-30 Sep.   2016

BERNY RIVIERE *3C4* (1.5km S Rural) *49.40603,
3.12860* **Camping La Croix du Vieux Pont,** Rue de la
Fabrique, 02290 Berny-Rivière 03 23 55 50 02; info@
la-croix-du-vieux-pont.com; www.la-croix-du-vieux-
pont.com

12 🏕 ♦♦ (htd) wo ♨ 🛁 ⚊ ⛵ MsP 🦋 🍴 🍽 🕀 ⚓ 🔺 ⚒
⚓ (covrd, htd)

On N31 bet Soissons & Compiègne. At site sp turn
onto D13, then at Vic-sur-Aisne take next R, R again
then L onto D91. Foll sp to site on o'skts of Berny.
5*, V lge, hdg, hdstg, pt shd, serviced pitches; EHU
(6A) €2.50 (poss rev pol, no earth & ltd supply); gas;
sw; TV; Eng spkn; adv bkg rec; ccard acc; games rm;
waterslide; gym; tennis; bike hire; horseriding; boating;
archery; fishing; golf; CKE. *"Pleasant, v lge, well-run,
clean site; busy LS; lge pitches, some rvside; excel for
families or older couples; friendly, helpful staff; vg san
facs, ltd LS; some sh stay pitches up steep bank; beauty
cent; some pitches worn/uneven end of ssn (2010);
some pitches liable to flood; many tour op statics high
ssn; site open all yr but no services Nov-Mar; excel;
tourers pitch on open area."* €37.00, P15.   2015

BERNY RIVIERE *3C4* (6km S Rural) *49.39280, 3.15161*
Camping La Halte de Mainville, 18 Chemin du Routy,
02290 Ressons-le-Long 03 23 74 26 69;
lahaltedemainville@wanadoo.fr; www.lahaltede
mainville.com.planete-moto.com

🏕 ♦♦ (htd) wo ♨ 🛁 ⚊ ⛵ MsP 🦋 🕀 ⚓ nr 🔺 ⚓ (htd) ⚓

Fr Soissons W on N31 dir Compiègne, in approx 8km
look for site sp on L. Clearly sp. 3*, Lge, mkd, hdg,
pt shd, EHU (10A) €3 (poss rev pol); bbq; 60% statics;
phone; Eng spkn; adv bkg rec; games area; tennis;
fishing; CKE. *"Pleasant, clean, conv NH; friendly,
helpful staff; 1 hr fr Disneyland; vg; lovely area."*
€21.50, 8 Jan-8 Dec.   2015

BESANCON *6G2* (6km NE Rural) *47.26472, 6.07255*
Camping de Besancon - La Plage, 12 Route de
Belfort, 25220 Chalezeule 03 81 88 04 26;
contact@campingdebesancon.com;
www.campingdebesancon.com

🏕 €1.35 ♦♦ (htd) wo ♨ 🛁 ⚊ ⛵ MsP 🕀 nr ⚓ ⚓ nr 🔺

Exit A36 junc 4 S; foll sp Montbéliard & Roulons
onto D683; site in 1.5km on R, 200m after rlwy
bdge; well sp fr D683. Fr Belfort 2.65m height
restriction; foll sp to Chalezeule & 300m after
supmkt turn L to rejoin D683, site in 200m on
rvside. 3*, Med, mkd, pt shd, terr, EHU (16A) (poss
rev pol); bbq; twin axles; 50% statics; bus to city;
Eng spkn; ccard acc; kayaking; CKE. *"Helpful staff;
htd pool adj; excel modern san facs; access to opp
side of dual c'way under sm tunnel, suggest going to
rndabt to make the turn; tram to city 1.5km uphill."*
€25.00, 15 Mar-31 Oct.   2018

FRANCE

BESSINES SUR GARTEMPE *7A3 (1.5km SW Urban)*
46.10013, 1.35423 **Camp Municipal Lac de Sagnat,**
Route de St Pardoux, 87250 Bessines-sur-Gartempe
05 55 76 01 66; ot.bessines@wanadoo.fr;
http://www.tourisme-hautevienne.co.uk/objet_
touristique/2570

Exit A20 junc 24 sp Bessines-sur-Gartempe onto
D220; then D27 sp lake. Foll sp to Bellevue
Restaurant. At rest, turn R foll site sp. Well sp
fr junc 24. 2*, Med, hdg, mkd, pt shd, pt sl, terr, EHU
(6A) inc; sw nr; TV; Eng spkn. *"Pretty site with lake
views; peaceful location; friendly staff; gd, clean san
facs; poss unkempt LS (Jun 2009); hotel for meals nrby;
conv NH A20."* €18.70, 15 Jun-15 Sep.   2020

BEZIERS *10F1 (10km NE Rural)* *43.39849, 3.37338*
Camping Le Rebau, 34290 Montblanc **04 67 98 50 78;**
gilbert@camping-lerebau.fr; www.camping-lerebau.fr

NE on N9 fr Béziers-Montpellier, turn R onto D18. Site
sp, narr ent 2.50m. 3*, Lge, hdstg, hdg, mkd, pt shd, EHU
(5A) €4.50; TV; 10% statics; phone; bus 1km; Eng spkn;
adv bkg acc; CKE. *"Gd site; tight ent & manoeuvring onto
pitches; some facs old, but modern shwrs; ltd facs LS, but
clean; helpful owner; gd pool; gd touring base; LS phone
ahead to check open."* €19.50, 1 May-31 Aug.   2020

BEZIERS *10F1 (7km SE Urban)* *43.3169, 3.2842*
Camping Les Berges du Canal, Promenade des
Vernets, 34420 Villeneuve-les-Béziers **04 67 39 36 09;**
contact@campinglbdc.com; www.campingles
bergesducanal.com

Fr A9 exit junc 35 & foll sp for Agde. Exit 1st
rndabt for D612 dir Béziers then 1st L onto D37 sp
Villneuve-les-Béziers. Foll site sp to site adj canal.
4*, Med, mkd, hdg, shd, EHU (16a) inc; 45% statics;
Eng spkn; adv bkg acc; bike hire; CKE. *"Pleasant site;
facs clean & modern but poss stretched in ssn; noisy, fr
rlwy yard; some pitches tight lge o'fits; pleasant stroll
along canal."* €28.00, 14 Mar-17 Oct.   2019

BEZIERS *10F1 (12km SW Rural)* *43.31864, 3.14276*
Camping Les Peupliers, 7 Promenade de l'Ancien Stade,
34440 Colombiers **04 67 37 05 26; contact@camping-**
colombiers.com; www.camping-colombiers.com

SW fr Béziers on D609 (N9) turn R on D162E & foll
sp to site using heavy vehicle rte. Cross canal bdge &
fork R; turn R & site on L. Easier ent fr D11 (Béziers-
Capestang) avoiding narr vill rds, turn L at rndabt at
end of dual c'way sp Colombiers; in 1km at rlwy bdge,
go strt on; in 100m turn L (bef canal bdge) where rd
turns sharp R. 3*, Med, mkd, pt shd, EHU (10A) €3.50
(inc in high ssn) (poss rev pol); gas; bbq; red long stay;
25% statics; adv bkg acc; CKE. *"Nr Canal du Midi away
fr busy beach sites; modern san facs; no twin axles; excel
walking & cycling; pleasant sm vill, conv NH; gd rest in vill;
diff for lge o'fits; touring pitches among statics; 45km to
stn for Carcassonne."* €28.50   2019

BIARRITZ *8F1 (4.6km S Coastal)* *43.45305, -1.57277*
Yelloh! Village Ilbarritz, Ave de Biarritz, 64210 Bidart
05 59 23 00 29; contact@camping-ilbarritz.com;
www.camping-ilbarritz.com

S fr Bayonne on D810, by-pass Biarritz. 1km after
A63 junc turn R at rndabt immed after Intermarché
on R; sp to Pavillon Royal. Site 1km on R sp.
4*, Lge, mkd, shd, pt sl, terr, EHU (10A) inc; gas; TV;
80% statics; phone; Eng spkn; adv bkg req; ccard acc;
games area; horseriding; bike hire; tennis; golf nr; CKE.
*"Attractive, mature site; lge pitches, need blocks as v
sl; narr access rds poss diff long o'fits; excel pool; gd
beaches nrby; gd."* €50.00, 27 Mar-5 Oct.   2015

> ## "We must tell the Club about that great site we found"
>
> Get your site reports in by mid-August and we'll
> do our best to get your updates into the next
> edition.

BIARRITZ *8F1 (5km S Coastal)* *43.43371, -1.59040*
Camping Ur-Onéa, Rue de la Chapelle, 64210 Bidart
05 59 26 53 61; contact@uronea.com;
www.uronea.com

Exit A63 junc 4 dir Bidart, fr Bidart on D810 sp
St Jean de Luz, L at traff lts in town where site sp,
then 2nd R, L at motel, site is 300m on L. Access
fr main rd a bit tricky, 2nd access further S is easier
for lge o'fits. 3*, Lge, hdstg, mkd, pt shd, terr, serviced
pitches; EHU (10A) inc; gas; bbq; TV; 20% statics;
phone; Eng spkn; adv bkg acc; ccard acc; CKE. *"Well-
kept site 600m fr Bidart; various pitch sizes, most not
terr; suitable for o'fits up to 8m; staff friendly & helpful;
excel, clean san facs; conv Pays Basque vills; new
covrd/open pool (2014)."*
€46.70, 6 Apr-22 Sep.   2019

BIARRITZ *8F1 (8.7km S Coastal)* *43.43838, -1.58184*
Village Camping Sunêlia Berrua, Rue Berrua, 64210
Bidart **05 59 54 96 66; contact@berrua.com;**
www.berrua.com

Exit A63 junc 4 dir Bidart, fr Bidart on D810 sp
St Jean de Luz, L at 1st traff lts, site sp. 4*, Lge, pt
shd, pt sl, EHU (6A) €6.20 (poss long lead req); gas;
bbq; TV; 50% statics; phone; bus 1km; Eng spkn; adv
bkg acc; ccard acc; tennis; bike hire; waterslide; golf
2km; archery; CKE. *"Busy, well-kept site in attractive
location; steam rm; excel, clean facs; pitches tight lge
o'fits; site rds narr, low trees, some high kerbs; muddy
after rain; gd rest; sh walk to vill; gd; pleasant staff."*
€46.00, 1 Apr-27 Sep.   2015

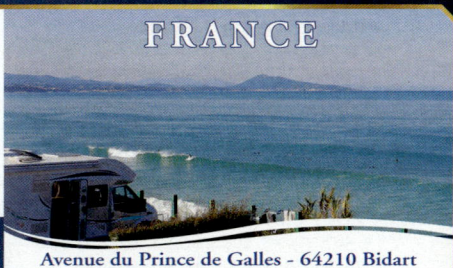
BIARRITZ *8F1* (2km SW Coastal) *43.4625, -1.5672*
Camping Biarritz, 28 Rue Harcet, 64200 Biarritz
05 59 23 00 12; info@biarritz-camping.fr;
www.biarritz-camping.fr

††† wo ♨ ♿ ⬛ ⊘ / ⵊ 🍴 ⊕ ⬛ ♨ ⚠ ⛱ ⚓ 🏊 (htd) ⬛ �🏖 sand 1km

S fr Bayonne on D810, by-pass Biarritz & cont to
junc of D810 coast rd sp Bidart & Biarritz; double
back on this rd, take 1st exit at next rndabt, 1st L dir
Biarritz Cent, foll sp to site in 2km.
Lge, mkd, pt shd, pt sl, terr, EHU (10A) €4; gas;
10% statics; bus at gate; adv bkg acc; ccard acc; tennis
4km; CKE. *"One of better sites in area, espec LS."*
€24.00, 12 May-14 Sep.   2016

BIARRITZ *8F1* (3.5km SW Coastal) *43.45525,
-1.58119* **Camping Pavillon Royal,** Ave du Prince
de Galles, 64210 Bidart 05 59 23 00 54; info@
pavillon-royal.com; www.pavillon-royal.com

††† wo ♨ ⬛ ♿ ⊘ / ⵊ 🍴 ⊕ ⬛ ♨ ⚠ ⚓ 🏊 (htd) ⬛

�🏖 sand adj

Exit A63/E4 junc 4; then take D810 S dir Bidart.
At rndabt after Intermarché supmkt turn R (sp
Biarritz). After 600m turn L at site sp.
4*, Lge, hdg, mkd, pt shd, pt sl, serviced pitches;
EHU (10A) inc (long lead poss req); gas; bbq; TV;
Eng spkn; adv bkg rec; ccard acc; tennis nr; golf
500m; games rm; horseriding 2km; bike rental; spa
treatments; massages; gym. *"Lovely, well-kept, busy
site in beautiful location beside beach; various pitch
sizes, some with sea views, some sm & diff lge o'fits;
direct access via steps to excel beach; fitness rm;
san facs poss irreg cleaning LS; mkt Sat; excel; adv
hkg rec as ess; no o'fits over 8m; avoid pitches on
perimeter fence as damage to vehicles fr stray golf
balls; vg, helpful, friendly staff; excel shwrs, wc, shop,
bar & rest."* **€64.00, 13 May-29 Sep, A06.**   **2019**

See advertisement

BIARRITZ *8F1* (4km SW Coastal) *43.44431, -1.58166*
Camping Erreka, Ave de Cumba, 64210 Bidart
05 59 54 93 64; erreka@seagreen.fr; www.seagreen-
campingerreka.com

††† wo ♨ ⬛ ♿ ⊘ / ⵊ 🦋 ⵊ 🍴 ⊕ ⬛ ♨ ⚠ ⚓ 🏊 ⬛ 🏖 sand 800m

Site at junc of D810 Biarritz by-pass & main rd into
town cent; well sp. 3*, Lge, pt shd, pt sl, terr, EHU
(6A) €4; gas; TV; 75% statics; adv bkg acc; ccard acc;
CKE. *"Some pitches sl & poss v diff to get into, rec
adv bkg to ensure suitable pitch; access rds v steep."*
€22.00, 16 Jun-16 Sep.   **2016**

BINIC *2E3* (1km S Coastal) *48.59216, -2.8238*
Camping Le Panoramic, Rue Gasselin, 22520 Binic
02 96 73 60 43; lepanoramic22@gmail.com;
www.lepanoramic.net

🐕 €2.50 †††(htd) wo ♨ ⬛ / 🦋 ⵊ 🍴 ⵊ ⬛ ♨ ⚓ 🏊(htd) ⬛

�🏖 sand 500m

D786 St Brieuc-Paimpol. 1st slip rd for Binic &
1st R up hill 100m, site sp. 3*, Med, mkd, pt shd,
pt sl, terr, EHU (10A) €5 (poss rev pol); gas; bbq;
75% statics; golf adj. *"Pleasant site; coastal path
nr; clean, excel facs, easy walk to beach & town."*
€30.00, 2 Apr-30 Sep.   **2016**

BINIC *2E3* (4km S Coastal) *48.57875, -2.78498*
Camping Le Roc de l'Hervieu, 19 Rue d'Estienne
d'Orves, 22590 Pordic 02 96 79 30 12; le.roc.de.
lhervieu@wanadoo.fr; www.campinglerocdel
hervieu.fr

††† wo ♨ ⬛ ♿ ⊘ / ⵊ 🦋 ⵊ 🍴 ⵊ ⚠ ⚓ 🏖 sand 600m

Site on E side of vill off N786, Binic-St Brieuc rd.
Turn E in cent of vill, sp to Les Madières then sp Le
Roc de l'Hervieu. 3*, Med, hdg, pt shd, EHU (10A)
€3.60; bbq; 10% statics; fishing. *"Gd walking; pleasant,
gd site."* **€21.00, 1 May-30 Sep.**   **2017**

BISCARROSSE *7D1* (3km N Coastal) *44.42955, -1.16792* **Campéole Camping Navarrosse,** 712 Chemin de Navarrosse, 40600 Biscarrosse 05 5809 84 32; navarrosse@campeole.com; www.campeole. co.uk/camping/landes/navarrosse-biscarrosse

♀ ♟ (htd) ♨ ⚲ ⚱ ⬅ 🖿 ⁄ 🅆 🦋 ♙ ♟ ℧ nr ⅋ 🝤 nr ⚠ ✒

Fr Biscarrosse N on D652 dir Sanguinet; 1km beyond turning to L to Biscarrosse-Plage, turn L onto D305 & foll sp to Navarrosse. 4*, V lge, mkd, pt shd, EHU (10A) inc (poss rev pol); bbq; sw nr; red long stay; TV; 40% statics; Eng spkn; ccard acc; games area; sailing; games rm; fishing; bike hire; tennis; Entertainment tent; Library; Inflatable structure; CKE. *"Pleasant site; vg for children; helpful staff; late arr area; gd walking; sailing lessons; cycle rtes; gd value."* **€33.00, 3 Apr-27 Sep.** 2020

BISCARROSSE *7D1* (4.5km N Rural) *44.42715, -1.16078* **Camping Bimbo,** 176 Chemin de Bimbo, 40600 Biscarrosse 05 58 09 82 33; info@camping bimbo.fr; www.campingbimbo.fr

♟ ♀ 🅆 ♨ ⚱ ⁄ ♙ ♟ ℧ 🝤 (htd) 🛁

Fr Biscarrosse take D652 N. At rndabt take 2nd exit (D305) sp Biscarrosse Lac. After 1.5km turn R twds Chemin de Bimbo, site on R in 500m. 4*, Med, shd, EHU (3-10A) inc (poss rev pol); 80% statics; adv bkg acc; games area; watersports 1km. *"Excel full facs site; beach 10km excel for surfing; bakery, pizzeria & creperie on site."* **€54.00, 1 Apr-30 Sep.** 2019

BISCARROSSE *7D1* (5km N Rural) *44.43535, -1.15496* **Camping Village Mayotte Vacances,** 368 Chemin des Roseaux, 40600 Biscarrosse 05 58 78 00 00; camping@ mayottevacances.com; www.mayottevacances.com

♀ €5 ♟ 🅆 ♨ ⚲ ⚱ ⁄ 🅼🅿 🦋 ♟ ℧ ⅋ 🝤 ⚠ ✒ ☇

Twd NE fr Biscarrosse on D652 L sp Navarrosse & at 1st fork R to Mayotte, foll camping sp. 4*, V lge, mkd, pt shd, EHU (10A) inc (poss rev pol); gas; bbq; sw nr; TV; 95% statics; Eng spkn; adv bkg rec; ccard acc; tennis; waterslide; games rm; sailing school; bike hire; jacuzzi; CKE. *"Excel leisure facs; vg for families; suitable o'fits up to 8m; rec."* **€43.00, 3 Apr-3 Oct.** 2016

BISCARROSSE *7D1* (8km NE Rural) *44.46230, -1.12900* **Camping de la Rive,** Route de Bordeaux, 40600 Biscarrosse 05 58 78 12 33; info@larive.fr; www.campinglarive.co.uk

♟ €13 ♀ (htd) 🅆 ♨ ⚲ ⚱ ⬅ 🖿 ⁄ 🅼🅿 ♙ ♟ ℧ ⅋ 🝤 ⚠ ✒
☇ (covrd, htd) 🛁

Fr Bordeaux on A63 dir Bayonne/San Sebastian; at junc 22 turn off onto A660; cont until 1st junc where turn L onto D216; cont for 17km to Sanguinet; cont on A652 for 3km; site sp on R nr Lake Cazaux. 4*, V lge, mkd, hdg, pt shd, EHU (6A) inc; gas; bbq (gas); sw nr; TV; 30% statics; phone; Eng spkn; adv bkg acc; ccard acc; games rm; jacuzzi; tennis; waterslide; bike hire; watersports; games area; CKE. *"On banks of Lake Cazaux-Sanguinet in delightful area; bustling site high ssn; many acitivies for all ages; no c'van/m'van over 9m; some pitches diff lge o'fits due trees; gd beaches; gd cycling; lovely rest, pleasant staff."* **€76.00, 12 Apr-30 Aug.** 2019

BISCARROSSE *7D1* (8km NW Coastal) *44.45804, -1.23968* **Campéole Camping Le Vivier,** 681 Rue du Tit, 40600 Biscarrosse-Plage 05 58 78 25 76; contact@ andretriganogroupe.com; www.campeole.co.uk

♟ €2.50 ♀ 🅆 ♨ ⚲ ⚱ ⬅ 🖿 ⁄ 🦋 ♙ ♟ ℧ ⅋ 🝤 ⚠ ✒ ☇ (htd) 🛁
🛁 sand 800m

Fr Arcachon & Pyla-sur-Mer, take D218, D83 to Biscarrosse Plage. Town o'skts site sp to R. Foll sps. 3*, Lge, pt shd, EHU (10A) inc (poss rev pol); 25% statics; ccard acc; fishing; bike hire; games rm; boating; tennis; horseriding nr. *"Sandy site in pine forest; access to beach via path thro dunes."* **€41.40, 28 Apr-17 Sep.** 2017

BIZE MINERVOIS *8F4* (0.2km SW Urban) *43.31584, 2.87070* **Camping De La Cesse,** Esplanade Champs de Foire, 11120 Bize-Minervois 04 68 46 14 40; marieange.lurqui@gmail.com; www.audetourisme.com

♟ €1.20 ♀ 🅆 ♨ ⚱ 🖿 ⁄ 🦋 ℧ nr 🝤 nr

Exit N fr D5/D11 Béziers-Carcassonne rd onto D26 to Bize-Minervois (D26 is 800m to E of D607); site in 1.8km on L, just bef rv bdge in S of vill. 1*, Sm, mkd, pt shd, EHU (5A) €2.30; bbq; phone; adv bkg acc; CKE. *"Peaceful, relaxing site; in need of TLC (2015)."* **€12.00, 1 May-30 Sep.** 2015

BLANC, LE *4H2* (2km E Rural) *46.63202, 1.09389* **Camping L'Ile d'Avant,** Route de Châteauroux, 36300 Le Blanc 02 54 37 88 22; info@tourisme-leblanc.fr; www.tourisme-leblanc.fr

♟ ♀ ♨ ⚱ 🖿 ⁄ 🅼🅿 🦋 ♟ nr ℧ nr 🝤 nr ⚠ ☇

Fr town cent take D951 twd St Gaultier/Argenton; site on R 1km after supmkt. 3*, Med, hdg, mkd, pt shd, EHU (6A) inc; bbq; adv bkg acc; fishing; tennis adj; Canoeing; Service area. *"Gd pitches; htd pool adj inc; adj sports field & club house; open Apr with adv bkg only, otherwise May."* **€14.00, 1 May-17 Sep.** 2020

BLANGY LE CHATEAU *3D1* (0.5km N Rural) *49.24670, 0.27370* **Camping Le Domaine du Lac,** 14130 Blangy-le-Château 02 31 64 62 00; info@domaine-du-lac.fr; www.domaine-du-lac.fr

♟ ♀ 🅆 ♨ ⚲ ⚱ ⁄ ♙ ♟ ℧ ⅋ 🝤

Fr Pont-l'Evêque & A13 S on D579 twd Lisieux. In 5km turn L onto D51 to Blangy where at fountain (rndabt) turn L, taking care. In 200m at end of vill turn L onto D140 Rte de Mesnil & site 200m on R. Site is 5km SE of Pont-l'Evêque. 3*, Med, mkd, pt shd, pt sl, EHU (6A) inc (long lead poss req); gas; bbq; 70% statics; adv bkg acc; ccard acc; games rm; tennis; lake fishing; CKE. *"Peaceful NH in lovely area; friendly British owner; poss uneven pitches; tired, access to pitches diff when wet; pretty vill; gd walks; conv Honfleur; 1hr to Le Havre ferry; NH only; mainly statics; facs poorly maintained."* **€24.00, 1 Apr-31 Oct.** 2019

BLANGY LE CHATEAU *3D1* (3km SE Rural) *49.22525, 0.30438* **Camping Le Brévedent,** 14130 Le Brévedent **02 31 64 72 88 or 02 31 64 21 50 (LS); contact@ campinglebrevedent.com; www.campingle brevedent.com**

♀♂ (htd) ⬚ ♨ ♿ ⛟ 🚿 ⊠ ∥ MSP ✂ ♈ ⌂ ① 🛈 ⛺ ⚓ ✦ 🏊 (htd) 🚲

Fr Pont l'Evêque & A13 go S on D579 twd Lisieux; after 5km turn L onto D51 twd Blangy-le-Château. In Blangy bear R at rndabt to stay on D51 & foll sp to Le Brévedent & Moyaux; site on L in just after le Breveden vill. 4*, Med, mkd, pt shd, pt sl, EHU (10A) (poss long leads req, poss rev pol); bbq; TV; 10% statics; phone; Eng spkn; adv bkg acc; ccard acc; horseriding 2km; games area; bike hire; tennis; games rm; golf 11km; lake fishing; kids' club; playground; CKE. *"Pleasant, busy site with all amenities, around lake in grnds of chateau; welcoming, helpful staff; no o'fits over 8m; some modern san facs, ltd LS; gd pool; rallies welcome; excel."* **€44.00, 13 Apr-15 Sep, N01.** **2019**

> ## "I need an on-site restaurant"
> We do our best to make sure site information is correct, but it is always best to check any must-have facilities are still available or will be open during your visit.

BLANGY SUR BRESLE *3C2* (2km SE Rural) *49.92378, 1.65693* **Camping Aux Cygnes d'Opale (formerly Municipal),** Zone de Loisirs, 76340 Blangy-sur-Bresle **02 35 94 55 65 or 09 72 32 88 40; contact@ auxcygnesdopale.fr; www.auxcygnesdopale.fr**

♈ €2 ♀♂ ⬚ ♨ ♿ ⛟ 🚿 ∥ MSP ♈ ⊺ nr ① nr ⛟ nr ⚓

Leave A28 at junc 5, R at T-junc onto D49, site on L in 800m. 3*, Med, mkd, unshd, EHU (5-16A) €3 (poss rev pol); bbq; 20% statics; phone; adv bkg rec; tennis nr; CKE. *"Attractive, well-kept site adj lakes; conv Calais, A28 & D928; gd san facs; adv bkg rec lge o'fits high ssn; no twin axles; pleasant & helpful warden; rec wait for warden for pitching; mini golf nr; poss waterlogged in wet (& ent refused); avoid during Int'l Petanque Competition 3rd w/end June on adj leisure cent; excel NH; new owners (2013), many improvements; new pool."* **€21.00, 1 Apr-31 Oct.** **2016**

BLANGY SUR BRESLE *3C2* (8km W Rural) *49.95430, 1.55098* **Camp Municipal La Forêt,** 76340 Bazinval **02 32 97 04 01; bazinval2@wanadoo.fr**

♀♂ ⬚ ∥ ♈ ⛟ nr ⚓

NW fr Blangy on D49 for 6km, then D149 to Bazinval. Site sp. 1*, Sm, hdg, pt shd, pt sl, EHU (10A) €4 (poss rev pol); twin axles; Eng spkn; games area; games rm; CKE. *"Gd san facs, poss inadequate; site yourself, warden calls early eve; poss travellers on site; NH only; lovely, peaceful site; conv Dieppe; vg."* **€10.40, 1 Apr-30 Oct.** **2018**

BLENEAU *4G3* (12km NE Rural) *47.75833, 3.09960* **Camping Le Bois Guillaume,** 89350 Villeneuve-les-Genêts **03 86 45 45 41; camping@bois-guillaume .com; www.bois-guillaume.com**

12 ♈ €1.40 ♀♂ (htd) ⊠ ⬚ ♿ ⛟ 🚿 ∥ MSP ♈ ⊺ ⚓ 🏊 (htd)

Fr W on D965 dir St Fargeau. At Mézilles take D7 thro Tannerre-en-Puisaye; stay on D7 & after 3.5km foll sp for site. Or fr A6 exit junc 18 onto D16 thro Charny, then turn L onto D119 to Champignelles; take D7 dir Tannere for approx 2km; turn R & foll sp to site. 4*, Med, hdstg, mkd, hdg, shd, EHU (5-10A) €3.10-4.60; gas; Eng spkn; tennis; bike hire; games area; CKE. *"Friendly staff; clean, tidy site; facs ltd LS; vg rest."* **€14.00** **2016**

BLERE *4G2* (0.6km E Urban) *47.32791, 0.99685* **Camping La Gâtine (Formaly Municipal),** Rue de Cdt Le Maître, 37150 Bléré **02 47 57 92 60; info@ campingblereplage.com**

♈ €1.20 ♀♂ ⊠ ⬚ ♿ ⛟ 🚿 ∥ MSP ♈ ⊺ nr ⛟ ⛟ nr

Exit A10 S of Tours onto A85 E. Exit A85 junc 11 dir Bléré. Site in 5km adj sports cent on S side of Rv Cher. 3*, Lge, mkd, pt shd, EHU (10A) €4 (poss rev pol & long lead poss req); bbq; twin axles; adv bkg acc; ccard acc; rv fishing adj; CKE. *"Excel, well-kept, peaceful, pleasant site; clean san facs, some dated & stretched when site full, some modernised; some dated EHU poss unrel in wet; gd cent for wine rtes & chateaux; htd pool adj high ssn; unrel opening dates LS; new management; looking a bit neglected (2017); excel cycle routes adj."* **€18.00, 1 Apr-10 Oct.** **2017**

> ## "Satellite navigation makes touring much easier"
> Remember most sat navs don't know if you're towing or in a larger vehicle – always use yours alongside maps and site directions.

BLOIS *4G2* (5km NE Rural) *47.605289, 1.374560* **Camping Le Val de Blois,** RD951 Lac de Loire 41350, Blois/Vineuil **02 54 79 93 57; contact@camping-loisir-blois.com; www.camping-loisir-blois.com**

♈ €1.20 ♀♂ (htd) ⊠ ⬚ ⛟ ∥ MSP ♈ ① 🛈 ⚓

Fr N exit 17 from A10 onto D200 thro Blois. Over bdge, turn off to D951. Site sp 3km to E. Fr S on d174, turn off D951 before bdge. Site sp 3km to E. 3*, Med, hdg, pt shd, pt sl, EHU 6A; gas; bbq (charcoal, elec, gas); sw nr; 10% statics; Eng spkn; ccard acc; bike hire; CKE. *"Situated on Loire rv; vast cycling area; facs stretched in high ssn; vg."* **€23.60, 30 Mar-12 Oct.** **2019**

BLOIS *4G2* (18km W Rural) *47.54427, 1.15712*
Ferme de Prunay, 41150 SEILLAC **09 53 86 02 01 or
06 98 99 09 86; contact@prunay.com; www.prunay.fr**

🛏🐕👫🚻 WD ⛺ 🔥 ♿ 🖊 ⛲ 🍴 🛒 🖼🏖 🚣 ⛵

Take exit Blois on the A10; foll dir for Angers
Chateau Renault until Molineuf, then Chambon
sur Cisse and Seillac, rd D131. 4*, Med, mkd, pt shd,
EHU (10A) inc; bbq; TV; Eng spkn; ccard acc; bike
hire; games area; fishing. *"In the heart of the Loire
Valley; spacious pitches; v nice site; san facs tired."*
€37.00, 31 Mar-3 Nov. 2019

BOEN SUR LIGNON *9B1* (1km S Urban) *45.73688,
4.00777* **Camping Municipal Domaine De Giraud,** Rue
de Camping, 42130 Boen Sur Lignon **04 77 97 39 96;
contact@camping-orangerie.com; www.camping-
orangerie.com**

🛏🐕👫🚻 WD ⛺ 🔥 ♿ 🖊 🖼

Fr Clermont Ferrand head E on D2089. Cont onto
D1089. Site well sp immed on exiting Boen sur
Lignon. Med, mkd, pt shd, pt sl, EHU (10A); bbq; twin
axles; TV; 4% statics; Eng spkn; games area; games
rm; CCI. *"Peaceful, well run site, 10 mins stroll fr town
cent with rest, bars, shops, supmkt & lndry; sports facs
nrby; vg."* **€18.60, 20 Mar-20 Oct.** 2019

BOIS DE CENE *2H4* (0.9km S Rural) *46.93395, -1.88728*
Camping Le Bois Joli, 2 Rue de Châteauneuf, 85710
Bois-de-Céné **02 51 68 20 05; contact@camping-
leboisjoli.com; www.camping-leboisjoli.com**

🛏🐕 €3.50 👫🚻 WD ⛺ 🖊 MP 🍴 🛒 nr 🖼🏖🚣 (covrd, htd) 🏊

Fr D21 turn R at church in cent of vill, site on R in
500m on rd D28. 3*, Med, hdg, pt shd, EHU (10A);
gas; bbq; 10% statics; phone; bus in vill; Eng spkn;
adv bkg acc; fishing; bike hire; games area; tennis;
CKE. *"Friendly, helpful owner; clean san facs; gd
walks; lovely pool; great site; ltd facs LS; rec; excel."*
€28.50, 1 Apr-10 Oct, A35. 2019

BOLLENE *9D2* (5.5km E Rural) *44.29811, 4.78645*
FFCC Camping et Centre Equestre La Simioune,
Quartier Guffiage, 84500 Bollène **04 90 30 44 62;
la-simioune@wanadoo.fr; www.la-simioune.fr**

🛏🐕 €2 👫🚻 WD ⛺ 🔥 🖊 🦋 🍴 � 🛒 nr 🖼🏖🚣🏊

Exit A7 junc 19 onto D994/D8 dir Carpentras (Ave
Salvatore Allende D8). At 3rd x-rd turn L into Ave
Alphonse Daudet dir Lambique & foll rd 3km to
sp for camping on L, then site 1km. 3*, Sm, shd,
pt sl, EHU (6A) €3; bbq; 10% statics; adv bkg rec;
horseriding; CKE. *"In pine forest; facs ltd in winter;
pony club for children & adults; NH only; lovely site."*
€24.00, 1 Mar-31 Oct. 2017

BOLLENE *9D2* (7km E Rural) *44.29124, 4.83837*
FFCC Camping Le Pont du Lez, Ave es Côtes du Rhône,
26790 Suze-la-Rousse **04 75 98 82 83; camping-le
pontdulez@wanadoo.fr**

🛏🐕 €1.40 👫 ⛺ 🖊 ⟲ 🍴 🛒 nr 🖼

E fr Bollène on D94 to Suze-la-Rousse; L in vill
sq; R immed bef rv bdge. 2*, Sm, pt shd, EHU
(6-10A) €3.40 (long lead poss req); TV; fishing;
games area; CKE. *"Lovely but decrepit (2009); basic,
clean facs - hot water to shwrs only; lovely area."*
€13.00, 1 Apr-30 Sep. 2017

BONIFACIO *10H2* (15km N Coastal) *41.47326, 9.26318*
Camping Rondinara, Suartone, 20169 Bonifacio **04 95
70 43 15; reception@rondinara.fr; www.rondinara.fr**

🛏🐕 €2.60 👫🚻 ⛺ 🖊 ⟲ 🦋 🍴 � 🛒 🖼🏖🚣⛵ sand 400m

Fr Bonifacio take N198 dir Porte-Vecchio for 10km,
then turn R onto D158 dir Suartone (lge camp
sp at turning). Site in 5km. NB D158 single track,
many bends & hills. 4*, Med, pt shd, pt sl, EHU (6A)
€3.60; bbq; 10% statics; Eng spkn; ccard acc; games
area; watersports; games rm; CKE. *"Excel rest;
idyllic location by bay; excel new san facs 2013; rd to
campsite steep and narr in places; adv bkg for mkd
pitches fr May."* **€35.70, 15 May-30 Sep.** 2019

> ## "There aren't many sites open at this time of year"
>
> If you're travelling outside peak season
> remember to call ahead to check site opening
> dates – even if the entry says 'open all year'.

BONNAC LA COTE *7B3* (1.4km S Rural) *45.93238,
1.28977* **Camping Le Château de Leychoisier,**
1 Route de Leychoisier, 87270 Bonnac-la-Côte
**05 55 39 93 43; contact@leychoisier.com;
chateau-de-leychoisier.pagesperso-orange.fr**

🛏🐕 €3 👫🚻 WD ⛺ 🔥 ♿ 🖊 MP 🍴 � 🛒 🖼🏖

Fr S on A20 exit junc 27 & L at T-junc onto D220.
At rndabt take 3rd exit then 1st L onto D97. At
mini-rndabt in Bonnac take 2nd exit, site on L in
1km. Fr N exit A20 junc 27, turn R at T-junc onto
D97, then as above. 5*, Med, mkd, hdg, pt shd, sl,
EHU (10A) inc; bbq (charcoal, gas); twin axles; TV;
phone; Eng spkn; adv bkg acc; ccard acc; games rm;
fishing; tennis; CKE. *"Peaceful site in grnds of chateau;
lge pitches; welcoming, friendly & helpful staff; no
o'fits over 20m; clean san facs but dated, unisex; excel
rest; extra for m'vans; blocks req some pitches; rallies
welcome; conv NH nr m'way; excel; ccard not acc for
1 night stay; access for lge o'fits diff; gd rest/pool
area; less commercial then other Les Castels sites."*
€34.00, 15 Apr-20 Sep, L11. 2017

BONNAL *6G2* (3.5km N Rural) *47.50777, 6.35583*
Camping Le Val de Bonnal, 1 Chemin du Moulin,
25680 Bonnal **03 81 86 90 87; www.camping-
valdebonnal.com or www.les-castels.com**

Fr N on D9 fr Vesoul or Villersexel to Esprels, turn
S onto D49 sp 'Val de Bonnal'. Fr S exit A36 junc
5 & turn N onto D50 sp Rougemont, site sp to N
of Rougemont. 4*, Lge, mkd, pt shd, EHU (5-10A)
inc (poss rev pol); gas; bbq; sw nr; twin axles; TV;
40% statics; Eng spkn; adv bkg acc; ccard acc; fishing;
golf 6km; games rm; gym; bike hire; waterslide;
canoe hire; watersports; CKE. *"Attractive, busy site;
lge accessible pitches; excel welcome; modern, clean
san facs; gd child activities; ltd facs LS; tour ops."*
€48.40, 7 May-6 Sep, J01. **2016**

BONNEVAL *4F2* (1km SE Rural) *48.17080, 1.38640*
Camping Le Bois Chièvre, Route de Vouvray,
St Maurice, 28800 Bonneval **02 37 47 54 01**

Rec app fr N (Chartres), or SE (D27 fr Patay/Orléans)
as app fr S thro town is narr & diff. Fr Chartres take
N10 into Bonneval & foll camp sp (mainly to L).
3*, Med, hdg, hdstg, mkd, shd, pt sl, EHU (6A) inc (rev
pol); bbq; 10% statics; Eng spkn; adv bkg acc; CKE.
*"Well-run, well-kept site in woodland; gd, lge pitches;
htd pool adj inc; friendly, helpful staff; vg facs but
poss stretched in ssn; vg NH for Le Havre or Dieppe."*
€17.00, 1 Apr-20 Oct. **2018**

BONNEVILLE *9A3* (0.5km NE Rural) *46.08206,
6.41288* **Camp Municipal Le Bois des Tours,** 314
Rue des Bairiers, 74130 Bonneville **04 50 97 04 31**

Fr A40 junc 16 take D1203, or fr Cluses take D1205
to Bonneville. Cross rv bdge into town cent; site sp.
2*, Med, pt shd, EHU (5A) €2.50; bbq; adv bkg acc;
Ironing room. *"Well-maintained, immac site; gd san
facs."* €8.00, 1 Jul-6 Sep. **2020**

BONNIERES SUR SEINE *3D2* (7km E Rural) *49.01646,
1.66256* **Camping Loisirs des Groux,** 1 Chemin de
L'ile, 78270 Mousseaux-sur-Seine **01 34 79 33 86;
www.campingdesgroux.com**

Fr W exit A13 junc 15 onto D113 dir Bonnières. Cont
thro Bonnières, turn L onto D37 Mousseaux/Base
de Loisirs. Cont strt on D37/D124/D125 & then turn
R & foll site sp. Fr E exit A13 junc 14 sp Bonnières
& foll sp Zone Industrielle. At rndabt take D113
Bonnières, then as above. 3*, Med, mkd, hdg, pt shd,
EHU (6A) €3.18; bbq; sw nr; 90% statics; Eng spkn;
adv bkg rec; ccard acc; games area; CKE. *"Conv Paris
(65km), Versailles, Rouen, Giverny; lge pitches; friendly,
helpful staff; basic, dated san facs; leisure cent inc pool
2km; poss clsd earlier than published dates - phone
ahead to check in LS; long winding track fr main rd;
poor quality."* €20.00, 15 Mar-30 Nov. **2016**

BONNIEUX *10E2* (1.6km W Rural) *43.81893, 5.31170*
Camp Municipal du Vallon, Route de Ménerbes,
84480 ~Bonnieux **04 90 75 86 14 or 06 48 08 46 79
(mob); contact@campinglevallon.com;
www.campinglevallon.com**

Fr Bonnieux take D3 twd Ménerbes, site sp on L
on leaving vill. 1*, Med, mkd, pt shd, terr, EHU (6-
10A) €3.80; Eng spkn; CKE. *"Beautiful, quaint, 'olde
worlde' site in wooded area; friendly warden; basic facs
but clean; gd walking & mountain biking; attractive
hilltop vill; gd touring base; gd rest in walking dist."*
€19.50, 15 Mar-15 Oct. **2015**

BONZEE *5D1* (1.6km E Rural) *49.09539, 5.61173*
Base de Loisirs du Colvert Les Eglantines, 55160
Bonzée **03 29 87 31 98; campingscolvert@free.fr;
http://base-de-loisirs-du-colvert.fr**

Fr Verdun take D903 twd Metz for 18km; in
Manheulles, turn R to Bonzée in 1km; at Bonzée turn
L for Fresnes; site on R, adj Camping Marguerites. Or
fr A4 exit junc 32 to Fresnes; then foll sp Bonzée.
3*, Med, hdg, mkd, pt shd, EHU (4-6A) €3.71-5.30; gas;
bbq; sw nr; twin axles; 80% statics; phone; Eng spkn;
adv bkg acc; ccard acc; boating adj; waterslide; fishing;
tennis 1.5km; CKE. *"Spacious pitches in well-planned
sites (2 sites together); facs ltd LS; v friendly staff."*
€15.50, 1 Apr-27 Sep. **2016**

> ## "That's changed – Should I let the Club know?"
>
> If you find something on site that's different
> from the site entry, fill in a report and let us
> know. See camc.com/europereport.

BORDEAUX *7C2* (7km N Rural) *44.89701, -0.58317*
Camping Le Village du Lac Bordeaux, Blvd Jacques
Chaban Delmas, 33520 Bordeaux-Bruges **05 57 87
70 60; contact@village-du-lac.com; www.camping-
bordeaux.com**

On ring rd A630 take exit 5 twd lake; site sp on N
side of lake, 500m N of Parc des Expositions.
4*, Lge, hdstg, mkd, pt shd, EHU (10A) inc; bbq; sw;
TV; 50% statics; bus/tram to city; Eng spkn; adv bkg
acc; ccard acc; fishing adj; games rm; bike hire; CKE.
*"Busy, poorly laid out, modern site; friendly staff;
san facs poss streched high ssn; plenty elec & water
pnts; excel rest; conv Bordeaux; easy access fr ring rd;
pitches poss soft and muddy after rain; bus/tram conn
to city; vg rest; gd unisex facs."* €34.00 **2017**

FRANCE

BORDEAUX *7C2* (4km S Urban) *44.75529, -0.62772*
Camping Beausoleil, 371 Cours du Général de Gaulle,
33170 Gradignan **05 56 89 17 66; campingbeausoleil@**
wanadoo.fr; www.camping-beausoleil-gradignan.fr

🏠12 🐕 €1 ♿(htd) 🚾 ♨ ⚶ ♿ ⁄ 🛒 👼 ⛱ nr ⒽBnr 🏊nr

Fr N take exit 16 fr Bordeaux ring rd onto D1010 sp
Gradignan. Fr S exit A63 junc 24 onto D211 to Jauge
then D1010 to Gradignan. Site S of Gradignan on
R after Beau Soleil complex, sp. 2*, Sm, mkd, hdstg,
hdg, pt shd, pt sl, EHU (6-10A) €1.50 -3 (poss rev pol);
bbq (elec, gas); sw nr; 70% statics; bus/tram 250m;
Eng spkn; adv bkg rec; CKE. *"Pleasant, family-run site;
helpful owners; vg, modern, clean san facs; ltd touring
pitches; sm pitches not suitable lge o'fits; adv bkg
rec; excel; gd sm site; booking necessary; htd pool &
waterslides 5km; highly rec; excel & cheap park & ride
tram sys 6km away; lovely quiet gdn site; easy bus rte
to city."* **€20.00**   **2017**

BOULOGNE SUR MER *3A2* (17km E Rural) *50.73337,
1.82440* **Camping à la Ferme Le Bois Groult (Leclercq),**
120 impasse du Bois Groult, 62142 Henneveux Le
Plouy **03 21 33 32 16; leclercq.gilbert0643@orange.fr;**
www.leboisgroult.fr

🏠12 🐕 €1 ♿♿ ⚶ ♿ ⁄ 👼 🎾 🏊nr

Take N42 fr Boulogne twd St Omer, take exit S dir
Desvres (D127). Immed at rndabt foll sp Colembert.
On ent Le Plouy turn R at the calvary & foll sp to
site in 1km. Sm, hdstg, pt shd, pt sl, EHU (6-10A)
€5; adv bkg acc. *"Charming, well-kept, peaceful CL-
type site; pleasant & helpful owner; no barrier; WWI
places of interest; easy access fr N42; ideal NH to/fr
ferry/tunnel; excel; v clean & tidy site; vg; shwrs €2."*
€15.00   **2018**

**"I like to fill in the reports as I
travel from site to site"**

You'll find report forms at the back of this
guide, or you can fill them in online at
camc.com/europereport.

BOULOGNE SUR MER *3A2* (8km SSW Coastal)
50.67128, 1.57079 **FFCC Camp Municipal La Falaise,**
Rue Charles Cazin, 62224 Equihen-Plage **03 21 31 22 61;**
camping.equihen.plage@orange.fr; www.camping-
equihen-plage.fr

🐕 €2.60 ♿♿ 🚾 ⚶ ♿ ⁄ 🛒 ⛱ 🏊(htd) 🍴 ⚓ sand 200m

Exit A16 junc 28 onto D901 dir Boulogne, then D940
S. Turn R to Condette then foll sp Equihen-Plage,
site sp in vill. Access fr D901 via narr rds.
3*, Med, hdg, pt shd, sl, terr, EHU (10-16A) inc (poss
rev pol); 85% statics; phone; adv bkg acc; ccard acc;
games rm; watersports; CKE. *"Pleasant, well-run site
in excel location, but poss windy; excel clean facs; sl
pitches poss diff long o'fits; steep rd to beach; gd site
approx 1hr fr Calais."* **€24.00, 25 Mar-3 Nov.**   **2019**

BOULOU, LE *8G4* (3.5km N Rural) *42.54157, 2.83431*
Camping Le Mas Llinas, 66165 Le Boulou
04 68 83 25 46; info@camping-mas-llinas.com;
www.camping-mas-llinas.com

🐕 €2.20 ♿♿(htd) 🚾 ⚶ ♿ ⁄ 🛒 ⛱ 🏊 🍴

Fr Perpignan, take D900 S; 1km N of Le Boulou turn
R at Intermarché supmkt 100m to mini rndabt, turn
L & foll sp to Mas-Llinas to site in 2km. Or fr A9 exit
43 & foll sp Perpignan thro Le Boulou. L at rndabt
adj Leclerc supmkt, site well sp. 3*, Med, pt shd, terr,
EHU (5-10A) €4.10-5.20; gas; bbq; TV; 10% statics;
phone; Eng spkn; adv bkg acc; adv bke hire; games area;
games rm; CKE. *"Friendly, welcoming owners; peaceful,
scenic site, mountain views; v peaceful; beware poss
high winds on high pitches; ltd water points at top
levels; ltd facs LS; facs clean; gd sized pitches; golden
orioles on site."* **€27.00, 1 Feb-30 Nov.**   **2017**

BOULOU, LE *8G4* (5km S Rural) *42.49083, 2.79777*
Camping Les Pins/Le Congo, Route de Céret, 66480
Maureillas-las-Illas, Pyrénées Orientales Occitanie
09 65 01 13 50; lespinslecongo@hotmail.fr;
https://www.campinglespinslecongo.com/en/

🐕 3,00 € ♿♿(htd) 🚾 ⚶ ♿ ⁄ 🛒 ⒽB 🏊nr ⛱ 🏊

Fr Le Boulou take D900 S, fork R after 2km onto
D618 dir Céret. Site on L 500m after Maureillas. 4*,
Med, hdg, shd, EHU (10A) €3.50; gas; bbq; 10% statics;
phone; Eng spkn; adv bkg acc; ccard acc; Gym; Bowling
green; Game room. *"Shabby and expensive, shwrs OK
(2010)."* **€23.00, 1 Apr-30 Oct.**   **2020**

BOULOU, LE *8G4* (4km SW Rural) *42.50664, 2.79502*
Camping de la Vallée, Route de Maureillas, 66490
St Jean-Pla-de-Corts **04 68 83 23 20; campingdela**
vallee@yahoo.fr; www.campingdelavallee.com

🐕 €2.50 ♿♿(htd) 🚾 ⚶ ♿ ⁄ 🛒 🏧 👼 🎾 🍴 ⒽB 🏊nr
⛱ ✎ 🏊

Exit A9 at Le Boulou. Turn W on D115. Turn L after
3km at rndabt, into St Jean-Pla-de-Corts, thro vill,
over bdge, site on L. 3*, Med, mkd, pt shd, EHU (5A)
€4; sw nr; red long stay; TV; 50% statics; phone; bus
adj; Eng spkn; adv bkg acc; ccard acc; fishing 1km;
archery; CKE. *"Lovely well-kept site; easy access lge,
well mkd pitches; friendly, helpful owners with gd local
info; excel san facs; conv NH fr A9 or longer; highly
rec."* **€24.60, 1 Apr-31 Oct.**   **2018**

BOULOU, LE *8G4* (4km W Rural) *42.50908, 2.78429*
FFCC Camping Les Casteillets, 66490 St Jean Pla-
de-Corts **04 68 83 26 83; jc@campinglescasteillets.**
com; www.campinglescasteillets.com

🏠12 ♿♿ 🚾 ⚶ ♿ ⁄ 🛒 👼 🎾 🍴 ⒽB 🏊 ⛱ ✎ 🏊

Exit A9 at Le Boulou; turn W on D115; after 3km
turn L immed after St Jean-Pla-de-Corts; site sp on
R in 400m. NB Narr app last 200m. 3*, Med, mkd, pt
shd, serviced pitches; EHU (6A) €3.30 (poss rev pol);
gas; red long stay; TV; 10% statics; Eng spkn; adv bkg
rec; tennis; games area. *"Lovely, friendly, scenic, well
run site; lge pitches; conv for touring & en rte NE Spain;
low lying; gd food in rest; gd."* **€28.00**   **2018**

BOURBON LANCY *9A1* (1km S Rural) *46.61949, 3.75506* **Camping Le Plan d'Eau du Breuil,** 71140 Bourbon Lancy **03 86 37 95 83 or 03 85 89 20 98; contact@aquadis-loisirs.com; www.aquadis-loisirs.com**

Site sp fr town, on lakeside. 3*, Sm, pt shd, pt sl, EHU (6A); bbq; TV; adv bkg acc; CKE. *"Excel; 2km to town; lake adj; bike rec."* **€16.00, 1 Jun-15 Sep.**   2017

BOURBON L'ARCHAMBAULT *9A1* (1km W Rural) *46.58058, 3.04804* **Camp Municipal de Bourbon l'Archambault,** 03160 Bourbon-l'Archambault **04 70 67 08 83 or 06 82 82 62 50; https://camping-municipal-de-bourbon-larchambault.business.site/**

Exit D953 at Bourbon-l'Archambault onto D1 northwards; in 400m turn L into Blvd Jean Bignon. Site sp. 2*, Lge, pt shd, sl, EHU (6-10A) €2-2.20; 75% statics; tennis nr. *"Beautifully laid-out in park surroundings; htd pool 300m; waterslide 300m; gd pitches; excel updated san facs (2013); charming town; excel."* **€6.40, 1 Mar-12 Nov.**   2019

BOURBOULE, LA *7B4* (3km NE Rural) *45.59680, 2.75130* **FFCC Camping Le Panoramique,** Le Pessy, 63150 Murat-le-Quaire **04 73 81 18 79; info@campingpanoramique.fr; www.campingpanoramique.fr**

Exit A89 junc 25; cont strt until junc with D922; turn R; in 3km turn R onto D219 dir Mont-Dore; in 5km pass thro Murat-le-Quaire; in 1km turn L in Le Pessy; site on L in 300m. Site well sp fr D922. 3*, Med, mkd, pt shd, terr, EHU (6-10A) €4.30-5.60; gas; 50% statics; phone; adv bkg acc; games rm; CKE. *"Site well set-out; mountain views; friendly, helpful recep; clean but dated facs; vg."* **€24.00, 15 Feb-15 Mar & 12 Apr-30 Sep.**   2016

BOURBOULE, LA *7B4* (1km E Rural) *45.58980, 2.7525210* **Camping Les Vernières,** 170 Avenue Maréchal de Lattre de Tassigny 63150 La Bourboule **047 38 110 20; contact@camping-la-bourboule.fr; www.camping-la-bourboule.fr**

Fr N on N89 or S on D922 turn E onto D130 dir Le Mont-Dore, site sp. 4*, Lge, hdg, pt shd, terr, EHU (10A) €3.50; Eng spkn; adv bkg acc; fishing nr. *"Lovely setting in mountains; gd clean facs; sh walk to fine spa town; gd family site; rec."* **€10.00, 9 Feb-30 Sep.**   2020

BOURBOULE, LA *7B4* (4km E Rural) *45.59456, 2.76347* **Camping Les Clarines,** 1424 Ave Maréchal Leclerc, 63150 La Bourboule **04 73 81 02 30; clarines.les@wanadoo.fr; www.camping-les-clarines.com**

Fr La Bourboule take D996/D88 on N bank of rv (old rd sp Piscine & Gare); fork L at exit fr town. Site sp on R, nr junc with D219. 3*, Lge, pt shd, terr, EHU (6-10A) €3.50-€5.80; gas; bbq; TV; adv bkg rec; games area; outdoor fitness space. *"Gd winter sports cent; excel htd facs."* **€16.00, 21 Dec-11 Oct.**   2020

BOURDEAUX *9D2* (1km SE Rural) *44.57854, 5.12791* **Camping Les Bois du Châtelas,** Route de Dieulefit, 26460 Bourdeaux **04 75 00 60 80; contact@chatelas.com; www.chatelas.com**

Fr N exit A7 m'way junc 16 onto D104, head twd Crest. Shortly bef Crest turn R onto D538 S thro Bourdeaux & cont dir Dienlefit (still on D538), site in 1km on L, well sp. 5*, Med, mkd, pt shd, terr, EHU (10A) inc; gas; bbq (elec, gas); cooking facs; TV; 30% statics; phone; Eng spkn; adv bkg req; ccard acc; games area; horseriding 5km; bike hire; games rm; waterslide; sauna; fitness rm; CKE. *"In lovely, scenic area; site on steep slope; no o'fits over 8m high ssn; gd walking."* **€34.70, 11 Apr-13 Sep, M11.**   2016

BOURG ACHARD *3D2* (1km W Rural) *49.35330, 0.80814* **Camping Le Clos Normand,** 235 Route de Pont Audemer, 27310 Bourg-Achard **02 32 56 34 84 or 06 40 25 53 14 (mob); contact@leclosnormand-camping.com; leclosnormand-camping.tr**

1km W of vill of Bourg-Achard, D675 Rouen-Pont Audemer or exit A13 at Bourg-Achard junc. 3*, Med, mkd, hdg, pt shd, pt sl, EHU (6A) €3.40 (poss rev pol & poss long lead req); gas; 10% statics; adv bkg acc; ccard acc; CKE. *"Vg, clean san facs; plenty hot water; many pitches uneven; gd; muddy when wet."* **€21.00, 15 Apr-30 Sep.**   2016

BOURG ARGENTAL *9C2* (2km E Rural) *45.29910, 4.58183* **Camping Domaine de l'Astrée,** L'Allier, 42220 Bourg-Argental **04 77 39 72 97 or 04 77 39 63 49 (TO); prl@bourgargental.fr**

S fr St Etienne on D1082 to Bourg-Argental, thro town, site well sp on R soon after rndabt & opp filling stn. Fr Annonay or Andance site on L of D1082 at start of Bourg-Argental, adj rv. 3*, Sm, mkd, hdstg, pt shd, EHU (4-6A) inc (long cable poss req); gas; bbq; 60% statics; phone; ccard acc; waterslide; games rm; tennis; fishing; bike hire; CKE. *"Pleasant site with modern facs; htd pool 600m; vg."* **€19.50**   2017

FRANCE

BOURG D'OISANS, LE *9C3* (1.5km NE Rural)
45.06557, 6.03980 **Camping à la Rencontre du Soleil,** Route de l'Alpe-d'Huez, La Sarenne, 38520 Le Bourg-d'Oisans **04 76 79 12 22 or 06 75 47 72 50; contact@ rencontresoleil.fr; www.rencontre-du-soleil.com**

Fr D1091 approx 800m E of town turn N onto D211, sp 'Alpe d'Huez'. In approx 500m cross sm bdge over Rv Sarennes, then turn immed L to site. (Take care not to overshoot ent, as poss diff to turn back). 5*, Med, hdg, mkd, pt shd, EHU (10A) inc; bbq; TV; 45% statics; adv bkg req; ccard acc; games rm; tennis; fishing; horseriding 1.5km; games area; CKE. *"Busy site with lovely views; various pitch sizes/shapes; excel, spotless san facs, some unisex; helpful owner; excel rest; La Marmotte cycle race (early Jul) & Tour de France usually pass thro area & access poss restricted; no o'fits over 7m high ssn; pitches poss flooded after heavy rain, but staff excel at responding; mkt Sat; highly rec."* **€38.00, 1 May-30 Sep.**   2020

BOURG D'OISANS, LE *9C3* (2km NE Rural) *45.06401, 6.03895* **Camping La Cascade,** Route de l'Alpe d'Huez, 38520 Le Bourg-d'Oisans **04 76 80 02 42; lacascade@ wanadoo.fr; www.lacascadesarenne.com**

Fr W drive thro Le Bourg-d'Oisans & cross bdge over Rv Romanche. Approx 800m E of town turn onto D211, sp Alpe d'Huez. Site on R in 600m. 4*, Med, mkd, pt shd, EHU (16A) €4.30; 10% statics; Eng spkn; adv bkg acc; ccard acc; CKE. *"V friendly, helpful staff; discounts for ski passes fr recep; modern san block, superb high pressure shwrs."* **€37.00, 1 Jan-30 Sep & 15 Dec-31 Dec.**   2015

BOURG D'OISANS, LE *9C3* (13km SE Rural) *44.98611, 6.12027* **Camping Le Champ du Moulin,** Bourg d'Arud, 38520 Vénosc **04 76 80 07 38; info@champ-du-moulin.com; www.champ-du-moulin.com**

On D1091 SE fr Le Bourg-d'Oisans sp Briançon for about 6km; turn R onto D530 twd La Bérarde & after 8km site sp. Turn R to site 350m after cable car stn beside Rv Vénéon. NB Site sp bef vill; do not cross rv on D530. 3*, Med, hdg, mkd, pt shd, EHU (6-10A) €7.20-9.80 (extra charge in winter, poss rev pol); gas; bbq; red long stay; TV; 20% statics; Eng spkn; adv bkg req; ccard acc; fishing nr; rafting nr; horseriding nr; sauna; games rm; tennis nr; CKE. *"Lovely, well-run site by alpine torrent (unguarded); friendly, helpful owners; ltd facs LS; htd pool adj; access to pitches poss diff lge o'fits; ideal for walking, climbing & relaxing; no o'fits over 10m; lots of outdoor activities to enjoy; cable car to Les Deux Alpes adj (closes end Aug); mkt Tue Vénosc (high ssn); highly rec."* **€29.00, 1 Jan-28 Apr, 1 Jun-15 Sep, 15 Dec-31 Dec, M03.**   2019

BOURG D'OISANS, LE *9C3* (4km NW Rural) *45.09000, 6.00750* **Camping Ferme Noémie,** Chemin Pierre Polycarpe, Les Sables, 38520 Le Bourg-d'Qisans **04 76 11 06 14 or 06 87 45 08 75 (mob); ferme. noemie@orange.fr; www.fermenoemie.com**

On D1091 Grenoble to Briançon; Les Sables is 4km bef Le Bourg-d'Oisans; turn L next to church, site in 400m. 2*, Sm, mkd, unshd, EHU (16A) €3.50; bbq (gas); red long stay; 25% statics; phone; bus 500m; adv bkg acc; ccard acc; cycling; fishing; games area; CKE. *"Simple site in superb location with excel facs; helpful British owners; lots of sports; skiing; walking; gd touring base lakes & Ecrins National Park; pool 3km; excel site."* **€29.00, 1 May-30 Oct.**   2017

BOURG D'OISANS, LE *9C3* (7km NW Rural) *45.11388, 6.00785* **RCN Camping Belledonne,** Rochetaillée, 38520 Le Bourg-d'Oisans **04 76 80 07 18; belledonne@rcn.fr; www.rcn-campings.fr**

Fr S of Grenoble take N85 to Vizille then D1091 twd Le Bourg-d'Oisans; in approx 25km in Rochetaillée turn L onto D526 sp Allemont. Site 100m on R. 4*, Med, hdg, shd, EHU (10A) inc; bbq; TV; Eng spkn; ccard acc; sauna; games area; tennis; games rm; fishing 500m; horseriding; windsurfing; CKE. *"Beautiful, well-run site in lovely location; no o'fits over 7.5m high ssn; friendly Dutch owners; access to many pitches tight; no twin axles; gd for teenagers; excel pool with views; many walks; gd touring base; La Marmotte cycle race (early Jun) & Tour de France usually pass thro area & access poss restricted; mkt Sat; excel new san facs (2018), gd rest; v helpful staff."* **€41.60, 11 May-2 Oct, M02.**   2018

BOURG EN BRESSE *9A2* (11km NE Rural) *46.29078, 5.29078* **Camp Municipal du Sevron,** Chemin du Moulin, 01370 St Etienne-du-Bois **04 74 24 05 47 or 06 47 97 50 73 (mob); campingdusevron@ gmail.com; www.campingdusevron.fr**

On D1083 at S end of vill of St Etienne-du-Bois on E side of rd. 3*, Sm, hdg, pt shd, EHU (10A) €2.05; 50% statics; Eng spkn; ccard acc; rv fishing; tennis. *"Gd NH; dated but clean facs; friendly; sm pitches; late arr get v sm pitches; poss rd & rlwy noise; gd shwrs & plenty hot water; gd facs."* **€17.00, 1 Mar-25 Oct.**   2018

BOURG ET COMIN 3D4 (0.5km NE Rural) 49.39871, 3.66072 **Camping de la Pointe,** 5 Rue de Moulins, 02160 Bourg-et-Comin **03 23 25 87 52; michel. pennec@9online.fr; www.tourisme-paysdelaon.com**

🏕12 🐕 €2 👫(htd) ⊞ 🚿 ♨ ⚿ 🅿 🦋 ⟙ ⟙ nr ⓗ ⛺

🏊(covrd, htd)

Leave A26/E17 at junc 14 & turn W along D925 dir Soissons for 15km. Site on R on ent vill. 2*, Sm, hdg, pt shd, EHU (6A) €3.20; bbq; phone; bus 500m; Eng spkn; adv bkg acc; CKE. "CL-type site in orchard; narr ent & access to pitches poss diff lge o'fits; most pitches sm & not suitable lge o'fits; EHU is only 2 pin; gd rest; gd walking area; 10 mins fr Parc Nautique de l'Ailette with watersports; conv Aisne Valley; bar 500m; v accommodating owner; htd pool OAY; wifi not reliable." €20.80   2018

"I need an on-site restaurant"

We do our best to make sure site information is correct, but it is always best to check any must-have facilities are still available or will be open during your visit.

BOURG MADAME 8H4 (6km NW Rural) 42.45979, 1.91075 **Camping Le Robinson,** 25 Ave Gare Internationale, 66760 Enveitg **04 68 04 80 38 or 06 11 81 25 46 (mob); lerobinson-cerdagne@ wanadoo.fr; www.robinson-cerdagne.com**

🏕12 🐕 €1.50 👫 ⊞ ♨ ⚿ 🅿 ⚿ ⓗ nr ⛺ 🎿 🏊

Fr Bourg-Madame, take N20 N twd Foix. Thro vill of Enveitg & turn L down Chemin de la Gare & L at camping sp. 2*, Lge, mkd, shd, pt sl, EHU (4-13A) €3-9; gas; bbq; TV; 10% statics; phone; adv bkg acc; games rm. "Beautiful setting; winter sports cent; conv Barcelona, Andorra; conv scenic rte train (Train Jaune); new management; new shwr block (excel)." €20.00   2015

BOURG ST ANDEOL 9D2 (1.8km N Rural) 44.38731, 4.64840 **Camping du Lion,** Quartier Ile Chenevrier, 07700 Bourg-St Andéol **04 75 54 53 20; contact@ campingdulion.com; www.campingdulion.com**

🐕 €3 👫 ⊞ ♨ ⚿ 🦋 ⟙ ⓘ 🅿 ⛺ 🏊

Exit A7 at junc 18 or 19 onto N7. At Pierrelatte turn W on D59 to Bourg-St Andéol. Site sp fr cent town dir Viviers. 3*, Med, mkd, shd, EHU (6A) €3; 10% statics; adv bkg acc; games rm; games area. "Peaceful site in woodland setting; muddy when wet; dir access to rv; highly rec; new san facs (2015)." €35.00, 1 Apr-30 Sep.   2016

BOURGES 4H3 (2km S Urban) 47.07228, 2.39497 **Camp Municipal Robinson,** 26 Blvd de l'Industrie, 18000 Bourges **02 48 20 16 85; camping@ ville-bourges.fr; www.ville-bourges.fr**

🐕 €2.15 👫(htd) ⊞ ♨ ♿ ⚿ 🅿 🦋 ⟙ ⟙ nr ⓗ ⛺

Exit A71/E11 at junc 7, foll sp Bourges Centre & bear R at 'Autres Directions' sp; foll site sp; site at traff lts on N side of S section of inner ring rd half-way bet junc with D2144 & D2076. NB: site access is via a loop - no L turn at traff lts, but rndabt just past site if turning missed. If on outer ring rd D400, app city on D2144 & then as above. Sp on app rds to site gd. 3*, Med, mkd, hdg, hdstg, pt shd, serviced pitches; EHU (10-16A) €3.40-8 (poss rev pol); bbq (elec, gas); red long stay; twin axles; bus adj; Eng spkn; ccard acc; CKE. "Attractive, well-kept, well-organised, busy, rvside site in gd location; helpful, friendly staff; pool 300m inc; excel, immac san facs; some v lge pitches, some sm & poss diff ent; most pitches hdstg; excel NH or longer; 20 min walk to historic town." €24.00, 30 Mar-28 Oct.   2018

BOURGUEIL 4G1 (0.8km S Rural) 47.26991, 0.16873 **Camp Municipal Parc Capitaine,** 37140 Bourgueil **02 47 97 85 62 or 02 47 97 25 00 LS; camping@bourgueil.fr; www.bourgueil.fr**

🐕 €1.50 👫 ⊞ ♨ ♿ ⚿ 🅿 🦋 ⟙ 🅿 nr ⛺

N on D749 fr junc 5 of A85, site 1km on R. Fr W (Longue) via D10 & by-pass, S at rndabt on D749 to site on L in 200m. Do not app fr N via D749 thro town cent. 3*, Med, hdg, mkd, pt shd, EHU (10A) €2.65 (poss long lead req); gas; bbq; sw; ccard acc; CKE. "Ideal cent Loire châteaux; 2 sites - one on R for tourers; excel; barrier ent & exit by code; office clsd 1230-1500 but warden lives upstairs; conv fr A85 & Loire valley; vg; san facs need refurb." €15.65, 1 May-15 Oct.   2019

BOUSSAC 7A4 (2km NE Rural) 46.37192, 2.20036 **Camping du Château de Poinsouze,** Route de la Châtre, 23600 Boussac-Bourg **05 55 65 02 21; camping-de-poinsouze@gmail.com; www.camping-de-poinsouze.com**

🐕 €3 👫 ⊞ ♨ ♿ ⚿ 🅿 🦋 ⟙ ⟙ ⓗ 🅿 ⛺ 🎿 🏊 🚣

Fr junc 10 on A71/E11 by-pass Montluçon via N145 dir Guéret; in 22km turn L onto D917 to Boussac; cont on D917 dir La Châtre; site 3km on L. Or fr Guéret on N145, exit Gouzon, at rndabt take D997 to Boussac, then as above. 4*, Med, mkd, unshd, pt sl, serviced pitches; EHU (6-20A) inc (poss rev pol); bbq; TV; 10% statics; Eng spkn; adv bkg req; ccard acc; horseriding 5km; games area; games rm; waterslide; lake fishing; golf 20km; bike hire; CKE. "Peaceful, relaxed site by lake in chateau grnds; well-kept & well-run; lge pitches, some sl; no o'fits over 15m; dogs not acc Jul/Aug welcoming, helpful owners; superb san facs; excel rest & snacks; gd for young children; gd walking." €39.00, 11 May-13 Sep, L16.   2019

FRANCE

BOUSSAC *7A4* (2km W Rural) *46.34938, 2.18662*
Camping Creuse-Nature (Naturist), Route de Bétête,
23600 Boussac **05 55 65 18 01; creuse-nature@
wanadoo.fr; www.creuse-nature.com**

🏕€5.50 ⵛ♿🚿🚮⊘❄🍽⊕🏖🛒🎻♨(covrd, htd) ⛵

Fr Boussac take D917 N twd La Châtre. In 500m turn
L (W) on D15 sp Bétête. Site on R in 2.5km, clearly
sp. 4*, Med, hdg, mkd, pt shd, pt sl, EHU (10A) €4.50
(poss long lead req); 10% statics; Eng spkn; adv bkg
acc; ccard acc; fishing; games area. *"Excel site in lovely
area; great pitches; charming & helpful owners; clean
facs; easy walk to town & interesting château; great
location."* €35.70, 1 Apr-15 Oct. 2019

BRACIEUX *4G2* (0.5km N Urban) *47.55060, 1.53743*
Camping Indigo les Châteaux, 11 Rue Roger Brun,
41250 Bracieux **02 54 46 41 84; chateaux@camping-
indigo.com; www.camping-indigo.com**

🏕€2.80 ⵛ♿🚿🚮⊘❄🦋⊕nr🛒🎻♨(covrd) ⛵

Fr S take D102 to Bracieux fr Cour-Cheverny. Fr N
exit Blois on D765 dir Romorantin; after 5km take
D923 to Bracieux & site on R on N o'skts of town
opp church, sp. 3*, Lge, hdg, mkd, hdstg, pt shd, EHU
(10A) €2.75 (poss long lead req); red long stay; TV;
10% statics; Eng spkn; adv bkg acc; ccard acc; tennis;
games rm; bike hire; CKE. *"Peaceful spot; attractive
forest area; busy high ssn; gd security; gd touring
base; gas 300m; bike tracks; well run site; all san
blocks replaced (2013); superb; excel, well run site."*
€32.00, 30 Mar-4 Nov. 2018

BRANTOME *7C3* (1km E Rural) *45.36074, 0.66035*
Camping Brantôme Peyrelevade, Ave André Maurois,
24310 Brantôme **05 53 05 75 24; info@camping-
dordogne.net; www.camping-dordogne.net**

🏕€2(htd) ⵛ♿🚿🚮⊘❄🦋⊕🍽🛒🎻nr♨⊘
⛱🏕sand adj

Fr N on D675 foll sp Centre Ville; ent vill & turn L
onto D78 Thiviers rd, site sp at turn; in 1km on R
past stadium opp g'ge. Fr S D939 foll sp 'Centre
Ville' fr rndabt N of town. Then L onto D78 Thiviers
rd & foll sp. Do not foll 'Centre Ville' sp fr rndabt
**S of town, use by-pass. Football stadium best ref
point for ent.** 3*, Lge, mkd, hdg, pt shd, EHU (10A)
inc; bbq; sw nr; 7% statics; Eng spkn; adv bkg acc;
ccard acc; tennis nr; CKE. *"Spacious, well-kept rvside
site; attractive courtyard layout; friendly, helpful
owners; excel, modern, gd san facs; facs stretched in
high ssn; grnd poss soft after heavy rain; 10 min walk to
lovely town (the Venice of Périgord); mkt Wed; games
area adj; beautiful countryside; gd walking & cycling;
excel; some pitches heavily shd; excel family camping."*
€26.00, 1 May-30 Sep. 2017

BRASSAC *8F4* (11km SE Rural) *43.59700, 2.60732*
Camping Le Rouquié, Lac de la Raviège, 81260
Lamontélarie **05 63 70 98 06; camping.rouquie@
wanadoo.fr; www.campingrouquie.fr**

🏕 ⵛ♿🚿🚮⊘❄🦋🍽🛒🎻♨

Fr Brassac take D62 to N side of Lac de la Raviège;
site on lakeside. 2*, Med, mkd, pt shd, terr, EHU
(3-6A) €4; bbq; sw; TV; 50% statics; adv bkg acc; ccard
acc; bike hire; watersports adj; games area; fishing;
sailing; CKE. *"Ltd facs LS; gd lake views; site needs
TLC."* €28.00, 1 May-31 Oct. 2019

BRASSAC *8F4* (5km S Rural) *43.60835, 2.47148·*
FFCC Camping Le Plô, Le Bourg, 81260 Le Bez
05 63 74 00 82; info@leplo.com; www.leplo.com

🏕€1.50 ⵛ♿🚿🚮⊘❄🦋🌿🛒🎻nr♨⛱

Fr Castres on D622 to Brassac; then D53 S to Le
Bez, site sp W of Le Bez. 3*, Med, mkd, pt shd, terr,
EHU (6A) €3; bbq; Eng spkn; adv bkg acc; games
area; games rm; bike hire; CKE. *"Lovely location;
well-equipped site; excel, clean san facs; friendly,
helpful Dutch owners; beautiful, historical area with
National Park; much wildlife; cafés & gd rest nrby; vg."*
€31.50, 1 May-30 Sep. 2019

BRAUCOURT *6E1* (5km SW Rural) *48.55425, 4.79235*
FLOWER Camping Presqu'île de Champaubert, Lac
du Der, 52290 Braucourt **03 25 04 13 20; camping-de-
braucourt@wanadoo.fr; www.lescampingsduder.
com or www.flowercampings.com**

🏕€1 ⵛ♿🚿🚮⊘❄🌿🍽⊕🛒♨

Fr St Dizier take D384 SW twd Montier-en-Der
& Troyes. In Braucourt R onto D153 sp Presq'ile
de Champaubert, site on L in 2km. Site situated
on Lac du Der-Chantecoq. 4*, Lge, mkd, hdg, shd,
serviced pitches; EHU (10A) €4 (rev pol); gas; sw nr;
TV; 60% statics; phone; ccard acc; boating; fishing;
watersports; CKE. *"Beautiful lge beach; birdwatching;
lge pitches; improved san facs; gates clsd 2230; ltd
spaces."* €26.00, 15 Apr-25 Nov. 2016

"Satellite navigation makes touring much easier"

Remember most sat navs don't know if you're
towing or in a larger vehicle – always use yours
alongside maps and site directions.

BRENGUES *7D4* (0.5km S Rural) *44.57509, 1.83261*
Camp Municipal de Brengues, 46320 Brengues
05 81 48 06 99

ⵛ♿🚿🚮⊘❄🍽⊕🛒nr♨

W fr Figeac on D13. After 6km turn L onto D41.
After 17km, turn L at x-rds with D38, site ent 100m
on R bef bdge over Rv Célé. 3*, Sm, mkd, pt shd,
EHU (10A) inc (rev pol); sw; tennis; CKE. *"Warden now
onsite."* €15.00, 1 Jun-30 Sep. 2018

BRESSE, LA *6F3* (3.2km E Rural) *47.99893, 6.91801*
FFCC Camp Municipal Le Haut des Bluches, 5 Route des Planches, 88250 La Bresse **03 29 25 64 80; www.hautdesbluches.com**

[icons]

Leave La Bresse on D34 Rte de la Schlucht. Site on R in 3km. 3*, Med, mkd, pt shd, terr, EHU (4-13A) €2-4.80; bbq; TV; 10% statics; Eng spkn; adv bkg acc; ccard acc; games rm; site clsd early Nov-mid Dec; games area; CKE. *"Excel site in attractive setting; NH area for m'vans; excel san facs; pool in vill; gd walks fr site; conv winter sports."* **€20.00**   2017

BRESSUIRE *4H1* (2.6km S Rural) *46.82923, -0.50223*
Camping Le Puy Rond, Allee du Puy Rond, Cornet, 79300 Bressuire **05 16 72 93 14 or 06 85 60 37 26 (mob); puyrondcamping@gmail.com; www.puyrond camping.com**

[icons]

Fr N149 foll site sp on rte 'Poids Lourds' to site on D38. Fr 'Centre Ville' foll sp for Fontenay-Le-Comte; turn R 100m after overhead bdge & go across junc to site. Well sp. 3*, Med, mkd, pt shd, pt sl, terr, EHU (6-10A) €5; bbq; red long stay; twin axles; 95% statics; Eng spkn; adv bkg acc; ccard acc; games rm; CKE. *"Gd touring base; friendly British owners; adv bkg ess for twin axles; winter storage avail; vg; poss rev pol."* **€21.00, 02 Mar-5 Nov.**   2020

BREST *2E2* (6.6km SW Coastal) *48.36544, -4.54163*
Camping du Goulet, Ste Anne-du-Porzic, 29200 Brest **02 98 45 86 84; campingdugoulet@wanadoo.fr; www.campingdugoulet.com**

[icons]

On D789 turn L at site sp. Approx 4km fr Brest after R bend at T junc, turn L & L again at site sp; down hill to site. 4*, Med, unshd, pt sl, terr, EHU (6-10A) €3-3.50; 15% statics; adv bkg acc; games area; games rm; waterslide; CKE. *"Excel site; great location; but to Centerville; P&R to city."* **€26.00**   2015

BRETENOUX *7C4* (0.2km N Urban) *44.91650, 1.83816*
Camping La Bourgnatelle, 46130 Bretenoux **05 65 10 89 04; contact@dordogne_vacances.fr; www.dordogne-vacances.fr**

[icons]

In town 100m fr D940. 4*, Lge, pt shd, EHU (5-10A) €3; adv bkg acc; canoe hire; rv; fishing. *"Lovely site along banks of Rv Cère; clean site; gd fishing; lovely town MD Tues."* **€25.00, 1 Apr-31 Oct.**   2019

BRETEUIL SUR L'ITON *4E2* (0.3km SSE Urban) *48.83175, 0.91258* **Camping Les Berges de l'Iton,** 53 rue du Fourneau, 27160 Breteuil-Iton **02 32 62 70 35 or 06 84 75 70 32 (mob); campinglesberges-de-liton@orange.fr; www.campinglesbergesde liton.com**

[icons]

Fr Evreux take D830 twd Conches-en-Ouche. L onto D840 to Breteuil, then foll sp for site. 3*, Med, hdg, mkd, hdstg, pt shd, pt sl, EHU (6A) inc; gas; bbq; 66% statics; adv bkg acc; INF; CCI. *"Well kept, landscaped site; gd NH; mkt on Wednesdays; helpful staff; vg."* **€23.70, 1 Apr-30 Sep.**   2019

BRETIGNOLLES SUR MER *2H3* (1km E Urban) *46.63583, -1.85861* **Camping La Trévillière,** Route de Bellevue, 85470 Bretignolles-sur-Mer **02 51 90 09 65 or 02 51 33 05 05; info@chadotel.com; La Trévillière**

[icons]

S along D38 fr St Gilles Croix-de-Vie twd Olonne-sur-Mer, site is sp to L in Bretignolles-sur-Mer. Site 1km fr town cent nr football stadium. Sp fr town cent. 4*, Lge, mkd, hdg, pt shd, serviced pitches; EHU (6A) inc; gas; bbq (gas); red long stay; TV; 70% statics; phone; Eng spkn; adv bkg acc; ccard acc; bike hire; waterslide; fishing; horseriding 5km; watersports 3km; games rm; CKE. *"Friendly, family site; lge pitches; no c'van/m'van over 8m high ssn; quiet; gd cycling area; salt marshes worth a visit; mkt Thu & Sun."* **€48.00, 5 Apr-20 Sep, A26.**   2018

BRETIGNOLLES SUR MER *2H3* (3.4km S Coastal) *46.603957, -1.840665* **Camping L'Ocean,** 17 ruc du Brandais, 85470 Brem-sur-Mer **02 51 90 59 16; contact@cybelevacances.com; www.campingde locean.fr**

[icons]

Fr La Roche-sur-Yon and Les Sables d'Olonne foll A87. Then D160. Take dir of Bretignolles-sur-Mer. 5*, Med, pt shd, bbq (gas); bus/train; adv bkg acc. *"Biggest indoor waterpark in Vendée; cycling rte fr site."* **NP 46, 6 Apr-3 Nov.**   2019

BRETIGNOLLES SUR MER *2H3* (4km S Coastal) *46.60413, -1.83231* **Camping Le Chaponnet,** 16 Rue du Chaponnet, 85470 Brem-sur-Mer **02 51 90 55 56; campingchaponnet@wanadoo.fr; www.le-chaponnet.com**

[icons]

Fr La Roche-sur-Yon on N160 dir Les Sables-d'Olonne. Turn R onto D87 thro St Mathurin vill & take 1st R (just after church) D38 dir L'Ile d'Olonne. Foll sp Brem-sur-Mer, go thro vill & foll sp 'Océan' (nr bakery & bar); turn L opp hairdresser, site in 50m along 1-way rd. 4*, Lge, hdg, pt shd, EHU (10A) inc; gas; bbq; TV; 75% statics; phone; adv bkg acc; ccard acc; gym; games area; sauna; bike hire; waterslide; games rm; jacuzzi; tennis; CKE. *"Gd beaches adj; vg."* **€34.00, 14 Apr-15 Sep, A05.**   2019

BRIANCON 9C4 (3.8km SW Rural) 44.87737, 6.61634
Camping Les Cinq Vallées, St Blaise, 05100
Briançon 04 92 21 06 27; infos@camping5vallees.
com; www.camping5vallees.com

♿♟♨♠⚓♻🚿/🛒MSP🌳♨️🍽️⑪🛖⚲▲🛶 (htd)

S of Briançon by N94 to vill St Blaise. Ent on L.
Med, pt shd, pt sl, EHU (10A) inc; TV; 80% statics;
games rm. "Vg site; traff noise barely noticeable; gd
shop on site with takeaway food; lge supmkt 2km."
€23.60, 1 Jun-30 Sep. 2015

BRIARE 4G3 (6km S Rural) 47.60018, 2.76101
Camping Municipal L'ecluse des Combles, Chemin
de Loire, 45360 Châtillon-sur-Loire 02 38 36 34 39
or 06 32 07 83 45; camping.chatillonsurloire@
orange.fr; www.camping.chatillon-sur-loire.com

🐕€1.20 ♟(htd) ♿♠⚓♻/🛒🦋🍽️nr ⑪nr 🛶nr ▲

SE fr Briare on N7, in 4km turn SW onto D50. Site
immed bef rv bdge on R. Care needed over bdge
after ent. 2*, Med, pt shd, terr, EHU (6A) inc; gas; bbq;
Eng spkn; fishing; games rm; CKE. "Basic site with
some nice pitches by Rv Loire & historic canal; pleasant
staff; right of way along rv bank passes thro site; mkt
2nd Thurs of month; vg; canal viaduct at Briare worth
visit; site neglected; pitch yourself; warden in off late
afternoon." €16.50, 1 Apr-31 Oct. 2017

BRIARE 4G3 (0.5km W Rural) 47.64137, 2.72560
Camping Le Martinet, Quai Tchékof, 45250 Briare
02 38 31 24 50 or 02 38 31 24 51; campingbriare@
recrea.fr; www.campinglemartinet.fr

🐕€1 ♟♿♠⚓♻/🦋🍽️nr ⑪nr 🛶nr

Exit N7 into Briare. Fr N immed R after canal bdge;
fr S L bef 2nd canal bdge; sp. 3*, Lge, mkd, unshd,
EHU (10A) €3.60; adv bkg acc; fishing adj. "Gd views
some pitches; pretty bars & rests along canal; gd
walking & cycling; interesting town; gates close 2200;
slightly neglected (2009); OK sh stay; san facs old style
but clean." €22.00, 30 Mar-30 Sep. 2018

BRIENNE LE CHATEAU 6E1 (6km S Rural) 48.34876,
4.52726 **Camping Le Tertre**, Route de Radonvilliers,
10500 Dienville 03 25 92 26 50; campingdutertre@
wanadoo.fr; www.campingdutertre.fr

🐕€1 ♟♿♠⚓♻/🛒MSP🦋♨️🍽️⑪🛖⚲▲🛶🚿(htd)🛶

On D443 S fr Brienne-le-Château; at Dienville turn
R at rndabt onto D11; site on R in 200m, sp. NB Site
opp Lake Amance harbour, foll sp 'Le Port'.
3*, Med, hdstg, hdg, mkd, pt shd, serviced pitches;
EHU (6-10A) €4 (poss long lead req); gas; bbq; TV;
10% statics; phone; bus 500m; Eng spkn; adv bkg acc;
ccard acc; games rm; fishing; games area; gym; CKE.
"Pleasant site 2 mins fr vill; man-made lake with sailing;
excel site for all watersports & other activities; cycle
tracks; vg; excel rest."
€25.00, 20 Mar-12 Oct. 2016

BRIGNOGAN PLAGES 1D2 (1km NW Coastal)
48.67278, -4.32916 **Camping de la Côte des
Légendes**, Keravezan, 29890 Brignogan-Plages
02 98 83 41 65; contact@campingcotedeslegendes.
com; www.campingcotedeslegendes.com

🐕€1.40 ♟♿♠⚓♻/🛒MSP🦋♨️🍽️⑪🛖⚲▲🛶🚿 sand adj

Fr Roscoff on D10, fr Brest on D788/770 or fr N12
exit dir Lesneven. In Brignogan foll sp Brignogan-
Plages & 'Centre Nautique'. 3*, Lge, hdg, hdstg, mkd,
pt shd, EHU (5-10A) €3.15-4.05 (poss rev pol); bbq; red
long stay; TV; 30% statics; phone; Eng spkn; adv bkg
acc; ccard acc; sailing; watersports; CKE. "On beautiful
sandy cove; friendly, helpful staff; site guarded 24 hrs;
ltd facs LS; vg touring base in interesting area; vg."
€20.00, 29 Mar-12 Nov. 2015

BRIGNOLES 10F3 (9km SE Rural) 43.33919, 6.12579
Camping La Vidaresse, 83136 Ste Anastasie-sur-Issole
04 94 72 21 75; info@campinglavidaresse.com;
www.campinglavidaresse.com

🐕€3 ♟♿♠⚓♻/🛒MSP🌳♨️🍽️⑪🛖⚲nr▲🛶🚿 (covrd, htd) 🛶

On DN7 2km W of Brignoles at rndabt take D43 dir
Toulon. In about 10km turn L at rndabt to D15. Do
not ent vill, go strt & site is approx 250m on R.
3*, Med, mkd, hdg, pt shd, terr, EHU (10A) €5 (poss
rev pol); gas; bbq (elec, gas); 40% statics; adv bkg acc;
ccard acc; tennis; fishing 200m; games area; CKE.
"Well-managed, family site in lovely area; peaceful;
friendly & helpful; facs adequate; excel pool; gd touring
base Haute Provence, Gorges du Verdon & Riviera;
vineyard adj; gd." €25.00, 20 Mar-30 Sep. 2019

BRILLANE, LA 10E3 (5km E Rural) 43.92282, 5.92369
Camping les Oliviers, Chemin St Sauveur, 04700
Oraison 04 92 78 20 00; camping-oraison@wanadoo.fr;
www.camping-oraison.fr

12 🐕€2.50 ♟♿♠⚓♻/🦋🍽️⑪🛖⚲▲🛶🚿

Exit A51 junc 19; take rd E to Oraison in 2km; site
sp in vill. 4*, Med, mkd, pt shd, pt sl, terr, EHU (16A)
€4.50; gas; TV; 10% statics; Eng spkn; adv bkg acc;
ccard acc; games area; bike hire; games rm; CKE.
"Pleasant, family-run site among olive trees; friendly,
helpful owners; walks fr site; conv Verdon gorge; adj
elec sub-stn, elec cables run over small pt of site, not
obtrusive; gd." €25.50 2015

BRILLANE, LA 10E3 (2.6km W Rural) 43.93305, 5.86777
Camping Le Moulin de Ventre, 04300 Niozelles
04 92 78 63 31 or 06 63 51 53 55 (mob); moulinde
ventre@gmail.com; www.moulin-de-ventre.com

🐕€3 ♟(htd) ♿♠⚓♻/🛒MSP🦋♨️🍽️⑪🛖⚲▲🛶🚿🛶

Exit A51 junc 19 at La Brillane; turn R onto D4096, then
L onto D4100 sp Niozelles & Forcalquier. Site in 3km
on L just after bdge, adj Rv Lauzon. 4*, Med, mkd, hdg,
pt shd, pt sl, serviced pitches; EHU (10A) inc; gas; bbq
(gas); twin axles; red long stay; TV; 10% statics; phone;
Eng spkn; adv bkg acc; ccard acc; rv fishing adj; games rm;
CKE. "Pleasant, peaceful, wooded site by lake & rv; rvside
pitches have drop to rv; excel touring base; boat hire adj;
lavendar fields in flower Jun/Jul; site neglected; poor san
facs." €38.50, 9 Apr-30 Sep. 2016

BRIONNE *3D2* (0.5km N Urban) *49.20256, 0.71554*
Camp Municipal La Vallée, Rue Marcel Nogrette,
27800 Brionne **02 32 44 80 35; www.ville-brionne.fr**

🐕 ♿ wc ⚓ 🚿 ⊿ ♨ MSP 🦋 ⊕ nr 🐟 nr ⚠

Fr D438 N or S on by-pass, turn N at D46 junc,
pass Carrefour supmkt on L & take 1st R, site on L.
2*, Sm, hdg, pt shd, EHU (8A) €3.45; gas; bbq; CKE.
*"Excel, well maintained site in lovely vill; gd san facs;
poss ltd LS; sh walk to supmkt; clean facs but ltd."*
€15.00, 30 Apr-30 Sep. 2019

"There aren't many sites open at this time of year"

If you're travelling outside peak season
remember to call ahead to check site opening
dates – even if the entry says 'open all year'.

BRIONNE *3D2* (6km N Rural) *49.24174, 0.70339*
Camp Municipal Les Marronniers, Rue Louise
Givon, 27290 Pont-Authou **02 32 42 75 06 or 06 27
25 21 45 (mob); lesmarronniers27@orange.fr or
campingmunicipaldesmarronniers@orange.fr;
www.normandie-accueil.fr**

12 🐕 €1.35 ♿ (htd) wc ⚓ 🚿 ⊿ ♨ 🦋 ⊕ nr 🐟 nr ⚠

Heading S on D438 take D130 just bef Brionne sp
Pont-Audemer (care req at bdge & rndabts). Site on
L in approx 5km, well sp on o'skts of Pont-Authou;
foll sp in vill. 2*, Med, mkd, hdstg, pt shd, EHU (10A)
€3.40 (poss rev pol); bbq; 50% statics; adv bkg acc;
fishing; bike hire; CKE. *"Useful, clean stop nr Rouen
& m'way; friendly recep; clean san facs; best pitches
far side of lake; few hdstg; adv bkg rec; some statics
unsightly; stream runs thro site; beautiful valley with
many historic towns & vills; excel walking; gd NH;
pretty but basic site; recep & security gate cls 1800 in
LS."* **€13.00** 2018

BRIONNE *3D2* (9km N Rural) *49.23648, 0.72265*
FFCC Camping Saint Nicolas (formerly Municipal),
15 Rue St Nicolas, 27800 Le Bec-Hellouin **02 32 44
83 55 or 06 84 75 70 32 (Mob); campingstnicolas@
orange.fr; www.campingsaintnicolas.fr**

🐕 €1.50 ♿ (htd) wc ⚓ 🚿 ⊿ ♨ MSP 🦋 ⊕ nr ⚠
🛝 (htd, indoor)

Exit A28 junc 13 onto D438 then take D581
to Malleville-sur-le-Bec; site on R 1km after
Malleville. Well sp. 4*, Med, pt shd, EHU (10A)
€3.50; bbq; 10% statics; tennis nr; horseriding nr;
CKE. *"Attractive, peaceful, well-kept site in pleasant
location; spacious pitches; friendly, helpful warden;
vg, clean san facs; gate clsd 2200-0700; gd dog walks;
vg cycling; attractive countryside; conv NH nr Calais;
rec; delightful vill; rec dir in book; vist to Abbey at Bec
Hellouin a must."* **€26.20, 27 Mar-11 Oct.** 2019

BRISSAC QUINCE *4G1* (2km NE Rural) *47.35944,
-0.43388* **Le Domaine de L'Etang,** Route de St
Mathurin, 49320 Brissac-Quincé **02 41 91 70 61;
info@campingetang.com; www.campingetang.com**

🐕 €2.10-9.10 ♿ (htd) wc ⚓ 🚿 ♿ ⊿ ♨ MSP 🦋 ⊕ 🍽 ⊗ ⊕ ⚓ 🛒
⚠ 🏊 (covrd, htd) 🛶

Fr N on A11, exit junc 14 onto N260 passing E of
Angers, following sp for Cholet/Poitiers. After x-ing
Rv Loire, foll sp to Brissac-Quincé on D748. Foll sp
for St Mathurin/Domaine de l'Etang on D55 to site.
4*, Med, hdstg, mkd, hdg, pt shd, serviced pitches;
EHU (10A) inc; gas; bbq (charcoal, gas); red long stay;
twin axles; TV; Eng spkn; adv bkg acc; ccard acc; bike
hire; waterslide; games rm; lake fishing; golf 8km;
CKE. *"Excel, well-cared for site amongst vineyards; lge
pitches; staff pleasant & helpful; clean, modern facs;
leisure facs gd for children; pleasant 15 min rvside walk
to Brissac-Quincé; wine tasting; gd touring base Loire
valley; mkt Thu; rec Apocalypse Tapestry at Chateau
d'Angers; gd for walks & sightseeing; extensive site."*
€36.00, 21 Apr-16 Sep, L15. 2019

BRISSAC QUINCE *4G1* (4km S Rural) *47.33317,
-0.43664* **Camping à la Ferme Domaine de la Belle
Etoile,** La Belle Etoile, 49320 Brissac-Quincé **06 62 32
99 40 (mob); vincent_esnou74@hotmail.com;
www.domaine-belle-etoile.fr**

♿ wc ⚓ 🚿 ⊿ ♨ 🦋 ⚠

Take D748 S fr Angers dir Poitiers. At D761 rndabt
cont on D748 sp N-D-d'Allençon. Site sp at 2nd
turn on L in 500m. Sm, pt shd, EHU (5A) €3; bbq; Eng
spkn. *"Excel CL-type site in vineyard with wine-tasting
& farm produce; clean, modern facs; troglodyte caves,
mushroom farms & château nrby; v friendly owners."*
€10.50, 1 Apr-1 Nov. 2015

"That's changed – Should I let the Club know?"

If you find something on site that's different
from the site entry, fill in a report and let us
know. See camc.com/europereport

BRIVE LA GAILLARDE *7C3* (19km SW Rural)
45.06942, 1.43060 **Camping La Magaudie,**
La Magaudie Ouest, 19600 Chartrier-Ferrière
**05 55 85 26 06 or 06 85 22 54 78; camping@
lamagaudie.com; www.lamagaudie.com**

🐕 €1.25 ♿ (htd) wc ⚓ 🚿 ⊿ ♨ 🦋 🍽 ⊗ ⊕ 🐟 nr ⚠ 🏊

Exit A20 junc 53 onto D920/D19 dir Chasteaux.
After rlwy bdge take 2nd L to Chartrier & foll blue
sps to site. NB Diff app climbing up narr lane with
no passing spaces for 1km. 1*, Sm, mkd, pt shd, sl,
EHU (10A) €3.50; bbq (gas); sw nr; 5% statics; Eng
spkn; adv bkg acc; CKE. *"Helpful Dutch owners; vg site
& facs but v ltd LS; rec arr early high ssn; excel; superb
rest; tranquil & relaxing."*
€23.00, 15 Apr-15 Apr. 2016

BROMMAT *7D4* (0.3km E Rural) *44.83083, 2.68638*
Camping Municipale, Le Bourg, 12600 Brommat
05 65 66 00 96; mairie-de.brommat@wanadoo.fr;
www.brommat.fr

Fr D98, cross rv bdge, cont uphill to Mairie. Turn R in front of Mairie and cont strt on. Campsite on R. Sm, hdg, pt shd, EHU (6A); sw nr; TV; bus 50m; adv bkg acc; tennis 2km; fishing; CCI. *"Beautiful adj walk; vg."* €13.00, 15 May-15 Sep. 2019

BROUSSES ET VILLARET *8F4* (0.5km S Rural) *43.33932, 2.25201* **Camping Le Martinet Rouge,** 11390 Brousses-et-Villaret 04 68 26 51 98 or 06 91 34 41 60 (mob); camping.lemartinetrouge@ orange.fr; www.camping-martinet.co.uk

Fr D118 Mazamet-Carcassonne, turn R 3km after Cuxac-Carbades onto D103; turn L in Brousses & foll sp. 3*, Med, hdg, pt shd, pt sl, EHU (6-10A); TV; 20% statics; phone; bus; Eng spkn; adv bkg acc; horseriding; waterslide; trout fishing; games area; canoeing; CKE. *"Helpful owners, great for walking or mountain biking; cather castles, abbeys & churchs, Canal du Midi; forest, lakes, rv & caverns; excel site."* €25.00, 9 Apr-19 Oct. 2019

BUGUE, LE *7C3* (1km SE Urban) *44.90980, 0.93160* **FFCC Camping Les Trois Caupain,** Le Port, 24260 Le Bugue Dordogne 05 53 07 24 60 or 06 85 48 44 25 (mob); info@camping-bugue. com; www.camping-des-trois-caupain.com

Exit Le Bugue town cent on D703 twd Campagne. Turn R at sp after 400m to site in 600m on rvside. 3*, Med, mkd, pt shd, EHU (6-16A) €4-4.30 (rev pol); gas; 25% statics; adv bkg acc. *"Beautiful, lovely, well run site; pleasant, helpful owners; cycle along rv to pretty town; excel; new pool; mkt in Le Bugue well worth a visit; rv adj; games area adj; ideal cent for touring the Dordogne region; lots of attractions; gd rest."* €21.00, 1 Apr-30 Oct. 2017

BUGUE, LE *7C3* (3km SE Rural) *44.90663, 0.97412* **Camping Le Val de la Marquise,** Le Petit Moulin, 24260 Campagne 05 53 54 74 10; contact@ levaldelamarquise.com; www.camping-dordogne-marquise.com

Fr D703 bet Le Bugue & Les Eyzies take D35 at Campagne dir St Cyprien, site sp. 4*, Med, mkd, pt shd, terr, EHU (10-15A); bbq; 5% statics; phone; Eng spkn; adv bkg acc; lake fishing; games area; CKE. *"Peaceful, attractive site; poss diff access to pitches for lge c'vans due narr site rds & low terrs; clean san facs; beautiful pool; Michelin starred rest nrby; brilliant site; great loc; excel fam facs; warm welcome fr new owner; pleasant town, great mkt; high rec."* €30.00, 28 Apr-30 Sep. 2018

BUGUE, LE *7C3* (6km SW Rural) *44.87990, 0.88576* **Camping du Port de Limeuil,** 24480 Alles-sur-Dordogne 05 53 63 29 76; didierbonvallet@aol.com; www.leportdelimeuil.com

Exit Le Bugue on D31 sp Le Buisson; in 4km turn R on D51 sp Limeuil; at 2km turn L over rv bdge; site on R after bdge. 3*, Med, hdg, mkd, pt shd, pt sl, serviced pitches; EHU (5A) €3.50; gas; bbq; 40% statics; Eng spkn; adv bkg acc; bike hire; canoe hire; games rm; CKE. *"Superb location & site for all ages; rv adj; lge pitches; clean san facs, ltd LS; tour ops."* €32.00, 26 Apr-23 Sep, A16. 2019

BUGUE, LE *7C3* (9km NW Rural) *44.95130, 0.85070* **Camping St Avit Loisirs,** 24260 St Avit-de-Vialard 05 53 02 64 00; contact@saint-avit-loisirs.com; www.saint-avit-loisirs.com or www.les-castels.com

Leave N89/E70 SE of Périgueux & turn S onto D710 for approx 32km; about 3km N of Le Bugue turn R sp St Avit-de-Vialard. Turn R in vill & cont for approx 1.5km, site on R. NB Narr, twisting app rd. 5*, Lge, hdg, pt shd, pt sl, EHU (6A) inc; gas; bbq; TV; adv bkg acc; ccard acc; games area; golf nr; bike hire; games rm; waterslide; horseriding nr; tennis; watersports nr; CKE. *"Excel, well-kept, well-run, busy site; gd sized pitches; friendly welcome; no o'fits over 7m; gd, clean san facs; archery nrby; gd touring base; conv for Lascaux; many static tents; amazing array of watersport facs."* €49.00, 26 Mar-24 Sep, D10. 2016

BUIS LES BARONNIES *9D2* (0.6km N Urban) *44.27558, 5.27830* **Camp Municipal,** Quartier du Jalinier, 26170 Buis-les-Baronnies 04 75 28 04 96 or 06 60 80 40 53 (mob)

Fr Vaison-la-Romaine S on D938; turn L onto D54/ D13/D5 to Buis-les-Baronnies; cont N onto D546; at bend turn R over rv bdge; turn L along rv, then 1st R. Site split into 2 either side of sw pool; recep in upper site. Med, hdg, mkd, pt shd, pt sl, EHU (6A) €3; 5% statics; phone; bus 300m; CKE. *"Lovely views; san facs dated but clean; not suitable lge o'fits but lger, more accessible pitches on lower level; attractive town; gd mkt Wed & Sat; fair; warden in off 1900-2000 only."* €11.50, 1 Mar-11 Nov. 2015

BUIS LES BARONNIES *9D2* (5km SW Rural) *44.25190, 5.24370* **Camping La Gautière,** La Penne-sur-l'Ouvèze, 26170 Buis-les-Baronnies **04 75 28 02 68; accueil@camping-lagautiere.com; www.camping-lagautiere.com**

🏕 €2.50 ♦♦ (htd) ♨ ▣ 🍴 🏊

On D5 Vaison-la-Romaine to Buis-les-Baronnies rd, on L. 3*, Sm, mkd, pt shd, EHU (3-10A) €3-4.60; gas; bbq; 5% statics; phone; bus adj; Eng spkn; adv bkg acc; ccard acc; games rm; fishing nr; horseriding nr; games area; CKE. "Beautiful situation; haphazard pitch size; diff for o'fits over 6m; climbing at Rocher St Julien & Gorges d'Ubrieux; helpful owners; ACSI acc; excel cycling." €24.50, 26 Mar-31 Oct. **2016**

> ## "We must tell the Club about that great site we found"
>
> Get your site reports in by mid-August and we'll do our best to get your updates into the next edition.

BURTONCOURT *5D2* (1km W Rural) *49.22485, 6.39929* **FFCC Camping La Croix du Bois Sacker,** 57220 Burtoncourt **03 87 35 74 08; camping.croixsacker@wanadoo.fr; www.campingcroixsacker.com**

🏕 €1.70 ♦♦ ♨ ⚏ 🍴 ⓗ nr 🏊 ⚎ ✎

Exit A4 junc 37 sp Argancy; at rndabt foll sp Malroy; at 2nd rndabt foll sp Chieuilles & cont to Vany; then take D3 for 12km dir Bouzonville; turn R onto D53A to Burtoncourt. 2*, Lge, hdstg, mkd, hdg, pt shd, terr, EHU (6A) inc; gas; TV; 10% statics; phone; bus 300m; Eng spkn; adv bkg acc; fishing; tennis; games area; CKE. "Lovely, wooded site in beautiful location; lge pitches; pleasant, friendly owners; clean san facs; forest walks; gd security; gd NH or sh stay en rte Alsace/Germany; conv Maginot Line; excel; Hachenberg Ouvrage tour highly rec (30km)." €20.00, 1 Apr-20 Oct. **2016**

BUXIERES-SOUS-MONTAIGUT *7A4* (3.8km SW Rural) *46.19271, 2.81994* **Camping Les Suchères,** Les Sucheres, 63700 Buxierères-sous-Montaigut **33 04 73 85 92 66; sucheres@gmail.com; www.campinglessucheres.com**

🏕 €1.50 ♦♦ ⚏ ♨ 🍴 ⓗ 🏊

Head SE on D92, cont on Buxières. Take Les Gouttes to Les Sucheres; 1st R onto Buxières; cont onto Les Gouttes after 7m turn R twd Les Sucheres, L twd Les Sucheres, 1st R onto Les Sucheres, turn L to stay on Les Sucheres, take the 1st L to stay on Les Sucheres; site on R. Sm, pt sl, EHU (6A) €3; bbq; TV; Eng spkn; CCI. "Helpful Dutch owners; lovely peaceful site; gd walking area; Montaigut within walking dist; shop; access to the site could be diff for lge o'fits as rd narr for last km; quiet." €27.80, 1 Apr-30 Sep. **2019**

BUZANCAIS *4H2* (0.5km N Urban) *46.89309, 1.41801* **Camp Municipal La Tête Noire,** Allée des Sports, 36500 Buzançais **06 59 88 78 32; buzancais@wanadoo.fr**

🏕 €1.50 ♦♦ ⚏ 🍴 🌐 🍴 nr ⓗ nr 🏊 nr ⚎ ✎

D943 fr Châteauroux thro town cent, cross rv, immed turn R into sports complex. 3*, Lge, hdstg, pt shd, EHU (16A) inc; red long stay; 10% statics; adv bkg acc; CKE. "Pleasant, peaceful, well-kept site on rv; clean facs; no access when office clsd but ample parking; no twin axles; pool 500m; gd fishing." €16.00, 15 Apr-15 Oct. **2019**

BUZANCY *5C1* (1.5km SW Rural) *49.42647, 4.93891* **Camping La Samaritaine,** 08240 **03 24 30 08 88; contact@camping-lasamaritaine.fr; www.camping-lasamaritaine.fr**

🏕 €2.20 ♦♦ ⚏ ♨ ♿ ▣ 🍴 🌐 🍴 ⓗ nr ⚎ 🏊 ⚎

Fr Sedan take D977 dir Vouziers for 23km. Turn L onto D12, cont to end & turn L onto D947 for Buzancy. On ent Buzancy in 100m turn 2nd R immed after g'ge on R sp Camping Stade. Foll sp to site on L past football pitches. 3*, Med, hdstg, mkd, hdg, pt shd, serviced pitches; EHU (10A) inc; bbq (charcoal, gas); sw nr; TV; 10% statics; phone; Eng spkn; adv bkg acc; tennis; games rm; horseriding nr; fishing; CKE. "Beautiful area for walking/cycling; library; helpful, pleasant staff; excel facs; ltd LS." €21.00, 19 Apr-13 Sep, L30. **2019**

CABANNES, LES *8G3* (2km SE Rural) *42.77444, 1.70328* **Camp Municipal La Coume,** 09310 Albiès **05 61 64 98 99; camping.albies@wanadoo.fr; www.pyrenees-ariegeoises.com/dormir/campings**

12 🏕 Free ♦♦ (htrl) ⚏ ♨ ♿ ▣ 🍴 🌐 ⓗ nr 🏊 nr

Site sp fr N20 in vill. 2*, Med, hdg, pt shd, pt sl, terr, EHU (5-10A) inc; bbq; 10% statics; fishing; games area. "Gd san facs; Rv Ariège 100m; not suitable for lge o'fits." €15.00 **2019**

CABOURG *3D1* (6km W Coastal) *49.28319, -0.19098* **Camping Le Point du Jour,** Route de Cabourg, 14810 Merville-Franceville-Plage **02 31 24 23 34; contact@camping-lepointdujour.com; www.camping-lepointdujour.com**

🏕 €3 ♦♦ (htd) ⚏ ♨ ♿ ▣ 🍴 🌐 🍴 🌐 ⓗ ⚎ 🏊 ⚎ ✎ 🏊 (covrd, htd) ☂ sand adj

Fr Ouistreham on D514 turn E at Bénouville onto D224, cross bdge onto D514, site on L dir Cabourg, 8km beyond Pegasus Bdge at far end of Merville. Or fr A13/D675 exit Dozulé dir Cabourg, then D514 to site. 4*, Med, hdg, pt shd, EHU (10A) inc; gas; bbq; red long stay; TV; 40% statics; bus; adv bkg acc; ccard acc; games rm; CKE. "Site with sea views; direct access to Sword Beach (D-Day) & sand dunes; conv Pegasus Bdge; some pitches might be diff for lge o'fits; open till 2300 for late ferry arr, v obliging; ent & exit diff; sm-med pitches, many sl; facs tired." €37.00, 30 Mar-4 Nov, N03. **2019**

CABOURG *3D1* (6km W Coastal) *49.28296, -0.19072*
Camping Village Ariane, 100 Route de Cabourg,
14810 Merville-Franceville-Plage **02 31 24 52 52;**
info@loisirs-ariane.com; www.camping-ariane.com

🐕€3 �(htd) wc ▲ ᬓ ♿ ⬛ ✎ ✿ ⑨ ⓣ ᕫ ⬛ nr ⛺ ✎
⚓ sand 300m

Fr Ouistreham on D514 turn E at Bénouville onto
D224, cross bdge onto D514 to site dir Cabourg. Or
fr A13/D675 exit Dozulé dir Cabourg, then D514 to
site. 3*, Lge, mkd, pt shd, EHU (6-10A) €4; gas; red
long stay; TV; 10% statics; Eng spkn; adv bkg acc;
games area; tennis nr; games rm; watersports nr; CKE.
€12.00, 1 Apr-5 Nov.   2018

CABRERETS *7D3* (1km NE Rural) *44.50771, 1.66234*
Camping Cantal, 46330 Cabrerets **05 65 31 26 61**

♯♯ wc ✎ ✿

Fr Cahors take D653 E for approx 15km bef turning
R onto D662 E thro Vers & St Géry. Turn L onto D41
to Cabrerets. Site 1km after vill on R.
2*, Sm, pt shd, pt sl, serviced pitches; EHU €2.50;
rv canoeing nr; CKE. *"Superb situation; v interesting
vill; peaceful site; warden calls; grnd slightly bumpy;
excel san facs; not suitable lge o'fits; conv Pech
Merle; gd cycling rte; quiet; friendly; overhanging
trees, care when pitching; unisex san facs; vg."*
€12.00, 1 Apr-15 Oct.   2017

CADENET *10E3* (5km N Rural) *43.767986, 5.372672*
Les Hautes Prairies, 28 route de Vaugines 84160,
Lourmarin **04 90 68 02 89; leshautesprairies@**
campasun.eu; www.campasun-lourmarin.eu

🐕€5 wc ▲ ᬓ ✿ ⑨ ⓣ ᕫ ⬛ nr ⛺ ✎

Fr D973 take exit to Cadenet. Fork L (eastbnd)
at rd junc twrds Lourmarin. In Lourmarin turn R
at 2nd rndabt. Site on R in 0.5km. 3*, Med, hdstg,
mkd, hdg, pt shd, pt sl, EHU (10A) inc; bbq (sep area);
twin axles; bus adj; Eng spkn; adv bkg acc; ccard
acc; jacuzzi; sm shop in recep; games area; CKE. *"Gd
gateway for Luberon area; lovely spacious site; v clean,
well maintained facs (new 2016); v helpful staff; gd
security (barrier); excel & enjoyable experience; excel."*
€45.00, 6 Apr-29 Sep.   2019

CADENET *10E3* (10km NE Rural) *43.76871,*
5.44970 **Camping Lou Badareu,** La Rasparine,
84160 Cucuron **04 90 77 21 46; contact@**
loubadareu.com; www.loubadareu.com

🐕€1.80 ♯♯ wc ▲ ᬓ ⬛ ✎ ᕫ ✿ ⛺ ✎

In Cadenet foll sp for church (église) onto D45 dir
Cucuron; S of Cucuron turn onto D27 (do not go
into town); site is E 1km. Well sp fr D27. 2*, Sm, mkd,
pt shd, pt sl, EHU (10A) €4.50 (long lead poss req);
own san rec; 10% statics; phone; CKE. *"Pretty farm
site in cherry orchard, vineyard and olive grove adj;
basic but adequate san facs; natural spring-fed pool;
friendly, helpful owner; sep access for high vans; lge
shd camping field."* **€16.70, 1 Apr-15 Oct.**   2017

CAEN *3D1* (20km N Coastal) *49.32551, -0.39010*
Sandaya La Côte de Nacre, 17 Rue du Général
Moulton, 14750 St Aubin-sur-Mer **02 31 97 14 45;**
cdn@sandaya.fr; www.sandaya.fr/cdn

🐕€5 ♯(htd) wc ▲ ᬓ ♿ ⬛ ✎ msp ✿ ⑨ ⓣ ⓣ ᕫ ⬛ ⛺ ✎
⬛(covrd, htd) ☵ ⚓ sand 500m

Fr Caen on D7 dir Douvres-la-Délivrande, Langrune-
sur-Mer & St Aubin. Site in St Aubin-sur-Mer on S
side of D514; clearly sp on o'skts. 5*, Lge, hdstg,
mkd, hdg, pt shd, EHU (10A); bbq (charcoal); TV;
70% statics; phone; Eng spkn; adv bkg rec; ccard
acc; sauna; waterslide; bike hire; games rm; tennis
200m; CKE. *"Ideal for families; lge pitches; conv Caen
ferry, Normandy beaches, WW2 sites; helpful staff;
excel modern san facs; poss waterlogging; gd cycle
tracks along sea front LS; easy walk into quiet vill;
vg; payment on arr, no refund for early dep; vg site."*
€25.50, 3 Apr-20 Sep, N11.   2019

CAGNES SUR MER *10E4* (4km N Rural) *43.68717,*
7.15589 **Camping Le Val Fleuri,** 139 Vallon-des-
Vaux, 06800 Cagnes-sur-Mer **04 93 31 21 74;**
valfleur2@wanadoo.fr; www.campingvalfleuri.fr

🐕€1.50 ♯♯ ▲ ✎ ⑨ ⓗ ᕫ ⬛ nr ⛺ ✎ ☵(htd) ⚓ shgl 4km

Fr Nice take D6007 W twd Cannes. On app Cagnes
turn R & foll sp Camping; site on R after 3km, well
sp. NB 3.3m height restriction on this rte.
3*, Sm, pt shd, terr, EHU (3-10A); Eng spkn; adv bkg
acc. *"Gd, clean, improving site, efficient NH; divided
by rd (not busy); some sm pitches; helpful, friendly
owners; bus to Nice; dated facs (2014); diff access lge
o'fits; no offsite parking."* **€31.00, 6 Apr-28 Sep.** 2019

CAGNES SUR MER *10E4* (5km S Coastal) *43.63128,*
7.12993 **Camping Parc des Maurettes,** 730 Ave du
Docteur Lefebvre, 06270 Villeneuve-Loubet
04 93 20 91 91; info@parcdesmaurettes.com;
www.parcdesmaurettes.com

🐕€4 ♯(htd) wc ▲ ᬓ ♿ ⬛ ✎ msp ✿ ⑨ ⓣ nr ⓗ ᕫ ⬛ ⛺
☵(htd, indoor) ⚓ shgl 1km

Fr Nice exit A8 junc 47, turn L onto D6007 dir
Antibes; foll sp Intermarché, then R into Rue des
Maurettes; site in 250m. N fr Cannes on A8 exit
Villeneuve-Loubet-Plage junc 46; foll D241 over
D6007 & rwly line, U-turn back over rwly line, then
R onto D6007 dir Antibes as above. NB Site on steep
cliff with narr winding rds packed with trees; diff
ent. 3*, Med, mkd, pt shd, terr, serviced pitches; EHU
(3-10A) €5.30; gas; bbq (charcoal, sep area); twin
axles; red long stay; TV (pitch); train Nice 400m; Eng
spkn; adv bkg rec; ccard acc; jacuzzi; CKE. *"Well-kept
site; variable pitch size/price; excel base for Nice,
Cannes, Antibes & Monaco; trains & bus fare gd value."*
€35.80, 10 Jan-15 Nov.   2019

CAGNES SUR MER *10E4 (7km S Rural) 43.62027, 7.12583* **Camping La Vieille Ferme,** 296 Blvd des Groules, 06270 Villeneuve-Loubet-Plage **04 93 33 41 44; info@vieilleferme.com; www.vieilleferme.com**

🏕12 🚗 €2.50 � (htd) 🅆 ⚓ ♿ 🖭 ⚙ 🍽 🏪 nr ⛺ 🏊 (covrd, htd) 🎣 ⛵ shgl 1km

Fr W (Cannes) take Antibes exit 44 fr A8, foll D35 dir Antibes 'Centre Ville'. At lge junc turn onto D6007, Ave de Nice, twd Biot & Villeneuve-Loubet sp Nice (rlwy line on R). Just after Marineland turn L onto Blvd des Groules. Fr E (Nice) leave A8 at junc 47 to join D6007 twd Antibes, take 3rd turning after Intermarché supmkt; site well sp fr D6007. 4*, Med, mkd, hdg, pt shd, pt sl, terr, serviced pitches; EHU (2A-10A) €3 - €7; gas; bbq (elec, gas); red long stay; TV; 40% statics; bus, train nr; Eng spkn; adv bkg acc; ccard acc; games rm. *"Peaceful, well-kept family-run site; well-drained pitches, some lge; san facs need refurb (2010); beach not suitable children & non-swimmers; no o'fits over 8m; excel pool; gd walking, cycling & dog walking as lge park adj; some aircraft & rd noise; vg value LS; excel; be wary of bike thieves; nice bar/rest; friendly staff; v quiet at night; bus & train nrby."* **€41.00, C22.** **2018**

CAGNES SUR MER *10E4 (1km NW Urban) 43.67159, 7.13845* **Camping Le Colombier,** 35 Chemin de Ste Colombe, 06800 Cagnes-sur-Mer **04 93 73 12 77; campinglecolombier06@gmail.com; www.camping lecolombier.com**

🏕 €2.50 ♣ (htd) 🅆 ⚓ ♫ 🖭 🦋 🛈 nr 🎣 🏪 nr ⛺ ⛵ 2.5km

N fr Cagnes cent foll 1-way system dir Vence. Half way up hill turn R at rndabt dir Cagnes-sur-Mer & R at next island. Site on L 300m, sp fr town cent. 3*, Sm, hdg, mkd, pt shd, EHU (2-16A) (poss rev pol) €2-8; red long stay; TV; 10% statics; phone; Eng spkn; bike hire; CKE. *"Friendly, family-run site; dogs not acc Jul/Aug; sm pool adj."* **€30.00, 1 Apr-1 Oct.** **2019**

CAGNES SUR MER *10E4 (4km NW Rural) 43.68272, 7.08391* **Camping Les Pinèdes,** Route de Pont de Pierre, 06480 La Colle-sur-Loup **04 93 32 98 94; info@lespinedes.com; www.lespinedes.com**

🏕 €3.60 ♣ 🅆 ⚓ ♫ 🦋 🍽 🛈 🎣 🏪 ⛺ ✎ 🏊 (htd) 🎣

Exit A8 junc 47; take D6007 dir Nice, then D2 sp Villeneuve-Loubet; turn R at rndabt sp Villeneuve-Loubet & cross rv bdge; go thro sh tunnel, other side is Cagnes-sur-Mer & rndabt; turn L onto D6 to Colle-sur-Loup; site on R sh dist after Colle-sur-Loup. NB Take 2nd turning into site (1st leads to rest). 4*, Lge, hdstg, mkd, hdg, pt shd, pt sl, terr, serviced pitches; EHU (6-10A) €4.60-5.90 (poss rev pol); bbq (elec, gas); sw nr; red long stay; TV; 20% statics; Eng spkn; adv bkg acc; ccard acc; rv fishing adj; games rm; archery; tennis adj; horseriding adj; games area; solarium; CKE. *"Excel, family-run site set in pine & oak trees; no c'vans over 6m (excluding towbar) & m'vans over 8m high ssn; helpful & friendly; spacious pitches; steep access to pitches - poss diff lge o'fits, help avail; adequate san facs; gd rest at site ent; highly rec; vg site has everything you need; spacious pitches; excel pool."* **€43.00, 1 Apr-30 Sep, C30.** **2019**

CAHORS *7D3 (2km N Urban) 44.46318, 1.44226* **Camping Rivière de Cabessut,** Rue de la Rivière, 46000 Cahors **05 65 30 06 30; contact@cabessut.com; www.cabessut.com**

🏕 €2 🅆 ⚓ ♿ 🖭 ♫ 🖭 🦋 🍽 🏪 ⛺ 🏊

Fr N or S on D820, at S end Cahors by-pass take L onto D620 sp Rodez. At traff lts by bdge do not cross rv but bear R on D911. In 1km at site sp turn L. Site on E bank of Rv Lot, well sp fr town. Site at end of long lane. 1.8km to site fr bdge (Pont Cabessut). (NB: Fr N if leaving A20 at J57 - Do not foll Sat Nav.) 3*, Med, hdg, mkd, pt shd, serviced pitches; EHU (10A) inc (poss rev pol); gas; bbq (gas); phone; bus to Cahors 600m; adv bkg req; CKE. *"Lovely, well-run site by rv; beautiful area; pleasant, mostly lge pitches, sm pitches diff access when site full; gd for children; walk to town by rv 1.8km; food mkt Wed, full mkt Sat; hypmkt 1.5km; excel san facs; well maintained site, helpful, commited owners; rv adj; great site with lge sunny or shd pitches; pre-ordered bread delivered daily; lge o'fits turned away if grnd is damp; adv bkg req Jul/Aug; free shuttle bus to Cahors 600m at park & ride."* **€26.00, 1 Apr-30 Sep.** **2019**

CAHORS *7D3 (8km N Rural) 44.52585, 1.46048* **Camping Les Graves,** 46090 St Pierre-Lafeuille **05 65 36 83 12; infos@camping-lesgraves.com; www.camping-lesgraves.com**

🏕 €1.50 ♣ 🅆 ⚓ ♫ 🖭 🍽 🛈 🎣 ⛺ 🏊

Leave A20 at junc 57 Cahors Nord onto D820. Foll sp St Pierre-Lafeuille; at N end of vill, site is opp L'Atrium wine cave. 3*, Med, hdg, pt shd, sl, EHU (6-10A) €2.50-3.50 (poss rev pol); 5% statics; Eng spkn; adv bkg rec; ccard acc; bike hire; CKE. *"Scenic site; lge pitches; poss clsd during/after wet weather due boggy grnd; disabled facs over stony rd & grass; ltd facs LS; conv A20; nice, quiet, clean site."* **€20.00, 1 Apr-31 Oct.** **2018**

CAHORS *7D3 (8km N Rural) 44.53136, 1.45926* **Camping Quercy-Vacances,** Mas de la Combe, 46090 St Pierre-Lafeuille **05 65 36 87 15; quercyvacances@ wanadoo.fr; www.quercy-vacances.com**

🏕 €1.50 ♣ 🅆 ⚓ ♫ 🖭 🦋 🍽 🛈 🎣 🏪 ⛺ ✎ 🏊 🎣

Heading N on D820, turn L at N end of St Pierre-Lafeuille turn W at site sp N of vill, site in 700m down lane. Site sp fr main rd. Fr A20 exit junc 57 & foll sp N20. 4*, Med, mkd, pt shd, pt sl, EHU (10A) €3.30-5.30; gas; twin axles; TV; 50% statics; phone; Eng spkn; adv bkg acc; ccard acc; games area; CKE. *"Pretty site; most pitches slightly sl; clean, modern san facs; poss unkempt LS; helpful owner; vg; tennis & horse riding nrby; gd for Cahors & Lot Valley."* **€23.00, 1 Apr-30 Sep.** **2017**

FRANCE

CAJARC *7D4* (6.4km NE Rural) *44.50612, 1.89667*
Camping Les Cournoulises, 46160 Montbrun
06 15 53 00 58 (mob); lescournoulises@sfr.fr;
http://lescournoulises.perso.sfr.fr

🐕 €0.50 ⚕ 🅆🅒 ♿ 🍽 🦋 ⊕ 🎣 🏊 ⛺

Fr Cahors foll D662 or fr Figeac D19. Foll D622
along N bank of R Lot for 6km. Site well sp on app.
2*, Sm, pt shd, EHU (6A) €3; bbq (charcoal,
sep area); twin axles; red long stay; bus adj; Eng
spkn; adv bkg acc; games area; canoe hire; tennis nr;
fishing; CKE. *"Lge pitches; teepee & trapper tents on
site (for hire); many attractions within 30km radius;
dir access to rv; fishing rods avail; friendly, helpful
owner; excel; paragliding; trekking; htd pool 6km;
beautiful site; spotless facs; wonderful; highly rec."*
€14.00, 1 Apr-10 Oct.   **2017**

CAJARC *7D4* (0.3km SW Urban) *44.48374, 1.83928*
Camp Municipal Le Terriol, Rue Le Terriol, 46160
Cajarc **05 65 40 72 74 or 05 65 40 65 20 (Mairie);**
mairie.cajarc@wanadoo.fr; www.cajarc.fr

🐕 🐕(cont) 🅆🅒 🍽 ♿ 🍽 🍽 🍸 nr ⊕ nr 🏊 nr ⛺

Fr Cahors dir Cajarc on D662 on L foll sp to site.
2*, Sm, hdstg, hdg, mkd, pt shd, EHU (10A) inc
(poss rev pol); bbq; phone; Eng spkn; adv bkg acc;
tennis 500m; CKE. *"Gd sized pitches; clean, basic
facs; lovely sm town on Rv Lot; pool 500m; vg."*
€15.50, 1 May-30 Sep.   **2017**

CAJARC *7D4* (6km W Rural) *44.4735, 1.7835*
Camping Ruisseau du Treil, 46160 Larnagol
05 65 31 23 39; contact@lotcamping.com;
www.lotcamping.com

🐕 €3.90 ⚕ 🅆🅒 🍽 ♿ 🍽 🍽 🦋 🍸 🎣 ⛺ 🚣

Exit A20 junc 57 onto D49 sp St Michel; in 4km turn
R onto D653; after 5.5km in Vers at mini-rndabt
turn L onto D662; site on L immed after leaving
Larnagol. Or fr Figeac foll D19 thro Cajarc. At top
of hill leaving Cajarc turn R onto D662 sp Cahors &
Larnagol. Site sp on R 300m bef Larnagol on blind
bend. 3*, Sm, mkd, pt shd, pt sl, EHU (6A) €4; bbq; sw
nr; TV; 4% statics; adv bkg acc; canoeing adj; fishing
adj; games rm; bike hire; horseriding; CKE. *"Beautiful,
spacious, peaceful site in lovely area; well-run; friendly,
helpful British owners; clean san facs but ltd when site
full; lge pitches poss uneven; many long-stay/returning
campers; library; guided walks; vg touring base; excel."*
€28.00, 8 May-8 Sep.   **2019**

CALAIS *3A3* (12km NE Coastal) *50.98907, 1.98545*
Les Argousiers, 766 rue des hemmes, 62215 Oye-
Plage **03 21 35 32 78; lesargousiers@wanadoo.fr;**
www.lesargousiers.com

🐕 €2 ⚕ 🅆🅒 🍽 ♿ 🍽 🍽 🦋 🏖 sand 2km

Take D940 fr A16 (exit 49) or Calais. In Oye-Plage,
turn L & foll sp for Les Argousiers Camping.
Sm, hdg, unshd, EHU; bbq; twin axles; 95% statics; bus
100m; CKE. *"Few touring pitches; gd NH; friendly &
helpful owners."* **€13.70, 1 Mar-31 Jan.**   **2015**

CALAIS *3A3* (13km SW Rural) *50.91160, 1.75127*
Camping Les Epinettes, Impasse de Mont Pinet,
62231 Peuplingues **03 21 85 21 39;**
lesepinettes@aol.com; www.lesepinettes.fr

🐕 €1.50 ⚕ 🅆🅒 🍽 ♿ 🍽 🦋 ⚐ ⊕ nr 🏊 ⛺ 🏖 sand 3km

A16 fr Calais to Boulogne, exit junc 40 W on D243
sp Peuplingues, go thro vill & foll sp; site on L in
3km. 2*, Lge, hdg, pt shd, pt sl, EHU (4-6A) €2.90-3.90;
bbq; 80% statics; phone; adv bkg acc; ccard acc; CKE.
*"Pleasant, easy-going, quiet site; conv NH for m'way,
ferries & tunnel; some pitches sm; san facs clean; when
bureau clsd, site yourself - warden calls eve or call at
cottage to pay; library; if arr late, park on grass verge
outside main gate - use facs excel elec, pay half price;
few touring pitches."*
€15.50, 1 Apr-31 Oct.   **2019**

CALAIS *3A3* (4km SW Coastal) *50.95677, 1.81101*
Camp du Fort Lapin, Route Provincial 940, 62231
Sangatte-Blériot Plage **03 21 97 67 77;**
**campingdufortlapin@orange.fr; www.campingdu
fortlapin.fr**

🐕 🐕 ⚕ 🅆🅒 🍽 ♿ 🍽 🍽 🦋 🍸 ⊕ 🍽 🏊 nr ⛺ 🏖 sand adj

Fr E exit junc 43 fr A16 Calais cent, dir beach
(Blériot-Plage). Turn L along coast onto D940 dir
Sangatte; site on R in dunes shortly after water
tower, opp sports cent; site sp fr D940. Fr S exit A16
junc 41 to Sangatte; at T-junc turn R onto D940;
site on L just bef water tower. 3*, Med, mkd, unshd,
pt sl, EHU (10A) inc (poss rev pol); bbq; 50% statics;
phone; bus; adv bkg acc; CKE. *"Conv ferry; warden
lives on site; rec arr bef 1700 high ssn; gates clsd
2300-0700; recep 0900-1200 & 1600-2000, barrier
clsd when recep clsd; ltd parking outside espec w/end
- phone ahead for access code; gd bus service; basic,
clean, adequate san facs (shwrs and lndry clsd after
2100); conv Auchan & Cité Europe shops; poss youth
groups high ssn; conv NH; close to beach; clean tidy
site; adequate facs; grnd v well drained; easy cycle into
Calais or walk along the promenade to the harbour
ent."* **€18.40, 1 Apr-31 Oct.**   **2018**

CALAIS *3A3* (5km W Coastal) *50.94610, 1.75798*
Camping des Noires Mottes, Rue Pierre Dupuy, 62231
Sangatte **03 21 82 04 75; campingdesnoiresmottes@
orange.fr; www.ville-sangatte.fr**

🐕 €1.30 ⚕ 🅆🅒 🍽 ♿ 🍽 🍽 🍽 🏖 nr ⛺ 🏖 sand 500m

Fr A16 exit junc 41 sp Sangatte onto D243, at T-junc
in vill turn R then R again bef monument.
3*, Lge, hdg, mkd, pt shd, pt sl, EHU (10A) €4.10;
90% statics; bus 500m; Eng spkn; adv bkg rec; CKE.
*"Conv ferries & Eurotunnel; lge pitches; san facs clean;
barrier - no arr bef office opens 1500 (1600 LS); san
facs clsd o'night & poss 1200-1600; some pitches
boggy when wet; windy spot; OK NH; well maintained
site."* **€23.60, 1 Apr-31 Oct.**   **2018**

CALAIS *3A3* (3km NW Coastal) *50.96603, 1.84370*
Aire Communale, Plage de Calais, Ave Raymond
Poincaré, 62100 Calais **03 21 97 89 79, 03 21 46 66 41
or 06 79 62 93 22 (mob); camping@marie-calais.fr**
🔟 👫 🅗 nr 🚮 nr

A16 exit junc 43 dir Blériot-Plage/Calais cent & foll
sp for beach (plage). Site nr harbour wall & Fort
Risban. Well sp fr town cent. Med,. *"M'vans only; well-
kept, busy site; gd NH to/fr ferries; obtain token/pass fr
Camp Municipal adj; warden calls to collect fee pm or
pay at Camp Municipal."* **€8.00** **2016**

CALAIS *3A3* (3km NW Coastal) *50.959323, 1.831833*
Camping Municipal Le Grande Gravelot, 62100
Calais **03 91 91 52 34; camping@mairie-calais.fr**
🐎 👫 🅦 🏊 ♨ ♿ 🚿 🍴 🅼🅿 🦋 ♒ ⛲250m

Head for Calais beach. Site at end of Port de
Plaisance dock on rd behind hses & flats o'look
beach. Med, mkd, hdg, unshd, EHU (16A) inc; twin
axles; TV; phone; bus; Eng spkn; adv bkg acc; sauna;
games rm; bike hire; CCI. *"Excel; aire de svr adj to site
all year round; site patrolled at night; local cafes nrby;
short walk to town."* **€17.00, 1 Apr-31 Oct.** **2018**

CAMARET SUR MER *2E1* (3km NE Coastal) *48.28070,
-4.56490* **Camping Le Grand Large,** Lambézen,
29570 Camaret-sur-Mer **02 98 27 91 41; contact@
campinglegrandlarge.com; www.campinglegrand
large.com**
🐎 €3 👫 🅦 🏊 ♨ ♿ 🚿 🍴 🅼🅿 🦋 ♒ 🍸 ⛱ 🚮 🅰 ⛴(htd) 🎣
⛲ shgl 500m

On D8 bet Crozen & Camaret, turn R at ent to
Camaret onto D355, sp Roscanvel. Foll sps to site in
3km. 4*, Med, hdg, mkd, pt shd, pt sl, EHU (10A) inc;
gas; bbq; TV; adv bkg acc; ccard acc; tennis; boating.
*"Coastal views fr some pitches, lovely beach; pleasant,
helpful owners; 45 min cliff top walk to town; excel;
excel location; do not arr bef 2pm if not prebooked."*
€28.00, 30 Mar-30 Sep. **2018**

CAMARET SUR MER *2E1* (4km NE Coastal) *48.28788,
-4.56540* **Camping Plage de Trez-Rouz,** Route de
Camaret à Roscanvel, 29160 Crozon **02 98 27 93 96;
contact@trezrouz.com; www.trezrouz.com**
🐎 €2.50 👫 🅦 🏊 ♨ ♿ 🚿 🍴 🅼🅿 🦋 ♒ 🅷 ⛱ 🚮 🅰 🎣(htd)
⛲ sand

Foll D8 to Camaret-sur-Mer & at rndabt turn N sp
Roscanvel/D355. Site on R in 3km. 3*, Med, hdg,
mkd, pt shd, pt sl, EHU (16A) €3.50; 10% statics; adv
bkg acc; horseriding 2km; tennis 500m; CKE. *"Great
position opp beach; conv for Presqu'île de Crozon; gd
facs but stretched high ssn; site scruffy LS; friendly
helpful owner; gd hot shwrs; gd 3km coastal path to
Camaret-sur-Mer."* **€27.10, 15 Mar-15 Oct.** **2020**

CAMBRAI *3B4* (2.5km W Urban) *50.17533, 3.21534*
FFCC Camp Municipal Les Trois Clochers, 77 Rue
Jean Goudé, 59400 Cambrai **03 27 70 91 64**
👫 (htd) 🅦 🏊 ♨ ♿ 🚿 🅼🅿 🅷 nr 🚮 nr

Exit A2 junc 14; at rndabt after slip rd (with 6 exits)
take D630 dir Cambrai; in 1km (by Buffalo Grill)
turn L onto D630; in 200m turn L onto D939; in
100m turn L into Rue Jean Goudé. Or fr Cambrai
W on D939; after x-ing rv bdge cont on D939 until
traff lts in 300m; go strt over traff lts, then in 100m
turn L into Rue Jean Goudé. Site sp fr all dirs on
ent town. 3*, Sm, hdg, unshd, EHU (5-8A) €2.50; Eng
spkn. *"Beautiful, well-kept site; gd, spacious pitches;
v conv Calais; early arr rec high ssn; v helpful, friendly
manager; gd san facs, ltd & stretched when site full;
interesting town; excel; 5 min walk to Aldi supmkt; hg
rec."* **€14.50, 15 Apr-15 Oct.** **2017**

CANCALE *2E4* (10km S Coastal) *48.61592, -1.85151*
Camping de l'Ile Verte, 42 Rue de l'Ile Verte, 35114
St Benoît-des-Ondes **02 99 58 62 55; camping-ile-
verte@sfr.fr; www.campingdelileverte.com**
🐎 €2.50 👫 (htd) 🅦 🏊 🚿 🅼🅿 🦋 ♒ 🍸 nr 🅷 nr 🚮 🅰 ⛲ sand adj

Site on S side of vill. Fr Cancale, take D76 SW for
approx 4km, then turn L onto D155 into St Benoît.
Foll site sp. 3*, Sm, hdg, pt shd, EHU (6A) €4
(poss rev pol); gas; 3% statics; phone; adv bkg acc;
CKE. *"Well-kept, tidy site on edge of vill; facs poss
stretched high ssn; big pitches but narr access rds."*
€28.00, 30 Mar-31 Oct. **2018**

CANCALE *2E4* (7km NW Coastal) *48.68861, -1.86833*
Camping Le Bois Pastel, 13 Rue de la Corgnais, 35260
Cancale **02 99 89 66 10; contact@campingbois
pastel.fr; www.campingboispastel.fr**
🐎 4€/day. 👫 🅦 🏊 ♨ ♿ 🚿 🅼🅿 🦋 ♒ 🍸 🅷 ⛱ 🚮 🅰
🎣(covrd, htd, indoor) ⛴ ⛲ sand 800m

Fr Cancale take D201 dir Pointe du Grouin & St Malo
by Rte Touristique. Site sp on L 2.5km after Pointe
du Grouin. 3*, Med, mkd, pt shd, EHU (6A) €4; bbq;
red long stay; 25% statics; adv bkg acc; ccard acc;
games area; games rm; fishing. *"Conv Mont-St Michel,
St Malo; gd touring base."*
€22.00, 3 Apr-4 Oct. **2020**

CANCON *7D3* (12km W Rural) *44.53461, 0.50555*
Camping Le Moulin, Lassalle, 47290 Monbahus
**05 53 01 68 87; info@lemoulin-monbahus.com;
www.lemoulin-monbahus.com**
🔟 🐎 👫 🅦 🏊 ♨ ♿ 🚿 ♒ 🅷 ⛱ 🚮 nr 🅰 🐕 ⛴(htd)

Fr N21 turn W at Cancon on D124 sp Miramont. In
7.5km at Monbahus pass thro vill cent take L turn,
still on D124 sp Tombeboeuf. In 3km lge grain silos
on L, site next on R. Sm, mkd, hdstg, pt shd, EHU
(5-10A) €3 (most pitches 5A only avail); bbq; Eng spkn;
adv bkg acc; bike hire; CKE. *"CL-type site in garden;
friendly British owners; bistro; clean, basic san facs; vg
pool; B & B avail; extra for twin axles over 5m; excel."*
€17.00 **2016**

CANDE SUR BEUVRON *4G2* (0.9km S Rural) *47.48952, 1.25834* **La Grande Tortue,** 3 Route de Pontlevoy, 41120 Candé-sur-Beuvron 02 54 44 15 20; camping@ grandetortue.com; www.grandetortue.com

🐕 €4.50 👫 (htd) 🚻 ♿ ⚡ 🅿 MSP 🦋 ⛲ 🍽 🍴 ⊛ 🛒 🏐 △ ✎ 🏊 (covrd, htd) ⛴

Exit A10 junc 17 (Blois) & foll 'Autres/Toutes Directions' or 'Vierzon' to cross Rv Loire; immed after bdge R onto D951/D971 dir Chaumont; ignore D173 R fork & foll D751 thro Chailles & Villelouet; R at rndabt to go thro Cande; fork L after Cande; site on L in abt 100m. 5*, Lge, hdstg, mkd, hdg, pt shd, pt sl, EHU (10A) €3.50; gas; bbq; TV; 50% statics; Eng spkn; adv bkg acc; ccard acc; bike hire; games area; CKE. *"Excel, rustic site amongst trees; poss diff access due trees; helpful staff; vg, clean san facs; gd pool; gd for children; gd cycling; gourmet rest by rv bdge in vill; conv Loire chateaux; gd rest."* €47.00, 4 Apr-13 Sep. **2019**

CANET PLAGE *10G1* (3km N Coastal) *42.70808, 3.03332* **Camping Le Brasilia,** 2 Ave des Anneux du Roussillon, 66140 Canet-en-Roussillon 04 68 80 23 82; info@lebrasilia.fr; www.brasilia.fr

🐕 €4 👫 🚻 🚿 ♿ ⚡ 🅿 MSP 🦋 ⛲ 🍴 ⊛ 🛒 △ ✎ 🏊 (htd) ⛴ 🏖 sand 150m

Exit A9 junc 41 sp Perpignan Nord & Rivesaltes onto D83 dir Le Barcarès & Canet for 10km; then take D81 dir Canet for 10km until lge rndabt which goes under D617 (do not foll sp to Canet to R) - cont round rndabt & foll sp Ste Marie-le-Mer (to go back the way you came). Then take 1st R sp Le Brasilia. 5*, V lge, mkd, hdg, pt shd, serviced pitches; EHU (10A) inc; gas; bbq (elec, gas); twin axles; TV; 35% statics; bus to Canet; Eng spkn; ccard acc; bike hire; tennis; fishing; archery; games rm; CKE. *"Excel, well-run, well laid-out site; gd sized pitches; friendly staff; immac san facs; excel facs, espec for families/ children/teenagers; rvside walk adj; conv day trips to Barcelona,Carcassonne etc; daily mkt in Canet except Mon."* €54.00, 12 Apr-4 Oct, C01. **2017**

CANET PLAGE *10G1* (3.5km N Coastal) *42.70905, 3.03285* **Camping Le Bosquet,** Ave des Anneaux du Roussillon, 66140 Canet-Plage 04 68 80 23 80; campinglebosquet@club-internet.fr; www.camping lebosquet.com

🐕 €3 👫 🚻 🚿 ♿ ⚡ 🅿 🦋 🍴 ⊛ 🛒 △ ✎ 🏊 🏖 sand 400m

Exit A9 junc 41 onto D83 dir Le Barcarès; then turn R onto D81 dir Canet; in Canet at lge rndabt go R round until exit dir Torreilles & Ste Marie; then immed after rndabt take sm rd on R; site sp. Or E on D617 fr Perpignan, turn L on D11 in Canet & foll sp. 3*, Med, hdg, mkd, pt shd, EHU (5A) €3.50; gas; bbq; TV; phone; bus adj; Eng spkn; ccard acc; games rm; games area; CKE. *"Family-run site nr excel sand beach; shops 2km - plenty of choice; gd touring base; vg."* €49.00, 6 Apr-5 Oct. **2019**

CANET PLAGE *10G1* (4km NE Coastal) *42.72724, 3.03377* **Camping La Pergola,** 66470 Ste Marie la Mer 02 51 20 41 94; contact@camp-atlantique.com; www.campinglapergola.com

👫 (cont) 🚿 ✎ 🛒 🏖 sand 500m

S fr Narbonne, exit N9 at Salses & foll D11 to St Marie-Plage for St Marie-sur-Mer. Site not sp but on D12 to coast. 3*, Lge, pt shd, EHU; gas; adv bkg acc. *"No lge o'fits; v tricky maneuvering as too many trees."* €39.00, 3 Apr-20 Sep. **2015**

CANET PLAGE *10G1* (4km W Urban) *42.70114, 2.99850* **Kawan Village Ma Prairie,** 1 Ave des Coteaux, 66140 Canet-en-Roussillon 04 68 73 26 17; ma.prairie@wanadoo.fr; www.maprairie.com

🐕 €5 👫 🚻 🚿 ♿ ⚡ 🅿 MSP 🦋 ⛲ 🍴 ⊛ 🛒 nr △ ✎ 🏊 ⛴ 🏖 sand 3km

Leave A9/E15 at junc 41, sp Perpignan Centre/ Canet-en-Roussillon. Take D83, then D81 until Canet-en-Roussillon. At rndabt, take D617 dir Perpignan & in about 500m leave at exit 5. Take D11 dir St Nazaire, pass under bdge & at rndabt turn R. Site on L. 4*, Lge, hdg, shd, serviced pitches; EHU (10A) inc; gas; bbq (elec, gas); TV; 20% statics; bus to town nr; Eng spkn; adv bkg req; ccard acc; waterslide; games rm; sailing; waterskiing; canoeing; CKE. *"Peaceful, popular site; friendly, helpful owners; o'fits 7.5m & over by request; reg bus to beach (Jul/Aug); daily mkt Perpignan; gd."* €51.00, 4 May-21 Sep, C05. **2019**

CANNET DES MAURES, LE *10F3* (4km N Rural) *43.42140, 6.33655* **FFCC Camping Domaine de la Cigalière,** Route du Thoronet, 83340 Le Cannet-des-Maures 04 94 73 81 06; www.domaine-lacigaliere.com

🐕 €2 👫 🚻 🚿 ♿ ⚡ 🅿 MSP 🍴 🛒 △ ✎ 🏊 (htd)

Exit A8 at Le Cannet-des-Maures onto D17 N dir Le Thoronet; site in 4km on R, sp. 3*, Med, hdg, mkd, hdstg, pt shd, pt sl, EHU (6A) €4; bbq (elec, gas); 20% statics; CKE. *"Peaceful site; lge pitches; St Tropez 44km; vg site."* €32.00, 1 Apr-1 Nov. **2019**

CANOURGUE, LA *9D1* (7.4km W Rural) *44.43638, 3.1475* **Municipal la Vallée,** Miége Rivière 48500 Canilhac 04 66 32 91 14 or 04 66 32 80 05; commune.canilhac@wanadoo.fr

🐕 €1 👫 🚻 🚿 ♿ ⚡ 🅿 🦋 ⛲ 🍴 🛒 △ 🏊 (htd) ⛴

Leave A75 at junc 40. Take D988 W, sp St Laurent d'Olt. Site on L at level x-ing after 10 mins. 2*, Sm, hdg, pt shd, EHU (16A) €3; bbq; TV; 10% statics; phone; adv bkg acc; games rm; fishing; CCI. *"Sm shop; supmkt 5km; next to rv (sw not allowed); horseriding nr; golf nr; canoeing nr; paint-balling & quad biking nrby; conv for Gorges du Tarn & Aubrac; St laurent d'Olt worth a visit."* €17.00, 13 Jun-15 Sep. **2019**

CANY BARVILLE 3C2 (3km N Rural) 49.80375, 0.64960 **Camping Maupassant,** 12 Route de la Folie, 76450 Vittefleur 02 35 97 97 14; campingmaupassant@orange.fr; www.camping-maupassant.com

🛖 🕴 (htd) WD ♨ 🛒 😊 💻 MSP 🦋 🛥

S fr St Valery-en-Caux on D925 dir Cany-Barville; site sp turning to R 700m bef Cany-Barville. 2*, Med, hdg, mkd, hdstg, pt shd, EHU (6A) €3.30; gas; bbq (charcoal); 10% statics; phone; adv bkg acc; CKE. "Friendly staff; gd NH; gd, clean site; 10 touring pitches." €20.00, 9 Mar-14 Dec. **2016**

CAPESTANG 10F1 (0.5km W Urban) 43.32759, 3.03865 **Camp Municipal de Tounel,** 1 Rue Georges Brassens, Ave de la République, 34310 Capestang 04 67 49 85 95; mairie@ville-capestang.fr; www.capestang.fr

🛖 🕴 (cont) WD ♨ ♿ 😊 💻 ⁄ ⑪ nr 🖳 nr 🏧

Fr Béziers on D11, turn R twd vill of Capestang, approx 1km after passing supmkt. Site on L in leisure park opp Gendamarie. 1*, Med, hdg, pt shd, EHU (6A) €3; tennis; bike hire; fishing. "300m fr Canal de Midi; excel walks or bike rides; lovely rest in vill; LS site yourself, fees collected; facs poss tired LS; poss diff access to pitches for long o'fits; ltd EHU; poss resident workers; NH only." €15.00, 1 May-30 Sep. **2019**

CARCASSONNE 8F4 (8.6km N Rural) 43.25999, 2.36509 **FFCC Camping Das Pinhiers,** Chemin du Pont Neuf, 11620 Villemoustaussou 04 68 47 81 90; campingdaspinhiers@wanadoo.fr; www.camping-carcassonne.net

🛖 €3 WD ♨ ♿ 😊 💻 ⁄ MSP 🦋 🍴 ⑪ 🖳 🏧 🛥

Exit A6 junc 23 Carcassonne Ouest & foll sp Mazamet on D118; R at rndabt with filling stn; turn R & foll camping sp. 3*, Med, hdg, shd, pt sl, EHU (10A) inc; 10% statics; bus 1 km; Eng spkn; adv bkg acc; ccard acc; CKE. "Diff to pitch lge vans due hdg pitches & sl; san facs basic & stretched high ssn; general area rather run down (2009); office clsd noon-2pm." €18.00, 1 Apr-31 Oct. **2015**

CARCASSONNE 8F4 (10km NE Rural) 43.28305, 2.44166 **Camping Le Moulin de Ste Anne,** Chemin de Ste Anne, 11600 Villegly-en-Minervois 04 68 72 20 80; contact@moulindesainteanne.com; www.moulinde sainteanne.com

🛖 €3.50 🕴 (cont, htd) WD ♨ ♿ 😊 💻 ⁄ 🦋 ⑪ 🍴 ⑪ 🖳 nr 🏧 🛥 (htd) 🍹

Leave A61 junc 23 Carcassone Ouest dir Mazamet; after approx 14km onto D620 to Villegly, site sp at ent to vill. NB Turning R off D620 hidden by trees, then over narr bdge; long o'fits need wide swing in. 4*, Med, mkd, hdg, pt shd, pt sl, terr, EHU (10A) inc; bbq (gas); red long stay; 25% statics; Eng spkn; adv bkg acc; ccard acc; games area; CKE. "Pretty, clean site; lge pitches; friendly, helpful owner; ltd san facs; pitches poss diff/muddy in wet; gd touring base; poss local youths congregate on motorbikes nrby in eve; min 3 nights high ssn; vg." €33.20, 17 Mar-30 Sep, C28. **2019**

CARCASSONNE 8F4 (10km E Rural) 43.21498, 2.47031 **Camping La Commanderie,** 6 Chemin Eglise, 11800 Rustiques 04 68 78 67 63 or 06 25 28 35 80 (mob); contact@campinglacommanderie.com; www.campinglacommanderie.com

🛖 €2 🕴 (htd) WD ♨ ♿ 😊 ⁄ 🦋 ⑪ 🍴 ⑪ 🖳 nr 🏧 🛥

Fr Carcassonne take D6113/D610 E to Trèbes (approx 8km); at Trèbes take D610 & after 2km L onto D906, then L onto D206; site on R; foll sp 'Rustiques'. Or fr A61 ext junc 24 onto D6113 to Trèbes & then as bef. 3*, Sm, mkd, pt shd, pt sl, EHU (6A) inc; 10% statics; phone; Eng spkn; adv bkg acc; ccard acc; CKE. "Pleasant, helpful owner & staff; modern san facs; patron sells own wines; gd cycling along canal fr Trèbes; conv A61; gd NH en rte Spain; superb refurbished pool; excel; quiet relaxing site; excel site improving year on year, running track and 12 fitness machines added this year." €25.00, 1 Apr-15 Oct. **2018**

CARCASSONNE 8F4 (7.6km E Rural) 43.20700, 2.44258 **FFCC Camping à l'Ombre des Micocouliers,** Chemin de la Lande, 11800 Trèbes 04 68 78 61 75; infos@campingmicocouliers.com; www.aude camping.com

🛖 €1.50 🕴 WD ♨ 😊 💻 ⁄ 🦋 ⑪ 🖳 🏧 🎣

Fr Carcassonne, take D6113 E for 6km to Trèbes; go under rlway bdge; fork L onto D610; turn R immed bef rv bdge; site on L in 200m. Fr W foll D6113 thro Trebes; at rndabt at E of town take last exit to L sp Sports Centre, site on R. 4*, Med, mkd, shd, EHU (6A); bbq; TV; phone; Eng spkn; rv fishing; CKE. "Pleasant, sandy site by rv; well shd; friendly & helpful staff; gd, clean but dated san facs, 1 block up 15 steps; ltd EHU; Trèbes in walking dist; vg cycling, 13 km cycle to Carcassonne along cana, bus for €1; gd base Canal du Midi; can be noisy fr local youths on mbikes; walk into town needs care with busy rd; lovely site; adv to arr early as popular site; site improved, new tiling & paint in toilet block (2015); v.busy." €26.00, 1 Apr-30 Sep. **2015**

CARCASSONNE 8F4 (6km S Rural) 43.17938, 2.37024 **Camping à l'Ombre des Oliviers,** Ave du Stade, 11570 Cazilhac 04 68 79 65 08 or 06 81 54 96 00 (mob); florian.romo@wanadoo.fr; www.alombredes oliviers.com

12 🛖 €2 🕴 ♨ ♿ 😊 💻 ⁄ 🦋 🍴 🖳 nr 🏧 🛥

Fr N & W exit Carcassonne by D6113 dir Narbonne. Cross rv & turn S onto D104, then D142/D56 to Cazilhac, site sp. 3*, Sm, pt shd, EHU (6-10A) €3 (poss rev pol); bbq; TV; 10% statics; adv bkg acc; games area; tennis; site clsd 1st week Jan. "Site in pleasant position; if office clsd phone owner on mob, or site yourself; helpful owners; v ltd facs LS; insufficient san facs when site full & ltd other facs; few water pnts; pitches poss muddy/soft when wet; bus to old city nrby; site very shabby (2014); san facs need maintenance (2015)." €23.00 **2015**

CARCASSONNE *8F4* (15km NW Rural) *43.29861, 2.22277* **Camping de Montolieu**, L'Olivier, 11170 Montolieu **04 68 76 95 01 or 06 31 90 31 92 (mob); nicole@camping-de-montolieu.com; www.camping-de-montolieu.com**

🐕 €2.50 ♦♦♦ WD ♠ ⚐ ♿ ◨ ✎ ⅋ ☂ nr ⊕ nr ☰ nr

Fr D6113 4km W Carcassonne, take D629 twd Montolieu; site on R in 2.5km after Moussoulens. Sp fr D6113, approx 5km dist. App thro Montolieu **not rec.** 3*, Sm, hdg, mkd, pt shd, EHU (5A) inc; gas; bbq; 10% statics; phone; adv bkg acc; games area; games rm; CKE. *"Well-run site in lovely countryside; pool 100m; manoeuvring tight; excel facs; conv Carcassonne; highly rec."*
€19.60, 25 Mar-31 Oct.   2019

CARCES *10F3* (0.5km SE Urban) *43.47350, 6.18826* **Camping Les Fouguières**, 165 chemin des Fouguières, 83570 Carcès **34 94 59 96 28 or 06 74 29 69 02 (mob); info@camping-les-fouguieres.com; www.camping-les-fouguieres.com**

🐕 €2 ♦♦♦ ♠ ♿ ✎ MSP 🦋 ♈ ☰ 🏊 (htd)

Exit A8 junc 35 at Brignoles onto D554 to Le Val; then take D562 to Carcès. Site sp off D13. Narr app rd, diff entry & exit for long o'fits. Med, pt shd, EHU (14A) €3; gas; sw nr; TV; 80% statics; phone; bus; Eng spkn; canoeing nr; fishing nr. *"Pleasant, clean, well-shd site; friendly, helpful owner; Rv Caramy runs thro site; interesting, medieval town; Lake Carcès 2km; don't miss Entrecasteaux chateau; mkt Sat; excel."*
€32.00, 10 Mar-30 Nov.   2019

CARENTAN *1D4* (0.6km NE Urban) *49.30864, -1.239117* **Camping Le Haut Dick**, 30 Chemin du Grand-Bas Pays, 50500 Carentan Les Marais **02 33 42 16 89; contact@camping-lehautdick.com; www.camping-lehautdick.com**

🐕 €2 ♦♦♦ WD ♠ ⚐ ♿ ◨ ✎ MSP 🦋 ♈ ☂ ⊕ 🍴 ☰ ⚲ 🏊 (covrd, htd, indoor) 🎿

Exit N13 at Carentan; clearly sp in town cent, nr pool, on L bank of canal, close to marina.Foll sp to Port de Plaisance. 3*, Med, mkd, hdg, pt shd, EHU (6A) €4 (rev pol); gas; bbq; 5% statics; phone; adv bkg acc; games rm; bike hire; ping pong; go-kart rental; CKE. *"Some pitches poss tight for lge o'fits; gd security; eve meals avail; gates locked 2200-0700; conv Cherbourg ferry & D-Day beaches; crazy golf; gd birdwatching & cycling; htd pool adj; mkt Mon."*
€25.50, 3 Apr-26 Sep.   2020

CARNAC *2G3* (1km N Rural) *47.59683, -3.06035* **Camping La Grande Métairie**, Route des Alignements de Kermario, 56342 Carnac **02 97 52 24 01; info@lagrandemetairie.com; www.lagrandemetairie.com**

🐕 €4 ♦♦♦ (htd) WD ♠ ⚐ ♿ ◨ ✎ MSP 🦋 ♈ ☂ ⊕ 🍴 ☰ ⚲ 🏊 (covrd, htd) 🎿 sand 2.5km

Fr Auray take N768 twd Quiberon. In 8km turn L onto D119 twd Carnac. La Métairie site sp 1km bef Carnac (at traff lts) turn L onto D196 to site on R in 1km. 4*, V lge, mkd, hdg, pt shd, EHU (6A) €3; gas; bbq; TV; 80% statics; Eng spkn; adv bkg acc; ccard acc; games rm; watersports 2.5km; sailing 2.5km; tennis; waterslide. *"Excel facs; vg pool complex; friendly, helpful staff; rec."* €42.00, 2 Apr-10 Sep.   2017

CARNAC *2G3* (3km N Rural) *47.60801, -3.09049* **Camping Les Bruyères**, Kerogile, 56340 Plouharnel **02 97 52 30 57; contact@camping-lesbruyeres.com; www.camping-lesbruyeres.com**

🐕 €2 ♦♦♦ (htd) WD ♠ ⚐ ♿ ◨ ✎ 🦋 ♈ ☂ ⊕ 🍴 ☰ ⚲ 🏊 sand 3km

Fr Vannes W on E60/N165, at Auray take D768 dir Quiberon. At rndabt approx 2km fr Plouharnel turn L into Rte du Hahon, site in 500m, sp.
3*, Med, hdstg, mkd, hdg, pt shd, EHU (6A) €3.70; bbq; TV; 30% statics; Eng spkn; adv bkg acc; ccard acc; tennis; games area; CKE. *"V pleasant, well-run, peaceful site; library; bicycles; pony rides; vg."*
€30.00, 6 Apr-29 Sep.   2019

CARNAC *2G3* (2km NE Rural) *47.60820, -3.06605* **Camping Le Moustoir**, 71 Route du Moustoir, 56340 Carnac **02 97 52 16 18; info@lemoustoir.com; www.lemoustoir.com**

🐕 €1 ♦♦♦ WD ♠ ⚐ ♿ ◨ ✎ MSP ♈ ☂ ⊕ 🍴 ☰ ⚲ 🏊 (covrd, htd) 🎿 sand 4km

Fr N165 take D768 at Auray dir Carnac & Quiberon. In 5km take D119 dir Carnac, site on L at ent to Carnac. 3*, Lge, mkd, hdg, pt shd, pt sl, EHU (10A) inc; bbq; TV; 60% statics; phone; Eng spkn; adv bkg acc; ccard acc; games area; waterslide; bike hire; tennis; CKE. *"Attractive, friendly, well-run site; facs clean but stretched; megaliths nrby; Sun mkt."*
€43.00, 14 Apr-9 Sep, B19.   2017

For a guide to symbols see the fold out on the rear cover

CARNAC *2G3* (2.4km NE Rural) *47.5964, -3.0617*
Camping Le Moulin de Kermaux, Route de Kerlescan, 56340 Carnac **02 97 52 15 90; moulin-de-kermaux@wanadoo.fr; www.camping-moulinkermaux.com**

🐕 €2.50 ♔(htd) ⊞ ☂ ⚲ ♿ 🖳 ⁄ MSP 🦋 ⛲ ▾ 🍴 🗗 ⚞ ♂
🏊(covrd, htd) 🛝 🏖 sand 3km

Fr Auray take D768 S sp Carnac, Quiberon. In 8km turn L onto D119 twds Carnac. 1km bef Carnac take D196 (Rte de Kerlescan) L to site in approx 500m opp round, stone observation tower for alignments. Fr St Trinite Sur Mer, take D781, cont to rndabt nr St Michel Tumulus on o'skirts of Carnac. Exit R onto D119. In 1km fork R onto D196, site on R in 1km.
3*, Med, hdg, mkd, pt shd, EHU (6A) €4 (poss rev pol); gas; bbq; TV; 50% statics; phone; bus adj; Eng spkn; adv bkg acc; ccard acc; sauna; waterslide; games area; jacuzzi; CKE. *"Well-kept, friendly, attractive site nr standing stones; many repeat visitors; excel."*
€38.00, 19 Apr-13 Sep.   **2015**

CARNAC *2G3* (3.5km NE Rural) *47.60198, -3.03672*
Camping de Kervilor, Route du Latz, 56470 La Trinité-sur-Mer **02 97 55 76 75; infos@camping-kervilor.com; www.camping-kervilor.com**

🐕 €2.90 ♔ ⊞ ☂ ⚲ ♿ 🖳 ⁄ MSP ⛲ ▾ 🍴 🗗 ⚞ ♂
🏊(covrd, htd) 🛝 🏖 sand 4km

Sp fr island in cent of Trinité-sur-Mer.
4*, Lge, hdstg, mkd, hdg, pt shd, EHU (6-10A) €3.85-4.35; gas; bbq; 5% statics; Eng spkn; adv bkg acc; ccard acc; waterslide; solarium; bike hire; games area; tennis; CKE. *"Busy, well-kept family site; lge pitches; clean dated unisex san facs; 20 min walk into La Trinité-sur-Mer (1.5km); gd cycling to Carnac & megaliths; great site; excel loc; easy walk to lovely town."*
€29.00, 1 Apr 18 Sep.   **2018**

"There aren't many sites open at this time of year"

If you're travelling outside peak season remember to call ahead to check site opening dates – even if the entry says 'open all year'.

CARNAC *2G3* (2km E Rural/Coastal) *47.5810, -3.0576*
Camping Les Druides, 55 Chemin de Beaumer, 56340 Carnac **02 97 52 08 18; contact@camping-les-druides.com; www.camping-les-druides.com**

🐕 €2.50 ♔ ⊞ ☂ ⚲ ♿ 🖳 ⁄ MSP 🦋 ⏀ nr ⚞ ♂ 🏊(htd)
🏖 sand 500m

Go E on seafront Carnac Plage to end; turn N onto Ave d'Orient; at junc with Rte de la Trinité-sur-Mer, turn L, then 1st R; site 1st on L in 300m.
3*, Med, hdg, pt shd, pt sl, EHU (6A) €3.70; TV; 5% statics; Eng spkn; adv bkg acc; ccard acc; games rm; CKE. *"Friendly welcome."*
€41.50, 13 Apr-3 Sep.   **2019**

CARNAC *2G3* (3km E Rural) *47.61122, -3.02908*
Camping du Lac, 56340 Carnac **02 97 55 78 78; info@lelac-carnac.com; www.lelac-carnac.com**

🐕 €2 ♔ ⊞ ☂ ⚲ ♿ 🖳 ⁄ MSP 🦋 ⏀ nr ⚞ ♂ 🗗 (htd)
🏖 sand 3km

Fr Auray (by-pass) take D768 sp Carnac; in 4km turn L on D186; after 4km look for C105 on L & foll sp to site. Fr E end of quay-side in La Trinité-sur-Mer take main Carnac rd & in 100m turn R onto D186; in 2km R on C105, R on C131; sp. 3*, Med, hdg, pt shd, pt sl, serviced pitches; EHU (6A) €3.60; gas; bbq; TV; 50% statics; phone; Eng spkn; adv bkg acc; ccard acc; bike hire; CKE. *"Excel, beautiful, woodland site o'looking tidal lake; helpful owner; clean, well-cared for; multi-sport court; fitness rm; superb pool; gd cycling & walking; vg; lovely sunsets & sunrises."*
€36.00, 1 Apr-30 Sep.   **2017**

CARNAC *2G3* (2km SE Coastal) *47.58116, -3.05804*
Camping Le Dolmen, Chemin de Beaumer, 56340 Carnac **02 97 52 12 35; contact@campingledolmen.com; www.campingledolmen.com**

🐕 €3 ♔(htd) ⊞ ☂ ⚲ ♿ 🖳 ⁄ MSP 🦋 ⛲ ⏀ ⚞ nr ⚞ ♂
🏊(htd) 🛝 🏖 sand 500m

Fr N on D768 twd Quiberon; turn L onto D781 twd La Trinité-sur-Mer. At Montauban turn R at rndabt dir Kerfraval & Beaumer, site in 700m, sp.
3*, Med, hdstg, mkd, hdg, pt shd, pt sl, EHU (10A) €4.70; bbq; 2% statics; adv bkg acc; ccard acc; games area; games rm; CKE. *"Excel, v friendly, clean, pleasant site; v well maintained; generous size pitches; modern, clean san facs; highly rec."*
€38.00, 2 Apr-23 Sep.   **2018**

CARNAC *2G3* (1km S Coastal) *47.57667, -3.06817*
Camping Les Menhirs, Allé saint michel, 56343 Carnac **02 97 52 94 67; contact@lesmenhirs.com; www.lesmenhirs.com**

♔ ⊞ ☂ ⚲ ♿ 🖳 ⁄ 🦋 ⚞ 🏊(htd) 🏖 sand 350m

Fr Auray foll sps to Carnac, Carnac Plage. Site past shopping cent rd on L, sp by camping sps.
4*, Lge, pt shd, pt sl, EHU (6A) €4.80; gas; 50% statics; adv bkg acc; sauna; jacuzzi; games rm. *"Extra charge for larger pitches; excel san facs; excel location, nr rest, shops & beach."*
€56.00, 1 Apr-30 Sep.   **2017**

CARNAC *2G3* (3.5km NW Rural) *47.59468, -3.09659*
Camping Les Goélands, Kerbachic, 56340 Plouharnel **02 97 52 31 92; contact@camping-lesgoelands.com; www.camping-lesgoelands.com**

🐕 €1 ♔ ⊞ 🖳 ⁄ ⚞ nr ⚞ ♂ 🏖 sand 3km

Take D768 fr Auray twd Quiberon. In Plouharnel turn L at rndabt by supmkt onto D781 to Carnac. Site sp to L in 500m. 2*, Med, pt shd, EHU (3-6A) €3.50; gas; adv bkg rec. *"Good facs; gd-sized pitches; gate clsd at 2200; nr beaches with bathing & gd yachting; bells fr adj abbey not too intrusive; conv for megalithic sites; high standard, pleasant, quiet site; facs basic; clean and tidy; new owners (2015)."*
€20.00, 1 Apr-31 Oct.   **2016**

FRANCE

CARNAC *2G3* (7.5km NW Rural) *47.62882, -3.14511*
Camping Les Mégalithes, Kerfélicité, 56410 Erdeven
02 97 55 68 76 or 02 97 55 68 09; campingdes
megalithes@orange.fr; www.campingdesmegalithes.fr

🐕 €1 ♿♿ (htd) 🅆♿ ♨ ⚲ 🚿 ⊘ ♫ 🦋 ⬤ 🍴 nr ⊕ nr 🐾 ⛺ 🛶
🛶 shgl 2km

Fr Carnac take D781 thro Plouharnel after further
4km; site on L in 500m. 3*, Med, hdg, mkd, pt shd,
pt sl, EHU (10A); twin axles; 40% statics; Eng spkn;
adv bkg acc; games area. *"Excel, peaceful, well
maintained site with lge pitches but poorly lit; poss
diff to manoeuvre lge c'vans; conv for megalithic
alignments; v clean facs; helpful & welcoming
staff; family run site; pool area beautiful but busy."*
€30.00, 1 May-21 Sep.   2015

CARPENTRAS *10E2* (7km N Rural) *44.09723, 5.03682*
Camping Le Brégoux, Chemin du Vas, 84810
Aubignan 04 90 62 62 50 or 04 90 67 10 13 (LS);
camping-lebregoux@wanadoo.fr; www.camping-
lebregoux.fr

🐕 €1.90 ♿♿ 🅆♿ ♨ ⚲ 🚿 ⊘ ♫ 🅼🆂🅿 ♫ 🍴 nr ⊕ nr 🐾 ⛺ ✏

Exit Carpentras on D7 sp Bollène. In Aubignan turn
R immed after x-ing bdge, 1st R again in approx
250m at Club de Badminton & foll site sp at fork.
2*, Lge, hdstg, mkd, hdg, pt shd, EHU (10A) €3.80
(poss long lead req); bbq; TV; 2% statics; phone;
Eng spkn; adv bkg acc; ccard acc; games rm; golf
nr; tennis; CKE. *"Popular site in beautiful area; lge
pitches & gd access; helpful, friendly staff; gates clsd
2200-0700; poss flooding in heavy
rain; pool 5km in ssn; excel walking & cycling nrby; gd
value; gd; san facs upgraded, modern & clean (2015)."*
€11.40, 1 Mar-31 Oct.   2015

CARPENTRAS *10E2* (6km S Urban) *43.99917, 5.06591*
Camp Municipal Coucourelle, Ave René Char, 84210
Pernes-les-Fontaines 04 90 66 45 55 or 04 90 61 31
67 (Mairie); camping@perneslesfontaines.fr;
www.tourisme-pernes.fr

🐕 €0.50 ♿♿ 🅆♿ ♨ ⚲ 🚿 ⊘ ♫ 🅼🆂🅿 🦋 ⊕ nr 🐾 nr ⛺

Take D938 fr Carpentras to Pernes-les-Fontaines;
then take D28 dir St Didier (Ave René Char pt of
D28). Site sp (some sps easily missed). Foll sp sports
complex, site at rear of sw pool.
2*, Sm, hdg, mkd, shd, EHU (10A) €3.50; bbq; adv
bkg acc; ccard acc; tennis adj; fishing 2.5km; CKE.
*"Pleasant, well-run site; views of Mont Ventoux; most
pitches lge but some sm & narr; excel clean facs;
m'vans can park adj to mv point free when site clsd;
pool 2.5km; gates close 1930; no twin axles; free use of
adj pool; attractive old town, easy parking; adv bkg rec
LS; vg."* €15.50, 1 Apr-30 Sep.   2016

CARPENTRAS *10E2* (4km SW Rural) *44.0398, 5.0009*
Camp Municipal de Bellerive, 54 Chemin de la
Ribière, 84170 Monteux 04 90 66 81 88 or
04 90 66 97 52 (TO); camping.bellerive@orange.fr;
www.provenceguide.com

🐕 €1 ♿♿ 🅆♿ ♨ ⚲ 🚿 ⊘ ♫ 🍴 nr ⊕ nr 🐾 nr ⛺

Site on N edge of Monteux cent, sp off ring rd
Monteux N, immed after rlwy x-ing. 2*, Sm, hdg,
mkd, hdstg, pt shd, serviced pitches; EHU (6-10A)
€2.50; red long stay; 10% statics; phone; bus; CKE.
*"Gd, busy, lovely site; rec arr early high ssn; helpful,
friendly, v helpful warden lives adj; gd security; vg,
clean, modern san facs; trees a problem for sat TV -
choose pitch carefully; park adj gd for children; 5 min
walk to vill; poss muddy when wet; poss some workers'
statics LS; Mistral blows early & late ssn; pool 4km;
gd touring base; free WiFi; no grey water drainage."*
€14.40, 1 Apr-15 Oct.   2018

CASSIS *10F3* (1.5km N Coastal) *43.22417, 5.54126*
Camping Les Cigales, 43 Ave de la Marne, 13260
Cassis 04 42 01 07 34; www.campingcassis.com

🐕 €1.10 ♿♿ 🅆♿ ♨ ⚲ 🚿 ⊘ ♫ 🍴 ⊕ 🐾 🐾 ⛺ 🛶 shgl 1.5km

App Cassis on D41E, then at 2nd rndabt exit D559
sp Cassis, then turn 1st R sp Les Calanques into Ave
de la Marne, site immed on R. Avoid town cent as
rds narr. 4*, Lge, hdg, mkd, hdstg, pt shd, pt sl, EHU
(3A) €2.60 (poss rev pol & poss long lead req); gas;
30% statics; phone; Eng spkn; ccard acc; CKE. *"Gd base
for Calanques; v busy w/ends; popular attractive resort,
but steep walk to camp site; poss tired san facs end
ssn; poss diff lge o'fits due trees; v strong pegs req to
penetrate hardcore; bus to Marseille cent fr campsite."*
€25.00, 15 Mar-15 Nov.   2019

CASTELJALOUX *7D2* (10km SE Rural) *44.27262, 0.18969*
Camping Moulin de Campech, 47160 Villefranche-du-
Queyran 05 53 88 72 43; camping@moulinde
campech.co.uk; www.moulindecampech.co.uk

🐕 €2.40 ♿♿ 🅆♿ ♨ ⚲ 🚿 ⊘ ♫ 🍴 ⊕ 🐾 🐾 ✏ 🛶 (htd)

Fr A62 exit junc 6 (sp Damazan & Aiguillon). Fr toll
booth take D8 SW sp Mont-de-Marsan. In 3km turn
R in Cap-du-Bosc onto D11 twd Casteljaloux. Site on
R in 4km. Or fr Casteljaloux S on D655 then SW on
D11 after 1.5km. Site on L after 9.5km.
3*, Sm, mkd, hdg, pt shd, EHU (6A) €4; bbq; phone;
adv bkg acc; ccard acc; lake fishing; games rm; golf
nr; CKE. *"Superb, peaceful rvside site in wooded valley;
well-run; lge pitches; friendly, helpful & welcoming
British owners; clean, dated san facs, needs refurb
(2014); gd pool; excel, gd value rest; BBQ suppers;
gd cycling; no o'fits over 8.2m; interesting area ideal
for nature lovers; excel site; many social events."*
€32.00, 1 Apr-7 Oct, D16.   2017

FRANCE

CASTELLANE *10E3* (2.7km SE Rural) *43.83833, 6.54194* **Camping La Ferme de Castellane,** Quartier La Lagne, 04120 Castellane **04 92 83 67 77; accueil@camping-la-ferme.com; www.camping-la-ferme.com**

🏕🐕€1 👫(wc) ⛺♨♿🚿🚮 /♨ 🦋 ⛲🍴 nr ⊕ nr 🛒 nr ⛰

Fr Castellane take D6085 dir Grasse. In 1km turn R (at Rest L'Escapade) then site in 1km, sp. Narr app rd with passing places. 3*, Sm, mkd, pt shd, terr, EHU €3.50; TV; 25% statics; Eng spkn; adv bkg acc; ccard acc; games rm; CKE. *"Vg, clean, friendly site; gd touring base; breakfast and BBQ evenings at rest."* **€17.00, 27 Mar-20 Sep.** **2016**

CASTELLANE *10E3* (0.3km SW Urban) *43.84623, 6.50995* **Camping Frédéric Mistral,** 12 Ave Frédéric Mistral, 04120 Castellane **04 92 83 62 27; www.camping-frederic-mistral.fr**

👫(htd) (wc) ⛺♿/♨ 🦋 ⛲🍴 ⊕ 🛒 🛒 nr

In town turn onto D952 sp Gorges-du-Verdon, site on L in 100m. 2*, Med, mkd, pt shd, serviced pitches; EHU (6A) €3 (poss rev pol); 2% statics; adv bkg acc; CKE. *"Friendly owners; pool 200m; gd san facs but poss stretched in ssn; gd base for gorges etc; gd."* **€21.00, 1 Mar-11 Nov.** **2017**

CASTELLANE *10E3* (0.5km SW Rural) *43.84570, 6.50447* **Camping Notre Dame,** Route des Gorges du Verdon, 04120 Castellane **04 92 83 63 02; camping-notredame@wanadoo.fr; www.camping-notredame.com**

🏕🐕 👫(wc) ⛺♿🚿🚮/♨ (MSP) 🍴 ⊕ nr 🛒 ⛰

N fr Grasse on D6085, turn L in Castellane at sq onto D952 to site on R in 500m. 3*, Sm, pt shd, EHU (6A) €3.50; gas; 20% statics; phone; Eng spkn; adv bkg acc; CKE. *"Ideal touring base; helpful owners; poss a bit unkempt early ssn; excel."* **€26.50, 1 Apr-8 Oct.** **2019**

CASTELLANE *10E3* (1.5km SW Rural) *43.83921, 6.49370* **Sandaya Domaine du Verdon,** D952, 04120 Castellane **04 92 83 61 29; ver@sandaya.fr; www.sandaya.co.uk**

🏕🐕€5 👫(wc) ⛺♨♿🚿🚮/♨ (MSP)🍴⊕🛒⛰ 🏊 🚣 (htd) 🚴

Fr Castellane take D952 SW twd Grand Canyon du Verdon & Moustiers-Ste Marie. After 1.5km turn L into site. NB To avoid Col de Lèques with hairpins use N202 & D955 fr Barrême instead of D6085. 4*, V lge, mkd, hdg, pt shd, serviced pitches; EHU (6A) inc; gas; bbq (elec, gas); sw; TV; 60% statics; Eng spkn; ccard acc; games rm; rv fishing adj; waterslide; canoeing; archery; games area; horseriding nr; CKE. *"Excel site by rv; no o'fits over 8m; gd sized pitches; gd, clean san facs, modern & dated blocks; quiet, rural walk to town; mkt Wed & Sat."* **€25.00, 12 Jun-14 Sep.** **2019**

CASTELNAUDARY *8F4* (7km E Rural) *43.31723, 2.01582* **FFCC Camping à la Ferme Domaine de la Capelle (Sabatte),** St Papoul, 11400 St Martin-Lalande **04 68 94 91 90; www.domaine-la-capelle.fr/en**

🏕🐕€1 👫(htd) (wc)♿🚮/♨ 🦋 🛒 nr

Fr D6113 Castelnaudary/Carcasonne, take D103 E & foll sp to St Papoul & site in 2km. Well sp. NB Ent poss awkward lge o'fits. Sm, hdg, mkd, pt shd, pt sl, EHU (4A) €2.50; bbq; phone; Eng spkn; CKE. *"Delightful, peaceful, spacious CL-type site; friendly, helpful owner; vg san facs, poss stretched when site full; ltd EHU; gd walking; nr St Papoul Cathar vill with abbey; ideal NH for Spain; excel; close to ind site, gd cycling."* **€14.50, 1 Apr-30 Sep.** **2016**

CASTIES LABRANDE *8F3* (1.5km W Rural) *43.32502, 0.99046* **Camping Le Casties,** Le Bas de Lebrande, 31430 Casties-Labrande **05 61 90 81 11; contact@camping-lecasties.fr; www.camping-lecasties.fr**

🏕🐕€1 👫(wc)⛺♨🚿🚮/♨ 🦋🍴♿⛰🏊🚣

S fr Toulouse, exit A64 junc 26 onto D626; after Pouy-de-Touges turn L onto & foll camping sp. 1*, Med, hdg, pt shd, EHU (5A) €1; bbq; 10% statics; phone; Eng spkn; adv bkg acc; ccard acc; tennis; fishing; CKE. *"Remote; lge hdg pitches; staff friendly & helpful; value for money; lovely pool; excel; new vg san facs (2013); v peaceful; sm farm for children."* **€12.50, 1 May-30 Sep.** **2019**

CASTILLON LA BATAILLE *7C2* (0.6km E Urban) *44.85350, -0.03550* **Camp Municipal La Pelouse,** Chemin de Halage, 33350 Castillon-la-Bataille **05 57 40 04 22 or 05 56 40 00 06 (Mairie)**

👫⛺/♨ 🦋 🛒

Site in town on N bank of Rv Dordogne. After x-ing rv on D17 fr S to N, take 1st avail rd on R to rv. 2*, Sm, shd, EHU (15A) inc; adv bkg acc; CKE. *"Peaceful, lovely site by rv; busy high ssn; pitches poss rough & muddy when wet; helpful warden; facs dated but clean; conv town; trans, St Emillion & wine area; gd NH."* **€17.00, 1 May-15 Oct.** **2018**

CASTRES *8F4* (2km NE Urban) *43.62054, 2.25401* **Camping de Gourjade,** Ave de Roquecourbe, 81100 Castres **05 63 59 33 51; contact@campingdegourjade.net; www.campingdegourjade.net**

🏕🐕€2 👫(wc)⛺♨🚿🚮/♨ (MSP) 🦋⛲⊕ nr 🛒⛰🚴

Leave Castres NE on D89 sp Rocquecourbe; site on R in 2km. Well sp. Ave de Roquecourbe is pt of D89. 3*, Med, hdg, pt shd, terr, EHU (6-16A) inc (poss rev pol); gas; bbq; 5% statics; bus; ccard acc; cycling; golf adj; CKE. *"Lovely site in beautiful park on Rv Agout; lge pitches; helpful staff; gd, tired clean san facs; 9 hole golf course adj; some lower pitches sl & poss soft; boat fr site to town; extra charge twin axles; gd security; poss groups workers LS; leisure cent & golf adj; vg cycling; highly rec; rest open evenings only; well run; excel for long or sh stay."* **€22.80, 1 Apr-30 Sep.** **2017**

CASTRIES 10E1 (2.6km NE Rural) 43.69406, 3.99585
Camping Domaine de Fondespierre, 277 Route de Fontmarie, 34160 Castries **04 67 91 20 03; accueil@ campingfondespierre.com; www.campingfondes pierre.com**

🐕 €3 ♿ (htd) WD ⛺ ♨ ⚲ 🚿 🏊 🦋 ☕ ♟ 🍴 ⊕ ♨ 🛝 ⛰ 🏊

Fr A9 exit junc 28 sp Vendargues, foll sp for Castries on D610. Cont thro Castries in dir of Sommieres. Aprox 1.5km past Castries turn L and foll camp sp. 3*, Med, hdstg, mkd, hdg, pt shd, terr, EHU (10A) inc (poss long lead req); bbq (sep area); sw nr; 40% statics; phone; Eng spkn; adv bkg acc; ccard acc; games area; tennis adj; bike hire; golf 2.5km; CKE. "Gd walking area; poss travellers & site poss unkempt LS; site rds narr with sharp, tree-lined bends - poss diff access to pitches for lge o'fits; NH; superb vill."
€34.00, 4 Jan-19 Dec. 2016

CAUDEBEC EN CAUX 3C2 (10km SE Urban) 49.48373, 0.77247 **Camp Municipal du Parc,** Rue Victor Hugo, 76940 La Mailleraye-sur-Seine **02 35 37 12 04; mairie-sg.lamaillerayesurseine@wanadoo.fr**

♿ WD ⛺ 🦋 ☕ 🍴 nr ⊕ nr 🛝 nr ⛰

Fr N on D131/D490 turn E onto D65. Or fr S on D913. Site sp in cent of town close to rv bank. 1*, Sm, hdg, pt shd, pt sl, EHU (6A) inc. "Pleasant, tidy site; site yourself, warden calls; adequate, clean san facs; gd walking area; vg NH."
€12.50, 1 Apr-30 Sep. 2015

CAUNES MINERVOIS 8F4 (1km S Rural) 43.32380, 2.52592 **Camp Municipal Les Courtals,** Ave du Stade, 11160 Caunes-Minervois **04 68 24 04 77 or 06 38 70 86 25; mairie.de.caunes@wanadoo.fr; www.odeaanaude.eu/catalogaude2/campsite-municipal-les-courtals-p-449.html**

♿ ⛺ 🦋 ☕ 🛝 ⛰

Sp fr D620 at stadium & adj rv. 1*, Sm, pt shd, EHU (4A) inc; phone; games area. "Pleasantly situated site; office opens 1800; gate locked 2100; site self, warden calls; pool 6km; rv adj; interesting town."
€12.00, 15 Jan-15 Dec. 2019

CAUSSADE 8E3 (1.8km N Urban) 44.16582, 1.54446 **Camp Municipal de la Piboulette,** Rue de la Piboulette, 82300 Caussade **05 63 93 09 07; secretariat@ mairie-caussade.com; www.mairie-caussade.fr**

🐕 €1.25 ♿ WD ⚲ 🚿 🦋 ☕ 🛝 ⛰

S on D820 fr Cahors (40km), turn L off D820 on ent Caussade onto D17 (Rte de Puylaroque). About 750m turn L (sp), site on R in 100m; lge grass stadium. 2*, Med, mkd, pt shd, serviced pitches; EHU (3A/8A) €1.90; adv bkg acc; CKE. "Pleasant site adj lake; spacious, mostly shd pitches; pleasant warden; excel, clean san facs, poss tired LS; sports cent adj; gates locked 2100 LS; easy 15 min walk to town; gd walks; pool on far side of stadium; gd cycling round lake; conv A20 & Gorges de l'Aveyron; vg mkt Mon; excel value; vg." **€10.00, 1 May-30 Sep.** 2015

CAUSSADE 8E3 (9km NE Rural) 44.18273, 1.60305 **Camping de Bois Redon,** 10 Chemin de Bonnet, 82240 Septfonds **05 63 64 92 49 or 06 78 35 79 97 (Mob); info@campingdeboisredon. com; www.campingdeboisredon.com**

12 🐕 €3 ♿ WD ⛺ ♨ ⚲ 🚿 🦋 ☕ 🍴 🛝 ⛰ 🏊

Exit A20 junc 59 to Caussade, then onto D926 to Septfonds (narr rds); after rndabt turn 3rd L; site sp. Site in 2km. One-way system when leaving site. 3*, Sm, mkd, pt shd, pt sl, EHU (10A) inc; bbq; 10% statics; Eng spkn; adv bkg req; bike hire; CKE. "Well-shd, spacious site in ancient oak forest with walks; charming Dutch owners; Septfonds nr with all facs; new shwrs (2013/14); enthusiastic owners continually making improvements; excel site; immac new san fac block." **€25.00** 2019

CAUSSADE 8E3 (10km NW Rural) 44.24323, 1.47735 **Camping Le Faillal,** 46 Blvd Pasteur, 82270 Montpezat-de-Quercy **05 63 02 07 08 or 07 68 59 25 32; contact@parcdufaillal.com; www.parcdufaillal.com**

12 🐕 €1.50 ♿ WD ⚲ 🚿 🦋 ☕ 🍴 🛝 nr ⛰ 🏊

N on D820, turn L onto D20, site clearly sp on R in 2km. (Do not take D38 bef D20 fr S). 2*, Med, hdg, pt shd, pt sl, terr, EHU (10A) €3.70; bbq; TV; phone; Eng spkn; adv bkg acc; games rm; tennis adj; games area; CKE. "Pretty, well-kept site; friendly, helpful staff; gd, clean san facs, poss ltd; super pool; many pitches unavail after heavy rain; access to some pitches diff; old town a 'must'; rec pay night bef dep; excel; horse drawn carriage rides, pony rides, kayaking, rafting, paintball." **€22.00** 2017

CAUTERETS 8G2 (2.5km NE Rural) 42.91092, -0.09934 **Camping GR10,** Route de Pierrefitte, 65110 Cauterets **06 20 30 25 85; contact@ gr10camping.com; www.gr10camping.com**

🐕 €1.30 ♿ (htd) WD ⛺ 🦋 ☕ 🛝 nr ⛰ 🏊 (htd)

N fr Cauterets on D920; site in 2.5km on R. Med, mkd, shd, terr, EHU €4; TV; 25% statics; Eng spkn; games rm; tennis; games area. "Pretty site; canyoning (guide on site); excel."
€20.00, 25 Jun-1 Sep. 2019

CAVAILLON 10E2 (8km E Rural) 43.84220, 5.13284 **Camp Municipal Les Royères du Prieuré,** La Combe-St Pierre, 84660 Maubec **04 90 76 50 34; camping.maubec@c-lmv.fr; www.campingmaubec-luberon.com**

🐕 €2 ♿ ⛺ 🦋 ☕ 🛝 nr ⛰

Heading E fr Cavaillon on D2, thro vill of Robion, in 400m at end vill sp turn R to Maubec. Site on R in 1km bef old vill. (Avoid any other rte with c'van). Diff access at ent, steep slope. Sm, pt shd, terr, EHU (6-10A) €5; 10% statics; CKE. "Awkward site for lge o'fits, otherwise vg; san facs stretched high ssn; conv A7; san facs refurbed; restful site; wine tasting on Tue eve." **€13.00, 1 Apr-15 Oct.** 2018

CAVAILLON *10E2 (1km S Rural) 43.82107, 5.03723*
Camp Municipal de la Durance, 495 Ave Boscodomini,
84300 Cavaillon **04 90 71 11 78; contact@camping-durance.com; www.camping-durance.com**

🏕 €1.50 🚻(htd) WD ♨ � ⅙ 🍴 🛒 nr 🏊

S of Cavaillon, nr Rv Durance. Fr A7 junc 25 foll
sp to town cent. In 200m R immed after x-ing rv.
Site sp (Municipal Camping) on L. 3*, Lge, pt shd,
EHU (4A-10A) €2.50- 6.50; TV; 30% statics; adv bkg
acc; tennis; fishing; games area. *"Site OK; gd NH
only; close to town; decent facs; reasonably priced."*
€18.60, 1 Apr-30 Sep.   2018

CAVAILLON *10E2 (9km S Rural) 43.78182, 5.04040*
Camping de la Vallée Heureuse, Quartier Lavau,
13660 Orgon **04 84 80 01 71; camping.valleeheureuse
@gmail.com; www.valleeheureuse.com**

🏕 €1.70 🚻 WD ♨ ☐ 🍴 MSP 🦋 ♈ 🍴 nr 🏊

Sp in Organ town cent. 3*, Lge, mkd, shd, terr, EHU
(16A); bbq; sw nr; TV; Eng spkn; adv bkg acc; CKE.
*"Site adj to old quarry in beautiful position; friendly,
helpful staff; superb san facs; gd pool; gd walking; café;
interesting area; conv m'way; isolated site; vill 1.5km."*
€25.00, 25 Mar-31 Oct.   2016

CAVAILLON *10E2 (12km SW Rural) 43.76058, 4.95154*
FFCC Camping Les Oliviers, Ave Jean Jaurès, 13810
Eygalières **04 90 95 91 86; campinglesoliviers13@
gmail.com; www.camping-les-oliviers.com**

🏕 €1 🚻(htd) ⅙ 🦋 ♈ 🍴 nr ⅙ nr 🛒 nr 🏕

Exit A7 junc 25; D99 dir St Rémy-de-Provence; in
8km camping sp on L; in vill well sp.
Sm, hdg, pt shd, EHU (6A) inc; bbq (elec, gas), adv bkg
acc. *"Lovely, friendly site in olive grove nr scenic vill;
quiet site; facs rustic but v clean; pitches cramped for
lge o'fits; simple site; diff acc for lge o'fits; free WiFi."*
€19.00, 30 Mar-30 Sep.   2018

CAVALAIRE SUR MER *10F4 (2km NE Rural) 43.18220,
6.51610* **Kawan Village Cros de Mouton,** Chemin de
Cros de Mouton, 83240 Cavalaire-sur-Mer **04 94 64
10 87 or 04 94 05 46 38; campingcrosdemouton@
wanadoo.fr; www.crosdemouton.com**

🏕 €2 🚻 WD ♨ ☐ MSP 🦋 ♈ 🍴 ⅚ 🛒 🏕 🏊(htd)

🏖 🏖 sand 1.8km

Exit A8 junc 36 dir Ste Maxime on D125/D25, foll
sp on D559 to Cavalaire-sur-Mer. Site sp on coast
app fr Grimaud/St Tropez & Le Lavandou; diff
access. 3*, Lge, mkd, shd, terr, serviced pitches; EHU
(10A); gas; TV; 10% statics; phone; Eng spkn; adv bkg
rec; ccard acc; bike hire; CKE. *"Attractive, well-run,
popular site in hills behind town - rec adv bkg even LS;
lge pitches avail; poss diff access to pitches due steep
site rds - help avail; pleasant, welcoming & efficient
staff; gd san facs; gd pool; vg rest & bar; buses to
St Tropez; excel; lovely views; steep walk fr town."*
€36.00, 21 Mar-31 Oct.   2015

CAVALAIRE SUR MER *10F4 (3km NE Coastal)
43.19450, 6.55495* **Sélection Camping,** 12 Blvd de la
Mer, 83420 La Croix-Valmer **04 94 55 10 30; camping-selection@wanadoo.fr; www.selectioncamping.com**

🏕 €4 🚻(htd) WD ♨ ☐ ⅙ 🍴 MSP 🦋 ♈ 🍴 ♈ ⅚ 🛒 🏕 🏊

🏊(htd) 🏖 🏖 sand 400m

Off N559 bet Cavalaire & La Croix-Valmer, 2km past
La Croix at rndabt turn R sp Barbigoua, site in 200m.
4*, Lge, mkd, hdg, shd, terr, EHU (10A) €5; gas; TV;
20% statics; phone; bus; Eng spkn; adv bkg req; games
area. *"Excel location; sm pitches; private bthrms avail;
dogs not acc Jul/Aug; vg san facs; excel pool; excel
site."* €35.00, 15 Mar-15 Oct.   2018

CAVALAIRE SUR MER *10F4 (0.9km S Urban) 43.16956,
6.53005* **Camping de La Baie,** Blvd Pasteur, 83240
Cavalaire-sur-Mer **04 94 64 08 15 or 04 94 64 08 10;
contact@camping-baie.com; www.camping-baie.com**

🏕 €4 🚻(htd) ♨ ☐ ⅙ 🍴 🦋 ♈ 🍴 ♈ ⅚ 🛒 🏕 🏊(htd) 🏖

🏖 sand 400m

Exit A8 sp Ste Maxime/St Tropez & foll D25 & D559
to Cavalaire. Site sp fr seafront. 4*, Lge, mkd, pt
shd, pt sl, EHU (10A) €6; bbq; 10% statics; Eng spkn;
adv bkg acc; ccard acc; sailing; games area; jacuzzi;
watersports; games rm. *"Well-run, busy site; pleasant
staff; excel pool & facs; nr shops, beach, marina & cafes;
cycle paths; gd location; diving 500m; sm pitches; narr
rd."* €55.00, 15 Mar-15 Nov.   2019

CAYEUX SUR MER *3B2 (4km NE Coastal) 50.20291,
1.52641* **Camping Les Galets de la Mollière,** Rue
Faidherbe, 80410 La Mollière-d'Aval **03 22 26 61 85;
info@campinglesgaletsdelamolliere.com;
www.campinglesgaletsdelamolliere.com**

🏕 €3 🚻 WD ♨ ☐ ⅙ 🍴 MSP 🦋 ♈ 🍴 ⅚ 🛒 🏕 🏊(htd)

🏖 🏖 sand 500m

Fr Cayeux-sur-Mer take D102 N along coast for 3km.
Site on R. 3*, Lge, mkd, pt shd, EHU (6A) inc; gas; bbq;
25% statics; games area; games rm; CKE. *"Spacious,
much improved, wooded site with lge pitches; barrier
clsd 2300-0700; pleasant staff; dirty pitches; unhelpful
staff; poor."* €33.00, 3 Apr-1 Nov.   2015

CAYLAR, LE *10E1 (4km SW Rural) 43.83629, 3.29045*
Camping Mas de Messier, St Félix-de-l'Héras, 34520
Le Caylar **04 67 44 52 63; info@masdemessier.com;
www.masdemessier.com**

🏕 🚻 WD ♨ ☐ ⅙ 🍴 🦋 ♈ 🛒 nr 🏕 🏊

Fr N exit A75 junc 49 onto D9 thro Le Caylar. Turn
R sp St Félix & foll sp St Félix-de-l'Héras; at x-rds
in St Félix turn R, site in 1km on L. Fr S exit A75
junc 50; foll sp to St Félix-de-l'Héras; at x-rds turn
R & as bef. Sm, hdg, pt shd, pt sl, EHU (10A) €3; Eng
spkn; adv bkg req; CKE. *"Excel views fr some pitches;
friendly, helpful Dutch owner; facs excel; access
unsuitable lge o'fits; meals avail some eves; gd walking;
excel long or sh stay; dogs free; low rates in LS."*
€23.00, 15 Apr-1 Oct.   2018

FRANCE

CAYLUS *8E4* (0.5km E Rural) *44.23368, 1.77636*
FFCC Camping de la Bonnette, 672 route de la
Bonnette, 82160 Caylus 05 63 65 70 20 or 06 07 34
61 99; info@campingbonnette.com;
www.campingbonnette.com

🐕 €1.50 ♙♙ �📅 ⚓ ♿ ➰ ⧗ ❄ ▽ 🍴 🛒nr ⛺ 🔧 ⛷

Fr A20 exit junc 59 dir Caylus; thro Caylus to g'ge
on L. Turn R in 1km over next crossrds & foll site sps
to site on R in 1km. 3*, Med, mkd, hdg, pt shd, EHU
(10A) €3.50; bbq; red long stay; 10% statics; Eng spkn;
adv bkg rec; games area. *"Nice, tidy, scenic site on edge
of medieval vill - worth a visit; friendly owner; pitches in
groups of 4, not v private."*
€19.00, 29 Mar-4 Oct. 2019

CEAUCE *4E1* (1km N Rural) *48.49812, -0.62481*
Camp Municipal de la Veillotière, Chemin de la
Veillotière, 61330 Ceaucé 02 33 38 31 19; mairie.
ceauce@wanadoo.fr; www.mairie-ceauce.fr

♙♙ 📅 ⚓ ♿ ➰ 🗺 ⧗ 🛒 ⛺

S fr Domfront on D962 dir Mayenne, at rndabt in
Ceaucé turn L. Site in 200m on R adj sm lake.
Sm, hdg, pt shd, pt sl, EHU (6A); fishing adj. *"Well-kept
site on edge vill; gd; nice as always; bar 200m; quiet
cycle rte to Ambrieves Les Vallees; warden calls eves,
otherwise visit mairie."*
€11.00, 1 May-30 Sep. 2019

"That's changed – Should I let the Club know?"

If you find something on site that's different
from the site entry, fill in a report and let us
know. See camc.com/europereport.

CERCY LA TOUR *4H4* (0.9km S Urban) *46.86680,
3.64328* **Camp Municipal Le Port,** 58360 Cercy-la-Tour
03 86 50 55 27 or 03 86 50 07 11 (Mairie)

🐕 🐕 ♙♙ 📅 ➰ ⧗

At Decize take D981 E; in 12 km L onto D37, then
L onto D10 to Cercy-la-Tour; site sp in vill. Adj
municipal pool, Rv Aron & canal. Med, hdstg, pt shd,
EHU inc; phone; Eng spkn; CKE. *"Clean & tidy site;
immac san facs; gd cycling/walking along canal; excel
value; excel."* **€9.00, 25 Apr-25 Oct.** 2017

CERESTE *10E3* (9km W Rural) *43.84361, 5.49666*
Camping à la Ferme (Bouscarle), Les Monguets,
84400 Castellet-en-Luberon 04 90 75 28 62

🐕 €1 ♙♙ 📅 ➰ ⧗

Fr W on D900 (Apt) ignore Camping à la Ferme sp
to R nr St Martin-de-Castillon (v narr rd). Cont 2km
to La Bègude & turn R onto D223 dir Le Boisset.
Site 3km on R, well sp. Sm, shd, pt sl, EHU (4A) €3
(long lead req); Eng spkn; adv bkg acc; CKE. *"Excel,
scenic CL-type site on fruit farm; friendly owners; excel
walking, cycling."* **€13.00, Easter-1 Nov.** 2015

CERET *8H4* (1km E Rural) *42.48981, 2.76305*
Camping Les Cerisiers, Mas de la Toure, 66400
Céret 09 70 35 00 30; www.campingcerisiers.fr

12 🐕 🐕 ♙♙ 📅 ⚓ ❄ ♿ ➰ ⧗ ❄ 🦋 ⧗ nr ⧗ nr ⛺ nr 🍴 ⛺ 🔧

Exit A9 junc 43 onto D115, turn off for cent of
Céret. Site is on D618 approx 800m E of Céret twd
Maureillas, sp. Tight ascent for lge o'fits.
2*, Med, mkd, shd, EHU (4A); gas; sw nr; TV;
60% statics; phone; site clsd Jan; CKE. *"Site in cherry
orchard; gd size pitches; facs dated & ltd LS; footpath
to attractive vill with modern art gallery; pool 600m;
conv Andorra, Perpignan, Collioure."* **€18.00** 2019

CERILLY *4H3* (10km N Rural) *46.68210, 2.78630*
Camping des Ecossais, La Salle, 03360 Isle-et-Bardais
04 70 66 62 57 or 04 70 67 50 96; ecossais@
campingstroncais.com; www.campingstroncais.com

🐕 €1.50 ♙♙ 📅 ⚓ ➰ 🗺 🦋 ⧗ ❄ 🍴 ⧗ nr 🛒 ⛺ ⛺

Fr Lurcy-Lévis take D978A SW, turn R onto D111 N
twd Isle-et-Bardais & foll camp sp. Ent tight.
2*, Med, hdg, pt shd, pt sl, EHU (10A) inc; bbq; sw; twin
axles; 10% statics; adv bkg acc; games area; games
rm; fishing; CKE. *"Excel; v busy high ssn; ltd facs LS;
gd cycling; site in oak forest; rec; mountain bike nec on
forest tracks."* **€12.00, 1 Apr-30 Sep.** 2016

CERNAY *6F3* (0.9km SW Urban) *47.80448, 7.16999*
Camping Les Cigognes (formerly Camping Les Acacias),
16 Rue René Guibert, 68700 Cernay 03 89 75 56 97;
campinglescigognes@orange.fr; www.camping-les-
cigognes.com

🐕 €1.20 ♙♙ 📅 ⚓ ♿ ➰ 🗺 🦋 ⧗ ❄ 🛒 🔧 ⛷

Fr N on D83 by-pass, exit Cernay Est. Turn R into
town at traff lts, immed L bef rv bdge, site sp on L;
well sp. 3*, Lge, mkd, pt shd, EHU (5A) €3.50 (poss rev
pol); red long stay; 25% statics; CKE. *"Friendly staff;
clean, tidy site; storks nesting over some pitches; sh
walk to town."* **€18.00, 1 Apr-30 Sep.** 2015

CERNAY LA VILLE *4E3* (0.8km NW Rural) *48.67630,
1.97208* **Cernay Vacances,** 37 Rue de la Ferme, 78720
Cernay-la-Ville 33 13 48 52 123; albert.koning@
free.fr; www.cernayvacances.com

12 🐕 🐕 ♙♙ 📅 ➰ 🦋

Fr Rouen take A13 twrds Paris, then A12 twrds
Rambouillet. Aft Leon de Bruxelles rest & metro
take exit Mesnil - St. Denis. At rndabt pass by D58
twrds le-Mesnil, dir Dampierre. In Dampierre turn R
onto D91 then L onto D149 twrds Senlisse. At top of
this rd turn onto D906, aft 500mtrs at Peugeot g'ge
turn R on Rue des Moulins strt to fm. Sm, pt shd,
EHU €4; cooking facs; Eng spkn; adv bkg acc; games
area. *"Vg."* **€16.00** 2017

CHABLIS *4F4* (0.6km SE Rural) *47.81376, 3.80563*
Camp Municipal Le Serein, Quai Paul Louis Courier,
89800 Chablis **03 86 42 44 39 or 03 86 42 80 80
(Mairie); mairie-chablis@chablis.net;
www.chablis.net**

🐕 €1.50 ♦♦♦ ♿ ⛱ 🚿 🍴 ℗ nr 🏧 nr 🏧

W fr Tonnere on D965; in approx 16km exit D965
for Chablis; in 300m, just bef x-ing Rv Serein, turn
L at camping sp onto Quai Paul Louis Courier; site
in 300m on R. 2*, Med, hdg, mkd, shd, EHU (5A)
€2; Eng spkn; adv bkg acc; CKE. *"Attractive, tidy
site; facs poss stretched high ssn; friendly & helpful
warden, calls 0800-1200 & 1600-2000; easy walk to
attractive town; vineyards & wine cellars nrby; excel
Sun mkt; warden attaches elec supply to locked post."*
€12.00, 2 Jun-15 Sep. 2016

CHAGNY *6H1* (0.7km W Urban) *46.91187, 4.74567*
Camping du Pâquier Fané, 20 Rue du Pâquier Fané,
71150 Chagny **03 85 87 21 42; camping-chagny@
orange.fr; www.campingchagny.com**

🐕 €1 ♦♦♦ ⬜ ♿ ⛱ 🚿 🍴 🍴 nr ℗ nr 🏧 nr 🏧

Clearly sp in town. 3*, Med, hdg, mkd, pt shd, EHU
(16A) inc; gas; Eng spkn; fishing; tennis adj; CKE.
*"Well laid-out, well-lit vg site; friendly, helpful resident
wardens; clean san facs; htd pool adj; many pitches sm
& diff med/lge o'fits; on wine rte; gd cycling nrby (voie
verte)."* **€24.60, 29 Mar-31 Oct.** 2019

CHAILLAC *7A3* (0.6km SW Rural) *46.43260, 1.29602*
Camp Municipal Les Vieux Chênes, 36310 Chaillac
**02 54 25 61 39 or 02 54 25 74 26 (Mairie); chaillac-
mairie@wanadoo.fr**

12 🐕 ♦♦♦ (htd) ⬜ ⛱ 🚿 🍴 🦋 🍴 nr ℗ nr 🏧 nr 🏧

Exit N20 S of Argenton-sur-Creuse at junc 20 onto
D36 to Chaillac. Thro vill, site 1st L after sq by
'Mairie', adj Lac du Rochegaudon. Fr S exit J21, take
D10 sp St Benoit du Sault. Fr there turn L onto D36
and foll instructions above. 3*, Sm, hdg, mkd, pt shd,
pt sl, EHU (16A) inc (poss rev pol); bbq; sw nr; Eng
spkn; adv bkg acc; waterslide; fishing adj; tennis adj;
CKE. *"Excel site, beautiful location, friendly wardens,
well kept san facs, gd local supmkt 2 mins walk (clsd
Mon); lake nrby."* **€11.40** 2018

CHALAIS *7C2* (10km NW Rural) *45.32758, -0.02385*
Chez Sarrazin, 16480 Brossac **05 45 78 21 57 or
07 80 52 27 32; chezsarrazin@yahoo.co.uk;
www.chezsarrazin.net**

🐕 €2 ♦♦♦ ⬜ ⛱ 🚿 🍴 🦋 🍴 🏧 🏊

N10 S fr Angouleme, leave exit for Barbezieux to
Brossac & Chalais on D731, 700m after rndabt at
Brossac Gare, L twd Brie Sous Chalais. After 1.4km R
at 4 wheelie bins sp Chez Sarrazin Camping.
Sm, shd, pt sl, EHU (10A); bbq; Eng spkn; adv bkg acc;
games area. *"Natural site in beautiful setting; many
historical vills; walks; san facs & pool excel; charming
& peaceful; excel; steep path to shwrs; helpful owners;
well equipped."* **€28.00, Easter-31 Oct.** 2017

CHALANDRAY *4H1* (0.8km N Rural) *46.66728,
-0.00214* **Camping du Bois de St Hilaire,** Rue de la
Gare, 86190 Chalandray **05 49 60 20 84 or 01246
852823 (UK); acceuil@camping-st-hilaire.com;
www.camping-st-hilaire.com**

🐕 €1 ♦♦♦ (htd) ⬜ ⛱ 🚿 🍴 MSP 🦋 🍴 🍴 🏧 nr 🏧 🏹
🏊 (htd)

Foll N149 bet Parthenay & Vouille; at xrds in vill,
turn N into Rue de la Gare (D24); site 750m on R
over rlwy line. 3*, Sm, mkd, hdg, shd, EHU (10A)
€3.95; bbq (charcoal, elec, gas); twin axles; TV; phone;
bus 750m; Eng spkn; adv bkg acc; ccard acc; tennis;
games rm; games area; mini golf; boules pitch; fire
pit; CCI. *"Friendly, helpful British owners; situated
in mature forest area, sh walk fr vill; 20 mins fr
Futuroscope; lge pitches; excel, clean site & pool; c'van
storage; poss muddy in wet weather; woodland walks;
excel bakery in vill."* **€25.00, 1 May-30 Sep.** 2019

**"I like to fill in the reports as I
travel from site to site"**

You'll find report forms at the back of this
guide, or you can fill them in online at
camc.com/europereport.

CHALLANS *2H4* (10km SE Rural) *46.81522, -1.77472*
Camping Domaine de Bellevue, Bellevue Du
Ligneron, 85670 Saint Christophe du Ligneron
**02 51 93 30 66 or 06 21 55 54 29 (mob); contact@
vendee-camping-bellevue.com; www.vendee-
camping-bellevue.com**

12 🐕 €3 ♦♦♦ ⛱ ♿ ⛱ 🚿 🍴 🍴 🏊 (htd)

Fr S: On Route National D948 exit Saint Christophe
du Lingeron; turn W in dir Saint Gilles Croix de Vie/
Commequirers; at rndbt cont strt on; take 2nd R
at Bellevue du Ligneron. 3*, Med, hdg, EHU (16) €4;
bbq; 50% statics; Eng spkn; adv bkg acc; ccard acc;
fishing; games rm; bike hire; CKE. *"Gd value for money;
in lovely Vendee region; gd fishing on site; new site with
friendly owners; takeaway; v lge pitches."*
€14.00 2016

CHALLANS *2H4* (4km S Rural) *46.81869, -1.88874*
FFCC Camping Le Ragis, Chemin de la Fradinière,
85300 Challans **02 51 68 08 49; info@camping-
leragis.com; www.camping leragis.com**

🐕 €4 ♦♦♦ (htd) ⬜ ⛱ ♿ 🚿 🍴 MSP 🦋 🍴 🍴 ℗ nr 🏧 🏧 🏧
🏊 (htd)

Fr Challans go S on D32 Rte Les Sables, turn R onto
Chemin de la Fradinière & foll sp.
3*, Lge, hdg, mkd, pt shd, EHU (10A) €4; gas; bbq;
twin axles; TV; 50% statics; bus 1km; Eng spkn; adv
bkg acc; ccard acc; waterslide; games area. *"Vg;
homegrown veg; tickets for Puy Du Fou; night car
park; conv Vendee coast; lake fishing; petanque;
traditional French site; kids club 4-10; v friendly staff."*
€25.00, 1 Apr-31 Oct. 2016

CHALON SUR SAONE *6H1* (3km E Rural) *46.78411, 4.87136* **Camping du Pont de Bourgogne,** Rue Julien Leneveu, 71380 St Marcel **03 85 48 26 86 or 03 85 94 16 90 (LS); campingchalon71@wanadoo.fr; www.camping-chalon.com**

🛉 €2.60 👫 (htd) 🚾 🛋 ♿ 🚮 ⁄ 💷 ♨ 🍴 🕙 🛒 🚲 ⚠

Fr A6 exit junc 26 (sp Chalon Sud) onto N80 E; foll sp Chalon-sur-Saône; at 1st rndabt go strt over (sp Louhans & St Marcel) & over flyover; take 4th exit on 2nd rndbt; immed after this rndabt fork R thro Les Chavannes (still on N80). Turn R at traff lts bef bdge. (DO NOT CROSS BDGE). Site in 500m. 3*, Med, hdg, mkd, hdstg, pt shd, terr, EHU (6-10A) inc (rev pol); gas; bbq; TV; 2% statics; Eng spkn; adv bkg acc; ccard acc; games rm; bike hire; canoeing nr; rv fishing; CKE. "Peaceful, well-run rvside site in gd location; lge pitches, some by rv; helpful, friendly staff; excel clean san facs; poss stretched high ssn; vg rest/bar; pool 500m; no o'fits over 12m; rvside walks; lovely town, 20 min walk; conv NH fr A6; vg; gd cycling; shopping ctr nrby." €30.70, 1 Apr-30 Sep, L17. 2019

CHALONNES SUR LOIRE *2G4* (1.5km E Rural) *47.35164, -0.74679* **Camping Les Portes de la Loire,** Le Candais, 49290 Chalonnes-sur-Loire **41 78 02 27; contact@lesportesdelaloire.fr**

🛉 👫 🏕 ♿ ⁄ 💷 🕙 ⚠

Fr D723 cross bdge to Challones. In town turn L sp Rochefort-Sur-Loire. Site on L of this rd in abt 1km. 3*, Lge, mkd, pt shd, EHU (10A) €3; bbq; twin axles; adv bkg acc. "Close to rv & town; peaceful setting; lge pitches; gd touring base; vg; excel san facs." €20.00, 1 May-30 Sep. 2016

CHALONNES SUR LOIRE *2G4* (10km NW Urban) *47.39211, -0.87082* **Camping La Promenade,** Quai des Mariniers, 49570 Montjean-sur-Loire **02 41 39 02 68 or 06 26 32 60 28 (mob); contact@campinglapromenade.com; www.campinglapromenade.com**

🛉 €2 👫 🚾 🏕 ♿ 🚮 ⁄ 🦋 📶 🍴 🕙 🛒 nr ⚠ ♨ 🏊 (htd)
🛁 ⛱ sand 600m

Exit Angers on N23 twd Nantes. Exit 1km beyond St Germain-des-Prés dir Montjean-sur-Loire. Cross rv then R on D210 to site in 500m. 3*, Lge, mkd, hdg, pt shd, EHU (10A) €4; gas; bbq; twin axles; TV; 30% statics; Eng spkn; adv bkg acc; ccard acc; games area; CKE. "Friendly, young owners; interesting sculptures in vill & at Ecomusée; gd for Loire cycling; diff exit to R for lge vehicles; fishing nr; on 'Loire á Vélo' route; vg value LS." €22.50, 1 Apr-30 Sep. 2020

CHALONS EN CHAMPAGNE *5D1* (3km S Urban) *48.93579, 4.38299* **Camping de Châlons en Champagne,** 11-15 Rue de Plaisance, 51000 Châlons-en-Champagne **03 26 68 38 00; camping.chalons@orange.fr; www.aquadis-loisirs.com**

🛉 €1.50 👫 (htd) 🚾 🏕 ♿ 🚮 ⁄ 💷 🦋 🕙 🛒 nr ⚠

Fr N on A26 exit junc 17, on D3 foll sp to Chalons en Champagne, then to Fagnières. Strt on at traff lts, then L at 1s rndabt. Turn R, sp Vitry le François, site sp. Fr S exit junc 18 onto D977, then D5 over rv & canal nr town cent; then foll site sp to R. Fr N44 S of Chalons go St Memmie; foll site sp. D977 fr N into Châlons, cont on main rd to traff lts at 6 x-rds & turn R, site well sp. Or exit A4 junc 27 onto N44; turn R at St Memmie; site sp. NB some sps in area still show old town name 'Châlons-sur-Marne'. Do not use SatNav. 4*, Med, hdg, mkd, hdstg, pt shd, EHU (6-10A) (poss long lead req & rev pol, 2 pin adapter req); bbq; red long stay; twin axles; TV; bus; Eng spkn; adv bkg acc; ccard acc; tennis; games area; CKE. "Popular site adj park; generous pitches, inc hdstg; rec arr early or phone ahead; check barrier arrangements if need early dep; gates shut 2130 LS & 2300 high ssn; ltd bus service; poss noisy high ssn - pop concerts in adj area; hypmkt 1km; flat walk to lovely, interesting town; conv touring base & NH; friendly helpful recep; seasonal workers in Sep; san facs neglected but clean." €35.00, 5 Mar-24 Aug. 2019

CHALUS *7B3* (10km NW Rural) *45.71540, 0.91956* **Camping Parc Verger,** Le Halte, 87150 Champagnac-la-Rivière, Limousin **0844 232 8500 (Fr UK) or 05 55 01 22 83 or 06 04 09 05 20 (mob); pvbureau@parcverger.com; www.parcverger.com**

12 🛉 👫 (htd) 🚾 🏕 ♿ 🚮 ⁄ 💷 🍴 nr 🕙 nr 🚲 🏊

N fr Châlus on D901; in 9km turn L onto D75 sp Champagnac-la-Rivière; site on L in 150m. Sm, mkd, hdstg, unshd, EHU (16A) inc; bbq; sw; twin axles; red long stay; bus 150m; Eng spkn; adv bkg acc; ccard acc; CKE. "Lovely site; welcoming, friendly, helpful British owners; lge pitches suitable for RVs; gd clean san facs, poss stretched high ssn; gd mkd walks nrby; 15km-long walk/cycle path adj (old rwly track); red grass pitch; excel local vet; excel area for walking; bike hire." €18.00 2016

CHAMBERY *9B3* (5km E Rural) *45.55151, 5.98416* **Camp Municipal Le Savoy,** Parc des Loisirs, Chemin des Fleurs, 73190 Challes-les-Eaux **04 79 72 97 31; www.camping-challesleseaux.com**

🛉 €1.40 👫 🚾 🏕 ♿ 🚮 🦋 🕙 nr 🚲 🛒 nr

On o'skts of town app fr Chambéry on D1006. Pass airfield, lake & tennis courts on L, L at traff lts just bef cent of Challes-les Eaux sp Parc de Loisirs, at Hôtel Les Neiges de France foll camp sp to site in 100m. Fr A41 exit junc 20, foll sp Challes-les-Eaux, then 'Centre Ville', then D1006 N. 3*, Med, hdstg, mkd, shd, serviced pitches; EHU (6-10A) €2.90; gas; sw nr; red long stay; bus; adv bkg acc; ccard acc; fishing adj; tennis adj. "Well-designed, well-run, clean site in beautiful setting; diff sized pitches; level (suitable wheelchairs); friendly, helpful staff; excel modern san facs; excel walking; well run site, rec hotel school rest in term time." €18.00, 1 Apr-8 Oct. 2017

CHAMBERY *9B3* (25km SW Rural) *45.53804, 5.79973*
Camping Les Peupliers, Lac d'Aiguebelette, 73610
Lépin-le-Lac **04 79 36 00 48 or 06 66 10 09 99 (mob);
info@camping-lespeupliers.net; www.camping-les
peupliers.net**

🐕 €1.20 ♟ ﾒ ⊞ 🚿 ♨ ✗ 🐾 ⛱ 🍴 ⊕nr 🍴 🛒nr ⛺

Exit A43 junc 12 & foll sp Lac d'Aiguebelette (D921).
Turn L at rndabt & foll rd on L of lake. Site on R after
sm vill. 2*, Lge, hdg, mkd, pt shd, EHU (6A) €3.50; sw
nr; ccard acc; fishing; CKE. *"Pleasant site in beautiful
setting, espec lakeside pitches; friendly, helpful owner;
busy w/ends."* **€19.00, 1 Apr-31 Oct.** **2015**

CHAMBON SUR LAC *7B4* (2km W Rural) *45.57127,
2.89067* **Camping de Serrette,** Serrette, 63790
Chambon-sur-La **04 73 88 67 67; camping.de.serrette
@wanadoo.fr; campingdeserrette.com**

🐕 €2.50 ♟ ﾒ ⊞ ♨ 🚿 ♿ 🚿 ✗ 🍴 ⊕ 🍴 🛒 ⛱ 🛶 🎣

Fr A75, exit 6, foll D996 dir Mont Dore. Foll site
sp after Lac Chambo. After 1.5km turn L onto
D636. Site on R. Sharp turn at ent. 3*, Sm, hdg,
mkd, pt shd, pt sl, terr, EHU (10A) €4.80; bbq; sw
nr; twin axles; TV; 50% statics; phone; Eng spkn;
adv bkg acc; table tennis; games rm; CKE. *"Excel
walking area; watersports on Lac Chambon; gd site."*
€26.70, 28 Apr-17 Sep. **2016**

CHAMONIX MONT BLANC *9B4* (3km NE Rural)
45.9378, 6.8925 **Camping La Mer de Glace,** 200 Chemin
de la Bagna, Praz de Chamonix, 74400 Chamonix
**04 50 53 44 03; info@chamonix-camp.com;
www.chamonix-camping.com**

🐕 ♟ (htd) ⊞ ﾒ ♨ ♿ 🚿 ✗ 🍴 🐾 ⛱ 🍴nr ⊕nr 🛒nr ⛺

Foll sp on D1506 thro Chamonix dir Argentière
& Swiss Frontier; site well sp on R in 3km but ent
under bdge 2.4m. Rec, to avoid low hdge cont to 1st
rndabt in Praz-de-Chamonix & foll sp to site (R at
rndabt). 3*, Med, mkd, hdg, hdstg, pt shd, pt sl, EHU
(10A) €3; bbq; bus & train 500m; Eng spkn; CKE. *"Well-
run, wooded site with superb views; sm pitches; helpful
staff; vg facs; bar 500m; v conv trains/buses; close to
Flégère lift; sports cent nr; htd pool 2km; path to town
via woods & rv; excel."*
€25.00, 4 May-9 Oct. **2016**

CHAMONIX MONT BLANC *9B4* (7km NE Rural)
45.97552, 6.92224 **Camping Le Glacier d'Argentière,**
161 Chemin des Chosalets, 74400 Argentière
**04 50 54 17 36; info@campingchamonix.com;
www.campingchamonix.com**

🐕 €0.50 ♟ ⊞ ﾒ ♿ 🚿 ✗ 🐾 ⛱ 🛒nr

On Chamonix-Argentière D1506 rd bef Argentière
take R fork twd Argentière cable car stn. Site
immed on R. 2*, Med, pt shd, pt sl, EHU (2-10A);
bbq; Eng spkn; adv bkg acc; games area; CKE.
*"Alpine excursions; cable cars adj; mountain views;
friendly, helpful owners; gd friendly site; Alpine
views; quiet relaxed site; bus stop 1 min; 10 min
walk to Argentiere Vill', train stn & cable car; mkd
paths fr site; free travel on local buses & trains inc."*
€24.00, 15 May-30 Sep. **2019**

CHAMONIX MONT BLANC *9B4* (1.6km SW Rural)
45.91466, 6.86138 **Camping Iles des Barrats,** 185
Chemin de l'Ile des Barrats, 74400 Chamonix
**04 50 53 51 44; campingiledesbarrats74@orange.fr;
www.campingdesbarrats.com**

🐕 €1 ♟ ⊞ ﾒ ♿ 🚿 ✗ 🐾 ⛱ 🛒nr

Fr Mont Blanc tunnel take 1st L on app Chamonix,
foll sp to hospital, site opp hospital. Do not go
into town. 3*, Sm, mkd, unshd, pt sl, EHU (5-10A)
€3.30-4.30; gas; sw nr; Eng spkn; adv bkg acc; CKE.
*"Great little site; superb mountain views; friendly family
owners; immac facs; 10 mins level walk to town; 10
mins cable car Mont Blanc; excel; bus & train pass fr
recep."* **€31.00, 1 Jun-23 Sep.** **2017**

"We must tell the Club about that great site we found"

Get your site reports in by mid-August and we'll
do our best to get your updates into the next
edition.

CHAMONIX MONT BLANC *9B4* (3.5km SW Rural)
45.90203, 6.83716 **Camping Les Deux Glaciers,**
80 Route des Tissières, Les Bossons, 74400
Chamonix **04 50 53 15 84; info@les2glaciers.com;
www.les2glaciers.com**

🐕 ♟ (htd) ⊞ ﾒ ♨ ♿ 🚿 ✗ 🍴 ⛱ ⊕ 🛒 ⛺

Exit Mont Blanc tunnel foll sps Geneva turn L on
D1506 (Chamonix-Geneva rd), in 2km turn R for Les
Bossons & L under bdge. Fr W foll sps Chamonix
& Mont Blanc tunnel. On dual c/way turn R at sp
`Les Bossons' & site after Mercure Hotel; adj Les
Cimes site; site clearly sp fr D1205. 3*, Med, pt
shd, sl, EHU (6-10A) €2.50-7; bus; Eng spkn; games
rm; table tennis; CKE. *"Pleasant, well-kept site in
wonderful location just under Mont Blanc; roomy
pitches; clean facs; poss diff site for lge o'fits over 6m;
if recep clsd pitch & wait until 1730; ideal for walking;
skating rink 4km; funicular adj to Glacier des Bossons;
rec arr early high ssn; pool 4km; highly rec; vg."*
€22.50, 1 Jan-15 Nov & 15 Dec-31 Dec. **2017**

CHANAC *9D1* (0.5km S Urban) *44.46519, 3.34670*
Camp Municipal La Vignogue, Rue de Plaisance,
48230 Chanac **04 66 48 24 09 or 06 82 93 60 68
(mob); gites-camping-chanac@orange.fr;
www.chanac.fr**

🐕 €1 ♟ (htd) ⊞ ﾒ ♨ 🚿 ✗ 🐾 ⛱ 🍴nr ⊕nr 🛒nr

Exit A75 junc 39.1 onto N88 to Chanac; site well
sp in vill. Sm, mkd, pt shd, pt sl, EHU (6A) inc;
bbq; 10% statics; Eng spkn; adv bkg acc. *"Excel;
bar 500m; pool adj; rec arr early (bef 1800)."*
€15.50, 15 Apr-30 Sep. **2017**

FRANCE

CHANTILLY *3D3* (5km NW Rural) *49.22571, 2.42862*
Camping Campix, 60340 St Leu d'Esserent
03 44 56 08 48; campix@orange.fr;
www.campingcampix.com

🏠 €2 🐕 (htd) 🚿 ♿ 🔌 🚰 / 🅿 🦋 ⛲ 🍴 ⓗ 🛒 🧺 ⛰ 🛶

Exit A1 junc 8 to Senlis; cont W fr Senlis on D924
thro Chantilly, x-ing Rv Oise to St Leu-d'Esserent;
leave town on D12 NW twd Cramoisy thro housing
est; foll site sp for 1km, winding app.
3*, Med, hdstg, mkd, shd, terr, EHU (6-10A) €3.50
(min 25m cable poss req); gas; bbq; sw nr; red long
stay; phone; Eng spkn; adv bkg acc; ccard acc; fishing;
games rm; CKE. "Beautiful, peaceful site in former
quarry - poss unguarded, vertical drops; helpful owner
& friendly staff; wide variety of pitches - narr, steep
access & o'hanging trees on some; conv Paris Parc
Astérix & Disneyland (Astérix tickets fr recep); sh walk
to vill; rec; gd facs; long elec leads maybe needed."
€27.00, 7 Mar-30 Nov. 2018

CHANTILLY *3D3* (7km NW Rural) *49.21225, 2.40270*
Camping L'Abbatiale, 39 Rue Salvador Allendé,
60340 St Leu-d'Esserent **03 44 56 38 76; contact@
camping-abbatiale.fr; www.camping-abbatiale.com**

12 🐕 (htd) 🚿 🔌 🚰 / 🅿 🦋 🍴 ⓗ nr 🧺 nr ⛰ 🛶 sandy 1km

S twds Paris on A1 exit Senlis; cont W fr Senlis on
D924/D44 thro Chantilly x-ing Rv Oise to St Leu-
d'Esserent; cont on D44, x-ing D603 which becomes
Rue Salvador Allendé in 700m; foll site sps; avoid rv
x-ing on D17 fr SW; v narr bdge. 3*, Sm, hdg, mkd,
hdstg, pt shd, EHU (3A) €2.50 (some rev pol); bbq (sep
area); twin axles; red long stay; phone; bus adj; Eng
spkn; adv bkg acc; ccard acc; games rm; games area.
"Chantilly & chateau interesting; conv for Chantilly,
Paris & L'oise Valley; gd walks nrby (woodland & rvside);
v friendly family owned & managed; lge nbr of statics
on site but does not detract fr touring pitches nor
impact on facs; best site in area." **€16.00** 2019

CHANTONNAY *2H4* (12km NE Rural) *46.75168,
-0.94568* **Camping La Baudonnière**, Route des
Salinières, 85110 Monsireigne **02 51 66 43 79;
tombann1962@gmail.com; www.labaudonniere.com**

12 🐕 (htd) 🚿 🔌 🚰 / 🅿 🦋 ⓗ 🛒 🧺 ⛰

Fr Chantonnay take D960B NE dir St Prouant &
Pouzauges. In St Prouant take D23 to Monsireigne.
Foll rd downhill, cross sm rv & as rd starts to climb
take 2nd L sp Reaumur; in 400m L onto Rue des
Salinières. Site on L in 800m. Sm, pt shd, pt sl, EHU
(10A) €4; bbq; Eng spkn; adv bkg acc; games rm;
tennis 2km. "V relaxing, peaceful, pretty CL-type site;
welcoming, friendly, helpful Irish owners; excel san
facs; conv Puy de Fou theme park; vg; v well kept site."
€22.00 2019

CHAPELLE D'ANGILLON, LA *4G3* (1km SE Rural)
47.36044, 2.44261 **Camping Paradis Nature
(formerly Municipal Les Murailles),** Route
d'Henrichemont, 18380 La Chapelle-d'Angillon
**06 70 29 52 00; christelle@camping-paradis-
nature.com; www.camping-paradis-nature.com**

🐕 🚿 🔌 🚰 / 🍴 ⓗ nr 🧺 nr ⛰

Fr Bourges or Aubigny-sur-Nère on D940, turn E
onto D926; turn onto D12 in vill, site on R, sp.
2*, Sm, pt shd, pt sl, EHU (6A) €3.20; bbq; 10% statics;
ccard acc; lake fishing adj; CKE. "Lake adj with
castle o'looking; quiet; vg; red for 3 nights or more."
€17.00, 1 Apr-24 Oct. 2015

CHAPELLE EN VERCORS, LA *9C3* (0.2km S Urban)
44.9695, 5.4156 **Camp Municipal Les Bruyères,**
Ave des Bruyères, 26420 La Chapelle-en-Vercors
04 75 48 21 46

🏠 €1 🐕 (htd) 🚿 🔌 🚰 / 🅿 🦋 🍴 nr ⓗ nr 🧺 nr ⛰

Take D518 N fr Die over Col de Rousset. Fr N on A49
exit 8 to N532 St Nazaire-en-Royans, then D76 thro
St Thomas-en-Royans, then D216 to St Laurent-en-
Royans. Take D2 round E flank of Combe Laval (2 sh
2-lane tunnels). Fr Col de la Machine foll D76 S 1km,
then D199 E over Col de Carri to La Chapelle. (D531
fr Villard de Lons, D76 over Combe Laval & D518
Grandes Goulet not suitable for c'vans & diff lge
m'vans due narr rds & tunnels & 5km of o'hanging
ledges.) 2*, Med, hdstg, pt shd, pt sl, EHU (6A); TV;
10% statics; adv bkg acc; cycling; fishing; horseriding;
CKE. "Excel base for beautiful Vercors plateau; friendly
welcome; climbing; pool 300m; excel value; choose
own pitch; clean & immac san facs; excel cycling; vg."
€13.50, 1 May-1 Oct. 2016

CHAPELLE HERMIER, LA *2H4* (4km SW Rural)
46.66652, -1.75543 **Camping Le Pin Parasol,**
Châteaulong, 85220 La Chapelle-Hermier
**02 51 34 64 72; contact@campingpinparasol.fr;
www.campingpinparasol.fr**

🐕 €6 🚿 🔌 🚰 / MSP 🦋 🍴 🍴 ⓗ nr 🛒 🧺 ⛰ ⚓
🛶 (htd) 🚤

Exit A83 junc 4 onto D763/D937 dir La Roche-sur-
Yon; turn R onto D948; at Aizenay turn R onto D6
twd St Gilles Croix-de-Vie; after 10km at x-rds turn
L onto D21; in La Chapelle-Hermier foll D42 twds
L'Aiguillon-sur-Vie; site sp in 4km. 5*, Lge, mkd, hdg,
unshd, pt sl, terr, EHU (16A) inc; gas; bbq; sw nr; TV;
45% statics; Eng spkn; adv bkg acc; ccard acc; games
rm; fishing 200m; excursions; fitness rm; archery; bike
hire; games area; waterslide; tennis; CKE. "On banks of
Lake Jaunay; access to lake down sm path; lge pitches;
friendly staff; no o'fits over 11m; boating 200m;
canoeing 200m; excel facs; adventure zone; lovely
pools; away fr crowds but close to beaches; pleasant
walks & cycle tracks around lake; beautiful site; v well
kept." **€42.00, May - September, A36.** 2019

CHARITE SUR LOIRE, LA *4G4* (0.5km W Urban)
47.17683, 3.01058 **FFCC Camp Municipal La Saulaie,**
Quai de la Saulaie, 58400 La Charité-sur-Loire **03 86
70 00 83 or 03 86 70 15 06 (LS); campinglasaulaie@
outlook.fr; www.campinglacharitesurloire.fr**

🏕 €1.50 ♿ 🚿 ⚐ ⛐ 🅿 🦋 ⚑ 🛒 nr

Exit A77 junc 30 & foll sp 'Centre Ville'. Turn L over
Rv Loire sp Bourges; take 2nd R bef next bdge.
Fr Bourges on N151, turn L immed after x-ing 1st
bdge over Rv Loire. Foll sp. NB Take care when
turn R over narr rv bdge when leaving site - v high
kerb. 3*, Med, mkd, pt shd, EHU (10A); sw nr; red long
stay; CKE. "*Lovely, well-kept site on rv island; warm
welcome, helpful staff; gd security; poss school groups
high ssn; LS phone to check open; beautiful town;
playgrnd & htd pool, paddling pool adj inc (pool opens
1 Jul); welcoming staff; new san facs (2016); site v well
maintained.*" **€21.00, 1 Apr-30 Sep.** 2018

CHARLEVILLE MEZIERES *5C1* (3.5km N Urban)
49.77813, 4.72245 **Camp Municipal Mont Olympe,**
Rue des Pâquis, 08000 Charleville-Mézières **03 24 33
23 60 or 03 24 32 44 80; camping-charleville
mezieres@wandadoo.fr**

🏕 €1.60 ♿ (htd) 🚿 ⚐ ⛐ 🅿 🦋 ⚑ 🛒 nr

Fr N43/E44 head for Hôtel de Ville, with Hôtel de
Ville on R, cont N along Ave des Arches, turn R
at 'Gare' sp & cross rv bdge. At 'Gare' turn sharp
L immed along Rue des Pâquis, site on L in 500m,
visible fr rd. Well sp fr town cent. 3*, Med, hdg, mkd,
hdstg, pt shd, serviced pitches; EHU (10A) €3.95; gas;
bbq; TV; 10% statics; Eng spkn; ccard acc; fishing;
boating; games rm; CKE. "*Lovely, spacious, well-kept
site on Rv Meuse; v lge pitches extra; helpful staff;
htd covrd pool adj; san facs clean, new (2018); useful
snack bar; easy walk to charming town; excel; NH for
m'van's.*" **€20.00, 1 Apr-30 Sep.** 2018

CHARLIEU *9A1* (1km E Urban) *46.15851, 4.18088*
FFCC Camp Municipal de la Douze, chemin du
Camping, 42190 Charlieu **04 77 72 86 01;
camp-charlieu@voila.fr**

🏕 ♿ (htd) 🚿 ⚐ ⛐ 🅿 🛒 nr

N fr Roanne on D482 to Pouilly-sous-Charlieu,
then E on D487 to Charlieu town cent, site sp in
town, by sw pool. NB Do not confuse with Camp
Municipal Pouilly-sous-Charlieu which is sp fr main
rd. 3*, Med, hdg, pt shd, EHU (6A) inc; sw nr; twin
axles; 5% statics; Eng spkn; adv bkg acc; boating
adj; fishing adj; games area; CKE. "*Gd clean new san
facs (2018); vg value; quiet; new cycle rte to Loire;
canal cycle paths; sw & tennis adj; historical town.*"
€16.00, 1 Apr-30 Sep. 2018

CHARMES *6E2* (1km N Rural) *48.37706, 6.28974*
Camp Municipal Les Iles, 20 Rue de l'Ecluse, 88130
Charmes **03 29 38 85 85 or 03 29 38 15 34;
andre.michel63@wanadoo.fr; www.ville-charmes.fr**

🏕 ♿ ♿ 🚿 ⚐ ⛐ 🅿 🦋 ⚑ 🛒 nr

Exit N57 for Charmes, site well sp on Rv Moselle.
Do not confuse with sp for 'Camping Cars'.
3*, Med, mkd, pt shd, EHU (10A) inc; gas; bbq; red long
stay; phone; Eng spkn; adv bkg acc; kayak hire; fishing;
CKE. "*Lovely site bet rv & canal; lge pitches; friendly
staff; footpath to town; m'van o'night area in town; vg
value; gd; v lge pitches.*"
€22.00, 1 Apr-15 Oct. 2019

> ## "I need an on-site restaurant"
>
> We do our best to make sure site information
> is correct, but it is always best to check any
> must-have facilities are still available or will
> be open during your visit.

CHARNY *4F3* (0.9km N Rural) *47.89078, 3.09419*
FFCC Camping des Platanes, 41 Route de la Mothe,
89120 Charny **03 86 91 83 60; info@campingles
platanes.fr; www.campinglesplatanes.fr**

🏕 €3 ♿ (htd) 🚿 ⚐ ⛐ 🅿 🦋 ⚑ 🛒 nr ⛽ 🛶

Exit A6 junc 18 onto D943 to Montargis. Turn S onto
D950 to Charny, site on R as ent vill; sp.
3*, Med, hdg, mkd, pt shd, serviced pitches; EHU (10A)
inc; gas; bbq; red long stay; TV; 60% statics; Eng spkn;
adv bkg acc; bike hire; tennis 500m; rv fishing 150m;
CKE. "*Pleasant, peaceful site; gd sized pitches; friendly,
helpful owners; excel, clean san facs; sh walk to vill; gd
walking; gd touring base.*" **€29.00, 1 Apr-30 Oct.** 2019

CHAROLLES *9A2* (0.5km E Rural) *46.43972, 4.28208*
FFCC Camp Municipal, Route de Viry, 71120
Charolles **03 85 24 04 90 or 32 17 10 10 62;
camping.charolles@orange.tr**

🏕 €1.50 ♿ (htd) 🚿 ⚐ ⛐ 🅿 🦋 ⚑ 🛒 nr ⛽ 🛶 (htd)
🛠

Exit N79 at E end of by-pass sp Vendenesse-lès-
Charolles; at rndabt foll camping sp; then sharp R
bottom hill bef town; site on L, next to Municipal
pool. 3*, Med, hdstg, hdg, mkd, pt shd, pt sl, EHU (6A)
€2; bbq; twin axles; 2% statics; adv bkg rec; ccard acc;
games rm; CKE. "*Well-kept site; sm pitches; friendly,
helpful warden; gd, modern san facs; pool adj high
ssn (proper sw trunks req); m'van area outside site;
negligible security; canoe's avail, launching stn to rv on
site; excel.*" **€14.00, 1 Apr-5 Oct.** 2018

CHARTRE SUR LE LOIR, LA *4F2* (0.5km W Rural) *47.73220, 0.57451* **Camping Le Vieux Moulin,** Chemin des Bergivaux, 72340 La Chartre-sur-le Loir **02 43 44 41 18; bordduloir@orange.fr**

🏠 €1.50 ♦♦♦ (htd) 🅆🄳 ⚷ ♿ 🚿 🖃 ⊘ ⅏ 🦋 ♈ ♉ 🎾 nr ⚠
🏊 (htd)

Sp fr D305 in town. Fr S exit A28 junc 27 onto D766 dir Beaumont-la-Ronce; then take D29 to La Chartre-sur-le Loir; go over rv, turn L immed after bdge. Fr N leave A20 at junc 24 & foll D304 to Chartre, site well sp on R bef bdge.

3*, Med, hdg, mkd, pt shd, EHU (5-10A) €4-5 (poss rev pol); bbq; TV; 20% statics; Eng spkn; adv bkg rec; 15% net CC members; rv fishing; bike hire; CKE. "Beautiful, well-kept rvside site; helpful, friendly staff; excel pool; gd for dogs; v lge MH's acc; gd base for chateaux, forest & Loir Valley; excel; pleasant walk to town." €24.00, 1 Mar-30 Nov.   2018

CHARTRES *4E2* (3km SE Urban) *48.43433, 1.49914* **Camping Les Bords de l'Eure,** 9 Rue de Launay, 28000 Chartres **02 37 28 79 43; ets-ya-roussel-montigny@orange.fr; www.camping-de-chartres.fr**

🏠 ♦♦♦ (htd) 🅆🄳 ⚷ ♿ 🖃 ⊘ ⅏ 🦋 ♉ 🎾 ⚠

Exit N123 ring rd at D935, R at T-junc dir Chartres; then R at 2nd traff lts dir Chartres immed after rlwy bdge; site on L in 400m; inside of ring rd. Also sp fr town cent on N154 fr N, foll sp town cent under 2 rlwy bdges, L at traff lts sp Orléans, after 1km site sp. Fr SE on N154 cross ring rd, foll site sp & turn L at 2nd traff lts; site on R. 3*, Med, mkd, hdg, shd, EHU (6A) inc (poss rev pol); bbq; 10% statics; Eng spkn; adv bkg acc; ccard acc; fishing; CKE. "Popular, spacious, pleasant, well laid-out, dir access to rv; unisex san facs clean but tired, stretched when busy; some pitches sl (gd lge o'fits; gates clsd 2200-0700; poss ssn workers; poss unkempt early ssn; when wet grnd soft & muddy in places; easy walk or cycle along rv to Chartres, well lit at night; rec Son et Lumière; ideal NH & longer; vg; attractive site, bottom of hill, some awkward pitches; friendly helpful staff; excel situation." €23.00, 1 Mar-31 Oct.   2019

CHASSENEUIL SUR BONNIEURE *7B3* (10km E Rural) *45.83283, 0.55811* **Camping Le Paradis,** Mareuil, 16270 Mazières **05 45 84 92 06 or 078 66 49 67 41 (mob); info@le-paradis-camping.com; www.le-paradis-camping.com**

12 🏠 ♦♦♦ (htd) 🅆🄳 ⚷ ♿ 🖃 ⊘ ⅏ 🦋 🎾 nr ⊕ nr ⚠

Fr Limoges W on N141 twd Angoulême, turn L at 1st traff lts in Roumazières-Loubert D161. Site sp in 2km at t-junc. 4*, Sm, hdstg, mkd, hdg, pt shd, EHU (10-16A) €5.50-8.50; bbq; sw nr; 20% statics; phone; bus 1km; adv bkg rec; fishing nr; tennis nr; games area; watersports 5km; CKE. "Clean, tranquil site; gd sized pitches; vg, immac san facs; welcoming, helpful British owners, helpful & friendly; gd touring base; adv bkg rec lge o'fits; excel; min €30 for 1 night stays; storage avail; highly rec." **€19.50**   2016

CHATAIGNERAIE, LA *2H4* (6km E Rural) *46.64854, -0.66580* **Camping La Viollière,** 85120 Breuil-Barret **02 51 87 44 82; vendeevacances@gmail.com; http://vendeevacances.googlepages.com/**

🏠 €1 🅆🄳 ⚷ ⊘ 🦋 ♉ nr ⊕ nr ⚠ nr

Take D949B E thro La Châtaigneraie for 5km. Cont thro Breuil-Barret & site 2nd R after passing under rlwy bdge. Sm, pt shd, pt sl, EHU (6A) inc (poss long lead req); bbq; Eng spkn; adv bkg acc. "Peaceful, relaxing CL-type site; v lge pitches with views; helpful British owners; excel." €18.00, Apr-Oct.   2019

CHATEAU ARNOUX *10E3* (3km NE Rural) *44.10476, 6.01680* **Camping Sunêlia L'Hippocampe,** Route Napoléon, 04290 Volonne **04 92 33 50 00; camping@l-hippocampe.com; www.l-hippocampe.com**

🏠 €2 🅆🄳 ⚷ ♿ 🖃 ⊘ ⅏ 🦋 ♈ ♉ 🎾 ⊕ ⚠ ➶ 🏊 (htd) ⛵

Exit A51 junc 21 onto D4085 12km S of Sisteron twd Volonne vill over rv. Turn R on D4 on ent vill & foll camp sp 1km. 4*, Lge, hdstg, mkd, hdg, pt shd, serviced pitches; EHU (10A) inc (poss rev pol); bbq (elec, gas); red long stay; TV; 10% statics; Eng spkn; adv bkg acc; ccard acc; canoeing; fishing; games area; waterslide; bike hire; rafting; tennis; games rm; CKE. "Pleasant, busy, well-run site; spacious, well-screened pitches; various pitch sizes/prices, some by lake; some pitches poss diff due trees; scruffy." €42.00, 25 Apr-30 Sep, C09.   2015

CHATEAU CHINON *4H4* (6km S Rural) *47.00587, 3.90548* **FFCC Camping L'Etang de la Fougeraie,** Hameau de Champs, 58120 St Léger-de-Fougeret **03 86 85 11 85; info@campingfougeraie.fr; www.campingfougeraie.com**

🏠 €1.70 ♦♦♦ 🅆🄳 ⚷ 🖃 ⊘ ⅏ 🦋 ♉ ⊕ ➶ ⚠ ⚠

Fr Château-Chinon S on D27; in approx 3km turn R onto D157 to St Léger-de-Fougeret; in vill foll sps S dir Onlay to site in 2.5km. 3*, Med, hdg, mkd, pt shd, terr, EHU (6A) €3.20; bbq; sw; TV; Eng spkn; games area; bike hire; games rm; fishing; CKE. "Beautiful, tranquil situation; most pitches lge & face lake; donkey rides; welcoming, efficient owners; facs at top of terr - poss stretched high ssn & ltd LS; gd rest; poss diff lge o'fits; pitches muddy when wet; excel." €29.00, 1 Apr-30 Sep, L24.   2019

CHATEAU DU LOIR *4G1* (8km E Rural) *47.71250, 0.49930* **Camping du Lac des Varennes,** Route de Port Gauthier, 72340 Marçon **02 43 44 13 72; contact@lacdesvarennes; www.lacdesvarennes.com**

🏠 €1.80 ♦♦♦ (htd) 🅆🄳 ⚷ ♿ 🖃 ⊘ ⅏ 🦋 ♈ ♉ 🎾 ⊕ ➶ ⚠ ⚠

Fr N on D338 fr Château-du-Loir dir Vendôme for 3km. Turn L onto D305 sp Marçon. In vill turn L onto D61 over bdge. Site on R by lake. 3*, Lge, hdg, hdstg, mkd, pt shd, EHU (10A) €3.40 (poss rev pol, poss long lead req); bbq; sw nr; red long stay; 11% statics; Eng spkn; adv bkg rec; ccard acc; boat hire; watersports; horseriding; tennis; bike hire; CKE. "Pretty site in lovely situation bet lake & rv; friendly, helpful staff; gd security; gd walks & cycling; san facs basic & unisex; LS off clsd 1200-1600; new owners (2016)." €20.00, 1 Apr-30 Oct.   2016

CHATEAU GONTIER *4F1* (2km N Urban) *47.83851, -0.69965* **Camping Le Parc,** 15 Route de Laval, 53200 Château-Gontier **02 43 07 35 60; camping.parc@ cc-chateau-gontier.fr; www.sudmayenne.com**

🔲 🐕 � (htd) WD ♨ ♿ ⚒ 🚿 MSP 🦋 ⟐ 🍽 nr ⚑ ✏

App Château-Gontier fr N on N162, at 1st rndabt on bypass take 1st exit. Site on R in 250m. 3*, Sm, mkd, pt shd, sl, EHU (6-10A) inc (rev pol); TV; 20% statics; ccard acc; tennis; fishing; games rm; CKE. *"V pleasant, beautiful site; most pitches sl, some o'look rv; superb clean unisex san facs; rvside path to attractive town; mkt Thurs; excel site, gd pitches; superb clean san facs; helpful staff; pool 800m; lots of activity on rv to watch."* **€18.00** 2018

CHATEAU GONTIER *4F1* (12km SE Rural) *47.74985, -0.64258* **Camping des Rivières,** Rue du Port, 53200 Daon **02 43 06 94 78; www.campingdaon.fr**

� WD ♨ ♿ ⚒ 🚿 ⚑ nr

On town side of rv bdge, turn down lane & site ent on R at bottom of hill. 2*, Med, pt shd, EHU (10A) €3; sw nr; adv bkg acc; tennis nr; CKE. *"Vg clean & well-cared for site; some pitches diff to access; mini golf nr; boating on adj Rv Mayenne; great san facs."* **€13.00, 1 Apr-30 Sep.** 2016

CHATEAU RENAULT *4G2* (7km S Urban) *47.54471, 0.88786* **Camp Municipal du Moulin,** Rue du Lavoir, 37110 Villedômer **02 47 55 05 50 or 02 47 55 00 04 (Mairie); mairie.villedomer@wanadoo.fr**

🐕 €1 � WD ⚒ 🚿 ⟐ nr ⊕ nr ⚑ nr

Fr A10 exit junc 18 onto D31 dir Château-Renault. Turn W onto D73 sp to Auzouer & Villedômer. Fr Château-Renault S on D910, site sp dir Villedômer. 1*, Sm, hdg, shd, EHU (10A) €3; adv bkg rec; rv fishing; fishing 2km. *"Gd, clean facs but old-fashioned; pitch yourself if warden not present; does not accept twin axles."* **€14.00, 15 Jun-15 Sep.** 2016

CHATEAU RENAULT *4G2* (0.5km W Urban) *47.59283, 0.90687* **Camp Municipal du Parc de Vauchevrier,** Rue Paul-Louis-Courier, 37110 Château-Renault **02 47 29 54 43 or 02 47 29 85 50 (LS); camping. vauchevrier@orange.fr; www.ville-chateau-renault.fr**

� WD ♨ ♿ ⚒ 🚿 MSP ⟐ nr ⊕ nr ⚑ nr ⚑ ⊼ (htd)

At Château-Renault foll sp to site 800m fr D910. If app fr a'route turn L on ent town & site on R of main rd adj Rv Brenne. 2*, Med, mkd, hdg, pt shd, EHU (6A) €2.20 (long lead poss req); tennis; fishing; CKE. *"Pleasant site by rv in park; lge pitches; friendly, helpful warden; clean, modern san facs; ltd LS; bar 300m; gd NH nr D910; no twin axles."* **€14.00, 1 May-15 Sep.** 2016

CHATEAUBRIANT *2F4* (1.5km S Urban) *47.70305, -1.37789* **Camp Municipal Les Briotais,** Rue de Tugny, 44110 Châteaubriant **02 40 81 14 38 or 02 40 81 02 32; h.menet@ville-chateaubriant.fr; www.tourisme-chateaubriant.fr/camping-municipal-des-briotais**

🐕 €0.35 � ♿ ⚒ 🚿 MSP ⟐ 🍽 nr ⊕ nr ⚑ nr

App fr Nantes (D178) site sp on S end of town. Or fr Angers on D963/D163 foll sp at 1st rndabt; fr town cent, foll sps thro town. 2*, Sm, hdg, pt shd, EHU €2.70; games area. *"11thC chateau in town; site locked o'night; site on municipal playing field; gd NH; pool in town."* **€6.00, 1 May-30 Sep.** 2016

CHATEAUDUN *4F2* (2km N Urban) *48.08008, 1.33141* **Camp Municipal Le Moulin à Tan,** Rue de Chollet, 28200 Châteaudun **02 37 45 05 34 or 02 37 45 22 46 (LS); tourisme-chateaudun@wanadoo.fr**

� WD ♨ ♿ ⚒ 🚿 ⊕ nr ⚑ nr ⚑

App Châteaudun fr N on N10; turn R onto D3955 at 2nd rndabt (supmkt & Buffalo Grill on L); L at next rndabt onto D955; in 800m turn L into Rue de Chollet. App Châteaudun fr S on N10, turn L onto D3955 & then as bef. Site adj Rv Loir & well sp fr D955. 2*, Med, mkd, pt shd, EHU (6A) inc; TV; 5% statics; fishing; games area; canoeing; CKE. *"Gd touring base; quiet/under-used LS; helpful warden; some night flying fr nrby military airfield; htd covrd pool 2km; security gate 2.1m height; no twin axles; gd; rec open fr 0700 - 2200; walks fr site; OK NH."* **€13.00, 1 Apr-30 Sep.** 2017

"Satellite navigation makes touring much easier"

Remember most sat navs don't know if you're towing or in a larger vehicle – always use yours alongside maps and site directions.

CHATEAULIN *2E2* (2km S Rural) *48.18754, -4.08515* **Camping La Pointe,** Route de St Coulitz, 29150 Châteaulin **02 98 86 51 53; lapointecamping@ gmail.com; www.lapointesuperbecamping.com**

🐕 €1 � WD ♨ ♿ ⚒ 🚿 MSP ⟐ 🍽 nr ⚑ nr ⚑

Exit N165 onto D887 to Châteaulin; in town cent, cross bdge & turn L along rv on D770; after approx 750m, turn L at sp for St Coulitz; in 100m turn R into site. NB if app fr S to Châteaulin on D770, do not attempt to turn R at sp for St Coulitz (tight turn); go into town & turn round. 3*, Med, hdg, mkd, hdstg, pt shd, pt sl, EHU (10A) €4 (poss rev pol); bbq; phone; Eng spkn; adv bkg acc; rv fishing nrby; games rm; bike hire; CKE. *"Charming, peaceful, spacious site in wooded setting; well-run; helpful & friendly British owners; immac san facs; rvside path to town; gd cycling, walking & fishing; gd touring base; excel well-kept & equipped site."* **€18.00, 15 Apr-15 Oct.** 2019

CHATEAUMEILLANT *7A4* (0.5km NW Rural) *46.56807, 2.18823* **Camp Municipal L'Etang Merlin,** Route de Vicq-Exemplet 18370 Chateaumeillant **02 48 61 31 38; www.camping-etangmerlin.e-monsite.com**

🐕 €1 🚻 WC ♨ ♿ 🚿 🛒 MSP 🦋 ☕ 📶 🍴 nr 🚰 🏊 (htd) 🛶

Rec app fr W to avoid narr town rds. Site sp fr rndabt at W end of town on D80 N of Châteaumeillant on lakeside. Fr Culan by pass town on D943, then as above. 3*, Sm, hdg, mkd, pt shd, serviced pitches; EHU (5A) inc; bbq; TV; Eng spkn; adv bkg acc; ccard acc; fishing; tennis adj; CKE. "Superb, well-kept site; lge pitches; friendly & helpful staff; basketball at sports complex adj; lake adj (no sw); rec arr early high ssn to secure pitch; easy walk to town." €11.50, 1 May-30 Sep.   2020

CHATEAUNEUF DU FAOU *2E2* (1km S Urban) *48.18306, -3.80986* **Gites & Camping de Penn ar Pont,** Rue de la Liberation, 29520 Chateauneuf du Faou **02 98 81 81 25 or 06 60 24 75 42; gites.pennarpont@ orange.fr; www.pennarpont.com**

🐕 €2 WC ♨ ⚡ 🦋 🍴 nr 🚰 nr

Take D36 S, go over bdge, site at 1st R turn. Sm, hdg, mkd, pt shd, terr, EHU (16A) €3.50; bbq; Eng spkn; adv bkg acc. "Steep rd on site, diff for lge o'fits; jazz fest last w/end of July; gd; san facs clean but needs upgrade; typical sm municipal site in beautiful setting." €15.00, 1 Apr-31 Oct.   2018

CHATEAUNEUF SUR LOIRE *4F3* (1km S Rural) *47.85643, 2.22426* **FFCC Camping de la Maltournée,** Route de Châteauneuf, 45110 Châteauneuf-sur-Loire **02 38 58 42 46 or 06 32 11 41 13 (mob); contact@ camping-chateauneufsurloire.fr; www.camping-chateauneufsurloire.com**

🐕 €1.50 🚻 (htd) WC ♨ ♿ ⚡ MSP 🦋 📶 🚰 🏕

S fr Chateauneuf cent, cross rv on D11; take 1st L, site in 300m on S bank of Rv Loire. 2*, Lge, pt shd, EHU (10A) inc; 75% statics; adv bkg acc; canoeing; CKE. "Well-kept, busy site; helpful, pleasant staff; clean, modern san facs; chem disp v basic via narr pipe; some m'van pitches beside rv; conv Orléans; security barrier; poss ssn workers; gd cycling base for Evro Velo." €18.00, 1 Apr-31 Oct.   2019

CHATEAUNEUF SUR LOIRE *4F3* (8.6km W Urban) *47.86884, 2.11597* **Camping de l'Isle aux Moulins,** Rue du 44ème Régiment d'Infanterie, 45150 Jargeau **02 38 59 70 04 or 02 54 22 26 61 (LS); camping. jargeau@orange.fr; www.jargeau.fr**

🐕 €1.20 🚻 (htd) WC ♨ ♿ ⚡ 🛒 / 🦋 📶 🍴 🅷 nr 🚰 nr 🏕 🚴

Exit Châteauneuf W on D960 dir Orléans; at St Denis-de l'Hôtel turn sharp L onto D921 to Jargeau over Loire bdge; immed after x-ing bdge turn R into Blvd Jeanne d'Arc sp Camping; in 200m cont strt on into Rue du 44ème Régiment d'Infanterie; site on R in 300m. Site clearly visible on R of bdge on W bank of rv. NB App rd & turning to site is v narr; do not arr 1200-1330 (lunch time) as parking diff. 2*, Lge, mkd, pt shd, pt sl, EHU (5A) €3.50; bbq; twin axles; red long stay; 2% statics; bus 500m; Eng spkn; adv bkg acc; ccard acc; bike hire; games area; rv fishing adj; CKE. "V pleasant rvside site; lge pitches amongst trees; friendly farming family; modern san facs; poss muddy when wet; pool adj; sh walk to sm town; conv for Oreans." €19.00, 1 Apr-31 Oct.   2015

CHATEAUPONSAC *7A3* (0.2km SW Rural) *46.13163, 1.27083* **Camping De La Gartempe,** Ave de Ventenat, 87290 Chateauponsac **05 55 76 55 33; campingdela gartempe@gmail.com;www.campingdelagartempe.fr**

12 🐕 €1 🚻 (htd) WC ♨ 🛒 🍴 🅷 ⚡ 🚰 nr 🏕 🚴

Fr N exit A20 junc 23.1 sp Châteauponsac; go thro vill, well sp on L on rvside. Fr S exit A20 junc 24 sp Châteauponsac & then as above. 3*, Sm, hdg, mkd, pt shd, terr, EHU (6A) €3 (poss rev pol); Eng spkn; adv bkg acc; kayaking; archery; CKE. "Pleasant site; gd san facs; pitches muddy in wet; not suitable lge m'vans; activities down steep hill by rv; poss noise fr parties in rest; children's activites; adj to holiday bungalows/ gites; helpful owners; nice vill." €16.00   2018

CHATEAUROUX *4H2* (2km N Rural) *46.82368, 1.69496* **Camp Municipal Le Rochat-Belle Isle,** Rue du Rochat, 36000 Châteauroux **06 02 71 14 55 or 02 54 08 96 29; campinglerochat@gmail.com;www.camping-lerochat.fr**

🐕 €1.50 🚻 WC ♨ ♿ ⚡ 🛒 MSP 🍴 🅷 nr 🚰 nr 🏕

Exit A20 junc 13 onto D943/N143 S; foll sp Châteauroux; site sp bef town. Site on banks of Rv Indre, just S of Lac de Belle-Isle. Sp in town. 3*, Med, pt shd, EHU (5-10A) inc; gas; Eng spkn. "Leisure park adj with pool & windsurfing on lake; friendly welcome & helpful; gd, modern, clean san facs; poss music till late w/end high ssn; poss travellers; pleasant walk into town along rv; lge brocante mkt 1st Sun of month Oct-Jul; vg; nice site; excel family site." €20.00, 25 Mar-23 Oct.   2017

★★★★
CAMPING AU PORT PUNAY

Cosy family campsite since 1964 ! Partly under large trees at 300m from the beach located in the heart of a small fisherman's village. An ideal choice for families with small children. Spacious camping pitches, sanitary block maintained to the highest standards, a brand new wellness center and the mobile homes are new from 2020 ! Wireless internet, daytrips and English spoken at reception. Shop with fresh bread, housewine and Pineau ! Don't forget your bikes, or hire them at reception : Châtelaillon and its surroundings can easily be discovered by bike !

Camping Au Port-Punay • Les Boucholeurs • 17340 CHATELAILLON-PLAGE
FRANCE • Tel. +33 (0)5 17 81 00 00 • Fax +33 (0)5 46 56 86 44
www.camping-port-punay.com • Email contact@camping-port-punay.com

---

CHATEL DE NEUVRE *9A1 (1.3km NE Rural) 46.4131, 3.31884* **Camping Deneuvre,** Route De Moulins, 03500 Châtel-de-Neuvre 04 70 42 04 51; campingde neuvre@wanadoo.fr; www.camping-deneuvre.fr

🏠 🐕 €1 ♦♦♦ 🛒 ♨ ⚓ ♿ 🚿 ⊘ ♯ ⊕ ♈ 🍴 ⊕ ♨ ⚓

S fr Moulins on D2009; sp N of vill on E side of D2009. 3*, Med, mkd, hdstg, pt shd, EHU (4A) inc; gas; Eng spkn; adv bkg acc; canoe hire; CKE. *"Site by Rv Allier in nature reserve; clean but not smart; useful NH without unhitching; friendly welcome; excel clean san facs; ltd facs LS; meals avail; splendid place for walking, fishing, cycling & birdwatching; diff ent/exit for lge o'fits; no twin axles."* **€20.00,** 1 Apr-30 Sep.   2016

CHATEL DE NEUVRE *9A1 (0.4km W Rural) 46.40320, 3.31350* **Canoe Camping la Courtine,** 7 Rue de St Laurant, 03500 Châtel-de-Neuvre 04 70 42 06 21; mail@camping-lacourtine.com; www.camping-lacourtine.com

12 🐕 ♦♦♦ (htd) ⊘ ♨ ⚓ ♿ 🚿 ⊘ ♯ MSP 🦋 ♈ 🍴 ⊕ nr ♨ 🏊 nr ⚓

Fr N on D2009 to cent of vill, turn L at x-rds onto D32; site in 500m. 2*, Sm, mkd, hdstg, pt shd, EHU (6-10A) €3-5 (poss rev pol); TV; Eng spkn; adv bkg acc; CKE. *"Friendly welcome; untidy ent masks v nice site; German family-owned site; access to Rv Allier for canoeing, fishing; walking in nature reserve; liable to flood & poss clsd LS, phone ahead to check; conv LS NH, lovely woodland setting."* **€17.00**   2018

CHATEL MONTAGNE *9A1 (0.5km W Rural) 46.11526, 3.67700* **Camping Retro Passion,** La Croix Cognat, 03250 Chatel Montagne 04 70 59 31 38; campingretro passion@gmail.com; www.camping-retro-passion.fr

🏠 🐕 ♦♦♦ WD ⊘ ♨ ⚓ ♿ 🚿 ⊘ ♯ MSP 🦋 ♈ 🍴 ♨ 🏊 ⚓

SW fr Lapalisse on D7, in 15km L on D25 to Chatel Montagne. Site on L bef vill. Sm, mkd, pt shd, pt sl, terr, EHU (6A); bbq; twin axles; TV; 5% statics; Eng spkn; adv bkg acc; games area; games rm; tennis 100m; bike hire; CKE. *"Vg."* **€18.00,** 15 Apr-31 Oct.   2015

CHATELAILLON PLAGE *7A1 (2km N Urban) 46.08632, -1.09489* **Camping L'Océan,** Ave d'Angoulins, 17340 Châtelaillon-Plage 05 46 56 87 97; reception@ oceancamping.fr; www.oceancamping.fr

🏠 🐕 €2 ♦♦♦ WD ⊘ ♨ ⚓ ♿ 🚿 ⊘ ⊕ nr ♈ 🏊 🏖 sand 500m

Fr La Rochelle take D602 to Châtelaillon-Plage, site sp on L in 300m (after passing g'ge & L'Abbaye camp site). 3*, Med, mkd, hdg, EHU (10A) €5; bbq; phone; bus; Eng spkn; ccard acc; waterslide; ice. *"Very nice, excel site; gd cycle rtes; top class facs; occasional noise fr rlwy & clay pigeon range; park & ride 400m; beautiful man made lake/beach; new owner (2017)."* **€33.00,** 20 May-23 Sep.   2017

CHATELAILLON PLAGE *7A1 (2.5km SE Coastal) 46.05491, -1.08331* **Camping Au Port Punay,** Les Boucholeurs, Allée Bernard Moreau, 17340 Châtelaillon-Plage 05 17 81 00 00; contact@ camping-port-punay.com; www.camping-port-punay.com

🏠 🐕 €3 ♦♦♦ ⊘ ♨ ⚓ ♿ 🚿 ⊘ ♯ 🦋 ♈ 🍴 ⊕ ♨ 🏊 nr ⚓ ♨ 🏊 🏖 sand 300m

Fr N exit D137 La Rochell-Rochefort rd onto D109; strt on at 1st rndabt, L at 2nd rndabt; then cont for 2.8km to end (harbour); turn L, keep R along narr one-way st; at next junc to L, site sp. Fr S exit D137 onto D203 sp Les Boucholeurs; at rndabt in 1km foll site sp to edge of Châtelaillon & turn R, foll sp. Site in 500m. 4*, Lge, pt shd, EHU (10A) €6; gas; TV; 25% statics; Eng spkn; adv bkg acc; bike hire; games area. *"Busy but quiet site; immac san facs; friendly, energetic, helpful owners; steel pegs req; sm pitches; excel; lovely area & location."* **€37.00,** 8 May-26 Sep.   2017

See advertisement

FRANCE

CHÂTEL-GUYON *9B1* (5km NW Rural) *45.91597, 3.07682* **Camping Le Ranch des Volcans (formerly Clos de Balanède),** Route de la Piscine, 63140 Châtel-Guyon **04 73 86 02 47; contact@ranchdesvolcans. com; www.ranchdesvolcans.com**

🐕 €1.50 👫🏻 ♿ 🚿 🛁 ♨ ⚡ 🍴 🍽 🛒 Ⓟ nr 🏪 ⛲ 🏊

Fr Riom take D227 to Châtelguyon, site on R on o'skts of town. **Tight turn into ent.** 3*, Lge, pt shd, pt sl, EHU (6A) inc; gas; red long stay; Eng spkn; adv bkg acc; tennis; poss open until 31 Dec. *"Pleasant, well-run site; san facs dated; some pitches steep & poss uneven; sh walk to town; m'vans/campers not allowed up to Puy-de-Dôme - must use bus provided; conv for A71, gd NH; gd quiet site; conv for Clermont-Ferrand and Puy de Dôme."* **€17.00, 4 Apr-1 Nov.** 2018

"That's changed – Should I let the Club know?"

If you find something on site that's different from the site entry, fill in a report and let us know. See camc.com/europereport.

CHATILLON EN DIOIS *9D3* (0.6km E Urban) *44.69450, 5.48817* **Camp Municipal Les Chaussières,** 26410 Châtillon-en-Diois **04 75 21 10 30 or 04 75 21 14 44 (Mairie); camping.chatillonendiois@wanadoo.fr; www.camping-chatillonendiois.com**

🐕 €2.10 👫🏻 🅆🄲 🚿 ♨ 🛒 🦋 🍴 🏪 nr Ⓟ 🏕 🌳

Fr Die take D93 S for 6km then L on D539 to Châtillon (8km) site sp on R on ent to town. 2*, Med, mkd, pt shd, EHU (10A) €3.60; bbq; 30% statics; phone; Eng spkn; adv bkg acc; ccard acc; ice; canoeing; fishing; cycling; horseriding; tennis; CKE. *"Wardens off site 1130- 1630; pool adj; pleasant sweet site, wardens friendly and helpful."* **€21.00, 1 Apr-13 Oct.** 2019

CHATILLON SUR CHALARONNE *9A2* (0.5km SE Urban) *46.11622, 4.96172* **FFCC Camp Municipal du Vieux Moulin,** Ave Jean Jaurès, 01400 Châtillon-sur-Chalaronne **04 74 55 04 79; camping@chatillon-sur-chalaronne.org; www.camping-vieuxmoulin.com**

🐕 €2 👫🏻 🅆🄲 🚿 ♨ 🛁 ♨ 🛒 🍴 🍽 nr Ⓟ 🏪 🏪 nr 🌳

Exit A6 junc 30 to Châtillon-sur-Chalaronne; pick up D7 on S site of vill; site on R in 400m. Ave Jean Jaurès is pt of D7. Site sp in town. 4*, Med, hdg, hdstg, shd, EHU (10A) €4 (long lead req on some pitches); 50% statics; phone; adv bkg acc; ccard acc; fishing; CKE. *"Lovely site in picturesque area; helpful warden; immac facs, ltd LS; check office opening hrs for early dep; leisure cent adj; if office clsd ring bell, warden will open barrier; lovely medieval town cent; pool adj inc; excel model rlwy; bar adj; mkt Sat; site remains excel, new municipal pool under construction next door."* **€25.80, 15 Apr-30 Sep.** 2019

CHATILLON SUR INDRE *4H2* (0.8km N Rural) *46.99116, 1.17382* **Les Rives de L'Indre (formerly municipal),** Rue de Moulin de la Grange, 36700 Châtillon-sur-Indre **07 61 39 81 62 or 02 54 38 17 86; camping-chatillon-sur-indre@orange.fr; www.chatillon-sur-indre.fr**

🐕 👫🏻 ♿ 🅆🄲 ♨ 🦋 Ⓗ nr 🏪 nr 🌳

Site well sp in vill. N twd Loches then foll sp. 3*, Med, mkd, hdg, pt shd, EHU (6A) €3; bbq; CKE. *"Lovely, relaxed, well-kept site; friendly, helpful warden; 4 chalets; gd, clean san facs; conv Loire chateaux; gd birdwatching area; interesting old town; htd pool 400m (proper sw trunks only); lge mkt Fri; excel value; call warden if barrier clsd; warden onsite 0800-1100/1630-2000."* **€12.00, 1 Apr-31 Oct.** 2017

CHATILLON SUR SEINE *6F1* (1km E Urban) *47.85955, 4.57975* **Camp Municipal Louis Rigoly,** Esplanade Saint Vorles, 21400 Châtillon-sur-Seine **03 80 91 03 05 or 03 80 91 13 19 (LS); contact@camping-chatillon surseine.com; camping-chatillonsurseine.com**

🐕 👫🏻 🅆🄲 🚿 🛁 ♨ 🦋 🍴 🏪 nr 🌳 🏊

Fr N, cross rv bdge (Seine); cont approx 400m twd town cent; at lge metal fountain forming rndabt turn L, foll sp to site. Fr S turn R & foll camping sp. Rec lge o'fits proceed thro town to metal fountain. Turn R & foll sp to site. 2*, Med, mkd, hdg, pt shd, pt sl, EHU (6A) €2.30-4.65; gas; Eng spkn; adv bkg acc; jacuzzi; tennis; fishing; CKE. *"Pretty site adj park; clean, tidy, well-spaced pitches; helpful, welcoming warden; htd pool adj; excel, clean new san facs (2016); gd access; easy walk to old town & famous museum housing Celtic Vix treasures; vg; excel disabled san facs."* **€17.30, 1 Apr-30 Sep.** 2017

CHATRE, LA *7A4* (3km N Rural) *46.60131, 1.97808* **Camp Municipal Solange-Sand,** Rue du Pont, 36400 Montgivray **02 54 06 10 34 or 02 54 06 10 36; mairie.montgivray@wanadoo.fr**

🐕 🐕 👫🏻 🅆🄲 ♨ 🛁 🚿 ♨ 🦋

Fr La Châtre take rd to Montgivray, foll camping sp. Fr Châteauroux on D943 SE twd La Châtre turn R 2km S of Nohant on D72. Site behind church. 2*, Med, mkd, pt shd, EHU (10A) inc (poss rev pol); bbq; CKE. *"Pleasant site in chateau grnds; new san facs (2016); gd access; warden calls am & pm; gd rest adj; gd walks; quiet but occ noise fr nrby hall; excel; v gd for stop over or sh stay; welcoming staff."* **€12.40, 15 Mar-15 Oct.** 2017

CHAUMONT *6F1* (1km NW Urban) *48.11790, 5.13334* **Camp Municipal Parc Ste Marie,** Rue des Tanneries, 52000 Chaumont **03 25 32 11 98 or 03 25 30 60 27 (Mairie); sports@ville-chaumont.fr**

🐕 €1.50 👫🏻 (cont) 🅆🄲 ♨ ♨ 🏪 nr 🌳

Site on Chaumont W by-pass joining N19 Troyes rd to N67 St Dizier rd. Do not try to app fr town cent. Exit A5 at exit 24, foll sp to town cent, bef town foll sp to site. 2*, Sm, hdg, mkd, pt shd, pt sl, EHU (10A) inc (poss long lead req); 20% statics; CKE. *"Rec arr early; care needed with steep access to some sl pitches; friendly warden; ent barrier under warden control at all times; gd NH; doesn't acc m'vans."* **€14.00, 2 May-30 Sep.** 2015

For a guide to symbols see the fold out on the rear cover

CHAUMONT SUR LOIRE *4G2* (1km NE Rural) *47.48444, 1.19417* **Camp Municipal Grosse Grève,** Ave des Trouillas, 41150 Chaumont-sur-Loire **02 54 20 95 22 or 02 54 20 98 41 (Mairie); mairie.chaumontsloire@ wanadoo.fr; www.camping-chaumont-sur-loire.com**

⛺👪(htd) ⬛ ♨ ♿ 🚻 🍴 ∀ nr ⊞ ♨

Fr N side of rv on D952 cross bdge to Chaumont on D1, turn R immed & R under bdge. Site sp in vill on D751. 2*, Med, pt shd, EHU (6-16A) €2-3.50 (poss long lead req); bbq; canoeing; tennis; fishing; bike hire; horseriding; CKE. *"Pleasant site by rv; gd, clean san facs; no twin axles; interesting chateau; cycle track along Loire; gd value; excel."* **€12.00, 29 Apr-30 Sep.** 2016

CHAUVIGNY *7A3* (1km E Urban) *46.57072, 0.65326* **Camp Municipal de la Fontaine,** Rue de la Fontaine, 86300 Chauvigny **05 49 45 99 10; camping-chauvigny@ cg86.fr; www.chauvigny.fr**

⛺ €1.80 👪(htd) ⬛ ♨ ♿ 🚿 ∥ MSP 🚻 nr ♨

N151 fr Poitiers to Chauvigny. Turn L in cent Chauvigny just bef gate. Site well sp fr Chauvigny. 3*, Med, pt shd, EHU (15A) inc; bbq; adv bkg acc; tennis 1km; bike hire; CKE. *"Popular; well-kept; well-run site adj park & lake; views of castle; lge pitches; helpful, friendly staff; excel immac san facs; o'night m'vans area; delightful walk to cent; mkts Tue, Thur & Sat; a real find; gd value; rec; vg; interesting town; gd touring base; €20 for barrier key; new ehu pnts & new barrier(2018)."* **€16.40, 1 Apr-30 Sep.** 2018

CHEF BOUTONNE *7A2* (2km W Rural) *46.10767, -0.09342* **Camping Le Moulin,** 1 Route de Niort, 79110 Chef-Boutonne **05 49 29 73 46 or 06 89 60 00 49 (mob); info@campingchef.com; www.campingchef.com**

12 ⛺ €1.50 👪(htd) ⬛ ♨ ♿ 🚿 ∥ 🦋 ♈ 🍴 ⊞ 🚻 nr ♨ 🖊 ≈ (htd)

Fr D950 to or fr Poitiers, turn E onto D740 to Chef-Boutonne, site on R. Fr N10 turn onto D948 to Sauzé-Vaussais then L onto D1 to Chef-Boutonne; then take D740 dir Brioux-sur-Boutonne; site on L. 3*, Sm, hdstg, mkd, hdg, pt shd, EHU (10A) bbq (charcoal, elec, gas); twin axles; red long stay; 10% statics; Eng spkn; adv bkg acc; ccard acc; ice; CKE. *"Well-kept site, lge pitches; friendly, helpful British owners; v gd rest; much bird life; conv Futuroscope & La Rochelle; vg; clean san facs refurbed with disabled facs (2018); peaceful; mv service pnt 1km; rest & bar refurb (2018); site acc rallies; excel; chge for wifi."* **€21.60** 2019

CHEMILLE *2G4* (1.5km SW Rural) *47.20182, -0.73486* **FFCC Camping Coulvée,** Route de Cholet, 49120 Chemillé **02 41 30 42 42 or 02 41 30 39 97 (Mairie); camping-chemille-49@wanadoo.fr; www.camping-coulvee-chemille.com**

⛺ €1.70 👪 ⬛ ♨ ♿ 🚿 ∥ MSP 🍴 ∀ 🐕 sand

Fr Chemillé dir Cholet on D160, turn R in 1km. 3*, Sm, hdg, pt shd, terr, EHU (10A) €3.60; bbq; sw; red long stay; Eng spkn; adv bkg acc; CKE. *"Clean facs; helpful staff; gd pitches, soft when wet; poss unrel opening dates; pedalos; mkt Thurs; mkd cycling and walking rtes fr site."* **€23.60, 1 May-15 Sep.** 2016

CHENONCEAUX *4G2* (1.5km E Rural) *47.32905, 1.08816* **Camping de l'Ecluse,** Route de la Plage, 37150 Chisseaux **02 47 23 87 10 or 06 15 83 21 20 (mob); sandrine@campingdelecluse-37.fr; www.campingdelecluse-37.fr**

⛺ €1.50 👪 ⬛ ♨ ♿ 🚿 ∥ 🍴 ∀ 🚻 nr ♨

E fr Chenonceaux on D176; cross bdge; immed hard R & foll rv bank; site in 300m. 2*, Med, mkd, pt shd, EHU (16A) €3.90 (rev pol); phone; Eng spkn; adv bkg acc; ccard acc; canoeing; watersports; fishing; CKE. *"Rv trips; fishing; gd walking; some rd/rlwy noise; gd."* **€12.50, 1 Mar-31 Oct.** 2019

CHENONCEAUX *4G2* (1.5km S Rural) *47.32765, 1.08936* **Camping Le Moulin Fort,** Pont de Chisseaux, 37150 Francueil **02 47 23 86 22; lemoulinfort@ wanadoo.fr; www.lemoulinfort.com**

⛺ €3 👪 ⬛ ♨ ♿ 🚿 🍴 ∥ ♈ ⊞ 🚻 🦋 ♨ ≈ 🚣

Exit A85 junc 11 N, then take D976 E dir Montrichard; site on S bank of Rv Cher just off D976. Fr Tours take D976 sp Vierzon; keep on D976 by-passing Bléré until sm rndabt (5km) where site sp to L twd rv. Take sm rd on R to site, bef actually x-ing bdge. Site well sp. 3*, Med, hdg, mkd, pt shd, EHU (6A) inc (long lead poss req); gas; bbq (charcoal, gas); TV; Eng spkn; adv bkg rec; ccard acc; games rm; bike hire; fishing; CKE. *"Lovely, well-kept site on rv bank; beautiful area; friendly, helpful British owners; gd san facs; easy access most pitches; many sm & v shady pitches; no o'fits over 8m high ssn; lge o'fits check in adv; some pitches suitable for lge o'fits; footpath by rv with view of chateau; gd cycle rtes; poss security probs due access to site fr rv bank; Fri mkt Montrichard & Sun mkt Amboise; excel; well laid site to rv view for many pitches; use of pool diff for those with red mobility due to poor design of ladder."* **€26.00, 7 May-27 Sep, L08.** 2019

> **"I like to fill in the reports as I travel from site to site"**
>
> You'll find report forms at the back of this guide, or you can fill them in online at camc.com/europereport.

CHERBOURG *1C4* (18km NE Coastal) *49.6928, -1.4387* **Camping De La Plage,** 2 Village de Fréval, 50840 Fermanville **02 33 54 38 84; campingdelaplage. fermanville@wanadoo.fr; www.campingdelaplage-fermanville.com**

⛺ €2.50 👪 ⬛ ♨ ∥ 🦋 ∀ 🚻 ♨ 🐕 300m, sand

Fr Cherbourg on D116 dir Barfleur, site in 12km on L. 3*, Med, hdg, unshd, EHU (10A); 70% statics; Eng spkn; adv bkg req. *"Friendly owner; conv for ferry & D-Day landing beaches; poss unrel opening dates; vg."* **€20.50, 1 Apr-15 Oct.** 2018

CHERBOURG *1C4* (10km E Coastal) *49.66720, -1.48772*
Camping L'Anse du Brick, 18 L'Anse du Brick, 50330 Maupertus-sur-Mer **02 33 54 33 57; contact@ adbcamping.com; www.anse-du-brick.com or www.les-castels.com**

🐕 €4.50 🏋️ 🚻 WC ♨ ♿ 🚿 🍴 ✉ MSP 🦋 ⛱ ℞ 🍽 🕤 🛝 ♨ ⛰ 🏊
🛶 (htd, indoor) 📶 🏖 sand adj

At rndabt at port take 2nd exit sp Caen, Rennes & Mont St Michel; at 2nd rndabt take 3rd exit sp Caen & Mont St Michel (N13); at 3rd rndabt take 2nd exit onto dual c'way sp St Lô, Caen (N13), Bretteville-sur-Mer; exit on D116 & foll sp thro Bretteville-en-Saire (take care lge speed hump in Le Becquet); turn R for site just after R-hand blind bend & turning for **Maupertus; up v steep incline.** 5*, Med, mkd, hdg, shd, sl, terr, serviced pitches; EHU (10A) inc (poss rev pol); gas; bbq; TV; adv bkg acc; ccard acc; archery; waterslide; bike hire; tennis; games rm; kayak rental; CKE. *"Attractive, well-kept site in beautiful setting; conv ferry; gd clean san facs; max 2 dogs per pitch; some pitches for lge o'fits; no o'fits over 8m; conv Landing Beaches, Barfleur, coastal nature reserve."* €53.00, 3 Apr-14 Sep, N14. **2019**

CHERBOURG *1C4* (3.6km NW Urban/Coastal) *49.65576, -1.65257* **Camp Municipal de la Saline**, Rue Jean Bart, 50120 Equeurdreville-Hainneville **02 33 93 88 33 or 02 33 53 96 00 (Mairie); mairie-equeurdreville@ dialoleane.com; www.equeurdreville.com**

12 🐕 €0.50 🏋️ (htd) WC ♨ 🚿 🍴 ✉ 🔌 ℞ nr 🕤 nr 🛝 nr 🏖 sand adj

Fr ferry terminal foll D901 & sp Beaumont-Hague. On dual c'way beside sea look out for site sp to L at traff lts. 2*, Med, mkd, hdg, hdstg, pt shd, pt sl, terr, EHU (10A) €4.56; 50% statics; phone; adv bkg acc; fishing; CKE. *"Sea views; boules & skateboard park adj; aquatic cent 500m; mv service pnt nr; cycle path to town; secured at night; excel NH for ferry."* €17.50 **2016**

CHEVERNY *4G2* (3km S Rural) *47.47798, 1.45070* **Camping Les Saules**, 102 Route de Contres, 41700 Cheverny **02 54 79 90 01; contact@camping-cheverny. com; www.camping-cheverny.com**

🐕 €2 🏋️ (htd) WC ♨ ♿ 🚿 🍴 🔌 MSP 🦋 ⛱ 🍽 🕤 🛝 ⛰
🏊 (htd) 🛁

Exit A10 junc 17 dir Blois Sud onto D765 to Romorantin. At Cour-Cheverny foll sp Cheverny & chateau. Fr S on D956 turn R onto D102 just N of Contres, site on L just bef Cheverny. Well sp fr all dirs. 4*, Lge, mkd, shd, EHU (10A) €3.50 (poss long lead req); gas; bbq; red long stay; TV; 2% statics; phone; Eng spkn; adv bkg rec; ccard acc; fishing; golf nr; games rm; tennis nr; excursions; bike hire; CKE. *"Beautiful, well-run site; friendly, welcoming, helpful owners; excel san facs; castle adj; excel pool; all pitches under trees; muddy after heavy rain; many excel cycle & walking rtes nr; Cheverny chateau worth visit; little train & boat rides; excel; gd rest."* €36.00, 1 Apr-17 Sep, L01. **2016**

CHINON *4G1* (0.5km SW Rural) *47.16397, 0.23377* **Camping de L'Ile Auger**, Quai Danton, 37500 Chinon **02 47 93 08 35; camping-chinon@cc-cvl.fr; www.camping-chinon.com**

🐕 €1.20 🏋️ WC ♨ ♿ 🚿 🍴 ✉ MSP 🦋 ⛱ 🍽 🛝 ⛰

On S side of rv at bdge. Fr S foll sp Chinon St Jacques; when app 2nd bdge on 1-way 'loop', avoid R lane indicated for x-ing bdge & cont strt past S end of main bdge to site on R. Fr N foll sp 'Centre Ville' round castle, cross bdge, site on R. Well sp in town & opp castle. 2*, Lge, hdg, mkd, pt shd, EHU (12A) inc (poss rev pol); red long stay; TV (pitch); phone; ccard acc; canoe hire; CKE. *"Excel, well-kept site in gd location; twin axles discretionary; poss midge prob; poss travellers; gd cycle rtes; gd views of chateau; rec; automatic ent barrier; htd pool 300m; well laid out; new san facs (2017); 5min walk to town; exc value; hg rec boat trip on Rv Vienne; gd value; gd touring base."* €16.00, 1 Apr-3 Oct. **2019**

CHINON *4G1* (14km NW Rural) *47.20693, 0.08127* **Camping Belle Rive**, 2 Route de Chinon, 37500 Candes-St Martin **02 47 97 46 03; contact@camping-candes.fr; www.camping-candes.fr**

🐕 €1.30 🏋️ WC ♨ ♿ 🚿 🔌 🦋 ⛱ 🍽 🕤 🛝 nr ⛰

Fr Chinon take D751. Site on R bef junc with D7, on S bank of Rv Vienne. 2*, Med, mkd, pt shd, EHU (16A) €3.10; sw nr; adv bkg acc; fishing adj; CKE. *"Pleasant rvside site; san facs on 2 floors, need update & poss stretched if site busy; conv Saumur & chateaux; excel location; scruffy & ill kempt site."* €16.00, 15 Apr-30 Sep. **2016**

CIOTAT, LA *10F3* (4km NE Coastal) *43.18733, 5.65810* **Campsite La Baie des Anges (formerly Les Oliviers)**, Chemin des Plaines Baronnes, 13600 La Ciotat **04 42 83 15 04; info@homair.com; www.camping-laciotat.fr or www.homair.com**

🐕 🏋️ WC ♨ 🚿 🔌 🍽 nr 🕤 nr 🛝 nr ⛰ 🏊 🏖 shgl 800m

Fr La Ciotat, foll D559 coast rd sp Bandol & Toulon. Site in 4km, look for lge sp on L. Caution x-ing dual c'way. 4*, V lge, shd, pt sl, terr, EHU (6A) (poss rev pol); gas; 80% statics; bus 300m; Eng spkn; adv bkg acc; ccard acc; tennis; CKE. *"Sea views many pitches; friendly staff; gd touring base; v nice."* €35.00, 12 Apr-1 Oct. **2019**

CIVRAY *7A2* (1km NE Urban) *46.15835, 0.30169* **Camping de Civray**, Route de Roche, 86400 Civray **05 17 34 50 02 or 06 08 51 88 80; campingdecivray@ gmail.com; www.camping-de-civray.com**

🐕 🏋️ WC ♨ 🚿 🔌 🦋 ⛱ 🍽 🕤 🛝 nr ⛰ 🏊 (htd)

Civray 9km E of N10 halfway bet Poitiers & Angoulême. Site outside town SE of junc of D1 & D148. Sp on D148 & on S by-pass. Avoid town cent narr rds. 2*, Med, pt shd, pt sl, EHU (6-10A) €3 (poss long lead req); bbq; sw nr; 50% statics; Eng spkn; ccard acc; golf; bike hire; fishing adj; CKE. *"Pleasant rvside site, walk to town; pitches soft when wet; vg rest; conv town cent; mkt Wed; vg; new owners; ltd san facs."* €15.00, 10 Apr-2 Nov. **2017**

CLAIRVAUX LES LACS *6H2* (1.2km SE Rural) *46.56431, 5.7562* **Yelloh! Village Le Fayolan,** Chemin de Langard, 39130 Clairvaux-les-Lacs **03 84 25 88 52; fayolan@ odesia.eu; www.campinglefayolan.fr or www.yellohvillage.co.uk**

♿€4 ⊞ ⚡♿♨ℐ ✉ 🍴 ⊘♨ 🎾 ⊞ ✎ ⛴(covrd, htd)

Fr town foll campsite sp, last site along lane adj to lake. 4*, V lge, mkd, hdg, pt shd, terr, serviced pitches; EHU (6A) inc (poss rev pol); gas; twin axles; TV; 16% statics; Eng spkn; adv bkg rec; ccard acc; waterslide; games rm; tennis 1km; bike hire; sauna; CKE. *"Excel, clean site; extra for lakeside pitches high ssn; pleasant sm town in easy walking dist; lovely area."* €48.00, 3 May-8 Sep, J11. **2019**

CLAIRVAUX LES LACS *6H2* (1km S Rural) *46.56761, 5.75480* **Camping La Grisière et Europe Vacances,** Chemin Langard, 39130 Clairvaux-les-Lacs **03 84 25 80 48; bailly@la-grisiere.com; www.la-grisiere.com**

♿€1.40 ♟(htd) ⊞ ⚡♿♨ℐ/MSP ✉ ⛴ 🍴 🎾 ⊞

Turn S off D678 in Clairvaux opp church onto D118; fork R in 500m & foll site sps to lake. Sp in vill. Camping La Grisière ent after Camping Les Lacs. 3*, V lge, mkd, pt shd, pt sl, EHU (6-10A) inc; bbq; sw nr; TV; 5% statics; phone; bus 700m; Eng spkn; ccard acc; bike hire; watersports; tennis 1km; fishing; canoe hire; CKE. *"Lovely views of lake in beautiful area; lge pitches; excel site; quiet; few facs."* €22.70, 1 May-15 Sep. **2017**

CLAIRVAUX LES LACS *6H2* (10km SW Rural) *46.52311, 5.67350* **Camping de Surchauffant,** Pont de la Pyle, 39270 La Tour-du-Meix **03 84 25 41 08; info@camping-surchauffant.fr; www.camping-surchauffant.fr**

♿€1.60 ♟♟⚡♿♨ℐ/MSP ✉ 🍴 ⊘♨🎾 ⛴ nr ⊞ ✎ 🛒⛴

Fr Clairvaux S on D27 or D49 to D470. Foll sp Lac de Vouglans, site sp. 3*, Med, mkd, pt shd, pt sl, EHU (6A) €3; bbq; TV; 10% statics; Eng spkn; adv bkg acc; ccard acc; watersports; sailing. *"Vg facs; lovely location; dir access to lake; hiiking trails."* €19.00, 22 Apr-10 Sep. **2016**

CLAIRVAUX LES LACS *6H2* (7km W Rural) *46.59976, 5.68824* **Camping Beauregard,** 2 Grande Rue, 39130 Mesnois **03 84 48 32 51; reception@juracamping beauregard.com; www.juracampingbeauregard.com**

♿€2.20 ♟(htd) ⊞ ⚡♿♨ℐ/ ✉ 🍴 nr ⊘♨ ⛴ nr ⊞
⛴(htd) ⛱sand 800m

S fr Lons-le-Saunier on D52/D678, about 1km bef Pont-de-Poitte turn L on D151. Site 1km on L opp rd junc to Pont-de-Poitte. 3*, Lge, hdg, mkd, hdstg, pl shd, pt sl, torr, EHU (6A) €4 (poss long lead req); gas; 10% statics; Eng spkn; adv bkg acc; tennis; bike hire; games rm. *"Super site, clean & well-run; different sized pitches; excel san facs, ltd LS; excel rest; kayaking nr; poss muddy when wet; new indoor pool with jacuzzi and sauna (2012), extremely gd quality."* €31.00, 28 Mar-30 Sep, J13. **2019**

CLAMECY *4G4* (1.3km SE Urban) *47.45133, 3.52770* **Camp Municipal du Pont-Picot,** Rue de Chevroches, 58500 Clamecy **07 86 86 14 31; clamecycamping@ orange.fr; www.clamecy.fr**

♟♟⚡♿♨ℐ/ ✉ 🍴 nr ⊞

On N151 fr S, exit N151 at rndabt 3km SW of town cent, cross level x-ing then R at rndabt on D23, take 1st L, site sp in 2.4km. Narr app rd. App fr N or E thro town not rec. Do not use sat nav thro town. 2*, Med, pt shd, pt sl, EHU (6A) inc; sw; CKE. *"Pleasant, peaceful site bet rv & canal in beautiful location; friendly, helpful staff; facs poss inadequate when busy; town 10 min walk on towpath; gd cycling; gd NH; narr bdge just bef ent."* €17.00, 1 Apr-30 Sep. **2019**

CLAYETTE, LA *9A2* (0.5km E Urban) *46.29159, 4.32020* **Camping des Bruyères,** 9 Route de Gibles, 71800 La Clayette **09 72 77 61 85 or 03 85 28 09 15; contact@ campingbruyeres.com; http://campingbruyeres.com**

♿€1.60 ♟♟(htd) ⊞ ⚡♿♨ℐ ✉ 🍴 🍴 nr ⛴ nr ⊞ ✎

Site on D79, 100m fr D987 & lake. 3*, Med, hdg, mkd, hdstg, shd, sl, EHU (6A) inc; gas; bbq; 10% statics; phone; adv bkg acc; boating; games area; tennis; CKE. *"Pleasant, well-kept site o'looking lake & chateau; friendly, helpful staff; gd-sized pitches; htd pool adj Jun-Aug inc; excel; 20 min walk to town; supmkt 10 min walk."* €25.00, 18 Apr-30 Sep. **2019**

CLECY *3D1* (1.4km E Rural) *48.91491, -0.47374* **FFCC Camping Les Rochers des Parcs,** La Cour, 14570 Clécy **02 31 69 70 36; camping.normandie@ gmail.com; www.camping-normandie-clecy.fr**

♿€1.60 ♟♟(htd) ⊞ ♿♨ℐ/MSP ✉ 🍴 🍴 ⊘♨ 🎾 ⛴ nr ⊞

Fr Condé take D562 dir Caen; turn R onto D133a sp Clécy & Le Vey; do not take turning to Clécy cent but cont downhill, past museum on L & then over bdge; turn R in 150m at campsite sp; site on R. 3*, Med, hdstg, mkd, pt shd, pt sl, EHU (6A) €3.50; bbq; red long stay; 10% statics; phone; Eng spkn; games area; bike hire; rv fishing. *"Lovely rvside situation; friendly, helpful owner; facs poss stretched high ssn & ltd LS; excel cent for walking."* €23.00, 1 Apr-30 Sep. **2018**

FRANCE

CLERMONT FERRAND *9B1* (16km SE Rural) *45.70027, 3.16953* **Camping Le Clos Auroy,** Rue de la Narse, 63670 Orcet **04 73 84 26 97; www.camping-le-clos-auroy.com**

[symbols] **12** €17.5 p/w (htd) [symbols] (htd)

S on A75 take exit 5 sp Orcet; foll D213 to Orcet for 2km, at rndabt onto D52, take 1st L, site on R. Do not foll SatNav to site. 4*, Med, hdstg, mkd, hdg, pt shd, terr, EHU (10A) inc; gas; red long stay; 10% statics; phone; Eng spkn; adv bkg acc; ccard acc; tennis; rv fishing 500m; CKE. "Excel, well-kept; site poss open all year; easy access; lge pitches, poss v high hedges; superb htd san facs; pitches by rv poss liable to flood; extra charge for sh stay m'vans; ltd fresh water points & diff to use for refill; vg winter site; interesting town; gd dog walks adj; snack & bar only open high ssn; vg value; helpful staff; gd site." €33.80   **2019**

CLERMONT FERRAND *9B1* (5km W Rural) *45.75845, 3.05453* **Huttopia Royat (was Camping Indigo Royat),** Route de Gravenoire, 63130 Royat **04 73 35 97 05; royat@camping-indigo.com; www.europe.huttopia.com**

[symbols] €4 (htd) [symbols] (htd)

Site diff to find fr Clermont-Ferrand cent. Fr N, leave A71 at Clermont-Ferrand. Foll sp Chamalières/Royat, then sp Royat. Go under rlwy bdge & pass thermal park on L. At mini-rndabt go L & up hill. At statue, turn L & go up long hill. Look for site sp & turn R. Site on R. NB Do not go down steep rd with traff calming. NB sat nav directs up v narr rds & steep hills. 4*, Lge, hdstg, mkd, pt shd, terr, serviced pitches; EHU (10A) €5.20; gas; bbq; TV; 10% statics; phone; Eng spkn; adv bkg acc; ccard acc; bike hire; tennis; CKE. "Excel, clean, spacious, lovely site; set on hillside in trees; gd size earth pitches; views at top levels over Clermont; clean san facs; facs ltd in LS; conv touring base; new recep; vg."
€40.00, 22 Mar-3 Nov, L18.   **2019**

CLISSON *2H4* (1.3km N Urban) *47.09582, -1.28216* **Camp Municipal du Vieux Moulin,** Rue de la Fontaine Câlin, Route de Nantes, 44190 Clisson **02 40 54 44 48 or 06 20 29 08 42 (mob); camping.clissonsevremaine.fr**

[symbols] €1.12 (htd) [symbols] nr [symbols] nr

1km NW of Clisson cent on main rd to Nantes, at rndabt. Look for old windmill nr ent on L of rd. Leclerc hypmkt on opp side of rd; site sp fr town cent. Narr ent. 3*, Sm, hdg, pt shd, pt sl, EHU 10A inc; TV; Eng spkn; adv bkg acc; fishing adj; boating; horseriding adj; tennis adj; game rm. "Gd municipal site; lge pitches; gd clean san facs; if office clsd pitch self, book in later; picturesque town 15 min walk; bar 500m; hypmkt 500m; mkd walks; interesting old town with castle ruins; next to retail park; excel rest in town." €24.50, 1 Mar-30 Nov.   **2018**

CLOYES SUR LE LOIR *4F2* (1km N Rural) *48.00240, 1.23304* **Parc de Loisirs Le Val Fleuri,** Route de Montigny, 28220 Cloyes-sur-le-Loir **02 37 98 50 53; info@val-fleuri.fr; www.val-fleuri.fr**

[symbols] €2 (htd) [symbols]

Located on L bank of Rv Loir off N10; site sp. 4*, Lge, hdg, pt shd, EHU (5A) inc; bbq; twin axles; 50% statics; phone; Eng spkn; adv bkg acc; ccard acc; waterslide; bike hire; €3; CKE. "Facs gd for children but ltd LS; well-run, pleasant site in wooded valley; site fees inc use of sm leisure park, pedalos & rowing boats on Rv Loir; vg san facs." €38.00, 15 Mar-15 Nov.   **2017**

"I need an on-site restaurant"

We do our best to make sure site information is correct, but it is always best to check any must-have facilities are still available or will be open during your visit.

CLUNY *9A2* (0.5km E Urban) *46.43086, 4.66756* **Camp Municipal St Vital,** 30 Rue de Griottons, 71250 Cluny **03 85 59 08 34; camping.st.vital@orange.fr; www.camping-cluny.blogspot.com**

[symbols] (htd) [symbols]

E fr Cluny on D15 (sp Azé & Camping) across narr rv bdge; in 200m turn R into Rue de Griottonste; site on L in 100m. Site adj sw pool. To avoid bdge app fr S on D15. 3*, Lge, mkd, hdstg, pt shd, sl, EHU (6A) €4.50 (poss rev pol); gas; bbq; twin axles; adv bkg rec; ccard acc; fishing; horseriding nr; bike hire; games rm; tennis. "Well-run, tidy site; helpful staff; gd clean san facs; cycle & walking rte adj (Voie Verte); frequent rlwy noise daytime; interesting town; htd pool adj inc; excel, reliable site; well organised and pleasant; busy site." €19.00, 26 Apr-5 Oct.   **2017**

CLUNY *9A2* (12km S Rural) *46.33744, 4.61123* **Camping du Lac,** 8 Rue du Port, 71520 St Point **03 85 50 52 31; reservation@campingsaintpoint.com; www.campingsaintpoint.com**

[symbols] €2 (htd) [symbols] nr [symbols]

Turn S off N79, Mâcon/Paray-le-Monial rd, turn L bef Ste Cécile on D22; site sp at junc; site 100m on R after St Point vill. 3*, Med, hdg, mkd, pt shd, pt sl, terr, EHU (16A) inc; bbq; sw nr; TV; 30% statics; phone; adv bkg acc; fishing; boat hire; tennis 4km; CKE. "Cluny attractive town & abbey; lge pitches; clean & basic san facs & ltd LS; lovely scenery & pleasant lake; on edge of Beaujolais; sp walks fr site; peaceful area with wooded hills & valleys." €17.60, 15 Apr-15 Oct.   **2018**

FRANCE

CLUSAZ, LA *9B3* (6km N Rural) *45.93972, 6.42777*
Camping L'Escale, Route de la Patinoire, 74450
Le Grand-Bornand **04 50 02 20 69; contact@
campingslescale.com; www.campinglescale.com**

🐕 €2.30 🛉🛉(htd) WD 🚿 ♿ 🗑 ⚒ 🍴 MJP ▽ 🍽 ① 🛒 🎿 nr ⚠
🏊(covrd, htd) 🛝

Exit A41 junc 17 onto D16/D909 E dir La Clusaz.
At St Jean-de-Sixt turn L at rndabt sp Le Grand
Bornand. After 1.5km foll camping sp on main rd
& at junc turn R sp for site & 'Vallée du Bouchet'.
Site is 1st exit R at rndabt at end of this rd. D4 S
fr Cluses not rec while towing as v steep & winding.
3*, Med, mkd, pt shd, pt sl, terr, EHU (10A) inc poss rev
pol); gas; bbq; TV; 20% statics; adv bkg req; ccard acc;
archery; tennis; fishing; games rm; CKE. "Family-run site
in scenic area; bike hire 250m; gd san facs; no c'vans over
8.5m or m'vans over 8m high ssn, Feb & wk of New Year;
serviced pitch in summer; vg rest; sh walk to attractive
vill; winter sports; free use htd ski/boot rm in winter;
boggy in wet weather; vg mkt Wed; excel site; ski bus; gd
sports facs." **€32.00, 1 Jan-12 Apr, 22 May-27 Sep
& 19 Dec-31 Dec, M07.** 2015

COEX *2H4* (2.5km W Rural) *46.67679, -1.76899*
RCN Camping La Ferme du Latois, 85220 Coëx
03 43 74 50 90; www.rcn.nl/fermedulatois

🐕 €5 🛉🛉(htd) WD 🚿 ♿ 🗑 ⚒ 🦋 ♀ 🍴 ▽ 🍽 ⚠ 🏊

Exit D948 at Aizenay onto D6 dir St Gilles-Croix-
de-Vie; at Coëx take D40 SW sp Brétignolles;
site in 1.5km on L. 4*, Lge, pt shd, EHU inc (poss
rev pol); bbq (gas); 20% statics; phone; Eng
spkn; adv bkg acc; games rm; games area; lake
fishing; bike hire. "Spacious pitches; cycle rtes adj;
conv Lac du Jaunay & Lac du Gué-Gorand; excel."
€41.00, 19 Apr-27 Sep. 2019

COGNAC *7B2* (2.5km NE Rural) *45.70920, -0.31284*
Camping de Cognac, Blvd de Châtenay, 16100 Cognac
**05 45 32 13 32; contact@campingdecognac.com;
www.campingdecognac.com**

🐕 €1.50 🛉🛉 WD 🚿 ♿ 🗑 ⚒ MJP ▽ ① 🛒 🎿 ⚠ 🛝 🏊

Fr N141 foll 'Camping' sp to town cent. Turn R at
'Speedy' g'ge, site immed on R in 2km after x-ing
rv; foll sp 'Base de Plein Air'. Take care ent barrier.
3*, Med, hdg, mkd, hdstg, pt shd, EHU (6A) inc (poss
long leads req & poss rev pol); bbq; red long stay;
5% statics; phone; bus; Eng spkn; adv bkg acc; ccard
acc; games area; rv boating; rv fishing; CKE. "Excel lge
park with many facs; helpful staff; clean modern san
facs but dated; gates clsd 2200-0700 (1800 LS); night
watchman high ssn; no twin axles; footpath to town;
conv Cognac distilleries (vouchers fr site recep); cycle
rte to town cent." **€22.40, 1 May-27 Sep.** 2018

COGNAC *7B2* (10km E Rural) *45.67160, -0.22718*
Camping De Bourg (formerly Camping du Port),
16200 Bourg-Charente **06 15 16 67 82 or
06 03 06 85 07 (mob)**

🐕 🛉🛉 WD 🚿 ♀ ① nr 🎿 nr

Exit N141 onto D158 dir Bourg-Charente; turn L
in 800m & site on R. Site sp fr D158. Chicane-type
ent gates. 1*, Sm, pt shd, pt sl, EHU (6A) €3; red
long stay; fishing; tennis. "Delightful site on banks
of Rv Charente; friendly staff; facs v basic & ltd but
clean, poss stretched high ssn; site on 2 levels, lower
one sl; gd walks & cycle path to Jarnac & Cognac; gd;
find placement, owner will call; vg value; v quiet site."
€10.00, 1 May-15 Sep. 2017

COGNAC *7B2* (16km E Urban) *45.67606, -0.17349*
FFCC Camping de l'Ile Madame, 16200 Gondeville
**06 26 91 40 92; campingilemadame@orange.fr;
camping-jarnac.jimdo.com**

🐕 €2.50 🛉🛉 🚿 ♿ ♀ ① nr 🎿 nr ⚠ 🛝 🏊

Turn E at S end of rv bdge at S end of town.
Fr Angoulême on N141, exit junc sp 'Jarnac Est'; foll
sp Jarnac thro 1 rndabt into Jarnac; at traff lts (LH
lane) turn L sp Tourist Info/Camping; cross rv bdge
& immed turn L to site. 3*, Lge, pt shd, EHU (6-10A)
€3.20 (rev pol); red long stay; TV; adv bkg acc; golf
nr; games area; CKE. "Pleasant, well-run site; gd sized
pitches; easy walk into Jarnac with shops & rests; gd
walks along rv; nr Courvoisier bottling plant; excel; boat
trips along rv; canoe hire nr; poss noise fr adj sports
grnd & disco; site redesigned & new san facs (2015)."
€14.00, 15 Apr-30 Sep. 2017

COGNAC LA FORET *7B3* (1.5km SW Rural) *45.82494,
0.99674* **Camping des Alouettes,** Les Alouettes,
87310 Cognac-la-Forêt **05 55 03 26 93; info@
camping-des-alouttes.com; www.camping-des-
alouettes.com**

🐕 €1 🛉🛉 WD 🚿 ♿ 🗑 ⚒ 🦋 ♀ 🍴 ▽ ① 🛒 🎿 nr ⚠ 🏊 🛝

Fr Aixe-sur-Vienne on D10, site W of Cognac-la-
Forêt on D10, sp to L. 3*, Med, hdg, pt shd, pt sl,
EHU (10A) €3; bbq; sw nr; 10% statics; Eng spkn;
adv bkg acc; tennis 700m; CKE. "Beautiful location;
friendly Dutch owners; conv war vill Oradour-
sur-Glane & Richard Lion Heart sites; excel facs,
peaceful, relaxing, vg site; lge pitches; well run site."
€23.00, 1 Apr-30 Sep. 2017

COLMAR *6F3* (2km E Urban) *48.07942, 7.38665*
Camping de l'Ill, 1 Allée du Camping, 68180
Horbourg-Wihr **03 89 41 15 94; colmar@camping-indigo.com; www.campingdelill.com**

🐕 €4.50 (htd) 👪 WD ♨ ♿ ⚑ ⚙ MSP 🦋 ♙ 🍴 ⊕ 🛒 🏪 ⚓ 🛶 (htd)

Exit A35 junc 25 onto D415, foll Freibourg sp. At 2nd rndabt turn L to Colmar cent, site on rvside on L bef bdge. 3*, Lge, hdstg, mkd, hdg, shd, pt sl, terr, EHU (10A) inc (poss rev pol); TV; 10% statics; bus/train to city cent; Eng spkn; adv bkg acc; ccard acc; bike hire; CKE. *"Lovely, clean, rvside site; excel san facs; gd rest; some pitches req steel pegs; much noise fr a'route; gd for town; sep area for NH, bus only to town, san facs tired, supmkt 900m."*
€22.50, 26 Mar-6 Jan, J12. 2019

COLMAR *6F3* (7km SW Rural) *48.04272, 7.29970*
Camping des Trois Châteaux, 10 Rue du Bassin, 68420 Eguisheim **03 89 23 19 39; reception@camping-eguisheim.fr; www.camping-eguisheim.fr**

🐕 €3 👪 WD ♨ ♿ ⚑ ⚙ MSP 🦋 ♙ 🍴 nr ⊕ nr 🛒 nr 🏪

Foll D83 S (Colmar by-pass) R at sp Eguisheim. R into vill to site at top of vill, foll camp sp. 3*, Med, mkd, pt shd, pt sl, terr, EHU (8-10A) €3-5 (poss rev pol); gas; adv bkg req; ccard acc; CKE. *"Popular, well-run, clean, busy site; no c'vans over 7m (inc draw bar); mv pitches flat but some c'van pitches sl & poss diff; gd touring base; weekly wine-tasting events; stork park adj; rec arr early; excel; cycle rte to cent of Colmar; gd."*
€23.80, 26 Mar-2 Nov & 25 Nov-24 Dec. 2019

COLMAR *6F3* (7km W Urban) *48.08517, 7.27253*
Camping Le Medieval (formerly Municipal Les Cigognes), Quai de la Fecht, 68230 Turckheim **03 89 27 02 00; reception@camping-turckheim.fr; en.camping-turckheim.fr**

🐕 €2.50 👪 (htd) WD ♨ ♿ ⚑ ⚙ MSP 🦋 ♙ 🛒 nr 🏪 ⚓ 🛶

Fr D83 twd Turchkeim turn W onto D11 to Turckheim. On ent vill, turn immed L down 1-way rd after x-ing rlwy lines. Do not cross rv bdge. Site on L bef bdge, adj stadium. 3*, Med, hdg, pt shd, EHU (16A) €4; bbq; twin axles; TV; bus adj, train 250m; Eng spkn; ccard acc; games rm; CKE. *"Lovely site with med pitches; cycle rtes nr; resident storks; sh walk to interesting, beautiful old vill with rests; gd touring base; gd, excel san facs; poss cr in June, high ssn & w/ends; new management (2016); friendly helpful staff; open 26 Dec-28 Dec for Christmas mkt; vg; close to historic sites and medieval castles; wine tasting & sales; great site; new shwr block (2017); cycle rte to Colmar & vineyards."*
€19.00, 7 Apr-23 Oct & 30 Nov-24 Dec. 2019

COLMARS *9D4* (2km SW Rural) *44.19148, 6.59690*
Camping Le Haut Verdon, 04370 Villars-Colmars **04 92 83 40 09; info@lehautverdon.com; www.lehautverdon.com**

🐕 €4 👪 (htd) WD ♨ ♿ ⚑ ⚙ MSP 🦋 ♙ 🍴 ⊕ 🛒 🏪 ⚓ 🛶 (htd) 🛏

Only app fr S on D955 & D908 fr St André-les-Alps thro Beauvezer. Clearly sp on ent Villars-Colmars on R. Do not take D908 via Annot/Le Fugeret with a caravan(Do not confuse with Municipal site approx 5km bef this site). 4*, Sm, mkd, hdstg, pt shd, EHU (6-10A) €3-4; gas; bbq; sw nr; twin axles; TV; 50% statics; 50m; adv bkg acc; rv fishing; games area; games rm; bike hire; CKE. *"Superb setting on Rv Verdon; gd, clean san facs; helpful staff; conv Colmars, flower meadows, Allos Lake; site nr Mercantour National Pk; scenic rte to Barcelonnette via Col d'Allos, not suitable for c'vans; ski area at Allos; gd."*
€28.00, 28 Apr-14 Oct. 2018

COMBOURG *2E4* (8km NE Rural) *48.45304, -1.65031*
Camping Le Bois Coudrais (Ybert), 35270 Cuguen **02 99 73 27 45; info@vacancebretagne.com; www.vacancebretagne.com**

🐕 👪 WD ♨ ⚑ ⚙ 🦋 ♙ 🍴 ⊕ 🏪 🛶 (htd)

Fr Combourg take D796 twd Pleine-Fougères, 5km out of Combourg turn L on D83 to Cuguen; 500m past Cuguen, turn L, site sp. Or fr Dol-de-Bretagne, take D795 then turn L onto D9 to Cuguen. Sm, hdg, pt shd, EHU (10A) €3; bbq (gas); twin axles; Eng spkn; adv bkg acc; ccard acc; golf nr; watersports nr; fishing nr; animal petting area; CCI. *"CL-type site, friendly British owners, gd clean facs, great for young children, sm animal-petting area, gd touring base; zoo nrby; adventure park nr; excel."*
€20.00, 8 May-8 Sep. 2019

COMBOURG *2E4* (6km SW Rural) *48.38090, -1.83290*
Camping Domaine du Logis, 35190 La Chapelle-aux-Filtzméens,Ille-et-Vilaine **02 99 45 25 45 or 06 85 78 69 71 (mob); domainedulogis@wanadoo.fr; www.domainedulogis.com**

🐕 €2 👪 WD ♨ ♿ ⚑ ⚙ 🦋 ♙ 🍴 ⊕ 🛒 🏪 nr ⚓ 🛶 🛶 (htd) 🛏

Fr N176 at junc for Dol-de-Bretagne branch R onto D155 sp Dol & take D795 S to Combourg. Then take D13 twd St Domineuc, go thro La Chapelle-aux-Filtzméens & site on R in 1km. 5*, Lge, mkd, hdg, pt shd, serviced pitches; EHU 16A; gas; bbq (elec, gas); twin axles; red long stay; TV; 10% statics; phone; Eng spkn; adv bkg rec; ccard acc; gym; games area; games rm; fishing nr; bike hire; fitness rm; CKE. *"Set in chateau grnds; lge flat grassy pitches; helpful, pleasant staff; gd, clean san facs; gd touring base, conv St Malo, Mont St Michel, Dinan & Channel Islands; mkt Mon; excel; no o'fits over 12m; beautiful; v child oriented; canoe 800m; superb pool; excel."*
€33.00, 1 Apr-2 Oct, B02. 2019

COMPS SUR ARTUBY 10E3 (1km NW Rural) *43.71543, 6.49862* **Camp Municipal du Pontet,** 83840 Comps-sur-Artuby **04 94 76 91 40; mairie.compsurartuby@wanadoo.fr**

🛏 👪 ⓌⒸ 🚿 ♿ 🏊 🛒 ⍰ 🍽 ♨ 🐕

Fr Comps-sur-Artuby take D71 sp Grand Canyon du Verdon. Site sp on R in 1km. 2*, Med, mkd, pt shd, terr, EHU (6A) €3; phone; CKE. *"Vg, well-laid out, wooded site; conv Gorges du Verdon; easy access; ltd san facs at top of site."* **€8.00, 1 May-31 Oct.** **2019**

CONCARNEAU 2F2 (6km S Coastal) *47.85628, -3.89999* **Camping Le Cabellou Plage,** Ave de Cabellou, Kersaux, 29185 Concarneau **02 98 97 37 41; info@le-cabellou-plage.com; www.le-cabellou-plage.com**

🛏 €4 👪(cont) ⓌⒸ 🚿 ♿ 🛗 🖥 ⍰ 🐾 ♨ 🍽 🛒 ⏏ 🏊(htd) 🚲

🏄 sand adj

Fr N165 turn onto D70 dir Concarneau. At 5th rndabt (Leclerc supmkt) foll dir Tregunc. After Moros bdge take 2nd exit at next rndabt dir Le Cabellou-Plage. Site sp on L. 4*, Lge, mkd, hdg, hdstg, pt shd, EHU (10A) inc; TV; 20% statics; bus at site ent; Eng spkn; adv bkg acc; ccard acc; games area; bike hire; games rm; watersports. *"Pleasant seaside site; vg san facs; gd walking fr site; gd for town via ferry."* **€36.00, 28 Apr-15 Sep, B34.** **2017**

> ## "There aren't many sites open at this time of year"
>
> If you're travelling outside peak season remember to call ahead to check site opening dates – even if the entry says 'open all year'.

CONCARNEAU 2F2 (1.5km NW Urban/Coastal) *47.8807, -3.9311* **Camping Les Sables Blancs,** Ave du Dorlett, 29900 Concarneau **02 98 97 16 44; contact@camping-lessablesblancs.com; www.camping-les-sablesblancs.com**

🛏 Free 👪(htd) ⓌⒸ 🚿 ♿ 🛗 🖥 ⍰ MP 🐾 ♨ 🍽 ⏏ 🛒nr ⏏ 🔥

🏊(htd) 🚲 🏄 sand 400m

Exit N165 to Concarneau dir 'Centre Ville'. Then foll sp 'La Côte' 300m after traff lts. Site on R, sp. 4*, Med, hdstg, mkd, hdg, pt shd, pt sl, terr, EHU (10A); bbq; red long stay; TV; 3% statics; phone; bus 300m; Eng spkn; adv bkg acc; ccard acc; jacuzzi; games rm; games area; CKE. *"Nice, clean, family site in woodland; many sm pitches; friendly staff; excel san facs; superb pool; gd rest; pleasant walk to town, 1.5km; mkt Mon & Thurs; vg; well run; some pitches uneven; steep walk to san facs."* **€32.00, 1 Apr-31 Oct.** **2019**

CONCARNEAU 2F2 (3km NW Coastal) *47.89054, 3.93847* **Camping Les Prés Verts aux 4 Sardines,** Kernous-Plage, 29900 Concarneau **02 98 97 09 74 or 07 87 90 90 01 (mob); info@presverts.com; www.presverts.com**

🛏 €2 👪 ⓌⒸ 🚿 ♿ 🖥 ⍰ ♨ ♨ ⏏nr 🏊(htd) 🚲

Exit N165 onto D70 dir Concarneau. At rndabt by Leclerc supmkt foll sp 'Centre Ville' (Town Centre) with Leclerc on L. Strt over at 2nd rndabt then bear R at the next rndabt onto Rue de Kerneach & down slope. Bear L at 1st rndabt & R at next. Keep R to join Rue des Sables Blancs, pass Hôtel l'Océan; site 3rd rd on L in 1.5km. 3*, Med, hdg, mkd, pt shd, pt sl, serviced pitches; EHU (6A-10A) inc (poss rev pol & long lead req); bbq (charcoal, gas); TV; 10% statics; adv bkg acc; ccard acc; games rm; horseriding 1km; sailing 1km. *"Peaceful, scenic, busy site; path to sandy cove below; gd sized pitches; lge pitches extra; family-run, friendly helpful staff; basic san facs, run down, ltd LS; poss unkempt LS; dir access to beach; no o'fits over 8m; gd touring base; walk along coastal path to Concarneau; mkt Mon & Fri; cycle track to old town (old rlwy track) 300m fr site; gd location."* **€28.00, 1 May-30 Sep, B24.** **2020**

CONDOM 8E2 (10km N Rural) *44.03324, 0.36614* **Camping Le Mouliat,** RD 219, 47600 Moncrabeau **05 53 65 43 28; contact@camping-le-mouliat.fr; www.camping-le-mouliat.fr**

🛏 👪 ⓌⒸ 🚿 ♿ 🖥 ⍰ MP ♨ 🍽 ⏏ 🏊

N fr Condom on D930 for 9.5km, then R on D219. Site on L in 0.5km, just bef rv bdge. 3*, Sm, hdg, mkd, pt shd, EHU €4.50; bbq; twin axles; 10% statics; games area; CKE. *"Quiet LS; conv for Condom/Nerac; takeaway; helpful, cheery owners; vg."* **€24.00, 1 May-1 Oct.** **2015**

> ## "That's changed – Should I let the Club know?"
>
> If you find something on site that's different from the site entry, fill in a report and let us know. See camc.com/europereport.

CONDOM 8E2 (4km NE Rural) *43.97491, 0.42038* **Camping à la Ferme (Rogalle),** Guinland, 32100 Condom **05 62 28 17 85; rogalle.guinland@wanadoo.fr; http://campingdeguinland.monsite-orange.fr**

🛏 👪 ⓌⒸ 🚿 ⍰ 🐾 ♨nr 🛒nr ⏏

NE fr Condom on D931, turn R onto D41. Pass water tower on R, site ent on L at bottom of hill just bef sm lake on R. Sm, shd, EHU (6-10A) €3; bbq; 10% statics; tennis nr. *"Vg CL-type site in pine grove; canoe hire nr; gd views; friendly owner; clean facs."* **€9.00, 1 Apr-30 Oct.** **2017**

CONDOM 8E2 (7.4km SE Rural) 43.92929, 0.42698
Ferme d'accueil de Bordeneuve, Bordeneuve Grazimis 32100 CONDOM +33 (0)5 62 28 07 09 or 06 35 23 90 83; fermedebordeneuve@gmail.com; www.campingde bordeneuve.fr

12 ⚡ WD ♨ ▣ / 🦋 🛒 nr

E fr Condom on D7 to Caussens; far end of vill turn R on D204, sp St Orens; in 1.2km turn R sp Béraut, bear R at fork, site on L in 400m. Also sp fr D654. Sm, pt shd, pt sl, EHU (12A) €2.50 (long lead poss req); adv bkg acc. *"Peaceful & secluded CL-type site; friendly owners; basic san facs; waymkd trails nr; phone ahead to check open LS - poss not open until Apr."*
€12.00 2020

CONDRIEU 9B2 (5.7km SE Rural) 45.42413, 4.78251
Camping Le Daxia, Route du Péage, 38370 St Clair-du-Rhône 04 74 56 39 20; info@campingledaxia.com; www.campingledaxia.com

🐕 €1.85 ⚡ WD ♨ ♿ ▣ / MSP 🦋 🍸 ⑭ 🛒 nr ⚓ 🛶

S fr Vienne on D386; turn L in Condieu sp D28 Les Roches-de-Condrieu & Le Péage-de-Roussillon; foll sp A7 Valance & 'Camping' onto D4. Site on L well sp fr Condrieu. 4*, Med, hdg, mkd, pt shd, EHU (5-10A) €2.40-2.85; bbq; adv bkg acc; games rm; CKE. *"Vg site; on edge of sm rv with beach."*
€23.00, 1 Apr-30 Sep. 2017

CONFOLENS 7A3 (0.5km N Rural) 46.01905, 0.67531
Camp Municipal des Ribières, Ave de St Germain, 16500 Confolens 05 45 85 35 27 or 05 45 84 01 97 (Mairie); contact@mairieconfolens.com; http://www.campingdesribieres.fr/

🐕 🛒 ⚡ WD ♨ ♿ ▣ / MSP 🛒 nr ⚓

Fr N foll D951 dir Confolens turn L sp St Germain-de-Confolens, site on R in 7km at edge of town bet rd & rv. NB Diff app fr S thro vill. 3*, Med, mkd, pt shd, EHU (16A); gas; bbq; sw nr; 3% statics; phone; Eng spkn; adv bkg req; bike hire; boating; fishing; games area. *"Interesting, pretty town; facs neglected & ltd LS; m'van o'night area outside site; pool 200m; warden calls am & pm; great site; lovely location; excel."* **€21.00, 1 Apr-1 Oct.** 2018

CONQUES 7D4 (8km E Rural) 44.55948, 2.46184
Camping L'Etang du Camp, 12320 Sénergues 05 65 46 01 95; info@etangducamp.fr; www.etangducamp.fr

🐕 €1.60 ⚡ WD ♨ ♿ ▣ / 🦋 🍸 🛒 🛝

Fr S on D901 dir Conques; at St Cyprien turn R onto D46 sp Sénergues; foll sp Sénergues up hill for 6km; 2nd L at the top; foll Camping sp. 3*, Med, mkd, hdg, pt shd, EHU Inc; bbq (charcoal); 10% statics; Eng spkn; adv bkg acc; fishing in private lake; ice; bike hire; games area; canoeing nr; games rm; CKE. *"Well-situated, well-kept site; quiet & relaxing; warm welcome, British owners; modern, clean san facs; gd base for touring, walking & cycling; htd pool 6km; conv Conques; highly rec; excel"*
€23.00, 1 Apr-30 Sep. 2019

CONQUET, LE 2E1 (2km N Coastal) 48.36748, -4.75990
Camping Les Blancs Sablons, 29217 Le Conquet 02 98 36 07 91; www.les-blancs-sablons.com

🛒 ⚡ WD ♨ ▣ / 🍸 nr ⑭ 🛒 ⚓ (htd) ☂ sand 100m

Exit Brest on D789 to Le Conquet. Turn R after 22km (1.8km bef Le Conquet) on D67 twd St Renan, turn L after 700m on D28 twd Ploumoguer. After 2km, turn L at x-rds twd Plage des Blancs Sablons, site on L in 1km. 2*, Lge, mkd, unshd, pt sl, EHU (16A) €3 (long lead poss req); adv bkg acc; ccard acc; CKE. *"Gd views fr some pitches; some soft pitches; ltd facs LS & dated but clean with gd hot water; bar 500m; lovely old fishing town."*
€21.00, 1 Apr-31 Oct. 2017

CORCIEUX *6F3* (1km ESE Rural) *48.16826, 6.89006*
Camping Le Clos de la Chaume, 671 Rue d'Alsace,
88430 Corcieux **03 29 50 76 76 or 06 85 19 62 55
(mob); info@camping-closdelachaume.com;
www.camping-closdelachaume.com**

🕭 €1.90 ♦♦♦ WD ♨ ♦ ♿ ▨ ✎ MP ❦ ♈ ▼ nr ⊕ nr ⤢ nr ⚠
⛵

Take D145 fr St Dié, then D8 thro Anould & bear R
onto D60. Site in 3km on R at ent to vill.
3*, Med, hdstg, mkd, hdg, pt shd, serviced pitches;
EHU (8-10A) €5; gas; bbq; red long stay; twin axles;
TV; 15% statics; phone; Eng spkn; adv bkg acc; ccard
acc; fishing; games area; games rm; CKE. "*Lovely,
peaceful site in beautiful area; stream runs thro;
friendly & helpful owners; bike hire 800m; san facs
poss stetched & busy high ssn; conv Gérardmer &
Alsace wine rte; excel; acess rd vg; highly rec; family
owned; v well run; excel covrd pool.*"
€29.60, 19 Apr-30 Sep, J08. 2019

See advertisement

CORDES SUR CIEL *8E4* (5km SE Rural) *44.04158,
2.01722* **Camping Redon,** Livers-Cazelles, 81170
Cordes-sur-Ciel **09 80 50 42 72 or 06 47 46 13 62
(mob); info@campredon.com; www.campredon.com**

🕭 €2.25 ♦♦♦ WD ♨ ♦ ♿ ▨ ✎ MP ❦ ♈ ▼ ⊕ ⤢ nr ⚠ ⛵

Off D600 Albi to Cordes rd. Exit on D107 to E.
Site sp. 3*, Sm, hdg, pt shd, pt sl, EHU (6-16A)
€4.25; gas; red long stay; TV; phone; bus 1km;
Eng spkn; adv bkg acc; CKE. "*Well-kept, well-run
site; views fr some pitches; friendly, helpful Dutch
owner; excel facs, poss stretched high ssn; ecological
septic tank - environmentally friendly liquid sold
on site; conv Bastides in area; highly rec; lovely.*"
€30.00, 22 Apr-22 Oct. 2017

"We must tell the Club about that great site we found"

Get your site reports in by mid-August and we'll
do our best to get your updates into the next
edition.

CORDES SUR CIEL *8E4* (3km W Rural) *44.06681,
1.92408* **Camping Le Garissou,** Les Cabannes, 81170
Cordes-sur-Ciel **05 63 56 27 14; contact@legarissou.fr;
www.legarissou.fr**

🕭 €1.50 ♦♦♦ ♨ ▨ ✎ ❦ ⤢ ⚠

Take D600 fr Cordes thro Les Cabanes; site sp
on L at bottom of hill, 1.5km after Les Cabanes.
3*, Med, mkd, pt shd, terr, EHU (6A) inc. "*Hilltop
site; pool complex adj; excel views; clean facs.*"
€16.50, 15 Mar-10 Nov. 2015

CORMATIN *9A2* (0.5km N Rural) *46.54841, 4.68351*
Camping Le Hameau des Champs, Route de Chalon,
71460 Cormatin **03 85 50 76 71; camping.cormatin@
wanadoo.fr; www.le-hameau-des-champs.com**

🕭 €1 ♦♦♦ (htd) WD ♨ ♦ ♿ ▨ ✎ MP ❦ ♈ ▼ ⊕ ⤢ nr ⚠

Fr Cluny N on D981 dir Cormatin for approx 14km,
site N of town sp on L, 300m after chateau. Look for
line of European flags. 3*, Sm, mkd, hdg, unshd, pt sl,
EHU (13A) €3.70 (long lead poss req); bbq (elec, gas);
cooking facs; sw nr; TV; 10% statics; phone; Eng spkn;
adv bkg acc; ccard acc; bike hire; CKE. "*Well-kept,
secure site in lovely countryside; welcoming, friendly
owner; lge pitches; ltd EHU, adv bkg rec; gd facs, poss
stretched high ssn; rest open LS; Voie Verte cycling rte
adj; excel municipal site; sm town but gd local store;
Chateau closeby.*" **€18.00, 1 Apr-30 Sep.** 2019

COSNE COURS SUR LOIRE *4G3* (5km SW Rural)
47.40923, 2.91792 **Camping de l'Ile,** Ile de Cosne,
18300 Bannay **03 86 24 48 43; camping.cosne@
aquadis-loisirs.com; www.aquadis-loisirs.com**

🕭 €0.90 ♦♦♦ (htd) WD ♨ ♿ ▨ ✎ MP ❦ ♈ ▼ ⊕ ⤢ ⚠ ✎ ⛵

Fr Cosne take Bourges rd, D955, over 1st half of
bdge, ent immed on L, 500m strt. On rv island.
3*, Lge, shd, EHU (10A) €4; bbq; TV; 10% statics; Eng
spkn; ccard acc; bike hire; CKE. "*Helpful staff; views
of Rv Loire; gd san facs; gd NH; supmkt Carrefour
closeby; gd rest opp; town within walking dist.*"
€24.00, 1 Apr-24 Oct. 2019

COULANGES SUR YONNE *4G4* (9km E Rural)
47.53610, 3.63326 **Camp Municipal Le Petit Port,**
89660 Châtel-Censoir **03 86 81 01 98 (Mairie) or
06 80 32 59 50 (mob); campinglepetitport@orange.fr
or mairie-de-chatel-censoir@wanadoo.fr;
www.chatel-censoir.com**

🕭 €0.50 ♦♦♦ WD ▨ ✎ ♈ ▼ ⤢ nr ⚠

Fr Auxerre or Clamecy on N151 at Coulanges
turn E onto D21, S side of rv & canal to Châtel-
Censoir; site sp. 1*, Med, pt shd, EHU (6A) €3 (poss
rev pol); bbq; sw nr; twin axles; 10% statics; phone;
Eng spkn; fishing adj; CKE. "*Attractive, peaceful site
bet rv & canal; friendly, busy resident warden; OK
san facs; some pitches muddy when wet; beautiful
area with gd cycling; concerts at w/ends; excel.*"
€8.50, 27 Apr-30 Sep. 2018

COULANGES SUR YONNE *4G4* (0.6km S Rural)
47.52269, 3.53817 **Camping des Berges de l'Yonne,**
89480 Coulanges-sur-Yonne **03 86 81 76 87;
lesbergesdelyonne@orange.fr**

🕭 ♦♦♦ WD ♨ ✎ ▼ ⤢ nr ⚠ ⛵

On N151 dir Nevers. 2*, Med, pt shd, EHU (10A)
€2.80; bbq; tennis; fishing. "*V pleasant site in beautiful
area; dated facs but adequate & clean; superb pool.*"
€14.40, 1 May-30 Sep. 2020

COULON *7A2* (0.8km N Rural) *46.32739, -0.58437*
Camp Municipal La Niquière, Route de Benet, 79510
Coulon 05 49 35 81 19 or 05 49 35 90 26 (Mairie);
tourisme.coulon79@orange.fr; www.ville-coulon.fr

🐕 €0.50 ♿♿ 🅿 ♨ ⚓ / 🔟 nr

Fr N148 at Benet take D1 to Coulon to site on L at
ent to Coulon. 2*, Sm, pt shd, EHU (10A) €3.10; gas;
boat hire. *"Well-kept site; dated but clean san facs;
sports facs adj; ent only with barrier card - collect fr
Mairie when site office clsd; 10 min walk to vill; gd
NH; gd ctr for Marais Poitevin; Coulon is a v attractive
town."* €16.00, 1 Apr-30 Sep.   2016

"I need an on-site restaurant"

We do our best to make sure site information
is correct, but it is always best to check any
must-have facilities are still available or will
be open during your visit.

COULON *7A2* (2km W Rural) *46.31444, -0.60888*
Camping La Venise Verte, 178 Route des Bords de
Sèvre, 79510 Coulon 05 49 35 90 36; accueil@camping-
laveniseverte.fr; www.camping-laveniseverte.fr

🐕 €2 ♿♿ 🅿 ♨ ♿ 🖥 / 🅼🅿 ♈ 🍽 🕙 🏧 🏕 🎣 ⚓ 🛒

Exit A83 junc 9 onto D148 to Benet. Turn R at
rndabt onto D25E sp Benet cent & foll sp for Coulon
thro Benet. In Coulon turn R at traff lts onto D123
sp Le Vanneau-Irleau & Arcais. Cont for approx 3km
with canal on L to site R bef canal bdge. Site sp.
4*, Med, mkd, pt shd, EHU (10A) inc (poss rev pol); bbq
(charcoal, gas); twin axles; 20% statics; phone; Eng
spkn; adv bkg acc; ccard acc; canoe hire; fishing; bike
hire; games rm; boating; CKE. *"Superb, peaceful eco
site in park-like setting; v friendly helpful owner; excel
facs; gd rest; gd sized pitches (some with reinforced
plastic grid), but some sm & diff due trees & posts;
ACSI; excel touring base for nature lovers; gd walking
& cycle paths beside waterways; pretty town; lovely
area; much revisited site; well placed pitches; gd facs;
beautiful, tranquil location; highly rec; excel family run
site; charming vill walkable."*
€30.50, 1 Apr-15 Oct, A37.   2019

COULON *7A2* (6km W Rural) *46.33020, -0.67524*
Camping Le Relais du Pêcheur, 85420 Le Mazeau
02 51 52 93 23; campinglerelaisdupecheur@orange.fr;
www.lerelaisdupecheur.fr

♿♿ 🅿 ♨ ♿ 🖥 / 🦋 ♈ 🔟 nr 🏕 🛒

Fr Fontenay-le-Comte take N148 SE. At Benet turn
R onto D25 thro vill to Le Mazeau. Turn L in vill then
R over canal bdge. Site on L in 500m. 2*, Med, hdg,
pt shd, EHU (16A) €3.50; Eng spkn; adv bkg acc; CKE.
*"Pleasant, clean site in delightful location; gd cyling
& walks; new owners, resident warden; facs being
updated (2016)."* €13.00, 1 Apr-15 Oct.   2017

COURBIAC *7D3* (1.7km W Rural) *44.37818, 1.01807*
FFCC Le Pouchou, 47370 Courbiac 05 53 40 72 68
or 06 42 83 37 62 (mob); lepouchou@gmail.com;
www.camping-le-pouchou.com

🐕 €1.80 ♿♿ 🅿 ♨ ♿ 🖥 / 🅼 ♈ 🍽 🏧 🏕 ⚓ 🛒

S fr Fumel on D102 thro Tournon-d'Agenais;
Courbiac sp to L on S side of town; site on R in
2.5km (1.5km bef Courbiac). 3*, Sm, pt shd, pt sl,
EHU (10A) €4 (poss rev pol); TV (pitch); 10% statics;
Eng spkn; adv bkg req; fishing; horseriding; bike hire;
site clsd 21 Dec-9 Jan; archery; CKE. *"Vg site in lovely
setting; lge pitches each with picnic table; many sl
pitches poss diff; gd, clean facs; gd views; friendly,
hospitable owners; gd cycling; peaceful location."*
€16.00, 1 Mar-30 Jun,
1 Jul-31 Aug, 1 Sep-30 Nov.   2019

COURPIERE *9B1* (5km NE Rural) *45.79199, 3.60583*
Camping Le Grün du Chignore, Les Plaines, 63120
Vollore-Ville 04 73 53 73 37; camping-du-chignore@
hotmail.fr; www.campingauvergne.fr

🐕 €1.50 ♿♿ 🅿 ♨ ♿ 🖥 / 🅼🅿 🦋 ♈ 🕙 🏧 🔟 nr 🏕 ⚓

D906 S fr Thiers; at Courpière turn L onto D7 to
Vollore-Ville; cont on D7 past vill; site on R in 500m.
2*, Sm, mkd, hdg, pt shd, EHU (10A) €4; bbq (sep
area); 10% statics; Eng spkn; adv bkg acc; ccard acc;
games area. *"Situated above fishing lake; rolling hills;
helpful & welcoming owners; facs poss stretched high
ssn; poss clsd on Weds in April; gd walks; chateau in
Vollore-Ville; bar pt of vill life; highly rec; excel; vg, new
deep pool; gd size level pitches; gd value pizza rest;
hiking guide maps at recep; excel value; some rd noise
on upper terrace."* €15.40, 1 Apr-31 Oct.   2018

COURSEULLES SUR MER *3D1* (8km SW Rural) *49.28949,
-0.52970* **Camp Municipal des Trois Rivières,**
Route de Tierceville, 14480 Creully 02 31 80 90 17;
contact@camping-les-3-rivieres.com; www.camping-
les-3-rivieres.com

🐕 €1.20 ♿♿ (htd) 🅿 ♨ ♿ 🖥 / 🦋 ♈ 🍽 nr 🕙 nr 🔟 nr 🏕
🏖 sand 5km

Fr Caen ring rd, exit junc 8 onto N13 dir Bayeux;
in 15km turn R onto D82 to Creully; site on R
500m past cent of Creully. 3*, Med, hdg, mkd, pt
shd, pt sl, EHU (10A) €4.10 (long leads req, poss rev
pol); bbq (charcoal, gas); twin axles; 9% statics; Eng
spkn; adv bkg acc; ccard acc; games area; games
rm; table tennis; tennis; CKE. *"Friendly, helpful
warden; facs not v clean, stretched high ssn; pool
5km; conv D-Day beaches, Bayeux; barrier clsd 1500-
1700; gd cycling; standard of maintenance is poor;
run down site and unkept (2019); many ssn vans."*
€20.40, 6 Apr-13 Oct.   2019

COURVILLE SUR EURE *4E2* (0.5km S Urban) *48.44629, 1.24157* **Camp Municipal Les Bords de l'Eure,** Ave Thiers, 28190 Courville-sur-Eure **02 37 23 76 38 or 02 37 18 07 90 (Mairie); secretaria-mairie@courville-sur-eure.fr; www.courville-sur-eure.fr**

(htd) nr nr

Turn N off D923 19km W of Chartres. Site on bank of rv. Foll sp. 2*, Med, hdg, pt shd, EHU (16A) €3.30. *"Lovely, peaceful rvside site; spacious pitches; friendly warden; no twin axles; Eng spkn; conv Chartres; mkt Thurs; easy walk into town; gd security, oniste warden; mv service pnt adj; pool 200m; site basic but lge pitches and v well kept; facs gd and spotless."* **€7.80, 30 Apr-18 Sep. 2016**

COUTRAS *7C2* (7.5km NW Rural) *45.07929, -0.20839* **Camping Le Chene du Lac,** 3 Lieu-dit Chateauneuf, 33230 Bayas **05 57 69 13 78 or 06 07 98 92 65 (mob); lechenedulac@orange.fr; www.camping-lechene dulac.com**

€2

Fr Coutras W on D10 to Guitres; N fr Guitres on D247 to Bayas; site 2km N of Bayas, sp. 3*, Sm, mkd, shd, EHU 6A; gas; bbq (elec); sw; 2% statics; Eng spkn; adv bkg acc; CCI. *"Helpful owner; pedalos & canoes adj; vg; red facs in winter; great site; friendly, helpful new owners; v relaxed atmosphere; lake adj; excel."* **€29.30, 1 Apr-31 Oct. 2019**

COUTURES *4G1* (1km NE Rural) *47.37440, -0.34690* **Camping Parc de Montsabert,** 49320 Coutures **02 41 57 91 63; camping@parcdemontsabert.com; www.parcdemontsabert.com**

€4 (htd) nr (covrd, htd)

Easy access on R side of Rv Loire bet Angers & Saumur. Take D751 to Coutures & fr town cent foll sp for site. 1st R after 'Tabac' & foll rd to site (1st on R bef chateau). 4*, Med, hdg, hdstg, mkd, pt shd, pt sl, serviced pitches; EHU (5-10A) inc; TV; 15% statics; phone; bus 1km; Eng spkn; adv bkg acc; ccard acc; bike hire; tennis; gym; games area; games rm; CKE. *"Ideal for chateaux & wine cellars; lge pitches."* **€29.00, 12 Apr-8 Sep. 2016**

COZES *7B1* (0.7km NW Urban) *45.58650, -0.83568* **Camping Le Sorlut (formerly Municipal),** Rue de Stade, 17120 Cozes **06 45 46 07 90 or 05 46 90 75 99; contact@camping-charente-maritime-cozes.com; www.camping-charente-maritime-cozes.com/**

nr

Fr bypass D730 turn into Cozes at Royan end. Foll sp for camping. Turn L at supmkt, site 400m on L. 2*, Med, mkd, pt shd, EHU (6A) €2.50; tennis; CKE. *"Pleasant site close to Royan; friendly, helpful warden; no twin axles; popular with long stay British; excel new san facs (2016); number plate recognition barrier."* **€16.00, 15 Apr-14 Oct. 2018**

CRAON *2F4* (1.7km E Urban) *47.84819, -0.94409* **Camp Municipal du Mûrier,** Rue Alain Gerbault, 53400 Craon **02 43 06 96 33 or 02 43 06 13 09 (Mairie); www.campingdecraon53.fr**

Fr Laval take D771 S to Craon. Site sp fr town cent. 3*, Sm, hdg, pt shd, EHU (6-10A) €2.90; red long stay; adv bkg acc; tennis. *"Lge pitches; easy walk to town; pool 200m; office clsd Tues & Sun LS, when barrier key req (2010); local chateau gardens; excel; new modern san block (2018)."* **€12.00, 1 May-21 Sep. 2018**

CREMIEU *9B2* (4km NW Rural) *45.74829, 5.22486* **Camping à la Ferme des Epinettes,** 11 Rue de l'Eglise, 38460 St Romain-de-Jalionas **04 74 90 94 90; info@camping-cremieu.com; www.camping-cremieu.com**

12 €1 (htd) nr

N fr Crémieu on D517; in 3km site sp on R, immed bef rndabt on edge of St Romain-de-Jalionas. 200m after turning R off D517 (into Rue de l'Eglise), turn L into Rue des Epinettes & site ent. Site on R in 100m. 1*, Sm, mkd, pt shd, EHU (16A); 20% statics; jacuzzi. *"Gd NH for interesting & historic town of Lyon and Crémieu; helpful owners; ltd facs LS; gd touring base; Pérouges worth visit; trams/metro fr Meyzieu to Lyon; rec; lovely, peaceful site; run down (2014); narr rds; statics mainly for workers; movers needed for lge o'fits; no resident warden."* **€17.00 2019**

"Satellite navigation makes touring much easier"

Remember most sat navs don't know if you're towing or in a larger vehicle – always use yours alongside maps and site directions.

CREON *7D2* (3km NW Rural) *44.78372, -0.37108* **FFCC Camping Caravaning Bel Air,** 150 Route Departementale 671, 33670 Créon **05 56 23 01 90 or 09 72 64 60 51; contact@camping-bel-air.com; www.camping-bel-air.com**

€2.50 (htd) nr

Fr A10/E70 at junc 24 take D936 E fr Bordeaux sp Bergerac. Approx 15km E turn SE onto D671 sp Créon & cont for 5km. Site on L, 1.5km after Lorient. 3*, Med, hdg, mkd, hdstg, pt shd, pt sl, EHU 5A-10A; bbq (elec, gas); TV; 60% statics; bus 300m; adv bkg acc; ccard acc; games area; games rm; CKE. *"Helpful owners; immac, modern san facs; rest sm & ltd; facs v ltd LS; no twin axles; some pitches v restricted and tight; phone ahead to check open LS; gd NH; poss music festival in next field; clsd to vehicles 2200-0800; poss rd noise; nr cycle path to Bordeaux and Sauverne; gd."* **€26.00, May-Oct. 2019**

FRANCE

CRESPIAN 10E1 (0.5km S Rural) 43.87850, 4.09590
Kawan Village Le Mas de Reilhe, 30260 Crespian
04 66 77 82 12; info@camping-mas-de-reilhe.fr;
www.camping-mas-de-reilhe.fr

🏕🐕€3 ♟(htd) 🚿♿🔊 MP 🦋 ♈♉🍸⊞⛽🏊⛺🖊 🏊(htd) ⛴

Exit A9 at Nîmes Ouest N onto N106 dir Alès for
5km. Fork R, then L over bdge onto D999 dir Le
Vigan. Foll rd for 24km, R at x-rds onto D6110 to
site on R just on ent Crespian. Take care - ent on a
bend on busy rd. 4*, Med, mkd, pt shd, pt sl, terr, EHU
(10A) inc; bbq (elec, gas); red long stay; TV; Eng spkn;
ccard acc; games area; table tennis; games rm; CKE.
"Quiet, relaxing & lovely site; friendly staff; no o'fits
over 7.5m; clean, modern excel san facs; wine-tasting
adj; conv Nîmes, Uzès & Cévennes National Park;
excel." €33.60, 23 Apr-29 Sep, C10.   2019

CREST 9D2 (1km SE Urban) 44.72410, 5.02755
Camping Les Clorinthes, Quai Soubeyran, 26400 Crest
04 75 25 05 28; clorinthes@wanadoo.fr;
www.lesclorinthes.com

🏕🐕€3-3.50 ♟♟🚿♿🔊🛁🦋♈🍸⊞⛽🖊🏊⛴

S fr Crest twd Nyons on D538, cross bdge cont to
rndabt,take last exit foll sp to site.
3*, Lge, hdg, hdstg, mkd, pt shd, EHU (6A) €4.20;
gas; sw nr; TV; 10% statics; phone; adv bkg acc;
CKE. "Well-maintained site in beautiful situation;
friendly, family run; dir access rv; gd, modern san
facs; easy walk or cycle to vill; sports complex
500m; mkt Tue & Sat, snacks and bar high ssn only."
€27.00, 28 Apr-14 Sep.   2015

CREVECOEUR LE GRAND 3C3 (13km SW Rural)
49.57569, 1.93899 **Camping du Vieux Moulin,**
2 Rue des Larris, 60690 Roy-Boissy 03 44 46 29 46

♟♟🚿♿🛁🖊🦋⛺

Fr Marseille-en-Beauvaisis SW onto D930 dir
Gournay-en-Bray; in 1.5km site sp to R at Roy-
Boissy. 1*, Sm, pt shd, EHU inc (poss rev pol);
10% statics; phone. "Farm site in area with few sites;
beautiful countryside; pitch yourself, owner calls eves;
excel." €10.00, 1 Apr-31 Oct.   2017

CRIEL SUR MER 3B2 (1.5km N Coastal) 50.02568,
1.30855 **FFCC Camp Municipal Le Mont Joli Bois,**
29 Rue de la Plage, 76910 Criel-sur-Mer 02 35 50 81 19
or 06 08 80 67 35 (mob); camping.criel@wanadoo.fr;
www.montjolibois.mobi

12 🐕€1.60 ♟♟(htd) 🚿♿🔊 MP 🦋♈🍸 nr ⊞ nr 🏊 nr ⛺

⛱shgl 500m

Fr D925 take D222 into Criel cent. Turn R opp
church into D126 for 1.6km to beach. Turn L then
immed R & foll beach rd to site in 1.5km.
3*, Med, hdg, mkd, pt shd, pt sl, terr, EHU (4-6A) €3-
4.60; TV; 50% statics; bus; CKE. "Lovely site, facs need
refurb." €14.50   2015

CROTOY, LE 3B2 (1.5km N Rural) 50.22968, 1.64140
Camping La Ferme de Tarteron, Route de Rue, 80550
Le Crotoy 03 22 27 06 75; contact@letarteron.fr;
www.letarteron.fr

♟♟🚿♿🛁🦋♈🍸🏊⛺🏊(htd) ⛱sand 1.5km

Fr A16 exit junc 24 onto D32, then D940 around
Rue twd Le Crotoy. Pass D4 dir St Firmin site on L.
3*, Med, hdg, mkd, pt shd, EHU (4-10A) €3.50-8; gas;
80% statics. "Conv Marquenterre bird park & steam
train fr Le Crotoy; v clean, basic san facs; 2km walk to
town, off rd; barrier ent."
€30.00, 1 Apr-31 Oct.   2018

CROTOY, LE 3B2 (3km N Rural/Coastal) 50.23905,
1.63182 **Camping Le Ridin,** Mayocq, 80550 Le Crotoy
03 22 27 03 22; info@yellohvillage-le-ridin.com;
www.campingleridin.com

🏕🐕€2 ♟(htd) 🚿♿🛁🖊 MP ♈🍸⊞⛽🏊⛺🖊🏊(htd)
⛴⛱sand 1km

Fr N exit A16 junc 24 dir Rue & Le Crotoy; at rndabt
on D940 on app to Le Crotoy take D4 (due W) sp
St Firmin; take 2nd rd to L, site sp. Or fr S exit A16
junc 23 onto D40/D940 to Le Crotoy; at rndabt
cont strt over onto D4; in 800m turn R; site on R
in 1km. NB Do not ent Le Crotoy town with c'van.
4*, Lge, hdstg, mkd, hdg, unshd, EHU (4-10A) €3-
5.50; gas; bbq; red long stay; TV; 60% statics; Eng
spkn; adv bkg acc; ccard acc; golf 10km; bike hire;
games rm; tennis 4km; gym; CKE. "Some sm, tight
pitches bet statics; narr site rds not suitable lge o'fits;
helpful staff; fitness rm; clean san facs, unisex LS; bird
sanctuary at Marquenterre; quiet except noise fr adj
gravel pit/lorries; Le Crotoy interesting town; vg site."
€30.00, 3 Apr-30 Sep.   2020

CROTOY, LE 3B2 (4km N Coastal) 50.24941, 1.61145
Camping Les Aubépines, 800 Rue de la Maye,
St Firmin, 80550 Le Crotoy 03 22 27 01 34;
lesaubepines@baiedesommepleinair.com;
www.baiedesommepleinair.com

🏕🐕€2 ♟♟(htd) 🚿♿🛁🖊🦋♈🏊⛺🖊🏊(htd) ⛴
⛱sand 1km

Exit A16 junc 23 to Le Crotoy via D40 & D940; then
foll sp St Firmin; site sp. Or exit A16 junc 24 onto
D32 dir Rue; by-pass Rue but take D4 to St Firmin;
sp 1 km after church. Site on rd to beach on W of
D4. 4*, Med, hdg, mkd, pt shd, EHU (3-10A) €3-8 (poss
long lead req); gas; bbq; 40% statics; phone; Eng spkn;
adv bkg acc; ccard acc; horseriding; bike hire; games
rm; CKE. "Peaceful, popular, well-run site; tourers
sited with statics; lovely pool; gd cycling & walking;
check office opening hrs for early dep; Marquenterre
ornithological park 3km; steam train 3km; excel."
€29.00, 25 Mar-1 Nov.   2016

CROZON *2E2* (6.5km E Coastal) *48.24204, -4.42932*
Camping L'Aber, Tal-ar-Groas,50 Route de la Plage de l'Aber, 29160 Crozon **02 98 27 02 96 or 06 75 62 39 07 (mob); contact@camping-aber.com; www.camping-aber.com**

🏕 €1.50 ♐♐♐ ♿ ᴊ ⊞ ▽ ⚑ ♨(htd) ⛱ sand 1km

On D887 turn S in Tal-ar-Groas foll camp sp to site in 1km on R. 3*, Med, mkd, pt shd, pt sl, terr, EHU (5A) €3.40; gas; 50% statics; adv bkg acc; fishing; sailing; windsurfing. *"Great views."*
€20.60, 1 Apr-31 Oct. 2017

CUISEAUX *9A2* (5km W Rural) *46.49570, 5.32662*
Camping Le Domaine de Louvarel, 71480 Champagnat **03 85 76 62 71; info@louvarel.com; www.louvarel.com**

🏕 €2 ♐♐♐(htd) ᴡᴅ ♨ ♿ ⊞ ᴊ ᴍᴘ ▽ ♈ ▽ ⑪ ♨ ∧ ⚑(htd)
⚒ ⛱ sand

Exit A39 junc 9 dir Cuiseaux; foll sp 'Base de Loisirs de Louvarel'. Or fr D1083 exit Champagnat & foll sp to site on lakeside. 3*, Med, mkd, hdg, pt shd, terr, EHU (10A) incl; bbq; sw nr; 7% statics; phone; Eng spkn; adv bkg acc; bike hire; games area; boating; fishing; CKE. *"Excel, clean site; helpful manager; o'night m'vans area; excel, immac san facs; nice rest & bar; gd walking; free use of canoes; busy."*
€34.00, 15 Apr-16 Sep. 2019

CUVILLY *3C3* (1.5km N Rural) *49.56750, 2.70790*
Camping de Sorel, 24 Rue St Claude, 60490 Orvillers-Sorel **03 44 85 02 74; contact@aestiva.fr; www.camping-sorel.com**

♐♐♐(htd) ᴡᴅ ♨ ♿ ⊞ ᴊ ᴍᴘ ▽ ♈ ▽ ⑪ ♨ ∧

Exit A1/E15 at junc 12 (Roye) S'bound or 11 (Ressons) N'bound. Site on E of D1017. 3*, Med, mkd, pt shd, EHU (10A) €3; bbq; TV; 50% statics; games area. *"Pleasant situation; conv NH A1 & Calais; friendly staff; facs need updating (2014); rec early arr in ssn; rv fishing 10km; busy at w/end; 30 mins Parc Astérix; plenty to visit."* **€21.00, 1 Feb-15 Dec.** 2019

DAMAZAN *7D2* (1.5km S Rural) *44.27966, 0.27739*
Camping Du Lac (formerly Municipal), Lac du Moulineau, 47160 Saint Pierre de Buzet **05 53 89 74 36 or 06 27 11 03 57; contact@campingdulac47.com; www.campingdulac47.com**

🏕 ♐♐♐ ᴡᴅ ♨ ♿ ⊞ ᴊ ♈ ▽ ⑪nr ♨nr ∧

Fr A62 take junc 6, turn R at rndabt onto D8; almost immed take slip rd sp Damazan/Buzet-dur-Baïse; at top take 2nd R sp Buzet (1st turning goes to lake only). Site 1km on R, sp fr rd. 2*, Sm, mkd, hdstg, hdg, pt shd, pt sl, EHU (10A) €3; bbq; sw nr; 2% statics; adv bkg acc; CKE. *"Pretty site by lake; helpful staff; next to cricket club; clean basic san facs; attractive Bastide town; conv NH; needs updating; fair; easy access fr a'route."* **€24.50, 1 Jul-31 Aug.** 2015

DANGE ST ROMAIN *4H2* (3km N Rural) *46.96944, 0.60399* **Camp Municipal,** 8 Rue des Buxières, 86220 Les Ormes **05 49 21 23 43; les-ormes@cg86.fr; www.tourisme-vienne.com**

🏕 €1.20 ♐♐♐ ᴡᴅ ♨ ♿ ⊞ ᴊ ▽ ♈ ♨ ⑪nr ♨ ∧

Turn W off D910 in cent Les Ormes onto D1a sp Vellèches & Marigny-Marmande, foll site sp to site on rv. 2*, Med, mkd, pt shd, pt sl, EHU (10A) inc; 10% statics; Eng spkn; adv bkg acc; tennis 100m; canoe launching area; CKE. *"Lovely, quiet, peaceful setting on rv bank; helpful warden; clean basic modern san facs; poss travellers; quiet vill in walking dist; chateau in walking dist; gd NH; vg."*
€11.00, 1 Apr-30 Sep. 2018

"There aren't many sites open at this time of year"

If you're travelling outside peak season remember to call ahead to check site opening dates – even if the entry says 'open all year'.

DAX *8E1* (1.5km W Rural) *43.71189, -1.07304*
Camping Les Chênes, Allée du Bois de Boulogne, 40100 Dax **05 58 90 05 53; campingleschenes@bala-dax.fr; www.camping-leschenes-dax.com**

🏕 €1.50 ♐♐♐(htd) ᴡᴅ ♨ ♿ ⊞ ᴊ ᴍᴘ ♈ ▽ ⑪nr ♨ ∧ ⚑

Fr D824 to Dax, foll sp Bois de Boulogne, cross rlwy bdge & rv bdge & foll camp sp on rv bank. Well sp. 4*, Lge, mkd, shd, serviced pitches; EHU (10A) inc; gas; bbq; TV; 80% statics; Eng spkn; adv bkg acc; ccard acc; games rm; bike hire; CKE. *"Excel position; easy walk along rv into town; poss noise fr school adj; conv thermal baths at Dax; modernised site with uptodate htd, clean san facs; lovely pool and child area; interesting spa town."* **€19.50, 15 Mar-31 Oct.** 2018

DAX *8E1* (11km W Rural) *43.68706, -1.14687*
FFCC Camping à la Ferme Bertranborde (Lafitte), 975 Route des Clarions, 40180 Rivière-Saas-et-Gourby **05 58 97 58 39; bertranborde@orange.fr**

12 ♐ €0.50 ♐♐♐ ᴡᴅ ♨ ᴊ ᴍᴘ ♈ ♨nr ∧

Turn S off D824 5km W of Dax onto D113, sp Angoumé; at x-rd in 2km turn R (by water tower); then immed L; site on R in 100m, well sp. Or fr N10/A63, exit junc 9 onto D824 dir Dax; in 5km turn R onto D113, then as bef. Sm, pt shd, pt sl, EHU (4-10A) €2.50-4.50; own san rec; bbq; Eng spkn; adv bkg acc; ice; CKE. *"Peaceful CL-type site; beautiful garden; friendly, helpful owners; meals on request; min 2 nights high ssn; poss travellers festival time; excel; lovely site."*
€16.40 2016

DAX *8E1* (3km NW Rural) *43.72020, -1.09365*
FFCC Camping Les Pins du Soleil, Route des Minières,
La Pince, 40990 St Paul-les-Dax **05 58 91 37 91;**
info@pinsoleil.com; www.pinsoleil.com

🐕 €2 ♿ (htd) 🚿 ⚓ ♿ 🍴 📶 ✉ ⚐ 🍸 ⊕ nr 🔥 🎣 🏕 ✂ 🏊 🛁

Exit N10 junc 11 sp Dax onto D16. Cross D824 & turn
R onto D459 S. Cross rndabt & cont on D459, Route
des Minières. Site sp in pine forest.
4*, Med, mkd, hdg, pt shd, pt sl, serviced pitches;
EHU (5A) €2; gas; bbq; red long stay; TV; 25% statics;
phone; Eng spkn; ccard acc; tennis 2km; games area;
bike hire. *"Nice, quiet site (LS); various pitch sizes,
some spacious; soft, sandy soil poss problem when
wet; helpful, friendly staff; excel pool; spa 2km; conv
Pyrenees & Biarritz; vg; not well maintained (2018); NH
only."* **€26.00, 1 Apr-31 Oct.** **2018**

DEAUVILLE *3D1* (3km S Urban) *49.32903, 0.08593*
Camping La Vallée de Deauville, Ave de la Vallée,
14800 St Arnoult **02 31 88 58 17; www.camping-
deauville.com**

🐕 €4.20 ♿ (htd) 🚿 ⚓ ♿ 🍴 🍸 ⊕ 🔥 🎣 🏕 ✂ 🏊 (covrd, htd) 🏖 sand 4km

Fr Deauville take D27 dir Caen, turn R onto D278 to
St Arnoult, foll site sp. 4*, Lge, hdg, mkd, hdstg, pt
shd, EHU (10A) inc; gas; 80% statics; phone; Eng spkn;
ccard acc; waterslide; games rm; lake fishing; CKE.
*"Easy access to beaches & resorts; conv Le Havre using
Pont de Normandie; lake walks & activities on site;
excel san facs."* **€36.60, 1 Apr-1 Nov.** **2019**

DECAZEVILLE *7D4* (9km NE Rural) *44.62920, 2.32030*
Camping La Plaine, Le Bourg, 12300 St Parthem
**05 65 64 05 24 or 05 65 43 03 99; infos@camping-
laplaine.fr; www.camping-laplaine.fr**

🐕 €1.50 ♿ 🚿 ⚓ ♿ 🍴 📶 🦋 🍸 ⊕ 🔥 🎣 🏕 ✂

N fr Decazeville on D963; in 6km over narr bdge
take 1st turn R onto D42 to St Parthem. Site 1km
past vill on R. 2*, Med, hdg, mkd, pt shd, EHU (6A) inc;
bbq; 5% statics; phone; Eng spkn; adv bkg acc; tennis;
CKE. *"Idyllic setting on banks of Rv Lot; friendly Dutch
owners; excel walking; vg."*
€24.50, 1 Apr-31 Oct. **2017**

DECAZEVILLE *7D4* (3km NW Rural) *44.58819,
2.22145* **FFCC Camping Le Roquelongue,** 12300
Boisse-Penchot **05 65 63 39 67; info@camping-
roquelongue.com; www.camping-roquelongue.com**

12 🐕 ♿ 🚿 ⚓ ♿ 🍴 📶 🦋 🍸 🎣 🏕 ✂ 🏊 (htd)

Fr D963 N fr Decazeville turn W onto D140 & D42
to Boisse-Penchot. Rte via D21 not rec (steep hill
& acute turn). Site mid-way bet Boisse-Penchot &
Livinhac-le-Haut on D42. 2*, Med, mkd, hdg, pt shd,
EHU (6-10A) €4.20-4.80; gas; 10% statics; phone; adv
bkg acc; canoeing; tennis; fishing; bike hire; CKE. *"Direct
access Rv Lot; pitches gd size; san facs clean; no twin
axles; excel base for Lot Valley."* **€18.30** **2016**

DEYME *8F3* (0.4km NE Rural) *43.48672, 1.5322*
Camping Les Violettes, Porte de Toulouse, 31450
Deyme **05 61 81 72 07; campinglesviolettes@
wanadoo.fr; www.campinglesviolettes.com**

12 🐕 €0.70 ♿ (htd) 🚿 ⚓ ♿ 📶 MSP 🦋 🍸 ⊕ 🔥 🏕

SE fr Toulouse to Carcassonne on N113, sp on L,
12km fr Toulouse (after passing Deyme sp).
2*, Med, mkd, hdstg, pt shd, EHU (6A) €4; bbq; TV;
60% statics; CKE. *"Helpful, friendly staff; facs run
down (Jun 2009); poss muddy when wet; 800m fr
Canal du Midi & 10km fr Space City; Park & Ride 2.5km
& metro to Toulouse; san facs updated (2018); sw pool
nrby."* **€25.00** **2018**

DIE *9D2* (1km NE Rural) *44.75444, 5.37778*
FFCC Camping Le Riou-Merle, Route de Romeyer,
26150 Die **04 75 22 21 31; lerioumerle@gmail.com;
www.camping-lerioumerle-drome.com**

🐕 €2 ♿ 🚿 ⚓ ♿ 🍴 🦋 🍸 ⊕ 🔥 nr 🏕 ✂

Fr Gap on D93 heading twd Valence. Cont on D93
twd town cent; R on D742 to Romeyer. Site on L
in 200m. On D93 fr Crest foll sp round town cent
onto D742. 3*, Med, pt shd, pt sl, EHU (10A) inc;
30% statics; Eng spkn; fishing. *"Clean, well laid out
site; friendly, helpful staff; gd san facs; 15 min walk to
attractive town with gd shops; gd base for touring; rec."*
€25.50, 1 Apr-15 Oct. **2018**

DIE *9D2* (2km NW Rural) *44.76250, 5.34674*
Camping de Chamarges, Route de Crest, 26150 Die
**04 75 22 14 13; campingchamarges@orange.fr;
www.camping-chamarges-die.fr**

🐕 €1.60 ♿ 🚿 ⚓ ♿ 🍴 🦋 🍸 ⊕ 🔥 nr 🏕 ✂

Foll D93 twd Valence, site on L by Rv Drôme.
2*, Med, mkd, pt shd, EHU (3-6A) €2.90-3.60; gas;
bbq (gas); sw nr; TV; phone; Eng spkn; adv bkg
rec; ccard acc; fishing; canoeing; table tennis; CKE.
"Beautiful mountainous area; vg; friendly owners."
€12.00, 1 Apr-13 Sep. **2020**

DIEPPE *3C2* (3km S Urban) *49.90040, 1.07472*
Camping Vitamin, 865 Chemin des Vertus, 76550 St
Aubin-sur-Scie **02 35 82 11 11; camping-vitamin@
wanadoo.fr; www.camping-vitamin.com**

🐕 €3 ♿ 🚿 📶 ✉ 🍴 🍸 🔥 nr 🏕 ✂ (covrd) 🛁 🏖 shgl 2km

Fr E or W leave Peripherique (D925) S at D927 (sp
Rouen). At rndabt take exit onto Canadiens Ave/
N27. About 850m take exit twrds Belvedere. Then R
onto Rue de la Briqueterie. Site on the R.
4*, Med, hdg, mkd, unshd, EHU (10A) inc; 80% statics;
adv bkg acc; ccard acc; games area; CKE. *"Lovely,
well-kept site; san facs immac; poss boggy in wet; conv
ferries; excel; auto barrier for early dep; v useful & gd
value; on bus rte to Dieppe; off clsd 1200-1430; lots of
statics & ssn workers; lge retail pk nrby; Aldi at ent; fully
equipped site; fair."* **€29.50, 31 Mar-1 Oct.** **2018**

DIEPPE *3C2* (5km S Rural) *49.87063, 1.14426*
Camping des 2 Rivières, 76880 Martigny
02 35 85 60 82; www.camping-2-rivieres.com

🐕 €1.70 ♿ 🚿 ⅃ 🦋 🛒 ⚠

Martigny vill on D154 S fr Dieppe. If appr fr Dieppe, ent is on L bef vill sp. Med, pt shd, EHU (6A) €3.05; adv bkg rec; horseriding nr; watersports nr. *"Attractive, pleasant, spacious site by lge lake; access poss diff long o'fits due parked vehicles; mountain biking nrby; Arques forest nrby; cycle paths; highly rec."* **€20.60, 31 Mar-08 Oct.** 2017

DIEPPE *3C2* (4km SW Rural) *49.89820, 1.05705*
Camping La Source, 63 Rue des Tisserands, Petit-Appeville, 76550 Hautot-sur-Mer **02 35 84 27 04; info@camping-la-source.fr; www.camping-la-source.fr**

🐕 €2.20 ♿ 🆆🅳 ♿ 🚿 ⅃ 🦋 ♈ 🍽 🛒 nr ⚠ 🎣 🏊 (htd)
🏖 sand 3km

Fr Dieppe ferry terminal foll sp Paris, take D925 W dir Fécamp. In 2km at Petit Appeville turn L, site in 800m on rvside. NB 4m bdge bef ent & narr rd to site - not suitable v lge o'fits. 3*, Med, mkd, pt shd, EHU (10A) €4.20; sw nr; TV; 10% statics; adv bkg acc; ccard acc; golf 4km; bike hire; games area; boating adj; games rm; fishing adj; CKE. *"Lovely, well-kept site in attractive setting; pleasant, vg, clean san facs; footpath to Le Plessis vill; gd cycling; excel NH for ferry; MH pitches sm, but backs onto delightful stream and fmland."* **€30.00, 15 Mar-15 Oct.** 2019

DIEPPE *3C2* (6km SW Rural) *49.90886, 1.04069*
Camping Marqueval, 1210 Rue de la Mer, 76550 Pourville-sur-Mer **02 35 82 66 46; contact@camping lemarqueval.com; www.campinglemarqueval.com**

🐕 €2 ♿ (htd) 🆆🅳 ♿ 🚿 ⅃ 🅼🆂🅿 🦋 ♈ 🍽 🛒 ⚠ 🎨
🏊 (htd) 🏖 sand 1.2km

Site well sp fr D75. 2*, Lge, mkd, hdg, pt shd, EHU (6A) €2.50; bbq; TV; 70% statics; Eng spkn; adv bkg acc; ccard acc; games rm; lake fishing; CKE. *"Attractive, well-kept site; san facs clean but tired; delightful coastal area close by; Bois Du Moutiers gdns highly rec; spa; dog walk on site."* **€28.00, 20 Mar-15 Oct.** 2017

DIEPPE *3C2* (9km SW Urban) *49.87297, 1.04497*
Camp Municipal du Colombier, 453 Rue Loucheur, 76550 Offranville **02 35 85 21 14**

♿ 🆆🅳 ♿ 🚿 ⅃ ♈ 🛒 🏖 shgl 5km

W fr Dieppe on D925, take L turn on D55 to Offranville, site clearly sp in vill to Parc du Colombier. NB Pt of site cul-de-sac, explore on foot bef towing in. 3*, Med, mkd, hdg, pt shd, EHU (10A) €2.20 (poss rev pol); gas; 80% statics; Eng spkn; CKE. *"Pleasant setting in ornamental gardens; vg clean site & facs; helpful staff; gates clsd 2200-0700; ask warden how to operate in his absence; conv ferries; easy walk to town; rec; gd site; michelin star rest adj."* **€21.00, 1 Apr-15 Oct.** 2017

DIEULEFIT *9D2* (1km SW Urban) *44.52129, 5.06126*
Le Domaine des Grands Prés, Chemin de la Bicoque, 26220 Dieulefit **04 75 49 94 36 or 06 30 57 08 43 (mob); info@lesgrandspres-dromeprovencale.com; www.lesgrandspres-dromeprovencale.com**

🐕 €2 ♿ 🆆🅳 ♿ 🚿 ⅃ 🦋 ♈ 🏊 🛒 🎨

Fr N of A7 take exit 17 twd Dieulefit/Montelimar. At rndabt, take 2nd exit onto N7. Turn L onto D74. Drive thro the vill of Souzet, La Batie-Rolland & la Begude de Mazenc. Campsite located bef town on S side of the rd on the R. 3*, Med, hdstg, mkd, pt shd, EHU (10A) €3.90; bbq; TV; bus 0.2km; Eng spkn; adv bkg acc; ccard acc; CCI. *"Site on o'skirts of vill (10 min walk) with all facs with unusual accomodations; attractive, well run site."* **€24.00, 20 Mar-1 Nov.** 2016

DIGOIN *9A1* (1km W Urban) *46.47985, 3.96780*
Camping de la Chevrette, 41 Rue de la Chevrette, 71160 Digoin **03 85 53 11 49; info@lachevrette.com; www.lachevrette.com**

🐕 €1 ♿ (htd) 🆆🅳 ♿ 🚿 ⅃ 🅼🆂🅿 🦋 ♈ 🍽 🛒 nr ⚠

Fr S exit N79/E62 at junc 24 sp Digoin-la-Grève D994, then on D979 cross bdge over Rv Loire. Take 1st L, sp campng/piscine. 3*, Med, hdstg, hdg, pt shd, pt sl, terr, EHU inc (10A) rev pol; 5% statics; Eng spkn; adv bkg acc; fishing; CKE. *"Pleasant, well-run site by rv; diff sized pitches, some lge; friendly, helpful owner; ltd facs LS; barrier clsd 2200-0700; htd pool adj; pleasant walk & dog walking by rv to town; lovely cycle rides along canals; gd NH; canoe hire avail."* **€22.00, 1 Apr-30 Sep.** 2018

> ## "That's changed – Should I let the Club know?"
>
> If you find something on site that's different from the site entry, fill in a report and let us know. See camc.com/europereport.

DIJON *6G1* (3km W Urban) *47.32127, 5.01108*
Camping du Lac Kir, 3 Blvd du Chanoine Kir, 21000 Dijon **03 80 30 54 01; reservation@camping-du-lac-dijon.com; www.camping-du-lac-dijon.com**

🐕 €2 ♿ 🆆🅳 🚿 ⅃ 🦋 🛒 nr

Site situated nr N5, Lac Kir. Fr Dijon ring rd take N5 exit (W) sp A38 twd Paris. At traff lts L sp A31, site immed on R under 3m high bdge. Do not tow thro town cent. 3*, Med, mkd, hdstg, pt shd, EHU (10-16A) inc (poss rev pol & long lead req); gas; sw; bus adj; Eng spkn; ccard acc; fishing; boating; CKE. *"Rvside path to town; wonderful surrounding area; proof of dog vaccination req, dogs must be on leads; easy bus to town; gd security; poss flooding; Aire for MH at ent (€10 per night); one point for chem disp."* **€20.00, 1 Apr-31 Oct.** 2017

FRANCE

DINAN *2E3* (3km N Rural) *48.48903, -2.00855*
Camping Beauséjour, La Hisse, 22100 St Samson-sur-Rance **02 96 39 53 27; beausejour-stsamson@orange.fr; www.beausejour-camping.com**

🐾 €2.05 ♨♿ 🚿♿ ᕯ♿ ⚥ / 🅿 MSP 🦋 ⛱ Ⴑ nr 🔺 ⚓ (htd)

Fr Dinan take N176/D766 N twd Dinard. In 3km turn R onto D12 dir Taden then foll sp thro Plouer-sur-Rance to La Hisse; site sp. Fr N exit N176/E401 dir Plouer-sur-Rance, then foll sp La Hisse. 3*, Med, hdg, mkd, pt shd, pt sl, EHU (10A) €3.45 (poss rev pol); red long stay; 40% statics; phone; Eng spkn; adv bkg acc; ccard acc; tennis; games area; sailing; CKE. "Pleasant, well-kept site; gd pool; quiet & spacious Jun & Sep; no twin axles; excel rv walks; excel well maintained site; footpath down to Rance and rvside walks; gd facs; off open 1000-1230 & 1600-1930; new plots may be diff for lge o'fits." €20.00, 1 May-30 Oct. **2019**

DINAN *2E3* (4km NE Rural) *48.47138, -2.02277*
Camping la Hallerais, 4 rue de la Robardais, 22100 Taden **02 96 39 15 93 or 02 96 87 63 50 (Mairie); contact@camping-lahallerais.com; www.camping-lahallerais.com**

🐾 ♨ (htd) WD ᕯ♿ 🚿♿ ⚥ / MSP 🦋 ⛱ Ⴑ nr 🔺 ⚓ ᕯ nr 🔺
Ⴑ (htd) 🏖 ⛱ shgl 10km

Fr Dinan take N176/D766 N twd Dinard. In 3km turn R onto D12 to Taden. Foll La Hallerais & Taden sp to site. Fr N176 take exit onto D166 dir Taden; turn onto D766 dir Taden, then L onto D12A sp Taden & Camping. At rndabt on ent Taden take 1st exit onto D12 sp Dinan; site rd is 500m on L. Do not ent Dinan. Site adj Rv Rance. 4*, Lge, mkd, pt shd, terr, serviced pitches; EHU (10A) inc (rev pol); gas; bbq; TV; 80% statics; Eng spkn; adv bkg acc; ccard acc; tennis; fishing; horseriding 500m; games rm. "Lovely site, well maintained; clean san facs; vg pool; phone ahead if arr late at night LS; ltd office hrs LS - report to bar; sh walk to Taden; rvside walk to Dinan medieval town; rv trips; no o'fits over 9m (check in adv rec); storage facs; gd walking, cycling; mkt Thur am & Fri eve; rec; excel; san facs refurb (2017); busy site; v helpful owner." €22.00, 14 Mar-15 Nov, B01. **2019**

DINAN *2E3* (0.9km S Urban) *48.44743, -2.04631*
Camp Municipal Châteaubriand, 103 Rue Châteaubriand, 22100 Dinan **02 96 39 11 96 or 02 96 39 22 43 (LS); campingmunicipaldinan@wanadoo.fr; www.brittanytourism.com**

🐾 €1.50 ♨♿ ᕯ 🚿 ⚥ / MSP ⛱ Ⴑ nr 🔺 nr ⚓ nr

Fr N176 (E or W) take slip rd for Dinan cent; at lge rndbt in cent take 2nd R; down hill to site on L (500m) after 2nd set of traff lts. 2*, Sm, mkd, pt shd, pt sl, EHU (6A) €2.70; bbq; phone; Eng spkn; adv bkg acc; ccard acc; games area; CKE. "Pleasant, helpful staff; high kerb onto pitches; poss mkt traders; opening dates vary each year; check time when barrier locked, espec LS; gd cent for Rance valley, St Malo & coast; gd location; bar adj; san facs old but clean; 20 min walk to chateau & town; excel position nr park; more level pitches in lower area of site beyond san block." €15.00, 1 Jun-30 Sep. **2017**

DINARD *2E3* (0km W Coastal) *48.6309, -2.08413*
Camping La Touesse, 171 Rue de la Ville Gehan, La Fourberie, 35800 St Lunaire **02 99 46 61 13; camping.la.touesse@wanadoo.fr; www.campinglatouesse.com**

🐾 €1.50 ♨♿ ᕯ♿ 🚿♿ ⚥ / MSP 🦋 ⛱ Ⴑ 🔺 ⚓ ᕯ sand 300m

Exit Dinard on St Lunaire coast rd D786, site sp. 3*, Med, mkd, pt shd, EHU (5-10A) €3.30-3.70; TV; adv bkg req; golf 2km; tennis 1.5km; CKE. "Vg well-kept site; gd beach & rocks nr; friendly recep." €30.00, 1 Apr-30 Sep. **2017**

DIVONNE LES BAINS *9A3* (3km N Rural) *46.37487, 6.12143* **Camping Huttopia Divonne-les-Bains,** Quartier Villard, 01220 Divonne-les-Bains **04 50 20 01 95; www.huttopia.com**

🐾 €5 ♨ (htd) WD ᕯ♿ 🚿♿ ⚥ / 🦋 ⛱ 🔆 🔺 ⚓ ᕯ 🔺 (htd) 🏊

Exit E62 dir Divonne-les-Bains approx 12km N of Geneva. Fr town on D984, foll sp to site. 3*, Lge, hdg, mkd, shd, sl, terr, EHU (4A) €5; gas; sw nr; TV; 50% statics; Eng spkn; adv bkg acc; ccard acc; tennis; games area; CKE. "Helpful owner; levellers req; Lake Geneva 8km; new recep & san facs renovated (2015)." €32.00, 19 Apr-29 Sep. **2019**

DOL DE BRETAGNE *2E4* (7km NE Coastal) *48.60052, -1.71182* **Camping de l'Aumône,** 35120 Cherrueix **02 99 48 84 82 or 06 48 64 60 16 (mob); laumone@orange.fr; www.camping-de-laumone.fr**

🐾 ♨♿ WD ᕯ♿ 🚿♿ ⚥ / MSP ⛱ 🔺 ⚓ ᕯ nr 🔺 ᕯ 1km

Exit D797 Pontorson-Cancale rd S onto D82, opp rd leading into vill of Cherrueix. Site in 100m. 3*, Med, unshd, EHU (10A) €3.50; gas; bbq; 20% statics; Eng spkn; adv bkg rec; bike hire; CKE. "Sm chateau; gd sized pitches; modern san facs; noise fr adj rd daytime; sand yachting nrby; beach not suitable for sw; vg; pleasant, friendly owners." €22.70, 15 Apr-6 Nov. **2017**

DOL DE BRETAGNE *2E4* (6km E Rural) *48.54941, -1.68386* **FFCC Camping du Vieux Chêne,** Le Motais, 35120 Baguer-Pican **02 99 48 09 55; vieux.chene@wanadoo.fr; www.camping-vieuxchene.fr**

🐾 €3 ♨♿ WD ᕯ♿ 🚿♿ ⚥ / 🦋 ⛱ 🔆 🔺 ⚓ ᕯ 🔺 ⚓ 🔺
Ⴑ (htd) 🏊

Leave N176 E of Dol on slip rd sp Baguer-Pican. At traff lts turn L thro vill, site on R of D576 at far end vill adj lake. 4*, Lge, mkd, hdg, pt shd, pt sl, EHU (10A) inc (poss rev pol & poss long cable req); gas; bbq (charcoal, gas); red long stay; TV; phone; Eng spkn; adv bkg acc; ccard acc; tennis; games rm; lake fishing; games area; horseriding; CKE. "Well-kept site in grnds of former farm; 3 sm unfenced lakes; plenty rm for pitch access; no o'fits over 7.5m high ssn; various pitch sizes, some sm & some with fruit trees; friendly & helpful staff; gd san facs; shop & rest ltd LS; mkt in Dol Sat; gd; boggy when wet." €30.00, 1 May-20 Sep. **2016**

DOL DE BRETAGNE *2E4* (7km SE Rural) *48.49150, -1.72990* **Les Ormes, Domaine & Resort,** 35120 Epiniac **02 99 73 53 60 or 02 99 73 53 01; info@lesormes.com; www.lesormes.com**

🛉🐕€3 🚐 wc 🏕♿🚿🗑/ 💧 ☂ 🅗🍴🛒🏪 ⚠ 🖊 🏊(htd) ⛵

Exit N176/E401 at W end of Dol-de-Bretagne; then S fr Dol on D795 twd Combourg & Rennes, in 7km site on L of rd, clearly sp. 5*, V lge, mkd, hdg, pt shd, pt sl, serviced pitches; EHU (6-16A) inc (poss long lead req); gas; bbq (charcoal, gas); TV; 80% statics; Eng spkn; adv bkg acc; ccard acc; lake fishing; bike hire; tennis; archery; golf; waterslide; canoeing; games rm; horseriding; CKE. *"Busy site set in well-kept chateau grnds; cricket; o'fits 8m & over by request only; helpful staff; clean san facs; covrd aquacentre; conv Mont St Michel, St Malo & Dinan; pedalos; disco at night; mkt Sat; golfing discount for campers; poss noisy (disco); excel all round."* **€64.00, 14 Apr-16 Sep, B08.** 2019

DOLE *6H2* (1.6km E Rural) *47.08937, 5.50339* **FFCC Camping Le Pasquier,** 18 Chemin Victor et Georges Thévenot, 39100 Dole **03 84 72 02 61; camping-pasquier@wanadoo.fr or lola@camping-le-pasquier.com; www.camping-le-pasquier.com**

🛉🐕€1.50 🛉👫(htd) wc 🚐🏕🗑/ 🅟 💧 🍴🛒🏪⚠🖊🏊

Fr A39 foll sp dir Dole & Le Pasquier. Fr all dir foll sp 'Centre ville' then foll site name sp & 'Stade Camping' in town; well sp. Site on rvside private rd. Narr app. 3*, Lge, hdg, mkd, pt shd, EHU (10A) inc (rev pol); twin axles; red long stay; 10% statics; Eng spkn; ccard acc; fishing; rv; CKE. *"Generous pitches; aqua park 2km; friendly recep; gd clean san facs; pleasant pool; walk along rv (otters!) into Dole; dir access rv 500m; mkt Tues, Thur, Sat; poss cr; lovely site."* **€23.00, 15 Mar-25 Oct.** 2019

> "I like to fill in the reports as I travel from site to site"
>
> You'll find report forms at the back of this guide, or you can fill them in online at camc.com/europereport.

DOMFRONT *4E1* (0.5km S Urban) *48.58808, -0.65045* **Camp Municipal Champ Passais,** 4 Rue du Champ Passais, 61700 Domfront **02 33 37 37 66 or 02 33 38 92 24 (LS); mairie-de-domfront@wanadoo.fr; http://camping-municipal-domfront.jimdo.com**

🛉🐕€0.80 🛉👫 wc 🚐🏕♿🗑/ 💧 ☂ 🅗nr ⛵nr

Fr N on D962 foll Laval sps into Domfront; then take D976 W dir Mont-St Michel; site turning in 400m on L; well sp bet old quarter & town cent. Fr S on D962 well sp fr edge of town. 2*, Sm, hdg, mkd, hdstg, pt shd, terr, EHU (10A) €3; TV; phone; Eng spkn; rv fishing nrby; CKE. *"Pleasant, well-kept terr site; helpful, charming staff; gd security; sh, steep walk to medieval town; no twin axles; vg; site still excel value; shade improving with growing trees."* **€7.30, 1 Apr-30 Sep.** 2018

DOMPIERRE LES ORMES *9A2* (0.5km NW Rural) *46.36369, 4.47460* **Camp Municipal Le Village des Meuniers,** 71520 Dompierre-les-Ormes **03 85 50 36 60; villagedesmeuniers@yahoo.fr; www.villagedes meuniers.com**

🛉🐕€2 🛉👫 wc 🏕♿🚿🗑/ 🅜🅢🅟 ☂ 💧 🍴🛒🏪⚠nr ⚠ 🖊 🏊(htd)

Fr A6 exit Mâcon Sud onto N79 dir Charolles. After approx 35km take slip rd onto D41 for Dompierre-les-Ormes. Well sp nr stadium. 4*, Med, hdg, mkd, pt shd, terr, serviced pitches; EHU (16A) €4.50; gas; adv bkg req; ccard acc; tennis; bike hire; waterslide; CKE. *"Excel, clean site with views; v lge pitches; o'flow field with full facs high ssn; facs stretched high ssn; excel for children; gd sp walks in area; pools, rest, bar etc used by public; free m'van hdstg outside site ent."* **€33.00, 12 Apr-20 Oct, L25.** 2019

DOMPIERRE SUR BESBRE *9A1* (1.5km S Urban) *46.51378, 3.68276* **Camp Municipal,** La Madeleine, Parc des Sports, 03290 Dompierre-sur-Besbre **04 70 34 55 57 or 04 70 48 11 39 (Mairie); camping@mairie-dsb.fr; www.dompierre-sur-besbre.fr**

🛉🐕€1 🛉👫(htd) wc 🚐🏕♿🗑/ 🅜 ☂ 💧 🍴🛒nr

At E end of town nr rv behind stadium; sp. 2*, Med, hdg, shd, pt sl, EHU (10A) inc; bbq; phone; Eng spkn; adv bkg acc; CKE. *"Smart, well-run, busy site; v well kept gd san facs, but poss stretched high ssn; excel sports complex; gd for Loire Valley, vineyards & chateaux; highly rec LS; excel; large easy acc pitches; gd adj park for dog walking; rv walks; cycling & running tracks; town v close; full sports facs adj; v friendly recep; rec."* **€12.00, 15 May-15 Sep.** 2016

DONJON, LE *9A1* (0.5km N Urban) *46.35317, 3.79188* **Camp Municipal,** 4 Chemin Denys Bournalot, 03130 Le Donjon **04 70 99 56 35 or 04 70 99 50 25 (Mairie); mairie-le-donjon@wanadoo.fr; www.allier-tourisme.com**

🛉🐕 🛉👫🏕🗑/ 🅜 ☂ 🍴🅗nr ⛵nr 🛒nr

Fr Lapalisse N on D994. Site sp fr town cent on D166 dir Monétay-sur-Loire. 2*, Sm, pt shd, pt sl, EHU (10A) €2.50; fishing 900m; windsurfing 900m; sailing 900m; CKE. **€8.00, 1 May-31 Oct.** 2016

DONZENAC *7C3* (1.5km S Rural) *45.21978, 1.51784* **FFCC Camping La Rivière,** Route d'Ussac, 19270 Donzenac **05 55 85 63 95; info@campingdonzenac.com; www.campinglariviere.jimdo.com**

🛉🐕€1.10 🛉👫 wc 🚐🏕♿🗑/ 💧 ☂ 🍴🛒🏪⚠ 🏊(htd)

Fr N exit A20 at junc 47 (do not use junc 48); take exit at rndabt dir Donzenac D920. In 3km on ent Donzenac keep on D920 & go down hill to rndabt. Take 2nd exit D170 sp Uzzac, site on R in 500m. NB Avoid app thro Donzenac as narr & diff for lge o'fits. Fr S exit junc 49 to Ussac. 3*, Med, mkd, pt shd, EHU (10A) €3.10; gas; TV; adv bkg rec; bike hire; games rm; fishing 5km; tennis; games area. *"Excel facs."* **€22.50, 2 May-30 Sep.** 2019

DORMANS *3D4* (9km NE Rural) 49.10638, 3.73380
Camping Rural (Nowack), 10 Rue de Bailly, 51700 Vandières **03 26 58 02 69 or 03 26 58 08 79;** champagne@nowack.fr; www.champagne-nowack.com

Fr N3, turn N at Port Binson, over Rv Marne, then turn W onto D1 for 3km, then N into Vandières. Site on R about 50m fr start of Rue Bailly, sp 'Champagne Nowack' or 'Camping Nowack.' Sm, pt shd, pt sl, EHU (6-10A) inc; bbq; TV; adv bkg acc; ccard acc; tennis 2km; fishing 1km; CKE. *"Charming, peaceful, CL-type site in orchard; friendly owners; lovely, well-kept, clean, modern san facs; fresh water tap beside chem disp; boating 6km; site poss muddy when wet; site pt of vineyard, poss grape pickers in Sep, champagne can be bought; pool 8km; excel value; excel."* €17.00, 1 Apr-1 Nov.   2018

DOUAI *3B4* (11km S Rural) 50.29004, 3.04945
FFCC Camp Municipal de la Sablière, Rue du 8 Mai 1945, 62490 Tortequesne **03 21 24 14 94;** camping@tortequesne.fr; www.tortequesne.fr

Fr D643 Douai-Cambrai rd; turn S onto D956 to Tortequesne where site sp. 2*, Sm, mkd, hdstg, hdg, pt shd, EHU (6A) €3; 80% statics; tennis; games area; CKE. *"Gd site; park & fishing adj; late night arr area; new & clean san facs (2014); recep open 10:00-12:00 and 16:30-20:00; walking in La Valée de la Sensée; family friendly site; barrier locked when warden leaves (am & pm)."* €15.00, 1 Apr-30 Sep.   2017

DOUAI *3B4* (12km S Rural) 50.27374, 3.10565
Camp Municipal Les Biselles, Chemin des Bisselles, 59151 Arleux **03 27 89 52 36 or 03 27 93 10 00;** office.tourisme@arleux.com

Exit A2 junc 14 at Cambrai & take D643 twd Douai, after 5km turn W at Bugnicourt to Arleux. Site sp in vill adj canal La Sensée. 3*, Lge, hdg, mkd, shd, EHU €6.85; 96% statics; phone; adv bkg acc; rv fishing; tennis 200m; games area. *"Very few touring pitches; basic san facs; gd cycling along canal."* €17.50, 1 Apr-31 Oct.   2015

DOUARNENEZ *2E2* (14km W Coastal) 48.08416, -4.48194 **Camping Pors Péron,** 29790 Beuzec-Cap-Sizun **02 98 70 40 24;** info@campingporsperon. com; www.campingporsperon.com

W fr Douarnenez take D7 sp Poullan-sur-Mer. Thro Poullan & in approx 4km turn R sp Pors-Piron, foll site & beach sp. Site bef Beuzec-Cap-Sizun vill. 2*, Med, hdg, mkd, pt shd, pt sl, EHU (10A) inc (long lead req); gas; bbq; 5% statics; adv bkg acc; bike hire; games area; CKE. *"Pleasant, quiet site nr beautiful sandy cove; friendly, helpful British owners; immac san facs, poss insufficient high ssn & long way fr some pitches; poss ltd privacy in ladies' facs; gd; excel site leaflet; gd pitches; excel well maintained site; highly rec; best pitches now taken up by cabins."* €25.40, 30 Mar-30 Sep.   2019

DOUARNENEZ *2E2* (2km W Rural) 48.09270, -4.35220
Camping de Trézulien, 14 Route de Trézulien, 29100 Douarnenez **02 98 74 12 30 or 06 80 01 17 98 (mob);** contact@camping-trezulien.com; www.camping-trezulien.com

Ent Douarnenez fr E on D7; foll sp 'Centre Ville'; turn L at traff lts sp to Tréboul. Cross rv bdge over le la Gare, at PO turn L, then 1st L. Turn R at island, foll site sp. 2*, Lge, pt shd, terr, EHU (10A) inc (poss rev pol, long lead req); gas. *"Pleasant site; steep hill fr ent to recep; 1km by foot to Les Sables Blancs; conv Pointe du Raz."* €25.50, 1 Apr-30 Sep.   2020

DOUARNENEZ *2E2* (4km W Urban) 48.09895, -4.36189
Camping de Kerleyou, 29100 Douarnenez-Tréboul **02 98 74 13 03;** info@camping-kerleyou.com; www.camping-kerleyou.com

Ent Douarnenez fr E on D7, soll sp 'Cent Ville', L at traff lts past Treboul. Cross over bdge into Ave la Gare, at PO turn L then 1st L, up hill, at rndabt take 3rd exit. Foll sp to site. 3*, Med, hdg, mkd, unshd, pt sl, EHU (10A); bbq; TV; 70% statics; phone; Eng spkn; adv bkg acc; games rm; games area. *"Excel."* €23.00, 9 Apr-20 Sep.   2015

DOUARNENEZ *2E2* (6km W Rural) 48.08166, -4.40722
Camping de la Baie de Douarnenez, Route de Douarnenez, 29100 Poullan-sur-Mer **02 98 74 26 39;** info@camping-douarnenez.com; www.camping-douarnenez.com or www.flowercampings.com

Fr E take circular rd around Douarnenez on D7/D765 dir Audierne & Poullan-sur-Mer, Tréboul & Pointe-du-Van. Site on L off D7 1km fr Poullan-sur-Mer vill, shortly after church spire becomes visible. 4*, Med, hdg, mkd, pt shd, EHU (10A) inc; gas; bbq (charcoal, gas); TV; Eng spkn; adv bkg acc; ccard acc; bike hire; watersports 4km; games area; tennis; games rm; lake fishing; pools; mini golf; CKE. *"Tranquil site in woodland; gd sized pitches; staff friendly; ltd facs LS; entmnt well away fr most pitches; gd for families; mkd walks, guided high ssn; no o'fits over 10m high ssn; statics (tour ops); mkt Mon & Fri; pools & water slides great fun."* €36.00, 5 Apr-15 Sep, B37.   2019

DOUCIER *6H2* (6km N Rural) *46.71221, 5.79709*
Camping du Gît, Monnet-le-Bourg, 39300 Montigny-sur-l'Ain **03 84 51 21 17 or 07 85 57 53 28 (off-season); olivierraph@orange.fr; www.campingdugit.com**

🏕 €2 ♦♦ WC ⚙ ♿ ⬇ 🚿 ⁄ 🦋 ⁂ 🍴 ⑪ ♨ 🛒 nr 🛝

W fr Champagnole on D471 foll sp Monnet-la-Ville, foll camp sp thro vill, turn L at x-rds to church; site immed afterwards on R behind church in Monnet-la-Ville (also known as Monnet-le-Bourg). 3*, Med, mkd, pt shd, pt sl, EHU (5A) €2.50; bbq; sw nr; TV; adv bkg acc; fishing 1.5km; games area; CKE. *"Peaceful site; beautiful views; kayaking 1.5km; lge pitches; gd san facs."* €12.00, 1 May-27 Sep. 2020

> ## "I need an on-site restaurant"
>
> We do our best to make sure site information is correct, but it is always best to check any must-have facilities are still available or will be open during your visit.

DOUE LA FONTAINE *4G1* (2km SW Rural) *47.17390, -0.34750* **Camping La Vallée des Vignes,** 49700 Concourson-sur-Layon **02 41 59 86 35; info@campingvdv.com; www.campingvdv.com**

🏕 €3 ♦♦ (htd) WC ♨ ♿ ⬇ ⁄ 🦋 🍴 ⑪ ♨ 🛒 🛝 🖌 🚣 (htd) 🪜

D960 fr Doué-la-Fontaine (dir Cholet) to Concourson-sur-Layon; site 1st R 250m after bdge on leaving Concourson-sur-Layon. Or fr Angers foll sp dir Cholet & Poitiers; then foll sp Doué-la-Fontaine. 4*, Med, mkd, pt shd, serviced pitches; EI IU (10A) €4, gas; bbq; red long stay; TV; 5% statics; bus; Eng spkn; adv bkg acc; ccard acc; bike hire; CKE. *"Peaceful site poss open all yr weather permitting - phone to check; vg, clean, well-maintained facs; pool open & htd early ssn; some pitches diff lge o'fits due o'hanging trees; conv for Loire chateaux & Futuroscope; new French owners (2016), v helpful."* €28.00, 1 Apr-30 Sep. 2017

DOUE LA FONTAINE *4G1* (18km W Rural) *47.18032, -0.43574* **Camping KathyDave,** Les Beauliers, 49540 La Fosse de Tigné **02 41 67 92 10 or 06 14 60 81 63 (mob); bookings@camping-kathydave.co.uk; www.camping-kathydave.co.uk**

🏕 🐕 ♦♦ (htd) WC ♨ ♿ ⬇ ⁄ 🦋 🍴 ⁂ nr ⑪ nr

Fr Doué-la-Fontaine on D84 to Tigne, turn S thro La Fosse-de-Tigné. Pass chateau, site sp on R. NB Tight turn in, access poss diff lge o'fits. Sm, mkd, pt shd, pt sl, EHU (8A) €3.50 (poss rev pol); bbq (gas); twin axles; Eng spkn; adv bkg acc; CKE. *"Tranquil, rural orchard site in picturesque area; welcoming, helpful, v friendly British owners; many regular visitors; gd san facs; some pitches restricted by trees; gd touring base; adults only preferred; phone ahead rec; excel; dogs free; sm CL type site in an old orchard; vg."* €13.00, 1 Jun-30 Sep. 2015

DOUE LA FONTAINE *4G1* (8km W Rural) *47.19355, -0.37075* **Camping Les Grésillons,** Chemin des Grésillons, 49700 St Georges-sur-Layon **02 41 50 02 32; camping.gresillon@wanadoo.fr; www.camping-gresillons.com**

🏕 ♦♦ (htd) WC ♨ ♿ ⬇ ⁄ 🦋 ⁂ nr ⑪ ♨ 🛒 🖌 🚣 (htd)

Fr Doué-la-Fontaine on D84, site sp. In St Georges-sur-Layon turn L opp church. 3*, Sm, hdg, hdstg, pt shd, terr, EHU (6-10A) €2.90-3.50; red long stay; 28% statics; Eng spkn; adv bkg acc; ccard acc; rv fishing 200m; games area; CKE. *"Delightful site in area of vineyards; friendly, helpful owner; gem of a site."* €20.00, 1 Apr-30 Sep. 2017

DOURDAN *4E3* (0.7km NE Urban) *48.52572, 2.02878* **Camping Les Petits Prés,** 11 Rue Pierre Mendès France, 91410 Dourdan **01 64 59 64 83 or 01 60 81 14 17; camping@mairie-dourdan.fr; www.camping-dourdan.com**

🏕 ♦♦ (htd) ⁄ 🍴 ⁂ nr ⑪ nr 🛒 nr 🛝 🚣

Exit A10 junc 10 dir Dourdan; foll by-pass sp Arpajon; after 5th rndabt site 200m on L. 3*, Med, mkd, unshd, pt sl, EHU (4A) €3.40; TV; 75% statics; Eng spkn; adv bkg acc; bread delivery Jul/Aug; meeting rm. *"Gd NH; friendly welcome; gas & supmkt 500m; clean dated san facs; ltd LS; pool 500m; town worth visit."* €14.00, 1 Apr-30 Sep. 2020

> ## "Satellite navigation makes touring much easier"
>
> Remember most sat navs don't know if you're towing or in a larger vehicle – always use yours alongside maps and site directions.

DOUSSARD *9B3* (3km N Rural) *45.80302, 6.20608* **Camping Le Taillefer,** 1530 Route de Chaparon, 74210 Doussard **04 50 44 30 30; info@campingletaillefer.com; www.campingletaillefer.com**

🏕 €2.50 ♦♦ WC ♨ ♿ ⬇ ⁄ 🦋 🍴 🛒 🛒 🐕 shgl 3km

Fr Annecy take D1508 twd Faverges & Albertville. At traff lts in Bredannaz turn R, then immed L for 1.5km; site immed on L by vill sp 'Chaparon'. Do NOT turn into ent by Bureau but stop on rd & ask for instructions as no access to pitches fr Bureau ent. Or, to avoid Annecy, fr Faverges, along D1508, turn L (sp Lathuile) after Complex Sportif at Bout-du-Lac. Turn R at rndabt (sp Chaparon), site is on R after 2.5km. 2*, Sm, mkd, pt shd, pt sl, terr, EHU (6A) €4.50 (check rev pol); bbq (charcoal, gas); sw nr; red long stay; TV; Eng spkn; adv bkg acc; games rm; bike hire; watersports 2km; sailing; tennis 100m; rafting. *"Peaceful, simple, family-run site nr Lake Annecy; fantastic mountain views; access some pitches poss diff due steep terraces; friendly, helpful owners; dated, clean san facs; no o'fits over 8m high ssn; canyoning; climbing; vg rest in easy walking dist; mkt Mon; worth another visit."* €34.00, 1 Apr-04 Nov, M06. 2019

FRANCE

DOUVILLE *7C3* (2km S Rural) *44.99271, 0.59853*
Camping Lestaubière, Pont-St Mamet, 24140
Douville 05 53 82 98 15 or 06 82 28 23 97;
lestaubiere@gmail.com; camping-lestaubiere.fr

🐕 €3.50 ⬛⬛⬛⬛⬛⬛⬛⬛⬛⬛⬛⬛⬛⬛⬛ (htd) ⬛

Well sp fr N & S on N21. Approx 21km N of
Bergerac. Exit fr N21 sp Pont St. Mamet. 3*, Med,
mkd, pt shd, EHU (6-10A) €4-5; gas; bbq; sw; twin
axles; TV; 10% statics; phone; Eng spkn; adv bkg acc;
ccard acc; tennis 5km; games area; lake fishing; games
rm; CKE. "Spacious, park-like site with beautiful views;
v lge pitches; owned by friendly, helpful Dutch couple;
twin axles (high ssn only); vg modern san facs; superb
out of ssn; site in 2 sep sections; a few v lge drive thro
pitches; excel." €35.00, 15 Apr-30 Sep. **2018**

DRAGUIGNAN *10F3* (4km S Rural) *43.51796, 6.47836*
Camping La Foux, Quartier La Foux, 83300 Draguignan
04 94 68 18 27; www.camping-lafoux.com

🐕 €3.90 ⬛⬛⬛⬛⬛⬛⬛⬛⬛⬛⬛

Fr A8, take Le Muy intersection onto N555 N to
Draguignan. Site ent on R at ent to town sp Sport
Centre Foux. Fr Draguignan, take N555 S; just after
'End of Draguignan' sp, double back at rndabt &
turn R. 2*, Lge, unshd, pt sl, EHU (4-10A) €3.50-5; TV;
fishing. "Friendly staff; v poor san facs; care needed
long vehicles on ent site; unshd, but many trees planted
(2011); poss flooding when wet; easy access to Riviera
coast." €16.00, 20 Jun-30 Sep. **2016**

DREUX *4E2* (9.5km NW Rural) *48.76149, 1.29041*
Camping Etangs de Marsalin, 3 Place du Général de
Gaulle, 28500 Vert-en-Drouais 02 37 82 92 23; contact
@campingdemarsalin.fr; www.campingdemarsalin.fr

12 🐕 ⬛⬛⬛ (htd) ⬛⬛⬛⬛⬛⬛⬛⬛ nr ⬛ nr ⬛⬛

Fr W onto N12 dir Dreux, cross dual c'way bef petrol
stn onto D152 to Vert-en-Drouais; on ent turn R to
church, site on L. Well sp. 2*, Med, hdg, mkd, hdstg, pt
shd, pt sl, EHU (6-10A), €4.60 (poss rev pol, long leads
poss req, avail at recep); 80% statics; Eng spkn; lake
fishing 2km; CKE. "Peaceful location; working families
on site; friendly, helpful staff; basic, clean san facs;
touring pitches at far end far fr facs; muddy when wet;
lovely vill; conv Versailles; NH only; site tidy and clean;
bar 100m; facs refurb (2016)." €18.00 **2018**

DUNKERQUE *3A3* (12km NE Coastal) *51.07600,
2.55524* **Camping Perroquet Plage,** 59123 Bray-Dunes
03 28 58 37 37; contact@campingleperroquet.com;
www.campingleperroquet.com

🐕 €0.50 ⬛⬛⬛ (htd) ⬛⬛⬛⬛⬛⬛⬛⬛⬛⬛⬛⬛ sand adj

On Dunkerque-Ostend D601, about 100m fr Belgian
frontier, thro vill on D947; cont 1km to traff lts, R
on D60 thro vill, past rlwy stn to site on L. NB Take
care some speed humps. 4*, V lge, hdstg, hdg, pt shd,
EHU (4A) €4.50; TV; 85% statics; Eng spkn; adv bkg
req; sauna; watersports; gym; tennis; mini-golf; CKE.
"Busy, well-kept site; lge pitches; if parked nr site ent, v
long walk to beach; lge bar & rest nr beach (long walk fr
ent); gd san facs, poss far; many local attractions; conv
NH for ferries; gd." €15.00, 1 Apr-20 Sept. **2020**

DUNKERQUE *3A3* (4.6km NE Coastal) *51.05171,
2.42025* **Camp Municipal La Licorne,** 1005 Blvd de
l'Europe, 59240 Dunkerque 03 28 69 26 68;
contact@campingdelalicorne.com; www.campingde
lalicorne.com

🐕 €0.90 ⬛⬛ (htd) ⬛⬛⬛⬛⬛⬛ MSP ⬛⬛⬛⬛⬛⬛ nr ⬛⬛
⬛ sand adj

Exit A16 junc 62 sp 'Malo'; at end of slip rd traff lts
turn L sp Malo-les-Bains; in 2km (at 5th traff lts)
turn R at camping sp; at 2nd traff lts past BP g'ge
turn L. Site on L (cont strt to rndabt & return on
opp side of dual c'way to ent). 3*, Lge, mkd, unshd,
pt sl, EHU (10A) (poss long lead); gas; 50% statics;
bus fr site ent; Eng spkn; adv bkg acc; ccard acc; clsd
2200-0700; CKE. "V gd, secure NH for ferries - obtain
gate code for early depart; pitches uneven; many
site rd humps; promenade along sea front to town
cent; site backs onto sand dunes & beach (used for
Dunkirk evacuation of Allied Forces in 1940); poss
windy; m'van o'night area; gd san facs; bus stop nr
site ent; very attractive site; site tired, clean san facs."
€25.00, 1 Apr-11 Nov. **2019**

DURAS *7D2* (0.5km N Rural) *44.68293, 0.18602*
Camping Le Cabri, Malherbe, Route de Savignac,
47120 Duras 05 53 20 16 67; info@lecabriresort.com;
www.lecabriresort.com

12 🐕 €3 ⬛⬛⬛ (htd) ⬛⬛⬛⬛⬛⬛⬛⬛⬛⬛⬛⬛⬛ nr ⬛
⬛⬛

Fr N on D708, turn R on ent Duras onto D203 at
mini-rndabt by tourist info shop; site in 800m.
Sm, hdg, hdstg, unshd, terr, EHU (4-10A) €3-5; bbq;
30% statics; bus 500m; Eng spkn; adv bkg acc; ccard
acc; games area; tennis 1km; games rm, mini-golf;
CKE. "Spacious site with wide views; lge pitches;
British owners (CC members); san facs poss tired high
ssn (2011); vg rest; Duras an attractive town; excel."
€17.00 **2020**

DURBAN CORBIERES *8G4* (0.5km N Rural) *43.00017,
2.81977* **Camping Municipal De Durban-Corbieres,**
Lespazo, 11360 Durhan-Corbieres 04 68 45 06 81 or
06 42 48 69 05; mairiededurham@orange.fr;
www.audetourisme.com

🐕 ⬛⬛⬛⬛⬛⬛⬛

Fr A61 take exit 25, foll D611 S across to Durban
Corbieres. Site sp on R on entering Vill. Sm, hdg, pt
shd, pt sl, EHU (10A); bbq; twin axles; 10% statics;
bus 0.5km; adv bkg acc; CCI. "Tranquil site surrounded
by rugged hills; pool 0.5km; Cathar castle in vill; vg."
€11.00, 15 Jun-15 Sep. **2019**

For a guide to symbols see the fold out on the rear cover

EAUX PUISEAUX *4F4* (1km SW Rural) *48.11696, 3.88317* **Camping à la Ferme des Haut Frênes (Lambert),** 6 Voie de Puiseaux, 10130 Eaux-Puiseaux 03 25 42 15 04; les.hauts.frenes@wanadoo.fr; www.les-hauts-frenes.com

12 € €2 ⛺ (htd) wc ♨ ♿ ⚲ ⚡ ⛺ ☂ nr ♿ ♨ nr ⚑

N fr St Florentin or S fr Troyes on N77. Ignore D374 but take next turning D111 in NW dir. Site in 2km; well sp. Long o'fits take care at ent gate.
3*, Med, hdstg, hdg, mkd, pt shd, EHU (6-15A) €2-3 (poss some rev pol); gas; bbq; red long stay; TV; Eng spkn; adv bkg acc; games rm; tennis 3km; CKE. *"Well-kept, tidy farm site in beautiful setting; lge, level pitches; helpful, friendly owners; gd san facs; meals on request; own facs adv high ssn; loyalty card; cider museum in vill; conv m'way; excl NH en rte S; super; v quiet site; gd."* **€18.00**   **2018**

ECHELLES, LES *9B3* (6km NE Rural) *45.45679, 5.81327* Camping La Bruyère, Hameau Côte Barrier, 73160 St Jean-de-Couz Chartreuse 04 79 65 79 11 or 04 79 65 74 27 (LS) or 06 29 47 27 43 (mob); camping-labruyere@orange.fr; www.campingsavoie.com

🐕 € €1 ⛺ wc ♨ ♿ ⚲ ⛺ ☂ ☂ (U) ♨ ♨ ⚑

Heading S on D1006 Chambéry-Lyon rd, after x-ing Col de Coux 15km S of Chambéry take D45 to St Jean-de-Couz; site sp. 2*, Med, hdg, pt shd, pt sl, EHU (4-10A) €2.90-5.90; gas; bbq; TV; 3% statics; adv bkg acc. *"Peaceful site; magnificent scenery; friendly, helpful owner; vg, clean facs; gd walking area; football; volleyball; Chartreuse caves open to public adj; vg base for touring Chartreuse mountains; video games; waymkd walks fr site; site well looked after; lovely."* **€15.00, 15 May-30 Sep.**   **2017**

ECHELLES, LES *9B3* (0.2km SE Urban) *45.43462, 5.75615* **Camping L'Arc-en-Ciel,** Chemin des Berges, 38380 Entre-Deux-Guiers 04 76 66 06 97; info@ camping-arc-en-ciel.com; www.camping-arc-en-ciel.com

🐕 € €1.10 ⛺ wc ♨ ♿ ⚲ ☂ nr (U) nr ♨ ⚑

Fr D520 turn W sp Entre-Deux-Guiers. On ent vill turn R into Ave de Montcelet dir Les Echelles & R again in 100m. Site sp fr D520. 3*, Med, hdg, mkd, pt shd, pt sl, EHU (2-4A) €2.50-4.30; gas; 40% statics; CKE. *"Conv La Chartreuse area with spectacular limestone gorges; gd."* **€20.00, 1 Apr-15 Oct.**   **2019**

ECHELLES, LES *9B3* (6km S Rural) *45.39107, 5.73656* **Camp Municipal Les Berges du Guiers,** Le Revol, 38380 St Laurent-du-Pont 04 76 55 20 63 or 04 76 06 22 55 (LS); camping.st-laurent-du-pont@ wanadoo.fr; www.camping-chartreuse.com

🐕 € €1 ⛺ wc ♨ ♿ ⚲ ⚡ ⛺ ☂ nr (U) nr ♨ nr ⚑

On D520 Chambéry-Voiron S fr Les Echelles. On ent St Laurent-du-Pont turn R just bef petrol stn on L. 2*, Sm, mkd, pt shd, EHU (5A) €3.50; bbq; Eng spkn; tennis 100m; CKE. *"Clean & well-kept; pool 300m; pleasant area; gates clsd 1100-1530; vg."* **€17.50, 15 Jun-15 Sep.**   **2017**

ECOMMOY *4F1* (0.4km NE Urban) *47.83367, 0.27985* **Camp Municipal Les Vaugeons,** 19 Rue de la Charité, 72220 Ecommoy 06 49 55 03 70; lau66san@aol.fr; www.camping-ecommoy.com

⛺ wc ♨ ♿ ⚲ ⚡ ⛺ ☂ nr ⚑

Heading S on D338 foll sp. Turn E at 2nd traff lts in vill; sp Stade & Camping. Also just off A28.
2*, Med, pt shd, pt sl, EHU (6A) €2.35; Eng spkn; adv bkg acc; tennis; CKE. *"Site full during Le Mans week (nr circuit); gd san facs; new arr no access when recep clsd, hrs 0900-1130 & 1500-2030; coarse sand/grass surface."* **€10.00, 1 May-30 Sep.**   **2019**

EGLETONS *7C4* (2km NE Rural) *45.41852, 2.06431* **Camping du Lac,** 10 Le Pont, 19300 Egleton 05 55 93 14 75; campingegletons@orange.fr; www.camping-egletons.com

12 🐕 € €1.30 ⛺ wc ♨ ♿ ⚲ ⚡ ⛺ ☂ ☂ Y (U) ♨ ♨ nr ⚑ ⚲ ⚓ ⚓

Fr Egletons on D1089 for approx 2km, site 300m past Hôtel Ibis on opp site of rd. 3*, Med, mkd, pt shd, terr, EHU (10A) inc; gas; sw nr; TV; 30% statics; phone; Eng spkn; fishing 300m; watersports 300m; CKE. *"Lovely, wooded site in attractive area; lge pitches; friendly owners; vg; san facs dated but clean."* **€13.00**   **2015**

EGUZON CHANTOME *7A3* (1.5km NE Urban) *46.44556, 1.58314* **Camping Eguzon La Garenne,** 1 Rue Yves Choplin, 36270 Eguzon-Chantôme 02 54 47 44 85; info@campinglagarenne.eu; www.campinglagarenne.eu

🐕 € €1.50 ⛺ wc ♨ ♿ ⚲ ⚡ MP ⛺ ☂ Y (U) ♨ ♨ nr ⚑ ⚲
⚓ (htd)

Exit A20 junc 20 onto D36 to Eguzon; on ent vill sq cont strt on, foll sp; site on L in 300m.
4*, Med, hdg, pt shd, pt sl, EHU (6-10A) inc; bbq; sw nr; TV; 3% statics; phone; Eng spkn; adv bkg acc; watersports 4km; cycling; CKE. *"All you need on site or in vill; excel; well run, attractive site; poss OAY; phone ahead; only 3 hdstg; gas 300m; site is improving; gd; clean, tidy; v friendly Dutch owners; ACSI acc."* **€26.00, 10 Mar-15 Oct.**   **2018**

ELNE *10G1* (3km E Coastal) *42.60695, 2.99098* **Camping Le Florida,** Route Latour-Bas-Elne, 66200 Elne 04 68 37 80 88; info@campingleflorida.com; www.campingleflorida.com

12 🐕 ⛺ wc ♨ ♿ ⚲ ⚡ MP ⛺ ☂ Y (U) nr ♨ ♨ nr ⚑ ⚲
⚓ ⚓ 🌲 sand 4km

Exit A9 junc 42 Perpignan-Sud onto D914 dir Argelès-sur-Mer. Exit D914 junc 7 onto D11 dir Elne Centre, then D40 sp St Cyprien to Latour-Bas-Elne, site sp. 4*, Lge, mkd, pt shd, EHU (6A) €4; bbq; TV; 70% statics; phone; Eng spkn; adv bkg acc; ccard acc; games area; games rm; tennis; CKE. *"Excel site; bus to beach high ssn."* **€43.00**   **2016**

ELNE 10G1 (4km S Rural) 42.57570, 2.96514
Kawan Village Le Haras, Domaine St Galdric, 66900
Palau-del-Vidre **04 68 22 14 50; contact@camping-
le-haras.com; www.camping-le-haras.com**

🐕€4 ⚫ WD ⚫ 🏊 🕳 ⚫ 🚿 ⚫ 🌡 ♨ ♈ 🍴 ⊞ 🏔 ⚓ 🏊

Exit A9 junc 42 sp Perpignan S dir Argelès-sur-Mer
on D900 (N9) & then D914; then exit D914 junc 9
onto D11 to Palau-del-Vidre. Site on L at ent
immed after low & narr rlwy bdge.
3*, Med, shd, EHU (10A) €5; bbq (elec, gas); TV;
10% statics; Eng spkn; adv bkg acc; ccard acc; tennis
1km; fishing 50m; archery; games rm; CKE. "Peaceful,
well-kept, family-owned site in wooded parkland;
helpful, friendly warden; san facs poss red LS; gd rest
& pool; 5 mins walk to delightful vill; no o'fits over 7m
high ssn; rds around site poss liable to flood in winter;
many walks in area; Collioure worth visit; conv Spanish
border; excel." €35.00, 1 Apr-30 Sep, C26.   2019

EMBRUN 9D3 (6km N Rural) 44.60290, 6.52150
FFCC Camping Les Cariamas, Fontmolines, 05380
Châteauroux-les-Alpes **04 92 43 22 63 or 06 30 11 30
57 (mob); contact@cariamas.fr; www.cariamas.fr**

12 🐕€4.50 👪 WD 🏊 🕳 ⚫ 🚿 MSP ♈ nr ♨ nr 🏊 🏔 🏊 (htd)

Fr Embrun on N94; in 6km slip rd R to Châteauroux
& foll sp to site. Site in 1km down narr but easy
lane. 3*, Med, mkd, pt shd, pt sl, terr, EHU (6A) €3.15;
bbq; sw nr; 20% statics; phone; Eng spkn; adv bkg acc;
ccard acc; watersports; bike hire; fishing; tennis 500m;
CKE. "Excel for watersports & walking; mountain views;
National Park 3km." €21.50   2020

EMBRUN 9D3 (3.5km S Urban) 44.54725, 6.48852
Camping le Petit Liou, Ancienne route de Baratier,
05200 Baratier **04 92 43 19 10; info@camping-
lepetitliou.fr; www.camping-lepetitliou.com**

🐕€1.50 👪 WD 🏊 🕳 ⚫ 🚿 MSP ♈ 🍴 🏊 🏔 🏊 (htd) 🏊

On N94 fr Gap to Briancon turn R at rndabt just bef
Embrun. First L after 150m then 1st R. Site on L in
250m, sp. 2*, Lge, mkd, hdg, pt shd, pt sl, EHU (3-10A)
€3.60-€4.20; bbq; 5% statics; Eng spkn; adv bkg acc;
games rm; bike hire; CKE. "Lovely mountain views; vg."
€22.00, 1 May-21 Sep.   2016

EMBRUN 9D3 (2.4km SW Urban) 44.55440, 6.48610
Camping La Vieille Ferme, La Clapière, 05200 Embrun
**04 92 43 04 08; info@campingembrun.com;
www.campingembrun.com**

🐕€3 👪 WD 🏊 🕳 ⚫ 🚿 MSP ♈ 🍴 🏊 nr 🏔 ⚓

On N94 fr Gap, at rndabt 3rd exit sp Embrun cross
Rv Durance then take 1st R, sp La Vielle Ferme,
keep L down narr lane, site ent on R. Access
poss diff for lge o'fits. 4*, Med, mkd, pt shd, EHU
(6-10A) €5-6 (pos rev pol); red long stay; Eng spkn;
adv bkg acc; rafting; watersports. "Friendly, Dutch
family-run site; canyoning; gd facs; pretty town."
€33.00, 26 Apr-1 Oct.   2015

EMBRY 3B3 (0.7km NW Rural) 50.49365, 1.96463
Aire de Service Camping-Cars d'Embryère, 62990
Embry **03 21 86 77 61**

12 👪 🕳 ⚫ 🚿 ⚫ MSP

N fr Embry site is just off D108 dir Hucqueliers
& Desvres. Sm, hdstg, EHU £2; bbq. "M'vans only;
modern, well-kept site; jetons fr ccard-operated
dispenser for services; conv Boulogne & Calais; simple
but well equipped; picnic area & gardens; lovely area."
€6.00   2015

ENTRAIGUES 9C3 (0.4km SW Rural) 44.90064, 5.94606
Camp Municipal Les Vigneaux, 38740 Entraigues
**04 76 30 17 05 or 06 43 76 22 66 (mob);
camping.murielbillard@orange.fr**

🐕€1 👪 🕳 ⚫ 🚿 ⚫ MSP 🦋 🏊 nr

S on D1085 (N85) fr La Mure, turn L on D114, fork
R on D26 to Valbonnais. This rd becomes D526.
Site on L on ent Entraigues, 4km beyond Lake
Valbonnais. Ent on bend in rd, more diff if ent
fr Bourg-d'Oisans. 2*, Sm, mkd, pt shd, EHU (6A) €2
(poss rev pol); red long stay; 15% statics; adv bkg acc;
fishing; CKE. "Clean facs; National Park adj; warden
visits am & pm." €14.00, 1 May-30 Sep.   2015

ENTRAYGUES SUR TRUYERE 7D4 (1.6km S Rural)
44.64218, 2.56406 **Camping Le Val de Saures
(formerly Municipal),** 12140 Entraygues-sur-Truyère
**05 65 44 56 92; info@camping-valdesaures.com;
www.camping-valdesaures.com**

🐕€1.50 👪 🕳 ⚫ 🚿 ⚫ 🦋 🏊 nr 🏔 ⚓

Fr town cent take D920 (twds Espalion) & in 200m
turn R over narr rv bdge and then R onto D904. In
200m fork R onto new rd and thro sports complex
to site. 3*, Med, mkd, pt shd, EHU (6A) €3.50;
10% statics; Eng spkn; ccard acc. "Pleasant, friendly,
gd site; in great situation; footbdge to town over rv; vg,
well-kept san facs; recep clsd Sun & pm Mon LS; pool adj;
gd touring base." €25.00, 3 June-22 Sep.   2019

EPERNAY 3D4 (1km NW Urban) 49.05734, 3.95042
Camp Municipal d'Epernay, Allées de Cumières, 51200
Epernay **03 26 55 32 14; camping.epernay@free.fr;
www.epernay.fr**

🐕€1.80 👪 (htd) WD 🏊 🕳 ⚫ 🚿 ⚫ MSP ♈ 🍴 🏊 🏊 🏔

Fr Reims take D951 twd Epernay, cross rv & turn
R at rndabt onto D301 sp Cumières (look for sp
'Stade Paul Chandon'), site sp. Site adj Stadium.
Avoid town at early eve rush hr. 2*, Med, hdg, mkd,
pt shd, EHU (10A) inc (poss long lead req); bbq;
red long stay; phone; Eng spkn; adv bkg acc; ccard
acc; fishing; tennis; bike hire; games area; canoeing;
CKE. "Attractive, well-run site on Rv Marne in lovely
location; generous pitches; friendly, helpful staff;
gd spacious san facs; barrier open 0800-2100 &
0700-2200 high ssn; parking outsite; rec arr early;
footpaths along rv into town; htd covrd pool 2km;
waterslide 2km; Mercier train tour with wine-tasting;
site used by grape pickers; no twin axles or c'vans
over 6m acc; gd value; boulangerie and cafe nrby."
€22.00, 28 Apr-1 Oct.   2017

FRANCE

EPESSES, LES *2H4* (0.5km N Rural) 46.88920, -0.89950
FFCC Camping La Bretèche, Base De Loisirs, 85590
LES EPESSES **02 51 20 41 94; contact@olela.fr;**
www.camping-la-breteche.com

🐕 € 5.00 / night 👫 ⓦⓓ ♿ ⛟ 🚻 ⋈ ◻ 🍴 🅟 △ 🚣
🏊 (htd)

Fr Les Herbiers foll D11 to Les Epesses. Turn N on
D752, site sp on R by lake - sp fr cent Les Epesses.
4*, Med, hdg, mkd, pt shd, EHU (10A) €3 (poss rev
pol); bbq; TV; 30% statics; Eng spkn; adv bkg acc;
ccard acc; fishing; horseriding; tennis; games room;
CKE. "Well-kept, well-run site; htd pool adj inc;
busy high ssn; helpful staff; plenty of attractions nr;
events staged in park by lake high ssn; conv Puy du
Fou; vg; no waste or water on site, long leads req."
€22.00, 4 Apr-1 Nov.   **2020**

EPINAL *6F2* (2km E Urban) 48.17930, 6.46780
Camping Parc du Château, 37 Rue du Petit Chaperon
Rouge, 88000 Epinal **03 29 34 43 65 or 03 29 82 49 41**
(LS); parcduchateau@orange.fr

12 🐕 €3 👫 (htd) ⓦⓓ ▲ ♿ ⛟ ⋈ ⓂⓈⓅ 🍴 △ 🚣

Sp fr town cent. Or fr N57 by-pass take exit sp
Razimont, site sp in 1km. 2*, Med, mkd, hdg, hdstg,
pt shd, terr, EHU (6-10A) €5-6; gas; bbq; red long
stay; TV; 20% statics; Eng spkn; adv bkg acc; ccard
acc; tennis; CKE. "Lge pitches; ltd facs LS; walk thro
park to town; helpful new owners who have improved
site; sep m'van park adj, fr €12; exceptionally clean."
€20.00   **2016**

EPINAL *6F2* (8km W Rural) 48.16701, 6.35975
Kawan Village Club Lac de Bouzey, 19 Rue du Lac,
88390 Sanchey **03 29 82 49 41; lacdebouzey@orange.fr;**
www.lacdebouzey.com

12 🐕 €4 👫 (htd) ⓦⓓ ▲ ♿ ⛟ ⋈ ⓂⓈⓅ 🦋 🍴 ⊕ 🅟 △ 🚣
🏊 (htd) 🏖

Fr Epinal take D460 sp Darney. In vill of Bouzey
turn L at camp sp. Site in few metres, by reservoir.
4*, Lge, mkd, hdg, hdstg, pt shd, pt sl, terr, EHU (10A)
€7; gas; bbq; red long stay; TV; 15% statics; phone;
Eng spkn; adv bkg acc; ccard acc; bike hire; fishing;
horseriding; games area; CKE. "Excel site; lake adj; sl
slightly but pitches fairly level; ACSI discount in LS; gd
cycling area; nice cycle ride to Epinal; pleasant position
opp lake." **€22.00**   **2016**

ERQUY *2E3* (3.6km NE Coastal) 48.64201, -2.42456
Camping Les Hautes Grées, Rue St Michel, Les Hôpitaux,
22430 Erquy **02 96 72 34 78; hautesgrees@wanadoo.fr;**
www.camping-hautes-grees.com

🐕 €1.70 👫 (htd) ⓦⓓ ♿ ⛟ ⋈ 🍴 ⊕ 🅟 △ 🚣 (htd)
🏖 sand 400m

Fr Erquy NE D786 dir Cap Fréhel & Les Hôpitaux sp
to site. 3*, Med, mkd, hdstg, hdg, pt shd, EHU (10A)
€4.70 (rec long lead); gas; bbq; TV; 10% statics; adv
bkg acc; ccard acc; gym; sauna; fishing; horseriding;
tennis; CKE. "Lovely, well-run site; well-kept pitches,
extra charge lge ones; helpful staff; modern facs; excel
site." **€26.00, 6 Apr-3 Oct.**   **2015**

ERQUY *2E3* (5km SSW Coastal) 48.604565, -2.489502
Camping La Vallée, St Pabu, 22430 Erquy
02 96 72 06 22; contact@campinglavallee.fr;
www.campinglavallee.fr

🐕 €2 👫 ⓦⓓ ♿ ⛟ ⋈ ⓂⓈⓅ 🦋 🍴 △ 🚣 500m

Foll d786 fr Val Andre twrds Erquy. As dual
c'way ends, becoming 2 way, turn L immed. Foll
sp for 750m. 3*, Sm, mkd, hdg, pt shd, terr, EHU
(10A) €4.50; bbq; 20% statics; Eng spkn; adv bkg
acc; sauna; games area; bike hire; CKE. "Vg site."
€26.60, 28 Apr-18 Sep.   **2018**

ERVY LE CHATEL *4F4* (1km E Rural) 48.04018, 3.91900
Camp Municipal Les Mottes, 10130 Ervy-le-Châtel
03 25 70 07 96 or 03 25 70 50 36 (Mairie); mairie-
ervy-le-chatel@wanadoo.fr; www.ervy-le-chatel.fr

🐕 €1.50 👫 ▲ ♿ ⋈ 🦋 🅟 nr △

Exit N77 sp Auxon (int'l camping sp Ervy-le-Châtel)
onto D374, then D92; site clearly sp.
2*, Med, pt shd, EHU (5A) €2.50; adv bkg acc; tennis;
rv fishing 300m; CKE. "Pleasant, well-kept, grassy
site; lge pitches; vg facs; v friendly, helpful staff; no
twin axles; rests in vill; rec; excel sm site; v clean."
€16.00, 15 May-4 Oct.   **2017**

ESPALION *7D4* (0.3km E Urban) 44.52176, 2.77098
Camping Roc de l'Arche, 12500 Espalion **05 65 44 06**
79; info@rocdelarche.com; www.rocdelarche.com

🐕 €0.50 👫 ▲ ♿ ⛟ ⋈ ⓂⓈⓅ 🦋 🅟 nr △

Sp in town off D920 & D921. Site on S banks of
Rv Lot 300m fr bdge in town. 2*, Med, hdg, mkd,
pt shd, EHU (6-10A); bbq; adv bkg acc; canoeing;
fishing; tennis. "Well-kept site; gd sized pitches, water
pnts to each; service rds narr; pool adj inc; friendly,
helpful warden; clean, modern san facs; excel."
€26.30, 6 May-13 Sep.   **2019**

"That's changed – Should I let the Club know?"

If you find something on site that's different
from the site entry, fill in a report and let us
know. See camc.com/europereport.

ESPALION *7D4* (5km E Rural) 44.51376, 2.81849
Camping Belle Rive, 40 rue du Terral Saint Come,
12500 Aveyron **06 98 22 91 59; bellerive12@**
orange.fr; www.camping-bellerive-aveyron.com

🐕 €0.70 👫 ▲ ♿ ⋈ ⓂⓈⓅ 🦋 🍴 ⊕ nr 🅟 nr

Fr Espalion take D987 to St Côme-d'Olt; cont thro
vill to x-rds at far side; turn R by cemetery (small
sp to site) down narr rd. Med, pt shd, EHU (6-10A)
inc (poss rev pol & long lead may be req); 10% statics;
Eng spkn. "Pleasant rvside site; friendly, helpful owner;
conv acc to delightful medieval vill; excel; gd walking/
driving." **€14.00, 1 May-30 Sep.**   **2015**

ESSAY *4E1* (0.6km S Rural) *48.53799, 0.24649*
FFCC Camp Municipal Les Charmilles, Route de Neuilly,
61500 Essay **02 33 29 15 46; lescharmillescamping@
gmail.com; www.camping-lescharmilles.com**

Exit A28 junc 18 (Alençon Nord) onto D31 to Essay
(sp L'Aigle); turn R in vill dir Neuilly-le-Bisson;
site on R in 400m. 2*, Sm, hdg, pt shd, EHU (6A) €3
(reverse pol); 50% statics; adv bkg acc. *"Lge pitches,
some diff to access; site yourself, warden calls in eve
to pay; historical vill; fair NH; no hot water; old style
European EHU."* **€10.00, 1 Apr-30 Sep.**   **2019**

ESTAGEL *8G4* (3km W Rural) *42.76566, 2.66583*
Camping La Tour de France (formerly La Tourèze),
Route d'Estagel, 66720 Latour-de-France **06 15 14 23 46;
camping.latoureze@wanadoo.fr; www.camping-la
tourdefrance.fr**

Fr D117 at Estagel turn S onto D612 then R onto
D17 to Latour. Site on R on ent to vill.
2*, Med, mkd, shd, EHU (10A) €3.50; sw nr; red long
stay; 13% statics; phone; Eng spkn; adv bkg acc;
ccard acc. *"Pretty vill & wine 'cave' in walking dist;
rec visit Rv Agly barrage nrby; htd pool 3km; helpful
staff; excel; peaceful; welcoming, helpful, young
owners; many ptiches with trees, diff for lge o'fits."*
€22.50, 1 Apr-14 Oct.   **2018**

ESTANG *8E2* (0.5km E Rural) *43.86493, -0.10321*
Camping Les Lacs de Courtès, Courtès, 32240 Estang
**05 62 09 61 98; contact@lacsdecourtes.com;
www.lacsdecourtes.com**

W fr Eauze site sp fr D30. Fr Mont-de-Marsan D932
take D1 to Villeneuve-de-Marsan, then D1/D30 to
Estang. 3*, Sm, hdg, mkd, pt shd, terr, EHU (6A) €3;
TV; 50% statics; Eng spkn; adv bkg acc; lake fishing;
tennis; games area. *"Gd family site; no bar/rest end of
Aug; excel walking area; area for m'vans open all yr; gd
rest in vill; vg."* **€28.00, 25 Apr-20 Oct.**   **2017**

ETRETAT *3C1* (5km E Rural) *49.69880, 0.27580*
Camping de l'Aiguille Creuse, 24 Rue de l'Aiguille,
76790 Les Loges **02 35 29 52 10; camping@aiguille
creuse.com; www.campingaiguillecreuse.com**

On S side of D940 in Les Loges; sp. 4*, Med, mkd,
unshd, EHU (10A) inc; bbq; TV; adv bkg acc; tennis;
games rm. *"Facs ltd LS; conv Etretat; gd; gd ctr for cliff
top walks and inland villages."*
€29.50, 1 Apr-16 Sep, N08.   **2018**

ETRETAT *3C1* (1km SE Urban/Coastal) *49.70053,
0.21428* **Camp Municipal,** 69 Rue Guy de Maupassant,
76790 Éetretat **02 35 27 07 67**

shgl 1krn

Fr Fécamp SW on D940 thro town cent of Etretat &
site on L. Or fr Le Havre R at 2nd traff lts; site on L
in 1km on D39. 2*, Med, mkd, hdstg, pt shd, pt sl, EHU
(6A) €6 (poss rev pol); gas; bbq; phone; ccard acc; CKE.
*"Busy, well-kept site; lge pitches; conv Le Havre ferry;
friendly & helpful staff; clean san facs but dated; level
walk to pleasant seaside resort, attractive beach nr;
gd cliff top walks nr; m'van o'night area adj (no EHU) open
all yr €8; early arr high ssn rec; excel; lovely site; clsd
1200-1500."* **€19.00, 1 Apr-15 Oct.**   **2018**

EU *3B2* (0.3km W Rural) *50.05065, 1.40996*
Camp Municipal du Parc du Chateau, Le Parc du Château,
76260 Eu **02 35 86 20 04; camping-du-chateau@
ville-eu.fr; www.ville-eu.fr**

shgl 3km

App fr Blangy on D1015 turn L at junc with D925
& foll camp sp to site in grnds of Hôtel de Ville
(chateau). Fr Abbeville on D925 fork R at 1st rndabt
in town S of rlwy then immed strt on over cobbled
rd to chateau walls. Turn R at chateau walls into
long, narr app rd thro trees. 2*, Med, hdstg, hdg, pt
shd, terr, EHU (16A) (poss rev pol); gas; 10% statics;
Eng spkn. *"Louis-Philippe museum in chateau; poor
san facs; easy uphill walk to town thro forest behind
chateau; Eu worth visit, an alt to seaside towns nrby;
vg Fri mkt; gd local dog walks; recep 0900-1200/1400-
2100; rec."* **€15.00, 1 Apr-31 Oct.**   **2019**

EVIAN LES BAINS *9A3* (6km W Rural) *46.39388,
6.52805* **FFCC Camping Les Huttins,** 350 Rue de la
Plaine, Amphion-les-Bains, 74500 Publier
**04 50 70 03 09; campingleshuttins@gmail.com;
www.camping-leshuttins.com**

Fr Thonon on D1005 twds Evian, at start of
Amphion turn L onto Rte du Plaine sp; ent 200m on
R after rndabt. Fr Evian on D1005 twds Thonon, at
end of Amphion turn R & foll sp. 2*, Med, mkd, shd,
EHU €3; gas; bbq; sw nr; TV; 5% statics; Eng spkn;
adv bkg acc; tennis adj. *"Spacious, simple, relaxed site
in beautiful area; hypmkt 300m; enthusiastic, helpful
owners; pool 200m; sports complex 200m; basic, clean
san facs; gd base for Lake Léman; poss unrel opening
dates - phone ahead; excel; site run by siblings."*
€22.40, 1 May-30 Sep.   **2019**

EVRON *4F1 (9km SE Rural) 48.09423, -0.35642*
Glamping Sainte-Suzanne (formerly Municipal),
10 Rue de la Croix Couverte, 53270 Ste Suzanne
02 43 10 49 60; contact@glamping-saintesuzanne.fr;
www.glamping-saintesuzanne.fr

Take D7 SW fr Evron sp Ste Suzanne. Site 800m S
(downhill) after this sm fortified town. 2*, Sm, mkd,
hdg, pt shd, pt sl, EHU (10A) inc; bbq; 25% statics; Eng
spkn; adv bkg acc; horseriding adj; CKE. *"Remodelled
site with new facs (2017); llovely area; unspoilt town &
castle with historic Eng conns; walking adj; 8 EHU pnts;
excel; rec."* **€10.00, 1 May-30 Sep.** 2017

EVRON *4F1 (1.6km SW Urban) 48.15077, -0.41223*
Camp Municipal de la Zone Verte, Blvd du Maréchal Juin,
53600 Evron **02 43 01 65 36; camping@evron.fr;**
www.camping.evron.fr

Site on ring rd 200 yards fr Super-U supmkt; clearly
sp fr all rds into town. 3*, Med, hdg, pt shd, EHU
(6-10A) €1.60-2.45; red long stay; 50% statics; adv bkg
acc. *"Attractive, peaceful, comfortable, well-kept site
with many flowers; gd, clean san facs; restricted recep
hrs in winter - warden on site lunchtime & early eve only;
poss maintenace issues early ssn (2011); no twin axles;
some worker's c'vans; sports complex adj; htd pool adj;
highly rec for sh or long stay; excel; gd value; san facs
dated (2015); gd dog walk."* **€10.00** 2015

EYMET *7D2 (5km SW Rural) 44.63211, 0.39977*
Camping Le Moulin Brûlé, 47800 Agnac **05 53 83 07 56;**
thebeales@wanadoo.fr; www.campingswfrance.co.uk

Fr S on D933 at Miramont-de-Guyenne (6km S of
Eymet) turn E onto D1; in 4km turn L onto C501 dir
Eymet; site on L in 2km. Or fr N approx 1km after
Eymet turn L onto C1 sp Chateau Pèchalbet. In
1.5km at x-rds turn L sp Bourgougnague, site on R in
2km. NB Narr lanes & bends on app. Sm, hdstg, mkd,
pt shd, sl, EHU (10-16A) €4; bbq (charcoal); 1% statics;
adv bkg rec; games area. *"Lovely, peaceful, well-kept
site in tranquil surroundings; friendly British owners;
gd clean san facs; gd cycling & walking; excel; animals
not permitted."* **€19.00, 1 May-15 Sep.** 2015

EYMET *7D2 (0.2km W Urban) 44.66923, 0.39615*
Camping du Château (formerly Municipal), Rue de la
Sole, 24500 Eymet **05 53 23 80 28 or 06 98 16 97 93
(mob); eymetcamping@aol.com; www.eymetcamping.fr**

Thro Miramont onto D933 to Eymet. Turn opp
Casino supmkt & foll sp to site. Sp on ent to Eymet
fr all dirs. 2*, Sm, mkd, hdg, pt shd, EHU (10A) €3
(poss rev pol); sw nr; red long stay; Eng spkn; adv
bkg acc; bike hire; boat hire; CKE. *"Lovely site by rv
behind medieval chateau; friendly, helpful owner;
clean but tired san facs; pool 1.5km; gas 300m; wine
tasting on site; lake nrby; Thur mkt; excel; peaceful
site nr lovely Bastide town; no arr bet 1200-1500."*
€11.50, 1 Apr-30 Sep. 2016

EYMOUTIERS *7B4 (8km N Rural) 45.80560, 1.84342*
Camping Les 2 Iles (formerly Municipal Les Peyrades),
Auphelle, Lac de Vassivière, 87470 Peyrat-le-Château
05 55 35 60 81; les2iles.camping@orange.fr;
www.campingslelacdevassiviere.jimdo.com

Fr Peyrat E on D13, at 5km sharp R onto D222 &
foll sp for Lac de Vassivière. At wide junc turn L,
site on R. Med, pt shd, pt sl, EHU (5A) €2.50; bbq;
sw nr; twin axles; 25% statics; Eng spkn; adv bkg
acc; games area; games rm. *"Helpful warden; some
pitches o'look lake; new fac block (2015); v gd."*
€20.70, 2 Apr-31 Oct. 2016

EYZIES DE TAYAC, LES *7C3 (5km NE Rural) 44.96935,
1.04623* **Camping Le Pigeonnier,** Le Bourg, 24620
Tursac **05 53 06 96 90; campinglepigeonnier@orange.fr;**
www.campinglepigeonnier.fr

NE fr Les Eyzies for 5km on D706 to Tursac; site is
200m fr Mairie in vill cent; ent tight.
2*, Sm, hdg, mkd, shd, pt sl, terr, EHU (10A) €3;
gas; sw nr; adv bkg acc; horseriding; fishing 1km;
bike hire; CKE. *"Freshwater pool (v cold), spacious,
grass pitches; facs poss stretched high ssn; canoeing
1km, v quiet hideaway site in busy area; chem disp in
vill; close to prehistoric sites; friendly Brit owners."*
€20.50, 1 Jun-15 Sep. 2020

FALAISE *3D1 (0.5km W Urban) 48.89545, -0.20476*
FFCC Camp Municipal du Château, 3 Rue du Val d'Ante,
14700 Falaise **02 31 90 16 55 or 02 31 90 30 90 (Mairie);**
camping@falaise.fr; www.falaise.fr/tourisme/
le-camping

Fr N on N158, at rndabt on o'skirts of town, turn
L into vill; at next rndabt by Super U go strt on; at
2nd mini-rndabt turn R; then sp on L after housing
estate. Or fr S on D958, at 1st rndabt foll sp town
cent & site. Cont down hill thro town then up hill
to 1st rndabt, site sp, then sp on L after housing
est. 2*, Med, hdg, mkd, pt shd, pt sl, terr, EHU (6-10A)
€4.20; bbq; red long stay; TV; TV (pitch); Eng spkn;
adv bkg acc; ccard acc; tennis; CKE. *"Lovely, peaceful,
well-kept site in pleasant surroundings; pitches poss
diff lge o'fits; htd pool in town; clean, well kept san
facs (lots of hot water) poss ltd LS & stretched high
ssn & clsd 2200-0800; pitch self & pay later; uphill
walk to town, birthplace of William the Conqueror;
vet in Falaise; mkt Sat am; excel; useful for ferry port."*
€19.00, 1 May-30 Sep. 2015

FANJEAUX *8F4* (2.5km S Rural) *43.16558, 2.02702*
FFCC Camping à la Ferme Les Brugues (Vialaret),
11270 Fanjeaux **04 68 24 77 37; lesbrugues@free.fr;**
http://lesbrugues.free.fr

🐕 👫 ⬚ ⛟ 🚿 🚽 ∥ 🦋 ♟ ♟ nr ⊞ nr 🛒 nr ⛺

Exit A61 junc 22 onto D4/D119 (dir Mirepoix) to
Fanjeaux; cont on D119 dir Mirepoix; at top of
hill turn L onto D102 sp La Courtète (past rest La
Table Cathare & fuel stn) & in 100m turn R to site in
2.5km. Site well sp fr Fanjeaux. Sm, hdg, mkd, shd,
pt sl, terr, EHU (10-16A) inc (rev pol); 10% statics;
Eng spkn; adv bkg acc; games rm; CKE. *"Delightful,
peaceful, 'off the beaten track' site adj sm lake; care
req sm children; well-kept; v lge pitches, some o'looking
lake; friendly, helpful owners; gd clean san facs; many
walks; beautful countryside; excel touring base; rec."*
€19.50, 1 Jun-30 Sep.   **2018**

FAVERGES *9B3* (7.3km NW Urban) *45.77510, 6.22585*
Camping La Serraz, Rue de la Poste, 74210 Doussard
04 50 44 30 68; info@campinglaserraz.com;
www.campinglaserraz.com

🐕 €2.50 👫 ⬚ 🚿 ♨ ⛟ 🚽 ∥ MP 🦋 ♟ ⊞ ⛺ 🚣 🏊 (htd) 🎣

Exit Annecy on D1508 twd Albertville. At foot of
lake ignore sp on R for Doussard Vill & take next
turn R. Site on L in 1km, bef PO, sp.
5*, Med, pt shd, EHU (16A) inc; bbq; sw nr; twin axles;
50% statics; Eng spkn; adv bkg acc; games area; bike
hire; games rm; sauna; CCI. *"Excel site; diving course
for 8-14 year olds in Jul & Aug; spa opening 2014."*
€47.00, 1 May-15 Sep.   **2019**

FAYENCE *10E4* (6km W Rural) *43.3500, 6.39590*
Camping La Tuquette (Naturist), The High Suanes
83440 Fayence **04 94 76 19 40; robert@tuquette.com;**
www.tuquette.com

🐕 €2 👫 ⬚ 🚿 ♨ 🚽 ∥ 🦋 ♟ ♟ ⊞ ⛺ 🏊 (htd)

Fr Fayence take N562. At km 64.2 sp turn R, site
ent 100m. 2*, Sm, mkd, pt shd, terr, EHU (6A) €4.60;
bbq; 10% statics; Eng spkn; adv bkg acc; INF card.
"Vg, lovely, clean site; friendly owners, family run."
€36.40, 10 Apr-26 Sep.   **2018**

FECAMP *3C1* (6km SE Rural) *49.74041, 0.41660*
Camping Les Falaises de Toussaint (formerly
Municipal Le Canada), D926 76400 Toussaint
02 35 29 78 34; info-lesfalaises@ka-vacances.com;
ka-vacances.com

🐕 👫 (htd) ⬚ 🚿 ♨ 🚽 ∥ 🦋 ♟ ♟ nr ⊞ nr 🛒 nr ⛺ ⛱ 4km

On D926 N of Toussaint. Sp fr main rd.
2*, Med, mkd, hdg, pt shd, pt sl, EHU (4-10A)
inc; bbq (gas); twin axles; 70% statics; Eng spkn;
adv bkg acc; games area; CKE. *"Lovely quiet
site; helpful warden; clean san facs; gd; excel."*
€20.00, 15 Mar-15 Nov.   **2019**

FERE, LA *3C4* (1.7km N Urban) *49.66554, 3.36205*
Camp Municipal du Marais de la Fontaine,
Rue Vauban, 02800 La Fère **03 23 56 82 94**

🐕 €1.20 👫 ⬚ 🚿 ♨ ∥ 🚽 nr ⊞ nr 🛒

S on D1044 (St Quentin to Laon); R onto D338; turn
E at rndabt; ignore 1st camping sp; turn N at next
rndabt; site sp. Or Exit A26 junc 12 onto D1032 SW;
in 2km turn R onto D35; in 4km pass under D1044; in
400m turn R; in 800m turn R at traff lts; foll over bdge
to sports complex. 2*, Sm, hdg, mkd, pt shd, EHU (15A)
€3.50; bbq; red long stay; adv bkg rec; CKE. *"Well-kept
site adj leisure cent; conv Calais, 2hrs 30mins; clean san
facs; pitching awkward due sm pitches & narr site rds;
warden lives adj site - on arr open double gates & ring
doorbell to register; htd covrd pool adj; gates shut 2200-
0700 - no vehicle/person access; avoid 1st w/end June
as Wine & Food Festival held on site; conv A26; gd NH;
generous sized pitches."* €14.00, 1 Apr-30 Sep.   **2015**

FERRIERES EN GATINAIS *4F3* (0.3km N Rural) *48.09198,
2.78482* **Camp Municipal Le Perray/Les Ferrières,**
Rue du Perray, 45210 Ferrières-en-Gâtinais **06 71 43
25 95 (mob) or 02 38 87 15 44 (Mairie); camping@
ferrieresengatinais.fr; www.ferrieresengatinais.fr**

👫 ⬚ 🚿 🚽 ∥ 🦋 ♟ ⊞ nr 🛒 nr 🛒

N fr Mantargis on N7; R onto D96/D32 sp Ferrières
& foll camp sp. 2*, Med, mkd, pt shd, EHU (10A)
inc; 50% statics; tennis; rv fishing adj. *"Vg site; direct
access to sm rv; sports facs adj; gd facs & security;
old pretty town with lovely church; supmkt clsd
Sun-Mon; pool adj; call to check if open; free WiFi;
off clsd 1200-1500, no access to site at this time."*
€12.00, 1 Apr-30 Oct.   **2018**

FERTE ST AUBIN, LA *4F3* (1km N Urban) *47.72553,
1.93565* **Camp Municipal Le Cosson,** Ave Löwendal,
45240 La Ferté-St Aubin **02 38 76 55 90; campingdu
cosson45@outlook.fr**

🐕 €2 👫 ⬚ 🚿 ∥ ♟ ⊞ nr 🛒 nr 🏊 (htd)

S fr Orléans on D2020; ent on R on N o'skts twd
Municipal pool. Turning onto Rue Lowendal.
2*, Sm, pt shd, EHU (6A) inc (poss rev pol); phone;
Eng spkn; fishing adj; CKE. *"Agreeable, spacious
site; friendly, helpful recep; clean, ltd facs; easy
walk to delightful town & gd rests; nr park &
chateau; poss travellers LS; conv A71; gd NH."*
€16.00, 26 Apr-29 Sep.   **2019**

FERTE VIDAME, LA *4E2* (1.2km SW Rural) *48.60760,
0.89005* **Camping Les Abrias du Perche,** Route de la
Lande, 28340 La Ferte Vidame **02 37 37 64 00;
info@campingperchenormandie.fr; www.campingper
chenormandie.fr**

🐕 €2.50 👫 ⬚ 🚿 ♨ 🚽 ∥ MP 🦋 ♟ ♟ ⊞ ⛺ 🏊 (covrd, htd)

Fr N12 take D45 (D24) twds Moussenvilliers and
la Ferte Vidame. Site on R (D15.1). Sm, mkd, hdstg,
pt shd, EHU (6A) €2.50; bbq; twin axles; 50% statics;
bus 1km; adv bkg acc; games rm; bike hire; CKE.
*"Close to sports ctr, forest walks and fishing; vg; max
2 dogs; fishing nr; long cable poss req; poss rev pol."*
€17.50, 1 Feb-31 Dec.   **2017**

FRANCE

FEUILLERES *3C3* (0.4km W Rural) *49.94851, 2.84364*
Camping du Château et de l'Oseraie, 12 Rue du Château, 80200 Feuillères **03 22 83 17 59 or 06 16 97 93 42 (mob-LS); jsg-bred@wanadoo.fr; www.camping-chateau-oseraie.com**

🐕 €1.20 [wc] ♨ ⚙ 🖵 🖉 [MP] 🛝 ▼ ⅊ ♿ ⚲ 🏊(htd)

Fr A1/E15 exit 13.1 Maurepas onto D938 dir Albert & then L onto D146; R at staggered x-rds in Feuillères (by church) & site on R in 500m. 3*, Med, hdg, mkd, hdstg, pt shd, EHU (10A) inc (poss rev pol); gas; bbq; red long stay; 10% statics; Eng spkn; adv bkg rec; ccard acc; games rm; fishing; tennis; games area; CKE. *"Excel, well-kept, well-run site; gd sized pitches; friendly staff; clean san facs; conv A1 a'route, WW1 battlefields & Disneyland Paris."* **€24.00, 15 Mar-31 Oct.** **2018**

FEURS *9B2* (1km N Urban) *45.75457, 4.22595*
Camp Municipal Le Palais, Route de Civens, 42110 Feurs **06 63 37 24 57; www.camping-rhonealpes.com**

🐕 €0.61 ♨(htd) [wc] ♨ ♿ 🖉 [MP] 🦋 🛝 ⅊ 🄰

Site sp fr D107 on N o'skts of town. Site in corner of sports campus next to Bouldrome. 3*, Lge, pt shd, EHU (6A) €3.05; gas; 80% statics; phone; CKE. *"Pleasant, spacious, beautifully-kept site; busy, espec w/ends; pool adj; clean san facs."* **€17.40, 1 Apr-31 Oct.** **2017**

FIGEAC *7D4* (2km E Rural) *44.60989, 2.05015*
Camping Caravanning Domaine Du Surgie, Base de Loisirs Surgié, 46100 Figeac **05 61 64 88 54; contact@ marc-montmija.com; www.domainedusurgie.com**

🐕 €2.50 ♨ [wc] ♨ ♿ 🖵 🖉 [MP] ▼ ⅊ 🄰 🛝 🄰 ⚲

Fr Figeac foll sp Rodez (on D840 S) to site by Rv Célé adj leisure complex. Foll sps 'Base Loisirs de Surgie'. Narr ent, light controlled. Or appr fr E on D840, immed after passing under rlwy arch a v sharp R turn into narr rd (keep R thro traff lts); site on L in 700m. NB Recep at beginning of rd to leisure cent & camping. 4*, Med, hdg, mkd, pt shd, EHU (10A) inc; red long stay; 30% statics; Eng spkn; adv bkg acc; boating; bike hire; tennis. *"Excel pool complex adj (free to campers, clsd Sundays); peaceful LS; pleasant 2km walk or car park just outside town; ent clsd 1200-1600 LS; adj rv unfenced; htd pool & waterslide adj; mkt Sat; rd noise nrby; lge plots; vg."* **€21.90, 25 Apr-30 Sept.** **2019**

FIGEAC *7D4* (7km SE Urban) *44.57328, 2.07296*
Camp Municipal Les Rives d'Olt, Blvd Paul-Ramadier, 12700 Capdenac-Gare **05 65 80 88 87 or 05 65 80 22 22 (Mairie); camping.capdenac@wanadoo.fr**

🐕 ♨ [wc] ♨ ♿ 🖉 [MP] 🦋 ▼nr ⑪nr ⅊nr 🄰

Fr Figeac on D840 dir Rodez; at Capdenac turn R onto D994 over rv bdge; immed after x-ing rv bdge turn R onto D86. Site in 200m on R by rv. 3*, Med, hdg, mkd, shd, EHU (9A) €2.90; TV; 5% statics; tennis adj; CKE. *"Site beside Rv Lot; ent clsd 1200-1600 LS; gd fishing, walking & cycling; gas adj; new security barrier."* **€11.00, 10 Apr-30 Sep.** **2017**

FISMES *3D4* (0.8km W Urban) *49.30944, 3.67138*
Camp Municipal de Fismes, Allée des Missions, 51170 Fismes **03 26 48 10 26; contact@fismes.fr; www.fismes.fr**

🐕 ♨ [wc] ♨ 🄰 🖉 ⅊nr

Fr Reims NW on N31. At Fismes do not ent town, but stay on N31 dir Soissons. Site on L down little lane at end of sports stadium wall. Or exit A4 junc 22 sp Soissons & Fismes & as bef. 2*, Sm, hdstg, unshd, EHU (12A) €3.50 (poss rev pol); bbq (elec, gas); train; adv bkg acc; games area; horseriding 5km; CKE. *"Vg site; gd, clean san facs; warden on site ltd hrs; gates locked 2200-0700; train to Reims nr; conv Laon, Epernay, Reims; mkt Sat am; vg NH; site clean and tidy; excel; site nr rd junc."* **€13.00, 1 May-15 Sep.** **2017**

FLECHE, LA *4G1* (10km E Rural) *47.70230, 0.07330*
Camp Municipal La Chabotière, Place des Tilleuls, 72800 Luché-Pringé **02 43 45 10 00; contact@ lachabotiere.com; www.lachabotiere.com or www.loir-valley.com**

🐕 €1.50 ♨ [wc] ♨ 🄰 ♿ 🖵 🖉 [MP] 🦋 ⅊nr 🄰

SW fr Le Mans on D323 twd La Flèche. At Clermont-Créans turn L on D13 to Luché-Pringé. Site sp. 3*, Med, mkd, hdg, pt shd, pt sl, EHU (10A) inc (poss rev pol); TV; 10% statics; phone; Eng spkn; adv bkg acc; bike hire; CKE. *"Lovely, well-kept site by Rv Loir; helpful, friendly warden; pool adj high ssn; clean, modern facs; gd site for children; many cycle rtes; conv chateaux; nice vill nrby; avoid Le Mans motor bike week - poss many bikers on site; excel."* **€16.00, 1 Apr-15 Oct.** **2018**

FLECHE, LA *4G1* (0.9km W Urban) *47.69514, -0.07936* **Camping Municipal de la Route d'Or,** Allée du Camping, 72200 La Flèche **02 43 94 55 90; info@ camping-laroutedor.com; camping-lafleche.com**

🐕 €1 ♨(htd) [wc] ♨ ♿ 🖉 [MP] 🛝 ⑪nr ⅊ 🄰 ⚲ 🏊(htd)

Fr NW dir Laval D306, keep to W of town, leave S on D306 twd Bauge; site on L after x-ing rv; sp. Fr S take dir for A11 & Laval, site clearly sp on R on rvside. 4*, Lge, mkd, hdstg, hdg, pt shd, EHU (10A) €3.80 (poss long lead req); gas; bbq; TV; phone; Eng spkn; adv bkg acc; ccard acc; fishing nr; canoeing nr; games area; tennis; CKE. *"Lovely, busy site in beautiful location by rv; well kept, run & maintained site; lge pitches; v friendly, welcoming, helpful staff; facs ltd LS; ring for ent code if office clsd; no twin axles; attractive, easy, sh walk across rv to attractive town; mkt Wed; rec; mkt Sun & Wed; defibrillator on site; new excel san facs (2016); recep clsd 1200-1400; gd value."* **€23.00, 13 Mar-2 Nov.** **2019**

FLERS *4E1* (3km E Urban) *48.75451, -0.54341*
Camping de la Fouquerie (formerly du Pays de Flers), 145 La Fouquerie 61100 Flers
02 33 65 35 00; campingflers@flers-agglo.fr; https://notre.guide/campingdelafouquerie/en

🐕🏠 ⌂ WD ♿ ♨ 🚻 ⚙ 🦋 ⛲ ⛺

Fr E on D924 thro town cent, site on L in 2 km. Fr W on D924 dir Centre Ville, site on R.
1*, Sm, pt shd, EHU (6A); bbq; 15% statics; Eng spkn; bike hire; games area; CCI. *"Easy walk to interesting town; excel."* **€12.00, 1 Apr-31 Oct.**   **2019**

FLEURAT *7A4* (1km E Rural) *46.24027, 1.68666*
Camping Les Boueix, Les Boueix, 23320 Fleurat
09 63 61 23 80; info@campinglesboueix.com; www.campinglesboueix.com

12 🐕🏠 ⌂ €1.50 🚻 WD ♨ ⚙

Fr N145 N onto D5 take slipway or D6 into Fleurat. Turn E at x-rds to Les Boueix then 2nd L. Site in middle of fork in rd. Sm, hdg, mkd, pt shd, sl, EHU (16A) €3.50 (€5 winter); bbq; Eng spkn; adv bkg acc; fishing; CKE. *"Beautiful, quiet & relaxing CL-type site; lge pitches with views; welcoming, helpful British owners; vg san facs; sl poss diff m'vans; well-stocked fishing lake nrby; lovely walks; ideal for beautiful Creuse Valley; rallies welcome; conv A20; highly rec."* **€16.00**   **2016**

FLEURIE *9A2* (0.7km S Rural) *46.18758, 4.69895*
Vivacamp La Grappe Fleurie, La Verne, 69820 Fleurie
04 74 69 80 07; info@beaujolais-camping.com; www.beaujolais-camping.fr

🐕🏠 ⌂ €3.10 🚻 WD ♨ ♿ ⚙ MSP ⛲ 🍴 ⓘ nr ♨ nr ⛺ ✎ 🏊

S dir Lyon on D906 turn R (W) at S end of Romanèche onto D32; 4km to vill of Fleurie (beware sharp turn in vill & narr rds) & foll site sp.
4*, Med, hdg, mkd, pt shd, terr, serviced pitches; EHU (10A) inc; gas; 10% statics; Eng spkn; adv bkg rec; ccard acc; tennis; CKE. *"Clean, well-run, busy site; friendly staff; excel san facs; lovely pool; gates & wash rms clsd 2200-0700; clean, spacious san facs; path to town thro vineyards (uphill); wine tasting; sm mkt Sat; excel."* **€27.00, 8 Apr-8 Oct.**   **2017**

FLORAC *9D1* (1km N Rural) *44.33569, 3.59002*
FFCC Camping Le Pont du Tarn, Route de Pont de Montvert, 48400 Florac **04 66 45 18 26 or 04 66 45 17 96 (LS); contact@camping-florac.com; www.camping-florac.com**

🐕🏠 ⌂ €2 🚻 (htd) WD ♨ 🚰 ⚙ MSP 🦋 ⛲ 🍴 ⓘ nr ♨ nr ⛺ 🏊

Exit Florac N on N106 & turn R in 500m by by-pass on D998; site on L in 300m. 3*, Lge, hdg, mkd, pt shd, EHU (10A) €4.20; bbq (charcoal, elec); sw nr; 60% statics; phone; Eng spkn; adv bkg rec; rv fishing adj; CKE. *"Nice, well-kept, well-run site in beautiful area; clean san facs, needs updating (2016); no twin axles; 20 min walk to town; gd touring base; lge pitches; lge mkt Thurs; vg value; excel site on rv; well situated."* **€28.50, 1 Apr-1 Nov.**   **2017**

FLORAC *9D1* (2.5km NE Rural) *44.34528, 3.61008*
FFCC Camping Chantemerle, La Pontèze, 48400 Bédouès **04 66 45 19 66 or 06 73 86 53 16 (mob); chante-merle@wanadoo.fr; www.camping-chantemerle.com**

🐕🏠 ⌂ €1.50 🚻 WD ♨ ⚙ 🦋 ⛲ ⛺ ⛺

Exit Florac N on N106; in 500m turn R onto D998; in 2.5km site on L, past Bédouès vill cent.
2*, Med, mkd, pt shd, pt sl, EHU (6A) €2.80; sw nr; 10% statics; Eng spkn; games rm; CKE. *"Lovely location; helpful owner; gd walking; conv Gorges du Tarn, Cévennes National Park; vg; water and EHU now avail on lower pitches; sm rest, home cooked food; excel site."* **€22.40, 14 Apr-16 Oct.**   **2017**

FLORAC *9D1* (4km NE Rural) *44.34433, 3.60533*
Camping Chon du Tarn, 48400 Bédouès
04 66 45 09 14; info@camping-chondutarn.com; www.camping-chondutarn.com

🐕🏠 ⌂ €1 🚻 WD ♨ ♿ ⚙ 🦋 🍴 ⓘ nr ⛺ ⛺

Exit Florac N on N106, turn R in 500m onto D998 (sp Pont de Monvert), site on L in 3km in vill.
2*, Med, mkd, pt shd, pt sl, terr, EHU (6A) €2 (poss rev pol); gas; sw; adv bkg acc; games area; CKE. *"Beautiful rvside site with views; helpful staff; clean dated san facs, ltd LS; conv Tarn Gorges, Causses & Cévennes National Park; lovely rural setting; excel."* **€18.10, 1 May-15 Oct.**   **2019**

FOIX *8G3* (2km N Rural) *42.98911, 1.61565*
Camping du Lac, Quartier Labarre, 09000 Foix
05 61 65 11 58; camping-du-lac@wanadoo.fr; www.campingdulac.com

12 🐕🏠 ⌂ €1.50 🚻 WD ♨ ♿ 🚰 ⚙ ⛲ 🍴 ⓘ ♨ nr ⛺ ⛺ ✎ 🏊 🛶

Fr N on N20 foll sp for 'Centre Ville', site on R in 2km. Fr S onto on N20 thro tunnel & take 1st exit N of Foix & foll sp 'Centre Ville', then as above. Site opp Chausson building materials store.
3*, Lge, mkd, pt shd, EHU (6A) inc; bbq; TV; 75% statics; bus to Foix adj (not Sun); Eng spkn; adv bkg rec; ccard acc; windsurfing; boating; tennis; CKE. *"Busy site w/end; quiet, spacious pitches on L of camp; modern san facs, poss stretched high ssn; site & facs poss uncared for early ssn (2011); gates clsd 2300-0700; pleasant town; NH only LS."* **€27.40**   **2017**

FOIX *8G3* (3km NW Rural) *42.97151, 1.57243*
Camp Municipal de Rieutort, 09000 Cos **05 61 65 39 79 or 06 71 18 10 38 (mob); bernard.blazy09@orange.fr; http://camping-municipal-cos09.fr**

12 🐕🏠 🚻 (htd) WD ♨ ♿ 🚰 ⚙ 🦋 ⓘ nr ⛺ nr ⛺ ✎

Fr Foix take D117 dir Tarbes. Turn R onto D17 then at rndabt onto D617, site on L in 3km. NB Narr app rds. 2*, Sm, pt shd, pt sl, serviced pitches; EHU (5A) €1.80; tennis; CKE. *"Pleasant site amongst trees with gd views; friendly, helpful warden; gd san facs, ltd LS; sm step into disabled facs; no c'vans over 6m."* **€11.00**   **2015**

FRANCE

FONTAINE SIMON *4E2* (0.8km N Rural) *48.51314, 1.01941* **Camping du Perche,** 3 Rue de la Ferrière, 28240 Fontaine-Simon **02 37 81 88 11 or 06 23 82 90 28 (mob); campingduperche@orange.fr; www.campingduperche.com**

12 🐕 €2 †ᵻ (htd) �owᴅ ♨ ⚷ 🖭 ∥ ꟿ 🦋 ⛾ 🛒 nr ⚏

Fr La Loupe on D929 take D25 N to Fontaine-Simon, site sp. 3*, Med, hdg, pt shd, pt sl, EHU €3.60; bbq; sw nr; 10% statics; adv bkg acc; fishing; CKE. *"Undulating, lakeside site; htd covrd pool adj; gd."* **€15.00**   2020

FONTAINEBLEAU *4E3* (5km NE Rural) *48.42215, 2.74872* **Camping Municipal de Samoreau (formerly Municipal Grange aux Dîmes),** Rue de l'Abreuvoir/Rue de l'Eglise, 77210 Samoreau **01 64 23 72 25 or 06 89 16 25 68; camping@samoreau.fr; www.samoreau.fr**

†ᵻ (htd) owᴅ ♨ ⚷ 🖭 ∥ ꟿ 🍸 nr ⑪ nr ⚏ 🛒 nr

Fr cent of Fontainebleau take D210 (dir Provins); in approx 4km at rndabt cross bdge over Rv Seine; take R at rndabt; site sp at end of rd thro Samoreau vill; site twd rv. 1*, Med, hdg, mkd, pt shd, pt sl, EHU (10A) inc (poss rev pol); phone; bus; adv bkg acc; CKE. *"Peaceful site in attractive location by Rv Seine; gd sized pitches; helpful staff; gd, immac san facs; adj vill hall poss noisy w/end; jazz festival late Jun; conv palace, Paris (by train) & Disneyland; clsd 2200-0700; excel; waterpoints around site could do with upgrade; bus stop adj; dedicated cycle route to Chateau."* **€22.00, 1 Mar-31 Oct.**   2019

FONTAINEBLEAU *4E3* (10km S Rural) *48.31740, 2.69650* **Camping Les Prés,** Chemin des Prés, 77880 Grez-sur-Loing **01 64 45 72 75; camping-grez@wanadoo.fr; www.camping-grez-fontainebleau.info**

🐕 †ᵻ owᴅ ♨ ⚷ 🖭 ∥ ꟿ 🍸 nr ⑪ nr ⚏ 🛒 ⚏

Fr Fontainebleau on D607 twd Nemours (S) for 8km; look for camping sps. At traff island turn L onto D40D, in 1km immed after x-ing bdge turn R; site on L. Do not tow into Grez-sur-Loing. 2*, Med, mkd, hdg, pt shd, EHU (5A) €3; gas; red long stay; 80% statics; phone; Eng spkn; adv bkg acc; ccard acc; fishing; canoe hire; bike hire; CKE. *"In attractive area; helpful British owner; 80% statics; site poss unkempt/scruffy end of ssn; vg."* **€17.00, 20 Mar-11 Nov.**   2017

FONTAINEBLEAU *4E3* (14km S Rural) *48.33362, 2.75386* **Camping Le Parc du Gué,** Route de Montigny, La Genevraye, 77690 Montigny-sur-Loing **01 64 45 87 79; contact@camping-parcdugue.com; www.camping-parcdugue.com**

🐕 €3.70 †ᵻ (htd) owᴅ ♨ ⚷ 🖭 ∥ 🦋 ⛾ 🍸 ⚏ 🛒 ⚏ 🛶 (htd) ⚏

Do not tow thro Montigny-sur-Loing, v narr tight turns. Site is E of Montigny, N of La Genevraye off D104. App fr S Nemours on D40, slow rd but safe, or fr NE, Moret-sur-Loing D606/D104. 2*, Lge, hdg, mkd, pt shd, EHU (10A) €3.60; bbq; sw nr; 70% statics; Eng spkn; adv bkg acc; ccard acc; fishing; games area; watersports; CKE. *"Beautiful, wooded country; kayaks; mkt Sat 2km; excel walking & cycling; new pool (2015); vg."* **€21.00, 15 Mar-30 Nov.**   2016

FONTENAY TRESIGNY *4E3* (7km NE Rural) *48.75050, 2.89728* **Camping des Quatre Vents,** 77610 Crèvecoeur-en-Brie **01 64 07 41 11; contact@caravaning-4vents.fr; www.caravaning-4vents.fr**

🐕 €3 †ᵻ (htd) owᴅ ♨ ⚷ 🖭 ∥ ꟿ 🦋 ⛾ 🛒 nr ⚏ 🛶

At Calais take A26/E15 dir Arras; at Arras take A1/E15 dir Paris; next take A104 dir A4 Metz/Nancy/Marne-la-Vallée, then A4 dir Metz/Nancy, exit junc 13 onto D231 dir Provins; after rndabt with lge monument turn R dir Crèvecoeur-en-Brie & foll site sp. Site in 13km. 3*, Lge, hdg, mkd, pt shd, serviced pitches; EHU (6A) inc; bbq; TV; 50% statics; phone; Eng spkn; adv bkg req; ccard acc; games rm; horseriding; games area; CKE. *"Friendly, well-run, beautiful site; lge, well-kept pitches; welcoming, helpful staff; san facs spacious & v clean; pleasant pool; conv Disneyland & Paris; poss muddy when wet; vg; beautiful countryside ideal for cycling; no o'fits over 10m high ssn; restful even in high ssn."* **€30.00, 20 Mar-1 Nov, P09.**   2016

FONTES *10F1* (0.9km N Rural) *43.54734, 3.37999* **FFCC Camping L'Evasion,** Route de Cabrières, 34320 Fontès **04 67 25 32 00; www.campingevasion.com**

🐕 €2.80 owᴅ ♨ ⚷ 🖭 ∥ 🦋 ⛾ 🍸 ⑪ ⚏ 🛶 🛒

Fr A75 exit junc 59 (Pézenas). At rndabt take D124 to Lézignan-la-Cèbe then fork L, cont on D124 to Fontès. In vill foll sp to site. 3*, Sm, mkd, hdg, pt shd, pt sl, EHU (10A) €3.50; gas; bbq; 75% statics; phone; adv bkg acc; CKE. *"Excel san facs; touring pitches amongst statics (long-term residents); helpful owners."* **€22.50, 14 Mar-2 Nov.**   2016

FORCALQUIER *10E3* (0.7km E Urban) *43.96206, 5.78718* **Camping Forcalquier,** Route de Sigonce, 04300 Forcalquier **04 92 75 27 94; info@camping-forcalquier.com; www.camping-forcalquier.com**

🐕 €4.50 †ᵻ owᴅ ♨ ⚷ 🖭 ∥ ꟿ 🦋 ⛾ 🍸 ⑪ ⚏ 🛒 nr ⚏ 🛶 (htd) ⚐

Fr A51 exit junc 19 La Brillane onto D4100 to Forcalquier. Site sp. 3*, Med, mkd, pt shd, pt sl, serviced pitches; EHU (10A) inc; bbq; TV; 10% statics; phone; Eng spkn; adv bkg acc; games area; CKE. *"Pleasant site in lovely location; excel m'van facs; access for lge o'fits & m'vans poss diff due v narr site rds & awkward corners; walking dist fr town cent; v friendly & helpful staff; famous lge mkt on Mon."* **€29.60, 3 Apr-30 Sep.**   2019

FORCALQUIER *10E3* (6.5km S Urban) *43.91096, 5.78210* **FFCC Camping l'Eau Vive,** 04300 Dauphin **04 92 79 51 91; info@leauvive.fr; www.leauvive.fr**

🐕 €3.50 †ᵻ (htd) owᴅ ♨ ⚷ ∥ 🦋 ⚏ 🛒 🛶 ⚏ 🛶 ⚐

S fr Forcalquier on D4100 dir Apt; in 2.5km turn L onto D13 (at Mane); site on R in 3km. Or fr D4096, turn onto D13 at Volx; site on L in 6km (800m past Dauphin). 3*, Med, mkd, shd, EHU (3-6A) €3.50-4.50; bbq (gas, sep area); TV; bus 800m; Eng spkn; adv bkg acc; games area; tennis; games rm; bike hire. *"Well-run, super site; helpful owners; vg pools; vg for children; excel."* **€23.50, 1 Apr-31 Sep.**   2016

FRANCE

FORCALQUIER 10E3 (4km NW Rural) 43.97235, 5.73800 Camping Le Domaine des Lauzons (Naturist), 04300 Limans 04 92 73 00 60; leslauzons@wanadoo.fr; www.camping-lauzons.com

🛉€4 🕴🕴 ⚏ ♨ ⚓ ⚐ ☐ ⊿ 🦋 ♈ ❡ 🍴 Ⓗ 🖼 ⚑ ⚒ (htd)

Exit A51 junc 19 onto N100 dir Avignon; in Forcalquier at rndabt turn L onto D950/D313 sp Banon; site on R in approx 6km. Lge site sp. Diff app. 4*, Med, mkd, pt shd, pt sl, terr, EHU (6A) €4.50; gas; bbq (charcoal, gas); TV; 25% statics; phone; Eng spkn; adv bkg acc; ccard acc; waterslide; games area; ice; sauna; games rm; INF card req; archery. "Pleasant site in wooded valley; wonderful scenery; excel family site; helpful, friendly staff; most san facs modern, ltd LS; excel pool area; walks fr site; Forcalquier lovely town; excel touring base; pony rides; many activities; access diff lge o'fits; tractor help avail; INF not compulsory." €37.60, 14 Apr-13 Oct. 2018

FORET FOUESNANT, LA 2F2 (2km SE Coastal) 47.89904, -3.96138 Camping Les Saules, 54 Route de la Plage, 29940 La Forêt-Fouesnant 02 98 56 98 57; info@ camping-les-saules.com; www.camping-les-saules.com

🛉€2.50 🕴🕴 (htd) ⚏ ♨ ⚓ ⚐ ☐ ⊿ MSP 🦋 ♈ 🍴 nr Ⓗ nr 🖼 nr ⚒ 🛥 sand 150m

Take N783 Concarneau-Quimper (by-pass) thro Le Poteau Vert, turn L at sp Kerleven. On ent vill, site on R opp Stereden Vor site. 3*, Lge, hdg, shd, pt sl, EHU (6A) €3; bbq; twin axles; TV; 60% statics; phone; bus adj; Eng spkn; adv bkg acc; ccard acc; games rm; sailing 150m; windsurfing 150m; fishing 150m; CKE. "Well run family site; many touring pitches with direct access to beach; yacht marina nrby-boat trips; gd walking on coastal path; excel." €27.00, 1 May-28 Sep. 2015

FORGES LES EAUX 3C2 (1km S Urban) 49.60603, 1.54302 Camp Municipal La Minière, 3 Blvd Nicolas Thiese, 76440 Forges-les-Eaux 02 35 90 53 91; campingforges@gmail.com; www.campingforges .com/en

🕴🕴 ♨ ⚓ ☐ ⊿ 🦋 🖼 nr

Fr Forges-les-Eaux cent, take D921 S sp Lyons-la-Forêt. In 750m turn R foll sp, camp on R in 150m. NB 3,500kg limit in town all dirs. 2*, Med, hdg, mkd, pt shd, pt sl, EHU (6A) inc (rev pol); CKE. "Well-presented site; mv service pnt adj; lge pitches; friendly warden; warm welcome; v basic, clean san facs; poss diff access some pitches; m'van o'night area opp; htd pool in town; pleasant town with excel WWII Resistance Museum; gd local vet; useful NH; gd access to town; dog walk on site." €17.00, 15 Mar-15 Oct. 2017

FOUGERES 2E4 (2.5km E Urban) 48.3544, -1.1795 Camp Municipal de Paron, Route de la Chapelle-Janson, 35300 Fougères 02 99 99 40 81; campingmunicipal 35@orange.fr; www.ot-fougeres.fr

🛉🐕 🕴🕴 ⚏ ♨ ⚓ ☐ ⊿ 🦋 ♈ Ⓗ nr 🖼 nr ⚑

Fr A84/E3 take junc 30 then ring rd E twd N12. Turn L at N12 & foll sp. Site on D17 sp R after Carrefour. Well sp on ring rd. 2*, Med, hdg, hdstg, pt shd, pt sl, serviced pitches; EHU (5-10A) €3.60-4.10 (poss rev pol); adv bkg acc; ccard acc; tennis; horseriding adj; CKE. "Well-kept site in pleasant parkland setting; lge pitches, poss soggy when wet; popular NH; helpful warden; gd clean facs; gates clsd 2200-0900 & 1230-1730 card pass avail, parking avail in adj car park; tours of 12thC castle; old town worth visit; Sat mkt; excel; excel san facs." €14.00, 27 Apr-16 Sep. 2018

FOURAS 7A1 (0.5km NE Coastal) 45.99264, -1.08680 Camp Municipal du Cadoret, Blvd de Chaterny, 17450 Fouras 05 46 82 19 19; campinglecadoret@fouras-les-bains.fr; www.campings-fouras.com

12 🛉€2.15 🕴🕴 ⚏ ♨ ⚓ ⚐ ☐ ⊿ 🍴 Ⓗ 🖼 nr ⚒ (htd) 🛥 🛶 sand adj

Fr Rochefort take N137, L onto D937 at Fouras, fork R at sp to site in 1km. At next rndabt take 3rd exit into Ave du Cadoret, then 1st R at next rndabt. 3*, Lge, hdg, mkd, pt shd, pt sl, EHU (6-10A) €3.50-5.40 (poss long lead req); gas; 50% statics; bus to La Rochelle, Rochefort, ferry to Ile d'Aix; Eng spkn; adv bkg acc; golf 5km; fishing; games area; tennis 1km; boating; CKE. "Popular, well-kept site; vg location; well shd; lge pitches; clean san facs, unisex LS; coastal footpath; pleasant town; a favourite; highly rec; gd conv site." €24.00 2019

FREJUS 10F4 (5km SW Rural) 43.39890, 6.67531 Camping Domaine de la Bergerie, Vallée-du-Fournel, Route du Col-du-Bougnon, 83520 Roquebrune-sur-Argens 04 98 11 45 45; info@domainelabergerie.com; www.domainelabergerie.com

🛉€6 🕴🕴 ⚏ ♨ ⚓ ⚐ ☐ ⊿ 🦋 ♈ 🍴 Ⓗ 🖼 ⚑ ⚒ 🛥 (covrd, htd) 🛶

On DN7 twd Fréjus, turn R onto D7 sp St Aygulf & Roquebrune-sur-Argens; after passing Roquebrune, site sp in approx 6km on R. 4*, V lge, mkd, hdg, pt shd, terr, serviced pitches; EHU (6A) inc (extra for 10A); gas; red long stay; 70% statics; Eng spkn; adv bkg acc; ccard acc; tennis; jacuzzi; sauna; archery; games area; lake fishing; waterslide. "Well-organised site; entmnt/activities for all ages; mini farm; early bkg ess for summer; excel." €47.00, 28 Apr-30 Sep. 2019

FREJUS *10F4* (11.6km W Rural) *43.44535, 6.65790*
Camping Le Moulin des Iscles, Chemin du Moulin des Iscles, 83520 Roquebrune-sur-Argens **04 94 45 70 74; moulin.iscles@wanadoo.fr; www.campingdes iscles.com**

♞ €2.50 ♟♟ (htd) ⱳ ♨ ⚲ ♿ ▣ ∕ ✿ ⍭ 🍽 ⑭ ♨🥾 ⚏ 🛠

Twd Fréjus on DN7, turn R onto D7 to St Aygulf sp Roquebrune. Site on L after passing thro Roquebrune vill. 3*, Med, mkd, shd, EHU (6A) €3.90; bbq; TV; 10% statics; adv bkg acc; ccard acc; games rm; rv fishing; canoeing. *"Excel well-kept, well-run site by rv; water skiing nrby; helpful owners; gd security."*
€28.00, 1 Apr-30 Sep.   2015

"Satellite navigation makes touring much easier"

Remember most sat navs don't know if you're towing or in a larger vehicle – always use yours alongside maps and site directions.

FREJUS *10F4* (4km NW Urban) *43.46616, 6.72203*
Camping La Baume - La Palmeraie, Route de Bagnoles, Rue des Combattants d'Afrique du Nord, 83600 Fréjus **04 94 19 88 88; reception@labaume-lapalmeraie.com; www.labaume-lapalmeraie.com**

♞ €6 ♟♟ (htd) ♨ ⚲ ▣ ∕♟ ⍭ 🍽 ⑭🥾 ⚏ 🛠

🏊 (covrd, htd, indoor) 🏖 sand 5km

Fr A8 exit junc 38 sp Fréjus cent. Fr E'bound dir foll Bagnols sp at 2 rndabts & Fréjus cent/Cais at 3rd. Fr W'bound dir foll Bagnols at 3 rndabts & Fréjus cent/Cais at 4th. Site on L in 300m.
4*, V lge, pt shd, pt sl, EHU (6A) inc; gas; 80% statics; adv bkg req; horseriding, tennis; waterslide; spa.
€51.00, 28 Mar-26 Sep.   2020

FREJUS *10F4* (6km NW Rural) *43.46944, 6.67805*
Camping La Bastiane, 1056 Chemin des Suvières, 83480 Puget-sur-Argens **04 94 55 55 94; info@ labastiane.com; www.labastiane.com**

♞ €4 ♟♟ ⱳ ♨ ⚲ ♿ ▣ ∕ ✿ ⍭ 🍽 ⑭🥾 ⚏ 🛠

🏊 (htd) 🚣

Exit A8 at junc 37 Puget/Fréjus. At DN7 turn R dir Le Muy & in 1km turn R immed after 2nd bdge. Foll sp to site. Fr DN7 turn L at traff lts in Puget, site is 2km N of Puget. 5*, Lge, mkd, hdg, shd, pt sl, EHU (10A) inc; bbq (elec); red long stay; TV; 40% statics; phone; Eng spkn; adv bkg acc; ccard acc; bike hire; tennis; games area; games rm; watersports; CKE. *"Excel, family-run, friendly site; cinema; car wash area; conv m'way (no m'way noise); clean san facs; gd rest."*
€50.20, 21 Apr-9 Oct.   2017

FRONTIGNAN *10F1* (6km S Coastal) *43.44970, 3.80540* **Sandaya Les Tamaris,** 140 Ave d'Ingril, 34110 Frontignan-Plage **04 67 43 44 77; tam@ sandaya.fr; www.sandaya.co.uk**

♞ €3 ♟♟ (htd) ⱳ ♨ ⚲ ♿ ▣ ∕ ᴹᴾ ✿ 🍽 ⑭🥾 ⚏ 🛠

🏊 (htd) 🚣 🏖 sand adj

Fr A9/E15 exit junc 32 St Jean-de-Védas & foll sp Sète. At next rndbt foll sp Sète N112. After approx 8km turn L sp Vic-la-Gardiole onto D114. Cross rlwy & Canal du Rhône. Pass Les Aresquiers-Plages & turn L in 500m, site sp on L in 500m.
Fr N on D613, take N300 to Sète; then N112 to Frontignan-Plage. 5*, Lge, hdstg, mkd, hdg, pt shd, serviced pitches; EHU (10A) inc; bbq; red long stay; TV; 50% statics; phone; adv bkg rec; ccard acc; lake fishing; bike hire; watersports; horseriding nr; games rm. *"Popular, family-run site; direct access to beach; sm pitches; archery; weights rm; friendly, helpful staff; gd clean san facs; vg for families; excel pool; late arr area; gd rest; lovely town; mkt Thu & Sat am; excel."*
€25.00, 03 Apr-27 Sep.   2019

FUMEL *7D3* (2km E Rural) *44.48929, 0.99704*
Camping de Condat/Les Catalpas, Path of the Plaine de Condat, 47500 Fumel **05 53 71 11 99 or 06 30 24 20 04; contact@les-catalpas.com; www.les-catalpas.com**

♞ ♟♟ (htd) ⱳ ♨ ⚲ ▣ ∕ ᴹᴾ ⍭ ⑭ nr 🥾 ⚏ nr ⚏ 🛠 🏊

Take D811 fr Fumel E twd Cahors. Clearly sp after Condat. 3*, Med, mkd, hdstg, pt shd, pt sl, EHU (10A) €3; bbq; TV; 15% statics; Eng spkn; adv bkg acc; fishing adj; CKE. *"New owners, friendly helpful, improvements to site, sec barrier, by rv."*
€21.00, 1 Apr-31 Oct.   2020

FUMEL *7D3* (8km E Rural) *44.49810, 1.06670*
Camping Le Ch'Timi, La Roque, 46700 Touzac **05 65 36 52 36; info@campinglechtimi.com; www.campinglechtimi.com**

♞ €1.90 ♟♟ ⱳ ♨ ⚲ ♿ ▣ ∕ ✿ ⍭ 🍽 ⑭♨🥾 ⚏ 🛠 🏊 🚣

Exit N20-E9 junc 57 onto D820 dir Cahors; turn R at rndabt onto D811 sp Villeneuve-sur-Lot; in Duravel take 3rd exit at rndabt onto D58, sp Vire-sur-Lot; in 2.5km cross bdge & turn R at rndabt onto D8, sp Touzac; site on R on rvside, on hill, in about 1.5km. Well sp. NB D8 not suitable lge c'vans or m'vans. 3*, Med, hdg, mkd, pt shd, pt sl, EHU (6A) €4.20; gas; bbq; twin axles; TV; 13% statics; phone; Eng spkn; adv bkg acc; ccard acc; tennis; games area; games rm; archery; bike hire; fishing 100m; CKE. *"Site in gd position; friendly, helpful Dutch owners; immac facs, ltd LS; rv nr site, down steep steps; access some pitches poss diff lge o'fits; no o'fits over 7m high ssn; canoeing 100m; wine-tasting tours; mkt Puy l'Evêque Tue; wonderful stay, rec; v well kept; rv view fr some pitches; ACSI acc."*
€28.00, 1 Apr-30 Sep, D05.   2015

FRANCE

GAILLAC *8E4* (5km E Urban) *43.90929, 1.98311*
Camping Les Pommiers, Aigueleze, 81600 Rivières
05 63 33 02 49; info@camping-lespommiers.com;
www.camping-lespommiers.com

🐕 €2 [symbols] (htd) [symbols]

Fr A68, Albi - Toulouse take exit 10, foll sp Espace
Loisirs d'Aigueleze. 3*, Med, hdstg, mkd, hdg, pt shd,
EHU (10-13A) €4.50; bbq; sw; twin axles; red long
stay; TV; 25% statics; phone; Eng spkn; adv bkg acc;
games area; bike hire; CCI. *"Visit Albi by sightseeing
boat on Rv Tarn or by train; canoe hire 150m; bike
hire 150m; vg; conv Albi, Cordes, P&R Toulose; excel;
well kept clean site; friendly, welcoming owners;
conv for bastide vill; sm eve mkt Mon in hg ssn nr."*
€27.00, 1 Apr-30 Sep. **2018**

GAILLAC *8E4* (2km W Urban) *43.89674, 1.88522*
FFCC Camping des Sources, 9 Ave Guynemer, 81600
Gaillac **05 63 57 18 30; camping-gaillac@orange.fr;**
www.camping-gaillac.fr

🐕 €2 (htd) [symbols] nr [symbols]

Exit A68 junc 9 onto D999 then in 3.5km at rndabt
turn onto D968 dir Gaillac. In 100m turn R immed
past Leclerc petrol stn, then L by Aldi. Site 200m on
R, well sp fr town cent. Sharp turn into ent.
3*, Med, hdg, hdstg, mkd, pt shd, terr, EHU (10A) €3;
TV; 10% statics; ccard acc; CKE. *"Peaceful, clean & tidy
site; friendly, helpful staff; gd, modern san facs; steep
walk to recep & bar but san facs at pitch level; purpose-
made dog-walk area; gd touring base Tarn & Albi region
& circular tour Bastides; cent of wine area; not suitable
lge o'fits; gd; call recep fr Aldi carpk to operate barrier."*
€14.50, 1 Apr-31 Oct. **2017**

GANGES *10E1* (7km E Rural) *43.92630, 3.78951*
Camp Municipal Le Grillon, Place de l'Eglise, 34190
Montoulieu **04 67 73 79 31 or 06 61 75 35 11;**
camping.montoulieu@sfr.fr; http://camping.
montoulieu.fr

12 🐕 [symbols] [symbols]

Fr Ganges take D999 E. At La Cadière-et-Cambo turn
R onto D195 (site sp). Site on R in 3km.
3*, Sm, hdstg, hdg, pt shd, pt sl, EHU (6A) inc;
40% statics. *"Gd cent for outdoor activities; gd, modern
facs; useful winter NH; fairly isolated."* **€17.60** **2019**

GANNAT *9A1* (10km W Rural) *46.11077, 3.08082*
Camp Municipal Les Nières, Rue des Nières, 03450
Ebreuil **04 70 90 70 60 or 04 70 90 71 33 (Mairie);**
contact@campingdesnieres.fr; www.camping-
sioule.fr

🐕 €3 [symbols] (cont) [symbols] nr [symbols] (htd)

Site 1km SW of Ebreuil, sp fr D915.
3*, Sm, shd, EHU (4-8A) €1.95-2.80; bbq; Eng
spkn; fishing; rv; tennis. *"Nice setting on Rv Sioule;
san facs dated but clean, poss stretched high ssn;
warden present 1700-2000 only LS; sh walk into vill."*
€8.00, 24 Apr-27 Sep. **2020**

GANNAT *9A1* (10km W Rural) *46.10838, 3.07347*
Camping La Filature de la Sioule, Route de Chouvigny,
03450 Ebreuil **04 70 90 72 01; camping.filature@
gmail.com; www.campingfilature.com**

🐕 [symbols] [symbols]

Fr A71 exit 12 (not 12.1); foll sp to Ebreuil, after rv
bdge in vill turn L onto D998 then cont onto D915.
Site on L in abt 1 km. 4*, Med, mkd, hdg, pt shd, EHU
(6A) €3.50; gas; bbq; red long stay; TV; 10% statics;
Eng spkn; adv bkg acc; ccard acc; canoeing;
horseriding; tennis 800m; bike hire; trout fishing; CKE.
*"Peaceful, pleasant rvside site in orchard; lge pitches;
helpful British owners; clean facs but tired, ltd LS; vg
value food high ssn (gd home cooking); vg walking
area; mv service pnt 800m; conv A71; no hdstg, v soft
grnd; poor water pressure in shwrs; site unkept (2015)."*
€26.00, 15 Apr-1 Oct. **2016**

GAP *9D3* (1.5km N Rural) *44.58030, 6.08270*
Camping Alpes-Dauphiné, Route Napoléon, 05000
Gap **04 92 51 29 95; info@alpesdauphine.com;**
www.alpesdauphine.com

🐕 €2.10 [symbols] (htd) [symbols] [symbols] (htd) [symbols]

On N85, sp. 4*, Med, hdstg, mkd, pt shd, pt sl, terr,
EHU (6A) €3; gas; TV; 20% statics; phone; Eng spkn;
adv bkg rec; ccard acc; games area; CKE. *"Pleasant site
with views; modern, well maintained san facs; m'vans
need levellers; gd touring base; lack of maintenance
early ssn (2011); conv NH; gd site; excel rest."*
€27.00, 15 Apr-20 Oct. **2017**

GAP *9D3* (10km S Rural) *44.45708, 6.04785*
Camping Le Chêne, Route de Marseille, 05130 Tallard
04 92 54 13 31; contact@camping-lechene.com;
www.camping-lechene.com

🐕 [symbols] nr [symbols] (htd)

Fr S take N85 twds Gap; turn R at traff lts onto
D942; site on R after 3km. Fr Gap take N85 S; turn L
at traff lts, D942; site on R 3km. 3*, Sm, mkd, hdstg,
pt shd, sl, terr, EHU (6A) €3.5; bbq (sep area); phone;
adv bkg acc; tennis; CKE. *"Poss unsuitable for lgs o'fits;
sm pitches; lovely setting; new san facs (2018), but ltd
for site size; site needs tlc."*
€13.00, 6 Apr-13 Oct. **2018**

GAVARNIE *8G2* (4km N Rural) *42.75896, 0.00069*
Camping Le Pain de Sucre, quartier Couret, 65120
Gavarnie **05 62 92 47 55 or 06 75 30 64 22 (mob);**
camping-gavarnie@wanadoo.fr or info@camping-
gavarnie.com; www.camping-gavarnie.com

🐕 €2.15 [symbols] [symbols] nr [symbols]

N of Gavarnie, across rv by sm bdge; clearly visible &
sp fr rd. 2*, Med, pt shd, EHU (2-10A) €2.30-6.50 (long
lead poss req); bbq; ccard acc. *"Gd base for walking;
gd facs; access to national park; vg; gd clean san facs;
fantastic view of Cirque."* **€20.00, 1 Jan-15 Apr,
1 Jun-30 Sep & 15 Dec-31 Dec.** **2016**

GENNES *4G1* (0.7km NE Rural) *47.34205, -0.22985*
Camping Au Bord de Loire, Ave des Cadets-de-Saumur, 49350 Gennes **02 41 38 04 67 or 06 95 00 24 87; contact@camping-auborddeloire.com; www.camping-auborddeloire.com**

🏕 €1.60 � WD ⏚ ♿ 🚿 ⊿ 🦋 ♈ 🍽 🍴 🔥 🛒 nr ♿ 🎣

At Rv Loire bdge cross S to Gennes on D751B. Site 200m on L. Ent to site thro bus terminus/car park on ent to Gennes. 2*, Med, pt shd, pt sl, EHU (10A) €3.40; bbq; red long stay; 2% statics; CKE. *"Delightful, relaxing, well-kept site by Rv Loire, spacious pitches, main san facs block up 18 steps, vg; htd pool in vill; Loire cycle rte passes gate; new san facs block (2015); v easy walk to vill."* **€16.80, 13 Apr-30 Sep.** 2018

"There aren't many sites open at this time of year"

If you're travelling outside peak season remember to call ahead to check site opening dates – even if the entry says 'open all year'.

GERARDMER *6F3* (7km E Rural) *48.06755, 6.94830*
FFCC Camping Les Jonquilles, Route du Lac, 88400 Xonrupt-Longemer **03 29 63 34 01; info@camping-jonquilles.com; www.camping-jonquilles.com**

🏕 €1.50 � WD ⏚ ♿ 🚿 ⊿ MSP 🦋 ♈ 🍴 ⊕ 🛒 ♿

Sp off D417 SE of Xonrupt-Longemer. Fr W thro Gérardmer on D417 (sp Colmar) in approx 1km over bdge & turn R at T-junc (still on D417). After 3km turn R opp hotel Auberge du Lac & almost immed R round W end of lake for 500m to T-junc, turn L, site on S bank 1km. 2^, Lge, mkd, unshd, pt sl, EHU (6-10A) €3.50-5.20; gas; sw nr; TV; 10% statics; phone; bus 1km; Eng spkn; adv bkg acc; ccard acc; sailing; fishing; CKE. *"Friendly, well-maintained, family-run site; gd views; poss uneven pitches; some noise fr entmnt at night; excel for Haute Vosges region; great lakeside site; busy rd."* **€18.00, 17 Apr-4 Oct.** 2015

GEX *9A3* (1.4km E Urban) *46.33430, 6.06744*
Camping Les Genêts, 400 Ave des Alpes, 01170 Gex **04 50 42 84 57 or 06 79 17 13 69 (mob); les.2b@hotmail.fr; www.gex.fr/decouvrir-gex/camping**

🏕 €1 � WD ⏚ ♿ 🚿 ⊿ 🦋 🍴 🛒 nr ♿

Fr all dir head for 'Centre Ville'; at rndabt take D984 twd Divonne/Lausanne. Site sp to R (tight turn) after rlwy sheds (poor sp in town) & Musée Sapeurs Pompiers. 3*, Med, hdg, hdstg, pt shd, pt sl, EHU (16A) €2.90; TV; phone; Eng spkn; adv bkg acc; games area; CKE. *"Excel, attractive, well-kept site; excel games facs/playgrnd; friendly, helpful staff; clean san facs; quiet with lots of privacy; conv Geneva; wifi in recep; gates clsd 2200-0800; 20 mins fr Geneva airport."* **€17.50, 1 May-31 Oct.** 2017

GIEN *4G3* (8km S Rural) *47.64152, 2.61528*
Les Bois du Bardelet, Route de Bourges, Poilly 45500 Gien **02 38 67 47 39; contact@bardelet.com; www.bardelet.com**

🏕 €4 � (htd) WD ⏚ ♿ 🚿 ⊿ MSP 🦋 ♈ 🍽 🍴 ⊕ 🛒 ♿ 🏊 (covrd, htd)

Fr Gien take D940 dir Bourges; turn R onto D53, then R again onto unclassified rd to go back across D940; foll sp to site on L side of this rd. Site well sp fr D940. 5*, Lge, hdstg, mkd, hdg, pt shd, pt sl, EHU (10-16A) inc (some rev pol); gas; bbq; red long stay; twin axles; TV; 17% statics; phone; adv bkg acc; ccard acc; archery; bike hire; fitness rm; jacuzzi; canoeing; games area; tennis; lake fishing; horseriding 5km; games rm; CKE. *"Pleasant, well-kept, well-run site; friendly welcome; modern, immac san facs, poss stretched high ssn; some pitches poss diff access; beautiful o'door pool; gd for young children; guided walks; remote site in countryside."* **€28.00, 3 Apr-30 Sep, L05.** 2019

GISORS *3D3* (7km SW Rural) *49.25639, 1.70174*
Camp Municipal de l'Aulnaie, Rue du Fond-de-l'Aulnaie, 27720 Dangu **02 32 55 43 42; etangcampingdangu@orange.fr; http://euredangu.e-monsite.com/**

🏕 €2.60 � (htd) WD ⏚ ♿ 🚿 ⊿ MSP 🍴 nr ⊕ nr ♿

On ent Gisors fr all dirs, take ring rd & exit dir Vernon D10, then L onto D181 dir Dangu. Site on L bef Dangu. Site sp fr D10. NB speed humps. 3*, Lge, mkd, pt shd, EHU (10A) €2.80; gas; sw; 90% statics; adv bkg acc; fishing; CKE. *"Lakeside site; Gisors attractive town; conv Giverny & Gisors local attractions; beautiful site."* **€14.00, 1 Apr-31 Oct.** 2019

GIVET *5B1* (0.5km N Urban) *50.14345, 4.82614*
Caravaning Municipal La Ballastière, 16 Rue Berthelot, 08600 Givet **03 24 42 30 20; sa.mairiegivet@wanadoo.fr; www.tourisme-champagne-ardenne.com**

12 🏕 €0.85 � (htd) WD ⏚ ♿ 🚿 ⊿ 🍴 nr ⊕ nr 🛒 nr ♿

Site at N end of town on lake. Foll 'Caravaning' sp fr W end of rv bdge or Dinant rd. 2*, Med, hdstg, hdg, mkd, pt shd, EHU (10A) inc; bbq; 60% statics; CKE. *"Nr Rv Meuse; adj sports & watersports complex; picturesque town; walking dist to shops & rest; vg; pool adj; conv for Rv Meuse cycleway; fair NH; scruffy & unkept san facs, rundown but clean (2018)."* **€9.00** 2018

GIVET *5B1* (2km SW Rural) *50.12993, 4.80721*
Camping Le Sanglier, 63 Rue des Grands Jardins, 08600 Rancennes **03 24 42 72 61 or 06 47 98 62 41 (mob); gilbert.gachet0455@orange.fr**

� WD ⏚ ⊿ 🦋 ♈ 🛒 ♿

Off D949 Givet to Beauraing. Immed after x-ing rv bdge turn R. Turn R again foll sp to site at end narr access rd on rvside. 1*, Sm, pt shd, pt sl, terr, EHU (4A); 60% statics; phone; Eng spkn; adv bkg acc; watersports; fishing; CKE. *"Gd touring base; clean, basic facs; gd NH."* **€9.00, 1 May-30 Sep.** 2015

GIVORS 9B2 (10km NW Urban) 45.61498, 4.67068
Camping La Trillonnière, Boulevard du General de
Gaulle, 69440 Mornant **04 82 29 21 89 or 04 78 44 16
47; contact@la-trillonniere.fr; www.la-trillonniere.fr**

🛠 €1 🚻 WC 🏕 ♿ 🚿 ⊟ 🖉 MP 🍴 ⓧ nr 🐕 nr 🏧

**Exit A7 at Givors & foll sp for St Etienne via D488,
thro Givors onto D2 till sp seen for Mornant via
D34, cont on D34 up hill for 7km, cross D342 &
cont 1km to o'skts of Mornant, L at junc island &
site on L.** 2*, Med, pt shd, pt sl, EHU (10A) inc; twin
axles; 20% statics; Eng spkn; adv bkg acc; CKE. "Well
managed, quiet site on edge of lovely vill in Monts
du Lyonnais; walks in hills; Lyon accessible by bus
(outsite gate) & metro; excell new san facs; 6 chalets."
€25.00, 15 May-30 Sep. 2018

GIVRE, LE 7A1 (1.5km S Rural) 46.44472, -1.39832
Camping La Grisse, 85540 Le Givre **02 51 30 83 03;
info@campinglagrisse.com; www.campinglagrisse.com**

12 🛠 €2 🚻 WC 🏕 ♿ 🚿 🖉 🍴 🏧

**Fr Luçon take D949 & turn L at junc with D747 (La
Tranche rd). Turn L in 3km & foll sps.** 3*, Sm, pt shd,
EHU (16A) €4; 50% statics; Eng spkn; adv bkg acc;
ccard acc; games area; CKE. "Peaceful, friendly, farm
site; lge pitches; clean, modern facs; beautiful area/
beach; gd for dogs; knowledgeable owner of local
area." **€29.00** 2017

GONDRIN 8E2 (3km SE Rural) 43.86936, 0.25844
Camping La Brouquère, Betbéze, 32330 Gondrin
**05 62 29 19 44; camping@brouquere.com;
www.brouquere.com**

🛠 €1 🚻 WC 🏕 ♿ 🚿 🖉 🦋 🍴 🏧

**Fr Condom S on D931; pass thro Gondrin & turn S
onto D113 dir Courrensan; site sp in 2km.**
Sm, mkd, shd, pt sl, EHU (10A) €2.50; bbq; TV; Eng
spkn; adv bkg acc; bike hire. "V quiet, CL-type site;
friendly Dutch owners; immac san facs; wine-tasting;
local produce, inc Armagnac; excel; adults only."
€17.00, 30 Apr-1 Oct. 2016

GORDES 10E2 (2km N Rural) 43.92689, 5.20207
Camping Les Sources, Route de Murs, 84220 Gordes
**04 90 71 12 48; contact@campingdessources.com;
www.campingdessources.com**

🛠 €5 🚻 WC 🏕 ♿ 🚿 🖉 🦋 🍴 ⓧ 🐕 🏧 ⚓

**Fr A7 junc 24, E on D973; then D22; then D900
twds Apt. After 18km at Coustellet turn N onto D2
then L on D15 twds Murs; site on L in 2km beyond
Gordes.** 2*, Med, mkd, hdstg, pt shd, terr, EHU (6A)
€4.40 (long lead poss req); red long stay; 25% statics;
Eng spkn; adv bkg acc; ccard acc; games rm; bike hire;
games area; CKE. "Lovely location & views; friendly
staff; modern, clean san facs; gd pool; access rds
narr; sm pitches v diff lge o'fits; ask for easy pitch &
inspect on foot; some steep rds to pitches as site on
hillside; 24 hr security barriers; gd walking; mkt Tues."
€37.70, 6 Apr-28 Sep. 2019

GOUAREC 2E3 (0.6km SW Rural) 48.22555, -3.18307
Camping Tost Aven, Au Bout du Pont, 22570 Gouarec
**02 96 24 87 86; bertrand.cocherel@orange.fr;
www.brittanycamping.com**

🛠 €1 🚻 WC 🏕 ♿ 🚿 🖉 🍴 nr ⓧ nr 🐕 nr 🏧 🖉

Sp fr town cent bet rv & canal. 2*, Med, pt shd,
EHU (10A) €2.40; bbq; sw nr; bus 200m; Eng
spkn; adv bkg acc; bike hire; canoe hire. "Clean,
relaxed, tidy site bet Nantes-Brest canal & rv on
edge of vill; gas adj; towpath for cycling; great!"
€12.00, 1 May-15 Sep. 2018

GOUDARGUES 10E2 (1km NE Rural) 44.22056,
4.47884 **Camping Les Amarines,** La Vérune Cornillon,
30630 Goudargues **04 66 82 24 92; les.amarines@
wanadoo.fr; www.campinglesamarines.com**

🛠 €3 🚻 (htd) 🏕 ♿ 🚿 ⊟ 🖉 🦋 🍴 🏧 🖉 🏊 (htd)

**Fr D980 foll sp onto D23 & site bet Cornillon &
Goudargues.** 3*, Med, hdg, mkd, shd, EHU (6A) €3.50;
adv bkg acc; rv fishing. "Lge pitches; site liable to flood
after heavy rain; excel."
€32.00, 1 Apr-1 Oct. 2019

GOURDON 7D3 (10km W Rural) 44.75491, 1.23999
Camping Le Convivial, La Gréze, 24250 St Martial de
Nabirat **05 53 28 43 15; contact@campingleconvivial
.com; www.campingleconvivial.com**

🛠 €1.60 🚻 (htd) WC 🏕 ♿ 🚿 ⊟ 🖉 🦋 🍴 ⓧ 🐕 nr 🏧 🖉

**SW fr Gourdon, take D673 twd Salviac. Bef Pont
Carral turn R onto D6 which becomes D46. Site
1.5km N St Martial on L.** Sm, hdg, pt shd, pt sl,
EHU (8A); bbq; twin axles; 25% statics; Eng spkn;
ccard acc; games area; fishing 1km; CCI. "Beautiful,
spacious site off tourist track; friendly & welcoming
owners; cycle trail in pretty valley of Céon nrby; vg."
€19.70, 1 Apr-31 Oct. 2019

GOUZON 7A4 (0.6km S Urban) 46.18785, 2.23913
Camp Municipal de la Voueize, 1 Ave de la Marche,
23230 Gouzon **05 55 81 73 22; camping-gouzon@
orange.fr; www.camping-lavoueize.fr**

🛠 €0.50 🚻 WC 🏕 ♿ 🚿 🖉 🦋 🍴 nr ⓧ nr 🐕 nr 🏧

**On E62/N145 Guéret/Montluçon exit at sp for Gouzon.
In cent of vill bear R past church & site is sp on edge of
Rv Voueize.** 2*, Sm, pt shd, EHU (10A) inc (poss rev pol);
adv bkg acc; golf 2km; bike hire; fishing. "Lovely aspect;
friendly recep; clean site; facs poss tired high ssn; gd
walking & cycling rtes; gd NH; birdwatching on lake 8km;
snacks/bar Jul & Aug only; gas adj; big trees; adj rv; san
facs tired." **€15.50, 1 May-16 Oct.** 2015

GRAMAT *7D4* (7km SE Rural) *44.74767, 1.79954*
Camping Le Teulière, L'Hôpital Beaulieu, 46500
Issendolus 05 65 40 86 71; laparro.mcv@free.fr;
http://laparro.mcv.free.fr

🏕 🚶 ⛟ 🚻 ⚥ 🌊 🍽 ⊕ 🛝 🛒 ⛰ ⛵

Site on R on D840 at L'Hôpital, clearly sp. Access
fr ent narr & tight corners, not for underpowered.
2*, Sm, pt shd, pt sl, EHU (20A) €2.65 (poss rev pol);
bbq; TV; 10% statics; adv bkg acc; tennis; fishing.
*"Conv Rocamadour; basic san facs; ltd facs LS; site rds
unmade, steep & narr - gd traction req; pitches muddy
when wet."* **€9.35**   **2016**

GRANDCAMP MAISY *1C4* (0.5km W Coastal) *49.38814,
-1.05204* **Camping Le Joncal,** Le Petit Nice, 14450
Grandcamp-Maisy 04 92 28 38 48; campingdu
joncal@hotmail.fr; www.campingdujoncal.com

🐕 €1.10 🚶 ⚥ 🌊 🍽 🅜🆂🅿 🦋 ⊕ nr 🛒 nr ⛵ sand adj

Ent on Grandcamp port dock area; visible fr vill.
Fr N13 take D199 sp Grandcamp-Maisy & foll Le
Port & Camping sps. 3*, Lge, hdg, mkd, pt shd,
EHU (6-10A) €5.40-7.50; gas; bbq; 80% statics; bus.
*"Conv for D Day beaches; some pitches at water's
edge; excel morning fish mkt close by; gd NH."*
€23.50, 1 Apr-30 Sep.   **2019**

GRANDE MOTTE, LA *10F1* (2km NW Coastal)
43.56440, 4.07528 **FFCC Camping La Petite Motte à
La Grande-Motte,** 195 Allée des Peupliers, 34280 La
Grande-Motte 04 67 56 54 75; camping.lagrandemotte@
ffcc.fr; www.camping-lapetitemotte.com

🐕 €4 🚶 ⛟ 🚻 ⚥ 🌊 🍽 🍽 🍽 🛒 ⊕ 🛒 ⛰ 🚴 ⛵ sand 700m

Exit A9 for Lunel or Montpellier Est to La Grande
Motte, site sp on D59 & D62 coast rd.
2*, Lge, shd, EHU (6A) €4.30; red long stay; twin axles;
10% statics; adv bkg acc; horseriding nr; watersports
nr; games area; tennis nr; golf nr; CKF. *"Walk to
beach thro ave of trees & footbdge over rds; helpful
staff; clean modern san facs; cycle rtes nrby; m'van
o'night area; vg; 2nd san fac modernised (2015)."*
€20.50, 29 Mar-30 Sep.   **2015**

GRANVILLE *1D4* (6km NE Coastal) *48.86976, -1.56380*
Kawan Village La Route Blanche, 6 La Route Blanche,
50290 Bréville-sur-Mer 02 33 50 23 31; larouteblanche
@camping-breville.com; www.campinglaroute
blanche.com

🐕 €3 🚶 (htd) 🆆🅳 ⛟ 🚻 ⚥ 🌊 🍽 🅜🆂🅿 🦋 🍽 🛒 ⛰ 🚴
⛵ (htd) 🏊 ⛵ sand 500m

Exit A84 junc 37 onto D924 dir Granville. Bef
Granville turn L onto D971, then L onto D114 which
joins D971e. Site on R bef golf club. Nr Bréville sm
airfield. 5*, Lge, hdstg, mkd, hdg, pt shd, serviced
pitches; EHU (6-10A) €4-5; gas; bbq; red long stay;
TV; 40% statics; phone; Eng spkn; adv bkg acc; ccard
acc; tennis nr; waterslide; sailing school; golf nr; games
area; CKE. *"Pleasant, busy site with vg clean facs; staff
friendly & helpful; disabled seatlift in pool; gd walking,
cycling & beach; pleasant old walled town & harbour;
vg."* **€39.50, 6 Apr-23 Sep.**   **2018**

GRANVILLE *1D4* (8km SE Rural) *48.79790, -1.5244*
Camping Le Château de Lez-Eaux, 50380 St Pair-sur-Mer
02 33 51 66 09; bonjour@lez-eaux.com;
www.lez-eaux.com

🐕 🚶 (htd) 🆆🅳 ⛟ 🚻 ⚥ 🌊 🍽 🅜🆂🅿 🦋 🍽 🛒 ⛰ 🛝
⛵ (covrd, htd) 🏊 ⛵ sand 4km

App site on D973 Granville to Avranches rd (not via
St Pair). Cont strt thro 1st rndabt & Geant and next
rndabt for 2km, site sp on R. 5*, Lge, mkd, pt shd, pt
sl, serviced pitches; EHU (10-16A) inc; bbq; twin axles;
TV; 80% statics; ccard acc; games rm; lake fishing;
bike hire; tennis; horseriding 4km; waterslide; games
area; CKE. *"Superb, beautiful site in grnds of chateau;
children's indoor aqua park; easy access; spacious
pitches, various prices; helpful & friendly staff; clean,
modern san facs; excel pool complex; gd for children;
boat hire 7km; great for dogs; gd cycling & gd cycle
rte to beach; gd touring base; conv Mont St Michel,
Dol & landing beaches; mkt Thu St Pair; highly rec."*
€46.00, 1 Apr-13 Sep, N02.   **2019**

GRASSE *10E4* (5.5km SE Urban) *43.63507, 6.94859*
Camping Caravaning La Paoute, 160 Route de
Cannes, 06130 Grasse 04 93 09 11 42; camppaoute@
hotmail.com; www.campinglapaoute.com

🏕 🐕 🚶 🆆🅳 ⛟ 🚻 ⚥ 🌊 🍽 🅜🆂🅿 🍽 🛒 🛒 nr ⛰ 🏊 (htd)

Sp fr Grasse town cent on Route de Cannes
(secondary rd to Cannes, NOT D6185), a 10 min
drive. 3*, Med, hdg, mkd, pt shd, sl, terr, EHU (10A) €4;
15% statics; bus 500m; games rm; CKE. *"Gd, quiet site;
m'vans acc out of ssn but adv bkg req."*
€31.00   **2019**

GRASSE *10E4* (8km S Rural) *43.60650, 6.90216*
Camping Le Parc des Monges, 635 Chemin du
Gabre, 06810 Auribeau-sur-Siagne 04 93 60 91 71;
parcdesmonges@dsonevacances.com;
www.parcdesmonges.com

🐕 €2.50 🚶 (htd) 🆆🅳 ⛟ 🚻 ⚥ 🌊 🍽 🅜🆂🅿 🦋 🍽 nr ⊕ 🛒 nr ⛰
🚴 🏊 (htd)

Exit A8 junc 40 or 41 onto D6007 dir Grasse; then
onto D109 becoming D9; foll sp to Auribeau-sur-
Siagne; site on rd to Le Gabre. 3*, Med, hdg, shd, EHU
(4-10A) €3.50-5.50; sw nr; 7% statics; phone; bus adj;
Eng spkn; adv bkg acc; ccard acc; ice; fishing nr
Jacuzzi onsite; Bowling alley; CKE. *"Vg site by
Rv Siagne; rv not accessible fr site; activities;
watch out for branches when manoeurvering."*
€23.00, 4 Apr-27 Sep.   **2020**

FRANCE

GRAVELINES *3A3* (4km NW Coastal) *51.00250, 2.09694* **Camping de la Plage,** 115 Rue du Maréchal-Foch, 59153 Grand-Fort-Philippe **03 28 65 31 95; campingdelaplage@campingvpa.fr; www.camping-de-la-plage.info**

🐕 €2 (htd) ♿ ⌷ ⌂ ⬚ ⟋ MSP 🦋 ⛱ 🎣 nr 🏔 🐾 ⛵ sand 500m

Exit A16 junc 51 dir Grand-Fort-Philippe; at o'skts of town turn R sp Camping ***; cont into town cent; foll rd along quayside; foll rd to L past lge crucifix; turn R at next x-rds; site on R. 3*, Med, hdg, hdstg, pt shd, terr, EHU (10A) €3.70 (poss long lead req); 20% statics; adv bkg acc; ccard acc; CKE. *"Various pitch sizes; ltd EHU; pleasant walk to sea front; night security guard; conv ferries; rec adv bkg; san facs excel; pool 3km; friendly, attractive site."* **€15.00, 1 Apr-31 Oct.** **2016**

GRAVESON *10E2* (2km SE Rural) *43.84408, 4.78080* **Camping Les Micocouliers,** 445 Route de Cassoulen, 13690 Graveson **04 90 95 81 49; micocou@free.fr; www.camping-les-micocouliers-provence.fr**

🐕 €2 ♿ ⌷ ⌂ ⬚ ⟋ MSP 🦋 ⛱ 🎣 nr ⊕ nr 🎣 ⛵

Leave A7 junc 25 onto D99 St Rémy-de-Provence then D5 N past Maillane, site on R. 3*, Med, hdg, mkd, unshd, EHU (4-13A) €4.40-7; bbq; 8% statics; phone; Eng spkn; adv bkg rec; bike hire; games area; tennis 1km; CKE. *"Peaceful but busy site; pretty & well-kept; friendly, helpful, welcoming owners; excel, immac san facs; lovely sm pool; vg cycling; attractive, interesting area; excel; additional san facs built (2014)."* **€31.00, 15 Mar-15 Oct.** **2016**

GRAY *6G2* (1km E Rural) *47.45207, 5.59999* **Camp Municipal Longue Rive,** Rue de la Plage, 70100 Gray **03 84 64 90 44; tourisme-gray@wanadoo.fr; www.ville-gray.fr**

🐕 €0.85 ♿ ⌷ ⬚ ⌂ ⟋ MSP ⛱ 🎣 nr ⊕ nr 🎣 nr 🏔

S on D67 to Gray. cross rv bdge, L at rndabt, after 300m sp La Plage. Well sp fr all rtes. 3*, Med, mkd, hdg, pt shd, EHU (10A) €2.45; gas; Eng spkn; tennis; boating; fishing; CKE. *"Lovely setting on Rv Saône; friendly recep; new high quality facs, poss stretched high ssn; twin axles; pool opp; many pitches waterlogged early ssn; several Bastide vills within cycling dist; NH only."* **€14.50, 15 Apr-30 Sep.** **2015**

GRENOBLE *9C3* (19km S Rural) *45.08553, 5.69872* **Camping à la Ferme Le Moulin de Tulette (Gaudin),** Route du Moulin de Tulette, 38760 Varces-Allières-et-Risset **06 37 74 61 70; campingdetulette@gmail.com; www.camping-moulindetulette.fr**

🐕 €1 ♿ ⌷ ⬚ ⌂ ⟋ 🦋 ⛱ 🎣 nr ⛵

Fr A51, exit junc 12 to join D1075 N, Varces in approx 2km. Turn R at traff lts & foll sp to site, (approx 2km fr D1075). If driving thro Grenoble look for sp Gap - D1075 diff to find; on ent Varce foll site sp. Sm, mkd, pt shd, pt sl, EHU (5-10A) inc; Eng spkn; adv bkg acc; CKE. *"Peaceful, picturesque, well-kept site with views; friendly, helpful owners; facs ltd but clean - stretched high ssn; gd base for touring/x-ing Alps; new lge pool."* **€19.00, 1 May-30 Sep.** **2015**

GRENOBLE *9C3* (4.5km SW Urban) *45.16687, 5.69897* **Camping Caravaning Les 3 Pucelles,** 58 Rue des Allobroges, 38180 Seyssins **04 76 96 45 73; amico.francoise@gmail.com; www.camping-trois-pucelles.com**

🔲12 ♿ (htd) ⌷ ⬚ ⌂ ⟋ 🍽 ⊕ 🎣 🏔 ⛵

On A480 in dir of rocade (by-pass) S exit 5B, on R after supmkt then foll sp to R then L. Clearly sp. Well sp fr m'way. Sm, hdg, hdstg, pt shd, EHU (16A) meter; 70% statics; phone; bus nr; CKE. *"Site pt of hotel campus run by friendly family; sm pitches; san facs need refurb; conv Grenoble by bus/tram; NH only; poorly maintained; tram to city 300m fr site."* **€21.00** **2015**

GREOUX LES BAINS *10E3* (1.2km S Rural) *43.75158, 5.88185* **Camping Le Verseau,** Route de St Pierre, 04800 Gréoux-les-Bains **04 92 77 67 10 or 06 22 72 93 25 (mob); info@camping-le-verseau.com; www.camping-le-verseau.com**

🐕 €2.50 ♿ ⌷ ⬚ ⌂ ⌂ ⟋ 🦋 🦜 ⛱ 🍽 ⊕ 🎣 nr 🏔 🐾 ⛵

Fr W on D952 to Gréoux. Go under bdge then bear L just bef petrol stn. Cross rv (narr bdge), site on R in 500m. 3*, Med, hdg, pt shd, pt sl, EHU (10A) €3.90; bbq (elec, gas); phone; adv bkg acc; tennis 1km; CKE. *"Friendly owners; interesting spa town; great views."* **€23.00, 1 Mar-31 Oct.** **2016**

GREZILLE *4G1* (1km E Rural) *47.32751, -0.33512* **Ferme du Bois Madame,** Frédéric Gauthier, 49320 Grézillé **02 41 54 20 97 or 06 87 23 32 55 (mob); ferme.boismadame@wanadoo.fr; www.fermedubois madame.com**

🔲12 🐕 €0.50 ♿ ⌷ ⬚ ⌂ ⟋ MSP

Turn L off D761 (Angers-Poitiers) in Les Alleuds sp Grézillé (D90); in 3.5km turn R sp Grézillé (D276); after 1.4km in Grézillé turn L and immed R sp Gennes (D176). Site on R in 1km. Sm, hdg, pt shd, EHU (10-12A); adv bkg acc; bike hire. *"Friendly welcome; CL feel to site but lge & more facs; working farm & stables; horse-drawn carrige trip avail in ssn; gd."* **€13.00** **2015**

GRIGNAN *9D2* (0.5km S Urban) *44.41731, 4.90950* **Camping de Grignan,** 2 Avenue de Grillon, 26230 Grignan **04 75 01 92 23; contact@campingde grignan.fr; www.campingdegrignan.fr**

🐕 ♿ ⌷ ⬚ ⌂ ⌂ ⟋ 🦋 ⛱ 🍽 ⛵ (htd) ♨

N7 S fr Montelimar on N7 N fr Orange, then D133 onto D541, dir Nyons for 17km. Grignan sp Camping Municipal in vill. Sm, lge, hdg, mkd, pt shd, EHU (6A); bbq; twin axles; bus; Eng spkn; adv bkg rec; CKE. *"10 min walk to town & Chateau and Saint Sauveur Church; excel."* **€16.00, 20 Apr-17 Sep.** **2017**

GRILLON *9D2* (1.5km S Rural) *44.38307, 4.93046*
Camping Le Garrigon, Chemin de Visan, 84600 Grillon
04 90 28 72 94; contact@camping-garrigon.com;
www.camping-garrigon.com

🏕️ 🚶 wc 🛒 ♿ 🚿 📶 ⚡ 🍴 🍽️ ℍ ⛽ 🏊 nr ⚠️ 🚣 (htd)

A7, exit Montelmar-Sud, twds Gap. Take D541 then
Grillon cent & foll sp to site. 4*, Med, mkd, pt shd,
EHU (10A); bbq (elec, gas); 10% statics; Eng spkn;
adv bkg acc; ccard acc; games rm; CKE. *"Pleasant
site in attractive area; nice pool; updated san facs
(2015); level but some rough or uneven grnd; vg."*
€28.50, 14 Mar-13 Nov.   2016

GRIMAUD *10F4* (6.8km E Coastal) *43.28205, 6.58614*
Camping de la Plage, 98 Route National, St Pons-les-
Mûres, 83310 Grimaud 04 94 56 31 15; campingplage
grimaud@wanadoo.fr; www.camping-de-la-plage.fr

🏕️ €2.20 🚶 wc ♿ 🚿 📶 🦋 🍴 🍽️ ℍ 🏊 ⚠️ ⚡ 🏄 sand

Fr St Maxime turn onto D559 sp to St Tropez; site
3km on L on both sides of rd (subway links both
parts). 3*, Lge, pt shd, EHU (4-16A) €4.70-14; gas; adv
bkg req; ccard acc; tennis; CKE. *"Pitches adj beach or in
shd woodland - some sm; site tired but lovely situation
& views compensate; clean facs, refurb 2015; cycle
tracks; site poss flooded after heavy rain; used every
yr for 44 yrs by one CC member (2011); conv for ferry
to St Tropez, rec as beautiful, helpful friendly efficient
staff."* €40.00, 11 Apr-13 Oct.   2019

GRIMAUD *10F4* (7.3km E Coastal) *43.283754, 6.591659*
Camping Les Mures, 2721 route du Littoral 83310,
Grimaud 04 94 56 16 97 or 04 94 56 16 17 (mob);
info@camping-des-mures.com; www.camping-des-
mures.com

🏕️ €3 (htd) 🛒 ♿ 🚿 📶 🍴 🍽️ ℍ 🏊 ⚠️ ⚡ 🏄 adj

Fr St Maxine take coast rd D559 twrds St Tropez.
Site on R after 5km. 4*, Lge, mkd, pt shd, pt sl, terr,
EHU 6-10A; bbq; twin axles; TV; 10% statics; phone;
bus adj; Eng spkn; adv bkg acc; games area; CCI.
*"Excel; gd access rds; site split both sides of rd; beach
pitches avail for extra cost; v friendly staff; gd rest;
ACSI acc."* €59.00, 6 Apr-13 Oct.   2019

GRUISSAN *10F1* (5km NE Coastal) *43.1358, 3.1424*
Camping Les Ayguades, Ave de la Jonque, 11430
Gruissan 04 68 49 81 59; infos@loisirs-vacances-
languedoc.com; www.camping-soleil-mer.com

🏕️ €2.50 🚶 (htd) wc 🛒 ♿ 🚿 📶 🦋 🍴 🍽️ ℍ 🏊 ⚠️ ⚡
🏊 🚣 sand adj

Exit A9 junc 37 onto D168/D32 sp Gruissan. In
10km turn L at island sp Les Ayguades, foll site
sp. 4*, Lge, mkd, hdg, unshd, EHU (6A) inc; TV;
75% statics; Eng spkn; adv bkg acc; ccard acc;
fitness rm; bike hire; sports grnd; CKE. *"Pleasant site;
extensive cycle network, 6 night min stay high ssn."*
€31.00, 20 Mar-8 Nov.   2020

GUDAS *8G3* (2km S Rural) *42.99269, 1.67830*
Camping Mille Fleurs (Naturist), Le Tuillier, 09120
Gudas 05 61 60 77 56; info@camping-millefleurs.
com; www.camping-millefleurs.com

🏕️ €2.25 🚶 wc 🛒 ♿ 🚿 📶 🦋 🍴 🍽️ ℍ 🏊

Do not use SatNav thro Dalou. App Foix on the N20
fr Toulouse foll sp Foix-Tarbes. Pass Camping du lac
on R, cont approx 2.2km, at traff lghts turn L sp D1
Laroque d'Olmes, Lieurac, l'Herm). Foll D1 for 6.5km
until junc D13 (Care req, sharp bend). Turn L sp Col
de Py, Mirepoix, cont past quarry, L fork (sp Gudas,
Varhilles). After 2km sp Millefleurs, le Tuilier, turn L
over bdge. Site in approx 2km bef Gudas.
1*, Sm, hdg, mkd, pt shd, pt sl, terr, EHU (6-10A)
€3.75; bbq; twin axles; phone; Eng spkn; adv bkg rec;
sauna; INF card req. *"Excel, scenic, beautiful, peaceful
site; lovely owners; gd pitches; 2 c'vans for hire; clean
facs; gd base Andorra, Toulouse & Carcassonne; great
touring base."* €29.00, 1 Apr-1 Nov.   2017

"We must tell the Club about that great site we found"

Get your site reports in by mid-August and we'll
do our best to get your updates into the next
edition.

GUEMENE PENFAO *2G4* (1km SE Rural) *47.62575,
-1.81857* **Flower Camping L'Hermitage,** 46 Ave du
Paradis, 44290 Guémené-Penfao 02 40 79 23 48;
camping.hermitage@wanadoo.fr; www.camping
lhermitage.com

🏕️ €2 🚶 wc 🛒 ♿ 🚿 📶 🦋 🍴 🍽️ ℍ 🏊 nr ⚠️ ⚡ 🚣

On D775 fr cent of Guémené-Penfao, dir
Châteaubriant for 500m, turn R, site sp.
3*, Med, hdstg, mkd, pt shd, EHU (6A) €3.50; gas;
bbq; sw nr; TV; 20% statics; phone; Eng spkn; adv bkg
acc; jacuzzi; games rm; waterslide; bike hire; fishing
300m; tennis; canoeing; games area; CKE. *"Gd walking
in area; htd covrd pool adj; site not ready early ssn."*
€22.50, 1 Apr-15 Oct.   2017

GUERANDE *2G3* (3km N Rural) *47.34954, -2.43170*
Camping La Fontaine, Kersavary, Route de St-Molf,
44350 Guérande 02 40 24 96 19 or 06 08 12 80 96
(mob); lafontaine.guerande@orange.fr;
www.camping-lafontaine.com

🏕️ €2 🚶 wc 🛒 ♿ 🚿 📶 🦋 🍴 ℍ nr ⚡ 🏊 nr ⚠️ 🏊 (htd) 🚣

Fr Guérande take N774 N sp La Roche-Bernard; in 1
km, opp windmill, fork L onto D233 sp St-Molf; site
on L in 500m. 3*, Med, hdg, hdstg, mkd, pt shd, EHU
(6A) €4; bbq; twin axles; 10% statics; Eng spkn; adv
bkg rec; games area; CKE. *"Pleasant, peaceful site; lge
pitches; helpful staff; san facs clean & new (2015); gd."*
€24.00, 3 Apr-18 Oct.   2016

FRANCE

GUERANDE *2G3* (7km W Coastal) *47.32856, -2.49907*
Camping Les Chardons Bleus, Blvd de la Grande
Falaise, 44420 La Turballe 02 40 62 80 60; campingles
chardonsbleus@mairielaturballe.fr; www.camping-
laturballe.fr

🏕 €5 🛉🛉 ᵂᶜ ᰔ ᵻ ⬅ 🍽 ⚡ ☂ ♨ 🍴 ♨ ᵻ 🐾 ⛺ 🌊 (htd) 🛶
🏖 sand adj

**Foll D99 to La Turballe. Site well sp fr town cent
along D92.** 3*, Lge, mkd, hdg, unshd, EHU (10A) inc
(poss rev pol, long lead poss req); gas; phone; Eng
spkn; ccard acc; CKE. *"Well-run, well-kept site in
great location; mv service pnt adj; warm welcome; gd,
clean san facs, poss stretched high ssn; ltd EHU when
full; variable opening dates, phone ahead early ssn;
nature reserve adj with bird life; superb beach adj, pt
naturist; walk along beach to pretty La Turballe with
rests; vg modern facs & pool area; pinewoods; gd kids
club for younger children; gd base for cycling, excel."*
€27.00, 1 Mar-29 Sep, A46. 2020

GUERET *7A4* (10km S Rural) *46.10257, 1.83528*
Camp Municipal Le Gué Levard, 5 Rue Gué Levard,
23000 La Chapelle-Taillefert 05 55 51 09 20 or
05 55 52 36 17 (Mairie); www.ot-gueret.fr

🏕 🛉🛉 ᵂᶜ ᰔ ⬅ 🍽 ᵻ 🦋 ⛺

**Take junc 48 fr N145 sp Tulle/Bourganeuf (D33 thro
Guéret); S on D940 fr Guéret, turn off at site sp. Foll
sp thro vill, well sp.** 1*, Sm, hdstg, pt shd, sl, terr, EHU
(16A) €2.50; bbq (sep area); 20% statics; adv bkg acc;
fishing in Rv Gartempe; CKE. *"Attractive, peaceful,
well-kept site hidden away; vg san facs; site yourself,
warden calls 1900; all pitches sl so m'van levelling diff;
gd auberge in vill (clsd most of Jul & Aug); gd walking;
sports facs nr; phone ahead to check open LS; excel
little site."* **€11.00, 1 Apr-1 Nov.** 2016

"I need an on-site restaurant"

We do our best to make sure site information
is correct, but it is always best to check any
must-have facilities are still available or will
be open during your visit.

GUERET *7A4* (1.4km W Rural) *46.16387, 1.85882*
Camp du Plan d'Eau de Courtille (formerly Municipal),
Rue Georges Aullon, 23000 Guéret 05 55 81 92 24

🏕 🐕 🛉🛉 ᵂᶜ ♨ ᰔ ⬅ 🍽 ᵻ ᴹˢᴾ 🦋 ᵻ ♨ nr 🐾 nr ⛺

**Fr W on N145 take D942 to town cent; then take
D914 W; take L turn bef lake sp; site in 1.5km along
lakeside rd with speed humps. Site sp.**
3*, Med, hdg, mkd, pt shd, pt sl, EHU (10A) inc; bbq;
sw; phone; watersports; CKE. *"Pleasant scenery; well-
managed site; beach sand; narr ent to pitches; mkd
walks nrby; pool 1.5km; ramps needed for m'vans; bread
delivered; busy NH."* **€20.00, 1 Apr-30 Sep.** 2018

GUIGNICOURT *3C4* (0.5km SE Urban) *49.43209,
3.97035* **Camping au Bord de l'Aisne (Formaly
Municipal),** 14b Rue des Godins, 02190 Guignicourt
03 23 79 74 58; campingguignicourt@orange.fr;
www.camping-aisne-picardie.fr

🏕 €1.70 🛉🛉 (htd) ᵂᶜ ᰔ ⬅ ᵻ ᴹˢᴾ 🦋 🍽 ᵻ ♨ nr 🐾 nr ⛺
🌊 (covrd, htd)

**Exit A26 junc 14 onto D925 to Guignicourt; after
passing under rlway bdge cont on D925 for 800m;
then turn R at Peugeot g'ge down narr rd to site
(12% descent at ent & ramp). Site sp in vill on rv
bank.** 4*, Med, mkd, hdg, pt shd, EHU (6-10A) inc
(poss rev pol, poss long cable req); bbq; red long stay;
20% statics; phone; train 500m; Eng spkn; adv bkg
acc; ccard acc; fishing; CKE. *"Pretty, well-kept/run,
excel site in beautiful setting on banks of rv; v pretty &
quiet; popular gd NH, conv A26; well-guarded; friendly,
v helpful staff; poss muddy when wet; pleasant town;
excel touring base Reims, Epernay; easy access despite
gradient; excel; v clean, refurbished & modern facs; facs
stretched in high ssn; fair."*
€31.00, 1 Apr-31 Oct, P02. 2019

GUILLESTRE *9D4* (1.8km SW Rural) *44.65854,
6.63836* **Camping La Rochette (formerly
Municipal),** 05600 Guillestre 04 92 45 02
15 or 06 62 17 02 15 (mob); guillestre@
aol.com; www.campingguillestre.com

🏕 🐕 🛉🛉 ᵂᶜ ᰔ ⬅ 🍽 🦋 🍴 ᵻ 🐾 ⛺ 🌊

**Exot N94 onto D902A to Guillestre. In 1km fork R on
side rd at camp sps. Site on L in 1km.** 3*, Lge, mkd, pt
shd, EHU (6-10A) €2.80-3.70; gas; bbq; phone; adv bkg
acc; tennis adj; fishing; games area. *"Spectacular views;
lge pitches; Dutch-owned site; helpful staff; superb
san facs; dir access to rv; public pool adj; conv Queyras
National Park."* **€19.50, 15 May-30 Sep.** 2015

GUILVINEC *2F2* (2.5km W Coastal) *47.80388,
-4.31222* **Camping la Plage,** Chemin des Allemands,
Penmarc'h, 29760 Guilvinec 02 98 58 61 90; info@
yellohvillage-la-plage.com; www.villagelaplage.com

🏕 €6 🛉🛉 ᵂᶜ ♨ ᰔ ⬅ 🍽 ᵻ ᴹˢᴾ 🦋 🍴 🍴 ♨ 🐾 ⛺ 🌊
🌊 (covrd, htd) 🛶 🏖 sand adj

**Fr Quimper, Pont l'Abbé on D785 SW to Plomeur;
turn S onto D57 sp Guilvinec. Bear R on app to town
& v soon after turn R sp Chapelle de Tremor. Foll
site to site in 1.5km.** 4*, Lge, pt shd, EHU (5A) inc;
gas; bbq; 60% statics; adv bkg acc; ccard acc; sauna;
fitness rm; archery; tennis; games rm; waterslide; bike
hire. *"Ideal for families; spacious pitches; no o'fits over
8m high ssn; site rds poss diff lge o'fits; excel touring
base; mkt Tue & Sun."*
€50.00, 12 Apr-14 Sep, B15. 2019

GUINES *3A3* (1km SW Rural) *50.86611, 1.85694*
Camping De La Bien Assise, Route D231 62340
Guînes **03 21 35 20 77; castels@bien-assise.com;**
www.camping-la-bien-assise.com

🐕 €3 (htd) 🚻 ♿ ⚡ 🚿 💧 ✉ 🅿 🛒 🍴 ⑪ 🎱 🏪 ✂
🏊 (covrd, htd) 🎱

Fr Calais or Boulogne, leave A16 at junc 43; foll
D305 then D127 to Guines; cont to junc with D231;
turn R (across S of vill and cont to rndabt) site ent
on L. Fr S (A26 or D943), take D231 to Guines.
5*, Lge, mkd, hdg, pt shd, pt sl, EHU (10A) inc (poss
rev pol); gas; bbq (charcoal, gas); red long stay; twin
axles; TV; 20% statics; Eng spkn; adv bkg req; ccard
acc; bike hire; games rm; horseriding 3km; waterslide;
golf nr; tennis; CKE. *"Pleasant, busy, excel site in grnds
of chateau; well-kept & well-run; gd sized pitches
with easy access; conv ferries - late arr area; pleasant,
cheerful, helpful staff; clean san facs, stretched when
site full; excel rest, clsd in Jan; vg pool complex;
grass pitches, some soft LS & boggy when wet; vet
in Ardres (9km), site will book for you; even if notice
says 'Complete' check for sh stay; mkt Fri; ACSI acc;
v popular NH stop; one san fac block newly refurb
(2016)."* **€36.20, 31 Mar-29 Sep, P05.** **2018**

GUISE *3C4* (0.5km SE Urban) *49.89488, 3.63372*
FFCC Camping de la Vallée de l'Oise, 33 Rue du
Camping, 02120 Guise **03 23 61 14 86**

🐕 🚻 ♿ 🚿 💧 ✉ 🦋 🛒 nr 🏪 ✂

Foll Vervin sp in town & camp clearly sp fr all dirs
in town. 3*, Lge, pt shd, EHU (6-10A) €5.50 (rev pol);
TV; 50% statics; Eng spkn; adv bkg acc; rv fishing adj;
bike hire; games rm; CKE. *"Spacious, beautifully kept,
friendly site; busy w/ends; gd san facs; barrier always
open, warden not always on site; canoe hire adj; if arr
late, pitch & pay next morning; interesting old town; gd
value."* **€19.00, 15 Apr-15 Oct.** **2018**

HAGUENAU *5D3* (2.6km SW Urban) *48.80233, 7.76439*
Camp Municipal Les Pins, 20 Rue de la Piscine,
67500 Haguenau **03 88 73 91 43 or 03 88 93 70 00;**
tourisme@ville-haguenau.fr; www.ville-haguenau.fr

🐕 €1 🚻 (htd) 🆆🅳 ♿ 🚿 💧 ✉ 🦋 🍴 nr ⑪ 🛒 nr 🏪

Fr S on D263, after passing Haguenau town sp turn
L at 2nd set of traff lts (opp Peugeot g'ge). Site sp
fr D263. 1*, Med, mkd, pt shd, terr, EHU (6A) inc; gas;
bbq; phone; bus 500m; Eng spkn; adv bkg acc; CKE.
*"Lge pitches; helpful staff; clean, modern san facs; meals
avail fr warden; grnd firm even after heavy rain; excel;
pleasant town."* **€13.00, 1 May-30 Sep.** **2016**

HAMBYE *1D4* (1.6km N Rural) *48.9600, -1.2600*
Camping aux Champs, 1 Rue de la Ripaudière,
50450 Hambye **02 33 90 06 98; michael.coles@
wanadoo.fr; www.campingauxchamps.com**

🐕 🚻 (htd) 🆆🅳 ♿ 🚿 ✉ 🍴 nr 🛒 nr

Exit A84 junc 38 onto D999 to Percy; then turn L
at town cent rndabt onto D58 to Hambye; at mkt
sq proceed to junc, strt sp Le Guislain, past Mairie;
site on R in 1.5 km on D51. Sm, hdstg, unshd, EHU
(10A) €3; red long stay; Eng spkn; adv bkg req; CKE.
*"Peaceful, well kept CL-type site; friendly, helpful
British owners; adults only; excel, clean san facs;
Hambye Abbey nrby; bell foundry at Villedieu-les-Poêls
worth visit; 1 dog only; conv ferry ports; a must if in
Normandy."* **€20.00, 1 Apr-30 Oct.** **2019**

HARDELOT PLAGE *3A2* (3km NE Urban) *50.64661,
1.62539* **Caravaning du Château d'Hardelot,**
21 Rue Nouvelle, 62360 Condette **03 21 87 59 59;**
contact@camping-caravaning-du-chateau.com;
www.camping-caravaning-du-chateau.com

🐕 🚻 🆆🅳 ♿ 🚿 💧 ✉ 🅼🅿 ✉ 🦋 nr 🏪 ✂ 🏊 sand 3km

Take D901 S fr Boulogne, R turn onto D940 dir Le
Touquet; then R at rndabt on D113 to Condette;
take 2nd turning to Château Camping, R at next
rndabt & site 400m on R. Fr S leave A16 at exit 27
to Neufchâtel-Hardelot, take D940 twd Condette &
turn L at 1st rndabt onto D113, then as above. Not
well sp last 3km. Tight turn into site ent. 3*, Med,
hdg, mkd, pt shd, pt sl, EHU (10A) €4.70 (poss rev pol);
30% statics; Eng spkn; adv bkg rec; horseriding; games
rm; tennis 500m; golf; CKE. *"Lovely, well-run, wooded
site; busy high ssn; vg LS; sm pitches; helpful, friendly
owners; sm multi-gym; clean, modern san facs; tight
access some pitches; conv Calais (site barrier opens
0800)."* **€28.60, 1 Apr-31 Oct.** **2016**

HARDINGHEN *3A3* (0.5km SE Rural) *50.79462,
1.81369* **Camping à la Ferme Les Piloteries,**
Rue de l'Eglise, 62132 Hardinghen **03 21 85 01 85;**
lespiloteries@free.fr; http://lespiloteries.free.fr

🚻 🆆🅳 ♿ ✉ 🦋 🏪

Fr N exit A16 junc 36 at Marquise onto D191 to
Hardinghen; turn R onto D127 (where D191 turns
sharp L); site in 1km (concealed ent). Sm, pt shd, pt
sl, EHU (6A) €2; bbq. *"Vg CL-type site; friendly owner;
lovely site; well looked after; rec; narr ent; gd NH."*
€11.00, 16 Apr-2 Oct. **2017**

HAUTEFORT *7C3* (3km NE Rural) *45.27248, 1.16861*
Camping Belle Vue, La Contie 24390 Boisseuilh
05 53 51 62 71 or 0117 230 2320 (fr UK); cbv@
dordogne-camping.org; www.dordogne-camping.org

🐕 €2 ♿ ⚦ wc ♨ ♿ 🍴 🆕 MP ☂ ♉ 🍴 ⊕ 🅿 🗻

Fr Limoges take D704 and cont until St Agnan. Take
turning for Hautefort and pass supmkt on L and the
Chateau on R. At next x-rds turn L onto D72 and cont
over 3 bdges until La Contie. Site is last hse on R.
Sm, shd, EHU (6A); bbq; twin axles; 25% statics; Eng
spkn; adv bkg acc; CKE. *"Beautiful views of chateau
Hautefort, illuminated at night; excel customer svrs;
breakfast delivered to pitch each morning; excel."*
€23.00, 1 May-30 Sep. 2017

HAUTEFORT *7C3* (4km NE Rural) *45.28081, 1.15917*
Camping La Grenouille, Brégérac, 24390 Hautefort
05 53 50 11 71; info@lagrenouillevacances.com;
www.lagrenouillevacances.com

🐕 ⚦ wc ♨ ♿ 🆕 ☂ ♉ ⊕ 🗻 🏕 🏊

Fr N on D704 at Cherveil-Cubas take D77 dir
Boisseuilh/Teillots. In 4km turn R & in 800m turn
L to site. Fr S on D704 at St Agnan take D62 sp
Hautefort/Badefols d'Ans. Pass 'Vival' (sm shop
on L) in Hautefort & turn L dir Boisseuilh. After 1st
bdge turn L to La Besse & site in 2km. Sm, pt shd, pt
sl, EHU (8A) €3.50; bbq; Eng spkn; adv bkg acc; ice;
CKE. *"Tranquil, scenic, well-kept CL type site; friendly,
helpful, Dutch owners; vg san facs; meals avail; goats,
guinea pigs, chickens in pens on site; gd walking; dogs
free; highly rec."* **€21.50, 22 Apr-15 Oct.** 2016

HAYE DU PUITS, LA *1D4* (6km N Urban) *49.38725,
-1.52755* **FFCC Camp Municipal du Vieux Château,**
Ave de la Division-Leclerc, 50390 St Sauveur-le-Vicomte
02 33 41 79 06; basedeloisirs@sslv.fr; www.ville-saint-
sauveur-le-vicomte.fr

🐕 €1.50 ♿ ♨ ♿ 🆕 ☂ ⊕ nr 🗻 nr 🗻

Fr Cherbourg on N13/D2 site on R after x-ing bdge
at St Sauveur-le-Vicomte, sp. 2*, Med, mkd, pt shd, pt
sl, EHU (10A) €2.40 (poss rev pol); bbq; TV; phone; adv
bkg acc; ccard acc; games area; games rm; tennis 1km;
CKE. *"Excel site in chateau grnds; friendly warden; gd
clean facs; ideal 1st stop fr Cherbourg; office open until
2200 for late arr; barrier clsd 2200-0800; vg auberge
opp; helpful warden; Eng not spkn; sh walk to friendly,
nice town."* **€14.00, 15 May-17 Sep.** 2017

HAYE DU PUITS, LA *1D4* (3km SW Rural) *49.27292,
-1.55896* **Camping La Bucaille,** 50250 Montgardon
02 33 07 46 38; info@labucaille.com; www.labucaille.com

🐕 wc ♨ 🆕 ☂ 🍴 nr ⊕ nr 🗻 nr 🏊 sand 4km

Fr Cherbourg S on N13 & D2 twd St Sauveur-le-
Vicomte, then D900 to La Haye-du-Puits. Fr cent of
La Haye turn onto D136 Rte de Bretteville-sur-Ay
for approx 2km, site sp at L turn, site on L.
Sm, pt shd, pt sl, EHU (10A) €5; bbq; adv bkg acc.
*"Pleasant quiet, 'hide-way' CL-type site; lge grassy
pitches; width restriction 3m; friendly British owners;
ideal for walking; dogs free; excel; peaceful, well kept
with super hosts."* **€17.00, 1 Apr-30 Sep.** 2016

HEMING *6E3* (5km SW Rural) *48.69130, 6.92769*
Camping Les Mouettes, 4 Rue de Diane Capelle,
57142 Gondrexange 03 87 25 06 01; otsi-gondrexange
.pagesperso-orange.fr

🐕 €1.55 ♿ (htd) wc ♨ ♿ 🆕 ☂ ♉ 🍴 nr ⊕ 🗻 nr 🗻

Exit Héming on N4 Strasbourg-Nancy. Foll sp
Gondrexange & site sp. App fr W on D955 turn to
site sp on L about 1km bef Héming.
2*, Lge, mkd, unshd, pt sl, EHU (16A) inc; sw nr;
60% statics; phone; Eng spkn; fishing adj; sailing adj;
bike hire; tennis; CKE. *"Pleasant site by lake; clean,
good facs."* **€18.00, 1 Apr-30 Sep.** 2019

HERBIGNAC *2G3* (0.3km E Rural) *47.44802, -2.31073*
Camp Le Ranrouet, 7 Allee des Pres Blancs, 44410
Herbignac 02 40 15 57 56; campingleranrouet@
orange.fr; www.camping-parc-de-la-briere.com

♿ ⚦ wc ♨ 🆕 ☂ 🍴 nr ⊕ nr 🗻 nr 🗻 🗻 (htd)

Site at intersection D774 & D33 on E edge of vill.
3*, Med, mkd, pt shd, EHU (6A); TV; CKE.
"Immac san facs; gd cent for Guérande."
€18.00, Easter-30 Oct. 2019

HERIC *2G4* (2km W Rural) *47.41329, -1.67050*
Camping La Pindière, La Denais, Route de la Fay-de-
Bretagne, 44810 Héric 06 63 78 57 44; contact@
camping-la-pindiere.com; www.camping-la-
pindiere.com

🔢 🐕 €1.40 ♿ ⚦ wc ♨ ♿ 🆕 MP ☂ ♉ 🍴 ⊕ 🗻 🗻 🗻
🗻 (htd) 🏊

Exit N137 twd Héric at traff lts in town, leave town
& turn W onto D16 (sp Camping). Site on L after
rndabt supmkt, turn at sp Notre Dames-des-Landes.
3*, Med, hdg, mkd, hdstg, pt shd, EHU (6-10A) €3.20-
4.80; gas; bbq (charcoal); twin axles; TV; 80% statics;
phone; Eng spkn; adv bkg rec; ccard acc; sports facs;
horseriding 200m; tennis; CKE. *"Pleasant site; lge,
grass pitches, soft in wet weather; warm welcome;
helpful owners; gd clean san facs; gd NH before St
Malo; gd walks."* **€22.50** 2019

HERISSON *7A4* (0.8km WNW Rural) *46.51055, 2.70576*
Camp Municipal de l'Aumance, Rue de Crochepot,
03190 Hérisson 04 70 06 88 22, 04 70 06 80 45 or
06 63 46 21 49 (mob); www.allier-tourisme.com

♿ ♨ 🆕 ☂ 🗻

Exit A71 junc 9 onto D2144 N; turn R onto D11 dir
Hérisson; immed bef T-junc with D3 turn L at blue
sp (high on L) into Rue de Crochepot; site on R down
hill. NB-Avoid towing thro town. 2*, Med, mkd, pt
shd, EHU (6A) €2.80; phone; games area. *"Delightful
rvside site; idyllic setting; old san facs but gd & clean;
warden calls eves; rec; peaceful and picturesque; easy
walk to vil; lovely site; sm gd supmkt & fuel at Vallons;
rv fishing reserved for campers - permit necessary;
remarkable value; site on 2 levels, higher level better in
wet weather."* **€8.00, 1 Apr-31 Oct.** 2016

For a guide to symbols see the fold out on the rear cover

FRANCE

HESDIN *3B3* (4km SE Rural) *50.35950, 2.07650*
Camping Rural St Ladre, 66 Rue Principale, 62770 St Georges **03 21 04 83 34; bd-martin@wanadoo.fr; http://martinbernard.monsite-orange.fr**

♿ WC ⚊ ♪ ➿

Fr Hesdin SE on D340 for 5.5km. Site on L after St Georges, ent narr lane next cottage on bend. Fr W on D939 or D349 foll sp Frévent, then St Georges. Sp to site poor. Sm, mkd, hdg, pt shd, EHU (5A) €2.40; adv bkg acc; CKE. *"Pleasant, peaceful, CL-type site in orchard; basic facs but clean; welcoming, pleasant owner; conv Channel ports, Agincourt & Crécy; usual agricultural noises; gd rests in Hesdin."* **€9.00, 1 May-30 Sep.** 2017

"That's changed – Should I let the Club know?"

If you find something on site that's different from the site entry, fill in a report and let us know. See camc.com/europereport.

HIRSON *3C4* (10km N Rural) *50.00585, 4.06195*
FFCC Camping Les Etangs des Moines, 100 rue des Etangs, 59610 Fourmies **03 27 63 05 26; contact@etangs-des-moines.fr**

🐕 €1 ♿ WC ⚊ ⚐ ♿ 🖥 ♪ MP 🍴 🛒 🖳 nr ⚠ 🚣 (htd)

Fr D1043 Hirson by-pass head N on D963 to Anor. Turn L onto D156 dir Fourmies, site sp on R on ent town. Site also well sp off D42 & thro Fourmies. 3*, Med, hdg, hdstg, pt shd, EHU (10A) €3.30; bbq; 80% statics; Eng spkn; CKE. *"Textile & eco museum in town; shwrs run down, other facs gd; vg."* **€15.00, 1 Apr-31 Oct.** 2019

HONFLEUR *3C1* (6km S Rural) *49.40083, 0.30638*
Camping Domaine Catinière, 910 Route de la Morelle, 27210 Fiquefleur-Equainville **02 32 57 63 51; info@camping-catiniere.com; www.camping-catiniere.com**

🐕 €2 ♿ WC ⚊ ♿ 🖥 ♪ 🍴 🛒 🖳 ⚠ ♪ 🚣 (htd)

Fr A29/Pont de Normandie (toll) bdge exit junc 3 sp Le Mans, pass under m'way onto D580/D180. In 3km go strt on at rndabt & in 100m bear R onto D22 dir Beuzeville; site sp on R in 500m. Do not app fr Beuzeville, c'vans not allowed in vill. 3*, Sm, hdg, mkd, pt shd, EHU (4A) inc or (8-13A) €1-1.50 (long lead poss req, poss rev pol); bbq; TV; 15% statics; Eng spkn; adv bkg rec; ccard acc; rv fishing; waterslide; games rm; CKE. *"Attractive, well-kept, busy site; pleasant, helpful, friendly owners; clean but dated unisex san facs, stretched high ssn & ltd LS; some pitches quite sm; unfenced stream on far boundary; gd touring base & NH; gd walks; easy parking for m'vans nr town; 20 mins to Le Havre ferry via Normandy bdge; no o'fits over 8.50m; conv A13; highly rec; lovely pool; ACSI acc."* **€32.00, 1 Apr-15 Oct, N16.** 2019

HONFLEUR *3C1* (3.5km SW Rural) *49.39777, 0.20861*
Camping La Briquerie, 14600 Equemauville **02 31 89 28 32; info@campinglabriquerie.com; www.campinglabriquerie.com**

🐕 €3 ♿ WC ⚊ ♿ ⚐ 🖥 ♪ MP 🅿 🍴 🍴 🖳 nr ⚠ ♪ 🚿 (htd) ⛱ sand 2.5km

Fr Honfleur head S on D579A. At rndabt cont strt onto D62, site on R. Fr S take D579 dir Honfleur Cent. Pass water tower n turn L at Intermarché rndabt, site on R in 300m. 5*, Lge, hdg, pt shd, EHU (5-10A) €4-5 (poss rev pol); gas; bbq; TV; 50% statics; bus nr; Eng spkn; adv bkg req; games rm; tennis 500m; horseriding 500m; fitness rm; waterslide; CKE. *"Lge pitches; staff helpful; gd clean san facs; late/early ferry arr; local vets geared up for dog inspections, etc; gd; cash only."* **€34.70, 1 Apr-30 Sep.** 2016

HONFLEUR *3C1* (1km NW Coastal) *49.42445, 0.22753* **Camping du Phare,** Blvd Charles V, 14600 Honfleur **02 98 83 45 06; camping.du.phare@orange.fr; www.camping-du-phare.com**

🐕 €3 ♿ WC ⚊ ♿ ♪ MP 🍴 🅿 nr 🛒 🖳 nr ⚠ ⛱ sand 100m

Fr N fr Pont de Normandie on D929 take D144; at ent to Honfleur keep harbour in R; turn R onto D513 sp Trouville-sur-Mer & Deauville (avoid town cent); fork L past old lighthouse to site entry thro parking area. Or fr E on D180; foll sp 'Cent Ville' then Vieux Bassin dir Trouville; at rectangular rndabt with fountain turn R sp Deauville & Trouville, then as above. 2*, Med, hdg, pt shd, EHU (16A) inc; gas; bbq; 10% statics; phone; Eng spkn; fishing; CKE. *"Gd clean site in excel location; conv NH Le Havre ferry; busy high ssn, rec arr early; friendly owners; san facs basic & tired but clean, ltd LS; barrier clsd 2200-0700; m'van pitches narr & adj busy rd; some soft, sandy pitches; easy walk to town/harbour; sep m'van Aire de Service nr harbour; new disabled san facs (2015); conv Honfleur by foot; nice site; own san facs rec."* **€23.00, 1 Apr-30 Sep.** 2017

HOULGATE *3D1* (1km E Coastal) *49.29390, -0.06820*
Camping La Vallée, 88 Rue de la Vallée, 14510 Houlgate **02 31 24 40 69; camping.lavallee@wanadoo.fr; www.campinglavallee.com**

🐕 €5 ♿ (htd) WC ⚊ ♿ 🖥 ♪ MP 🍴 🅿 🛒 🖳 ⚠ ♪ 🚣 (covrd, htd) 🛁 ⛱ sand 900m

Exit junc 29 or 29a fr A13 onto D45 to Houlgate. Or fr Deauville take D513 W. Bef Houlgate sp, turn L & foll sp to site. 5*, Lge, mkd, hdg, pt shd, pt sl, terr, serviced pitches; EHU (6A) inc; gas; TV; 85% statics; Eng spkn; adv bkg req; ccard acc; games rm; bike hire; waterslide; lake fishing 2km; tennis; golf 1km; CKE. *"Superb, busy site; friendly recep; clean san facs; some pitches poss sm for lge o'fits; sep area m'vans; 1,5km walk to sandy beach and town; bkg fee; ACSI acc; fam/child orientated site."* **€47.00, 1 Apr-1 Nov.** 2019

HOURTIN *7C1* (10km W Coastal) *45.22296, -1.16472*
Camping La Côte d'Argent, Rue de la Côte d'Argent,
33990 Hourtin-Plage **05 56 09 10 25; info@cca33.com;
www.cca33.com**

€5.50 (covrd, htd) sand 300m

On D1215 at Lesparre-Médoc take D3 Hourtin,
D101 to Hourtin-Plage, site sp. 4*, V lge, mkd, shd,
pt sl, terr, EHU (10A) inc; bbq; sw nr; red long stay;
30% statics; phone; Eng spkn; adv bkg acc; ccard
acc; bike hire; watersports; horseriding; fishing 4km;
games area; ice; waterslide; games rm; jacuzzi;
CKE. "Pleasant, peaceful site in pine trees & dunes;
poss steel pegs req; conv Médoc region chateaux
& vineyards; ideal for surfers & beach lovers."
€53.00, 14 May-18 Sep. 2017

See advertisement

HUELGOAT *2E2* (3km E Rural) *48.36275, -3.71532*
FFCC Camping La Rivière d'Argent, La Coudraie,
29690 Huelgoat **02 98 99 72 50; contact@
larivieredargent.com; www.larivieredargent.com**

€2.30 nr (covrd, htd, indoor)

Sp fr town cent on D769A sp Poullaouen & Carhaix.
2*, Med, mkd, hdg, shd, EHU (6-10A) €3.70; red
long stay; adv bkg acc; tennis. "Lovely wooded site
on rv bank; some rvside pitches; gd walks with maps
provided; san facs updated (2017) well maintained, v
clean; gd unisex facs; site self; poss rev pol; excel dog
walks fr site; v friendly & helpful new owners (2018);
excel." **€22.10, 1 Apr-30 Sep.** 2019

HYERES *10F3* (9km S Coastal) *43.02980, 6.15490*
Camping La Tour Fondue, Ave des Arbanais, 83400
Giens **04 94 58 22 86; info@camping-latourfondue.
com; www.camping-latourfondue.com**

€3 adj

D97 fr Hyères, site sp. Med, hdg, pt shd, pt sl, terr,
EHU (6A) €4.70; 10% statics; Eng spkn; adv bkg
acc; ccard acc; games area. "Pleasant, sister site
of Camping Presqu'île de Giens with easier access;
sm pitches; no dogs on beach; only water point at
'Sanitaires' (by recep); superb new san facs (2014)."
€36.00, 23 Mar-3 Nov. 2019

Make sure you check any essential information with the site before you travel

ILE BOUCHARD, L' *4H1* (0.5km N Urban) *47.12166, 0.42857* **Camping Les Bords de Vienne,** 4 Allée du Camping, 37220 L'Ile-Bouchard 02 47 95 23 59; info@campingbordsdevienne.com; www.camping bordsdevienne.com

🛉 €1.50 ‼ WD ♨ ᵬ ♿ 🖥 ⋮ 🦋 ☂ nr ⛰ 🛝

On N bank of Rv Vienne 100m E of rd bdge nr junc of D757 & D760. Fr E, turn L bet supmkt & pharmacy. 3*, Med, mkd, pt shd, pt sl, EHU (6-16A) €3.50; gas; sw nr; red long stay; 10% statics; Eng spkn; adv bkg acc; ccard acc; tennis 500m; CKE. *"Lovely, clean rvside site; attractive location; poss travellers; conv Loire chateaux."* **€28.00, 15 Mar-25 Oct.** 2019

> ## "We must tell the Club about that great site we found"
>
> Get your site reports in by mid-August and we'll do our best to get your updates into the next edition.

ILLIERS COMBRAY *4E2* (2km SW Rural) *48.28667, 1.22697* **FLOWER Camping Le Bois Fleuri,** Route de Brou, 28120 Illiers-Combray 02 37 24 03 04; infos@camping-chartres.com; www.camping-chartres.com or www.flowercampings.com

🛉 €4 ⛺ (htd) WD ♨ ᵬ ♿ 🖥 ⋮ 🦋 ⓨ ☂ nr ᵬ ☂ nr ⛰ ✎ 🛝

S on D921 fr Illiers for 2km twd Brou. Site on L. 3*, Med, hdg, hdstg, pt shd, serviced pitches; EHU (6A) €3.50; gas; 30% statics; adv bkg acc; fishing adj; games area; CKE. *"Many pitches wooded & with flowers, popular NH; excel san facs; ltd water/EHU; htd pool 200m; uneven grnd makes access diff; gd security; excel cycle path to vill."* **€23.00, 1 Apr-31 Oct.** 2018

INGRANDES *4H2* (1km N Rural) *46.88700, 0.58800* **Camping Le Petit Trianon de St Ustre,** 1 Rue du Moulin de St Ustre, 86220 Ingrandes-sur-Vienne 05 49 02 61 47; contact@domaine-petit-trianon.com; www.petit-trianon.com

🛉 €3 ‼ WD ♨ ᵬ ♿ 🖥 ⋮ MSP 🦋 🌐 ⓨ Ⓗ ᵬ ☂ ⛰ ✎
🏊 (htd) 🛝

Leave A10/E5 at Châtellerault Nord exit 26 & foll sp Tours. Cross rv heading N on D910 twd Tours & Dangé-St Romain. At 2nd traff lts in Ingrandes (by church), turn R. Cross rlwy line & turn L at site sp in 300m. After 1.5km turn R at site sp, site at top of hill. NB Site ent narr, poss diff lge o'fits. 4*, Med, mkd, pt shd, pt sl, EHU (10A) inc; gas; bbq; TV; Eng spkn; adv bkg acc; ccard acc; horseriding 1km; rv fishing 3km; games rm; tennis 1.5km; bike hire; games area; CKE. *"Lovely site in chateau grnds; charming old buildings; gd sized pitches; friendly, helpful staff; excel facs."* **€38.85, 6 Apr-24 Sep, L07.** 2019

ISIGNY SUR MER *1D4* (0.5km NW Rural) *49.31872, -1.10825* **Camping Le Fanal,** Rue du Fanal, 14230 Isigny-sur-Mer 02 31 21 33 20; info@camping-lefanal.com; http://www.camping-normandie-fanal.fr

🛉 €5 ‼ WD ♨ ᵬ ♿ 🖥 ⋮ MSP 🦋 🌐 ⓨ Ⓣ Ⓗ ᵬ ☂ ⛰ ✎
🏊 (htd, indoor) 🛝

Fr N13 exit into Isigny, site immed N of town. Foll sp to 'Stade' in town, (just after sq & church on narr rd just bef R turn). 4*, Med, hdg, mkd, pt shd, EHU (16A) inc (long cable poss req); TV; 50% statics; phone; adv bkg acc; ccard acc; games rm; horseriding; tennis; games area; lake fishing adj; CKE. *"Friendly staff; aqua park; poss boggy in wet weather; vg site."* **€30.50, 1 Apr-30 Sep.** 2020

ISLE JOURDAIN, L' *8F3* (0.5km NW Urban) *43.61569, 1.07839* **Camping Municipal du Pont Tourné,** 32600 L'Isle Jourdain 05 62 07 25 44

🛉 ‼ WD ♨ ᵬ ⋮ MSP 🦋

Exit N124 to town cent. Site well sp. Med, mkd, shd, EHU (10A); bbq; adv bkg acc; CCI. *"Sports ctr adj to site; shop nr; vg; security barrier; excel Sat mkt; wifi avail at TO; vg walking & cycling; lakes next to site; v relaxing; hg rec."* **€12.80, 6 Jul-1 Sep.** 2017

ISLE SUR LA SORGUE, L' *10E2* (6.5km E Rural) *43.91087, 5.10665* **Camping La Coutelière,** Route de Fontaine-de-Vaucluse, 84800 Lagnes 04 90 20 33 97; info@camping-lacouteliere.com; www.camping-lacouteliere.com

🛉 €4.50 ‼ ♨ ᵬ ♿ 🖥 ⋮ 🦋 ⓨ Ⓗ ᵬ ⛰ ✎ 🏊

Leave L'Isle-sur-la-Sorgue by D900 dir Apt, fork L after 2km sp Fontaine-de-Vaucluse. Site on L on D24 bef ent Fontaine. 3*, Med, hdg, shd, EHU (10A) €4.40; 40% statics; phone; Eng spkn; adv bkg acc; canoeing nr; tennis; CKE. *"Attractive, busy site by rv; walking/cycling on canal towpath; 2km easy cycle ride to Fontaine; ltd san facs LS; poss unkept LS; lovely area; gd."* **€32.00, 1 Apr-10 Oct.** 2015

> ## "I need an on-site restaurant"
>
> We do our best to make sure site information is correct, but it is always best to check any must-have facilities are still available or will be open during your visit.

ISLE SUR LE DOUBS, L' *6G2* (0.4km N Rural) *47.45288, 6.58338* **Camping Les Lûmes,** 10 Rue des Lûmes, 25250 L'Isle-sur-le-Doubs 03 81 92 73 05 or 06 85 42 97 81; contact@les-lumes.com; www.les-lumes.com

🛉 €1.20 ‼ WD ♨ ⋮ ☂ ⛰

Well sp fr town edge on D683 bef rv bdge. 3*, Med, pt shd, EHU (10A) €4 (long lead req & poss rev pol; sw; 20% statics; Eng spkn; adv bkg acc; CKE. *"Busy site; san facs need upgrade & up steps; gd."* **€13.50, 1 May-30 Sep.** 2018

FRANCE

ISPAGNAC *9D1* (1km W Rural) *44.37232, 3.53035*
FFCC Camp Municipal Le Pré Morjal, 48320 Ispagnac
04 66 45 43 57; lepremorjal@gmail.com;
www.campingdupremorjal.com

🏕 €1.20 ♀♀(htd) [WD] ♨ ♿ 🚽 ♨ / ⊞ 🦋 ♈ 🛒 Ⓗ 🛒 nr ♨ 🏔 🛶

On D907B 500m W of town, turn L off D907B
& then 200m on R, sp. 3*, Med, hdg, pt shd, EHU
(10-16A) €3; bbq; sw nr; TV; games area; games rm.
"Lovely family site; gd sized pitches on rocky base,
poss muddy when wet; pool 50m inc; friendly staff; gd
rvside walks; vg base for Tarn & Joute Gorges; early
ssn poss unkempt & irreg cleaning of san facs (2010)."
€23.50, 1 Apr-31 Oct.   2019

ISSOIRE *9B1* (3km E Rural) *45.55113, 3.27423*
FFCC Camp Municipal du Mas, Ave du Dr Bienfait,
63500 Issoire **06 09 80 52 63 or 04 73 89 03 59 or
04 73 89 03 54 (LS); camping-mas@wanadoo.fr;**
www.camping-issoire.com

🏕 €0.70 ♀♀(htd) [WD] ♨ ♿ 🚽 ♨ / ⊞ [MP] 🦋 ♈ 🍷 nr Ⓗ nr 🛒
🛒 nr 🏔

Fr Clermont-Ferrand S on A75/E11 take exit 12 sp
Issoire; turn L over a'route sp Orbeil; at rndabt, take
1st exit & foll site sp. 3*, Med, hdg, mkd, pt shd, pt
sl, serviced pitches; EHU (10-13A) inc; bbq (elec, gas);
red long stay; TV; 5% statics; phone; Eng spkn; adv
bkg rec; ccard acc; fishing adj; tennis 500m; boule;
ten pin bowling; CKE. "Lovely, well-kept, basic site in
park-like location; lge pitches; helpful warden; new,
modern san facs; site poss boggy after rain; conv A75;
excel touring base or NH; easy cycle rte to Issoire; vg."
€19.90, 1 Apr-3 Nov.   2019

ISSOIRE *9B1* (11km S Rural) *45.47373, 3.27161*
Camping Les Loges, 63340 Nonette **04 73 71 65 82;**
campingnonette@lesloges.com; www.lesloges.com

🏕 €3 ♀♀ [WD] ♨ 🚽 ♨ / ♈ 🍷 Ⓗ 🛒 🏔 🛶 (htd)

Exit 17 fr A75 onto D214 sp Le Breuil, dir Nonette.
Turn L in 2km, cross rv & turn L to site. Site perched
on conical hill. Steep app. 3*, Med, hdg, mkd, pt shd,
EHU (10A) €3.50; gas; bbq; sw nr; TV; 30% statics; adv
bkg acc; sports facs; volleyball; pétanque; table tennis;
games area; bouncy castle; games rm; fishing adj;
CKE. "Friendly site; conv Massif Cent & A75; gd NH."
€21.00, 30 Mar-30 Sep.   2020

ISSOUDUN *4H3* (3km N Rural) *46.96361, 1.99011*
Camp Municipal Les Taupeaux, 37 Route de Reuilly,
36100 Issoudun **02 54 03 13 46 or 02 54 21 74 02;**
tourisme@issoudun.fr; www.issoudun.fr

🏕 ♀♀ 🚽 / 🦋 🏔

Fr Bourges SW on N151, site sp fr Issoudun on D16
nr Carrefour supmkt. Sm, hdg, mkd, pt shd, EHU
€3.70. "Pleasant site off RR; mv service pnt adj; conv
A71 & N151." €11.00, 15 May-15 Sep.   2016

JARD SUR MER *7A1* (2km NE Rural) *46.42624, -1.56564*
Camping La Mouette Cendrée, Les Malécots, 85520
St Vincent-sur-Jard **02 51 33 59 04; camping.mc@
orange.fr; www.mouettecendree.com**

🏕 €3 [WD] ♨ ♿ 🚽 / ♈ 🛒 nr 🏔 🛶 🛶 🏊 sand 2km

Fr Les Sables-d'Olonne take D949 SE to Talmont-
St-Hilaire; then take D21 to Jard-sur-Mer; at rndabt
stay on D21 (taking 2nd exit dir La Tranche-sur-Mer
& Maison de- Clemanceau); in 500m turn L onto
D19 sp St Hilaire-la-Forêt & foll site sps. Site on L in
700m. 3*, Med, hdg, mkd, pt shd, EHU (10A) inc; bbq
(elec, gas); 30% statics; Eng spkn; adv bkg acc; ccard
acc; golf 10km; waterslide; windsurfing 2km; fishing;
horseriding 500m; bike hire; games rm; CKE. "Busy site
high ssn; gd pitches; welcoming, helpful owners; san
facs poss stretched when site full; no o'fits over 7.5m
high ssn; vg pool; gd woodland walks & cycle rtes nr;
mkt Mon." €27.50, 1 Apr-30 Sept, A20.   2018

JARD SUR MER *7A1* (2km SE Coastal) *46.41980, -1.52580*
Camping La Bolée d'Air, Route du Bouil, Route de
Longeville, 85520 St Vincent-sur-Jard **02 51 90 36 05
or 02 51 33 05 05; info@chadotel.com;**
www.chadotel.com

🏕 €3.90 ♀♀(htd) [WD] ♨ ♿ 🚽 ♨ / ♈ 🍷 🛒 🏔 🛶
🏊 (covrd, htd) 🛶 sand 900m

Fr A11 junc 14 dir Angers. Take N160 to La Roche-
sur-Yon & then D747 dir La Tranche-sur-Mer to
Moutier-les-Mauxfaits. At Moutiers take D19 to
St Hilaire-la-Forêt & then L to St Vincent-sur-Jard. In
St Vincent turn L by church sp Longeville-sur-Mer,
site on R in 1km. 4*, Lge, mkd, hdg, pt shd, serviced
pitches; EHU (10A) inc; gas; bbq (charcoal, gas); red
long stay; TV; 25% statics; Eng spkn; adv bkg acc;
ccard acc; sauna; bike hire; games rm; waterslide;
jacuzzi; tennis; CKE. "Popular, v busy site high ssn; mkt
Sun; no o'fits over 8m; whirlpool; access some pitches
poss diff lge o'fits; excel."
€39.00, 1 Apr-24 Sep, A31.   2018

JAULNY *5D2* (0.5km S Rural) *48.96578, 5.88524*
Camping La Pelouse, Chemin de Fey, 54470 Jaulny
03 83 81 91 67; info@campingdelapelouse.com;
www.campingdelapelouse.com

🏕 €2 ♀♀ 🚽 ♨ / 🍷 Ⓗ 🏔 🛶 (htd)

SW fr Metz on D657, cross rv at Corny-sur-Moselle
onto D6/D1; in 1.5km turn R onto D952 dir Waville
& Thiaucourt-Regniéville; in 6km turn L onto D28
dir Thiaucourt-Regniéville; cont on D28 to Jaulny;
site sp to L in Jaulny. 3*, Med, pt shd, sl, EHU (6A)
€4; bbq; sw nr; TV; 80% statics; adv bkg acc; fishing;
volleyball; table tennis; CKE. "Vg site; friendly owner
and staff; basic san facs, poss stretched high ssn;
no fresh or waste water facs for m'vans; conv NH."
€20.60, 1 Apr-30 Sep.   2020

JAUNAY CLAN *4H1 (7km NE Rural) 46.72015, 0.45982*
Camping Lac de St Cyr, 86130 St Cyr **05 49 62 57 22;**
contact@campinglacdesaintcyr.com; www.camping
lacdesaintcyr.com

🐕 €3 [icons]

Fr A10 take Châtellerault Sud exit & take D910
dir Poitiers; at Beaumont turn L at traff lts for
St Cyr; foll camp sp in leisure complex (Parc
Loisirs) by lakeside - R turn for camping. Or fr S
take Futuroscope exit to D910. 4*, Lge, mkd, hdg,
pt shd, pt sl, serviced pitches; EHU (10A) inc (poss
rev pol); gas; bbq; sw; red long stay; TV; 15% statics;
Eng spkn; adv bkg acc; ccard acc; games area; boat
hire; golf adj; watersports; games rm; fishing; sailing;
canoeing; tennis; fitness rm; bike hire; CKE. *"Excel,
well-kept site in leisure complex; lovely setting by lake;
gd sized pitches; helpful recep; no o'fits over 8m; gd,
clean san facs, poss stretched high ssn; gd rest; some
pitches poss diff lge o'fits; rec long o'fits unhitch at
barrier due R-angle turn at barrier - poss diff long o'fits;
Futuroscope approx 13km; highly rec; excel site; gd size
pitches; friendly helpful staff."*
€33.00, 30 Mar-30 Sep, L09. 2017

JAUNAY CLAN *4H1 (2km SE Urban) 46.66401, 0.39466*
Kawan Village Le Futuriste, Rue du Château, 86130
St Georges-les-Baillargeaux **05 49 52 47 52; camping-
le-futuriste@wanadoo.fr; www.camping-le-
futuriste.fr**

12 🐕 €2.50 (htd) [icons] (covrd, htd)

On A10 fr N or S, take Futuroscope exit 28; fr toll
booth at 1st rndabt take 2nd exit. Thro tech park
twd St Georges. At rndabt under D910 take slip rd
N onto D910. After 150m exit D910 onto D20, foll
sp. At 1st rndabt bear R, over rlwy, cross sm rv &
up hill, site on R. 4*, Med, mkd, hdg, pt shd, serviced
pitches; EHU (6A) inc (check earth & poss rev pol); gas;
bbq; TV; 10% statics; Eng spkn; adv bkg acc; ccard
acc; games area; games rm; lake fishing; waterslide;
CKE. *"Lovely, busy, secure site; well-kept; friendly,
helpful family owners; vg clean facs, ltd LS - facs block
clsd 2200-0700; vg pool; vg for families; hypmkt 2km;
ideal touring base for Poitiers & Futuroscope (tickets fr
recep); vg value, espec in winter; conv a'route; excel."*
€33.00 2017

JAUNAY CLAN *4H1 (5km SE Rural) 46.65464,
0.37786* **Camp Municipal Parc des Ecluzelles,**
Rue Leclanché, 86360 Chasseneuil-du-Poitou
**05 49 62 58 85 or 05 49 52 77 19 (LS); maire@
mairie-chasseneuildupoitou.fr; www.ville-
chasseneuil-du-poitou.fr**

🐕 [icons] nr

Fr A10 or D910 N or Poitiers take Futuroscope exit
28/18. Take Chasseneuil rd, sp in town to site.
2*, Sm, mkd, hdstg, pt shd, EHU (8A) inc; bbq.
*"Vg, clean site; lge pitches; conv Futuroscope;
immac; htd pool adj inc; v simple site with the vg
san facs, helpful staff; gd bus service into the city."*
€19.50, 11 Apr-27 Sep. 2015

JOIGNY *4F4 (8km E Urban) 47.955286, 3.507431*
Camping Les Confluents, Allée Léo Lagrange, 89400
Migennes **03 86 80 94 55; contact@les-confluents.com;
www.les-confluents.com**

🐕 €1 (htd) [icons]

A6 exit at junc 19 Auxerre Nord onto N6 & foll sp to
Migennes & site, well sp. 3*, Med, hdstg, mkd, hdg, pt
shd, EHU (6-10A) €3.50-4.90; gas; bbq; red long stay;
TV; 8% statics; phone; bus 10 mins; adv bkg acc; ccard
acc; bike hire; watersports 300m; games area; canoe
hire; volleyball; ping pong; bowling green; library; CKE.
*"Friendly, family-run, clean site nr canal & indust area;
no twin axles; medieval castle, wine cellars, potteries
nrby; walking dist to Migennes; mkt Thurs; excel."*
€24.00, 28 Mar-1 Nov. 2020

JOIGNY *4F4 (2km W Rural) 47.98143, 3.37439*
FFCC Camp Municipal, 68 Quai d'Epizy, 89300 Joigny
**03 86 62 07 55; camping.joigny@orange.fr;
www.ville-joigny.fr/index.php**

[icons] nr [icons] nr

Fr A6 exit junc 18 or 19 to Joigny cent. Fr cent,
over brdg, turn L onto D959; turn R in filter lane
at traff lts. Foll sp to site. 2*, Sm, hdg, hdstg,
pt shd, EHU (10A) inc; sw nr; fishing adj; tennis;
horseriding; CKE. *"V busy site; liable to flood in wet
weather; v helpful warden; pool 4km; interesting
town; v modern clean san facs; quiet in May; some
sm pitches; v helpful warden; local wine avail to buy."*
€13.40, 1 May-30 Sep. 2018

JONZAC *7B2 (4km SW Rural) 45.42916, -0.44833*
FFCC Camping Les Castors, 8 Rue Clavelaud, St Simon
de Bordes, 17500 Jonzac **05 46 48 25 65; camping-
les-castors@wanadoo.fr; www.campingcastors.com**

🐕 €1.60 [icons] (covrd)

Fr Jonzac take D19 S twds Montendre, after approx
2km, immed after ring rd rndabt, turn R into minor
rd. Site ent adj. 4*, Med, hdg, hdstg, pt shd, EHU
(6-10A) €4.20-4.90; sw nr; TV; 50% statics; CKE.
*"Peaceful, friendly, well-maintained site; gd facs;
excel pool; gd; ent & exit gate can be diff for c'vans."*
€17.60, 15 Mar-30 Oct. 2015

JOSSELIN *2F3 (1.5km W Rural) 47.95230, -2.57338*
Domaine de Kerelly, Le bas de la lande, 56120 Guégon
**02 97 22 22 20 or 06 27 57 22 79 (mob); domaine
dekerelly@orange.fr; www.camping-josselin.com**

🐕 [icons] nr [icons]

Exit N24 by-pass W of town sp Guégon; foll sp 1km;
do not attempt to cross Josselin cent fr E to W. Site
on D724 just S of Rv Oust (canal).
3*, Med, hdg, pt shd, terr, EHU (6-10A) €3.80-4.50;
bbq; TV; phone; Eng spkn; adv bkg acc; ccard acc; bike
hire; CKE. *"Vg, clean san facs; site rds steep; pleasant
walks; poss diff if wet; walk to Josselin, chateau & old
houses; gd cycling; family run; gd food; mini golf."*
€20.00, 1 Apr-31 Oct. 2018

JUMIEGES *3C2* (1km E Rural) *49.43490, 0.82970*
Camping de la Forêt, Rue Mainberte, 76480 Jumièges
02 35 37 93 43; info@campinglaforet.com;
www.campinglaforet.com

🐕 ♟️ (htd) WD ♨️ 🛒 ♿ 🖥️ ⏳ MSP 🦋 👘 ⓗ nr 🔔 ▦ 🏊 (htd) 🗒️

Exit A13 junc 25 onto D313/D490 N to Pont de
Brotonne. Cross Pont de Brotonne & immed turn R
onto D982 sp Le Trait. Cont thro town & in 1km turn
R onto D143 sp Yainville & Jumièges. In Jumièges
turn L at x-rds after cemetary & church, site on R
in 1km. NB M'vans under 3.5t & 3m height can take
ferry fr Port Jumièges - if towing do not use sat nav
dirs. 4*, Med, mkd, hdg, pt shd, EHU (10A) €5 (poss rev
pol); gas; bbq; TV; 30% statics; phone; bus to Rouen;
adv bkg acc; ccard acc; watersports; bike hire; games
rm; fishing; tennis; games area. *"Nice site, well-situated
in National Park; busy; some sm pitches; gd, clean san
facs but poss stretched high ssn; interesting vill; conv
Paris & Giverny; no o'fits over 7m high ssn; gd walking,
cycling; ferries across Rv Seine; gd for dogs; children
loved it."* €29.00, 1 Apr-31 Oct, N15. **2017**

KAYSERSBERG *6F3* (1km NW Rural) *48.14899, 7.25405*
Camping Municipal de Kayserberg, Rue des Acacias,
68240 Kaysersberg 03 89 47 14 47 or 03 89 78 11 11
(Mairie); camping@villekaysersberg.fr;
www.camping-kaysersberg.com

🐕 €2 ♟️ WD ♨️ 🛒 ♿ 🖥️ 🦋 👘 🔔 nr ▦

Fr A35/N83 exit junc 23 onto D4 sp Sigolsheim &
Kaysersberg; bear L onto N415 bypass dir St Dié;
site sp 100m past junc with D28. Or SE fr St Dié on
N415 over Col du Bonhomme; turn L into Rue des
Acacias just bef junc with D28. 4*, Med, hdg, mkd,
pt shd, EHU (8-13A) inc (may need cable); gas; TV;
fishing adj; tennis adj. *"Excel, well-kept, busy site; rec
arr early high ssn; no dogs Jul/Aug; many gd sized
pitches; friendly staff; clean san facs; rv walk to lovely
town, birth place Albert Schweitzer; bread delivery;
many mkd walks/cycle rts; Le Linge WWI battle grnd nr
Orbey; excel site; if arr when clsd, choose pitch nbr bef
registering; recep clsd 12-14pm, no access to site at
this time."* €18.60, 1 Apr-30 Sep. **2019**

KAYSERSBERG *6F3* (7km NW Rural) *48.18148,
7.18449* **Camping Les Verts Bois,** 3 Rue de la Fonderie,
68240 Fréland 03 89 47 57 25 or 06 81 71 89 38 (mob);
gildas.douault@sfr.fr; www.camping-lesvertsbois.com

🐕 €0.70 ♟️ (htd) WD ♨️ 🖥️ 🦋 👘 ⓗ 🔔 nr

Sp off N415 Colmar/St Dié rd bet Lapoutroie &
Kaysersberg. Site approx 5km after turn fr main
rd on D11 at far end of vill. Turn L into rd to site
when D11 doubles back on itself. 2*, Sm, pt shd, pt
sl, terr, EHU (6-10A) €2.70-3.20; gas; bbq; Eng spkn;
adv bkg acc; ccard acc; CKE. *"Lovely site in beautiful,
peaceful setting adj rv; friendly welcome; excel;
fishing & bird watching; cheese farms 2 miles away; a
must for cheese lovers; v helpful owners; excel rest."*
€19.00, 1 Apr-31 Oct. **2019**

KRUTH *6F3* (2km N Rural) *47.94355, 6.95418*
Camping du Schlossberg, 19 rue du Bourbach, 68820
Kruth 03 89 82 26 76; camping@schlossberg.fr;
www.schlossberg.fr

🐕 ♟️ WD ♨️ 🛒 ♿ 🖥️ 🦋 👘 ⓗ 🍴 🔔 ▦

Fr N66 turn N on D13 for Fellering and Kruth.
Leaving Kruth twd Wildenstein, turn L at camping
sp. Foll rd round and turn R bef no entry sp.
3*, Lge, mkd, pt shd, pt sl, EHU (6A) €3; 20% statics;
phone; Eng spkn; adv bkg acc; games area; games
rm; CKE. *"Boules & quoytes on site; Go Ape 2km;
lake with peddleoes; walking; castle ruins; excel."*
€17.00, 1 Apr-7 Oct. **2015**

LABENNE *8E1* (4km S Rural) *43.56470, -1.45240*
Camping du Lac, 518 Rue de Janin, 40440 Ondres
05 59 45 28 45 or 06 80 26 91 51 (mob); contact@
camping-du-lac.fr; www.camping-du-lac.fr

🐕 €5 ♟️ (htd) WD ♨️ 🛒 ♿ 🖥️ 🦋 👘 ⓗ 🔔 nr ▦ 🏊

🏖️ sand 4km

Fr N exit A63 junc 8 onto N10 S. Turn R just N of
Ondres sp Ondres-Plage, at rndabt turn L & foll site
sp. Fr S exit A63 junc 7 onto N10 to Ondres. Cont
thro town cent & turn L at town boundary, then as
above; tight turns thro housing est.
3*, Med, hdg, mkd, pt shd, terr, EHU (10A) €4; gas; red
long stay; 60% statics; phone; Eng spkn; adv bkg req;
bike hire; fishing; boating; games area; CKE. *"Peaceful,
charming lakeside site by lake; twin axles LS only; gd
welcome; helpful staff; ltd facs LS; vg pool; excel."*
€45.00, 21 Mar-2 Oct. **2017**

LABENNE *8E1* (3km SW Coastal) *43.59533, -1.45651*
Camping Le Sylvamar, Ave de l'Océan, 40530 Labenne
05 59 45 75 16; camping@sylvamar.fr; www.sylvamar.fr
or www.yellohvillage.co.uk

♟️ WD ♨️ 🛒 ♿ 🖥️ 🦋 👘 🍴 🔔 nr ▦ 🏊 🗒️

🏖️ sand 800m

Exit A63 junc 7 onto D85; then take N10 N to
Labenne; turn L onto D126; site sp. Lge, hdg, mkd, pt
shd, serviced pitches; EHU (10A) inc; bbq; 50% statics;
Eng spkn; adv bkg acc; ccard acc; waterslide; CKE.
*"Site amongst pine trees; sauna; spa; creche; sandy
pitches; fitness rm; beauty cent; gd location; vg facs."*
€43.00, 9 Apr-25 Sep. **2017**

LACANAU OCEAN *7C1* (1km N Coastal) *45.00823, -1.19322* **Airotel Camping de l'Océan**, 24 Rue du Repos, 33680 Lacanau-Océan 05 56 03 24 45; airotel.lacanau@wanadoo.fr; www.airotel-ocean.com

🐕 €4 ♨ WD ♨ ⚲ / ✿ 🍴 Ⓓ ⚑ 🍴 ✿ 🏖 sand 600m

On ent town at end of sq in front of bus stn turn R, fork R & foll sp to site (next to Camping Grand Pins). 4*, Lge, pt shd, pt sl, EHU (15A) inc; gas; TV; adv bkg acc; fishing; watersports; bike hire; tennis. *"Attractive site/holiday vill in pine woods behind sand dunes; surfing school nrby; care in choosing pitch due soft sand; gd, modern san facs; some pitches tight access."* **€33.00, Easter-27 Sep.** 2017

See advertisement

LACANAU OCEAN *7C1* (5km SE Rural) *44.98620, -1.13410* **Camping Le Tedey**, Par Le Moutchic, Route de Longarisse, 33680 Lacanau-Ocean 05 56 03 00 15; camping@le-tedey.com; www.le-tedey.com

♨ WD ♨ ⚲ ♨ ⚲ / MSP ✿ 🍴 Ⓓ 🍴 ⚑ 🏖 ✿

Fr Bordeaux take D6 to Lacanau & on twd Lacanau-Océan. On exit Moutchic take L fork twd Longarisse. Ent in 2km well sp on L. 3*, V lge, mkd, shd, EHU (10A) €4.30; gas; sw nr; TV; 10% statics; Eng spkn; adv bkg rec; ccard acc; bike hire; boating; golf 5km; CKE. *"Peaceful, friendly, family-run site in pine woods - avoid tree sap; golf nr; gd cycle tracks; no EHU for pitches adj beach; access diff some pitches; excel site."* **€35.60, 25 Apr-19 Sep.** 2019

LACAPELLE VIESCAMP *7C4* (1.6km SW Rural) *44.91272, 2.24853* **Camping La Presqu'île du Puech des Ouilhes**, 15150 Lacapelle-Viescamp 04 71 46 42 38 or 06 80 37 15 61 (mob); contact@cantal-camping.fr; www.camping-lac-auvergne.com

🐕 €2 ♨ WD ♨ ⚲ ♨ ⚲ / ✿ 🍴 Ⓓ 🍴 nr ♨ ⚑ 🏖 ✿ sand adj

W fr Aurillac on D120; at St Paul-des-Landes turn S onto D53 then D18 to Lacapelle-Viescamp. Foll sp Base de Loisirs, Plage-du-Puech des Ouilhes & Camping. Site beside Lake St Etienne-Cantalès. 3*, Med, hdstg, hdg, mkd, pt shd, EHU (16A) €3; sw nr; 10% statics; Eng spkn; fishing; canoeing; tennis; games rm; watersports. *"Friendly, helpful young owners; excel."* **€19.00, 15 Jun-15 Sep.** 2019

LACAUNE *8E4* (6km E Rural) *43.69280, 2.73790*
Camping Domaine Le Clôt, Les Vidals, 81230 Lacaune
05 63 37 03 59; campingleclot@orange.fr;
www.pageloisirs.com/le-clot

🐕 €1.50 ♿(htd) 🅆 ♨ ♿ 🚿 ∅ 🦋 ⊕ ⓡ ⚂ nr ⚠

Fr Castres to Lacaune on D622. Cont on D622 past
Lacaune then turn R onto unclassified rd to Les
Vidals. Site sp 500m on L after Les Vidals. 2*, Sm, pt
shd, terr, EHU (6-10A) €3.25-4; Eng spkn; CKE. "Excel
site; modern, immac san facs; gd views; gd walking in
Monts de Lacaune; lake sw 12km; fishing 12km; sailing
12km; windsurfing 12km; friendly Dutch owner; site rd
steep & narr; vg rest." **€22.00, 15 Apr-15 Oct.** 2016

LAGRASSE *8F4* (0.7km N Rural) *43.09516, 2.61893*
Camp Municipal de Boucocers, Route de Ribaute,
11220 Lagrasse **04 68 43 10 05 or 04 68 43 15 18;**
mairielagrasse@wanadoo.fr; www.audetourisme.com

🐕 €2.10 ♿ 🅆 ♨ ♿ ∅ 🛁 ⊕ nr ⚂ nr

1km on D212 fr Lagrasse to Fabrezan (N).
1*, Sm, hdstg, pt shd, pt sl, EHU (15A) €2.80; sw nr;
phone; adv bkg acc; CKE. "At cent of 'off-the-beaten-
track' beautiful touring area; helpful warden; simple but
gd san facs; gd walking; path down to lagrasse cent;
o'looks superb medieval town; rec arr early; hillside
walk into vill needs care; site run down at then of ssn;
no entry barrier, site self, pay when warden calls; excel,
well kept site; Lagrasse Abbey & town worth a visit."
€15.00, 15 Mar-15 Oct. 2018

LAGUEPIE *8E4* (1km E Rural) *44.14780, 1.97892*
Camp Municipal Les Tilleuls, 82250 Laguépie
05 63 30 22 32 or 05 63 30 20 81 (Mairie); camping.
lestilleuls0837@orange.fr; www.camping-les-
tilleuls.com

🐕 ♿ ♨ ♿ ∅ 🦋 ⍟ nr ⚂ nr ⚠

Exit Cordes on D922 N to Laguépie; turn R at bdge,
still on D922 sp Villefranche; site sp to R in 500m;
tight turn into narr lane. NB App thro Laguépie poss
diff lge o'fits. Med, pt shd, terr, EHU (10A) €2.70; sw;
TV; 44% statics; phone; adv bkg acc; canoe hire; fishing;
tennis; games area. "Attractive setting on Rv Viaur;
friendly welcome; excel playgrnd; gd touring base; conv
Aveyron gorges." **€14.00, May-Oct.** 2018

LAGUIOLE *7D4* (0.5km NE Rural) *44.68158, 2.85440*
Camp Municipal Les Monts D'Aubrac, 12210 Laguiole
05 65 44 39 72 or 05 65 51 26 30 (LS); http://
campinglesmontsdaubraclaguiole.jimdo.com

🐕 ♿ 🅆 ♨ ∅ 🛁 🦋 ⍟ nr ⊕ nr ⚂ nr

E of Laguiole on D15 at top of hill. Fr S on D921 turn
R at rndabt bef ent to town. Site sp.
Med, hdg, mkd, pt shd, pt sl, EHU (16A) inc; phone;
CKE. "Clean & well cared for site; pleasant vill."
€19.00, 15 May-15 Sep. 2019

LAISSAC *7D4* (3km SE Rural) *44.36525, 2.85090*
FLOWER Camping La Grange de Monteillac, Chemin
de Monteillac, 12310 Sévérac-l'Eglise **05 65 70 21 00**
or 06 87 46 90 83 (mob); info@le-grange-de-
monteillac.com; www.la-grange-de-monteillac.com
or www.flowercampings.com

🐕 €1.50 ♿ 🅆 ♨ ♿ ∅ 🦋 ⍟ ⚂ ⚠ 🖊 🛷 🏊

Fr A75, at junc 42, go W on N88 twds Rodez; after
approx 22km; bef Laissac; turn L twds Sévérac-
l'Eglise; site sp. 4*, Med, hdg, mkd, unshd, pt sl, terr,
EHU (6A) inc (long lead poss req); TV; 10% statics;
phone; Eng spkn; adv bkg rec; bike hire; tennis;
horseriding; CKE. "Beautiful, excel site; bar & shops
high ssn." **€41.00, 24 May-15 Sep.** 2019

LALINDE *7C3* (2km E Urban) *44.83956, 0.76298*
Camping Moulin de la Guillou, 24150 LALINDE,
Dordogne **05 53 58 31 84 or 05 53 73 44 60 (Mairie);**
moulindelaguillou@ville-lalinde.fr; www.moulinde
laguillou.fr

🐕 €2 ♿ ♨ ♿ ∅ ⍟ ⚂ nr ⚠ 🖊 🛷

Take D703 E fr Lalinde (Rv Dordogne on R) &
keep strt where rd turns L over canal bdge. Site in
300m; sp. 2*, Med, shd, EHU (5A) €2.60; sw nr; adv
bkg rec; tennis adj; fishing adj. "Charming, peaceful
site on bank of Rv Dordogne; lovely views; clean
san facs, in need of upgrade; poss travellers; vg."
€15.00, 1 May-30 Sep. 2020

LALLEY *9D3* (0.3km S Rural) *44.75490, 5.67940*
Camping Belle Roche, Chemin de Combe Morée,
38930 Lalley **04 76 34 75 33; contact@campingbelle**
roche.com; www.campingbelleroche.com

🐕 €1.50 ♿ 🅆 ♨ ♿ ∅ 🛁 🦋 ⍟ ▾ ⊕ ⚂ ⚂ nr ⚠ 🖊
🛷 (htd)

Off D1075 at D66 for Mens; down long hill into
Lalley. Site on R thro vill. 3*, Med, hdstg, hdg, pt
shd, pt sl, EHU (10A) €4 (poss rev pol, poss long lead
req); gas; bbq; TV; 10% statics; adv bkg acc; ccard
acc; games area; tennis 500m; CKE. "Well-kept, scenic
site; spacious pitches but little shd; friendly, welcoming
owners; clean, vg modern san facs, poss stretched high
ssn; pleasant pool area; nr Vercors National Park; vg
walking/cycling; don't miss The Little Train of La Mure;
conv NH; v nice site; highly rec superb in every way."
€29.50, 31 Mar-14 Oct. 2019

LAMALOU LES BAINS *10F1* (2km SE Rural) *43.57631,
3.06842* **Camping Domaine de Gatinié,** Route de Gatinié,
34600 Les Aires **04 67 95 71 95 or 04 67 28 41 69 (LS);**
gatinie@wanadoo.fr; www.domainegatinie.com

🐕 €2 ♿ 🅆 ♨ ♿ ∅ 🦋 ⍟ ⊕ ⚂ ⚠ 🖊 🛷 🏊 ⛲

Fr D908 fr Lamalou-les-Bains or Hérépian dir
Poujol-sur-Orb, site sp. Fr D160 cross rv to D908
then as above. 3*, Med, hdg, mkd, pt shd, pt sl,
EHU (6A) inc; bbq; sw nr; red long stay; 10% statics;
Eng spkn; adv bkg acc; fishing; horseriding 2km;
tennis 2km; canoeing; games area; golf 2km; CKE.
"Beautiful, peaceful situation; many leisure activities;
vg; helpful staff, leafy pleasant site in a lovely area."
€19.00, 1 Apr-31 Oct. 2019

LAMASTRE 9C2 (5km NE Rural) 45.01173, 4.62410
Camping Les Roches, 07270 Le Crestet **04 75 06 20 20;**
camproches@nordnet.fr; www.campinglesroches.com

🐕 €4.50 ♂♀ WD ♨ ♿ 🛒 ✉ MSP 🦋 ☂ Y ⊕ 🏪 🏟 🏊 (htd)

Take D534 fr Tournon-sur-Rhône dir Lamastre. 3km
fr vill. Do not use Sat Nav. Sm, hdstg, mkd, pt shd,
terr, EHU (6A) €4.50; bbq; sw nr; TV; 30% statics;
bus 1km; Eng spkn; adv bkg acc; ccard acc; games
area; tennis 3km; fishing 500m; CKE. "Friendly
family-run site; clean facs; lovely views; gd base for
touring medieval vills; gd walking; site rd steep; on
hillside abv rv valley; diff for lge o'fits; excel rest."
€23.50, 1 May-30 Sep.   2019

"That's changed – Should I let the Club know?"

If you find something on site that's different
from the site entry, fill in a report and let us
know. See camc.com/europereport

LANDEDA 2E1 (2km NW Coastal) 48.59333, -4.60333
Camping des Abers, 51 Toull Tréaz, Plage de Ste
Marguerite, 29870 Landéda **02 98 04 93 35; info@
camping-des-abers.com; www.camping-des-abers.com**

🐕 €2.50 ♂♀ WD ♨ ♿ 🛒 ✉ MSP 🦋 ☂ Y ⊕ nr 🏪 🏟 🏊
⛱ sand adj

Exit N12/E50 at junc with D788 & take D13 to
Lannilis. Then take D128A to Landéda & foll green
site sp. 4*, Lge, mkd, hdg, pt shd, terr, EHU (10A)
€3 (long lead poss req); gas; bbq; red long stay; TV;
10% statics; Eng spkn; adv bkg rec; ccard acc; bike hire;
fishing; games rm; classes; CKE. "Attractive, landscaped
site on wild coast; views fr high pitches; friendly, helpful
manager; san facs clean, some new, others old; some
pitches muddy when wet; no o'fits over 8m high ssn;
access to many pitches by grass tracks, some sl; gd
walks, cycling; excel; some problems with voltage."
€22.50, 1 May-30 Sep, B30.   2019

LANDIVISIAU 2E2 (9.3km NE Urban) 48.57724,
-4.03006 **Camp Municipal Lanorgant,** 29420 Plouvorn
**02 98 61 32 40 (Mairie); www.plouvorn.com/aire-de-
camping-cars**

♂♀ ♨ ✉ MSP 🦋 Y ⊕ nr 🏪 nr 🏟 ⛱ sand

Fr Landivisiau, take D69 N twd Roscoff. In 8km
turn R onto D19 twd Morlaix. Site sp, in 700m
turn R. NB Care req entry/exit, poss diff lge o'fits.
2*, Sm, hdg, mkd, pt shd, terr, EHU (10A) inc; bbq;
sw, adv bkg acc; tennis; fishing; canoe hire. "Ideal
NH for ferries; lge pitches; sailboards hire; nr lake."
€5.20, 26 Jun-15 Sep.   2016

LANGEAC 9C1 (0.8km NE Rural) 45.10251, 3.49980
Camp Municipal du Pradeau/Des Gorges de l'Allier,
43300 Langeac **04 71 77 05 01; infos@camping
langeac.com; www.campinglangeac.com**

🐕 €1.05 ♂♀ WD ♨ ♿ 🛒 ✉ MSP 🦋 ☂ Y ⊕ nr 🏪 🏟 nr 🏊

Exit N102 onto D56 sp Langeac; in 7km join D585
into Langeac; pass under rlwy; at 2nd rndabt in 1km
turn L to site, just bef junc with D590. Fr S on D950
to Langeac, take 1st R after rv bdge; then 1st exit
at rndabt in 100m. 3*, Lge, pt shd, EHU (10A) €2.60
(poss long lead req); sw nr; TV; 10% statics; phone;
bus 1km; Eng spkn; bike hire; fishing adj; canoeing adj;
CKE. "Beautiful location on Rv Allier; tourist train thro
Gorges d'Allier fr Langeac; walking rtes adj; barrier to
site poss clsd after sept 11am-5pm; gd san facs; gd
local mkt; excel NH." €13.00, 1 Apr-31 Oct.   2015

LANGOGNE 9D1 (2km W Rural) 44.73180, 3.83995
Camping Les Terrasses du Lac, 48300 Naussac
04 66 69 29 62; info@naussac.com; www.naussac.com

🐕 €3.30 ♂♀ WD ♨ ♿ 🛒 ✉ MSP 🦋 ☂ Y ⊕ 🏪 nr 🏟 🏊
🏊 ⛴

S fr Le Puy-en-Velay on N88. At Langogne take D26
to lakeside, site sp. 3*, Lge, pt shd, terr, EHU (6A)
€2.50; bbq; sw nr; TV; 10% statics; phone; Eng spkn;
adv bkg acc; horseriding 3km; games area; sailing
school; bike hire; golf 1km; watersports adj; CKE.
"Vg views; steep hill bet recep & pitches; vg cycling &
walking." €23.30, 15 Apr-1 Oct.   2018

LANGRES 6F1 (6km E Rural) 47.87190, 5.38120
Kawan Village Le Lac de la Liez, Rue des Voiliers,
52200 Peigney **03 25 90 27 79; contact@camping-
liez.fr; www.campingliez.com**

🐕 €3 ♂♀ (htd) WD ♨ ♿ 🛒 ✉ MSP 🦋 Y ⊕ 🏪 🏟 🏊
🏊 (covrd, htd) ⛴

Exit A31 at junc 7 (Langres Nord) onto DN19; at
Langres turn L at traff lts onto D74 sp Vesoul,
Mulhouse, Le Lac de la Liez; at rndabt go strt on
sp Epinal, Nancy; after Champigny-lès-Langres
cross over rlwy bdge & canal turning R onto D52
sp Peigney, Lac de la Liez; in 3km bear R onto D284
sp Langres Sud & Lac de la Liez; site on R in 800m.
Well sp fr N & S. 5*, Lge, mkd, hdg, hdstg, pt shd,
terr, EHU (10A) €5.50; bbq; sw nr; TV; 15% statics;
phone; Eng spkn; ccard acc; bike hire; sauna; golf
10km; boat hire; watersports; fishing; horseriding
10km; tennis; games rm; CKE. "Popular, well-run,
secure site; lake views fr some pitches; various sized
pitches; helpful, friendly staff; san facs ltd LS; blocks
poss req some pitches; some sm pitches & narr access
rds diff manoeuvre lge o'fits; no o'fits over 10m; spa;
vg rest; rec arr bef 1600 high ssn; gd walks & cycle rte
by picturesque lake; interesting & historic town; poor."
€37.00, 1 Apr-25 Sep, J05.   2016

LANGRES *6F1* (15km S Rural) *47.74036, 5.30727*
Camping du Lac, 14 rue Cototte, 52190 Villegusien le
Lac 25 88 45 24; richard-emmanuel@hotmail.fr;
www.tourisme-langres.com

Take N19, foll N19 to Ave du Capitaine Baudoin,
then foll Ave du Général de Gaulle, foll D974 to D26
in Villegusien-le-Lac, cont on D26, turn L onto D26,
turn L, turn R,site on L. 1*, Med, mkd, shd, pt sl, EHU;
bbq (gas); sw; twin axles; adv bkg acc; windsurfing;
trekking; games rm; tennis; fishing; sailing. "V pleasant
site in lovely setting, some slight rd noise; beach
lifeguard." **€22.00, 15 Mar-30 Oct.**   2019

LANGRES *6F1* (7.5km S Rural) *47.81210, 5.32080*
Camping de la Croix d'Arles, 52200 Bourg 03 25 88
24 02; croix.arles@yahoo.fr; www.campingdelacroix
darles.com

Site is 4km S of Langres on W side of D974 (1km S of
junc of D974 with D428). Site opp junc of D51 with
D974. Fr Dijon poss no L turn off D974 - can pull
into indust est N of site & return to site, but memb
reported that L turn now poss (2011). 3*, Med, hdg,
mkd, hdstg, pt shd, pt sl, EHU (10A) €4 (poss rev pol)
(long cable req); phone; Eng spkn; ccard acc; CKE.
"Popular site, fills up quickly after 1600; friendly staff;
some lovely secluded pitches in woodland; gd san facs;
access poss diff lge o'fits; muddy after rain; unkempt
LS; poss haphazard pitching when full; conv NH Langres
historic town; nice, sm rest on site; easy to reach."
€22.00, 15 Mar-31 Oct.   2018

LANGRES *6F1* (1km SW Urban) *47.86038, 5.32894*
Camp Municipal Navarre, 9 Blvd Maréchal de Lattre
de Tassigny, 52200 Langres 03 25 87 37 92 or
06 10 74 10 16; contact@campingnavarre.fr;
www.camping-navarre-langres.fr

App fr N or S on D619/D674, cont on main rd until lge
rndabt at top of hill & go thro town arched gateway;
site well sp fr there. NB Diff access for lge o'fits thro
walled town but easy access fr D619. Med, pt shd,
pt sl, EHU (10A) €3.10 (long lead req & poss rev pol);
bbq; phone; Eng spkn; CKE. "Well-situated, busy NH,
gd views fr some pitches; on arr site self & see warden;
rec arr bef 1630; helpful staff; excel, modern unisex
san facs; lovely walk round citadel ramparts; delightful
town; vg site, views and location; warden mulit-lingual
and helpful; conv for shops, rest, Friday mkt, cathedral."
€18.30, 10 Mar-5 Nov.   2017

LANGRES *6F1* (13km SW Rural) *47.79528, 5.23278*
Camping de la Croisée, 3 Route De Auberive, 52250
Flagey 03 25 88 01 26; yannick.durenne52@orange.fr;
www.campingdelacroisee.com

Exit A31 at J6 direction Langres D428. Campsite 1km
on L (opp junc to Flagey). Med, hdstg, hdg, mkd, pt shd,
bbq (charcoal, gas); ccard acc; red low ssn.. "Conv NH stop
as 2km fr A31 m'way; farm animals; gd." **€17.00**   2018

LANILDUT *2E1* (1km N Coastal) *48.48012, -4.75184*
Camping du Tromeur, 11 Route du Camping, 29840
Lanildut 02 98 04 31 13; contact@tromeur.fr;
www.tromeur.fr

Site well sp on app rds to vill. 2*, Med, EHU €3 (poss
long lead req & poss rev pol); bbq; phone. "Clean,
sheltered site; san facs gd; harbour & sm beach; LS
warden am & pm only - site yourself; wooded walk into
vil." **€15.00, 1 May-30 Sep.**   2019

LANLOUP *2E3* (0.4km W Rural) *48.71369, -2.96711*
FFCC Camping Le Neptune, 22580 Lanloup
02 96 22 33 35; contact@leneptune.com;
www.leneptune.com

sand 2km

Take D786 fr St Brieuc or Paimpol to Lanloup, site
sp. NB Take care sat nav dirs (2011).
3*, Med, mkd, hdg, pt shd, EHU inc; gas; bbq; TV;
15% statics; phone; Eng spkn; adv bkg acc; horseriding
4km; bike hire; tennis 300m; CKE. "Excel, well-
maintained site nr beautiful coast; various pitch sizes;
clean san facs; friendly, helpful owner; highly rec."
€30.00, 31 Mar-9 Oct.   2017

LANNE *8F2* (1km NW Rural) *43.17067, 0.00186*
Camping La Bergerie, 79 Rue des Chênes, 65380
Lanne 05 62 45 40 05; camping-la-bergerie@
orange.com; www.camping-la-bergerie.com

Fr Lourdes take N21 N dir Tarbes; turn R onto D16
(Rue des Chênes) dir Lanne; site on R in 200m.
3*, Med, mkd, shd, EHU (10A) €3.8 (poss rev pol); gas;
bus 200m; Eng spkn; adv bkg acc; tennis; CKE. "Well-
run site; friendly owners; some rd noise & aircraft noise
at night; gd san facs; poss unkempt LS; poss flooding
wet weather." **€19.00, 15 Mar-15 Oct.**   2017

LANNION *1D2* (9km NNW Coastal) *48.73833,
-3.54500* **FFCC Camping Les Plages de Beg-Léguer,**
Route de la Côte, 22300 Lannion 02 96 47 25 00;
info@campingdesplages.com; www.campingdes
plages.com

(covrd, htd)   sand 500m

Fr Lannion take rd out of town twd Trébeurden
then twd Servel on D65, then head SW off that
rd twd Beg Léguer (sp). 3*, Lge, mkd, hdg, pt shd,
EHU (6A) €3.50 (poss long lead req); gas; red long
stay; TV; 20% statics; phone; bus 400m; Eng spkn;
adv bkg acc; ccard acc; windsurfing; fishing; sailing;
tennis; CKE. "Pleasant, peaceful, well-run family site;
charming French owner who speaks excel Eng; superb
pool complex & vg children's play area; lge grass
pitches; immac, modern san facs; one of the best sites
in France; many superb rest in nrby seaside resorts;
stunning beaches; cliftop location; adj to GR34 coastal
path; phone LS; excel, fam oriented facs; conv for
beach." **€31.70, 29 May-22 Sep.**   2019

FRANCE

LANSLEBOURG MONT CENIS 9C4 (0.3km SW Rural) 45.28417, 6.87380 **Camp Municipal Les Balmasses,** Chemin du Pavon, 73480 Lanslebourg-Mont-Cenis 06 38 28 92 84; info@camping-les-balmasses.com; www.camping-les-balmasses.com

Fr Modane, site on R on rv on ent to town. 2*, Med, mkd, pt shd, EHU (6-10A) €4.50-5.40; bbq; phone; Eng spkn; CKE. *"Pleasant, quiet site by rv; mountain views; clean facs; conv NH bef/after Col du Mont-Cenis."* **€14.00, 1 Jun-20 Sep.** 2019

LAON 3C4 (3km W Rural) 49.56190, 3.59583 **Camp La Chênaie (formerly Municipal),** Allée de la Chênaie, 02000 Laon 03 23 23 38 63 or 03 23 20 25 56; contact.camping.laon@gmail.com; www.camping-aisne.fr

Exit A26 junc 13 onto N2 sp Laon; in 10km at junc with D1044 (4th rndabt) turn sp Semilly/Laon, then L at next rndabt into site rd. Site well sp. 3*, Sm, hdstg, mkd, hdg, pt shd, sl, terr, EHU (10A) €5.10 (poss rev pol); bbq; red long stay; twin axles; 10% statics; phone; Eng spkn; adv bkg acc; fishing 50m; CKE. *"Peaceful, pleasant site in gd location; popular NH; well-mkd pitches - lgest at end of site rd; pool (2.5km); extremely helpful staff; no twin axles; if travelling Sept phone to check site open; m'van parking nr cathedral; vg; woodland glades; gd NH; site now privately owned; 20min walk up steep path to historic town."* **€23.90, 1 Apr-30 Sep.** 2019

LAPALISSE 9A1 (0.3km S Urban) 46.24322, 3.63950 **Camping de la Route Bleue,** Rue des Vignes, 03120 Lapalisse 04 70 99 26 31, 04 70 99 76 29 or 04 70 99 08 39 (LS); contact@lapalissetourisme.com; www.lapalisse-tourisme.com

S fr Moulins on N7; at rndabt junc with D907 just bef Lapalisse, take 3rd exit onto Ave due Huit Mai 1945 (to town cent), foll rd for 1.5km, over rv bdg, round RH bend onto Rue des Vignes, site on R in 500m. 3*, Med, mkd, pt shd, EHU (6-9A) €2.40; Eng spkn; CKE. *"Popular, excel NH off N7 in pleasant parkland setting; gd clean san facs; pleasant 10 min walk thro adj park to town; no twin axles; poss flooding after heavy rain; adequate sans but need upgrade."* **€11.90, 28 Apr-15 Oct.** 2019

LARGENTIERE 9D2 (5km SE Rural) 44.50347, 4.29430 **Camping Les Châtaigniers,** Le Mas-de-Peyrot, 07110 Laurac-en-Vivarais 04 75 36 86 26; chataigniers@hotmail.com; www.chataigniers-laurac.com

Fr Aubenas S on D104 dir Alès; site sp fr D104. Site on one of minor rds leading to Laurac-en-Vivarais. 3*, Med, mkd, pt shd, pt sl, EHU (10A) €3; bbq (gas); 15% statics; adv bkg acc. *"Attractive, great, clean site; some pitches deep shd; sun area; gd pool; sh uphill walk to vill shops & auberge; vg."* **€25.00, 1 Apr-30 Sep.** 2016

LARGENTIERE 9D2 (1.6km NW Rural) 44.56120, 4.28615 **Domaine Les Ranchisses,** Route de Rocher, Chassiers, 07110 Largentière 04 75 88 31 97; reception@lesranchisses.fr; www.lesranchisses.fr

Exit A7/E15 junct 17/18 (Montelimar N or S) on to N7 dir Montelimar to take N102. Fr Aubenas S on D104 sp Alès. 1km after vill of Uzer turn R onto D5 to Largentière. Go thro Largentière on D5 in dir Rocher/Valgorge; site on L in 1.5km. DO NOT use D103 bet Lachapelle-Aubenas & Largentière - too steep & narr for lge vehicles & c'vans. NB Not rec to use sat nav dirs to this site. 4*, Lge, mkd, pt shd, EHU (10A) inc; gas; bbq (elec, gas); sw; TV; 30% statics; adv bkg req; ccard acc; games rm; fishing; tennis; bike hire; games area; canoeing. *"Lovely, well-run, busy site adj vineyard; gd sized pitches; friendly, helpful staff; gd, immac san facs; o'fits over 7m by request; excel rest & takeaway; lovely pools; gd choice of sporting activities; wellness cent; poss muddy when wet; noisy rd adj to S end of site; mkt Tues am; first class; 5 star site in lovely location."* **€56.00, 13 Apr-21 Sep, C32.** 2019

LARUNS 8G2 (0.8km S Rural) 42.98241, -0.41591 **Camping Les Gaves,** Quartier Pon, 64440 Laruns 05 59 05 32 37; campingdesgaves@wanadoo.fr; www.campingdesgaves.com

Site on S edge of town, N of Hôtel Le Lorry & bdge. Fr town sq cont on Rte d'Espagne (narr exit fr sq) to end of 1-way system. After Elf & Total stns turn L at site sp immed bef bdge (high fir tree each side of bdge ent). Ignore 1st site on L. At v constricted T-junc at ent to quartier 'Pon', turn R & foll rd into site. App no suitable lge o'fits. 3*, Med, mkd, pt shd, serviced pitches; EHU (3-10A) €2.60-4.50; TV; 75% statics; fishing; games area; games rm; rv fishing adj; CKE. *"Beautiful, lovely site; nr vill; htd covrd pool 800m; facs tired (2015); level walk to vill."* **€24.00** 2015

LAURENS 10F1 (1km S Rural) 43.53620, 3.18583 **Camping L'Oliveraie,** Chemin de Bédarieux, 34480 Laurens 04 67 90 24 36; oliveraie@free.fr; www.oliveraie.com

Clearly sp on D909 Béziers to Bédarieux rd. Sp reads Loisirs de L'Oliveraie. 3*, Med, mkd, hdstg, pt shd, terr, EHU (10A) €3.20-4.60 (poss rev pol); TV; 30% statics; phone; adv bkg acc; ccard acc; site clsd 15 Dec-15 Jan; games rm; CKE. *"Helpful staff; gd, clean san facs; sauna high ssn; site becoming tatty (2011); in wine-producing area; gd winter NH."* **€35.00** 2019

LAVAL *2F4* (17km N Rural) *48.17467, -0.78785*
Camp Municipal Le Pont, 53240 Andouillé
02 43 69 72 72 (Mairie)

Fr Laval N on D31 dir Ernée. In 8km turn R onto D115 to Andouillé. Site on L bef hill to vill cent. 2*, Sm, hdg, pt shd, EHU (3A) inc. "Pretty, busy, basic site; vg, clean san facs; warden on site am & pm; site liable to flood." **€6.00, 1 Apr-31 Oct.** 2015

LAVANDOU, LE *10F3* (2km S Coastal) *43.11800, 6.35210* **Camping du Domaine,** La Favière, 2581 Route de Bénat, 83230 Bormes-les-Mimosas
04 94 71 03 12; mail@campdudomaine.com; www.campdudomaine.com

App Le Lavandou fr Hyères on D98 & turn R on o'skts of town clearly sp La Favière. Site on L in 2.3km about 200m after ent to Domaine La Favière (wine sales) - ignore 1st lge winery. If app fr E do not go thro Le Levandou, but stay on D559 until sp to La Favière. 4*, V lge, mkd, pt shd, terr, EHU (10A) inc (long lead poss req); gas; bbq (gas); TV; 10% statics; phone; Eng spkn; adv bkg req; ccard acc; tennis; games rm; CKE. "Lge pitches, some with many trees & some adj beach (direct access); well-organised site with excel facs; gd walking & attractions in area." **€55.00, 4 Apr-31 Oct.** 2019

See advertisement

LAVANDOU, LE *10F3* (2.7km W Urban) *43.13630, 6.35439* **Camping St Pons,** Ave Maréchal Juin, 83960 Le Lavandou **04 94 71 03 93; campingstpons@netcourrier.com; www.campingstpons.com**

App fr W on D98 via La Londe. At Bormes keep R onto D559. At 1st rndabt turn R sp La Favière, at 2nd rndabt turn R, then 1st L. Site on L in 200m. 2*, Med, mkd, shd, EHU (6A) inc; 10% statics; phone; Eng spkn; CKE. "Much improved site; helpful owner." **€26.00, 29 Apr-1 Oct.** 2017

LAVANDOU, LE *10F3* (8km NW Rural) *43.16262, 6.32152* **Camping Manjastre,** 150 Chemin des Girolles, 83230 Bormes-les-Mimosas **04 94 71 03 28; manjastre@infonie.fr; www.campingmanjastre.com**

App fr W on D98 about 3km NE of where N559 branches off SE to Le Lavandou. Fr E site is 2km beyond Bormes/Collobrières x-rds; sp. 3*, Lge, mkd, hdg, pt shd, sl, terr, EHU (10A) €4.70; bbq; TV; 10% statics; Eng spkn; adv bkg acc; CKE. "Lovely site in vineyard on steep hillside with 3 san facs blocks; dohs not acc Jul/Aug; c'vans taken in & out by tractor; facs poss stretched in ssn; winter storage avail." **€30.00** 2015

LAVELANET *8G4* (1km SW Urban) *42.92340, 1.84477* **Camping Le Pré Cathare,** Rue Jacquard, 09300 Lavelanet **05 61 01 55 54; leprecathare@orange.fr; www.leprecathare.fr**

Fr Lavelanet, take D117 twd Foix & foll sp (foll sp for sports complex). Adj 'piscine'. 3*, Med, mkd, pt shd, EHU (15A) €3; bbq; TV; 80% statics; adv bkg acc; games area; tennis 800m; CKE. "Gd sized pitches, some with mountain views; excel san facs; poss open in winter with adv bkg; pool adj; gates locked 2200; quiet town; vg." **€20.00, 15 Mar-31 Oct.** 2017

LE BUISSON *9D1* (10km NNE Rural) *44.705795, 3.282804* **Camping Municipal Aumont Aubrac,** D809 48130 Peyre en Aubrac **04 66 42 80 02; www.ot-aumont-aubrac.fr**

Travelling on A75 between Millau and St Flour South. Leave at J35. Med, pt shd, EHU 6A; twin axles; CKE. "V pleasant quiet campsite; perfect for NH; gd walk in area; vg." **€12.00, 1 Jun-30 Sep.** 2019

LEGE *2H4* (10km SW Rural) *46.82121, -1.64844* **Camp Municipal Les Blés d'Or,** 10 rue de la Piscine, 85670 Grand'Landes **02 51 98 51 86; mairiegrandlandes@wanadoo.fr; www.vendee-tourisme.com**

Take D753 fr Legé twd St Jean-de-Monts. In 4km turn S on D81 & foll sp. Fr S on D978, turn W sp Grand-Landes. 3km N of Palluau. 2*, Sm, pt shd, pt sl, EHU (16A) €2.30; gas; 30% statics; Eng spkn; adv bkg acc. "V pleasant site; height barrier only, cars 24hr access; immac but dated facs; pay at Mairie adj; v useful." **€10.50** 2017

LEGE-CAP-FERRET *7D1* (6km W Coastal) *44.73443, -1.1960* **Camping Les Viviers,** Ave Léon Lesca, Claouey, 33950 Lège-Cap-Ferret **05 56 60 70 04; reception@lesviviers.com; www.lesviviers.com**

Fr N exit A10/A630 W of Bordeaux onto D106 sp Cap-Ferret. Foll D106 thro Arès & vill of Claouey on W side of Bassin d'Arcachon, site on L after LH bend (approx 1.5km after Claouey). 4*, V lge, mkd, hdg, pt shd, EHU (10A) inc; gas; bbq (elec, gas); red long stay; TV; 27% statics; bus; Eng spkn; adv bkg req; ccard acc; games rm; sauna; windsurfing; fishing; tennis; waterslide; games area; bike hire; sailing; CKE. "Sand pitches, various positions & prices; clean san facs; sea water lagoon with private sand beach adj; cinema; vg leisure facs and waterpark on site; free night bus along peninsular; vg site." **€50.00, 28 Mar-13 Sep.** 2016

LEMPDES SUR ALLAGNON 9C1 (1.2km N Rural)
45.38699, 3.26598 **Camping Le Pont d'Allagnon
(formerly CM au Delà de l'Eau),** Rue René Filiol, off
Route de Chambezon, 43410 Lempdes-sur-Allagnon
**04 71 76 53 69; centre.auvergne.camping@
orange.fr; www.campingenauvergne.com**

Going S on A75 exit junc 19 (ltd access) onto D909;
turn R on D654 bef vill, site sp at junc. Or fr junc 20
going N; foll sp. Site just outside vill. 3*, Med, hdg, pt
shd, EHU (16A) €3.40; phone; adv bkg acc; ccard acc;
games rm; tennis; rv fishing; games area. *"Pleasant
site in beautiful area; pool 100m; conv NH A75; gd."*
€25.00, 28 Mar-19 Oct. 2019

LEON 8E1 (4km N Rural) 43.90260, -1.31030
Camping Sandaya Le Col Vert, Lac de Léon, 40560
Vielle-St Girons **05 58 42 94 06; www.sandaya.co.uk/
our-campsites/le-col-vert**

€4.70 (covrd, htd)

Exit N10 junc 12; at Castets-des-Landes turn R onto
D42 to Vielle-St Girons. In vill turn L onto D652
twd Léon sp Soustons. In 4km, bef Vielle, take 2nd
of 2 RH turns twd Lac de Léon. Site on R at end
of rd in 1.5km. 4*, V lge, shd, serviced pitches; EHU
(3A) inc; gas; bbq (elec, gas); sw nr; red long stay;
TV; 60% statics; adv bkg acc; ccard acc; canoeing nr;
games rm; windsurfing nr; archery; tennis; sailing nr;
bike hire; fishing nr; horseriding; CKE. *"Lakeside site in
pine forest; fitness rm; some pitches 800m fr facs; ideal
for children & teenagers; wellness cent; no c'van/m'van
over 6.5m; daily mkt in Léon in ssn; excel location."*
€64.00, 12 Apr-7 Sep, A08. 2019

LEON *8E1* (9km NW Coastal) *43.90830, -1.36380*
Domaine Naturiste Arna (Naturist), Arnaouthot,
5006 Route de Pichelèbe, 40560 Vielle-St Girons
05 58 49 11 11; contact@arna.com; www.arna.com

🏕🐕 €3.50 ♿ WC ♨ ♿ 🚿 🔌 ⊘ 🦋 ♈ ▽ 🕐 🍴 🛒 🛍 🏔 ⚠
🏊(covrd, htd) 🚣 ⛱ sand adj

Fr St Girons turn R onto D328 at Vielle sp Pichelèbe.
Site in 5km on R. 3*, Lge, hdstg, shd, pt sl, EHU
(3-10A) €4.50-6.10 inc; gas; bbq (elec, gas); red long
stay; TV; 80% statics; Eng spkn; adv bkg acc; ccard
acc; games area; golf nr; bike hire; waterslide; games
rm; tennis; watersports 5km; archery. *"Excel site in
pine forest; Arna Forme Spa; some pitches soft sand;
clean san facs, ltd LS; no o'fits over 6.5m; lake adj;
spa cent; excel LS site; access lge o'fits poss diff due
trees; superb beach; daily mkt in Léon in ssn; new
hdstg pitches with elec/water for MH's; great facs."*
€40.00, 9 Apr-25 Sep. **2018**

LERAN *8G4* (2km E Rural) *42.98368, 1.93516*
Camping La Régate, Route du Lac, 09600 Léran
**05 61 03 09 17 or 06 08 48 08 63 (mob); contact@
campinglaregate.com; www.campinglaregate.com**

🏕🐕 €1 ♿ WC ♨ ♿ 🚿 🔌 ⊘ 🦋 ♈ ▽ 🕐 nr 🛍 nr

Fr Lavelanet go N on D625, turn R onto D28 & cont
to Léran. Site sp fr vill. Ent easily missed - rd past
it is dead end. 3*, Med, hdg, mkd, shd, terr, EHU (8A)
€3.70; bbq; 10% statics; phone; adv bkg acc; ccard acc;
watersports. *"Conv Montségur chateau; leisure cent
nr; pony trekking; clean san facs; lake adj; gd location;
pool adj; mkd walking & cycle rtes around adj lake."*
€33.60, 30 Mar-26 Oct. **2019**

LES MOUTIERS EN RETZ *2H3* (4km SSE Coastal)
47.036544, -1.984846 **Domaine du Collet,** Route
Verte 44760 Les Moutiers-en-Retz
**00 33 2 40 21 40 92; contact@domaine-du-collet.com;
www.domaine-du-collet.com**

🏕🐕 €5 ♿ WC ♨ ♿ 🚿 🔌 MSP 🦋 ♈ ▽ 🕐 🏔 🚣 🏊(covrd, htd)
🚣 ⛱ 100m

SW fr Nantes on D723, after 9km turn L D751 sp
Noirmoutier; in abt 8km at Port-Saint-Père turn L
sp D758/Noirmoutier; in abt 18km foll D758 thro
Bourgneuf-en-Retz (beware narr sharp turn); at
mini-rndabt go L onto D758; at rndabt take 2nd exit
sp Port du Collet; in abt 2km turn R over bdge; aft
1km fork R and site on R aft 1km. 4*, Lge, pt shd, TV;
70% statics; games rm. *"Very quiet; gd for families."*
€40.00, 1 Apr - 31 Oct, B36. **2019**

LESCHERAINES *9B3* (2.5km SE Rural) *45.70279,
6.11158* **Camp Municipal de l'Ile,** Base de Loisirs,
Les Iles du Chéran, 73340 Lescheraines **04 79 63 80 00;
contact@savoie-camping.com; www.iles-du-
cheran.com**

🏕🐕 €1.50 ♿ WC ♨ ♿ 🚿 🔌 ⊘ MSP 🦋 ♈ ▽ 🕐 nr 🛒 🛍 🏔 🚣

Fr Lescheraines foll sp for Base de Loisirs.
3*, Lge, mkd, pt shd, EHU (6-10A) €2.40-3.50; bbq; sw;
5% statics; phone; Eng spkn; boat hire; fishing; canoe
hire; CKE. *"Beautiful, scenic, lakeside setting; v helpful
staff; gd walks."* **€16.50, 19 Apr-28 Sep.** **2019**

LESPERON *8E1* (4km SW Rural) *43.96657, -1.12940*
Le Laha Camping (formerly Parc de Couchoy), 3000
Route de Linxe, 40260 Lesperon **05 58 89 60 15;
www.lelaha.com**

🏕🐕 €1 ♿ WC ♨ ♿ 🚿 🔌 ⊘ 🦋 ♈ ▽ 🕐 nr 🛍 🏔 🚣

Exit N10 junc 13 to D41 sp Lesperon; in 1km turn L,
thro vill of Lesperon; L at junc onto D331; bottom
of hill turn R & immed L; site on R in 3km dir Linxe.
3*, Sm, mkd, pt shd, EHU (6A); gas; bbq (elec, gas); sw
nr; red long stay; twin axles; 10% statics; phone; Eng
spkn; adv bkg acc; ccard acc; CKE. *"Lovely but isolated
site on edge of wine country; gd facs on lakes for
sailing, windsurfing; British owners; clean san facs; vg;
new owners."* **€27.50, Apr-Oct.** **2019**

"We must tell the Club about that great site we found"

Get your site reports in by mid-August and we'll
do our best to get your updates into the next
edition.

LEZIGNAN CORBIERES *8F4* (10km S Rural)
43.11727, 2.73609 **Camping Le Pinada,** Villerouge
la Crémade, 11200 Fabrezan **04 68 43 32 29;
contact@lepinada.com; www.lepinada.com**

🏕🐕 €3 ♿ WC ♨ ♿ 🚿 🔌 ⊘ 🦋 ♈ ▽ 🕐 🛒 🛍 🏔 🚣 🏊 🚣

Fr Lézignan-Corbières on D611 S, pass airfield & fork
L thro Ferrals-les-Corbières (steep, narr) on D106.
Site sp & on L after 4km. Alt rte to avoid narr rd thro
Ferrals: exit A61 junc 25 & foll D611 thro Fabrezan.
At T-junc turn L onto D613 & after 2km turn L onto
D106. Site on R after Villerouge-la-Crémade.
3*, Med, hdg, mkd, shd, pt sl, terr, EHU (6A)
€5; bbq; sw nr; TV; 25% statics; Eng spkn; adv
bkg req; fishing 3km; games area; tennis; CKE.
*"Friendly owners; gd base for Carcassonne & Med
coast; bkg fee; well-run site; dated san facs; excel."*
€18.50, 1 Mar-30 Oct. **2020**

LEZIGNAN CORBIERES *8F4* (1km NW Urban) *43.20475,
2.75255* **Camp Municipal de la Pinède,** Ave Gaston
Bonheur, 11200 Lézignan-Corbières **04 68 27 05 08;
reception@campinglapinede.fr; www.campingla
pinede.fr**

🏕🐕 €2.10 ♿ WC ♨ ♿ 🚿 🔌 ⊘ MSP 🦋 ♈ ▽ 🕐 🛍 nr

On D6113 fr Carcassonne to Narbonne on N of rd;
foll 'Piscine' & 'Restaurant Le Patio' sp.
3*, Med, hdstg, hdg, pt shd, pt sl, terr, EHU (6A) inc; gas;
bbq (gas); 5% statics; adv bkg acc; tennis; CKE. *"Well-
run, clean, popular site; helpful, friendly staff; gd san
facs; gd m'van facs; htd pool adj; some pitches diff due
high kerb; no o'fits over 5m; superb pool; mkt Wed; gd
touring base or NH."* **€19.00, 1 Apr-30 Oct.** **2015**

FRANCE

LICQUES *3A3* (2.5km E Rural) *50.77905, 1.95567* **Camping-Caravaning Le Canchy,** Rue de Canchy, 62850 Licques **03 21 82 63 41 or 06 88 70 66 79;** campinglecanchylicques@orange.fr; www.camping-lecanchy.com

🐕 ♿ wc 🚿 ♿ 🛒 🚮 ♪ 🍽 ⬆ (H) 🅿 🚗 nr ⛽ ✒

Fr Calais D127 to Guînes, then D215 sp Licques; site sp in vill on D191; site on L in 1km with narr app rd. Or fr Ardres take D224 to Liques then as above. Or A26 fr Calais exit junc 2 onto D217 dir Zouafques/Tournehem/Licques. Foll site sp in vill.
2*, Med, mkd, hdg, pt shd, EHU (6A) €3.70; bbq; 50% statics; Eng spkn; adv bkg acc; ccard acc; fishing nr; CKE. *"Busy site; friendly, helpful owners; dated san facs; ltd LS; gd walking/cycling; conv Calais & ferries; vg."* **€18.00, 30 Mar-3 Nov.** **2020**

LICQUES *3A3* (1.8km SE Rural) *50.77974, 1.94766* **Camping Les Pommiers des Trois Pays,** 273 Rue du Breuil, 62850 Licques **03 21 35 02 02; contact@pommiers-3pays.com; www.pommiers-3pays.com**

🐕 €1 ♿ wc 🚿 ♿ 🛒 🚮 ♪ MSP 🦋 🍽 ⬆ (H) 🚗 nr ⛽ ✒ 🏊 (covrd, htd)

Fr Calais to Guînes on D127 then on D215 to Licques; take D191 fr vill & foll sp; site on L in 1km. Or exit A26 junc 2 onto D217 to Licques; turn L onto D215; cont strt on & site on L on far side of vill. NB sloping ent, long o'fits beware grounding.
4*, Med, mkd, hdg, pt shd, sl, EHU (16A) €4.80; bbq; red long stay; TV; 65% statics; Eng spkn; adv bkg acc; ccard acc; games rm; golf 25km; fishing 2km; sailing 25km; games area. *"Site v full early Jun, adv bkg rec; lge pitches; friendly, helpful owners; gd quality facs, ltd LS, rest clsd; gd beaches nr; gd walking; conv Calais/Dunkerque ferries; gd; excel san facs; busy, well-run site; sm pool for children; clean facs; only 0.75h fr Calais ferry."* **€29.00, 15 Mar-31 Oct.** **2019**

LIGNY EN BARROIS *6E1* (0.5km W Rural) *48.68615, 5.31666* **Camp Municipal Chartel,** Rue des Etats-Unis, 55500 Ligny-en-Barrois **03 29 77 09 36 or 03 29 78 02 22 (Mairie); mairie@lignyenbarrois.fr; http://www.lignyenbarrois.com/wp/tourisme/camping-municipal/**

🐕 ♿ (cont) wc 🚮 ♪ 🚗 nr ⛽

If app fr E, leave N4 at Ligny-en-Barrois N exit, turn S twd town; in approx 500m turn R at junc (bef rd narr); foll sm sp, site 500m on L. If app fr W, leave N4 at exit W of town onto N135 (Rue des Etats-Unis); site sp on R. 2*, Sm, hdstg, pt shd, terr, EHU inc; own san rec; sw nr; Eng spkn; fishing 500m; CKE. *"Poss diff lge o'fits; modern san facs; further modernisation planned (2010); gd NH; great site and location."* **€11.00, 1 May-30 Sep.** **2020**

LIGNY LE CHATEL *4F4* (0.5km SW Rural) *47.89542, 3.75288* **Camp Municipal La Noue Marrou,** 89144 Ligny-le-Châtel **03 86 47 56 99 or 03 86 47 41 20 (Mairie); camping.lignylechatel@orange.fr; www.mairie-ligny-le-chatel-89.fr**

🐕 ♿ wc 🚿 ♿ 🛒 🚮 ♪ MSP 🦋 🍽 ⬆ (H) 🚗 🚮

Exit A6 at junc 20 Auxerre S onto D965 to Chablis. In Chablis cross rv & turn L onto D91 dir Ligny. On ent Ligny turn L onto D8 at junc after Maximart. Cross sm rv, foll sp to site on L in 200m. 2*, Sm, mkd, pt shd, EHU (16A) inc; bbq (charcoal, elec, gas); sw nr; phone; bus 200m; Eng spkn; ccard acc; tennis; games area; CKE. *"Well-run site; lge pitches; no twin axles; v welcoming, friendly warden lives on site; san facs dated but clean; pleasant vill with gd rests; popular NH; excel."* **€12.00, 15 Apr-1 Oct.** **2019**

LIGUEIL *4H2* (2km N Rural) *47.05469, 0.84615* **Camping de la Touche,** Ferme de la Touche, 37240 Liqueil **02 47 59 54 94; booklatouche@hotmail.co.uk; www.theloirevalley.com**

12 🐕 ♿ wc 🚮 ♪ 🍽 ⬆ (H) 🚗 🚮

Fr Loches SW on D31; turn L at x-rds with white cross on R 2km after Ciran; in 500m turn R, site on R bef hotel. Fr A10 exit junc 25 Ste Maure-de-Touraine & foll sp to Ligueil; then take D31 dir Loches; turn L at white cross. Sm, mkd, hdstg, pt shd, EHU (10A) €5; adv bkg acc; ccard acc; bike hire; fishing; CKE. *"Well-maintained, relaxed CL-type site; lge pitches; welcoming, helpful British owners; c'van storage; excel san facs; gd walking & touring base; dogs free; much wild life; conv m'way; gd; cycling dist fr pleasant vill."* **€15.50** **2015**

LILLEBONNE *3C2* (4km W Rural) *49.53024, 0.49763* **Camping Hameau des Forges,** 76170 St Antoine la-Forêt **02 35 39 80 28 or 02 35 91 48 30**

12 🐕 ♿ wc 🚮 ♪ 🦋

Fr Le Havre take rd twds Tancarville bdge, D982 into Lillebonne, D81 W to site on R in 4km (pt winding rd). Fr S over Tancarville bdge onto D910 sp Bolbec. At 2nd rndabt turn R onto D81, site 5km on L. NB Concealed ent by notice board and post-box. 1*, Med, pt shd, EHU (5A) inc; 90% statics; adv bkg acc; CKE. *"Basic, clean, open site; staff welcoming & helpful; poss statics only LS & facs ltd; site muddy when wet; conv NH for Le Havre ferries late arr & early dep; Roman amphitheatre in town worth visit; site & facs tired (2019); fair."* **€16.40** **2019**

LIMOGNE EN QUERCY *7D4* (0.6km W Rural) *44.39571, 1.76396* **Camp Municipal Bel-Air,** 46260 Limogne-en-Quercy **05 65 24 32 75 or 06 84 27 22 95; camping.lebelair@free.fr; www.camping-le-bel-air.fr**

♿ 🚿 ♪ 🦋 🍽 nr 🚗 🏊

E fr Cahors on D911 just bef Limogne vill. W fr Villefranche on D911 just past vill; 3 ents about 50m apart. 3*, Sm, mkd, shd, sl, EHU (6A) inc; adv bkg rec. *"Friendly welcome; if warden absent, site yourself; pleasant vill."* **€18.00, 1 Apr-1 Oct.** **2019**

FRANCE

LISIEUX *3D1* (2km N Rural) *49.16515, 0.22054*
Camp Municipal de La Vallée, 9 Rue de la Vallée, 14100 Lisieux **02 31 62 00 40 or 02 31 48 18 10 (LS); tourisme@cclisieuxpaysdauge.fr; www.lisieux-tourisme.com**

[icons] nr [icons] nr [icons] nr

N on D579 fr Lisieux twd Pont l'Evêque. Approx 500m N of Lisieux take L to Coquainvilliers onto D48 & foll sp for Camping (turn L back in Lisieux dir). Site on D48 parallel to main rd. On app to site look for Volvo dealer & Super U supmkt. 3*, Med, hdstg, pt shd, EHU (6A) €2.50-4.50; gas; 20% statics; bus fr ent; CKE. "Interesting town, childhood home of St Thérèse; helpful warden; v clean san facs; gd." €14.30, 1 May-30 Sep. **2017**

"I need an on-site restaurant"

We do our best to make sure site information is correct, but it is always best to check any must-have facilities are still available or will be open during your visit.

LISLE *7C3* (6km SW Rural) *45.25731, 0.49573*
Camp Municipal Le Pré Sec, 24350 Tocane-St Apre **05 53 90 40 60 or 05 53 90 70 29; commune-de-tocane-st-apre@orange.fr; www.campingdupresec.com**

[icons] nr

Fr Ribérac E on D710 sp Brantôme. Fr E or W at Tocane St Apre, take bypass rd at rndabt. Site sp at both rndabts - dist 500m. Site is on N side of D710 (fr Riberac dir, there is a gab bet cent reservation to turn L.) Ent thro lge car park for Tocan Sports, barrier to site 100m back. 3*, Med, hdg, shd, EHU (6-10A) €1.80; bbq; twin axles; 10% statics; phone; bus 200m; Eng spkn; adv bkg acc; CKE. "Gd; canoeing nrby on Rv Dronne." €10.00, 2 May-30 Sep. **2019**

LOCHES *4H2* (1km S Urban) *47.12255, 1.00175*
Camping La Citadelle (formerly Kawan Vill), Ave Aristide Briand, 37600 Loches **02 47 59 05 91 or 06 21 37 93 06 (mob); camping@lacitadelle.com; www.lacitadelle.com**

[icons] €3 (htd) [icons] (htd)

Fr any dir take by-pass to S end of town & leave at Leclerc rndabt for city cent; site well sp on R in 800m. 4*, Lge, mkd, hdg, pt shd, EHU (10A) €5 (poss rev pol) (poss long lead req); gas; bbq; red long stay; TV; 30% statics; Eng spkn; adv bkg rec; ccard acc; golf 9km; tennis nr; boating; games area; bike hire; fishing; CKE. "Attractive, well-kept, busy site nr beautiful old town; views of citadel; gd sized pitches, poss uneven; helpful staff; facs poss stretched; barrier clsd 2200-0800; poss no night security (2010); rvside walk into town; poss mosquitoes; site muddy after heavy rain; mkt Wed & Sat am; excel site; lge serviced pitches; sh walk to a beautiful medieval town; new san facs; 3 pool complex." €32.50, 29 Mar-30 Sep. **2019**

LOCMARIAQUER *2G3* (2km NW Coastal) *47.57982, -2.97394* **Camping Lann Brick,** Lieu Dit Lann-Brick, 56740 Locmariaquer **02 97 57 32 79 or 06 42 22 29 69 (mob); camping.lanbrick@wanadoo.fr; www.camping-lannbrick.com**

[icons] €2.60 (cont) [icons] nr [icons] (htd) [icons] 0.5km

N165/E60, exit Crach via D28 dir Locmariaquer. L Onto D781. Sp on R 2km bef Locmariaquer. 3*, Med, mkd, hdg, shd, EHU (6/10A); bbq; twin axles; TV; 40% statics; phone; bus adj; Eng spkn; adv bkg acc; ccard acc; bike hire; CKE. "Gd; quiet well managed site; helpful & friendly owners; facs well maintained & spotless; easy walk to beach; delightful site; gd location for Gulf of Morbihan; easy cycle rte; hg hdg." €27.60, 16 Mar-31 Oct. **2019**

LOCQUIREC *2E2* (2km SW Coastal) *48.67940, -3.65320* **Camping Municipal Du fond de la Baie,** Route de Plestin, 29241 Locquirec **02 98 67 40 85; campingdufonddelabaie@gmail.com; www.campinglocquirec.com**

12 [icons] €1 [icons] [icons] sand adj

Fr D786 Morlaix-Lannion, turn L (traff lts) at Plestin-Les-Graves onto D42. At T junc on reaching Bay turn L onto D64. Site on R on app Locquirec. 2*, Lge, mkd, pt shd, gas; bbq; twin axles; 6% statics; phone; bus adj; Eng spkn; adv bkg acc; ccard acc. "Beautifully situated beachside site; vill 1.5km; flat site; fishing, boating & shellfishing; gd." €19.00 **2016**

LODEVE *10E1* (3km S Urban) *43.71247, 3.32179* **Camping Les Vals,** 2000 route de Puech, 34700 Lodève **04 30 40 17 80 or 06 04 01 18 78; campinglesvals@yahoo.fr; www.camping-les-vals.org**

[icons]

Fr N: A75 exit 52 dir Lodéve. Foll av. Fumel, not the cent. R over Vinas bdge dir Puech. Fr S: A75 exit 53 dir Lodéve cent dir Puech on Vinas bdge. 2km on the D148. 3*, Med, hdg, mkd, pt shd, pt sl, terr, EHU (6A); sw nr; TV; 30% statics; phone; Eng spkn; adv bkg acc; games area; watersports adj; games rm; bike hire; tennis; rv fishing adj; CKE. "Gd site; v ltd facs LS." €26.00, 15 Apr-30 Oct. **2015**

LODEVE *10E1* (9km S Rural) *43.67182, 3.35429* **Camp Municipal Les Vailhés,** Baie des Vailhes, Lac du Salagou, 34700 Lodève **04 11 95 01 82; camping@lodevoisetlarzac.fr; www.campinglesvailhes.com**

[icons]

Fr N exit A75 junc 54 onto D148 dir Octon & Lac du Salagou. Foll site sp. Fr S exit A75 junc 55. 3*, Lge, hdg, mkd, pt shd, terr, EHU (16A) inc; bbq; sw; 20% statics; Eng spkn; fishing; watersports; CKE. "Peaceful, remote site by lake; pleasant staff; no facs nrby; excel walks; gd." €8.00, 1 Apr-30 Sep. **2018**

LONGEVILLE SUR MER *7A1* (3km SW Coastal) *46.41310, -1.52280* **Camping Les Brunelles,** Rue de la Parée, Le Bouil, 85560 Longeville-sur-Mer **02 51 33 50 75; camping@les-brunelles.com; www.les-brunelles.com**

🐕 €5.50 ♨ ⛺ ♿ 🚿 🖭 MSP 🍴 🍽 Ⅲ nr 🎣 🛶 ♠ ✎
🏊 (covrd, htd) 🛶 ⛱ sand 800m

Site bet Longeville-sur-Mer & Jard-sur-Mer; foll D21. 4*, Lge, mkd, pt shd, pt sl, serviced pitches; EHU (10A) inc; TV; 75% statics; Eng spkn; adv bkg acc; ccard acc; gym; sauna; bike hire; horseriding 2km; games area; waterslide; watersports; tennis; golf 15km. *"Gd san facs."* **€25.00, 7 Apr-22 Sep, A02.** 2017

LONS LE SAUNIER *6H2* (2.7km NE Rural) *46.68437, 5.56843* **Camping La Marjorie,** 640 Blvd de l'Europe, 39000 Lons-le-Saunier **03 84 24 26 94; info@camping-marjorie.com; www.camping-marjorie.com**

🐕 €2.60 ♨ WD ⛺ ♿ 🚿 🖭 🍴 🍽 🛶 ♠ Ⅲ 🏊 (covrd, htd)

Site clearly sp in town on D1083 twd Besançon. Fr N bear R dir 'Piscine', cross under D1083 to site. 4*, Lge, hdg, hdstg, pt shd, terr, EHU (10A) inc (poss rev pol); gas; twin axles; phone; Eng spkn; ccard acc; golf 8km; games area; CKE. *"Lovely site in beautiful area; conv location; lge pitches; welcoming, friendly, helpful owners; excel, spotless san facs; 20 mins walk to interesting old town & Laughing Cow Museum; ideal touring base; rec; excel; by busy main rd; well run; aquatic cent adj; red facs in LS; upper terr nr to superior facs; long lead poss needed."* **€25.00, 1 Apr-15 Oct.** 2019

LORIENT *2F2* (6km N Rural) *47.82041, -3.40689* **Camping Ty Nénez,** Route de Lorient, 56620 Pont-Scorff **02 97 32 51 16; contact@camping-tynenez.com; www.lorient-camping.com**

12 🐕 €1 ♨ (htd) WD ⛺ ♿ 🚿 🖭 MSP 🦋 🍴 🍽 Ⅲ nr
🏊 (htd)

N fr N165 on D6, look for sp Quéven in approx 5km on R. If missed, cont for 1km & turn around at rndabt. Site sp fr Pont Scorff. 3*, Med, hdg, pt shd, EHU (16A) €3; bbq; 10% statics; Eng spkn; adv bkg acc; games area. *"Site barrier locked 2200-0800; excel LS; peaceful NH; tidy, organised site; excel htd facs; gd base for S Brittany."* **€29.00** 2017

LORIENT *2F2* (10km NE Rural) *47.80582, -3.28347* **Camping d'Hennebont (formerly Municipal St Caradec),** Quai St Caradec, 56700 Hennebont **07 88 41 06 41 or 02 97 36 21 73; campinghennebont @gmail.com; campinghennebont.wixsite.com/bretagne**

🐕 ♨ WD ⛺ ♿ 🚿 🖭 MSP 🦋 🍴 🍽 nr ♠

Fr S on D781 to Hennebont. In town cent turn L & cross bdge, then sharp R along Rv Blavet for 1km. On R on rv bank. 2*, Med, mkd, pt shd, EHU inc; 10% statics; Eng spkn; adv bkg acc; bike hire; CKE. *"Pretty site; excel fishing; peaceful; pleasant sh walk into sm town; site barrier locked 2200-0700; tel on arri; excel customer care."* **€13.00, 1 Apr-15 Sep.** 2019

LOUDEAC *2E3* (2km E Urban) *48.17764, -2.72834* **Campsite Seasonova Aquarev,** Les Ponts es Bigots, 22600 Loudéac **02 96 26 21 92; contact@camping-aquarev.com; www.vacances-seasonova.com**

🐕 ♨ ⛺ ♿ 🚿 🖭 MSP 🍴 🍽 Ⅲ

Fr Loudeac take N164 twrds Rennes. Site on L by lake. 2*, Med, mkd, pt shd, EHU (10A) inc; 10% statics; adv bkg acc; games area; CKE. *"Walks; tennis; fishing; archery; vg."* **€19.00, 31 Mar-15 Oct.** 2017

LOUDUN *4H1* (1km W Rural) *47.00379, 0.06337* **Camp Municipal de Beausoleil,** Chemin de l'Etang, 86200 Loudun **05 49 98 14 22 or 05 49 98 15 38; mairie@ville-loudun.fr; www.ville-loudun.fr**

♨ ⛺ ♿ 🚿 / 🦋 🍽 nr Ⅲ

On main rte fr Poitiers to Saumur/Le Mans; N on D347 around Loudun, foll sp; turn L just N of level x-ing, then on R approx 250m. 3*, Sm, hdg, mkd, pt shd, terr, EHU (10A) inc; bus adj; Eng spkn; lake fishing adj; CKE. *"Beautiful, well-kept site; lge pitches; site yourself, warden calls am & pm; friendly & helpful; excel; long way fr the town."* **€22.00, 15 May-31 Aug.** 2019

LOUHANS *6H1* (2km W Urban) *46.62286, 5.21733* **Camping Les 3 Rivieres Louhans,** 10, Chemin de la Chapellerie, 71500 Louhans **03 85 75 19 02 or 03 85 76 75 10 (Mairie); campinglhs@gmail.com; www.camping-louhans.com/**

🐕 Free ♨ WD ⛺ ♿ 🚿 / 🍴 🍽 🕙 ♠ Ⅲ 🏊 (covrd)

In Louhans foll sp for Romenay on D971. Go under rlwy & over rv. Site on L just after stadium. 3*, Med, hdg, mkd, hdstg, shd, EHU €3.60; bbq; sw nr; adv bkg acc; Tennis, volleyball, table tennis; CKE. *"Rv location; clean & well-appointed; sports complex adj; lovely cycling area; tennis courts adj; mv service pnt nr; lge town mkt Mon am; poss travellers; vg."* **€7.40, 28 Mar-30 Sep.** 2020

LOURDES *8F2* (1km N Urban) *43.09697, -0.04336* **Camping de la Poste,** 26 Rue de Langelle, 65100 Lourdes **05 62 94 40 35**

♨ ⛺ ♿ / 🖭 🦋

Fr NW take D940/D914 sp Centre Ville. At traff lts turn R. Go under rlwy bdge, at rndabt take 2nd exit sp Centre Ville. In 400m at La Poste turn L into Rue de Langelle. Site on R in 400m sp "Camping". Entry thro archway. Fr NE take N21/D914 sp Cent Ville. Sm, pt shd, EHU (3-10A); train 500m, bus 1km; adv bkg acc; CKE. *"Well supervised by friendly, helpful owners; excel food mkt; basic facs; gd NH."* **€12.50, 1 Apr-30 Sep.** 2016

LOURDES *8F2* (1km NE Urban) *43.10247, -0.02789*
Camping de Sarsan, 4 Ave Jean Moulin, 65100 Lourdes
05 62 94 43 09 or 06 07 94 36 74 (mob); camping.
sarsan@wanadoo.fr; www.camping-sarsan.fr

🐕 🏕 👫 wc 🚿 ⬛ 🏊 ⁄ MSF 🦋 ♀ 🛒 ⚓ 🛶

Fr N on N21 past airport, on app to Lourdes turn
L sp 'Zone Indust du Monge'. Pass Cmp Le Moulin
du Monge & foll site sp for approx 2km. Site on L
immed after x-rds. 3*, Med, pt shd, pt sl, EHU (4-10A)
pos rev pol €2.50-4.60; TV; 10% statics; adv bkg acc;
games rm; games area. *"Easy 25min walk to town
cent."* **€13.00, 1 Apr-15 Oct.**   **2020**

LOURDES *8F2* (3km W Rural) *43.09561, -0.07463*
Camping La Forêt, Route de la Forêt, 65100 Lourdes
05 62 94 04 38; hello@camping-hautes-pyrenees.com;
www.camping-hautes-pyrenees.com

🐕 🏕 👫 ♿ ⬛ ⁄ MSF 🦋 ♀ 🍴 Ⓗ 🛒 ⚓ 🛶 🎿

Fr N on N21 exit onto D914 to Lourdes; on ent
Lourdes turn L off D914 under rlwy bdge dir Cent
Ville & hospital; in 100m turn R onto Rue de Pau sp
St Pé & Bétharram; in 1km turn L over rv bdge; site
in 1km. 3*, Med, mkd, pt shd, EHU (3-10A) €2.60-
7.60; gas; bbq; 10% statics; phone; Eng spkn; adv
bkg acc; ccard acc; CKE. *"Lovely site; helpful owners;
conv town cent & grotto (1km); poss open outside
stated dates - adv bkg req; ideal site to visit Lourdes."*
€30.00, 25 Mar-31 Oct.   **2019**

LOUVIE JUZON *8F2* (1km E Rural) *43.08940,*
-0.41019 **FFCC Camping Le Rey,** Quartier Listo, Route
de Lourdes, 64260 Louvie-Juzon **05 59 05 78 52;**
nadia@camping-pyrenees-ossau.com; www.camping-
pyrenees-ossau.com

🐕 €2 👫(htd) wc 🚿 ♿ ⬛ ⁄ 🦋 ♀ Ⓗ 🛒 nr ♨ 🛒 nr ⚓ 🎿 🛶

Site on L at top of hill E fr Louvie; v steep app.
3*, Sm, mkd, pt shd, pt sl, EHU (6A) €3.30; 50% statics;
phone; adv bkg acc; site clsd last 2 weeks Nov &
last 2 weeks Jan; watersports nr; fishing nr; games
area; CKE. *"Fascinating area; chateau nr; lovely,
friendly site; not all facs open in LS; nice town."*
€22.00, 1 Jan-15 Jan, 1 Feb-15 Nov &
1 Dec-31 Dec.   **2015**

LOUVIERS *3D2* (3.5km W Rural) *49.21490, 1.13279*
Camping Le Bel Air, Route de la Haye-Malherbe,
Hameau de St-Lubin, 27400 Louviers **02 32 40 10 77;**
contact@camping-lebelair.fr; www.camping-lebelair.fr

🐕 €2.50 👫 wc 🚿 ⬛ ⁄ MSF 🦋 ♀ 🛒 nr ⚓ 🛶 (htd)

Site well sp in Louviers. Fr cent foll D81 W for 2.5km
dir La Haye-Malherbe; twisting rd uphill; site on R.
Or if travelling S leave A13 at junc 19 to Louviers &
as bef. NB In town cent look for sm green sp after
Ecole Communale (on L) & bef Jardin Public - a
narr rd (1-way) & easy to miss. 3*, Med, mkd, hdg,
hdstg, shd, EHU (6A) €4.90; gas; 30% statics; Eng
spkn; adv bkg acc; ccard acc; CKE. *"Access to pitches
diff long o'fits, poss mover req; check barrier opening
times; bowling; poss NH only (2013); gd site and
dog walks on site; handy for Newhaven Dieppe rte."*
€24.00, 15 Mar-15 Oct.   **2016**

LUCHON *8G3* (2km N Rural) *42.80806, 0.59667*
Camping Pradelongue, 31110 Moustajon
05 61 79 86 44; contact@camping-pradelongue.com;
www.camping-pradelongue.com

🐕 €2 👫 wc 🚿 ♿ ⬛ ⁄ 🦋 ♀ 🛒 nr ⚓ 🛶 (htd)

Site is on D125c on W of D125 main rd fr Luchon.
Ent at Moustajon/Antignac going S. Site adj
Intermarché; sp. 4*, Lge, mkd, hdg, pt shd, EHU (2-
10A) €2-4; bbq; 10% statics; Eng spkn; adv bkg acc;
ccard acc; games area; CKE. *"Excel, well-run, tidy, big
site; mountain views; gd sized pitches; friendly, helpful
owners; rec; excel clean san facs; big supmkt adj;
20mins walk to lovely town; excel for walking, mountain
& rd cycling."* **€26.00, 1 Apr-30 Sep.**   **2015**

LUCON *7A1* (11km E Rural) *46.46745, -1.02792*
Camp Municipal Le Vieux Chêne, Rue du Port,
85370 Nalliers **02 51 30 91 98 or 02 51 30 90 71;**
nalliers.mairie@wanadoo.fr

👫 wc 🚿 ⬛ ⁄ 🦋 🛒 nr ⚓

Fr Luçon E on D949 dir Fontenay-le-Comte;
500m after ent Nalliers turn R onto D10 (Rue de
Brantome); after level x-ing cont strt on for 50m
(leaving D10); then Rue du Port on L. Site sp on
D949 but easy to miss. 2*, Sm, hdg, mkd, pt shd,
EHU (4-13A) €3.90; adv bkg acc; CKE. *"Excel, clean
site; site yourself on lge pitch; in LS contact Mairie
for ent to site; vg NH; conv for rd to Bordeaux."*
€14.50, 15 May-15 Sep.   **2015**

LUCON *7A1* (17km SE Rural) *46.39174, -01.01952*
Camping l'île Cariot, Rue Du 8 Mai, 85450 Chaillé-
les-Marais **02 5156 7527; camping.ilecariot@**
gmail.com; camping-chaille-les-marais.com

🐕 €1.65 👫(htd) wc 🚿 ♿ ⬛ ⁄ MSF 🦋 ♀ 🍴 🛒 nr ⚓
🛶 (htd)

In Chaille take D25, sp in town. 3*, Sm, mkd, pt shd,
EHU (10A) €3.90; bbq; TV; bus adj; Eng spkn; adv bkg
acc; games area; games rm; CKE. *"Cycle & walking rtes
fr site; nr 'Green Venice'; free canoeing on canal; excel."*
€19.00, 1 Apr-30 Sep.   **2016**

LUDE, LE *4G1* (1km NE Rural) *47.65094, 0.16221*
Camp Municipal au Bord du Loir, Route du Mans,
72800 Le Lude **02 43 94 67 70; camping@ville-**
lelude.fr; www.camping-lelude.com

🐕 👫 wc 🚿 ⬛ ⁄ 🦋 ♀ Ⓗ nr 🛒 nr ⚓ 🛶 🎿

Fr town cent take D305 (E); in 1km take D307 (N) sp
'Le Mans'; site immed on L. Well sp. Fr E on D305,
avoid cent of Vaas, use HGV route. 3*, Med, mkd,
hdg, pt shd, EHU (10A) inc; bbq (gas); TV; 10% statics;
phone; Eng spkn; adv bkg acc; ccard acc; fishing;
cycling; tennis; canoeing; CKE. *"Well-kept, well-run
site; warm welcome, helpful staff; modern san facs; vg
walk to town; Château du Lude & excel rest nrby; highly
rec; gd."* **€13.00, 1 Apr-4 Oct.**   **2016**

LUNEL *10E2* (3km S Rural) *43.65666, 4.14111*
Camping Le Bon Port, 383 Chemin de Mas St Angé, 34400 Lunel **04 67 71 15 65; contact@camping bonport.com; www.campingbonport.com**

🐾 €3.50 ♂♀ ⛺ ♿ ☕ 🚿 ⊿ ◨ ♨ ⛲ 🍽 ⊗ ⓘ 🛒 🎯 🛶 ⚓ 🏊

Exit A9 junc 27 S dir La Grande Motte, D61. **Site sp on L.** 4*, Lge, mkd, hdg, pt shd, EHU (5A) €4; bbq (gas); TV; 50% statics; adv bkg acc; games area; waterslide. *"Site scruffy; ltd facs out of ssn; narr site rds; new leisure pools being completed (2015)."*
€37.00, 4 Apr-30 Sep. **2015**

> ## "Satellite navigation makes touring much easier"
>
> Remember most sat navs don't know if you're towing or in a larger vehicle – always use yours alongside maps and site directions.

LUSIGNAN *7A2* (0.5km N Rural) *46.43712, 0.12369*
Camp Municipal de Vauchiron, Chemin de la Plage, 86600 Lusignan **05 49 43 30 08 or 05 49 43 31 48 (Mairie); lusignan@cg86.fr; www.lusignan.fr**

🐾 ♂♀ ⊿ ⛺ ♿ ☕ 🚿 ⊿ ◨ ⛲ 🍽 nr 🛒 🎯nr 🏊

Site sp fr D611, 22km SW of Poitiers; foll camp sp in Lusignan to rvside. 2*, Med, pt shd, EHU (15A) €2.40 (poss rev pol); bbq; sw nr; phone; adv bkg acc; ccard acc; fishing; boat hire; CKE. *"Beautiful, peaceful site in spacious park; lge pitches; forest & rv walks adj; friendly, helpful resident warden; excel clean san facs; steep walk to historic town; highly rec; rv fishing."*
€13.50, 15 Apr-30 Sep. **2017**

LUSSAC LES CHATEAUX *7A3* (13km SW Rural) *46.32231, 0.67384* **Camp Municipal du Renard,** 8 route de la Mairie, 86150 Queaux **05 49 48 48 32 or 05 49 48 48 08 (Mairie); contact@queaux.fr; www.queaux.fr**

♂♀ ⊿ ⛺ ⊿ 🅼 🦋 🍽 🎯nr ⚓ 🏊

Fr Lussac cross rv bdge sp Poitiers & immed turn L. Foll sp to Gouex & Queaux. Site on D25 S of vill. 2*, Med, mkd, pt shd, pt sl, EHU (6A) €2.50; 10% statics; Eng spkn. *"Lovely rvside site nr pleasant vill; manned high ssn or apply to Mairie."* **€9.00, 15 Jun-15 Sep.** **2017**

LUSSAC LES CHATEAUX *7A3* (6km SW Rural) *46.36912, 0.69330* **Camp Municipal du Moulin Beau,** 86320 Gouex **05 49 48 46 14; www.tourisme-vienne.com**

🐾 ♂♀ ⛺ ⊿ 🦋 🎯

Fr Lussac on N147/E62 dir Poitiers, cross rv bdge sp Poitiers & immed turn L on D25; foll sp to Gouex; site on L in 4km at sw pool/camping sp. Sm, pt shd, EHU (15A) €1.60 (check pol); Tennis; CKE. *"Excel site on bank Rv Vienne; bakery in vill; facs clean but ltd; bollards at site ent, care needed if van over 7m or twin axles; pool 300m; highly rec."*
€4.00, 15 Jun-15 Sep. **2020**

LUXEUIL LES BAINS *6F2* (0.5km N Rural) *47.82315, 6.38200* **FFCC Camping du Domaine de Chatigny,** 14 Rue Grammont, 70300 Luxeuil-les-Bains **03 84 93 97 97; camping.lechatigny@ chainethermale.fr; www.domaine-du-chatigny.com**

🐾 €1.70 ♂♀ (htd) ⊿ ⛺ ♿ ☕ 🚿 ⊿ 🅼 ⛲ 🍽 ⊗ ⓘ 🛒 🎯 ⚓ 🛶

N fr Vesoul on N57; turn L at rndabt into Luxeuil-les-Bains; foll Camping sp. Vehicular access fr Rue Ste Anne. 3*, Med, hdstg, mkd, hdg, pt shd, terr, EHU (16A) €3.50-4.50; gas; bbq; TV; 20% statics; bus 300m; Eng spkn; adv bkg acc; ccard acc; CKE. *"New (2009), high standard site; indoor tennis court; gd."*
€8.00, 1 Mar-31 Oct. **2019**

LUZ ST SAUVEUR *8G2* (1km N Rural) *42.88140, -0.01258* **Airotel Camping Pyrénées,** 46 Ave du Barège, La Ferme Theil, 65120 Esquièze-Sère **05 62 92 89 18; contact@airotel-pyrenees.com; www.airotel-pyrenees.com**

🐾 €1.50 ♂♀ (htd) ⊿ ⛺ ♿ ☕ 🚿 ⊿ 🅼 🦋 ⛲ 🍽 ⊗ ⓘ 🛒 🎯 ⚓ 🏊
🏊 (covrd)

On main rd fr Lourdes to Luz on L past Int'l Campsite. L U-turn into ent archway needs care - use full width of rd & forecourt. 5*, Med, mkd, shd, pt sl, EHU (3-10A) €3.50-6.50 (rev pol); gas; TV; 30% statics; Eng spkn; adv bkg acc; ccard acc; horseriding; sauna; site clsd Oct & Nov; fishing; CKE. *"Beautiful area; facs poss stretched high ssn; ski in winter; walking; excel walking & wildlife; lovely vill; well organised; ACSI discount."*
€37.00, 1 May-24 Sep. **2017**

LUZ ST SAUVEUR *8G2* (0.2km E Urban) *42.87342, -0.00057* **Camping Toy,** 17 Place du 8 mai 1945, 65120 Luz Saint Sauveur **05 62 92 86 85; campingtoy@gmail.com; www.camping-toy.com**

12 🐾 ♂♀ ⊿ ⛺ ♿ ☕ ⊿ 🦋 ⛲ 🍽 nr ⓘnr 🎯nr ⚓

Fr Lourdes D921, at Luz St Sauveur turn L onto sq after x-ing rv. Site in 100m. Med, mkd, shd, pt sl, EHU (1-10A); bbq; bus adj; Eng spkn. *"In cent of town; helpful, friendly owners; pool 0.5km; magnificent views; gd walking/cycling area; st foot of Col du Tourmalet; excel."* **€15.00** **2015**

LUZ ST SAUVEUR *8G2* (2km NW Rural) *42.88218, -0.02270* **Camping Le Pyrénévasion,** Route de Luz-Andiden 65120 Sazos **05 62 92 91 54; camping-pyrenevasion@wanadoo.fr; www.campingpyrene vasion.com**

12 🐾 €2.50 ♂♀ (htd) ⊿ ⛺ ♿ ☕ 🚿 ⊿ 🦋 ⛲ 🍽 ⊗ ⓘ 🛒 🎯 ⚓
🏊 🛶

Fr Lourdes S on D921 twd Gavarnie. Shortly bef Luz-St Sauveur after petrol stn & campsites sp, take R fork onto D12 sp Sazos. Cont thro vill & turn R sp Luz-Andiden, then immed R again sp Sazos (D12) & Luz-Andiden. Cont uphill, site on R just after Sazon sp. 3*, Med, mkd, hdg, pt shd, EHU (3A/6A/10A) €3.5/€7/€8; gas; bbq (charcoal, elec, gas); 60% statics; Eng spkn; fishing; games rm; site clsd 20 Oct-19 Nov. *"Fair site in mountains; no o'fits over 7.5m high ssn; long, steep trek to/fr shops."* **€28.00** **2017**

LUZY *4H4* (1km NE Rural) *46.79622, 3.97685*
Camping La Bédure, Route d'Autun, 58170 Luzy
**03 86 30 68 27; info@campinglabedure.com;
www.campinglabedure.com**

🐕 €1.50 👥 ▲ ♿ ⚡ ✉ 🦋 ⛺ nr ⚠

Foll sps on D981 to site. 2*, Med, mkd, pt shd, pt
sl, EHU (6A) €3 (poss rev pol); Eng spkn. *"Pleasant
site; pool adj; gd walking & touring base; adjoins Lidl."*
€18.60, 14 Apr-30 Sep. **2018**

LYON *9B2* (8km NW Urban) *45.81948, 4.76168*
Camping de Lyon, Ave de la Porte de Lyon, 69570
Dardilly **04 78 35 64 55; contact@camping-lyon.com;
www.camping-lyon.com**

12 🐕 €4,70 👥 (htd) WD ▲ ♿ 🚻 ⚡ ✉ 🛒 ⛱ 🍽 ⓗ ⛺ nr ⚠ 🚣 (htd)

Fr D306 Paris rd, take Limonest-Dardilly-Porte de
Lyon exit at Auchan supmkt. Fr A6 exit junc 33 Porte
de Lyon. Site on W side of A6 adj m'way & close to
junc, foll sp (poss obscured by trees) for 'Complexe
Touristique'. Fr E take N ring rd dir Roanne, Paris,
then as above. 4*, Lge, hdstg, mkd, hdg, pt shd, serviced
pitches; EHU (10A) inc; twin axles; TV; 10% statics;
phone; bus/train to city nr; Eng spkn; adv bkg acc; ccard
acc; games rm; CKE. *"Well-run, secure site; Lyon easy by
bus & metro, tickets can be bought fr recep; bar 100m; gd
touring base for interesting area; helpful recep; gd, clean
san facs; gas 100m; cafes nrby."* **€30.00** **2019**

MACHECOUL *2H4* (0.5km SE Urban) *46.98987,
-1.81562* **Camp Municipal La Rabine,** Allée de la
Rabine, 44270 Machecoul **02 40 02 30 48 or
06 08 49 22 88; camprabine@wanadoo.fr;
camping-la-rabine.com**

🐕 €0.90 👥 WD ▲ ♿ 🚻 ⚡ ✉ 🦋 ⛺ nr ⚠ ✏

Sp fr most dirs. Look out for prominent twin-spired
church in cent; take sm one-way rd that leads away
fr spire end; site on R in 400m.
2*, Med, pt shd, EHU (4-13A) €2-3.20; bbq (gas); adv
bkg acc. *"Pleasant site with lge generous size pitches
& gd facs; excel base for birdwatching & cycling over
marshes; pleasant town; mkt Wed & Sat; pool adj;
lovely friendly well managed site; excel facs; lovely site
rv fishing."* **€15.00, 1 Apr-30 Sep.** **2017**

MACON *9A2* (4km N Urban) *46.33023, 4.84491*
Camp Municipal Les Varennes, 1 Route des Grandes
Varennes, Sancé, 71000 Mâcon **03 85 38 16 22 or
03 85 38 54 08; camping@ville-macon.fr;
www.macon.fr/Tourisme/Camping**

🐕 €1.40 👥 (htd) WD ▲ ♿ 🚻 ⚡ ✉ 🛒 ⛱ 🍽 ⓗ 🎣 ⛺ ⚠ 🚣

Fr both N & S exit A6 junc 28 & cont S on N6 twd
Mâcon; site on L in approx 3km, sp. (Fr S, leaving A6
at junc 28 avoids long trip thro town).
4*, Lge, mkd, pt shd, pt sl, EHU (5-10A) inc (poss rev
pol); gas; red long stay; twin axles; TV; phone; bus; Eng
spkn; adv bkg acc; ccard acc; golf 6km; tennis 1km; CKE.
*"Well-kept, busy NH nr A6; rec arr early as poss full after
1800; friendly staff; vg, immac san facs; hypmkt 1km;
excel rest; gates clsd 2200-0630; poss flooding bottom
end of site; long level walk to town; excel; perfect new
facs (2014)."* **€27.00, 15 Mar-31 Oct.** **2019**

MACON *9A2* (8km S Rural) *46.25167, 4.82610*
Base de loisirs du lac de Cormoranche, Les Luizant,
01290 Cormoranche-sur-Saône **03 85 23 97 10;
contact@lac-cormoranche.com; www.lac-
cormoranche.com**

🐕 €2.20 👥 (htd) WD ▲ ♿ 🚻 ⚡ ✉ MP 🦋 ⛱ 🍽 ⓗ 🎣 🛒 ⛺ ⚠ 🚣 ✏ 🚴

Exit A26 junc 29 sp Mâcon Sud onto N6 S to
Crêches-sur-Saône. Turn L in town at traff lts onto
D31 sp Cormoranche, then D51A. Cross rv, site sp
on L. Alt rte: exit N6 in Mâcon & turn E onto D1079
dir St Laurent-sur-Saône then take D933 S to Pont-
de-Veyle. Cont on D933 & foll sp to Cormoranche.
4*, Med, hdg, mkd, pt shd, EHU (10A) inc; bbq; sw nr;
TV; 25% statics; Eng spkn; adv bkg acc; ccard acc;
fishing; bike hire; CKE. *"Spacious pitches, some with
narr access; vg; tight access to some pitches; gd for
families."* **€31.40, 1 May-30 Sep.** **2019**

MAICHE *6G3* (1km S Rural) *47.24705, 6.79952*
Camp Municipal St Michel, 23 Rue St Michel, 25120
Maîche **03 81 64 12 56 or 03 81 64 03 01 (Mairie);
contact@mairie-maiche.fr; www.mairie-maiche.fr**

12 🐕 👥 (htd) WD ▲ ♿ 🚻 ⚡ ✉ ⛺ nr ⚠

Fr S turn R off D437 onto D442. App on D464 L on
o'skts of town. Sp fr both dir. 3*, Med, pt shd, sl,
terr, EHU (6A) inc; 10% statics; phone; adv bkg acc;
games area; site clsd 3rd week Nov & Dec; games rm.
*"Beautiful, neat, well-run site with lovely views; many
trees & wild flowers; lower pitches are quieter; pool adj;
clean facs; phone ahead LS to check open; gd walks in
woods."* **€18.00** **2017**

"There aren't many sites open at this time of year"

If you're travelling outside peak season
remember to call ahead to check site opening
dates – even if the entry says 'open all year'.

MAILLEZAIS *7A2* (0.4km S Rural) *46.36921, -0.74054*
Camp Municipal de l'Autize, Rue du Champ de Foire,
85420 Maillezais **02 51 00 70 79 or 06 43 19 14 90
(mob); camping.lautize@orange.fr; www.maillezais.fr**

👥 WD ▲ ♿ 🚻 ⚡ ✉ 🦋 ⛱ ⛺ nr ⚠

Fr Fontenay take D148 twd Niort; after 9km, turn R
onto D15 to Maillezais; pass church in vill on L, site
on R after 200m. Or fr A83, exit junc 9 onto D148,
then D15 (do not use v minor rds, as poss directed
by sat nav). 3*, Sm, hdg, mkd, pt shd, EHU (4-13A)
€3-5; twin axles; TV; adv bkg acc; ccard acc; games
rm; games area; CKE. *"Lovely, clean site; spacious
pitches, gd views fr some; friendly, helpful warden;
excel, immac san facs; warden calls am & pm; some
low branches (2010); excel mkd cycle paths; conv
Marais Poitevin area & Venise Verte; nrby abbey worth
a visit; vg NH fr A83; excel; boat rides fr Vieux Port."*
€17.00, 1 Jun-30 Sep. **2018**

MAILLY LE CHATEAU *4G4* (5km S Rural) *47.56267, 3.64671* **Camping Merry Sur Yonne (formerly Municipal Escale),** 5 Impasse de Sables, 89660 Merry-sur-Yonne **03 86 34 59 55; gite.merrysuryonne@wanadoo.fr; www.campingmerrysuryonne.com**

🏕 12 🐕 ♿ wd ⚓ ♨ ⚲ ♿ ∥ MSP 🦋 ♈ 🍴 ⊕ ⚓ 🅿 ⛰

Fr N on D100, turn R over bdge, sp Merry Sur Yonne. At t-junc in vill turn L. At end of vill bear L at war memorial into site. 2*, Med, hdstg, mkd, pt shd, EHU; bbq; cooking facs; sw nr; twin axles; Eng spkn; adv bkg acc; games rm; games area; CCI. *"New British owners; takeaway; beautiful location nr rv and canal; canal walks adj; excel."* **€15.00**   2016

MAINTENON *4E2* (6km NW Rural) *48.60890, 1.54760* **Camping Les Ilots de St Val,** Le Haut Bourray, 28130 Villiers-le-Morhier **02 37 82 71 30; lesilots@camping lesilotsdestval.com; www.campinglesilotsdestval.com**

🏕 €2 🏕(htd) wd ⚓ ⚲ ∥ MSP 🦋 ♈ ⚓ nr ⛰

Take D983 N fr Maintenon twd Nogent-le-Roi, in 5km 2nd L onto D101 sp Néron/Vacheresses-les-Basses/Camping to site in 1km on L at top of hill. NB New by-pass around Nogent le Roi fr N. 3*, Lge, hdg, mkd, hdstg, pt shd, EHU (6-10A) €4-7; gas; bbq; red long stay; 50% statics; Eng spkn; adv bkg acc; games rm; rv fishing 1km; tennis; CKE. *"Pleasant, peaceful site in open countryside; lge private pitches; some vg, modern san facs; helpful staff; gd value site; conv Chartres, Versailles, Maintenon Château, train to Paris; dog walking fr the site is gd; improved access for lge o'fits; pool 4km; phone ahead late Dec to mid Feb as site may be clsd to tourers."* **€32.00, 1 Feb 22 Dec**   2016

MALAUCENE *10E2* (4km N Rural) *44.20101, 5.12535* **Camping La Saousse,** La Madelaine, 84340 Malaucène **04 90 65 14 02; lcamping.lasaousse@orange.fr; www.lasaousse.com**

🐕 🏕 wd ⚓ ⚲ ∥ 🦋 ♈ ⊕ nr ⚓ nr

Fr Malaucène take D938 N dir Vaison-la-Romaine & after 3km turn R onto D13 dir Entrechaux where site sp. After 1km turn R, site 1st on R. Sm, hdg, shd, terr, EHU (5A) €2.50; bbq; adv bkg rec; CKE. *"CL-type site o'looking vineyards with views to Mt Ventoux; some pitches in woods with steep incline - rec pitch on lower level for easy access; friendly, helpful owners; pool 4km; basic, clean facs; v peaceful, excel."* **€14.00, 1 Apr-30 Sep.**   2020

MALBUISSON *6H2* (1.4km SW Urban) *46.79176, 6.29257* **Camping Les Fuvettes,** 24 Route de la Plage et des Perrières, 25160 Malbuisson **03 81 69 31 50; les-fuvettes@wanadoo.fr; www.camping-fuvettes.com**

🐕 €1.50 🏕(htd) ⚓ ⚲ ∥ 🦋 🍴 ⊕ ⚓ 🅿 ⛰

Site 19km S of Pontarlier on N57 & D437 to Malbuisson, thro town, R down rd to Plage. 3*, Lge, pt shd, pt sl, EHU (4-6A) €3.60-4; gas; sw; 30% statics; fishing; games rm; boating; CKE. *"Popular, lakeside, family site; mkd walks/cycle paths in adj woods; petting zoo (llamas etc) nrby."* **€28.00, 5 Apr-30 Sep.**   2019

MALENE, LA *9D1* (0.2km W Rural) *44.30120, 3.31923* **FFCC Camp Municipal Le Pradet,** 48210 La Malène **04 66 48 58 55 or 04 66 48 51 16 (LS); camping.lamalene@gmail.com; www.gorgesdutarn-camping.com**

🐕 €0.30 🏕 wd ⚓ ⚲ ∥ 🦋 ♈ 🍴 nr ⊕ nr ⚓ nr ⛰

W fr La Malène on D907B dir Les Vignes. Site on L in 200m. Well sp. 2*, Sm, hdstg, mkd, pt shd, pt sl, EHU (10A) €2.50; bbq; sw; phone; adv bkg acc; ccard acc; fishing; CKE. *"Kayak hire; boat trips fr vill; helpful warden; excel; v narr pitches; rvside site; steep slope down to recep; spectacular scenery."* **€27.00, 1 Apr-30 Sep.**   2017

MALESHERBES *4E3* (5km S Rural) *48.25659, 2.43574* **FFCC Camping Ile de Boulancourt,** 6 Allée des Marronniers, 77760 Boulancourt **01 64 24 13 38; info@camping-iledeboulancourt.com; www.camping-iledeboulancourt.com**

🏕 12 🐕 €1 🏕(htd) wd ⚓ ⚲ ∥ MSP 🦋 ⊕ ⚓ ⛰

Exit A6 at junc 14 Ury & Fontainebleau. SW on D152 to Malesherbes; S on D410 for 5km into Boulancourt. Site sp fr D410 & in vill. 3*, Med, pt shd, EHU (3-6A) €2.70; bbq; 90% statics; Eng spkn; waterslide 5km; fishing 3km; tennis; CKE. *"Attractive rv thro site; well-maintained facs, ltd LS; sep field for tourers; friendly, helpful staff; golf course in vill; chateau nr; excel."* **€15.70**   2016

MALESTROIT *2F3* (0.5km E Urban) *47.80865, -2.37922* **Camp Municipal de la Daufresne,** Chemin des Tanneurs, 56140 Malestroit **02 97 75 13 33 or 02 97 75 11 75 (Mairie); etat.civil@malestroit.fr; www.villede malestroit.bzh**

🐕 🏕 wd ⚓ ♿ ⚲ ∥ 🚐 ♈ 🍴 nr ⊕ nr ⚓ nr ⛰

S fr Ploërmel on N166 dir Vannes for 9km. Turn L onto D764 to Malestroit; site sp just off Blvd du Pont Neuf on E bank of Rv Oust, not well sp. 2*, Sm, hdg, pt shd, EHU (10A) €2.70 (poss long lead req); adv bkg acc; ccard acc; rv fishing adj; tennis; canoeing nr; CKE. *"Pleasant site in excel location; narr site rds, some pitches poss diff to manoeuvre; no twin axles, clean san facs, basic but ok, poss stretched high ssn; canal towpath adj; gd cycle rtes; Museum of Breton Resistance in St Marcel; v nice, pretty site, highly rec."* **€10.00, 1 May-15 Sep.**   2017

MAMERS *4E1* (0.5km N Rural) *48.35778, 0.37181* **Camp Municipal du Saosnois,** Route de Contilly, 72600 Mamers **02 43 97 68 30; camping.mamers@free.fr; www.mairie-mamers.fr**

🐕 €0.50 🏕(htd) ⚓ ♿ ⚲ ∥ MSP 🦋 ⚓ ⚓

Fr W on D311, at rndabt at top of hill on circular rd, turn R (sp); then easy L (sp). Fr E on D311, strt thro rndabt (at Super U), ignore 1st camping sp, turn R at traff its & 2nd camping sp; at mini-rndabt turn L, sp Contilly; see lake & site. 3*, Sm, hdg, hdstg, pt shd, pt sl, terr, EHU (10A) inc (long lead poss req); TV; 30% statics; adv bkg acc; games area; CKE. *"Well-kept, secure site; admittance LS 1700-1900 only; Mamers pretty; pool 200m; lakeside; easy walk to town."* **€15.00, 15 Apr-30 Sep.**   2016

MANDRES AUX QUATRE TOURS *5D2* (2km S Rural) *48.82739, 5.78936* **Camp Municipal Orée de la Forêt de la Reine,** Route Forêt de la Reine, 54470 Mandres-aux-Quatre-Tours **03 83 23 17 31; mandres.54470@ wandoo.fr**

🛒 🚿 ♿ WD 🚾 ⚘ 🦋 ⛺

On D958 Commercy to Pont-à-Mousson, sp as Camping Mandres. Turn R at sp in Beaumont & foll sp to vill Mandres-aux-Quatre-Tours.
1*, Sm, mkd, hdg, pt shd, EHU (10A) inc (poss long lead req); red long stay; 10% statics; tennis; sailing 500m; watersports 500m; horseriding adj. *"Gd, peaceful site; basic san facs; site poss muddy when wet; gd birdwatching, walking, cycling; popular NH."*
€17.00, 1 Apr-31 Oct. 2018

"That's changed – Should I let the Club know?"

If you find something on site that's different from the site entry, fill in a report and let us know. See camc.com/europereport.

MANOSQUE *10E3* (4km E Rural) *43.82352, 5.85424* **Camping Oxygene,** 04210 Valensole **04 92 72 41 77; info@camping-oxygene.com; www.camping-oxygene.com**

🛒 €2.50 🚿 ♿ WD 🅿 ⚘ 🦋 ⛺ 🛥

Exit A51 junc 18 onto D907 E dir Vinon-sur-Verdon; in 1km turn L at rndabt onto D4 N dir Oraison; site in 2.5km on L, at Les Chabrands, just bef Villedieu. Med, hdg, mkd, pt shd, EHU (6-10A) €3.50-4.50; bbq (elec, gas); gym; horseriding nr; games area. *"Peaceful, well-kept site with hill views; excel well-run site; vg pool; many places of interest nrby, inc Gorges du Verdon; canyoning, angling & rafting nr; paragliding nr; vg farm shop nr."* **€33.50, 20 Apr-17 Sep.** 2019

MANS, LE *4F1* (7.6km NE Rural) *48.01904, 0.27996* **Camping Le Pont Romain,** Allée des Ormeaux, Lieu-dit La Châtaigneraie, 72530 Yvré-l'Evêque **02 43 82 25 39; contact@campinglepontromain.fr**

🛒 €1 🚿 (htd) WD 🚾 ♿ 🅿 ⚘ 🦋 ⛺ 🛥 (htd)

Fr Le Mans take D314 to Yvré-l'Evêque - but do not ent town; just after rv bdge take 1st L into Allée des Ormeaux; site on L in 800m. Or exit A28 junc 23 onto D314 dir 'Le Mans Cent'; site on R just bef Yvré-l'Evêque. Avoid direct rte into vill over bridge.
4*, Med, hdstg, mkd, hdg, pt shd, EHU (16A) inc; gas; bbq; 15% statics; phone; bus; Eng spkn; adv bkg acc; games rm; CKE. *"Excel modern san facs; sep car park; conv Le Mans & m'way; vg; uneven pitches, need TLC; pleasant rural site; easy access to city; recep open 0830-1200 & 1430-2000; gd; bus to Le Mans 1.5km; beautiful site; easy access to bus; excel pitches; gd MV service pnt."* **€28.60, 13 Mar-8 Nov.** 2019

MANS, LE *4F1* (20km SW Urban) *47.889024, 0.033594* **Camp Municipal Le Port,** Ave de la Piscine, 72210 La Suze-sur-Sarthe **02 43 77 32 74 or 02 43 77 39 48; contact@lasuzero.fr; www.lasuze.fr**

12 🛒 €0.45 🚿 WD 🚾 ♿ 🅿 ⚘ MP ⛺ 🛥 ⛺ (htd)

Fr A11 take exit 9 twrds Tours/Allonnes on A11.1, 1st exit on rndabt onto D309. Foll sp to La Suze Sur Sarthe on D233. Cross rlwy and turn L as you come into town, foll sp for MH. Turn R into Ave de la Piscine, then right into parking area. Pay at barrier to be let thro to site. 2*, Med, mkd, pt shd, EHU (10A) €2.30; bbq; red long stay; rv adj; own san; tennis; adv bkg; fishing. *"Narr gate to site; ample hdstg for m'vans in adj car park."* **€4.50** 2018

MANSLE *7B2* (0.4km NE Urban) *45.87841, 0.18175* **Camp Municipal Le Champion,** Rue de Watlington, 16230 Mansle **05 45 20 31 41 or 05 45 22 20 43; mairie.mansle@wanadoo.fr; www.mansle.fr**

🚿 ♿ WD 🚾 ♿ 🅿 ⚘ 🦋 🍴 nr ⛺ 🛥 nr ⛺ 🖊

N on N10 fr Angoulême, foll sp Mansle Ville. Leave N10 at exit to N of town, site rd on L, well sp. Rec ent/leave fr N as rte thro town diff due to parked cars. Site beside Rv Charente. 3*, Med, hdg, pt shd, EHU (16A) €2.80 (poss long lead req); bbq; sw nr; 5% statics; phone; Eng spkn; adv bkg acc; fishing; boating adj; CKE. *"Popular, peaceful, well-kept NH nr N10; lge pitches, choose own; helpful warden; immac san facs; grnd poss boggy after heavy rain; mkt Tues, Fri am; great site in excel location, well run; vg; gd rest; easy walk to town."* **€16.40, 15 May-15 Sep.** 2017

"I like to fill in the reports as I travel from site to site"

You'll find report forms at the back of this guide, or you can fill them in online at camc.com/europereport.

MANSLE *7B2* (10km SE Rural) *45.84137, 0.27319* **Camping Devezeau,** 16230 St Angeau **05 45 94 63 09; ask@campingdevezeau.com; www.campingde vezeau.com**

12 🛒 🚿 (htd) WD ♿ 🅿 ⚘ 🦋 ⛺ 🍴 ⛺ 🛥 nr ⛺

N or S on N10 exit Mansle; in cent vill at traff lts foll sp twd La Rochefoucauld (D6); past Super U supmkt; over bdge; 1st R onto D6. In approx 9km at T-junc turn R, site sp. App down narr rd.
2*, Sm, hdstg, hdg, pt shd, sl, EHU (6A-10A) €2; gas; bbq; twin axles; 25% statics; Eng spkn; adv bkg acc; cycling; canoeing; horseriding; fishing; CKE. *"Nice CL-type site; v friendly British owners; excel san facs modernised (2015); traction diff in wet (4x4 avail); blocks & steel pegs needed; gd cycling country; phone ahead in winter; lovely tranquil site; walking; vg; friendly atmosphere; bar snacks & English breakfast."* **€20.00** 2017

MARANS *7A1* (1km N Rural) 46.31682, -0.99158
Camp Municipal Le Bois Dinot, Route de Nantes, 17230 Marans 05 46 01 10 51; campingmarans@orange.fr; www.ville-marans.fr

🏕 €1.10 ⵛ⚅ / ⛲ ⛳ nr ⊕ nr ≋ nr

Heading S, site on L of D137 bef ent Marans. Heading N, site is well sp on R 300m after supmkt on L. 3*, Lge, shd, EHU (6-10A) €3; red long stay; Eng spkn; adv bkg rec; fishing; boat hire; CKE. *"Well-kept, wooded site; v helpful, efficient staff; quieter pitches at back of site; vg pool adj; poss mosquitoes; gd cycling; mkt Tues & Sat; excel; v clean san facs; grass pitch avail subj to rainfall; woodland pitches quietest; poss diff lger o'fits."* €16.50, 1 Apr-30 Sep. 2019

> **"We must tell the Club about that great site we found"**
>
> Get your site reports in by mid-August and we'll do our best to get your updates into the next edition.

MARCIGNY *9A1* (7km W Rural) 46.26489, 3.95756
Camping La Motte aux Merles, 71110 Artaix 03 85 25 37 67; campingpicard@yahoo.fr

🏕 €1 ⵛ⚅ / ⛲ ⛳ 🦋 ⛳ ⊕ ≋

Leave D982 (Digoin-Roanne) at Marcigny by-pass. Take D989 twd Lapalisse. In 2km at Chambilly cont on D990, site sp in 5km on L, 200m down side rd. Sm, pt shd, pt sl, EHU (8A) €2.40; bbq; fishing nr; tennis nr; golf nr. *"Friendly owners, gd sightseeing in peaceful area; site diff in wet; excel."* €10.00, 1 Apr-31 Oct. 2020

MARENNES *7B1* (10.5km SE Rural) 45.77324, -0.96301 **Camping Le Valerick,** La Petite Mauvinière, 17600 St Sornin 05 46 85 15 95; camplevalerick@aol.com; www.camping-le-valerick.fr

🏕 €1.40 ⵛ(htd) ⚅ / 🦋 ⛳ ⛲ ≋ ⊕

Fr Marennes take D728 sp Saintes for 10km; L to St Sornin; site sp in vill. Fr Saintes D728 W for 26km; take 2nd R turn R in vill D118, site on L sp La Gripperie. 2*, Sm, mkd, pt shd, pt sl, EHU (4-6A) €3-€3.70 (poss rev pol); bbq (charcoal, gas); adv bkg acc; ccard acc; CKE. *"Nice, friendly site; gd san facs; plenty of bird life - herons, storks etc; poss mosquito problem; excel; spotless san facs; lge pitches; v warm welcome; highly rec."* €19.00, 1 Apr-30 Sep. 2019

MARENNES *7B1* (5km SE Rural) 45.81083, -1.06027 **Camping Séquoia Parc,** La Josephtrie, 17320 St Just-Luzac 05 46 85 55 55; info@sequoiaparc.com; www.sequoiaparc.com

🏕 €7 ⚅ ⛲ ⚅ / ⛲ ⛳ ⊕ ≋ ⊕ ≋ 🦋

Fr A10/E05 m'way exit at Saintes, foll sp Royan (N150) turning off onto D728 twd Marennes & Ile d'Oléron; site sp to R off D728, just after leaving St Just-Luzac. Or fr Rochefort take D733 & D123 S; just bef Marennes turn L on D241 sp St Just-Luzac. Best ent to site fr D728, well sp fr each dir. 5*, Lge, mkd, hdg, unshd, sl, serviced pitches; EHU (6A) inc (poss rev pol); gas; bbq; red long stay; TV; 60% statics; adv bkg acc; ccard acc; fishing 1.5km; bike hire; watersports 3km; games area; horseriding; tennis; games rm; CKE. *"High standard site; aqua park: o'fits over 8m on request; max 1 dog; waterslides, waterjets & whirlpool; barrier clsd 2230-0700; 3 pools (2 htd); lge pitches; cash machine; clean san facs; superb pools; excel free club for children."* €54.00, 5 May-5 Sep, A28. 2019

MARENNES *7B1* (2km NW Coastal) 45.83139, -1.15092 **Camp Municipal La Giroflée,** 17560 Bourcefranc-le-Chapus 05 46 85 06 43 or 05 46 85 02 02 (Mairie); campinglagiroflee@orange.fr; www.bourcefranc-le-chapus.fr

ⵛ ⛲ ⚅ / 🦋 ⛳ nr ⊕ ≋ adj

Fr Saintes on D728/D26 to Boucefranc, turn L at traff lts. Site on L after 1km (after sailing school) opp beach. 2*, Med, pt shd, EHU (6A) €3. €7.60, 1 May-30 Sep. 2017

MAREUIL *7B2* (5km N Rural) 45.49504, 0.44860 **FFCC Camping Les Graulges,** Le Bourg, 24340 Les Graulges 05 53 60 74 73; info@lesgraulges.com; www.lesgraulges.com

🏕 €2 ⵛ ⚅ ⛲ ⚅ / 🦋 ⛳ ⊕ ≋

Fr D939 at Mareuil turn L onto D708 & foll sp to Les Graulges in 5km. 1*, Sm, mkd, pt shd, pt sl, terr, EHU (6A) €3.50; bbq; red long stay; TV; 10% statics; Eng spkn; adv bkg acc; lake fishing. *"Tranquil site in forested area; ideal touring base; friendly Dutch owners; excel rest; not suitable for elderly; pool dirty; lge dog lives on site (2012)."* €20.50, 1 Apr-30 Sep. 2020

MAREUIL *7B2* (4km SE Rural) 45.44481, 0.50474 **Camping L'Etang Bleu,** 24340 Vieux-Mareuil 05 53 60 92 70; letangbleu@ornage.fr; www.letangbleu.com

🏕 €3 ⵛ ⚅ ⛲ ⚅ / ⛲ ⛳ ⊕ ≋ ⊕ ≋

On D939 Angoulême-Périgueux rd, after 5km turn L cent of Vieux-Mareuil onto D93, foll camping sp to site in 2km. Narr app thro vill, care needed. 2*, Lge, hdg, mkd, pt shd, EHU 6-10A (poss rev pol); gas; bbq; TV; 10% statics; adv bkg acc; ccard acc; lake fishing 500m; CKE. *"Pleasant site in unspoilt countryside; lge pitches, but narr site rds; access diff lge o'fits without mover; friendly British owners; gd san facs, ltd LS; gd walking/cycling area; excel."* €23.50, 1 Apr-20 Oct. 2018

MAREUIL *7B2* (8km SE Rural) *45.42429, 0.53070*
Camping La Charrue, Les Chambarrières, 24340
Vieux-Mareuil **05 53 56 65 59; bookings@lacharrue.
biz** or **clive.davie@sfr.fr; www.lacharrue.biz**

🐕 ♿ ♨ wc ♨ 🚿 ⛴ 〆 〒 nr ⊕ nr ♨ 🏊 nr 🎭 🛝 🏖 sand nrby

SE fr Angoulême on D939 sp Périgueux to
Mareuil. Fr Mareuil stay on D939 twds Brantôme,
thro Vieux-Mareuil then in 2km site immed on L
after passing a lge lay-by on R with white stone
chippings. Awkward turn. Sm, mkd, pt shd, EHU
(4A) €3; bbq; red long stay; adv bkg req; watersports
nr; fishing 3km; bike hire; golf nr; CKE. *"CL-type site
in Regional Park; friendly, helpful British owners; no
dogs high ssn; bar 500m; immac facs; gd touring base
for beautiful area; lakes nrby; B&B & gites avail; excel."*
€14.50, 1 May-31 Oct. **2015**

MARNAY (HAUTE SAONE) *6G2* (0.5km SE Urban)
47.28975, 5.77628 **Camping Vert Lagon,** Route de
Besançon, 70150 Marnay **03 84 31 73 16** or **06 40 78
58 13; accueil@camping-vertlagon.com;
www.camping-vertlagon.com**

🐕 €1 ♿ wc ♨ 🚿 ♿ 〆 〆 MSP 🦋 〒 〒 ⊕ nr ♨ 🛝 nr 🎭
🏊 (htd)

Fr N stay on D67 Marnay by-pass; ignore old
camping sp into town. Proceed to S of town on
by-pass then turn L at junc. Bef bdge in 1km take
gravel rd on S side, round under bdge to site (app
thro town fr N v narr). 4*, Med, hdg, mkd, pt shd, EHU
(10A) €4; bbq; 40% statics; adv bkg acc; ccard acc;
games area; canoeing; fishing; CKE. *"Pleasant, popular,
family site by Rv Ognon; gd san facs; lake adj; tree-top
walks; vg."* **€21.00, 2 May-30 Sep.** **2017**

> ## "I need an on-site restaurant"
>
> We do our best to make sure site information
> is correct, but it is always best to check any
> must-have facilities are still available or will
> be open during your visit.

MARQUION *3B4* (2.7km NE Rural) *50.22280, 3.10863*
FFCC Camping de l'Epinette, 7 Rue du Calvaire,
62860 Sauchy-Lestrée **03 21 59 50 13; lepinette62@
wanadoo.fr; www.lepinette62.com**

🐕 ♿ wc ♨ 🚿 〆 🛒 nr 🎭

Fr A26 exit junc 8 onto D939 to Marquion. On ent
Marquion turn R at x-rds to Sauchy-Lestrée; on
ent vill turn R at 1st T-junc & site on L in 100m.
Fr Cambrai take D939 twd Arras, then as above.
2*, Sm, pt shd, pt sl, EHU (10A) €3 (poss rev pol); own
san rec; gas; 80% statics; adv bkg acc; games area;
CKE. *"Charming, well-kept site in tranquil spot; sm CL-
type area for tourers; clean, simple, dated but adequate
facs, no facs LS, NH only; levelling blocks ess for
m'vans; conv Calais/Dunkerque; quiet but some military
aircraft noise; WW1 cemetary nr; gd value; popular
excel NH."* **€15.00, 1 Apr-31 Oct.** **2019**

MARQUISE *3A3* (5km SW Rural) *50.78389, 1.66917*
FFCC Camping L'Escale, 15 Route Nationale, 62250
Wacquinghen **03 21 32 00 69; camp-escale@
wanadoo.fr; www.escale-camping.fr**

🐕 ♿ (cont) wc ♨ 🚿 ♿ 〆 〆 MSP 🦋 〒 🍴 ⊕ ♨ 🎭 🛝 🖌

Fr A16 S fr Calais exit junc 34. Fr A16 N fr Boulogne
exit junc 33. Foll sp. 3*, Lge, pt shd, EHU (4A) €3.50
(poss rev pol); gas; 90% statics; ccard acc. *"Pleasant,
busy site; open 24 hrs; conv NH nr ferries, A16,
Channel tunnel & WW2 coastal defences; o'fits staying
1 night pitch on meadow at front of site for ease of
exit (but some noise fr m'way); m'van 'aire' open all
yr; vg; site relandscaped (2017), vg; comfort pitches."*
€25.00, 1 Apr-15 Oct. **2017**

MARSANNE *9D2* (2.5km NE Rural) *44.65769, 4.89098*
Camping Les Bastets, Quartier Les Bastets, 26740
Marsanne **04 75 90 35 03; contact@campingles
bastets.com; www.campinglesbastets.com**

🐕 €4 ♿ (htd) wc ♨ 🚿 ♿ 〆 〆 MSP 🦋 〒 〒 ⊕ ♨ 🛝 🖌 🏊

Exit A7 junc 17 onto N7; pass thro Les Tourettes &
La Coucourde to Marsanne. In La Coucourde turn L
onto D74 & in 6km L onto D105 thro Marsanne. Site
sp fr N on D105. App fr N on D57 not rec. 4*, Med,
hdg, pt shd, sl, terr, EHU (10A); bbq; TV; 10% statics;
Eng spkn; adv bkg acc; games rm; archery; bike hire;
games area. *"Pleasant site; gd views; beautiful area;
vg; infinity pool with views over Valdaine Plaine; 30
new easy access level hdg pitches, some in woods;
welcoming site; mini golf, golf 10km; highly rec."*
€24.50, 1 Apr-1 Oct. **2016**

MARSEILLAN PLAGE *10F1* (7km SE Coastal) *43.31904,
3.55655* **Flower Camping Robinson,** Quai de Plaisance,
34340 Marseillan Plage **04 67 21 90 07; reception@
camping-robinson.com; www.camping-robinson.com**

♿ wc ♨ 🚿 ♿ 〆 MSP 〒 🍴 ♨ 🎭 🛝 opp

Fr Agde take D612 twds Sete. In Marseillan Plage
cont on D612 & cross canal bdge. In abt 300m turn
R and foll sp to site. 3*, Med, mkd, pt shd, EHU (10A);
twin axles; 33% statics; Eng spkn; adv bkg acc; games
area; CKE. *"Gd."* **€38.00, 23 Apr-23 Sep.** **2016**

MARSEILLAN PLAGE *10F1* (1km SW Coastal) *43.31275,
3.54638* **Camping La Créole,** 74 Ave des Campings,
34340 Marseillan-Plage **04 67 21 92 69; contact@
campinglacreole.com; www.campinglacreole.com**

🐕 €4 ♿ wc ♨ 🚿 ♿ 〆 〆 MSP 🦋 〒 〒 nr ⊕ nr ♨ 🛝 🎭 🖌
🏖 sand adj

Fr Agde-Sète rd N112, turn S at rndabt onto D51
& foll sp thro town. Narr ent easily missed among
lger sites. 3*, Med, mkd, hdstg, hdg, pt shd, EHU (6A)
€3.50; 10% statics; phone; adv bkg acc; ccard acc;
tennis 1km; games area; CKE. *"Vg, well-kept site; min
stay 7 nights Jul-Aug; dir access to excel beach; naturist
beach 600m."* **€34.50, 28 Mar-11 Oct.** **2020**

FRANCE

MARSEILLAN PLAGE *10F1* (1.3km SW Coastal)
43.31036, 3.54601 **Camping La Plage,** 69 Chemin du
Pairollet, 34340 Marseillan-Plage **04 67 21 92 54;**
info@laplage-camping.net; www.laplage-camping.net

🛉€4 🛉🛉 WC 🚿 ♿ 🅿 / MSP 🦋 ▼ ⊕ 🏛 🏊 sand adj

On D612 fr Agde to Sète, turn R at rndabt dir
Marseillan-Plage. Foll sp for site at 2nd rndabt.
Site on L in 150m. 3*, Med, hdg, pt shd, EHU (10A)
inc; gas; bbq; TV; 1% statics; phone; Eng spkn; adv bkg
acc; ccard acc; games area; watersports; CKE. "Excel,
popular, family-run site; superb beach; extra for beach
front pitches; sm pitches, some off o'fits; gd,
friendly atmosphere." **€42.00, 14 Mar-31 Oct.**   **2015**

MARTRES TOLOSANE *8F3* (1.5km S Rural) *43.19060,
1.01840* **Camping Le Moulin,** 31220 Martres-Tolosane
05 61 98 86 40; info@domainelemoulin.com; www.
domainelemoulin.com or www.campinglemoulin.
com/en/toulouse-campsite-france/

🛉€3 🛉🛉 WC 🚿 ♿ 🅿 / MSP 🦋 🍴 ▼ 🏛 nr 🏔 🏊 (htd)
🛶

Exit A64 junc 22 (fr N or S) & foll camping sps. Site
sp adj Rv Garonne. 4*, Med, hdg, pt shd, pt sl, EHU
(6-10A) €4-6; gas; bbq; red long stay; TV; 20% statics;
Eng spkn; adv bkg rec; ccard acc; games area; tennis;
games rm; bike hire; rv fishing adj; outdoor fitness;
canoeing; massages; canoeing; CKE. "Excel, well-
maintained site; friendly welcome; gd, modern san facs;
water on all pitches; gd touring base for Spain, Lourdes,
etc." **€26.90, 1 Apr-27 Sep, D28.**   **2019**

"Satellite navigation makes touring much easier"

Remember most sat navs don't know if you're
towing or in a larger vehicle – always use yours
alongside maps and site directions.

MARVEJOLS *9D1* (1km NE Rural) *44.55077, 3.30440*
Camping Village Le Coulagnet, Quartier de l'Empery,
48100 Marvejols **04 66 32 03 69**

🛉🛉 🚿 ♿ 🅿 / 🦋 🏛 🏔 🏊

Exit A75 junc 38 onto D900 & N9. Foll E ring rd
onto D999, cont over rv & foll sp to site; no R turn
into site, cont 500m to Aire de Retournement, &
turn L into site. Foll sp 'VVF', camping pt of same
complex. NB U-turn bef ent impossible long o'fits;
nasty speed humps on app rd. 2*, Sm, hdg, pt shd,
EHU (5A) inc (poss rev pol); bbq (sep area); TV;
50% statics; phone; Eng spkn; adv bkg acc; ccard acc;
games rm; tennis; games area. "Well equiped site; san
facs immac; sep area for tourers; interesting walled
town; rv adj; excel; ent too tight to make u-turn."
€21.00, 5 May-15 Sep.   **2019**

MASEVAUX *6F3* (1km N Urban) *47.77820, 6.99090*
Camping Les Rives de la Doller (formerly de Masevaux),
3 Rue du Stade, 68290 Masevaux **03 89 39 83 94 or
06 33 49 44 88 (mob);** www.masevaux-camping.fr

🛉€0.50 🛉🛉 (htd) WC 🚿 ♿ 🅿 / MSP 🦋 🍴 ▼ 🏛 nr 🏔 🏊

Fr N83 Colmar-Belfort rd take N466 W to Masevaux;
site sp. NB D14 fr Thann to Masevaux narr & steep
- not suitable c'vans. 3*, Med, mkd, pt shd, EHU
(3-6A) €3.20-3.80; red long stay; TV; 40% statics;
Eng spkn; adv bkg acc; ccard acc; CKE. "Pleasant
walks; htd pool adj; interesting town - annual staging
of Passion Play; helpful, friendly owners; excel facs;
sports complex adj; gd cycle rtes; excel; gd site in nice
little town; supmkt nrby; close to Ballon d'Alsace."
€20.00, 1 Apr-19 Oct.   **2019**

MASSERET *7B3* (11km N Rural) *45.61142, 1.50110*
Camping de Montréal, Rue du Petit Moulin, 87380 St
Germain-les-Belles **05 55 71 86 20;** contact@camping
demontreal.com; www.campingdemontreal.com

12 🛉€2.60 🛉🛉 (htd) WC 🚿 ♿ 🅿 / MSP 🦋 🍴 ▼ ⊕ 🏛 nr 🏔
🏊 / 🛶 (htd)

S fr Limoges on A20; exit junc 42 onto D7B to
St Germain-les-Belles; turn R onto D216; site on L in
500m. Site sp in vill. NB Care needed due narr rds.
3*, Mkd, mkd, hdg, pt shd, terr, EHU (10A) €3; bbq; sw
nr; 12% statics; phone; Eng spkn; adv bkg acc; ccard
acc; tennis; fishing; watersports; CKE. "Peaceful, lovely,
well-run site in attractive setting o'looking lake; excel,
modern, spotless san facs; bike hire 1km; conv A20;
a gem of a site; gd rest; vg NH; shops 10 min walk."
€19.00   **2018**

MASSEUBE *8F3* (0.4km E Rural) *43.42914, 0.58516*
Camping Berges du Gers, Route de Simorre, 32140
Masseube **05 62 66 01 75;** camping.masseube@
orange.fr; www.camping-masseube-lesbergesdugers.fr

🛉 🛉🛉 WC 🚿 ♿ 🅿 / 🦋 🍴 ▼ nr ⊕ nr 🏛 nr 🏔 🏊

S fr Auch on D929 to Masseube; turn L onto D27 dir
Simorre; site on L in 500m. 3*, Med, shd, EHU (6A) €3;
bbq; TV; 10% statics; Eng spkn; adv bkg acc; ccard acc;
games area; tennis; bike hire; games rm; CKE. "Well-run
site in pleasant setting; security barrier; htd pool adj;
access to rv; vg." **€13.00, 1 May-31 Oct.**   **2017**

MASSEUBE *8F3* (2km E Rural) *43.42748, 0.61142*
Camping Aux Mêmes, 32140 Bellegarde **05 62 66 91 45
or 06 83 62 02 22;** info@gascogne-camping.fr;
www.gascogne-camping.fr

🛉 🛉🛉 WC 🚿 ♿ 🅿 / 🦋 🍴 ▼ 🏛 🏔 🏊

Fr Masseube take D27 E dir Simorre & Bellegarde; in
2.5km turn L (having past sports stadium & driven
up hill thro trees); site is 1st farm on R in 300m.
Site sp. 3*, Sm, unshd, pt sl, EHU (6A) €3; bbq; TV;
Eng spkn; adv bkg acc; tennis nr; canoeing; games rm;
sailing nr; golf nr; watersports; bike hire; windsurfing
nr; fishing. "Excel; v friendly & helpful Eng owners."
€25.00, 1 Apr-15 Sep.   **2017**

MATHES, LES *7B1* (1km WSW Urban) *45.71517, -1.15520* **Camping Monplaisir,** 26 avenue de la Palmyre, 17250 Les Mathes **05 46 22 50 31; camping-monplaisir@orange.fr; www.camping monplaisirlesmathes.fr**

🐕 👫 ⚓ ♿ 🚻 ⁄ MP 🦋 ▾ 🍴 nr ⊕ nr 🅰 🛒 nr ⛱ ⛲

🛶 beach 3.5km

Fr Saujon take D14 to the o'skirts of Tremblade, avoid vill of Arvert & Etaule if towing c'van, rd surface poor & narr. At rndabt take D25 for a sh dist & take L onto D268 twrds La Palmyre. Cont along D141 to o'skirts of Les Mathes, then L at rndabt. Site on L within approx 450m opp cycle hire. 3*, Med, pt shd, pt sl, EHU €4.50; bbq; TV; Eng spkn; ccard acc; games area; games rm. *"Bike hire nrby; crazy golf & childrens car track on site; friendly family owned site, clean & tidy; gd cycle tracks in area; bar 300m; zoo 4km; vg; v clean san facs; open mkt in vill most days."* €20.00, Apr-Sep. **2016**

MATHES, LES *7B1* (3.5km N Rural) *45.72980, -1.17929* **Camping Sandaya L'Orée du Bois,** 225 Route de la Bouverie, La Fouasse, 17570 Les Mathes **05 46 22 42 43; www.sandaya.fr/nos-campings/l-oree-du-bois**

🐕 €3.60 👫 WD ⚓ ♿ 🚻 ⁄ MP 🦋 ▾ 🍴 ⊕ 🅰 🛒 ⛱ ✎

🏊 (htd) 🛶 sand 4km

Fr A10 to Saintes, then dir Royan. Fr Royan take D25 thro St Palais & La Palmyre twd Phare de la Coubre. Cont 4km past Phare & turn R on D268 to La Fouasse. Site on R in 4km. 4*, Lge, hdstg, mkd, hdg, pt shd, EHU (6A) inc; gas; bbq; red long stay; TV; 50% statics; Eng spkn; adv bkg rec; ccard acc; games rm; bike hire; waterslide; games area; golf 20km; tennis; CKE. *"Well-kept site in pine wood; local beaches ideal for sw & surfing; helpful staff; excel pool area; private san facs some pitches; zoo in La Palmyre worth visit; excel."* €40.00, 24 May-14 Sep. **2019**

MATHES, LES *7B1* (1km SW Rural) *45.70256, -1.15638* **Camping Palmyre Loisirs,** 28 Ave des Mathes, 17570 La Palmyre **05 46 23 67 66; www.palmyreloisirs.com**

🐕 €4.50 👫 ⚓ ⁄ 🦋 ▾ 🍴 ⊕ 🅰 🛒 ⛱ 🛶 sand 3km

S fr La Tremblade on D14; at Arvert take D141 SW thro Les Mathes; site on L of rd 1km fr Les Mathes. Lge, pt shd, EHU (6A) inc; adv bkg acc. *"Excel new san facs; new pool complex for 2015; 1 dog per pitch; pitches away fr bar/rest are quiet; barrier clsd 12-6am."* €51.50, Apr-Sep. **2015**

MATOUR *9A2* (1km W Rural) *46.305161, 4.482047* **Camp Municipal Le Paluet,** 2 Rue de la Piscine, 71520 Matour **03 86 37 95 83; contact@aquadis-loisirs.com; http://www.matour.fr/en/welcome-to-matour/**

🐕 👫 WD ⚓ ♿ 🚻 ⁄ MP 🦋 ▾ 🍴 ⊕ nr 🅰 🛒 ⛱ ✎ 🏊 (htd)

On W o'skts of Matour off Rte de la Clayette D987. 3*, Med, hdg, mkd, pt shd, EHU (10A) inc; bbq; TV; Eng spkn; adv bkg acc; ccard acc; lake fishing adj; tennis; games area; waterslide; badminton; volleyball; ping pong; CKE. *"Conv touring vineyards; highly rec; facs poss inadequate high ssn."* €18.50, 1 Apr-25 Oct. **2020**

MAUBEUGE *3B4* (10km NE Rural) *50.34525, 4.02842* **Camping Les Avallées,** 19 Rue du Faubourg, 59600 Villers-Sire-Nicole **03 27 67 92 56; loisirs-les-avallees @wanadoo.fr; www.loisirs-les-avallees.fr**

🐕 👫 WD ⚓ ♿ 🚻 ⁄ 🦋 ▾ 🍴 ⊕ 🅰 🛒 ⛱

N fr Maubeuge on N2; in 5km R onto D159 to Villers-Sire-Nicole. Site well sp. Last 4km narr country rd. 1*, Lge, pt shd, pt sl, terr, EHU (4A) €2; bbq; 80% statics. *"Friendly owners; lake fishing; no twin axles; vg; lovely site."* €11.00, 1 Apr-14 Oct. **2015**

> ## "There aren't many sites open at this time of year"
>
> If you're travelling outside peak season remember to call ahead to check site opening dates – even if the entry says 'open all year'.

MAULEON LICHARRE *8F1* (2km S Rural) *43.20795, -0.89695* **Camping Uhaitza Le Saison,** Route de Libarrenx, 64130 Mauléon-Licharre **05 59 28 18 79; camping.uhaitza@wanadoo.fr; www.camping-uhaitza.com**

🐕 €2 👫 ⚓ ♿ 🚻 ⁄ MP 🦋 ▾ 🍴 ⊕ 🛒 nr ⛱

Fr Sauveterre take D936 twd Oloron. In 500m turn R onto D23 to Mauléon, then take D918 dir Tardets, site on R. 3*, Sm, hdg, mkd, pt shd, EHU (6A) €2.65-4.90; bbq; 10% statics; adv bkg acc; tennis 2km; rv fishing adj; games rm; CKE. *"Lovely, quiet site beside rv; lge pitches; friendly owners."* €25.00, 1 Apr-15 Oct. **2015**

MAURS *7D4* (0.8km S Rural) *44.70522, 2.20586* **Camp Municipal Le Vert,** Route de Decazeville, 15600 Maurs **04 71 49 04 15 or 06 75 46 74 17; camping@ ville-maurs.fr; www.ville-maurs.fr/tourisme/camping**

👫 WD ⚓ ♿ 🚻 ⁄ 🦋 🛒 nr ⛱ 🏊

Fr Maurs take D663 dir Decazeville. Site on L 400m after level x-ing thro sports complex. Narr ent. 3*, Med, mkd, shd, EHU (15A) inc; adv bkg acc; rv fishing; tennis. *"V pleasant on side of rv; sports complex adj; friendly helpful warden."* €11.00, 2 May-30 Sep. **2019**

MAYENNE *4E1* (2km N Rural) *48.31350, -0.61296* **Camp Municipal du Gué St Léonard,** 818 Rue de St Léonard, 53100 Mayenne **02 43 04 57 14 or 02 43 04 19 37; www.campingduguesaintleonard.fr**

👫 (htd) WD ♿ 🚻 ⁄ ⊕ nr 🅰 🛒 ⛱ ✎ (htd)

Fr N, sp to E of D23 & well sp fr cent of Mayenne on rvside. 3*, Med, hdg, mkd, pt shd, serviced pitches; EHU (10A) €2.20; bbq; twin axles; 8% statics; phone; adv bkg acc; rv fishing adj; CKE. *"Peaceful, well-kept site by rv; pleasant location adj parkland walks; modern san facs with piping hot water; some pitches sm & access poss diff; vg value."* €13.70, 15 Mar-30 Sep. **2015**

MAZAMET *8F4* (1.5km E Urban) 43.49634, 2.39075
FFCC Camp Municipal de la Lauze, Chemin de la
Lauze, 81200 Mazamet **05 63 61 24 69; contact@
camping-mazamet.com; www.camping-mazamet.com**

Exit Mazamet dir St Pons on D612, site on R past
rugby grnd. 3*, Med, hdstg, pt shd, pt sl, EHU (15A)
€3.50; bbq; red long stay; adv bkg acc; tennis; CKE.
*"Well-kept site in 2 adj parts, 1 flat & other sl; office
thro gateway - warden needed for access; htd pool
adj; san facs excel; gd touring base 'Black Mountain'
region."* **€12.00, 1 Jun-30 Sep.** 2019

MEAUX *3D3* (4km NE Rural) 49.00301, 2.94139
Camping Village Parisien, Route des Otages, 77910
Varreddes **02 51 20 41 94; direction@villageparisien.
com; http://villageparisien.camp-atlantique.nl**

Fr Meaux foll sp on D405 dir Soissons then
Varreddes, site sp on D121 dir Congis. 4*, Med, mkd,
hdg, pt shd, EHU (6A) €2; gas; bbq; red long stay; TV;
85% statics; Eng spkn; adv bkg acc; waterslide; games
area; golf 5km; tennis; games rm; fishing; bike hire;
CKE. *"Conv Paris cent (drive to metro), Parc Astérix &
Disneyland - tickets avail fr site; friendly, helpful staff;
cash only; sm pitches; narr site rds; v busy, well-used
site."* **€41.00, 1 Apr-5 Nov.** 2017

MEAUX *3D3* (10km SW Rural) 48.91333, 2.73416
Camping L'International de Jablines, 77450 Jablines
**01 60 26 09 37; welcome@camping-jablines.com;
www.camping-jablines.com**

Fr N on A1 then A104 exit Claye Souilly. Fr E on A4
then A104 exit Meaux. Fr S on A6, A86, A4, A104
exit Meaux. Site well sp 'Base de Loisirs de Jablines'.
3*, Lge, mkd, pt shd, pt sl, EHU (10A) inc; bbq; sw
nr; bus to Eurodisney; Eng spkn; adv bkg req; ccard
acc; horseriding; windsurfing; bike hire; tennis 500m;
fishing; sailing; CKE. *"Clean, well-run, well-guarded site;
vg pitches; pelasant staff; san facs poss tired high ssn;
ideal for Disneyland (tickets for sale), Paris & Versaille."*
€28.00, 31 Mar-29 Sep. 2017

MEES, LES *10E3* (11km S Rural) 43.95377, 5.93304
Camping Les Olivettes, Hameau-Les-Pourcelles,
04190 Les Mées **04 92 34 18 97; campingolivette@
club-internet.fr; www.campingolivettes.com**

Exit A51 junc 20 (fr N) or 19 (fr S) & cross Rv
Durance onto D4. Site bet Oraison & Les Mées.
Turn onto D754 to Les Pourcelles & foll site sp.
3*, Sm, hdg, mkd, pt shd, pt sl, terr, EHU (6-10A)
€4.90; 5% statics; Eng spkn; adv bkg acc. *"Views
over beautiful area; friendly owners; occasional
out of ssn pitches avail; unrel opening; vg."*
€33.50, 29 Apr-30 Sep. 2016

MEGEVE *9B3* (2km SW Rural) 45.84120, 6.58887
FFCC Camping Gai Séjour, 332 Route de
Cassioz, 74120 Megève **04 50 21 22 58**

On D1212 Flumet-Megève rd, site on R 1km after
Praz-sur-Arly, well sp. 2*, Med, mkd, pt shd, sl, EHU
(4A); Eng spkn; adv bkg acc; CKE. *"Pleasant site
with gd views, lge pitches; gd walks; 40km fr Mont
Blanc; helpful owners; no free parking in Megeve."*
€15.00, 6 Jan-15 Sep. 2019

MEHUN SUR YEVRE *4H3* (0.5km N Urban) 47.14797,
2.21725 **Camp Municipal,** Ave Jean Châtelet, 18500
Mehun-sur-Yèvre **02 48 57 44 51 or 02 48 57 30 25
(Mairie); www.ville-mehun-sur-yevre.fr/Le-camping**

Leave A71 junc 6 onto D2076 (N76) dir Bourges.
App Mehun & turn L into site at 2nd traff lts. Ave
Jean Châtelet is pt of D2076. 2*, Sm, mkd, pt shd,
EHU (6A) €2.80 (poss rev pol & long lead req some
pitches); twin axles; tennis adj. *"Excel NH conv for
m'way; clean, modern san facs; water pnts poss long
walk; gates locked 2200-0700 (high ssn); facs open to
elements; pool adj; town rather run down, nice park."*
€13.00, 8 May-30 Sep. 2017

MELE SUR SARTHE, LE *4E1* (0.5km SE Rural) 48.50831,
0.36298 **Camp Intercommunal La Prairie,** La
Bretèche, St Julien-Sarthe, 61170 Le Mêle-sur-Sarthe
02 33 27 18 74

Turn off N12 onto D4; site sp in vill.
2*, Med, mkd, pt shd, EHU (6A) inc; adv bkg acc;
sailing; tennis; CKE. *"Pt of excel sports complex; vg."*
€11.00, 1 May-30 Sep. 2019

MELISEY *6F2* (0.5km E Rural) 47.75484, 6.58683
Camping La Bergereine, 17bis Route des
Vosges, 70270 Mélisey **06 23 36 87 16 (mob);
isabelle.schweizer0704@orange.fr**

Fr Lure (or by-pass) take D486 dir Le Thillot; site sp.
1*, Sm, pt shd, EHU inc; gas; 25% statics; adv bkg acc;
rv fishing adj; CKE. *"Ok NH; simple farm site; leisure
cent 500m; attractive scenery; improvd san block; pool
500m; v scruffy."* **€8.00, 1 Apr-30 Sep.** 2015

MELISEY *6F2* (8km E Rural) 47.75525, 6.65273
Camping La Broche, Le Voluet, 70270 Fresse
03 84 63 31 40; www.camping-broche.com

Fr Lure head NE on D486 twd Melisey. Fr Mélisey
stay on D486 twd Le Thillot, in 2.5km turn R onto
D97 dir Plancher-les-Mines. In approx 5.5km
site sp on R in Fresse. 2*, Sm, mkd, pt shd, pt sl,
terr, EHU (10A) €2.50; bbq; sw nr; 10% statics;
phone; adv bkg acc; games rm; fishing adj; ice;
games area; CKE. *"Secluded, relaxing site next to
lake, in attractive setting in regional park; friendly
owner; conv Rte of 1000 lakes; great site; vg."*
€12.00, 15 Apr-15 Oct. 2015

MELLE *7A2* (11km SW Rural) *46.14421, -0.21983* **Camp Municipal,** Rue des Merlonges, 79170 Brioux-sur-Boutonne 05 49 07 50 46

🏕🚲♨🚐⚡🦋🎾 nr ⛱

On ent Brioux fr Melle on D150 turn R immed over bdge; site on R in 100m. 1*, Sm, pt shd, EHU (6A) €1.80. *"Pleasant rural setting; tidy, well-cared for site; ltd facs but clean; choose own pitch & pay at Mairie on dep if no warden; conv for town; great value; vg sh stay/NH."* **€8.00, 1 Apr-31 Oct.** 2018

MENDE *9D1* (3km W Rural) *44.51409, 3.47363* **Camping Tivoli,** Route des Gorges du Tarn, 48000 Mende 04 66 65 31 10; camping.tivoli0601@ orange.fr; www.camping-tivoli.com

12 🏕€1 🏕🚲♨🚐⚡🦋🎾🍴⛱⛺🏊

Sp fr N88, turn R 300m downhill (narr but easy rd). Site adj Rv Lot. 3*, Med, pt shd, EHU (6A) inc; TV; 10% statics; adv bkg rec; rv fishing. *"Gd site nr town at back of cent commerciale; hypmkt 1km; v narr ent with little rm to park."* **€20.00** 2015

"That's changed – Should I let the Club know?"

If you find something on site that's different from the site entry, fill in a report and let us know. See camc.com/europereport.

MERDRIGNAC *2E3* (2km N Rural) *48.19786, -2.41622* **Camping Le Val de Landrouët,** 14 rue du Gouède, 22230 Merdrignac 02 96 28 47 98; contact@ valdelandrouet.com; www.valdelandrouet.com

🏕🐕🚲♨🚐⚡🦋🍴⛱ nr 🏊 (htd)

Sp fr town cent, 500m fr town on D793 twd Broons, site on L. Med, hdg, mkd, pt shd, pt sl, EHU (4A) €3; bbq; sw nr; twin axles; 5% statics; bus adj; adv bkg acc; ccard acc; fishing; tennis; CKE. *"Superb, spacious site; mv service pnt (emptying only); gd touring ctr; activities adj; excel."* **€19.00, 30 Apr-30 Sep.** 2019

MERENS LES VALS *8G4* (1km W Rural) *42.64633, 1.83083* **Camp Municipal Ville de Bau,** Ville de Bau, 09110 Mérens-les-Vals 05 61 02 85 40 or 05 61 64 33 77; camping.merens@wanadoo.fr; merenslesvals.fr

12 🐕€0.70 🏕(htd)♨🚐⚡🦋🎾🍴⛱

Fr Ax-les-Thermes on N20 sp Andorra past Mérens-les-Vals turn R nr start of dual c'way sp Camp Municipal. Site on R in 800m. 3*, Med, hdg, EHU (6-10A) inc (poss rev pol); bbq; 20% statics; ccard acc; CKE. *"Excel site; gd clean san facs; gd walks fr site; conv Andorra, Tunnel de Puymorens; all pitches have water taps; pool 8km; lovely walk fr site past Eglise Romane in vill to hot spring with natural bathing pools."* **€17.00** 2017

MERS LES BAINS *3B2* (1.5km NE Rural) *50.07730, 1.41540* **Flower Camping Le Rompval,** Lieudit Blengues, 154 Rue André Dumont, 80350 Mers-les-Bains 02 35 84 43 21 or 06 50 02 79 57 (mob); www.camping-lerompval.com

🏕€3 🏕(htd) 🚲♨🚐⚡🚐⚡🦋🎾🍴⛱⛺🏊
🏊(covrd, htd) ⛱ sand 2.5km

Fr Calais on A16, exit junc 23 at Abbeville onto A28. In 5km exit junc 2 onto D925 dir Friville-Escarbotin, Le Tréport. In approx 20km at rndabt junc with D19 foll sp Ault & at next rndabt take D940 twd Mers-les-Bains. In St Quentin-la-Motte turn R, site on R, sp. Fr S on A28 exit junc 5 onto D1015 to Mers-les-Bains & foll sp Blengues & site. 3*, Med, hdstg, mkd, hdg, unshd, EHU (6-13A) €4-6.50; gas; bbq; red long stay; TV; 25% statics; Eng spkn; adv bkg acc; ccard acc; tennis 3km; games rm; bike hire; games area; CKE. *"Vg site; library; gd facs."* **€28.80, 5 Apr-3 Nov.** 2019

MESNIL ST PERE *6F1* (2km NE Rural) *48.26329, 4.34633* **Kawan Village Camping Lac d'Orient,** Rue du Lac, 10140 Mesnil-St Père 03 25 40 61 85 or 03 85 72 27 21 (LS); info@camping-lacdorient.com; www.camping-lacdorient.com

🏕€3 🏕(htd) 🚲♨🚐⚡🚐⚡🦋🎾🍴⛱ nr ⛺🏊
🏊(covrd, htd) ⛱

On D619 foll sps Lac de la Forêt d'Orient. Approx 10km fr Vendeuvre or 20km fr Troyes turn N on D43A, to Mesnil-St Père; site sp. Sp at ent to site: 'Camping Lac d'Orient' (with 'Kawan Village' in v sm lettering). 4*, Lge, hdstg, hdg, mkd, pt shd, pt sl, EHU (10A) inc; bbq; sw nr; 10% statics; phone; Eng spkn; adv bkg acc; ccard acc; watersports 500m; games rm; fishing; games area; tennis; jacuzzi; CKE. *"Peaceful site with mature trees next to lake & forest; lge pitches; 1st class san facs; no o'fits over 10m high ssn; poss muddy when wet; conv Nigloland theme park & Champagne area; conv A26; excel spacious site; excel cycle rte; private san facs some pitches; fantastic rest over looking lake; vg."* **€36.00, 9 Apr-23 Sep, J07.** 2016

MESSANGES *8E1* (2km SW Coastal) *43.79790, -1.40135* **Airotel Camping Le Vieux Port,** Plage Sud, 40660 Messanges 01 76 76 70 00; contact@ levieuxport.com; www.levieuxport.com

🏕€5.50 🏕🚲♨🚐⚡🚐⚡🦋🎾🍴⛱⛺🏊
🏊(htd) 🏊 ⛱ sand 400m

Fr S take D652 past Vieux-Boucau; site sp. Turn W at Super U rndabt. 5*, V lge, hdstg, mkd, shd, EHU (6A) inc; gas; bbq; red long stay; TV; 10% statics; Eng spkn; adv bkg acc; ccard acc; horseriding; waterslide; tennis; bike hire; games area; CKE. *"V pleasant, clean site; dir access to sand beach; quad bikes; superb, v lge pool complex; excel touring base."* **€85.00, 24 Mar-4 Nov, A14.** 2017

METZ *5D2* (1.5km NW Urban) *49.12402, 6.16917*
Camp Municipal Metz-Plage, Allée de Metz-Plage, 57000 Metz **03 87 68 26 48; campingmetz@ mairie-metz.fr; www.metz.fr**

🐕 €0.60 ♗♖ [WD] ⛟♿🔥🚿🖉 [MSP] 🛜 ⏰🍴🛒⚓ 🎢

Fr W exit A31 junc 33 Metz-Nord/Pontiffroy exit; cross rv bdges Pont Canal & Pont des Morts; then immed turn L into Allée de Metz-Plage; site in 200m (or after leaving A31 at junc 33, at rndabt turn R & foll sps). Fr E foll 'Autres Directions' over A31 & Rv Moselle, then as above. 3*, Lge, mkd, hdstg, pt shd, pt sl, EHU (10A) inc (poss rev pol); twin axles; Eng spkn; adv bkg acc; ccard acc; rv fishing adj; CKE. *"Spacious, well-situated on rv with views; some gd sized pitches; helpful staff; poss long walk to san facs; rv unfenced; facs stretched if site full; early arr ess high ssn; vg; fac's need updating; wifi in designated areas; pool adj; excel."* €24.00, 15 Apr-30 Sep. **2019**

MEYRAS *9 D2* (4.7km SE Rural) *44.66480, 4.29409*
Camping La Charderie, 410 route de Bayzan, 07380 Pont-de-Labeaume **04 75 38 00 52; la.charderie@ wanadoo.fr; www.camping-lacharderie.com**

🐕 ♗♖ ⛟♿🔥🚿🖉 [MSP] 🛜 🍴⚓ 🎢 river sand beach

Fr Aubenas twrds Le Puy-en-Velay on the N102. At Pont de Labeaume, R over narr stone bdge. Site on R in 200m. 3*, Sm, mkd, pt shd, pt sl, EHU 10A (€4.50); gas; bbq (elec); sw; Eng spkn; adv bkg acc; ccard acc; games area; games rm; CCI. *"Excel; gd walks."* €27.70, 18 Apr-3 Oct. **2019**

MEYRUEIS *10E1* (0.5km E Rural) *44.18075, 3.43540*
Camping Le Jardin des Cevennes, Route de la Brèze, 48150 Meyrueis **04 66 45 60 51; infocamping@ jardindescevennes.com; www.campinglejardin descevennes.com/**

🐕 €1 ♗♖ [WD] ⛟♿🔥🚿🖉 [MSP] 🛜 🍴 ⏰nr ⚓🎢🖌🏊(htd)

Fr W on D907 dir Gorges de la Jonte into Meyrueis. Foll sp Château d'Ayres & site. 3*, Med, hdg, mkd, pt shd, pt sl, EHU (6A) €3; bbq; 15% statics; phone; Eng spkn; adv bkg acc; ccard acc; games rm; games area; bike hire; CKE. *"Helpful owners; rec."* €26.50, 27 Apr-25 Sep. **2020**

MEZE *10F1* (3km N Rural) *43.44541, 3.61595*
Camp Municipal Loupian, Route de Mèze, 34140 Loupian **04 67 43 57 67 or 04 67 43 82 07 (LS); camping@loupian.fr; www.loupian.fr**

🐕 €1 ♗♖ [WD] ⛟♿🔥🚿🖉 🍴⚓🎢🖌🏊 sand 3km

Fr Mèze tak D613 & turn L at 1st Loupian sp, then foll sp for site. 3*, Med, mkd, hdg, pt shd, EHU (6A); bbq; phone; Eng spkn; adv bkg acc; tennis; CKE. *"Pleasant site in popular area; plenty shd; friendly, helpful staff; vg san facs; takeaway; gd beaches; excel fisherman's rest; gd rests at Mèze & Bouzigues; superb cycling on old rlwy rte fr site to Mèze (Voie Verte); rec; cent to main attractions; gd value site; vg."* €19.00, 6 Apr-14 Oct. **2019**

MEZOS *8E1* (1km SE Rural) *44.07980, -1.16090*
Le Village Tropical Sen Yan, 40170 Mézos, Landes **05 58 42 60 05; reception@sen-yan.com; www.sen-yan.com**

🐕 €6 ♗♖ [WD] ⛟♿🔥🚿🖉 🦋 🛜🍷 ⏰🍴⚓🛒🎢🖌
🏊 (covrd, htd, indoor) 🚣

Fr Bordeaux on N10 in 100km at Laharie turn W onto D38 dir Mimizan; in 12km turn L onto D63 to Mézos; turn L at mini-rndabt; site on L in approx 2km. Site 1.5km fr D63/D38 junc NE of Mézos. 5*, Lge, mkd, hdg, shd, EHU (6A) inc; gas; bbq (gas); TV; 80% statics; phone; Eng spkn; adv bkg acc; ccard acc; waterslide; tennis; watersports 15km; jacuzzi; bike hire; rv fishing adj; games rm; sauna; CKE. *"Attractive, restful site; many plants, inc banana trees; fitness cent; no o'fits over 8m; canoe hire 1km; modern, many sports & games; clean san facs; excel facs for families; mkt Mimizan Fri & Morcenx Wed."* €47.00, 1 Jun-9 Sep. **2020**

MILLAS *8G4* (7km SW Urban) *42.67165, 2.62907*
Camp Municipal Le Colomer, Rue Colonel Fabien, 66130 Ile-sur-Tet **04 68 84 72 40; camping@ ille-sur-tet.com; www.ille-sur-tet.com**

🐕 €1.50 ♗♖ ⛟🔥🖉 🎢

Exit N116 on NE of town, R twds Ille sur Tet on D916, L at next rndabt foll sp to site. Med, hdg, pt shd, EHU (10A) €4; 30% statics; bus adj; train 0.5km; Eng spkn; adv bkg req; games area; CKE. *"Conv for Les Orgues cliffs & Prieure de Serrabone; gd rests in attractive town; pool 200m; adj rlwy not busy but conv for Perpignan; vg."* €11.30, 1 Nov-30 Sep. **2016**

> ## "I like to fill in the reports as I travel from site to site"
>
> You'll find report forms at the back of this guide, or you can fill them in online at camc.com/europereport.

MILLAU *10E1* (7km N Rural) *44.15188, 3.09899*
Camping La Belle Etoile (formerly d'Aguessac), Chemin des Prades, 12520 Aguessac **05 65 72 91 07 ou 06 72 23 10 56 (mob); contact@camping-labelleetoile.fr; www.camping-labelleetoile.fr**

🐕 €2 ♗♖ [WD] ⛟♿🖉 🦋 🛜🍷🍴nr 🖌

Site on N907 in vill; ent on R v soon after level x-ing when app fr Millau. 2*, Med, mkd, pt shd, EHU (6A) inc; gas; canoeing; games area; rv fishing adj; CKE. *"Nice, spacious, clean rvside site; gd position with mountain views; gd sized pitches; helpful & friendly staff; public footpath thro site along rv to picturesque vill; poss youth groups high ssn; sports grnd adj; excel touring base; vg location; vg quiet site."* €23.00, 27 Apr-30 Sep. **2019**

MILLAU *10E1* (1.6km NE Rural) *44.10640, 3.08800*
Camping Les Erables, Route de Millau-Plage, 12100
Millau 05 65 59 15 13; camping-les-erables@
orange.fr; www.campingleserables.fr

♦ €1.20 ♦♦ (htd) 🚿 ⏣ ♿ 🛒 🖊 🍴 ☂ ⛱ 🏔 🖌

Exit Millau on D991 (sp Nant) over Rv Tarn bdge;
take L at island sp to Millau-Plage & site on L
immed after Camping du Viaduc & bef Camping
Larribal. On ent Millau fr N or S foll sps 'Campings'.
3*, Med, mkd, hdg, shd, EHU (10A) €3 (rev pol);
bbq; sw nr; TV; phone; Eng spkn; adv bkg acc; ccard
acc; canoeing adj; CKE. *"Peaceful, well-kept, clean
site on banks of Rv Tarn; lge shd pitches; friendly,
helpful owners; excel modern san facs; some
pitches poss diff lge o'fits; excel walking; beavers
nrby; Millau Viaduct Vistor Cent a must; excel."*
€21.00, 1 Apr-30 Sep. 2017

MILLAU *10E1* (2km NE Urban) *44.10240, 3.09100*
Camping Indigo Millau, Ave de l'Aigoual, 12100 Millau
05 65 61 18 83; millau@camping-indigo.com;
www.camping-indigo.com or www.europe.huttopia.
com/site/camping-millau

♦ €4.60 ♦♦ ⏣ 🚿 🖊 ⛱ 🐟 ⛱ 🏔 🖌 (htd) 🛍

Fr N exit A75 junc 45 to Millau. Turn L at 2nd traff
island sp 'Camping'. Site on R over bdge in 200m.
Fr S exit A75 junc 47 onto D809 & cross rv on by-
pass, turn R at 1st traff island sp Nant on D991,
cross bdge, site on R in 200m, sp. Site a S confluence
of Rv Dourbie & Rv Tarn. 3*, Med, mkd, shd, pt sl,
EHU (5A) €3.50; gas; sw nr; 10% statics; Eng spkn;
adv bkg acc; fishing nr; games; CKE. *"Excel site; gd
san facs, renovated 2015; hang-gliding nrby; pleasant,
helpful owner; canoe hire nr; conv Tarn Gorges; lge mkt
Fri."* **€28.90, 19 Apr-29 Sep, D17.** 2019

MILLAU *10E1* (1km E Rural) *44.10166, 3.09611*
Camping Les Rivages, Ave de l'Aigoual, 12100 Millau
05 65 61 01 07 or 06 10 75 65 94 (mob); info@
campinglesrivages.com; www.campinglesrivages.com
♦ €4 ♦♦ (htd) 🚿 ⏣ ♿ 🛒 🖊 ⛱ 🍴 ☂ 🏔 🖌 🏊

Fr Millau take D991 dir Nant (sp Gorges de la
Dourbie & Campings). Cross Rv Tarn & cont on this
rd, site is 500m after bdge on R. 4*, Lge, pt shd,
serviced pitches; EHU (10A) inc (poss rev pol); bbq; sw
nr; red long stay; twin axles; TV; 10% statics; phone;
Eng spkn; adv bkg acc; ccard acc; canoeing nr; squash;
fishing; games area; tennis; games rm; CKE. *"Pleasant,
busy, scenic site - esp rv/side pitches; helpful & friendly
staff; immac, clean san facs; vg rest/snack bar - home
cooked & inexpensive; gd security; views of Millau
viaduct; hang-gliding; spa; easy access to town; mkt
Wed & Fri; pleasant cycle ride along rvbank; v nice site."*
€37.00, 15 Apr-30 Sep, D20. 2015

MIMIZAN PLAGE *7D1* (0.7km E Coastal) *44.21629,
-1.28584* **Camping de la Plage,** Blvd d'Atlantique,
40200 Mimizan-Plage 05 58 09 00 32; contact@
mimizan-camping.com; www.mimizan-camping.com

♦ €1.80 ♦♦ ⏣ ♿ 🛒 🖊 ⛱ 🍴 ☂ 🏔 ⛱ 🖌 sand 850m

Turn off N10 at Labouheyre on D626 to Mimizan
(28km). Approx 5km after Mimizan turn R. Site
in approx 500m. 3*, V lge, shd, pt sl, EHU (10A)
inc; bbq; 20% statics; games area. *"Gd facs; town
nrby; big busy coastal site; many cycle paths; excel."*
€24.00, 7 Apr-30 Sep. 2018

MIMIZAN PLAGE *7D1* (3km E Coastal) *44.20420,
-1.2908* **Club Marina-Landes,** Rue Marina, 40202
Mimizan-Plage-Sud 05 58 09 12 66; contact@
clubmarina.com; www.marinalandes.com

♦ €5 ♦♦ ⏣ 🚿 ♿ 🛒 🖊 ⛱ 🦋 🍴 ☂ 🍺 🏔 🖌
🏊 (covrd, htd) 🛍 sand 500m

Turn R off N10 at Labouheyre onto D626 to Mimizan
(28km). Approx 5km fr Mimizan-Plage turn L at
Camping Marina sp on dual c'way. Site sp on S bank
of rv. 4*, V lge, hdg, hdstg, pt shd, EHU (10A) €7; gas;
bbq; TV; 10% statics; Eng spkn; adv bkg acc; ccard acc;
ice; golf 7km; games area; horseriding; games rm; bike
hire; waterslide; fitness rm; tennis; CKE. *"Excursions to
Dax, Biarritz & Bordeaux areas; excel leisure facs; excel;
great location."* **€61.00, 15 May-16 Sep.** 2017

MIRAMBEAU *7C2* (0.5km N Urban) *45.37822,
-0.56874* **Camp Municipal Le Carrelet,** 92 Ave de la
République, 17150 Mirambeau 06 71 77 30 38 or
05 46 70 26 99; campingcarrelet@hotmail.fr;
www.mirambeau-tourisme.fr

♦ ♦♦ (cont) 🖊 ⛱ 🦋 ⛱ nr

Exit 37 fr A10 onto D730/D137 dir Mirambeau. Site
opp Super U supmkt, behind TO.
2*, Sm, pt shd, pt sl, EHU (10A) inc; gas; 80% statics;
phone; ccard acc. *"Basic site; clean but tired facs;
obliging warden; site yourself & warden calls evening; v
muddy when wet; poss neglected LS; conv NH for A10;
no longer a campsite; now a camperstop (2019); toilet
block clsd; Ccd payment at machine allws access."*
€8.00, 1 Apr-31 Oct. 2019

MIRAMBEAU *7C2* (15km W Coastal) *45.38333,
-0.72250* **Camping L'Estuaire,** La Grange Godinet,
17150 St Thomas-de-Cônac 05 46 86 08 20;
info@lestuaire.com; www.lestuaire.com

12 ♦ €4 ♦♦ (htd) 🚿 ⏣ ♿ 🛒 🖊 ⛱ 🦋 🍴 ☂ 🍺 🏔 🖌
🏊 🛍

Exit A10 junc 37 Mirambeau onto D730 dir Royan.
At St Ciers-du-Taillon foll sp St Thomas-de-Cônac,
site sp. 4*, Lge, hdg, mkd, unshd, EHU (16A) inc; bbq;
TV; 60% statics; adv bkg acc; games area; gym; bike
hire; watersports nr; fishing; tennis. *"Interesting area nr
Gironde estuary; gd walking & cycling."*
€20.00 2016

Make sure you check any essential information with the site before you travel

MIRAMONT DE GUYENNE *7D2* (7km NW Rural) *44.62877, 0.29135* **Camp Municipal Le Dropt,** Rue du Pont, 47800 Allemans-du-Dropt **05 53 20 25 59 or 05 53 20 23 37 (Mairie)**

Fr D668 site well sp in vill. Sm, shd, EHU (20A) €2; canoeing; kayaking; CKE. *"Attractive site on opp side of Rv Dropt to vill; friendly warden; ltd pitches for c'vans & lge o'fits due trees & o'hanging branches; basic but clean facs; excel."* **€7.00, 1 Apr-15 Oct.**   **2019**

"We must tell the Club about that great site we found"

Get your site reports in by mid-August and we'll do our best to get your updates into the next edition.

MIRANDE *8F2* (0.5km E Rural) *43.51432, 0.40990* **Camp Municipal L'Ile du Pont,** Au Batardeau, 32300 Mirande **05 62 66 64 11; info@camping-gers.com; www.groupevla.fr**

On N21 Auch-Tarbes, foll sp to site on island in Rv Grande Baise. 3*, Med, pt shd, EHU (6A) inc; bbq; 20% statics; adv bkg rec; bike hire; games rm; sailing; canoeing; windsurfing; tennis; waterslide; fishing; CKE. *"Excel site; helpful staff; quiet location; 5min walk to town; gd stopover if heading to pyrenees."* **€20.00, 15 Apr-30 Sep.**   **2016**

MIREPOIX (ARIEGE) *8F4* (1km E Rural) *43.08871, 1.88585* **Camping Les Nysades,** Route de Limoux, 09500 Mirepoix **05 61 60 28 63; campinglesnysades@ orange.fr; www.camping-mirepoix-ariege.com**

E fr Pamiers on D119 to Mirepoix. Site well sp on D626. 2*, Med, hdg, mkd, shd, EHU (6A) €3.50; 10% statics; fishing 1km; tennis. *"Lge pitches; san facs ok; site a bit tired; interesting medieval town; mkt Mon rec; gd little site, walks along rv; barrier open 0700-2300, if warden not on site he will collect fees later."* **€15.00, 16 Apri-31 Oct.**   **2017**

MIRMANDE *9D2* (3km SE Rural) *44.68705, 4.85444* **Camping La Poche,** 26270 Mirmande **04 75 63 02 88; camping@la-poche.com; wwwcamping-lapoche.com**

Fr N on N7, 3km after Loriol turn L onto D57 sp Mirmande. Site sp in 7km on L. Fr S on N7 turn R onto D204 in Saulce & foll sp. 3*, Med, hdg, hdstg, mkd, shd, terr, EHU (6A) €3; TV; 90% statics; adv bkg acc; games area; CKE. *"Pleasant, scenic, gd site in wooded valley; gd walking/cycling; v friendly, helpful Dutch owners."* **€26.00, 1 Apr-1 Oct.**   **2015**

MODANE *9C4* (12km ENE Rural) *45.22870, 6.78116* **Camp Municipal Val d'Ambin,** Plan de l'Eglise, 73500 Bramans-le-Verney **04 79 05 03 05 or 06 16 51 90 91 (mob); campingbramans@gmail.com; www.camping-bramansvanoise.com**

10km after Modane on D1006 twd Lanslebourg, take 2nd turning R twd vill of Bramans, & foll camping sp, site by church. App fr Lanslebourg, after 12km turn L at camping sp on D306 at end of vill. 2*, Med, unshd, EHU (12-16A) €3.70-5.20; bbq; TV; games area. *"Away-fr-it-all site worth the climb; beautiful area, mountain views; gd dog walk adj; excel, brilliant site; great for walkers & outdoor enthusiasts; v well rec; friendly staff."* **€17.00, 20 Apr-30 Oct.**   **2015**

MOISSAC *8E3* (2km S Rural) *44.09664, 1.08878* **Camping Le Moulin du Bidounet,** St Benoît, 82200 Moissac **05 63 32 52 52; info@camping-moissac.com; www.camping-moissac.com**

Exit A62/E72 at junc 9 at Castelsarrasin onto D813 dir Moissac. Or fr N on D813 cross Rv Tarn, turn L at 1st rndabt & foll camp sp, site on L by rv. NB Height restriction 3.05m for tunnel at ent & tight turn lge o'fits. 3*, Med, hdg, mkd, hdstg, shd, EHU (6A) €3.10; bbq; red long stay; 10% statics; phone; Eng spkn; adv bkg acc; ccard acc; canoe hire; fishing; bike hire; watersports; boat hire; CKE. *"Excel, pleasant, rvside site in lovely area; extra for twin axles; helpful staff; basic, clean san facs; conv lovely town & abbey; gd fishing; walking/cycling; vg cycle track by canal; gd NH; entry tight for lge o'fits; passport identity needed."* **€24.20, 1 Apr-30 Sep.**   **2019**

MOLIETS ET MAA *8E1* (2km W Coastal) *43.85166, -1.38375* **Camping Les Cigales,** Ave de l'Océan, 40660 Moliets-Plage **05 58 48 51 18; reception@ camping-les-cigales.fr; www.camping-les-cigales.fr**

In Moliets-et-Maa, turn W for Moliets-Plage, site on R in vill. 3*, Med, shd, pt sl, EHU (5A) €3.50; bbq; TV; 80% statics; adv bkg acc; ccard acc; games area; CKE. *"Site in pine wood - sandy soil; narr access tracks; excel beach & surfing; many shops, rests 100m; gd forest walk to N."* **€30.70, 1 Apr-30 Sep.**   **2019**

MOLIETS ET MAA *8E1* (2km W Coastal) *43.85210, -1.38730* **Camping St Martin,** Ave de l'Océan 40660 Moliets-Plage **05 58 48 52 30; contact@camping-saint-martin.fr; www.camping-saint-martin.fr**

On N10 exit for Léon, Moliets-et-Maa. At Moliets foll sp to Moliets-Plage. Camp site after Les Cigales, by beach. 4*, V lge, mkd, hdg, pt shd, pt sl, terr, serviced pitches; EHU (10A) €5.30; gas; TV; Eng spkn; adv bkg rec; ccard acc; games area; jacuzzi; tennis nr; watersports; golf nr; sauna; CKE. *"Excel family site; cycle paths; vg san facs; gd for teenagers; gd cycling, walking."* **€43.00, 8 Apr-1 Nov.**   **2017**

MOLSHEIM *6E3* (0.9km SE Urban) *48.54124, 7.50003*
Camp Municipal de Molsheim, 6 Rue des Sports,
67120 Molsheim **03 88 49 82 45 or 03 88 49 58 58**
(LS); camping-molsheim@orange.fr;
www.mairie-molsheim.fr

🏕 €1.30 👪 ⚿ 🏊 ♿ 🚻 ♨ ⚲

On ent town fr Obernai on D1422 site sp on R
immed after x-ing sm rv bdge. 2*, Med, mkd, pt
shd, EHU (10A) €3.40; bbq; train to Strasbourg
700m; Eng spkn; adv bkg acc; bike hire; CKE.
"Pleasant site; excel san facs; pool adj; easy walk to
town cent & shops; Bugatti museum in town; vg."
€18.00, 7 Apr-29 Oct.   2017

MONESTIER DE CLERMONT *9C3* (0.7km SW Urban)
44.91515, 5.62809 **Camping Les Portes du Trièves,**
Chemin de Chambons, 38650 Monestier-de-Clermont
04 76 34 01 24 or 04 76 34 06 20 (LS);
camping.lesportesdutrieves@wanadoo.fr;
www.campingisere.com

🏕 👪 (htd) ⚿ 🏊 ♿ 🚻 ♨ ⚲ 🦋 ♨ ♀ nr ♨ nr 🛒 nr ⛺

Turn W off D1075. Sp in vill. 700m up hill adj sw
pool & school. Fr Grenoble take A51 to S end of vill
& foll sps to site. 3*, Sm, hdg, hdstg, mkd, pt shd, terr,
EHU (10A); red long stay; bus 500m; Eng spkn; adv
bkg acc; tennis adj; games rm; CKE. "Attractive, immac,
well-run site; friendly, helpful staff; clean san facs but
sm; watersports at lake; htd pool 200m; spectacular
countryside; train to Grenoble; gd NH; off clsd 1200-
1530, site self." €15.00, 1 May-30 Sep.   2015

MONETIER LES BAINS, LE *9C3* (1km NW Rural)
44.98059, 6.49537 **Camp Municipal Les Deux**
Glaciers, 05220 Le Monêtier-les-Bains **07 89 56 58 77;**
camping.monetier@orange.fr; www.monetier.com

🏕 €1 👪 (htd) ⚿ 🏊 ♿ 🚻 ♨ ⚲ ♀ nr ♨ nr 🛒 nr ⛺

On D1091 12km NW of Briançon; pass thro Le
Monêtier-les-Bains, in 1km site sp on L. 2*, Med, hdstg,
mkd, shd, terr, EHU (16A) €3.50; bus 1km; adv bkg acc;
CKE. "Excel, scenic site bef x-ing Montgenèvre pass; gd
base for Ecrins National Park; easy access fr D1091;
footpath to vill; v friendly helpful staff; immac gd facs;
excel for hiking, cycling, wildlife & flowers; fantastic loc;
clean." €15.50, 1 Jun-30 Sep.   2017

MONISTROL D'ALLIER *9C1* (4km N Rural) *44.99148,*
3.67781 **Camp Municipal Le Marchat,** 43580
St Privat-d'Allier **04 71 57 22 13; info@mairie-**
saintprivatdallier.fr; www.mairie-saintprivatdallier.fr

👪 ⚿ ♿ 🚻 ⚲ ♀ nr 🛒 nr ⛺

Fr Le Puy-en-Velay W on D589. Turn R in cent of
vill at petrol stn, site on R in 200m. 2*, Sm, hdg, shd,
terr, EHU (10A) €1.10. "Beautifully-kept, superb sm
site; friendly warden; not suitable lge o'fits; bars & shop
within 200mtrs." €6.00, 1 May-1 Nov.   2018

MONISTROL SUR LOIRE *9C1* (7km SE Rural)
45.21630, 4.21240 **Kawan Village Camping de**
Vaubarlet, 43600 Ste Sigolène **04 71 66 64 95;**
camping@vaubarlet.com; www.vaubarlet.com

🏕 €1 👪 ⚿ 🏊 ♿ 🚻 ♨ ⚲ MSP 🦋 ♨ ♀ ♨ 🍴 ♨ 🛒 ⛺
🏊 (htd) 🏊

Fr Monistrol take D44 SE twd Ste Sigolène & turn
R into vill. In vill take D43 dir Grazac for 6km. Site
by Rv Dunière, ent L bef bdge. Site well sp fr vill.
4*, Med, mkd, pt shd, EHU (6A) €3 (poss rev pol); bbq;
sw nr; TV; 15% statics; phone; Eng spkn; adv bkg acc;
ccard acc; trout fishing; games area; bike hire; CKE.
"Friendly, helpful staff; well-run site; excel, spotless
san facs; interesting museums nrby; ideal for families."
€33.00, 27 Apr-30 Sep, L23.   2019

"I need an on-site restaurant"

We do our best to make sure site information
is correct, but it is always best to check any
must-have facilities are still available or will
be open during your visit.

MONISTROL SUR LOIRE *9C1* (8km NW Urban)
45.31087, 4.12004 **Camping Municipal La Garenne,**
Route du Camping, 43210 Bas-en-Basset
04 71 66 72 37 or 04 71 66 70 01; contact@
basenbasset.fr; www.basenbasset.fr

🏕 👪 ⚿ 🏊 ♿ 🚻 ♨ ⚲ MSP 🦋 ♨ ♀ 🍴 ♨ nr ⛺ 🏊 (htd)

Fr N88 take the S exit (D47) sp Monistrol-sur-Loire.
L at 1st rndabt; downhill on D12 dir Gourdon &
Bas-en-Basset. Immed after Rv Loire turn R on
D46. At rndabt turn R & foll sp to site. Med, hdg,
mkd, pt shd, EHU (10A); bbq; twin axles; 95% statics;
phone; games rm; games area; CKE. "Fishing adj;
bustling static site, sm quiet area next to rv for tourers;
takeaway; clean modern san facs; vg value; gd NH."
€7.00, 15 Apr-30 Sep.   2015

MONNERVILLE *4E3* (2km S Rural) *48.33256, 2.04702*
Camping Le Bois de la Justice, Méréville, 91930
Monnerville **01 64 95 05 34; leboisdelajustice@**
gmail.com; www.campingleboisdelajustice.com

🏕 €1 👪 (htd) ⚿ 🏊 ♿ 🚻 ♨ ⚲ 🦋 ♀ 🍴 ♨ ⛺ 🏊 (htd)

Fr N20 S of Etampes, turn onto D18 at Monnerville,
site well sp. Long narr app rd. 3*, Med, hdg, mkd,
pt shd, pt sl, EHU (5A) inc; bbq; cooking facs; TV;
50% statics; phone; Eng spkn; adv bkg acc; ccard acc;
tennis; games area. "Delightful woodland oasis in open
countryside; beware caterpillars in spring (poisonous
to dogs); friendly welcome; clean san facs; ideal for
Chartres, Fontainebleau, Orléans, Paris or excel NH just
off N20; excel." €25.00, 7 Feb-24 Nov.   2015

MONPAZIER 7D3 (3km SW Rural) 44.65875, 0.87925
Camping Moulin de David, Route de Villeréal, 24540 Gaugeac-Monpazier 05 53 22 65 25; contact@ moulindedavid.com; www.moulindedavid.com

🐕 €3 🚻(htd) ⬜ ♨ ⚲ ♿ 🚰 ⋔ MSP 🦋 ⛲ 🍽 ⑪ 🛒 🔥 ⚱ 🚿 🏊 🎣

Fr Monpazier, take D2 SW twd Villeréal, site sp on L after 3km. Narr app rds. 4*, Lge, mkd, hdg, pt shd, serviced pitches; EHU (10A) inc gas; bbq; sw; TV; 80% statics; Eng spkn; adv bkg acc; ccard acc; games rm; waterslide; archery; bike hire; tennis; fishing adj; games area; CKE. *"Charming site nr lovely town; welcoming, helpful owners; excel facs, ltd LS; poss mosquitoes nr rv thro site; mkt Thur Monpazier; highly rec; v rural; superb rest."* **€31.00, 1 May-15 Sep.** 2019

MONT DORE, LE 7B4 (4km SE Rural) 45.571474, 2.817692 **Domaine de la Grande Cascade,** Route de Besse, 63240 Le Mont-Dore 04 73 65 06 23; contact@ camping-grandecascade.com; www.camping-grandecascade.com

🐕 €1 🚻 ⬜ ♨ ⚲ ♿ 🚰 ⋔ MSP 🦋 ⛲ 🔥

Fr Le Mont-Dore take D36 (12% incline) via col rte twd Besse-en-Chandesse. Site on R visible fr rd after 4km. App fairly steep & winding with poor surface. 2*, Med, mkd, hdg, pt shd, pt sl, EHU (6A); cooking facs; 5% statics; Eng spkn; adv bkg acc; games area; CKE. *"Excel; simple with magnificent, stunning mountain views; walk to waterfall; modern clean san facs; helpful staff."* **€15.00, 1 Jun-30 Sep.** 2018

MONT LOUIS 8G4 (5km W Rural) 42.50636, 2.04671 **Camping Huttopia Font-Romeu,** Route de Mont-Louis, 66120 Font-Romeu 04 68 30 09 32; font-romeu@huttopia.com; www.huttopia.com

🐕 €3.50 🚻(htd) ♨ 🚰 ⋔ 🦋 ⛲ 🍽 ⑪ 🛒 ⚱ 🏊(htd) 🎣

W fr Mont-Louis on D618. Site on L bef Font-Romeu, opp stadium. Fr Aix-les-Thermes or Puigcerdà turn E at Ur up longish hill, thro town to site on R at o'skts. Lge, pt shd, sl, EHU (6-10A) €4.20-6.20; 10% statics; phone; adv bkg acc; tennis 500m; horseriding 1km. *"Gd cent for mountain walks; site at 1800m altitude."* **€30.50, 29 May-15 Sep, D29.** 2019

MONT ST MICHEL, LE 2E4 (10km E Rural) 48.62822, -1.41508 **Camping St Michel,** Route du Mont-St Michel, 50220 Courtils 02 33 70 96 90; infos@campingsaint michel.com; www.campingsaintmichel.com

🐕 €2-3 🚻(htd) ⬜ ♨ ⚲ ♿ 🚰 ⋔ MSP 🦋 ⛲ 🍽 🛒 ⋔ ⚱ 🏊(htd)

Fr A84 exit J33. Foll sp for Courtils on Mont St Michel rd. Site on L at far end of vill. 3*, Med, mkd, hdg, pt shd, pt sl, EHU (6A) €3.50; gas; bbq; TV; 40% statics; phone; bus adj; Eng spkn; adv bkg acc; ccard acc; bike hire; games area; games rm; CKE. *"Excel, flat site; helpful, friendly owner; excel modern san facs (unisex); cycle paths adj; gd NH for St Malo; attractive; vg."* **€29.00, 31 Mar-1 Nov.** 2017

MONTAIGU 2H4 (10km SE Rural) 46.93769, -1.21975 **Camping L'Eden,** La Raillière, 85600 La Boissière-de-Montaigu 02 51 41 62 32; contact@ camping-domaine-eden.fr; www.domaine-eden.fr

12 🐕 €2 🚻 ⚲ ♿ 🚰 ⋔ 🍽 ⑪ 🛒 ⚱ 🔥 🏊 🎣(htd)

Fr Montaigu S on D137, in 8km turn E on D62, thro Le Pont-Legé. Site sp on L off D62. 3*, Med, mkd, shd, EHU (10A) inc; gas; TV; 40% statics; adv bkg acc; tennis; CKE. *"Pleasant, quiet site in woodlands; site poss open all year; clean facs; motor mover useful; site looking a bit tired."* **€23.00** 2017

MONTBARD 6G1 (1km N Urban) 47.6314, 4.33303 **Camp Municipal Les Treilles,** Rue Michel Servet, 21500 Montbard 03 80 92 69 50; camping. montbard@wanadoo.fr; www.montbard.com

🐕 €2 🚻 ⬜ ⚲ ♿ 🚰 ⋔ 🛒 nr 🔥

Lies off N side D980. Camping sp clearly indicated on all app including by-pass. Turn onto by-pass at traff lts at rndabt at junc of D905 & D980. Site nr pool. 3*, Med, hdg, pt shd, EHU (16A) €4; bbq; sw nr; phone; bike hire; CKE. *"Pleasant & well-kept site; gd pitches; lge, smart san facs; poss contract worker campers; pool complex adj inc; quiet but rd/rlwy noise at far end; interesting area; excel NH."* **€20.00, 26 Mar-30 Oct.** 2016

MONTBARREY 6H2 (1km SW Rural) 47.01230, 5.63161 **FLOWER Camping Les Trois Ours,** 28 Rue du Pont, 39380 Montbarrey 03 84 81 50 45; h.rabbe@orange.fr; www.camping-les3ours-jura.com or www.flowercampings.com

🐕 🚻(htd) ⬜ ♨ ⚲ ♿ 🚰 ⋔ MSP 🦋 ⛲ 🍽 ⑪ 🛒 nr 🔥 🏊

Exit A39 junc onto D905 E; 1km after Mont-sur-Vaudrey on D472 turn L dir Montbarrey. Cross rv, site on L at rvside on edge of vill. 3*, Med, mkd, hdg, shd, EHU (10A) inc; bbq; TV; 10% statics; phone; bus; Eng spkn; adv bkg acc; ccard acc; games rm. *"Improvements planned; vg walking/cycling fr site; excel menu in rest."* **€25.00, 13 Apr-28 Sep.** 2019

MONTBAZON 4G2 (0.8km N Rural) 47.29044, 0.71595 **Camping La Vallée de l'Indre (formerly de la Grange Rouge),** parc la Grange Rouge, 37250 Montbazon 02 47 26 06 43; contact@camping-montbazon.com; www.camping-montbazon.com

🐕 €2 🚻 ⬜ ⚲ ♿ 🚰 ⋔ 🦋 🍽 nr ⑪ nr 🛒 nr 🔥 🏊(htd)

On D910 thro Montbazon fr S to N, after x-ing bdge (pt of D910) immed turn L to site. Clearly visible & clearly sp on W side of rd at N end of town. 3*, Med, mkd, pt shd, EHU (10A) €4; TV; 10% statics; Eng spkn; adv bkg acc; ccard acc; fishing; tennis; CKE. *"Lovely, spacious rvside site in pretty town (walkable); helpful, friendly owner; bar adj; conv Tours & a'routes; facs being renewed (2019)."* **€22.80, 1 Apr-11 Oct.** 2019

MONTBERT *2H4* (0.5km SE Rural) *47.05133, -1.47930*
Camping Le Relais des Garennes (Gendron), La
Bauche Coiffée, 44140 Montbert **02 40 04 78 73;**
lerelaisdesgarennes@gmail.com; www.camping-le
relaisdesgarennes.com

🐕 (htd) ⊞ ♨ ♨ ⚠ 🗑 🚿 ♿ 🛝 ♒ ⛱

Fr Nantes on N937 dir La Roche, at Geneston turn
L dir Montbert & foll site sp. Or fr Nantes on N137
dir La Rochelle turn R at Aigrefeuille-sur-Maine for
Montbert. Sm, mkd, pt shd, pt sl, EHU (10A) inc; Eng
spkn; adv bkg acc; lake fishing adj; tennis nr; CKE.
*"Peaceful, picturesque site; lge pitches; friendly owners;
immac facs, but no individual wash rms; rabbits &
hens on site; toys for children; many attractions nrby;
pleasant walk to town; gd value; sports facs nrby;
excel; highly rec; bus avail to Nantes fr vill; excel."*
€13.00, 1 Jun-30 Sep. 2018

MONTBRISON *9B1* (1.5km S Urban) *45.59133,*
4.07806 **Camp Municipal Le Surizet,** 31 Rue du
Surizet, Moingt, 42600 Montbrison **04 77 58 08 30**

🐕 €0.85 ♦♦♦ ⊞ ♨ ⚠ 🗑 ♿ 🛝 🦋 🐾 nr ⛱ 🚣

Fr St Etienne on D8, at rndabt junc with D204 turn
L sp St Anthème & Ambert. Cross rlwy & turn R in
400m, site sp. 3*, Med, pt shd, EHU (5-10A) inc; bbq;
10% statics; bus (every hr); adv bkg acc; fishing; tennis
2km; CKE. *"Pleasant, well-kept site; no twin axles; vg
value; highly rec NH or sh stay; bird reserve (20km)."*
€13.00, 15 Apr-15 Oct. 2017

> ## "Satellite navigation makes touring much easier"
>
> Remember most sat navs don't know if you're
> towing or in a larger vehicle – always use yours
> alongside maps and site directions.

MONTBRON *7B3* (6km SE Rural) *45.65972, 0.55805*
Camping Les Gorges du Chambon, Le Chambon,
16220 Eymouthiers **05 45 70 71 70; info@**
gorgesduchambon.fr; www.gorgesduchambon.fr

🐕 €6 ♦♦♦ (htd) ⊞ ♨ ♨ ⚠ 🗑 🚿 ♿ 🛝 🦋 ♒ 🍽 ⊞ ⊕ 🐾 ⛱ ⚠ 🚴 🚣 🛶

Fr N141 turn SE onto D6 at La Rochefoucauld;
cont on D6 out of Montbron; after 5km turn L at La
Tricherie onto D163; foll camp sp to site in approx
1.9km. NB Fr La Tricherie narr in places & some sharp
bends. 4*, Med, hdstg, mkd, pt shd, pt sl, EHU (10A)
inc; gas; bbq (charcoal, gas); red long stay; twin axles;
TV; 25% statics; Eng spkn; adv bkg acc; ccard acc;
horseriding nr; games rm; tennis; bike hire; games area;
golf nr; canoe hire; rv fishing; CKE. *"Beautiful, 'away
fr it all', scenic site in grnds of old farm; welcoming,
helpful & friendly staff; lge pitches but some sl; excel
san facs; superb rest; gd mkd walks; birdwatching &
wildlife; poss motorbike rally on site end June; excel."*
€45.00, 19 Apr-13 Sep, D11. 2019

MONTECH *8E3* (1km E Rural) *43.96608, 1.24003*
Camping de Montech (formerly Camping Paradis),
Chemin de la Pierre, 82700 Montech
05 63 31 14 29; contact@camping-montech.fr;
www.camping-montech.fr

🐕 €2.80 ♦♦♦ ⊞ ♨ ⚠ 🗑 🚿 🍽 MP 🍽 ⊞ ⚠ 🐾 ⛱ ⚠ 🚣

Exit A20 junc 65 Montauban Sud onto D928 dir
Auch. In Montech turn R just bef canal, site well
sp. 3*, Lge, hdg, mkd, unshd, EHU (16A) €4; bbq;
twin axles; 60% statics; Eng spkn; adv bkg acc;
games area; lake fishing nrby; CKE. *"Gd cycle paths."*
€24.00, 1 Mar-31 Oct. 2019

MONTENDRE *7C2* (4km NW Rural) *45.30037, -0.43495*
Camping Twin Lakes, La Faïencérie, 17130 Souméras
05 46 49 77 12 or 0114 2463800 (UK); twinlakesinfo
@hotmail.co.uk; www.twinlakesfrance.com

12 🐕 €1.50 ♦♦♦ ⊞ ♨ ⚠ 🗑 🚿 ♿ 🦋 🍽 ⊞ 🐾 nr ⚠ (htd) 🚣

Exit N10/E606 at Montlieu-la-Garde onto D730 thro
Montendre dir Mirambeau; go past Souméras vill
on R, site sp on L. Or exit A10 junc 37; turn R onto
D730; at rndabt turn R onto N137; in Mirambeau
turn L onto D730; site on R in approx 14 km.
Sm, hdg, pt shd, pt sl, EHU (10-16A) €3; gas; bbq; red
long stay; TV; 15% statics; Eng spkn; adv bkg acc; clsd
15 Dec-5 Jan; lake fishing; games rm. *"Vg British-
owned site; meals arranged; gd touring base; vg; best
to pitch on field beside lake."* **€25.00** 2017

MONTESQUIOU *8F2* (4km W Rural) *43.57705,*
0.29111 **Camping l'Anjou,** L'Anjou 32320
Montesquiou **05 62 70 95 24; clemens.van-**
voorst@wanadoo.fr; www.camping-anjou.com

🐕 €2.50 ♦♦♦ ⊞ ♨ ⚠ ♿ 🗑 🚿 MP 🍽 ⊞ 🐾 🚣 🛶

Campsite is bet Montesquiou & Bassoues on the
D943. Site is well mkd. A sm lane leads to site ent. 1*,
Sm, hdg, hdstg, mkd, pt shd, pt sl, EHU (6A) €2.50; bbq;
50% statics; Eng spkn; adv bkg acc; games area; playgd;
CCI. *"Excel; no twin axles; friendly welcoming owners;
mini farm; ideally situated for those attending Marciac
Jazz Festival."* **€19.50, 1 May-30 Sep.** 2015

MONTFAUCON *7D3* (3km W Rural) *44.69197, 1.53480*
Kawan Village Domaine de la Faurie, 46240
Séniergues **05 65 21 14 36; contact@camping-**
lafaurie.com; www.camping-lafaurie.com

🐕 €3 ♦♦♦ (htd) ⊞ ♨ ♨ ⚠ 🗑 🚿 ♿ 🛝 🦋 ♒ ⊞ 🐾 ⚠ 🚣 (htd) 🛶

Fr N20 turn E onto D2 sp Montfaucon, or fr A20 exit
junc 56. In 5km site sp. Rd to site (off D2) is 500m
long, single-track with passing places & steep but
passable. Well sp fr A20.
4*, Med, mkd, pt shd, pt sl, terr, EHU (6-10A) €4.50-
6.70; twin axles; TV; 30% statics; Eng spkn; adv bkg
acc; ccard acc; games area; bike hire. *"Superb, pretty
site with great views; quiet & peaceful; lge pitches;
excel facs & rest; gd touring base; poss intermittent
elec supply some pitches (2010); many walks; conv
A20; award winning site; one of the best sites."*
€30.00, 5 Apr-31 Oct. 2015

MONTFERRAND 8F4 (4.8km N Rural) 43.39007, 1.82788 **FFCC Domaine St Laurent,** Les Touzets, 11320 Montferrand 04 68 60 15 80 or 06 76 60 58 42 (mob); info@camping-carcassonne-toulouse. com; www.camping-carcassonne-toulouse.com

🐕€2 ♛♛ WD ♨ 🖥 ✗ 🐾 ♈ ♐ Y 🈂 🖳 🛒 ⚓ 🏊

S fr Toulouse on N113/D1113 past Villefranche-de-Lauragais. Turn L onto D43 for 4.2km; then R to St Laurent. Or turn L onto D218 bypassing Montferrand & cont directly to St Laurent; turn L at church. Site well sp. 3*, Sm, hdg, pt shd, EHU (6A) inc; TV; 10% statics; Eng spkn; adv bkg acc; tennis; bike hire; games rm; sauna; archery. "Attractive, peaceful, well-kept site; clean san facs; friendly owners; gd views; woodland walks; vg site but narr access rds." €26.00, 1 Apr-15 Oct. 2017

"There aren't many sites open at this time of year"

If you're travelling outside peak season remember to call ahead to check site opening dates – even if the entry says 'open all year'.

MONTFERRAND 8F4 (6km SE Rural) 43.31451, 1.80246 **Camping Le Cathare,** Château de la Barthe, 11410 Belflou 04 68 60 32 49; contact@camping-lecathare.com; www.auberge-lecathare.com

🐕€3.25 ♛♛ WD ♨ ✗ 🐾 ♈ Y 🈂 ⚓ 🛶 shgl

Fr Villefranche-de-Lauragais on N113/D6113, foll D622 sp Toulouse/Carcassonne over rlwy, canal, then immed L on D625 for 7km. Thro St Michel-de-Lanes then take D33 to Belflou; foll sp to Le Cathare. 3*, Sm, mkd, pt shd, EHU (3-10A) €3-7.50; bbq; sw nr; 10% statics; boules pitch; mini golf; common rm; CKE. "Poss long walk to basic san facs - sh timer for lts & might prefer to use your own facs; Cent Nautique on lake; dramatic position o'looking lake." €18.00, 15 Apr-15 Nov. 2020

MONTIGNAC 7C3 (7km E Rural) 45.05375, 1.23980 **Yelloh! Village Lascaux Vacances,** Route des Malénies, 24290 St Amand-de-Coly 05 53 50 81 57; mail@campinglascauxvacances.com; www.camping lascauxvacances.com or www.yellohvillage.co.uk

🐕€4 ♛♛ WD ♨ ♨ 🖥 ✗ 🐾 MP 🦋 ♈ Y 🈂 🖳 🛒 ⚓ 🏊 🛶

Exit A89 junc 17 (Peyrignac) SE onto D6089 to Le Lardin-St Lazare. Join D62 S to Coly & then foll sp to Saint Amand-de-Coly. Site well sp. 3*, Med, mkd, hdg, pt shd, EHU (10A) inc; bbq; red long stay; TV; 60% statics; phone; adv bkg acc; ccard acc; fishing nr; waterslide; games area; sauna; games rm. "Excel, peaceful, renovated site in superb location; warm welcome; lge pitches; excel touring base." €33.00, 15 Apr-11 Sep. 2017

MONTIGNAC 7C3 (8km SE Rural) 45.07211, 1.23431 **Camping La Tournerie Ferme,** La Tournerie, 24290 Aubas 05 53 51 04 16; la-tournerie@orange.fr; www.la-tournerie.com

🐕 ♛♛ (htd) WD ♨ ♨ 🖥 ✗ 🐾 Y 🈂 🖳 🈂 nr

Fr Montignac on D704 dir Sarlat-la-Canéda; in 5.5km turn L onto C1 sp St Amand-de-Coly; in 1.6km at x-rds turn L sp Malardel & Drouille; in 400m at Y-junc foll rd to R sp Manardel & La Genèbre; cont on this rd ignoring minor rds; in 1.6km at elongated junc take rd to R of post box; immed after passing Le Treuil farm on R turn R at x-rds La Tournerie. Site opp farm. Sm, hdstg, unshd, sl, terr, EHU (6A) inc; bbq; twin axles; Eng spkn; adv bkg req. "Lovely, tranquil site; adults only; lge pitches with beautiful views; friendly, helpful British owners (CC members); excel san facs; request detailed dirs or see website - sat nav not rec; excel touring base; excel site; fenced dog pitches." €23.00, 1 Mar-30 Nov. 2016

MONTIGNAC 7C3 (0.5km S Urban) 45.05980, 1.15860 **Camping Le Moulin du Bleufond,** Ave Aristide Briand, 24290 Montignac 05 53 51 83 95; info@bleufond.com; www.bleufond.com

🐕€3 ♛♛ (htd) ♨ ♨ 🖥 ✗ 🐾 ♈ Y 🈂 🖳 🛒 ⚓ 🏊 (htd) 🛒

S on D704, cross bdge in town & turn R immed of rv on D65; site sp in 500m nr stadium, adj Rv Vezere. 3*, Med, hdg, pt shd, EHU (10A) €3.50; bbq; red long stay; TV; adv bkg acc; ccard acc; fishing; tennis adj; wellness area with jacuzzi and sauna (additional charge and reservation required); table football; table tennis; pinball machine; bowling. "Pleasant site; pleasant, helpful owners; facs excel; poss diff lge o'fits due trees; conv Lascaux caves & town; gd walking area; lovely site." €31.40, 31 Mar-14 Oct. 2020

"That's changed – Should I let the Club know?"

If you find something on site that's different from the site entry, fill in a report and let us know. See camc.com/europereport.

MONTIGNAC 7C3 (9km S Rural) 45.01765, 1.18811 **FFCC Camping La Fage,** 24290 La Chapelle-Aubareil 05 53 50 76 50 or 06 87 37 5 891 (Mob); contact@ camping-lafage.com; www.camping-lafage.com

🐕€1.80 ♛♛ ♨ ♨ 🖥 ✗ 🐾 MP 🦋 ♈ Y 🈂 🖳 🛒 ⚓ 🏊 (htd) 🛒

Fr Montignac take D704 twd Sarlat. In about 8km turn R onto La Chapelle-Aubareil & foll camp sp. 4*, Med, hdstg, pt shd, pt sl, EHU (10A); bbq; TV; 30% statics; adv bkg acc; games area; CKE. "Excel site; helpful owners; vg, clean san facs; red facs LS; gd rest at auberge in vill; conv Lascaux 2 & other pre-historic sites; gd walking." €30.00, 11 Apr-10 Oct. 2015

MONTIGNAC *7C3* (14km SW Rural) *45.00178, 1.07155* **Camping Le Paradis,** La Reybeyrolle, 24290 St Léon-sur-Vézère **05 53 50 72 64; le-paradis@ perigord.com; www.le-paradis.fr**

🐕 €2.50 ♂♀ (htd) [WD] ⚓ ♿ ♨ [MP] ♚ ℗ 🍴 ♨ ⚒ 🏊 🛝 ✏
🚣 (htd, indoor) 🏖 🛶 adj

On W bank of Rv Vézère on D706 Montignac-Les Eyzies rd, 1km fr Le Moustier. D706 poss rough rd. 5*, Med, hdg, pt shd, EHU (10A); bbq; sw; red long stay; TV; 25% statics; phone; Eng spkn; adv bkg acc; ccard acc; boat hire; tennis; fishing; sauna; games area; bike hire; CKE. "Excel, high standard site in gd location; friendly, conscientious Dutch owners; immac san facs; gd pool, rest & takeaway; vg for families; tropical vegetation around pitches, grnds like a garden; excel, espec LS; ACSI acc."
€38.00, 1 Apr-20 Oct, D30. 2017

See advertisement

MONTLUCON *7A4* (12km NW Rural) *46.37795, 2.46695* **Camp Municipal Le Moulin de Lyon,** 03380 Huriel **06 11 75 05 63 or 04 70 28 60 08 (Mairie); mairie.huriel@wanadoo.fr**

♂♀ [WD] ⚓ 🛒 🦋 ♨ 🍴 nr 🛝 🏊

Exit A71 junc 10 & foll sp Domérat, then D916 to Huriel. Site well sp. Or fr N D943 turn SW at La Chapelaude to Huriel on D40, foll sp to site. Last km single track (but can pass on level grass) with steep incline to site ent. Site adj Rv Magieure. 2*, Med, hdg, pt shd, pt sl, EHU (10A) inc (poss rev pol); gas; bbq; TV; 10% statics; Eng spkn; lake fishing; tennis. "Peaceful, wooded site in lovely setting by lake; well-kept; friendly; site yourself, warden calls am & pm; no apparent security; uphill walk to vill (1km); lovely quiet site, clean facs." **€9.00, 15 Apr-15 Oct.** 2016

MONTMAUR *9D3* (7km SE Rural) *44.55003, 5.95114* **Camping au Blanc Manteau,** Route de Céüse, 05400 Manteyer **92 57 82 56 or 92 57 85 89; pierre.wampach @wanadoo.fr; www.campingaublancmanteau.fr**

[12] ♂♀ (htd) [WD] ⚓ ♨ 🛒 ♨ 🦋 🍴 ⚒ nr 🛝 🏊 (htd)

Take D994 fr Veynes twd Gap, past Montmaur; site sp fr vill of La Roche-des-Arnauds on D18 in 1km. 3*, Sm, mkd, pt shd, EHU (10A) €5.35; adv bkg rec; tennis. "Gd sized pitches; pleasant owner; pretty, in wooded area with beautiful views of mountains."
€24.00 2019

MONTMEDY *5C1* (0.7km NW Urban) *49.52126, 5.36090* **Camp Municipal La Citadelle,** Rue Vauban, 55600 Montmédy **03 29 80 10 40 (Mairie); mairie. montmedy@wanadoo.fr; www.montmedy.fr**

🐕 €2.24 ♂♀ [WD] ⚓ 🦋 🦋 🛝 🏊

Fr D643 foll sp to Montmédy cent & foll site sp. Steep app. 2*, Sm, hdg, pt shd, pt sl, EHU (4-10A) €2.80-3.97; red long stay; CKE. "Warden calls am & pm; facs clean, ltd LS; nr Montmedy Haut fortified town; 10A hook-up not avail high ssn; vg; lovely, delightful little site; gd views." **€9.60, 1 May-30 Sep.** 2019

MONTMORILLON *7A3* (0.8km S Urban) *46.42035, 0.87554* **Camp Municipal de l'Allochon,** 31 Ave Fernand Tribot, 86500 Montmorillon **05 49 91 02 33 or 05 49 91 13 99 (Mairie); www.montmorillon.fr**

🐕 ♂♀ (htd) ⚓ 🛒 ♨ [MP] ♚ 🍴 ℗ nr 🛝 🏊

On D54 to Le Dorat, approx 400m SE fr main rd bdge over rv at S of town. Site on L. Fr S v sharp RH turn into site. 3*, Med, mkd, pt shd, terr, EHU (10A); bbq; TV; Eng spkn; adv bkg acc; ccard acc; games area; fishing; CKE. "Delightful, peaceful, well-kept site; lge pitches; friendly, hard-working warden; gd touring base; vg value; v clean facs, old but working shwrs; htd covrd pool adj; relaxing; rec; security barrier; gd walking area, maps fr TO; ltd facs LS." **€12.00, 1 Mar-31 Oct.** 2018

FRANCE

MONTOIRE SUR LE LOIR *4F2* (0.5km S Rural) *47.74750, 0.86351* **Camp Municipal Les Reclusages,** Ave des Reclusages, 41800 Montoire-sur-le Loir **02 54 85 02 53; camping.reclusages@orange.fr; www.mairie-montoire.fr**

🐕 €0.97 👫 wc ♨ ⚲ ♿ 🚿 ⊿ MSP 🦋 👍 🍴 🛒🐟 nr ⛺

Foll site sp, out of town sq, over rv bdge & 1st L on blind corner at foot of old castle. 3*, Med, mkd, pt shd, EHU (6-10A) €3.10-3.93; 5% statics; Eng spkn; adv bkg acc; ccard acc; canoeing; fishing; CKE. "Lovely location nr Rv Loir; peaceful, well-kept, secure site; some rvside pitches; friendly, helpful warden; excel clean san facs, ltd LS; gd cycling; conv troglodyte vills; excel; pleasant sh walk into town across rv; htd pool adj; attractive town; Int'l Folk Festival mid Aug." **€14.00, 1 Apr-30 Sep.** 2017

> ## "I like to fill in the reports as I travel from site to site"
> You'll find report forms at the back of this guide, or you can fill them in online at camc.com/europereport.

MONTPELLIER *10F1* (8km N Rural) *43.65135, 3.89630* **Sandaya Le Plein Air des Chênes,** 531 Avenue Georges France, 34830 Clapiers **04 67 02 02 53; pac@ sandaya.fr; www.sandaya.co.uk**

🐕 €5 👫 ♨ ♿ 🚿 ⊿ 🦋 👍 🍴 ⊕ 🛒 ⅲ ⛺ 🏊 🎣

Exit A9 junc 28 onto N113/D65 twd Montpellier. Leave at junc with D21 sp Jacou & Teyran, site sp on L. NB Site ent/exit v narr & no place to stop when leaving. 4*, Med, mkd, pt shd, pt sl, terr, serviced pitches; EHU (10A) inc; gas; red long stay; 75% statics; horseriding; tennis; games area; waterslide. "Vg site; site rds tight for lge o'fits; private san facs some pitches (extra charge), pitches muddy in wet." **€25.00, 3 Apr-13 Sep.** 2019

MONTPON MENESTEROL *7C2* (1km N Rural) *45.01280, 0.15828* **Camping La Cigaline,** 1 Rue de la Paix, Route de Ribérac, 24700 Montpon-Ménestérol **05 53 80 22 16; contact@lacigaline.fr; www.lacigaline.fr**

🐕 €1.50 👫 wc ♨ ⚲ 🚿 ⊿ 🦋 👍 🍴 ⊕ 🛒 nr ⛺

Fr Montpon town cent traff lts take D730 N to Ménestérol. Site on L bef bdge beside Rv Isle. 3*, Med, hdg, mkd, shd, EHU (10A) inc; bbq; sw nr; 1% statics; train 1km; Eng spkn; adv bkg acc; ccard acc; fishing; tennis 200m; boat hire; CKE. "Gd touring base for St Emilion region; gd walking, cycling; vg; new young owners (2014); leisure park nrby; bike hire 500m; gd food in bar/rest; terr o'looks rv; site improving." **€19.60, 6 Apr-30 Sep.** 2019

MONTREJEAU *8F3* (7km S Rural) *43.02864, 0.57852* **Camping Es Pibous,** Chemin de St Just, 31510 St Bertrand-de-Comminges **05 61 88 31 42; contact@ es-pibous.fr; www.espibous.fr**

🐕 👫(htd) wc ♨ ⚲ ♿ 🚿 ⊿ MSP 🦋 🍴 nr ⊕ nr 🛒 ⛺ 🏊

Turn S fr D817 onto D825 sp Bagnères-de-Luchon & Espagne. Foll past 'Super U' to lge rndabt & turn R sp St Bertrand-de-Comminges/Valcabrère then at 1st traff lts turn R & foll sp for St Bertrand. Turn R off N125 onto D825 to roman excavation site. Site on L. Or exit A64 junc 17 onto A645 sp Bagnères-de-Luchon to lge rndabt, then as above. 3*, Med, mkd, hdg, pt shd, EHU (10A) inc; gas; TV; 20% statics; adv bkg acc; ccard acc; fishing 3km; tennis 3km. "Peaceful, friendly site; pitches among trees; clean dated san facs, ltd LS; lndry is owner's washing machine, not always avail (2010); gd touring area nr mountains; picturesque town in walking dist." **€20.40, 1 Apr-31 Oct.** 2017

MONTREJEAU *8F3* (1km W Rural) *43.08624, 0.55414* **Camping Couleurs Garonne (formerly Camping Les Hortensias),** Route de Tarbes, 31210 Montréjeau **05 61 88 52 30; campingcouleursgaronne@ orange.fr; www.campingcouleursgaronne.com**

👫 wc ♨ ⊿ 🛒 nr ⛺

Fr St Gaudens on D817, R at foot of steep hill, sp 'Tarbes Poids Lourds' to avoid Montréjeau cent. Site on L in 1km. On W o'skirts of town, well sp on rd to Tarbes. Sm, pt shd, EHU (15A) inc; bbq; CKE. "Gd NH; no twin axles; spacious grassy site; friendly." **€15.00, 15 Apr-31 Oct.** 2015

> ## "We must tell the Club about that great site we found"
> Get your site reports in by mid-August and we'll do our best to get your updates into the next edition.

MONTRESOR *4H2* (3km W Rural) *47.15782, 1.16026* **Camping Les Coteaux du Lac,** 37460 Chemillé-sur-Indrois **02 47 92 77 83; lescoteauxdulac@ wanadoo.fr; www.lescoteauxdulac.com**

🐕 €1.70 👫 wc ♨ ⚲ ♿ 🚿 ⊿ MSP 🦋 👍 🍴 ⊕ 🛒 ⛺ ✏ 🏊 (htd) 🎣

Fr Loches on D764; then D10 dir Montrésor; cont to Chemillé-sur-Indrois. 4*, Med, pt sl, EHU (6A) €3.90; bbq; TV; phone; Eng spkn; fishing; games rm; boating. "Excel setting by lake; immac, modern san facs; beautiful vill 600m; trekking in Val d'Indrois; 3km along cycle track (old rlwy)." **€34.00, 3 Mar-15 Oct.** 2019

FRANCE

MONTREUIL *3B3* (0.5km W Rural) *50.46853, 1.76280* **FFCC Camping La Fontaine des Clercs,** 1 Rue de l'Eglise, 62170 Montreuil **03 21 06 07 28; desmarest. mi@wanadoo.fr; www.campinglafontainedesclercs.fr**

🏕12 🐕 €2 🛉🛉 (htd) 🚐 ♨ ⚕ MSP 🦋 ⛨ 🛒nr

Fr N or S turn SW off D901 at rndabt onto D349 to Montreuil; turn R immed after rlwy x-ing (onto Rue des Préaux); in 120m turn R; site in 100m on R; sp on Rv Canche. Or take 2nd R ALMOST immed after (20m) rlwy-xing (onto Grande Ville Basse); in 50m fork R (Rue de l'Eglise); site in 200m on R. NB Poss difff access lge o'fits. 3*, Med, mkd, hdstg, pt shd, pt sl, terr, EHU (6-10A) €3.70-€4.80; bbq; 60% statics; adv bkg rec; rv fishing adj; site clsd over New Year; games rm; CKE. *"Busy, basic site in beautiful spot; helpful, friendly owner; gd san facs; steep & narr site rd with tight turns to terr pitches, some sm; pool 1.5km; not suitable lge o'fits; some generous pitches beside rv; vet in Montreuil; attractive, historic town with amazing restaurants- uphill walk; conv NH Le Touquet, beaches & ferry; wine society outlet; excel site; some Eng spkn."* €19.50 **2017**

MONTREUIL BELLAY *4H1* (1km W Urban) *47.13191, -0.15897* **Camping Les Nobis D'Anjou,** Rue Georges Girouy, 49260 Montreuil-Bellay **02 41 52 33 66; camping-les-nobis@orange.fr; www.campingles nobis.com**

🐕 🛉🛉 ♨ ⚕ ♿ 🚐 ♨ MSP 🦋 ⛨ 🍴 🛒 🛖 ♨ (htd)

Fr S on D938 turn L immed on ent town boundary & foll rd for 1km to site; sp fr all dir. Fr N on D347 ignore 1st camping sp & cont on D347 to 2nd rndabt & foll sp. Fr NW on D761 turn R onto D347 sp Thouars to next rndabt, foll site sp. 4*, Lge, hdg, mkd, pt shd, EHU (10A) €3 (poss long cable req, rev pol); gas; red long stay; TV; 50% statics; phone; Eng spkn; adv bkg acc; ccard acc; bike hire; CKE. *"Spacious site bet castle & rv; gd, modern san facs; local chateaux & town worth exploring; 'aire de service' for m'vans adj; gd patissiere in town; some pitches o'look rv Thouet; extremely well managed, friendly site; nr Saumur vineyards; excel."* €29.00, 31 Mar-30 Sep. **2018**

MONTREVEL EN BRESSE *9A2* (0.5km E Rural) *46.201520, 5.136681* **Camping La Plaine Tonique,** Base de loisirs - 599, route d'Etrez - 01340 Malafretaz **04 74 30 80 52; contact@laplainetonique.com; www.laplaine tonique.com**

🐕 €4 🛉🛉 ♨ ♨ ⚕ ♿ 🚐 ♨ MSP 🦋 ⛨ 🍴 ♨ 🛒 🛖 ♨ 🖊 ♨ (covrd, htd) 🕮 🏃

Exit A40 junc 5 Bourg-en-Bresse N onto D975; at Montrevel-en-Bresse turn E onto D28 dir Etrez & Marboz; site sp on L in 400m. Or exit A6 junc 27 Tournus S onto D975. 4*, V lge, hdg, mkd, shd, EHU (10A) inc; bbq; sw nr; Eng spkn; adv bkg acc; ccard acc; waterslide; fishing; watersports; bike hire; games area; tennis. *"Excel, busy, family site; superb leisure facs; mountain biking; archery; vg clean san facs; some pitches boggy after rain."* €30.00, 22 Apr-6 Sep. **2020**

MONTRICHARD *4G2* (1km S Rural) *47.33384, 1.18766* **Camping Couleurs du Monde,** 1 Rond Point de Montparnasse, 41400 Faverolles-sur-Cher **02 54 32 06 08 or 06 74 79 56 29 (mob); touraine-vacances@ wanadoo.fr; www.camping-couleurs-du-monde.com**

🐕 €2 🛉🛉 🚐 ♨ ♨ ♿ 🚐 ♨ MSP 🦋 ⛨ 🍴 ♨ 🛒 🛖nr ⚑ 🖊 ♨ (htd) 🕮

E fr Tours on D796 thro Bléré; at Montrichard turn S on D764 twd Faverolles-sur-Cher, site 200m fr junc, adj to Carrefour supmkt - on L by 2nd rndabt. 4*, Med, mkd, hdstg, pt shd, EHU (10A) €4; bbq; sw nr; TV; Eng spkn; adv bkg acc; ccard acc; tennis 500m; games rm; sauna; bike hire; games area; waterslide 500m; CKE. *"Level site in gd location nr vineyards; beauty cent; gd sports activities; vg; excel facs; gd sw pool with canopy; ideal for exploring Cher & Loire Valley."* €30.00, 31 Mar-29 Sep. **2017**

MONTRICOUX *8E3* (0.5km W Rural) *44.07660, 1.61103* **FFCC Camping Le Clos Lalande,** Route de Bioule, 82800 Montricoux **06 49 27 48 28; contact@ camping-lecloslalande.com; www.camping-leclos lalande.com**

🐕 €2.50 🛉🛉 🚐 ♨ ♨ ♿ 🚐 ♨ MSP ⛨ 🍴 ♨ 🛒 🛖nr ⚑ 🏃

Fr A20 exit junc 59 to Caussade; fr Caussade take D964 to Montricoux, where site well sp. 3*, Med, hdg, mkd, pt shd, EHU (6A) €3.60; bbq; TV; 10% statics; phone; bus 400m; Eng spkn; adv bkg rec; games area; rv fishing 400m; canoe hire; watersports; tennis; bike hire; CKE. *"Peaceful, quiet, well-kept site by rv at mouth of Aveyron gorges; beautiful area, inc Bastide vills; great family site; friendly, helpful owners; mkt Weds; easy walk to town; highly rec."* €25.40, 30 Mar-6 Oct. **2019**

MONTROLLET *7B3* (0.1km N Rural) *45.98316, 0.89702* **Camping Auberge La Marchadaine,** Beaulieu, 16420 Montrollet **05 45 71 09 88 or 06 63 07 82 48 (mob); aubergedelamarchadaine@gmail.com**

🐕 🛉🛉 🚐 ♨ ♨ ⚕ ♨ MSP 🦋 ⛨ 🍴 ♨ 🛒 ⚑

N fr St Junien on D675, turn W onto D82 to Montrollet. Auberge sp in vill. Sm, pt shd, EHU (6A) inc; gas; bbq; twin axles; phone; adv bkg acc; games area; fishing; CKE. *"Delightful CL-type site nr beautiful lake; vg rest; many mkd walks; Oradour sur Glane nrby (wartime museum); Vienne rv; gd; rund down (2017)."* €12.00 **2017**

MONTSAUCHE LES SETTONS *4G4* (5.4km SE Rural) *47.19276, 4.06047* **FFCC Camping de la Plage des Settons,** Rive Gauche, Lac des Settons, 58230 Montsauche-les-Settons **03 86 84 51 99; camping@ settons-tourisme.com; www.settons-tourisme.com**

🐕 🛉🛉 🚐 ♨ ♨ ♨ MSP ♨ 🛒nr ⚑

Fr Montsauche foll sp Château-Chinon. In 500m fork L to Les Settons. After 2km foll sp for Rive Gauche, after 1km L at bend for site. 3*, Med, hdg, mkd, pt shd, terr, EHU (4A) inc (long lead req); bbq; sw; Eng spkn; ccard acc; bike hire; fishing; CKE. *"In cent of Parc du Morvan; lake adj; direct access to Lac des Settons; pedalos; access rd busy pm."* €20.00, 15 Apr-15 Oct. **2015**

MONTSAUCHE LES SETTONS *4G4* (7km SE Rural) *47.18175, 4.05293* **FFCC Camping Les Mésanges,** Rive Gauche, 58230 Montsauche-les-Settons **03 86 84 55 77; info@campinglesmesanges.fr; www.campinglesmesanges.fr**

🐕 €0.80 🏕️🔥♿🚿🅿️♨️💧 MP 💧 ⓗ nr 🍴🛒🏭

Fr Montsauche take D193 twds Les Settons, just bef Les Settons fork R onto D520 dir Chevigny. After 1km turn L and foll sp to site on R on W side of lake. 3*, Med, mkd, shd, pt sl, terr, EHU (16A) inc; gas; sw; Eng spkn; adv bkg acc; games rm; fishing; games area; CKE. *"Beautiful site; well-maintained; gd for families - lge play areas; excel."* **€22.00, 14 May-15 Sep.** 2015

MONTSAUCHE LES SETTONS *4G4* (7.6km SE Rural) *47.18578, 4.07056* **Camping Plage du Midi,** Lac des Settons Les Branlasses, 58230 Montsauche-les-Settons **03 86 84 51 97; campplagedumidi@aol.com; www.settons-camping.com**

🐕 €1 👫(htd) WD 🏕️🔥♿🚿🅿️💧 MP 🍴♨️🍴ⓗ nr 🛒🏭🎣 🏊(covrd, htd) 🏖️sand adj

Fr Salieu take D977 bis to Montsauche, then D193 'Rive Droite' to Les Settons for 5km. Cont a further 3km & take R fork sp 'Les Branlasses' Cent du Sport. Site on L after 500m at lakeside. 3*, Med, mkd, pt shd, terr, EHU (10A) €3.60; gas; bbq; sw; phone; Eng spkn; adv bkg acc; ccard acc; horseriding 2km; watersports; bike hire; CKE. *"Site in gd situation; muddy when wet."* **€20.00, 19 Apr-15 Sep.** 2015

MONTSOREAU *4G1* (1.3km NW Rural) *47.21805, 0.05270* **Camping L'Isle Verte,** Ave de la Loire, 49730 Montsoreau **02 41 51 76 60 or 02 41 67 37 81; isleverte@cvtloisirs.fr; www.campingisleverte.com**

🐕 €2 👫 WD 🏕️🔥♿🚿🅿️💧 MP 🍴♨️🍴🛒nr 🏭🎣🏊🛶

At Saumur on S side of rv turn R immed bef bdge over Rv Loire; foll sp to Chinon & site. Fr N foll sp for Fontevraud & Chinon fr Rv Loire bdge; site on D947 in vill on banks of Loire opp 'Charcuterie' shop. 4*, Med, mkd, pt shd, EHU (16A) poss long lead req; gas; TV; 20% statics; bus to Saumur; Eng spkn; adv bkg rec; ccard acc; games area; rv fishing; bike hire; watersports; golf 13km; tennis; CKE. *"Pleasant rvside site in beautiful situation; v busy high ssn; various sized/shaped pitches; car hire; adequate san facs, poss irreg cleaning LS; vg rest; barrier clsd 2200-0700; gd security; pleasant vill; gd; excel; helpful staff."* **€38.50, 3 Apr-14 Oct, L34.** 2019

MOREE *4F2* (2.5km SW Urban) *47.88932, 1.20109* **Camping La Maladrerie,** Rue du Plessis, 41160 Fréteval **06 50 23 11 88 or 06 67 31 55 52**

👫 WD 🏕️🔥♿🚿🅿️💧 🍴🛒nr 🏭🛶

E fr Le Mans on D357 to Fréteval; turn L in vill. Sp. 3*, Med, mkd, pt shd, EHU (4-6A) €1.55-2.30; gas; bbq; sw nr; 60% statics; Eng spkn; ccard acc; lake fishing; CKE. *"Delightful, well-kept, quiet site; friendly owner; unisex wc; poss ltd facs LS; site was a medieval leper colony; new owners but site still run down (2017)."* **€12.00, 1 Apr-30 Oct.** 2017

MORESTEL *9B3* (8km S Urban) *45.63521, 5.57231* **Camping Couleur Nature (formerly Les Avenières),** 6 Rue du Stade, 38630 Les Avenières **04 74 33 92 92; camping@lesavenieres.fr; www.camping-couleur-nature.fr**

🐕 👫(htd) WD 🏕️🔥♿🚿🅿️💧 MP 🍴♨️ⓗ🍴🏭🛶🎣

S fr Morestel on D1075, turn onto D40 to Les Avenières, site well sp. 3*, Med, hdg, mkd, hdstg, pt shd, EHU (10A); bbq; sw nr; TV; 35% statics; phone; adv bkg acc; ccard acc; CKE. *"Phone ahead LS to check open; pool adj; noise fr adj stadium."* **€27.00, 1 May-30 Sep.** 2019

MORLAIX *2E2* (13km N Coastal) *48.65950, -3.84847* **Camping De La Baie de Terenez,** 29252 Plouezoch **02 98 67 26 80; contact@campingbaiedeterenez.com; www.campingbaiedeterenez.com**

🐕 👫🔥♿🚿🅿️💧 MP 🦋♨️🍴🛒🏭🛶(htd) 🏖️sand 2km

Take D46 on exit Morlaix, turn L on D76 to site. 3*, Lge, pt shd, pt sl, EHU (10A) inc; gas; TV; adv bkg acc; fishing; windsurfing; games rm. *Quiet, rural site; variety of plants & trees; coastal path adj;* **€26.50, 4 Apr-27 Sep.** 2019

MORLAIX *2E2* (11km E Rural) *48.60283, -3.73833* **Camping Aire Naturelle la Ferme de Croas Men (Cotty),** Garlan, 29610 Plouigneau **02 98 79 11 50; info@ferme-de-croasmen.com; www.ferme-de-croasmen.com**

🐕 €1 👫 WD 🏕️🔥♿🚿💧 MP 🦋🛒🏭

Fr D712 rndabt W of Plouigneau twd Morlaix (exit fr N12) 2km R sp Garlan; thro Garlan site 1km on L, well sp. Sm, hdg, pt shd, serviced pitches; EHU (6A) €3.50; 10% statics; Eng spkn; horseriding 200m; CKE. *"Lovely, well-kept CL-type farm site; excel facs; farm museum, donkey/tractor rides; ideal for children; produce avail inc cider & crêpes; vg."* **€19.00, 1 Apr-31 Oct.** 2017

MORTAIN *2E4* (12km S Rural) *48.57039, -0.94883* **Camping Les Taupinières,** La Raisnais, 50140 Notre-Dame-du-Touchet **02 33 69 49 36 or 06 33 26 78 82 (mob); belinfrance@fsmail.net; www.les taupinieres.com**

🐕 👫 WD 🏕️💧 MP 🍴♨️ⓗ nr 🛒nr

Fr Mortain S on D977 sp St Hilaire-du-Harcouët; shortly after rndabt take 2nd L at auberge to Notre-Dame-deTouchet. In vill turn L at PO, sp Le Teilleul D184, then 2nd R sp La Raisnais. Site at end of lane on R (haycart on front lawn). Sm, hdstg, pt shd, pt sl, EHU (10A) inc (poss long lead req); adv bkg acc. *"Pleasant, tranquil, spacious CL-type site adj farm; lovely outlook; washing machine on request; adults only; NB no wc or shwrs Dec-Feb but water & EHU all year; DVD library; friendly, helpful British owners; htd pool 8km; well-kept, clean san facs; adv bkg rec; highly rec."* **€15.00, 1 Mar-31 Oct.** 2017

MOSNAC *7B2* (0km E Rural) 45.50557, -0.52304
Camp Municipal Les Bords de la Seugne, 34 Rue de la Seugne, 17240 Mosnac 05 46 70 48 45; mosnac@mairie17.com

🐕 ♀♀♀ (htd) ♨ ♿ ✉ 🦋

Fr Pons S on N137 for 4.5km; L on D134 to Mosnac; foll sp to site behind church. 2*, Sm, mkd, pt shd, EHU (10A) inc; gas; red long stay; Eng spkn; adv bkg acc; CKE. *"Charming, clean, neat site in sm hamlet; site yourself, warden calls; helpful staff; excel, spotless san facs; conv Saintes, Cognac & Royan."*
€13.50, 1 May-30 Sep. 2017

MOTHE ACHARD, LA *2H4* (5km NW Rural) 46.65285, -1.74759 **Camping La Guyonnière,** 85150 St Julien-des-Landes 02 51 46 62 59; info@laguyonniere.com; www.laguyonniere.com

🐕 €4 ♀♀♀ WC ♿ 🔥 ♨ ∥ 🍴 🍽 ⑭ 🎱 🏖 ⚠ ⛵ (covrd, htd)

Leave A83 junc 5 onto D160 W twd La Roche-sur-Yon. Foll ring rd N & cont on D160 twd Les Sables-d'Olonne. Leave dual c'way foll sp La Mothe-Achard, then take D12 thro St Julien-des-Landes twd La Chaize-Giraud. Site sp on R.
3*, Lge, hdg, pt shd, pt sl, EHU (6A) €3.50 (long lead rec); gas; bbq; TV; 10% statics; phone; Eng spkn; adv bkg acc; ccard acc; waterpark; lake fishing 400m; waterslide; windsurfing 400m; bike hire. *"V lge pitches; canoe hire 400m; gd views; friendly owners; gd walking area."* €23.50, 26 Apr-28 Sep, A12. 2019

> ## "I need an on-site restaurant"
> We do our best to make sure site information is correct, but it is always best to check any must-have facilities are still available or will be open during your visit.

MOTHE ACHARD, LA *2H4* (6km NW Rural) 46.64469, -1.73346 **FLOWER Camping La Bretonnière,** 85150 St Julien-des-Landes 02 51 46 62 44 or 06 14 18 26 42 (mob); camp.la-bretonniere@wanadoo.fr; www.la-bretonniere.com or www.flowercampings.com

🐕 €2-5 ♀♀♀ WC ♨ ♿ 🔥 ∥ 🦋 🍽 ⑭ nr 🍴 ⚠ ✒ ⛵ (covrd, htd)

Fr La Roche-sur-Yon take D160 to La Mothe-Achard, then D12 dir St Gilles-Croix-de-Vie. Site on R 2km after St Julien. 4*, Med, mkd, pt shd, pt sl, EHU (6-12A) €2-4.50; bbq; sw nr; TV; 20% statics; Eng spkn; adv bkg acc; ccard acc; bike hire; fishing; ice; games area; sailing 2km; tennis; games rm; CKE. *"Excel, friendly site adj dairy farm; v lge pitches; san facs stretched in high ssn; 10 mins fr Bretignolles-sur-Mer sand dunes."* €33.00, 9 Apr-30 Sep. 2017

MOTHE ACHARD, LA *2H4* (7km NW Rural) 46.66280, -1.71380 **Camping La Garangeoire,** 85150 St Julien-des-Landes 02 51 46 65 39; info@garangeoire.com; www.camping-la-garangeoire.com or www.les-castels.com

🐕 €5 ♀♀♀ WC ♿ 🔥 ♨ ∥ 🦋 ⑭ 🍴 🍽 ⑭ 🎱 🏖 ⚠ ✒ ⛵ (covrd, htd) 🛶

Site sp fr La Mothe-Achard. At La Mothe-Achard take D12 for 5km to St Julien, D21 for 2km to site. Or fr Aizenay W on D6 turn L dir La Chapelle-Hermier. Site on L, well sp. 5*, Lge, mkd, hdg, shd, pt sl, serviced pitches; EHU (16A) inc (poss rev pol); gas; bbq (gas); red long stay; twin axles; TV; 50% statics; phone; Eng spkn; adv bkg rec; ccard acc; lake fishing; games rm; waterslide; bike hire; games area; tennis; horseriding; webcam computer; CKE. *"Busy, well-run site set in chateau parkland; some v lge pitches; pleasant helpful owners; excel, clean facs; gd for families & all ages; pitches quiet - entmnt well away fr pitches; super site; gd site in every way."* €37.00, 7 May -20 Sep. 2020

MOULINS *9A1* (21km N Rural) 46.709544, 3.323283 **Camping Municipal des Baillys,** Les Bailly, 58390 Dornes 06 74 82 04 02

12 🐕 ♀♀♀ WC ♨ ∥ 🦋 🍴 nr ⑭ nr 🏖 nr

On the D22 bet Dornes and Chantenay Saint Imbert. 2nd turning on the left after Dornes. Sm, pt shd, EHU; adv bkg acc. *"O'looking fishing lake (no sw); v welcoming warden; no fixed pitches but warden allocates; vg."* €11.00 2019

MOURIES *10E2* (2km E Rural) 43.68207, 4.91769 **Camping à la Ferme Les Amandaies (Crouau),** Mas de Bou Malek, 13890 Mouriès 04 90 47 50 59; www.les-amandaies.fr

12 🐕 ♀♀♀ ∥ 🦋

Fr Mouriès take D17 E sp Salon-de-Provence. Site sp on R 200m past D5 junc. Foll site sp to farm in 2km. Sm, pt shd, EHU €2 (rec long lead) (poss rev pol); bbq. *"Simple CL-type site; a few lge pitches; friendly owners; dated, dimly-lit san facs; conv coast & Avignon; book in using intercom on LH wall at ent to shwr block."* €15.40 2018

MOURIES *10E2* (7km NW Urban) 43.72138, 4.80950 **Camp Municipal Les Romarins,** Route de St Rémy-de-Provence, 13520 Maussane-les-Alpilles 04 90 54 33 60; camping-municipal-maussane@wanadoo.fr; www.maussane.com

🐕 €3 ♀♀♀ WC ♨ ♿ 🔥 ∥ 🦋 🍽 🏖 nr

Fr Mouriès N on D17, turn onto D5 on o'skts of vill dir St Rémy-de-Provence, turn immed L site on R adj municipal pool. 4*, Med, hdg, mkd, pt shd, EHU (10A) €3.80; red long stay; twin axles; TV; phone; bus in ssn; Eng spkn; adv bkg rec; ccard acc; bike hire; games area; games rm; tennis; CKE. *"Well-kept, well-run site in lovely area; on edge of vill; excel san facs; pool adj inc; some pitches diff m'vans due low trees; gd security; in Natural Park; hiking; mountain biking; excel."* €26.00, 15 Mar-3 Nov. 2017

MOUSTIERS STE MARIE *10E3* (0.5km W Rural)
43.84497, 6.21555 **Camping Manaysse,** 04360
Moustiers-Ste Marie **04 92 74 66 71; manaysse@
orange.fr; www.camping-manaysse.com**

🐕 €1.40 ♿♿♿ WC ♨ ♿ ⚲ ⬛ MSP 🦋 ☂ 🛒 nr ⚘

Fr Riez take D952 E, pass g'ge on L & turn L at 1st
rndabt for Moustiers; site on L off RH bend; strongly
advised not to app Moustiers fr E (fr Castellane,
D952 or fr Comps, D71) as these rds are diff for lge
vehicles/c'vans - not for the faint-hearted.
2*, Med, mkd, pt shd, pt sl, EHU (6-10A) €2.50-3.50;
bbq; adv bkg acc; ccard acc; volleyball court; field balls;
ping pong tables; CKE. *"Welcoming, family-run site;
super views; gd unisex san facs; cherry trees on site -
avoid parking under during early Jun; steep walk into vill;
lge o'fits do not attempt 1-way system thro vill, park &
walk; gd."* **€14.00, 28 Mar-1 Nov.** 2020

MOUSTIERS STE MARIE *10E3* (1km W Rural)
43.84371, 6.21475 **FFCC Camping St Jean,** Route de
Riez, 04360 Moustiers-Ste Marie **04 92 74 66 85;
camping-saint-jean@wanadoo.fr; www.camping-
st-jean.com**

🐕 €2.10 ♿♿♿ (htd) WC ♨ ♿ ⚲ ⬛ ⚲ 🦋 ☂ 🛒 ⚘

On D952 opp Renault g'ge & petrol stn.
3*, Med, hdg, pt shd, pt sl, EHU (6-10A) €3.60-4.70;
gas; bbq (elec, gas); sw nr; TV; 10% statics; Eng
spkn; adv bkg acc; ccard acc; games rm; fishing;
games area; CKE. *"Excel site in lovely location by rv;
climbing nr; dated san facs (2010); boating 4km; some
pitches diff lge o'fits; easy uphill walk to beautiful
vill; conv Gorges du Verdon; cycle rtes; gd value."*
€23.00, 28 Mar-11 Oct. 2015

MOYAUX *3D1* (3.4km NE Rural) *49.20860, 0.39230*
Camping Château Le Colombier, Chemin du Val Séry,
14590 Moyaux **02 31 63 63 08; mail@camping-le
colombier.com; www.camping-normandie-
lecolombier.com**

🐕 ♿♿♿ WC ♨ ♿ ⚲ ⬛ ⚲ MSP 🦋 ☂ 🍽 🔵 🛒 ⚘ 🛶 🐎 (htd)

Fr Pont de Normandie on A29, at junc with A13
branch R sp Caen. At junc with A132 branch R &
foll sp Lisieux, D579. Turn L onto D51 sp Blangy-le-
Château. Immed on leaving Moyaux turn L onto D143
& foll sp to site on R in 3km. 4*, Lge, mkd, pt shd, EHU
(10A) inc (poss lead req); gas; bbq; red long stay; TV;
30% statics; phone; Eng spkn; adv bkg acc; ccard acc;
excursions; games rm; bike hire; tennis; horseriding nr;
games area; CKE. *"Beautiful, peaceful, spacious site in
chateau grnds; ltd san facs LS; lge pool, but no shd, seats
or sunshades around; vg for children; gd shop & crêperie;
some static tents/tour ops; shgl paths poss diff some
wheelchairs/pushchairs; if dep bef 0800 must move to
car park o'night; mkt Sun; gd site; some pitches boggy
when wet; no o'fits over 7m high ssn; gd facs; excel
site to explore Normandy landing beaches; easy walk
to vill with shops and rest and sh drive to larger town,
lovely site, v helpful owners; poss travellers on site."*
€33.70, 19 Apr-29 Sep, N04. 2019

MUIDES SUR LOIRE *4G2* (1km N Rural) *47.67191,
1.52596* **Camp Municipal Belle Vue,** Ave de la Loire,
41500 Muides-sur-Loire **02 54 87 01 56 or 02 54 87 50 08
(Mairie); contact.muides@orange.fr; www.muides.fr**

🐕 €2.55 ♿♿♿ WC ♨ ♿ ⚲ ⬛ ⚲ MSP 🦋 ⓗ nr 🛒 ⚘

Fr A10/E5/E60 exit junc 16 S onto D205. Turn R onto
D2152 then D112 over rv. Site on S bank of rv on
D112 W of bdge. Tight U-turn into site fr N.
2*, Med, mkd, pt shd, EHU (6A) €4.80 (poss long lead
req),(poss rev pol); sw nr; rv fishing adj; cycling; CKE.
*"Neat, clean, basic, spacious site; ladies shwrs need
upgade (2011); vehicle barrier; gd views over rv; some
pitches by fast-flowing (unfenced) rv; little shd; excel
cycling; site self when off clsd (open 0800-1000 &
1700-1900)."* **€14.00, 1 May-15 Sep.** 2018

MUIDES SUR LOIRE *4G2* (0.5km S Rural) *47.66611,
1.52916* **Sandaya Château des Marais,** 27 Rue de
Chambord, 41500 Muides-sur-Loire **02 54 87 05 42;
mar@sandaya.fr; www.sandaya.co.uk**

🐕 €5 ♿♿♿ (htd) WC ♨ ♿ ⚲ ⬛ ⚲ MSP ☂ 🍽 🔵 🛒 ⚘ 🛶 (covrd, htd)
🚣

Exit A10 at junc 16 sp Chambord & take D2152 sp
Mer, Chambord, Blois. At Mer take D112 & cross
Rv Loire; at Muides-sur-Loire x-rds cont strt on
for 800m; then turn R at Camping sp; site on R in
800m. 5*, Lge, mkd, shd, pt sl, serviced pitches; EHU
(6A) inc (poss rev pol); gas; bbq (charcoal); twin axles;
TV; 65% statics; Eng spkn; adv bkg acc; ccard acc;
watersports nr; lake fishing; games area; bike hire;
waterslide; tennis; jacuzzi; games rm; sauna; CKE.
*"Busy lively site in wooded area in chateau grnds;
gd sized pitches; excel, clean san facs; friendly staff;
plenty of gd quality children's play equipment; sh walk
to rv; conv Loire chateaux; plenty to do in area; mkt
Sat Blois; pitches grass, can be a problem when wet."*
€25.00, 3 Apr-20 Sep, L10. 2019

MULHOUSE *6F3* (10km SW Rural) *47.72225, 7.22590*
FFCC Camping Parc La Chaumière, 62 Rue de
Galfingue, 68990 Heimsbrunn **03 89 81 93 43 or
03 89 81 93 21; reception@camping-lachaumiere.
com; www.camping-lachaumiere.com**

12 🐕 €1 ♿♿♿ (htd) WC ♨ ♿ ⚲ ⬛ ⚲ MSP 🦋 ☂ 🛒 nr ⚘ 🚣

Exit A36 junc 15; turn L over m'way; at rndabt exit
on D166 sp Heimsbrunn; in vill turn R at rndabt; site
end of houses on R. 2*, Med, hdg, hdstg, mkd, pt shd,
pt sl, EHU (10A) €3.50 (poss rev pol); bbq; twin axles;
50% statics; phone; bus 1km; Eng spkn; adv bkg acc;
ccard acc; CKE. *"Sm pitches not suitable long o'fits;
beautiful wine vills on La Route des Vins; museum
of trains & cars in Mulhouse; conv; vg san facs."*
€11.00 2015

FRANCE

MULHOUSE *6F3* *(2km SW Rural)* *47.73405, 7.3235*
Camping de l'Ill, 1 Rue de Pierre Coubertin,
68100 Mulhouse **03 89 06 20 66; campingdelill@
wanadoo.fr; www.camping-de-lill.com**

🛉 €1.50 ♦♦ 🚿 ♿ ⚐ 🐾 ⓗ nr 🗗 🐟 nr ⚓

Fr A36 take Mulhouse/Dornach exit & foll sp
Brunstatt at 1st traff lts. At 2nd traff lts turn
R, foll University/Brunstatt/Camping sps, site
approx 2.5km on rvside. 3*, Lge, mkd, pt shd, pt
sl, EHU (10A); gas; tram 500m; CKE. *"Welcoming
recep; cycle/walk along rv to town cent; OK NH."*
€22.30, 1 Apr-30 Sep. 2017

MULHOUSE *6F3* *(30km W Rural)* *47.73554, 7.01497*
Flower Camping du Lac de la Seigneurie, 3 Rue de la
Seigneurie, 90110 Leval **03 84 23 00 13; contact@
camping-lac-seigneurie.com; www.camping-lac-
seigneurie.com**

🛉 ♦♦ 🚿 ♿ ⚐ 🐾 🍸 ⓗ 🐟 ⚓ (htd) 🏊

Off N83 dir Belfort-Mulhouse. D11 NW
Petitefontaine twds Roughmont sp to Leval.
3*, Med, hdg, mkd, pt shd, pt sl, EHU (6-10A); bbq;
6% statics; adv bkg acc; ccard acc; games area.
€21.00, 1 Apr-31 Oct. 2016

MUNSTER *6F3* *(13km SW Rural)* *47.98250, 7.01865*
Camp Municipal de Mittlach Langenwasen,
68380 Mittlach **03 89 77 63 77; mairiemittlach@
wanadoo.fr; www.mittlach.fr**

🛉 €0.80 ♦♦ 🚿 ♿ ⚐ 🐾 🦋 🐟 🪜

Fr Munster on D10 to Metzeral then R onto D10.
Site at end rd in 6km. 1*, Med, mkd, hdg, pt shd,
pt sl, EHU (6-10A) €2.45-6; gas; 10% statics; Eng
spkn; adv bkg acc; CKE. *"Peaceful, wooded site at
bottom of valley; helpful staff; san facs gd & clean;
gd walking base; plenty of interest locally; excel."*
€14.00, 20 Apr-10 Oct. 2015

MUNSTER *6F3* *(2km SW Rural)* *48.03105, 7.11350*
FFCC Camping Les Amis de la Nature, 4 Rue du Château,
68140 Luttenbach-près-Munster **03 89 77 38 60;
an-munster@wanadoo.fr; www.camping-an.fr**

🛉 €1.50 ♦♦ (htd) 🚿 ♿ ⚐ 🐾 🦋 🍸 ⓗ 🐟 🪜 ✏
⚓ (htd)

Fr Munster take D10 sp Luttenbach; site sp.
3*, Lge, mkd, pt shd, EHU (4-6A) €3.25-4.40/6.20;
bbq; TV; 50% statics; Eng spkn; ccard acc; sauna;
fishing; tennis 1km; games area. *"Lovely setting
by stream; dir access to rv; gd value; new san facs
(2017); pleasant walk to town; excel rest; gd touring
area."* **€16.50, 21 Mar-11 Nov.** 2018

MURAT *7C4* *(5km SW Rural)* *45.07781, 2.83047*
Aire Naturelle Municipal, 15300 Albepierre-Bredons
04 71 20 20 49

🛉 🐾 ⚐ ♿ ⚐ 🐾 🦋 🍸 nr ⓗ nr 🐟 nr

SW fr Murat on D39 dir Prat-de-Bouc; site sp fr cent
of Albepierre. Sm, pt shd, EHU (10A) €2; CKE. *"Excel,
peaceful location; basic, clean facs; warden visits am &
pm; bar 300m; vg walking amidst extinct volcanoes; gd;
beautiful sm friendly site."*
€9.00, 15 Jun-15 Sep. 2016

MUROL *7B4* *(1km S Rural)* *45.57400, 2.95735*
FFCC Camp Le Repos du Baladin, Groire, 63790 Murol
**04 73 88 61 93; reposbaladin@free.fr; www.camping-
auvergne-france.com**

🛉 €3 ♦♦ (htd) 🚿 ♿ ⚐ 🐾 🍸 🐟 nr ⚓ 🏊 (htd)

Fr D996 at Murol foll sp 'Groire' to E, site on R in
1.5km just after vill. 3*, Med, hdg, mkd, shd, pt sl, terr,
EHU (6A); sw nr; Eng spkn; sauna; CKE. *"Lovely site with
immac san facs; friendly, helpful owners; easy walk into
town thro fields."* **€28.00, 29 Apr-16 Sep.** 2018

MUROL *7B4* *(2km W Rural)* *45.57516, 2.91428*
Camping Le Pré Bas, 63790 Chambon-sur-Lac
**04 73 88 63 04; prebas@campingauvergne.com;
www.campingauvergne.com**

🛉 €2.10 ♦♦ 🚿 ♿ ⚐ 🐾 🦋 🍸 ⓗ 🐟 ⚓ ✏
🏊 (covrd, htd) 🏊

Take D996 W fr Murol twd Mont-Dore. Site 1.5km on
L, twd lake. 5*, Lge, mkd, hdg, pt shd, pt sl, serviced
pitches; EHU (6A) €4.70; bbq; sw; TV; 40% statics;
phone; Eng spkn; adv bkg acc; games area; waterslide;
ice; fitness room; CKE. *"Excel family-run site by Lac
Chambon; library; superb views; friendly, helpful staff;
immac san facs; excel pool complex; rock pegs ess;
access to sm pitches poss diff lge o'fits; excel walking
area."* **€24.00, 25 Apr-13 Sep.** 2020

MUROL *7B4* *(5km W Rural)* *45.56979, 2.90185*
Camping Les Bombes (formerly Municipal), Chemin
de Pétary, 63790 Chambon-sur-Lac **04 73 88 64 03
or 06 88 33 25 94 (mob); lesbombes@orange.fr;
www.camping-les-bombes.com**

🛉 €5 ♦♦ 🚿 ♿ ⚐ 🐾 🦋 🍸 ⓗ 🐟 ⚓ (htd) 🏊

Site is on D996. Nr exit fr vill Chambon. Well
sp. 3*, Med, mkd, pt shd, EHU (6A) €4.50; bbq; sw
nr; TV; 5% statics; phone; Eng spkn; adv bkg acc;
homeball; mini golf; playhse for kids; soccer field;
volleyball; terrain balls; table tennis; chess; bowling;
CKE. *"Beautiful area; gd, clean, well-maintained facs
stretched in high ssn; lge pitches; friendly, helpful
owners; excel."* **€24.00, 30 Apr-13 Sep.** 2020

MUZILLAC *2G3* (8km SW Coastal) *47.51780, -2.55539*
Camping Ty Breiz, 15 Grande Rue, Kervoyal, 56750
Damgan **02 97 41 13 47; campingtybreiz@orange.fr;**
www.campingtybreiz.com

🐕 €1.50 👪♿⚓♿♿/🚿🏕 sand 300m

Fr Muzillac on D153 dir Damgan, turn S for
Kervoyal; site on L opp sm church. 2*, Med, hdg,
mkd, pt shd, EHU (6-10A) €3-3.50; bbq; TV; Eng
spkn; adv bkg rec; ccard acc; table tennis; CKE.
*"Pleasant, welcoming, family-run site; excel san
facs; quiet; cycle path to Damgan; mkt Wed; vg."*
€21.00, 1 Apr-31 Oct. 2020

NAJAC *8E4* (1.7km W Rural) *44.22011, 1.96985*
Camping Le Païsserou, 12270 Najac **05 65 29 73 96;**
campingnajac@gmail.com; www.campingnajac.com

🐕 €2 WD ⚓♿/🦋 ⅋ ⓘ ♿ ⛱ nr 🏊 (htd)

Take D922 fr Villefranche-de-Rouergue. Turn R on
D39 at La Fouillade to Najac. Site by rv, sp in vill. Or
fr A20 exit junc 59 onto D926. At Caylus take D84
to Najac. All appr v steep. 3*, Med, hdg, shd, EHU €3;
bbq; 10% statics; phone; Eng spkn; adv bkg acc; tennis
adj; CKE. *"Conv for Aveyron gorges; friendly owners;
ltd facs LS; lovely vill; unrel opening LS, phone ahead;
htd covrd pool adj (free); site yourself if recep clsd, avail
pitches listed."* **€23.00, 1 May-30 Sep.** 2020

NAMPONT ST MARTIN *3B3* (3km W Rural) *50.33595,
1.71230* **La Ferme des Aulnes,** 1 Rue du Marais,
Fresne-sur-Authie, 80120 Nampont-St Martin
**03 22 29 22 69 or 06 22 41 86 54 (mob LS); contact@
fermedesaulnes.com; www.fermedesaulnes.com**

🐕 €4 👪(htd) WD ⚓♿♿/🦋 MSP 🦋 ⅋ Y ⓘ ♿ ⛱ nr 🛖 🎿
🎣 (covrd, htd)

D901 S fr Montreull 13km thro Nampont-St Firmin
to Nampont-St Martin; turn R in vill onto D485; site
in 3km; sp fr D901. 4*, Med, hdg, pt shd, pt sl, EHU
(6-10A) €6-12; bbq (charcoal, gas); TV; 80% statics;
Eng spkn; adv bkg acc; games area; golf 1km; archery;
CKE. *"Attractive site nr Calais; some pitches sm, some
very sl; friendly welcoming staff; clsd 2200-0800;
cinema rm; old fm bldgs retain character of an old
fmstead; clean san facs."*
€32.50, 1 Apr-31 Oct, P13. 2017

NANCAY *4G3* (0.9km NW Rural) *47.35215, 2.18522*
Camp Municipal des Pins, Route de Salbris, La Chaux,
18330 Nançay **02 48 51 81 80 or 02 48 51 81 35
(Mairie); campingdenancay@orange.fr;
www.nancay.a3w.fr**

👪(htd) WD ⚓♿/🦋 🦋 ⛱ nr 🛖

Site on D944 fr Salbris twd Bourges on L immed
bef ent Nançay. 2*, Med, mkd, hdstg, shd, EHU (6A)
inc; gas; adv bkg acc; golf 2km; fishing; tennis; CKE.
*"Lovely spot in pine woods; friendly recep; clean san
facs; poor site lighting; beautiful vill; gd walking; rec
open am and pm."* **€8.50, 1 May-30 Sep.** 2017

NANCY *6E2* (6.5km SW Rural) *48.65730, 6.14028*
Campéole Le Brabois, 2301 Ave Paul Muller,
54600 Villers-lès-Nancy **03 83 27 18 28; brabois@
campeole.com; www.campeole.nl/le-brabois**

🐕 €2.60 👪(htd) WD ⚓♿/🚿 ⓘ ♿ 🛖 🛖

Fr A33 exit junc 2b sp Brabois onto D974 dir Nancy;
after 400m turn L at 2nd traff lts; at slip rd after 2nd
further traff lts turn R on slip rd & site on R; site well
sp. 3*, Lge, mkd, pt shd, EHU (4-15A) €4.50-5.25 (poss
rev pol)(ask for pitch with 15A if req); gas; bbq; TV;
10% statics; bus adj; Eng spkn; adv bkg acc; ccard acc;
games area; CKE. *"Popular, well-run site; mostly lge
pitches, but some sm, all grass; supmkt & petrol 2km;
friendly, helpful staff; gd, clean, all new san facs; no
twin axles over 5.5m (m'vans OK); interesting town; rec
arr early; vg NH; excel."*
€21.30, 30 Mar-14 Oct, J03. 2018

"Satellite navigation makes touring much easier"

Remember most sat navs don't know if you're
towing or in a larger vehicle – always use yours
alongside maps and site directions.

NANCY *6E2* (10km NW Rural) *48.74733, 6.05700*
Camping Les Boucles de la Moselle, Ave Eugène
Lerebourg, 54460 Liverdun **03 83 24 43 78 or
06 03 27 69 71 (mob); francis.iung@orange.fr**

🐕 €1.20 👪(htd) ⚓♿/🚿 Y ⓘ ♿ 🛖 🛖 ⅋ 🎿

Fr A31 exit junc 22 to Frouard. In Frouard bear L
onto D90 to Liverdun; cross rv bdge (sp Liverdun);
under rlwy bdge L at traff lts, thro town, fork L &
foll sp to site by on rvside by sports area. Do not
turn L at site exit when towing. 2*, Lge, pt shd, EHU
(6A) €3.20; 10% statics; CKE. *"Lovely site & area;
helpful staff; Nancy worth visit; pleasant rvside site."*
€23.00, 1 May-30 Sep. 2017

NANT *10E1* (2km N Rural) *44.03578, 3.29008*
Camping Le Roc Qui Parle, Les Cuns, 12230 Nant
**05 65 62 22 05; contact@camping-roc-qui-parle-
aveyron.fr; www.camping-roc-qui-parle-aveyron.fr**

🐕 👪 WD ⚓♿/🦋 MSP 🦋 🍴 🛖 🛖

Fr Millau take D991E to site passing Val de
Cantobre. Fr La Cavalerie take D999E to Nant & at
T-junc on o'skts of Nant turn N; Millau & Les Cuns
approx 2km; site on R. NB Steep decent into site.
3*, Med, hdg, mkd, pt shd, pt sl, serviced pitches;
EHU (10A) €3.50; bbq; sw; adv bkg acc; fishing; CKE.
*"Excel, well-run site in magnificent surroundings; lge
pitches with views; warm welcome, friendly & helpful;
excel facs; rv walk; rec; same price year round."*
€15.00, 13 Mar-21 Oct. 2016

NANT *10E1* (11km E Rural) *44.01117, 3.20457*
Camping La Dourbie, Route de Nant, 12230 Saint-Jean-du-Bruel, Aveyron **05 65 46 06 40; camping ladourbie@orange.fr; www.camping-dourbie-aveyron.com**

🏕🐕💶 ♿ WD ☂ ♿ 🚿 ✉ MSP 👁 🍽 🛝 🏊 (htd)

Fr A75 take exit 47, twrds La cavalerie, Nat, St-Eulalie-de-Cernon. At rndabt take 3rd exit onto D999, go thro next rndabt, turn R cont D999 to site. 4*, Med, hdg, pt shd, EHU (10A); bbq; 20% statics; canoeing. *"Excel site, such a lot to do & see; very friendly; bungee jumping; paragliding; clean san facs; spa; 1 dog per pitch; rest open Fri & Sat nights in LS."* **€25.00, 14 Apr-30 Sep.** **2018**

NANT *10E1* (1km S Rural) *44.01698, 3.30125*
Camping Les Deux Vallées, 12230 Nant **05 65 62 26 89 or 05 65 62 10 40; contact@lesdeuxcallees.com; www.lesdeuxvallees.com**

🏕💶€1 👁 WD ☂ ♿ 🚿 ✉ MSP 🦋 🍽 👁 🛒 ⚓ nr 🛝 ✏

Exit A75 junc 47 onto D999 for 14km to Nant; site sp. 3*, Med, mkd, pt shd, serviced pitches; EHU (6A) €2 (poss rev pol); own san req; TV; phone; adv bkg acc; rv fishing; CKE. *"Peaceful, well-kept, scenic site; friendly; clean, modern san facs; pool 500m; 15 mins walk fr vill cent; gd walking; rec."* **€21.50, 15 Apr-17 Oct.** **2016**

NANT *10E1* (0.7km SW Rural) *44.02105, 3.29390*
Camping Les Vernèdes, Route St Martin-Le Bourg, 12230 Nant **05 65 62 15 19; http://patocheperso.pagesperso-orange.fr/camping/accueil.htm**

🏕🐕 WD ☂ ♿ 🚿 ✉ 🦋 🛝

Site sp fr vill cent. 1*, Sm, shd, EHU (10A) inc (long lead req); bbq; Eng spkn; adv bkg acc; CKE. *"Orchard site set in beautiful location; pleasant stroll to Nant cent; gd trout rest adj; gd touring base; very helpful owners; excel and great site to stay on; CL style, not modern but idyilic; gd rest next door."* **€13.50, 1 Mar-31 Oct.** **2015**

NANTES *2G4* (3km N Urban) *47.24261, -1.55703*
Nantes Camping, 21 Blvd de Petit Port, 44300 Nantes **02 40 74 47 94; nantes-camping@nge-nantes.fr; www.nantes-camping.fr**

12 🐕💶€3.10 👁 (htd) WD ☂ ♿ 🚿 ✉ MSP 🦋 🍽 🛒
🛝 ✏

Fr ring rd exit junc 39 sp Porte de la Chapelle & foll sp Cent Ville, Camping Petit Port or University when ent o'skts of Nantes. Site ent opp Hippodrome & nr racecourse & university; well sp. Take care tram lines. 5*, Lge, mkd, hdg, hdstg, pt shd, serviced pitches; EHU (16A) €5; gas; bbq (charcoal); twin axles; red long stay; TV; 30% statics; bus & tram to city cent adj; Eng spkn; adv bkg req; ccard acc; bike hire; CKE. *"Well kept and maintained; htd covrd pool adj; waterslide adj inc; excel san facs; tram stop next to site, easy access to Nantes cent; excel site, great location; o'night m'van area; ACSI red LS; popular; recep clsd 1230-1500."* **€41.00** **2018**

NANTES *2G4* (6km E Rural) *47.25416, -1.45361*
Camping Belle Rivière, Route des Perrières, 44980 Ste Luce-sur-Loire **02 40 25 85 81; belleriviere@wanadoo.fr; www.camping-belleriviere.com**

12 🐕💶€1.45 👁 (htd) WD ☂ ♿ 🚿 ✉ 👁 nr ⚓ nr 🛝

Fr 'Nantes Périphérique Est' take exit 43 (at Porte d'Anjou) onto A811; exit A811 junc 24 dir Thouaré-sur-Loire on D68; at double rndabt by car showroom turn S & foll sp over rlwy bdge; site sp. Fr E via D68, thro Thouaré dir Ste Luce; at double rndabt by car showroom, S over rlwy bdge twd rv; site sp. 3*, Med, mkd, hdstg, hdg, pt shd, EHU (3-10A) €2.70-3.90 (extra charge in winter); gas; bbq; 50% statics; Eng spkn; adv bkg acc; CKE. *"Beautifully-kept site; helpful owners; gd clean san facs; rvside walks; conv Nantes Périphérique & city cent; gd touring base; excel."* **€17.00** **2017**

> ## "There aren't many sites open at this time of year"
>
> If you're travelling outside peak season remember to call ahead to check site opening dates – even if the entry says 'open all year'.

NANTUA *9A3* (1km W Urban) *46.14999, 5.60017*
Camping du Signal, 17 Ave du Camping, 01130 Nantua **04 74 75 02 09 or 06 71 76 36 17 (mob); contact@camping-nantua.fr; www.camping-nantua.fr**

🏕 👁 🚿 ✉ MSP 🦋 👁 🛒 ⚓ nr 🛝

E on D1084 fr Pont d'Ain, rd passes alongside Nantua lake on R. At end of lake bef ent town turn R & foll sps. 2*, Sm, mkd, hdg, unshd, EHU (16A) €3 (rev pol); sw nr; 10% statics. *"Attractive, spacious, well-kept site in lovely setting; nice lrg pitches; friendly staff; town & shops mins away; conv for m'way; sports cent nr; Lidl store 3 mins away; gd shwrs."* **€17.60, 1 Apr-31 Oct.** **2017**

NARBONNE *10F1* (6km S Rural) *43.13662, 3.02595*
Village-Camping Les Mimosas, Chaussée de Mandirac, 11100 Narbonne **04 68 49 03 72; info@lesmimosas.com; www.lesmimosas.com**

🏕💶€4 👁 (htd) WD ☂ ♿ 🚿 ✉ 🦋 🍽 👁 🛒 🛝 ✏
🏊 (htd) 🎣

Leave A9 junc 38 at Narbonne Sud & at rndabt foll sp La Nautique. Turn L opp ent to Camping La Nautique & foll sp Mandirac & site. 4*, Lge, mkd, hdg, hdstg, pt shd, serviced pitches; EHU (6A) inc; gas; bbq (elec, gas); red long stay; TV; 6% statics; Eng spkn; adv bkg acc; ccard acc; sauna; games rm; horseriding adj; lake fishing 300m; waterslide; bike hire; rv fishing adj; jacuzzi; watersports; games area; gym; tennis; CKE. *"Attractive site, lge pitches; gd choice of pitches; friendly, helpful staff; vg san facs; poss ltd LS; excel pool complex; vg for children; lge o'fits rec phone in adv high ssn; excel touring base in historic area; gd birdwatching; cycle path to Narbonne."* **€46.00, 17 Mar-31 Oct, C35.** **2017**

For a guide to symbols see the fold out on the rear cover

NARBONNE *10F1 (12km SW Rural) 43.16296, 2.89186* **Camping La Figurotta,** Route de Narbonne, 11200 Bizanet **04 68 45 16 26 or 06 88 16 12 30 (mob); camping.figurotta@gmail.com; www.camping-figurotta.com**

12 ♉ €3 ♟(htd) ⬜ ⛅ ♿ 🚿 🚽 ♥ ⛲ ☂ Ⓗ 🛒 🎮 ⚠ 🏊

Exit A9 at Narbonne Sud onto slip rd N9/D6113 twd Lézignan-Corbières; in 3km at new rndabt head L twd D613 & then D224 sp Bizanet & site. App fr W not rec due narr D rds. 1*, Sm, mkd, hdstg, shd, pt sl, terr, EHU (4-10A) €2.50-3.50 (poss long lead req); gas; red long stay; 5% statics; phone; Eng spkn; adv bkg acc; games area; CKE. *"Pleasant, simple, well-run, scenic site; friendly & helpful owners; sm dogs only; gd pool with new snack bar o'looking; gusty & stony site - steel pegs req; excel drainage; gd NH en rte Spain; vg; new san facs (2018)."* **€25.00** 2018

NARBONNE *10F1 (4km SW Urban) 43.14702, 3.00424* **Camping La Nautique,** Chemin de la Nautique,11100 Narbonne **04 68 90 48 19; info@campinglanautique.com; www.campinglanautique.com**

♉ €6 ♟ ⬜ ⛅ ♿ 🚿 🚽 ♥ MSP ☂ ⛲ ☂ Ⓗ 🛒 🎮 ⚠ ✂ 🏊 (htd) 🏛

Exit junc 38 fr A9 at Narbonne Sud. After toll take last rndabt exit & foll sp La Nautique. Site on R 2.5km fr A9 exit. 4*, Lge, hdstg, mkd, hdg, pt shd, EHU (10A) inc; gas; bbq (elec); red long stay; 30% statics; Eng spkn; adv bkg acc; ccard acc; waterslide; windsurfing; canoeing; tennis; CKE. *"Helpful, friendly Dutch owners; caution - hot water very hot; individual san facs on each pitch inc; some pitches lge but narr; steel pegs req; pitches sheltered but some muddy after heavy rain; excel rest; many sports activities avail; cycle trips; gd walks nrby."* **€47.70, 1 Mar-31 Oct, C07.** 2018

NARBONNE PLAGE *10F1 (8km NE Coastal) 43.20592, 3.21056* **Camping La Grande Cosse,** St Pierre-sur-Mer, 11560 Fleury-d'Aude **04 68 33 61 87; grande-cosse@franceloc.fr; www.camping-grandecosse.fr**

♉ €9 ♟ ⬜ ⛅ ♿ 🚿 🚽 ♥ MSP ☂ ⛲ ☂ Ⓗ 🛒 🎮 ⚠ ✂ 🏊 (htd)

🏖 sand 300m

Exit A9 junc 37 & foll sp Narbonne-Plage. Cont thro Narbonne-Plage to St Pierre-sur-Mer, pass municipal site & turn R twd L'Oustalet, site sp. 4*, Lge, hdg, mkd, pt shd, serviced pitches; EHU (10A); gas; red long stay; TV; 20% statics; phone; Eng spkn; adv bkg acc; ccard acc; boat hire; INF card req; games rm; fishing; games area; tennis; gym. *"Excel; gd pitches; helpful, friendly staff; excel san facs; lovely walk to beach thro lagoons & dunes (poss flooded early ssn); mosquitoes poss problem Jun-Sep; ACSI; flood risk after heavy rain; gd mkt St Pierre-sur-Mer; access rds can be diff, very narr, new owners, no longer a naturist site (2017)."* **€50.00, 15 Apr-30 Oct.** 2017

NASBINALS *9D1 (1km N Rural) 44.67016, 3.04036* **Camp Municipal,** Route de St Urcize, 48260 Nasbinals **02 46 32 51 87 or 04 66 32 50 17; mairie.nasbinals@laposte.net; www.mairie-nasbinals.info**

♉ ♟(htd) ⬜ ⛅ ♿ 🚿 🚽 ♥ MSP ☂ Ⓗ nr 🛒 nr

Fr A75 exit 36 to Aumont-Aubrac, then W on D987 to Nasbinals. Turn R onto D12, site sp. Med, pt shd, pt sl, EHU (16A) €3; bbq; CKE. *"Lovely location; gd views; no shd; facs inadequate peak ssn; excel communal rm."* **€12.00, 15 May-30 Sep.** 2016

NAVARRENX *8F1 (0.2km S Urban) 43.31988, -0.76143* **Camping Beau Rivage,** Allée des Marronniers, 64190 Navarrenx **05 59 66 10 00; beaucamping@free.fr; www.beaucamping.com**

♉ €1.50 ♟(htd) ⬜ ⛅ ♿ 🚿 🚽 ♥ ⛲ ☂ ☂ ☂ nr Ⓗ nr 🛒 🎮 nr ⚠ 🏊

Fr E exit A64 junc 9 at Artix onto D281 dir Mourenx, then Navarrenx. Fr N on D947 thro Orthez to Navarrenx (D947 fr Orthez much improved). Site well sp bet walled (Bastide) town & rv. 3*, Med, hdstg, hdg, mkd, pt shd, pt sl, terr, serviced pitches; EHU (6-10A) inc; bbq; 15% statics; phone; Eng spkn; adv bkg acc; ccard acc; rv fishing; games rm; rafting; tennis; CKE. *"Lovely, peaceful, well-run site; no o'fits over 9m high ssn; nr interesting walled town; helpful, friendly, British owners; bike hire in town; clean san facs; gd pool; bar 300m; gd area for walking, cycling; conv local shops & rests; mkt Wed; rec; outstanding."* **€28.70, 25 Mar-8 Oct, D26.** 2017

NAY *8F2 (2km N Rural) 43.20027, -0.25722* **Camping Les Ô Kiri,** Ave du Lac, 64800 Baudreix **05 59 92 97 73; contact@lesokiri.com; www.lesokiri.com**

♉ €2 ♟(htd) ⬜ ⛅ ♿ 🚿 🚽 ♥ MSP ☂ ⛲ ☂ Ⓗ 🛒 🎮 ⚠

Exit A64 junc 10 onto Pau ring rd D317 S, then D938 dir Nay & Lourdes. Exit sp Baudreix & in 2km turn R at rndabt & foll sp to lake & site. 4*, Med, hdg, mkd, pt shd, EHU (6-10A) €4-5.50; bbq; sw; 50% statics; adv bkg acc; ccard acc; tennis; waterslide; bike hire. *"Conv Biarritz, N Spain & Pyrennees; lake sw complex booking ess; on arr use carpark for recep; excel rest; superb lake facs; picturesque; basic but OK san facs, poss stretched if site full."* **€19.50, 1 Apr-30 Sep.** 2019

NEBOUZAT *9B1 (2km NW Rural) 45.72569, 2.89008* **Camping Les Domes,** Les Quatre Routes de Nébouzat, 63210 Nébouzat **04 73 87 14 06 or 04 73 93 21 02 (LS); camping-les-domes@wanadoo.fr; www.les-domes.com**

♉ ♟ ⬜ ⛅ ♿ ♥ ⛲ ☂ 🎮 ⚠ ✂ 🏊 (covrd, htd)

Exit 5 fr A75 onto D213 twd Col de la Ventouse; turn L on D2089 sp Tulle. Do not ent vill of Nébouzat but cont for 1km. Take L onto D216 sp Orcival then immed L. Site on L in 100m. 3*, Med, mkd, hdstg, pt shd, EHU (10-15A) €6 (poss long lead req); gas; TV; phone; Eng spkn; adv bkg acc; sailing; windsurfing; CKE. *"Immac site; walking; boules area; warm welcome; friendly, helpful staff; sm pitches; gd san facs; conv Vulcania; excel rest nrby; gd base for Auvergne."* **€26.50, 23 Apr-3 Oct.** 2016

NERAC *8E2* (6km SW Rural) *44.09948, 0.31028*
Aire Naturelle Les Contes d'Albret, 47600 Nérac
05 53 65 18 73 or 06 84 70 07 78; lescontesdalbret
@orange.fr; www.albret.com

🚻 (htd) 🛁 ♿ 🚿 💧 ❄ 🐾 🅿 ⏸ ⛺

Exit A62 junc 7 onto D931 to Laplume. Then turn
W onto D15 & D656 to Nérac. Cont on D656 dir
Mézin & foll site sp 'Les Contes d'Albert' to end
of rd in 3km. Sm, pt shd, pt sl, EHU (6A) €2; Eng
spkn; adv bkg acc; kayaking. *"Vg, peaceful, CL-
type site; farm shop; excel views; glorious garden."*
€17.00, 1 May-30 Sep.   2019

NERET *4H3* (3km N Rural) *46.58885, 2.13425*
Campsite Le Bonhomme, Mulles 36400 Neret
02 54 31 46 11; info@camping-lebonhomme.com;
www.camping-lebonhomme.com

🚻 🛁 🅦🅓 🚿 💧 🅼🅢🅟 🐾 🅟 ⏸

Fr Vierzon on the A20 take exit 12 to Chateauroux,
then the D943 twds Montlucon.Turn L at Neret
exit and foll Aire Naturelle signs. Site is 2km
beyond Neret on L. 2*, Sm, mkd, hdstg, pt shd, sl,
EHU (16A); bbq; Eng spkn; adv bkg acc; games area.
"Excel; lovely rural, quiet site; food avail fr owners."
€20.50, 1 Apr-1 Oct.   2016

NEUF BRISACH *6F3* (1km E Urban) *48.01638, 7.53565*
Camp Municipal Vauban, Entrée Porte de Bâle,
68600 Neuf-Brisach 03 89 72 54 25 or 03 89 72 51 68
(Mairie); contact@camping-vauban.fr;
www.camping-vauban.fr

🐾 €1 🚻 🛁 💧 🅼🅢🅟 🦋 🅿 nr ⛺

Fr D415 (Colmar-Freiburg) at E of Neuf-Brisach turn
NE on D1 bis (sp Neuf-Brisach & Camping Vauban).
At next junc turn L & immed R into site rd.
2*, Med, pt shd, EHU (10A) €4; 5% statics; adv bkg acc;
CKE. *"Gd, well-run site; fascinating ramparts around
town; lge pitches; friendly, helpful staff; excel cycle rtes
fr site along Rhine & thro historic vill; pool 3km; site
won many awards; long elec leads req; ideal long stay;
supmkt 2km."* €17.00, 1 Apr-31 Oct.   2018

NEUF BRISACH *6F3* (6km SE Rural) *47.97988, 7.59639*
FFCC Camping L'Orée du Bois, 5 Rue du Bouleau,
68600 Geiswasser 03 89 72 80 13; valerie.schappler@
orange.fr; valerieschappler1.wixsite.com/camping
aloreedubois

🐾 🚻 (htd) 🅦🅓 🛁 ♿ 🚿 💧 🦋 🅿 ⛺

Site in vill cent; rd name on bungalow; ent bet
bungalow & vegetable garden - tight turn, watch
out bungalow gutters. 1*, Sm, hdg, pt shd, EHU
(10A) €3.60; bbq; 60% statics; bus adj; Eng spkn; adv
bkg acc; CKE. *"Gd touring base; friendly owner; gd."*
€6.60, 1 Apr-30 Sep.   2017

NEUFCHATEL EN BRAY *3C2* (1.4km NW Urban)
49.73781, 1.42803 **Camping Sainte Claire,** 19 rue
Grande Flandre, 76270 Neufchâtel-en-Bray
02 35 93 03 93 or 06 20 12 20 98 (mob); fancelot@
wanadoo.fr; www.camping-sainte-claire.com

🐾 🚻 🅦🅓 🛁 ♿ 🚿 💧 🅼🅢🅟 ⛲ ⏸ 🅿 ⛺

Fr N & S exit A28 junc 9 onto D928 sp Neufchâtel;
in 1km at mini rndabt at bottom hill, turn L into
Rue de la Grande Flandre, foll Leclerk supmkt sp;
cont past supmkt for 400m to Rue Ste Claire. (NB
Motorvan aire immed bef site ent, do not turn in by
mistake as there are charges). 3*, Med, hdstg, mkd,
hdg, pt shd, pt sl, terr, serviced pitches; EHU (6-10A)
inc; bbq; red long stay; twin axles; 20% statics; phone;
bus 400m; Eng spkn; adv bkg acc; ccard acc; bike hire;
fishing; CKE. *"Beautiful, spacious, well-run, well-kept,
busy site by rv; lge, med & sm pitches; not all pitches
have 10A, poss 6A pitches better; friendly, helpful
owner; excel clean san facs - poss long walk LS; wet rm
for disabled; wheelchair access/easy walking; pleasant
walk along cycle rte (old rlwy line) to town & vet; Sat
mkt; conv Le Havre/Dieppe ferries & A28; sep o'night
area; some drive-thro pitches; gd value sh or long stay;
popular NH; excel; nice site as always; Aire for m'vans
now open adj (OAY, €12, all hdstg, full facs, 10A elec &
acc ccards only); busy, efficient site; gd easy access fr
a'route; ent tight for lge o'fits; best book for twin axles;
excel rest; adj 40km greenway cycle ride; ACSI acc; lge
Leclerc nrby."* €17.00, 1 Apr-15 Oct.   2019

NEUNG SUR BEUVRON *4G3* (0.5km NE Rural) *47.53893,
1.81488* **FFCC Camp Municipal de la Varenne,** 34
Rue de Veilleas, 41210 Neung-sur-Beuvron 02 54 83
68 52 or 06 27 92 39 14 (mob); camping.lavarenne@
wanadoo.fr; www.neung-sur-beuvron.fr/camping

🐾 🚻 🅦🅓 🛁 💧 🅼🅢🅟 🦋 ⏸ nr ⏸ nr 🅿 nr ⛺

On A10 heading S take Orléans Sud exit & join N20
S. At end of La Ferté-St Aubin take D922 SW twd
Romorantin-Lanthenay. In 20km R onto D925 to
Neung. Turn R at church pedestrian x-ing in cent of
vill ('stade' sp), R at fork (white, iron cross) & site
on R in 1km. Site by rvside. Fr A71 exit junc 3 onto
D923; turn R onto D925 & as above.
2*, Sm, mkd, hdg, pt shd, pt sl, EHU (6A) €3.10; gas;
10% statics; Eng spkn; adv bkg acc; ccard acc; tennis.
*"Friendly, helpful warden; gd, immac facs; lge pitches;
barrier clsd 2200-0800; vg cent for hiking, cycling,
birdwatching; mkt Sat; excel well maintained site."*
€12.00, Easter-20 Oct.   2017

NEUVE LYRE, LA *3D2* (0.4km W Urban) *48.90750,
0.74486* **Camp Municipal La Salle,** Rue de l'Union,
27330 La Neuve-Lyre 02 32 60 14 98 or 02 32 30
50 01 (Mairie); mairie.la-neuve-lyre@wanadoo.fr

🐾 🚻 🅦🅓 🛁 ♿ 💧 🅼🅢🅟 🦋 🅿 nr

Fr NE on D830 into vill turn R at church (sp not
visible), fr S (Rugles) foll sp. Well sp fr vill.
1*, Med, pt shd, EHU (5A) inc (poss long lead req);
2% statics; fishing; CKE. *"Delightful, peaceful, clean
site; site yourself, warden calls; excel sh stay/NH."*
€10.00, 15 Mar-15 Oct.   2017

NEUVIC (CORREZE) *7C4* (4km N Rural) *45.38245, 2.22901* **Camping Domaine de Mialaret,** Route d'Egletons, 19160 Neuvic 05 55 46 02 50; info@lemialaret.com; www.lemialaret.com

🏕🏃👫(htd) 🚿♨🅿♿🏊📶 🦋 🍴🍺♨🛒🎣🏛⛰🛶

Fr N on A89 exit 23 twds St Angel then D171 to Neuvic or foll sp fr Neuvic on D991. 4*, Med, hdg, pt shd, pt sl, EHU (10A) €3-4; red long stay; TV; 30% statics; phone; bus 4km; Eng spkn; adv bkg acc; games rm; watersports nr; CKE. "Excel site in grnds of chateau; 2 carp fishing pools; charming owner, friendly staff; facs ltd LS; blocks req most pitches; mini farm; walking tours; mountain bike trails; children's mini zoo & rare sheep breeds nrby." €42.60, 26 Apr-5 Oct. 2019

NEVERS *4H4* (1km S Rural) *46.98210, 3.16110* **FFCC Camping de Nevers,** Rue de la Jonction, 58000 Nevers 03 86 36 40 75; campingdenevers@orange.fr; www.aquadis-loisirs.com/camping-de-nevers

🏕€1.50 👫(cont) 🚿♨🅿♿🛒📶 🍴🍺♨nr🛒nr🏛

🏖 sand 200m

Fr E exit A77 junc 37 & foll dir 'Cent Ville'. Site on R immed bef bdge over Rv Loire. Fr W (Bourges) on D976 foll sp 'Nevers Centre' onto D907. In approx 3km bef bdge turn R, site on L. 3*, Sm, hdstg, mkd, hdg, shd, pt sl, terr, EHU (10A); bbq; TV; 3% statics; phone; bus 20m; Eng spkn; adv bkg acc; ccard acc; rv fishing; bike hire; CKE. "Pleasant, scenic site on bank of Rv Loire; on 3 levels - ltd EHU on lower; gd clean san facs, poss stretched high ssn; cycle paths along Loire; no twin axles; poss noisy when events at Nevers Magny-Cours racing circuit; gd site; easy walk over bdge to interesting town; nr town; excel recep staff; ltd no of elec pitches, arr early." €23.00, 2 Mar-2 Nov. 2018

NEVERS *4H4* (7km NW Urban) *47.01222, 3.07822* **FFCC Camping La Loire,** 2 Rue de la Folie, 58600 Fourchambault 03 86 60 81 59 or 06 11 05 18 69 (mob); campingdelaloire@dbmail.com; www.camping-de-loire.fr.st

🏕€0.50 👫🚿♨🅿♿🛒📶🍴♨nr🛒nr

Fr Nevers on D40 thro town, site on L bef rv bdge. 2*, Med, pt shd, EHU (6-10A) €3-4.50; bbq; red long stay; bus; CKE. "Friendly, helpful staff; rv adj; san facs need update & poss unclean; NH only." €17.50, 9 Apr-31 Oct. 2017

NEXON *7B3* (6km SSW Rural) *45.63471, 1.16176* **Flower Camping L'Air Du Lac,** Impasse du Lac, Plaisance, 87800 St Hilaire-les-Places 05 55 58 79 18; campinglairdulac@flowercampings.com; www.campinglairdulac.com

🏕€2🚿🅿♿🛒📶🦋♨🍴🛒🏛🏊🛶adj

S fr Nexon on D11. Soon after ent St Hilaire-les-Places take a L sp Lac Plaisance & Camping. Site adj to lake. 3*, Med, hdg, shd, pt sl, EHU (10A) inc; bbq; sw; TV; 20% statics; Eng spkn; adv bkg acc; ccard acc; games rm; games area; CKE. "Pleasant site adj to lake sw beach; dep req; very helpful staff; gd sized pitches; clean facs; vg for families; interesting touring area; excel." €14.50, 15 Apr-30 Sep. 2017

NIEDERBRONN LES BAINS *5D3* (1.5km SW Rural) *48.92958, 7.60428* **Camping Oasis Oberbronn,** 3 Rue de Frohret, 67110 Oberbronn 03 88 09 71 96; contact@opale-dmcc.com; www.opale-dmcc.fr

🏕€2.65 👫🚿♨🅿♿🛒📶 🦋 🍴♨🛒🏛⛰🛶(covrd, htd) 🏊

Fr D1062 turn S on D28 away fr Niederbronn; thro Oberbronn, site sp. 3*, Lge, mkd, pt shd, pt sl, EHU (6A) €4.30; bbq; red long stay; 20% statics; adv bkg rec; ccard acc; golf; cycling; fishing 2km; sauna; games rm; clsd 1200-1300; tennis; CKE. "Vg site with views; pt of leisure complex; sl area for tourers; horseriding rtes; some san facs tired; walking; wellness cent; fitness rm; site gravel paths not suitable wheelchair users." €15.00, 1 Apr-30 Sep. 2016

> ## "That's changed – Should I let the Club know?"
>
> If you find something on site that's different from the site entry, fill in a report and let us know. See camc.com/europereport.

NIMES *10E2* (8km S Rural) *43.78776, 4.35196* **Camp La Bastide (formerly Municipal),** route de Générac, 30900 Nîmes 04 66 62 05 82; bastide@capfun.com; www.camping-nimes.com

12 🏕€2.70 👫(htd) 🚿♨🅿♿🛒📶 🦋♨🍴♨🛒 🏊nr 🏛

Fr A9 exit junc 25 onto A54 dir Arles; in 2km exit A54 junc 1 onto D42 sp St Gilles; in 1.5km (at 2nd rndabt) turn R onto D135; in 2.5km at rndabt turn R onto D13; site on L. Or N fr Montpellier on N113/D6113 to Nimes; at Périphique Sud turn S onto D13 sp Générac; site on R 500m after rndabt junc with D613. Site well sp fr town cent. 4*, Lge, hdg, mkd, hdstg, shd, EHU (10A) inc; gas; TV; 50% statics; phone; bus; Eng spkn; adv bkg acc; games area; CKE. "Excel, well-run site; lge pitches; friendly, helpful recep; Nîmes 20 mins by bus fr site; gd site; exciting water complex; vg bistro on site; child's entmnt; old san facs; busy, used by workers; gd NH." €27.50 2019

NOIRETABLE *9B1* (1km S Rural) *45.80817, 3.76844* **Camp Municipal de la Roche,** Route de la Roche, 42440 Noiretable 04 77 24 72 68; www.noiretable.fr/plan_eau_camping_Roche.aspx

👫(htd) 🚿♨🍴nr🛒nr🏛

Leave A72/E70 junc 4 sp Noiretable; thro toll & turn SW onto D53. Ignore narr tourist rte sp to W; cont downhill to T-junc & turn R onto D1089. Take next L & site on R in 750m. 2*, Sm, hdstg, mkd, pt shd, pt sl, terr, EHU (10A) €2.80; own san rec; 40% statics; Eng spkn. "Warden lives on site, but barrier poss locked LS; recep open 0900-1230, 1800-1930; camperstop 100m; lake adj; €3 for water & chem disp, token fr site." €10.00, 1 Apr-1 Nov. 2017

NOIRMOUTIER EN L'ILE *2H3* (2km E Coastal) *46.99697, -2.22057* **Huttopia Noirmoutier,** Bois de la Chaize, 23 Rue des Sableaux, 85330 Noirmoutier-en-l'Ile **02 51 39 06 24; www.europe.huttopia.com**

🐕 €4.50 WD ♨ ♿ 🚫 ⚟ ♪ MP ✕ 🦋 ♈ 🍴 🛶 sand adj

Ent Noirmoutier on D948, strt on over bdge & foll sp for Bois-de-la-Chaize, then 'campings'.
2*, Lge, pt shd, EHU (10A); 10% statics; phone; adv bkg acc; bike hire; fishing; boat launch; CKE. *"Peaceful site in pine forest nr salt water marshes; gd for children."* €32.00, 1 Apr-1 Oct, A45.   2017

NOIRMOUTIER EN L'ILE *2H3* (10km SE Coastal) *46.94503, -2.18542* **Sandaya Domaine le Midi,** 17 Rue du Camping, 85630 Barbâtre **02 51 39 63 74; mid@sandaya.fr; www.sandaya.co.uk**

🐕 €5 ♨ ♿ 🚫 ⚟ ♪ 🦋 ♈ 🍴 🛶 ☀ (htd) 🏊
☂ sand adj

Cross to island by Passage du Gois D948 (low tide - 2.5 hrs per day) or bdge D38. Turn L after 2.5km off dual c'way to Barbâtre. Site sp N thro vill.
5*, Lge, pt shd, pt sl, EHU (10A) inc; gas; bbq (gas); 45% statics; ccard acc; games area; tennis. *"Gd site; sandy but firm pitches; food, wine and pool only avail high ssn."* €25.00, 3 Apr-13 Sep.   2019

NOLAY *6H1* (1km NW Rural) *46.95084, 4.62266* **Camping La Bruyère,** Rue du Moulin Larché, 21340 Nolay **03 80 21 87 59 or 06 88 16 06 18 (mob); www.nolay.com/fr/?/Logement/Les-campings**

12 ♨ (htd) WD ♨ ♿ ⚟ ♪ MP ♈ 🍴 nr ♈ nr ♈ nr

Fr Beaune take D973 W dir Autun. In approx 20km, arr in vill of Nolay & cont on D973 thro vill. Site on L in 1km after vill, opp supmkt. 3*, Sm, mkd, hdg, pt shd, terr, EHU (10-12A) €3.60-4; bbq; 10% statics; bus adj; Eng spkn; ccard acc; CKE. *"Lovely, peaceful, well-kept site; friendly staff; gd, clean san facs, poss stretched if site busy; poss grape pickers in Sep; poss school & youth groups; attractive walk to bustling old town; gd touring base in wine area or NH; excel."* €19.00   2016

NONANCOURT *4E2* (4km E Urban) *48.76410, 1.23686* **Camp Municipal du Pré de l'Eglise,** Rue Pré de l'Eglise, 28380 St Rémy-sur-Avre **02 37 48 93 87 or 02 37 62 52 00 (LS); mairiesaintremy2@wanadoo.fr; www.ville-st-remy-sur-avre.fr**

🐕 ♨ WD ♨ ♿ 🚫 ⚟ ♪ ♈ nr

Fr Dreux take N12 W to St Rémy; strt over 1st rndabt & at traff lts complex in 500m turn R & then immed R & foll site sp. Fr Evreux (W) on N12 to St Rémy; after x-ing rv bdge at traff lts complex strt ahead to rndabt (no L turn at traff lts), then immed R at end rv bdge to cross N12 as above. Site clearly sp in vill cent, sp 'Oscar' is for sports cent adj. NB Speed ramps on site app rd. 3*, Sm, mkd, hdg, pt shd, EHU (6-10A) €2.83 (poss rev pol); TV; phone; Eng spkn; adv bkg rec; tennis adj; fishing adj; CKE. *"Pleasant, popular, well-kept NH nr rv; welcoming warden; clean, fair facs, some modern, ltd LS; no twin axles (but negotiable); some pitches poss diff access; factory adj poss noisy; vill in walking dist; a gd find; Carrefour with fuel 1km; excel site in middle of vill; site van, warden will call."* €14.60, 1 Apr-30 Sep.   2017

NONTRON *7B3* (11km NE Rural) *45.55138, 0.79472* **Kawan Village Le Château Le Verdoyer,** 24470 Champs-Romain **05 53 56 94 64; chateau@verdoyer.fr; www.verdoyer.fr**

🐕 €3 ♨ WD ♨ ♿ 🚫 ⚟ ♪ MP 🦋 ♈ 🍴 🛶 ☀ (covrd, htd) 🏊

Fr Limoges on N21 twd Périgueux. At Châlus turn R sp Nontron (D6 bis-D85). After approx 18km turn L twd Champs Romain on D96 to site on L in 2km.
4*, Lge, hdg, pt shd, terr, EHU (5-10A) inc (poss rev pol); gas; bbq (charcoal, gas); TV; 20% statics; phone; Eng spkn; adv bkg acc; ccard acc; lake fishing; games rm; waterslide; bike hire; tennis; golf 25km; boating; CKE. *"Peaceful, Dutch-run site in grnds of chateau; B&B in chateau; lovely location; no o'fits over 10m; gd sized pitches, but terr; friendly staff; superb facs; poss steep access some pitches; grnd hard, but awnings poss; excel; highly rec."* €30.00, 20 Apr-30 Sep, D21.   2019

NONTRON *7B3* (8km NE Rural) *45.56185, 0.71979* **Camping Manzac Ferme,** Manzac, 24300 Augignac **05 53 56 31 34; info@manzac-ferme.com; www.manzac-ferme.com**

🐕 ♨ (htd) WD ♨ ♿ ⚟ ♪ 🦋 ♈ ♈ nr ♈ nr

Fr Nontron take D675 N dir Rochechouart & after 7km on ent Augignac turn R sp Abjat-sur-Bandiat then immed R sp Manzac. Site on R 3.5km.
Sm, mkd, hdstg, pt shd, pt sl, EHU (6A) inc; bbq; sw nr; Eng spkn; adv bkg acc; rv fishing; CKE. *"Superb, peaceful, well-kept CL-type, adults only site; helpful British owners; dogs by prior arrangement; excel san facs; phone ahead in winter; ideal for birdwatching & wildlife; highly rec; most pitches in dense shd; excel."* €24.00, 15 May-15 Sep.   2016

NONTRON *7B3* (1km S Urban) *45.51992, 0.65876*
Camping de Nontron, St Martiel-de-Valette, 24300
Nontron **05 53 56 02 04 or 06 30 66 25 74 (mob);**
camping-de-nontron@orange.fr; www.camping
denontron.com

[icons] **12** ⛺ €1 ♦♦(htd) ▦ ♨ ✎ MP ✿ ⊤ nr ⑪ nr ⚲ nr ⚏ ✏ ⬚

Thro Nontron S twd Brantôme on D675. Site on
o'skts of town on L nr stadium. **Sp.** Med, mkd, hdg, pt
shd, EHU (10A) €3.50; gas; TV; Eng spkn; games area;
games rm; CKE. *"Pleasant owners; site clsd mid-Dec
to early Jan; excel, modern san facs; gd touring base;
town 1km walk along footpath."* **€22.50**   **2018**

NORT SUR ERDRE *2G4* (1km S Rural) *47.42770,
-1.49877* **Camping Seasonova du Port Mulon,**
Rue des Mares Noires, 44390 Nort-sur-Erdre **02 36
81 00 01 or 02 40 72 23 57; contact@camping-
portmulon.com; www.camping-portmulon.com**

[icons] ⛺ €0.90 ♦♦ ▦ ♨ ✎ ✿ ⚲ nr ⚏

Sp fr all ents to town; foll 'Camping' & 'Hippodrome'
sp. NB: C'vans banned fr town cent, look for diversion
sp. 3*, Med, shd, EHU (6A) €2.40; adv bkg acc; fishing;
boating; tennis; CKE. *"Delightful, spacious, under-used
site; gd walking & cycling area, espec along Nantes canal
& Rv Erdre; Barrier perm locked, access when warden on
site only; new site rd & toilet block (2014); friendly staff."*
€22.00, 1 Apr-31 Oct.   **2019**

NOUAN LE FUZELIER *4G3* (0.7km S Urban) *47.53328,
2.03508* **Camping La Grande Sologne,** Rue des Peupliers,
41600 Nouan-le-Fuzelier **02 54 88 70 22; info@
campingrandesologne.com; www.campingrande
sologne.com**

[icons] ⛺ €1 ♦♦ ▦ ♨ ♿ ✎ MP ✿ ⛱ ⚲ nr ⚏

On E side of D2020, at S end of Nouan opp rlwy stn.
Sp fr town cent & opp rlwy stn. NB sat nav not rec.
3*, Med, mkd, pt shd, EHU (10A) €3; red long stay;
2% statics; Eng spkn; adv bkg acc; golf 15km; tennis;
fishing; games area; CKE. *"Pretty site adj lake (no sw);
some pitches boggy when wet; facs poss stretched high
ssn; ltd facs end of ssn & poss unclean; htd pool adj;
public park at ent to site, but quiet; red arr early; excel
NH; phone for entry LS; excel site; office open 0700-
1500; voucher for nrby sw pool; san facs dated; friendly
owners."* **€24.50, 1 Apr-15 Oct.**   **2019**

NOUVION EN THIERACHE, LE *3B4* (2km S Rural)
50.00538, 3.78292 **Camp Municipal du Lac de Condé,**
Promenade Henri d'Orléans, Rue de Guise (Le Lac),
02170 Le Nouvion-en-Thiérache **03 23 98 98 58;
campinglacdeconde@gmail.com; www.camping-
thierache.com**

[icons] ⛺ €0.80 ♦♦ WD ▦ ♿ ✎ MP ⊤ nr ⑪ nr ⚲ nr ⚏

Sp fr cent of Le Nouvion fr D1043 on D26, dir Guise
opp chateau. 2*, Sm, hdstg, hdg, mkd, pt shd, pt sl,
EHU (4-8A) €2.50; bbq; red long stay; 70% statics;
phone; Eng spkn; adv bkg acc; ccard acc; tennis nr;
horseriding nr; CKE. *"Beautiful, spacious, lakeside
site; busy even LS - rec phone ahead; gd sized pitches;
warm welcome, staff helpful; htd pool adj; gd san
facs; gd for families; canoe hire nr; some pitches not
suitable m'vans due slope; muddy when wet; walk
around lake; conv NH; excel; coarse fishing in adj lake."*
€12.50, 1 Apr-30 Sep.   **2017**

NOYON *3C3* (4.5km E Rural) *49.58882, 3.04370*
FFCC Camping L'Etang du Moulin, 54 Rue du Moulin,
60400 Salency **03 44 09 99 81**

[icons] **12** ⛺ €1 ♦♦(htd) WD ▦ ♿ ✎ MP ✿ ⊤ ⑪ nr ⚲ nr ⚏

Take D1032 fr Noyon dir Chauny. On ent Salency
turn L & foll site sp. Site in 1km. 2*, Sm, shd, pt sl,
EHU (10A) €1.60; gas; bbq; 75% statics; fishing; tennis;
CKE. *"Site adj to fishing lake; gd facs; very clean & tidy;
elec french 2 pin; security barrier card; pool 3km; v
quiet location."* **€13.00**   **2016**

NOYON *3C3* (10km S Rural) *49.50667, 3.01765*
FFCC Camping Les Araucarias, 870 Rue du Général
Leclerc, 60170 Carlepont **03 44 75 27 39; camping-
les-araucarias@wanadoo.fr; www.camping-les-
araucarias.com**

[icons] ⛺ €1 ♦♦(htd) WD ▦ ♨ ♿ ✎ MP ✿ ⊤ nr ⑪ nr ⚲ nr ⚏

Fr S, fr A1 exit junc 9 or 10 for Compiègne. There
take D130 sp Tracy-le-Val & Carlepont. Site on L
100m fr Carlepont vill sp. Or fr N on D934 Noyon-
Soissons rd take D130 dir Carlepont & Tracy-le-Val.
Site on R after vill on SW twd Compiegne not well
sp. 2*, Sm, mkd, pt shd, pt sl, EHU (6-10A) €3 (poss
rev pol); gas; bbq; 80% statics; Eng spkn; adv bkg
acc; CKE. *"Secluded site, previously an arboretum;
close Parc Astérix & La Mer-de-Sable (theme park);
85km Disneyland; san facs poss scruffy LS; vg."*
€12.50, 1 Apr-31 Oct.   **2016**

NUITS ST GEORGES *6G1* (5km S Urban) *47.10323,
4.94148* **Camping Le Moulin de Prissey,** 14 rue du
Moulin de Prissey, 21700 Premeaux-Prissey
**03 80 62 31 15; cpg.moulin.prissey@free.fr;
www.cpg-moulin-prissey.fr**

[icons] ⛺ €0.90 ♦♦ WD ▦ ♿ ✎ MP ⊤ nr ⑪ nr ⚲ nr ⚏

Fr A31 take D8 to Nuits St Georges then D974 twrds
Beaune. After Premeaux turn L onto D115E. Thro
Prissey and site on R. 3*, Sm, mkd, pt shd, pt sl, EHU
(6A) inc; gas; bbq; adv bkg acc; ccard acc; CKE. *"Popular
NH - arr early; sm pitches; access poss diff lge o'fits;
basic facs; gd cycling; noisy rlwy adj; site well laid out &
tidy (2015)."* **€20.00, 4 Apr-15 Oct.**   **2019**

NYONS *9D2* (1km NE Rural) *44.36523, 5.15365*
Camping Les Clos, Route de Gap, 26110 Nyons
04 75 26 29 90; info@campinglesclos.com;
www.campinglesclos.com

🏕 €2.20 👫 🚾 🏊 ♿ 🍴 ⬛ 🍽 Ⓗ 🛒 🧺 nr 🎐 🛶 🚲 ⛷

Fr rndabt in town cent take D94 sp Gap & site on
R in 1km. 4*, Med, hdg, mkd, hdstg, pt shd, EHU
(10A) inc; gas; bbq (elec, gas); 20% statics; phone;
Eng spkn; adv bkg acc; ccard acc; rv; fishing; CKE.
*"Quiet, well-kept site in lovely area; friendly, helpful
staff; excel touring base; 20 min walk to town
along quiet side rd; mkt Thu & Sat; popular site."*
€22.00, 1 Apr-30 Sep.   2019

NYONS *9D2* (12km NE Rural) *44.42569, 5.21904*
Camping de Trente Pas, 26110 St Ferréol-Trente-Pas
04 75 27 70 69; contact@campingtrentepas.com;
www.campingtrentepas.com

🏕 €2 👫 🏊 ⬛ 🍴 🍽 Ⓗ nr 🧺 nr 🎐 🚲 ⛷

Exit A7 junc 19 Bollène onto D994 & D94. L on
D70 to St Ferréol-Trente-Pas. Site 100m fr vill on
banks of stream. 2*, Med, shd, EHU (6A) €3.10; TV;
5% statics; bike hire; tennis; games rm; horseriding
4km. *"Peaceful site nr rv; scenic area, views fr site; gd,
clean san facs; gd pool; on flood plain; excel value; rec."*
€22.80, 1 May-31 Aug.   2017

NYONS *9D2* (12km NE Rural) *44.43507, 5.21248*
FFCC Camping Le Pilat, 26110 St Ferréol-Trente-Pas
04 75 27 72 09; info@campinglepilat.com;
www.campinglepilat.com

🏕 €3.50 high ssn 👫 🚾 🏊 ♿ 🍴 ⬛ 🎐 🍽 🛒 🧺 🎐 🚲
⛷ (htd) 🛶

Fr D94 N or Nyons turn N at La Bonté onto D70 to
St Ferréol, site sp 1km N of vill.
3*, Med, hdg, shd, EHU (6A) €4; bbq; red long stay;
TV; 25% statics; phone; Eng spkn; games area, ping
pong table.; CKE. *"Site among lavender fields; pleasant,
helpful owners; gd clean san facs; outdoor gym; gd
walking & off-rd cycling; Thurs mkt Nyons; excel."*
€23.60, 1 Apr-30 Sep.   2020

NYONS *9D2* (18km E Rural) *44.34319, 5.28357*
Camp Municipal Les Cigales, Allée des Platanes, 26110
Ste Jalle **04 75 27 34 88 or 04 75 27 32 78 (mairie);**
mairie.saintejalle@orange.fr

🏕 👫 🚾 🏊 ⬛ 🍴 🍽 nr Ⓗ 🧺 nr 🎐

Fr Nyons take D94 dir Serres; in 10 km at Curnier
turn R onto D64 to Ste-Jalle. In vill turn R onto D108
dir Buis-les-Baronnies. Site on R in 300m. NB Dist by
rd fr Nyons is 20km. 2*, Sm, hdg, pt shd, EHU (10A)
€2.20; 15% statics; adv bkg acc. *"Vg site in attractive
old vill; friendly warden; facs dated but clean."*
€13.00, 1 May-30 Sep.   2016

OBERNAI *6E3* (16.5km ESE Urban) *48.41413,
7.66983* **Camping Municipal Le Wagerlott,** 1 rue de
la Sucrerie, 67150 Erstein **33 88 98 09 88 or 33 88
98 14 33 (Municipal);** campingerstein@gmail.com

🏕 €2.30 👫 (htd) 🏊 ⬛ 🍽 🍴 Ⓗ nr 🧺 nr 🎐

Fr Strasbourg on A35 then D1083. R onto D426.
At rndabt turn L then 1st R to site. Med, mkd,
hdg, unshd, EHU (16A) €3.50; 50% statics; phone;
Eng spkn; adv bkg acc; ccard acc. *"Gd municipal
site; cls to Strasbourg; gd cycle rts; clean facs."*
€16.00, 1 Apr-30 Sep.   2018

OBERNAI *6E3* (1.5km W Urban) *48.46460, 7.46750*
Camp Municipal Le Vallon de l'Ehn, 1 Rue de Berlin,
67210 Obernai **03 88 95 38 48;** camping@
obernai.fr; www.obernai.fr

🏕 €1.10 👫 (htd) 🚾 🏊 ⬛ 🍴 🍽 MP 🎐 🍽 🧺 🎐

Fr N exit A35 junc 11 onto D426 sp Obernai. Foll
D426 W around Obernai & foll sp Mont St Odile
& Camping VVF; at final rndabt turn R & immed L
to site. Fr S on A35 exit junc 12 sp Obernai. At 3rd
rndabt turn L onto D426 Ottrott-Mont Ste Odile
(look for sp Camping VVF). Do not tow into
Obernai. 3*, Lge, hdstg, mkd, pt shd, pt sl, serviced
pitches; EHU (10-16A) €4.50; bbq; twin axles; red
long stay; phone; bus to Strasbourg & Obernai adj,
train; Eng spkn; adv bkg acc; ccard acc; horseriding
adj; tennis adj; CKE. *"Attractive, well-kept, busy site
on edge of picturesque town; sm pitches; welcoming,
helpful staff; superb, excel, modern clean san facs;
no entry after 1930; rec arr early high ssn; lge pool
200m; 10% red CC members LS; c'vans, m'vans & tents
all sep areas; excel bus/train links; ideal NH; highly rec;
very well run, gd site; office clsd 1230-1400; popular."*
€21.00, 1 Jan-8 Jan & 17 Mar-31 Dec.   2017

OCTON *10F1* (2km NE Rural) *43.65948, 3.32052*
Camping Le Village du Bosc (Naturist), Chemin
de Ricazouls, 34800 Octon **04 67 96 07 37;**
r.villagedubosc@free.net; www.villagedubosc.net

🏕 €3 👫 🚾 🏊 ♿ 🍴 ⬛ 🎐 🍽 🍽 🛒 Ⓗ 🛒 🧺 🎐 🛶 (htd)

Exit 54 or 55 fr N9/A75 dir Octon onto D148, foll
sp to Ricazouls/site. 2*, Med, hdg, mkd, pt shd, pt sl,
terr, EHU (10A)inc; sw; red long stay; TV; 5% statics;
Eng spkn; adv bkg acc; watersports; INF card; games
area; games rm. *"Lovely, quiet site with wooded walks;
friendly owners; clean facs; tight turns on terr access
for lge o'fits; Octon vill pretty; wheelchair facs in san
facs."* €30.00, 21 Apr-30 Sep.   2017

OLARGUES *8F4* (0.4km N Rural) *43.55798, 2.91440*
Camp Municipal Le Baoüs, 34390 Olargues **04 67 97
71 50;** otsi.olargues@wanadoo.fr; www.olargues.org

👫 (cont) 🚾 🎐 🍴 🍽 🛒 🧺 nr 🎐

Take D908 W fr Bédarieux, site immed bef ent
Olargues. Site sp over sm bdge on L. At end of bdge
turn R to site. Last 50m rough track & narr turn into
site. 2*, Sm, pt shd, EHU (6A); adv bkg req; canoeing;
bike hire. *"Helpful warden; hill climb to services block;
site poss flooded by Rv Jaur in spring; sh walk to
amazing hilltop vill."* **1 Jul-15 Sep.**   2019

OLLIERGUES *9B1* (4km N Rural) *45.69008, 3.63289*
Camping Les Chelles, 63880 Olliergues **04 73 95 54 34;**
info@camping-les-chelles.com; www.camping-les-chelles.com

🐕 €1 ♦♦ wo ♿ ♨ 🚿 ⧖ ⦿ 🍽 👶 🛒 nr ⚠ 🏊 (htd)

Fr Olliergues take D37 N up hill dir Le Brugeron; then sharp L onto D87 dir La Chabasse; site sp. 3*, Med, hdg, mkd, shd, terr, EHU (15A) €2.80; TV; phone; Eng spkn; adv bkg acc; ccard acc; games area; games rm. *"Facs excel for families with young children; enthusiastic, helpful & kind Dutch owners; gd walking; gd touring base; excel.* €19.00, 1 Apr-31 Oct.   2015

OLONZAC *8F4* (9km E Rural) *43.28372, 2.82688*
FFCC Camping Les Auberges, 11120 Pouzols-Minervois **04 68 46 26 50; vero.pradal@neuf.fr; www.camping lesauberges.hubside.fr**

🐕 ♦♦ wo 🚿 ⧖ 🚿 🦋 ⦿ 🍽 🛒 nr ⚠ 🏊

Fr D5 site 500m S of vill of Pouzols-Minervois. 2*, Sm, mkd, pt shd, EHU (5A) €3.50; bbq; 30% statics; Eng spkn; adv bkg rec; tennis; CKE. *"V popular site; friendly owners; gas adj; sm Sat mkt at 'cave' opp."* €16.00, 1 Apr-1 Nov.   2020

OLORON STE MARIE *8F2* (3km SW Urban) *43.17886, -0.62328* **Camping Pyrenees Nature (formerly Gîtes du Stade),** Chemin de Lagravette, 64400 Oloron-Ste Marie **05 59 39 11 26; camping.pyrenees.nature@gmail.com; www.campingpyreneesnature.fr**

12 🐕 €1.20 ♦♦ wo ♿ 🚿 🚿 🦋 ⦿ 🍽 🛒 nr ⚠ 🏊

Fr N on ring rd foll sp to Saragosse (Spain); at rndabt take 2nd exit onto D6 still sp Saragosse, site sp on R just after sports field. Fr S on D55 join ring rd & turn W at rndabt by McDonalds; sp. 3*, Med, hdg, mkd, pt shd, EHU (6-10A) €4-6 (some rev pol); bbq; sw nr; twin axles; TV; adv bkg acc; tennis; rv fishing 1km; bike hire; CKE. *"Well-kept site; lge pitches; helpful staff; clean facs but ltd LS & stretched high ssn; take care low tree; grnd poss soft & damp after rain; barrier clsd 1200-1500; excel base for Pyrenees; pool adj; gd walking."* €23.60   2019

ONESSE ET LAHARIE *8E1* (0.5km N Rural) *44.06344, -1.07257* **FFCC Camping Le Bienvenu,** 259 Route de Mimizan, 40110 Onesse-et-Laharie **05 58 07 30 49 or 06 81 32 12 56 (mob); www.camping-onesse.fr**

🐕 €1 ♦♦ wo 🚿 🚿 🦋 ⦿ 🍽 ⦿ nr 🛒 nr ⚠

On N10 Bordeaux-Bayonne rd, turn W onto D38 at Laharie. Site in 5km. 2*, Med, mkd, pt shd, EHU (10A) €4; red long stay; TV; 10% statics; adv bkg acc; CKE. *"Well-run, nice, family site; gd facs; very helpful staff."* €18.00, 1 Mar-30 Sep.   2019

ONZAIN *4G2* (6km W Rural) *47.51030, 1.10400*
Yelloh! Village Le Parc du Val de Loire, 155 Route de Fleuray, 41150 Mesland **02 54 70 27 18; parcduvaldeloire@orange.fr; www.parcduvalde loire.com or www.yellohvillage.co.uk**

🐕 €4 ♦♦ wo ♿ 🚿 ⧖ 🚿 mp 🦋 ⦿ 🍽 👶 🛒 nr ⚠ 🏊 (covrd, htd) 🎣

Fr Blois take D952 SW twd Amboise. Approx 16km outside Blois turn R to Onzain & foll sp to Mesland; go thro Mesland vill & turn L dir Fleuray; site on R after 1.5km. 4*, Lge, hdg, mkd, pt shd, pt sl, serviced pitches; EHU (10A) inc; gas; bbq (charcoal, gas); TV; 30% statics; Eng spkn; adv bkg acc; ccard acc; waterslide; bike hire; tennis; games area; games rm; CKE. *"Secluded site; wine-tasting; excursions to vineyards; mkt Thur Onzain; excel."* €35.00, 11 Apr-20 Sep, L02.   2016

ORANGE *10E2* (12km NE Rural) *44.16222, 4.93531*
Camping des Favards (formerly Aire Naturelle Domaine), 1335 Route d'Orange, 84150 Violès **04 90 70 90 93; campingfavards@gmail.com; www.favards.com**

🐕 €1.70-€1.90 ♦♦ (htd) 🚿 ⧖ 🚿 🦋 ⦿ 🍽 ⚠ 🏊

Fr N exit A7 junc 19 Bollène. Foll D8 dir Carpentras & Violès. In Violès foll dir Orange & look for camp sp. Fr S exit A7 junc 22 sp Carpentras, take dir Avignon, then dir Vaison-la-Romaine to Violès. Avoid cent of Orange when towing. 3*, Sm, hdg, mkd, unshd, EHU (6-10A) €3.65 (poss rev pol); Eng spkn; adv bkg acc; ccard acc; CKE. *"Well-kept site; excel pitches - some very lge (extra charge); superb san facs; poss stretched; wine-tasting on site high ssn; gd touring base; poss dust clouds fr Mistral wind; pitches muddy when wet; gd."* €23.60, 13 Apr-30 Sep.   2018

ORBEC *3D1* (1.5km N Urban) *49.02829, 0.40857*
Camp Municipal Les Capucins, Rue des Frères Bigot, 14290 Orbec **02 31 32 76 22; camping.sivom@orange.fr**

🐕 ♦♦ wo 🚿 🚿 🦋 🛒 nr ⚠

Exit A28 junc 15 to Orbec; on ent town foll site sp. If app fr D519 or D819 steep drag up to site & care req down to town. 2*, Sm, pt shd, EHU (10A) €2. *"Well-kept site; site yourself if office clsd; san facs old but clean; no twin axles; access easy for lge o'fits; delightful countryside; excel."* €12.00, 25 May-8 Sep.   2015

ORBEY *6F3* (7km SE Rural) *48.09198, 7.19741*
Camping des Deux Hohnack, Giragoutte 68910 Labaroche **03 89 49 83 72; camping-labaroche@orange.fr; www.camping-labaroche.fr**

🐕 €1 ♦♦ wo 🚿 ⧖ 🚿 🦋 🍽 ⦿ ⚠

Fr Colmar take D11 thro Turckheim (do not turn off on D10). Cont thro Trois Epis. At fork turn L sp Linge. In half km turn R. 2*, Med, mkd, hdg, hdstg, pt shd, pt sl, EHU (6A) €4; bbq; TV; games area; CKE. *"Gd walks; rural museum at Labaroche 1.5km; vg."* €17.50, 1 Apr-30 Sep.   2015

FRANCE

ORLEANS

ORLEANS *4F3* (11km E Rural) *47.88830, 2.02744*
Camp Municipal Les Pâtures, 55 Chemin du Port,
45430 Chécy **02 38 91 13 27; camping@checy.fr;
www.checy.fr**

🏕 €1 ♨ wc ♿ 🚿 🔥 🚮 MP 🐾 nr

Take D960 E twd Châteauneuf. In Chécy, foll site
sp. Access thro town via narr rds. 2*, Sm, hdg, pt
shd, EHU (16A) €3.80; bbq; twin axles; red long stay;
Eng spkn; adv bkg acc; fishing; golf 5km; tennis; CKE.
*"Excel, well-run site on Rv Loire; vg location; friendly,
helpful warden; gd san facs; conv Orléans, park & ride
tram; poss open bef & after dates given; popular NH."*
€19.00, 12 May-25 Sep. 2018

ORLEANS *4F3* (5km S Rural) *47.85603, 1.92555*
Camp Municipal d'Olivet, Rue du Pont-Bouchet,
45160 Olivet **02 38 63 53 94; infos@camping-
olivet.org; www.camping-olivet.org**

🏕 €2 (htd) ♨ wc 🚿 ♿ 🔥 🚮 MP 🐾 🏊 ⛱

To avoid height restriction, best app fr A71 exit junc 2
onto N271 dir Orléans-La Source. Cont on N271 until
rd crosses N20 into Rue de Bourges. Pass commercial
estate & hotel on L & turn L at traff lts into Rue de
Châteauroux. Pass university (Parc Technologique),
cross tramway & turn L at traff lts onto D14, Rue de
la Source, then in 500m turn R (watch for pharmacy
on L & green site sp) into Rue du Pont-Bouchet
(narr rd). Site well sp on D14. NB Beware height
restrictions on junc underpasses in Orléans cent.
2*, Sm, hdg, pt shd, pt sl, EHU (16A) €3.10 (rev pol); bus
400m; Eng spkn; adv bkg rec; CKE. *"Well-run, busy site
by Rv Loiret; friendly; excel clean san facs; guided tours
of Orléans by site staff; gd walking; vineyards nr; vg."*
€21.70, 1 Apr-30 Sep. 2018

ORNANS *6G2* (1km E Rural) *47.10064, 6.16036*
Camping La Roche d'Ully, Allée de la Tour de
Peiltz, 25290 Ornans **03 81 57 17 79; contact@
larochedully.com; www.camping-larochedully.com**

🏕 €3 (htd) wc 🚿 ♿ 🔥 🚮 MP 🦋 ⛱ 🍽 🕐 🐾 ⛱
🏊 (covrd, htd) 🛁

Fr Ornans foll blue sps to site nr rvside.
4*, Med, mkd, unshd, EHU (10A) €4; bbq; 20% statics;
adv bkg acc; ccard acc; rv fishing; bike hire; sauna;
canoeing; games area. *"Pleasant, family-run site in gd
location in rv valley; popular with students; some noise
in ssn."* **€36.00, 2 Apr-9 Oct.** 2016

ORPIERRE *9D3* (0.5km E Rural) *44.31110, 5.69650*
Camping Les Princes d'Orange, Flonsaine, 05700
Orpierre **04 92 66 22 53; campingorpierre@orange.fr;
www.campingorpierre.com**

🏕 €1.60 ♨ wc 🚿 ♿ 🔥 🚮 MP 🍽 🐾 ⛱ 🏊 (htd)

N75 S fr Serres for 11km to Eyguians. Turn R in
Eyguians onto D30, 8km to Orpierre, turn L in vill
to site (sp). 4*, Med, mkd, hdstg, pt shd, pt sl, terr,
EHU (10A) €4.50; gas; TV; 10% statics; adv bkg
acc; fishing; games area; waterslide; tennis. *"Rock-
climbing area; gd walking; beautiful, interesting vill."*
€46.40, 1 Apr-3 Nov. 2019

OUISTREHAM *3D1* (1km S Urban) *49.26909,
-0.25498* **Camping Le Riva Bella,** Rue de la Haie
Breton, 14150 Ouistreham **02 31 97 12 66; camping-
rivabella@vacances-seasonova.com; www.
vacances-seasonova.com/camping-riva-bella**

🏕 €1.50 ♨ (htd) wc 🚿 ♿ 🔥 🚮 MP 🦋 🍽 🐾 ⛱ 🏊 ⚓
(htd) ⛱ sand 1.8km

Fr ferry terminal foll sp Caen on D84 (Rue de l'Yser/
Ave du Grand Large); in approx 1.5km site sp at
rndabt; take 3rd exit. 3*, Lge, hdg, pt shd, EHU (10A)
inc; gas; twin axles; 40% statics; bus; Eng spkn; adv
bkg acc; ccard acc; games area; tennis; bike hire; CKE.
*"V conv for late or early ferry (5 mins to terminal),
site stays open for late Brittany ferry; busy high ssn;
gd sized pitches; sandy soil; gates open 0630-2300
(dep out of hrs, by request); opens for late arr; no twin
axles; nice walk/cycle along canal to town; wonderful
beaches; interesting area; mkt Thur; conv & sep area
for NH without unhitching; British twin axle c'vans acc;
gd for long stay; takeaway food and bread shop on site;
new management has improved site (2017); new san
facs & pool."* **€34.00, 1 Apr-30 Oct, N10.** 2019

> ## "I need an on-site restaurant"
>
> We do our best to make sure site information
> is correct, but it is always best to check any
> must-have facilities are still available or will
> be open during your visit.

OUISTREHAM *3D1* (7km S Rural) *49.23838, -0.25763*
FFCC Camping des Capucines, rue de la Côte Fleurie,
14860 Ranville **02 31 78 69 82; campingdescapucines.
14@orange.fr; www.campingdescapucines.com**

12 🏕 €1.80 ♨ (htd) wc 🚿 ♿ 🔥 🚮 MP 🦋 🍽 🐾 nr ⛱
⛱ sand 3km

App Caen fr E or W, take Blvd Péripherique Nord,
then exit 3a sp Ouistreham car ferry (D515). In
approx 8.5km turn R onto D514 sp Cabourg, cross
Pegasus Bdge & foll sp Ranville across 2 rndabts;
at x-rds in 500m turn L (at sm campsite sp); site
in 300m on L. Fr Ouistreham foll D514 dir Caborg
to Pegasus Bdge, then as above. 3*, Med, hdg,
mkd, pt shd, terr, EHU (10A) inc (poss rev pol); gas;
60% statics; phone; bus 500m; Eng spkn; adv bkg rec;
ccard acc. *"Well established site in pleasant position;
some pitches sm, best pitches without ehu; gd clean
san facs but dated; barrier open 0600-2400 but if clsd
LS use intercom at recep; conv ferries (if arr late fr
ferry, phone in adv for pitch number & barrier code);
take care o'hanging trees; conv vill, Pegasus Bdge,
museum & war cemetery; vg, quiet well run site;
hypmkt 4.8km; site run down in LS; reliable freq visited
stop nr port."* **€21.40** 2019

372   For a guide to symbols see the fold out on the rear cover

OUISTREHAM *3D1* (5km SW Urban) *49.24970, -0.27190* **Camping Les Hautes Coutures,** avenue de la Côte de Nacre, 14970 Bénouville **02 31 44 73 08 or 06 07 25 26 90 (mob LS); info@campinghautes coutures.com; www.campinghautescoutures.com**

🚐 €3 👫(htd) 🗼 ♨ ⚲ ♿ 🚿 🗑 ⭐ 🛒 🍴 🕐 ♨ 🎿 ⛏

🏊(covrd, htd) 🗼 2km

Leave Ouistreham ferry & foll sp Caen & A13 over 2 rndabts. After 2nd rndabt join dual c'way. Leave at 1st exit (D35) sp St Aubin d'Arquenay & ZA de Bénouville. Turn R at end of slip rd, then L at T-junc; site in 200m uphill on R. Or fr Caen twd port on dual c'way, site has own exit shortly after Pegasus Memorial Bdge exit; site clearly visible on R of dual c'way. 4*, Lge, hdg, pt shd, pt sl, EHU (10A) €5.50 (rev pol)(adaptors avail €18); bbq; TV; 30% statics; Eng spkn; adv bkg acc; ccard acc; jacuzzi; golf 4km; bike hire; fishing; horseriding 1km; games rm; windsurfing 1km; waterslide; CKE. *"Busy, poss noisy holiday complex o'looking Caen Canal; friendly staff; sm pitches; access tight some pitches when busy; recep 0800-2000 high ssn, but staff will open for late ferry arr if req in adv; no o'fits over 12m high ssn; ltd EHU (2009); cycle path to Caen; daily mkt in Ouistreham; conv NH; access to pitches diff as high kerbs, some pitches on steep slopes; excel pool."* **€35.00, 25 Mar-25 Sep.** 2016

OUNANS *6H2* (1km N Rural) *47.00290, 5.66550* **Huttopia La Plage Blanche,** 3 Rue de la Plage, 39380 Ounans **03 84 37 69 63; plageblanche@ camping-indigo.com; europe.huttopia.com/en/site/ la-plage-blanche**

🚐 €2 👫 🗑 ♨ ⚲ ♿ 🚿 🗑 ⭐ 🛒 🍴 🕐 ♨ 🎿 ⛏ 🎿

Exit A39 junc 6 sp Dole Cent. Foll N5 SE for 18km dir Pontarlier. After passing Souvans, turn L on D472 sp Mont-sous-Vaudrey. Foll sp to Ounans. Site well sp in vill. 3*, Lge, mkd, hdstg, pt shd, EHU (6A) €4 (poss rev pol); sw nr; TV; 1% statics; Eng spkn; adv bkg rec; ccard acc; lake fishing; bike hire; horseriding; canoeing; CKE. *"Superb rvside pitches; trout & carp fishing; friendly recep; excel san facs, recently updated (2013); gd rest; excel."* **€27.90, 19 Apr-22 Sep, J02.** 2019

OUST *8G3* (12km SE Rural) *42.81105, 1.25558* **Camping Le Montagnou,** Route de Guzet, 09140 Le Trein-d'Ustou **05 61 66 94 97 or 06 07 85 37 65; campinglemontagnou@wanadoo.fr; www.lemontagnou.com**

🚐 €1.50 👫(htd) 🗑 ♨ ⚲ ♿ 🚿 🗑 ⭐ 🛒 🍴 🕐 nr 🎿 ⛏ 🎿

Fr St Girons S on D618 & D3 to Oust. Fr Oust SE on D3 & D8 thro Seix & at Pont de la Taule turn L onto D8 twd Le Trein-d'Ustou. Site on L just bef vill, sp. 3*, Med, hdg, pt shd, EHU (6-10A) €3.50-5.50; bbq; sw nr; 30% statics; phone; adv bkg acc; ccard acc; tennis; fishing; CKE. *"Well-situated, well-run, delightful rvside site; mountain views; skiing 9km; gd sized pitches; friendly, helpful French owners; gd walking; highly rec."* **€22.00, 1 Jan-31 Oct & 1 Dec-31 Dec.** 2015

OUST *8G3* (0.6km S Rural) *42.87042, 1.21947* **Camping Les Quatre Saisons,** Route d'Aulus-les-Bains, 09140 Oust **05 61 96 55 55; camping.ariege@gmail.com; www.camping4saisons.com**

12 🚐 €1.50 👫(htd) 🗑 ♨ ⚲ ♿ 🚿 🗑 ⭐ 🛒 🍴 🕐 nr 🎿 ⛏

Take D618 S fr St Girons; then D3 to Oust; on N o'skts of town turn L (sp Aulus) onto D32; in 1km site on R nr Rv Garbet. 3*, Med, hdg, pt shd, EHU (10A) inc; TV; 25% statics; phone; Eng spkn; adv bkg rec; ccard acc; games area; CKE. *"In beautiful, unspoilt area; friendly site; excel boulangerie 5mins walk on footpath to vill; excel."* **€20.00** 2016

OYONNAX *9A3* (13km E Rural) *46.25530, 5.55705* **Camping Les Gorges de l'Oignin,** Rue du Lac, 01580 Matafelon-Granges **04 74 76 80 97; camping.lesgorges deloignin@wanadoo.fr; www.gorges-de-loignin.com**

🚐 €2.40 👫(htd) 🗑 ♨ ⚲ ♿ 🚿 🗑 ⭐ 🛒 🍴 🕐 ♨ 🎿 ⛏ 🎿 🎿

Exit A404 junc 9 onto D979 dir Bourg-en-Bresse; in 700m turn R onto D18 to Matafelon-Granges; foll sp. NB Fr Oyonnax 22km by rd. 3*, Med, hdg, mkd, hdstg, pt shd, terr, EHU (10A) €3.40; bbq; sw nr; TV; 10% statics; phone; Eng spkn; adv bkg acc; games area; CKE. *"Beautiful site on lake - boat launching; friendly, helpful staff; Jura National Park; Rv Ain gorges; excel."* **€29.00, 15 Apr-20 Sep.** 2015

PACAUDIERE, LA *9A1* (0.2km E Rural) *46.17512, 3.87639* **Camp Municipal Beausoleil,** Route de Vivans, 42310 La Pacaudière **04 77 64 11 50 or 04 77 64 30 18 (Mairie); lapacaudiere@wanadoo.fr; www.camping-rhonealpes.com**

👫 🗑 ♨ ⚲ 🚿 🗑 ⭐ 🛒 🍴 🎿

NW on N7 Roanne to Lapalisse; turn R in La Pacaudière, D35; site well sp; fork R in 50m; site ent in 400m. 2*, Sm, hdg, hdstg, unshd, sl, EHU (10A); gas; TV. *"Pleasant NH in beautiful countryside; public pool high ssn; ltd facs LS; interesting area; Sat mkt."* **€15.50, 1 May-30 Sep.** 2017

PAIMPOL *1D3* (2.5km SE Coastal) *48.76966, -3.02209* **Camp Municipal Crukin,** Rue de Crukin, Kérity, 22500 Paimpol **02 96 20 78 47 or 02 96 55 31 70 (Mairie); contact@camping-paimpol.com; www.camping-paimpol.com**

🚐 €2.10 👫(htd) 🗑 ♨ ⚲ ♿ 🚿 🗑 ⭐ 🛒 🍴 nr 🎿

🗼 shgl 250m

On D786 fr St Brieuc/Paimpol, site sp in vill of Kérity 80m off main rd shortly bef abbey. 2*, Med, hdg, pt shd, EHU (6A) €3.90 (poss rev pol); TV; 10% statics; bus 100m; watersports; fishing; CKE. *"Sep m'van area; Beaufort Abbey nrby; excel sh stay/NH; plenty of space; facs ltd LS; walk to town along coast rd gd views; site unkept; boggy when wet; gd; tourist train runs past site ent to/fr Paimpol, hourly svrs."* **€23.00, 1 Apr-30 Sep.** 2018

FRANCE

PALAVAS LES FLOTS 10F1 (1km NE Coastal) 43.53346, 3.94820 **Camping Montpellier Plage,** 95 Ave St Maurice, 34250 Palavas-les-Flots **04 67 68 00 91; camping.montpellier.plage@wanadoo.fr; www.camping-montpellier-plage.com**

🐕 ♿ WC ♿ ⚲ ⚐ ✉ MP Ⓣ ⓘ ⛽ 🛒 ⚓ ⛵ 🏊 sand adj

Site on D21ES on o'skts of vill twd Carnon. 3*, V lge, mkd, pt shd, EHU (4A) inc; gas; bbq; 50% statics; bus high ssn; Eng spkn; adv bkg rec; games area; CKE. *"Gd location;spa facs; basic san facs, but lge pitches & friendliness of site outweigh this; gd security; poss somewhat unkempt; easy walk into Palavas - interesting sm port; flamingoes on adjoining lake; gd."* €36.00, 16 Apr-18 Sep. 2017

PARAY LE MONIAL 9A1 (1km NW Urban) 46.45750, 4.10472 **Camping de Mambré,** Route du Gué-Léger, 71600 Paray-le-Monial **03 85 88 89 20; camping. plm@gmail.com; www.campingdemambre.com**

🐕 €2 ♿ WC ⚓ ♿ ⚐ ✉ 🦋 Ⓣ ⚓ 🛒 ⚓ ⛵

Fr N79 Moulin to Mâcon; site at W end of town; just after level x-ing turn NE into Rte du Gué-Léger. Turn R into site after x-ing rv; well sp. 4*, Lge, mkd, pt shd, EHU (10A) €3.40; CKE. *"Paray-le-Monial is pilgrimage cent; ltd facs & poorly maintained LS (2011); no designated fresh water pnts (2011); 15min walk to town along rv; excel cycling cent."* €22.50, 2 May-30 Sep. 2019

PARENTIS EN BORN 7D1 (6km SW Rural) 44.34562, -1.09241 **Camping L'Arbre d'Or,** 75 Route du Lac, 40160 Landes **05 58 78 41 50; contact@arbre-dor. com; www.arbre-dor.com**

🐕 ♿ WC ⚓ ♿ ⚲ ⚐ ✉ 🦋 ⚓ Ⓣ ⓘ 🛒 ⚓ nr ⚓ ✂ 🏊

Leave the Bordeaux m'way A63/N10 in Liposthey and drive twds Parentis (D43). The campsite is sp in Parentis. 4*, Med, mkd, pt shd, EHU inc (10A); bbq; sw nr; twin axles; 25% statics; phone; Eng spkn; adv bkg acc; ccard acc; games area; CKE. *"Vg; lake 500m fr site, watersports in lake; v friendly mgmt; bike hire."* €30.00, 1 Apr-30 Oct. 2017

PARENTIS EN BORN 7D1 (3km NW Rural) 44.35153, -1.10959 **Camping Calède,** Quartier Lahitte, 40160 Parentis-en-Born **05 58 78 44 63; contact@ camping-calede.com; www.camping-calede.com**

🐕 €0.50 ♿ WC ⚓ ♿ ⚐ ✉ 🦋 Ⓣ ⚓ 🛒 nr ⚓

Exit N10 junc 17 onto D43 to Parentis-en-Born; then take D652 dir Biscarrosse; site in 3km on L. Sp adj lake. 2*, Med, hdg, pt shd, EHU (10A) €3.30; gas; bbq; sw nr; phone; Eng spkn; adv bkg acc; sailing; fishing; CKE. *"Peaceful site in remote location; well-kept pitches & san facs; friendly, helpful staff; site yourself if office clsd; rec."* €22.00, 6 Apr-26 Oct. 2019

PARIS 3D3 (11km W Urban) 48.86843, 2.23471 **Camping Indigo Paris Bois de Boulogne,** 2 Allée du Bord de l'Eau, 75016 Paris **01 45 24 30 00; paris@ camping-indigo.com; www.camping-indigo.com or www.campingparis.fr**

12 ♿ €4.70 ♿ (htd) WC ⚓ ♿ ⚐ ✉ MP 🌿 Ⓗ nr 🛒 nr ⚓

Site bet bdge of Puteaux & bdge of Suresnes. App fr A1: take Blvd Périphérique W to Bois de Boulogne exit at Porte Maillot; foll camp sp. App fr A6: Blvd Périphérique W to Porte Dauphine exit at Porte Maillot; foll camp sp. App fr Pont de Sèvres (A10, A11): on bdge take R lane & take 2nd rd R mkd Neuilly-sur-Seine; rd runs parallel to Seine; cont to site ent. App fr A13: after St Cloud Tunnel foll sp twd Paris; immed after x-ing Rv Seine, 1st R sp Bois de Boulogne; foll camp sps; traff lts at site ent. NB Sharp turn to site, poorly sp fr N - watch for lge 'Parking Borne de l'Eau 200m'. 4*, V lge, hdg, mkd, hdstg, pt shd, pt sl, EHU (10A) €6.20; gas; twin axles; TV; 10% statics; phone; bus to metro; Eng spkn; adv bkg rec; ccard acc; CKE. *"Busy site in excel location; easy access A13; conv cent Paris - Metro Porte Maillot 4km; some v sm pitches; walk over Suresne bdge for shops, food mkt, supmkt etc; some tour ops on site; gd security; refurbished san facs (2014); vg; food truck; new rest (2015)."* €40.20, P18. 2019

PARIS 3D3 (22km NW Urban) 48.94001, 2.14563 **Sandaya Paris Maisons Laffitte,** 1 Rue Johnson, 78600 Maisons-Laffitte **01 39 12 21 91; pml@ sandaya.fr; www.sandaya..co.uk**

🐕 €5 ♿ (htd) WC ⚓ ♿ ⚐ ✉ 🦋 Ⓣ ⓘ ⚓ 🛒 ⚓

Easy access fr A13 sp Poissy; take D308 to Maisons-Laffitte; foll site sp bef town cent. Fr A15 take N184 S fr Poissy, foll sp St Germain; approx 6km after x-ing Rv Seine & approx 300m after x-ing lge steel bdge, take L lane ready for L turn onto D308 to Maison-Laffitte; foll camp sp. Or D301 to St Denis, then A86 exit Bezons, then dir Poissy, Noailles, Sartrouville & Maisons-Laffitte. NB Narr app rd diff due parked cars & high kerbs. 4*, Lge, hdg, mkd, pt shd, serviced pitches; EHU (10-16A); gas; TV; 40% statics; Eng spkn; adv bkg acc; ccard acc; games area; CKE. *"V busy, popular site on island in Rv Seine; ideal for visiting Paris (20 min by RER), Disneyland & Versailles; RER stn 1km; mobilis ticket covers rlwy, metro & bus for day in Paris; friendly, helpful staff; poss ltd facs LS."* €25.00, 3 Apr-1 Nov, P03. 2019

PARTHENAY *4H1* (1km SW Urban) *46.64160, -0.26740*
Camping Flower du Bois Vert, 14 Rue Boisseau, Le Tallud, 79200 Parthenay 05 49 64 78 43; camping boisvert@orange.fr; www.camping-boisvert.com

🏕🏕 (htd) 🇼🇩 ▦ ♨ ⚙ ✉ 🅿 ⊞ 🦋 ♒ ⊤ ⦿ ♿ 🏃 ▱ ✂ 🏊 (htd) ⛵

Site on D743 to Niort. Sp fr N & S. Fr S 1km bef town turn L at sp La Roche-sur-Yon immed after rv bdge turn R; site on R in 500m. 4*, Med, hdg, hdstg, mkd, pt shd, pt sl, EHU (6 or 10A) inc; bbq; TV; 10% statics; phone; adv bkg acc; fishing; games rm; bike hire; tennis; boating; CKE. "1 hr rvside walk to town; m'van o'night area adj; noisy nr main rd & bar; Wed mkt; gd NH to Spain; conv Futuroscope; new facs, plenty hot water; well spaced hdg grass pitches; excel facs."
€28.50, 4 Apr-31 Oct. **2017**

PARTHENAY *4H1* (9km W Urban) *46.62214, -0.35139*
Camp Municipal Les Peupliers, 79130 Azay-sur-Thouet 05 49 95 37 13 (Mairie); mairie-azaysurthouet@ cc-parthenay.fr; www.tourisme-gatine.com

🏕🏕 ▦ ✉ 🦋 ♒ nr ▱

Fr Parthenay take D949 dir Secondigny to Azay-sur-Thouet; turn L onto D139 dir St Pardoux; site on L in 200m. Site adj stadium on rvside. 2*, Sm, mkd, pt shd, EHU (10A) €3.50; bbq. "Pleasant, peaceful site; barrier open ltd hrs; clean dated san facs; poss inadequate number high ssn; MH area outside of campsite; gd." **€9.00, 15 Jun-30 Sep.** **2017**

PARTHENAY *4H1* (9km W Rural) *46.65738, -0.34816*
FFCC Camping La Chagnée (Baudoin), 79450 St Aubin le Cloud 05 49 95 31 44 or 06 71 10 09 66 (mob); gerard.baudoin3@wanadoo.fr; www.lachagnee vacances.fr

12 🐕 🏕🏕 🇼🇩 ▦ ♨ ⚙ 🅿 ✉ 🦋 🎭 nr

Fr Parthenay on D949BIS dir Secondigny. Turn R in Azay-sur-Thouet onto D139 dir St Aubin, site on R in 2km, look for 'Gîte' sp. 3*, Sm, hdg, pt shd, terr, EHU (10A) €3.50; Eng spkn; fishing. "Charming, CL-type organic fm site o'looking lake; friendly, extremely helpful & welcoming owners; v clean, modern facs; OAY providing use own san in winter; maps loaned for walks; excel; m'van only during period Nov-Mar; fmhse meal avail weekly; vg lake fishing; rec." **€15.00** **2017**

PAU *8F2* (5km E Rural) *43.28909, -0.26985*
FFCC Camping Les Sapins, Route de Tarbes, 64320 Ousse 05 59 81 79 03 or 05 59 81 74 21 (LS); lessapins64@orange.fr

12 🏕🏕 ▦ ✉ 🅿 ⦿ nr 🎭 nr

Site adj Hôtel des Sapins on S side of D817 (Pau-Tarbes rd). 3*, Sm, pt shd, EHU (4-10A) inc; fishing. "Popular, pleasant NH; red facs LS; helpful owners; NH only; bus svrs infrequent." **€17.00** **2019**

PAU *8F2* (6km W Rural) *43.32081, -0.45096*
Camping Le Terrier, Ave du Vert-Galant, 64230 Lescar 05 59 81 01 82; camping.terrier@wanadoo.fr; www.camping-terrier64.com

12 🐕 🏕🏕 (htd) 🇼🇩 ▦ ♨ ⚙ 🅿 ✉ 🦋 ♒ ⊤ ⦿ ♿ 🏃 ▱ ✂ 🏃 (covrd) ⛵

Exit A64 junc 9.1 onto D817; in 3km, at rndabt junc with D509, turn L onto Blvd de L'Europe; in 1.5km at rndabt turn R onto Av du Vert Galant; site on R in 1km, 200m bef rv bdge. NB. If app on Av du Galant fr S, rec cont to next rndabt & app fr opp dir due tight, concealed ent. 3*, Med, mkd, hdg, shd, EHU 6A; gas; bbq (elec); TV; 50% statics; bus; adv bkg acc; ccard acc; car wash; rv fishing adj; tennis; games rm; CCI. "Gd base for Pau & district; helpful new owners (2010); improved access (2011); vg clean san facs; excel food; no twin axles; 2 golf courses nr; excel." **€21.00** **2019**

"There aren't many sites open at this time of year"

If you're travelling outside peak season remember to call ahead to check site opening dates – even if the entry says 'open all year'.

PAUILLAC *7C2* (1km S Rural) *45.18515, -0.74218*
FFCC Camp Municipal Les Gabarreys, Route de la Rivière, 33250 Pauillac 05 56 59 10 03 or 05 56 73 30 50; camping.les.gabarreys@wanadoo.fr; www.pauillac-medoc.com

🐕 €3 🏕🏕 🇼🇩 ▦ ♨ 🅿 ✉ 🦋 🎭 nr ▱

On ent Pauillac on D206, turn R at rndabt, sp site. On app Quays, turn R bef 'Maison du Vin'. Site on L in 1km. 4*, Med, hdg, hdstg, mkd, pt shd, EHU (5-10A) €5-6; bbq; TV; 6% statics; Eng spkn; adv bkg acc; ccard acc; games rm; CKE. "Peaceful, well-kept, well-equipped site on estuary; nice clean san facs; conv wine chateaux; cycle rtes; mkt Sat; excel." **€23.00, 3 Apr-8 Oct.** **2017**

PAYRAC *7D3* (1km N Rural) *44.80574, 1.47479*
Camping Panoramic, Route de Loupiac, 46350 Payrac-en-Quercy 05 65 37 98 45 or 06 17 95 63 21; info@campingpanoramic.com; www.camping panoramic.com

12 🏕🏕 (htd) 🇼🇩 ▦ ♨ ⚙ 🅿 ✉ 🦋 🎭 ♒ ⊤ ⦿ ⊞ 🦋 nr ▱ ✂

N fr Payrac on D820, turn L onto D147 sp Loupiac (200m after 'end of vill' sp), site 300m on R. 2*, Sm, hdstg, pt shd, pt sl, EHU (5A) €3 (poss rev pol); gas; bbq; sw nr; TV; 10% statics; phone; Eng spkn; adv bkg acc; bike hire; canoe hire; CKE. "Well-run, clean site; OK san facs - poss inadequate if site full; poss muddy in bad weather but hdstg avail; pool 400m; friendly, helpful Dutch owner; gd walking; excel winter NH." **€15.00** **2019**

PEILLAC *2F3* (2km N Rural) *47.72635, -2.21430*
Camp Municipal du Pont d'Oust, 56220 Peillac 02 99
91 39 33 or 02 99 91 26 76 (Mairie); www.peillac.fr

⛺ (htd) 🚽 ♿ 🚿 🍽 🛒 ℉ nr ⊕ nr 🛖 nr

SW fr La Gacilly on D777; in 6km turn L onto D14 sp
Les Fougerêts; cont thro Les Fougerêts, site on R in
1km opp canal. Or N fr Peillac on D14, folls sp Pont
d'Oust; site on L. 2*, Med, pt shd, EHU (10A) €3.20
(poss rev pol); bbq. *"Nice, peaceful site by Rv Oust &
canal; spacious pitches, soft when wet; helpful warden
calls, site yourself; v flat, ideal for cycling; pretty vill;
vg; mkd cycling and walking rtes fr site; pool adj; pay at
Mairie during May."* €12.70, 1 May-30 Sep.   2017

PELUSSIN *9B2* (1km SE Rural) *45.41375, 4.69143*
Camping Bel'Epoque du Pilat, La Vialle, Route de
Malleval, 42410 Pélussin 04 74 87 66 60; contact@
camping-belepoque.fr; www.camping-belepoque.fr

🐕 €2.50 ⛺ (htd) 🅱 🚽 ♿ 🚿 🍽 🛒 🦋 🎣 ℉ ⊕ 🛖 nr 🖊 🛶
🏊 (htd) 🚣

Exit A7 junc 10 just S of Lyon foll N86 dir Serrières; in
Chavanay turn R onto D7 to Pélussin, then at rndabt
turn L and foll D79 S & foll site sp. Rec do not use sat
nav! 3*, Sm, hdg, pt shd, pt sl, EHU (6A) €3.50; gas; bbq;
phone; train 10km; Eng spkn; adv bkg acc; ccard acc;
games area; tennis; CKE. *"In nature reserve; excel touring
base; vg walking; vg, peaceful site; supmkt in Pelussin;
friendly, helpful owners."* €28.00, 1 Apr-30 Sep.   2017

PENESTIN *2G3* (3km E Rural) *47.47687, -2.45204*
Camping Les Pins, Chemin du Val au Bois de la
Lande, 56760 Pénestin 02 99 90 33 13; camping.
lespins@wanadoo.fr; www.camping-despins.fr

🐕 €1.50 ⛺ (htd) 🅱 🚽 ♿ 🚿 🍽 🛒 🎣 ℉ 🍽 🚲 🛖 🖊
🏊 (covrd, htd) 🚣 🏖 sand 3km

Fr Roche-Bernard take D34 dir Pénestin, 2km
bef town turn L sp Camping Les Pins. Site on R in
250m. 2*, Med, mkd, hdg, pt shd, pt sl, EHU (10A)
€3; bbq; red long stay; twin axles; TV; 33% statics;
Eng spkn; adv bkg acc; waterslide; games area; bike
hire; games rm; CKE. *"Sun mkt; excel; fab countryside;
sandy beaches nrby; gd facs, exceptionally clean; gd
welcome."* €26.00, 1 Apr-18 Oct.   2015

PENESTIN *2G3* (3km S Coastal) *47.44527, -2.48416*
Camping Les Iles, La Pointe du Bile, 56760 Pénestin
02 99 90 30 24; reservation@camping-lesiles.fr;
www.camping-des-iles.fr

🐕 €3.90 ⛺ 🅱 🚽 ♿ 🚿 🍽 🛒 🍽 ⊕ 🚲 🛖 🖊 🛶 (htd)
🚣 🏖 sand direct access

Fr La Roche Bernard take D34 to Pénestin; cont
on D201 for 2.5km & foll site sp. 4*, Lge, mkd, hdg,
pt shd, serviced pitches; EHU (10A) inc (poss rev
pol); gas; bbq (charcoal, elec); TV; 10% statics; Eng
spkn; adv bkg acc; ccard acc; bike hire; waterslide;
fishing adj; horseriding; tennis; games rm; CKE.
*"Lovely site o'looking sea; no o'fits over 7m high ssn;
direct access to shoreline; some pitches sm; max 1
dog; helpful staff; clean modern unisex san facs; mkt
Sun (also Wed in Jul/Aug); gd cycling, walking; vg."*
€45.00, 12 Apr-30 Sep, B06.   2019

PERIERS *1D4* (6km NE Rural) *49.21581, -1.35093*
Camping Le Clos Castel, 50500 Raids 02 33 17 23 61
or 07789 227484 (mob); lecloscastel@live.com;
www.camping-france-normandy.com

12 🐕 ⛺ 🅱 🚽 ♿ 🚿 🍽 🛒 🍽 nr

S fr Carentan on D791 to Raids; cont past vill on
D791 for 300m; turn R to site, ent on R in 100m. Or
N fr Periers on D791; turn L 300m bef Raids & then
as bef. Site well sp. Sm, hdstg, unshd, EHU (6A) inc;
bbq; Eng spkn; adv bkg acc. *"Site has B&B; helpful
British owners; dogs free; conv D-day beaches; excel."*
€17.50   2016

PERIERS *1D4* (5km SE Rural) *49.16638, -1.34916*
FFCC Aire Naturelle Municipale Le Clos Vert, 50190
St Martin-d'Aubigny 02 33 46 57 03 or 02 33 07 73 92
(Mairie); mairie-st-martin-daubigny@wanadoo.fr;
www.gites-de-france-manche.com

⛺ 🅱 🚽 ♿ 🚿 🍽 🛒 🦋 ℉ nr ⊕ nr 🛖 nr 🖊

E fr Périers on D900 dir St Lô; in 4km turn R sp
St Martin-d'Aubigny; site on L in 500m adj church.
Sm, pt shd, EHU (6A) €2.50; bbq; golf 2km; fishing
2km; tennis 2km; CKE. *"Charming, sm, well-kept, useful
site; facs basic but OK; easy 70km run to Cherbourg;
no twin axles; basic quiet site in vill, bar & rest within
walking dist; conv for ports; pay at Marie if no one calls
for payment."* €10.50, 15 Apr-15 Oct.   2018

PERIGUEUX *7C3* (13km NE Rural) *45.21975, 0.86383*
Camping Le Bois du Coderc, Route des Gaunies,
24420 Antonne-et-Trigonant 05 53 05 99 83; coderc-
camping@wanadoo.fr; www.campinglecoderc.com

12 🐕 €1 ⛺ 🅱 🚽 ♿ 🚿 🍽 🛒 🦋 🍽 ℉ ⊕ nr 🛖 nr 🖊
🏊 (htd) 🛶 shgl adj

NE fr Périgueux on N21 twd Limoges, thro Antonne
approx 1km turn R at x-rds bet car park & rest. Site
in 500m. 3*, Med, hdg, pt shd, EHU (10A) inc; bbq;
sw nr; TV; 10% statics; phone; Eng spkn; adv bkg acc;
ccard acc; games rm; ice; games area; CKE. *"Secluded,
pleasant, peaceful site; most pitches spacious; rallies
welcome; gd value, inc rest; highly rec; quiet; well
maintained; excel site; view of website a must; gd
birdwatching; v helpful owners, v eager to please; excel
htd pool; excel wifi fr some pitches; new san block
(2018); excel."* €22.00   2018

PERIGUEUX *7C3* (20km SE Rural) *45.13165, 0.92867*
Camping de la Pélonie, La Bourgie, 24330 St Antoine-
d'Auberoche 05 53 07 55 78; info@campinglapelonie.
com; www.lapelonie.com

🐕 €2 ⛺ 🅱 🚽 ♿ 🚿 🍽 🍽 ℉ 🚲 🛖 🖊 🏊 (htd) 🚣

Fr Périgueux on A89 twd Brive; 5km past St Pierre-
de-Chignac, site sp on L; turn L at picnic area - go
under rlwy bdge; site ent on L. 3*, Med, mkd, pt
shd, EHU (10A) €3.80 (poss req long cable); gas;
TV; 20% statics; phone; Eng spkn; adv bkg acc;
ccard acc; CKE. *"Delightful site; pleasant, welcoming
owners; gd, clean, well kept facs; excel facs for
children; some pitches diff lge o'fits; gd touring base."*
€22.00, 18 Apr-10 Oct.   2015

PERIGUEUX *7C3* (8km SE Rural) *45.14900, 0.77880*
Camping Le Grand Dague, Route du Grand Dague,
24750 Atur **05 53 04 21 01; info@legranddague.fr;**
www.legranddague.fr

[icons] €2 (htd) [icons] (htd) [icon]

Fr cent Périgueux, take N21 & A89 twd Brive. Fork
L onto D2 to Atur (main rd bears R). In Atur turn L
after bar/tabac; foll site sp for 2.5km.
4*, Lge, shd, pt sl, EHU (6A) inc; bbq; TV; 70% statics;
phone; Eng spkn; adv bkg acc; ccard acc; games rm;
bike hire; games area; CKE. *"Gd family site; friendly
owners; site immac, even end of ssn; poss unkempt
early ssn; lots to do; ltd touring pitches; excel."*
€39.00, 22 Apr-25 Sep.   **2016**

PERONNE *3C3* (0.9km NE Urban) *49.93424, 2.94140*
Camp Municipal du Brochet, Rue Georges Clémenceau,
80200 Péronne **03 22 84 02 35; peter.v.gent@orange.fr**

[icons] [icon] nr [icon] nr [icon]

Fr N on D1017 turn R into town. L at lights & L
immed after footbdge. 1st R & site on L. Well sp
fr all dirs. Go to town cent then foll 'Intn'l Camping
Site' sps. 1*, Sm, hdstg, pt shd, pt sl, terr, EHU (16A)
inc; phone; bus 500m; Eng spkn; adv bkg acc; CKE.
*"Pleasant, basic site nr park & attractive town; grass
pitches soft when wet; rec arr early high ssn; conv WW1
museum; NH, vg."* **€16.00, 8 Apr-30 Oct.**   **2015**

PERONNE *3C3* (2.6km S Rural) *49.91805, 2.93227*
Camping du Port de Plaisance, Route de Paris,
80200 Péronne **03 22 84 19 31; contact@camping-
plaisance.com; www.camping-plaisance.com**

[icons] €1.30 (htd) [icons] nr [icons] (htrl)

Exit A1/E15 junc 13 dir Peronne on D1029 to D1017.
Site on L o'looking canal. Well sp fr all dirs.
3*, Med, mkd, pt shd, EHU (6-10A) €4.30-7.95 (some
rev pol & long lead poss req); red long stay; Eng
spkn; ccard acc; jacuzzi; fishing. *"Popular NH; helpful,
pleasant staff & owners; gd play park & pool; gates
locked 2200-0800 - when clsd, park outside; vg rest adj;
rec visit to war museum in Péronne castle; popular with
ralliers; facs need upgrading; vg site, pleasant situation
nr a canal; gd size pitches; gd dog walk along canal;
hypmkt 3km; san facs clean but tired; site self if recep
clsd."* **€27.00, 1 Mar-31 Oct.**   **2017**

PERONNE *3C3* (2km NW Rural) *49.94409, 2.90826*
Camping La Tortille, L'Orgibet, 80200 Cléry-sur-Somme
**03 22 83 17 59 or 03 22 84 10 45 (LS); jsg-bred@
wanadoo.fr**

[icons] €1.30 [icons] nr [icon]

Exit A1/E15 junc 13.1 onto D938 to Cléry, dir Péronne.
Site sp on rvside in 5km. 2*, Med, hdstg, hdg, pt shd,
EHU (10A) €3.60; bbq; red long stay; 10% statics; adv
bkg acc; rv fishing; games area; CKE. *"Peaceful site;
sm, uneven pitches; clean modern san facs; conv for A1
m'way."* **€21.50, 1 Apr-31 Oct.**   **2017**

PERPIGNAN *8G4* (6km S Rural) *42.63754, 2.89819*
Camping Les Rives du Lac, Chemin de la Serre, 66180
Villeneuve-de-la-Raho **04 68 55 83 51; camping.
villeneuveraho@wanadoo.fr**

[icons] €1.60 (htd) [icons] (htd) [icon] 1.5km

Fr A9 exit Perpignan Sud, dir Porte d'Espagne. In
3km turn R onto N9 dir Le Boulou. In 1km after
Auchan supmkt take slip rd to N91 dir Villeneuve-
de-la-Raho. In 2km rd becomes D39, turn R to
site, site on L in 1km. Beware ford on D39 in v wet
weather (usually dry). 2*, Med, hdstg, mkd, pt shd,
pt sl, EHU (6A) inc; bbq (elec, gas); sw nr; 10% statics;
phone; Eng spkn; adv bkg acc; ccard acc; tennis 2km;
watersports 1.5km; fishing 1.5km; CKE. *"Lakeside site
with views; poor san facs & insufficient for site size;
busy cycling/jogging path adj; conv trips to Spain; busy
public beach nr."* **€20.00, 15 Mar-15 Nov.**   **2019**

PERROS GUIREC *1D2* (1km SE Coastal) *48.79657,
-3.42689* **Camp Municipal Ernest Renan,** 22700
Louannec **02 96 23 11 78; www.camping-louannec.fr**

[icons] €1.35 [icons] [icon] (htd) sand adj

1km W of Louannec on D6. 3*, Lge, unshd, EHU
(6A) inc; gas; TV; Eng spkn; adv bkg acc; watersports
adj; fishing adj; games rm. *"Well-kept site; pitches on
seashore; clean san facs; clsd 1200-1530, little parking
space outside; highly rec."*
€17.00, 1 Jun-30 Sep.   **2017**

PERROS GUIREC *1D2* (3km NW Coastal) *48.82798,
-3.47623* **Sandaya Le Ranolien,** Boulevard du Semaphore,
Ploumanac'h, 22700 Perros-Guirec **02 96 91 65 65;
ranolien@sandaya.fr; www.sanraya.co.uk**

[icons] €5 (htd) [icons] (covrd, htd) sand

At Perros-Guirec harbour turn R at Marina foll sp
Trégastel. Up hill above coast into Perros Guirec
town. Cont strt thro traff lts & into La Clarté vill;
strt at traff lts & sharp R at Camping & Le Ranolien
sp. Ent shortly on L. Foll Trégastel sp all way.
5*, V lge, mkd, pt shd, pt sl, serviced pitches; EHU
(16A) inc; 75% statics; Eng spkn; adv bkg acc; ccard
acc; waterslide; horseriding; fishing; tennis; golf. *"Excel
beaches; spa; many tour op statics; vg coastal walks
nrby."* **€25.00, 10 Apr-18 Sep.**   **2019**

PERTUIS *10E3* (8km N Rural) *43.75860, 5.50407*
Camping de La Bonde, 84240 Cabrières-d'Aigues
**04 90 77 63 64; campingdelabonde@wanadoo.fr;
www.campingdelabonde.com**

[icons] 12 [icons] €1.80 [icons] [icon]

NE fr Pertuis on D956, fork L onto D9 (sp Cabrières
& Etang de la Bonde). At x-rds in 8km turn R onto
D27. Site on L in 200m. 2*, Med, pt shd, EHU (6A)
(poss rev pol) €3.20; gas; sw; 80% statics; adv bkg
acc; ccard acc; tennis; fishing; watersports; games
area; CKE. *"Lovely lakeside & beach; ltd facs LS; phone
ahead to check site open; pool 8km; gd cycling area."*
€18.00   **2017**

PESMES 6G2 (0.5km S Rural) 47.27612, 5.56451
Camp Municipal La Colombière, Route de Dole, 70140
Pesmes 03 84 31 20 15; campcolombiere@aol.com

🏕🐕 €1.20 ♿ �📶 🏊 🍴 ⏰ nr 🛒 nr

On D475 halfway bet Gray & Dole. S fr Pesmes
immed on L after x-ing rv bdge. N fr Dole, site
sp on R immed bef rest at rv bdge. 2*, Med, hdg,
pt shd, EHU (6-10A) €2.30-3.60; phone; Eng spkn;
adv bkg rec; ccard acc; bike hire. "Picturesque vill;
helpful, friendly staff; gd san facs; vg; no twin axles."
€12.60, 1 May-31 Oct.   2018

PEYRELEAU 10E1 (1.2km NW Rural) 44.19810,
3.19442 **FFCC Camping Les Bords du Tarn,** 12720
Mostuéjouls 05 65 62 62 94; lesbordsdutarn@
orange.fr; www.campinglesbordsdutarn.com

🏕🐕 €2 ♿ �📶 🏊 ♿ 🍽 / 🌳 ⛱ 🍴 ⏰ 🛒 ⛰ 🚴 ♨ (htd)

Exit A75 junc 44.1 onto D29 to Aguessac; turn L onto
D907 dir Le Rozier & Peyreleau; site on R 1km bef Le
Rozier. NB Do not use exit 44 fr A75 (as sat nav might
instruct). 3*, Med, mkd, pt shd, pt sl, EHU (10A) €3.50;
bbq (charcoal, gas); sw nr; 10% statics; phone; Eng spkn;
adv bkg acc; ccard acc; cycling; fishing; games rm; canoe
hire; tennis; CKE. "Site in beautiful area by rv; some v lge
pitches; climbing; gd for rv sports; paragliding; modern
san facs; gd walking; conv Gorges du Tarn & Gorges de la
Jonte; excel." €36.00, 16 Jun-2 Sep.   2019

PEZENAS 10F1 (0.5km SW Urban) 43.45419, 3.41573
Campotel Municipal de Castelsec, Chemin de Castelsec,
34120 Pézenas 04 67 98 04 02; contact@camping-
pezenas.com; www.camping-gites-herault.com

🏕🐕 €1.40 ♿ �📶 🏊 ♿ 🍽 / 🌳 🍴 ⏰ 🛒 nr ⛰

Fr Béziers take N9 to Pézenas; foll Cent Ville sps
fr rndabt at edge of town onto Route de Béziers;
in 600m at next rndabt (at junc with D13) go strt
over into Ave de Verdun; in 400m take 1st L after
McDonalds & pharmacy at ent to Carrefour supmkt;
foll Campotel sps; site on L in 300m. 2*, Sm, mkd, pt
shd, pt sl, terr, EHU (10A) €2.90; TV; 30% statics; adv
bkg acc; tennis adj; CKE. "Great little site; friendly staff;
some pitches unsuitable lge o'fits; easy walk/cycle to
interesting town; toy museum worth visit; vg; updated
san facs (2019)." €16.00, 1 Apr-30 Oct.   2019

PHALSBOURG 5D3 (3km N Rural) 48.78300, 7.25020
FFCC Camping de Bouleaux (CC de F), 5 Rue des Trois
Journeaux, 57370 Vilsberg 03 87 24 18 72; info@
campinglesbouleaux.fr; www.campinglesbouleaux.fr
or www.campingclub.asso.fr

🏕🐕 €2 ♿ �📶 🏊 ♿ 🍽 / 🅿 🌳 🍴 ⛰

Fr A4 exit junc 44 dir Phalsbourg. At x-rds turn L
sp D661 Sarreguemines. Site on R in 2km. NB Site
ent off steep descent on D661. Lge o'fits take care
leaving site & turning L - watch rear overhangs.
3*, Lge, pt shd, EHU (6A) inc; bbq; 15% statics; phone;
Eng spkn; adv bkg acc; CKE. "Peaceful, well-kept site;
welcoming, helpful Dutch owners; barrier clsd 1930;
gd facs; access to some pitches poss diff, some uneven;
conv m'way & NH to/fr Germany/Austria; gd NH."
€18.50, 1 Apr-18 Oct.   2015

PHALSBOURG 5D3 (6km SW Rural) 48.71922, 7.22643
Camping du Plan Incliné, Hoffmuhl, 57820 Henridorff
03 87 25 30 13 or 06 71 21 86 91 (mob); camping
planincline@wanadoo.fr; www.campingplanincline.fr

🏕🐕 €1 ♿ ⏰ 🏊 ♿ 🍽 / 🍴 ⏰ 🛒 nr ⛰ ♨ 🏊

Exit A4 at junc 44. In Phalsbourg take D38 twds
Lutzelbourg; turn R onto D98 dir Arzviller & foll sp
to Henridorff & site on R adj rv (narr ent).
3*, Med, hdg, hdstg, pt shd, EHU (6A) €3; gas; sw nr;
red long stay; 60% statics; phone; Eng spkn; adv bkg
acc; fishing adj; boating adj; CKE. "In wooded valley;
friendly, helpful owner; vg rest; grnd soft when wet;
cycle path to Strasbourg; adj to unique canal; poss dif
ent for lge units; v poor, run-down site; gd for NH or
short stay." €18.40, 1 Apr-15 Oct.   2018

PICQUIGNY 3C3 (0.3km E Urban) 49.9445, 2.1458
Camping De L'Abime (formerly Municipal), 66 Rue
du Marais, 80310 Picquigny 03 22 51 25 83 or 06 51
64 40 25; contact@campingdelabime-picquigny.fr;
www.campingdelabime-picquigny.fr

🏕🐕 ♿ ⏰ 🏊 ♿ / 🌳 🍴 nr ⛰

Site sp fr town cent. 2*, Med, pt shd, EHU (10A)
inc; 80% statics; adv bkg rec; rv; fishing. "Pleasant,
well laid out site; gd, clean, modern san facs; some
shd pitches bet statics; occasional noise fr rlwy line;
WW1 war cemetery nr town; nice, small, simple
site; easy walking dist fr town; many places to visit."
€26.00, 1 Apr-31 Oct.   2018

PIERRE BUFFIERE 7B3 (2km SE Rural) 45.68937,
1.37101 **Camp Intercommunal Chabanas,** 87260
Pierre-Buffière 05 55 00 96 43; www.pierre-buffiere.com

🏕🐕 €1.14 ♿ ⏰ 🏊 ♿ / 🌳 🍴 nr ⛰

Approx 20km S of Limoges on A20, take exit 40 onto
D420 S bound; site on L in 500m. Foll sps for 'Stade-
Chabanas'. 3*, Med, hdg, mkd, pt shd, pt sl, EHU (10A)
inc (poss rev pol); phone; adv bkg acc; fishing; CKE.
"Clean, quiet site; helpful staff; excel clean san facs;
some pitches diff for lge o'fits; no twin axles; warden
on site 1600-2200, but gate poss locked all day LS
(code issued, phone ahead); conv Limoges; excel NH
fr A20; conv for Oradour Sur Glane; gd size plots."
€13.00, 15 May-30 Sep.   2018

PIERREFITTE SUR SAULDRE 4G3 (6km NE Rural)
47.54444, 2.19138 **Sandaya Les Alicourts,** Domaine
des Alicourts, 41300 Pierrefitte-sur-Sauldre 02 54 88
63 34; www.sandaya.fr/nos-campings/les-alicourts

🏕🐕 €7 ♿ ⏰ 🏊 ♿ / 🅿 🍴 🍴 ⏰ 🛒 🛒 ⛰ ♨

Fr S of Lamotte-Beuvron, turn L on D923. After
14km turn R on D24E sp Pierrefitte. After 750m turn
L, foll sp to site approx 750m on R. 5*, Med, pt shd,
EHU (6A) inc; bbq; sw; 10% statics; Eng spkn; adv bkg
acc; ccard acc; waterslide; bike hire; games rm; tennis;
CKE. "Excel, peaceful site; skating rink; kayak/pedalo
hire; extra for lakeside pitches; fitness cent; gd, clean
facs; v lge pitches." €56.00, 4 May-1 Sep, L22.   2019

PIERREFONDS *3D3* (0.5km N Urban) *49.35427, 2.97564* **Camping Le Coeur de la Foret (formerly Municipal de Batigny),** 34 Rue de l'Armistice, 60350 Pierrefonds **03 44 42 80 83 or 06 45 31 64 21 (mob); contact@lecoeurdelaforet.fr; www.lecoeurdelaforet.fr**

🐕 €1 � (htd) WD 🚿 🔽 ⚓ / MSP ⓗ nr ⚓nr

Take D973 fr Compiegne; after 14km site on L adj sp for Pierrefonds at ent to vill. 3*, Med, hdg, pt shd, serviced pitches; EHU (10A) €2.80 (poss rev pol); red long stay; adv bkg acc; CKE. "Attractive, well-run, busy site; tight pitches for lge o'fits; clean san facs; poss unkempt LS; site yourself if recep clsd; cycle rte to Compiegne; nr Armistice train & museum; gd site; walking dist to vill, Chateau Pierrefonds; bike rental avail." **€20.40, 6 Apr-30 Sep.** 2019

PIEUX, LES *1C4* (3km SW Coastal) *49.49444, -1.84194* **Le Grand Large,** 11 Route de Grand Large, 50340 Les Pieux **02 33 52 40 75; info@legrandlarge.com; www.legrandlarge.com**

🐕 ♟ (htd) WD 🚿 ⚓ 🔽 / MSP 🦋 ♈ ⓩ ⓗ nr ⚓ 🔀 / 🏊 (htd, indoor) 🛒 🏖 sand adj

Fr ferry at 1st rndabt take 1st exit sp Cent Ville. Closer to town cent foll old N13 sp Caen. In about 1.5km branch R onto D900 then L onto D650 sp Carteret. Foll this rd past Les Pieux, cont on D650 to sp Super U. Turn R & foll site sp onto D517, then D117 for 3km until reaching beach rd to site, site on L in 2km. 4*, Lge, hdg, mkd, pt shd, EHU (10A) €6.50; gas; bbq; red long stay; TV; 40% statics; phone; Eng spkn; adv bkg acc; ccard acc; tennis; horseriding 4km; games rm; outdoor games. "Well-run site; rec for families; 1 dog per pitch; dir access to superb lge beach; friendly staff; clean modern san facs; o'fits over 8m by request; barrier clsd 22.00-08.00; conv Cherbourg ferries but arr not rec after dark due sm country lanes; outside pitches avail for early dep for ferries; mkt Fri." **€38.00, 4 Apr-20 Sep, N07.** 2019

PISSOS *7D1* (0.5km E Rural) *44.30469, -0.76817* **Camp Municipal l'Arriu,** 40410 Pissos **05 58 08 90 38 or 05 58 04 41 40 (LS); mairie@pissos.fr; www.pissos.fr**

♟ 🔽 / 🏊

Fr N exit N10 junc 18 onto D834 to Pissos; at x-rds turn L onto D43 sp Sore; site on R in 500m, sp. 3*, Med, shd, EHU (6A) inc; red long stay; ice; rv fishing 300m. "Lge pitches; pool 500m; excel." **€15.00, 1 Jul-15 Sep.** 2019

PITHIVIERS *4F3* (8km S Rural) *48.10365, 2.24142* **Camping Le Clos des Tourterelles,** Rue des Rendillons, 45300 Bouzonville-aux-Bois **02 38 33 01 00 or 06 79 48 36 18 (mob); leclosdestourterelles@sfr.fr; www.camping-clos-tourterelles.fr**

12 ♟ (htd) WD 🚿 ⚓ 🔽 / 🦋 🔀

S fr Pithiviers on D921 twds Jargeau; enter Bouzonville; turn R immed bef cafe; site 500m on R; sp in vill. 2*, Med, pt shd, EHU (16A) inc; 90% statics; adv bkg acc; CKE. "Ltd space for tourers - phone ahead rec; friendly, helpful owners; gd NH; cash only." **€15.00** 2019

PLAISANCE *8F2* (0.5km S Urban) *43.92511, 2.54616* **Camping Municipal Le Moulin De L'Horte,** 12550 Plaisance **05 65 99 72 07 or 05 65 99 75 07; mairie.plaisance12@laposte.net**

🐕 ♟ ⚓ 🔽 / 🦋 ♈ 🏊

Fr D999 Albi-Millau, exit at D127 to Plaisance. R onto D77. Site on R after bdge. 1*, Sm, mkd, pt shd, EHU (6A); gas; bbq; sw nr; twin axles; TV; 10% statics; phone; Eng spkn; adv bkg acc; games rm. " Vg, great quiet site with rv adj to swim in; excel rest & café nrby 0.2km; sm town but v pleasant." **€12.00, 15 Jun-15 Sep.** 2019

PLESTIN LES GREVES *2E2* (4km NE Coastal) *48.66805, -3.60060* **Camp Municipal St Efflam,** Rue Lan-Carré, 22310 Plestin-les-Grèves **02 96 35 62 15; campingmunicipalplestin@wanadoo.fr; www.camping-municipal-bretagne.com**

🐕 €1.30 ♟ WD ⚓ 🔽 / 🔽 ♈ ⓗ ⚓ nr 🔀 🏖 sand 150m

Fr Morlaix on D786 thro Plestin-les-Grèves; foll D786 sp St Efflam down hill to bay; site on R 850m along bay; sp. 3*, Lge, mkd, pt shd, pt sl, terr, EHU (10A) €2.50; gas; bbq; sw nr; Eng spkn; adv bkg req; ccard acc; boating adj; fishing adj; CKE. "Excel; helpful recep; v well kept; modern san facs; municipal pool on site; superb beach nrby; grass pitches liable to waterlogging in wet weather." **€14.00, 26 Mar-3 Oct.** 2016

"That's changed – Should I let the Club know?"

If you find something on site that's different from the site entry, fill in a report and let us know. See camc.com/europereport.

PLOERMEL *2F3* (7.6km N Rural) *47.98425, -2.38191* **FFCC Camping Parc Merlin l'Enchanteur,** 8 Rue du Pont, Vallée de l'Yvel, 56800 Loyat **02 97 93 05 52 or 02 97 73 89 45; camelotpark@wanadoo.fr; www.campingmerlin.com**

12 🐕 €2 ♟ (htd) WD ⚓ 🔽 / MSP 🦋 ♈ ⓩ ⓗ nr ⚓ 🏊 (covrd, htd)

Fr Ploërmel take D766 N sp St Malo. In 5km turn L to Loyat. Site on L on ent vill opp g'ge, adj sm lake. 2*, Med, hdg, mkd, pt shd, EHU (10-16A) €3.50-6 (poss rev pol); gas; bbq; sw nr; red long stay; 10% statics; adv bkg acc; ccard acc; games area; tennis; bike hire; fishing; watersports 4km; CKE. "Peaceful site; spacious pitches; welcoming British owners; vg clean facs; gd indoor pool; poss soggy in winter; new 60km tarmac cycle trail adj; conv Château Josselin, Lizio & Brocéliande forest with legend of King Arthur; pleasant site; excel walking and cycling; site rather unkept." **€20.00** 2018

PLOERMEL *2F3* (10km S Rural) *47.86354, -2.44612*
Camping Domaine du Roc, Rue Beaurivage, 56460 Le
Roc-St André **02 97 74 91 07 or 06 48 07 68 05 (mob);**
contact@domaine-du-roc.com; www.domaine-du-
roc.com

🏕️⁺₃ ♟♟♟ ♨ ⏦ ♿ 🚿 ♫ 🦋 ⚑ Ⴌ nr ⒽⒾ nr 🛖 nr ⛫ 🏊 (covrd, htd)

Fr N on N166 turn R onto D764/D4 to Le Roc-St
André. Site in approx 3km at end of bdge over
Nantes & Brest Canal. 2*, Med, mkd, hdg, pt shd,
EHU (6A) €3.50; bbq; 50% statics; adv bkg acc; ccard
acc; CKE. "Peaceful, well-situated site; gd touring
base; excel cycle rtes adj canal; v helpful staff."
€18.00, 1 Apr-1 Nov. 2015

PLOERMEL *2F3* (10km NW Rural) *47.96932, -2.47010*
Camping La Vallée du Ninian, Route du Lac, Le
Rocher, 56800 Taupont **02 97 93 53 01; infos@
camping-ninian.com; www.camping-ninian.com**

🏕️⁺₁ ♟♟♟ Ⓦ ♨ ⏦ ♿ 🚿 ♫ 🦋 ⚑ Ⴌ ⛫ ✎ 🛷 (htd) 🛶

🏊 sand 4km

Fr Ploërmel cent foll sp to Taupont or Lac au Duc;
N on D8. Thro vill Taupont take L hand turn sp La
Vallée du Ninian; site on L 1km fr Helléan.
3*, Sm, hdg, pt shd, EHU (3-10A) €2-3.50; sw nr; adv
bkg rec; watersports 4km. "Farm produce; helpful,
friendly owners; peaceful; gd facs for children; vg."
€21.50, 1 Apr-30 Sep. 2015

PLOMBIERES LES BAINS *6F2* (10km S Rural)
47.92460, 6.47545 **Camp Municipal Le Val d'Ajol,**
Rue des Oeuvres, 88340 Le Val-d'Ajol **03 29 66 55 17;**
camping@valdajol.fr; www.valdajol.fr

🏕️ ♟♟♟ Ⓦ ♨ ♿ ♫ ⚑ 🦋 📶 Ⴌ nr

Fr N on N57 after Plombières-les-Bains turn onto
D20 sp Le Val-d'Ajol. Site sps in vill. 2*, Sm, hdg,
pt shd, EHU (6A) €2.50; TV; phone; adv bkg acc;
CKE. "Excel site; excel, clean san facs; vg touring
base; lovely; htd covrd pool adj; attractive area."
€13.00, 15 Apr-30 Sep. 2017

PLONEVEZ PORZAY *2E2* (3km W Coastal)
48.14458, -4.26915 **Camping La Plage de Tréguer,**
Plage de Ste Anne-la-Palud, 29550 Plonévez-
Porzay **02 98 92 53 52; camping-treguer-plage@
wanadoo.fr; www.camping-treguer-plage.com**

🏕️⁺₂.₂₀ ♟♟♟ (htd) Ⓦ ♨ ⏦ ♿ 🚿 ♫ ᴹˢᶠ 🦋 ⏦ 🥘 Ⴌ nr ⛫ ⚑

🏊 (indoor) 🛷 🏖️ sand adj

On D107 S fr Châteaulin. After 8km turn R to
Ste Anne-la-Palud & foll sp. 2*, Lge, mkd, hdg,
unshd, EHU (10A) €5; gas; bbq; TV; 10% statics; Eng
spkn; adv bkg acc; ccard acc; games area; games rm;
CKE. "Well-situated touring base; vg, friendly site;
excel beach with direct access; new san facs (2019)."
€31.90, 27 Apr-21 Sep. 2019

PLOUGASNOU *1D2* (1.5km SE Rural) *48.68548,
-3.78530* **Camping Le Trégor,** 130 route du Cosquerou,
29630 Plougasnou **02 98 67 37 64; bookings@
campingdutregor.com; www.campingdutregor.com**

🏕️⁺₁ ♟♟♟ Ⓦ ♨ ⏦ ♫ 🦋 Ⴌ nr ⛺ sand 1.2km

At junc of D46 to Plougasnou. Site is on L just bef
town sp. Sm, mkd, hdg, pt shd, EHU (6-10A) inc; gas;
bbq; sw nr; 40% statics; adv bkg acc; watersports 3km;
CKE. "Well-run site in beautiful area; dated but clean
facs; ideal for walking, cycling & fishing; conv Roscoff
ferries & Morlaix; phone if req NH after end Oct."
€15.00, Easter-11 Nov. 2019

PLOUGASTEL DAOULAS *2E2* (5km NE Coastal)
48.40134, -4.35419 **Camping Saint Jean,** 29470
Plougastel-Daoulas **02 98 40 32 90; info@camping
saintjean.com; www.campingsaintjean.com**

🏕️⁺₂ ♟♟♟ (htd) Ⓦ ♨ ⏦ ♿ 🚿 ♫ ᴹˢᶠ 🦋 📶 ♆ ⏦ 🥘 ⛫ ⚑

🏊 (covrd, htd) 🛷

Fr Brest, take N165 E for approx 12km then leave
m'way after Plougastel exit & foll sp. Site in 2km
at end of rd by rv. 4*, Med, hdstg, hdg, pt shd, pt sl,
terr, EHU (6A) €3 (poss rev pol); TV; 10% statics;
waterslide; games area. "Nice site by rv; steep in
places; gd facs." €25.00, 11 Apr-26 Sep. 2015

PLOUGUENAST *2E3* (2km NW Rural) *48.28653,
-2.72145* **Pinábre Camping & Caravaning,** Lingouet
22150 **02 96 26 80 04; campgite-brittany.com**

♟♟♟ Ⓦ ♨ ⏦ ♫ ⚑ 📶

Site is 50 miles fr St. Malo ferry port, bet Loudeac
and Moncontour off the D768. Sm, pt shd, pt sl,
EHU (16A) €3; bbq; Eng spkn; adv bkg acc; CKE. "Gd
for walks & cycling; sm friendly site; excel facs; close
to N & S coast; open plan, grassy site; quiet; excel."
€12.00, Apr-Sep. 2018

PLOUGUERNEAU *2E2* (3km N Coastal) *48.63048,
-4.52402* **Camping La Grève Blanche,** St Michel, 29880
Plouguerneau **02 98 04 70 35 or 02 98 04 63 97 (LS);**
lroudaut@free.fr; www.campinggreveblanche.com

🏕️ ♟♟♟ (htd) Ⓦ ♨ ⏦ ♫ ⚑ 🦋 📶 ♆ ⏦ Ⴌ nr ⛫ ⚑ 🏖️ sand

Fr Lannilis D13 to Plouguerneau, D32 sp La
Grève, St Michel (look out for lorry rte sp). Avoid
Plouguerneau vill when towing - tight RH bend.
2*, Med, mkd, hdg, unshd, pt sl, terr, EHU (9A) €2.80
(long cable poss req, rev pol); bbq (charcoal, elec, gas);
twin axles; 20% statics; bus adj; Eng spkn; adv bkg acc;
games area; games rm; CCI. "Excel location; sea views;
helpful staff; facs clean & well-kept; LS recep open
eves only; in fog lighthse sounds all night otherwise
quiet; walking coastal rte; san facs clean but dated."
€16.50, 23 Mar-8 Oct. 2018

PLOUGUERNEAU *2E2* (7km NE Coastal) *48.63112, -4.44972* **Camping du Vougot**, Route de Prat-Leden, 29880 Plouguerneau **02 98 25 61 51; campingdu vougot@hotmail.fr; www.campingplageduvougot.com**

🏕 €2.60 � WC ♨ ⅙ 🖥 🗗 🖉 MSP 🦋 ⛱ 🎣 🏊 ≋ sand 250m

Fr N12 at Landerneau exit N onto D770 to Lesneven, then D28/D32 to Plouguerneau. Fr Plouguerneau take D10 dir Guisseny then turn W onto D52 dir Grève-du-Vougot, site sp.

3*, Med, hdg, mkd, pt shd, EHU (10A) €3.30; red long stay; 30% statics; adv bkg acc; ccard acc; watersports nr; CKE. "Gd walking (GR34); interesting area; excel touring base; excel site; v lge pitches; friendly staff."
€20.60, 4 Apr-24 Oct. 2015

PLOUHARNEL *2F3* (7km S Coastal) *47.55458, -3.13198* **Camping Municipal De Penthievre**, Avenue Duquesne, Penthievre 56510 St Pierre, Quiberon **02 07 52 33 86; www.saintpierrequiberon.fr**

🏕 €1.04 � WC ♨ ⅙ 🖥 🗗 🖉 MSP 🦋 ⛱ 🍴 🚻 🛒 ⌂ 🏊 🖉 🎣 adj

Take D768 fr N165 at Auray dir Quiberon. Foll sp at Penthievre. V lge, pt shd, pt sl, EHU (10A) €1.83; gas; bbq; twin axles; phone; bus; train; Eng spkn; ccard acc; games area. "Traditional French municipal; v friendly; ideal watersports & cycling; coastal scenery; Quiberon magnificent; rests, mkt; park & ride; ideal base for visiting southern Brittany; pool 6km; excel."
€15.00, 1 Apr-30 Sep. 2016

POET LAVAL, LE *9D2* (2km SE Rural) *44.52889, 5.02300* **Camp Municipal Lorette**, 26160 Le Poët-Laval **04 75 91 00 62 or 04 75 46 44 12 (Mairie); camping. lorette@wanadoo.fr; www.campinglorette.fr**

🏕 €1.80 � (htd) WC ♨ ⅙ 🖥 🗗 🖉 MSP 🦋 ⛱ 🍴 🚻 🛒 ⌂ 🏊

Site 4km W of Dieulefit on D540. 2*, Sm, mkd, pt shd, pt sl, EHU (1A) €3; bus; Eng spkn; adv bkg acc; ccard acc; tennis; CKE. "Well-kept site with views; lge pitches; clean, modern facs; nr lavender fields (Jun/Jul); mkt in Dieulefit Fri; excel; gd welcome."
€12.50, 1 May-30 Sep. 2016

POILLY-LEZ-GIEN *4G3* (3km S Rural) *47.68233, 2.62289* **Camping Touristique de Gien**, Rue des Iris, 45500 Poilly-lez-Gien **02 38 67 12 50; info@ camping-gien.com; www.camping-gien.com**

🏕 €2 � (htd) WC ♨ ⅙ 🖥 🗗 🖉 MSP 🦋 ⛱ 🍴 🚻 🛒 ⌂ 🏊 🖉 🏊 (covrd) WC

Off D952 Orléans-Nevers rd; turn R over old rv bdge in Gien & then R again onto D951; site on R on Rv Loire. Alt dir fr D940 (Argent-sur-Sauldre - Gien) at rndbt take rd sp Gien. Take L at traff lts bef old bdge; site on R, 1km S of rv. 3*, Lge, hdstg, mkd, hdg, pt shd, pt sl, EHU (10A) €5; bbq; sw nr; red long stay; TV; 20% statics; phone; Eng spkn; adv bkg acc; ccard acc; tennis; canoeing; games rm; bike hire; CKE. "Lovely rvside site; views of old bdge & town some pitches; excel staff; gd san facs; vg facs; no sw allowed in rv; easy walk to town across bdge; porcelain factory 'seconds'; vg value; gd rest; san facs unisex; excel site, highly rec; nice situation; bar adj; gas adj; flock of sheep/goats traverse the site daily." **€27.00, 9 Mar-31 Oct.** 2019

POITIERS *7A2* (12km N Rural) *46.65611, 0.30194* **Camping du Futur,** 9 Rue des Bois, 86170 Avanton **05 49 54 09 67; contact@camping-du-futur.com; www.camping-du-futur.com**

🏕 €1.50 � WC ♨ ⅙ 🖥 🗗 🖉 MSP 🦋 ⛱ 🍴 🚻 nr 🛒 nr ⌂ 🏊

Exit A10 junc 28. After toll take 1st exit at rndabt sp Avanton. Site well sp fr Avanton, but care needed thro Martigny & hotel complex. 3*, Med, hdg, mkd, pt shd, EHU (6-10A) €3.50-3.8; TV; adv bkg acc; games area; games rm; CKE. "Attractive, spacious site in rural setting; well-kept & well-run; helpful French owners; vg clean san facs; ltd early ssn; c'van storage; 5 mins Futuroscope & A10; ideal NH or longer; bread, pastries and breakfast can be ordered; mv service pnt; nr Futurscope attraction; ltd shd; lovely & peaceful; quiet parkland setting; conv for Poitiers; excel."
€19.00, 1 Apr-31 Oct. 2016

POITIERS *7A2* (4.5km S Rural) *46.54367, 0.33230* **Saint-Benoît Camping,** 2 Rue de Passe Lourdain, 86280 St Benoît **05 49 88 48 55; camping.stbenoit@ orange.fr; www.ville-saint-benoit.fr**

🏕 €0.50 � ♨ 🖉 🍴 nr ⌂ nr 🛒 nr ⌂

Fr N or S turn W off D741 to St Benoît, site well sp. 2*, Med, mkd, pt shd, EHU (4A) €3; adv bkg acc; rv fishing adj; watersports adj; CKE. "Pleasant 10 min walk into vill; gd cheap bus service fr vill to Poitiers."
€16.00, 1 Jun-6 Sep. 2015

POIX DE PICARDIE *3C3* (0.3km SW Rural) *49.77621, 1.97467* **Camp Municipal Le Dois des Pêcheurs,** Route de Forges-les-Eaux, 80290 Poix-de-Picardie **03 22 90 11 71 or 03 22 90 32 90 (Mairie); camping@ ville-poix-de-picardie.fr; www.ville-poix-de-picardie.fr**

🏕 €1.50 � WC ♨ ⅙ 🖥 🗗 🖉 MSP 🦋 ⛱ 🍴 nr 🚻 nr 🛒 nr ⌂

Fr town cent on D901 dir Beauvais, in 100m turn R onto D919 opp Citroën agent sp Camping; site on R in 500m. Fr Beauvais, turn L at bottom of steep hill opp Citroën agent; site in 500m on R. 3*, Med, hdg, mkd, hdstg, pt shd, EHU (6A) €4 (poss long lead req); bbq; red long stay; TV; Eng spkn; adv bkg acc; rv fishing adj; tennis 800m; bike hire; games rm; CKE. "Pleasant, peaceful, tidy site in delightful area; v clean modern san facs; htd covrd pool 800m; gd touring base; vg walking & cycling; bar 500m; train to Amiens; lovely mkt Sun; rec; every 3rd night free; gas 300m; sh walk to town and supmkt; vg."
€18.00, 1 Apr-30 Sep. 2018

FRANCE

POLIGNY *6H2* (1km SW Rural) *46.83455, 5.69840*
Camp Communautaire de la Croix du Dan, 39800
Poligny 03 84 37 01 35; cccgrimont@wanadoo.fr;
www.ville-poligny.fr

🐕 ♿ WD ♨ ᕳ ☄ / 🦋 🛒 nr ⛺

Fr SW on N83 turn R at rndabt sp 'Centre'; site
on R immed bef town sp Poligny. Fr N & NW take
D905 into & thro town cent (no L turn on N83 S of
Poligny), then foll sp Lons-Le Saunier. Site on L bef
sportsgrnd - look for m'van sp. Do not overshoot
ent, as diff to see. N5 fr E not rec as steep & hairpins.
2*, Med, mkd, pt shd, EHU (10A) €6.40; twin axles;
phone; Eng spkn; CKE. "Excel, clean, tidy site; helpful
warden; pretty town; if recep clsd ring number on board
to open barrier." €15.00, 15 Jun-20 Sep.   2017

PONS (CHARENTE MARITIME) *7B2* (0.5km W Urban)
45.57791, -0.55552 **Camp Municipal Le Paradis,**
1 Ave de Poitou, 17800 Pons 05 46 91 36 72;
campingmunicipalpons@voila.fr; www.pons-ville.org

🐕 €1.76 ♿ ♨ ᕳ / MP 🎱 🛒 nr

Well sp fr town o'skts. 3*, Med, mkd, pt shd, EHU (6-
10A) inc (poss rev pol); TV; Eng spkn; rv fishing 200m.
"Excel site in attractive grnds; helpful, friendly, super
wardens; interesting town; conv for Saintes, Cognac,
Royan; free wifi in snack bar; gd sized pitches; pool
100m; waterslide 100m; easy walk to old city; excel;
some rd noise." €22.00, 1 May-30 Sep.   2019

PONT AUDEMER *3D2* (2km NW Rural) *49.36660,
0.48739* **Camp Municipal Risle-Seine Les Etangs,**
19 Route des Etangs, 27500 Toutainville
02 32 42 46 65; camping@ville-pont-audemer.fr;
www.ville-pont-audemer.fr

🐕 ♿ WD ♨ ᕳ ☄ / MP 🦋 🎱 🛒 nr ⛺

Fr Le Havre on A131/E05 cross rv at Pont de
Normandie (toll). Take D580 & at junc 3 branch R
& take 2nd exit onto D22 sp Beuzeville. At edge of
Fiquefleur take D180, then D675 dir Pont-Audemer.
In Toutainville foll site sp, turn L just bef A13
underpass, then immed R. Site approx 2km on R.
3*, Med, mkd, hdg, pt shd, serviced pitches; EHU
(5-10A) €3.95; bbq; red long stay; TV; bus; Eng spkn;
adv bkg acc; ccard acc; fishing; bike hire; watersports;
games area; tennis 1.5km; games rm; canoeing.
"Lovely, well-run site; helpful warden; barrier clsd
2200-0830 but flexible for ferry; many leisure
activities; htd pool 1.5km; poss school groups at w/end;
vg for dogs; 1hr Le Havre ferry; Fri mkt Pont-Audemer;
conv NH; excel; facs stretched LS; boggy when wet;
pitches are narr which means car has to go at the front
of your pitch." €21.00, 25 Mar-31 Oct, N13.   2016

PONT AVEN *2F2* (13km N Rural) *47.92512,
-3.68888* **Camping Les Genêts d'Or,** KermerourPont
Kereon 29380 Bannalec 02 98 39 54 35; info@
holidaybrittany.com; www.holidaybrittany.com

🐕 €1.50 ♿ WD ♨ ᕳ / 🍽 🅗 🛒 nr ⛺

Fr Pont Aven/Bannalec exit on N165 N to Bannalec
on D4; after rlwy x-ing turn R sp Quimperlé. In 1km
turn R, sp Le Trévoux; site on L 500m.
3*, Sm, hdg, mkd, pt shd, pt sl, EHU (6A) €3.50; bbq
(gas); red long stay; 10% statics; Eng spkn; adv bkg
acc; games rm; bike hire; CKE. "Lovely, peaceful, well-
kept site in orchard; ACSI acc; lge pitches; welcoming,
helpful, friendly, lovely British owners; immac san facs;
Bannalec in walking dist; lovely area - excel touring
base; highly rec." €19.00, 31 May-30 Sep.   2015

PONT AVEN *2F2* (10km S Coastal) *47.80492, -3.74510*
Camping Le St Nicolas, Port Manec'h, 29920 Névez
05 47 74 30 72; reservation@cote-o.fr; www.cote-o.
fr/port-manech

🐕 €1.70 WD ♨ ᕳ ☄ / 🦋 🍽 nr 🅗 nr ⛺ 🏊 (htd) 🛁

⛱ sand 200m

Take D783 W fr Pont-Aven for 2km, turn L onto D77
S thro Névez to Port Manech. Site well sp. Narr app
to site. 3*, Lge, hdg, mkd, pt shd, pt sl, EHU (6-10A)
€3.70-4.70; gas; TV; Eng spkn; adv bkg acc; ccard
acc; tennis nr; games rm; watersports; games area;
horseriding nr; CKE. "Pleasant, wooded site; friendly
owners; sh walk to beach & cliff walks; gd touring base;
NH nr Le Havre." €29.00, 1 May-19 Sep.   2019

PONT AVEN *2F2* (11km SSW Coastal) *47.79640,
-3.77489* **Camping Les Chaumières,** 24 Hameau
de Kerascoët, 29920 Névez 02 98 06 73 06; info@
camping-des-chaumieres.com; www.camping-des-
chaumieres.com

🐕 €1.50 ♿ WD ♨ ᕳ ☄ / MP 🦋 🛒 nr 🅗 nr 🛒 nr ⛺ ⛱ sand 800m

S fr Pont-Aven thro Névez to Kerascoët.
2*, Med, hdg, mkd, pt shd, serviced pitches; EHU
(4-10A) €3.40-4.30; bbq; Eng spkn; adv bkg req; CKE.
"Excel, well-organised, peaceful, beautiful site; immac
facs poss stretched high ssn; gd play & games areas;
sandy bay/beaches, cliff walks; san facs refurbished and
upgraded; highly rec; friendly owner; recep clsd LS, but
owner avail via mob." €18.00, 15 May-19 Sep.   2018

PONT AVEN *2F2* (6km SW Coastal) *47.79906, -3.79033*
Sandaya Deux Fontaines, Raguenès, 29920 Névez
02 98 06 81 91; fon@sandaya.fr; www.sandaya.co.uk

🐕 €5 ♿ ♨ ᕳ ☄ / 🍽 🛒 🏊 (htd) ⛱ sand 4km

Leave N165/E60 at Kérampaou foll sp D24 twds
Pont Aven. In approx 4.5km turn R (S) foll sp Névez
then Raguenès. Site 3km fr Névez. 4*, Lge, mkd,
pt shd, EHU (10A) inc; bbq (charcoal); 80% statics;
adv bkg acc; tennis. "Busy high ssn; popular with
British families; o'night facs for m'vans; 25 meter
conn lead req'd; price inc waterpark acc & kids club."
€33.00, 10 Apr-13 Sep.   2019

FRANCE

PONT AVEN 2F2 (8km SW Coastal) 47.79597, -3.79877 **Camping du Vieux Verger,** Raguenès-Plage, 29920 Névez **02 98 06 86 08; contact@campingduvieux verger.com; www.campingduvieuxverger.com**

🛉🐎 ⓦⓓ ♿ ⌿ 🦋 ⊕ 🛒 🏊 ⛵ sand 500m

Fr Pont-Aven take D783 dir Concarneau; in 2.5km L onto D77 to Névez; foll sp Raguenès-Plage; 1st site on R. Foll 'Vieux Verger' sps. 2*, Med, hdg, mkd, pt shd, EHU (4-10A) €3.20-4.20 (poss rev pol); phone; CKE. *"Well-run, well-kept site with pool & waterslides; statics (sep area); highly rec LS; excel; gd for young children; excel site; gd value; many attractive beaches nrby."* €23.70, 14 Apr-15 Sep. 2018

> ## "We must tell the Club about that great site we found"
>
> Get your site reports in by mid-August and we'll do our best to get your updates into the next edition.

PONT AVEN 2F2 (8km SW Coastal) 47.79330, -3.80110 **Camping Raguenès-Plage,** 19 Rue des Îles à Raguenès, 29920 Névez **02 98 06 80 69; leraguenesplage@ orange.fr; www.camping-le-raguenes-plage.com**

🛉🐎 €3.20 🛉🛉 (htd) ⓦⓓ ♿ ⌿ 🦋 🍽 🏊 ⛵ sand adj (covrd, htd)

Fr Pont-Aven take D783 dir Trégunc; in 2.5km turn L for Névez, foll sps to Raguenès fr Névez. Or fr N165 take D24 at Kérampaou exit; in 3km turn R to Nizon; at church in vill turn R onto D77 to Névez; site on L 3km after Névez. 4*, Lge, mkd, hdstg, pt shd, EHU (6-15A) €4-6.90; gas; bbq; 20% statics; Eng spkn; adv bkg rec; ccard acc; games rm; watersports school adj; sauna; tennis nr; bike hire; games area; waterslide; horseriding; CKE. *"Pretty, wooded, family-run site; trampoline; statics sep area; private path to beach; clean facs; 1st class site."* €33.00, 20 Apr-30 Sep, B12. 2017

See advertisement

PONT D'AIN 9A2 (1.4km SE Urban) 46.04680, 5.34446 **Camping de l'Oiselon,** Rue E'mile Lebreüs, 01160 Pont-d'Ain **04 74 39 05 23; campingoiselon@ free.fr; www.campingpontdain.e-monsite.com**

🛉🐎 🛉🛉 ⓦⓓ ♿ 🚿 🦋 ⊕ 🛒 🏊 ⛵ ⌿ 🚣

Fr A42 exit Pont-d'Ain foll D90 to vill. In vill cent turn R on D1075. Turn L immed after x-ing Rv L'Ain. Foll rd passing tennis club on L. Site on L, clearly sp. 3*, Lge, pt shd, EHU (6-10A) €2.40-3.10 (poss rev pol); bbq; sw; 30% statics; Eng spkn; adv bkg acc; fishing; canoeing; tennis adj; games area; horseriding 5km; bike hire; CKE. *"Gd, well-run site with easy access, v lge; helpful, friendly staff; gd clean san facs; cash only; site needs TLC (early ssn 2010); gd NH; excel site."* €17.50, 17 Mar-14 Oct. 2018

PONT DE L'ARCHE 3D2 (0.8km N Urban) 49.3060, 1.1546 **Camp Municipal Eure et Seine,** Quai Maréchal Foch, 27340 Pont-de-l'Arche **02 35 23 06 71 or 02 32 98 90 70 (Mairie); campeure@pontdelarche.fr; www.pontdelarche.fr**

🛉🐎 €1.50 🛉🛉 ⓦⓓ ♿ ⌿ 🍽 🛒 nr 🏕

Fr Rouen S on D6015 turn 1st L after x-ing rv bdge, drive downhill then L under bdge & strt on for 300m (foll Camping Car sp at traff lts, do not go into town), site on R. Restricted width on app. Or exit A13 junc 20 onto D321 to Pont-de-l'Arche; turn L at War Memorial onto Place du Souvenir; in 300m to R at rv; site on L in 200m. 2*, Med, mkd, pt shd, EHU (6-10A) inc; red long stay; TV; 4% statics; phone; adv bkg rec; ccard acc; rv fishing adj; CKE. *"Pleasant, peaceful, clean rvside site in attractive medieval town; sm pitches; helpful warden; gd, modern san facs; recep 1000-1200 & 1600-2000; access only after 1600, Aire outside site accessible 24/7; many shops clsd Wed pm; bus fr town to Rouen; popular NH & longer; beautiful site nr Gothic church; excel; superb setting; v busy so arrive early or ring ahead; sh walk to town; o'night parking for M'van outside site €5 pn "* €12.00, 1 Apr-30 Oct. 2019

PONT DE SALARS *7D4* (1.5km N Rural) *44.29150, 2.72571* **Parc Camping du Lac,** 12290 Pont-de-Salars **05 65 46 84 86; contact@parc-du-lac.com; www.campingpontdesalars.fr**

Fr Rodez on D911 La Primaube-Millau rd, turn L bef ent Pont-de-Salars. Site sp. 3*, Lge, mkd, pt shd, pt sl, terr, EHU (3-6A) €2.50-3.50; gas; bbq; sw; TV; 90% statics; phone; adv bkg acc; ccard acc; fishing; sailing. *"Beautiful situation; poor for c'vans, OK m'vans; diff lge o'fits; blocks req; site poss unclean end of ssn; ltd facs."* **€17.00, 1 Jun-30 Sep.** 2017

PONT DE SALARS *7D4* (8km S Rural) *44.21500, 2.77777* **Camping Soleil Levant,** Lac de Pareloup, 12290 Canet-de-Salars **05 65 46 03 65; contact@ camping-soleil-levant.com; www.camping-soleil-levant.com**

Exit A75 junc 44.1 onto D911 to Pont-de-Salars, then S on D993 dir Salles-Curan. Site in 8km bef bdge on L. 3*, Lge, mkd, pt shd, pt sl, terr, EHU (6A) inc; gas; bbq; sw nr; TV; 50% statics; Eng spkn; adv bkg acc; ccard acc; watersports; games area; tennis; games rm; fishing; CKE. *"Lovely lakeside site; excel san facs; vg; well run by friendly couple."* **€30.00, 1 May-30 Sep.** 2017

PONT DE VAUX *9A2* (4km NE Rural) *46.44394, 4.98313* **Camping Les Ripettes,** St Bénigne, 01190 Chavannes-sur-Reyssouze **03 85 30 66 58; info@ camping-les-ripettes.com; camping-les-ripettes. pagesperso-orange.fr**

Take D2 fr Pont-de-Vaux sp St Trivier-des-Courtes for 3km. Immed after water tower on R turn L onto D58 sp Romenay, then immed L. Site well sp on L in 100m. 3*, Med, hdg, mkd, pt shd, pt sl, EHU (10A) €4; 1% statics; phone; Eng spkn; adv bkg rec; ccard acc; games area; CKE. *"Lovely, popular site in beautiful location; spacious pitches; friendly, helpful owner; immac facs; gd pool area; gd touring base; hard to beat; ACSI card acc; one of the best; cycle rte maps at TO in Pont de Vaux; memb of La Via Natura; promoting many eco ideas; excel."* **€23.70, 1 Apr-30 Sep.** 2018

PONT DE VAUX *9A2* (0.5km W Urban) *46.42979, 004.93296* **Camping Champ d'Été,** Lieu-dit Champ D'Été, 01190 Reyssouze **0033 385 23 96 10; info@ camping-champ-dete.com; www.camping-champ-dete.com**

Fr A6 N J27, take D906 dir Pont-de-Vaux. In town, foll Base-de-Loisirs & camping sp. 4*, Med, hdstg, mkd, pt shd, EHU (10A) inc; bbq; TV; 20% statics; bus adj; Eng spkn; adv bkg acc; ccard acc; games rm; CKE. *"Walking dist to town; adj to pk & free sw pool; v clean san facs; friendly owners; htd pool adj; gd for touring Burgundy area; gd for long or sh stays; some pitches tight for lge o'fits; vg."* **€23.00, 25 Mar-15 Oct.** 2016

PONT DU CHATEAU *9B1* (5km SSW Urban) *45.77546, 3.24197* **Camping Les Ombrages,** Rue Pont du Château, 63111 Dallet **04 73 83 10 97; lesombrages@hotmail.com; www.lesombrages.nl**

E fr Clermont Ferrand on D769; 200m bef x-ing Rv Allier turn R onto D783/D769A; 50m after x-ring rv turn L into Rue Pont du Château; site on L in 400m. 3*, Sm, shd, EHU (6A) (rev pol) €3.50; sw nr; TV; canoeing; fishing; games rm. *"Peaceful, pretty, gd site; excel pitches by rv; gd for fishing & canoeing; mosquitoes; gd san facs."* **€25.00, 14 May-15 Sep.** 2015

PONT FARCY *1D4* (0.5km N Rural) *47.46810, 4.35709* **Camp Municipal Pont-Farcy,** Quai de la Vire, 14380 Pont-Farcy **02 31 68 32 06 or 02 31 68 86 48; pontfarcy@free.fr; www.pont-farcy.fr**

Leave A84 junc 39 onto D21 to Pont-Farcy; site on L at ent to vill. 3*, Med, hdg, mkd, pt shd, terr, EHU (10A) €2.50; 30% statics; phone; adv bkg acc; boating adj; rv fishing adj; tennis; bike hire; CKE. *"Barrier poss locked periods during day but parking avail; bar 500m; helpful, friendly warden; clean facs; mosquitoes at dusk."* **€12.50, 3 April-30 Sep.** 2019

PONT L'ABBE *2F2* (7km S Rural) *47.81241, -4.22147* **Camping L'Océan Breton,** Route Kerlut, 29740 Lesconil **02 98 82 23 89; info@yellohvillage-loceanbreton. com; www.camping-bretagne-oceanbreton.fr or www.yellohvillage.co.uk**

Fr Pont l'Abbé S on D102 to Plobannalec & head for Lesconil; site on L after supmkt. 4*, Lge, hdstg, mkd, hdg, pt shd, serviced pitches; EHU (5A) inc; gas; red long stay; 80% statics; phone; Eng spkn; adv bkg acc; ccard acc; tennis; games area; sauna; waterslide; bike hire; kids clubs; bowling; adventure trail; CKE. *"Excel site for families; fitness rm; spacious pitches."* **€50.00, 06 Apr-15 Sep, B39.** 2019

PONT L'ABBE *2F2* (8.6km S Rural/Coastal) *47.79715, -4.22868* **Camping des Dunes,** 67 Rue Paul Langevin, 29740 Plobannalec-Lesconil **02 98 87 81 78; contact@ camping-desdunes.com; www.camping-desdunes.com**

Fr Pont l'Abbé, S on D102 for 5km to Plobannalec; over x-rds; in 1km turn R, 100m after sports field; green sp to site in 1km. 3*, Med, hdg, mkd, pt shd, EHU (8A) €3.70; bbq; adv bkg acc; ccard acc; games area; games rm; CKE. *"Helpful owner; nr fishing port; gd walking, cycling & birdwatching; site gd for children; access to beach with amazing granite rock formations; red early ssn; well cared for."* **€25.70, 30 Mar-29 Sep.** 2019

PONT L'ABBE *2F2* (10km NW Rural) *47.89462, -4.32863* **Camping Kerlaz,** Route de la Mer, 29670 Tréguennec **02 98 87 76 79; contact@kerlaz.com; www.kerlaz.com**

🐕 €1.30 👥 WC 🚿 🚯 ⚡ MSP 🦋 🚲 ♿ nr 🏧 🏊 (covrd, htd)

⛱ sand 2km

Fr Plonéour-Lanvern take D156 SW to Tréguennec. 3*, Med, hdg, pt shd, EHU (10A); bbq; 30% statics; Eng spkn; adv bkg acc; ccard acc; bike hire. *"Nice, friendly site; pleasant owners; attractive site; gd for cycling."* **€24.00, 1 Apr-30 Sep.** **2017**

PONT ST ESPRIT *9D2* (10km NW Rural) *44.29808, 4.56535* **Camping Les Cigales,** 30760 Aiguèze **04 66 82 18 52; www.camping-cigales.fr**

12 🐕 €2 🚿 🚯 ⚡ MSP 🍴 ♿ nr 🏧 nr 🏊 (htd)

N fr Pont-St Esprit on D6086 take D901 NW twd Barjac & D141 to St Martin-d'Ardèche. Site on L bef rv bdge. Avoid app fr St Martin-d'Ardèche over narr suspension bdge. Care at ent. Diff for lge units. 2*, Sm, mkd, shd, EHU (4-10A) €3.13-5.88; gas; bbq; sw nr; 25% statics; adv bkg acc; ccard acc; CKE. *"Helpful, friendly owner; easy walk to St Martin-d'Ardèche."* **€21.00** **2015**

PONT ST ESPRIT *9D2* (6km NW Rural) *44.30388, 4.58443* **Camping Le Pontet,** 07700 St Martin-d'Ardèche **04 75 04 63 07 or 04 75 98 76 24; contact@campinglepontet.com; www.campinglepontet.com**

🐕 €3 👥 WC 🚿 🚯 ⚡ MSP 🦋 🍴 🍺 ♿ 🏧 🏊 🏊

N86 N of Pont-St Esprit; turn L onto D290 at sp Gorges de l'Ardèche & St Martin-d'Ardèche, site on R after 3km, sp. 3*, Med, mkd, pt shd, EHU (6A) €3.60 (rev pol); gas; sw nr; 5% statics; phone; Eng spkn; adv bkg acc; CKE. *"Vg; helpful owners; peaceful out of ssn; facs stretched when busy; online bkg fee €10."* **€22.00, 8 Apr-25 Sep.** **2017**

PONT ST ESPRIT *9D2* (8km NW Rural) *44.34423, 4.60434* **FFCC Camping Les Truffières,** 201 Route de St Ramèze, 07700 St Marcel-d'Ardèche **04 75 04 68 35 or 06 82 01 28 30 (mob); soulier.valerie@wanadoo.fr; www.camping-les-truffieres.com**

12 🐕 €1.60 👥 (htd) 🚿 🚯 ⚡ 🦋 🍴 🍺 ♿ nr 🏧 🏊

S fr Bourg-St Andéol, turn W on D201; in vill foll sp to site located approx 3km W of vill. 2*, Med, mkd, pt shd, terr, EHU (6A) €6.60 (poss rev pol); gas; 70% statics; adv bkg acc; CKE. *"Friendly owners; glorious views; gd san facs; conv NH nr A7; v pleasant; tricky without motor mover (trees)."* **€17.00** **2017**

PONT ST ESPRIT *9D2* (9km NW Rural) *44.30043, 4.57069* **Camping Indigo Le Moulin,** 07700 St Martin-d'Ardèche **04 75 04 66 20; moulin@camping-indigo.com; europe.huttopia.com/site/camping-le-moulin-ardeche**

🐕 €4 👥 (htd) WC 🚿 ♿ 🚯 ⚡ MSP 🦋 🍺 🍴 ♿ nr 🏧 🏊 🏊 🏊 (htd) 🏊

Exit A7 junc 19 to Bollène, then D994 to Pont-St Esprit & D6068/D86 to St Just. Turn L onto D290 to St Martin in 4km. Site on L on rvside. 3*, Med, pt shd, pt sl, EHU (10A) €4.90; sw nr; TV; 5% statics; phone; Eng spkn; ccard acc; canoe hire; games area; tennis 500m; bike hire; fishing. *"Friendly site; gd modern san facs; footpath to vill; quiet low ssn; gd local walks; rec."* **€38.50, 30 Apr-28 Sep.** **2019**

PONTAILLER SUR SAONE *6G1* (0.8km E Rural) *47.30817, 5.42518* **Camping La Chanoie,** 46 Rue de la Chanoie, 21270 Pontailler-sur-Saône **03 80 67 21 98; camping.municipal1@orange.fr; www.camping-lachanoie.com**

🐕 €1.55 👥 (htd) WC 🚿 ♿ 🚯 ⚡ MSP 🦋 🍴 🍺 🏧 nr 🏧

E fr Pontailler-sur-Saône on D959; pass town hall & TO on R; after bdg take 1st L sp Camping; site in 500m. Fr W on D959 turn R bef bdg & bef ent town. 3*, Med, hdg, mkd, pt shd, EHU (6-10A) €2.85-4.10; bbq; sw nr; red long stay; 80% statics; bus; adv bkg acc; games area; tennis; watersports adj; games rm; fishing adj; CKE. *"Attractive sm town; polite & helpful owner; clean san facs; poss stretched high ssn; vg; OK NH."* **€17.30, 15 Mar-15 Oct.** **2019**

PONTARLIER *6H2* (1km SE Rural) *46.90024, 6.37425* **FFCC Camping Le Larmont,** Rue du Toulombief, 25300 Pontarlier **03 81 46 23 33; lelarmont.pontarlier@wanadoo.fr; www.camping-pontarlier.fr**

🐕 €1 👥 (htd) WC 🚿 ♿ 🚯 ⚡ MSP 🍴 🍺 🏧

Leave N57 at Pontarlier Gare & foll site sp. Site uphill, turning nr Nestlé factory. 3*, Med, hdstg, unshd, terr, EHU (10A) €4; gas; 20% statics; Eng spkn; adv bkg acc; horseriding adj; CKE. *"Friendly; easy access; clean san facs; ltd pitches for awnings; site self out of office hrs; skiing winter; well-behaved zebra on site; excel; horseriding next to site; rec."* **€22.50, 1 Jan-11 Nov.** **2019**

PONTARLIER 6H2 (12km S Rural) 46.81176, 6.30326
Camp Municipal, 8 Rue du Port, 25160 St Point-Lac
03 81 69 61 64 or 03 81 69 62 08 (Mairie); camping-saintpointlac@orange.fr; www.camping-saintpointlac.fr

🐕 €1.50 ♀♂(htd) 🚾 ♿ 🚿 🍽 MSP 🦋 ⚲ 🍴 ⓗ nr 🐟 🅿 ⛾ 🛶 🛷 adj

Exit Pontarlier S on N57 dir Lausanne, turn R on D437 dir Malbuisson; in 6km turn R onto D129 thro Les Grangettes to St Point-Lac. Site sp on L.
3*, Med, mkd, hdstg, pt shd, EHU (16A) €4.50; bbq; 5% statics; Eng spkn; adv bkg rec; ccard acc; games area; CKE. "Delightful, well-kept lakeside site in beautiful position; sm pitches, some may be diff for large units to get in in; friendly staff; vg, clean san facs; m'van o'night area with facs opp; gd fishing, walking, birdwatching; sw; gd touring; rec adv bkg wkends/high ssn; excel." €20.00, 1 May-30 Sep. 2017

PONTAUBAULT 2E4 (0km W Urban) 48.62983, -1.35205 **Camping La Vallée de la Sélune,** 7 Rue Maréchal Leclerc, 50220 Pontaubault 02 33 60 39 00; campselune@wanadoo.fr; www.camping-manche.com

🐕 €1.30 ♀♂ 🚾 ♿ 🚿 🍽 ⚲ 🍴 🐟 🛶 🛷

Foll sp to Pontaubault (well sp fr all dirs). In vill head twd Avranches. Turn L immed bef bdge over Rv Sélune. In 100m turn L, site strt in 100m, well sp. 2*, Med, mkd, pt shd, pt sl, EHU (10A) inc; red long stay; 10% statics; adv bkg rec; ccard acc; horseriding nr; fishing adj; golf nr; tennis adj; CKE. "Relaxing, clean, tidy, pleasant site in sm vill; vg, clean san facs; conv Mont St Michel & Cherbourg ferries; gd NH; cycling nr; friendly Yorkshire owner; on cycle rte." €15.00, 1 Apr-20 Oct. 2018

"Satellite navigation makes touring much easier"

Remember most sat navs don't know if you're towing or in a larger vehicle – always use yours alongside maps and site directions.

PONTCHATEAU 2G3 (7km W Rural) 47.44106, -2.15981 **Le Château du Deffay,** Ste Reine-de-Bretagne, 44160 Pontchâteau 02 40 88 00 57; info@camping-le-deffay.com; www.camping-le-deffay.com

🐕 €1 ♀♂ 🚾 ♿ 🚿 🍽 ⚲ 🦋 ⚲ 🍴 ⓗ 🐟 🛶 🛷 🏊(covrd, htd) ♨

Leave N165 at junc 13 onto D33 twd Herbignac. Site on R approx 1.5km after Le Calvaire de la Madeleine x-rds, 270m past Chateau ent. Site sp fr by-pass. 4*, Lge, mkd, hdg, pt shd, pt sl, terr, EHU (10A); bbq (charcoal, gas); TV; 40% statics; Eng spkn; adv bkg acc; ccard acc; lake fishing; bike hire; tennis; games rm; golf 10km; CKE. "Excel, beautiful site with trees in grnds of chateau by lake; free pedalos; friendly, helpful, welcoming staff; excel clean san facs; some pitches lakeside & not fenced; mkt Mon; gd value rest." €38.00, 1 May-30 Sep, B25. 2019

PONTGIBAUD 7B4 (0.2km S Rural) 45.82978, 2.84517 **FFCC Camp Municipal La Palle,** 3 Avenue du General de Gaulle, 63230 Pontgibaud 04 73 88 96 99 or 04 73 88 70 42 (LS); mairie.pontgibaud@wanadoo.fr; www.ville-pontgibaud.fr/camping-municipal

🐕 ♀♂ (htd) 🚾 🚿 🍽 ⚲ 🍴 ⛾ 🛶

At W end of Pontgibaud turn S over bdge on D986 & site in 500m on L, past site for La Palle Chalets. 3*, Med, hdg, mkd, hdstg, pt shd, EHU (10-16A) inc; bbq; sw nr; red long stay; Eng spkn; adv bkg acc; games area; tennis 400m; CKE. "Pleasant, clean, tidy site nr sm rv; helpful staff; pop concerts once a week high ssn; conv Vulcania exhibition cent; bike hire 400m; v lge hdg plots; minimal rd & rlwy noise; well maintained; friendly; easy flat walk to town; gd base for Puy de Dome." €17.00, 15 Apr-30 Sep. 2018

PONTORSON 2E4 (0.9km NW Rural) 48.55805, -1.51444 **Camping Haliotis,** Chemin des Soupirs, 50170 Pontorson 02 33 68 11 59; camping.haliotis@wanadoo.fr; www.camping-haliotis-mont-saint-michel.com

🐕 €2 ♀♂(htd) 🚾 🚿 ♿ 🍽 ⚲ MSP 🍴 ⓗ nr 🐟 🛶 🛷 (htd) ⚓

Exit A84 junc 33 onto N175 dir Pontorson; foll sp Cent Ville/Mont-St-Michel. Site well sp. 3*, Lge, mkd, hdg, pt shd, pt sl, EHU (10-16A) inc (poss rev pol); gas; bbq; 25% statics; phone; bus 400m; Eng spkn; adv bkg rec; ccard acc; boating; games area; tennis; rv fishing; games rm; bike hire; sauna; CKE. "Popular, well-kept, busy, superb site; lge pitches; friendly, helpful owners; immac, unisex san facs; lovely pool & bar; rvside walk to town; cycle rte/bus to Mont St Michel; highly rec; serviced pitches; pitches with private bthrms avail; spa; library; avoid pitches 77-89 due to noise fr bins; excel." €30.00, 30 Mar-4 Nov, N17. 2018

PONTORSON 2E4 (8km NW Rural) 48.59415, -1.59855 **Camping Les Couesnons,** Route de St Malo, 35610 Roz-sur-Couesnon 02 99 80 26 86; contact@les-couesnons.com; www.lescouesnons.com

🐕 €2 ♀♂(htd) 🚾 🚿 ♿ 🍽 ⚲ 🦋 ⚲ 🍴 ⓗ 🐟 🛶

Exit N175/N176 NW onto D797 dir St Malo on coastal rd; site sp 700m past Roz-sur-Couesnon on R. Turn R at Les Couesnons Rest. Site behind. 3*, Sm, hdg, mkd, pt shd, EHU (6A) €3; bbq (charcoal, gas); red long stay; TV; 10% statics; Eng spkn; adv bkg acc; ccard acc; games rm; games area; CKE. "Excel site; Mont St Michel 8km; ACSI acc; vg, spotless, htd facs; gd rest & bar; highly rec." €23.00, 1 Apr-31 Oct. 2017

PONTRIEUX *2E3* *(0.5km W Rural)* *48.69493, –3.16365*
Camping de Traou Mélédern (Moisan), Traou Mélédern, 22260 Pontrieux **02 96 95 69 27; campingpontrieux@ free.fr; www.camping-pontrieux.com**

N on D787 fr Guingamp; on ent town sq turn sharp L sp Traou Mélédern, cross rv bdge & turn R alongside church. Site in 400m. Access poss diff for lge o'fits; steep exit on 1-way system.
2*, Med, mkd, hdg, pt shd, pt sl, EHU (8A) €3.50; bbq; phone; Eng spkn; adv bkg acc; CKE. *"In orchard; excel touring base; friendly owner; quiet but some daytime factory noise; steep junc nr site poss problem for lge o'fits; gd."* **€17.50** **2016**

PORGE, LE *7C1* *(9km W Coastal)* *44.89430, –1.20181*
Camping La Grigne, Ave de l'Océan, 33680 Le Porge **05 56 26 54 88; info@lagrigne.com; www.camping-leporge.fr**

Fr Bordeaux ring rd take N215 twd Lacaneau. In 22km at Ste Hélène D5 to Saumos & onto Le Porge. Site on L of rd to Porge-Océan in approx 9km. 3*, V lge, mkd, shd, pt sl, terr, EHU (10A) €5; gas; red long stay; TV; adv bkg acc; tennis; games area. *"Vg facs; great beach; excel cycle path network."* **€22.00, 1 Apr-30 Sep.** **2016**

PORNIC *2G3* *(4km E Rural)* *47.11885, –2.07296*
Camping Le Patisseau, 29 Rue du Patisseau, 44210 Pornic **02 40 82 10 39; contact@lepatisseau.com; www.lepatisseau.com**

Fr N or S on D213, take slip rd D751 Nantes. At rndabt take exit sp to Le Patisseau, foll sp.
4*, Med, mkd, hdstg, hdg, pt shd, pt sl, EHU (6A) inc; bbq; TV; 35% statics; Eng spkn; adv bkg rec; ccard acc; sauna; fitness rm; waterslide; golf 2km; tennis 1km; bike hire; games area; games rm; jacuzzi. *"Excel, modern, family site; modern san facs block - lovely shwrs; 1hr walk on path fr back of site to Pornic."* **€42.00, 7 Apr-12 Sep.** **2017**

PORNIC *2G3* *(6km SE Rural/Coastal)* *47.08450, –2.03650* **Camping Les Ecureuils,** 24 Ave Gilbert Burlot, 44760 La Bernerie-en-Retz **02 40 82 76 95; camping.les-ecureuils@wanadoo.fr; www.camping-les-ecureuils.com**

Fr Pornic take D13 S for 5km, then D66 for 1km; site sp. 4*, Lge, hdg, pt shd, pt sl, EHU (10A) inc; bbq; 30% statics; Eng spkn; adv bkg acc; ccard acc; waterslide; golf 5km; tennis; CKE. *"Excel; children's club; v clean modern san facs; hg rec."* **€48.00, 1 Apr-30 Sep, L29.** **2019**

PORNIC *2G3* *(10km S Coastal)* *47.07500, –2.00741*
Campsite Les Brillas, Le Bois des Treans, 44760 Les Moutiers-en-Retz **02 40 82 79 78; info@camping lesbrillas.com; www.campinglesbrillas.com**

Fr Nantes ring rd, take D723 SW. Take exit D751 twd Pornic. Turn L on D66. Foll sp. 3*, Med, mkd, hdg, EHU (6A); Eng spkn; CCI. *"Sm coastal vill; easy walk to beach; excel; lovely location & beach; basic facs."* **€31.00, 14 Apr-1 Oct.** **2017**

PORNIC *2G3* *(5km W Rural)* *47.14079, –2.15306*
Camping La Tabardière, 44770 La Plaine-sur-Mer **02 40 21 58 83; info@camping-la-tabardiere.com; www.camping-la-tabardiere.com**

(covrd, htd) sand 3km

Take D13 NW out of Pornic sp Préfailles & La Plaine-sur-Mer. In about 5.5km turn R (nr water tower). Foll sps to site, about 1km fr main rd. NB C'vans not allowed in Pornic town cent, use by-pass. 4*, Lge, hdstg, mkd, hdg, pt shd, terr, serviced pitches; EHU (8A) €5; gas; bbq (charcoal, gas); TV; 40% statics; Eng spkn; adv bkg acc; ccard acc; tennis; games rm; fishing 3km; waterslide; horseriding 5km; CKE. *"Excel, peaceful site; multi-sport area; no o'fits over 7.5m high ssn; vg facs for families; v clean unisex san facs; gates clsd 2230-0800; recep clsd lunchtime."* **€47.00, 12 Apr-20 Sep, B31.** **2019**

> ## "There aren't many sites open at this time of year"
>
> If you're travelling outside peak season remember to call ahead to check site opening dates – even if the entry says 'open all year'.

PORNIC *2G3* *(9km NW Coastal)* *47.15995, –2.16813*
Camping Thar-Cor, 43 Ave du Cormier, 44730 St Michel-Chef-Chef **02 40 27 82 81; camping@ letharcor.com; www.camping-le-thar-cor.com**

sand 200m

Fr Pornic take D213 twds Saint Michel Chef Chef. Turn L onto Rue de la Dalonnerie. L at rndabt onto D96. Foll sp to site. Lge, mkd, hdg, pt shd, EHU (10A) €5; bbq; twin axles; TV; 50% statics; phone; Eng spkn; adv bkg rec; ccard acc; games area. *"Vg town site, mkt at Tharon-Plage high ssn; 200m to promenade & sandy beach; friendly staff; mainly French; beach excel."* **€26.50, 10 Apr-25 Sep.** **2016**

FRANCE

PORT EN BESSIN HUPPAIN *3D1* (1km N Coastal) *49.34693, -0.77095* **Camping Port'land,** Chemin du Sémaphore, 14520 Port-en-Bessin **02 31 51 07 06; campingportland@wanadoo.fr; www.camping-portland.com**

🐕 €3 👫 (htd) 🆆 ♿ 🛒 ▥ ⊘ MꝒ 🦋 🍴 ℗ 🛢 🎣 ⚒ 🖌
♨ (covrd, htd) 🏖 ⛱ sand 4km

Site sp fr D514 W of Port-en-Bessin. 4*, Lge, mkd, hdg, hdstg, pt shd, EHU (16A) €5; bbq; red long stay; TV; 30% statics; Eng spkn; adv bkg acc; ccard acc; waterslide; tennis 800m; games area; games rm; CKE. *"Pleasant site; friendly, helpful staff; vg san facs; extra charge lger pitches; excel touring base for landing beaches etc; well kept clean, well spaced lge hdged pitches; well positioned for Bayeaux, Arromanche and D Day museums and cemetaries."* €37.50, 1 Apr-30 Oct, N09. **2016**

PORT LESNEY *6H2* (0.2km N Rural) *47.00358, 5.82366* **Camping Les Radeliers,** 1 Rue Edgar Faure, 39600 Port-Lesney **03 84 73 81 44; camp.portlesney@aliceadsl.fr; www.camping-les-radeliers.com**

🐕 €2 👫 🆆 🛒 ♿ 🛢 ▥ 🦋 🍴 nr ℗ nr 🎣 nr ⚒

N fr Arbois on N83, cross junc with D472 & turn L in 1.5km sp Port-Lesney. Site sp. 3*, Med, mkd, pt shd, EHU (13A) €4; sw nr; twin axles; 2% statics; bus adj; Eng spkn; adv bkg acc; canoeing; kayak hire; CKE. *"Tranquil site in delightful rvside setting; helpful staff; poss youth groups high ssn; gd walking & cycling; Salt Mine Museum in Salins-les-Bains worth visit; canyoning; bar 200m; plenty rvside pitches."* €23.00, 1 May-30 Sep. **2016**

PORT SUR SAONE *6F2* (0.8km S Rural) *47.68056, 6.03937* **Camp Municipal Parc de la Maladière,** 70170 Port-sur-Saône **03 84 78 18 00 (Mairie); serviceculturel@gmail.com; www.ville-port-sur-saone.fr**

👫 (cont) 🆆 🛢 ♿ 🛒 ▥ 🦋 🍴 nr ℗ nr 🎣 nr ⚒

Take N19 SE fr Langres or NW fr Vesoul. Site sp in vill bet rv & canal off D6 at municipal bathing area. 2*, Med, hdg, pt shd, EHU (6A) €3 (poss rev pol); own san rec; adv bkg acc; ccard acc; fishing; tennis; CKE. *"Peaceful site on island; rvside cycle path; gd walks; gd sh stay/NH; san facs basic & tired; pool adj; 25m cable needed; vg value."* €15.40, 15 May-15 Sep. **2017**

PORT VENDRES *10G1* (2km E Urban) *42.51775, 3.11314* **Aire Communale des Tamarins,** Route de la Jetée, 66660 Port-Vendres **04 68 82 07 54**

12 👫 🆆 MꝒ 🍴 nr ℗ nr 🎣 nr ⛱ shgl 100m

Fr D914 at Port-Vendres at Banyuls side of town turn N on D86B sp Port de Commerce & Aire de Camping-Cars. Foll sp to site on R in 700m. Sm, hdstg, pt shd, own san req. *"NH, m'vans only; walking dist rlwy stn; a bit run down (Jun 2009); gd; payment collected am; popular."* €10.00 **2016**

PORTIRAGNES PLAGE *10F1* (2km NE Coastal) *43.29138, 3.37333* **Camping Les Mimosas,** Port Cassafières, 34420 Portiragnes-Plage **04 67 90 92 92; info@mimosas.fr or les.mimosas.portiragnes@wanadoo.fr; www.mimosas.com**

🐕 €5.50 👫 🆆 🛒 ♿ 🛢 ▥ ⊘ MꝒ 🦋 🍴 ℗ 🛢 🎣 ⚒ 🖌 🏊
🏖 ⛱ sand 1km

Exit A9 junc 35 Béziers Est & take N112 sp Vias, Agde. After 3km at rndabt foll sp Portiragnes & cont along side of Canal du Midi. Cross canal, site sp. 4*, Lge, hdstg, mkd, pt shd, EHU (6-10A) €4; gas; bbq (gas); 50% statics; Eng spkn; adv bkg acc; ccard acc; games area; jacuzzi; sauna; games rm; waterslide; bike hire; CKE. *"Excel touring base in interesting area; friendly welcome; superb waterpark; fitness rm; private san facs avail; 4 star site; gd for families."* €51.90, 1 Jun-7 Sep, C35. **2019**

POSES *3D2* (1.6km SE Urban) *49.29552, 1.24914* **Base de Loisirs,** Rue du Souvenir French, 27740 Poses **02 32 59 13 13; lery.poses@wanadoo.fr; www.lery-poses.fr**

👫 🆆 🛢 ▥ ⛱

Fr Poses head NE on Rue du Bac twrd Rue das Masures, take 1st R onto Rue des Masures, turn R onto Rue du Roussillon, after 350m turn L onto Rue du Souvenir Francais, site aftr 220m on L. Lge, pt shd, EHU (16A); table tennis; canoeing. *"Gd san facs; gravel rdway throughout site; water ski; hiking; pedalo hire; mini golf; site adj to & overlooking the Rv Seine with direct access to the rvside; plenty of pitches for tourers; beach volleyball; supmkt 5km; older san block needs updating (2018)."* €15.00, 1 Apr-31 Oct. **2018**

"That's changed – Should I let the Club know?"

If you find something on site that's different from the site entry, fill in a report and let us know. See camc.com/europereport.

POUILLY EN AUXOIS *6G1* (0.8km NW Urban) *47.26534, 4.54804* **Camping Vert Auxois,** 15 Voûte du Canal du Bourgogne, 21320 Pouilly-en-Auxois **03 80 90 71 89; contact@camping-vert-auxois.com; www.camping-vert-auxois.fr**

🐕 👫 🆆 ♿ 🛒 🛢 ▥ ⊘ MꝒ 🦋 🍴 ℗ 🛢 🎣 ⚒

Exit A6 at Dijon/Pouilly-en-Auxois onto A38. Exit A38 at junc 24. Thro vill & turn L after church on R, site sp adj Burgandy canal. 3*, Sm, hdg, pt shd, EHU (6-10A) long cable req; 10% statics; bus 300m; Eng spkn; adv bkg acc; ccard acc; rv fishing adj; CKE. *"Beautiful position, relaxed & peaceful; lge pitches, unusual layout; run by delightful, friendly couple; gd cycling; interesting area; sh walk to sm town; vg; san facs poss stretched."* €23.00, 1 Apr-7 Oct. **2018**

For a guide to symbols see the fold out on the rear cover

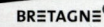

FRANCE

POUILLY SUR LOIRE *4G3* (1km N Rural) *47.28742, 2.94427* **Camp Municipal Le Malaga,** Rue des Champs-sur-Loire, Les Loges, 58150 Pouilly-sur-Loire **03 33 86 39 12 55; www.ot-pouillysurloire.fr**

Fr S exit A77 junc 26 onto D28a, turn L onto D59/D4289 W, bef rv bdge turn R, site in 1km on rv. Fr N on ent vill turn R at site sp into narr rd. Turn R along rv as above. 3*, Med, pt shd, EHU (10A) inc (poss long lead req & poss rev pol); bbq; phone; Eng spkn. *"Beautifully kept site on banks of Loire; busy NH; spacious but uneven pitches; mixed reports san facs; poss youth groups; beautiful area; wine tasting nrby; no twin axles or o'fits over 5m; poss mosquitoes; excel; delightful site adj to the Loire, spacious and leafy areas, wonderful wines in Pouilly and Sancerre, excel museum closeby."* **€16.00, 1 May-30 Sep.** **2019**

POULDU, LE *2F2* (0.3km N Coastal) *47.76850, -3.54540* **Camping Les Embruns,** 2 Rue du Philosophe Alain, Clohars-Carnoët, 29360 Le Pouldu **02 98 39 91 07; camping-les-embruns@wanadoo.fr; www.camping-les-embruns.com**

Exit N165 dir Quimperlé Cent, onto D16 to Clohars-Carnoët. Cont on D16/D24/D1214 to Le Pouldu. Site on R on ent 1-way traff system. Site sp. 4*, Lge, hdstg, mkd, hdg, pt shd, terr, serviced pitches; EHU (10A) inc; gas; bbq; TV; 40% statics; bus nrby; Eng spkn; adv bkg acc; ccard acc; watersports; games area; tennis; horseriding nr; tennis 200m; games rm; bike hire; fishing; CKE. *"Excel family-run site in great location; children's farm; luxury pitches extra charge; friendly, helpful owners; vg clean san facs; superb facs; gd walking along coastal paths; cycle rtes; great for dogs; town was home of Paul Gauguin; highly rec."* **€31.50, 10 Apr-19 Sep.** **2019**

See advertisement

POULDU, LE *2F2* (2km N Coastal) *47.78401, -3.54463* **FFCC Camping de Croas An Ter,** Quelvez, Le Pouldu, 29360 Clohars-Carnoët **02 98 39 94 19 or 06 24 88 68 20 (mob); campingcroasanter@orange.fr; www.campingcroasanter.com**

On D49 fr Quimperlé to Le Pouldu. Site on L 3km after junc with D224. 2*, Med, pt shd, pt sl, EHU (6A) €3.20; Eng spkn; CKE. *"Lge pitches; friendly owners; cash only; gd bathing & sailing; walks in wood & rv fr site; Tues mkt; vg."* **€13.60, 1 May-15 Sep.** **2016**

PRADES *8G4* (10km NE Urban) *42.64269, 2.53367* **Camping Lac De Vinca (formerly Municipal Les Escoumes),** Rue des Escoumes, 66320 Vinça **04 68 05 84 78 or 06 72 32 27 07 (mob); campinglesescoumes@orange.fr; www.camping-lac-de-vinca.com**

Fr Prades take N116 E twd Perpignan. Vinca on R about 5m from Prades outskirts. Ignore 1st R into Vinca - narr rds. Take 2nd R then foll sp. 2*, Med, mkd, pt shd, pt sl, EHU (6-10A) €3; gas; sw; 20% statics; Eng spkn; fishing; bike hire. *"Beautiful, quiet, excel site; helpful staff; gd sized pitches; gd touring base; lake not suitable for toddlers (no sand, entry via steps); rec."* **€17.00, 1 Apr-31 Oct.** **2019**

PRALOGNAN LA VANOISE *9B4* (13.7km NW Rural) *45.44274, 6.64874* **Camping Huttopia Bozel en Vanoise (formerly Municipal),** Route de Chevelu, 73350 Bozel **04 79 41 70 83; camping.lechevelu.bozel@gmail.com; www.camping-bozel.com**

Foll D915 thro Bozel dir Pralognan. Site on R immed beyond vill. 2*, Med, mkd, hdstg, shd, pt sl, terr, EHU (6-10A) €3.50-4.50; sw nr; phone; Eng spkn; adv bkg acc; lake fishing 1km; CKE. *"In wood by rv; excel walking & climbing; vg; pleasant vill; lunchtime rest v popular with locals."* **€18.40, 1 Jun-30 Sep.** **2019**

PRAZ SUR ARLY *9B3* (0.6km W Urban) *45.83628, 6.56747* **Chantalouette,** 384 Route du Val d'arly, 74120 Praz sur Arly **04 50 21 90 25 or 06 70 06 19 71 (mob); chantalouette@prazarly.fr; www.prazarly.fr**

12 🐕 €0.40 ♿(htd) WD 🚿 🖳 ⊞ 🦋 ♍ 🍴 nr ⊕ nr 🛒 nr

On D1212, Ugine to Megeve. Site on L at southern end of vill. Sm, hdstg, pt shd, EHU (6-10A) €4.60-€8.50; gas; twin axles; bus adj; Eng spkn; adv bkg acc; ccard acc; games rm; CKE. *"Walking dist to ski bus; vg."* **€19.00** 2015

PREMERY *4G4* (1km NW Urban) *47.17804, 3.33692* **Camp Municipal Le Plan D'eau (Les Prés de la Ville),** 58700 Prémery **03 86 37 99 42 or 03 86 68 12 40 (Mairie); mairie-premery@wanadoo.fr; www.mairie-premery.fr**

♿ WD 🚿 ⅙ ♍ 🦋 🛒 nr

N fr Nevers on D977 to Prémery; turn R after 2nd rndabt. Site sp on D977. Med, pt shd, EHU (8-10A) €1-1.80; sw nr; red long stay; adv bkg acc; tennis adj; boating; fishing. *"Lovely, well-run lakeside site in town park; lake adj; clean, excl, htd, unisex san facs; popular NH; nice walk to interesting town; poss mkt traders; excel value."* **€9.30,** 1 May-30 Sep. 2016

PRESSAC *7A3* (8km SW Rural) *46.09696, 0.48081* **Camping Rural des Marronniers,** La Bussière, 16490 Pleuville **05 45 71 42 19; campingruraldes marronniers@gmail.com; www.campingruraldes marronniers.com**

12 🐕 Free ♿(htd) WD 🚿 ⅙ 🖳 ⊞ ♍ 🦋 ♍ 🍴 nr 🛒 nr ⚓ 🛶

S fr Poitiers on D741 to Pressac; turn R onto D34 to Pleuville then turn onto D30 dir Charroux, site on L in 1.5km - look for sp La Bussière. Sm, unshd, pt sl, EHU (10A) inc; bbq; twin axles; adv bkg acc; games rm; CKE. *"Friendly, British-owned, peaceful, lovely sm CL-type farm site; open field - chickens & ducks roaming; gd touring base; ideal for exploring SW France; fam/couples welcome; excel."* **€15.00** 2019

PRIVAS *9D2* (1.5km S Urban) *44.72668, 4.59730* **Kawan Village Ardèche Camping,** Blvd de Paste, Quartier Ouvèze, 07000 Privas **04 75 64 05 80; jcray@wanadoo.fr; www.ardechecamping.fr**

🐕 €3.30 ♿ WD 🚿 ⅙ 🖳 ⊞ MP ♍ ⊕ 🦈 🛒 nr ⚓ 🏊 🛶(htd) 🛝

Exit A7 junc 16 dir Privas. App Privas cross rv bdge & at rndabt take 2nd exit. Site ent opp supmkt, sp. 4*, Lge, mkd, pt shd, pt sl, EHU (10A) inc; bbq; red long stay; TV; 80% statics; Eng spkn; adv bkg acc; ccard acc; rv fishing; tennis adj; CKE. *"Very gd, friendly owners; gd rest and shady pitches; interesting area to visit; pleasant site; walk to town up extremely steep rd."* **€33.00,** 11 Apr-27 Sep. 2015

PUGET THENIERS *10E4* (2km NW Rural) *43.95801, 6.85980* **Camping L'Origan (Naturist),** 2160 Route de Savé, 06260 Puget-Théniers **04 93 05 06 00; origan@orange.fr; www.origan-village.com**

🐕 €2.50 ♿(htd) 🏔 ⅙ 🖳 ♍ 🍴 ⊕ 🦈 🛒 ⚓ 🛶(htd) 🛝

On N202 fr Entrevaux (dir Nice) at Puget-Théniers, immed turn L at rlwy x-ing (sp), site approx 1km up track. 3*, Med, hdg, mkd, hdstg, pt shd, pt sl, terr, EHU (6A) €4; bbq; TV; 50% statics; phone; train to Nice; Eng spkn; adv bkg acc; ccard acc; INF card; tennis; fishing; waterslide; sauna; archery. *"Sm pitches not suitable o'fits over 6m; hilly site but pitches level; san facs dated (2018); interesting area; great views; ent noise poss high ssn; attractive bar/rest; tourist steam train bet Puget-Theniers & Annot on certain days."* **€36.00,** Easter-3 Oct. 2018

PUIMOISSON *10E3* (6.5km NE Rural) *43.89836, 6.18011* **Camping à la Ferme Vauvenières (Sauvaire),** 04410 St Jurs **06 50 74 37 11; ferme.de.vauvenieres@ gmail.com; www.ferme-de-vauvenieres.fr**

🐕 €0.75 ♿ WD 🏔 ⅙ ♍ 🦋 ⊕ 🛒 nr

Fr Riez take D953 N to 1km beyond Puimoisson then fork R onto D108 sp St Jurs & site sp. Sm, pt shd, EHU (6A) €2.90; bbq; sw nr; Eng spkn; adv bkg acc; games area; CKE. *"Peaceful, basic site off beaten track; wonderful views; lavendar fields; friendly Dutch owner; clean san facs, poss stretched if site full; gd for mountain walking; D17 to Majastres v narr; vg mkt on Wed & Sat in Riez; sm supmkt at filling stn at ent Puimoisson; v lge mkd pitches."* **€18.00,** 1 Apr-15 Oct. 2019

PUIVERT *8G4* (0.5km S Rural) *42.91596, 2.0441* **Camping de Puivert,** Fontclaire, 11230 Puivert **04 68 20 00 58 or 06 22 45 15 74 (mob); camping-de-puivert@orange.fr; www.campings11.fr**

🐕 ♿ WD 🏔 🖳 ♍ 🦋 ♍ 🍴 ⊕ nr ⅙ 🛒 ♍

Take D117 W fr Quillan dir Lavelanet for 16km; at Puivert turn L onto D16; site in 500m by lake; well sp. Or E fr Foix on D117 for 45km; at Puivert turn R onto D16 & as bef. 2*, Med, hdg, hdstg, pt shd, terr, EHU (16A) €3; bbq (sep area); sw nr; fishing adj. *"Attractive area; lge pitches, some lakeside, some hill views; dated san facs but adequate & clean; museum in vill; chateau nrby; vg."* **€19.00,** 20 Apr-20 Sep. 2019

PUY EN VELAY, LE *9C1* (0.5km N Urban) *45.05014, 3.88044* **Camping de Bouthezard,** Chemin de Bouthezàrd, Ave d'Aiguilhe, 43000 Le Puy-en-Velay **04 71 09 55 09 or 06 15 08 23 59 (mob); camping.puyenvelay@aquadis-loisirs.com; www.aquadis-loisirs.com/camping-de-bouthezard**

🐕 €2 ♟♟♟ [WD] 🏕 ♨ ᕫ 🖫 ∕ [MSP] 📶 🛢 🛒 ⚠

Fr Le Puy heading NW on N102 to city cent; look for sp Clermont & Vichy; turn R at traff lts in Place Carnot at sp for Valence; site on L on bank of rv. Site ent immed opp Chapel St Michel & 200m fr volcanic core. 3*, Med, hdg, pt shd, EHU (10A) inc (rev pol); sw nr; bus stn 1.5km; Eng spkn; adv bkg acc; tennis adj; games rm; CKE. "Popular, well-kept site in gd location; busy - rec arr early; efficient staff; gates clsd 2100-0700 LS; no twin axles; may flood & grnd soft in v heavy rain; unrel opening dates - phone ahead LS; vg touring base on pilgrim rte to Spain; immac; very helpful owners; spectacular town; highly rec; pool adj; excel." **€18.00, 1 Apr-24 Oct.** 2019

PUY EN VELAY, LE *9C1* (9km N Rural) *45.12473, 3.92177* **Camp Municipal Les Longes,** Route des Rosières, 43800 Lavoûte-sur-Loire **04 71 08 18 79; campinglavoutesurloire@orange.fr; www.lavoutesurloire.fr**

🐕 €1.50 ♟♟♟ 🏕 ♨ ᕫ 🖫 ∕ [MSP] 🦋 ⚠

Fr Le Puy take N on D103 sp Lavoûte & Retournac. In Lavoûte turn R onto D7 bef rv bdge, site on L in 1km on rvside. 3*, Med, mkd, shd, EHU (6A) €2.50; sw nr; tennis; fishing 50m. "Gd, friendly site; gd walking; lovely quiet site by Haute Loire; san facs clean; rec; mostly statics." **€17.00, 1 May-14 Sep.** 2017

PUY EN VELAY, LE *9C1* (3km E Urban) *45.04431, 3.93030* **Camp Municipal d'Audinet,** Ave des Sports, 43700 Brives-Charensac **04 71 09 10 18; camping. audinet@wanadoo.fr; www.camping-audinet.fr**

♟♟♟ [WD] 🏕 ♨ ᕫ 🖫 ∕ [MSP] 🦋 ☂ 🛢 🛒 ⚠ 🛶

Fr Le Puy foll green sp E twd Valence. Fr S on N88 foll sp twd Valence & on E side of town foll white sp. 3*, Lge, pt shd, EHU (6A) €3.30; bbq; sw; red long stay; bus to town; fishing. "Spacious site on rvside; friendly, helpful staff; gd san facs, poss stretched high ssn; poss travellers - but not a prob; no twin axles; vg; 12 min bus to town every 1/2 hr." **€19.00, 30 Apr-17 Sep.** 2017

PUYSSEGUR *8E3* (0.2km N Rural) *43.75064, 1.06065* **FFCC Camping Namasté,** 31480 Puysségur **05 61 85 77 84; contact@camping-namaste.com; www.camping-namaste.com**

🐕 €1.50 ♟♟♟ 🏕 ♨ ᕫ 🖫 ∕ 🦋 ☂ 🛢 🛒 ⚠ 🖊 🛶 ⛵

Fr Toulouse NW on N224/D1 sp Cadours; at Puysségur in 30km foll Camping Namasté sp. (Puysségur is 1km NE of Cadours). 4*, Sm, pt shd, EHU (4-10A) €3-5; bbq; 10% statics; sauna; bike hire; games area; games rm; fishing. **€30.00, 1 May-15 Oct.** 2019

PYLA SUR MER *7D1* (7km S Coastal) *44.58517, -1.20868* **Camping Village Centre La Forêt,** Route de Biscarosse, 33115 Pyla-sur-Mer **05 56 22 73 28; contact@village-center.com; www.village-center.com**

🐕 €2 [WD] 🏕 ♨ ᕫ 🖫 ∕ [MSP] ☂ 🛢 🛒 ⚓ 🏖 sand 600m

Fr Bordeaux app Arcachon on A660 by-pass rd; at La Teste-de-Buch at rndabt foll sp for Dune du Pilat & 'campings'. At T-junc in 4km turn L; foll 'plage' & camping sp on D218. Site on R. 3*, Lge, hdg, mkd, shd, sl, EHU (6A) inc; bbq; 80% statics; adv bkg acc; ccard acc; solarium; tennis; bike hire; CKE. "Forest setting at foot of sand dune (own steps); well-organised; many facs; hang-gliding, surfing, sailing, cycle rtes nrby." **€20.00, 4 Apr-20 Sep.** 2018

"We must tell the Club about that great site we found"

Get your site reports in by mid-August and we'll do our best to get your updates into the next edition.

PYLA SUR MER *7D1* (8km S Rural/Coastal) *44.57474, -1.22217* **Yelloh! Village Panorama du Pyla,** Route de Biscarosse, 33115 Pyla-sur-Mer **05 56 22 10 44; mail@ camping-panorama.com; www.camping-panorama. com or www.yellohvillage.co.uk**

🐕 €5 ♟♟♟ [WD] 🏕 ♨ ᕫ 🖫 ∕ [MSP] ☂ 🛢 🛒 ⚠ 🖊 (htd) 🛶 sand adj

App Arcachon fr Bordeaux on A63/A660, at rndabt foll sp for Dune-du-Pilat & 'campings'. Foll sp for 'plage' & 'campings' on D218. Site on R next to Camping Le Petit Nice. 4*, Lge, mkd, hdstg, shd, sl, terr, EHU (3-10A) inc; gas; bbq; TV; 20% statics; Eng spkn; games area; tennis; games rm; sauna; waterslide; CKE. "Pleasant site on wooded dune; pitches clsd together; adv bkg not acc; some pitches poor; direct steep access to excel beach; site rds v narr; ltd pitches for v lge o'fits; some pitches sandy; gd facs; paragliding adj." **€46.00, 9 Apr-3 Oct.** 2016

QUETTEHOU *1C4* (2.5km E Urban/Coastal) *49.58520, -1.26858* **Camping La Gallouette,** Rue de la Gallouette, 50550 St Vaast-la-Hougue **02 33 54 20 57; contact@ camping-lagallouette.fr; www.camping-lagallouette.fr**

🐕 €1.80 ♟♟♟ [WD] 🏕 ♨ ᕫ 🖫 ∕ [MSP] 🦋 ☂ 🛢 🛒 ⚠ 🛶 (htd) 🏖 sand 300m

E fr Quettehou on D1, site sp in St Vaast-la-Houge to S of town. 4*, Lge, hdg, mkd, pt shd, EHU (6-10A) €3.80-4.60; gas; bbq; 10% statics; phone; adv bkg acc; games area; games rm; CKE. "Lovely friendly site; some lge pitches; gd range of facs; sh walk to interesting town; excel site." **€31.00, 1 Apr-30 Sep.** 2017

QUIBERON *2G3* (3.6km N Coastal) *47.49978, -3.12021* **Camping Do Mi Si La Mi,** 31 Rue de la Vierge, 56170 Quiberon **02 97 50 22 52; camping@ domisilami.com; www.domisilami.com**

🐕 €2.40 ♂♀ ⓌⒸ ♨ ⚲ ♿ 🚮 ⊘ 🦋 ⓜ 🍴 nr 🛒 nr ⛺

🛶 shgl 100m

Take D768 down Quiberon Peninsular, 3km after St Pierre-Quiberon & shortly after sp for rlwy level x-ing turn L into Rue de la Vierge, site on R in 400m. 3*, Lge, hdg, mkd, pt shd, pt sl, serviced pitches; EHU (3-10A) €2.80-4.30; gas; bbq; 40% statics; Eng spkn; ccard acc; bike hire; tennis nr; horseriding nr; sailing nr; games area; CKE. *"Gd touring base; vg; excel site; great location; excel rest."* **€32.00, 31 Mar-30 Sep.** 2018

QUIBERON *2G3* (1.5km SE Rural/Coastal) *47.47641, -3.10441* **Camping Le Bois d'Amour,** Rue St Clément, 56170 Quiberon **02 97 50 13 52; camping. boisdamour@flowercampings.com; www.quiberon-camping.com**

🐕 €5 ♂♀ ⓌⒸ ♨ ⚲ ♿ 🚮 ⊘ ⓜ 🦋 🍴 ♿ 🚲 🛒 ⛺ ✎ 🏊 (htd)

🛶 200m

Exit N165 at Auray onto D768. In Quiberon foll sp 'Thalassothérapie', site sp. 3*, Lge, mkd, hdg, pt shd, EHU (16A) €5; gas; bbq; Eng spkn; adv bkg acc; ccard acc; tennis; horseriding; bike hire; games area; CKE. *"Shwrs clean but hot water can be temperamental; lovely friendly clubhse with reasonable food prices."* **€20.00, 2 Apr-24 Sep.** 2016

QUIBERON *2G3* (2km SE Coastal) *47.47424, -3.10563* **Camp Municipal Le Goviro,** Blvd du Goviro, 56170 Quiberon **02 97 50 13 54 or 02 97 30 24 00 (LS); www.ville-quiberon.fr**

🐕 €1.65 ♂♀ ⓌⒸ ♿ 🚮 ⊘ ⓜ 🦋 ♿ nr ⛺ 🛶 sand adj

Fr D768 at Quiberon foll sp Port Maria & 'Cent Thalassothérapie'. Site 1km on L nr Sofitel hotel. 2*, Lge, hdg, mkd, pt shd, terr, EHU (13A) €3; gas; fishing adj; watersports adj. *"Popular, well-run site in excel location; lovely bay, gd sea views & coastal path into town; smallish pitches; clean, adequate san facs; ltd LS."* **€16.00, 1 Apr-12 Oct.** 2015

QUILLAN *8G4* (1.2km W Urban) *42.87358, 2.17565* **FFCC Camp Municipal La Sapinette,** 21 Ave René Delpech, 11500 Quillan **04 68 20 13 52; camping sapinette@wanadoo.fr; www.camping-la-sapinette.com**

🐕 €1.60 ♂♀ (htd) ⓌⒸ ♨ ♿ ⊘ 🦋 ⓟ 🛒 nr ⛺ 🏊

Foll D118 fr Carcassonne to Quillan; turn R at 2nd traff lts in town cent; site sp in town. 3*, Med, mkd, hdstg, hdg, pt shd, sl, terr, EHU (6A) €3.10; TV; 25% statics; adv bkg acc; ccard acc; CKE. *"Gd touring base; sm pitches, some level, mostly sl; early arr rec; helpful staff; san facs a little tired; excel pool; site poss tired end ssn; mkt Wed & Sat; leisure cent 500m; vet adj; highly rec; 15min walk to nice town."* **€25.00, 1 Apr-30 Oct.** 2016

QUIMPER *2F2* (10km SE Rural) *47.94133, -4.02453* **Camping de Keromen,** 38 Rue de Cornouaille, 29170 Saint-Evarzec **02 98 64 09 59; contact@campingde keromen.fr; www.campingdekeromen.fr**

🐕 ♂♀ ⓌⒸ ♨ ♿ ⊘ 🦋 ⓟ ⛺

Heading S fr Quimper on D783 at end of dual c'way fork R sp Evarzec. Cont over mini rndabt, site on R in 1.5km, well sp. Med, mkd, hdg, pt shd, EHU (10A); twin axles; TV; 40% statics; bus; adv bkg acc; games area; games rm. *"Adj lake area; donkeys & goats in enclosure; free fishing on sm lake; gd."* **€18.50, 1 Apr-30 Oct.** 2017

QUIMPER *2F2* (9km SE Rural) *47.93811, -3.99959* **Camping Vert de Creac'h-Lann (Hemidy),** 202 Route de Concarneau, 29170 St Evarzec **02 98 56 29 88 or 06 68 46 97 25 (mob); contact@campingvert creachlann.com; www.campingvertcreachlann.com**

🐕 ♂♀ ⓌⒸ ♨ 🚮 ⊘ ⓜ 🦋 ⓟ ♿ nr ⛺ nr ⛺ (htd)

S fr Quimper on D783, 1.5km fr St Evarzec rndabt at brow of hill (easily missed). Sm, hdg, pt shd, pt sl, EHU (4-13A) €3-3.50; bbq; 60% statics; Eng spkn; adv bkg acc; games rm. *"Lovely spacious site; lge pitches; friendly, helpful owner; gd playgrnd; poss to stay after end Sep by arrangement; lovely old town; gd touring base; daily mkt; excel."* **€13.00, 1 Jun-30 Sep.** 2017

QUIMPER *2F2* (3.5km S Rural) *47.97685, -4.11060* **Camping L'Orangerie de Lanniron,** Château de Lanniron, 29000 Quimper **02 98 90 62 02; camping@ lanniron.com; www.lanniron.com**

🐕 €5.70 ♂♀ ⓌⒸ ♨ ⚲ ♿ 🚮 ⊘ ⓜ ⓟ 🍴 ♿ 🚲 ⛺ ✎ 🏊 (htd) 🚣

Fr Rennes/Lorient: on N165 Rennes-Quimper, Quimper-Centre, Quimper-Sud exit, foll dir Pont l'Abbé on S bypass until exit sp Camping de Lanninon on R. At top of slip rd turn L & foll site sp, under bypass then 2nd R to site. Recep at Old Farm 500m bef site. 5*, Lge, mkd, pt shd, serviced pitches; EHU (10A) inc; gas; bbq; TV; 40% statics; phone; bus; Eng spkn; adv bkg acc; ccard acc; bike hire; tennis; golf; canoeing; rv fishing; games rm; CKE. *"Excel, busy, family-run site in grnds of chateau by Rv Odet; 9-hole golf on site; aqua park; well-spaced pitches; vg san facs; vg leisure facs; easy walk to town."* **€37.00, 31 Mar-5 Nov, B21.** 2018

QUIMPER *2F2* (2.6km W Urban) *47.99198, -4.12536* **Camp Municipal Bois du Séminaire,** Ave des Oiseaux, 29000 Quimper **02 98 55 61 09; camping-municipal@ quimper.bzh; www.mairie-quimper.fr**

♂♀ ⓌⒸ ♨ ♿ ⊘ 🦋 🍴 ⓟ nr 🛒 nr

Fr E on D765 to Quimper, bear L on 1-way system along rv. In 1km bear R over rv into Blvd de Boulguinan - D785. In 500m turn R onto Blvd de France (lge junc). In 1km bear R into Ave des Oiseaux, site on R in front of Auberge de Jeunesse. Med, hdg, pt shd, terr, EHU (5A) €3.30; bbq; 10% statics; phone; bus adj; ccard acc; CKE. *"Conv NH/ sh stay."* **€12.00, 1 Jun-30 Sep.** 2015

For a guide to symbols see the fold out on the rear cover

QUIMPERLE *2F2* (7km NE Rural) *47.90468, -3.47477* **Camping Le Ty-Nadan,** Route d'Arzano, 29310 Locunolé **17 46 78 51 00 or 02 98 71 75 47; info@tynadan-vacances.fr; www.irisparc.co.uk**

🐕 €5.50 � (htd) ⬛ ⛲ ♿ ⬛ 🚿 🚮 ♨ 🍴 🍺 ⛽ 🛒 ⚒ ⚞ ⛷ (covrd, htd) 🚣

To avoid Quimperlé cent exit N165 dir Quimperlé. As ent town turn R onto D22 dir Arzano. In 9km turn L at W end of Arzano (un-numbered rd) sp Locunolé & Camping Ty Nadan; site on L just after x-ing Rv Elle. Or fr Roscoff on D69 S join N165/E60 but take care at uneven level x-ing at Pen-ar-Hoat 11km after Sizun. 5*, Lge, mkd, hdg, pt shd, serviced pitches; EHU (10A) inc (long lead poss req); gas; bbq (charcoal, gas); TV; 40% statics; Eng spkn; adv bkg acc; ccard acc; waterslide; games area; horseriding; rv fishing adj; tennis; archery; games rm; sauna; bike hire; canoeing adj; CKE. *"Excel, peaceful site by rv; pitches poss narr for lge o'fits; friendly staff; spa; no o'fits over 8.5m high ssn; barrier clsd 2300-0800; many activities; gd touring base."* **€46.00, 18 Apr-31 Aug, B20.** **2019**

"I need an on-site restaurant"

We do our best to make sure site information is correct, but it is always best to check any must-have facilities are still available or will be open during your visit.

QUINTIN *2E3* (0.6km SE Urban) *48.40128, -2.90672* **Camp Municipal du Lac,** Chemin des Côtes, 22800 Quintin **02 96 74 92 54 or 02 96 74 84 01 (Mairie); mairie@quintin.fr; www.quintin.fr**

♨♨ ⛲ ♿ 🚿 🚮 ⚒ ♨ 🍴 ⛽ nr 🛒 nr ⚞

Fr N exit D790 at rndabt & foll sp 'Cent Ville'; at 2nd rndabt site sp; site on L 200m after 5th ped x-ing (narr rd, easy to miss). Fr S on D790 do not take slip rd (D7) but cont to rndabt - narr rds in town; then as above. Site N (100m) of town gardens & boating lake. 2*, Sm, pt shd, pt sl, EHU (6A) €2.80; bbq; fishing. *"Fair site; helpful warden; poss insufficient of security (2011); interesting town."* **€8.50, 15 Apr-30 Sep.** **2016**

RABASTENS *8E3* (2km NW Rural) *43.83090, 1.69805* **Camp Municipal des Auzerals,** Route de Grazac, 81800 Rabastens **05 63 33 70 36 or 06 23 81 85 69 (mob); mairie.rabastens@libertysurf.fr**

♨♨ ⬛ ⛲ ⬛ 🚮 ⚒ ♨ nr 🛒 nr ⚞

Exit A68 junc 7 onto D12. In Rabastens town cent foll sp dir Grazac, site sp. 1*, Sm, hdg, mkd, pt shd, pt sl, terr, EHU (10A) inc; CKE. *"Attractive lakeside site; facs old but clean; office 0900-1200 & 1500-1900, otherwise height barrier in place; conv m'way NH; pool adj high ssn; highly rec; gd hedges around plots; call to check if site open."* **€11.00, 1 Apr-30 Sep.** **2017**

RAMBOUILLET *4E3* (3km SE Rural) *48.6252, 1.84495* **Camping Huttopia Rambouillet,** Route du Château d'Eau, 78120 Rambouillet **01 30 41 07 34; rambouillet@huttopia.com; www.huttopia.com**

🐕 €4.20 (htd) ⬛ ⛲ ♿ ⬛ 🚿 🚮 ⚞ ♨ 🍴 ⛽ 🛒 ⚞

Fr N exit D910 at 'Rambouillet Eveuses' & foll sp to site in 2.5km. Fr S exit at 'Rambouillet Cent' & foll sp to site back onto D910 (in opp dir), exit 'Rambouillet Eveuses' as above. Avoid Rambouillet town cent. 3*, Lge, hdg, pt shd, EHU (10A) inc; bbq (elec, gas); 10% statics; phone; Eng spkn; adv bkg rec; ccard acc; fishing adj; sep car park; CKE. *"Excel, busy, wooded site; conv Paris by train - parking at stn 3km; gd cycling rtes; interesting town."* **€41.00, 30 Mar-3 Nov, P17.** **2017**

RAON L'ETAPE *6E3* (2km SE Rural) *48.39474, 6.86232* **Camping Vosgina,** 1 Rue la Cheville, 88420 Moyenmoutier **03 29 41 47 63; info@camping-vosgina.com; www.camping-vosgina.com**

🐕 €1.50 ♨♨ ⬛ ⛲ ⬛ 🚮 ⚞ ♨ 🍴 ⛽

On N59 St Dié-Lunéville rd, take exit mkd Senones, Moyenmoutier. At rndabt take rd twd St Blaise & foll camping sp. Site is on minor rd parallel with N59 bet Moyenmoutier & Raon. 2*, Med, hdg, pt shd, terr, EHU (4-10A) €3-6; gas; TV; 20% statics; Eng spkn; adv bkg acc; ccard acc; CKE. *"Gd site for quiet holiday in a non-touristy area of Alsace; friendly recep; lovely countryside; many cycle/walking rtes in area; barrier clsd 2200-0700; park like setting; beautifully maintained; friendly Swiss owners; excel for sh stay or NH."* **€20.00, 25 Mar-31 Oct.** **2016**

"Satellite navigation makes touring much easier"

Remember most sat navs don't know if you're towing or in a larger vehicle – always use yours alongside maps and site directions.

RAON L'ETAPE *6E3* (9km S Rural) *48.36355, 6.83861* **Camping Beaulieu-sur-l'Eau,** 41 Rue de Trieuche, 88480 Etival-Clairefontaine **03 29 41 53 51; camping-beaulieu-vosges@orange.fr; www.camping-beaulieu-vosges.com**

12 🐕 ♨♨ (htd) ⛲ 🚮 ⚞ ♨ 🍴 ⛽ nr 🛒 ⚞

SE fr Baccarat on N59 turn R in vill of Etival-Clairefontaine on D424 sp Rambervillers & Epinal & foll sp for 3km. Ent on L. 2*, Med, mkd, pt shd, terr, EHU (4-10A) €3.05-7.90; gas; sw nr; 10% statics; adv bkg rec; CKE. *"Lovely, peaceful, clean site; 80% statics; dedicated touring area; gd rural views."* **€10.50** **2015**

RAUZAN *7D2* (0.2km N Rural) *44.78237, -0.12712*
Camping du Vieux Château, 6 Blabot-Bas, 33420
Rauzan 05 57 84 15 38; contact@vieuxchateau.fr;
www.camping-levieuxchateau.com

Fr Libourne S on D670, site is on D123 about 1.5km
fr D670, sp. 3*, Sm, mkd, shd, EHU (6A) €5 (poss
rev pol); gas; TV; 10% statics; Eng spkn; adv bkg acc;
ccard acc; tennis; bike hire; horseriding; CKE. "Lovely
site but take care tree roots on pitches; quiet wooded
area; pleasant family run site; helpful owners; basic
san facs - ltd LS & poss not well-maintained, & poss
stretched high ssn; access to some pitches diff when
wet; conv vineyards; walking dist to vill; nice sw pool;
wine-tasting; TV rm & bar open to 9pm; events avail."
€27.00, 30 Mar-18 Oct.   2018

REALMONT *8E4* (2.5km SW Rural) *43.77092, 2.16336*
Camp Municipal La Batisse, Route Graulhet, 81120
Réalmont 05 63 55 50 41; camping-realmont@
wanadoo.fr; www.realmont.fr/decouvrir/camping-
municipal-realmont

On D612 fr Albi heading S thro Réalmont. On exit
Réalmont turn R on D631 where site sp. Site 1.5km
on L on Rv Dadou. 2*, Sm, pt shd, EHU (3A) inc; gas;
10% statics; rv fishing adj. "Pleasant, peaceful, well-kept
site in rv valley; friendly, pleasant warden; dated but
clean san facs; nr Albi-Castres cycle rte; excel value; mkt
Wed; gd; hg rec." €12.00, 1 Apr-30 Sep.   2017

REGUINY *2F3* (1km S Urban) *47.96928, -2.74083*
Camp Municipal de l'Etang, Rue de la Piscine, 56500
Réguiny 02 97 38 66 11; mairie.requiny@wanadoo.fr;
www.reguiny.com

On D764 fr Pontivy to Ploërmel, turn R into D11
to Réguiny then foll sp. 2*, Med, pt shd, EHU (10A)
€2.50; phone; Eng spkn; ccard acc. "Gd facs; htd pool
500m; gd touring base; deposit for gate remote control
(€100); v pleasant site; rec rest in vill; gd acc to S
Brittany." €10.40, 15 Jun-15 Sep.   2018

REIMS *3D4* (19km SE Rural) *49.16687, 4.21416*
**Camping Intercommunalité Val de Vesle (formerly
Municipal),** 8 Rue de Routoir, Courmelois, 51360
Val-de-Vesle 03 26 03 91 79; valdevesle.camping@
orange.fr; www.reims-tourism.com

Fr Reims twd Châlons-en-Champagne on D944, turn
L by camp sp on D326 to Val-de-Vesle, foll camp sp;
look for tall grain silos by canal. NB do not turn L
bef D326 due narr lane. 2*, Med, mkd, shd, EHU (6-
10A) €3 (long lead poss req); bbq; adv bkg acc; ccard
acc; rv fishing; CKE. "Charming, well-kept, busy site
amongst trees; popular NH, rec arrive early; informal
pitching; friendly, helpful staff; new security gate,
booking in req for code (2011); in sm vill (no shops);
poss mosquito prob; cycle rte to Reims along canal; gd
touring base; lge pitches; lovely, clean facs; well sp fr
D944." €15.00, 1 Apr-15 Oct.   2018

REMOULINS *10E2* (2km NW Rural) *43.94805,
4.54583* **Camping La Sousta,** Ave du Pont
de Gard, 30210 Remoulins 04 66 37 12 80;
info@lasousta.fr; www.lasousta.fr

Fr A9 exit Remoulins, foll sp for Nîmes, then sp
'Pont du Gard par Rive Droite' thro town. Immed
over rv bdge turn R sp 'Pont du Gard etc'; site on R
800m fr Pont du Gard. 4*, Lge, hdstg, mkd, shd, pt sl,
EHU (6A); gas; bbq (sep area); sw nr; TV; 20% statics;
Eng spkn; adv bkg acc; ccard acc; bike hire; fishing;
watersports; tennis; CKE. "Friendly, helpful staff;
poss diff lge o'fits due trees; excel touring base; in
walking dist Pont-du-Gard; set in lovely woodland
with plenty of shd; vg; can be dry & dusty in Jul & Aug;
bar & rest open in LS; sw pool clsd until 5th May."
€34.00, 12 Mar-1 Nov.   2018

REMOULINS *10E2* (4km NW Rural) *43.95594, 4.51588*
Camping International Les Gorges du Gardon,
Chemin de la Barque Vieille, Route d'Uzès, 30210
Vers-Pont-du-Gard 04 66 22 81 81; camping.
international@wanadoo.fr; www.le-camping-
international.com

Exit A9 junc 23 Remoulins & head NW twd Uzès
on D981. Pass turn for Pont-du-Gard & site on L
in 1.5km. Or fr E on N100 turn N onto D6086 then
D19A to Pont-du-Gard (avoiding Remoulins cent).
4*, Lge, mkd, hdg, pt shd, EHU (6A) inc; gas; sw nr;
red long stay; TV; 10% statics; Eng spkn; adv bkg
acc; ccard acc; tennis; games rm; boating; fishing;
games area; CKE. "Beautiful location; many sm pitches
- some lge pitches to back of site; friendly, cheerful
owners; excel san facs, ltd LS; no winch axles or o'fits
over 5m; beavers in rv; site poss subject to flooding
& evacuation; superb; conv for the Pont du Gard,
thoroughly rec staying several nights, unique site."
€29.00, 15 Mar-30 Sep, C18.   2018

RENNES *2F4* (4km NE Urban) *48.13529, -1.64597*
Camp Municipal des Gayeulles, Rue du Maurice
Audin, 35700 Rennes 02 99 36 91 22; info@camping-
rennes.com; www.camping-rennes.com

Exit Rennes ring rd N136 junc 14 dir Maurepas
& Maison Blanche, foll sp 'Les Gayeules' & site.
Narr app to site. 3*, Med, mkd, hdstg, pt shd, pt sl,
serviced pitches; EHU (10A) inc; bbq; red long stay;
phone; bus; Eng spkn; adv bkg acc; ccard acc; tennis
nr; CKE. "Lovely, well-kept, well-run site adj activity
park; friendly, helpful staff; lge pitches; slight sl for
m'vans; 1st class facs; office clsd 1200-1400; reg bus
to Rennes, a lovely city; sm m'van Aire de Service adj;
excel; mini golf nr; archery nrby; no dogs allowed in
park adj; m'van o'night area; pool adj; noise fr disco
& football; great location; new san facs close to ent."
€19.00   2018

REOLE, LA *7D2* (1.6km SE Urban) *44.57778, -0.03360* **Camp Municipal La Rouergue,** Bords de Garonne, 33190 La Réole **05 56 61 13 55; lareole@ entredeuxmers.com; www.entredeuxmers.com**

🐕 €2 ♦♦♦ 🏍 ⬛

On N113 bet Bordeaux & Agen or exit A62 at junc 4. In La Réole foll sps S on D9 to site on L immed after x-ing suspension bdge. 2*, Med, pt shd, EHU (3A) inc; gas; boating; fishing. *"Resident warden; 2m barrier clsd 1200-1500; pool 500m; Sat mkt on rv bank."* **€16.00, 1 May-30 Sep.** 2015

"There aren't many sites open at this time of year"

If you're travelling outside peak season remember to call ahead to check site opening dates – even if the entry says 'open all year'.

RETHEL *5C1* (19km E Urban) *49.48234, 4.57589* **Camping Le Vallage (formerly Municipal),** 38 Chemin de l'Assaut, 08130 Attigny **03 24 71 23 06; camping. levallage@orange.f; www.camping-levallage.fr**

🐕 ♦♦♦ WD 🏍 ⬛ ⬛ 🏍 🐕 nr ⬛

E on D983 fr Rethel to Attigny; fr town cent take D987 twd Charleville; over rv bdge; 2nd turn on L; sp. 2*, Med, mkd, hdg, hdstg, pt shd, EHU (10A) inc; 50% statics; phone; fishing; tennis; CKE. *"Lovely quiet site; lge pitches; sports facs adj; helpful staff; pool adj; gd facs."* **€16.00, 1 Apr-15 Oct.** 2015

RFVEL *8F1* (0.5km E Urban) *43.45454, 2.01515* **Camp Municipal Le Moulin du Roy,** Tuilerie de Chazottes, off Ave de Sorèze, 31250 Revel **05 61 83 32 47 or 05 62 18 71 40 (Mairie); mairie@mairie-revel.fr; www.tourisme-revel.com**

🐕 €0.90 🏍 🏍 ⬛ 🐕 nr ⬛

Fr Revel ring rd take D1/D85 dir Sorèze, site sp. 2*, Med, hdg, pt shd, EHU €320; sw nr; phone; bus; Eng spkn; tennis adj; CKE. *"Pleasant, immac site; htd pool adj; helpful staff; Sat mkt; vg."* **€16.00, 2 Jun-7 Sep.** 2017

REVEL *8F4* (6km E Urban) *43.45446, 2.06953* **Camping St Martin,** Les Vigariés, 81540 Sorèze **05 63 50 20 19; campingsaintmartin@gmail.com; www.campingsaintmartin.com**

🐕 €1.50 ♦♦♦ WD 🏍 ⬛ ⬛ 🐕 🦋 🏍 Y 🏍 ⬛ ⬛ 🐕 ⬛

Fr Revel take D85 sp Sorèze; site sp on N side of vill; turn L at traff lts; site on R in 100m. 3*, Sm, mkd, hdstg, hdg, pt shd, EHU (10A) €3.60; bbq; sw nr; TV; 20% statics; tennis; games rm; CKE. *"Vg, well-kept site; friendly staff; excel san facs; fascinating medieval town; nr Bassin de St Ferréol; excel mkt in Revel; rec; noise fr adj sports facs & pitches nr san fac beware of being hit by footballs."* **€24.60, 30 Mar-14 Oct.** 2017

REVIGNY SUR ORNAIN *5D1* (0.4km S Urban) *48.82663, 4.98412* **Camp Municipal du Moulin des Gravières,** Rue du Stade, 55800 Revigny-sur-Ornain **03 29 78 73 34; contact@ot-revigny-ornain.fr; www.ot-revigny-ornain.fr**

🐕 ♦♦♦ WD 🏍 ⬛ 🏍 ⬛ 🏍 MSP 🦋 🐕 nr ⬛

N fr Bar-le-Duc on D994 to Revigny-sur-Ornain; fr town cent take D995 twd Vitry-le-François. Site on R, sp. 2*, Sm, mkd, hdg, pt shd, EHU (6A) €2.70; TV; 3% statics; Eng spkn; adv bkg acc; CKE. *"Pleasant, well-kept site; lge pitches; vg, modern facs; trout stream runs thro site; bike hire in town; tennis in town; gd cycling along canal; mkt Wed adj; highly rec; excel site, beautifully kept; park like setting; far better than any other municipal site we have stayed on."* **€13.00, 1 May-30 Sep.** 2018

RHINAU *6E3* (0.5km NW Rural) *48.32123, 7.69788* **Camping Ferme des Tuileries,** 1 Rue des Tuileries, 67860 Rhinau **03 88 74 60 45 or 06 85 74 98 97; camping.fermetuileries@neuf.fr; www.fermedes tuileries.com**

♦♦♦ WD 🏍 🏍 ⬛ 🏍 MSP 🦋 Y Y ⬛ 🏍 🐕 nr ⬛ 🏍 🏊 (htd)

Take D1083 (between Strasbourg and Selestat). Exit at Benfield or Sand and take D5 through Boofzheim to Rhinau. Site sp. 3*, Med, hdstg, mkd, pt shd, EHU (6A) €3.20; gas; bbq; sw; 20% statics; Eng spkn; games area; games rm; bike hire; tennis. *"Spacious site with excel facs; regimented; free ferry across Rv Rhine adj; vg; excel for cycling; hdstdg for MH's."* **€16.50, 1 Apr-30 Sep.** 2018

RIBEAUVILLE *6E3* (2km E Urban) *48.19490, 7.33648* **Camp Municipal Pierre-de-Coubertin,** Rue de Landau, 68150 Ribeauville **03 89 73 66 71; camping.ribeauville@ wanadoo.fr; www.camping-alsace.com**

🐕 €1 ♦♦♦ (htd) WD 🏍 🏍 ⬛ 🏍 🦋 Y 🏍

Exit N83 junc 20 at Ribeauville onto D106 & foll rd to o'skts; at traff lts turn R & then immed R again. Site on R in 500m. Camp at sports grnd nr Lycée. 4*, Lge, mkd, pt shd, pt sl, EHU (16A) €3.50; gas; CKF *"Well-run site; friendly, helpful staff; park outside site bef checking in; clean, excel san facs; resident storks; gd size pitches; gd touring base; mkt Sat; pool adj; highly rec; excel."* **€17.00, 15 Mar-15 Nov.** 2017

RIBEAUVILLE *6E3* (4.5km S Rural) *48.16200, 7.31691* **Camping de Riquewihr,** 1 Route du Vin, 68340 Riquewihr **03 89 47 90 08; camping.riquewihr@wanadoo.fr; www.ribeauville-riquewihr.com**

🐕 €1.20 ♦♦♦ (htd) WD 🏍 🏍 ⬛ 🏍 MSP Y 🐕 nr ⬛

Fr Strasbourg on N83/E25, take junc 21 (fr opp dir take junc 22) to Blebenheim/Riquewihr. D416 & D3 thro Blebenheim. At T-junc turn R onto D1B, site on R at rndabt. 4*, Lge, mkd, hdg, hdstg, pt shd, pt sl, EHU (6A) €3.50 (poss rev pol); gas; ccard acc; tennis; CKE. *"Rec arr early; friendly staff; san facs clean; gd for sm children; lovely town; games area adj; m'van o'night area; office clsd 1200-1400."* **€21.00, 28 Mar-31 Dec.** 2015

RIBERAC *7C2* (0.5km N Rural) *45.25755, 0.34128*
Camp Municipal La Dronne, Route d'Angoulême,
24600 Ribérac **05 53 92 41 61; ot.riberac@perigord.tm.fr**

🐕 €0.50 ♿ 🚿 ♿ 🔌 🍴 ✗ ♨ 🛒 nr ⛺

Site on W of main rd D708 immed N of bdge over
Rv Dronne on o'skts of Ribérac. 2*, Med, hdg, pt shd,
EHU (10A) €2.50. "Vg, well-run site; pitches in cent
hdgd & shady; facs gd & clean but inadequate high ssn;
Fri mkt." **€14.00, 1 Jun-15 Sep.** **2017**

RIBES *9D2* (0.7km S Rural) *44.29545, 4.12436*
Camping Les Cruses, Ribes 07260 Joyeuse
33 04 75 39 54 69; **les-cruses@wanadoo.fr;**
www.campinglescruses.com

🐕 €3 ♿ (htd) 🚿 ♿ 🔌 🍴 MSP 🦋 📶 🍴 🍺 ⛺ ✏ 🛶 🏊 1km

Head NW on rue du Mas de Laffont twd Le Chateâu
after 120m turn L onto Le Chateâu. Turn R onto
D550, sharp R twds Laffont, L onto Laffont, sharp
R twd D450 after 40m turn L onto D450. Sm, mkd,
shd, EHU (10A) €4.30; bbq; TV; Eng spkn; adv bkg acc;
ccard acc; games area; CCI. "Excel on site pool and
jacuzz; v helpful and friendly owners; nr lively town and
places to see." **€31.70, 1 Apr-30 Sep.** **2019**

RIEL LES EAUX *6F1* (2km W Rural) *47.97050, 4.64990*
Camp Municipal du Plan d'Eau, 21570 Riel-les-Eaux
03 80 93 72 76; **bar-camping-du-marais@wanadoo.fr**

♿ 🚿 ♿ 🔌 🍴 ✗ ♨ 🍴 🛶 ⛺

NE fr Châtillon-sur-Seine on D965 twd Chaumont:
after 6km turn N onto D13 at Brion-sur-Ource; cont
thro Belan-sur-Ource. Site almost opp junc with D22
turning to Riel-les-Eaux; site well sp. 2*, Sm, mkd,
pt shd, EHU (6A) €3; Eng spkn; fishing; CKE. "Conv
Champagne area; lake adj; excel; vg, simple site; lge
hdg pitches." **€12.00, 1 Apr-31 Oct.** **2015**

RIEUX *2G3* (0.5km E Urban) *47.59801, -02.10131*
Le Parc du Château, 56350 Rieux, France **02999
19785; contact@mariederriex.fr; rieux-morbihan.fr**

🐕 🐎 🚿 ♿ 🔌 🍴 MSP 🍴 ♨ ⛺

Turn R off D114 at R angled bend E of town.
Sm, hdg, mkd, pt shd, terr, EHU (10A) €2.60; bbq;
TV; 5% statics; phone; bus 200m; Eng spkn; adv
bkg acc; canoeing; fishing; sailing; tennis; CKE.
"Beside Vilaine canal; pretty, well kept site; vg."
€13.40, 1 Apr-31 Oct. **2016**

RIEZ *10E3* (0.8km SE Urban) *43.81306, 6.09931*
Camping Rose de Provence, Rue Edouard Dauphin,
04500 Riez **04 92 77 75 45; info@rose-de-provence.com;
www.rose-de-provence.com**

🐕 €1.60-2.10 ♿ 🚿 ♿ 🔌 🍴 🍴 nr ♨ nr ⛺

Exit A51 junc 18 onto D82 to Gréoux-les-Bains then
D952 to Riez. On reaching Riez strt across rndabt,
at T-junc turn L & immed R, site sp. 3*, Med, mkd,
pt shd, EHU (6A) inc (rev pol); 5% statics; phone; adv
bkg acc; tennis adj; CKE. "Beautiful, well-kept site;
helpful, friendly owners; gd san facs; nice vill; conv
Verdon Gorge; mkd walks around vill; trampoline &
gym equipmnt; gate clse 1230-1500 & 2100-0830."
€21.00, 12 Apr-1 Oct. **2015**

RILLE *4G1* (4km W Rural) *47.45750, 0.21840*
Camping Huttopia Rillé, Base de Loisirs de Pincemaille,
Lac de Rillé, 37340 Rillé **02 47 24 62 97; rille@
huttopia.com; www.huttopia.com**

🐕 €3.50 ♿ (htd) 🚿 ♿ 🔌 🍴 ✗ 🍸 ♨ 🍴 ⛺ 🏊 (htd)

Fr N or S D749 to Rillé, foll sp to Lac de Pincemaille,
site sp on S side of lake. 3*, Med, shd, EHU (6-10A)
€4.20-6.20; sw nr; 10% statics; adv bkg rec; sep car
park; watersports; fishing; games rm; tennis. "Peaceful
site; vg walking; excel." **€38.00, 13 Apr-29 Sep.** **2019**

RIOM *9B1* (6km NW Rural) *45.90614, 3.06041*
Camping de la Croze, St Hippolyte, 63140 Châtel-
Guyon **04 73 86 08 27 or 06 87 14 43 62 (mob);
info@campingcroze.com; www.campingcroze.com**

🐕 €1.80 ♿ (htd) 🚿 🔌 🍴 ✗ 🦋 📶 🍴 nr ⛺ 🏊 (htd)

Fr A71 exit junc 13; ring rd around Riom sp
Châtel-Guyon to Mozac, then D455. Site L bef ent
St Hippolyte. Fr Volvic on D986 turn L at rndabt
after Leclerc supmkt & L again to D455. NB Not rec
to tow thro Riom. 3*, Lge, mkd, pt shd, pt sl, EHU
(6-10A) €3.80; 10% statics; CKE. "Gd sightseeing area;
mini-bus to Châtel-Guyon (2km) high ssn; vg; supmkt
nrby; gd rest." **€18.50, 26 Mar-30 Oct.** **2017**

RIOM ES MONTAGNES *7C4* (0.9km E Rural) *45.28214,
2.66707* **Camp Municipal Le Sédour,** 15400
Riom-ès-Montagnes **04 71 78 05 71**

♿ 🚿 ♿ 🔌 🍴 MSP 🍴 nr ⛺

Site on W of D678 Riom N to Condat rd, 500m out of
town over bdge, sp fr all dirs, opp Clinique du Haut
Cantal. 3*, Med, mkd, pt shd, pt sl, EHU (6A); bbq;
twin axles; TV; Eng spkn; adv bkg acc; games area. "Vg;
takeaway." **€16.00, 1 May-30 Sep.** **2015**

RIOZ *6G2* (0.9km E Rural) *47.42525, 6.07524*
Camp Municipal du Lac, Rue de la Faïencerie, 70190
Rioz **03 84 91 91 59, 03 84 91 84 84 (Mairie) or 06 33
78 63 75 (mob); camping@rioz.fr; camping.rioz.fr**

🐕 €1.50 ♿ (htd) 🚿 🔌 🦋 ♨ nr 🛒 nr ⛺

Site sp off D15. 3*, Med, hdstg, hdg, pt shd, EHU
(16A) €2.50; gas. "Site yourself, warden calls; some
lge pitches; gd facs; pool adj; footpath to vill shops."
€10.40, 1 Apr-30 Sep. **2016**

RIVIERE SUR TARN *10E1* (2km E Rural) *44.19100,
3.15675* **FLOWER Camping Le Peyrelade,** Route des
Gorges du Tarn, 12640 Rivière-sur-Tarn **05 65 62 62 54;
campingpeyrelade@orange.fr; www.camping
peyrelade.com or www.flowercampings.com**

🐕 €2 ♿ 🚿 ♿ 🔌 🍴 MSP ✗ 🍸 🍴 ♨ ⛺ ✏ 🏊 (htd)

Exit A75 junc 44.1 to Aguessac, then take D907
N thro Rivière-sur-Tarn to site in 2km. Fr Millau
drive N on N9 to Aguessac, then onto D907 thro
Rivière-sur-Tarn, & site sp on R. 4*, Lge, mkd, hdg,
shd, terr, EHU (6A) €4; gas; bbq; cooking facs; sw nr;
TV; phone; bus; adv bkg acc; ccard acc; canoeing;
games rm; CKE. "Excel touring base in interesting area;
bike hire 100m; lovely quiet site with pitches next to Rv
Tarn; gd pool; excel facs; rvside pitches extra charge."
€46.90, 12 May-15 Sep. **2019**

For a guide to symbols see the fold out on the rear cover

FRANCE

RIVIERE SUR TARN *10E1* (0.4km SW Rural) *44.18530, 3.13060* **Camping Les Peupliers,** Rue de la Combe, 12640 Rivière-sur-Tarn **05 65 59 85 17; lespeupliers 12640@orange.fr; www.campinglespeupliers.fr**

🐕 €3 ♨ ♿ WD ♨ ⛱ 🚿 🚽 ✉ MAP 🦋 ♫ 🍽 🛈 🍴 🛒 nr 🏭 🏊 ⚓ (htd) 🚣

Heading N on N9 turn R dir Aguessac onto D907 twd Rivière-sur-Tarn. Site on R bef vill. Or fr A75 exit junc 44.1 sp Aguessac/Gorges du Tarn. In Aguessac, foll sp Rivière-sur-Tarn for 5km, site clearly sp. 4*, Med, hdstg, mkd, hdg, pt shd, EHU (6A) inc; gas; bbq; sw nr; TV; 10% statics; Eng spkn; adv bkg acc; ccard acc; canoeing; fishing; horseriding; waterslide; games area; tennis; watersports; CKE. *"Lovely rural site alongside rv Tarn; friendly staff and owners; beautiful scenery; kayaking avail; adv bkg rec; excel site for gorges."* **€34.00, 1 Apr-30 Sep.** **2015**

ROANNE *9A1* (5km SW Rural) *45.98830, 4.04531* **Camping L'Orée du Lac,** 68 Route du Barrage, 42300 Villerest **04 77 69 60 88; loreedulac@wanadoo.fr; www.loreedulac.net**

🐕 €1 ♨ WD ⛱ ♫ 🦋 ♫ 🍽 🛈 🍴 🛒 nr 🏭 🏊 ⚓

Take D53 SW fr Roanne to Villerest; site sp in vill. 3*, Sm, mkd, pt shd, pt sl, EHU (6A) €3.50; sw; TV; phone; Eng spkn; adv bkg rec; watersports; fishing; CKE. *"Attractive, lovely site nr medieval vill; much of site diff lge/med o'fits; lower pt of site diff when wet; sandy sw beach 800m on lake; gd facs; helpful owners."* **€24.00, 14 Apr-28 Oct.** **2019**

ROCAMADOUR *7D3* (2.7km N Rural) *44.81040, 1.61615* **FFCC Camping Ferme Branche,** Route de Souillac, Les Campagnes, 46500 Rocamadour **05 65 33 63 37 or 06 75 19 69 90 (mob); campingferme branche@yahoo.fr; www.campingfermebranche.com**

🐕 ♨ ⛱ 🚿 🚽 ✉ MAP 🦋 🛒 nr 🏭

Site on D247, 1km N of Rocamadour. Sm, pt shd, EHU (6A) €2; bbq; phone. *"Lovely, open, spacious site; gd, clean facs; gd for dogs (free); nr chateau; facs stretched in ssn; friendly owner; great site for price."* **€8.50, 10 Apr-15 Nov** **2015**

ROCHE BERNARD, LA *2G3* (0.3km NW Urban) *47.51946, -2.30517* **Camp Municipal Le Patis,** Chemin du Patis, 56130 La Roche-Bernard **02 99 90 60 13 or 02 99 90 60 51 (Mairie); camping.lrb56@gmail.com; www.laroche-bernard.com/camping-le-patis**

🐕 €2.30 ♨ (cont) WD ♨ ♿ 🚽 ✉ MAP 🦋 🛈 nr 🛒 nr 🏭

Leave N165 junc 17 (fr N) junc 15 (fr S) & foll marina sp. NB Arr/exit OK on mkt day (Thurs) if avoid town cent. 3*, Med, hdstg, hdg, mkd, pt shd, EHU (6A); red long stay; Eng spkn; adv bkg acc; ccard acc; boating adj; games area; sailing adj. *"Excel clean site in lovely spot on rv bank; helpful staff; facs poss stretched high ssn; grass pitches poss soft - heavy o'fits phone ahead in wet weather; Thurs mkt; m'van o'night area; organic mkt Sat; ancient, pretty town up steep hill; gd walks; yacht harbour adj; highly rec."* **€20.00, 15 Mar-14 Oct.** **2019**

ROCHE CHALAIS, LA *7C2* (0.5km S Rural) *45.14892, -0.00245* **Camp Municipal Les Gerbes,** Rue de la Dronne, 24490 La Roche-Chalais **05 53 91 40 65 or 06 38 82 40 08 (mob); campinggerbes@orange.fr**

♨ ⛱ 🚿 🚽 ✉ 🛒 nr 🏭

Fr S on D674 turn sharp L in vill at site sp. Site on R in 500m. Fr N take Coutras-Libourne rd thro vill; site sp on L beyond sm indus est. 3*, Med, mkd, pt shd, terr, EHU (5-10A) €2.60-3.60 (poss rev pol); sw nr; red long stay; adv bkg acc; canoeing adj; fishing adj; boating adj; CKE. *"Pleasant, well-kept, well-run site nr rv; gd sized pitches, some rvside; leisure pk 5km; gd clean san facs; rec pitch N side of site to avoid factory noise; mkt Sat am; rec."* **€14.00, 15 Apr-30 Sep.** **2019**

ROCHE POSAY, LA *4H2* (1.5km N Rural) *46.7989, 0.80961* **Camping La Roche-Posay,** Route de Lésigny. 86270 La Roche-Posay **05 49 86 21 23; info@laroche posay-vacances.com; www.larocheposay-vacances.com**

🐕 €3 ♨ (htd) ⛱ 🚿 🚽 ✉ MAP 🍽 🛈 🍴 🛒 nr 🏭 🏊 (covrd, htd)

On A10 take exit 26 Châtellerault-Nord, La Roche-Posay; foll sp La Roche-Posay; foll the D725 to La Roche-Possay; at rndabt foll sp for 'Camping-Hippodrome'. 4*, Lge, mkd, hdg, shd, serviced pitches; EHU (10A) inc; gas; bbq (elec, gas); sw nr; red long stay; 40% statics; Eng spkn; adv bkg acc; bike hire; fishing 1.5km; tennis; waterslide; CKE. *"Excel, popular, well-maintained site; aquatic park; 1st class facs; barrier locks automatically 2300; parking avail outside; walk to town on busy rd with no pavement; spa town."* **€42.00, 7 Apr-23 Sep, L21.** **2019**

"That's changed – Should I let the Club know?"

If you find something on site that's different from the site entry, fill in a report and let us know. See camc.com/europereport.

ROCHE SUR YON, LA *2H4* (8.2km SW Rural) *46.62281, 1.44983* **Campilo,** L'Auroire, 85430 Aubigny **02 51 31 68 45; accueil@campilo.com; www.campilo.com**

12 🐕 €3 WD ♨ ♿ 🚽 ✉ 🍽 🏭 🏊

Take Rue du Maréchal Joffre, D248 Rue du Maréchal Lyautey and D747 to Les Gâts in Aubign, take Rue des Mésanges and Le Champt des Landes to La Guyonnière, turn R onto Les Gâts, turn L onto Route de l'Auroire, cont onto Rue des Mésanges, turn L onto Le Champt des Landes, take the 2nd R onto La Guyonnière. Med, mkd, pt shd, sl, EHU (10A); bbq; Eng spkn. *"Tow cars not allowed besides c'vans sep car park; fishing lake on site; walks and cycling rtes; lge sports area; bicycles; sm gym; friendly staff; new san facs and pool."* **€26.00** **2019**

FRANCE

ROCHEFORT *7B1* (1km S Urban) 45.93013, -0.95826
Camping Municipal Le Rayonnement, 3, Avenue de la Fosse Aux Mâts, 17300 Rochefort 05 46 82 67 70; camping.municipal@ville-rochefort.fr; www.ville-rochefort.fr/decouvrir/camping

🏕 €1.05 👪 🗄 WC ♨ ⚒ ⅃ ✓ nr ⚓ 🔥

Exit E602 at junc 31 & take D733 dir Rochefort. At rndabt by McDonalds, take D733 dir Royan. Cont on D733. At rndabt with plane take 3rd exit onto Bd Edouard Pouzet. At rndabt take 3rd exit onto Bd de la Résistance, at next rndabt take 1st exit & then turn L onto ave de la Fosse aux Mâts. Site on L. Med, hdg, hdstg, shd, EHU (15A) inc; bbq; TV; 15% statics; phone; bus 100m; Eng spkn; adv bkg rec; games rm; bike hire. *"Bikes hire free; rv Charente & cycle path to cent 800m away; v helpful staff; no c'vans over 6m & twin axles; san facs v clean; Ecolabel campsite; vg; excel transporter bdge & access to town; excel."* €18.00, 27 Feb-3 Dec. 2016

ROCHEFORT *7B1* (8km W Coastal) 45.94828, -1.09592
Camp Municipal de la Garenne, Ave de l'Ile-Madame, 17730 Port-des-Barques 05 46 84 80 66 or 06 08 57 08 75 (mob); camping@ville-portdesbarques.fr; www.camping-municipal-portdesbarques.com

🏕 €1.26 👪 WC ♨ ⚒ ⅃ ✓ MSP 🦋 ♟ nr 🍴 ⅃ ⚓ nr 🔥 ⛵ (htd) 🏖 shgl adj

Fr Rochefort S on D773, cross Rv Charente bdge & take 1st exit sp Soubise & Ile Madame. Cont strt thro Port-des-Barques, site on L opp causeway to Ile-Madame. 3*, Lge, mkd, unshd, EHU (10A) inc; red long stay; 25% statics; phone; bus adj; adv bkg acc; ccard acc; CKE. *"Pleasant site; lge pitches; pitches a little scruffy, but level; facs dated but clean; refurb (2016) nice location to sea."* €22.00, 1 Apr-31 Oct. 2017

> **"I like to fill in the reports as I travel from site to site"**
>
> You'll find report forms at the back of this guide, or you can fill them in online at camc.com/europereport.

ROCHEFORT EN TERRE *2F3* (9.8km NE Urban) 47.74455, -2.25997 **Camp Municipal de La Digue,** Route 77 Le Guélin, 56200 St Martin sur Oust 02 99 91 55 76 or 02 99 91 49 45; st-martin-oust@wanadoo.fr; www.tourismebretagne.fr

🏕 €0.50 👪 ⚒ ✓ 🔥 ⚓ nr 🔥

On D873 14km N of Redon at Gacilly, turn W onto D777 twd Rochefort-en-Terre; site sp in 10km in St Martin. 2*, Med, pt shd, EHU (3-5A) €3.20; bbq; adv bkg acc; rv fishing 50m. *"Towpath walks to vill & shops; clean facs but ltd LS; well-maintained site; site yourself, warden calls am & eve; excel, refurbished facs (2013)."* €10.00, 1 May-30 Sep. 2018

ROCHEFORT EN TERRE *2F3* (0.6km S Rural) 47.695193, -2.349117 **Camping Au Gré des Vents (formerly du Moulin Neuf),** Chemin de Bogeais, Route de Limerzel, 56220 Rochefort-en-Terre 02 97 43 37 52; gredesvents@orange.fr; www.campingaugredesvents.com

🏕 €3 👪 WC ⚒ ♨ ⅃ ✓ MSP 🦋 ⅃ nr ⚓ nr 🔥 (htd)

Fr Redon W on D775 twd Vannes, approx 23km turn R onto D774 sp Rochefort-en-Terre; immed after vill limit sp, turn sharp L up slope to ent. NB Do not drive thro vill. 3*, Med, hdg, mkd, pt shd, pt sl, terr, EHU ltd (10A) €4.50; bbq; sw nr; 10% statics; adv bkg acc; ccard acc; games area; CKE. *"Peaceful base for touring area; helpful, lovely owners; no vehicle movement or shwrs 2200-0700 (0800 LS), but wcs open; no twin axles; excel; bit scruffy; v nr vill."* €26.00, 31 Mar-30 Sep. 2019

ROCHEFORT SUR LOIRE *4G1* (0.5km N Urban) 47.36021, -0.65611 **Camping Seasonova Les Plages de Loire,** route de Savennières, 49190 Rochefort-sur-Loire 02 41 68 55 91; www.camping-lesplagesdeloire.com

🏕 €2 👪 (htd) WC ⚒ ♨ ⅃ ✓ 🦋 🍴 ⅃ ⚓ 🔥

Fr Angers: S on A87. Exit 24 onto D160 dir Beaulieu for 1km. At rndabt 1st R onto D54 to Rochfort. Thro town cent over rv. Site on L. Med, EHU (10A); twin axles; 10% statics; Eng spkn; adv bkg acc; CKE. *"New site, nice facs up steps; interesting area."* €19.00, 3 Apr-1 Nov. 2015

ROCHELLE, LA *7A1* (12km N Rural/Coastal) 46.25239, -1.11972 **Camp Municipal Les Misottes,** 46 Rue de l'Océan, 17137 Esnandes 07 68 16 70 20 or 05 46 01 32 13; www.campinglesmisottes.fr

🏕 €2.50 👪 (cont) ⚒ ✓ MSP 🦋 🍴 ⅃ ⚓ nr 🔥 ⛷ 🏖 shgl 2km

Fr N on D938 or N1327 turn W at Marans onto D105. In 7.5km turn S onto D9 then D202 to Esnandes. Enter vill, at x-rds strt, site on R in 200m. Fr La Rochelle D105 N to cent Esnandes, site sp. 2*, Med, mkd, pt shd, EHU (10A) €3; 5% statics; Eng spkn; adv bkg acc; fishing; CKE. *"Site on the edge of marshlands; v nice & quiet; excel bus svrs; canal fishing; liable to flood; vg; new manager (2018) enthusiastic and determined to update site; v clean basic san facs; vg for La Rochelle and area; rec for sh stay; san facs tired."* €15.50, 1 Apr-15 Oct. 2019

ROCHELLE, LA *7A1* (5km S Rural/Coastal) 46.11659, -1.11939 **Camping Les Sables,** Chemin du Pontreau, 17440 Aytré 05 46 45 40 30; camping_les_sables@yahoo.fr; www.camping-les-sables.com

🏕 €1.50 👪 WC ⚒ ♨ ⅃ ✓ MSP 🍴 ⅃ ⚓ 🔥 ⚒ ⛵ (covrd, htd) 🏖

Fr S (Rochefort) on D137, exit sp Aytré. At 2nd traff lts turn L & foll site sp. Lge, hdg, pt shd, EHU (6A) €3; bbq; 50% statics; phone; Eng spkn; adv bkg acc; ccard acc; bike hire; games area; games rm; waterslide; CKE. *"Vg."* €35.00, 1 May-15 Oct. 2017

ROCROI *5C1* (12km SE Rural) 49.87200, 4.60446
Camp Départemental du Lac des Vieilles Forges,
08500 Les Mazures **03 24 40 17 31; cmpingvieilles
forges@cg08.fr**

🛖 🐕 €1 ♀♀(htd) 🏊 ♿ 🖥 🚿 MP 🦋 🎣 🛒 ⚠ 🚴

Fr Rocroi take D1 & D988 for Les Mazures/Renwez.
Turn R D40 at sp Les Vieilles Forges. Site on R nr
lakeside. 3*, Lge, mkd, hdstg, shd, pt sl, EHU (6-10A)
€2.50-4.30 (long leads req); sw; TV; 20% statics; adv
bkg acc; bike hire; boating; tennis; fishing. *"Attractive
walks; lake views fr some pitches; vg site; recep clsd
1200-1500."* **€20.00, 11 Apr-15 Sep.** 2016

RODEZ *7D4* (1km NE Urban) 44.35323, 2.58708
Camp Municipal Layoule, 12000 Rodez **05 65 67 09 52;
contact@mairie-rodez.fr**

🛖 🐕 ♀♀ WC 🏊 ♿ 🖥 🚿 MP 🦋 🛒 nr ⚠

Clearly sp in Rodez town cent & all app rds. Access
at bottom steep hill thro residential area.
4*, Med, hdg, hdstg, mkd, pt shd, EHU (6A) inc; phone;
bus adj; golf nr; tennis nr; CKE. *"Site by lake & rv; gd
sized pitches; helpful warden; clean facs; steep walk
to historic town; gates clsd 2000-0700; ent is down
steep twisty rds & exit is up the same hill; interesting
wild life; gd walks & cycling; excel NH; excel for town."*
€14.00, 1 May-30 Sep. 2018

ROHAN *2F3* (0.2km NW Rural) 48.07078, -2.75525
Camp Municipal du Val d'Oust, Rue de St Gouvry,
56580 Rohan **02 97 51 57 58 or 02 97 51 50 33 (Mairie);
mairie.rohan@wanadoo.fr; www.morbihan.com**

🐕 €0.90 ♀♀ WC 🏊 ♿ 🚿 🍴 ⏰ nr 🛒 nr ⚠

Rue de St Gouvry runs NW fr Rohan parallel to D11,
but other side of canal. 2*, Sm, mkd, pt shd, EHU
€3.10; bbq; phone; adv bkg acc; CKE. *"Pleasant site
beside Nantes/Brest canal; gd cycling; market in vill;
some rd noise."* **€12.00, 1 Jun-15 Sep.** 2018

ROMIEU, LA *8E2* (0.3km NE Rural) 43.98299, 0.50183
Kawan Village Le Camp de Florence, 32480 La Romieu
**05 62 28 15 58; info@lecampdeflorence.com;
www.lecampdeflorence.com**

🛖 🐕 €2.30 ♀♀ WC 🏊 ♨ ♿ 🖥 🚿 MP 🦋 🍴
🍽 ⏰ nr 🍴 🛒 nr ⚠ 🎿 🚣 ⛵

Take D931 N fr Condom & turn R onto D41, where
La Romieu sp next to radio mast. Go thro La Romieu
& turn L at sp just bef leaving vill. 4*, Lge, hdstg,
hdg, pt shd, EHU (10A) inc (poss rev pol); bbq; twin
axles; TV; 80% statics; Eng spkn; adv bkg req; ccard
acc; bike hire; games area; games rm; tennis; CKE.
*"Peaceful, Dutch-run site in pleasant location; gd sized
pitches, most with views; welcoming, helpful staff;
waterslide; jacuzzi; leisure complex 500m; gd clean
san facs; gd rest; poss muddy when wet; archery;
some noise fr disco, ask for pitch away fr bar; rest
in 16thC farmhouse; gd pool but take care sl ent;
gd cycling; historic 11thC vill; mkt Wed Condom."*
€36.60, 28 Apr-24 Sep, D19. 2017

ROMORANTIN LANTHENAY *4G2* (1km E Urban)
47.35486, 1.75568 **Camping de Tournefeuille,**
Rue de Long Eaton, 41200 Romorantin-Lanthenay
**02 54 76 16 60; romo2015@outlook.fr;
www.campingromorantin.com**

🛖 🐕 €1.80 ♀♀(htd) 🏊 🚿 🦋 🍽 🍴 🛒 nr ⚠ 🎿

Fr town cent on D724 to Salbis, foll sp thro several
traff lts over bdge turn R into Rue de Long-Eaton,
site sp. 3*, Med, pt shd, EHU (6A) inc; gas; bbq;
TV; ccard acc; fishing; bike hire. *"Rv walk to town
rec; pool adj; excel modern san facs; helpful staff."*
€30.00, 1 Apr-31 Oct. 2019

ROSANS *9D3* (2.5km SW Rural) 44.38273, 5.46172
Camping des Rosieres, Quartier des Coings, 05150
Rosans **04 92 66 62 06 or 06 70 10 69 99 (mob);
contact@camping-rosieres.com; www.camping-
rosieres.com/fr**

🛖 🐕 ♀♀ WC 🏊 🚿 🍴 ♀ 🍽 🍴 🖥 ⚠ 🚴 🎿(htd)

On D94 Nyons to Gap on RH side just prior to ent
Rosans. 3*, Sm, hdg, shd, EHU (6A); twin axles; Eng
spkn; adv bkg acc; games area; CKE. *"Horseriding;
canyoning; tennis; boules; steep narr rd fr recep & sw
pool to pitches; gd."* **€24.00, 1 May-30 Sep.** 2017

ROSCOFF *1D2* (7km SW Rural/Coastal) 48.67246,
-4.05326 **Camp Municipal du Bois de la Palud,** 29250
Plougoulm **02 98 29 81 82 or 02 98 29 90 76 (Mairie);
contact@plougoulm.bzh; www.plougoulm.bzh**

♀♀ WC 🏊 ♿ 🖥 🚿 🦋 🛒 nr ⚠ 🏖 sand 500m

Fr D58 turn W on D10 sp Cléder/Plouescat; after
3km on ent Plougoulm foll sp to site.
2*, Sm, mkd, hdg, pt shd, terr, EHU (8A) €3.50; phone;
Eng spkn; adv bkg acc; ccard acc; CKE. *"Clean, tidy
site in delightful area; lovely views to sandy inlet;
conv ferry; if arr late, site yourself; warden calls am &
pm; access all hrs with c'van; walk in first, turning diff
inside; also lower field with EHU; sh walk to vill; excel;
late arr & late dep; beautiful beaches to the west."*
€14.00, 15 Jun-4 Sep. 2016

ROSIERS SUR LOIRE, LES *4G1* (6km NW Rural)
47.39231, -0.27381 **Camping Port St Maur,** 49250
La Ménitré **02 41 45 60 80; 0611417561@sfr.fr**

🛖 🐕 €1 ♀♀ WC 🏊 ♿ 🖥 🚿 🍴 ⏰ 🍴 🛒 nr ⚠ 🚴

Exit Les Rosiers on D952 sp Angers. At rndabt 3km
past St Mathhurin sur Loire take 1st exit sp Port
St Maur. Site on R in 200m. 2*, Med, mkd, pt shd, EHU
(5A) inc; bbq; 10% statics; Eng spkn. *"Access to san
facs by steps; helpful warden; boat trips on Loire; lovely
rvside setting with view of St Maur Abbey; gd walking &
cycling; gd."* **€12.50, 1 May-15 Sep.** 2016

FRANCE

ROSNAY *4H2* (0.8km N Rural) *46.70647, 1.21161*
Camp Municipal Les Millots, Route de St Michel-en-Brenne, 36300 Rosnay 02 54 37 80 17 **(Mairie);**
rosnay-mairie@wanadoo.fr

🏕👫👬 (htd) WD ♿ ♨ 🚿 ♿ 🚻 ⧖ 🦋 ⊞nr 🚲nr ⛺

NE on D27 fr Le Blanc to Rosnay; site sp 500m N of Rosnay on D44. 2*, Sm, mkd, pt shd, EHU (6-10A) inc (poss rev pol); bbq; phone; adv bkg acc; lake fishing; tennis; cycling; CKE. *"Lovely, tranquil, popular site; well-kept; excel modern san facs; warden collects fees twice daily; lakeside walks; excel walking, cycling, birdwatching & fishing; gd base for exploring Brenne National Park; vg value; excel; friendly."*
€11.40, 16 Feb-15 Nov. 2018

ROUEN *3C2* (5km E Urban) *49.43154, 1.15387*
Camping L'Aubette, 23 Rue du Vert- Buisson, 76160 St Léger-du-Bourg-Denis 02 32 08 47 69;
campingaubette@gmail.com; www.rouentourisme.com

12 👫👬 Free 👫👬 WD ♨ ♿ ♿ 🚻 ⊞nr

Fr Rouen E on N31 dir Darnétal & Beauvais; in 1km cont strt on onto D42/D138 dir St Léger-du-Bourg-Denis; in 400m turn L onto Rue du Vert Buisson; site on r in 800m just past stop sp. Site well sp as 'Camping' fr Rouen cent. 2*, Med, pt shd, pt sl, terr, EHU 4A; bbq; 40% statics; bus 150m; CKE. *"In attractive rv valley; conv city cent; conv bus to town; v ltd touring pitches; cash only; v basic site, gd NH only; v poor."* **€15.00** 2019

ROUEN *3C2* (14km NW Rural) *49.50553, 0.98409*
Camping Les Nenuphars, 765 Rue des Deux Tilleuls, Le Bout du Haut, 76480 Roumare 02 35 33 80 75;
www.camping-les-nenuphars.com

🏕 €1.70 👫👬 WD ♨ ♿ ⧖ ⛺

S on D6015/A150 dir Rouen, foll sp Roumare & site. Fr Rouen take A150/D6015 N to St Jean-du-Cardonnay; turn L to Roumare; site sp. 500m bef Roumare. 2*, Med, mkd, hdg, pt shd, pt sl, EHU (5-10A); twin axles; phone; bus 1km; Eng spkn; adv bkg acc; games area; CKE. *"Pleasant grassy site, handy for Rouen; v ltd sports facs; lge pitches; vg."*
€18.00, 28 Mar-15 Dec. 2015

ROYAN *7B1* (9km NE Rural) *45.64796, -0.95847*
FFCC Camping Le Bois Roland, 82 Route de Royan, 17600 Médis 05 46 05 47 58; contact@le-bois-roland.com; www.le-bois-roland.com

🏕 €2.80 👫👬 WD ♨ ♿ ♿ 🚻 ⧖ 🦋 🍽 Y 🚲 🚲 ⧖ 🏊 🚲 ⛵ 🏖sand 4km

On N150 Saintes-Royan rd, site sp on R 100m beyond Médis vill sp. 3*, Med, pt shd, EHU (5-10A) €4.20-5.20; gas; TV; phone; Eng spkn; adv bkg acc; ccard acc; CKE. *"Attractive, wooded site; friendly, family-run; facs poss stretched high ssn; waiting area avail; vg; shop/rest/bar open in July when tradsmn will call."* **€19.00, 1 May-30 Sep.** 2015

ROYAN *7B1* (1.7km SE Coastal) *45.61817, -1.00425*
Camping La Triloterie, 44 ter, Ave Aliénor d'Aquitaine, 17200 Royan 05 46 05 26 91; info@campingroyan.com; www.campingroyan.com

12 🏕 €1.50 👫👬 (htd) WD ♨ ♿ 🚻 🚲 🍴 Y 🚲 ⊞nr 🏊 🚲 🚲 sand 900m

Fr Royan PO, foll sp Bordeaux N730, on E of rd. 2*, Med, shd, EHU (4-12A) €4-6 (poss rev pol); bbq; 10% statics; phone; waterslide. *"Excel site; conv for Royan town cent & St George de Didonne; site a bit tired, ok for NH."* **€23.00** 2017

ROYAN *7B1* (16km SE Coastal) *45.55713, -0.94655*
Camping Soleil Levant, Allée de la Langée, 17132 Meschers-sur-Gironde 05 46 02 76 62; info@camping-soleillevant.com; www.camping-soleillevant.com

🏕 €3.50 👫👬 WD ♨ ♿ 🦋 Y 🍴 🚲 ⧖ 🚲 🏖 🏊 sand 1.5km

Take D145 coast rd fr Royan to Talmont. At Meschers turn R foll camp sp twd port; sp. 4*, Med, pt shd, EHU (10A) €5.10; 20% statics; adv bkg acc; ccard acc; horseriding adj; watersports adj; CKE. *"Gd, busy site; v clean san facs; port & rest 300m; vill shop & daily mkt 500m; visits to Cognac & Bordeaux distilleries; v friendly, helpful family run site."* **€31.00, 1 Apr-30 Sep.** 2015

ROYAN *7B1* (5km SE Coastal) *45.58345, -0.98720*
Camping Bois Soleil, 2 Ave de Suzac, 17110 St Georges-de-Didonne 05 46 05 05 94; camping.bois.soleil@wanadoo.fr; www.bois-soleil.com

🏕 €3 (not acc end Jun-Aug inc) 👫👬 (htd) WD ♨ ♿ ♿ 🚻 🍴 ⧖ 🍴 🚲 ⧖ 🏊 🚲 (htd) 🚲 🏖sand adj

Fr A10 exit junc 35 dir Saintes & Royan; on app Royan foll St Georges-de-Didonne sp onto bypass D25/D730/D25/D25E; go over 2 rndabts (with underpass bet); at 3rd rndabt turn L sp Meschers-sur-Gironde; site on R in 500m. Site well sp. 4*, Lge, hdstg, mkd, hdg, pt shd, terr, EHU (6A) inc (poss rev pol); gas; bbq (gas); TV; 30% statics; phone; Eng spkn; adv bkg rec; ccard acc; bike hire; tennis; games area; CKE. *"Superb wooded site in vg location nr beach; popular & busy; generous pitches, some sandy; excel, clean san facs; vg shop & rest; many sandy beaches nrby."* **€42.00, 2 Apr-9 Oct.** 2019

ROYAN *7B1* (4km NW Urban/Coastal) *45.6309, -1.0498* **Campéole Camping Clairefontaine,** 6 Rue du Colonel Lachaud, Pontaillac, 17200 Royan 05 46 39 08 11; clairefontaine@campeole.com; www.camping-clairefontaine.com or www.campeole.com

🏕 €3 👫👬 WD ♨ ♿ 🚻 ⧖ 🦋 🍴 Y ⧖ 🚲 🚲 ⧖ 🏊 🏖sand 300m

Foll Pontaillac sp fr Royan. Site sp in Clairefontaine (& Pontaillac). 4*, Lge, mkd, pt shd, serviced pitches; EHU (10A); gas; bbq; TV; 80% statics; phone; Eng spkn; adv bkg req; ccard acc; tennis; CKE. *"Lovely coastline; gd for family holiday; helpful owner; clean, unisex san facs; ltd touring pitches, some sm; gd security; site poss dusty; vg walking & cycling; casino 300m; coastal path Pontaillac to Royan; gd site; easy walk/bike/bus into town; nice sw; bar & shop onsite; conv for city; vg."* **€41.00, 31 Mar-1 Oct.** 2017

ROYBON *9C2* (1.6km S Rural) *45.24639, 5.24806*
Camping de Roybon, Route de St Antoine, 38940
Roybon 04 76 36 23 67 or 06 86 64 55 47;
campingroybon38@gmail.com; www.camping
roybon.com

🐕 €2.65 ♦♦ wc ♨ ♿ / ♨ 🔌nr ⚏

Fr Roybon go S on D71 & foll sp. 2*, Med, mkd, pt shd,
pt sl, EHU (10A) €3.50; sw nr; adv bkg acc; watersports
adj. *"V peaceful; gd, modern facs new; vg; can be boggy
when wet."* **€18.40, 1 May-30 Sep.** **2016**

ROYERE DE VASSIVIERE *7B4* (6km SW Rural)
45.78869, 1.89855 **Camping Les Terrasses du Lac,**
Vauveix, 23460 Royère-de-Vassivière 05 55 64 76 77;
lesterrasses.camping@free.fr; www.campings-
vassiviere.com

🐕 €1 ♦♦ (htd) wc ♨ ♿ / 🦋 🍽 nr ⊕nr 🏖 adj

Fr Eymoutiers take D43 for approx 10km then
take D36 to Vauveix & foll sp. 1*, Med, mkd,
hdg, pt shd, terr, EHU (10A) €3.10 (poss rev pol);
TV; 50% statics; cycling; horseriding; watersports
adj; CKE. *"Helpful staff; walking; lovely setting."*
€22.00, 2 Apr-31 Oct. **2017**

RUE *3B2* (6km N Rural) *50.31367, 1.69472*
Kawan Village Le Val d'Authie, 20 Route de Vercourt,
80120 Villers-sur-Authie 03 22 29 92 47; camping@
valdauthie.fr; www.valdauthie.fr

🐕 €1.50 ♦♦ (htd) wc ♨ ♿ 🚿 / MP 🦋 🍽 ⊕ 🔌 ⚏ 🏊
🏊 (covrd, htd) 🚣

Exit 24 on A16 twrds Vron, foll sp Camping Vercourt
thro town. 5*, Lge, mkd, hdg, pt shd, pt sl, EHU
(6-10A) (rev pol); gas; TV; 60% statics; phone; Eng
spkn; adv bkg acc; ccard acc; games area; games rm;
fitness rm; tennis; CKE. *"Set in pleasant countryside;
sauna; steam rm; helpful, friendly owners; clean,
unisex facs & spacious shwrs; sm sep area for tourers,
but many touring pitches bet statics (2009); poss diff
for lge o'fits; gd pool; v cr & noisy high ssn; excel."*
€31.00, 1 Apr-30 Sep. **2017**

RUE *3B2* (4km SE Rural) *50.25278, 1.71224*
Camping de la Mottelette, Ferme de la Mottelette,
80120 Forest-Montiers 03 22 28 32 33 or
06 72 85 73 77 (mob); contact@la-mottelette.com;
www.la-mottelette.com

🐕 €1 wc ♨ ♿ / 🦋 🔌nr ⚏

Exit A16 junc 24 onto D32 dir Rue & L Crotoy;
at rndabt junc with D235 cont on D32; site on
L in 1.5km. Site sp on leaving A16. 2*, Sm, mkd,
hdg, unshd, EHU (6A) €4; bbq; 50% statics; Eng
spkn; adv bkg acc; games area; games rm; CKE.
*"Basic, CL type, clean site on wkg frm; welcoming,
friendly owners; mkt Sat; conv A16; gd touring base
or NH; vg; pleasant atmosphere; new facs (2015)."*
€20.00, 1 Apr-31 Oct. **2017**

RUFFEC *7A2* (3km SE Rural) *46.01500, 0.21304*
Camping Le Réjallant, Les Grands Champs, 16700
Condac 05 45 31 29 06 or 06 58 12 88 18; contact@
camping-du-rejallant.com; www.camping-du-
rejallant.com

12 🐕 ♦♦ wc ♨ ♿ / 🦋 🕯 ⊕nr ⚏ ⚏

Site sp fr N10 & fr town. App 1km fr turn-off.
3*, Med, hdg, mkd, shd, pt sl, EHU (10A) inc; sw nr; Eng
spkn; fishing 100m; CKE. *"Friendly, sm nbr of touring
sites; lovely vill 2km, gd Leclerc and Lidl supmkt;
gd pool; clean facs; bar 100m; great for families."*
€21.00 **2019**

RUMILLY *9B3* (3.5km S Rural) *45.84083, 5.96277*
Camping Le Madrid, Route de St Félix, 74150 Rumilly
04 50 01 12 57; contact@camping-le-madrid.com

🐕 €2 ♦♦ (htd) wc ♨ ♿ / MP 🦋 🕯 🍽 ⊕ 🔌 ⚏nr ⚏ 🏊
🏊 🚣

S fr Rumilly on D910, take D3 L dir St Marcel for
approx 600m & at 2nd rndabt turn R, site sp.
3*, Med, hdstg, hdg, mkd, pt shd, EHU (6-10A)
€2.80-4.30; bbq; 50% statics; adv bkg acc; games
rm; fishing; bike hire; games area. *"Pleasant owners;
chosen for proximity to m'way; ideal for NH."*
€28.00, 1 Apr-31 Oct. **2019**

RUOMS *9D2* (4km SW Urban) *44.43101, 4.32945*
Camping La Chapoulière, 07120 Ruoms 04 75 39 64 98
or 04 75 93 90 72; camping@lachapouliere.com;
www.lachapouliere.com

🐕 €3.50 ♦♦ ♨ ♿ / ♨ 🦋 🕯 🍽 ⊕ 🔌 ⚏ 🏊 🚣 🚣

Exit Ruoms S on D579. At junc 2km S, foll D111 sp
St Ambroix. Site 1.5km fr junc. 3*, Med, mkd, shd,
pt sl, EHU (6A) €4.60; gas; sw nr; TV; Eng spkn; adv
bkg rec; games area; tennis 2km; canoeing; fishing
adj. *"Beautiful pitches on rv bank; friendly; ltd facs LS;
vg; excel modern san facs; lge pitches demarcated by
trees."* **€37.00, Easter-30 Sep.** **2019**

SABLE SUR SARTHE *4F1* (0.5km S Rural) *47.83101,
-0.33177* **Camp Municipal de l'Hippodrome,** Allée du
Québec, 72300 Sable-sur-Sarthe 02 43 95 42 61;
camping@sablesursarthe.fr; camping.sablesursarthe.fr

♦♦ ♨ ♿ / 🦋 ⚏ ⚏ 🚣 🚣

Sp in town (foll sm, white sp with c'van symbols
or Hippodrome). Fr N on D306; at traff lts at junc
with D309, go strt over & under rlwy brdg sp Centre
Ville; foll camping sps. 3*, Med, hdg, pt shd, EHU
(15A) €2.40; gas; bbq; red long stay; TV; Eng spkn;
ccard acc; boat hire; canoeing; rv fishing; bike hire.
*"Excel site next to racecourse; gd, clean facs; helpful
staff; conv for town; some pitches diff for lge fits."*
€16.40, 3 Apr-15 Oct. **2018**

SABLES D'OLONNE, LES 7A1 (10km ESE Coastal)
46.471521, -1.725812 **Camping Bel Air,** 6 allee de la Chevreuse, Chateau d'Olonne 85180 **02 51 22 09 67; dubelair@cybelevacances.com; www.campingdu belair.com**

🏕 €6 🚿 🔖 ⚐ ⚒ (covrd, htd) 🏖 sand

Fr La Roche-sur-Yon take D160 twrds Les Sables d'Olonne. Take D949 twrds Niort then the D2949 on Avenue de Talmont. At rndabt take D32A, 3rd exit on Rue du Brandais. Turn R onto Chemin de Bel air. Med, pt shd, bbq (gas); adv bkg acc. €46.00, 1 Apr-1 Nov. **2019**

SABLES D'OR LES PINS 2E3 (1km NW Rural/ Coastal) 48.63230, -2.41229 **Camping Les Salines,** Rue du Lac, 22240 Plurien **02 96 72 17 40 or 06 28 22 43 36; campinglessalinesplurien@ gmail.com; www.campinglessalines.fr**

🏕 €0.50 👫 ⓌⒸ 🚿 ♿ 🔖 ⚐ 🐾 🛒 nr 🅿 🏖 sand 400m

Fr D786 turn N at Plurien onto D34 to Sables-d'Or. In 1km turn L & site on L after 200m. 2*, Med, pt shd, pt sl, terr, EHU (6A) €2.35; phone; Eng spkn; adv bkg acc; CKE. *"Lovely, quiet, tranquile hillside site; some sea views; vg san facs; gates clsd 2200-0700; no pitching when office clsd, but lge car park opp; excel access to nature reserve & beautiful beaches; enthusiastic, helpful new owners (2017); lge pitches; lovely estuary walks; conv St Malo; wonderful coast; highly rec."* €16.00, 1 Apr-12 Nov. **2017**

SAILLANS 9D2 (1.6km W Rural) 44.69511, 5.18124 **Camping Les Chapelains,** 26340 Saillans **04 75 21 55 47; camping@chapelains.fr; www.chapelains.fr**

🏕 🐕 👫 🔖 ⚐ 🐾 Ⓒ ⓪ 🛒 🅿 🏖 shgl

Fr W on D93 turn onto D493. Site well sp just bef Saillans vill boundary adj Rv Drôme. Sm, hdg, mkd, pt shd, EHU (4-10A); gas; Eng spkn; adv bkg acc; games area; CKE. *"Attractive, well-run rvside site; some v sm pitches; friendly, helpful warden; rv walk to vill; rest open LS; san facs clean & updated (2015); gd."* €22.60, 18 Apr-15 Sep. **2015**

ST AIGNAN SUR CHER 4G2 (9km N Rural) 47.32361, 1.36983 **FFCC Camping Domaine du Bien Vivre,** 13-15 Route du Petit Village, 41140 St Romain-sur-Cher **02 54 71 73 74; domainedubienvivre@free.fr; www.domainedubienvivre.fr**

🔢12 🐕 👫 ⓌⒸ 🔖 ⚐ 🐾 Ⓒ nr 🛒 nr 🅿

Fr St Aignan-sur-Cher N on D675; in 6km in St Romain-sur-Cher site sp to L; foll sps for 3km. Sm, mkd, pt shd, pt sl, EHU (6A) inc; bbq; Eng spkn; ccard acc; CKE. *"A vineyard site; helpful owner; ltd facs in winter; sale of wines; conv Blois; gd."* €16.50 **2016**

ST AIGNAN SUR CHER 4G2 (1.6km SE Rural) 47.26530, 1.38875 **Camping Les Cochards,** 1 Rue du Camping, Seigy, 41110 St Aignan-sur-Cher **02 54 75 15 59 or 06 72 09 45 24 (mob); camping@ lesclochards.com; www.lescochards.com**

🏕 €1.60 👫 (htd) ⓌⒸ 🔖 ♿ 🔖 ⚐ 🐾 🛒 🏖 🍴 🐾 🅿 🛒 🅿 ⚒

On D17 heading SE fr St Aignan twd Seigy on S bank of Rv Cher. 4*, Lge, mkd, pt shd, EHU (5-10A) €4.50; bbq; sw nr; TV; 20% statics; phone; Eng spkn; ccard acc; games area; horseriding 3km; rv fishing; canoeing; CKE. *"Attractive, open site; helpful owners; gd san facs; recep clsd 2000; some pitches waterlogged after rain; easy walk to attractive town; excel; discount vouchers avail for local attractions; san facs being upgraded (2015)."* €28.00, 1 Apr-15 Oct. **2015**

ST AMAND EN PUISAYE 4G4 (0.5km NE Urban) 47.53294, 3.07333 **Camp Municipal La Vrille,** Route de St Sauveur, 58310 St Amand-en-Puisaye **03 86 39 72 21 or 03 86 39 63 72 (Mairie); saintam.mairie@ wanadoo.fr; www.ot-puisaye-nivernaise.fr**

👫 🔖 ⚐ 🍴 nr Ⓒ nr 🛒 nr

Fr N7 take D957 Neuvy-sur-Loire to St Amand, at rd junc in vill take D955 sp St Sauveur-en-Puisaye, site on R in 500m; clearly sp on all app to vill. 2*, Sm, mkd, pt shd, EHU €2.30; sailing adj; fishing in adj reservoir. *"Vg simple site; gates clsd 2200-0700."* €12.50, 1 Jun-30 Sep. **2015**

ST AMAND LES EAUX 3B4 (4km SE Rural) 50.43535, 3.46290 **FFCC Camping du Mont des Bruyères,** 806 Rue Basly, 59230 St Amand-les-Eaux **03 27 48 56 87; info@campingmontdesbruyeres.com; www.camping montdesbruyeres.com**

🏕 €1.50 👫 (htd) 🔖 ⚐ 🐾 🛒 🐾 🍴 🐾 🛒 🅿

Exit A23 m'way at junc 5 or 6 onto ring rd D169, site sp. Fr N exit E42 junc 31 onto N52/N507 then D169. Avoid St Amand cent. 4*, Med, mkd, hdg, shd, pt sl, terr, EHU (6A-10A) inc; bbq; 60% statics; adv bkg acc; CKE. *"Attractive site on forest edge; most touring pitches under trees; access to some pitches diff due slopes; gd cycling; excel birdlife on site; fac gd & clean."* €24.00, 15 Mar-30 Oct. **2015**

ST AMAND MONTROND 4H3 (3km SW Rural) 46.71258, 2.49000 **Camp Municipal La Roche,** Rue de la Roche, 18200 St Amand-Montrond **02 48 96 09 36; camping-la-roche@wanadoo.fr; www.st-amand-tourisme.com**

🏕 👫 (htd) ⓌⒸ 🔖 ⚐ 🐾 🍴 🐾 🛒 nr 🅿 ⚒

Exit A71/E11 junc 8 dir St Amand-Montrond on D300. Then foll sp to Montluçon on D2144 until rndabt on canal, turn R onto Quai Pluviôse/Rue de la Roche, site on R. Site sp on far side of town. 3*, Med, shd, pt sl, EHU (6A) €2.90 (poss rev pol); phone; rv fishing; tennis; CKE. *"Popular NH, rec arr by 1700 high ssn; helpful warden; clean facs; tight for lge o'fits; rvside walk to pleasant town; gd."* €17.00, 1 Apr-30 Sep. **2015**

ST ANDRE DE CUBZAC *7C2* (4km NW Rural)
45.00703, -0.47724 **FFCC Camping Le Port Neuf,**
1125 Route du Port Neuf, 33240 St André-de-Cubzac
**05 57 43 16 44; contact@camping-port-neuf.com;
www.camping-port-neuf.com**

🐕 €1 (htd) 🚻 ⓌⒹ ♿ 🏊 🛒 ⊘ ⓂⓅ 🍴 ⑪ 🏍 ⛴

Fr A10 or N10 take exit sp St André. Well sp
fr St André (narr rds) on D669. 2*, Sm, mkd, hdg,
hdstg, pt shd, EHU (6A) €3.50 (poss long lead
req); train to Bordeaux fr vill; Eng spkn; adv bkg
acc; bike hire; lake fishing 100m; boating 100m;
horseriding nr; CKE. *"Lovely spot; friendly, helpful
staff; san facs clean; pedalo hire; scruffy site (2015)."*
€15.00, 1 May-30 Sep.   **2016**

STE ANNE D'AURAY *2F3* (1.6km SW Rural) *47.69842,
-2.96226* **Camp Municipal du Motten,** Allée des Pins,
56400 Ste Anne-d'Auray **02 97 57 60 27 or 02 97 57
63 91; contact@sainte-anne-auray.com or
campingmotten@orange.fr; www.sainte-anne-
auray.com**

🐕 🚻 ⓌⒹ 🏊 ♿ 🛒 ⊘ 🦋 Ⓨ 🏍 🛒nr ⛺

Fr W on N165 take D17bis N to St Anne-d'Auray;
then L onto D19 to town. This rte avoids Pluneret.
Foll site sp. 2*, Med, mkd, pt shd, EHU (10A) inc; TV;
Eng spkn; adv bkg acc; tennis; games area. *"Peaceful,
well-kept site; best pitches immed R after ent;
welcoming, helpful warden; gd clean san facs; excel
touring base; conv Basilica Ste Anne d'Auray; excel."*
€16.00, 13 Jun-14 Sep.   **2015**

**"We must tell the Club about
that great site we found"**

Get your site reports in by mid-August and we'll
do our best to get your updates into the next
edition.

ST ANTONIN NOBLE VAL *8E4* (1.5km N Rural)
44.1595, 1.7564 **FFCC Camp Municipal Le Ponget,**
Route de Caylus, 82140 St Antonin-Noble-Val
**05 63 68 21 13 or 05 63 30 60 23 (Mairie);
camping-leponget@wanadoo.fr**

🐕 €1.20 🚻 (htd) 🏊 ♿ ⊘ Ⓜ Ⓟ 🦋 Ⓨ nr ⑪ nr 🛒nr ⛺

Fr Caylus take D19 S to St Antonin; site on R, well
sp. 2*, Sm, hdg, pt shd, EHU (3-6A) €2.50-3.70; gas;
sw nr; phone; CKE. *"Well-kept site adj sports field;
modern san facs; poss diff lge o'fits; gd walking; vg
friendly site; excel mkt Sun; discount for 7 days; lovely
medival town; gd for Aveyron Gorges & Bastide towns."*
€11.70, 2 May-30 Sep.   **2017**

ST AUBIN DU CORMIER *2E4* (0.3km E Urban)
48.25990, -1.39609 **Camp Municipal de l'Etang,** Rue
de l'Etang, 35140 St Aubin-du-Cormier **02 99 39 10 42
(Mairie); mairie@ville-staubinducormier.fr;
www.saint-aubin-du-cormier.bzh/accueil**

🐕 €0.65 🚻 ⓌⒹ 🏊 ♿ 🛒 ⊘ 🦋 🛒nr

NE fr Rennes on A84; in 20km exit junc 28 dir
St Aubin-du-Cormier. Foll sp 'Centre Ville' then site
sp. Poss diff for lge o'fits - narr app. 2*, Sm, mkd,
pt shd, pt sl, terr, EHU (6A) inc; bbq (charcoal, elec,
gas); 10% statics; adv bkg acc; lake fishing; Jeu de
boules alleys; mkd walking rtes nrby; CKE. *"Pleasant,
beautifully kept site adj lake; friendly; forest walks &
around lake; pretty vill, with excel shops; mkt Thur; vet
1km; lovely site; san facs; vg disabled facs; recycling;
dog health certs check on ent; excel for sh or long stay;
suitable for v sm vans or MHs; narr angled ent thro
stone pillars."* **€15.00, 27 Apr-29 Sep.**   **2015**

ST AVOLD *5D2* (2km N Urban) *49.11017, 6.71059*
FFCC Camping Le Felsberg, Centre International
de Séjour, Rue en Verrerie, 57500 St Avold
**03 87 92 75 05; cis.stavold@wanadoo.fr;
www.mairie-saint-avold.fr**

12 🐕 €1 🚻 ⓌⒹ 🏊 ♿ 🛒 ⊘ ⓂⓅ ⑪ 🛒nr ⛺

Fr N on A4 exit junc 39 onto D633 to St Avold,
stay in L hand lane at 2nd traff lts & turn L; pass
under D603 for 2km & turn R. Site well sp in &
around town; app up steep incline. 3*, Sm, hdstg,
hdg, mkd, pt shd, pt sl, EHU (6-10A) €3-5; red long
stay; 50% statics; adv bkg acc; ccard acc; CKE.
*"German border 10km; sm pitches; gd facs; coal mine
& archaeological park nrby worth visit; hypmkt 1.5km;
awkward, heavy duty security gate at site ent; conv NH
nr m'way; gd; walking dist of town facs."*
€14.00   **2015**

ST AYGULF *10F4* (0.5km N Coastal) *43.39151,
6.72648* **Camping de St Aygulf Plage,** 270 Ave
Salvarelli, 83370 St Aygulf Plage **04 94 17 62 49 or 06
12 44 36 52 (mob); info@campingdesaintaygulf.fr;
www.campingdesaintaygulf.fr**

🐕 €3 🚻 ⓌⒹ 🏊 🛒 ⊘ 🍴 ⑪ 🛒 ⛺ 🏍 🏄 🌲 sand adj

Fr Roquebrunne on D7 at rndabt 100m after vill
sp St Aygulf take 3rd exit leading to Rue Roger
Martin du Gard. Keep turning L. Fr Fréjus on D559,
rd bends R after bdge over beach access, turn R
bef rd climbs to L. 2*, V lge, hdg, mkd, shd, EHU
(5A) €3.50; gas; red long stay; twin axles; adv bkg
acc; ccard acc; fishing; watersports nr; games area;
CKE. *"Gd; shop clsd LS; sports facs nrby; pool (2017)."*
€34.00, 1 Apr-28 Oct.   **2017**

ST AYGULF *10F4* (5km NW Rural) *43.41626, 6.70598* **Camping L'Etoile d'Argens,** Chemin des Etangs, 83370 St Aygulf **04 94 81 01 41; info@ etoiledargens.com; www.etoiledargens.com**

€5 (htd)

sand 3km

Exit A8 at junc 37 Puget-sur-Argens onto DN7 to Fréjus & D559 to St Aygulf, or fr DN7 take D7 to St Aygulf by-passing Fréjus & turn onto D8 to site. 4*, Lge, mkd, hdg, shd, serviced pitches; EHU (10A) inc; gas; 40% statics; Eng spkn; adv bkg acc; ccard acc; tennis; rv fishing; archery; golf 1.5km; CKE. *"Friendly, helpful owners; gd facs, poss unclean LS; excel pool complex; ferry down rv to beach in ssn; vg."* **€59.00, 1 Apr-30 Sep.** 2015

ST BENOIT SUR LOIRE *4F3* (0.5km SE Rural) *47.80711, 2.29528* **FFCC Camping Le Port,** Rue du Port, 45730 St Benoît-sur-Loire **02 38 35 12 34; contact@campingleport.fr**

(htd) nr nr sand adj

Fr Orléans take N60 & bypass Châteauneuf-sur-Loire. Take D60 twd Sully-sur-Loire to St Benoît-sur-Loire. Foll sp fr vill, site on L side of 1-way rd. 2*, Sm, pt shd, pt sl, EHU (13A) €2.50; bbq; sw nr; fishing adj; canoeing adj; CKE. *"Gd cycling, walking; pleasant town; splendid views over Loire fr some pitches, others in wooded area; excel."* **€20.00, 1 May-30 Sep.** 2019

ST BREVIN LES PINS *2G3* (2km N Coastal) *47.26553, -2.16918* **FFCC Camping de Mindin,** 32-40 Ave du Bois, 44250 St Brévin-les-Pins **02 40 27 46 41; info@ camping-de-mindin.com; www.camping-de-mindin.com**

12 €2.35 (htd) (htd)

sand adj

On beach rd at N end of St Brevin. 3*, Med, shd, EHU (16A) €5.05; 80% statics; adv bkg acc; ccard acc; CKE. *"Sm, sandy pitches; 6 touring pitches, area unkept; san facs being updated."* **€16.80** 2017

ST BREVIN LES PINS *2G3* (2.4km S Coastal) *47.23514, -2.16739* **Camping Le Fief,** 57 Chemin du Fief, 44250 St Brévin-les-Pins **02 40 27 23 86; camping@ lefief.com; www.lefief.com**

€7 (covrd, htd) sand 800m

Fr Nantes dir St Nazaire. After St Nazaire bdge S on D213. Pass Leclerc & exit sp St Brévin-l'Océan/La Courance. At rndabt foll sp Le Fief. 4*, Lge, hdstg, mkd, pt shd, EHU (8A) €6; gas; bbq (charcoal, gas); red long stay; TV; 30% statics; Eng spkn; adv bkg acc; ccard acc; sauna; gym; games area; waterslide; games rm; jacuzzi; CKE. *"Excel for families; wellness cent; fitness rm; waterpark & waterslide etc adj; vg leisure facs."* **€41.00, 4 Apr-20 Sep.** 2019

See advertisement

"I need an on-site restaurant"

We do our best to make sure site information is correct, but it is always best to check any must-have facilities are still available or will be open during your visit.

ST BRIAC SUR MER *2E3* (1km N Urban) *48.62765, -2.13056* **FFCC Camping Emeraude,** 7 Chemin de la Souris, 35800 St Briac-sur-Mer **02 99 88 34 55; emeraude@seagreen.fr; www.seagreen-camping emeraude.com**

€2.50 (htd)

700m

SW fr Dinard to St Lunaire on N786, after passing Dinard golf course, site is sp to L. 3*, Lge, hdg, pt shd, EHU (6A) €3.80; gas; 40% statics; adv bkg acc; bike hire; games area; waterpark; games rm. *"Excel, well-run site, quiet LS."* **€26.00, 3 Apr-19 Sep.** 2016

For a guide to symbols see the fold out on the rear cover

ST BRIAC SUR MER *2E3* (0.5km S Coastal) *48.61493, -2.12779* **Camping Le Pont Laurin,** Route de la Vallée Gatorge, 35800 St Briac-sur-Mer **02 99 88 34 64; lepontlaurin@ouest-camping.com; www.ouest-camping.com**

🛏 €1.50 ♦♦♦ WD ♨ ♣ ♿ ▣ ∥ MP 🦋 ♈ 🍴 🛒 ⚏ 🌳 sand 1km

Fr St Briac, 500m S on D3. 2*, Lge, hdstg, hdg, mkd, pt shd, EHU (10A) €3 (poss rev pol); 40% statics; Eng spkn; adv bkg acc; ccard acc; games area; sailing; tennis nr; CKE. *"Peaceful site; welcoming, helpful staff; clean, modern san facs; excel beaches; canoe hire nr; sports cent adj; gd walking; walking dist to shops, rest etc; interesting town; highly rec."* **€26.00, 1 Apr-30 Sep.** 2017

ST BRIEUC *2E3* (2km S Rural) *48.50066, -2.75938* **Camping des Vallées,** Blvd Paul-Doumer, 22000 St Brieuc **02 96 94 05 05; campingdesvallees@ wanadoo.fr; www.camping-desvallees.com**

🛏 €2.40 ♦♦♦ WD ♨ ♣ ♿ ▣ ∥ MP 🦋 ♈ 🍴 🛒 ⚏ 🌳 sand 3km

Fr N12 take exit sp D700 Trégueux, Pleufragan & foll sp 'Des Vallées'. Site nr Parc de Brézillet. 3*, Sm, hdstg, mkd, hdg, pt shd, EHU (10A) €4; 25% statics; Eng spkn; adv bkg acc; waterslide adj; CKE. *"High kerbs to pitches; htd pool adj; excel."* **€25.00, 2 Mar-18 Dec.** 2015

"Satellite navigation makes touring much easier"

Remember most sat navs don't know if you're towing or in a larger vehicle – always use yours alongside maps and site directions.

ST CALAIS *4F2* (0.5km N Urban) *47.92691, 0.74413* **Camp Municipal du Lac,** Rue du Lac, 72120 St Calais **02 43 35 04 81; campingstcalais@orange.fr**

🛏 ♦♦♦ WD ♨ ♿ ▣ ∥ MP 🦋 ♈ nr 🛒 nr 🌳

E fr Le Mans on D357 to St Calais; after sharp (90 degree) L/H bend away fr town cent take L/H lane for next junc in 100m; do not foll D357 bend to R but go strt ahead on D429; in 200m turn R onto sm rd sp 'Conflans/Plan d'Eau'. Site on R after football grnd. Fr N exit A11 junc 5 onto D1 to St Calais; turn R onto D357 dir Le Mans; in 200m turn R onto D429 N; in 400m turn R into sm rd sp 'Confland/ Plan d'Eau to site; leave D357 at R angle bend by Champion supmkt; site in 100m. Site by lake on N edge of town, well sp fr cent. Ent easy to miss. 3*, Med, hdg, mkd, pt shd, EHU (6A) inc; bbq; sw nr; 10% statics; adv bkg acc; CKE. *"Delightful, well-kept site; friendly, helpful warden; spacious pitches, espec nr lake; easy rvside walk to town; pool adj; gd touring base; excel; immac old style san facs; gd stopover."* **€14.00, 26 Mar-15 Oct.** 2019

ST CAST LE GUILDO *2E3* (0.5km N Coastal) *48.63690, -2.26900* **Camping Le Châtelet,** Rue des Nouettes, 22380 St Cast-le-Guildo **02 96 41 96 33; info@ lechatelet.com; www.lechatelet.com**

🛏 €4.20 ♦♦♦ WD ♨ ♣ ♿ ▣ ∥ MP 🦋 ♈ 🍴 🛒 ⚏ 🌳 🏊‍ 🚣 (covrd, htd) 🚣 sand 300m

Site sp fr all dir & in St Cast-le-Guildo but best rte: fr D786 at Matignon take D13 into St Cast-le-Guildo, turn L after Intermarché supmkt on R; foll sm site sp. Or app on D19 fr St Jaguel. Care needed down ramp to main site. (NB Avoid Matignon cent Wed due to mkt). 5*, Lge, mkd, hdg, pt shd, pt sl, terr, EHU (10A) inc; gas; bbq (charcoal, elec); TV; 50% statics; adv bkg acc; ccard acc; games rm; golf 2km; fishing. *"Site o'looks coast; o'fits over 7m by req; extra for sea view pitches; gd for families; helpful staff; modern unisex san facs; bike hire 500m; gates clsd 2230-0700; access to some pitches diff lge o'fits; mkt Mon; excel site."* **€50.00, 16 Apr-15 Sep, B11.** 2017

ST CAST LE GUILDO *2E3* (3.5km S Rural) *48.58441, -2.25691* **Camping Le Château de Galinée,** Rue de Galinée, 22380 St Cast-le-Guildo **02 96 41 10 56; contact@ chateaudegalinee.com; www.chateaudegalinee.com**

🛏 €4.50 ♦♦♦ (htd) ♨ ♣ ♿ ▣ ∥ MP 🦋 ♈ 🍴 ⊞ 🛒 ⚏ 🌳 🏊‍ (covrd, htd, indoor) 🚣 sand 4km

W fr St Malo on D168 thro Ploubalay. At La Ville-es-Comte branch onto D786 & go thro Notre Dame-du-Guildo. Approx 2km after Notre Dame-du-Guildo turn 3rd L into Rue de Galinée & foll sp to site. Do not go into St Cast. 4*, Lge, mkd, hdg, pt shd, EHU (10A) inc; bbq; cooking facs; red long stay; TV; 30% statics; Eng spkn; adv bkg acc; ccard acc; sauna; games area, waterslide; horseriding 6km; games rm; tennis; golf 3km; fishing; mini golf; CKE. *"Peaceful, family site in lovely area; spacious, well laid-out pitches; helpful staff; modern, clean, excel san facs; pitches poss muddy after rain; fishing pond; excel rest; mkt Fri & Mon; identity bracelet to be worn at all times."* **€54.50, 10 May-5 Sep, B27.** 2019

ST CAST LE GUILDO *2E3* (6km SW Rural) *48.59111, -2.29578* **Camping Le Vallon aux Merlettes,** Route de Lamballe, 22550 Matignon **02 96 80 37 99; contact@ campingdematignon.com; www.campingde matignon.com**

🛏 €0.75 ♦♦♦ (cont) WD ♨ ♿ ▣ ∥ MP 🦋 ♈ 🛒 ⚏ 🌳 🏊‍

Fr E & W take D786 to Matignon; 500m fr town cent turn SW on D13 twds Lamballe. 3*, Med, pt shd, pt sl, EHU (8A); gas; 10% statics; adv bkg rec; tennis; CKE. *"Lovely site on playing fields outside attractive town; vg clean facs; new hard working private owners (2015); excel & popular."* **€19.00, 4 Apr-30 Sep.** 2015

ST CHELY D'APCHER *9D1 (3km N Rural) 44.81644, 3.27074* **Cosy Camping (formerly Municipal Croix des Anglais,** 48200 St Chély-d'Apcher **06 42 10 49 04; cosycamping48@gmail.com; cosy-camping.com**

🚐€1 ♂♀ Wo ♿ ℗ 🚿 MSP ⊗ ⚲ ⵜ nr ℗ nr ⬛ nr ⬥

Fr N on A75 J33 onto D809, 2nd exit of rndabt, site 100m on L. Fr S J34 onto D809 thro vill dir Clermont Ferand. Site 1km on R after vill. 2*, Med, hdg, pt shd, EHU (10A) inc; twin axles; TV; 5% statics; Eng spkn; adv bkg acc; games area; games rm; CKE. *"Friendly, helpful staff; gd walks; gd NH/long stay; horse riding adj; gd."* **€14.00, 1 Apr-6 Oct.** 2018

ST CHELY D'APCHER *9D1 (10km E Rural) 44.77506, 3.37203* **Camping Le Galier,** Route de St Chély, 48120 St Alban-sur-Limagnole **04 66 31 58 80; accueil@ campinglegalier.fr; campinglozere.net/en**

🚐€1.60 ♂♀ (htd) Wo ♿ ℗ 🚿 ⊗ ⚲ ⵜ ☐ ⬛ nr ⬥ ⬤ ⬢

Exit A75 junc 34 onto D806, then E on D987 for 3km. Site 1.5km SW of St Alban on rvside. 2*, Sm, mkd, pt sl, EHU (6A) inc; bbq; 10% statics; Eng spkn; adv bkg acc; tennis 800m; games rm; CKE. *"Lovely, quiet setting by rv; friendly owners; clean san facs - stretched high ssn, ltd LS; gd walking, fishing; vg NH; rec; pretty site with rv running thro; grass pitches."* **€19.00, 1 Mar-30 Sep.** 2015

ST CHINIAN *10F1 (2km W Rural) 43.42082, 2.93395* **Camp Municipal Les Terrasses,** Route de St Pons, 34360 St Chinian **04 67 38 28 28 (Mairie); mairie@ saintchinian.fr; www.campinglesterrasses.net**

♂♀ ⚲ 🚿 ⚲ ⬤ ⬛ nr ⬥

On main Béziers-St Pons rd, D612, heading W on o'skts of St Chinian. Site on L. Med, unshd, terr, EHU (10A) €4. *"Attractive site with gd views; sm pitches; diff access some pitches; terraced site; quiet until school hols; pool; friendly hosts."* **€12.00, 1 Apr-6 Nov.** 2016

ST CHRISTOPHE *7A3 (2.5km NE Rural) 46.01467, 0.87679* **Camping En Campagne,** Essubras, 16420 St Christophe **05 45 31 67 57; info@encampagne.com; www.encampagne.com**

🚐€2 ♂♀ (htd) Wo ⚲ 🚿 ♿ ⊗ 🚿 MSP ⚲ ⬤ ⚲ ⬥ ℗ ⬛ ⬢

⬥ (covrd, htd) ⬢

Fr Bellac take D675 direction Saint-Junien. In Chene Pignier turn R on D9/D82 to Confolens. In Saint-Christophe turn R on D330 to Nouic. Site on L in 2.6km. 3*, Sm, mkd, hdg, pt shd, EHU (6-10A) inc; bbq; Eng spkn; adv bkg acc; games area; games rm; bike hire; pingpong table; petanque court; CCI. *"Vg; tourist attractions info avail; hiking/biking rtes; excel."* **€23.80, 1 Apr-1 Oct.** 2018

ST CIRQ LAPOPIE *7D3 (2.5km S Rural) 44.44871, 1.67468* **FFCC Camping La Truffière,** Route de Concots, 46330 St Cirq-Lapopie **05 65 30 20 22; contact@ camping-truffiere.com; www.camping-truffiere.com**

🚐€1.50 ♂♀ (htd) Wo ⚲ 🚿 ♿ ⊗ 🚿 MSP ⚲ ⵜ ℗ ⬤ ⬛ ⬥ 🏊

⬥ (htd) ⬢

Take D911, Cahors to Villefranche rd; in 20km turn N onto D42 at Concots dir St Cirq for 8km - site clearly sp. NB Do not app fr St Cirq-Lapopie. 3*, Med, shd, pt sl, terr, EHU (10A) €4; TV; phone; Eng spkn; adv bkg acc; ccard acc; fishing 3km; bike hire; CKE. *"Well-kept site in gd location; friendly owners; excel but dated san facs (2014), ltd LS; most pitches in forest clearings; muddy when wet; lovely pool; gd; 2m fr fairytale vill of St Cirq Lapopie, a must see; site 11m fr nearest supmkt."* **€25.00, 1 Apr-30 Sep.** 2019

ST CLAUDE *9A3 (2km S Rural) 46.37153, 5.87171* **Campsite Flower Camping Le Martinet,** 12 le Martinet, 39200 St Claude **03 84 45 00 40 or 03 84 41 42 62 (LS); contact@camping-saint-claude.fr; www.camping-saint-claude.fr**

♂♀ Wo ⚲ 🚿 ⚲ ⬤ ⬥ ⬛ nr

On ent town foll 1-way, under bdge mkd 4.1m high, then take R turn 'Centre Ville' lane to next traff lts. Turn R then immed L sp Genève, turn R 300m after Fiat g'ge onto D290, site on R. 3*, Med, pt shd, EHU (5A) €2.30; gas; Eng spkn; adv bkg acc; ccard acc; tennis; fishing; CKE. *"Site now pt of Flower camping group (2014), completely renovated; htd pool adj; has 3 modern san blocks; excel walking; v attractive town; gd."* **€23.00, 1 Apr-30 Sep.** 2019

ST CYPRIEN PLAGE *10G1 (3km S Coastal) 42.59939, 3.03761* **Camping Cala Gogo,** Ave Armand Lanoux, Les Capellans, 66750 St Cyprien-Plage **04 68 21 07 12; contact@camping-le-calagogo.fr; www.camping-le-calagogo.fr**

🚐€3-4 ♂♀ (htd) Wo ⚲ 🚿 ♿ ⊗ 🚿 MSP ⵜ ℗ ⬤ ⚲ ⬛ ⬥ 🏊 🏊

⬥ ⬢ sand adj

Exit A9 at Perpignan Nord onto D617 to Canet-Plage, then D81; site sp bet St Cyprien-Plage & Argelès-Plage dir Les Capellans. 5*, V lge, hdg, mkd, pt shd, EHU (6A) €2-4; TV; 30% statics; Eng spkn; adv bkg acc; ccard acc; tennis; games area; CKE. *"Excel site; gd pitches; lovely beach; v helpful staff."* **€48.00, 8 Apr-30 Sep.** 2017

ST DENIS D'OLERON *7A1 (3.7km S Coastal) 46.00480, -1.38480* **Camping Les Seulières,** 1371 Rue des Seulières, 17650 Saint-Denis-d'Oléron **33 546 479 051; campinglesseulieres@wanadoo.fr; www.campingles seulieres.com**

🚐€2 ♂♀ ⚲ 🚿 ♿ ⊗ 🚿 ⚲ ⬤ ⚲ ⵜ ⬛ nr 🏊 ⬥ ⬢ sand 0.3km

Fr D734 Cheray-Saint-Denis-d'Oleron. L twd La Jausiere, cont onto Grande Rue a Chaucre and foll sp to campsite. 2*, Med, mkd, pt shd, EHU (10A); gas; 45% statics; Eng spkn; adv bkg acc; ccard acc; CCI. *"Very nice beach; sep cycling rtes (plan provided)."* **€24.00, 1 Apr-30 Oct.** 2019

ST DONAT SUR L'HERBASSE *9C2* (0.5km S Rural)
45.11916, 4.99290 **Camping Domaine Les Ulèzes,**
Route de Romans, 26260 St Donat-sur-l'Herbasse
04 75 47 83 20; contact@domaine-des-ulezes.com;
www.domaine-des-ulezes.com

🐕 €2 [icons] (htd)

Exit A7 junc 13 onto D532 dir Romans-sur-Isère. In
5km turn N onto D67 thro St Donat. Site on edge of
vill off D53 dir Peyrins, well sp. 4*, Med, mkd, hdg,
pt shd, EHU (6-10A) €3.50-4.50; bbq (elec, gas); TV;
10% statics; Eng spkn; adv bkg acc; ccard acc; games
rm; ice; games area; CKE. *"Lovely rvside site; gd size
pitches; immac; excel facs; welcoming, friendly owners;
canal-side walk to town; gd touring base; vg; rec;
serviced pitches."* **€32.30, 1 Apr-31 Oct.**   2019

> ## "There aren't many sites open at this time of year"
>
> If you're travelling outside peak season
> remember to call ahead to check site opening
> dates – even if the entry says 'open all year'.

ST EMILION *7C2* (3km N Rural) *44.91695, -0.14160*
Camping Yelloh Saint Emilion, 2 lieu dit Les Combes,
33330 St Emilion **05 57 24 75 80; info@camping-**
saint-emilion.com; www.camping-saint-emilion.com

🐕 €4 [icons] (htd)
[icon]

NB Trailer c'vans not permitted in cent of
St Emilion. Fr A10 exit junc 39a sp Libourne onto
D670. In Libourne turn E on D243 twd St Emilion. On
o'skts of St Emilion turn L onto D122 dir Lussac &
Montagne; site on R by lake in 3km. Or fr S, foll site
sp off D670 to Libourne, nr Les Bigaroux. NB D122 S
of St Emilion unsuitable for c'vans.

4*, Lge, hdg, hdstg, mkd, shd, EHU (10A) inc; gas; bbq
(gas); TV; 10% statics; phone; Eng spkn; adv bkg acc;
ccard acc; horseriding 8km; games rm; waterslide; bike
hire; watersports nr; tennis; canoeing; fishing; CKE.
*"Lovely, peaceful, well-run lakeside site; owners friendly
& helpful; gd sized & shd pitches; pedalos avail; suitable
lge o'fits; no o'fits over 10m; mountain bike circuit;
clean, modern san facs but inadequate; free shuttle bus
service to St Emilion; gd cycle rtes; poss boggy when
wet; excel."* **€40.00, 28 Apr-25 Sep, D08.**   2017

ST EMILION *7C2* (9km SE Rural) *44.85138, -0.10683*
Aire St Emilion Domaine du Château Gerbaud,
33000 St Pey-d'Armens **06 03 27 00 32 (mob);**
contact@chateau-gerbaud.com; www.chateau-
gerbaud.com

12 [MSP]

Fr Libourne SE on D670/D936 dir Castillon-la-
Bataille. In St Pey-d'Armens at bar/tabac foll sp
Château Gerbaud vineyard. Eng spkn. *"Parking for
max 48 hrs; friendly, lovely site among the vines."*
€5.00   2016

ST FARGEAU *4G4* (6km SE Rural) *47.60941, 3.11961*
Camp Municipal La Calangue, 89170 St Fargeau
03 86 74 04 55; campingmunicipallacalangue@
nordnet.fr; www.camping-lacalangue.fr

🐕 [icons] (htd) [icons] nr [icon]

Take D85 fr St-Fargeau, after 1km turn R on D185,
after 2km turn R onto D485. Site on L (by circus)
after 2 km. 3*, Lge, mkd, shd, EHU (6-10A) €3.80; bbq;
sw nr; twin axles; 2% statics; adv bkg rec; canoeing;
games area; horseriding nr; fishing; CKE. *"Pleasant site
in woods; tight manoeuvring round trees; sm pitches;
gd; shops & rest 6km; conv for Guedelon; san facs not
clean."* **€10.50, 1 Apr-30 Sep.**   2015

ST FLORENTIN *4F4* (1km S Rural) *47.99252, 3.73450*
Camping L'Armançon, 89600 St Florentin **03 86 35 08**
03 13 or 03 86 35 11 86 (mob); ot.saint-florentin@
wanadoo.fr; www.camping-saint-florentin.fr

🐕 €0.20 [icons] (cont) [icons]

N fr Auxerre on N77 site on R app rv bdge S of town.
Fr N pass traff islands, exit town up slope, x-ing
canal & rv. Site immed on S side of rv bdge - turn R
immed at end of bdg then under bdg to site. Site
well sp fr all dirs. 2*, Med, hdg, pt shd, pt sl, EHU
(10A) inc (poss long lead req); gas; fishing. *"Well-kept
site; excel, lge pitches; friendly manager; dated but
clean san facs; diff, steep exit to main rd; gd NH."*
€14.50, 2 Apr-11 Oct.   2015

ST FLOUR *9C1* (4km N Rural) *45.05120, 3.10778*
Camping International La Roche Murat, N9 15100
St Flour **04 71 60 43 63; courrier@camping-saint-**
flour.com; www.camping-saint-flour.com

🐕 [icons] (htd) [icons] nr [icon]

Fr N or S on A75 exit junc 28; sp off rndabt on
St Flour side of m'way. Site ent visible 150m
fr rndabt. 3*, Med, hdg, mkd, pt shd, terr, EHU (16A)
inc (poss rev pol); gas; Eng spkn; adv bkg acc; CKE.
*"Busy site with gd views; sunny & secluded pitches; gd,
clean facs; some pitches sm; when pitches waterlogged
use site rds; old town high on hill worth visit; excel
touring cent & conv NH fr A75; vg; v clean facs."*
€16.50, 1 Apr-1 Nov.   2016

ST FORT SUR GIRONDE *7B2* (4km SW Rural) *45.43278,
-0.75185* **Camping Port Maubert,** 8 Rue de Chassillac,
17240 St Fort-sur-Gironde **05 46 04 78 86; bourdieu.**
jean-luc@wanadoo.fr; www.campingportmaubert.com

🐕 €2 [icons] [icons] nr [icon]

Exit A10 junc 37 onto D730 dir Royan. Foll sp Port
Maubert & site. 2*, Sm, hdg, mkd, shd, EHU (10A)
€3.50; gas; bbq; red long stay; TV; 10% statics; Eng
spkn; adv bkg acc; ccard acc; bike hire; games rm;
CKE. *"Pleasant, well-run site; LS ltd facs, OK NH."*
€12.40, 1 Apr-30 Oct.   2019

STE FOY LA GRANDE *7C2* (1km NE Rural) *44.84426, 0.22468* **Camping de la Bastide,** Allée du Camping, 2 Les Tuileries, Pineuilh, 33220 Ste Foy-la-Grande **05 57 46 13 84; contact@camping-bastide.com; www.camping-bastide.com**

[icons]

Fr W go thro town & turn off at D130 to site, well sp on Rv Dordogne. 3*, Med, mkd, pt shd, EHU (10A) €3 (poss rev pol); 10% statics; phone; Eng spkn; adv bkg acc; ccard acc; canoeing; games rm; jacuzzi; fishing; CKE. *"Pretty, well-cared for site; sm pitches; helpful, lovely British owners; immac, modern san facs; high kerb stones onto pitches - poss diff lge o'fits; mkt Sat; excel; ACSI acc; walking dist to supmkt & town; v clean site; v peaceful."* **€25.00, 1 Apr-31 Oct.** 2019

ST GALMIER *9B2* (2km E Rural) *45.59266, 4.33528* **Campéole Camping Val de Coise,** Route de la Thiéry, 42330 St Galmier **04 77 54 14 82; val-de-coise@campeole.com; www.campeole-valdecoise.com or www.campeole.com**

[icons] €2.60

Fr St Etienne take D1082 N. In 7km turn R onto D12 sp St Galmier; after x-ing rv bdge on o'skirts of vill turn R & foll Camping sp for 2km. Or fr N on D1082 look for sp to St Galmier about 1.5km S of Montrond-les-Bains & turn L onto D6 to St Galmier. On D12 in St Galmier at floral rndabt with fountain if app fr N go L & fr S go R, uphill & foll site sp. Site approx 1.5km fr rndabt.
4*, Med, hdstg, mkd, pt shd, pt sl, EHU (16A) €4.10; gas; bbq; TV; 20% statics; phone; Eng spkn; adv bkg acc; ccard acc; bike hire; tennis 2km; fishing; games area; games rm; CKE. *"Pleasant rvside site; helpful staff; facs poss stretched high ssn; highly rec; mainly statics."* **€21.50, 11 Apr-11 Oct.** 2015

> ## "That's changed – Should I let the Club know?"
>
> If you find something on site that's different from the site entry, fill in a report and let us know. See camc.com/europereport.

ST GAULTIER *4H2* (0.3km W Rural) *46.63470, 1.42172* **Camp Municipal L'Illon,** Rue de Limage, 36800 St Gaultier **02 54 47 11 22 or 02 54 01 66 00 (Mairie); st-gaultier.mairie@wanadoo.fr; www.mairie-saintgaultier.fr**

[icons] nr

Site well sp in town. V narr thro town - best app fr W. NB App down sh, steep hill with sharp R turn into site ent. 2*, Med, mkd, pt shd, pt sl, EHU inc; gas; rv; fishing 50m. *"Lovely, peaceful setting nr rv; site ent poss too narr for twin axles/lge o'fits; gd cycle path on old rlwy track nrby; site now has barriers, if off clse call warden; gd."* **€13.00, Easter-30 Sep.** 2016

ST GENIX SUR GUIERS *9B3* (0.3km SE Urban) *45.58878, 5.64252* **Les Bords du Guiers,** Route de Pont Beauvoisin, 73240 Saint Genix sur Guiers **04 76 31 71 40; info@lesbordsduguiers.com; www.lesbordsduguiers.com**

[icons]

On reaching vill on D1516 foll sp Le-Pont-de-Beauvoisin, site 300m on R. Med, mkd, hdg, pt shd, EHU (8-10A); bbq; twin axles; Eng spkn; games area; games rm. *"Excel, quiet site; bike hire; v helpful owners; gd base for site seeing or star watching; town cent 5 mins walk; mkt day Wed."* **€22.00, 13 Apr-21 Sep.** 2019

ST GEORGES DU VIEVRE *3D2* (0.2km W Rural) *49.24248, 0.58040* **Camp Municipal du Vièvre,** Route de Noards, 27450 St Georges-du-Vièvre **02 32 42 76 79 or 02 32 56 34 29 (LS); camping. stgeorgesduvievre@wanadoo.fr; www.saintgeorges duvievre.org**

[icons] (htd) nr

Fr traff lts on D130 in Pont Authou turn W onto D137 to St Georges-du-Vièvre; turn L after town square uphill sp camping; site 200m on L. If app fr S on N138 at Bernay take D834 sp Le Havre to Lieurey. Turn R onto D137 to St Georges, then turn R at camping sp by sw pool. 2*, Sm, hdg, pt shd, serviced pitches; EHU (5A) inc; bbq; sw nr; Eng spkn; adv bkg rec; bike hire; tennis 50m; CKE. *"Peaceful; gd facs & pitches; pool 150m; well-run site; interesting area; gd cycling; vg; basic but attractive site on edge of v picturesque vill; gd sized pitches."* **€11.00, 1 Apr-30 Sep.** 2018

ST GEORGES LES BAILLARGEAUX *4H1* (1km S Rural) *46.66452, 0.39477* **Camping Le Futuriste,** Rue du Château, 86130 St Georges-les-Baillargeaux **05 49 52 47 52; camping-le-futuriste.@wanadoo.fr; www.camping-le-futuriste.fr**

[icons] €2.50 (htd) (covrd, htd)

On A10 fr N or S, take Futuroscope exit 28; fr toll booth at 1st rndabt take 2nd exit. Thro tech park twd St Georges. At rndabt take D910 take slip rd N onto D910. After 150m exit D910 onto D20, foll sp. At 1st rndabt bear R, over rlwy, cross sm rv & up hill, site on R. 4*, Med, hdg, mkd, pt shd, serviced pitches; EHU (6A) inc (check earth & poss rev pol); gas; bbq; twin axles; TV; 10% statics; Eng spkn; adv bkg acc; ccard acc; games area; waterslide; games rm; lake fishing; CKE. *"Lovely, busy, secure site; well-kept; friendly, helpful family owners; vg clean facs, ltd LS - facs block clsd 2200-0700; vg poolwith waterslide for kids & adults; hypmkt 2km; vg for families; ideal touring base for Poitiers & Futuroscope (tickets fr recep); vg value, espec in winter; conv a'route; excel."* **€33.00** 2017

ST GERVAIS LES BAINS *9B4* (2.6km S Rural) *45.87333, 6.72000* **Camping Les Dômes de Miage,** 197 Route des Contamines, 74170 St Gervais-les-Bains **04 50 93 45 96; info@camping-mont-blanc.com; www.natureandlodge.fr**

🏕 €2 ♨ (htd) 🚐 🛂 ♿ 🔥 🚿 / 🦋 ☁ 🍴 nr ⚓ 🚲 🞜

Exit A40 junc 21; fr N thro St Gervais, at sm rndabt in cent foll sp Les Contamines onto D902, site 2km on L. 4*, Med, mkd, pt shd, EHU (6A) €3.50 (poss rev pol); gas; bbq; TV; bus adj; Eng spkn; adv bkg req; ccard acc; tennis 800m; fishing 1km; games area; CKE. *"Superb, well-kept, perfect, family-owned site in beautiful location at base of Mt Blanc; welcoming, helpful & friendly; lux chalet to rent; bike hire 800m; immac san facs; conv Tramway du Mont Blanc excursions; mkt Thurs; bkg fee; htd pool 800m; excel; free bus service to delightful sm town."* **€31.00, 15 May-16 Sep.**   **2017**

ST GILLES *10E2* (0.3km SW Urban) *43.67569, 4.42946* **Camping de la Chicanette,** Rue de la Chicanette, 30800 St Gilles **04 66 87 28 32; camping@camping lachicanette.fr; www.campinglachicanette.fr**

🏕 €2 ♨ 🚐 🛂 🚿 / 🦋 🍴 ⚓ nr 🞜 🚲 🞜

Site on D6572 W fr Arles, sp in cent of town, behind Auberge de la Chicanette. Narr app rd, tight turn to ent. 3*, Med, hdg, pt shd, EHU (6A) €3 (rev pol); 20% statics; CKE. *"Useful site; sm pitches; facs poss stretched high ssn; site poss unkempt LS; interesting old town; bus to Nîmes; mkt Sun."* **€22.00, 1 Apr-30 Oct.**   **2015**

ST GILLES CROIX DE VIE *2H3* (4km SE Coastal) *46.67095, -1.90874* **Camping Les Cyprès,** 41 Rue du Pont du Jaunay, 85800 St Gilles-Croix-de-Vie **02 51 55 38 98; contact@camping-lescypres85.com; www.camping-lescypres85.com/en**

🏕 €3.30 ♨ 🚐 🛂 ♿ 🔥 🚿 / 🗺 🦋 🍴 ⚓ 🚲 🞜 🞜 (covrd, htd)

🏖 sand 600m

Site on S end of St Gilles-Croix-de-Vie off D38, after rndabt sp Le Jaunay turn sharp L - hard to spot. 3*, Lge, hdg, shd, EHU (10A) €3; gas; red long stay; 12% statics; Eng spkn; adv bkg req; ccard acc; CKE. *"Excel for family hols; family-run site; red facs LS; footpath along rv to town cent; busy & noisy in high ssn."* **€33.00, 9 Apr-28 Sep.**   **2019**

ST GIRONS PLAGE *8E1* (1km E Coastal) *43.95105, -1.35276* **Camping Eurosol,** Route de la Plage, 40560 St Girons-Plage **05 58 47 90 14 or 05 58 56 54 90; contact@camping-eurosol.com; www.camping-eurosol.com**

🏕 €4 ♨ 🚐 🛂 ♿ 🔥 🚿 / 🦋 ☁ ⚓ 🚲 🞜 🖉 🞜 🞜

🏖 sand 700m

Turn W off D652 at St Girons on D42. Site on L in 4km. 4*, Lge, pt shd, pt sl, serviced pitches; EHU (10A) inc; gas; TV; 10% statics; tennis; games rm; bike hire; games area; horseriding adj. *"Pitches poss tight for long vans; excel for beach."* **€43.00, 10 May-13 Sep,** A27.   **2017**

See advertisement

STE HERMINE *2H4* (11km NE Rural) *46.59764, -0.96947* **FFCC Camping Le Colombier (Naturist),** 85210 St Martin-Lars **02 51 27 83 84; info@lecolombier-naturisme.com; www.lecolombier-naturisme.com**

🏕 €4.50 ♨ 🚐 🛂 ♿ 🔥 🚿 / 🦋 ☁ 🍴 🞜 ⚓ 🚲 nr 🞜 🞜

Fr junc 7 of A83 take D137 N; 3km past Ste Hermine turn R onto D52 to Le Poteau; turn L onto D10 to St Martin-Lars; 150m past St Martin-Lars turn R sp Le Colombier. Site ent on L in 200m. 4*, Lge, hdg, mkd, hdstg, pt shd, pt sl, EHU (16A) €4.50; gas; 50% statics; Eng spkn; adv bkg acc; ccard acc; jacuzzi; sauna. *"Well-run site; diff areas diff character; lge pitches; friendly Dutch owners; san facs clean but tired; gd walking in site grnds & local area; conv Mervent National Park; excel; superb facs; gd loc."* **€29.00, 1 Apr-1 Oct.**   **2018**

ST HILAIRE DE RIEZ *2H3 (6km N Rural) 46.76332, -1.95839* **Camping La Puerta del Sol,** 7 Chemin des Hommeaux, 85270 St Hilaire-de-Riez **02 51 49 10 10; info@campinglapuertadelsol.com; www.campingla puertadelsol.com**

🏕 €4 ⓦ ♨ ♿ 🚿 💳 🖉 ⚌ 🦋 ♈ ♟ ♟ 🍴 🎏 🐕 🛒 ⚠ ✂ 🛶 (htd)
🛥 🏖 sand 4.5km

N on D38 fr Les Sables-d'Olonne; exit onto D69 sp Soullans, Challans, Le Pissot. At next rndabt take 3rd exit & foll lge sp to site. Site on R in 1.5km. 4*, Lge, hdg, mkd, pt shd, pt sl, serviced pitches; EHU (10A) inc (poss rev pol); bbq (elec, gas); TV; 50% statics; Eng spkn; adv bkg acc; ccard acc; tennis; games area; watersports 5km; horseriding; sauna; games rm; jacuzzi; bike hire; waterslide; fishing 2km; golf; CKE. "Vg site; med sized pitches, some diff lge o'fits due odd shape; clean san facs; gd for families; no o'fits over 10m high ssn; gd touring base; lovely pools and playgrnd." **€33.00, 1 Apr-30 Sep.** 2016

ST HILAIRE DE RIEZ *2H3 (3.5km W Coastal) 46.72289, -1.97931* **Camp Municipal de La Plage de Riez,** Allée de la Plage de Riez, Ave des Mimosas, 85270 St Hilaire-de-Riez **02 51 54 36 59; www.souslespins.com**

🏕 €3.90 ⚌ ⚌ ♨ 🖉 ♟ ♟ 🍴 🐕 🛒 ⚠ ✂ 🛶 sand adj

Fr St Hilaire take D6A sp Sion-sur-l'Océan. Turn R at traff lts into Ave des Mimosas, site 1st L. 3*, V lge, mkd, shd, pt sl, serviced pitches; EHU (10A) €3.40; gas; TV; 30% statics; Eng spkn; bike hire. "Vg for dogs; pool 5km; exceptionally helpful manager." **€22.00, 30 Mar-31 Oct.** 2016

ST HILAIRE DU HARCOUET *2E4 (1km W Urban) 48.58105, -1.09771* **FFCC Camp Municipal de la Sélune,** 50600 St Hilaire-du-Harcouët **02 33 49 43 74 or 02 33 49 70 06; info@st-hilaire.fr; www.st-hilaire.fr**

🏕 €0.70 ⚌ ⓦ ♨ 🖉 ♟ ♟ 🐕 nr ⚠

Sp on N side of N176 twd Mont St Michel/St Malo/Dinan, on W side of town; well sp. 3*, Med, hdg, pt shd, pt sl, EHU (16A) €1.95; red long stay; CKE. "Peaceful, beautifully maintained site; pool 300m; easy access; helpful, pleasant warden; superb san facs; gate locked 2200-0730; excel." **€22.50, 23 Apr-16 Sep.** 2019

ST HILAIRE LA PALUD *7A2 (4km NW Rural) 46.28386, -0.74344* **Flower Camping Le Lidon,** Le Lidon, 79210 St Hilaire-la-Palud **05 49 35 33 64; info@le-lidon.com; www.le-lidon.com**

🏕 €2.50 ⚌ ⓦ ♨ ♿ 🚿 🖉 ⚌ MSP 🦋 ♟ ♟ 🍴 🎏 🐕 🛒 ⚠ ✂ 🛶 (htd) 🛥

Exit A10 junc 33 onto E601 then N248 & N11 S. At Epannes foll D1 N to Sansais, then D3 to St Hilaire-la-Palud. Foll sp Canal du Mignon & site. NB Access to site over narr angled bdge, extreme care needed - v diff lge o'fits. 3*, Med, mkd, hdg, pt shd, EHU (10A) inc; bbq; 5% statics; Eng spkn; adv bkg acc; ccard acc; canoe hire; ice; rv fishing; bike hire; CKE. "Secluded site in Marais Poitevin Regional Park (marsh land); gd sized pitches; excel clean san facs; gd walking, cycling, birdwatching; vg; might not be suitable for lge o'fits due to many trees." **€20.00, 11 Apr-19 Sep.** 2015

ST HONORE LES BAINS *4H4 (0.5km W Urban) 46.90413, 3.83919* **Camp Municipal Plateau du Guet,** 13 Rue Eugène Collin, 58360 St Honoré-les-Bains **03 86 30 76 00 or 03 86 30 74 87 (Mairie); mairie-de-st-honore-les-bains@wanadoo.fr; www.st-honore-les-bains.com**

⚌ (htd) ♨ ♿ 🖉 ⚌ MSP ♈ ♟ nr 🎏 nr 🐕 nr ⚠

On D985 fr Luzy to St Honoré-les-Bains. In cent vill turn L on D106 twd Vandenesse. Site on L in 150m. Or N fr Château-Chinon 27km. Then D985 to St Honoré. 2*, Med, mkd, hdstg, pt shd, terr, EHU (10A) €2.90; adv bkg acc; CKE. "Gd, modern san facs (part unisex); htd pool 300m; pleasant, conv site town; gd walking; get barrier key for early dep." **€8.60, 1 Apr-26 Oct.** 2019

ST HONORE LES BAINS *4H4 (1.5km W Rural) 46.90680, 3.82843* **Camping & Gîtes Les Bains,** 15 Ave Jean Mermoz, 58360 St Honoré-les-Bains **03 86 30 73 44; campinglesbains@gmail.com; www.campinglesbains.com**

🐕 ⚌ ⓦ ♨ ♿ 🚿 🖉 ⚌ 🦋 ♟ ♟ 🍴 🎏 🐕 nr ⚠ ✂ 🛶 🛥

Fr St Honoré-les-Bains foll site sp as 'Village des Bains' fr town cent on D106 twd Vandenesse. 3*, Med, mkd, hdg, hdstg, pt shd, pt sl, EHU (10A) €4; gas; bbq; twin axles; TV; 20% statics; phone; Eng spkn; adv bkg acc; ccard acc; bike hire; fishing; horseriding 300m; tennis; games rm; waterslide; CKE. "Helpful staff; poor maintenance & san facs need refurb; gd walking; sm pitches & poss waterlogged after rain; mkt Thu; new British owners." **€20.80, 1 Apr-31 Oct.** 2015

> ## "We must tell the Club about that great site we found"
>
> Get your site reports in by mid-August and we'll do our best to get your updates into the next edition.

ST JEAN D'ANGELY *7B2 (3km WNW Rural) 45.94868, -0.53645* **Camping Val de Boutonne,** 56 Quai de Bernouet, 17400 St Jean-d'Angély **05 46 32 26 16; info@camping-charente-maritime-17.com; www.campingcharentemaritime17.com**

🐕 €2 ⚌ ⓦ ♨ ♿ 🚿 🖉 ⚌ MSP 🦋 ♟ nr 🎏 nr 🐕 nr ⚠

Exit A10 at junc 34; head SE on D939; turn R at 1st rndabt into town. Site sp. 3*, Med, mkd, shd, EHU (10A) €4; red long stay; TV; 10% statics; Eng spkn; adv bkg acc; ccard acc; CKE. "Pleasant, friendly, well-kept site by Rv Boutonne; helpful owners; aquatic cent 500m; lovely pool, strict rules, men must wear speedos; gd, clean san facs, outdated; poss open in Oct - phone ahead; vg; lake with sm boating facs; rec; gd NH just off the A10; 10min walk to historic town; lge Sat mkt; no admittance until 14:30; gd rests." **€19.50, 1 Apr-30 Sep.** 2018

ST JEAN DE LUZ *8F1* (2km NE Coastal) *43.40563, -1.64216* **Camping de la Ferme Erromardie,** 40 Chemin d'Erromardie, 64500 St Jean-de-Luz **05 59 26 34 26; contact@camping-erromardie.com; www.camping-erromardie.com**

🏕 €3 🚻 WC ♨ 🛒 ♿ 📶 ⚡ ♨ 🍽 🛢 Ⓗ ⛱ ⛰ 🏖 sand adj

Exit A63 junc 3 onto D810 sp St Jean-de-Luz. After 1km cross rlwy and turn immed sharp R sp Erromardie. Site ent on R in 3km just bef rest/ bar. 4*, Lge, hdg, mkd, shd, EHU (6-16A) inc; gas; 80% statics; Eng spkn; adv bkg acc; CKE. *"Well-run, popular site; cheerful, helpful staff; ltd water pnts in 2nd field; lovely, sandy beaches; coastal walk into St Jean-de-Luz; Basque museum nrby; site in 3 sections, lge o'fits should ask for pitch on touring field; excel modern san facs."* **€45.00, 15 Mar-30 Sep.**   2019

See advertisement

ST JEAN DE LUZ *8F1* (3km NE Coastal) *43.40549, -1.64222* **Camping Bord de Mer,** 71 chemin d'Erromardie, 64500 St Jean-de-Luz **05 59 26 24 61; bord-de-mer64@orange.fr; www.camping-le-bord-de-mer.fr**

🏕 🚻 WC ♨ 🛒 ♿ 📶 ⚡ MSP 🦋 🍽 🛢 ⛱ sand adj

Exit A63 junc 3 onto D810 dir St Jean-de-Luz. In 1km cross rlwy & immed turn sharp R sp Erromardie. Site on sharp turn L bef beach. Ent by plastic chain fence bef ent to prom, but easy to miss. App poss diff lge o'fits due hairpin turn - drive on to car park where may be poss to turn. 3*, Med, hdg, pt sl, EHU (10A) €3,50; bbq. *"Nice site in excel position; owner connects EHU; cliff walk to town; NH en rte Spain; san facs refurbished; wonderful location; site on 2 levels, sea views on top level."* **€34.00, 10 Apr-1 Nov.**   2015

ST JEAN DE LUZ *8F1* (10km SE Rural) *43.35748, -1.57465* **Camping d'Ibarron,** 64310 St Pée-sur-Nivelle **05 59 54 10 43; camping.dibarron@wanadoo.fr; www.camping-ibarron.com**

🐕 €1.60 🚻 WC ♿ 🛒 📶 ⚡ 🦋 ♨ 🛢 🏊 ⛰ 🏖

Fr St Jean take D918 twd St Pée, site 2km bef St Pée on R of rd. 3*, Lge, shd, EHU (6A) €3.95; TV; 5% statics; phone; Eng spkn; adv bkg acc; games rm; CKE. *"Well-kept site in scenic location; spacious pitches; welcoming, helpful owner; gd san facs; on main rd & no footpath to vill; walk along rv into vill; mkt Sat; excel."* **€29.00, 23 Apr-30 Sep.**   2017

ST JEAN DE LUZ *8F1* (8km SE Rural) *43.34591, -1.61724* **Camping Chourio,** Luberriaga, 64310 Ascain **05 59 54 06 31 or 05 59 54 04 32; www.tourisme-aquitaine.fr**

🚻 WC ♨ 🛒 MSP 🦋 🍽 nr Ⓗ nr

Fr St Jean-de-Luz take D918 sp Ascain. In 6km turn R at traff lts, in 250m over rv bdge & turn L at mini-rndabt. Site sp in town. 1*, Med, pt shd, EHU (6A) €2.80; phone; CKE. *"Friendly, family-owned, relaxed site in lovely countryside; conv Spanish border; Tues & Sat mkt St Jean-de-Luz; vg; v helpful owners; bar only 300mtrs."* **€12.00, 20 Mar-15 Nov.**   2018

ST JEAN DE LUZ *8F1* (3km SW Rural) *43.37064,
-1.68629* **Camping Larrouleta,** 210 Route de Socoa,
64122 Urrugne 05 59 47 37 84; info@larrouleta.com;
www.larrouleta.com

12 🐕 €2 (htd) WD ⚓ ♿ 🚿 ♨ 🍴 ⛲ 🎿 🛝 ✏

🏊 (covrd, htd) ⛱ sand 3km

Exit A63 junc 2 St Jean-de-Luz Sud. Pass under
D810 & take 1st L sp Urrugne. Loop back up to
N10 & turn R, site sp in 500m. Or fr S on D810,
2km beyond Urrugne vill (by-pass vill), turn L into
minor rd, site 50m on R. 3*, Lge, hdstg, mkd, hdg,
pt shd, EHU (10A) inc (poss rev pol); gas; sw; phone;
bus 200m; Eng spkn; adv bkg req; ccard acc; games
area; boating; tennis; fishing; CKE. *"Pleasant, well-
run family site nr lake; satisfactory san facs (unisex
LS) & pool; friendly & helpful (ask for dir on dep to
avoid dangerous bend); some pitches unrel in wet but
can park on site rds/hdstg; poss ltd facs LS; conv A63,
Biarritz & en rte Spain; excel; conv m'way & hypmkt/
fuel 1.5km; nice walk to Urrugne & St Jean to Luz;
lots of hot water shwrs."* **€33.00** 2019

See advertisement

ST JEAN DE LUZ *8F1* (9km SW Rural) *43.33277,
-1.68527* **Le Camping du Col d'Ibardin,** Route d'Ascain,
64122 Urrugne 05 59 54 31 21; info@col-ibardin.com;
www.col-ibardin.com

🐕 €3 🚻 WD ⚓ ♿ 🚿 ♨ 🦋 ♈ 🍴 ⛲ 🎿 ⛰ ✏ 🏊 (htd) 🛶

Exit A63 junc 2, ignore slip rd to R 50m, turn L & in
100m turn R onto D810 S. In 2km at rndabt foll sp
Col d'Ibardin, Ascain; after 4km site on R immed
past minor rd to Col d'Ibardin. 3*, Med, mkd, hdstg,
hdg, pt shd, pt sl, terr, serviced pitches; EHU (10A)
inc; gas; bbq; red long stay; TV; 50% statics; phone;
Eng spkn; adv bkg acc; ccard acc; games rm; tennis;
games area; CKE. *"Lovely, well-run site in woodland;
fair sized pitches; helpful, friendly owner; gd san facs;
pleasant bar/rest; mountain rlwy nr; gd touring base for
Pyrenees & N Spain; excel."*
€50.00, 1 Apr-1 Oct, A15. 2017

ST JEAN DE MAURIENNE *9C3* (1km SE Urban)
45.27034, 6.35023 **Camp Municipal des Grands Cols,**
422 Ave du Mont-Cenis, 73300 St Jean-de-Maurienne
09 52 17 46 55; info@campingdesgrandscols.com;
www.campingdesgrandscols.com

🐕 €1 🚻 WD ⚓ 🚿 ♨ MBP 🦋 ♈ 🍴 ⛲ nr 🚲

Site sp fr D1006 in St Jean-de-Maurienne; site
behind shops 100m fr town cent behind trees/
parking. 4*, Med, hdg, mkd, hdstg, pt shd, pt sl,
serviced pitches; EHU (16A) €3; TV; Eng spkn;
games rm; CKE. *"Warm welcome; helpful staff;
clean san facs; pool 1.5km; interesting town; excel
for serious cycling; gd NH for Fréjus tunnel; excel."*
€24.00, 10 May-22 Sep. 2019

ST JEAN DE MONTS *2H3* (8km SE Coastal) *46.75638,
-2.00749* **Camping La Yole,** Chemin des Bosses, Orouët,
85160 St Jean-de-Monts 02 51 58 67 17; contact@
la-yole.com; www.vendee-camping.eu

🐕 €7 🚻 WD ⚓ ♿ 🚿 ♨ ♈ 🍴 ⛲ 🎿 ⛰ ✏ 🏊 (covrd, htd)
🏊 ⛱ sand 2km

Take D38 S fr St Jean-de-Monts dir Les Sable
d'Olonne & Orouet. At Orouet turn R at L'Oasis rest
dir Mouette; in 1.5km turn L at campsite sp; site on L.
Situated bet D38 & coast, 1km fr Plage des Mouettes.
On arr, park in carpark on R bef registering. 4*, Lge,
mkd, hdg, pt shd, serviced pitches; EHU (10A) inc; bbq
(gas); TV; 80% statics; Eng spkn; adv bkg req; ccard acc;
tennis; watersports 6km; fishing; jacuzzi; games rm;
waterslide; horseriding 3km; CKE. *"Busy, gd, well-run
site; no o'fits over 8m; sm dogs only; san facs clean, not
spacious; excel cycle paths; mkt Wed & Sat; vg; friendly
& helpful staff."* €46.00, 11 Apr-24 Sep, A23. 2018

ST JEAN DE MONTS *2H3* (2.5km NW Coastal) *46.80311, -2.09300* **La Prairie,** 146 Rue du Moulin Casse, 85160 Saint-Jean-de-Monts **02 51 58 16 04; contact@campingprairie.com; campingprairie.com**

🏕🏍🚹♿ ⓌⒸ ♨🛁⛽🅿🚿✉ 🎾 🍴 ⊛🛒⚓🚣🏊⛵ 🏖 sand

Fr St Jean de Monts take D38 twds Notre Dame de Monts. Site abt 1.5km N of St Jean de Monts. Foll sp. Sm, mkd, pt shd, EHU (6A); bbq; twin axles; 40% statics; bus adj; Eng spkn; adv bkg acc; bike hire; games rm; sauna; games area. "Gd site." €34.00, 1 Apr-9 Oct.   2016

ST JEAN DE MONTS *2H3* (4km NW Coastal) *46.80978, -2.10971* **Camping Les Places Dorées,** Route de Notre Dame de Monts, 85160 St Jean-de-Monts **02 51 59 02 93 or 02 40 73 03 70 (LS); abridespins@aol.com; www.placesdorees.com**

🏕€2.80 🚹♿ ⓌⒸ ♨🛁🅿🚿✉ 🦋 ⊛🛒⚓nr 🏊 (htd) 🏖 sand 800m

Fr Nantes dir Challons & St Jean-de-Monts. Then dir Notre Dame-de-Monts. 4*, Med, shd, pt sl, EHU (10A) inc; gas; Eng spkn; adv bkg acc; games area; games rm; waterslide; CKE. "Vg; free entmnt children/adults; organised excursions; friendly family-run site; mountain views." €32.00, 1 Jun-10 Sep.   2016

ST JEAN DE MONTS *2H3* (6km NW Coastal) *46.81831, -2.13006* **Camping La Forêt,** 190 Chemin de la Rive, 85160 St Jean-de-Monts **02 51 58 84 63; camping-la-foret@wanadoo.fr; www.hpa-laforet.com**

🏕€2.50 🚹♿ ⓌⒸ ♨🛁🅿🚿✉ 🦋🛒⚓🏛🏊 (htd) 🏖 sand 500m

Fr St Jean-de-Monts, take D38 twd Notre-Dame-de-Monts for 6km, over rndabt then turn L (last turning bef Notre-Dame-de-Monts) sp Pont d'Yeu, then immed L, site on L in 200m, on parallel rd to main rd. 4*, Med, mkd, hdg, pt shd, EHU (10A) €3.80; gas; bbq; IV; 30% statics; phone; Eng spkn; adv bkg acc; horseriding nr; CKE. "Friendly, helpful owners; clean san facs; not suitable twin axles; some pitches diff c'vans; excl; great cycling area fr site." €36.00, 1 May-20 Sep.   2015

ST JEAN PIED DE PORT *8F1* (0.6km S Urban) *43.16126, -1.23662* **Camp Municipal de Plaza Berri,** Ave de Fronton, 64220 St Jean-Pied-de-Port **05 59 37 11 19 or 05 59 37 00 92; mairie.stjeanpieddeport@ wanadoo.fr; www.saintjeanpieddeport-paysbasque-tourisme.com**

🚹♿ ⓌⒸ ♨🛁🅿✉ 🦋🛒nr

Fr N on D933 thro town & cross rv. In 50m bear L at sm rndabt, site in 200m, sp. Enquire at Hôtel de Ville (Town Hall) off ssn. Narr app rds. 1*, Med, mkd, pt shd, pt sl, EHU (5A) €2.50 (poss rev pol); CKE. "Nice site; busy, rec arr early high ssn; dogs; friendly warden; if recep unmanned, site yourself & report later; san facs still need refurb (2015); gd walks & scenery; used by walkers on pilgrim rte; pelota court adj; mkt Mon; gd NH; pool 500m; lovely site." €13.00, 23 Apr-1 Nov.   2016

ST JEAN PIED DE PORT *8F1* (3km W Rural) *43.17745, -1.25970* **Camping Narbaïtz Vacances Pyrénées Basques,** Route de Bayonne, 64220 Ascarat **05 59 37 10 13 or 06 09 39 30 42 (mob); camping-narbaitz@ wanadoo.fr; www.camping-narbaitz.com**

🏕🏍 🚹♿(htd) ⓌⒸ ♨🛁♿🅿🚿✉ 🦋 🍴🛒⚓🏛🏊(htd)

Site on L of D918 St Jean to Bayonne 3km fr St Jean, sp. 4*, Med, hdg, mkd, pt shd, pt sl, EHU (6-10A) €4.50-5.50 (poss rev pol); 5% statics; phone; Eng spkn; adv bkg acc; ccard acc; trout fishing; kayaking; canoeing; cycling; CKE. "Attractive, clean, pleasant, family-run site; lovely views; helpful owners; vg facs; rec m'vans use top of site when wet; nr Spanish border (cheaper petrol); excel; gd san facs." €41.00, 29 Apr-24 Sep.   2017

ST JEAN PIED DE PORT *8F1* (2.4km NW Rural) *43.17304, -1.25416* **Europ Camping,** 64220 Ascarat **05 59 37 12 78; europcamping64@orange.fr; www.europ-camping.com**

🏕€2.50 🚹♿ ⓌⒸ ♨🛁♿🅿🚿✉ 🦋 🍴⊛🛒⚓nr 🏛🏊🛒

Site on D918 bet Uhart-Cize & Ascarat. Well sp. 4*, Med, hdg, mkd, pt shd, EHU (6A) €4 (poss rev pol); 30% statics; adv bkg acc; ccard acc; sauna; games area; games rm; CKE. "Beautiful location; helpful staff; ltd facs LS; only basic food in bar/rest; grnd v soft when wet; vg." €33.00, 4 Apr-30 Sep.   2016

"That's changed – Should I let the Club know?"

If you find something on site that's different from the site entry, fill in a report and let us know. See camc.com/europereport.

ST JULIEN EN GENEVOIS *9A3* (5km SE Rural) *46.12015, 6.10565* **Kawan Village La Colombière,** 166 Chemin Neuf-Chef-Lieu, 74160 Neydens **04 50 35 13 14; la.colombiere@wanadoo.fr; www.camping-la-colombiere.com**

🏕€2.50 🚹(htd) ⓌⒸ ♨🛁♿🅿✉ 🎾 🍴⊛🛒⚓🏛🚿 🏊(covrd, htd) 🛒

Exit A40 junc 13 onto D1201 dir Cruseilles; in 1.75km turn L to Neydens; turn R at church; site on R in 200m. Site sp. NB: Do not go into St Julien-en-Genevois when towing. 4*, Med, hdstg, hdg, mkd, pt shd, pt sl, EHU (6-10A) inc, extra for 15A; gas; bbq; TV; 10% statics; Eng spkn; adv bkg acc; ccard acc; bike hire; lake fishing 1km; games rm; CKE. "Family-owned site; friendly, helpful staff; boggy after heavy rain; farm produce; conv Geneva - guided tours high ssn; no o'fits over 10m high ssn; park & ride bus; open for m'vans all year; gd NH; excel; highly rec." €39.70, 1 Apr-31 Oct, M08.   2017

ST JUNIEN *7B3* (4km E Rural) *45.88078, 0.96539*
FFCC Camp Municipal de Chambery, 87200 St
Brice-sur-Vienne **05 55 02 42 92; mairiest-brice@
wanadoo.fr; www.tourismelimousin.com**

🏕🐕 (htd) ⚓🍴🖪 ⊘ nr ⛺

Fr St Junien take D32 E sp St Brice & St Victurnien;
on leaving St Brice on D32 turn L & foll sp; site on
L in 500m, on E edge of vill. Or app on D32 fr E,
turn R onto C2 bef St Brice-sur-Vienne town sp, sp
'Campings & Gite Rural'. 2*, Sm, hdg, mkd, hdstg, pt
shd, pt sl, serviced pitches; EHU (10A) €3.40; adv bkg
acc; CKE. *"Peaceful, clean site in park; spacious pitches
o'look lake & countryside; site opening office open
1hr am & pm; barrier clsd 2200-0700; conv Oradour-
sur-Glane; excel; beautiful location; excel san facs;
each pitch has own tap & drain; call to check if open."*
€10.00, 1 May-1 Sep. **2019**

ST JUST (CANTAL) *9C1* (0.5km W Urban) *44.89035,
3.21079* **FFCC Camp Municipal,** 15320 St Just
**04 71 73 72 57, 04 71 73 70 48 or 06 31 47 05 15
(mob); info@saintjust.com; www.saintjust.com**

🏕🐕🚻 (htd) 🅆🅞⚓🖪⊘🍴 🦋🍽🎪🛒🛎nr ⛴

Exit junc 31 fr A75, foll sp St Chély-d'Apcher D909;
turn W onto D448 twds St Just (approx 6km); sp
with gd access. 3*, Med, mkd, pt shd, pt sl, terr, EHU
(10A) €2.30; red long stay; phone; Eng spkn; ccard
acc; tennis; bike hire; fishing. *"Vg site; friendly, helpful
warden; ltd facs LS; excel tennis & pool; gd touring base;
area for m'vans."* **€10.20, Easter-30 Sep.** **2017**

ST JUSTIN *8E2* (2.5km NW Rural) *44.00166, -0.23502*
Camping Le Pin, Route de Roquefort, 40240 St Justin
**05 58 44 88 91; camping.lepin@orange.fr;
www.campinglepin.com**

🏕🐕 €2.50 🚻🅆🅞⚓🖪♿🖪⊘🍴🦋🍽🍸🎪🛒🛎⛺🚲⛴

Fr D933 in St Justin take D626 sp Requefort, site
on L in 2km (sp says 3). 3*, Sm, hdg, mkd, pt shd,
EHU (6-10A) inc; bbq; TV; 10% statics; Eng spkn;
adv bkg acc; rv fishing 2km; games area; bike hire;
horseriding; CKE. *"Pleasant, spacious site; new facs
(2016); beautiful vill; rustic wooded setting; gd
welcome; helpful owner; bread avail daily; sm pond,
free fishing for campers; highly rec; excel modern clean
san facs; Bastide town nrby; conv to & fr Spain; excel."*
€23.60, 3 Mar-1 Dec. **2019**

ST LARY SOULAN *8G2* (4km NE Rural) *42.84482,
0.33836* **Camping Le Lustou,** 89 Chemin d'Agos, 65170
Vielle-Aure **05 62 39 40 64; contact@lustou.com;
www.lustou.com**

🔟🏕🐕 €1.80 🚻 (htd) 🅆🅞⚓🖪♿🖪⊘🍴 🦋🍽🍸🎪🛒🛎nr ⛺

Exit A64 junc 16 & head S on D929. Thro Arreau &
Guchen turn R onto D19 dir Vielle-Aure. Site on R
just bef Agos. 3*, Med, hdg, pt shd, pt sl, EHU (6-10A)
€6.80; gas; bbq; TV; 5% statics; phone; adv bkg acc;
canoeing nr; fishing nr; tennis nr; games area; CKE.
*"Organised walks in mountains by owner; excel skiing;
immac facs; communal meals organised weekly (high
ssn); excel site."* **€19.00** **2016**

ST LAURENT DE CERIS *7B3* (4.6km NE Rural) *45.95902,
0.52880* **Camp Laurent,** Le Fournet, 16450 St Laurent
de Ceris Charente **06 02 22 37 15; lecamplaurent@
gmail.com**

🔟🏕🐕🚻🅆🅞⚓🖪♿🖪⊘🍴🥋🦋🎪🍽🍸🛎🎪nr🛎⛴

Fr St Claud on D174. Fr St Laurent de Ceris turn R
at rest onto D15. Take 2nd L on D345, Le Fournet
sp at junc. Site on R in about 1km. Sm, pt shd, pt sl,
EHU (10A) €3; bbq; twin axles; Eng spkn; adv bkg acc.
*"Adults only site; suitable for all units; Eng owners;
beside sm rv; v clean facs; helpful, friendly welcome;
lakes with beach nrby; new owners; ideal walking &
cycling country."* **€25.00** **2015**

ST LAURENT EN GRANDVAUX *6H2* (0.5km SE Rural)
46.57645, 5.96214 **Camp Municipal Le Champs de
Mars,** 8 Rue du Camping, 39150 St Laurent-en-Grandvaux
**03 84 60 19 30 or 06 03 61 06 61; champmars.camping
@wanadoo.fr or champmars.camping@orange.fr;
www.st-laurent39.fr**

🏕🐕🚻 (htd) 🅆🅞⚓🖪♿🖪⊘🍴🍽 🦋🛎nr ⛺

E thro St Laurent on N5 twd Morez, site on R,
sp 'Caravaneige' at ent. 2*, Med, mkd, hdstg,
pt shd, pt sl, serviced pitches; EHU (4-10A) €5-
6.4; TV; 20% statics; phone; adv bkg acc; CKE.
"Gd site; peaceful LS; gd NH; friendly staff."
€13.80, 1 Jan-30 Sep. **2019**

**"I like to fill in the reports as I
travel from site to site"**

You'll find report forms at the back of this
guide, or you can fill them in online at
camc.com/europereport.

ST LAURENT SUR SEVRE *2H4* (1km W Rural)
46.95790, -0.90290 **Camping Le Rouge Gorge,**
Route de la Verrie, 85290 St Laurent-sur-Sèvre
**02 51 67 86 39; campinglerougegorge@wanadoo.fr;
www.camping-lerougegorge-vendee.com**

🏕🐕 €2.10 🚻 (htd) 🅆🅞⚓🖪♿🖪⊘🍴 🦋🍽🍸🎪🛒🛎⛺⛴🛏

Fr Cholet on N160 dir La Roche-sur-Yon; at
Mortagne-sur-Sèvre take N149 to St Laurent-sur-
Sèvre. In St Laurent foll sp La Verrie on D111.
Site on R at top of hill. Or take 762 S fr Cholet to
St Laurent. Site sp in town. 3*, Med, hdg, mkd, pt
shd, pt sl, EHU (4-13A) €2.95-4.10; 30% statics; adv
bkg acc; lake fishing 800m; golf 15km; games area;
CKE. *"Peaceful family site; woodland walks & mountain
biking; attractive sm town; close to Puy du Fou Theme
Park."* **€24.00, 1 Apr-30 Sep.** **2017**

ST LEONARD DE NOBLAT *7B3* (15km N Rural) *45.94311, 1.51459* **Camping Pont du Dognon (formerly Municipal),** 87240 St Laurent-les-Eglises 06 75 73 25 30 or 05 55 56 57 25; www.aupont dudognon.fr

🐕 €2 ♟♟♟(htd) ⓦⓓ ♨ ⬛ 🗑 ⊘ 🍴 ☕ ⑪ 🛒 💧 ⚠ 🚲 ⚡ 🛶 shgl

Take D941 fr St Léonard-de-Noblat; after 1.5km turn L (N) on D19 thro Le Châtenet-en-Dognon. Site in approx 4km, bef St Laurent-les-Eglises. 3*, Med, mkd, hdg, pt shd, terr, EHU (6-16A) €3.50; gas; bbq; twin axles; adv bkg acc; tennis; bike hire; canoeing. *"Vg site."* **€13.00, 2 Apr-1 Oct.** **2016**

ST LOUIS *6G3* (2km N Rural) *47.59428, 7.58930* **Camping au Petit Port,** 10 Allée des Marronniers, 68330 Huningue 03 89 69 05 25 or 03 89 70 01 71; contact@campinghuningue.fr; www.camping huningue.fr

🐕 ♟♟♟ ⓦⓓ ♨ ⊘ ⑤ 🗑 ⊘ 🍴 🌊 🛒 ⚠ nr 🍴 ⑪ ⊘ 💧 nr ⚠

S fr Mulhouse on A35, exit onto D105 & foll sps to Huningue; after level x-ing site sp on rvside. 2*, Med, pt shd, EHU (6A) €3; bbq; cooking facs; TV; 50% statics; bus to Basle; Eng spkn; adv bkg acc; games rm; bike hire; CKE. *"Excel NH on banks of Rv Rhine; helpful staff; htd pool 2km; clean facs; poss diff access lge o'fits; bar 500m; canoeing."* **€20.00, 15 Apr-15 Oct.** **2018**

ST MAIXENT L'ECOLE *7A2* (1.5km SW Urban) *46.40836, -0.21856* **Camp Municipal du Panier Fleuri,** Rue Paul Drévin, 79400 St Maixent-l'Ecole 05 49 05 53 21

🐕 ♟♟♟ ♨ ⊘ 🛒 ⚠ 🍴 ⑪ 🍴 nr ⑪ nr ⚠

Take D611 twd Niort, at 2nd set of traff lts nr top of hill out of town turn L. Foll camping sps into ent. 3*, Med, mkd, pt shd, pt sl, EHU (10A); tennis. *"Warden on site am & eve, if office locked go to hse nr wc block; ltd/basic facs LS, htd pool adj; interesting town; NH en rte Spain; immac new htd san facs (2014)."* **€10.50, 1 Apr-15 Oct.** **2019**

"We must tell the Club about that great site we found"

Get your site reports in by mid-August and we'll do our best to get your updates into the next edition.

ST MALO *2E4* (10km NE Rural) *48.67368, -1.92732* **Camping a la ferme La Vignette,** 35350 St Coulomb 02 99 89 08 42; francoise.morin600@orange.fr; www.facebook.com/campinglavignette

12 🐕 ♟♟♟ ⓦⓓ ⊘ 🌊 ⚠ 1km

Fr St Malo foll D355 E twds St Coulomb. Just bef vill turn L, sp 'Camping a la ferme'. Site in 400m on R. Sm, pt shd, pt sl, EHU (10A). *"Vg site."* **€14.00** **2015**

ST MALO *2E4* (11km NE Coastal) *48.69000, -1.94200* **Camping des Chevrets,** La Guimorais, 35350 St Coulomb 02 99 89 01 90; contact@campingdes chevrets.fr; www.campingdeschevrets.fr

🐕 ♟♟♟ ⓦⓓ ♨ ⊘ ⑤ 🗑 ⊘ 🛒 🍴 ⑪ 🌊 🍴 ☕ ⑪ ⊘ 🛒 💧 ⚠ 🛶 🌊 sand adj

St Malo to Cancale coast rd D201; La Guimorais on L 3km E of Rothéneuf, strt thro vill; fairly narr app. 3*, V lge, hdg, mkd, pt shd, pt sl, EHU (6A) €3.35 (poss rev pol); gas; bbq; red long stay; 50% statics; Eng spkn; adv bkg acc; ccard acc; games area; bike hire; CKE. *"Vg, beautiful location with 2 bays; vg, busy, well run site; bus fr St Malo to Cancale in the summer; statics in sep area; vg value LS; vg facs; conv for ferry."* **€28.00, 30 Mar-16 Oct.** **2017**

ST MALO *2E4* (5km SE Rural) *48.60916, -1.98663* **Camping Le P'tit Bois,** La Chalandouze, 35430 St Jouan-des-Guérets 02 99 21 14 30; camping.ptitbois @wanadoo.fr; www.ptitbois.com

🐕 €4-6 ♟♟♟ ⓦⓓ ♨ ⊘ ⑤ 🗑 ⊘ 🍴 ⑪ 🌊 🍴 ☕ ⑪ 🛒 💧 ⚠ 🚲 🌊 (covrd, htd) 🚿 🌊 sand 2km

Fr St Malo take D137 dir Rennes; after o'skts of St Malo turn R twd St Jouan-des-Guérets, site sp. 4*, Lge, mkd, hdg, pt shd, serviced pitches; EHU (10A) inc; gas; bbq (elec, gas); TV; 75% statics; adv bkg acc; ccard acc; waterslide; games rm; tennis; bike hire; watersports 2km; CKE. *"Well-kept, well-run site; lge o'fits by request; busy even LS; min 3 persons high ssn; tidal rv fishing 2km; jacuzzi; turkish bath; friendly, helpful staff; gd clean san facs, one block unisex; some narr site rds poss diff lge o'fits; conv Le Mont-St Michel & ferries; excel."* **€52.00, 11 Apr-20 Sep, B03.** **2019**

ST MALO *2E4* (2.7km S Coastal) *48.63558, -2.02731* **Camp Municipal Cité d'Alet,** Allée Gaston Buy, Saint-Servan 35400 St Malo 02 99 81 60 91 or 02 99 40 71 11 (LS); camping@ville-saint-malo.fr; www.ville-saint-malo.fr/campings

🐕 €2.95 ♟♟♟ ⓦⓓ ⊘ 🛒 ⚠ 🍴 ⑪ nr ⑪ 💧 nr ⚠ 🌊 sand 500m

Fr ferry terminal go twd St Malo, site sp at rndabt immed past docks. Fr all other dir foll sp for port/ferry, then site sp. Site off Place St Pierre, St Servan-sur-Mer. App thro old pt of city poss diff for lge o'fits. 2*, Lge, hdstg, pt shd, pt sl, EHU (10A) inc (poss rev pol & long elec cable poss req); bbq (charcoal, elec, gas); twin axles; phone; bus 1km; Eng spkn; adv bkg acc; ccard acc; CKE. *"Well-run, scenic site; staff helpful & friendly; sm pitches, access to some diff lge o'fits; san facs basic but OK (poss v slippery); WW2 museum adj; noise fr harbour when foggy; mkt Fri; parts of site steep, lovely walks, cliff top views of Dinard & St Malo, walk to St Malo worth while; site feels cosy."* **€22.50, 26 Apr-21 May & 1 Jul-25 Sep.** **2018**

ST MALO *2E4* (6km S Rural) *48.61469, -1.98663*
Camping Domaine de la Ville Huchet, Rue de la
Passagère, Quelmer, 35400 St Malo **02 99 81 11 83;**
info@lavillehuchet.com; www.lavillehuchet.com

🛍 €3.50 👥 WC ♨ ♿ 🚿 ♨ / MBP 🦋 ♨ 🍸 ⊕ ♨ 🛒 ⚠ ✎
🏊 (covrd, htd) 🛁 🏖 sand 4km

Fr ferry port, foll sps for D137 dir Rennes; site sp
fr 'Madeleine' rndabt on leaving St Malo. Or fr S
on D137 take D301 sp St Malo cent. Take 1st exit
at next 2 rndabts (thro indus est) & cont on this rd
(sharp R-hand bend), then under bdge, site on R.
Fr S head N on D137, merge onto D301, at rndabt
take 1st exit onto Rue de la Grassinais, thro next
rndabt. At next rndabt take 1st exit. Site on the
L. 4*, Lge, hdg, mkd, pt shd, pt sl, EHU (6A) inc;
bbq (charcoal, gas, sep area); TV; 40% statics; Eng
spkn; adv bkg acc; waterpark; games area; games
rm. *"Spacious site in grnds of sm chateau; helpful
team; modern san facs; no o'fits over 7.4m except by
request; lge pitches avail; some pitches v shady; conv
ferries & Mont St Michel; excel; bus to St Malo adj."*
€40.70, 4 Apr-20 Sep, B32.   2019

See advertisement

STE MARIE AUX MINES *6E3* (1.7km SW Urban)
48.23520, 7.16995 **FFCC Camping Les Reflets du Val
d'Argent,** 20 Rue d'Untergrombach, 68160 Ste Marie-
aux-Mines **03 89 58 64 31; reflets@calixo.net;**
www.les-reflets.com

12 🛍 €3.50 👥 (htd) WC ♨ ♿ 🚿 ♨ / MBP 🦋 ♨ 🍸 ⊕ ♨ 🛒 ⚠

Fr Sélestat N59 into Ste Marie. Go thro vill to traff
lts & turn L. 1km to site; sp. 3*, Med, hdg, mkd, pt shd,
pt sl, EHU (5-15A) €3.30-9.90; bbq; TV; 5% statics;
phone; adv bkg acc; games rm; CKE. *"Pleasant site;
winter skiing 5km; new san facs; grnds could be
improved."* **€21.00**   2015

STE MARIE DU MONT *1D4* (3km SE Coastal) *49.36564,
-1.17721* **Camping La Baie des Veys,** Le Grand Vey,
50480 Ste Marie-du-Mont **02 33 71 56 90 or
06 09 82 61 82 (mob); jerome.etasse@orange.fr;
www.campinglabaiedesveys.com**

🛍 €1.50 👥 WC ♨ ♿ 🚿 / 🦋 ♨ 🍸 🛒 ♨ 🏊 (htd)

N of Carentan exit N13 onto D913 thro Ste Marie-
du-Mont. At lge calvary 2km after vill, turn R
onto D115 sp Le Grand Vey. Turn R at sea edge,
site on R in 100m. 3*, Med, hdg, mkd, pt shd, EHU
(10A) €4; bbq; 10% statics; Eng spkn; adv bkg acc;
bike hire. *"Site beside salt flats; helpful, friendly
owners; gd birdwatching, fishing; conv Utah Beach,
D-Day museums etc; nature reserve adj; nice site"*
€29.00, 1 Apr-26 Sep.   2019

STES MARIES DE LA MER *10F2* (0.8km E Coastal)
43.45633, 4.43576 **Camping La Brise,** Rue Marcel
Carrière, 13460 Les Stes Maries-de-la-Mer
**04 90 97 84 67; info@camping-labrise.fr;
www.camping-labrise.fr**

🛍 €5.20 👥 (htd) ♨ ♿ 🚿 / MBP ♨ ⊕ nr 🛒 ♨ ✎ 🏊 (htd) 🛁 🏖 adj

Sp on o'skts on all rds. Take N570 fr Arles or D58
fr Aigues-Mortes. 3*, V lge, unshd, EHU (16A) €4.90;
bbq; TV; 10% statics; fishing; site clsd mid-Nov to
mid-Dec. *"Gd facs; v cr Aug; poss mosquitoes; gd
security; beach improved with breakwaters; m'vans
can use free municipal car park with facs; fitness
area; recep open fr 0900-1700 but clsd 1200-1400;
vg winter NH; pitches poorly mrkd, dirty & dusty."*
€17.00, 1 Jan-12 Nov & 15 Dec-31 Dec.   2016

STES MARIES DE LA MER *10F2* (2.6km W Coastal) *43.45014, 4.40163* **Camping Le Clos du Rhône,** Route d'Aigues-Mortes, 13460 Stes Maries-de-la-Mer **04 90 97 85 99; info@camping-leclos.fr; www.camping-leclos.fr**

€6 (htd) sand

Fr Arles take D570 to Stes Maries; fr Aigues Mortes, D58/D570. 4*, Lge, mkd, pt shd, serviced pitches; EHU (16A) inc; gas; bbq; cooking facs; twin axles; TV; 30% statics; phone; Eng spkn; adv bkg acc; ccard acc; horseriding adj; games area; games rm; bike hire; waterslide; CKE. *"Excel pool & facs; san facs clean, poss ltd & stretched LS; popular with families; private gate to beach; mosquitoes; rv boat trips adj; off rd bike & foot paths to town; vg."* **€33.00, 3 Apr-1 Nov.** **2019**

ST MARTIN DES BESACES *1D4* (1.2km W Rural) *49.00889, -0.85955* **Camping Sous Les Etoiles,** La Groudière, 14350 St Martin-des-Besaces Calvados **08 09 48 62 or 06 37 87 99 53; info@sous-les-etoiles.camp; www.sous-les-etoiles.camp**

(htd)

Fr Caen SW on A84 dir Rennes, Villers-Bocage & exit junc 41 to St Martin-des-Besaces. At traff lts in vill turn R. Site on L at end of Vill after gge after 500m. Fr Cherbourg foll sp St Lô onto m'way. After Torini-sur-Vire at junc with A84 foll sp Caen & exit J41, then as above. 2*, Sm, hdg, pt shd, pt sl, serviced pitches; EHU (6A) (poss rev pol); bbq; red long stay; twin axles; TV; Eng spkn; adv bkg acc; ccard acc; fishing; cycling; games rm; CKE. *"Pleasant CL-type orchard site; no arr bef 1400; lge pitches with garden; 'super' pitches extra cost; B&B in farmhouse; equestrian trails; lake adj; suitable for rallies up to 30 vans; c'van storage; war museum in vill; conv Caen ferries; new excel san facs (2019);excep helpful, new English owners (2018); easy reach of D Day beaches, Bayeaux, Falaises and Villers Bocage; excel."* **€25.00, 1 Mar-31 Oct.** **2019**

ST MARTIN EN CAMPAGNE *3B2* (2km N Coastal) *49.96631, 1.20469* **Camping Domaine Les Goélands,** Rue des Grèbes, 76370 St Martin-en-Campagne **02 35 83 82 90; domainelesgoelands@orange.fr; www.camping-les-goelands.fr**

€2 (htd) nr nr shgl 500m

Fr Dieppe foll D925 twd Le Tréport & Abbeville. Turn L at rndabt on D113 twd St Martin-en-Campagne. Cont thro vill to St Martin-Plage (approx 3km) & foll 'Camping' sp to site on L. 4*, Lge, hdg, hdstg, mkd, pt shd, pt sl, terr, serviced pitches; EHU (16A) inc (poss rev pol); gas; bbq; TV; 40% statics; Eng spkn; adv bkg acc; ccard acc; bike hire; waterslide 1km; tennis; fishing; CKE. *"Gd touring area; ltd recep hrs LS; no late arr area; poss resident workers LS; mkt Dieppe Sat; golf 20km; horseriding 15km; vg site; immac modern san facs(2017); v helpful recep."* **€23.00, 1 Apr-31 Oct.** **2017**

ST MARTIN SUR LA CHAMBRE *9B3* (0.5km N Rural) *45.36883, 6.31458* **Camping Le Petit Nice,** Notre Dame-de-Cruet, 73130 St Martin-sur-la-Chambre **04 79 56 37 72 or 06 76 29 19 39 (mob); campinglepetitnice@yahoo.fr; www.campinglepetitnice.com**

12 €1 (htd)

Fr N on A43 exit junc 26 & foll sp to cent of La Chambre, thro town to rndabt & turn R into Rue Notre Dame-du-Cruet. Foll site sp & in 2km turn R thro housing, site on L in 200m. 3*, Sm, pt shd, terr, EHU (3-10A); 80% statics; Eng spkn; adv bkg acc; CKE. *"By stream with mountain views; clean, dated facs; gd location for hilly cycling; fair."* **€16.00** **2016**

"Satellite navigation makes touring much easier"

Remember most sat navs don't know if you're towing or in a larger vehicle – always use yours alongside maps and site directions.

ST MARTIN SUR LA CHAMBRE *9B3* (1km SW Rural) *45.36146, 6.31300* **Camping Le Bois Joli,** 73130 St Martin-sur-la-Chambre **04 79 56 21 28; camping.le.bois.joli@wanadoo.fr; www.campingleboisjoli.com**

€4

Leave A43 at junc 26 onto D213 sp La Chambre & Col de la Madeleine; foll camping sp (rd narr & winding in places); site on L. 2*, Med, mkd, pt shd, pt sl, terr, EHU (6A) inc; gas; bbq; red long stay; 20% statics; phone; Eng spkn; adv bkg acc; fishing; CKE. *"Helpful staff; mountain scenery; gd walking, skiing; guided walks; ltd facs LS; conv Fréjus Tunnel."* **€13.00, 5 Apr-6 Oct, A35.** **2017**

STE MAURE DE TOURAINE *4H2* (6km NE Rural) *47.14831, 0.65453* **Camping Le Parc de Fierbois,** 37800 Ste Catherine-de-Fierbois **02 47 65 43 35; contact@fierbois.com; www.fierbois.com or www.les-castels.com**

(covrd, htd)

S on D910 fr Tours, thro Montbazon & cont twd Ste Maure & Châtellerault. About 16km outside Montbazon nr vill of Ste Catherine look for site sp. Turn L off main rd & foll sp to site. Or exit A10 junc 25 onto D760E, then D910 N sp Tours; in 6.5 km turn R to Ste Catherine-de-Fierbois; site on L 1.5km past vill. 4*, Lge, hdg, mkd, pt shd, EHU (10A) €5; bbq; twin axles; TV; Eng spkn; adv bkg acc; ccard acc; games area; waterslide; tennis; bike hire; games rm; boating; fishing; CKE. *"Excel, well-kept family site; helpful staff; gd touring base; peaceful LS; rec."* **€44.00, 19 May-6 Sep, L20.** **2017**

FRANCE

STE MAURE DE TOURAINE *4H2* (1.5km SE Rural)
47.10483, 0.62574 **Camp Municipal Marans,** Rue de Toizelet, 37800 Ste-Maure-de-Touraine **02 47 65 44 93 or 06 72 18 05 41; www.tourisme-saintemaurede touraine.fr**

🐕 €1.42 ♨♿ 🆆🅳 ⛺ 🅿 ♿ ⚡ 〽 🦋 ☂ 🍴 nr ⊕ 🛒 nr ⛰

Fr A10 take Ste Maure exit junc 25 & foll D760 twd Loches. At 4th rndabt turn L & then immed R. Site on R in 500m. Site sp fr m'way. 2*, Med, mkd, pt shd, EHU (10A) €3.20 (poss long cables req); bbq; phone; Eng spkn; adv bkg acc; fishing; tennis. *"Well-kept, basic site; cheerful staff; gd, clean facs - poss stretched when busy; pool 1.5km; if office clsd site yourself; barrier down 2200-0700; roller blade court; late arr area outside barrier; no twin axles; poss travellers in sep area; vg; wifi around office area; lovely peaceful site."* €9.00, 10 Apr-30 Sep. **2017**

STE MAURE DE TOURAINE *4H2* (1.5km S Rural)
47.10861, 0.61440 **Aire de Service Camping-Cars Bois de Chaudron,** 37800 Ste-Maure-de-Touraine **02 47 34 06 04**

🔟 ♨⛺ 🔌 〽 🅿

Fr S on D910 dir Tours, as ent town, site on R adj junc at traff lts; sm sp on dual-c'way. Sm, EHU €2 (on only some pitches); Eng spkn. *"M'vans only; New Aire de Service (2009); warden calls; conv N/S journeys; easy to park; level, grass; friendly."* €5.00 **2017**

STE MAURE DE TOURAINE *4H2* (10km W Rural)
47.10705, 0.51016 **Camping du Château de la Rolandière,** 37220 Trogues **02 47 58 53 71; contact@larolandiere.com; www.larolandiere.com**

🐕 €3 ♨♿ 🆆🅳 ⛺ 🅿 ♿ 🔌 〽 🦋 🅿 ⚡ 🍴 🛒 nr ⛰ 🛶 (htd) 📶

Exit A10 junc 25 onto D760 dir Chinon & L'Ile-Bouchard. Site sp on S side of rd in 5.5km. 4*, Sm, mkd, hdg, pt shd, pt sl, EHU (10A) €4.40 (poss long lead req); bbq; TV; Eng spkn; adv bkg acc; games area; games rm; CKE. *"Beautiful, well-maintained, family-run site in chateau grnds; friendly, helpful owners; gd clean san facs; excel for young families, sh or long stay; gd dog walking; conv Loire chateaux; excel pool & sports field; highly rec; Villandry gdns to N; Richlieu worth a visit; secluded and peaceful; gd size pool; football pitch & games for children; great location for Loire chateaux; gd for o'night stay."* €24.00, 30 Apr-18 Sep. **2016**

ST MAURICE LES CHARENCEY *4E2* (0km N Rural)
48.64747, 0.75575 **Camp Municipal de la Poste,** Rue de Brest, 61190 St Maurice-lès-Charencey **02 33 25 72 98; mairie.stmaurice-charencey@wanadoo.fr**

🔟 ♨⛺ 🔌 〽 🍴 nr ⊕ nr 🛒

Vill on N12 halfway bet Verneuil-sur-Avre & Mortagne-au-Perche. Site in vill cent, opp Mairie & church. 2*, Sm, hdg, mkd, EHU; bbq; 50% statics; phone; fishing. *"Phone ahead LS to check open; helpful warden; facs basic but adequate; gd NH; lake adj; site self; gd site."* €7.60 **2016**

SAINT MAURICE SOUS LES COTES *5D2* (0.4km N Rural) *49.01796, 5.67539* **Camping Du Bois Joli,** 12 rue haute Gaston Parant, 55210 St Maurice-sous-les-Côtes **03 29 89 33 32; campingduboisjoli@voila.fr; www.forest-campingbj.com**

🐕 ♨♿ ⛺ ♿ 🔌 〽 🍴 nr ⊕ nr ⛰

Well sp in vill. If app on D23, turn R at t-junc & foll sp. Sm, pt shd, sl, EHU (7A) €2.20 (ltd points, long cable useful); bbq; Eng spkn. *"Conv Verdun & WW1 sites; gd view during World Air Balloon Festival."* €14.80, 1 Apr-15 Oct. **2019**

ST MAURICE SUR MOSELLE *6F3* (4.5km NE Urban) *47.88888, 6.85758* **Sunêlia Domaine de Champé,** 14 Rue des Champs Navés, 88540 Bussang **03 29 61 61 51; info@domaine-de-champe.com; domaine-de-champe.fr**

🐕 €3 ♨ (htd) 🆆🅳 ⛺ ♿ 🖥 🔌 〽 🦋 🅿 ⊕ 🛒 nr ⛰ 🖊 🛶 (covrd, htd) 📶

Fr N66/E512 in Bussang, site sp fr town sq. Opp Avia filling stn. 3*, Med, mkd, pt shd, pt sl, terr, EHU (6-10A) €5-6; bbq; TV; 50% statics; phone; bus 1km; Eng spkn; adv bkg acc; ccard acc; sauna; waterslide; games rm; bike hire; tennis; games area; CKE. *"Excel site behind hospital grnds; lovely views; welcoming, helpful owners; fitness rm; immac, state of art facs; vg rest; excel walks, cycle path; hg rec."* €34.00, 1 Apr-15 Nov. **2019**

ST MAURICE SUR MOSELLE *6F3* (14km E Rural) *47.88170, 6.94435* **Camp Municipal Bénélux-Bâle,** Rue de la Scierie, 68121 Urbès **03 89 82 78 76 or 03 89 82 60 91 (Mairie); mairie.urbes@wanadoo.fr; camping-urbes.fr**

🐕 ♨ (htd) 🆆🅳 ⛺ ♿ 🔌 〽 🦋 ⚡ 🍴 🅿 ⊕ ⛰ 🖊

Site off N66 on N side of rd at foot of hill rising W out of Urbès. At foot of Col de Bessang. Fr Bussang on N66, immed on ent Urbes turn L doubling back & foll rd, site on L. 2*, Lge, mkd, pt shd, EHU (6-10A) €6.80; bbq; sw nr; 10% statics; phone; adv bkg rec; fishing adj; games area; CKE. *"Gd sh stay/ NH; beautiful area; friendly, welcoming staff; meals avil on site; facs bit cramped & ltd with poor shwrs; horse riding; hang gliding; cycle paths fr site; walks."* €9.00, 1 May-30 Sep. **2017**

ST MAURICE SUR MOSELLE *6F3* (1.7km W Rural) *47.8555, 6.8117* **Camping Les Deux Ballons,** 17 Rue du Stade, 88560 St Maurice-sur-Moselle **03 29 25 17 14; stan0268@orange.fr; www.camping-deux-ballons.fr**

🐕 €3.20 ♨♿ 🆆🅳 ⛺ ♿ 🔌 〽 🦋 ⚡ 🍴 🛒 nr 🏊

On N66 on E side of rd in vill, site on L bef petrol stn. Clearly sp. 3*, Lge, mkd, pt shd, pt sl, EHU (4-15A) €4.15-5.20; gas; TV; phone; Eng spkn; adv bkg acc; waterslide; tennis; games rm; CKE. *"Some pitches sm; excel site & facs; cycle path fr site."* €32.00, 19 Apr-27 Sep. **2015**

ST MAXIMIN LA STE BAUME *10F3* (3km S Rural) *43.42848, 5.86498* **Camping Caravaning Le Provençal,** Route de Mazauges, 83470 St Maximin-la-Ste Baume **04 94 78 16 97; camping.provencal@ wanadoo.fr; www.camping-le-provencal.com**

Exit St Maximin on N560 S twd Marseilles. After 1km turn L onto D64. Site on R after 2km. 3*, Lge, mkd, shd, pt sl, EHU (6-10A) €3.40-4.40; gas; TV; 40% statics; adv bkg acc; CKE. *"Gd NH; easy access fr A8."* **€29.00, 1 Apr-30 Sep.** 2019

SAINT MEEN LE GRAND *2E3* (1km S Urban) *48.183972, -2.188716* **Camping Municipal,** 35290 Saint-Meen-le-Grand **02 99 09 60 61**

On N164 E or W leave at junc to E of town D125. Turn L at rndabt and foll rd for 1km. Site on L after gge by level x-ing. Sm, mkd, hdg, pt shd, pt sl, EHU 4A; own san rec; bbq; twin axles; bus; Eng spkn. *"Gd site for NH; facs basic, not v clean; if barrier down phone for warden, only 2 mins away."* **€6.00, 1 Jun-30Sep.** 2019

SAINT MEEN LE GRAND *2E3* (1km S Urban) *48.183972, -2.188716* **Camping Municipal,** 35290 Saint-Meen-le-Grand **02 99 09 60 61**

On N164 E or W leave at junc to E of town D125. Turn L at rndabt and foll rd for 1km. Site on L after gge by level x-ing. Sm, mkd, hdg, pt shd, pt sl, EHU 4A; own san rec; bbq; twin axles; bus; Eng spkn. *"Gd site for NH; facs basic, not v clean; if barrier down phone for warden, only 2 mins away."* **€6.00, 1 Jun-30Sep.** 2019

STE MENEHOULD *5D1* (1km E Rural) *49.08937, 4.90969* **Camp Municipal de la Grelette,** Chemin de l'Alleval, 51800 Ste Menéhould **03 26 60 24 76; mairie@ste-menehould.fr; www.ste-menehould.fr**

Exit A4 junc 29 to Ste Menéhould; foll sp 'Centre Ville' thro town to Mairie & cent sq on D3; then foll sp 'Piscine' & 'Camping' on D3; cont uphill with rlwy on R; turn R over narr rlwy bdge, then L to site in 200m. 2*, Sm, pt shd, pt sl, EHU (10A) €4; Eng spkn; adv bkg acc; CKE. *"Delightful site; helpful warden 0830-1000 & 1700-1930, gate open at other times, access to o'fits over 2m poss restricted; confirm dep with warden; vg, clean but dated san facs(2017); interesting old town; well maintained site; new indoor pool opened nrby; conv for Reims & Verdun; ok for NH; park away fr bungalows."* **€16.00, 1 May-30 Sep.** 2019

STE MERE EGLISE *1C4* (9.5km NE Coastal) *49.46650, -1.23540* **Camping Le Cormoran,** 2 Rue du Cormoran, 50480 Ravenoville-Plage **02 33 41 33 94; lecormoran@wanadoo.fr; www.lecormoran.com**

(covrd, htd) sand adj

NE on D15 fr Ste Mère-Eglise to Ravenoville, turn L onto D14 then R back onto D15 to Ravenoville Plage. Turn R on D421, Rte d'Utah Beach, site on R in 1km. Or fr N13 sp C2 Fresville & ent Ste Mère-Eglise, then take D15. 5*, Lge, mkd, hdstg, hdg, unshd, EHU (6A) inc; gas; bbq (charcoal, gas); twin axles; TV; 60% statics; Eng spkn; adv bkg acc; ccard acc; jacuzzi; games rm; archery; tennis; bike hire; games area; horseriding; sauna; CKE. *"Popular, family-run site; lge pitches; warm welcome, helpful recep; well-kept san facs, poss tired end of ssn; poss v windy; vg children's facs; special pitches for early dep for ferry; m'van o'night area; excel."* **€33.00, 31 Mar-30 Sep, N12.** 2017

STE MERE EGLISE *1C4* (0.7km E Urban) *49.41006, -1.31078* **Camping De Sainte-Mere Eglise (formerly Municipal),** 6 Rue due 505eme Airborne, 50480 Ste Mère-Eglise **02 33 41 35 22; www.camping-sainte-mere.fr**

Fr Cherbourg S on N13 to cent of Ste Mère-Eglise (avoiding by-pass); at vill sq turn L on D17 to site, next adj sports grnd. 3*, Med, hdstg, pt shd, pt sl, EHU (12A) €4 (poss rev pol); bbq; 5% statics; phone; Eng spkn; adv bkg acc; games rm; bike hire; tennis; CKE. *"Nice, basic site; clean facs; friendly warden; if warden absent site yourself & pay later; conv ferries & D-Day beaches etc; gates open 6am for early dep; rec; san facs improving (2014)."* **€22.00, 15 Mar-1 Oct.** 2015

ST MICHEL EN GREVE *2E2* (1km NE Coastal) *48.69277, -3.55694* **Camping Les Capucines,** Voie Romaine, Kervourdon, 22300 Trédez-Locquémeau **02 96 35 72 28; les.capucines@wanadoo.fr; www.lescapucines.fr**

(covrd, htd) sand 1km

Fr Lannion on D786 SW twd St Michel-en-Grève, sp Morlaix; in approx 700m, after steep descent & 'Landebouch' sp, turn R & R again in 100m at x-rds. Fr Roscoff take D58 to join N12 at junc 17; NE of Morlaix at next junc turn onto D786 twd Lannion; site down narr app rd on L on leaving St Michel-en-Grève (slow down at town exit sp), then R at x-rds. 4*, Med, hdg, mkd, pt shd, pt sl, serviced pitches; EHU (10A) inc; gas; bbq (charcoal, gas); red long stay; TV; 15% statics; phone; Eng spkn; adv bkg acc; ccard acc; games area; watersports 1km; bike hire; games rm; CKE. *"Excel, peaceful, well-kept site; no o'fits over 9.5m high ssn; gd sized pitches; helpful owners; clean san facs; gd pool; gd touring base; mkt Lannion Thu."* **€30.00, 1 Apr-30 Sep, B13.** 2017

ST NAZAIRE LE DESERT 9D2 (0.2km E Rural) 44.56952, 5.27750 **Camp Municipal**, 26340 St Nazaire-le-Désert **04 75 26 42 99 or 04 75 27 52 31 (LS); info@ camping-stnazaire.com; www.campingstnazaire.fr**

🐕 €2 ♟ WC ♨ ♿ ⛲ 🍴 ℗ 🛒 nr 🏕 🏊 (htd)

Well sp in St Nazaire-le-Désert. 2*, Med, mkd, shd, terr, EHU €3.50; own san rec; bbq; phone; Eng spkn; adv bkg rec; games rm. *"Busy, friendly site in beautiful location; v lge o'fits poss diff to pitch; gd."* €15.00, 1 May-30 Sep. 2016

ST NECTAIRE 9B1 (1km S Rural) 45.57541, 2.99942 **Camping La Vallée Verte**, Route des Granges, 63710 St Nectaire **04 73 88 52 68; lavalleeverte@ neuf.fr; www.valleeverte.com**

🐕 €3 ♟ (htd) WC ♨ ♿ ⛲ 🚿 🛒 🦋 🍴 🛒 🏕

Fr A75 exit junc 6 onto D978 & D996 to St Nectaire. On ent o'skts St Nectaire turn L immed at site sp, site in 300m. 3*, Med, pt shd, EHU (5-8A) €3-3.50; sw nr; 20% statics; phone; Eng spkn; adv bkg acc; CKE. *"Vg, friendly, well-maintained, family-run site."* €21.00, 15 Apr-18 Sep. 2017

> ## "There aren't many sites open at this time of year"
>
> If you're travelling outside peak season remember to call ahead to check site opening dates – even if the entry says 'open all year'.

ST OMER 3A3 (15km NE Rural) 50.80152, 2.33924 **Camping La Chaumière**, 529 Langhemast Straete, 59285 Buysscheure **03 28 43 03 57; camping. lachaumiere@wanadoo.fr; www.campingla chaumiere.com**

🐕 €1 ♟ WC ♨ ♿ ⛲ 🚿 🛒 🦋 🍴 ℗ 🛒 nr 🏕 🏊 (htd) 🛗

Take D928 fr St Omer (see NOTE) twd Bergues & Watten & foll sp St Momelin. Stay on rd until Lederzeele & turn R onto D26 twds Cassel. After approx 2km turn R just bef rlwy bdge sp Buysscheure & site. Turn L after church, R, then site on L 500m. Single-track rd after church. NOTE on D928 fr St Omer height limit 3m; use adj level x-ing sp rte for vehicles over 3m. NB app fr Cassel diff, espec for wide or long o'fits; also rd thro Cassel cobbled & poss more diff to find. 3*, Sm, hdstg, hdg, mkd, unshd, pt sl, EHU (6A) inc; bbq; TV; Eng spkn; adv bkg acc; archery; bike hire; lake fishing; CKE. *"Lovely, well-kept site; friendly, welcoming, family-run; conv ferries - but poss no exit bef 0800; gd sized pitches - some may req o'fit manhandling due hedges; gd san facs, ltd in number, stretched when site full; no arr bef 12 noon; close to WW1/WW2 sites; local vet; excel; gd bar & food; rest open only w/end in LS."* €23.00, 1 Apr-30 Sep. 2015

ST OMER 3A3 (11km E Rural) 50.73490, 2.37463 **FFCC Camping Le Bloem Straete,** 1 Rue Bloemstraete, 59173 Renescure **03 28 49 85 65 or 06 50 01 08 16 (mob); lebloemstraete@ gmail.com; www.lebloemstraete.fr**

🐕 ♟ (htd) WC ♨ ♿ ⛲ 🚿 🦋 🍴 ℗ nr 🛒 nr 🏕

E fr St Omer on D642 thro Renescure dir Hazebrouck; turn L (site sp) onto D406 Rue André Coo on bend on leaving Renescure; over level x-ing; site on L thro gates. 3*, Sm, hdstg, hdg, mkd, pt shd, EHU (2-6A) €2.50 (poss rev pol); bbq (charcoal, gas); 20% statics; Eng spkn; adv bkg acc; tennis; games area; CKE. *"Conv Calais ferry & tourist sites; manoeuvring poss diff due high kerbs; m'van area; site clean and tidy; worth finding!; excel facs; easy access to ports; new owners, v helpful & planning on improving site (2015)."* €27.00, 15 Apr-15 Oct. 2016

ST OMER 3A3 (6.5km E Urban) 50.74612, 2.30566 **Camp Municipal Beauséjour,** Rue Michelet, 62510 Arques **03 21 88 53 66; camping@ville-arques.fr; www.camping-arques.fr**

🐕 ♟ WC ♨ ♿ ⛲ 🚿 🛒 🍴 ℗ nr 🛒 nr 🏕

Fr junc 4 of A26 foll sp Arques to town cent. Foll sp Hazebrouck. After x-ing canal site sp 'Camping ***' on L. NB Drive 25m bef correct turning to site. Site signs sm and easily missed. 4*, Med, mkd, hdg, EHU (6-10A) €3 (poss rev pol); bbq; 80% statics; phone; Eng spkn; adv bkg acc; ccard acc; lake fishing; CKE. *"Neat, tidy site; well-run; lge pitches but tight access; friendly, helpful warden; excel, clean facs; m'van o'night area adj (no EHU); gd cycling along canal; lakes & nature park nrby; conv Cristal d'Arques; canal lift & preserved rlwy in town; Calais & Dunkerque 50 mins drive; useful NH; vg."* €17.50, 1 Apr-31 Oct. 2019

ST OMER 3A3 (10km NW Rural) 50.81890, 2.17870 **Kawan Village Château du Gandspette,** 133 Rue du Gandspette, 62910 Eperlecques **03 21 93 43 93; contact@chateau-gandspette.com; www.chateau-gandspette.com**

🐕 €2.50 ♟ WC ♨ ♿ ⛲ 🚿 🛒 🦋 🍴 ℗ 🛒 nr 🏕 🏊 (htd)

Fr Calais SE on A26/E15 exit junc 2 onto D943 foll sp Nordausques-St Omer. 1.5km after Nordausques turn L onto D221 twd Eperlecques; site 5km on L. Do not ent Eperlecques. (Larger o'fts should cont on D943 fr Nordausques to Tilques; at rndabt foll sp for Dunkerque (D300) then D221 dir Eperlecques, site on R. 4*, Med, hdstg, mkd, hdg, pt shd, pt sl, EHU (6A) €5.20 (some rev pol); gas; bbq (charcoal, gas); TV; 15% statics; phone; Eng spkn; adv bkg acc; ccard acc; tennis; bike hire; fishing 3km; golf 5km; games rm; horseriding 5km; playground; CKE. *"Beautiful, well-kept, busy site; spacious, mainly sl pitches; charming, helpful friendly owners; superb, clean san facs; excel rest; site poss muddy in wet; gd for dogs; no o'fits over 8m; rec visit WW2 'Le Blockhaus' nr site; conv A26; highly rec; conv for ferry to Dover; spectacular location; excel ctr for visits & activities; vg; security guard with dog; excel site."* €34.00, 1 Apr-30 Sep, P08. 2018

ST PALAIS SUR MER *7B1* (7km N Rural) *45.67550, -1.09670* **Camping Le Logis du Breuil,** 17570 St Augustin **05 46 23 23 45; info@logis-du-breuil.com; www.logis-du-breuil.com**

€4.20 ⚹ sand 5km

N150 to Royan, then D25 dir St Palais-sur-Mer. Strt on at 1st rndabt & 2nd rndabt; at next rndabt take 2nd exit dir St Palais-sur-Mer. At next traff lts turn R dir St Augustin onto D145; site on L. NB sat nav can direct thro diff & narr alt rte. 3*, Lge, mkd, pt shd, pt sl, serviced pitches; EHU (6-10A) €6-8 (50m cable poss req); gas; bbq (elec, gas); TV; 10% statics; phone; Eng spkn; adv bkg acc; ccard acc; tennis; fishing 1km; golf 3km; excursions; games area; bike hire; games rm; horseriding 400m; CKE. *"Nice peaceful site; lge pitches in wooded area; gd alt to cr beach sites; friendly owner; san facs clean; no c'vans over 12m; gd for young families; excel."* **€38.04, 5 May-30 Sep, A04.**   2019

ST PALAIS SUR MER *7B1* (0.5km NE Coastal) *45.64245, -1.07677* **Camping de Bernezac,** 2 Ave de Bernezac, 17420 St Palais-sur-Mer **05 46 39 00 71; acccf-bernezac@acccf.com; bernezac.acccf.com**

€1 Nr adj

Leave A10 at junc 35 fr N. N150 then D25, at 2nd rndabt take 3rd exit (Rue de la Roche), cross 2 rndabts then L onto Ave de Bernezac. Site on R in under 1km. 3*, Med, hdg, mkd, pt shd, pt sl, serviced pitches; EHU (6A) €4.60 (poss rev pol); bbq; twin axles; TV; 60% statics; Eng spkn; adv bkg acc; lake fishing 1km; games area. *"Helpful, friendly staff; clean, spacious pitches; new shwrs (2016); free wifi; cycle rtes nr; sm quiet site; direct access to beach; pleasant coastal walks; off rd bike rides fr beach gate; lots of activities in area; vg."* **€33.00, 15 Mar-15 Oct.**   2017

ST PALAIS SUR MER *7B1* (1.5km E Rural/Coastal) *45.64656, -1.07300* **Camping Les Ormeaux,** 44 Ave de Bernezac, 17420 St Palais-sur-Mer **05 46 39 02 07; campingormeaux@aliceadsl.fr; www.camping-ormeaux.com**

€4 (htd) sand 800m

Foll sp fr D25 Royan-St Palais rd. Rec app ent fr R. Ent & camp rds narr. 3*, Lge, pt shd, EHU (6-10A) €7.50; gas; TV; 98% statics. *"Ltd touring area & access diff for lge o'fits or m'vans - tents or sm m'vans only; one of the best campsites we have stayed in; clean spacious pitches; amazing staff, new san facs; dir access to 41km cycle rtes, mostly off-rd; no TV on pitches."* **€25.00, 1 Apr-31 Oct.**   2016

ST PALAIS SUR MER *7B1* (2km E Coastal) *45.64396, -1.06325* **Camping Le Val Vert,** 108 Ave Frédéric Garnier, 17640 Vaux-sur-Mer **05 46 38 25 51; camping-val-vert@wanadoo.fr; www.val-vert.com**

€4.50 (htd) sand 900m

Fr Saintes on N150 dir Royan; join D25 dir St Palais-sur-Mer; turn L at rndabt sp Vaux-sur-Mer & Centre Hospitaliers; at traff lts ahead; at 2nd rndabt take 3rd exit & then turn immed R. Site on R in 500m. 3*, Med, hdg, EHU (10A) inc; gas; bbq (elec, gas); adv bkg acc; ccard acc; tennis 400m; bike hire; horseriding 5km; games rm; fishing; watersports; games area; golf 5km. *"Well-kept, family-run site; no o'fits over 6.5m high ssn; gd sized pitches; unisex san facs; a stream runs alongside site; sh walk to pleasant vill; daily mkt in Royan."* **€39.72, 27 Apr-30 Sep, A25.**   2019

ST PALAIS SUR MER *7B1* (2km SE Urban/Coastal) *45.64272, -1.07183* **Camping Nauzan-Plage,** 39 Ave de Nauzan-Plage, 17640 Vaux-sur-Mer **05 46 38 29 13; info@campinglenauzanplage.com; www.campinglenauzanplage.com**

€5 sand 450m

Take either coast rd or inland rd fr Royan to Vaux-sur-Mer; site not well sp. 4*, Lge, mkd, pt shd, EHU (10A) €5.50; gas; red long stay; TV; 10% statics; adv bkg rec; tennis 200m; games rm; CKE. *"Gd site, busy high ssn; helpful staff; gd cycling rte; pt of Flower Camping group."* **€45.00, 1 Apr-15 Oct.**   2017

ST PALAIS SUR MER *7B1* (3km NW Coastal) *45.6500, -1.1193* **Camping La Côte de Beauté,** 157 Ave de la Grande Côte, 17420 St Palais-sur-Mer **05 46 23 20 59; campingcotedebeaute@wanadoo.fr; www.camping-cote-de-beaute.com**

€3 (htd) sand 200m

Fr St Palais-sur-Mer foll sp to La Tremblade & Ronce-les-Bains. Site on D25, 50m fr beach, look for twin flagpoles of Camping Le Puits de l'Auture & lge neon sp on R; site in 50m. 3*, Med, hdg, shd, EHU (6A) €4.20; 10% statics; adv bkg acc; tennis adj; golf 2km. *"Clean, tidy site; friendly staff; steep descent to beach opp - better beach 600m twd La Tremblade; bike hire adj; cycle track to St Palais & Pontaillac; town 3km; clean san facs; gd pitches."* **€26.00, 1 May-30 Sep.**   2017

FRANCE

ST PALAIS SUR MER *7B1* (6.5km NW Coastal) *45.64930, -1.11785* **Camping Le Puits de l'Auture,** La Grande Côte, 17420 St Palais-sur-Mer 05 46 23 20 31; contact@camping-puitsdelauture.com; www.camping-puitsdelauture.com

🚻 (htd) 🚿♿🏪🍴♨️♟️🌴🍺🏊🎾◐ (htd) ⛱ sand adj

Fr Royan take D25 onto new rd past St Palais foll sp for La Palmyre. At 1-way section turn back L sp La Grande Côte & site is 800m; rd runs close to sea, flags at ent. 4*, Lge, pt shd, serviced pitches; EHU (10A) inc; gas; 25% statics; Eng spkn; adv bkg rec; ccard acc; fishing; games area; CKE. *"Well-maintained, well laid-out, excel site; san facs stretched high ssn & 'tired'; poss cr but carefully controlled; friendly, helpful staff; gd cycle paths."* €38.00, 28 Apr-3 Oct. 2016

ST PANTALEON LES VIGNES *9D2* (2km E Rural) *44.39752, 5.06099* **Camping Les Cyprès,** Hameau Font de Barral, 26770 Saint Pantaleon les Vignes 06 81 53 78 03 or 06 82 27 19 14; contact@lescyprescamping.com; www.lescypres-camping.com

🐕€1.80 🚻 WC ♿🍴♨️🦋♟️◐ nr 🏊nr 🏪

D541 fir Nyons. Fr highway A7 exit Montélimar-Sud Bollène or Orange Cent. 1*, Sm, pt shd, pt sl, EHU (4,6,10A) €2.50-3.60; bbq; twin axles; games rm. *"Beautiful surroundings; friendly owners."* €11.00, 1 Apr-31 Oct. 2019

ST PARDOUX *7A3* (1.6km S Rural) *46.04955, 1.27893* **Campsite de Fréaudour,** Site de Freaudour 87250 St Pardoux 05 55 76 57 22; camping.freaudour@orange.fr; www.aquadis-loisirs.com

🐕🚻 WC 🏪♨️♟️🍴🏊🏪🚣

Fr A20 dir Limonges, take exit 25, onto D219. Cont onto D44 thro Razes & foll sp to Lac De Saint-Pardoux. Turn R onto D103A to Freaudour. 4*, Med, mkd, pt shd, EHU (6A); bbq; TV; 20% statics; Eng spkn; adv bkg rec; games area. *"Fair site."* €20.40, 1 Apr-27 Oct. 2019

ST PAUL DE FENOUILLET *8G4* (0.4km S Rural) *42.80762, 2.50235* **Camping de l'Agly,** Ave 16 Août 1944, 66220 St Paul-de-Fenouillet 04 68 59 09 09; contact@camping-agly.com; www.camping-agly.com

12 🐕🚻 WC 🏪♿♨️🦋🏊nr

Heading W on D117; turn L at traff lts in St Paul; site on R in 200m, well sp. 2*, Sm, mkd, hdg, pt shd, pt sl, EHU (16A) €4.50; sw nr; site clsd Jan; CKE. *"Vg site; friendly warden; mountain scenery; gd climbing & cycling; conv for Château's Payrepertuse & Quéribus; sm pitches, diff access for lge o'fits; conv NH."* €16.00 2017

ST PAUL EN FORET *10E4* (3.5km N Rural) *43.58449, 6.69016* **Camping Le Parc,** Quartier Trestaure, 83440 St-Paul-en-Forêt 04 94 76 15 35; contact@campingleparc.com; www.campingleparc.com

🐕€4.50 🚻 (htd) WC 🏪♿🍴♨️📶MSP 🦋♟️🍴🍺◐🏊🏪🏪🚣♨ 🏊 (htd) 🎣

Exit A8 at junc 39, foll D37 (dir Fayence) for 8.4km to lge rndabt on D562. Take 3rd exit at rndabt (sp draguignan/Fayence). Foll D562 for 4.8km thro 4 more rndabts. At 5th rndabt (Intermarche Supmkt on L) take 3rd exit D562 sp Draguignan. After 4.2km take 3rd exit at rndabt onto D4, after 2km turn L at bus stop. Foll rd to site. 4*, Sm, mkd, shd, sl, EHU (10A) €5 high ssn only; twin axles; TV; 65% statics; phone; Eng spkn; adv bkg acc; games rm; fishing; games area; tennis; CKE. *"Conv hill vills of Provence; gd rests in St Paul; many medieval vill; excel."* €29.00, 2 Apr-30 Sep. 2016

ST PAULIEN *9C1* (2.5km SW Rural) *45.12041, 3.79357* **Camping de la Rochelambert,** 43350 St Paulien 04 71 00 54 02; infos@camping-rochelambert.com; www.camping-rochelambert.com

🐕€1.50 🚻 WC ♿🏪♨️📶🦋♟️🍴🍺🏪nr 🏪🚣🏊🎣

Fr St Paulien take D13; turn L onto D25 sp La Rochelambert; site on L in 1.5km. 4*, Med, mkd, pt shd, terr, EHU (10A) €3.10; bbq; 15% statics; phone; Eng spkn; adv bkg acc; tennis; CKE. *"Gd touring base; gd walking & fishing; app poss diff lge/long o'fits; gd."* €23.80, 1 Apr-30 Sep. 2019

> ## "We must tell the Club about that great site we found"
>
> Get your site reports in by mid-August and we'll do our best to get your updates into the next edition.

ST PHILBERT DE GRAND LIEU *2H4* (1km N Rural) *47.04202, -1.64021* **Camping La Boulogne,** 1 Ave de Nantes, 44310 St Philbert-de-Grand-Lieu 32 40 78 88 79; accueil@camping-la-boulogne.com

🐕€1 🚻 WC 🏪♨️🍴♟️🍴🍺🏪nr 🏪🚣

Fr Nantes on A83 exit junc 1 or 2 onto D178 - D117 dir St Philbert; turn L onto D65 (Ave de Nantes) to St Philbert; site on R in 500m adj rv & sp. Or fr Machecoul take bypass to St Philbert & then D65 as narr rds thro town. 2*, Med, hdg, mkd, pt shd, EHU (6A) inc; bbq; 10% statics; phone; bus adj; Eng spkn; adv bkg acc; ccard acc; fishing; games area; CKE. *"Well-kept, secure site; htd covrd pool 200m; lake adj; new enthusiastic, helpful owners (2010); gd; ACSI acc."* €13.50, 1 Apr-31 Oct. 2016

ST PIERRE EN PORT *3C2* (0.5km N Coastal)
49.80943, 0.49354 **Les Falaises,** 130 rue du Camping,
76540 St Pierre-en-Port **02 35 29 51 58; lesfalaises@
cegetel.net; www.campinglesfalaises.com**

🐕 ♿ ⭘ ♿ ⚲ ⊞ ♿ ⌳ ⬚ MSP 🦋 ♈ 🍽 🎿 🛒 nr 🏕 ⛺2km

Fr D925 turn onto D79 bet St Valery & Fecamp. Site
sp in St Pierre. 2*, Med, hdg, unshd, EHU (10A); bbq;
60% statics; bus 0.5km; Eng spkn; games area; games
rm; CKE. *"Cliff top site; path to beach steep with
steps; narr app rd; facs dated but clean; well kept site;
takeaway snacks avail high ssn only; v quiet, pleasant
site; gd."* €19.00, 1 Apr-5 Oct.   2017

"I need an on-site restaurant"

We do our best to make sure site information
is correct, but it is always best to check any
must-have facilities are still available or will
be open during your visit.

ST PIERRE LE MOUTIER *4H4* (8km SW Rural)
46.75722, 3.03328 **Camp Municipal de St Mayeul,**
Rue de Saint-Mayeul, 03320 Le Veurdre
**04 70 66 40 67 (Mairie); mairie.le.veurdre@
wanadoo.fr; www.allier-tourisme.com**

♿ ⚲ ⊞ ⌳ 🦋 nr

Fr N7 at St Pierre-le-Moûtier SW onto D978A to Le
Veurdre. Site sp on far side of Le Veurdre.
2*, Sm, hdg, mkd, pt shd, pt sl, EHU €4; bbq; adv bkg
acc. *"Pleasant spot; site yourself, warden calls; friendly
staff; clean, basic facs; shops in pleasant vill; rec NH;
vg."* €11.40, 1 May-15 Sep.   2018

ST POL DE LEON *1D2* (2km E Coastal) *48.69103,
-3.96730* **Camping Ar Kleguer,** Plage de Ste Anne,
29250 St Pol-de-Léon **02 98 69 18 81; info@camping-
ar-kleguer.com; www.camping-ar-kleguer.com**

🐕 €2.80 ♿ WD ⭘ ♿ ⚲ ⊞ ⌳ MSP ♈ 🍽 🎿 🛒 nr ⛱ (htd) 🏊 ⛱ adj

In St Pol-de-Léon foll Centre Ville sp. At cathedral
sq (2 towers) with cathedral on L descend hill & in
150m, bef church with tall belfry, turn L foll Plage &
camping sp. On reaching sea turn L (N); site at end,
well sp. NB Narr, busy rds in town.
4*, Med, mkd, pt shd, pt sl, terr, EHU (10A) (long
lead poss req); 40% statics; adv bkg acc, waterslide;
games rm; tennis; CKE. *"Well-kept, attractive
site; modern facs; gd views; conv Roscoff ferry."*
€31.00, 2 Apr-25 Sep.   2015

ST POL DE LEON *1D2* (2km E Coastal) *48.69355,
-3.96930* **Camping de Trologot,** Grève du Man,
29250 St Pol-de-Léon **02 98 69 06 26 or 06 62 16 39 30
(mob); camping-trologot@wanadoo.fr;
www.camping-trologot.com**

🐕 €2.40 ♿ WD ⭘ ♿ ⚲ ⊞ ⌳ MSP 🦋 ♈ 🍽 ℍ nr
🎿 🛒 ⛱ ⚓ 🛷 (htd) 🏊 ⛱ sand adj

Fr the port of Roscoff take D58 go briefly on the D769
then back on to the D58 foll the sp to Morlaix over
six rndabts (approx 4miles/6.5km). Just after passing
under a rlwy bdge, take the exit for the D769 (sp St Pol
de Léon, Kerlaudy, Penzé) then turn L. Stay on the
D769 for 1.8 km, just past the graveyard turn R at the
rndabt and go strt over the next rndabt (sp Campings/
Plage) at the end of the rd turn L and the turning for
the site will be on L after 1km and is sp. Do not use sat
nav. Fr the E on the N12 take the exit for the D19 (sp
Morlaix St pol de Leon) at the rndabt take the 2nd exit
cont twds St-Pol-de Leon on the D58. Take the exit
to the D769 (SP St-Pol-de Leon) then foll above dirs
fr the graveyard. 3*, Med, mkd, hdg, pt shd, EHU (10A)
€4.50; bbq (charcoal, gas); red long stay; TV; 20% statics;
adv bkg acc; ccard acc; games rm; bouncy castle; CKE.
*"Lovely, well-kept site; ideal NH for Roscoff ferry; gd sized
pitches; helpful owners; clean, modern san facs; no o'fits
over 7m high ssn; gd for family beach holiday; peaceful
area, many walks nrby; beautiful town; gd cycling area; hg
rec; excel."* €21.90, 31 March-27 Oct, B29.   2019

"Satellite navigation makes touring much easier"

Remember most sat navs don't know if you're
towing or in a larger vehicle – always use yours
alongside maps and site directions.

ST POL DE LEON *1D2* (5km SE Coastal) *48.65805,
-3.92805* **Les Mouettes,** La Grande Grève, 29660
Carantec **02 98 67 02 46; camping@les-mouettes.
com; www.les-mouettes.com**

🐕 €6 ♿ WD ⭘ ♿ ⚲ ⊞ ⌳ MSP ♈ 🍽 🎿 🛒 ⛱ 🏕 🖌 🛷 (covrd, htd)
🏊 ⛱ shgl 1km

Fr Morlaix take D58 N sp Roscoff; at lge rndabt turn
R sp Carantec on D173; turn L at 1st rndabt; strt on
at 2nd & 3rd rndabt past Casino supmkt; turn L next
rndabt; site on L. Or fr Roscoff take D58 sp Mortaix,
then D173 to Carantec; foll sp town cent, then site.
5*, Lge, mkd, pt shd, EHU (10A) inc (poss rev pol); gas;
bbq (charcoal); TV; 50% statics; Eng spkn; adv bkg acc;
ccard acc; tennis; bike hire; fishing; games area; golf
1.5km; waterslide; games rm; CKE. *"Attractive site
with sea views; no o'fits over 8m; clean, modern san
facs; sauna; jaccuzi; impressive pool complex; plenty to
do on site; mkt Thu; noise fr boatyard; conv Carnac."*
€60.00, 20 Apr-10 Sep, B14.   2019

ST POL DE LEON *1D2* (9km SE Rural) *48.64912, -3.92126* **Camping Les Hortensias (Jacq),** Kermen, 29660 Carantec **02 98 67 08 63 or 02 98 67 96 34; contact@leshortensias.fr; www.leshortensias.fr**

🐕 €0.80 ♦♦♦ [wc] ♨ 🚿 🚻 🍴 [MSP] 🦋 🛒 nr 🏕 ⚓ 2.5km

Fr Roscoff on D58 dir Morlaix. Turn L after approx 10km onto D173, then turn R at 1st rndabt, site in 200m, site sp. Sm, mkd, unshd, EHU (6A) €3; adv bkg acc; CKE. "Conv Roscoff ferry; views of bay; friendly staff; poss unkempt LS; organic produce in shop; gd touring base; no gates allows early deparature; excel NH; no o'fits over 6m." €12.50, 1 May-30 Sep. 2015

ST PONS DE THOMIERES *8F4* (2km E Rural) *43.49055, 2.78527* **Camping Village Les Cerisiers du Jaur,** Les Marbrières-du-Jaur, Route de Bédarieux, 34220 St Pons-de-Thomières **04 67 95 30 33; info@cerisierdujaur.com; www.cerisierdujaur.com**

🐕 €1.50 ♦♦♦ [wc] ♨ 🚿 🚻 🍴 [MSP] 🦋 ⛳ nr 🔱 🛒 ⚓ 🏄

Fr Castres on D612 to St Pons; go thro town cent under rlwy bdge; turn L onto D908 sp Olargues. Site on R in 500m. 3*, Med, mkd, hdg, pt shd, terr, EHU (10A) €4; bbq; phone; Eng spkn; ccard acc; games area; bike hire; CKE. "Excel site nr Rv Jaur; welcoming, friendly, helpful owner; cycle rte fr site; an oasis!; hot water not v hot; expensive in LS; san facs unkept." €33.00, 29 Mar-26 Oct. 2017

ST POURCAIN SUR SIOULE *9A1* (0.7km SE Urban) *46.30643, 3.29207* **Camp Municipal de l'île de la Ronde,** Quai de la Ronde, 03500 St Pourçain-sur-Sioule **04 70 35 13 69 or 04 70 45 35 27; camping.ronde@ville-saint-pourcain-sur-sioule.com; www.ville-saint-pourcain-sur-sioule.com**

🐕 0,50 € ♦♦♦ [wc] ♨ 🚿 🚻 🍴 [MSP] 🦋 🛒 nr 🏕

On D2009, 31km S of Moulins; in St Pourçain-sur-Sioule town cent turn R immed bef rv bdge; site ent on L in 100m. NB Sp in town easily missed. 3*, Med, hdg, pt shd, EHU (10A) inc; adv bkg acc; CKE. "Well-run, magnificent, busy, pleasant site in pretty town; extra charge for lger pitches; barrier clsd 2000-0800; gd rest nr; mkt Sat; great value; excel; recep and barrier clsd 1200-1400; 2 supmkt in town; 2 pin adapter ess; set amongst trees; walks/rvside path adj; san facs stretched at times; gd value." €14.00, 3 Apr-5 Oct. 2019

ST QUAY PORTRIEUX *2E3* (3km NW Coastal) *48.66269, -2.84550* **Camping Bellevue,** 68 Blvd du Littoral, 22410 St Quay-Portrieux **02 96 70 41 84; info@campingbellevue.net; www.campingbellevue.net**

🐕 ♦♦♦ [wc] ♨ 🚿 🚻 🍴 [MSP] 🦋 ⛳ 🔱 🛒 ⚓ 🏄 (htd) 🏊 🏖 sand adj

Foll D786 thro St Quay-Portrieux twd Paimpol; turn R at traff lts sp St Quay-Portrieux; foll site sp; site in 2.5km. 3*, Lge, hdg, hdstg, mkd, pt shd, pt sl, terr, EHU (6A) €3; gas; bbq; TV; 8% statics; Eng spkn; adv bkg acc; ccard acc; games area; golf 3km; CKE. "Beautiful position with sea views; direct access to sm cove; friendly staff; gd, clean facs; vg; excel pool; gd exercise area for dogs." €23.00, 8 May-15 Sep, B05. 2015

ST QUENTIN *3C4* (12km SW Urban) *49.78222, 3.21333*
Camping du Vivier aux Carpes, 10 Rue Charles Voyeux, 02790 Seraucourt-le-Grand **03 23 60 50 10; contact@ camping-picardie.com; www.camping-picardie.com**

🐕 €1.50 ♂♀ WD ♨ ♿ ⊟ ✉ MSP 🦋 ♔ ⬚ 🏪 🎢

Fr A26 take exit 11 St Quentin/Soissons; S 4km on D1 dir Tergnier/Soissons. Fork R onto D8 to Essigny-le-Grand & in vill foll camping sp W to Seraucourt. Fr St Quentin, S 10km on D930 to Roupy, E on D32 5km to Seraucourt-le-Grand. Site N of Seraucourt on D321. Narr ent fr rd unsuitable lge o'fits.
3*, Med, hdg, mkd, hdstg, pt shd, EHU (10A) inc (poss rev pol); gas; bbq; 30% statics; Eng spkn; adv bkg acc; tennis adj; golf adj; horseriding adj; games rm; CKE. *"Delightful, lovely, well-run site; busy, even LS - rec arr early; ltd hdstg; peaceful LS; gd, lge pitches; narr site rds; friendly, helpful staff; pitches by lake poss boggy when wet; poss flooding; mkd footpaths round lakes; vg angling; mosquito probs; Disneyland 90 mins; conv Channel ports; c'van storage; warn staff night bef if v early dep; excel; facs stretched but clean & gd; lovely cycle rte along canal to St Quentin; nice bistro in vill; new coded security barrier (2015)."*
€23.50, 20 Mar-19 Oct, P14. 2019

ST QUENTIN EN TOURMONT *3B2* (0.5km S Rural) *50.26895, 1.60263* **Camping Le Champ Neuf,** 8 Rue du Champ Neuf, 80120 St Quentin-en-Tourmont **03 22 25 07 94; campinglechampneuf@ orange.fr; www.camping-lechampneuf.com**

🐕 €1.50 ♂♀(htd) WD ♨ ♿ ⊟ ✉ 🦋 ♔ Y ⬚ 🏪 🎢 ⚓(covrd, htd) 🚿 🏖2km

Exit D1001 or A16 onto D32 to Rue, take D940 around Rue & foll sp St Quentin-en-Tourmont, Parc Ornithologique & Domaine du Marquenterre to site. Site sp fr D204. 3*, Lge, mkd, hdg, pt shd, EHU (5-10A) inc; bbq; 80% statics; phone; adv bkg acc; ccard acc; horseriding 500m; bike hire; games area. *"Excel Ornithological Park nrby; well-kept, pleasant site; friendly, helpful owner; gd cycle paths."*
€30.00, 1 Apr-1 Nov. 2017

See advertisement

ST RAPHAEL *10F4* (8.6km WSW Coastal) *43.408915, 6.708677* **Camping Sandaya Rivièra d'Azur,** 189 Les Grands Chat.de Villepey, RD7 83370, Saint Aygulf **04 11 32 90 00; www.sandaya.fr/nos-campings/ riviera-d-azur**

🐕 ♂♀ WD ♨ ♿ ⊟ ✉ 🦋 ♔ Y ⬚ 🏪 🎢 ⚓(htd) 🛁 🏖 sandy 2.5km

Leave A8 exit 36 Le Muy on N555 twrds Draguignan then N7 twrds Frejus. R on d7 sp St Aygulf. Site on R in 2.5km before town. 5*, Mkd, EHU 10A; bbq (elec, gas); Eng spkn; adv bkg rec; ccard acc; bike hire; beauty ctr; fishing; tennis; security.
€74.00, 31 Mar-14 Oct. 2019

ST RAPHAEL *10F4* (4.5km N Rural) *43.44611, 6.80610* **Sandaya Douce Quiétude,** 3435 Blvd Jacques Baudino, 83700 St Raphaël **04 94 44 30 00; dou@sandaya.fr; www.sandaya.co.uk**

🐕 €5 ♂♀(htd) WD ♨ ♿ ⊟ ✉ 🦋 ♔ Y ⬚ 🏪 🎢 🚿(htd) 🛁 🏖 sand 2km

Exit A8 at junc 38 onto D37 then D100 sp Agay. Foll sp Valescure-Boulouris, site sp. NB c'vans not permitted on St Raphaël seafront. 4*, Lge, hdstg, mkd, hdg, pt shd, pt sl, serviced pitches; EHU (10A) inc; gas; bbq (gas); TV; phone; bus; Eng spkn; adv bkg acc; ccard acc; games area; gym; waterslide; games rm; bike hire; mini golf; CKE. *"Lge pitches; excel facs; takeway; disco nightly high ssn; many tour ops statics; sm touring pitches mostly amongst statics; vg."*
€24.00, 30 Apr-8 Oct. 2019

ST REMY DE PROVENCE *10E2* (0.5km NE Rural) *43.79622, 4.83878* **FFCC Camping Le Mas de Nicolas,** Ave Plaisance-du-Touch, 13210 St Rémy-de-Provence **04 90 92 27 05; contact@camping-masdenicolas.com; www.camping-masdenicolas.com**

🐕 €2.15-€2.80 ♂♀(htd) WD ♨ ♿ ⊟ ✉ MSP 🦋 ♔ Y ⬚ 🏪 🎢 🚿 🏖(htd)

Fr town ctr take D99 eastwards for abt 0.5km. Turn L at 2nd rndabt & foll sp to campsite. 4*, Lge, hdg, mkd, hdstg, pt shd, EHU (6A) €3.80; bbq; TV; TV (pitch); 20% statics; bus 1km; Eng spkn; adv bkg req; ccard acc; games area; games rm; CKE. *"Family-owned site; gd clean modern san facs; some pitches diff access long o'fits; excel; v helpful staff; interesting town."* **€33.00, 1 Apr-14 Oct.** 2017

ST REMY DE PROVENCE *10E2* (0.9km E Urban) *43.78836, 4.84093* **Camping Pégomas,** Ave Jean Moulin, 13210 St Rémy-de-Provence **04 90 92 01 21; contact@campingpegomas.com; www.camping pegomas.com**

🐕 €1.70 ♂♀(htd) WD ♨ ♿ ⊟ ✉ MSP 🦋 ♔ Y ⬚ 🏪nr 🎢 🚿 🏖

On D99 fr W dir Cavaillon, ignore R fork to St Rémy 'Centre Ville' (& sat nav!). Pass twin stone sculptures on rndabt, at 2nd rndabt turn into Ave Jean Moulin, site on R in 400m - v sharp turn into site. Fr E Exit A7 junc 25 on D99 W dir St Rémy. Ignore sp 'Centre Ville', pass under aquaduct & across rndabt. At next rndabt turn L into Ave Jean Moulin, then as above. Do not attempt to tow thro town.
3*, Med, hdg, mkd, shd, EHU (6A) €3.50 (poss rev pol & long lead req); gas; TV; phone; Eng spkn; adv bkg acc; ccard acc; games area; CKE. *"Well-run, busy site; clean san facs; lge o'fits poss diff some sm pitches; gd pool; gd touring base; recep clsd 2000 hrs, lge lay-by outside; mkt Wed am; excel for walking; lovely site."*
€31.00, 15 Mar-24 Oct. 2015

ST REMY DE PROVENCE *10E2* (2km NW Rural) *43.7967, 4.82378* **Camping Monplaisir,** Chemin Monplaisir, 13210 St Rémy-de-Provence 04 90 92 22 70; reception@camping-monplaisir.fr; www.camping-monplaisir.fr

Exit D99 at St Rémy onto D5 going NW dir Maillane, in 110m turn L & foll sp in 500m. Avoid going thro town. 4*, Med, hdstg, hdg, shd, EHU (10A) inc; gas; bbq (elec, gas); red long stay; phone; bus 1km; Eng spkn; adv bkg acc; ccard acc; bike hire; CKE. *"Immac, well-run site; mostly gd sized pitches; clean, modern san facs; gd touring base; highly rec; site clsd last Sat in Oct; excel site; lovely pool; walk to nice town; fills up quickly."* €41.00, 10 Mar-19 Oct. 2017

See advertisement

ST ROME DE TARN *8E4* (0.3km N Rural) *44.05302, 2.89978* **Camping de la Cascade des Naisses,** Route du Pont, 12490 St Rome-de-Tarn 05 65 62 56 59; contact@camping-cascade-aveyron.com; www.camping-cascade-aveyron.com

Fr Millau take D992 to St Georges-de-Luzençon, turn R onto D73 & foll sp to St Rome. In St Rome turn R along Ave du Pont-du-Tarn, site sp. Diff, steep app for sm/underpowered car+c'van o'fits. 4*, Med, hdg, hdstg, mkd, pt shd, terr, EHU (6A) inc; own san req; 40% statics; Eng spkn; adv bkg acc; boating; rv fishing; tennis; bike hire; CKE. *"Lovely rvside pitches; pleasant vill; friendly, helpful staff; each level has a wc but steep walk to shwr block; owners will site vans; conv Millau viaduct; excel tranquil, scenic site."* €35.00 2016

ST SAVIN *7A3* (0.5km N Rural) *46.56892, 0.86772* **Camping du Moulin de la Gassotte,** 10 Rue de la Gassotte, 86310 St Savin-sur-Gartempe 05 49 48 18 02; camping@moulindelagassotte.fr; www.moulindelagassotte.fr

E fr Chauvigny on D951 to St Savin; fr St Savin N on D11; well sp. Fr S on D5 cross rv; meet D951, turn R & site on R. Fr S on D11 use 'poids lourds' (heavy vehicles) rec rte to meet D951. 2*, Sm, pt shd, EHU (12A) inc; bbq; TV; rv fishing adj; CKE. *"Beautiful, peaceful, park like site by rv; views of Abbey; helpful warden; san facs old but clean; sh walk to vill; murals in Abbey restored by UNESCO; defined pitches."* €13.40, 8 May-30 Sep. 2019

> ## "I like to fill in the reports as I travel from site to site"
>
> You'll find report forms at the back of this guide, or you can fill them in online at camc.com/europereport.

ST SEINE L'ABBAYE *6G1* (1.8km SE Rural) *47.44073, 4.79236* **Camp Municipal,** Rue de la Foire aux Vaches, 21440 St Seine-l'Abbaye 03 80 35 00 09 or 03 80 35 01 64 (Mairie)

On D971 in vill of St Seine-l'Abbaye, turn N onto D16. Turn R uphill, sp camping & turn R thro gateway in stone wall. Narr rds in vill. Or fr N on D974, avoiding Dijon, turn R onto D959 at Til-Châtel, then D901 Moloy/Lamargelle. Turn L in Lamargelle onto D16 St Seine-l'Abbaye. Turn L uphill at edge of vill & as above (avoids narr rds). 1*, Sm, hdstg, pt sl, EHU (10A) €2.50 (rev pol); CKE. *"Pleasantly situated & peaceful site; basic but immac san facs; fees collected fr 1900 hrs; lovely vill; conv Dijon or as NH; pool 4km; excel; not suitable for o'fits over 7m."* €12.00, 1 May-30 Sep. 2015

STE SEVERE SUR INDRE *7A4* (6km SE Rural)
46.471980, 2.148024 **Camping La Grange Pérassay,** Le Bourg, 36160 Pérassay **02 54 30 87 73 or 06 86 34 68 52 (mob); guy.timothy@orange.fr; www.lagrangecamping.com**

🐕🏕⬛ WD ⬛♿🚿⬛/🦋♟🏊

Fr Ste Sévère take D917 S & after approx 6km turn L onto D71 sp Pérassay. Site on L in cent of vill. 1*, Sm, pt shd, pt sl, EHU (10A); bbq; 1% statics; Eng spkn; adv bkg acc; bike hire. *"Lovely CL-type site in quiet location; friendly British owners; vg san facs; vg; field for exercising dogs; gd walks direct fr site; countryside views."* **€17.00, 1 Apr-31 Oct.** **2019**

ST SYMPHORIEN *7D2* (1km S Rural) *44.41831, -0.49232* **Camping Vert Bord'Eau (formerly Camping La Hure),** Route de Sore, 33113 St Symphorien **05 56 25 79 54 or 06 07 08 37 28 (mob); camping@ vertbordeau.com; www.vertbordeau.com**

🐕 €1.30 🏕(htd) WD ⬛♿🚿⬛/🦋♟🏊⬛⬛🏊🏊⬛

S thro Langon on app. Foll sp Villandraut, St Symphorien. Sp fr vill 1km S on D220, opp **Intermarché.** 2*, Sm, shd, EHU (10A) €2.50; 80% statics; Eng spkn; adv bkg acc; games area; tennis; rv fishing. *"Helpful staff; basic facs; site in pinewoods; gd cycling, walks, beaches; vg cycle path run thro St Symphorien, gd level surface thro woods and vineyard; excel."* **€23.40, 2 Apr-29 Oct.** **2016**

ST TROPEZ *10F4* (11km SW Rural) *43.21804, 6.57830* **Camping Moulin de Verdagne,** Route du Brost, 83580 Gassin **04 91 09 10 27; www.domaine-verdagne.com**

🐕 €3 🏕⬛🚿⬛/🦋⬛♟⬛🏊⬛nr ⬛🏊🏊sand 5km

Foll N559 N fr Cavalaire for 6km. Take 1st R after town traff lts in La Croix-Valmer, site sp. Site in 2km, surrounded by vineyards. Rough app rd/ track. 3*, Med, mkd, pt shd, terr, EHU (6A) €4; red long stay; 60% statics; phone; Eng spkn; ccard acc. *"Vg, lovely site; tight bends & narr pitches poss diff long o'fits; pool 2m deep; c'van best app fr La Croix vill; new owners (2016); helpful; new pool (2017)."* **€37.50, 1 Apr-31 Oct.** **2017**

ST VALERY SUR SOMME *3B2* (4.6km S Rural) *50.15333, 1.63583* **Le Domaine du Château de Drancourt,** 80230 Estréboeuf **03 22 26 93 45; chateau.drancourt @wanadoo.fr; www.chateau-drancourt.fr**

🐕 €3.80 🏕 WD ⬛🚿⬛♿🚿⬛/🦋♟⬛🏊🏊⬛/🏊(covrd, htd) 🏊

Exit A28/E402 junc 1 at Abbeville onto D40 twd Noyelles-sur-Mer. At rndabt with D940 turn L sp St Valery-sur-Somme. At next rndabt go strt over dir Le Tréport, then at next rndabt at junc with D48 take last exit (sp Estréboeuf), turn immed L & foll sps to site. NB.1-way system at recep area. 5*, Lge, mkd, hdg, pt shd, pt sl, EHU (10A) inc (poss rev pol); gas; bbq; 80% statics; Eng spkn; adv bkg acc; ccard acc; bike hire; fishing adj; golf driving range; tennis; horseriding 12km; games rm; watersports 2km; CKE. *"Conv, busy, popular NH in grnds of chateau; friendly staff; facs poss stretched when site full; red facs LS; bird sanctuary in estuary nrby; gd."* **€40.00, 13 Apr-24 Sep, P06.** **2017**

ST VALERY SUR SOMME *3B2* (1km SW Urban/Coastal) *50.18331, 1.61786* **Camping Le Walric,** Route d'Eu, 80230 St Valery-sur-Somme **03 22 26 81 97; info@ campinglewalric.com; www.campinglewalric.com**

🐕 €3 🏕 WD ⬛🚿⬛♿🚿⬛/MSP ♟🏊🏊⬛🏊⬛(htd) 🏊

Ringrd round St Valery D940 dir Le Tréport. Cont to 3rd rndabt (1st rndabt Carrefour supmkt on L) 3km & take 1st exit (R) sp St Valery & Cap Hornu D3. Site on R in 2km at ent to town sp. 4*, Lge, hdstg, hdg, mkd, pt shd, EHU (6A) inc; gas; bbq; red long stay; 70% statics; phone; Eng spkn; adv bkg acc; ccard acc; tennis; games area; bike hire; games rm; boat hire; fishing; CKE. *"Well-kept, well-run, busy site in excel location; clean dated san facs; cycle rtes, canal track; steam train; beach nrby; delightful medieval town; mkt Sun; excel; easy to find."* **€37.00, 1 Apr-30 Oct.** **2017**

> **"We must tell the Club about that great site we found"**
>
> Get your site reports in by mid-August and we'll do our best to get your updates into the next edition.

ST VALERY SUR SOMME *3B2* (1km W Urban) *50.18447, 1.62263* **Camping de la Croix l'Abbé,** Place de la Croix l'Abbé, 80230 St Valery-sur-Somme **03 22 60 81 46; w.a.georges@wanadoo.fr**

🏕 WD ⬛🚿⬛/🦋⬛♟🏊🏊nr ⬛🏊(covrd, htd) 🏊shgl 1km

Ringrd round St Valery D940 dir Le Tréport. Cont to 2nd rndabt (1st rndabt Champion supmkt on L) 3km & take exit sp St Valery & Cap Hornu D3. Site 250m beyond Camping Le Walric. Lge, mkd, hdg, unshd, pt sl, EHU (10A) inc; TV; 90% statics; bus adj; Eng spkn. *"San facs needs updating (2017); gd location for walk to town; sh stay/NH only; super town; rec steam rlwy to Le Crotoy."* **€20.00, 1 Apr-30 Nov.** **2017**

ST VALLIER *9C2* (2km N Rural) *45.18767, 4.81225* **Camp Municipal Les Iles de Silon,** 26240 St Vallier **04 75 23 22 17 or 04 73 23 07 66; camping.saintvallier@ orange.fr; www.saintvallier.fr/decouvrir/camping**

🐕 €2.30 🏕 WD ⬛🚿⬛♿/♟🏊🏊⬛

On N7 just N of town, clearly sp in both dirs on rvside. 3*, Med, hdg, pt shd, EHU (10A) €2.30 (poss long cable req); bbq; 10% statics; Eng spkn; adv bkg acc; ccard acc; watersports; tennis adj; CKE. *"Attractive, gd quality site; views over rv; lge pitches; friendly warden; gd immac san facs; rec arr bef 1600 high ssn; gd value; cycle/walking track adj, along Rhône; excel well managed site; vg facs and staff; free WiFi."* **€13.00, 15 Mar-15 Nov.** **2018**

FRANCE

ST VINCENT DE BARRES *9D2* (1km SW Rural) *44.65659, 4.69330* **Camping Le Rieutord,** 07210 St Vincent-de-Barrès **04 75 20 86 17; campinglerieutord@ orange.fr; www.camping-le-rieutord.com**

🐕 €2 ♀♂ (htd) 🔥 🛁 ♿ 🦋 ♈ 🍴 🏪 🛒 ⚓ ⛴

Fr N exit A7 junc 16 Loriol onto D104 & foll sp Le Pouzin then Chomérac (do not foll 1st sp St Vincent-de-Barrès - narr rd). At rndabt foll D2 dir Le Teil-Montélimar for 6km. When arr at St Vincent (vill on L), turn R & foll site sp for 1.5km. Fr S exit junc 18 Montélimar Sud, foll sps Montélimar then Privas. Cross Rv Rhône, go thro Rochemaure sp Privas. At Meysse turn L after bdge dir Privas. Foll D2 for 4.5km then turn L dir St Bauzile to site in 3km. 2*, Med, hdg, pt shd, pt sl, EHU (16A) €3; cooking facs; 10% statics; Eng spkn; adv bkg acc; tennis; games area; waterslide; CKE. *"Tranquil site in beautiful setting nr old walled town; pleasant owners; no c'vans over 6m or twin axles; gd touring base; tired end of ssn."* **€20.00, 4 Apr-31 Oct.** **2019**

"I need an on-site restaurant"

We do our best to make sure site information is correct, but it is always best to check any must-have facilities are still available or will be open during your visit.

SAINTES *7B2* (0.5km N Urban) *45.75511, -0.62871* **Camp Municipal au Fil de l'Eau,** 6 Rue de Courbiac, 17100 Saintes **05 46 93 08 00 or 06 75 24 91 96 (mob); contact@camping-saintes-17.com; www.camping-saintes-17.com**

🐕 €1.60 ♀♂ 🚾 🔥 🛁 ♿ 🦋 ♈ 🍴 🏪 🛒 ⚓ ⛴

Well sp as 'Camping Municipal' fr rndbts on by-pass N & S on D150 & D137 (thro indus area), adj rv. If app fr W on D128 (N side of Saintes), turn R at rndabt onto Rue de l'Abbatoir; in 800m turn L into Rue de Courbiac; site on R in 200m. NB 1st Mon in month st mkt & many rds clsd. 3*, Lge, pt shd, EHU (10A) €3.60; bbq; sw nr; red long stay; Eng spkn; adv bkg acc; ccard acc; boating adj; fishing adj; CKE. *"Excel site; vg; clean, upgraded (2019) san facs; excel rest; grnd poss boggy when wet; gd touring base; mkt Wed & Sat; easy walk to attractive Roman town; huge open site, efficent recep; friendly staff; gd NH just off A10; rest clsd on Sundays;spacious, well positioned for town."* **€21.00, 20 Apr-15 Oct.** **2019**

SALBRIS *4G3* (1km N Urban) *47.43006, 2.05427* **Camping de Sologne,** 8 Allée de la Sauldre, Route de Pierrefitte, 41300 Salbris **02 54 97 06 38; campingdes ologne@wanadoo.fr; www.campingdesologne.fr**

🐕 €1 ♀♂ 🚾 🔥 🛁 ♿ 🛒 ♈ 🍴 🏪 🛒 nr ⛺

Fr N exit A71 J4. Take D724 bypass (2nd exit on rndabt). At next rndabt take D2020 N sp Salbris. Cont thro town. After x-ing bdge at next traffl lts turn R onto D55 (Rte de Perrelefitte). Impass de la Sauldre leading to Allee de la Sauldre is 2nd turning on R in 200m (narr and easy to miss). Fr S to avoid Peage leave A71 at J5. Take D2020 N to Salbris then as abv. 3*, Med, mkd, hdg, pt shd, EHU (10A) inc (some rev pol); gas; TV; 25% statics; phone; Eng spkn; adv bkg acc; ccard acc; fishing; boat hire; CKE. *"Excel, well-kept site in pleasant lakeside location; friendly, helpful owners; karting 6km; lake adj; gd san facs poss stretched if site busy & ltd LS; gd rest; gd dog walks adj; conv NH for m'way; hypmkt 1km; beautiful site; easy access to town; new shwr block (2015); ACSI accepted."* **€25.00, 1 Apr-30 Sep.** **2019**

SALERS *7C4* (0.8km NE Rural) *45.14756, 2.49857* **Camp Municipal Le Mouriol,** Route de Puy-Mary, 15140 Salers **04 71 40 73 09 or 04 71 40 72 33 (Mairie); www.salers.fr**

🐕 ♀♂ 🚾 🔥 🛁 ♿ 🛒 🦋 ♈ 🍴 nr ⊕ nr 🛒 nr ⛺

Take D922 SE fr Mauriac dir Aurillac; turn onto D680 E dir Salers; site 1km NE of Salers on D680 dir Puy Mary, opp Hôtel Le Gerfaut; sp fr all dir. 2*, Med, hdg, mkd, pt shd, sl, EHU (16A) €4.60 (long lead poss req); bbq; red long stay; phone; bus 1km; tennis; CKE. *"Generous pitches; san facs gd but stretched if site full; peaceful LS; hill walking; excel cycling & walking; beautiful medieval vill; vg; well kept; footpath fr site to Salers."* **€19.80, 1 Apr-30 Oct.** **2017**

SALERS *7C4* (0.8km W Rural) *45.13304, 2.48762* **Camping à la Ferme (Fruquière),** Apcher, 15140 Salers **04 71 40 72 26**

🐕 ♀♂ 🔥 🛁 ♈ 🦋 🛒 nr

D922 S fr Mauriac for 17km; L on D680 sp Salers; in lane on R sp Apcher - immed after passing Salers town sp. Sm, pt shd, EHU (10A) €2.30; CKE. *"Sm farm, CL type site; welcoming, friendly owner; excel clean san facs, plenty hot water; beautiful countryside; gd; run down end of ssn."* **€10.00, 1 May-30 Sep.** **2017**

SALIES DE BEARN *8F1* (3km S Rural) *43.45277, -0.92055* **Domaine d'Esperbasque,** Chemin de Lagisquet, 64270 Salies de Béarn **05 59 38 21 04; info@esperbasque.com; www.esperbasque.com**

🐕 €1.50-€3.50 ♀♂ 🚾 🔥 🛁 ♿ 🛒 MP 🦋 ♈ 🍴 ⊕ 🛒 nr ⛺ ⚓ ⛴

Site well sp on D933. E of rd bet Salies de Bearn and Sauveterre. Fr N pass the site, turn at next exit & app fr southern side. 2*, Med, hdstg, mkd, pt shd, sl, terr, EHU (6A) €3.50; bbq; twin axles; TV; Eng spkn; adv bkg acc; ccard acc; games area; games rm; CKE. *"Gd touring; horse riding at site highly rec; excel; go-karts; petanque; scenic, rural, visits to wine growers & Salies de Bearn; gd."* **€23.40, 1 Mar-31 Oct.** **2017**

SALIES DU SALAT *8F3* (2km S Rural) *43.07621, 0.94683*
Complex Touristique de la Justale, Chemin de St
Jean, 31260 Mane **05 61 90 68 18; contact@village-
vacances-mane.fr; www.village-vacances-mane.fr**

🐕 €1.20 ♟♦♦ wc ♨ ⚿ 🖭 ♈ ⬛nr ⚏ 🏊

Fr A64 exit 20 onto D117, turn R in vill at sp 'Village
de Vacances'. Site on R in approx 500m. 2*, Sm, pt
shd, EHU (6A) €3.60 (poss rev pol); TV; phone; adv bkg
rec; horseriding; tennis; fishing. *"Lovely, peaceful site;
lge pitches; helpful staff; excel facs; signage poss diff to
foll."* **€16.00, 1 Apr-31 Oct.** **2019**

SALINS LES BAINS *6H2* (0.5km N Rural) *46.94650,
5.87896* **Camp Municipal,** 39110 Salins-les-Bains
**03 84 37 92 70; campingsalins.kanak.fr; www.salins
camping.com**

♟♦♦ ♨ ⚿ ⚿ ⬛nr ⚏

SE fr Besançon on N83. At Mouchard take D472 E
to Salins. Turn L at rndabt at N of Salins, well sp
nr old stn. If app fr E take 2nd exit fr rndabt (blind
app). 2*, Sm, pt shd, EHU (10A) €3.10; 10% statics;
adv bkg acc. *"Well-run site; clean, modern san facs;
excel touring base N Jura; not often visited by British;
far end of site quieter; htd pool adj; gd NH; barrier
locked 1000-0700; chalets being built (2016)."*
€13.50, 31 Mar-1 Oct. **2017**

SALLANCHES *9A3* (4km SE Rural) *45.92388, 6.65042*
Camping Village Center Les Iles, Lac de Passy
245 Chemin de la Cavettaz, 74190 Passy
04 30 05 15 04; www.campinglesiles.fr

🐕 €3 ♟♦♦ ♨ ⚿ ⚿ 🖭 ⚿ 🦋 ⬛ ⚏ 🏊 (htd)

E fr Geneva on A40, exit junc 21 onto D339 dir
Passy; in 400m turn L onto DJ9 dir Sallanches; at
rndabt in 1.5km turn L onto D199 dir Domancy;
immed after rlwy x-ing in 500m turn R into Chemin
de Mont Blanc Plage; site at end of rd in 1km. Or E
fr Sallanches on D1205 dir Chamonix; in 3km turn
L (1st into filter to turn L) onto D199; in 1km turn L
immed bef level x-ing; site at end of rd. 3*, Lge, mkd,
hdg, pt shd, EHU (8A) inc; sw nr; phone; Eng spkn; adv
bkg acc; ccard acc; fishing; CKE. *"Mountain views; conv
Chamonix; vg site; v overgrown; nr rlwy and m'way;
pitches bare of grass, some v muddy after rain, v shady;
not rec."* **€16.00, 1 Apr-1 Oct.** **2016**

SALLES (GIRONDE) *7D1* (4km SW Rural) *44.52039,
-0.89631* **Camping Le Bilos,** 37 Route de Bilos, 33770
Salles **05 56 88 36 53 or 06 25 70 17 46 (mob);
lebilos@aol.com; www.lebilos.wixsite.com/
camping-lebilos**

12 🐕 ♟♦♦ (htd) wc ♨ ⚿ 🦋 ⚏ ⬛

Exit A63 junc 21; foll sp Salles on D3; turn L onto
D108/D108E3 sp Lugos; pass Carrefour supmkt on
R; in 2km bear R & site on R in 2km. 2*, Med, pt shd,
EHU (6A) inc; gas; bbq (sep area); 80% statics; adv
bkg acc. *"Pleasant, peaceful site in pine forest; sm,
well-drained pitches, ltd space for tourers, friendly
owners, old but clean san facs, ltd LS, cycle lane thro
forest, vg NH en rte Spain; friendly welcome; site cr."*
€22.40 **2019**

SALLES CURAN *8E4* (2km NW Rural) *44.18933,
2.76693* **Camping Les Genêts,** Lac de Pareloup,
12410 Salles-Curan **05 65 46 35 34; contact@
camping-les-genets.fr; www.camping-les-genets.fr**

🐕 €4 ♟♦♦ ♨ ⚿ ⚿ 🖭 ♈ Ⴅ ⊕ ⚿ ⚏ 🏊 (htd) ⚏

🐕 and lake adj. to site

Fr D911 Rodez-Millau rd take D993 S for approx
9km, then R onto D577, site sp on R by lake.
4*, Lge, shd, pt sl, EHU (10A) inc; sw; red long stay;
40% statics; adv bkg acc; fishing; sailing; bike hire;
games area. *"Beautiful area; ltd facs LS; excel site."*
€36.00, 25 Apr - 22 Sep, D07. **2019**

SALON DE PROVENCE *10E2* (5km NW Rural)
43.67820, 5.06480 **Camping Nostradamus,**
Route d'Eyguières, 13300 Salon-de-Provence
**04 90 56 08 36; gilles.nostra@gmail.fr;
www.camping-nostradamus.com**

🐕 €3 ♟♦♦ wc ♨ ⚿ 🖭 🦋 ♈
Ⴅ ⊕ ⚿ ⬛nr ⚏ 🖋 🏊 ⚏

Exit A54/E80 junc 13 onto D569 N sp Eyguières.
After approx 1.5km turn R opp airfield onto D72d,
site on R in approx 4km just bef T-junc. Or fr N exit
A7 junc 26 dir Salon-de-Provence. Turn R onto D17
for 5km dir Eyguières, then L onto D72, site on L.
3*, Med, mkd, hdg, pt shd, EHU (4-6A) €2.95-5.15;
gas; bbq; TV; 15% statics; phone; Eng spkn; adv bkg
req; ccard acc; games area; CKE. *"Pleasant site; busy
high ssn; welcoming owner with vg sense of humour!;
bkg fee; poss diff access lge o'fits; dusty when dry; gd
walking."* **€24.00, 1 Mar-30 Oct.** **2019**

SAMOENS *9A3* (6km W Rural) *46.08944, 6.67874*
Camp Municipal Lac et Montagne, 74440 Verchaix
06 79 57 69 59; www.verchaix.com

12 🐕 €1.40 ♨ ⚿ 🦋 ♈nr ⊕nr ⬛nr ⚏

Fr Taninges take D907 sp Samoëns for 6km, site to
R of main rd in Verchaix. 2*, Med, shd, EHU (10A)
€4.10; 10% statics; phone; adv bkg acc; tennis. *"Gd
touring base; clean facs; rv & lake adj; barrier locked
2200-0700."* **€21.00** **2016**

SANCERRE *4G3* (4km N Rural) *47.34215, 2.86571*
Flower Camping Les Portes de Sancerre, Quai de
Loire, 18300 St Satur **02 48 72 10 88; camping.
sancerre@flowercampings.com; www.camping-
cher-sancerre.com**

🐕 €2 ♟♦♦ wc ♨ ⚿ 🖭 ♈ ⊕nr ⬛nr ⚏ 🖋

Fr Sancerre on D955 thro cent St Satur &
St Thibault. Turn L immed bef Loire bdge. Site on R
in 100m. 3*, Med, hdg, shd, EHU (16A) inc (long lead
poss req); sw; TV; 50% statics; Eng spkn; adv bkg acc;
bike hire; games area; tennis; CKE. *"Nice site; some
pitches sm, some with rv view; friendly & helpful staff;
pool adj; canoe hire adj; gd clean excel san facs, rec own
in peak ssn; rvside walks; gd touring cent; vg; highly rec;
gd rest nrby."* **€23.00, 1 Apr-1 Oct.** **2017**

SANCERRE *4G3* (9.4km SW Rural) *47.30353, 2.74555* **Camping Crezancy en Sancerre,** 9 Route de Veagues, 18300 Crezancy en Sancerre 06 12 55 69 98; campingcrezancy@orange.fr

Fr Sancerre take D955 dir Bourges. In 5km turn R onto D22 sp Crezancy, Henrichement. After 5km at vill turn L onto D86 for Veagues. Site 100m on L. Sm, hdg, mkd, shd, EHU (6A); bbq; cooking facs; twin axles; phone; bus 100m; Eng spkn; adv bkg acc; CKE. *"Site in Sancerre vineyards with wine tasting & to buy; gd walks & cycling, but a bit hilly; easy acc to Sancerre and The Loire; hospitable site manager; excel; lovely sm friendly site; indiv hdg bays, rural, quiet & clean; new shwrs (2016)."* **€10.00, 1 Apr-31 Oct.**   2017

SANGUINET *7D1* (2km SW Rural) *44.48402, -1.09098* **Camping Les Grands Pins,** Ave de Losa, Route du Lac, 40460 Sanguinet 05 58 78 61 74; info@campingles grandspins.com; www.campinglesgrandspins.com

Foll Le Lac sp at rndabt in Sanguinet. Turn L at lakeside. Site on L in 450m opp yacht club. 3*, Lge, hdg, shd, EHU (3-10A) inc; sw nr; TV; 50% statics; Eng spkn; adv bkg acc; canoeing; bike hire; fishing; tennis; boating; windsurfing; CKE. *"Clean site; rest & bar poss clsd LS; parking for m'vans adj."* **€37.00, 1 Apr-31 Oct.**   2016

SANGUINET *7D1* (1.5km W Rural) *44.483045, -1.088951* **Sandaya Sanguinet Plage,** 1039 Avenue de Losa, 40460 Sanguinet 05 58 76 61 74; sap@ sandaya.fr; www.sandaya.co.uk

Foll Le Lac sp at rndabt in Sanguinet, turn L on lakeside, site on L in 600m. 5*, Lge, mkd, pt shd, EHU (10A); sw nr; twin axles; 80% statics; Eng spkn; games rm; games area; sailing nr; bike hire; watersports; CKE. *"Spacious site; cycle path around lake; watersports on lake; friendly, helpful staff."* **€36.00, 03 Apr-27 Sep.**   2019

SARLAT LA CANEDA *7C3* (10km NE Rural) *44.95778, 1.27280* **Sandaya Les Péneyrals,** Le Poujol, 24590 St Crépin-et-Carlucet 05 53 28 85 71; pen@sandaya.fr; www.sandaya.co.uk

Fr Sarlat N on D704; D60 E dir Salignac-Eyvignes to Le Poujol; S to St Crépin. Site sp. 5*, Lge, hdg, pt shd, pt sl, terr, serviced pitches; EHU (5-10A); bbq (gas); 50% statics; Eng spkn; adv bkg acc; ccard acc; games area; waterslide; fishing; tennis. *"Friendly owners; superb family & touring site; excel aquatic ctr; some pitches require mover."* **€25.00, 10 Apr-13 Sep, A18.**   2019

SARLAT LA CANEDA *7C3* (8km NE Rural) *44.90404, 1.28210* **Camping Les Grottes de Roffy,** 24200 Ste Nathalène 05 53 59 15 61; contact@roffy.fr; www.roffy.fr

Fr N end of Sarlat take D47 NE for Ste Nathalène. Site on R 1km bef vill. Or fr A20 exit junc 55 onto ND804/D703 dir Carlux. Turn R onto D61B then D47 to Ste Nathalène, site thro vill on L. 4*, Lge, mkd, hdg, pt shd, terr, EHU (6A) €3; gas; bbq; 40% statics; Eng spkn; adv bkg rec; canoeing; games rm; tennis; bike hire; games area; CKE. *"Excel rest, bar & shop; extra for 'comfort' pitches; helpful staff; lovely site."* **€33.50, 25 Apr-13 Sep.**   2015

SARLAT LA CANEDA *7C3* (9.7km NE Rural) *44.91905, 1.27789* **Camping Domaine des Mathévies,** Les Mathévies, 24200 Ste Nathalène 05 53 59 20 86 or 06 14 10 95 86 (mob); info@mathevies.com; www.mathevies.com

Exit A20 junc 55 Souillac & foll sp Roufillac. At Roufillac, foll sp to Carlux & cont to Ste Nathalène, site sp N of Ste Nathèlene. 2*, Sm, hdg, mkd, pt shd, EHU (10A) €4; TV (pitch); 10% statics; adv bkg acc; tennis; games area; playground; games rm. *"Gd, British-owned site; lge pitches, most with views; max. 2 dogs per pitch; excel site; gd for kids."* **€35.00, 18 May-21 Sep, D04.**   2019

SARLAT LA CANEDA *7C3* (2km E Rural) *44.89328, 1.22756* **Camping Indigo Sarlat Les Périères,** Rue Jean Gabin, 24200 Sarlat-la-Canéda 05 53 59 05 84; sarlat@camping-indigo.com; www.camping-indigo.com

Site on R of D47 to Proissans & Ste Nathalène. NB steep access rds. 4*, Med, mkd, shd, terr, EHU (6A); gas; bbq (charcoal, gas); 10% statics; Eng spkn; adv bkg acc; ccard acc; games rm; sauna; tennis. *"Lovely site; friendly, helpful staff; san facs clean; excel pool complex; steep site rds; access poss diff med & lge o'fits; excel; great facs & location; v easy walk to Old City; site extended (2015); new san facs (2016); excel site."* **€37.00, 24 Mar-2 Nov.**   2015

SARLAT LA CANEDA *7C3* (20km E Rural) *44.86732, 1.35796* **Camping Les Ombrages,** Rouffillac, 24370 Carlux 09 53 53 25 55; ombragesperigord@ free.fr; www.ombrages.fr

12km W thro Souillac on D703. Turn L at x-rds in Rouffillac & immed turn L bef rv bdge into site. 2*, Med, mkd, pt shd, EHU (6A) €2.70; bbq; sw nr; TV; 2% statics; phone; Eng spkn; adv bkg acc; ccard acc; fishing; tennis; bike hire; games area; canoe hire; CKE. *"Pleasant, well-kept, rvside site; enthusiastic new owners live on site; pitching poss diff due trees; san facs (open air) poss stretched high ssn; cycle track; vg; lovely peaceful site; pool adj; lots of entmnt."* **€20.00, 19 Apr-15 Oct.**   2015

Caudon 24200 VITRAC – France
info@labouysse.com – www.labouysse.com

Site owned by French family. English spoken.

Along the river Dordogne near the well known Caudon rock,
direct access to beach area where you can swim or go canoeing.
Beautiful site near Montfort château, Sarlat (6km.) and many
other Dordogne sights.
Green pitches, with trees and hedges giving some shade.
Lovely swimming pool. A wide range of accommodations available
(country cottages, mobile homes, gîtes and pitches).
On the site: grocery's, bar and snack bar (open from 15th June
until 31st August) – washing machine, dryer and iron - WiFi

SARLAT LA CANEDA 7C3 (11km SE Rural) 44.83274,
1.26626 **Camping Le Plein Air des Bories,** 24200
Carsac-Aillac **05 53 28 15 67; camping.lesbories@
wanadoo.fr; www.camping-desbories.com**

🐕 €3 ♟♟♟ ♨ ♿ ⚲ ☕ ✉ ≈ 🦋 ⛵ 🏓 🏊 ⛷ (htd)

Take D704 SE fr Sarlat sp Gourdon; diff RH turn
to site after Carsac vill. Easier access on D703
fr Vitrac. 3*, Med, shd, pt sl, EHU (16A) €4.50; gas;
sw; Eng spkn; canoe hire; fishing; boating; tennis
700m; CKE. "Clean, shady rvside site; friendly owners."
€24.00, 1 Jun-15 Sep. 2018

SARLAT LA CANEDA 7C3 (10km S Rural) 44.82525,
1.25360 **Domaine de Soleil-Plage,** Caudon-par-
Montfort, 24200 Vitrac **05 53 28 33 33; info@
soleilplage.fr; www.soleilplage.fr**

🐕 €3.50 ♟♟♟ (htd) ⬜ ♨ ♿ ⚲ ☕ ✉ ≈ 🦋 ⛵ ⛺ ☕ ⚌ 🏓 ⛺ ✏
🏊 (htd) 🚿

On D46, 6km S of Sarlat twd Vitrac, turn L onto
D703 to Château Montfort, R to site dir Caudon, sp.
Site beyond Camping La Bouysse on rvside, 2km E
of Vitrac. If coming fr Souillac on D703, when app
Montfort rd v narr with overhanging rock faces. Narr
access rds on site. 5*, Lge, hdg, pt shd, serviced pitches;
EHU (16A) inc (poss rev pol); gas; bbq; TV; 45% statics;
phone; Eng spkn; adv bkg req; ccard acc; waterslide;
bike hire; tennis; golf 1km; canoeing; rv fishing adj;
horseriding 5km; games rm; CKE. "Lovely site in
beautiful location; friendly, welcoming owner; variety of
pitches - extra for serviced/rvside (shady); no o'fits over
7m Jun-Aug; san facs clean; superb aquatic complex;
poss muddy when wet; red groups; highly rec; first class
comprehensive site; poss best site we've ever stayed
at; lge private pitches; lovely cycling, but some on fairly
steep rds." **€43.70, 8 Apr-29 Sep, D15.** 2019

SARLAT LA CANEDA 7C3 (12km S Rural) 44.79175,
1.16266 **Camping Bel Ombrage,** 24250 St Cybranet
**05 53 28 34 14; belombrage@wanadoo.fr;
www.belombrage.com**

🐕 ♟♟♟ ⬜ ♨ ♿ ⚲ ☕ ✉ 🦋 ⚌ ♟ ☕ nr ⚌ nr ⛺ 🏊 ⛷ ⛱

Fr Sarlat take D46 sp Bergerac, rd then conts as
D57; after 8km turn L at Vézac sp Castelnaund.
After 1.6km at T-junc turn L onto D703 & in 180m
turn R onto D57. Cont thro Castelnaund on D57; site
on L in 3km. 3*, Lge, hdg, shd, EHU (10A) inc; bbq; sw;
red long stay; TV; adv bkg acc; ccard acc; tennis 800m;
horseriding 2km; fishing; games area; bike hire; games
rm; CKE. "Attractive, well-run site by rv; popular with
British; lge pitches; no o'fits over 8m high ssn; modern
san facs; peaceful early ssn; library; ideal base for
Dordogne; mkt Thur; excel."
€25.00, 1 Jun-5 Sep, D01. 2017

SARLAT LA CANEDA 7C3 (6km S Rural) 44.82375,
1.25080 **Camping La Bouysse de Caudon,** 24200
Vitrac **05 53 28 33 05; info@labouysse.com;
www.labouysse.com**

🐕 €3.50 ♟♟♟ ⬜ ♨ ♿ ⚲ ☕ ✉ 🦋 ⚌ ♟ ☕ ⚌ 🏓 ⛺ 🏊 ⛷ (htd)
🚿

S fr Sarlat on D46 dir Vitrac. At Vitrac 'port'
bef bdge turn L onto D703 sp Carsac. In 2km
turn R & foll site sp, site on L. Well sp. 3*, Med,
mkd, hdg, pt shd, EHU (10A) €5.80; gas; bbq; sw;
8% statics; phone; Eng spkn; adv bkg req; ccard
acc; canoe hire; tennis; fishing; games area; CKE.
"Beautiful family-run site on Rv Dordogne; helpful
owner; plenty gd clean san facs; gd access rv beach;
muddy when wet; many Bastides in area; excel."
€25.80, 12 Apr-17 Sep. 2019

See advertisement

SARLAT LA CANEDA *7D3* (18km SSW Rural) *44.76762, 1.17590* **Camping Le Moulin de Paulhiac, 24250 Daglan 05 53 28 20 88; francis.armagnac@ wanadoo.fr; www.moulin-de-paulhiac.com**

D57 SW fr Sarlat, across rv into St Cybranet & site in 2km. Fr Souillac W on D703 alongside Rv Dordogne; x-ing rv onto D46 (nr Domme) & D50, to site. Med, mkd, hdg, shd, EHU (6-10A) €3.70-4.40; gas; TV; 20% statics; Eng spkn; adv bkg acc; ccard acc; canoeing; waterslide; rv fishing adj; CKE. *"Pretty site; friendly, helpful staff; vg fruit/veg mkt Sun in vill; highly rec."* **€25.00, 15 May-16 Sep.** 2020

See advertisement

SARLAT LA CANEDA *7C3* (10km SW Rural) *44.83819, 1.14846* **Camping Le Capeyrou, 24220 Beynac-et-Cazenac 05 53 29 54 95; lecapeyrou@ wanadoo.fr; www.campinglecapeyrou.com**

Fr W on D703 on R (opp sm supmkt & baker) immed past vill of Beynac. Or fr N on D57 fr Sarlat; in vill immed on L on rv. 3*, Med, hdg, hdstg, pt shd, EHU (6-10A) €3.50-4.20; Eng spkn; adv bkg acc; ccard acc. *"View of chateau most pitches; helpful, friendly owners; clean san facs; excel lge pool; rvside walk to attractive vill; excel NH; canoeing, hot air ballooning; v muddy when wet."* **€28.00, Apr-30 Sep.** 2015

SARLAT LA CANEDA *7C3* (10km SW Rural) *44.80519, 1.15852* **Camping Maisonneuve, Vallée de Céou, 24250 Castelnaud-la-Chapelle 05 53 29 51 29; contact@campingmaisonneuve.com; www.camping maisonneuve.com**

Take D57 SW fr Sarlat sp Beynac. Cross Rv Dordogne at Castelnaud; site sp 500m on L out of Castelnaud on D57 twd Daglan. Foll narr rd across bdge (or alt ent - cont on D57 for 2km, sp on L for c'vans). 3*, Med, hdstg, mkd, hdg, pt shd, EHU (6-10A) €3.10-6.40; gas; bbq; sw; TV; 10% statics; Eng spkn; adv bkg req; ccard acc; rv; games rm; tennis 2km; bike hire; fishing; CKE. *"Vg, spacious site; helpful owners; excel, modern, clean facs; gd walks, cycling; outstanding."* **€26.70, Apr-Oct.** 2019

SARLAT LA CANEDA *7C3* (12km SW Rural) *44.82585, 1.15322* **Camping La Cabane, 24220 Vézac 05 53 29 52 28; contact@lacabanedordogne.com; www.lacabanedordogne.com**

Fr Sarlat-La-Canéda take D57 thro Vézac. On leaving Vézac turn L immed bef rlwy bdge, site sp on R on bank of Rv Dordogne. 2*, Lge, hdg, mkd, pt shd, EHU (6-10A) €2.60-3.15; gas; bbq; sw nr; TV; 10% statics; phone; Eng spkn; adv bkg acc; ccard acc; CKE. *"Well-shd, rvside site; lge pitches; clean facs; friendly, helpful family owners; rvside walk to Beynac Château; gd; 2nd san facs block modernised (2015)."* **€18.00, 1 Apr-30 Sep.** 2015

For a guide to symbols see the fold out on the rear cover

SARLAT LA CANEDA *7C3* (9km W Rural) *44.90805, 1.11527* **Camping Le Moulin du Roch,** Le Roch, Route des Eyzies, 24200 Sarlat-la-Canéda 05 53 59 20 27; moulin.du.roch@wanadoo.fr; www.moulin-du-roch.com or www.les-castels.com
🏕 (htd) 🚐 ♨ ⚓ ♿ ⬛ ✉ 🧺 🦋 ⛱ 🍽 🔟 🅿 🛒 ⚒ 🏊 (htd) ⚓

Fr A20 take exit 55 at Souillac dir Sarlat. Head for D704 twds Sarlat La Caneda. At rndabt in Sarlat (just under rlwy viaduct) take 2nd exit onto bypass. Take 2nd exit at next rndabt staying on D704. At next rndabt take 2nd exit onto D6 dir Les Eyzies (becomes D47). Site on L in approx 9 km on D47. Fr N on D704 to Sarlat, turn R at hypmkt, then as above. 5*, Lge, mkd, hdg, pt shd, terr, serviced pitches; EHU (6A) inc; gas; bbq (charcoal, gas); red long stay; twin axles; TV; 45% statics; Eng spkn; adv bkg rec; ccard acc; horseriding nr; games rm; canoeing nr; lake fishing; outdoor sports; playground; CKE. *"Well-run, family owned site; lge pitches; clean facs but poss long, steep walk; some noise fr adj rd; gd rest & pool; m'vans poss not acc after prolonged heavy rain due soft grnd; mkt Sat."* €52.00, 25 May-22 Sep, D02. **2019**

SARZEAU *2G3* (8km SE Coastal) *47.50551, -2.68308* **Camping Manoir de Ker An Poul,** 1 Route de la Grée, Penvins, 56370 Sarzeau 02 57 62 04 65; manoirdeker anpoul@wanadoo.fr; www.manoirdekeranpoul.com
🏕 €4 🏕 (htd) 🚐 ♨ ⚓ ♿ ⬛ ✉ 🦋 🍽 🔟 nr 🅿 🛒 ⚒ 🏊 (htd, indoor) ⛱ sand 1km

Fr E exit N165 1km E of Muzillac, sp Sarzeau D20 & cont approx 20km to junc of D20 & D199, S on D199 sp Penvins. Fr W, 6km E of Vannes, exit N165 onto N780 sp Sarzeau, in 9.5km S onto D199 sp Penvins. 4*, Lge, hdg, pt shd, pt sl, EHU (6-10A) €4; bbq; TV; 30% statics; Eng spkn; adv bkg acc; tennis; games area; bike hire; CKE. *"Spacious pitches; warm welcome; excel staff; no dog walk on site; san facs recently renovated (2015); noisy weekend nr pool, quieter mid week."* €41.00, 7 Apr-23 Sep. **2018**

SARZEAU *2G3* (2.5km S Coastal) *47.50720, -2.76083* **Camping La Ferme de Lann Hoëdic,** Rue Jean de la Fontaine, Route de Roaliguen, 56370 Sarzeau 02 97 48 01 73; contact@camping-lannhoedic.fr; www.camping-lannhoedic.fr
🏕 €2.60 🏕 (htd) 🚐 ♨ ⚓ ♿ ⬛ ✉ 🧺 🦋 🍽 🔟 nr 🅿 nr 🛒 nr 🛖 ⛱ sand 800m

Fr Vannes on N165 turn onto D780 dir Sarzeau. Do not ent Sarzeau, but at Super U rndabt foll sp Le Roaliguen. After 1.5km turn L to Lann Hoëdic. 3*, Med, mkd, pt shd, EHU (16A) €4.10; gas; 10% statics; phone; Eng spkn; adv bkg acc; ccard acc; bike hire; CKE. *"Peaceful, well-managed, popular, family-run site; warm welcome; excel, clean facs; beautiful coastline - beaches & dunes; highly rec; gd cycling routes."* €24.50, 28 Mar-01 Nov. **2020**

SAULIEU *6G1* (1km N Rural) *47.28936, 4.22401* **Camping de Saulieu,** Route de Paris, 21210 Saulieu 03 80 64 16 19; camping.salieu@wanadoo.fr; www.aquadis-loisirs.com
🏕 €1.50 🏕 (htd) 🚐 ♨ ⚓ ♿ ⬛ ✉ 🧺 🍽 🔟 🅿 🛒 🛖 🏊 ⚓

On D906 on L of rd on ent fr N. Sp.

3*, Lge, hdg, mkd, pt shd, pt sl, EHU (10A) €3.90; gas; adv bkg acc; tennis; lake fishing; CKE. *"Nr town but rural feel; quiet at far end of site, away fr pool & playgrnd; no twin axles; many rests in town; gd walking area; gd."* €21.70, 8 Apr-3 Nov. **2019**

SAUMUR *4G1* (2km N Urban) *47.25990, -0.06440* **Flower Camping de L'Ile d'Offard,** Rue de Verden, 49400 Saumur 02 41 40 30 00 or 02 52 56 03 11; iledoffard@flowercampings.com; www.saumur-camping.com or www.flowercampings.com
🏕 €3 🏕 (htd) 🚐 ♨ ⚓ ♿ ⬛ ✉ 🧺 🍽 🔟 🅿 🛒 🛖 ⚒ 🏊 (htd) ⚓

Exit A85 junc 3 onto D347 and then D347E; ent town past rlwy stn & cross Rv Loire bdge; turn L immed over bdge & alongside rv. At rndabt turn L & take 1st L to site; foll sp. Site on island facing Saumur castle. 4*, Lge, hdstg, mkd, hdg, pt shd, pt sl, EHU (10A) (poss rev pol); gas; sw nr; TV; 20% statics; Eng spkn; adv bkg req; ccard acc; tennis; boating adj; fishing adj; games area; jacuzzi; bike hire; CKE. *"Pleasant, busy, well-run site; ideal for children; hdstg pitches in winter; helpful staff; clean, most pitches lge but some v sm pitches bet statics - lge o'fits check in advance; gd bar & rest; can be muddy when wet; gd cycle rtes; nice rvside and bdge walk to town; excel, but busy; great facs; easy acc to city; san facs refurb, modern & clean (2015); recep clsd 1200-1400; lovely loc; gd base for visiting Loire Valley; 35 placement municiple area adj, acc by card; v welcoming."* €40.00, 14 Mar-18 Oct. **2019**

> ## "There aren't many sites open at this time of year"
>
> If you're travelling outside peak season remember to call ahead to check site opening dates – even if the entry says 'open all year'.

SAUMUR *4G1* (7km NF Rural) *47.29937, -0.01218* **Camping Le Pô Doré,** 49650 Allonnes 02 41 38 78 80 or 06 09 26 31 28 (mob); camping.du.po.dore @wanadoo.fr; www.camping-lepodore.com
🏕 €1.50 🏕 🚐 ♨ ♿ ⬛ ✉ 🧺 🍽 🔟 🅿 🛒 ⚒ 🏊 (htd)

NE fr Saumur on N347 & turn R onto D10. Site 3km W of Allonnes on R. 4*, Med, mkd, hdg, hdstg, pt shd, EHU (6-10A) €3-4 (poss rev pol); 25% statics; phone; Eng spkn; ccard acc; bike hire; CKE. *"Gd, clean & tidy site; helpful staff; dirty, sandy soil; conv wine rtes, caves, museums & a'route; conv NH/sh stay; excel san facs; spectacular laggon."* €29.00, 15 Mar-15 Nov. **2017**

FRANCE

SAUMUR *4G1* (6km E Rural) *47.24755, -0.00033*
Camping Domaine de la Brèche, 5 Impasse de la
Brèche, 49730 Varennes-sur-Loire **02 41 51 22 92;**
mail@etang-breche.com; www.domainedela
breche.com

🏕 👫 ⅏ ♨ ♿ ⬆ ✐ ⚐ ♟ 🍴 🕙 📶 🛒 △ ✐ 🎿 (htd)

Exit 3 of A85, then D767 & D347 twrds Saumur, then
D952 twd Tours & site sp fr either dir. Site on N side
of rd (6km W of Varennes) app fr lge lay-by giving
easy ent. 5*, Lge, hdg, pt shd, serviced pitches; EHU
(16A); gas; TV; 50% statics; phone; Eng spkn; adv bkg
rec; ccard acc; waterslide; tennis; bike hire; games rm;
CKE. *"Spacious site & pitches; well-organised; excel
facs; auto barrier clsd 2300-0700; helpful staff; excel."*
€48.00, 14 Apr-09 Sep, A32.   **2019**

SAUMUR *4G1* (7.5km NW Rural) *47.29440, -0.14120*
Camping de Chantepie, Route de Chantepie, 49400
St Hilaire-St Florent **02 41 67 95 34;** info@camping
chantepie.com; www.campingchantepie.com

🏕 €4 👫 (htd) ⅏ ♨ ♿ ⬆ ⚐ ✐ 🦋 ♟ 🍴 🛒 △ ✐
🎿 (covrd, htd) ♿

Fr Saumer take D751 on S bank of Rv Loire sp
Gennes. Turn L 3km N of St Hilaire-St-Florent just
bef lge sp for a supmkt & bef mushroom museum.
Site sp. Or fr N after x-ing rv on N347, take turn sp
St Hilaire-St-Florent & join D751 for Gennes; site is
3km N of St Hilaire-St Florent, well sp fr D751. NB
Easy to miss turning. 5*, Lge, mkd, hdg, pt shd, EHU
(10A) inc (poss rev pol); gas; bbq; TV; 10% statics;
Eng spkn; adv bkg acc; ccard acc; golf 2km; games
rm; horseriding 5km; tennis 2km; bike hire; fishing;
CKE. *"Excel well-run site nr rv; well-spaced, lge pitches,
some with excel rv views, ltd; access to some pitches
diff lge o'fits; friendly, helpful staff; no o'fits over
10m; boating 5km; excel san facs, conv Loire cycle
rte; mkt Sat Saumur; excel views, bar & rest; excel
cycle track; TV recep may be diff due to many trees."*
€39.00, 4 May-26 Sep, L06.   **2016**

SAUMUR *4G1* (9km NW Rural) *47.30982, -0.14492*
**Camping Terre d'Entente (formerly La Croix
Rouge),** Lieu dit de la Croix Rouge, 49160 St Martin-
de-la-Place **09 72 30 31 72 or 07 70 07 69 37;**
contact@terre-dentente.fr; terre-dentente.fr

🏕 €1.50 👫 ⅏ ♨ ♿ ⬆ ⚐ ✐ ♟ 🦋 ✐ 🍴 nr 🕙 nr 🛒 nr △

Exit A85 junc 3 sp Saumur. Take slip rd immed bef
bdge then L sp 'Angers Touristique'. Site on L at vill
sp. Fr Saumur take D347 N across rv then turn L
onto D952 dir Angers. At St Martin-de-la-Place foll
sp for site. 2*, Med, mkd, pt shd, EHU (6-10A) €3-4; sw
nr; bus 150m; Eng spkn; adv bkg acc; sailing adj; CKE.
*"Beautiful, tranquil site on Rv Loire; friendly, helpful
owners; 26 steps to spacious san facs; disabled facs at
grnd level; 2m high security fence by rv; barrier clsd
2200-0700; no twin axles; conv Saumur; bar 200m; v
pleasant site; poor."* **€18.00, 8 Apr-30 Sep.**   **2017**

SAVENAY *2G3* (2.5km E Rural) *47.35651, -1.92136*
Camp Municipal du Lac de Savenay, Route du Lac,
44260 Savenay **02 40 58 31 76;** www.camping-lac-
savenay.fr

🏕 €1.20 👫 (htd) ♨ ♿ ⬆ ⚐ ✐ 🦋 ♟ △

Site well sp in Savenay. Can avoid Savenay Town
by turning off N165 SW of town on new rd, dir
LAC. 2*, Med, mkd, pt shd, terr; EHU (10A) €2.07;
Eng spkn; fishing. *"Vg, clean site in attractive
lakeside park; lge pitches; gas adj; pool adj; excel
modern san block; terr pitches req long elec leads."*
€26.00, 1 Mar-31 Oct.   **2016**

SAVERNE *6E3* (2km SW Urban) *48.73329, 7.35371*
**Camping Les Portes d'Alsace (formerly Camping
de Saverne),** Rue du Père Libermann, 67700 Saverne
03 88 91 35 65; contact@camping-lesportesdalsace.
com; www.vacances-seasonova.com

🏕 €1.60 👫 (htd) ⅏ ♨ ♿ ⬆ ⚐ ✐ 📶 🕙 ♟ nr △

Take Saverne exit fr A4, junc 45. Site well sp nr town
cent. 3*, Med, hdg, mkd, hdstg, pt shd, pt sl, terr, EHU
(6-10A) €3.10-5.70 (poss rev pol); 20% statics; adv
bkg acc; ccard acc; CKE. *"Pleasant, busy, well-run site;
pitches mostly terr; warm welcome, friendly staff; long
steep walk back fr town; m'van aire de service nr ent;
trains to Strasbourg fr town; poss travellers; v gd."*
€27.50, 26 Mar-1 Nov, J06.   **2018**

SEES *4E1* (1km S Urban) *48.59875, 0.17103*
Camp Municipal Le Clos Normand, Ave du 8 mai
1945, 61500 Sées **02 33 28 87 37 or 02 33 28 74 79
(LS); contact@camping-sees.fr; www.ville-sees.fr**

🏕 €1.25 👫 ⅏ ♨ ♿ ⬆ ⚐ ✐ 🕙 🍴 nr 🕙 nr 🛒 nr △

C'vans & lge m'vans best app fr S - twd rndabt
at S end of by-pass (rec use this rndabt as other
rtes diff & narr). Well sp. Narr ent. 3*, Sm, hdg, pt
shd, EHU (10A) €2.50; gas; 10% statics; Eng spkn;
adv bkg acc; fishing; CKE. *"Spacious, well-cared for
pitches; helpful, friendly warden; gd san facs, poss
stretched if site full; excel mv service pnt; gates clsd
2100 (2000 LS); easy walk to town; shop nr; vg."*
€13.00, 16 Apr-30 Sep.   **2018**

SEGRE *2F4* (7km NW Rural) *47.71003, -0.95165*
Camping Parc de St Blaise, 49520 Noyant-la-
Gravoyère **02 41 26 43 48;** parcsaintblaise49@
gmail.com; www.campingsaintblaise.fr

🏕 👫 ⅏ ♿ ⬆ ✐ 🍴 🛒 △ ✐

Fr Segré take D775 dir Pouancé to Noyant, site/park
sp in vill on R. 2*, Sm, hdg, pt shd, terr, EHU (6A) inc;
sw nr; phone; horseriding; fishing; CKE. *"Clean, well-
maintained site in leisure park; gd views; aquatic park;
slate mine worth visit."* **€11.00, 15 Jun-30 Sep.**   **2019**

SEILHAC *7C4 (4km SW Rural) 45.35018, 1.64642*
Camp Municipal du Pilard, La Barthe, 19700
Lagraulière 05 55 73 71 04; mairie.lagrauliere@
wanadoo.fr; www.lagrauliere.correze.net

🐕 €1 ♿ WD ♨ ⚲ ❄ 🦋 ⊤ nr ⊕ nr 🛒 nr ⛆

Exit A20 junc 46 onto D34 to Lagraulière, site sp.
NB Lge o'fits rec take D44 & D167E fr Seilhac.
2*, Sm, mkd, pt shd, EHU (3-6A) €3 (poss rev pol); bbq;
Eng spkn; tennis; CKE. *"Quiet, clean site nr pleasant
interesting vill; htd pool adj; warden calls; mkts on
Thurs."* €10.00, 15 Jun-15 Sep. **2019**

> ## "That's changed – Should I let the Club know?"
>
> If you find something on site that's different
> from the site entry, fill in a report and let us
> know. See camc.com/europereport.

SEISSAN *8F3 (2km WNW Rural) 43.49554, 0.57815*
Domaine Lacs de Gascogne, Route Du Lac, 32260
Seissan 05 62 66 27 94; info@domainelacsde
gascogne.eu; www.domainelacsdegascogne.eu

🐕 €3 WD ⚲ 🛒 ∥ MP ⊕ ⊤ 🛒 ⛆ 🏊

V lge, mkd, pt shd, pt sl, EHU (16A); bbq; twin
axles; TV; 25% statics; bus 2km; Eng spkn; adv
bkg acc; HCAP ltd; bike hire; games area; showrs;
games rm; pool paddling; CKE. *"Tennis, separate
carpk; walks; watersports; 1 dog per pitch; tourist
attractions; table tennis; pool; sauna; carp fishing; vg."*
€32.00, 31 Mar-30 Sep. **2018**

SELESTAT *6E3 (7km N Rural) 48.30647, 7.50057*
Camping Rural (Weiss), 17 Rue du Buhl, 67600
Ebersheim 06 85 10 95 54; theo.sonntag@wanadoo.fr

🐕 ♿ ⚲ ❄ ∥ 🦋 🛒 nr

Fr S or N on N83 in vill of Ebersheim foll green
Camping Rural sps. Sm, pt shd, EHU (16A) inc; bbq;
cooking facs; bus 0.5km; Eng spkn; adv bkg acc;
CKE. *"Gd touring base; friendly, helpful staff; excel
Boulangerie in vill; dogs free; site self, staff visit pm;
excel for sh or lg stay."* €13.00, 15 Jun-15 Sep. **2019**

SELESTAT *6E3 (1km SW Urban) 48.25470, 7.44781*
Camp Municipal Les Cigognes, Rue de la 1ère
D.F.L, 67600 Sélestat 03 88 92 03 98; camping@
ville-selestat.fr; http://camping.selestat.fr

🐕 €1 ♿ WD ⚲ ❄ ∥ MP 🦋 ⊕ ⊤ nr ⊕ nr 🛒 ⛆ 🏊

Site sp D1083 & D424. Fr S town cent turn E off
D1083 & foll sps to site adj schools & playing
fields. 2*, Med, mkd, pt shd, EHU (6-16A) inc;
gas; train to Strasbourg nrby; Eng spkn; adv bkg
rec; CKE. *"Great, well-run site; helpful staff; pool
300m; some noise fr local football area; excel new
san blocks; easy walk to old town; mkt Sat; rec."*
€15.50, 1 Apr-15 Oct & 15 Nov-24 Dec. **2016**

SEMUR EN AUXOIS *6G1 (3.5km S Rural) 47.46812,
4.35589* **FFCC Camping Lac de Pont,** 16 Rue du Lac,
21140 Pont-et-Massène 03 80 97 01 26 or 03 80 97 01
26 (LS); contact@camping-lacdepont.fr or camping-
lacdepont@orange.fr; www.campinglacdepont.fr

12 🐕 €2 WD ⚲ 🛒 ❄ ∥ MP ⊕ ⊤ ⊕ nr 🛒 ⛆

Exit A6 junc 23 twd Semur-en-Auxois on D980; after sh
dist turn R sp 'Lac de Pont' D103. 3*, Med, hdg, pt shd,
pt sl, EHU (6A) €3.50; gas; bbq; sw nr; phone; Eng spkn;
ccard acc; tennis; watersports; games rm; bike hire; CKE.
*"Warm welcome, helpful owners; generous pitches, some
shady; san facs dated; vg for teenagers - games/meeting
rm; 'Petit Train' goes round site & into Semur; cycle rte/
walks adj; gd touring base; nr A6 m'way; diving platform;
walled, medieval town; muddy pitches; site neglected
(2017), NH only."* €15.00 **2017**

SENNECEY LE GRAND *6H1 (7km E Rural) 46.65480,
4.94461* **Château de L'Epervière,** Rue du Château,
71240 Gigny-sur-Saône 03 85 94 16 90; info@domaine
-eperviere.com; www.domaine-eperviere.com

🐕 €3 ♿ (htd) WD ⚲ 🛒 ♿ ∥ MP 🦋 ⊕ ⊤ ⊕ 🛒 🛆 ⛆ ∥
🏊 (covrd, htd) 🖼

Fr N exit A6 junc 26 (Chalon Sud) onto N6 dir Mâcon
& Tournus; at Sennecey-le-Grand turn E onto D18 sp
Gigny-sur-Saône; site sp 1km S of Gigny-sur-Saône. Or
fr S exit A6 junc 27 (Tournus) onto N6 N to Sennecey-
le-Grand, then as above. NB Diff to find signs fr main
rd. 5*, Lge, hdstg, hdg, mkd, pt shd, EHU (6A) inc; gas;
bbq; TV; Eng spkn; adv bkg acc; ccard acc; sauna; bike
hire; tennis 400m; fishing; games rm; jacuzzi; CKE.
*"Superb, spacious, well-run site in grnds of chateau nr
sm lake; lovely, lge pitches; warm welcome, pleasant
staff; excel san facs; gd pools & rest, vg for families;
wine tasting; tour op statics; lake nrby; interesting wild
life; no o'fits over 18m high ssn; boggy when wet; conv
NH fr a'route; fantastic site; level pitches; great facs."*
€40.00, 1 Apr-30 Sep, L12. **2016**

SENNECEY LE GRAND *6H1 (5km NW Rural)
46.67160, 4.83301* **Camping La Héronnière,**
Les Lacs de Laives, 71240 Laives 03 85 44 98 85;
camping.laives@wanadoo.fr; www.camping-
laheronniere.com

🐕 €1.60 ♿ ⚲ ❄ ∥ MP 🦋 ⊕ nr 🛒 ⛆ 🏊 (htd)

Exit A6 junc 26 (fr N) or junc 27 (fr S) onto N6. Turn
W at Sennecey-le-Grand to Laives. Foll sp 'Lacs
de Laives'. Sp on D18. 3*, Med, hdg, mkd, hdstg, pt
shd, EHU (6A) €4.80; sw nr; Eng spkn; adv bkg acc;
fishing; windsurfing; bike hire; watersports; CKE.
*"Lovely, level, lakeside site; busy NH; may fill up after
1500; popular with bikers; vg; pretty site; laid back
helpful staff; gd NH; romantic rest by lakeside 3 mins
walk (high ssn); excel facs; san facs ok but dirty."*
€27.00, 3 Mar-4 Nov. **2018**

FRANCE

★★★★★

Le Sérignan Plage

yelloh! VILLAGE

Happy parents nature reserve

Between Camargue and Spain, in the heart of a region rich in colours and flavours, Yelloh! Village Le Sérignan-Plage stretches along a large sandy beach that gently plunges into the Mediterranean. In this oasis of greenery, a warm, friendly team welcomes you for family holidays with many aquatic areas, entertainment for all and quality accommodation.
An incomparable atmosphere emanates from this place, to be discovered, which has received numerous distinctions.

info@leserignanplage.com - www.leserignanplage.com
Sérignan Plage - France - Tel : +33 4 67 32 35 33

SENS *4F4 (1km S Urban) 48.18312, 3.28803*
Camp Municipal Entre Deux Vannes, Ave de Senigallia, 89100 Sens **03 86 65 64 71 or 03 86 65 37 42 (LS); http://ville-sens.fr**

D606/D1060 S of town. Take D606a sp sens. Site on R in 600m. 2*, Med, mkd, pt shd, EHU (16A) inc; adv bkg rec; ccard acc; CKE. *"Excel site; opp rv & superb park area; friendly, helpful warden; san facs old but clean; gate locked 2200; easy walk to town; ensure height barrier moved bef ent."* €13.50, 15 May-15 Sep. 2019

SERIGNAC *7D3 (5km W Rural) 44.43103, 1.06902*
Camping Le Clos Barrat (Naturist), 46700 Sérignac **06 47 50 09 78 or 04 74 24 60 82; info@leclosbarrat.fr; www.leclosbarrat.fr**

Fr Fumel by-pass turn S on D139 to Montayral, rd cont but becomes D4. Site sp bet Mauroux & St Matré. 3*, Med, mkd, pt shd, pt sl, EHU (6A) inc; own san rec; gas; bbq (gas); twin axles; TV; 2% statics; phone; Eng spkn; adv bkg acc; ccard acc; games rm; CKE. *"Nr Rv Lot; INF card req - can be bought on site; new owners (2015); helpful staff; excel & friendly site; beautiful area."* €29.00, 1 May-25 Sep. 2017

SERIGNAN PLAGE *10F1 (1km W Coastal)*
43.26398, 3.3210 **Sérignan Plage,** Les Orpelières, 34410 Sérignan-Plage **04 67 32 35 33; info@leserignanplage.com; www.leserignanplage.com**

Exit A9 junc 35. After toll turn L at traff lts onto N112 & at 1st rndabt strt on to D64. In 5km turn L onto D37E Sérignan-Plage, turn R on narr 1-way rd to site. Adj to Camping Sérignan-Plage Nature (Naturist site). 3*, V lge, mkd, hdg, pt shd, EHU (5A) inc; gas; bbq; sw; TV; 80% statics; Eng spkn; adv bkg acc; tennis; horseriding; CKE. *"Busy, even LS; excel pool; Club Nautique - sw, sailing & water-ski tuition on private beach; use of naturist private beach & facs adj; some tourers amongst statics & sm sep touring area."* €78.00, 24 Apr-28 Sept. 2019

See advertisement

SERIGNAN PLAGE *10F1* (1.6km W Coastal) *43.26308, 3.31976* **Camping Le Sérignan-Plage Nature (Naturist),** Les Orpelière, 34410 Sérignan-Plage **04 67 32 09 61; info@leserignannature.com; www.leserignannature.com**

🐕 €6 [wc] � ⚷ ⊗ 🚿 / [MP] ⚑ 🍽 ⚗ 🛒 🏪 ⚠ 🏊 ⚲ sand

Exit A9 junc 36 Beziers Est onto D64. At Sérignan town turn L on D37E to Sérignan-Plage. After 4km turn R on dual c'way. At T-junc turn L & immed L again in 50m to site. 3*, Lge, mkd, pt shd, EHU (5A) inc (poss rev pol); gas; bbq; red long stay; TV; 75% statics; Eng spkn; adv bkg rec; golf 15km; bike hire; CKE. *"Lovely, clean site & facs; max 2 dogs; helpful staff; Cmp Le Sérignan Plage (non-naturist) adj with use of same private beach & facs; pool also shared - for naturists' use 1000-1200 only; beauty cent; cycle rtes adj; excel."* **€68.00, 24 Apr-28 Sept.** 2019

SERRES *9D3* (1.4km S Rural) *44.41941, 5.71840* **Camping des Barillons,** Route de Nice, 05700 Serres **04 92 67 17 35 or 06 30 50 31 58; campingdes barillons@free.fr; campingdesbarillons.free.fr**

🐕 €1.60 [wc] ⚷ 🚿 / ⚑ 🍽 ⚗ ⚠ ⚲ (covrd, htd)

D4075 dir Sistoron fr town ctr. Sm, pt shd, EHU (6A); bbq; adv bkg acc.; CKE. *"Gd."* **€20.00, 1 Apr-30 Sep.** 2017

SERRIERES *9C2* (3km W Rural) *45.30872, 4.74622* **Camping Le Bas Larin,** 88 Route de Larin Le Bas, 07340 Félines **04 75 34 87 93 or 06 80 05 13 89 (mob); camping.baslarin@wanadoo.fr; www.camping-bas-larin.com**

🐕 ⚥ [wc] ⚷ ⅊ 🚿 / ⚑ 🍽 ⊗ 🛒 nr ⚠ 🏊 ⚲ 🍴

Exit A7 junc 12 Chanas or fr N7, exit at Serrières onto D1082; cross canal & rv; cont over rndabt up winding hill, camp on L nr hill top. Sp fr N7 & D1082, but easily missed - foll sp Safari de Peaugres. 3*, Med, shd, terr, EHU (4-10A) €2.50-3.80; 10% statics; Eng spkn; games area; games rm; CKE. *"Friendly, family-run site; beautiful views; helpful staff; easy access pitches; popular with Dutch; excel; v nice site but ent to pitches may be diff."* **€18.50, 1 Apr-30 Sep.** 2018

SEVERAC LE CHATEAU *9D1* (15km SE Rural) *44.27302, 3.21538* **Camp Municipal,** 48500 St Rome-de-Dolan **04 66 44 03 81 or 04 66 48 83 59; camping-stromededolan@orange.fr; www.saint-rome-de-dolan.com**

🐕 €0.80 ⚥ [wc] ⚷ ⅊ / 🦋 ⚑ 🍽 ⊗ nr 🛒 nr ⚠

Exit A75 junc 42 to Sévérac, then take D995 fr Séverac-le-Château then E thro Le Massegros to St Rome-de-Dolan. Site on R at ent to vill, sp. NB Rec not to use GPS. 2*, Sm, pt shd, pt sl, terr, EHU (6A); bbq; sw nr; Eng spkn; adv bkg acc; CKE. *"Simple, well-kept, well-run site in beautiful location nr Gorges du Tarn; fantastic views some pitches; friendly, helpful warden; clean san facs; some pitches sm & need mover; bird watching, inc vultures; walking; highly rec."* **€13.50, 1 May-30 Sep.** 2015

SEVERAC LE CHATEAU *9D1* (1km SW Urban) *44.31841, 3.06412* **FFCC Camping Les Calquières,** Ave Jean Moulin, 12150 Sévérac-le-Château **05 65 47 64 82; contact@camping-calquieres.com; www.camping-calquieres.com**

🐕 €1.50 ⚥ (htd) ⚷ 🚿 ♿ 🚿 / [MP] ⚑ 🍽 ⊗ 🛒 nr ⚠ ⚲ (covrd, htd)

Exit A75 junc 42 sp Sévérac & Rodez; foll 'Camping' sps to avoid narr town rds. 4*, Med, hdg, pt shd, serviced pitches; EHU (6-16A) €4.20 (poss long lead & rev pol); bbq; red long stay; 10% statics; adv bkg acc; tennis; fishing; games area; CKE. *"Lovely, spacious site with gd views; lge pitches; friendly, v helpful owners; v gd touring base & NH; conv A75; busy NH, espec w/end; gd for main holiday stay; new excel san facs (2015); vg rest; chge for wifi."* **€28.50, 1 Apr-30 Sep.** 2018

SEYNE *9D3* (0.8km S Rural) *44.34270, 6.35896* **Camping Les Prairies,** Haute Gréyère, 04140 Seyne-les-Alpes **04 92 35 10 21; info@campinglesprairies. com; www.campinglesprairies.com**

🐕 €2 ⚥ (htd) [wc] ⚷ 🚿 ♿ 🚿 / [MP] 🦋 🍽 ⊗ nr 🛒 nr ⚠ ⚲ (htd)

Fr Digne-les-Bains, take D900 N to Seyne. Turn L on ent Seyne onto D7, site sp beside Rv La Blanche. 3*, Med, mkd, pt shd, EHU (10A) €3.50; gas; bbq; phone; Eng spkn; adv bkg acc; ccard acc; tennis 300m; horseriding 500m; CKE. *"Immac, tidy, peaceful site; excel; beautifully sited and maintained; rest fr mid June; highly rec."* **€26.80, 7 May-7 Sep.** 2019

SEZANNE *4E4* (2km NW Rural) *48.72115, 3.70247* **Camp Municipal,** Route de Launat, 51120 Sézanne **03 26 80 57 00 or 03 26 80 57 00 (mob); campingdesezanne@wanadoo.fr**

🐕 €1.05 ⚥ ⚷ ♿ / ⊗ nr 🛒 nr ⚠

W'bound on N4 Sézanne by-pass onto D373 & foll site sp. Fr E turn R at 1st junc on Sézanne bypass & foll sps 'Camping & Piscine'. Avoid town cent. 2*, Med, pt shd, sl, serviced pitches; EHU (10A) inc; waterslide; CKE. *"Nice, well-kept site, v busy high ssn; generous pitches, some v sl; helpful manager; excel, immac san facs; levelling blocks req some pitches; request gate opening/closing at back bungalow of 2 opp site; nice vill; vg; well run site; pool adj; excel value; barrier clsd until 1500 unless adj pool open."* **€11.00, 1 Apr-30 Sep.** 2018

SIERCK LES BAINS *5C2* (6km SW Rural) *49.426188, 6.300037* **Camp Municipal de Malling,** 2 rue du plan d'eau 57480 Malling **03 82 50 12 97; camping.malling@orange.fr; www.malling.fr/camping**

🐕 €2 ⚥ [wc] ⚷ / 🍽 nr ⊗ nr ⅊

W of D654, well sp. Lge, mkd, pt shd, EHU 4A; bbq; sw; adv bkg acc. *"Beautifully situated between Plan d'eau and Rv Moselle; v helpful staff; v clearly sp fr D654; lovely site with wildlife on lake."* **€15.00, 1 Apr-30 Sep.** 2019

FRANCE

SIERCK LES BAINS *5C2* (1.7km W Rural) *49.44544, 6.34899* **Camp Municipal les Tilleuls,** Allée des Tilleuls, 57480 Sierck-les-Bains **03 82 83 72 39; camping@siercklesbains.fr; www.siercklesbains.fr**

Fr S on D654 turn L onto D64 sp Contz. Fr Schengen (Lux) turn L immed bef Moselle Bdge sp Contz. Well sp on banks of Moselle. 3*, Sm, hdg, mkd, pt shd, EHU (16A); bbq; Eng spkn; adv bkg acc; bike hire; CKE. *"Excel site."* **€14.00, 1 May-15 Oct.** **2019**

SIGEAN *10G1* (5km N Rural) *43.06633, 2.94100* **Camping La Grange Neuve,** 17 La Grange Neuve Nord, 11130 Sigean **04 68 48 58 70; info@camping-sigean.com; www.campingsigean.com**

sand 5km

Exit junc 39 fr A9; pass over A9 (fr N) then 1st R sp La Réserve Africaine, then turn R just bef entering Sigean sp La Grange Neuve. 3*, Med, hdstg, hdg, mkd, pt shd, pt sl, terr, EHU (6A) inc; TV; 5% statics; adv bkg acc; waterslide; CKE. *"Easy access; gd san facs; excel pool; ltd facs LS; phone ahead to check open LS; gd NH."* **€30.00** **2017**

SIGEAN *10G1* (10km S Rural) *42.95800, 2.99586* **Camping Le Clapotis (Naturist),** 11480 La Palme **04 68 48 15 40 or 05 56 73 73 73; info@leclapotis.com; www.leclapotis.com**

€2 (cont)

On D6009 S fr Narbonne turn L 8km S of Sigean. After 350m turn R at camping sp. Site in 150m. Final app rd narr but negotiable for lge vans. 2*, Lge, mkd, pt shd, EHU (4A) €4; gas; 80% statics; Eng spkn; adv bkg acc; ccard acc; games area; tennis. *"Pleasant, basic, friendly site; sm pitches; Naturists INF card req; helpful owners; san facs dated but clean; gd pool; poss strong winds - gd windsurfing; La Palme vill 15 mins walk; great location."* **€31.00, 11 Apr-10 Oct.** **2017**

SIGNY L'ABBAYE *5C1* (0.6km N Urban) *49.70123, 4.41971* **Camp Municipal de l'Abbaye,** 08460 Signy-l'Abbaye **03 24 52 87 73; mairie-signy-l.abbaye@wanadoo.fr; www.sud-ardennes-tourisme.com**

€0.60 (htd) nr nr

Take D985 N twd Belgium fr Rethel to Signy-l'Abbaye. Foll sp fr town cent to Stade & Camping. Site by sports stadium. 2*, Sm, hdstg, hdg, pt shd, pt sl, EHU (10A) €3.20 (poss rev pol); Eng spkn; adv bkg acc; rv fishing adj; CKE. *"Lovely site in gd location; friendly warden; sports cent adj; san facs excel (shared with public); strong awning pegs req on gravel hdg pitches, or can park on open grassed area."* **€6.40, 1 May-30 Sep.** **2016**

SIGOULES *7D2* (1.5km N Rural) *44.77135, 0.41076* **Camping Pomport Beach,** Route de la Gardonnette, 24240 Pomport-Sigoulès **05 24 10 61 13; info@pomport-beach.com; www.pomport-beach.com**

nr (htd)

S fr Bergerac take D933 S. After 6km at top of hill turn R by La Grappe d'Or Rest onto D17 sp Pomport/Sigoulès. Thro Pomport, site at bottom of hill on R by lake. 4*, Med, mkd, shd, pt sl, EHU (6A); bbq (charcoal, gas); sw nr; TV; 25% statics; phone; Eng spkn; adv bkg rec; ccard acc; lake; fishing; tennis; canoeing; games area; bike hire; games rm; CKE. *"Barrier ent; gd security; gd site; 2 san facs blocks, clean and up to date (2019); kids loved the site; rec."* **€37.50, 4 May-8 Sep.** **2019**

SILLE LE GUILLAUME *4F1* (3km N Rural) *48.20352, -0.12774* **Camping Indigo Les Mollières,** Sillé-Plage, 72140 Sillé-le-Guillaume **02 43 20 16 12; molieres@camping-indigo.com; www.camping-indigo.com**

(htd) (htd)

Fr Sillé-le-Guillaume take D5 N, D203 to site. 3*, Med, shd, EHU (13A) inc; sw; 10% statics; ccard acc; watersports; fishing; bike hire; games area. *"Site in pine forest; gd dog walk around lake."* **€25.00, 30 Apr-28 Sep.** **2015**

"We must tell the Club about that great site we found"

Get your site reports in by mid-August and we'll do our best to get your updates into the next edition.

SILLE LE GUILLAUME *4F1* (2km NW Rural) *48.18943, -0.14130* **Camping Les Tournesols,** Route de Mayenne, Le Grez, 72140 Sillé-le-Guillaume **02 43 20 12 69; campinglestournesols@orange.fr; www.campinglestournesols.com**

€2

Exit Sillé on D304/D35 sp Mayenne; in 2km at x-rds turn R; site in 150m on L, easily visible & sp. 3*, Med, hdg, mkd, pt shd, pt sl, EHU (6A) inc (poss long lead req); bbq (gas); sw nr; red long stay; TV; 20% statics; Eng spkn; adv bkg acc; ccard acc; bike hire; fishing 1km; CKE. *"Beautiful site; friendly owners; facs dated but spotless; rabies cert req for dogs; badminton; bouncy castle; pleasant town; canoeing 2km; mini golf; football; volleyball; jeux de boules; conv Le Mans; gd; welcoming, helpful owner; excel value; pretty, 'natural' site; onsite family owners."* **€18.00, 1 May-30 Sep.** **2016**

SILLE LE PHILIPPE *4F1* (1.4km W Rural) *48.10880, 0.33730* **Camping Le Château de Chanteloup,** Parc de l'Epau Sarl, 72460 Sillé-le-Philippe **02 43 27 51 07 or 02 43 89 66 47; chanteloup.souffront@ wanadoo.fr; www.chateau-de-chanteloup.com**

🐕€2 👫(htd) 🚐 ♿ ⚓ 🚿 🍴 ▢ ☕ 🔌 ⊕ 🦋 🎯 🛒 ⚠ 🏕

Leave A11/E50 at junc 7 Sp Le Mans Z1 Nord. After toll turn L onto N338. Foll this & turn L onto D313 sp Coulaines, Mamers & Ballon. Take D301 (at lge supmkt) & in approx 13km site is sp just after ent to Sillé-le-Philippe. Avoid cent Sillé-le-Philippe.

5*, Med, mkd, pt shd, pt sl, EHU (10A) €4 (poss rev pol); gas; bbq; twin axles; TV; Eng spkn; adv bkg acc; ccard acc; golf 10km; games area; lake fishing; games rm; horseriding 10km; CKE. *"Lovely, tranquil, spacious site in chateau grnds; pleasant, helpful staff; some pitches in wooded areas poss tight lge o'fits; gd rest; twin axles & lge o'fits by request; gd for Le Mans; sep o'night area with elec & water; rec; no facs to drain waste water fr m'van; higher charge during Le Mans events; excel san facs; clean & well maintained park."*
€46.50, 29 May-31 Aug, L13. 2019

SISTERON *10E3* (2.5km N Rural) *44.21467, 5.93643* **Camp Municipal Les Prés Hauts,** 44 Chemin des Prés Hauts, 04200 Sisteron **04 92 61 00 37 or 04 92 61 19 69; camping@sisteron.fr; www.camping-sisteron.fr**

🐕€2 👫 🚐 ♿ ⚓ 🍴 🦋 🛒 ⚠ 🏊

On W of D951. 4*, Lge, hdg, pt shd, pt sl, serviced pitches; EHU (10A) inc; Eng spkn; ccard acc; fishing; tennis; CKE. *"Lovely, well-kept, busy, excel site; excel location, gd views; lge pitches & gd for m'vans; site yourself LS; vg facs, ltd LS; interesting old town, gd mkt; conv a'route; vg; ent Barrier clsd at 2000; stunning pool; huge pitches; gd facs; friendly helpful staff; handy for m'way; 30min walk to Sisteron."*
€21.50, 1 Apr-30 Sep. 2019

SIZUN *2E2* (1km S Rural) *48.40038, -4.07635* **Camp Municipal du Gollen,** 29450 Sizun **02 98 24 11 43 or 02 98 68 80 13 (Mairie); mairie.sizun@wanadoo.fr; www.mairie-sizun.fr**

👫 🚐 🚿 🦋 🛒 nr ⚠

Fr Roscoff take D788 SW onto D69 to Landivisiau, D30 & D764 to Sizun. In Sizun take D18 at rndabt. At end of by-pass, at next rndabt, take 3rd exit. Site adj pool. 2*, Sm, pt shd, EHU (10A) €3 (poss rev pol); phone; CKE. *"Lovely little site; simple & restful by rv in nature park; friendly recep; htd pool adj high ssn; site yourself if warden not avail; vg."*
€13.50, 16 Apr-30 Sep. 2017

SOISSONS *3D4* (2km N Urban) *49.39295, 3.32701* **Camp Municipal du Mail,** 14 Ave du Mail, 02200 Soissons **03 23 74 52 69; campingdumail@gmail.com or camping@ville-soissons.fr; www.tourisme-soissons.fr**

🐕€1 👫 (htd) 🚐 ♿ ⚓ 🚿 🍴 ▢ 🦋 🎯 🛒 nr ⚠ 🏕

Fr N on D1; foll town cent sp to 1st rndabt; turn R, cross rv & immed R into Ave du Mail. Foll sp 'Camping Piscine'. Site well sp beside sw pool. Rd humps & tight ent on last 500m of access rd. (Poss to avoid tight ent by going 150m to rndabt & returning). Or fr S on D1, turn R sp Centre Ville along Ave de Château-Thiery; at 3rd rndabt turn R into Rue du Général Leclerc to Place de la Republique; cont strt over into Blvd Gambette for 500m, then turn L into Ave de l'Aisne, leading into Ave du Petit Mail; then as above.

3*, Med, hdg, mkd, hdstg, pt shd, EHU (6A) €3.15 (poss rev pol); bbq; 5% statics; phone; ccard acc; bike hire; clsd 1 Jan & 25 Dec; CKE. *"Pleasant, excel, clean & well-run site in interesting area; gd sized pitches, some nr rv; poss muddy, park on site rds in winter; m'van pitches all hdstg; helpful, friendly staff; gd clean, modern san facs, updated (2015); rvside walks/cycling; gate clsd 2200-0700; pool adj; lge mkt Wed & Sat; vg winter NH; conv for town (15mins)."*
€16.00, 2 Jan-24 Dec & 26 Dec-31 Dec. 2019

SOMMIERES *10E1* (2km SE Rural) *43.77550, 4.09280* **Camping Domaine de Massereau,** 1990 Route d'Aubais, 30250 Sommières **04 66 53 11 20 or 06 03 31 27 21 (mob); camping@massereau.com; www.massereau.com**

🐕€3.90 👫 🚐 ⚓ ♿ 🚿 🍴 ▢ 🅿 🦋 🎯 🍴 🔌 ⊕ 🛒 ⚠ 🏕 🚣 🏊

Exit A9 junc 26 at Gallargues, foll sp Sommières; site sp on D12. NB Danger of grounding at ent fr D12. Use this rte 24/7 - 03/08 (due to festival in Sommières). Otherwise exit A9 junc 27 onto D34 to Sommières, foll sps to "Centre Historique" dir Aubias; cross bdge (sharp turn) & turn R onto D12; site on L in 3km. 5*, Med, mkd, hdg, pt shd, pt sl, serviced pitches; EHU (16A) inc; gas; bbq (gas); sw nr; TV; 50% statics; phone; Eng spkn; adv bkg acc; ccard acc; games rm; jacuzzi; bike hire; waterslide; canoeing nr; sauna; games area; tennis; horseriding nr; CKE. *"Lovely, tranquil, well-run site adj vineyard; lge pitches, some uneven; pleasant, cheerful staff; running track; no o'fits over 7m high ssn; trampoline; modern san facs; narr site rds, sl/uneven pitches & trees diff lge o'fits; tight ents, diff without mover; excel; pool not htd."*
€54.80, 04 Apr-30 Sep, C33. 2019

FRANCE

SOMMIERES *10E1* (3km SE Rural) *43.76120, 4.11961*
Camping Les Chênes, Les Teullières Basses, 30250
Junas **04 66 80 99 07 or 06 03 29 36 32 (mob);**
chenes@wanadoo.fr; www.camping-les-chenes.com

🏕€4 ♀♀ WC ⚠ ♨ 🚿 🗑 🅿 ✗ 🦋 ♥ 🕭 🏕 🛶

Fr Sommières take D12 S (sp Gallargues) 3km to
junc with D140 L (N) for 1km. Site on R 300m up
side rd. Sp. 2*, Med, mkd, pt shd, pt sl, EHU (10A)
€5.40 (long lead poss req); gas; bbq (charcoal, gas);
sw nr; 10% statics; adv bkg acc; games area; sep
car park; CKE. *"Gd shd; gd san facs; friendly, helpful
staff; vg; 2km fr disused rlwy cycle track; vg site."*
€23.40, 7 Apr-14 Oct.   2018

SOMMIERES *10E1* (6km SE Urban) *43.77052,
4.12592* **Camping L'Olivier**, 112 Route de Congénies
Junas, 30250 Sommières **04 66 80 39 52; camping.
lolivier@wanadoo.fr; www.campinglolivier.fr**

🏕(€3) ♀♀ WC ⚠ ♨ 🚿 🗑 ✗ MSP 🦋 ♥ 🕭 🏕 nr 🏕 🛶 🗑

Fr Nîmes, take D40 twd Sommieres. At Congenies
take D140 L to Junas, site sp in vill. 3*, Sm, mkd, pt
shd, pt sl, EHU (6-10A) €5, poss inc on certain pitches;
cooking facs; 40% statics; phone; Eng spkn; adv bkg
acc; fishing; tennis; games area; CKE. *"Excel home
made pizzas; jazz festival in summer; elec BBQ for
hire; excel; lovely site; ping pong; entmnt (Thur eves);
trampoline; homemade jams & olive oil for sale; less
than 1km fr Nimes-Sommiere Voie Verte; mini golf;
new owners (2017)."* **€24.30, 30 Mar-20 Oct.**   2017

SOMMIERES *10E1* (0.5km NW Urban) *43.78672,
4.08702* **Camp Municipal Le Garanel**, 110 Rue
Eugène Rouché, 30250 Sommières **04 66 80 33 49;
campingmunicipal.sommieres@wanadoo.fr;
www.sommieres.fr**

🏕€2 ♀♀ (htd) WC ⚠ ♨ 🚿 🗑 ✗ MSP 🕭 nr ⓗ nr 🏕 nr 🛶

Fr S on A9 exit junc 27 N & foll D34 then take D610
twd Sommières. By-pass town on D610, over rv
bdge; turn R for D40, Rue Condamine. After L
turn for Nîmes pull out to make sharp R turn sp
'Camping Arena' (easy to miss this R turn). At T-junc
turn R, site thro car park. Fr N on D610 turn L at
4th junc sp 'Ville Vieille' & site adj rv. Site sp fr D610
fr N. NB Narr rds nr site. 2*, Sm, hdg, mkd, pt shd,
EHU (10A) inc; bbq; bus 500m; Eng spkn; adv bkg
acc; tennis adj; CKE. *"Well-kept site in great location
nr medieval town cent & rv; some open views; friendly,
helpful warden; nice sm pool; poss some workers'
statics LS; rv walks; bar 200m; Voie Verte cycle rte;
interesting town & area; site subject to flooding at any
time; mkt Sat; twin axle restrictions; diff in/out for
lge o'fits; email for avail in Jul/Aug; san facs updated
(2018)."* **€18.50, 1 Apr-30 Sep.**   2018

SONZAY *4G1* (0.5km W Rural) *47.52620, 0.45070*
Kawan Village L'Arada Parc, 88 Rue de la Baratière,
37360 Sonzay **02 47 24 72 69; info@laradaparc.com;
www.laradaparc.com**

🏕€3 ♀♀ WC ⚠ ♨ 🚿 🗑 ♿ 🅿 ✗ MSP 🦋 ♥ 🕭 🏐 ⓗ 🏕 🏕 🛶
🐕 (covrd, htd) 🏊

Fr N exit A28 junc 27 to Neuillé-Pont-Pierre; then
D766 & D6 to Sonzay; turn R in town cent. Site on
R on o'skirts immed past new houses; sp. Fr S & E
use Sat Nav. 4*, Med, mkd, hdg, pt shd, pt sl, serviced
pitches; EHU (10A) inc (poss rev pol); gas; bbq; red
long stay; TV; 15% statics; phone; bus to Tours; Eng
spkn; adv bkg acc; ccard acc; bike hire; rv fishing
500m; gym; games area; CKE. *"Peaceful, well-kept
site; spa; friendly, helpful owners & staff; clean, modern
facs; gd views; vg rest; poss diff for lge o'fits when
site full/cr; barrier clsd 2300-0800; many walks, inc in
attractive orchards; 60km fr Le Mans circuit; rec; gd
size pitches; bread to order; gd NH en route Spain."*
€36.00, 1 Apr-30 Sept.   2019

SORGUES *10E2* (7.4km NW Rural) *44.04163, 4.82493*
Camping L'Art de Vivre, Islon St Luc, 84230 Châteauneuf-
du-Pape **04 90 02 65 43; contact@camping-
artdevivre.com; www.camping-artdevivre.com**

🏕€2.50 ♀♀ WC ⚠ ♨ 🚿 🗑 ✗ MSP 🕭 🏐 ⓗ 🏕 🛶

Exit A7 junc 22 onto D907 S dir Sorgues; in 11km
(just bef Sorgues) turn R onto D17 dir Châteauneuf-
du-Pape; in 4km, bef vill, turn L at site sp; site in
1km. Site well fr D17. 2*, Med, mkd, shd, EHU (10A)
€4; bbq; Eng spkn; ccard acc; games area; games
rm. *"Site situated in woodland nr rv; new enthusiastic
owners (2011); gd walks & cycling; wine-growing
area; m'van o'night area; gd; pleasant site; gd rest."*
€26.00, 4 Apr-27 Sep.   2015

SOSPEL *10E4* (4km NW Rural) *43.89702, 7.41685*
Camping Domaine Ste Madeleine, Route de Moulinet,
06380 Sospel **04 93 04 10 48; camp@camping-
sainte-madeleine.com; www.camping-sainte-
madeleine.com**

🏕€1.50 ♀♀ WC ⚠ ♨ 🚿 🗑 ✗ MSP 🦋 🛶

Take D2566 fr Sospel NW to Turini & site 4km on
L; sp fr town. Rd to site fr Menton steep with many
hairpins. 3*, Med, mkd, shd, pt sl, terr, EHU (10A)
€2.90; gas; Eng spkn; adv bkg rec; CKE. *"Friendly, busy
site; gd pool but has no shallow end; stunning scenery;
beautifully kept site; gd, immac facs; v well run."*
€25.40, 28 Mar-3 Oct.   2018

SOUILLAC *7C3* (9km N Rural) *44.95178, 1.46547*
Camping Le Lac Rouge, 46200, Lachapelle Auzac
**06 82 92 55 67 or 06 82 92 55 67 (mob); jo.camping
lelacrouge@gmail.com**

🏕♀♀ WC ⚠ ♨ 🚿 🗑 ✗ 🕭 🏕

Fr Souillac foll D15, sp Salignac, at La Forge turn R
on D15 sp Gignac. Site on R by junc for Lhom, 500m
past golf club. Sm, pt shd, pt sl, EHU inc; bbq; twin
axles; 50% statics; adv bkg acc; games area; CKE. *"Gd
site."* **€14.00, 1 Apr-31 Oct.**   2015

SOUILLAC *7C3* (1km W Urban) *44.88895, 1.47418*
FLOWER Camping Les Ondines, Ave de Sarlat, 46200
Souillac **05 65 37 86 44 or 06 33 54 32 00; camping.
les.ondines@flowercampings.com; www.camping-
lesondines.com or www.flowercampings.com**

🏕🐕 €2 🚻 ⓌⒹ ♨ ♿ 🅿/ 🦋 ⌕ 🍴 Ⓘ nr 🍴 🎠 ⚠ ⚡ (htd)

Leave A20 junc 55. D804 then D820 to Souillac. In
cent of town turn W onto D804 to Sarlat. In 225m
turn R into Rue des Ondines. Site on R after 200m
(opp Quercyland). 3*, Lge, mkd, pt shd, EHU (6A)
inc; bbq; 10% statics; phone; Eng spkn; horseriding;
tennis; canoeing; fishing; CKE. *"Gd touring base nr rv;
helpful staff; clean facs; conv NH Rocamadour & caves;
easy access fr A20/D820; aquatic park nrby; vg; ACSI
accepted."* **€27.00, 1 May-28 Sep.** 2019

SOUILLAC *7C3* (8km NW Rural) *44.94510, 1.44140*
Domaine de la Paille Basse, 46200 Souillac
**05 65 37 85 48; info@lapaillebasse.com;
www.lapaillebasse.com**

🏕🐕 €4 🚻 ⓌⒹ ♨ ♿ 🅿/ 🅼🆂🅿 🦋 ⌕ 🍴 Ⓘ 🍴 🎠 ⚠ ⚡ 🏊 🛶

Exit Souillac by D15 sp Salignac, turn onto D165 at
Bourzolles foll sp to site in 3km. NB Narr app, few
passing places. 4*, Lge, hdg, pt shd, terr, EHU (3-10A)
€4-6; gas; bbq; TV; adv bkg acc; ccard acc; golf 5km;
tennis; bike hire; games area; waterslide. *"Excel site
in remote location; friendly, helpful staff; clean facs;
organised outdoor activities; cinema rm; some shwrs
unisex; restored medieval vill."*
€25.00, 15 May-14 Sep, D06. 2016

"There aren't many sites open at this time of year"

If you're travelling outside peak season
remember to call ahead to check site opening
dates – even if the entry says 'open all year'.

SOULAC SUR MER *7B1* (13km S Coastal) *45.41600,
-0.12930* **Centre Naturiste Euronat (Naturist),**
33590 Grayan-l'Hôpital **05 56 09 33 33;
info@euronat.fr; www.euronat.fr**

🏕🐕 €3 🚻 (htd) ⓌⒹ ♨ ♿ 🅿/ 🅼🆂🅿 🦋 ⌕ 🍴 Ⓘ 🍴 🎠 ⚠ ⚡
🏊 (covrd, htd) 🏖 sand adj

Fr Soulac, take D101 twd Montalivet, turn W at
camp sp onto rd leading direct to site. Fr Bordeaux,
take D1215 sp Le Verdon-sur-Mer. Approx 8km
after Lesparre-Médoc turn L onto D102. In Venday-
Montalivet bear R onto D101. In 7.5km turn L sp
Euronat. 4*, V lge, hdstg, mkd, shd, serviced pitches;
EHU (10A) inc; gas; bbq; TV; 30% statics; phone; Eng
spkn; adv bkg acc; bike hire; horseriding; tennis; archery;
INF card req; golf driving range. *"Expensive, but well
worth it; cinema; thalassotherapy & beauty treatment
cent; gd lge pitches, many with elec/water; shwrs basic/
dated; excel."* **€55.50, 1 Apr-29 Oct.** 2017

SOULAC SUR MER *7B1* (5km SSW Coastal) *45.480917,
-1.145109* **Sandaya Soulac Plage,** Lieu-dit l'Amelie,
33780 Soulac-sur-Mer **05 56 09 87 27; sp@sandaya.fr;
www.sandaya.co.uk**

🏕🐕 €5 🚻 (htd) ⓌⒹ ♨ ♿ 🅿/ 🅼🆂🅿 🦋 ⌕ 🍴 Ⓘ 🍴 🎠 ⚠ ⚡
🏊 (covrd, htd) 🏖 sand adj

Fr S on D1215 dir Le Verdon, turn R onto D1E4
dir Soulac-sur-Mer, in 1.8km turn R onto Av de
L'Europe sp Centre Ville & Plages. At rndabt go
R sp plages, site sp. 4*, V lge, hdg, mkd, pt shd,
EHU (10A) inc; bbq (gas); 60% statics; adv bkg acc;
sauna; tennis. *"Excel site; direct access to beach."*
€25.00, 10 Apr-13 Sep. 2019

SOULAC SUR MER *7B1* (1.5km SW Coastal)
45.49958, -1.13899 **Camping Les Sables d'Argent,**
Blvd de l'Amélie, 33780 Soulac-sur-Mer **05 56 09 82
87; sables@lelilhan.com; www.sables-d-argent.com**

🏕🐕 €2.95 🚻 ♨ 🅿/ 🍴 Ⓘ 🍴 🎠 ⚠ ⚡ 🏖 sand adj

Drive S fr Soulac twd L'Amélie-sur-Mer. Clearly
sp on R. 3*, Med, mkd, pt shd, pt sl, EHU (10A) inc
(poss long lead req); TV; 60% statics; tennis; fishing.
*"Nice area, but major erosion of coast so no access to
beach; poss diff lge o'fits; Soulac sm, lively mkt town."*
€25.00, 1 Apr-30 Sep. 2018

SOUSTONS *8E1* (6.5km NE Rural) *43.78430, -1.30473*
Camping Azu'Rivage, 720 Route des Campings,
40140 Azur **05 58 48 30 72; info@campingazurivage.
com; www.campingazurivage.com**

🏕🐕 €2 🚻 ♨ ♿ 🅿/ Ⓘ 🍴 🎠 ⚠ ⚡ 🏊 🛶

Exit m'way A10 at exit Magescq & take D150 W for
8km to Azur, site sp fr church adj La Paillotte.
3*, Med, pt shd, EHU (10A) €7.40; sw; red long stay;
TV; 80% statics; adv bkg acc; ccard acc; boating;
tennis; watersports. *"Delightful forest setting
adj lake; v busy high ssn; san facs poss stretched
high ssn; rec; lovely pool; no easy access to lake;
v few touring pitches; heavily commercialised."*
€29.00, 15 May-30 Sep. 2019

SOUSTONS *8E1* (9km W Coastal) *43.75579, -1.35384*
Camping Sandaya Souston Village, 63 Avenue
de Port d'Albret, 40140 Soustons **05 58 77 70 00;
www.sandaya.fr/nos-campings/soustons-village**

♿ Ⓘ 🍴 🎠 ⚠ ⚡ (htd, indoor) 🏖

Head S on N10. Leave at Magesq exit and head for
Soustons on D116. Then follow sp. 5*, TV; adv bkg
rec; Ccard acc; bike hire; fishing; watersports; spa;
games area; gym; cinema. **14 Apr-1 Oct.** 2019

STENAY *5C1* (0.3km W Urban) *49.49083, 5.18333*
Port de Plaisance - Motor Caravan Parking Area,
Rue du Port, 55700 Stenay **03 29 80 64 22 or
03 29 74 87 54; otsistenayaccueil@orange.fr**

12 ♨ 🅿/ 🅼🆂🅿 🦋 Ⓘ nr 🍴 nr

Off D947 fr town cent. Foll sp to rv port. NB M'vans
only. Sm, hdstg, EHU (6A) inc. *"Adj to rv; excel san
facs; NH only; sh walk to Beer Museum, rest, shop."*
€8.00 2015

STRASBOURG *6E3* (3km W Urban) *48.57537, 7.71724*
Camping Indigo Strasbourg, 9 rue de l'Auberge de
Jeunesse, 67200 Strasbourg **03 88 30 19 96; info@
camping-strasbourg.com; www.camping-
strasbourg.com**

Fr A35 exit junc 4, then foll (white) sp to Montagne
Verte. Then foll D392 to site. 4*, Lge, hdg, pt shd,
pt sl, EHU (10A); bbq; twin axles; red long stay; TV;
50% statics; bus; Eng spkn; adv bkg req; bike hire;
games area; games rm; CKE. *"Excel site; site renovated
(2015); bus/tram/cycle path to city; v busy."*
€30.00, J10. 2019

SULLY SUR LOIRE *4F3* (2km NW Rural) *47.77180,
2.36200* **Camping Le Jardin de Sully,** 1 Route Orleans,
45600 Saint-Pere-Sur-Loire **02 38 67 10 84 or 07 81
11 47 65 (mob); lejardindesully@gmail.com;
www.camping-bord-de-loire.com**

Fr N on D948 to Sully then turn R at rndabt immed
bef x-ing bdge over Rv Loire onto D60 in St Père-
sur-Loire, dir Châteauneuf-sur-Loire. Sp to site in
200m. Fr S thro Sully on D948, cross Rv Loire & turn
L at rndabt onto D60. Well sp fr town. 3*, Med, mkd,
hdstg, hdg, pt shd, serviced pitches; EHU (10-16A)
inc (poss rev pol); gas; bbq; red long stay; TV (pitch)
18% statics; phone; bus; Eng spkn; adv bkg rec; ccard
acc; tennis; bike hire; games rm; CKE. *"Pleasant, well-
kept, well laid-out site on rvside adj nature reserve;
pleasant walk along rv to town; long dist footpath
(grande randonnée) along Loire passes site; gd dog
walks; htd covrd pool 500m; gd cycling; gd winter
site & NH en rte S; recep might be clsd LS, need to
phone for barrier code ent; fairy-tale chateau in Sully;
gd loc; helpful, friendly new owner keen to bring the
standards up; excel new san fac (2018); excel; poss cr."*
€19.00 2019

SURGERES *7A2* (0.7km S Urban) *46.10180, -0.75376*
Camping de La Gères, 10 Rue de la Gères,
17700 Surgères **05 46 07 79 97 or 06 64 03 89 32
(mob); contact@campingdelageres.com;
www.campingdelageres.com**

Site sp in Surgères, on banks of Rv Gères, &
fr Surgères by-pass. 3*, Sm, mkd, hdg, shd, EHU (6A)
€3.50; bbq; phone; ccard acc; tennis 800m; CKE. *"Adj
to park; m'vans extra charge; poss travellers; excel;
park with rv walks, shops and rests via traff free walk in
town cent."* **€20.00, 12 Jan-11 Dec.** 2015

SURGERES *7A2* (13km SW Rural) *46.07123,
-0.86742* **Aire Naturelle de Loisirs,** Le Pré Marechat,
17290 Landrais **46 27 87 29 or 46 27 73 69**

Fr D911 dir Rochefort, turn R at Muron onto D112
sp Landrais. Foll camping sp (not Loisirs). Site on L
at NW end of vill. Sm, mkd, hdg, shd, bbq; twin axles;
adv bkg acc; games area. *"Delightful peaceful site conv
for La Rochells & Rochefort; site yourself & pay at Marie
or staff; vg."* **€9.50, 15 Jun-15 Sep.** 2015

SURIS *7B3* (1km N Rural) *45.85925, 0.63739*
Camping La Blanchie, 16270 Suris **05 45 89 33 19
or 06 35 43 21 39 (mob); contact@lablanchie.co.uk;
www.lablanchie.co.uk**

Fr N141 halfway bet Angoulême & Limoges take
D52 S at La Péruse to Suris; in 3km turn E up a narr
lane to site. 2*, Sm, hdstg, pt shd, pt sl, EHU (10A) €4;
bbq; sw nr; twin axles; red long stay; 10% statics; Eng
spkn; adv bkg acc; golf nr; tennis nr; CKE. *"Welcoming,
friendly British owners; clean site in lovely area;
Futuroscope nrby; ltd facs; c'van storage; gd touring
base; poor."* **€20.40, 1 Apr-30 Sep.** 2019

SURZUR *2G3* (2km NE Urban) *47.58775, -2.61913*
Camping Ty-Coët, 38 rue du Bois, 56450 Surzur
**02 97 42 09 05; contact@camping-tycoet.com;
www.camping-tycoet.com**

N165/E60 Vannes-Nantes. Take Exit 22. D183 twd
Surzur. At rndabt bef Surzur cont onto D183, then
1st L onto Rue des Lutins. Foll sp to site.
3*, Med, hdg, mkd, pt shd, EHU (16A) €3.20; bbq; sw
nr; twin axles; 30% statics; bus 0.5km; Eng spkn; adv
bkg acc; games rm; games area; CCI. *"BBQ except
Jul & Aug; conv for Golfe de Morbihan; gd mkt in
Vannes (Sat & Tue); lovely, quiet, well-kept site with
super clean san facs; excel; gd touring area; v pleasant
warden."* **€18.60, 1 Mar-15 Nov.** 2015

TAGNIERE, LA *6H1* (2km SW Rural) *46.77728,
3.56283* **Camping Le Paroy,** 71190 La Tagnière
**03 85 54 59 27 or 603 56 64 82 (mob); info@
campingleparoy.com; www.campingleparoy.com**

Fr Autun SW on D681, after 11km S on D994.
3km after Etang L onto D224 to La Tagniere
and foll sp. Sm, hdg, pt shd, terr, EHU (10A) €4;
bbq; twin axles; TV; Eng spkn; adv bkg acc; bike
hire; CKE. *"Fishing at Sm adj lake; takeaway; vg."*
€23.00, 1 Apr-30 Sep. 2015

TAIN L'HERMITAGE *9C2* (5km NE Rural) *45.10715, 4.89105* **Camping Chante-Merle,** 26600 Chantemerle-les-Blés **04 75 07 49 73; campingchantemerle@wanadoo.fr; www.campingchante-merle.fr**

🐕 12 €2 ♦♦(htd) WD ▥ ♿ ⬛ ⤋ ✈ ☂ ♍ ▽ ⑪ ⬛ ♨ nr ⌂ ⛵

Exit A7 at Tain-l'Hermitage. After exit toll turn L twd town, next turn R (D109) to Chantemerle; site sp. Cont for 5km, site on L. 3*, Sm, hdg, mkd, pt shd, serviced pitches; EHU (10A) €4.50; 10% statics; adv bkg req; tennis 500m; site clsd Jan; CKE. *"Helpful manager; popular site; excel facs."* **€23.00** **2017**

TAIN L'HERMITAGE *9C2* (1.4km S Urban) *45.06727, 4.84880* **Camp Municipal Les Lucs,** 24 Ave du Président Roosevelt, 26600 Tain-l'Hermitage **04 75 08 32 82; camping.tainlhermitage@orange.fr; www.camping-tain.fr/en**

🐕 €1.40 ♦♦(htd) WD ▥ ♿ ⬛ ⤋ ✈ ♍ ⑪ nr ♨ nr ⌂

Fr N or S exit A7 junc 13 dir Tain-l'Hermitage onto N7. Cont N twd town cent; at fuel stn on R & Netto supmkt sp prepare to turn L in 80m; ent to site in 35m. Fr N on N7 prepare to turn R after fuel stn on R. Site alongside Rv Rhône via gates (locked o/night). Well sp adj sw pool/petrol stn. 3*, Med, mkd, hdstg, hdg, pt shd, EHU (6A) inc (poss rev pol); phone; Eng spkn; CKE. *"Pretty, well-kept, well-run site by Rhône; lovely views; secure site; friendly staff; excel, clean san facs; no twin axles, no c'vans over 5.5m & no m'vans over 6m (poss high ssn only); rvside walk to town; Valrhona chocolate factory shop nrby; mkt Sat; gd touring base; popular NH; highly rec; access gate with PIN; v sm pitches."* **€22.00, 1 Mar-31 Oct.** **2019**

TALMONT SAINT HILAIRE *7A1* (8km WSW Coastal) *46.451713, -1.702118* **Camping Sandaya Le Littoral,** Le Porteau 85440, Talmont-St-Hilaire **02 51 22 04 64; www.sandaya.fr/nos-campings/le-littoral**

🐕 ♦♦(htd) WD ▥ ♿ ⬛ ⤋ ✈ ☂ ♍ ▽ ⑪ ⬛ ⌂ ♨ ⛵(htd) ⊞

🏕 shgl

Fr Talmont-St-Hilaire to Les Sables d'Olonne on D949. Turn L after racecourse. Site sp. 5*, Mkd, pt shd, EHU 10A; gas; bbq (elec, gas); twin axles; Eng spkn; adv bkg rec; ccard acc; bike hire; fishing; scuba diving; games rm; security. **€56.00, 5 Apr-7 Sep.** **2019**

TANINGES *9A3* (1km S Rural) *46.09899, 6.58806* **Camp Municipal des Thézières,** Les Vernays-sous-la-Ville, 74440 Taninges **04 50 34 25 59; camping.taninges@wanadoo.fr**

🐕 12 €1.30 ♦♦(htd) WD ▥ ♿ ⬛ ⤋ ✈ ♍ ☂ ▽ nr ⑪ ♨ ⌂

Take D902 N fr Cluses; site 1km S of Taninges on L - just after 'Taninges' sp on ent town boundary; sp Camping-Caravaneige. 2*, Lge, pt shd, EHU (6-10A) €2.50-4; bbq; TV; phone; Eng spkn; ccard acc; tennis; CKE. *"Splendid site with magnificent views; pool at Samoens 11km; peaceful & well-kept; lge pitches; friendly, helpful staff; excel facs; conv for N Haute Savoie & Switzerland to Lake Geneva; excel; wooded site; bit of rd noise."* **€13.40** **2017**

TARASCON *10E2* (5km SE Rural) *43.76744, 4.69331* **Camping St Gabriel,** Route de Fontvieille, 13150 Tarascon **04 90 91 19 83; contact@campingsaintgabriel.com; www.campingsaintgabriel.com**

🐕 €2 ♦♦(htd) WD ▥ ♿ ⬛ ⤋ MSP ✈ ♍ ▽ ⑪ ⬛ ♨ ⌂ ⛵(htd)

Take D970 fr Tarascon, at rndabt take D33 sp Fontvieille, site sp 100m on R. 3*, Med, hdg, shd, EHU (6A) €3.3; gas; TV; 30% statics; adv bkg acc; games rm; site clsd mid-Feb & Xmas/New Year; rv fishing; CKE. *"Well-kept, charming site; excel base for Camargue & Arles; modern san facs; sm pitches poss not suitable lge o'fits; gd; 10 min walk into cent."* **€27.00, 14 Mar-14 Nov.** **2016**

TARASCON SUR ARIEGE *8G3* (2km SE Rural) *42.83981, 1.61215* **Kawan Village Le Pré-Lombard,** Route d'Ussat, 09400 Tarascon-sur-Ariège **05 61 05 61 94; leprelombard@wanadoo.fr; www.prelombard.com**

🐕 €4 ♦♦(htd) WD ▥ ♿ ⬛ ⤋ MSP ✈ ☂ ♍ ▽ ⑪ ⬛ ♨ ⌂ ✎ ⛵(htd) ⊞

Travelling S twd Andorra join N20 to Tarascon. Approx 17km S of Foix after 3 rndabts & x-ing a bdge, at 4th rndabt turn L, after rlwy on D618 foll site sp. This rte avoids cent of Tarascon. 4*, Lge, hdg, mkd, pt shd, EHU (10A) inc; gas; bbq; sw nr; TV; 50% statics; Eng spkn; adv bkg rec; ccard acc; rv fishing adj; games rm; bike hire; archery; tennis; CKE. *"Busy, well-run, family site in lovely location by rv; spacious pitches; helpful owner; san facs tired (2015), poss stretched high ssn; no o'fits over 6m; plenty for teenagers to do; canyoning & climbing nrby; gd base for exploring area; excel winter NH en rte to Spain; kayaking adj; poss rallies LS; excel; nice walk to town."* **€38.60, 2 Mar-4 Oct.** **2015**

TARASCON SUR ARIEGE *8G3* (3km SW Rural) *42.81311, 1.58908* **Camping Les Grottes,** Dumaines de la Hille, 09400 Alliat **05 61 05 88 21; info@campingdesgrottes.com; www.campingdesgrottes.com**

🐕 €2 ♦♦(htd) WD ▥ ⤋ ✈ MSP ♍ ▽ ⑪ nr ⬛ ♨ ⌂ ⛵(htd) ⊞

S fr Foix on N20 dir Andorra, turn R onto D8 just past Tarascon-sur-Ariège sp Niaux/Vicdessos. Site on R in 2km. 3*, Med, hdg, hdstg, mkd, pt shd, EHU (6-10A) €2; TV; 20% statics; phone; adv bkg acc; waterslide; games area. *"Lovely, peaceful site in valley; ideal NH for Andorra or long stay; Miglos Castle & Niaux cave nr; excel modern san facs; excel."* **€28.00, 1 Mar-15 Oct.** **2017**

TARDETS SORHOLUS *8F1* (1km S Rural) *43.11143, -0.86362* **Camping du Pont d'Abense,** 64470 Tardets-Sorholus **05 59 28 58 76 or 06 78 73 53 59 (mob); camping.abense@wanadoo.fr; www.camping-pontabense.com**

🐕 12 €2 ♦♦ WD ⬛ ⤋ ✈ ♍ ☂ nr ⑪ ♨ nr

Take D918 S to Tardets, turn R to cross bdge onto D57. Site sp on R. Tardets cent narr. 2*, Med, shd, EHU (3A) €3.20; 10% statics; adv bkg acc; rv fishing nr; CKE. *"Informal pitching; facs old; gd birdwatching; lovely, quaint site, a gem; nr gorges; heavenly!"* **€26.00** **2017**

TEICH, LE *7D1* (1.8km W Rural) *44.63980, -1.04272*
Camping Ker Helen, Ave de la Côte d'Argent, 33470
Le Teich 05 56 66 03 79; camping.kerhelen@
wanadoo.fr; www.kerhelen.com

†⁺(htd) ⊞ ⚓ ♿ ⚓ ⚐ / ⛟ ⛲ ☂ ⛱ (⋅) ⏛ ⚑ ⚓

Fr A63 take A660 dir Arcachon & exit junc 2 onto D3
then D650 thru Le Teich. Site sp on L.
3*, Med, hdg, pt shd, EHU (10A) €3.70; TV;
75% statics; adv bkg acc; canoeing; horseriding; CKE.
*"Less cr than coastal sites in Arcachon region; bird
reserve nrby; vg; rest and snacks bar only open in July
and August."* €25.30, 16 Apr-16 Oct.   **2015**

TELGRUC SUR MER *2E2* (1km S Coastal) *48.22386,
-4.37223* **Camping Le Panoramic,** 130 Route de la
Plage, 29560 Telgruc-sur-Mer 02 98 27 78 41;
info@camping-panoramic.com; www.camping-
panoramic.com

⛟ €4 †⁺ ⊞ ⚓ ♿ ⚓ ⚐ / ⛟ ⛲ ☂ ⛱ (⋅) ⚑ ⏛ ⚓(htd)
⚐ ⛱ sand 700m

Fr D887 Crozon-Châteaulin rd, turn W on D208 twd
Trez-Bellec Plage, site sp on R in approx 1.5km.
4*, Med, hdg, mkd, pt shd, terr, EHU (6-10A) inc;
bbq; TV; 10% statics; adv bkg acc; ccard acc; jacuzzi;
bike hire; tennis; games rm; CKE. *"Vg, well-run,
welcoming site; access to pitches poss diff due trees
& narr site rds; rec; some facs tired need updating;
sea views; excel rest, pool & all facs; helpful owner."*
€26.50, 1 May-15 Sep.   **2019**

THANN *6F3* (9km NW Rural) *47.85071, 7.03058*
FFCC Camping La Mine d'Argent, Rue des Mines,
68690 Moosch 03 89 82 30 66 or 03 89 60 34 74;
moosch@camping-la-mine-argent.com;
www.camping-la-mine-argent.com

⛟ €0.60 †⁺ ⊞ ⚓ ⚐ / ⛟ ☂ ⚓nr ⏛

Turn L off N66 Thann-Thillot rd in cent of Moosch
opp church; foll sps for 1.5km, ent on R, narr app.
2*, Med, mkd, pt shd, pt sl, terr, EHU (6-10A) €3-
5.60; gas; 10% statics; phone; adv bkg acc; ccard
acc; CKE. *"Well-kept site in wooded valley; busy
w/end; helpful staff; excel walking; highly rec."*
€12.50, 5 Apr-15 Oct.   **2015**

THENON *7C3* (3km SE Rural) *45.11883, 1.09119*
Camping Le Verdoyant, Route de Montignac,
24210 Thenon 05 53 05 20 78; contact@camping
leverdoyant.fr; www.campingleverdoyant.fr

⛟ €1.75 †⁺ ⊞ ⚓ ♿ ⚓ ⚐ / ⛟ ⛲ ☂ ⛱ (⋅) ⚓nr ⏛

Sp fr A89, take D67 fr Thenon to Montignac.
Site on R in 4km. 3*, Med, mkd, pt shd, sl, terr,
EHU (10A) inc; gas; 20% statics; Eng spkn; adv bkg
acc; lake fishing; CKE. *"Beautiful setting away fr
tourist bustle; friendly owners; excel base for area."*
€20.20, 4 Apr-30 Sep.   **2019**

THIEZAC *7C4* (0.5km E Rural) *45.01360, 2.67027*
Camping La Bédisse, 3 Rue de la Bédisse, 15800
Thiézac 0471 47 00 41; camping.thiezac@orange.
fr; camping-thiezac.pagesperso-orange.fr

⏱ ⚓ ♿ ⚓ ⚐ / ⛟ ⛱ ⚑ ⏛

Fr Murat, take N122 twds Vic sur Cere & Aurillac. In
approx 24km foll sp to Thiezac. Site posted fr vill
cent. EHU €4; bbq; sw; twin axles; 10% statics; Eng
spkn; adv bkg acc; games area; CKE. *"Tennis court;
lovely rvside site; sh uphill walk to vill & shops; view of
mountains; gd walks; rec; excel."* €13.00   **2016**

THILLOT, LE *6F3* (3.7km NNE Rural) *47.90694,
6.78138* **Camping l'Oree du Bois,** 51 Bis Grande
Rue, 88160 Le Ménil 03 29 25 04 88; contact@
loree-du-bois.fr; www.loree-du-bois.fr

⏱ ⚓ €1 †⁺ ⊞ ♿ ⚓ ⚐ / ⛟ (⋅) ⏛

Fr N66 bet Ramonchamp & St Maurice, in Le Thillot
turn L (N) on D486. After 3km ent Le Menil. In middle
of vill, immed opp church turn L to enter site behind
hse selling honey. Gd sp after Le Thillot.
Sm, unshd, terr, EHU (10A) €5; 75% statics; phone; bus;
Eng spkn; adv bkg acc; games rm; games area; CKE. *"Gd
walking & cycling, mkd trails fr site; htd pool adj; access
to winter sports nrby; vg."* €18.00   **2015**

THIONVILLE *5C2* (0.5km NE Urban) *49.36127,
6.17534* **Camp Municipal Touristique,** 6 Rue du
Parc, 57100 Thionville 03 82 53 83 75; camping.
municipal@mairie-thionville.fr; www.thionville.
fr/fr/content/camping-municipal-touristique-1

⛟ €1.20 †⁺ ⊞ ⚓ ♿ ⚐ / ⛟ ⛱ ☂nr (⋅)nr ⚓nr ⏛

Exit A31 at sp Thionville Cent; foll sp 'Centre Ville';
foll site sp dir Manom. 2*, Sm, hdstg, mkd, pt shd,
EHU (3-10A) €2.40-4.65; red long stay; Eng spkn;
adv bkg acc; fishing; boating; CKE. *"Well-kept site;
some rvside pitches which can be noisy in eve; friendly
warden; gd san facs; rec arr early high ssn; 5 min walk
thro lovely adj park to town; vg; walk alongside rv as
adj."* €16.50, 1 May-30 Sep.   **2017**

THIVIERS *7C3* (7km N Rural) *45.47390, 0.93808*
Camping La Petite Lande, Lieu-dite La Petitie Lande,
24800 St Jory-de-Chalais 09 64 44 82 79; info@
la-petite-lande.com; www.la-petite-lande.com

⏱ ⚓ €1 †⁺(htd) ⊞ ⚓ ♿ ⚐ / ⛟ ☂ (⋅)nr ⚓nr ⏛ ⚓

N fr Thiviers on D21; in 6km turn L after La Poste
onto unclassified rd sp 'La Petite Lande' campsite;
foll sps to site in 500m. Sm, unshd, EHU (6-10A)
€3.75; bbq; Eng spkn; ccard acc. *"Relaxing, CL-type
site; new site (2011); helpful Dutch owners; vg, clean
facs plans to expand."* €11.00   **2016**

FRANCE

THIVIERS 7C3 (2km E Rural) 45.41299, 0.93209
Camping Le Repaire, Ave de Verdun, 24800 Thiviers
05 53 52 69 75; contact@camping-le-repaire.fr;
www.camping-le-repaire.fr

N21 to Thiviers; at rndabt take D707 E dir
Lanouaille; site in 1.5km on R. 3*, Med, mkd, hdg,
pt shd, pt sl, terr, EHU (12A) €3; bbq; TV; 5% statics;
phone; Eng spkn; adv bkg acc; games rm; lake fishing;
CKE. "Lovely site, one of best in area; friendly owners;
clean san facs; some pitches unrel in wet weather;
excel; v nice tree shd plots."
€20.00, 1 Apr-4 Nov. 2017

"That's changed – Should I let the Club know?"

If you find something on site that's different
from the site entry, fill in a report and let us
know. See camc.com/europereport.

THONNANCE LES MOULINS 6E1 (2km W Rural)
48.40630, 5.27110 **Camping La Forge de Ste
Marie,** 52230 Thonnance-les-Moulins 03 25 94
42 00; info@laforgedesaintemarie.com; www.
laforgedesaintemarie.com or www.les-castels.com

Fr N67 exit sp Joinville-Est, foll D60 NE sp
Vaucouleurs. In 500m turn R onto D427 sp Poissons
& Neufchâteau. Site on R in 11km. NB Swing wide
at turn into site fr main c'way, not fr what appears
to be a run in. Site ent narr. 5*, Lge, hdg, mkd, pt shd,
pt sl, terr, serviced pitches; EHU (6A) inc; gas; bbq;
TV; 25% statics; phone; Eng spkn; adv bkg acc; ccard
acc; games rm; bike hire; boating; lake fishing; games
area; CKE. "Vg, well-kept, busy site; friendly, helpful
owners; freshwater fishing; access poss diff to some
terr pitches/sharp bends on site rds; muddy after rain;
vg rest; no o'fits over 8m; mkt Fri; lovely spacious, well
run site, beautiful area; swing wide at ent; poss no mob
phone recep; san facs fair."
€40.00, 18 Apr-4 Sep, J04. 2015

THONON LES BAINS 9A3 (3km NE Rural) 46.39944,
6.50416 **Camping Le Saint Disdille,** 117 Ave de St
Disdille, 74200 Thonon-Les-Bains 04 50 71 14 11;
camping@disdille.com; www.disdille.com

Exit A41/A40 junc 14 Annemasse onto D1005
& foll sp Thonon twd Evian. At Vongy rndabt
foll sp St Disdille & site. Site 200m fr Lake
Geneva. 3*, V lge, mkd, shd, EHU (6-10A) €4;
gas; bbq; sw nr; 30% statics; adv bkg req; ccard
acc; fishing; watersports; tennis; games area;
bike hire; games rm; CKE. "Well-situated; well-
equipped site; gd touring base for v nice area."
€33.50, 1 Apr-30 Sep. 2019

See advertisement

THONON LES BAINS 9A3 (13km W Rural) 46.35638,
6.35250 **Campéole Camping La Pinède,** 74140
Excenevex 04 50 72 85 05 or 04 50 72 81 27
(Mairie); pinede@campeole.com; www.camping-
lac-leman.info or www.campeole.com

sand adj

On D1005 to Geneva, 10km fr Thonon, turn R
at Camping sp. 3*, V lge, mkd, shd, EHU (10A)
€4.10; gas; bbq; sw nr; TV; 75% statics; adv
bkg acc; horseriding 1km; games area; tennis;
watersports adj; fishing adj. "Excel lakeside site;
friendly & efficient staff; ltd touring emplacements."
€30.00, 28 Apr-30 Sep. 2016

"I like to fill in the reports as I travel from site to site"

You'll find report forms at the back of this
guide, or you can fill them in online at
camc.com/europereport.

FRANCE

THURY HARCOURT *3D1* (0.9km NE Rural) *48.98930, -0.46966* **FFCC Camping Vallée du Traspy,** Rue du Pont Benoît, 14220 Thury-Harcourt **02 31 29 90 86; contact@campingdutraspy.com; www.camping dutraspy.com**

🅟 €2.90 👪 �🔲 ⛺ ♨ ♿ 🍽 ⋪ 🦋 🍸 🛒 nr ⚠ ✦

App fr N on D562 fr Caen, take L fork into town after pool complex. In 100m turn L at Hôtel de la Poste, 1st L to site, clearly sp adj Rv Orne. 3*, Med, mkd, pt shd, terr, EHU (4A) inc; gas; bbq; 20% statics; phone; Eng spkn; adv bkg rec; fishing; canoeing; CKE. *"Friendly owners; well-maintained pitches; o'night m'vans area; gd walking; site under new management with some refurbishment (2014); rec."* **€25.00, 1 Apr-30 Sep.** **2019**

TIL CHATEL *6G1* (2km E Rural) *47.53042, 5.18700* **Camping Les Sapins,** 21120 Til-Châtel **03 80 95 16 68; www.restaurantlessapins.eresto.net**

👪 ⛺ ♿ ⋪ 🦋 🛒 nr

Leave A31 junc 5 onto D974 dir Til-Châtel. Site on R in 500m adj Rest Les Sapins. 1*, Sm, pt shd, pt sl, serviced pitches; EHU (10A) inc; Eng spkn; adv bkg acc; CKE. *"Clean, CL type site; basic san facs; no twin axles; conv NH fr a'route."* **€16.50, 1 Apr-30 Sep.** **2016**

TINTENIAC *2E4* (0.5km N Rural) *48.33111, -1.83315* **Camp Municipal du Pont L'Abbesse,** Rue du 8 Mai 1945, 35190 Tinténiac **02 99 68 09 91 or 02 99 68 02 15 (Mairie)**

👪 (htd) ⛺ ♿ ⋪ 🦋 🍸 nr 🕧 nr 🛒 nr ⚠

Fr D137 turn E onto D20 to Tinténiac; go strt thro vill to canal; sp just bef canal bdge; turn L. Site behind Brit Hôtel La Guinguette, on Canal d'Ille et Rance. 2*, Sm, hdg, mkd, pt shd, pt sl, EHU inc; 10% statics; fishing; CKE. *"Delightful, busy site; gd san facs; lovely walks/cycling along canal; vg; unreliable end of ssn closing; clsd at night by barrier; NH."* **€10.00, 1 Mar-30 Sep.** **2017**

TINTENIAC *2E4* (2km S Rural) *48.31058, -1.82027* **Camping Les Peupliers,** Manoir de la Besnelais, 35190 Tinténiac **02 99 45 49 75; contact@domaine lespeupliers.fr; www.domainelespeupliers.fr**

🐕 €1.60 👪 �🔲 ⛺ ♨ ♿ 🍽 ⋪ 🗺 ♔ 🍸 🕧 🚲 🛒 nr ⚠ 🛶 (htd)

On D137 Rennes to St Malo rd; after Hédé foll rd to Tinténiac about 2km; site on main rd on R, sp. 3*, Med, hdg, mkd, pt shd, pt sl, EHU (6A) €2.90 (poss rev pol); TV; 30% statics; phone; adv bkg acc; games area; tennis; lake fishing; CKE. *"Pleasant, quiet, well-kept site; gd pool & park; on pilgrim rte to Spain; conv for acc to canal."* **€25.50, 1 Apr-1 Oct.** **2018**

TONNERRE *4F4* (1.5km NE Urban) *47.86003, 3.98429* **Camp Municipal de la Cascade,** Ave Aristide Briand, 89700 Tonnerre **03 86 55 15 44 or 03 86 55 22 55 (Mairie); ot.tonnerre@wanadoo.fr; www.tonnerre.fr (NO LONGER ACTIVE)**

👪 (htd) ⛲ ⛺ ♨ ♿ 🍽 ⋪ 🗺 ♔ 🍸 🛒 ⚠ ✦

Best app via D905 (E by-pass); turn at rndabt twd town cent L after x-ing 1st rv bdge. Foll site sp to avoid low bdge (height 2.9m, width 2.4m). On banks of Rv Armançon & nr Canal de l'Yonne, 100m fr junc D905 & D944. 2*, Med, pt shd, EHU 3 euros; bbq; sw nr; TV; 10% statics; Eng spkn; adv bkg acc; ccard acc; fishing; CKE. *"Pleasant, spacious, shady site in arboretum; friendly warden; lge pitches; excel clean san facs; often damp underfoot; no twin axles; interesting town; gd cycling/walking along canal; conv site; excel."* **€15.00, 6 Apr-13 Oct.** **2019**

TORIGNI SUR VIRE *1D4* (1km S Rural) *49.02833, -0.97194* **Camping Le Lac des Charmilles,** Route de Vire, 50160 Torigni-sur-Vire **02 33 75 85 05 or 06 09 35 29 94; contact@camping-lacdescharmilles. com; www.camping-lacdescharmilles.com**

🐕 €3 👪 (htd) ⛺ ♨ ♿ 🍽 ⋪ 🗺 ♔ 🍸 🕧 🚲 🛒 ⚠ 🛶 (htd)

Exit A84 junc 40 onto D974 dir Torigni-sur-Vire/St Lô; site on R in 4km. Opp municipal stadium. 3*, Med, hdstg, mkd, hdg, pt shd, pt sl, EHU (10A) inc (long lead poss req); gas; bbq; sw nr; twin axles; TV; 30% statics; phone; Eng spkn; adv bkg acc; ccard acc; games area; bike hire; games rm; CKE. *"Lovely, well-kept, well-laid out site; clean, modern san facs, new shwr (2016); attractive, interesting town; excel; excel shopping in the town within walking dist; v helpful,friendly new owner (2016); picturesque lakes; tree-lined walks."* **€31.00, 1 Apr-30 Sep.** **2019**

TORREILLES PLAGE *10G1* (0.9km N Coastal) *42.76750, 3.02972* **Camping Sunêlia Les Tropiques,** Blvd de la Méditerranée, 66440 Torreilles-Plage **04 68 28 05 09; contact@campinglestropiques.com; www.camping lestropiques.com**

🐕 €4 👪 ⛺ ♨ ♿ 🍽 ⋪ 🗺 ♔ 🍸 🕧 🚲 🛒 ⚠ ✦ 🛶 🖐

🏖 sand 400m

Exit A9 junc 41 onto D83 E dir Le Barcarès, then D81 dir Canet-Plage. At 1st rndabt turn L onto D11 sp Torreilles-Plage, site sp. 4*, Lge, mkd, hdg, shd, EHU (6A) inc; gas; red long stay; TV; 80% statics; Eng spkn; ccard acc; waterslide; gym; bike hire; tennis; games area; CKE. *"Vg family site; excel leisure & san facs."* **€48.50, 9 Apr-1 Oct.** **2017**

TOUCY *4F4* (0.7km S Urban) *47.73159, 3.29677* **Camping des Quatre Merlettes,** Rue du Pâtis, 89130 Toucy **03 86 44 13 84; 4merlettestoucy@orange.fr; www.ville-toucy.fr/public/?code=camping-municipal**

👪 ⛺ ♿ ⋪ 🗺 🛒 nr 🛶 (htd)

On D3, 25km SW of Auxerre to Toucy. After rv x-ing take 1st L sp 'Base de Loisirs'. Site on S bank of Rv Quanne. 2*, Med, pt shd, EHU (8A) €3.50; 10% statics; adv bkg acc; fishing. *"Pleasant vill; pleasant, helpful warden; no twin axles; mkt Sat; rests in walking dist; gd."* **€12.00, 1 Apr-14 Oct.** **2016**

TOUL *6E2* (10km E Rural) *48.65281, 5.99260*
Camping de Villey-le-Sec, 34 Rue de la Gare, 54840 Villey-le-Sec **03 83 63 64 28; info@camping villeylesec.com; www.campingvilleylesec.com**

🏕 €1.80 ♨ WD ⚒ ♿ 🚿 ✉ MP ❄ 🦋 🍴 ⓖ ♨ 🛒 ⚠

Exit Toul E on D909 or exit A31 junc 15 ondo D400 (W, in dir Hôpital Jeanne d'Arc); at rndabt turn L onto D909 to Villey-le-Sec; in vill site S by Rv Moselle, sp. V steep app rd. 3*, Med, hdg, mkd, hdstg, pt shd, EHU (6-10A) €3.70-4.50; gas; bbq; red long stay; phone; Eng spkn; ccard acc; games area. *"Peaceful, well-kept site on rvside; lovely location; lge pitches; friendly; vg san facs, poss stretched; gd cycle paths; popular NH, ess arr bef 1800 high ssn."* **€22.00, 1 Apr-15 Oct.** 2015

TOULOUSE *8F3* (5km N Urban) *43.65569, 1.41585*
Camping Toulouse Le Rupé, 21 Chemin du Pont de Rupé, 31200 Toulouse **05 61 70 07 35; campingle rupe31@wanadoo.fr; www.camping-toulouse.com**

12 🏕 €1.50 ♨ (htd) WD ⚒ ♿ 🚿 ✉ MP ❄ 🍴 ⓖ ♨ 🛒 ⚠

N fr Toulouse on D820, sp. Poss tricky app fr N for long vans, suggest cont past Pont de Rupé traff lts to next rndabt & double back to turn. Fr S on ring rd exit junc 33A (after junc 12), turn immed R & foll sp. 3*, Lge, hdg, mkd, hdstg, pt shd, EHU (10A) inc; TV; 50% statics; phone; bus; Eng spkn; ccard acc; games rm; lake fishing; CKE. *"If site clsd 1200-1500, park in layby just bef site & use speakerphone; gd clean san facs; rock pegs poss req; ssn workers camp opp but no probs, site security excel; conv Airbus factory tours; space theme park 10km; well maintained; v helpful staff; ideal for dogs, children or walkers."* **€27.20** 2019

TOUQUET PARIS PLAGE, LE *3B2* (2km S Coastal)
50.51091, 1.58867 **Camping Caravaning Municipal Stoneham,** Ave François Godin, 62520 Le Touquet-Paris-Plage **03 21 05 16 55; caravaning. stoneham@letouquet.com; www.letouquet.com**

🏕 €2 ♨ ⚒ ✉ 🛒 nr ⚠ 🏖 sand 1km

Fr Etaples on D939; stay in L-hand lane at traff lts dir airport & cont strt on (Ave du Général de Gaulle); L at traff lts sp Golf (Ave du Golf); foll rd to rndabt; turn R onto Ave François Godin (site sp); at next rndabt site on R. Or cont another 500m along Ave du Général de Gaulle to x-rds; turn L into Ave Louis Quetelart; in 500m at T-junc turn L into Ave François Godin; site on L in 200m. 2*, Lge, hdg, mkd, pt shd, EHU (16A) €5.80 (poss rev pol); 82% statics; adv bkg rec; ccard acc; CKE. *"Pleasant & well kept site; conv for town; helpful staff; excel facs; recep closes 1800 (LS 2010); htd pool 2km; m'van 'aires' nr harbour & equestrian cent; mkt Thu/Sat; walking & cycle paths to South Beach; town has many rest; gd sh stay."* **€26.40, 2 Feb-15 Nov.** 2017

TOUQUIN *4E4* (2.5km W Rural) *48.73305, 3.04697*
Camping Les Etangs Fleuris, Route de la Couture, 77131 Touquin **01 64 04 16 36; contact@etangs-fleuris.com; www.etangsfleuris.com**

🏕 €1.50 ♨ (htd) WD ⚒ ✉ ❄ 🦋 ♨ 🍴 ♨ 🛒 ⚠ 🚴 🏊 (htd) ⛵

On D231 fr Provins, turn R to Touquin. Turn sharp R in vill & foll sp to site on R in approx 2km. Or fr Coulommiers, take D402 SW twd Mauperthuis, after Mauperthuis L twd Touquin. Foll sp in vill. NB Beware two unmkd speed bumps on entering vill. 3*, Med, hdstg, mkd, hdg, pt shd, EHU (10A) inc; gas; bbq; TV; 20% statics; phone; adv bkg acc; ccard acc; games rm; fishing; games area; CKE. *"Peaceful site; no twin axles high ssn; conv Paris & Disneyland; helpful, supportive staff; no noise after 11pm."* **€30.00, 13 Apr-14 Sep.** 2019

"We must tell the Club about that great site we found"

Get your site reports in by mid-August and we'll do our best to get your updates into the next edition.

TOURNON SUR RHONE *9C2* (0.4km N Rural)
45.07000, 4.83000 **FFCC Camping de Tournon HPA,** 1 Promenade Roche-de-France, 07300 Tournon-sur-Rhône **04 75 08 05 28; camping@ camping-tournon.com; www.camping-tournon.fr**

12 🏕 €2 ♨ (htd) WD ⚒ ♿ 🚿 ✉ MP 🍴 nr ♨ ⓖ nr 🛒 nr ⚠

Fr Tain l'Hermitage cross Rhône, turn R onto D86; in approx 1km R at end of car park; turn L after 50m, site on R on Rv Rhône. Or fr N on D86, sp on L by car park. 3*, Med, shd, EHU (6-10A) €4-6.50; gas; red long stay; 10% statics; phone; Eng spkn; adv bkg rec; canoeing; CKE. *"Pleasant, well-kept site in wooded location; rvside pitches; friendly owners; clean, dated san facs (unisex LS); m'van o'night area; c'van storage avail; some sm pitches & narr site rds poss diff lge o'fits; gd security; footbdge to Tain-l'Hermitage; fr mid-Jun rock concerts poss held nrby at w/end; gd; conv NH; interesting old town."* **€24.00** 2016

TOURNON SUR RHONE *9C2* (6km N Rural)
45.12116, 4.80023 **FFCC Camping L'Iserand,** Rue Royal, 07610 Vion **04 75 08 01 73; camping@ iserand.com; www.iserandcampingardeche.com**

🐕 🏕 €3 ♨ (htd) WD ⚒ ♿ 🚿 ✉ MP 🍴 ⓖ ♨ 🛒 🚴 🏊 🚣

Take D86 N fr Tournon, site 1km N of Vion on L. 3*, Med, mkd, hdg, pt shd, sl, terr, EHU (10A) €3; gas; bbq; TV; 20% statics; phone; bus 1km; Eng spkn; adv bkg acc; bike hire; CKE. *"Excel site; friendly owner lives on site - will take LS visitors."* **€16.00, 7 Apr-15 Sep.** 2018

TOURNUS *9A2* (1km N Urban) 46.57244, 4.90854
Camping de Tournus, 14 Rue des Canes, 71700
Tournus **03 85 51 16 58; camping-tournus@orange.fr;**
www.camping-tournus.com

🐕 €2.60 ♂♀ ⬜ ♿ 🅿 🍴 🛉 📶 ☂ ▽ 🍴 ⛰

Fr N6 at N of town turn E opp rlwy stn & rest 'Le
Terminus;' foll site sp. 3*, Med, hdstg, mkd, pt shd,
pt sl, EHU (10A) €4.70 (long lead poss req)(poss
rev pol); gas; bbq; TV; Eng spkn; rv fishing 100m;
CKE. *"Peaceful, rvside site in nice position; popular
NH, conv A6 - rec arr early; helpful staff; clean
facs poss stretched high ssn & ltd LS; htd pools adj;
poss extra charge twin axles; rv walk into town; gd
cycling nrby; quiet but rd & rlwy noise some pitches;
abbey worth visit; vg; well kept site; helpful staff."*
€27.00, 1 Apr-30 Sep. 2017

TOURNUS *9A2* (9km S Rural) 46.48768, 4.91286
Camping International d'Uchizy - Le National 6,
71700 Uchizy **03 85 40 53 90; camping.uchizylen6@**
wanadoo.fr; www.camping-lenational6.com

🐕 €1 ♂♀ ⛺ ✗ 🚲 ⛰ 🍴 ⛱

Exit A6 junc 27 & foll N6 S; sp on L, turn L over
rwly bdge on lane to site on L. Adj Rv Saône.
2*, Med, shd, EHU (6A) €3.90; gas; adv bkg acc;
fishing; boat hire. *"Attractive, well-maintained site;
gd, modern san facs; pitches soft & muddy in rain;
cash only; arr early for rvside pitch; lovely position."*
€26.40, 1 Apr-30 Sep. 2017

TOURS *4G2* (8km E Rural) 47.40226, 0.77845
Camping Les Acacias, Rue Berthe Morisot, 37700
La Ville-aux-Dames **02 47 44 08 16; contact@**
camping-tours.fr; www.camping-tours.fr

12 🐕 €2 ♂♀ (htd) ⬜ ⛺ ✗ ♿ 🅿 🍴 📶 🛉 ① 🍴 nr ⛰

Fr Tours take D751 E sp Amboise; after 6km at
rndabt where La Ville-aux-Dames sp to R, go strt
on for 200m, then turn R, site sp. 3*, Med, hdg, mkd,
hdstg, pt shd, EHU (10A) inc; bbq; red long stay;
10% statics; bus nr; Eng spkn; adv bkg acc; ccard acc;
tennis 600m; fishing 100m; games area; bike hire; CKE.
*"Well-kept, well-run, level site; excel san facs, ltd LS;
conv town cent; fitness trail; many long-term residents;
gd site; conv NH; lovely friendly helpful owners;
mountain bike circuit; lge supmkt nr; bus to city nr; pool
500m; gd for long or sh stays; country park adj for dog
walks; gd for Chateaux."* €32.00, L03. 2019

TOURS *4G2* (8km E Rural) 47.39273, 0.81085
Camping Les Peupliers, 37270 Montlouis-sur-Loire
02 47 50 81 90; aquadis1@wanadoo.fr;
www.aquadis-loisirs.com

🐕 €1.90 ♂♀ (htd) ⬜ ⛺ ✗ ♿ 🅿 🍴 📶 🍴 nr ⛰

On D751, 2km W of vill of Montlouis. Fr N foll sp to
Vouvray (keep on N side of Rv Loire to avoid Tours)
& cross rv by bdge to Montlouis. Sp at last min. NB
App fr E a 'Q-turn' to get into site.
3*, Lge, hdg, pt shd, EHU (6A) €2; 12% statics; Eng
spkn; adv bkg acc; ccard acc; tennis; CKE. *"Clean,
tidy site; poss clsd mid-Oct; lge pitches; mkt Sun in
Amboise; vg."* €19.60, 8 Apr-27 Oct. 2019

TOURS *4G2* (8km SW Urban) 47.35530, 0.63401
Camping La Mignardière, 22 Ave des Aubépines,
37510 Ballan-Miré **02 47 73 31 00; info@mignardiere.**
com; www.mignardiere.com

🐕 ♂♀ (htd) ⬜ ⛺ ✗ ♿ 🅿 🍴 📶 ☂ 🍴 nr ⛰ ⛰ 🏊 (covrd, htd)

Fr A10 exit junc 24 onto N585 & D37 by-pass. At exit
for Joué-lès-Tours foll sp Ballan-Miré onto D751.
Turn R at 1st set traff lts & foll site sp to W of lake.
4*, Lge, hdstg, mkd, hdg, pt shd, serviced pitches; EHU
(6-10A) €3.50; bbq; TV; phone; Eng spkn; adv bkg acc;
squash; bike hire; tennis; windsurfing 1km; fishing
1km; CKE. *"Conv Loire valley & chateaux; friendly,
helpful staff; unisex facs LS; gd cycle paths; vg site; rec;
bar 200m; gd san facs; v conv for bus/tram to Tours."*
€27.00, 1 Apr-25 Sep. 2018

TOURS *4G2* (10km W Rural) 47.35054, 0.54964
Camp La Confluence, Route du Bray, 37510
Savonnières **02 47 50 00 25; contact@campingla**
confluence.fr; www.onlycamp.fr

🐕 €1.20 ♂♀ ⬜ ⛺ ✗ ♿ 🅿 🍴 📶 🦋 🍴 nr ① nr 🍴 nr ⛰

Fr Tours take D7 on S of Rv Cher. Site on R on ent
Savonnières on rvside. 3*, Med, hdstg, hdg, mkd,
pt shd, EHU (10A) €4.20; bbq; phone; bus 200m;
Eng spkn; adv bkg acc; tennis adj; canoe hire; CKE.
*"Well-kept, clean, pleasant site; friendly, efficient
staff; modern unisex san facs (a bit dated, 2018);
some pitches narr & awnings diff; lovely vill with basic
facs; gd touring base; gd birdwatching, cycling; bar
adj; highly rec; gd touring base; on cycle rte; Vallendry
Chateau 3.5km."* €25.00, 30 Apr-30 Sep. 2019

TRANCHE SUR MER, LA *7A1* (0.5km E Coastal)
46.34945, -1.43280 **Camping Bel,** Rue de Bottereau,
85360 La Tranche-sur-Mer **02 51 30 47 39;**
campbel@wanadoo.fr; www.campingbel.com

♂♀ ⬜ ⛺ ✗ ♿ 🅿 🦋 🍴 ① nr ⛰ 🍴 nr ⛰ ▽ ⛱

Ent La Tranche on D747, take 2nd R at rndabt, R
at traff lts, ent on L. 4*, Med, hdg, mkd, pt shd, EHU
(10A) inc; TV; phone; Eng spkn; adv bkg acc; table
tennis; CKE. *"Ideal for families with young children;
bike hire nrby; adv bkg is only for current year."*
€36.00, May- Sep, A34. 2019

TRANCHE SUR MER, LA *7A1* (3km E Coastal)
46.34810, -1.38730 **Camping du Jard,** 123 Blvd
du Lattre de Tassigny, 85360 La Tranche-sur-Mer
**02 51 27 43 79; info@campingdujard.fr;
www.campingdujard.fr**

⚌ (covrd, htd)

sand 700m

Foll D747 S fr La Roche-sur-Yon twd La Tranche; at
rndabt on o'skirts of La Tranche turn L onto D46 sp
La Faute-sur-Mer; cont for approx 5km. At rndabt
turn R sp La Faute-sur-Mer 'par la côte'; then R at
next rndabt onto D46 sp La Tranche-sur-Mer 'par la
côte' & La Grière-Plage (ignore all previous La Grière
sps); site on R in 1km. Rough app rd.
4*, Lge, mkd, hdg, pt shd, serviced pitches; EHU (10A)
inc; bbq (charcoal, gas); red long stay; TV; 75% statics;
Eng spkn; adv bkg acc; ccard acc; horseriding 10km;
games area; bike hire; games rm; waterslide; tennis; golf
20km; sauna; CKE. *"Lovely, well-run, clean & tidy site;
busy high ssn; gd sized pitches, some sm; gd, well-kept
san facs; fitness cent; no c'vans over 8m high ssn; gd
pool; superb beach across busy coastal rd; easy parking
at other beaches; poss flooding in wet weather; mkt Tue
& Sat."* €36.00, 17 May-12 Sep, A03. **2018**

TREBEURDEN *1D2* (3.5km NW Coastal) *48.79905,
-3.58386* **Camp Municipal Le Dourlin,** L'Île Grande,
22560 Pleumeur-Bodou **02 96 91 92 41 or 02 96
23 91 17 (Mairie); infos.tourisme@pleumeur-
bodou.com; www.pleumeur-bodou.com**

€0.60 nr shgl adj

Off D788 N fr Trébeurden. Foll minor rd thro vill
to site on coast. Well sp. 2*, Med, mkd, unshd, EHU
(6A) €2.35; bbq; phone; bus; Eng spkn; sailing; games
area; fishing; CKE. *"Popular site in excel location - fine
sea views; excel facs; gd walking, cycling; ornithological
cent nr; 8km circular coast rd round peninsula;
gd; lovely coastal walk; well stocked shop in vill."*
€9.00, 30 Apr-27 Sep. **2017**

TREGASTEL *1D2* (3km NE Coastal) *48.82549,
-3.49135* **Tourony Camping,** 105 Rue de Poul-
Palud, 22730 Trégastel **02 96 23 86 61; contact@
camping-tourony.com; www.camping-tourony.com**

€1.50 nr sand adj

On D788 fr Trébeurden dir Perros Guirec, site on
R immed after exit Trégastel town sp & immed
bef bdge over Traouieros inlet, opp Port de
Ploumanac'h. 3*, Med, hdg, mkd, pt shd, EHU (6A)
€3; gas; bbq; red long stay; TV; 15% statics; Eng spkn;
adv bkg acc; ccard acc; tennis; bike hire; games area;
horseriding nr; lake fishing; golf nr; CKE. *"Pleasant,
lovely sm site in gd location; friendly, helpful staff;
gd touring base Granit Rose coast; sm pitches dif
for lge o'fits; clean but dated san facs (2015)."*
€25.00, 31 Mar-22 Sep. **2018**

TREGASTEL *1D2* (3.8km SW Rural/Coastal)
48.80995, -3.54140 **Camping du Port,** 3 Chemin
des Douaniers, 22560 Landrellec **02 96 23 87 79 or
06 73 78 32 64 (mob); renseignements@camping-
du-port-22.com; www.camping-du-port-22.com**

€2.50 (htd)

sand

Turn off D788 to Landrellec & foll rd thro vill past
shop for 100m, take care tight turn L. Site in 500m.
4*, Med, mkd, hdg, pt shd, pt sl, serviced pitches; EHU
(10-15A) €3.20-3.50; gas; bbq; TV; 25% statics; Eng
spkn; adv bkg acc; ccard acc; waterskiing; games rm;
bike hire; boating; fishing; CKE. *"Immac, family-owned
site; beautiful location; direct access beach; beach front
pitches extra charge but narr; coastal path runs thro
site; lots of lovely beaches nrby; telecoms museum
worth visit; excel."* €22.00, 21 Mar-8 Nov. **2015**

TREGUNC *2F2* (3.5km SW Coastal) *47.83384,
-3.89173* **Camping La Plage Loc'h Ven,** Plage
de Pendruc, 29910 Trégunc **02 98 50 26 20;
contact@lochven.com; www.lochven.com**

€1.60 (htd) nr nr shgl adj

Fr N165 exit at Kérampaou sp Trégunc. At rndbt
W of Trégunc foll Loc'h Ven sp thro Lambell,
site on coast. 2*, Med, hdg, mkd, pt shd, pt sl, EHU
(4-10A) €3.50-4.70; gas; TV; 40% statics; Eng spkn;
adv bkg acc; games area. *"Easy walk to beach,
rock pools & coastal footpath; helpful owners."*
€18.50, 28 Apr-20 Sep. **2019**

"Satellite navigation makes touring much easier"

Remember most sat navs don't know if you're
towing or in a larger vehicle – always use yours
alongside maps and site directions.

TREPORT, LE *3B2* (1km N Urban) *50.05805,
1.38860* **Camp Municipal Les Boucaniers,** Rue Pierre
Mendès-France, 76470 Le Tréport **02 35 86 35 47;
camping@ville-le-treport.fr; www.ville-le-treport.fr**

€1.60 (htd) sand 2km

Fr Eu take minor rd sp to Le Tréport under low
bdge. On ent o'skts of Le Tréport, turn R at traff lts,
camp ent 100m on R. Site nr stadium.
3*, Lge, hdstg, pt shd, EHU (6A) inc; TV; 10% statics;
games rm. *"Busy, well-kept, well-run site; some lge
pitches; gd, clean san facs; gd sep m'van area; lots to
see in Le Tréport; m'van Aire de Service adj; gd value;
excel; check elec lead is long enough bef unhitching."*
€18.80, 28 Mar-30 Sep. **2019**

TREPT *9B2* (3km E Rural) *45.68701, 5.35190*
Camping les 3 Lacs du Soleil, La Plaine de Serrières,
38460 Trept 04 74 92 92 06; info@les3lacsdusoleil.
com; www.camping-les3lacsdusoleil.com

[icons] €2.50 [icons]

Exit A432 at junc 3 or 3 & head twd Crémieu then
Morestel. Trept bet these 2 towns on D517, site sp
by lakes. 4*, Lge, pt shd, EHU (6A) inc; bbq (gas); sw
nr; TV; 5% statics; phone; Eng spkn; adv bkg acc; ccard
acc; waterslide; fishing; tennis; games area; archery;
horseriding 2km. *"Gd family site; gd, modern san
facs; fitness rm; lge & busy site with lots of activities."*
€38.00, 27 Apr-8 Sep.   2019

TRETS *10F3* (4km SW Rural) *43.44178, 5.62847*
Camping Le Devançon, Chemin de Pourachon, 13790
Peynier 04 42 53 10 06; reservation@ledevancon.fr;
www.ledevancon.fr

[icons] €1 [icons]

Leave A8 at Canet or Pas-de-Trets or leave D6 at
Trets & take D908 to Peynier. In vill cont on D908 sp
Marseille. Site on R at end vill after g'ge.
3*, Med, mkd, hdstg, shd, pt sl, EHU (3-10A) €3-5;
gas; bbq; red long stay; TV; 50% statics; Eng spkn;
adv bkg acc; ccard acc; tennis; CKE. *"Excel facs & site;
helpful owner; poss diff manoeuvring onto pitches
for lge o'fits; few water points; gd touring area."*
€27.00, 1 Mar-5 Nov.   2017

TREVIERES *1D4* (1.4km NE Rural) *49.31308, -0.90578*
Camp Municipal Sous Les Pommiers, Rue du Pont de
la Barre, 14710 Trévières 02 31 92 89 24 or
06 24 06 10 92; mairie@ville-trevieres.fr;
http://trevieres.eu/camping-municipal/

[icons] (cont) [icons]

Turn S off N13 onto D30 sp Trévières. Site on
R on ent to vill. 2*, Med, mkd, hdg, pt shd, EHU
(10A) €3; adv bkg rec; rv fishing adj; CKE. *"Delightful
site in apple orchard; lge pitches; vg san facs; conv
D-Day beaches; excel site; sm town in walking dist."*
€14.00, 1 Apr-30 Sep.   2019

TRIE-SUR-BAISE *8F2* (22km WNW Urban) *43.388595,
0.155504* **Camping Municipal La Galotte,** 44 Rue
de Mirande, 65140 Rabastens de Bigorre
05 62 36 57 64 or 06 10 35 34 95; camping.
lagalotte@gmail.com; www.camping-lagalotte.com

[icons]

Turn R (fr Tarbes, S) in ctr of Rabastens-de-Bigorre
and foll N21. Site on R on outskirts of town abt
1km. Sm, shd, EHU (10A); gas; bbq (charcoal, elec,
gas, sep area); twin axles; Eng spkn; adv bkg acc; CKE.
"Gd, basic site on edge of vill; suitable for short stays."
NP 19.8, 1 Apr-30 Sep.   2018

TROYES *4E4* (3km NE Urban) *48.31150, 4.09630*
Camp Municipal de Troyes, 7 Rue Roger Salengro,
10150 Pont-Ste Marie 03 25 81 02 64; info@
troyescamping.net; www.troyescamping.net

[icons] €1.15 (htd) [icons] (htd)

Fr N exit A26 junc 22 onto D677. site on R opp stadium
& adj Esso g'ge, just pass junc with D960. Fr S exit
A26 junc 23 for Pont-Ste-Mairie. Pont-Ste-Marie & site
'municipal' well sp fr all dirs & in town. NB Queues
form onto rd outside site, use Esso g'ge to turn if
queue too long. 3*, Med, hdstg, hdg, mkd, pt shd, EHU
(10A) (long lead poss req); gas; bbq; red long stay; TV;
bus opp; Eng spkn; adv bkg acc; ccard acc; games area;
bike hire; games rm; CKE. *"Busy, popular, transit site in
parkland - rec arr early; can be noisy at w/ends; vg pool;
some lge pitches; some pitches soft when wet; diff access
some pitches; twin axles acc at recep's discretion; red facs
LS; takeaway; Troyes Cathedral, museums & old quarter
worth visit; Lac d'Orient & Lac du Temple nrby; conv NH;
gd rest by rv bdge 3 min fr site; conv for m'way; pleasant
friendly site; clean facs; excel snacks/rest; stay 7 nights
pay for 6."* €27.00, 1 Apr-16 Oct.   2017

TROYES *4E4* (16km E Rural) *48.28998, 4.28279*
Camping La Fromentelle, Ferme Fromentelle, 10220
Dosches 03 25 41 52 67; www.tourisme-champagne-
ardenne.com

[icons] €1.50 [icons] sand 5km

Exit A26 junc 23 onto D619 dir Bar-sur-Aube. In
8.5km turn L onto D1 sp Géraudot (take care bends).
Site on L in 5km. 2*, Sm, mkd, pt shd, pt sl, EHU (6-
10A) €3 (long lead poss req)(poss rev pol); bbq; sw nr;
adv bkg acc; games area; CKE. *"Beautiful, lovely farm/
CL-type site in old orchard; well-kept & well-run; warm
welcome, charming owner; v clean san facs; gd for
birdwatching, sailing, watersports on lakes; excel cycle
tracks; nr nature reserve, lakes & forest; conv A26;
excel spacious pitches; gd facs; some rd noise; hg rec
old town in Troyes."* €15.00, 30 Apr-15 Oct.   2018

TROYES *4E4* (14km SE Rural) *48.20106, 4.16620*
Le Base de Loisirs au Plan d'Eau 'Les Terres Rouges',
10390 Cléry 06 70 00 76 75; terres-rouges@
wanadoo.fr; www.les-terres-rouges.com

[icons] (htd) [icons]

Exit A5 junc 21 onto D671 S dir Bar-sur-Seine &
Dijon; site on R in 3.5km. Or SE fr Troyes on D671
dir Bar-sur-Seine, foll sp Cléry; then as bef. Site
well sp. App over gravel track thro gravel quarry
area. 2*, Sm, hdstg, pt shd, EHU (5-10A) €3.20
(poss rev pol); sw; 10% statics; phone; adv bkg acc;
tennis; waterskiing; fishing; boating; CKE. *"Gd, basic
NH; clean, v basic san facs; friendly, helpful new
owners(2017); gate opens 0600, recep clsd 1900;
conv fr a'route to Calais; commuter traff noise."*
€19.00, 2 April-30 Sep.   2017

TUCHAN *8G4 (1km S Rural) 42.88302, 2.71861*
Camping La Peiriere, route de Paziols, 11350 Tuchan
04 68 45 46 50; lapeiriere@lapeiriere.com;
www.lapeiriere.com

🛠🐕€3 ♙♟ WD ♨⚓♿ 🖭✗ 🎐 ⛱ 🍴🎣 ⛵ 🎿

Fr Tuchan dir Paziols on L, 200m fr edge of town.
Med, hdg, mkd, shd, EHU (9A); bbq; 10% statics; bus
adj; Eng spkn; adv bkg acc; CKE. *"Mini farm & free lake
fishing on site; excel base; access rds are v tight; vg."*
€26.00, 1 Apr-30 Sep. 2016

URCAY *4H3 (6km NE Rural) 46.6430, 2.6620*
Camping Champ de la Chapelle, St Bonnet-Tronçais,
03360 Braize 00 33 470 07 82 46; simon.swinn@sfr.fr;
www.champdelachapelle.com

🛠🐕€1 ♙♟ WD 🖭✗ 🎐 🍴 ⑪nr 🎣 🎿 ⛱ ⛵

Fr D2144 take D978A for Tronçais. 1.5km on L
fr rndabt(Montaloyer) x-ing D28. Site sp.
3*, Med, mkd, pt shd, pt sl, EHU (10A) inc; sw nr;
10% statics; Eng spkn; adv bkg acc; ccard acc; games
area; CKE. *"Excel walking & flora/fauna in ancient oak
forest; some lge pitches; peaceful site; new British
owner (2016)."* **€22.00, 14 Apr-17 Oct.** 2019

> ## "There aren't many sites open at this time of year"
> If you're travelling outside peak season remember to call ahead to check site opening dates – even if the entry says 'open all year'.

URDOS *8G2 (0.5km N Rural) 42.87705, -0.55670*
Camp Municipal Le Gave d'Aspe, 64490 Urdos
05 59 34 88 26; guittonb@hotmail.com

♙♟ WD ♨✗ 🖭 🍴 nr ⑪ 🎣 nr ⛱ 🎿

Turn W off N134 onto site access rd by disused Urdos
stn approx 1km bef vill, clear sp. Other access rds
in vill v diff lge o'fits. 2*, Sm, mkd, pt shd, pt sl, EHU
(10A) €2.40; bbq; phone; Eng spkn; adv bkg acc; ccard
acc; rv; CKE. *"Adj Rv Aspe; 14km fr Col du Somport/
Tunnel; surrounded by mountains; conv x-ing into Spain;
vg; lovely sm site; beautiful mountain scenery; gd facs;
gd walking."* **€16.00, 1 May-15 Sep.** 2017

URT *8F1 (0.9km E Rural) 43.49353, -1.27960*
Camping Ferme Mimizan, 64240 Urt
05 59 56 21 51; contact@lafermedemimizan.fr;
www.lafermedemimizan.fr

12 ♙♟ ♨✗ 🍴 ⛱ 🎿 🎐

E fr Bayonne on A64/E80, exit junc 4 sp Urt; in vill
turn sharp R at PO & foll sps; site on R in 1km. Fr N
on D12 cross Rv Adour by metal bdge & turn L
immed past church, site on R in 1.5km.
2*, Med, pt shd, EHU (10A) €3.50; 10% statics; adv
bkg acc; CKE. *"V peaceful out of ssn; friendly owners;
gd walking & cycling; conv coast & Pyrenees; gd NH."*
€19.50 2017

UZERCHE *7B3 (8km NE Rural) 45.45200, 1.65056*
Camping Aimée Porcher (Naturist), 19140 Pingrieux
Eyburie 05 55 73 20 97 or 06 01 11 51 90;
aimeeporcher@hotmail.com; www.aimee-porcher.com

🛠🐕 ♙♟ WD ♨⚓♿ 🖭✗ 🦋 ⑪ 🍴🎣 ⛱

Fr Uzerche take D3 NE to Eyburie & in Eyburie
turn R at site sp (Cheyron/Pingrieux). In 1km turn
L at site sp; site at end of narr lane. 2*, Sm, mkd,
pt shd, terr, EHU (6A) (poss long lead req); bbq;
sw nr; red long stay; adv bkg acc; games area; INF
card. *"Beautiful views; wonderful location; INF not
req; excel san facs; spacious pitches; basic; site rd
steep in places; superb; v friendly Dutch owners."*
€26.50, 20 May-11 Sep. 2017

UZES *10E2 (2km E Rural) 44.03202, 4.45557*
Camping Le Moulin Neuf, 30700 St Quentin-la-
Poterie 04 66 22 17 21; lemoulinneuf@yahoo.fr;
www.le-moulin-neuf.fr

🐕€1.50 ♙♟ WD ♨⚓ 🖭✗ 🖭 🦋 ⑪ 🍴🎣 🎿 ⛱ ⛵ (htd)

N fr Uzès on D982; after 3km turn L onto D5; in
1.5km fork R, keeping on D5; in 200m turn R onto
D405 (Chemin du Moulin Neuf); site on L in 500m.
3*, Med, mkd, pt shd, EHU (5A) €3.50; 10% statics;
fishing; horseriding; bike hire; tennis. *"Site off beaten
track; busy high ssn, rec phone in adv; conv touring
base; o'night m'van area; barrier clsd 2230-0700; poss
mosquito problem; Uzès a lovely town; wonderful
helpful staff; excel facs."* **€24.50, 1 Apr-22 Sep.** 2017

VAISON LA ROMAINE *9D2 (1.5km NE Urban)
44.24472, 5.07861* **Camping du Théâtre Romain,**
Chemin du Brusquet, 84110 Vaison-la-Romaine
04 90 28 78 66; info@camping-theatre.com;
www.camping-theatre.com

🛠🐕€2 ♙♟ (htd) WD ♨⚓♿ 🖭✗ 🖭 🦋 ⑪ 🍴 🎣 nr ⛱ 🎿

Fr D975, cont onto Ave de Martigny to Chemin du
Brusquet. Foll sp for Théâtre Romain & site. Ent to
Chemin du Busquet on rndabt at Théâtre Romain.
Or site sp off Orange-Nyons rd thro town (do not
ent town cent). 4*, Med, hdg, mkd, pt shd, serviced
pitches; EHU (5-10A); bbq; 10% statics, Eng spkn;
adv bkg req; ccard acc; games rm; CKE. *"Excel, well-
kept, friendly site; busy LS due long stay residents,
rec book in adv; mainly gd sized pitches but some sm;
most pitches suitable m'vans; clean, unisex san facs;
attractive town; mkt Tues; highly rec; excel as usual;
old Roman town cent, 10 mins walk fr campsite; conv
for town; refurbed sw & new paddling pool (2016); long
stay red."* **€28.00, 15 Mar-5 Nov.** 2019

> ## "That's changed – Should I let the Club know?"
> If you find something on site that's different from the site entry, fill in a report and let us know. See camc.com/europereport.

VAISON LA ROMAINE *9D2* (3.7km SE Rural)
44.22357, 5.10428 **Camping Le Voconce,** route de
St Marcellin, 84110 St Marcellin **04 90 36 28 10;**
contact@camping-voconce.com; www.camping-
voconce.com

🐕 €3-4 [WC] ♨ ♿ 🚿 ⊞ ⊘ 🦋 ♛ 🍴 ⛱ 🛒nr 🏛 ✂ ⛷

**Fr Vaison S on D977. Turn L onto D938 after 1km.
Turn R onto D151 after 0.5km to St Marcellin-
les-Vaison. Turn R at rndabt by a chapel & foll sp
to site.** 3*, Med, mkd, hdg, pt shd, EHU (10A) €5;
gas; 15% statics; Eng spkn; adv bkg acc; ccard acc;
games area; CKE. *"Tranquil site bet 2 vineyards;
friendly, fam run site; vg base for cycling, walking
& exploring; boules; great views; acc to rv; vg."*
€24.00, 1 Apr-15 Oct. 2016

VAL D'ISERE *9B4* (1km E Rural) *45.44622, 6.99218*
Camping Les Richardes, Le Laisinant, 73150 Val-
d'Isère **04 79 06 26 60;** campinglesrichardes@free.fr;
www.campinglesrichardes.free.fr

🐕 €0.50 ♀♂ ♨ ♿ 🦋

**Leave Val d'Isère going E twds Col de l'Iseran on
D902, site on R 1.5km bef Le Fornet vill.**
1*, Med, unshd, pt sl, EHU (3-6A) €1.90-3.80;
CKE. *"Peaceful site; pool 1.5km; delightful owner."*
€13.00, 15 Jun-15 Sep. 2016

VALENCAY *4H2* (1.7km W Urban) *47.15656, 1.55202*
Camp Municipal Les Chênes, Route de Loches, 36600
Valençay **02 54 00 03 92 or 02 54 00 32 32;**
www.valencay.fr

🐕 ♀♂ [WC] ♨ ♿ ⊘ 🦋 🛒nr 🏛

**App town fr E on D960 or N/S on D956, foll sp for
D960 Luçay-le-Mâle. D960 is next L in town. Foll
sp for pool & camping. Site adj pool mkd by flags.**
3*, Sm, hdg, mkd, pt shd, EHU (6A) €3.20 (poss rev
pol); bbq; red long stay; TV; adv bkg acc; fishing;
tennis adj; CKE. *"Excel, well-kept site in parkland with
lake; lge pitches; gd, clean facs; poss muddy after
heavy rain; htd pool adj (high ssn); gate clsd 2100-
0700; sh walk to impressive chateau; day's drive to
Calais or Le Havre ferries; motor museum & vill 1km."*
€15.00, 1 May-30 Sep. 2015

VALENCE *9C2* (8.5km N Rural) *44.99723, 4.89383*
Camping Le Soleil Fruité, Les Pêches, 26300
Chateauneuf-sur-Isère **04 75 84 19 70;** contact@
lesoleilfruite.com; www.lesoleilfruite.com

🐕 €2 ♀♂ [WC] ♨ ♿ 🚿 ⊞ ⊘ /~ 🦋 ♛ 🍴 ⊕ 🍽 🏛 ✂ ⛷ 🛶

**Exit A7 junc 14 Valence Nord onto D67 sp
Chateauneuf-sur-Isère, site sp to W of vill. Alt rte
foll N7 turn onto D877 twrds Chateauneuf and
foll sp to campsite.** 4*, Med, hdg, mkd, pt shd, EHU
(10A) €4; bbq; TV; 15% statics; phone; Eng spkn;
adv bkg acc; ccard acc; CKE. *"Vg, family-run site; lge
pitches; friendly owner; no dogs high ssn; excel, clean,
modern san facs; rest/takeaway open early Jun (2011);
ltd water pnts; cycle friendly; gd bar/rest; smart
site; v busy HS; gd for families with young children."*
€33.00, 26 Apr-15 Sep. 2016

VALENCE *9C2* (9km NW Rural) *45.00726, 4.84862*
Camp Municipal Les Vernes, 26600 La Roche-de-Glun
04 75 84 54 11 or 04 75 84 60 52 (Mairie); mairie.
rdg@wanadoo.fr; www.ladrometourisme.com

♀♂ [WC] ♨ ♿ ⊘ /~ 🦋 🛒nr

**Turn W off N7 at Pont-d'Isère. On ent La Roche-de-
Glun foll camping sp.** 4*, Sm, mkd, hdg, shd, serviced
pitches; EHU (10A) €1.40; bbq; 50% statics; phone;
adv bkg acc; CKE. *"Pleasant site; friendly resident
warden; htd pool adj in ssn inc; sports cent adj; gd,
clean san facs; vg municipal pool adj; barrier clsd 2200-
0700; vg value; vg NH."*
€17.00, 1 May-30 Sep. 2015

VALLOIRE *9C3* (0.5km N Rural) *45.17000, 6.42960*
Camp Caravaneige Municipal Ste Thècle, Route des
Villards, 73450 Valloire **04 79 83 30 11;** camping-
caravaneige@valloire.net; www.valloire.net

🐕 ♀♂ (htd) [WC] ♨ ♿ 🚿 ⊘ /MP 🦋 ♛ 🍴 🛒nr ⊕nr 🛒nr 🏛 ⛷ 🛷

**Exit A43 junc 29 onto D306 to St Michel-de-
Maurienne, then onto D902 to Valloire. At
vill mkt turn R over rv to site. Climb fr valley
15% gradient max.** 3*, Med, hdstg, mkd, unshd,
EHU (13A) €3.60; red long stay; TV; bus; Eng
spkn; adv bkg acc; ccard acc; waterslide; tennis;
fishing. *"Superb mountain scenery for walking &
cycling; fitness rm; bar 200m; excel, well kept site."*
€20.00, 12 Dec-23 Apr & 1 Jun-30 Sep. 2015

VALLON EN SULLY *7A4* (1.2km SE Rural) *46.53019,
2.61447* **Camp Municipal Les Soupirs,** Allée des
Soupirs, 03190 Vallon-en-Sully **04 70 06 50 96 or 04
70 06 50 10 (LS);** mairie.vallonensully@wanadoo.fr

🐕 ♀♂ (cont) [WC] ♨ ⊘ 🦋 🍴nr ⊕nr 🛒nr

**N fr Montluçon on D2144; in 23km at traff lts where
D11 crosses D2144 turn L & foll camping sp for
Vallon-en-Sully. After bdge over Rv Cher turn L in
50m. Site in 500m. If N or S on A71 exit at junc 9
Vallon-en-Sully; turn N on D2144; in 3km at traff
lts turn L.** 2*, Med, pt shd, EHU (6-20A) €2-4; TV;
bus 500m; adv bkg acc. *"Peaceful, spacious site on
banks of rv & canal; immac san facs; lge pitches; risk
of flooding in wet; gd cycling along canal; gd NH; vg."*
€10.40, 1 Jul-12 Sep. 2017

VALLON PONT D'ARC *9D2* (1km SE Rural) *44.39777,
4.39861* **Camping Nature Park L'Ardéchois,** Route
des Gorges de l'Ardèche, 07150 Vallon-Pont-d'Arc
04 75 88 06 63; info@ardechois-camping.com;
www.ardechois-camping.com

🐕 €9 ♀♂ (htd) [WC] ♨ ♿ 🚿 ⊞ ⊘ /~ /MP 🦋 ♛ 🍴 ⊕ 🍽 🏛 ✂
⛷ (htd) 🛶

**Fr Vallon take D290 Rte des Gorges & site on R bet
rd & rv.** 5*, Lge, hdstg, mkd, hdg, shd, pt sl, serviced
pitches; EHU (6-10A) inc; gas; bbq; TV; Eng spkn; adv
bkg acc; ccard acc; tennis; bike hire; canoeing; games
area; CKE. *"Spectacular scenery; private bthrm avail
(by reservation); excel rvside site; helpful staff; price
depends on size of pitch; gd san facs; 5 star site."*
€60.00, 4 Apr-10 Sep, M14. 2019

VALLON PONT D'ARC *9D2* (1.5km SE Rural) *44.39467, 4.39909* **Mondial Camping,** Route des Gorges, 07150 Vallon-Pont-d'Arc **04 75 88 00 44; reserv-info@mondial-camping.com; www.mondial-camping.com**

🐕 €4.50 👪 (htd) WD ♨ ♿ 🚻 ⊒ ⚊ MSP 🦋 ♥ 🍴 ⑭ 🏪 🛒 ⛺ ✐ 🏊 (htd) 🛶

Fr N exit A7 Montélimar Nord junc 17 onto N7 then N102 dir Le Teil, Villeneuve-de-Berg. Turn S onto D103/D579 dir Vogüé, Ruoms then Vallon-Pont-d'Arc. Take D290, Rte des Gorges de l'Ardèche to site in 1.5km. Fr S exit A7 junc 19 at Bollène, dir Bourg-St Andéol, then D4 to St Remèze & Vallon-Pont-d'Arc. App to Vallon fr E thro Gorges de l'Ardeche not rec. 4*, Lge, mkd, hdg, shd, serviced pitches; EHU (6-10A) inc; gas; TV; 10% statics; phone; Eng spkn; adv bkg acc; ccard acc; tennis adj; canoeing; games rm; CKE. *"Dir access to rv, Ardèche gorges & canoe facs; gd touring base; waterslides & aqua park; excel site."* **€42.00, 1 Apr-30 Sep.** 2017

> ## "I like to fill in the reports as I travel from site to site"
>
> You'll find report forms at the back of this guide, or you can fill them in online at camc.com/europereport.

VALLON PONT D'ARC *9D2* (4.6km S Rural) *44.39333, 4.39465* **Camping Le Clapas,** La Vernède, 07150 Salavas **04 75 37 14 76; contact@camping le clapas.com; www.camping-le-clapas.com**

🐕 €2 👪 WD ♨ ♿ 🚻 ⊒ ⚊ MSP 🦋 ♥ 🍴 ⑭ nr 🏪 🛒 ⛺ ✐

D579 S fr Vallon-Pont-d'Arc to Salavas; 250m after Salavas turn L. Well sp. Med, mkd, shd, pt sl, EHU (10A) €3; bbq (elec, gas); sw; TV; Eng spkn; adv bkg acc; ccard acc; games rm; rafting; fishing; canoeing; games area; CKE. *"Beautiful, well-kept site by Rv Ardèche with beach; friendly, helpful staff; poss diff lge o'fits; canyoning; conv Ardèche Gorges; excel; French adaptor needed, site sells or loans."* **€27.50, 17 Apr-27 Sep.** 2015

VALLON PONT D'ARC *9D2* (2km W Rural) *44.41517, 4.37796* **Domaine de L'Esquiras,** chemin du Fez, 07150 Vallon-Pont-d'Arc **04 75 88 04 16; esquiras@orange.fr; www.camping-esquiras.com**

🐕 €3.50 👪 WD ♨ ♿ 🚻 ⊒ ⚊ MSP 🦋 ♥ 🍴 ⑭ 🏪 🛒 ✐ 🏊

Fr Ruoms L at rndabt bef the Lidl nr the vill. Foll sp. Fr Vallon foll dir Ruoms. R after Lidl. 4*, Med, mkd, pt shd, pt sl, gas; twin axles; TV; phone; Eng spkn; adv bkg acc; ccard acc; games area; games rm; CKE. *"Lovely vill (10 min walk) with lots of bars & rest; caving, climbing or kayaking; excel; ACSI acc."* **€40.00, 25 Mar-30 Sep.** 2016

VALLON PONT D'ARC *9D2* (4km W Rural) *44.41251, 4.35018* **Camping L'Arc en Ciel,** Route de Ruoms, Les Mazes, 07150 Vallon-Pont-d'Arc **04 75 88 04 65; camping.arcenciel@wanadoo.fr; www.arcenciel-camping.com**

🐕 €3.50 👪 WD ♨ ♿ 🚻 ⊒ ⚊ 🦋 ♥ 🍴 ⑭ 🏪 🛒 ⛺ ✐ 🏊 🛶

Fr Ruoms take D579 dir Vallon. After 4km bear R for Les Mazes. Pass thro vill & in about 1.7km bear L at camp sp. 3*, Lge, pt shd, pt sl, EHU (10A) €4; bbq (elec, gas); 10% statics; bus; adv bkg acc; ccard acc; games rm; rv; canoeing; horseriding nr; tennis nr; fishing. *"Pleasant site on rv bank; excel; some pitches diff to access."* **€41.00, 29 Apr-18 Sep.** 2016

VALLORCINE *9A4* (1km SE Rural) *46.0242, 6.92370* **Camping des Montets,** Le Buet, 74660 Vallorcine **06 79 02 18 81; b.stam@orange.fr; http://camping-montets.com**

🐕 👪 WD ♨ 🚻 ⊒ ⚊ 🦋 ⑭ 🏪 🛒 nr

N fr Chamonix on D1506 via Col de Montets; Le Buet 2km S of Vallorcine; site sp nr Le Buet stn. Fr Martigny (Switzerland) cross border via Col de la Forclaz; then D1506 to Vallorcine; cont to Le Buet in 1km. 2*, Med, hdg, mkd, pt shd, EHU (3-6A) €2-3; red long stay; train 500m; Eng spkn; tennis adj; CKE. *"Site with spectacular views; friendly owners; ltd flat pitches for o'fits (others for tents in field), rec phone ahead; clean san facs; excel walking direct fr site; free train pass to Chamonix; vg."* **€16.00, 1 Jun-15 Sep.** 2016

VALRAS PLAGE *7E3* (2.5km SW Coastal) *43.227408, 3.243536* **Camping Sandaya Blue Bayou,** Vendres Plage Ouest 34350, Valras-Plage **04 67 37 41 97 or 04 11 32 90 00; www.sandaya.fr/nos-campings/blue-bayou**

🐕 👪 (htd) WD ♨ ♿ 🚻 ⊒ ⚊ 🦋 ♥ 🍴 ⑭ 🏪 🛒 ⛺ ✐ 🏊 (htd) 🛶 ⛱ sandy 0.5

Take exit 36 off the A9. Then onto the D64 twrds Vendres-Plage. 5*, Mkd, unshd, EHU 10A; bbq (elec, gas); TV; Eng spkn; ccard acc; bike hire; beauty ctr; fishing; watersports. **€67.00, 12 Apr-14 Sep.** 2019

VALRAS PLAGE *10F1* (3km SW Coastal) *43.23101, 3.25330* **Sandaya Les Vagues,** Chemin des Montilles, 34350 Vendres-Plage **04 67 37 03 62; vag@sandaya.fr; www.sandaya.co.uk**

🐕 €5 👪 ♨ ♿ 🚻 ⊒ ⚊ 🍴 ⑭ 🏪 🛒 ⛺ ✐ 🏊 (htd) 🛶 ⛱ sand 400m

Exit A9 junc 36 onto D64 to Valras-Plage then Vendres-Plage. Site sp. 4*, Lge, pt shd, EHU (10A) inc; bbq (sep area); TV; 75% statics; Eng spkn; adv bkg acc; games area; horseriding 5km; waterslide; jacuzzi. *"Recep helpful; clean san facs; wave machine excel."* **€25.00, 20 May-13 Sep.** 2019

FRANCE

VALRAS PLAGE *10F1* (6km NW Rural) *43.29273, 3.26710* **Camping La Gabinelle,** 7 Rue de la Grille, 34410 Sauvian **04 67 39 50 87; info@lagabinelle.com; www.lagabinelle.com**

🐕 €3.50 ♙♙ 🅆🄳 ♿ 🍴 🅷 🦋 ♈ ⒽⓁ nr 🍸 🔌 nr ⛺ 🚲 🛶
⛵ sand 5km

Exit A9 at Béziers Ouest, turn R twd beaches sp S to Sauvian on D19. Site 500m on L thro town. 3*, Med, pt shd, EHU (6A) €3; red long stay; TV; adv bkg acc; fishing 1km; tennis; games area; games rm. *"Friendly, helpful staff; suitable lge m'vans; canoeing 2km; LS ltd san facs & poss unkempt; sh walk to delightful old vill; popular; bar/pool shut LS."* €13.80, 12 Apr-12 Sep. 2016

VALREAS *9D2* (1km N Rural) *44.39264, 4.99245* **Camping La Coronne,** Route de Pègue, 84600 Valréas **04 88 70 00 13; contact@lacoronne.com; www.vaucluse-camping.fr**

🐕 €4 ♙♙ 🅆🄳 ♨ ♿ 🍴 ♈ 🌐 🦋 ♈ 🍸 ⒽⓁ 🐎 🚲 ⛺ 🚲 🛶
Fr Nyons take D538 W to Valréas. Exit town on D10 rd to Taulignan, immed after x-ing bdge over Rv Coronne turn R into D196 sp Le Pègue. Site on R in 100m on rvside. Sp app fr E but easy to miss; app fr W; well sp in Valréas. 3*, Med, hdg, mkd, pt shd, EHU (6A) inc; gas; bbq; TV; phone; Eng spkn; adv bkg acc; ccard acc; fishing. CKE. *"Sm pitches; excel pool; facs need refurb & poss unclean; site clsd 2200-0700."* €25.70, 31 Mar-15 Oct. 2017

VANDENESSE EN AUXOIS *6G1* (2.5km NE Rural) *47.23661, 4.62880* **Camping Le Lac de Panthier,** 21320 Vandenesse-en-Auxois **03 80 49 21 94; info@lac-de-panthier.com; www.lac-de-panthier.com**

🐕 €3 ♙♙ 🅆🄳 ♨ ♿ 🍴 ♈ 🍸 ⒽⓁ 🐎 ⛺ 🚲 🛶 (covrd, htd) 🏊
Exit A6 junc 24 (A38) at Pouilly-en-Auxois; foll D16/D18 to Vandenesse; turn L on D977bis, cross canal bdge & cont strt for 3km to site on L. Fr SW (Autun) on D981 approx 12km after Arnay-le-Duc turn R onto D994 sp Châteauneuf. At x-rds cont onto D977bis then as above. 4*, Lge, hdg, mkd, pt shd, pt sl, terr, EHU (6A) inc (some rev pol); bbq; TV (pitch); adv bkg req; fishing; waterslide; bike hire; sauna; CKE. *"Lovely area; Oct open Fri, Sat & Sun; views fr higher pitches; well-run site operating with Les Voiliers adj; lge pitches, most sl & blocks req; facs poss stretched high ssn, adequate; gd cycling & walks round lake; popular NH; vg."* €28.00, 1 Apr-28 Sep, L31. 2019

VANNES *2F3* (3km S Rural) *47.62754, -2.74117* **FFCC Camping Moulin de Cantizac,** 2 Rue des Orchidées, 56860 Séné **02 98 92 53 52; info@camping-vannes.com; www.camping-vannes.com**

12 🐕 €2.30 ♙♙ 🅆🄳 ♨ ♿ 🍴 🦋 ♈ 🐎 ⛺ 🚲 🛶 (htd)
⛵ sand 4km

S fr Vannes on D199 twds Séné. Site on L at rndabt beside rv. 3*, Med, hdg, pt shd, pt sl, EHU (10A) €3.90; gas; 50% statics; ccard acc; games rm; boating; games area. *"Superb cent for birdwatching; excel new facs; buses to Vannes."* €29.00 2019

VANNES *2F3* (4km SW Coastal) *47.63365, -2.78008* **Flower Camping Le Conleau (formerly Municipal),** 188 Ave Maréchal Juin, 56000 Vannes **02 97 63 13 88; camping.conleau@flowercampings.com; en.vannes-camping.com**

🐕 €3 ♙♙ 🅆🄳 ♨ ♿ 🍴 ♈ 🌐 🦋 ♈ 🍸 🐎 ⛺ 🚲 🛶 (covrd, htd) 🏊
⛵ sand 300m

Exit N165 at Vannes Ouest junc; Conleau sp on R. Site twd end of rd on R. If on N165 fr Auray take 1st exit sp Vannes & at 2nd rndabt R (sp) to avoid town cent. C'vans not allowed thro town cent. 4*, Lge, mkd, hdg, pt shd, pt sl, EHU (6A) €3.50 (some rev pol); bbq; twin axles; TV; 20% statics; phone; bus adj; Eng spkn; adv bkg acc; ccard acc; games area; bike hire; CKE. *"Most pitches sl; sep area for m'vans by rd - little shd & poss long walk to san facs; v busy/noisy in high ssn; sea water pool nr; lovely easy walk to Port Conleau; site full of atmosphere - rec; excel; great location & facs."* €32.00, 1 Apr-1 Oct. 2017

VANNES *2F3* (5km SW Coastal) *47.62190, -2.80056* **Camping de Penboch,** 9 Chemin de Penboch, 56610 Arradon **02 97 44 71 29; camping.penboch@orange.fr; www.camping-penboch.fr**

🐕 €3.50 ♙♙ 🅆🄳 ♨ ♿ 🍴 ♈ 🌐 🦋 ♈ 🍸 🐎 ⛺
🏊 (covrd, htd, indoor) 🚲 ⛵ sand 200m

Exit Brest-Nantes N165 Vannes by-pass at junc with D127 sp Ploeren & Arradon. Foll sp Arradon. Site well sp. 4*, Lge, mkd, hdg, pt shd, EHU (10A) inc (poss rev pol); gas; bbq; TV; 10% statics; Eng spkn; adv bkg rec; ccard acc; games rm; waterslide; games area; playground; CKE. *"Excel site; gd clean san facs; bike hire 2km; some pitches sm; steel pegs req; o'flow area with facs; no o'fits over 7m high ssn; plenty for youngsters; 20 mins walk to Arradon; gd coast walks."* €41.00, 12 Apr-26 Sep, B33. 2019

VANS, LES *9D1* (2.5km E Rural) *44.40953, 4.16768* **Camping Domaine des Chênes,** 07140 Chassagnes-Haut **04 75 37 34 35; reception@domaine-des-chenes.fr; www.domaine-des-chenes.fr**

🐕 €2.50 ♙♙ ♨ ♿ 🍴 🌐 🦋 🍸 ⒽⓁ 🐎 ⛺ 🚲
Fr town cent take D104A dir Aubenas. After Peugeot g'ge turn R onto D295 at garden cent twd Chassagnes. Site on L after 2km; sp adj Rv Chassezac. 3*, Med, pt shd, pt sl, terr, EHU (10A) inc; bbq; 80% statics; adv bkg acc; ccard acc; rv fishing 500m; CKE. *"Lovely shady site; ideal for birdwatchers; gd rest; rec."* €18.00, 4 Apr-27 Sep. 2016

VARENNES EN ARGONNE *5D1* (0.4km N Rural)
49.22935, 5.03424 **Camp Municipal Le Pâquis,**
Rue St Jean, 55270 Varennes-en-Argonne
**03 29 80 71 01 (Mairie); mairievarennesenargonne@
wanadoo.fr; www.varennesenargonne.fr/
pages/annexe/reglement-du-camping**
🐕 €0.40 ♂♀ 🏕 🔥 🚿 🗑 ∥ 🦋 🚲 nr

On D946 Vouziers/Clermont-en-Argonne rd; sp
by bdge in vill, on banks of Rv Aire, 200m N of
bdge. NB Ignore sp by bdge to Camping Lac Vert
(not nr). 2*, Med, pt shd, EHU (6-16A) €3.65; bbq;
Eng spkn; rv fishing. *"Pleasant site with gd facs;
gd (hilly) cycle ride taking in US WWI cemetary."*
€14.60, 31 Mar-6 Oct. 2019

VARILHES *8G3* (0.4km NE Urban) *43.04714, 1.63096*
FFCC Camp Municipal du Parc du Château,
Ave de 8 Mai 1945, 09120 Varilhes **05 61 67 42 84
or 05 61 60 55 54 (TO); campingdevarilhes@
orange.fr; www.campingdevarilhes.com**
12 🐕 ♂♀(htd) 🏕 🔥 🚿 🗑 ∥ MP 🦋 ♈ 🍽 🚲 nr 🕙 nr 🚲 nr 🌊

Exit N20/E9 at sp Varilhes. Turn N in town on D624.
Site 250m on L (sp) just bef leisure cent adj Rv
Ariège. 2*, Med, mkd, pt shd, terr, EHU (5-10A) €5.90-
6.40; 20% statics; adv bkg acc; rv fishing adj; games
area. *"Shwr & sinks locked 2100-0700; hot water
unreliable."* **€13.00** 2018

VARILHES *8G3* (3km NW Rural) *43.06258, 1.62101*
FFCC Camping Les Mijeannes, Route de Ferriès, 09120
Rieux-de-Pelleport **05 61 60 82 23; www.vap-camping.fr**
12 🐕 €1.10 ♂♀(htd) WD 🔥 ∥ MP 🦋 ♈ 🍽 🍺 🌊

Exit N20 sp Varilhes; on app Varilhes cent join 1-way
system; 1st R at Hôtel de Ville; over rv bdge; foll
camp sps; site 2km on R. 3*, Med, hdg, pt shd, EHU
(10A) €4.60; bbq; TV; Eng spkn; adv bkg acc; fishing;
games area; CKE. *"Peaceful site by rv, on island formed
by rv; ACSI; helpful owner; kids club; badminton; gd size
pitches; excel san facs; weekly theme nights high ssn;
volley; excel; ltd facs LS."* **€27.00** 2017

VATAN *4H3* (9km N Rural) *47.13479, 1.85121*
Camp Municipal St Phalier, 2 Chemin Trompe-Souris,
18310 Graçay **02 48 51 24 14 or 02 48 51 42 07
(Mairie); camping-gracay@wanadoo.fr;
www.camping.gracay.info**
🐕 €1.02 ♂♀ WD 🏕 ∥ 🦋 🌊

Leave A20 at junc 9 & take D83 to Graçay. On
o'skts of vill turn L & immed turn L foll sp to Cent
Omnisport & site. 2*, Sm, pt shd, EHU (10A) €2.69;
phone; Eng spkn; fishing; CKE. *"Lovely, peaceful,
well-kept, pleasant site by sm unfenced lake & park;
plenty of space lge o'fits - site yourself; excel clean
san facs; poss travellers, but no problem; rest nr; bar
nr; pool adj; shop nr; vill in walking dist; gd NH fr A20."*
€8.70, 1 Apr-15 Sep. 2016

VATAN *4H3* (0.5km W Urban) *47.07131, 1.80573*
Camp Municipal de la Ruelle au Loup, Rue du Collège,
36150 Vatan **02 54 49 91 37 or 02 54 49 76 31 (Mairie);
vatan-mairie1@wanadoo.fr; www.vatan-en-berry.com**
♂♀ 🏕 🔥 🚿 🗑 ∥ 🦋 🕙 nr 🚲 nr 🌊

Exit A20 junc 10 onto D922 to town cent. Take D2
dir Guilly & foll site sp - 2nd on L (easily missed).
2*, Med, hdg, mkd, pt shd, EHU (10A) inc (rev pol);
adv bkg acc; CKE. *"Pleasant, well-kept, beautiful site
in park o'looking lake; spacious pitches; v clean, gd san
facs (2019); twin axles; warden onsite daytime into
early eve; easy access fr a'route; pool adj; conv Loire
chateaux."* **€17.00, 15 Apr-15 Sep.** 2019

VAUVERT *10E2* (6km SE Rural) *43.65440, 4.29610*
FLOWER Camping Le Mas de Mourgues,
Gallician, 30600 Vauvert **04 66 73 30 88; info@
masdemourgues.com; www.masdemourgues.com**
or www.flowercampings.com
🐕 €3 ♂♀ WD 🔥 🚿 🗑 ∥ MP 🦋 🌊

Exit A9 junc 26 onto D6313/D6572. Site on L at x-rds
with D779 sp to Gallician & Stes Marie-de-la-Mer.
2*, Med, mkd, pt shd, EHU (6A) inc; bbq; 15% statics;
phone; Eng spkn; adv bkg acc; ccard acc; games area;
CKE. *"Enthusiastic, helpful British owners; some diff,
long narr pitches; grnd stony; rd & farming noise; clean
facs but poss stretched high ssn; excel pool; excel
cycling; vg site."* **€27.00, 15 Mar-15 Oct.** 2015

VENAREY LES LAUMES *6G1* (0.6km W Urban)
47.54448, 4.45043 **Camp Municipal Alésia,** Rue du
Docteur Roux, 21150 Venarey-les-Laumes **03 80 96
07 76 or 03 80 96 01 59 (Mairie); camping@ville-
venareyleslaumes.fr; www.venareyleslaumes.fr**
🐕 €1 ♂♀(htd) 🏕 🔥 🚿 ∥ 🚲 nr 🌊

SE fr Montbard on D905, site well sp fr Venarey on
D954. 3*, Med, mkd, hdg, hdstg, pt shd, EHU (16A) €3;
bbq; sw; red long stay; TV; 10% statics; phone; Eng
spkn; adv bkg acc; ccard acc; bike hire; CKE. *"Well-kept
site in scenic area; lge pitches; pleasant wardens; gd,
sm htd refurbished san facs; barrier clsd 2200-0700;
cycle tracks to Canal de Bourgogne, ltd facs in LS."*
€14.70, 1 Apr-15 Oct. 2015

VENCE *10E4* (3km W Rural) *43.7117, 7.0905*
Camping Domaine La Bergerie, 1330 Chemin
de la Sine, 06140 Vence **04 93 58 09 36; info@
camping-domainedelabergerie.com; www.
camping-domainedelabergerie.com**
🐕 ♂♀ WD 🏕 🔥 🚿 🗑 ∥ MP 🦋 🍽 🕙 🚲 🌊 🍺 🎣

Fr A8 exit junc 47 & foll sp Vence thro Cagnes-sur-
Mer. Take detour to W around Vence foll sp Grasse/
Tourrettes-sur-Loup. At rndabt beyond viaduct take
last exit, foll site sp S thro La Sine town; long, narr
rd to site, up driveway on R.
3*, Lge, mkd, hdstg, shd, pt sl, EHU (5A); gas; bbq
(gas); red long stay; Eng spkn; adv bkg acc; ccard acc;
lake fishing; games area; tennis; CKE. *"Shady site;
helpful staff; clean san facs; no twin axles or c'vans
over 5m; gd dog walks; Vence lovely & excel touring
base."* **€33.40, 25 Mar-16 Oct.** 2019

VENDAYS MONTALIVET *7C1* (8.6km W Coastal)
45.36325, -1.14496 **Camping CHM Montalivet
(Naturist),** 46 Ave de l'Europe, 33930 Vendays-
Montalivet **05 33 09 20 92; infos@socnat.fr;
www.chm-montalivet.com**

12 🐕 €6.90 ♿ WD 🚿 🔥 ♿ ⚡ 🚐 MSF 🦋 ⌂ 🍽 🍷
🔥 ♨ 🛒 ⛱ 🏖 ⛱ (htd) 🚣 sand adj

D101 fr Soulac to Vendays-Montalivet; D102 to
Montalivet-les-Bains; site bef ent to vill; turn L
at petrol stn; site 1km on R. 3*, V lge, hdstg, mkd,
pt shd, pt sl, EHU (6A) inc; gas; red long stay; TV;
50% statics; phone; Eng spkn; adv bkg acc; ccard acc;
games rm; bike hire; INF card; games area. *"Vast,
peaceful site in pine forest; superb lge naturist beach
adj; excel facs for children of all ages; vg; excel; hdstg
with elec for MH's."* **€48.00** 2018

VENDOIRE *7B2* (3km W Rural) *45.40860, 0.28079*
Camping du Petit Lion, 24320 Vendoire
**05 53 91 00 74; contact@camping-petit-lion.com;
www.camping-petit-lion.com**

12 🐕 €3 ♿ (htd) 🚿 🔥 ♿ ⚡ 🚐 🦋 🍷 🍽 ♨ 🛒 ⛱ 🏖 ⛱

S fr Angoulême on D939 or D674, take D5 to
Villebois-Lavalette, then D17 to Gurat. Then take
D102 to Vendoire, site sp. 1*, Sm, hdg, hdstg, pt shd,
EHU (10A) €4; 10% statics; adv bkg acc; lake fishing;
tennis; CKE. *"British owners; rally fields."*
€17.00 2016

"I need an on-site restaurant"

We do our best to make sure site information
is correct, but it is always best to check any
must-have facilities are still available or will
be open during your visit.

VENDOME *4F2* (0.5km E Urban) *47.79122,
1.07586* **Camping au Coeur de Vendôme,** Rue
Geoffroy-Martel, 41100 Vendôme **02 54 77 00 27
or 09 70 35 83 31; aucoeurdevendome@camp-
in-ouest.com; www.aucoeurdevendome.com**

🐕 €2.50 ♿ WD 🚿 🔥 ♿ ⚡ 🚐 🦋 🍷 nr ♨ nr 🛒 nr ⛱

Fr N10 by-pass foll sp for town cent; in town foll
sp Camping; site adj to pool 500m. 3*, Lge, mkd, pt
shd, EHU (10A) inc; bbq; red long stay; 5% statics;
phone; Eng spkn; rv fishing adj; tennis; CKE. *"Pleasant
rvside setting; clean san facs - a trek fr outer pitches;
sports cent, pool & theatre adj; statics sep area;
recep 0900-2100; htd pool adj; games area adj;
barrier clsd 2200-0630; vg; friendly; bar 500m; level
site; narr ent/exit over bdge, poss diff for lge o'fits."*
€20.00, 15 Apr-30 Oct. 2017

VERDUN *5D1* (2km SW Urban) *49.15428, 5.36598*
Camping Les Breuils, 8 Allée des Breuils, 55100
Verdun **03 29 86 15 31; contact@camping-
lesbreuils.com; www.camping-lesbreuils.com**

🐕 €2.10 ♿ WD 🚿 🔥 ♿ ⚡ 🚐 🦋 MSF 🍷 🍽 ♨ 🛒 ⛱ 🏖 🚣

Fr W (Paris) on A4/E50, exit junc 30 onto D1916/
D603/D330; cont over rndabt junc with D34 onto
D330; at next rndabt in 100m turn R into Allée
des Breuils. Or fr E (Metz) exit junc 31 onto D964/
D330; cont on D330 past junc with D34A; at rndabt
in 150m turn L into Allée des Breuils. Site sp nr
Citadel. Avoid Verdun town cent due to 1-way rds.
Allée des Breuils runs parallel to D34 on E side of
rwly. Site well sp fr D603 & all other dirs. Steepish
ent. 3*, Lge, hdg, mkd, hdstg, pt shd, pt sl, EHU (16A)
€4.55 (poss some rev pol); gas; red long stay; phone;
Eng spkn; adv bkg rec; ccard acc; fishing; bike hire;
waterslide; CKE. *"Pleasant, clean, well-kept, lovely,
busy site; grass pitches beside lge pond, some lge; poss
long walk to water taps; some site rds tight for lge
o'fits; gd pool; poss lge youth groups Sept; interesting
historial town; cycle rtes around WWI battlefields;
easy walk to Citadel with WWI museum; excel; gd
rest; friendly staff; sports cent; bus tours fr site;
san facs block refurbished (2018); facs expanding."*
€25.00, 15 Mar-15 Oct. 2018

VERDUN SUR LE DOUBS *6H1* (0.5km W Rural)
46.90259, 5.01777 **Camp Municipal La Plage,** Quai du
Doubs Prolongé, 71350 Verdun-sur-le-Doubs **03 85 91
55 50 or 03 85 91 52 52; mairie.verdunsurledoubs@
wanadoo.fr; www.tourisme-verdun-en-bourgogne.com**

🐕 €1 ♿ WD 🚿 🚐 🦋 🍷 🍽 nr ♨ nr 🛒 nr ⛱

SE on D970 fr Beaune to Verdun-sur-le-Doubs &
foll sp in town. Or on D973 or N73 twd Chalon
fr Seurre, turn R onto D115 to Verdun; site on bank
of Rv Saône. 2*, Lge, mkd, shd, pt sl, EHU (10A) €2.10;
bbq; phone; waterslide; tennis; fishing. *"Lovely rvside
location; lge pitches; helpful warden; interesting sm
town; confluence of 3 rvs: La Saône, Le Doubs & La
Dheune; htd pool adj; fishermen's paradise; excel."*
€16.50, 1 May-15 Sep. 2017

VERMENTON *4G4* (0.9km S Rural) *47.65897, 3.73087*
Camp Municipal Les Coullemières,
route de Coullemières, 89270 Vermenton
**03 86 81 53 02; contact@camping-vermenton.com;
www.camping-vermenton.com**

🐕 €1 ♿ (htd) WD 🚿 🔥 ♿ ⚡ 🚐 🦋 🍷 ♨ nr 🛒 nr ⛱

Lies W of D606 - turn off D606 into Rue Pasteur
(tight turn & narr rd), strt on at x-rds into Ave de la
Gare. Turn R at stn, L over level x-ing. Well sp in vill
adj to rv but sps low down & easy to miss.
3*, Med, mkd, hdg, pt shd, EHU (6A) inc; TV;
5% statics; bus; adv bkg rec; ccard acc; fishing;
boating; tennis; bike hire. *"Peaceful, well-run rvside
site; excel san facs; absolutely immac; weight limit on
access rds & pitches; no twin axles; gd walks & cycling;
conv Chablis vineyards; town with 12thC church; excel
site; staff helpful; delightful site in interesting area."*
€17.00, 1 Apr-30 Sep. 2019

VERNANTES *4G1* (7km NW Rural) *47.43717, 0.00641*
Camping La Fortinerie, La Fortinerie, 49390 Mouliherne
02 41 67 59 76; north.john.a@gmail.com;
www.lafortinerie.com

🐕 ⚌ WC ♨ ♿ ⚊ 🦋 ⑪nr 🏊nr

Fr Vernantes take D58 dir Mouliherne; opp Château
Loroux (Plaissance) turn L; at x-rds turn R, site over
1.5km on L. Sm, pt shd, EHU (16A) €5 (poss rev pol);
bbq; adv bkg acc. *"Peaceful CL-type site; only sound
is crickets!;dogs by prior arrangement; lge pitches;
helpful, friendly British owners; B&B avail; beautiful
chateau town; conv Loire valley & vineyards; excel."*
€12.00, 1 May-30 Sep.   2016

VERNET LES BAINS *8G4* (4km S Rural) *42.53330,
2.39847* **Domaine-St-Martin,** 6 Boulevard de la
Cascade 66820 Casteil **04 68 05 52 09;**
info@domainestmartin.com

🐕 ⚌ WC ♨ ♿ ⚊ 🦋 ♟ ⍾ ⑪ 🏊nr ⚏ ⛵

Fr Prade to Villefranche on N116. Twd Vernet-les-
Bains/Casteil at rndabt. Sp to campsite.
3*, Med, mkd, hdstg, shd, terr, EHU (10A); bbq; cooking
facs; TV; 20% statics; phone; bus adj; Eng spkn; adv bkg
acc; games rm; CCI. *"Mountain hiking/biking; Grottoes
6km; Abbey in vill; friendly, helpful staff; excel rest; vg."*
€29.70, 31 Mar-31 Oct.   2019

VERNET LES BAINS *8G4* (8km NW Rural) *42.56255,
2.36050* **Camping Le Rotja,** Ave de la Rotja, 66820
Fuilla **04 68 96 52 75; info@camping-lerotja.com;**
www.camping-lerotja.com

🐕 €2 ⚌ (htd) WC ♨ ♿ ⚊ 🦋 ⑪nr ⍾ 🏊nr ⚏ ⛵

Take N116 fr Prades dir Mont-Louis, 500m after
Villefranche-de-Conflens turn L onto D6 sp Fuilla;
in 3km just bef church, turn R at sp to site. D6
narr but passing places. 3*, Sm, mkd, pt shd, pt sl,
terr, EHU (10A) €3.25; gas; bbq (gas); red long stay;
10% statics; phone; Eng spkn; adv bkg acc; ccard
acc; CKE. *"Peaceful site; views of Mount Canigou;
friendly, helpful Dutch owners; gd hiking/walks."*
€27.50, 1 Apr-17 Oct.   2015

VERNET, LE *9D3* (0.8km N Rural) *44.28170,
6.39080* **Camping Lou Passavous,** Route de
Roussimat, 04140 Le Vernet **04 92 35 14 67;**
loupassavous@orange.fr; www.loupassavous.com

🐕 €1.50 ⚌ (htd) WC ♨ ♿ ⚊ 🦋 ♟ ⍾ ⑪ 🏊 ⚏ ✏ ⛵

Fr N on A51 exit junc 21 Volonne onto N85 sp
Digne. Fr Digne N on D900 to Le Vernet; site on
R. Fr S exit A51 junc 20 Les Mées onto D4, then
N85 E to Digne, then as above. 3*, Sm, pt shd, pt
sl, EHU (6A) €4; TV; 10% statics; Eng spkn; adv bkg
acc; fishing; games area; CKE. *"Scenic location; gd,
clean facs; Dutch owners; gd walking, mkd walks
fr site, escorted walks by owner; excel; highly rec."*
€24.00, 1 May-15 Sep.   2016

VERNON *3D2* (2km W Rural) *49.09625, 1.43851*
Camping Les Fosses Rouges, Chemin de Réanville,
27950 St Marcel **02 32 51 59 86 or 06 22 42 19 11 (LS);**
camping@cape27.fr; www.cape27.fr

🐕 €0.50 ⚌ (htd) WC ♨ ♿ ⚊ 🦋 🏊nr ⚏

Exit A13/E5 junc 16 dir Vernon onto D181; in 2km
at rndabt turn L onto D64e dir St Marcel; in 2km at
5-exit rndabt take 1st R onto Chemin de Réanville
(D64) & foll camping sp. At 1st major bend to R,
cont strt ahead, site on L in 50m.
2*, Med, mkd, pt shd, pt sl, EHU (6-10A) €3.20-4.20;
gas; bbq; 10% statics; adv bkg acc; CKE. *"Well-kept,
well-run scenic site; gd clean san facs but tired; parking
for m'vans at St Marcel - cont past site over rndabt
for 900m, turn sharp L past hotel on R & parking
on R; lovely little vill; conv Giverny, but access diff
lge o'fits; pool 4km; gd size pitches; peaceful site."*
€11.00, 1 Mar-31 Oct.   2017

VERSAILLES *4E3* (3km E Urban) *48.79455, 2.16038*
Camping Huttopia Versailles, 31 Rue Berthelot,
Porchefontaine, 78000 Versailles **01 39 51 23 61;**
versailles@huttopia.com; www.huttopia.com

🐕 €4 ⚌ (htd) WC ♨ ♿ ⚊ MSP 🦋 ♟ ⑪ ⍾ 🏊nr ⚏
🏊 (htd)

Foll sp to Château de Versailles; fr main ent
take Ave de Paris dir Porchefontaine & turn R
immed after twin gate lodges; sp. Narr access
rd due parked cars & sharp bends. No sp rec use
sat nav. 3*, Lge, mkd, pt shd, pt sl, terr, EHU inc
(6-10A) €4.60-6.80; gas; bbq; red long stay; TV;
20% statics; bus 500m; Eng spkn; adv bkg acc; ccard
acc; bike hire; games area; CKE. *"Wooded site; sm,
sl, uneven pitches poss diff lge o'fits; friendly, helpful
staff, excel, clean san facs; stretched high ssn; conv
Paris trains & Versailles Château; bus 171 to town."*
€45.50, 24 Mar-2 Nov, P19.   2016

VERTEILLAC *3 B3* (3km W Rural) *45.340833, 0.340833*
HighThorn At Haute Epine, 24320 St Martial
Viveyrols **05 53 91 11 83 or 06 82 30 80 60 (mob);**
info@highthorn.com; www.highthorn.com

🐕 ⚌ (htd) WC ♨ ♿ ⚊ MSP 🦋 ♟ ⍾nr ⑪ 🏊nr ⚏ 🏊 (htd)

Fr Vertaillac foll D97 W for 2km. Then turn L at
x-rds, S for 200m to site. Sm, hdg, unshd, serviced
pitches; EHU 10A; bbq (charcoal, elec, gas); cooking
facs; sw nr; twin axles; bus; Eng spkn; adv bkg
rec; ccard acc. *"Adults only; tranquil site; only 4
pitches, each with own enclosed secure bathroom;
separate utility and freezer rm; pick of fruit and
veg in gdn; plenty of rest in area; lge shopping area
and mkts in Riberac (12km); many beautiful vill,
historic towns and vineyards to visit; owners live on
site, friendly and welcoming, runs rest onsite only
avail to site guest; dog sitting avail; hg rec; excel."*
€36.75, 1 May-30 Sep.   2019

VERVINS *3C4* (8.5km N Rural) *49.90676, 3.91977*
FFCC Camping du Val d'Oise, 3 Rue du Mont
d'Origny, 02580 Etréaupont **03 23 97 48 04;**
www.campingduvaldoisern2.com

🐕 €0.30 ⚥ 🅆🄳 📷 ♨ ⁄ 🕮 🦋 ♿ 🍴 nr ⛺

Site to E of Etréaupont off N2, Mons-Reims rd.
Site adj football pitch on banks of Rv Oise. Well sp
fr main rd. 2*, Sm, mkd, hdg, pt shd, EHU (10A) €4
(poss rev pol); Eng spkn; adv bkg acc; rv fishing adj;
tennis; CKE. *"Pretty, tidy site; sports field adj; warm
welcome; v clean san facs; site self if recep clsd; conv
rte to Zeebrugge ferry (approx 200km); gd walking
& cycling; gd; delightful site; canoe hire adj; vg."*
€16.00, 1 Apr-31 Oct. 2017

VESOUL *6G2* (3km W Rural) *47.63026, 6.12858*
Camping International du Lac, Ave des Rives
du Lac, 70000 Vesoul **03 84 76 22 86; camping_
dulac@yahoo.fr; www.camping-vesoul.com**

12 🐕 €2 ⚥ (htd) ♨ ♿ 🅆🄳 📷 ⁄ 🕮 🍴 🍽 ♿ 🍴 nr ⛺

2km fr D619, sp fr W end of by-pass, pass indus est
to lge lake on W o'skts. Ent opp Peugeot/Citroën
factory on lakeside. 3*, Lge, mkd, pt shd, EHU (6A)
€3; gas; 10% statics; adv bkg acc; ccard acc; tennis;
fishing; waterslide 300m; games area; CKE. *"Super
site screened fr indus est by trees; pool & paddling pool
300m; site clsd mid-Dec to early Jan; gd size pitches
but poss soft after rain; excel aqua park nr; gd cycle
rtes; vg."* **€19.00** 2016

VEULES LES ROSES *3C2* (0.3km S Rural/Coastal)
49.87586, 0.80314 **Camping Les Mouettes,**
7 Ave Jean Moulin, 76980 Veules-les-Roses **02 35
97 61 98; camping.les.mouettes0509@orange.
fr; www.camping-lesmouettes-normandie.com**

🐕 €2 ⚥ (htd) 🅆🄳 ♨ ♿ 🅆🄳 ⁄ 🕮 🦋 ⁄ 🍴 🍽 ⛺ ⁄
🏊 (covrd, htd) 🏖 🏖 shgl 800m

On ent vill fr Dieppe on D925, turn R onto D68, site
in 500m up hill (14%). 3*, Lge, hdg, mkd, pt shd, EHU
(6A) €4.70; gas; bbq; red long stay; TV; 10% statics;
Eng spkn; adv bkg acc; ccard acc; games area; games
rm; fitness rm; CKE. *"Pleasant area; peaceful, well-
kept site; vg; site a bit scruffy start of ssn (2017)."*
€29.30, 1 Apr-15 Oct. 2017

VEZELAY *4G4* (4.6km S Rural) *47.45675, 3.78768*
FFCC Camping de Vézelay L'Ermitage, 1 Route
de l'Étang, 89450 Vézelay **03 86 33 24 18; auberge.
jeunesse.vezelay@orange.fr; www.camping-
auberge-vezelay.com**

⚥ 🅆🄳 📷 ⁄ 🕮 🦋 🍴 nr

Foll sp fr cent of Vézelay to 'Camping Vézelay' &
Youth Hostel. 1*, Sm, pt shd, pt sl, serviced pitches;
EHU (4-6A) €3; Eng spkn; CKE. *"Pleasant, peaceful,
scenic site; welcoming; gd, clean facs; some pitches diff
lge o'fits & blocks req; recep eve only - site self & sign
in when open; some pitches muddy after heavy rain;
Vézelay the starting point of one of the pilgrim rtes -
superb abbey; excel."* **€8.50, 1 Apr-31 Oct.** 2015

VIAS *10F1* (3km S Coastal) *43.29055, 3.39863*
Camping Californie Plage, 34450 Vias-Plage
**04 67 21 64 69; info@californie-plage.fr;
www.californie-plage.fr**

🐕 €4.60 ⚥ 🅆🄳 ♨ ♿ 🅆🄳 ⁄ 🕮 🍴 🍽 🍴 🍽 ♿ 🍴
⛺ ⁄ 🏊 (covrd, htd) 🏊 🏖 sand adj

W fr Agde on D612 to Vias; turn S in town & foll sps
'Mer' over canal bdge & sp to site. 4*, Lge, mkd, shd,
EHU (5-10A) €1.50-3.50; gas; TV; 10% statics; Eng
spkn; adv bkg acc; ccard acc; bike hire; waterslide; CKE.
€33.00, 1 Apr-30 Oct. 2016

VIAS *10F1* (3km S Coastal) *43.29083, 3.41783*
Yelloh! Village Le Club Farret, Farinette-Plage,
34450 Vias-Plage **04 67 21 64 45; info@
farret.com; www.camping-farret.com**

🐕 €6 ⚥ 🅆🄳 ♨ ♿ 🅆🄳 ⁄ 🕮 🦋 🍴 🍽 🍴 🍽 ⛺ ⁄ 🍴 (htd)
🏊 sand adj

Fr A9, exit Agde junc 34. Foll sp Vias-Plage on
D137. Sp fr cent of Vias-Plage on L, immed after
Gendarmerie. 4*, V lge, mkd, pt shd, EHU (6A) inc;
gas; TV; 10% statics; Eng spkn; adv bkg acc; ccard acc;
games rm; bike hire; fitness rm; games area; tennis;
watersports; CKE. *"Excel facs, entmnt; excursions; gd
security."* **€65.00, 12 Apr-29 Sep.** 2017

VIAS *10F1* (3km W Rural) *43.31222, 3.36320*
Camping Sunêlia Le Domaine de la Dragonnière,
34450 Vias **04 67 01 03 10; contact@dragonniere.
com; www.dragonniere.com**

🐕 €5 ⚥ 🅆🄳 ♨ ♿ 🅆🄳 ⁄ 🕮 🍴 🍽 🍴 🍽 ⛺ ⁄ 🍴 (htd)
🏊 sand 3km

Exit A9 junc 35 onto D64 twd Valras-Plage, then
D612 dir Agde & Vias. Site on R bef Vias. Or exit junc
34 onto D612A. At Vias turn R onto D612 sp Béziers,
site on L. NB Take care high speed humps at sh
intervals. 4*, V lge, mkd, hdg, pt shd, EHU (16A) inc;
gas; bbq; TV; 80% statics; phone; Eng spkn; adv bkg
acc; ccard acc; games area; spa; bike hire; tennis; CKE.
*"Vg site; excel for children & teenagers high ssn; Canal
du Midi nrby; opp Béziers airport; free bus to beach;
site poss flooded after heavy rain; touring pitches
have individual shwr block on pitch; v busy at w/ends."*
€85.00, 5 Apr-3 Nov, C06. 2016

VICHY *9A1* (4km S Rural) *46.11555, 3.43006*
Camping Beau Rivage, Rue Claude Decloître, 03700
Bellerive-sur-Allier **04 70 32 26 85; camping-beaurivage
@wanadoo.fr; www.camping-beaurivage.com**

🐕 €1 ⚥ 🅆🄳 ♨ ♿ 🅆🄳 ⁄ 🕮 🦋 🍴 🍽 🍴 🍽 ⛺ ⁄ 🏊 (covrd, htd)

Fr Vichy cross rv bdge over Rv Allier onto D1093,
turn L at rndabt foll sp Campings, sp to Beau
Rivage. Site on L on rv bank, past Cmp Les Acacias.
4*, Med, shd, EHU (10A) €3.10; gas; bbq; TV;
50% statics; tennis 2km; games area; bike hire;
archery; waterslide; canoeing; fishing. *"Lovely
rvside site, but no rv sw allowed; lge o'fits have
diff pitching; easy cycle ride to lovely city."*
€23.60, 1 Apr-8 Oct. 2016

VICHY 9A1 (4km S Urban) 46.10756, 3.43670
FFCC Camping La Croix St Martin, Allée du Camping, 99 Ave des Graviers, 03200 Abrest **04 70 32 67 74 or 06 10 94 70 90 (mob); camping-vichy@orange.fr; www.camping-vichy.com**

🐕 ♦♦♦ ⓦⒹ ♨ ♿ ⬛ ⁄ ⓂⓈⓅ 🦋 ☂ 🄌 🛶 (htd) 🛗

Exit D906 at Abrest onto D426 N (Ave des Graviers); in 900m turn L into Allée du Camping. Site sp fr D906, both N & S of Abrest. 3*, Med, mkd, hdg, pt shd, EHU (10A) €3.80; 15% statics; phone; Eng spkn; adv bkg acc; ccard acc; games area; CKE. "*Gd cycling along rv allier thro Vichy; san facs clean; well maintained, well run, attractive site; friendly staff; flat walking dist fr a v attractive town; free wifi over all site; pool now covrd.*" **€20.00, 2 Apr-2 Oct.** 2015

VICHY 9A1 (1km SW Rural) 46.11648, 3.42560
Camping Les Acacias, Rue Claude Decloître, 03700 Bellerive-sur-Allier **04 70 32 36 22; camping-acacias03@orange.fr; www.camping-acacias.com**

🐕 €1 ⓦⒹ ♨ ♿ ⁄ ☂ 🄌 nr 🄌 🛶

Cross bdge to Bellerive fr Vichy & foll Hauterive sp onto D1093. Strt over at 1st rndabt & turn L at 2nd rndabt onto D131 dir Hauterive. At 3rd rndabt turn L sp 'piscine'. Foll sm camping sps along rv side. Or fr S leave D906 at St Yorre & cross Rv Allier, then foll sp to Bellerive. Site sp at rndabt on app to Bellerive adj Rv Allier. On final app, at sp showing site in either dir, keep L & foll site sp along rv bank to recep. NB Many other sites in area, foll sp carefully. 4*, Med, mkd, hdg, shd, EHU (10A) €3.40; gas; bbq; TV; 20% statics; adv bkg acc; ccard acc; boating; fishing; CKE. "*Well-run site; helpful owner; gd san facs; free Vichy Célestins water at spring in lovely town.*" **€19.00, 7 Apr-7 Oct.** 2015

VIERZON 4G3 (2.5km SW Urban) 47.20937, 2.08079
Camp O'village Vierzon (formerly Municipal), Route de Bellon, 18100 Vierzon **02 48 53 99 89; contact@campovillage.com; www.campovillage.com**

🐕 ♦♦♦ ⓦⒹ ♨ ♿ ⁄ ⓂⓈⓅ ☂ 🍴 🄌 🄌 nr 🄌

Fr N on A71 take A20 dir Châteauroux, leave at junc 7 onto D2020 & then D27 dir Bourges; pass Intermarché supmkt on L, after next traff lts turn L into Route de Bellon; site in 1km on R, sp. NB Do not go into town cent. 2*, Med, hdg, mkd, pt shd, pt sl, EHU (6A) €3 (some rev pol); gas; bbq (elec, gas); phone; Eng spkn; adv bkg acc; boat hire; fishing; CKE. "*Attractive, well-kept site by rv; gd sized pitches but some poss diff to negotiate; nice little rest o'looking rv; gates clsd 2300-0700; helpful staff; poss travellers; ideal NH; gd site; friendly recep; new facs, v clean (2017).*" **€23.50, 15 Jun-14 Sep.** 2019

VIEURE 7A4 (2km NE Rural) 46.50305, 2.90754
Plan d'eau de Vieure, La Borde, 03430 Vieure **04 70 02 04 46 or 09 60 36 53 41; plandeau03@orange.fr; www.locationschaletscampingdelaborde.fr**

🐕 ♦♦♦ ♨ ♿ ⬛ ⁄ 🦋 ☂ 🍴 🄌 🄌 🄌

Exit A71-E11 at junc 10. Take D94 NE to Cosne d'Allier, then R onto D11. L onto D459, 1st R onto La Bordé. Foll sp to campsite. Med, hdg, pt shd, pt sl, EHU (10A) €3.10; sw; twin axles; 35% statics; phone; ccard acc; CCI. "*Large, open & shd pitches; dated san facs; v pleasant remote site by lake; fishing & canoeing; family friendly; gd.*" **€11.50, 11 Apr-30 Sep.** 2019

VIHIERS 4G1 (15km SE Rural) 47.07419, -0.41104
Camping Le Serpolin, St Pierre-à-Champ, 49560 Cléré-sur-Layon **02 41 52 43 08; info@loirecamping.com; www.loirecamping.com**

12 🐕 ♦♦♦ (htd) ⓦⒹ ♨ ⁄ 🦋 ☂ 🄌 🛶

Take D748 S fr Vihiers by-pass sp Argenton Château. In 2km turn L at sp Cléré-sur-Layon onto D54. Cont thro vill to 1st mkd x-rd, turn R, site last house along this lane. Sm, hdstg, pt shd, EHU (10A) €4; bbq; Eng spkn; adv bkg rec; bike hire; fishing; CKE. "*Peaceful, CL-type site; clean san facs; helpful British owners; dogs free; rallies by arrangement; conv chateaux; Futuroscope; vg.*" **€15.00** 2015

VILLARD DE LANS 9C3 (1.5km N Rural) 45.07750, 5.55620 **Camping Caravaneige L'Oursière,** 38250 Villard-de-Lans **04 76 95 14 77; oursiere@franceloc.fr; www.camping-oursiere.fr**

12 🐕 €5 ♦♦♦ (htd) ♨ ♿ ⬛ ⁄ ⓂⓈⓅ 🦋 ☂ 🄌 🛶 🄌

Site clearly visible on app to town fr D531 Gorges d'Engins rd (13km SW Grenoble). App fr W on D531 not rec for c'vans & m'vans due o'hangs. 3*, Lge, unshd, terr, EHU (10A) €4-6; gas; bbq; 20% statics; Eng spkn; adv bkg acc; ccard acc; CKE. "*Excel all winter sports; friendly owners; drying rm; san facs need upgrade (2010); pool 800m; waterpark 800m; new htd indoor sw pool (2015).*" **€26.00** 2016

VILLARD DE LANS 9C3 (12km N Rural) 45.12951, 5.53215 **Camping Caravaneige Les Buissonnets,** 38112 Méaudre **04 76 95 21 04; camping-les-buissonnets@wanadoo.fr; www.camping-les-buissonnets.com**

♦♦♦ (htd) ⓦⒹ ♿ ♨ ⬛ ⁄ ⓂⓈⓅ 🦋 🄌 nr 🄌 nr 🄌

Fr Grenoble take D1532 to Sassenage then D531 to Lans-en-Vercors. Turn R at rndabt onto D106 twrds Meaudre. Turn L just bef rndabt in vill off D106. Approx 30km SW of Grenoble by rd & 18km as crow flies. 3*, Med, unshd, sl, EHU (6-10A) €4-6; bus to ski slopes; games area; clsd 1 Dec-10 Nov. "*Gd skiing cent; conv touring Vercours; levellers ess; highly rec; friendly, v well managed site; higher price in winter; pool 300m; lovely area; slightly sl, levelling necessary; v pleasant.*" **€21.00, 1 Jan-31 Oct & 12 Dec-31 Dec.** 2017

VILLARS LES DOMBES *9A2* (0.2km S Urban)
45.99763, 5.03163 **Camping Le Nid du Parc (formerly Parc des Oiseaux),** 164 Ave des Nations, 01330 Villars-les-Dombes **04 74 98 00 21; camping@ parcdesoiseaux.com; www.leniddparc.com**

🏕 €3 🏕 ⛺ ♿ 🚿 🧺 ♨ 🍽 ⓦ 🛒 🛒 nr 🎪 ✏ 🏊

N fr Lyon on N83, site in town cent on R by sw pool. 4*, Lge, hdstg, pt shd, EHU (10A) €4.50; bbq (gas); 60% statics; games area; rv fishing adj; bike hire; tennis. *"Excel site; lge pitches; modern, gd san facs; htd pool adj inc; gd security; bird park 10 mins walk; popular NH."* €33.50, 29 Mar-11 Nov. **2019**

"Satellite navigation makes touring much easier"

Remember most sat navs don't know if you're towing or in a larger vehicle – always use yours alongside maps and site directions.

VILLEDIEU LES POELES *1D4* (0.6km S Urban)
48.83638, -1.21694 **Camping Les Chevaliers de Malte,** 2 Impasse Pré de la Rose, 50800 Villedieu-les-Poêles **02 33 59 49 04; contact@camping-deschevaliers. com; www.camping-deschevaliers.com**

🏕 €1.50 🏕 (htd) ⓦ ⛺ ♿ 🚿 🧺 ♨ 🍽 ⓦ 🐾 🏕 🍽 🛒 nr 🎪 ✏ 🏊 (htd)

Exit A84 junc 38 onto D999 twd Villedieu, then R onto D975 & R onto D924 to avoid town cent. Foll sp fr car park on R after x-ing rv. Site behind PO & cinema. 3*, Med, hdstg, hdg, mkd, pt shd, EHU (6A) inc (poss rev pol); bbq; TV; 40% statics; phone; Eng spkn; adv bkg acc; games area; boating; games rm; rv fishing; tennis; CKE. *"Peaceful, lovely site; lge pitches but kerbs poss diff lger o'fits; interesting historic town; avoid arr Tue am due mkt; conv A84 & Cherbourg ferry; vg; gd modern facs, all new; well worth a visit to town; excel site; rest extended 2011; staff v helpful; bell foundry worth a visit; new owners (2016); vg."* €28.00, 1 Apr-15 Oct. **2017**

VILLEFORT (LOZERE) *9D1* (0.6km S Rural) *44.43536, 3.93323* **Le Mas Les Sédariès,** Ave des Cévennes, 48800 Villefort **04 66 46 25 20; vacances48@ gmail.com; www.sedaries.com**

🏕 €1 🏕 ⓦ ⛺ ♨ 🐾 🍽 nr ⓦ nr 🛒 nr

On D906 heading S fr Villefort twd Alès. 2*, Sm, pt shd, terr, EHU (6A) €2; bbq; sw nr; phone; fishing 2km; CKE. *"Attractive, scenic site; bureau clsd 1000-1830; privately owned now (2014); not many touring places."* €15.00, 1 Jun-30 Sep. **2019**

VILLEFRANCHE DE LAURAGAIS *8F3* (8km SW Rural) *43.35498, 1.64862* **Camping Le Lac de la Thésauque,** Nailloux, 31560 Montgeard **05 61 81 34 67; camping@ thesauque.com; www.camping-thesauque.com**

12 🐕 🏕 (htd) ⓦ ⛺ ♿ 🚿 🧺 ♨ 🍽 🛒 🛒 🎪 🏊

Fr S exit A61 at Villefrance-de-Lauragais junc 20 onto D622, foll sp Auterive then Lac after Gardouch vill, site sp. Fr N turn off A61 at 1st junc after tolls S of Toulouse onto A66 (sp Foix). Leave A66 at junc 1 & foll sp Nailloux. Turn L on ent vill onto D662 & in 2km turn R onto D25 & immed R to site, sp. 3*, Med, mkd, hdstg, pt shd, terr, EHU (10A) inc; bbq; 70% statics; ccard acc; boating; fishing; tennis; CKE. *"Scenic, peaceful location; conv NH for A61; helpful owners; ltd facs LS; gd security; steep app to sm terr pitches poss diff lge o'fits; facs basic but adequate."* €24.00 **2019**

VILLEFRANCHE DE ROUERGUE *7D4* (9km SE Rural) *44.26695, 2.11575* **Camping Le Muret,** 12200 St Salvadou **05 65 81 80 69 or 05 65 29 84 87; info@lemuret.com; www.lemuret.com**

🏕 €2 🏕 ⛺ ♿ 🚿 🧺 🦋 ♨ 🍽 🛒 🛒 🏊

Fr Villefranche on D911 twd Millau, R on D905A sp camping & foll camping sp 7km. 3*, Sm, mkd, hdg, shd, EHU (16A) €4.50; red long stay; phone; adv bkg acc; fishing; CKE. *"Lovely setting; gas & ice at farm; lake adj; gd sized pitches."* €23.00, 5 Apr-22 Oct. **2017**

VILLEFRANCHE DU PERIGORD *7D3* (8km SW Rural) *44.59025, 1.04799* **Moulin du Périé Camping - Caravaning,** 47500 Sauveterre-la-Lémance **05 53 40 67 26; moulinduperie@wanadoo.fr; www.camping-moulin-perie.com or www.flowercampings.com**

🏕 €4.60 🏕 ⓦ ⛺ ♿ 🚿 🧺 ♨ 🐾 🍽 🛒 🛒 🏊 🏊

Fr N fr Villefranche-du-Périgord take D710 S dir Fumel. At Sauveterre-la-Lémance turn L at traff lts, cross level x-ing & in 400m turn L sp Loubejac & site; site on R in 4km. Tight ent bet tall hedges 2.6m apart for 30m. Fr E fr Cahors on D660 & turn L onto D46 sp Loubejac. Cont thro Loubejac & turn L at T-junc, foll sp Sauveterre. Site on R in 4km. 4*, Med, pt shd, pt sl, EHU (6-10A) €3 (poss rev pol); gas; bbq; TV; 25% statics; Eng spkn; adv bkg rec; ccard acc; tennis 3km; bike hire; archery; trout fishing; games rm; CKE. *"Beautiful, well-run site in grnds of old mill; welcoming, friendly family owners; clean, dated san facs; vg rest; site rds narr, not suitable v lge o'fits; gd touring base; excel; poor maintenance (2015)."* €30.00, 13 May-16 Sep. **2015**

VILLEFRANCHE SUR CHER *4G3* (8km SE Rural) *47.26917, 1.86265* **FFCC Camp Municipal Val Rose,** Rue du Val Rose, 41320 Mennetou-sur-Cher 02 54 98 11 02 or 02 54 98 01 19 (Mairie); mairie. mennetou@wanadoo.fr; http://mennetou.fr/ tourisme/se-loger-restauration/camping-municipal

🐕 €0.20 ♂♀(htd) ⬛ ♿ ⬛ ✉ ⬛ 🦋 ⊕ nr ⬛ nr ⛺

Site sp fr D976/D2076 fr Villefranche (sm white sp); site on R in SW side of vill of Mennetou. To avoid narr bdge in town fr N76 onto A20, just outside town, turn imm R, site sp after L turn. 2*, Sm, pt shd, EHU (4A); Eng spkn; adv bkg acc. "Pleasant, well-kept site; friendly, helpful warden; excel, spotless san facs; excel lndry; pretty, walled town 5 mins walk along canal; mkt Thurs; htd pool adj; vg value; access for lge o'fits diff; excel NH." **€13.00, 13 May-18 Sep.**   2018

VILLEFRANCHE SUR SAONE *9B2* (10km E Rural) *45.99104, 4.81802* **FFCC Camp Municipal le Bois de la Dame,** 590 Chemin du Bois de la Dame, 01480 Ars-sur-Formans 04 74 00 77 23 or 04 74 00 71 84 (Mairie); camping.boisdeladame@orange.fr; www.ars-village.fr

🐕 €3 ♂♀(cont) ⬛ ⬛ ♿ ⬛ ✉/⬛ ⛰

Exit A6 junc 31.1 or 31.2 onto D131/D44 E dir Villars-les-Dombes. Site 500m W of Ars-sur-Formans on lake, sp. 2*, Med, mkd, pt shd, pt sl, terr, EHU (10-16A) €3-5; 60% statics; adv bkg rec; lake fishing; tennis court; CKE. "Average site, but pretty & interesting vill; ltd facs LS; no twin axles; higher pitches have unguarded precipices; gd." **€19.90, 2 Apr-30 Oct.**   2019

"There aren't many sites open at this time of year"

If you're travelling outside peak season remember to call ahead to check site opening dates – even if the entry says 'open all year'.

VILLEFRANCHE SUR SAONE *9B2* (10km SE Rural) *45.93978, 4.76811* **Camping Kanopee (formerly Municipal La Petite Saône),** Rue Robert Baltié, 01600 Trévoux 04 74 08 44 83; contact@kanopee-village.com; www.kanopee-village.com

🐕 ♂♀♿ ⬛ ✉/ 🦋 ⬛ nr ⛺ ⬛

Fr Villefranche take D306 S to Anse. Turn L onto D39/D6 for Trévoux, site sp in town, on bank of Rv Saône. 3*, Lge, pt shd, EHU (6A) inc; sw nr; 75% statics; adv bkg req; rv fishing adj; CKE. "Spacious rvside site nr vill; helpful staff; well maintained; access poss diff lge o'fits due statics; gd cycling rtes nrby; Trévoux interesting history; m'van o'night area at ent; excel shwr blocks; Aire at ent to camp; vg." **€28.00, 1 Apr-30 Sep.**   2018

VILLEFRANCHE SUR SAONE *9B2* (5km SE Rural) *45.97243, 4.75237* **Camp Municipal La Plage Plan d'Eau,** 2788 Route de Riottier, 69400 Villefranche-sur-Saône 04 74 65 33 48; campingvillefranche@voila.fr; www.villefranche.net

♂♀ ⬛ ⬛ ♿ ⬛ ✉/⬛ 🦋 ⬛ ♟ ⬛ ⬛ nr

Exit A6 junc 31.2 Villefranche. Fr N turn R at rndabt, cross over a'route & str over next rndabt; cont to site on R bef Rv Saône. Or fr S turn R at rndabt & cont to site as above. Look for sp on rndabt. 3*, Med, shd, EHU (10A); gas; sw nr; 10% statics; adv bkg acc; ccard acc; fishing; CKE. "Busy site in gd position; easy access & nr m'way but quiet; a bit run down; gd rvside walking; NH only; san facs clean (2015); card ent sys." **€22.00, 1 May-30 Sep.**   2015

VILLENEUVE SUR LOT *7D3* (3km S Urban) *44.39483, 0.68680* **Camping Lot et Bastides,** Allée de Malbentre, 47300 Pujols 05 53 36 86 79 or 06 14 13 78 93 (mob); contact@camping-lot-et-bastides.fr; www.camping-lot-et-bastides.fr

🐕 €2 ♂♀ ⬛ ⬛ ♿ ⬛ ✉ ⬛ 🦋 ♟ ⬛ ⬛ ⛺ ⬛

Fr Villeneuve Sur Lot on D911 take L onto D118. At rndabt take 1st exit onto D911. Turn L onto Rue du General. Site on the R. 3*, Med, hdg, pt shd, EHU (16A); bbq; twin axles; 25% statics; bus adj; adv bkg acc; ccard acc; games area; CCI. "New site 2012; neat and clean; views of Pujols, most beautiful vill in France; lots to see & do in area; v scenic; friendly staff; bike hire." **€24.00, 30 Mar-2 Nov.**   2019

VILLEREAL *7D3* (9km SE Rural) *44.61426, 0.81889* **Camping Fontaine du Roc,** Les Moulalies, 47210 Dévillac 05 53 36 08 16; reception@fontaineduroc.com; www.fontaineduroc.com

🐕 €3.50 ♂♀ ⬛ ⬛ ✉/ ♟ ⬛ ⊕ ⬛ ⬛ ⬛ ⬛

Fr Villeréal take D255 sp Dévillac, just beyond Dévillac at x-rds turn L & L again sp Estrade; site on L in 500m. 3*, Med, mkd, hdstg, hdg, pt shd, EHU (5-10A) €3.50-4.50 gas; bbq; red long stay; TV; 2% statics; phone; Eng spkn; adv bkg acc; fishing 500m; bike hire; games rm; CKE. "Peaceful, well-cared for site; helpful owner; lge pitches; ACSI acc (LS); excel." **€15.00, 1 Apr-15 Oct.**   2016

VILLEREAL *7D3* (3km NW Rural) *44.65253, 0.72375* **Camping de Bergougne,** 47210 Rives 05 53 36 01 30; info@camping-de-bergougne.com; www.camping-de-bergougne.com/camping/

🐕 ♂♀ ⬛ ⬛ ⬛ ♿ ⬛ ✉/ 🦋 ⬛ ⊕ ⬛ ⬛ nr ⛺ ⬛ ⬛(htd) ⬛

Fr Villeréal, take D207 NW sp Issigeac/Bergerac. In 1km turn L onto D250 W sp Doudrac. Foll sm green sp to site. 3*, Med, mkd, hdg, pt shd, pt sl, terr, EHU (6A) inc; gas; bbq (sep area); TV; 15% statics; Eng spkn; adv bkg acc; ccard acc; games rm; fishing; games area; CKE. "Vg site; small café; bread del in Jul & Aug; friendly welcoming new owners; occasional events in bar/rest; v peaceful rustic ambience; vg." **€24.00, 1 May-30 Sep.**   2018

VILLERSEXEL *6G2* (1km N Rural) *47.55763, 6.43628*
Camping Le Chapeau Chinois, 92 Rue du Chapeau Chinois, 70110 Villersexel 03 84 63 40 60; contact@camping-villersexel.eu; camping-villersexel.eu

🐕 ♟ ⛟ WD ♨ ♿ 🅿 ⊿ MSP 🦋 ⛲ ⛱ nr ⅃ nr ⚏

Leave vill on D468 N, site on R immed after rv bdge. 3*, Med, hdg, mkd, pt shd, EHU (10A) €3.30; bbq; sw; 5% statics; Eng spkn; adv bkg acc; games area; CKE. "Vg." **€19.00, 1 Apr-6 Oct.** **2016**

VILLIERS SUR ORGE *4E3* (0.6km SE Urban) *48.65527, 2.30409* **Camping Le Beau Village,** 1 Voie des Prés, 91700 Villiers-sur-Orge 01 60 16 17 86; contact@campingparis.com; www.campingparis.com

12 ♟ €2 ♟(htd) ⛟ ♨ 🅿 ⊿ MSP 🦋 ⛲ ⛱ nr ⚏

Fr S on N20 turn off onto D35 heading E twrds Villiers sur Orge. Cont strt on to traff lts & sm Renault g'ge, turn R alongside rv. Turn just bef St Genieve des Bois. 3*, Med, hdg, pt shd, EHU (10A) (poss rev pol); gas; bbq; phone; train 700m; games rm; kayaking; fishing. "Pleasant, well-run site; conv Paris; some statics/chalets; ltd space for lge o'fits; helpful staff." **€22.00** **2017**

VIMOUTIERS *3D1* (0.6km N Urban) *48.93236, 0.19646* Camp Municipal La Campière, Ave Dr Dentu, 61120 Vimoutiers 02 33 39 18 86 (Mairie); campingmunicipal vimoutiers@wanadoo.fr; www.vimoutiers.fr

🐕 €1.50 ♟(htd) WD ♨ ♿ 🅿 ⊿ ⒽH nr 🅰 ⅃ nr ⚏

App Vimoutiers fr N on on D579/D979/D916, site on R 300m after passing junc with D16; turn R at flag poles (200m after Avia petrol stn). Or appr fr Gacé on D979 turn L at flag poles (on D916 just bef junc with D16). Site nr stadium & not well sp. 2*, Sm, hdg, pt shd, EHU (6A) €2.85; sw nr; 10% statics; adv bkg acc; tennis; bike hire; rv fishing 2km; CKE. "Excel, well-maintained, pretty site at cent of Camembert cheese industry; helpful, friendly warden; sports facs 2km; vg, clean san facs; noise fr nrby factory; boating 2km; unrel opening dates - phone ahead LS; attractive town; gd value." **€13.00, 1 Apr-31 Oct.** **2018**

VIRIEU LE GRAND *9B3* (5km NE Rural) *45.87483, 5.68428* **Camping Le Vaugrais,** Chemin de Vaugrais, 01510 Artemare 04 79 87 37 34; contact@camping-le-vaugrais.fr; www.camping-savoie-levaugrais.com

🐕 €1 ♟ WD ♨ ♿ 🅿 ⊿ MSP 🦋 ⛲ ⛱ ⒽH nr 🅰 ⅃ nr ⚏ 🛶

N fr Belley on D1504 then D904 to Artemare; sp in vill. Well sp fr D904 on rvside. 3*, Sm, hdg, pt shd, EHU (10A); bbq; 10% statics; Eng spkn; adv bkg acc; fishing; CKE. "Charming site in gd location; some lge pitches with views; friendly owners; clean san facs, poss inadequate high ssn; nice pool; Artemare within walking dist; gd food at hotel in town; vg local walks; excel; app over narr bdge; gd views; highly rec." **€25.00, 1 Mar-1 Dec, M12.** **2016**

VITRE *2 F4* (2.7km SSE Urban) *48.11000, -1.19891* **Camping Municipal de Vitre 109,** 109 Boulevard des Richter's, 35500 Vitre 02 99 75 25 28; camping@marie-vitre

🐕 ♟ ⛟ WD ♨ ♿ 🅿 ⊿ MSP 🦋 ⛲ ⛱ ⚏

Fr Vitre ring rd D173 take D88 heading SE sp Argentre du P. Site on L in 450m. Well sp. Sm, hdg, pt shd, EHU 10A (€2.60); bbq (charcoal, elec, gas); sw nr; bus fr site ent; public pool 1km; CKE. "Interesting, attractive medieval town; quiet cycling rds nrby; excel." **€12.20, 1 Mar-15 Dec.** **2017**

VITRY LE FRANCOIS *6E1* (6km SE Rural) *48.69673, 4.63039* **Aire Naturelle Camping Nature (Scherschell),** 13 Rue de l'Evangile, 51300 Luxémont-et-Villotte 03 26 72 61 14 or 06 83 42 83 53 (mob); eric.scherschell@wanadoo.fr; www.camping-nature.net

🐕 €1 ♟ WD ♨ 🅿 ⊿ MSP 🦋 ⛱ ⚏

Fr N44 at rndabt take N4 sp St Dizier. Take exit sp Luxemont. At rndabt take 1st exit D396, at next rndabt take 4th exit sp Luxemont (D316). After 2.1km turn R, site on L in 100km. Sm, hdstg, shd, pt sl, EHU (6A) inc (poss rev pol & long lead req); bbq; sw nr; Eng spkn; adv bkg acc; fishing; CKE. "Delightful, CL-type site; well-kept & immac; helpful, friendly owners; gd, clean unisex san facs; nr canal & cycle paths; interesting area to visit; excel; poss mosquitoes." **€15.40, 1 May-15 Oct.** **2019**

VOLLORE-VILLE *9B1* (1km NE Rural) *45.79199, 3.60583* **Camping Des Plaines,** Le Grun de Chignore, Les Plaines, 63120 Vollore-Ville 04 73 53 73 37; jenny-loisel@orange.fr; www.campingauvergne.fr

12 ♟ ♨ ♿ 🅿 ⊿ 🦋 ⛲ ⛱ ⒽH nr 🅰 ⅃ nr ⚏ 🛶

Leave A89/E70 at junc 29 onto D906 S to Courpiere. Fr Courpiere take D7 to Vollore-Ville. Site on the R at turning to Chabrier. 2*, Sm, hdg, mkd, pt shd, gas; bbq; twin axles; 20% statics; adv bkg acc; ccard acc; CKE. "Excel, well-kept little site; friendly owners; pleasant vill; conv for A89/E70." **€15.00** **2019**

VOLVIC *9B1* (0.7km E Urban) *45.87208, 3.04591* **Camp Municipal Pierre et Sources,** Rue de Chancelas, 63530 Volvic 04 73 33 50 16; camping@ville-volvic.fr; www.ville-volvic.fr

🐕 €1.50 ♟(htd) WD ♨ ⊿ MSP 🦋 🏊

Exit Riom on D986: foll sp for Pontgibaud & Volvic. Site sp to R on app to town. 3*, Sm, shd, EHU (12A) €3.50; 10% statics; Eng spkn; adv bkg acc. "Pleasant, tidy site with lovely views; welcoming & helpful; excel, clean san facs; access some pitches poss diff, particularly for lge o'fits; conv Volvic factory tour; no access for new arrivals when off is clsd." **€20.00, 1 May-30 Sep.** **2018**

VOREY 9C1 (0.4km SW Rural) 45.18576, 3.90679
Camping Les Moulettes, Chemin de Félines, 43800
Vorey-sur-Arzon 04 71 03 70 48 or 04 71 03 79 49;
contact@camping-les-moulettes.fr;
www.camping-les-moulettes.fr

🐾 €1.50 ♦♦♦ ⚓ ❄ ♿ ✎ 🦋 ♈ ⛲ ⓘ ♨ ⬛nr ⚠ ⛵ 🛶

Fr Le Puy take D103 sp Vorey. Site sp in vill; L
in main sq. 4*, Sm, hdg, pt shd, EHU (10A) €3.50;
10% statics; Eng spkn; adv bkg acc; fishing adj;
waterslide; games area. "Peaceful site by rv; gd sized
pitched, many on rv bank; friendly owners; gd quality
rest acc rv." **€23.50, May-Sep.** 2015

VOUECOURT 6E1 (0.1km E Rural) 48.26774, 5.13671
Camp Municipal Rives de Marne, Rue de Verdun
52320 Vouécourt 06 78 52 50 54 or 03 25 02 44 46 46;
commune.vouecourt@bbox.fr; www.camping
vouecourt.sopixi.fr

🐾 ♦♦♦ 🆆 ⚓ ❄ ♿ ✎ ♈ ⓘnr ⬛nr ⚠

N fr Chaumont on N67; sp to site in 17km; thro vill
by Rv Marne; site on L bef main rv bdge, almost
opp Mairie; well sp. 2*, Sm, mkd, pt shd, EHU (10A)
€2.50 (poss rev pol); gas; adv bkg acc; ccard acc;
fishing; CKE. "Lovely, peaceful, rvside site; gd sized
pitches; friendly warden calls pm; clean; rv poss floods
in winter; forest walks & cycling; popular NH; new excel
san facs (2015); crowded; excel."
€15.00, 29 Apr-30 Sep. 2017

VOULTE SUR RHONE, LA 9D2 (5km N Rural)
44.82663, 4.76171 **Camping La Garenne,** Quartier La
Garenne, 07800 St Laurent-du-Pape 04 75 62 24 62;
info@lagarenne.org; www.campinglagarenne-
ardeche.fr

🐾 €2.50 ♦♦♦ 🆆 ⚓ ❄ ♿ ✎ 🦋 ♈ ⛲ ⓘ ♨ ⬛ ⚠ ⚡ 🛶

Well sp fr La Voulte. Fr Valence S on D86 La Voulte,
approx 15km turn W onto D120; 300m after
St Laurent-du-Pape cent, turn R bef PO.
3*, Med, pt shd, terr, EHU (6A) inc (poss rev pol);
gas; red long stay; Eng spkn; adv bkg acc; bike
hire; CKE. "Popular site; friendly, helpful Dutch
owners; views fr terr pitches; gd clean san facs; sh
walk to vill, vg; In cycling dist of the Dolce Via rte."
€37.00, 1 Apr-1 Oct. 2015

VRAIGNES EN VERMANDOIS 3C4 (0.2km N Rural)
49.88538, 3.06623 **Camping des Hortensias,**
22 Rue Basse, 80240 Vraignes-en-Vermandois
03 22 85 64 68; campinghortensias@free.fr;
www.campinghortensias.com

12 🐾 €2 ♦♦♦(htd) 🆆 ⚓ ❄ ✎ ♈ ⓘ ♈nr ⬛nr

Fr N on A1/E15 take exit 13 onto D1029 sp
St Quentin; strt rd 16km until rndabt, take D15
(Vraignes) exit; site sp 1st on R in vill. Or fr S & A26,
take junc 10 onto D1029 sp Péronne; after 15km
at rndabt take D15 as bef. 2*, Sm, hdg, hdstg, pt
shd, EHU (4-8A) €2.50-4.50 (poss long lead req); bbq;
red long stay; 10% statics; CKE. "Lovely farm site;
sm pitches, poss muddy when wet; helpful, friendly
owners; vg, clean san facs; conv for Somme battlefields
& m'way; excel; rec torch." **€13.00** 2016

WASSELONNE 6E3 (1km W Urban) 48.63739,
7.43209 **FFCC Camp Municipal,** Rue des Sapins,
67310 Wasselonne 03 88 87 00 08; camping-
wasselonne@wanadoo.fr; www.suisse-alsace.com

🐾 €0.60 ♦♦♦ ⚓ ❄ 🆆 ✎ 🦋 ♈ ⛲ ⓘ ♨ ⬛ ⚠ 🛷(covrd, htd)

Fr D1004 take D244 to site. 2*, Med, mkd, pt shd,
terr, EHU (5-10A) €2.30-3.70; gas; 30% statics; CKE.
"Pleasant, pretty town; facs excel; cycle rte & bus (adj)
to Strasbourg; gd NH."
€17.00, 15 Apr-15 Oct. 2017

WATTEN 3A3 (0.6km N Urban) 50.83521, 2.21047
Camping Le Val Joly (Le Val Joli), Rue de Aa, 59143
Watten 03 21 88 23 26 or 03 21 88 24 75;
www.campings-nord.com

🐾 €1.55 ♦♦♦ 🆆 ⚓ ❄ ✎ ⬛nr ⚠

NW fr St Omer on D943; N of Tilques turn N onto
D300; in 5km at rndabt turn R onto D207 sp Watten;
at T-junc turn L onto D213; cross rv brdg & turn
L in 500m at camping sp. 2*, Med, mkd, pt shd,
EHU (10A) €3.70; 90% statics; adv bkg acc; fishing.
"Spacious, attractive, well-kept site; conv NH for
ferries; welcoming, friendly, helpful owner; basic, clean
san facs; secure gates, locked 2200-0700, but off rd
parking; cycling along rv/canal; no site lighting (2010);
few touring pitches - arr early or phone ahead high ssn;
access to rv walk; glass works at Arques; vet nr; vg."
€12.00, 1 Apr-31 Oct. 2019

WIMEREUX 3A2 (1.5km S Coastal) 50.75277, 1.60722
Caravaning L'Eté Indien, Hameau de Honvault,
62930 Wimereux 03 21 30 22 50; ete.indien@
wanadoo.fr; www.eteindien-wimereux.com

12 🐾 ⛹ ♦♦♦ 🆆 ⚓ ❄ ♿ ✎ 🅼 ♈ ⛲ ⓘ ♨ ⬛ ⚠ ⚡ 🛶(htd) 🎣

⛱ sand 1.5km

Fr Calais on A16 exit junc 32 sp Wimereux Sud. Thro
Terlincthun R after x-ing rlwy, site in 700m on R (do
not enter 1st site, correct site is the 2nd one clearly
sp above gate with site name) - narr, v rough rd.
4*, Med, unshd, pt sl, terr, serviced pitches; EHU (10A)
inc; gas; bbq (gas); red long stay; 90% statics; phone;
Eng spkn; adv bkg acc; games area; games rm. "Conv
A16, Calais ferries; rec LS phone to check site open;
ltd touring pitches & poss steep; muddy & unpleasant
in winter; rlwy runs along one side of site; NH only if
desperate!; new sw pool and MV area; gd clean facs
(2012); poor facs for waste water." **€28.00** 2019

WINGEN SUR MODER 5D3 (1.3km S Rural) 48.91565,
7.36934 **Camp Municipal/Aire Naturelle,**
Rue de Zittersheim, 67290 Wingen-sur-Moder
03 88 89 71 27 (Mairie); mairie@wingensurmoder.fr;
www.wingensurmoder.fr

♦♦♦ 🆆 ⚓ ✎ ♈ ⓘnr ⬛nr

W fr Haguenau on D919 to W end Wingen-sur-
Moder. Site sp by rlwy arch. Sm, mkd, pt shd, terr,
EHU (13A); Eng spkn; adv bkg acc; CKE. "Excel,
peaceful site but adj sports field poss used by youth
groups/motorbikers high ssn; clean facs; warden calls
am & pm; gd walking/cycling; pitch layout plan at the
gate." **€11.50, 1 May-30 Sep.** 2015

FRANCE

WISSANT *3A2 (7.6km NE Coastal) 50.91226, 1.72054* **Camping Les Erables,** 23 Rue du Château d'Eau, 62179 Escalles **03 21 85 25 36; boutroy.les-erables@wanadoo.fr; www.camping-les-erables.fr**

🐕 👫(htd) 🚾 🏕 ♿ 🅿/ MP ⊞nr ♨nr ⚓ sand 2km

Fr A16 take exit 40 onto D243 thro Peuplingues. Site sp to L on ent Escalles (on sharp R bend). Steep ent. Don't be put off by No Entry sp - 1-way system for c'vans on app rd. 1*, Sm, mkd, hdstg, pt shd, terr, EHU (6-10A) €3.50-€4.50; bbq; phone; Eng spkn; adv bkg rec; CKE. *"Lovely, well-kept open site with great views; family owned; spacious pitches but poss haphazard pitching; immac, modern facs; gates open 0800-2200; 2 pitches for disabled visitors with san facs; coast walks; sh walk to vill; private san facs extra; conv tunnel & ferries; gd site with view of Channel; excel grass pitch site; friendly, welcoming, helpful owners; popular site; ideal NH."* **€18.00, 23 Mar-11 Nov.** **2019**

YPORT *3C1 (0.9km SE Rural) 49.73221, 0.32098* **Camp Municipal La Chenaie,** Rue Henri-Simon, 76111 Yport **02 35 27 33 56; www.camping-normandie-yport.com**

👫 🏕 🅿/ 🦋 ♨nr ⚓ shgl 1km

Take D940 fr Fécamp SW, D211 to Yport to site. 3*, Med, pt shd, EHU (10A); 80% statics. *"Conv Le Havre."* **€33.00, 31 Mar-30 Sep.** **2018**

CORSICA

GHISONACCIA *10H2 (4km E Coastal) 41.99850, 9.44220* **Camping Arinella Bianca,** Route de la Mer, Bruschetto, 20240 Ghisonaccia **04 95 56 04 78; arinella@arinellabianca.com; www.arinellabianca.com**

🐕 €6 👫 🚾 🏕 ♿ 🅿/ MP ⊞ Y ♨ 🛖 🔥 ⚓ 🏊 (htd) 🛶
⚓ sand adj

S fr Bastia on N193/N198 approx 70km to Ghisonaccia. At Ghisonaccia foll sp opp pharmacy to beach (plage) & Rte de la Mer. In 3km turn R at rndabt & site well sp. NB When towing keep to main, coastal rds. 4*, Lge, mkd, hdg, shd, EHU (6A) €5.50 (poss rev pol); gas; bbq; TV; 45% statics; Eng spkn; adv bkg acc; ccard acc; games area; horseriding adj; games rm; bike hire; fishing; watersports; tennis; CKE. *"Clean, well-run site; attractive lake in cent; trees make access to pitches diff; helpful owner & staff."* **€38.00, 16 Apr-30 Sep.** **2016**

PIETRACORBARA *10G2 (4km SE Coastal) 42.83908, 9.4736* **Camping La Pietra,** Marine de Pietracorbara, 20233 Pietracorbara **04 95 35 27 49; lapietra@wanadoo.fr; www.la-pietra.com**

🐕 €3.50 👫(htd) 🏕 ♿ 🅿/ Y ⊞ Y ♨ 🛖 ⚓ 🏊 ⚓ sand 600m

Fr Bastia on D80 N. In 20km ent vill & turn L onto D232. Site on R in 1km at marina beach. Well sp. 3*, Med, mkd, hdg, shd, EHU (20A) €3.60; bbq; TV; bus nr; Eng spkn; ccard acc; bike fishing; tennis; CKE. *"Generous pitches; helpful owners; excel facs; beautiful pool; gd beach rest."* **€29.80, 20 Mar-4 Nov.** **2017**

PORTO VECCHIO *10H2 (7.3km N Rural) 41.646168, 9.296385* **Camping Cupulatta,** 20170 Porto Vecchio **06 12 81 50 89; www.campingcorse-cupulatta.com**

🐕 €2 👫 (cont) 🚾 🏕 ♿ 🅿/ ⊞nr ⚓ 🏊 🛶 ⚓ 10km shgl

Fr Lecci on N198 (T10). Site on R after dbl bdge direction Porto Vecchio in 4km. 3*, Sm, mkd, pt shd, EHU (6A) €4; bbq (elec, gas); twin axles; 90% statics; phone; adv bkg acc; CKE. *"Driving distance fr coast with all facs; close to scenic mountains; rest on access rd; gd."* **€25.00, 1 Apr-31 Sep.** **2019**

SOLENZARA *10H2 (12km W Rural) 41.83495, 9.32144* **Camping U Ponte Grossu,** Route de Bavella, 20145 Sari-Solenzara **04 95 48 26 61 or 06 64 79 80 46 (mob); lucchinitoussaint[at]gmail.com; www.uponte grossu.com**

🐕 👫 🚾 🏕 ♿ 🅿/ MP Y ♨ 🛖

Fr N198, take D268 to U Ponte Grossu. Sm, mkd, pt shd, terr, EHU (6A); adv bkg acc; CCI. *"Site alongside rv; rv adj; canyoning; rafting; access to fab mountain areas; vg."* **€26.50, 1 May-20 Sep.** **2019**

ILE DE RE

ARS EN RE *7A1 (0.4km S Coastal) 46.20395, -1.52014* **FFCC Camping du Soleil,** 57 Route de la Grange, 17590 Ars-en-Ré **05 46 29 40 62; contact@ campdusoleil.com; www.campdusoleil.com**

🐕 €3.20 👫 🚾 🏕 ♿ 🅿/ MP Y ⊞ ♨ 🛖 🔥 ⚓ 🏊 (htd) 🛶
⚓ sand 400m

On ent Ars-en-Ré on D735, pass Citroën g'ge & in 700m take 3rd L dir Plage de la Grange. Site sp. 3*, Med, mkd, hdg, shd, EHU (4-10A) €3.70-4.90; bbq (elec, gas); TV; 35% statics; phone; adv bkg acc; games area; bike hire; tennis; CKE. *"Pleasant, pretty site with pines & bamboo; helpful, friendly staff; gd pool; gd cycling & walking; sm pitches tight."* **€48.00, 1 Apr-1 Oct.** **2017**

ARS EN RE *7A1 (1.6km SW Coastal) 46.20282, -1.52733* **Camping Essi,** 15 Route de la Pointe de Grignon, 17590 Ars-en-Ré **05 46 29 44 73 or 05 46 29 46 09 (LS); camping.essi@wanadoo.fr; www.campingessi.com**

🐕 €2.10 👫(htd) 🚾 🏕 ♿ 🅿/ MP 🦋 Y 🛖 ⚓ 🏊

D735 to Ars-en-Ré; do not enter town; turn L at supmkt. Site sp. 3*, Med, hdg, pt shd, EHU (5-10A) €3.95-5.60; bbq; 20% statics; phone; Eng spkn; adv bkg acc; bike hire; watersports; CKE. *"Attractive waterfront town; excel beaches 2km; gd cycling; gd oysters; vg; well run & clean facs."* **€28.50, 1 Apr-31 Oct.** **2015**

FRANCE

ARS EN RE *7A1 (0.3km NW Coastal) 46.21130, -1.53017* **Camping Le Cormoran,** Route de Radia, 17590 Ars-en-Ré **05 46 29 46 04; info@cormoran.com; www.cormoran.com**

🐕 €5.00 👫 wc 🚿 🔥 ♿ 🏪 ∥ MP 🦋 ▼ ⑪ 🍴 🛒 nr 🎡 🚴
🏊(htd) 🏖500m

Fr La Rochelle take D735 onto Ile-de-Ré, site sp fr Ars-en-Ré. 4*, Med, hdstg, hdg, mkd, pt shd, EHU (10A) €6; 10% statics; Eng spkn; adv bkg acc; ccard acc; games rm; sauna; golf 10km; bike hire; tennis; games area; CKE. *"Delightful vill; vg site."* €49.00, 1 Apr-30 Sep. **2019**

COUARDE SUR MER, LA *7A1 (5km SE Coastal) 46.17405, -1.37865* **Sunêlia Parc Club Interlude,** 8 Route de Gros Jonc, 17580 Le Bois-Plage-en-Ré **05 46 09 18 22; infos@interlude.fr; www.interlude.fr**

🐕 €8 (htd) wc 🚿 🔥 ♿ 🏪 ∥ MP 🦋 ⑪ ▼ ⑪ 🛒 🎡
🏊(covrd, htd) 🏖sand

Fr toll bdge at La Rochelle foll D201 to Gros-Jonc. Turn L at rndabt at site sp. Site 400m on L. 4*, Lge, hdg, hdstg, mkd, pt shd, serviced pitches; EHU (10A) inc; gas; bbq; TV; 45% statics; Eng spkn; adv bkg req; bike hire; watersports; fitness rm; boat hire; solarium; sauna; tennis nr; games area; jacuzzi. *"Excel, well-run, clean, relaxing site; busy but not noisy; vg facs; some sm, sandy pitches - extra for lger; gd rest; nrby beaches excel; o'night m'vans area; walk to great beach; gd atmosphere, entmnt and shop."* €50.00, 11 Apr-20 Sep. **2016**

COUARDE SUR MER, LA *7A1 (1km W Urban/Coastal) 46.19348, -1.43427* **Camp Municipal Le Remondeau,** 12 Route Petite Noue, 17670 La Couarde-sur-Mer **05 46 29 84 27; campingleremondeau@wanadoo.fr; www.leremondeau.fr**

🐕 €3 (htd) wc 🔥 ♿ 🏪 ∥ MP 🦋 ⑪ 🎡 🏖sand adj

Fr toll bdge foll D735 to rndabt on W side of La Couarde-sur-Mer & take D201. Foll sp to site. 3*, Lge, pt shd, pt sl, EHU (10A) €4.70; bbq; red long stay; 10% statics; Eng spkn, CKE. *"Vg site; great cycling base."* €25.00, 15 Mar-7 Nov. **2018**

COUARDE SUR MER, LA *7A1 (3.6km NW Coastal) 46.20408, -1.46740* **Camping de l'Océan,** 50 Route d'Ars, 17670 La Couarde-sur-Mer **05 46 29 87 70; info@campingocean.com; www.campingocean.com**

🐕 €5 👫 (htd) wc 🚿 🔥 ♿ 🏪 ∥ MP ⑪ ▼ ⑪ 🛒 🎡 🚴
🏊(htd) 📷 🏖sand adj

Fr La Rochelle take D735 over bdge to Ile de Ré. Past St Martin-de-Re & La Couarde twd Ars-en-Ré. Site on R, 2.5km after La Couarde. 3*, Lge, mkd, hdg, shd, EHU (10A) €5.50; 40% statics; phone; Eng spkn; adv bkg acc; ccard acc; bike hire; games area; golf 6km; tennis; watersports; horseriding 1.5km; CKE. *"Popular site in superb location; some sm pitches with diff access; site rds & ent to pitches narr; rd noisy; gd, clean san facs; friendly staff; twin axles not rec; recep clsd 1230-1400, if clsd, park in yard facing recep; gd walking & cycling; excel; toll fee to island €16."* €39.00, 16 Apr-18 Sep. **2015**

ST CLEMENT DES BALEINES *7A1 (0.5km E Rural/Coastal) 46.24041, -1.56070* **Camping Les Baleines,** Chemin Devaude, 17590 St. Clement-des-Baleines **05 46 29 40 76; camping.lesbaleines@ wanadoo.fr; www.camping-lesbaleines.com**

🐕 €2-€3 👫 wc 🚿 🔥 ♿ 🏪 ∥ MP ▼ ▼ nr ⑪ nr 🛒 nr 🎡 🏖sand adj

Fr bdge foll sp for Phare De Baleines. Sp 500m bef lighthouse. Do not foll sat nav. Narr vill rds. 3*, Lge, hdg, mkd, pt shd, EHU (10A) €5-6; bbq; twin axles; TV; 10% statics; phone; bus 200m; Eng spkn; ccard acc; games area; games rm; CKE. *"Vg, quiet site in natural surroundings; helpful staff; clean modern shwrs; direct access to beach; bar 500m; 5mins walk to lighthouse."* €42.00, 27 Apr-21 Sep. **2019**

STE MARIE DE RE *7A1 (4km NW Coastal) 46.16112, -1.35428* **Camping Les Grenettes,** Route De l'Ermitage, 17740 Ste Marie De Re **05 46 30 22 47; contact@ hotel-les-grenettes.com; www.campingles grenettes.com**

12 🐕 €4 👫 wc 🚿 🔥 ∥ MP ⑪ 🛒 🎡 🚴 📷 🏊 🏖200m

Foll sp for D201 'Itinéraire Sud' after toll bdge in the dir of Le Bois-de-Plage; after approx 2km turn L. 2*, Med, mkd, pt shd, EHU (6A) €4.50; gas; bbq; TV; Eng spkn; adv bkg acc; ccard acc; tennis; fishing; waterslide; bike hire. *"Nice site close to sea; vg rest; many facs, but stretched in high ssn."* €44.00 **2016**

ST MARTIN DE RE *7A1 (4km E Urban/Coastal) 46.18194, -1.33110* **Flower Camping de Bel Air,** Route de la Noué, 17630 La Flotte-en-Ré **05 46 09 63 10; camping.bel-air@flowercampings.com; www.bel-air-camping.com**

👫 wc 🚿 🔥 ♿ 🏪 ∥ MP 🦋 ⑪ ▼ ⑪ 🎡 🚴 🏖800m

Fr toll bdge take D735 to La Flotte. Turn R at rndabt to town into Route de la Noué, site sp. 3*, Lge, hdg, mkd, pt shd, EHU (6A) €3.84; phone; adv bkg acc; games rm; tennis. *"Walk to shops, harbour, beach etc; gd; friendly staff; toll bdge €8 winter ssn, €16 summer ssn."* €29.00, 30 Mar-3 Nov. **2015**

ST MARTIN DE RE *7A1 (0.5km S Urban) 46.19913, -1.36682* **Camp Municipal Les Remparts,** Rue Les Remparts, 17410 St Martin-de-Ré **05 46 09 21 96; camping.stmartindere@wanadoo.fr; www.saint-martin-de-re.fr**

🐕 €2 👫 wc 🚿 🔥 ♿ 🏪 ∥ MP 🦋 🛒 🎡 🏖sand 1.3km

Foll D735 fr toll bdge to St Martin; sp in town fr both ends. 2*, Med, mkd, hdg, pt shd, pt sl, EHU (10A) €3.70; bbq; Eng spkn; adv bkg acc; ccard acc; CKE. *"Busy site in brilliant location; san facs dated but clean; gd basic rest; poss children's groups mid-ssn; some pitches boggy when wet; gd cycling; site poss unkempt end ssn; vg mkt; beautiful situation on o'skirts of a lovely town, gd size pitches; pool 3km; superb position."* €25.00, 12 Mar-18 Nov. **2017**

FRANCE

ILE D'OLERON

BREE LES BAINS, LA *7A1* (0.8km NW Coastal)
46.01861, -1.35446 **Camp Municipal Le Planginot,**
Allée du Gai Séjour, 17840 La Brée-les-Bains
05 46 47 82 18; camping.planginot@orange.fr;
www.labreelesbains.com

🏕€2 (htd) [WD] ♨ ♿ ⊟ ⁄ [MSP] 🦋 ⊕ 🛒 ♨ ⊼ adj

N fr St Pierre d'Oléron on D734, turn R for La Brée
on D273, site sp (if sp diff to see - foll 'plage' sp).
2*, Lge, mkd, pt shd, EHU (10A) €3.60; 15% statics;
Eng spkn; adv bkg acc. "Well-kept site in quiet location;
friendly, helpful staff; gd cycling; daily mkt nrby; gd."
€15.00, 15 Mar-15 Oct.   2015

CHATEAU D'OLERON, LE *7B1* (2.5km NW Coastal)
45.90415, -1.21525 **Camping La Brande,** Route des
Huîtres, 17480 Le Château-d'Oléron **05 46 47 62 37;**
info@camping-labrande.com; www.camping-
labrande.com or www.campings-oleron.com

🏕€3 ♟ ♨ ♿ ⊟ ⁄ [MSP] ♒ ⊤ ⊕ 🛒 ♨
⊼ ⚓ (covrd, htd) ⊼ sand 300m

Cross bdge on D26, turn R & go thro Le Château-
d'Oléron. Foll Rte des Huîtres to La Gaconnière
to site. 5*, Lge, shd, EHU (6-10A) €4-6; gas; bbq;
TV; 60% statics; Eng spkn; adv bkg acc; ccard acc;
tennis; golf 6km; games area; sep car park; bike
hire; waterslide; CKE. "Pleasant owners; pitches at
far end adj oyster farm - some noise fr pumps & poss
mosquitoes; sauna; steam rm; 10 min cycle ride into
town; vg." €44.00, 1 Apr-5 Nov.   2017

"That's changed – Should I let the Club know?"

If you find something on site that's different
from the site entry, fill in a report and let us
know. See camc.com/europereport.

ST GEORGES D'OLERON *7A1* (7km E Coastal)
45.96820, -1.24483 **Camp Atlantique Signol,** Ave des
Albatros, Boyardville, 17190 St Georges-d'Oléron
02 51 20 41 94; contact@signol.com; signol.camp-
atlantique.co.uk/en

🏕€4 ♟ [WD] ♨ ♿ ⊟ ⁄ [MSP] ⊤ ⊕ 🛒 ♨ ⊼ ⚓ (htd, indoor)
⛵ ⊼ sand 800m

Cross bdge onto Ile d'Oléron & cont on main rd
twd St Pierre-d'Oléron. Turn R at Dolus-d'Oléron
for Boyardville & foll sp in vill. 4*, Lge, hdg, mkd, pt
shd, pt sl, EHU (6A); gas; 70% statics; Eng spkn; adv
bkg acc. "Size of pitches variable; san facs stretched
in high ssn; impressive pool complex; narr site rds;1
dog per pitch; gd site & facs; vg activities for kids; low
overhanging branches."
€22.00, 3 Apr-20 Sep.   2017

ST GEORGES D'OLERON *7A1* (2km SE Rural)
45.96796, -1.31874 **Camping Le Domaine d'Oléron,**
La Jousselinière, 17190 St Georges-d'Oléron
05 46 76 54 97 or 02 51 33 05 05 (LS); info@
chadotel.com; www.chadotel.com

🏕€3.90 [WD] ♟ ♨ ♿ ⊟ ⁄ [MSP] 🦋 ⊤ ♒ ⊕ 🛒 ♨ ⊼ ⚓ ⛵ ⚓
⊼ sand 3km

After x-ing Viaduct (bdge) onto island foll sp dir
St Pierre d'Oléron & St Georges d'Oléron on D734;
turn R on rndabt immed see Leclerc supmkt on R; at
next rndabt turn L sp 'Le Bois Fleury'; pass airfield
'Bois 'Fleury' on R; take next R & then immed L. Site
on L in 500m. 4*, Lge, mkd, hdg, pt shd, terr, EHU
(6A) inc; gas; bbq (gas, sep area); red long stay; TV;
40% statics; Eng spkn; adv bkg rec; ccard acc; bike
hire; games area; games rm; waterslide; CKE. "Popular,
well-organised, clean site; friendly, helpful staff; lovely
pool; no o'fits over 8m high ssn; max 1 dog; cycle paths;
fair." €42.14, 1 Apr-30 Sep, A41.   2019

"I like to fill in the reports as I travel from site to site"

You'll find report forms at the back of this
guide, or you can fill them in online at
camc.com/europereport.

ST GEORGES D'OLERON *7A1* (6km SW Coastal)
45.95386, -1.37932 **Camping Les Gros Joncs,** Les
Sables Vigniers, 17190 St Georges-d'Oléron **05 46 76
52 29;** info@camping-les-gros-joncs.com;
www.camping-les-gros-joncs.com

[12] 🏕 ♟ €3 ♟ ♨ ♿ ⊟ ⁄ 🦋 ⊤ ⊕ 🛒 ♨ ⊼ ⚓ (htd) ⛵
⊼ shgl 200m

Fr bdge D734 to St Pierre, at 2nd traff lts (police
stn) turn L to La Cotinière 4km, at x-rds turn R
dir Domino (Ave De Pins) for 5km. Site on L past
Le Suroit. 5*, V lge, pt shd, EHU (10A) €3; TV;
10% statics; adv bkg acc; games area; jacuzzi. "Excel
pool; beach sand 1km; hydrotherapy sprays; great
location; clean facs; rec." **€50.00**   2016

ST GEORGES D'OLERON *7A1* (7km SW Coastal)
45.94756, -1.37386 **Camping Le Suroit,** L'Ileau de la
Grande Côte, 17190 St Georges-d'Oléron
05 46 47 07 25 or 06 80 10 93 18 (mob); camping@
lesuroit.fr; www.camping-lesuroit.com

🏕€5 ♟ (htd) ♨ ♿ ⊟ ⁄ 🦋 ⊤ ⊕ 🛒 ♨ ⊼
⚓ (covrd, htd) ⊼ sand adj

Fr Domino cent foll sp for beach, turn L for L'Ileau.
Strt at x-rds. Fork L for La Cotinière, site on R in
150m. 4*, Lge, mkd, shd, EHU (10A) €4.50; gas; bbq;
TV; 10% statics; adv bkg acc; ccard acc; bike hire;
games area; tennis; CKE. "Excel, well-organised site."
€35.00, 1 Apr-33 Sep.   2015

ST PIERRE D'OLERON *7B1* (4km SW Coastal)
45.92315, -1.34130 **Camping Le Sous Bois,**
avenue des Pins, 17310 Saint Pierre d'Oleron
05 46 47 22 46; resa.lesousbois@orange.fr;
www.camping-lesousbois-oleron.com

🐕 €4 ♦♦ WD ♨ ♿ 🖰 ⁄ 🖤 🍽 nr 🛒 nr 🏄

Fr St Pierre take D274 to La Cotiniere. In La
Cotiniere foll dir L'lleau, turn R onto Ave des Pins.
Campsite 500m out of town on R. 3*, Med, mkd, hdg,
pt shd, EHU (3A, 6A-10A) €5-7; Eng spkn; adv bkg
acc; sauna; games area; beac 200m. *"Gd cycle tracks;
sailing school; jet ski; equestrian ctr in Cotiniere; conv
location; bar 20m; vg."*
€33.50, 1 Apr-31 Oct. 2016

ST PIERRE D'OLERON *7B1* (3.5km W Coastal)
45.92394, -1.34273 **FFCC Camp Municipal La
Fauche Prère,** Ave des Pins, La Cotinière, 17310
St Pierre d'Oléron **05 46 47 10 53; camping@
saintpierreoleron.com; www.saintpierreoleron.com**

🐕 €2 ♦♦ WD ♨ ♿ 🖰 ⁄ MP 🛒 🏔 ⛵ sand adj

Fr bdge foll D734 N to St Pierre-d'Oléron. Turn L
onto D274 for La Cotinière, site bef vill on L, sp.
Med, mkd, shd, pt sl, EHU (12A) €4.10; CKE. *"Direct
access to beach; most pitches sandy; gd; lovely site
amongst pine trees; new san facs (2017); quiet."*
€22.00, 1 Apr-30 Sep. 2017

ST TROJAN LES BAINS *7B1* (1.5km SW Rural)
45.82947, -1.21632 **Flower Camping St-Tro'Park
(formerly Camping La Combinette),** 36 Ave des
Bris, 17370 St Trojan-les-Bains **05 46 76 00 47;**
info@st-tro-park.com; www.st-tro-park.com

🐕 ♦♦ ♨ ♿ 🖰 ⁄ 🦋 🍴 ⊞ 🛒 🏔 🏄 ⛵ 🎿 2km

Fr toll bdge stay on D26 for 1km, L onto D275 &
L onto D126 to St Trojan-les-Bains. Strt ahead at
rndabt with figure sculpture, then R at next rndabt
sp Campings. In 1km turn L at rd fork, site on R in
1km. 4*, Lge, shd, EHU (5-10A) (poss rev pol); gas;
games area; bike hire. *"Gd touring base; some super
pitches; poss flooding in heavy rain; lovely site amongst
pine trees; sauna; spa; gym; new san facs (2017); vg."*
€35.00, 15 Apr-15 Oct. 2017

CANILLO (ANDORRA) *8G3* (0.3km ENE Urban)
42.56740, 1.60235 **Camping Pla,** Ctra General s/n,
AD100 Canillo **601 283; www.facebook.com/
paco.cristina**

12 🐕 ♦♦ (htd) WD ♨ ♿ 🖰 ⁄ 🍽 ⊞ nr 🏔

App Canillo fr S, pass Tarrado petrol stn on R; take
1st exit at 1st rndabt opp lge hotel, over bdge &
turn L to site. Med, mkd, pt shd, EHU (5-10A) €3; gas;
75% statics; bus adj; Eng spkn; adv bkg acc. *"Excel
location for skiing but poss unkempt/untidy LS; htd
covrd pool in town; sports facs in town; ski lift 100m."*
€14.00 2016

"We must tell the Club about that great site we found"

Get your site reports in by mid-August and we'll
do our best to get your updates into the next
edition.

MASSANA, LA (ANDORRA) *8G3* (2km N Rural)
42.56601, 1.52448 **Camping Borda d'Ansalonga,**
Ctra General del Serrat, AD300 Ordino **850 374;**
www.campingbordaansalonga.com

🐕 ♦♦ (htd) WD ♨ ♿ 🖰 ⁄ 🦢 🍽 ⊞ 🛒 🏔 🎿

Fr Andorra-la-Vella foll sp La Massana & Ordino. Turn
L twd El Serrat, site on R, well sp. Lge, pt shd, EHU
(10A) €5.60; gas; bbq; phone; Eng spkn; games rm; CKE.
*"Statics moved to storage area in summer; winter statics
for skiers; quieter than sites on main thro rte."*
€24.00, 17 Oct-25 Apr & 15 Jun-15 Sep. 2016

FRANCE

Sites in Andorra

CANILLO (ANDORRA) *8G3* (0.3km ENE Urban) *42.56740, 1.60235* **Camping Pla,** Ctra General s/n, AD100 Canillo **601 283; www.facebook.com/ paco.cristina**

12 ⛺ ♀♂(htd) WD ▲ ♨ ⊟ ⊬ Ψ ⊕ nr ⛰

App Canillo fr S, pass Tarrado petrol stn on R; take 1st exit at 1st rndabt opp lge hotel, over bdge & turn L to site. Med, mkd, pt shd, EHU (5-10A) €3; gas; 75% statics; bus adj; Eng spkn; adv bkg acc. *"Excel location for skiing but poss unkempt/untidy LS; htd covrd pool in town; sports facs in town; ski lift 100m."* **€14.00**   **2016**

MASSANA, LA (ANDORRA) *8G3* (2km N Rural) *42.56601, 1.52448* **Camping Borda d'Ansalonga,** Ctra General del Serrat, AD300 Ordino **850 374; www.campingbordaansalonga.com**

⛺ ♀♂(htd) WD ▲ ♨ ⊟ ⊬ 🦋 Ψ ⊕ 🐕 ⛰ 🛶

Fr Andorra-la-Vella foll sp La Massana & Ordino. Turn L twd El Serrat, site on R, well sp. Lge, pt shd, EHU (10A) €5.60; gas; bbq; phone; Eng spkn; games rm; CKE. *"Statics moved to storage area in summer; winter statics for skiers; quieter than sites on main thro rte."* **€24.00, 17 Oct-25 Apr & 15 Jun-15 Sep.**   **2016**

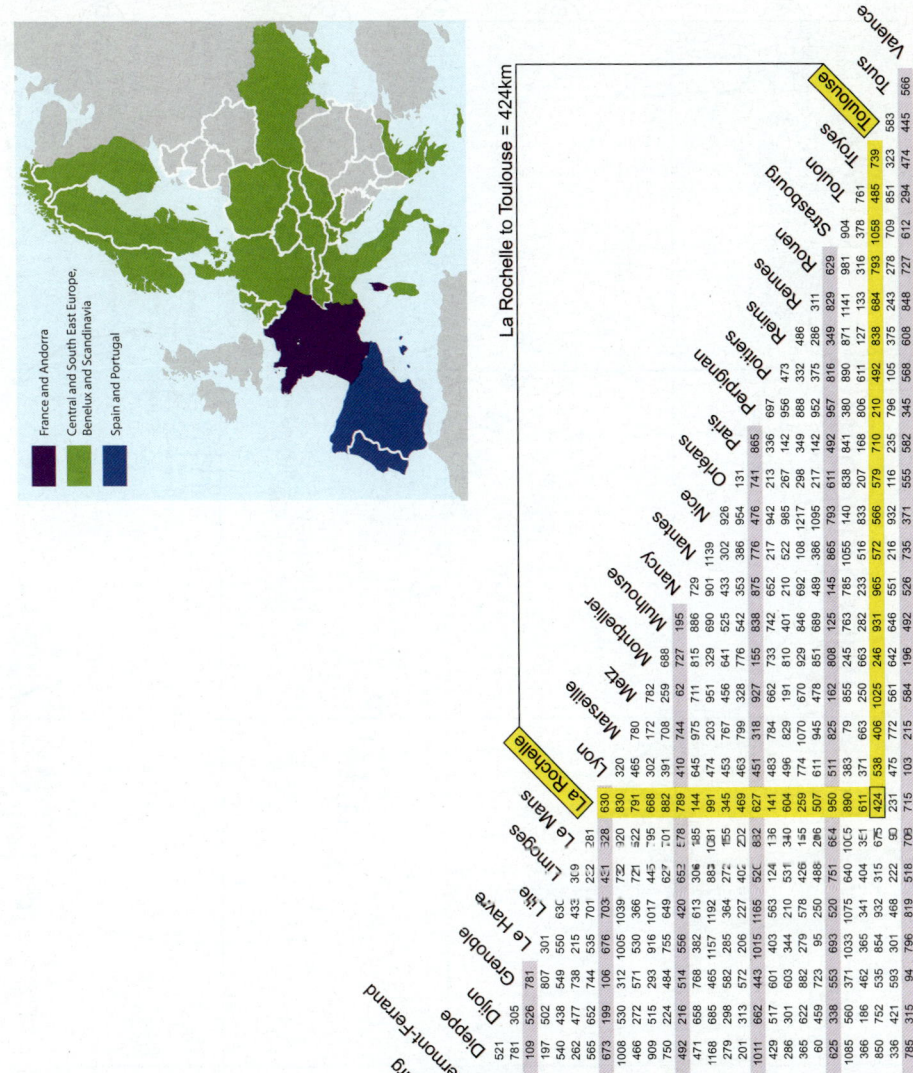

France and Andorra

Central and South East Europe, Benelux and Scandinavia

Spain and Portugal

La Rochelle to Toulouse = 424km

Andorra-la-Vella · Annecy · Bayonne · Besançon · Bordeaux · Bourges · Brest · Caen · Calais · Cherbourg · Clermont-Ferrand · Dieppe · Dijon · Grenoble · Le Havre · Lille · Limoges · Le Mans · La Rochelle · Lyon · Marseille · Metz · Montpellier · Mulhouse · Nancy · Nantes · Nice · Orléans · Paris · Perpignan · Poitiers · Reims · Rennes · Rouen · Strasbourg · Toulon · Troyes · Toulouse · Tours · Valence

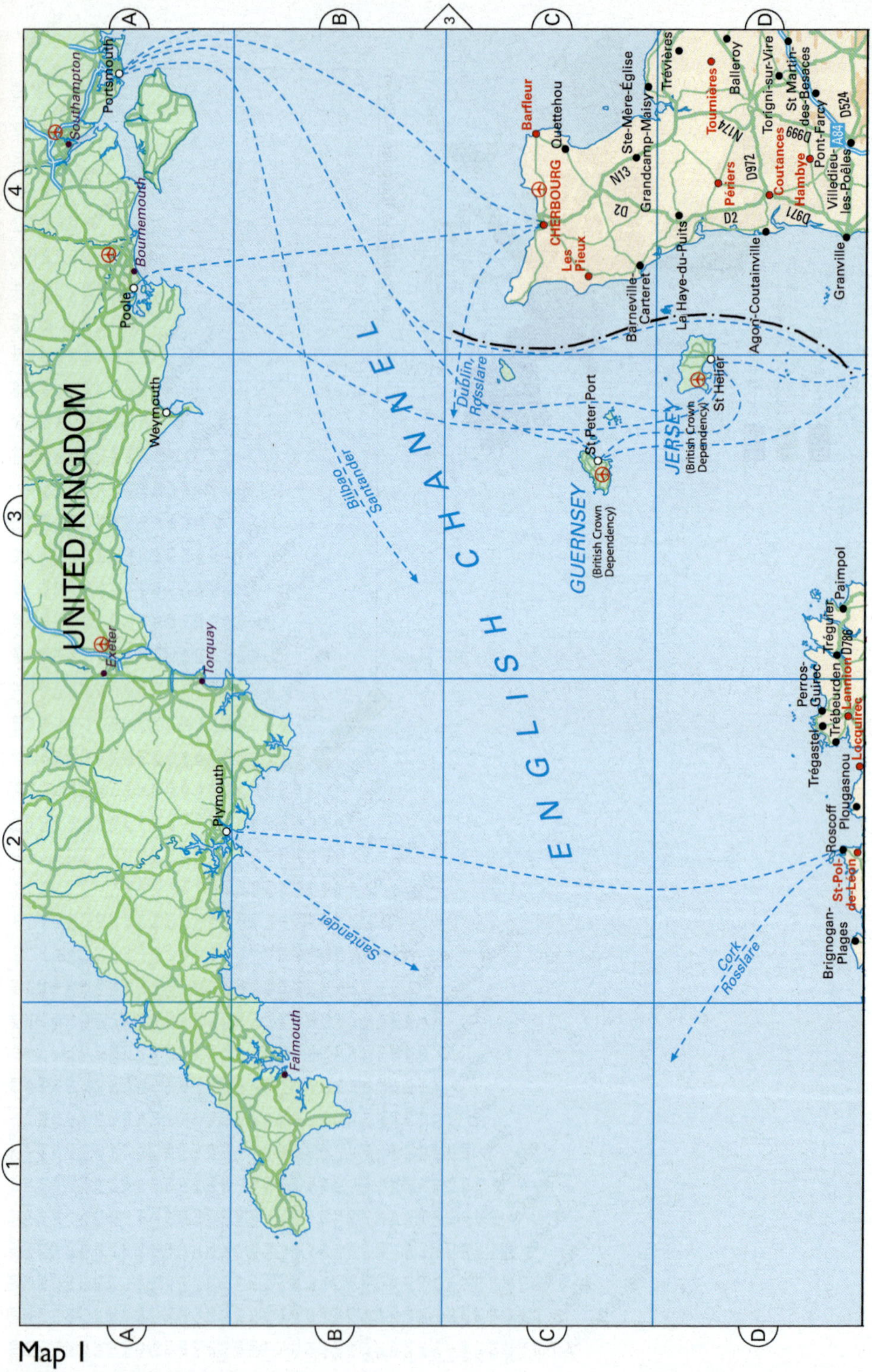

UNITED KINGDOM

Southampton
Portsmouth
Bournemouth
Poole
Weymouth
Exeter
Torquay
Plymouth
Falmouth

ENGLISH CHANNEL

Bilbao
Santander
Dublin
Rosslare
Santander
Cork
Rosslare

Barfleur
Quettehou
CHERBOURG
Les Pieux
Ste-Mère-Église
Grandcamp-Maisy
N13
D2
Barneville-Carteret
La Haye-du-Puits
Trévières
Tournières
Balleroy
Torigni-sur-Vire
St-Martin-des-Besaces
N174
D999
Pont-Farcy
Villedieu-les-Poêles
D524
A84
Périers
Coutances
Hambye
D972
D971
D2
Agon-Coutainville
Granville

GUERNSEY
(British Crown Dependency)
St Peter Port

JERSEY
(British Crown Dependency)
St Helier

Perros-Guirec
Trégastel
Trébeurden
Tréguier
Paimpol
Lannion
D786
Lézardrieux
Plougasnou
Roscoff
St-Pol-de-Léon
Brignogan-Plages

Map I

FRANCE

BAY OF BISCAY

Motorways
Major roads
Main Roads

All year site(s)
Seasonal site(s)
No sites listed
200m +
0–200m

© Collins Bartholomew Ltd 2021

Map 2

471

Map 3

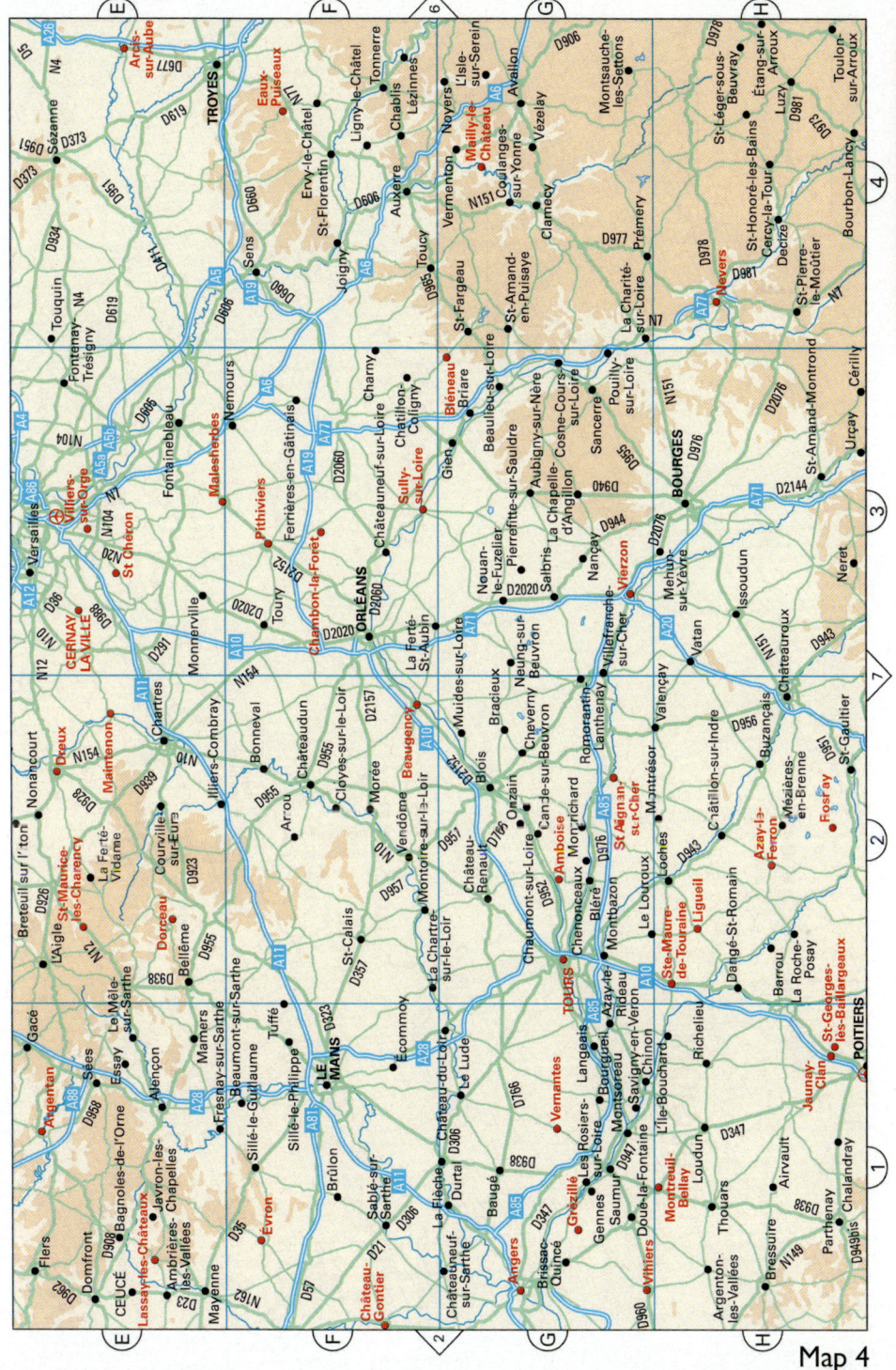

FRANCE

Map 4

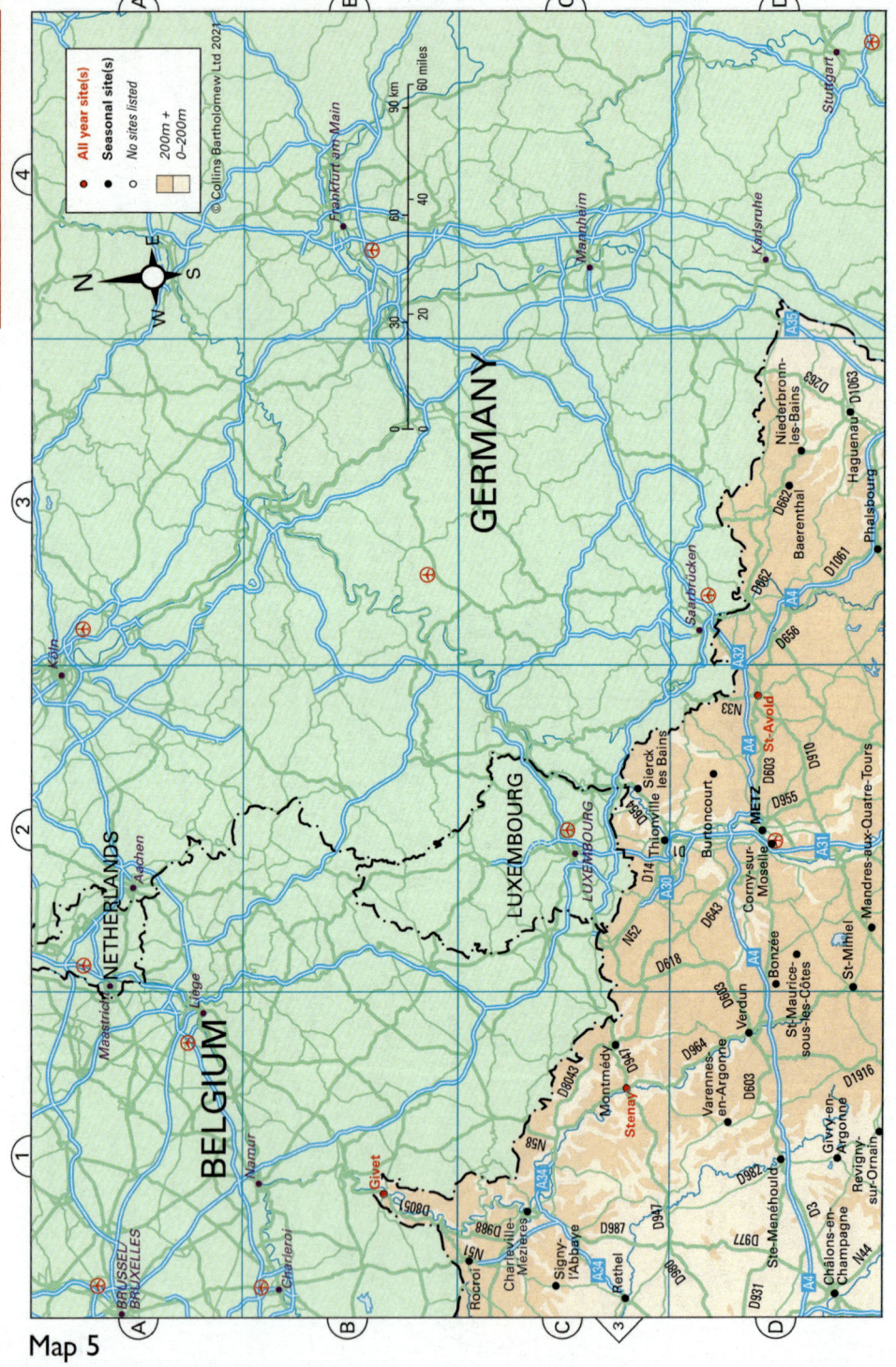

FRANCE

Map 5

474

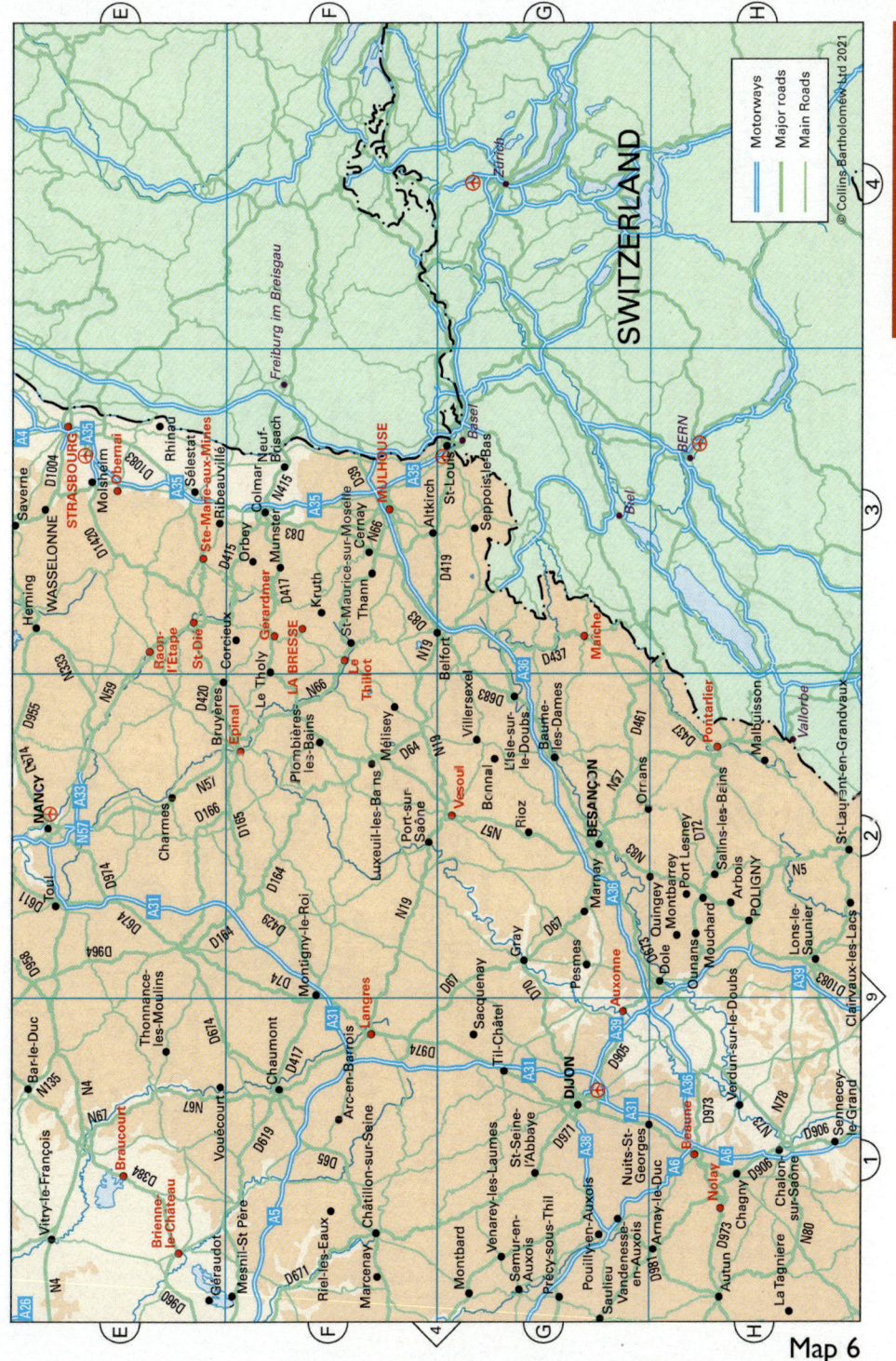

FRANCE

© Collins Bartholomew Ltd 2021

Motorways
Major roads
Main Roads

SWITZERLAND

Map 6

475

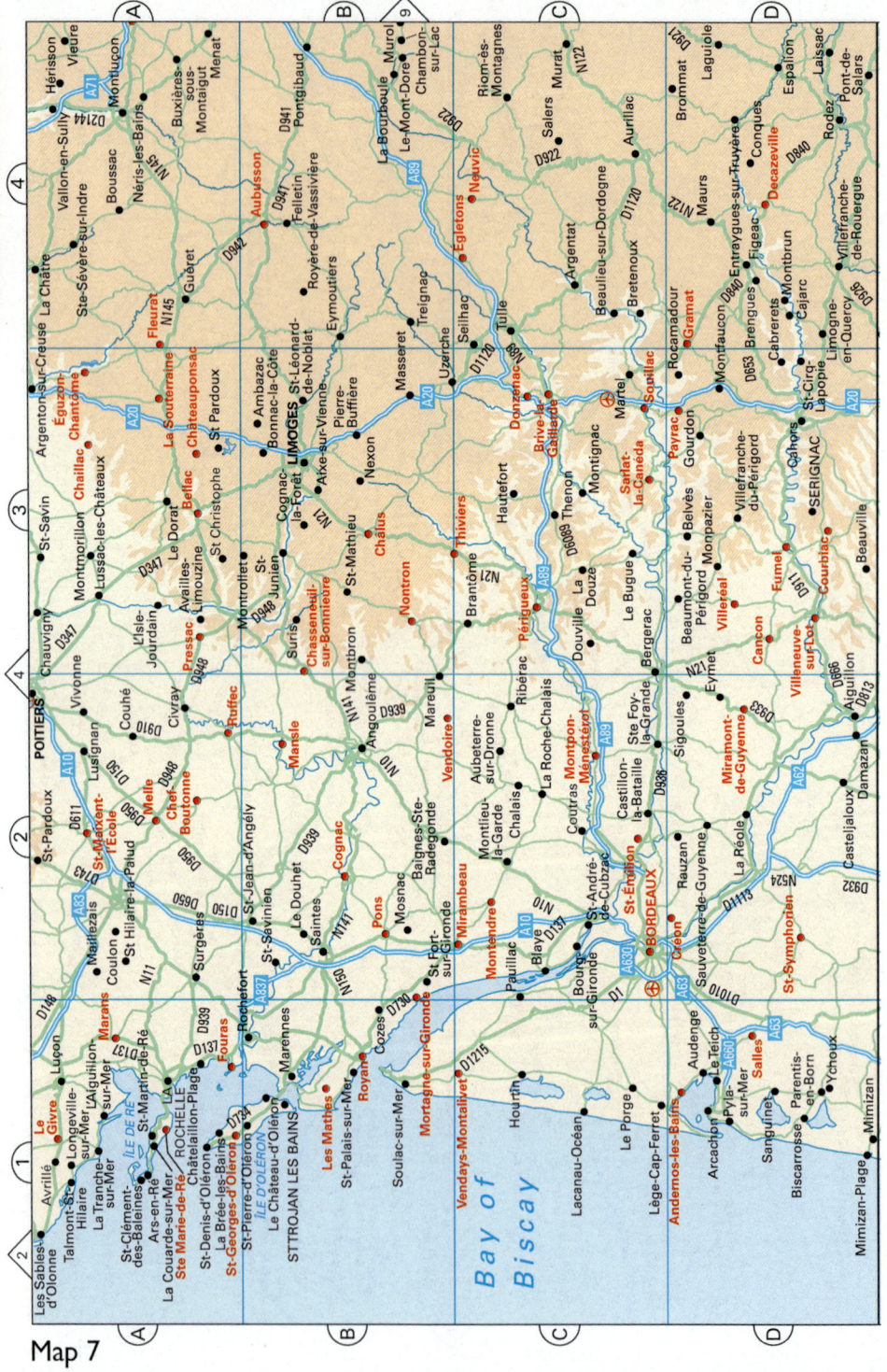

FRANCE

Map 7

476

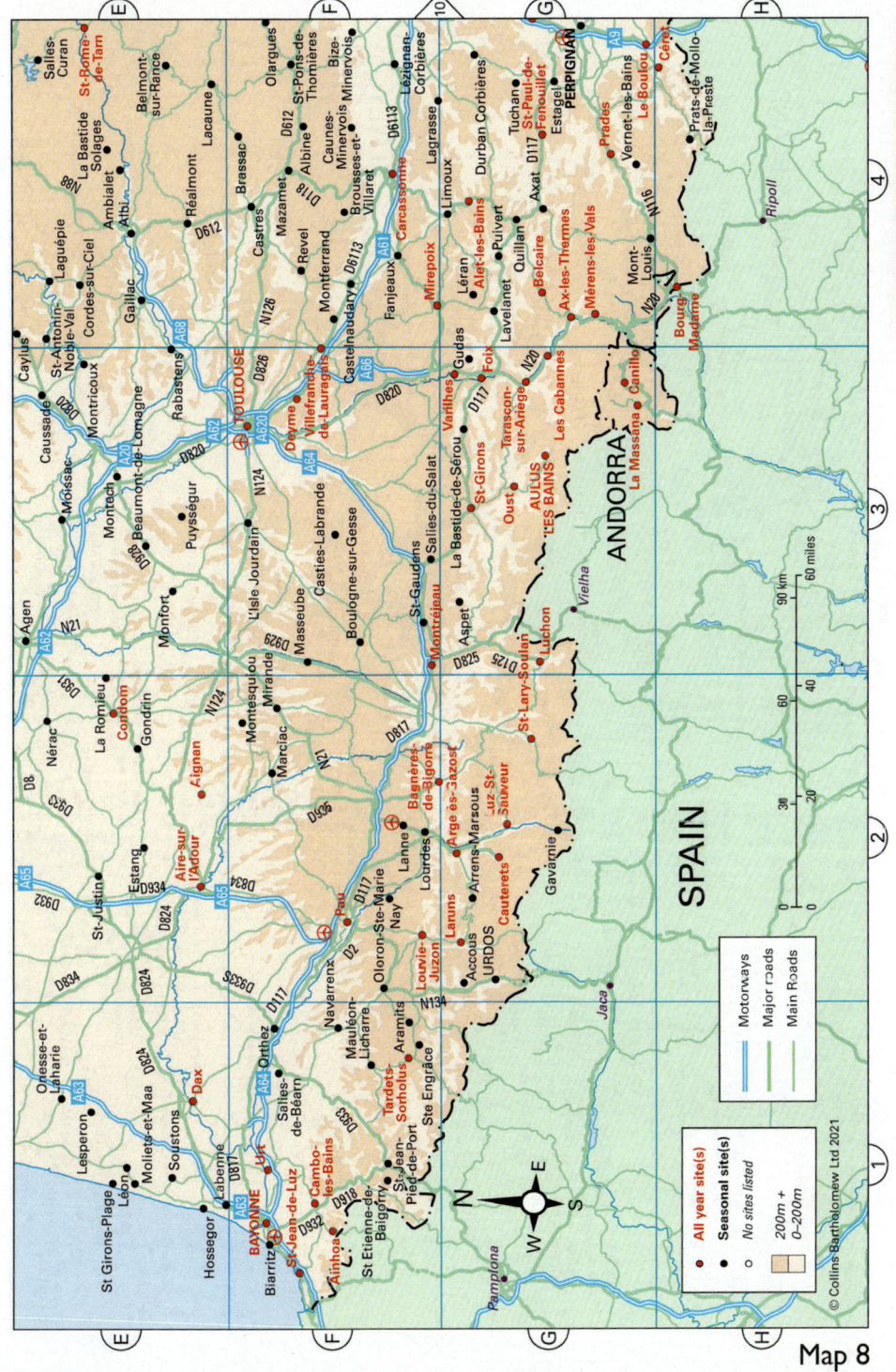

Map 8

Map 9

© Collins Bartholomew Ltd 2021

Motorways
Major roads
Main Roads

All year site(s)
Seasonal site(s)
No sites listed

200m +
0–200m

MEDITERRANEAN SEA

CORSICA

Corse

SPAIN

Map 10

Germany

Cologne

Shutterstock/mapman

Highlights

Home to beautiful landscapes, architectural delights and diverse cities, Germany has a rich culture and history for you to discover. Berlin is undoubtedly one of the culture and arts capitals of the world, while the picturesque timbered villages and castles have inspired countless works of literature, film and art.

Often thought of as the home of beer and bratwurst, Germany has much more to offer on a gastronomic level, with Riesling wine, Black Forest Gateaux and Stollen just some of the treats that are waiting to be discovered and enjoyed.

Germany is the home of the modern car, and its automobile industry is one of the most innovative in the world. BMW, Audi, Porsche and Mercedes all have museums to visit.

Oktoberfest, the largest beer festival in the world, is held annually in Munich and attracts people from around the globe. This 17-day festival only serves traditional beers that are brewed within Munich city limits.

Major towns and cities

- Berlin – this capital is an exciting city of culture and science.
- Hamburg – enjoy stunning and varied architecture in this gorgeous city.
- Munich – a magnificent city of culture and technology.
- Cologne – this city is brimming with bars, restaurants and pubs.

Attractions

- Neuschwanstein, Füssen – this fairytale castle inspired Sleeping Beauty's palace.
- Holstentor, Lübeck – a UNESCO relic of the medieval city fortifications.
- Cologne Cathedral – This gothic cathedral is Germany's most visited landmark.
- Lindau – an enchanting island town boasting beautiful architecture and wonderful gardens.

Find out more

www.germany.travel
E: hallo@visitberlin.de T: 0049 (0) 69 97 46 40

Country Information

Population (approx): 81million

Capital: Berlin (population approx 3.4 million)

Area: 357,050 sq km

Bordered by: Austria, Belgium, Czech Republic, Denmark, France, Luxembourg, Netherlands, Poland, Switzerland

Terrain: Lowlands in north; uplands/industrialised belt in the centre; highlands, forests and Bavarian alps in the south

Climate: Temperate throughout the year; warm summers and cold winters; rain throughout the year

Coastline: 2,389km

Highest Point: Zugspitze 2,962m

Language: German

Local Time: GMT or BST + 1, i.e. 1 hour ahead of the UK all year

Currency: Euros divided into 100 cents; £1 = €1.14, €1 = £0.88 (Feb 2021)

Emergency numbers: Police 112; Fire brigade 112; Ambulance 112. Operators speak English

Public Holidays 2021: Jan 1, 6; Apr 2, 5; May 1, 13, 24; June 1; Aug 15; Oct 3, 31; Nov 1; Dec 25, 26.

Public holidays vary according to region. The dates shown here may not be celebrated throughout the country. School summer holidays also vary by region but are roughly July to mid/end Aug or Aug to mid Sept.

Entry Formalities

British and Irish passport holders may stay for up to 90 days in any 180 day period without a visa. Following Brexit you may be asked to show a return or onward ticket at the border to confirm your length of stay, or to prove that you have enough money for your stay.

Your passport will need to have a minimum of 6 months' validity remaining, and be less than 10 years old (even if it has over 6 months left).

Visitors arriving at a campsite or hotel must complete a registration form.

Regulations for Pets

Certain breeds of dogs, such as pit bull terriers and American Staffordshire terriers, are prohibited from entering Germany unless you have a Certificate of Personality Test, which must be given by a vet on entering Germany. Other breeds such as Dobermann, Mastiff and Rottweiler may need to be kept on a lead and muzzled in public, including in your car. You are advised to contact the German embassy in London before making travel arrangements for your dog and check the latest available information from your vet or from the PETS Helpline on 0370 241 1710.

Medical Services

Local state health insurance fund offices offer assistance round-the-clock and telephone numbers can be found in the local telephone directory. EU citizens are entitled to free or subsidised emergency care from doctors contracted to the state health care system on presentation of a European Health Insurance Card (EHIC). Private treatment by doctors or dentists is not refundable under the German health service. You will be liable for a percentage of prescribed medication charges at pharmacies and this is also non-refundable. Pharmacies offer an all-night and Sunday service and the address of the nearest out-of-hours branch will be displayed on the door of every pharmacy.

There is a fixed daily charge for a stay in hospital (treatment is free for anyone under 18 years of age) which is not refundable. If you are required to pay an additional patient contribution for treatment then reduced charges apply to holders of an EHIC. For refunds of these additional charges you should apply with original receipts to a local state health insurance fund office.

Opening Hours

Banks: Mon-Fri 8.30am-12.30pm & 1.30pm-3.30pm (to 5pm or 6pm on Thurs).

Museums: Check locally as times vary.

Post Offices: Mon-Fri 7/8am-6/8pm; Sat 8am-12pm.

Shops: Mon-Fri 8/9am-6pm/8pm. Sat 8/9am-12/4pm; bakers may be open Sun mornings.

Safety and Security

Most visits to Germany are trouble free but visitors should take the usual commonsense precautions against mugging, pickpocketing and bag snatching, particularly in areas around railway stations, airports in large cities and at Christmas markets. Do not leave valuables unattended.

Germany shares with the rest of Europe a general threat from terrorism. Attacks could be indiscriminate and against civilian targets in public places, including tourist sites. You should maintain a high level of vigilance at all times.

British Embassy

WILHELMSTRASSE 70, D-10117 BERLIN
Tel: (030) 204570,
www.ukingermany.fco.gov.uk/en/

British Consulates-General

OststraBe 86, 40210
DÜSSELDORF
Tel: (0211) 94480

MÖHLSTRASSE 5, 81675 MÜNCHEN
Tel: (089) 211090

Irish Embassy

JÄGERSTRASSE 51, 10117 BERLIN
Tel: (030) 220720
www.embassyofireland.de

There are also Irish Honorary Consulates in Frankfurt, Hamburg, Köln (Cologne) and München (Munich).

Documents

Passport

It is a legal requirement to carry your passport at all times. German police have the right to ask to see identification and for British citizens the only acceptable form of ID is a valid passport.

Money

The major debit and credit cards, including American Express, are widely accepted by shops, hotels, restaurants and petrol stations. However, you may find that credit cards are not as widely accepted in smaller establishments as they are in the UK, including many shops and campsites, due to the high charges imposed on retailers, and debit cards are preferred. Cash machines are widespread and have instructions in English.

British visitors have been arrested for possession of counterfeit currency and the authorities advise against changing money anywhere other than at banks or legitimate bureaux de change.

Carry your credit card issuers'/banks' 24-hour UK contact numbers in case of loss or theft of your cards.

Vehicle(s)

Carry your valid driving licence, insurance and vehicle documents with you in your vehicle at all times. It is particularly important to carry your vehicle registration document V5C, as you will need it if entering a low emission zone (see later in this chapter for more information).

If you are driving a hired or borrowed vehicle, you must be in possession of a letter of authorisation from the owner or a hire agreement.

Driving

Roads in Germany are of an excellent standard but speed limits are higher than in the UK and the accident rate is greater. Drivers undertaking long journeys in or through Germany should plan their journeys carefully and take frequent breaks.

Accidents

In the event of a road accident the police must always be called even if there are no injuries.

Alcohol

The maximum permitted level of alcohol is 50 milligrams per 100 millilitres of blood, i.e. lower than that in the UK (80 milligrams). For novice drivers who have held a driving licence for less than two years, and for drivers under the age of 21, no alcohol is permitted in the bloodstream. Penalties for driving under the influence of alcohol or drugs are severe.

Breakdown Service

The motoring organisation Allgemeiner Deutscher Automobil-Club (ADAC) operates road patrols on motorways and in the event of a breakdown, assistance can be obtained by calling from emergency phones placed every 2 km. Members of clubs affiliated to the AIT or FIA, such as The Caravan and Motorhome Club, must ask specifically for roadside assistance to be provided by ADAC as they should be able to receive assistance free of charge. You must pay for replacement parts and towing. ADAC breakdown vehicles are yellow and marked 'ADAC Strassenwacht'.

If ADAC Strassenwacht vehicles are not available, firms under contract to ADAC provide towing and roadside assistance, against payment. Vehicles used by firms under contract to ADAC are marked 'Strassendienst im Auftrag des ADAC'.

On other roads the ADAC breakdown service can be reached 24 hours a day by telephoning 01802-22 22 22 (local call rates) or 22 22 22 from a mobile phone.

Child Restraint Systems

Children under three years of age must be placed in an approved child restraint and cannot be transported in a vehicle otherwise. Children of three years and over must travel in the rear of vehicles. Children under 12 years old and 1.5 metres in height must be seated in an approved child restraint. If a child restraint won't fit into the vehicle because other children are using a child restraint, then children of three years and over must use a seat belt or other safety device attached to the seat.

Fuel

Most petrol stations are open from 8am to 8pm. In large cities many are open 24 hours. In the east there are fewer petrol stations than in the south and west. Some have automatic pumps operated using credit cards.

LPG (autogas or flussiggas) is widely available. You can view a list of approximately 800 outlets throughout the country, including those near motorways, from the website www.autogastanken.de (follow the links under 'Tanken' and 'Tankstellan-Karte'). On some stretches of motorway petrol stations may be few and far between, e.g. the A45, A42 and A3 to the Dutch border, and it is advisable not to let your fuel tank run low.

Lights

Dipped headlights are recommended at all times and must always be used in tunnels, as well as when visibility is poor and during periods of bad weather. Bulbs are more likely to fail with constant use and you are recommended to carry spares.

Low Emission Zones

A large number of German cities and towns now require motorists to purchase a 'Pollution Badge' (Umwelt Plakette) in the form of a windscreen sticker in order to enter city centre 'Umwelt' or green zones. The areas where restrictions apply are indicated by signs showing coloured vignettes, the colour of the vignette issued (red, yellow or green) depending on your vehicle's engine type and its Euro emission rating.

You must present your vehicle registration document, V5C, at an 'Umwelt Plakette' sales outlet, which can be found at vehicle repair centres, car dealers, MOT (Tüv) stations and vehicle licensing offices and it is understood that badges are also available from ATU motoring supplies shops. The cost varies between €5 and €10 + VAT and postage.

Failure to display a badge could result in a fine of €40. Enforcement is managed by the police, local authorities and traffic wardens. Older vehicles without a catalytic converter or a particulate filter (generally emission-rated Euro 1) will not be issued with a badge and will not be permitted to enter the centres of those cities and towns participating in the scheme.

Visit www.lowemissionzones.eu or www.umwelt-plakette.de (you may also be able to purchase your badge here before you travel to Germany).

Motorways

With around 12,845 toll free kilometres, Germany's motorways (autobahns) constitute one of the world's most advanced and efficient systems. For a complete list of autobahns, including the location of all junctions and roadworks in progress, see www.autobahn-online.de

Some motorways are so heavily used by lorries that the inside lane has become heavily rutted. These parallel ruts are potentially dangerous for caravans travelling at high speed and vigilance is necessary.

It is understood that the A44 and A7 are particularly prone to this problem. Caution also needs to be exercised when driving on the concrete surfaces of major roads.

On motorways emergency telephones are placed at 2 km intervals; some have one button to request breakdown assistance and another to summon an ambulance. Other telephones connect the caller to a rescue control centre. A vehicle that has broken down on a motorway must be towed away to the nearest exit.

There are hundreds of motorway service areas offering, at the very least, a petrol station and a restaurant or cafeteria. Tourist information boards are posted in all the modern motorway service areas. Recent visitors have reported an increase in service facilities just off Autobahn exit ramps, in particular with 'Autohof' (truck stops). The facilities at Autohofs are reported to be comparable to service areas, but usually with considerably lower prices.

Parking

Zigzag lines on the carriageway indicate a stopping (waiting) and parking prohibition, e.g. at bus stops, narrow roads and places with poor visibility, but double or single yellow lines are not used. Instead look out for 'no stopping', 'parking prohibited' or 'no parking' signs.

Except for one-way streets, parking is only permitted on the right-hand side. Do not park in the opposite direction to traffic flow. Parking meters and parking disc schemes are in operation and discs may be bought in local shops or service stations.

Priority

At crossroads and junctions, where no priority is indicated, traffic coming from the right has priority. Trams do not have absolute priority over other vehicles but priority must be given to passengers getting on or off stationary trams. Trams in two-way streets must be overtaken on the right. Drivers must give way to a bus whose driver has indicated his intention to pull away from the kerb. Do not overtake a stationary school bus which has stopped to let passengers on or off. This may be indicated by a red flashing light on the bus.

Traffic already on a roundabout has right of way, except when signs show otherwise. Drivers must use their indicators when leaving a roundabout, not when entering.

Always stop to allow pedestrians to cross at marked pedestrian crossings. In residential areas where traffic-calming zones exist, pedestrians are allowed to use the whole street, so drive with great care.

Road Signs and Markings

Most German road signs and markings conform to the international pattern. Other road signs that may be encountered are:

Keep distance shown

Street lights not on all night

Lower speed limit applies in the wet

Recommended route on motorways

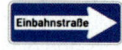
One way street

Tram or bus stop

German	English Translation
Einsatzfahrzeuge Frei	Emergency vehicles only
Fahrbahnwechsel	Change traffic lane
Freie Fahrt	Road clear
Frostchaden	Frost damage
Gefährlich	Danger
Glatteisgefahr	Ice on the road
Notruf	Emergency roadside telephone
Radweg Kreuzt	Cycle-track crossing
Rollsplitt	Loose grit
Stau	Traffic jam
Strassenschaden	Road damage
Umleitung	Diversion
Vorsicht	Caution

Road signs on motorways are blue and white, whereas on B roads (Bundesstrasse) they are orange and black. If you are planning a route through Germany using E road numbers, be aware that E roads may be poorly signposted and you may have to navigate using national A or B road numbers.

Speed Limits

	Open Road (kmph)	Motorway (kmph)
Solo Car	100	130
Car towing caravan/trailer	80*	80
Motorhome under 3500kg	100	130
Motorhome 3500-7500kg	80	100

* 100 km/h (62 mph) if your car and caravan passes a TUV test in Germany (test costs €70 and takes 2 hours to complete)

There is a speed limit of 50 km/h (31 mph) in built-up areas for all types of motor vehicles, unless otherwise indicated by road signs. A built-up area starts from the town name sign at the beginning of a town or village.

The number of sections of autobahn with de-restricted zones, i.e. no upper speed limit, is diminishing and the volume of traffic makes high speed motoring virtually impossible. Regulations on many stretches of two-lane motorway restrict lorries, together with cars towing caravans, from overtaking.

Speed cameras are frequently in use but they may be deliberately hidden behind crash barriers or in mobile units. A GPS navigation system which indicates the location of fixed speed cameras must have the function deactivated. The use of radar detectors is prohibited.

A car towing a caravan or trailer is prohibited to 80km/h (50 mph) on motorways and other main roads. You may occasionally see car/caravan combinations displaying a sign indicating that their maximum permitted speed is 100 km/h (62 mph). This is only permitted for vehicles that have passed a TUV test in Germany, who will then need to apply for a sticker at a Zulassungsstelle. The application process can be complicated as some Zulassungsstelles will insist they see a registration certificate for your caravan.

Obtaining a 100km/h sticker without a registration certificate is best done in Aachen as they are the only Zulassungsstelle familiar with this process. If you are having difficulty at a different Zulassungsstelle ask them to call the Zulassungsstelle in Aachen to confirm that a registration document is not required.

In bad weather when visibility is below 50 metres, the maximum speed limit is 50 km/h (31 mph) on all roads.

Towing

Drivers of cars towing caravans and other slow-moving vehicles must leave enough space in front of them for an overtaking vehicle to get into that space, or they must pull over from time to time to let other vehicles pass.

If you are towing a car behind a motorhome, our advice would be to use a trailer with all four wheels of the car off the ground. Although Germany doesn't have a specific law banning A-frames, they do have a law which prohibits a motor vehicle towing another motor vehicle.Outside built-up areas the speed limit for such vehicle combinations is 80 km/h (50 mph) or 60 km/h (37 mph) for vehicles over 3,500 kg.

Traffic Jams

Roads leading to popular destinations in Denmark, the Alps and Adriatic Coast become very congested during the busy holiday period of July and August and on public holidays. In those periods traffic jams of up to 60 km are not unheard of.

Congestion is likely on the A3 and A5 north-south routes. Traffic jams are also likely to occur on the A7 Kassel-Denmark, the A8 Stuttgart-Munich-Salzburg and on the A2 and A9 to Berlin. Other cities where congestion may occur are Würzburg, Nürnberg (Nuremberg), Munich and Hamburg. Alternative routes, known as U routes, have been devised; those leading to the south or west have even numbers and those leading to the north or east have odd numbers. These U routes often detour over secondary roads to the following motorway junction and the acquisition of a good road map or atlas is recommended.

ADAC employs 'Stauberater' (traffic jam advisors) who are recognisable by their bright yellow motorbikes. They assist motorists stuck in traffic and will advise on alternative routes.

Upgrading of motorways to Berlin from the west and improvements to many roads in the old east German suburbs may result in diversions and delays, and worsened traffic congestion.

Violation of Traffic Regulations

Police are empowered to impose and collect small on-the-spot fines for contravention of traffic regulations. Fines vary according to the gravity of the offence and have in recent years been increased dramatically for motorists caught speeding in a built-up area (over 50 km/h – 31 mph). A deposit may be required against higher fines and failure to pay may cause the vehicle to be confiscated.

It is an offence to use abusive language, or make rude gestures in Germany, including to other drivers while driving. It is also an offence to stop on the hard shoulder of a motorway except in the case of mechanical failure - please note that running out of fuel is not classed as a mechanical failure so you may be liable for a fine of up to €20 if you do run out of fuel and stop on the hard shoulder.

It is illegal for pedestrians to cross a road when the red pedestrian light is displayed, even if there is no traffic approaching the crossing. Offenders could be fined and will find themselves liable to all costs in the event of an accident.

Winter Driving

All vehicles, including those registered outside Germany, must be fitted with winter tyres (or all season tyres) during winter conditions, bearing the mark 'M+S' (Mud + Snow) or the snowflake symbol. Failure to use them can result in a fine and penalty points. There must also be anti-freeze in the windscreen cleaning fluid.

The use of snow chains is permitted and for vehicles fitted with them there is a maximum speed limit of 50 km/h (31 mph).
In mountainous areas the requirement for chains is indicated by signs. The use of spiked tyres is not authorised.

Essential Equipment

First Aid Kit

Drivers of German registered vehicles must carry a first aid kit but this is not a legal requirement for foreign visitors.

Lights

Dipped headlights are recommended at all times and must always be used in tunnels, as well as when visibility is poor and during periods of bad weather. Bulbs are more likely to fail with constant use and you are recommended to carry spares.

Touring

German food is generally of high quality and offers great regional range and diversity. In the country there is at least one inn – 'gasthof' or 'gasthaus' – in virtually every village. A service charge is usually included in restaurant bills but it is usual to leave some small change or round up the bill by 5-10% if satisfied with the service.

Smoking is generally banned on public transport and in restaurants and bars, but regulations vary from state to state.

The German National Tourist Board (GNTB) produces guides to walking and cycle paths throughout the country, as well as an extensive range of other brochures and guides. The individual tourist offices for the 16 federal states can also supply a wealth of information about events, attractions and tourist opportunities within their local regions. Obtain contact details from the GNTO.

Christmas markets are an essential part of the run-up to the festive season and they range in size from a few booths in small towns and villages, to hundreds of stalls and booths in large cities. The markets generally run from mid November to 22 or 23 December.

There are 32 UNESCO World Heritage sites in Germany, including the cities of Lübeck, Potsdam and Weimar, the cathedrals of Aachen, Cologne and Speyer, together with numerous other venues of great architectural and archaeological interest.

The Berlin Welcome Card is valid for 2, 3 or 5 days and includes free bus and train travel (including free travel for three accompanying children up to the age of 14), as well as discounted or free entrance to museums, and discounts on tours, boat trips, restaurants and theatres. It can be extended to include Potsdam and the Museuminsel and is available from tourist information centres, hotels and public transport centres or from www.visitberlin.de. A 3 day museum card – SchauLUST-MuseenBERLIN – is also available, valid in more than 60 national museums in and around the city.

Other cities, groups of cities or regions also offer Welcome Cards, including Bonn, Cologne, Dresden, Düsseldorf, Frankfurt, Hamburg, Heidelberg and Munich. These give discounts on public transport, museums, shopping, dining and attractions. Enquire at a local tourist office or at the German National Tourist Office in London.

Camping and Caravanning

There are approximately 3,500 campsites in Germany, which are generally open from April to October. Many (mostly in winter sports areas) stay open in winter and have all the necessary facilities for winter sports enthusiasts. Sites may have a very high proportion of statics, usually in a separate area. In the high summer season visitors should either start looking for a pitch early in the afternoon or book in advance.

Campsites are usually well equipped with modern sanitary facilities, shops and leisure amenities, etc. Some sites impose a charge for handling rubbish, commonly €1 to €2 a day. Separate containers for recycling glass, plastic, etc, are now the norm.

A daily tourist tax may also be payable of up to €2 or €3 per person per night.

Naturism is popular, particularly in eastern Germany, and sites which accept naturists will generally display a sign 'FKK'.

Many sites close for a two hour period between noon and 3pm (known as Mittagsruhe) and you may find barriers down so that vehicles cannot be moved on or off the site during this period. Some sites provide a waiting area but where a site entrance is off a busy road parking or turning may be difficult.

For a list of small sites (up to 150 pitches) see www.kleincamp.de

Casual/wild camping is discouraged and is not allowed in forests and nature reserves. In the case of private property permission to pitch a tent or park a caravan should be obtained in advance from the owners, or on common land or state property, from the local town hall or police station.

Cycling

There is an extensive network of over 70,000 km of cycle routes across all regions. Children under eight years are not allowed to cycle on the road. Under 10 year olds may ride on the pavement but must give way to pedestrians and dismount to cross the road. Bicycles must have front and rear lights and a bell.

Cyclists can be fined €25 for using a mobile phone while cycling and €10 for using earphones.

Electricity and Gas

Current on campsites varies between 2 and 16 amps, 6 to 10 amps being the most common. Plugs have two round pins. Most campsites have CEE connections.

Many sites make a one-off charge – usually €1 or €2 however long your stay – for connection to the electricity supply, which is then metered at a rate per kilowatt hour (kwh) of approximately €0.50-€0.70, with or without an additional daily charge. This connection charge can make one night stays expensive. During the summer you may find only a flat, daily charge for electricity of €2-€5, the supply being metered during the rest of the year.

Campingaz is available and the blue cylinders in general used throughout Europe may be exchanged for German cylinders which are green-grey. At some campsites in winter sports areas a direct connection with the gas mains ring is available and the supply is metered.

Public Transport

Most major German cities have underground (U-bahn), urban railway (S-bahn), bus and tram systems whose convenience and punctuality are renowned. Pay your fare prior to boarding public transport using the automated ticketing machines. Your ticket must then be date stamped separately using the machines on board the vehicle or at the entry gates at major stops. Daily tickets permit the use of trains, buses and trams.

A number of car ferries operate across the Weser and Elbe rivers which allow easy touring north of Bremen and Hamburg. Routes across the Weser include Blexen to Bremerhavn, Brake to Sandstedt and Berne to Farge. The Weser Tunnel (B437) connects the villages of Rodenkirchen and Dedesdorf, offering an easy connection between the cities of Bremerhaven and Nordenham. Across the Elbe there is a car ferry route between Wischhafen and Glückstadt. An international ferry route operates all year across Lake Constance (Bodensee) between Konstanz and Meersburg. There is also a route between Friedrichshafen and Romanshorn in Switzerland.

Neuschwanstein Castle

Shutterstock/ Yevhenii Chulovskyi

AACHEN *1A4* (18km SE Rural) *50.69944, 6.22194*
Camping Vichtbachtal, Vichtbachstrasse 10, 52159
Roetgen-Mulartshütte **(02408) 5131; camping@
vichtbachtal.de; www.vichtbachtal.de**

12 ♀♀ wo ⚡ ☐ ⟋ MSP 🦋 ⊕ nr 🏖 ⚞

On E40/A44 exit junc 3 Aachen/Brand onto B258
dir Kornelimünster. In 5km at R-hand bend turn L
sp Mulartshütte. Thro Venwegen. Site ent on L 50m
bef T-junc app Mulartshütte, site sp. 3*, Med, shd, pt
sl, EHU (16A) €1.50 or metered (rev pol); 80% statics;
site clsd Nov; CKE. *"Sm area for tourers; v friendly
Eng spkn owners; gd site for visiting Aachen; gd walks
adj; gd bus service to Aachen; v pretty wooded area."*
€21.50   2016

AACHEN *1A4* (3.5km SE Urban) *50.76140, 6.10285*
Aachen Platz für Camping, Branderhoferweg 11,
52066 Aachen-Burtscheid **(0241) 6088057; mail@
aachen-camping.de; www.aachen-camping.de**

12 🐕 ♀♀(htd) wo ⚡ ☐ ⟋ MSP

Exit A44 junc 2 onto L233 Monschauerstrasse dir
Aachen. In 3.8km at outer ring rd Adenauer Allee
L260 turn R, then in 800m L at 2nd traff lts onto
Branderhoferweg twd Beverau. Site on R at bottom
of hill. 2*, Sm, mkd, hdstg, pt shd, EHU (16A) inc; bus
500m; Eng spkn. *"Nice, clean, well-run municipal site;
gd, modern san facs; max stay 5 nights; excel o'night
stop; rec arr bef 1600 high ssn; ideal Xmas mkts; gd
conv site; close to city cent; open access site; fair."*
€15.00   2015

"There aren't many sites open at this time of year"

If you're travelling outside peak season
remember to call ahead to check site opening
dates – even if the entry says 'open all year'.

ALPIRSBACH *3C3* (2km N Rural) *48.35576, 8.41224*
Camping Alpirsbach, Grezenbühler Weg 18-20,
72275 Alpirsbach **(07444) 6313; info@camping-
alpirsbach.de; www.camping-alpirsbach.de**

12 🐕 €1 ♀♀ wo ⚡ ☐ ⅄ ⟋ MSP 🦋 ⏑ ⊕ 🏖 ⚞

On B294 leave Alpirsbach twds Freudenstadt.
1st site sp on L. 4*, Med, pt shd, serviced pitches;
EHU (16A) metered; gas; red long stay; 10% statics;
Eng spkn; tennis; golf 5km; CKE. *"Excel site; helpful,
informative & friendly owner; vg welcome, free bottle
of local beer per person; immac san facs; gd rest; gd
walking; o'night area for m'vans €10; guest card for
free transport on some local transport; some rvside
pitches (v shd)."* **€30.00**   2019

ALSFELD *1D4* (11km W Rural) *50.73638, 9.15222*
Camping Heimertshausen, Ehringshäuserstrasse,
36320 Kirtorf-Heimertshausen **(06635) 206;
info@campingplatz-heimertshausen.de;
campingplatz-heimertshausen.de**

🐕 €1 ♀♀ wo ⚡ ☐ ⟋ 🦋 ⊕ ⏑ 🏖 ⚞

Exit A5 junc 3 Alsfeld West onto B49 dir Frankfurt.
Turn R in vill of Romrod to Heimertshausen & L to
site. Site also sp fr B62. Med, shd, EHU (10-16A) €2
or metered; 65% statics; Eng spkn; adv bkg acc; CKE.
*"Beautiful, wooded area; lovely 'hunting lodge' type
cosy rest; bar/food open Jul/Aug; clsd 1300-1500
& 2200-0800; htd pool adj; o'night m'vans area; site
run down (2015); facs dated but clean & adequate."*
€27.50, 1 Apr-30 Sep.   2015

ALTENBERG *4G1* (1km W Rural) *50.76666, 13.74666*
Camping Kleiner Galgenteich (Naturist), Galgenteich
3, 01773 Altenberg **(035056) 31995; mail@camping-
erzgebirge.de; www.camping-erzgebirge.de**

12 🐕 €1 ♀♀ wo ⚡ ☐ ⟋ MSP 🦋 ⏑ ⊕ 🏖 ⚞

Leave A4 at Dresden-Nord onto B170 sp Zinnwald
then Altenberg. On SW side of B170; clearly sp. Lge,
pt shd, pt sl, EHU (10A) metered + conn fee; sw nr;
50% statics; sailing adj. *"Sep area for naturists; ski lift
500m; site clsd in Nov."* **€21.00**   2016

ALTENBURG *2F4* (12km NNE Rural) *51.045799,
12.500404* See Camping Altenburgh-Pahna, 04617
Pahna **(03434) 351914; camping-pahna@t-online.de;
www.camping-pahna.de**

12 🐕 €2.50 ♀♀(htd) wo ⚡ ☐ ⅄ ⟋ MSP ⏑ ⏇ ⊕ ⚓ 🏖 ⚞

A4 exit 60 (Ronneburg) then B7 to Altenburg. B93
direction Leipzig, right B7 direction Frohburg, foll sp
at Eschefeld. 4*, V lge, pt shd, serviced pitches; EHU
€2; bbq; cooking facs; sw; red long stay; 25% statics;
Eng spkn; adv bkg acc; lake adj; games area; CKE. *"Vg;
nature walks; conv Dresden, Leipzig & Colditz; quiet LS
but busy on w/ends and hg ssn."* **€24.00**   2019

ALTENKIRCHEN *2F1* (9km W Coastal) *54.62905,
13.22281* Caravancamp Ostseeblick, Seestr. 39a,
18556 Dranske **(03839) 18196; www.caravancamp-
ostseeblick.de**

🐕 ♀♀ wo ⚡ ☐ ⏑ ⟋ MSP ⏇

Clearly sp fr main rd bet Kuhle & Dranske. Sm,
hdstg, hdg, mkd, pt shd, EHU €2.50; twin axles;
20% statics; Eng spkn; adv bkg rec. *"Excel; sea adj."*
€23.00, 1 Apr-31 Oct.   2017

ALTENSTEIG *3C3* (3km W Rural) *48.58456, 8.57866*
Schwarzwald Camping Altensteig, Im Oberen Tal 3-5,
72213 Altensteig (07453) 8415; info@schwarzwald
camping.de; www.schwarzwaldcamping.de

🚐 🐕 €2 ♟ WD ♿ 🚲 ✉ 🦋 ⛄ ⛳

Take Obere Talstrasse (L362) due W fr town ctr. Aft
2km site on L. Easy access. Sm, pt shd, EHU; bbq;
twin axles; 75% statics; Eng spkn; games area. *"Gd;
table tennis, beach volleyball, boating, walking fr site;
Black Forest; cross country skiing."* **€23.00**   2017

AUGSBURG *4E3* (7km N Rural) *48.41168, 10.92371*
Camping Bella Augusta, Mühlhauserstrasse 54B,
86169 Augsburg-Ost (0821) 707575; info@
caravaningpark.de; www.caravaningpark.de

🚐 🐕 €2.55 ♟ WD ♿ 🚲 ✉ MSP ⛳ nr ⛄ ⛲ 🏛

Exit A8/E52 junc 73 dir Neuburg to N, site sp.
2*, Lge, pt shd, EHU (10A) inc; sw nr; 80% statics;
ccard acc; boating. *"V busy NH; excel rest; camping
equipment shop on site; vg san facs but site looking
a little run down; noise fr a'bahn; cycle track to town
(map fr recep); vg; nice lake."* **€31.00**   2019

AUGSBURG *4E3* (8km N Rural) *48.43194, 10.92388*
Camping Ludwigshof am See, Augsburgerstrasse 36,
86444 Mühlhausen-Affing (08207) 961724; info@
campingludwigshof.de; www.campingludwigshof.de

🐕 €2 ♟ WD ♿ 🚲 ✉ MSP ⛳ ⛄ 🔔 nr 🏛

Exit A8/E52 junc 73at Augsburg Ost/Pöttmes exit;
foll sp Pöttmes; site sp on L on lakeside. 3*, Lge,
unshd, EHU (16A) €3.50 (long cable req); bbq; sw; twin
axles; red long stay; 70% statics; bus; Eng spkn; ccard
acc; tennis; CKE. *"Pleasant site; unmkd field for tourers,
close to san facs; both 6A panel & 16A panels for EHU
-16A only accepts German type of plug; beautiful clean,
modern facs; nr A8 m'way; conv NH on way to E Italy;
clsd 1300-1500; gd for long stay, special rates can be
negotiated; poss need long cable as EHU in corner of
field."* **€31.50, 1 Apr-31 Oct.**   2018

AUGSBURG *4E3* (9km NE Rural) *48.4375, 10.92916*
Lech Camping, Seeweg 6, 86444 Affing-Mühlhausen
(08207) 2200; info@lech-camping.de; www.lech-
camping.de

🐕 €3 ♟ (htd) WD ♿ 🚲 ✉ MSP ⛳ ⛄ 🔔 nr

Exit A8/E52 at junc 73 Augsburg-Ost; take rd N sp
Pöttmes; site 3km on R. 5*, Sm, hdstg, mkd, pt shd,
EHU (16A); bbq; sw nr; bus to Augsburg, train Munich;
Eng spkn; adv bkg rec; ccard acc; boating. *"Lovely,
well-ordered site; friendly, helpful owners; excel san
facs; gd play area; deposit for san facs key; camping
accessory shop on site; cycle rte to Augsburg; excel
NH for A8; excel site espec lakeside pitch; statics (sep
area); c'vans close together; constant rd noise; recep
shut 12-2pm."* **€36.50, 15 Apr-15 Sep, G19.**   2018

BAD ABBACH *4F3* (6km W Rural) *48.93686, 12.01992*
Campingplatz Freizeitinsel, Inselstraße 1a, D93077
Bad Abbach (09405) 9570401 or (0176) 96631729;
info@campingplatz-freizeitinsel.de; www.camping
platz-freizeitinsel.de

♟ WD ♿ 🚲 ✉ MSP 🦋 ⛳ ⛄ 🏛

A93 Regensburg, exit Pentling B16 dir twrds
Kelheim. Cont on B16 past Bad Abbach and take
next exit R to Poikam/Inselbad. Over rv and foll
rd round to R past Poikam sp. At junc turn R sp
Inselbad. Site on R. Med, mkd, EHU; bbq; cooking
facs; sw nr; twin axles; 20% statics; Eng spkn; adv
bkg acc; bike hire; CKE. *"New (2014) family run
developing site; vg, modern, clean facs; some deluxe
serviced pitches avail with supp; gd area for touring,
cycling & walking; nrby lake, sw & thermal baths; gd
rest in vill 1km; train to Regensburg 1km; excel site."*
€28.00, 25 Mar-31 Oct & 27 Nov-18 Dec.   2017

BAD BIRNBACH *4G3* (800km N Rural) *48.450201,
13.094024* **Camping Theresienhof,** Breindoblweg 6,
84364 Bad Birnbach (08563) 963244; www.camping-
theresienhof.de

🚐 🐕 ♟ (htd) WD ♿ 🚲 ✉ MSP 🦋

Off B388 W fr A3 fr Schaarding. Hdstg, mkd, pt shd,
terr, EHU (16A); bbq (charcoal, elec, gas); cooking
facs; twin axles; adv bkg rec; bike hire. *"Ideal stopover."*
NP 26.9   2019

BAD BRAMSTEDT *1D2* (1km N Rural) *53.9283, 9.8901*
Kur-Camping Roland, Kielerstrasse 52,24576 Bad
Bramstedt (04192) 6723

🐕 €2 ♟ WD ♿ 🚲 ✉ ⛄ nr 🔔

Exit A7 junc 17 dir Bad Bremstedt; site sp, ent
immed at Nissan g'ge at top of hill at start of dual
c'way. Fr N exit A7 junc 16 dir Bad Bremstedt;
site on L in 4km. 3*, Sm, shd, EHU (6-16A) €2 &
metered; Eng spkn; CKE. *"Excel CL-type site; friendly
owner; EHU not rec if site v full; gd sh stay/NH."*
€24.00, 1 Apr-31 Oct.   2017

BAD DOBERAN *2F1* (10km N Coastal) *54.15250,
11.89972* **Ferien-Camp Börgerende (Part Naturist),**
Deichstrasse 16, 18211 Börgerende (038203) 81126;
info@ostseeferiencamp.de; www.ostseeferien
camp.de

🐕 €4 ♟ WD ♿ 🚲 ✉ MSP 🦋 ⛳ ⛄ 🔔 🏛 ✏
🏖 shgl adj

In Bad Doberan, turn L off B105 sp Warnemunde.
In 4km in Rethwisch, turn L sp Börgerende. In 3km
turn R at site sp. 5*, V lge, hdg, unshd, EHU (10-16A)
€3; cooking facs; 10% statics; phone; bus 500m;
Eng spkn; games area; bike hire; sauna; CKE. *"Excel
beaches; o'night m'vans area; cycle paths; sep naturist
beach; excel site."* **€35.00, 21 Mar-30 Oct.**   2016

BAD DURKHEIM *3C2* (3km NE Rural) *49.47361, 8.19166* **Knaus Campingplatz Bad Dürkheim,** In den Almen 3, 67098 Bad Dürkheim **(06322) 61356; badduerkheim@knauscamp.de; www.knauscamp.de**

🏕 12 ♟ (htd) ⓦⓓ ♨ ♿ ♿ 🛒 ⚐ ℳⓈℙ 🅗 🏊 🆎 ⚓ sand adj

Fr S on A61/E31 exit junc 60 onto A650/B37 twds Bad Dürkheim. At 2nd traff lts turn R, site sp nr local airfield. Fr N on A6 exit junc 19 onto B271 to Bad Dürkheim. At traff lts after Ungstein turn L dir Lugwigshafen, at next traff lts turn L, then 1st R. Site at end of rd. Ent strictly controlled. Site well sp fr all dir on town o'skts. 4*, V lge, mkd, pt shd, EHU (16A) €2.50; gas; bbq; sw nr; red long stay; TV; 45% statics; phone; bus; Eng spkn; tennis; bike hire; sauna; solarium; golf 8km; games area; CKE. *"Well-equipped, busy site in vineyards; sm, well-worn pitches; some modern san facs - all clean; m'van o'night facs; no access 1300-1500; gd pool in Bad Dürkheim; wine-fest & wurst-fest Sep excel; conv NH Bavaria & Austria."* **€36.50** 2015

"That's changed – Should I let the Club know?"

If you find something on site that's different from the site entry, fill in a report and let us know. See camc.com/europereport.

BAD DURKHEIM *3C2* (3km S Rural) *49.43741, 8.17036* **Campingplatz im Burgtal,** Waldstrasse 105, 67157 Wachenheim **(06322) 9580-801; touristinfo@vg-wachenheim.de; www.wachenheim.de**

🏕 🐕 €1 ♟ ⓦⓓ ♨ ♿ 🛒 ⚐ ℳⓈℙ 🦋 🍽 🍸 🅗 🏊 🆎

Fr Bad Dürkheim, take B271 S dir Neustadt for approx 2km. After passing Villa Rustica rest area, turn L for Wachenheim, then R. Go strt at traff lts, up hill thro vill (narr). Site on L. Med, hdg, mkd, hdstg, pt shd, serviced pitches; EHU (16A) inc; 50% statics; tennis; golf 12km; CKE. *"Forest walks in Pfalz National Park; in heart of wine-tasting country; v busy during wine festival - adv bkg rec; helpful owners; gd facs; site bit shabby (2017); upper area unshd."* **€27.50, 1 Mar-30 Nov.** 2019

BAD EMS *3B2* (7km E Rural) *50.32773, 7.75483* **Camping Lahn-Beach,** Hallgarten 16, 56132 Dausenau **(02603) 13964; info@canutours.de; www.campingplatz-dausenau.de**

🐕 ♟ ⓦⓓ ♨ 🛒 ⚐ ℳⓈℙ 🅗 🆎 🏊 🆎 nr 🆎

Foll rv E fr Bad Ems twd Nassau on B260/417. At ent to vill of Dausenau turn R over bdge, site visible on S bank of Lahn Rv. Med, pt shd, EHU (6-16A) metered + conn fee; 40% statics; adv bkg acc; bike hire; boat launch; sep car park. *"Pleasant situation; interesting rv traff & sightseeing around Lahn Valley; liable to flood at v high water; gd san facs."* **€23.50, 1 Apr-31 Oct.** 2015

BAD FALLINGBOSTEL *1D2* (3km NE Rural) *52.87686, 9.73147* **Camping Bohmeschlucht,** Vierde 22, D 29683 Fallingbostel-Vierde **(05162) 5604; campingplatz-hoehmeschlucht@t-online.de; www.boehmeschlucht.de**

🏕 12 🐕 ♟ ⓦⓓ ♨ ♿ 🛒 ⚐ ℳⓈℙ 🦋 🍽 🍸 🅗 🏊 🆎 nr 🆎

A7 junc 47 Bad Fallingbostel. Foll sp Dorfmark/Soltau. On leaving Fallingbostel, go strt at rndabt and cont for approx 1 km. Site sp on R. 4*, Med, mkd, pt shd, EHU (16A) - €2; bbq; sw; 60% statics; Eng spkn; adv bkg acc; games rm. *"Excel walking, cycling & boat/canoe tours fr site; vg rest; library; helpful staff; excel for exploring Luneburger Heide, Hamburg or Walsrode Bird Park; excel site."* **€21.00** 2019

BAD FUSSING *4G3* (3km S Urban) *48.33236, 13.31577* **Fuchs Kur Camping,** Falkenstraße 14, 94072 Bad Fussing **(0853) 7356; info@kurcamping-fuchs.de; www.kurcamping-fuchs.de**

🏕 12 🐕 €2 ♟ ⓦⓓ ♿ ⚐ 🦋 🅗 🆎

Fr A3 Nurnberg-Passau, take exit 118 dir Egglfing. Foll sp. 4*, Med, mkd, hdstg, EHU inc; 10% statics; Eng spkn; adv bkg acc; ccard acc; CKE. *"Gd NH; gd value; vg."* **€23.00** 2015

BAD FUSSING *4G3* (3km S Rural) *48.33255, 13.31440* **Kur-Camping Max,** Falkenstrasse 12, 94072 Egglfing-Bad Füssing **(08537) 96170; info@campingmax.de; www.campingmax.de**

🏕 12 🐕 €2 ♟ (htd) ⓦⓓ ♨ ♿ 🛒 ⚐ ℳⓈℙ 🦋 🍽 🍸 🅗 nr ⚓ 🏊 🆎 🖊

Across frontier & bdge fr Obernberg in Austria. Site sp in Egglfing. On B12 Schärding to Simbach turn L immed bef vill of Tutting sp Obernberg. Site on R after 7km, sp. 5*, Med, pt shd, EHU (16A) metered + conn fee; cooking facs; sw; TV; 20% statics; fishing; golf 2km; tennis 2km; bike hire; CKE. *"Gd rest for snacks & meals on site; well managed site; excel clean facs; wellness cent; thermal facs in Bad Füssing; pool 3km; private san facs avail; new indoor thermal bath & outdoor sw pool (2014)."* **€22.60** 2019

BAD GANDERSHEIM *1D3* (2km E Rural) *51.86694, 10.04972* **Kur-Campingpark,** 37581 Bad Gandersheim **(05382) 1595; info@camping-bad-gandersheim.de; www.camping-bad-gandersheim.de**

🏕 12 🐕 €1 ♟ ⓦⓓ ♨ ♿ 🛒 ⚐ ℳⓈℙ 🦋 🅗 ⚓ 🏊 🆎

Exit A7/E45 at junc 67 onto B64 dir Holzminden & Bad Gandersheim. Site on R shortly after Seboldshausen. 4*, Lge, pt shd, EHU (10A) metered + conn fee; 40% statics; bike hire. *"Excel; pool 1.5km; always plenty of space; sep o'night area."* **€25.00** 2019

BAD HONNEF *1B4* (9km E Rural) *50.65027, 7.30166*
Camping Jillieshof, Ginsterbergweg 6, 53604 Bad
Honnef-Aegidienberg **(02224) 972066; information@
camping-jillieshof.de; www.camping-jillieshof.de**

🛿 €2 ⚥ ⛺ ♨ ⚒ 🦋 ⚓ ⛟

Exit E35/A3 junc 34 & foll sp Bad Honnef. In Himburg
bef pedestrian traff lts turn L, then R. Site in 300m.
3*, Lge, mkd, pt shd, sl, EHU (16A) €2 or metered;
85% statics; Eng spkn; fishing. *"Excel facs; pool 9km;
gated."* **€17.50** 2020

BAD KOSEN *2E4* (1.5km S Rural) *51.12285, 11.71743*
Camping an der Rudelsburg, 06628 Bad Kösen
**(034463) 28705; campkoesen@aol.com;
www.campingbadkoesen.de**

🐕 €2 ⚥ ♨ ⚒ 🛒 ⟟ ▾ 🍴 ⊕nr ⚓nr ⛟

Site sp fr town. 4*, Med, pt shd, EHU (16A) metered +
conn fee; gas; 10% statics; CKE. *"O'night m'vans area."*
€24.40, 23 Mar-1 Nov. 2016

BAD KREUZNACH *3C2* (8km N Rural) *49.88383,
7.85712* **Campingplatz Lindelgrund,** Im Lindelgrund 1,
55452 Guldental **(06707) 633; info@lindelgrund.de;
www.lindelgrund.de**

🐕 €1.50 ⚥ ♨ ▾ 🦋 ⊕ ⚓ ⛟

Fr A61 exit junc 47 for Windesheim. In cent immed
after level x-ing, turn L & pass thro Guldental.
Site sp on R in 500m. Sm, hdstg, pt shd, terr, EHU
(10-16A) €2 or metered; red long stay; 60% statics;
tennis; golf 12km. *"Lovely, peaceful site; friendly,
helpful staff; wine sold on site; narr gauge rlwy &
museum adj; gd NH; htd covrd pool 2km; san facs nr
touring pitches; conv base for Rhine & Mosel Valleys."*
€22.00, 1 Mar-15 Dec. 2016

BAD NEUENAHR AHRWEILER *3B1* (8km W Rural)
50.53400, 7.04800 **Camping Dernau,** Ahrweg 2, 53507
Dernau **(02643) 8517; www.camping-dernau.de**

🐕 €1 ⚥ (htd) ♨ ▾ ▾ ⚒ ⚓nr ⛟

Exit A61 junc 30 for Ahrweiler. Fr Ahrweiler on
B267 W to Dernau, cross rv bef Dernau & turn L
into Ahrweg, site sp. 3*, Sm, hdstg, shd, EHU (16A)
€2; bus, train. *"In beautiful Ahr valley - gd wine area;
train to Ahrweiler Markt rec; immac, modern san facs; v
nice."* **€17.00, 1 Apr-31 Oct.** 2019

BAD RIPPOLDSAU *3C3* (7km S Rural) *48.38396,
8.30168* **Schwarzwaldcamping Alisehof,**
Rippoldsauerstrasse 8, 77776 Bad Rippoldsau-
Schapbach **(07839) 203; camping@alisehof.de;
www.alisehof.de**

🛿 €2 ⚥ (htd) ♨ ♨ ⚒ 🛒 ▾ 🦋 Y 🍴 ⚒ ⚓ ⛟ ✎

Exit A5/E35 junc 55 Offenburg onto B33 dir
Gengenbach & Hausach to Wolfach. At end of
Wolfach vill turn N dir Bad Rippoldsau. Site on
R over wooden bdge after vill of Schapbach. 2
steep passes fr other dir. 5*, Med, mkd, pt shd, pt
sl, serviced pitches; EHU (16A) metered + conn fee;
gas; red long stay; 20% statics; phone; Eng spkn;
adv bkg acc; CKE. *"Highly rec; clean, friendly site; site
clsd 1230-1430; many gd walks in area; not a NH."*
€28.20 2019

BAD SCHANDAU *2G4* (3km E Rural) *50.92996,
14.19301* **Campingplatz Ostrauer Mühle,**
Kirnitzschtal, 01814 Bad Schandau, Sachsen
**+49 35022 - 42742; campmuehle@hotmail.com;
www.ostrauer-muehle.de**

🛿 €2 ⚥ ♨ ♨ ⚒ ▾ 🦋 ⊕ ⚓ ⛟

SE fr Dresden on B172 for 40km (Pirna-Schmilka).
In Bad Schandau turn E twds Hinterhermsdorf; site
in approx 3km. Med, pt shd, terr, EHU (10A) €1.75 +
conn fee; sep car park; CKE. *"In National Park; superb
walking area; rec arr early high ssn; site yourself if
office clsd on arr."* **€18.50** 2020

BAD SEGEBERG *1D2* (5km NE Rural) *53.96131,
10.33685* **Klüthseecamp Seeblick,** Stripdorfer Weg,
Klüthseehof 2, 23795 Klein Rönnau **(04551) 82368;
info@kluethseecamp.de; www.kluethseecamp.de**

🐕 €2 ⚥ ♨ ♨ ⚒ 🛒 ▾ 🦋 ⚑ ⊕ ⚒ ⛟ ⚊ (htd)

Exit A21 junc 13 at Bad Sedgeberg Süd onto
B432; turn L sp Bad Sedgeberg; cont on B432
dir Scharbeutz & Puttgarden thro Klein Rönnau,
look out for sp, site on R. 5*, V lge, pt shd, serviced
pitches; EHU (16A) inc; gas; bbq; sw nr; twin
axles; TV; 75% statics; bus adj, train to Hamburg,
Lübeck; Eng spkn; adv bkg acc; ccard acc; fishing;
golf 6km; games rm; horseriding; tennis; bike hire;
CKE. *"Spacious, well-kept nr lakeside site; relaxing
atmosphere; lge pitches; sauna; steam rm; helpful staff;
gd facs & pool; site clsd Feb; wide range of activities;
spa; gd cycling, walking; conv Hamburg, Lübeck;
excel; peaceful 50 min lakeside walk to town; excel."*
€25.00, 1 Jan-31 Jan & 1 Mar-31 Dec, G12. 2018

BAD TÖLZ *4E4* (7km S Rural) 47.70721, 11.55023
Alpen-Camping Arzbach, Alpenbadstrasse 20, 83646
Arzbach **(08042) 8408; info@alpen-campingplatz.de;
www.alpen-campingplatz.de**

🔢 🐕 👫 WD ⛲ ♨ 🚿 ♿ 🍽 ⊘ 🦋 ⍩ 🍴 ⊕ 🛒nr 🏕 ⛵ (covrd)

S fr Bad Tölz on B13. Exit Lenggries, turn R to cross
rv & R on Wackersburgerstrasse twds Arzbach; in
5km on ent Arzbach turn L. Site ent past sw pool. 3*,
Med, hdstg, pt shd, EHU (10-16A) €2; gas; bbq; sw nr;
twin axles; 50% statics; bus 300m; Eng spkn; adv bkg
acc; tennis 100m; CKE. *"Gd walking, touring Bavarian
lakes, excel facs & rest; care needed with lge c'vans due
trees & hedges; vg site with superb rest; easy eccess to
Munich; excel."* **€24.00**   **2018**

BAD URACH *3D3* (11km E Rural) 48.48598, 9.50761
Camping Lauberg, Hinter Lau 3, 72587 Römerstein-
Böhringen **(07382) 1509; info@lauberg.de;
www.lauberg.de**

🔢 🐕 €1.50 👫 (htd) WD ⛲ ♿ 🍽 ⊘ 🦋 🍴 ⊕ 🛒 🏕

Fr Bad Urach, take rd twd Grabenstetten & foll sp to
Böhringen, then sp to site. NB Rd to Grabenstetten
avoids long, steep climb on B28. 3*, Med, mkd,
unshd, terr, serviced pitches; EHU (16A) metered +
conn fee; bbq; red long stay; 80% statics; adv bkg acc.
*"Ideal walking area, castles, caves, Bad Urach baths;
winter sports; htd pool 9km; ski lift 5km."* **€16.50**
                                                                               2015

BAD WILDBAD IM SCHWARZWALD *3C3* (9km E
Rural) 48.73745, 8.57623 **Camping Kleinenzhof,**
Kleinenzhof 1, 75323 Bad Wildbad **(07081) 3435;
info@kleinenzhof.de; www.kleinenzhof.de**

🔢 🐕 €2.90 👫 WD ⛲ ♨ 🚿 ♿ 🍽 ⊘ 🦋 ⊕ 🚣 🛒 🏕 ⚓ ⛵ (covrd, htd)

Fr Calmbach foll B294 5km S. Site sp on R, in rv
valley. Fr Bad Wildbad site is on L. 5*, Lge, pt shd, pt
sl, serviced pitches; EHU (16A) metered + conn fee;
gas; red long stay; 80% statics, adv bkg acc; sauna;
bike hire. *"Nature trails fr site; o'night m'vans area; clsd
1300-1500; mountain views; distillery on site; modern
san facs; ski lift 8km; sm pitches."* **€27.80**   **2018**

BAD WILDBAD IM SCHWARZWALD *3C3* (7km S
Rural) 48.69777, 8.52027 **Camping Kälbermühle,**
Kälbermühlenweg 57, 75323 Bad Wildbad **(07085)
7322 or 7353; information@kaelbermuehle.de**

🔢 🐕 €0.80 👫 WD ⛲ ♨ 🍽 ⊘ 🦋 🏕

Take Enzklösterle rd S fr Bad Wildbad, site sp on
rv bank. 2*, Med, pt shd, EHU (16A) metered + conn
fee; 60% statics; bus; adv bkg acc. *"Friendly owners;
beautifully kept, peaceful site; superb rest; mkd forest
walks; gd; no cc/debit cards."* **€23.00**   **2015**

BAMBERG *4E2* (5km S Rural) 49.86138, 10.91583
Camping Insel, Am Campingplatz 1, 96049 Bamberg-
Bug **(0951) 56320; buero@campinginsel.de;
www.campinginsel.de**

🔢 🐕 €1.10 (htd) WD ⛲ ♨ ♿ 🍽 ⊘ 🦋 🛒 🏕 🍴 🍴 🏕

Exit A70/E48 junc 16 or A73 exit Bamberg-Süd onto
B22 dir Würzburg. Site on L of rd along Rv Regnitz.
Bug sm vill suburb of Bamburg to S of rv. Fr S on
A3 exit junc 79 dir Bamberg. In 12km turn L dir
Pettstadt; turn R at rndabt, site in 2km. 4*, Lge, pt
shd, EHU (16A) metered (long lead poss req); gas; red
long stay; TV; 20% statics; bus to Bamburg; Eng spkn;
clsd 1300-1500 & 2300-0700; CKE. *"Lovely historic
town, Unesco; cash only; rvside site; excel cycle facs
to town; bus to town €1.50; excel, modern san facs;
family run site; gd rest; beautiful walk thro park by
rvside; UNESCO World Heritage town; new lgr san facs
for 2015."* **€29.50**   **2015**

"I need an on-site restaurant"

We do our best to make sure site information
is correct, but it is always best to check any
must-have facilities are still available or will
be open during your visit.

BENSERSIEL *1B2* (0km W Coastal) 53.67531, 7.57001
Familien & Kurcampingplatz Bensersiel, 26427
Esens-Bensersiel **(04971) 917121; info@bensersiel.de;
www.bensersiel.de**

👫 WD ⛲ ♨ ♿ 🍽 ⊘ MSP ⊕ 🚣 🛒 🏕 ⚓ ⛵ (htd) 🏖 adj

Fr B210 turn N at Ogenhargen; thro Esens to
Bensersiel. Site adj to harbour in cent of vill -
clearly sp. V lge, unshd, EHU (16A) €2.50; gas; TV;
70% statics; adv bkg acc; tennis; bike hire; games area.
*"Cycling country; spa cent nrby; gd boat trips; gd san
facs; open site adj sea; gd access vill, rests & island
ferries; elec metered after 3 days - if staying longer,
check meter on arr."* **€17.00, Easter-15 Oct.**   **2017**

BERCHTESGADEN *4G4* (5km NE Rural) 47.64742,
13.03993 **Camping Allweglehen,** Allweggasse 4,
83471 Berchtesgaden-Untersalzberg **(08652) 2396;
camping@allweglehen.de; www.allweglehen.de**

🔢 🐕 €2.95 👫 WD ⛲ ♨ 🚿 ♿ 🍽 ⊘ 🦋 ⍩ 🍴 ⊕ 🛒 🏕
⚓ ⛵ (htd)

On R of rd B305 Berchtesgaden dir Salzburg, immed
after ent Unterau; sp. App v steep in places with
hairpin bend; gd power/weight ratio needed. 4*, Lge,
hdstg, pt shd, pt sl, terr, serviced pitches; EHU (16A)
metered + conn fee; 20% statics; phone; bus 500m;
adv bkg rec; ccard acc; CKE. *"Gd touring/walking
cent; wonderful views some pitches; cycles; beautiful
scenery; Hitler's Eagles' Nest worth visit (rd opens mid-
May) - bus fr Obersalzburg; ski lift; site rds poss o'grown
& uneven; steep app some pitches - risk of grounding
for long o'fits; friendly, family-run site; excel rest."*
€45.50   **2019**

GERMANY

BERGEN *1D3* (9km E Rural) *52.80443, 10.10376*
Camping am Örtzetal, Dicksbarg 46, 29320 Oldendorf
(05052) 3072; www.campingplatz-oldendorf.de

Fr S, exit A7/E45 junc 52 dir Celle, in 5km turn L sp
Winsen, Belsen & Bergen. Fr N exit A7/E45 at junc
45 onto B3 to Bergen. Foll rd to Bergen. In Bergen
foll sp Hermannsburg. In about 7km at T-junc turn
R, then 1st L sp Eschede & Oldendorf. In Oldendorf
turn L at 2nd x-rds. Site on R in 1km. Lge, pt shd,
EHU (6A) metered + conn fee; 40% statics; phone;
bike hire; CKE. *"Ideal for walking & cycling on Lüneburg
Heath; welcoming, friendly owner; conv Belsen memorial;
htd pool 4km; peaceful site; barrier clsd 1300-
1500."* **€17.00**   **2016**

"Satellite navigation makes touring much easier"

Remember most sat navs don't know if you're
towing or in a larger vehicle – always use yours
alongside maps and site directions.

BERLIN *2G3* (23km SW Rural) *52.4650, 13.16638*
DCC Campingplatz Gatow, Kladower Damm 207-213,
14089 Berlin-Gatow **(030) 3654340;
gatow@dccberlin.de; www.dccberlin.de**
sand 1km

Fr A10 to W of Berlin turn E on rd 5 sp Spandau/
Centrum. Go twd city cent & after 14km turn R
onto Gatowerstrasse (Esso g'ge) sp Kladow/Gatow.
Site 6.5km on L almost opp Kaserne (barracks). 3*,
Med, pt shd, EHU (10-16A) metered + conn fee; gas;
60% statics; bus at gate; Eng spkn; CKE. *"Excel site;
bus tickets fr friendly recep; frequent bus to Berlin cent
at gate; highly rec; excel, clean san facs; bicycles can be
taken on nrby Kladow ferry to Wannsee S Bahn; gates
close bet 1300 & 1500 and at 2200; rec."* **€26.50 2016**

BERLIN *2G3* (26km SW Rural) *52.55111, 13.24900*
City Campingplatz Hettler & Lange, Bäkehang 9a,
14532 Kleinmachnow-Dreilinden **(033203) 79684;
kleinmachnow@city-camping-berlin.de;
www.city-camping-berlin.de**

Fr S exit A115/E51 junc 5 sp Kleinmachnow, turn
L at T-junc & cont to rndabt. Turn L & foll site sp in
800m. 3*, Lge, pt shd, pt sl, EHU (6A) €2.50; gas; sw
nr; phone; bus nr; Eng spkn; adv bkg acc; boat hire;
CKE. *"Excel location on canal side; immac, modern san
facs; twin axles by arrangement; gd walking in woods;
gd public transport conv Berlin 45 mins - parking at
Wannsee S-bahn (family ticket avail for bus & train); v
busy sandy site under trees; 20 min walk to bus stop;
vg."* **€24.00**   **2018**

BERLIN *2G3* (13km NW Urban) *52.54861, 13.25694*
City-Camping Hettler & Lange, Gartenfelderstrasse
1, 13599 Berlin-Spandau **(030) 33503633; spandau@
city-camping-berlin.de; www.hettler-lange.de**

Fr N on A111/A115/E26 exit junc 10 sp Tegel Airport
& head W on Saatwinkler Damm. Fr S on A100 exit
junc 11 onto Saatwinkler Damm. Cont 3.2km to
traff lts, turn R, then R again immed bef 2nd bdge.
Site on island in rv. Med, shd, pt sl, EHU (16A) €2; Eng
spkn; ccard acc; CKE. *"Conv Berlin; 15 min walk to bus
stn; gd location beside a canal but aircraft noise; gd
san facs; NH/sh stay only; poss to cycle along canal to
Potsdam."* **€22.50**   **2019**

BERNKASTEL KUES *3B2* (2km SW Rural) *49.90883,
7.05600* **Knaus Campingpark (formerly Kueser
Werth Camping),** Am Hafen 2, 54470 Bernkastel-
Kues **(06531) 8200; www.knauscamp.de**

A'bahn A1/48 (E44) exit Salmtal; join rd sp
Bernkastel. Bef rv bdge turn L sp Lieser, thro Lieser
cont by rv to ent on R for boat harbour, foll camping
sp to marina. Diff access via narr single-track rd.
3*, Lge, mkd, pt shd, EHU (16A); bbq; 10% statics;
bus 1km; Eng spkn; adv bkg acc; CKE. *"Excel cent
for touring Mosel Valley; covrd pool 2km; Bernkastel
delightful sm town with gd parking, sailing, boat
excursions, wine cent; cycle lanes; site low on rv bank
- poss flooding in bad weather; efficient staff; gd site;
not rec for NH/sh stay high ssn as pitches & position
poor; san facs old but gd condition; newly taken over by
Knaus."* **€22.00, 1 Apr-31 Oct.**   **2017**

"There aren't many sites open at this time of year"

If you're travelling outside peak season
remember to call ahead to check site opening
dates – even if the entry says 'open all year'.

BERNKASTEL KUES *3B2* (3km NW Rural) *49.93736,
7.04853* **Camping Schenk,** Hauptstrasse 165, 54470
Bernkastel-Wehlen **(06531) 8176; info@camping-
schenk.de; www.camping-schenk.com**

On Trier/Koblenz rd B53, exit Kues heading N
on L bank of rv & site on R in 4km at Wehlen,
sp. Steep each end. Med, mkd, hdstg, pt shd, pt sl, terr,
serviced pitches; EHU (16A) metered + conn fee;
gas; 40% statics; phone; bus; Eng spkn; adv bkg acc;
CKE. *"In apple orchard on Rv Mosel; price according
to pitch size; friendly helpful owners; debit cards
acc; pool deep - not suitable non-swimmers; poorly
ventilated san facs; rv walks & cycle path to town."*
€21.00, 19 Mar-31 Oct.   **2016**

BERNKASTEL KUES *3B2* (4km NW Rural) *49.94122, 7.04653* **Weingut Studert-Prum,** Uferallee 22, 54470 Bernkastel Kues **(06531) 2487; info@studert-pruem.de; www.studert-pruem.com**

🏕 ⚐ WD MSP ⚑ ⛐ Ⓨ nr Ⓗ nr 🛒 nr

Fr Bernkastel-Kues, co N on W Bank of Rv Mosel, site on R in 4km at ent to Wehlen. Adj to Camp Schenk. Sm, hdstg, mkd, unshd, terr, own san rec; adv bkg acc. *"M'homes only; no san facs; terr site with lovely views of Rv Mosel; covrd pool 2km; vineyards; sh walk to pretty vill; walk/cycle path by rv; boat trips; wineries; excel."* **€10.00, 1 Apr-31 Oct.** 2016

BIELEFELD *1C3* (8km SW Rural) *52.00624, 8.45681* **Campingpark Meyer Zu Bentrup,** Vogelweide 9, 33649 Bielefeld **(0521) 4592233; bielefeld@meyer-zu-bentrup.de; www.camping-bielefeld.de**

🏕 ⚐ €2 ⚌ WD ⛐ ⚒ ⚐ MSP 🦋 ⚐ Ⓨ ⚐

Fr N or S on A2 - At interchange 21 take A33 Osnabruck. Cont till m'way ends, cont onto A61 dir Bielefeld. After 2km take A68 exit, dir Osnabruck/Halle West. Site on L after 3km. 3*, Lge, unshd, pt sl, EHU (10-16A) €1.50; cooking facs; 70% statics; games area; games rm; CKE. *"Vg; immac but dated san facs (2015); conv for Bielefeld; well maintained; warm welcome; excel shop at adj fruit farm."* **€25.00, 1 Mar-30 Nov.** 2018

BINGEN *3C2* (3km E Urban) *49.97029, 7.93916* **Camping Hindenburgbrucke,** Bornstrasse 22, 55411 Kempton-Bingen **(06721) 17160; bauer@bauer-schorsch.de; www.bauer-schorsch.de**

⚌ WD ⛐ ⚒ ⚐ Ⓨ Ⓗ ⚐ ⚑

Foll rd on Rhine twd Mainz, site on L bef traff lts. Turn into tarmac rd, bear R, L under rlwy bdge, strt to site ent by Rhine. Lge, hdg, unshd, EHU (watch rev pol); bbq; twin axles; 40% statics; bus/train adj. *"Open site on W bank of Rhein; staff conn elec pnts; lovely position for sh stay; mosquitoes abound; close to Rüdesheim-Bingen ferry, vineyards, castles, cruising."* **€19.00, 1 May-31 Oct.** 2019

BINZ *2G1* (6km NW Coastal) *54.44817, 13.56152* **Wohnmobil-Oase Rügen,** Proraer Chaussee 60, 18609 Ostseebad Binz OT Prora **+49 (0) 38393. 699 777; info@wohnmobilstellplatz-ruegen.de; www.wohnmobilstellplatz-ruegen.de**

12 🏕 ⚌(htd) WD ⛐ ⚐ ⚐ MSP ⚐

Fr Binz foll coast rd to Prora, site on L past traff lts. Med, hdstg, pt shd, EHU (16A); gas; bus/tram adj; Eng spkn. *"Vg site; m'vans only; track to beach."* **€15.00** 2020

BITBURG *3B2* (10km W Rural) *49.95895, 6.42454* **Prümtal Camping,** In der Klaus 5, 54636 Oberweis **(06527) 92920; info@pruemtal.de; www.pruemtal.de**

12 🏕 €2.10 (htd) ⚒ ⛐ ⚐ ⚐ Ⓨ Ⓨ ⚐ 🛒 ⚑ ⚐

On B50 Bitburg-Vianden rd. On ent Oberweis sharp RH bend immed L bef rv bdge - sp recreational facs or sp Köhler Stuben Restaurant-Bierstube. V lge, pt shd, EHU (16A) €2.75 or metered; 60% statics; Eng spkn; adv bkg acc; ccard acc; bike hire; CKE. *"Excel facs; san facs stretched high ssn; vg rest."* **€26.00** 2020

BONN *1B4* (13km SE Rural) *50.65388, 7.20111* **Camping Genienau,** Im Frankenkeller 49, 53179 Bonn-Mehlem **(0228) 344949; genienau@freenet.de**

12 🏕 €2 ⚒ WD ⛐ ⚐ ⚐ Ⓗ nr 🛒 nr

Fr B9 dir Mehlem, site sp on Rv Rhine, S of Mehlem. Med, pt shd, EHU (6A) €3 or metered; 60% statics; bus; Eng spkn; CKE. *"Excel site on rv bank; liable to flood when rv v high; nr ferry to cross Rhine; late arr no problem; san facs up steps but disabled facs at grnd level; lots to see & do."* **€20.00** 2016

BOPPARD *3B2* (6km NE Rural) *50.24888, 7.62638* **Camping Sonneneck,** 56154 Boppard **(06742) 2121; kontakt@camping-sonneneck.de; www.camping park-sonneneck.de**

🏕 €2.40 ⚒ WD ⛐ ⚐ ⚐ MSP Ⓨ Ⓗ ⚐ 🛒 ⚐ ⚑ shgl nr

On Koblenz-Mainz rd B9, on W bank of Rhine, in vill of Spay. 4*, Lge, mkd, pt shd, serviced pitches; EHU (4A) €2.50; gas; 10% statics; phone; Eng spkn; fishing; sauna; CKE. *"V pleasant staff; night watchman; clean san facs, poss long way fr pitches; ltd waste water points; extra for rvside pitch; crazy golf; 18-hole golf 2km; site poss liable to flood; gd cycle path along Rhine; gd NH."* **€25.00, 1 Apr-31 Oct.** 2015

BRANDENBURG AN DER HAVEL *2F3* (9km E Rural) *52.39833, 12.43665* **Camping und Ferienpark am Plauer See,** Plauer Landstrasse 200, 14774 Brandenburg **33 81 80 45 44; info@camping-plauersee.de; www.camping-plauersee.de**

12 🏕 ⚐ ⚒ WD ⛐ ⚐ ⚐ ⚐ 🦋 Ⓨ Ⓗ ⚐ ⚑

Fr A2 take 102 to Brandenburg. L onto 1, cont 4km. Just after sp for Plauerhof is a campsite sp. Turn L & foll rd for 1.5km to site on the side of lake. Med, mkd, pt shd, pt sl, EHU (10A) €1.90; bbq; 75% statics; Eng spkn; adv bkg acc; games area; bike hire; CCI. *"Next to sm lake; boat, cycles & BBQ hire; nr historic town of Brandenburg; vg site, mainly statics but tourers and MH given gd pitches next to lake; gd rest and bar; rec Potsdam."* **€33.00** 2019

BRAUNEBERG *3B2* (0.9km W Rural) *49.90564, 6.97603* **Wohnmobilstellplatz Brauneberger Juffer,** Moselweinstraße 101, 54472 Brauneberg **6534 933 333; mfrollison@yahoo.co.uk or info@ brauneberg.de; www.brauneberg.de**

🔢12 🐕 ⓦ ♦ ⭢ 🦋

Fr NE of A1 take exit 127-Klausen onto L47 twds Mulheim. Cont onto L158, then turn L onto B53. Supermkt 20m fr site ent which is down side rd twds rv. Sm, mkd, hdg, hdstg, pt shd, EHU (16A); bbq; sw nr; bus 100m; Eng spkn. *"Aire-type site; no adv bkg; Gd cycle paths along rv; vg site."* **€10.00** 2019

BRAUNLAGE *2E4* (12km SE Rural) *51.65697, 10.66786* **Campingplatz am Bärenbache,** Bärenbachweg 10, 38700 Hohegeiss **(05583) 1306; campingplatz-hohegeiss@t-online.de; www.campingplatz-hohegeiss.de**

🔢12 🐕 €1.50 👫(htd) ⓦ ♦ ⭢ ♿ 🔲 ⬇ 🅿 🦋 ⛱ ♈ 🍴 ⒽⓃ ⛽ 🅱nr
⚠ 🏊(htd) 🎣

Fr Braunlage S on B4 thro Hohegeiss; site sp on L downhill (15%) on edge of town. 4*, Med, hdg, mkd, pt shd, terr, EHU (10A); bbq; cooking facs; 10% statics; Eng spkn; adv bkg acc; bike hire. *"Gd walking; friendly; walking dist to vill; vg."* **€22.50** 2019

BREISACH AM RHEIN *3B4* (7km E Rural) *48.03104, 7.65781* **Kaiserstuhl Camping,** Nachwaid 5, 79241 Ihringen **(07668) 950065; info@kaiserstuhl camping.de; www.kaiserstuhlcamping.de**

🐕 €2.50 👫 ⓦ ♦ ⭢ ♿ 🔲 🅿 🦋 ♈ 🍴 Ⓗnr ⛽ 🅱nr ⚠

Fr S exit A5/E35 junc 64a, foll sp twds Breisach, then camping sp to Ihringen. At Ihringen site sp dir Merdingen. Fr N exit junc 60 & foll sp. Med, unshd, EHU (16A) metered + conn fee; red long stay; 10% statics; tennis adj; golf 8km; CKE. *"Can get cr in high ssn; htd pool adj."* **€32.00,** 15 Mar-31 Oct. 2019

BREMEN *1C2* (16km SW Rural) *53.01055, 8.68972* **Marchencamping (formerly Camp Wienberg),** Zum Steller See 83, 28816 Stuhr-Gross Mackenstedt **(04206) 9191; info@maerchen-camping.com; maerchen-camping.com**

🔢12 🐕 €2 👫(htd) ⓦ ♦ ⭢ 🔲 🅿 🅼🅿 ♈ 🍴 Ⓗ ⛽ 🅱 ⚠ 🏊 ⛵

Exit A1/E37 junc 58a onto B322 sp Stuhr/ Delmenhorst. Foll Camping Steller See sp. Sp also call site Marchen Camping. Lge, mkd, hdstg, pt shd, pt sl, EHU (16A) metered or €3; TV; 50% statics; Eng spkn; adv bkg acc; ccard acc; bike hire; CKE. *"Helpful staff; basic facs; gd."* **€20.50** 2018

BREMEN *1C2* (17km SW Rural) *53.00694, 8.69277* **Campingplatz Steller See,** Zum Stellersee 15, 28817 Stuhr-Gross Mackenstedt **(04206) 6490; steller.see@t-online.de; www.steller-see.de**

👫(htd) ⓦ ♦ ⭢ ♿ 🔲 🅿 🅼🅿 ♈ 🍴 Ⓗ ⛽ 🅱nr ⚠ 🎣

Exit A1/E37 junc 58a onto B322 sp Stuhr/ Delmenhorst. Foll site sp. 3*, Lge, unshd, EHU (10-16A) inc; gas; bbq; sw nr; red long stay; 80% statics; phone; adv bkg acc; ccard acc; games area; CKE. *"Site officially clsd but owner may accommodate you; well-appointed, clean, lakeside site; immac san facs; friendly owners; conv NH fr m'way & for trams to Bremen; gd space, easy to position; vg."* **€35.00,** 1 Apr-3 Oct. 2018

BREMEN *1C2* (5km NW Rural) *53.11483, 8.83263* **Camping Hanse (formerly Camping am Stadtwaldsee),** Hochschulring 1, 28359 Bremen **(0421)30746825**

🔢12 🐕 €4 👫(htd) ⓦ ♦ ⭢ ♿ 🔲 🅿 🅼🅿 ♈ 🍴 Ⓗ ⛽ 🅱 ⚠

Fr A27 take exit 19 for Universitat, foll sp for Universitat and camping. Site on L in 1km after leaving University area. 3*, Lge, hdstg, mkd, pt shd, EHU (16A) metered; gas; bbq; cooking facs; sw nr; red long stay; 10% statics; phone; bus 100m; Eng spkn; adv bkg acc; ccard acc; CKE. *"Excel, spacious lakeside site; superb san facs; cycle path to beautiful city; gd bus service; v gd rest adj; spacious pitches but unkept & poorly maintained."* **€35.50** 2017

BRIESELANG *2F3* (5km W Rural) *52.57138, 12.96583* **Campingplatz Zeestow im Havelland,** 11 Brieselanger strasse, 14665 Brieselang **(033234) 88634; info@ campingplatz-zeestow.de; www.campingplatz-zeestow.de**

🔢12 🐕 €2 👫 ⓦ ♦ ♿ 🔲 🅿 ♈ Ⓗ 🅱

Exit A10/E55 junc 27; turn W dir Wustermark; site on L after canal bdge in 500m. 3*, Lge, unshd, pt sl, EHU (16A) metered; gas; 75% statics; bus; CKE. *"Gd NH nr a'bahn; facs dated but clean; 13km fr Berlin & 25km fr Potsdam; fair."* **€14.00** 2016

BRUGGEN *1A4* (2km SE Rural) *51.23416, 6.19815* **Camping-Forst Laarer See,** Brüggenerstrasse 27, 41372 Niederkrüchten **(02163) 8461 or 0172 7630591 (mob); info@campingforst-laarersee. com; www.campingforst-laarersee.com**

🔢12 🐕 €1 👫(htd) ⓦ ♦ ⭢ ♿ 🔲 🅿 🅼🅿 🦋 ♈ Ⓗnr ⛽ 🅱nr ⚠

Fr A52 junc 3 or A61 junc 3 - take B221 to Brüggen, turn R at 1st traff lts into site. Lge, pt shd, pt sl, EHU (16A) inc; bbq; 80% statics; Eng spkn; adv bkg acc; games area; CKE. *"Unspoilt area nr pretty town; many leisure amenities nr site - gd for children; vg site; ltd touring pitches; pleasant site with lake; walking/bike paths."* **€21.00** 2016

BUHL *3C3* (7km NW Rural) *48.72719, 8.08074*
Ferienpark & Campingplatz Adam, Campingstrasse 1,
77815 Bühl-Oberbruch **(07223) 23194; info@camping
platz-adam.de; www.campingplatz-adam.de**

Exit A5 at Bühl take sp Lichtenau & foll sp thro
Oberbruch, then L twd Moos to site in 500m. If app
on rd 3 take rd sp W to Rheinmünster N of Bühl. Site
sp to S at W end of Oberbruch. 4*, Lge, mkd, hdstg,
pt shd, serviced pitches; EHU (10A) €3; sw; red long
stay; 60% statics; Eng spkn; adv bkg acc; ccard acc;
sailing; tennis; fishing; boating; CKE. *"Excel, clean san
facs; conv for Strasbourg, Baden-Baden & Black Forest
visits; o'night area tarmac car park; extra for lakeside
pitches; if recep clsd use area outside gate; vg; excel
camp with own lake; gd rest; friendly staff; handy for
m'way but still quiet; o'night tarmac area excel for NH
but worth a longer stay; highly rec; 45 mins to Europe
Pk."* **€28.00** 2017

BURGEN *3B2* (0.6km N Rural) *50.21457, 7.38976*
Camping Burgen, 56332 Burgen **(02605) 2396; info@
camping-burgen.de; www.camping-burgen.de**

Leave A61 at J39; foll B411 twds Dieblich to reach S
bank of Mosel; turn L and foll B49 for approx 12km;
site on L bet rd and rv bef vill. Sat nav uses rte thro
vill, not suitable. 4*, Med, mkd, unshd, EHU (10A)
metered + conn fee (poss rev pol); gas; 30% statics;
Eng spkn; boat launch; CKE. *"Scenic area; ideal for
touring Mosel, Rhine & Koblenz areas; gd shop; poss
liable to flood; lovely, clean site; gd san facs; rec."*
€23.00, 11 Apr-19 Oct. 2019

CALW *3C3* (12km SW Rural) *48.67766, 8.68990*
Camping Erbenwald, 75387 Neubulach-Liebelsberg
**(07053) 7382; info@camping-erbenwald.de;
www.camping-erbenwald.de**

On B463 S fr Calw, take R slip rd sp Neubulach to
go over main rd. Foll Neubulach sp until camping sp
at R junc. Site well sp. 4*, Lge, mkd, hdg, pt shd, EHU
(10A) metered; 60% statics; phone; Eng spkn; adv bkg
acc; games area. *"Gd size pitches; child-friendly site;
no vehicles in or out fr 1300-1500; excel; cash only."*
€22.00 2019

CANOW *2F2* (2km E Rural) *53.19636, 12.93116*
Camping Pälitzsee, Am Canower See 165, 17255
Canow **(039828) 20220; info@mecklenburg-
tourist.de; www.mecklenburg-tourist.de**

Fr N on B198 turn S dir Rheinsberg to Canow vill,
site sp. Lge, pt shd, EHU (16A) metered or €3; sw;
50% statics; adv bkg acc; boating. *"Canow charming
vill; vg touring base for lakes."* **€20.00** 2016

CHEMNITZ *2F4* (10km SW Rural) *50.76583, 13.01444*
Waldcampingplatz Erzgebirgsblick, An der
Dittersdorfer Höhe 1, 09439 Amtsberg **(0371)
7750833; info@waldcamping-erzgebirge.de;
www.waldcamping-erzgebirge.de**

Fr A4 take A72 S & exit junc 15. Foll sp 'Centrum'
& join 'Südring' ring rd. Turn onto B174 & foll sp
Marienberg twd junc with B180. Site sp 500m
fr junc. Med, mkd, pt shd, EHU (16A) metered; gas;
red long stay; TV; bus 800m; Eng spkn; games area;
site clsd 6-27 Nov; CKE. *"Gd san facs; relaxing site; gd
walking; dogs free; vg standard of site."* **€17.00** 2016

CHIEMING *4F4* (2km NW Rural) *47.902103,
12.519891* **Camping Seehäusl,** Beim Seehäusl 1,
83339 Chieming **(8664) 303; www.camping-
seehaeusl.de**

J109 N off A8 twrds Chieming. Foll sp. Diff access
for v lge o'fits (narr lane) 4*, Med, hdstg, mkd, pt shd,
EHU (16A); bbq (elec, gas); sw nr; twin axles; Eng spkn;
adv bkg rec; ccard acc; fishing; watersports. *"Gd san
facs."* **€32.50, 1 Apr-1 Oct.** 2019

COBURG *4E2* (15km SW Rural) *50.19433, 10.83809*
Campingplatz Sonnland, Bahnhofstrasse 154,
96145 Sesslach **(09569) 220; info@camping-
sonnland.de; www.camping-sonnland.de**

Exit A73 junc 10 Ebersdorf onto B303 W. Then at
Niederfüllbach turn S onto B4, then turn W dir
Sesslach. Site sp N of Sesslach dir Hattersdorf; turn
R at sp opp filling stn, site in 150m. Med, mkd, hdstg,
pt shd, terr, serviced pitches; EHU (16A) metered; bbq;
sw; 70% statics; adv bkg acc; CKE. *"Sesslach unspoilt,
medieval, walled town; site well laid-out."* **€21.50** 2016

COCHEM *3B2* (1.5km N Rural) *50.15731, 7.17360*
Campingplatz am Freizeitzentrum,
Moritzburgerstrasse 1, 56812 Cochem **(02671) 4409;
info@campingplatz-cochem.de; www.campingplatz-
cochem.de**

On rd B49 fr Koblenz, on ent town go under 1st
rv bdge then turn R over same bdge. Foll site sp.
3*, Lge, mkd, pt shd, pt sl, EHU (10-16A) €2.50 +
conn fee (some rev pol); gas; 10% statics; bike hire;
CKE. *"Gd, clean site adj Rv Mosel; pitches tight &
poss diff access fr site rds; gd for children; easy walk
along rv to town; train to Koblenz, Trier, Mainz."*
€23.00, 1 Apr-31 Oct. 2016

COCHEM *3B2* (6km SE Rural) *50.10999, 7.23542*
Campingplatz Happy-Holiday, Moselweinstrasse,
56821 Ellenz-Poltersdorf **(02673) 1272;**
www.camping-happy-holiday.de

€1.50 (htd)

Fr Cochem, take B49 S to Ellenz; site sp on bank
of Rv Mosel. Med, shd, pt sl, EHU (6A) metered; gas;
70% statics; Eng spkn; fishing; watersports. *"Pleasant
situation; gd value rest; pool 300m; clean facs; conv
touring base."* **€19.50, 1 Apr-31 Oct.** **2019**

COCHEM *3B2* (7km SE Rural) *50.08231, 7.20796*
Camping Holländischer Hof, Am Campingplatz 1,
56820 Senheim **(02673) 4660;** info@moselcamping.
com; https://www.moselcamping.com

Fr Cochem take B49 twd Traben-Trarbach; after
approx 15km turn L over rv bdge sp Senheim; site
on rv island. 4*, Med, mkd, pt shd, EHU (6-10A)
metered; gas; sw nr; red long stay; 20% statics;
phone; Eng spkn; adv bkg acc; tennis; CKE. *"Pleasant,
well-run site; beautiful location; helpful staff; sm
pitches on loose pebbles; excel cycle paths; poss
flooding when wet weather/high water; poss overcr."*
€16.00, 9 Apr-31 Oct. **2020**

COCHEM *3B2* (7km SE Rural) *50.13253, 7.23029*
Campingplatz Bruttig, Am Moselufer, 56814 Bruttig-
Fankel **(02671) 915429; www.campingplatz-bruttig.de**

(htd)

Leave Cochem on B49 twd Trier. In 8km turn L over
bdge to Bruttig-Fankel. Thro vill, site on R on banks
Rv Mosel. Sm, mkd, pt shd, EHU (16A) metered; sw nr;
50% statics; phone; Eng spkn. *"Pleasant site in pretty
vill; gd walking, cycling; Mosel boat trips fr Bruttig."*
€16.00, Easter-31 Oct. **2016**

COCHEM *3B2* (15km S Rural) *50.09162, 7.16319*
Campingplatz zum Feuerberg, 56814 Ediger-Eller
(02675) 701; info@zum-feuerberg.de; www.zum-
feuerberg.de

€2 nr

On A49 fr Cochem to Bernkastel Kues, just bef vill
of Ediger on L - 17km by rd. Lge, mkd, hdg, EHU
(16A) metered + conn fee; gas; 40% statics; phone;
bus, train to Cochem; Eng spkn; adv bkg acc; bike
hire; CKE. *"Well-kept site in lovely area; charming vill;
boat mooring; helpful staff; facs at 1st floor level, via
key (deposit); gd selection of rests & pubs; rv bus high
ssn; gd touring base; gd; pitches next to rv cost more."*
€23.00, 18 Mar-31 Oct. **2016**

COLBITZ *2E3* (3km NE Rural) *52.33158, 11.63123*
Campingplatz Heide-Camp, Angerschestrasse,
39326 Colbitz **(039207) 80291;** info@heide-
camp-colbitz.de; www.heide-camp-colbitz.de

12 €2.80 nr nr

Exit A2/E30 junc 70 onto B189 N dir Stendal.
In Colbitz foll sp Angern. Site in 2km.
4*, Lge, mkd, pt shd, EHU (6-16A) metered + conn
fee; gas; 20% statics; Eng spkn; adv bkg acc; ccard
acc; games area; CKE. *"Site on woodland, lge pitches."*
€19.00 **2019**

"That's changed – Should I let the Club know?"

If you find something on site that's different
from the site entry, fill in a report and let us
know. See camc.com/europereport.

COLDITZ *2F4* (4km E Rural) *51.13083, 12.83305*
Campingplatz am Waldbad, Im Tiergarten 5, 04680
Colditz **(034381) 43122;** info@campingplatz-
colditz.de; www.campingplatz-colditz.de

€1 nr

Fr Leipzig A14 to Grimma, foll B107 to Colditz.
Cross rv, foll B176 sp Dobeln. Turn L immed bef
town exit sp. After 1km turn R at camping sp.
Foll track thro woods for 500m, site on R immed
after sw pool. 4*, Med, pt shd, pt sl, EHU (10A) inc;
30% statics; phone; Eng spkn; sauna; CKE. *"V nice
peaceful site; gd clean facs; gd value; tight turn into
site fr narr rd; helpful, friendly manager & staff; 30 mins
walk to Colditz Castle; leisure cent adj; sm rest 200m;
new chem point."* **€19.00, 1 Apr-30 Sep.** **2015**

CREGLINGEN *3D2* (3.5km S Rural) *49.43945,
10.04210* **Campingpark Romantische Strasse,**
Münster 67, 97993 Creglingen-Münster **(07933)
20289;** camping.hausotter@web.de; www.camping-
romantische-strasse.de

€1 (htd) nr

(covrd, htd)

Fr E43 exit A7/junc 105 at Uffenheim. At edge of
Uffenheim turn R in dir of Bad Mergentheim; in
approx 17km at T-junc turn L for Creglingen, thro
vill & then R sp Münster with camping sp - approx
8km further. Site on R after Münster. (Avoid rte bet
Rothenburg & Creglingen as includes some v narr
vills & coaches). 4*, Med, pt shd, serviced pitches;
EHU (6A) €2.20; bbq; 20% statics; phone; sauna; bike
hire; lake fishing; CKE. *"Site ent needs care; helpful
owner; lovely welcome; excel rest & facs; Romantische
Strasse with interesting medieval churches locally;
gd cent for historic towns; clsd 1300-1500; gd value;
facs stretched high ssn; poss long walk fr facs."*
€24.00, 15 Mar-15 Nov. **2017**

DAUN *3B2* (19km SE Rural) *50.13111, 6.93331*
Feriendorf Pulvermaar, Auf der Maarhöhe,
Vulkanstrasse, 54558 Gillenfeld **(06573) 287;
info@feriendorf-pulvermaar.de; www.feriendorf-
pulvermaar.de**

🏕 ♞ €1 ♦♦♦ WD 📶 🖥 ✐ ✗ ♨ 🔥 🛈 ♨

Fr A1/A48/E44 exit junc 121 onto B421 dir Zell/
Mosel. After approx 5km turn R to Pulvemaar,
site sp nr lakeside. 3*, Med, pt shd, sl, EHU (16A)
metered + conn fee; bbq; 60% statics; Eng spkn; adv
bkg acc; fishing adj; games area; CKE. *"Conv Mosel
valley & Weinstrasse; attractive site; helpful owner."*
€21.00 2016

DETTELBACH *3D2* (6km S Rural) *49.82603, 10.20083*
Camping Katzenkopf, Am See, 97334 Sommerach
**(09381) 9215; info@camping-katzenkopf.de;
www.camping-katzenkopf.de**

🏕 ♞ €2 ♦♦♦ WD 📶 ♨ 🖥 ✐ ✗ MSP 🦋 🛈 ♨ 🛈

Fr A7/E45 junc 101 dir Volkach. Cross rv & foll sp
S to Sommerach, site sp. Fr S exit A3/E43 junc 74
dir Volkach & foll sp. NB Town unsuitable c'vans;
foll site sps bef town ent (beware - sat nav rte poss
thro town). Lge, pt shd, EHU (16A) €2.50 or metered;
gas; sw; red long stay; ccard acc; boating; golf 10km;
fishing; CKE. *"Beautiful surroundings; sm pitches; clean,
modern facs; m'van o'night area outside site; barrier
clsd 1300-1500; easy walk to wine-growing vill; gd rest;
gd NH nr A3."* **€21.60, 1 Apr-25 Oct.** 2020

> ## "I like to fill in the reports as I travel from site to site"
>
> You'll find report forms at the back of this guide, or you can fill them in online at camc.com/europereport.

DINKELSBUHL *3D3* (2km NNE Rural) *49.08194,
10.33416* **DCC Campingpark Romantische Strasse,**
Kobeltsmühle6, 91550 Dinkelsbühl **(09851) 7817;
campdinkelsbuehl@aol.com; www.campingplatz-
dinkelsbuehl.de**

🏕 ♞ €1 ♦♦♦ WD 📶 ♨ 🖥 ✐ ✗ MSP 🦋 🛈 ♈ 🛈 ♨ 🛈

On Rothenburg-Dinkelsbühl rd 25. Turn sharp L at
camp sp immed bef rlwy x-ing (at Jet petrol stn) at
N end of town. Site on R in 1km on lakeside. Or exit
A7/E43 junc 112; turn R at T-junc. Site well sp. 4*,
Lge, mkd, pt shd, terr, EHU (10-16A) metered; gas;
sw; 40% statics; phone; adv bkg acc; ccard acc; site
clsd 1300-1500 & 2200-0800; boating; dog wash; CKE.
*"Pitches poss long way fr san facs; gd, modern san facs;
NH area with easy access; close to beautiful medieval
town (25min walk); m'van o'night area with EHU; quiet,
peaceful, well-equipped & well-managed site; excel
rest; gd cycle paths in area; gd; recep open 9-1230 &
1500-1700."* **€23.00** 2019

DONAUESCHINGEN *3C4* (7km SE Rural) *47.93754,
8.53422* **Riedsee-Camping,** Am Riedsee 11, 78166
Donaueschingen **(0771) 5511; info@riedsee-
camping.de; www.riedsee-camping.de**

🏕 ♞ €3.50 ♦♦♦ WD 📶 ♿ ♨ 🖥 ✐ ✗ MSP ♈ 🛈 ♨ 🐟

Fr Donaueschingen on B31 to Pfohren vill, site sp.
Lge, mkd, pt shd, EHU (16A) metered, €0.50 (check
for rev pol); sw; 90% statics; Eng spkn; ccard acc; bike
hire; golf 9km; boating; tennis; CKE. *"Vg facs; clean,
well-run site; sm pitches; site busy at w/end; office clsd
Mon (poss LS only); gd value rest; conv Danube cycle
way."* **€24.00** 2016

DONAUWORTH *4E3* (5km SE Rural) *48.67660,
10.84100* **Donau-Lech Camping,** Campingweg 1,
86698 Eggelstetten **(09090) 4046; info@donau-
lech-camping.de; www.donau-lech-camping.de**

🏕 ♞ €2.20 ♦♦♦(htd) WD 📶 ♨ 🖥 ✐ ✗ MSP 🦋 ♈ 🛈 nr ♨ nr 🛈

Fr B2 take Eggelstetten exit & foll sp to vill. Site
immed bef vill on R, foll 'Int'l Camping' sp. 4*, Med,
hdg, mkd, hdstg, pt shd, EHU (16A) inc (some rev pol);
gas; sw; 80% statics; phone; Eng spkn; adv bkg acc;
archery; golf nr; boat hire; site clsd Nov; fishing nr;
horseriding nr; CKE. *"Superb, well-maintained, site but
poss unkempt & boggy LS; ltd area for tourers; friendly,
helpful staff & owner; facs clean but update req; owner
sites vans; conv base for touring Danube & Romantic
Rd; nr Danube cycle way."* **€25.00** 2019

DORTMUND *1B4* (10km SE Rural) *51.42078, 7.49514*
Camping Hohensyburg, Syburger Dorfstrasse 69,
44265 Dortmund-Hohensyburg **(0231) 774374;
info@camping-hohensyburg.de; www.camping-
hohensyburg.de**

🏕 ♞ €3 ♦♦♦ WD 📶 ♨ 🖥 ✐ ✗ MSP 🦋 ♈ 🛈 ♨ 🛈

Exit Dortmund a'bahn ring at Dortmund Sud onto
B54 sp Hohensyburg. Foll dual c'way S & strt at next
traff lts. Turn L twd Hohensyburg, up hill to Y junc.
Turn L (camping sp) & cont over hill to Gasthof.
Turn R immed bef Gasthof down narr, steep rd
(sharp bends) to site in 100m. Lge, pt shd, pt sl, EHU
(16A) €2.50 or metered; bbq; twin axles; 80% statics;
Eng spkn; adv bkg acc; golf 3km; boat launch. *"Lovely,
friendly site; narr lane at ent not suitable lge o'fits;
excel, clean san facs; gd; lge site; immac san facs."*
€26.50 2016

DORUM *1C2* (6km NE Coastal) *53.73938, 8.51680*
Knaus Campingpark Dorum, Am Kuterhafen,
27632 Dorum/Neufeld **0049 4741 5020; dorum@
knauscamp.de; www.knauscamp.de**

🏕 ♦♦♦ WD 📶 ♨ 🖥 ✐ MSP ♨ 🛈 ♈ adj

Fr A27 Bremerhaven-Cuxhaven, take exit 4 to
Dorum. Then foll signs to Dorum-Neufeld. Cont
over dyke to harbour, campsite on R. Lge, unshd,
EHU (6A); twin axles; 40% statics; bus 0.5km; Eng
spkn; adv bkg acc; bike hire; CCI. *"Vg; temporary ssnal
site; scenic fishing port."* **€41.00, 1 Apr-30 Sep.** 2019

DRANSFELD *1D4* (1km S Rural) *51.49177, 9.76180*
Camping am Hohen Hagen, Hoher-Hagenstrasse 12,
37127 Dransfeld **(05502) 2147; mail@campingplatz-dransfeld.de; www.campingplatz-dransfeld.de**

Exit A7 junc 73 onto B3 to Dransfeld; foll sp to S of
town & site. 5*, Lge, mkd, pt shd, terr, EHU (16A) inc;
gas; bbq; cooking facs; 95% statics; Eng spkn; ccard
acc; waterslide; sauna; games area; tennis 100m.
*"Beautiful area; gd san facs; o'night m'vans area; diff
after heavy rain; helpful staff."* **€38.00** **2016**

DRESDEN *2G4* (7km N Rural) *51.13833, 13.71861*
Camping Dresden Nord, Sandweg, 01471
Volkersdorf **(035207) 81469; kontakt@dresden-camping.com; www.cbm-camping.de/dd-nord**

Exit A4/E40 junc 81A (Dresden-Flughafen) onto
S81 W - Wilschdorfer Landstrasse. In approx 600m
turn R at x-rds dir Volkersdorf, then L to site on
lakeside, sp. 3*, Med, hdg, shd, pt sl, EHU (16A) €2.70
or mtrd (poss rev pol); bbq; sw; 60% statics; adv bkg
acc; CKE. *"Gd; touring pitch at lake v attractive; san
facs v clean but poss a bit distant; little Eng spkn."*
€18.00, 1 Apr-31 Oct. **2019**

DRESDEN *2G4* (17km NE Rural) *51.12027, 13.98000*
Camping- und Freizeitpark Lux Oase, Arnsdorfer
strasse 1, 01900 Kleinröhrsdorf **(035952) 56666;
info@luxoase.de; www.luxoase.de**

Leave A4/E40 at junc 85 dir Radeberg. S to
Leppersdorf, Kleinröhrsdorf. Sp on L end vill, well sp
fr a'bahn. 5*, Lge, mkd, pt shd, serviced pitches; EHU
(10A) inc; gas; bbq; sw nr; red long stay; twin axles; TV;
30% statics; bus to city; Eng spkn; ccard acc; fishing;
games area; horseriding; bike hire; sauna; games rm;
CKE. *"Excel site by lake; vg san facs; new luxury san
facs 2011; v helpful staff; gd rest; site bus to Dresden
Tues - 15 mins walk to reg bus; fitness cent; weekly bus
to Prague fr site & other attractions in easy reach; new
spa 2013."* **€33.60, 1 Jan-31Dec, G14.** **2019**

DRESDEN *2G4* (16km SE Rural) *50.99839, 13.86919*
Campingplatz Wostra, At 7 Wostra, 01259 Dresden
**(351) 20278678; cp-wostra@dresden.de;
https://www.dresden.de/de/leben/sport-und-freizeit/
sport/campingplatz.php**

Take exit 6 fr E55 Prague-Dresden in dir of Pirna,
then take B172 Dresden-Pirna to Heidenau, foll
sp to site. Med, pt shd, EHU (16A); bbq (sep area);
cooking facs; twin axles; bus/tram adj; Eng spkn; ccard
acc; games rm; table tennis; CKE. *"Excel quiet site."*
€20.00, 6 Apr-1 Nov. **2020**

DRESDEN *2G4* (7km S Urban) *51.01416, 13.7500*
Campingplatz Mockritz, Boderitzerstrasse 30,
01217 Dresden-Mockritz **(0351) 4715250; camping-dresden@t-online.de; www.camping-dresden.de**

Exit E65/A17 junc 3 onto B170 N sp Dresden. In
approx 1.5km turn E at traff lts sp Zschernitz, site
sp. 2*, Med, mkd, pt shd, pt sl, EHU (10A) €2.70;
5% statics; bus; Eng spkn; adv bkg rec; site clsd
Christmas to end Jan; CKE. *"V conv city cent & buses;
poss muddy after rain; helpful staff; excel; office clsd
1300-1600 find a pitch and inform recep; highly rec."*
€21.00, 1 Jan-31 Jan, 16 Feb-31 Dec. **2016**

DUSSELDORF *1B4* (19.5km NNW Urban) *51.30180,
6.72560* **Rheincamping Meerbusch,** Zur Rheinfähre
21, 40668 Meerbusch **(02150) 911877; info@
rheincamping.com; www.rheincamping.com**

Exit A44 junc 28, turn R twd Strümp. Thro vill, turn
L at sp for Kaiserswerth ferry, site on rv. Lge, pt shd,
EHU (10A) €3.50; gas; bbq; 40% statics; Eng spkn;
adv bkg acc; boat launch; CKE. *"Pleasant, busy, well-organised, open site with gd views of Rv Rhine; all facs
up steps; ferry x-ring rv, then tram/train to Dusseldorf;
ferry/tram; site may flood when rv at high level; long
lead req'd; gd NH."* **€28.00, 4 Apr-12 Oct.** **2019**

ECHTERNACHERBRUCK *3A2* (1km SW Rural) *49.81240,
6.43160* **Camping Freibad Echternacherbrück,**
Mindenerstrasse 18, 54668 Echternacherbrück
**(06525) 340; info@echternacherbrueck.de;
www.echternacherbrueck.de**

Fr Bitburg on B257/E29 site is at Lux'burg border,
sp. Fr Trier take A64 dir Luxembourg; exit junc
15 onto N10 to Echternacherbrück; cross bdg
dir Bitburg, then 1st L sp camping & foll sp. 4*,
Lge, pt shd, EHU (10A) €2.70 + conn fee; sw nr; TV;
30% statics; Eng spkn; games area; boat hire; tennis
400m; horseriding 4km; bike hire; waterslide; CKE.
*"Poss flooding in v wet weather; private bthrms avail;
excel facs; o'night m'van area; gd, well-organised site;
gd bus service to Luxembourg and Trier; ACSI card acc;
rvside pitches lger."* **€29.00, 18 Mar-15 Oct.** **2016**

ECKERNFORDE *1D1* (12km NE Coastal) *54.50280,
9.95802* **Ostsee-Camping Gut Ludwigsburg,**
Ludwigsburg 4, 24369 Waabs **(49043) 58370;
info@ostseecamping-ludwigsburg.de;
www.ostseecamping-ludwigsburg.de**

Fr Eckernforde take coastal rd NE, sp Ludwigsburg
& Waabs. Site sp in approx 12km on R; turn R down
single track rd. Site in 2km. Lge, mkd, hdstg, pt shd,
EHU (16A) €3; bbq; twin axles; TV; 60% statics; Eng
spkn; games area; games rm; CKE. *"Fishing in lake adj;
excel san facs; horseriding & watersports adj; gd
walking and cycling rtes nrby; gd site."*
€26.00, 28 Mar-1 Oct. **2019**

EGING AM SEE *4G3* (1km NE Rural) *48.72135, 13.26540* **Bavaria Kur-Sport-Campingpark,** Grafenauerstrasse 31, 94535 Eging **(08544) 8089; info@bavaria-camping.de; www.bavaria-camping.de**

12 €2.60 (htd)

Exit A3 junc 113 at Garham dir Eging, site sp in 4.5km twd Thurmansbang. 4*, Med, mkd, hdg, hdstg, pt shd, pt sl, terr, EHU (16A) €2.50; sw nr; TV; 20% statics; Eng spkn; ccard acc; games area; golf 10km; fishing; bike hire; tennis; CKE. *"Lovely site nr Bavarian National Park; gd walking/cycling fr site; htd pool 700m; Wild West theme town, Pullman City, 2.5km; vg NH & longer; adj to Danube llz cycleway and other cycleways."* **€29.00** **2015**

EISENACH *1D4* (10km S Rural) *50.90888, 10.29916* **Campingplatz Eisenach am Altenberger See,** Am Altenberger See, 99819 Wilhelmsthal **(03691) 215637; campingpark-eisenach@t-online.de; www.camping park-eisenach.de**

€2

Leave E40/A4 at junc 39 Eisenach Ost onto B19 sp Meiningen; site 2km S of Wilhelmsthal, sp. Med, hdstg, pt shd, pt sl, serviced pitches; EHU (16A) inc; 80% statics; bus to Eisenach nr; ccard acc; sauna; boating; site clsd Nov; CKE. *"Helpful staff; clsd 1300-1500; conv Wartburg & Thuringer Wald, Bach & Luther houses in Eisenach; lake adj; lge carpk in town suitable for MH's."* **€25.50, 1 Jan-31 Oct & 1 Dec-31 Dec.** **2017**

ERFURT *4E1* (10km NW Urban) *51.03895, 10.97870* **Campingplatz "Erfurt am See",** Steinfeld 4, 99189 Erfurt-Kühnhausen **(0176) 517 52386; mail@erfurtamsee.de; www.erfurtamsee.de**

12 (htd) adj

Fr A71 take exit 9 twds Kühnhausen. Turn L onto August-Röbling-Straße. Turn L onto Kühnhäuser Str, turn R onto Steinfeld, site on L. Med, unshd, pt sl, EHU; train 1km; CKE. *"Basic clean site bet angling & sw lakes; conv for visiting Erfurt; no laundry rm; gd site."* **€19.50** **2018**

ERLANGEN *4E2* (7km NW Rural) *49.63194, 10.9425* **Camping Rangau,** Campingstrasse 44, 91056 Erlangen-Dechsendorf **(09135) 8866; infos@ camping-rangau.de; www.camping-rangau.de**

€2.50 (htd) nr

Fr A3/E45 exit junc 81 & foll camp sp. At 1st traff lts turn L, strt on at next traff lts, then L at next traff lts, site sp. 4*, Med, pt shd, EHU (6A) €3 (long lead poss req); sw; red long stay; Eng spkn; adv bkg acc; ccard acc; boat hire; CKE. *"Gd site, espec for families; clean facs; welcoming & well-run; some sm pitches; popular NH - overflow onto adj sports field; vg, busy NH; arrive early; gates clsd 1300-1500 & 2200 hrs; dog wash facs."* **€28.50, 1 Apr-15 Oct.** **2019**

ESSEN *1B4* (8km S Urban) *51.38444, 6.99388* **DCC Campingpark Stadtcamping,** Im Löwental 67, 45239 Essen-Werden **(0201) 492978; essen@knauscamp.de; www.dcc-stadtcamping-essen-werden.de**

12

Exit A52 junc 28 onto B224 S dir Solingen. Turn R bef bdge over Rv Ruhr at traff lts & immed sharp R into Löwental, site sp. 3*, Med, hdstg, mkd, pt shd, EHU (16A) metered; gas; 95% statics; phone; Eng spkn; adv bkg acc; games area; games rm. *"Rv trips; poss ssn workers; site clsd 1300-1500 & 2130-0700; car park adj; gd."* **€27.30** **2016**

EXTERTAL *1C3* (3km SW Rural) *52.05118, 9.10223* **Camping Extertal,** Eimke 4, 32699 Extertal-Eimke **(05262) 3307; info@campingpark-extertal.de; www.campingpark-extertal.de**

12 €1.50 (htd) nr

Fr Rinteln on B238 S twd Barntrup; about 1.5km S Bösingfeld turn L at sp to site over level x-ing. 4*, Med, mkd, hdg, pt shd, pt sl, serviced pitches; EHU (16A) €1.50 or metered; gas; cooking facs; sw; red long stay; 90% statics; bus adj; Eng spkn; games rm; CKE. *"Gd site; dry & well-drained in v wet weather; all facs clean; forest walks & cycle paths fr site; 80 touring pitches; gd facs; some rd noise in day; clsd 1300-1500."* **€15.50** **2015**

FASSBERG *1D2* (6km E Rural) *52.87593, 10.22718* **Ferienpark Heidesee (Part Naturist),** Lüneburger-Heidesee, 29328 Fassberg-Oberohe **(05827) 970546; heidesee@ferienpark.de; www.campingheidesee.com**

12 €2 (htd)

Leave A7/E45 at exit 44 onto B71. Turn S to Müden, then dir Unterlüss. Foll site sp. V lge, pt shd, terr, EHU (10A) €3; gas; sw; 65% statics; Eng spkn; ccard acc; sauna; bike hire; fishing; horseriding; tennis; games rm; CKE. *"Naturist camping in sep area; long leads maybe req; pool 250m; friendly helpful staff; places of interest nrby; private bthrms avail; gd mkd cycling and walking rtes fr site."* **€21.00** **2019**

FELDBERG *2G2* (2km NE Rural) *53.34548, 13.45626* **Camping am Bauernhof,** Hof Eichholz 1-8, 17258 Feldberg **(039831) 21084; info@campingplatz-feldberg.de; www.campingplatz-am-bauernhof.de**

12 €3 nr

Fr B198 at Möllenbeck turn dir Feldburg, thro Feldburg dir Prenzlau, site sp. 4*, Med, mkd, unshd, pt sl, EHU (16A) metered + conn fee; sw; 30% statics; fishing; CKE. *"Well-situated, vg site among lakes; many cycle paths in area."* **€18.00** **2016**

FICHTELBERG *4F2* (2.5km N Rural) *50.01673,*
11.85525 **Kur-Camping Fichtelsee,** Fichtelseestrasse
30, 95686 Fichtelberg **(09272) 801; info@camping-**
fichtelsee.de; www.camping-fichtelsee.de

🏕 €2.50 ♀♀ WC ♿ ⚆ 🚿 ✓ MSP ☂ ☃ nr 🛒 nr ⚒ ✦

Exit junc 39 fr A9/E51. Foll B303 twd Marktredwitz.
After Bischofsgrün take R turn sp Fichtelberg, site
on L in 1km. 4*, Lge, mkd, hdstg, pt shd, pt sl, terr,
EHU (16A) metered + conn fee (poss rev pol); TV;
20% statics; phone; Eng spkn; ccard acc; site clsd 7
Nov-15 Dec; dog wash; CKE. *"Gd cent for walking in*
pine forests round lake & winter sports; peaceful site;
pool 800m; barrier clsd 1230-1430; excel san facs."
€25.00, 1 Jan-31 Oct, 6 Dec-31 Dec. **2018**

FINSTERAU *4G3* (1km N Rural) *48.94091, 13.57180*
Camping Nationalpark-Ost, Buchwaldstrasse 52,
94151 Finsterau **(08557) 768; berghof-frank@berghof-**
frank.de; www.camping-nationalpark-ost.de

12 🏕 €2 ♀♀ WC ♿ ⚆ 🚿 ✓ ☂ 🛒 nr

Fr B12 turn N dir Mauth. Cont to Finsterau & site
1km adj parking for National Park. Sm, pt shd,
EHU (6-16A) metered + conn fee or €2.50; gas; TV;
CKE. *"Gd walking & mountain biking; site in beautiful*
Bavarian forest." **€17.60** **2016**

FLENSBURG *1 D1* (7.4km S Rural) *54.74445, 9.43812*
Jarplund Campsite, Europastrasse 80, 24976
Handewitt **(04619) 79024; campingplatz.jarplund@**
web.de; www.campingplatz-jarplund.de

🏕 €1 ♀♀ WC ♿ ⚆ 🚿 ✓ MSP ☂ ☃ ☂ Y nr ⚆ nr 🛒 ⚒ ⚓

Due S on Flensburg on old main road to Jarplund,
Oeversee. Med, hdg, mkd, pt shd, EHU 10A (€2.50);
bbq; cooking facs; Eng spkn; adv bkg acc; ccard acc.
"Conv for historic Flensburg port; sm supmkt next
door; pool not always filled; gd NH/short stay; gd".
€24.00, 15 Mar-15 Nov. **2018**

FRANKFURT AM MAIN *3C2* (8km NE Rural)
50.81700, 8.46550 **Campingplatz Mainkur,**
Frankfurter Landstraße 107, 63477 Maintal **(069)-**
412193; info@campingplatz-mainkur.de;
www.campingplatz-mainkur.de

🏕 ♀♀♀ ♿ ⚆ 🚿 MSP Y 🛒 ⚒ ⚏

Fr Frankfurt head NE B4 and Hanua cross over
A661 and cont over 8 sets of traff lts pass car
showrooms and Bauhaus on L. 100m aft flyover
bear R into single track tarmac rd to site. Sp on B8/
B4. Med, mkd, pt shd, bbq; 35% statics; Eng spkn;
adv bkg acc; boating; lounge with sm library. *"Family*
run site o'looking rv; conv for Frankfurt; vg, rec."
€28.00, 1 Apr-30 Sept. **2020**

FREIBURG IM BREISGAU *3B4* (21km NE Rural)
48.02318, 8.03253 **Camping Steingrubenhof,**
Haldenweg 3, 79271 St Peter **(07660) 210; info@**
camping-steingrubenhof.de; www.camping-
steingrubenhof.de

🏕 €2.50 ♀♀♀ WC ♿ ⚆ 🚿 ✓ MSP ☂ ☃ Y nr ⚆ nr 🛒 ⚏

Exit A5 junc 61 onto B294. Turn R sp St Peter.
Steep hill to site on L at top of hill. Or fr B31 dir
Donaueschingen, after 4km outside Freiburg
turn N sp St Peter; by-pass vill on main rd, turn
L under bdge 1st R. Fr other dir by-pass St Peter
heading for Glottertal; site on R 200m after rd
bdge on by-pass. Med, hdg, mkd, hdstg, unshd,
terr, serviced pitches; EHU (16A) €2.50; bbq; red
long stay; 70% statics; phone; Eng spkn; adv bkg
acc; ccard acc; CKE. *"Peaceful site in heart of Black*
Forest; wonderful location; pleasant staff; immac
facs; gate clsd 1200-1400 & 2200-0800; v diff to
manoeuvre twin axle vans onto pitches as narr access
paths; pitches are sm & few for tourers; great site."
€25.00, 1 Jan-10 Nov & 15 Dec-31 Dec. **2019**

FREIBURG IM BREISGAU *3B4* (4km E Rural) *47.99250,*
7.87330 **Camping Hirzberg,** Kartäuserstrasse 99,
79104 Freiburg-im-Breisgau **(0761) 35054; hirzburg@**
freiburg-camping.de; www.freiburg-camping.de

12 🏕 €1 ♀♀♀ (htd) WC ♿ ⚆ 🚿 ✓ MSP ☂ ☃ Y ⚆ ♿ 🛒 ⚏

Exit A5 at Freiburg-Mitte & foll B31 past town cent
sp Freiburg, Titisee. Foll camping sp twd Freiburg-
Ebnet, nr rocky slopes on R. Then approx 2.5km on
narr, winding rd. Site on R just after start of blocks
of flats on L. Med, pt shd, pt sl, terr, EHU (10A) €2.50;
gas; bbq; 40% statics; bus 300m; Eng spkn; adv bkg
acc; bike hire; CKE. *"Pleasant, v helpful owner; site*
clsd 2000 - ltd outside parking; gd cycle path & easy
walk to town; busy in high ssn; clsd 1300-1500; pool
500m; excel, v clean & modern san facs; gd value rest."
€31.00 **2018**

FREIBURG IM BREISGAU *3B4* (11km SE Rural) *47.96015,*
7.95001 **Camping Kirchzarten,** Dietenbacherstrasse 17,
79199 Kirchzarten **(07661) 9040910; info@camping-**
kirchzarten.de; www.camping-kirchzarten.de

12 🏕 €2.50 ♀♀♀ (htd) WC ♿ ⚆ 🚿 ✓ MSP
☂ Y ⚆ nr ♿ 🛒 nr ⚏ ✦

Sp fr Freiburg-Titisee rd 31; into Kirchzarten; site sp
fr town cent. 5*, Lge, mkd, pt shd, serviced pitches;
EHU (16A) €2.50 or metered; bbq; red long stay;
20% statics; train 500m; Eng spkn; adv bkg rec; ccard
acc; tennis adj; CKE. *"Gd size pitches; choose pitch*
then register at office (clse fr 1200-1400); spacious,
well-kept site; office clsd 1300-1430; Quickstop o'night
area; excel san facs; gd rest; 3 htd pools adj; winter
sports area; site fees inc free bus & train travel in Black
Forest region; helpful staff; dogs not acc Jul/Aug."
€35.00 **2016**

GERMANY

FREUDENSTADT *3C3* (8km ENE Rural) *48.48011, 8.5005* **Höhencamping Königskanzel,** Freizeitweg 1, 72280 Dornstetten-Hallwangen **(07443) 6730; info@ camping-koenigskanzel.de; www.camping-koenigs kanzel.de**

Fr Freudenstadt head E on rte 28 foll sp Stuttgart for 7km. Camping sp on R, sharp R turn foll sp, sharp L on narr, winding track to site in 200m. Fr Nagold on R28, 7km fr Freudenstadt fork L; sp as bef. NB: 1st sharp R turn is v sharp - take care. Med, hdg, pt shd, pt sl, terr, serviced pitches; EHU (10A) metered; gas; bbq; red long stay; 60% statics; phone; Eng spkn; adv bkg req; site clsd 3 Nov-15 Dec; golf 7km; sauna; bike hire; CKE. *"Pleasant owners; friendly welcome; excel shwr facs, inc for dogs; well run family site; hill top location with gd views of Black Forest; bkg fee; ski lift 7km; recep clsd 1300-1400; excel value rest."* **€30.40** **2019**

"We must tell the Club about that great site we found"

Get your site reports in by mid-August and we'll do our best to get your updates into the next edition.

FREUDENSTADT *3C3* (5km W Rural) *48.45840, 8.37255* **Camping Langenwald,** Strassburgerstrasse 167, 72250 Freudenstadt-Langenwald **(07441) 2862; info@camping-langenwald.de; www.camping-langenwald.de**

Foll sp fr town on B28 dir Strassburg. 5*, Med, pt shd, terr, serviced pitches; EHU (16A) metered; gas; red long stay; 10% statics; Eng spkn; ccard acc; bike hire; golf 4km; CKE. *"Gd, clean san facs & site; woodland walks fr site; gd rest; friendly owners."* **€30.00, 26 Mar-1 Nov.** **2016**

FRICKENHAUSEN AM MAIN *3D2* (1km W Rural) *49.66916, 10.07444* **Knaus Campingpark Frickenhausen,** Ochsenfurterstrasse 49, 97252 Frickenhausen/Ochsenfurt **(09331) 3171; info@ knauscamp.de; www.knauscamp.de**

Turn off B13 at N end of bdge over Rv Main in Ochsenfurt & foll camping sp. 4*, Lge, hdg, mkd, pt shd, serviced pitches; EHU (16A) €2.40 or metered; gas; red long stay; TV; 40% statics; Eng spkn; adv bkg acc; bike hire. *"Vg, well-managed site on rv island; excel, clean facs; located on Romantischestrasse with many medieval vills; site clsd 1300-1500; v clean, cared for site; gd rest; friendly staff; gd sized pitches; site clsed bet 1-3pm."* **€32.60** **2018**

FRIEDRICHSHAFEN *3D4* (10km W Coastal) *47.66583, 9.37694* **Campingplatz Schloss Helmsdorf,** Friedrichshafenerstrasse, 88090 Immenstaad-am-Bodensee **(07545) 6252; info@schloss-helmsdorf.org; www.schloss-helmsdorf.org**

Site sp fr B31 bet Meersburg & Friedrichshafen at Immenstaad. Lge, pt shd, pt sl, EHU (6A) €2.50; sw; 80% statics; windsurfing; boating. *"Vg, well-run site; gd position on lakeside; gd, clean san facs; helpful owners; sh walk to lake ferry; no dogs high ssn; Zeppelin & Dornier museums 8km level bike rte."* **€32.00, 25 Mar-9 Oct.** **2016**

FRIEDRICHSHAFEN *3D4* (8km W Rural) *47.66896, 9.40253* **Camping Fischbach,** Grenzösch 3, 88048 Friedrichschafen-Fischbach **(07541) 42059; info@ camping-fischbach.de; www.camping-fischbach.de**

Take B31 fr Friedrichhafen to Meersburg. Site sp on L at end of vill. Turning lane avail for easy access off busy rd. 3*, Med, hdstg, mkd, pt shd, EHU (10-16A) €2 (poss rev pol); sw nr; 40% statics; phone; Eng spkn; CKE. *"Tranquil, relaxing site; some lake view pitches, worth the extra; excel, clean, modern san facs; ferries to Konstanz nrby; Zeppelin/Dornier museums nrby; cr; on Lake Constance cycle rte."* **€27.00, 14 Apr-8 Oct.** **2017**

FRIESOYTHE *1C2* (13km SE Rural) *52.93703, 7.92923* **Campingplatz Wilken,** Thülsfelder Str. 3, 26169 Friesoythe **04 49 52 61; info@camping-wilken.de; www.camping-wilken.de**

Fr B72 Cloppenburg-Friesoythe. After 13km turn L onto Thülsfelder Straße. Site next to Thülsfeld Reservoir on L. Lge, mkd, hdstg, unshd, EHU (16A) metered. *"Excel site for long stay; spacious pitches; v clean san facs; would rec."* **€13.50** **2019**

FUSSEN *4E4* (6km N Rural) *47.61553, 10.7230* **Camping Magdalena am Forggensee,** Bachtalstrasse 10, 87669 Osterreinen **(08362) 4931; campingplatz.magdalena@t-online.de; www.sonnenhof-am-forggensee.de**

Fr Füssen take rd 16 sp Kaufbeuren & Forggensee for 5km; R sp Osterreinen for 500m; L at T-junc foll site sp; site on R in 50m; app rd steep with sharp bends. Site well sp. 3*, Med, hdg, mkd, pt shd, terr, EHU (10A) metered + conn fee; gas; 40% statics; Eng spkn; adv bkg rec; sailing; watersports; CKE. *"Ltd touring pitches; superb views over lake; peaceful; gd site; sm pitches; conv for Zugspitze, Royal Castles, Oberammergau; lakeside cycle track to Füssen & to Neuschwanstein Castle."* **€23.90, 1 Apr-31 Oct.** **2019**

FUSSEN *4E4* (6km NE Rural) *47.59638, 10.73861*
Camping Brunnen, Seestrasse 81, 87645 Brunnen
**(08362) 8273; info@camping-brunnen.de;
www.camping-brunnen.de**

12 🐕 €4.50 [wc] ♿ 🚿 ⚷ ⚌ MSP 🏕 nr ⊕ nr 🛒 🚲 ⛺adj

S on rte 17 twd Füssen turn R in vill of Schwangau
N to Brunnen; turn R at ent to vill at Spar shop, site
clearly sp. Fr Füssen N on B17; turn L in Schwangau;
well sp on lakeside. 5*, Lge, mkd, hdstg, pt shd, pt
sl, serviced pitches; EHU (10-16A) metered + conn
fee; gas; sw nr; bus; Eng spkn; adv bkg acc; ccard
acc; bike hire; golf 3km; site clsd 5 Nov-20 Dec; CKE.
*"Lovely location, next to lake; o'fits poss tightly packed;
steel pegs ess; excel san facs; some pitches cramped;
gd for Royal castles; gd cycle rtes; 10% red visits to
Neuschwanstein Castle nrby; gates clsd 2200-0700;
excel, busy, vg site; yachting in Lake Forggensee adj;
handy rest, supmkt & g'ge."* **€38.00** **2019**

FUSSEN *4E4* (5km NW Rural) *47.60198, 10.68333*
Camping Hopfensee, Fischerbichl 17/Uferstrasse,
87629 Hopfen-am-See **(08362) 917710;
info@camping-hopfensee.de; www.camping-
hopfensee.com**

🐕 €4.15 ♿ [wc] ⚷ ♿ 🚿 ⚌ MSP 🦋 ♨ 🏕 ⊕ 🛒 🚲 ⛺ ✎
🏊(covrd, htd)

Fr Füssen N on B16 twd Kaufbeuren in 2km L on
rd sp Hopfen-am-See, site at ent to vill on L thro
c'van car park. Lge, hdstg, mkd, pt shd, serviced
pitches; EHU (16A) metered; gas; sw nr; free bus
to Füssen; Eng spkn; adv bkg rec; sauna; boating;
fishing; CKE. *"Gd location; excel facs; helpful staff;
gd rest on site; no tents allowed except for awnings;
tight squeeze in high ssn; vans need manhandling;
fitness cent; solarium; winter sports area; gd walking
& cycling; lakeside pitches rec; excel; highly rec;
5 star facs; WiFi €2 per day; recep clsd 12-2pm."*
€43.00, 1 Jan-4 Nov & 15 Dec-31 Dec. **2018**

GANDERKESEE *1C2* (7km W Rural) *53.04666, 8.46388*
Ferienpark Falkensteinsee, Am Falkensteinsee 1,
27777 Ganderkesee-Steinkimmen **(04222) 9470077;
camping@falkensteinsee.de; www.falkensteinsee.de**

12 🐕 €1.50 ♿ ♿ 🚿 ⚌ MSP 🦋 ⊕ nr 🛒 🚲 ⛺

Exit A28/E22 junc 18 dir Habbrügge. Site on R in 2km.
4*, Lge, pt shd, EHU (16A) €3.50 or metered; sw nr;
70% statics; Eng spkn; golf 8km; sauna; CKE. *"Conv
Oldenburg & Bremen; new owners; completely refurb
(2015); lake sw with 2 sandy beaches; pleasant holiday
park; well organised; o'night m'van area; friendly staff;
sep naturist beach; new facs & v high quality; excel; sep
sw area for dogs."* **€21.50** **2016**

GARTOW *2E2* (4km NW Rural) *53.03972, 11.41583*
Camping Laascher See, Ortsteil Laasche 13, 29471
Gartow (05846) 342; pewsdorf@campingplatz-
laascher-see.de; www.elbtalaue-camping.de

🐕 €1.50 ♿ ♿ 🚿 ⚷ ⚌ MSP 🦋 🏕 ⊕ nr 🛒 nr ⛺

Fr S on B493 to Gartow, turn N on L256
(Rondelerstrasse) dir Gartower See & Laasche
See, site sp on R. Or E fr Dennenberg on L256
dir Gorleben & Gartow, site sp approx 5km after
Gorleben. Med, hdg, pt shd, pt sl, EHU (6A) inc; sw nr;
60% statics; adv bkg acc; CKE. *"Pleasant owners; clean,
modern san facs; vg."* **€19.50, 1 Apr-31 Oct.** **2016**

GEESTHACHT *1D2* (9km SW Rural) *53.42465,
10.29470* **Campingplatz Stover Strand International,**
Stover Strand 10, 21423 Drage **(04177) 430; info@
camping-stover-strand.de; www.camping-stover-
strand.de**

12 🐕 €2 (htd) ♿ [wc] 🚿 ⚷ ♿ 🚿 ⚌ MSP 🦋 ♨ 🏕 ⊕ 🛒 🚲 ⛺ ✎

Fr N on A25 to Geesthacht, then B404 dir Winsen
to Stove. Site at end Stover Strand on banks of
Rv Elbe. Fr S on A7 to Maschen, then A250 to
Winsen then B404, as above. 5*, V lge, mkd, pt shd,
EHU (6-16A) €2 or metered; bbq; cooking facs; sw;
80% statics; adv bkg acc; ccard acc; bike hire; fishing;
games area; watersports; CKE. *"Excel rvside site;
marina; site clsd 1300-1500; Hamburg Card avail."*
€20.00 **2020**

GEMUNDEN AM MAIN *3D2* (5km W Rural) *50.05260,
9.65656* **Spessart-Camping Schönrain,** Schönrain
strasse 4-18, 97737 Gemünden-Hofstetten **(09351)
8645; info@spessart-camping.de; www.spessart-
camping.de**

🐕 €2.80 ♿ (htd) [wc] ♿ 🚿 ⚌ MSP 🦋 🏕 ⊕ 🛒 🚲 ⛺ 🍽

Rd B26 to Gemünden, cross Rv Main & turn R
dir Hofstetten, site sp. 5*, Lge, hdg, mkd, hdstg,
pt shd, terr, EHU (10A) metered + conn fee €2.15;
TV; 50% statics; phone; Eng spkn; bike hire; sauna;
fitness rm; solarium; games area; CKE. *"Clean, well-
kept, wooded site; interesting towns nrby; variable
pitch sizes/prices; excel; v well kept new facs block;
welcoming."* **€25.00, 1 Apr-30 Sep.** **2019**

GERSFELD (RHON) *3D2* (2.5km N Rural) *50.46223,
9.91953* **Camping Hochrhön,** Schachen 13, 36129
Gersfeld-Schachen **(06654) 7836; info@camping-
hochrhoen.de; www.rhoenline.de/camping-hochrhoen**

12 🐕 €1 [wc] ♿ 🚿 ⚌ MSP ⊕ nr 🛒 nr ⛺

Exit A7 exit Fulda-Süd S onto B27/B279 to Gersfeld,
then B284 sp Ehrenberg, Turn L dir Schachen, foll
sp to site. 3*, Med, hdg, mkd, hdstg, pt shd, EHU
(16A) metered; 10% statics; CKE. *"Conv for gliding
& air sports at Wasswerkuppe; ski lift 3km; friendly."*
€18.00 **2020**

GLUCKSBURG (OSTSEE) *1D1* (6km NE Coastal) *54.85901, 9.59109* **Ostseecamp,** An der Promenade 1, 24960 Glücksburg-Holnis **(04631) 622071; info@ostseecamp-holnis.de; www.ostseecamp-holnis.de**

🛗 €2.50 ♟♟ (htd) 🅆 ♨ ⚲ ♿ 🖵 ⚟ MP 🦋 ♈
⊕ nr ⬧ 🏊 ⛰ ⤢ ⛵ 🛥 sand adj

Fr Flensburg on rd 199 turn off thro Glücksburg & further 6km to Holnis. 4*, Med, hdstg, mkd, pt shd, EHU (16A) €3; bbq; cooking facs; 30% statics; adv bkg acc; windsurfing 1km; fishing; bike hire; CKE. "Lovely coastal loc; v friendly staff; clean facs." **€29.00, 28 Mar-16 Oct.** **2016**

GOPPINGEN *3D3* (13.5km SW Rural) *48.63946, 9.55508* **Campingplatz Aichelberg,** Bunzenberg 1, 73101 Aichelberg **(07164) 2700**

🛗 €2 ♟♟ 🅆 ⚟ 🦋 ♈ ⊕ nr 🏊

Exit E52/A8 junc 58 sp Aichelberg-Goppingen & foll sp to camp site in 1km. 3*, Med, pt shd, EHU (10A) €2; 80% statics; adv bkg acc. "Fills up after 1600 hrs but gd overflow field with EHU for NH; family-run site; new excel facs; owner helpful; nr A8; gd conv NH." **€20.00, 7 Apr-8 Oct.** **2017**

GOSLAR *1D3* (4km SW Rural) *51.88958, 10.39889* **Campingplatz Sennhütte,** Clausthalerstrasse 28, 38644 Goslar **(05321) 22498; sennhuette@camping platz-goslar.de; www.campingplatz-goslar.de**

12 🛗 ♟♟ 🅆 ♨ 🖵 ⚟ ⊕ 🏊

Fr Goslar on B241 twd Clausthal, Zellerfeld site on R in 2km. Ent thro car pk of Hotel Sennhütte. 2*, Med, pt shd, EHU (16A) metered + €2 conn fee (poss long lead req); 30% statics; bus at ent to town; ccard acc. "Gd NH/sh stay nr beautiful town." **€21.00** **2018**

GRAFENDORF *JD2* (11km SE Rural) *50.106/8, 9.78241* **Camping Rossmühle,** Rossmühle 797782 Gräfendorf-Weickersgrüben **(09357) 1210; www.campingplatz-rossmuehle.de**

12 🛗 €2 ♟♟ 🅆 ♨ ⚲ ♿ 🖵 ⚟ MP 🦋 ♈ ⊕ 🏊 ⛰ ⤢

Exit A7 junc 96 onto B27 sp Karlstadt. At Hammelburg foll sps to Gräfendorf & site in 8km on rvside, beyond Weickersgrüben. 3*, Lge, mkd, pt shd, terr, EHU (6-10A) €2; TV; 50% statics; adv bkg acc; bike hire; canoe hire; watersports; solarium. "Poss liable to flooding after heavy rain; o'night m'vans area; clean san facs; fitness rm; excel; cycle rte tourers sep fr statics." **€18.00** **2020**

GREFRATH *1A4* (4km N Rural) *51.36492, 6.32328* **Campingplatz Waldfrieden,** An de Paas 13, 47929 Grefrath-Vinkrath **(02158) 3855; info@ferienpark-waldfrieden.de; www.ferienpark-waldfrieden.de**

12 🛗 €2 ♟♟ (htd) 🅆 ♨ 🖵 ⚟ MP 🦋 🏊 nr ⛰

Fr A40-E34 S to Duisburg; turn S at exit 3 sp Grefrath; site sp on L in 3km; 1km down side rd beside Am Blumenfeld. 4*, Lge, hdg, hdstg, pt shd, EHU (10A) €3.50; gas; sw nr; 80% statics; Eng spkn; CKE. "Conv NH North Sea ports; WWII cemetaries at Reichswald; sw pools 1.5km; site over-used & weary; site clsd 1300-1500." **€17.50** **2018**

GREIFSWALD *2G1* (16km NE Coastal) *54.12666, 13.52196* **Campingplatz Loissin (Part Naturist),** 17509 Loissin **(038352) 243; info@campingplatz-loissin.de; www.campingplatz-loissin.de**

🛗 €2 ♟♟ 🅆 ♨ ⚲ ♿ ⚟ MP 🦋 ♈ 🍽 ⊕ ⬧ 🏊 ⛰ 🛥 🛥 sand adj

Fr Greifswald E to Kemnitz, then head N twds Loissin; site on coast N, well sp fr the vill. 3*, Lge, mkd, pt shd, EHU (16A) inc; 40% statics; adv bkg acc; games area; windsurfing; clsd 1300-1430 & 2200-0800; bike hire; CKE. "Vg site; approx 40km to foot x-ing fr car park to Poland for shopping; excel san facs; sep naturist beach; main attraction is immed proximity to sea." **€22.00, 1 Apr-31 Oct.** **2018**

GREVEN *1B3* (6km SW Rural) *52.08328, 7.55806* **Campingplatz Westheide,** Altenbergerstrasse 23, 48268 Greven **(02571) 560701; kontakt@camping platz-westheide.de; www.campingplatz-westheide.de**

12 🛗 €1 (htd) 🅆 ♨ ⚲ ♿ ⚟ 🦋 🍽 ⛰ ⬧ 🛥 sand adj

Exit A1 junc 76 onto B481 around E side of Greven, then turn L onto B219 for 2km. Turn R onto L555 Nordwalderstrasse & in 2km at Westerode turn L into Altenbergerstrasse, site on L in 1km. Med, hdg, pt shd, EHU (16A) metered; 80% statics; ccard acc; games rm; fishing; CKE. "Gd for sh stay; lake adj; walks around lake." **€18.00** **2016**

GYHUM *1D2* (4km SE Rural) *53.19308, 9.33638* **Waldcamping Hesedorf,** Zum Waldbad 3, 27404 Gyhum-Hesedorf **(04286) 2252; info@waldcamping-hesedorf.de; www.waldcamping-hesedorf.de**

12 🛗 €0.50 ♟♟ (htd) 🅆 ♨ ⚲ ⚟ MP 🦋 ♈ ⊕ 🏊 nr ⛰

Exit A1/E22 junc 49 in dir Zeven. In 1km turn R sp Gyhum & foll site sp to Hesedorf. Med, unshd, EHU (16A) inc; 70% statics; Eng spkn; CKE. "Clean, well-kept site; attractive area; htd pool 150m inc; gd rest; lge sep area for tourers; barrier clsd 1300-1500; dated san facs but clean; gd NH." **€20.00** **2019**

HAMBURG *1D2* (7km NW Urban) *53.5900, 9.93083* **Campingplatz Buchholz,** Keilerstrasse 374, 22525 Hamburg-Stellingen **(040) 5404532; info@camping-buchholz.de; www.camping-buchholz.de**

12 🛗 €4 ♟♟ 🅆 ♨ ♿ ⚟ 🍽 ⊕ nr 🏊 nr

Exit A7/E45 junc 26 & foll dir 'Innenstadt' - city cent. Site sp in 600m on L. Sm, hdg, mkd, hdstg, pt shd, EHU (16A) €4; 10% statics; bus, train nr; adv bkg acc. "Fair NH nr a'bahn & Hamburg cent; conv transport to city - tickets fr recep; friendly management; sm pitches; busy site, rec arr early; diff access for lge o'fits." **€35.00** **2019**

GERMANY

HAMBURG *1D2* (9km NW Urban) *53.64916, 9.92970* **Knaus Campingpark Hamburg,** Wunderbrunnen 2, 22457 Hamburg **(040) 5594225; service@campingplatz-hamburg.de; www.campingplatz-hamburg.de**

[12] 🐕 €3.50 🚻 [WD] 🚿 ♿ 🧺 ⚡ [MSP] 🦋 🍸 🍴 nr 🛒 🛝 ⛺

Heading N on A7 exit junc 23 to Schnelsen Nord; L at traff lts, foll sp Ikea & site behind Ikea. 4*, Med, mkd, pt shd, EHU (6A) inc; TV; phone; bus to city; Eng spkn; ccard acc; CKE. *"Useful NH; helpful staff; stn adj; gates clsd 2200 hrs & 1300-1600 LS; elec pylons & cables cross site; deposit for key to san facs & el box; 3-day Hamburg card excel value."* **€43.50** **2019**

HAMELN *1D3* (2km W Urban) *52.10916, 9.3475* **Campingplatz zum Fährhaus,** Uferstrasse 80, 31785 Hameln **(05151) 67489; info@campingplatz-hameln.de; www.campingplatz-hameln.de**

[12] 🐕 €1 🚻 (htd) [WD] 🚿 ♿ 🧺 ⚡ [MSP] 🦋 🍸 🍴 🛝 nr

Fr A2/E30 at Bad Eilsen junc 35 onto B83 to Hameln on NE side of Rv Weser; in town foll sp Detmold/ Paderborn; cross bdge to SW side (use Thiewall Brücke); turn R on minor rd twd Rinteln; foll site sp. 3*, Med, unshd, EHU (10-16A); 20% statics; phone; clsd 1300-1430; CKE. *"Picturesque & historic district; open-air performance of Pied Piper in town on Sun to mid-Sep; sm pitches & poss uneven; helpful, lovely owner; san facs refurb, best in Europe!(2017); gd cycle paths by rv to town; site beautifully kept."* **€18.50** **2017**

HAMELN *1D3* (8km W Rural) *52.10725, 9.29588* **Camping am Waldbad,** Pferdeweg 2, 31787 Halvestorf **(05158) 2774; info@campingamwaldbad.de; www.campingamwaldbad.de**

🐕 🚻 [WD] 🚿 ♿ 🧺 ⚡ 🦋 🛒 🛝 nr ⛺ 🏊 (htd) ♨

Fr Hameln on B83 dir Rinteln. In approx 10km turn L, cross rv & foll sp Halvestorf & site. 4*, Med, unshd, pt sl, EHU (16A) €2; 80% statics; adv bkg acc. *"Pleasant site - better than site in Hameln; gd facs."* **€19.00, 1 Apr-31 Oct.** **2018**

HAMM *1B3* (13km E Rural) *51.6939, 7.9710* **Camping Uentrop,** Dolbergerstrasse 80, 59510 Lippetal-Lippborg **(02388) 437 or (0172) 2300747; info@camping-helbach.de; www.camping-helbach.de**

[12] 🐕 €2 🚻 (htd) [WD] 🚿 🧺 ⚡ 🍴 nr 🛝 nr ⛺

Exit A2/E34 junc 19, site sp; behind Hotel Helbach 1km fr a'bahn. 3*, Lge, pt shd, pt sl, EHU (16A) €2; gas; 90% statics; Eng spkn; ccard acc. *"Friendly; gd security; barrier clsd 1300-1500 & 2200-0500; fair NH."* **€18.00** **2016**

HAMMELBACH *3C2* (0.6km S Rural) *49.63277, 8.83000* **Camping Park Hammelbach,** Gasse 17, 64689 Grasellenbach/Hammelbach **(06253) 3831; info@camping-hammelbach.de; www.camping-hammelbach.de**

🐕 €2.50 🚻 (htd) [WD] 🚿 👪 ♿ 🧺 ⚡ [MSP] 🦋 📶 🍸 nr 🍴 nr 🛝 nr

Exit A5/E35 exit junc 31 onto B460 E. Turn S in Weschnitz to Hammelbach & foll site sp. 5*, Med, hdg, pt shd, EHU (16A) metered; gas; bbq; 70% statics; bus 300m; Eng spkn; adv bkg acc; ccard acc; CKE. *"Excel family run site with views; sauna adj; v pleasant, helpful staff; red for snrs; conv Heidelberg; immac hotel like san facs; htd pool 300m; well up to CC standards."* **€24.50, 1 Apr-31 Oct.** **2019**

HANNOVER *1D3* (14km NE Urban) *52.45383, 9.85611* **Campingplatz Parksee Lohne,** Alter Postweg 12, 30916 Isernhagen **05139 88260; parksee-lohne@t-online.de; www.parksee-lohne.de**

🐕 🚻 (htd) [WD] 🚿 👪 ♿ 🧺 [MSP] 🦋 🍸 🍴 🛒

Fr A2 take exit 46 to Altwarmbüchen. Cont onto K114, turn R onto Alter Postweg & foll sp to campsite. V lge, pt shd, cooking facs; 95% statics; Eng spkn. *"Vg site; next to golf course; excel san facs; narr cobbled rd 1/2 m; under flight path, but quiet at night."* **€29.60, 1 Apr-15 Oct.** **2019**

HANNOVER *1D3* (16km SE Rural) *52.30447, 9.86216* **Camping Birkensee,** 30880 Laatzen **(0511) 529962; birkensee@camping-laatzen.de; www.camping-laatzen.de**

[12] 🐕 €2.50 🚻 [WD] 🚿 ♿ 🧺 ⚡ [MSP] 🍸 🛒 ⛺ 🏊 (covrd)

Fr N leave A7 junc 59 dir Laatzen, turn R, then turn L & site well sp on L after traff lts. Fr S exit junc 60 twd Laatzen, site sp on L on lakeside. 3*, Lge, pt shd, EHU (10A) €2.50 (poss rev pol); sw; 60% statics; Eng spkn; fishing; games area; sauna; CKE. *"Gd, clean facs; sm touring area; site needs TLC; v helpful staff."* **€27.00** **2019**

HANNOVER *1D3* (10km S Rural) *52.30133, 9.74716* **Campingplatz Arnumer See,** Osterbruchweg 5, 30966 Hemmingen-Arnum **(05101) 3534; info@camping-hannover.de; www.camping-hannover.de**

[12] 🐕 €1.50 🚻 (htd) [WD] 🚿 👪 🧺 ⚡ [MSP] 🦋 📶 🍸 🍴 🛒 🛝 nr ⛺

Leave A7 junc 59 onto B443 dir Pattensen, then B3 dir Hannover. Site sp in Hemmingen dir Wilkenburg. 4*, Lge, hdg, mkd, pt shd, EHU (16A) €3; gas; cooking facs; sw; 95% statics; bus to Hannover 1.5km; tennis; fishing; bike hire; CKE. *"Friendly staff; excel, modern, clean san facs; sm area for tourers - gd size open pitches; gd lake sw & boating; insect repellent ess!"* **€31.00** **2019**

 Make sure you check any essential information with the site before you travel

HANNOVER *1D3 (16km NW Rural) 52.42083, 9.54638* **Camping Blauer See,** Am Blauen See 119, 30823 Garbsen **(05137) 89960; info@camping-blauer-see.de; www.camping-blauer-see.de**

🏕 12 🐕 €2.50 👫(htd) 📶 ♨ ⚲ ♿ 🚿 ∕ ᴹˢᴾ 🍴 ① ♨ 🛒 ⛺

Fr W exit A2 at junc 41 onto Garbsen rest area. Thro service area, at exit turn R, at T-junc turn R (Alt Garbson). All sp with int'l camp sp. Fr E exit junc 40, cross a'bahn & go back to junc 41, then as above. Lge, hdstg, pt shd, serviced pitches; EHU (16A) €2.70; gas; bbq; sw nr; 90% statics; phone; bus to Hannover 1.5km; Eng spkn; ccard acc; watersports adj; CKE. *"Excel san facs; well-organised site; helpful staff; conv bus/train to Hannover; barrier clsd 2300-0500 & 1300-1500; rec pitch by lake."* **€29.00**　　　　2019

HANNOVERSCH MUNDEN *1D4 (0.9km W Rural) 51.41666, 9.64750* **Campingplatz Grüne Insel Tanzwerder,** Tanzwerder 1, 34346 Hannoversch-Münden **(05541) 12257; info@busch-freizeit.de; www.busch-freizeit.de**

🐕 €2 👫 📶 ♨ 🚿 ∕ ᴹˢᴾ 🍴 ① nr 🛒 nr ⛺

A7/E45 exit junc 76 onto B496 to Hann-Münden. Cross bdge & site sp on an island on Rv Fulda next to town cent. App over narr swing bdge. Fr junc 75 foll sp to Hann-Münden. At Aral g'ge in town take next L & foll sp to site (sp Weserstein). 3*, Med, mkd, pt shd, EHU (16A) metered + conn fee; red long stay; Eng spkn; adv bkg acc; CKE. *"Pleasant, well looked after site on island bordered by rv both sides; noisy bdge traff; easy stroll to historic old town."* **€21.00, 1 Apr-16 Oct.**　　　　2016

HARZGERODE *2E4 (8km SW Rural) 51.60833, 11.08444* **Ferienpark Birnbaumteich,** Birnbaumteich 1, 06493 Neudorf Harzgerode **(03948) 46243; info@ferienpark-birnbaumteich.de; www.ferienpark-birnbaumteich.de**

🏕 12 🐕 €4 👫 📶 ♨ ⚲ ♿ ∕ ᴹˢᴾ 🍴 🍴 ① ♨ 🛒 ⛺ ✂

Fr Harzgerode on B242 dir Halle, after 1km turn R, dir Stolberg. In 4.3km after Neudorf turn R at camping sp. Site 1km on R. 3*, Med, pt shd, pt sl, EHU (16A) €3; bbq; sw; twin axles; 50% statics; phone; bus 1km; Eng spkn; adv bkg acc; games rm; sauna; games area; CKE. *"Forest walk & bike trails; steam rlwy 3km; interesting towns nrby; vg."* **€24.00**　　　　2015

HATTINGEN *1B4 (3km NW Urban) 51.40611, 7.17027* **Camping Ruhrbrücke,** Ruhrstrasse 6, 45529 Hattingen **(02324) 80038; info@camping-hattingen.de; www.camping-hattingen.de**

🐕 €2 👫(htd) 📶 ♨ ♿ ∕ 🦋 🍴 nr ① nr 🛒 ⛺

Fr A40 bet Essen & Bochum exit junc 29 dir Höntrop & Hattingen. Foll sp Hattingen on L651 & B1, site sp bef rv bdge. 3*, Med, unshd, pt sl, EHU (16A) €3; bbq; sw nr; phone; bus, train adj; Eng spkn; adv bkg acc; windsurfing adj; canoeing adj; CKE. *"Beautiful rvside setting; plentiful, clean facs; friendly owner; excel cycle tracks."* **€18.00, 1 Apr-20 Oct.**　　　　2016

HAUSEN IM TAL *3C4 (0.1km E Rural) 48.08365, 9.04290* **Camping Wagenburg,** Kirchstr. 24, 88631 Beuron / i Tal Hausen **(07579) 559; info@camping-wagenburg.de; www.camping-wagenburg.de**

🐕 €1.50 👫 📶 ♨ ♿ ∕ ᴹˢᴾ 🍴 ① nr 🛒 nr ⛺

Fr E on B32 stay on Sigmaringen bypass and take minor rd L227 sp Gutenstein/Beuron to Hausen, site in vill beside Rv Donau. 3*, Med, hdstg, pt shd, EHU (16A) metered + conn fee; sw nr; red long stay; TV; Eng spkn; adv bkg acc; tennis 300m. *"Beautiful location in Danube Gorge; friendly, helpful owner; clsd 1230-1430; poss flooding in wet weather/high rv level; gd walking/cycling; vg; excel site gd for walking cycling; rv canoeing."* **€26.00, 30 Apr-22 Sep.**　　　　2020

HECHTHAUSEN *1D2 (4km SW Rural) 53.62525, 9.20298* **Ferienpark & Campingpark Geesthof,** Am Ferienpark 1, 21755 Hechthausen-Klint **(04774) 512; info@geesthof.de; www.geesthof.de**

🏕 12 🐕 €2 👫 📶 ♨ ⚲ ♿ ∕ ᴹˢᴾ 🦋 🍴 ♈ ① ♨ 🛒 ⛺ ✂ 🚣(covrd, htd) 🎣

Site sp on B73 rd to Lamstedt. 3*, Med, hdg, mkd, pt shd, EHU (10A) €2; 60% statics; Eng spkn; boat hire; waterslide; watersports; fishing; bike hire; sauna. *"Superb site with mature trees around pitches; peaceful surroundings adj to rv, lake & woods; friendly staff."* **€22.50**　　　　2015

> ## "I need an on-site restaurant"
>
> We do our best to make sure site information is correct, but it is always best to check any must-have facilities are still available or will be open during your visit.

HEIDELBERG *3C2 (10km E Rural) 49.40175, 8.77916* **Campingplatz Haide,** Ziegelhäuser Landstrasse 91, 69151 Neckargemünd **(06223) 2111; info@camping-haide.de; www.camping-haide.de**

🐕 €2 👫 📶 ♨ ⚲ ∕ ᴹˢᴾ ♈ ① ♨ 🛒 nr ⛺

Take B37 fr Heidelberg, cross Rv Neckar by Ziegelhausen bdge by slip rd on R (avoid vill narr rd); foll site sp. Site on R bet rv & rd 1km W of Neckergemünd on rvside. Lge, hdstg, unshd, EHU (6A) €2.50 (long lead req); 5% statics; Eng spkn; bike hire; CKE. *"Conv Neckar Valley & Heidelberg; some rd, rlwy (daytime) & rv noise; NH/sh stay only; long attractive site along rv."* **€20.30, 1 Apr-31 Oct.**　　2016

HEIDELBERG *3C2* (12km E Urban) 49.39638, 8.79472
Campingplatz an der Friedensbrücke, Falltorstrasse 4, 69151 Neckargemünd (06223) 2178; nfo@camping platz-am-neckar.de; www.campingplatz-am-neckar.de

🏕 €1.50 👫 (htd) 🅆🅾 ♨ 🚿 ♿ 🖤 ∥ 🆖 ⛺ 🍽 ㉆ nr 🐾

Exit Heidelberg on S side of rv on B37; on ent Neckargemünd site sp to L (grey sp) mkd Poststrasse; site adj rv bdge. Fr S on B45 turn L sp Heidelberg, then R at camping sp. Fr A6 exit junc 33 onto B45 sp Neckargemünd, then as above. Foll sp - do not foll sat nav. 4*, Lge, unshd, EHU (6-16A) €5 or metered (poss rev pol); gas; TV; phone; Eng spkn; adv bkg acc; tennis. "Gd location by busy rv, poss liable to flood; immac, well-run, relaxing site; ask for rvside pitch (sm) - extra charge; transport to Heidelberg by boat, bus & train 10 mins walk fr site; owner will site o'fits; warm welcome; helpful staff; kayaking 500m; no plastic grndsheets; 26 steps up to main san facs; pool adj; gd rvside walks & cycling; TO 500m; gd NH facs, nr ent; recep clsd 1-3pm; Wifi €2 per day." €27.00, 1 Apr-21 Oct. **2018**

HEIDENAU *1D2* (2.6km W Rural) 53.30851, 9.62038
Ferienzentrum Heidenau, Minkens Fuhren, 21258 Heidenau (04182) 4272 or 4861; info@ferienzentrum-heidenau.de; www.ferienzentrum-heidenau.de

12 👫 (htd) ♨ 🖤 ∥ 🆖 🦋 ㊝ 🍽 ㉆ 🐾 🏔 🛶 (htd)

Exit A1 Hamburg-Bremen m'way junc 46 to Heidenau; foll sp. 4*, Lge, pt shd, EHU (16A) €2.50 (poss long lead req); bbq (sep area); 75% statics; phone; Eng spkn; sauna; cycling; games area; tennis; lake fishing; CKE. "Pleasant, wooded site; tourers on grass areas by lakes; clean, modern facs; ltd shop; gd; visa ccards not acc; pitches maybe unusable in v wet weather." €26.00 **2016**

HERSBRUCK *4E2* (6km E Rural) 49.51884, 11.49200
Pegnitz Camping, Eschenbacherweg 4, 91224 Hohenstadt (09154) 1500; camping.mueller@t-online.de; www.urlaub.nuernberger-land.de

👫 🅆🅾 ♨ 🖤 ∥ 🆖 ⒽⒸ nr 🐾 nr

Exit A9 junc 49 onto B14 dir Hersbruck & Sulzbach-Rosenberg. By-pass Hersbruck & after 8km turn L sp Hohenstadt. Bef vill, cross rv bdge & immed turn R at site sp. 3*, Med, pt shd, EHU (10A) inc; gas; 10% statics; train nr; Eng spkn; adv bkg acc; bike hire; CKE. "Lovely, peaceful, friendly site; gd walking & cycling area; helpful owner; vg san facs; train to Nuremberg; gd; stn 200m; recep clsd 1230-1330, waiting area outside." €19.50, 1 Mar-31 Oct. **2019**

HOCHDONN *1D1* (1.5km E Rural) 54.02395, 9.29381
Campingplatz Klein Westerland, Zur Holstenau 1, 25712 Hochdonn 04948 252345; info@campingplatz-klein-westerland.de; www.campingplatz-klein-westerland.de

🏕 €1.50 👫 ♨ 🖤 ∥ 🍽 Ⓗ 🐾

Fr A23, take exit 5 to Süderhastedt. Turn L on 431 to Hochdonn. Site sp. Canal ferry maybe diff for trailer c'vans, steep ramps. Med, pt shd, EHU; 70% statics; gd. "Interesting canal traff & lge locks at Brunsbüttel, 20km S; noisy, passing ships; only site on the Northsea-Baltic sea canal." €18.00, 1 Apr-31 Oct. **2016**

HOF *4F2* (10km NW Rural) 50.37494, 11.83804
Camping Auensee, 95189 Joditz-Köditz (09295) 381; rathaus@gemeinde-koeditz.de; www.gemeinde-koeditz.de

12 🏕 €1.50 👫 ♨ 🖤 ∥ 🆖 🦋 ㊝ 🐾 nr 🏔

Exit A9 at junc 31 Berg/Bad Steben. Turn R fr m'way & in 200m L to Joditz, foll site sp in vill (1-way ent/exit to site). 3*, Med, unshd, terr, EHU (16A) €1.80 or metered; sw; 75% statics; tennis; fishing; clsd 1230-1500; CKE. €16.00 **2016**

HOLZMINDEN *1D3* (10km N Rural) 51.88618, 9.44335 **Weserbergland Camping,** Weserstrasse 66, 37649 Heinsen (05535) 8733; info@weserbergland-camping.de; www.weserbergland-camping.de

🏕 €3 👫 (htd) 🅆🅾 ♨ 🚿 ♿ 🖤 ∥ 🦋 ㊝ 🍽 Ⓗ 🐾 nr 🏔 🎣 🛶 (htd)

Fr Holzminden on B83 twd Hameln, site sp in Heinsen cent twd rv bank. 3*, Med, pt shd, pt sl, EHU (10A) €1.90; gas; twin axles; red long stay; 50% statics; Eng spkn; adv bkg acc; ccard acc; bike hire; sauna; games area; CKE. "Beautiful site on rv bank; gd modern san facs (2015); gd area for walking/cycling; gd local bus service; accomodating owner; excel." €23.00, 1 Apr-31 Oct. **2015**

HOOKSIEL *1C2* (2km N Coastal) 53.64100, 8.03400
Nordsee Camping Hooksiel (Part Naturist), Bäderstrasse, 26434 Wangerland (04425) 958080; info@wangerland.de; www.wangerland.de

🏕 €3.10 👫 🅆🅾 ♨ 🚿 ♿ 🖤 ∥ 🆖 🦋 ㊝ Ⓗ 🐾 🏔 🎣 🐎

Exit A29 at junc 4 sp Fedderwarden to N. Thro Hooksiel, site sp 1.5km. 4*, V lge, hdstg, unshd, EHU (6-10A) inc; gas; 50% statics; bike hire; fishing; games area; watersports; sailing. "Main san facs excel but up 2 flights steps - otherwise facs in Portakabin; naturist site adj with same facs." €24.00, 25 Mar-17 Oct. **2016**

GERMANY

HORB AM NECKAR *3C3* (4km W Rural) *48.44513, 8.67300* **Camping Schüttehof,** Schütteberg 7-9, 72160 Horb-am-Neckar **(07451) 3951; camping-schuettehof@t-online.de; www.camping-schuettehof.de**

12 ⌂ €2 ⇋ ⓦ ⚓ ♨ ∥ 🦋 ⛲ ⓗ ▣ ⏧ ⚒ (htd) 🏊

Fr A81/E41 exit junc 30; take Freudenstadt rd out of Horb site sp. Med, mkd, pt shd, pt sl, EHU (16A) metered + conn fee; gas; 75% statics; adv bkg acc. *"Horb delightful Black Forest town; site close to saw mill & could be noisy; steep path to town; site clsd 1230-1430; superb, new, state of the art facs; peaceful; v pleasant helpful staff."* **€18.50**   **2017**

HOXTER *1D3* (2km S Rural) *51.76658, 9.38308* **Wesercamping Höxter,** Sportzentrum 4, 37671 Höxter **(05271) 2589; info@campingplatz-hoexter.de; www.campingplatz-hoexter.de**

⌂ €1.50 ⇋ ⓦ ⚓ ∥ 🦋 ♨ ⓗ ⚒ ⏧

Fr B83/64 turn E over rv sp Boffzen, turn R & site sp almost on rv bank. Turn R in 300m at green sp, turn L in car park. Med, pt shd, EHU (10-16A) €2; 60% statics; CKE. *"Lge open area for tourers; clsd 1300-1500; spaces beside rv; easy walk along rv to town."* **€19.50, 15 Mar-15 Oct.**   **2019**

"That's changed – Should I let the Club know?"

If you find something on site that's different from the site entry, fill in a report and let us know. See camc.com/europereport.

HUCKESWAGEN *1B4* (4km NF Rural) *51.15269, 7.36557* **Campingplatz Beverblick,** Grossberghausen 29, Mickenhagen, 42499 Hückeswagen **(02192) 83389; info@beverblick.de; www.beverblick.de**

12 ⌂ ⇋ (htd) ⓦ ⚓ ∥ 🦋 ▣ ⓗ ⚒

Fr B237 in Hückeswagen at traff lts take B483 sp Radevormwald. Over rv & in 500m turn R sp Mickenhagen. In 3km strt on (no thro rd), turn R after 1km, site on R. Steep app. Med, hdstg, unshd, pt sl, EHU (10A) metered; 90% statics. *"Few touring pitches; helpful owners; gd rest & bar; gd touring base; vg."* **€15.00**   **2020**

HUNFELD *1D4* (5km SW Rural) *50.65333, 9.72388* **Knaus Campingpark Praforst,** Dr Detlev-Rudelsdorff Allee 6, 36088 Hünfeld **(06652) 749090; huenfeld@knauscamp.de; www.knauscamp.de/huenfeld-praforst**

12 ⌂ €2 ⇋ ⓦ ⚓ ♨ ∥ 🦋 ▣ ⏧ ⚒ ⏧

Exit A7 junc 90 dir Hünfeld, foll sp thro golf complex. 5*, Med, mkd, pt shd, pt sl, EHU (16A) metered or €3.50; 40% statics; fishing; golf adj; games area; games rm. *"Excel san facs; gd walking/cycling."* **€33.00**   **2018**

IDAR OBERSTEIN *3B2* (15km N Rural) *49.80455, 7.26986* **Camping Harfenmühle,** 55758 Asbacherhütte **(06786) 7076; mail@harfenmuehle.de; www.camping-harfenmuehle.de**

12 ⌂ €3 ⇋ ⓦ ⚓ ⚑ ∥ MSP ♨ ⓣ 🍴 ⓗ ⛲ ⚒ ⏧

Fr rte 41 fr Idar twd Kirn, turn L at traff lts at Fischbach by-pass sp Herrstein/Morbach, site 3km past Herrstein vill. Sharp turn to site. 4*, Med, pt shd, EHU (16A) metered; gas; sw nr; TV; 50% statics; phone; Eng spkn; adv bkg acc; tennis; games rm; sauna; fishing; games area; golf 10km; CKE. *"Vg rest; o'night m'vans area; gd san facs but poss inadequate in high ssn; sep area late arr; barrier clsd 2200; gd site."* **€31.00**   **2019**

ILLERTISSEN *3D4* (11km S Rural) *48.14138, 10.10665* **Camping Christophorus Illertal,** Werte 6, 88486 Kirchberg-Sinningen **(07354) 663; info@camping-christophorus.de; www.camping-christophorus.de**

12 ⌂ €3.50 ⇋ (htd) ⓦ ⚓ ♨ ∥ ⓗ ⛲ ⚒ ⏧ ⚒ (covrd)

Exit A7/E43 junc 125 at Altenstadt. In cent of town turn L, then R immed after level x-ing. Foll site sp. 4*, Lge, pt shd, EHU (16A) €2.50 or metered; sw nr; 80% statics; Eng spkn; adv bkg acc; bike hire; fishing; sauna; CKE. *"Gd site; sm sep area for tourers; excel san facs."* **€26.00**   **2017**

ILLERTISSEN *3D4* (2km SW Rural) *48.21221, 10.08773* **Camping Illertissen,** Dietenheimerstrasse 91, 89257 Illertissen **(07303) 7888; campingplatz-illertissen@t-online.de; www.camping-illertissen.de**

⌂ €2 ⇋ ⓦ ⚓ ⚑ ∥ 🦋 ⓗ nr ⛲ ⚒ ⏧

Leave A7 at junc 124, twd Illertissen/Dietenheim; after rlwy x-ing turn R then L foll site sp. Off main rd B19 fr Neu Ulm-Memmingen fr N, turn R in Illertissen, toll sp. 3*, Sm, mkd, pt shd, terr, EHU (16A) €2 or metered; gas; 65% statics; ccard acc; CKE. *"Trains to Ulm & Kempten; 20 mins walk to town or cycle track; some pitches poss unrel in wet; site clsd bet 1300-1500 & 2200-0700; obliging owner; conv a'bahn; vg."* **€24.50, 1 Apr-31 Oct.**   **2018**

IMMENSTADT IM ALLGAU *3D4* (3km NW Rural) *47.57255, 10.19358* **Buchers Alpsee Camping,** Seestrasse 25, 87509 Bühl-am-Alpsee **(08323) 7726; mail@alpsee-camping.de; www.alpsee-camping.de**

12 ⌂ €3 ⇋ ⚓ ♨ ∥ 🦋 ⓗ ⚒ ⏧

Fr Immenstadt, W on B308; turn R dir Isny & Missen. In 1.3km turn L sp Bühl & site sp. 2*, Lge, unshd, EHU (16A) €2.50 (poss rev pol); gas; sw nr; Eng spkn; adv bkg acc. *"Lake sm but pleasant; gd mountain walks; friendly welcome; ski lift 3km; excel site, first class facs."* **€45.00**   **2019**

INGOLSTADT *4E3* (4.5km E Rural) *48.75416, 11.46277* **Campingpark Am Auwaldsee,** 85053 Ingolstadt **(0841) 9611616; ingolstadt@azur-camping.de; www.azur-camping.de**

12 €3.50 WD MSP nr

Exit A9/E45 junc 62 Ingolstadt Süd, foll sp for camp site & Auwaldsee. Lge, pt shd, EHU (10A) inc; gas; sw; 50% statics; bus; adv bkg rec; fishing; boating. *"Wooded site by lake; useful NH nr m'way; modern & clean san facs; gd location; excel facs; gd rest; excel."* **€27.00, G07.** **2018**

"I like to fill in the reports as I travel from site to site"

You'll find report forms at the back of this guide, or you can fill them in online at camc.com/europereport.

INZELL *4F4* (0.8km SW Rural) *47.76722, 12.75341* **Camping Lindlbauer,** Kreuzfeldstraße 44, 83334 Inzell **08665 928 99 88; info@camping-inzell.de; www.camping-inzell.de**

12 €4 (htd) WD MSP (covrd, htd)

Fr A8 exit 112 Traunstein-Siegsdorf. Take B306 twds Inzell. Foll sp in vill to campsite. Med, hdstg, mkd, unshd, terr, EHU (16A); twin axles; bus adj; Eng spkn; adv bkg acc; games area; CCI. *"Excel site; beautiful views; friendly, family run site; excel location for walking & cycling."* **€44.70** **2019**

JENA *2E4* (2km NE Rural) *50.93583, 11.60833* **Campingplatz Unter dem Jenzig,** Am Erlkönig 3, 07749 Jena **(03641) 666688; post@camping-jena.com; www.camping-jena.com**

12 €1 WD MSP nr nr

Exit A4/E40 junc 54 to Jena, then B88 for 4m N dir Naumberg. Turn R just outside Jena at campsite sp, R over blue bdge; site nr sports stadium/sw pool on L, sp. Med, unshd, EHU (10A) €2.50; phone; bus 1km; Eng spkn; adv bkg acc. *"Gd san facs in Portakabin; pool adj; sh walk to interesting town; gd cycle paths."* **€17.00** **2019**

JESTETTEN *3C4* (0.8km SW Urban) *47.64802, 8.56648* **Campingplatz & Schwimmbad,** Waldshuterstrasse 13, 79798 Jestetten **(07745) 1220; info@jestetten.de; www.jestetten.de**

(htd) WD nr nr (htd)

Site in town on B27 main rd, sp. Sm, pt shd, pt sl, EHU (10A) metered; bus at gate, train 500m; Eng spkn; adv bkg acc. *"Gd for walk or train Rhine Falls & Switzerland; shwr token inc; friendly; site in Schwimmbad grnds."* **€22.00, Mid May-Mid Sep.** **2015**

KALKAR *1A3* (5km N Rural) *51.76100, 6.28483* **Freitzeitpark Wisseler See,** Zum Wisseler-See 15, 47546 Kalkar-Wissel **(02824) 96310; info@wisseler-see.de; www.wisseler-see.de**

12 €3 WD MSP

Fr A3 take junc 4 onto B67 dir Kalkar & Wissel. Fr Kleve take B57 SE for 8km twd Kalkar, E to Wissel & foll camp sp. V lge, mkd, hdg, pt shd, serviced pitches; EHU (16A) inc; 75% statics; Eng spkn; adv bkg rec; bike hire; games area; watersports; tennis. *"Commercialised & regimented but conv NH Rotterdam ferry; gd facs; gd for children & teenagers."* **€25.00** **2016**

KAMENZ *2G4* (7km NE Rural) *51.30465, 14.15272* **Campingplatz Deutschbaselitz,** Grossteichstrasse 30, 01917 Kamenz **(03578) 301489; info@campingplatz-deutschbaselitz.com; www.campingplatz-deutschbaselitz.com**

(htd) WD MSP

Fr Kamenz N on rd S95 dir Wittichenau; at Schiedel turn R twd lake, site sp. 3*, Med, pt shd, EHU (16A) €3; bbq; cooking facs; sw; 10% statics; adv bkg acc; bike hire; games area; watersports; games rm; CKE. **€23.00, 1 Mar-31 Oct.** **2016**

KARLSHAGEN *2G1* (2km E Coastal) *54.11769, 13.84477* **Dünencamp,** Zeltplatzstraße; 17449 Ostseebad; Karlshagen **038371 20291; camping@karlshagen.de; www.duenencamp.de**

12 €4 (htd) WD MSP adj

Site sp fr Karlshagen along Zeltplatzstrasse. Lge, mkd, shd, pt sl, EHU (16A) €2 (or metered); phone; Eng spkn. *"Site has direct access to long clean sandy beach; long mains lead may be needed for some pitches; conv for visiting Peenemünde; gd site."* **€26.00** **2016**

"We must tell the Club about that great site we found"

Get your site reports in by mid-August and we'll do our best to get your updates into the next edition.

KARLSRUHE *3C3* (7km E Rural) *49.00788, 8.48303* **Azur Campingpark Turmbergblick,** Tiengenerstrasse 40, 76227 Karlsruhe-Durlach **(0721) 497236; karlsruhe@azur-camping.de; www.azur-camping.de**

€3.50 (htd) WD MSP

Exit A5/E35 junc 44 dir Durlach/Grötzingen onto B10 & foll sp to site 3km. Lge, mkd, pt shd, EHU (10A) €3 (long lead poss req); gas; 20% statics; Eng spkn; adv bkg acc; ccard acc; tennis; CKE. *"NH conv to a'bahn; adequate, clean san facs; clsd 1230-1400; expensive for average site; Karlsruhe worth a visit."* **€32.00, 1 Apr-31 Oct.** **2016**

KASSEL *1D4* (22km S Rural) *51.17757, 9.47781*
Camping Fuldaschleife, zum Bruch 6, 34302
Guxhagen-Büchenwerra **(0566) 5961044; info@
fuldaschleife.de; www.fuldaschleife.de**

🏕 €1.50 ♟(htd) ⬜ ⚓ ♨ 🚿 ⊟ ♿ ⵏ 🍴 ⒣ ♨ 🛒 nr 🏔 🚣

Exit A7 at J81 twrds Guxhagen. Foll sp. Site in 4km.
4*, Sm, mkd, pt shd, bbq; twin axles; 60% statics;
bus adj; Eng spkn; adv bkg acc; ccard acc; games
area; CKE. *"Pleasant site adj rv; helpful staff; boating,
canoeing & cycling rtes fr site; Hann Munden &
Gottingen worth visiting; conv for N, S, E & W Germany;
excel."* **€22.00, 1 Mar-31 Oct.** **2016**

KASTELLAUN *3B2* (0.8km SE Rural) *50.06846,
7.45382* **Burgstadt Camping Park,** Südstrasse 34,
56288 Kastellaun **(06762) 40800; info@burgstadt.de;
www.burgstadt.de**

12 🏕 €2 ♟(htd) ⬜ ⚓ ♨ 🚿 ⊟ ♿ ⵏ 🦋 ⒣ ♨ 🍴 ⒣ 🏔

Exit A61 junc 42 dir Emmelshausen onto L206/L213
for 1.2km; turn L onto B327; cont for 13.5km to
Kastellaun. Site adj hotel on B237. Med, mkd, hdstg,
unshd, terr, EHU (16A) metered; bbq; Eng spkn; adv
bkg acc; ccard acc; tennis nr; sauna; solarium; CKE.
*"Lge pitches; clean site; excel, clean san facs; o'night
m'van area; helpful staff; conv touring base; htd covrd
pool 300m; riding & kayaking nrby; fitness & beauty
cent in hotel adj; excel; v peaceful."* **€24.00** **2015**

KEHL *3B3* (3km S Urban) *48.5615, 7.80861* DCC
Campingpark Kehl-Strassburg, Rheindammstrasse 1,
77694 Kehl-Kronenhof **(07851) 2603; Campingpark
Kehl@aol.com; www.campingplatz-kehl.de**

🏕 €2 ♟(htd) ⬜ ⚓ ♿ ⊟ ⵏ ♨ ⒣ 🛒 🏔

Fr A5/E35, take exit 54 onto B28 at Appenweier
twd Kehl & foll site sp. 4*, Lge, pt shd, EHU (16A)
metered + conn fee (long lead poss req); gas,
15% statics; bus 1km; Eng spkn; adv bkg acc; ccard
acc; CKE *"Peaceful site adj Rv Rhine; excel rest &
modern san facs; sm pitches; pleasant rv walk & cycle
paths to town; sw pool adj; barrier clsd 1300-1500."*
€25.00, 15 Mar-31 Oct. **2019**

KELBRA *2E4* (2km W Rural) *51.42551, 11.00307*
Seecamping Kelbra, Langestrasse 150, 06537 Kelbra
(034651) 45290; info@seecampingkelbra.de

12 🏕 €2 ♟(htd) ⬜ ⚓ ⵏ 🦋 🍴 ⒣ ♨ 🛒 🏔 🚣 sand 1km

Exit A38 at Berga (bet junc 12 & 14); on app to
town turn L at traff lts onto B85 to Kelbra; go
thro chicane in vill, then R onto L234/L1040 dir
Sonderhausen; site sp. L234 is Langestrasse. Lge,
unshd, pt sl, EHU (16A) €2; bbq (elec, gas); sw nr; TV;
phone; bus adj; Eng spkn; adv bkg acc; games area;
CKE. *"Gd touring base & walking area; boat hire on site;
vg; 2 toilet blocks now (2015); NH outside main gates."*
€18.50 **2015**

KEMPTEN (ALLGAU) *3D4* (25km E Rural) *47.80283,
10.55377* **Camping Platz Elbsee,** Am Elbsee 3, 87648
Aitrang **08 34 32 48; info@elbsee.de; www.elbsee.de**

12 🏕 €4.50 ♟(htd) ⬜ ⚓ ♨ 🚿 ⊟ ♿ ⵏ 🦋 ♨ ⒣ ♨ 🛒 🏔 🚣

S on A7. Take J134 dir Marktoberdorf on B12. Take
exit twd Unterthingau on OAL10. Turn L on OAL3,
cont onto OAL 5. Turn R on Am Elbsee. Foll sp.
5*, Lge, hdg, mkd, hdstg, pt shd, EHU (16A); bbq;
cooking facs; twin axles; bus 0.75km; Eng spkn; adv
bkg acc; ccard acc; games rm; CCI. *"Excel site; gd
base; lake adj; many local historical places & amazing
architecture; camp has much to offer - peace & quiet,
spa art, yoga."* **€29.70** **2019**

KINDING *4E3* (5km E Rural) *49.00328, 11.45200*
Camping Kratzmühle, Mühlweg 2, 85125 Kinding-
Pfraundorf **(08461) 64170; info@kratzmuehle.de;
www.kratzmuehle.de**

12 🏕 €2 ♟(htd) ⬜ ⚓ ♨ 🚿 ⊟ ⵏ 🦋 ♨ ⒣ 🛒 🏔

Exit A9/E45 junc 58, dir Beilngries. Site sp. 4*,
Lge, pt shd, serviced pitches; EHU (16A) €2.50; gas;
cooking facs; sw nr; red long stay; 40% statics; adv
bkg acc; ccard acc; games area; sauna; CKE. *"Beautiful
situation; conv NH for a'bahn; ideal boating & bathing,
public access to lake; clsd 1300-1500; poss mosquito
prob; helpful staff."* **€26.00** **2018**

KIRCHHEIM *1D4* (5km SW Rural) *50.81435, 9.51805*
Camping Seepark, Reimboldshäuserstraße, 36275
Kirchheim **(06628) 1525; info@campseepark.de;
www.campseepark.de**

12 🏕 ♟(htd) ⬜ ⚓ ♿ ⊟ ⵏ 🦋 🍴 ⒣ ♨ 🛒 🏔 🚣 (covrd)

Exit A7 at Kirchheim junc 87, site clearly sp. 5*,
Lge, mkd, pt shd, pt sl, terr, EHU (16A) €3 metered;
gas; sw; red long stay; 50% statics; phone; bus 500m;
adv bkg acc; ccard acc; sauna; golf 3km; games area;
tennis; CKF *"Gd walking; helpful owner; o'night m'vans
area; excel site - leisure facs pt of lge hotel complex;
NH only."* **€26.00** **2017**

KIRKEL *3B3* (1km S Urban) *49.28175, 7.22860*
Caravanplatz Mühlenweiher, Unnerweg 5c,
66459 Kirkel-Neuhäusel **(06849) 1810555; info@
camping-kirkel.de; www.caravanplatz-kirkel.de**

12 🏕 €1.15 ♟(htd) ⬜ ⚓ ♿ ⊟ ⵏ 🍴 ⒣ 🛒 nr

Fr A6 junc 7 & fr A8 junc 28, take dir into town & foll
sp for 'schwimmbad'. Site on L past pool, well sp.
3*, Med, hdstg, mkd, pt shd, EHU (10A) €3 or metered
+ conn fee (poss rev pol); gas; TV (pitch); 60% statics;
phone; CKE. *"Gd welcome; excel area for cycling; noise
fr pool & church bells all night; pool adj; site/office clsd
1230-1500."* **€15.00** **2016**

GERMANY

KITZINGEN 3D2 (3km E Urban) 49.73233, 10.16833
Camping Schiefer Turm, Marktbreiter Straße 20,
97318 Kitzingen-Hohenfeld (09321) 33125; info@
camping-kitzingen.de; www.camping-kitzingen.de

🌳♿ €1.50 🚻 wc ♨ ⚫ ⁄ MsP ⊕ ♨ 🛒

Fr A3 take exit junc 74 sp Kitzingen/Schwarzach
or exit 72 Würzburg-Ost, or fr A7 exit junc 103
Kitzingen. Site sp in town 'Schwimmbad'. 3*, Med,
mkd, pt shd, EHU (16A) €2 or metered; gas; bus; ccard
acc. *"Bird reserve; pleasant town in evening; gd cycling;
busy NH high ssn; san facs up steps; excel Lido adj."*
€18.00, 1 Apr-11 Oct. 2020

KOBLENZ 3B2 (4km NE Urban) 50.36611, 7.60361
Camping Rhein-Mosel, Schartwiesenweg 6, 56070
Koblenz-Lützel (0261) 82719; info@camping-
rhein-mosel.de; www.camping-rhein-mosel.de

🌳♿ wc ♨ ⚫ ⁄ MsP ⚫ ⊕ ♨ 🛒

Fr Koblenz heading N on B9 turn off dual c'way at
sp for Neuendorf just bef Mosel rv bdge; foll sp to
Neuendorf vill. Or heading S on B9 exit dual c'way
at camping sp (2nd sp) bef Koblenz; fr Koblenz cent
foll sp for 'Altstadt' until Baldwinbrücke (bdge);
N over bdge instead of foll sp along S bank of Rv
Mosel; R after bdge, then foll sp; site on N side of
junc Rhine/Mosel rvs. 2*, Lge, hdstg, pt shd, pt sl,
EHU (6-16A) €2.05 or metered (long lead poss req);
cooking facs; Eng spkn; adv bkg rec; CKE. *"Pleasant,
informal site in beautiful location; muddy in wet; staff
helpful; no veh acc after 2200; adj ferry to city & easy
cycle rte; mkt Sat; sep dog shwrs; flea mkt Sun; 'Rhine
in Flames' fireworks 2nd Sat in Aug - watch fr site;
MH stopover called Knaus Campingpark just outside
main gates, basic price €12.50, both sites under same
owner."* €33.00, 1 May-20 Oct. 2016

KOBLENZ 3B2 (12km SW Urban) 50.30972, 7.50166
**Campinginsel Winningen (previously Campingplatz
Ziehfurt),** Inselweg 10, 56333 Winningen (02606) 357
or 1800; ferieninsel-winningen@t-online.de;
www.mosel-camping.com

🌳 €3 🚻 wc ♨ ⚫ ⁄ MsP ⊕ ♨ 🛒 ⚫

Exit A61/E31 junc 38 to Winningen. In Winningen
turn R twds Cochem B416, then L at sw pool. In
approx 100m turn R and then in 700m turn L over
bdge to site recep. Lge, pt shd, EHU (16A) €2.50;
50% statics; Eng spkn. *"Cent of wine-growing country;
boat trips avail fr Koblenz; cycle rtes; scenic area;
poss flooding if v high water; pool 300m; lively site
when busy; gd, modern san facs up steep steps but
poss stretched when busy; excel rest; excel site."*
€25.00, 1 May-1 Oct. 2017

KOBLENZ 3B2 (8km SW Rural) 50.33194, 7.55277
Camping Gülser Moselbogen, Am Gülser
Moselbogen 20, 56072 Koblenz-Güls (0261) 44474;
info@moselbogen.de; www.moselbogen.de

12 🌳 €4 (htd) wc ♨ ♿ ⚫ ⁄ MsP ⊕ nr 🛒 nr ⚫

Fr A61/E31 exit 38 dir Koblenz/Metternich. After
400m turn R at rndabt dir Winningen. Stay on
this rd to T-junc in Winningen, turn L dir Koblenz-
Güls, site sp on R in 3km. 4*, Med, hdg, mkd, pt
shd, EHU (16A) €1.50 + conn fee; gas; TV (pitch);
50% statics; phone; Eng spkn; adv bkg acc; ccard acc;
bike hire; CKE. *"High quality, high-tech san facs; no
vehicles 1200-1400; poss subject to flooding; excel."*
€28.00 2019

> ## "I need an on-site restaurant"
>
> We do our best to make sure site information
> is correct, but it is always best to check any
> must-have facilities are still available or will
> be open during your visit.

KOLN 1B4 (4km NE Urban) 50.96305, 6.98361
Reisemobilhafen Köln, An der Schanz, 50735 Köln
017 84674591 (mob); info@reisemobilhafen-koeln.de

12 🌳 ⁄ MsP 🛒 nr ⊕ nr ⚫ nr

Fr A1 Köln ring rd exit junc 100 dir Köln 'Zentrum'
until reach rv. Turn L & foll sp to site. M'vans only.
Sm, mkd, hdstg, EHU (10A) €1 for 12 hrs; own san req;
bus, train nr. *"Adj Rv Rhine; must have change for elec
& water (metered) - €0.50, parking (€10 note) etc; easy
access to city cent; site is unmanned; cycle rte to city,
zoo & botanic gdns."* €10.00 2017

KOLN 1B4 (8km SE Rural) 50.8909, 7.02306
Campingplatz Berger, Uferstrasse 71, 50996
Köln-Rodenkirchen (0221) 9355240; camping.
berger@t-online.de; www.camping-berger-koeln.de

12 🌳 €1 🚻(htd) wc ♨ ♿ ⚫ ⁄ MsP 🦋 ⊕ ♨ ⚫ 🛒

Fr A4 turn S onto A555 at Köln-Sud exit 12. Leave
A555 at Rodenkirchen exit 3. At 1st junc foll site
sp to R. Fr A3 Frankfurt/Köln a'bahn, take A4 twd
Aachen (Köln ring rd); exit at Köln Sud; foll sp
Bayenthal; at lge rndabt turn R sp Rheinufer & R
again at camp sp, under a'bahn. App rd narr & lined
with parked cars. Lge, pt shd, EHU (4-10A) €1.50; gas;
cooking facs; red long stay; 80% statics; phone; bus
500m; Eng spkn; ccard acc; bike hire; CKE. *"Pleasant,
popular, wooded site on banks of Rhine; rvside pitches
best; excel rest; helpful staff; gd dog walking; cycle
path to city cent; conv cathedral, zoo & museums;
some noise fr Rhine barges; don't arr early eve at w/end
as narr app rd v busy; pitches poss muddy after rain;
san facs up steps - poss clsd 2300-0600; gd site; vg
facs; need car/bike to get around."* €28.00 2018

KOLN *1B4* (6km S Urban) *50.90263, 6.99070*
Campingplatz der Stadt Köln, Weidenweg 35, 51105 Köln-Poll **(0221)** 831966; info@camping-koeln.de; www.camping-koeln.de

€2.50 (htd) nr

Exit fr A4 (E40) at junc 13 for Köln-Poll-Porz at E end of bdge over Rv Rhine, 3km S of city. At end of slip rd, turn L twd Poll & Köln. Cont about 1000m turn L at sp just bef level x-ing, then foll site sp. Narr lane to ent. Lge, pt shd, EHU (10A) €3.50 (some rev pol & long lead poss req); gas; cooking facs; phone; Eng spkn; CKE. *"Tram to city over rv bdge; rural site in urban setting on bank of Rv Rhine & subject to flooding; clsd 1230-1430; gd undercover cooking facs; gd refurbished san facs on 1st floor; friendly site; v busy at w/end; rvside cycle track to city; cycle theft a problem (store in caged kitchen o'night); friendly owner; site in green zone."* **€29.40, 1 Apr-15 Oct.** 2016

KONIGSSEE *4G4* (1km N Rural) *47.5992, 12.98933*
Camping Mühlleiten, Königsseerstrasse 70, 83471 Königssee **(08652)** 4584; info@muehlleiten.eu; www.camping-muehlleiten.de

12 €2.50 nr 1km

On R of B20 Berchtesgaden-Königssee. 3*, Med, unshd, EHU (16A) €3 or metered; gas; golf 6km; CKE. *"Beautiful area; friendly staff; excel san facs; excel site with mixed MH's, c'van and camping; walking trails; free/red bus fares with visitor card; ski lift 500m; off clsd 1200-1500 daily."* **€30.00** 2016

KONIGSSEE *4G4* (2km N Rural) *47.59445, 12.98583*
Camping Grafenlehen, Königsseer Fussweg 71, 83471 Königssee **(08652)** 6554488; camping-grafenlehen@t-online.de; www.camping-grafenlehen.de

€2 (htd) MSP nr

On B20 fr Berchtesgaden 5km to Königssee. Where car park with traff lts is ahead, turn R sp Schönau, site on R. Lge, pt shd, terr, EHU (16A) metered; 10% statics; site clsd Nov to mid-Dec; CKE. *"Pleasant site; spectacular views; gd san facs; superb walking; cycle path by rv; gd value rest; 30 mins drive Salzburg Park & Ride; conv Berchtesgaden."* **€31.00, 1 Jan-1 Nov & 15 Dec-31 Dec.** 2015

KONIGSTEIN *2G4* (1km E Rural) *50.92222, 14.08833*
Camping Königstein, Schandauerstrasse 25e, 01824 Königstein **(035021)** 68224; info@camping-koenigstein.de; www.camping-koenigstein.de

€3 MSP nr

Foll B172 SE fr Dresden/Pirna. Site 500m past Königstein rlwy stn. Turn L over rlwy x-ing & R into site ent on Rv Elbe. 3*, Med, unshd, pt sl, EHU (10-16A) €2.60; gas; red long stay; 15% statics; adv bkg acc; sep car park. *"Gd san facs; lovely location nr national parks & Czech border; on Elbe cycle path; frequent trains to Dresden; boat trips; gates clsd 1300-1500; dogs not acc Jul/Aug; site updated to hg std (2018)."* **€24.00, 25 Mar-31 Oct.** 2018

KONIGSTEIN *2G4* (3km E Rural) *50.91500, 14.10730*
Caravan Camping Sächsische Schweiz, Dorfplatz 181d, 01824 Kurort-Gohrisch **350 21 59107;** Info@caravan-camping-saechsischeschweiz.de; www.caravan-camping-saechsischeschweiz.de

12 €2 nr

Fr Königstein foll B172 E dir Bad Schandau. Fork R dir Gohrisch for 2.5km, turn L into Dorfplatz & foll site sp. Med, hdstg, hdg, mkd, pt shd, pt sl, EHU (16A) metered; bbq; cooking facs; red long stay; TV (pitch); 5% statics; bus 500m; Eng spkn; adv bkg acc; bike hire; games area; sauna. *"Excel site; gd touring base; htd covrd pool 4km; interesting area; guided walks."* **€22.00** 2020

KONSTANZ *3D4* (13km N Rural) *47.74596, 9.14701*
Camping Klausenhorn, Hornwiesenstrasse, 78465 Dingelsdorf **(07533)** 6372; info@camping-klausenhorn.de; www.camping-klausenhorn.de

(htd) nr

Site sp N of Dingelsdorf on lakeside. 4*, Lge, hdstg, mkd, pt shd, EHU (10A) inc; bbq; 50% statics; bus 500m; Eng spkn; adv bkg acc; ccard acc; boating; games area; sep car park; CKE. *"Excel site; lake adj; 1st class san facs; v helpful recep; free bus svrs fr site."* **€30.00, 27 Mar-5 Oct.** 2016

KONSTANZ *3D4* (12km W Rural) *47.69871, 9.04603*
Camping Sandseele, Bradlengasse 24, 78479 Niederzell **(07534)** 7384; info@sandseele.de; www.sandseele.de

MSP

Clearly sp off B33 Konstanz-Radolfzell rd. Foll sp on island & sm multiple sp. Lge, pt shd, EHU (16A) €3.50; gas; sw; 30% statics; watersports. *"Insect repellent rec, excel san facs; sep car park high ssn; excel walking & cycling all over island; poor layout."* **€33.00, 18 Mar-9 Oct.** 2016

KRANICHFELD *2E4* (4km NW Rural) *50.87216, 11.17843* **Campingplatz Stausee Hohenfelden,** 99448 Hohenfelden **(036450)** 42081; info@stausee-hohenfelden.de; www.stausee-hohenfelden.de

12 €2.50

Fr A4/E40 take exit 47a S twd Kranichfeld. Site clearly sp by lake along rough rd. 4*, V lge, mkd, pt shd, pt sl, terr, EHU (10A) €4.50; bbq; cooking facs; sw; red long stay; 50% statics; adv bkg acc; ccard acc; bike hire; boating; lake adj; CKE. *"Woodland, lakeside walks; gd."* **€24.00** 2019

GERMANY

KRESSBRONN AM BODENSEE *3D4* (9km NE Rural)
47.63395, 9.6477 **Gutshof-Camping,** Badhütten 1,
88069 Laimnau **(07543) 96330; gutshof.camping@
t-online.de; www.gutshof-camping.de**

Fr Kressbronn take B467 to Tettnang & Ravensburg.
In 3km immed after x-ing Rv Argen turn R & site
sp for approx 3km. Take care on final app rd. Dark,
steep and twisty, great care needed. 4*, V lge, mkd,
hdg, pt shd, serviced pitches; EHU (16A) metered;
gas; red long stay; 40% statics; adv bkg acc; CKE. *"Sep
area for naturists; gd facs; v rural site; clean, quiet &
pleasant; excel."* €29.00, 7 Apr-3 Oct, G15.   2016

KRESSBRONN AM BODENSEE *3D4* (2km SW Rural)
47.58718, 9.58281 **Campingplatz Irisweise,** Tunau 16,
88079 Kressbronn **(07543) 8010; info@campingplatz-
irisweise.de; www.campingplatz-irisweise.de**

Fr E or W take exit off B31 bypass for Kressbronn,
site well sp. 4*, Lge, hdg, mkd, pt shd, EHU (10A)
metered + conn fee; gas; bbq; sw nr; 10% statics;
phone; Eng spkn; watersports; sailing; CKE. *"Steamer
trips on lake; no car access 2100-0700, park outside
site; sep naturist beach; excel san facs but some dist fr
touring pitches; gd."* €28.00, 22 Mar-21 Oct.   2019

KRUMBACH *4E4* (7km SW Rural) *48.22720, 10.29280*
See Camping Günztal, Oberrieder Weiherstrasse 5,
86488 Breitenthal **(08282) 881870;
info@see-camping-guenztal.de; www.see-camping-
guenztal.de**

W fr Krumbach on rd 2018, in Breitenthal turn S twd
Oberried & Oberrieder Weiher, site sp on lakeside.
Med, hdstg, mkd, pt shd, EHU (10A) inc; bbq; sw; TV;
30% statics; adv bkg acc; games area; watersports;
fishing. €21.00, 15 Apr-30 Oct.   2016

KULMBACH *4E2* (11km NE Rural) *50.16050, 11.51605*
Campingplatz Stadtsteinach, Badstrasse 5, 95346
Stadtsteinach **(09225) 800394; info@campingplatz-
stadtsteinach.de; www.campingplatz-stadtsteinach.de**

Fr Kulmbach take B289 to Untersteinach (8km);
turn L to Stadtsteinach; turn R at camping sp &
foll rd for 1km. Site also sp fr N side of town on
B303. Or fr A9/E51 exit junc 39 onto B303 NW
to Stadtsteinach. 4*, Med, mkd, pt shd, pt sl, EHU
(6-16A) €2.50; bbq (charcoal, gas); sw; 60% statics;
Eng spkn; adv bkg acc; ccard acc; rv fishing; bike
hire; tennis; CKE. *"Excel site in beautiful countryside;
htd pool adj; excel, modern facs; highly rec."*
€24.00, 1 Mar-1 Nov.   2019

LAHNSTEIN *3B2* (3km E Urban) *50.30565, 7.61313*
Kur-Campingplatz Burg Lahneck, Am Burgweg,
56112 Lahnstein-Oberlahnstein **(02621) 2765;
http://www.camping-burg-lahneck.de**

Take B42 fr Koblenz over Lahn Rv, if fr low bdge
turn L immed after church & sp fr there; if fr high
level bdge thro sh tunnel turn L at 1st rd on L sp
to Burg-Lahneck - site sp on L. 4*, Med, pt shd, pt sl,
EHU (16A) metered + conn fee; 10% statics; Eng spkn.
*"Gd views over Rhine; scenic area; delightful, helpful
owner v particular about pitching; gd size pitches;
immac, well-run site."* €21.50, 29 Mar-3 Nov.   2020

LAHNSTEIN *3B2* (6km SE Urban) *50.27393, 7.64098*
Campingplatz Uferwiese, Am Campingplatz 1,
56338 Braubach **(02627) 8762; uferwiese@web.de;
www.campingplatz-braubach.de**

Take B42 S twd Rüdesheim. Site behind hotel
opp church. Med, shd, EHU (16A) €2 (poss rev pol);
50% statics; bus; CKE. *"Scenic on Rv Rhine; poss
flooding after heavy rain; gd san facs; no shd on rvside
pitches."* €21.50, 15 Apr-25 Oct.   2015

LAHR (SCHWARZWALD) *3B3* (9km SE Rural)
48.29999, 7.94395 **Ferienparadies Schwarzwälder
Hof,** Tretenhofstrasse 76, 77960 Seelbach **(07823)
960950; info@spacamping.de; www.campingplatz-
schwarzwaelder-hof.de**

Fr A5 take exit 56 to Lahr. In 5km turn R twd
Seelbach & Schuttertal. Thro town & site on S o'skts
of Seelbach just after town boundary. 5*, Med, mkd,
hdstg, pt shd, pt sl, terr, serviced pitches; EHU (10A)
metered + conn fee; gas; 10% statics; Eng spkn; adv
bkg req; ccard acc; CKE. *"Vg touring base; o'night
m'vans area; well-laid out pitches & excel facs; many
gd mkd walks; lake adj; htd pool adj; gd programme of
events in Seelbach; within easy reach of Strasbourg."*
€37.00   2015

LAICHINGEN *3D3* (6km SE Rural) *48.47560, 9.7458*
Camping & Freizeitzentrum Heidehof, Heidehof
strasse 50, 89150 Laichingen-Machtolsheim
**(07333) 6408; info@heidenhof.info; www.camping-
heidehof.de**

Exit A8 junc 61 dir Merklingen. At T-junc turn R sp
Laichingen. In 3km site sp to L. 4*, V lge, hdg, mkd,
hdstg, pt shd, pt sl, EHU (10-16A) €2 or metered;
gas; red long stay; 95% statics; adv bkg acc; bike hire;
sauna; CKE. *"Blaubeuren Abbey & Blautopf (blue pool
of glacial origin) worth visit; sep area for o'nighters
immed bef main camp ent - poss current when wet; hdstg
pitches sm & sl; vg rest; gd NH; clean modern facs; lack
of elec boxes; no water taps excep at facs; whole site
on uneven sl; arr early to get nr elec."* **€27.50   2019**

LANDSBERG AM LECH *4E4* (4km SE Rural) 48.03195, 10.88526 **DCC Campingpark Romantik am Lech,** Pössinger Au 1, 86899 Landsberg-am-Lech **(08191) 47505; campingparkgmbh@aol.com; www.camping platz-landsberg.de**

[icons] 12 🐕 €1 👪 WD ▲ & 🚻 ✏ MSP 🦋 ⊤ ⓗ nr 🍖 🗜 nr ⛺

Not rec to tow thro Landsberg. If app fr S, get onto rd fr Weilheim & foll sp on app to Landsberg. Fr other dir, exit junc 26 fr a'bahn A96 Landsberg Ost, then app town via Muchenstrasse. Foll sp dir Weilheim, after 400m turn R & foll site sp. 4*, Lge, mkd, hdg, pt shd, pt sl, EHU (16A) metered (some rev pol); gas; 50% statics; Eng spkn; adv bkg acc; tennis; bike hire; CKE. *"V pleasant site; excel, clean facs; nature reserve on 2 sides; gd walking & cycling; attractive old town; pool 3km; site clsd 1300-1500 & 2200-0700."* **€19.00** 2015

LANDSHUT *4F3* (3km NE Urban) 48.55455, 12.1795 **Camping Landshut,** Breslauerstrasse 122, 84028 Landshut **(0871) 53366; www.landshut.de**

[icons] 🐕 €1.50 👪 WD ▲ & 🚻 ✏ MSP 🦋 ⊤ ⓗ nr 🍖 🗜 nr

Fr A92/E53 exit junc 14 onto B299 dir Landshut N. After approx 5km turn L at int'l camping sp & foll site sp. 2*, Med, pt shd, EHU (16A) €2.50; bbq; 10% statics; CKE. *"Well-run, friendly site; gd san facs; htd pool 3km; beautiful medieval town & castle - easy cycle rte."* **€17.00, 1 Apr-30 Sep.** 2016

LECHBRUCK *4E4* (3km NE Rural) 47.71169, 10.81872 **Via Claudia Camping,** Via Claudia 6, 86983 Lechbruck **(08862) 8426; info@camping-lechbruck.de; www.via-claudia-camping.de**

[icons] 12 🐕 €3.50 👪 WD ▲ & 🚻 ✏ MSP 🦋 ♈ ⊤ ⓗ 🍖 ⛺ ✎

A7 exit 138 Nesselwang. Sp Seeg, foll Oa1 round Seeg to Roßhaupten. Then B16 sp Markt-Oberdorf. 1st exit to Lechbruck. Thro Lechbruch to site on R by lake. 4*, Lge, hdstg, mkd, pt shd, terr, EHU (10-16A) €2.65; gas; sw; twin axles; red long stay; TV; 50% statics; Eng spkn; adv bkg acc; ccard acc; watersports; games rm; CKE. *"Pleasant, peaceful, lakeside site; o'night m'van area; fac to a high standard; pool 500m; mini golf; gd welcome; v helpful; volleyball; archery; cont investment in site fr new owners; bus 1.5km; watersports; mountain tours; hiking; cycle trails; model aircraft; spa; rafting; traditional craft demos; skiing; local historic buildings; excel."* **€34.00** 2018

LEER (OSTFRIESLAND) *1B2* (7km W Rural) 53.22416, 7.41891 **Camping Ems-Marina Bingum,** Marinastrasse 14-16, 26789 Leer-Bingum **(0491) 64447; into-camping-bingum@t-online.de; www.ems-marina-bingum.de**

[icons] 12 🐕 €3.50 👪 WD ▲ & 🚻 ✏ MSP 🦋 ⓗ 🍖 🗜 nr ⛺

Leave A32/E12 junc 12; site 500m S of Bingum; well sp. Lge, pt shd, EHU (16A) €2.50 or metered; gas; red long stay; 65% statics; adv bkg acc; bike hire; CKE. *"Gate clsd 1230-1500."* **€23.00** 2016

LEIPHEIM *3D3* (3.5km NNW Rural) 48.46566, 10.2035 **Camping Schwarzfelder Hof,** Schwarzfelderweg 3, Riedheim, 89340 Leipheim **(08221) 72628; info@ schwarzfelder-hof.de; www.schwarzfelder-hof.de**

[icons] 12 🐕 €3.90 (htd) WD ▲ & 🚻 ✏ 🦋 ⊤ ⓗ nr 🍖 🗜 nr ⛺

Fr A8 exit junc 66 Leipheim onto B10. In Leipheim foll sp Langenau & Riedheim, site sp. Do not confuse with Laupheim 25km S of Ulm on B30. Sm, hdstg, pt shd, serviced pitches; EHU (16A) €2.50; bbq; 50% statics; train 1km; Eng spkn. *"Peaceful, delightful, farm-based site on site of old quarry; ideal for children & adults; welcoming, helpful owner; lge pitches; vg san facs but ltd; farm animals & riding for children; conv Ulm; recep open 0800-1000 & 1730-2000; poss noisy youth groups; conv NH for m'way."* **€25.50** 2019

LEIPZIG *2F4* (7km NW Urban) 51.37030, 12.31375 **Campingplatz Auensee,** Gustav-Esche Strasse 5, 04159 Leipzig **(0341) 4651600; leipzig@knauscamp.de; www.camping-auensee.de**

[icons] 12 🐕 €2 (htd) WD ▲ & 🚻 ✏ MSP ⊤ 🍖 🗜 nr ⛺

Fr A9/E51 exit junc 16 onto B6 two Leipzig. In Leipzig-Wahren turn R at 'Rathaus' sp Leutzsch (camping symbol), site on R in 1.5km, sp. 4*, Lge, hdstg, mkd, pt shd, EHU (16A) €3; bbq; cooking facs; TV; phone; bus; Eng spkn; adv bkg acc; ccard acc; CKE. *"Roomy, well-run, clean site; plentiful, excel, modern san facs; gd size pitches; friendly, helpful staff; Lake Auensee 500m; tram 1.5km; 10 mins walk to tram for city cent or bus stop at site ent; excel."* **€29.00** 2018

LEMGO *1C3* (0.6km E Urban) 52.02503, 8.90874 **Campingpark Lemgo,** Regenstorstrasse 10, 32657 Lemgo **(05261) 14858; info@camping-lemgo.de; www.camping-lemgo.de**

[icons] 12 🐕 €2 👪 🚻 ✏ ⓗ nr 🗜 nr ⛺

Exit A2 junc 28 onto L712N to Lemgo; at traff lts turn L following L712; at rndbt take Bismarckstrasse exit; at traff lts turn R into Regenstorstrasse. Site sp. 3*, Med, pt shd, EHU (6A) metered + conn fee; 25% statics; adv bkg rec. *"Pleasant site in cent of lovely medieval town; o'night m'vans area; pool 200m; sm, modern, clean san facs."* **€26.60** 2019

LIETZOW *2G1* (0.2km N Coastal) 54.48358, 13.50846 **Störtebecker Camp,** Gästehaus Lietzow, Waldstraße 59a, 18528 Lietzow 038302 2166; info@lietzow.net; **www.lietzow.net**

[icons] 🐕 €2.50 👪 WD ▲ 🚻 ✏ ⓗ 🍖 🐾 250m

On rd 96, E22 fr Stralsund to ferry harbour at Sassnitz; when you arr at Lietzow site sp 'Gästehaus Lietzow' on RH side of rd; sh, steep incline fr main rd. Med, hdg, pt shd, EHU inc; gas; adv bkg rec; CKE. *"Pleasant, beautifully kept sm site in woodland; cent for the island, sightseeing & useful stopover nr ferry point; MV waste; many mkd cycle rtes around island; charming greens; excel san facs; sh walk to delightful coast."* **€33.50, 29 Mar-15 Oct.** 2015

GERMANY

LIMBURG AN DER LAHN *3C2* (2km SSW Urban)
50.38916, 8.07333 **Lahn Camping,** Schleusenweg
16, 65549 Limburg-an-der-Lahn **(06431) 22610;
info@lahncamping.de; www.lahncamping.de**

🏕 €1.50 🛊🛉 WD 🚿 ♿ 🏪 🧺 ⚙ MP ⊕ 🎣 ⚂

**Exit A3/E35 junc 42 Limburg Nord, site sp. By Rv
Lahn in town, easy access.** 3*, Lge, pt shd, EHU
(6A) €2.60 (long lead poss req); gas; sw; 20% statics;
bus; Eng spkn; fishing; CKE. *"Busy, well-organised
site; delightful location by rv; sm pitches - some
poss diff to manoeuvre; gd views; friendly staff; poss
flooding in wet weather; htd pool 100m; sh walk to
interesting town; gates clsd 1300-1500; useful NH."*
€19.90, 28 Mar-27 Oct. **2019**

LIMBURG AN DER LAHN *3C2* (9km SW Rural)
50.38151, 8.00046 **Camping Oranienstein,**
Strandbadweg, 65582 Diez **(06432) 2122; info@
camping-diez.de; www.camping-diez.de**

🏕 🛊🛉 WD 🚿 ♿ 🧺 ⚙ MP ⊕ ⚂ ⚂

**In Diez on L bank of Lahn. Exit A3 junc 41 Diez or
junc 43 Limburg-Süd. Site sp 1km bef Diez, 8km fr
a'bahn.** 3*, Lge, pt shd, EHU (6A) inc; gas; 60% statics;
adv bkg acc; ccard acc; bike hire; watersports; CKE.
"Pleasant vill; gd rests; hot water metered; gd NH."
€20.00, 1 Apr-31 Oct. **2015**

LINDAU (BODENSEE) *3D4* (5km NE Rural) *47.58509,
9.70667* **Campingpark Gitzenweiler Hof,** Gitzenweiler
88, 88131 Lindau-Gitzenweiler **(08382) 94940; info@
gitzenweiler-hof.de; www.gitzenweiler-hof.de**

12 🐕 €3.50 🛊🛉 WD 🚿 ♿ 🏪 🧺 ⚙ ⊕ ⚂ ⚂ ⚂ ⚂

**Exit A96/E43/E54 junc 4 onto B12 sp Lindau. Turn
off immed after vill of Oberreitnau twd Rehlings.
Site well sp fr all dirs.** Lge, mkd, pt shd, pt sl, serviced
pitches; EHU (6-16A) inc; gas; red long stay; TV;
50% statics; bus 1km; Eng spkn; adv bkg acc; boating;
fishing; CKE. *"Well-run, busy site in scenic area; gd
facs; friendly staff; excel site for children; max 2 dogs;
o'night facs for m'vans; gd cycling; poss prone to
flooding after v heavy rain; pitches poorly maintained;
poss cr."* **€36.00, G18.** **2019**

LINDAU (BODENSEE) *3D4* (9km SE Coastal) *47.53758,
9.73143* **Park-Camping Lindau am See,** Fraunhofer
strasse 20, 88131 Lindau-Zech **(08382) 72236;
info@park-camping.de; www.park-camping.de**

🏕 €3 🛊🛉 WD 🚿 ♿ 🧺 ⚙ ⊕ 🎣 ⚂ ⚂ ⚂ shgl

**On B31 fr Bregenz to Lindau, 200m after customs
turn L to site in 150m; ent could be missed; mini-
mkt on corner; ent rd crosses main rlwy line with
auto barriers. B31 fr Friedrichshafen, site well sp
fr o'skts of Lindau.** 4*, Lge, hdstg, mkd, pt shd, EHU
(10A) €1 (long lead poss req); sw; 20% statics; Eng
spkn; bike hire; golf 3km. *"Busy site; immac san facs;
sh stay pitches poss diff to manoeuvre as v cramped;
office/gate clsd 1300-1400; staff helpful; m'van o'night
area €10; shwr rm for dogs; excel walking in Pfänder
area; excel; Korridor scheme round Bregenz abolished;
Pfander tunnels complete; Austria m'way vignette req;
cyc rtes fr site."* **€33.50, 25 Mar-10 Nov.** **2018**

LINDAUNIS *1D1* (1km SSW Rural) *54.58626, 9.8173*
Camping Lindaunis, Schleistrasse 1, 24392 Lindaunis
**(04641) 7317; info@camping-lindaunis.de;
www.camping-lindaunis.de**

🏕 €2 🛊🛉 (htd) WD 🚿 ♿ 🏪 🧺 ⚙ 🦋 ⚘ ⊕ 🍺 🎣 ⚂ ⚂ ⚂

**Exit A7/E45 junc 5 onto B201 sp Brebel &
Süderbrarup. At Brebel turn R & foll dir Lindaunis,
site approx 12km on R beside Schlei Fjord.** 3*, Lge,
hdg, mkd, pt shd, terr, EHU (16A); bbq; twin axles; TV;
80% statics; Eng spkn; adv bkg rec; games area; boat
hire; games rm; boating; fishing; bike hire; canoeing;
CKE. *"Vg, family-run site ideally placed for exploring
Schlei fjord & conv Danish border; lakeside setting; boat
& canoe rentals; gd walks & cycle rtes; attractive area;
vg."* **€23.00, 28 Mar-15 Oct.** **2016**

LINGERHAHN *3B2* (1km NE Rural) *50.09980,
7.57330* **Campingpark am Mühlenteich,** Am
Mühlenteich 1, 56291 Lingerhahn **(06746) 533;
info@muehlenteich.de; www.muehlenteich.de**

12 🐕 €3.50 🛊🛉 WD 🚿 ♿ 🏪 🧺 ⚙ MP 🦋 ⊕ ⚂ ⚂ ⚂ ⚂

**Exit A61/E31 exit junc 44 to Laudert & Lingerhahn.
In Lingerhahn foll sp Pfalzfeld, site sp.** 4*, Lge,
unshd, serviced pitches; EHU (6A) €2; 75% statics;
adv bkg acc; golf 12km; tennis; CKE. *"Delightful rest
& beer garden; ent clsd 1300-1500 & 2200; excel site."*
€22.50 **2019**

LIPPSTADT *1C4* (8km NE Rural) *51.70095, 8.40808*
Campingparadies Lippstadter Seenplatte, Seeufer
Straße 16, 59558 Lippstadt **02 948 22 53; info@
camping-lippstadt.de; www.camping-lippstadt.de**

🏕 €2.50 🛊🛉 WD 🚿 ♿ 🧺 ⚙ MP ⚂ ⚂

**Turn R off B55 to Lipperode. In town turn R onto
Niederdedinghauser. After 2.5km turn L onto
Seeuferstraße. Site 200m on R.** Sm, mkd, pt shd, EHU
(16A); twin axles; 25% statics; bus 200m; adv bkg acc;
bike hire; CCI. *" Vg site; fishing in adj lake; excel modern
facs; lge pitches; friendly owners; Paderborn lovely city;
off clsd 1230-1430."* **€23.00, 1 Mar-31 Oct.** **2018**

LORCH *3C2* (6km SE Rural) *50.01820, 7.85493*
Naturpark Camping Suleika, Im Bodenthal 2, 65391
Lorch-bei-Rüdesheim **(06726) 839402; info@
suleika-camping.de; www.suleika-camping.de**

🏕 €2 🛊🛉 🚿 ♿ 🧺 ⚙ 🦋 ⊕ ⚂ 🎣 ⚂

**Site off B42 on E bank of Rv Rhine, 3km NW of
Assmannshausen. 3km SE of Lorch foll sp over rlwy
x-ing on narr winding, steep rd thro vineyards to
site. App poss diff & dangerous for lge o'fits.** Sm, pt
shd, pt sl, terr, serviced pitches; EHU (16A) metered
+ conn fee; bike hire; sep car park; CKE. *"Vg site in
magnificent setting; excursions by Rhine steamer, local
places of interest, wine district; access & exit 1-way
system; helpful staff; excel rest; environmentally
friendly."* **€23.00, 15 Mar-1 Nov.** **2015**

LOWENSTEIN *3D3* (4km N Rural) *49.11697, 9.38321*
Camping Heilbronn Breitenauer See, 74245
Löwenstein **(07130) 8558; info@breitenauer-see.de;
www.breitenauer-see.de**

12 ♞ €5 ♦♦ (htd) wo ♨ ⚲ ♿ ◻ ⁄ 🐕 ☓ 🦋 Y ⊕ ⚒ 🛒 ⚠ ⚓

**Exit m'way A81 (E41) at J10, Weinsberg/Ellhofen
& on B39 twd Löwenstein/Schwäbisch Hall; site in
approx 8km.** 5*, V lge, mkd, pt shd, EHU (16A) €2
or metered + conn fee; gas; sw nr; red long stay; 50%
statics; Eng spkn; adv bkg acc; ccard acc; golf 15km;
boating; watersports; dog wash; CKE. *"Lake walks;
beautiful location; pleasant site close to A6 & A81;
all facs highest quality & superb; some fully serviced
pitches; excel."* **€25.00** **2015**

LUBBEN *2G3* (1km S Urban) *51.93641, 13.89490*
Spreewald Camping, Am Burglehn 218, 15907 Lübben
**(03546) 7053 or 3335 or 8874; info@spreewald-
camping-luebben.de; www.spreewald-camping-
luebben.de**

♞ ♦♦ wo ♨ ⚲ ◻ ⁄ MSP 🦋 🐕 ⊕ 🛒 nr ⚠

**Fr N on A13 exit junc 7 at Freiwalde onto B115
twd Lübben. In town cent turn R to stay on
B115 sp Lübbenau. Site on L - well sp. Or fr S
exit junc 8 onto B87 to Lübben. Cross rlwy, cont
along Luckauerstrasse. Turn R at traff lts into
Puschkinstrasse, sp Cottbus. Site on L, well sp.**
Lge, pt shd, EHU (10A) metered; gas; 20% statics;
adv bkg acc; CKE. *"Excel location; modern, clean facs;
dogs free; excel cycle rtes; adj rv for boating; conv for
Berlin."* **€27.00, 15 Mar-31 Oct.** **2015**

LUBECK *2E2* (6km W Rural) *53.86943, 10.63086*
Campingplatz Lübeck-Schönböcken, Steinrader
Damm 12, 23556 Lübeck-Schönböcken **(0451)
893090; Info@camping-luebeck.de;
www.camping-luebeck.de**

12 ♞ ♦♦ wo ♨ ⚲ ◻ ⁄ MSP 🦋 🐕 🛒 ⚠

**Fr A1 exit junc 23 on sh slip rd, stay in L lane, foll
sp to Schönböcken & then camp sp (not v obvious);
turn R at traff lts bef Dornbreite, site in 1km on L.**
3*, Med, unshd, pt sl, EHU (6A) inc; gas; bbq; bus to
town; Eng spkn; ccard acc; games rm; CKE. *"Helpful
owners; busy site; gd san facs but poss stretched if site
full; conv Travemünde ferries; Lübeck interesting town;
cycle path to town; vg; nice place; gd hypmkt nr; gd
site; gd bus service to fascinating town."* **€24.00** **2019**

LUNEBURG *1D2* (6km S Rural) *53.20925, 10.41000*
Camping Rote Schleuse, Rote Schleuse 4, 21335
Lüneburg **(04131) 791500; kontakt@camp-rote-
schleuse.de; www.camproteschleuse.de**

12 ♞ €1 ♦♦ wo ♨ ⚲ ♿ ◻ ⁄ 🐕 Y ⊕ nr ☓ 🛒 ⚠ ⚓

**Exit A250 junc 4 onto Neu Häcklingen twd
Lüneburg. Site sp to R in 300m.** 3*, Med, pt shd,
EHU (16A) €2.50 or metered; bbq; 60% statics; bus fr
site ent; Eng spkn; adv bkg acc; ccard acc; games rm;
bike hire. *"Pleasant, friendly owners; clsd 1300-1500;
interesting town; gd rest."* **€25.80** **2018**

LUTHERSTADT WITTENBERG *2F3* (5km S Rural)
51.85465, 12.64563 **Marina-Camp Elbe,** Brückenkopf
1, 06888 Lutherstadt-Wittenberg **(03491) 4540; info@
marina-camp-elbe.de; www.marina-camp-elbe.de**

12 ♞ €1.50 ♦♦ wo ♨ ⚲ ◻ ⁄ MSP 🦋 🐕 🛒 nr

Site on S side of Elbe bdge on B2 dir Leipzig; well sp.
5*, Med, pt shd, serviced pitches; EHU (16A) €2.50; gas;
bbq; cooking facs; TV; bus at gate; ccard acc; bike hire;
sauna; CKE. *"Delightful rvside site; marina adj; excel,
modern san facs."* **€27.00** **2017**

MAGDEBURG *2E3* (15km N Rural) *52.21888,
11.65944* **Campingplatz Barleber See,**
Wiedersdorferstrasse, 39126 Magdeburg **(0391)
503244; campingplatz@cvbs.de; www.cvbs.de**

♞ €2 ♦♦ wo ♨ ⚲ ◻ ⁄ MSP 🐕 🛒 Y ⊕ ☓ ⚠ ☓ ⚓ sand adj

**Exit A2/E30 junc 71 sp Rothensee-Barleber See; site
1km N of a'bahn.** 4*, Lge, mkd, pt shd, EHU (10A) €2;
gas; sw; red long stay; 80% statics; Eng spkn; bike hire;
CKE. *"Gd beach & watersports; pleasant site; gd sports
facs; gd touring base; v noisy due to adj gravel quarry;
unhelpful staff; v busy at w/end; crowded beach."*
€22.00, 15 Apr-1 Oct. **2018**

> ## "There aren't many sites open at this time of year"
>
> If you're travelling outside peak season
> remember to call ahead to check site opening
> dates – even if the entry says 'open all year'.

MALLISS *2E2* (2km SE Rural) *53.19596, 11.34046*
Camping am Wiesengrund, Am Kanal 4, 19294
Malliss **(038750) 21060; sielaff-camping@t-online.de;
www.camping-malliss.m-vp.de**

12 ♞ €2.50 ♦♦ wo ♨ ⚲ ◻ ⁄ MSP 🦋 Y ⊕ nr ☓ 🛒 ⚠

Sp in Malliss on rd 191 fr Ludwigslust to Uelzen.
4*, Sm, pt shd, EHU (16A) €2; gas; sw nr; 30% statics;
phone; watersports; bike hire; CKE. *"Well-run,
pleasant, family site; beautiful surroundings; barrier
clsd 1200-1400; m'van o'night facs; visit Ludwigslust
Palace & Dömitz Fortress; vg; lovely site and v friendly
staff."* **€16.50** **2020**

MALSCH *3C3* (4km S Rural) *48.86165, 8.33789*
Campingpark Bergwiesen, Waldenfelsstrasse 1,
76316 Malsch **(07246) 1467; email@campingpark-
bergwiesen.eu; www.campingpark-bergwiesen.eu**

12 ♞ €2 ♦♦ wo ♨ ⚲ ◻ ⁄ 🦋 Y ⊕ 🛒 nr ⚠

**Fr Karlsruhe on B3 thro Malsch vill over level x-ing
to Waldprechtsweier. Foll site sp, take care tight L
turn & steep app thro residential area.** 4*, Lge, mkd,
hdg, hdstg, pt shd, terr, serviced pitches; EHU (16A);
gas; sw nr; 80% statics; Eng spkn; adv bkg req; CKE.
*"1st class facs; well-run site in beautiful forest setting;
v friendly site & owner; not rec for long o'fits or lge
m'vans; gd walks fr site; no wifi."* **€19.00** **2016**

MANNHEIM *3C2* (8km S Urban) *49.44841, 8.44806*
Camping am Strandbad, Strandbadweg 1, 68199
Mannheim-Neckarau **(0176) 55422268;**
cfsm.mannheim@googlemail.com;
www.campingplatz-mannheim-strandbad.de

⊗ €1.50 ♦♦ ⚓ 🚿 ✉ ⧄ MSP ⍩ 🍴 ⊕ nr 🍴 nr

Exit A6 Karlsruhe-Frankfurt at AB Kreuz Mannheim
(junc 27) L onto A656 Mannheim-Neckarau. Exit junc
2 onto B36 dir Neckarau, site sp. 2*, Med, pt shd, EHU
(16A) metered; gas; sw; 60% statics; CKE. *"Some noise
fr barges on Rhine & factories opp; poss flooding at
high water; interesting area; barrier down & recep clsd
1200-1500."* **€20.00, 1 Apr-15 Oct.** **2019**

MARKTHEIDENFELD *3D2* (5km S Rural) *49.81885,
9.58851* **Camping Main-Spessart-Park,** Spessart
strasse 30, 97855 Triefenstein-Lengfurt **(09395) 1079;**
info@camping-main-spessart.de; www.camping-
main-spessart.de

12 ⊗ €2.50 ♦♦ ⚓ 🚿 ✉ ⧄ MSP ⊕ 🍴 ⧄

Exit A3/E41 junc 65 or 66 sp Lengfurt. In Lengfurt
foll sp Marktheidenfeld; site in 1km. 5*, Lge, pt shd,
pt sl, terr, serviced pitches; EHU (6-10A) €3; 50%
statics; Eng spkn; adv bkg acc; ccard acc; watersports;
CKE. *"Excel, high quality site; vg rest; vg san facs; easy
access A4; sep NH area; helpful owners; access diff
parts of site due steep terrs; busy site; pool adj; gd
facs."* **€24.00** **2016**

MEDELBY *1D1* (0.7km W Rural) *54.81490, 9.16361*
Camping Kawan Mitte, Sonnenhügel 1, 24994
Medelby **(04605) 189391;** info@camping-mitte.de;
www.camping-mitte.de

12 ♞ (htd) ⊗ MSP ⚓ 🚿 ⅏ ✉ ⧄ 🦋 ⍩ ⊕ nr 🍴 ⧄ 🛶 (htd)

Exit A7 junc 2 onto B199 dir Niebüll to Wallsbüll,
turn N dir Medelby, site sp. 5*, Lge, mkd, pt shd, EHU
(16A) metered; bbq; cooking facs; TV; 20% statics; adv
bkg acc; fitness rm; horseriding 600m; sauna; games
area; bike hire; golf 12km; CKE. *"Conv m'way & Danish
border; vg."* **€29.00** **2017**

MELLE *1C3* (8km NW Rural) *52.22428, 8.2661*
Campingplatz Grönegau-Park Ludwigsee,
Nemdenerstrasse 12, 49326 Melle **(05402) 2132;**
info@ludwigsee.de; www.ludwigsee.de

12 ⊗ €3 ♦♦ MSP ⚓ 🚿 ✉ ⧄ MSP ⍩ 🍴 🍴 ⊕ 🍴 nr ⧄ 🖊

Exit A30/E30 junc 22 twd Bad Essen, site sp on
lakeside. 4*, Lge, hdg, mkd, pt shd, EHU (10A) inc;
sw; 80% statics; adv bkg acc; ccard acc; games area;
bike hire; CKE. *"Beautiful & pleasant site; sep car park;
barrier clsd 1300-1500; helpful owners; sep area for
tourers."* **€30.00** **2019**

MENDIG *3B2* (7km N Rural) *50.42151, 7.26448*
Camping Laacher See, Am Laacher See, 56653
Wassenach **(02636) 2485;** info@camping-
laacher-see.de; www.camping-laacher-see.de

⊗ €4 (htd) ⊗ ⚓ 🚿 ⅏ ✉ ⧄ 🦋 ⍩ 🍴 ⊕ 🍴 🍴 ⧄

Fr A61, exit junc 34 Mendig. Foll tents sp to Maria
Laach. Site on Laacher See. 4*, Lge, mkd, hdg, hdstg,
pt shd, pt sl, terr, EHU (16A) metered + conn fee;
gas; sw; 50% statics; bus 500m; Eng spkn; adv bkg·
acc; ccard acc; fishing; sailing; CKE. *"Beautiful, neat,
clean, relaxing site; all pitches lake views; busy at w/
end; modern, outstanding san facs; gd woodland walks,
cycling & sw; excel sailing facs & sw; excel site & rest;
close to m'way; rec; helpful staff; avoid arr bet 11am-
2pm when recep clsd."* **€29.00, 29 Mar-25 Sep.** **2018**

MENDIG *3B2* (2km NNW Rural) *50.38646, 7.27237*
Camping Siesta, Laacherseestrasse 6, 56743 Mendig
(02652) 1432; service@campingsiesta.de;
www.campingsiesta.de

12 ⊗ €2 ⊗ MSP ⚓ 🚿 ✉ ⧄ 🍴 ⊕ ⧄ 🛶

Fr A61 exit junc 34 for Mendig dir Maria Laach; foll
camp sps; site on R in 300m by ent to car park.
3*, Med, hdg, pt shd, sl, EHU (16A) €2.5; gas;
60% statics; Eng spkn; CKE. *"Useful NH; easy access
fr A61; owner helpful in siting NH o'fits; longest
waterslide in Europe; gd base for region's castles &
wines; friendly owners; spotless site; gd rest; site has
so much more to offer than only a NH; v welcoming; vg
refurbished; new san facs (2014)."* **€24.00** **2019**

MESCHEDE *1C4* (10km S Rural) *51.29835, 8.26425*
Knaus Campingpark Hennesee, Mielinghausen 7,
59872 Meschede **(0291) 952720;** hennesee@
knauscamp.de; www.knauscamp.de

12 ⊗ €3.80 ♦♦ ⊗ MSP ⚓ 🚿 ✉ ⧄ 🦋 ⍩ 🍴 ⊕ 🍴 🍴 ⧄ 🖊

S fr Meschede on B55 for 7km; at sp for
Erholungszentrum & Remblinghausen turn L over
Lake Hennesee, site on L in 500m, sp. 5*, Lge, mkd,
pt shd, terr, serviced pitches; EHU (6A) conn fee; gas;
sw nr; 60% statics; Eng spkn; adv bkg acc; bike hire;
sauna; CKE. *"Conv Sauerland mountains & lakes; 50m
elec cable advisable; vg."* **€28.70** **2020**

METTINGEN *1B3* (2km SW Rural) *52.31251, 7.76202*
Camping Zur Schönen Aussicht, Schwarzestrasse 73,
49497 Mettingen **(05452) 606;** info@camping-
schoene-aussicht.de; www.camping-schoene-
aussicht.de

12 ♦♦ ⊗ ⚓ 🚿 ✉ ⧄ MSP ⍩ 🍴 ⊕ 🍴 ⧄ 🖊 (covrd, htd)

Exit A30 junc 12 dir Mettingen. Go thro town cent,
uphill turn L at traff lts, site sp. 3*, Med, mkd, hdg, pt
shd, pt sl, EHU (10A) €3 or metered; 50% statics; Eng
spkn; adv bkg acc; CKE. *"Nice, friendly site; gd walking,
cycling; easy walk to town; gd facs."* **€27.50** **2015**

MITTENWALD *4E4* (4km N Rural) *47.47290, 11.27729*
Naturcamping Isarhorn, Am Horn 4, 82481 Mittenwald
**(08823) 5216; camping@mittenwald.de;
www.camping-isarhorn.de**

🐕 €4.50 � WD ♨ ♿ ✉ ✗ MSP 🦋 ⚕ 📶 🎣 ⚓

E fr Garmisch-Partenkirchen on rd 2; at Krün turn
S on D2/E533 dir Mittenwald. Site on R in approx
2km at int'l camping sp. Ent on R fr main rd. NB:
Rd thro to Innsbruck via Zirlerberg improved & no
longer clsd to c'vans descending S; long & steep;
low gear; not to be attempted N. 4*, Lge, hdstg,
pt shd, EHU (16A) inc; bbq; bus adj; Eng spkn; ccard
acc; tennis; site clsd 1 Nov-mid Dec; site clsd 1300-
1500 & 2200-0700; canoeing. *"Relaxed, secluded
site in pines; mountain views; excel base for walking;
htd covrd pool 4km; cycle track to attractive town;
poss some noise fr nrby military base; ski lift; owner v
keen on recycling waste; facs gd, warm and modern;
highly rec; v conv NH en route to Italy; helpful staff."*
€36.00, 1 Jan - 4 Nov. 2019

MITTENWALD *4E4* (8km N Rural) *47.49040,
11.25438* **Alpen-Caravanpark Tennsee,** Am
Tennsee 1, 82493 Klais-Krün **(08825) 170; info@
camping-tennsee.de; www.camping-tennsee.de**

🐕 €3.30 ♦♦♦ (htd) WD ♨ ♿ ✉ ✗ MSP 🍽 ⚕ 🎣 ⚓ 🏛 ✏

N fr Mittenwald on main Innsbruck-Garmisch rd
turn off for Krun, foll Tennsee & site sp. 2km SE of
Klais, not well sp. 5*, Lge, mkd, hdstg, pt shd, terr,
serviced pitches; EHU (16A) metered; gas; phone; Eng
spkn; adv bkg acc; ccard acc; bike hire; CKE. *"Excel
area for Bavarian Alps, Tirol; barrier clsd 1200-1500;
gd size pitches; ski lift 2.5km; red snr citizens; vg, clean,
friendly, family-run site; price inc use of tourist buses."*
€35.00, 1 Jan-2 Nov, 18 Dec-31 Dec. 2016

"That's changed – Should I let the Club know?"

If you find something on site that's different
from the site entry, fill in a report and let us
know. See camc.com/europereport.

MITTERTEICH *4F2* (3km NW Rural) *49.97311,
12.22497* **Campingplatz Großbüchlberg,**
Großbüchlberg 32, 95666 Mitterteich **09633 40 06 73;
camping@freizeithugl.de; www.freizeithugl.de**

12 🐕 €1.50 ♦♦♦ (htd) WD ♨ ♿ ✉ ✗ MSP 🍽 ⚕ 🍽 🎣 ⚓ 🏛

Fr A93 Marktredwitz-Mitterteich take exit 16
Mitterteich. At xrds in town cent foll Freizeithugl
signs. Turn L after 200m twds Grossbuchberg. Foll
sp. 5*, Med, hdg, mkd, hdstg, pt shd, pt sl, terr, EHU
(16A); twin axles; TV; bus adj; Eng spkn; adv bkg acc;
ccard acc; CCI. *"Excel site; superb htd san facs; close
to mini golf, toboggan run, etc; extensive views; v
friendly."* **€25.00** 2019

MONTABAUR *3C2* (8km E Rural) *50.43761, 7.90498*
Camping Eisenbachtal, 56412 Girod **(06485) 766**

12 🐕 €2 ♦♦♦ (htd) WD ♨ ♿ ✉ ✗ MSP 🦋 ⚕ nr ⚓

S on A3/E35 exit junc 41 dir Montabaur; at Girod
turn L to site, well sp. Med, hdg, mkd, hdstg, pt
shd, pt sl, serviced pitches; EHU (10A) inc (poss rev
pol); gas; sw nr; red long stay; 75% statics; Eng spkn;
adv bkg acc; CKE. *"Beautiful, well-equipped site in
Naturpark Nassau; conv NH fr a'bahn & worth longer
stay; friendly, welcoming staff; gd for nature lovers
& children; gd walking & cycling; adj rest excel; site
clsd 1300-1500 but car park opp; conv Rhine & Mosel
valleys."* **€18.00** 2019

MORFELDEN *3C2* (3km E Rural) *49.97986, 8.59461*
Campingplatz Mörfelden, Am Zeltzplatz 5-15, 64546
Mörfelden-Walldorf **(06105) 22289; info@camping
platz-moerfelden.de; www.campingplatz-
moerfelden.de**

12 🐕 €1.50 ♦♦♦ ♨ ♿ ✉ ✗ MSP 🦋 ⚕ 📶 ⚓

Fr A5 exit 24, turn W on 486 twds Morfelden.
In 200m turn L, opp Holiday Inn. Site on R in 100m.
3*, Med, pt shd, EHU (16A) metered or €2.50; gas;
phone; Eng spkn. *"Conv NH/sh stay for Frankfurt;
excel, modern san facs; helpful owner; vg."*
€26.50 2016

MORFELDEN *3C2* (9km S Rural) *49.94461, 8.60544*
Campingplatz Am Steinrodsee, Triftweg 33, 64331
Weiterstadt **06150 53593; rezeption.koehres@t-
online.de; www.camping-steinrodsee.de**

🐕 ♦♦♦ (htd) WD ♨ ♿ ✉ ✗ MSP 🦋 ⚕ 🍽 ⚓ 🏛

Leave A5 twds Darmstadt at exit 25. L at 2nd
traff lts onto L3113. Turn R in 5km & foll signs. 4*,
Lge, mkd, hdg, pt shd, EHU (16A), bbq; twin axles;
60% statics; CCI. *"Vg site; quiet with some aircraft &
m'way noise; clean, tidy, well regulated site; immac san
facs; conv for Darmstadt."* **€23.00, 1 Jan-31 Oct.**
2015

MORITZBURG *4G1* (3km S Rural) *51.1450, 13.67444*
Campingplatz Bad Sonnenland, Dresdnerstrasse
115, 01468 Moritzburg **(0351) 8305495; bad-
sonnenland@t-online.de; www.bad-sonnenland.de**

🐕 €3 ♦♦♦ WD ♨ ♿ ✉ ✗ MSP 🍽 ⚕ 🎣 ⚓ 🏛

Leave A4/E40 exit 80. Turn R sp Moritzburg, foll site
sp thro Reichenberg. Site on L 3km bef Moritzburg.
Lge, pt shd, EHU (16A) €2.50; gas; sw nr; bus to
Dresden; Eng spkn; ccard acc; games area; games rm;
CKE. *"Scenic area; friendly staff; excel, immac facs;
site clsd 1300-1500 & 2200-0700; also holiday vill with
many huts; conv Dresden, Meissen; narr gauge steam
train Dresden-Moritzburg; day trip to Prague; statics
(sep area); many mkd walking & cycling rtes in area;
Schloss Moritzburg in vill; vg site; poss cr high ssn."*
€22.00, 1 Apr-31 Oct. 2015

MUHLBERG *2E4* (1.6km NW Rural) *50.87516, 10.80843* **Campingplatz Drei Gleichen,** Am Gut Ringhofen, 99869 Mühlberg **(036256) 22715; service@campingplatz-muehlberg.de; www.campingplatz-muehlberg.de**

12 🐕 €2.20 � WD ▲ ᐸ 🖆 ✎ MSP 🦋 ♈ 🗑 nr 🐾 nr ⚠

Leave A4/E40 at junc 43 (Wandersleben) S twds Mühlberg; site well sp in 2km on rd to Wechmar. Med, hdg, mkd, unshd, pt sl, EHU (16A) €1.80 + conn fee; sw nr; 50% statics; adv bkg acc; CKE. *"Gd facs; helpful staff; site clsd 1300-1500; conv a'bahn."* **€16.00** 2015

"I like to fill in the reports as I travel from site to site"

You'll find report forms at the back of this guide, or you can fill them in online at camc.com/europereport.

MUNCHEN *4E4* (12km NW Urban) *48.19888, 11.49694* **Campingplatz Nord-West,** Auf den Schrederwiesen 3, 80995 München-Moosach **(089) 1506936; info@campingplatz-nord-west.de; www.campingplatz-nord-west.de**

12 🐕 €2 ♴ (htd) WD ▲ ᐸ 🖆 ✎ MSP 🦋 ♈ 🗑 nr 🐾 ✎

Fr N exit A99 junc 10 Lugwigsfeld onto B304 S - Dachauerstrasse, sp München. Turn L in approx 800m at traff lts. Turn R at T-junc to site on R. Med, hdstg, shd, EHU (10-16A) €5 or metered; 50% statics; phone; bus to city; Eng spkn; adv bkg acc; ccard acc; CKE. *"Friendly, helpful welcome; enquire about public transport tickets; ltd facs LS; Dachau - pretty town 10km; gd; Dachau Concentration Camp Memorial worth a visit."* **€23.20** 2017

MUNCHEN *4E4* (17km NW Rural) *48.19821, 11.41161* **Campingplatz am Langwieder See,** Eschenrieder strasse 119, 81249 München-Langwied **(089) 8641566; info@camping-langwieder-see.de; www.camping-langwieder-see.de**

12 🐕 €1.70 ♴ (htd) WD ▲ 🖆 ✎ ♈ 🗑 🐾

Exit A8 junc 80 at Langwieder See & foll sp Dachau; site within 200m. Fr ring rd A99 junc 8 join A8 to N, then as above. Med, hdstg, pt shd, EHU (10A) metered + conn fee €1; gas; sw nr; 95% statics; Eng spkn; CKE. *"Pleasant owners; tourers in a row outside recep area parked v close together; v sm pitches, mostly on gravel; gd san facs; site used by workers; easy access to Munich by train fr Dachau; lge free car park at stn; NH/sh stay only."* **€21.50** 2016

MUNSTER *1B3* (9km SE Rural) *51.94638, 7.69027* **Camping Münster,** Laerer Wersuefer 7, 48157 Münster **(0251) 311982; mail@campingplatz-muenster.de; www.campingplatz-muenster.de**

12 🐕 €3 ♴ (htd) WD ▲ ᐸ 🖆 ✎ MSP 🦋 ♈ 🗑 🐾 ⚠

Fr A43 exit junc 2 or A1/E37 exit junc 78 onto B51 dir Münster then Bielefeld. On leaving built-up area, turn R after TV mast on R. Cross Rv Werse & turn L at 1st traff lts, site sp. (Site is also sp fr Münster S by-pass). 5*, Lge, mkd, hdstg, pt shd, serviced pitches; EHU (16A) inc; bbq; twin axles; 50% statics; bus 150m; Eng spkn; adv bkg acc; ccard acc; tennis; bike hire; fishing; CKE. *"Excel; quiet mid wk; Münster very interesting; radio/TV mast useful landmark fr S; gd cycle rtes; o'night m'van area; barrier clsd 1300-1500; htd pool adj; vg site, tokens for shwrs; sep motor parking outside camp; excel for bus to Munster; helpful staff; clean facs & plentiful; well organised; pitches cramped; gd rest."* **€24.00** 2016

MUNSTERTAL *3B4* (2km WNW Rural) *47.85995, 7.76370* **Feriencamping Münstertal,** Dietzelbach strasse 6, 79244 Münstertal **(07636) 7080; info@camping-muenstertal.de; www.camping-muenstertal.de**

12 🐕 €3.50 ♴ WD ▲ ᐸ 🖆 ✎ MSP 🦋 ♈ 🗑 🐾 ⚠ ✎
🏊 (covrd, htd)

Exit A5 junc 64a at Bad Krozingen-Staufen-Münstertal. By-pass Stauffen & foll Münstertal sps. Site on L 1.5km past Camping Belchenblick off rd L123. 5*, Lge, mkd, shd, serviced pitches; EHU (16A) metered; gas; red long stay; TV (pitch); 10% statics; phone; adv bkg rec; fishing; tennis; horseriding; games area; games rm; CKE. *"Superb, well-managed site; luxurious, clean facs; beauty treatments avail; winter sports nrby; ski lift 10km; sauna; steam rm; solarium; private bthrms avail; many organised activities for all family; gd walking; vg rest; conv Freiburg & Black Forest; new premium pitches (2016); rlwy stn 200m; gates clsd 1300-1430 & 2200-0730; m'van o'night area; friendly staff."* **€36.50** 2017

MURNAU AM STAFFELSEE *4E4* (3.5km NW Rural) *47.68493, 11.17918* **Camping Halbinsel Burg,** Burgweg 41, 82418 Murnau-Seehausen **(08841) 9870; info@camping-staffelsee.de; www.camping-staffelsee.de**

♴ WD ▲ ᐸ 🖆 ✎ MSP 🗑 🐾 ⚠ ✎

Exit A95 junc 9 Sindelsdorf/Peissenberg to Murnau. Site sp at traff lts in cent of Murnau, dir Seehausen. 3*, Med, pt shd, EHU (16A) €2.50; sw; 20% statics; watersports; CKE. *"Wonderful sw & boating; pleasant, lovely, well-equipped site in superb location for alps, lakes & local amenities."* **€26.00, 6 Jan-25 Oct.** 2019

NAUMBURG (HESSEN) *1C4* (0.8km NW Rural) *51.25070, 9.16060* **Camping in Naumburg (formerly Kneipp Kur Camping),** Am Schwimmbad 12, 34311 Naumburg **(05625) 9239670 or 0170 4418621 (mob); info@camping-naumburg.de; www.camping-naumburg.de**

12 €2.50 (htd)

Exit A44 junc 67 onto B251 thro Istha. At Bründersen foll sp Altenstadt & Naumburg. Foll int'l camping sp, well sp. 4*, Med, mkd, unshd, terr, EHU (16A) €2 or metered (poss rev pol); bbq; cooking facs; twin axles; 30% statics; bus 500m; Eng spkn; adv bkg acc; games area; golf 15km; tennis; horseriding 5km; CKE. *"Charming site; excel, modern san facs; spacious pitches; friendly, helpful staff; interesting town; clsd 1300-1500; gd walks fr site; spa treatments; rec; nr pool, smkt, Dambusters Dam; pool adj; new management."* **€22.00** **2015**

NENNIG *3A2* (1.6km N Rural) *49.54195, 6.37126* **Mosel-Camping Dreiländereck,** Am Moselufer, 66706 Perl-Nennig **(06866) 322; info@mosel-camping.de; www.mosel-camping.de**

€1 (htd) nr

Site on bank of Mosel opp Remich (Luxembourg), access on R just bef bdge (fr German side). Fr Luxembourg cross rv bdge, turn L after former border post cont to rv & turn L under bldg; site is ahead. Med, unshd, EHU (16A) inc; bbq; red long stay; 65% statics; phone; Eng spkn; adv bkg acc; golf 15km; cycling; fishing; CKE. *"Nice, lovely site; dishwashing & chem disp adj; ltd, tired facs; conv vineyards, Roman mosaic floor in Nennig; cycle track along rv; sh walk to Remich; friendly welcome."* **€19.40, 1 Apr-15 Oct.** **2018**

"We must tell the Club about that great site we found"

Get your site reports in by mid-August and we'll do our best to get your updates into the next edition.

NENNIG *3A2* (1.8km N Rural) *49.54331, 6.37207* **Camping Mosella am Rothaus (formerly Moselplatz),** Zur Moselbrücke 15, 66706 Perl-Nennig **(06866) 510 or 26660222 (Lux'bourg); info@mosel-camping.de**

(htd) nr

Site on bank of Mosel opp Remich (Luxembourg), access on R just bef bdge. Fr Luxembourg cross rv bdge, turn L after former border post, site is ahead, opp Mosel-Camping Dreiländereck. Med, hdg, pt shd, EHU (10A) inc; bbq; 50% statics; bus 100m; Eng spkn; CKE. *"Lovely, well placed site by rv for sh or long stay; helpful, friendly owner; ltd facs, a bit tired; rest nr; rvside pitch sm extra charge; gd touring base; frequent bus to Luxembourg City."* **€22.60, 1 Apr-15 Oct.** **2017**

NEUMARKT IN DER OBERPFALZ *4E3* (10km N Rural) *49.32944, 11.42876* **Campingplatz Berg,** Hausheimerstrasse 31, 92348 Berg **(09189) 1581; campingplatz-herteis@t-online.de; www.camping-in-berg.de**

12 €2 nr nr

Exit A3 junc 91 & foll sp Berg bei Neumarkt. In cent of Berg, turn R, site on R in 800m, sp. On ent turn R to tourers area & walk to recep. 3*, Med, unshd, pt sl, EHU (20A) €2.50; 60% statics; Eng spkn; golf 8km. *"Well-run, friendly, family-owned site; excel san facs; sh walk to Berg cent; excel touring base; gd NH fr m'way; pleasant views of countryside; canal walk."* **€20.00** **2016**

"I need an on-site restaurant"

We do our best to make sure site information is correct, but it is always best to check any must-have facilities are still available or will be open during your visit.

NEUMUNSTER *1D1* (6km SW Rural) *54.04636, 9.92306* **Familien-Camping Forellensee,** Humboldredder 5, 24634 Padenstedt **(04321) 82697; info@familien-campingplatz.de; www.familien-campingplatz.de**

12 €1.50 nr

Exit A7 junc 14 for Padenstedt, join dual c'way for 1km & turn L sp Centrum. In 1km turn L at traff lts sp Padenstedt for 3km, under m'way. Site on L in vill. 4*, Lge, mkd, pt shd, EHU (16A) €3.50 or metered; sw; 75% statics; phone; Eng spkn; tennis; trout fishing; games area; CKE. *"Gd NH; conv for trains to Hamburg/ Lübeck; swimming lake with section for dogs."* **€26.00** **2019**

NEUREICHENAU *4G3* (8km E Urban) *48.74861, 13.81694* **Knaus Campingpark Lackenhäuser,** Lackenhäuser 127, 94089 Neureichenau **(08583) 311; lackenhaeuser@knauscamp.de; www.knauscamp.de**

12 €2.50 (htd)

Leave A3/E56 at junc 14 (Aicha-vorm Wald) & go E for 50km via Waldkirchen, Jandelsbrunn, Gsenget & Klafferstrasse to Lackenhäuser. 4*, Lge, hdg, mkd, pt shd, pt sl, terr, serviced pitches; EHU (16A) €2.60 or metered; gas; bbq; red long stay; TV; 40% statics; adv bkg acc; ccard acc; horseriding adj; fishing; tennis 500m; games rm; sauna; bike hire. *"Lge site with little waterfalls & walkways; ski lift on site - equipment for hire; mv service pnt diff to access; excel shop; 2km to 3 point border with Austria & Czech Republic; excursions booked; solarium; hairdresser; recep clsd 1200-1500 & after 1800."* **€34.00** **2016**

GERMANY

NEUSTADT *3C2* (10km SW Rural) *49.30083, 8.09027*
Campingplatz Wappenschmiede, Talstrasse 60, 67487
St Martin **(06323) 6435; cpwappenschmiede@
hotmail.de; www.campingplatz-wappenschmiede.
beep.de**

🐶 🏕 ⚓ 🍴 ⓘ 🖦nr ⛰

Exit A65 at junc 13 or 14 to Maikammer, then foll
sp St Martin & site (blue/white or yellow/brown
sp). At end houses take 1st L into touring area (do
not go up hill to statics area). 2*, Sm, shd, EHU €2;
red long stay; 50% statics; Eng spkn; adv bkg acc;
CKE. *"Poss long walk to facs; friendly site; St Martin
very picturesque; gd rests; gd walking area; gd site."*
€20.00, 1 Apr-1 Nov. 2015

NEUSTADT AN DER AISCH *4E2* (9km N Rural)
49.64058, 10.59975 **Campingplatz Münchsteinach,**
Badstrasse 10, 91481 Münchsteinach **(09166) 750;
gemeinde@muenchsteinach.de; www.muench
steinach.de**

12 🐶 €2 ⚓ ⓘnr

Turn NW fr rd 470 Neustadt-Höchstadt at camp sp
8km fr Neustadt & thro Gutenstetten. Int'l camping
sp in 5km turn R, foll camp sp. Lge, unshd, EHU (16A)
metered; red long stay; 60% statics; CKE. *"Sm touring
area; clean facs; pool adj; site muddy when wet."*
€11.00 2016

NEUSTADT/HARZ *2E4* (2km NW Rural) *51.56897,
10.82836* **Campingplatz am Waldbad,** An der Burg 3,
99762 Neustadt/Harz **036331 479891; info@
neustadt-harz-camping.de; www.neustadt-harz-
camping.de**

12 🐶 €2 (htd)

Fr A38, exit J10 for B243 to Nordhausen. Turn L
onto B4 dir Niedersachswerfen. Turn R onto L1037,
L onto Osteroder Straße and R onto Klostergasse.
Foll sp to campsite. 4*, Med, hdg, pt shd, pt sl, EHU
(10A) metered + con fee; twin axles; 50% statics;
adv bkg acc; games area; CCI. *"Gd site; conv for Harz;
helpful owners; vg san facs."* **€18.90** 2019

NEUSTRELITZ *2F2* (10km SW Rural) *53.30895,
13.00305* **Camping- und Ferienpark Havelberge,** An
der Havelbergen 1, 17237 Gross Quassow **(03981)
24790; info@haveltourist.de; www.haveltourist.de**

🐶 ⓘ

Fr Neustrelitz foll sp to Userin on L25 & bef Userin
turn L sp Gross Quassow. Turn S in vill at camping
sp, cross rlwy line & rv, sm ent in 1.5km. Site 1.7km S
of Gross Quassow twd lake, sp. 5*, Lge, pt shd, pt sl,
EHU (16A) €2.90; sw; 30% statics; watersports; sauna;
bike hire. *"Lovely wooded area; poss diff lge o'fits; not
rec as NH."* **€33.40, 01 Apr-03 Nov, G11.** 2016

NIESKY *2H4* (3km W Rural) *51.30156, 14.80302*
Campingplatz Tonschächte (Part Naturist),
Raschkestrasse, 02906 Niesky **(03588) 205771;
info@campingplatz-tonschacht.de; campingplatz-
tonschacht.de**

🐶 ⓘnr

Leave A4/E40 at junc 93 onto B115 sp Niesky; cont
on B115 site sp on L; do not go into Niesky but stay
on B115. 2*, Lge, shd, EHU (10A); 50% statics; games
area. *"Conv Polish border x-ing & a'bahn; sep naturist
area."* **€12.50, 15 Apr-15 Oct.** 2016

NORDEN *1B2* (5km W Coastal) *53.60471, 7.13863*
Nordsee-Camp Norddeich, Deichstrasse 21, 26506
Norden-Norddeich **(04931) 8073; info@nordsee-
camp.de; www.Nordsee-Camp.de**

🐶 €3.80 ⓘ 200m

Off B70 N of Norden. Well sp. V lge, mkd, pt shd,
EHU (6A) €2.20; 25% statics; ccard acc; fishing; bike
hire; CKE. *"Immac san facs; friendly atmosphere;
day trips to Frisian Islands; excel rest; vg site."*
€20.80, 8 Mar-25 Oct. 2016

NURNBERG *4E2* (12km W Rural) *49.43174, 10.92541*
Camping Zur Mühle, Seewaldstraße 75, 90513
Zirndorf/Leichendorf **(0911) 693801; camping.
walther@t-online.de; www.camping-zur-muehle.de**

🐶 €2 (htd) ⓘ

Head W on Adlerstraße twd Stangengäßchen,
cont onto Josephspl, then Vordere Lederg. Cont
onto Schlotfegerg then onto Fürther Tor; Cont
onto Dennerstraße then slight R onto Am Plärrer.
Cont onto Rothenburger Str, turn L to stay on
Rothenburger. Turn R twd Seewaldstraße, keep R.
Site on L. Med, mkd, pt shd, EHU metered; bbq; ccard
acc; CKE. *"Mastercard acc not Visa; local style rest in
traditional building on site; conv for visiting Nurnberg;
vg site."* **€24.00, 1 Apr-31 Dec.** 2019

OBERAMMERGAU *4E4* (1km S Rural) *47.58988,
11.0696* **Campingpark Oberammergau,**
Ettalerstrasse 56B, 82487 Oberammergau **(08822)
94105; info@camping-oberammergau.de;
www.campingpark-oberammergau.de**

12 🐶 €2 ⓘnr 🖦nr ⛰

Fr S turn R off B23, site on L in 1km. Fr N turn L at
2nd Oberammergau sp. Do not ent vill fr N - keep to
bypass. 4*, Med, hdstg, hdg, mkd, pt shd, EHU (16A)
metered + conn fee; gas; red long stay; 25% statics;
bus; Eng spkn; adv bkg rec; sep car park; bike hire;
CKE. *"Plenty of space; helpful recep; excel san facs;
excel rest adj; easy walk to vill; well run site, visitor tax
does not apply to one night stays."* **€29.00** 2017

OBERSTDORF *3D4* (2km N Rural) *47.42370, 10.27843*
Rubi-Camp, Rubingerstrasse 34, 87561 Oberstdorf
(08322) 959202; info@rubi-camp.de; www.rubi-camp.de

🔢12 🐕 €4 ♦♦ (htd) 🆆 ⚓ ♿ 🚿 🚮 ⭐ 🦋 🍸 ⑭ 🍴 🛒 nr ⛺

Fr Sonthofen on B19, just bef Oberstdorf at rndabt take exit sp Reichenbach, Rubi. Site in 1km over level x-ing, 2nd site on R. 5*, Med, hdstg, unshd, serviced pitches; EHU (8A) metered; bbq; TV; 10% statics; phone; bus; Eng spkn; adv bkg acc; site clsd Nov; CKE. *"Well-run, well-maintained site; immac facs; block paved paths to pitches; block hdstg with grass growing thro; ski lift 1km; excel scenery; excel facs; easy 20 min level walk to town."* **€38.80**   **2019**

OBERSTDORF *3D4* (3km N Rural) *47.42300, 10.27720*
Campingplatz Oberstdorf, Rubingerstrasse 16, 87561 Oberstdorf **(08322) 6525; camping-oberstdorf@t-online.de; www.camping-oberstdorf.de**

🐕 €0.50 ♦♦ 🆆 ⚓ 🚿 🚮 ⭐ 🍴 🛒 nr

Fr B19 dir Oberstdorf, foll site sp. 3*, Med, hdstg, serviced pitches; EHU (10A) metered; 45% statics; golf 5km. *"Cable cars to Nebelhorn & Fellhorn in town; ski lift 3km; ski bus; Oberstdorf pedestrianised with elec buses fr o'skirts; vg."*
€32.00, 1 Jan-31 Oct, 15 Dec-31 Dec.   **2017**

OBERWESEL *3B2* (7.6km SE Rural) *50.05111, 7.7750*
Camping Sonnenstrand, Strandbadweg 9, 55422 Bacharach **(06743) 1752; info@camping-sonnenstrand.de; www.camping-rhein.de**

🐕 €1 ♦♦ 🆆 ⚓ ♿ 🚿 🚮 ⭐ 🍴 🛒 ⛺ 🛶 adj

S on A61. Exit 44 Laudert via Oberwesel to Bacharach (B9). Turn Sat Nav off after Laudert. Foll sp to Oberwesel-Bacharach. Med, mkd, hdstg, pt shd, EHU (6A); bbq; red long stay; twin axles; 25% statics; Eng spkn, boating; golf 6km; games area; bike hire; games rm; CKE. *"Helpful, knowledgeable owner; poss lge groups m'cyclists; scenic area; busy, noisy rvside site; sm pitches; wine cellar visits; shwrs/san facs ltd & poss stretched high ssn; plenty of rv activities; excel rest; sh walk to sm medieval town; sh stay/NH; gd."*
€19.50, 25 Mar-31 Oct.   **2016**

OBERWESEL *3B2* (0.9km S Urban) *50.10251, 7.73664*
Camping Schönburgblick, Am Hafendamm 1, 55430 Oberwesel **(06744) 714501; camping-oberwesel@t-online.de; www.camping-oberwesel.de**

♦♦ 🆆 ⚓ 🚮 ⭐ 🍸 ⑭ nr 🛒 nr

Fr A61/E31 exit sp Oberwesel, site sp on L at ent to sports stadium, on rvside. Sm, pt shd, EHU (6A) €4.20; red long stay; adv bkg acc; tennis adj; CKE. *"Clean, modern san facs in Portacabins - stretched when site full; o'night m'vans area; rv trips, cycling, walking."* **€23.40, 17 Mar-1 Nov.**   **2017**

OBERWESEL *3B2* (9km NW Rural) *50.14976, 7.69478*
Camping Friedenau, Gründelbach 103, 56329 St Goar-am-Rhein **(06741) 368; info@camping-friedenau.de; www.camping-friedenau.de**

🔢12 🐕 €2 ♦♦ 🆆 ⚓ ♿ 🚿 🚮 ⭐ 🦋 💧 ⑭ 🍴 🛒 nr

App on B9 fr Boppard or Bingen; turn under rlwy bdge 1km N of St Goar; keep L; site on L in 1km. NB - do not app fr J43 off m'way. 3*, Sm, shd, pt sl, EHU (16A) €2.50; gas; bus; Eng spkn; CKE. *"Quieter than other sites in area - uphill fr busy Rhine & resorts; some pitches uneven & poss diff after heavy rain; vg welcome; easy walk or cycle to rv town; country walks fr site; relaxed atmosphere; pool 1.5km; friendly staff; gd bar/rest; san fac gd; great views fr Rheinfels Castle; in very pleasant valley; washing up and lndry facs in female toilet block."* **€21.50**   **2016**

"Satellite navigation makes touring much easier"

Remember most sat navs don't know if you're towing or in a larger vehicle – always use yours alongside maps and site directions.

OLPE *1B4* (8km N Rural) *51.0736, 7.8564* **Feriencamp Biggesee - Vier Jahreszeiten,** Am Sonderner Kopf 3, 57462 Olpe-Sondern **(02761) 944111; info@camping-sondern.de; www.camping-biggesee.de**

🔢12 🐕 €4.50 ♦♦ 🆆 ⚓ ♿ 🚿 🚮 ⭐ 🦋 💧 🍸 ⑭ 🍴 🛒 ⛺ 🚴

Exit A45/E41 junc 18 & foll sp to Biggesee. Pass both turnings to Sondern. Take next R in 200m, Ent on R in 100m. NB. Other sites on lake. 4*, Lge, mkd, pt shd, terr, EHU (16A) inc; gas; cooking facs; sw nr; 20% statics; Eng spkn; adv bkg acc; sauna; tennis; watersports inc diving; solarium; bike hire; CKE. *"Gd facs; well-organised site; barrier clsd 1300-1500 & 2200-0700; rollerskating rink; conv Panorama Theme Park & Cologne; vg cycling area; footpaths."* **€31.50**   **2019**

ORTRAND *2G4* (2km E Rural) *51.37265, 13.77956*
Ferienpark Dresden, Am Bad 1, 01990 Ortrand 35 75 56 20 00; ferienpark-dresden@themencamping.de; www.themencamping.de

🔢12 🐕 €2 ♦♦ 🆆 ⚓ ♿ 🚿 🚮 ⭐ 🦋 💧 🍸 ⑭ 🍴 🛒 ⛺ 🚴
🛶 (htd) 🎿

A13 Berlin-Dresden. Take exit 18 - Ortrand. At rndabt take 2nd exit (L55) & foll signs to camp site 2km. Note tight turn L after passing thro indus units. Med, mkd, unshd, EHU (16A) €1.50; bbq; cooking facs; twin axles; TV; 30% statics; phone; Eng spkn; adv bkg acc; bike hire; games area; waterslide; games rm; CCI. *"Vg site; volleyball; fishing adj; cls to mkd cycle rtes; sep car park with hook-ups for late arrs."* **€33.70**   **2019**

OSNABRUCK *1C3* (14km SW Rural) *52.22944, 7.89027* **Regenbogen-Camp Tecklenburg,** Grafenstrasse 31, 49545 Leeden **(05405) 1007; www.regenbogen.ag**

12 🐕 €4 ♀♀ WD ♨ ♿ 🖥 ✉ MSP 🦋 ⊕ 🦮 ▲ 🛝 ✏ 🚣 (covrd, htd) 🛁

Exit A1/E37 junc 73 or fr A30/E30 junc 13; foll sp to Tecklenburg, then Leeden & foll site sp. V lge, pt shd, pt sl, serviced pitches; EHU (16A) €2.90; 45% statics; adv bkg acc; ccard acc; bike hire; games area; CKE. *"Gd views; o'night area for m'vans open all yr; site clsd 1 Nov-15 Dec; clsd 1300-1500; excel san facs; gd rest."* €36.50   2018

OSTERODE AM HARZ *1D4* (2km E Rural) *51.72779, 10.28281* **Camping Eulenburg,** Scheerenbergstrasse 100, 37520 Osterode-am-Harz **(05522) 6611; ferien@ eulenburg-camping.de; www.eulenburg-camping.de**

12 🐕 €2 ♀♀ (htd) WD ♨ ♿ 🖥 ✉ MSP 🦋 ⊕ 🍴 ⊕ 🦮 nr

▲ 🚣 🛁

Take B498 fr Osterode cent, cross by-pass at traff lts. Site on R in 1.5km. Med, hdstg, mkd, hdg, pt shd, serviced pitches; EHU (6-16A) metered + conn fee; gas; bbq (charcoal, sep area); red long stay; 50% statics; Eng spkn; CKE. *"Beautiful old town; gd cent for Harz mountains; walks to lake fr site; motorhome stellplatze adj."* €21.00   2015

PAPENBURG *1B2* (1km S Rural) *53.06481, 7.42691* **Camping Poggenpoel,** Am Poggenpoel, 26871 Papenburg **(04961) 974026; campingpcp@ aol.com; www.papenburg-camping.de**

12 🐕 €2.50 ♀♀ (htd) WD ♨ ♿ 🖥 ✉ MSP 🦋 🍴 ⊕ 🦮

Fr B70, site sp fr town. 4*, Med, pt shd, EHU (10A) inc; sw nr; red long stay; TV (pitch); 40% statics; phone; games area; golf 1km; CKE. *"O'night facs for m'vans."* €27.50   2016

PAPPENHEIM *4E3* (1.8km N Rural) *48.93471, 10.96993* **Camping Pappenheim,** Badweg 1, 91788 Pappenheim **(09143) 1275; info@camping-pappenheim.de; www.camping-pappenheim.de**

🐕 €1 ♀♀ WD ♨ ✉ MSP 🦋 ⊕ nr 🦮 🛁

B2 heading S, site sp after passing thro Weissenburg, on edge of Pappenheim. Med, pt shd, EHU (16A) €2; sw; 25% statics; Eng spkn. *"Mountain views; excel site in historical town; castle worth visiting; grass pitches; san facs dated."* €20.00, 1 Apr-25 Oct.   2017

PASSAU *4G3* (10km NW Rural) *48.60605, 13.34583* **Drei-Flüsse Campingplatz,** Am Sonnenhang 8, 94113 Irring **(08546) 633; dreifluessecamping@t-online. de; www.dreifluessecamping.privat.t-online.de**

🐕 €1.50 ♀♀ WD ♿ 🖥 ✉ MSP ⊕ 🦮 ▲ 🏊 (covrd)

On A3/E56, junc 115 (Passau Nord); foll sps to site. 3*, Med, pt shd, pt sl, terr, serviced pitches; EHU (16A) €4; gas; bbq; red long stay; phone; bus 200m; adv bkg acc; ccard acc; CKE. *"Interesting grotto on site; gd rest; rec arr early; facs need updating; poor surface drainage after heavy rain; interesting town at confluence of 3 rvs; on Danube cycle way; conv NH fr A3/E56."* €28.00, 1 Apr-31 Oct.   2019

PFALZFELD *3B2* (1km SW Rural) *50.10612, 7.56804* **Country-Camping Schinderhannes,** Hausbayer strasse, 56291 Hausbay **(06746) 8005440; info@ countrycamping.de; www.countrycamping.de**

12 🐕 €2 ♀♀ (htd) WD ♨ ♿ 🖥 MSP 🦋 ⊕ 🍴 ⊕ 🦮 nr

Fr A61/E31 exit J43, foll sps for 3km to Pfalzfeld & onto Hausbay, site sp. 4*, Med, mkd, hdstg, pt shd, terr, EHU (6-16A) inc; sw; twin axles; 10% statics; adv bkg acc; ccard acc; fishing; games rm; tennis; CKE. *"Pleasant, peaceful, clean site; spacious pitches, some far fr san facs; helpful, friendly staff; sep NH area; excel, immac san facs; htd pool 8km; scenic area close Rv Rhine; vg cycle track; nice area for walking; conv m'way; excel NH with sep area to stay hitched-on; wonderful touring area; excel."* €26.00   2019

PFORZHEIM *3C3* (13km S Rural) *48.81800, 8.73400* **International Camping Schwarzwald,** Freibadweg 4, 75242 Neuhausen-Schellbronn **(07234) 6517; fam. frech@t-online.de; www.camping-schwarzwald.de**

12 ♀♀ WD ♿ 🖥 ✉ MSP 🦋 ⊕ 🍴 ⊕ 🦮 🛝 ▲ ✏

Fr W on A8 exit junc 43 for Pforzheim; fr E exit junc 45. In town cent take rd 463 sp Calw, but immed after end of town sp take minor rd L thro Huchenfeld up hill to Schellbronn; go R in vill. Site in vill of Schellbronn on N side of rd to Bad Liebenzell - sp at church on R. 4*, Lge, pt shd, pt sl, EHU (17A) €2 or metered; gas; red long stay; 80% statics; bus; adv bkg acc; bike hire; CKE. *"Scenic area; dance & fitness cent; no vehicle access after 2200; htd pool adj; v clean, well-maintained site; vg san facs; excel rest/takeaway; v rural."* €22.00   2016

PIELENHOFEN *4F3* (2km S Rural) *49.05896, 11.95820*
Campingplatz Naabtal, Distelhausen 2, 93188
Pielenhofen (09409) 373; camping-pielenhofen@t-
online.de; www.camping-pielenhofen.de

🕙 🐕 €2.20 ♂♀(htd) 🗷 ♨ ♿ 🖭 ✗ 🦋 🍽 ⒣ 🏊 ⚲

Exit A3/E56 junc 97 onto B8 dir Etterzhausen. Thro
Etterzhausen turn L to Pielenhofen/Amberg. In
Pielenhofen turn R over bdge. Lge, mkd, pt shd, EHU
(10A) metered + conn fee €0.60; gas; 65% statics; Eng
spkn; sauna; solarium; bike hire; games area; tennis;
CKE. *"In beautiful valley; helpful warden; v nice site in
gd location; liable to flooding; gd rv access for boating;
family-run site; lots of facs; skittle alley; summer
curling rink; spacious pitches; gd rest; conv Regensburg;
busy site."* **€17.60** 2015

PIRMASENS *3B3* (20km NE Rural) *49.27546, 7.72121*
Camping Clausensee, 67714 Waldfischbach-Burgalben
(06333) 5744; info@campingclausensee.de;
www.campingclausensee.de

🕙 🐕 €4.20 ♂♀(htd) 🗷 ♨ ♿ 🖭 ✗ 🦋 🍽 ⒣ 🏊 ⚲

Leave a'bahn A6 at junc 15 Kaiserslautern West;
S onto B270 for 22km. E 9km on minor rd sp
Leimen, site sp. 4*, Lge, mkd, pt shd, serviced pitches;
EHU (6-16A) inc; gas; bbq; sw nr; red long stay;
TV; 50% statics; Eng spkn; adv bkg acc; ccard acc;
fishing; games rm; boating; CKE. *"Peaceful situation
in Pfalzerwald Park; helpful staff; clean san facs; busy
at w/ends; gd walking & cycling; gd; lovely setting
on shore of Lake Clausensee; noisy at wkends when
permanent o'fits inhabited."* **€31.50** 2016

**"I like to fill in the reports as I
travel from site to site"**

You'll find report forms at the back of this
guide, or you can fill them in online at
camc.com/europereport.

PORTA WESTFALICA *1C3* (8km SW Rural) *52.22146,
8.83995* **Camping Grosser Weserbogen,** Zum
Südlichen See 1, 32457 Porta Westfalica (05731)
6188 or 6189; info@grosserweserbogen.de;
www.grosserweserbogen.de

🕙 🐕 €1.50 ♂♀ 🗷 ♨ ♿ 🖭 ✗ 🦋 ⒣ 🍽 ⒣ 🏊 ⚲

Fr E30/A2 exit junc 33, foll sp to Vennebeck &
Costedt. Site 12km by rd fr Bad Oeynhausen. Site
sp fr m'way. 4*, Lge, mkd, hdstg, pt shd, EHU (16A)
€2.90; bbq; sw nr; twin axles; Eng spkn; adv bkg acc;
ccard acc; fishing; watersports; games rm; CKE. *"Site
in cent of wildlife reserve; v tranquil, lovely lakeside
location; gd base Teutoburger Wald & Weser valley;
barrier clsd 1300-1500 & o'night; 80% statics; lge area
for tourers; gd for families; excel san facs & rest; shwrs
charged to electronic card; level access; highly rec."*
€27.00 2016

POTSDAM *2F3* (10km SW Rural) *52.36088, 12.94663*
Camping Riegelspitze, Fercherstrasse, 14542
Werder-Petzow (03327) 42397; info@campingplatz-
riegelspitze.de; www.campingplatz-riegelspitze.de

🐕 €3 ♂♀ 🖭 ♨ ♿ 🖭 ✗ 🦋 🍽 ⒣ 🏊 ⚲

Fr A10/E55 Berlin ring a'bahn take exit 22 dir
Glindow or Werder exits & foll sp to Werder; then
foll B1 for 1.5km twd Potsdam, R after
Strengbrücke bdge twd Petzow. 4*, Lge, pt shd, terr,
EHU (16A) €0.50 (poss rev pol & long lead req); sw;
50% statics; bus; Eng spkn; adv bkg acc; watersports;
bike hire; CKE. *"Friendly recep; haphazard pitching;
no dogs high ssn; transport tickets fr recep; recep
clsd 1300-1500 and 2200-0700; bus outside site;
Sanssouci visit a must; train to Berlin £6; vg."*
€26.50, 1 Apr-25 Oct. 2016

POTSDAM *2F3* (10km SW Rural) *52.35278,
12.98981* **Naturcampingplatz Himmelreich,**
Wentorfinsel, 14548 Caputh (033209) 70475;
info@berlin-potsdam-camping.de; www.berlin-
potsdam-camping.de

🐕 €2 ♂♀(htd) 🖭 ♨ ♿ 🖭 ✗ 🍽 ⒣ 🏊

Exit A10 junc 20 or 23 to Glindow. Take B1 to
Geltow, turn L immed after rlwy x-ring & foll sp
Caputh. Do not foll sat nav. 3*, Lge, shd, EHU (10A)
€1.50 (poss rev-pol); 65% statics; phone; adv bkg acc;
boat hire; CKE. *"Lovely position on waterfront, ferry
750m; modern san facs; poss haphazard pitching; cycle
rtes & walks; lake adj; 2 pin adaptor needed for some
pitches."* **€30.00, 1 Apr-31 Oct.** 2015

POTSDAM *2F3* (7km SW Rural) *52.36055, 13.00722*
Camping Sanssouci, An der Pirschheide 41, 14471
Potsdam (0331) 9510988; info@camping-potsdam.de;
www.camping-potsdam.de

🐕 €4.90 ♂♀ 🖭 ♨ ♿ 🖭 ✗ 🦋 ⒣ 🍽 ⒣ 🏊 ⚲

Fr A10 Berlin ring rd take exit 22 at Gross Kreutz
onto B1 twd Potsdam cent for approx 17km, past
Werder (Havel) & Geltow. Site sp approx 2km after
Geltow immed bef rlwy bdge. 5*, Lge, shd, serviced
pitches; EHU (6A) inc (poss rev pol); gas; bbq; sw nr;
25% statics; Eng spkn; adv bkg acc; horseriding 8km;
games rm; bike hire; watersports; fishing; CKE. *"V
helpful, friendly owners; lovely area; sandy pitches;
poss diff lge o'fits manoeuvring round trees; excel
clean facs inc music & underfloor heating; camp
bus to/fr stn; gate clsd 1300-1500; fitness cent; gd
security; covrd pool 200m; conv Schlosses & Berlin
by rail - minibus to stn; excel site and rest; 5 star facs;
sm pitches; site & rest cash only; gate opens 7.30am;
new kitchen, washup and dog shwr (2016); rec."*
€36.00, 18 Mar-2 Jan, G16. 2016

POTTENSTEIN *4E2* (3km NW Rural) *49.77942, 11.38411* **Feriencampingplatz Bärenschlucht,** 12 Weidmannsgesees, 91278 Pottenstein **(09243) 206;** info@baerenschlucht-camping.de; www.baeren schlucht-camping.de

12 🐕 €1.90 👫(htd) WD ♨ ☵ ♿ 🚐 ♦ MSP 🦋 ⛾ (H) 🅿nr

Exit A9 junc 44 onto B470 dir Forchheim; cont past Pottenstein; site in 2km on R. Med, pt shd, pt sl, EHU (8-16A) €1.90; gas; cooking facs; 40% statics. *"A naturalized quarry surrounded by trees & rocky cliffs; vg; scenic area; local caves & climbing; excel local rest and san facs; adv bkg via email."* **€20.00**   **2016**

PREETZ *1D1* (6km SE Rural) *54.21073, 10.31720* **Camp Lanker See,** Gläserkoppel 3, 24211 Preetz-Gläserkoppel **(04342) 81513; camp@lankersee.de;** www.camp-lankersee.de

🐕 €1 👫 WD ♨ ♦ 🦋 ⛾ (H) 🅿 🛝

Sp off B76 bet Preetz & Plön. 4*, Lge, mkd, pt shd, terr, EHU (6A) metered; sw; 10% statics; phone; adv bkg acc; ccard acc; horseriding; boating; CKE. *"Barrier clsd 1300-1500 & o'night; gd."* **€19.00, 1 Apr-31 Oct.**   **2016**

PRUM *3A2* (2km NE Rural) *50.21906, 6.43811* **Waldcamping Prüm,** 54591 Prüm **(06551) 2481;** info@waldcamping-pruem.de; www.waldcamping-pruem.de

12 👫 €2.50 👫 WD ♨ ☵ ♿ 🚐 ♦ MSP 🦋 ♈ (H) 🅿nr 🛌 🛝 ✎

Site sp fr town cent dir Dausfeld. 4*, Med, pt shd, EHU (10-16A) inc; gas; 60% statics; Eng spkn; adv bkg acc; ccard acc; tennis adj; bike hire; CKE. *"Pleasant site in lovely surroundings; pool complex adj; friendly staff; clean facs; m'van o'night facs; ski lift 2km; o'night facs for m'vans; do not arr bef 1900 on Sundays due local rd closures for family cycling event."* **€28.20**   **2019**

QUEDLINBURG *2E3* (10km SW Urban) *51.75614, 11.04956* **Kloster Camping Thale,** Burghardt Wilsdorf, Wendhusenstraße 3, 06502 Thale **(03947) 63185;** info@klostercamping-thale.de; www.kloster camping-thale.de

12 👫(htd) WD ♨ ☵ ♦ MSP 🦋 ⛾ (H) 🅿 🅿nr 🛝

Head S twds Steinholzstraße. 1st R onto Steinholzstraße. Bear L onto Stauffenberg-Platz. Turn L onto Weststraße cont onto Wipertistraße for 1.4km then onto Unter der Altenburg. Cont onto K2356, turn L onto Thalenser Str. Cont onto L240 then turn L onto L92. After 1.4km turn L onto Schmiedestraße. Then R onto Breiteweg & bear R onto Wendhusenstraße. Site on LH side. Med, mkd, hdstg, pt shd, EHU (10A) €2.50; 10% statics; bus 0.3km; CKE. *"San facs excel; lovely site with gdn & lake."* **€27.00**   **2018**

RADEVORMWALD *1B4* (5km SW Rural) *51.18498, 7.31362* **Camping-Ferienpark Kräwinkel,** Kräwinkel 1, 42477 Radevormwald **(02195) 6887899; info@** ferienpark.de

12 🐕 €2 👫(htd) WD ♨ ♿ ♦ 🦋 ⛾ (H) 🛝

Exit A1 at junc 95B, take B229 sp Radevormwald, foll B229 for 6km over lake bdge to 1st rndabt, R sp Heide & Kräwinkel, site on L in 3km. Sm, hdg, pt shd, terr, EHU (20A) inc; sw nr; 80% statics; Eng spkn; adv bkg acc; CKE. *"Lge pitches; pleasant area; key needed for all facs €10 deposit; friendly owner; call nbr on noticeboard for access."* **€16.00**   **2017**

RADOLFZELL AM BODENSEE *3C4* (16km S Rural) *47.65972, 8.93388* **Campingplatz Wangen,** Seeweg 32, 78337 Öhningen-Wangen **(07735) 919675; info@** camping-wangen.de; www.camping-wangen.de

🐕 €2 👫 WD ♨ ☵ ♿ 🚐 ♦ MSP 🦋 ♈ ⛾ (H) 🅿 🅿nr 🛝

Site in Wangen vill, 5km E of Stein am Rhien. 4*, Med, hdstg, pt shd, EHU (10A) metered + conn fee; bbq; sw nr; twin axles; 40% statics; phone; Eng spkn; adv bkg acc; games area; fishing; CKE. *"Lovely scenery; site in vill but quiet; dogs by prior arrangement only; helpful recep; gd cycling & sw; lake steamer trips; Stein-am-Rhein 5km; watersports in adj lake."* **€22.00, 3 Apr-3 Oct.**   **2019**

RADOLFZELL AM BODENSEE *3C4* (6km SW Urban) *47.72942, 9.02432* **Campingplatz Willam,** 78315 Markelfingen **(049) 7533 6211; info@campingplatz-willam.de;** www.campingplatz-willam.de

👫 WD ♨ ♦ ⛾ (H) 🛝 🅿adj

Fr S on A81 at junc 40 take A98 for 9m, at end of m'way turn L, site ent on L in 0.75m. Lge, mkd, pt shd, EHU (€0.7/kWh); gas; bbq; Eng spkn; boat hire; CKE. *"Gd site; cycle track; modern san facs; some noise fr rlwy; 2.6m low bdge nr site ent (can be avoided)."* **€20.50, 23 Mar-3 Oct.**   **2016**

RAVENSBURG *3D4* (13km SW Rural) *47.73935, 9.47187* **Camping am Bauernhof,** St Georg Strasse 8, 88094 Oberteuringen-Neuhaus **(07546) 2446;** kramer@camping-am-bauernhof.de; www.camping-am-bauernhof.de

🐕 €2 👫 WD ♨ ♿ ♦ 🦋 🅿nr 🛝

Fr Ravensburg twd Meersburg on B33. In Neuhaus foll sp on R; site bef chapel. Sm, pt shd, EHU (10A) €2.50; bbq; sw; 20% statics; Eng spkn; games rm; CKE. *"CL-type but with full facs inc shwrs for wheelchair users; vg, clean, modern san facs; volleyball; relaxed atmosphere; gd cycling area; farm with animals, fruit, distillery, herb garden, barn; sm lake on site; pre order fresh rolls/bread daily; excel site; lots of interest for kids; sep park for m'van on hdstg; friendly, helpful owners."* **€22.50, 28 Mar-15 Sep.**   **2015**

REGENSBURG *4F3* (5km NW Urban) *49.02779, 12.05899* **Azur Campingpark Regensburg,** Weinweg 40, 93049 Regensburg **(0941) 270025; regensburg@azur-camping.de; www.azur-camping.de**

🏕 12 🐕 €3.50 👪 (htd) 🚿 ♨ ♿ 🚮 ⊘ 🏧 MSP 🦋 ♈ 🍽 🕐 🅿 🅰

Fr A93/E50 exit junc 40 Regensburg W, dir Weiden; turn W away fr town onto dual c'way; R at traff lts, site sp fr next T-junc. Lge, hdstg, pt shd, EHU (10A) €3 (poss long lead req); 40% statics; phone; bus at site ent; bike hire; CKE. *"Helpful owner; vg facs; gd, clean san facs, lge block unisex; covrd pool 300m; sm pitches poss diff lge o'fits; dist bet units minimal; o'night m'vans area; cycle path into town along Rv Danube; gates clsd 1300-1500 & 2200-0800; gd."* **€31.00**

2015

REINSBERG *2G4* (1km W Rural) *51.00381, 13.36012* **Campingplatz Reinsberg,** Badstrasse 17, 19629 Reinsberg **(037324) 82268; campingplatz-reinsberg@web.de; www.campingplatz-reinsberg.de**

🐕 €2 👪 (htd) 🚿 ♨ ♿ 🚮 ⊘ 🦋 ♈ 🍽 nr 🕐 nr 🅰

Exit A4/E40 junc 75 Nossen. Take 1st R to Siebenlehn & foll sp Reinsberg. In Reinsberg take 1st R sp camping & 'freibad' to site. 3*, Med, pt shd, EHU (16A) €2; 40% statics; phone; Eng spkn; adv bkg acc. *"Friendly, helpful owner; sports facs adj; excel san facs; gd walking; conv Meissen, Dresden & Freiberg; v clean; peaceful; pool adj; gd for dogs, walks and cycling."* **€16.00, 25 Mar-31 Oct.**

2016

REMAGEN *3B1* (1km ENE Urban) *50.57666, 7.25083* **Campingplatz Goldene Meile,** Simrockweg 9-13, 53424 Remagen **(02642) 22222; info@camping-goldene-meile.de; www.camping-goldene-meile.de**

🏕 12 🐕 €1.70 👪 🚿 ♨ ♿ 🚮 ⊘ MSP ♈ 🍽 🕐 🅿 🅰

Fr A61 exit dir Remagen onto B266; foll sp 'Rheinfähre Linz'; in Kripp turn L, site sp. Or fr B266 1km beyond Bad Bodendorf at rndabt take B9 (dir Bonn & Remagen); in 1km take exit Remagen Süd; foll sp to sports cent/camping. Site adj Luddendorf Bdge. Fr S on A48 exit junc 10 onto B9 twd Bonn. Site sp in 22km after junc with B266. 4*, Lge, hdstg, hdg, mkd, pt shd, serviced pitches; EHU (16A) €2.60 (50m cable rec some pitches); gas; 50% statics; train into Bonn; Eng spkn; adv bkg acc; bike hire; CKE. *"Tourers on flat field away fr rvbank; sm pitches tightly packed in high ssn; gd rest; helpful staff; EHU up ladder; access to facs not gd; cycle path along Rhine; m'van o'night area adj; site clsd 1300-1500; vg, well-organised site; pool adj; interesting old town."* **€27.50**

2018

RERIK *2E1* (1km NE Urban) *54.11133, 11.63234* **Campingpark Ostseebad Rerik,** Straße am Zeltplatz 18230 Ostseebad Rerik **038296 75720; info@campingpark-rerik.de; www.campingpark-rerik.de**

🏕 12 🐕 €3 👪 (htd) 🚿 ♨ ♿ 🚮 ⊘ 🦋 ♈ 🍽 🕐 🅰 🛶

Fr A20 junc 12 to Kröpelin on L12 thro Kröelin twrds Rerik then foll sp to site. 5*, Med, hdg, mkd, pt shd, EHU (16A); Eng spkn; ccard acc. *"Gd site; new modern facs."* **€27.00**

2016

RETGENDORF *2E2* (4.6km N Rural) *53.75194, 11.49638* **Seecamping Flessenow,** Am Schweriner See 1A, 19067 Flessenow **(03866) 81491; info@seecamping.de; www.seecamping.de**

🐕 👪 (htd) 🚿 ♨ ♿ 🚮 ⊘ MSP 🦋 ♈ 🍽 🅰

Exit A14 at junc 4 Schwerin-Nord onto B104 dir Schwerin. In 2km turn R along lakeside sp Retgendorf & Flessenow, site in approx 10km. 4*, Med, mkd, pt shd, EHU (10A) €2.50; gas; bbq (charcoal); sw nr; twin axles; TV; 50% statics; phone; bus adj; adv bkg acc; ccard acc; watersports; games area; CKE. *"Fair site in gd location; gd long stay for touring."* **€30.00, 30 Mar-14 Oct.**

2018

RHEINMUNSTER *3C3* (1km NW Rural) *48.77330, 8.04041* **Freizeitcenter Oberrhein,** Am Campingpark 1, 77836 Rheinmünster-Stollhofen **(07227) 2500; info@freizeitcenter-oberrhein.de; www.freizeitcenter-oberrhein.de**

🏕 12 🐕 €4.50 👪 🚿 ♨ ♿ 🚮 ⊘ MSP 🦋 ♈ 🍽 🕐 🅿 🅰 ⚓

Exit A5 junc 51 at Baden Baden/Iffezheim sp to join B500. At traff lts turn L onto B36 dir Hügelsheim & Kehl. In 8km turn R at rndabt immed on ent Stollhofen & cont to end of lane. 5*, V lge, mkd, hdg, pt shd, serviced pitches; EHU (16A) €2.50 + conn fee; gas; sw; 70% statics; phone; Eng spkn; adv bkg acc; ccard acc; watersports; windsurfing; golf 6km; tennis; fishing; bike hire. *"Conv touring base Baden-Baden, Strasbourg; Black Forest; helpful, nice staff; clsd 1300-1500; m'van o'night area outside site; excel san facs; highly rec; some lovely lakeside pitches; gd cycling by Rhine."* **€32.00**

2015

RIBNITZ DAMGARTEN *2F1* (13km NE Coastal) *54.28194, 12.31250* **Camping in Neuhaus,** Birkenallee 10, 18347 Dierhagen-Neuhaus **(038226) 539930; ostsee@camping-neuhaus.de; www.camping-neuhaus.de**

🏕 12 🐕 €3 👪 (htd) 🚿 ♨ ♿ 🚮 ⊘ 🦋 ♈ 🍽 nr 🅰 🛶 100m

Exit E55/A19 junc 6 onto B105 N. At Altheide turn N thro Klockenhagen dir Dierhagen, then turn L at camping sp & foll site sp to sea. Med, hdg, pt shd, EHU (16A); 40% statics; adv bkg acc. *"Friendly site; vg."* **€28.00**

2016

RIBNITZ DAMGARTEN *2F1* (13km NW Coastal) *54.29188, 12.34375* **Ostseecamp Dierhagen,** Ernst Moritz Arndt Strasse, 18347 Dierhagen-Strand **(038226) 80778; info@ostseecamp-dierhagen.de; www.ostseecamp-dierhagen.de**

🐕 €2.80 👪 🚿 ♨ ♿ 🚮 ⊘ 🦋 nr 🅰 🛶 sand 800m

Take B105 fr Rostock dir Stralsund. Bef Ribnitz, turn L sp Dierhagen & Wustrow & cont for 5km to traff lts & camp sp. Turn L to site on R in 300m. Lge, pt shd, EHU (6A) €3; gas; 20% statics; phone; adv bkg req; bike hire. *"Site low-lying, poss v wet after heavy rain; bkg fee; charge for chem disp."* **€34.00, 15 Mar-31 Oct.**

2016

GERMANY

RIEGEL AM KAISERSTUHL *3B4* (1.5km N Rural) *48.16463, 7.74008* **Camping Müller-See,** Zum Müller-See 1, 79359 Riegel-am-Kaiserstuhl **(07642) 3694; info@muellersee.de; www.muellersee.de**

†‖‖ (htd) ⬚ ♨ ⚲ ♿ 🖃 ⊿ ✎ ❦ ➊ nr ➋ nr 🏕

Exit A5/E35 at junc 59 dir Riegel, foll site sp. 4*, Med, pt shd, EHU (16A) €2; sw nr; phone; CKE. *"Excel cycle paths in area; excel san facs; gd NH; train to Freiburg; sep excel MH area (unshd, €10 inc acc to all facs); elec fr pay boxes."* **€25.00, 1 Apr-31 Oct.** **2019**

RIESTE *1C3* (0.2km W Rural) *52.48555, 7.99003* **Alfsee Ferien- und Erholungspark,** Am Campingpark 10, 49597 Rieste **(05464) 92120; info@alfsee.de; www.alfsee.de**

12 ⊿ €5 †‖‖ (htd) ⬚ ♨ ⚲ ♿ 🖃 ⊿ ✎ ❦ ➊ ❦ ❦ ➋ 🏕

Exit A1/E37 junc 67; site in 10km, sp. 5*, V lge, mkd, pt shd, EHU (16A) metered; sw nr; 50% statics; phone; Eng spkn; ccard acc; tennis; watersports; bike hire; CKE. *"Site pt of lge watersports complex; modern san facs; gd for famiies, conv for Osnotbruk old town; excel pitch; vg facs; may be noisy."* **€37.30** **2019**

ROSENHEIM *4F4* (9km N Rural) *47.92518, 12.13571* **Camping Erlensee,** Rosenheimerstrasse 63, 83135 Schechen **(08039) 1695; campingplatz-erlensee@t-online.de; www.camping-erlensee.de**

12 ⊿ €2 †‖‖ ⬚ ♨ ♿ 🖃 ⊿ ✎ ❦ ➊ ➋ nr

Exit A8 junc 102, avoid Rosenheim town cent foll B15 sp Landshut. Site on E side of B15 at S end Schechen. 3*, Med, pt shd, serviced pitches; EHU (16A) €2; sw; 60% statics; Eng spkn; adv bkg acc; CKE. *"Pleasant, gd & simple site; helpful owners; excel facs; mosquito prob."* **€25.00** **2019**

ROSENHEIM *4F4* (14km SW Rural) *47.78978, 12.00575* **Kaiser Camping (formerly known as Tenda-Park),** Reithof 2, 83075 Bad Feilnbach **(08066) 884400; info@kaiser-camping.com; www.kaiser-camping.com**

12 ⊿ €3 †‖‖ ⬚ ♨ ⚲ ♿ 🖃 ⊿ ✎ ❦ ⊿ ➊ ➋ 🏕 ✎ ⚲ (htd) ⚒

Take exit 100 fr A8/E45/E52 & foll sp to Brannenburg. Site in 5km on R, 1km N of Bad Feilnbach. 4*, V lge, pt shd, EHU (16A) €2 or metered + conn fee (poss rev pol); gas; 80% statics; Eng spkn; adv bkg acc; bike hire. *"V busy, clean, well-run site; pleasant, wooded pitches; useful NH; pleasant helpful staff; some of the best san facs; ski lift 12km; discount vouchers for local shops/rest."* **€32.00** **2017**

ROSTOCK *2F1* (23.5km NNE Rural/Coastal) *54.194259, 12.155333* **Camp & Ferienpark Markgrafenheide,** Budentannenweg 2, 18146 Markgrafenheide **(938166) 11510 or (45448) 00313; info@baltic-freizeit.de; www.baltic-freizeit.de**

12 ⊿ †‖‖ ⬚ ♨ 🖃 ⊿ ✎ ❦ ➊ ➋ ⚲ ➋

🏕 ⚲ (covrd, htd) ⚲ 100m

Take B105/E22 fr Rostock twrds Stralsund. Aft 9km exit twrds Markgrafenheide & Niederhagen. Aft 3.5km turn L. Aft approx 4km sharp R, site immed on L. Lge, mkd, shd, EHU (16A); bbq; TV; Eng spkn; adv bkg acc; sauna; games area; bike hire; CKE. *"Vg site; 20mins fr ferry terminal; max 2 dog; wellness ctr."* **€36.50** **2018**

ROTHENBURG OB DER TAUBER *3D2* (3km NW Rural) *49.38805, 10.16638* **Camping Tauber-Idyll,** Detwang 28, 91541 Rothenburg-ob-der-Tauber **(09861) 3177 or 6463; camping-tauber-idyll@t-online.de; www.rothenburg.de/tauberidyll**

✎ €1 †‖‖ (htd) ⬚ ♨ ⊿ ✎ ❦ ➊ nr ➋

NW on Rothenburg-Bad Mergentheim rd in vill of Detwang. Sp. Site behind inn nr church. Care on tight R turn into ent. Sm, pt shd, EHU (6-16A) €2 or metered + conn fee; gas; bus; Eng spkn; adv bkg rec; bike hire. *"Church clock chimes each hr; clsd to vehicles 2200-0800; old walled town, gd cent for Romantische Strasse & Hohenlohe Plain; owners helpful, friendly; pleasant, peaceful, excel site; gd, clean san facs; sm c'van pitches at busy times; gd walking & cycle rte along valley; playgrnd at church; rec."* **€20.00, 23 Mar-31 Oct.** **2018**

ROTHENBURG OB DER TAUBER *3D2* (3km NW Rural) *49.38888, 10.16722* **Campingplatz Tauber-Romantik,** Detwang 39, 91541 Rothenburg-ob-der-Tauber **(09861) 6191; info@camping-tauber romantik.de; www.camping-tauberromantik.de**

✎ €2 †‖‖ (htd) ⬚ ♨ ⚲ ♿ 🖃 ⊿ ✎ ❦ ✎ ➊ nr ⚲ ➋ 🏕

NW on Rothenburg-Bad Mergentheim rd in vill of Detwang; turn L at camp sp & immed R; site sp fr Rothenburg. Sharp turn into site ent. Med, mkd, hdstg, pt shd, pt sl, terr, EHU (16A) €2.40; gas; 10% statics; phone; bus adj; Eng spkn; adv bkg acc; ccard acc; CKE. *"Pleasant, gd value site; excel, clean, vg facs; gd sized pitches; picturesque town; gd cycle rte; pleasant atmosphere; gd facs for children; conv NH for Rothenburg, Austria, Italy; busy over festival w/ends; vg; well managed."* **€24.00, 15 Mar-4 Nov & 30 Nov-7 Jan.** **2017**

RUDESHEIM *3C2* (3km E Urban) *49.97944, 7.95777* **Camping Geisenheim Rheingau,** Am Campingplatz 1, 65366 Geisenheim **(06722) 75600; campingplatz geisenheim@t-online.de; www.rheingau-camping.de**

✎ €1.50 †‖‖ (htd) ⬚ ♨ ⚲ ♿ 🖃 ⊿ ✎ ❦ ➊ ➋ nr 🏕

Well sp fr B42, on rvside. 3*, Lge, mkd, pt shd, EHU (16A) metered 1 + 0.76 per kWh; bbq; 50% statics; bus adj; Eng spkn; adv bkg acc; games area; CKE. *"Vg site bet Rv Rhine & vineyards; walks and cycling by rv; lots to do."* **€25.00, 15 Mar-31 Oct.** **2017**

RUDESHEIM *3C2* (2km SE Urban) 49.97777, 7.94083
Camping am Rhein, Auf der Lach, 65385 Rüdesheim-am-Rhein **(06722) 2528 or 49299 (LS);** info@camping platz-ruedesheim.de; www.campingplatz-ruedesheim.de

🛖 €3 ♦♦(htd) 🆆 ♨ ᕒ ᕗ ⬛ ⁄ 🆖 𝖸 🕀nr ⚏ ⚑

Fr Koblenz (N) on B42 pass car ferry to Bingen on app to Rüdesheim; turn L & over rlwy x-ing, foll Rheinstrasse & rlwy E for 1km; cont under rlwy bdge, turn R sp to Car Park 6; turn R at T-junc, pass coach park; turn L at x-rds & foll rd to site on R. When arr via Bingen ferry turn R onto B42 & foll above dir fr level x-ing. Fr S on B42 ent Rüdesheim, turn L immed after o'head rlwy bdge (2.8m); foll camping sp. Lge, pt shd, EHU (10A) inc (poss rev pol & poss long lead req); gas; bbq (charcoal, gas); bus 500m; Eng spkn; adv bkg acc; horseriding 4km; tennis adj; bike hire; CKE. *"Pleasant, busy, family-run, well-kept site; gd, clean modern facs; poss long walk to water supply; pleasant 1km walk/cycleway by rv to town; warden sites you & connects elec - no mkd pitches; perforated grnd sheets only allowed; recep 0800-2200; rallies welcome; htd pool, paddling pool adj; Harley Davidson w/end bike festival in June; no o'fits over 11m; pool adj; shwrs far; pleasant loc by rv; shops conv."* **€31.00,** 1 May-3 Oct, G08. 2016

SAARBURG *3B2* (5km S Urban) 49.59937, 6.54143
Camping Leukbachtal, 54439 Saarburg **(06581) 2228;** service@campingleukbachtal.de; www.camping leukbachtal.de

🛖 €2 ♦♦ 🆆 ♨ ⁄ 🦋 🕈 🕀 ⚏nr ⚑

Fr B51 Trier-Sarbrucken rd on S end Saarburg ring rd, take exit sp Nennig, Wincheringen, site sp. Site on o'skirts of Saarburg on L of B407. 3*, Med, hdg, pt shd, EHU (6A); bbq; sw nr; Eng spkn; adv bkg acc; CKE. *"Gd walking area; m'van o'night rate; interesting scenic town; vg."* **€19.70,** 19 Mar-15 Oct. 2016

SAARBURG *3B2* (3km W Rural) 49.60083, 6.52833
Campingplatz Waldfrieden, Im Fichtenhain 4, 54439 Saarburg **(06581) 2255;** info@campingwaldfrieden.de; www.campingwaldfrieden.de

12 🛖 €2 ♦♦ 🆆 ♨ ᕒ ⁄ 🆖 🦋 🕈 𝖸 ⚏ ⏣nr ⚑

Fr B51/B407 bypass foll sp 'krankenhaus' (hospital). Site sp off L132. 4*, Med, hdg, hdstg, pt shd, pt sl, serviced pitches; EHU (16A) metered; gas; bbq; cooking facs; red long stay; TV; 60% statics; Eng spkn; adv bkg acc; bike hire; CKE. *"Highly rec; helpful owners; warm welcome; clean facs; pitches poss tight lge o'fits; Aldi & Rewe supmkt 1km."* **€24.00** 2016

SAARBURG *3B2* (4km NW Rural) 49.62010, 6.54274
Camping Landal Warsberg, In den Urlaub, 54439 Saarburg **31-(0)70 300 35 06;** warsberg@landal.de; www.landal.de

🛖 €3 ♦♦ 🆆 ♨ ᕒ ᕗ ⬛ ⁄ 🆖 𝖸 🕀 ⚏ ⚑ 🏊 (covrd, htd)

Fr Trier foll B51 S and turn at rd sp Saarbrücken at Konz, after 25km on leaving Ayl vill turn R sp Saarburg. Cont over bdge turn R sp Centre. At rndabt turn L thro cent, at rndabt L into rd sp Warsburg, after 300m turn L uphill sp Landal. 5*, V lge, mkd, pt shd, pt sl, EHU (6A) inc; gas; bbq; ccard acc; games rm; tennis; bike hire. *"Excel; gd san facs; chem disp diff to use; excel pool; site clsd 1300-1500; chairlift to attractive town cent; gd views; many activities all ages."* **€32.00,** 3 Apr-9 Nov. 2020

SAARLOUIS *3B2* (11km NW Rural) 49.36732, 6.66043
Camping Siersburg, Zum Niedwehr 1, 66780 Siersburg **(06835) 2100;** info@campingplatz-siersburg.de; www.campingplatz-siersburg.de

🛖 €2 ♦♦ 🆆 ♨ ⁄ 🦋 🕈 ⚏ ⚑

Fr Saarlouis, leave A8 at junc 7, foll Rehlingen, turn off to Siersburg. Foll sp in Siersburg for site thro town to o'skirts. Lge, mkd, pt shd, EHU (16A); bbq; twin axles; Eng spkn; games area. *"Spacious site in rv Nied; walking & cycling rtes nrby; ruined castle in town; vg."* **€19.00,** 1 Apr-31 Oct. 2015

SAARLOUIS *3B2* (2km NW Urban) 49.31833, 6.73972
Campingpark Saarlouis Dr Ernst Dadder, Marschall-Ney-Weg 2, 66740 Saarlouis **(06831) 3691;** info@campingplatz-saarlouis.de; www.campingplatz-saarlouis.de

🛖 €0.60 ♦♦ ♨ ⁄ 🆖 🦋 🕈 ⚏nr

Exit A620/E29 junc 2. Foll sp to city cent. At 500m approx turn L at traff lts sp 'Schiffanlegestelle'. At 500m approx site on R. 3*, Med, pt shd, EHU (16A) €2.30 or metered; gas; red long stay; 50% statics; Eng spkn; adv bkg acc; ccard acc; CKE. *"Castles, Roman remains, ruins & forest rds at Saarland & Saarbrücken; htd pool 150m; beautifully situated & clean; conv for A8; 15min walk to town; friendly, helpful owner; gd rest; cycle rte along R Saar; recep clsd 1200-1400."* **€21.00,** 15 Mar-31 Oct. 2018

SALEM *3D4* (2.6km NE Rural) 47.76926, 9.30693
Gern-Campinghof Salem, Weildorferstrasse 46, 88682 Salem-Neufrach **(07553) 829695;** info@campinghof-salem.de; www.campinghof-salem.de

🛖 €2 ♦♦(htd) 🆆 ♨ ᕒ ⁄ 🦋 𝖸 🕀nr ⚑

Site well sp on all app to Neufrach on rvside. 4*, Med, mkd, unshd, pt sl, EHU (16A) €2; gas; bbq; cooking facs; sw nr; TV (pitch); 5% statics; phone; bus; Eng spkn; adv bkg acc; ccard acc; tennis; games rm; CKE. *"Excel touring base for Lake Constance away fr busy lakeside sites; htd covrd pool 4km; barrier clsd 1230-1500 & 2200-0700; avoid pitches by recep - noise & dust; gd, clean san facs; friendly, helpful owners; no dogs Jul/Aug; gd for families; vg."* **€25.50,** 1 Apr-31 Oct. 2018

SCHILLINGSFURST *3D3* (2km S Rural) *49.27353, 10.26587* **Campingplatz Frankenhöhe,** Fischhaus 2, 91583 Schillingsfürst (09868) 5111; info@camping platz-frankenhoehe.de; www.campingplatz-frankenhoehe.de

🗓12 🐕 €1.50 (htd) �🅆ⅅ ♨ ♿ 🆗 ⅋ MSP ⅋ ⅟⅟ ₐₙ 🔥 /Λ\

Fr A7/E43 exit junc 109; fr A6/E50 exit junc 49. Site situated bet Dombühl & Schillingsfürst. 3*, Med, pt shd, pt sl, EHU (16A) €2.50 or metered + conn fee; gas; sw nr; red long stay; 40% statics; phone; adv bkg acc; CKE. *"Very clean facs; barrier clsd 1300-1500 & 2100-0700; poss unkempt early ssn (2009); gd cycle paths; ACSI prices; gd NH."* **€21.00** **2017**

SCHILTACH *3C3* (0.8km W Urban) *48.29061, 8.33746* **Camping Schiltach,** Bahnhofstrasse 6, 77761 Schiltach (07836) 7289; campingplatz-schiltach@t-online.de

⅟⅟ (htd) ⅁ ♨ ♿ 🆗 ⅋ MSP ⅟⅟ ⅍ ⅟⅟ ₐₙ 🔥 /Λ\

Site on B294 sp on ent to vill; short, steep ent & sharp turns. 3*, Sm, mkd, pt shd, EHU (16A) metered + conn fee; bbq; 2% statics; phone; train 200m; Eng spkn; adv bkg acc; CKE. *"Vg, clean, tidy site on rv bank adj indus est; covrd pool 2km; recep clsd 1230-1430; picturesque vill; disused rlwy bdge over pt of site, 2.6m headrm; friendly staff."* **€21.70, 1 Apr-10 Oct.** **2016**

SCHLEIDEN *3B1* (6km NW Rural) *50.52752, 6.41195* **Camping Schafbachmühle,** 53937 Schleiden-Harperscheid (02485) 268; info@schafbachmuehle.de; www.schafbachmuehle.de

🗓12 🐕 €2.20 ⅟⅟ (htd) ⅁ ♨ ♿ 🆗 ⅋ MSP ⅟⅟ 🔥 /Λ\

Fr Schleiden take B258 twd Monschau. In 3.5km turn R sp Schafbachmühle. Site in 2.5km on L. Med, hdstg, mkd, pt shd, terr, EHU (10A) metered + conn fee; bbq; 60% statics; phone; Eng spkn; adv bkg acc; games area. *"Tranquil site; gd for touring Eifel, Mosel Valley, Rhine Valley."* **€20.50** **2016**

SCHLESWIG *1D1* (6km S Rural) *54.50111, 9.57027* **Wikinger Camping Haithabu,** 24866 Haddeby (04621) 32450; info@campingplatz-haithabu.de; www.campingplatz-haithabu.de

🐕 €2 ⅟⅟ ⅁ ♨ ♿ 🆗 ⅋ MSP ⅟⅟ ⅟⅟ ₐₙ 🔥 /Λ\

Leave A7/45 N & S junc 6. Travel E two Schleswig & turn R onto B76 sp Kiel & Eckernförde. Site on L in 2km sp. Med, pt shd, EHU (16A) €2; bbq; sw nr; 10% statics; bus; Eng spkn; adv bkg acc; fishing; bike hire; CKE. *"Lovely site on rv with lovely views; foot & cycle paths to Schleswig (4.5km) & ferry; gd area for children; Schloss Gottorf worth visit; boating facs; vg Viking museum adj; shwrs newly refurb (2015); boating; gd."* **€23.00, 1 Mar-31 Oct.** **2017**

SCHOMBERG *3C3* (2km N Rural) *48.79820, 8.63623* **Höhen-Camping,** Schömbergstrasse 32, 75328 Langenbrand (07084) 6131; info@hoehencamping.de; www.hoehencamping.de

🗓12 🐕 €2 ⅟⅟ (htd) ⅁ ♨ ♿ 🆗 ⅋ ⅟⅟ ⅟⅟ ₐₙ /Λ\

Fr N exit A8 junc 43 Pforzheim, take B463 dir Calw. Turn R sp Schömberg & foll sp Langenbrand. 5*, Med, hdg, mkd, pt shd, pt sl, EHU (10-16A) €3; TV; 70% statics; phone; adv bkg acc; CKE. *"Clean, well-maintained site in N of Black Forest; no recep, ring bell on house adj site ent; blocks req for sl pitches; vg site with excel san facs."* **€20.00** **2018**

SCHONAU IM SCHWARZWALD *3B4* (1km N Rural) *47.79127, 7.90076* **Camping Schönenbuchen,** Friedrichstrasse 58, 79677 Schönau (07673) 7610; info@camping-schoenau.de; www.camping-schoenau.de

🗓12 🐕 €1 ⅟⅟ ⅁ ♨ ♿ 🆗 ⅋ MSP ⅟⅟ ⅍ ⅟⅟ ₐₙ /Λ\ ⅟⅟ (htd)

Fr Lörrach on B317 dir Todtnau for approx 23km. Site thro Schönau main rd on R on rvside, ent thro car park. Narr access diff for l'ge o'fits. 3*, Med, hdg, pt shd, EHU inc (16A) (poss rev pol); sw nr; red long stay; 70% statics; adv bkg acc; watersports adj; bike hire; horseriding; sauna; tennis; CKE. *"Friendly staff; site poss not well-kept; gd walking & cycling; lovely old town."* **€25.00** **2019**

SCHUTTORF *1B3* (2km N Rural) *52.33960, 7.22617* **Camping Quendorfer See,** Weiße Riete 3, 48465 Schüttorf 05923 90 29 39; info@camping-schuettorf.de; www.camping-schuettorf.de

🐕 €2 ⅟⅟ (htd) ⅁ ♨ ♿ 🆗 ⅋ MSP ⅟⅟ ⅍ ⅟⅟ ₐₙ /Λ\

A1/A30, exit J4 Schüttorf-Nord. Or A31 exit J28 Schüttorf-Ost twds town cent. Foll sp to site. Sm, hdg, mkd, unshd, EHU (16A); sw nr; twin axles; adv bkg acc; ccard acc; games area; CCI. *"Excel site; immac san facs; mostly fully serviced pitches; conv NH for ferries fr Holland; flat cycling & walking."* **€26.50, 1 Apr-31 Oct.** **2019**

SCHWAAN *2F2* (3.6km S Rural) *53.92346, 12.10688* **Camping Schwaan,** Güstrowerstrasse 54/Sandgarten 17, 18258 Schwaan (03844) 813716; info@camping platz-schwaan.de; www.campingplatz-schwaan.de

🐕 €2 ⅟⅟ (htd) ⅁ ♨ ♿ 🆗 ⅋ MSP ⅟⅟ ⅍ ⅟⅟ ₐₙ /Λ\ ⅋

Fr A20 exit junc 13 to Schwaan, site sp. Fr A19 exit junc 11 dir Bad Doberan & Schwaan. Site adj Rv Warnow. 4*, Lge, mkd, pt shd, EHU (16A) €2.20 or metered; cooking facs; TV; 30% statics; adv bkg acc; sauna; site clsd 21 Dec-4 Jan; canoeing; games area; bike hire; tennis 700m; boat hire. *"Pleasant rvside site; gd touring base; tight app thro Schwaan town (esp fr N)."* **€21.00, 1 Mar-31 Oct.** **2019**

SCHWÄBISCH HALL *3D3* (2km S Urban) *49.09868, 9.74288* **Camping am Steinbacher See,** Mühlsteige 26, 74523 Schwäbisch Hall-Steinbach **(0791) 2984; thomas.seitel@t-online.de; www.camping-schwaebisch-hall.de**

🐕 €2 ♿ (htd) 🚿 ⛱ ⚓ 🔥 MP 🍽 🕖 nr ♿ 🛒 nr ⚠

Fr A6/E50 exit junc 43 fr W or junc 42 fr E & foll permanent diversion via new B19 rd. At x-rds at lge Lidl store, turn L twds town and foll sp S to Comburg & site. 4*, Med, mkd, pt shd, EHU (10A) metered + conn fee; bbq; 50% statics; Eng spkn; adv bkg acc; bike hire; CKE. *"Lovely well kept idiosyncratic site; friendly; clsd 1300-1500; walking dist to interesting medieval town; cycle track to town."* **€22.00, 15 Mar-15 Oct.** 2015

SCHWEICH *3B2* (1.6km S Urban) *49.81459, 6.75019* **Campingplatz zum Fährturm,** Am Yachthafen, 54338 Schweich **(06502) 91300; camping@kreusch.de; www.kreusch.de**

🐕 ♿ 🚿 ⛱ ⚓ 🔥 MP 🦋 🍽 🕖 ♿ 🛒 nr ⚠

Fr exit 129 or 130 fr A1/E44. Site by rv bank by bdge into town, sp. 4*, Lge, mkd, pt shd, EHU (16A) €1.60; gas; bbq; twin axles; bus to Trier nr; Eng spkn; adv bkg acc; bike hire; watersports; CKE. *"Poss long wait for conn to EHU; poss long walk to san facs - dated; m'van o'night area outside site - no EHU; sports cent adj; on banks of Mosel with cycle rte; yacht/boating harbour adj; gd rest/bar; pool adj; vg."* **€20.00, 8 Apr-21 Oct.** 2017

SCHWEPPENHAUSEN *3B2* (1km N Rural) *49.93392, 7.79194* **Campingplatz Aumühle,** Naheweinstraße 65, 55444 Schweppenhausen **06724 602392; info@camping-aumuehle.de**

🐕 ♿ (htd) ♿ ⛱ 🔥 🔥 🦋 🍽 🕖 ♿ ⚠

Fr A61 take exit 47 - Waldlaubersheim. Foll signs to Schweppenhausen. Sp to camp site. Med, mkd, pt shd, EHU (10A); twin axles; 50% statics; Eng spkn; adv bkg acc; CKE. *"V gd site; cycle rtes fr site; v helpful Dutch owners; gd san facs; touring vans in sep area nr m'way; excel NH; gd base for Rhine."* **€21.50, 1 Apr-31 Oct.** 2018

SCHWERIN *2E2* (10km N Rural) *53.69725, 11.43715* **Ferienpark Seehof,** Am Zeltzplatz 1, 19069 Seehof **(0385) 512540; info@ferienparkseehof.de; www.ferienparkseehof.de**

12 🐕 €1 ♿ ♿ ⛱ 🔥 MP 🍽 🕖 ♿ 🛒 ⚠ 🚲 🏄 sand

Take B106 N fr Schwerin for approx 5km: turn R at city boundary & site within 5km at end of vill, sp. 4*, Lge, pt shd, pt sl, serviced pitches; EHU (4A) inc (poss rev pol); gas; sw; 30% statics; adv bkg acc; ccard acc; sailing school; bike hire; windsurfing. *"Lge pitches; vg."* **€33.00** 2015

SEEBURG *2E4* (1km NW Rural) *51.49400, 11.69400* **Camping Seeburg am Süsser See,** Nordstrand 1, 06317 Seeburg **(034774) 28281; info@campingplatz-seeburg.de; www.campingplatz-seeburg.de**

12 🐕 €1.20 ♿ ♿ ⛱ 🔥 🔥 🕖 nr ⚠

W fr Halle on B80 twd Eisleben, sp fr Seeburg. Site on N shore of Lake Süsser See. 2*, Lge, pt shd, EHU (16A) €1.10; sw; 95% statics; fishing. *"Attractive, busy site by lake; excel base for medieval towns nr & 'Martin Luther country'; gd; nice site by lake; not many pitches; new immac facs (2015)."* **€19.60** 2015

SEEFELD *4E4* (1.3km W Rural) *48.030463, 11.199018* **Camping Am Pilsensee,** Am Pilseesee 2, 82229 Seefeld am Pilsensee **(08152) 7232; info@camping-pilsensee.de; www.camping-pilsensee.de**

12 🐕 ♿ ♿ ⛱ ⚓ 🔥 🔥 MP 🍷 🍽 🕖 ♿ 🛒 ⚠

W on 96 fr Munchi, exit 31, turn R onto 2349. Aft abt 6km turn R onto 2068. Cont for 4.5km, site 500m S of junc with 2070 to Seefeld to the R. V lge, mkd, hdg, pt shd, EHU (10A); bbq; sw; twin axles; TV; 80% statics; phone; Eng spkn; adv bkg acc; games area; CKE. *"Gd site; boat hire on lake; Andechs monastery nrby."* **€26.00** 2018

SEESHAUPT *4E4* (4km E Rural) *47.82651, 11.33906* **Camping beim Fischer,** Buchscharnstrasse 10, 82541 St Heinrich **(08801) 802; info@camping-beim-fischer.de; www.camping-beim-fischer.de**

12 🐕 ♿ (htd) ♿ ⛱ ⚓ 🔥 🔥 🦋 🍽 nr 🕖 nr ⚠

Exit A95 junc 7 & foll sp Seeshaupt for 1.6km to T-junc. Turn R, site in 200m on R. 4*, Med, mkd, unshd, EHU (16A) metered; gas; sw nr; TV; 45% statics; bus adj; Eng spkn; adv bkg acc; games area; CKE. *"Well-maintained, friendly, lovely, honest family-run site; immac facs; conv Munich & Bavarian castles."* **€26.40** 2019

SIGMARINGEN *3D4* (2km SW Urban) *48.08366, 9.20794* **Erlebnis-Camp Sigmaringen,** Georg-Zimmererstrasse 6, 72488 Sigmaringen **(07571) 50411; info@outandback.de; www.erlebnis-camp.de**

12 🐕 €1 ♿ ♿ ⛱ ⚓ 🔥 🔥 MP 🍷 🕖 nr ⚠

App town fr N or SW, ent town over Danube bdge, turn R into car pk (camp sp). To far end of car park, turn R in front of supmkt. Ent camp fr far end. Site adj to stadium by rv, sp fr town. 4*, Med, pt shd, EHU (6-16A) €3; 10% statics; bike hire; CKE. *"On Danube cycle way; gd outdoor activities; lovely site; htd pool 300m; clsd 12-1400; new facs; new ent."* **€26.50** 2015

SIMMERATH *1A4* (8km E Rural) *50.61777, 6.37690* **Camping Rursee,** Seerandweg 26, D 52152 Simmerath/Rurberg **(02473) 2365; info@camping-rursee.de; http://camping-rursee.de**

♿ ♿ ⛱ 🔥 🍽 ♿ ⚠

Fr Simmerath L166 to Kesternich; R on 266 for 1 km; then L on L166 twds Rurberg. L on L128 twds Woffelsbach then sp R to site. Sm, mkd, unshd, EHU €3; games area. **€18.50, 1 Apr-Nov.** 2019

GERMANY

SOEST *1C4* (12km S Rural) *51.47722, 8.10055*
Camping Delecke-Südufer, Arnsbergerstrasse 8, 59519 Möhnesee-Delecke **(02924) 8784210; info@ campingplatz-moehnesee.de; www.campingplatz-moehnesee.de**

12 🚫 ⛺ 👤 ♿ 🚿 ⬜ *nr* 🚽 ☕ 🪨

Exit A44/E331 at junc 56 onto B229 sp Arnsberg/ Mohnesee. Cont to lake, cross bdge. At next junc turn L & site immed on L, sp. 4*, Med, hdg, unshd, pt sl, EHU (16A); sw nr; 50% statics; phone; Eng spkn; adv bkg acc; clsd 1300-1500 & 2000-0800; boating; CKE. *"Excel site on boating lake; san facs locked o'night; gd walking & sailing; v busy at w/ends; gd disable facs."* **€25.00** **2016**

SOTTRUM *1D2* (5km SW Rural) *53.08335, 9.17697*
Camping-Paradies Grüner Jäger, Everinghauser Dorfstrsse 17, 27367 Sottrum/Everinghausen **(04205) 319113; info@camping-paradies.de; www.camping-paradies.de**

12 🐕 €2 👤 *(htd)* ⬜ ⛺ ♿ ⬜ ⬜ 🍴 ⛲ 🛒 🚽 🪨 ⛵ 🎣

Exit A1 junc 50 at Stuckenborstel onto B75 dir Rotenburg. In approx 500m turn R & foll sp Everinghausen. Site in 4km. Med, mkd, unshd, EHU (16A) inc; bbq; 30% statics; Eng spkn; CKE. *"Excel NH; new superb facs block (2016)."* **€31.00** **2019**

SPEYER *3C3* (3km N Rural) *49.33600, 8.44300*
Camping Speyer, Am Rübsamenwühl 31, 67346 Speyer **(06232) 42228; info@camping-speyer.de; www.camping-speyer.de**

🐕 €2 ⛺ ⬜ 🍴 🛒 🚽 🪨

Fr Mannheim or Karlsruhe take rd 9 to exit Speyer Nord dir Speyer. At 3rd traff lts turn L into Auestrasse, then at 2nd rndabt L into Am Rübsamenwühl. Site in 500m. Sm, mkd, EHU €3; sw; red long stay; 90% statics. *"Speyer pleasant town, cathedral & Technik Museum worth visit; v basic site; scruffy & not well-kept; fair NH/sh stay."* **€29.00, 15 Mar-25 Sep.** **2019**

SPEYER *3C3* (1km SE Urban) *49.31250, 8.44916*
Camping Technik Museum, Am Technik Museum 1, Geibstrasse, 67346 Speyer **(06232) 67100; info@hotel-speyer.de; www.hotel-speyer.de**

12 🐕 👤 *(htd)* ⬜ ⛺ ♿ ⬜ 🛒 *nr* 🪨 *nr* 🚽 *nr*

Exit A61/E34 at junc 64, foll sp to museum. Med, unshd, EHU inc (10A); bus; Eng spkn; adv bkg acc; ccard acc. *"Book in at hotel adj; 3 nights max stay; excel museum & IMAX cinema on site; conv Speyer cent and cathedral; dogs free; site unkept; excel san facs; 24hr CCTV controlled ent gate."* **€22.00** **2016**

STAUFEN IM BREISGAU *3B4* (1.4km SE Rural) *47.87194, 7.73583* **Ferien-Campingplatz Belchenblick,** Münstertälerstrasse 43, 79219 Staufen-im-Breisgau **(07633) 7045; info@camping-belchenblick.de; www.camping-belchenblick.de**

12 ⬜ €2.50 👤 ⬜ ⛺ ♿ 🚿 ⬜ ⬜ 🍴 🍴 🚽 *nr* 🚽 🪨 🎣

⛷ *(htd, indoor)*

Exit A5/E35 junc 64a dir Bad Krozingen-Staufen-Münstertal. Avoid Staufen cent, foll Münstertal sp. Camp on L 500m past Staufen. Visibility restricted fr Münstertal dir. 4*, Lge, pt shd, EHU (16A) metered; gas; bbq; TV; 60% statics; phone; Eng spkn; adv bkg rec; horseriding 500m; games rm; bike hire; sauna; tennis nr; CKE. *"Well-run, family-owned site; some pitches sm; no o'fits over 8m high ssn; no veh access 1230-1500 & night time - parking area avail; strict pitching rules; beautiful area & Staufen pleasant town; beware train app round blind corner at x-ing; gd walking, cycling, horseriding; san facs tired, need refurbishing (2013); better cheaper sites close by."* **€30.00, G02.** **2015**

STOCKACH *3C4* (7.5km SSW Rural) *47.80860, 8.97000* **Campinggarten Wahlwies,** Stahringerstrasse 50, 78333 Stockach-Wahlwies **(07771) 3511; info@camping-wahlwies.de; www.camping-wahlwies.de**

🐕 👤 ⬜ ⛺ ⬜ 🛒 ⬜ 🦋 🍴 🚽 🪨 *nr*

Exit A98 junc 12 Stockach West onto B313 to Wahlwies. In vill turn L immed after level x-ing, site on R bef next level x-ing, sp. 3*, Med, pt shd, EHU (16A) €2; sw nr; 50% statics; phone; Eng spkn; adv bkg rec; CKE. *"Pleasantly situated, orchard site 6km fr Bodensee; friendly, helpful staff; female san facs inadequate; gd touring cent; gd local train service; excel cycle tracks."* **€23.00, 1 Jan-15 Nov & 15 Dec-31 Dec.** **2016**

"I need an on-site restaurant"

We do our best to make sure site information is correct, but it is always best to check any must-have facilities are still available or will be open during your visit.

STOCKACH *3C4* (2.5km SW Urban) *47.84194, 8.99500* **Camping Papiermühle,** Johann Glatt Strasse 3, 78333 Stockach **(07771) 9190490; campingpark-stockach@web.de; www.campingpark-stockach-de.webnode.com**

🐕 €2.20 👤 *(htd)* ⬜ ⛺ ♿ ⬜ 🛒 ⬜ 🦋 🍴 🚽 *nr* 🪨 ⛲

Fr Stockach at junc rndabt of B31 & B313, turn L (E) to Caramobil C'van Sales Depot. Site adj under same management. Med, mkd, hdstg, pt shd, pt sl, terr, EHU (6A) €2; bbq; 50% statics; phone; bus 200m; Eng spkn; adv bkg acc; ccard acc; CKE. *"Sep m'van area adj; v clean facs; helpful staff; conv location for town; gd walking & cycling; vg site."* **€21.50, 1 Mar-30 Nov.** **2016**

STRAUBING *4F3* (1km N Urban) 48.89346, 12.5766
Camping Straubing, Wundermühlweg 9, 94315
Straubing **(09421) 89794; info@campingplatz
straubing.de; www.campingplatzstraubing.de**

🏕 🐕 ♿ 🛁 ⚒ 🚿 💬 MSP 🍴 🍷 ⊕ 🛒 nr ⚠

Fr A3/E56 exit junc 105 or 106 to Straubing. Foll
sp over Danube bdge, site sp on R in approx 1km.
Also foll sp to stadium. 4*, Med, shd, EHU (16A)
inc; bbq; cooking facs; sw nr; twin axles; phone; bus;
adv bkg acc; golf 2km; CKE. *"Gd, clean, well-kept
site In grnds of sports stadium; quaint town with
attractive shops; gd san facs; pool 5km; conv Danube
cycle way; easy walk to town; dogs not acc Aug;
excel stop over fr A3, gd for longer breaks; excel."*
€23.50, 1 May-15 Oct.   2018

> ## "Satellite navigation makes touring much easier"
>
> Remember most sat navs don't know if you're
> towing or in a larger vehicle – always use yours
> alongside maps and site directions.

STUTTGART *3D3* (5km E Urban) 48.79395, 9.21911
Campingplatz Cannstatter Wasen, Mercedesstrasse
40, 70372 Stuttgart **(0711) 556696; info@camping
platz-stuttgart.de; www.campingplatz-stuttgart.de**

12 🐕 €3 👪 (htd) WD 🛁 ♿ 🚿 💬 MSP ⊕ 🛒 nr ⚠

Fr B10 foll sp for stadium & Mercedes museum &
then foll camping sp. Access poss diff when major
events in park adj. Lge, hdstg, pt shd, serviced pitches;
EHU (16A) metered + conn fee; bbq; bus nr; Eng spkn;
adv bkg acc; ccard acc; CKE. *"Helpful staff; clean san
facs (2015); town cent best by train, tickets fr recep;
cycle ride to town thro park; Mercedes museum 15
mins walk; fr Sep site/office open 0800-1000 & 1700-
1900 only; site within low emission zone; camping field
for tents."* €22.00   2016

SULZBURG *3B4* (1.5km SE Rural) 47.83583, 7.72333
Terrassen-Camping Alte Sägemühle, Badstrasse 57,
79295 Sulzburg **(07634) 551181; info@camping-alte-
saegemuehle.de; www.camping-alte-saegemuehle.de**

12 🐕 €2 👪 (htd) WD 🛁 🚿 💬 MSP 🦋 🍴 nr ⊕ nr 🛒

Exit A5 junc 64a to Heitersheim & Sulzburg. Fr cent
of Sulzburg, foll camp sps SE past timber yard on rd
to Bad Sulzburg hotel. 3*, Sm, mkd, pt shd, terr, EHU
(16A) metered + conn fee; bbq; sw nr; 10% statics;
Eng spkn; CKE. *"Excel san facs, poss long walk; v
friendly, helpful owners site van with tractor; restful
site in beautiful hilly countryside; gd walks, cycling."*
€26.00   2016

SULZBURG *3B4* (1km NW Rural) 47.84778, 7.69848
Camping Sulzbachtal, Sonnmatt 4, 79295 Sulzburg
**(07634) 592568; a-z@camping-sulzbachtal.de;
www.camping-sulzbachtal.de**

12 🐕 €2.60 (htd) WD 🛁 ♿ 🚿 💬 MSP 🦋 🍴 🍷 ⊕ nr 🛒 nr
⚠ 🏊

Fr A5/E35 exit junc 64a Bad Krozingen onto L120/
L123 dir Staufen-in-Breisgau. Cont on L125, site sp
on L. 5*, Med, mkd, hdstg, pt shd, terr, serviced
pitches; EHU (16A) metered; red long stay; 10%
statics; phone; Eng spkn; adv bkg acc; ccard acc;
tennis; CKE. *"Gd base for S Black Forest & Vosges; well
laid-out site; clean facs; conv m'way; 45 mins to Basel;
helpful, pleasant owners; ask about bus/train pass;
m'van o'night facs; high standards; well maintained;
excel san facs; lge pitches; in wine growing area; excel
walks."* €35.40   2019

TENGEN *3C4* (1km NW Rural) 47.82365, 8.65296
Hegau Familien-Camping, An der Sonnenhalde 1,
78250 Tengen **(07736) 92470; info@hegau-camping.
de; www.hegau-camping.de**

12 🐕 €4 👪 (htd) WD 🛁 ♿ 🚿 💬 MSP 🦋 🍴 🍷 ⊕ 🛒 ⚠ ✎
🏊 (covrd, htd) 🛝

Exit A81 junc 39 thro Engen dir Tengen, site sp.
5*, Lge, hdstg, mkd, pt shd, pt sl, serviced pitches;
EHU (16A) metered or €2; gas; sw; red long stay;
40% statics; bus 500m; Eng spkn; adv bkg acc; ccard
acc; tennis adj; sauna; games area; horseriding 2km;
bike hire; games rm; canoeing; dog shwr; CKE. *"Site of
high standard; fairly isolated; gd family facs; clsd 1230-
1430; o'night m'vans area; excel; same price in high ssn;
beautifully maintained; well run; 1st rate pool complex;
wonderful children's play facs; rec."* €42.00   2016

TITISEE NEUSTADT *3C4* (7km SW Rural) 47.88693,
8.13776 **Terrassencamping Sandbank,** Seerundweg 9,
79822 Titisee-Neustadt **(07651) 8243 or 8166; info@
camping-sandbank.de; www.camping-sandbank.de**

🐕 €1.50 👪 (htd) WD 🛁 ♿ 🚿 💬 MSP 🍴 ⊕ 🛒 ⚠

Fr rte 31 Freiberg-Donauschingen turn S into
Titisee. Fork R after car park on R, foll sp for
Bruderhalde thro town. After youth hostel fork
L & foll sp at T junc. 4*, Lge, mkd, hdstg, terr, EHU
(16A) €1.40; sw; red long stay; 50% statics; Eng
spkn; ccard acc; boating; bike hire; CKE. *"Ltd touring
pitches; steel pegs ess; clean, well-run, well laid-out
site in gd position; terr gives gd lake views; helpful
owner; m'van welcome; larger pitches avail at extra cost;
gd touring base for Black Forest; gd walks round
lake; lakeside walk into town thru woods (approx
30 mins); ask for Konus card for free travel on local
buses; clsd 1200-1400; excel; rd to site tarmaced."*
€25.50, 1 Apr-18 Oct.   2016

GERMANY

TITISEE NEUSTADT *3C4 (7.6km SW Rural) 47.89516, 8.13789* **Camping Bühlhof,** Bühlhofweg 13, 79822 Titisee-Neustadt **(07652) 1606 or (01713) 634160 (mob);** info@camping-buehlhof.de; www.camping-buehlhof.de

12 ⚹ €2.30 [wc] ⚐ ♨ ♿ ⟲ ∥ [MSP] 🦋 ☂ (H) nr ⛺

Take rd 31 out of Freiburg to Titisee; R fork on ent Titisee; bear R to side of lake, site on R after end of Titisee, up steep but surfaced hill, sharp bends. 2*, Lge, mkd, pt shd, pt sl, terr, serviced pitches; EHU (16A) €1.80; gas; bbq; 30% statics; Eng spkn; horseriding; boat hire; site clsd Nov to mid-Dec; tennis; watersports; CKE. *"Beautiful situation on hillside above Lake Titisee; 300m fr Lake Titisee (but no access; recep 0700-2200; lower terr gravel & 50% statics; top terr for tents & vans without elec; winter sports area, ski lift 6km; pitches sm; woodland walks; pleasant walk to town; gd san facs."* **€25.50**   **2017**

TITISEE NEUSTADT *3C4 (8.6km SW Rural) 47.88633, 8.13055* **Camping Bankenhof,** Bruderhalde 31a, 79822 Titisee-Neustadt **(07652) 1351;** info@camping-bankenhof.de; www.camping-bankenhof.de

12 ⚹ €2.80 ♦♦♦ [wc] ♨ ♿ ⟲ ∥ [MSP] 🦋 ☂ ⚑ (H) ☂ ⛺ ✂

Fr B31 Frieberg-Donaueschingen, turn S into Tittisee & fork R after car park on R, foll sp Bruderhalde thro town. In 2.5km fork L after youth hostel; foll sp to site in 200m. If app Titisee fr Donausechingen (B31) do not take Titisee P sp exit but exit with int'l camping sp only, then as above. 4*, Lge, mkd, hdstg, pt shd, EHU (10A) metered (poss rev pol); gas; sw nr; 20% statics; Eng spkn; adv bkg acc; ccard acc; bike hire; CKE. *"Gd walk to town & in forest; o'night area for m'vans €12 - dogs free in this area; lovely scenery; helpful staff; vg san facs; excel rest; most pitches gravel; boat launch 200m; ask at recep for red/free tickets on public transport; excel, well-run, clean site, some pitches narr."* **€28.00**   **2015**

TRAUNSTEIN *4F4 (8km SW Rural) 47.81116, 12.5890* **Camping Wagnerhof,** Campingstrasse 11, 83346 Bergen **(08662) 8557;** info@camping-bergen.de; www.camping-bergen.de

12 ⚹ €2 ♦♦♦ [wc] ⟲ ∥ [MSP] 🦋 (H) nr ☂ ⛺ ⛷ shgl 10km

Exit A8/E52/E60 junc 110. On ent Bergen take 2nd R turn (sp). 4*, Med, mkd, pt shd, EHU (16A) metered; red long stay; 30% statics; Eng spkn; adv bkg acc; tennis; site clsd 1230-1500; CKE. *"Excel, v clean, pleasant site in beautiful location; htd pool adj; debit & euro card acc; helpful owner; when not full owner tries to offer pitches with empty pitches adjoining; conv a'bahn; cable car to Hockfelln."* **€23.50**   **2019**

TRAVEMUNDE *2E2 (4km SW Rural) 53.94196, 10.84417* **Camping Ivendorf,** Frankenkrogweg 2, 23570 Ivendorf **(04502) 4865;** mail@camping-travemuende.de; www.camping-travemuende.de

12 ⚹ €2 ♦♦♦ [wc] ♨ ♿ ⟲ ∥ (H) nr ☂ ⛺

Fr A1 exit junc 19 take B226 to Ivendorf, then B75 dir Travemünde, site well sp. 3*, Med, mkd, pt shd, EHU €3.50 or metered; 10% statics; CKE. *"Sep disabled pitches; conv ferries to/fr Sweden; pool 4km; easy access to Lübeck, a beautiful city."* **€23.00**   **2016**

TRIER *3B2 (2km SW Urban) 49.74385, 6.62523* **Camping Treviris,** Luxemburgerstrasse 81, 54290 Trier **(0651) 8200911;** info@camping-treviris.de; www.camping-treviris.de

⚹ €1.70 ♦♦♦ [wc] ♨ ♿ ⟲ ∥ 🦋 ☂ ⚑ (H) ☂ nr ⛺

On E side of Rv Mosel on A1/A603/B49/B51 cross to W side of rv on Konrad Adenauerbrücke. Cont in R lane & foll sp Koln/Aachen - Luxemburgerstrasse. In 500m turn R to site, site on R. Well sp fr W bank of rv. Med, mkd, pt shd, EHU (10A) metered; bbq; bus 200m; ccard acc; site clsd 1-10 Jan; CKE. *"Cycle/walk to town cent; m'van park adj open all yr - ltd facs; clean, modern, clean san facs; swipe card for all facs; elec pylon in cent of site; gd touring base; gd sh stay/NH; well placed; sm pitches; 20min walk to city."* **€24.00, 18 Mar-30 Oct.**   **2018**

TRIER *3B2 (9km SW Rural) 49.70555, 6.55333* **Campingplatz Igel,** Moselstrasse, 54298 Igel **(06501) 12944;** info@camping-igel.de; www.camping-igel.de

⚹ €2 ♦♦♦ (htd) [wc] ♨ ⟲ ∥ [MSP] ☂ ⚑ nr ⛺

SW on A49 Luxembourg rd fr Trier; in cent of lge vill, turn L by Sparkasse Bank, thro narr tunnel (3.6m max height); in 200m turn L along rv bank; site 300m on L; café serves as recep. Med, pt shd, EHU (6A) €2 (poss rev pol); 90% statics; lake fishing adj; CKE. *"Excel, friendly, well-run site; immac san facs; gd rest; ltd touring pitches; rv bank foot & cycle path to Trier; conv Roman amphitheatre in Trier (bus/train); close to Luxembourg border for cheap petrol; conv for bus into Trier."* **€19.00, 1 Apr-31 Oct.**   **2019**

TRIER *3B2* (15km W Rural) *49.75416, 6.50333*
Campingplatz Alter Bahnhof-Metzdorf, Uferstrasse 42, 54308 Langsur-Metzdorf **(06501) 12626; info@ camping-metzdorf.de; www.camping-metzdorf.de**

⊞12 🐕 €1 ♟(htd) 🅆 ⇌ ᚛ 🚻 🚿 ✎ MSP 🦋 ♀ 🍴 ⊕ 🏧 ⁄⁀

Fr W leave A64/E44 junc 15 & foll sp Wasserbillig; at T-junc in Wasserbillig turn L onto B49 sp Trier. Ignore campsite in 500m. On ent Germany at end of bdge turn sharp L onto B418 sp Ralingen/ Metternich. In 3km turn L sp Metzdorf; in 750m turn L, site in 750m. Fr N (Bitburg) join A64 at junc 3 sp Luxembourg, then as above. Fr SE on A1/E422 join A602 (Trier) & approx 1km past end of a'bahn turn R over Kaiser Wilhelm Bdge sp A64 Lux'bourg) & immed L at end of bdge. In 9km in Wasserbillig turn R under rlwy bdge & keep R on B418 sp Ralingen/ Mesenich. In 3km turn L sp Melzdorf, in 750m turn L, site in 750m. Do not use sat nav if app fr the E. 3*, Med, pt shd, pt sl, EHU (6-16A) €2 or metered (10A); red long stay; 75% statics; phone; bus 500m; Eng spkn; adv bkg acc; CKE. *"Rvside location; gd san facs but poss long walk & steep climb; m'van o'night €9; cycle rte to Trier; vg NH."* **€17.50**   2015

TRITTENHEIM *3B2* (4km N Urban) *49.84933, 6.89283*
Camping Neumagen-Dhron, Moselstrasse 100, 54347 Neumagen-Dhron **(06507) 5249; camping-neumagen@ t-online.de; www.campingneumagen.de**

🐕 🚻 🅆 ⇌ ᚛ 🚿 ✎ ♀ 🍴 ⊕ 🏧 ⁄⁀

On B53 fr Trittenheim twd Piesport. Immed after x-ing rv turn R, then R again sp Neumagen. Site sp in vill on rvside. 3*, Med, mkd, pt shd, EHU (6A) metered + conn fee; bbq; 40% statics; adv bkg acc; boating; fishing; CKE. *"Gd; site clsd if rv in flood; marina adj; rvside park; excel site; interesting Roman town; poss noise fr adj rest; main san facs up 25 steps; Hot water 7am-9pm."* **€22.00,** 1 Apr-31 Oct.   2017

TRITTENHEIM *3B2* (8km S Rural) *49.79956, 6.92715*
Campingplatz Moselhöhe, Bucherweg 1, 54426 Heidenburg **(06509) 99016; vandijk1968@hotmail. com; www.moselhohe.de**

⊞12 🐕 €1.70 ♟(htd) 🅆 ⇌ ᚛ 🚿 ✎ MSP ♀ 🍴 ⊕ nr 🏧 ᚛ nr ⁄⁀ ⊞

Leave A1/E422 at junc 131, foll sp twd Thalfang. After 4km take 2nd L over bdge sp Heidenburg (2 hairpin bends). Thro Büdlich to Heidenbrug, foll sp in vill. 4*, Med, mkd, unshd, terr, serviced pitches; EHU (16A) metered; red long stay; 25% statics; Eng spkn; adv bkg acc; ccard acc; site clsd mid-Nov to mid-Dec; games rm; CKE. *"Excel, clean, hilltop site surrounded by meadows; well-maintained; generous terraces; excel san facs; water & waste disposal points nr every pitch; wonderful views; v friendly owner; conv Rv Mosel attractions 4km."* **€19.00**   2015

TUBINGEN *3C3* (5km SW Rural) *48.51008, 9.03525*
Neckarcamping Tübingen, Rappenberghalde 61, 72070 Tübingen **(07071) 43145; mail@neckar camping.de; www.neckarcamping.de**

🐕 €1.50 🅆 ⇌ ᚛ 🚿 ✎ MSP ⊕ 🏧 🦺 ⁄⁀

B28 to Tübingen, site well sp fr main rds. Site on N bank of Rv Neckar. 3*, Med, pt shd, EHU (6A) metered + conn fee (rev pol); 70% statics; bike hire; clsd 1230-1430 & 2200-0800; CKE. *"Easy walk to attractive old town & lge pool complex; Neckar cycle path rn; cramped pitches; NH only; bus stop nr camp ent."* **€27.00,** 1 Apr-30 Oct.   2017

UBERLINGEN *3D4* (3km SE Coastal) *47.75186, 9.19315* **Campingplatz Nell,** Zur Barbe 7, 88662 Überlingen-Nussdorf **(07551) 4254; info@camping platz-nell.de; www.campingplatz-nell.de**

🚻 🅆 ⇌ ᚛ ✎ 🦋 🍴 nr ⊕ nr 🏧 ᚛ nr

Exit B31 to Nussdorf. In vill cent turn L under rlwy bdge at 2nd campsite sp, site on R on lakeside. Sm, pt shd, EHU (10A) metered; bbq; sw nr; adv bkg acc. *"Beautifully-kept site; friendly owner; all amenities nr; gd cycling; excel; lge plots; cash only; ltd places for tourers so arrive early."* **€21.00,** 21 Mar-20 Oct.   2016

UBERLINGEN *3D4* (13km NW Rural) *47.81720, 9.03802* **Campingplatz Schachenhorn,** Radolfzeller Str. 23, 78351 Bodman-Ludwigshafen **07773 9376851; info@camping-schachenhorn.de; www.camping-schachenhorn.de**

🐕 🚻 🅆 ⇌ ᚛ 🚿 ✎ ♀ 🍴 ⊕ ⁄⁀

Exit A98/E54 junc 12 onto B34. Site sp 1.5km on Bodensee fr Ludwigshafen. Med, pt shd, EHU (16A); bbq; sw nr; twin axles; TV; 20% statics; Eng spkn; games rm. *"Taken over in 2013, formerly Camping See-Ende; lovely location at W end of Bodensee; excel san facs; many cycle paths; bit disorganised; poss muddy after rain; rec visit Mainau Gdns."* **€30.00,** 15 Mar-15 Oct.   2016

UBERLINGEN *3D4* (3km NW Rural) *47.77081, 9.13813* **Campingplatz Überlingen,** Bahnhofstrasse 57, 88662 Überlingen **(07551) 64583; infocampingpark-ueberlingen.de; www.campingpark-ueberlingen.de**

🐕 €2.50 🚻(htd) 🅆 ⇌ ᚛ ✎ 🍴 ⊕ 🏧 🦺 ⁄⁀

Heading SE on B31, bef Überlingen turn R at sp Campingplatz Goldbach down slip rd; after 1.75km turn R; foll rd parallel with rlwy; after level x-ing site immed on R by lakeside. 1*, Lge, pt shd, pt sl, EHU (16A) metered; gas; bbq; sw nr; red long stay; 30% statics; bus; Eng spkn; boating adj; CKE. *"Extra for lake pitches; high ssn poss diff for lge c'vans to manoeuvre; gd rest; strict rule no vehicles in after 2230; rec arr early to secure pitch; boat to Insel Mainau fr site."* **€23.50,** 1 Apr-9 Oct.   2018

UBERSEE *4F4* (4km N Rural) *47.8412, 12.47166* **Chiemsee-Campingplatz Rödlgries,** Rödlgries 1, 83236 Übersee-Feldwies **(08642) 470; info@ chiemsee-camping.de; www.chiemsee-camping.de**

🐕 €2.50 (htd) ⚭ ⚓ 🚿 ❄ MSP 🦋 ⍟ ⊕ ⚑ ♿ 🏔 ⚓ 🛶 shgl

Exit A8/E52 junc 108 Übersee, foll sp Chiemseestrand, veer L at wooden sp of sites. 4*, V lge, mkd, hdstg, pt shd, serviced pitches; EHU (16A) metered + conn fee; gas; sw; phone; adv bkg acc; boating. *"Superb facs; vg for children; highly rec; extra for lakeside/serviced pitches; dogs by prior agreement in Jul/Aug; vg touring base; v conv nr A8; cycle track around lake; excel; lge level pitches."* **€32.50, 1 Apr-31 Oct.** **2015**

ÜBERSEE *4F4* (16km W Rural) *47.816891, 12.363742* **Camping Mariengrund,** Prienerstr. 42, D-83233 Bernau am Chiemsee **(08051) 7894; mariengrund@ aol.com; campingplatz-mariengrund.de**

12 🐕 ⚭ ⚓ 🚿 ❄ MSP ⍟ ⚑ nr

Exit m'waysp Bernau. Turn twrds Prien. Ent to site v sharp R immed after Munich slip rd. Lge o'fits can cont twrds Prien and u turn at next rndabt. Hdstg, pt shd, EHU (16A) inc; bbq (charcoal, elec, gas); sw nr; Eng spkn; adv bkg acc; ccard acc. *"Hdstng area sometimes crowded with NH'ers; facs basic but ok; vast numbers of flies & mosquitoes in summer; fair."* **€31.00** **2019**

VLOTHO *1C3* (5km NE Rural) *52.17388, 8.90666* **Camping Sonnenwiese,** Borlefzen 1, 32602 Vlotho **(05733) 8217; info@sonnenwiese.com; www.sonnenwiese.com**

12 🐕 €2.20 (htd) ⚭ ⚓ ♿ 🚿 ❄ MSP 🦋 📶 ⍟ ⊕ ⚑ 🏔 ⚓ 🛶

Fr S exit A2 junc 31 to Vlotho; cross rv bdge (Mindenerstrasse) & in 500m turn R into Rintelnerstrasse to site - 2 sites share same access. Fr N exit A2 junc 32 to Vlotho; turn L bef bdge into Rintelner Strasse. 4*, Lge, hdstg, unshd, serviced pitches; EHU (10A) inc; bbq; sw; TV (pitch); 75% statics; phone; Eng spkn; adv bkg acc; games rm; CKE. *"Excel site; v helpful staff, abundant wildlife; rv adj for boats/canoes; recep clsd 1300-1500."* **€25.50** **2016**

VOLKACH *3D2* (2km NW Rural) *49.869215, 10.214989* **Campingplatz Ankergrund,** Fahrerstraße 7, 97332 Volkach am Main **(09381) 6713 or (09381) 4114; info@campingplatz-ankergrund.de; www.campingplatz-ankergrund.de**

🐕 €3.50 ⚭ ⚓ ♿ 🚿 ❄ MSP 📶 ⍟ ⚑

Exit A3 J74 sp Kitzingen/Schwarzach/Volkach. Site sp in town approx 10km fr A3. Med, mkd, hdg, pt shd, EHU (10A) €0.60kwh; bbq; sw nr; red long stay; twin axles; 25% statics; 800m; adv bkg acc; games area; CKE. *"Excel; super pitches avail with rv view; adj to Rv Main; sports ctr nrby with pool; san facs raised with disabled access via lift; in wine area; excel cycling & walking; gd rests; gd supmkt."* **€24.00, 1 Apr-21 Oct.** **2018**

WALDBREITBACH *3B1* (1.5km NE Rural) *50.55389, 7.42518* **Campingplatz Wiedhof,** Wiedhof 1, 56588 Waldbreitbach **(02638) 4258; camping@wiedhof.de; www.wiedhof.de**

🐕 ⚭ MSP ⚓ ❄ ⚑ 🛶 🏔

Exit A3 junc 36 onto B256 W to Bonefeld, then take L257 Kurtscheiderstrasse to Niederbreitbach, then L255 to Waldbreitbach, site sp on rvside. This rte avoids steep hills. Sm, unshd, EHU (10A) inc; bbq; TV; 80% statics; adv bkg acc; fishing; CKE. *"Conv A3 m'way; vg, peaceful site; gd walks, quiet site next to local town."* **€13.00, 1 Apr-31 Oct.** **2015**

WALDMUNCHEN *4F2* (3km N Rural) *49.39598, 12.69913* **Campsite Ferienpark Perlsee (formerly Camping am Perlsee),** Alte Ziegelhütte 6, 93449 Waldmünchen **(09972) 1469; info@ferienpark-perlsee.de; www.ferienpark-perlsee.de**

12 🐕 €2 (htd) ⚭ ⚓ ♿ 🚿 ❄ MSP ⍟ ⊕ ⚑ ♿ 🏔

N fr Cham on B22 to Schontal, NE to Waldmünchen for 10km. Foll site sp 2km. 4*, Med, hdg, mkd, pt shd, terr, EHU (16A) metered; bbq; sw nr; 50% statics; games area; watersports; CKE. *"Vg san facs; superb site; long leads poss req."* **€25.30** **2019**

WALKENRIED *2E4* (1km NE Rural) *51.58944, 10.62472* **Knaus Campingpark Walkenried,** Ellricherstrasse 7, 37445 Walkenried **(05525) 778; walkenried@knauscamp.de; www.knauscamp.de**

12 🐕 €2.80 ⚭ ⚓ ♿ 🚿 ❄ MSP 🦋 ⍟ ⊕ ⚑ ♿ 🏔 ⚓ (covrd, htd)

A7, exit Seesen, then B243 to Herzberg-Bad Sachsa-Walkenried, sp. 4*, Lge, mkd, pt shd, pt sl, terr, EHU (6-10A) €2.40; gas; red long stay; TV; 20% statics; Eng spkn; adv bkg acc; games area; solarium; site clsd Nov; sauna. *"Vg rest; winter sports; lovely old vill; excel site."* **€32.50** **2018**

WARNITZ *2G2* (0.7km S Rural) *53.17754, 13.87400* **Camping Oberuckersee,** Lindenallee 2, 17291 Warnitz **(039863) 459; info@camping-oberuckersee. de; www.camping-oberuckersee.de**

🐕 €2 ⚭ ⚓ ♿ 🚿 ❄ MSP 🦋 ⊕ nr ⚑ nr 🏔

Fr A11/E28 exit 7. Site sp fr Warnitz on lakeside. 3*, Lge, shd, pt sl, EHU (10A) €2; sw; TV; 50% statics; fishing; bike hire; boating. *"Lovely site in pine trees on edge lge lake; conv NH en rte to Poland; deposit for san facs key; clsd 1300-1500; gd cycle rte nrby."* **€16.00, 1 Apr-5 Oct.** **2016**

WEIKERSHEIM *3D2* (4km S Rural) *49.45640, 9.92565* **Camping Schwabenmühle,** Weikersheimer Straße 21, 97990 Weikersheim **07934 99 22 23; info@camping-schwabenmuehle.de; www.camping-schwabenmuehle.de**

🐕 €1 ⚭ ⚓ ♿ 🚿 ❄ MSP 📶 ⍟ 🏔

Fr Weikersheim twd Laudenbach, site on R in 3km. 4*, Med, hdg, mkd, hdstg, pt shd, EHU (16A); twin axles; Eng spkn; bike hire; CCI. *"Excel; bread can be ordered."* **€26.00, 17 Apr-12 Oct.** **2019**

WEILBURG *3C1* (4km SW Rural) 50.4757, 8.23966
Campingplatz Odersbach, Runkelerstrasse 5A,
35781 Weilburg-Odersbach **(06471) 7620; info@
camping-odersbach.de; www.camping-odersbach.de**

🐕 €1 ♯♯ ♿ 🚿 ∥ 🦋 ☂ ℗ nr ♨ ⛴ ⚠ ⛵ ⚓

Fr Limburg exit B49 sp Weilburg & Bad Homburg,
turn S (R) opp Shell stn at top of hill at Weilburg
o'skts. Site on L at foot of hill in Odersbach. 4*, Lge,
unshd, EHU (16A) metered + conn fee; 75% statics;
ccard acc; boating; bike hire; golf 8km; CKE.
€25.00, 1 Apr-31 Oct.   **2019**

WEIMAR *2E4* (12km S Rural) 50.92456, 11.34785
Camping Mittleres Ilmtal, Auf den Butterberge 1,
99438 Oettern **(036453) 80264; weil-camping@
freenet.de; www.camping-oettern.de**

🐕 €2 ♯♯ 🆆 🚿 ∥ 🦋 ☂ ℗ ♨

Exit A4/E40 junc 50 & foll B87 to SW to Oettern,
take 1st L after narr bdge, site on L in 600m along
narr rd, sp 'Camperbaude'. 2*, Med, hdstg, pt shd,
pt sl, terr, EHU (16A) €2; 50% statics; phone. "Conv
Weimar & Buchenwald; recep open 0800-1000 & 1700-
2000; welcoming; gd NH/sh stay; v pleasant rural site;
gd walking & cycling fr site; statics (sep area); helpful
manager; no public transport."
€20.50, 15 Apr-31 Oct.   **2016**

WEINHEIM *3C2* (9km N Rural) 49.59776, 8.64013
Camping Wiesensee, Ulmenweg 7, 69502 Hemsbach
**(06201) 72619; familie.herwig@camping-wiesensee.
de; www.camping-wiesensee.de**

12 🐕 €2 ♯♯ 🆆 🚿 ♿ 🚿 ∥ 🅼 ♨ ⚠

Exit A5/E35 junc 32; foll sp Hemsbach. On ent vill
strt at 1st rndbt & traff lts, at 2nd rndabt turn L
& foll camping sp about 1km. 4*, Lge, hdg, pt shd,
serviced pitches; EHU (16A) €1.90 or metered + conn
fee; gas; sw; 75% statics; Eng spkn; adv bkg rec;
boating; tennis 100m; golf 12km; hike hire. "Superb
facs to CC standard; htd pool 100m; friendly welcome;
helpful staff; supmkt in walking dist; gd NH for A5."
€21.50   **2019**

WERNIGERODE *2E3* (5km SE Rural) 51.81530,
10.81359 **Campingplatz Alte Waldmuhle,** Mühlental
78, 38855 Wernigerode **(03943) 266399; info@
altewaldmuehle.de; www.altewaldmuehle.de**

🐕 €1.50 ♯♯ 🆆 🚿 ♿ 🚿 ∥ 🦋 ☂ ℗ ♨ ⚠

Fr Wernigerode foll B244 SE to Elbingerode. Site on
R on edge of Wernigerode. Med, hdstg, pt shd, EHU
(10A) inc; bbq; twin axles; TV; bus 200m; Eng spkn;
adv bkg acc; games rm; CKE. "Basic san facs; gd rest;
bus free into town; beautiful town, castle & Harz rlwy
stns." **€23.00, 1 May-31 Oct.**   **2016**

WERTACH *4E4* (1km NE Rural) 47.60861, 10.41750
Camping Waldesruh, Bahnhofstrasse 19, 87497
Wertach **(08365) 1004; info@camping-wertach.de;
www.camping-wertach.de**

12 🐕 €2.50 ♯♯ (htd) 🆆 🚿 ♿ 🚿 ∥ 🅼 🦋 ☂ nr ℗ nr
⛴ nr ⚠

Fr A7 exit junc 137 at Oy & take B310 dir Wertach;
2km bef Wertach turn R into Bahnhofstrasse & foll
site sp. 4*, Med, mkd, pt shd, pt sl, EHU (16A) metered;
gas; bbq; sw nr; red long stay; TV; 50% statics; phone;
bus; Eng spkn; adv bkg acc; games area; games rm;
CKE. "V picturesque area; friendly site; gd walks; winter
sports site & conv NH in rte Austria/Italy." **€22.50**
2015

WERTHEIM *3D2* (11km NE Rural) 49.78097, 9.56553
Campingpark Wertheim-Bettingen, Geiselbrunnweg
31, 97877 Wertheim-Bettingen **(09342) 7077;
info@campingpark-wertheim-bettingen.de;
www.campingpark-wertheim-bettingen.de**

🐕 €2 ♯♯ 🆆 🚿 ♿ 🚿 ∥ 🦋 ☂ ℗ ♨ ⚠

Fr A3/E41 exit junc 66 - 2nd Wertheim exit; then
turn off to vill of Bettingen; site sp. 4*, Med, pt shd,
pt sl, EHU (10A) inc (long lead req for rvside pitches);
gas; red long stay; 80% statics; Eng spkn; adv bkg acc;
ccard acc; bike hire; boating; fishing; CKE. "On bank
of Rv Main; conv, popular NH for A3 - rec arr early;
NH tourers on sep, lge, level meadow outside main
site (but within barrier); gd rest; htd pool; paddling
pool adj; waterslide adj; fuel stn nrby; effcnt check-in."
€25.50, 1 Apr-1 Nov.   **2019**

WESEL *1B3* (3km W Rural) 51.66795, 6.55620
Erholungszentrum Grav-Insel, 46487 Wesel-Flüren
**(0281) 972830; info@grav-insel.com; www.grav-
insel.com**

12 🐕 €1 ♯♯ 🆆 🚿 ♿ 🚿 ∥ 🅼 ☂ ℗ ♨ ⛴ ⚠ ✏

Exit A3/E35 junc 6 dir Wesel. Then foll sp Rees
& Flüren, site sp. 4*, V lge, unshd, EHU (10A) inc;
65% statics; Eng spkn; tennis 3km; boat hire; fishing;
games area; bike hire; watersports; golf 7km. "Rv
Rhine adj; many activities; gd touring base; htd pool
3km; modern san facs but pss far fr pitches; v lge site
with comprehensive facs & v well kept; poss cr during
high ssn; excel shwrs in main building." **€23.50**   **2019**

WESTERSTEDE *1C2* (1km S Rural) *53.2508, 7.93506*
Camping Westerstede, Süderstrasse 2, 26655
Westerstede **(04488) 78234; camping@westerstede.
de; www.westerstede.de/camping**

12 ♦♦♦ (htd) wo ♿ 🚿 ♨ MSP 🦋 ⊕ nr ⚠

Exit E35/A28 junc 6 to Westerstede; cont thro town
dir Bad Zwischenahn on L815 for 1km; then foll
L815 to L onto Oldenburgerstrasse (rd conts strt
on as L821); in 200m turn L to site. 3*, Med, hdstg,
mkd, pt shd, EHU (9A) inc; bus, train 400m; Eng spkn;
CKE. "*Pleasant, friendly, relaxing, well-managed site;
clsd 1300-1500; sm pitches; outer field (nr mv svc pnt
and rest) cheaper but rd noise and abt 100mtrs fr facs;
o'night m'van facs; gd touring base; many cycle paths;
gd town for shopping; gd midway stop to/fr Denmark.*"
€15.50 2016

WETTRINGEN *1B3* (10km N Rural) *52.27408, 7.3204*
Campingplatz Haddorfer Seen, Haddorf 59, 48493
Wettringen **(05973) 2742; info@campingplatz-
haddorf.de; www.campingplatz-haddorf.de**

12 🐕 €3 ♦♦♦ (htd) wo ♨ ♿ ♨ MSP 🦋 ⊞ ⊕ 🔋 ⚠

Exit A30 junc 7 at Rheine Nord dir Neuenklrchen. At
end city limits turn R dir Salzbergen then L in 4km &
foll site sp. 4*, V lge, mkd, pt shd, EHU (16A) metered
+ conn fee; sw; 90% statics; adv bkg acc; fishing; boat
hire; games area; watersports; CKE. "*Family-friendly
site; modern san facs; gd bistro; gd walking, cycling.*"
€24.00 2016

WETZLAR *3C1* (13km SW Rural) *50.51155, 8.38293*
Campingpark Braunfels, Am Weiherstieg 2, 35619
Braunfels **(06442) 4366; www.braunfels.de**

12 🐕 €1 ♦♦♦ wo ♨ ♿ ♨ 🦋 ⊕ 🔋 nr

Take B49 fr Wetzlar to Braunfels. Site on R at S end
of town. 2*, Med, hdg, mkd, pt shd, pt sl, EHU (16A)
metered + conn fee; 60% statics; adv bkg acc; tennis
300m; horseriding 1km. "*Braunfels beautiful health
resort in easy reach Taunus mountains; htd pool 200m;
fair NH.*" **€20.00** 2015

WIESLOCH *3C3* (8km NW Urban) *49.31643, 8.63481*
Campingplatz Walldorf-Astoria, Schwetzingerstrasse
98, 69190 Walldorf **(06227) 9195**

♦♦♦ wo ♨ ♿ ♨ MSP ⊕ 🔋

Fr A5, exit junc 39 for Walldorf & Wiesloch; take
B291/L598 N sp Walldorf Nord; in 2km turn R onto
Schwetzingerstrasse; site sp in 250m. 3*, Med, pt
shd, EHU (16A) €2.50; 50% statics; Eng spkn; CKE.
"*Vg rest on site; sm zoo & sports complex adj; bus to
Heidelberg at gate; gates clsd 1200-1500; indoor pool
200m; excel NH/sh stay, busy; rec arr bef 1700 high
ssn; conv for Hockenheim Circuit; gd rest; hard working
fam run site; Heidelberg & Speyer worth visiting.*"
€18.00, 15 Apr-15 Oct. 2015

WILDESHAUSEN *1C2* (6km W Rural) *52.89916,
8.35444* **Camping Auetal,** Aumühlerstrasse 75,
27793 Aumühle **(04431) 1851**

12 ♦♦♦ ♿ 🚿 ♨ ♨ Y ⊕ ⚠

Exit a'bahn A1/E37 junc 61. Take rd B213 E; site on L
in 1.5km. 2*, Sm, pt shd, EHU (16A) €1.50; bbq; sw nr;
CKE. "*Statics site but sm field for tourers; vg rest; NH
only.*" **€16.00** 2015

WINTRICH *3B2* (30km NE Rural) *49.96541, 7.10537*
Mosel Stellplatz Wintrich, Rissbacherstraße 155,
56841 Traben-Trarbach **06542 9691728; info@alf.
moselcampingplatz.de; www.mosel-camping-platz.de**

12 🐕 ♦♦♦ wo ♨ ♨ 🦋 ☷

Fr S of A1 take exit 125 Wittlich-Mitte for B50 twds
Wittlich. Merge onto B49, cont onto L55 to Urzig,
then turn R onto B53 & foll sp to camp. 4*, Med, shd,
EHU (6A). "*Vg site.*" **€8.00** 2019

WISMAR *2E2* (0.4km S Urban) *53.89388, 11.45166*
Wohnmobilpark Westhafen, Schiffbauerdamm 12,
23966 Wismar **(01723) 905368 or 884003; info@
wohnmobilpark-wismar.de; www.wohnmobilpark-
wismar.de**

12 ♦♦♦ ♨ ♨ ⊕ nr 🔋 nr

Exit A20/E22 junc 8 to cent of Wismar; foll sp to
'hafen', site sp. 4*, Sm, hdstg, unshd, EHU (10A) €1
for 8 hrs; adv bkg acc. "*Superb NH in stunning town;
quayside noise; m'vans only - no c'vans allowed.*"
€9.00 2016

WISMAR *2E2* (9km NW Coastal) *53.93441, 11.37160*
Ostsee Camping, Sandstrasse 19c, 23968 Zierow
**(038428) 63820; info@ostsee-camping.de;
www.ostsee-camping.de**

12 🐕 €2.70 ♦♦♦ (htd) wo ♨ ♿ ♨ MSP ☷ ⊕ 🔋 ⚠ 🏕 adj

Fr Wismar-Lübeck rd B105/22 to Gägelow, turn
N to Zierow; thro vill to site at end of rd. 4*, V lge,
unshd, EHU (16A) €2.80; TV; 75% statics; games
area; sauna; horseriding adj; bike hire; CKE. "*Busy site
in superb location; gd san facs; a first class campsite.*"
€32.00 2016

WISSEN *1B4* (3km SW Rural) *50.76108, 7.72086* **Zum
Hahnhof,** Paffrather Str. 192, 57537 Wissen **49 27 42
56 10; info@zumhahnhof.de; www.zum-hahnhof.de**

12 🐕 ♦♦♦ ♨ ♨ ♿ ♨ MSP 🦋 Y ⊕ ⚠

Take B62 twds Roth. After 1km turn R onto
Koblenzer Str (rd doubles back onto overpass) then
1st R onto Nistertais Str. Site approx 3km on R. Sm,
hdstg, pt shd, terr, EHU (6A) €1.50; bbq; sw nr; twin
axles; TV; 25% statics; Eng spkn; adv bkg acc; CKE.
"*Modern san facs, very clean; some hdstg pitches, rest
in meadow - long elec leads req; app rd (K133) fairly
narr in places; gd site.*" **€10.00** 2016

WITZENHAUSEN *1D4* (2km N Rural) *51.3499, 9.86916* **Camping Werratal,** Am Sande 11, 37213 Witzenhausen (05542) 1465; info@campingplatz-werratal.de; www.campingplatz-werratal.de

🏕 12 🐕 €2.30 👫 wc ⚓ 🚮 ♿ ⚙ 🛒 ⓗ nr 🚂 🏛

Exit A7/E45 junc 75 to Witzenhausen. Cross rv & immed R foll sp rte around town cent. Site nr rv, sp. 3*, Med, unshd, EHU (16A) €2.30; red long stay; 50% statics; bike hire. *"Clean, pleasant, family-run site; htd covrd pool 200m; poss flooding at high water; easy walk to town; some rd & rlwy noise."* **€20.00**　　　2015

WOLFSBURG *2E3* (3km NE Urban) *52.4316, 10.8158* **Camping am Allersee,** In den Allerwiesen 5, 38446 Wolfsburg (05361) 63395; allerseecamping@gmx.de; www.camping-allersee.de

🏕 12 🐕 €1 👫 (htd) wc ⚓ ♿ 🚮 ♿ 🛒 Ⓨ ⓗ nr 🏛 ✂ 🛥 adj

Exit A39 junc 5 twd Zentrum, foll sp VW Autostadt until start of flyover, keep R and foll sp. 3*, Med, mkd, hdstg, pt shd, EHU (10A) €2.50 or metered; cooking facs; sw nr; 80% statics; Eng spkn; adv bkg acc; sailing; clsd 1300-1500 & 2200-0700; canoeing. *"Vg, clean site beside lake; conv VW factory visits (not w/end or bank hols) - check time of tour in Eng; o'night m'vans area; gd lake perimeter path adj; friendly, helpful owners; ice rink & indoor water cent other side of lake."* **€19.00**　　　2016

WURZBURG *3D2* (6km NE Urban) *49.83286, 9.99783* **Camping Estenfeld,** Maidbronnerstrasse 38, 97230 Estenfeld (09305) 228; cplestenfeld@freenet.de; www.camping-estenfeld.de

🏕 🐕 €1.50 👫 wc ⚓ 🚮 ♿ 🦋 Ⓨ ⓗ nr 🚂 🏛

Exit A7/E45 junc 101. Foll sp to Estenfeld & site sp. Sm, hdstg, pt shd, EHU (16A) €2.50 or metered & conn fee; red long stay; 10% statics; Eng spkn; CKE. *"Helpful owner; clsd 1300-1500; clean, tidy site; rec NH."* **€21.50, 29 May-14 Oct.**　　　2019

WUSTENWELSBERG *4E2* (0.5km SE Rural) *50.13750, 10.82777* **Camping Rückert-Klause,** Haus Nr 16, 96190 Wüstenwelsberg (09533) 288

🏕 🐕 👫 wc ⚓ 🚮 ♿ 🦋 Ⓨ 🚂 nr 🏛

Fr Coburg on B4, turn W at Kaltenbrunn; site sp thro Untermerzbach & Obermerzbach. Or fr B279 fr Bamberg to Bad Königshofen, turn R just S of Pfarrweisch, sp. Sm, pt shd, pt sl, EHU (16A) metered + conn fee; 50% statics; Eng spkn; adv bkg acc; games rm; CKE. *"Many castles nrby; beautiful countryside; super situation."* **€18.00, 1 Apr-31 Oct.**　　　2016

ZELL *3B2* (9km W Rural) *50.03305, 7.11527* **Camping Moselland,** Im Planters, 56862 Pünderich (06542) 2618; www.campingplatz-moselland.de

🏕 🐕 €2 👫 wc ⚓ 🚮 ♿ 🦋 Ⓨ 🏗 ♿ 🏛

Foll Rv Mosel S fr Zell on B53. In 6km turn R sp Pünderich & site. Turn immed L, then immed R & foll narr rd to site in 1km. Med, mkd, pt shd, EHU (16A) metered + conn fee; 30% statics; phone; Eng spkn; adv bkg acc; boat launch. *"Pleasant rvside site in vineyards & orchards; vg; various odd rules."* **€18.00, 1 Apr-1 Nov.**　　　2015

ZELL *3B2* (6km NW Rural) *50.05391, 7.13041* **Bären Camp,** Am Moselufer 1-3, 56859 Bullay (06542) 900097; info@baeren-camp.de; www.baeren-camp.de

🏕 🐕 €2 👫 wc ⚓ 🏗 ♿ 🚮 ♿ 🛒 🦋 🚂 🏛

Exit A1 junc 125 at Wittlich onto B49 to Alf. At Alf cross rv to Bullay & foll sp to site. 4*, Med, pt shd, EHU (16A) metered; bbq; Eng spkn. *"Conv Cochem, Bernkastel-Kues; gd cycling along tow-path; extra for rvside pitch; recep clsd 1230-1400; narr rd to recep; friendly staff; gd location on the Mosel."* **€28.50, 18 Apr-10 Nov.**　　　2019

ZEVEN *1D2* (2km NE Urban) *53.30401, 9.29793* **Campingplatz Sonnenkamp Zeven,** Sonnenkamp 10, 27404 Zeven (04281) 951345; info@campingplatz-sonnenkamp.de; www.campingplatz-zeven.de

🏕 12 🐕 €0.50 👫 (htd) ⚓ 🏗 ♿ 🚮 ♿ 🛒 🦋
♿ Ⓨ ⓗ 🚂 🏛 ✂ 🛥 🏊

Fr A1 exit 47 or 49 to Zeven. Fr Zeven dir Heeslingen/Buxtehude rd, site sp fr all dir twd stadium. 5*, Lge, hdstg, mkd, unshd, EHU (16A) metered; gas; 75% statics; phone; Eng spkn; adv bkg acc; ccard acc; bike hire; games area; tennis; games rm; sauna; CKE. *"Sports facs adj."* **€22.60**　　　2016

FEHMARN ISLAND

WULFEN *2E1* (0.6km E Coastal) *54.40611, 11.1772* **Camping-und Ferienpark Wulfener Hals (Part Naturist),** Wulfener Hals Weg, 23769 Wulfen (04371) 86280; camping@wulfenerhals.de; www.wulfenerhals.de

🏕 🐕 €10 👫 (htd) wc ⚓ 🏗 ♿ 🚮 ♿ 🛒 ♿ Ⓨ
ⓗ 🏊 🚂 🏛 ✂ 🛥 🏊 sand adj

Turn off B207/E47 to Avendorf, site sp. 5*, V lge, mkd, shd, serviced pitches; EHU (160A) inc; gas; 20% statics; phone; adv bkg acc; ccard acc; golf adj; sauna; watersports; sailing; CKE. *"Excel."* **€56.00, 24 Mar-5 Nov, G10.**　　　2017

ZIERENBERG *1D4* (1km E Rural) *51.36809, 9.31494*
Campingplatz Zur Warme, Im Nordbruch 2, 34289
Zierenberg (05606) 3966; campingplatz-zierenberg@
t-online.de; www.campingplatz-zierenberg.de

Exit A44 at junc 67 to Zierenberg. In vill cent foll
sp for Freizeit Centrum. Site on R on leaving vill,
well sp. 4*, Med, mkd, hdstg, unshd, EHU (16A) €1.70
or metered; TV; 75% statics; Eng spkn; adv bkg acc;
fishing. *"Scenic, well-kept site with stream & sm lake
adj; clean, modern facs but poss stretched if site full."*
€16.50   2016

ZINGST AM DARSS *2F1* (3km W Coastal) *54.44055,
12.66031* **Camping am Freesenbruch,** Am Bahndamm
1, 18374 Zingst-am-Darss (038232) 15786; info@
camping-zingst.de; www.camping-zingst.de

On rd 105/E22 at Löbnitz take rd thro Barth to
Zingst; site on coast rd. 4*, Lge, mkd, pt shd, EHU
(16A) metered + conn fee; 20% statics; ccard acc; games area; bike hire; CKE. *"Well-
maintained site in National Park; sep car park; o'night
facs for m'vans; sep fr beach by sea wall & rd; well-
maintained; card operated barrier."* €36.00   2016

> ## "I like to fill in the reports as I travel from site to site"
> You'll find report forms at the back of this guide, or you can fill them in online at camc.com/europereport.

ZISLOW *2F2* (2km N Rural) *53.44555, 12.31083*
Naturcamping Zwei Seen, Waldchaussee 2, 17209
Zislow (039924) 2550; info@zwei-seen-natur
camping.de; www.zwei-seen-naturcamping.de

A19/E55 exit 17 dir Adamshoffnung. Turn R at x-rds
in 4km. Site sp. Also sp fr W of Stuer on B198.
3*, Lge, pt shd, EHU (6A) €2; sw; 40% statics; phone;
Eng spkn; adv bkg acc; ccard acc; games area; bike
hire; watersports; CKE. *"Ideal for country lovers;
remote spot; vg lakeside pitches."* €22.70   2016

ZITTAU *2H4* (3km W Rural) *50.8943, 14.77005* **See-
Camping Zittauer Gebirge,** Zur Landesgartenschau 2,
02785 Olbersdorf (03583) 69629-2; info@seecamping-
zittau.com; www.seecamping-zittau.com

Fr Zittau foll Olbersdorfer See sp, site on lakeside.
3*, Lge, unshd, sl, EHU (10A) €2; sw nr; 10% statics;
Eng spkn; ccard acc; CKE. *"Excel san facs; excel
base for hill walking; close Polish & Czech borders."*
€23.00   2016

RUGEN ISLAND

ALTEFAHR *2F1* (1km NW Coastal) *54.33200,
13.12206* **Sund Camp,** Am Kurpark 1, 18573 Altefähr
(038306) 75483; info@sund-camp.de; www.sund-
camp.de

Fr Stralsund, cross bdge on B96 to Rügen Island.
Foll sp to Altefähr. Site well sp fr vill. Med, mkd,
pt shd, EHU (16A) inc (poss rev pol); red long stay;
TV; 15% statics; phone; sep car park; bike hire. *"Conv
Rugen Is (walks, cycle tracks, beaches, steam rlwy);
easy walk to vill & harbour; splendid, but busy island;
well worth visit; ferry to Stralsund Altstadt nrby; excel,
friendly site; muddy when wet; excel, clean san facs; ltd
nbr of touring pitches."* €24.00   2015

BINZ *2G1* (3km NW Coastal) *54.42315, 13.57808*
Camping Meier, Proraer Chaussee 30, 18609 Prora
(038393) 2085; info@camping-meier-ruegen.de;
www.camping-meier-ruegen.de

On B96 Stralsund to Bergen cont on 196 to Karow.
Turn L on 196a to Prora, at traff lts turn R onto L29
to Binz. After 1.5km at camp sp turn R thro wood to
site. Med, mkd, pt shd, EHU (6A) €2.50; red long stay;
phone; adv bkg req; ccard acc; bike hire; tennis. *"Gd
location for touring Rügen area; gd sandy beach 5-10
min walk thro woods; bkg fee; vg rest; vg san facs."*
€30.00, 13 Mar-1 Nov.   2016

SYLT ISLAND

WESTERLAND *1C1* (5km N Coastal) *54.94251, 8.32685*
Camping Wenningstedt, Am Dorfteich, 25996
Wenningstedt (04651) 944004; camp@wenningstedt.
de; www.campingplatz.wenningstedt.de

Fr Westerland foll sp to Wenningstedt or List. Site
app rd on sharp bend bef Wenningstedt. 4*, Lge,
unshd, pt sl, EHU (16A) metered; adv bkg acc; fishing
300m. €27.00, Easter-31 Oct.   2016

ZWEIBRUCKEN *3B3* (17km SW Rural) *49.15888,
7.24388* **Camping Walsheim(formerly Camping
am Schwimmbad),** Am Campingplatz 1, 66453
Gersheim-Walsheim (06843) 800180; info@
campingwalsheim.de; www.campingwalsheim.de

Fr A8/E50 exit junc 9 onto B423 dor Blieskastel. In
Webenheim turn L twd Gersheim, after 11km turn
L for Walsheim. Site on L beyond vill. 3*, Med, pt
shd, pt sl, EHU €2 or metered (10A); bbq; 85% statics;
phone; adv bkg acc; CKE. *"Helpful warden; htd pool
adj; sep area for tourers; pleasant countryside; walking
& cycle paths nr; site barrier clsd 1300-1500 & 2200."*
€19.00, 15 Mar-31 Oct.   2019

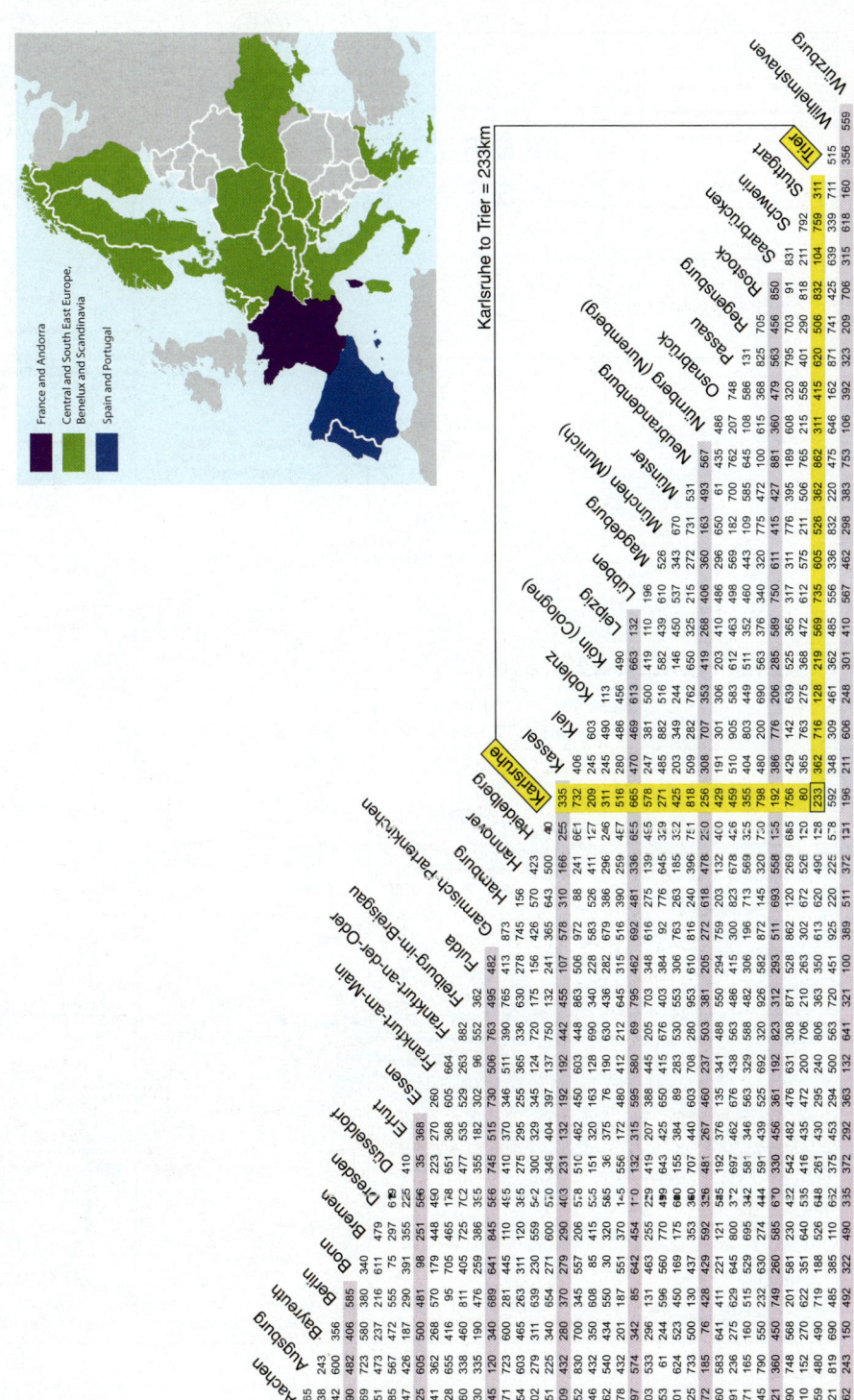

France and Andorra

Central and South East Europe, Benelux and Scandinavia

Spain and Portugal

Karlsruhe to Trier = 233km

GERMANY

Map 1

542

Map 2

Map 3

544

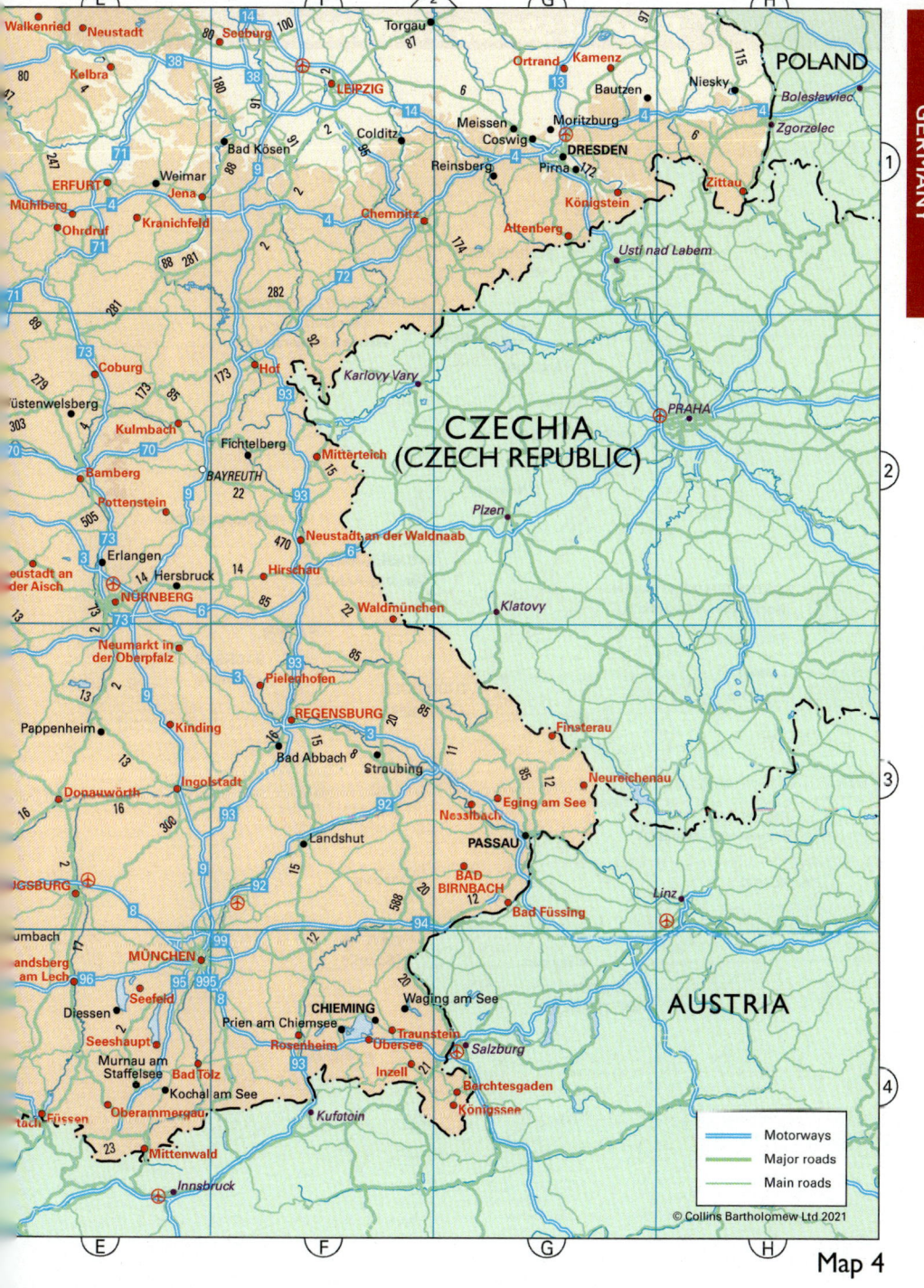

Map 4

GERMANY

SCHLESWIG-HOLSTEIN

MECKLENBURG-VORPOMMERN
(Mecklenburg-Western Pomerania)

• Hamburg

HAMBURG

BREMEN • Bremen

NIEDERSACHSEN
(Lower Saxony)

BERLIN

• Berlin

• Hannover

BRANDENBURG

NORDRHEIN-WESTFALEN
(North Rhine-Westphalia)

SACHSEN-ANHALT
(Saxony-Anhalt)

• Düsseldorf

• Leipzig

• Köln

SACHSEN
(Saxony)

• Dresden

• Bonn

THÜRINGEN
(Thuringia)

HESSEN
(Hesse)

• Frankfurt-am-Main

RHEINLAND-PFALZ
(Rhineland-Palatinate)

SAARLAND

• Nürnberg

• Stuttgart

BAYERN
(Bavaria)

BADEN-WÜRTTEMBERG

• München

Greece

Piraeus, Athens

Shutterstock/NAPA

Highlights

Whether you want to marvel at ancient ruins, lay on an idyllic sandy beach or sample local dishes, Greece is undoubtedly the place to be.

From rugged hillsides to the sparkling blue waters of the Mediterranean, this is a country steeped in myths of gods and heroes. The country is also famed for the friendly and hospitable nature of its people, so you're sure to receive a warm welcome.

Music is an integral part of Greek society and laïkó is a modern folk music genre that boomed in the 1960s and 70s. There are now many different forms of this music, but it still retains a sense of being a song of the people.

Greece can be considered the birthplace of wine, and the origins of wine-making in Greece go back well over 6000 years. Although not as well-known as other European nations for its wine, Greece has a thriving industry and the local varieties pair up well with food dishes from the same area.

Major towns and cities

- Athens – the cradle of Western civilization and one of the world's oldest cities.
- Thessalonika – a charming city filled with museums to explore.
- Patras – this amazing city is home to fascinating sites from ancient times.
- Larissa – surrounded by mountains and home to several ancient sites.

Attractions

- The Acropolis, Athens – an ancient citadel containing the Parthenon and other ruins.
- Meteora – stunning monasteries built on natural sandstone pillars.
- Delphi – this site boasts some of Greece's most important ancient ruins.
- Cape Sounion – fantastic views over the Aegean and the ruins of an ancient temple.

Find out more

www.visitgreece.gr
E: info@gnto.gr T: 0030 (0) 21 03 31 05 29

Country Information

Population (approx): 10.8 million

Capital: Athens

Area: 131,957 sq km

Bordered by: Albania, Bulgaria, Macedonia, Turkey

Coastline: 13,676km

Terrain: Mainly mountain ranges extending into the sea as peninsulas and chains of islands

Climate: Warm Mediterranean climate; hot, dry summers; mild, wet winters in the south, colder in the north; rainy season November to March; winter temperatures can be severe in the mountains

Highest Point: Mount Olympus 2,919m

Language: Greek

Local Time: GMT or BST + 2, i.e. 2 hours ahead of the UK all year

Currency: Euros divided into 100 cents; £1 = €1.14, €1 = £0.88 (Feb 2021)

Emergency numbers: Police 100; Fire brigade 199; Ambulance 166. Operators speak English. Dial 171 for emergency tourist police.

Public Holidays 2021: Jan 1, 6; Mar 15, 25; Apr 30; May 1, 3; Jun 21; Aug 15; Oct 28; Dec 25, 26.

School summer holidays run from the beginning of July to the first week in September.

Border Posts

Borders may be crossed only on official routes with a Customs office. These are usually open day and night. Customs offices at ports are open from 7.30am to 3pm Monday to Friday.

Entry Formalities

British and Irish passport holders may stay for up to 90 days in any 180 day period without a visa. Following Brexit you may be asked to show a return or onward ticket at the border to confirm your length of stay, or to prove that you have enough money for your stay.

Your passport will need to have a minimum of 6 months' validity remaining, and be less than 10 years old (even if it has over 6 months left).

Visitors arriving at a campsite or hotel must complete a registration form.

Medical Services

For minor complaints seek help at a pharmacy (farmakio). In major cities there is usually one member of staff in a pharmacy who speaks English. You should have no difficulty finding an English speaking doctor in large towns and resorts.

Medications containing codeine are restricted. If you are taking any medication containing it, you should carry a letter from your doctor and take no more than one month's supply into the country.

There are numerous public and private hospitals and medical centres of varying standards. Wards may be crowded and the standards of nursing and after care, particularly in the public health sector, are generally below what is normally acceptable in Britain. Doctors and facilities are generally good on the mainland, but may be limited on the islands. The public ambulance service will normally respond to any accident but there are severe shortages of ambulances on some islands.

Emergency treatment at public medical clinics (yiatria) and in state hospitals registered by the Greek Social Security Institute, IKA-ETAM, is free on presentation of a European Health Insurance Card (EHIC) but you may face a long wait. You will be charged for prescriptions so keep the adhesive labels from the medicines packages in order to claim a refund at an IKA-ETAM office. See www.ika.gr for a list of local offices.

You may consult a doctor or dentist privately but you will have to present your EHIC and pay all charges up front. You can then claim back the charges later from the IKA-ETAM.

If staying near a beach, ensure that you have plenty of insect repellent as sand flies are prevalent. Do not be tempted to befriend stray dogs as they often harbour diseases which may be passed to humans.

Opening Hours

Banks: Mon-Fri 8am-2pm (1.30pm on Friday); 8am-6pm in tourist areas.

Museums: Check locally for opening hours. Normally closed on Mon or Tues and some bank holidays.

Post Offices: Mon-Fri 8am-2pm; 8am-7pm

in tourist areas; many in Athens open Sat mornings in summer.

Shops: Mon-Fri 8am/8.30am/9am-2pm/4.30pm & on some days 5pm-8.30pm; Sat 8.30am-3pm; check as hours vary according to season.

Safety and Security

Normally visits to Greece are trouble-free, but the tourist season results in an increase in incidents of theft of passports, wallets, handbags, etc, particularly in areas or at events where crowds gather.

Take care when visiting well-known historical sites; they are the favoured haunts of pickpockets, bag-snatchers and muggers. Women should not walk alone at night and lone visitors are strongly advised never to accept lifts from strangers or passing acquaintances at any time.

Since banking services were restricted in 2015, the FCO has recommended that you take enough cash to cover your needs while you are in Greece. If you are carrying large amounts of cash, make sure you take safety precautions. Be aware that tourists are expected to be carrying larger amounts of money, making them potential targets for thieves.

Multi-lingual tourist police are available in most resorts offering information and help; they can be recognised by a 'Tourist Police' badge, together with a white cap band. There is also a 24-hour emergency helpline for tourists; dial 171 from anywhere in Greece.

Certain areas near the Greek borders are militarily sensitive and you should not take photographs or take notes near military or official installations. Seek permission before photographing individuals.

There is a general threat from domestic terrorism. Attacks could be indiscriminate and against civilian targets in public places. Public protests are a standard feature of Greek politics and it is wise to avoid public gatherings and demonstrations. Domestic anarchist groups remain active but their actions are primarily directed against the Greek state.

During especially hot and dry periods there is a danger of forest fires. Take care when visiting or driving through woodland areas.

Ensure that cigarette ends are properly extinguished, do not light barbecues and do not leave rubbish or empty bottles behind.

Some motorists have encountered stowaway attempts while waiting to board ferries to Italy from Patras. Keep a watch on your vehicle(s).

In order to comply with the law, always ensure that you obtain a receipt for goods purchased.

British Embassy

1 PLOUTARCHOU STREET
106 75 ATHENS
Tel: (210) 7272600
www.ukingreece.fco.gov.uk

There are also British Consulates/Vice-Consulates/Honorary Consulates in Corfu, Heraklion (Crete), Rhodes and Zakynthos.

Irish Embassy

7 LEOF.VAS
KONSTANTINOU, 106 74 ATHENA
Tel: (210) 7232771
www.embassyofireland.gr

There are also Honorary Consulates in Corfu, Crete, Rhodes and Thessaloniki.

Documents

Money

Major credit cards are accepted in hotels, restaurants and shops and at some petrol stations. They may not be accepted at shops in small towns or villages. There is an extensive network of cash machines in major cities.

Carry your credit card issuers'/banks' 24-hour UK contact numbers in case of loss or theft.

Passport

Carry your passport at all times as a means of identification.

Vehicle(s)

Carry your vehicle registration certificate (V5C), insurance certificate and MOT certificate (if applicable) at all times.

Driving

Accidents

It is not essential to call the police in the case of an accident causing material damage only, however motorists are advised to call at the nearest police station to give a description of the incident to the authorities.

Whenever an accident causes physical injury, drivers are required to stop immediately to give assistance to the injured and call the police. Drivers who fail to do this are liable to imprisonment for up to three years.

If a visiting motorist has an accident, especially one causing injuries, they should inform the motoring organisation, ELPA, preferably at its head office in Athens, on (210) 6068800, email: info@elpa.gr, as they should be able to offer you assistance.

Alcohol

The maximum permitted level of alcohol is 50 milligrams in 100 millilitres of blood, i.e. lower than that permitted in the UK (80 milligrams). A level of 20 milligrams in 100 millilitres of blood applies to drivers who have held a driving licence for less than two years and to motorcyclists. Police carry out random breath tests and refusal to take a test when asked by the police, and/or driving while over the legal limit, can incur high fines, withdrawal of your driving licence and even imprisonment.

Breakdown Service

The Automobile & Touring Club of Greece (ELPA) operates a roadside assistance service (OVELPA) 24 hours a day on all mainland Greek roads as well as on most islands. The number to dial from most towns in Greece is 10400.

Members of AIT/FIA affiliated clubs, such as The Caravan and Motorhome Club, should present their valid membership card in order to qualify for reduced charges for on-the-spot assistance and towing. Payment by credit card is accepted.

Child Restraint System

Children under three years of age must be seated in a suitable and approved child restraint. Children between the ages of 3 and 11 years old that are less than 1.35 metres in height must be seated in an appropriate child restraint for their size. From 12 years old children that are over 1.35 metres in height can wear an adult seat belt.

A rear facing child restraint can be placed in the front seat only if the airbag is deactivated.

Fuel

Petrol stations are usually open from 7am to 7pm; a few are open 24 hours. Some will accept credit cards but those offering cut-price fuel are unlikely to do so. In rural areas petrol stations may close in the evening and at weekends, so keep your tank topped up. There are no automatic petrol pumps operated with either credit cards or bank notes.

LPG (autogas) is available from a limited number of outlets.

Motorways

There are over 2,000 km of motorways in Greece.Service areas provide petrol, a cafeteria and shops. The main motorways are A1 Agean, A2 Egnatia,A6 Attiki, A7 Peloponissos, A8 Pathe, A29 Kastorias. For further information visit www.greek-motorway.net.

Motorway Tolls

Tolls are charged according to vehicle classification and distance travelled. By European standards the tolls are generally quite low. Cash is the preferred means of payment.

The Egnatia Highway

The 804 km Egnatia Highway (the A2), part of European route E90 linking the port of Igoumenitsa with the Turkish border at Kipoi, has undergone extensive upgrade and improvement in recent years. The route includes many bridges and tunnels with frequent emergency telephones for which the number to call from a landline or mobile phone is 1077. The road provides a continuous high speed link from west to east and will eventually connect with Istanbul. An electronic toll collection system is planned for the future.

Patras – Antirrio Bridge

A 2.8 km long toll suspension bridge between Rio (near Patras) and Antirrio links the Peloponnese with western central Greece and is part of the A8/E55 motorway. It has cut the journey time across the Gulf of Corinth – formerly only possible by ferry – to just five minutes. Tolls are charged.

Preveza – Aktio Tunnel

This undersea toll tunnel links Preveza with Aktio near Agios Nikolaos on the E55 along the west coast of mainland Greece and is part of a relatively fast, scenic route south from Igoumenitsa to central and southern regions.

Parking

Parking is only permitted in the Athens 'Green Zone' where there are parking meters. Special parking sites in other areas are reserved for short-term parking for tourists.

There may be signs on the side of the road indicating where vehicles should be parked. Parking restrictions are indicated by yellow lines at the side of the road. The police are entitled to remove vehicles. They can also confiscate the number plates of vehicles parked illegally and, while this usually applies only to Greek-registered vehicles, drivers of foreign registered vehicles should nevertheless avoid illegal parking.

Parking is not permitted within three metres of a fire hydrant, five metres of an intersection, stop sign or traffic light, and fifteen metres of a bus stop, tram stop and level crossings.

Roads

The surfaces of all major roads and of the majority of other roads are in good condition. Some mountain roads, however, may be in poor condition and drivers must beware of unexpected potholes (especially on corners), precipitous, unguarded drops and single-carriageway bridges. Even on narrow mountain roads you may well encounter buses and coaches.

British motorists visiting Greece should be extra vigilant in view of the high incidence of road accidents. Driving standards are generally poorer than in the UK and you may well have to contend with dangerous overtaking, tailgating, weaving motorcycles and scooters, constant use of the horn, roaming pedestrians and generally erratic driving. Greece has one of the highest rate of road fatalities in Europe and overtaking and speeding are common causes of accidents, particularly on single lane carriageways. Drive carefully and be aware of other drivers at all times.

August is the busiest month of the year for traffic and the A1/E75 between Athens and Thessalonika is recognised as one of the most dangerous routes, together with the road running through the Erimanthos mountains south of Kalavrita. Mountain roads in general can be dangerous owing to narrow carriageways, blind bends and unprotected embankments, so keep your speed down.

You are strongly advised against hiring motorcycles, scooters and mopeds, as drivers of these modes of transport are particularly at risk. The wearing of crash helmets is a legal requirement. Never hand over your passport when hiring a vehicle.

Greece has a high level of pedestrian fatalities. Where there is a shortage of parking spaces drivers park on pavements so pedestrians are forced to walk in the road. Collisions between pedestrians and motorcycles are common.

Road Signs and Markings

Road signs conform to international conventions. Motorway signs have white lettering on a green background, signs on other roads are on a blue background. All motorways, major and secondary roads are signposted in Greek and English.

Some open roads have a white line on the nearside, and slower-moving vehicles are expected to pull across it to allow vehicles to overtake.

Speed Limits

	Open Road (km/h)	Motorway (km/h)
Car Solo	90-110	130
Car towing caravan/trailer	80	80
Motorhome under 3500kg	80	90
Motorhome 3500-7500kg	80	80

Traffic Jams

There is heavy rush hour traffic in and around the major cities and traffic jams are the norm in central Athens any time of day. During the summer months traffic to the coast may be heavy, particularly at weekends. Traffic jams may be encountered on the A1/E75 Athens to Thessalonika road and on the A8/E65 Athens to Patras road. Traffic may also be heavy near the ferry terminals to Italy and you should allow plenty of time when travelling to catch a ferry. Delays can be expected at border crossings to Turkey and Bulgaria.

Violation of Traffic Regulations

The Greek police are authorised to impose fines in cases of violation of traffic regulations, but they are not allowed to collect fines on the spot. Motorists must pay fines within ten days, otherwise legal proceedings will be started.

Essential Equipment

First Aid Kit

All vehicles must carry a first aid kit.

Fire Extinguisher

All vehicles must carry a fire extinguisher.

Warning Triangles

The placing of a warning triangle is compulsory in the event of an accident or a breakdown. It must be placed 100 metres behind the vehicle.

Touring

Mainland Greece and most of the Greek islands that are popular with British tourists are in seismically active zones, and small earth tremors are common. Serious earthquakes are less frequent but can, and do, occur.

Smoking is prohibited in bars and restaurants. In restaurants, if the bill does not include a service charge, it is usual to leave a 10 to 20% tip. Taxi drivers do not normally expect a tip but it is customary to round up the fare.

The best known local wine is retsina but there is also a wide range of non-resinated wines. Beer is brewed under licence from German and Danish breweries; Ouzo is a popular and strong aniseed-flavoured aperitif.

The major Greek ports are Corfu, Igoumenitsa, Patras, Piraeus and Rhodes. Ferry services link these ports with Cyprus, Israel, Italy and Turkey. The routes from Ancona and Venice in Italy to Patras and Igoumenitsa are very popular and advance booking is recommended.

For further information contact:

VIAMARE LTD
SUITE 108
582 Honeypot Lane
STANMORE
MIDDX
HA7 1JY
Tel: 020 8206 3420,
www.viamare.com
Email: ferries@viamare.com

Some ferries on routes from Italy to Greece have 'camping on board' facilities whereby passengers can sleep in their outfits. Mains hook-ups, t showers and toilets are available.

There are several World Heritage Sites in Greece (with more under consideration), including such famous sites as the Acropolis in Athens, the archaeological sites at Olympia and Mistras, and the old towns of Corfu and Rhodes. See www.worldheritagesite.org for more information. When visiting churches and monasteries dress conservatively, i.e. long trousers for men and no shorts, sleeveless T-shirts or short skirts for women.

Camping and Caravanning

There are over 300 campsites licensed by the Greek National Tourist Office. These can be recognised by a sign displaying the organisation's blue emblem. Most are open from April until the end of October, but those near popular tourist areas stay open all year. There are other unlicensed sites but visitors to them cannot be assured of safe water treatment, fire prevention measures or swimming pool inspection.

Casual/wild camping is not allowed outside official sites in Greece.

Electricity and Gas

Usually current on campsites varies between 4 and 16 amps. Plugs have two round pins. There are few CEE connections.

The full range of Campingaz cylinders are available from hypermarkets and other shops, but when purchasing a cylinder you may not be given a refundable deposit receipt.

Public Transport

Greece has a modern, integrated public transport system, including an extensive metro, bus, tram and suburban railway network in and around Athens – see www.ametro.gr for a metro map.

Buy bus/tram tickets from special booths at bus stops, newspaper kiosks or from metro stations. A ticket is valid for a travel time of 90 minutes.

Taxis are relatively cheap. All licensed taxis are yellow and are equipped with meters (the fare is charged per kilometre) and display a card detailing tariffs and surcharges. In certain tourist areas, you may be asked to pay a predetermined (standard) amount for a ride to a specific destination. Taxis run on a share basis, so they often pick up other passengers on the journey.

There are many ferry and hydrofoil services from Piraeus to the Greek islands and between islands.

Meteora Monasteries

Shutterstock/ Ihor Pasternak

ALEXANDROUPOLI *C1 (2km W Coastal) 40.84679, 25.85614* **Camping Alexandroupolis Beach,** Makris Ave, 68100 Alexandroupolis **(25510) 28735; camping@ditea.gr; www.ditea.gr**

🏕12 ♀♂ wc ⚲ ⚟ 🐕 ❀ 🍴 🚻 🎣 ⛱ sand adj

Site on coast - after drainage channel, at 2nd set traff lts close together. Lge, mkd, hdstg, hdg, shd, EHU (8A) €3.60; gas; 20% statics; phone; Eng spkn; watersports; games area; tennis; CKE. *"Spacious, secure, well-run site; clean, hot shwrs; easy walk to pleasant town cent; site a little tired (2019); ACSI acc."* **€22.00** 2019

ATHINA *B3 (7km NW Urban) 38.00916, 23.67236* **Camping Athens,** 198-200 Athinon Ave, 12136 Athens **(210) 5814114 or 5814101 winter; info@camping athens.com.gr; www.campingathens.com.gr**

🏕12 🐕 ♀♂ wc ⚲ ⚟ MP 🍴 🎣

Fr Corinth on E94 m'way/highway, stay on this rd to Athens o'skts; site is approx 4km past Dafni Monastery, set back on L of multi-lane rd, sh dist beyond end of underpass. Go past site to next traff lts where U-turn permitted. Fr N use old national rd (junc 8 if on toll m'way). Med, pt shd, EHU (16A) €4; TV; bus to Athens; ccard acc. *"V dusty but well-managed site; gd san facs but poss insufficient high ssn; helpful staff; bus tickets to Athens sold; visitors rec not to use sat nav to find site, as it misdirects!"* **€33.00** 2019

DELFI *B2 (2km W Rural) 38.4836, 22.4755* **Camping Apollon,** 33054 Delfi **(22650) 82762 or 82750; apollon4@otenet.gr; www.apolloncamping.gr**

🏕12 🐕 ♀♂ wc ⚲ ⚟ 🐕 ❀ 🍴 ⛱ 🎣

Site on N48 fr Delfi twd Itea & 1st of number of campsites on this rd. Site 25km fr Parnassus ski cent. 3*, Med, mkd, pt shd, pt sl, terr, EHU (16A) €3; gas; TV; 30% statics; phone; adv bkg acc; ccard acc; bike hire; CKE. *"Magnificent views over mountains & Gulf of Corinth; Harmonie Group site; site cooler than some other sites due to its elevation; vg site; popular with groups of students; vg campsite."* **€30.00** 2015

DELFI *B2 (5km W Rural) 38.47868, 22.47461* **Camping Delphi,** Itea Road, 33054 Delfi **(22650) 82745; info@ delphicamping.com; www.delphicamping.com**

🐕 ♀♂ wc ⚲ ⚟ MP 🍴 🎣

App fr Itea-Amfissa rd or Levadia; well sp. Med, shd, terr, EHU (16A) €3.90; gas; TV; phone; bus to Delfi; adv bkg acc; ccard acc; tennis; CKE. *"Visit grotto, refuge of Parnassus; Delfi archaeological sites 3km; friendly, helpful staff; Sunshine Group site; magnificent views; gd pool; dogs free; tired facs; 20% discount for Minoan Line ticketholders; delightful site; san facs bit tired but clean & tidy; excel site."* **€29.00, 1 Apr-31 Oct.** 2019

DELFI *B2 (8.5km W Rural) 38.47305, 22.45926* **Chrissa Camping,** 33055 Chrissa **(22650) 82050; info@chrissacamping.gr; www.chrissacamping.gr**

🏕12 ♀♂ wc ⚲ ⚟ 🐕 ❀ 🍴 🍴 🎣 ⛱ 🎣 shgl 10km

1st site on Itea to Delfi rd, sp. 4*, Med, shd, pt sl, terr, EHU (10A) €4 first 4KWh/day then metered; gas; TV; adv bkg acc; ccard acc; games area; tennis 300m; CKE. *"Excel, scenic site."* **€21.50** 2017

DREPANO *B3 (12km E Coastal) 37.49710, 22.99028* **Iria Beach Camping,** Iria Beach 21060, Nafplio 02 75 20 94 253; iriabeach@naf.forthnet.gr; www.iriabeach.com

🏕12 🐕 ♀♂ wc ⚲ ⚟ ❀ 🍴 🎣 ⛱ 🎣 adj

Fr Drepano head E on Epar. Od. Drepanou-Kantias. Cont onto Kantias-Irion. 800m after Iria Beach Hotel turn R. Site on L after 1.5km. Med, hdstg, shd, EHU (16A); bbq; cooking facs; twin axles; TV; 5% statics; Eng spkn; adv bkg acc; CCI. *"Opp beach; gd sw; site quiet & relaxing; helpful staff; vg site."* **€25.00** 2019

"We must tell the Club about that great site we found"

Get your site reports in by mid-August and we'll do our best to get your updates into the next edition.

EGIO *B2 (13km NW Coastal) 38.32078, 21.97195* **Tsoli's Camping,** Lambíri Egion, 25100 Lambiri **(26910) 31469 or 31621**

🏕12 🐕 ♀♂ wc ⚲ ⚟ 🍴 🎣 ⛱ ❀ 🎣 shgl adj

Fr Athens: A8/E65 exit Kamaras, site clearly sp 1km W of Lambiri. Fr Patras: Leave A8/E65 at exit Longos, take the Old Nat. On L in 1.5km after Lampiri. Med, hdstg, shd, EHU (16A) inc; gas; bbq; TV; 10% statics; phone; bus; Eng spkn; adv bkg acc; ccard acc; sep car park; boat launch; fishing; watersports; CKE. *"Bus & train service to Athens & Patras; gd site with gd facs in delightful position; few shd pitches for tourers & poss diff for high o'fits."* **€24.00** 2015

FINIKOUNDAS *A3 (1km W Coastal) 36.80555, 21.79583* **Camping Thines,** 24006 Finikoundas **(27230) 71200; thines@otenet.gr; www.finikounda.com**

🏕12 🐕 ♀♂ wc ⚲ ⚟ 🐕 ❀ 🍴 🎣 ⛱ 🎣 sand adj

Fr Methoni dir Finikoundas, turn R 1km bef vill, site on L. Sm, hdg, mkd, hdstg, pt shd, EHU (6-10A); gas; bbq; cooking facs; TV; Eng spkn; ccard acc; boat launch; CKE. *"Excel facs; helpful, friendly management; wonderful scenery & beach; red winter long stay; lovely vill in walking dist; beautiful site."* **€26.50** 2015

GERAKINI *B2* (3km SE Coastal) *40.26464, 23.46338*
Camping Kouyoni, 63100 Gerakini **(23710) 52226;**
info@kouyoni.gr; www.kouyoni.gr

🐕 👫 wc 🚿 🏕 🚮 ✗ 🦋 🍴 ♿ ⊕ 🛒 🏪 ⚓ 🛶 ⬆ 🌳 sand adj

Take main rd S fr Thessaloniki to Nea Moudania,
then turn E twd Sithonia. Site is 18km on that rd
past Gerakini on R, past filling stn. Well sp. Med,
hdg, mkd, shd, pt sl, EHU (16A) €3.30; bbq; red long
stay; TV; 30% statics; phone; adv bkg acc; games area;
boat launch; CKE. *"Gd touring base set in olive grove;
friendly owner; gd facs; gd beach; influx of w/enders
high ssn."* **€29.00, 1 May-30 Sep.** 2016

GITHIO *B3* (5km SSW Coastal) *36.73055, 22.55305*
Camping Meltemi, Mavrovouni Gytheio Lakonias
23200 **(02733) 023260; info@campingmeltemi.gr;**
www.campingmeltemi.gr

🐕 👫 wc 🏕 🚮 ✗ MP ♿ ⊕ 🛒 🏪 ⬆ 🛶 🌳 20m

Site is approx 3km S of Githio on the L of the
rd to Areopoli. Lge, mkd, shd, EHU (16A); bbq;
cooking facs; twin axles; TV; phone; Eng spkn;
adv bkg acc; waterslide; games area; CKE. *"Beach
volleyball, tennis, table tennis & basketball court; vg."*
€26.00, 1 Apr-31 Oct. 2015

IGOUMENITSA *A2* (10km S Coastal) *39.46346,
20.26037* **Camping Elena's Beach,** 46100 Platariá
**(26650) 71414; bteo@altecnet.gr or info@
campingelena.gr; www.epirus.com/campingelena**

🐕 👫 wc 🏕 🚮 🚾 ✗ 🍴 ⊕ 🛒 🏪 🌳 🛶 shgl adj

Sp on Igoumenitsa-Preveza rd, 2km NW of Platariá.
Med, hdstg, pt shd, terr, EHU (5A) inc; gas; bbq; red
long stay; 10% statics; phone; bus; adv bkg acc; CKE.
*"Well-maintained, family-run, friendly site; clean,
modern san facs; beautiful location with pitches
next to sea; excel rest; conv ferries Corfu, Paxos."*
€26.50, 1 Apr-31 Oct. 2019

> ## "I need an on-site restaurant"
>
> We do our best to make sure site information
> is correct, but it is always best to check any
> must-have facilities are still available or will
> be open during your visit.

IGOUMENITSA *A2* (5km W Coastal) *39.51014,
20.22133* **Camping Drepanos,** Beach Drepanos,
46100 Igoumenitsa **(26650) 26980; camping@
drepano.gr; www.drepano.gr**

12 🐕 👫 wc 🏕 🚮 🚾 MP 🍴 ⊕ 🛒 🏪 nr 🌳 🛶 sand

Fr Igoumenitsa take coast rd N. Foll sp for Drepanos
Beach. Fr either port turn L and head N up coast.
Med, hdstg, pt shd, sl, bbq; twin axles; 10% statics;
bus adj; Eng spkn; adv bkg acc; CKE. *"Beside nature
reserve; amazing sunsets; friendly; dated san facs;
attractive walks/cycle; vg."* **€33.00** 2019

IOANINA *A2* (2km NW Urban) *39.67799, 20.84279*
Camping Limnopoula, Kanari 10, 45000 Ioanina
(26510) 25265

🐕 👫 wc 🏕 🚮 ✗ 🦋 🍴 nr ⊕ nr 🛒 🏪

At Ioanina Nautical Club on Igoumenitsa rd at W
o'skts of town on rd that runs along lake fr citadel;
site well sp fr all dirs. Med, pt shd, EHU (10A) inc; gas;
bbq; phone; Eng spkn; watersports. *"Beautiful situation
on lake, mountain views; excel touring base; helpful
staff; gd facs; clean; may close earlier; adv bkg acc 1-2
days ahead only LS; popular with groups LS; dogs free;
vg."* **€27.00, 1 Apr-15 Oct.** 2015

> ## "Satellite navigation makes touring much easier"
>
> Remember most sat navs don't know if you're
> towing or in a larger vehicle – always use yours
> alongside maps and site directions.

KALAMBAKA *A2* (4km SE Rural) *39.68250, 21.65510*
Camping Philoxenia, 42200 Kalambaka **(24320)
24466; philoxeniacamp@ath.forthnet.gr**

🐕 👫 (htd) wc 🏕 ♿ 🚮 ✗ MP 🦋 🍴 ⊕ nr 🛒 🏪 🌳 🛶 ⬆

Site on N side of E92 Trikala rd, behind barrier.
3*, Med, hdstg, shd, EHU (6A) inc; gas; bbq; cooking
facs; TV; 30% statics; Eng spkn; adv bkg acc; ccard acc;
waterslide; bike hire; CKE. *"Interesting area esp during
Easter religious festivals; Still open 2016 but call bef
travelling."* **€20.00, 1 Mar-30 Nov.** 2017

KALAMBAKA *A2* (2km NW Rural) *39.71315,
21.61588* **Camping Vrachos,** Meteoron Street,
42200 Kastraki **(24320) 22293; tsourvaka@
yahoo.gr; www.campingkastraki.com**

12 🐕 👫 wc 🏕 ♿ 🚮 🚾 MP 🦋 🍴 ⊕ 🛒 🏪 🌳 🛶 (htd)

Fr cent of Kalambaka take rd at app to vill of
Kastraki. Site is 2km N of E92. Med, hdstg, mkd, hdg,
pt shd, pt sl, terr, EHU (16A) inc; gas; bbq; cooking
facs; twin axles; TV; phone; bus adj; train 1km; Eng
spkn; adv bkg acc; CKE. *"V friendly management;
clean san facs; vg views fr some pitches; ltd facs open
in winter; dogs free; Harmonie Group site; conv for
monasteries, tour bus fr camp."* **€19.00** 2017

KAVALA *C1* (4km SW Urban/Coastal) *40.91573,
24.37851* **Camping Multiplex Batis,** 65000 Kavala
(2510) 245918; nfo@batis-sa.gr; www.batis-sa.gr

12 👫 (htd) wc 🏕 ♿ 🚮 ✗ 🍴 ⊕ 🛒 🏪 🛶 ⬆ 🌳 sand adj

On W app to town on old coast rd, ent on a curving
hill. Med, hdg, mkd, shd, pt sl, EHU (6A) €4; phone;
bus; Eng spkn; adv bkg acc; ccard acc; CKE. *"Beautiful
location but v developed; conv ferry to Thassos &
archaeological sites; clean facs but site poss unkempt
LS; vg."* **€26.00** 2016

KORINTHOS B3 (7km W Urban/Coastal) *37.93470, 22.86543* **Blue Dolphin Camping,** 20011 Lecheon Korinth **(27410) 25766 or 25767; info@camping-blue-dolphin.gr; www.camping-blue-dolphin.gr**

🏕 ⛺ 🚹 WC ♨ 🚿 ♿ ⊘ 🏊 🍴 🍸 🛈 🅿 🛒 🏧 ⚲ shgl

Best app fr E to avoid town; Fr A8 exit sp Ancient Corinth, then N (R) to T-junc end of rd, W (R) past pipe factory, sp 400m N (R) at bottom of bdge sl. Fr W take exit sp Ancient Corinth after toll point. Fr Old National rd turn N (L) immed over rlwy bdge bef pipe factory. Fr Corinth foll old National rd twd Patras, past pipe factory. Med, mkd, hdstg, pt shd, EHU (6A) €3.50; gas; bbq; TV; Eng spkn; ccard acc; games area; CKE. *"V obliging, friendly owners; Sunshine Group site; pleasant site; sm pitches; lovely site by sea."* **€23.00, 1 Apr-31 Oct.** 2015

KYLLINI A3 (10km S Coastal) *37.88539, 21.11175* **Campsite Melissa,** 27050 Kastro Kyllinis Ilia **02 62 30 95 213; camping_melissa@yahoo.gr**

🏕 ⛺ 🚹 WC ♨ 🚿 ♿ ⊘ MSP ⚲ 🍴 🍸 🛈 🛒 🏧 ⚲

S fr Patras twd Pygros on E55. Turn R twds Lehena after 58km marker. Foll signs to Kastro Kyllinis. Med, hdg, shd, EHU (10A); bbq; cooking facs; twin axles; TV; 2% statics; Eng spkn; adv bkg acc; CCI. *"Great campsite to chill; excel rest, bar & shop; lovely sandy beach; excel sw; fabulous views across the bay."* **€25.00, 1 Apr-31 Oct.** 2019

KYLLINI A3 (17km S Coastal) *37.83828, 21.12972* **Camping Aginara Beach,** Lygia, 27050 Loutra Kyllinis **(26230) 96211; info@camping-aginara.gr; www.camping-aginara.gr**

12 ⚲ 🚹 WC ♨ 🚿 ♿ ⊘ 🏊 ⚲ 🍴 🍸 🛈 🅿 🛒 🏧 ⚲ shgl adj

S fr Patras on E55 twds Pyrgos; exit Gastouni & turn W thro Vartholomio twd Loutra Kyllinis; turn L about 3km bef Kyllinis then foll sps. 3*, Lge, hdg, hdstg, shd, pt sl, EHU (10A); gas; bbq; TV; 25% statics; phone; Eng spkn; adv bkg acc; ccard acc; watersports; CKE. *"Friendly proprietor; excel, modern facs; site on lovely beach; beautiful views."* **€28.00** 2019

METHONI A3 (1km ESE Coastal) *36.81736, 21.71515* **Camp Methoni,** 24006 Methoni **(27230) 31188**

🏕 ⚲ 🚹 🚿 ⊘ 🍸 🛈 🅿 🏧 ⚲ sand

Fr Pylos on rd 9, strt thro Methoni to beach, turn E along beach, site sp. 2*, Med, hdstg, pt shd, EHU (10A) inc; bbq; phone; Eng spkn; adv bkg acc; CKE. *"Superb Venetian castle; close to pleasant vill; park away fr taverna & rd to avoid noise; excel sw; v dusty site; clean san facs; new owner & undergoing renovations (2013); quiet & gd site."* **€21.40, 1 May-31 Oct.** 2019

MIKINES B3 (0.1km E Urban) *37.71922, 22.74676* **Camping Mikines/Mykenae,** 21200 Mikines **(27510) 76247; dars@arg.forthnet.gr; www.ecogriek.nl**

12 ⚲ 🚹 WC ♨ 🚿 ♿ ⊘ 🍴 🛒 nr

In town of Mikines (Mycenae) nr bus stop. On R as heading to archeological site, sp. 2*, Sm, hdstg, mkd, pt shd, EHU (10A) €4.50; Eng spkn; CKE. *"Quaint family-run site; v warm welcome; conv ancient Mycenae; meals served; friendly staff; vg."* **€21.00** 2019

PARGA A2 (2km W Coastal) *39.28550, 20.38997* **Camping Valtos,** Valtos Beach, 48060 Parga **(26840) 31287; info@campingvaltos.gr; www.camping valtos.gr**

🏕 ⚲ 🚹 WC ♨ 🚿 ⊘ 🍴 🍸 🛈 🅿 🛒 ⚲ sand adj

Foll sp fr Parga twd Valtos Beach, site sp. Site at far end of beach behind bar/club. Med, mkd, shd, pt sl, EHU (10A); Eng spkn; CKE. *"Helpful owners; gd walking area; steep walk to town; poor san facs."* **€28.50, 1 May-30 Sep.** 2016

PLAKA LITOHORO B2 (10km N Coastal) *40.18230, 22.55885* **Camping Stani,** 60200 Kalivia Varikou **(23520) 61277**

12 ⚲ 🚹 WC ♨ 🚿 ⊘ 🍸 🛈 🅿 🛒

Leave E75 (Athens-Thessaloniki) at N Efesos/Variko, foll sp Varikou & site. Lge, mkd, shd, EHU; TV; phone; CKE. *"Ltd facs LS; conv Dion; fair site."* **€22.00** 2019

PYLOS A3 (7km N Coastal) *36.94784, 21.70635* **Camping Navarino Beach,** 24001 Gialova **(27230) 22973; info@navarino-beach.gr; www.navarino-beach.gr**

12 ⚲ 🚹 WC ♨ 🚿 ⊘ MSP ⚲ 🍸 🛈 🅿 🛒 nr 🏧 ⚲

Fr Pylos N twds Kiparissia for 5km around Navarino Bay, site at S end of Gialova vill; sp. Med, hdstg, pt shd, EHU (16A) €4; gas; bbq; cooking facs; red long stay; bus; Eng spkn; adv bkg acc; ccard acc; windsurfing; boat launch; CKE. *"Management v helpful; gd, clean, modern facs; several rest & shops in easy walking dist; some pitches on beach; vg."* **€32.50** 2019

SPARTI B3 (5km W Rural) *37.06941, 22.38163* **Camping Castle View,** 23100 Mistras **(27310) 83303; info@castleview.gr; www.castleview.gr**

🏕 ⚲ 🚹 WC ♨ 🚿 ⊘ 🍴 🍸 🛈 🅿 🛒 🏧 🏊

Fr Kalamata take 1st turning to Mistras, past castle then thro vill dir Sparti. Site in approx 1km on L, well sp. 3*, Med, pt shd, EHU (16A) inc; gas; TV; 10% statics; phone; Eng spkn; CKE. *"Gd clean facs; gd rest; close to archaeological remains; helpful owner."* **€26.00, 1 Apr-20 Oct.** 2016

STYLIDA *B2* (4km SE Coastal) *38.89638, 22.65555*
Camping Interstation, Rd Athens-Thessalonika, Km 230, 35300 Stylida **(22380) 23828; www.campinginterstation.com**

🔢12 🐕 🏕️ 🚻 ♿ 🛒 💧 ⚊ 🦋 🌐 🍴 🏛️ ✂️ ⛱️ adj

Fr Lamia take rd E to Stylis; cont for further 3km & site situated to side of dual-c'way opp petrol stn. Med, shd, EHU (16A); gas; TV; 10% statics; Eng spkn; adv bkg acc; tennis; watersports; CKE. *"Day visitors have access to beach via site; do not confuse with Cmp Paras adj - not rec; Sunshine Camping Group site; poss poor san facs LS; NH only."* **€27.40** **2017**

VARTHOLOMIO *A3* (10km SW Coastal) *37.83555, 21.13333* **Camping Ionion Beach,** 27050 Glifa **(26230) 96828; ioniongr@otenet.gr; www.ionion-beach.gr**

🔢12 🐕 🏕️ (htd) 🚻 ♿ 🛒 💧 ⚊ 🦋 🍴 🍸 🌐 🍴 nr 🏛️ ⚊ ⛱️ adj

Fr E55 Patras-Pirgos rd turn W to Gastouni, Ligia & Glifa, then Glifa Beach. Site is 1km SW of Glifa. Med, hdg, hdstg, pt shd, serviced pitches; EHU (16A); gas; bbq; TV; Eng spkn; adv bkg acc; ccard acc; watersports; games area; CKE. *"Excel, well-run site; superb facs."* **€30.60** **2016**

VIVARI *B3* (1km E Coastal) *37.53421, 22.93179* **Camping Lefka Beach,** 21100 Drepanon Vivari **(27520) 92334; info@camping-lefka.gr; www.camping-lefka.gr**

🐕 🏕️ 🚻 ⚊ 🛒 💧 ✂️ 🍸 🌐 🍴 ⛱️ 20m

On the Nafplio-Drepanon-Iria rd. About 1km on the R after vill of Vivari. Foll sp. Med, mkd, hdstg, shd, terr, EHU (16A); bbq; twin axles; TV; Eng spkn; adv bkg acc; CKE. *"Beautiful views of bay fr site; close to antiquities; vg."* **€28.00, 1 Apr-10 Nov.** **2015**

VOLOS *B2* (18km SE Coastal) *39.31027, 23.10972* **Camping Sikia,** 37300 Kato Gatzea **(24230) 22279 or 22081; info@camping-sikia.gr; www.camping-sikia.gr**

🔢12 🐕 🏕️ 🚻 🛒 ⚊ 💧 ⚊ 🦋 🍴 🌐 🍴 ✂️ ⛱️ shgl

Fr Volos take coast rd S to Kato Gatzea site on R, sp immed next to Camping Hellas. Med, shd, terr, EHU (16A) €3; gas; red long stay; 20% statics; phone; Eng spkn; adv bkg acc; ccard acc; CKE. *"Highly rec; some beautiful, but sm, pitches with sea views; Sunshine Group site; excel, friendly family-run site; v clean; v helpful staff; take care o'hanging trees."* **€24.00** **2016**

ZACHARO *A3* (8km S Coastal) *37.41068, 21.66850* **Camping Tholo Beach,** Tholo, 27054 Zacharo **(26250) 61345 or 33454 (winter); campingtholo@hotmail.com**

🐕 🏕️ 🚻 🛒 ⚊ 💧 ✂️ 🦋 🍴 🍸 🌐 🍴 🏛️ ⛱️ sand adj

S fr Pyrgos on E55 dir Kyparissia, 8km S of Zacharo turn R to Tholo. Site sp in 500m on L. Med, shd, EHU €4; bbq; TV; Eng spkn; adv bkg acc; CKE. *"Excel, quiet, clean site; gd, clean san facs; friendly staff; excel sandy beach where loggerhead turtles lay eggs; dolphins off shore; san facs need updating; great location; excel mkt on Tuesdays; Ancient Olympia about an hr's drive."* **€24.50, 1 May-30 Oct.** **2015**

GREEK ISLANDS

AGIA GALINI (CRETE) *C4* (2km E Rural/Coastal) *35.10004, 24.69514* **Camping No Problem!,** 74056 Agia Galini **(28320) 91386; www.agia-galini.com**

🔢12 🐕 🏕️ 🚻 🛒 ♿ 🛒 💧 ✂️ 🅿️ 🍴 🍸
🌐 🍴 ⚊ 🏊 ⚊ ⛱️ shgl 500m

Site sp on Tympaki rd. Sm, mkd, pt shd, EHU (6A) €4; bbq; 10% statics; bus 500m; Eng spkn; adv bkg acc. *"Vg, family-run site; dogs free; gd walks."* **€22.00** **2016**

ERETRIA (EVIA) *B2* (11km NE Coastal) *38.39148, 23.77562* **Milos Camping,** 34008 Eretria **(22290) 60420; info@camping-in-evia.gr; www.camping-in-evia.gr**

🐕 🏕️ 🚻 🛒 ⚊ 💧 ✂️ 🅿️ 🦋 🍴 🍸 🌐 🍴 🏛️ ⛱️ shgl adj

Fr Chalkida for 20km; ignore any previous sp for Milos Camping. Med, mkd, pt shd, terr, EHU (16A) inc; gas; bbq; TV; 70% statics; phone; Eng spkn; CKE. *"Friendly site; excel rest; rather scruffy (5/09) but gd san facs."* **€25.00, 15 Apr-30 Sep.** **2015**

> ## "There aren't many sites open at this time of year"
>
> If you're travelling outside peak season remember to call ahead to check site opening dates – even if the entry says 'open all year'.

LEFKADA (LEFKAS) *A2* (26km SE Coastal) *38.67511, 20.71475* **Camping Santa Maura,** Dessimi, 31100 Vlycho **(26450) 95007, (00306) 976085621, (00306) 932902309; campingsantamavra@yahoo.gr; www.campingsantamaura.com**

🐕 🏕️ 🚻 🛒 ⚊ 💧 ✂️ 🦋 🍸 🌐 🍴 ⚊ ⛱️ shgl adj

Take coast rd S fr Lefkada to Vlycho, turn L for Dessimi, site in 2.5km (after Camping Dessimi). Access via v steep hill - severe gradients both sides. 3*, Med, mkd, pt shd, terr, EHU (6A) inc; gas; bbq; TV; phone; CKE. *"Excel site & beach; gd, clean san facs; friendly owners; pls call for prices."* **1 Apr-31 Oct.** **2016**

PEFKARI (THASSOS) *C2* (0.3km W Coastal) *40.61630, 24.60021* **Camping Pefkari Beach,** 64002 Pefkari **(25930) 51190; info@camping-pefkari.gr; www.camping-pefkari.gr**

🛒 ⚊ 💧 ✂️ 🦋 🍸 🌐 🍴 ⚊ ⛱️ sand adj

SW fr Thassos port approx 43km to Limenaria, Pefkari is next sm vill. Site well sp in vill. Med, hdstg, pt shd, EHU (6A) €2.90; own san req; bbq; 5% statics; bus 1km; Eng spkn; CKE. *"Lovely spot; worth putting up with poor, dated san facs; gd local rest; vg; improving site; beautiful; easy walk to Pefkari and Potos; excel on site rest; lovely spot."* **€31.00, 1 May-30 Sep.** **2019**

GREECE

RETHYMNO (CRETE) *C4* (3km E Coastal) *35.36795, 24.51487* **Camping Elizabeth,** Ionias 84 Terma, 74100 Missiria **(28310) 28694; info@camping-elizabeth.net; camping-elizabeth.net**

12 🕊 👫 WD ⚓ ♿ 🛒 ⁄ MP 🛍 🍴 ⊕ 🅰 🐾 ⚑ adj

W fr Iraklio/Heraklion exit Platanes/Arkadi. Site **1km bef Platanes, on R on sh unsurfaced rd.** Lge, hdg, shd, EHU (12A) inc; bbq; cooking facs; 3% statics; phone; bus 500m; Eng spkn; adv bkg acc; CKE. *"Gd walking on mkd rtes; gd cycling; excursion programme; vg; san facs tired."* **€28.50** 2019

TINOS (TINOS) *C3* (0.5km E Coastal) *37.53994, 25.16377* **Tinos Camping Bungalows,** Louizas Sohou 5, 84200 Tinos **(22830) 22344 or 23548; tinoscamping@thn.forthnet.gr; tinoscamping.gr**

🕊 👫 WD ⚓ ♿ 🛒 ⁄ ⊕ 🅰 🐾 ⚑ shgl 500m

Clearly sp fr port. Sm, hdg, mkd, hdstg, shd, EHU €4.50; bbq; cooking facs; red long stay; phone; Eng spkn; adv bkg acc; ccard acc; CKE. *"1,600 Venetian dovecots & 600 churches on island; monastery with healing icon."* **€21.50, 1 May-31 Oct.** 2016

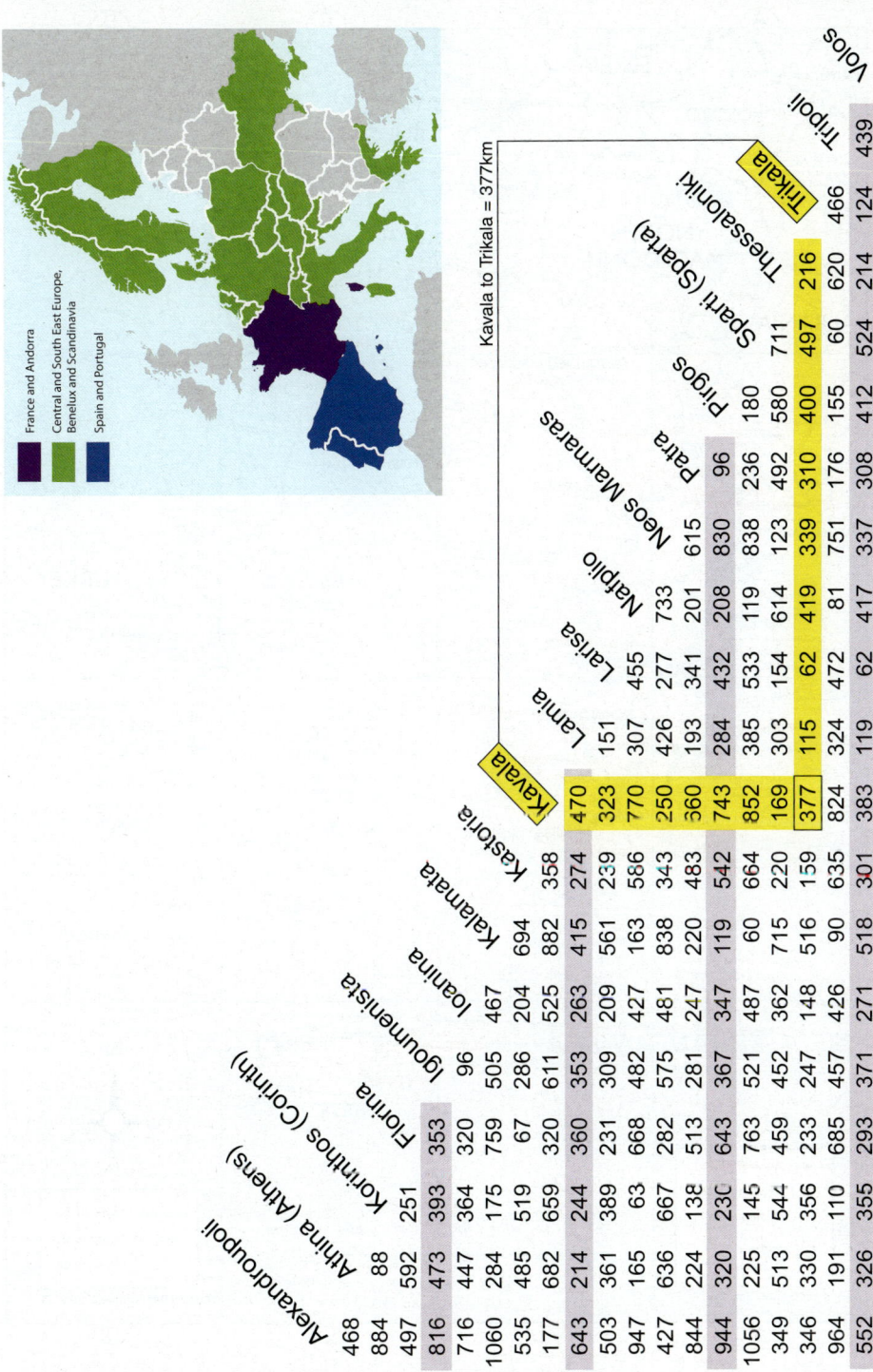

GREECE

Hungary

Budapest

Shutterstock/ ZGPhotography

Highlights

Hungary is home to some of the most dramatic and exotic architecture found in Europe, with buildings spanning from the Art Nouveau era to Ancient Rome. Turkish, Slavic, Magyar and Roman influences entwine with its own unique culture to make Hungary a fascinating place.

There are more medicinal spas in Hungary than anywhere else in Europe and spa culture is an important part both of tourism and everyday life. You can enjoy spas that range from traditional bathhouses to modern wellness centres that cater for the whole family.

Many folk festivals are celebrated in Hungary throughout the year, the biggest of which is the Festival of Folk Arts/Crafts held every August in Buda Castle. Thousands of visitors attend to view the fantastic traditional crafts on offer.

One of the most renowned crafts is pottery making, with Hungary having a long tradition of creating both fine porcelain, such as Herend, and tiling and stoneware.

Major towns and cities

- Budapest – an enchanting city full of galleries, theatres and museums.
- Debrecen – this former capital is one of Hungary's most important cultural centres.
- Pécs – an ancient city with countless things to see and do.
- Eger – a city famous for its fine red wines.

Attractions

- Fisherman's Bastion, Budapest – enjoy unmatched views over the city.
- Hungarian Parliament Building, Budapest – a magnificent building on the banks of the Danube.
- Lake Hévíz – one of the largest thermal lakes in the world with its own unique ecosystem.
- Esztergom Basilica – a spectacularly enormous cathedral with Renaissance art.

Find out more

www.gotohungary.com
E: info@mtu.gov.hu T: 0036 (0) 14 88 87 00

Country Information

Population (approx): 9.9 million

Capital: Budapest

Area: 93,000 sq km

Bordered by: Austria, Croatia, Romania, Serbia, Slovakia, Slovenia, Ukraine

Terrain: Mostly flat and rolling plains; hills and low mountains to the north

Climate: Temperate, continental climate; cold, cloudy winters; warm, sunny summers; changeable in spring and early summer with heavy rain and storms. The best times to visit are spring and autumn

Highest Point: Kekes 1,014m

Language: Hungarian

Local Time: GMT or BST + 1, i.e. 1 hour ahead of the UK all year

Currency: Forint (HUF); £1 = HUF 413, HUF 1000 = £2.42 (Feb 2021)

Emergency numbers: Police 107; Fire brigade 105; Ambulance 104. Operators speak English.

Public Holidays 2021: Jan 1; Mar 15; Apr 2, 4, 5; May 1, 23, 24; Aug 20; Oct 23; Nov 1; Dec 24, 25, 26.

School summer holidays are from mid-June to the end of August

Entry Formalities

British and Irish passport holders may stay for up to 90 days in any 180 day period without a visa. Following Brexit you may be asked to show a return or onward ticket at the border to confirm your length of stay, or to prove that you have enough money for your stay.

Your passport will need to have a minimum of 6 months' validity remaining, and be less than 10 years old (even if it has over 6 months left).

Visitors arriving at a campsite or hotel must complete a registration form.

Medical Services

British nationals may obtain emergency medical and dental treatment from practitioners contracted to the national health insurance scheme, Országos Egészségbiztosítási (OEP), together with emergency hospital treatment, on presentation of a European Health Insurance Card (EHIC) and a British passport.

Fees are payable for treatment and prescribed medicines, and are not refundable in Hungary. You may be able to apply for reimbursement when back in the UK.

Pharmacies (gyógyszertár) are well stocked. The location of the nearest all-night pharmacy is displayed on the door of every pharmacy.

Opening Hours

Banks: Mon-Thurs 8am-3pm. Fri 8am - 1pm. Hours may vary slightly.

Museums: Tue-Sun 10am-6pm; closed Mon.

Post Offices: Mon-Fri 8am-6pm; post office at Budapest open Mon-Sat 7am-9pm.

Shops: Mon-Fri 10am-6pm (supermarkets from 7am-7pm with some grocery stores open 24 hours); open half day Saturdays.

Safety and Security

Petty theft in Budapest is common in areas frequented by tourists, particularly on busy public transport, at markets and at popular tourist sites. Beware of pickpockets and bag snatchers.

Do not carry large amounts of cash. Take care when receiving bank notes and change as some that are no longer valid are still in circulation, e.g. HUF 200 notes were withdrawn in 2009. There has been a small number of instances of taxi drivers deliberately passing these notes to tourists. Be aware especially when paying with a HUF 10,000 or 20,000 bank note.

Theft of and from vehicles is common. Do not leave your belongings, car registration documents or mobile phones in your car and ensure that it is properly locked with the alarm on, even if leaving it for just a moment. Beware of contrived 'incidents', particularly on the Vienna-Budapest motorway, designed to stop motorists and expose them to robbery.

Visitors have reported in the past that motorists may be pestered at service areas on the Vienna to Budapest motorway by people insisting on washing windscreens and demanding money.

During the summer season in Budapest, uniformed tourist police patrol the most frequently visited areas of the city. Criminals sometimes pose as tourist police and ask for visitors' money, credit cards or travel documents in order to check them. Always ensure that a uniformed police officer is wearing a badge displaying the word 'Rendörség' and a five-digit identification number, together with a name badge. Plain clothes police carry a badge and an ID card with picture, hologram and rank. If in doubt, insist on going to the nearest police station.

There are still occasional incidents of exorbitant overcharging in certain restaurants, bars and clubs in Budapest, accompanied by threats of violence. Individuals who have been unable to settle their bill have frequently been accompanied by the establishment's security guards to a cash machine and made to withdraw funds. Visitors are advised to ask for a menu and only order items which are priced realistically. A five digit price for one dish is too high. Never accept menus which do not display prices and check your bill carefully.

Taxi drivers are sometimes accomplices to these frauds, receiving 'commission' for recommending restaurants and bars which charge extortionate prices to visitors. Never ask a taxi driver to recommend a bar, club or restaurant. If a driver takes you to one or you are approached on the street with an invitation to an unfamiliar bar or restaurant, you should treat such advice with extreme caution.

Do not change money or get involved in gambling in the street; which are both illegal.

If you need help, go to the nearest police station or the Tourist Information Point open 8am - 8pm, Deák Ferenc Square, 1052 Budapest, Sütő Street 2 (1) 438 8080

There is a low threat from terrorism.

British Embassy

FUGE UTCA 5-7 BUDAPEST 1022
Tel: (1) 2662888
www.ukinhungary.fco.gov.uk

Irish Embassy

SZABADSÁG TÉR 7, BANK CENTRE, GRANIT TOWER, V. FLOOR
1054 BUDAPEST
Tel: (1) 3014960
www.embassyofireland.hu

Documents

Money

Hungarian currency is available from banks in Austria before crossing the border. For emergency cash reserves, it is advisable to have euros, rather than sterling. Foreign currency is best exchanged at banks as they are not allowed to charge commission. Private bureaux de change do charge commission, but the rate of exchange may be better.

Credit cards are accepted at many outlets in large towns and cities and cash dispensers, 'bankomats', are widespread even in small towns. There is a high incidence of credit card fraud and payment in cash wherever possible is advisable. Carry your credit card issuers'/banks' 24 hour UK contact numbers separately in case of loss or theft of your cards.

Recent visitors report that some newer types of debit and credit cards issued in the UK do not work in certain cash machines in Hungary. The banks are working on a solution but, in the meantime, if you encounter this problem you should try a cash machine at a different bank. It is possible to obtain cash from post offices with a debit or credit card.

Euros are widely accepted in shops and restaurants frequented by tourists, but check the exchange rate.

When leaving Hungary on the MI motorway (Budapest-Vienna), it is important to change back your forints on the Hungarian side of the border by crossing the carriageway to the left at the designated crossing-point, as visitors report that there are no facilities on the right hand side and none on the other side in Austria.

Passport

Carry your passport at all times. A photocopy is not acceptable.

Vehicle(s)

Carry your vehicle registration certificate (V5C), vehicle insurance certificate and MOT certificate (if applicable) with you when driving.

Driving

Accidents

Accidents causing damage to vehicles or injury to persons must be reported to the nearest police station and to the Hungarian State Insurance Company (Hungária Biztosító) within 24 hours. The police will issue a statement which you may be asked to show when leaving the country.

If entering Hungary with a conspicuously damaged vehicle, it is recommended that you obtain a report confirming the damage from the police in the country where the damage occurred, otherwise difficulties may arise when leaving Hungary.

Alcohol

It is illegal to drive after consuming any alcohol whatsoever.

Breakdown Service

The motoring organisation, Magyar Autóklub (MAK), operates a breakdown service 24 hours a day on all roads. Drivers in need of assistance should telephone 188 or (1) 3451680. The number (1) is the area code for Budapest. On motorways emergency phones are placed at 2km intervals.

MAK road patrol cars are yellow and marked 'Segélyszolgálat'. Their registration numbers begin with the letters MAK.

The roadside breakdown service is chargeable, higher charges applying at night. There is a scale of charges by vehicle weight and distance for towing vehicles to a garage. Payment is required in cash.

Child Restraint System

Children under the height of 1.5m must be seated in a suitable child restraint system appropriate for their size in the rear of the vehicle.

If no child restraint is available a child over 3 who is over 1.35m in height may travel in the rear seat with a seatbelt. Children younger or shorter than this may not ever travel without a suitable restraint system in the vehicle.

Fuel

Leaded petrol is no longer available. The sign 'Ólommentes üzemanyag' or 'Bleifrei 95' indicates unleaded petrol. LPG is widely available.

Most petrol stations are open from 6am to 8pm. Along motorways and in large towns they are often open 24 hours. Some petrol stations accept credit and debit cards but cash is the most usual means of payment.

Lights

Outside built-up areas dipped headlights are compulsory at all times, regardless of weather conditions. Bulbs are more likely to fail with constant use and you are recommended to carry spares. At night in built-up areas dipped headlights must be used as full beam is prohibited.

Headlight flashing often means that a driver is giving way, but do not carry out a manoeuvre unless you are sure that this is the case.

Motorways

All motorways (autópálya) and main connecting roads run to or from Budapest. In recent years the road network has been extended and improved and there are now approximately 1500 kilometres of motorway and dual carriageways or semi-motorways. However, most roads are still single carriageway, single lane and care is recommended. The M0 motorway is a 75km ringroad around Budapest which links the M1, M7, M6, M5 and Highway 11. The recently built Megyeri Bridge on the Danube is part of the M0 and its opening has considerably reduced traffic congestion to the north of Budapest.

Emergency corridors are compulsory on motorways and dual carriageways. Drivers are required to create a precautionary emergency corridor to provide access for emergency vehicles whenever congestion occurs. Drivers in the left-hand lane must move as far over to the left as possible, and drivers in the central and right-hand lanes must move as far over to the right as possible.

Motorway Vignettes

Approximately 30% of motorways are toll-free; otherwise you must purchase an electronic vignette (matrica) or e-vignette (sticker) before entering the motorway.

They are available online, from motorway customer service offices and at large petrol

stations near the motorways.
You can pay in forints or by credit card.

Leaflets are distributed to motorists at the border and a telephone information centre is available in Hungary – tel 36 58 75 00. Vignettes should only be purchased from outlets where the prices are clearly displayed at the set rates. For full details (in English), including how to buy online and toll-free sections, see www.motorway.hu

When purchasing an e-vignette a confirmation message will be sent or a coupon issued and this must be kept for a year after its expiry date. There is no need to display the vignette in your windscreen as the motorway authorities check all vehicles electronically (without the need for you to stop your vehicle) and verify registration number, category of toll paid and validity of an e-vignette. Charges in forints (2015 charges, subject to change) are shown below:

Category of Vehicle	Period of Validity	
	10 Days	1 month
Vehicle up to 3,500kg with or without caravan or trailer	2,975	4,780
Motorhome	5,950	9,560

Since the beginning of 2013 Hungary's State Motorway Management company (AAK) have been imposing on-the-spot fines for motorists who do not have a vignette. Fines amount to HUF 14,875 (around £40) for vehicles under 3,500kg or HUF 66,925 (around £178) for vehicles between 3,500kg and 7,500kg if paid within 30 days. 78% of the motorists fined so far have been foreign nationals, so ensure you have a vignette before travelling on motorways.

Parking

Zigzag lines on the carriageway and road signs indicate a stopping/parking prohibition. Illegally-parked vehicles will be towed away or clamped. On two-way roads, vehicles must park in the direction of traffic; they may park on either side in one-way streets. In certain circumstances, parking on the pavement is allowed.

Budapest is divided into various time restricted parking zones (maximum three hours) where tickets must be purchased from Monday to Friday from a machine. For longer periods you are advised to use 'Park and Ride' car parks located near major metro stations and bus terminals.

Priority

Pedestrians have priority over traffic at pedestrian crossings and at intersections. They do not have priority on the roadway between central tram loading islands and pavements, and drivers must exercise care on these sections. Major roads are indicated by a priority road ahead sign. At the intersection of two roads of equal importance, where there is no sign, vehicles coming from the right have priority. Trams and buses have priority at any intersection on any road and buses have right of way when leaving bus stops after the driver has signalled his intention to pull out.

Roads

Hungary has a good system of well surfaced main roads and driving standards are higher than in many other parts of Europe. There are few dual carriageways and care is required, therefore, when overtaking with a right-hand drive vehicle. Extra care is required on provincial roads which may be badly lit, poorly maintained and narrow. In the countryside at night be on the alert for unlit cycles and horse drawn vehicles

Road Signs and Markings

Road signs and markings conform to international conventions. Square green road signs indicate the number of km to the next town. At traffic lights a flashing amber light indicates a dangerous intersection. Destination signs feature road numbers rather than the names of towns, so it is essential to equip yourself with an up-to-date road map or atlas. Signs for motorways have white lettering on a blue background; on other roads signs are white and green.

Speed Limits

	Open Road (km/h)	Motorway (km/h)
Car Solo	90-110	130
Car towing caravan/trailer	70	80
Motorhome under 3500kg	90-110	130
Motorhome 3500-7500kg	70	80

A speed limit of 30 km/h (18 mph) is in force in many residential, city centre and tourist resort areas.

Traffic Jams

Roads around Budapest are busy on Friday and Sunday afternoons. In the holiday season roads to Lake Balaton (M7) and around the lake (N7 and N71) may be congested. There are regular traffic hold ups at weekends at the border crossings to Austria, the Czech Republic and Serbia. Motorway traffic information (in English) is available on www.motorway.hu

Violation of Traffic Regulations

The police make spot vehicle document checks and are keen to enforce speed limits. They are permitted to impose on-the-spot fines of up to HUF300,000. Credit cards are accepted for the payment of fines in some circumstances.

Winter Driving

The use of snow chains can be made compulsory on some roads when there is severe winter weather.

Essential Equipment

First Aid Kit

It is a legal requirement that all vehicles should carry a first aid kit.

Reflective Jackets/Waistcoats

If your vehicle is immobilised on the carriageway outside a built-up area, or if visibility is poor, you must wear a reflective jacket or waistcoat when getting out of your vehicle. Passengers who leave the vehicle, for example, to assist with a repair, should also wear one. Keep the jackets inside your vehicle, not in the boot.

In addition, pedestrians and cyclists walking or cycling at night or in poor visibility along unlit roads outside a built-up area must also wear a reflective jacket.

Warning Triangles

In the event of accident, it is compulsory to place a warning triangle 100 metres behind the vehicle on motorways and 50 metres on other roads.

Touring

Hungary boasts eight World Heritage sites including the national park at Aggtelek which contains Europe's largest cave network, the Christian cemetery at Pécs and the monastery at Pannonhalma. Lake Balaton, the largest lake in Central Europe, offers swimming, sailing, fishing and windsurfing. With 200km of sandy shoreline and shallow warm waters, it is very popular with families.

A Budapest Card is available, allowing unlimited travel on public transport for two or three consecutive days, free city walking tours, discounted entry to museums and other attractions, plus discounts on many guided tours, events, shops and restaurants. Cards are available from metro stations, tourist information offices, many travel agencies, hotels, museums and main Budapest transport ticket offices, as well as from the Hungarian National Tourist Office in London. You can also order online from www.budapest-card.com.

A tip of 10-15% of the bill is expected in restaurants. Check your bill first to ensure that a service charge has not already been added.

Hungarian is a notoriously difficult language for native English speakers to decipher and pronounce. English is not widely spoken in rural areas, but it is becoming increasingly widespread elsewhere as it is now taught in schools. German is widely spoken and a dictionary may be helpful.

Camping and Caravanning

There are approximately 100 organised campsites in Hungary rated from 1 to 4 stars. These are generally well signposted off main routes, with the site name shown below a blue camping sign. Most campsites open from May to September and the most popular sites are situated by Lake Balaton and the Danube. A Camping Key Europe (CKE) or Camping Card International (CCI) is essential.

Facilities vary from site to site, but visitors will find it useful to carry their own flat universal sink plug. There has been much improvement in recent years in the general standard of campsites, but communal changing areas for showers are not uncommon. Many sites have communal kitchen facilities which enable visitors to make great savings on their own gas supply.

Many campsites require payment in cash. Prices have risen sharply in recent years. Therefore, prices in this guide for sites not reported on for some time might not reflect the current prices.

Casual/wild camping is prohibited.

Cycling

There are approximately 2,000km of cycle tracks, 100km of which are in Budapest and 200km around Lake Balaton. Tourinform offices in Hungary provide maps of cycling routes.

Children under 14 years are not allowed to ride on the road and all cyclists must wear a reflective jacket at night and in poor daytime visibility.

Electricity and Gas

Current on campsites varies between 6 and 16 amps. Plugs have two round pins. There are some sites that do not have CEE connections.

Only non-returnable and/or non-exchangeable Campingaz cylinders are available.

Public Transport & Local Travel

Cars are not permitted within the Castle District and on Margaret Island in Budapest. It is advisable to use public transport when travelling into the city and there is an excellent network of bus, tram and metro routes (BKV). All public transport in Hungary is free for over 65s, and this also applies to foreign visitors with proof of age (passport).

There are a number of ticket options, including family tickets, 1, 3 and 7 day tickets, and they can be bought at metro stations, ticket machines, tobacconists and newsagents. Validate your bus and metro tickets before use at each stage of your journey and every time you change metro lines at the red machines provided. Tickets are often checked on vehicles or at metro station exits by controllers wearing arm bands and carrying photo ID. For further information on public transport in Budapest see www.bkv.hu

As a general rule, it is better to phone for taxis operated by reputable local companies, rather than flag them down in the street, and always ensure that fares are metered. A tip of approximately 10% of the fare is customary.

Mahart, the Hungarian Shipping Company, operates a regular hydrofoil service from April to October along the Danube between Budapest and Vienna. The journey lasts six hours and covers 288km.

Local companies Legenda (www.legenda.hu) and Mahart also offer city cruises between May and October, as well as regular trips to tourist attractions outside Budapest, such as Szentendre, Visegrád and Esztergom.

A ferry service takes cars across Lake Balaton from Szántód to Tihany. There are crossings every 10 minutes from June to September and every hour during the low season. Regular bus and train services link the towns and villages along the lakeside.

AGGTELEK A3 (1km NW Rural) 48.47094, 20.49446
Baradla Camping, Baradla Oldal 1, 3759 Aggtelek
(06) 308619427; szallas@anp.hu

†↟† ⚑ ⩘ ✉ 🍴 Ⴑ nr ④nr ⏶

Fr Slovakia turn off E571/A50 at Plesivec onto rd
587 S via Dlha Ves to border x-ing. Cont S for approx
800m & hotel/campsite complex is on L. Fr Miskolc
45km N on rte 26, turn onto rte 27 sp Perkupa then
foll sp Nemzeti National Park & Aggtelek. Site sp in
vill. 1*, Med, pt shd, pt sl, EHU (16A) inc; bbq; cooking
facs; 10% statics. *"Gd NH to/fr Slovakia; ent to lge
Barlang Caves system adj; facs poss stretched high
ssn."* **HUF 4366, 15 Apr-15 Oct.** 2016

BALATONAKALI C1 (1km SW Rural) 46.87939,
17.74190 **Balatontourist Camping Levendula
(Naturist),** Hókuli u 25, 8243 Balatonakali **36 30 309
7797; info@levendulacamp.com; levendulacamp.com**

🐾 HUF950 †↟† ⓌⒹ ▲ Ⴑ ⊟ ⩘ ᵐᴾ ᵠ 🍴 ④ Ⓓ Ⴊ ⏶

NE on rte 71 on N shore of Lake Balaton twds
Tihany. Site sp on W app to Balatonakali. Turn R
twds lake; go over level x-ing, site ent on R.
3*, Med, mkd, pt shd, EHU (4A) inc; gas; sw; TV; Eng
spkn; adv bkg acc; ccard acc; fishing; games area; bike
hire; windsurfing school; sauna; CKE. *"Superb site."*
HUF 7500, 7 May-12 Sep. 2016

BALATONFURED C2 (9km NE Rural) 46.99184,
17.98698 **Présház Camping,** Présház út 1, 8226
Alsóörs **(87) 447736**

⑫ 🐾 †↟† ⓌⒹ ▲ ⩘ ✉

Rd 71 fr Balatonfüred, site just past vill of Alsóörs
on L. Sm, pt shd, pt sl, EHU (10A) inc; sw nr; games
area. *"Vg, lovely, CL-type site in orchard of wine shop;
friendly owner; wine-tasting; paid in Euros but Forint
preferred; sighting of wild boar nrby!"* **HUF 4360**
2015

BUDAPEST B2 (14km N Rural) 47.6013, 19.0191
Jumbo Camping, Budakalászi út 23, 2096 Üröm
**(26) 351251; jumbo@campingbudapest.com;
www.jumbocamping.hu**

🐾 †↟† ⓌⒹ ▲ ⊟ ⩘ ✉ 🍴 ④ nr Ⴊ Ⴑ nr ⏶ ⚓ (htd)

Best app fr N on rd 10 or 11. Fr M1 take Zsámbék exit
thro Perbál to join rd 10 & turn W twd Budapest. After
Pilisvörösvar turn L in 8km sp Üröm Site well sp.
3*, Med, hdg, hdstg, pt shd, pt sl, terr, EHU (6-10A) inc;
TV; 10% statics; bus to Budapest fr vill; Eng spkn; adv
bkg acc. *"Highly rec; clean, modern facs; immac, family-
run site, v helpful."* **HUF 6495, 1 Apr-31 Oct.** 2017

BUDAPEST B2 (10km E Urban) 47.50421, 19.15834
Camping Arena, Pilisi Str 7, 1106 Budapest **06 30 29
691 29; info@budapestcamping.hu; www.budapest
camping.hu**

⑫ 🐾 †↟† ⓌⒹ ▲ Ⴑ ⊟ ⩘ ✉ ᵠ

Do not use Sat Nav. Leave M0 at exit 60 Kistarcsa
& foll Rd 3 twd city cent for 7.5km. Turn L just bef
rlwy bdge. Site 200m on R. Sm, hdg, pt shd, EHU
(16A) inc; cooking facs; 10% statics; bus 400m; Eng
spkn; adv bkg acc; CCI. *"Some rlwy & aircraft noise;
supmkt 400m; shopping arcade 1km; metro 1km; rec
all day travel card for metro, trams & busses; vg; v
helpful staff."* **HUF 7650** 2019

BUDAPEST B2 (7km WNW Rural) 47.514437,
18.972951 **Ave Natura Camping,** Csermely u. 3, 1121
Budapest **(36) 12003470 or (36) 705507069;
campingavenatura@gmail.com; www.camping
avenatura.hu**

🐾 †↟† ⓌⒹ ▲ ⊟ ⩘ ✉ ᵐᴾ ⚑ ᵠ

Fr Austria via M1/M7 fr Balaton exit 14 Budakeszi.
Fr M0, foll rd to end then Route 1 direction
Budakeszi. Fr Budakeszi foll camping sp. Fr city
to Moskva Ter then foll sp. Sm, hdstg, hdg, pt shd,
terr, EHU (16A) HUF1200; bbq; cooking facs; phone;
bus 300m; Eng spkn; adv bkg acc; CKE. *"Guaranteed
warm and informative welcome by family run peaceful,
wooded site; 10min downhill walk to bus into Budapest;
vg."* **HUF 5800, 1 Apr-31 Oct.** 2018

BUK B1 (4km E Rural) 47.38433, 16.79051 **Romantik
Camping,** Thermál Krt 12, 9740 Bükfürdö **(94) 558050;
info@romantikcamping.com;
www.romantikcamping.com**

⑫ 🐾 €2 †↟† (htd) ⓌⒹ ▲ Ⴑ ⊟ ⩘ ✉ ᵐᴾ ⚑ 🍴 nr ④ Ⴉ ⏶ ⧆ ⚞

Fr Sopron on rte 84 twd Lake Balaton for approx
45km, foll sp & exit Bükfürdö. After service stn turn
R then cont for 5km sp Thermalbad & site.
3*, Lge, pt shd, EHU (10-16A) metered; red long stay;
10% statics; adv bkg acc; ccard acc; bike hire; tennis
500m; CKE. *"Quiet and peaceful an ideal place to
unwind; thermal cent 500m."* **HUF 5604** 2015

CSERKESZOLO C3 (0.8km S Urban) 46.86386,
20.2019 **Thermal Camping Cserkeszölö,** Beton út
5, 5465 Cserkeszölö **(6) 56568450; hotelcamping@
cserkeszolo.hu; www.touring-hotel.hu/en**

⑫ 🐾 †↟† (htd) ⓌⒹ ▲ ⊟ ⩘ ✉ ᵐᴾ ⚑ ④ Ⴉ Ⴑ nr ⚞ (covrd, htd) 🛁

On rte 44 bet Kecskemet & Kunszentmárton. Site
sp in Cserkeszölö. 4*, Lge, pt shd, EHU (10A) inc;
bbq; cooking facs; 10% statics; phone; bus 200m;
waterslide; sauna; tennis; games area; CKE. *"Use
of sw pools & thermal pools inc in site fee; gd."*
HUF 6226 2016

DOMOS *B2* (0.5km E Rural) *47.7661, 18.91495* **Dömös Camping,** Dömös Dunapart, 2027 Dömös **(33) 482319; info@domoscamping.hu; www.domoscamping.hu**

🐕 HUF500 ♂♀ WC ♨ 🚿 🗑 ✎ 🍴 ⊕ ♿ ⛰ 🏊 🛒

On rd 11 fr Budapest, site on R on ent Dömös, adj Rv Danube. 3*, Med, hdg, pt shd, EHU (10A) HUF950; cooking facs; red long stay; TV; phone; bus to Budapest; Eng spkn; adv bkg acc; CKE. *"Delightful site with views Danube bend; spacious pitches - lower ones poss subject to flooding; excel, clean facs & rest."* **HUF 6150, 1 May-30 Sep.** **2017**

DUNAFOLDVAR *C2* (2km NE Rural) *46.81227, 18.92664* **Kék-Duna Camping,** Hösök Tere 23, 7020 Dunaföldvár **(75) 541107; ddifzrt@freemail.hu**

12 ♂♀ ♨ 🗑 ✎ 🦋 ⊕ 🏊 🛒 (covrd) 🛶

Fr rndabt S of Dunaföldvár turn twd town cent. At traff lts turn R down to rv, then turn L, under green bdge & foll towpath 300m to site. 2*, Sm, shd, EHU (16A) inc; bbq; adv bkg acc; fishing; bike hire; tennis; watersports; CKE. *"Pleasant position o'looking Danube; adequate, clean san facs but dated; gd touring base Transdanubia."* **HUF 4100** **2016**

GYOR *B1* (7km NE Rural) *47.72547, 17.71446* **Piheno Camping,** Weg 10, 9011 Gyor **(96) 523008; piheno@piheno.hu; www.piheno.hu**

🐕 HUF1000 ♂♀ (htd) WC ♨ 🗑 ✎ 🍴 ⊕ ⛰ 🏊 🛒

E fr Gyor on rte 1 twds Budapest, stay on rte 1 for Komarom. Site on L 3km past m'way (M1) junc. Sm, hdg, mkd, pt shd, pt sl, EHU (16A); gas; bbq; cooking facs; TV; 10% statics; phone; bus; Eng spkn; adv bkg acc; ccard acc; CKE. *"Gd facs; fair."* **HUF 4593, 1 May-30 Sep.** **2017**

HAJDUSZOBOSZLO *B4* (2km N Urban) *47.45756, 21.39396* **Thermál Camping,** Böszörményi út 35A, 4200 Hajdúszoboszló **(52) 558552; thermalcamping@ hungarospa.hu; www.hungarospa.hu**

12 🐕 HUF440 ♂♀ ♨ 🗑 ✎ MSP ⊕ ♿ 🏊 ⛰ 🛒

Fr W on rte 4/E573 thro town, site sp on L. Fr Debrecen, turn R 500m past Camping Hadjdútourist on lakeside. 3*, Lge, hdg, pt shd, EHU (12A) inc; bbq; cooking facs; TV; phone; Eng spkn; ccard acc; waterslide; CKE. *"Pleasant site; htd covrd pool adj; sm naturist island in lake; thermal baths adj."* **HUF 9136** **2016**

JASZAPATI *B3* (1.5km S Urban) *47.50537, 20.14012* **Tölgyes Strand Camping,** Gyöngyvirág u 11, 5130 Jászapáti **(57) 441187; info@tolgyesstrand.hu; www.tolgyesstrand.hu**

🐕 ♂♀ WC ♨ 🗑 ✎ MSP 🍴 ⊕ ♿ 🏊 (covrd, htd)

Fr Budapest E on M3, exit at Hatvan & take rd 32 to Jászberény then foll rd 31 to Jászapáti. Site sp fr town cent. 3*, Med, mkd, pt shd, EHU (10A); TV; 10% statics; adv bkg acc; games area; site clsd 1 Nov to mid-Dec; bike hire; tennis 200m. *"Gd, modern facs."* **1 Apr-30 Nov.** **2016**

KESZTHELY *C1* (8.5km N Rural) *46.80803, 17.21248* **Camping Panoráma,** Köz 1, 8372 Cserszegtomaj **(83) 314412; matuska78@freemail.hu; www.panorama camping.com**

🐕 €1 ♂♀ (htd) WC ♨ 🗑 ✎ 🦋 ⊕ 🛒 nr

Exit Keszthely by direct rd to Sümeg. After turn to Hévíz (Thermal Spa). Clearly sp on R of side rd. 3*, Med, pt shd, terr, EHU (16A) €2.50; sw nr; TV; 30% statics; phone; CKE. *"Conv Lake Balaton area; v friendly & clean; remedial massage avail; gd views."* **HUF 4000, 1 Apr-31 Oct.** **2015**

MANFA *D2* (18km NE Rural) *46.23372, 18.30844* **Campsite Mare Vara,** Varvolgyi utca 2, 7332 Magyaregregy **(72) 420126; info@camping-marevara.com; www.camping-marevara.com**

🐕 ♂♀ (htd) WC ♨ 🚿 ♿ 🗑 ✎ 🦋 🍴 🏊 ⛰

Fr Pecs head N on 6. Turn L onto Cseresznyes ut, which then becomes Komlo-Zobakpuszta. In 6.8km turn R onto Varvolgyi u. Site in 120m. Sm, pt shd, pt sl, EHU (10A) inc; bbq; 1% statics; Eng spkn; adv bkg acc; games area; CKE. *"Dutch owners, warm welcome; ample space to pitch; almost an orchard setting; vg."* **HUF 5499, 15 Apr-30 Sep.** **2015**

MATRAFURED *B3* (4km N Rural) *47.84416, 19.95725* **Mátra Camping Sástó,** Farkas út 4, 3232 Mátrafüred **(37) 374025; www.matrakemping.hu**

🐕 ♂♀ ♨ ✎ 🍴 nr ⊕ nr 🛒 nr

Take rte 24 N fr Gyöngyös. Site on L 2km after Mátrafüred. 4*, Med, hdstg, pt shd, pt sl, EHU (10A) inc; cooking facs; TV; 10% statics; ccard acc. *"Site pt of controlled sports complex; vg secure site."* **HUF 5543, 1 Apr-31 Oct.** **2016**

MOSONMAGYAROVAR *B1* (1km E Urban) *47.87718, 17.27874* **Termál Aqua Camping,** Kigyó út 1, 9200 Mosonmagyaróvár **(96) 579168; aquahotel@t-online.hu; www.tha.hu**

🐕 €2 ♂♀ (htd) WC ♨ 🗑 ✎ MSP 🍴 ⊕ ♿ 🛒 nr

Foll sp fr town cent to Termál Hotel Aqua; site in grnds, just behind lge thermal baths. Sm, hdg, mkd, shd, EHU €3; bbq; cooking facs; phone; bus, train 1km; Eng spkn. *"Vg site; htd covrd thermal adj; pool adj; price inc ent to thermals & sauna."* **HUF 9028, 1 Apr-30 Oct.** **2016**

MOSONMAGYAROVAR *B1* (3km SE Urban) *47.84224, 17.28591* **Camping Kis-Duna,** Gabonakpart 6, 9200 Mosonmagyaróvár **(96) 216433**

12 🐕 HUF500 ♂♀ WC ♨ 🗑 ✎ 🛒 nr

Site on L of M1 Mosonmagyaróvár-Györ in grnds of motel & rest, 15km fr border. 2*, Sm, hdstg, unshd, EHU (16A) HUF500; TV. *"Gd, clean, facs; thermal pool 2.5km; rest gd but busy; gd alt to Bratislava site (Slovakia); ideal NH."* **HUF 6113** **2018**

PAPA *B1* (2km N Urban) *47.33797, 17.47367* **Termál Camping Pápa,** Várkert út 7, 8500 Pápa **36 89 320 735; info@thermalkemping.hu; www.thermalkemping.hu**

12 ⊟ €2 ♦♦(htd) WD ♨ ⚓ ♿ ⬛ / MSP ✖ ⚑ ⓘ ⓐ ▣ nr ⌂ ✎ ⟴

Fr 83 exit at Gyori Way. Foll sp. Lge, hdstg, mkd, hdg, pt shd, EHU (16A); gas; bbq; cooking facs; sw nr; twin axles; 20% statics; phone; bus 500m; Eng spkn; adv bkg acc; games rm; games area; CCI. *"Onsite kids club; boccia; basketball; archery; disco adj; thermal baths with indoor & outdoor pools, slides; excel; htd pool adj; well managed site; gd area for long stay & touring; very helpful staff."* **HUF 11570** **2019**

"I like to fill in the reports as I travel from site to site"

You'll find report forms at the back of this guide, or you can fill them in online at camc.com/europereport.

SAROSPATAK *A4* (2km NE Rural) *48.33274, 21.58245* **Tengerszem Camping,** Herceg Ferenc ut 2, 3950 Sárospatak **(47) 312744; info@tengerszem-camping.hu; www.tengerszem-camping.hu**

♦♦♦ / ⬛ MSP ▣ ⌖

NW fr Tokaj on R38; then NE on R37 to Sárospatak; foll camp sp. 3*, Med, hdg, pt shd, EHU (10A) inc; TV; games area; tennis; CKE. *"Refurbished thermal sw baths next door; gd site for mountains."* **HUF 6441,** 30 Apr-15 Oct. **2016**

SARVAR *B1* (2km SE Urban) *47.24671, 16.9473* **Sárvár Thermal Camping,** Vadkert út 1, 9600 Sárvár **(95) 523610; info@thermalcamping.com; www.thermalcamping.com**

12 ⊟ €2 ♦♦(htd) WD ♨ ⚓ ♿ ⬛ / MSP ✖ ⚑ ⓘ nr ▣ ⌂ ⟴

E fr Szombathely via rtes 86 & 88. Site on Sopron-Lake Balaton rte 84. 4*, Med, hdstg, pt shd, EHU (16A) €3; bbq; cooking facs; red long stay; 10% statics; ccard acc; waterslide; lake fishing; tennis 500m; sauna; CKE. *"Barrier clsd 1330-1500; htd thermal pools adj; private san facs avail; free ent to spa & fitness cent adj."* **HUF 13007** **2016**

SOPRON *B1* (8km SE Rural) *47.6525, 16.6575* **Kurcamping Castrum Balf-Sopron,** Fürdő Sor 59-61, 9494 Balf **(99) 339124; balfcamping@gmail.com; sopron-balf-camping.hu**

⊟ €2.50 ♦♦(htd) WD ♨ ⬛ / ⓘ nr ▣ nr ⌖

On rte 84 S of Sopron turn E sp Balf. In 2km turn N sp Sopron & foll sps. Site at W end Balf vill. 3*, Med, hdg, mkd, pt shd, EHU (6A) HUF800; TV; phone; Eng spkn; ccard acc; bike hire; sauna; CKE. *"Thermal baths avail; Tesco hypmkt on app to Sopron 6km, with ATM; pitches uneven; ltd facs LS & poss unkempt; poss cold shwrs; site in need of maintenance; overpriced NH."* **HUF 4770,** 1 Apr-31 Oct. **2016**

SZIGETVAR *D1* (14km E Rural) *46.059598, 17.933796* **Camping Idyll,** Petofi S.u.28, 7912 Nagyvaty **(73) 546612; info@campingidyll.hu; www.campingidyll.hu**

⊟ ♦♦♦ WD ♿ ⬛ / ✖ ⚑ ⓘ

Rte 6 Szigetvar to Pecs. Turn L to Nagyvaty after km marker 222. Foll sp fr vill. Sm, hdstg, hdg, pt shd, EHU (6-10A); bbq; red long stay; twin axles; TV; 10% statics; bus 500m; Eng spkn; adv bkg acc; Spa 12km; CCI. *"Local walks, cycle rides fr site; clse to Rv Drava nature & forest area; excel."* **HUF 6302,** 1 May-1 Oct. **2018**

TATABANYA *B2* (14km N Rural) *47.6679, 18.3090* **Fényes Camping,** Környei út 24, 2890 Tata **(34) 481208; fenyesfurdo@tata.hu; www.fenyesfurdo.hu**

⊟ HUF500 ♦♦♦ / ⓘ ▣ ⌂ ⌖

Exit junc 67 fr M1 to Tata town cent; foll sp for 3km E to site. Lge, shd, EHU; own san rec; Eng spkn; games area; CKE. *"Tata interesting town; fair site set in lge park."* **HUF 1800,** 1 May-15 Sep. **2016**

TOKAJ *A4* (1km NE Rural) *48.12306, 21.41806* **Tiszavirág Camping,** Horgász út 11a, 3910 Tokaj **(06) 709344175; tiszavir@axelero.hu; www.tokaj.hu**

⊟ HUF400 WD ♨ ⬛ / ✖ ⚑ ▣ nr

Fr town cent turn E over rv on rte 38 sp Nyiregyháza. Camp ent 100m over bdge on L. Med, shd, EHU (10A) HUF450; fishing. *"On rv bank; wine cellars in walking dist; ltd facs on Sun."* **HUF 4200,** 1 Apr-30 Oct. **2015**

TURISTVANDI *A4* (1km SW Rural) *48.04710, 22.64300* **Vizimalom Camping,** Malom út 3, 4944 Túristvándi **(30) 289 9808; turvizimalom@ freemail.hu; www.turvizimalom.hu**

⊟ ♦♦♦ / ✖ ⚑ ⓘ ▣ nr ⌂

Fr Fehérgyarmat foll rd 491 NE for 4km to Penyige, turn L to Túristvándi. After approx 12km site on R adj 18thC water mill on Rv Túr. Sm, hdstg, pt shd, EHU (10A); bbq; TV; games rm; canoeing; games area. *"Excel location; no hdstg."* **HUF 5853,** 1 Mar-1 Nov. **2016**

ZALAKAROS *C1* (3km S Rural) *46.53165, 17.12443* **Kurcamping Castrum,** Ady Endre út, 8754 Galambok **(93) 358610; zalakaros@castrum.eu; www.castrum-group.hu**

⊟ ♦♦(htd) WD ♨ ⬛ / ✖ ⚑ ⓘ ⓐ ▣ nr ⌖ (covrd, htd)

Fr rte 7 N dir Zalakaros, site sp. 4*, Med, mkd, hdg, pt shd, EHU (6A) inc; bbq; 10% statics; bus; ccard acc; sauna; CKE. *"Thermal complex 2km."* **HUF 8000,** 1 Mar-31 Oct. **2016**

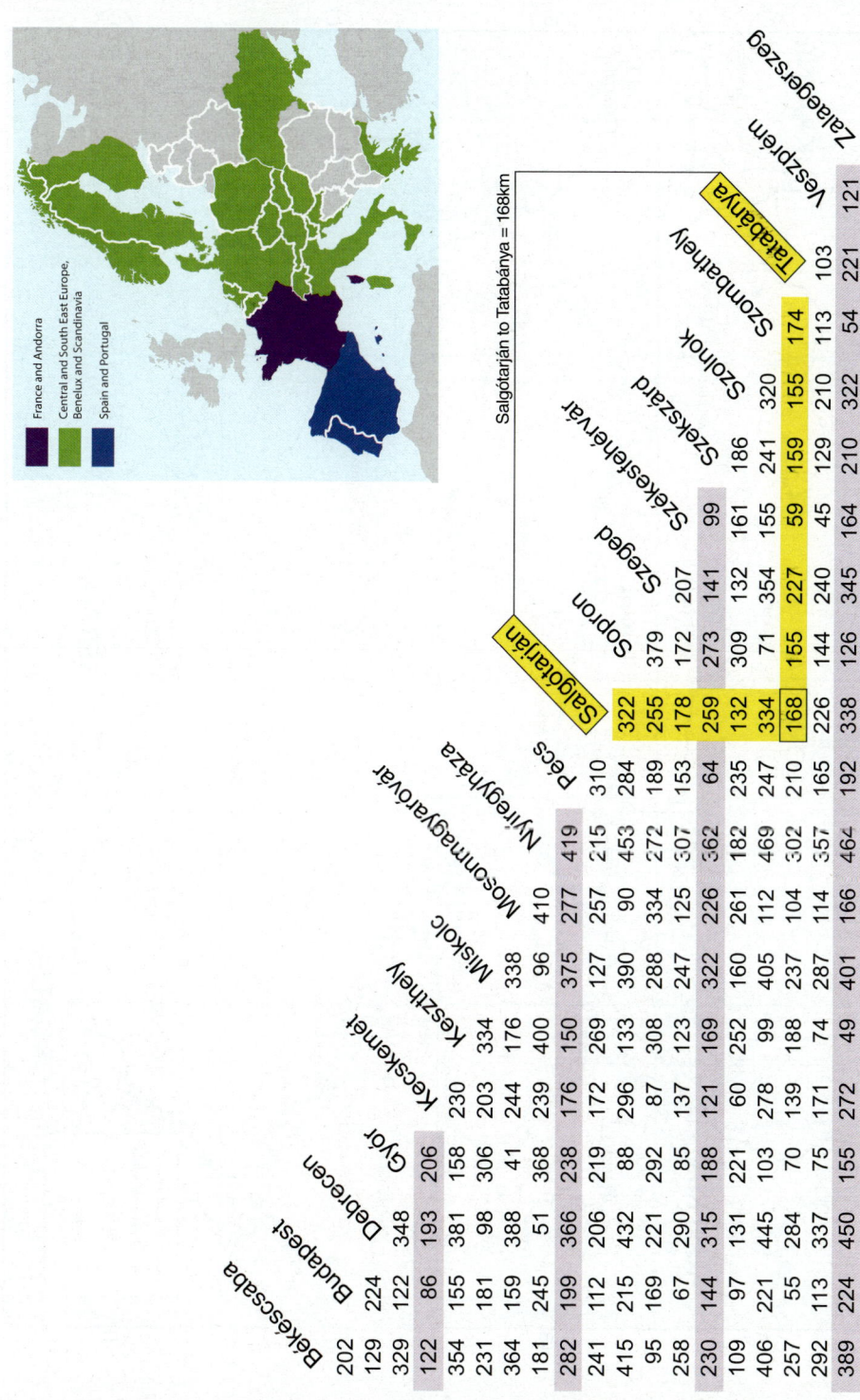

Map legend:
- France and Andorra
- Central and South East Europe, Benelux and Scandinavia
- Spain and Portugal

Salgótarján to Tatabánya = 168km

Distance chart (km)

To ↓ / From →	Békéscsaba	Budapest	Debrecen	Győr	Kecskemét	Keszthely	Miskolc	Mosonmagyaróvár	Nyíregyháza	Pécs	Salgótarján	Sopron	Szeged	Székesfehérvár	Székszárd	Szolnok	Szombathely	Tatabánya	Veszprém
Budapest	224																		
Debrecen	129	231																	
Győr	329	122	306																
Kecskemét	122	86	193	206															
Keszthely	354	185	381	158	230														
Miskolc	231	181	98	306	203	334													
Mosonmagyaróvár	364	159	388	41	277	176	338												
Nyíregyháza	181	245	51	368	252	400	96	410											
Pécs	282	199	366	238	176	133	334	277	419										
Salgótarján	241	112	206	219	150	269	90	257	215	310									
Sopron	415	215	432	88	296	133	390	90	453	284	322								
Szeged	95	169	206	292	88	288	247	334	272	189	255	379							
Székesfehérvár	258	67	221	85	99	133	237	125	307	153	178	172	207						
Székszárd	230	144	290	221	121	169	288	307	362	64	259	273	141	99					
Szolnok	109	97	131	172	60	252	160	261	182	235	132	309	132	161	155				
Szombathely	406	221	445	103	278	99	405	112	469	247	334	71	354	155	241	320			
Tatabánya	257	55	284	75	139	188	237	104	302	210	168	155	240	45	129	155	174		
Veszprém	292	113	337	70	171	74	287	114	357	165	226	144	210	164	129	113	103	54	
Zalaegerszeg	389	224	450	155	272	49	401	166	464	192	338	126	345	164	210	210	54	221	121

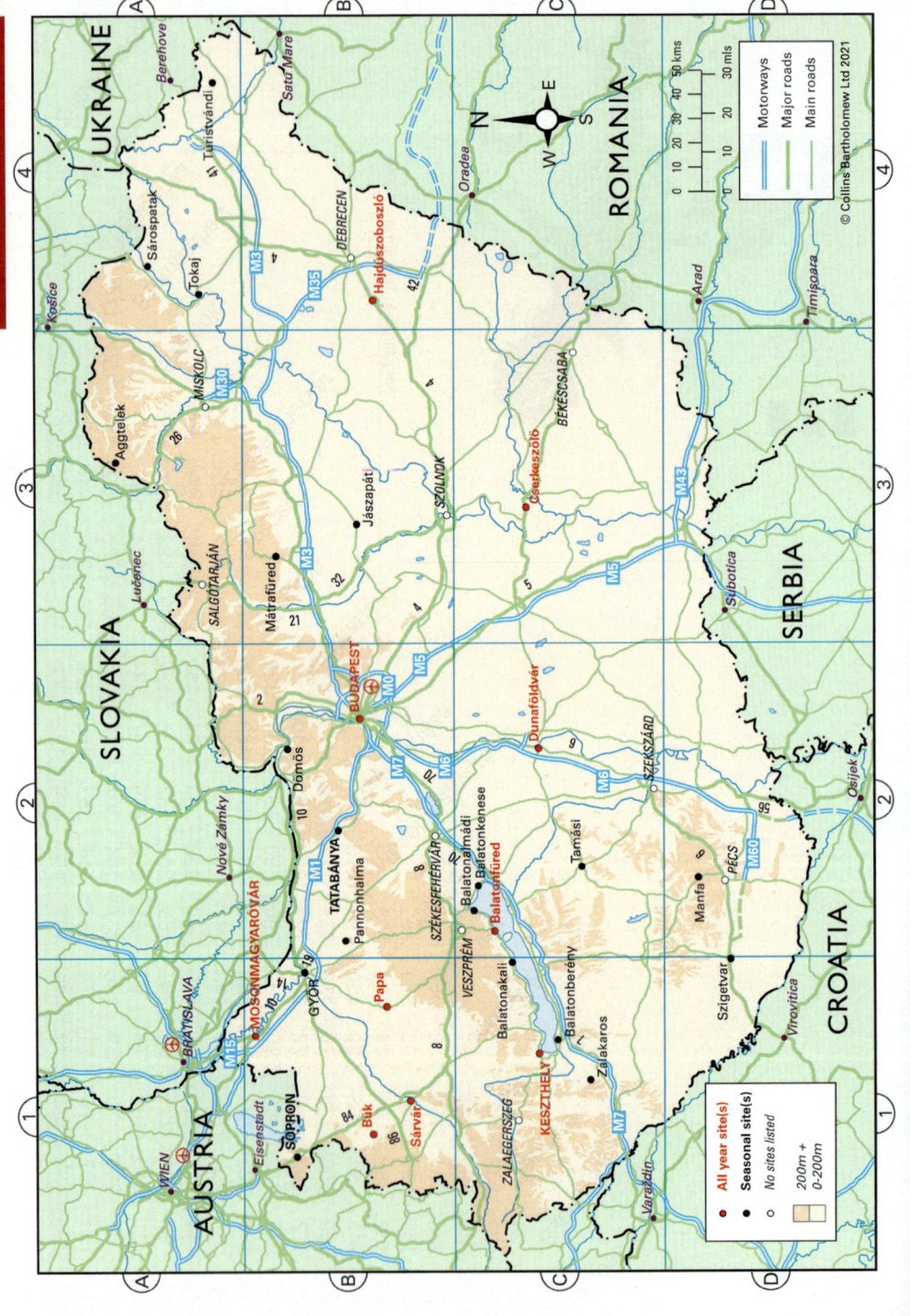

© Collins Bartholomew Ltd 2021

	Motorways
	Major roads
	Main roads

All year site(s)

Seasonal site(s)

No sites listed

- • All year site(s)
- • Seasonal site(s)
- ○ No sites listed

200m +
0–200m

Italy

Montepulciano, Tuscany

Shutterstock/Jarek Pawlak

Highlights

One of the greatest cultural jewels in Europe's crown has to be Italy. It is a country alive with art and fashion that is envied across the world, and boasts some of the most extraordinary architectural masterpieces in existence.

Alongside the grandeur is a country with great natural diversity, from the snow-capped Alps in the north to the stunning Mediterranean coastline. The variety of local customs and traditions encountered through the different regions are always captivating.

Italy is often considered the fashion capital of the world, and leather working has often been at the forefront of its fashion industry. The Italian tanning industry is considered a world leader and there are many products available from bags to belts which showcase this skill.

Italy is also a country of celebration, with hundreds of festivals and carnivals taking place. One of the most famous is the Carnival of Venice, where traditional masks and costumes are worn by attendees.

Major towns and cities

- Rome – this remarkable city is known as the "Capital of the World".
- Milan – a global centre of fashion and known for its exquisite galleries.
- Turin – famous for its baroque architecture and monuments.
- Naples – boasting a wealth of historical buildings from a variety of periods.

Attractions

- Venice – one of the world's most beautiful cities and boasting a wealth of historic sites.
- Santa Maria del Fiore, Florence – one of the most recognisable cathedrals that houses several important works of art.
- Pompeii – the remains of an ancient Roman town in the shadow of Mount Vesuvius.
- Cinque Terre – five beautiful and traditional villages that lie on the Italian Riviera.

Find out more

www.enit.it
E: sedecentrale@enit.it T: 0039 (0) 06 49 711

Country Information

Population (approx): 61.8 million

Capital: Rome

Area: 301,318 sq km (inc Sardinia & Sicily)

Bordered by: France, Switzerland, Austria, Slovenia

Terrain: Mountainous in the north descending to rolling hills in the centre; some plains and coastal lowlands

Climate: Predominantly Mediterranean climate, alpine in the far north, hot and dry in the south

Coastline: 7,600km

Highest Point: Monte Bianco (Mont Blanc) 4,810m

Language: Italian, German (in the northern Alps)

Local Time: GMT or BST + 1, i.e. 1 hour ahead of the UK all year

Currency: Euros divided into 100 cents; £1 = €1.14, €1 = £0.88 (Feb 2021)

Emergency numbers: Police 113; Fire brigade 115; Ambulance 118

Public Holidays 2021: Jan 1, 6; Apr 4, 5, 25; May 1; Jun 2; Aug 15; Nov 1; Dec 8, 25, 26.

Each locality also celebrates its patron saint's day. School summer holidays run from mid June to mid September.

Entry Formalities

British and Irish passport holders may stay for up to 90 days in any 180 day period without a visa. Following Brexit you may be asked to show a return or onward ticket at the border to confirm your length of stay, or to prove that you have enough money for your stay.

Your passport will need to have a minimum of 6 months' validity remaining, and be less than 10 years old (even if it has over 6 months left).

Visitors arriving at a campsite or hotel must complete a registration form.

Medical Services

Ask at a pharmacy (farmacia) for the nearest doctor registered with the state health care scheme (SSN) or look in the telephone directory under 'Unita Sanitaria Locale'. The services of a national health service doctor are normally free of charge.

A European Health Insurance Card (EHIC) entitles you to emergency treatment and medication at local rates and to hospital treatment under the state healthcare scheme. Any charges you do incur are non-refundable in Italy but you may be able to make a claim on your return to the UK. Dental treatment is expensive and you will be charged the full fee.

Emergency services (Guardia Medica) are available at weekends and at night and there are first aid posts at major train stations and airports. Staff at pharmacies can advise on minor ailments and at least one pharmacy remains open 24 hours in major towns.

Opening Hours

Banks: Mon-Fri 8.30am-1.30pm & 3pm-4pm.

Museums: Check locally as may vary. The Vatican museums and Sistine Chapel are not open to visitors Sun. Visitors under 18 or over 60 are admitted free to State museums on production of a passport.

Post Offices: Mon-Fri 8.30am-2pm/5.30pm, Sat 8.30am-12 noon.

Shops: Mon-Sat 8.30am/9am-1pm & 3.30pm/ 4pm-7.30pm/8pm. In southern Italy and tourist areas shops may stay open later. There is no lunch time closing in large cities. Shops are closed half a day each week (variable by region).

Regulations for Pets

All dogs, including those temporarily imported, must be on a leash at all times. It is advisable to carry a muzzle as the police/ authorities can insist on your dog wearing one if they consider your dog to be dangerous. Some sites and some public transport operators insist that all dogs are muzzled at all times - check local requirements on arrival.

A domestic animal may be transported in a car provided it does not distract the driver. More than one animal may be transported provided they are kept in the rear of the car, separated from the driver by bars, or kept in special cages.

Safety and Security

Most visits to Italy are trouble free and, in general, levels of crime are low, but visitors should take care on public transport and in crowded areas where pickpockets and bag snatchers may operate. In Rome take particular care around the main railway station, Roma Termini, and on the bus to and from St Peter's Square. Also take care in and around railway stations in large cities. Be particularly wary of groups of children who may try to distract your attention while attempting to steal from you. Do not carry your passport, credit cards and cash all together in one bag or pocket and only carry what you need for the day. Do not wear expensive jewellery, particularly in the south of Italy.

Take care in bars and don't leave drinks unattended. Recently there have been cases of drinks being spiked. Check prices before ordering food and insist on seeing a priced menu. Be particularly careful when ordering items, such as lobster, which are charged by weight.

When driving in towns keep your car windows shut and doors locked and never leave valuables on display. Around Rome and Naples moped riders may attempt to snatch bags from stationary cars at traffic lights. Always lock your vehicle and never leave valuables in it, even if you will only be away for a short time or are nearby. Avoid leaving luggage in cars for any length of time or overnight.

Increasingly robberies are taking place from cars at rest stops and service stations on motorways. Treat offers of help with caution, for example with a flat tyre, particularly on the motorway, as sometimes the tyre will have been punctured deliberately.

Do not be tempted to enter or bathe in Italy's many fountains – there are heavy fines if you do. Dress conservatively when visiting places of worship, i.e. cover shoulders and upper arms and do not wear shorts. Avoid queues in the peak season by visiting early.

The authorities are making strenuous efforts to stamp out the illegal production and sale of counterfeit goods. Illegal traders operate on the streets of all major cities, particularly tourist cities such as Florence and Rome. You are advised not to buy from them at the risk of incurring a fine.

Italy shares with the rest of Europe a general threat from terrorism. Attacks could be indiscriminate and against civilian targets in public places, including tourist sites.

There continue to be isolated cases of domestic terrorism by extreme left wing and secessionist groups, aimed primarily at official Italian targets.

British Embassy

VIA XX SETTEMBRE 80A, I-00187 ROMA RM
Tel: 06 4220 0001 (24 hour emergency number)
www.ukinitaly.fco.gov.uk/en

British Consulate-General

VIA SAN PAOLO 7, I-20121 MILANO MI
Tel: 02 7230 01
There is also a British Consulates in Naples.

Irish Embassy

VILLA SPADA, VIA GIACOMO MEDICI
1 - 00153 ROMA
Tel: 06 5852 381
www.embassyofireland.it
There is also an Irish Honorary Consulate in Milan.

Documents

Driving Licence

The standard pink UK paper driving licence is recognised in Italy but holders of the old-style green UK licence are recommended to change it for a photocard licence. Alternatively an International Driving Permit may be purchased from the AA, the RAC or selected Post Offices.

Money

There are few bureaux de change, so change cash at a bank.

Major credit cards are widely accepted including at petrol stations, but not as widely as in some other European countries. Automatic cash machines (Bancomat) are widespread. Carry your credit card issuers'/banks' 24-hour UK contact numbers in case of loss or theft of your cards.

Vehicle(s)

You must be able to present to the police on demand your vehicle and insurance documents, i.e. vehicle registration certificate (V5C), insurance certificate and MOT certificate (if applicable) and, if you are not the owner of your vehicle(s), authorisation for its use from the owner.

Driving

Alcohol

The maximum permitted level of alcohol is 50 milligrams in 100 millilitres of blood, i.e. less than in the UK (80 milligrams). For drivers with less than three years' driving experience, the limit is zero. It is advisable to adopt the 'no drink and drive' rule as penalties are severe.

Breakdown Service

The motoring organisation, Automobile Club d'Italia (ACI) operates a breakdown service 24 hours a day throughout Italy, including San Marino and Vatican City. Telephone 803116 from a landline or mobile phone. ACI staff speak English. This number also gives access to the ACI emergency information service, operated by multi-lingual staff, for urgent medical or legal advice. There are emergency phones placed every 2km on motorways.

On all roads, including motorways, standard charges are made for assistance and/or recovering a vehicle weighing up to 2,500kg to the nearest ACI garage. Higher charges apply for vehicles over 2,500kg, at night, over weekends and public holidays and for towing to anywhere other than the nearest ACI garage. Payment is required in cash.

Road police, 'Polizia Stradale', constantly patrol all roads and motorways and can assist when vehicles break down.

Congestion Charge

To access the historical centre of Milan (Area C) from 7.30am – 7.30pm on Monday, Tuesday, Wednesday and Friday and from 7.30am- 6pm on Thursday you must pay a fee of €5 a day.

You can buy a ticket for entrance from parking meters, newsagents and some ATM points or online at www.areac.it – tickets must then be activated on the day before you plan to drive into the area. You can activate the ticket via text message or telephone. Visit the above website address to find out more. Petrol vehicles classed as Euro 0 and diesel vehicles in classes Euro 0 - 3 are not allowed to enter Area C at all during the above times.

Child Restraint System

Children travelling in UK registered vehicles must be secured according to UK legislation.

Fuel

Unleaded petrol is sold from pumps marked 'Super Unleaded' or 'Super Sensa Piombo'. Diesel is called 'gasolio' and LPG is known as 'gas auto' or 'GPL'.

Fuel is sold 24 hours a day on motorways but elsewhere petrol stations may close for an extended lunch break and overnight from approximately 7pm. Opening hours are clearly displayed, as are the addresses of the nearest garages which are open.

Major credit cards are accepted, but possibly not in rural areas, so always carry some cash. Look for the 'Carta Si' sign. Recent visitors report that many petrol stations in rural areas and on major routes between towns are now unmanned and automated. Payment may be made with bank notes but the machines will usually only accept credit cards issued by Italian banks.

Lights

It is compulsory for all vehicles to have dipped headlights at all times when driving outside built-up areas, on motorways and major roads, when driving in tunnels and when visibility is poor, e.g. in rain or snow. Bulbs are more likely to fail with constant use so you are advised to carry spares.

Low Emission Zones

Many Italian cities and towns operate low emission zones. They often affect all vehicles, but rules vary from city to city. For more information visit www.lowemissionzones.eu.

Motorways

There are approximately 6,700km of motorway (autostrade) in Italy. Tolls (pedaggio) are levied on most of them. On some motorways, tolls are payable at intermediate toll booths for each section of the motorway used. On a few others the toll must be paid on entering the motorway.

Motorway Tolls

Category A — Cars with height from front axle less than 1.30m.

Category B — Motor vehicles with 2 axles with height from front axle over 1.30m including motorhomes.

Category C — Motor vehicles with 3 axles, e.g. car plus caravan.

Category D — Motor vehicles with 4 axles, e.g. car plus twin-axle caravan.

To calculate the tolls payable and find traffic and motorway services information see www.autostrade.it which allows you to enter your route and class of vehicle.

Tolls can prove to be expensive especially over long distances.

Cash (euro only), debit and credit cards are accepted. Credit cards are also accepted for payment in the Fréjus, Mont-Blanc and Grand St Bernard tunnels. However, visitors advise that on some stretches of motorway automated pay desks which accept credit cards will only do so for solo vehicles. If you are towing a caravan it is advisable to have cash available as you may need to pass through the manned white channel for cash payments.

The prepaid Viacard, available in values of €25, €50 and €75, is also accepted on the majority of motorways and is obtainable from motorway toll booths, service areas and PuntoBlu points of sale along the motorways. The card may be used for any vehicle. When leaving a motorway on which the Viacard is accepted (use the blue or white lanes – do not use the yellow 'Telepass' lanes), insert your entry ticket and card into the machine or give them to the attendant who will deduct the amount due. A Viacard is valid until the credit expires and may be used on a subsequent visit to Italy but cannot be refunded. Viacards are not accepted on Sicilian motorways.

Overtaking

On roads with three traffic lanes, the middle lane is reserved for overtaking, but overtaking is only allowed if a vehicle travelling in the opposite direction is not already overtaking.

When pulling out to overtake on motorways check for cars travelling at well over the maximum speed limit of 130km/h (81 mph).

Parking

In major towns there are parking zones where payment is required and these are indicated by blue road signs. Pay either at a machine with coins or buy a card from local tobacconists or newspaper shops and display it inside your vehicle. Some cities also have green zones where parking is prohibited on working days during the morning and afternoon rush hours.

Parking against the traffic flow and parking on the pavement are not allowed. Illegally parked vehicles may be clamped or towed away.

Priority

In general, priority must be given to traffic coming from the right except if indicated by road signs. At traffic lights a flashing amber light indicates that traffic must slow down and proceed with caution, respecting the priority rules.

Roads

The road network is of a high standard and main and secondary roads are generally good. Many main roads are winding and hilly but provide a more interesting route than the motorways. Stopping places for refreshments may be few and far between in some areas.

Standards of driving may be erratic, especially overtaking, and lane discipline poor; some roads have a particularly bad reputation for accidents. Those where special vigilance is called for include the Via Aurelia between Rome and Pisa, which is mostly two lane and is extremely busy at weekends, the A12 to the north with its series of tunnels and curves, the A1 between Florence and Bologna, the Rome ring road, roads around Naples and Palermo, and mountain roads in the south and in Sicily.

Road Signs and Markings

Road signs conform to international standards. White lettering on a green background indicates motorways (autostrada), whereas state and provincial roads outside built-up areas have white lettering on a blue background.

Snow chains
required

Horizontal
traffic light

Carabinieri
(police)

Ecopass
zone (Milan)

Other frequently encountered signs include
the following:

Italian	English Translation
Attenzione	Caution
Autocarro	Lorries
Coda	Traffic jam
Curva pericolosa	Dangerous bend
Destra	Right
Deviazione	Diversion
Divieto di accesso	No entry
Divieto di sorpasso	No overtaking
Divieto di sosta	No parking
Ghiaia	Gravel
Incidente	Accident
Incrocio	Crossroads
Lavori in corso	Roadworks ahead
Pericoloso	Danger
Rallentare	Slow down
Restringimento	Narrow lane
Senso unico	One-way street
Senso vietato	No entry
Sinistra	Left
Sosta autorizzata	Parking permitted (times shown)
Sosta aietata	No parking
Svolta	Bend
Uscita	Exit
Vietato ingresso veicili	No entry for vehicles

A single or double unbroken line in the centre
of the carriageway must not be crossed.

Speed Limits

	Open Road (km/h)	Motorway (km/h)
Car Solo	90-110	130
Car towing caravan/trailer	70	80
Motorhome under 3500kg	90-110	130
Motorhome 3500-7500kg	80	100

Motorhomes over 3,500kg are restricted to
80 km/h (50 mph) outside built-up areas and
100 km/h (62 mph) on motorways.

Speed on some sections of Italian motorways
is electronically controlled. When you leave
a motorway the toll booth calculates the
distance a vehicle has travelled and the
journey time. The police are automatically
informed if speeding has taken place, and
fines are imposed.

In bad weather the maximum speed is 90
km/h
(56 mph) on roads outside built-up areas and
110 km/h (68 mph) on motorways.

The transportation or use of radar detectors is
prohibited.

Traffic Jams

During the summer months, particularly
at weekends, the roads to the Ligurian and
Adriatic coasts and to the Italian lakes are
particularly busy, as are the narrow roads
around the lakes. Travelling mid week may
help a little. Bottlenecks are likely to occur
on the A1 north-south motorway at stretches
between Milan and Bologna, Rioveggio and
Incisa and on the ring road around Rome.
Other traffic jams occur on the A14 to the
Adriatic coast; on the A4 between Milan
and Brescia caused by heavy traffic to Lakes
Iseo and Garda; the A11 Florence to Pisa
(before the A12 junction); the A12 Rome
to Civitavecchia; the A23 Udine to Tarvisio
and before the tunnels on the A26 between
Alessandria and Voltri.

Italians traditionally go on holiday during the
first weekend of August when traffic density
is at its worst. Traffic jams regularly occur on
the ring roads for Milan, Rome and Naples.

Violation of Traffic Regulations

The police may impose on the spot fines, which are particularly heavy for speeding and drink and/or drug related driving offences. Payment is required in cash and a receipt must be given. It can take up to a year for notice of a traffic violation and resulting fine to reach the owner of a foreign registered vehicle.

Winter Driving

In the area of Val d'Aosta vehicles must be equipped with winter tyres or snow chains must be carried between 15 October and 15 April. This rule may apply in other areas and over other periods as conditions dictate.

Essential Equipment

Reflective Jackets/Waistcoats

If your vehicle is immobilised on the carriageway outside a built-up area at night, or in poor visibility, you must wear a reflective jacket or waistcoat when getting out of your vehicle. This rule also applies to passengers who may leave the vehicle, for example, to assist with a repair. Keep the jackets to hand inside your vehicle, not in the boot.

Warning Triangle

At night a warning triangle must be used to give advance warning of any vehicle parked outside a built-up area near a bend, or on a hill if rear side lights have failed, or in fog. Place the triangle at least 50 metres behind the vehicle (100 metres on motorways). Failure to use a triangle may result in a fine.

Touring

Italy's great cities, with their religious, artistic and historic treasures, are high on the short break list and are worthy destinations in their own right. Visitors over 65 often qualify for reduced or free entrance to museums and other attractions, so carry your passport as proof of age.

In Rome an Archaeological Card is available, valid for up to seven days, offering entry (ahead of any queues) to many of the most famous sites, together with discounts on guided tours. The cards are available from participating sites and museums.

Smoking is not permitted in public places including restaurants and bars.

In bars prices shown are for drinks taken standing at the bar. Prices are higher if you are seated at a table. In restaurants a service or cover charge is usually added to the bill but it is customary to add 50 cents or €1 per person if you are happy with the service provided. Not all restaurants accept credit cards; check before ordering.

The east coast of Italy has many holiday resorts with fine, sandy beaches, from Ravenna, to Pescara and beyond. However, most beaches in Italy are commercially managed and unless a campsite or hotel has its own private beach, be prepared to pay to enjoy a day by the sea. By law a part of every beach must have free access, but usually it is the least attractive part.

Many parts of Italy lie on a major seismic fault line and tremors and minor earthquakes are common. Visitors climbing Mount Etna should follow the marked routes and heed the advice of guides. There is also ongoing low-intensity volcanic activity on the island of Stromboli.

Visitors to Venice should note that parts of the city are liable to flood in late autumn and early spring.

There are more than 40 World Heritage Sites in Italy (more than any other country) including the historic centres of Florence, Siena, Naples, Pienza, Urbino and the Vatican City.

The Vatican museums and Sistine Chapel are closed on Sundays, except on the last Sunday of the month. When visiting art galleries in Florence, in particular the Uffizi and Accademia, you are advised to buy timed tickets in advance, either online or in person. Otherwise you will encounter long queues.

There are numerous ferry services transporting passengers and vehicles between Italy and neighbouring countries. Major ports of departure for Croatia, Greece and Turkey are Ancona, Bari, Brindisi, Trieste and Venice. Services also operate to Corsica from Citavecchia, Genoa, Livorno, Porto Torres (Sardinia), Santa Teresa di Gallura (Sardinia) and Savona.

For further information contact:

VIAMARE LTD
SUITE 108, 582 HONEYPOT LANE
STANMORE
MIDDX HA7 1JS
Tel: 020 8206 3420, Fax: 020 8206 1332
www.viamare.com
Email: ferries@viamare.com

If you are planning a skiing holiday contact the Italian State Tourist Board for advice on safety and weather conditions before travelling.

Italy has introduced a law requiring skiers and snowboarders to carry tracking equipment if going off-piste. The law also obliges children up to 14 years of age to wear a helmet. There are plans for snowboarders to be banned from certain slopes, check local news for updates.

Camping and Caravanning

There are approximately 2,000 organised and supervised campsites in Italy. They are usually well signposted and are open from April to September. Advance booking is recommended in high season, especially by the lakes and along the Adriatic coast. About 20% of campsites are open all year including some in the mountains and around large towns. Campsites organised by the Touring Club Italiano (TCI) and the Federcampeggio are particularly well equipped.

In general pitch sizes are small at about 80 square metres and it may be difficult to fit a large outfit plus an awning onto a pitch. You will frequently find that hot water is supplied to showers only, for which you will be charged. Published opening and closing dates may be unreliable - phone ahead if travelling during the low season.

It is not compulsory to have a Camping Key Europe (CKE) or Camping Card International (CCI), but it is recommended as a means of identification. If for any reason details are missing from the CKE or CCI a site will insist on holding a visitor's passport instead.

Casual camping is not recommended and is not permitted in national parks or in state forests.

Motorhomes

Many local authorities permit motorhomes to park overnight in specially designated places known as 'Camper Stops' or 'Aree di Sosta' and a list of their locations and the services provided are contained in a number of publications and on a number of websites including the French 'Guide Officiel Aires de Service Camping-Car' published by the Fédération Française de Camping et de Caravaning, www.ffcc.fr. You will also find a list of 'Camper Stops' on www.turismoitinerante.com.

Transportation of bicycles

An overhanging load must be indicated by an aluminium square panel (panello) measuring 50cm x 50cm with reflective red and white diagonal stripes. The load must not exceed 30% of the length of the vehicle, may only overhang at the rear and the regulation applies to a car or caravan carrying bicycles at the rear or windsurf boards on the roof. A fine may be imposed for failure to display the approved sign which is made by Fiamma and in the UK may be purchased from or ordered through motorhome or caravan dealers/accessory shops. For a list of Fiamma stockists please see www.fiamma.com.

At night, outside built up areas, cyclists must wear a reflective jacket and must ride in single file.

Electricity and Gas

Current at campsites varies between 2 and 16 amps and often it is very low, offering a maximum of only 4 amps across the whole site. Many sites have CEE connections. Plugs have three round pins in line.

Campingaz cylinders are generally available, except in the south of Italy, Sardinia and Sicily where exchange may be difficult outside of marinas and holiday resorts.

Public Transport & Local Travel

Traffic is restricted in the historical centre of most Italian cities in order to reduce congestion and pollution levels, and you are advised to use out of centre car parks and public transport. The boundaries of historic centres are usually marked with signs displaying the letters ZTL (zona traffico limitato). A crossed hammer on the sign means the restriction does not apply on Sundays and public holidays. Do not pass the ZTL sign as your registration number is likely to be caught on camera and fined. Fines are around €100 each time you enter a ZTL.

In addition many northern Italian regions have banned traffic, except buses and taxis, in town and city centres on Sundays.

Public transport is usually cheap and efficient. All the major cities have extensive bus networks and Messina, Milan, Padova, Rome and Turin also have trams. At present only Rome and Milan have an underground network and Perugia has a 'minimetro'. Bus and metro tickets cannot be purchased on board and must be obtained prior to boarding from newsagents, tobacconists, ticket kiosks or bars. Books of tickets and daily, weekly and monthly passes are also available. Validate your ticket at the yellow machines positioned at the entrance to platforms in railway stations, in the entrance hall of metro stations and on board buses and trams. Officials patrol all means of public transport and will issue an on the spot fine if you do not hold a validated ticket. Tickets for buses and the metro tend to be time limited (75 minutes) and it is therefore necessary to complete your journey within the allotted time and purchase a new ticket for any additional travel.

Only use taxis which are officially licensed. They will have a neon taxi sign on the roof and are generally white or yellow. Also ensure that the meter in the taxi has been reset before starting your journey. Fares are quite high and there are additional charges for luggage and pets, at night and on public holidays. A tip is expected (up to 10%) and this is sometimes already added to the fares for foreigners.

Car ferry services operate between Venice and the Lido, the Italian mainland and the Aeolian Islands, Sardinia, Sicily, Elba and Capri, Corsica (France) and on Lakes Maggiore, Como and Garda. Parking in Venice is very difficult; instead park at a mainland car park and use a bus or ferry to the city. However, be aware that thieves may operate in car parks in Mestre. Driving and parking in Naples are not recommended in any circumstances.

Cars towing caravans are prohibited from using the S163 south of Naples because it is narrow and has many bends. Motorhomes are prohibited in summer between Positano and Vietri-a-Mare.

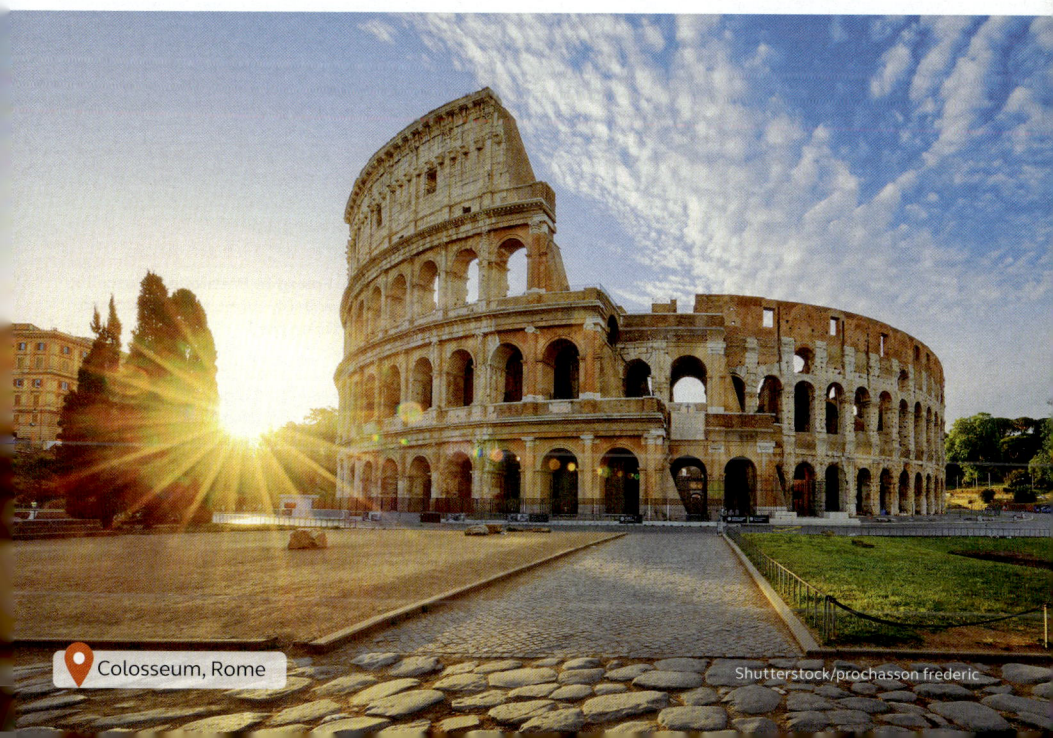

Colosseum, Rome

Shutterstock/prochasson frederic

AGEROLA *3A3* (3.5km SE Urban) *40.62537, 14.56761*
Camping Beata Solitudo, Piazza Generale Avitabile 4, San Lazzaro, 80051 Agerola (NA) **081 8025048; beatasol@gmail.com; www.beatasolitudo.it**

12 | 🐎 | 👫(cont) | wc | 🚿 | 🍴 | MP | 🦋 | ⚐ | ⟁ | 🍵 nr | ⊕ nr | 🅿 nr | ⛲

Exit A3/S145 at Castellammare-di-Stabia & foll dirs S on S366 to Agerola. Turn L sp San Lazzaro, site in vill sq - narr access rds. Do not app via Amalfi coast rd. Sm, shd, terr, EHU (3A) inc; 70% statics; bus adj; Eng spkn; adv bkg acc; CKE. "Vg access to Amalfi coast via bus; site at 650m - sea views; v helpful owner; bungalows & hostel accomm avail in restored castle building on site; vg but suitable m'vans only; facs tired."
€20.00   2016

ALBA *1B2* (1km SW Urban) *44.68507, 8.01019*
Camping Village Alba, Corso Piave 219, San Cassiano, 12051 Alba (CN) **0173 280972; info@albavillage hotel.it; www.albavillagehotel.it**

12 | 🐎 | 👫(htd) | wc | ♿ | 🚿 | 🍴 | 🦋 | ⚐ | ⟨Y⟩ | ⊕ nr | 🚣

Fr A21 exit Asti Est onto S231 to Alba ring rd. Take Corso Piave dir Roddi & Castiglione Falletto, site sp (Campo Sportivo) on L - red block. Or fr A6 exit at SP662 & foll sp Cherasco & Marene, then at rndabt foll sp Pollenza, then Roddi. Fr Roddi site sp dir Alba. 3*, Med, mkd, hdg, pt shd, EHU (16A) €2.50; bbq; red long stay; bus; Eng spkn; adv bkg acc; ccard acc; games area; bike hire; CKE. "Excel, friendly, clean site; mv service pnt adj; open country to rear; htd pool adj; vg facs; some statics or apartmnts; sports cent adj; conv Barolo vineyards; attractive town & area; camper van stop adj €5." **€30.00**   2017

ALBEROBELLO *3A4* (1.5km N Rural) *40.80194, 17.25055* **Camping Dei Trulli,** Via Castellana Grotte, Km 1.5, 70011 Alberobello (BA) **0804 323699; info@ campingdeitrulli.it; www.campingdeitrulli.com**

👫 | 🚿 | 🍴 | MP | ⚐ | ⟨Y⟩ | ⊕ | 🚣 | 🅿 | ✏ | 🚣

Fr Alberobello, site sp on R. Lift barrier to ent if clsd. 3*, Med, mkd, hdstg, pt shd, EHU (6A) €2.50; red long stay; phone; Eng spkn; ccard acc; bike hire; CKE. "Gd touring base; some pitches sm due to trees; mv service pnt nr; ltd, basic facs LS; hot water to shwrs only; site run-down." **€29.50,** 1 Apr-30 Oct.   2019

ALBEROBELLO *3A4* (1km S Rural) *40.77507, 17.24040* **Camping Bosco Selva,** 27 Via Bosco Selva, 70011 Alberobello (BA) **080 4323726; info@camping boscoselva.it; www.campingboscoselva.it**

12 | 👫 | wc | 🚿 | 🍴 | MP | 🦋 | ⚐ | ⟨Y⟩ | ⊕ nr | 🚣

Sp fr S172/S239 Alberobello ring rd. 3*, Med, hdstg, shd, pt sl, EHU (2A) inc; Eng spkn; CKE. "In heart of 'Trulli' region of sm beehive-shaped houses; wooded site; friendly owner; vg facs; v nice site; tennis courts; walks in forest adj." **€23.00**   2019

AOSTA *1B1* (5km SW Rural) *45.71706, 7.26161*
Camping Monte Bianco, St Maurice 15, 11010 Sarre (AO) **0165 258514; info@campingmontebianco.it; www.campingmontebianco.it**

👫 | wc | 🚿 | 🍴 | MP | 🦋 | ⚐ | ⟨Y⟩ nr | ⊕ nr | 🅿 nr | ⛲

Fr A5/E25 exit Aosta W twd Aosta, site on R, well sp. Fr Mont Blanc tunnel on S26 site on R at Sarre 500m past St Maurice sp. W fr Aosta, site on L 100m past boundary sp St Maurice/Sarre, yellow sp. Turn into site poss tight for lge o'fits. 2*, Sm, pt shd, terr, EHU (6-10A) €2.80; gas; red long stay; phone; bus fr site to Aosta; Eng spkn; adv bkg acc; CKE. "Sm, gd, family-run site set in orchard on rv; friendly, helpful; excel tourist info; beautiful alpine scenery & walks; last tunnel is close to exit when coming fr Mont Blanc do not rely on sat nav to restart in time; bar 100m; pool 4km; pleasant site; supmkt 2km; fascinating walled Roman town; many archaeological sites to visit."
€25.00, 15 May-30 Sep.   2018

ARCO *2D1* (6km SSW Coastal) *45.87614, 10.86779*
Camping Bellavista, Via Gardesana, 31 - Arco **0464 505644; www.camping-bellavista.it**

🐎 €3.50 | 👫 | wc | 🚿 | ♿ | 🍴 | MP | ⚐ | ⟨Y⟩ | ⊕ | 🅿 | 🚣 | 🚴

Fr A22 take exit for Roveretto Sud-Lago di Garda; at rndabt take 4th exit twrds Riva Del Garda; in 3km turn L onto SS240. After town cent in 8km take L into site bef lakeside tunnel, just after Lidl supmkt on L. Med, mkd, shd, EHU (3A) inc; bbq; twin axles; phone; bus 100m; Eng spkn; bike hire. "Lakeside; v busy but v pleasant site; direct access to beach; takeaway; excel, immac san facs; vg & reasonable rest; next to supmkt; town cent 5 min walk along lakeside path; vg touring area for northern towns of lake Garda; excel site." **€38.00,** 1 Apr-30 Oct.   2019

AREZZO *1D3* (10km SW Rural) *43.44982, 11.78990*
Camping Villaggio Le Ginestre, Loc Ruscello 100, 52100 Arezzo **0575 363566; info@campingle ginestre.it; www.campingleginestre.it**

🐎 | 👫(htd) | wc | 🚿 | ♿ | 🍴 | MP | ⚐ | ⟨Y⟩ | ⊕ | 🅿 nr | ⛲ | 🚣

Onto A1 sp Arezzo. Foll sp to Battifolle & Ruscello, proceed for 2km to rndabt, turn L to Ruscello and foll sp to site which is on the L. 3*, Med, hdstg, pt shd, pt sl, terr, EHU (5-10A) inc; 5% statics; bus; adv bkg acc; ccard acc; tennis; site clsd Jan; games area; games rm; CKE. "Pleasant tiered grassy site with views; friendly owner; gd rest (clsd Mon); trains fr Arezzo to Florence, Rome etc; gd touring base/NH."
€29.00, 1 Mar-5 Nov.   2018

ARONA *1B1* (8km N Rural) *45.81583, 8.54992*
Camping Solcio, Via al Campeggio, 28040 Solcio-de-Lesa (NO) **0322 7497; info@campingsolcio.com; www.campingsolcio.com**

🐕 €3.80 (htd) ⚏ ♨ 🛁 ⁄ 🅼🅿 ♟ 🍴 🕙 🅟 🛒 ⚓ 🏄

Foll S33 N fr Arona, thro Meina campsite on R of rd app Solcio; well sp, adj boatyard. 2*, Med, mkd, pt shd, EHU (6A) inc; gas; bbq; sw nr; red long stay; 40% statics; phone; Eng spkn; adv bkg acc; fishing; boat hire; watersports; CKE. *"Gd site adj lake; some sm pitches; premium for lakeside pitches; gd rest; gd cent for area; conv Stresa and Borromeo Islands; friendly; highly rec; beach has permanent wooden parasols; immac san facs; lovely site."*
€39.40, 8 Mar-22 Oct. 2018

ARSIE *1D1* (3km S Rural) *45.96333, 11.76027*
Camping Al Lago, Via Campagna 14, 32030 Rocca di Arsie (BL) **0439 58540; info@campingallago.bl.it; www.campingallago.bl.it**

🐕 ♀️ 🚻 ⚏ ♨ 🦋 ⁄ 🍴 🕙 🛒nr 🏔

Fr Trento on S47, turn E dir Feltre/Belluno rd SS50B, take 1st exit after long tunnel. Fr Belluno on S50 & S50B take Arsié exit & foll site sp. 2*, Med, pt shd, EHU (4A) inc; gas; sw nr; 15% statics; phone; adv bkg acc; ccard acc; CKE. *"Excel, well-run, clean, tidy site in unspoilt area of historical & cultural interest; simple facs, basic but clean; boat hire locally; ent clsd 1400-1530 & 0000-0800; passport req to register."*
€26.00, 20 Apr-18 Sep. 2016

> ## "We must tell the Club about that great site we found"
>
> Get your site reports in by mid-August and we'll do our best to get your updates into the next edition.

ASSISI *2E3* (1km SE Rural) *43.06605, 12.63056*
Camping Fontemaggio, Via Eremo delle Carceri, 24 Assisi 06081 (PG) **075 813636 or 812317; info@fontemaggio.it; www.fontemaggio.it**

12 🐕 🚻 (htd) ⚏ ♨ ⚭ 🛁 ⁄ 🅼🅿 🦋 🍴 🕙 🛒

Fr Perugia on S75, turn L onto rd SS147 twd Assisi; keeping Assisi walls on L past coach car park & foll sp to Porta Nuova. In sq at front of gate turn R & foll sp to Eremo delle Carceri, Foligno & Cmp Fontemaggio. Foll sp 1km to sq in front of next gate, turn R (sharp hairpin), site sp 800m on R at gate with narr arch, site 800m on R. Diff long, winding uphill app; recep in hotel. Pls do not use sat nav. 2*, Lge, hdstg, pt shd, terr, serviced pitches; EHU (6A) inc (long lead rec); gas; TV (pitch); 10% statics; phone; Eng spkn; adv bkg acc; ccard acc; CKE. *"Lovely, spacious site in olive grove; views; footpath to attractive town; steep site rds diff when wet; order bread at hotel recep; htd pool 3km; firefly displays on site; facs tired; great rest."* **€25.50** 2015

ASSISI *2E3* (3km W Rural) *43.07611, 12.57361*
Green Village Assisi (Formerly Camping Assisi), Via San Giovanni Campiglione 110, 06081 Assisi (PG) **075 813710 or 075 816813; prenotazioni@greenvillageassisi.it; www.greenvillageassisi.it**

🐕 €2 🚻 ⚏ ⚭ 🛁 🗑 ⁄ 🅼🅿 🦋 ♟ 🍴 🕙 🅟 🛒 🏔 🏊

Fr Perugia SS75 to Ospedalicchio, then SS147 twd Assisi. Site well sp on R bef Assisi. Fr Assisi take SS147 to Perugia. Site on L in 3km adj Hotel Green. 3*, Lge, mkd, shd, EHU 6A inc; gas; 40% statics; phone; bus; Eng spkn; adv bkg rec; ccard acc; tennis; car wash; CKE. *"Helpful staff; minibus to Assisi; lovely, tidy, clean site; busy even in LS; immac san facs; gd rest; sm pitches; caves at Genga worth visit; excel; 10% red on next site if pt of same chain; v conv for visiting local area."* **€46.00, 1 Apr-2 Nov.** 2019

ASTI *1B2* (15km S Rural) *44.79688, 8.24183*
International Camping Le Fonti, Via Alle Fontane 54, 14041 Agliano Terme **0141 954820; info@campingle fonti.eu; www.campinglefonti.eu**

🐕 ♀️ 🚻 ⚏ ♨ ⚭ 🛁 🗑 ⁄ 🅼🅿 ♟ 🍴 🕙 🅟 🛒 🏔 🏊 (htd) 🛶

Fr A21 Torino to Alessandria exit Asti Est, dir Alba. Then Isola d'Asti exit, rd 456. Camp sp at the end of Montegrosso d'Asti vill, R twds Agliano Terme. 3*, Med, mkd, shd, terr, EHU (6A); bbq; twin axles; TV; 10% statics; Eng spkn; games area. *"Beautiful (if challenging) area for cycling; v friendly & helpful staff; some pitches small & diff to access; v gd."*
€28.50, 25 Mar-30 Oct. 2016

ASTI *1B2* (2km NW Rural) *44.94087, 8.18726*
Camping Umberto Cagni, Loc Valmanera 152, 14100 Asti **0141 271238; info@campingcagniasti.it; www.campingcagniasti.it**

🐕 €2 🚻 ♨ ⁄ 🍴 🕙 🅟 🛒 🏄

Leave A21 at Asti E. Foll sp to Asti. At beg of town cntre with Asti Service Stn on L; turn R foll sp to camping site. 2*, Med, shd, pt sl, EHU €3; 50% statics; games area; CKE. *"Fair NH/sh stay; friendly staff; not suitable lge o'fits; poss travellers; gates clsd 1300-1500."* **€23.50, 1 Apr-30 Sep.** 2020

BARDOLINO *1D2* (2km S Rural) *45.52525, 10.72977*
Camping Cisano/San Vito, Via Peschiera 48, 37011 Cisano (VR) **045 6229098; cisano@camping-cisano.it; www.camping-cisano.it**

🚻 ⚏ ♨ ⚭ 🛁 ⁄ 🅼🅿 🦋 🍴 🕙 🅟 🛒 ⚓ 🏄 🏊 ⛵

Sites on S boundary of Cisano, on SE shore of Lake Garda. 5*, V lge, mkd, shd, sl, terr, EHU (16A) inc; gas; sw nr; TV; Eng spkn; windsurfing; canoeing; waterskiing; waterslide; bike hire; games area; tennis. *"Two lovely, clean, lakeside sites run as one - San Vito smaller/quieter; helpful staff; san facs in need of refurb; some pitches diff access & chocks req; passport req at site check-in; Verona Opera excursions arranged high ssn; gd; v popular; helpful staff; gd walking/cycling; gd rest."* **€50.00, 17 Mar-8 Oct.** 2018

BARDONECCHIA *1A2* (5km SW Rural) *45.04954, 6.66510* **Camping Bokki,** Loc Pian del Colle, 10052 Bardonecchia (TO) **0122 99893; info@bokki.it; www.bokki.it**

12 ⊗ €1 ⊛(htd) ⊠ ⊕ ⊕ ⊟ / ⊠ ❀ ℧ ⊕ ⊕ nr ⚏

Fr A32 ent Bardonecchia & foll sp Melezet. After Melezet foll rd uphill for 1.5km. Bokki is 2nd site on R. 2*, Med, mkd, pt shd, pt sl, EHU (2A) inc; sw nr; TV; 95% statics; phone; Eng spkn; adv bkg acc; CKE. "Helpful owners; beautiful location; conv Fréjus tunnel; diff ent to v sm sl, uneven pitch; no red in LS." **€31.00** **2019**

"I need an on-site restaurant"

We do our best to make sure site information is correct, but it is always best to check any must-have facilities are still available or will be open during your visit.

BAROLO *1B2* (1km W Rural) *44.61246, 7.92106* **Camping Sole Langhe,** Piazza della Vite e Del Vino, Frazione Vergne, 12060 Barolo (CN) **0173 560510; info@solelanghe.com; www.campingsolelanghe.it**

⊗ ⊛ ⊠ ⊕ ⊟ / ⊠ ❀ ℧ nr ⚏ ⚏

Fr S exit A6 E sp Carru. At Carru turn N onto SP12 & foll sp Barolo. Site sp on ent Barolo. Sm, hdg, pt shd, EHU (6A) inc; bbq; Eng spkn; games area. "Lovely orchard site in cent Barolo wine region; v helpful owner; highly rec." **€26.00, 1 Mar-30 Nov.** **2017**

BARREA *2F4* (2km S Rural) *41.74978, 13.99128* **Camping La Genziana,** Loc Tre Croci 1, 67030 Barrea (AQ) **0864 88101; pasettanet@tiscalinet.it; www.campinglagenzianapasetta.it**

⊗ €3 ⊛ ⊠ ⊕ ⊟ / ⊠ ❀ ℧ nr ⚏ ⚏

Fr S83 to S end Lago di Barrea, thro Barrea S, site immed on L on uphill L-hand bend. 2*, Med, mkd, pt shd, terr, EHU (3A) €2.60; bbq; sw nr; bus; Eng spkn; adv bkg acc. "Knowledgeable owner; delightful site; excel area cycling; trekking, skiing; ltd shops Barrea 10 mins walk; conv Abruzzi National Park; updated facs (2015)." **€33.50, 5 Apr-20 Oct.** **2016**

BASCHI *2E3* (13km NE Rural) *42.70722, 12.2920* **Camping Il Falcone,** Loc Vallonganino 2A, Loc Civitella-del-Lago, 05023 Baschi (TR) **0744 950249; info@campingilfalcone.com; www.campingilfalcone.com**

⊗ ⊛ ⊠ ⊕ ⊕ ⊟ / ℧ ⚏ ⚏

Fr Orvieto take SS205 dir Baschi then S448 alongside Lago di Corbaro. Turn R sp Civitella. Uphill for 4km to site. 2*, Sm, hdstg, mkd, pt shd, terr, EHU (3A) inc; gas; bbq; red long stay; TV; Eng spkn; adv bkg acc; ccard acc; games rm; sep car park; CKE. "Lovely site in olive grove & woods; quiet; excel clean san facs; some pitches poss diff lge o'fits." **€32.00, 1 Apr-30 Sep.** **2018**

BELLAGIO *1C1* (1.8km S Rural) *45.97093, 9.25381* **Clarke Camping,** Via Valassina 170/C, 22021 Bellagio, Como **031 951325; elizabethclarke54@icloud.com; www.bellagio-camping.com**

⊛ ⊠ ⊕ / ⊠ ❀ ℧ ℧ nr ⊕ nr ⚏ nr

Fr Como, on arr in Bellagio foll sp Lecco to R, foll site sps uphill. Narr rds & site ent. Med, pt shd, terr, EHU (16A) €2; sw nr. "Friendly British owner; views over lake; uphill walk fr town to campsite; town is on lakeside; site & ent not suitable for o'fits over 7m; ferries, water taxis 1.5km; no twin axles; beautiful, peaceful site; basic san facs but clean; use vehicle ferry fr Cadenabbis or Varenne €20 for m'van & 2 people, then foll dirs." **€34.00, 1 May-20 Sep.** **2016**

BELLARIA *2E2* (2km NE Coastal) *44.16076, 12.44836* **Happy Camping Village,** Via Panzini 228, San Mauro a Mare, 47814 Bellaria (RN) **0541 346102; info@happycamping.it; www.happycamping.it**

12 ⊗ €6 ⊛ ⊠ ⊕ ⊕ ⊟ / ⊠ ℧ ℧ ⊕ ⚏ ⚏ ⚏ ⚏

⊕ sand adj

Fr A14 exit Rimini Nord onto S16 N. Turn off dir San Mauro Mare & Bellaria Cagnona, foll sp Aquabell Waterpark. Over rlwy x-ing, turn R, site on L. 4*, Lge, mkd, hdstg, pt shd, pt sl, EHU (8-10A) €3.50; gas; TV; 40% statics; phone; Eng spkn; adv bkg acc; tennis; games area; games rm; CKE. "Conv Rimini, San Marino; variable size pitches; clean, private beach; pool clsd 1300-1530 & after 1900; lge shopping cent & cinema complex 2km; Bellaria pleasant resort with port & marina." **€39.00** **2020**

BERGAMO *2C1* (25km N Rural) *45.78866, 9.94705* **Camping La Tartufaia,** Via Nazionale 2519, 24060 Ranzanico al Lago di Endine **39 035 819 259; info@latartufaia.com; www.latartufaia.com**

⊗ ⊛ ⊠ ⊕ ⊕ ⊟ / ⊠ ℧ ℧ ⊕ ⚏ nr ⚏ ⊕ adj

Fr A4 Milan-Venice, exit at Seriate. Take SS42 dir Lovere. Campsite on L past Ranzanico exit. 3*, Med, mkd, hdstg, pt shd, terr, EHU (6A) inc; gas; bbq; sw nr; twin axles; bus adj; Eng spkn; ccard acc; games rm; CCI. "Excel site; beautiful views over lake & mountains; gd bus conns; foothpath around lake; v friendly & helpful owners." **€41.50, 1 May-22 Sep.** **2019**

BEVAGNA *2E3* (4.5km SW Rural) *42.91236, 12.58622* **Camping Pian di Boccio,** Via Pian de Boccio 10, 06031 Bevagna **0742 360 164; info@piandiboccio.com; www.piandiboccio.com**

⊗ ⊛ ⊠ ⊕ ⊕ ⊟ / ⊠ ❀ ℧ ℧ ⚏ ⚏ (htd) ⊕

Fr Foligno to Bevagna in c'van strt on S316 & turn R after 3km, foll signs. In car - just past Bevagna 1st rd on the R past the bdge. 3*, Med, hdg, hdstg, shd, pt sl, terr, EHU (6A); phone; Eng spkn; adv bkg acc; games rm; games area. "Excel site; beautiful location; conv for Assis and historic hill towns; dated san facs." **€26.50, 1 Apr-30 Sep.** **2015**

BIBIONE *2E1* (6km W Coastal) *45.63055, 12.99444*
Camping Village Capalonga, Viale della Laguna 16,
30020 Bibione-Pineda (VE) **0431 438351 or 0431
447190 LS; capalonga@bibionemare.com;
www.capalonga.com**

♦♦ ⓦⓓ ♨ ♥ ⚅ ⛱ / ⓂⓈⓅ ✈ 🦋 ♈ ♈ ⓣ ⓗ ⓐ ⛟ ⚠ ✦ ⚓ ⚓sand adj

Well sp approx 6km fr Bibione dir Bibione Pineda.
4*, V lge, EHU (10A) inc; gas; bbq; TV; 25% statics;
phone; adv bkg acc; ccard acc; excursions; watersports;
games rm; archery; horseriding 6km; fishing; golf
10km; tennis. *"Well-organised site; gd for families;
various activities; extra for pitches on beach; spacious,
clean san facs; no o'fits over 10m high ssn; rest
o'looking lagoon; blue flag sand beach; voracious
mosquitoes!"* **€52.00, 24 Apr-21 Sep, Y15.   2016**

BIELLA *1B1* (88km NNW Rural) *45.84781, 7.93980*
Campeggio Alagna, Localita Miniere, 3, 13020 Riva
Valdobbia VC **0163 922947; info@campeggioalagna.
it; www.campeggioalagna.it**

⑫ ♞ ⓦⓓ ♨ ⚅ / 🦋 ✈ ⓗ ⛟ ⚠

**Site on R hand side up valley on the S299 at Riva
Valdobbia, just bef Alagna Valsesia.** 2*, Sm, shd,
EHU; twin axles; phone; bus adj; Eng spkn; adv bkg
acc; ccard acc; games area. *"Excel site."* **€20.00   2016**

BOLOGNA *1D2* (2km NE Rural) *44.52333, 11.37388*
Centro Turistico Campeggio Città di Bologna, Via
Romita 12/4a, 40127 Bologna **051 325016; info@
hotelcamping.com; www.hotelcamping.com**

♞ €2 ♦♦(htd) ⓦⓓ ♨ ⚅ ⛱ / ⓂⓈⓅ ♈ ✈ ⓗ ⓐ ⛟ ⚠ ⚓

**Access is fr A14 Bologna to Ancona. Leave at junc
7 sp Fiera & Via Stalingrado. Can be accessed fr the
parallel 'Tangenziale' at same junc. Sp at 1st junc
after toll.** 3*, Med, mkd, pt shd, EHU (6A) inc; bbq
(charcoal, gas); red long stay; TV; bus to city; Eng spkn;
adv bkg acc; ccard acc; site clsd 20 Dec-9 Jan; games
rm; CKE. *"Conv Bologna Trade Fair & Exhibition cent;
friendly, helpful staff; excel, clean san facs; fitness cent;
excel pool; tourist pitches at rear nr san facs block; no
o'fits over 15m on hdstg & over 9m on grass; gd bus
service fr ent into city; access to pitches poss diff lge
o'fits; sat nav dir may take you down narr rds; poss
lots mosquitoes; excel site."* **€36.00, 20 Jan-18 Dec,
Y14.   2019**

BOLSENA *1D3* (2km S Rural) *42.62722, 11.99444*
Camping Village Lido di Bolsena, Via Cassia, Km
111, 01023 Bolsena (VT) **0761 799258; info@
bolsenacamping.it; www.bolsenacamping.it**

♦♦ ⓦⓓ ♨ ⚅ / ⓂⓈⓅ 🦋 ✈ ⓗ ⓐ ⛟ ⚠ ✦ ⚓ ⚓sand adj

**Fr S on a'strada A1 foll sp Viterbo & Lago di Bolsena,
then take SR2 N to site; sp. Fr N exit A1 at Orvieto
onto SS71 to Bolsena. At traff lts in cent of town
turn L, site on R in approx 2km.** 4*, V lge, pt shd,
EHU (3A) inc (poss rev pol); gas; sw; 10% statics;
phone; Eng spkn; adv bkg acc; tennis; games area; sep
car park; bike hire; watersports. *"Beautiful lakeside
location; gd size pitches; all facs excel; cycle path
around lake to town; private bthrms avail; sm dogs acc;
charge for pool."* **€34.50, 18 Apr-30 Sep.   2019**

BOLSENA *1D3* (1.8km SW Rural) *42.63039, 11.99802*
Camping Le Calle, Via Cassia, Km 111.2, 01023
Bolsena (VT) **0761 797041**

♞ €2 ♦♦ ⓦⓓ ♨ ⚅ ⛱ / ⓂⓈⓅ 🦋 ⓗnr

**On S2 bet Lido Camping Vill & Camping Blu, ent by
Fornacella rest.** Sm, mkd, pt shd, EHU (6A) inc; sw nr;
adv bkg acc; CKE. *"Family-run CL-type 'Agrituristico'
site; friendly, helpful owners offer own produce inc
wine & olive oil; vg san facs; foot/cycle path to Bolsena;
excel sm site."* **€17.00, 1 Mar-31 Oct.   2015**

BOLZANO/BOZEN *1D1* (10km S Rural) *46.42982,
11.34357* **Camping-Park Steiner,** Kennedystrasse
32, 39055 Laives/Leifers (BZ) **0471 950105; info@
campingsteiner.com; www.campingsteiner.com**

♞ €5 ♦♦(htd) ⓦⓓ ♨ ♥ ⚅ ⛱ / ⓂⓈⓅ ♈ ✈ ⓗ ⓐ ⛟ ⚠ ⚓(covrd)

**Fr N take Bolzano/Bozen-Sud exit fr A22/E45 & pick
up rd S12 twd Trento to site; site on R on ent Laives
at N edge of vill. Fr S leave A22 at junc for Egna
onto rd S12 dir Bolzano. Poorly sp.** 3*, Lge, hdg, mkd,
shd, pt sl, EHU (6A) inc; gas; TV; 10% statics; phone;
Eng spkn; adv bkg rec; bike hire; CKE. *"Pleasant,
well-run, excel site on edge of Dolomites; attractive
pitches; helpful staff; gd, clean, modern san facs;
gates clsd 1300-1500 & 2200-0700; no dogs high
ssn; beautiful area; vg walking; well stocked shop;
highly rec; easy 5 min walk into town; excel rest;
busy in high ssn; excel value transport passes fr TO."*
€40.00, 12 Mar-31 Oct.   2016

BOLZANO/BOZEN *1D1* (2km NW Rural) *46.50333,
11.3000* **Camping Moosbauer,** Via San Maurizio 83,
39100 Bolzano **0471 918492; info@moosbauer.com;
www.moosbauer.com**

⑫ ♞ €4 ♦♦(htd) ⓦⓓ ♨ ♥ ⚅ ⛱ / ⓂⓈⓅ 🦋 ✈ ⓗ ⓐ ⛟ ⚠ ✦
⚓(htd)

**Exit A22/E45 at Bolzano Sud exit & take S38 N dir
Merano (keep L after toll booths). After tunnel
take 1st exit sp Eppan & hospital, & turn L at top of
feeder rd sp Bolzano. After approx 2km at island
past 08 G'ge turn L & foll site sp. Site on R in 1km
by bus stop on S38, sp.** 4*, Med, hdstg, mkd, hdg, pt
shd, pt sl, serviced pitches; EHU (5A) inc; TV (pitch);
bus; Eng spkn; adv bkg acc; games rm; CKE. *"Popular,
well-maintained, attractive site; gd welcome fr friendly
owners; pitches narr; excel, modern san facs; gate shut
1300-1500; bus service adj for archaeological museum
(unique ice man); gd cent for walks in Dolomites."*
€34.00   2020

BORGO SAN LORENZO *1D3* (7km SE Rural) *43.93087,
11.46426* **Camping Vicchio Ponte,** Via Costoli 16,
50039 Vicchio **055 8448306; info@campingvecchio
ponte.it; www.campingvecchioponte.it**

♞ ♦♦(cont) ⓦⓓ ⚅ / ⓂⓈⓅ 🦋 ✈nr ⓗnr ⛟nr

On SP551 adj to sw pool in Vicchio. 3*, Med, pt shd,
EHU (4A) inc; train to Florence 1km; Eng spkn; CKE.
*"Simple, municipal site; htd pool adj inc in price; v clean
san facs; v helpful staff."* **€24.00, 1 Jun-15 Sep.**
**   2016**

ITALY

BORGO SAN LORENZO *1D3* (5km W Rural)
43.96144, 11.30918 **Camping Mugello Verde,** Via
Massorondinaio 39, 50038 San Piero-a-Sieve (FI)
**055 848511; mugelloverde@florencecamping.
com; www.florencecamping.com**

♀♀ (htd) ⬜ ⬛ ⚲ ⟵ ⚙ ⚕ ⬛ ✈ ❀ ⚖ Ⲡ ⬛ ⬛ ⚠ ⚒ ⚲

Exit A1 at Barberino exit & foll Barberino sp twd
San Piero-a-Sieve & Borgo San Lorenzo. Turn S on
S65 twd Florence. Site sp immed after Cafaggiolo.
3*, Lge, pt shd, sl, terr, EHU (6A) inc; gas; 50% statics;
bus/train; ccard acc; tennis; bike hire; CKE. *"Hillside
site; bus to Florence high ssn (fr vill LS) or 20 mins
drive; hard grnd diff for awnings; poss long walk to
recep & shop; helpful, friendly, gd, clean san facs;
avoid early Jun - Italian Grand Prix!."*
€34.00, 16 Mar-3 Nov.   2019

BORGO SAN LORENZO *1D3* (28km NW Rural)
44.09810, 011.26836 **Camping La Futa,** Via Bruscoli
Futa, 889/h, Firenzuola **3289248746; info@camping
lafuta.it; www.campinglafuta.it**

♀€2 ♀♀ ⬜ ⬛ ⚲ ⟵ ⚙ ⚕ ⬛ ✈ ⚖ ⬛ ⬛ ⚒ ⚲ (htd)

A1 Bologna to Firenze - exit Roncobiaccio SS65 to
Passo Della Futa. Site close to pass. 2*, Med, mkd, pt
shd, terr, EHU (10A); bbq; twin axles; TV; 25% statics;
phone; Eng spkn; adv bkg acc; games rm; games area;
CKE. *"Excel site."* **€28.00, 15 Apr-30 Sep.**   2016

BRACCIANO *2E4* (3km N Rural) *42.1300, 12.17333*
Kwan Village Roma Flash Sporting, Via Settevene
Palo 42, 00062 Bracciano **0699 805458 or 3389
951738 LS; info@romaflash.it; www.romaflash.it**

♀€5.50 ♀♀ ⬜ ⬛ ⚲ ⚕ ⬛ ⬛ ✈ ❀ ⚖ Ⲡ ⬛ ⬛ ⚠ ⚒ ⚲

Fr A1 exit at Magliano Sabina dir Civita Castellana.
Then foll sp Nepi, Sutri, Trevignano & Bracciano.
Sp on lakeside rd N of Bracciano. 3*, Lge, mkd,
pt shd, EHU (6A) inc; bbq (charcoal, gas); sw; TV;
5% statics; bus to Bracciano, bus/train to Rome; Eng
spkn; ccard acc; games rm; sauna; horseriding 4km;
bike hire; fishing; watersports; tennis. *"Attractive,
well-kept lakeside site; clean, modern san facs; fitness
cent; no o'fits over 12m; sep car park; conv Rome."*
€42.00, 1 Apr-29 Sep, Y16.   2020

CANAZEI *1D1* (2km W Rural) *46.47479, 11.74067*
Camping Miravalle, Strèda de Greva 39, 38031
Campitello-di-Fassa (TN) **0462 750502; info@
campingmiravalle.it; www.campingmiravalle.it**

♀€4 ♀♀ ⬜ ⬛ ⚲ ⟵ ⚙ ⚕ ⬛ ✈ ❀ ⚖ ⬛ nr ⬛ nr

In vill cent on rte 48 site sp down side rd. 3*, Lge,
unshd, sl, EHU (6A) inc (poss rev pol), extra €2 for 6A;
Eng spkn; adv bkg acc; ccard acc; CKE. *"Excel new san
facs 2015; conv cable car."* **€37.00, 1 Jan-30 Mar,
1 Jun-30 Sep & 1 Dec-31 Dec.**   2015

CANNOBIO *1C1* (0.5km N Urban) *46.06678, 8.69507*
Camping Del Sole, Via Sotto i Chiosi 81/A, 28822
Cannobio (VB) **0323 70732; info@campingsole.it;
www.campingsole.it**

♀€3 ♀♀ ⬜ ⬛ ⚲ ⟵ ⚙ ⚕ ⬛ ✈ ❀ ⚖ Ⲡ ⬛ nr ⚠ ⚲

Fr S fr A26 foll Verbania sp then sp Cannobio or
Locarno. Ent vill, over cobbles, 2nd R in 750m.
Bef rv bdge immed sharp R under main rd, site
on L after quick R turn. Fr N ent Cannobio, 1st L
after x-ing rv, then as above. 2*, Lge, hdg, mkd,
hdstg, pt shd, EHU (4A) €3; gas; sw nr; red long stay;
60% statics; Eng spkn; CKE. *"Attractive vill & lake
frontage; friendly, family-run site; poss tight access
some pitches; lovely pool area; cramped pitches; diff to
park m'van; dated clean san facs; close to town; fair."*
€34.00, 1 Mar-3 Nov.   2019

CANNOBIO *1C1* (1km N Rural) *46.07791, 8.69345*
Villaggio Camping Bosco, Punta Bragone, 28822
Cannobio (VB) **0323 71597; bosco@boschetto
holiday.it; www.boschettoholiday.it/bosco**

♀€4 ♀♀ ⬜ ⬛ ⚲ ⟵ ⚙ ⚕ ⬛ ✈ ⚖ ⬛ ⬛ ⚲ shgl

On W side of lakeshore rd bet Cannobio & Swiss
frontier. Sh steep app to site & hairpin bend fr narr
rd, unsuitable for car/c'van o'fits & diff for m'vans.
2*, Med, pt shd, terr, EHU (3A) €3.90; gas; bbq;
sw; Eng spkn; adv bkg rec; CKE. *"All pitches with
magnificent lake view; beautiful town; hot water to
shwrs only."* **€32.30, 1 Apr-22 Oct.**   2017

CANNOBIO *1C1* (1.5km SW Rural) *46.05756, 8.67831*
Camping Valle Romantica, Via Valle Cannobina,
28822 Cannobio (VB) **0323 71249; valleromantica@
riviera-valleromantica.com; www.riviera-valle
romantica.com**

♀€4 ♀♀ ⬜ ⬛ ⚲ ⟵ ⚙ ⚕ ⬛ ✈ ❀ ⚖ ⬛ ⬛ ⚠ ⚲

Turn W on S o'skirts of Cannobio, sp Valle
Cannobina. In 1.5km at fork keep L. Site immed
on R. On ent site cont to bottom of hill to park &
walk back to recep. 2*, Lge, hdg, mkd, pt shd, pt sl,
terr, EHU (4-6A) €4.50; 25% statics; adv bkg acc; golf
12km. *"Vg; some sm pitches; particularly helpful&
friendly staff; narr site rds poss diff m'vans; masses
of flowers; beautiful situation; footpath to town,
poss cr high ssn; v well kept; req to show passport."*
€41.50, 1 Apr-11 Sep.   2017

CAORLE *2E2* (5km SW Coastal) *45.56694, 12.79416*
Camping Villaggio San Francesco, Via Selva Rosata
1, Duna Verde, 30020 Porto-Santa-Margherita (VE)
**0421 299333; info@villaggiostrancesco.com;
www.villaggiosfrancesco.com**

♀€3 ♀♀ ⬜ ⬛ ⚲ ⟵ ⚙ ⚕ ⬛ ✈ ❀ ⚖ Ⲡ ⬛ ⬛ ⚒ ⚲ adj

Fr A4/E70 exit Santo Stino di Livenza, then dir
Caorle. By-pass town & cont on coast rd, site sp on
L. 4*, V lge, shd, EHU (6A) inc; gas; TV; 60% statics;
phone; waterslide; windsurfing; games area; solarium;
bike hire; games rm; tennis; boat hire; waterskiing;
CKE. *"Excel family facs; min 2 nights' stay."*
€44.60, 24 Apr-25 Sep.   2016

CAPRAROLA *2E4* (6km NW Rural) *42.33504, 12.20488* **Camping Natura,** Loc Sciente Le Coste, 01032 Caprarola (VT) **333 2505792; campingnatura@gmail. com; www.camping-natura.com**

🐕€3 ♀♀ WC ♨ ♿ / MP 🦋 ♈ 🍽 🛒 🚣

Fr Viterbo take Via Cimina sp Ronciglione. After approx 19km bef Ronciglione turn R sp Nature Reserve Lago di Vico, in 200m turn R, site sp on R in 3km. 3*, Med, mkd, pt shd, EHU (4A) €3; sw nr; ccard acc. *"Friendly site; guided walks in nature reserve; run down LS & ltd facs."* **€18.00, Easter-30 Sep.** 2020

CASALBORDINO *2F4* (7km NE Coastal) *42.20018, 14.60897* **Camping Village Santo Stefano,** S16, Km 498, 66020 Marina-di-Casalbordino (CH) **0873 918118; info@campingsantostefano.com; www.camping santostefano.com**

♀♀ WC ♨ ♈ 🍽 ⊕ 🛒 🚣 ⚽ / 🦋 🏊 🛝 🅿adj

Exit A14 Vasto N onto S16 dir Pescara, site at km 498 on R. 3*, Med, mkd, shd, EHU (6A) inc; 10% statics; Eng spkn; adv bkg acc; CKE. *"Pleasant, well-maintained, family-run site; sm pitches; beautiful private beach & pool area; gd rest."* **€48.00, 21 Apr-23 Sep.** 2019

CASTELSANTANGELO SUL NERA *2E3* (4km S Rural) *42.88223, 13.18181* **Camping Monte Prata,** Loc. Schianceto, 62030 Castel S Angelo Sul Nera **33 86 54 49 24 or 33 32 95 18 60 (mob); sostare@camping monteprata.it; www.campingmonteprata.it**

🐕 ♀♀ (htd) WC ♨ ♿ / 🦋 🐾 ♈ ⊕ 🛒 🚣 🏊

Fr SP209 Muccia-Visso. Thro Visso on the Strada Provinciale 134 twds Castelsantangelo Sur Nera. Aft vill slight R onto SP 136. Campsite on L after vill of Gualdo. 3*, Med, mkd, hdstg, pt shd, terr, EHU; bbq; Eng spkn; ccard acc; games area. *"Gd site; excel position nr top of Monte Prata; guided walks & other excursions fr site in Nat Park."* **€33.00, 15 Jun-15 Sep.** 2019

CASTIGLIONE DEL LAGO *2E3* (1km N Rural) *43.13460, 12.04383* **Camping Listro,** Via Lungolago, Lido Arezzo, 06061 Castiglione-del-Lago (PG) **075 951193; listro@ listro.it; www.listro.it**

♀♀ WC ♨ ♿ 🛒 / ♈ ⊕ nr 🚣 🏊

Fr N A1 Val di Chiana exit 75 bis Perugia, site clearly sp on N edge of town on lakeside. 2*, Med, mkd, pt shd, EHU (3A) inc (poss rev pol); gas; sw nr; red long stay; Eng spkn; adv bkg acc; ccard acc; tennis nr; bike hire; CKE. *"On W shore of Lake Trasimeno; facs stretched when site full; v helpful staff; sand beach & lake sw adj; bus to Perugia; rlwy stn 1km for train to Rome; 'tree fluff' a problem in spring; new san facs (2016); poor elecs."* **€22.30, 1 Apr-30 Sep.** 2016

CAVALLINO *2E2* (2.5km S Coastal) *45.46726, 12.53006* **Union Lido Park & Resort,** Via Fausta 258, 30013 Cavallino (VE) **041 968080 or 2575111; info@unionlido.com; www.unionlido.com**

♀♀ (htd) WC ♨ ♿ 🛒 / MP ♈ ♈ 🍽 ⊕ 🚣 🏊 ⚽ 🏊 🚣

Exit a'strada A4 (Mestre-Trieste) at exit for airport or Quarto d'Altino & foll sp for Jesolo & then Punta Sabbiono; site on L 2.5km after Cavallino. V lge, mkd, shd, serviced pitches; EHU (6A) inc; gas; 50% statics; Eng spkn; adv bkg acc; ccard acc; gym; bike hire; watersports; horseriding; tennis; boating; golf; sauna; fishing. *"Variable pitch size; sat TV; late arr (after 2100) area with EHU; min stay 7 days high ssn; children's lagoon with slides; some pitches soft sand (a spade useful!); church; banking facs; Italian lessons; wellness cent; many long-stay campers; skating rink; hairdresser; babysitting; no admissions 1230-1500 (poss busy w/end); excursions; varied entmnt programme high ssn; well-organised, well-run; clean facs; worth every penny! excel."* **€66.00, 21 Apr-10 Oct.** 2017

CAVALLINO *2E2* (5km SW Coastal) *45.45638, 12.4960* **Camping Enzo Stella Maris,** Via delle Batterie 100, 30013 Cavallino-Treporti (VE) **041 966030; info@enzostellamaris.com; www.enzostellamaris.com**

♀♀ WC ♨ ♿ 🛒 / MP 🦋 ♈ ♈ 🍽 ⊕ 🛒 🚣 🏊 / 🏊 (htd) 🅿 sand adj

Exit A4 at sp for airport. Foll sp Jesolo, Cavallino, Punta Sabbioni rd SW. Site sp after Ca'Ballarin. 5*, Lge, mkd, pt shd, serviced pitches; EHU (10A) inc; gas; red long stay; TV; 25% statics; phone; Eng spkn; ccard acc; fitness rm; clsd 1230-1600 & 2300-0700; games area; CKE. *"Well-run, friendly, family-owned site; excel facs; beware mosquitoes; indoor htd pool; wellness cent; €30 in LS."* **€60.00, 29 Apr-22 Oct.** 2017

CAVALLINO *2E2* (6km SW Coastal) *45.44872, 12.47116* **Camping Dei Fiori,** Via Vettor Pisani 52, 30010 Cavallino-Treporti (VE) **041 966448; fiori@vacanze-natura.it; www.deifiori.it**

♀♀ WC ♨ ♿ / MP 🦋 ♈ ♈ 🍽 ⊕ 🛒 🚣 🏊 ⚽ 🏊 🅿 sand adj

Fr Lido di Jesolo foll sp to Cavallino; site on L approx 6km past Cavallino & bef Ca'Vio. 4*, Lge, mkd, shd, serviced pitches; EHU (5A) inc (poss rev pol); gas; red long stay; Eng spkn; adv bkg req; ccard acc; games area. *"V clean & quiet even in Aug; excel facs & amenities; conv water bus stop at Port Sabbioni; hydro massage therapy; 3/5 day min stay med/high ssn; highly rec; excel."* **€22.50, 19 Apr-30 Sep.** 2016

CECINA *1D3* (3km NW Coastal) *43.31850, 10.47440*
Camping Mareblu, Via dei Campilunghi, Mazzanta,
57023 Cecina Mare (Li) 0586 629191; info@camping
mareblu.com; www.campingmareblu.com

🐕 🏕 ᴡᴄ 🏊 ᴊ ♿ 🚿 ⚡ ᴍsᴘ ⛱ ♈ ⑪ 🍴 🎿 ᴧ 🏊 🚣 🌲 sand adj

Fr S on SS1 exit sp Cecina Nord & foll dir Mazzanta,
site sp. Fr N exit sp Vada then Mazzanta. 3*, Lge,
hdg, mkd, pt shd, EHU (3A) inc; gas; bbq (gas);
10% statics; phone; Eng spkn; adv bkg acc; ccard acc;
CKE. *"Lge pitches; gd facs & pool area; car must be
parked in sep car park; no dogs Jul/Aug; ATM; well-
organised, friendly site."* €42.50, 1 Apr-21 Oct.   2017

CERVIA *2E2* (3.6km S Coastal) *44.24760, 12.35901*
Camping Adriatico, Via Pinarella 90, 48015 Cervia (RA)
0544 71537; info@campingadriatico.net; www.camping
adriatico.net

🐕 €6 🏕 ᴡᴄ 🏊 ♿ 🚿 ⚡ 🍴 ⑪ 🎿 ᴧ 🏊 🚣 (htd) 🌲 sand 600m

On SS16 S fr Cervia twd Pinarella, turn L at km post
175, over rlwy line & take 1st R, site sp. 3*, Lge, shd,
EHU (6A) inc; TV; 40% statics; Eng spkn; adv bkg acc;
ccard acc; fishing; tennis 900m; golf 5km; CKE. *"V
pleasant site; friendly staff; gd san facs; excel pizza at
rest; ACSI acc."* €33.70, 14 Apr-19 Sep.   2016

CESENATICO *2E2* (2km N Coastal) *44.21584, 12.37798*
Camping Zadina, Via Mazzini 184, 47042 Cesenatico
(FC) 0547 82310; info@campingzadina.it;
www.campingzadina.it

🐕 €7 🏕 ᴡᴄ 🏊 ♿ 🚿 ⚡ ᴍsᴘ ⛱ ♈ ⑪ 🎿 ᴧ 🚣 🌲 sand

Leave A14 at Cesena Sud; foll sp Cesenático; after
10.5km turn R at T-junc onto SS16; after 2km fork L
over level x-ing; site on L. Lge, mkd, pt shd, terr, EHU
(6A) inc; gas; bbq; 80% statics; Eng spkn; adv bkg acc;
sep car park; fishing. *"Sea water canal runs thro site;
pitches poss tight lge o'fits; gd."*
€43.00, 18 Apr-22 Sep.   2019

CHIOGGIA *2E2* (2km E Urban/Coastal) *45.19027,
12.30361* **Camping Miramare,** Via A. Barbarigo 103,
30015 Sottomarina (VE) 041 490610; campmir@tin.it;
www.miramarecamping.com

🐕 €3.50 🏕 ᴡᴄ 🏊 ♿ 🚿 ⚡ ᴍsᴘ ⛱ ♈ ⑪ 🎿 ᴧ 🚣 🌲 sand

Fr SS309 foll sp Sottomarina. In town foll brown
sp to site. 3*, Lge, mkd, pt shd, EHU (6A) inc; gas;
75% statics; adv bkg acc; ccard acc; games area; CKE.
*"Busy site; friendly staff; gd entmnt facs for children;
cycle tracks to picturesque Chioggia; site 10 min walk fr
ferry point and beach or free shuttle bus service until
mid Sept; free sun umbrella for the beach front; rec;
visit Venice by bus/ferry; pitches generous; private
beach beautifully kept; site rest vg."*
€38.00, 19 Apr-24 Sep.   2018

CHIUSA/KLAUSEN *1D1* (0.7km E Rural) *46.64119,
11.57332* **Camping Gamp,** Via Griesbruck 10, 39043
Chiusa/Klausen (BZ) 0472 847425; info@camping-
gamp.com; www.camping-gamp.com

12 🐕 €3.50 🏕 (htd) ᴡᴄ 🏊 ♿ 🚿 ⚡ ᴍsᴘ ⛱ ♈ ⑪ 🎿 ᴧ 🏊

Exit A22 Chiusa/Klausen & bear L at end of slip rd
(sp Val Gardena). Site on L at rd fork 800m, sp.
3*, Sm, mkd, pt shd, EHU (6A) €2.60; TV (pitch);
phone; Eng spkn; CKE. *"Excel cent for mountain
walks; Chiusa attractive town; immac facs, sep m'van
o'night area; busy site; table tennis; htd ski & boot rm;
some pitches sm for lge o'fits; sep m'van o'night facs;
discount with Camping Euro card."* €34.00   2019

COMO *1C1* (5km S Urban) *45.78385, 9.06034*
**Camping No Stress (formerly International Camp-
Sud),** Breccia, Via Cecilio, 22100 Como 031 521435;
campingint@hotmail.com; camping-internazionale.
business.site

🐕 €2 🏕 🏊 🚿 ⚡ ♈ ⑪ 🎿 ᴧ 🏊

Fr E to Como, on SS35 Milano rd foll sp a'strada
Milano; site on Como side of rndabt at junc S35 &
S432; ent/exit diff unless turn R. Or take 2nd exit off
m'way after border (Como S), site sp.
2*, Med, pt shd, pt sl, EHU (4-6A) €2.50 (rev pol); gas;
ccard acc; golf 5km; bike hire. *"Conv NH for m'way."*
€24.00, 1 Apr-31 Oct.   2019

CORIGLIANO CALABRO *3A4* (10km N Coastal)
39.69130, 16.52233 **Camping Thurium,** Contrada
Ricota Grande, 87060 Ricota Grande (CS) 0983 851101;
info@campingthurium.com;
www.campingthurium.com

12 🐕 €4.80 🏕 ᴡᴄ 🏊 ♿ 🚿 ⚡ ᴍsᴘ ⛱ ♈ ⑪ 🎿 ᴧ 🏊 🚣 🌲 sand adj

Exit SS106 at km stone 21. Site sp on gd app rd for
2km. Rd narr and bumpy in places. Do not foll sat
nav. 4*, Lge, mkd, pt shd, EHU inc (3-6A); gas; twin
axles; 20% statics; Eng spkn; games area; tennis;
bike hire; CKE. *"Vg well-run site; windsurfing lessons;
site rdways narr on corner, tight for lge o'fits; fair."*
€49.00   2019

CORIGLIANO CALABRO *3A4* (7km N Coastal)
39.70333, 16.52583 **Camping Onda Azzurra,**
Contrada Foggia, 87064 Corigliano-Calabro (CS) 0983
851157; info@onda-azzurra.it; www.onda-azzurra.it

12 🐕 €3 🏕 (htd) ᴡᴄ 🏊 ♿ 🚿 ⚡ ♈ ⑪ 🎿 ᴧ 🌲 sand adj

On SS106-bis Taranto to Crotone rd, after turn off
for Sibari, cont S for 6km. Turn L at 4 lge sp on 1
notice board by lge sep building, 2km to site on
beach. 3*, Lge, mkd, pt shd, EHU (6-10A) €3-4; red long
stay; 10% statics; adv bkg acc; ccard acc; tennis; bike
hire; CKE. *"Excel, well-run site all ssns - facs open all
yr; popular long stay; clean facs; lge pitches; water not
drinkable; v friendly helpful owner; popular in winter;
special meals Xmas/New Year; site conv Sybaris &
Rossano; high standard site; excel friendly welcome;
free acitivities LS."* €31.00   2019

CORIGLIANO CALABRO *3A4* (8km N Coastal) *39.68141, 16.52160* **Camping Il Salice,** Contrada da Ricota Grande, 87064 Corigliano-Calabro (CS) **0983 851169; info@salicevacanze.it; www.salice vacanze.it**

⏹12 🐕 €4 � (htd) [wc] 🚿♨️🔥🚮✎ 🏪 🍴 ⊕🏖🛒 ⚲ 🏄

🌲 sand adj

Exit A3 dir Sibari onto SS106 bis coast rd dir Crotone. At 19km marker after water tower on L, turn L sp Il Salice - 1.5km to new access rd to site on L. Site sp easily missed. 4*, Lge, mkd, hdstg, pt shd, pt sl, serviced pitches; EHU (3-6A) inc; gas; bbq; TV; 70% statics; phone; Eng spkn; watersports; games area; tennis; games rm; bike hire; CKE. *"Narr rds thro vill to site - care needed when busy; v popular, well-run winter destination; haphazard siting in pine trees; clean, private beach; modern san facs; ltd facs LS; big price red LS; scenic area."* **€48.00** 2020

CORTINA D'AMPEZZO *2E1* (3.5km S Rural) *46.51858, 12.1370* **Camping Dolomiti,** Via Campo di Sotto, 32043 Cortina-d'Ampezzo (BL) **0436 2485; campeggio dolomiti@tin.it; www.campeggiodolomiti.it**

🐕 � (htd) [wc] 🚿♨️🔥✎ 🦋 🍴 ⊕nr 🛒 ⚲🏪 🏄 (htd)

2km S of Cortina turn R off S51. Site beyond Camping Cortina & Rocchetta. 4*, Lge, mkd, pt shd, EHU (4A) inc (check earth); gas; 10% statics; phone; bus; Eng spkn; ccard acc; games area; games rm. *"Superb scenery in mountains, gd walks; cycle rte into Cortina; helpful owner; beautiful setting; choice of open meadow or shd woodland pitches; gd facs; excel shwrs."* **€24.00, 1 Jun-20 Sep.** 2019

"Satellite navigation makes touring much easier"

Remember most sat navs don't know if you're towing or in a larger vehicle – always use yours alongside maps and site directions.

CORVARA IN BADIA *1D1* (2km W Rural) *46.55111, 11.8575* **Camping Colfosco,** Via Sorega 15, 39030 Corvara-in-Badia (BZ) **0471 836515; info@camping colfosco.org; www.campingcolfosco.org**

🐕 €4 � [wc] 🚿♨️✎ 🍴 🦋 🍴 ⊕nr 🛒 🏪

Leave A22 (m'way fr Brenner) at Bressanone exit foll E66/S49 E. At San Lorenzo turn S on S244 for 28km to Corvara. In town turn R dir Colfosco, foll sp. 1*, Lge, hdstg, unshd, pt sl, EHU (16A) €0.70 per kWh; bbq; twin axles; Eng spkn; adv bkg acc; ccard acc, sep car park; golf 4km; site clsd 1200-1500; games rm. *"Fine scenery & walks; well-managed site; sh walk to vill; gd base for skiing (ski in & out of site) & mountain biking; ski lift 300m; ski bus; lift/bus passes avail; vg san facs; somewhat bleak hdstg area; site lies at 5000ft - cool nights; cycle track, walking routes nr; gd base for Passo Pordoi; vg."* **€35.50, 5 Jan-6 Apr & 7 Jun-20 Dec.** 2018

COURMAYEUR *1A1* (6.2km NE Rural) *45.83293, 6.99095* **Campsite Grandes Jorasses,** Via per la Val Ferret 53, 11013 Courmayeur (Valle d'Aosta) **0165 869708; info@grandesjorasses.com; www.grandes jorasses.com**

� [wc] 🚿♨️🔥🚮✎🏪 🍴🍴 ⊕🏖🛒

Foll the brown 'Val Ferret' signs bet Courmayeur and the Mont Blanc tunnel, and the campsite is located a few km on the L of the rd. Med, hdstg, pt shd,; games rm; CKE. *"Beautiful site at the foot of Mt Blanc; nature trails thro forest; trekking expeditions arranged; gd rest."* **€26.00, 20 Jun-15 Sep.** 2019

"There aren't many sites open at this time of year"

If you're travelling outside peak season remember to call ahead to check site opening dates – even if the entry says 'open all year'.

COURMAYEUR *1A1* (6km SE Rural) *45.76333, 7.01055* **Camping Arc en Ciel,** Loc Feysoulles, 11017 Morgex (AO) **0165 809257; info@ campingarcenciel.it; www.campingarcenciel.it**

⏹12 🐕 €1 � (htd) [wc] 🚿♨️🔥🚮✎🏪 🦋 🍴 ⊕ 🛒 nr

Fr A5/E25 take Morgex exit, turn L to vill & foll sp dir Dailley. Site in 1km on L, sp. Fr tunnel take SS25 to Morgex, then as above. 1*, Med, pt shd, terr, EHU (3-6A) €1-€2; bbq; 30% statics; adv bkg acc; ccard acc; sep car park; site clsd 6 Nov-8 Dec; rafting; CKE. *"Gd, clean san facs; views Mont Blanc fr some pitches; vg; ski lift 8km; mountain climbing; ski bus; views of the mountains marvellous; helpful manager."* **€27.00** 2019

DEIVA MARINA *1C2* (3km E Coastal) *44.22476, 9.55146* **Villaggio Camping Valdeiva,** Loc Ronco, 19013 Deiva-Marina (SP) **0187 824174; camping@ valdeiva.it; www.valdeiva.it**

🐕 � [wc] 🚿♨️✎🍴 🍴 ⊕🛒🏪 🏄 🏖 🐕 shgl 3km

Fr A12 exit Deiva Marina, site sp on L in approx 4km by town sp. 3*, Med, mkd, hdstg, pt shd, pt sl, EHU (3-6A) inc; bbq; TV (pitch); 90% statics; phone; bus to stn; Eng spkn; adv bkg rec; ccard acc; CKE. *"Free minibus to stn - conv Cinque Terre or Portofino; helpful, friendly staff; gd rest; sep car park high ssn; excel walking; v quiet LS & shwrs ltd; gd facs; can be long waits at rest; late night disco."* **€36.00, 1 Jan-8 Jan, 5 Feb-15 Nov & 3 Dec-31 Dec.** 2019

ITALY

DESENZANO DEL GARDA *1D2* (5km SE Rural)
45.46565, 10.59443 **Camping San Francesco,** Strada
V San Francesco, 25015 Desenzano-del-Garda (BS)
**030 9110245; booking@campingsanfrancesco.com;
www.campingsanfrancesco.com**

🐕 👫 WC 🛁 ♿ 🖥 ✎ 🍴 🛒 🏧 ⛺ 🎿 🏊

E fr Milan on A4 a'strada take exit Sirmione & foll sp
twd Sirmione town; join S11 twd Desenzano & after
Garden Center Flowers site 1st campsite on R after
rndabt; site sp twd lake bet Sirmione & Desanzano.
Or fr Desenzano, site just after Rivoltella. 5*, Lge,
mkd, shd, pt sl, EHU (6A) inc; gas; bbq (charcoal, gas);
sw; TV; 50% statics; phone; Eng spkn; adv bkg acc;
ccard acc; games area; sailing; boat hire; windsurfing;
canoe hire; golf 10km; fishing; bike hire; tennis; CKE.
*"Lovely lakeside pitches for tourers (extra); no o'fits
over 6m high ssn; muddy if wet; poss diff lge o'fits due
trees; helpful staff; well managed site; gd position
on edge of lake; recep clsd 1300-1500 & no vehicle
movement; handy for local bus; excel site; v clean facs;
gd rest."* **€53.70, 1 Apr-30 Sep.** 2019

DIANO MARINA *1B3* (4km NE Coastal) *43.92177,
8.10831* **Camping del Mare,** Via alla Foce 29, 18010
Cervo (IM) **0183 400130 or 0183 405556; info@
campingdelmare-cervo.com; www.campingdelmare-
cervo.com**

🐕 👫 WC 🛁 ♿ 🖥 ✎ 🦋 🍴 🛒 🏊 shgl adj

Exit A10/E80 at San Bartolomeo/Cervo onto Via
Aurelia. Turn L at traff lts twd Cervo. Sp adj rv bdge.
R turn acute - long o'fits app fr NE. 2*, Med, hdstg,
hdg, mkd, shd, EHU (6A) €2; gas; TV; 40% statics;
phone; Eng spkn; adv bkg rec; ccard acc. *"Immac site;
spacious pitches; friendly, helpful staff; picturesque
beach & perched vill (Cervo); easy walk San Bartolomeo;
gd mkts; highly rec site; pitches close together; office
closes 1200-1500."* **€45.00, 1 Apr-15 Oct.** 2019

"That's changed – Should I let the Club know?"

If you find something on site that's different
from the site entry, fill in a report and let us
know. See camc.com/europereport.

EDOLO *1D1* (1.5km W Rural) *46.17648, 10.31333*
Camping Adamello, Via Campeggio 10, Loc Nembra,
25048 Edolo (BS) **0364 71694 or 0333 8275354;
info@campingadamello.it; www.campingadamello.it**

12 🐕 €3 👫 WC 🛁 ♿ 🖥 🦋 🍴 ⊕nr 🛒

On rd 39 fr Edolo to Aprica; after 1.5km turn sharp L
down narr lane by rest; camping sp on rd; diff app.
3*, Med, pt shd, pt sl, terr, EHU (6A) €1.50; 50% statics.
*"Useful NH; beautiful mountain site; steep rds all round;
v diff app fr W; quiet for couples; nothing for children."*
€27.00 2016

FALZE DI PIAVE *2E1* (0.7km S Rural) *45.85674,
12.16565* **Parking Le Grave,** Via Passo Barca, 31020
Falze-di-Piave (TV) **0390 43886896; belleluigi@
libero.it; www.legrave.it**

12 WC ✎ 🦋 ⛺

Fr A27 exit Conegliano & turn R onto SP15 then
SS13 to Susegana. At Ponte-della-Priula turn onto
SP34 to Falze-di-Piave. Fr town cent turn L just past
war memorial into Via Passo Barca, site on R.
Sm, unshd, EHU (4A) inc; bbq. *"CL-type site in
delightful area; no wc or shwrs; friendly, helpful owner;
gd walking/cycling; wine tasting last w/end May."*
€10.00 2016

FERRARA *1D2* (3km NE Rural) *44.85303, 11.63328*
Campeggio Comunale Estense, Via Gramicia 76,
44100 Ferrara **0532 752396; campeggio.estense@
freeinternet.it or idem@libero.it**

12 🐕 €1.50 👫 (htd) WC 🛁 ♿ ✎ 🦋 ⊕nr 🛒nr

Exit A13 Ferrara N. After Motel Nord Ovest on L
turn L at next traff lts into Via Porta Catena. Rd
is 500m fr city wall around town; foll brown/
yellow sps - well sp fr all dirs. 3*, Med, pt shd, EHU
(6A) €3.50; Eng spkn; ccard acc; golf adj; site clsd
early-Jan to end-Feb; bike hire; CKE. *"Peaceful, well-
kept, clean site; helpful staff; lge pitches; ltd privacy
in shwrs; pool in park nrby; interesting, beautiful
town; gd cycle tracks round town; some stored
c'vans; rlwy stn in town for trains to Venice; gd NH;
watch out for low branches when driving thro site."*
€24.50, 1 Jan-11 Jan & 1 Mar-31 Dec. 2016

FIANO ROMANO *2E4* (2km W Rural) *42.15167,
12.57670* **Camping I Pini,** Via delle Sassete 1/A, 00065
Fiano-Romano **0765 453349; ipini@camping.it;
www.camping.it/roma/ipini**

🐕 €2 👫 (htd) WC 🛁 ♿ 🖥 ✎ 🦋 🍴 ⊕ 🏧 🎿 ⛺ 🏊

Fr A1/E35 exit sp Roma Nord/Fiano Romano (use
R-hand lane for cash toll), foll sp Fiano at rndabt.
Take 1st exit at next rndabt sp I Pini & stay on this
rd for approx 2km. Take 2nd exit at next rndabt, L
at T-junc under bdge, site sp on R. 4*, Med, mkd, hdg,
pt shd, pt sl, terr, EHU (6A) inc (poss rev pol); bbq;
TV; 60% statics; phone; bus; Eng spkn; adv bkg acc;
ccard acc; fishing; games rm; tennis; horseriding nr;
bike hire; CKE. *"Well-run, clean, excel san facs; helpful,
friendly staff; excel rest; access poss diff lge o'fits;
kerbs to all pitches; most pitches slope badly side to
side req double height ramps; no o'fits over 10m high
ssn; excursions by coach inc daily to Rome or gd train
service; super site."* **€37.50, 18 Apr-30 Sep, Y13.**
2019

FIE/VOLS *1D1* (3km N Rural) *46.53334, 11.53335*
Camping Alpe di Siusi/Seiser Alm, Loc San Constantino 16, 39050 Fiè-allo-Sciliar/Völs-am-Schlern (BZ) **0471 706459; info@camping-seiseralm.com; www.camping-seiseralm.com**

🐕 €4.50 ⛺🚿(htd) 🏪 ♨ 🚰 🚮 ♿ MSP 🦋 🛝 🍴 ⑭ 🅿️ 🛒 ⚠

Leave Bolzano on SS12 (not A22) sp Brixen & Brenner. After approx 7km take L fork in tunnel mouth sp Tiers, Fiè. Foll rd thro Fiè, site in 3km dir Castelrotto, sp on L. 4*, Lge, mkd, hdstg, unshd, terr, EHU (16A) metered; TV (pitch); 20% statics; phone; bus; Eng spkn; adv bkg acc; golf 1km; sauna; site clsd 5 Nov to 20 Dec; CKE. *"Well-organised site with gd views; impressive, luxury undergrnd san facs block; private san facs avail; vg walking/skiing; an amazing experience; v popular site; efficiently run!"*
€47.00, 1 Jan-2 Nov & 20 Dec-31 Dec. 2019

> ## "I like to fill in the reports as I travel from site to site"
>
> You'll find report forms at the back of this guide, or you can fill them in online at camc.com/europereport.

FIESOLE *1D3* (1km NE Rural) *43.80666, 11.30638*
Camping Panoramico, Via Peramonda 1, 50014 Fiesole (FI) **055 599069; panoramico@florence village.com; https://www.campingpanoramico fiesole.com/en/**

12 🐕 👫 WD 🏪 ♨ 🚰 ♿ 🚮 MSP 🦋 🍴 ⑭ 🛒 ⚠ 🏊

Foll sp for Fiesole & Camping Panoramico fr Florence; site on R. Rd to Fiesole v hilly & narr thro busy tourist area. 3*, Lge, pt shd, terr, EHU (3A) inc; gas; 20% statics; Bus; Eng spkn; ccard acc. *"Access v diff - more suitable tenters; site soggy in wet; ltd water points; Florence 20 mins bus but 1.5km steep walk to stop; excel views; excel site."* **€39.00** 2020

FIGLINE VALDARNO *1D3* (20km SW Rural) *43.53847, 11.41380* **Camping Orlando in Chianti,** Localita Caffggiolo, 52022 Cavriglia **055 967 422; info@ campingorlandoinchianti.it; www.campingorlando inchianti.it**

👫 WD 🏪 ♿ 🚮 MSP 🦋 🍴 ⑭ 🛒 🏊

Fr A1 Firenze-Roma, exit Incisa. Foll Figline Val d'Arno. Dir Greve in Chianti, exit at Lucolena, then foll signs to 'Piano Orlando Parco Cavriglia'. Med, hdstg, mkd, shd, pt sl, EHU (16A); bbq; 10% statics; Eng spkn; adv bkg acc; CCI. *"Vg site; excel priced rest; rural; v friendly staff."* **€40.00, 25 May-13 Oct.** 2019

FIGLINE VALDARNO *1D3* (2.5km W Rural) *43.61111, 11.44940* **Camping Norcenni Girasole Club,** Via Norcenni 7, 50063 Figline-Valdarno (FI) **055 915141; girasole@ecvacanze.it; www.ecvacanze.it**

🐕 👫 WD 🏪 ♨ ♿ 🚰 🚮 MSP 🍴 ⑭ 🛒 ⚠ 🏊 (covrd) 🏖

Fr a'strada A1, dir Rome, take exit 24 (sp Incisa SS69) to Figline-Valdarno; turn R in vill & foll sp to Greve; site sp Girasole; steep app rd to site with some twists for 3km. 4*, V lge, hdg, pt shd, terr, EHU (6A) inc; gas; bbq; twin axles; TV; bus to Florence; Eng spkn; adv bkg acc; ccard acc; sauna; horseriding; games area; tennis; excursions; jacuzzi; games rm; bike hire. *"Excel, well-run site; some pitches sm; fitness cent; steep site rds poss diff lge o'fits; private bthrm extra; steel pegs rec; upper level pool area excel for children; site clsd 1330-1530; site hilly; gd touring base."* **€50.00, 19 Apr-13 Oct, Y07.** 2017

FINALE LIGURE *1B2* (1.5km N Rural) *44.18395, 8.35349* **Eurocamping Calvisio,** Via Calvisio 37, 17024 Finale-Ligure (SV) **019 601240; info@ eurocampingcalvisio.it; www.eurocampingcalvisio.it**

🐕 👫 WD 🏪 ♿ 🚰 🚮 🦋 🍴 ⑭ 🛒 ⚠ 🏊 🏖

⛺ sand 2km

On SS1 Savona-Imperia, turn R at ent to Finale-Ligure; sp to site in Calvisio vill. 3*, Med, mkd, hdg, shd, EHU (6A) inc; 80% statics; adv bkg acc; ccard acc; solarium. *"Security guard at night; sep car park high ssn; clean, well-maintained san facs."*
€54.50, Easter-5 Nov. 2016

FIRENZE *1D3* (24km SE Rural) *43.70138, 11.40527* **Camping Village Il Poggetto,** Strada Provinciale Nr1 Aretina Km14, 50067 Troghi **055 8307323; info@campingilpoggetto.com; www.campingil poggetto.com**

🐕 €2.20 👫 WD 🏪 ♨ ♿ 🚰 🚮 MSP 🦋 🍴 ⑭ 🛒 ⚠ 🏊

Fr S on E35/A1 a'strada take Incisa exit & turn L dir Incisa. After 400m turn R dir Firenze, site in 5km on L. Fr N on A1 exit Firenze-Sud dir Bagno a Ripoli/S. Donato; go thro S. Donato to Troghi, site on R, well sp. Narr, hilly app rd & sharp turn - app fr S easier. Lge, mkd, hdg, pt shd, pt sl, terr, EHU (7A) inc (poss rev pol); gas; red long stay; 5% statics; phone; bus adj; Eng spkn; adv bkg req; ccard acc; table tennis; bike hire; CKE. *"Superb, picturesque, family-run site in attractive location inc vineyard; clean, modern facs; lovely pool; bus to Florence 45mins - tickets fr recep; trains fr Incisa Valdarno (free parking at stn); excursions; gd rest; LS offers for long stay (7+ days); money exchange; vg site; helpful staff; private san facs avail; lge o'fits come fr S; highly rec."*
€37.00, 1 Apr-15 Oct. 2017

FORNI DI SOPRA *2E1* (2km E Rural) *46.42564, 12.56928* **Camping Tornerai,** Stinsans. Via Nazionale, 33024 Forni-di-Sopra (UD) **0433 88035; www.camping tornerai.it**

🏠 12 🐕 €2 👫(cont) ⓦ 〰️ 🦋

Site sp on SS52 Tolmezzo-Pieve di Cadore rd, 2km E of Forni-di-Sopra (approx 35km by rd fr Pieve-di-Cadore). Sm, pt shd, pt sl, EHU (2A) €1 (extra for 6A) (long lead poss req); 50% statics; Eng spkn; ccard acc. *"Conv CL-type site for Forni-di-Sopra chairlift & Passo-della-Mauria; gd san facs."* **€20.00** 2016

GALLIPOLI *3A4* (4km SE Coastal) *39.99870, 18.02590* **Camping Baia di Gallipoli,** Litoranea per Santa Maria di Leuca, 73014 Gallipoli (LE) **0833 273210 or 338 8322910 LS; info@baiadigallipoli.com; www.baiadi gallipoli.com**

🐕 €3 👫(htd) ⓦ 🍽️ ♿ 🗑️ 〰️ 🦋 🎱 ♟️ 🍸
🅿️ 🍴 🦋 🏔️ ♿ 🛶 🐕 sand 800m

Fr Brindisi/Lecce take S101 to Gallipoli. Exit at sp Matino-Lido Pizzo & foll sp to slte, on coast rd bet Gallipoli & Sta Maria di Leuca. 4*, V lge, pt shd, EHU (6A) inc; bbq; TV; ccard acc; tennis; excursions; games area; sep car park. *"Gd site; small dogs only."* **€32.00, 1 Apr-31 Oct.** 2019

GENOVA *1C2* (15km W Coastal) *44.41437, 8.70475* **Caravan Park La Vesima,** Via Aurelia, Km 547, 16100 Arenzano (GE) **010 6199672; info@caravanpark lavesima.it; www.caravanparklavesima.it**

🏠 12 👫(htd) ⓦ 🍽️ ♿ 🗑️ 〰️ 🍸 🅿️ 🍴 🦋 🛶 shgl adj

E of Arenzano on coast rd, clearly sp. Or leave A10 at Arenzano & go E on coast rd. 2*, Med, mkd, hdstg, unshd, EHU (3A) inc (poss rev pol); gas; 90% statics; Eng spkn; adv bkg acc; CKE. *"Useful LS NH/sh stay; gd security; gd, clean san facs; v cr, noisy high ssn; some pitches sm; vg site."* **€35.00** 2018

GOLDRAIN *1D1* (1km SW Urban) *46.61762, 10.81859* **Camping Cevedale,** Via Val Venosta 59, 39021 Goldrain **0473 742132; info@camping-cevedale.com; www.camping-cevedale.com**

🐕 €4 👫 ⓦ 🍽️ ♿ 🗑️ 〰️ 🦋 🍽️ 🦋 (covrd, htd)

SS38 Merano-Silandro, pass Latsch/Laces to rndabt sp Goldrain/Martelltal, sp on R (do not confuse vill of Lasa/Laas). Med, hdg, pt shd, EHU (6A); bbq; phone; bus/train 50m; Eng spkn; adv bkg acc. *"Excel site."* **€35.50, 15 Mar-7 Nov.** 2015

GOREGLIA ANTELMINELLI *1D2* (0.8km N Rural) *44.06642, 10.52879* **Camping Pian d'Amora,** Via Crocifisso, Loc. Pian d'Amora, 55025 Coreglia Antelminelli **0583 78334; info@campingpiandamora. nl; www.campingpiandamora.nl**

👫 ⓦ 🍽️ ♿ 🗑️ 〰️ 🦋 🍸 🅿️ 🏔️ 🛶 (covrd, htd)

Fr A11 at Lucca foll sp Val Gaifagnama SS12. After 30km at Piano di Coreglia turn N on minor rd 7km to Coreglia Antelminelli. Site top of town. Sm, shd, terr, EHU (10A); Eng spkn; adv bkg acc. *"Beautiful historic hill top town, 5 min walk; gd walking area; conv Lucca; sm c'vans rec; excel."* **€35.50, 15 Apr-1 Oct.** 2015

GRAVEDONA *1C1* (3km SW Rural) *46.13268, 9.28954* **Camping Magic Lake,** Via Vigna del Lago 60, 22014 Dongo (CO) **034 480282; camping@magiclake.it; www.magiclake.it**

🐕 €3 👫(htd) ⓦ 🍽️ ♿ 🗑️ 〰️ MSP 🦋 🍸 🅿️ 🦋 nr ⛺

Site sp on S340d adj Lake Como. 2*, Sm, pt shd, pt sl, EHU (6A) inc; bbq; sw nr; red long stay; TV; 40% statics; bus 100m; Eng spkn; adv bkg acc; CKE. *"Excel, friendly, family-run site; walk, cycle to adj vills along lake; excel facs; v clean mod facs; bike/kayak hire on site; bike repairs on site; helpful staff."* **€30.00, 1 Apr-10 Oct.** 2016

GUBBIO *2E3* (1.2km W Urban) *43.35213, 12.56704* **Camping Parking Gubbio,** Via Bottagnone 06024 Area Communale P4 **07 59 27 20 37**

🏠 12 ⓦ MSP

Head NW on SR298 twd Via Bruno Buozzi, at rndbt take 2nd exit onto Viale Parruccini cont for 500m, take 1st exit at rndabt onto Viale Leonardo da Vinci, after 250m turn L onto Via Botagore. Sm, pt shd,. *"Only campervan parking allowed; no san facs; gd NH; historical town worth a visit."* **€5.00** 2019

IDRO *1D1* (2km NE Rural) *45.7540, 10.4981* **Rio Vantone,** Via Vantone 45, 25074 Idro (BS) **0365 83125; idro@azur-camping.de; www.idrosee.eu**

🐕 €5 👫 ⓦ 🍽️ ♿ 🗑️ 〰️ MSP 🦋 🍸 🅿️ 🍴 🦋 🏔️ ♿ 🛶

Fr Brescia, take S237 N. At S tip of Lago d'Idro, turn E to Idro. thro Crone, on E shore of lake, thro sh tunnel, site 1km on L, last of 3 sites. 4*, Lge, shd, serviced pitches; EHU (6A) inc; gas; TV; phone; adv bkg acc; ccard acc; games area; boat hire; windsurfing; bike hire; tennis; CKE. *"Idyllic on lakeside with beautiful scenery; lake adj; superb san facs; excel."* **€45.00, 20 Apr-30 Sept, Y08.** 2017

IMPERIA *1B3* (1km SW Coastal) *43.86952, 7.99810* **Camping de Wijnstok,** Via Poggi 2, 18100 Porto-Maurizio (IM) **0183 64986; info@campingdewijnstok. com; www.campingdewijnstok.com**

🏠 12 🐕 👫 ⓦ 🍽️ ♿ 🗑️ 〰️ 🦋 🍸 🅿️ 🍴 🦋 nr 🛶 shgl 500m

Exit A10/E80 Imperia W twds sea, take coast rd SS1 Via Aurelia dir San Remo. At km 651/1 turn dir Poggi, site sp. Med, shd, EHU (3A) €2; gas; TV; 80% statics; phone; ccard acc; sep car park; site clsd mid-Dec to mid-Jan. *"Shabby facs ltd LS; sm pitches diff for lge o'fits; sh walk to town; NH only."* **€31.00** 2016

ISEO *1C1* (0.5km NE Rural) *45.66416, 10.05722*
Camping Iseo, Via Antonioli 57, 25049 Iseo (BS) **030 980213; info@campingiseo.it; www.campingiseo.com**

🐕 €3.50 ♿ 🚿 ♿ 🚻 🔌 nr 🦋 ⛽ ⟁ ① nr ⟐ 📶 nr ⟁ 🌊
🌡️adj

Fr A4 exit sp Rovato & immed foll brown sp Lago d'Iseo. Site well sp in vill. 3*, Med, hdg, pt shd, serviced pitches; EHU (6-10A) €2; gas; 10% statics; phone; Eng spkn; adv bkg acc; windsurfing; golf 3km (red for campers); games area; bike hire; CKE. "V scenic; friendly, welcoming owner; well-organised, smart site; sm pitches; extra for lakeside pitches; well-maintained, clean facs but ltd; cruises on lake; many rests nr; excel; site next to a rlwy line, poss sm noise; sm pitches." **€37.00, 1 Apr-1 Nov.** **2017**

ISEO *1C1* (0.5km NE Rural) *45.66388, 10.05638*
Camping Punta d'Oro, Via Antonioli 51-53, 25049 Iseo (BS) **030 980084; info@camping-puntadoro.com; www.puntadoro.com**

🐕 €5 ♿ 🚿 ♿ 🚻 🔌 ⛽ ⟁ ① nr ⟐ 📶 nr ⟁ 🌡️shgl

Fr Brescia-Boario Terme into Iseo, look for `Camping d'Iseo' sp on corner; after 200m cross rlwy, 1st R to site in 400m on lakeside. Med, pt shd, pt sl, EHU (4A) inc; sw; Eng spkn; boating; golf 6km; CKE. "Gd security; beautiful area; friendly family run site, eager to help." **€35.50, 1 Apr-15 Oct.** **2017**

ISEO *1C1* (1km NE Rural) *45.66527, 10.06277*
Camping Quai, Via Antonioli 73, 25049 Iseo (BS) **030 9821610; info@campingquai.it; www.campingquai.it**

🐕 🐕 ♿ 🚿 ♿ 🔌 ⛽ ⟁ ① nr ⟐ 📶 nr ⟁

Fr Brescia-Boario Terme rd by-passing Iseo, take NE exit; look for 'Camping d'Iseo' sp on corner. After 200m cross rlwy, site sp (sps obscured - go slow). Site adj Punta d'Oro on lakeside. 3*, Med, mkd, shd, EHU (4A) inc (poss rev pol); bbq; sw nr; red long stay; 25% statics; phone; bus, train 1km; Eng spkn; adv bkg acc, ccard acc; watersports; boat launch; sep car park; games area. "Well-kept; lake views fr some pitches; helpful manager; some noise fr nrby rlwy." **€35.00, 20 Apr-20 Sep.** **2019**

ISEO *2F2* (1km E Urban) *45.66700, 10.06766* **Camping Covelo,** Via Covelo 18, 25049 Iseo **030 982 13 05; info@campingcovelo.it; www.campingcovelo.it**

🐕 €3.50 ♿ 🚿 🔌 ⛽ ⟁ ① ⟐ 📶

Fr A4 Bergamo-Brescia, take exit Palazzolo/SP469. Cont Onto SP12. At rndabt take 2nd exit SPxi. Take 3rd exit at next rndabt and foll sp to camp. Med, pt shd, EHU (6A); sw nr; Eng spkn; adv bkg acc; ccard acc; games area. "Excel site; v well run; adj to lake; beautiful views; range of watersports; v helpful staff." **€36.00, 18 Apr-3 Nov.** **2019**

ISEO *1C1* (1.5km W Rural) *45.65689, 10.03739*
Camping Del Sole, Via per Rovato 26, 25049 Iseo (BS) **030 980288; info@campingdelsole.it; www.camping delsole.it**

🐕 €3.50 ♿ 🚿 ♿ 🚻 🔌 📶 🦋 ⛽ ⟁ ① ⟐ 📶 ⟁ 🌊(htd) 🌡️

Exit Brescia-Milan a'strada at Rivato-Lago d'Iseo exit & foll sp to Iseo. At complex rd junc with rndabts on Iseo o'skirts, site ent on L (lge sp). Site bet lakeside & rd, bef API petrol stn on R. 4*, Lge, mkd, shd, EHU (6A) inc; sw; TV; 75% statics; Eng spkn; adv bkg acc; ccard acc; sep car park; bike hire; waterskiing; tennis; games area. "Glorious views; excel facs; htd private bthrms avail; well-run, pleasant, popular lakeside site; pitches poss closely packed; ltd waste/water disposal; no dogs high ssn; narr site rds." **€46.00, 15 Apr-25 Sep.** **2017**

ISEO *1C1* (1.5km W Rural) *45.65690, 10.03429*
Camping Sassabanek, Via Colombera 2, 25049 Iseo (BS) **030 980300; sassabanek@sassabanek.it; www.sassabanek.it**

♿ 🚿 ♿ 🔌 📶 🦋 ⛽ ① ⟐ 📶 ⟁ 🌊 🌡️

On periphery of Iseo by lakeside. 4*, Lge, pt shd, EHU (6A) inc; gas; bbq; TV; 50% statics; phone; adv bkg acc; ccard acc; boating; sep car park; bike hire; tennis; windsurfing; sauna. "Clean facs; sh walk to pretty lakeside & vill; helpful staff; gd NH/sh stay; nice location; cramped pitches; vg." **€39.00, 1 Apr-30 Sep.** **2017**

> ## "I need an on-site restaurant"
>
> We do our best to make sure site information is correct, but it is always best to check any must-have facilities are still available or will be open during your visit.

LAZISE *1D2* (1.5km N Urban) *45.50807, 10.73166*
Camping Lazise Campeggio Comunale (former Municipale), Via Roma 1,37017 Lazise (VR) **045 7580020; camping.municipale@comune.lazise.vr.it; www.comune.lazise.vr.it**

🐕 €3 ♿ 🚿 ♿ 🔌 📶 🦋 ⟁ nr ① nr ⟐ nr

N on S249 fr Peschiera, thro Pacengo & Lazise, at rndabt cont on S249 then turn L into Via Roma. Site sp at end of rd. Care req in 100m, sharp R turn; site ent pt hidden. 2*, Med, hdg, mkd, pt shd, EHU (10A) inc; sw nr; 5% statics; Eng spkn; ccard acc. "Gd touring cent; some pitches v muddy; gd, clean facs; friendly staff; avoid arr bef 1500 Wed (mkt on app rd); easy walk along lake to interesting sm town." **€33.00, 22 Mar-2 Nov.** **2018**

ITALY

LAZISE *1D2* (0.9km S Rural) *45.49861, 10.7375*
Camping Du Parc, Via Gardesana, 110 I, 37017 Lazise
(VR) **045 7580127; duparc@campingduparc.com;
www.campingduparc.com**

€5.70

Site on W side of lakeside rd SR249. 3*, Lge, hdg, pt
shd, pt sl, EHU (5A) inc (rev pol); sw; 15% statics; Eng
spkn; adv bkg acc; ccard acc; boat hire; waterslide;
gym; bike hire; watersports. *"Sh walk to old town &
ferry terminal; lovely lakeside position; excel, well-
maintained site; vg san facs; gd size pitches, some
on lake - long walk to water point; vg pizzeria & pool;
quiet; ideal for families; gd security; Magic of Europe
discount; vg; site improved every year; most pitches
have water & drain."* **€50.00, 15 Mar-4 Nov.**   2017

LAZISE *1D2* (1.5km S Rural) *45.49277, 10.73305*
Camping La Quercia, Loc Bottona, 37017 Lazise (VR)
**045 6470577; laquercia@laquercia.it;
www.laquercia.it**

€6.90 (htd)

sand

Exit A22/E45 at Affi/Lago di Garda Sud or exit A4/
E70 at Peschiera-del-Garda. Site on SR249, on SE
shore of lake. 4*, V lge, hdg, mkd, shd, pt sl, EHU (6A)
inc; gas; 15% statics; phone; adv bkg rec; watersports;
jacuzzi; gym; waterslide; games area; tennis. *"Superb
site for family holidays; many excel sports & leisure
facs; vehicle safety checks for cars/m'vans; some
pitches on lakeside; easy walk to town along beach;
highly rec."* **€61.00, 26 Mar-11 Oct.**   2020

LAZISE *1D2* (3.5km S Urban) *45.47912, 10.72635*
Camping Amici di Lazise, Loc Fossalta Nuova, Strada
del Roccolo 8, 37017 Lazise (VR) **045 6490146; info@
campingamicidilazise.it; www.campingamicidilazise.it**

12   €4.50

shgl 300m

S fr Lazise, immed bef high rest with Greek columns
(bef Gardaland) take side rd on R, site on R. 3*, Med,
pt shd, serviced pitches; EHU (6A) inc; 40% statics;
Eng spkn; adv bkg acc. *"Gd; nice friendly site; gd pool;
noise fr theme pk next door."* **€34.00**   2016

LECCE *3A4* (10km W Rural) *40.36417, 18.09889*
Camping Lecce Namaste, 73100 Lecce **0832 329647;
info@camping-lecce.it; www.camping-lecce.it**

12   nr

Fr Lecce ring rd exit junc 15 W dir Novoli, in 5km
immed after (abandoned) sm petrol stn turn R at
sp Namaste. App rd to site potholed/gravelled. Site
may appear clsd - sound horn for attention. Sm,
hdstg, shd, EHU (10A) inc; bus to Lecce. *"Gd, clean
site but dated facs; conv for Baroque city of Lecce &
coast around heel of Italy."* **€21.00**   2015

LECCO *1C1* (6km S Coastal) *45.81555, 9.39969*
Camping Village Riviera, Via Foppaola 113, 23852,
Garlate **0341 680346; info@campingvillageriviera.
com; www.campingvillageriviera.com**

(htd)   nr

Head S on SS36, take exit Pescate/Lecco, cont strt,
at rndbt take 3rd exit onto Via Roma, over rndbt,
cont onto Via Statale, turn L onto Via Foppaola, site
on L. Sm, hdg, pt shd, pt sl, EHU (10A); bbq (sep area);
sw; bus; adv bkg acc; CKE. *"Lake location with free
kayak, pedalo, gym, site poor; facs dirty and unkept
(2019); very noisy day and night."* **€25.00**   2019

LECCO *1C1* (4km W Rural) *45.81730, 9.34307*
Camping Due Laghi, Via Isella 34, 23862 Civate (LC)
**0341 550101; erealin@tin.it; www.duelaghicamping.
com**

€3   (cont)

S side of Lecco-Como rd on lake. Use slip rd mkd
Isella/Civate. Turn L at T-junc, then L over bdge; foll
v narr app rd to site, sp. 2*, Med, shd, pt sl, EHU (10A)
inc; gas; 80% statics; Eng spkn; games area. *"Lovely
lakeside pitches; gd facs; quiet except weekends; app to
site is v narr."* **€29.00, 28 Mar-15 Sep.**   2019

LEVANTO *1C2* (0.4km SE Urban/Coastal) *44.16656,
9.61366* **Camping Acqua Dolce,** Via Guido Semenza 5,
19015 Levanto (SP) **0187 808465; mail@camping
acquadolce.com; www.campingacquadolce.com**

12   nr   sand 300m

Site sp fr town cent, app rd to Levanto steep &
winding. Site ent steep. Pls do not use sat nav fr
town. 1*, Med, hdstg, mkd, shd, terr, serviced pitches;
EHU (6A) €2.50 (rev pol); phone; Eng spkn; adv bkg
acc; ccard acc; site clsd mid-Jan to end Feb; sep car
park. *"Site ent poss diff; sm pitches; vg, modern san
facs but unisex; o'fits parked v close high ssn; pool
250m; not rec c'vans over 6m; gd touring base Cinque
Terre vills; gd walks fr site; lovely, clean beach; easy
walk to boat terminal & rlwy stn."* **€38.50**   2015

LEVICO TERME *1D1* (1km S Rural) *46.00638,
11.28944* **Camping Lago Levico,** Via Pleina 5, 38056
Levico-Terme (TN) **0461 706934; info@camping
levico.com; www.campinglevico.com**

€2-6

shgl 200m

Foll sp to Levico fr A22 or SS12 onto SS27; site sp.
Lge, mkd, shd, serviced pitches; EHU (6A) inc; gas;
bbq; 30% statics; adv bkg acc; golf 7km. *"Health
spa nr; vg; supp for lakeside pitch (no dogs on these
pitches)."* **€38.00, 1 Apr-10 Oct.**   2017

LEVICO TERME *1D1* (5km SW Rural) *46.00392, 11.25838* **Camping Spiaggia,** Viale Venezia 12, 38050 Calceranica al Lago (TN) **0461 723037; info@ campingspiaggia.net; www.campingspiaggia.net**

Foll sp to Levico fr Trento; after exit rd turn L & in 400m turn L foll sp to site. Site after Camping Jolly on S side of lake. Med, mkd, hdg, pt shd, EHU inc; sw nr; 10% statics; Eng spkn. *"Gd site; private san facs avail; new san facs (2015) & private bthrms."* **€22.50, 10 Apr-27 Sep.** 2015

LEVICO TERME *1D1* (6km SW Urban) *46.00574, 11.24698* **Camping Penisola Verde,** Via Penisola Verde, 5 38050 Galceranica Al Lago **0461 723272; info@penisolaverde.it; www.penisolaverde.it**

Exit Trento-Padova SS47 either end of lake for Calceranica. Turn W in vill at camping sp, over rlwy x-ing and immed L to lakeside site. 2*, Med, mkd, hdstg, pt shd, EHU (6A); bbq; sw; twin axles; 10% statics; train 200m, bus 100m; Eng spkn; adv bkg acc; games area. *"Mountain views across lake; beach has sep area for sw, fishing & boating; excel."* **€36.00, 9 May-13 Sep.** 2015

LIDO DI JESOLO *2E2* (5.8km NE Coastal) *45.52862, 12.69693* **Campsite Parco Capraro,** Via Corer 2 ramo, 4 30016 Lido di Jesolo **0421 961073; info@parco capraro.it; www.parcocapraro.it**

Fr Jesolo head NE on Via Roma Destra twrds Via Giotto da Bondone. Cont onto Via Loghetto, then onto Via Cà Gamba, L onto Via Corer. Site on L. 3*, Lge, pt shd, EHU (16A); bbq; twin axles; TV; Eng spkn; games rm; bike hire. *"Vg; v well kept family site; public transport 1km; takeaway; path thro sm pine forest leads to beach & bus stop to cent of town; vg rest/bar; superb sw pool."* **€41.00, 5 Apr-15 Sep.** 2019

LIMONE SUL GARDA *1D1* (0.7km S Rural) *45.80555, 10.7875* **Camping Garda,** Via 4 Novembre, 25010 Limone-sul-Garda (TN) **0365 954550; horstmann. hotel@tin.it**

Site sp fr SS45b. 3*, Sm, hdstg, mkd, pt shd, pt sl, terr, EHU (3A) €1; sw; 10% statics; Eng spkn; adv bkg acc; bike hire; CKE. *"Splendid views; v friendly owner; clean, well-kept site adj to lake; excel pool; tired facs but OK (2014)."* **€38.00, 1 Apr-31 Oct.** 2015

LUCCA *1D3* (0.8km NW Urban) *43.85000, 10.48583* **Camper Il Serchio,** Via del Tiro a Segno 704, Santa Anna, 55100 Lucca (LU) **0583 317385; info@ camperilserchio.it; www.camperilserchio.it**

Sp fr main rds to Lucca & fr town. Gd access rds. Med, hdg, mkd, hdstg, pt shd, EHU (5A) inc; bbq; Shuttle service to the city centre; adv bkg acc; bike hire; tennis opp. *"Attractive pitches; mainly for m'vans - not suitable lge car/c'van o'fits or lge tents; games area opp; vg site."* **€25.00** 2020

LUINO *1C1* (6km N Rural) *46.04189, 8.73279* **Camping Lido Boschetto Holiday,** Via Pietraperzia 13, 21010 Maccagno (VA) **0332 560250; lido@ boschettoholiday.it; www.boschettoholiday.it/lido**

On E shore of Lake Maggiore on SS394 bet Bellinzona & Laveno. Fr Luino pass under 2 rlwy bdges & foll sp L twd lake, site clearly sp. Med, pt shd, EHU (3-4A) €3.50 (poss rev pol); sw nr; 4% statics; adv bkg acc; ccard acc; watersports; CKE. *"Hydrofoil/ ferries fr vill to all parts of lake; trains to Locarno; barrier clsd 1300-1500, no place to pk outside; well kept."* **€31.00, 31 Mar-22 Oct.** 2017

MAGIONE *2E3* (10km S Rural) *43.08140, 12.14340* **Camping Polvese,** Via della Sapienza - Sant'Arcangelo di Magione - 06063 **075 848078; polvese@polvese.com; www.polvese.com**

Fr A1 exit dir Lake Trasimeno to Castiglione-del-Lago, then S599 to San Arcangelo. 3*, Med, mkd, pt shd, EHU (10A) inc; gas; red long stay; 40% statics; phone; adv bkg acc; lake fishing; bike hire; games area; watersports; CKE. *"Gd touring base for Umbria; lakeside pitches avail; helpful staff."* **€22.00, 1 Apr-30 Sep.** 2020

MALCESINE *1D1* (0km N Urban) *45.76583, 10.81096* **Camping Villaggio Turistico Priori,** Via Navene 31, 37018 Malcesine (VR) **045 7400503; info@appartement-prioriantonio.it; www.appartement-prioriantonio.it**

Well sp in town cent. Take care if app fr N. 1*, Sm, mkd, hdstg, pt shd, pt sl, terr, EHU (3A) inc; sw nr; phone; Eng spkn; adv bkg acc; CKE. *"Vg; conv all amenities & Monte Baldo funicular."* **€24.00, 15 Apr-16 Oct.** 2016

MALCESINE *1D1* (3km N Rural) 45.78971, 10.82609
Camping Martora, Campagnola, Martora 2, 37018
Malcesine (VR) **045 4856733 or 338 1453795;**
martora@martora.it; www.martora.it

♦♦ �ⓦ ⌂ ✗ ⌁ 🦋 ⍨ ⑪ nr

On E side of lake on rd SS249 at km 86/11. Ent up
concrete rd bet iron gates at 'Prinz Blau' sp. 2*, Med,
mkd, pt shd, pt sl, EHU (4A) inc; sw nr; 10% statics;
adv bkg acc; windsurfing adj. *"Lakeside cycle path to
town."* **€27.00, 1 Apr-3 Oct.** **2016**

MALS/MALLES VENOSTA *1D1* (3km S Rural) 46.67305,
10.5700 **Campingpark Gloria Vallis,** Wiesenweg 5,
39020 Glurns/Glorenza (BZ) **0473 835160;**
info@gloriavallis.it; www.gloriavallis.it

🐕 €4 ♦♦ (htd) ⓦ ⌂ ♨ ⌂ 🖥 ⌁ ⍨ 🦋 ⍨ ⚓ 🌊 ⚠ ✈

Sp on rd S41 E of Glorenza. 4*, Med, mkd, unshd, terr,
EHU (10A) inc; gas; 5% statics; phone; Eng spkn; adv
bkg acc; ccard acc; tennis; games area; CKE. *"Excel
mountain views; dog shwr rm; higher prices in winter;
excel well run site; serviced pitches; 7 day travel pass in
'all inc' package."* **€37.00, 23 Mar-31 Oct.** **2016**

MANERBA DEL GARDA *1D2* (2.5km N Rural) 45.56333,
10.56611 **Camping San Biagio,** Via Cavalle 19,
25080 Manerba-del-Garda (BS) **0365 551549; info@
campingsanbiagio.net; www.campingsanbiagio.net**

🐕 €5 ♦♦ (htd) ⌂ ♨ ⌂ 🖥 ⌁ 🦋 ⍨ ⍨ ⑪ ⚓ 🌊 ⚠

Fr S572 rd turn E at sp Manerba, site sp 1.5km N
fr Manerba. 3*, Lge, hdstg, mkd, shd, terr, EHU (16A)
metered; bbq; sw; Eng spkn; adv bkg acc; ccard acc.
*"Terr pitches with views over Lake Garda; v clean,
modern san facs; easily got twin axle into lge pitch
(reserved); beautiful site; extra for lakeside pitches; gd
cent for touring area - Verona, Mantua, Sigurta, Torri."*
€31.00, 23 Mar-30 Sep. **2016**

MANERBA DEL GARDA *1D2* (3km S Rural) 45.52555,
10.54333 **Camping Fontanelle,** Via del Magone 13,
25080 Moniga-del-Garda (BS) **0365 502079; info@
campingfontanelle.it; www.campingfontanelle.it**

🐕 €7 ♦♦ ⓦ ⌂ ♨ ⌂ 🖥 ⌁ ⍨ ⍨ ⑪ ⚓ 🌊 ⚠ ✈ 🛥 ⛵

Exit A4 m'way dir Desenzano del Garda & foll sp
Salo. In 10km arr at Moniga del Garda take 2nd exit
off 1st rndabt twd Salo, then 1st R into Via Roma sp
Moniga Centro. Immed after 'Api' g'ge on L turn R
into into Via Caccinelli; at end of this narr rd turn R
into Via del Magone; site on L by lake. Access poss
diff lge o'fits due narr vill rds. 4*, Lge, mkd, pt shd,
sl, terr, EHU (6A) inc; gas; bbq (charcoal, gas); sw;
TV; 20% statics; phone; Eng spkn; adv bkg acc; ccard
acc; tennis; fishing; golf 5km; games rm; horseriding
8km; watersports; boat trips; CKE. *"Vg site; excursions
to Venice, Florence, Verona; bike hire 2km; friendly,
helpful staff; excel san facs; no o'fits over 6.5m high
ssn; levellers needed all pitches; extra for lakeside
pitches; pitches poss tight lge o'fits due trees; mkt Mon;
lovely site."* **€45.00, 18 Apr-26 Sep, Y01.** **2017**

MANFREDONIA *2G4* (10.5km SSW Coastal)
41.55477, 15.88794 **Camping Lido Salpi,** SS159
delle Saline Km 6,200, 71043 Manfredonia **0884
571160; lidosalpi@alice.it; www.lidosalpi.it**

🔢12 ♦♦ ⓦ ⌂ ♨ ⌂ 🖥 ⌁ ⍨ ⍨ ⑪ ⚓ 🌊 ⛵

Head S on A14, exit at Foggia dir Manfredonia/
SS89. Take ramp to Manfredonia Sud and cont strt.
Turn R onto SS159, site on the R. Sm, mkd, pt shd,
EHU (6A) €2; bbq; twin axles; 10% statics; bus 0.5km;
Eng spkn. *"V well located for San Giovanni Rotondo &
Gargano; gd o'night stop fr A14; some pitches awkward
for lge o'fits due to trees & site furniture; gd site."*
€24.00 **2019**

MARINA DI MINTURNO *2F4* (6km SE Coastal)
41.20731, 13.79138 **Camping Villlagio Baia Domizia,**
Via Pietre Bianche, 81030 Baia-Domizia (CE) **0823
930164; info@baiadomizia.it; www.baiadomizia.it**

♦♦ ⓦ ⌂ ♨ ⌂ 🖥 ⌁ 🦋 ⍨ ⑪ ⚓ 🌊 ✈ sand adj

Exit A1 at Cassino onto S630, twd Minturno on
S7 & S7quater, turn off at km 2, then foll sp Baia
Domizia, site in 1.5km N of Baia-Domizia. 4*, V lge,
hdg, shd, EHU ('10A) inc (poss rev pol); gas; TV; ccard
acc; boat hire; windsurfing; games area; tennis; bike
hire. *"Excel facs; 30/7-16/8 min 7 night stay; site clsd
1400-1600 but adequate parking area; top class site
with all facs; gd security."* **€56.00, 19 Apr-23 Sep,
Y10.** **2017**

MARINA DI MONTENERO *2F4* (1km NW Coastal)
42.06500, 14.77700 **Centro Vacanze Molise,** SS
Adriatica, Km 525, 86036 Montenero di Bisaccia
**0873 803570 or 3385 408323 (mob); info@
campingmolise.it; www.campingmolise.it**

🐕 €1 ♦♦ ⓦ ⌂ ♨ ⌂ 🖥 ⌁ ⍨ ⍨ ⑪ ⚓ 🌊 ✈ sand adj

Exit A14 at Vasto Sud to SS16 dir S. On R Centro
Commerciale Costa Verde, site opp on L. 4*, Med,
mkd, pt shd, EHU (3A) inc; gas; phone; bus; Eng
spkn; adv bkg acc; games area; tennis; CKE. *"Excel
site; helpful staff; vg beach; Aqualand Water Park nr;
Tremiti Isands rec; gd touring base; conv for m'way
A14."* **€33.00, 1 Jun-8 Sep.** **2015**

MARTINSICURO *2F3* (1km S Urban/Coastal)
42.88027, 13.92055 **Camping Riva Nuova,**
Via dei Pioppi 6, 64014 Martinsicuro (TE) **0861
797515; info@rivanuova.it; www.rivanuova.it**

♦♦ ⓦ ⌂ ♨ ⌂ 🖥 ⌁ ⍨ ⍨ ⑪ ⚓ 🌊 ⚠ ✈ 🛥 🚲 ⛵ sand adj

Fr N exit A14/E55 sp San Benedetto-del-Tronto
onto S16 dir Pescara to Martinsicuro, site sp.
3*, Lge, shd, EHU inc; TV; adv bkg acc; ccard acc;
games area; excursions; gym; watersports; bike hire.
"San facs were exceptionally gd & spotless; quiet."
€43.00, 14 May-18 Sep. **2016**

MENAGGIO *1C1* (0.5km N Rural) *46.02516, 9.23996*
Camping Europa, Loc Leray, Via dei Cipressi 12, 22017 Menaggio (CO) **344 31187; europamenaggio@
hotmail.it**

🐕 🕎 ♨ 🛁 🍽 🍽 ⑪ nr 🛶 🏊

On ent Menaggio fr S (Como) on S240 turn R & foll 'Campeggio' sp along lakeside prom. On ent fr N turn L at 'Campeggio' sp, pass site ent & turn in boatyard. 1*, Sm, mkd, pt shd, terr, EHU; sw; 80% statics; Eng spkn; adv bkg acc; bike hire; boat hire; CKE. *"V sm pitches cramped high ssn; narr site rds diff for lge o'fits; old-fashioned facs but clean; poor security; helpful owner; m'vans rec to arr full of water & empty of waste; hardly any rd noise, Menaggio delightful place; v friendly."*
€26.50, 25 Mar-30 Sep. 2016

"Satellite navigation makes touring much easier"

Remember most sat navs don't know if you're towing or in a larger vehicle – always use yours alongside maps and site directions.

MERANO/MERAN *1D1* (5km E Rural) *46.67144, 11.20091* **Camping Hermitage,** Via Val di Nova 29, 39012 Meran **0473 232191; info@einsiedler.com; www.einsiedler.com**

🐕 €3 🕎 🛁 ♨ 🛁 🍽 🦋 ♈ 🍽 ⑪ 🛶 🏊

Exit SS38 at Meran Süd & foll sp twds Merano to Meran 2000 past Trautmannsdorf. **Site sp.** 4*, Med, mkd, hdstg, pt shd, terr, EHU (10-16A); bbq; twin axles; phone; bus 100m; adv bkg acc; bike hire; sauna. *"Tennis; serviced pitches; mountain views; hotel facs avail to campers; forest walk; ACSI site; excel."*
€40.00, 8 Apr 5 Nov. 2018

MERANO/MERAN *1D1* (1km S Urban) *46.66361, 11.15638* **Camping Merano,** Via Piave/Piavestrasse 44, 39012 Merano/Meran (BZ) **0473 231249; info@meran.eu; www.merano-suedtirol.it**

12 🐕 €3.30 🕎 🛁 ♨ 🛁 🍽 🍽 ⑪ nr 🏊 🏊 (htd)

Exit S38 at Merano Sud & foll rd into town. Brown site sps to Camping & Tennis (no name at main juncs in town cent). Site ent mkd 'Camping Tennis'. Site also sp fr N. 3*, Med, hdstg, pt shd, EHU (6A) €3; red long stay; phone; tennis adj; CKE. *"Sh walk to town cent; fine site surrounded by spectacular mountain scenery; helpful staff; pitches soft after rain; gd clean san facs; helpful staff; 10% surcharge for 1 night; excel thermal baths; take car pk ticket to acc site recep at barrier, ticket to exit car park provided free at recep."*
€29.00 2015

MERANO/MERAN *1D1* (15km S Rural) *46.59861, 11.14527* **Camping Völlan,** Zehentweg 6, 39011 Völlan/Foiana **0473 568056; info@camping-voellan. com; www.camping-voellan.com**

🐕 €3 🕎 🛁 ♨ 🛁 🍽 🦋 ⑪ nr 🏊 🏔 🏊

Leave S38 dual c'way (Merano-Bolzano) S of Merano sp Lana. Drive thro Lana, turn uphill sp Gampenpass. Turn R sp Foliana/Völlan & foll sp to site. 3*, Sm, mkd, pt shd, terr, serviced pitches; EHU (4A) €2.50; 10% statics; phone; Eng spkn; golf 6km; CKE. *"Long drag up to site fr Lana, but worth it; beautiful situation o'looking Adige Valley; excel facs & pool; barriers clsd 1300-1500 & 2200-0700; v helpful owners; some pitches with steep acc & tight for lge units."* **€42.80, 23 Mar-4 Nov.** 2019

MESTRE *2E2* (3km E Urban) *45.48098, 12.27516* **Venezia Camping Village,** Via Orlanda 8/C, 30170 Mestre/Venezia (VE) **041 5312828; info@ veneziavillage.it; www.veneziavillage.it**

🐕 €2 🕎 (htd) 🛁 🛁 ♨ 🛁 ♿ 🛁 🍽 🍽 🦋 ♈ 🍽 🛶 🏊 🏔

🏊 (htd, indoor)

On A4 fr Milan/Padova take exit SS11 dir Venice. Exit SS11 for SS14 dir Trieste & airport. 200m after Agip g'ge on R watch for sp and take 1st exit R fr rdbt bet two major dealerships. Keep in R lane all way to site. 2*, Med, hdstg, hdg, pt shd, EHU (6A) inc (poss rev pol); gas; bbq (charcoal, elec, gas); sw nr; red long stay; twin axles; 10% statics; bus to Venice; Eng spkn; adv bkg acc; ccard acc; CKE. *"V conv Venice - tickets/maps fr recep; clean, well-run site; popular with m'vans; friendly, helpful owners; pitches cramped when site full; mosquitoes; pool 3km; bus to Pizzale Roma fr campsite; excel."* **€44.70, 22 Feb-31 Dec.** 2019

"There aren't many sites open at this time of year"

If you're travelling outside peak season remember to call ahead to check site opening dates – even if the entry says 'open all year'.

MESTRE *2E2* (4km E Urban) *45.48425, 12.28227* **Camping Rialto,** 16 Via Orlanda, Loc Campalto, 30175 Mestre (VE) **041 5420295; rialto@camping.it; www.campingrialto.com**

🐕 €3 🕎 🛁 ♨ 🛁 🍽 ♈ 🏊

Fr A4 take Marco Polo Airport exit, then fork R onto SS14 dir Venice. Site on L 1km past Campalto opp lge car sales area, well sp. Do not enter Mestre. Med, pt shd, EHU (15A) €1.50; phone; bus to Venice; Eng spkn; adv bkg acc; CKE. *"Site in need of refurb but v conv Venice; bus tickets fr recep; friendly, helpful staff; vg san facs, vg rest; rec."* **€33.00, 7 Apr-31 Oct.** 2019

MESTRE *2E2* (5.5km SW Urban) *45.47138, 12.21166*
Camping Jolly delle Querce, Via G De Marchi 7,
30175 Marghera (VE) **041 920312; campingjolly@
ecvacanze.it; www.ecvacanze.it**

App fr Milan, exit A4/E70 immed after toll, sp Mestre/
Ferrovia/Marghera, then onto SS309 at rndabt sp
Chioggia, then 1st R, site sp on R. 2*, Med, hdg, hdstg,
mkd, unshd, EHU (4-16A) inc (rev pol); gas; bbq; twin
axles; 50% statics; Eng spkn; adv bkg acc. *"Bus to
Venice 15 min walk; excel modern facs block; v noisy
fr adj airport & m'way; beach volleyball court;
hydromassage tub; gd."* **€38.00**   2016

MILANO *1C2* (8km W Urban) *45.47390, 9.08233*
Camping Citta di Milano, Via Gaetano Airaghi 61,
20153 Milano **0248 207017; info@campingmilano.it;
www.campingmilano.it**

Fr E35/E62/A50 Tangentiale Ovest ring rd take
Settimo-Milanese exit & foll sp San Siro along Via
Novara (SS11). Turn R in 2km at Shell petrol stn,
then R at traff lts in 500m & L to site in 600m. Site
ent at Gardaland Waterpark, poorly sp. 4*, Lge, mkd,
hdstg, pt shd, EHU (6A) inc; phone; bus 500m; Eng
spkn; ccard acc; CKE. *"Gd san facs; noise fr adj concerts
high ssn; conv bus/metro Milan; penned animals for kid
to enjoy; rd, aircraft noise, disco at w/end & waterpark
adj; gd security; peacocks roaming site; excel well
organised site; gd for NH; wet, muddy in winter."*
€34.00   2019

MONTEFORTINO *2E3* (0.8km W Rural) *42.94495,
13.34017* **Camping Sibilla,** Via Tenna, 63858
Montefortino FM **3387695040; info@campingsibilla.it;
www.campingsibilla.it**

A14 exit Civitanova Marche. M'way Macerata take
Sarnano exit and on to Amondola. Foll sp for
Montefortino. In about 5km, fork R after IP g'ge.
Site 200m on L. Med, mkd, hdstg, pt shd, terr, EHU
(6A) inc; bbq; twin axles; TV; bus 0.8km; Eng spkn;
adv bkg acc; CKE. *"New site opened June 2016;
great mountain views; family owned; excel site."*
€25.00, 1 May-10 Nov.   2016

NATURNO/NATURNS *1D1* (0.5km S Rural) *46.6475,
11.00722* **Camping Adler,** Via Lido 14, 39025 Naturno
(BZ) **0473 667242; info@campingadler.com;
www.campingadler.com**

Fr E on SS38 turn L at rndabt into Naturno, L at traff
lts & foll sp to site. Fr W after passing thro tunnel
bypass, turn R at rndabt then as above. 4*, Med, mkd,
pt shd, EHU (4-6A) €3.90; twin axles; TV; 10% statics;
bus/train 500m; Eng spkn; adv bkg acc; ccard acc; CKE.
*"Well-kept site; conv town cent; gd hill walks; htd pool
300m; friendly staff; off clsd 1230-1500; cable car nrby;
excel."* **€33.00, 15 Mar-15 Nov.**   2015

NICOTERA *3B4* (3km S Coastal) *38.50755, 15.92666*
Camping Villaggio Mimosa, Mortelletto, 89844
Nicotera Marina (VV) **0963 81397; info@villaggio
mimosa.com**

sand adj

Exit A3/E45 at Rosarno exit. Cross S18 & site sp dir
San Ferdinando Porto. Foll sp on SP50 for approx
7km. 3*, Sm, mkd, pt shd, EHU (12A); gas; twin
axles; 40% statics; Eng spkn; games area; tennis; bike
hire; boat hire; windsurfing; CKE. *"Some pitches have
tight corners for lge o'fits; gd site."* **€42.00**   2019

ORBETELLO *1D4* (5.5km N Coastal) *42.46341, 11.18597*
Camping Village Obertello, Strada Gianella 166, 58015
Orbetello **0564 820 201; orbetellocampingvillage@
clubdelsole.com; www.orbetellocampingvillage.it**

adj

Fr SS1 Aurelia take exit Albinia. Cont twds Porto
Santo Stefano. Campsite on L after 5km. V lge,
hdstg, mkd, pt shd, EHU (6A); bbq; cooking facs; TV;
Eng spkn; adv bkg acc; games area; bike hire; CCI.
€62.00, 19 Apr-27 Sep.   2019

ORBETELLO *1D4* (7km N Coastal) *42.49611, 11.19416*
Argentario Camping Village, Torre Saline, 58010
Albinia (GR) **+39 0564 870068; info@argentario
campingvillage.com; www.argentariocamping
village.com**

shgl

Turn W off Via Aurelia at 150km mark, sp Porto
S. Stefano, site on R, clearly sp in 500m. Ignore
sps Zona Camping. 1*, Lge, mkd, shd, EHU (6A) inc;
90% statics; phone; adv bkg acc; games area; boat
hire; sep car park. *"Better suited for campervans and
tent; san facs due for upgrade; excel rest; easy access
to beach."* **€42.00, 1 Apr-30 Sep.**   2020

ORTA SAN GIULIO *1B1* (0.5km N Rural) *45.80125,
8.42093* **Camping Orta,** Via Domodossola 28, Loc
Bagnera, 28016 Orta San Giulio (NO) **0322 90267;
info@campingorta.it; www.campingorta.it**

Fr Omegna take rd on SS229 for 10km to km 44.5
sp Novara. Site both sides of rd 500m bef rndabt
at Orta x-rds. Recep on L if heading S; poor access
immed off rd. Med, pt shd, pt sl, terr, EHU (3-6A)
€2.50; gas; sw nr; Eng spkn; adv bkg acc. *"Popular site
in beautiful location; sm pitches; narr site rds & tight
corners; arr early for lakeside pitch (extra charge);
slipway to lake; friendly, helpful owner; Orta a gem;
waterskiing; noise fr Beach Club at night; €4.50 for
lakeside pitches; lakeside walk round peninsular;
rec Sacre Monte for St Francis."*
€38.00, 8 Mar-31 Dec.   2019

ORTA SAN GIULIO *1B1* (2km N Rural) *45.81212, 8.41076* **Camping Verde Lago,** Corso Roma 76, 28028 Pettenasco (NO) **0323 89257; campingverdelago@ campingverdelago.it; www.campingverdelago.it**

Site bet SS229 & lake at km 46, 500m S of Pettenasco on Orta Lake. Gd access. Sm, pt shd, pt sl, EHU (6A) €2.50; bbq; sw nr; TV; 60% statics; Eng spkn; ccard acc; games rm. "Vg family-run site; friendly, helpful; clean facs but dated; beach; boat mooring; recep 0930-1200 & 1630-1900; excel rest; beautiful setting by lake; if visiting Orta by car take lots of €1 coins for parking; excel." **€38.00, 25 Mar-16 Oct.**
2016

OSTRA *2E3* (0.2km SW Rural) *43.61032, 13.15351* **Camping 'L Prè,** Viale Matteotti 45, 60010 Ostra (AN) **071 68045; info@lpre.it; www.lpre.it**

Exit A14 at Senigallia onto S360. After approx 10km turn R to Ostra. Sp in vill. 2*, Sm, pt shd, terr, EHU (3A) €2.50; red long stay; games rm. "Gd san facs; very friendly owners; lovely, quiet, simple site with easy access Ancona, Esini Valley; beautiful views over valley; gd for cyclists; gd place to relax after Venice." **€24.00, 1 Apr-30 Sep.**
2019

PAESTUM *3A3* (4km N Coastal) *40.42780, 14.98244* **Camping Villaggio Ulisse,** Via Ponte di Ferro, 84063 Paestum (SA) **0828 851095; info@campingulisse.com; www.campingulisse.com**

Foll site sp in cent Paestum, well sp. 3*, Lge, shd, EHU (3A) inc; 80% statics; games area; CKE. "Direct access to beautiful beach; gd, clean, lovely, friendly site; cash only; gd rest." **€36.00, 1 Apr-30 Sep.** 2018

PAESTUM *3A3* (5km WNW Coastal) *40.42896, 14.98214* **Campsite Athena,** Via Ponte di Ferro, 84063 Paestum **0828 851105; vathena@tiscali.it; www.campingathena.com**

Site 50km S of Salerno. Foll a'strada to Battipaglia onto main rd to Paestum. Head S on SS18. At rndabt take 1st exit onto SP276, then at next rndabt take 1st exit onto Via della Repubblica. Go thro 1 rndabt, turn L onto SP175, at rndabt take 1st exit onto Via Marittima, L onto Via Poseidonia and 1st L onto Via Ponte di Ferro. Site on R. 3*, Med, pt shd, EHU (5A); twin axles; Eng spkn; CKE. "Gd site, direct access to beach; takeaway." **€36.00, 1 Apr-31 Oct.** 2019

PAESTUM *3A3* (5km NW Coastal) *40.41330, 14.99140* **Camping Villaggio Dei Pini,** Via Torre, 84063 Paestum (SA) **0828 811030; info@campingvillaggiodeipini. com; www.campingvillaggiodeipini.com**

Site 50km S of Salerno in vill of Torre-de-Paestum. Foll a'strada to Battipaglia onto main rd to Paestum, site sp bef Paestum on rd S18, foll to beach. 3*, Med, hdg, mkd, shd, EHU (6A) inc; bbq; 30% statics; phone; adv bkg acc; ccard acc; games area; CKE. "Historical ruins nr; narr access rd fr vill due parked cars; lge o'fits may grnd at ent; some sm pitches - c'vans manhandled onto pitches; no dogs Jul/Aug; pleasant site by beach; gd rest; helpful owner; rec." **€45.00** 2019

PALMI *3B4* (7km N Coastal) *38.39317, 15.86280* **Sosta Camper Prajola,** Lungomare Costa Viola, 4, 89015 Palmi RC **03662 529692; sostacamper.praiola@gmail.com**

Sp fr camp site San Fantino (Palmi), on beach front, down the hill in 2km. Sm, hdstg, pt shd, EHU (6A); bbq; twin axles. "Gd basic NH to & fr Sicily; fair." 2016

"That's changed – Should I let the Club know?"

If you find something on site that's different from the site entry, fill in a report and let us know. See camc.com/europereport.

PALMI *3B4* (9.5km N Coastal) *38.40676, 15.86912* **Villaggio Camping La Quiete,** Contrada Scinà, 89015 Palmi (RC) **0966 479400; info@villaggiola quiete.it; www.villaggiolaquiete.it**

N fr Lido-di-Palmi on Contrada Pietrenere coast rd dir Gioia Tauro, site sp. 3*, Lge, hdstg, pt shd, EHU (10A) €3; gas; red long stay; 5% statics; phone; Eng spkn; adv bkg acc; ccard acc; CKE. "Sm pitches; fair sh stay/NH; friendly owner; pitches in ctr of little cottages." **€30.00, 1 May-31 Oct.** 2018

PASSIGNANO SUL TRASIMENO *2E3* (1km E Rural) *43.18338, 12.15085* **Camping Kursaal,** Viale Europa 24, 06065 Passignano-sul-Trasimeno (PG) **075 828085; info@campingkursaal.it; www.camping kursaal.it**

Fr Perugia on S75 to Lake Trasimeno. Exit at Passignano-Est twd lake; site on L past level x-ing adj hotel, well sp. 3*, Med, mkd, hdg, pt shd, pt sl, EHU (6A) €2 (poss rev pol); TV; phone; Eng spkn; adv bkg req; ccard acc; bike hire; CKE. "Pleasant, lovely site in gd position; vg rest; some pitches have lake view; ltd space & pitches tight; gd clean site; vg san facs; great pool." **€36.00, 24 Mar-04 Nov.** 2018

PERTICARA *2E3* (2km N Rural) *43.89608, 12.24302*
Camping Perticara, Via Serra Masini 10/d, 47863
Perticara (PS) **0335 7062260; info@camping
perticara.com; www.campingperticara.com**

✦ ♂♀† (htd) WD ⚒ ♿ ▣ ∥ MSP ➶ ♈ Ⴒ ⅄ ∄ ⅏ ◭ ✎ ♒ ⚓

Fr A14 at Rimini take S258 to Novafeltria. Foll sp
Perticara & site. Steep, hairpins on pt of rte.
3*, Med, hdstg, hdg, mkd, unshd, terr, serviced
pitches; EHU (10A) inc; gas; TV; 5% statics; phone;
bus; Eng spkn; adv bkg acc; ccard acc; CKE. *"Clean,
well-maintained, scenic site; hospitable Dutch owners;
many activities arranged; immac san facs; poss diff
egress to SW (hairpins with passing places) - staff help
with 4x4 if necessary; rough terrain; excel; well run."*
€38.00, 13 May-20 Sep. **2016**

PESCHIERA DEL GARDA *1D2* (1km N Urban)
45.44780, 10.70195 **Camping del Garda,** Via Marzan 6,
37019 Castelnuovo-del-Garda (VR) **045 7551682;
info@camping-delgarda.com;
www.campingdelgarda.it**

♂♀† WD ⚒ ♿ ▣ ∥ MSP ➶ ♈ Ⴒ ⅄ ① ∄ ⅏ ◭ ✎ ♒ ⚓ shgl

Exit A4/E70 dir Peschiera onto SR249 dir Lazise.
Turn L in 500m dir Lido Campanello, site in 1km on
L on lakeside. 4*, V lge, shd, EHU (4A) inc; gas; sw;
60% statics; phone; adv bkg acc; games area; tennis.
*"Busy, well-organised site; helpful staff, discount
snr citizens; gd rest; walking & cycling rtes adj; conv
Verona."* **€60.00, 1 Apr-5 Nov.** **2017**

PESCHIERA DEL GARDA *1D2* (1km N Rural) *45.46722,
10.71638* **Eurocamping Pacengo,** Via del Porto 13,
37010 Pacengo (VR) **045 7590012; info@eurocamping
pacengo.it; www.eurocampingpacengo.it**

✦ €2.40 ♂♀† WD ⚒ ♿ ▣ ∥ MSP ➶ ♈ Ⴒ ⅄ ① ∄ ⅏ ◭ ✎

On SS249 fr Peschiera foll sp to Gardaland, Pacengo
in 1km. Turn L at traff lts in cent of vill, site on L. 3*,
Lge, mkd, pt shd, sl, EHU (4A) inc; sw nr; 25% statics;
phone; Eng spkn; adv bkg acc; boat launch; CKE.
*"Well-equipped site on shore Lake Garda; helpful staff;
some sm pitches; pool adj; espec gd end of ssn; excel
rest; conv Verona."* **€36.50, 11 Apr-30 Sep.** **2019**

PESCHIERA DEL GARDA *1D2* (6km NE Rural)
45.46472, 10.71416 **Camping Le Palme,** Via del
Tronchetto 2, 37017 Pacengo (VR) **045 7590019;
info@lepalmecamping.it; www.lepalmecamping.it**

✦ €4.60 ♂♀† WD ⚒ ♿ ▣ ∥ ♈ Ⴒ ① nr ∄ ⅏ ◭ ✎ ♒ (htd) ⚓

A4/E70 exit at Peschiera onto SS249, sp Lazise. Site
sp bef Pacengo in approx 5km. 3*, Lge, mkd, pt shd,
terr, serviced pitches; EHU (6A) inc; sw nr; 40% statics;
Eng spkn; adv bkg acc; ccard acc; waterslide. *"Well-
maintained site; excel, clean facs; extra for lakeside
pitches; helpful staff; sh walk to vill; 4 theme parks nr;
excel."* **€37.00, 27 Mar-26 Oct.** **2015**

PESCHIERA DEL GARDA *1D2* (6km W Coastal)
45.45120, 10.66557 **Camping Wien,** Loc. Fornaci,
37019 Peschiera (VR) **045 7550379; info@camping
wien.it**

✦ ♂♀† WD ⚒ ♿ ▣ ∥ MSP ➶ ♈ ⅄ ① ∄ ⅏ ◭ ✎ ♒ ⚓ shgl adj

On Verona-Brescia rd (not a'strada) W of Peschiera,
turn R at San Benedetto, turn R 400m after traff
lts, site has 2 ents 100m apart. Med, mkd, hdstg, shd,
pt sl, EHU inc (3A); gas; red long stay; 50% statics;
phone; bus adj; Eng spkn; adv bkg acc; boating; games
area; fishing; ice; CKE. *"Wonderful pool o'looking Lake
Garda; walking/cycle path into town; vg site; busy high
ssn."* **€40.00, 9 Apr-30 Sep.** **2017**

PESCHIERA DEL GARDA *1D2* (2km NW Urban)
45.44825, 10.66978 **Camping San Benedetto,** Strada
Bergamini 14, 37019 San Benedetto (VR)
**045 7550544; info@campingsanbenedetto.it;
www.campingsanbenedetto.it**

✦ €1.50-2 ♂♀† ⚒ ▣ ∥ MSP ➶ ♈ Ⴒ ⅄ ① ∄ ⅏ ◭ ✎ ♒ ⚓

Exit A4/E70 dir Peschiera-del-Garda, turn N at traff
lts in cent of vill, site on lake at km 274/V111 on rd
S11. 3*, Lge, shd, pt sl, EHU (3A) inc; 30% statics; adv
bkg acc; games area; bike hire; boat hire; canoeing;
windsurfing. *"Pleasant, well-run; sm harbour; site clsd
1300-1500; excel modern rest beside lake; excel new
san facs (2017)."* **€44.60, 1 Apr-8 Oct.** **2017**

PIEVE TESINO *1D1* (6km N Rural) *46.11361,
11.61944* **Villaggio Camping Valmalene,** Loc
Valmalene, 38050 Pieve-Tesino (TN) **0461 594214;
info@valmalene.com; www.valmalene.com**

12 ✦ €5 ♂♀† (htd) ⚒ ♿ ▣ ∥ MSP ➶ ♈ Ⴒ ⅄ ① ∄ ⅏ ◭
♒ (htd) ⚓

Fr Trento E for 50km on S47. Turn N at Strigno to
Pieve-Tesino, site sp. 3*, Med, mkd, pt shd, EHU inc;
10% statics; adv bkg rec; ccard acc; site clsd Nov;
sauna; fitness rm; bike hire; games area; tennis. *"Gd
base for summer & winter hols; private bthrms avail."*
€32.00 **2016**

PISA *1C3* (0.5km N Urban) **Camper Parking,** Via di
Pratale 78, 56100 Pisa, Toscane **+39050555678**

12 ✦ ♿ MSP ➶ ♈ Ⴒ nr ① nr ∄

On Via Aurelia SS1 fork R app Pisa, then turn E
approx 1km N of Arno Rv, sp camping. After 1km
turn L into Via Pietrasantina. Site on R behind lge
Tamoil petrol stn, sp coach parking. Max height
under rlwy bdge 3.30m. C'vans acc. Lge, hdstg,
unshd, own san req; bus adj. *"Excel NH; parking within
walking dist of leaning tower; water & waste inc;
plenty of space; san facs open at café opp during day."*
€12.00 **2020**

PISA *1C3* (1km N Urban) *43.72416, 10.3830* **Camp Torre Pendente,** Viale delle Cascine 86, 56122 Pisa **050 561704; info@campingtorrependente.com; www.campingtorrependente.com**

🐕 €1.60 ♦♦ WC ≛ ♨ ♿ ⊟ ✉ MSP ♈ ❦ Ⴑ 🅿 ⚓ 🛝 ⛱

Exit A12/E80 Pisa Nord onto Via Aurelia (SS1). After 8km & after x-ing rlwy bdge, turn L after passing Pisa sp at traff lts. Site on L, sp. 1*, Lge, mkd, pt shd, EHU (5A) inc (poss rev pol); gas; bbq; red long stay; TV; phone; Eng spkn; ccard acc; bike hire; CKE. *"Gd base Pisa; leaning tower 15 mins walk; immac, modern, well-maintained san facs; private san facs avail; pitches typically 50sqm; poss diff due narr site rds & corners; many pitches shd by netting; site rds muddy after rain; friendly staff; excel, well-run site; 300m fr Pisa San Rossore rlwy stn, trains to Lucca etc."* **€39.00, 1 Apr-4 Nov.** **2019**

PISTOIA *1D3* (10km S Rural) *43.84174, 10.91049* **Camping Barco Reale,** Via Nardini 11, 51030 San Baronto-Lamporecchio (PT) **0573 88332; info@barcoreale.com; www.barcoreale.com**

🐕 ♦♦ WC ≛ ♨ ♿ ⊟ ✏ MSP 🦋 ♈ ❦ Ⴑ ⑪ 🅿 ⚓ 🛝 ✎ ⛱

Leave A11 at Pistoia junc onto P9 & foll sp to Vinci, Empoli & Lamporecchio to San Baronto. In vill turn into rd by Monti Hotel & Rest, site sp. Last 3km steep climb. 4*, Lge, mkd, shd, pt sl, terr, serviced pitches; EHU (3-6A) inc (poss rev pol); gas; red long stay; phone; Eng spkn; adv bkg req; ccard acc; bike hire; games area; CKE. *"Excel site in Tuscan hills; helpful staff; gd touring base; excel mother & fam bthrm; vg rest; poss diff access some pitches but towing help provided on request; unsuitable lge o'fits; well-organised walking & bus trips; excel pool."* **€45.50, 1 Apr-30 Sep.** **2019**

POGGIBONSI *1DJ* (12km N Rural) *43.58198, 11.13001* **Camping Panorama Del Chianti,** Via Marcialla 349, 50020 Marcialla-Certaldo (FI) **0571 669334; info@campingchianti.it; www.camping chianti.it**

🐕 €2 ♦♦ WC ✏ MSP ♈ Ⴑ nr ⑪ nr 🅿 nr ⛱

Fr Florence-Siena a'strada exit sp Tavarnelle. On reaching Tavernelle turn R sp Tutti Direzione/ Certaldo & foll by-pass to far end of town. Turn R sp to Marcialla, in Marcialla turn R to Fiano, site in 1km. NB Some steep hairpins app site fr E. 2*, Med, mkd, hdstg, pt shd, terr, EHU (3A) inc; red long stay; phone; Eng spkn; adv bkg acc; bike hire; CKE. *"Gd tourist info (in Eng); sports facs in area; cultural sites; helpful staff; friendly owner; san facs clean - hot water to shwrs only; 4 excel rests nr; panoramic views; midway bet Siena & Florence; popular site - arr early to get pitch; facs need updating."* **€36.00, 1 Apr-1 Nov.** **2019**

POMPEI *3A3* (1km S Urban) *40.74638, 14.48388* **Camping Spartacus,** Loc Pompei Scavi, Via Plinio 127, 80045 Pompei (NA) **081 8624078; staff@ campingspartacus.it; www.campingspartacus.it**

12 ♦♦ WC ≛ ♨ ⊟ ✏ MSP ♈ Ⴑ nr

Fr N on A3 exit Pompei Ovest. At T-junc turn L & site on R just after passing under rlwy bdge. Fr S exit Pompei Est & foll sp Pompei Scavi (ruins). Sat nav may lead to low bdge. 3*, Sm, mkd, shd, EHU (5A) €2.3.(poss rev pol); gas; TV; Eng spkn; adv bkg acc; ccard acc; CKE. *"Nice, family-run, welcoming site, 50m fr historical ruins; conv train to Naples, boats to Capri; stray dogs poss roam site & ruins; v popular with students high ssn; rest, snacks, bar in high ssn; best of 3 town sites; gd site for exploring area; friendly owners; clean san facs; steep access rd."* **€34.00** **2015**

PORLEZZA *1C1* (4km E Rural) *46.04074, 9.16827* **Camping Ranocchio,** Via Al Lago 7,22010 Loc Piano di Porlezza, Carlazzo (CO) **0344 70385 or 62611; campeggioranocchio@gmail.com; www.camping ranocchio.com**

🐕 €2 (htd) ♦♦ WC ≛ ♨ ♿ ⊟ ✏ MSP 🦋 ♈ ❦ Ⴑ ⑪ 🅿 ⚓ 🛝 ⛱ 🛶

On main rd bet Menaggio & Porlezza. Ent in vill of Piano on S side. Sp. Steep app in Lugano with hairpin bends; 15% gradient. V narr rd fr Lugano - clsd to c'vans at peak times. 2*, Lge, mkd, unshd, pt sl, terr, EHU inc (6A); gas; sw; TV; Eng spkn; horseriding 2km; fishing; CKE. *"Friendly recep; gd for exploring Como & Lugano; steamer trips on both lakes; lovely, v attractive site; helpful recep; excel corner shop & rest; vg."* **€29.50, 1 Apr-30 Sep.** **2019**

PORTO RECANATI *2F3* (4km N Coastal) *43.47123, 13.64150* **Camping Bellamare,** Lungomare Scarfiotti 13, 62017 Porto-Recanati (MC) **071 976628; info@bellamare.it; www.bellamare.it**

♦♦ WC ≛ ♿ ✏ ♈ ❦ Ⴑ ⑪ 🅿 ⚓ 🛝 ✎ 🛶 🖼 ⛵ shgl

Exit A14/E55 Loreto/Porto-Recanati; foll sp Numana & Sirolo; camp on R in 4km on coast rd. 3*, Lge, unshd, EHU (6A) €3; gas; 10% statics; phone; Eng spkn; ccard acc; games area; games rm; bike hire; CKE. *"V well-run & laid out site on beach; NH tariff of €17-28 (inc elec) for a pitch at the edge of the site but OK; beach access; gd facs & security."* **€39.00, 29 Mar-7 Oct.** **2018**

PORTOFERRAIO *1C3* (9km E Rural) *42.80072, 10.36452* **Rosselba Le Palme,** Loc. Ottone 3, 57037 Elba Portoferraio **0565 933 101; info@ rosselbalepalme.it; www.rosselbalepalme.it**

♦♦ WC ≛ ♨ ✏ MSP 🦋 ♈ ❦ Ⴑ ⑪ 🅿 ⚓ 🛝 ✎ 🛶 ⛵ sand 0.5km

Fr ferry terminal foll signs 'tutti direzioni'. At 3rd rndabt head twds Porto Azzurro. Take L fork to Bagnaia. Site sp. 3*, Sm, hdg, pt shd, terr, EHU (6A); twin axles; 80% statics; bus adj; Eng spkn; adv bkg acc; CCI. *"Ferry service fr Piombino every 1/2 hr; statics enhance site facs."* **€55.00, 20 Apr-30 Sep.** **2019**

POZZA DI FASSA *1D1* (0.5km SW Rural) *46.42638, 11.68527* **Camping Catinaccio Rosengarten,** Via Avisio 15, 38036 Pozza-di-Fassa (TN) **0462 763305; info@catinacciorosengarten.com; www.catinacciorosengarten.com**

🐕 €4 ♟️ 🚿 ⛺ ♿ ✉️ 🧺 🦋 ♈ 🍴 nr ⓗ nr 🧺 nr

Fr S SS48 site sp just after San Giovanni. 1*, Lge, hdstg, pt shd, EHU (2A) inc (extra for higher amperage); red long stay; 30% statics; Eng spkn; adv bkg req; ccard acc; site clsd Oct; CKE. *"Superb scenery; helpful staff; luxury san facs; free taxi (2018) to Vigo di Fassa cable car; ski lift 1km; pool 300m; excel site; v convly sited for access to vill & public transport; 20 min walk to Buffaure cable car; ski bus; off clsd 1230-1500."* **€35.50, 1 Jan-30 Apr, 1 Jun-15 Oct, 1 Dec-31 Dec.**
2018

PRATO ALLO STELVIO *1D1* (0.5km NW Rural) *46.62472, 10.59388* **Camping Kiefernhain,** Via Pineta 37, 39026 Prato-allo-Stélvio (BZ) **0473 616422; reception@camping-kiefernhain.it; www.camping-kiefernhain.it**

🐕 €4 ♟️ 🚿 ⛺ ♿ 🚽 ✉️ 🧺 🦋 ♈ 🍴 ⓗ nr 🧺 🧺 🏔️ 🛝 (htd)

Fr rd S40 turn SW at Spondigna onto rd S38 dir Stélvio, site sp in vill. Lge, mkd, pt shd, EHU (6A) €2.50; bbq; red long stay; phone; Eng spkn; adv bkg rec; waterslide; dog shwrs. *"V modern, clean san facs; superb views; sports cent adj; private bthrms avail; facs stretched high ssn; vg value."* **€52.50, 1 May-4 Oct.**
2019

PRECI *2E3* (3km NW Rural) *42.88808, 13.01483* **Camping Il Collaccio,** 06047 Castelvecchio-di-Preci (PG) **0743 665108; info@ilcollaccio.com; www.ilcollaccio.com**

🐕 ♟️ (htd) 🚿 ⛺ ♿ 🚽 ✉️ 🧺 🦋 🍴 ⓗ 🧺 🏔️ 🛝

S fr Assisi on S75 & S3, turn off E sp Norcia, Cascia. Then foll sp for Visso on S209. In approx 30km turn R for Preci, then L, site sp. Rte is hilly.
4*, Med, mkd, pt shd, terr, EHU (6A) inc (long lead poss req); TV; 20% statics; phone; Eng spkn; adv bkg acc; ccard acc; bike hire; horseriding; tennis; games area; CKE. *"Beautiful views; well-maintained, clean site; pleasant rest; maganificent pool area; sm pitches; gd walking in Monti Sibillini National Park; paragliding; conv Assisi & historic hill towns; excel; well run."* **€35.00, 1 Apr-30 Sep.**
2015

PREDAZZO *1D1* (2.5km E Rural) *46.31027, 11.63138* **Camping Valle Verde,** Loc Ischia 2, Sotto Sassa, 38037 Predazzo (TN) **0462 502394; info@campingvalleverde.it; www.campingvalleverde.it**

🐕 €3.50 ♟️ (htd) 🚿 ⛺ ♿ ✉️ 🧺 🦋 ♈ 🍴 ⓗ 🛝 🏔️

Exit A22 dir Ora onto rd S48 dir Cavalese/Predazzo. Fr Predazzo take SS50 E, turn R in 1.5km, site on L in 500m. 2*, Med, mkd, pt shd, pt sl, EHU (6A) €2; bbq; sw nr; twin axles; 5% statics; bus 0.5km; Eng spkn; adv bkg acc; ccard acc; games area. *"Excel; bus & cable car rides; walks, cycle tracks & mountain climbs nrby; mini train adj; beautiful site."* **€32.00, 28 Apr-30 Sep.**
2018

PUNTA SABBIONI *2E2* (0.7km S Coastal) *45.44141, 12.42127* **arking Dante Alighieri,** Lungomare Dante Alighieri 26, 30010 Punta-Sabbioni (VE) **+390412909711**

🐕 ♟️ 🚿 ⛺ 🚽 ✉️ 🧺 🦋 🍴 nr ⓗ nr 🧺 nr

Take rd Jesolo to Punta-Sabbioni, pass all camps & go to end of peninsula. Turn L at boat piers & foll rd alongside beach; site on L just bef Camping Miramare. Sm, pt shd, EHU (8A) inc; bus 500m; Eng spkn. *"M'vans only; friendly, helpful owner; 10 min walk for boats to Venice; vg."* **€23.00**
2020

PUNTA SABBIONI *2E2* (1.6km SSW Coastal) *45.44035, 12.4211* **Camping Miramare,** Lungomare Dante Alighieri 29, 30013 Punta-Sabbioni (VE) **041 966150; info@camping-miramare.it; www.miramarevenezia.it**

🐕 €4 ♟️ (htd) 🚿 ⛺ ♿ 🚽 ✉️ 🧺 🦋 ♈ ⓗ nr 🧺 🏔️ 🏊

Take rd Jesolo to Punta-Sabbioni, pass all camps & go to end of peninsula. Turn L at boat piers & foll rd alongside beach; site 500m on L. 3*, Med, hdg, mkd, pt shd, EHU (6A) inc (rev pol); gas; phone; Eng spkn; adv bkg acc; ccard acc. *"Excel, well-organised, helpful, caring, friendly family-owned site - 10 mins walk for Venice (tickets fr recep) - can leave bikes at terminal; gd security; new pt of site v pleasant wooded area; clean facs; poss mosquito problem; min 3 nights stay high ssn; superior to other sites in area; min stay 2 nights Jul/Aug; sm dogs only; don't miss camping supmkt on way in - an Aladdin's cave; bus to beach; avoid dep on Sat due traff; ferry; Magic of Italy site; highly rec, reasonable mob home rentals; excel staff; close to beach and ferries."* **€41.40, 1 Apr-3 Nov.**
2019

PUNTA SABBIONI *2E2* (1km SW Rural) *45.44236, 12.42251* **Al Batèo,** via Lungomare Dante Alighieri 19/A, 30013 Cavallino Treporti Venice **040 5301 455 or 041 5301 564; info@albateo.it; www.albateo.it**

12️⃣ 🐕 ♟️ (htd) 🚿 ⛺ ✉️ 🧺 🦋 🧺

Take rd Jesolo to Punta Sabbioni and go to end of the peninsula. Turn L at boat piers and foll rd along side beach. Site 300 on L. Sm, hdg, shd, bus; Eng spkn; adv bkg acc. *"M'vans only; gd value; Vapporetti to Venice 300m."* **€25.00**
2019

RAPALLO *1C2* (2km N Urban) *44.35805, 9.2100*
Camping Miraflores, Via Savagna 10, 16035 Rapallo
(GE) **0185 263000; info@campingmiraflores.it;**
www.campingmiraflores.it

🏕 ♀♂ ⬜ ⚓ ♿ 🖥 ⁄ ᴹˢᴾ ▾ Ⓗ 🍴 🐕 nr ⛺ 🛶

Exit A12/E80 at Rapallo. In 100m fr toll gate sharp
L across main rd, sharp L again, site sp 200m on R.
Site almost immed beside toll gate but not easily
seen. Sp fr town. 1*, Med, hdg, mkd, hdstg, pt shd,
terr, EHU (3A) €1.80; gas; red long stay; 10% statics;
bus 200m to stn & town cent; ccard acc; sep car park;
CKE. *"Excel htd pool adj; gd, modern san facs, refurb
(2018); grass pitches for tents, earth only for m'vans &
c'vans; v noisy & dusty as under m'way; v friendly staff;
ferries to Portofino fr town; conv NH; rec phone ahead
if lge o'fit."* **€32.00, 1 Mar-31 Dec.** **2018**

RAPALLO *1C2* (2.5km W Urban) *44.35691, 9.1992*
Camping Rapallo, Via San Lazzaro 4, 16035 Rapallo
(GE) **0185 262018; campingrapallo@libero.it;**
www.campingrapallo.it

🏕 ♀♂ ⬜ ⚓ ♿ 🖥 ⁄ ᴹˢᴾ ▾ Ⓗ nr 🐕 nr ⛺ (htd) 🏔 shgl 2.5km

Exit A12/E80 dir Rapallo, turn immed R on leaving
tolls. Site sp in 500m on L at bend (care), over bdge
then R. Narr app rd. Site sp. 2*, Med, hdg, mkd, pt
shd, EHU (3A) €2.20; gas; 10% statics; bus (tickets
fr recep); Eng spkn; adv bkg acc; ccard acc; bike hire;
CKE. *"Clean, family-run site; conv Portofino (boat trip)
& train to Cinque Terre; beautiful coastlline; shwrs clsd
during day but hot shwrs at pool; v busy public hols -
adv bkg rec; awkward exit, not suitable for lge o'fits;
NH only."* **€28.50, 15 Mar-15 Nov.** **2019**

RAVENNA *2E2* (10.6km E Coastal) *44.43335,
12.29680* **Camping Park Adriano,** Via dei Campeggi 7,
48122 Punta-Marina-Terme (RN) **0544 437230; info@
adrianocampingvillage.com; www.campingadriano.
com**

🏕 €3 ♀♂ ⬜ ⚓ ♿ 🖥 ⁄ ᴹˢᴾ ♈ ▾ Ⓗ 🍴 🐕 ⛺ 🏔 🏖 🛶 300m

Fr S309 Ravenna-Venezia rd foll sp to Lido Adriano.
Site at N end of Lido. 4*, Lge, shd, EHU (5A) inc
(poss rev pol/no earth); bbq; TV; 70% statics; bus to
Ravenna; Eng spkn; adv bkg acc; ccard acc; bike hire;
golf 10km; CKE. *"Site in pine forest; excel san facs;
ATM; sh walk to beach."* **€43.00, 20 Apr-18 Sep. 2015**

RHEMES ST GEORGE *1B1* (3km N Rural) *45.64966,
7.15150* **Camping Val di Rhemes,** Loc Voix 1, 11010
Rhêmes-St George (AO) **0165 907648; info@camping
valdirhemes.com; www.campingvaldirhemes.com**

🏕 €2.50 ♀♂ ⬜ (htd) ⚓ ♿ 🖥 ⁄ ᴹˢᴾ 🦋 ♈ ▾ 🏔

Fr S26 or A54/E25 turn S at Introd dir Rhêmes-St
George & Rhêmes-Notre-Dame; site on R in 10km
past PO; app is diff climb with hairpins. 2*, Med, pt
shd, pt sl, EHU (2-6A) €2; 10% statics; Eng spkn; adv
bkg acc; ccard acc; CCI. *"Peaceful, family-run site;
nr Gran Paradiso National Park; gd walking; excel."*
€26.40, 20 May-10 Sep. **2019**

RIVA DEL GARDA *1D1* (2.5km E Rural) *45.88111,
10.86194* **Camping Monte Brione,** Via Brione 32,
38066 Riva-del-Garda (TN) **0464 520885; info@
campingbrione.com; www.campingbrione.com**

🏕 €4 ♀♂ ⬜ ⚓ ♿ 🖥 ⁄ ᴹˢᴾ 🦋 ♈ ▾ Ⓗ nr 🐕 ⛺ 🏔 🛶 (htd)

Exit A22 Garda Nord onto SS240 to Torbole & Riva;
on app to Riva thro open-sided tunnel; immed R
after enclosed tunnel opp Marina; site ent 700m on
R. 4*, Med, mkd, pt shd, terr, EHU (6A) inc; gas; bbq;
sw nr; Eng spkn; adv bkg acc; ccard acc; watersports;
bike hire; solarium; CKE. *"Olive groves adj; barriers clsd
1300-1500 & 2300-0700; pleasant site with lge pitches;
gd, modern san facs."* **€31.50, 15 Apr-16 Oct.** **2016**

ROMA *2E4* (9km N Rural) *42.00353, 12.45283* **Happy
Village & Camping,** Via Prato della Corte 1915,
00123 Roma **06 33626401 or 06 33614596; info@
happycamping.net; www.happycamping.net**

🏕 ♀♂ ⬜ ⚓ ♿ 🖥 ⁄ ᴹˢᴾ ▾ Ⓗ 🍴 🐕 ⛺ 🛶

Take exit 5 fr Rome ring rd sp Viterbo. Site sp on
ring rd, fr N & S on dual c'way Rome/Viterbo at 1st
exit N of ring rd. 3*, Lge, pt shd, terr, EHU (6A) inc;
gas; bbq; 10% statics; train into Rome; adv bkg acc;
ccard acc; CKE. *"Friendly, busy site in hills; sm pitches;
vg rest; mini bus shuttle to train stn; gd site; v nice well
kept site; steep access rd."* **€25.00, 1 Mar-6 Jan.**
2015

ROMA *2E4* (10km SW Rural) *41.77730, 12.39605*
Camping Fabulous, Via Cristoforo Colombo, Km 18,
00125 Acilia (RM) **06 5259354; fabulous@ecvacanze.
it; www.ecvacanze.it**

🏕 €1.50 ♀♂ (htd) ⚓ ♿ 🖥 ⁄ ▾ Ⓗ 🍴 🐕 ⛺ 🏊 🛶 🏖

Exit junc 27 fr Rome ring rd into Via C Colombo. At
18km marker turn R at traff lts, site 200m on R. V
lge, mkd, shd, pt sl, EHU (6-10A) inc; bbq; 80% statics;
phone; bus on main rd, Eng spkn; adv bkg acc; ccard
acc; tennis; games area; waterslide; CKE. *"Set in
pinewoods; gd sh stay; ltd facs in LS, helpful staff."*
€40.00, 14 Apr-31 Oct. **2017**

ROSETO DEGLI ABRUZZI *2F3* (3km S Coastal)
42.65748, 14.03568 **Eurcamping Roseto,** Lungomare
Trieste Sud 90, 64026 Roseto-degli-Abruzzi (TE) **085
8993179; info@eurcamping.it; www.eurcamping.it**

🏕 €5 ♀♂ ⬜ ⚓ ♿ 🖥 ⁄ ᴹˢᴾ ♈ ▾ Ⓗ 🍴 🐕 ⛺ 🏊 🏖 🛶
🏔 shgl adj

Fr A14 exit dir Roseto-degli-Abruzzi to SS16.
At rndabt turn R, next L & under rlwy bdge to
promenade. Turn R at sea front, site at end of
promenade. 3*, Med, hdg, mkd, shd, EHU (3A) inc;
20% statics; Eng spkn; adv bkg acc; bike hire; tennis;
games area; CKE. *"Phone to check if open LS; gates
close 2300; pitches poss flood after heavy rainfall;
Roseto excel resort."* **€43.50, 1 May-24 Oct.** **2015**

ITALY

SALBERTRAND *1A2* (1km SW Rural) *45.06200, 6.86821* **Camping Gran Bosco,** SS24, Km 75, Monginevro, 10050 Salbertrand (TO) **0122 854653; info@campinggranbosco.it; www.campinggran bosco.it**

12 ♀♂ (htd) 🚾 🛁 ♿ ⓦ MP Ⓨ Ⓖ nr 🛒 🔥 ✗

Leave A32/E70 (Torino-Fréjus Tunnel) at Oulx Ouest junc & foll SS24/SS335 sp Salbertrand. Site sp 1.5km twd Salbertrand at km 75. Fr S (Briançon in France) on N94/SS24 to Oulx cent, foll SS24 thro town & foll sp Salbertrand, then as above. 3*, Lge, pt shd, EHU (3-6A) inc; gas; 80% statics; ccard acc; tennis; games area. *"Beautiful setting; excel NH bef/after Fréjus Tunnel or pass to/fr Briançon; gates open 0830-2300; excel, modern, clean san facs; sm pitches; grnd soft in wet - no hdstg; conv for m'way; popular with m'cyclists but quiet at night."* **€29.00**   **2016**

SALSOMAGGIORE TERME *1C2* (3km E Rural) *44.80635, 10.00931* **Camping Arizona,** Via Tabiano 42, 43039 Tabiano-Salsomaggiore Terme (PR) **0524 565648; info@camping-arizona.it; www.camping-arizona.it**

🐕€3 ♀♂ 🚾 🛁 ♿ ♿ ✗ MP 🦮 Ⓨ Ⓖ 🛒 🔥 ✗ 🛶

Fr fidenza foll sp Salsomaggiore and then at rndabt to Tabiano. Go thro Tabiano and site 500m on L. 4*, Lge, shd, pt sl, EHU (3A) inc (rev pol); 30% statics; phone; bus to Salsomaggiore; waterslide; games area; jacuzzi; sep car park; games rm; tennis; bike hire; golf 7km; fishing. *"Vg site; friendly, helpful staff; interesting, smart spa town; excel touring base; gd for families; san facs vg; best campsite shop; vg rest."* **€37.00, 1 Apr-6 Oct.**   **2019**

SAN FELICE DEL BENACO *1D2* (1km E Rural) *45.58500, 10.56583* **Camping Fornella,** Via Fornella 1, 25010 San Felice-del-Benaco (BS) **0365 62294; fornella@fornella.it; www.fornella.it**

🐕€7 ♀♂ (htd) 🚾 🛁 ♿ ♿ ✗ MP 🦮 Ⓨ Ⓖ 🛒 🔥 ✗ 🛶 🚣

N fr Desenzano on S572 twd Salo. Turn R to San Felice-del-Benaco, over x-rds & take 2nd R turn at sp to site. R into app rd, L into site. Rd narr but accessible. Avoid vill cent, site sp (with several others) fr vill by-pass just bef g'ge. 5*, Lge, pt shd, pt sl, terr, EHU (6A) inc; gas; bbq (charcoal); sw; TV; 20% statics; Eng spkn; adv bkg acc; ccard acc; games area; bike hire; games rm; boat hire; windsurfing; tennis; fishing; CKE. *"Family-run site in vg location by Lake Garda; park outside until checked in; recep 0800-1200 & 1400-2000; no o'fits over 7m high ssn; sep car park; excel pool; extra for lge pitches & lakeside pitches; excursions to Venice, Florence & Verona opera; excel rest; gd san facs."* **€54.40, 13 Apr-13 Oct, Y11.**   **2019**

SAN MARINO *2E3* (7km N Rural) *43.95990, 12.46090* **Centro Vacanze San Marino,** Strada San Michele 50, 47893 Cailungo, Repubblica di San Marino **0549 903964; info@centrovacanzesanmarino.com; www.centrovacanzesanmarino.com**

12 🐕€5 ♀♂ (htd) 🚾 🛁 ♿ ♿ ✗ MP 🦮 🐾 Ⓨ Ⓖ 🛒 🔥 ✗ 🛶 (htd) 🚣

Exit A14 at Rimini Sud, foll rd S72 to San Marino. Pass under 2 curved footbdges, then 800m after 2nd & 13km after leaving a'strada, fork R. Cont uphill for 1.5km then turn R at Brico building, site sp. Steep long-haul climb. 4*, Lge, hdstg, hdg, pt shd, terr, serviced pitches; EHU (6A) inc (poss rev pol); bbq; cooking facs; red long stay; TV (pitch); 10% statics; bus; Eng spkn; adv bkg acc; ccard acc; bike hire; games area; tennis; CKE. *"V busy at w/end - rec arr early; superb hill fort town; excel rest & pool; sm pitches; conv Rimini 24km; solarium; mini zoo; excel, clean site; bus calls at site ent for San Marino."* **€37.00, Y04.**   **2019**

SAN MICHELE ALL'ADIGE *1D1* (3km SW Rural) *46.16789, 11.11452* **Camping Moser,** Via Nazionale 64, 38015 Nave San Felice (TN) **0461 870248**

🐕 ♀♂ 🚾 ✗ Ⓨ Ⓖ 🛒 nr

12km N of Trento on SS12. Sm, mkd, shd, EHU inc; bus 500m; Eng spkn; adv bkg acc; ccard acc. *"Gd, friendly NH; site run by Hotel Moser (well sp on S12); scruffy & run down but busy; new san facs block almost completed (2014)."* **€18.00, 1 May-31 Oct.**   **2015**

SAN REMO *1B3* (2.5km W Coastal) *43.802393, 7.745345* **Camping Villaggio Dei Fiori,** Via Tiro a Volo 3, 18038 San Remo (IM) **0184 660635; info@villaggiodeifiori.it; www.villaggiodeifiori.it**

♀♂ (htd) 🚾 🛁 ♿ ♿ ✗ MP Ⓨ Ⓖ 🛒 nr 🔥 ✗ 🛶 (htd) 🌴 shgl adj

Fr A10/E80 take Arma-di-Taggia exit & foll sp San Remo Centro. At SS1 coast rd turn R sp Ventimiglia. At 2.5km look for red/yellow Billa supmkt sp on R; 50m past sp take L fork, site on L in 50m. Fr W on A10 take 1st exit dir San Remo - winding rd. Turn R & site on L after Stands supmkt. Fr Ventimiglia on SS1, 150m past San Remo boundary sp turn sharp R (poss diff lge o'fits) to site. 4*, Lge, hdstg, mkd, hdg, pt shd, terr, EHU (3-6A) €4-7; bbq (gas); cooking facs; twin axles; red long stay; 60% statics; phone; train to Monaco & bus San Remo nr; Eng spkn; adv bkg rec; ccard acc; games area; tennis; bike hire; CKE. *"Gd location; well-kept, tidy, paved site; vg, clean facs; beach not suitable for sw; some pitches superb sea views (extra charge), some sm; rd & fairgrnd noise; lge o'fits not acc high ssn as sm pitches; vg rest; conv Monaco; gates locked at night."* **€73.00, 15 Jun-31 Dec.**   **2018**

SAN VALENTINO ALLA MUTA *1D1* (0.7km N Rural) *46.7700, 10.5325* **Camping Thöni,** Landstrasse 83, 39020 St Valentin-an-der-Haide, Graun **0473 634020; thoeni.h@rolmail.net; www.camping-thoeni.it**

12 🐕 ⛺(htd) 🚿 🅿 🛒 ☂ 🍴 nr ♨ nr 🛒 nr

N twd Austrian border site on L on edge of vill on S edge of Lago di Resia. 2*, Sm, unshd, pt sl, EHU 6-16A; site clsd Nov. *"Conv sh stay/NH en rte Austria; cycle rte around lake; scenic area; off open 0900-1000 & 1700-1800; numbered pitches; views; walking rte rnd Haidensee below vill; cable car opens late June."* €26.00   2018

"We must tell the Club about that great site we found"

Get your site reports in by mid-August and we'll do our best to get your updates into the next edition.

SARNANO *2E3* (3km SSW Rural) *43.01743, 13.28358* **Quattro Stagioni,** Contrada Brilli, 62028 Sarnano **0733 651147; quattrostagioni@camping.it; www.camping4stagioni.it**

12 🐕 🛖 ⛺ 🚿 ♿ 🍴 ☂ 🍴 🍴 ♨ 🛒 🛒 🚲

A14 exit Civitanova Marche. M'way to Macerata as far as Sarnano exit. In Sarnano turn R at sq, foll main rd. Site approx 3km outside Sarnano to the W. 3*, Sm, mkd, pt shd, pt sl, EHU; bbq; twin axles; 60% statics; Eng spkn; adv bkg acc; games area; CKE. *"Fair site."* €30.00   2019

SARTEANO *1D3* (0km W Rural) *42.9875, 11.86444* **Camping Parco Delle Piscine,** Via del Bagno Santo, 53047 Sarteano (SI) **0578 26971; info@parcodelle piscine.it; www.parcodellepiscine.it**

⛺ 🚿 🛖 ♿ 🍴 🚐 🍴 ☂ 🍴 ♨ 🛒 nr 🍴 🚲 🍴

Exit A1/E35 onto S478 at Chiusi & foll sp to Sarteano. Site at W end of vill, sp. 4*, Lge, pt shd, serviced pitches; EHU (6A) inc; 50% statics; Eng spkn; ccard acc; solarium; tennis. *"Clean, well-run; security guard 24 hrs; no vehicles during quiet periods 1400-1600 & 2300-0700; poss long walk to wc/shwrs; Florence 90 mins on m'way, Siena 1 hr; site at 600m, so cool at night; excl."* €70.00, 14 Apr-30 Sep, Y17.
                                                          2017

SARZANA *1C2* (4km SE Coastal) *44.076651, 9.981182* **Camping Iron Gate Marina 3B,** Viale XXV Aprile 54 19038, Sarzana **0187 676370; info@marina3b.it; www.marina3b.com**

🐕 ⛺(htd) 🚿 🛖 ♿ 🍴 🚐 ☂ 🍴 ♨ 🍴 🚲 🚲1km

Fr A12 exit Sarzana dir S. TR at 4th rndabt (2nd after dble rndabt). 3.1 km or R. Lge, mkd, shd, 65% statics; Eng spkn; ccard acc. *"VG, nice site; gd facs; conv for Cinque Terre towns."* €20.00, 15 Mar-30 Sep.   2019

SARZANA *1C2* (8km S Rural/Coastal) *44.07638, 9.97027* **Camping River,** Loc Armezzone, 19031 Ameglia (SP) **0187 65920; info@campingriver.com; www.campingriver.com**

🐕 €3 ⛺ 🚿 🛖 ♿ 🍴 🚐 🍴 ☂ 🍴 ♨ 🚐 🛒 nr 🏔 🍴 🚲 🍴 🚲2km

Exit A12 at Sarzana & foll sp Ameglia & Bocca di Magra on SP432. In 7km turn L into Via Crociata to site (blue sp). Narr app rd with few passing places. 3*, Lge, mkd, pt shd, EHU (3-6A) inc; TV; 50% statics; adv bkg acc; bike hire; games area; tennis 200m; boat hire; golf driving range; rv fishing; horseriding 200m; sauna. *"Gd touring base Cinque Terre; pleasant, helpful staff; vg, well-situated site; gd shop & rest; bus to beach; nice location by rv; dated facs; gd pools."* €44.00, 12 Apr-30 Sep.   2019

SAVONA *1B2* (13km SW Coastal) *44.224200, 8.41032* **Camping Leo,** Via Siaggia 4, 17028 Spotorno **019 745184; info@campingleo.it; www.campingleo.it**

🐕 ⛺ 🚿 🛖 ♿ 🍴 🚐 🍴 ☂ ♨ 🛒 nr 🏔

Leave A10 sp S8 Spotorno. Immed after rlwy bdge turn R at rndabt into site. Med, hdstg, pt shd, serviced pitches; EHU (3A); bbq (gas, sep area); sw nr; 500m; Eng spkn; adv bkg rec; games area; bike hire. *"Excel."* €25.00, 1 Feb-4 Nov.   2019

SAVONA *1B2* (13km SW Coastal) *44.22731, 8.40795* **Camping Rustia,** Via La Torre 4, 17028 Spotorno (SV) **019 745042 or 019 741446; info@ campingrustia.it; www.campingrustia.it**

🐕 ⛺ 🚿 🛖 ♿ 🍴 🍴 ♨ nr 🛒 🚲 🚲sand 600m

Exit A10/E80 for Spotorno, site sp on app rd to m'way. V steep app rd. C'vans returning to m'way use ent at Albissola Marina. 1*, Lge, shd, EHU (3A) €3; 30% statics; Eng spkn; ccard acc. *"Site diff for lge o'fits due narr paths & many trees - manhandling necessary onto pitches, gd san facs; gates locked at night; busy, well laid out site, helpful staff."* €32.00, 1 Mar-30 Sep.   2015

SENIGALLIA *2E3* (1km S Coastal) *43.70416, 13.23805* **Villaggio Turistico Camping Summerland,** Via Francesco Podesti, 236 Senigallia P.Iva 00207190422 **071 7926816; info@camping summerland.it; www.campingsummerland.it**

🐕 (except Jul/Aug) ⛺(cont) 🛖 🚿 ♿ 🍴 🚐 🍴 🍴 ♨ 🚐 🛒 🏔 🍴 🍴 🚲 🚲200m

Exit A14/E55 onto SS16 to Senigallia S. Site on R after lge car park at side of rd. 4*, Lge, shd, EHU (5A) €2.50; gas; TV; 10% statics; adv bkg rec; games area; sep car park; tennis. €42.00, 1 Jun-15 Sep.   2020

ITALY

SESTO CALENDE *1B1* (4km N Rural) *45.74892, 8.59698* **Camping Okay Lido,** Via per Angera 115, Loc Lisanza, 21018 Sesto Calende (VA) **0331 974235; campingokay@camping-okay.com; www.camping-okay.com**

Exit A8 at Sesto Calende onto SP69 N dir Angera, **site sp.** 4*, Med, mkd, pt shd, terr, EHU (6A) €3; sw; TV; 10% statics; Eng spkn; adv bkg acc; watersports; games rm; games area. *"Friendly, welcoming site; private san facs avail; NH pitches by lakeside; gd NH for Amsterdam ferry."* **€42.00, 30 Mar-13 Oct.** 2019

SESTO CALENDE *1B1* (7.5km N Rural) *45.82712, 8.62722* **International Camping Ispra,** Via Carducci, 21027 Ispra (VA) **0332 780458; info@international campingispra.it; www.internationalcampingispra.it**

Site 1km NE of Ispra on E side of lake. 4*, Med, shd, terr, EHU (6A) €3; own san req; bbq; sw; TV; 90% statics; Eng spkn; adv bkg acc, fishing; boating; games area; CKE. *"Gd views of lake; muddy beach; vg rest; nice, peaceful site; friendly, helpful staff; lovely situation on banks of Lake Maggiore; well run; loud music fr bar till midnight."* **€32.00, 18 Mar-2 Nov.** 2016

SESTO/SEXTEN *2E1* (3km SE Rural) *46.66806, 12.39935* **Caravan Park Sexten,** St. Josefstr. 54, 39030 Sexten / Moos **0474 710444; info@ caravanparksexten.it; www.caravanparksexten.it**

Fr S49 take S52 SE fr San Candido thro Sexten & Moos. After sh, steep climb site on W of S52 midway bet Moos & Kreuzberg pass. 4*, Lge, mkd, pt shd, pt sl, serviced pitches; EHU (16A) metered; gas; TV; Eng spkn; adv bkg acc; tennis; sauna; solarium; CKE. *"Excel, clean facs; Waldbad worth visit; rock climbing wall; lovely scenery; mountain walks; beauty & wellness treatments; v popular & busy site; private bthrms avail; winter sports; v well managed & equipped; rest worth a visit."* **€54.70, Y03.** 2019

SETTIMO VITTONE *1B1* (2.5km N Rural) *45.56474, 7.81668* **Camping Mombarone,** Torre Daniele, 10010 Settimo-Vittone (TO) **0125 757907; info@ campingmombarone.it; www.campingmombarone.it**

On E side of Ivrea-Aosta rd (SS26), 100m S of Pont-St Martin. Exit A5 at Quincinetto, turn R onto SP69 across bdge, R at end onto SP26 & site on L in 150m. (App fr S, sp at ent but if overshoot go on 100m to rndabt to turn). Tight ent off busy rd. 2*, Med, pt shd, pt sl, EHU (6A) €2.50; 80% statics; games area; CKE. *"Gd base Aosta valley; superb views; Quincinetto medieval vill walking dist; lovely, grassy, well-kept site; ltd space for tourers; v pleasant, helpful owner who speaks gd Eng, friendly welcome; san facs immac; gd NH; rlwy stn nrby."* **€22.50** 2019

SIBARI *3A4* (4km E Coastal) *39.77944, 16.47889* **Camping Villaggio Pineta di Sibari,** 87070 Sibari (CS) **0981 74135; info@pinetadisibari.it; www.pinetadisibari.it**

Exit A3 at Frascineto onto SS106, then exit at Villapiana-Scalo. Site sp on beach. 3*, Lge, pt shd, EHU (4A) inc; TV; 20% statics; ccard acc; tennis; bike hire. *"Vg beach; site in pine forest; noisy bar/music; gd touring base; watch out for low bdge on app."* **€44.00, 19 Apr-29 Sep.** 2019

SIENA *1D3* (7.4km N Urban) *43.33750, 11.33055* **Camping Siena Colleverde,** Via Scacciapensieri 47, 53100 Siena **0577 334080; info@sienacamping.com; www.sienacamping.com**

Site sp ('Camping' or symbol) on all app to Siena, foll sp for 'Ospedale' (hospital). Use exit Siena Nord & foll site sp, but take care as some sp misleadingly positioned. 3*, Lge, hdg, mkd, hdstg, pt shd, pt sl, terr, EHU (10A) inc; gas; TV; phone; bus; Eng spkn; adv bkg acc; CKE. *"Attractive location; gd views old town wall fr upper pitches (no shd); excel touring base; upgraded, well-run site - gd, well kept; modern san facs; easy access by bus to town fr site ent; excel; pt of 'We Love Camping' group; some lge unmkd pitches."* **€37.00, 1 Mar-31 Dec.** 2015

SIENA *1D3* (21km W Rural) *43.2815, 11.21905* **Camping La Montagnola,** Strada della Montagnola 139, 53100 Sovicille (SI) **0577 314473; info@camping lamontagnola.it; www.campinglamontagnola.it**

Fr N on S2 or S on S223 site well sp fr junc with S73. Avoid Siena town cent. 2*, Med, hdstg, mkd, pt shd, terr, EHU (6A) inc; gas; 7% statics; phone; bus to Siena; Eng spkn; adv bkg rec; ccard acc; games area; sep car park; CKE. *"Super site; sm pitches; sharp stone chippings on hdstg pitches; v clean facs; vg refuge fr summer heat in wooded hills; facs poss stretched high ssn & rubbish bins o'flowing; gd walks fr site (booklet fr recep); Magic of Italy disc, conv bus service to Siena fr site."* **€29.00, 1 Apr-30 Sep.** 2015

SIRMIONE *2G2* (3km E Coastal) *45.45738, 10.64025* **Camping Tiglio,** Loc. Punta Grò, 25019 Sirmione **030 990 4009; info@campingtiglio.it; www.campingtiglio.it**

A4 Milan-Verona, exit Sirmione. 1st exit at rndabt onto SP13. 1st exit at next rndabt. Turn L twds Via San Martino. 1st exit at rndabt onto Via Verona. Foll sp to camp. Lge, mkd, shd, EHU inc (4A); bbq; twin axles; 50% statics; bus adj; Eng spkn; adv bkg acc; ccard acc; CKE. *"Gd site; noisy & busy but friendly; on bus rte to Verona."* **€36.00, 18 Apr-30 Sep.** 2019

SIRMIONE *1D2* (3km S Rural) *45.46845, 10.61028*
Camping Sirmione, Via Sirmioncino 9, 25010
Colombare-di-Sirmione (BS) **030 99 04 665; info@
camping-sirmione.it; www.camping-sirmione.it**

Exit S11 at traff lts sp Sirmione, in 500m R at site sp.
3*, Lge, mkd, hdstg, pt shd, pt sl, EHU (6A) inc; sw;
30% statics; adv bkg acc; ccard acc; games area;
watersports. *"Excel lakeside site; facs poss stretched
when site busy; excel rest, bar, pool & san facs; lovely
walk to Sirmione; highly rec."*
€43.60, 17 Apr-5 Oct.   2019

SORRENTO *3A3* (3km N Coastal) *40.63541, 14.41758*
Camping I Pini, Corso Italia 242, 80063 Piano-di-
Sorrento (NA) **081 8786891; info@campingipini.com;
www.campingipini.com**

S fr Naples on A3; Exit A3 sp Castellammare di Stabia
& take SS145 sp to Sorrento; pass thro vill of Meta;
site on R immed over bdge; lge sp on main rd.
1*, Med, hdg, mkd, pt shd, pt sl, EHU (4A) inc; red long
stay; 50% statics; bus 50m; Eng spkn; adv bkg acc;
ccard acc; CKE. *"Spacious site in mountains bet 2 vills;
pool restricted to campers; sh walk to public transport
to sites of interest; best site in Sorrento to avoid
narr gridlocked rds; old, tired facs (2013); tight narr
pitches."* €47.50   2019

SORRENTO *3A3* (2km W Coastal) *40.62818, 14.35816*
Camping Villaggio Santa Fortunata, Via Capo 39,
80067 Capo-de-Sorrento (NA) **081 8073579 or 081
8073574; info@santafortunata.com; www.santa
fortunata.com**

Only app fr a'strada, exit Castellamare. Foll sp into
Sorrento then sp Massa-Lubrense. Site poorly sp
fr Sorrento on R, gd wide ent. 1*, V lge, mkd, hdg,
shd, pt sl, terr, EHU (6A) inc; gas; red long stay; TV;
50% statics; phone; bus adj; Eng spkn; sep car park;
CKE. *"Gd, clean facs; pitches sm for lge o'fits (7m+)
& poss dusty; bus fr gate, ticket fr recep; boat trips
to Capri fr site beach; noisy nr gd rest, disco & 18-30
tours; many scruffy statics; facs dated; steep access
& tight hairpins to some pitches; friendly, vg site."*
€46.00, 30 Mar-3 Nov.   2019

SPERLONGA *2E4* (1km SE Coastal) *41.25514,
13.44625* **Camping Villaggio Nord-Sud,** Via Flacca,
Km 15.5, 04029 Sperlonga (LT) **0771 548255; info@
campingnordsud.it; www.campingnordsud.it**

Site on seaward side of S213 at km post 15.9. Lge
sp visible fr both dirs. Lge, mkd, hdstg, shd, EHU
(4A) inc; 10% statics; adv bkg acc; tennis; games
area; windsurfing; fitness rm. *"Mostly statics but
great location; pleasant site; picturesque beach."*
€48.00, 1 Apr-31 Oct.   2016

STRESA *1B1* (3.4km NW Urban) *45.91246, 8.50410*
Camping Parisi, Via Piave 50, 28831 Baveno (VB)
**0323 924160; campingparisi@tiscalinet.it;
www.campingparisi.it**

Exit A26 at Baveno, after x-ing bdge on o'skirts
Baveno, turn L off main rd bet Hotel Simplon & Agip
g'ge & foll sp. Fr Stresa drive thro Baveno. At end of
prom, take R fork at Dino Hotel up a minor 1-way
rd (poss congested by parked cars); foll Parisi sp. 2*,
Med, pt shd, pt sl, EHU (6A) €3.50; sw; 10% statics;
phone; bus; Eng spkn; adv bkg acc; boat launch;
fishing; CKE. *"Well-managed site on Lake Maggiore;
fine views; extra for lakeside pitches; frequent lake
steamers nr site; gd rests adj; long hose rec for m'van
fill up; sm pitches; busy at w/end; sw in lake - supervise
children; many repeat visitors; bar adj; clean facs;
welcoming recep; conv base for visiting Borromeo
Islands."* €34.00, 25 Mar-30 Sep.   2015

STRESA *1B1* (4km NW Rural) *45.91185, 8.48913*
Camping Tranquilla, Via Cave 2, Oltrefuime, 28831
Baveno (VB) **0323 923452; info@tranquilla.com;
www.tranquilla.com**

Fr N go into Baveno & turn R 200m past Hotel
Splendide; fr S turn L immed after x-ing bdge. Foll
brown sp to site up steep hill 1km. 2*, Med, hdg,
mkd, hdstg, pt shd, pt sl, terr, serviced pitches; EHU
(6A) €2.60; red long stay; 25% statics; train to Milan
2km; Eng spkn; adv bkg acc; watersports; bike hire;
car wash; CKE. *"Clean, comfortable, well-managed,
pleasant, family-owned site; entmnt (w/end); v helpful
staff; sm pitches; conv Lake Maggiore; day trip by train
to Milan."* €33.50, 19 Mar-16 Oct.   2016

TORBOLE *1D1* (0.4km N Urban) *45.8725, 10.87361*
Camping Al Porto, Via Al Cor, 38069 Tórbole (TN)
**0464 505891; info@campingalporto.it;
www.campingalporto.it**

On ent Tórbole fr S take rd twd Riva-del-Garda
for approx 600m. Petrol stn & car park on R, turn
L into narr lane after shops; site sp. 3*, Med, mkd,
pt shd, EHU (5A) inc; bbq; sw nr; red long stay;
watersports; CKE. *"Excel san facs; excel site; secure;
helpful staff; vill has many rest & sportlng locations."*
€39.00, 10 Apr-3 Nov.   2019

TRAFOI *1D1* (0.9km S Rural) *46.54332, 10.50750*
Camping Trafoi, Drei Brunnen Weg 1, 39020 Trafoi
**0473 611533; info@camping-trafoi.com;
www.camping-trafoi.com**

Fr SS40 turn SW at Spondigna onto SS38 dir
Stelvio to Trafoi. Site thro vill sp on L. Sm, pt shd,
pt sl, EHU (4A); bbq; bus 500m; Eng spkn. *"Excel
cycle rtes, mountaineering; chair lift for skiing; excel."*
€30.00, 15 Jun-15 Sep.   2015

TRENTO *1D1* (12km NW Rural) *46.11111, 11.04805*
Camping Laghi di Lamar, Via alla Selva Faeda 15,
38070 Terlago (TN) **0461 860423; campeggio@
laghidilamar.com; www.laghidilamar.com**

🏕 €2.50 ⚹⚹ ⬛ ♨ ⬛ ✉ MSP 📶 ♍ 🍽 ⊕ ♿ 🎿

Head W fr Trento for 10km on SS45b dir Riva-del-
Garda/Brescia. Turn R twd Monte-Terlago; site sp
on R. Last section via SS45 v steep. 3*, Med, pt shd,
terr, EHU (10A) inc; gas; bbq; sw nr; TV; 30% statics;
phone; Eng spkn; ccard acc; games rm; bike hire;
games area; CKE. *"Excel site; excel new san facs."*
€35.00, 1 Apr-30 Oct. **2017**

"I need an on-site restaurant"

We do our best to make sure site information
is correct, but it is always best to check any
must-have facilities are still available or will
be open during your visit.

TRIESTE *2F1* (5.5km N Rural) *45.67974, 13.78387*
Camping Obelisco, Strada Nuova Opicina 37, 34016
Opicina (TS) **040 212744; campeggioobelisco@
gmail.com; www.campeggioobelisco.it**

12 🏕 €2.50 ⚹⚹ (cont) ♨ ✉ MSP 🦋 🍽 nr ⊕ ♿ 🏛

Sp fr S58. 2*, Med, hdstg, shd, pt sl, terr, EHU €2.50;
own san req; 95% statics; Eng spkn; CKE. *"V steep,
narr, twisting ent/exit to site - suitable sm c'vans only
& diff in wet; excel views Trieste harbour; interesting
tram ride into city fr obelisk; demanding up hill walk to
top of site, both Turkish & European wcs."* **€18.00**
2016

TROPEA *3B4* (7km NE Coastal) *38.70610, 15.97024*
Villaggio Camping Sambalon, Via del Mare,
89868 Marina-di-Zambrone (VV) **0963 392828;
info@sambalon.com; www.sambalon.com**

🏕 ⚹⚹ ⬛ ♨ ✉ MSP 🦋 ♍ 🍽 ⊕ ♿ 🎣 🏛 🏊 sand adj

Fr N exit A3 at Pizzo Calabro onto S522 dir Tropea
for 20km. Foll sp Marina di Zambrone & site. 4*,
Med, mkd, hdstg, pt shd, EHU; TV; 10% statics; adv
bkg acc. **€46.50, 20 May-23 Sep.** **2020**

URBISAGLIA *2E3* (5km NE Rural) *43.21136, 13.41544*
Centro Agrituristico La Fontana, Via Selva 8, Abbadia-
di-Fiastra, 62010 La Fontana (MC) **0733 514002**

12 ⚹⚹ ⬛ ♨ ⬛ ♿ ✉ MSP 🦋 🍽 ⊕ ♿ 🏛

Fr SP77 turn S to Abbadia-di-Fiastra onto SP78.
On reaching Abbadia turn L & immed R, then uphill
above Monastery for 2km & foll sp to site on R just
after sharp RH bend. Sm, pt shd, terr, EHU (6A) inc;
bbq; TV (pitch); minigolf; ping pong. *"Fair sh stay/NH;
CL-type site on farm; not suitable lge o'fits; attactive
countryside; v helpful owners."* **€21.00** **2020**

VENEZIA *2E2* (18km SW Coastal) *45.41916, 12.25666*
Camping Fusina, Via Moranzani, 93, 30176 Fusina
**041 5470055; info@campingfusina.com;
www.campingfusina.com**

12 🏕 ⚹⚹ (htd) ⬛ ♨ ⬛ ♿ ✉ MSP 🦋 ♍ 🍽 ⊕ ♿ 🎣 🏛 🏊 🚣

Exit A4 at sp Ravenna/Chiogga onto SS309 S, & foll
sp to site. Take care when turning into rd leading
to Fusina as L-hand turning lane used by locals for
o'taking. 3*, Lge, pt shd, EHU (6A) inc (poss rev pol);
gas; TV; 50% statics; ccard acc; games area; boat
hire; CKE. *"Pleasant, busy site; some pitches o'looking
lagoon; many backpackers, educational groups & 18-
30s; gd san facs; gd public transport/boat dir to Venice;
ferry to Greece adj; helpful staff; poss mosquitoes;
some ship & aircraft noise + noise fr bar & adj indus
complex; some pitches diff due trees & soft when wet;
ltd facs LS & poss travellers; new sw."* **€35.00** **2019**

VENEZIA *2E2* (16km W Rural) *45.45222, 12.18305*
Camping Serenissima, Via Padana 334/A, 30176
Malcontenta **041 5386498 or 041 921850; info@
campingserenissima.it; www.campingserenissima.com**

🐕 ⚹⚹ (htd) ⬛ ♨ ⬛ ♿ ✉ MSP 🦋 ♍ 🍽 ⊕ ♿ 🏛

Exit A4 at Oriago/Mira exit. At 1st rndabt foll sp
Ravenna/Venezia; at next rndabt take 1st exit sp
Padova/Riviera del Brenta (SR11) twd Oriago. Rv
on L, site on R in approx 2km. 3*, Med, mkd, pt shd,
EHU (10-16A) inc; gas; 25% statics; phone; Eng spkn;
adv bkg acc; ccard acc; boat hire; bike hire; CKE. *"Bus
to Venice/Padua - buy tickets on site; friendly, helpful
owners; efficient recep; some sm pitches; excel, v clean
san facs; poss mosquitoes; conv Padova; highly rec for
Venice; supmkt 3km; vg."* **€34.00, 26 Mar-5 Nov.**
2018

"Satellite navigation makes touring much easier"

Remember most sat navs don't know if you're
towing or in a larger vehicle – always use yours
alongside maps and site directions.

VERBANIA *1B1* (6km W Rural) *45.93731, 8.48615*
Camping Conca d'Oro, Via 42 Martiri 26, 28835
Feriolo di Baveno (VB) **0323 28116; info@concadoro.
it; www.concadoro.it**

🏕 €5 ⚹⚹ ⬛ ♨ ⬛ ♿ ✉ MSP 🦋 ♍ 🍽 ⊕ ♿ 🏛 🏊 🎿 sand adj

Foll S33 NW fr Stresa, thro Bavena to Feriolo. At
traff lts in Feriolo fork R, sp Verbania & in 800m
immed over rv bdge, turn R into site. Clearly sp.
3*, Lge, mkd, shd, pt sl, EHU (6A) inc; 10% statics;
Eng spkn; adv bkg acc; ccard acc; games area;
windsurfing; bike hire; CKE. *"Helpful staff; excel,
clean, modern san facs; discount for local services;
dogs not acc Jul/Aug; extra for lakeside pitches;
excel, v well run site; beautiful location; busy site."*
€48.00, 1 Apr-10 Sep. **2019**

VERBANIA *1B1* (9km NW Urban) *45.96111, 8.45694*
Camping Lago delle Fate, La Quartina, Via Pallanza 22, 28802 Mergozzo (VB) **0323 80326; info@lagodel lefate.com; www.lagodellefate.com**

� (cont) WD ♨ ✖ ◪ ▣ ✗ ╱ ⛺ Ⓨ ☇ nr ❤ nr ⛵ shgl

1km E of vill of Mergozzo which is 2nd L after exit Gravellona on S34 to Verbania. 2*, Med, hdstg, pt shd, EHU (6A); gas; bbq; sw; twin axles; 10% statics; Eng spkn; adv bkg acc; boat hire; CKE. "*Extra charge for lakeside pitches, slightly bigger with superb views; gd sh stay; town, 5 min walk; gd walking & cycling.*"
€43.00, 2 Apr-4 Oct. 2015

VERONA *1D2* (1.5km N Rural) *45.44985, 11.00415*
Camping San Pietro, Via Castel San Pietro 2, 37129 Verona **045 592037; info@campingcastelsanpietro. com; www.campingcastelsanpietro.com**

⛺ � (cont) WD ♨ ✖ ◪ ▣ ╱ ⛺ Ⓨ nr ❤

Exit A4/E70 to San Martino-Buon-Albergo & foll S11 dir Verona cent, site sp adj Castel San Pietro.
1*, Sm, mkd, hdstg, shd, EHU; bbq; 10% statics; bus 1km; adv bkg req. "*Basic site in park, more suited to tents or sm m'vans only; no vehicles/o'fits over 7m; beautiful views over city; easy walk to town cent, but many steps or use funicular 300mtrs; poor & ltd san facs.*" **€41.00, 2 May-30 Sep.** 2018

"There aren't many sites open at this time of year"

If you're travelling outside peak season remember to call ahead to check site opening dates – even if the entry says 'open all year'.

VERONA *1D2* (15km W Rural) *45.44557, 10.83447*
Camping El Bacàn, Via Verona 11, 37010 Palazzolo di Sona (VR) **348 9317204; info@el-bacan.it; www.el-bacan.it**

12 ♘ � (cont) WD ♨ ✖ ◪ ▣ ╱ ✖ ⛺ Ⓨ nr Ⓗ nr ❤ ⚠

Exit A4 onto A22 N & foll sp for Brescia (W) on SR11. Site in 7km on R, sp 150m bef site ent. Sm, hdg, mkd, pt shd, EHU (16A) inc; bbq; TV; bus 1km; Eng spkn; adv bkg acc; ccard acc; CKE. "*Charming, pleasant site on wkg farm; conv Verona, Lake Garda; friendly owner & staff; excel farm shop; highly rec; easy access; vg; gd san facs.*" **€23.00** 2017

VERONA *1D2* (7km W Rural) *45.446075, 10.918951*
Agricamping Corte Finiletto, Strada Bresciana 41, 37139 Verona **340 6075017; info@cortefiniletto.it; www.cortefiniletto.it**

12 � WD ♨ ╱ MSP ⛺ ⚠

Exit A4 onto A22 N & foll sp for Brescia (W) on SR11. Site approx 3km on R. Lge sp with flags flying. Sm, mkd, pt shd, EHU (6A) inc; bbq; bus; Eng spkn; adv bkg acc; ccard acc. "*Kiwi fruit fm; site OAY except for 1st 2 weeks in Nov (harvest time); gd.*" **€25.50** 2018

VIAREGGIO *1C3* (2km S Coastal) *43.85133, 10.25963*
Camping Viareggio, Via Comparini 1, 55049 Viareggio (LU) **0584 391012; info@camping viareggio.it; www.campingviareggio.it**

♘ €4 � WD ♨ ✖ ◪ ▣ ╱ MSP ✖ ⛺ Ⓨ Ⓗ ❤ ⚠ ⛵ 800m

Fr sea front at Viareggio, take rd on canal sp Livorno; after x-ing canal bdge turn L (but not immed on canal) & 2nd R to site in 2km. 1*, Lge, shd, EHU (4A) (poss rev pol); gas; TV; phone; adv bkg acc; games area; CKE. "*Gd site & facs; no dogs Aug; hot water to shwrs only; cycle rte/footpath to town.*"
€32.00, 19 Apr-30 Sep. 2019

VIAREGGIO *1C3* (5km S Coastal) *43.82920, 10.2727*
Camping Italia, Viale dei Tigli 52, 55048 Torre-del-Lago Puccini (LU) **0584 359828; info@camping italia.net; www.campingitalia.net**

♘ � WD ♨ ✖ ◪ ▣ ╱ MSP ⛺ Ⓨ Ⓗ ❤ ⚠ ✗ ⛵ ⛱ sand 1.5km

Fr A12 N exit sp Viareggio, fr S exit Pisa N onto SS1 & turn twd Torre del Lago at S junc, site well sp thro vill. Do not turn L at vill cent but cont for 2km N, then L at rlwy bdge. At rndabt turn L, site on R in 250m. Avoid Viareggio town cent. Med, shd, EHU (6A) €1.30; gas; TV; 10% statics; Eng spkn; adv bkg acc; ccard acc; sep car park; bike hire; tennis. "*Vg for Lucca - Puccini's birthplace; bus tickets fr site for Pisa & Lucca; dogs not acc Jun-Aug; some pitches diff for lge o'fits due trees & low branches; gd clean facs; poss problem with mosquitoes.*"
€32.50, 17 Apr-27 Sep. 2019

VICENZA *1D2* (9km SE Urban) *45.5175, 11.60222*
Camping Vicenza, Strada Pelosa 239, 36100 Vicenza **0444 582311; info@campingvicenza.it; www.campingvicenza.it**

� WD ♨ ✖ ◪ ▣ ╱ MSP ⛺ Ⓨ Ⓗ nr ❤ nr ⚠ ✗

Exit A4 Vicenza Est dir Torri di Quartesole; turn R immed after toll; site on L 300m fr Vicenza exit, hidden behind Viest Quality Inn. Fr city foll sp Padua & a'strada; sp. 4*, Med, pt shd, pt sl, EHU (3A) inc (rev pol); bbq; red long stay; TV; bus; Eng spkn; adv bkg acc; ccard acc; bike hire; tennis; CKE. "*Cycle path to interesting town; functional site; clean san facs; friendly, helpful staff; pleasant site.*"
€38.00, 1 Apr-18 Oct. 2016

VIESTE *2G4* (2km N Coastal) *41.89901, 16.14964*
Camping Punta Lunga, Loc Defensola, 71019 Vieste (FG) **0884 706031 or 03466 403894; info@puntalung.it; www.puntalunga.it**

� (htd) WD ♨ ✖ ◪ ▣ ╱ MSP ✖ ⛺ Ⓨ Ⓗ ❤ ⚠ ✗ ⛵ adj

N fr Vieste 1.5km fr end of long beach, turn R at traff lts down narr lane. Site sp. 3*, Lge, mkd, pt shd, terr, EHU (3-5A) inc; gas; TV; 15% statics; phone; bus; Eng spkn; adv bkg acc; ccard acc; canoeing; windsurfing; sep car park; bike hire; CKE. "*Friendly, helpful staff; well-run site on lovely cove; tight pitches - beware pitch marker posts; v clean facs; rec use bottled water; beautiful coastal area; statics sep area; gd rest; lovely cove; excel beaches.*"
€49.00, 30 May-15 Sep. 2019

VIPITENO/STERZING *1D1* (1km S Urban) *46.88737, 11.43098* **Autoporto,** 00098 Vipiteno **0472 760620; info@hotel-brenner.com**

⟦12⟧ ⟦icons⟧ nr ⟦icon⟧ nr

S fr Brenner Pass approx 17km, take exit immed bef toll booths Vipiteno & foll sp 'Autoporto'. Site well sp fr toll booth - 500m. Can also be accessed fr SS12. Push button on site barrier if office clsd. Med, hdstg, pt shd, EHU inc. *"Excel NH for c'vans or m'vans; conv Austrian border; all facs in services."* **€15.00**   2015

VOLTERRA *1D3* (1km NW Rural) *43.41271, 10.8509* **Camping Le Balze,** Via di Mandringa 15, 56048 Volterra (PI) **0588 87880; campinglebalze@hotmail.it; www.campinglebalze.com**

⟦icons⟧ nr ⟦icons⟧

Take Pisa rd (S68) fr town; site clearly sp ('Camping' or symbol) after 1km. Watch out for R turn at sharp L corner. 2*, Med, pt shd, pt sl, terr, EHU (6A) inc; gas; bus adj; Eng spkn; ccard acc; CKE. *"Beautifully situated with views of Volterra & hills; gd, adequate san facs; select own pitch; Etruscan walls just outside site; excel site; helpful staff."* **€33.00, 1 Apr-15 Oct.**   2018

ELBA ISLAND

MARINA DI CAMPO *1C3* (0km E Coastal) *42.75194, 10.24472* **Camping Ville degli Ulivi,** Via della Foce 89, 57034 Marina-di-Campo nell'Elba (LI) **0565 976098; info@villedegliulivi.it; www.villedegliulivi.it**

⟦icons⟧ (€6, dog shwrs) ⟦icons⟧ sand adj

Fr Portoferraio take rd sp 'tutti le direzione', then foll sp Procchio, Marina-di-Campo & La Foce, site sp. 3*, Lge, pt shd, EHU (4A) €2.50; gas; 30% statics; adv bkg acc; ccard acc; horseriding 2km; archery; tennis 300m; bike hire; waterslide; golf 15km; watersports. *"Lovely, well-preserved island; gd, v clean, modern site."* **€54.50, 21 Apr-20 Oct.**   2020

SARDINIA

ALGHERO *3A1* (1.5km N Coastal) *40.57916, 8.31222* **Camping La Mariposa,** Via Lido 22, 07041 Alghero (SS) **079 9950480; info@lamariposa.it; www.lamariposa.it**

⟦icons⟧ sand adj

N fr Alghero on coast rd dir Fertilia. Site on L just beyond pool. 3*, Lge, hdstg, pt shd, pt sl, terr, EHU (6-10A) €3; gas; bbq; TV; 20% statics; bus nr; Eng spkn; ccard acc; bike hire; watersports; games rm; sep car park; CKE. *"Lovely wooded site; gd clean facs; gd security; friendly staff; boat fr Alghero to caves at Cape Caccia or by rd + 625 steps."* **€41.00, 1 Apr-15 Oct.**   2016

CAGLIARI *3B1* (1km SE Urban) *39.21129, 9.12883* **Camper Cagliari Park,** 13 Via Stanislao Caboni, 09125 Cagliari **329 6713141 or 070 303147 or 0328 3348847 (mob); info@campercagliaripark.it; www.campercagliaripark.it**

⟦12⟧ ⟦icons⟧ WD ⟦icon⟧

Well sp on main rds into Cagliari. Sm, unshd, EHU (10A) €4; bus 200m; Eng spkn; CKE. *"Gd secure site; v helpful owner; walking dist historical cent, rests etc; c'vans enquire 1st."* **€21.00**   2019

DORGALI *3A2* (7km W Coastal) *40.28486, 9.63370* **Camping Villaggio Calagonone,** Via Collodi 1, 08022 Cala-Gonone (NU) **0784 93476; info@calagononecamping.com; www.calagononecamping.com**

⟦icons⟧ €5 ⟦icons⟧ WD ⟦icons⟧ MSP ⟦icons⟧ shgl 400m

Fr S125 turn E twd Cala Gonone, thro tunnel. Site sp on L of main rd. 4*, Med, shd, terr, EHU (6A) €5; bbq; 30% statics; phone; adv bkg acc; ccard acc; games area; tennis. *"Beautiful situation in pine forest on edge of pretty town; nrby coves & grottoes accessible by boat or on foot."* **€44.00, 1 Apr-3 Nov.**   2019

NARBOLIA *3A1* (6km W Coastal) *40.06956, 8.48375* **Camping Nurapolis,** Loc Is Arenas, 09070 Narbolia (OR) **0783 52283 or 348 8080839(mob); info@nurapolis.it; www.nurapolis.it**

⟦12⟧ ⟦icons⟧ sand adj

Fr Oristano take sp to Cuglier on rd SS292i. Site sp fr rd approx 5km fr S. Caterina-di-Pittinura. 3*, Lge, pt shd, EHU (3A) €3; gas; adv bkg acc; ccard acc; tennis; watersports; CKE. *"Site in pine forest; many sports, guided walks Easter to Oct; very pleasant owners."* **€36.50**   2019

PORTO SAN PAOLO *3A2* (2km S Coastal) *40.85870, 9.64296* **Camping Tavolara,** Loc Porto Taverna, 07020 Loiri-Porta San Paolo (SS) **0789 40166; info@camping-tavolara.it; www.camping-tavolara.it**

⟦icons⟧ €3 ⟦icons⟧ WD ⟦icons⟧ MSP ⟦icons⟧ sand 500m

On SS125, sp. 3*, Lge, hdg, unshd, EHU (3-6A) €3.50; 25% statics; Eng spkn; adv bkg acc; ccard acc; tennis; bike hire; site clsd Dec & early Jan; CKE. *"Friendly staff; conv ferries & boat trips; pleasant, well managed site; 16km fr Olbia ferries; lovely beach; siesta 1:30-3:30pm; vg."* **€50.00, 19 Apr-13 Oct.**   2019

PORTO TORRES *3A1* (7km E Coastal) *40.81607, 8.48541* **Camping Golfo dell'Asinara-Cristina,** Loc Platamona, 07037 Sorso (SS) **079 310230; info@ campingasinara.it; www.campingasinara.it**

⟦icons⟧ MSP ⟦icons⟧ sand adj

Foll coast rd SP81 E fr Porto-Torres to site. Sp. 4*, Lge, pt shd, EHU (4A) €4; gas; red long stay; 40% statics; ccard acc; bike hire; tennis; games area; sep car park; CKE. *"Gd position."* **€35.00, 15 May-30 Sep.**   2016

PULA *3B1* (4km S Coastal) *38.96779, 8.97799*
Camping Flumendosa, Santa Margherita, Km 33.800, 09010 Pula (CA) **070 4615332 or 392 9623094; info@campingflumendosa.com; www.camping flumendosa.com**

🛉 €2.50 👫 (htd) 🚿 ♨ 🚻 ♿ 🍴 ⚙ ⁄ MP 🦋 ♈ 🍷 ⑪ 🛒 ⚘ 🛶
🏖 sand

Fr Cagliari take SS195 past Pula, sp. Turn L, foll track for 500m to site ent. Lge, hdstg, mkd, pt shd, EHU (8A); gas; bbq; cooking facs; TV; 30% statics; Eng spkn; adv bkg acc; ccard acc; fishing; guided walks; jeu de boules alley; beach volleyball. *"Beautiful coastline; excel for children; sand flies abound; good, pleasant, friendly site; gd bar/rest; rec Nora for Roman city & beach; conv for lovely coast to W."* **€43.00, 1 Apr-13 Nov.** 2019

TONARA *3A1* (0.9km NE Rural) *40.02812, 9.17647*
Camping Sa Colonia, Via Muggianeddu 4, 08039 Tonara (NU) **03921 282340; info@camping sacolonia.it**

12 👫 🚿 ♨ ⁄ 🦋 🍷 ⑪ 🛒 nr ⛰

Fr S fr Cagliari on SS128/SS295, site sp. Sp rte unsuitable lge car + c'van o'fits or v lge m'vans. Avoid town cent rds - v narr & steep. Med, mkd, shd, terr, EHU (5A) inc; Eng spkn; CKE. *"Mountain scenery; rds gd but steep, twisty & slow; welcoming owners."* **€20.00** 2016

SICILY

ACIREALE *3C4* (1.5km NE Coastal) *37.62015, 15.17320*
La Timpa International Camping, Via Santa Maria La Scala 25, 95024 Acireale **095 7648155; info@ campinglatimpa.com; www.campinglatimpa.com**

12 🛉 €4 👫 🚿 ♨ ♿ ⁄ 🍷 ⑪ 🛒 ⛰ 🏖 adj

Exit A18/E45 onto rd S114 dir Acireale. Foll sp for Santa Maria La Scala; site on L after 1.5km; steep & diff access rds. 3*, Med, pt shd, EHU (6A) €3.50, 60% statics; ccard acc; sep car park; CKE. *"Lovely site in orchard, o'looking sea, surfaced in black volcanic ash; hot & cold shwrs; no dogs Jul/Aug; chem displ; trips to Etna; lift down to rocky beach; sh, steep walk to vill & harbour; v quiet; gd rest."* **€30.50** 2018

AGRIGENTO *3C3* (8km S Urban/Coastal) *37.26936, 13.58299* **Camping Valle dei Templi,** Viale Emporium 95, 92100 San Leone **0922 411115; info@camping velledeitempli.com; www.campingvalledeitempli. com**

12 🛉 👫 🚿 ♨ ♿ 🍴 ⁄ MP 🍷 ⑪ 🛒 nr 🏖 800m

Sp S of Agrigento, foll sp San Leone, site on L bef beach. Lge, hdstg, pt shd, pt sl, terr, EHU (6A) €3; red long stay; 20% statics; bus; Eng spkn; adv bkg acc; ccard acc; tennis; bike hire; site clsd 8 Dec-15 Jan; CKE. *"Gd modern facs; friendly staff; bus to temples fr site ent."* **€40.50** 2018

AVOLA *3C4* (4km N Coastal) *36.93631, 15.17462*
Camping Sabbiadoro, Via Chiusa di Carlo 45, 96012 Avola (SR) **0931 822415; info@campeggio sabbiadoro.com; www.campeggiosabbiadoro.com**

12 🛉 👫 🚿 ♨ ⁄ MP 🦋 ♈ 🍷 🛒 🏖 sand

Fr N exit A18/E45 at Cassibile onto S115 dir Avola, site sp in 4km. Last 500m on narr, winding rd. 3*, Med, mkd, shd, pt sl, terr, EHU (2A) €4; 20% statics; phone; adv bkg acc; ccard acc; horseriding. *"V attractive site with clean, ltd facs; rec visit Noto; well run; dir access to beach; sep car park Jul-Aug; poss muddy pitches after heavy rain."* **€41.00** 2019

AVOLA *3C4* (5km NE Coastal) *36.93853, 15.17756*
Camping Paradiso del Mare, Contrada Gallinara Fondolupo, 96012 Avola (SR) **0931 561147; info@ paradisodelmare.com; www.paradisodelmare.com**

🛉 👫 🚿 ♨ ♿ ⁄ 🦋 🍷 ⑪ nr 🛒 🏖 adj

Best app fr N on S115 fr Siracusa, site on L, well sp. Tight turn if app fr Avola. 2*, Sm, mkd, pt shd, EHU (5A) €3; bus 200m; Eng spkn; CKE. *"Pleasant lovely site by beautiful beach; friendly helpful owners."* **€27.50, 14 Apr-31 Oct.** 2018

> ## "That's changed – Should I let the Club know?"
>
> If you find something on site that's different from the site entry, fill in a report and let us know. See camc.com/europereport.

CASTELLAMMARE DEL GOLFO *3C3* (1km E Coastal) *38.02393, 12.89348* **Nausicaa Camping,** C/da Spiaggia-Plaia, Loc Forgia, 91014 Castellammare-del-Golfo (TP) **0924 33030; info@nausicaa-camping.it; www.nausicaa-camping.it**

👫 🚿 ♨ ⁄ 🦋 ⑪ nr 🛒 ⛰ 🏖 sand adj

Site 1km E fr Castellammare on R of rte 187. Well sp. Awkward ent for lge o'fits as steep ramp. 3*, Sm, hdstg, mkd, pt shd, EHU €3; gas; 10% statics; ccard acc; tennis; CKF *"Nr Roman temple at Segesta; gd 1st stop fr Palermo if touring historical sites; lovely site on cliff; easy walk to town & access to beach."* **€41.00, 1 Apr-15 Oct.** 2018

CASTELVETRANO *3C3* (13km SE Coastal) *37.59571, 12.84139* **Camping Athena,** Loc Marinella, Contrada Garraffo, 91022 Castelvetrano (TP) **0924 46132; info@campingathenaselinunte.it; www.camping athenaselinunte.it**

12 🛉 👫 🚿 ♨ ⁄ MP 🍷 ⑪ 🛒 nr 🏖 sand 800m

Exit SS115 (Castelvetrano-Sciacca) at sp to Selinunte, site on L bef Selinunte. 1*, Sm, hdstg, pt shd, EHU (10A) inc; bbq; phone; ccard acc; CKE. *"Can take lger o'fits than Maggiolino site; conv temples at Selinunte; excel facs; gd rest adj."* **€18.00** 2020

CATANIA *3C4* (6km NE Coastal) *37.53279, 15.12012*
Camping Jonio, Loc Ognina, Via Villini a Mare 2,
95126 Catania **095 491139; info@campingjonio.com;
www.campingjonio.com**

🏕12 🐕 ♀♂ wc ⚓ ♿ 🚿 ⊟ ∿ MSP 🍴 ☂ ⊕ ♨ 🛒 ⛵ nr ⛱shgl

SS114 N of Catania, exit Ognina. Fr the Catania ring
rd, take exit Catania Centro (San Gregorio) and then
Catania E. Foll sp to site. 3*, Med, hdstg, pt shd, terr,
EHU (6A) €4; gas; bbq; twin axles; 20% statics; bus to
Catania; Eng spkn; adv bkg acc; ccard acc; waterskiing;
games area; sep car park; CKE. *"Mt Etna 45 mins
drive N; owner v helpful; some pitches sm; subways,
scubadiving; gd."* **€39.00**   **2016**

CEFALU *3B3* (3km W Coastal) *38.02703, 13.98283*
Camping Costa Ponente, C de Ogliastrillo, 90015
Cefalù (PA) **0921 420085; info@camping-costa
ponente.com; http://camping-costaponente.com**

🐕 €3.50 ♀♂ wc ⚓ ♿ 🚿 ∿ 🍴 ☂ ⊕ 🛒 ⛵ ⛱sand

Fr Palermo E twd Cefalù, on rd SS113 at km stone
190.3, site sp. Lge, hdstg, shd, terr, EHU rev pol
(3A) €5; gas; 10% statics; bus nr; ccard acc; tennis;
CKE. *"Sep car park (high ssn); dogs not acc Aug."*
€30.00, 1 Apr-31 Oct.   **2020**

CEFALU *3B3* (5km W Rural) *38.02700, 13.98247*
Camping Sanfilippo, Ogliastrillo SS113, 90015 Cefalù
**0921 420 184; info@campingsanfilippo.com;
www.campingsanfilippo.com**

🐕 €3.50 ♀♂ wc ⚓ ♿ 🚿 ⊟ ∿ MSP 🦋 ☂ 🛒 ⛱ 150m

Fr Palermo E twds Cafalu on rd SS113. 2*, Med,
hdstg, mkd, shd, terr, EHU (4A) inc; bbq; twin axles;
50% statics; bus 300m; Eng spkn; adv bkg acc;
games area; games rm; CCI. *"Vg, beautiful site; sea
views fr some pitches; newly renovated (2016)."*
€28.50, 1 Apr-31 Oct.   **2018**

MARINA DI RAGUSA *3C3* (2km E Coastal) *36.78116,
14.56697* **Camping Baia del Sole,** Lungomare Andrea
Doria, 97010 Marina-di-Ragusa (RG) **03495 116018 or
03393 471986; info@campingbaiadelsole.it;
www.campingbaiadelsole.it**

🏕12 ♀♂ ⚓ ⊟ 🍴 ☂ ⊕ 🛒 ⊞ ⛵ ⛱adj

Foll sp in Marina di Ragusa for Hotel Baia del Sole.
Site in hotel grnds on dual c'way on seafront.
3*, Med, shd, EHU (4A) inc; adv bkg acc; ccard acc; bike
hire; tennis. *"Go to recep 1st; no height barrier; sep car
park; v quiet."* **€19.00**   **2018**

MENFI *3C3* (6km S Coastal) *37.56500, 12.96416*
Camping La Palma, Contrada Fiore, Via delle Palme
29, 92013 Menfi (AG) **0925 78392; campinglapalma@
libero.it; www.campinglapalma.com**

🏕12 🐕 ♀♂ wc ⚓ ♿ 🚿 ∿ 🦋 ☂ ⊕ 🛒 ⊞ ⛵ ⛱sand adj

Foll sp fr SS115 past Menfi to coast. In abt 3-4km
look for campsite sp. 1*, Med, hdstg, shd, EHU 16A;
gas; bbq; twin axles; TV; 5% statics; Eng spkn; adv bkg
acc; games area; CKE. *"Lovely, unspoilt quiet beach
(blue flag) with dunes; v helpful owner & staff; family
run site; excel."* **€30.00**   **2018**

MILAZZO *3B4* (2km N Coastal) *38.26090, 15.24335*
Camping Villaggio Riva Smeralda, Strada
Panoramica 64, 98057 Milazzo (ME) **090 9282980;
info@rivasmeralda.it; www.rivasmeralda.it**

🏕12 ♀♂ wc ⚓ ♿ 🚿 ∿ MSP 🍴 ☂ ⊕ 🛒 ⛵ ⊞ ⚓ 🌊 ⛱shgl adj

Clearly sp in Milazzo; foll sp Capo-di-Milazzo. Diff
app. 1*, Med, hdstg, shd, pt sl, terr, EHU (6A) €3; bbq;
twin axles; 5% statics; Eng spkn; adv bkg acc; CKE. *"Gd
base for trips to adj isles; site a bit run down; 1 in 5 sl
access to pitches, ltd turning space; best for sm m'vans;
diving cent on site; excel; v nice site with beautiful
views of sea; pitches tight; extremely helpful owners;
€3 a night to leave camper to go to Aeolian Islands; vg."*
€33.50   **2017**

PALERMO *3B3* (16km NW Urban/Coastal) *38.19805,
13.28083* **Camping Degli Ulivi,** Via Pegaso 25, 90148
Sferracavallo (PA) **091 533021 or 091 530247;
mporion@libero.it; www.campingdegliulivi.com**

🏕12 🐕 ♀♂ wc ⚓ ♿ 🚿 ∿ MSP 🦋 ☂ 🛒 nr ⛱ ⛱shgl 300m

Fr W on A29 exit sp Tommaso & foll dual c'way
twd Mondello. Do U-turn at 1st opportunity to
Sferracavallo. Downhill thro vill, site sp, R turn off
hg street. 1*, Sm, hdg, pt shd, pt sl, EHU (6-10A) €3;
bbq; twin axles; 10% statics; bus to Palermo; Eng spkn;
sep car park; CKE. *"Helpful staff; pleasant ambience;
beach sand 700m; well-maintained site nr nature park -
excel views, popular site."* **€20.50**   **2016**

PATTI *B4* (4.8km NNW Coastal) *38.169266, 14.948943*
Camping IL Cicero, Via Pola 98, 98063 San Giorgio
**094 139551 or 347 9989530; info@ilcicero.it;
www.ilcicero.it**

🐕 ♀♂(htd) wc ∿ MSP 🦋 ☂ 🍴 ⊕ nr 🛒 nr ⚓
⛱sand; adj

Fr E90 take SS113 to San Giorgio. Site on seafront.
Med, mkd, shd, EHU (6A) inc; twin axles; 20% statics;
0.5km; games area; games rm. *"V friendly, helpful
staff; gd for kids; vg site."* **€36.00, 1 May-30 Sep. 2018**

PIAZZA ARMERINA *3C3* (4km SE Rural) *37.20239,
14.23155* **Camping Agriturismo Agricasale,** C da
Ciavarini, 94015 Piazza-Armerina (EN) **0935 686034;
www.agricasale.it**

🏕12 🐕 ♀♂ wc ⚓ ♿ 🚿 ∿ MSP 🦋 🍴 ⊕ 🛒 nr ⊞ ⚓

In Piazza-Armerina town foll sp twd Mirabella but at
rndabt with stone cross bear R (red fox sign) & foll
red fox down nar rd to wooded site. Park with care.
Sm, pt shd, pt sl, EHU (4A) inc; bbq; TV; Eng spkn;
adv bkg acc; CKE. *"Excel site close Palazzo Romana
mosaics; pony-trekking, archery & other activities high
ssn; all inc rate of €50 avail per day inc excel banquet;
site run down."* **€15.00**   **2019**

PUNTA BRACCETTO *3C3* (0km E Urban/Coastal) *36.81713, 14.46736* **Camping Scarabeo,** Via dei Canaletti 120, Punta-Braccetto, 97017 Santa Croce Camerina (RG) **0932 918096; info@scarabeo camping.it; www.scarabeocamping.it**

🏕 🐕 €2.50 🚻 wc ♨ ♿ 🚿 🚮 ♨ MSP 🦋 ⛺ ℗ nr ⑪ nr 🛒 ♠ 🏕 sand adj

W fr Marina di Ragusa on SP80/SC25 coast rd. **Site sp.** 2*, Sm, hdstg, hdg, pt shd, pt sl, EHU (3-6A); bbq; red long stay; twin axles; 5% statics; phone; Eng spkn; adv bkg acc; ccard acc; CKE. *"Beautiful situation; private bthrm €4; well-maintained, friendly, family-run site; gd, clean, modern facs; vg security; friendly, helpful staff; cars parked sep across rd; excel."* **€41.50** 2017

PUNTA BRACCETTO *3C3* (0km S Urban/Coastal) *36.81722, 14.46583* **Camping Luminoso,** Viale dei Canalotti, 97017 Punta Braccetto - Santa Croce Camerina (RG) **0932 918401; info@camping luminoso.com; www.campingluminoso.com**

🏕 🐕 🚻 wc ♨ ♿ 🚿 🚮 ♨ MSP 🦋 ℗ ⛺ ⑪ ♠ 🏕 sand adj

W fr Marina di Ragusa on SP80/SC25 coast rd. **Site sp.** 3*, Med, mkd, hdstg, shd, EHU (6A) €5; TV; adv bkg rec; ccard acc; bike hire; CKE. *"Well-run site in gd location; easy access to pitches - suitable lge o'fits/m'vans; excel; modern, immac facs; spacious level hdstg pitches; reliable wifi; helpful English manager; private bthrms avail; direct access to sandy beach; mob shops call daily; ideal long stay in winter."* **€46.00** 2019

PUNTA BRACCETTO *3C3* (4km SW Coastal) *36.81661, 14.46895* **Camping Baia Dei Coralli,** Punta Braccetto, 97017 Santa Croce Camerina **0932 91 81 92; info@baiadeicoralli.it; www.baiadeicoralli.it**

🏕 🐕 🚻 wc ♨ ♿ 🚿 🚮 ♨ MSP 🦋 ℗ ⛺ ⑪ 🧺 🛒 ♠ 🏊 🏕 sand

Fr Agrigento take SS115 twds Sircusa to Gela. Turn L onto SP14, cont onto SP13. At rndabt take 3rd exit onto SP20, R onto SP85, L twd Strada Regionale 25. R onto Strada Regionale 24. Campsite on L. 3*, Lge, hdg, hdstg, unshd, EHU (6A); bbq; twin axles; TV; bus; Eng spkn; adv bkg acc; ccard acc; CCI. *"Excel site; v busy in summer."* **€35.00** 2019

SAN VITO LO CAPO *3B3* (3km S Coastal) *38.15067, 12.73184* **El Bahira Camping Village,** Contrada Salinella, 91010 San-Vito-lo-Capo (TP) **0923 972577; info@elbahira.it; www.elbahira.it**

🏕 🚻 wc ♿ 🚿 🚮 ♨ 🦋 ⛺ ⑪ 🧺 🛒 ♠ 🏊 ⛵ 🏕 shgl adj

W fr Palermo on A29 dir Trapani. Exit at Castellammare del Golfo onto SS187, then turn N onto SP16 sp San Vito-lo-Capo. At Isolidda foll site **sp.** 4*, Lge, mkd, shd, EHU (6A) inc; bbq; TV; 10% statics; phone; bus nr; Eng spkn; ccard acc; watersports; games rm; sep car park; tennis; excursions; games area; CKE. *"Excel, secure site in vg location; gd facs for families; san facs tired need updating (2014)."* **€26.00** 2019

SECCAGRANDE *3C3* (2km SE Coastal) *37.43833, 13.2450* **Kamemi Camping Village,** Contrada Camemi Superiore, 92016 Seccagrande-di-Ribera (AG) **0925 69212; info@kamemicamping.it; www.kamemicamping.it**

🏕 🐕 🚻 ♨ ♿ 🚿 🚮 ♨ ⛺ ℗ 🧺 ♠ 🏕 sand 1km

Foll sp fr S115 to Seccagrande & site. 2*, Med, hdstg, pt shd, EHU (6A) €5; 40% statics; Eng spkn; adv bkg rec; tennis; games area. **€37.00** 2019

SIRACUSA *3C4* (4km SW Rural) *37.03841, 15.25063* **Camping Agritourist Rinaura,** Strada Laganelli, Loc Rinaura, SS115, 96100 Siracusa **0931 721224; sindona.marina@virgilio.it; www.campingrinaura.it**

🏕 🚻 wc ♨ ♿ 🚮 ⛺ ⑪ nr 🛒 ♠ 🏕 sand 2km

S fr Siracusa on S115 twd Avola. Turn R 300m past Hotel Albatros then immed R after rlwy x-ing. Narr lane to site in 300m. 2*, Lge, pt shd, EHU (16A) €3; red long stay; phone; bus 1km; Eng spkn; adv bkg acc; bike hire; CKE. *"CL-type site in lge orchard; basic but adequate san facs; rather neglected LS; helpful owners."* **€27.00** 2019

TAORMINA *3C4* (10km NE Coastal) *37.93159, 15.35560* **Camping La Focetta Sicula,** Via Torrente Agro, 98030 Sant' Alessio Siculo (ME) **0942 751657; info@lafocetta.it; www.lafocetta.it**

🏕 🐕 🚻 wc ♨ ♿ 🚿 🚮 ♨ MSP 🦋 ⛺ ℗ ⑪ 🧺 🛒 ♠ 🏕 sand

A'strada fr Messina to Catania, exit Roccalumera. SS114 thro Sta Teresa-di-Riva to vill of Sant' Alessio-Siculo. Sp at beg of vill. NB Many towns poorly sp. 2*, Med, mkd, pt shd, EHU (6A) €3 gas; red long stay; sep car park; bike hire; games area; CKE. *"Popular winter site; v helpful owner."* **€26.00** 2018

TAORMINA *3C4* (12km S Coastal) *37.74928, 15.20616* **Camping Mokambo,** Via Spiaggia 211, Fondachello, 95016 Máscali (CT) **095 938731; info@campingmokambo.it; www.campingmokambo.it**

🐕 🚻 wc ♨ ♿ 🚮 ♨ ⑪ nr 🛒 nr ♠ 🏕 adj

Exit A18/E45 at Fiumefreddo & take S114 sp Catania. In Máscali turn L twd Fondachello. At Fondachello turn R & foll site sp, site 1km on R. 2*, Med, hdstg, pt shd, EHU (3A) €4; bbq; 10% statics; Eng spkn; adv bkg acc; ccard acc; games area; CKE. *"Gd views Etna; conv beach & Taormina; wifi unreliable; no dogs Jul/Aug; poor."* **€43.20, 1 Apr-30 Sep.** 2017

TAORMINA *3C4* (7km SW Coastal) *37.8047, 15.2444* **Camping Internazionale Almoetia,** Via San Marco 19, 95011 Calatabiano (CT) **095 641936; camping almoetia@virgilio.it; www.campingalmoetia.it**

🏕 🐕 🚻 wc ♨ ♿ 🚿 🚮 ♨ 🦋 ⛺ ⑪ 🧺 🛒 🏕 shgl 500m

Exit a'strada dir Giardini Naxos. Turn S onto S114 dir Catania, foll sp L onto Via San Marco, site clearly **sp.** 2*, Med, pt shd, EHU (6A) €2.50; gas; bbq; red long stay; TV; phone; adv bkg acc; bike hire; canoeing; tennis; CKE. *"Conv Etna, Taormina; surrounded by orchards; used by tour groups in motor hotels; site well kept; excel facs; lovely beach nrby."* **€27.00** 2020

Map 1

Map 2

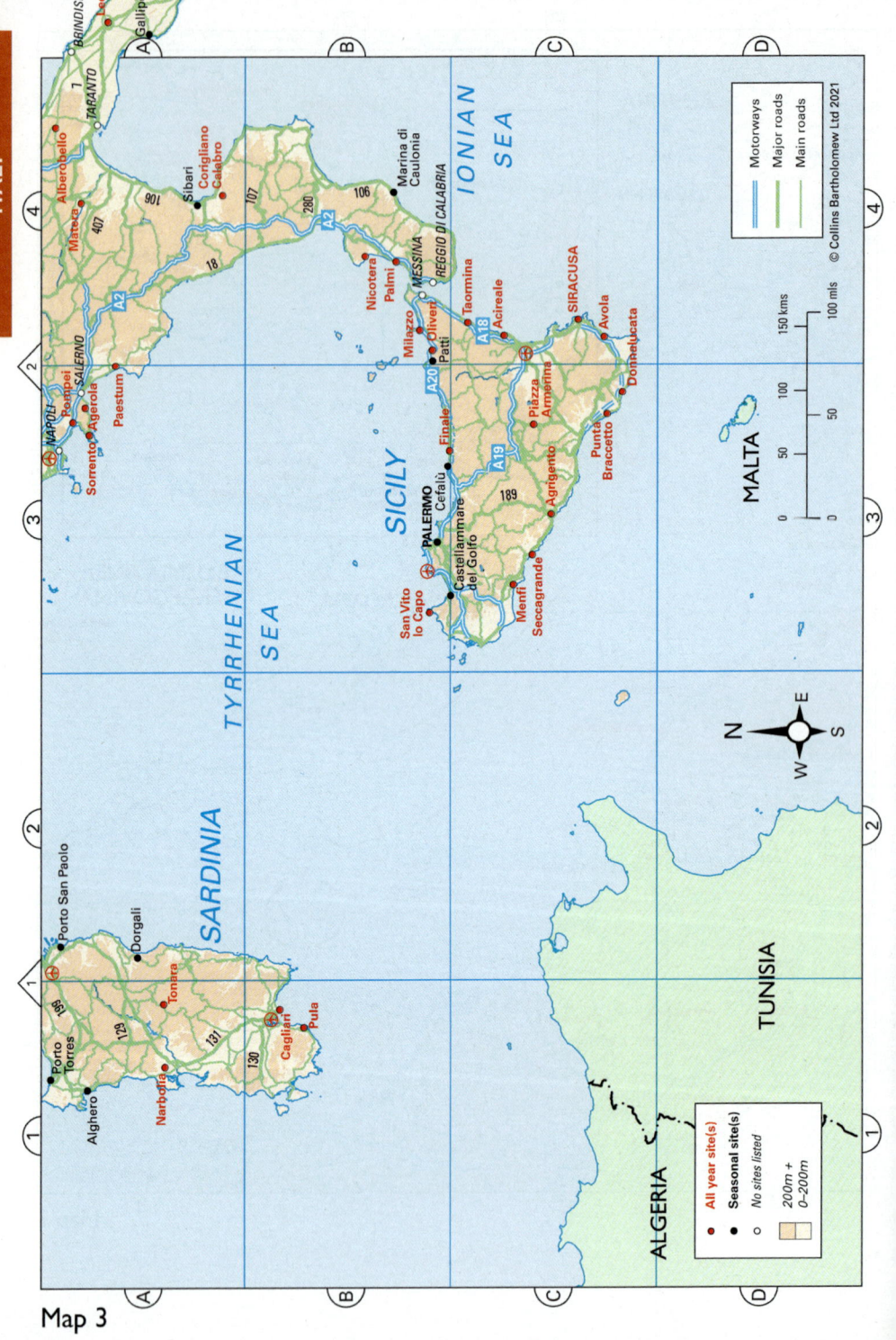

Map 3

ABRUZZO
Chieti
L'Aquila
Pescara
Teramo

BASILICATA
Matera
Potenza

CALABRIA
Catanzaro
Cosenza
Crotone
Reggio di Calabria
Vibo Valentia

CAMPANIA
Avellino
Benevento
Caserta
Napoli
Salerno

EMILIA-ROMAGNA
Bologna
Ferrara
Forli
Modena
Parma
Piacenza
Ravenna
Reggio Emilia
Rimini

FRIULI-VENEZIA GIULIA
Gorizia
Pordenone
Trieste
Udine

LAZIO
Frosinone
Latina
Rieti
Roma
Viterbo

LIGURIA
Genova
Imperia
La Spezia
Savona

LOMBARDIA
Bergamo
Brescia
Como
Cremona
Lecco
Lodi
Mantova
Milano
Pavia
Sondrio
Varese

MARCHE
Ancona
Ascoli Piceno
Macerata
Pesaro e Urbino

MOLISE
Campobasso
Isernia

PIEMONTE
Alessandria
Asti
Biella
Cuneo
Novara
Torino
Verbano-Cusio-Ossola
Vercelli

PUGLIA
Bari
Brindisi
Foggia
Lecce
Taranto

SARDEGNA
Cagliari
Nuoro
Oristano
Sassari

SICILIA
Agrigento
Caltanissetta
Catania
Enna
Messina
Palermo
Ragusa
Siracusa
Trapani

TOSCANA
Arezzo
Firenze
Grosseto
Livorno
Lucca
Massa Carrara
Pisa
Pistoia
Prato
Siena

TRENTINO-ALTO ADIGE
Bolzano
Trento

UMBRIA
Perugia
Terni

VALLE D'AOSTA
Aosta/Aoste

VENETO
Belluno
Padova
Rovigo
Treviso
Venezia
Verona
Vicenza

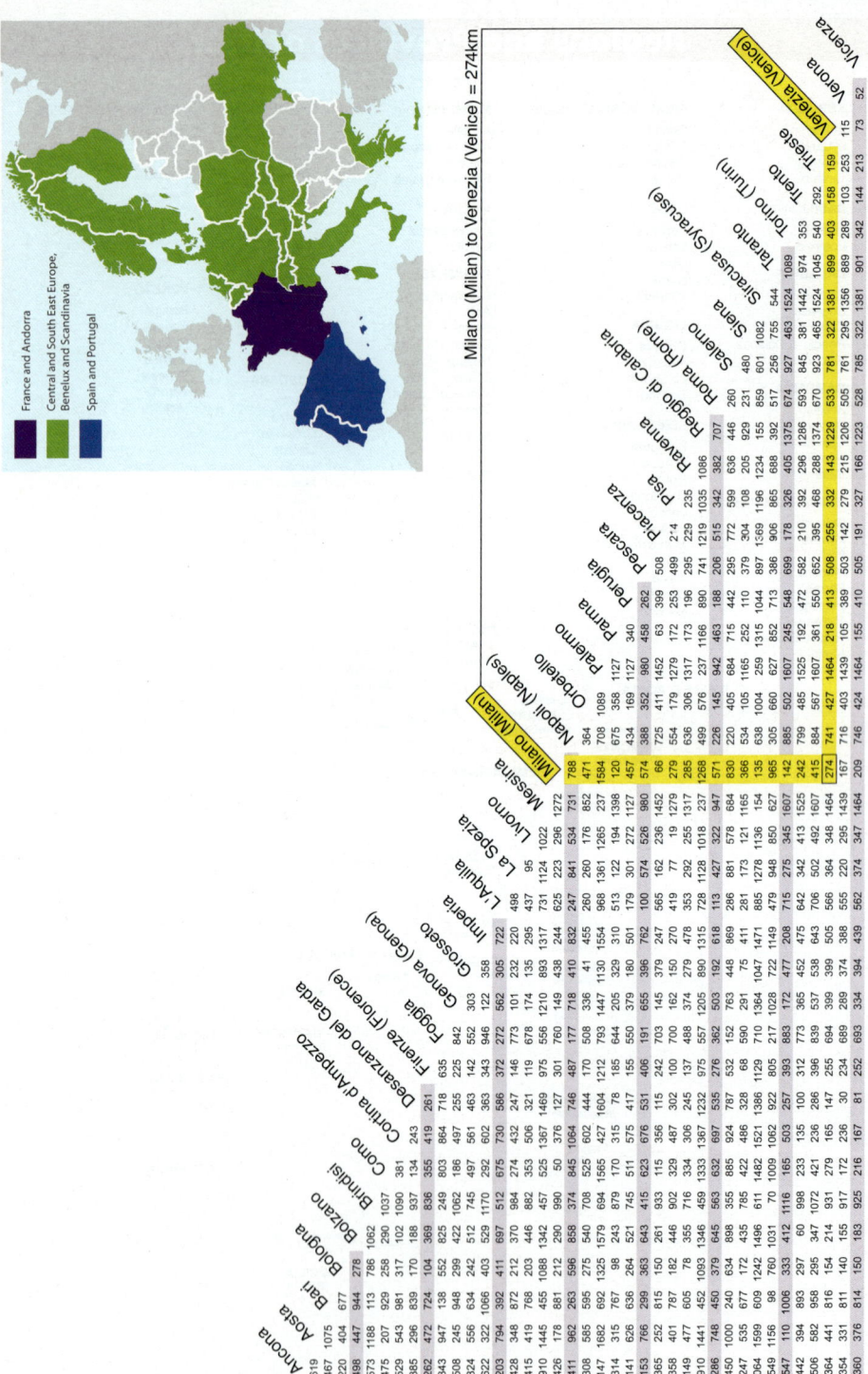

France and Andorra

Central and South East Europe, Benelux and Scandinavia

Spain and Portugal

Milano (Milan) to Venezia (Venice) = 274km

Luxembourg

Vianden Castle

Highlights

Although a tiny country just over 50 miles long, Luxembourg is an economic powerhouse. Luxembourg City is famous for its stunning, medieval old town and for the number of notable museums and galleries that it boasts

Most of the country is rural, and the beautiful landscapes vary from the micro-gorges of Müllerthal to the vineyards of the Moselle wine region.

Luxembourg cuisine is heavily influenced by its neighbours and in particular has many Germanic influences. Judd mat Gaardebounen, a smoked collar of pork with broad beans, is a particularly popular meal and is widely recognised as one of the country's national dishes.

The Festival of Wiltz is an annual affair that celebrates some of the most talented international musicians. With its open air setting and castle backdrop, it attracts large audiences each year and is considered to be a cultural highlight.

Major towns and cities

- Luxembourg City – this fascinating capital offers UNESCo sites and gastronomy.
- Esch-sur-Alzette – this city has the longest shopping street in the country.
- Diekirck – a city with charming old streets.
- Dudelange – a cultural centre with lots to see including Mount St. Jean.

Attractions

- Mullerthal Trail – explore 112km of varied landscape, from forests to rock formations.
- Vianden Castle, Vianden – a grand building that originates from the 10th century.
- National Museum of Art and History, Luxembourg City – enjoy a fascinating range of exhibitions from archaeology to fine arts.
- Holy Ghost Citadel, Luxembourg City – a majestic fortress with stunning views.

Find out more

www.visitluxembourg.lu
E: info@visitluxembourg.lu
T: +352 (0) 42 82 82 10

Country Information

Population (approx): 570,000

Capital: Luxembourg City

Area: 2,586 sq km

Bordered by: Belgium, France, Germany

Terrain: Rolling hills to north with broad, shallow valleys; steep slope to Moselle valley in south-east

Climate: Temperate climate without extremes of heat or cold; mild winters; warm, wet summers; July and August are the hottest months; May and June have the most hours of sunshine.

Highest Point: Kneiff 560m

Languages: French, German, Lëtzebuergesch (Luxembourgish)

Local Time: GMT or BST + 1, i.e. 1 hour ahead of the UK all year

Currency: Euros divided into 100 cents; £1 = €1.14, €1 = £0.88 (Feb 2021)

Emergency numbers: Police 113; Fire brigade 112; Ambulance 112. Operators speak English

Public Holidays 2021: Jan 1; Apr 4, 5; May 1, 9, 13, 24; Jun 23; Aug 15; Nov 1; Dec 25, 26.

There are other dates such as Luxembourg City Fete and 2 Nov which are not official holidays but many businesses, banks and shops may close. School summer holidays run from mid-July to mid-September.

Entry Formalities

British and Irish passport holders may stay for up to 90 days in any 180 day period without a visa. Following Brexit you may be asked to show a return or onward ticket at the border to confirm your length of stay, or to prove that you have enough money for your stay.

Your passport will need to have a minimum of 6 months' validity remaining, and be less than 10 years old (even if it has over 6 months left).

Visitors arriving at a campsite or hotel must complete a registration form.

Medical Services

Emergency medical treatment is available on presentation of a European Health Insurance Card (EHIC) but you will be charged both for treatment and prescriptions. Refunds can be obtained from a local sickness insurance fund office, Caisse de Maladie des Ouvriers (CMO). Emergency hospital treatment is normally free apart from a non-refundable standard daily fee.

Opening Hours

Banks: Mon-Fri 8.30am-12 noon & 1.30pm-4.30pm.Some stay open to 6pm and open Sat 9am-12 noon.

Museums: Tue-Sun 10am-6pm, Thurs late opening 5pm-8pm (check locally); most close Mon.

Post Offices: Mon-Fri 8am-12 noon & 1.30pm-4.30pm/5pm; the central post office in Luxembourg City is open 7am-7pm Mon to Fri & 7am-5pm Sat.

Shops: Mon-Sat 9am/10am-6pm/6.30pm. Some close for lunch and Mon mornings. Large malls may be open to 8pm or 9pm.

Safety and Security

There are few reports of crime but visitors should take the usual commonsense precautions against pickpockets. Do not leave valuables in your car.

Luxembourg shares with the rest of Europe an underlying threat from terrorism. Attacks could be indiscriminate and against civilian targets in public places, including tourist sites.

British Embassy

BOULEVARD JOSEPH II, L-1840 LUXEMBOURG
Tel: 22 98 64
www.ukinluxembourg.fco.gov.uk

Irish Embassy

Résidence Christina (2nd floor)

28 ROUTE D'ARLON, L-1140 LUXEMBOURG
Tel: 450 6101
www.embassyofireland.lu

Documents

Money

Major credit cards are widely accepted although there are often minimum amount requirements. Cash machines are widespread. Carry your credit card issuers'/banks' 24-hour UK contact numbers in case of loss or theft of your cards.

Passport

When driving it is easy to cross into neighbouring countries without realising it. Although you are unlikely to be asked for it, you must have your valid passport with you.

Vehicle(s)

Drivers of foreign-registered vehicles must be able to produce on demand a current driving licence, vehicle registration document (V5C) insurance certificate, insurance certificate and MOT certificate (if applicable).

Driving

Alcohol

The maximum permitted level of alcohol is 50 milligrams in 100 millilitres of blood, i.e. lower than that permitted in the UK (80 milligrams). For drivers who have held a driving licence for less than two years the permitted level is 20 milligrams i.e. virtually nil. Breath tests are compulsory following serious road accidents and road offences.

Breakdown Service

A 24-hour breakdown service 'Service Routier' is operated by the Automobile Club De Grand-Duche de Luxembourg (ACL) on all roads, telephone 26000. Operators speak English. Payment by credit card is accepted.

Child Restraint System

Children under the age of 3 years old must be seated in an approved child restraint system. Children from the ages of 3 to 17 and/or under the height of 1.5m must be seated in an appropriate restraint system. If they are over 36kg in weight they can use a seat belt but only if they are in the rear of the vehicle.

Rear-facing child restraint systems are not allowed on seats with front airbags unless the airbag has been deactivated.

Fuel

Petrol stations are generally open from 8am to 8pm with 24 hour service on motorways. Most accept credit cards. It is illegal to carry petrol in a can.

LPG is available at a handful of petrol stations – see www.mylpg.eu and use the drop down menu listed under LPG stations.

Motorways

There are approximately 152km of motorways, all of which are toll-free for private vehicles. Motorway service areas are situated at Capellen on the A6 near Mamer, at Pontpierre on the A4, and at Berchem near Bettenbourg on the A3.

Emergency telephones are situated every 1.5km along main roads and motorways and link motorists to the 'Protection Civile'.

Overtaking

When overtaking at night outside built-up areas it is compulsory to flash headlights.

Parking

Parking is prohibited where there are yellow lines or zigzag white lines. Blue zone parking areas exist in Luxembourg City, Esch-sur-Elzette, Dudelange and Wiltz. Parking discs are available from the ACL, police stations, tourist offices and shops. Parking meters operate in Luxembourg City. Police will clamp or remove illegally parked vehicles.

There are free car parks two to three kilometres outside Luxembourg City and Esch-sur-Elzette from which regular buses leave for the city.

If there is no public lighting when parking on a public road sidelights must be switched on.

Priority

Where two roads of the same category intersect, traffic from the right has priority. In towns give priority to traffic coming from the right, unless there is a 'priority road' sign (yellow diamond with white border) indicating that the driver using that road has right of way.

Road Signs and Markings

Road signs and markings conform to international standards and are shown in French and German. Traffic lights pass from red immediately to green (no red and amber phase). A flashing amber light allows traffic to turn in the direction indicated, traffic permitting. In Luxembourg City some bus lanes and cycle lanes are marked in red.

Speed Limits

	Open Road (km/h)	Motorway (km/h)
Car Solo	90	130
Car towing caravan/trailer	75	90
Motorhome under 3500kg	90	130
Motorhome 3500-7500kg	90	130

The solo car top speed of 130 km/h (80 mph) is reduced to 110 km/h (68 mph) in wet weather.

The speed limit for drivers who have held a licence for less than a year is 90 km/h (56 mph) on motorways and 75 km/h (47 mph) outside built-up areas. In some residential areas called 'Zones de Rencontre' the maximum permitted speed is 20 km/h (13 mph).

Traffic Jams

Many people travel through Luxembourg in order to take advantage of cheaper fuel and queues at petrol stations often cause jams, in particular along the 'petrol route' past Martelange (N4 in Belgium), at Dudelange on the A3/E25 at the Belgium-Luxembourg border, and near Steinfort on the A6.

Other bottlenecks occur, particularly during weekends in July and August, at the junctions on the A1/E44 near Gasperich to the south of Luxembourg City, and the exit from the A3/E25 at Dudelange. To avoid traffic jams between Luxembourg City and Thionville (France), leave the western ring road around Luxembourg and take the A4 to Esch-sur-Alzette and then the D16. When past Aumetz join the N52 which then connects to the A30 to Metz.

The website www.cita.lu provides webcam views of all motorways and traffic information.

Violation of Traffic Regulations

Police officers may impose on the spot fines for infringement of regulations. These must be settled in cash and a receipt given. Non-residents of Luxembourg can receive penalty points for serious infringements of traffic law.

Winter Driving

Vehicles are required to have M&S (Mud and Snow) marked tyres fitted when driving in wintery conditions (frost, snow, ice etc.). This regulation applies to all drivers, regardless of where the vehicle is registered.

Essential Equipment

Lights

The use of dipped headlights in the daytime is recommended for all vehicles.

Reflective Jacket/Waistcoat

It is compulsory to wear a reflective jacket when getting out of your vehicle on a motorway or main road. Pedestrians walking at night or in bad visibility outside built-up areas must also wear one.

Warning Triangle

A warning triangle must be used if the vehicle is immobilised on the roadway.

Touring

Luxembourg is the only Grand Duchy in the world and measures a maximum of 81km (51 miles) from north to south and 51km (32 miles) from east to west. The fortifications and old town of Luxembourg City have been designated as a UNESCO World Heritage site.

Smoking is not allowed in bars and restaurants. A service charge is usually added to restaurant bills and it is normal practice to leave a little extra if the service is good.

The Luxembourg Card is valid for one, two or three days, and entitles the holder to free public transport, admission to numerous museums and tourist attractions, and discounts on sightseeing trips. It is available from tourist offices, campsites, hotels, information and public transport offices as well as from participating attractions. You can also buy it online at www.ont.lu.

There are many marked walking trails throughout the country – see www.hiking-in-luxembourg.co.uk for full details. A Christmas market is held in the pedestrianised Place d'Armes in Luxembourg City. Others are held in towns and villages throughout the country.

French is the official language, but Luxembourgish is the language most commonly used. English is widely spoken in Luxembourg City, but less so elsewhere.

Camping and Caravanning

There are approximately 120 campsites in Luxembourg; most are open from April to October. Apart from in the industrial south, campsites are found all over the country. The Ardennes, the river banks along the Moselle and the Sûre and the immediate surroundings of Luxembourg City are particularly popular.

Casual/wild camping is only permitted with a tent, not a caravan, but permission must first be sought from the landowner.

Motorhomes

Many campsites have motorhome amenities and some offer Quick Stop overnight facilities at reduced rates.

Electricity and Gas

Most campsites have a supply of between 6 and 16 amps and many have CEE connections.

Plugs have two round pins. The full range of Campingaz cylinders is widely available.

Public Transport & Local Travel

A transport network ticket (billet réseau) is available at railway stations throughout the country and at the airport. It allows unlimited travel on city buses, trains and country coaches for one day (until 8am the next morning) throughout Luxembourg. Public transport maps can be downloaded from the Luxembourg Tourist Office website, www.luxembourg.co.uk

Luxembourg is a compact city and walking around it is easy and pleasant. It is served by an efficient network of buses. You can buy bus tickets valid either for two hours (billet de courte durée) or one day (billet de longue durée). A discount is offered on a block of 10 tickets. Tickets must be validated at the machines on buses and train platforms. Dogs are allowed free of charge on city buses. People over 65 years of age may qualify for travel concessions; show your passport as proof of age.

Luxembourg City

Shutterstock/Rudy Balasko

BORN SUR SURE *C3* (0.5km NE Rural) *49.76081, 6.51672* **Camping Officiel Born-Sûre,** 9 Rue du Camping, 6660 Born-sur-Sûre tel 730144; syndicat@ gmx.lu; www.camping-born.lu

🐕 €2.50 ♦♦♦ wc 🏕 ♿ 🚿 🗑 🚮 🍴 ⛱ 🍽 ⊞ 🛶

E along E44 sp Trier; leave immed bef ent Germany. On N10 go N sp Echternach; ignore sat nav & drive to end of vill, site sp. Med, mkd, pt shd, EHU (6A); bbq; 70% statics; phone; Eng spkn; adv bkg acc; ccard acc; boating; fishing; CKE. *"Gd, clean site; all tourers on rvside; htd pool 8km; if barrier clsd find contact in bar; excel."* **€23.00, 1 Apr-1 Oct.** **2019**

CLERVAUX *B2* (16km SW Rural) *49.97045, 5.93450* **Camping Kaul,** Rue Joseph Simon, 9554 Wiltz tel 9503591; info@kaul.lu; www.kaul.lu

🐕 €1.50 ♦♦♦ (htd) wc 🏕 ♿ 🚿 🗑 🚮 MP 🦋 🛶 🚃 ⼊

Turn N off rd 15 (Bastogne-Ettelbruck) to Wiltz, foll sp N to Ville Basse & Camping. Lge, mkd, unshd, EHU (6-10A) €2.50-2.75; gas; adv bkg rec; tennis; waterslide. *"Gd site; pitches tight for awnings if site full; excel san facs & takeaway; pool adj; local children use playgrnd."* **€30.00, 15 Feb-31 Dec.** **2019**

DIEKIRCH *C2* (0.5km SE Urban) *49.86635, 6.16513* **Camping de la Sûre,** 23, route de la Sûre – L-9390 Reisdorf tel +352 691 84 96 66; info@ campingdelasure.lu; https://campingdelasure.lu

🐕 €2 ♦♦♦ (htd) wc 🏕 ♿ 🚿 🗑 🚮 🦋 🍽 🚃 nr ⼊

Fr town cent take N14 twds Larochette, then 1st L after x-ing rv bdge. Well sp. Lge, mkd, pt shd, EHU (10A) €2.50; 50% statics; Eng spkn; adv bkg acc; ccard acc; CKE. *"Nice welcome; excel, clean facs; m'van o'night area outside gates; pleasant rvside site 5 mins walk fr town cent; pool 200m; vg touring base, Battle of Bulge Museum nrby."* **€20.50, 1 Apr-30 Sep.** **2020**

DIEKIRCH *C2* (0.9km S Rural) *49.86768, 6.16984* **Camping op der Sauer,** Route de Gilsdorf, L 9234 Diekirch tel 808590; info@campsauer.lu; www.campsauer.lu

🐕 €2.50 ♦♦♦ (htd) wc 🗑 🚮 🍴 🍽 ⊞ 🛶 🚃 ⼊

On rd 14 to Larochette, on S o'skts of Diekirch. 1st L after x-ing rv bdge, site well sp on L past Camping de la Sûre and behind sports facs. Lge, mkd, pt shd, EHU (6A) €3; gas; bus 800m; Eng spkn; adv bkg acc; CKE. *"On banks Rv Sûre; sh walk/cycle to town; spacious site; friendly owners; ltd facs LS; gd, basic site; helpful recep; pool 400m; clean san facs with plenty of hot water; vet is 20 mins walk."* **€21.00, 1 Mar-31 Oct.** **2015**

ECHTERNACH *C3* (2km SE Rural) *49.79681, 6.43122* **Camping Alferweiher,** Alferweiher 1, 6412 Echternach tel 720271; info@camping-alferweiher.lu; www.camping-alferweiher.lu

🐕 €2 ♦♦♦ (htd) wc 🏕 ♿ 🚿 🗑 🚮 MP 🦋 🍽 🚃 ⼊ 🛶

Fr S on N10 turn R at traff lts & pictogram fishing/ camping. Then L at sp to Alferweiher. 3*, Lge, mkd, pt shd, EHU (10A) €2.75; gas; TV; Eng spkn; adv bkg acc; bike hire; CKE. *"Gd walking; office open 0900-1300 & 1400-1800; if shut site yourself - elec boxes not locked; hot water in individ cubicles in san facs block only, other basins cold water; popular site but in need of some tlc (2017)."* **€24.00, 21 Apr-17 Sep.** **2017**

ECHTERNACH *C3* (6km NW Rural) *49.81958, 6.34737* **Camping Belle-Vue 2000,** 29 Rue de Consdorf, 6551 Berdorf tel 790635 or 808149; campbv2000@gmail.com

12 🐕 ♦♦♦ (htd) wc 🏕 ♿ 🚿 🚮 🦋 🚃 ⼊

Nr cent of vill on rd to Consdorf. 2nd of 3 adj sites with facs on L on way out of vill. Lge, hdg, pt shd, terr, EHU (6A) €2.5; gas; bbq; 50% statics; phone; adv bkg acc; games rm; CKE. *"Gd walking; attractive vill with gd rests; open in Jan only if no snow; pitches poss soft after rain; pool 500m; owner's son now running & improving site (2017)."* **€19.00** **2017**

ECHTERNACH *C3* (6km NW Rural) *49.81904, 6.34694* **Camping Bon Repos,** 39 Rue de Consdorf, 6551 Berdorf tel 790631; irma@bonrepos.lu; www.bonrepos.lu

♦♦♦ (htd) wc 🏕 ♿ 🚿 🚮 🦋 🍴 🍽 ⊞ nr 🚃 nr ⼊

In cent Echternach at x-rds take Vianden rd, then in 2km turn L to Berdorf thro vill twds Consdorf. Site nr cent vill on L adj Camping Belle-Vue. Fr Luxembourg thro Consdorf to Berdorf, site on R on ent to vill, clearly sp. Med, hdg, mkd, pt shd, pt sl, terr, EHU (16A) €2.80 (poss rev pol); gas; red long stay; TV; bus 100m; Eng spkn; adv bkg acc; games rm; CKE. *"Clean, tidy site - best in area; clean facs; helpful, friendly owners; some pitches sm; forest walks fr site; conv for trips to Germany; pool 5km; pleasant site but v small pitches."* **€18.00, 1 Apr-4 Nov.** **2017**

ESCH SUR SURE *B2* (1km SE Rural) *49.90693, 5.94220* **Camping Im Aal,** 7 Rue du Moulin, 9650 Esch-sur-Sûre tel 839514; info@camping-im-aal.lu; www.campingaal.lu

🐕 €2 ♦♦♦ (htd) wc 🏕 ♿ 🚿 🗑 🚮 🦋 🍽 🚃 ⼊

Fr N turn R off N15 onto N27 sp Esch-sur-Sûre. Pass thro sh tunnel, site on L in 500m on banks of Rv Sûre. 3*, Lge, hdg, mkd, pt shd, pt sl, EHU (6A) €2; 50% statics; Eng spkn; site clsd 1 Jan-14 Feb; fishing; CKE. *"Well-kept, clean site; gd welcome; gd, modern facs; some rvside pitches; walks along towpath & in woods; cash only; gd for wheelchair users; gd fishing, walking; gd NH & longer; vg."* **€27.00, 12 Feb-11 Dec.** **2019**

ETTELBRUCK *B2* (4km E Rural) *49.85043, 6.13461*
Camping Gritt, 2 Rue Gritt, 9161 Ingeldorf **tel 802018;**
info@camping-gritt.lu; www.camping-gritt.lu

🐕 €2 �(htd) WD ⚊ ♨ ♿ ▣ ⊿ MP 🦋 ♈ ▼ 🛒 ⚓ nr ⚙ ✎

On N15 fr Bastogne turn R at rndabt in Ettelbrück
sp Diekirch, go under A7 sp Diekirch. In 3km at end
of elevated section foll slip rd sp Diekirch,
Ettelbrück, Ingeldorf. At rndabt take 2nd exit sp
Ingledorf, site on R over narr rv bdge. Fr Diekirch on
N7 fork L twd Ingeldorf. Site on L over rv bdge.
Lge, mkd, pt shd, EHU (6A) €2.80; gas; bbq; sw nr;
twin axles; TV; 30% statics; bus/train to Luxembourg
City; Eng spkn; adv bkg acc; games rm; tennis nr;
fishing nr; CKE. *"Peaceful site; helpful, welcoming
Dutch owners; lge pitches with open aspect; gd,
modern san facs; recep 0900-1800 high ssn; canoe
hire nr; red for groups; pitching still OK after
heavy rain; on banks of Rv Sûre (swift-flowing &
unfenced); gd walking & sightseeing; rest vg; vg site."*
€28.00, 17 Apr-27 Oct. 2019

ETTELBRUCK *B2* (1.5km W Rural) *49.84600, 6.08193*
Camping Ettelbruck (formerly Kalkesdelt),
88 Chemin du Camping, 9022 Ettelbrück **tel 00 352
81 21 85; ellen.ringelberg@gmx.de; www.camping
ettelbruck.com**

🐕 €2.50 �(htd) WD ⚊ ♨ ♿ ▣ ⊿ MP 🦋 ▼ 🛒 ⚓ ⚙

Exit Ettelbrück on Bastogne rd N15. Site visible as
app town; approx 200m fr town cent fork L into
lane, turn R at sp at foot of hill, steep & narr rd.
Site sp fr town. 4*, Lge, mkd, pt shd, terr, EHU (16A)
€2.90; TV; 15% statics; phone; Eng spkn; adv bkg
acc; CKE. *"Gd, well-maintained, friendly, family-run
site in woods; excel san facs; lge pitches; gd walks;
train to Luxembourg city fr town; pool 3km; vg rest."*
€30.00, 1 Apr-1 Oct. 2016

GREVENMACHER *C3* (0.8km N Urban) *49.68302,
6.44891* **Camping La Route du Vin,** 10 route du Vin,
L 6794 Grevenmacher **tel 750234 or 758275;
campvin@pt.lu; grevenmacher-tourist.lu/
unterkuenfte/camping**

🐕 €1 ♈♈ WD ♿ ▣ ⊿ 🛒 ▼ 🛒 ⚓ nr 🛒 nr ✎

Fr E44/A1 exit junc 14 onto N1 to Grevenmacher.
After 1km turn R at T-junc opp Esso g'ge. Site sp in
town, ent off rndabt. Med, mkd, pt shd, pt sl, EHU
(16A) €2.50; 60% statics; Eng spkn; adv bkg acc;
games area; games rm; tennis; CKE. *"Easy walk to
town cent; wine festival in Sep; pleasant, well kept site;
excel new san facs (2015); boat trips; rvside walks;
excel base for touring Moselle & Luxembourg; pool adj;
views; helpful staff; excel."* **€19.40, 1 Apr-30 Sep.**
2017

KAUTENBACH *B2* (1km E Rural) *49.95387, 6.02730*
Camping Kautenbach, An der Weierbaach, 9663
Kautenbach **tel 950303; campkaut@pt.lu;
www.campingkautenbach.lu**

12 🐕 ♈♈(htd) WD ⚊ ♨ ♿ ▣ ⊿ 🛒 ▼ ⚓ ⚓ ⚙ ✎

Travelling E fr Bastogne on N84, approx 5km after
Luxembourg border take N26 to Wiltz & foll sp to
Kautenbach/Kiischpelt. In 10km turn L over bdge
into vill, site sp 800m. 3*, Lge, mkd, pt shd, EHU (6A)
inc; gas; bbq; TV; 20% statics; phone; Eng spkn; adv
bkg acc; ccard acc; site clsd 21 Dec-14 Jan; bike hire.
*"Gd for walking & mountain biking; long site along
beautiful, secluded rv valley."* **€26.00** 2016

LAROCHETTE *C3* (2km W Rural) *49.78525, 6.21010*
Iris Parc Camping Birkelt, 1 Um Birkelt, 7633
Larochette **tel 879040; info@camping-birkelt.lu;
www.camping-birkelt.lu**

🐕 €2.50 ♈♈(htd) WD ⚊ ♨ ♿ ▣ ⊿ MP 🦋 ▼ ⚓ ⚓ ⚙ ✎
🏊(covrd, htd) 🛒

Fr Diekirch take N14 to Larochette; turn R in town
on CR118 (N8), foll sp for Mersch. At top of hill foll
site sp. Fr Luxembourg take N7 foll sp for Mersch &
Ettelbruck (ignore Larochette sp bef Mersch). Turn
R bef rv bdge at Mersch onto CR118 & foll rd to
o'skts of town. Site on R beyond municipal sports
cent - fairly steep, winding app rd. 5*, Lge, mkd,
hdg, pt shd, pt sl, serviced pitches; EHU (16A) inc;
gas; bbq (charcoal, gas); TV; 50% statics; Eng spkn;
ccard acc; golf 5km; tennis; games rm; horseriding;
bike hire; sauna; fishing; games area; CKE. *"Excel,
well-kept, busy site in pleasant wooded hilltop location;
friendly, helpful staff; ideal for families; fitness rm;
no o'fits over 9m; canoeing 5km; gd san facs, poss
stretched high ssn; access poss diff lge o'fits, care req;
late arr report to rest/bar; gd bar & rest, open in LS."*
€39.00, 12 Apr-29 Sep, H08. 2019

LAROCHETTE *C3* (7km W Rural) *49.78521, 6.16596*
Camping Nommerlayen, Rue Nommerlayen, 7465
Nommern **tel 878078; info@nommerlayen-ec.lu;
www.nommerlayen-ec.lu**

🐕 €3 ♈♈(htd) WD ⚊ ♨ ♿ ▣ ⊿ MP 🦋 ♈ ▼ ⚓ ⚓ ⚙ ✎
🏊(htd) 🛒

N7 Luxembourg to Diekirch. At Mersch N8 E dir
Larochette & Nommern. Site is 1km S of Nommern.
5*, Lge, hdg, mkd, pt shd, terr, EHU (10A) inc; gas;
TV; 40% statics; Eng spkn; adv bkg acc; sauna; games
rm; tennis; bike hire; games area. *"Superb site & facs;
private bthrms avail; ideal for families; acc to some
pitches diff, site staff will help."* **€40.00, 1 Mar-5 Nov,
H20.** 2018

LAROCHETTE *C3* (3km NW Rural) *49.79991, 6.19816*
Camping auf Kengert, Kengert, 7633 Larochette
tel 837186; info@kengert.lu; www.kengert.lu

🚐 €2 ♗♗ (htd) 🅆 ♨ ⚲ ♿ 🖭 ⋁ ⬛ 🦋 ♕ 🍴 🛈 🎣 🗼 ⛰ 🛶 (htd)

N8 dir Mersch, CR19 dir Schrondweiler. Site sp
fr cent Larochette. 5*, Lge, mkd, shd, sl, EHU (4-16A)
€2; gas; 10% statics; Eng spkn; adv bkg acc; solarium;
sauna; CKE. *"Vg facs; Luxembourg Card (red on
attractions & public transport) avail at recep; peaceful,
friendly site; indoor playgrnd; excel rest; gd local walks/
cycle rtes; ltd hdstg for MH's."*
€34.50, 1 Mar-8 Nov. 2017

> ## "I like to fill in the reports as I travel from site to site"
>
> You'll find report forms at the back of this guide, or you can fill them in online at camc.com/europereport.

LIELER *B2* (0.5km SW Rural) *50.12365, 6.10509*
Camping Trois Frontières, Hauptstroos 12, 9972
Lieler **tel** 998608; info@troisfrontieres.lu;
www.troisfrontieres.lu

12 🚐 €2.20 ♗♗ (htd) 🅆 ♨ ⚲ ♿ 🖭 ⋁ ⬛ 🦋 ♕ 🍴 🛈 🎣 ⛰ ♒ 🛶 🗼

Fr N7/E421 turn E sp Lieler, site sp. 4*, Med, mkd,
pt shd, EHU (6A) €2.75; TV; 10% statics; adv bkg acc;
bike hire; games area; games rm. *"V pleasant site; gd
touring base; site under new ownership (2014); ACSI
registered; discount in LS."* **€32.80** 2019

LUXEMBOURG CITY *C3* (7km S Rural) *49.57220, 6.10857* **Camping Kockelscheuer,** 22 Route de
Bettembourg, 1899 Kockelscheuer **tel** 471815;
caravani@pt.lu; www.ccclv.lu/site/index.php/en

🚐 ♗♗ (htd) 🅆 ♨ ⚲ ♿ 🖭 ⋁ ⬛ 🦋 ♕ 🍴 🛈 nr 🎣 🗼 ⛰

Fr N on A6 then A4 exit junc 1 sp Leudelange/
Kockelscheuer, at top of slip rd turn L N4. After
about 1.5km turn R N186 sp Bettembourg/
Kockelscheuer & foll camp sp. Foll sp 'Park & Ride',
site is 1st R. Fr S exit A3 junc 2 sp Bettembourg &
Kockelscheuer. In 700m turn R dir Kockelscheuer &
in 3km turn L & foll site sp, rd numberd CR196.
4*, Lge, hdg, mkd, pt shd, terr, EHU (10-16A) metered
(check pol); gas; TV (pitch); bus to city 400m (tickets
fr site recep); Eng spkn; adv bkg acc; CKE. *"Rec arr
early afternoon as popular; well-run, clean, pretty site;
helpful, pleasant staff; office & gates clsd 1200-1400
& 2230-0700; gd san facs; pitch access on lower level
needs care; gd size pitches on terr; poss boggy after
rain; sports complex adj; gd dog walks nrby; useful NH
for Zeebrugge; pool 4km; excel site; poss to cycle into
Luxembourg city."* **€18.50, 24 Mar-31 Oct.** 2018

LUXEMBOURG CITY *C3* (9km S Rural) *49.56907, 6.16010* **Camping Bon Accueil,** 2 Rue du Camping,
5815 Alzingen **tel** 367069; www.camping-alzingen.lu

🚐 €3 ♗♗ (htd) 🅆 ♨ ⚲ ♿ 🖭 ⋁ ⬛ 🦋 ♕ 🍴 🛈 🎣 🗼 ⛰

Fr Luxembourg city take A3/E25 S, exit junc 1 sp
Hespérange. Cont thro town to Alzingen, site sp
on R after Mairie, well sp. Med, hdg, mkd, hdstg,
pt shd, EHU (16A) inc (poss rev pol); gas; bbq; twin
axles; phone; bus to city adj; Eng spkn; adv bkg acc;
ccard acc; games area; CCI. *"Pleasant, open, clean, tidy
site; gd size pitches; friendly staff; vg, clean, modern
san facs; hot water metered; lovely gardens adj; clsd
1200-1400 - ltd waiting space; excel base for city;
spotlessly clean; vg site; pool 3km; rec arrive early."*
€16.00, 1 Apr-15 Oct. 2015

MERSCH *B3* (2km SW Urban) *49.74339, 6.08963*
Camping Um Krounebierg, Rue du Camping, 7572
Mersch **tel** 352329756; contact@camping
krounebierg.lu; www.campingkrounebierg.lu

🚐 €2.50 ♗♗ (htd) 🅆 ♨ ⚲ ♿ 🖭 ⋁ ⬛ 🦋 ♕ 🍴 🛈 🎣 🗼 ⛰ 🗼

In Mersch town cent fr main N7 foll site ss. Fr A7,
exit Kopstal dir Mersch, then foll site sps. 5*, Lge,
mkd, hdstg, hdg, pt shd, pt sl, terr, EHU (10A) inc; gas;
bbq; twin axles; TV; 20% statics; phone; Eng spkn; adv
bkg acc; tennis. *"Gd touring & walking cent; conv for
trains to Luxembourg City; htd covrd pool adj; warden v
helpful - only on site 2 hrs morning & 2 hrs evening LS;
site guarded; excel clean facs; skate park; nice site close
to a pleasant town; well laid out; beautiful location; san
facs clean."* **€35.00, 25 Mar-31 Oct.** 2017

REISDORF *C2* (0.1km W Urban) *49.86958, 6.26746*
Camping De La Sure, 23 Route de la Sure, L-9390
Reisdorf **tel** 661-151358; reisdorfcamp@gmail.com;
www.campingdelasure.lu

🚐 🐕 🅆 ♨ ⚲ ♿ 🖭 ⋁ ⬛ 🦋 ♕ 🍴 🛈 🎣 nr ⛰

Reisdorf is bet Diekirch & Echternach. Site sp off
the N10 in Reisdorf. NB-2nd site on L after the bdge
driving fr Diekirch. Med, pt shd, EHU (10A); bbq
(charcoal, gas); TV; 10% statics; bus adj; Eng spkn;
adv bkg acc; games area; games rm; CKE. *"V friendly
& helpful; gd cycle paths along rv; ACSI; site being
upgraded to a hg standard (2015); vg; lovely site by rv;
easy walk to town."* **€27.00, 30 Mar-16 Oct.** 2018

REMICH *C3* (4km S Rural) *49.5106, 6.36302*
Camping Le Port, 5447 Schwebsange **tel** 23664460;
commune@wellenstein.lu or info@camping-port.lu

🚐 🐕 🅆 ♨ ⚲ ♿ 🖭 ⋁ ⬛ 🍴 🛈 nr ⛰

Fr Remich take N10 S on W bank of Moselle. Site
1km E of Schwebsange. Or fr S leave A13 at junc 13
onto N10. Site sp. Lge, mkd, pt shd, serviced pitches;
EHU (10A) inc; gas; 80% statics; Eng spkn; adv bkg
rec; CKE. *"Busy transit site for Austria/Italy; clean facs;
helpful staff; office open 0800-1200, 1350-1800; rd,
rv & port noise; sep area for m'vans on far side of port;
marina & rv activities; red facs LS; pool 4km; gd cycle
rtes fr site."* **€20.50, 1 Apr-31 Oct.** 2018

SEPTFONTAINES *B3 (2.5km NE Rural) 49.69274, 5.98514* **Camping Simmerschmelz,** Rue de Simmerschmelz 1, 8363 Septfontaines **tel 307072; info@simmerschmelz.com; simmerschmelz.com**

Head NE fr Arlon sp Mersch. In 4km at Gaichel (Bel/Lux frontier) foll valley of Rv Eisch thro Hobscheid, Septfontaines & in 2km at rd junc turn R. Site on L in 100m. Or fr E25 m'way exit at Windhof. Head N to Koerich & onto Septfontaines, as above. Med, pt shd, pt sl, EHU (6A) €2.50; gas; TV; 40% statics; phone; Eng spkn; adv bkg acc. *"Pleasant site in valley, wet in winter; 1 hdstg pitch; helpful owner."* **€25.80** 2017

TROISVIERGES *B2 (0.4km S Urban) 50.11908, 6.00251* **Camping Troisvierges (formerly Walensbongert),** Rue de Binsfeld, 9912 Troisvierges **tel 997141; info@camping-troisvierges.lu; www.camping-troisvierges.lu**

Fr Belgium on E42/A27 exit at junc 15 St Vith on N62 sp Troisvierges. Site sp. 1*, Med, hdg, mkd, pt shd, EHU (16A) €2.50; 10% statics; phone; train 1km; Eng spkn; adv bkg acc; ccard acc; games rm; tennis; CKE. *"Pretty town; pools adj; gd hiking; charming, helpful owners."* **€23.50, 1 Apr-30 Sep.** 2019

> ## "We must tell the Club about that great site we found"
>
> Get your site reports in by mid-August and we'll do our best to get your updates into the next edition.

VIANDEN *C2 (1km E Rural) 49.93213, 6.21554* **Camping op dem Deich,** Rue Neugarten, 9420 Vianden

Fr Dickirch take N19 E for 3km. Turn L on N17 to Vianden. Site sp 500m fr town cent twd Bitburg. 1*, Sm, hdstg, unshd, EHU (16A) inc. *"Site no longer camp site but an Aire de Service for MH's; 16 hdstdg pitches with ehu; water, waste and cassette services avail at ent; payment by machine; €15 per 24hrs; all pitches line the rv bank; easy walk to sm town with cafes, rest & shops as well as castles; excel scenery."* **€15.00** 2018

VIANDEN *C2 (2km SE Rural) 49.92673, 6.21990* **Camping du Moulin,** Rue de Bettel, 9415 Vianden **tel 834501; campingdumoulin@vianden-info.lu; www.campingdumoulin-vianden.lu**

Fr Diekirch take N17 dir Vianden. In 8km at Fouhren take rd N17B sp Bettel then sp Vianden. Site on R behind yellow Vianden sp. Lge, mkd, pt shd, EHU (10-16A) €2.20; TV (pitch); phone; Eng spkn; CKE. *"Lovely location; spacious pitches, some on rv bank; gd, modern san facs; superb children's san facs; rv adj; interesting area; rec."* **€24.00, 14 Apr-3 Apr.** 2017

WASSERBILLIG *C3 (2km SW Rural) 49.70241, 6.47717* **Camping Mertert,** Rue du Parc, 6684 Mertert **tel 748174**

On E of rte 1 (Wasserbillig-Luxembourg), clearly sp in both dir. Immed R after rlwy x-ing. Site on rv. 3*, Med, mkd, shd, EHU (10A) inc; 70% statics; buses & trains nr; adv bkg acc. *"Grassed tourer area open fr Apr, but owner allows pitching on tarmac rd adj office; excel, clean facs; scruffy statics area; sm boating pond; pool 4km; recep clsd 1300-1500; vg."* **€12.50, 15 Apr-15 Oct.** 2019

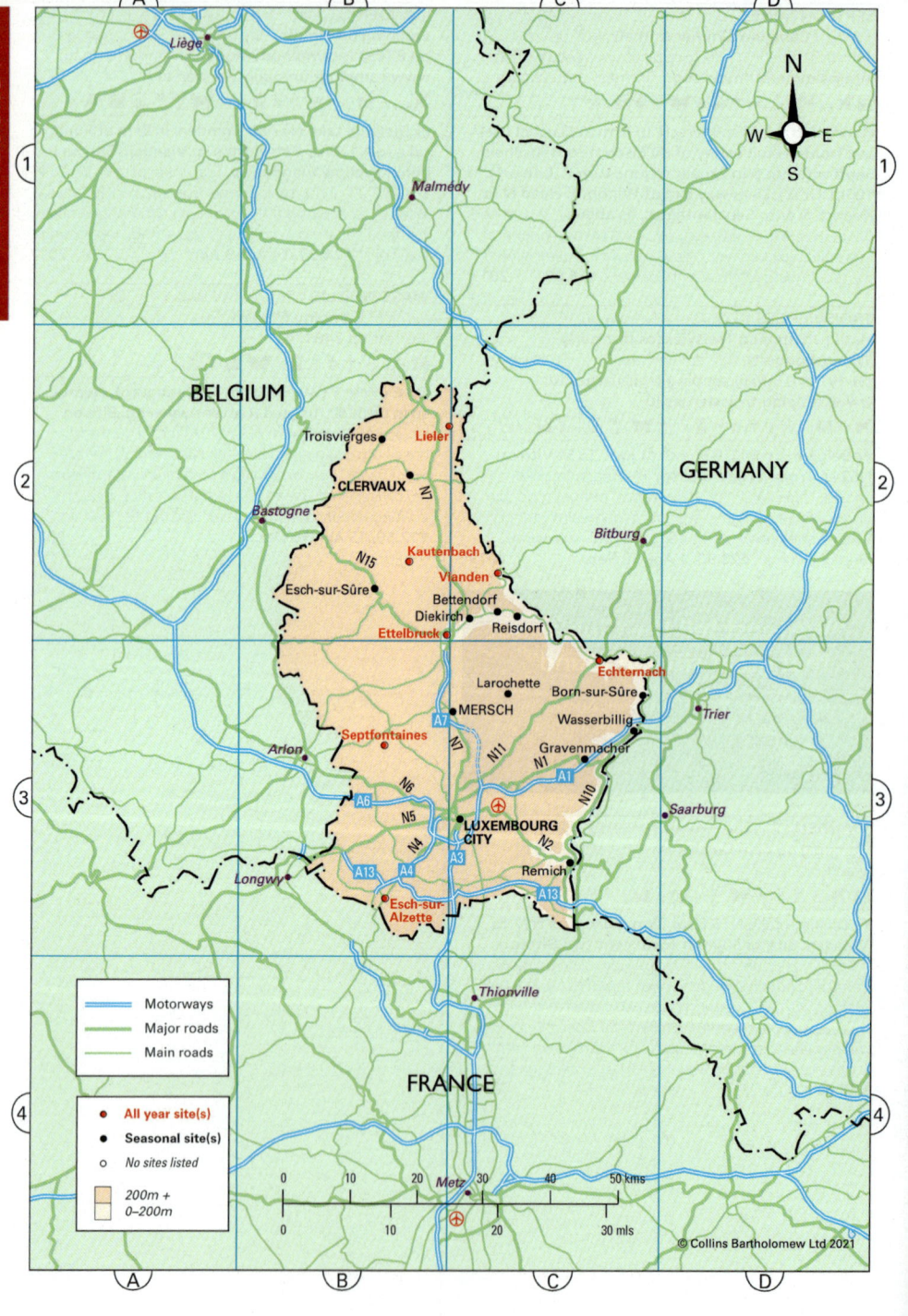

Motorways
Major roads
Main roads

All year site(s)
Seasonal site(s)
No sites listed
200m +
0–200m

© Collins Bartholomew Ltd 2021

Amsterdam

Shutterstock/Yasonya

Highlights

With a flat landscape that's covered in tulips and windmills, the Netherlands is an enchanting country to explore and is ideal for cyclists. Amsterdam is often the main draw for tourists, and is the home of several museums, including one dedicated to Van Gogh.

The Netherlands is also well known for its beaches, and the coast is a great place to visit for nature lover and sports enthusiasts alike.

The Netherlands has produced some of the greatest painters in the world, from Rembrandt to Vermeer and Van Gogh to Escher. The Mauritschuis in The Hague houses many famous works of art from the Dutch golden age and is well worth a visit.

Christmas is a time of great celebration for the Dutch, with Sinterklaas a traditional holiday figure based on Saint Nicholas. The giving of gifts on December 5th is a long-held tradition, as is the Sinterklaas parade in mid-November, which is broadcast live on national TV.

Major towns and cities

- Amsterdam – this beautiful capital is filled with canals, galleries and pretty buildings.
- Rotterdam – a city famous for its museums and landmark architecture.
- The Hague – a historic city of political and cultural significance.
- Leiden – home of the oldest university in the Netherlands the birthplace of Rembrandt.

Attractions

- Keukenhof, Lisse – one of the world's largest flower gardens and a must-see in the spring.
- Hoge Veluwe, Gelderland – this National Park is a great place for walking or cycling.
- Rijksmuseum, Amsterdam – a national museum dedicated to arts and history.
- Kinderdijk - a beautiful village with the largest collection of old windmills in the Netherlands.

Find out more

www.holland.com
E: info@holland.com T: 0031 (0) 70 37 05 705

Country Information

Population (approx): 16.9million

Capital: Amsterdam

Area: 33,939 sqkm

Bordered by: Belgium, Germany

Terrain: Mostly coastal lowland and reclaimed land (polders) dissected by rivers and canals; hills in the south-east

Climate: Temperate maritime climate; warm, changeable summers; cold/mild winters; spring is the driest season

Coastline: 451km

Highest Point: Vaalserberg 322m

Language: Dutch

Local Time: GMT or BST + 1, i.e. 1 hour ahead of the UK all year

Currency: Euros divided into 100 cents; £1 = €1.14, €1 = £0.88 (Feb 2021)

Emergency numbers: Police 112; Fire brigade 112; Ambulance 112. Operators speak English

Public Holidays 2021: Jan 1; Apr 4, 5, 27; May 5, 13, 23, 24; Dec 25, 26

School summer holidays vary by region, but are roughly early/mid July to end August/early September

Entry Formalities

British and Irish passport holders may stay for up to 90 days in any 180 day period without a visa. Following Brexit you may be asked to show a return or onward ticket at the border to confirm your length of stay, or to prove that you have enough money for your stay.

Your passport will need to have a minimum of 6 months' validity remaining, and be less than 10 years old (even if it has over 6 months left).

Visitors arriving at a campsite or hotel must complete a registration form.

Medical Services

Pharmacies (apotheek) dispense prescriptions whereas drugstores (drogisterij) sell only over-the-counter remedies. Pharmacies may require a photocopy of the details on your European Health Insurance Card (EHIC). You will need to show your EHIC to obtain treatment by a doctor contracted to the state health care system (AGIS Zorgverzekeringen) and you will probably have to pay a fee.

You will be charged for emergency dental treatment. Charges for prescriptions vary. Treatment refunds are obtained from AGIS.

Inpatient hospital treatment is free provided it is authorised by AGIS. Local state health insurance fund offices can give advice on obtaining emergency medical services and provide names and addresses of doctors, health centres and hospitals. Tourist Information offices also keep lists of local doctors.

Opening Hours

Banks: Mon-Fri 9am-4pm/5pm (some open Sat).

Museums: Tue-Fri 10am-5pm; Sat & Sun 11am/1pm-5pm.

Post Offices: Mon-Fri 9am-5pm; some Sat 9am-12 noon/1.30pm.

Shops: Mon-Fri 8am/8.30am-6pm/8pm; Sat 8am/8.30am-4pm/5pm; late night shopping in many towns on Thursday or Friday to 9pm. Shops close one day or half day in the week in addition to Sunday.

Safety and Security

In relative terms there is little crime but visitors should take the usual precautions in central Amsterdam (particularly in and around Central Station), in Rotterdam and The Hague. As in many large cities, pickpocketing and bag snatching are more common. Pickpockets operate on trams, especially on numbers 2 and 5 in Amsterdam.

Ensure you keep your valuables safely with you at all times and do not leave them unattended or hanging on the back of a chair. Bicycle theft is a common occurrence in the major cities.

Fake, plain clothes policemen carrying badges are in action pretending to be investigating counterfeit money and false credit cards. Dutch police do not have badges and plain clothes police will rarely carry out this kind of inspection. Always ask for identity, check it thoroughly and do not allow yourself to be intimidated. Call 0900 8844 to contact the nearest police station if you are concerned or suspicious.

Several deaths occur each year due to drowning in canals. Take particular care when driving, cycling or walking alongside canals.

Avoid confrontation with anyone offering to sell you drugs and stay away from quiet or dark alleys, particularly late at night.

There have been incidences of drinks being spiked in city centre locations. Always be aware of your drink and do not leave it unattended. Young women and lone travellers need to be especially vigilant in these situations.

The Netherlands shares with the rest of Europe a general threat from terrorism. Attacks could be indiscriminate and against civilian targets in public places, including tourist sites.

British Embassy

LANGE VOORHOUT 10, 2514 ED THE HAAG
Tel: (070) 4270427
www.ukinnl.fco.gov.uk

British Consulate-General

KONINGSLAAN 44,1075 AE AMSTERDAM
Tel: (020) 6764343

Irish Embassy

SCHEVENINGSEWEG 112, 2584 AE THE HAGUE
Tel: (070) 3630993
www.embassyofireland.nl

Documents

Passport

Everyone from the age of 14 is required to show a valid identity document to police officers on request and you should, therefore, carry your passport at all times.

Vehicle(s)

When driving carry your driving licence, vehicle registration certificate (V5C), insurance certificate and MOT certificate, if applicable. If driving a vehicle that does not belong to you, carry a letter of authority from the owner.

Money

Money may be exchanged at main border crossing posts, major post offices, banks, VVV tourist information offices and some ANWB offices. Other bureaux de change may not give such favourable rates.

The major credit and debit cards are widely accepted but supermarkets will not generally accept credit cards. As a precaution carry enough cash to cover your purchases as you may find that debit cards issued by banks outside the Netherlands are not accepted. Cash machines are widespread.

Driving

The Dutch drive assertively and are not renowned for their road courtesy. Pedestrians should be very careful when crossing roads, including on zebra crossings.

Accidents

All accidents which cause injuries or major damage must be reported to the police. Drivers involved in an accident must exchange their identity details and their insurance company contact information.

Alcohol

The maximum permitted level of alcohol is 50 milligrams in 100 millilitres of blood, i.e. lower than that permitted in the UK (80 milligrams). Penalties for driving under the influence of alcohol can be severe. A lower level of 20 milligrams applies to drivers who have held a driving licence for less than five years. It is wisest to adopt a 'no drinking and driving' rule.

Breakdown Service

There are emergency telephones every 2km on all motorways and they are directly linked to the nearest breakdown centre.

ANWB, the motoring and leisure organisation, has a road patrol service which operates 24 hours a day on all roads. Drivers requiring assistance may call the 'Wegenwacht' road patrol centre by telephoning 088 2692888. Alternatively call the ANWB Emergency Centre on (070) 3141414.

Charges apply for breakdown assistance and towing is charged according to distance and time of day. Members of clubs affiliated to the AIT/FIA, such as The Caravan and Motorhome Club, incur lower charges. Payment by credit card is accepted. In some areas the ANWB Wegenwacht has contracts with local garages to provide assistance to its members and affiliates.

Child Restraint System

Children under the age of 18 years, measuring less than 1.35m must be seated in an approved child restraint adapted to their size (ECE 44/03 or 44/04 safety approved). Children under 3 years old are able to travel in the front if they are seated in a rear facing child seat with the airbag deactivated, and under no circumstances are they allowed to travel in a car with no child restraint system fitted.

Fuel

Unleaded petrol is available from green pumps marked 'Loodvrije Benzine'. LPG (autogas) is widely available along main roads and motorways.

Petrol stations along motorways and main roads and in main towns are open 24 hours, except in parts of the north of the country where they close at 11pm. Credit cards are accepted but some all night petrol stations only have automatic pumps which may operate with bank notes only.

Lights

The use of dipped headlights during the day is recommended.

Low Emission Zones

Low Emission Zones are in operation in 16 cities in the Netherlands. Restrictions only apply to freight vehicles over 3500kg, however currently all foreign vehicles are able to enter the Low Emission Zone without any restrictions. Before you travel check www.urbanaccessregulations.eu

Motorways

There are over 2,750 kilometres of toll-free motorway. There are rest areas along the motorways, most of which have a petrol station and a small shop. Tolls are charged on some bridges and tunnels, notably the Westerschelde Toll Tunnel. This road tunnel links Terneuzen (north of Gent) and Ellewoutsdijk (south of Goes) across the Westerschelde. It provides a short, fast route between Channel ports and the road network in the west of the country. The tunnel is 6.6km long (just over 4 miles) and the toll for a car + caravan (maximum height 3m measured from front axle) is €7.45 and for a motorhome €7.45 height under 2.5m) or €18.20 (height over 3m)

(all prices for 2015). Credit cards are accepted. For more information go to www.westerscheldetunnel.nl.

Parking

Parking meters or discs are in use in many towns allowing parking for between 30 minutes and two or three hours; discs can be obtained from local shops. A sign 'parkeerschijf' indicates times when a disc is compulsory. Paid parking is expensive and there are insufficient parking spaces to meet demand. Clamping and towing away of vehicles are commonplace and fines are high. Check signs for the precise times you are allowed to park, particularly on main roads in Amsterdam.

Priority

Yellow diamond shaped signs with a white border indicate priority roads. In the absence of such signs drivers must give way to all traffic approaching from the right. At the intersection of two roads of the same class where there are no signs, traffic from the right has priority.

At junctions marked with a 'priority road ahead' sign, a stop sign or a line of white painted triangles ('shark's teeth') across the road, drivers must give way to all vehicles on the priority road, including bicycles and mopeds.

Be particularly careful when using roundabouts as on some you have the right of way when on them, but on others you must give way to vehicles entering the roundabout, i.e. on your right.

Trams have priority at the intersection of roads of equal importance, but they must give way to traffic on priority roads. If a tram or bus stops in the middle of the road to allow passengers on and off, you must stop. Buses have right of way over all other vehicles when leaving bus stops in built-up areas.

Roads

Roads are generally good and well maintained, but are overcrowded and are frequently subject to strong winds. Most cities have a policy of reducing the amount of nonessential traffic within their boundaries. Narrowing roads, obstacles, traffic lights and speed cameras are often in place to achieve this.

Road Signs and Markings

National motorways are distinguished by red signs, and prefixed with the letter A, whereas European motorways have green signs and are prefixed E. Dual carriageways and other main roads have yellow signs with the letter N and secondary roads are prefixed B.

In general road signs and markings conform to international standards. The following are some road signs which may also be seen:

Cycle path

Cycle route

District Numbers

Hard shoulder open as rush-hour lane

Dutch	English Translation
Afrit	Exit
Doorgaand verkeer gestremd	No throughway
Drempels	Humps
Langzaam rijden	Slow down
Omleiding	Detour
Oprit	Entrance
Ousteek u lichten	Switch on lights
Parkeerplaats	Parking
Pas op!	Attention
Stop-verbod	No parking
Wegomlegging	Detour
Werk in uitvoering	Road works
Woonerven	Slow down (in built-up area)

A continuous central white line should not be crossed even to make a left turn.

Speed Limits

	Open Road (km/h)	Motorway (km/h)
Car Solo	80-100	130*
Car towing caravan/trailer	80-90	90
Motorhome under 3500kg	80-100	130*
Motorhome 3500-7500kg	80	80

*Unless otherwise indicated.

Be vigilant and observe the overhead illuminated lane indicators when they are in use, as speed limits on motorways are variable. Speed cameras, speed traps and unmarked police vehicles are widely used. Radar detectors are illegal, with use resulting in a heavy fine.

Motorhomes over 3,500kg are restricted to 50 km/h (31 mph) in built-up areas and to 80 km/h (50 mph) on all other roads. The beginning of a built up area is indicated by a rectangular blue sign with the name of the locality in white. The end of a built up area is indicated by the same sign with a white diagonal lines across it.

Traffic Jams

The greatest traffic congestion occurs on weekdays at rush hours around the major cities of Amsterdam, Den Bosch, Eindhoven, Rotterdam, Utrecht, The Hague and Eindhoven.

Summer holidays in the Netherlands are staggered and, as a result, traffic congestion is not too severe. However during the Christmas, Easter and Whitsun holiday periods, traffic jams are common and bottlenecks regularly occur on the A2 (Maastricht to Amsterdam), the A12 (Utrecht to the German border) and on the A50 (Arnhem to Apeldoorn). Roads to the Zeeland coast, e.g. the A58, N57 and N59, may become congested during periods of fine weather.

Many Germans head for the Netherlands on their own public holidays and the roads are particularly busy during these periods.

Violation of Traffic Regulations

Police are empowered to impose on-the-spot fines (or confiscate vehicles) for violation of traffic regulations and fines for speeding can be severe. If you are fined always ask for a receipt.

Touring

The southern Netherlands is the most densely populated part of the country but, despite the modern sprawl, ancient towns such as Dordrecht, Gouda, Delft and Leiden have retained their individuality and charm. Rotterdam is a modern, commercial centre and a tour of its harbour – the busiest in Europe – makes a fascinating excursion. The scenery in the north of the country is the most typically Dutch – vast, flat landscapes, largely reclaimed from the sea, dotted with windmills.

Some of the most charming towns and villages are Marken, Volendam and Alkmaar (famous for its cheese market). Aalsmeer, situated south of Amsterdam, stages the world's largest daily flower auction.

It is worth spending time to visit the hilly provinces in the east such as Gelderland, known for its castles, country houses and its major city, Arnhem, which has many links with the Second World War. Overijssel is a region of great variety and the old Hanseatic towns of Zwolle and Kampen have splendid quays and historic buildings. Friesland is the Netherland's lake district.

An Amsterdam Card entitles you to free admission to many of the city's famous museums, including the Rijksmuseum and Van Gogh Museum, and to discounts in many restaurants, shops, attractions and at Park & Ride car parks. It also entitles you to discounts on tours as well as free travel on public transport and a free canal cruise. The Card is valid for one, two or three days and is available from tourist information offices, some Shell petrol stations, Canal Bus kiosks, Park & Ride car parks and some hotels. Alternatively purchase online from www.iamsterdamcard.com

Service charges are included in restaurant bills and tips are not necessary. Smoking is not permitted in bars or restaurants.

Spring is one of the most popular times to visit the Netherlands, in particular the famous Keukenhof Gardens near Lisse, open from 24 March to 16 May in 2016, see www.keukenhof.nl. Visitors enjoy a display of over seven million flowering bulbs, trees and shrubs. Special events take place here at other times of the year, including a National Bulb Market in October.

Camping and Caravanning

There are approximately 2,500 officially classified campsites which offer a wide variety of facilities. Most are well equipped with modern sanitary facilities and they generally have a bar, shop and leisure facilities.

A number of sites require cars to be parked on a separate area away from pitches and this can present a problem for motorhomes. Some sites allow motorhomes to park on pitches without restrictions, but others will only accept them on pitches if they are not moved during the duration of your stay. Check before booking in.

A tourist tax is levied at campsites of approximately €1.00 per person per night. It is not generally included in the prices quoted in the Site Entry listings which follow this chapter.

The periods over, and immediately after, the Ascension Day holiday and the Whitsun weekend are very busy for Dutch sites and you can expect to find many of them full. Advance booking is highly recommended.

Casual/wild camping is prohibited as is overnight camping by the roadside or in car parks. There are overnight parking places specifically for motorhomes all over the country – see the website of the Camper Club Nederland, www.campervriendelijk.nl and look under 'camperplaatsen NL' or write to CCN at Postbus 115, 7480 AC Haaksbergen, tel:(0)634 492 913. Alternatively see www.campercontact.nl or email cnn@camperclubnetherland.nl

Many campsites also have motorhome amenities and some offer Quick Stop overnight facilities at reduced rates.

Cycling

There are twice as many bicycles as cars in the Netherlands and as a result cyclists are catered for better than in any other country. There are 15,000 km of well-maintained cycle tracks in both town and country, all marked with red and white road signs and mushroom-shaped posts indicating the quickest and/or most scenic routes. Local tourist information centres (VVV) sell maps of a wide range of cycling tours and cycling fact sheets and maps are available from the Netherlands Board of Tourism in London. Motorists should expect to encounter heavy cycle traffic, particularly during rush hours.

Obligatory separate bicycle lanes for cyclists are indicated by circular blue signs displaying a white bicycle. Small oblong signs with the word 'fietspad' or 'rijwielpad' indicate optional bicycle lanes. White bicycles and dotted white lines painted on the road surface indicate cycle lanes which may be used by motor vehicles providing they do not obstruct cyclists. Cycle lanes marked by continuous white lines are prohibited for use by motor vehicles.

Cyclists must obey traffic light signals at crossroads and junctions; elsewhere, where no traffic lights are in operation, they must give way to traffic from the right.

Cycle tracks are also used by mobility scooters and mopeds. Pedestrians should be especially cautious when crossing roads, especially on zebra crossings. Look out for both cyclists and riders of mopeds, who often ignore traffic rules as well as red lights. In Amsterdam in particular, many cyclists do not use lights at night.

Bicycles may be carried on the roof of a car providing the total height does not exceed 4 metres. They may also be carried at the rear providing the width does not extend more than 20cm beyond the width of the vehicle.

Electricity and Gas

Most campsites have a supply ranging from 4 to 10 amps and almost all have CEE connections. Plugs have two round pins.

The full range of Campingaz cylinders is available.

Public Transport

There is an excellent network of buses and trams, together with metro systems in Amsterdam (called the GVB), Rotterdam and The Hague. An electronic card 'OV Chipkaart' is gradually replacing the previous system of 'Strippenkaart' which were strips of 15 or 45 tickets valid throughout the country.

OV-Chip cards can be bought at vending machines at stations or ticket offices and on board buses and trams and are available for periods from one hour to seven days allowing unlimited travel on trams, buses and the metro. Children under 12 and people over the age of 65 qualify for reduced fares (show your passport as proof of age). See www.gvb.nl for more information.

Tickets must be validated before travel either at the yellow machines on trams and at metro stations or by your bus driver or conductor.

In Amsterdam canal transport includes a regular canal shuttle between Centraal Station and the Rijksmuseum. A 'circle tram' travels from Centraal Station through the centre of Amsterdam past a number of local visitor attractions, such as Anne Frank's house, the Rijksmuseum, Van Gogh museum and Rembrandthuis.

There are Park & Ride facilities at most railway stations. Secure parking is also offered at 'transferiums', a scheme offering reasonably priced guarded parking in secure areas on the outskirts of major towns with easy access by road and close to public transport hubs. Transferiums have heated waiting rooms and rest rooms as well as information for travellers, and some even have a shop.

Frequent car ferry services operate on routes to the Frisian (or Wadden) Islands off the north west coast, for example, from Den Helder to Texel Island, Harlingen to Terschelling Island and Holwerd to Ameland Island. Other islands in the group do not allow cars but there are passenger ferry services. In the summer island-hopping round tickets are available to foot passengers and cyclists and are popular for exploring the country.

ALKMAAR *B2* (7.7km W Rural/Coastal) *52.634290, 4.660384* **De Markiess,** Driehuizerweg 1A, 1934 PR Egmond aan den Hoef **(072) 5062274; info@demarkiess.nl; www.demarkiess.nl**

🐴 �†(htd) 🅆 ♨ ♿ 🚿 ✗ ♨ 🦋 ⛱ 🍴 nr ⑪ nr 🛱 nr ⅏

⚓ 2km; sand

N9 W of Alkmaar. Take Egmond sp. Turn R aft petrol stn. Foll sp to site. Med, unshd, EHU (6A) inc; bbq; TV; bus 2km; Eng spkn; games rm. *"One of best maintained sites; grass like bowling green; no grass cuttings left; spotless facs; recycling; excel."* €24.00, 30 Mar-30 Sep.   2018

ALKMAAR *B2* (2.6km NW Urban) *52 64205, 4.72407* **Camping Alkmaar,** Bergerweg 201, 1817 ML Alkmaar **(072) 5116924; info@campingalkmaar.nl; www.campingalkmaar.nl**

🐴 €3 �†(htd) 🅆 ♨ ♿ 🚿 ♨ 🅼🆂🅿 🦋 🛱 nr ⅏

Fr W ring rd (Martin Luther Kingweg) foll Bergen sp, bear R at T-junc & site 150m on L. Site well sp. Med, hdstg, mkd, pt shd, EHU (4-10A) inc; bbq; TV (pitch); 10% statics; bus at gate; Eng spkn; adv bkg acc; ccard acc; golf 2km; CKE. *"Clean, friendly site; decent sized pitches; buses to town; 20 min walk to town cent; cheese mkt on Friday in ssn; pool adj; vg cycling rte into centre; cash/mastercard; gd san facs."* €29.00, 1 Mar-1 Oct.   2019

ALMERE *C3* (7km W Rural) *52.35688, 5.22505* **Camping Waterhout,** Archerpad 6, 1324 ZZ Almere **(036) 5470632; info@waterhout.nl; www.waterhout.nl**

🐴 €2.50 �† 🅆 ♨ 🚿 ♨ ✗ 🍴 ⑪ 🛱 ⅏ ✂

Exit A6 junc 4, site sp fr slip rd on S edge Weerwater. Med, mkd, shd, EHU (10A) inc; sw nr; TV; 30% statics; phone; bus 200m; Eng spkn; adv bkg acc; CKE. *"Well laid-out site; conv Amsterdam by bus or train - 30 mins; Almere ultra-modern city."* €27.00, 19 Apr-27 Oct.   2019

AMERSFOORT *C3* (11km S Rural) *52.07975, 5.38151* **Vakantiepark De Heigraaf,** De Haygraeff 9, 3931 ML Woudenberg **(033) 2865066; info@heigraaf.nl; www.heigraaf.nl**

�†(htd) 🅆 ♨ ♿ 🚿 ♨ 🅼🆂🅿 🦋 🍴 ⑪ 🛱 ⅏ ✂

Exit A12 at Maarn junc 21 or junc 22 & foll sp to site on N224, 2km W of Woudenberg. V lge, mkd, pt shd, EHU (4-6A) inc; sw nr; 50% statics; phone; bus 500m; Eng spkn; adv bkg acc. *"Vg, well-managed site; modern san facs; well run site, does not accept Visa."* €20.00, 26 Mar-30 Sep.   2020

AMSTERDAM *B3* (12km N Rural) *52.43649, 4.91445* **Camping Het Rietveen,** Noordeinde 130, 1121 AL Landsmeer **(020) 4821468; info@campinghetrietveen.nl; www.campinghetrietveen.nl**

12 🐴 ♿ �† 🅆 ♨ ✗ ♨ 🍴 nr ⑪ nr 🛱 nr

Fr A10 ring rd exit junc 117. At junc off slip rd turn L dir Landsmeer, site sp. Sm, mkd, EHU (10A) inc; sw; bus to Amsterdam 200m; Eng spkn; tennis; adv bkg adv; fishing; bike hire; CKE. *"Vg, pretty lakeside site, like lge CL, in well-kept vill; no recep - site yourself & owner will call; sep field avail for rallies; excel touring base; city 30 mins by bus; san facs inadequate; no wifi; dogs free."* €27.00   2018

AMSTERDAM *B3* (5km NE Urban) *52.38907, 4.92532* **Camping Vliegenbos,** Meeuwenlaan 138, 1022 AM Amsterdam **(020) 6368855; vliegenbos@ noord.amsterdam.nl; www.vliegenbos.com**

�†(htd) 🅆 ♨ ♿ 🚿 ♨ ✗ 🅼🆂🅿 🍴 ⑪ nr ♨ 🛱

Fr A10 Amsterdam ring rd, take exit S116 Amsterdam Noord, at 2nd slip rd turn R sp Noord over rndabt, turn L at next rndabt, then immed sharp R, L onto service rd, site sp. 2*, Lge, hdstg, pt shd, pt sl, EHU (6A) inc; gas; phone; bus to city nr; Eng spkn; ccard acc. *"Sm pitches mainly for tents; ltd EHU; m'vans & c'vans park outside barrier; friendly staff; pool 1.5km; bus tickets to city cent fr recep; cycle path to city cent via free ferry; clean, modern san facs; v well set up."* €30.00, 1 Apr-1 Oct.   2016

AMSTERDAM *B3* (6km E Urban) *52.36555, 4.95829* **Camping Zeeburg,** Zuider Ijdijk 20, 1095 KN Amsterdam **(020) 6944430; info@campingzeeburg.nl; www.campingzeeburg.nl**

12 🐴 €3 �† 🅆 ♨ ✗ ♨ 🅼🆂🅿 ♨ ♨ 🛱

Fr A10 ring rd exit at S114 & foll site sps. Lge, unshd, EHU (6-16A) inc; gas; 10% statics; bus/tram to city nr; adv bkg rec; bike hire. *"Used mainly by tents in summer, but rest of year suitable for c'vans; conv city cent."* €29.00   2016

AMSTERDAM *B3* (12km SE Urban) *52.31258, 4.99035* **Gaasper Camping,** Loosdrechtdreef 7, 1108 AZ Amsterdam-Zuidoost **(020) 6967326; info@ gaaspercamping.nl; www.gaaspercamping.nl**

🐴 €2.50 �†(htd) 🅆 ♨ ✗ 🅼🆂🅿 🦋 🍴 ⑪ ♨ 🛱 ⅏

Fr A2 take A9 E sp Amersfoort. After about 5km take 3rd exit sp Gaasperplas/Weesp S113. Cross S113 into site, sp. 2*, Lge, hdg, mkd, hdstg, pt shd, serviced pitches; EHU (10A) €3.50 (care needed); gas; 20% statics; Eng spkn; CKE. *"Immac site set in beautiful parkland; well-run with strict rules; night guard at barrier (high ssn); vans must be manhandled onto pitch (help avail); high ssn arr early to ensure pitch - no adv bkg for fewer than 7 nights; metro 5 mins walk (tickets fr site recep); poss cold shwrs & ltd shop LS; gd security; well run site; conv for metro; adv bkg rec high ssn."* €30.00, 1 Jan-4 Jan, 15 Mar-1 Nov, 28 Dec-31 Dec.   2017

AMSTERDAM *B3* (15km SW Rural) *52.29366, 4.82316*
Camping Het Amsterdamse Bos, Kleine Noorddijk 1,
1187 NZ Amstelveen **(020) 6416868; info@camping
amsterdam.com; www.campingamsterdamsebos.
com**

🐕€3 ♿(htd) ⚿ ♨ ♿ 🍴 ✉ 🚰 💈 ▼ Ⓣ Ⓗ 💧 🛒

Foll A10 & A4 twd Schiphol Airport. Fr junc on A4 &
A9 m'way, take A9 E twd Amstelveen; at next exit
(junc 6) exit sp Aalsmeer. Foll Aalsmeer sp for 1km
bearing R at traff lts then at next traff lts turn L
over canal bdge onto N231. In 1.5km turn L at 2nd
traff lts into site. Fr S exit A4 junc 3 onto N201 dir
Hilversum (ignore other camp sps). Turn L onto
N231 dir Amstelveen, at rd junc Bovenkirk take
N231 dir Schiphol, site on R in 200m, sp.
1*, V lge, pt shd, EHU (10A) €4.50; gas; 20% statics;
bus to city; Eng spkn; adv bkg acc; ccard acc; CKE.
*"Conv Amsterdam by bus - tickets sold on site; poss
migrant workers resident on site; san facs stretched
high ssn; gd walking & cycling paths; spectacular
daily flower auctions at Aalsmeer; waterpark nr; conv
bulbfields."* **€25.50, 18 Mar-3 Nov.** **2019**

ANNEN *D2* (3.7km S Rural) *53.03017, 6.73912*
De Baldwin Hoeve, Annerweg 9, 9463 TB Eext
**05 92 27 16 29; baldwinhoeve@hetnet.nl;
www.baldwinhoeve.nl**

12 🐕 ♿ ⚿ ♨ ✉ 🚰 ▼

Fr N34 take Annen exit. Turn R onto Anlooerweg.
At rndabt take R dir Eext. Bef underpass take
sm service rd on L to campsite. Sm, mkd, unshd,
EHU (10A); bbq; twin axles; bus adj; Eng spkn; adv
bkg acc; CCI. *"CL type farm site with excel san facs;
friendly owners; horses & other livestock; lg group
accomodation avail; vg."* **€16.50** **2019**

> ## "I need an on-site restaurant"
> We do our best to make sure site information
> is correct, but it is always best to check any
> must-have facilities are still available or will
> be open during your visit.

APELDOORN *C3* (10km N Rural) *52.29066, 5.94520*
Camping De Helfterkamp, Gortelseweg 24, 8171 RA
Vaassen **(0578) 571839; info@helfterkamp.nl;
www.helfterkamp.nl**

🐕€1.75 ♿(htd) ⚿ ♨ ♿ 🍴 ✉ 🚰 ▼ ♈ 🛒 ⁄!\

Leave A50 junc 26; foll sp to Vaassen; site sp on ent
to town - 2.5km W of Vaassen. Med, mkd, pt shd,
EHU (16A) metered (poss rev pol); gas; sw nr; red long
stay; 40% statics; phone; Eng spkn; adv bkg req; ccard
acc; bike hire; CKE. *"Excel, immac, well-maintained,
busy site in beautiful woodland area; key for shwrs
& hot water; v friendly owners; conv for Apeldoorn/
Arnhem areas & De Hooge Veluwe National Park; gd
walking/cycling."* **€25.00, 1 Mar-31 Oct.** **2017**

APELDOORN *C3* (10km S Rural) *52.11771, 5.90641*
Camping De Pampel, Woeste Hoefweg 35, 7351 TN
Hoenderloo **(055) 3781760; info@pampel.nl;
www.pampel.nl**

12 🐕€3 ♿(htd) ⚿ ♨ ♿ 🍴 ✉ 🚰 ▼ ♈ Ⓣ Ⓗ 💧 🛒 ⁄!\ 🛶

Exit A1 Amersfoort-Apeldoorn m'way at junc 19
Hoenderloo. Fr Hoenderloo dir Loenen, site sp. Lge,
mkd, hdg, pt shd, serviced pitches; EHU (6-16A); adv
bkg req; bike hire. *"V pleasant setting 2km fr National
Park; go-kart hire; excel facs; free 1-day bus ticket;
private bthrms avail; some site rds diff for lge o'fits; vg
for children; no dogs high ssn; many mkd walks/cycle
paths; friendly staff."* **€32.30** **2018**

APPELSCHA *D2* (4.5km S Rural) *52.92134, 6.34447*
Boscamping Appelscha, Oude Willem 3, 8426 SM
Appelscha **(0516) 431391; info@boscamping
appelscha.nl; www.campingalkenhaer.nl**

♿ ⚿ ♨ ♿ 🍴 ✉ 🚰 ▼ ♈ 💧 ⁄!\ 🛶

A28 junc 31 sp Drachten. Turn L onto N381. About
13km turn L onto Oude Willem then take 3rd R,
site on L. Lge, mkd, pt shd, EHU (16A); 60% statics;
Eng spkn; CKE. *"Neat, friendly, well run site; takeaway;
many walking, cycling & riding trails in nrby national
park; vg site."* **€24.50, 1 Apr-1 Oct.** **2019**

ARNHEM *C3* (6km W Rural) *51.99365, 5.82203*
Camping Aan Veluwe, Sportlaan 1, 6861 AG
Oosterbeek **(0224) 563109; info@aannoordzee.nl;
www.aanveluwe.nl**

🐕€1.80 ♿(htd) ⚿ ♨ ✉ 🚰 ▼ ♈ Ⓣ 🛒 ⁄!\

Fr S fr Nijmegen, cross new bdge at Arnhem. Foll
Oosterbeek sp for 5km, cont past memorial in
Oosterbeek, in 1km turn R at rndabt, 500m L to site.
Or fr A50 exit junc 19 onto N225 twd Osterbeek/
Arnhem. In 3km at rndabt turn L, site on L in 500m.
Med, pt shd, pt sl, EHU (16A) inc; gas; red long stay;
10% statics; adv bkg acc; sep car park. *"Conv Airborne
Museum & Cemetery & Dutch Open Air Museum; sports
club bar open to site guests; shwr facs for each pitch;
pool 3km; lovely walks."* **€21.00, 29 Mar-28 Oct.**
2019

ARNHEM *C3* (5km NW Rural) *52.0072, 5.8714*
Camping Warnsborn, Bakenbergseweg 257, 6816 PB
Arnhem **(026) 4423469; info@campingwarnsborn.nl;
www.campingwarnsborn.nl**

🐕€3 ♿(htd) ⚿ ♨ ♿ 🍴 ✉ 🚰 ▼ ♈ 💧 Ⓗnr 🛒 ⁄!\

Fr Utrecht on E35/A12, exit junc 25 Ede (if coming
fr opp dir, beware unnumbered m'way junc 200m
prior to junc 25). Take N224 dual c'way twd Arnhem
& foll sp Burgers Zoo, site sp. Beware oncoming
traff & sleeping policeman nr site ent. Med, pt shd,
EHU (6A) inc; gas; bbq; red long stay; 5% statics;
phone; bus 100m; Eng spkn; adv bkg acc; ccard acc;
CKE. *"Excel, spacious, clean, well-maintained, wooded
site; san facs clean; friendly, helpful family owners &
staff; airborne museum & cemetery; cycle rtes direct fr
site; conv Hooge Veluwe National Park & Kröller-Müller
museum (Van Gogh paintings); super site but busy; bus
into Arnhem."* **€19.50, 24 Mar-30 Oct.** **2016**

ASSEN *D2* (16km NW Rural) *53.07783, 6.44870*
Camping de Norgerberg, Langeloërweg 63. 9331
VA Norg **(0592) 612281; info@norgerberg.nl;**
www.norgerberg.nl

🐕 €2.30 👫(htd) WD ♨ ♿ ⚷ 🖥 ✉ MSP 🦋 ⵜ 🍸 ⑪ ⛱ 🪑 ⛺ ⚒

Fr Leeuwarden, N31 S to junc 30(20km). Then N381
sp Emmen for 10km, L twrds Waskemeer/Norg on
N917. Turn L at Norg onto N373. Site on L in 1km.
Med, hdg, mkd, pt shd, EHU (10A); gas; bbq; TV; bus
adj; Eng spkn; adv bkg acc; games area; games rm;
CCI. *"Vg cycling trails including forest; easy access to
town, rest & shops; excel."* **€28.00, 27 Mar-1 Nov.**
2015

BERGEN OP ZOOM *B4* (5km SE Rural) *51.46913,
4.32236* **Camping Uit en Thuis,** Heimolen 56,
4625 DD Bergen op Zoom **(0164) 233391; info@
campinguitenthuis.nl; www.campinguitenthuis.nl**

🐕 €2.80 👫(htd) WD ♨ ♿ ⚷ 🖥 ✉ MSP 🦋 🍸 ⑪ ⛱ ⛺

Exit A4/E312 at junc 29 sp Huijbergen & foll site sp.
Lge, hdg, pt shd, EHU (4-6A) €2; red long stay; TV;
75% statics; Eng spkn; adv bkg acc; tennis; games
area; CKE. *"Spacious site in woodland; gd cycle paths to
pleasant town; sep mv places; excel site, v pretty; lge
pitches."* **€22.00, 1 Apr-1 Oct.** 2017

BLADEL *C4* (1.6km S Rural) *51.35388, 5.22254* **Mini-
Camping De Hooiberg,** Bredasebaan 20, 5531 NB
Bladel **(0497) 369619 or 06 54341822 (mob); info@
minicampingdehooiberg.nl; www.minicamping
dehooiberg.nl**

🐕 👫(htd) WD ♨ ♿ 🖥 ✉ 🦋

Exit A67 junc 32 onto N284 to Bladel, turn L at traff
lts to Bladel-Zuid, site on L in 2km. Sm, pt shd, EHU
(6A) inc; bus adj; Eng spkn; adv bkg acc; sep car park.
*"Gd, quiet site; clean san fac; v friendly owner; dogs
free; farm shop selling local produce adj; 10 mins fr
A67; conv NH & for Eindhoven & Efteling theme park."*
€18.00, 15 Mar-31 Oct. 2019

BLADEL *C4* (3km S Rural) *51.34325, 5.22740*
Camping De Achterste Hoef, Troprijt 10, 5531 NA
Bladel **(0497) 381579; info@achterstehoef.nl;**
www.achterstehoef.nl

🐕 👫(htd) WD ♨ ♿ ⚷ 🖥 ✉ MSP 🍸 ⑪ ⛱ ⛺ ⚒
🛶 (covrd, htd) 🎿

Fr A67 exit junc 32 onto N284 to Bladel, then
Bladel-Zuid, site sp. 5*, V lge, pt shd, EHU (6A) inc;
70% statics; adv bkg acc; ccard acc; waterslide; games
area; tennis; games rm; bike hire. *"Private san facs
avail."* **€41.70, 5 Apr-29 Sep.** 2019

BOURTANGE *D2* (1km NW Rural) *53.01014, 7.18494*
NCC Camping 't Plathuis, Bourtangerkanaal Noord 1,
9545 VJ Bourtange **(0599) 354383; info@plathuis.nl;**
www.plathuis.nl

🐕 👫(htd) WD ♨ ♿ ⚷ 🖥 ✉ MSP 🦋 ⵜ 🍸 ⑪ ⛱ ⛺

Exit A47 junc 47 onto N368 sp Blijham to
Vlagtwedde. Turn L onto N365 to Bourtange, site sp
on R. Med, hdg, pt shd, EHU 10; bbq; cooking facs; sw;
TV; 50% statics; phone; bus; Eng spkn; adv bkg acc;
ccard acc; canoe hire; games area; bike hire; fishing;
CKE. *"Site adj historic fortress; town 2km fr German
border; level pitches, some hdstdng but mainly grass;
peaceful atmosphere; gd, clean facs; sm family run
site next to marina; cafe at recep; vg; tv recep (Astra)."*
€28.30, 1 Apr-31 Oct. 2019

BRIELLE *B3* (1km E Urban) *51.90666, 4.17527*
Camping de Meeuw, Batterijweg 1, 3231 AA Brielle
(0181) 412777; info@demeeuw.nl; www.demeeuw.nl

🐕 €3.75 👫 WD ♨ ♿ ⚷ 🖥 ✉ 🦋 🍸 ⑪ ⛱ ⛺ ⚒ 🌊 sand

On A15/N57 foll sp to Brielle. Turn R after passing
thro town gates & foll sp to site. Lge, pt shd, EHU
(10A) €2 (poss rev pol); gas; 70% statics; phone; Eng
spkn; bike hire; CKE. *"Historic fortified town; attractive
area for tourers; conv Europoort ferry terminal; gd NH/
sh stay; phone warden fr recep when arr after 5pm."*
€28.00, 31 Mar-30 Oct. 2017

CADZAND *A4* (2km SE Rural) *51.36099, 3.42503*
Camping De Wielewaal, Zuidzandseweg 20, 4506
HC Cadzand **(0117) 391216; info@
campingwielewaal.nl; www.campingwielewaal.nl**

🐕 €2 👫 WD ♨ ♿ ⚷ 🖥 ✉ 🦋 ⵜ 🍸 nr ⑪ nr ⛱ nr ⛺ ⚒ 🌊 3km

Head to Cadzand. Travel 1km SE, site ent on L,
3km NW of Zuidzande. Med, hdg, mkd, pt shd,
EHU; bbq; Eng spkn; adv bkg acc; ccard acc; games
rm. *"Many cycle tracks; walks fr site; friendly,
helpful owners; windmill 1km; highly rec; excel."*
€18.70, 19 Mar-31 Oct. 2016

CADZAND *A4* (5km S Rural/Coastal) *51.344562,
3.429860* **Minicamping de Hullu,** Kokersweg 1, 4505
PK Zuidzande **(3111) 7452842; www.campingde
hullu.nl**

🐕 👫(htd) WD ♨ ♿ 🖥 ✉ MSP 🦋 ⵜ 🌊 4km

Do not use SatNav. Fr Bruge A11 (new) N253 to
Oostburg. N674 thro Zuidzande. Site on L. Sm, shd,
EHU (6A) inc; bbq; Eng spkn; adv bkg acc; games
area. *"Excel; feels like camping in gdn of stately home;
16 vans when full; views; lawned; no passing traff;
spacious."* **NP 20, 20 Apr-15 Sep.** 2018

CALLANTSOOG *B2* (2.5km NE Coastal) *52.84627, 4.71549* **Camping Tempelhof,** Westerweg 2, 1759 JD Callantsoog **(0224) 581522; info@tempelhof.nl; www.tempelhof.nl**

🏕 **12** €3.50 ♂♀ (htd) 🅦 ⚘ ♨ ♿ 🖥 ✉ 🅟 ❦ 🍸 🄷 🍴 ⛰ ✂
🏊 (covrd, htd) 🎣 🏖 sand 1km

Fr A9 Alkmaar-Den Helder exit Callantsoog, site sp to NE of vill. 5*, Lge, mkd, pt shd, serviced pitches; EHU (10A) inc; gas; TV (pitch); 50% statics; phone; adv bkg rec; sauna; gym; bike hire; games area; tennis. *"Superb, well-run site & facs; private bthrms avail; ACSI acc."* **€43.00** 2017

CALLANTSOOG *B2* (3km NE Coastal) *52.84143, 4.71909* **NCC Camping De Ooster Nollen,** Westerweg 8, 1759 JD Callantsoog **(0224) 581281 or 561351; info@denollen.nl; www.denollen.nl**

🐕 €3 ♂♀ (htd) 🅦 ⚘ ♨ ♿ ✉ 🅟 🦋 🍸 🄷 🍴 🛒 ⛰ ✂
🏖 sand 1.5km

N fr Alkmaar on A9; turn L sp Callantsoog. Site sp 1km E of Callantsoog. Lge, mkd, pt shd, EHU (10A) inc; gas; red long stay; TV; 40% statics; phone; Eng spkn; adv bkg acc; ccard acc; bike hire; games area; CKE. *"Nature area nr; cheese mkt; clean & superb san facs; pool 400m; supmkt 3km."* **€34.00, 1 Apr-29 Oct.** 2017

DELFT *B3* (4km NE Urban) *52.01769, 4.37945* **Camping Delftse Hout,** Korftlaan 5, 2616 LJ Delft **(015) 2130040; info@delftsehout.nl; www.delftse hout.co.uk**

🐕 €3.25 ♂♀ (htd) 🅦 ⚘ ♨ ♿ 🖥 ✉ 🅟 🍸 🄷 🍴 🛒 ⛰ ✂
🏊 (htd) 🎣

Fr Hook of Holland take N220 twd Rotterdam; after Maasdijk turn R onto A20 m'way. Take A13 twd Den Haag at v lge Kleinpolderplein interchange. Take exit 9 sp Delft (Ikea on R). Turn R twrds Ikea then L at rndabt. Foll sp. Do not use Sat Nav. 4*, Lge, hdstg, mkd, hdg, pt shd, EHU (10A) inc; gas; bbq; red long stay; TV; 50% statics; phone; bus to Delft; Eng spkn; adv bkg rec; ccard acc; bike hire; fishing nr; golf 5km; watersports nr; games rm; CKE. *"Located by pleasant park; gd quality, secure, busy site with excel facs; Holland Tulip Parcs site; helpful, friendly staff; little shd; no o'fits over 7.5m; excursions by hike & on foot; easy access Delft cent; sm m'van o'night area outside site; mkt Thur; excel; site clean & well maintained; gd rest; vg play areas for kids; flea mkt on Sat; gd tram and train svcs to the Hague, Leiden and Gouda fr Delft stn; gd sized pitches; vg MH svr pnt; well stocked shop."* **€37.60, 22 Mar-3 Nov, H06.** 2019

DELFT *B3* (9.4km SW Rural) *51.95450, 4.28833* **Hoeve Bouwlust,** Oostgaag 31, 3155 CE Maasland **(0105) 912775; info@hoevebouwlust.nl; www.hoevebouwlust.nl**

♂♀ 🅦 ⚘ ♨ ✉ 🅟 🍸 🄷 🍴 ⛰

Fr Hofh on A20 turn N at junc 7. Go thro Maasland on N468. Site on L in 3km. Sm, hdg, pt shd, EHU; bbq; twin axles; 10% statics; bus adj; Eng spkn; adv bkg acc; CKE. *"Lots of outdoor activities inc tandem, boating & scotters; v friendly & helpful owners; vg site."* **€19.00, 1 Apr-31 Oct.** 2018

DEN HELDER *B2* (3.5km SW Coastal) *52.93672, 4.73377* **Camping de Donkere Duinen,** Jan Verfailleweg 616, 1783 BW Den Helder **(0223) 614731; info@donkereduinen.nl; www.donkereduinen.nl**

🐕 €2.75 ♂♀ 🅦 ⚘ ♨ ♿ ✉ 🅟 🍸 🛒 nr ⛰ 🏖 sand 800m

Fr S turn L off N9 sp Julianadorp (Schoolweg), strt over at x-rds in Julianadorp (Van Foreestweg). Turn R at t-junc onto N502, site on L in approx 4km. 2*, Lge, pt shd, EHU (4-16A) inc; gas; 10% statics; Eng spkn; adv bkg req; ccard acc; tennis; bike hire; CKE. *"V helpful owner; excel walking/cycling; ferry to Texel Is; bkg fee; lge naval museum & submarine; opp Heldersee Valley Adventure (treetop) Pk."* **€25.50, 13 Apr-12 Sep.** 2017

DENEKAMP *D3* (4km NE Rural) *52.39190, 7.04890* **Camping De Papillon,** Kanaalweg 30, 7591 NH Denekamp **(0541) 351670; info@depapillon.nl; www.depapillon.nl**

🐕 €4.50 ♂♀ (htd) 🅦 ⚘ ♨ ♿ 🖥 ✉ 🅟 🦋
🍸 🄷 🍴 🛒 ⛰ 🏊 (covrd, htd)

Fr A1 take exit 32 onto N342 Oldenzaal-Denekamp, dir Nordhorn, site sp on left just bef German border. 4*, Lge, mkd, hdg, pt shd, EHU (6-10A) inc; gas; hbq; sw; red long stay; TV; 5% statics; phone; Eng spkn; tennis; pool paddling; bike hire. *"Super, clean site; friendly site; helpful owners; man-made lake; vg."* **€35.00, 29 Mar-30 Sep, H18.** 2018

DEVENTER *C3* (11km E Rural) *52.25591, 6.29205* **Camping De Flierweide,** Traasterdijk 16, 7437 Bathmen **31 570 541478; info@flierweide.nl; www.flierweide.nl**

🐕 ♂♀ 🅦 ⚘ ♨ ♿ 🖥 ✉ 🅟 🦋 🍸 ⛰

Fr A1 junc 25 dir Bathmen. After 1km turn R sp De Flierweide, 800m L onto Laurensweg, thro vill. Cross rlwy, 1st R ontp Traasterdijk. Site on R after 500m at fm buildings. Med, hdg, mkd, hdstg, pt shd, EHU (4-16A) €2.50; bbq; red long stay; 1% statics; Eng spkn; adv bkg acc; bike hire; games area; CKE. *"Walking & cycle rtes; golf nr; boules onsite; excel."* **€23.00, 15 Mar-1 Nov.** 2016

DIEREN *C3 (2.5km NW Rural) 52.06908, 6.07705* **De Jutberg Vakantiedorp,** Jutberg 78, 6957 DP Laag-Soeren **03 13 61 92 20; jutberg@ardoer.com; www.ardoer.com/jutberg**

🔟 🐕 👫 (htd) 🚿 ♿ ⚐ 🚮 ⫽ 🦋 ⛽ 🍴
🅗 ♨ 🚯 ⛰ 🎿 🏊 (covrd, htd)

Fr A12 take exit 27 onto the A348. Turn L on the N348 into Dieren. Turn L at petrol stn, cont for 2.7km. Foll sp to site. V lge, mkd, shd, pt sl, EHU (6A); bbq; Eng spkn; adv bkg acc; games rm; games area; CCI. "Hugh pitches, fully serviced; v lively but not noisy; excursions for adults & kids in summer; wet weather diversions; excel san facs; extensive cycle paths thro countryside & forest; excel site." **€35.20**   **2019**

DOKKUM *C2 (0.4km E Urban) 53.32611, 6.00468* **Camping Harddraverspark,** Harddraversdijk 1a, 9101 XA Dokkum **(0519) 294445; info@camping dokkum.nl; www.campingdokkum.nl**

🐕 €2 👫 🚿 ⛰ ♿ ⚐ 🚮 ⫽ 🦋 🍴 nr 🅗 nr 🚮 ⛰

Best app fr E fr ring rd N361 onto Harddraversdijk alongside rv, site sp. Do not app thro town - narr rds. Med, hdg, mkd, hdstg, pt shd, EHU (6A) €2.50; gas; Eng spkn; tennis. "Excel location in cent of pleasant town; conv for ferry to Ameland Island (12km)." **€19.00, 1 Apr-31 Oct.**   **2015**

DORDRECHT *B3 (13km N Rural) 51.89530, 4.72209* **Camping en Feestzall Landhoeve,** Lekdijk 15, 2957 CA Nieuw-Lekkerland **(3184) 684137 or (316) 40487201; info@landhoeve.info; www.landhoeve.com**

🐕 👫 (htd) 🚿 ⛰ ♿ ⫽ 🦋 🍴

Fr A15 take exit 23. Take 2nd exit at rndabt and then 3rd exit at next rndabt twrds New Lekkerland. Turn R onto the N480 twrds Streefkerk. Then L onto Zijdeweg & L again at the end of rd. Site in 400mtrs. Sm, unshd, EHU; bbq; Eng spkn; adv bkg acc. "New htd toilet block (2017); views; 19 windmills at Kinderdijk nrby, Unesco site; like lge CL; vg." **€22.00, 1 Apr-1 Oct.**   **2017**

DORDRECHT *B3 (3km SE Rural) 51.80738, 4.71862* **Camping Het Loze Vissertje,** Loswalweg 3, 3315 LB Dordrecht **(078) 6162751; info@campinghet vissertje.nl; www.campinghetvissertje.nl**

🐕 €1 👫 🚿 ⛰ ⫽ 🦋 🍴

Fr Rotterdam across Brienenoord Bdge foll sp Gorinchem & Nijmegen A15. Exit junc 23 Papendrecht & turn R onto N3 until exit Werkendam. Turn R & foll sp 'Het Vissertje'. Sm, pt shd, EHU (6A) inc; red long stay; 20% statics; Eng spkn. "Lovely, delightful site; friendly, helpful manager; modern, clean san facs; gd cycle rtes nr; vg; easy acc to town on local train." **€21.00, 15 Apr-15 Sep.**   **2019**

DRACHTEN *C2 (10km W Rural) 53.09696, 5.94695* **Camping De Veenhoop Watersport & Recreatie,** Eijzengapaed 5, 9215 VV De Veenhoop **(0512) 462289; info@de-veenhoop.nl; www.de-veenhoop.nl**

🐕 👫 (htd) 🚿 ⛰ ⫽ 🦋 🅗 nr 🚮 nr ⛰

Exit A7 junc 28 dir Nij Beets, foll De Veenhoop sp to site. Or exit A32 junc 13 & turn W for approx 6km via Aldeboarn. Turn L at Pieter's Rest to De Veenhoop, site on L bef sm bdge. Med, pt shd, EHU (6-10A) €4; bbq; sw; 50% statics; bus adj; Eng spkn; adv bkg acc; boat hire. "Excel, peaceful, friendly site; helpful owners; clean & well-maintained; excel sailing, cycling, walking; well situated for lakes & N N'lands; gd NH & longer stays; MH beware some soft (peat) grnd." **€24.00, 1 Apr-1 Oct.**   **2018**

DROONENBURGH *C3 (3km NNW Rural) 51.90416, 5.98529* **Camping de Waay,** Rijndijk 67A, 6686 MC Doornenburg **(048) 1421256; info@de-waay.nl; www.de-waay.nl**

🐕 👫 🚿 ⛰ ♿ ⚐ 🚮 ⫽ 🍴 🅗 ♨ 🚯 ⛰ 🏊 (htd) 🛒

A325 S fr Arnhem for 12km turn R onto A15 twrds Tiel, take exit N839 Bemmel. At t-junc foll sp to Gendt. In Gendt take N838. Foll ANWB de Waay sp twrds Angeren. Turn R onto the dyke and site on R. Sm, pt shd, EHU 6A; bbq; TV; 60% statics; Eng spkn; adv bkg acc; waterslide; games rm; bike hire; games area; CKE. "V helpful staff; takeaway; gd for Arnhem & Nijmegen; ACSI acc; vg." **€33.50, 25 Mar-1 Oct.**   **2016**

DWINGELOO *D2 (2km SE Rural) 52.82216, 6.39258* **Camping De Olde Bârgen,** Oude Hoogeveensedijk 1, 7991 PD Dwingeloo **(0521) 597261; info@ oldebargen.nl; www.oldebargen.nl**

🔟 🐕 €2 👫 🚿 ⛰ ♿ ⚐ 🚮 ⫽ 🦋 🍴 🚯 nr ⛰

Exit A28 Zwolle/Assen rd at Spier, turn W sp Dwingeloo, site clearly sp, in wooded area. Sm, mkd, pt shd, EHU (4-6A) inc; 10% statics; Eng spkn; adv bkg acc; CKE. "Excel, v clean, well-run site on N side Dwingelderveld National Park; gd for walkers & cyclists; v friendly, helpful owners; pool 1.5km; delightful, quiet sitewarden avail 1 hr each morning LS; pitch & pay next day." **€21.00**   **2017**

EDAM *B2 (2km NE Coastal) 52.51853, 5.07286* **Camping Strandbad Edam,** Zeevangszeedijk 7A, 1135 PZ Edam **(0299) 371994; info@camping strandbad.nl; www.campingstrandbad.nl**

👫 (htd) 🚿 ⛰ ♿ ⚐ 🚮 ⫽ 🦋 🍴 🅗 ♨ 🚯 ⛰ 🛒 ⛵ sand adj

Foll N247 Amsterdam-Hoorn; after sp for Edam foll site sp. At traff lts in Edam keep on N247 past bus stn on R, then R at next rndabt. Last 100m to site is single track opp marina. Access thro public car park. 2*, Lge, pt shd, EHU (10A) €2.90; gas; red long stay; TV; 40% statics; phone; Eng spkn; adv bkg acc; ccard acc; watersports; bike hire. "Walking dist Edam; landing stage for boats; excel san facs; pool 3km; sm, poss cramped pitches high ssn." **€20.00, 1 Apr-30 Sep.**   **2018**

EDAM *B2* (2.5km NE Coastal) *52.52472, 5.06472*
Camping Zeevangshoeve, Zeevangszeedijk 5-C, 1135
PZ Edam **(061) 7864374; info@zeevangshoeve.nl;**
www.zeevangshoeve.nl

🐕 €1.50 ♦♦ WD ♨ ♿ ⅃ MP ♐ opp

Foll coast rd out of Nof old part of Edam past
marina along edge of the Markermeer dyke. Site is
on L opp the Zeedijk. Sm, pt shd, EHU 6A; bbq; Eng
spkn; adv bkg acc. *"Easy walk/cycle to historic cent of
Edam; vg."* **€20.00, 30 Mar-31 Oct.** **2018**

EERSEL *C4* (4km SE Rural) *51.33635, 5.35552*
Camping De Paal, De Paaldreef 14, 5571 TN Bergeijk
(0497) 571977; info@depaal.nl; www.depaal.nl

🐕 €5 ♦♦ (htd) WD ♨ ♿ ⅃ MP ♐ Ⓗ 🎱 ♿
🎿 (covrd, htd)

Fr A67/E34 Antwerp/Eindoven exit junc 32 sp Eersel
& bear R onto N284 & stay in R-hand lane. At rndabt
take 1st exit onto Eijkereind. In 500m after rndbt
turn L at traff lts & foll rd around R & L bend. Take
R turn sp Bergeijk after lge church (sm sp on sharp
L bend). After approx 5km turn L into site rd. 5*,
V lge, pt shd, EHU (6A) inc; gas; bbq (charcoal, gas);
TV; 10% statics; phone; games rm; sep car park; bike
hire; tennis; watersports 10km; fishing; horseriding
500m; sauna. *"Excel, family-run site set in woodland;
espec gd for young children; lge pitches in groups with
sep sm play areas; excursions; recep 0900-1800; sm
children's zoo; fitness cent; no o'fits over 8m high ssn;
conv Efteling theme park, Hilvarenbeek safari park,
Oisterwijk bird park; mkt Mon & Tue pm; 1st class facs."*
€25.00, 25 Mar-30 Oct, H04. **2016**

EINDHOVEN *C4* (16km S Rural) *51.32887, 5.46160*
Recreatiepark Brugse Heide, Maastrichterweg 183,
5556 VB Valkenswaard **(040) 2018304; info@
vakantieparkbrugseheide.nl; www.vakantiepark
brugseheide.nl**

🐕 ♦♦ (htd) WD ♨ ♿ ⅃ MP ♐ Ⓗ 🎱 nr 🎿 (htd)

S fr Elndhoven, exit Waalre; take N69
Valkenswaard; drive thro to rndabt, turn L. At
next rndabt strt ahead, at next rndabt turn R,
foll sp Achel. Site on L in 1km. 3*, Lge, mkd, shd,
serviced pitches; EHU (6A) inc (rev pol); gas; bbq; TV;
40% statics; phone; Eng spkn; adv bkg acc; ccard acc;
bike hire. *"Excel, friendly site; gd NH en rte Germany;
excel san facs."* **€34.00, 18 Mar-31 Oct.** **2016**

EMMEN *D2* (6km N Rural) *52.82861, 6.85714*
Vakantiecentrum De Fruithof, Melkweg 2, 7871 PE
Klijndijk **(0591) 512427; infofruithof.nl;
www.fruithof.nl**

🐕 ♦♦ (htd) WD ♨ ♿ ⅃ MP ♐ Ⓗ 🎱 🎿 (htd)

On N34 N fr Emmen dir Borger, turn R sp Klijndijk,
foll site sp. 5*, Lge, mkd, hdg, pt shd, serviced pitches;
EHU (6A) inc; gas; bbq; sw nr; red long stay; TV;
50% statics; Eng spkn; adv bkg acc; tennis; games
area; bike hire; CKE. *"Excel; v lge busy site; gd san
facs."* **€38.80, 5 Apr-23 Sep.** **2019**

ENKHUIZEN *C2* (1km N Coastal) *52.70888, 5.28830*
Camping De Vest, Noorderweg 31, 1601 PC Enkhuizen
**(0228) 321221; info@campingdevest.nl;
www.campingdevest.nl**

🐕 ♦♦♦ WD ♨ ⅃ ♐ sand 800m

When N302 turns R at traff lts, keep strt on to
T-junc. Foll site sp to R, site on R in 50m. Sm, pt
shd, EHU (4A) inc; 25% statics; Eng spkn; adv bkg acc.
*"Gates clsd 2300-0800; easy walk to town cent; lively
jazz festival last w/end in May; facs old but clean, well-
kept - poss stretched when site full; site inside town
walls."* **€21.00, 30 Mar-30 Sep.** **2018**

ENSCHEDE *D3* (6km E Urban) *52.21034, 6.95127*
Euregio Camping de Twentse Es, Keppelerdijk 200,
7534 PA Enschede **(053) 4611372; info@twentse-es.nl;
www.twentse-es.nl**

12 🐕 ♦♦ (htd) WD ♨ ⅃ MP ♐ Ⓗ 🎱 🎿

Fr Germany, cross border at Gronau on B54/N35;
twd Enschede. In 2.5km turn R into Oostweg, then
in 2km turn R into Gronausestraat, then in 800m
turn R into Esmarkelaan. Foll rd thro residential
area, turn L at end, site on R. Not rec to foll sat nav
due rd building, rec foll rd signs. 3*, Lge, pt shd, EHU
(10A) inc; gas; TV; 70% statics; adv bkg acc; ccard acc;
bike hire; games area; CKE. *"Excel site; modern facs;
15% discount with CCI card; local tourist tax of €0.76
pppn."* **€24.00** **2018**

EXLOO *D2* (2km SE Rural) *52.86841, 6.88496*
Camping Exloo, Valtherweg 37, 7875 TA Exloo **05 91
54 91 47 or 05 91 56 40 14; info@campingexloo.nl;
www.campingexloo.nl**

12 🐕 €1 ♦♦ WD ♨ ♿ ⅃ MP 🦋 ♐

N34 fr Groningen, exit Exloo. Turn R after vill twd
Valthe. Site 2km on L. Sm, pt shd, EHU (6A); bbq;
twin axles; TV; Eng spkn; adv bkg acc; CCI. *"Friendly
recreation rm; vg site."* **€20.20** **2019**

GENDT *C3* (1km E Rural) *51.87599, 5.98900*
Waalstrand Camping, Waaldijk 23, 6691 MB Gendt
**(0481) 421604; info@waalstrand.nl;
www.waalstrand.nl**

🐕 €3 ♦♦ WD ♿ ⅃ ♐ Ⓗ 🎱 🎿

Exit A15 to Bemmel, then Gendt. In Gendt foll sp to
site on Rv Waal. Med, mkd, unshd, terr, EHU (6A) inc;
gas; TV (pitch); 50% statics; Eng spkn; adv bkg acc;
bike hire; tennis. *"Excel, well-kept site; clean, modern
san facs; interesting rv traff; v friendly owners; lovely
position; gd walks; 6 fully serviced camper van pitches;
good views; excel site."* **€29.50, 1 Apr-30 Sep.** **2018**

GORINCHEM *B3* (13km E Rural) *51.81845, 5.12563*
Camping De Zwaan, Waaldijk 56, 4171 CG Herwijnen
(0418) 582354; info@rivierenland.biz;
http://www.rivierenland.nl

👤🚿 ⭕ ♨ 🚻 ⚖ nr 🏕

Exit A15 at junc 29 dir Herwijnen. In Herwijnen turn
R at T-junc sp Brakel. Turn L in 500m (Molenstraat).
At T-junc turn R (Waaldijk), site on L in 150m on
Rv Waal. Sm, pt shd, EHU (4A) inc; 75% statics;
Eng spkn; adv bkg rec; CKE. *"Helpful owners; rv
adj; ltd but clean facs; 66 m fr Amsterdam ferry."*
€13.00, 15 Apr-15 Oct. 2020

GOUDA *B3* (10km E Rural) *52.01719, 4.82943*
Camping De Mulderije, Hekendorpsebuurt 33, 3467
PA Hekendorp **(0348) 563233 or 06 20680521
(mob); info@demulderije.nl; demulderije.nl**

12 👤 👥🚿 ♨ ♿ ⚖ ✉ 🦋 nr ⑪ nr ⚖ nr

Exit A12 junc 14 Woerden onto N204 S. In 5km
turn R to Oudewater N228. Cont dir Hekendorp &
in approx 2km site sp on R. Narr rd to site. 1*, Sm,
hdstg, pt shd, EHU (6A) inc; Eng spkn. *"Vg, clean,
friendly site in nature reserve; cycle or boat to Gouda;
facs clean attractive position; gd base; narr rd to site
not suitable for lge o'fits; no passing places; do not use
sat nav."* **€17.00** 2017

GOUDA *B3* (2km E Urban) *52.01226, 4.71544*
Klein Amerika Parking, 2806 Gouda

12 👥🚿 ⭕ ✉

500m fr Gouda town cent, sp off Blekerssingel/
Fluwelensingel. EHU (16A). *"30 spaces in car pk at
Klein Amerika supervised by Gouda City Council; 12
EHU sockets; max stay 3 days; normal car parking fees
applicable; poorly maintained."* **€8.00** 2016

GRONINGEN *D2* (6km SW Urban) *53.20128, 6.53577*
Camping Stadspark, Campinglaan 6, 9727 KH
Groningen **(050) 5251624; info@campingstadspark.
nl; www.campingstadspark.nl**

👤 €2 👥🚿 ⭕ ♨ 🚻 ⚖ ✉ 🦋 🍴 ⚖ 🏕

Take exit 36-A (dir Drachten) and foll 'Stadspark'.
In the park go to the L and foll the sp. Fr Drachten/
Winsum, take exit 36. 2*, Med, shd, EHU (6A) €2.50
(poss rev pol); gas; TV; 20% statics; phone; Eng spkn;
adv bkg acc; bike hire; sep car park. *"Municipal site adj
parkland with gd sports facs; park & ride into town;
plenty of space, tents & vans mixed; extensive cycle
paths; car park adj to each set of pitches; gd san facs;
well run site; interesting town; pool 3km; friendly
helpful staff."* **€24.00, 15 Mar-15 Oct.** 2017

GULPEN *C4* (1.5km S Rural) *50.80720, 5.89430*
Panorama Camping Gulperberg, Berghem 1, 6271
NP Gulpen **(043) 4502330; info@gulperberg.nl;**
www.gulperberg.nl

👤 €4.50 👥 (htd) ⭕ ♨ ♿ ✉ ⚖ 🦋 ⛪ 🍴 ⑪ ♨ ⚖ nr 🏕 🚣 🛶

Fr Maastricht on N278 twd Aachen. At 1st traff lts
in Gulpen turn sharp R & foll site sp for 2km (past
sports complex). Narr final app. 4*, Lge, hdstg,
mkd, pt shd, terr, EHU (10A) inc; gas; bbq; TV (pitch)
10% statics; phone; Eng spkn; adv bkg acc; games
area; bike hire; CKE. *"Nr Maastricht with gd walking/
views; mkd cycle rtes & footpaths; modern, clean facs
- poss long walk; beautiful views; v popular site, busy
even in LS; excel."* **€37.00, 17 Mar-3 Nov, H12.** 2017

HARDERWIJK *C3* (13.6km W Rural) *52.340102,
5.505166* **Camping Het Groene Bos,** Green
Woudseweg 98, 3896 LS Zeewolde **(036) 5236366;**
info@hetgroenebos.nl; www.hetgroenebos.nl

👥 (htd) ⭕ ♨ ♨ ⚖ ✉ 🦋 ♨ 🏕

Off A305 on minor rd between Kampen & A27. Exit
A27 J26 onto 305. Med, mkd, hdg, pt shd, EHU inc;
Eng spkn; CKE. *"Vg site; surrounded by woodland."*
€21.60, 1 Apr-11 Oct. 2018

HARLINGEN *C2* (2km SW Coastal) *53.16253, 5.41653*
Camping De Zeehoeve, Westerzeedijk 45, 8862 PK
Harlingen **(0517) 413465; info@zeehoeve.nl;**
www.zeehoeve.nl

👤 €3.50 👥 (htd) ⭕ ♨ ♿ ✉ ⚖ ✉ 🍴 ⑪ ♨ ⚖ nr 🏕 ✏ ⚓ adj

Leave N31 N'bound at sp Kimswerd. At rndabt
turn L under N31 & foll site sp. Site on R in 1.6km.
3*, Lge, mkd, EHU (6A) inc; gas; TV; 30% statics;
phone; Eng spkn; ccard acc; fishing; bike hire; games
area; watersports. *"Roomy, well-maintained, well run,
open site; clean modern facs; easy walk to historic
town & harbour; interesting area; vg; ACSI acc."*
€26.00, 1 Apr-31 Oct. 2018

HAVELTE *D2* (1km SE Rural) *52.76820, 6.24987*
Campsite Jelly's Hoeve, Raadhuislaan 2, 7971 CT
Havelte **(052) 1342808; info@jellyshoeve.nl;**
www.jellyshoeve.nl

👤 €2 👥🚿 ⭕ ♨ ♿ ✉ ✉ 🦋 ♨

Take exit 4 on A32. Then N371 twrds Havelte/
Diever. After 4km cross the bdge and take immed
R, foll rd for 1km. Turn L at canal bdge, bear R &
after 75m turn R. Site on R after 100m. Sm, mkd,
hdg, pt shd, EHU (10A) €2; bbq; twin axles; Eng spkn;
games area. *"Plenty of walks & cycle tracks; excel."*
€21.00, 1 Apr-30 Sep. 2015

HELDEN *C4* (2km E Rural) *51.31813, 6.0235* **Camping De Heldense Bossen,** De Heldense Bossen 6, 5988 NH Helden **07 73 07 24 76; heldensebossen@ ardoer.com; www.ardoer.com/heldensebossen**

🐕 👭 WD 🏕 🚿 ♿ 🍽 ∥ MSP 👣 ▼ 🍴 ⊕ 🛒 ⚑ 🏔 ⚓ (covrd, htd) ♨

Fr A67 Eindhoven-Venlo, take exit 38 (Helden). Turn R onto N277 twds Maasbreeseweg. Cont onto N562. Fr Helden dir Kessel. Turn L after 1km. Campsite **1km further on.** 5*, V lge, mkd, pt shd, EHU (10A); bbq; twin axles; 65% statics; Eng spkn; adv bkg acc; games area; waterslide; bike hire; CCI. *"Excel site."* **€34.50, 29 Mar-27 Oct.** 2019

HENGELO *D3* (7km W Rural) *52.25451, 6.72704* **Park Camping Mooi Delden,** De Mors 6, 7491 DZ Delden **(074) 3761922; info@parkcamping.nl; www.parkcamping.nl**

🐕 €3.15 👭 (htd) WD 🏕 🚿 ♿ 🍽 ∥ 🦋 ▼ 🛒 ⚑ 🏔 ⚓

Exit A35 junc 28 onto N346 dir Delden. Fr Delden-Oost, site sp. Site ent is R-hand of 2 via barrier (use intercom on arr.) If you have a high vehicle take the turning after Delden-Oost to avoid low rail bdge (3.2m); turn L immed aft lge rv bdge & **foll site sp.** 3*, Med, mkd, pt shd, EHU (6-10A) €3.40 (poss rev pol); 50% statics; Eng spkn; adv bkg acc; tennis. *"Ideal for touring beautiful pt of Holland; sports complex adj; pleasant, well-kept site; clean facs."* **€28.00, 25 Mar-1 Oct.** 2016

HEUMEN *C3* (2km NW Rural) *51.76890, 5.82140* **Camping Heumens Bos,** Vosseneindseweg 46, 6582 BR Heumen **(024) 3581481; info@heumensbos.nl; www.heumensbos.nl**

12 🐕 €4 👭 (htd) WD 🏕 🚿 ♿ 🍽 ∥ MSP 🦋 👣 ▼ 🍴 ⊕ 🛒 ⚑ 🏔 ∥ ⚓ (covrd, htd) ♨

Take A73/E31 Nijmegen-Venlo m'way, leave at exit 3 sp Heumen/Overasselt. Do not re-cross m'way. After 500m turn R at camp sp. Site on R in approx **1.5km, 1km S of Heumen.** 5*, V lge, mkd, hdg, shd, EHU (6A) inc; gas; bbq; sw nr; TV; 60% statics; phone; Eng spkn; adv bkg acc; ccard acc; games area; horseriding 100m; games rm; bike hire; tennis; fishing 2km; watersports 6km; jacuzzi; sep car park; CCI. *"Excel, busy, family-run site; modern san facs; lots to do on site & in area - info fr recep; no o'fits over 14m; ideal for Arnhem; WW2 museums nr; activities in ssn; extra €3 for m'vans; noise fr bar high ssn; mkt Sat & Mon in Nijmegen."* **€31.50, H01.** 2019

HOEK *A4* (7km W Rural) *51.31464, 3.72618* **Oostappen Vakantiepark Marina Beach (formerly Braakman),** Middenweg 1, 4542 PN Hoek **(0115) 481730; info@vakantieparkmarinabeach.nl; www.vakantieparkmarinabeach.nl**

🐕 €5 👭 (htd) WD 🏕 🚿 ♿ 🍽 ∥ ▼ 🍴 ⊕ 🛒 ⚑ 🏔 ∥ ⚓

Sp fr N61. V lge, mkd, pt shd, serviced pitches; EHU (4A) inc; gas; TV (pitch); 50% statics; phone; Eng spkn; adv bkg acc; ccard acc; squash; sailing; tennis. *"Excel for families; lake beach; extensive recreation facs; conv Bruges/Antwerp; extra for lake view pitches."* **€46.00, 18 Mar-31 Oct.** 2016

HOEK VAN HOLLAND *B3* (1.5km N Urban) *51.98953, 4.12767* **Camping Hoek van Holland,** Wierstraat 100, 3151 VP Hoek van Holland **(0174) 382550; info@campinghoekvanholland.nl; www.camping hoekvanholland.nl**

👭 (htd) WD 🏕 🚿 ♿ 🍽 🦋 ▼ ⊕ 🛒 ⚑ 🏔 ∥ ⚓ 👣 sand nrby

Fr ferry foll N211/220 Rotterdam. After 2.4km turn L, 50m bef petrol stn on R, sp 'Camping Strand', site **400m on R.** 3*, Lge, mkd, hdstg, pt shd, EHU (6A) inc; gas; TV; 60% statics; phone; bus; Eng spkn; sep car park; bike hire; tennis; CKE. *"Open 0800-2300; modern san facs but poss inadequate when site full & long walk fr m'van area; conv ferry; mind speed bumps."* **€37.50, 1 Mar-31 Oct.** 2019

HOEK VAN HOLLAND *B3* (3km N Coastal) *51.99685, 4.13347* **Camping Jagtveld,** Nieuwlandsedijk 41, KV 2691 'S-Gravenzande **(0174) 413479; info@jagtveld.nl; www.jagtveld.nl**

👭 WD 🏕 🍽 ∥ 🦋 ▼ 🛒 ⚑ 🏔 ∥ 👣 sand 400m

Fr ferry foll N211/220 sp Rotterdam. After 3.2km, turn L at junc with traff lts gantry into cul-de-sac. **Site 200m on L.** 2*, Med, unshd, EHU (16A) poss rev pol €2; gas; 80% statics; phone; Eng spkn; sep car park. *"Ideal for ferry port; conv Den Haag & Delft; gd, clean, level, family-run site; diff when wet; helpful owners; excel 8km long beach."* **€33.30, 1 Apr-1 Oct.** 2019

HOEK VAN HOLLAND *B3* (3.4km N Rural/Coastal) *52.002950, 4.138390* **Strandpark Vlugtenburg,** 't Louwtje 10, 2691 KR/'s-Gravenzande **(017) 4412420**

12 🐕 👭 WD 🏕 🚿 ♿ 🍽 ∥ MSP 👣 ▼ 🍴 ⊕ 🛒 ⚑ 👣 sand; adj

Fr ferry take N211. After passing N220 junc. After tight R-hand bend immed take L between petrol stn & bus shelter. Lge, mkd, unshd, EHU (16A) inc; bbq; 70% statics (sep area); bus adj; Eng spkn; adv bkg acc; ccard acc. *"Vg site; excel for kite & wind surfing; restrictions on dog breeds - check bef travel; conv fr ferry; easy for Delft, The Hague."* **€36.20** 2018

HOORN *B2* (5km SW Rural) *52.63085, 5.00920* **Camping 't Venhop,** De Hulk 6a, 1622GJ, Berkhout **(0229) 551371; info@venhop.nl; www.venhop.nl**

12 🐕 €1.50 👭 (htd) WD 🏕 ∥ 🦋 👣 ▼ nr ⊕ nr 🛒 🏔

Fr A7, exit junc 7 dir Avenhorn. Turn L under A7, site **sp on R.** Med, mkd, hdg, pt shd, serviced pitches; EHU (10A) inc; 60% statics; Eng spkn; ccard acc; sep car park; boat, electric bike & scooter hire; CKE. *"Friendly owner; pleasant, well-run site nr canal; full facs LS; vg, delightful waterside camp; fishing in canal fr some pitches."* **€27.00** 2019

KATWIJK AAN ZEE *B3* (6km E Rural) *52.19990, 4.45625* **Camping Koningshof**, Elsgeesterweg 8, 2331 NW Rijnsburg **(071) 4026051; info@ koningshofholland.nl; www.koningshofholland.nl**

🐾 €3.25 ♟(htd) �│wc⏐ ♨ ⚲ ♿ 🖲 ⟋ ⏐MSP⏐ ❦ ♈ ⟁ ⒣ ⓓ ⚓ ♋ ⟁
♒ ⛷(covrd, htd) ⛵ ⎍ 🏖 sand 5km

Fr A44 (Den Haag/Wassenaar-Amsterdam) exit junc 7 (Rijnsburg-Oegstgeest). In Rijnsburg cont twd Noordwijk. Foll blue & white sps thro Rijnsburg, across a bdge & then R twd Voorhout. Site in 2km. 4*, Lge, hdstg, mkd, hdg, pt shd, EHU (16A) inc; gas; bbq; red long stay; TV (pitch); 35% statics; phone; Eng spkn; adv bkg acc; games rm; bike hire; fishing; tennis; CKE. *"Vg, well-run, busy, friendly site; o'fits over 8m by request; gd for families; excel rest; Holland Tulip Parcs site; excel facs & pool; recep 0900-1230 & 1330-2000 high ssn; sep car park for some pitches; useful tour base for bulb fields; mkt Tues; well maintained; close to beaches and town; rec cash as few cards acc."* **€35.00, 17 Apr-3 Nov, H03.**   **2019**

KORTGENE *A3* (0.5km S Rural) *51.55446, 3.80483* **Camping Villa Park de Pardakreek**, Havenweg 1, NL 4484, N Beevland **0113-302051; paardekreek@ ardoer.com; www.ardoer.com/nl/camping/ paardekreek**

🐾 ♟ ⏐wc⏐ ♨ ⚲ ♿ 🖲 ⟋ ⏐MSP⏐ ❦ ♈ ♈ ⓓ ⚓ ♋ ⟁ ♒

Take the N256 to Zierikzee, exit Kortgene foll sps to camp. Med, hdg, mkd, pt shd, EHU (16A); bbq; 40% statics; bus 0.5km; Eng spkn; sauna; games rm; CKE. *"Excel site; boat slipway & storage; adj Lake Veerse Meer; lake adj; water playgrnd; many places to visit."* **€43.00, 27 Mar-1 Nov.**   **2015**

KOUDUM *C2* (2km S Rural) *52.90290, 5.46625* **Kawan Village De Kuilart**, De Kuilart 1, 8723 CG Koudum **(0514) 522221; info@kuilart.nl; www.kuilart.nl**

⓬ 🐾 €3.35 ♟(htd) ♨ ⚲ ♿ 🖲 ⟋ ⏐MSP⏐ ❦ ♈ ♈ ⓓ ⚓ ♋ ⟁
♒⛷(covrd, htd)

Fr A50 exit sp Lemmer/Balk. Foll N359 over Galamadammen bdge, site sp. 5*, Lge, mkd, pt shd, serviced pitches; EHU (6-16A) €1.50-3.60; gas; TV; 50% statics; phone; Eng spkn; adv bkg acc; sailing; watersports; sauna; games area; sep car park; waterslide; CKE. *"Holland Tulip Parcs site; dogs by prior agreement only; private bthrms some pitches; marina."* **€26.00**   **2016**

LAUWERSOOG *D1* (0.5km SE Coastal) *53.40250, 6.21740* **Camping Beleef Lauwersoog**, Strandweg 5, 9976 VS Lauwersoog **(0519) 349133; info@ lauwersoog.nl; www.lauwersoog.nl**

⓬ 🐾 €4.75 ♟(htd) ⏐wc⏐ ♨ ⚲ ♿ 🖲 ⟋ ⏐MSP⏐ ❦ ♈ ♈ ⓓ ⚓ ♋ ⟁
♒ ⛷

Fr N355 Leeuwarden-Groningen rd, take N361 Dokkum exit. Foll rd to Lauwersoog, site sp. 4*, V lge, unshd, serviced pitches; EHU (10A) inc; gas; TV; 50% statics; phone; Eng spkn; adv bkg acc; ccard acc; bike hire; tennis; sep car park; CKE. *"Excel, well-maintained site; Holland Tulip Parcs site; vg rest; gd facs; next to historic boat harbour."* **€28.50**   **2017**

LEEK *D2* (1.6km N Rural) *53.171114, 6.382174* **Landgoedcamping Nienoord**, Midwolderweg 19, 9351 PG Leek **(0159) 4580898; info@camping nienoord; www.campingnienoord.nl**

🐾 ♟ ⏐wc⏐ ♨ ⚲ ♿ 🖲 ⟋ ⏐MSP⏐ ❦ ♈ ⓓ ♋ nr

A7 exit 34 Leek. Foll sp immed; Ent to site along slip rd. Med, hdstg, mkd, pt shd, EHU (10A); Eng spkn; ccard acc. *"Site on edge of Nienoord pk; gd fr cycling or walks; vg."* **€22.00, 30 Mar-31 Oct.**   **2019**

LEEUWARDEN *C2* (7km W Rural) *53.19484, 5.73785* **Minicamping Van Harinxma**, Marssummerdyk 7, 9033 WD Deinnum **0031 (0) 58 215 04 98; Info@ minicamping-van-Harinxma.nl; www.minicamping-van-harinxma.nl**

🐾 ♟ ⏐wc⏐ ♨ 🖲 ⟋ ⚓ ♋ ⟁

Fr S: take N31/N32 twrds Leeuwarden. Turn L on N31 sp Harlingen, turn R to Masum-Harlingen, and imm R sp Ritsumazijl. Foll rd turn L at T- junc, then fork L into no thro rd. Site on L. Sm, hdg, pt shd, EHU (6A); twin axles; TV; Eng spkn; adv bkg rec; CKE. *"Vg; billiards; fishing fr site."* **€12.00, 15 Mar-15 Oct.**   **2020**

LEIDEN *B3* (8km N Rural) *52.20984, 4.51370* **Camping De Wasbeek**, Wasbeeklaan 5b, 2361 HG Warmond **(071) 3011380; dewasbeek@hetnet.nl**

🐾 ♟ ⏐wc⏐ ♨ 🖲 ❦ ♈ ⏐ nr ⓓ nr ♋ nr

Exit A44 junc 4 dir Warmond; in 200m turn L into Wasbeeklaan, then R in 50m. Site sp. Sm, pt shd, bbq; 40% statics; bus 500m; Eng spkn; adv bkg acc; sep car park. *"Attractive, lawned site close to bulb fields; m'vans by arrangement; friendly, helpful staff; some aircraft noise; gd cycling (track to Leiden); dogs free; fishing; boating; birdwatching; lovely sm tidy site; nice area."* **€26.00, 1 Apr-1 Oct.**   **2019**

LISSE *B3* (6km S Rural) *52.22175, 4.55418* **Camping De Hof van Eeden**, Hellegatspolder 2, 2160 AZ Lisse **(0252) 212573; info@dehofvaneeden.nl; www.dehofvaneeden.nl**

♟ ⏐wc⏐ ♨ ⟋ ♈ ⓓ ♋

Exit A44 junc 3 & turn N onto N208 dir Lisse. Turn R at rest on R bef 1st set traff lts into narr rd, foll rd to end (under A44) to site. 3*, Sm, unshd, EHU (16A) inc; 90% statics; Eng spkn. *"Gd CL-type site, space for 10 tourers (sep area) - rec phone or email bef arr; interesting location by waterway & lifting rlwy bdge; conv Keukenhof; helpful owners; cycling ctr among bulb fields & around lake; excel site; lots of room for MH."* **€17.50, 15 Apr-15 Oct.**   **2018**

MAASTRICHT *C4* (10km E Rural) *50.84468, 5.77994* **Boerderijcamping Gasthoes**, Gasthuis 1, 6268 NN Bemelen **(043) 4071346 or (06) 54717951; info@ boerderijcamping-gasthoes.nl; www.boerderij camping-gasthoes.nl**

⓬ 🐾 ♟ ⏐wc⏐ ♨ ⚲ ♿ ⟋ ❦

Head for Bemelen, site is sp. Sm, pt shd, EHU (10A); bbq; twin axles; bus; Eng spkn; adv bkg acc; CKE. *"Excel."* **€18.00**   **2017**

MAURIK *C3* (2km NE Rural) *51.97605, 5.43020*
Recreatiepark Eiland van Maurik, Rijnbandijk 20, 4021 GH Maurik **(0344) 691502; receptie@ eilandvanmaurik.nl; www.eilandvanmaurik.nl**

🐕 €4 ♟(htd) 🚾 🏕 🔥 ♿ ✎ MSP 🦋 ☘ ♈ 🍴 (H) 🎿 📷 ⚠ ✏

Exit A15 junc 33 at Tiel onto B835 N & foll sp to Maurik & site on rvside. Or exit A2 junc 13 at Culembourg onto N320 to Maurik. 4*, Lge, pt shd, EHU (10A) inc; gas; TV; 50% statics; Eng spkn; adv bkg acc; tennis; fishing; horseriding; games area; watersports. *"Covrd play area; Holland Tulip Parcs site."* **€42.00, 29 Mar-1 Nov.** 2019

MEERSSEN *C4* (1.6km ESE Rural) *50.87851, 5.77112*
Camping Meerssen, Houthemerweg 95, 6231 KT Meerssen **(0433) 654743 or (0651) 970389; info@ campingmeerssen.nl; www.campingmeerssen.nl**

🐕 ♟ 🚾 🏕 ✎ MSP ♈ 🍴 nr (H) nr 📷 nr

Fr Eindhoven A2, take exit 51, foll Valkenburg sp. Take A79 to Hellen exit 2 Meerssen. L at junc after 400m, site on R. Sm, mkd, pt shd, EHU (6A); gas; bbq; twin axles; 2% statics; Eng spkn. *"Nice, peaceful & relaxing site; v popular with Dutch people; cent for touring the area; excel site."* **€35.00, 1 Apr-30 Sep.** 2019

> **"Satellite navigation makes touring much easier"**
>
> Remember most sat navs don't know if you're towing or in a larger vehicle – always use yours alongside maps and site directions

MEPPEL *C2* (15km W Rural) *52.72164, 6.07484*
Passantenhaven Zuiderkluft, Jonenweg, 8355 LG Giethoorn **(0521) 362312**

♟ 🚾 🏕 ✎ MSP 🦋

Turn off N334 sp Dwarsgracht, over lifting bdge, 1st L over bdge, 1st L again, site on R. Sm, unshd, EHU (10A) metered; Eng spkn. *"M'vans only; site run by VVV (tourist board) for m'vans only; ltd EHU; walking dist fr delightful vill on water; all svrs accessed by smartcard purchased from machine on site; CC only."* **€11.00, 1 Apr-1 Nov.** 2018

MIDDELBURG *A4* (8km N Rural) *51.55005, 3.64022*
Mini Camping Hoekvliet, Meiwerfweg 3, 4352 SC Gapinge **(0118) 501615 or (0621) 957185; copgapinge@zeelandnet.nl; www.hoekvliet.nl**

🐕 €1 ♟ 🚾 🏕 🔥 ♿ ✎ 🦋 ♈ 🍴 nr (H) nr ⚠ 🏖 sand 5km

Fr Middleburg turn R off N57 at traff lts sp Veere & Gapinge, site sp after Gapinge vill. Sm, mkd, hdstg, pt shd, EHU (10A) inc; bbq; TV (pitch); 20% statics; Eng spkn; bike hire; CKE. *"Superb little (25 o'fits) farm site; excel, modern san facs; sep car park; helpful owner; immac san facs; fully serviced pitches; great value."* **€23.00, 1 Apr-31 Oct.** 2017

MIDDELBURG *A4* (7km NE Rural) *51.53863, 3.65394*
Minicamping Trouw Vóór Goud, Veerseweg 66, 4351 SJ Veere **(0118) 501373; info@trouwvoorgoud.nl; www.trouwvoorgoud.nl**

🐕 €0.80 ♟ 🚾 🏕 ✎ 🦋 ⚠

Take Veere rd N out of Middleburg. Site on L in 4km, bef lge g'ge, sp 'Minicamping'. 1.5km SW of Veere. Sm, pt shd, EHU (6A) €4.95; 10% statics; Eng spkn. *"Excel facs; friendly, tidy, spacious, CL-type site; walking dist Veere; no wifi."* **€16.00, 15 Mar-31 Oct.** 2018

MIDWOLDA *D2* (2km W Urban) *53.18900, 6.99053*
Camping de Bouwte, Hoofdweg 20A, 9681 AH Midwolda **05 97 59 17 06; info@campingdebouwte.nl; www.campingdebouwte.nl**

🐕 €1.75 ♟ 🚾 🏕 🔥 ♿ ✎ ♈ 🍴 (H) 📷 ⚠ ✏

Via A7 dir Groningen-Winschoten or via N33 Assen-Delfzil, then onto A7. Exit 45 Scheemda-Midwolda. Foll camping signs. Turn R at traff lts, site on R in 500m. Med, pt shd, EHU (10A); bbq; sw; twin axles; TV; 50% statics; phone; bus adj; Eng spkn; adv bkg acc; bike hire; games area; games rm; CCI. *"Vg walking/ cycling area with mkd rtes; horseriding 1km; WWll Museum in vill; watersports on Oldambtmeer 2km; vg site."* **€25.00, 29 Mar-21 Oct.** 2019

MIERLO *C4* (1.5km S Rural) *51.43250, 5.61694*
Camping De Sprink, Kasteelweg 21, 5731 PK Mierlo **(0492) 661503; info@campingdesprink.nl; www.campingdesprink.nl**

🐕 €0.75 ♟ 🚾 🏕 🔥 ♿ ✎ MSP 🦋 ♈ 🍴 🎿 📷 nr ⚠

Take A67 and exit at Geldrop/Mierlo. Foll sp for Mierlo. Turn R at rndabt onto Santheuvel West fr Geldropseweg. R onto Heer de Heuschweg, R onto Kasteelweg. Site on the L. Med, mkd, hdstg, unshd, EHU (6A); bbq; Eng spkn; adv bkg acc. *"Friendly, helpful staff; all facs immac; excel."* **€20.00, 31 Mar-30 Oct.** 2017

NOORDWIJK AAN ZEE *B3* (5km NE Urban) *52.26580, 4.47376* **De Wijde Blick,** Schulpweg 60, 2211 XM Noordwijkerhout **(0252) 372246; info@bungalow parkdewijdeblick.nl; www.bungalowparkdewijde blick.nl**

12 ♟ 🚾 🏕 ✎ MSP ♈ ⚠ 🏖 2km

Fr Hague exit L fr N206 at Noordwijkerhout Zuid. Shortly turn R at rndabt 1.3km, turn L at rndabt. Site on Rin 1km (1st bldg after felds). Med, mkd, unshd, EHU; 90% statics; train 10km; Eng spkn; CKE. *"Site with bungalows + statics; very clean facs; friendly, helpful staff; excel wifi; conv for Keukenhof; Flora Holland at Aalsmeer nrby; train to Amsterdam; excel."* **€25.00** 2017

OIRSCHOT *C3* (1km N Rural) *51.51684, 5.30854*
Camping De Bocht, Oude Grintweg 69, 5688 MB
Oirschot **(0499) 550855; info@campingdebocht.nl;
www.campingdebocht.nl**

🔟 🐕 €2.50 ♿(htd) 📶 ⚓ ⛱ ♿ 🖥 ⚡ 🦋 ♈ 🍽 🛈 🎣 🏧 nr 🚴 ⛴

Fr A58/E312 take exit 8 to Oirschot. Site in 4km on
Boxtel rd. Site sp. 3*, Med, hdg, shd, EHU (10A) €3;
gas; TV; 60% statics; phone; Eng spkn; adv bkg acc;
bike hire. *"Gd touring base; gd for families; pleasant
town; helpful family run site."* **€30.50** 2019

OMMEN *D2* (6km W Rural) *52.51911, 6.36461*
Resort de Arendshorst, Arendshorsterweg 3A,
7731 RC Ommen **(0529) 453248; info@resort-de-
arendshorst.nl; www.resort-de-arendshorst.nl**

🔟 🐕 €4 ♿(htd) 📶 ⚓ ⛱ ♿ 🖥 ⚡ 🦋 ♈ 🍽 🛈 🎣 🏧 🏊 ⛴

W fr Ommen on N34/N340 turn L at site sp, then
500m along lane past farm, site on rvside. 5*, Lge,
mkd, pt shd, serviced pitches; EHU (10A) inc; gas; sw;
red long stay; TV; 50% statics; phone; Eng spkn; adv
bkg req; bike hire; games area; CKE. *"Beautiful area;
bkg fee; many cycle rtes; pool 3km; gd children's facs."*
€39.00, H02. 2017

OMMEN *D2* (4km WNW Rural) *52.532519, 6.385082*
Boerderijcamping Het Varsenerveld, Emslandweg 14,
7731 RP Ommen **(0529) 453300; boerderijcamping@
varsenerveld.nl; www.varsenerveld.nl**

🔟 🐕 ♿(htd) 📶 ⚓ ⚡ 🦋 ♈ 🏊

W fr Ommen on N340 turn R after 2km at 1st minor
x-rds. Take 2nd L and site on L at flagpole. Sm, pt
shd, EHU (10A); bbq (charcoal, gas); twin axles; bus
2km; Eng spkn; adv bkg acc; ccard acc. *"Wkg fm;
goats and chickens contained within child petting area;
excel."* **€21.00** 2019

OOSTERHOUT *B3* (6km W Rural) *51.64658, 4.80818*
Koeckers Camping 't Kopske, Ruitersspoor 75, 4911
BA Den Hout **(0613) 142151; info@campingtkopske.
nl; www.campingtkopske.nl**

♿ 📶 ⚓ 🦋 🍽 🛈

Leave A59 at junc 32 to Oosterhout W. At rndabt
take R for Den Hout. In Den Hout R opp Church.
1st site on L after 1km. Sm, mkd, unshd, Eng
spkn. *"Gd cycling area; activity ctr; rest nr; gd."*
€19.00, 26 Mar-2 Oct. 2016

OOTMARSUM *D3* (2.5km S Rural) *52.38959, 6.90016*
Camping De Haer, Rossummerstraat 22, 7636 PL
Agelo **0541 291847; info@dehaer.nl; www.dehaer.nl**

🐕 €1.50 ♿ 📶 ⚓ ⛱ ♿ 🖥 ⚡ ♈ 🍽 🛈 🎣 🏧

Site sp 3km S of Ootmarsum. Lge, hdg, mkd, pt
shd, EHU (6-10A); bbq; twin axles; TV; 30% statics;
bus adj; Eng spkn; adv bkg acc; games rm; bike hire;
games area; CKE. *"Many cycle paths fr site; vg."*
€21.00, 1 Apr-1 Nov. 2016

OPENDE *D2* (3km SE Rural) *53.16465, 6.22275*
NCC Camping de Watermolen, Openderweg 26,
9865 XE Opende **(0594) 659144; info@campingde
watermolen.nl; www.campingdewatermolen.nl**

🐕 €2.50 ♿(htd) 📶 ⚓ 🖥 ⚡ 🅿 🦋 ♈ 🍽 🛈 🎣 🏧 nr 🏊 ⛴

Exit A7 junc 32 dir Kornhorn. In Noordwijk turn L at
church & in 2 km turn R into Openderweg. Site in
700m on L. Med, hdstg, mkd, pt shd, EHU (16A); bbq;
sw; twin axles; TV; 10% statics; phone; Eng spkn; adv
bkg acc; ccard acc; CKE. *"Friendly owners; pt of site
for NCC members - CMC members welcome but must
book ahead; brilliant site with lakes to walk around &
woods; hide for bird watching; dogs not acc high ssn;
excel; fishing on site; bike hire; €10 dep for key; car free
pitches."* **€25.30, 1 Apr-1 Oct.** 2017

OTTERLO *C3* (2km S Rural) *52.08657, 5.76934*
Europarcs Resort De Wije Werelt, Arnhemseweg
100-102, 6731 BV Otterlo **(0880) 708090; kcc@euro
parcs.nl; www.europarcs.nl/vakantiepark/resort-de-
wije-werelt**

🔟 🐕 €4 ♿(htd) 📶 ⚓ ⛱ 🖥 ⚡ 🅿 🦋 ♈ 🍽 🛈 🎣 🏧 🏊 ⛴

Exit A50 junc 22 dir Hoenderlo & N304 to Otterlo.
Site on R after Camping de Zanding. 4*, Lge, mkd,
unshd, EHU (6-10A) inc; 40% statics; phone; Eng spkn;
adv bkg acc; ccard acc; games area. *"Excel, well-run
site; immac, gd san facs; vg for families; conv Arnhem;
gd access to Kroller-Muller Museum; helpful staff."*
€35.00 2019

OTTERLO *C3* (2km NW Rural) *52.10878, 5.76040*
Camping 't Kikkergat, Lange Heideweg 7, 6731 EG
Otterlo **(0318) 591794; contact@kikkergat.nl;
www.kikkergat.nl**

🔟 🐕 ♿ 📶 ⚓ ⛱ ♿ 🖥 ⚡ 🅿 ♈ 🍽 🏧

Exit A1/E30 at J17 dir Harskamp. Site on R in 12km,
unmade rd. Sm, pt shd, EHU (10A); twin axles; Eng
spkn; adv bkg acc; CKE. *"Excel site."* **€18.00** 2017

PANNINGEN *C4* (4km NW Rural) *51.34894, 5.96111*
Beringerzand Camping, Heide 5, 5981 NX Panningen
**07 73 07 20 95; info@beringerzand.nl;
www.beringerzand.nl**

🔟 🐕 €4.85 ♿ 📶 ⚓ ⛱ 🖥 ⚡ 🅿 ♈ 🍽 🛈 🎣 🏧 🏊 (covrd, htd)
⛴

Fr A67 exit at junc 38 twd S, dir Koningslust/
Panningen. Site is 3km NW Panningen, down narr
lane thro asparagus fields. Med, mkd, pt shd, EHU
(10A); bbq; twin axles; Eng spkn; adv bkg rec; games
rm; games area; bike hire; waterslide. *"Max 2 dogs per
pitch."* **€36.80** 2019

RENSWOUDE C3 (2km NE Rural) 52.08435, 5.55069
Camping de Grebbelinie, Ubbeschoterweg 12, 3927
CJ Renswoude **(0318) 591073; info@campingde
grebbelinie.nl; www.campingdegrebbelinie.nl**

🌲🐕 €1.75 ♀♀ (htd) 🆆 ♨ 🍴 ⚷ ♿ ⚘ ⚘ ♈ nr ⓗ nr ⚘ nr ⛺

Head NW on Dorpsstraat/N224, at rndabt take 1st
exit onto Barneveldsestraat, turn R onto Bekerweg,
R onto Ubbeschoterweg then turn L. Site on the R.
Med, unshd, EHU; Eng spkn; adv bkg acc; games area;
CKE. *"Friendly owners; excel cycling with cycle rte adj;
conv for Arnhem & Utrecht; peaceful site on former
farm; in open countryside; excel value for money."*
€22.60, 19 Mar-15 Oct. **2016**

RIJSSEN D3 (7km S Rural) 52.265473, 6.520075
Camping De Bovenberg, Bovenbergweg 14, 7475
ST/Markelo **(0547) 361781; info@debovenberg.nl;
www.debovenberg.nl**

♀♀ (htd) 🆆 ♨ 🍴 ⚷ ⚘ 🌲 ♈ ⛺ 🚲 🐕 sand; adj

Fr A1 J26, foll sp for Markelo. Site name on brown
sp. Med, hdstg, mkd, hdg, pt shd, EHU (10A) inc;
5% statics; Eng spkn; CKE. *"Vg; ideal for restful stay;
gd NH; away fr rd noise; ideal cycling area; Markelo
nrby."* **NP 24.4, 30 Mar-16 Oct.** **2018**

ROCKANJE A3 (2km NW Coastal) 51.88000, 4.05422
Molecaten Park Waterbos, Duinrand 11, 3235 CC
Rockanje **(0181) 401900; info@waterboscamping.nl;
www.waterboscamping.nl**

♀♀ (htd) 🆆 ♨ 🍴 ⚷ ⚘ ♿ 🌲 ♈ ⚘ 🐕 ⛺ 🚲 🐕 sand 1km

Site clearly sp fr Rockanje vill. 4*, Lge, hdg, pt shd,
EHU (6A) inc; TV (pitch); 80% statics; phone; adv bkg
acc; CKE. *"Lovely base for Voorne area; private san facs
avail."* **€33.00, 25 Mar-31 Oct.** **2016**

ROERMOND C4 (15km W Rural) 51.20947, 5.83008
Camping Geelenhoof, Grathemerweg 16, 6037 NR
Kelpen-Oler (Limburg) **(0495) 651858;
info@geelenhoof.nl; www.geelenhoof.nl**

🐕 €2.50 ♀♀ (htd) 🆆 ♨ 🍴 ⚷ ⚘ 🌲 ♈ ♈ ⓗ ⚘ ⛺

1km S of Kelpen-Oler; bet Roermond & Weert; exit
N280 foll sp; well mkd. Med, mkd, hdg, pt shd, EHU
(6A) €3; Eng spkn; adv bkg acc; games area; games rm;
CKE. *"Cars not to be parked with c'van; dogs on req;
vg site; semi serviced pitches; sep NH; keycard barrier;
no twin axles; lake fishing; warm welcome; excel site."*
€25.00, 1 Mar-31 Oct. **2017**

ROOSENDAAL B3 (7km S Rural) 51.49430, 4.48536
Camping Zonneland, Turfvaartsestraat 6, 4709 PB
Nispen **(0165) 365429; info@zonneland.nl;
www.zonneland.nl**

♀♀ 🆆 ♨ 🍴 ⚷ ⚘ 🌲 ♈ ♈ 🐕 ⚘ ⛺ 🚲 🐕 (htd)

Take A58 exit 24 onto N262 dir Nispen. Foll site sps.
3*, Lge, hdstg, shd, EHU (4-10A) €2; 80% statics;
phone; Eng spkn; adv bkg acc; ccard acc.
€19.00, 16 Mar-28 Oct. **2020**

ROTTERDAM B3 (17km SE Rural) 51.83454, 4.54673
Camping De Oude Maas, Achterzeedijk 1A, 2991 SB
Barendrecht **(078) 6772445; www.campingdeoude
maas.nl**

12 🐕 ♀♀ (htd) 🆆 ♨ 🍴 ⚷ ♿ 🌲 ⚘ MSP ⚘ 🐕 🐕 ⛺

Leave A29 (Rotterdam-Bergen op Zoom) junc 20
Barendrecht, foll sp for Heerjansdam, site sp. Fr A16
(Breda-Dordrecht) foll Europort sp, then Zierikzee,
Barendrecht, site sp. 3*, Lge, pt shd, EHU (10A) inc;
TV; 80% statics; phone; ccard acc. *"Excel site on Rv
Maas inc sm marina & joins rec park; excel facs; some
pitches rough & long way fr facs; ferry fr site in ssn;
check recep opening time if planning dep bef midday
(espec Sun) for return of deposit & barrier key (€35);
entry via new ent past old."* **€22.00** **2016**

ROTTERDAM B3 (3km W Urban) 51.93100, 4.44200
Stadscamping Rotterdam, Kanaalweg 84, 3041 JE
Rotterdam **(010) 4153440; info@stadscamping-
rotterdam.nl; www.stadscamping-rotterdam.nl**

12 🐕 €2 ♀♀ 🆆 ♨ 🍴 ⚷ ♿ 🌲 ⚘ ♈ ♈ 🐕 🐕

Adj to junc of A13 & A20, take slip rd sp Rotterdam
Centrum & Camping Kanaalweg sp to site. Dist
fr m'way 2.5km with 3 L turns. 2*, Lge, pt shd, EHU
(6A) €3.75; gas; bus; adv bkg acc; ccard acc. *"Gd bus
service to city cent; few water taps; pool 500m; friendly
staff."* **€25.00** **2016**

SCHIMMERT C4 (0.6km E Rural) 50.90746, 5.83122
Camping Mareveld, Mareweg 23, 6333 BR Schimmert
South Limburg **(045) 4041269; info@mareveld.nl;
www.campingmareveld.nl**

12 🐕 €1.75 ♀♀ (htd) 🆆 ♨ 🍴 ⚷ ♈ ♈ ⓗ ⚘ (htd)

A76 exit Spaubeek, turn R twd Schimmert. 2nd on
the L in Schimmert. Campsite sp. Sm, pt shd, EHU
(6A) €2.10, TV; 80% statics; Eng spkn; adv bkg acc;
games area. *"Gd cycling/walking fr site; gd site; popular
with families; open plan, grassy site."* **€24.00** **2019**

SEVENUM C4 (5km SW Rural) 51.38310, 5.97590
Camping De Schatberg, Midden Peelweg 1, 5975 MZ
Sevenum **(077) 4677777; receptie@schatberg.nl;
www.schatberg.nl**

12 🐕 ♀♀ (htd) 🆆 ♨ 🍴 ⚷ ♿ 🌲 ⚘ MSP ⚘ ♈ ⓗ 🐕 🐕 ⚘ ⛺
🏊 (covrd, htd) 🎣

Fr A2/A67 exit junc 38 for Helden; foll sp Sevenum
& site by sm lake. 5*, V lge, shd, EHU (6-10A) inc;
gas; sw; TV; 60% statics; phone; Eng spkn; adv bkg
acc; fishing; bike hire; waterslide; games area; tennis;
jacuzzi; sauna; watersports; CKE. *"Excel leisure facs,
espec for children; sep pitches for dogs; private san
facs some pitches; vg site but impersonal; Holland Tulip
Parcs site; tourers pitched amongst statics; Venlo Sat
mkt worth visit."* **€41.00** **2019**

'S-HEERENBERG D3 (3km W Rural) 51.87795, 6.21125 **Camping Brockhausen,** Eltenseweg 20, 7039 CV Stokkum **(0314) 661212; campingbrockhausen@ gmail.com; www.brockhausen.nl**

🐕 €3.45 ♿ (htd) ⓌⒹ ♨ ♿ 🚿 ╱ 🦋 🛒 nr 🎢

Fr A12 exit junc sp 's-Heerenberg, cont past 's-Heerenberg sp & pick up sp to Stokkum & site on L. 2*, Med, mkd, pt shd, EHU (4-6A) inc; TV (pitch); 40% statics; Eng spkn; adv bkg acc. "V clean, eco-friendly site; facs charged on electronic key; friendly, helpful staff; lovely area walking, cycling; excel." €24.00, 1 Apr-31 Oct. 2020

'S-HERTOGENBOSCH C3 (10km E Rural) 51.6938, 5.4148 **Camping de Hooghe Heide,** Werstkant 17, 5258 TC Berlicum **(073) 5031522; info@ hoogheheide.nl; www.hoogheheide.nl**

🐕 €4.25 ♿ ⓌⒹ ♨ ♿ 🚿 ╱ 🦋 🎮 🛒 🎢 🚣

Fr A59/A2 circular rd around 's-Hertogenbosch exit junc 21 dir Berlicum. Foll sp Berlicum & site. Site is NE of Berlicum. 4*, Med, mkd, pt shd, EHU (10A) €3; TV; 70% statics; phone; Eng spkn; adv bkg req; games area; CKE. "Nice, peaceful wooded site; narr site rds for lge o'fits; tourers on open field; excel." €32.40, 26 Mar-1 Nov. 2016

'S-HERTOGENBOSCH C3 (10km SW Rural) 51.65507, 5.23520 **Topparken Résidence de Leuvert,** Loverensestraat 11, 5266 Cromvoirt **088 5002473; info@deleuvert.nl; www.deleuvert.nl**

🐕 ♿ ⓌⒹ ♨ ♿ 🚿 ╱ 🦋 🎮 🍴 🛒 🎢 🖊 🎣 (htd) 🚣

Exit for Cromvoirt fr A59 or A65. Med, mkd, pt shd, EHU (10A) inc; bbq; twin axles; TV; 75% statics; bus 0.5km; Eng spkn; adv bkg acc; games area; games rm; CKE. "Gd bus access to 's-Hertogenbosch; vg site." €28.40, 1 Jan-31 Oct. 2016

SINT OEDENRODE C3 (3km N Rural) 51.57800, 5.4400 **NCC Camping 't Roois Klumpke,** Vliegden 1, 5491 VS Sint Oedenrode **(0413) 474702; www.ncc.nl**

12 ♿ (htd) ⓌⒹ ♨ ♿ 🚿 ╱ 🦋

Exit A2 junc 26 to Sint Oedenrode; site sp on Schijndel rd - 100m bef Camping Kienehoef turn R onto Vliegden, site 400m on L. Med, mkd, pt shd, EHU (10A); bbq; Eng spkn; adv bkg acc; CKE. "Members only - CC members welcome but must pre-book; shop, rest, snacks avail at Camping de Kienehoef; run by volunteers; spacious; woodland." **€11.00** 2017

SINT OEDENRODE C3 (3.7km SE Urban) 51.54780, 5.48703 **Camping De Graspol,** Bakkerpad 17, 5492 TL Sint Oedenrode **(0413) 474133 or (0653) 224220; info@campingdegraspol.nl; www.campingde graspol.nl**

🐕 ♿ (htd) ⓌⒹ ♨ ♿ 🚿 ╱ ⓂⓅ 🦋 🍴

Fr A50 take exit St Oedenrode, dir Nijnsel. Foll sp to site. Med, mkd, pt shd, EHU (16A); gas; bbq; red long stay; TV; Eng spkn; adv bkg rec; bike hire; fishing; games rm. "Well kept; gd for NH or longer; ACSI; warm welcome; wild flower nature walk." €35.50, 1 Mar-1 Oct. 2019

SNEEK C2 (2km E Urban) 53.03557, 5.67630 **Jachthaven Camping De Domp,** De Domp 4, 8605 CP Sneek **(0515) 412559; www.dedomp.nl**

🐕 ♿ (htd) ⓌⒹ ♨ ♿ 🚿 ╱ ⓂⓅ 🍴 🍴 🔟 🛒 nr 🎢

Fr cent of Sneek on Leeuwarden rd, turn R sp De Domp. 3*, Med, pt shd, serviced pitches; EHU (16A) inc; gas; Eng spkn; adv bkg acc; boating; sep car park. "Many canals in Sneek; marina on site; easy walk to pleasant town; gd cycling cent; v helpful staff." €24.50, 25 Mar-1 Nov. 2018

STEENBERGEN B3 (5km NW Rural) 51.60887, 4.27303 **Camping De Uitwijk,** Dorpsweg 136, 4655 AH De Heen **(0167) 560000; info@de-uitwijk.nl; www.campingdeuitwijk.nl**

🐕 €3.20 ♿ (htd) ⓌⒹ ♨ ♿ 🚿 ╱ ⓂⓅ 🍴 🍴 🔟 🛒 nr 🎢 🖊

Fr N259 at Steenbergen turn W onto N257 dir Zierikzee. In 2km turn N thro De Heen & turn R at T-junc. Site recep on R, site on L. Do not take c'van to recep, but ent site, park on R & walk back. Med, mkd, pt shd, EHU (4-10A) inc; TV (pitch); 60% statics; bus 750m; Eng spkn; adv bkg acc; games rm; CKE. "Pleasant, well run, quiet site adj marina; friendly staff; excel; excel cycle rtes; conv for ferry." €24.00, 23 Mar-29 Sep. 2019

TUITJENHORN B2 (4km SE Rural) 52.73495, 4.77612 **Campingpark de Bongerd,** Bongerdlaan 3, 1747 CA Tuitjenhorn **(0226) 391481; info@bongerd.nl; www.bongerd.nl**

🐕 €1.90 ♿ (htd) ⓌⒹ ♨ ♿ 🚿 ╱ 🦋 🍴 🍴 🔟 🛒 🎢 🖊 🎣 (covrd, htd) 🚣

N fr Alkmaar on N245, exit at Dirkshorn & foll sp to site. 5*, V lge, mkd, pt shd, EHU (10A) inc; gas; bbq; 60% statics; Eng spkn; adv bkg acc; ccard acc; games area; lake fishing; bike hire; waterslide; tennis. "Excel, attractive family site; vg facs." €56.50, 5 Apr-1 Oct. 2019

UDEN C3 (14km E Rural) 51.66309, 5.77641 **Mini Camping Boszicht,** Tipweg 10, 5455 RC Wilbertoord **(0485) 451565 or (06) 12957217; boszicht-wilbertoord@planet.nl; www.boszichtcamping.nl**

🐕 €2 ♿ ♨ 🚿 ╱ 🦋 🍴 🔟 nr 🎢

Fr 's-Hertogenbosch on N279 dir Helmond. At Veghel turn L onto N265. Bef Uden turn R onto N264 to Wilbertoord in 11km. Sm, hdg, mkd, unshd, EHU (6A) metered; Eng spkn; games area. "Family-run farm site in woodland; conv Arnhem, Nijmegen; delightful site." **€17.00**, 20 Mar-19 Oct. 2016

UTRECHT *B3* (10km NE Rural) *52.13123, 5.22024*
Camping Bospark Bilthoven, Burg van der Borchlaan 7, 3722 GZ Bilthoven **(030) 2286777; info@ bosparkbilthoven.nl; www.bosparkbilthoven.nl**

🐕 €3.50 ♟♟ (htd) ⬜ ♨ ⚲ ⬛ 🚿 ✚ 🍽 🛒 nr 🏠 🏊 (htd)

Exit A28/E30 Utrecht-Amersfoort at exit sp De Bilt & strt to Bilthoven. Approx 3km after leaving m'way (400m S of level x-ing) turn R sp De Bospark Bilthoven. At edge of town foll sps twd lge brown tower & golf course. Site on L. 2*, V lge, pt shd, serviced pitches; EHU (4-6A) inc (poss rev pol); gas; TV; 60% statics; phone; Eng spkn; adv bkg acc. *"Helpful management; quiet but some noise fr air base; 20 mins walk to stn for trains to Utrecht cent; few facs for size of site."* **€29.40, 29 Mar-20 Oct.** **2018**

VAALS *C4* (1.5km N Rural) *50.78159, 6.00694*
Camping Hoeve de Gastmolen, Lemierserberg 23, 6291 NM Vaals **(043) 3065755; info@gastmolen.nl; www.gastmolen.nl**

🐕 €2.70 ♟♟ ⬜ ♨ 🚿 ✚ 🦋 ⏱ nr 🛒 nr 🏠

Fr A76 exit at Knooppunt Bocholtz onto N281 SW to join N278, turn L twd Aachen. Site on L just bef 1st rndabt as ent Vaals. 2*, Med, mkd, hdg, pt shd, pt sl, EHU (6A) €2.70; 10% statics; bus 500m; Eng spkn; adv bkg rec; sep car park; CKE. *"Sm rural site; conv Aachen; vg san facs; diff in wet - tractor avail; mosquitoes; Drielandenpunt 4km, in walking dist (where Netherlands, Germany & Belgium meet); excel."* **€20.50, 25 Mar-31 Oct.** **2016**

VALKENBURG AAN DE GEUL *C4* (13km N Rural) *50.94973, 5.87883* **De Botkoel,** Kerkpad 2, 6155 KJ Puth **(0464) 432374; camping@botkoel.nl; www.botkoel.nl**

🐕 ♟♟ (htd) ⬜ ♨ ⚲ ♿ ⬛ 🚿 ✚ 🛒 🚲 nr ⏱ nr 🛒 ⌂ 🏠 🏊

Fr W on A2 exit at J4 sp Schinnen. At end of rd turn L, cross x-rds and turn R again on the R until you cross rlwy x-ing, then R on the R. Cont on Stn Street until T-junc, turn L twrds Puth. Uphill to Puth then turn R. At S-turn, turn R into narr rd. Site 200m on L. Sm, unshd, pt sl, terr, EHU; bbq; twin axles; train 1km; Eng spkn; adv bkg acc; games area; CKE. *"Site on fruit fm; views; bike hire; clean facs, rebuilt 2017; excel; conv for Sittard, Maastricht & Aachen; vg; Zoover award site."* **€22.50, 15 Mar-31 Oct.** **2018**

VALKENBURG AAN DE GEUL *C4* (2km N Rural) *50.88013, 5.83466* **Familie Camping De Bron,** Stoepertweg 5, 6301 WP Valkenburg **(045) 4059292; info@camping-debron.nl; www.camping-debron.nl**

🐕 €3.50 ♟♟ (htd) ⬜ ♨ ⚲ ♿ ⬛ 🚿 ✚ 🛒 🍽 ⌂ 🛒 🏠 🚲 🏊

Fr A79 exit junc 4 dir Hulsberg. Take 3rd exit fr rndabt onto N298, across next rndabt, then L onto N584, site sp. Fr A76 exit junc 3 dir Schimmert, foll sp Valkenburg & site. 4*, Lge, mkd, pt shd, EHU (4-6A) €3-4.50; TV; 30% statics; phone; adv bkg acc; bike hire; games area; CKE. *"Vg, well laid-out site; gd facs; muddy in wet weather; 2 pools with lots of equipment for kids; statics hidden away in the greenery; helpful staff."* **€30.00, 1 Apr-20 Dec.** **2019**

VALKENBURG AAN DE GEUL *C4* (3km S Urban) *50.85972, 5.83138* **Stadscamping Den Driesch,** Heunsbergerweg 1, 6301 BN Valkenburg **(043) 6012025; info@campingdendriesch.nl; www.campingdendriesch.nl**

🐕 €3 ♟♟ (htd) ⬜ ♨ ⚲ 🚿 ✚ 🛒 🦋 ⌂ nr 🛒 🛒

Fr A2 dir Maastricht exit sp Valkenburg-Cauberg. Foll sp Valkenburg N590 & take turning sp Sibbe-Margraten. At rndabt foll sp Valkenburg, pass coal mine & turn R in 250m into sm, sl, unmkd ent. Steep turn off main rd into ent. NB L turn into site diff - proceed to rndabt at top of hill & return downhill to site. 2*, Med, hdstg, mkd, pt shd, pt sl, terr, EHU (10A) inc; 10% statics; phone; Eng spkn; adv bkg acc; ccard acc; bike hire; CKE. *"Castle & caves adj; other attractions nr; gd Xmas mkts in caves; easy access Maastricht by bus/train; vg."* **€42.00, 23 Mar-31 Dec, H10.** **2017**

VALKENBURG AAN DE GEUL *C4* (1km SW Rural) *50.85672, 5.81891* **Camping De Cauberg,** Rijksweg 171, 6325 AD Valkenburg **(043) 6012344; info@ campingdecauberg.nl; www.campingdecauberg.nl**

🐕 €3.10 ♟♟ (htd) ⬜ ♨ ⚲ ⬛ 🚿 ✚ 🦋 🍽 ⌂ 🛒 🏠

Exit A79 sp Valkenburg, foll Sibbe & Margraten sp to town cent. Take R fork in town sp De Cauberg, site on R at top of hill just past end Valkenburg sp. Med, mkd, shd, pt sl, EHU (10A) inc; red long stay; 10% statics; phone; bus; Eng spkn; adv bkg acc; site clsd 1-15 Nov; CKE. *"Excel pool 1km; excel, modern, clean san facs; htd pool 1km; friendly, helpful owner; conv Maastricht; many rests, cafes in Valkenburg."* **€33.00, 22 Mar-27 Oct & 16 Nov-23 Dec.** **2019**

VENLO *D4* (10km NW Rural) *51.42029, 6.10675* **Camping Californië,** Horsterweg 3, 5971 ND Grubbenvorst **(077) 3662049; info@limburgse camping.nl; www.limburgsecamping.nl**

♟♟ (htd) ⬜ ♨ ⚲ 🚿 ✚ 🛒 🦋 🏠

Exit A73 at Grubbenvorst junc 12 dir Sevenum, site sp. Med, pt shd, EHU (4-10A); Eng spkn. *"Pleasant, peaceful, warm welcome; unisex shwrs; CL style site with grass cut reg."* **€18.00, 15 Mar-15 Oct.** **2019**

VIERHUIZEN *D1* (0.3km E Rural) *53.36011, 6.29505* **Camping Lauwerszee,** Hoofdstraat 49, 9975 VR Vierhuizen **05 95 40 16 57; info@camping-lauwerszee.nl; www.camping-lauwerszee.nl**

🐕 ♟♟ ⬜ ♨ ♿ ⬛ 🚿 ✚ 🛒 🍽 ⏱ 🍽 ⌂ 🏠

Fr A7/E22 Amsterdam-Groningen take exit 33 Oude Riet onto N388 Grijpskerk. Turn L on N355 then R onto N388. 2.5km after Zoutcamp turn L to Vierhuizen. Site on R in 1km. Med, mkd, hdg, pt shd, EHU (6A); bbq; twin axles; bus 0.5km; Eng spkn; adv bkg acc; bike hire; CCI. *"Sep field with lge pitches avail for CC memb at red price; helpful owner; vg."* **€21.00, 1 Apr-1 Nov.** **2019**

NETHERLANDS

VORDEN

VORDEN D3 (5km SE Rural) 52.08379, 6.35510
't Lebbink, Lindense Enkweg 1, 7251NH Vorden (0575)
556680; harmsen@tlebbink.nl; www.tlebbink.nl

🅃 🕴 🛉 WD ⚊ 🏊 ♿ 🚽 ⁄ 🦋 ⛲

Fr Vordon N316 S for 1.6km. L onto Lindeseweg
for 3km to Linde. L just bef windmill along access
rd to campsite on R. Med, hdg, mkd, pt shd, EHU
(6-16A); bbq; twin axles; adv bkg acc; bike hire;
CKE. "On numbered cycle rte & walking rte; vg."
€16.00, 15 Mar-1 Nov. 2015

WASSENAAR

WASSENAAR B3 (1km NW Rural) 52.14638, 4.38750
Camping Duinrell, Duinrell 1, 2242 JP Wassenaar
(070) 5155147 or (070) 5155255; touroperator@
duinrell.nl; www.duinrell.nl

12 🐕 €6 🕴🛉 (htd) WD ⚊ 🏊 ♿ 🚽 ⁄ MSP 🦋 ⛲ 🍴 🍹 🍷 🔌 🛒 🛥 🅿
🎣 🚣 (covrd) 🧺 ⛳ sand 3km

Fr Rotterdam in dir Den Haag on A13/E19, then on
A4/E19 foll sp for Amsterdam. On A4 keep R onto
A12 in dir Voorburg/Den Haag. At end m'way turn
R onto N44 sp Wassenaar. In 8km turn L at traff
lts immed bef Mercedes g'ge, foll site sp. On arr at
site foll sp to campsite not coach park. Not rec to
arrive mid-afternoon/early evening due to heavy
traff leaving amusement park. 4*, V lge, mkd, hdg,
pt shd, serviced pitches; EHU (6A) inc; gas; bbq; TV;
30% statics; phone; Eng spkn; adv bkg acc; ccard acc;
waterslide; tennis; sauna; golf 1km; fishing nr; bike
hire; games rm; horseriding nr. "Popular, busy site;
no o'fits over 7.75m high ssn; some pitches poss diff
access, check bef siting; superb, modern facs; tropical
indoor pool; free ent adj amusement park; private san
facs avail; sep car park for some pitches; vg security;
excel." €33.50, H13. 2016

WEZUPERBRUG

WEZUPERBRUG D2 (9km SW Rural) 52.77911,
6.68607 Camping De Bronzen Emmer, Mepperstraat
41, 7855 TA Meppen (0591) 371543; info@de-
bronzen-emmer.nl; www.bronzenemmer.nl

🅃 🕴🛉 (htd) WD ⚊ 🏊 ♿ 🚽 ⁄ 🦋 ⛲ 🍴 🔌 🛒 🛥 nr 🅿
🚣 (covrd, htd)

Exit the A37 at Oosterhesselen (N854) twrds
Meppen. Foll sp to site. Lge, mkd, pt shd, EHU (10A)
€0.40/Kwh; gas; TV; 10% statics; Eng spkn; adv bkg
acc; tennis; games area; games rm. "Cycling off-rd to
supmkt; friendly, family site; excel facs; sauna; excel."
€34.00, 1 Apr-28 Oct. 2017

WINTERSWIJK

WINTERSWIJK D3 (5km N Rural) 52.00878, 6.73850
Poelhuis Boerderijcamping, Poolserweg 3, 7104 DC
Winterswijk (0543) 569246; info@poelhuis.nl;
www.poelhuis.nl

🕴🛉 WD ⚊ ♿ 🚽 ⁄ 🦋 ⛲

N on Meddosweg to Meddo, R on Wandersweg to
x-rds, Poolseweg, L and site on R in 500m. Sm, mkd,
hdstg, pt shd, EHU (6A); bbq; TV; Eng spkn; adv bkg
acc; bike hire; games rm; CKE. "Numbered cycle rte;
close to German border; flamingo nature park with
walking rtes; vg." €18.00, 15 Mar-31 Oct. 2015

WOERDEN

WOERDEN B3 (4km NE Rural) 52.09280, 4.88530
Camping Batenstein, Van Helvoortlaan 37, 3443
AP Woerden (0348) 421320; campingbatenstein@
planet.nl; www.camping-batenstein.nl

🅃 €1.50 🕴🛉 WD ⚊ 🏊 ♿ 🚽 ⁄ MSP 🦋 ⛲ 🔌 🛒 nr 🛥 🚣 (covrd, htd)
🧺

Fr A12 exit junc 14 sp Woerden. Twd cent of town,
L at rndabt, R at next rndabt, thro rlwy tunnel. L
at traff lts, L again at next traff lts, R at camping
sp. Ent narr & sm sp. 1*, Med, pt shd, EHU (6-10A)
inc; gas; red long stay; 75% statics; phone; bus
750m; Eng spkn; adv bkg acc; ccard acc; sep car park;
waterslide; sauna; games area; CKE. "Gd touring
base; Al conn by site staff only (locked boxes); san
facs cramped but gd quality & clean; conv for ferries."
€20.80, 29 Mar-27 Oct. 2019

> ## "That's changed – Should I let the Club know?"
>
> If you find something on site that's different
> from the site entry, fill in a report and let us
> know. See camc.com/europereport.

AMELAND ISLAND

BUREN

BUREN C1 (1km N Coastal) 53.45355, 5.80460
Camping Klein Vaarwater, Klein Vaarwaterweg 114,
9164 ME Buren (0519) 542156; info@kleinvaarwater.
nl; www.kleinvaarwater.nl

12 🕴🛉 (htd) WD ⚊ ♿ 🚽 ⁄ MSP 🍷 🔌 🛒 🛥 🅿 🎣
🚣 (covrd, htd) 🧺 ⛳ sand 800m

Take ferry fr Holwerd to Nes on Ameland Island.
Turn R at rndabt twd Buren & strt on to supmkt.
At 3-lane intersection turn L twd beach rd & site.
4*, Med, mkd, pt shd, EHU (16A); gas; bbq; TV;
75% statics; adv bkg acc; tennis; fitness rm; games
area; waterslide. "Nature park adj; site in dunes &
forest; ATM; Holland Tulip Parcs site; 10-pin bowling."
€20.00 2016

ZANDVOORT

ZANDVOORT B3 (5km N Coastal) 52.40415, 4.55180
Kennemer Duincamping De Lakens, Zeeweg 60,
2051 EC Bloemendaal aan Zee (023) 5411570;
delakens@kennemerduincampings.nl;
www.kennemerduincampings.nl

🕴🛉 (htd) WD ⚊ ♿ 🚽 ⁄ MSP 🦋 ⛲ 🔌 🛒 🛥 🅿 ⛱ sand 200m

Site sp N of Zaandvoort on coast rd, site in sand
dunes. 4*, V lge, unshd, EHU (4-10A) inc; gas; TV;
50% statics; Eng spkn; adv bkg rec; ccard acc;
horseriding 300m; games area; windsurfing 2km. "V
busy May/June public holidays; gd facs; excel walking,
cycling fr site; welcoming helpful staff; excel spar shop;
gd position in National Park; pool 4km; gd for
sightseeing in Amsterdam, Haarlem, Aalsmeer flower
mkt as well as outdoor pursuits."
€54.00, 29 Mar-28 Oct. 2019

ZEVENAAR *C3* (8km S Rural) *51.89666, 6.07041*
Camping De Rijnstrangen, Beuningsestraat 4,
6913 KH Aerdt **(0316) 371941 or (0612) 559464;**
info@derijnstrangen.nl; www.derijnstrangen.nl

12 ♂♀(htd) wc ♨ ⚓ ♿ ▣ ♪ MP ❀ ♔ ⚏ nr

Exit A12 junc 29 onto N 336 Elten & Lobith. At sp
Aerdt turn R onto dyke (narr) & cont approx 1.5km
to church. Turn L in 100m, site on R (500m W of
Aerdt). Sm, hdg, mkd, hdstg, pt shd, EHU (6A); bbq;
cooking facs; twin axles; Eng spkn; adv bkg acc; games
rm; bike hire; CKE. *"Friendly, welcoming, helpful
owners; gd cycling area with numbered rte; excel htd
facs; excel; sep carpark."* **€20.50** 2018

ZIERIKZEE *A3* (5km N Rural) *51.68048, 3.89847*
Mini-Camping Appelgaerd, Zandweg 6, 4321 TA
Kerkwerve **(0614) 449924; info@appelgaerd.nl;**
www.appelgaerd.nl

♂ ♂♀ wc ♿ ♨ ♪ MP ❀ ♔ ⚏ ⌂ ⚏4km

Fr Zierikzee take N59 dir Serooskerke. Immed
turn R onto Zandwek. Cont for 3km, site on L bef
vill of Kerkwerve. Sm, hdg, pt shd, EHU (6A) inc;
bbq; twin axles; bus 250m; Eng spkn; adv bkg acc.
"Gd cycling, walking & bird watching area; excel site."
€20.50, 1 Apr-30 Oct. 2019

TERSCHELLING ISLAND

OOSTEREND *C1* (0.2km N Rural) *53.40562, 5.37947*
Camping 't Wantij, Oosterend 41, 8897 HX Oosterend
**(0562) 448522 or (06) 20396345 (mob); info@
wantij-terschelling.nl; www.wantij-terschelling.nl**

12 ♂ €1.75 ♂♀(htd) wc ♨ ♿ ♪ ❀ ♔
♔ nr ⊕ nr ⚏ nr ⌂ ⚏ sand 2km

Fr Harlingen to Terschelling by ferry. Take rd to
Oosterend, site ent on L 250m after vill sp, past
bus stop & phone box. Sm, mkd, pt shd, EHU (6A)
€3 (poss rev pol); cooking facs; TV; bus adj; Eng spkn;
adv bkg acc; CKE. *"Gd area for birdwatching; many
cycle/foot paths across dunes; horsedrawn vehicles for
conducted tours; Elvis memorabilia 2km at Heartbreak
Hotel - rest on stilts; excel site."* **€18.00** 2016

TEXEL ISLAND

DE KOOG *B2* (0.5km E Rural) *53.09610, 4.76500*
**Camping Coogherveld Texel (formerly De Luwe
Boshoek),** Kamperfoelieweg 3, 1796 MT De Koog
02 22 31 77 28; www.coogherveld-texel.nl

♂ ♂♀(htd) wc ♨ ⚓ ♿ ♪ ❀ ⚏ nr ⚏ sandy 1km

Fr ferry take 501 to De Koog. Sp after ref point 17. R
at De Zwaluw Hotel. Site on L after 100m. Med, mkd,
unshd, EHU (16A); bbq; 10% statics. *"Excel; gd base to
stay; bike hire 0.5 km."* **€32.50, 12 Apr-25 Oct.** 2019

DEN BURG *B2* (16km N Rural) *53.16987, 4.86072*
Camping de Hoek, Vuurtorenweg 83, 1795 LK De
Cocksdorp **(0222) 316236; saaldehoek@tele2.nl;**
www.campingdehoek.nl

♂ ♂♀(htd) wc ♨ ▣ ♪ MP ❀ ♔ ⊕ nr ⚏ nr ⚏ sandy 1km

Take the main rd fr ferry to top of island, past exit
35, site on L nr end of rd. Sm, pt shd, EHU (16A);
bbq; Eng spkn; adv bkg acc. *"Farm site; beatifully
kept; lovely fam; by rd but v quiet; cycle path; excel."*
€25.00, 1 Apr-1 Oct. 2017

ZUIDWOLDE *D2* (2km S Rural) *52.65822, 6.42726*
NCC Camping De Krententerp, Ekelenbergweg 2,
7921 RH Zuidwolde DR **(0528) 372847; zuidwolde@
ncc.nl; www.ncc.nl**

♂ ♂♀(htd) wc ♨ ▣ ♪ ❀ ♔ nr ⊕ nr ⚏ nr ⌂

Fr S fr Zwolle exit A28 junc 22 dir Dedemsvaart.
Turn L at Balkbrug onto N48, then L at junc
Alteveer-Linde to site. Sm, mkd, shd, EHU (4A) €2.75
(long lead poss req); bus 200m; adv bkg acc. *"Peaceful
site; friendly, helpful staff; CC members welcome;
phone ahead bet 1700 & 1800; htd covrd pool 2km;
excel cycling, walking; Zuidwolde beautiful town."*
€12.50, 1 Apr-31 Oct. 2016

> ## "I like to fill in the reports as I travel from site to site"
>
> You'll find report forms at the back of this guide, or you can fill them in online at camc.com/europereport.

ZWOLLE *C2* (5km NE Urban) *52.53690, 6.12954*
Camping De Agnietenberg, Haersterveerweg 27,
8034 PJ Zwolle **(038) 4531530; info@camping
agnietenberg.nl; www.campingagnietenberg.nl**

♂ €3.50 ♂♀(htd) wc ♨ ⚓ ♪ MP ❀ ♔ ♔ ⊕ ⚏ ⌂ ♪ ⚲

N fr Zwolle on A28 exit junc 20 Zwolle Oost & turn
R at end of slip rd then immed L. In 400m turn L at
traff lts into Haersterveerweg & foll site sp. Lge,
mkd, pt shd, EHU (10A); bbq; sw nr; TV; 60% statics;
Eng spkn; ccard acc; fishing; tennis. *"Excel, family site
in pleasant area; gd walking, cycling, water recreation;
cars parked in sep areas; single track rd to site."*
€30.00, 29 Mar-31 Oct. 2019

ZWOLLE *C2* (6.5km E Urban) *52.524253, 6.167658*
Vecht & Zo, Hessenweg 14, 8028 PA Zwolle **(06)
24332462; info@vechtenzo.nl; www.vechtenzo.nl**

♂ ♂♀(htd) wc ♨ ♿ ♪ MP ❀ ♔ ⚏ ⊕ ⌂

Fr J21 on A28 N of Zwolle take N340 in 2km R
at sp onto cycleway (row of shops). Sm, mkd, pt
shd, EHU (6A) inc (rev pol); bbq; sw; Eng spkn; adv
bkg acc; games area; canoes. *"Gd for Gelderland,
Kampen, Zwolle; traff noise in day; spotless facs; vg."*
€20.00, 1 Apr-31 Oct. 2018

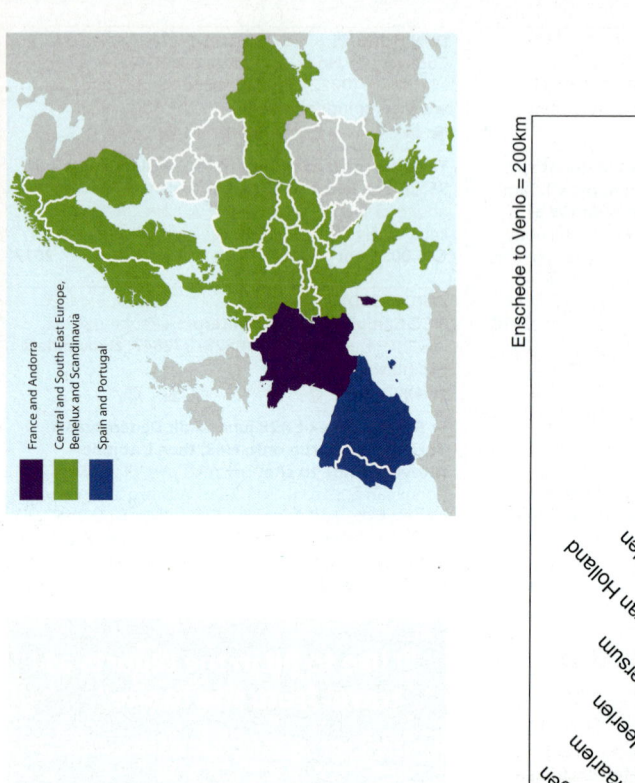

Legend:
- France and Andorra
- Central and South East Europe, Benelux and Scandinavia
- Spain and Portugal

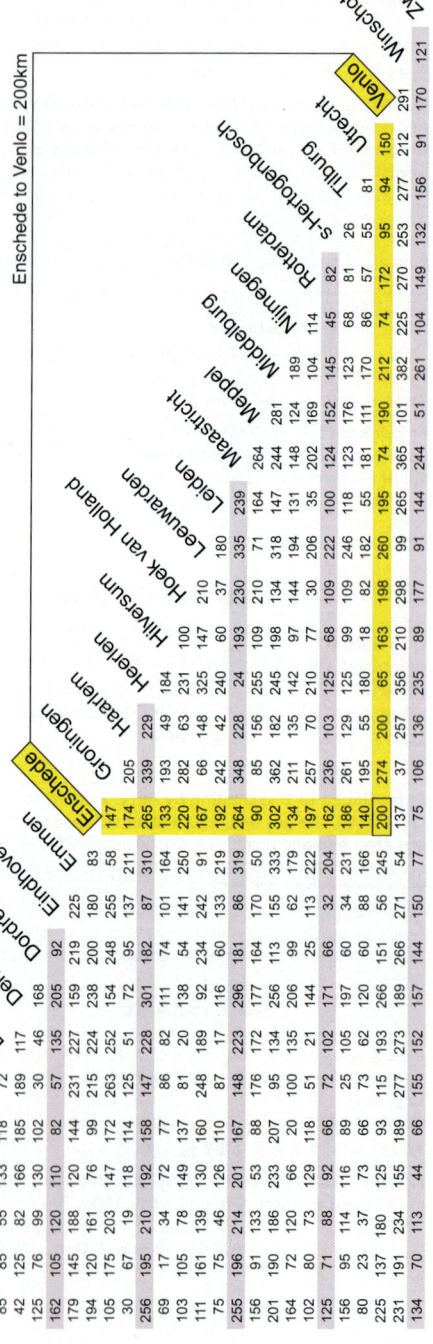

Enschede to Venlo = 200km

Road distance chart (km). City labels along the diagonal (listed from top-right to bottom-left): Zwolle, Winschoten, Venlo, Utrecht, Tilburg, s-Hertogenbosch, Rotterdam, Nijmegen, Middelburg, Meppel, Maastricht, Leiden, Leeuwarden, Hoek van Holland, Hilversum, Heerlen, Haarlem, Groningen, Enschede, Emmen, Eindhoven, Dordrecht, Den Helder, Den Haag (The Hague), Breda, Arnhem, Apeldoorn, Amsterdam, Amersfoort, Alkmaar.

Distances by origin city (read down the chart):

- **Alkmaar:** 83, 40, 120, 141, 145, 85, 42, 125, 162, 179, 194, 105, 30, 256, 69, 103, 111, 75, 255, 196, 156, 201, 164, 102, 125, 156, 80, 225, 231, 134
- **Amersfoort:** 47, 99, 87, 51, 89, 55, 82, 76, 105, 145, 120, 161, 175, 67, 195, 17, 78, 139, 46, 214, 190, 133, 186, 120, 73, 95, 137, 23, 191, 70
- **Amsterdam:** 25, 141, 111, 133, 118, 185, 72, 189, 120, 161, 203, 76, 67, 147, 172, 130, 160, 126, 110, 192, 186, 233, 207, 66, 20, 114, 93, 155, 189, 113
- **Apeldoorn:** 110, 82, 144, 99, 215, 263, 147, 203, 146, 76, 99, 130, 114, 118, 72, 149, 160, 248, 110, 57, 86, 88, 95, 134, 95, 20, 66, 125, 234, 66
- **Arnhem:** 57, 120, 144, 227, 224, 252, 154, 248, 189, 17, 60, 116, 87, 146, 82, 20, 81, 100, 135, 228, 176, 172, 134, 256, 95, 21, 73, 189, 277, 155
- **Breda:** 72, 189, 117, 72, 135, 205, 30, 46, 168, 57, 182, 228, 147, 223, 201, 158, 148, 110, 248, 147, 77, 86, 95, 51, 144, 152, 102, 273, 266, 152
- **Den Haag (The Hague):** 46, 30, 255, 200, 248, 154, 238, 224, 205, 159, 182, 301, 111, 177, 82, 74, 20, 54, 92, 234, 164, 172, 134, 266, 151, 189, 193, 273, 157, 144
- **Den Helder:** 92, 182, 181, 164, 101, 74, 138, 54, 248, 95, 66, 164, 60, 116, 182, 177, 82, 25, 66, 171, 113, 164, 256, 113, 99, 25, 144, 102, 266, 150
- **Dordrecht:** 87, 310, 255, 180, 225, 219, 159, 92, 58, 141, 250, 179, 62, 242, 91, 133, 219, 58, 83, 231, 88, 120, 197, 266, 271, 150, 144, 177, 91, 54
- **Eindhoven:** 86, 319, 296, 211, 87, 137, 95, 60, 170, 50, 333, 222, 32, 204, 231, 245, 166, 88, 56, 271, 77, 54, 106, 137, 75
- **Emmen:** 264, 192, 167, 220, 133, 265, 174, 147, 186, 90, 302, 134, 197, 162, 140, 200, 274, 37, 106, 75
- **Enschede:** 147, 174, 265, 133, 220, 167, 192, 264, 90, 302, 134, 197, 162, 186, 140, 200, 274, 37, 106, 75
- **Groningen:** 229, 184, 49, 63, 325, 240, 42, 228, 255, 182, 245, 211, 135, 70, 148, 66, 282, 231, 193, 339, 205
- **Haarlem:** 24, 193, 103, 129, 125, 180, 55, 257, 356, 210, 235, 136, 257, 101, 209, 382, 225, 104, 149, 132
- **Heerlen:** 222, 109, 246, 118, 99, 82, 18, 109, 198, 298, 89, 177, 91, 235, 101, 261, 244, 51
- **Hilversum:** 100, 210, 68, 109, 125, 246, 55, 163, 298, 210, 89, 177, 91, 144
- **Hoek van Holland:** 37, 180, 202, 246, 118, 99, 65, 195, 265, 99, 91, 144
- **Leeuwarden:** 131, 206, 181, 182, 74, 198, 260, 318, 194, 131, 35, 147
- **Leiden:** 148, 152, 111, 190, 195, 147, 148, 202, 169, 264, 244, 281
- **Maastricht:** 124, 123, 176, 74, 212, 225, 382, 261, 104, 149
- **Meppel:** 45, 68, 86, 170, 123, 170, 189, 104, 152, 145
- **Middelburg:** 82, 57, 55, 86, 95, 57, 81, 123, 45, 145
- **Nijmegen:** 26, 55, 95, 172, 95, 81, 68, 176, 123
- **Rotterdam:** 81, 253, 270, 225, 277, 253, 132
- **s-Hertogenbosch:** 94, 81, 212, 277, 156
- **Tilburg:** 150, 277, 212, 156, 91
- **Utrecht:** 150, 277, 212, 156
- **Venlo:** 291, 170
- **Winschoten:** 121
- **Zwolle:** —

NETHERLANDS

653

Norway

Bergen

Shutterstock/Grisha Bruev

Highlights

Home to soaring fjords, glaciers and polar bears juxtaposed with cosmopolitan cities and vibrant festivals, Norway truly is a remarkable country. The natural landscape must rank as one of the most beautiful in the world, it is easy to see why people become entranced.

With a rich culture spanning centuries from the ancient Vikings to the present day, and plenty of legends, folklore and fairytales in between, Norway is a magical place that invariably delights and inspires its visitors.

The Nobel Peace Prize has, since its inception, been awarded in Oslo by the Norwegian Nobel Committee. Oslo City Hall, where the ceremony is held, is now one of Norway's most famous buildings.

As a country steeped in myths and legends, Norway has a vibrant heritage of story-telling. Trolls are some of the most talked about fairytale creatures, and statues, books and pictures of them can be found all over the country.

Major towns and cities

- Oslo – Norway's capital city hosts numerous festivals throughout the year.
- Bergen – a colourful and peaceful city surrounded by mountains.
- Trondheim – home to the world's most northerly medieval cathedral.
- Drammen – a city with plenty of attractions such as the oldest brewery in Norway.

Attractions

- Heddal Stave Church, Notodden – Norway's largest medieval wooden church.
- Geirangerfjord, Sunnmøre – one of Norway's most breathtaking fjords and a UNESCO site.
- Jostedal Glacier – Europe's largest glacier and an outstanding natural environment.
- The Royal Palace, Oslo - take a tour through some of the most beautiful state rooms.

Find out more

www.visitnorway.com
E: info@visitoslo.com T: 0047 (0) 22 00 25 00

Country Information

Population (approx): 5.3 million

Capital: Oslo

Area: 328,878 sqkm

Bordered by: Finland, Russia, Sweden

Terrain: Mostly high plateaux and mountain ranges broken by fertile valleys; deeply indented coastline; arctic tundra in the north

Climate: Moderate climate along coastal areas; more extreme inland with snowy/rainy winters; arctic conditions in the north; summers can be unpredictable and May and June can be cool

Coastline: 25,148km (including islands/fjords)

Highest Point: Galdhøpiggen 2,469m

Language: Norwegian; Sami in some areas

Local Time: GMT or BST + 1, i.e. 1 hour ahead of the UK all year

Currency: Krone (NOK) divided into 100 øre; £1 = NOK 11.83, NOK 10 = £0.85 (Feb 2021)

Emergency numbers: Police 112, with mobile phone 911; Fire brigade 110; Ambulance 113. From a mobile phone dial 112 for any service.

Public Holidays 2021: Jan 1; Apr 1, 2, 4, 5; May 1, 13, 17, 23, 24; Dec 25, 26.

School summer holidays run from mid-June to mid-August.

Border Posts

Borders with Sweden and Finland may be crossed on all main roads. Storskog on the E105, east of Kirkenes, is the only border crossing for tourist traffic from Norway into Russia (visa required).

Duty-Free Allowances

Norway isn't a member of the EU and therefore it is possible to import goods duty-free into the country from the EU. Duty-free allowances, which are strictly enforced, are as follows:

- 200 cigarettes or 250gm tobacco
- 1 litre spirits and 1½ litres wine
- or 1 litre spirits and 3.5 litres beer
- or 3 litres wine and 2 litres beer
- or 5 litres beer

Goods to the value of NOK 6,000 (including alcohol and tobacco products)

Visitors must be aged 20 years and over to import spirits and 18 years and over for wine, beer and cigarettes.

Entry Formalities

Holders of British and Irish passports may visit Norway for up to three months without a visa.

Food and Medicines

Up to 10kg (combined weight) of meat, meat products and cheese can be imported into Norway from EU countries for personal consumption. The import of potatoes is not permitted but you can take in up to 10kg of fruit, berries and other vegetables. Visitors may only take in medicines for their own personal use with a covering letter from a doctor stating their requirements.

Medical Services

British visitors are entitled to the same basic emergency medical and dental treatment as Norwegian citizens, on production of a UK passport or European Health Insurance Card (EHIC), but you will have to pay the standard fees. Ensure you consult a doctor who has a reimbursement arrangement with the NAV (Norwegian Employment and Welfare Organisation). Hotels and tourist offices have lists of local doctors and dentists.

You will have to pay in full for most prescribed medicines which are available from pharmacies (apotek). Emergency in-patient hospital treatment at public hospitals, including necessary medication, is free of charge but you will have to pay for out-patient treatment. NAV Health Service Agencies will reimburse any payments that are refundable.

Mosquitos and midges may be a nuisance at certain times of the year, especially near lakes.

Money

Travellers may import or export currency up to the equivalent of NOK 25,000 in Norwegian and/or foreign notes and coins. Any amount above this must be declared to Customs.

Opening Hours

Banks: Mon-Fri 8am-3.30pm and some open until 5pm on Thurs.

Museums: 9am/10am-4pm/5pm; no regular closing day.

Post Offices: Mon-Fri 8am/8.30am-4pm/5pm; Sat 8am-1pm.

Shops: Mon-Fri 9am-4pm/5pm (Thurs until 6pm/8pm); Sat 9am/10am-1pm/3pm. Some supermarkets and shopping centres are open longer and some open Sun.

Refund of VAT on Export

Some shops have a blue and red sign in their window indicating that visitors may purchase goods free of VAT. For visitors from the UK the purchase price of individual items (exclusive of VAT) must be at least NOK 250. Shop assistants will issue a voucher and on departure from Norway visitors must present goods and vouchers at a tax-free counter situated on ferries, at airports and at main border crossings where a refund of 11-18% will be made.

Regulations for Pets

For details of the regulations regarding the import of pets into Norway, see website www.mattilsynet.no (English option) or contact the Norwegian Embassy in London.

Safety and Security

Norway is considered to have lower crime rates than some other European countries, even in the large cities, however you should always take the usual precautions against pickpockets and petty theft, especially in crowded areas. Do not leave valuables in your vehicle.

Following some recent incidents of robbery, the police are warning motorists not to stop in lay-bys overnight. The Norwegian Automobile Association, Norges Automobilforbund (NAF), has also sent out warnings to campsites urging campers to be careful.

If you plan to go off the beaten track or out to sea you should take local advice about weather conditions, have suitable specialist equipment and respect warning signs. Because of Norway's northerly latitude the weather can change rapidly, producing sudden arctic conditions on exposed mountains – even in summer. The winter is long (it can last well into April) and temperatures can drop to minus 25º celcius and below, plus any wind chill factor.

Norway shares with the rest of Europe an underlying threat from terrorism. Attacks could be indiscriminate and against civilian targets in public places, including tourist sites.

British Embassy

THOMAS HEFTYES GATE 8, OSLO
Tel: 23 13 27 00
www.ukinnorway.fco.gov.uk/en/

Irish Embassy

HAAKON VIIS GATE 1, N-0244 OSLO
Tel: 22 01 72 00
www.embassyofireland.no

Documents

Money

Norway is expensive; bring or have electronic access to plenty of money, especially if you are intending to eat and drink in restaurants and bars.

Bank opening hours are shorter than in the UK, especially in summer, but cash machines are widespread. Bureaux de change are found in banks, post offices, airports, stations, hotels and some tourist offices.

The major credit cards are widely accepted (although some supermarkets and petrol stations do not accept credit cards) and may be used at cash machines (minibanks) throughout the country. In remote areas banks and cash machines may be few and far between.

It is advisable to carry your passport or photocard driving licence if paying with a credit card as you may well be asked for photographic proof of your identity. Carry your credit card issuers'/banks' 24-hour UK contact numbers in case of loss or theft of your cards.

Vehicle(s)

Carry your vehicle registration document (V5C), insurance certificate and MOT certificate (if applicable). If driving a borrowed vehicle carry a letter of authority from the owner.

Driving

Alcohol

Norwegian law is very strict: do not drink and drive. Fines and imprisonment await those who exceed the legal limit of 20 milligrams of alcohol in 100 millilitres of blood, which is considerably lower than that permitted in the UK (80 milligrams), and equates to virtually zero for at least 12 hours before driving. Random roadside breath tests are frequent.

If you are involved in a road accident which causes damage to property or vehicles or injuries you should not drink any alcohol for six hours following the accident as the police may wish to carry out blood alcohol tests.

If purchasing medicines in Norway you should be aware that some containing alcohol should be avoided if you intend to drive. These are marked with a red triangle.

Breakdown Service

Norges Automobilforbund (NAF) operates a 24-hour breakdown service nationwide. Call 08505 from a landline or 0926 08505 from a mobile phone. Emergency yellow telephones have been installed on difficult stretches of road.

NAF Veipatrulje (road patrols) operates from mid-June to mid-August on mountain passes and in remote areas but in Oslo, Stavanger and Bergen, they operate all year round.

If you're a member of The Caravan and Motorhome Club show your membership card in order to benefit from special NAF rates for breakdown assistance. Some breakdown vehicles have credit card payment terminals; otherwise payment is required in cash.

Child Restraint System

Children of four years and under 135cm must be seated in a special child restraint system. If in a rear facing system on the front seat, the airbag must be deactivated. A child between 135-150cm should use a booster seat with an adult seatbelt.

All child restraints must conform to ECE R44-03 or 04 regulations.

Fuel

Prices vary according to region - they are slightly higher in the north and in mountainous areas. Prices can also vary on different days and fuel tends to be cheaper on Sunday and Monday. There are automatic petrol pumps where payment is made by credit card or cash.

Petrol stations are generally open from 7am to 10pm on weekdays, but in cities you might find some open 24 hours. Petrol stations maybe scarce, particularly in the north.

Unleaded petrol is dispensed from pumps marked 'Blyfri'. Not all petrol stations stock diesel. If you fill up with it, ensure that you use the correct pump and do not inadvertently fill with 'Afgift Diesel' (red diesel for agricultural vehicles). LPG is available at a limited number of outlets – see www.visitnorway.com for a list.

Lights

The use of dipped headlights is compulsory at all times, regardless of weather conditions. Bulbs are more likely to fail with constant use and it is recommended that you carry spares.

Mountain Passes

Always check that any mountain passes you intend to use are open. Some high mountain roads close during the winter, the duration of the closure depending on weather conditions, but many others remain open all year. Other passes may close at short notice, at night or during periods of bad weather. Yellow emergency telephones are installed on mountain passes.

The Norwegian Tourist Board can provide a list of roads which normally close in winter, or contact the Road User Information Centre (Vegtrafikksentralen) for information about roads, road conditions, mountain passes, tunnels, border crossings, etc. The Centre is open round the clock all year, telephone 02030 within Norway or (0047) 91 50 20 30 from abroad. Alternatively a list of roads that are closed in winter or which have limited accessibility can be found at www.vegvesen.no/en/traffic and click on Truckers' Guide, or email firmapost@vegvesen.no

Motorways

There are 300km of 4 lane motorways signposted by the prefix A, which are situated around the towns of Bergen and Oslo. In addition there are category B motorways with 2 lanes. There are normally no emergency telephones on motorways.

There are many toll roads throughout the country and most have an electronic toll system. Vehicles are categorised as follows:

Class 1 – Motorcycles.

Class 2 – Car, with or without trailer, with a total weight less than 3,500kg and maximum length of 6m.

Class 3 – Vehicle with or without trailer and a total weight of more than 3,500kg or between 6m and 12.4m in length.

Motorway tolls

If you have not registered your credit card under the Visitors' Payment scheme (see below) you would normally pass through tolls in the lanes marked 'Mynt/Coin' or 'Manuell'. You either pay manually or at a coin machine – keep a supply of small change handy as it is understood that the machines do not issue change. Most toll roads have a facility for credit card payment. Drivers of vehicles over 3,500kg must drive through the 'Manuell' lane.

Don't be tempted to pass through unmanned tolls without paying, as checks are made. However, many toll road operators have installed fully automatic toll stations – AutoPASS – where a sign indicates that you should not stop. Drivers without an AutoPASS can stop and pay at Esso stations (following the 'KR-Service' signs) within three days of being eligible to pay a toll, or they will receive an invoice at their home address. This also applies to drivers of foreign-registered vehicles.

Alternatively, and more conveniently, there is now a 'Visitors' Payment' system for which you register and pay NOK 300 (vehicles below 3,500kg) or NOK 1,000 (over 3,500kg) by credit card. You specify how long your account is to be operative (maximum three months) and it is then automatically debited when you pass a pay point. Three months after your 'Visitors' Payment' has expired your account will be credited with any balance remaining. See www.autopass.no (English option) for more information and to open an account.

This system means you can drive through all toll roads in the AutoPASS lane and pay automatically at toll stations and pay points

Parking

A white line on the edge of the carriageway indicates a parking restriction. Do not park on main roads if visibility is restricted or where there is a sign 'All Stans Førbudt' (no stopping allowed). If you do so you may have your vehicle towed away. Parking regulations in towns are very strict and offences are invariably subject to fines. Pay and display car parks are in use in the main towns.

Priority

Priority roads (main roads) are indicated by a road sign bearing a yellow diamond on a white background. A black diagonal bar through the sign indicates the end of the priority rule. If you are not travelling on a priority road then vehicles coming from the right have priority. Traffic already on a roundabout has priority and trams always have priority.

Narrow roads have passing places (møteplass) to allow vehicles to pass. The driver on the side of the road where there is a passing place must stop for an oncoming vehicle. However heavy goods vehicles tend to take right of way on narrow roads, especially if travelling uphill, and it may be necessary to reverse to a passing place to allow one to pass.

Roads

The standard of roads is generally good but stretches of major roads may be bumpy and rutted as a result of use by heavy freight traffic. Caravanners in particular should take care to avoid wheels being caught in ruts.

Some roads are narrow, especially in the mountains, and may not have a central yellow line. State roads are shown in red on maps and are asphalted but may not have kerbs and may, therefore, easily become cracked and rutted. Many roads have barriers mounted close to the side of the road.

Secondary roads have a gravel surface that can be tricky when wet and may be in poor condition for some weeks during and after the spring thaw.

Don't assume that roads with an E prefix are major roads - sections of the E39, for example, are single-track with passing places. The E6 road is asphalted all the way to the Swedish border in the south and to Kirkenes in the north.

Some roads in the fjord region have many hairpin bends and can be challenging. Roads may narrow to a single carriageway and single-track bridges often have no advance warning.

Gradients on main highways are generally moderate, not over 10%, but the inside of hairpin bends may be much steeper. There is a gradient of 20% on the E68 from Gudvangen (on the southern tip of the Sognefjord) to Stalheim, but a tunnel under the steepest section of the Stalheim road eliminates this difficult section.

Maps showing roads closed to caravans and those only recommended for use by experienced caravanners, together with rest stops, may be obtained from the Norwegian Tourist Board, Norwegian local road authority offices and from the NAF.

Because of the nature of the country's roads – and the beauty of the scenery – average daily mileage may be less than anticipated. Major repairs to roads and tunnels take place during the summer months and traffic controls may cause delays. Ferries make up an integral part of a number of routes, particularly when travelling north along the coast.

Care should be taken to avoid collisions with elk, deer and reindeer, particularly at dawn and dusk. Accidents involving any kind of animal must be reported to the police.

A number of roads are closed in winter, including the E69 to the North Cape, due to snow conditions; some do not open until late May or early June.

Road Signs and Markings

European highways are prefixed with the letter E and are indicated by signs bearing white letters and figures on a green background, national highways (Riksvei or Stamvei) are indicated by black figures prefixed Rv on a yellow background and local, county roads (Fylkesvei) by black figures on a white background. County road numbers do not generally appear on maps.

Lines in the middle of the carriageway are yellow. Bus, cycle and taxi lanes are marked in white.

Some signs have been introduced, for example a square blue sign showing a car and '2+' in white means that cars carrying more than two people can use bus lanes. Square signs indicate the presence of speed cameras, small rectangular signs indicate the exit numbers on highways and main roads, and a number of triangular signs with a yellow background indicate a temporary danger. Signs advising maximum speeds on bends, obstructions, etc, should be respected.

In addition to international road signs, the following signs may also be seen:

Passing place

Place of intrest

Norwegian	English Translation
All stans førbudt	No stopping allowed
Arbeide pa vegen	Roadworks ahead
Enveiskjøring	One-way traffic
Ikke møte	No passing, single line traffic
Kjør sakte	Drive slowly
Løs grus	Loose chippings
Møteplass	Passing place
Omkjøring	Diversion
Rasteplass	Lay-by

Speed Limits

	Open Road (km/h)	Motorway (km/h)
Car Solo	80	90-100
Car towing caravan/ trailer	80	80
Motorhome under 3500kg	80	90-100
Motorhome 3500-7500kg	80	80

Drivers should pay close attention to speed limits, which are in general significantly lower than in the UK. Fines for exceeding speed limits are high and often have to be paid on the spot. Radar detectors are illegal.

In residential areas the speed limit may be as low as 30 km/h (18 mph). Frequent speed controls are in operation. Ramps and speed control bumps are not always signposted.

Vehicles over 3,500kg are restricted to 80 km/h (50 mph) on motorways and highways, regardless of signs showing higher general limits.

Tolls

Toll ring roads are in place around major cities charging drivers to take their vehicles into city centres. There are 3 zones (rings) of toll points in Oslo. In the outer zone you are only charged on entry. In the two inner zones you are charged every time you pass a toll point. Surcharges apply from 6.30-9am and 3-5pm, and for diesel vehicles - see www.fjellinjen.no/private/prices for full details.

Because of the mountainous terrain and the numerous fjords and streams, there are many bridges and tunnels where tolls are normally payable. Tunnels may be narrow and unlit and care is needed when suddenly entering an unlit tunnel from bright daylight. Alternative routes to avoid tolls can be full of obstacles which are not marked on a map, e.g. narrow stretches with sharp turns and/or poor road surface, and are best avoided.

Svinesund Bridge

There is a 700 metre long bridge linking Norway and Sweden on the E6 at Svinesund (Sweden) – the busiest border crossing between the two countries. Tolls are NOK20 for vehicles up to 3,500kg and NOK100 for vehicles over 3,500kgs (2019 prices).

Towing

Drivers of cars and caravans with a combined length of more than 12.4 metres must check from the list of national highways and/or municipal roads may not be allowed on some routes.

You can check this information with the Road User Information Centre (Vegtrafikksentralen), tel: 02030 within Norway or (0047) 91 50 20 30 from abroad, www.vegvesen.no/en/Traffic and click on Truckers' Guide, or from the Norwegian Tourist Board or NAF. For a motorhome the maximum length is 12 metres.

Any vehicle towing must have extended towing mirrors fitted.

Some secondary roads have a maximum width of less than 2.55 metres. If your caravan is wider than 2.3 metres and more than 50cm wider than your car, white reflectors must be mounted on the front of your car mirrors. More information is available from the Road User Information Centre.

It is understood that the Rv55 from Sogndal to Lom and the Rv63 north from Geiranger are not suitable for caravans exceeding 5 metres in length, or those without an adequate power/weight ratio.

Traffic Jams

Roads in general are rarely busy but the roads in and around the cities of Oslo, Bergen, Kristiansand and Trondheim suffer traffic jams during rush hours and at the beginning and end of the holiday season. The E6 Oslo-Svinesund road at the border with Sweden and the E18 Oslo-Kristiansand road are generally busy during the June to August holiday period. During the summer you should also expect delays at ferry terminals.

Tunnels

The road network includes approximately 950 tunnels, most of which can be found in the counties of Hordaland and Sogn og Fjordane in western Norway. Most tunnels are illuminated and about half are ventilated. There are emergency telephones at the entrance to tunnels and inside them. Tunnels also have refuges which can be used by motorists in the event of an emergency.

Laersdal Tunnel

The Lærsdal road tunnel links the Rv50 from just east of Aurlandsvangen to the E16 east of Lærdalsoyri, by-passing the ferry link from Gudvangen to Lærsdal. The toll-free 24.5km long tunnel is illuminated and ventilated throughout and has a number of caverns at regular intervals which act as turning points and, it is reported, help dispel any feelings of claustrophobia. An alternative route is to take the Rødnes tunnel and then the Rv53, but this involves a steep climb beyond Øvre Ardal.

Lofoten and Vesterålen Islands

The Lofoten Islands can be reached by ferries from Bodø & Skutvik and the Vesteralen Islands can be reached by road (E10) west of Narvik. The individual islands of the Lofoten and Vesterålen groups are connected to each other by bridge or tunnel and the two groups of islands are linked by the E10 Lofast route from Gullesfjordbotn in Vesterålen to Fiskebøl in Lofoten. This route was formerly only possible by ferry.

Oslo Tunnel

A 3km long toll-free tunnel runs from east to west Oslo.

Violation of Traffic Regulations

The police are empowered to impose and collect on-the-spot fines for infringement of traffic regulations.

where there is no option for manual payment. You do not need an AutoPASS tag which is designed for residents and long-stay visitors and for which you have to enter into a contract.

Winter Driving

Vehicles with a total weight of 3,500kg or more must carry chains during the winter season, regardless of road conditions. Checks are often carried out.

Generally spiked tyres can be used from 1st November to the first Sunday after Easter. In an effort to discourage the use of spiked tyres in Bergen, Oslo and Trondheim a tax is levied on vehicles equipped with them. For vehicles up to 3,500kg the tax is NOK 30 for one day and NOK 400 for a month. For vehicles over 3,500kg the fee is doubled. Daily permits are available from vending machines along major roads into the city marked 'Frisk luft I byen'. Vehicles over 3,500 kg must be equipped with winter tyres on all axles between 15th November and 31st March.

Essential Equipment

Reflective Jacket/Waistcoat

Owners of vehicles registered in Norway are required to carry a reflective jacket to be worn if their vehicle is immobilised on the carriageway following a breakdown or accident. This legislation does not yet apply to foreign registered vehicles but you are strongly advised to carry at least one such jacket. Passengers who leave the vehicle, for example to assist with a repair, should also wear one.

Warning Triangle

An warning triangle must be used if the vehicle has broken down, punctures or is involved in an accident, and could cause danger to other road users.

Touring

International ferry services operate between Norway and Denmark, Germany, Iceland and Sweden. Routes from Harwich to Denmark and Newcastle to the Netherlands are in operation as gateways to Europe and, in addition, a daily overnight ferry service connects Copenhagen and Oslo.

A green 'i' sign indicates a tourist information office which is open all year with extended opening hours in summer, whereas a red sign means that the office is only open during the summer season.

Norwegians take their school and industrial holidays from mid-June to mid-August; travelling outside this season will ensure that facilities are less crowded and more economically priced. Winter brings the inevitable snowfall with some of the most reliable snow conditions in Europe. The winter sports season is from November to April.

Alta, on the coast north of the Arctic Circle, boasts the most extensive prehistoric rock carvings in Europe and has been declared a UNESCO World Heritage Site. Other World Heritage Sites include Geirangerfjord, Nærøyfjord, Bryggen in Bergen and the wooden buildings in Røros.

City cards are available for Oslo and Bergen, giving unlimited free travel on public transport, free public parking and free or discounted admission to museums and tourist attractions. They can be bought from tourist information centres, hotels and campsites in or near the city, from some kiosks or online at www.visitoslo.com or www.visitbergen.com.

Wine and spirits are only available from special, state-owned shops (vinmonopolet) usually found in larger towns, and are expensive, as are cigarettes. Beer is available from supermarkets. Smoking in bars, restaurants and public places is prohibited. Tipping is not expected in restaurants.

English is widely spoken, often fluently, by virtually everyone under the age of 60.

Camping and Caravanning

There are more than 1,000 campsites in Norway which are classified 1 to 5 stars and which are generally open between June and mid August. A camping guide listing 300 sites is available from the Norwegian Automobile Association, Norges Automobilforbund (NAF), see www.nafcamp.no. The Norwegian Tourist Board also distributes a camping guide free of charge – see www.camping.no. Most 3 star sites and all 4 and 5 star sites have sanitary facilities for the disabled and all classified sites have cooking facilities.

Many sites do not open until mid-June and do not fully function until the beginning of July, particularly if the winter has been prolonged. Sites with published opening dates earlier than June may not open on time if the weather has been particularly bad and if, for example, there has been heavy rain and flooding near rivers or lakes where campsites are situated. Campsites which are open all year will usually have very limited facilities for most of the year outside the short holiday season.

Facilities vary; in main tourist centres there are large, well-equipped sites with good sanitary facilities, grocery shops, leisure facilities and attendants permanently on duty. Sites are generally maintained to a high standard of cleanliness. In more remote areas, sites are small and facilities can be very simple.

Many small campsites have no chemical disposal point. Roadside notice boards at the entrance to each local area (kommune) indicate campsites, chemical disposal points (normally sited at petrol stations) and other local amenities. These disposal facilities are usually coin-operated and have instructions in English. In some areas in the north, there may be no adequate arrangements for the disposal of waste water, either on site or in the immediate area, and you are advised enquire when arriving at a campsite.

The Camping Key Europe, which replaced the Camping Card Scandinavia (CCS) in 2012, may be required at some sites. You can buy the Camping Key Europe on arrival at your first site and will be issued with a temporary card. Alternatively, you can order the card before you travel from www.camping.no/en/cke and click on 'Bestillig av Kort' where you can then select to view the order form in English. If ordering in advance allow at least three weeks for the card to arrive.

There are many sites on the E6 to the North Cape, seldom more than 30km apart. These sites may be subject to road noise. Caravans are allowed to stay at the North Cape but no facilities are available – see Nordkapp later in this chapter and in the Site Entry listing.

In the short summer season campsites can be crowded and facilities stretched and you are recommended to arrive before 3pm (many sites have a latest arrival time of 4pm) in order to have a better choice of pitches and have the opportunity to erect an awning.

Casual/wild camping is not actively encouraged but the Norwegian 'Right of Access' allows visitors to explore the countryside freely, except for cultivated land, farmland, gardens, nurseries, etc. Off-road driving is not allowed. Visitors must respect nature and take their rubbish away with them when they leave. Open fires (which include Primus stoves) are prohibited in forests or on open land between 15 April and 15 September.

Cycling

Cyclists are fairly well catered for and some areas, such as Vestfold, Rogaland and the Lillehammer area, have a well-developed network of cycle paths. Some old roads have been converted into cycle paths in the mountains and along western fjords. Paths run through magnificent scenery in the Lofoten and Vesterålen Islands in particular, and from Haugastøl in the Hardangervidda National Park to Flåm. A number of tunnels are prohibited to cyclists, but local detours are generally signposted. Information is available at www.cyclingnorway.no

Electricity and Gas

Campsites usually have a minimum 10 amp supply. Plugs are the continental type and have two round pins plus two earth strips. Some sites do not yet have CEE connections. It is recommended that you take an extension cable of at least 50 metres.

There are often problems with both polarity and the earthing of the electrical supply on some sites. Due to its mountainous nature, Norway's electricity supply network is quite different from that found elsewhere in Europe. There is no national grid and electricity systems vary from place to place throughout the country.

Any polarity testing system is likely to give false readings. It is understood that progress is being made to improve and standardise the electrical supply throughout the country but you should exercise caution and, if in any doubt, ask site staff to demonstrate the integrity of the earthing system before connecting.

Propane gas cylinders are generally widely available from Esso and Statoil petrol stations. You will need to buy an appropriate adaptor, available from camping shops or Statoil garages. AGA AS dealers will allow you to sell back propane cylinders within six months of purchase prior to leaving Norway at approximately 80% of the purchase price. It is understood that Statoil garages no longer buy them back. Some Statoil garages and AGA AS dealers will exchange Swedish Primus propane cylinders for their Norwegian version but will not accept other foreign propane cylinders. There is no refund for the adaptor.

Gas supplies can be conserved by taking advantage of the kitchens and/or cooking facilities available at classified campsites, and using electrical hook-ups at every opportunity.

Motorhomes

Many towns provide parking places for motorhomes close to city centres, known as Bobil Parks, which are open in June, July and August. In general these parking areas provide limited facilities and car and caravan outfits are not permitted. Details, where known, are listed in the Site Entry pages.

Apart from at campsites, motorhome service points are reported to be few and far between and are generally to be found at petrol stations, where water refill may also be available.

The Midnight Sun and Northern Lights

The best time to experience the midnight sun is early or high summer. The sun does not sink below the horizon at the North Cape (Nordkapp) from the second week in May to the last week in July.

Midsummer Night's Eve is celebrated all over the country with thousands of bonfires along the fjords.

You can hope to see the Northern Lights (Aurora Borealis) between November and February depending on weather conditions. You need to go north of the Arctic Circle, which crosses Norway, just south of Bodø on the Nordland coast. Occasionally the Northern Lights may be seen in southern Norway.

North Cape (Nordkapp)

A tunnel links the island of Magerøya, on which the North Cape is situated, to the mainland.

North Cape is open from the beginning of May until the end of September. It is possible to visit in winter; contact the Nordkapp Tourist Office, www.nordkapp.no or tel: (0047) 78 47 70 30. This is a tourist centre where there are exhibitions, displays, restaurants, shops and a post office, as well as an area of hardstanding for parking. This charge covers a stay of up to 48 hours. More information is given in the campsite entry for Nordkapp or on the website www.nordnorge.com. There are no cash machines at North Cape but credit cards are accepted in shops and restaurants, as are euros and sterling.

The true northernmost point of Norway is in fact at Knivskjellodden on a peninsular to the west of North Cape which is marked by a modest monument and a wooden box where you can record your name in a log book. It is possible to walk the 18km round trip from a car park on the E69 to Knivskjellodden but the walk should not be undertaken lightly. Later you can claim a certificate to mark your achievement from the tourist office in Honningsvåg by quoting the reference number of your signed entry in the log book.

The Order of Bluenosed Caravanners

Visitors to the Arctic Circle from anywhere in the world may apply for membership of the Order of Bluenosed Caravanners which will be recognised by the issue of a certificate by the International Caravanning Association (ICA).

For more information contact bluenosed@icacaravanning.org and attach a photograph of yourselves and your outfit under any Arctic Circle signpost, together with the date and country of crossing and the names of those who made the crossing.

This service is free to members of the ICA (annual membership £20); the fee for non-members is £5. Plastic decals for your outfit, indicating membership of the Order, are also available at a cost of £4. For more information see www.icacaravanning.org

Public Transport

The public transport network is excellent and efficient with bus routes extending to remote villages. For economical travel buy a 24 hour bus pass (campsites often sell them), valid when stamped for the first time. Many train routes run through very scenic countryside and special offers and discounts mean that train travel is reasonably priced. Only Oslo has a metro system. Trams operate in Bergen and Trondheim.

Using domestic public ferry services is often the quickest way of travelling around Norway and from place to place along the coast and within fjords. Most operate from very early in the morning until late at night. Booking is not normally necessary except in the height of the holiday season when there may be long queues to the more popular destinations. However, internal ferries can be expensive in high season and you may wish to plan your route carefully in order to avoid them.

The ultimate ferry journey is the Norwegian steamer trip (hurtigrute) up the coast from Bergen to Kirkenes. A daily service operates in both directions and the steamer stops at about 30 ports on the way. The round trip lasts eleven days.

The scenic round trip from Bergen or Oslo, 'Norway in a Nutshell', takes you through some of the most beautiful scenery in the country. It combines rail, boat and coach travel on the scenic Bergen railway, the breathtaking Flåm Railway, and takes in the Aurlandsfjord, the narrow Naerøyfjord and the steep Stalheimskleiva. Further details are available from the Norwegian Tourist Board.

You can safely hail a taxi off the street or take one from a taxi stand. Most drivers speak English and all taxis are equipped for taking payment by credit card.

Flam

ALESUND *1B1* (1km N Coastal) *62.47571, 6.15688*
Ålesund Bobilsenter, Storgata 39, 6015 Ålesund
(Møre og Romsdal)

♦ ♦ ♦ / MP

Foll coast to N of town cent & m'van sps; well sp.
Sm, hdstg, unshd, EHU; ccard acc. *"No on-site warden;*
motor c'vans only; site on water's edge adj sea wall;
conv town cent; v nice facs in wonderful location."
NOK 200, May-Sep. **2019**

ALESUND *1B1* (3km E Urban/Coastal) *62.46986,*
6.19839 **Volsdalen Camping,** Sjømannsveien, 6008
Ålesund (Møre og Romsdal) **tel 70 12 58 90; post@
volsdalencamping.no; www.volsdalencamping.no**

♦ ♦ ♦ ♦ (htd) ♦ ♦ ♦ ♦ / MP ♦ ♦ ♦ ♦

**Foll Rv136 two Centrum, ignore 1st camping sp
(Prinsen), take 2nd site sp Volsdalsberga to exit
R, up slip rd. At top turn L over E136 then immed
R, site on L.** 3*, Sm, mkd, hdstg, unshd, terr, EHU
(10A) NOK30 (no earth); gas; cooking facs; red long
stay; TV; 40% statics; bus 600m; Eng spkn; adv bkg
acc; ccard acc. *"Stunning location; some pitches
o'looking fjord; sm pitches not suitable lge o'fits high
ssn; 75% travellers; site unkempt; new san facs being
built (2013); rec NH; only site for c'van nr Alesund,
so adv bkg strongly advised; town 30 min walk."*
NOK 350, 1 May-1 Sep. **2019**

ALTA *2G1* (6km S Rural) *69.92904, 23.26136* **Alta
River Camping,** Steinfossveien 5, 9518 Øvre Alta
(Finnmark) **tel 07 94 03 27 99; post@alta-river
camping.no; www.alta-river-camping.no**

12 ♦ ♦ (htd) ♦ ♦ ♦ ♦ / MP ♦ ♦ ♦ /

**Fr E6 (by-passing Alta), take E93 S sp Kautokeino.
Site clearly sp on L (opp information board).** Med,
pt shd, EHU (10-16A) NOK30; cooking facs; TV; Eng
spkn; adv bkg acc; ccard acc; sauna; CKE. *"Excel facs;
o'looks salmon rv; pitches not mkd and close together,
some hdstg; elec point poss no earth; facs dated but
clean; elec poss no earth."* **NOK 279** **2019**

ALTA *2G1* (7km S Rural) *69.92735, 23.27075* **Alta
Strand Camping & Apartments,** Stenfossveien 29,
9518 Øvre Alta (Finnmark) **tel 78 43 40 22; mail@
altacamping.no; www.altacamping.no**

12 ♦ ♦ ♦ (htd) ♦ ♦ ♦ ♦ ♦ / MP ♦ ♦ ♦ ♦ nr /

**Fr E6 (W of Alta) take Rv93 S sp Kautokeino. Three
sites adj in 3km on L, clearly sp, Strand is last one.**
3*, Sm, hdstg, unshd, EHU (16A) NOK50 (poss no
earth); bbq; cooking facs; twin axles; 20% statics;
phone; Eng spkn; adv bkg acc; ccard acc; sauna; car
wash; CKE. *"Gd for visiting rock carvings; midnight sun
visible fr nrby Alta museum; excel."* **NOK 272** **2017**

ALVDAL *1C2* (5km NE Rural) *62.13115, 10.56896*
Gjelten Bru Camping, 2560 Alvdal (Hedmark) **tel
62 48 74 44; www.nafcamp.com/gjelten-camping**

12 ♦ ♦ ♦ ♦ ♦ ♦ ♦ / MP ♦ ♦

**Fr Rv3 join rd 29 at Alvdal. Cross rv opp general
store to site on rv bank.** 3*, Sm, mkd, pt shd, EHU
(10A) NOK40; Eng spkn; fishing; games area. *"V
pleasant site; friendly owner."* **NOK 237** **2016**

ANDALSNES *1B1* (11km S Rural) *62.4940, 7.75846*
Trollveggen Camping, Horgheimseidet, 6300
Åndalsnes (Møre og Romsdal) **tel 07 40 09 20 02;
post@trollveggen.no; www.trollveggen.com**

♦ ♦ ♦ (htd) ♦ ♦ ♦ ♦ ♦ / ♦ ♦ ♦ ♦ nr /

Sp on W side of E136, dir Dombås. 3*, Sm, mkd, pt
shd, terr, EHU (16A) NOK40; bbq; cooking facs; Eng
spkn; adv bkg acc; ccard acc; fishing; bike hire; golf
10km. *"Friendly, family-run site; excel touring base;
outstanding scenery; at foot of Trollveggen wall - shd
fr late afternoon; ideal site for walking in Romsdal; on
Trollsteig classic rte."* **NOK 294, 10 May-20 Sep.**
2019

ANDALSNES *1B1* (3km S Rural) *62.55223, 7.70394*
Åndalsnes Camping & Motell, 6300 Åndalsnes (Møre
og Romsdal) **tel 71 22 16 29; epost@andalsnes-
camping.no; www.andalsnes-camping.com**

♦ ♦ ♦ ♦ ♦ ♦ / MP ♦ ♦ ♦

**Foll E136 to o'skirts of Åndalsnes. Foll sp Ålesund
x-ing rv bdge twd W & L immed.** Lge, pt shd, EHU
(10-16A) NOK40 (check earth); TV; ccard acc; fishing;
boating; CKE. *"Excel facs; rvside, excel mountain
scenery; nr Troll Rd & Wall; nice site; grnd can be
soft; poss long lead req (poss no earth); gd cent site."*
NOK 284, 1 May-30 Sep. **2019**

ANDALSNES *1B1* (23km NW Rural/Coastal) *62.58720,
7.53004* **Saltkjelsnes Camping,** N-6350 Eidsbygda
**tel 71 22 39 00; camping@saltkjelsnes.no;
www.saltkjelsnes.no**

♦ ♦ ♦ (htd) ♦ ♦ ♦ / MP ♦ ♦

FV64 twds Molde, site on L sp Eidsbyga. 3*, Sm, pt
shd, pt sl, terr, EHU (10A) 40 NOK; bbq; cooking facs;
twin axles; 60% statics; Eng spkn; boat hire; fishing.
*"Lovely location; site small & space ltd, but 1st class
facs; Rodven Stavkirke 10km; vg."*
NOK 287, 1 Apr-1 Oct. **2015**

BARDU *2 F2* (2km N Rural) *68.87647, 18.36256*
Bardu Camping & Turistsenter, Idrettsveien 2, 9360
Bardu (Troms) **tel 77 61 23 00 or 97 41 87 82;
haukland@live.no; www.barducamping.no**

12 ♦ ♦ ♦ (htd) ♦ ♦ ♦ ♦ / MP ♦ ♦ ♦ nr /

Site sp fr E6, N of Setermoen. 3*, Med, pt shd, EHU
(10A) NOK50; phone; tennis. *"In valley surrounded by
mountains; scruffy but useful NH; only acc Norwegian
cc."* **NOK 255** **2018**

NORWAY

BERGEN *1A3* (21km E Rural) *60.37381, 5.45768* **Lone Camping,** Hardangerveien 697, 5268 Haukeland (Horda-Rogaland) **tel 55 39 29 60; booking@lone camping.no; www.lonecamping.no**

†1† WD ⚫ 🅿 ✉ MSP 🦋 ⵏ ⛺ 🏔

Fr N on E39 until junc with E16. foll sp Voss to rndabt junc with Rv580 sp Nesttun. Foll Rv580 S for approx 5km, site sp on L. Fr S on E39 until Nesttun, foll Rv580 N sp Indre Arna for approx 6km, site sp on R. Recep is sm bureau adj g'ge or, if unmanned, in g'ge. Do NOT go into Bergen city cent. Site is 20km by rd fr Bergen. 3*, Lge, hdstg, pt shd, pt sl, EHU (16A) NOK40; gas; sw; red long stay; TV; 10% statics; phone; bus to Bergen; Eng spkn; ccard acc; site clsd 5 Nov-19 Dec & New Year; fishing; boating; CKE. *"Well-organised; helpful staff; peaceful lakeside setting; superb views; lakeside pitches diff when wet; bus at camp ent for Bergen (35 mins)."* NOK 326, 5 Jan-19 Apr & 29 Apr-20 Dec.   2019

BERGEN *1A3* (17km SE Rural) *60.35220, 5.43520* **Bratland Camping,** Bratlandsveien 6, 5268 Haukeland (Hordaland) **tel 55 10 13 38 & 92 61 52 00 (mob); post@bratlandcamping.no; www.bratlandcamping.no**

†1† WD ⚫ 🅿 ✉ MSP 🖳 ⛺

Fr N on E39 until junc with E16, foll sp Voss to rndabt junc with Rv580 sp Nesttun. Foll Rv580 S for approx 4km; site sp on L. Fr Voss on E16, emerge fr tunnel to rndabt, turn L onto Rv580. Then as above. Site 16km by rd fr Bergen. 3*, Sm, hdstg, unshd, EHU (10A) NOK40; cooking facs; TV; 10% statics; bus to Bergen at site ent; Eng spkn; ccard acc; CKE. *"Clean, family-run site; gd, modern san facs; v helpful, friendly owners; conv Bergen, nrby stave church & Grieg's home; great loc."* NOK 267, 1 May-15 Sep.   2016

BERLEVAG *2H1* (0.6km E Coastal) *70.85716, 29.09933* **Berlevåg Pensjonat Camping,** Havnagata 8, 9980 Berlevåg (Finnmark) **tel 41 54 42 55; post@ berlevag-pensjonat.no; www.berlevag-pensjonat.no**

†1† (htd) WD ⚫ 🅿 ✉ MSP 🖳 ⛺ nr 🏔 🐎

Leave E6 at Tanabru, foll Rv890 to Berlevåg. Site at beg of vill. 3*, Sm, unshd, EHU (16A) NOK40; bbq; cooking facs; TV; phone; Eng spkn; adv bkg acc; ccard acc; CKE. *"Busy fishing port on edge of Barents Sea; museum, glassworks, WW2 resistance history; v helpful staff as site is also TO; site will open outside Jun-Sep on request if contacted ahead; library & lounge; rec arr early; excel site."* NOK 237, 1 Jun-30 Sep.   2016

BIRTAVARRE *2G1* (0.7km S Rural) *69.49051, 20.82976* **Camping Birtavarre (TR34),** 9147 Birtavarre (Troms) **tel 47 40 00 34 34; https://eng.high-north.com/camp-birtavarre/**

†1† WD ⚫ 🅿 ✉ MSP 🖳 nr

On E6 Olderdalen to Nordkjsobotn, sp. Or foll sp fr vill. 3*, Med, unshd, EHU NOK45; cooking facs; sw; Eng spkn; ccard acc; CKE. *"Basic site; OK for NH."* NOK 195, 1 May-15 Oct.   2019

BO *1C3* (9km SE Rural) *59.38478, 9.18171* **Teksten Camping AS,** Strannavegen 140, 3810 Gvary **tel 35 95 55 96; teksten@barnascamping.no; www.barnas camping.no**

†1† (htd) WD ⚫ 🅿 ✉ MSP 🦋 ⛺

On 36 dir Skien. Go thro Gvarv. Site sp on L. 700m fr main rd by rv. Med, mkd, pt shd, terr, cooking facs; sw nr; twin axles; 30% statics; Eng spkn; adv bkg acc; ccard acc; games area; games rm; CKE. *"Vg site for children."* NOK 258, 1 May-9 Sep.   2015

BODO *2F2* (11km NE Coastal) *67.34136, 14.51261* **Geitvågen Bad & Camping,** Geitvagen, 8001 Bodø (Nordland) **tel 47 40 04 97 50; post@geitvaagen.no**

🐎 †1† WD ⚫ 🅿 ✉ MSP 🦋 🚣 🎣 adj

On ent Bodø on Rv80, turn R onto Rv834 sp Kjerringøy. After 10km turn L at sp, pass car park on R. 1*, Med, mkd, hdg, pt shd, pt sl, terr, EHU 10A (NOK30); cooking facs; sw; twin axles; Eng spkn; adv bkg acc; ccard acc. *"Arr early for pitch with sea view for midnight sun; on rd to Kjerringoy ferry; some pitches hidden among trees with sea views; salwater lagoon; facs adequate but tired; fair."* NOK 210, 1 Jun-31 Aug.   2019

BODO *2F2* (28km SE Coastal) *67.23545, 14.62125* **Saltstraumen Camping,** Knapplund, 8056 Saltstraumen (Nordland) **tel 75 58 75 60; saltstraumen@pluscamp.no; www.saltstraumen-camping.no**

12 🐎 †1† (htd) WD ⚫ 🅿 ✉ MSP 🦋 (I) nr 🎣 nr 🏔

Fr Bodø take Rv80 for 19km; turn S onto rte 17 at Løding; site sp in Saltstraumen. 3*, Med, hdstg, unshd, EHU (16A) NOK30; gas; bbq; cooking facs; twin axles; TV; 50% statics; phone; bus 300m; Eng spkn; adv bkg acc; ccard acc; fishing; bike hire; boating; CKE. *"5 min walk to Mælstrom, the 'angler's paradise'; v busy high ssn - rec arr early; site a bit tired."* NOK 330   2019

BREMSNES *1B1* (6km W Coastal) *63.08043, 7.59535* **Skjerneset Brygge Camping,** Ekkilsøy, 6530 Averøy (Møre og Romsdal) **tel 71 51 18 94; info@skjerneset. com; www.skjerneset.com**

12 †1† (htd) WD ⚫ 🅿 ✉ 🦋 🚣

Foll sp to Ekkilsøya Island on Rv64 (off Averøy Island). Site on R over bdge. Sm, hdstg, pt shd, EHU (10-16A) NOK30; cooking facs; TV (pitch); boat hire; fishing. *"Charming, clean, peaceful site adj working harbour; beautiful outlook; apartments to rent; basic san facs; waterside pitches - unfenced deep water in places; museum adj."* NOK 200   2015

BRONNOYSUND *2E3* (14km SW Coastal) *65.39340, 12.09920* **Torghatten Camping,** 8900 Torghatten (Nordland) **tel 75 02 54 95; post@torghatten.net; www.rv17.no/torghatten-camping/**

🏕12 ⛺ wc ♿ 🚿 🧺 ⚡ msp 🦋 🐕 🍽 🛝 🏪 🛶 🚤adj

Fr Rv17 onto Rv76 to Brønnøysund, foll sp Torghatten. Site at base of Torghatten mountain. Sm, unshd, pt sl, EHU (16A) NOK30; phone; bus; Eng spkn. *"Take care speed humps in/out Brønnøysund; sea water pool adj; vg."* **NOK 280**   2019

BRUFLAT *1C2* (10km SE Rural) *60.82932, 9.75050* **Etna Familiecamping,** Maslangrudvegen 50, 2890 Etnedal **tel 61 12 17 55 or 94 81 90 56 (mob); info@etnacamping.no; www.etnacamping.no**

🏕12 ♀♂(htd) wc ⛺ ♿ 🧺 ⚡ msp 🦋 🐕 🛶

Fr Gjovik, W on 33 past Dokka. Site on R approx 2 km past 251. Downhill to ent. Lge, pt shd, pt sl, terr, twin axles; TV; 20% statics; Eng spkn; adv bkg acc; ccard acc; games rm; CKE. *"Relaxing site; sep area for touring; may need long lead, some still 2 pin; vg."* **NOK 276**   2015

BUD *1B1* (1km SE Coastal) *62.9040, 6.92866* **PlusCamp Bud (MR11),** 6430 Bud (Møre og Romsdal) **tel 71 26 10 23 or 97 70 05 44 (mob); bud@pluscamp. no; www.budcamping.no**

🐕 ♀♂(htd) wc ⛺ ♿ 🚿 🧺 ⚡ msp 🦋 🍽 🏪 🛝 🏪 🛶 🛝sand adj

Site on Rv664, sp fr Bud. 4*, Med, unshd, pt sl, EHU (16A) NOK40; cooking facs; TV; 50% statics; Eng spkn; ccard acc; fishing; boat hire; CKE. *"Waterfront site with beautiful views; 20 min walk to vill shops/ rest; gd facs; gd location for start of Atlantic Highway, National Tourist Rte & for cycling, vg site."* **NOK 270, 20 Apr-1 Oct.**   2015

BYGLANDSFJORD *1B4* (3km N Rural) *58.68895, 7.80322* **Neset Camping,** 4741 Byglandsfjord (Aust-Agder) **tel 37 93 40 50; post@neset.no; www.neset.no**

🏕12 🐕 ♀♂(htd) wc ⛺ ♿ 🚿 🧺 ⚡ msp 🦋 🍽 ⏚nr 🏪 🛝 🛶 🏪

N on Rv9 fr Evje, thro Byglandsfjord, site on L. 4*, Lge, unshd, pt sl, EHU (10A) NOK30; gas; bbq; cooking facs; sw nr; TV; 40% statics; Eng spkn; adv bkg acc; ccard acc; windsurfing; bike hire; fishing; sauna; boat hire. *"Wonderful location on lakeside; elk safaris; walks; rafting nr; check elec earth."* **NOK 352**   2019

BYRKJELO *1B2* (0.3km S Rural) *61.73026, 6.50843* **Byrkjelo Camping & Hytter,** 6826 Byrkjelo (Sogn og Fjordane) **tel 91 73 65 97; mail@byrkjelo-camping.no; www.byrkjelo-camping.tefre.com**

♀♂ wc ⛺ ♿ 🚿 🧺 ⚡ 🦋 🍽 🏪 ⏚nr 🛝 ⏚nr 🏪 🛶(htd) 🎣

Fr S site ent on L as ent town, clearly sp. 3*, Sm, hdstg, pt shd, EHU (10A) NOK30; cooking facs; 25% statics; phone; Eng spkn; adv bkg acc; ccard acc; solarium; fishing; cycling; CKE. *"Horseriding, mountain & glacier walking; excel, well kept site; great facs."* **NOK 278, 1 May-24 Sep.**   2019

DRAMMEN *1C3* (25km SE Coastal) *59.60003, 10.40383* **Homannsberget Camping,** Strømmveien 55, 3060 Svelvik (Vestfold) **tel 33 77 25 63 or 91 30 98 52 (mob); post@homannsberget.no; www.homannsberget.no**

⛺ 🧺 ⚡ msp 🦋 🍽 ♈ 🍽 🛝 🏪 🛶 🛝adj

Head SW on E18, take exit 25 twr Svelvik/RV319, at rndabt take 3rd exit onto E134. At next rndabt take 1st exit onto Bjørnsons gate/Rv282. Turn L onto Havnegata/Rv319. Cont on Rv319, go thro 1 rndabt. Site on the L. Med, mkd, unshd, EHU; twin axles; adv bkg acc; ccard acc; games area; CKE. *"Vg site; train stn within 20 mins; site is also a strawberry farm & orchard."* **NOK 245, 1 May-1 Sep.**   2019

EDLAND *1B3* (6km E Rural) *59.72378, 7.69712* **Velemoen Camping,** 3895 Edland Vinje i Telemark **tel 35 07 01 09 or 90 89 40 49 (mob); velemoen@ frisurf.no; www.velemoen.no**

🐕 ♀♂ ⛺ ♿ 🧺 ⚡ 🦋 🍽 🏪nr 🛝

Fr E site on L off E134 bef Edland; Fr W site is on R, 8km after Haukeligrend on Lake Tveitevatnet. 2*, Sm, hdstg, unshd, pt sl, EHU (16A, no earth); bbq; cooking facs; sw nr; red long stay; twin axles; TV; 10% statics; phone; Eng spkn; adv bkg acc. *"V helpful owner; immac san facs; beautiful lakeside/ mountain location; on S side of Hardangervidda National Park; on main E-W rte Oslo-Bergen; excel."* **NOK 250, 15 May-1 Oct.**   2017

EIDFJORD *1B3* (7km SE Rural) *60.42563, 7.12318* **Sæbø Camping (HO11),** 5784 Øvre-Eidfjord (Hordaland) **tel 53 66 59 27 or 55 10 20 48; scampi@online.no; www.saebocamping.com**

♀♂(htd) wc ⛺ ♿ 🧺 ⚡ msp 🦋 🍽 🏪 🛝

Site N of Rv7 bet Eidfjord & Geilo, 2nd on L after tunnel & bdge; clearly sp. 3*, Med, pt shd, EHU (10A) NOK40 (earth fault); cooking facs; boating; CKE. *"Vg; beautiful lakeside setting; adj to excel nature cent with museum/shop/theatre; clean san facs; helpful staff; gd location for walking & cycling."* **NOK 240, 1 May-30 Sep.**   2019

ELVERUM *1D2* (2km S Rural) *60.86701, 11.55623* **Elverum Camping,** Halvdan Gransvei 6, 2407 Elverum (Hedmark) **tel 62 41 67 16; booking@ elverumcamping.no; www.elverumcamping.no**

🏕12 🐕 ♀♂(htd) wc ⛺ 🧺 ⚡ msp 🦋 🍽 ♈ 🍽 ⏚nr 🏪nr 🏪

Site sp fr Rv20 dir Kongsvinger. Lge, pt shd, EHU (10A); bbq; 20% statics; phone; Eng spkn; adv bkg acc. *"Vg; museum of forestry adj; rlwy museum at Hamar (30km)."* **NOK 300**   2019

FAGERNES *1C2* (0.6km S Rural) *60.98189, 9.23125*
Camping Fagernes, Tyinvegen 23, 2900 Fagernes
(Oppland) **tel 61 36 05 10; post@fagernes-camping.
no; www.fagernes-camping.no**

12 ♀♀ (htd) wo ♨ ♣ ♿ ⚲ ✉ Ⓣ ⓐ ♨ ⚲ ⚏

Site on N side of Fagernes on E16. 4*, Lge, hdg, pt
shd, pt sl, EHU (10-16A) NOK30; cooking facs; sw;
TV; 90% statics; phone; Eng spkn; ccard acc; cycling;
fishing; CKE. *"Helpful owner; car wash; activity cent;
ltd water pnts; Valdres folk museum park adj highly rec;
fjord views; skiing; excel new san facs & site refurbished
(2015); vg."* **NOK 275**   **2015**

FARSUND *1A4* (6km S Coastal) *58.0663, 6.7957*
Lomsesanden Familiecamping, Loshavneveien 228,
4550 Farsund (Vest-Agder) **tel 38 39 09 13; e-vetlan@
online.no; www.lomsesanden.no**

♀ ♀♀ wo ♨ ♣ ⚲ ✉ ⚲ ⚏ ♨ sand adj

Exit E39 at Lyngdal onto Rv43 to Farsund & foll
camp sps. (NB Rv465 fr Kvinesdal not suitable for
c'vans.) 2*, Med, pt shd, EHU (10A) NOK45; TV;
95% statics; Eng spkn; adv bkg rec; ccard acc; fishing.
"Gd site in beautiful location."
NOK 200, 1 May-15 Sep.   **2016**

"We must tell the Club about that great site we found"

Get your site reports in by mid-August and we'll
do our best to get your updates into the next
edition.

FAUSKE *2F2* (5km S Urban) *67.23988, 15.41961*
Fauske Camping & Motel, Leivset, 8201 Fauske
(Nordland) **tel 75 64 84 01; fausm@online.no**

12 ♀ ♀♀ ♨ ♣ ⚲ ✉ ♨ ⚲ nr ⚏

Fr S site on R of E6, approx 6km fr exit of Kvenflåg
rd tunnel, & 2km bef Finneid town board. Fr N site
on L approx 1km after rv bdge. 3*, Sm, pt shd, sl,
EHU (10A) NOK40; cooking facs; sw nr; Eng spkn; adv
bkg acc; ccard acc; fishing; cycling. *"Vg; phone ahead
LS to check open; v close to E6 rd."* **NOK 267**   **2016**

FJAERLAND *1B2* (4km N Rural) *61.42758, 6.76211*
Bøyum Camping, 5855 Fjærland (Sogn og Fjordane)
**tel 57 69 32 52; post@boyumcamping.no;
www.boyumcamping.no**

12 ♀♀ (htd) wo ♨ ⚲ ✉ ⚲ ♨ ⚏

On Rv5 Sogndal to Skei. Shortly after end of toll
tunnel on L, well sp. 4*, Sm, hdstg, unshd, EHU;
cooking facs; TV; 30% statics; phone; Eng spkn; adv
bkg acc; ccard acc; bike hire; CKE. *"Adj glacier museum,
conv for glacier & fjord trips; beautiful location nr fjord
(no views); visit Mundal for 2nd hand books; helpful
owner; superb, clean site; vg."* **NOK 270**   **2017**

FLAM *1B2* (1km WNW Urban) *60.86296, 7.10985*
Flåm Camping, Nedre Brekkevegen 12, 5743 Flåm
(Sogn og Fjordane) **tel 57 63 21 21; camping@
flaam-camping.no; www.flaam-camping.no**

♀ ♀♀ (htd) wo ♨ ♣ ⚲ ✉ ⚲ MSP ⚏ nr Ⓗ nr ⚏ ⚏

Fr Lærdal Tunnel cont on E16 thro 2 more tunnels.
At end of 2nd tunnel (Fretheim Tunnel) turn L
immed to Sentrum. Turn L at x-rds, site on L.
4*, Med, hdstg, pt shd, pt sl, terr, serviced pitches;
EHU (10A) inc; bbq; cooking facs; red long stay;
phone; Eng spkn; ccard acc; bike hire; boating;
fishing; watersports; CKE. *"Well-kept, friendly, busy,
family-run site; no o'fits over 8.5m; excel san facs;
conv mountain walks, excel location for Flambana
rlwy, Aurlandsvangen 7km - gd shops; gd cycling base;
excel."* **NOK 300, 1 Mar-31 Oct.**   **2015**

FLEKKEFJORD *1A4* (6km ESE Rural) *58.28868,
6.7173* **Egenes Camping (VA7),** 4400 Flekkefjord
(Vest-Agder) **tel 38 32 01 48; post@egenescamping.
no; http://2017.egenescamping.no/**

12 ♀♀ (htd) wo ♨ ♣ ⚲ ✉ ⚲ MSP ♨ ⚲ ⚏

Located N of E39 dir Seland. 4*, Med, mkd, pt shd,
EHU (5A) NOK40; TV; 75% statics; phone; ccard acc;
CKE. *"Ltd facs LS; overflow car park area with facs for
tourers 0.5km; lovely situation."* **NOK 250**   **2019**

FLORO *1A2* (2km E Coastal) *61.59420, 5.07244*
Pluscamp Krokane (SF15), Strandgt 30, 6900 Florø
(Sogn og Fjordane) **tel 57 75 22 50; post@krocamp.no;
www.krocamp.no**

12 ♀♀ (htd) wo ♨ ♣ ⚲ ✉ ⚲ MSP ⚲ Ⓣ nr Ⓗ nr ⚲ nr ⚏
♨ sand adj

On Rv5 Forde to Florø, on ent town turn L at rndabt
sp Krokane, then immed R & foll rd to coast. Turn
L, pass marina to site, sp. Steep ent/exit. Sm, hdstg,
pt shd, pt sl, EHU (10A) NOK30; 80% statics; phone;
bus; Eng spkn; boat hire; fishing; CKE. *"V sm area for
tourers; Florø interesting fishing town with boat trips
etc."* **NOK 130**   **2016**

FREDRIKSTAD *1C4* (16km SE Coastal) *59.13942,
11.03855* **Bevo Camping,** Bevoveien 31, 1634 Gamle
Fredrikstad **tel 69 34 92 15; info@bevo.no;
www.bevo.no**

♀♀ wo ♨ ✉ ⚲ ♨ ⚲ ♨ sand adj

Avoid app fr Fredrikstad. Fr E6 junc 4, take RV110
(Fredrikstad) then L on RV111 & L on RV107
(Torsnesveien). Foll signs to campsite. 3*, Sm, mkd,
pt shd, EHU; CCI. *"Isolated site on Oslo Fjord; 15 mins
to Gamle Frederikstad by car."*
NOK 280, 28 Apr-8 Sep.   **2019**

GEILO *1B3* (2km NE Rural) *60.54422, 8.23637* **Øen Turistsenter & Geilo Vandrerhjem,** Lienvegen 139, 3580 Geilo **tel 32 08 70 60; post@oenturist.no; www.oenturist.no**

Fr Geilo on Rv.7 twds Gol. Turn L onto Lienvegen & site. Med, hdg, pt shd, pt sl, EHU (10A) 30 NOK; bbq; cooking facs; 30% statics; Eng spkn; sauna; CKE. *"Vg site."* **NOK 230** 2015

GEIRANGER *1B1* (0.4km S Rural) *62.09998, 7.20421* **Camping Geiranger,** 6216 Geiranger (Møre og Romsdal) **tel 70 26 31 20; post@geirangercamping.no; www.geirangercamping.no**

Site on fjord edge in vill. On Rv63 Eidsdal-Geiranger take lower rd thro vill to site on R & on both sides of rv. Rv63 not suitable for c'vans - steep hill & hairpins, use ferry fr Hellesylt. 2*, Lge, unshd, pt sl, EHU ltd (16A) NOK35; bbq; cooking facs; Eng spkn; ccard acc; CKE. *"Busy site in superb location, gd touring base, gd boat trips on fjord, facs (inc EHU) ltd if site full; gd facs."* **NOK 270, 10 May-20 Sep.** 2015

GEIRANGER *1B1* (2km NNW Rural) *62.11548, 7.18437* **Grande Hytteutleige og Camping,** 6216 Geiranger (Møre og Romsdal) **tel 70 26 30 68; office@grande-hytteutleige.no; www.grande-hytteutleige.no**

Head N on Rv63, in 2.3km turn L at the foot of zigzags, then 1st R. Site on the L. Sm, pt sl, EHU (16A); cooking facs; Eng spkn; ccard acc. *"Friendly staff; conv for Fjord cruise, vg site."* **NOK 310, 15 May-15 Sep.** 2019

GOL *1C2* (3km S Rural) *60.70023, 9.00416* **Gol Campingsenter (BU17),** Heradvegen 7, 3550 Gol (Buskerud) **tel 32 07 41 44; gol@pluscamp.no; www.golcamp.no**

Ent on R of Rv7 fr Gol twd Nesbyen. 4*, Lge, unshd, pt sl, EHU (16A) inc; gas; cooking facs; sw nr; I V; ccard acc; sauna; games area; CKE. *"Excel; lge extn with full facs across main rd - modern & clean."* **NOK 245** 2016

GOL *1C2* (2km SW Rural) *60.69161, 8.91909* **Personbråten Camping,** 3550 Gol (Buskerud) **tel 90 78 32 73; leif.personbraten@c2i.net**

Fr Gol to Geilo on Rv7, on L on rvside. 2*, Med, pt shd, EHU (10A); bbq; cooking facs; sw nr; Eng spkn; adv bkg acc; fishing; cycling; CKE. *"On rvside; v pleasant; poss noise fr rd & rv; honesty box if office unmanned; excel NH."* **NOK 217** 2016

GRIMSBU *1C2* (0km N Rural) *62.15546, 10.17198* **Grimsbu Turistsenter,** 2582 Grimsbu (Oppland) **tel 62 49 35 29; mail@grimsbu.no; www.grimsbu.no**

On Rv29 11km E of Folldal, well sp. 4*, Med, pt shd, pt sl, EHU (16A) NOK30; bbq; cooking facs; sw nr; TV; Eng spkn; adv bkg acc; ccard acc; sauna; boat hire; bike hire; rv fishing. *"Family-run site; fitness rm; private san facs avail; beautiful situation."* **NOK 310** 2019

GRIMSTAD *1B4* (5km NE Coastal) *58.36888, 8.63722* **Moysand Familiecamping,** Moy, 4885 Grimstad (Aust-Agder) **tel 90 53 55 93; mail@moysand-familie camping.no; www.moysand-familiecamping.no**

Exit A18 junc 78 onto Rv420 E twd Fevik. Foll site sp on rd to Riksveien, site 2km after Riksveien. Lge, mkd, pt shd, EHU metered; bbq; cooking facs; TV; 10% statics; adv bkg acc; fishing; boat hire. *"Private san facs avail."* **NOK 190** 2016

GRONG *2E3* (2km S Rural) *64.4604, 12.3137* **Langnes Camping,** 7870 Grong (Nord-Trøndelag) **tel 47 68 83 33; post@langnescamping.no; langnescamping.no**

N on E6 turn off S of bdge over rv on by-pass, site sp. 4*, Med, mkd, hdstg, unshd, EHU (10A) NOK50; bbq; cooking facs; sw nr; TV; 10% statics; Eng spkn; adv bkg acc; games area; rv fishing; games rm. *"Helpful staff; drying rm for skiers; pleasant, family-run site; Quick Stop pitches; free phone to owner if site clsd; gd facs; access via gravel track."* **NOK 296, 1 Jun-31 Aug.** 2018

GUDVANGEN *1B2* (1km SW Rural) *60.87206, 6.82873* **Vang Camping,** 5747 Gudvangen (Sogn og Fjordane) **tel 57 63 39 26; post@vang-camping.no; www.vang-camping.no**

At S end of of Nærøy Fjord on E16 at edge of vill. 3*, Sm, hdstg, unshd, EHU (16A) NOK30 (poss no earth); Eng spkn; CKE. *"Immac site in beautiful valley with waterfalls; spectacular scenery; cruises on adj fjord; bus to Flam; poor san facs (2015)."* **NOK 225, 1 May-15 Sep.** 2015

HELLESYLT *1B1* (0.4km S Coastal) *62.08329, 6.87224* **Hellesylt Camping,** 6218 Hellesylt (Møre og Romsdal) **tel 90 20 68 85; postmottak@hellesyltturistsenter.no; www.hellesyltturistsenter.no**

Site on edge of fjord, sp fr cent of vill dir Geiranger. 2*, Sm, unshd, EHU (10A) NOK30; 40% statics; Eng spkn; adv bkg acc; CKE. *"Conv ferry to Geiranger; adj fjord surrounded by mountains - great views; gd rest in local hotel; beautiful church nr."* **NOK 140, 15 Apr-30 Sep.** 2019

HONNINGSVAG 2H1 (8km NW Coastal) 71.02625, 25.89091 Nordkapp Camping, 9751 Honningsvåg (Finnmark) tel 78 47 33 77; post@nordkappcamping.no; www.nordkappcamping.no

🐾 NOK10 ♀♂(htd) ⓌⒹ �/ ♿ ⌂ ⚏ ∥ MSP 🦋 ⚐

En rte Nordkapp on E69, site clearly sp. 3*, Sm, unshd, EHU (16A) NOK40; bbq; cooking facs; twin axles; 10% statics; bus 100m; Eng spkn; ccard acc; CKE. *"Vg; reindeer on site."* **NOK 319, 1 May-30 Sep.**　　　　2017

HORTEN 1C3 (3km S Rural/Coastal) 59.39776, 10.47582 Rørestrand Camping, Parkveien 34, 3186 Horten (Vestfold) tel 33 07 33 40; booking@rorestrandcamping.no; rorestrandcamping.no

🐾 ♀♂(htd) ⓌⒹ ⚏ ♿ ⌂ ⚏ ∥ 🦋 ⚏ 🐚 ⼕

Fr Horten foll Rv19 for 500m S to rndabt, then **foll sp.** 3*, Sm, unshd, sl, EHU (10A) NOK40; 90% statics; phone; Eng spkn; ccard acc; games area; CKE. *"Conv NH en rte Oslo; facs stretched high ssn."* **NOK 250, 1 May-15 Sep.**　　　　2016

JORPELAND 1A3 (5km SE Rural) 58.99925, 6.0922 Preikestolen Camping (RO17), Preikestolvegan 97, 4100 Jørpeland (Horda-Rogaland) tel 47 48 19 39 50; info@preikestolencamping.com; www.preikestolencamping.com

12 🐾 ♀♂ ⓌⒹ ⚏ ♿ ⌂ ⚏ ∥ MSP 🦋 Y ⚏ ⚐ 🐚 ⼕

Fr S exit Rv13 to Preikestolen to R, site sp. Rd narr **in places, care needed.** Med, hdstg, unshd, EHU (16A) NOK40; sw nr; red long stay; phone; bus to Preikestolen parking; Eng spkn; adv bkg acc; ccard acc; games area; CKE. *"Marvellous views; poss walk to Pulpit Rock but not easy; conv Stavanger by ferry; excel facs, esp shwrs; midge repellent ess; long lead poss needed; poss no earth."* **NOK 322**　　　　2016

KARASJOK 2H1 (1km SW Rural) 69.46888, 25.48908 Camping Karasjok, Kautokeinoveien, 9730 Karasjok (Finnmark) tel 97 07 22 25; karasjokcamping@runbox.no or booking@karacamp.no

12 ♀♂(htd) ⓌⒹ ⚏ ♿ ⌂ ⚏ ∥ 🦋 ⚐ 🐚 nr ⼕

Sp in town; fr x-rds in town & N of rv bdge take Rv92 W dir Kautokeino, site 900m on L. 3*, Sm, pt shd, EHU (10A) NOK40; Eng spkn; adv bkg acc; ccard acc; CKE. *"Youth hostel & cabins on site; gd, clean site & facs; lge pitches suitable RVs & lge o'fits; sh walk to Sami park & museum."* **NOK 241**　　　　2018

KAUTOKEINO 2G1 (2.5km S Rural) 68.99760, 23.03662 Arctic Motell & Kautokeino Camping, Suomaluodda 16, 9520 Kautokeino (Finnmark) tel 78 48 54 00; samicamp@me.com; www.kautokeinocamping.no

12 ♀♂(htd) ⚏ ⚏ ∥ 🦋 ⚏ 🐚

Well sp fr Rv93. Sm, unshd, pt sl, EHU (10A); 20% statics; Eng spkn. *"No chem disp; Juhls silver gallery worth visit; gd, friendly site."* **NOK 325**　2019

KILBOGHAMN 2E2 (3km S Coastal) 66.50667, 13.21608 Polar Camp, 8754 Kilboghamn (Nordland) tel 75 09 71 86; post@polarcamp.com or booking@polarcamp.com; www.polarcamp.com

12 ♀♂ ⓌⒹ ⚏ ♿ ⌂ ⚏ ∥ 🦋 ⚐ Y ⚏ 🐚 ⼕ ⚓ shgl adj

N on Rv17 sp to L just bef Kilboghamn ferry. Sm, hdstg, unshd, terr, EHU (10A); 10% statics; phone; Eng spkn; fishing. *"Superb location on Arctic Circle; ltd san facs in high ssn; fishing/boat trips arranged; helpful owner; v welcoming."* **NOK 300**　　　　2018

KIRKENES 2H1 (92km SSW Rural) 69.21283, 29.15560 Ovre Pasvik Camping, Vaggetem, 9925 Svanvik tel 95 91 13 05; atle.randa@pasvikcamping.no; www.pasvikcamping.no

🐾 ♀♂ ⚏ ⚏ ∥ ⚐

On the R of Rte 885. Sp fr rd. Sm, hdstg, pt shd, pt sl, EHU; bbq; cooking facs; 50% statics; Eng spkn; sauna; CKE. *"Clean facs, dated & basic; gd for birdwatching; fishing; canoeing; gd."* **NOK 250, Mid Apr-Mid Oct.**　　　　2016

KONGSBERG 1C3 (7km N Rural) 59.71683, 9.61133 Pikerfoss Camping, Svendsplassveien 2, 3614 Kongsberg (Buskerud) tel 32 72 49 78 or 91 19 07 41; mail@pikerfoss.no or erikfred@online.no; www.pikerfoss.no

12 ♀♂(htd) ⓌⒹ ⚏ ⚏ ∥ 🦋 ⼕

Fr E134 in Kongsberg turn N bef x-ring rv & go N bet rv (on L) & rlwy line (on R) on Bærvergrendveien. Site on R just after x-ing rlwy line. Sm, mkd, pt shd, EHU (10A) NOK30; 75% statics; Eng spkn; ccard acc. *"Modern, clean facs; lge pitches; facs stretched high ssn; excel."* **NOK 160**　　　　2019

KONGSVINGER 1D3 (10km S Rural) 60.11786, 12.05208 Sigernessjøen Familiecamping, Strenelsrud Gård, Arko-Vegen, 2210 Granli (Hedmark) tel 40 60 11 22; post@sigernescamp.no; www.sigernescamp.no

♀♂(htd) ⓌⒹ ⚏ ⚏ ∥ 🦋 ⚐ ⼕

On N side of Rv2 Kongsvinger to Swedish border, **well sp.** 3*, Med, pt shd, pt sl, EHU (10A) NOK40; sw nr; 30% statics; Eng spkn; golf adj. *"Gd."* **NOK 250, 1 May-30 Sep.**　　　　2018

KOPPANG 1D2 (3km W Rural) 61.57163, 11.01745 Camping Koppang, 2480 Koppang (Hedmark) tel 62 46 02 34; info@koppangcamping.no; www.koppangcamping.no

🐾 ♀♂ ⓌⒹ ⚏ ♿ ⌂ ⚏ ∥ MSP 🦋 ⚏ ⚐ nr 🐚 ⼕

Fr Rv3, 25km S of Atna, turn onto Rv30; site on L immed bef rv bdge. 4*, Med, pt shd, pt sl, EHU (16A) NOK30; gas; cooking facs; TV; 10% statics; Eng spkn; adv bkg acc; ccard acc; fishing. **NOK 256, 1 May-30 Sep.**　　　　2018

KRISTIANSAND *1B4* (12km E Rural) *58.12187, 8.06568* **Kristiansand Feriesenter,** Dvergsnesveien 571, 4639 Kristiansand (Vest-Agder) **tel 38 04 19 80; post@kristiansandferiesenter.no; www.dvergsnestangen.no**

♿ (htd) ⓦ ♨ ⚲ ♿ ▣ ⁄ ⓂⓈⓅ 🦋 ⚓ 🛒 ⚠

Turn S off E18 jnc 91, 6km E of Kristiansand after Varoddbrua onto Rv401, cont for 5.5km foll sps to site. Rd narr last 3km. 5*, Lge, mkd, shd, sl, EHU (16A) inc; cooking facs; sw; TV; phone; ccard acc; boat hire; fishing; CKE. *"Gd NH; conv for ferry (20 mins); beautiful location; helpful, friendly staff."* NOK 506, 16 Apr-16 Sep. 2019

> ## "I need an on-site restaurant"
>
> We do our best to make sure site information is correct, but it is always best to check any must-have facilities are still available or will be open during your visit.

KROKSTRANDA *2F2* (0.3km SE Rural) *66.46233, 15.09344* **Krokstrand Camping,** Saltfjellveien 1573, 8630 Krokstranda (Nordland) **tel 75 16 60 02; toverakvaag@msn.com**

♿ (htd) ⓦ ♨ ⚲ ▣ ⁄ 🦋 ⑪ ⚓ 🛒 ⚠

Nr Krokstrand bdge on E6, 18km S of Artic Circle & approx 50km N of Mo i Rana. 2*, Med, pt shd, pt sl, EHU (10A) NOK40; cooking facs; 20% statics; phone; train; Eng spkn; adv bkg acc; ccard acc; fishing; CKE. *"Conv Polar Circle Cent; gd; recep in café opp."* NOK 256, 1 Jun-20 Sep. 2018

KVISVIKA *1R1* (8km NE Coastal) *63.10910, 8.07875* **Magnillen Camping,** 6674 Kvisvika (Møre og Romsdal) **tel 71 53 23 59; jarl-mo@online.no; www.magnillen.no**

♿ ⓦ ♨ ♿ ▣ ⁄ ⓂⓈⓅ 🦋 ⚓ ⚠

Fr W turn L off E39 approx 5km after Vettafjellet (N); thro Kvisvika & after another 9km turn L into site; sp. Sm, unshd, serviced pitches; EHU (10A) NOK30; gas; bbq; sw nr; red long stay; 50% statics; Eng spkn; adv bkg acc; ccard acc; boat hire; CKE. *"Site adj sm harbour; gd views."* **NOK 170** 2016

LAERDALSOYRI *1B2* (26km E Rural) *61.06725, 7.82170* **Borgund Hyttesenter and Camping,** 6888 Borgund in Laerdal **tel 57 66 81 71 or 90 62 08 59 (mob); ovoldum@alb.no; hyttesenter.com**

⑫ ☩ ♿ ⓦ ♿ ▣ ⁄ ⓂⓈⓅ ⑪ ⚠

Site on L of E16 just aft Borgunds Tunnel. Well sp in adv aft rd to Borgund Stave Church. Sm, hdstg, unshd, EHU (16A) no earth; bbq; cooking facs; red long stay; TV; 10% statics; phone; bus 500m; Eng spkn; adv bkg acc; bike hire. *"Gd for Borgund Stave Church, Laerdal tunnel, Glacier ctr & historic rtes; gd."* NOK 220 2017

LAERDALSOYRI *1B2* (0.8km NW Rural/Coastal) *61.10056, 7.47031* **Lærdal Ferie & Fritidspark,** Grandavegen 5, 6886 Lærdal (Sogn og Fjordane) **tel 57 66 66 95; info@laerdalferiepark.com; www.laerdalferiepark.com**

☩ ♿ (htd) ⓦ ♨ ⚲ ♿ ▣ ⁄ ⓂⓈⓅ 🦋 ⑪ 🍽 ⑪ ⚓ 🛒 ⚠ 🌳 shgl adj

Site on N side of Lærdal off Rv5/E16 adj Sognefjord. 4*, Med, unshd, EHU NOK40 (poss no earth); bbq; cooking facs; red long stay; TV; phone; Eng spkn; ccard acc; games rm; bike hire; golf 12km; boat hire; games area; tennis; CKE. *"Modern, clean, gd value site; excel san & cooking facs; lovely location adj fjord ferry terminal & nr attractive vill; gd touring base; friendly, helpful owners - will open on request outside dates shown; nice site next to Fjord; 10% discount for CAMC members; nr worlds longest tunnel."* NOK 270, 27 Mar-25 Oct. 2019

LANGFJORDBOTN *2G1* (1km S Rural) *70.02781, 22.2817* **Altafjord Camping,** 9545 Langfjordbotn (Finnmark) **tel 78 43 80 00; booking@altafjord-camping.no; www.altafjord-camping.no**

☩ ♿ (htd) ⓦ ♨ ▣ ⁄ 🦋 ⑪ 🛒 nr 🌳 shgl

On E6, 600m S of exit to Bognelv, site adj to fjord across E6, sp. Dist by rd fr Alta 80km. 3*, Med, hdstg, unshd, terr, serviced pitches; EHU (16A); gas; cooking facs; sw; TV; 50% statics; phone; Eng spkn; ccard acc; fishing; sauna; bike hire. *"Friendly owner; excel views; boat hire; mountaineering."* NOK 271, 1 Jun-1 Sep. 2016

LARVIK *1C4* (1km S Urban) *59.04902, 10.03330* **Larvic Bobilparkering,** Tollerudden, Larvik (Vestfold) **www.bobilplassen.no**

⑫ ☩ ⁄ 🦋

Fr E18 exit at Rv303 twd Larvik. At rndabt take 1st exit onto Strandpromenaden. Sm, hdstg, unshd, EHU (3A); bbq. *"Gd; parking lot for m'vans; NH only; 8 mkd pitches, honesty box for payment."* **NOK 137** 2016

LILLEHAMMER *1C2* (10km S Urban) *61.10275, 10.46278* **Camping Lillehammer,** Dampsagveien 47, 2609 Lillehammer (Oppland) **tel 61 25 33 33; resepsjon@lillehammer-camping.no; www.lillehammer-camping.no**

⑫ ☩ ♿ ⓦ ♨ ⚲ ♿ ▣ ⁄ ⓂⓈⓅ 🦋 ⑪ 🛒 nr ⚠

Exit E6 at Lillehammer Sentrum. Turn 1st R at 1st rndabt, foll rd around Strandtorget shopping cent, cont approx 1.5km along lakeside rd. 4*, Med, hdstg, mkd, unshd, EHU (10A) inc (check earth); gas; TV; phone; Eng spkn; adv bkg acc; ccard acc; CKE. *"Excel san facs, site adj Lake Mjøsa; gd views, conv town & skiing areas; site adj to c'van cent, spare parts etc; facs need updating."* **NOK 300** 2016

LOM *1C2* (0.1km E Rural) *61.83812, 8.56969*
Camping Nordal Turistsenter, 2686 Lom (Oppland)
tel 61 21 93 00; booking@nordalturistsenter.no;
www.nordalturistsenter.no

🐕 👫 (htd) 🅆🅓 ♨ ♿ ♿ ✉ 🅼🅿 🍸 🅗 ⌇ nr 🏕

In cent Lom at x-rds R of Rv15. Ent by rndabt bet
Esso stn & recep. Site at foot of Sognefjell Pass.
4*, Med, pt shd, EHU (10A) (no earth); cooking facs;
TV; 10% statics; Eng spkn; adv bkg acc; ccard acc;
sauna; CKE. *"Split level site; bottom level quiet; top
level adj to recep - often noisy due to rd noise & w/
end coach parties; gd, modern san facs; mosquitoes
troublesome in hot weather; busy tourist area; pleasant
site; nice vill."* **NOK 356, 15 May-30 Sep.** **2015**

LUNDE *1C3* (0.8km W Rural) *59.29844, 9.09041*
Telemark Kanalcamping, Slusevegen 21, 3825
Lunde **tel 91 57 54 21; post@kanalcamping.no;**
www.kanalcamping.no

🐕 👫 🅆🅓 ♨ ♿ ♿ ✉ 🅼🅿 ⌇

Fr Rv 359 foll sp to Lunde slues. Site on L 1km fr
cent of Lunde. Med, hdstg, unshd, sl, EHU (16A); bbq;
twin axles; bus/train 1km; Eng spkn; adv bkg acc; boat
hire; CKE. *"Site on Telemark canal; lovely position;
gd cycling/walking; lake adj; site & san facs being
developed, current san facs adequate (2015); vg."*
NOK 210, Mar-Sep. **2015**

MALVIK *1D1* (2km E Rural) *63.43243, 10.70778*
Storsand Gård Camping (ST68), 7563 Malvik (Sør-
Trøndelag) **tel 73 97 63 60; post@storsandcamping.
no; www.storsandcamping.no**

👫 🅆🅓 ♨ ♿ ✉ 🅼 🏕 🐟 shgl

On N side of E6 N, site sp. Rec use E6 toll rd fr S, 2nd
exit after tunnel. Many lge speed humps on local
rd Rv950, care needed. 4*, Lge, unshd, EHU (16A);
cooking facs; TV; 10% statics; phone; games area;
fishing. **NOK 364, 15 May-1 Sep.** **2015**

MALVIK *1D1* (2km W Coastal) *63.44064, 10.63978*
Vikhammer Camping, Vikhammerløkka 4, 7560
Vikhammer **tel 73 97 61 64; vikcampi@online.no;**
www.vikhammer.no

12 🐕 👫 (htd) 🅆🅓 ♨ ♿ ✉ 🅼🅿 ⌇ 🅗 🅼 nr

E fr Trondheim on E6. Immed bef toll plaza take
ramp sp Vikhammer/Ransheim & turn R, then foll
sp Vikhammer. After 6km at traff lts cont strt on
Rv950 to rndabt & take 3rd exit sp motel & site.
Fr N exit E6 after airport sp Hell, then Malvik/
Hommelvik. Then take Rv950 to site. NB Many lge
speed humps on Rv950, care req. RV950 appears as
24 on Sat Nav. 3*, Sm, unshd, terr, EHU (16A) NOK30,
no earth; bbq; 75% statics; phone; bus adj; Eng spkn;
adv bkg acc; ccard acc; CKE. *"Insuffiicient san facs;
site muddy after rain; migrant workers in statics."*
NOK 240 **2015**

MANDAL *1B4* (3.5km N Rural) *58.04213, 7.49436*
Sandnes Camping, Holumsveien 133, 4516 Mandal
(Vest-Agder) **tel 98 88 73 66; sandnescamping@
online.no; www.sandnescamping.com**

🐕 👫 (htd) 🅆🅓 ♨ ♿ ✉ 🅼🅿 🐾 ⌇ 🅗 nr 🅼 nr 🐟 sand 2.5km

On E39 Kristiansand to Stavanger. Turn N onto
Rv455, site on R 1.4km. 3*, Med, hdstg, pt shd, EHU
(16A) NOK40 (poss rev pol); bbq; cooking facs; sw
nr; 5% statics; phone; Eng spkn; adv bkg acc; fishing;
boating; CKE. *"Excel, well-kept site; friendly, helpful
owners; superb scenery; nature trails thro adj pine
forest; Mandal pretty town with longest sandy beach in
Norway, conv Kristiansand ferry & Lindesnes, Norway's
most S point."* **NOK 284, 1 May-1 Sep.** **2019**

MAURVANGEN *1C2* (0.1km SW Rural) *61.48838,
8.84176* **Maurvangen Hyttegrend Camping,**
Besseggen Fjellpark, 2680 Maurvangen VÅGÅ
(Oppland) **tel 61 23 89 22; post@maurvangen.no;**
www.maurvangen.no

12 👫 🅆🅓 ♨ ♿ ✉ 🅼🅿 🐾 ⌇ 🅗 🅳 🅼 🏕

At rv bdge turn off Rv51. Foll sp. Med, hdstg, pt shd,
pt sl, EHU (10A) inc; bbq; cooking facs; sw nr; TV;
phone; Eng spkn; adv bkg acc; cycling; fishing; CKE.
*"White water rafting; gd views; rd 51 poss clsd Nov to
mid-May; gd hill walking cent; lovely site."*
NOK 300 **2016**

MELHUS *1C1* (8km NW Coastal) *63.32635, 10.21564*
Øysand Camping (ST38), Øysandan, 7224 Melhus
(Sør-Trøndelag) **tel 72 87 24 15 or 92 08 71 74 (mob);**
post@oysandcamping.no; www.oysandcamping.no

🐕 👫 🅆🅓 ♨ ♿ ✉ ⌇ 🍸 🅗 🅼 🏕 🐟 adj

Fr Melhus, N on E6; then L (W) onto E39; site sp.
2*, Med, mkd, unshd, EHU (10A) NOK50; bbq; cooking
facs; sw nr; red long stay; phone; Eng spkn; ccard acc;
games area; fishing adj; boating adj; CKE. *"Fair site
with gd views; facs stretched if full; next to Fjord;
beach open to day trippers; barrier clsd at night."*
NOK 240, 1 May-1 Sep. **2019**

MO I RANA *2F2* (17km SW Rural) *66.23307,
13.89178* **Yttervik Camping,** Sørlandsveien 874, 8617
Dalsgrenda (Nordland) **tel 75 16 45 65 or 90 98 73 55
(mob); ranjas@online.no; www.yttervikcamping.no**

🐕 👫 (htd) 🅆🅓 ♨ ✉ 🐾 ⌇ 🅼 🏕

Sp S of Mo i Rana, on W side of E6, cross sm bdge
over rlwy, diff for long o'fits. Sm, mkd, hdstg, unshd,
EHU (16A) NOK 50 (no earth); 50% statics; Eng
spkn; adv bkg acc; ccard acc; fishing; CKE. *"Pleasant
location on edge fjord; friendly owners; clean, small
well-run site; gd new facs (2015); rd works on E6, easier
access to site in 2017; kitchen/diner; some road noise."*
NOK 250, 1 Jun-15 Sep. **2018**

MOLDE *1B1* (4km E Rural) *62.74258, 7.2333* **Camping Kviltorp,** Fannestrandveien 140, 6400 Molde (Møre og Romsdal) **tel 71 21 17 42 or 47 90 14 83 05 (mob); kviltorp.camping@online.no; www.kviltorpcamping.no**

On app fr S, Rv64 (toll) turn L onto E39/Rv62, site on L, sp. Nr airport. 3*, Med, pt shd, pt sl, EHU (16A) NOK35; gas; sw nr; TV; phone; Eng spkn; ccard acc; solarium; boating; fishing; CKE. *"Conv Molde; adj Romsdal Fjord (some pitches avail on fjord-side); wonderful mountain views; excel, clean facs; poor security - site open to rd on 1 side; helpful owners; aircraft & rd noise; gd site; pool 3km; cycle track into Molde."* **NOK 370** **2019**

MOSJOEN *2E3* (2km E Rural) *65.83453, 13.21971* **Mosjøen Camping & Hotel,** Kippermoen, 8657 Mosjøen (Nordland) **tel 75 17 79 00; mosjoen-camping@hotmail.com; www.mosjoencamping.no**

E6 by-passes town, well sp on W side of E6 by rndabt. Fr S only mkd by flag 500m bef rndabt at start Mosjøen bypass. 4*, Med, hdstg, unshd, terr, EHU (16A) NOK40; twin axles; TV; 40% statics; phone; Eng spkn; adv bkg acc; ccard acc; games rm; CKE. *"Clean, v basic san facs; gd site; gd kitchen facs and san facs, friendly staff; lge spmkt nrby; pizza rest; bowling alley; lively local ctr; gd."* **NOK 298** **2017**

NORDKAPP *2H1* (0.1km S Rural/Coastal) *71.16795, 25.78174* **Nordkapphallen Carpark,** 9764 Nordkapp (Finnmark) **tel 78 47 68 60; nordkapphallen@rica.no; www.rica.no**

N on E69. Hdstg, unshd, pt sl, own san req. *"NOK 285 per person for 24hrs (max stay); no other o'night or site charges; 1 Nov-1 Apr private vehicles not permitted - buses in convoy (daily) only; price inc visit to Nordkapp Cent; no facs; very exposed gravel surface; excel for viewing midnight sun."* **NOK 285** **2019**

NOTODDEN *1C3* (1km W Rural) *59.55850, 9.24878* **Notodden Bobilcamp,** Nesøya 11, 3674 Notodden **tel 47 35 01 33 10; notcamp@notoddencamping.com; www.notoddencamping.com**

1km W of Notodden on the E134. Sm, hdstg, pt shd, bus/tram 1km. *"City run stop over; low charge for all facs except electric; no one on site, owner calls in evening."* **NOK 130** **2019**

ODDA *1A3* (2km S Rural) *60.0533, 6.5426* **Odda Camping,** Jordalsveien 29, 5750 Odda (Hordaland) **tel 94 14 12 79; post@oddacamping.no; www.oddacamping.no**

Sp on Rv13; adj sports complex, nr lakeside. 3*, Med, pt shd, EHU (16A) NOK40; bbq; Eng spkn; games area; bike hire; watersports; lake fishing. *"Beautiful area; nr Hardanger Fjord; watersports with canoes for hire; private san facs avail; owner owns a guesthouse where you can use wifi & organise trips."* **NOK 150** **2016**

OPPDAL *1C1* (13km SW Rural) *62.49886, 9.58853* **Magalaupe Camping,** 7340 Oppdal (Sør-Trøndelag) **tel 72 42 46 84 or 99 25 99 93 (mob); anja.moene@gmail.com; www.magalaupe.no**

On W side of E6 Dombås to Trondheim rd, sp on side of Rv Driva. 2*, Med, unshd, pt sl, EHU (10-16A) NOK20; cooking facs; TV; 10% statics; Eng spkn; sauna; bike hire; fishing. *"Sh walk to waterfalls; musk oxen safaries run by owner; excel; facs satisfactory; quiet site."* **NOK 158** **2015**

OPPDAL *1C1* (12km W Rural) *62.61640, 9.47845* **Trollheimsporten Turistsenter Bobil Plass,** Festa, 7340 Oppdal **tel 47 48464241 or 41339130; turist@oppdal.com; campingoppdal.no**

In Oppal on E6 take turning onto Rte 70. Site on R of Rte 70 in about 15km. Sm, hdstg, pt sl, EHU; TV; 50% statics; Eng spkn. *"This site is only for MH; vg."* **NOK 150** **2016**

OPPDAL *1C1* (36.4km W Rural) *62.54191, 9.10602* **Gjora Camping,** Fjellgardsvegen 35, 6613 **tel 71 69 41 49 or 91 73 79 75; endre@nisja.no**

35km W of Oppdal on Rv70. 1km fr Gjora centre. 3*, Sm, pt shd, EHU 10A (NOK45); cooking facs; twin axles; Eng spkn; adv bkg acc; ccard acc. *"In deep wooded valley on N side of Dovrefjell national pk; gd walking area, especially to Amotan waterfalls; many traditional wooden fmhses nrby; comfortable kitchen/diner; vg."* **NOK 175, 1 May-1 Oct.** **2018**

ORNES *2E2* (7km NW Rural) *66.91327, 13.62995* **Reipa Camping,** N 8146 Reipa **tel 75 75 57 74 or 90 95 60 47; post@reipacamping.com; www.reipacamping.com**

Head NE on Havneveien twd Chr. Tidemanns vei/Rv17, then turn R onto Havneveien/Fv456. Sm, EHU inc (16A); Eng spkn; adv bkg acc; ccard acc; CKE. *"Gd NH on classic Rv17."* **NOK 230** **2019**

OS I OSTERDALEN *1D1* (2km NE Rural) *62.50430, 11.25938* **Røste Hyttetun & Camping,** 2550 Os I Østerdalen (Sør-Trøndelag) **tel 62 49 70 55; post@ rostecamping.no; www.rostecamping.no**

Sp on Rv30. 3*, Sm, EHU NOK40; cooking facs; TV; 10% statics; fishing 150m. **NOK 207**   **2016**

OSLO *1C3* (5km W Urban) *59.91802, 10.67554* **Sjølyst Marina Campervan Parking,** Drammensveien 160, Sjølyst Båtopplag, 0273 Oslo **tel 22 50 91 93; post@bobilparkering.no; www.bobilparkering.no**

Fr E exit E18 at junc after Bygdøy (museums) junc. At rndabt take last exit, go under E18 & into site. Fr W leave E18 at Sjølyst junc, at bottom of slip rd turn R into site. Sm, hdstg, unshd, EHU inc; own san rec; bbq; bus adj; Eng spkn; clsd 2300-0700. *"Gd, basic site, pt of marina; m'vans only - pay at machine; san facs clsd o'night; 30 min walk city cent."* **NOK 300, 1 Jun-15 Sep.**   **2016**

OSLO *1C3* (9km NW Urban) *59.9623, 10.6429* **NAF Camping Bogstad,** Ankerveien 117, Røa, 0766 Oslo **tel 22 51 08 00; bogstad@naf.no; www.bogstad camping.no**

Fr N on E16 cont to E18 & turn E twd Oslo. After approx 7km exit & proceed N twds Røa and Bogstad. Site sp adj Oslo golf club. 4*, V lge, mkd, pt shd, pt sl, EHU (10A) NOK50 (long lead poss req); 25% statics; bus to Oslo 100m; Eng spkn; adv bkg acc; ccard acc; CKE. *"Beautiful area with walking trails; avoid area of site with statics & many ssn workers (behind recep); far end OK with lake views; modern, clean san facs; helpful staff; recep open 24 hrs; conv Oslo cent; bus stop nrby, bus every 10 mins; lake nrby; 30 mins to cent; gd."* **NOK 434**   **2019**

"Satellite navigation makes touring much easier"

Remember most sat navs don't know if you're towing or in a larger vehicle – always use yours alongside maps and site directions.

OYSTESE *1A3* (2.4km SSW Coastal) *60.36828, 6.18969* **Hardanger Feriesenter,** Hardangerfjordvegen 341, 5600 Norheimsund **tel 92 05 09 55; booking@ hardangerferiesenter.no; www.hardanger-resort.com**

Directly at Rv7 in Kvam, app 2.5km E of Norheimsund on the shores of Hardangerfjord. Sm, unshd, pt sl, EHU (10A); bbq; cooking facs; 50% statics; Eng spkn; CKE. *"Boat hire & pier on site; vg."* **NOK 250**   **2015**

PORSGRUNN *1C4* (5km SE Rural) *59.11183, 9.71208* **Camping Olavsberget,** Nystrandveien 64, 3944 Porsgrunn (Vestfold) **tel 35 51 12 05; irene@olavsbergetcamping.no**

Leave E18 at Eidanger onto Rv354 N; foll camp sp for 1km; site on L. Fr Porsgrunn foll Rv36 S; just bef E18 junc turn L; foll sp as above. Med, unshd, pt sl, EHU (16A) NOK30 (no earth); 60% statics; Eng spkn; CKE. *"Well-run site; public access to beach thro site; gd walks in wood; visits to Maritime Brevik & mineral mine, Porsgrunn porcelain factory & shop, Telemark Canal inc boat tour."* **NOK 200**   **2019**

RANDSVERK *1C2* (0.8km NE Rural) *61.73016, 9.08155* **Randsverk Camping,** Fjellvegen 1972 Randsverk (Oppland) **tel 61 23 87 45; randsverk. kiosk@c2i.net; www.randsverk-camping.no**

Heading S on Rv51, 20km fr junc with Rv15, site on L on ent vill of Randsverk. Med, hdstg, unshd, sl, terr, EHU (10A) inc (long lead poss req); bbq; cooking facs; twin axles; Eng spkn. *"V scenic rds; excel area for walking or driving excursions; excel san facs; vg site in area."* **NOK 270**   **2015**

RISOR *1C4* (18km SW Coastal) *58.69083, 9.16333* **Sørlandet Feriecenter,** Sandnes, 4950 Risør **tel 37 15 40 80; sorferie@online.no; www.sorlandet-feriesenter.no**

Fr N take E18 to Sørlandsporten then Rv416 to Risør, then Rv411 to Laget. Foll sp Sørlandet. Fr S exit E18 at Tvedestrand & cont to Laget, then foll site sp. Site is 20km by rd fr Risør. 4*, Med, mkd, pt shd, EHU inc; cooking facs; TV (pitch); 10% statics; Eng spkn; adv bkg acc; bike hire; games rm; boat hire; tennis 1km; watersports. *"Fitness rm; private san facs avail."* **NOK 392**   **2019**

RODBERG *1C3* (6.5km SE Rural) *60.23533, 9.0040* **Fjordgløtt Camping,** Vrenne, 3630 Rødberg (Buskerud) **tel 32 74 13 35 or 97 15 96 53 (mob); info@fjordglott.net; www.fjordglott.net**

Fr Rødberg on Rv40 dir Kongsberg, take R turn sp Vrenne, cross bdge & foll sp past power stn. 4*, Med, mkd, pt shd, terr, serviced pitches; EHU (16A) NOK30; sw; 40% statics; phone; Eng spkn; ccard acc; fishing; sauna; CKE. *"Lovely views of fjord; excel facs; well kept."* **NOK 268**   **2019**

ROLDAL *1B3* (0.5km E Rural) *59.83103, 6.82888* **Røldal Hyttegrend & Camping,** Kyrkjevegen 49, 5760 Røldal (Hordaland) **tel 07 90 05 44 64; adm@ roldal-camping.no; www.roldal-camping.no**

Fr E on E134 turn L on ent vill, site sp. 4*, Sm, pt shd, EHU (10A) NOK30; gas; cooking facs; sw nr; TV; 20% statics; phone; Eng spkn; adv bkg acc; ccard acc; CKE. *"Gd walking, angling."* **NOK 206**   **2019**

ROLDAL *1B3* (1km SW Rural) *59.83012, 6.81061*
Seim Camping, 5760 Røldal (Horda-Rogaland) **tel
53 64 73 71 or 97 53 35 17 (mob) or 90 91 90 63
(mob); seim@seimcamp.no; www.seimcamp.no**

12 ♞ �(htd) WD ⚲ ♁ ♿ ▣ ✎ Ⴤnr Ⴤnr ☶nr ♨

App fr SW on E134, site sp at ent town. Turn R off
main rd & R again. 3*, Med, pt shd, pt sl, EHU (20A)
NOK40; Eng spkn; boating; fishing; CKE. *"Gd walks;
beautiful views; prehistoric burial mounds & museum
on site; poss rd noise."* **NOK 258** **2019**

ROROS *1D1* (0.6km S Urban) *62.57078, 11.38295*
Idrettsparken Hotel & Camping, Øra 25, 7374 Røros
(Sør-Trøndelag) **tel 72 41 10 89; ihotell@online.no;
www.idrettsparken.no**

♙♙(htd) ⚲ ♿ ✎ ☶ Ⴤnr

Heading twd Trondheim on Rv30 to Røros cent, turn
L at rndabt into Peter Møllersvei, over rlwy line, L
again & foll sp to site. Sm, unshd, EHU (16A) NOK35.
*"Tours of museums & mines; nature reserve & nature
park nr; no chem disp - use dump point at fire stn on
Rv30; fair NH."* **NOK 300, 1 May-30 Sep.** **2019**

RORVIK *2E3* (2km NE Coastal) *64.8729, 11.2609*
Nesset Camping, Engan, 7900 Rørvik (Nord-Trøndelag)
tel 74 39 06 60

♙♙(htd) WD ⚲ ✎ ☶

Fr cent of Rørvik on Rv770, foll sp to site. Med,
hdstg, hdg, pt shd, pt sl, terr, EHU (10A); sw nr;
10% statics; Eng spkn. *"Many pitches with fjord view;
facs stretched high ssn; beware of speed bumps on app
rd."* **NOK 250, May-Sep.** **2019**

SARPSBORG *1C3* (10km NW Rural) *59.31800,
10.98049* **Utne Camping,** Desideriasvei 43, 1719
Greaker **tel 47 69 14 71 26; post@utnecamping.no;
www.utnecamping.no**

12 ♞ ♙♙(htd) WD ⚲ ♨ ✎ ☶ ♈ ♨

Leave E6 at junc 9 sp Sollikrysset. Take 118 S
(Desiderias vei), 2km to site on R. 3*, Sm, unshd, pt
sl, EHU (10A) NOK60; bbq; twin axles; TV; bus adj; Eng
spkn; adv bkg acc; ccard acc; games area; CKE. *"Conv
acc fr E6; pleasant open site; excel."* **NOK 294** **2017**

SKARNES *1D3* (10km SW Rural) *60.19910, 11.58054*
Sanngrund Camping, Oslovegen 910, 2100 Skarnes
(Hedmark) **tel 62 96 46 60; booking@sanngrund.no;
www.sanngrund.no**

12 ♙♙(htd) WD ⚲ ♁ ♿ ▣ ✎ ⑪ ♨ ♨

Fr Skarnes foll Rv2 S; site sp on L. Sm, mkd, pt shd,
EHU inc; bbq; cooking facs; sw nr; TV; 50% statics; Eng
spkn; fishing adj; CKE. *"Conv NH to/fr Oslo (approx
70km); pleasant rest; fair site."* **NOK 235** **2016**

SKARSVAG *2G1* (1km SW Coastal) *71.1073, 25.81238*
Kirkeporten Camping, 9763 Skarsvåg (Finnmark)
**tel 90 96 06 48; kipo@kirkeporten.no;
www.kirkeporten.no**

♙♙(htd) WD ⚲ ♿ ✎ MSP ☶ ♈ ♈ ⑪ ♨

Foll E69 fr Honningsvåg for 20km to Skarsvåg junc;
site sp at junc & on L after 2km immed bef vill.
3*, Sm, hdstg, unshd, pt sl, EHU (16A) NOK35; TV; Eng
spkn; adv bkg acc; ccard acc; sauna; CKE. *"Site on edge
sm fishing vill 10km fr N Cape, ringed by mountains;
exposed location; claims to be world's most N site;
helpful, knowledgeable owner; vg rest; clean facs
but stretched if site full; poss reindeer on site; highly
rec; arr early; camping area extended & modernised
(2016)."* **NOK 247, 15 May-15 Sep.** **2016**

SKIBOTN *2G1* (1km SE Rural) *69.38166, 20.29528*
Olderelv Camping (TR30), 9048 Skibotn (Troms)
**tel 77 71 54 44 or 91 13 17 00 (mob); firmapost@
olderelv.no; www.olderelv.no**

♞ ♙♙(htd) WD ⚲ ♁ ♿ ▣ ✎ ☶ ♈ ♈ ♨ ♨ ♨

W of E6 1km N of junc at E8. 4*, Lge, mkd, hdstg,
unshd, pt sl, EHU (16A) NOK40; bbq; cooking facs;
twin axles; 80% statics; phone; Eng spkn; adv bkg acc;
ccard acc; solarium; sauna. *"Well-maintained & clean;
dryest area of Troms; vg walking; v busy; vg; car wash."*
NOK 290, 15 May-1 Sep. **2019**

SOGNDALSFJORA *1B2* (4.5km SE Coastal) *61.2118,
7.12106* **Camping Kjørnes,** 6856 Sogndal (Sogn og
Fjordane) **tel 57 67 45 80 or 975 44 156 (mob);
camping@kjornes.no; www.kjornes.no**

12 ♞ ♙♙(htd) WD ⚲ ♁ ♿ ▣ ✎ MSP ♈ ⑪nr ☶nr ♨ ♨adj

Fr W foll sp in Sogndal for Kaupanger/Lærdal (Rv5)
over bdge. Fr E (Rv55) turn L at T-junc with rd 5 over
bdge. Site on R; sharp R turn into narr lane (passing
places); site ent on R in approx 500m. 4*, Med, hdstg,
unshd, pt sl, terr, EHU (10-16A) NOK40 (no earth);
cooking facs; twin axles; red long stay; 20% statics;
phone; bus 500m; Eng spkn; adv bkg acc; ccard acc;
boat launch; fishing; CKE. *"Useful for ferries; stunning
location on edge of fjord; superb san facs, the best!;
excel site; v highly rec."* **NOK 290** **2019**

STAVANGER *1A3* (3.5km SW Rural) *58.9525, 5.71388*
Mosvangen Camping, Henrik Ibsens Gate, 4021
Stavanger (Rogaland) **tel 51 53 29 71;
info@mosvangencamping.no; www.
mosvangencamping.no**

♞ ♙♙(htd) WD ⚲ ♁ ♿ ▣ ✎ MSP ☶ ⑪ii ☶ii ♨

Fr Stavanger foll sp E39/Rv510; site well sp.
Fr Sandnes on E39 exit Ullandhaug; foll camp sp.
Med, hdstg, pt shd, sl, EHU (10A) NOK40 (no earth
& poss intermittent supply); cooking facs; sw nr;
phone; bus; Eng spkn; ccard acc; CKE. *"Excel for
wooden city of Stavanger; easy, pleasant walk
to town cent; soft grnd in wet weather; facs well
used but clean but stretched when site full; helpful
manager; excel rustic type of site; bus to cent nr ent."*
NOK 250, 1 Apr-1 Oct. **2016**

STEINKJER *2E3* (14km N Rural) *64.10977, 11.57816*
Follingstua Camping, Haugåshalla 6, 7732 Steinkjer (Nord-Trøndelag) **tel 74 14 71 90; post@follingstua. no; www.follingstua.com**

12 🐕 ♦♦♦ (htd) WC ▲ ♿ 🖥 ✏ MSP 🦋 ♗ 🍴 ⓘ ♨ 🏔

N on E6, site on R, well sp. 3*, Sm, mkd, hdstg, unshd, terr, EHU (16A) NOK40; bbq; twin axles; TV; 60% statics; phone; bus 200m; Eng spkn; adv bkg acc; bike hire; boating; fishing. "Excel san facs down 10 steps; lake adj; some lakeside pitches; nr Gold Rd tour of local craft & food producers; excel." **NOK 292**
2017

STEINKJER *2E3* (2km E Urban) *64.02246, 11.50745*
Camping Guldbergaunet, Elvenget 34, 7716 Steinkjer (Nord-Trøndelag) **tel 74 16 20 45; g-book@online.no; guldbergaunetcamping.no**

12 🐕 ♦♦♦ (htd) WC ▲ ♿ 🖥 ✏ MSP 🦋 ♗ 🍴 nr ⓘ nr 🖥 nr 🏔

E fr town cent on E6. Foll Rv762 at 2km L past school. Site at end. 3*, Med, mkd, pt shd, pt sl, EHU 10; bbq; cooking facs; sw nr; twin axles; Eng spkn; adv bkg acc; ccard acc; fishing. "On peninsula bet two rvs; friendly; gd NH; facs up stairs; 10 mins walk to town along rv; gd." **NOK 240**
2019

STORJORD *2F2* (1km SSE Rural) *66.81317, 15.40055*
Saltdal Turistsenter, 8255 Storjord (Nordland) **tel 75 68 24 50; firmapost@saltdal-turistsenter.no; www.saltdal-turistsenter.no**

12 ♦♦♦ (htd) WC ▲ ♿ 🖥 ✏ MSP 🦋 ♗ ⓘ ♨ 🖥 🏔

Site is 35km S of Rognan by-pass on E6, 700m N of junc of Rv77, adj filling stn. Med, mkd, hdstg, pt shd, terr, EHU (10A) NOK25; bbq; cooking facs; 99% statics; phone; Eng spkn; adv bkg acc; CKE. "M'way-style service stn & lorry park; tightly packed cabins & statics; 10 pitches only for tourers; excel rv walks fr site; beautiful area; NH only; secure barrier; clean facs, could be stretched if full." **NOK 305**   **2019**

STRYN *1B2* (10km E Rural) *61.93347, 6.88640*
Mindresunde Camping (SF43), 6783 Stryn (Sogn og Fjordane) **tel 57 87 75 32 or 41 56 63 16 (mob); post@mindresunde.no; www.mindresunde.no**

♦♦♦ (htd) WC ▲ ♿ 🖥 ✏ MSP 🖥 🏔 ✈ shgl

2nd site on Rv15 on N side of rd. 3*, Sm, mkd, unshd, pt sl, EHU inc (earth prob); TV; Eng spkn; adv bkg acc; car wash; CKE. "Well-kept, pleasant site; many pitches on lake; friendly staff; site yourself; vg views; excel facs; conv Geiranger, Briksdal glacier & Strynefjellet summer ski cent; gd walking." **NOK 289,** 1 May-31 Oct.   **2019**

STRYN *1B2* (12km E Rural) *61.9314, 6.92121*
Strynsvatn Camping, Meland, 6783 Stryn (Sogn og Fjordane) **tel 57 87 75 43; camping@strynsvatn.no; www.strynsvatn.no**

♦♦♦ (htd) WC ▲ ♿ ✏ MSP 🦋 ♗ 🖥 🏔

On Rv15 Lom to Stryn, on L. 4*, Sm, unshd, terr, EHU (10A) inc (poss earth fault); TV; 20% statics; Eng spkn; adv bkg acc; ccard acc; sauna; CKE. "Superb site; lake adj; excel facs & v clean, gd views/walking; v friendly owners." **NOK 247,** 1 May-30 Sep.   **2016**

TANA *2H1* (5km SE Rural) *70.1663, 28.2279*
Tana Familiecamping, Skiippagurra, 9845 Tana (Finnmark) **tel 78 92 86 30; tana@famcamp.net**

♦♦♦ (htd) WC ▲ 🖥 ✏ MSP 🦋 ⓗ 🏔

On ent Tana fr W, cross bdge on E6, heading E sp Kirkenes; site on L in approx 4km. 3*, Sm, unshd, pt sl, EHU (16A); bbq; Eng spkn; ccard acc; sauna. **NOK 217,** 20 May-1 Oct.   **2016**

TENNEVOLL *2F2* (5km SW Rural) *68.67881, 17.91421* **Lapphaugen Turiststasjon,** General Fleischers Vei 365, 9357 Tennevoll **tel 77 17 71 27; postmaster@lapphaugen.no; www.lapphaugen.no**

🐕 ♦♦♦ ▲ ♿ 🖥 ✏ MSP 🖥 ♨ 🏔

On the L of E6 approx 60km N of Narvik. Sm, hdstg, unshd, pt sl, terr, EHU (16A) NOK40; bbq; cooking facs; twin axles; red long stay; 50% statics; Eng spkn; adv bkg acc. "Gd." **NOK 200,** 12 Feb-16 Dec.   **2017**

TINN AUSTBYGD *1B3* (8km S Rural) *59.98903, 8.81665* **Sandviken Camping (TE13),** 3650 Tinn Austbygd (Telemark) **tel 35 09 81 73; post@ sandviken-camping.no; www.sandviken-camping.no**

12 🐕 ♦♦♦ (htd) WC ▲ ♿ 🖥 ✏ 🖥 🏔

Site is off Rv364 on L after passing thro Tinn Austbygd. 4*, Med, pt shd, EHU (10A) NOK35 (check earth); gas; bbq; cooking facs; sw; TV; 10% statics; phone; Eng spkn; games area; boat hire; sauna; games rm; CKE. "Superb, peaceful location at head of Lake Tinnsjø; sh walk thro woods to shops & bank; conv for museum at Rjukan heavy water plant." **NOK 245**
2016

TJOTTA *2E3* (26km N Rural) *65.94692, 12.46255*
Sandnessjøen Camping, Steiro, 8800 Sandnessjøen, Norge **tel 97 56 20 50 or 75 04 54 40; post@ssj.no; www.ssj.no**

🐕 ♦♦♦ (htd) WC ▲ ♿ 🖥 ✏

Head NW on Rv17 twrds Parkveien. Site is on R. Sm, unshd, pt sl, EHU; bbq; cooking facs; Eng spkn; ccard acc. "Excel san facs; fjord views; gd hiking & fishing; excel site." **NOK 250,** 1 May-31 Aug.   **2019**

TOSBOTN *2 E3* (550km E Rural) *65.32508, 12.97020*
Tosbotn Camping, Tosbotn, 8960 Tosbotnet **tel 75 02 61 50; mhermann1955@gmail.com; tosbotn-camping.no**

12 🐕 ♦♦♦ WC ▲ 🖥 ✏ MSP 🦋 ♗ ✈ shingle (1km)

In Tosbotn, sp off Fv76. 25km W of E6, 70km E Bronnoysund. Sm, pt shd, EHU 10A (NOK30); bbq; sw nr; twin axles; Eng spkn; adv bkg acc; ccard acc. "V ltd area for campers; boats for hire; facs poor; NH only." **NOK 220**
2018

TREUNGEN *1B4* (18km N Rural) *59.15560, 8.50611*
Søftestad Camping, Nissedal, 3855 Treungen (Aust-
Agder) **tel 41 92 76 20; www.facebook.com/Softestad**

⊞ ⌗ 🚿 ♿ 🗑 ⚲ 🦋 ⛺

N fr Kristiansand on Rv41 to Treungen, then
alongside E edge of Nisser Water to Nissedal,
site sp. Sm, shd, EHU (10A) inc; bbq; red long stay;
phone; bus adj; Eng spkn; adv bkg acc; CKE. *"Close to
Telemarken heavy water plant; beautiful alt rte N fr
Kristiansand - rd suitable for towed c'vans; gorgeous
views over lake."* **NOK 162, 1 May-1 Sep.**   **2019**

TROGSTAD *1D3* (6km N Rural) *59.68888, 11.29275*
Olberg Camping, Olberg, 1860 Trøgstad (Østfold)
tel 07 41 76 56 72

⊞ (htd) ⌗ 🚿 ♿ 🗑 ⚲ 🦋 ⛺ 🚣 🎣 3km

Fr Mysen on E18 go N on Rv22 for approx 20km dir
Lillestrøm. Site is 2km 2 of Båstad. 3*, Sm, hdg, pt
shd, EHU (10-16A) NOK35; bbq; red long stay; TV;
phone; Eng spkn; adv bkg acc; ccard acc; tennis 200m;
fishing; CKE. *"Site on lge, working farm with elk safaris;
local bread & crafts; farm museum; conv Oslo (40km);
v helpful staff; ice-skating; gd for NH or longer."*
NOK 274, 1 May-1 Oct.   **2019**

> ## "There aren't many sites open at this time of year"
>
> If you're travelling outside peak season
> remember to call ahead to check site opening
> dates – even if the entry says 'open all year'.

TROMSO *2F1* (27km NE Coastal) *69.77765, 19.38273*
Skittenelv Camping, Ullstindveien 736, 9022
Krokelvdalen (Troms) **tel 46 85 80 00; post@
skittenelvcamping.no; www.skittenelvcamping.no**

🐕 ⌗ (htd) ⊞ 🚿 ♿ 🗑 ⚲ 🦋 🍴 🎣 🛒 ⛴ (htd) 🛶

Fr S end of Tromsø Bdge on E8, foll sps to Kroken
& Oldervik. Site on N side of rd Fv53. 4*, Med, hdstg,
unshd, EHU (10A) NOK50; bbq; TV; 10% statics;
ccard acc; waterslide; fishing; sauna; games rm; CKE.
*"Beautiful situation on edge of fjord; arctic sea birds;
some facs dated but nice; location o'looking Fjord."*
NOK 320, 15 May-30 Sep.   **2019**

TROMSO *2F1* (5km E Rural) *69.64735, 19.01505*
Tromsø Camping, 9020 Tromsdalen (Troms)
**tel 77 63 80 37; post@tromsocamping.no;
www.tromsocamping.no**

12 🐕 ⌗ ⊞ 🚿 ⚲ 🗑 🍴 🛒 ⛺

At rndabt on edge of Tromsø take 2nd exit under
E8 bdge. Shortly turn R & foll sp. Do not cross narr
bdge but turn R then fork L to site. 3*, Sm, unshd,
EHU (10-16A) NOK50; Eng spkn; CKE. *"V busy site;
surrounded by fast rv after rain; poss mkt traders
on site; rec visit to Arctic church at midnight; many
improvements; excel san facs (2016)."* **NOK 356**
                              2016

TRONDHEIM *1C1* (14km W Rural) *63.45004,
10.20230* **Flakk Camping (ST19),** 7070 Flakk (Sør-
Trøndelag) **tel 07 94 05 46 85; contact@flakk-
camping.no; www.flakk-camping.no**

🐕 ⌗ ⊞ 🚿 ♿ 🗑 ⚲ 🛒 🛒 nr

Fr N on E6 to Trondheim cent, then foll sp Fosen
onto Rv715 W; site sp & adj Flakk ferry terminal; fr S
to Trondheim take Rv707 to site & ferry. 3*, Med,
unshd, pt sl, EHU (10A) NOK40 (check earth); bus to
city; Eng spkn; adv bkg acc; ccard acc; CKE. *"V well-
kept site; clean facs; pleasant view over fjord; parts
poss muddy after rain; site by ferry terminal (Need to
be on R), some ferry noise at night; helpful owner; no
earth on elec."* **NOK 361, 1 May-1 Sep.**   **2019**

ULSVAG *2F2* (3km NE Coastal) *68.13273, 15.89699*
Sorkil Fjordcamping, Sorkil 8276 **tel 75 77 16 60 or
41 66 08 42 (mob); kontakt@sorkil.no;
www.sorkil.no**

⌗ (htd) ⊞ 🚿 🗑 ⚲ 🦋 🍴 🛒 adj

Head NE fr Ulsvag on E6, turn R in abt 2.7km onto
site. Sm, mkd, unshd, pt sl, EHU (16A) NOK40; bbq;
Eng spkn. *"Lovely site S of ferry; adj Fjord excel for
midnight sun and fishing."* **1 May-30 Sep.**   **2019**

UTVIKA *1C3* (0.5km N Rural) *60.02972, 10.26316*
Utvika Camping (BU14), Utstranda 263, 3531
Utvika (Buskerud) **tel 32 16 06 70; post@utvika.no;
www.utvika.no**

⌗ ⊞ 🚿 ♿ 🗑 ⚲ 🛒 🦋 🍴 🛒 ⛺

Site on loop rd fr E16 N of Nes twd Hønefoss.
Site sp but sp opp site ent v sm. Med, mkd, hdstg,
unshd, pt sl, EHU (10A) NOK30; sw nr; twin axles;
TV (pitch); 80% statics; Eng spkn; adv bkg acc; CKE.
*"Conv Oslo (40km) & better than Oslo city sites,
busy, friendly site; san facs inadequate when busy."*
NOK 289, 1 May-1 Oct.   **2017**

VADSO *2H1* (18km W Coastal) *70.11935, 29.33155*
Vestre Jakobselv Camping, Lilledalsveien 6, 9801
Vestre Jakobselv (Finnmark) **tel 78 95 60 64;
post@vj-camping.no; www.vj-camping.no**

12 🐕 ⌗ ⊞ 🚿 ♿ 🗑 ⚲ 🦋 🛒 nr

E fr Tana for approx 50km on E6/E75 dir Vadsø, site
sp, 1km N of Vestre Jakobselv. Sm, hdstg, pt shd,
EHU (10A) NOK40; cooking facs; 10% statics; bus
1km; Eng spkn; ccard acc; CKE. *"Conv Vadsø & Vardø -
interesting towns."* **NOK 150**   **2016**

VAGAMO *1C2* (1km S Rural) *61.86950, 9.10291*
Smedsmo Camping, Vågåvegen 80, 2680 Vågåmo
(Oppland) **tel 61 23 74 50; smedsmo@online.no**

🐕 ⌗ ⊞ 🚿 ♿ 🗑 ⚲ ⛺

Behind petrol stn on Rv15 twd Lom. 3*, Med, hdstg,
unshd, EHU (16A) NOK40; bbq; cooking facs; twin
axles; TV; 50% statics; Eng spkn; ccard acc; CKE.
"Gd touring base; site now sep fr g'ge; fair."
NOK 290, 1 May-30 Sep.   **2017**

VALLE *1B3* (12km N Rural) *59.2441, 7.4753*
Flateland Camping & Hyttesenter, 4747 Valle
(Aust-Agder) **tel 95 00 55 00; flateland.camping@
broadpark.no; www.flatelandcamping.no**

🐕 ♦♦♦(htd) ⬜ ▱ ◢ ▱ 🦋 ♈ 🛒nr ⛺

On W side of Rv9 to Bykle, 1km N of junc with Rv45
Dalen. 2*, Med, pt shd, pt sl, EHU (10A) NOK30; bbq;
cooking facs; 20% statics; Eng spkn; ccard acc; boat
hire; CKE. *"Pleasant; site yourself; fee collected pm;
water trampolin; rvside walks; climbing; excel site."*
NOK 160, 1 Jun-1 Sep.   **2019**

VANG *1B2* (1.7km NW Rural) *61.13032, 8.54352*
Bøflaten Camping, 2975 Vang I Valdres (Sogn og
Fjordane) **tel 61 36 74 20; info@boflaten.com;
www.boflaten.com**

12 🐕 ♦♦♦ ⬜ ▱ ♿ ◢ 🦋 ♈ 🛒nr ⛺

Sp on E16 55km NW of Fagernes. 4*, Sm, pt shd,
EHU (10A) NOK40; bbq (charcoal, gas); cooking facs;
sw nr; twin axles; 10% statics; phone; Eng spkn;
ccard acc; games area; CKE. *"Beautiful area; lakeside;
useful NH & gd winter sports site; walks nrby; guided
excursions; boat, canoe, bike & TV hire; excel."*
NOK 237   **2016**

VANGSNES *1B2* (0km N Rural/Coastal) *61.17483,
6.63729* **Solvang Camping & Motel,** 6894 Vangsnes
(Sogn og Fjordane) **tel 57 69 66 20; post@
solvangcamping.com; www.solvangcamping.com**

12 ♦♦♦ ▲ ♿ ◢ ▱ ◢ 🍽 🍺 🛒nr ⛺ 🏊

Site at end of peninsula, on S side of Sognefjord on
Rv13, immed overlkg ferry terminal. 4*, Sm, pt shd,
sl, EHU NOK30; sw; TV; boating; fishing. *"Wonderful
views; useful sh stay/NH for x-ing Sognefjord; some
noise fr ferries; delightful."* **NOK 185**   **2016**

VANGSNES *1B2* (3km S Rural) *61.14515, 6.62330*
Tveit Camping (SF32), 6894 Vangsnes (Sogn og
Fjordane) **tel 57 69 66 00; tveitca@online.no;
www.tveitcamping.no**

🐕 ♦♦♦(htd) ⬜ ▲ ♿ ◢ ▱ MSP 🦋 ♈ 🍺nr 🛒nr ⛺

On Rv13; sp. 3*, Sm, pt shd, terr, EHU (10A) NOK25;
red long stay; TV; 30% statics; phone; boating; bike
hire; boat hire; CKE. *"Sw poss off rocky shore; views of
Sognefjord."* **NOK 192, 1 May-1 Oct.**   **2016**

VASSENDEN *1A2* (2km SW Rural) *61.48785,
6.08366* **PlusCamp Jølstraholmen,** 6847 Vassenden
(Sogn og Fjordane) **tel 95 29 78 79; post@
jolstraholmen.no; www.jolstraholmen.no**

12 🐕 ♦♦♦(htd) ⬜ ▲ ♿ ◢ ▱ MSP 🦋 🍺 🛒 ⛺ 🖼

On R of E39, site is 2km SW of Vassenden at Statoil
petrol stn. 4*, Med, hdg, pt shd, pt sl, terr, EHU (10-
16A) NOK40; bbq; sw; TV (pitch); 70% statics; Eng
spkn; ccard acc; fishing; CKE. *"Rv flows thro site; gd
facs; ski lift 500m; friendly site; ltd facs for tourers;
NH."* **NOK 286**   **2016**

VEGA *2E3* (6km S Rural) *65.64353, 11.95110* **Vega
Camping,** 8980 Vega **tel 47 94 35 00 80; post@
vegacamping.no; www.vegacamping.no**

12 🐕 ♦♦♦(htd) ⬜ ◢ ▱ 🦋

Fr Fv90 head NW, take 1st L onto Fv90, turn L twd
Fv84, turn R onto Fv84. After 1.6km turn L, then
take 2nd L. Site in 450m. Sm, unshd, EHU (16A) inc;
cooking facs; sw; Eng spkn. *"Island ideal for cycling/
walking; Elder Duck cent; beautiful location; cash only;
excel site."* **NOK 250**   **2019**

VESTBY *1C3* (3km N Rural) *59.62620, 10.73126*
Vestby Gjestegard & Hyttepark, Hytteveien 11,
1540 Vestby **tel 47 64 95 98 00; info@vestbyhytte
park.co; www.vestbyhyttepark.no**

12 ♦♦♦ ▲ ◢ ◢ ⛺

Junc 17 on E6. Foll sp. Site behind Esso stn on W
of E6. Sm, hdstg, unshd, pt sl, 90% statics; Eng spkn;
ccard acc; CKE. *"Limited touring space, mainly chalets;
NH only."* **NOK 210**   **2016**

VIKOYRI *1B2* (0.2km N Rural) *61.08884, 6.57721*
Vik Camping, 6891 Vikøyri (Sogn og Fjordane)
tel 57 69 51 25; grolilje@hotmail.com

🐕 ♦♦♦(htd) ⬜ ▲ ◢ ◢ ▱ ♈ 🛒nr

Sp in cent of Vikøyri dir Ligtvor; 67km N of Voss on
Rv13. 2*, Sm, unshd, EHU (10A) (no earth); Eng spkn;
CKE. *"Conv for ferry fr Vangsnes, easier access than
other sites; gd NH."* **NOK 178, 1 May-30 Sep.**   **2016**

VOSS *1A2* (0.3km S Rural) *60.62476, 6.42235*
Voss Camping, Prestegardsmoen 40, 5700 Voss
(Hordaland) **tel 56 51 15 97; post@vosscamping.no;
www.vosscamping.no**

♦♦♦(htd) ⬜ ▲ ◢ ▱ 🛒nr ⛺ 🏊(htd)

Exit town on E16 & camping sp; by lake nr cent of
Voss; app fr W on E16, site visible by lake on R; 2nd
turn on R in town to site in 300m. Sm, mkd, hdstg,
pt shd, terr, EHU (10A) NOK45; 10% statics; phone;
Eng spkn; ccard acc; watersports; bike hire; boat hire;
CKE. *"Excel cent for fjords; cable car stn in walking dist;
tourist bureau; lake adj; most pitches hdstg gravel but
narr/sm."* **NOK 408, 1 May-1 Oct.**   **2019**

LOFOTEN ISLANDS

RAMBERG *2E2* (7km W Rural) *68.0975, 13.1619*
Strand & Skærgårdscamping, 8387 Fredvang
**tel 76 09 42 33 or 76 09 46 46; mail@fredvang
camping.no; www.fredvangcamp.no**

♦♦♦(htd) ⬜ ▲ ◢ ▱ MSP ◢ 🐟 sand adj

Foll Fredvang sp fr E10; site sp in vill cent.
Sm, unshd, EHU (16A) NOK25; cooking facs; TV
(pitch); Eng spkn; boat launch; boat hire; washing
machine NOK20; dryer NOK20; CKE. *"View of midnight
sun; surrounded by sand beach, sea & mountains;
peaceful; gd san facs, tired (unisex), stretched when
busy; friendly."* **NOK 300, 20 May-31 Aug.**   **2019**

SORVAGEN *2E2* (3km N Coastal) *67.90017, 13.04656*
Moskenes Camping, 8392 Sørvågen **tel 99 48 94 05;**
info@moskenescamping.no; www.moskenes
camping.no

♚♟ (htd) ⬛ 🔲 ⊘ 🏕 🦋 📶 ♈ 🍽 ⬛nr

Fr ferry turn L, then immed R opp terminal exit, site
up sh unmade rd, sp. Med, hdstg, unshd, terr, EHU
(16A) NOK20 (no earth); Eng spkn. *"Excel NH; gd san
facs."* **NOK 283, 1 May-15 Sep.**   **2018**

"That's changed – Should I let the Club know?"

If you find something on site that's different
from the site entry, fill in a report and let us
know. See camc.com/europereport.

STAMSUND *2F2* (15km N Rural/Coastal) *68.20429,*
13.88580 **Brustranda Sjøcamping,** Rolfsfjord, 8356
Leknes **tel 76 08 71 00; post@brustranda.no;**
www.brustranda.no

🐴 ♚♟ ⬛ 🏕 ⊘ ⊙ 🔲 ⊘ 🦋 ♈ ⬛ 🏊 shgl adj

Take E10 W fr Svolvaer ferry for approx 19km. After
3rd bdge turn L onto Rv815. Site on L in 22km.
4*, Sm, pt shd, EHU (10A) NOK50 (poss rev pol);
30% statics; Eng spkn; boat hire; fishing. *"Idyllic
setting; mountain views; beach sand 2km; v helpful
staff; san facs stretched when site full; highly rec."*
NOK 200, 1 Jun-31 Aug.   **2018**

SVOLVAER *2F2* (15km W Coastal) *68.20573,*
14.42576 **Sandvika Fjord & Sjøhuscamping (N09),**
Ørsvågveien 45, 8310 Kabelvåg **tel 76 07 81 45;**
post@sandvika-camping.no; www.sandvika-
camping.no

♚♟ ⬛ 🏕 ⊙ ⊘ 🔲 ⊘ 🏕 🦋 ♈ ⊙ ⬛ 🏊 ⬛ 🛶

Sp on S of E10; app lane thro 1 other site. 4*, Lge,
mkd, unshd, terr, EHU (16A) NOK35 (poss rev pol); TV;
phone; bus nr; Eng spkn; ccard acc; fishing; sauna; bike
hire; boating. *"Ideal for trip thro Lofoten Islands; conv
Svolvær main fishing port; vg; beautiful views; helpful
staff; currency exchange; san facs stretched in high
ssn."* **NOK 330, 15 Apr-30 Sep.**   **2019**

SVOLVAER *2F2* (26km NW Coastal) *68.27619,*
14.30207 **Rystad Lofoten Camping,** Brennaveien 235,
8313 Kleppstad **tel 47 91658954; kwes_8@hotmail.
com; www.rystadcamping.com**

♚♟ ⬛ 🏕 ⊘ 🔲 ⊘ 🦋 ♈

Foll E10 W out of Svolvaer. Just bef bdge to
Grimsoya Island turn R, sp to Rystad. Site sp fr this
junc, about 2km on L. Sm, pt sl, EHU; bbq; sw nr;
Eng spkn; CKE. *"Gd for birdwatching; lovely sea
views; gd for photographing midnight sun; vg site."*
NOK 220, 1 May-30 Sep.   **2016**

RUNDE ISLAND

RUNDE *1A1* (4km NW Rural/Coastal) *62.40416,*
5.62525 **Camping Goksøyr,** 6096 Runde (Møre og
Romsdal) **tel 70 08 59 05 or 924 12 298 (mob);**
camping@goksoyr.no; www.goksoeyr-camping.com

⬛12 ♚♟ ⬛ 🏕 ⊙ 🔲 ⊘ 🏕 🦋 🐕 ⬛

Take causeway/bdge to Runde Island. Turn R off
bdge & foll rd round island, thro tunnel. Rd ends 1km
after site. 3*, Sm, hdstg, unshd, EHU (16A) NOK30;
phone; Eng spkn; adv bkg acc; fishing; bike hire; CKE.
*"Excel birdwatching (inc puffins); site on water's edge;
boat trips avail; basic facs poss inadequate when site
full; owner helps with pitching; vg."* **NOK 222**   **2019**

VESTERALEN ISLANDS

ANDENES *2F1* (21km SW Coastal) *69.20410,*
15.84674 **Stave Camping & Hot Pools,** Stave 8489
Nordmela **tel 92 60 12 57; info@stavecamping.no;**
www.stavecamping.no

♚♟ (htd) ⬛ 🏕 ⊘ ♈ ♉ adj

Head S on Storgata/Rv82 twds Stadionveien,
cont to foll Rv82, turn R onto Fv976, bear L onto
Laksebakkveien, cont onto Fv976; site on L.
Sm, unshd, EHU (16A) 40NOK; cooking facs; Eng spkn;
ccard acc. *"Excel for midnight sun, hot tubs 250NOK
pn."* **NOK 268, 17 May-1 Sep.**   **2019**

ANDENES *2F1* (9.6km SW Coastal) *69.27552,*
15.96372 **Midnattsol Camping,** Gardsveien 8, 8481
Bleik **tel 47 47 84 32 19; midnattsol.camping@
gmail.com; www.midnattsolcamping.com**

⬛12 🐕 ♚♟ ⬛ 🏕 ⊙ 🔲 ⊘ 🦋 ♈ ⛰ ♉ sand

Take Rte 02 S. Then turn R onto Rte 976 sp Bleik.
Site at side of Rte 976 just bef Bleik. Med, mkd,
unshd, terr, EHU 16A (NOK50); bbq; cooking facs;
TV; Eng spkn; adv bkg acc; recep open 0930-1200;
CKE. *"Sea adj; walks; birdwatching; conv for puffin &
whale safaris & fishing boat trips; golf & sports grnd
adj; lovely site; sea views; friendly owner; lovely setting
bet mountain & sea; easy walk to vill shop; excel."*
NOK 235   **2019**

GULLESFJORDBOTN *2F2* (1km NW Coastal)
68.53213, 15.72611 **Gullesfjordbotn Camping,**
Våtvoll, 8409 Gullesfjordbotn **tel 47 91 59 75 50;**
post@gullesfjordcamping.no; www.gullesfjord
camping.no

♚♟ (htd) ⬛ 🏕 ⊘ 🔲 ⊘ 🦋 ♉ shgl adj

Fr S on E10 then rd 85. At rndabt just bef
Gullesfjordbotn take 2nd exit sp Sortland rd 85.
Site on R 1km, well sp. 3*, Sm, hdstg, unshd, EHU
(16A, poss rev pol) NOK50; cooking facs; phone;
Eng spkn; ccard acc; fishing; boat hire; sauna; CKE.
*"On edge of fjord; liable to flood after heavy rain;
mountain views; gd san facs; friendly owners."*
NOK 256, 15 May-15 Sep.   **2018**

HARSTAD *2F2* (5km S Coastal) *68.77231, 16.57878*
Harstad Camping, Nessevegen 55, 9411 Harstad
tel 77 07 36 62; postmaster@harstad-camping.no;
www.harstad-camping.no

12 ♦♦ WD ♨ ♿ ▭ ∥ ✿ ♔ ⊕ nr ⛴ ⛺

Sp fr E10/Rv83. 3*, Med, unshd, pt sl, EHU (16A)
NOK50; ccard acc; fishing; boating; CKE. *"San
facs poss stretched high ssn; lovely situation."*
NOK 315   **2019**

> ## "I like to fill in the reports as I travel from site to site"
>
> You'll find report forms at the back of this guide, or you can fill them in online at camc.com/europereport.

RISOYHAMN *2F1* (13km S Coastal) *68.88408,
15.60304* **Andøy Friluftssenter & Camping,**
Buksnesfjord, 8484 Risøyhamn **tel 76 14 88 04;**
**firmapost@andoy-friluftssenter.no; www.andoy-
friluftssenter.no**

12 ♦♦ (htd) WD ♨ ♿ ▭ ∥ ✿ ⊕ ⛺

Exit E10 onto Rv82 sp Sortland; in 31km at bdge
to Sortland do not cross bdge but cont N on Rv82
sp Andenes. Site on R in 38km at Buknesfjord.
Sm, hdstg, unshd, pt sl, EHU (10A) NOK50; sw;
50% statics; Eng spkn; adv bkg acc; ccard acc; fishing;
CKE. *"Lake fishing; guided mountain walks; easy access
for whale-watching; v clean facs; gourmet meals."*
NOK 250   **2016**

SORTLAND *2F2* (2km NW Rural) *68.70286, 15.3919*
Camping Sortland & Motel, Vesterveien 51, 8400
Sortland **tel 76 11 03 00; hj.bergseng@sortland-
camping.no; www.sortland-camping.no**

12 ♦♦ WD ♨ ♿ ▭ ∥ ✿ ♔ ♪ ⛴ ⛺

Exit E10 onto Rv82/85 sp Sortland; in 31km turn L
over bdge to Sortland, L again at end bdge. Site sp
in approx 1km immed past church. Foll rd uphill for
1km, site on R. 4*, Med, hdstg, pt shd, EHU (16A) (no
earth) NOK30; gas; cooking facs; TV; phone; Eng spkn;
ccard acc; fishing; cycling; gym; solarium; boating;
CKE. *"Basic, clean site; v helpful staff; gd base to tour
islands; walking; skiing; facs stretched when full; red
facs LS."* **NOK 250**   **2019**

STO *2F1* (0.7km W Coastal) *69.01922, 15.10894*
Stø Bobilcamp, 8438 Stø **tel 97 63 36 48;**
stobobilcamp@gmail.com; www.stobobilcamp.no

♦♦ (htd) WD ♨ ♿ ∥ MSP ✿ ⊕ ⛴

Site sp fr cent of Stø. Sm, hdstg, unshd, EHU
(16A) NOK30; cooking facs; 10% statics; Eng spkn;
fishing; bike hire. *"View of midnight sun; 10min
walk to whale boat safari; coastal walks, Queen
Sonja's walk fr site, v scenic but poss strenuous; facs
stretched high ssn; site open to public for parking."*
NOK 130, 1 May-10 Sep.   **2016**

> ## "We must tell the Club about that great site we found"
>
> Get your site reports in by mid-August and we'll do our best to get your updates into the next edition.

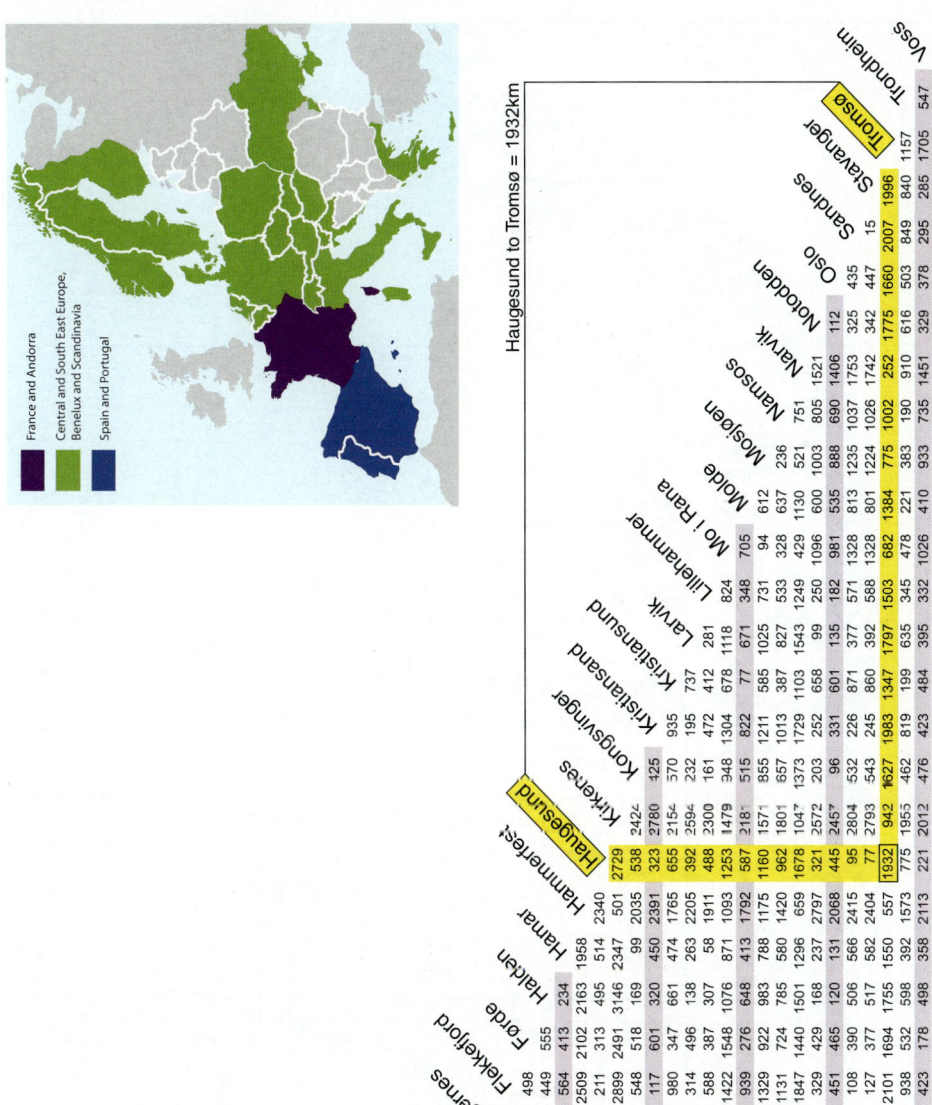

Legend:
- France and Andorra
- Central and South East Europe, Benelux and Scandinavia
- Spain and Portugal

Haugesund to Tromsø = 1932km

City distance chart (diagonal labels):

Voss, Trondheim, Tromsø, Stavanger, Sandnes, Oslo, Notodden, Narvik, Namsos, Mosjøen, Molde, Mo i Rana, Lillehammer, Larvik, Kristiansund, Kristiansand, Kongsvinger, Kirkenes, Haugesund, Hammerfest, Hamar, Halden, Førde, Flekkefjord, Fagernes, Drammen, Bodø, Bergen, Arendal, Ålesund

NORWAY

Map 1

▲ see map 2

© Collins Bartholomew Ltd 2021

682

Motorways
Major roads
Main roads

All year site(s)
Seasonal site(s)
No sites listed

200m +
0–200m

0   50   100   150 kms
0   50   100 mls

NORWEGIAN
SEA

Arctic Circle

N
W   E
S

see map 1

SWEDEN

FINLAND

GULF
OF
BOTHNIA

Nordkapp
Skarsvåg
Hønningsvåg
Berlevåg
HAMMERFEST
Tana
Vadsø
Langfjordbotn
Alta
Utsjoki
KIRKENES
TROMSØ
Birtavarre
Skibotn
Karasjok
Andenes
Stø
Risøyhamn
Sortland
Harstad
TENNEVOLL
Kautokeino
Ivalo
NARVIK
Kaaresuvanto
Ramberg
Stamsund
Svolvær
Ulvåg
Skutvika
Muonio
Sørvågen
BODØ
Fauske
Ørnes
Storjord
Krokstranda
Kilboghamn
Storforshei
MO I RANA
Gällivare
Rovaniemi
MOSJØEN
Vega
Arvidsjaur
Luleå
Bronnoysund
Forbotn
Storuman
Skellefteå
Oulu
Rørvik
Kolvereid
NAMSOS
Grong
Steinkjer
Umeå
TRONDHEIM

Vesterålen
Lofoten

1

2

3

4

© Collins Bartholomew Ltd 2021

Map 2

Poland

Gdansk

Shutterstock/Patryk Kosmider

Highlights

Poland is a country with a deep sense of history, cultural identity and resilience that has been built over thousands of years. The historic and beautiful centre of Kraków is a must see, while the engaging and fascinating museums of Warsaw are also a fantastic experience.

For those looking for relaxation, the Polish countryside is peaceful and unspoilt. There are many hiking trails scattered around the country taking you alongside rivers, through thick forests and around mountains.

Amber, sometimes called the gold of the Baltic, has been crafted in Poland for centuries. Amber products are still produced and sold with the best place to shop being Cloth Hall in the heart of Kraków.

Poland has been producing vodka since the early Middle Ages, and is the birthplace of this spirit. The vodka distilled in Poland is considered some of the finest in the world and vodka tasting events are held around the country.

Major towns and cities

- Warsaw – Poland's capital and the largest city in the country.
- Kraków – a charming and beautiful place that has retained its historic feel.
- Gdansk - a pretty seaside city with a rich history and heritage.
- Wrocław – a city with plenty of landmarks and wonderful buildings.

Attractions

- Main Square, Kraków – a bustling, medieval market square filled with historic buildings and monuments.
- Białowi¿ea Forest – the remains of a primeval forest, home to European bison, ancient oaks and a magical beauty.
- Wieliczka Salt Mine – discover a fascinating mix of history, art and industry in one of Poland's oldest salt mines.

Find out more

www.poland.travel
E: pot@pot.gov.pl
T: 0048 (0) 22 53 67 070

Country Information

Population (approx): 38.3 million

Capital: Warsaw

Area: 312,685 sq km

Bordered by: Belarus, Czech Republic, Germany, Lithuania, Russia, Slovakia, Ukraine

Terrain: Mostly flat plain with many lakes; mountains along southern border

Climate: Changeable continental climate with cold, often severe winters and hot summers; rainfall spread throughout the year; late spring and early autumn are the best times to visit

Coastline: 440km

Highest Point: Rysy 2,499m

Language: Polish

Local Time: GMT or BST + 1, i.e. 1 hour ahead of the UK all year

Currency: Zloty (PLN) divided into 100 groszy; £1 = PLN 5.20; PLN10 = £1.92 (Feb 2021)

Emergency numbers: Police 997; Fire brigade 998; Ambulance 999. Call 112 for any service.

Public Holidays 2021: Jan 1, 6; Apr 4, 5; May 1, 3 (Constitution Day), 23; Jun 3; Aug 15; Nov 1, 11 (Independence Day); Dec 25, 26.

School summer holidays run from the last week of June to the end of August.

Border Posts

British and Irish passport holders may stay for up to 90 days in any 180 day period without a visa. Following Brexit you may be asked to show a return or onward ticket at the border to confirm your length of stay, or to prove that you have enough money for your stay.

Your passport will need to have a minimum of 6 months' validity remaining, and be less than 10 years old (even if it has over 6 months left).

Visitors arriving at a campsite or hotel must complete a registration form.

Entry Formalities

British and Irish passport holders may visit Poland for up to three months without a visa. At campsites reception staff should look after any required registration with local authorities.

Medical Services

For simple complaints and basic advice visit a pharmacy (apteka). In general, medical facilities are comparatively inexpensive and of a good standard. Medical staff are well qualified. English is not always widely spoken so you may face language difficulties.

You will need a European Health Insurance Card (EHIC) to obtain emergency treatment from doctors, dentists and hospitals contracted to the state health care system, the NFZ. Reimbursements for any charges that you incur can be claimed from the NFZ office in Warsaw. You will have to pay a proportion of the cost of prescriptions, which is not refundable in Poland.

Private health clinics, found in large cities, offer a good standard of medical care.

Opening Hours

Banks: Mon-Fri 9am-4pm; Sat 9am-1pm.

Museums:Tue-Sun 10am-5pm; closed Mon.

Post Offices: Mon-Fri 8am-6pm; Sat 8am-2pm (on rota basis).

Shops: Mon-Fri 11am-8pm; Sat 9am-2pm/4pm; food shops open and close earlier; supermarkets open until 9pm/10pm.

Safety and Security

Most visits to Poland are trouble free and violent crime is rare, but there is a risk of robbery in tourist areas, particularly near hotels, at main railway stations and on public transport. Passengers are most at risk when boarding and leaving trains or trams. Avoid walking alone at night, particularly in dark or poorly-lit streets or in public parks.

Some tourists have been the target of a scam in which men claiming to be plain clothes police officers ask visitors to show their identity documents and bank cards, and then ask for their PIN(s).

Theft of and from vehicles is common so do not leave vehicle documentation or valuables in your car. Foreign registered cars may be targeted, especially in large, busy supermarket car parks.

Cases have been reported of vehicles with foreign number plates being stopped by gangs posing as police officers, either claiming a routine traffic control or at the scene of fake accidents, particularly in rural and tourist areas. If in doubt, when flagged down keep all doors and windows locked, remain in your vehicle and ask to see identification. The motoring organisation, PZM, advises that any car or document inspection performed outside built-up areas can only be carried out by uniformed police officers and at night these officials must use a police patrol car. Although police officers do not have to be in uniform within built-up areas, they must always present their police identity card. More details are available to motorists at Polish road borders.

An emergency helpline has been set up to assist visitors who have been victims of crime or who require assistance tel: 0800 200300 (freephone) or +48 608 599999 (mobile number). The helpline operates from 1 June to 30 September between 10am and 10pm.

Do not leave drinks or food unattended or accept drinks from strangers. There has been a small number of reports of drinks being spiked and of visitors having their valuables stolen whilst drugged.

British Embassy

UL KAWALERII 12
00-468 WARSZAWA
Tel: (022) 3110000
www.ukinpoland.fco.gov.uk

Irish Embassy

UL MYSIA 5, 00-496 WARSZAWA
Tel: (022) 5642200
www.embassyofireland.pl.

Documents

Driving Licence

The standard pink UK paper driving licence is recognised, but if you hold the old style green UK licence or a Northern Irish licence you are advised to update it to a photocard licence in order to avoid any local difficulties.

Passport

You should carry your passport with you at all times.

Vehicle(s)

You must carry your original vehicle registration certificate (V5C), insurance documentation and MOT certificate (if applicable) at all times. You may be asked for these if you are stopped by the police and, in particular, when crossing borders. If you do not own the vehicle(s) you will need a letter of authority from the owner, together with the vehicle's original documentation.

Money

Cash can easily be obtained from ATMs in banks and shopping centres. ATMs offer an English option.

Major credit cards are widely accepted in hotels, restaurants and shops but you may find that supermarkets do not accept them. Take particular care with credit/debit cards and don't lose sight of them during transactions.

Sterling and euros are readily accepted at exchange bureaux but Scottish and Northern Irish bank notes are not generally recognised and you may have difficulties trying to exchange them.

Carry your credit card issuers'/banks' 24-hour UK contact numbers in case of loss or theft of your cards.

Driving

Poland is a major route for heavy vehicles travelling between eastern and western Europe and driving can be hazardous. There are few dual carriageways and even main roads between large towns can be narrow and poorly surfaced. Slow moving agricultural and horse-drawn vehicles are common in rural areas. Street lighting is weak even in major cities.

Local driving standards are poor and speed limits, traffic lights and road signs are often ignored. Drivers rarely indicate before manoeuvring and you may encounter aggressive tailgating, overtaking on blind bends and overtaking on the inside. Take particular care on national holiday weekends when there is a surge in road accidents.

It isn't advisable to drive a right hand drive vehicle alone for long distances or to drive long distances at night.

At dusk watch out for cyclists riding without lights along the edge of the road or on its shoulder.

Hitchhikers use an up and down motion of the hand to ask for a lift. This may be confused with flagging down.

Accidents

Drivers involved in accidents must call the police, obtain an official record of damages and forward it to the insurance company of the Polish driver involved (if applicable). Members of AIT/FIA affiliated clubs, such as The Caravan and Motorhome Club, can obtain help from the touring office ('Autotour') of the Polish motoring organisation, Polski Zwiazek Motorowy (PZM), tel: (022) 8496904 or (022) 8499361.

If people are injured, you must call an ambulance or doctor. By law, it is an offence for a driver not to obtain first aid for accident victims or to leave the scene of an accident. In such circumstances the authorities may withdraw a tourist's passport and driving licence, vehicle registration certificate or even the vehicle itself and the penalties can be a prison sentence and a fine.

Alcohol

The permitted level of alcohol is 20 milligrams in 100 millilitres of blood, which in practice equates to zero. At the request of the police or if an accident has occurred a driver must undergo a blood test which, if positive, may lead to a prison sentence, withdrawal of driving licence and a fine. Penalty points will be notified to the authorities in the motorist's home country.

Breakdown Service

The toll free telephone number for breakdown assistance throughout the country is 981.

The PZM runs a breakdown service covering the entire country 24 hours a day. Members of AIT and FIA affiliated clubs, such as The Caravan and Motorhome Club, should call the PZM Emergency Centre on (022) 5328433. Staff speak English. Roadside assistance must be paid for in cash.

Child Restraint System

Children under the age of 12 years old and under the height of 1.5m must use a suitable restraint system that has been adapted to their size. It is prohibited to place a child in a rear facing seat in the front of the vehicle if the car is equipped with airbags.

Fuel

The usual opening hours for petrol stations are from 8am to 7pm; many on main roads and international routes and in large towns are open 24 hours. Credit cards are widely accepted. LPG (Autogas) is widely available from service stations.

Motorways and Tolls

There are approximately 3000km of motorways in Poland. Tolls are levied on sections and vary in price, for example, the A1 Rusocin to Nowe Marzy is PLN 41.80 (2015 prices) for a car towing a caravan weighing under 3500kg.

An electronic toll system is in place for vehicles which weigh over 3,500kg, including motorhomes and car and caravan combinations if the total weight is over 3,500kg. These vehicles will need to be equipped with an electronic device called a viaBOX. Visit www.viatoll.pl/en and select the 'Trucks' option for details of toll costs for motorhomes and car/caravan combinations weighing over 3500kg.

An electronic option is also available for vehicles and car/caravan combinations which weigh under 3500kg - go to the above website and choose the 'Cars' options for details.

There are emergency telephones every 2km along motorways. Recent visitors report that newer stretches of motorway have rest areas with chemical disposal and waste water disposal facilities.

Parking

There are parking meters in many towns and signs display parking restrictions or prohibitions. There are many supervised car parks charging an hourly rate. Illegally parked cars causing an obstruction may be towed away and impounded, in which case the driver will be fined. Wheel clamps are in use.

Sidelights must be used when parking in unlit streets during the hours of darkness.

Priority

Priority should be given to traffic coming from the right at intersections of roads of equal importance, however vehicles on rails always have priority. At roundabouts traffic already on a roundabout has priority.

Give way to buses pulling out from bus stops. Trams have priority over other vehicles at all times. Where there is no central reservation or island you should stop to allow passengers alighting from trams to cross to the pavement.

Roads

All roads are hard surfaced and the majority of them are asphalted. However, actual road surfaces may be poor; even some major roads are constructed of cement or cobbles and heavily rutted. Average journey speed is about 50 km/h (31 mph).

Some roads, notably those running into Warsaw, have a two metre wide strip on the nearside to pull onto in order to allow other vehicles to overtake. Oncoming lorries expect other motorists to pull over when they are overtaking.

Overtake trams on the right unless in a one-way street.

Road Signs and Markings

Road signs and markings conform to international standards. Motorway and national road numbers are indicated in red and white, and local roads by yellow signs with black numbering. Signs on motorways are blue with white lettering and on main roads they are green and white.

The following road signs may be seen:

Polish	English Translation
Rondzie	Roundabout
Wstep szbroniony	No Entry
Wyjscie	Exit

You may also encounter the following:

Crossroads and road junctions may not be marked with white 'stop' lines, and other road markings in general may be well worn and all but invisible, so always take extra care.

Speed Limits

Paid parking between 7am and 6pm

Residential area-predestrians have priority

Toll road

Rutted road

Droga kręta
Winding road

Emergency vehicles

	Open Road (km/h)	Motorway (km/h)
Car Solo	90	140
Car towing caravan/trailer	70	80
Motorhome under 3500kg	90	140
Motorhome 3500-7500kg	70	80

In built up areas the speed limit is 50 km/h (31 mph) between 5am and 11pm, and 60 km/h (37 mph) between 11pm and 5am.

For vehicles over 3,500kg all speed limits are the same as for a car and caravan outfit. In residential zones indicated by entry/exit signs, the maximum speed is 20 km/h (13 mph). The use of radar detectors is illegal.

Traffic Lights

Look out for a small, non-illuminated green arrow under traffic lights, which permits a right turn against a red traffic light if the junction is clear.

Violation of Traffic Regulations

Motorists must not cross a road's solid central white line or even allow wheels to run on it. Radar speed traps are frequently in place on blind corners where speed restrictions apply. Police are very keen to enforce traffic regulations with verbal warnings and/or on the spot fines. Fines are heavy and drivers of foreign registered vehicles will be required to pay in cash. Always obtain an official receipt.

Touring

The national drinks of Poland include varieties of vodka and plum brandy. When dining and drinking in restaurants it is usual to leave a tip of between 10 to 15%.

There are over 9,000 lakes in Poland, mostly in the north. The regions of Western Pomerania, Kaszubia and Mazuria are a paradise for sailing enthusiasts, anglers and nature lovers. In order to protect areas of natural beauty, national parks and nature reserves have been created, two of the most interesting of which are the Tatra National Park covering the whole of the Polish Tatra mountains, and the Slowinksi National Park with its 'shifting' sand dunes.

There are 14 UNESCO World Heritage sites including the restored historic centres of Warsaw and Kraków, the medieval, walled town of Toruń and Auschwitz Concentration Camp. Other towns worth a visit are Chopin's birthplace at Zelazowa Wola, Wieliczka with its salt mines where statues and a chapel are carved out of salt, and Wrocław.

White and brown signs in cities and near sites of interest indicate architectural and natural landmarks, places of religious worship, etc. Each sign includes not only information on the name of and distance to a particular attraction, but also a pictogram of the attraction, e.g. Jasna Góra monastery. Themed routes, such as the trail of the wooden churches in the Małopolska Region (south of Kraków), are marked in a similar way.

A Warsaw Tourist Card and a Kraków Tourist Card are available, both valid for up to three days and offering free travel on public transport and free entry to many museums, together with discounts at selected restaurants and shops and on sightseeing and local excursions. Buy the cards from tourist information centres, travel agents or hotels.

The Polish people are generally friendly, helpful and polite. English is becoming increasingly widely spoken in major cities.

Camping and Caravanning

There are around 250 organised campsites throughout Poland, with the most attractive areas being the Mazurian lake district and along the coast. Campsites are usually open from the beginning of May or June to the middle or end of September, but the season only really starts towards the end of June. Until then facilities may be very limited and grass may not be cut, etc.

You can download details of approximately 160 sites (including GPS co-ordinates) from the website of the Polish Federation of Camping & Caravanning, www.pfcc.eu

Campsites are classified from one to four stars. Category one sites provide larger pitches and better amenities, but it may still be advisable to use your own facilities. There are also some basic sites which are not supervised and are equipped only with drinking water, toilets and washing facilities. Sites may be in need of modernisation but, on the whole, sanitary facilities are clean although they may provide little privacy. Some new sites are being built to higher standards. A site may close earlier than its published date if the weather is bad.

Many sites are not signposted from main roads and may be difficult to find. It is advisable to obtain a large scale atlas or good maps of the areas to be visited and not rely on one map covering the whole of Poland.

Casual/wild camping is not recommended and is prohibited in national parks (except on organised sites) and in sand dunes along the coast.

Cycling

There are several long-distance cycle routes using a combination of roads with light motor traffic, forest trails or tracks along waterways. There are some cycle lanes on main roads where cyclists must ride in single file.

Electricity and Gas

The current on most campsites is 10 amps. Plugs have two round pins. There are some CEE connections.

It is understood that both propane and butane supplies are widely available, but cylinders are not exchangeable and it may be necessary to refill. The Caravan and Motorhome Club does not recommend this practice and you should aim to take enough gas to last during your stay. Some campsites have kitchens which you may use to conserve your gas supplies.

Public Transport & Local Travel

For security reasons recent visitors recommend using guarded car parks such as those in Warsaw on the embankment below the Old Town, in the Palace of Culture and near the Tomb of the Unknown Soldier.

Use only taxis from official ranks whose vehicles have the name and telephone number of the taxi company on the door and on the roof (beside the occupied/unoccupied light). They also display a rate card in the window of the vehicle. Taxis with a crest but no company name are not officially registered.

There are frequent ferries from Gydnia, Swinoujscie and Gdansk to Denmark, Germany and Sweden.

Passenger ferries operate along the Baltic Coast, on the Mazurian lakes and on some rivers, for example, between Warsaw and Gdansk.

There is a metro system in Warsaw. It is possible to buy a daily or weekly tourist pass which is valid for all means of public transport – bus, tram and metro. Buy tickets at newspaper stands and kiosks displaying a sign 'bilety'. Tickets must be punched before travelling at the yellow machines at the entrance to metro stations or on board buses and trams. You will incur an on the spot fine if you are caught travelling without a valid ticket.

Niedzica castle

BIALOWIEZA *B4* (3km W Rural) *52.69395, 23.83088*
Camping U Michała (No. 124), ul Krzyże 11, 17-230 Białowieża **(085) 6812703; info@bialowieza-forest. com; http://bialowieza-forest.com/miejsce/ camping-u-michala-bialowieza**

Exit Bielsk Podlaski onto rd 689; cont past Hajnówka for 17m; site on R at end of vill. Sm, mkd, pt shd, EHU (16A); bike hire. *"Gd san facs."*
PLN 50, 15 Apr-30 Sep. 2016

CZESTOCHOWA *C3* (4km W Urban) *50.81122, 19.09131* **Camping Oleńka (No. 76),** ul Oleńki 10, 42-200 Częstochowa **(034) 3606066; camping@ mosir.pl; www.mosir.pl**

Fr A1/E75 foll sp Jasna Góra monastery, pick up sm white camping sp to site. Lge, pt shd, EHU (20A); TV; 20% statics; phone; Eng spkn; ccard acc; CKE. *"Guided tours; monastery worth visit; gd NH/sh stay nr Jasna Góra & Black Madonna painting; poor security; san facs unclean & poorly maintained."*
PLN 58, 1 May-15 Oct. 2016

ELK *A3* (3km SW Urban) *53.81545, 22.35215*
Camping Plaża Miejska (No. 62), ul Parkowa 2, 19-300 Ełk **(087) 6109700; mosir@elk.com.pl; http://mosir.elk.pl/plaza-miejska/camping/**

Fr town cent on rd 16 take rd 65/669 dir Białystok. After 200m cross rv & immed turn R, site 100m on l. 3*, Sm, mkd, hdstg, pt shd, EHU (10A) inc; cooking facs; sw nr; CKE. *"Gd security; well-maintained, clean site adj town cent & attractive lake; gd touring base lake district."* **PLN 65, 1 Jun-1 Sep.** 2016

JELENIA GORA *C2* (2km SE Urban) *50.89638, 15.74266* **Auto-Camping Park (No. 130),** ul Sudecka 42, 58-500 Jelenia Góra **(075) 7524525; campingpark@ interia.pl; www.camping.karkonosz.pl**

In town foll sp to Karpacz on rd 367. Site 100m fr hotel. Well sp. Med, hdstg, pt shd, terr, EHU (6-10A) PLN10 (poss rev pol); TV; 20% statics; adv bkg acc; ccard acc; CKE. *"Conv Karkanosze mountains & Czech border; well-run, clean, neat site nr hotel with gd, modern facs; 20 min walk to pleasant town; pool 500m; sports facs 500m; staff friendly, helpful & obliging; conv NH; gd facs."* **PLN 53** 2015

KARTUZY *A2* (9km W Rural) *54.31983, 18.11736*
Camping Tarnowa (No. 181), Zawory 47A, 83-333 Chmielno **(058) 6842535; camping@tarnowa.pl; www.tarnowa.pl**

Fr Gdańsk take rd 7 & rd 211 to Kartuzy, cont for approx 4km on 211. Turn L for Chmielno; site sp fr vill on lakeside along narr, bumpy app rd. Med, unshd, terr, EHU (10-16A) inc; bbq; sw nr; bus station 1KM away; Eng spkn; sauna; boat hire; bike hire; CKE. *"Attractive, well-kept site in beautiful location; friendly owner; not suitable lge o'fits; v nice site; shop 0.5m."* **PLN 54** 2020

KATOWICE *D3* (4km SE Rural) *50.24355, 19.04795*
Camping Dolina Trzech Statow (No. 215), ul Trzech Stawow 23, 40-291 Katowice **(032) 2565939 or (032) 2555388; camping@mosir.katowice.pl; camping.mosir.katowice.pl**

Exit A4 at junc Murckowska & foll sp on rd 86 Sosnowiec. In 500m turn R & foll site sp. Med, shd, pt sl, EHU (16A) PLN2.50/kwh; cooking facs; Eng spkn; adv bkg acc; ccard acc; tennis; CKE. *"V clean facs but basic & little privacy; vg."* **PLN 45, 1 May-30 Sep.** 2016

KAZIMIERZ DOLNY *C3* (2km N Rural) *51.33106, 21.95879* **Campsite Pielak,** Pulawska 82, 24-120 Kazimierz Dolny (Lubelskie) **(069) 1047409**

Site sp on the S824 300m N of the town. Sm, pt shd, pt sl, EHU (16A); bbq; cooking facs; twin axles; bus adj; Eng spkn; kayaking; CCI. *"V friendly owners, warm welcome; pool 50m; walking dist to town; close to rv; open grassy site; historic town; excel."*
PLN 72, 1 May-30 Oct. 2016

KLODZKO *D2* (13km W Urban) *50.41502, 16.51335*
Camping Polanica-Zdroj (No. 169), ul Sportowa 7, 57-320 Polanica-Zdrój **(074) 8681210; osir.polanica@ neostrada.pl; www.osir.polanica.net/pl**

Foll sp fr rd 8/E67. Site is 1km N of Polanica-Zdrój. Med, pt shd, EHU (6A) PLN9.50; Eng spkn; ccard acc; tennis; CKE. *"Well-run site; clean san facs; helpful warden; many statics adj; easy walk to pleasant spa town - many rests/cafés; wifi free in recep."*
PLN 69.3 2019

KRAKOW *D3* (5km N Urban) *50.09454, 19.94127*
Camping Clepardia (No. 103), ul Pachońskiego
28A, 31-223 Kraków **(012) 4159672; clepardia@
gmail.com; www.clepardia.com.pl**

🐕 🏕 ⬜wd 🚿 🖪 🚽 ⚓ ⑪ nr 🚽 nr

Fr Kraków cent take rd 7/E77 N twds Warsaw for
3km. Turn L onto rd 79 'Opolska' & foll sp 'Domki
Kempingowe - Bungalows'. Fr A4/E40 exit onto
E462 then S on rd 79 'Pasternik' thro to 'J Conrada
& foll sp. Site is nr lge Elea supmkt & Clepardia
Basen (sw pools). Med, mkd, pt shd, EHU (6A) PLN12;
phone; bus 250m; Eng spkn; CKE. *"Busy site with
tightly packed pitches - rec arr bef 1700 high ssn to
secure pitch; excel, clean, modern san facs; ltd EHU
if site full; muddy in wet weather; dogs free; pool adj;
friendly, helpful staff; gd security; well maintained."*
PLN 94, 15 Apr-15 Oct. **2017**

KRAKOW *D3* (7km SW Rural) *50.04638, 19.88111*
Camping Smok (No. 46), ul Kamedulska 18, 30-252
Kraków **48 12 429 88 00; info@smok.krakow.pl;
www.smok.krakow.pl**

12 🐕 PLN5 🏕 ⬜wd 🚿 🖪 🚽 ⚓ MP 🦋 🌊 ⑪ nr 🚽 🏔

Fr Kraków W ring rd site sp as No 46. Fr S 1st exit
immed after x-ing rv onto rd 780 twd Kraków.
3*, Med, shd, pt sl, EHU (5-10A) PLN12; red long stay;
Eng spkn; adv bkg rec; windsurfing 6km; CKE. *"On rd
to Auschwitz; salt mine at Wieliczka; friendly, well-kept
site; spotless san facs; lower field (m'vans) poss muddy
after rain - tractor tow avail; poss rallies on site; gd tour
base; frequent bus to Krakow connects with trams to
cent; cycle rte to cent; gd security; tours with pick-up fr
site; excel; v helpful and friendly."* **PLN 111** **2018**

LANCUT *D3* (2km E Urban) *50.070940, 22.254689*
Camping Lancut, ul. Kazimierza Wielkiego 20, 37-
100 Łańcut **(604) 915112 or (602) 252909; biuro@
campinglancut.pl; www.campinglancut.pl**

🐕 PLN 5 🏕 ⬜wd 🚿 🖪 🚽 ⚓ MP ⚲ 🍽 ⑪ nr 🚽 nr

On 94 between Rzeszow and Przeworks. Sm, mkd,
hdg, pt shd, serviced pitches; EHU; bbq (charcoal,
elec, gas, sep area); cooking facs; twin axles; red long
stay; phone; bus; Eng spkn; adv bkg acc. *"Excel; lots
to see locally; bike ride off rd; lovely site, 2 years old
(2019); modern; helpful American owner; v well kept."*
PLN 51, 1 Apr-30 Oct. **2019**

LEBA *A2* (2km NE Urban) *54.76580, 17.57145*
Camping Przymorze Nr. 48, ul. Nadmorska 9, 84-360
Leba **059 866 1304; biuro@camping.leba.pl;
http://camping-leba.pl/kamery.asp**

🐕 🏕 (htd) ⬜wd 🚿 ♿ 🖪 🚽 ⚓ MP 🦋 ⚲ 🚽 🏔 ⛵ sand 0.5km

Take DW214 dir Leba, at rndabt take 1st exit onto
aleja swietego Jakuba. Turn R onto Nadmorska
& foll sp to camp. Lge, mkd, pt shd, EHU; bbq; TV;
10% statics; phone; bus adj; Eng spkn; ccard acc; CCI.
*"Excel site; shops & rest in walking dist; interesting
harbour with fresh fish for sale; windsurfing; lovely
sandy beach."* **PLN 110, 1 May-30 Sep.** **2019**

LEGNICA *C2* (13km SE Rural) *51.14216, 16.24006*
Camping Legnickie Pole (No. 234), Ul Henryka
Brodatego 7, 59-241 Legnickie Pole **(076) 8582397;
osir.legnica@wp.pl; www.osir.legnica.pl**

🐕 PLN8 🏕 🚿 ♿ ⚲ 🍽 🚽 nr 🏛

Fr A4/E40 fr Görlitz take exit dir Legnickie Pole/
Jawor, foll sp to vill & site. Sharp L turn after leaving
main rd. Site sp on S o'skirts of Legnica on E65 &
fr m'way. Sm, pt shd, EHU (10A) inc; CKE. *"Helpful,
friendly welcome; clean, basic facs (hot water to shwrs
only); poss diff after heavy rain; gd NH on way S;
pleasant vill."* **PLN 44, 1 May-30 Sep.** **2017**

LEZAJSK *C4* (12km ENE Rural) *50.280257,
22.514233* **Pole Biwakowe Laguna,** 37-303
Kuryłówka **(602) 717262; marianszktanny.wp.pl**

🐕 🏕 (htd) 🚿 🖪 🚽 ⚲ 🍽 ⑪ nr 🚽 nr 🏔 ⚓ sand adj

Thro Kurylowka town. At edge of town foll sp left
to Ozanna-Stron. Site on L. 5*, Sm, pt shd, EHU
(16A); bbq (charcoal, elec, gas); cooking facs; sw; twin
axles; bus; Eng spkn; adv bkg acc; games area. *"Site on
lakeside; fishing; grass mowed short; peaceful; Lezajsk
monastery 20 mins; cycle path around lake; v friendly;
sailing ok; vg."* **PLN 30, 1 May-30 Sep.** **2019**

"I need an on-site restaurant"

We do our best to make sure site information
is correct, but it is always best to check any
must-have facilities are still available or will
be open during your visit.

LUBLIN *C4* (8km S Rural) *51.19186, 22.52725*
Camping Graf Marina (No. 65), ul Kręznicka 6,
20-518 Lublin **(081) 7441070 or (0607) 455320;
info@graf-marina.pl; grafmarina.obitur.pl**

🏕 🚿 ⚓ ⚲ ⑪ 🚽 nr

Take rd 19 S & cross rlwy line; lge parking area
after 1.8km then L after 300m (no sp but leads to
Zemborzyce); in 5km cross rlwy then L at T-junc; site
on R in 5km on lakeside. Med, mkd, hdg, unshd, EHU
(10A); own san req; sw nr; Eng spkn; CKE. *"Marina adj;
sailing; fishing; site run down (early ssn 2011); sodden
after rain."* **PLN 71, 1 May-30 Sep.** **2016**

MRAGOWO *A3* (11km N Rural) *53.94278, 21.32001*
Camping Seeblick, Ruska Wieś 1, 11-700 Mrągowo
**(089) 7413155; marian.seeblick@gmail.com;
www.campingpension.de**

12 🐕 (if on a lead) 🏕 (htd) ⬜wd 🚿 🖪 🚽 ⚓ 🦋 ⚲ 🍽 ⑪ nr 🚶

Fr Mrągowo N on rd 591 dir Ketrzyn, site sp. 3*, Med,
pt shd, terr, EHU inc; sw; Eng spkn; boating; games
area; tennis. *"Gd but ltd san facs; lots for kids to do;
shop nr."* **PLN 50** **2020**

NIEDZICA *D3* (3.5km SE Urban) *49.40477, 20.33411*
Camping Polana Sosny (No. 38), Osiedle Na Polanie
Sosny, 34-441 Niedzica **(018) 2629403;**
polana.sosny@niedzica.pl; www.niedzica.pl

12 ♦♦(htd) wo ▲ ♣ ♿ ▣ ✗ 🦋 ⬤ ⓗ nr 🔌 🔋 nr

Rte 969 fr Nowy Targ. At Dębno turn R & foll sp to
border (lake on L). At 11km pass castle & 1st dam
on L twds 2nd Dunajec dam. Site sp. 2*, Sm, mkd,
unshd, EHU inc; cooking facs; red long stay; phone;
adv bkg acc; watersports; games area; CKE. *"Beautiful,
well-maintained site in superb location; friendly, helpful
staff; clean, modern san facs; excel walks in mountains;
2km to Slovakian border; quiet but noise fr dam; vg
touring base."* **PLN 50**   **2016**

OSWIECIM *D3* (4km S Rural) *50.02262, 19.19891*
Centre for Dialogue & Prayer in Auschwitz, ul
Maksymiliana Kolbego 1, 32-600 Oświęcim **(033)**
8431000; biuro@centrum-dialogu.oswiecim.pl;
www.centrum-dialogu.oswiecim.pl

12 ♦♦ ▲ ♿ ✗ ⓗ 🔋 nr

700m fr Auschwitz 1 museum car park on parallel rd
to S, on forecourt of hotel-like building. Sm, hdstg,
unshd, EHU inc; bbq; phone; Eng spkn; CKE. *"Conv
Auschwitz museum & Auschwitz-Birkenau (3km); clean,
modern, lovely site on lawn & among trees; all site
powered; gd, clean san facs, similar quality to UK CC
sites; friendly, helpful staff; very nice site; excel facs; a
gem of a site; highly rec."* **PLN 84**   **2018**

POZNAN *B2* (5km E Urban) *52.40343, 16.98399*
Camping Malta (No. 155), ul Krańcowa 98, 61-036
Poznań-Malta **(061) 8766203; camping@malta.
poznan.pl; www.poznan.pl**

12 ♦♦(htd) wo ▲ ♿ ✗ 🦋 ▼ 🔋

Fr A2/E30 Poznań bypass leave at rte 2/11 dir
Poznań. Turn R at traff lts onto rte 5/F261 sp Malta,
Zoo & camping, site sp. 4*, Sm, hdg, pt shd, EHU
(16A) inc; 80% statics; tram to city; Eng spkn; ccard
acc; CKE. *"Clean tidy site on lake with sports but poss
unkempt pitches LS; 6 tram stops to Poznań Sq; vg 24-
hr security; lake adj; helpful staff; site amongst sports
facs by lake."* **PLN 102**   **2019**

SANDOMIERZ *C3* (1km E Urban) *50.68010, 21.75502*
Camping Browarny (No. 201), ul Żwirki I Wigury 1,
27-600 Sandomierz **(015) 8332703; wmajsak@
poczta.fm; www.majsak.pl**

🐕 ♦♦ wo ▲ ♿ ✗ Msp ⓗ ▼ ⓗ nr 🔋 nr ⚲

Diff app to site off dual c'way. App on rd 77 fr N only.
Avoid town ctr, 2.5 tonne weight limit. 3*, Sm, pt shd,
EHU (16A) PLN10; bbq; cooking facs; phone; bus adj;
Eng spkn; adv bkg acc; games rm; CKE. *"Attractive sm
town in walking dist; vg site; helpful staff; red for 'vans
under 5mtrs."* **PLN 57, 1 May-30 Sep.**   **2017**

SOPOT *A2* (2km N Urban) *54.46136, 18.5556*
Camping Kamienny Potok (No. 19), Metropolis Sopot
Recreation Center Al. Niepodległości 899 81-861 Sopot
**(058) 5500445; metropolis.polmetro@camping
sopot.pl; www.kemping19.cba.pl**

♦♦ wo ▲ ▣ ✗ ⓨ ▼ ⓗ nr 🔋 nr ⚲

Fr Gdańsk rte 27 twds Sopot. Site on R just behind
Shell petrol stn. Fr N on rte 6/E28 turn S at Gdynia,
onto new section of E28, for 7.5km. Turn L onto rte
220 by 'Euromarket' for 5km. Turn R onto rte 27
(S) twd Gdańsk & site nr Shell g'ge on opp c'way.
Lge, mkd, pt shd, EHU (2-20A) PLN10; TV; phone;
ccard acc; CKE. *"Pleasant site; friendly & helpful
staff; frequent trains for Gdansk 250m; modern,
clean san facs; gd security; gd walking/cycling track
into town; busy site; upgrades in process (2012)."*
PLN 72, 1 May-30 Sep.   **2020**

SUWALKI *A3* (11km SE Rural) *54.0767, 23.0742*
Kajaki Camping Pokoje, 16-412 Stary Folwark 44,
Wigry **(087) 5637789; wigry@wigry.info;
www.wigry.info**

♦♦ wo ▲ ▣ ✗ 🦋 ⓨ

Fr Suwalki take 653 dir Sejny. In about 11km turn
R in Stary Folwark at PTTK sp. Site on R in approx
100m. Sm, unshd, EHU (10A) inc; bbq; sw nr; Eng
spkn. *"Nr lake in National Park; kayaking fr site; vg site."*
PLN 40, 1 May-30 Sep.   **2016**

SWIECIE *B2* (1km S Urban) *53.40321, 18.45574*
Camping Zamek (No. 54), Zamkowa Street 10,
86-100 Świecie **(052) 3311726 or 604 993 070;
recepcja@camping-zamek.pl; www.camping-
zamek.pl**

🐕 ♦♦ ▲ ▣ ✗ 🦋 ▼ 🔋 ⚲

S fr Gdańsk on E75 take rd 1 to Chełmno & Świecie.
Cross Rv Wisła & L at x-rds in Świecie cent; site sp
at traff lts. 1*, Med, shd, EHU (10A); own san rec;
50% statics; phone; games area; fishing. *"Interesting
town & churches; helpful staff; in castle grnds (tower
visible fr rd); if gate clsd, ring bell on L; new tolet block
(2012)."* **PLN 25, 1 May-15 Sep.**   **2020**

SWINOUJSCIE *A1* (2km N Coastal) *53.91709,
14.25693* **Camping Relax (No. 44),** ul Słowackiego
1, 72-600 Świnoujście **(097) 3213912; relax@osir.
swinoujscie.pl; www.camping-relax.com.pl**

12 ♦♦ ▲ ▣ ✗ 🦋 ⓨ 🔋 nr ⚲ 🏊200m

Fr E rd 3/E65 cross rv on free ferry. Fr town cent N
for 500m. No vehicle border x-ing fr W. 3*, V lge,
shd, EHU (16A) PLN10; cooking facs; phone; adv bkg
acc; ccard acc; games rm. *"Nice town; gd beach; gd
walking; site popular with families; red snr citizens."*
PLN 65   **2020**

POLAND

SZCZECIN/STETTIN *B1* (8km SE Rural) *53.39505, 14.63640* **Marina Camping (No. 25),** ul Przestrzenna 23, 70-800 Szczecin-Dabie **(091) 4601165; camping. marina@pro.onet.pl; www.campingmarina.pl**

12 🐕 ♿ ♨️(htd) ♨️ ⚓ 🚿 ⚡ 🛒 ▣ 🍽️ 🍴 ⏱️ 🛢️ 🅿️ nr

Fr E28/A6 take A10 sp Szczecin. Immed after rlwy bdge turn R sp Dąbie. At traff lts in cent Dąbie turn L, site on R in approx 2km on lake. 3*, Med, pt shd, EHU (6A) inc; sw; bus to Stettin; tennis; boat hire; games area; CKE. *"Pleasant, lakeside site; clean, modern san facs but inadequate if site full; bus tickets fr recep; helpful staff; vg site on lake side."* **PLN 85** **2018**

TORUN *B2* (2km S Urban) *53.00062, 18.60847* **Camping Tramp (No. 33),** ul Kujawska 14, 87-100 Toruń **(056) 6547187; tramp@mosir.torun.pl; www.mosir.torun.pl**

12 🐕 PLN4.50 ♿ ♨️ ⚓ 🚿 ⚡ 🛒 🍴 ⏱️ ⑩ nr 🛢️ 🅿️ nr

Cross bdge S of town & take 1st L at traff lts, site sp in 500m on rvside. 3*, Med, shd, EHU (10A) inc; 10% statics; games area; CKE. *"Noisy, busy site but reasonable; walking dist fr interesting old town across bdge; gd security; NH/sh stay only."* **PLN 76** **2018**

WARSZAWA *B3* (13km SE Urban) *52.17798, 21.14727* **Camping Wok (No. 90),** ul Odrębna 16, 04-867 Warszawa **(022) 6127951; wok@campingwok. warszawa.pl; www.campingwok.warszawa.pl**

♿♨️(htd) 🛒 ⚓ 🚿 ⚡ 🛒 🐕 🍴 ⏱️ ⑩ nr 🛢️ 🅿️ nr 🏔️

Fr city cent or fr W on E30, take bdge on E30 over Rv Wisła to E side of rv. Then take rte 801 for approx 8km (dual c'way). At rndabt double back for 600m & take 3rd R into Odrębna. Site 200m on R. 4*, Sm, shd, EHU (10-16A) PLN15; gas; bbq; cooking facs; TV; bus/tram adj; Eng spkn; adv bkg acc; ccard acc; games area; CKE. *"Lovely little site; v secure; spotless, modern san facs; helpful staff."* **PLN 125, 1 Apr-31 Oct.** **2018**

WARSZAWA *B3* (17km W Rural) *52.23066, 20.79196* **Campsite Kaputy 222,** Sochaczewska 222, 05-850 Kreczki, (Mazowieckie) **(860) 1088112; biuro@ camping222.pl; www.camping222.pl**

🐕 PLN5 ♿(htd) 🛒 ⚓ 🚿 ⚡ 🛒 🐕 ♨️

Head S on SS36, take exit Pescate twd Pescate/ Lecco/Malgrate/SS583/Bellagio/Calco, cont strt; at rndabt take 3rd exit via Roma, go thro 1 rndabt; cont onto Via Statale, turn L onto Via Foppaola, site on L. Med, mkd, EHU 15PLN; bus adj; Eng spkn; CCI. *"Fishing lake on site; NH or visit to Warsaw; excel san facs; bread on site; clean, spacious site & easy to find."* **PLN 138, 15 Apr-30 Sep.** **2019**

WARSZAWA *B3* (4km W Urban) *52.2144, 20.96575* **Majawa Camping (No. 123),** ul Bitwy Warszawskiej 19/20, 02-366 Warszawa-Szczęśliwice **(022) 8229121; biuro@majawa.pl; www.majawa.pl**

♿♨️ 🛒 ⚓ 🚿 ⚡ 🐕 🐾 ⏱️ nr 🛢️ 🅿️ nr

Fr W on E30/rd 2 at junc with E67/rd 8 rd goes S thro tunnel under rlwy then strt on under new over-pass. Site on R in 100m. On E67/rd 8 fr Wrocław app concrete monument 3m high in middle of tramway; turn L at traff lts. Hotel Vera on R, site on L. Fr cent of Warsaw, take rd no. 7/8 700m twds Katowice. Not v well sp fr cent of town. Ent & exit diff due v busy rd. 1*, Sm, pt shd, EHU (6A) PLN15; bbq; 10% statics; phone; bus 500m; Eng spkn; ccard acc; tennis; CKE. *"Easy access to Warsaw & Royal Castle; gd meals at adj bowling alley or Vera hotel; poss lge rallies on site; friendly; poor condition but well positioned to get into city."* **PLN 138, 1 May-30 Sep.** **2019**

WEGORZEWO *A3* (4km SE Rural) *54.18647, 21.77018* **Camping Rusałka (No. 175),** 11-600 Węgorzewo warmińsko-mazurskie Polska **(087) 4272191; camping@cmazur.pl; www.cmazur.pl**

🐕 ♿♨️ 🛒 ⚓ 🚿 ⚡ 🍽️ 🍴 ⏱️ ⑩ 🛢️ 🅿️ nr 🛢️ nr

Fr rte 63 fr Giżycko to Węgorzewo turn W approx 3km SW of Węgorzewo. Foll sp to site. 2*, Lge, pt shd, EHU PLN8; sw nr; 80% statics; sailing; fishing. *"Lovely pt of Lake District; delightful situation; all facs at top of steep hill."* **PLN 48, 1 May-30 Sep.** **2020**

WIELICZKA *D3* (1.5km SE Urban) *49.98273, 20.07611* **Motel Camping Wierzynka,** ul Wierzynka 9, 32-020 Wieliczka **(012) 2783614; motel@nawierzynka.pl; www.nawierzynka.pl**

♿♨️ ⚓ ⚡ 🐕 ⏱️ 🍴 ⑩ 🛢️ 🅿️ nr

Site sp fr E40/rte 4 about 2km fr salt mine. Sm, hdstg, pt shd, pt sl, EHU (10A) PLN10 (rev pol); bus to Krakow, train 1km; Eng spkn; ccard acc; bike hire; CKE. *"10 pitches in pleasant setting; helpful staff; facs basic but clean; shwrs erratic; 2km fr salt mines; vg site, local to salt mines; shwr portacabin, but clean."* **PLN 80, 1 May-30 Sep.** **2019**

WROCLAW *C2* (4km NE Urban) *51.11722, 17.09138* **Stadion Olimpijski Camp (No. 117),** ul Padarewskiego 35, 51-620 Wrocław **(071) 3484651**

🐕 ♿♨️ ⚓ ⚡ 🍴 ⑩ nr 🛢️ 🅿️ nr 🏔️

Fr A4 into Wrocław foll N8 sp Warszawa thro city. On N8 dir Warszawa, pass McDonalds, at fork in rd take Sienkiewicza to end, then Rozyckiego to stadium, site on R. If poss foll sp 'stadium' to camp; head for lighting towers of sports stadium if seen thro trees. 2*, Lge, pt shd, EHU (16A) PLN7.50; bbq; 10% statics; phone; tram nr; CKE. *"San facs basic but clean; site run down (2017); gd security; poss noise fr stadium; v conv for city; stop for tram v handy; pool 700m; carpk outside site."* **PLN 77, 1 May-15 Oct.** **2018**

ZAKOPANE *D3* (4km NE Rural) *49.32415, 19.98506*
Camping Harenda (No. 160), Oś Harenda 51B, 34-500
Zakopane **(018) 2014700; harenda51b@gmail.com;
www.harenda.tatrynet.pl**

12 🐾 ♦♦♦ (htd) WD ♨ 🏊 ⩘ MSP ♈ ⊕ 🛒 nr ⚠

On main rd to Zakopane fr N, after town sp turn R
into petrol stn with McDonalds. Cont to R, pass
Cmp Ustep on L then turn L over rv bdge to site in
200m on R. 2*, Med, pt shd, pt sl, EHU (10A) PLN10
(long lead req); bbq; Eng spkn; CKE. *"Gd views Tatra
mountains fr site; superb walking; poss rallies on site;
poss unkempt LS; laundry done at modest cost; vg
rest; rafting (not white water) on Dunajec Rv; Nowy
Targ rec; lower site poss muddy in wet weather."*
PLN 52 2019

"Satellite navigation makes touring much easier"

Remember most sat navs don't know if you're
towing or in a larger vehicle – always use yours
alongside maps and site directions.

ZAKOPANE *D3* (4km NE Rural) *49.32229, 19.98550*
Camping Ustup (No. 207), ul Ustup K/5, 34-500
Zakopane-Ustup **(08667) 477791; camping.ustup@
gmail.com**

♦♦♦ WD ♨ 🏊 ⩘ ✿ ⊕ nr 🛒 nr ⚠

Turn R off Kraków-Zakopane rd 47 at petrol stn/
McDonalds just after 1st town sp. Turn R again
immed (also sp Cmg Harenda), site on L in 200m.
Sm, unshd, pt sl, EHU (10A) inc; bus to town cent; adv
bkg acc; CKE. *"Ideal cent for Tatra region; mountain
views; excel, family-run site; v welcoming, friendly
& helpful owner (ltd Eng); vg, clean san facs; grassy
pitches; coach tours arranged fr adj g'ge info desk."*
PLN 81, 1 May-30 Sep. 2019

ZAKOPANE *D3* (3km SE Urban) *49.2830, 19.9690*
Camping Pod Krokwia (No. 97), ul Żeromskiego 26,
34-500 Zakopane **(018) 2012256; camp@podkrokwia.
pl; www.podkrokwia.pl**

12 🐾 PLN5 ♦♦♦ WD ♨ 🏊 ⩘ ✿ ♈ ⟟ nr ⊕ 🛒 nr ⚠

Sp fr town cent. Fr N 2nd exit at 1st rndbt; strt over
at 2nd rndbt; turn R at 3rd rndabt, then R in 250m.
Site on L. 3*, Lge, hdstg, shd, pt sl, EHU (10A) inc; bbq
cooking facs; TV; phone; bus to Kraków; Eng spkn;
tennis adj; CKE. *"Lge tent area; few mkd pitches; poss
scruffy LS; poor san facs; conv town cent; ski slopes
& cable cars; rafting on rapids; muddy when set; conv
Tatra Mountains; mountain walks; town v touristy; vg
loc; ltd facs; free gas stove."* **PLN 65.4** 2020

ZAMOSC *C4* (1km SW Rural) *50.71919, 23.23908*
Camping Duet (No. 253), ul Królowej Jadwigi 14,
22-400 Zamość **(084) 6392499; duet@virgo.com.pl**

12 🐾 ♦♦♦ WD ♨ 🏊 ⩘ ✿ ⟟ ⊕ 🛒

Fr Zamość cent W on rd 74, site on R bef Castorama.
1*, Sm, pt shd, EHU PLN12; 10% statics; CKE. *"Walk
to attractive town; pool 150m; fair sh stay/NH."*
PLN 59 2016

ZGORZELEC *C1* (1km N Urban) *51.15957, 15.00069*
Camping Zgorzelec, ul Lubańska 1a, 59-900 Zgorzelec
**(075) 7752436; it@zgorzelec.eu; https://www.it.
zgorzelec.pl**

12 ♦♦♦ ⩘

Ent Zgorzelec fr Germany & foll rd sp Zagan. Turn L
at traff lts at BP g'ge INTO Lubanska rd sp 351 site
on R after 560m, bef downwards hill. Only sp is at
camp gate. Sm, unshd, pt sl, EHU inc; CKE. *"Conv NH."*
PLN 60 2020

Legend:
- France and Andorra
- Central and South East Europe, Benelux and Scandinavia
- Spain and Portugal

Koszalin to Warszawa (Warsaw) = 436km

Biala Podlaska	Bialystok	Bielsko-Biala	Bydgoszcz	Czestochowa	Elblag	Gdansk	Gorzów Wielkopolski	Jelenia Góra	Katowice	Kielce	Koszalin	Kraków	Legnica	Lódz	Lublin	Olsztyn	Plock	Poznan	Przemysl	Radom	Rzeszów	Suwalki	Swinoujscie	Szczecin	Torun	Warszawa (Warsaw)	Wroclaw	Zamosc	Zielona Góra
149																													
472	543																												
412	392	447																											
365	410	133	314																										
404	320	584	171	451																									
461	379	617	167	473	59																								
596	603	496	214	415	333	315																							
605	641	348	344	285	515	513	251																						
416	485	58	391	75	524	545	456	327																					
262	365	207	348	124	461	482	480	415	156																				
596	570	618	198	508	247	188	215	461	560	543																			
376	477	86	434	114	567	565	529	403	75	114	621																		
567	603	301	288	247	460	455	219	56	291	371	405	341																	
286	322	252	203	121	325	342	341	313	196	143	395	222	273																
127	260	362	421	288	441	500	596	537	323	167	595	269	499	242															
305	223	537	217	401	99	156	431	536	479	392	344	501	482	279	372														
267	270	363	150	230	234	276	346	385	305	231	340	327	340	104	271	177													
470	488	387	131	289	300	296	131	226	333	354	241	405	170	210	465	323	215												
312	445	319	588	342	622	685	721	618	322	241	778	243	580	384	185	555	444	595											
184	285	285	322	181	383	444	487	430	232	78	512	192	392	137	107	316	179	358	268										
297	430	238	513	272	585	642	639	542	243	165	710	165	503	306	170	514	378	517	78	199									
269	117	631	417	497	277	336	613	722	571	449	524	565	675	414	379	200	336	525	562	370	549								
730	701	676	312	586	400	341	179	429	636	651	151	701	397	508	728	491	462	297	892	634	816	667							
677	656	603	267	520	374	351	105	356	561	585	160	634	324	446	683	484	415	234	832	585	750	651	110						
366	347	422	46	290	167	181	260	366	364	307	236	384	312	159	375	172	104	150	542	278	472	370	356	313					
157	188	355	252	222	280	338	439	452	297	183	436	294	415	136	161	212	112	310	346	103	299	274	601	524	211				
496	532	230	265	176	436	432	268	109	199	300	420	267	69	204	428	442	276	178	511	321	435	614	442	371	289	344			
180	334	392	514	335	532	589	683	624	367	211	686	320	582	329	90	459	360	554	148	196	155	447	815	770	463	249	508		
570	601	387	259	328	430	411	109	142	358	420	322	427	111	301	542	453	351	130	663	433	586	653	290	212	281	413	159	629	

Motorways
Major roads
Main roads

© Collins Bartholomew Ltd 2021

50 kms
30 mls

LITHUANIA
VILNIUS
Marijampolė

RUSSIA
Kaliningrad

BALTIC SEA

BORNHOLM
(Denmark)
Sassnitz

Rostock
Greifswald
Sassnitz

BELARUS
Slonim
Hrodna
Białowieża
Brest

UKRAINE
Kovel'

SUWAŁKI
Ełk
Ruciane-Nida
Mikołajki
Frombork
Morąg
OLSZTYN
PŁOCK

BIAŁYSTOK
BIAŁA
PODLASKA

LUBLIN
ZAMOŚĆ
Zamość 17

LEZAJSK
Przeworsk
LANCUT
RZESZÓW
Tarnów

SANDOMIERZ
Sandomierz
RADOM
Kazimierz
Dolny
KIELCE

WARSZAWA

ŁÓDŹ

CZĘSTOCHOWA
KATOWICE
Oświęcim
KRAKÓW
Wieliczka
BIELSKO-BIAŁA
Niedzica
Zakopane
Żilina

SLOVAKIA

GDAŃSK
Łeba
Ustka
Mielno
Kołobrzeg
KOSZALIN

TORUŃ
BYDGOSZCZ

POZNAŃ
Lutichów

WROCŁAW
LEGNICA
Kłodzko
JELENIA
GÓRA
Karpacz
ZIELONA GÓRA
Liberec
Hradec
Králové

SZCZECIN
GORZÓW
WIELKOPOLSKI
Sulecin
ŚWINOUJŚCIE
Pasewalk
Frankfurt
an der Oder
Cottbus
Görlitz

PRAHA
CZECHIA
(CZECH REPUBLIC)
Ostrava

GERMANY
BERLIN
Dresden

N
W   E
S

Red: All year site(s)
Black: Seasonal site(s)
○ No sites listed
200m +
0–200m

● All year site(s)
● Seasonal site(s)
○ No sites listed

697

Azenhas do Mar

Shutterstock/Sean Pavone

Highlights

With around 3000 hours of sunshine a year, 850 kilometres of spectacular beaches and a wonderfully vibrant and varied landscape, Portugal is a visitor's paradise.

The country has been heavily influenced by its nautical tradition and position on the Atlantic. Many local delicacies are fish-based dishes, such as grilled sardines and salt cod, while some of Portugal's most splendid architecture date from when it was a global maritime empire.

Ceramic tiles, or azelujos, are a common element of Portuguese designs. Often depicting aspects of Portuguese culture and history, these tiles are both beautiful and functional, and are a significant part of Portugal's heritage.

Portugal is the birthplace of port, and the Douro region is one of the oldest protected wine regions in the world. Taking its name from the city of Porto, this smooth, fortified wine is exclusively produced in the Duoro Valley of Northern Portugal.

Major towns and cities

- Lisbon – Portugal's capital is known for its museums and café culture.
- Porto – an extravagant city filled with beautiful and colourful sights.
- Braga – an ancient city with filled with churches and Roman ruins.
- Faro – the prefect base to explore the Algarve.

Attractions

- Jerónimos Monastery – this UNESCO heritage site houses two museums.
- Guimarães Castle – this medieval castle is known as the Cradle of Portugal.
- National Palace of Pena – a striking palace filled with wonderful works of art.
- Lisbon Oceanarium – enjoy stunning living ocean exhibits.

Find out more

www.visitportugal.com
E: info@visitportugal.com T: (0)1 21 11 40 200

Country Information

Population (approx): 10.8 million

Capital: Lisbon

Area: 92,100 sq km (inc Azores and Madeira)

Bordered by: Spain

Terrain: Rolling plains in south; mountainous and forested north of River Tagus

Climate: Temperate climate with no extremes of temperature; wet winters in the north influenced by the Gulf Stream; elsewhere Mediterranean with hot, dry summers and short, mild winters

Coastline: 1,794km

Highest Point (mainland Portugal): Monte Torre 1,993m

Language: Portuguese

Local Time: GMT or BST, i.e. the same as the UK all year

Currency: Euros divided into 100 cents; £1 = €1.14, €1 = £0.88 (Feb 2021)

Emergency numbers: Police 112; Fire brigade 112; Ambulance 112

Public Holidays 2021: Jan 1; Apr 2, 4, 25; May 1; Jun 3, 10 (National Day); Aug 15; Oct 5; Nov 1; Dec 1, 8, 25.

Other holidays and saints' days are celebrated according to region. School summer holidays run from the end of June to the end of August.

Entry Formalities

British and Irish passport holders may stay for up to 90 days in any 180 day period without a visa. Following Brexit you may be asked to show a return or onward ticket at the border to confirm your length of stay, or to prove that you have enough money for your stay.

Your passport will need to have a minimum of 6 months' validity remaining, and be less than 10 years old (even if it has over 6 months left).

Visitors arriving at a campsite or hotel must complete a registration form.

Medical Services

For treatment of minor conditions go to a pharmacy (farmacia). Staff are generally well trained and are qualified to dispense drugs, which may only be available on prescription in Britain. In large towns there is usually at least one pharmacy whose staff speak English, and all have information posted on the door indicating the nearest pharmacy open at night. All municipalities have a health centre.

State emergency health care and hospital treatment is free on production of a European Health Insurance Card (EHIC). You will have to pay for items such as X-rays, laboratory tests and prescribed medicines as well as dental treatment. Refunds can be claimed from local offices of the Administracão Regional de Saúde (regional health service).

For serious illness you can obtain the name of an English speaking doctor from the local police station or tourist office or from a British or American consulate.

Normal precautions should be taken to avoid mosquito bites, including the use of insect repellents, especially at night.

Opening Hours

Banks: Mon-Fri 8.30am-3pm; some banks in city centres are open until 6pm.

Museums: Tue-Sun 10am-5pm/6pm; closed Mon and may close 12.30pm-2pm.

Post Offices: Mon-Fri 9am-6pm; may close for an hour at lunch.

Shops: Mon-Fri 9am-1pm & 3pm-7pm, Sat 9am-1pm; large supermarkets open Mon-Sun 9am/9.30am 10pm/11pm.

Safety and Security

The crime rate is low but pickpocketing, bag snatching and thefts from cars can occur in major tourist areas. Be vigilant on public transport, at crowded tourist sites and in public parks where it is wise to go in pairs. Keep car windows closed and doors locked while driving in urban areas at night. There has been an increase in reported cases of items stolen from vehicles in car parks. Thieves distract drivers by asking for directions, for example, or other information. Be cautious if you are approached in this way in a car park.

Take care of your belongings at all times. Do not leave your bag on the chair beside you, under the table or hanging on your chair while you eat in a restaurant or café.

Death by drowning occurs every year on Portuguese beaches. Warning flags should be taken very seriously. A red flag indicates danger and you should not enter the water. If a yellow flag is flying you may paddle at the water's edge, but you may not swim. A green flag indicates that it is safe to swim, and a chequered flag means that the lifeguard is temporarily absent. Do not swim from beaches which are not manned by lifeguards. The police may fine bathers who disobey warning flags.

During long, hot, dry periods forest fires can occur, especially in northern and central parts of the country. Take care when visiting or driving through woodland areas: ensure that cigarettes are extinguished properly, do not light barbecues, and do not leave empty bottles behind.

Portugal shares with the rest of Europe an underlying threat from terrorism. Attacks could be indiscriminate and against civilian targets in public places including tourist sites.

British Embassy

RUA DE SÃO BERNARDO 33,
1249-082 LISBOA
Tel: 21 392 4000
www.ukinportugal.fco.gov.uk
There is also a British Consulate in Portimão.

Irish Embassy

VENIDA DA LIBERDADE No 200, 4th FLOOR
1250-147 LISBON
Tel: 213 308 200
www.embassyofireland.pt

Documents

Driving Licence

All valid UK driving licences should be accepted in Portugal but holders of an older all green style licence are advised to update it to a photocard before travelling. Alternatively carry an International Driving Permit, available from the AA, the RAC or selected Post Offices.

Passport

You must carry proof of identity which includes a photograph and signature, e.g. a passport or photocard licence, at all times.

Vehicle(s)

When driving you must carry your vehicle registration certificate (V5C), proof of insurance and MOT certificate (if applicable). There are heavy on the spot fines for those who fail to do so.

Money

The major credit cards are widely accepted and there are cash machines (Multibanco) throughout the country. A tax of €0.50 may be added to credit card transactions, especially at petrol stations. Carry your credit card issuers'/banks' 24 hour UK contact numbers in case of loss or theft.

Driving

Many Portuguese drive erratically and vigilance is advised. By comparison with the UK, the accident rate is high. Particular blackspots are the N125 along the south coast, especially in the busy holiday season, and the coast road between Lisbon and Cascais. In rural areas you may encounter horse drawn carts and flocks of sheep or goats. Otherwise there are no special difficulties in driving except in Lisbon and Porto, which are unlimited 'free-for-alls'.

Accidents

The police must be called in the case of injury or significant material damage.

Alcohol

The maximum permitted level of alcohol is 50 milligrams in 100 millilitres of blood, i.e. lower than permitted in the UK (80 milligrams). For newly qualified drivers (those with under 3 year's experience), the legal limit is 20 milligrams per 100 millilitres of blood. It is advisable to adopt the 'no drink-driving' rule at all times.

Breakdown Service

The Automovel Club de Portugal (ACP) operates a 24 hour breakdown service covering all roads in mainland Portugal. Its vehicles are coloured red and white. Emergency telephones are located at 2km intervals on main roads and motorways. To contact the ACP breakdown service call +351 219 429113 from a mobile or 707 509510 from a landline.

The breakdown service comprises on the spot repairs taking up to a maximum of 45 minutes and, if necessary, the towing of vehicles. The charges for breakdown assistance and towing vary according to distance, time of day and day of the week, plus motorway tolls if applicable. Payment by credit card is accepted.

Alternatively, on motorways breakdown vehicles belonging to the motorway companies (their emergency numbers are displayed on boards along the motorways) and police patrols (GNR/Brigada de Trânsito) can assist motorists.

Child Restraint System

Children under 12 years of age and less than 1.35m in height are not allowed to travel in the front passenger seat. They must be seated in a child restraint system adapted to their size and weight in the rear of the vehicle, unless the vehicle only has two seats, or if the vehicle is not fitted with seat belts.

Children under the age of 3 years old can be seated in the front passenger seat as long as they are in a suitable rear facing child restraint system and the airbag has been deactivated.

Fuel

Credit cards are accepted at most filling stations but a small extra charge may be added and a tax of €0.50 is added to credit card transactions. There are no automatic petrol pumps. LPG (gáz liquido) is widely available.

Low Emission Zone

There is a Low Emission Zone in operation in Lisbon. There are 2 different zones within the city. In zone 1 vehicles must meet European Emission Standard 2 (EURO 3) and in zone 2 vehicles must meet EURO 2 standard. For more information visit www.lowemissionzones.eu

Motorways

Portugal has more than 2,600km of motorways (auto-estradas), with tolls (portagem) payable on most sections. Take care not to use the 'Via Verde' green lanes reserved for motorists who subscribe to the automatic payment system – be sure to go through a ticket booth lane where applicable, or one equipped with the new electronic toll system.

Dual carriageways (auto vias) are toll free and look similar to motoways, but speed limits are lower.

It is permitted to spend the night on a motorway rest or service area with a caravan, although The Caravan and Motorhome Club does not recommend this practice for security reasons. Toll tickets are only valid for 12 hours and fines are incurred if this is exceeded.

Vehicle are classified for tolls as follows:

Class 1   Vehicle with or without trailer with height from front axle less than 1.10m.

Class 2   Vehicle with 2 axles, with or without trailer, with height from front axle over 1.10m.

Class 3   Vehicle or vehicle combination with 3 axles, with height from front axle over 1.10m.

Class 4* Vehicle or vehicle combination with 4 or more axles with height from front axle over 1.10m.

* Drivers of high vehicles of the Range Rover/ Jeep variety, together with some MPVs, and towing a twin axle caravan pay Class 4 tolls.

Mountain Roads and Passes

There are no mountain passes or tunnels in Portugal. Roads through the Serra da Estrela near Guarda and Covilha may be temporarily obstructed for short periods after heavy snow.

Parking

In most cases vehicles must be parked facing in the same direction as moving traffic. Parking is very limited in the centre of main towns and cities and 'blue zone' parking schemes operate. Illegally parked vehicles may be towed away or clamped. Parking in Portuguese is 'estacionamento'.

Priority

In general at intersections and road junctions, road users must give way to vehicles approaching from the right, unless signs indicate otherwise. At roundabouts vehicles already on the roundabout, i.e. on the left, have right of way.

Do not pass stationary trams at a tram stop until you are certain that all passengers have finished entering or leaving the tram.

Roads

Roads are surfaced with asphalt, concrete or stone setts. Main roads generally are well surfaced and may be three lanes wide, the middle lane being used for overtaking in either direction.

Roads in the south of the country are generally in good condition, but some sections in the north are in a poor state. Roads in many towns and villages are often cobbled and rough.

Drivers entering Portugal from Zamora in Spain will notice an apparently shorter route on the CL527/N221 road via Mogadouro. Although this is actually the signposted route, the road surface is poor in places and this route is not recommended for trailer caravans. The recommended route is via the N122/IP4 to Bragança.

Road Signs and Markings

Road signs conform to international standards. Road markings are white or yellow. Signs on motorways (auto-estrada) are blue and on regional roads they are white with black lettering. Roads are classified as follows:

Code	Road Type
AE	Motorways
IP	Principal routes
IC	Complementary routes
EN	National roads
EM	Municipal roads
CM	Other municipal roads

Signs you might encounter are as follows:

Portuguese	English Translation
Atalho	Detour
Entrada	Entrance
Estação de gasolina	Petrol station
Estacão de policia	Police station
Estacionamento	Parking
Estrada con portagem	Toll road
Saida	Exit

Speed Limits

	Open Road (km/h)	Motorway (km/h)
Car Solo	90-100	120
Car towing caravan/ trailer	70-80	100
Motorhome under 3500kg	90-100	120
Motorhome 3500-7500kg	70-90	100

Drivers must maintain a speed between 40 km/h (25 mph) and 60 km/h (37 mph) on the 25th April Bridge over the River Tagus in Lisbon. Speed limits are electronically controlled.

Visitors who have held a driving licence for less than one year must not exceed 90 km/h (56 mph) on any road subject to higher limits.

In built-up areas there is a speed limit of 50 km/h.

It is prohibited to use a radar detector or to have one installed in a vehicle.

Towing

Motorhomes are permitted to tow a car on a four wheel trailer, i.e. with all four wheels of the car off the ground. Towing a car on an A-frame (two back wheels on the ground) is not permitted.

Traffic Jams

Traffic jams are most likely to be encountered around Lisbon and Porto and on roads to the coast, such as the A1 Lisbon-Porto and the A2 Lisbon-Setúbal, which are very busy on Friday evenings and Saturday mornings. The peak times for holiday traffic are the last weekend in June and the first and last weekends in July and August.

Around Lisbon bottlenecks occur on bridges across the River Tagus, the N6 to Cascais, the A1 to Vila Franca de Xira, the N8 to Loures and on the N10 from Setúbal via Almada.

Around Porto you may find traffic jams on the IC1 on the Arribada Bridge and at Vila Nova de Gaia, the A28/IC1 from Póvoa de Varzim and near Vila de Conde, and on the N13, N14 and the N15.

Major motorways are equipped with suspended signs which indicate the recommended route to take when there is traffic congestion.

Traffic Lights

There is no amber signal after the red. A flashing amber light indicates 'caution' and a flashing or constant red light indicates 'stop'. In Lisbon there are separate traffic lights in bus lanes.

Violation of Traffic Regulations

Speeding, illegal parking and other infringements of traffic regulations are heavily penalised.

You may incur a fine for crossing a continuous single or double white or yellow line in the centre of the road when overtaking or when executing a left turn into or off a main road, despite the lack of any other 'no left turn' signs. If necessary, drive on to a roundabout or junction to turn, or turn right as directed by arrows.

The police are authorised to impose on the spot fines and a receipt must be given. Most police vehicles are now equipped with portable credit card machines to facilitate immediate payment of fines.

Tolls

An electronic toll collecting system was introduced in Portugal during 2010. The following motorways have tolls but no toll booths: A27, A28, A24, A41, A42, A25, A29, A23, A13, A8, A19, A33, A22 and parts of the A17 and A4. Tolls for these motorways can be paid by one of the following options:

If you are crossing the border from Spain on the A24, A25 or A22 or the A28 (via the EN13) then you can use the EASYToll welcome points. You can input your credit card details and the machine reads and then matches your credit/debit card to your number-plate, tolls are deducted automatically from your credit card, and the EASYToll machine will issue you a 30 day receipt as proof that you have paid.

If you are entering Portugal on a road that does not have an EASYToll machine you can register on-line or at a CTT post office and purchase either €5, €10, €20 or €40 worth of tolls. You can purchase a virtual prepaid ticket

up to 6 times a year. For more information visit www.ctt.pt – you can select 'ENG' at the top left of the screen to see the site in English.

Alternatively you can get a temporary device (DT) available from some motorway service stations, post offices and Via Verde offices.

A deposit of €27.50 is payable when you hire the DT and this is refundable when you return it to any of the outlets mentioned above. If you use a debit card, toll costs will automatically be debited from your card. If you pay cash you will be required to preload the DT. For further information see www.visitportugal.com and see the heading 'All about Portugal' then 'Useful Information'.

On motorways where this system applies you will see a sign: 'Lanço Com Portagem' or 'Electronic Toll Only', together with details of the tolls charged. Drivers caught using these roads without a DT will incur a minimum fine of €25.

The toll roads A1 to A15 and A21 continue to have manned toll booths. Most, but not all, accept credit cards or cash.

Toll Bridges

The 2km long 25th April Bridge in Lisbon crosses the River Tagus. Tolls are charged for vehicles travelling in a south-north direction only. Tolls also apply on the Vasco da Gama Bridge, north of Lisbon, but again only to vehicles travelling in a south-north direction. Overhead panels indicate the maximum permitted speed in each lane and, when in use, override other speed limit signs.

In case of breakdown, or if you need assistance, you should try to stop in the emergency hard shoulder areas, wait inside your vehicle and switch on your hazard warning lights until a patrol arrives. Emergency telephones are placed at frequent intervals. It is prohibited to carry out repairs, to push vehicles physically or to walk on the bridges.

Essential Equipment

Reflective Jackets/Waistcoats

If your vehicle is immobilised on the carriageway you should wear a reflective jacket or waistcoat when getting out of your vehicle. This is a legal requirement for residents of Portugal and is recommended for visitors. Passengers who leave a vehicle, for example, to assist with a repair, should also wear one. Keep the jackets within easy reach inside your vehicle, not in the boot.

Warning Triangles

Use a warning triangle if, for any reason, a stationary vehicle is not visible for at least 100 metres. In addition, hazard warning lights must be used if a vehicle is causing an obstruction or danger to other road users.

Touring

Some English is spoken in large cities and tourist areas. Elsewhere a knowledge of French could be useful.

A Lisboa Card valid for 24, 48 or 72 hours, entitles the holder to free unrestricted access to public transport, including trains to Cascais and Sintra, free entry to a number of museums, monuments and other places of interest in Lisbon and surrounding areas, as well as discounts in shops and places offering services to tourists. These cards are obtainable from tourist information offices, travel agents, some hotels and Carris ticket booths, or by visiting www.welovecitycards.com

Do ensure when eating out that you understand exactly what you are paying for; appetisers put on the table are not free. Service is included in the bill, but it is customary to tip 5 to 10% of the total if you have received good service. Rules on smoking in restaurants and bars vary according to the size of the premises. The areas where clients are allowed to smoke are indicated by signs and there must be adequate ventilation. Each town in Portugal devotes several days in the year to local celebrations which are invariably lively and colourful. Carnivals and festivals during the period before Lent, during Holy Week and during the grape harvest can be particularly spectacular.

Camping and Caravanning

There are numerous campsites in Portugal, and many of these are situated along the coast. Sites are rated from 1 to 4 stars.

There are 22 privately owned campsites in the Orbitur chain. Caravanners can join the Orbitur Camping Club for discounts of at least 15% at these sites. The joining fee is €21, with a 50% discount for senior citizens. You can buy membership at Orbitur sites or www.orbitur. com. Casual/wild camping is not permitted.

Motorhomes

A number of local authorities now provide dedicated short stay areas for motorhomes called 'Áreas de Serviço'. It is rare that yours will be the only motorhome staying on such areas, but take sensible precautions and avoid any that are isolated.

Cycling

In Lisbon there are cycle lanes in Campo Grande gardens, also from Torre de Belém to Cais do Sodré (7km) along the River Tagus, and between Cascais and Guincho. Elsewhere in the country there are few cycle lanes.

Transportation of Bicycles

Legislation stipulates that the exterior dimensions of a vehicle should not be exceeded and, in practice, this means that only caravans or motorhomes are allowed to carry bicycles/motorbikes at the rear of the vehicle. Bicycles may not extend beyond the width of the vehicle or more than 45cms from the back. However, bicycles may be transported on the roof of cars provided that an overall height of 4 metres is not exceeded. Cars carrying bicycles/motorbikes on the back may be subject to a fine.

If you are planning to travel from Spain to Portugal please note that slightly different regulations apply and these are set out in the Spain Country Introduction.

Electricity and Gas

Usually current on campsites varies between 6 and 15 amps. Plugs have two round pins. CEE connections are commonplace.

The full range of Campingaz cylinders is available.

Public Transport

A passenger and vehicle ferry crosses the River Sado estuary from Setúbal to Tróia and there are frequent ferry and catamaran services for cars and passengers across the River Tagus from various points in Lisbon including Belém and Cais do Sodré.

Both Lisbon and Porto have metro systems operating from 6am to 1am. For routes and fares information see www.metrolisboa.pt and www.metrodoporto.pt (English versions).

Throughout the country buses are cheap, regular and mostly on time, with every town connected. In Lisbon the extensive bus and tram network is operated by Carris, together with one lift and three funiculars which tackle the city's steepest hills. Buy single journey tickets on board from bus drivers or buy a rechargeable 'Sete Colinas' or Via Viagem card for use on buses and the metro.

In Porto buy a 'Euro' bus ticket, which can be charged with various amounts, from metro stations and transport offices. Validate tickets for each journey at machines on the buses. 'Andante' tickets are valid on the metro and on buses. Porto also has a passenger lift and a funicular so that you can avoid the steep walk to and from the riverside.

Taxis are usually a cream. In cities they charge a standard, metered fare; outside they may run on the meter or charge a flat rate. Agree a price for your journey before setting off.

Lisbon

Shutterstock/Balate Dorin

ALANDROAL *C3* (13km S Rural) *38.60645, -7.34674* **Camping Rosário,** Monte das Mimosas, Rosário, 7250-999 Alandroal **268 459566; info@camping rosario.com; www.campingrosario.com**

🐕 €1 ♦♦♦ WD ≛ ⚘ / 🦋 🍸 ⑪ ⚓ nr ⚑

Fr E exit IP7/A6 at Elvas W junc 9; at 3rd rndabt take exit sp Espanha, immed 1st R dir Juromenha & Redondo. Onto N373 until exit Rosário. Fr W exit IP7/A6 junc 8 at Borba onto N255 to Alandroal, then N373 E sp Elvas. After 1.5km turn R to Rosário & foll sp to site. Sm, hdstg, pt shd, pt sl, EHU (6A) €2.35; sw nr; red long stay; TV; Eng spkn; adv bkg acc; boating; fishing; CKE. *"Remote site beside Alqueva Dam; excel touring base; dogs not acc Jul/Aug; ltd to 50 people max; excel site; idyllic; peaceful; clean & well maintained; v helpful owner."* **€22.50, 2 Jan-30 Sep.**   2019

ALBUFEIRA *B4* (3km N Urban) *37.10617, -8.25395* **Camping Albufeira,** Estrada de Ferreiras, 8200-555 Albufeira **289 587629 or 289 587630; geral@campingalbufeira.net or info@ campingalbufeira.net; www.campingalbufeira.net**

12 🐕 ♦♦♦ WD ≛ ⚘ & 🖩 / MSP 🦋 🍸 ⑪ ♨ ⚓ ⚑ /🏊

🏄 sand 1.5km

Exit IP1/E1 sp Albufeira onto N125/N395 dir Albufeira; camp on L, sp. 4*, V lge, mkd, pt shd, pt sl, EHU (10-12A) €3; gas; red long stay; TV; 20% statics; phone; bus adj; Eng spkn; ccard acc; games area; games rm; bike hire; tennis; CKE. *"Friendly, secure site; excel pool area/bar; some pitches lge enough for US RVs; car wash; cash machine; security patrols; disco (soundproofed); sports park; pitches on lower pt of site prone to flooding in heavy rain; conv beach & town; poss lge rallies during Jan-Apr; camp bus to town high ssn."* **€27.60**   2016

See advertisement

ALCACER DO SAL *B3* (1km NW Rural) *38.38027, -8.51583* **Parque de Campismo Municipal de Alcácer do Sal,** Olival do Outeiro, 7580-125 Alcácer do Sal **265 612303; cmalcacer@mail.telepac.pt**

🐕 ♦♦♦ WD ≛ ⚘ & 🖩 / MSP ⚘ 🍸 nr ⑪ nr ⚓ nr ⚑

Heading S on A2/IP1 turn L twd Alcácer do Sal on N5. Site on R 1km fr Alcácer do Sal. Sp at rndabt. Site behind supmkt. 2*, Sm, hdg, mkd, pt shd, pt sl, EHU (6-12A) €1.50 (rev pol); bbq; phone; bus 50m; Eng spkn; ccard acc; games area; clsd mid-Dec to mid-Jan; CKE. *"In rice growing area - major mosquito prob; historic town; spacious pitches; pool, paddling pool adj; poss full in winter - rec phone ahead; pleasant site behing supmkt; wifi at recep; san facs tired & not clean."* **€13.70, 15 Jan-15 Dec.**   2017

"There aren't many sites open at this time of year"

If you're travelling outside peak season remember to call ahead to check site opening dates – even if the entry says 'open all year'.

ALCOBACA *B2* (3km S Rural) *39.52611, -8.96583* **Camping Silveira,** Capuchos, 2460-479 Alcobaça **262 509573; campingsilveira@gmail.com; www.campingsilveira.com**

🐕 €1 ♦♦♦ ≛ ⚘ / 🦋 🍸 nr ⑪ nr ⚓ nr

S fr Alcobaça on N 8-6 sp Evora de Alcobaça. Site on L in 3km after Capuchos. 1*, Med, hdg, shd, pt sl, EHU (6A) €3; bbq; bus 500m; Eng spkn; adv bkg acc; games rm; badminton; sm library; WiFi access pnt. *"Vg, wooded, CL-type site; friendly owner; gd views; excel facs; pool 3km; excel touring base; site access extremely tight; site overgrown and unkept; Monastry Santa Maria in Alcobaca a must see; fair."* **€13.00, 15 May-15 Sep.**   2019

AMARANTE *C1* (3km NE Rural) *41.27805, -8.07027*
Camping Penedo da Rainha, Rua Pedro Alveollos, Gatão, 4600-099 Amarante **255 437630 or 915 493330; ccporto@sapo.pt or geral@amarante camping.com; www.amarantecamping.com**

🐕 👭 WD ♨ ⚓ 🚿 🚽 / MSP 🦋 🍴 ⊕ 🛒 ⚠ 🚲 ♨

Fr IP4 Vila Real to Porto foll sp to Amarante & N15. On N15 cross bdge for Porto & immed take R slip rd. Foll sp thro junc & up rv to site. 2*, Lge, hdstg, shd, pt sl, terr, EHU (10A) inc; TV; phone; bus to Porto fr Amarante; Eng spkn; adv bkg acc; games rm; rv fishing adj; canoeing; cycling; CKE. *"Well-run site in steep woodland/parkland - take advice or survey rte bef driving to pitch; excel facs but some pitches far fr facs; few touring pitches; friendly, helpful recep; plenty of shd; conv Amarante old town & Douro Valley; Sat mkt; not suitable for long o'fits, better for MH's; beautiful cycle route on old rlwy."* **€21.50, 1 Jan-30 Nov.** 2019

ARCO DE BAULHE *C1* (0.3km NE Rural) *41.48659, -7.95845* **Arco Unipessoal,** Lugar das Cruzes, 4860-067 Arco de Baúlhe (Costa Verde) **(351) 968176246; campismoarco@hotmail.com**

🐕 👭 WD ♨ 🚿 / 🍴 ⊕ (htd) ♨

Dir A7 exit 12 Mondm/Cabeceiras, 2nd R at rndabt dir Arco de Baulhe. Call and they will lead you in. V narr rd access, no mv's over 7m. Med, pt shd, terr, EHU (6A); bbq; TV; Eng spkn; adv bkg rec; rv. *"New site run by couple with 20 yrs experience; quiet; centrally located for historic towns & nature parks; gd rest; lovely well maintained site with view; excel facs; 100m fr vill cent; beautiful mountain area."* **€23.00, 3 Apr-1 Oct.** 2019

"That's changed – Should I let the Club know?"

If you find something on site that's different from the site entry, fill in a report and let us know. See camc.com/europereport.

ARGANIL *C2* (3km N Rural) *40.2418, -8.06746* **Camp Municipal de Arganil,** 3300-432 Sarzedo **235 205706; camping@cm-arganil.pt; www.cm-arganil.pt**

🐕 👭 WD ♨ ⚓ 🚿 / MSP 🦋 🍴 ⊕ 🛒 ⚠ ♨

Fr Coimbra on N17 twd Guarda; after 50km turn S sp Arganil on N342-4; site on L in 4km in o'skts of Sarzedo bef rv bdge; avoid Góis to Arganil rd fr SW. 2*, Med, pt shd, pt sl, terr, EHU (5-15A) €2.40; gas; bbq; red long stay; TV; phone; Eng spkn; ccard acc; canoeing adj; games area; fishing adj; CKE. *"Vg, well-run site; friendly owner; fine views; gd cent for touring; gd walks; ski in Serra da Estrela 50km Dec/Jan; interesting town; gd mkt (Thu)."* **€12.50, 1 Mar-31 Oct.** 2016

AVEIRO *B2* (14km SW Coastal) *40.59960, -8.74981* **Camping Costa Nova,** Estrada da Vagueira, Quinta dos Patos, 3830-453 Ílhavo **234 393220; info@camping costanova.com; www.campingcostanova.com**

🐕 €1.40 👭 (htd) WD ♨ ⚓ 🚿 🚽 / MSP 🦋 🍴 ⊕ 🛒 ⚠ 🚲 ♨ sand

Site on Barra-Vagueira coast rd 1km on R after Costa Nova. 2*, V lge, mkd, unshd, EHU (2-6A) €2.40; gas; bbq; red long stay; TV; 10% statics; phone; Eng spkn; adv bkg acc; ccard acc; games rm; site clsd Jan; fishing; bike hire; games area; CKE. *"Superb, peaceful site adj nature reserve; helpful staff; gd, hot water to shwrs only; sm pitches; sep car park high ssn; pool 4km; vg; excel cycle track fr site."* **€22.50, 21 Mar-1 Oct.** 2019

AVEIRO *B2* (10km W Coastal) *40.63861, -8.74500* **Parque de Campismo Praia da Barra,** Rua Diogo Cão 125, Praia da Barra, 3830-772 Gafanha da Nazaré **(234) 369425 or (929) 056884 (mobile); info@ campingbarra.com; www.campingbarra.com**

12 🐕 €1.90 👭 WD ♨ ⚓ 🚿 🚽 / MSP 🦋 ♟ 🍴 ⊕ 🛒 ⚠ 🚲

♨ sand 200m

Fr Aveiro foll sp to Barra on A25/IP5; foll sp to site. 3*, Lge, mkd, shd, EHU (6-10A) inc; gas; bbq; TV; 90% statics; phone; bus adj; Eng spkn; adv bkg acc; bike hire; games area; games rm; CKE. *"Well-situated site with some pitches in pine trees; recep open 0900-2200; pool 400m; old san facs; m'homes may have to park clse together on hardstanding area in LS; may be rd noise in some areas."* **€22.60** 2019

BRAGANCA *D1* (6km N Rural) *41.84361, -6.74722* **Inatel Parque Campismo Bragança,** Estrada de Rabal, 5300-671 Meixedo **351 273 326 080 or 351 96 420 66 22; campismobraganca@gmail.com; www campismo embraganca.com**

🐕 👭 WD ♨ ⚓ 🚽 / 🦋 🍴 ⊕ 🛒 ⚠

Fr Bragança N for 6km on N103.7 twd Spanish border. Site on R, sp Inatel. 2*, Med, hdstg, pt shd, pt sl, terr, EHU (6A) inc; gas; bus; Eng spkn; bike hire; fishing. *"On S boundary of National Park; rv runs thro site; friendly staff; gd rest; vg facs; lovely location by rv; sm, crowded; no pitch markings."* **€21.00, 1 Jun-15 Sep.** 2019

BRAGANCA *D1* (12km W Rural) *41.84879, -6.86120* **Cepo Verde Camping,** Gondesende, 5300-561 Bragança **273 999371; cepoverde@montesinho.com; www.montesinho.com/cepoverde-campismo**

12 🐕 €3.50 👭 WD ♨ ⚓ 🚿 / ⚓ 🦋 🍴 ⊕ 🛒 ⚠

Fr Spain take IP4 twrds Vinhais/Chaves to skirt Bragança. Site sp fr IP4 ring rd. R off N103, foll lane & turn R at sp. NB Camping sp to rd 103-7 leads to different site (Sabor) N of city. 3*, Med, mkd, hdstg, pt shd, terr, EHU (6A) inc (poss rev pol & long lead poss req); bbq; phone; bus 1km; Eng spkn; adv bkg acc; ccard acc; CKE. *"Remote, friendly, v pleasant, scenic site adj Montesinho National Park; vg value; gd modern san facs; staff v helpful; gd rest with vegetarian options; gd base for Montesinho area; highly rec; v attractive site."* **€24.80** 2018

CAMINHA *B1* (3km SW Coastal) *41.86611, -8.85888* **Camping ORBITUR-Caminha,** Mata do Camarido, N13, Km 90, 4910-180 Caminha **258 921295; infocaminha@orbitur.pt; www.orbitur.pt**

🏕12 🐕 €1.50 ♂♀ WD ♿ 🚿 🚮 MSP ✉ ☕ 🍽 ⓗ 🛒 ⚠

🏖 sand 150m

Foll seafront rd N13/E1 fr Caminha dir Viana/Porto, at sp Foz do Minho turn R, site in approx 1km. Long o'fits take care at ent. 2*, Med, shd, terr, EHU (5-15A) €3-4; gas; red long stay; TV; 5% statics; Eng spkn; adv bkg acc; ccard acc; fishing; bike hire; CKE. *"Pleasant, woodland site; pool 2.5km; care in shwrs - turn cold water on 1st as hot poss scalding; Gerês National Park & Viana do Castelo worth visit; poss to cycle to Caminha; vg site, nr attractive beach and sh walk to pleasant town."* **€38.60** 2017

CAMPO MAIOR *C3* (2km SE Rural) *39.00833, -7.04833* **Camping Rural Os Anjos,** Estrada da Senhora da Saúde, 7371-909 Campo Maior **268 688138 or 965 236625 (mob); info@campingosanjos.com; www.campingosanjos.com**

🏕12 🐕 €1 ♂♀ WD ♿ 🚿 🚮 ✉ 🍽 🛒nr 🏊

Fr Elvas foll rd N373 to Campo Maior. Foll sm sp thro vill pass green tree and football stadium. Site on L down country lane. Sm, hdstg, pt shd, terr, EHU (6A) €2.60; bbq; TV; phone; Eng spkn; adv bkg rec; games rm; games area; CKE. *"Excel, lovely, peaceful site; v helpful, friendly, caring Dutch owners; gd touring base for unspoiled, diverse area; conv Spanish border, Badajoz & Elvas; 15 Nov-15 Feb open with adv bkg only; max 1 dog per pitch; Campo Maior beautiful, white town; LS call or email bef arr; gd walks & bike rides; v clean shwrs; lake sw 8km; fishing 8km; watersports 8km; modern facs; fantastic views; excel."* **€17.50** 2019

CASCAIS *A3* (7km NW Urban/Coastal) *38.72166, -9.46666* **Camping ORBITUR-Guincho,** Lugar de Areia, EN 247-6, Guincho 2750-053 Cascais **(214) 870450; infoguincho@orbitur.pt; www.orbitur.pt/camping-orbitur-guincho**

🏕12 🐕 €3 ♂♀ WD 🚿 🚮 ♿ ✉ MSP ☕ 🍽 ⓗ 🛒 ⚠ 🏊

🏖 sand 800m

Fr Lisbon take A5 W, at end m'way foll sp twd Cascais. At 1st rndabt turn R sp Birre & Campismo. Foll sp for 2.5km. Steep traff calming hump - care needed. 2*, V lge, mkd, hdg, shd, terr, EHU (6A) inc; gas; bbq; red long stay; twin axles; TV (pitch); 50% statics; phone; Eng spkn; adv bkg acc; ccard acc; games rm; horseriding 500m; tennis; watersports 1km; car wash; fishing 1km; golf 3km; bike hire; CKE. *"Sandy, wooded site behind dunes; poss stretched & v busy high ssn; poss diff lge o'fits due trees; steep rd to beach; gd san facs, gd value rest; vg LS; buses for Cascais for train to Lisbon; beautiful coastline within 20 min walk; rec lge o'fits prebook to ensure suitable pitch."* **€37.00,, E10.** 2017

CASTELO DE VIDE *C3* (7km SW Rural) *39.39805, -7.48722* **Camping Quinta do Pomarinho,** N246, Km 16.5, Castelo de Vide **(00351) 965 755 341; info@pomarinho.com; www.pomarinho.com**

🏕12 🐕 ♂♀ 🚿 🚮 ✉ ☕ 🍽 🛒nr ⚠

On N246 at km 16.5 by bus stop, turn into dirt track. Site in 500m. Sm, mkd, hdstg, unshd, EHU (6A) €2.50-3.50; bus adj; Eng spkn; adv bkg acc; bike hire. *"On edge of Serra de São Mamede National Park; gd walking, fishing, birdwatching, cycling; vg; gd views twd Serra de Sao Marmede; recep clsd 1-3pm; not many ehu or flat lge pitches."* **€16.50** 2019

CASTRO VERDE *C4* (1km N Urban) *37.704976, -8.087696* **Parque Campismo Castro Verde,** Rua Timor Lorosae 7780, Castro Verde **286 320150; parque.campismo@cm-castroverde.pt; https://cm-castroverde.pt/pt/553/parque-de-campismo-municipal.aspx**

🏕12 🐕 ♂♀ WD 🚿 🚮 ✉ ☕ 🍽 🛒nr ⚠

Sp fr Castro Verde town. Med, hdstg, pt shd, pt sl, EHU; gas; twin axles; TV; Eng spkn; CCI. *"Vg site."* 2019

CELORICO DE BASTO *C1* (0.7km NW Rural) *41.39026, -8.00581* **Parque de Campismo de Celorico de Basto,** Adaufe-Gemeos, 4890-361 Celorico de Basto **(255) 323340 or 964-064436 (mob); www.facebook.com/Celoricocamping/**

🏕12 🐕 €1.80 ♂♀ WD 🚿 🚮 ✉ MSP ☕ 🍽 ⓗ 🛒 ⚠ 🚣

E fr Guimarães exit A7/IC5 S sp Vila Nune (bef x-ing rv). Foll sp Fermil & Celorico de Basto, site sp. Rte narr and winding or take the N210 fr Amarente and foll sp to site. 3*, Med, mkd, hdstg, shd, EHU (6-16A) €2-3.20; gas; bbq; sw nr; red long stay; TV; 10% statics; phone; ccard acc; games area; fishing adj; CKE. *"Peaceful, well-run site; gd facs; pool 500m; gd cycling and walking; vg."* **€16.00** 2019

CHAVES *C1* (6km S Rural) *41.70166, -7.50055* **Camp Municipal Quinta do Rebentão,** Vila Nova de Veiga, 5400-764 Chaves **276 322733; parquedecampismo@chaves.pt; www.ccchaves.com**

🐕 ♂♀ WD 🚿 🚮 ♿ ✉ MSP ☕ 🍽 🛒nr ⚠

Fr o'skts Chaves take N2 S. After about 3km in vill of Vila Nova de Veiga turn E at sp thro new estate, site in about 500m. 1*, Med, hdstg, pt shd, terr, EHU (6A) inc; bbq; sw nr; phone; bus 800m; Eng spkn; adv bkg acc; bike hire; fishing 4km; games rm; CKE. *"Gd site in lovely valley but remote; excel helpful, friendly staff; facs block quite a hike fr some terr pitches, old but clean facs; Chaves interesting, historical Roman town; baker visits every morn; vg rest (clsd Mon in LS) & bar; site clsd Dec; pool adj; easy access; wifi at recep."* **€15.00, 1 Feb-30 Nov.** 2019

COIMBRA *B2* (6km SE Urban) *40.18888, -8.39944*
Coimbra Camping, Rua de Escola, Alto do Areeiro, Santo António dos Olivais, 3030-011 Coimbra
239 086902; geral@cacampings.com; www.coimbra camping.com

12 🐕 €2.90 👥 (htd) ⓦ ⌂ ♨ ⚲ ♿ ⊟ ∥ ᴍsᴘ 🦋 ⛱ ☂ ⑭ 🎣 🛒 ⚂

Fr S on AP1/IP1 at junc 11 turn twd Lousa & in 1km turn twd Coimbra on IC2. In 9.5km turn R at rndabt onto Ponte Rainha, strt on at 3 rndabts along Avda Mendes Silva. Then turn R along Estrada des Beiras & cross rndabt to Rua de Escola. Or fr N17 dir Beira foll sp sports stadium/campismo. Fr N ent Coimbra on IC2, turn L onto ring rd & foll Campismo sps.
4*, V lge, hdstg, pt shd, pt sl, terr, EHU (6A) inc (rev pol); gas; bbq; sw nr; red long stay; TV; 10% statics; bus 100m; Eng spkn; adv bkg acc; ccard acc; bike hire; games area; tennis; games rm; sauna; CKE. "Vg site & facs; health club; pool adj; v interesting, lively university town; supmkt & fuel nrby." **€23.70**   2019

COIMBRAO *B2* (0.5km NW Urban) *39.90027, -8.88805*
Camping Coimbrão, 185 Travessa do Gomes, 2425-452 Coimbrão **244 606007; campingcoimbrao@web.de**

12 👥 ⓦ ⌂ ♿ ⊟ ∥ ᴍsᴘ 🦋 ⛱ 🛒 Nr ⚂ ⚂

Site down lane in vill cent. Care needed lge o'fits, but site worth the effort. Sm, unshd, EHU (6-10A) €2.20-3.30; bbq; sw nr; red long stay; TV; bus 200m; Eng spkn; fishing 4km. "Excel site; helpful & friendly staff; gd touring base; gd loc for exploring; office open 0800-1200 & 1500-2200; canoeing 4km; German owners." **€16.70**   2017

COVILHA *C2* (48km NW Rural) *40.40406, -7.58770*
Vale do Rossim, Penhas Douradas, 6270 Gouveia
275 981 029; vrecoresort@gmail.com; valedorossimecoresort.com

12 🐕 👥 (htd) ⓦ ⌂ ♨ ⚲ ⊟ ∥ ᴍsᴘ 🦋 ⛱ ☂ ⑭ ✏

20km W on N232 fr Manteigas. Turn L at sp. Site 1km at end of rd. Sm, pt shd, pt sl, EHU (6A) €3.50; gas; bbq; sw nr; twin axles; phone; Eng spkn; adv bkg acc; ccard acc. "High in mountains by lake wth beaches; sw, kayaking, biking, climbing, walking; rest & bar by lake; peaceful, rural site in beautiful surroundings; friendly, helpful staff; vg." **€11.00**   2016

ELVAS *C3* (2km SW Urban) *38.87305, -7.1800* **Parque de Campismo da Piedade,** 7350-901 Elvas **268 628997 or 268 622877**

🐕 👥 ⓦ ⌂ ⊟ ∥ ⛱ ⑭ 🛒 Nr ⚂

Exit IP7/E90 junc 9 or 12 & foll site sp dir Estremoz. 1*, Med, mkd, hdstg, pt shd, sl, EHU (16A) inc; gas; bbq; phone; bus 500m; CKE. "Attractive aqueduct & walls; Piedade church & relics adj; traditional shops; pleasant walk to town; v quiet site, even high ssn; adequate san facs; conv NH en rte Algarve; c'vans parked to cls; noisy; facs need updating."
€20.00, 1 Apr-15 Sep.   2018

ERMIDAS SADO *B4* (11km W Rural) *38.01805, -8.48500* **Camping Monte Naturista O Barão (Naturist),** Foros do Barão, 7566-909 Ermidas-Sado
936710623 (mob); info@montenaturista.com; www.montenaturista.com

12 🐕 €1 👥 ⓦ ⌂ ♨ ⚲ ♿ ⊟ ∥ ᴍsᴘ 🦋 ⛱ ☂ 🏊

Fr A2 turn W onto N121 thro Ermidas-Sado twd Santiago do Cacém. At x-rds nr Arelãos turn R at bus stop (km 17.5) dir Barão. Site in 1km along unmade rd. Sm, mkd, pt shd, pt sl, EHU (6A) €3.20; bbq; red long stay; TV; 10% statics; Eng spkn; adv bkg acc; ccard acc; games area; CKE. "Gd, peaceful 'retreat-type' site in beautiful wooded area; meals Tue, Thurs, Sat & Sun; friendly atmosphere; spacious pitches - sun or shd; rec." **€22.50**   2016

EVORA *C3* (3km SW Urban) *38.55722, -7.92583* **Camping Orbitur Evora,** Estrada das Alcaçovas, Herdade Esparragosa, 7005-206 Évora **(266) 705190; infoevora@orbitur.pt; www.orbitur.pt**

12 🐕 €4.15 👥 👥 ⌂ ♿ ∥ ᴍsᴘ 🦋 ⛱ ☂ 🎣 🛒 ⚂ 🏊 🖐

Fr N foll N18 & by-pass, then foll sps for Lisbon rd at each rndabt or traff lts. Fr town cent take N380 SW sp Alcaçovas, foll site sp, site in 2km. NB Narr gate to site. 3*, Med, mkd, hdstg, pt shd, pt sl, EHU (16A) inc (long lead poss req, rev pol); gas; red long stay; TV; phone; bus; Eng spkn; adv bkg acc; ccard acc; games area; car wash; tennis; CKE. "Conv town cent, Évora World Heritage site with wealth of monuments & prehistoric sites nrby; cycle path to town; free car parks just outside town walls; poss flooding some pitches after heavy rain; beautiful site; gd sized pitches; helpful staff; bread to order; gd cycle track on old rlwy; recently improved EHU and water points (2020); vg, clean san facs; poor water pressure in shwrs." **€33.80**   2020

EVORAMONTE *C3* (6km NE Rural) *38.79276, -7.68701* **Camping Alentejo,** Novo Horizonte, 7100-300 Evoramonte **268 959283 or 936 799249 (mob); info@campingalentejo.com; www.camping alentejo.com**

12 🐕 €1 👥 ⓦ ⌂ ♿ ⊟ ∥ ᴍsᴘ 🦋 ⛱ 🏊

Fr E exit A6/E90 junc 7 Estremoz onto N18 dir Evora. Site in 8km at km 236. Sm, hdstg, pt shd, terr, EHU (16A) inc; bbq; bus adj; Eng spkn; adv bkg acc; horseriding; CKE. "Excel site; gd birdwatching, v friendly and helpful owner; conv NH on the way to S; easy parking; excel modern clean facs; gd library in off; bus stop outside gate to Evora; care req ent site; MH stay at lower price if no hookups; improved site; gd; secure." **€15.00**   2018

FIGUEIRA DA FOZ *B2* (7km S Urban/Coastal) *40.11861, -8.85666* **Camping ORBITUR-Gala,** N109, Km 4, Gala, 3090-458 Figueira da Foz **233 431231; infogala@orbitur.pt; www.orbitur.pt**

🏕 🐕 €1.50 WD ♨ ♿ 🚿 ✉ MSP 🛒 🍽 ⓦ 🎣 🅿 ⚠ ✍ 🛶 (htd)

🧺 ⛱ sand 400m

Fr Figueira da Foz on N109 dir Leiria for 3.5km. After Gala site on R in approx 400m. Ignore sp on R 'Campismo' after long bdge. 3*, Lge, hdstg, shd, terr, EHU (6-10A) €3-4; gas; bbq; red long stay; TV; 80% statics; phone; Eng spkn; adv bkg acc; ccard acc; fishing 1km; car wash; tennis; games rm; CKE. *"Gd, renovated site adj busy rd; luxury san facs (furthest fr recep); excel pool; busy site; in pine woods."* €29.00 2016

GERES *C1* (2km N Rural) *41.73777, -8.15805* **Vidoeiro Camping,** Lugar do Vidoeiro, 4845-081 Gerês **253 391289; gerescamping@gmail.com; www.vidoeiro gerescamping.com**

🏕 🐕 WD ♨ ♿ 🚿 ✍ 🦋 ⓦ 🍽 Nr ⓦ Nr 🛶

NE fr Braga take N103 twds Chaves for 25km. 1km past Cerdeirinhas turn L twds Gerês onto N308. Site on L 2km after Caldos do Gerês. Steep rds with hairpins. Cross bdge & reservoir, foll camp sps. 2*, Lge, hdstg, mkd, pt shd, terr, EHU (10A) inc; bbq; sw nr; phone. *"Attractive, wooded site in National Park; gd, clean facs; thermal spa in Gerês; pool 500m; diff access for lge o'fits, mountain rd; gd walks direct fr site."* €22.00, 15 May-15 Oct. 2019

GERES *C1* (14km NW Rural) *41.76305, -8.19111* **Parque de Campismo de Cerdeira,** Rue de Cerdeira 400, Campo do Gerês, 4840-030 Terras do Bouro **(253) 351005; info@parquecerdeira. com; www.parquecerdeira.com**

🏕 🐕 €3 👫 WD ♨ ♿ 🚿 ✍ 🛒 🍽 ⓦ 🅿 ⚠ ✍

Fr N103 Braga-Chaves rd, 28km E of Braga turn N onto N304 at sp to Poussada. Cont N for 18km to Campo de Gerês. Site in 1km; well sp. 3*, V lge, shd, EHU (5-10A) €4; gas; sw; TV; 10% statics; bus 500m; Eng spkn; ccard acc; canoeing; bike hire; fishing 2km; CKE. *"Beautiful scenery; unspoilt area; fascinating old vills nrby & gd walking; ltd facs LS; Nat pk campsite; wooded site; san facs modern & clean."* €30.00 2018

GOUVEIA *C2* (7km NE Rural) *40.52083, -7.54149* **Camping Quinta das Cegonhas,** 6290-122 Nabaínhos **238 745886; cegonhas@cegonhas.com; www.cegonhas.com**

🏕 🐕 €1.10 👫 WD ♨ ♿ 🚿 ✍ MSP 🦋 🍽 ⓦ 🅿 Nr ⚠ ✍ 🛶

Turn S at 114km post on N17 Seia-Celorico da Beira. Site sp thro Melo vill. Sm, pt shd, EHU (6-10A) inc; red long stay; TV; bus 400m; Eng spkn; adv bkg acc; games rm; CKE. *"Vg, well-run, busy site in grnds of vill manor house; friendly Dutch owners; beautiful sm village location conv Torre & Serra da Estrella; guided walks; excel walks; highly rec; beautiful views; great stargazing opps; bread to order; follow dir given as a 1 dir ent."* €24.50 2019

GUIMARAES *B1* (32km E Rural) *41.46150, -8.01120* **Quinta Valbom,** Quintã 4890-505 Ribas **351 253 653 048; info@quintavalbom.nl; www.quintavalbom.nl**

🏕 🐕 👫 ♿ 🚿 ✉ ✍ 🦋 ⓦ 🍽 🛶

Fr Guimaraes take A7 SE. Exit 11 onto N206 Fafe/ Gandarela. Turn R bef tunnel twds Ribas. Foll blue & red signs of campsite. Med, mkd, pt shd, terr, EHU (10A); bbq; twin axles; Eng spkn; adv bkg acc; CCI. *"Very nice site; friendly, extremely helpful Dutch owners; quiet surroundings; lots of space in beautiful setting; if driving c'van, park at white chapel and call campsite for their 4WD assistance up last bit of steep hill; owner won't acc c'vans over 6mtrs."* €26.70, 1 Apr-1 Oct. 2017

GUIMARAES *B1* (6km SE Rural) *41.42833, -8.26861* **Camping Parque da Penha,** Penha-Costa, 4800-026 Guimarães **253 515912 or 253 515085; geral@turipenha.pt; www.turipenha.pt**

🏕 🐕 👫 ♿ ✍ 🍽 ⓦ Nr ⚠ 🛶

Take N101 SE fr Guimarães sp Felgueiras. Turn R at sp for Nascente/Penha. Site sp. Lge, hdstg, shd, pt sl, terr, EHU (6A) inc; gas; phone; bus; Eng spkn; adv bkg acc; fishing; car wash; CKE. *"Excel v helpful staff; gd but dated san facs; lower terrs not suitable lge o'fits; densely wooded hilltop site; conv Guimarães World Heritage site European City of Culture 2012; cable car down to Guimaraes costs €5 return; excel rest; m'homes must park v close together on higher lvl hard stndng."* €19.00, 1 May-15 Sep. 2019

LAGOS *B4* (7km W Rural/Coastal) *37.10095, -8.73220* **Camping Turiscampo,** N125 Espiche, 8600-109 Luz-Lagos **282 789265; info@turiscampo.com; www.turiscampo.com**

🏕 🐕 €1.50 👫 (htd) WD ♨ ♿ 🚿 ✉ MSP 🦋 ⓦ 🍽 🅿 ⚠ ✍ 🧺 ⛱ sand 2km

Exit A22/IC4 junc 1 to Lagos then N125 fr Lagos dir Sagres, site 3km on R. 4*, Lge, hdstg, mkd, hdg, shd, pt sl, terr, EHU (6A) inc - extra for 10A; gas; bbq; red long stay; TV; 25% statics; phone; bus to Lagos 100m; Eng spkn; adv bkg acc; ccard acc; games area; tennis 2km; bike hire; games rm; fishing 2.5km; CKE. *"Superb, well-run, busy site; fitness cent; v popular for winter stays & rallies; all facs (inc excel pool) open all yr; gd san facs; helpful staff; lovely vill, beach & views; varied & interesting area, Luz worth visit; vg."* €44.00, E07. 2019

See advertisement opposite

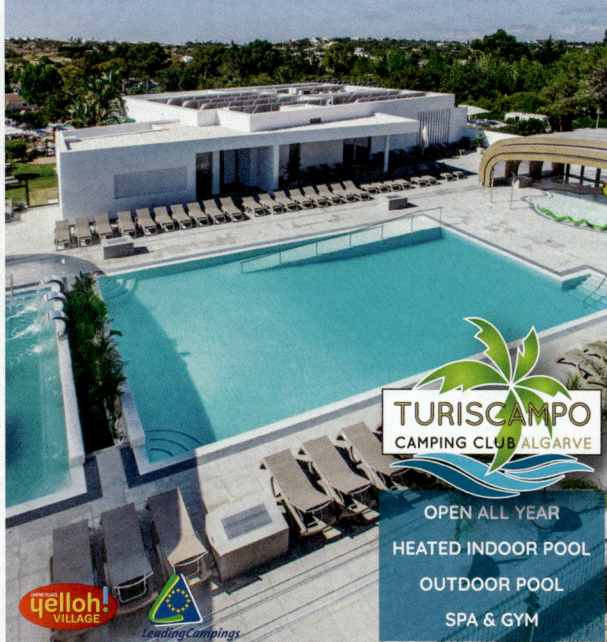

LAMAS DE MOURO *C1 (2km S Rural) 42.03587, -8.19644* **Camping Lamas de Mouro,** 4960-170 Lamas de Mouro **(251) 466041; geral@camping-lamas.com; www.camping-lamas.com**

12 ★ ⛺ ♦♦♦ wn ▲ 🖎 / ⟨⟩ ❤ ⵉ ⟨Ḣ⟩ ⛴ ⚑ ⚞ ⚄

Fr N202 at Melgaco foll sp Peneda- Gerês National Park, cont R to rd sp Porta de Lamas de Mouro. Cont 1km past park info office, site on L in pine woods. 2*, Med, pt shd, EHU (10A) €3; cooking facs; phone; bus 1km; CKE. *"Ideal for walking in National Park; natural pool."* **€15.00**   **2017**

LAMEGO *C1 (0.5km NW Urban) 41.09017, -7.82212* **Camping Lamego,** EN2 Lugar da Raposeira, 5101-909 Lamego **351 969 021 408; campinglamego@gmail.com; campinglamego.wix.com**

12 ♦♦♦ (htd) wn ▲ ⊝ 🖎 / mʀp ❤ ⵉ ⟨Ḣ⟩ ⛴

Foll N225. Turn L onto N2. Sm, hdstg, pt shd, EHU (6A) €4; Eng spkn. *"Easy walk to Bom Jesus do Monte; site only suitable for MH's; san facs new & excel (2016); v friendly owners; excel."* **€15.00**   **2016**

LISBOA *B3 (17km SW Coastal) 38.653909, -9.238510* **Camping ORBITUR-Costa de Caparica,** Ave Afonso de Albuquerque, Quinta de S. António, 2825-450 Costa de Caparica **212 901366 or 903894; caparica@orbitur.pt, www.orbitur.pt**

12 ★ ⛺ ♦♦♦ wn ▲ ♿ 🖎 / mʀp ⟨Ḣ⟩ ❤ ⵉ ⟨Ḣ⟩ ⛴ ⚑ ⚞ ⚅ ⛱ sand 1km

Take A2/IP7 S fr Lisbon; after Rv Tagus bdge turn W to Costa de Caparica. At end of rd turn N twd **Trafaria, & site on L. Well sp fr a'strada.** 3*, Lge, mkd, hdg, shd, terr, EHU (6A) €3; gas; bbq; red long stay; TV; 75% statics; phone; bus to Lisbon; Eng spkn; adv bkg acc; ccard acc; car wash; games rm; tennis; fishing; CKE. *"Gd, clean, well run site; heavy traff into city; rec use free parking at Monument to the Discoveries & tram to city cent; ferry to Belém; ltd facs LS; pleasant, helpful staff; pool 800m; aircraft noise early am & late pm."* **€44.00**   **2019**

Make sure you check any essential information with the site before you travel

PORTUGAL

LISBOA *B3* (9km W Urban) *38.72472, -9.20805*
Parque Municipal de Campismo de Monsanto, Estrada da Circunvalação, 1400-061 Lisboa **(217) 628200; info@lisboacamping.com; www.lisboa camping.com**

€2.90 (htd)

Fr W on A5 foll sp Parque Florestal de Monsanto/ Buraca. Fr S on A2, cross toll bdge & foll sp for Sintra; join expressway, foll up hill; site well sp; stay in RH lane. Fr N on A1 pass airport, take Benfica exit & foll sp under m'way to site. Site sp fr all major rds. Avoid rush hrs! 4*, V lge, hdstg, mkd, pt shd, pt sl, terr, serviced pitches; EHU (6-16A) inc; gas; TV; 5% statics; bus to city; Eng spkn; adv bkg acc; ccard acc; tennis; CKE. *"Well laid-out, spacious, guarded site in trees; bank; PO; car wash; ltd mv service pnt; san facs poss stretched when site full but rel and reg cleaned in LS; friendly, helpful staff; in high ssn some o'fits placed on sl forest area (quiet); few pitches take awning; excel excursions booked at TO on site; reg bus service to town; excel rest; bus to Lisbon; san facs dated; expensive for low ssn."* **€40.00**   **2019**

LOURICAL *B2* (5km SW Rural) *39.99149, -8.78880*
Campismo O Tamanco, Rua do Louriçal 11, Casas Brancas, 3105-158 Louriçal **236 952551; tamanco@ me.com; www.campismo-o-tamanco.com**

(htd)

sand 5km

S on N109 fr Figuera da Foz S twds Leiria foll sp at rndabt Matos do Corrico onto N342 to Louriçal. Site 800m on L. 3*, Med, hdstg, hdg, mkd, pt shd, EHU inc (6A) €2.25-3.50; gas; bbq; sw nr; red long stay; twin axles; 5% statics; bus 500m; Eng spkn; adv bkg acc; CKE. *"Excel; friendly Dutch owners; chickens & ducks roaming site; superb mkt on Sun at Louriçal; a bit of real Portugal; gd touring site; mkd walks thro pine woods; v clean; relaxed; sm farm animal area."* **€25.00**   **2016**

MEDA *C2* (0.5km N Urban) *40.96972, -7.25916*
Parque de Campismo Municipal, Av. Professor Adriano Vasco Rodrigues, 6430 Mêda **(351) 925 480 500 or (351) 279 883 270; campismo@cm-meda.pt; www.cm-meda.pt/turismo/Paginas/Parque_ Camsimo.aspx**

Head N fr cent of town, take 1st R, take 1st L & site on L within the Meda Sports Complex. Sm, hdstg, pt shd, pt sl,. *"Pt of the Municipal Sports Complex with facs avail; conv for town cent & historic ctr; lovely sm site; lge pitches; some pull thro; blocks esential; clean modern san facs."* **€16.00**   **2017**

MONTARGIL *B3* (4km N Rural) *39.10083, -8.14472*
Camping ORBITUR, Baragem de Montargil, N2, 7425-017 Montargil **242 901207; infomontargil@ orbitur.pt; www.orbitur.pt**

€1.50

Fr N251 Coruche to Vimiero rd, turn N on N2, over dam at Barragem de Montargil. Fr Ponte de Sor S on N2 until 3km fr Montargil. Site clearly sp bet rd & lake. 3*, Med, hdstg, mkd, pt shd, terr, EHU (6-10A) €3-4; gas; bbq; red long stay; TV (pitch); 60% statics; phone; Eng spkn; adv bkg acc; ccard acc; fishing; car wash; tennis; games rm; boating; watersports; CKE. *"Friendly site in beautiful area."* **€26.70**   **2016**

NAZARE *B2* (2km N Rural) *39.62036, -9.05630*
Camping Vale Paraíso, N242, 2450-138 Nazaré **262 561800; info@valeparaiso-naturpark.com; www.valeparaiso-naturpark.com**

€2.10

sand 2km

Site thro pine reserve on N242 fr Nazaré to Leiria. 3*, V lge, hdstg, mkd, shd, terr, EHU (4-10A) €3; gas; red long stay; TV; 20% statics; bus; Eng spkn; adv bkg acc; ccard acc; games area; games rm; bike hire; site clsd 19-26 Dec; fishing; CKE. *"Gd, clean site; well run; gd security; pitches vary in size & price, & divided by concrete walls, poss not suitable lge o'fits, bus outside gates to Nazare, exit down steep hill."* **€23.60**   **2017**

ODIVELAS *B3* (8km NE Rural) *38.18361, -8.10361*
Camping Markádia, Barragem de Odivelas, 7920-999 Alvito **(284) 763141; info@markadia.pt; www.markadia.pt/camping**

(except Jul-Aug)

sand 500m

Fr Ferreira do Alentejo on N2 N twd Torrão. After Odivelas turn R onto N257 twd Alvito & turn R twd Barragem de Odivels. Site in 7km, clearly sp. 3*, Med, hdstg, pt shd, pt sl, EHU (16A) inc; gas; sw nr; phone; adv bkg acc; horseriding; boating; fishing; car wash; tennis; CKE. *"Beautiful, secluded site on banks of reservoir; spacious pitches; pool 50m; gd rest; site lighting low but san facs well lit; excel walking, cycling, birdwatching; wonderful; unmarked sites; long el cable ess."* **€32.00**   **2019**

OLHAO *C4* (2km NE Rural) *37.03527, -7.82250*
Camping Olhão, Pinheiros do Marim, 8700-912 Olhão **289 700300; parque.campismo@sbsi.pt; www.sbsi.pt**

€1.60   1.5km

Turn S twd coast fr N125 1.5km E of Olhão by filling stn. Clearly sp on S side of N125, adj Ria Formosa National Park. 3*, V lge, mkd, hdg, shd, pt sl, EHU (6A) €2.40; gas; red long stay; TV; 75% statics; phone; bus adj, train 1.5km; Eng spkn; adv bkg acc; ccard acc; tennis; games area; horseriding 1km; bike hire; games rm; CKE. *"Pleasant, helpful staff; sep car park for some pitches; car wash; security guard; excel pool; gd san facs; very popular long stay LS; many sm sandy pitches, some diff access for lge o'fits; gd for cycling, birdwatching; ferry to islands."* **€22.30**   **2019**

OLIVEIRA DO HOSPITAL *C2* (9km NE Rural) *40.40338, -7.82684* **Camping Toca da Raposa,** 3405-351 Meruge **238 601547 or 926 704218 (mob); campingtocada raposa@gmail.com; toca-da-raposa.com**

🏕🐕👪 wo ♿ & ⚡ 🚿 msp 🦋 ☕ 🍴 ⊕ ♨ △ 🏊

Fr N: N170 Oliveira Do Hospital head SW. Drive thro EM540-2, EM503-1, R. Principal, Estr. Principal and EM504-3 to Coimbra. Foll sp to site. Sm, hdg, pt shd, pt sl, terr, EHU (6A) €2.50; gas; bus; Eng spkn. *"Charming; lovely pool; bar & eve meals; friendly Dutch owner; vg."* **€18.50, 15 Mar-1 Nov.**   **2017**

ORTIGA *C3* (6km SE Rural) *39.48277, -8.00305* **Parque Campismo de Ortiga,** Estrada da Barragem, 6120-525 Ortiga **241 573464; campismo@cm-macao.pt**

12 🐕 👪 wo ♿ & 🚿 ⚡ 🍴 🍴nr ⊕nr 🏊nr △

Exit A23/IP6 junc 12 S to Ortiga. Thro Ortiga & foll site sp for 1.5km. Site beside dam. Sm, mkd, hdstg, pt shd, terr, EHU (10A) €1.50; bbq; sw nr; TV; 50% statics; Eng spkn; watersports; CKE. *"Lovely site in gd position; useful NH; dogs free; lge o'fits should avoid acc thro town."* **€21.00**   **2016**

OURIQUE *B4* (10km S Rural) *37.5675, -8.2644* **Camping Serro da Bica,** Horta da Bica, Aldeia de Palheiros, 7670-202 Ourique **286 516750; info@ serrodabica.com; www.serrodabica.com**

12 🐕 2 max 👪 (htd) wo ♿ 🚿 ⚡ 🍴 msp 🦋 ☕ 🍴

Fr N of IC1 turn R at km post 679.4 & foll sp to site. Fr S go past km post & do U-turn at turn off for Castro da Cola, then as above. 1*, Med, pt shd, pt sl, terr, EHU (10A) €2.50; gas; bbq (elec, gas); red long stay; bus 800m; Eng spkn; adv bkg acc; CKE. *"Pretty, relaxing site; gd walking; v friendly owners; spotless facs; excel."* **€21.30**   **2019**

PENACOVA *B2* (3km N Rural) *40.27916, -8.26805* **Camp Municipal de Camp de Penacova (Vila Nova),** Rua dos Barqueiros, Vila Nova, 3360-204 Penacova **919 121967; penaparque2@iol.pt**

👪 🚿 ⚡ 🍴 ☕ 🍴 ⊕nr ♨ 🏊nr △

IP3 fr Coimbra, exit junc 11, cross Rv Mondego N of Penacova & foll to sp to Vila Nova & site. Med, pt shd, EHU (6A) €1; bbq; sw nr; TV; phone; bus 150m; Eng spkn; bike hire; fishing; CKE. *"Open, attractive site."* **€20.00, 31 May-30 Sep.**   **2017**

PONTE DA BARCA *B1* (11km E Rural) *41.82376, -8.31723* **Camping Lima Escape (formerly Entre-Ambos-os-Rios),** Lugar da Igreja, Entre-Ambos-os-Rios, 4980-613 Ponte da Barca **258 588361 or 964 969309; info@lima-escape.pt; www.lima-escape.pt**

🏕🐕 €0.60 👪 🚿 ⚡ 🍴 ☕ 🍴 ⊕nr ♨ 🏊nr △ 🚣

N203 E fr Ponte da Barca, pass ent sp for vill. Site sp N twd Rv Lima, after 1st bdge. 2*, Lge, shd, pt sl, EHU (6A) €1.20; gas; TV; phone; bus 100m; adv bkg acc; fishing; canoeing; CKE. *"Beautiful, clean, well run & maintained site in pine trees; well situated for National Park; vg rest."*
€29.00, 2 Jan-10 Nov, 1 Dec-30 Dec.   **2019**

PORTO *B1* (17km N Coastal) *41.2675, -8.71972* **Camping Orbitur-Angeiras,** Rua de Angeiras, Matosinhos, 4455-039 Lavra **229 270571; infoangeiras@orbitur.pt; www.orbitur.pt**

12 🐕 €1.50 👪 🚿 ♿ & 🚿 ⚡ 🍴 msp ☕ 🍴 ⊕ 🏊 △ 🏄 🚣

🛶 🌳 sand 400m

Fr ICI/A28 take turn-off sp Lavra, site sp at end of slip rd. Site in approx 3km - app rd potholed & cobbled. 3*, Lge, shd, pt sl, EHU (6A) €3-4 (check earth); gas; bbq; red long stay; TV (pitch); 70% statics; phone; bus to Porto at site ent; Eng spkn; adv bkg acc; ccard acc; car wash; games area; tennis; games rm; fishing; CKE. *"Friendly & helpful staff; gd rest; gd pitches in trees ahead of site but ltd space lge o'fits; ssnl statics all yr; fish & veg mkt in Matosinhos; excel new san facs (2015); vg pool; poss noisy on Sat nights (beach parties)."* **€40.70**   **2017**

PORTO *B1* (32km SE Rural) *41.03972, -8.42666* **Campidouro Parque de Medas,** Lugar do Gavinho, 4515-397 Medas-Gondomar **224 760162; geral@ campidouro.pt; www.campidouro.pt**

12 🐕 👪 wo 🚿 ♿ & 🚿 ⚡ 🍴 msp 🦋 ☕ 🍴 ⊕ 🏊 △ 🏄 🚣 🛶

Take N12 dir Gondomar off A1. Almost immed take R exit sp Entre-os-Rios. In approx 14km. Sp for Medas on R, thro hamlet & forest for 3km & foll sp for site on R. Long, steep app. New concrete access/site rds. 3*, Lge, mkd, hdstg, pt shd, terr, serviced pitches; EHU (6A) inc (poss rev pol); gas; bbq; sw; TV; 90% statics; phone; bus to Porto; Eng spkn; adv bkg acc; ccard acc; games rm; tennis; boating; fishing; CKE. *"Beautiful site on Rv Douro; helpful owners; gd rest; clean facs; sm level area (poss cr by rv & pool) for tourers - poss noisy at night & water logged after heavy rain; bus to Porto (just outside site) rec as parking diff (ltd buses at w/end)."*
€26.00   **2016**

PORTO *B1* (9km SW Urban/Coastal) *41.10777, -8.65611* **Camping ORBITUR-Madalena,** Rua do Cerro 608, Praia da Madalena, 4405-736 Vila Nova de Gaia **(227) 122520; infomadalena@orbitur.pt; www.orbitur.pt**

12 🐕 €4.10 👪 wo 🚿 ♿ & 🚿 ⚡ 🍴 msp ☕ 🍴 ⊕ 🏊 △ 🏄 🚣

🛶 🌳 sand 250m

Fr Porto ring rd IC1/A44 take A29 exit dir Espinho. In 1km take exit slip rd sp Madalena opp Volvo agent. Watch for either 'Campismo' or 'Orbitur' sp to site along winding, cobbled rd (beware campismo sp may take you to another site nrby). 4*, Lge, pt shd, pt sl, terr, EHU (6A)inc; gas; bbq; red long stay; TV; 40% statics; phone; bus to Porto; Eng spkn; adv bkg acc; ccard acc; car wash; games area; tennis; games rm; CKE. *"Site in forest; slight aircraft noise; some uneven pitches; pitches not mkd out; excel bus to Porto cent fr site ent takes 40 mins - do not take c'van into Porto; facs fine & avail LS."* **€27.50**   **2019**

SAGRES *B4* (1km N Coastal) *37.02305, -8.94555*
Camping ORBITUR-Sagres, Cerro das Moitas, 8650-998 Vila de Sagres **282 624371; infosagres@orbitur.pt; www.orbitur.pt**

12 🐕 €1.50 ♦♦♦ wd ♿ 🔥 ⊘ ⁄ MSP 🦋 ♈ 🍸 ⑪ ♨ 🗲 ⚠

🏕 sand 2km

On N268 to Cape St Vincent; well sp. 2*, Lge, hdg, mkd, hdstg, pt shd, EHU (6-10A) €3-4; gas; bbq; red long stay; TV; Eng spkn; adv bkg acc; ccard acc; bike hire; car wash; games rm. *"Vg, clean, tidy site in pine trees; helpful staff; hot water to shwrs only; cliff walks; gd rest; v windy site; new san facs ok; all pitches sl."* **€33.80** **2019**

SANTIAGO DO CACEM *B4* (17km NW Coastal) *38.10777, -8.78690* **Camping Lagoa de Santo Andre,** Lagoa de Santo Andre, 7500-024 Vila Nova de Santo Andre **269 708550**

♦♦♦ 🏕 ⁄ 🍸 ⑪ 🗲

Take N261 sp Melides out of town & foll sps to Lagoa de Santo Andre to site on L of rd. On shore but fenced off fr unsafe banks of lagoon. 1*, Med, pt shd, pt sl, EHU inc (4-6A); sw; boating; fishing. *"Ltd facs LS."* **€19.50, 1 Jan-23 Dec, 26 Dec-31 Dec.** **2019**

SANTO ANTONIO DAS AREIAS *C3* (5km N Rural) *39.41370, -7.37575* **Quinta Do Maral (Naturist),** PO Box 57, Cubecudos, 7330-205 Santo Antonio das Areias **(963) 462169; info@quintadomaral.com; www.quintadomaral.com**

12 🐕 ♦♦♦ wd 🏕 ♿ ⊘ ⁄ MSP 🦋 ♈ 🍸 ♨ 🏊

Take N359 twds Santo Antonio Das Areias/Beira. Pass turn off to Santo Antonio in dir to Beira. At Ranginha turn L to Cubecudos. Turn R past vill sp by a school bldg, keep on this rd for 1.7km. Campsite on L, white hse with blue stripe. Do not use sat nav as they lead to unsuitable rds. Sm, hdg, pt shd, EHU (6-16A); bbq; twin axles; red long stay; TV; 5% statics; Eng spkn; adv bkg rec. *"In S Mamede nature park; vill & castle of Marvao an hr's walk; young, friendly owners; excel."* **€18.50** **2016**

SANTO ANTONIO DAS AREIAS *C3* (0km S Rural) *39.40992, -7.34075* **Camping Asseiceira,** Asseiceira, 7330-204 Santo António das Areias **(245) 992940 or (960) 150352 (mob); gary-campingasseiceira@hotmail.com; www.campingasseiceira.com**

🐕 ♦♦♦ wd 🏕 ♿ ⁄ ♈ 🍸 ⑪ nr ♨ 🗲 nr 🏊

Fr N246-1 turn off sp Marvão/Santo António das Areias. Turn L to Santo António das Areias then 1st R on ent town then immed R again, up sm hill to rndabt. At rndabt turn R then at next rndabt cont strt on. There is a petrol stn on R, cont down hill for 400m. Site on L. Sm, pt shd, pt sl, EHU (10A) €4; bus 1km; CKE. *"Attractive area; peaceful, well-equipped, remote site among olive trees; clean, tidy; gd for walking, birdwatching; helpful, friendly, British owners; excel san facs, maintained to a high standard; nr Spanish border; excel; ideal cent for walking, cycling, visit hilltop castle Marvao; access & pitches poss tight for lge o'fits."* **€19.00, 1 Jan-31 Oct.** **2019**

SAO MARCOS DA SERRA *B4* (5km SE Rural) *37.3350, -8.3467* **Campismo Rural Quinta Odelouca,** Vale Grande de Baixo, CxP 644-S, 8375-215 São Marcos da Serra **282 361718 or 915 656685; info@quintaodelouca.com; www.quintaodelouca.com**

🐕 €1 ♦♦♦ wd 🏕 ♿ ⊘ ⁄ ♨ 🗲

Fr N (Ourique) on IC1 pass São Marcos da Serra & in approx 2.5km turn R & cross blue rlwy bdge. At bottom turn L & at cont until turn R for Vale Grande (paved rd changes to unmade). Foll sp to site. Fr S exit A22 junc 9 onto IC1 dir Ourique. Pass São Bartolomeu de Messines & at km 710.5 turn L & cross blue rlwy bdge, then as above. 2*, Sm, pt shd, terr, EHU (6-10A) €3.50; bbq (elec, gas, sep area); sw; twin axles; Eng spkn; adv bkg rec; CKE. *"Helpful, friendly Dutch owners; beautiful views; gd walks; vg; v little shd; access via bad rd; excel; internet free but unreliable and weak signal; fantastic location & facs."* **€23.00, 1 Feb-30 Sep.** **2019**

SAO PEDRO DE MOEL *B2* (1km E Urban/Coastal) *39.75861, -9.02583* **Camping ORBITUR-São Pedro de Moel,** Rua Volta do Sete, São Pedro de Moel, 2430 Marinha Grande **244 599168; infospedro@orbitur.pt; www.orbitur.pt**

12 🐕 €4.10 ♦♦♦ wd ♿ 🔥 ⊘ ⁄ MSP 🦋 ♈ 🍸 ⑪ ♨ 🗲 ⚠ ✂

🏊 (htd) 📶 🏕 sand 500m

Site at end of rd fr Marinha Grande to beach; turn R at 1st rndabt on ent vill. 3*, V lge, hdstg, mkd, hdg, shd, terr, EHU (6A) inc (poss rev pol); gas; bbq; red long stay; TV (pitch); 10% statics; phone; Eng spkn; adv bkg acc; ccard acc; waterslide; fishing; car wash; tennis; games rm; bike hire; CKE. *"Friendly, well-run, clean site in pine woods; easy walk to shops, rests; heavy surf; gd cycling to beaches; tracks alng coast & inland; São Pedro smart resort; ltd facs LS site in attractive area and well run; bread to order; pitches soft sand & sl."* **€34.00,, W18.** **2019**

SAO TEOTONIO *B4* (7km W Coastal) *37.52560, -8.77560* **Parque de Campismo da Zambujeira,** Praia da Zambujeira, 7630-740 Zambujeira do Mar **(283) 958 407; info@campingzambujeira; www.campingzambujeira.com**

🐕 €4 ♦♦♦ wd 🏕 ⁄ MSP 🍸 ⑪ ♨ 🗲 ⚠ 🏕 sand 1km

S on N120 twd Lagos, turn W when level with São Teotónio on unclassified rd to Zambujeira. Site on L in 7km, bef vill. 2*, V lge, pt shd, pt sl, EHU (6-10A) €3.50; gas; red long stay; TV; phone; bus adj; Eng spkn; tennis. *"Welcoming, friendly owners; in pleasant rural setting; hot water to shwrs only; sh walk to unspoilt vill with some shops & rest; cliff walks; nice site; pool gd; rest food basic; vg facs; v clean site; gd beaches & walks."* **€18.00, 1 Apr-31 Oct.** **2019**

SERPA *C4* (1km SW Urban) *37.94090, -7.60404*
Parque Municipal de Campismo Serpa, Rua da Eira
São Pedro, 7830-303 Serpa **284 540193; parque**
campismoserpa@cm-serpa.pt; www.cm-serpa.pt
12 🐕 ♦♦ wc ♨ ⚓ 🚻 💧 ⁄ ♈ ⊤ ⊕ nr 🛒 nr

Fr IP8 take 1st sp for town; site well sp fr most dirs
- opp sw pool. Do not ent walled town. Med, pt shd,
pt sl, EHU (6A) €1.25; gas; bbq; sw nr; 20% statics;
phone; adv bkg acc; CKE. *"Popular gd site; daily mkt*
500m; pool adj; simple, high quality facs; interesting,
historic town; main site ent may be clsd due to
improvement wrks; rec phone ahead bef arr (2019)."
€10.00 2019

TAVIRA *C4* (5km E Rural/Coastal) *37.14506, -7.60223*
Camping Ria Formosa, Quinta da Gomeira, 8800-591
Cabanas-Tavira **281 328887; info@campingria**
formosa.com; www.campingriaformosa.com
12 🐕 €2 ♦♦ (htd) wc ♨ ⚓ 🚻 💧 ⁄ 🦋 ♈ ⊤ ⊕ 🛒 🛒 ⚠
🏊 🛁 🏖 sand 1.2km

Fr spain onto A22 take exit junc 17 (bef tolls)
Fr N125 turn S at Conceição dir 'Cabanas Tavira' &
'Campismo'. Cross rlwy line & turn L to site, sp.
3*, V lge, hdstg, mkd, pt shd, terr, EHU (16A) €3; gas;
bbq; red long stay; TV; bus 100m, train 100m; Eng
spkn; adv bkg acc; ccard acc; games area; car wash;
bike hire; CKE. *"Excel, comfortable site; friendly,*
welcoming owner & staff; vg, modern san facs;
various pitch sizes; cycle path to Tavira, excel facs."
€24.00 2019

TOMAR *B2* (9km NE Rural) *39.63833, -8.33694*
Camping Pelinos, Casal das Aboboreiras, 2300-093
Tomar **249 301814; info@campingpelinos.com;**
www.campingpelinos.com
🐕 ♦♦ wc ♨ ⚓ 🚻 💧 ⁄ 🦋 ♈ ⊤ ⊕ 🛒 🛒

N fr Tomar on N110, turn R to Calçadas at traff lts
opp g'ge, foll site sp. Steep descent to site. 1*, Sm,
pt shd, sl, terr, EHU (6A); bbq (elec, gas); TV; phone;
bus 100m; Eng spkn; adv bkg acc; table tennis; CKE.
"Lake sw, watersports & fishing 7km; vg; lovely site; no
shops nrby; v helpful Dutch couple; dogs 2 max; walks
fr site; ltd wifi on pitch." **€20.50, 15 Mar-1 Oct.** 2019

TOMAR *B2* (1km NW Urban) *39.60694, -8.41027*
Campismo Parque Municipal, 2300-000 Tomar **249**
329824 or 249 329800 (town hall); presidencia@
cm-tomar.pt; www.cm-tomar.pt
12 🐕 ♦♦ wc ♨ ⚓ 🚻 msp 🦋 ♈ ⊤ nr ⊕ 🛒 ⚠

Fr S on N110 foll sp to town cent at far end of
stadium. Fr N (Coimbra) on N110 turn R immed
bef bdge. Site well sp fr all dirs. Med, mkd, pt shd,
bbq; TV; Eng spkn; adv bkg acc; ccard acc; CKE.
"Useful base for touring Alcobaca, Batalha & historic
monuments in Tomar; conv Fatima; Convento de
Cristo worth visit; vg; lovely walk to charming rvside
town; easy access for lge vehicle; sh walk thro gdns
to Knights Templar castle; pool adj; no longer a camp
site: now a free camperstop (2019); all facs avail but
no hot water; no security; v rundown site; clean san
facs." 2019

TORRES NOVAS *B2* (13.5km SE Urban) *39.400100,*
-8.485829 **Parque De Campismo Municipal Da**
Golega, Largo do Parque de Campismo 7, 2150-269
Golega **249 979003; cm-golega.pt**
12 🐕 €1.77 ♨ 🚻 ⁄ ⊕ nr 🛒 nr

Sp fr main rd. Med, pt shd, EHU (10A); twin axles; Eng
spkn. *"Vg; ideal for visiting lovely nature reserve; easy*
walk to town." **€10.00** 2019

VIANA DO CASTELO *B1* (4.6km S Urban/Coastal)
41.67888, -8.82583 **Camping ORBITUR-Viana do**
Castelo, Rua Diogo Álvares, Cabedelo, 4935-161
Darque **258 322167; infoviana@orbitur.pt;**
www.orbitur.pt
🐕 €2.20 ♦♦ wc ♨ ⚓ 🚻 💧 ⁄ msp 🦋 ♈ ⊤ ⊕ 🛒 🛒 ⚠ ✎
🏊 (htd) 🏖 sand adj

Exit IC1 junc 11 to W sp Darque, Cabedelo, foll sp
to site in park. 3*, Lge, mkd, shd, pt sl, EHU (6A) inc;
gas; bbq; red long stay; TV; phone; Eng spkn; adv bkg
acc; ccard acc; surfing; fishing; car wash; CKE. *"Site in*
pine woods; friendly staff; gd facs; plenty of shd; major
festival in Viana 3rd w/end in Aug; lge mkt in town Fri;
sm passenger ferry over Rv Lima to town high ssn; ferry
rec'd over cycling due to busy narr rds; Santa Luzia
worth visit." **€42.00, 1 Feb-3 Nov.** 2019

VILA NOVA DE CERVEIRA *B1* (5km E Rural)
41.94362, -8.69365 **Parque de Campismo Convívio,**
Rua de Badão, 1 Bacelo, 4920-020 Candemil **251**
794404; info@campingconvivio.net; www.camping
convivio.net
🐕 €1.10 ♦♦ wc ♨ ⚓ 🚻 💧 ⁄ 🦋 ♈ ⊤ ⊕ 🏊

Fr Vila Nova de Cerveira dir Candemil on N13/N302,
turn L at Bacelo, site sp. Sm, pt shd, terr, EHU (6A);
bbq; red long stay; Eng spkn; adv bkg acc; games rm;
CKE. *"V helpful Dutch owners; gd area to visit; vg."*
€21.00, 1 Mar-15 Oct. 2017

Camping Milfontes

beautiful beaches - pure air

Servicestation for Motorhomes
Supermarket - Mobile Homes
Bungalows - Restaurant
Laundry

Near the town center - shops open all year!

www.campingmilfontes.com
geral@parquemilfontes.com
Tel.: +351 283 996 140

VILA NOVA DE MILFONTES *B4* (1km N Coastal) *37.73194, -8.78277* **Camping Milfontes,** Apartado 81, 7645-300 Vila Nova de Milfontes **(283) 996140; reservas@campingmilfontes.com; www.camping milfontes.com**

S fr Sines on N120/IC4 for 22km; turn R at Cercal on N390 SW for Milfontes on banks of Rio Mira; **clear sp.** 3*, V lge, hdg, mkd, pt shd, EHU (6A) inc (long lead poss req); gas; TV; 80% statics; phone; bus 600m; ccard acc; CKE. *"Pitching poss diff for lge o'fits due trees & statics; supmkt & mkt 5 mins walk; nr fishing vill at mouth Rv Mira with beaches & sailing on rv; pleasant site; helpful staff; gd cycle ride to Porto Corvo; attractive town; gd coastal walks; chge for pool; site on edge of lovely vill."* **€25.60** **2019**

See advertisement

VILA REAL *C1* (1km NE Urban) *41.30361, -7.73694* **Camping Vila Real,** Rua Dr Manuel Cardona, 5000-558 Vila Real **259 324724**

On IP4/E82 take Vila Real N exit & head S into town. Foll 'Centro' sp to Galp g'ge; at Galp g'ge rndabt, turn L & in 30m turn L again. Site at end of rd in 400m. Site sp fr all dirs. 2*, Med, pt shd, pt sl, terr, EHU (6A); gas; bbq; 10% statics; phone; bus 150m; tennis; CKE. *"Conv upper Douro; pool complex adj; gd facs ltd when site full; gd mkt in town (15 min walk); Lamego well worth a visit; excel rest adj."* **€18.70,** 1 Feb-31 Dec. **2017**

VILA REAL DE SANTO ANTONIO *C4* (14km W Rural) *37.18649, -7.55003* **Camping Caliço Park,** Sitio do Caliço, 8900-907 Vila Nova de Cacela **281 951195; geral@calico-park.com; www.calico-park.com**

On N side of N125 Vila Real to Faro rd. Sp on main rd & in Vila Nova de Cacela vill, visible fr rd. 1*, Lge, hdstg, shd, pt sl, terr, EHU (6A) €2.80; gas; red long stay; 80% statics; phone; Eng spkn; adv bkg acc; ccard acc; bike hire; CKE. *"Friendly staff; noisy in ssn & rd noise; not suitable for m'vans or tourers in wet conditions - ltd touring pitches & poss diff access; gd NH."* **€17.00** **2016**

VILA REAL DE SANTO ANTONIO *C4* (3km W Coastal) *37.17972, -7.44361* **Parque Municipal de Campismo,** 8900 Monte Gordo **281 510970; geral@cm-vrsa.pt; http://www.cm-vrsa.pt/pt/menu/459/parque-de-campismo.aspx**

Fr Faro on N125 turn R sp Monte Gordo. Site on sea front in 500m. Or fr Spain over bdge at border, exit junc 9 to Vila Real over rlwy line. Strt over rndabt & turn R at T-junc, site sp just bef ent town. 1*, shd, Pt sl, EHU (10A) €1.90 (long cable poss req); gas; bbq; red long stay; TV; 10% statics; phone; bus, train to Faro 3km; Eng spkn; ccard acc; canoeing; CKE. *"Former campsite now MH stop; sp through town; san facs avail but shwrs cold water; MH svr pnt."* **€13.50** **2019**

VILAMOURA *B4* (4.8km N Rural) *37.112371, -8.106409* **Vilamoura Rustic Motorhome Aire,** N125 436A, 8100 Consiguinte, Loule **289 149315 or 918 721948 (mob) or 917 428356 (mob); info@vilamoura-rustic-motorhome-aire.com; www.vilamoura-rustic-motorhome-aire.com**

Fr A22 (tollrd) take exit for Quarteria and drive for 3km for exit Quarteira/Portimao. Turn R at exit to join N125 and drive for approx 6km W direct to site. Sm, hdstg, pt shd, EHU (6A) €0.50 per KW; bbq; twin axles; TV; bus 200m; Eng spkn; adv bkg acc; games area; bike hire. *"Boutique, adults only (18+), MH & c'van Aire; outdoor cinema; Sky Sports; events throughout the year; vg; run by past CAMC memb."* **€10.00** **2019**

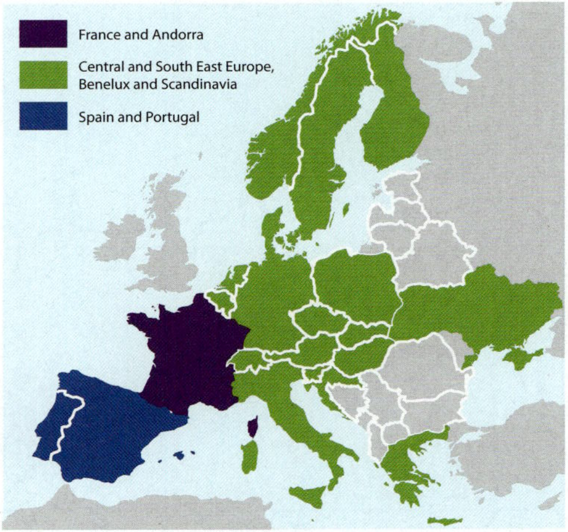
France and Andorra
Central and South East Europe, Benelux and Scandinavia
Spain and Portugal

Miranda do Douro to Vila Real de Santo António = 688km

	Aveiro	Beja	Braga	Bragança	Castelo Branco	Chaves	Coimbra	Elvas	Évora	Faro	Fundão	Guarda	Leiria	Lisboa (Lisbon)	Miranda do Douro	Mourão	Portalegre	Portimão	Porto	Sagres	Santarém	Setúbal	Sines	Valença	Viana do Castelo	Vila Formoso	Vila Real	Vila Real de Santo António	Vila Verde de Ficalho
Beja	408																												
Braga	129	500																											
Bragança	285	558	214																										
Castelo Branco	225	274	318	288																									
Chaves	235	630	140	106	341																								
Coimbra	77	339	186	298	156	260																							
Elvas	379	162	478	445	155	456	253																						
Évora	325	77	432	485	198	513	258	84																					
Faro	535	164	639	732	442	723	468	328	245																				
Fundão	227	317	263	253	43	175	150	198	239	483																			
Guarda	163	361	263	200	92	240	156	247	290	538	57																		
Leiria	143	276	248	368	174	327	77	252	201	417	199	230																	
Lisboa (Lisbon)	273	179	383	503	247	480	206	206	131	295	300	362	146																
Miranda do Douro	320	572	280	76	287	180	313	442	487	732	252	195	387	607															
Mourão	365	110	490	533	260	575	322	101	66	276	303	356	265	193	552														
Portalegre	258	180	365	382	94	440	191	64	105	351	136	185	167	216	382	173													
Portimão	508	105	607	680	379	725	443	267	185	61	465	476	381	295	682	215	288												
Porto	74	445	65	219	261	170	121	364	372	578	208	209	191	317	254	407	303	552											
Sagres	556	153	655	728	407	773	491	315	233	109	513	524	429	343	730	263	336	48	600										
Santarém	205	198	310	426	177	388	140	174	120	338	220	292	78	80	445	186	148	336	251	384									
Setúbal	309	144	418	525	261	500	240	171	96	260	347	391	182	47	576	161	195	260	355	308	113								
Sines	390	99	497	609	305	570	323	193	109	201	348	397	262	162	592	209	214	140	433	147	184	119							
Valença	180	560	66	280	373	208	241	529	487	696	365	316	297	436	352	544	418	658	116	706	364	466	548						
Viana do Castelo	147	520	50	264	342	192	196	437	446	651	314	283	263	395	340	509	379	625	77	673	322	423	507	51					
Vila Formoso	193	400	290	226	135	269	190	290	271	575	111	44	259	428	175	336	228	507	240	555	333	439	380	358	342				
Vila Real	163	560	95	119	268	643	190	425	448	641	222	166	262	412	188	510	363	660	100	708	321	432	506	165	150	200			
Vila Real de Santo António	594	120	693	688	396	815	529	284	200	66	560	492	463	350	688	234	308	126	639	174	400	312	264	761	728	535	742		
Vila Verde de Ficalho	465	60	560	626	334	680	399	222	140	230	377	430	338	241	627	68	246	182	511	230	261	204	160	622	583	460	614	183	
Viseu	84	445	191	220	171	173	89	326	341	547	77	77	161	330	234	401	259	650	132	698	219	321	404	255	237	107	99	562	501

Legend:
- Motorways
- Major roads
- Main Roads
- ● All year site(s)
- ● Seasonal site(s)
- ○ No sites listed
- 200m +
- 0–200m

0   30   60   90   120   150 km
0   20   40   60   80   100 miles

© Collins Bartholomew Ltd 2021

Slovakia

Štrbské Pleso

Shutterstock/Mike Mareen

Highlights

Well known for the sheer volume of castles to be found, Slovakia is a country rich in culture. It retains much of its sense of tradition, both in its beautiful medieval towns such as Levoča or Bardejov and in the small villages dotted around the countryside.

A relatively small country with an untamed and diverse wilderness, Slovakia is a great place for those wanting to experience new and different landscapes on a daily basis.

Slovakia has a rich tradition of folklore, and festivals celebrating local folk customs are found throughout the country. The oldest of these is held in Východná, and showcases parades, music, costumes and local crafts.

There are several speciality foods found in Slovakia, one of which is bryndza, a creamy sheep's cheese known for its strong smell. It is the main ingredient of Bryndzové Halušky, a dish made of potato dumplings, bryndza and bacon and considered the national speciality.

Major towns and cities

- Bratislava – a unique capital with a hill-top castle overlooking the city.
- Košice – the well-preserved historical centre is full of heritage sites.
- Prešov – a tourist favourite with many attractions.
- Žilina – packed with museums and historic buildings.

Attractions

- Tatras National Park – with a rich variety of flora and fauna there is plenty to discover in this gorgeous landscape.
- Spiš Castle – the sprawling remains of a 12th century castle that now houses a fascinating museum.
- Nedbalka Gallery, Bratislava – admire the works of Slovakian artists from the 19th century to the present day.

Find out more

www.slovakia.travel
E: touristinfo@visitbratislavia.com
T: 0042 (0) 14 84 13 61 46

Country Information

Population (approx): 5.4 million

Capital: Bratislava

Area: 49,036 sq km

Bordered by: Austria, Czech Republic, Hungary, Poland, Ukraine

Terrain: Rugged mountains in the centre and north; lowlands in the south

Climate: Continental climate; warm, showery summers; cold, cloudy, snowy winters; best months to visit are May, June and September

Highest Point: Gerlachovský štít 2,655m

Languages: Slovak, Hungarian, German

Local Time: GMT or BST + 1, i.e. 1 hour ahead of the UK all year

Currency: Euros divided into 100 cents; £1 = €1.14, €1 = £0.88 (Feb 2021)

Emergency numbers: Police 112; Fire brigade 112; Ambulance 112

Public Holidays 2021: Jan 1, 6; Apr 2, 5; May 1, 8; Jul 5; Aug 29; Sep 1, 15; Nov 1, 17; Dec 24, 25, 26.

School summer holidays are from the beginning of July to the end of August

Entry Formalities

British and Irish passport holders may stay for up to 90 days in any 180 day period without a visa. Following Brexit you may be asked to show a return or onward ticket at the border to confirm your length of stay, or to prove that you have enough money for your stay.

Your passport will need to have a minimum of 6 months' validity remaining, and be less than 10 years old (even if it has over 6 months left).

Visitors arriving at a campsite or hotel must complete a registration form. All foreign visitors are required to show proof of medical insurance cover on entry.

Medical Services

Medical facilities are variable. Whereas the standard of care from doctors is good, many hospitals suffer from a lack of maintenance. The biggest problem you will probably encounter is language, as nurses and ancillary workers may not speak English.

There is a reciprocal health care agreement with the UK for urgent medical treatment and you should present a European Health Insurance Card (EHIC). Emergency treatment is from doctors and dentists contracted to the Slovak health insurance system, but you will be asked for payment and follow on costs could be considerable. Hospital patients are required to make a financial contribution towards costs. Charges incurred are not refundable in Slovakia.

A 24 hour first aid service exists in provincial and district towns, as well as in some small communities. For minor ailments, the first call should be to a pharmacy (lekáreň) where staff are qualified to give advice and may be able to prescribe drugs normally available only on prescription in the UK.

Hepatitis A immunisation is advised for long stay travellers to rural areas, and those who plan to travel outside tourist areas.

Opening Hours

Banks: Mon-Fri 8am-3pm/5pm.

Museums: Tue-Sun 10am-5pm; closed Mon.

Post Offices: Mon-Fri 8am-6pm; Sat 8am-1pm.

Shops: Mon-Fri 7am-6pm; Sat 7am-12 noon. Hypermarkets usually open Sun.

Food Shops: Mon-Fri 7am-6pm; Sat 7am-12pm.

Department Stores - Mon-Sat 9am-9pm

Safety and Security

Most visits to Slovakia are trouble free. However, there is a risk of being a victim of petty theft, particularly in Bratislava, and pickpocketing is common at tourist attractions and in some bars. When placing your jacket on the back of a chair in a restaurant make sure you don't leave valuables in the pockets. Don't put handbags on the floor or under chairs, where they may be vulnerable to theft. There have been occurrences in Bratislava of visitors being offered 'spiked' drinks and subsequently being robbed.

Visitors entering Slovakia via the border crossings on the D2 and D4 motorways should be extremely vigilant. While you leave your vehicle to buy petrol or a motorway vignette, a tyre may be deliberately damaged. Once you are back on the road and have driven a few kilometres other motorists will flag you down under the pretext of offering assistance. In these circumstances you should stay in your vehicle with the doors locked and call the police (dial 112) or the emergency service of the Slovensky Autoturist Klub (SATC) on 18124 or (02) 68249211.

Robberies from parked cars are on the increase. Cameras, mobile phones and tablets are as attractive as cash and credit cards; don't leave them or other valuables unattended.

If you intend to ski or hike in the Slovak mountains you are recommended to have sufficient insurance to cover rescue costs should the Slovak Mountain Rescue (HZS) be called out. Take heed of any instructions issued by HZS; if you ignore their advice you may be liable to a heavy fine.

Taking photos of anything that could be perceived as a military establishment or of security interest may result in problems with the authorities.

Slovakia shares with the rest of Europe an underlying threat from terrorism. Attacks, although unlikely, could be indiscriminate and against civilian targets, including places frequented by tourists.

British Embassy

PANSKA 16, 81101 BRATISLAVA
Tel: (02) 59982000
www.ukinslovakia.fco.gov.uk/en/

Irish Embassy

MOSTOVA 2, 81102 BRATISLAVA
Tel: (02) 32338700
www.embassyofireland.sk

Documents

Passport

Carry your passport at all times as it is an offence to be without it and you may be fined and held in custody for up to 24 hours. Keep a photocopy of the details page separately. Ensure your passport is in a presentable state as the authorities can refuse you entry if it is worn or damaged or looks as if it may have been tampered with.

Vehicle(s)

You should carry your vehicle registration certificate (V5C), at all times together with your driving licence, insurance certificate and your vehicle's MOT certificate (if applicable). Fines may be imposed by police patrols if you cannot produce these documents on request.

Money

Exchange kiosks often offer poor exchange rates and there is a risk of being robbed by thieves nearby. Scottish and Northern Irish bank notes will not be exchanged.

Cash machines which accept UK debit or credit cards are common but do not rely on finding one in remote areas. Shops, particularly in the main tourist areas, increasingly accept credit cards but are sometimes reluctant to accept cards issued by foreign banks. If you intend to pay for something by card do check first that the shop will accept it and that it can be read. You should also check your statements carefully for transactions you did not make.

Driving

The standard of driving is not high and sometimes aggressive with drivers going too fast, especially in bad weather, tailgating and overtaking dangerously. Drive defensively and allow yourself more 'thinking time'. Beware of oncoming cars overtaking on your side of the road, especially on bends and hills.

Accidents

If your vehicle is damaged when you enter Slovakia the border authorities must issue a certificate confirming the visible damage. While in the country if an accident causes bodily injury or material damage exceeding a value of approximately €4,000 it must be reported to the police immediately. If a vehicle is only slightly damaged both drivers should complete a European Accident Report. In the case of foreign motorists driving vehicles registered abroad, it is advisable to report the accident to the police who will issue a certificate which will facilitate the exportation of the vehicle.

Alcohol

Slovakia has a policy of zero tolerance for drinking or consuming drugs before driving. There is no permitted level of alcohol in the bloodstream. Police carry out random breath tests and you will be heavily penalised if there is any trace of alcohol in your system.

Breakdown Service

The motoring organisation, Slovensky Autoturist Klub (SATC), operates an emergency centre which can be contacted 24 hours a day by dialling (0)18124 or (02) 68249211. Operators speak English.

Child Restraint System

Children under the age of 12 years and anyone under 1.5m in height must not travel in the front seat of a vehicle. Child restraint seats must be used for any children weighing less than 36kg.

Fuel

Diesel is sold in service stations with the sign 'TT Diesel' or 'Nafta'. LPG is widely available and is sold under the name ECO Auto-gas or ECO Car-Gas – see www.lpg.szm.sk/slovensko_5.pdf for a list of outlets. If driving a vehicle converted to use LPG you must be in possession of a safety certificate covering the combustion equipment in your vehicle.

Some service stations on international roads and in main towns are open 24 hours but in other areas they may close by 6pm. Credit cards are generally accepted. Service stations may be hard to find in rural areas.

Lights

All vehicles must use dipped headlights at all times.

Motorways

There are 432km of motorways. Bratislava has direct motorway connections with Prague and Vienna and a new motorway is planned to connect it with Budapest.

Emergency phones are placed along motorways and callers are connected directly to the police.

Vehicles using motorways and selected highways must display a vignette (windscreen sticker), which may be purchased at border crossings, petrol stations and post offices. Charges for vehicles up to 3,500kg with or without a caravan or trailer are as follows (2015 prices): €10 for a period of 10 days and €14 for one month. Fines are payable for non-display and old stickers must be removed. The road from the Austrian border crossing at Berg to Bratislava is free of charge.

Motorhomes over 3,500kg are considered private vehicles and can buy the above vignettes as long as you are able to show the Vehicle Registration Certificate (V5) and it shows that the vehicle has fewer than 9 seats. Without the V5, drivers of vehicles over 3,500kg must pay motorway tolls by means of an electronic toll collection unit fitted to their vehicle. Tolls vary according to distance driven, vehicle weight and emissions classification. For information see www.emyto.sk or telephone 00421 235 111111.

Parking

Visitors are warned to park only in officially controlled parking areas since cars belonging to tourists may be targeted for robbery. There are many restrictions on parking in Bratislava and fines are imposed. Wheel clamps are used in main towns and vehicles may be towed.

Continuous white/yellow lines indicate that parking is prohibited and broken white/yellow lines indicate parking restrictions.

Priority

At uncontrolled crossroads or intersections not marked by a priority sign, priority must be given to vehicles coming from the right. Drivers must not enter an intersection unless the exit beyond the crossing is clear.

Drivers must slow down and, if necessary, stop to allow buses and trams to move off from stops and to allow buses to merge with general traffic at the end of a bus lane. A tram turning right and crossing the line of travel of a vehicle moving on its right has priority once the driver has signalled his intention to turn. Trams must be overtaken on the right but do not overtake near a tram refuge.

Roads

Roads are relatively quiet and are generally well maintained. They often follow routes through towns and villages, resulting in sharp bends and reduced speed limits.

Many main roads, although reasonably good, have only a single carriageway in each direction making overtaking difficult.

In winter, north-south routes through Slovakia can be challenging as they pass through mountain ranges. The passes of Donovaly (Ružomberok to Banská Bystrica), Veľký Šturec (Martin to Banská Bystrica), and Čertovica (Liptovský Mikuláš to Brezno) are the most frequented. Slow moving vehicles travelling uphill should pull over at suitable stopping places to allow vehicles to pass.

Road Signs and Markings

Road signs and markings conform to international standards. The following signs may also be seen:

Slovak	English Translation
Dialkova premavka	By-pass
Hnemocnica	Hospital
Jednosmerny premavka	One-way traffic
Obchadzka	Diversion
Průjezd zakázaný	Closed to all vehicles
Zákaz parkovania	No parking
Zákaz vjazdu	No entry

Signs indicating motorways are red and white and signs on motorways or semi motorways have a green or blue background; on other roads signs have a blue background.

Sat Nav/GPS Device

A GPS device must not be placed in the middle of the windscreen where it will impede the driver's view.

Speed Limits

	Open Road (km/h)	Motorway (km/h)
Car Solo	90	130
Car towing caravan/trailer	90	90
Motorhome under 3500kg	90	130
Motorhome 3500-7500kg	80	90

Motorhomes over 3,500kg are restricted to 80/90 km/h (56 mph) on motorways and to 80 km/h (50 mph) on other main roads and dual carriageways. Do not exceed 30 km/h (18 mph) when approaching and going over level crossings.

Speed limits are strictly enforced. Carrying and/or use of radar detectors is prohibited.

Traffic Lights

A green arrow together with a red or amber light indicates that drivers may turn in the direction indicated by the arrow provided they give way to other traffic and to pedestrians. A green arrow accompanied by an amber light in the form of a walking figure means that pedestrians have right of way.

Violation of Traffic Regulations

Police are empowered to collect on the spot fines for contravention of driving regulations. An official receipt should be obtained.

Winter Driving

In winter equip your vehicle(s) for severe driving conditions and fit winter tyres, which are compulsory when roads are covered in snow or ice. Carry snow chains and use them when there is enough snow to protect the road surface.

Essential Equipment

First aid kit

A first aid kit is compulsory in all vehicles.

Reflective Jacket/Waistcoat

If your vehicle is immobilised on the carriageway outside a built up area, or if visibility is poor, you must wear a reflective jacket or waistcoat when getting out of your vehicle. Passengers who leave the vehicle, for example, to assist with a repair, should also wear one.

Warning Triangles

Carry a warning triangle which, in an emergency or in case of breakdown, must be placed at least 100 metres behind your vehicle on motorways and highways, and 50 metres behind on other roads.

The triangle may be placed closer to the vehicle in built-up areas. Drivers may use hazard-warning lights until the triangle is in position.

In case of breakdown, vehicles left on the edge of the carriageway will be towed away after three hours by the organisation in charge of the motorway or road at the owner's expense.

Touring

Smoking is not allowed on the premises where food is served and a partial smoking ban is in force in some bars and cafés which have a dedicated area for smokers. A tip of between 5 to 10% is usual in restaurants. It is normal to give taxi drivers a small tip by rounding up fares to the nearest 50 cents.

Mains water is heavily chlorinated and may cause stomach upsets. Bottled water is available.

The highest peaks of the Tatras mountains are covered with snow for approximately four months of the year and offer ample scope for winter sports. There are plenty of cableways and ski-lifts.

There are a number of UNESCO World Heritage sites in Slovakia including the town of Bardejov, the mining centre of Banská Štiavnica, the 'gingerbread houses' of Vlkolínec village, Spiš Castle, wooden churches in the Carpathian mountains and the caves of Aggtelek Karst and Slovak Karst.

Slovakia has over a thousand curative mineral and thermal springs, together with extensive deposits of high quality healing peat and mud reputed to cure a variety of diseases and ailments. Visitors from all over the world attend these spas every year.

The Bratislava City Card valid for one, two or three days, offers discounts and benefits at approximately 60 attractions and at restaurants and cafés. In addition, it offers free access to public transport and a free one hour walking tour of the Old Town. The card can be obtained at tourist information centres, at the central railway station and at hotels.

In general Slovakia does not cater for the physically handicapped. For example, it is normal for cars to park on the pavement and dropped kerbs are perceived as helping drivers to achieve this without damaging tyres or suspension! Public transport invariably requires large steps to be climbed and bus and tram drivers tend to accelerate from stops at great speed, catching passengers by surprise. Access to most buildings is by steps, rather than ramps. However effort is now being taken to make buildings more accessible.

German is the most common second language, English is not widely understood or spoken.

Camping and Caravanning

There are approximately 175 campsites (Kemping or Autocamp) which are classified into four categories. Sites generally open from mid-June until mid-September, although some are open all year. The season is slow to get going and sites which claim to open in May may not do so or offer only minimal facilities.

Campsites' standards vary and facilities may be basic. Many consist mainly of cabins and chalets in various states of repair, while others form part of the facilities offered by hotels, guest houses or leisure/thermal spa complexes. Casual/wild camping is not permitted; it is prohibited to sleep in a caravan or motorhome outside a campsite.

Campsite prices and the cost of living are still relatively low. Some of the prices shown in the campsite entries have been directly converted from prices previously shown in koruna (crowns) and rounded up. You may find actual prices somewhat higher now that the official currency is the euro. Prices charged include a tourist tax.

Cycling

There are a number of long distance cycle tracks throughout the country (visit the website www.slovakia.travel for more information) including alongside the River Danube between Bratislava and the Gabčikovo Dam.

Cyclists must ride in single file on the right hand side of the road or may use the verge outside built up areas. Children under 10 years of age may not ride on the road unless accompanied by a person over 15 years of age.

Electricity and Gas

Usually the current on campsites varies between 10 and 16 amps. Plugs have two round pins. Some campsites, but not all, have CEE connections.

It is not possible to purchase Campingaz International or any other of the gas cylinders normally available in the UK. Sufficient supplies for your stay should be taken with you. Many sites have communal kitchen facilities which enable visitors to make great savings on their own gas supply.

Public Transport

From April to September hydrofoil services operate from Bratislava to Vienna and Budapest.

In Bratislava bus, trolley bus and tram tickets are valid for periods of up to 60 minutes, extending to up to 90 minutes at night and weekends. Buy them from kiosks and yellow ticket machines. Alternatively you can buy tickets valid for one or several city zones for a fixed period, e.g. 24, 48 or 72 hours or for seven days. Ensure that you validate your ticket on boarding the bus or tram.

Passengers aged 70 and over travel free; carry your passport as proof of age. You must buy a ticket for dogs travelling on public transport and they must be muzzled. You must also purchase a ticket for large items of luggage. See www.imhd.zoznam.sk/ba for more information.

Bratislava

Shutterstock/TTstudio

BANSKA BYSTRICA *B2* (11km W Rural) *48.7540, 19.0552* **Autocamping Tajov,** 97634 Tajov **(048) 4197320; ks.rovdyklev@rovdyklev; www.velkydvor. sk/en**

12 ♿ (htd) 👥 ⚡ 🎿 ⛱ 🦋 ♟ 🍴 ⓗ nr ♨ 🛒 🎢

Fr Tajov dir Kordíky. Site well sp 2km NW of Tajov. Sm, unshd, pt sl, EHU (6-10A) inc; TV; bus; CKE. *"Lovely setting in wooded valley; friendly welcome."* **€16.00** 2016

BANSKÁ ŠTIAVNICA *C2* (6.7km E Rural) *48.447462, 18.983303* **Camping Studenec,** 969 01 Banský Studenec **907 418 033 or 907 746 303; info@ campingstudenec.eu; www.campingstudenec.eu**

🐕 ♿ WD ⚡ 🦋 ♟

Fr Banska Stiavnica take 2536 (sp Bansky Studenec) for 5km. At end of vill turn L sp Studenec. At next junc go strt on gravel track for 50m. Sm, unshd, pt sl, EHU (16A); bbq; cooking facs; sw nr; bus 500m; Eng spkn. *"Well run new (2018) site; excel facs; extensive views; rural walks & biking; conv Bansky Stiavnica; poss open off ssn esp w/ends; excel."* **€21.00, 1 Jul-31 Aug.** 2018

BRATISLAVA *C1* (9km NE Urban) *48.18801, 17.18488* **Autocamping Zlaté Piesky,** Senecká Cesta 12, 82104 Bratislava **(02) 44257373 or 44450592; kempi@ netax.sk; www.intercamp.sk**

🐕 €2 ♿ ⛱ ♟ 🍴 ⓗ ♨ 🛒 🎢 🚲

Exit D1/E75 junc sp Zlaté Piesky. Site on S side of rd 61 (E75) at NE edge of Bratislava. Look for pedestrian bdge over rd to tram terminus, ent thro adj traff lts. If x-ing Bratislava foll sp for Žilina. In summer a 2nd, quieter, drier site is opened. For 1st site turn L when ent leisure complex; for 2nd site carry strt on then turn R. Med, shd, EHU (10A) €3 (long lead poss req); sw; phone; tram to city; Eng spkn; golf 10km; tennis; fishing; CKE. *"Basic site on lge leisure complex; no privacy in shwrs; ltd hot water; muddy in wet; security guard at night & secure rm for bikes etc but reg, major security problems as site grnds open to public; pedalos on lake; helpful, friendly staff; interesting city."* **€13.00, 1 May-15 Oct.** 2016

LEVOCA *B3* (5km N Rural) *49.04982, 20.58727* **Autocamping Levočská Dolina,** 05401 Levoča **(053) 4512705 or 4512701; rzlevoca@pobox.sk**

12 🐕 €1.50 ♿ WD ⚡ 🦋 🍴 ⓗ ♨ 🛒 nr 🎢

Site on E side of minor rd 533 running N fr E50 at Dolina to Levočská Dolina. Steep ent; ltd access lge o'fits. Med, pt shd, sl, EHU (16A) €3; TV; Eng spkn; CKE. *"Diff in wet weather due v sl grnd; friendly staff; interesting old town; ski lift 2.5km; Spišský Hrad castle worth visit; walks in forests around site."* **€18.00** 2016

LIPTOVSKY MIKULAS *B3* (11km NW Rural) *49.13608, 19.5125* **Resort Villa Betula (formerly Penzión),** 03223 Liptovský Sielnica **(907) 812327; villabetula@ villabetula.sk; www.villabetula.sk**

12 🐕 €7 ♿ WD ⚡ ♟ 🦋 ♟ 🍴 ⓗ 🎢

Fr rd 18/E50 exit onto R584 to Liptovský Mikuláš, site on N of lake 6km past Autocamp. 3*, Med, unshd, EHU (10A) inc; sw nr; phone; Eng spkn; ccard acc; bike hire; jacuzzi; sauna; CKE. *"Family-friendly, gem of a site in wonderful area of lakes, mountains & forest; welcoming, helpful owners; v clean & well-kept; vg rest; site at rear of hotel; excel for long or sh stay."* **€26.00** 2015

MARTIN *B2* (5km NW Rural) *49.1082, 18.89888* **Autocamping Turiec,** Kolónia Hviezda 92, 03608 Martin **(421) 907 539178; recepcia@autocamping turiec.sk; www.autocampingturiec.sk**

🐕 €0.70 ♿ WD ⛱ ♟ MP 🦋 ♟ 🍴 ♨ 🛒 nr

Site in town of Vrútky 3km NW of Martin. Foll Autocamping Turiec sps fr rd 18/E50 Žilina-Poprad. Site approx 1km S of this rd on o'skts Vrútky. 3*, Med, pt shd, sl, EHU (10A); 50% statics; Eng spkn; adv bkg acc; CKE. *"Warm welcome; excel security; pleasant wooded setting; excel art galleries/museums in Martin; vg."* **€17.00, 1 May-31 Oct.** 2018

> ## "There aren't many sites open at this time of year"
>
> If you're travelling outside peak season remember to call ahead to check site opening dates – even if the entry says 'open all year'.

NITRIANSKE RUDNO *B2* (1km N Rural) *48.80457, 18.47601* **Autocamping Nitrianske Rudno,** 97226 Nitrianske Rudno **(090) 5204739; info@camping-nrudno.sk; www.camping-nrudno.sk**

🐕 €1 ♿ ⛱ ♟ 🦋 ♟ 🍴 🍴 ♨ 🎢 🚲

E fr Bánovce & Dolné Vestenice on rd 50, turn N onto rd 574. Site on shore of Lake Nitrianske Rudno, sp in vill. 2*, Med, pt shd, EHU €2.50; cooking facs; sw; 10% statics; adv bkg acc; watersports; games area; CKE. *"Welcoming, helpful owner; pleasant location."* **€13.00, 1 Jun-30 Sep.** 2016

PIESTANY *B1* (2.6km S Urban) *48.576469, 17.833889*
Camping Pullman, Cesta Janka Alexyho 2, 92101
Piešťany **(033) 7623563; info@campingpiestany.sk;**
www.campingpiestany.sk

🐕 🏕 🚾 ⚡ 🅿 🍴 ⛱ 🏊

On rd 507 500m S of junc with 499 (immed E of rv
bdge). Sm, unshd, EHU (6A); bbq; cooking facs; TV;
20% statics; train 2km; Eng spkn; adv bkg acc; games
rm; bike hire; CCI. *"Canoeing on rv adj; rvside walk to
town; reg trains to Bratislava 50mins (taxi to stn €8 or
free parking nr stn); pleasant parks in town ctr; bar/rest
in town; vg."* **€15.00, 15 Apr-15 Oct.** 2018

"That's changed – Should I let the Club know?"

If you find something on site that's different
from the site entry, fill in a report and let us
know. See camc.com/europereport.

PREŠOV *B4* (13km W Rural) *49.00386, 21.08145*
Autokemping A Motorest Kemp, Chminianske Nová
Ves, District Prešov 082 33 **0517 795190 or 0905
191056 (mob); kemppo@kemppo.sk; www.kemppo.sk**

🐕 €2 🏕 🏕 🚾 ⚡ 🦋 🍴 ⓗ ♨ ⛱

Fr W on Rte 18/D1/E50, take exit twd Vit'az/
Hrabkov, site on R. Sm, pt shd, EHU €4; gas; bbq;
cooking facs; twin axles; Eng spkn; ccard acc; games
area; CKE. *"Site behind motorest Kemp on Rte 18;
campers kitchen; recep in rest; 5 chalets for rent on
site; fair site."* **€15.00, Feb-Dec.** 2019

ROZNAVA *B3* (6km E Rural) *48.64920, 20.59796*
Autocamping Krásnohorské, Hradná 475, 04941
Krásnohorské Podhradie **(058) 7325457**

🏕 🏕

E fr Rožňava on rd 50/E571 foll sp Krásnohorské
Podhradie. Site under shadow of castle. Sm, pt shd,
80% statics. *"Lovely setting in pine woods; primitive
facs but plenty of hot water; conv for cave visits."*
€10.00 2020

TATRANSKA LOMNICA *B3* (2.5km ESE Rural)
49.15830, 20.30979 **Intercamp Tatranec,** 05960
Tatranská Lomnica **(052) 4467092; hoteltatranec@
hoteltatranec.com**

12 🏕 🚾 🏕 🏕 ⚡ 🦋 🅿 🍴 ⓗ ♨ ⛱ ✏

NE fr Poprad on rd 67, after 8km turn L over level
**x-ing, thro Vel'ká Lomnica twds Tatranská Lomnica
on rd 540. Site on L.** 3*, Lge, unshd, pt sl, EHU (6A)
inc; Eng spkn; adv bkg acc; CKE. *"Superb views of High
Tatras; conv cable car, train etc; excel base for walking
& holiday resort; hotel adj; poor, dated facs & ltd
privacy."* **€18.50** 2015

TERCHOVA *B2* (3km SW Rural) *49.24779, 18.98866*
Autocamp Belá, Nižné Kamence, 01305 Belá **(041)
5695135 or (905) 742514; camp@bela.sk;**
www.campingbela.eu

🐕 €1 🏕 🚾 🏕 🏕 ⚡ 🦋 ⓗ ♨ ⛱

Fr Zilina foll rd 583 twd Terchová. Site on L 3km
after vill of Belá. 2*, Med, pt shd, EHU (10A) €3; bbq;
cooking facs; 10% statics; tennis. *"Delightful rvside
site; gd welcome; clean, modern san facs; conv walking
in Malá Fatra mountains."* **€11.50, 1 May-15 Oct.**
2016

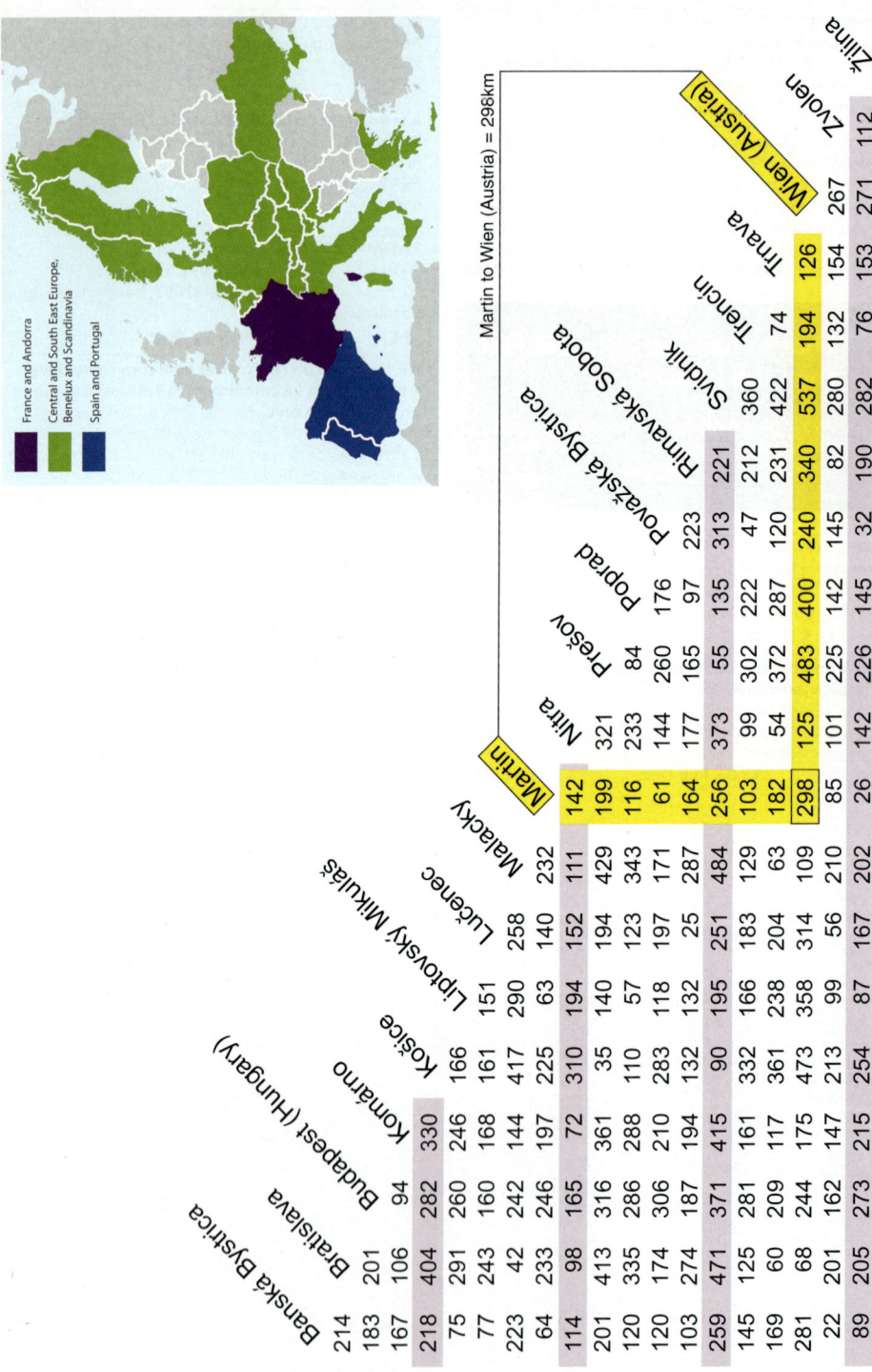

Map legend:
- France and Andorra
- Central and South East Europe, Benelux and Scandinavia
- Spain and Portugal

Martin to Wien (Austria) = 298km

Road-distance chart (km). Values are read as the distance between the row city and the column city.

Key to column headers: BB = Banská Bystrica · BA = Bratislava · BU = Budapest (Hungary) · KN = Komárno · KE = Košice · LM = Liptovský Mikuláš · LC = Lučenec · ML = Malacky · MT = Martin · NR = Nitra · PO = Prešov · PP = Poprad · PB = Považská Bystrica · RS = Rimavská Sobota · SK = Svidník · TN = Trenčín · TT = Trnava · WN = Wien (Austria) · ZV = Zvolen

	BB	BA	BU	KN	KE	LM	LC	ML	MT	NR	PO	PP	PB	RS	SK	TN	TT	WN	ZV
Bratislava	214																		
Budapest (Hungary)	183	162																	
Komárno	167	106	94																
Košice	218	417	260	290															
Liptovský Mikuláš	75	290	290	240	151														
Lučenec	77	246	144	160	140	140													
Malacky	223	35	246	130	440	360	258												
Martin	64	215	288	168	230	76	140	256											
Nitra	114	94	165	72	310	194	152	111	142										
Prešov	201	413	316	361	35	140	194	429	199	321									
Poprad	120	335	286	288	110	57	123	343	116	233	84								
Považská Bystrica	120	174	306	210	283	118	197	171	61	144	260	176							
Rimavská Sobota	103	287	194	210	132	132	25	287	164	177	165	97	223						
Svidník	259	471	371	415	90	195	251	484	256	373	55	135	313	221					
Trenčín	145	125	281	161	332	166	183	129	103	99	302	222	47	212	360				
Trnava	169	60	209	117	361	238	204	63	182	54	372	287	120	231	422	74			
Wien (Austria)	281	68	244	175	473	358	314	109	298	125	483	400	240	340	537	194	126		
Zvolen	22	201	162	147	213	99	56	210	85	101	225	142	145	82	280	132	154	267	
Žilina	89	205	273	215	254	87	167	202	26	142	226	145	32	190	282	76	153	271	112

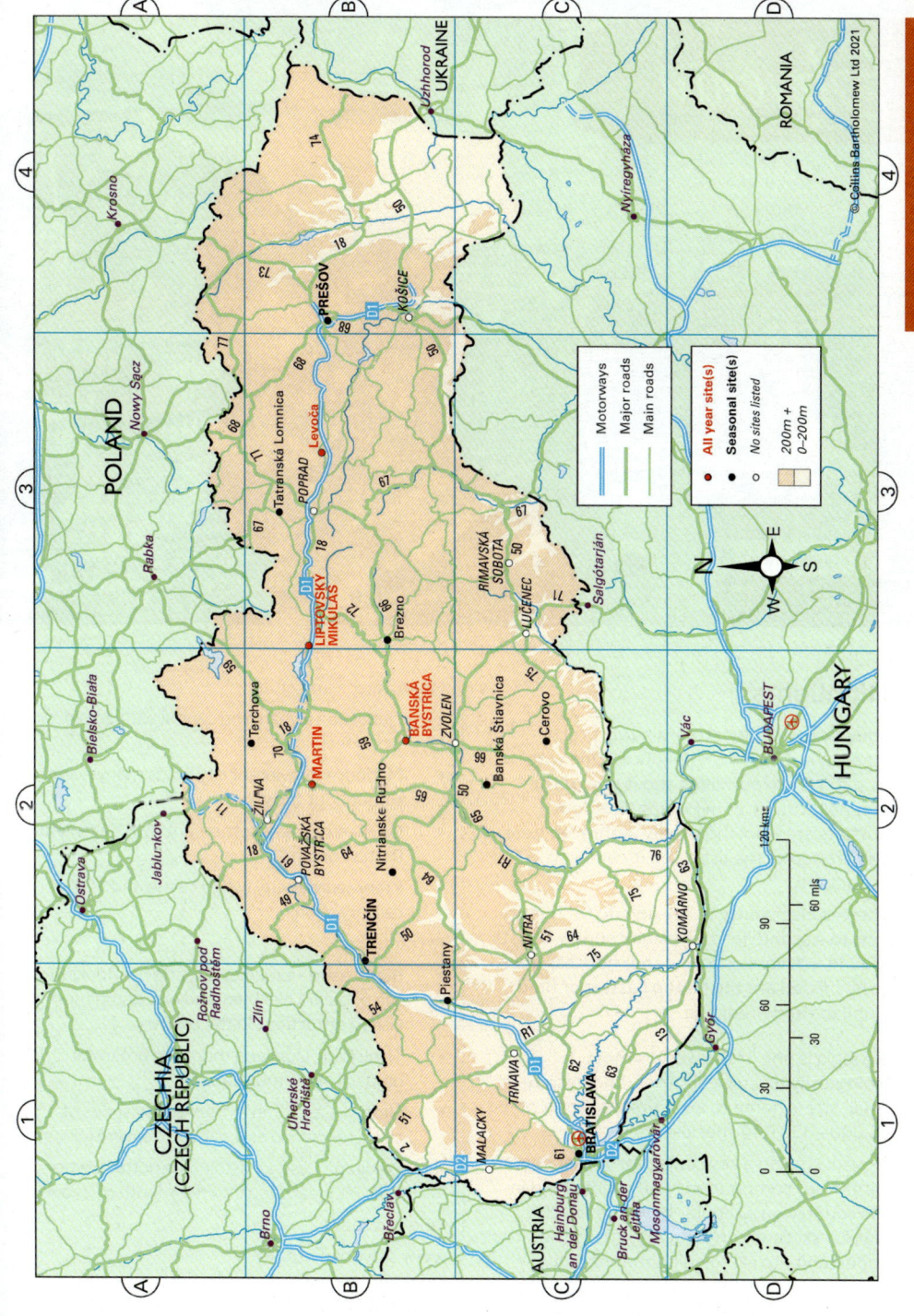

© Collins Bartholomew Ltd 2021

Legend

Motorways
Major roads
Main roads

All year site(s)
Seasonal site(s)
No sites listed
200m +
0–200m

POLAND

UKRAINE

ROMANIA

CZECHIA
(CZECH REPUBLIC)

AUSTRIA

HUNGARY

BRATISLAVA

PREŠOV

KOŠICE

POPRAD

Levoča

LIPTOVSKÝ MIKULÁŠ

MARTIN

BANSKÁ BYSTRICA

ZVOLEN

Brezno

Terchová

ŽILINA

POVAŽSKÁ BYSTRICA

TRENČÍN

Nitrianske Rudno

Banská Štiavnica

Cerovo

RIMAVSKÁ SOBOTA

LUČENEC

Salgótarján

BUDAPEST

Vác

KOMÁRNO

Győr

NITRA

Piešťany

TRNAVA

MALACKY

Mosonmagyaróvár

Bruck an der Leitha

Hainburg an der Donau

Tatranská Lomnica

Krosno

Nowy Sącz

Rabka

Bielsko-Biała

Jabłunkov

Ostrava

Rožnov pod Radhoštěm

Zlín

Uherské Hradiště

Brno

Břeclav

Nyíregyháza

Užhhorod

120 km's

60 ml's

0   30   60   90

0   30   60

Slovenia

Ljubljana

Shutterstock/Matej Kastelic

Highlights

Equipped with an extraordinarily pretty landscape, Slovenia is deeply in tune with its natural surroundings and is one of the greenest countries in Europe. Outdoor pursuits are wholeheartedly embraced here and are top of the list when it comes to attractions.

There is also plenty to see and do for history fans to see and do - this small country boasts around 500 castles and manor houses. Not to be missed are the hilltop castles of Bled, Ljubljana and Predjama.

Slovenia is one of the world's most biologically diverse countries, and despite its small size is home to an estimated total of 45,000 – 120,000 species.

Slovenia is also a key centre for winter sports, with major competitions and events held in the country on a regular basis. Kanin, the highest ski centre in Slovenia, offers the opportunity to ski to neighbouring Italy.

Major towns and cities

- Ljubljana – a charming capital with an old-world feel.
- Maribor – this vibrant city holds many events throughout the year.
- Celje – an ancient settlement with Celtic and Roman origins.
- Kranj – a lively city with a castle and 14th century church.

Attractions

- Bled Castle – a medieval castle overlooking the popular Lake Bled, and one of the most visited attractions in the country.
- Tivoli Park, Ljubljana - home to botanical gardens and a museum.
- Škocjan Caves – an extraordinary series of caves renowned as a natural treasure.
- Predjama Castle, Postojna – a gothic castle built 700 years ago into the mouth of a cave.

Find out more

www.slovenia.info
E: info@slovenia.info
T: 0038 (0) 61 58 98 550

Country Information

Population (approx): 2 million

Capital: Ljubljana

Area: 20,273 sqkm

Bordered by: Austria, Croatia, Hungary, Italy

Coastline: 46.6km

Terrain: Coastal strip on the Adriatic; alpine mountains in west and north; many rivers and forests

Climate: Mediterranean climate on the coast; hot summers and cold winters in the plateaux and valleys in the east; spring and early autumn are the best times to visit

Highest Point: Triglav 2,864m

Languages: Slovenian; Serbo-Croat

Local Time: GMT or BST + 1, i.e. 1 hour ahead of the UK all year

Currency: Euros divided into 100 cents; £1 = €1.14, €1 = £0.88 (Feb 2021)

Emergency numbers: Police 113; Fire brigade 112; Ambulance 112. Operators speak English

Public Holidays 2021: Jan 1, 2; Feb 8; Apr 4, 5 27; May 1, 2, 23; Jun 25; Aug 15; Oct 31; Nov 1; Dec 25, 26.

School summer holidays are from the last week in June to the end of August

Entry Formalities

British and Irish passport holders may stay for up to 90 days in any 180 day period without a visa. Following Brexit you may be asked to show a return or onward ticket at the border to confirm your length of stay, or to prove that you have enough money for your stay.

Your passport will need to have a minimum of 6 months' validity remaining, and be less than 10 years old (even if it has over 6 months left).

All foreign nationals must register with the police within three days of arrival in Slovenia. Campsites carry out registration formalities, but if you are staying with friends or family you or your host will need to visit the nearest police station to register your presence in the country.

Medical Services

British visitors may obtain emergency medical, hospital and dental treatment from practitioners registered with the public health service, Health Institute of Slovenia (HIIS) on presentation of a European Health Insurance Card (EHIC). You will have to make a contribution towards costs which will not be refunded in Slovenia. Full fees are payable for private medical and dental treatment.

Health resorts and spas are popular and the medical profession uses them extensively for treatment of a wide variety of complaints.

Opening Hours

Banks: Mon-Fri 9am-12 noon & 2pm-5pm; closed Sat/Sun

Museums: Tues-Sun 9/10am-5/6pm. Most closed Mon.

Post Offices: Mon-Fri 8am-6pm; Sat 8am-12noon.

Shops: Mon-Fri 8am-7pm/9pm; Sat 8am-1pm.

Safety and Security

Slovenia is relatively safe for visitors but the usual sensible precautions should be taken against pickpockets in large towns and cities. Do not leave valuables in your car.

Western Slovenia is on an earthquake fault line and is subject to occasional tremors.

If you are planning a skiing or mountaineering holiday, contact the Slovenian Tourist Board for advice on weather and safety conditions before travelling. You should follow all safety instructions meticulously, given the danger of avalanches in some areas. Off-piste skiing is highly dangerous.

There is a low threat from terrorism but attacks could be indiscriminate and against civilian targets, including places frequented by tourists.

British Embassy

4TH FLOOR, TRG REPUBLIKE 3, 1000 LJUBLJANA
Tel: (01) 2003910
www.ukinslovenia.fco.gov.uk/en

Irish Embassy

Palaca Kapitelj, 1st floor
POLJANSKI NASIP 6
1000 Ljubljana
Tel: (01) 3008970
www.embassyofireland.si

Documents

Driving Licence

All European countries recognise the EU format paper UK driving licence introduced in 1990. However, it is a legal requirement to show your driving license with a form of photographic identification, such as your passport, if your driving licence does not include a photograph.

Passport

Carry a copy of your passport at all times as a form of identification.

Vehicle(s)

You should carry your vehicle documentation, i.e. vehicle registration certificate (V5C), insurance certificate, MOT certificate (if applicable) and driver's licence.

If you are driving a hired or borrowed vehicle, you must be in possession of a letter of authorisation from the owner or a hire agreement.

Money

Cash machines are widespread and the major credit cards are widely accepted. Carry your credit card issuers'/banks' 24-hour UK contact numbers in case of loss or theft of your cards.

Driving

Accidents

Any visible damage to a vehicle entering Slovenia must be certified by authorities at the border. All drivers involved in an accident while in the country should inform the police and obtain a written report (Potrdilo). Drivers of vehicles which have been damaged will need to present this police report to Customs on departure.

Alcohol

The maximum permitted level of alcohol is 50 milligrams in 100 millilitres of blood, i.e. lower than the limit in the UK (80 milligrams). If a driver is under the age of 21 or has held a driving licence for less than three years the permitted level of alcohol is zero. The police carry out tests at random.

Breakdown Service

The motoring organisation, Avto-Moto Zveza Slovenije (AMZS), operates a 24 hour breakdown service which can be contacted by telephoning 1987. On motorways, using a mobile phone, call the AMZS Alarm Centre in Ljubljana on (01) 5305353 or use the emergency telephones and ask for AMZS assistance.

Charges apply for repairs or towing, plus supplements at night, weekends and on public holidays. Credit cards are accepted.

Child Restraint System

Children under 12 years of age and under the height of 1.5 metres must use a suitable child restraint system for their size and age.

Fuel

Petrol stations are generally open from 7am to 8pm Monday to Saturday. Many near border crossings, on motorways and near large towns are open 24 hours. Credit cards are accepted. It is understood that few petrol stations sell LPG.

Lights

Dipped headlights are compulsory at all times, regardless of weather conditions. Bulbs are more likely to fail with constant use and you are required to carry spares. Hazard warning lights must be used when reversing.

Motorways

There are about 620km of motorways (autoceste) and expressways (hitre ceste) with more under construction. For more information about motorways see the website www.dars.si.

There are service areas and petrol stations along the motorways and emergency telephones are situated every 2km.

Emergency corridors are compulsory on motorways and dual carriageways. Drivers are required to create a precautionary emergency corridor to provide access for emergency vehicles whenever congestion occurs. Drivers in the left-hand lane must move as far over to the left as possible, and drivers in the central and right-hand lanes must move as far over to the right as possible.

Motorway Tolls

Drivers of vehicles weighing up to 3,500kg must purchase a vignette (windscreen sticker) for use on motorways and expressways. Caravans/trailers don't need an additional vignette and the weight of the caravan/trailer isn't taken into account. The vignette is available from petrol stations in Slovenia, neighbouring countries and at border posts. The cost of a 7 day vignette is €15, 1 month is €30 and an annual is €110 (2015 charges). For vehicles over 3,500kg tolls are payable with cash or credit card.

Karawanken Tunnel

The 8km Karawanken Tunnel links the E61/A11 in Austria and E61/A2 in Slovenia. The toll is €7.20 for car and caravan or motorhome up to 3,500kg and €9.38 for a motorhome over 3,500kg (2018 charges).

Parking

Parking meters are used in towns. In city centres white lines indicate that parking is permitted for a maximum of two hours between 7am and 7pm, a parking ticket must be purchased from a machine. Blue lines indicate places where parking is allowed free of charge for up to 30 minutes. Vehicles parked illegally may be towed away or clamped.

Priority

At intersections drivers must give way to traffic from the right, unless a priority road is indicated. The same rule applies to roundabouts, i.e. traffic entering a roundabout has priority.

Roads

Slovenia has a well-developed road system, and international and main roads are in good condition. Secondary roads may still be poorly maintained and generally unlit. Minor roads are often gravelled and are known locally as 'white roads'. Road numbers are rarely mentioned on road signs and it is advisable to navigate using place names in the direction you are travelling.

Roadside verges are uncommon, or may be lined with bollards which make pulling over difficult. Where there is a hard shoulder it is usual for slow vehicles to pull over to allow faster traffic to overtake.

The capital, Ljubljana, can be reached from Munich, Milan, Vienna and Budapest in less than five hours. There are numerous border crossings for entry into Slovenia.

Care should be taken, especially on narrow secondary roads, where tailgating and overtaking on blind bends are not unknown. Drive defensively and take extra care when driving at night. Be prepared for severe weather in winter.

Information on roads may be obtained by telephoning the AMZS Information Centre on (01) 5305300.

Road Signs and Markings

Road signs conform to international standards. Motorway signs have a green background and national road signs a blue background. On your travels you may see the following signs:

| Mountain pass | School area | Toll: Vignette/card or cash |

Speed Limits

	Open Road (km/h)	Motorway (km/h)
Car Solo	90-110	130
Car towing caravan/trailer	90	100
Motorhome under 3500kg	90-110	130
Vehicle over 3500-7500kg	80	80

Motorhomes over 3,500kg are restricted to 80 km/h (50 mph) on open roads, including motorways. Other speed limits are the same as for solo cars.

Areas where speed is restricted to 30 km/h (18 mph) are indicated by the sign 'Zone 30'. In bad weather when visibility is reduced to 50 metres the maximum speed limit is 50 km/h (31 mph).

Traffic Jams

Slovenia is a major international through-route and bottlenecks do occur on the roads to and from Ljubljana, such as the E61/A2 from Jesinice and the E57 from Maribor. Traffic queues can be expected from May to August on the roads around Lake Bled and to the Adriatic and on the E70/A1 motorway near the Razdrto toll station and near Kozina and Koper. Tailbacks also occur at border posts near the Karawanken Tunnel, Ljubelj and Šentilj/Spielfeld particularly at weekends. The motoring organisation, AMZS, provides traffic information in English – telephone (01) 5305300 or see their website www.amzs.si.

Violation of Traffic Regulations

The police have powers to stop drivers and levy heavy on-the-spot fines, including penalties for speeding, driving under the influence of alcohol and for using mobile phones without properly installed wireless headsets (bluetooth). Jaywalking is an offence and you could be fined if caught. Fines must be paid in local currency and you should obtain an official receipt.

Winter Driving

From 15 November to 15 March, and beyond those dates during winter weather conditions (snowfalls, black ice, etc), private cars and vehicles up to 3,500kg must have winter tyres on all four wheels or, alternatively, carry snow chains. Minimum tread depth of tyres is 3mm.

Essential Equipment

First aid kit

Although a first aid kit is not compulsory in all vehicles, it is recommended.

Reflective Jacket/Waistcoat

In the event of vehicle breakdown on a motorway, anyone who leaves the vehicle must wear a reflective jacket.

Warning Triangles

Vehicles towing a trailer must carry two warning triangles (single vehicles require only one). In the event of a breakdown to vehicle and trailer combinations, one triangle must be placed at the rear of the towed vehicle and another at the front of the towing vehicle at a distance which ensures maximum safety and visibility. At night, drivers must use hazard warning lights or a torch in addition to the warning triangles.

Touring

A 10% tip is usual in restaurants and for taxi drivers.

The capital, Ljubljana, is a gem of a city with many Baroque and Art Nouveau influences. The works of the world renowned architect Jože Plecnik are among the finest urban monuments in the city. A Ljubljana Card is available for one, two or three days and offers free travel on city buses, tourist boat trips, the funicular, guided tours and the tourist train to Ljubljana Castle, plus free admission to museums and discounts at a wide range of shops, restaurants and bars. You can buy the card at the main bus and railway stations, hotels and tourist information centres or from www.visitljubljana.si.

Visit the largest cave in Europe is situated at Postojna, south west of Ljubljana. Also worth visiting are the mountains, rivers and woods of Triglav National Park, which covers the major part of the Julian Alps, together with the oldest town in Slovenia, Ptuj, and the city of Maribor. In Lipica take a guided tour around the stud, home to the world famous Lipizzaner horses.

There is a hydrofoil service between Portorož and Venice from April to November.

Slovenian is the official language although most Slovenians speak at least one other major European language and many, especially the young, speak English.

Camping and Caravanning

There are over 60 organised campsites in Slovenia rated one to five stars. They are usually open from May to October but a few are open all year. Standards of sites and their sanitary facilities are generally good. Campsites on the coast consist mostly of statics and can be overcrowded during the peak summer season. Casual/wild camping is not permitted.

Cycling

There are some cycle lanes which are also used by mopeds. Cyclists under the age of 15 must wear a safety helmet.

If using a vehicle bike carrier which overhangs by over one metre at the rear of a vehicle, you need to affix a 30cm square red flag or panel. At night the overhanging load must be indicated by a red light and a reflector. Loads may only project rearwards; they must not overhang the sides of vehicles.

Electricity and Gas

Usually the current on campsites varies between 6 and 16 amps. Plugs have two round pins. Hook-up points on most campsites conform to CEE standards.

Campingaz cylinders cannot be purchased or exchanged. Recent visitors report that it is possible to have gas cylinders refilled at premises on Verovškova Ulica 70, Ljubljana. The company's name is Butan-Plin. However, The Caravan and Motorhome Club does not recommend this practice and you should aim to take enough gas to last during your stay.

Public Transport

There is an extensive bus network in Ljubljana. Buy a yellow 'top-up' Urbana card for a one-off payment of €2 from news-stands, tobacconists, tourist information offices or the central bus station and add credit (between €1 and €50) at the same locations or at the green Urbanomati machines around the city. When boarding a bus simply touch the card to one of the card readers at the front of the bus and €1.20 will be deducted allowing 90 minutes of unlimited travel regardless of how many changes you make. Taxis are generally safe, clean and reliable. Fares are metered. For longer distances ordering a taxi by phone will attract lower rates.

Lake Bled

Shutterstock/Zdenek Matyas Photography

BLED *B2* (12.5km SE Rural) *46.326170, 14.234771*
Turistična kmetija Hribar, Brezje 14, 4243 Brezje
(04) 0260414; breda.policar@gmail.com;
www.turisticna-kmetija-hribar.si

12 ♦♦ WD ▲ 🔌 ✗ MSP 🦋 ⟟ 🍴 nr (H) 🏖 nr

Exit m'way sp Brezje and turn L to Brezje. Turn R at rndabt sp Brezje. On reaching Brezje bear R and cont past firestn. At T-junc turn R. Cont for 300m (ignoring Sat Nav) until you see sm residential carpk on R. Now turn sharp L and go straight thro metal gates to site. Sm, pt shd, EHU (16A) €3.50; bbq (charcoal, elec, gas); cooking facs; red long stay; 5% statics; bus 1km; Eng spkn; adv bkg acc; ccard acc. **€24.40** **2019**

BLED *B2* (4km SE Rural) *46.35527, 14.14833*
Camping Šobec, Šobčeva Cesta 25, 4248 Lesce
(04) 5353700; sobec@siol.net; www.sobec.si

🐕 €3.50 ♦♦ WD ▲ 🔌 🏖 ✗ MSP ⟟ 🍴 (H) 🏖 🏖 ▵

Exit rte 1 at Lesce, site sp. 5*, Lge, pt shd, pt sl, EHU (16A) €3.70 (poss long lead req); red long stay; TV; Eng spkn; ccard acc; bike hire; CKE. *"Excel, tranquil rvside site in wooded area surrounded by rv; friendly, helpful staff; lge pitches; clean san facs; gd rest; gd walking/cycling; many sports & activities; real camping atmosphere, plenty of space; def rec; rv pool; beautiful area; conv NH en-rte to Croatia."* **€35.00, 15 Apr-1 Oct.** **2017**

BLED *B2* (4km SW Rural) *46.36155, 14.08066*
Camping Bled, Kidričeva 10c, SI 4260 Bled **04 5752000; info@camping-bled.com; www.camping-bled.com**

🐕 €3 ♦♦ WD ▲ ♿ 🏖 ✗ MSP ⟟ 🍴 nr 🏖 🏖 nr ▵ 🖊 🏊 shgl

Fr Ljubljana take E16/A2 & exit dir Bled/Lesce. At rndabt take 2nd exit for Bled & cont along rd 209. In Bled take rd around lake on L (lake on R), site sp - winding rd. 5*, Lge, mkd, pt shd, pt sl, EHU (16A) inc (long lead req some pitches - fr recep); gas; bbq; sw nr; twin axles; red long stay; TV; bus to Ljubljana adj; Eng spkn; ccard acc; games rm; fishing; white water rafting; games area; horseriding; bike hire; dog shwrs; CKE. *"Beautifully situated nr lake; m'van & car wash; busy, popular, well-run site; well-drained in bad weather altho lower pitches poss muddy; v gd, modern, clean san facs, stretched in ssn; helpful, efficient, friendly staff; spa cent nrby; paragliding; conv Vintgar Gorge, Bled Castle, Lake Bohinj, Dragna Valley; excel walking/cycling around lake; excel rest; arr acc anytime; free WiFi throughout site."* **€34.00, 1 Apr-15 Oct, X03.** **2018**

See advertisement

BOHINJSKA BISTRICA *B1* (0.8km NW Rural)
46.27438, 13.94798 **Camping Danica Bohinj,**
Triglavska 60, 4264 Bohinjska Bistrica **(04) 5721702; info@camp-danica.si; www.camp-danica.si**

12 ♦♦ €2 ♦♦ WD ▲ 🔌 ✗ MSP 🦋 ⟟ 🍴 (H) 🏖 🏖 nr 🖊

Site on o'skts of vill clearly sp. 3*, Med, pt shd, EHU (6A) inc (long lead poss req); gas; red long stay; 10% statics; Eng spkn; ccard acc; tennis; canoe hire; kayak hire; fishing; CCI. *"Excel site, spacious, open, attractive site in beautiful valley; fly-fishing; gd walking & climbing; gd, clean san facs but poss stretched high ssn; conv bus to Ljubljana & Lake Bohinji."* **€33.00** **2018**

KAMNIK *B2* (1km NE Urban) *46.22724, 14.61902*
Kamp Resnik, Nevlje 1a, 1240 Kamnik **(01) 8317314;**
info@kampresnik.com; www.kampresnik.com

Fr Ljubljana foll rd sp Celje then turn N for Kamnik.
Fr Kemnik by-pass (E side of rv) bear R thro 2 sets
traff lts, site 200m on L just after sports cent - site
ent not obvious, turn bef zebra x-ing opp pub. Fr E
on rd 414, site sp. 2*, Med, pt shd, EHU (10A) €3;
gas; 5% statics; bus; Eng spkn; adv bkg acc; ccard
acc; golf nr; CKE. *"Conv Ljubljana & Kamnik Alps;
friendly staff; pleasant, well-kept; thermal spa nrby;
pool adj; new excel extra shwrs (2018); views of
Kamniska Alps; short stroll into town; rly stn 1km."*
€17.00, 1 May-30 Sep.   2019

KOBARID *B1* (1km NE Rural) *46.25070, 13.58664*
Kamp Koren, Drežniške Ravne 33, 5222 Kobarid **(05)
3891311;** info@kamp-koren.si; www.kamp-koren.si

Turn E fr main rd in town, site well sp dir Drežnica.
4*, Med, pt shd, EHU (16A) €4; red long stay; TV; Eng
spkn; ccard acc; bike hire; canoeing; CKE. *"Vg, clean
facs but stretched; friendly, helpful staff; pitches
cramped; pleasant location in beautiful rv valley; excel
walk to waterfall (3hrs); WW1 museum in town; lge
elec lead poss req."* €30.00   2017

KOPER *D1* (7km N Coastal) *45.57818, 13.73573*
Camping Adria, Jadranska Zesta 25, 6280 Ankaran
(05) 6637350; camp@adria-ankaran.si;
www.adria-ankaran.si

Fr A1/E70/E61 onto rd 10 then rd 406 to Ankaran.
Or cross Italian border at Lazzaretto & foll sp to site
in 3km. Site sp in vill. 4*, Lge, mkd, shd, EHU (10A)
€3; bbq; 60% statics; bus 500m; ccard acc; tennis;
bike hire; waterslide; sauna. *"Old town of Koper worth
a visit, 1 Olympic-size pool; Vinakoper winery rec N of
site on dual c'way; poss noisy groups high ssn; insect
repellent req; private san facs avail; clean san facs but
red LS; gd rest; has beach but not picturesque; vg."*
€35.00, 8 Apr-15 Oct.   2018

KRANJSKA GORA *B1* (14km E Rural) *46.46446,
13.95773* **Camping Kamne,** Dovje 9, 4281 Mojstrana
(04) 5891105; info@campingkamne.com;
www.campingkamne.com

Sp fr rd 201 bet Jesenice & Kranjska Gora, 2km E
of Mojstrana. Do not go thro vill of Dovje. 3*, Sm,
hdstg, pt shd, terr, EHU (6A) €2.50-3.50; red long stay;
TV; 10% statics; bus to Kranjska Gora fr site; Eng spkn;
bike hire; tennis; fishing; CKE. *"Conv Triglav National
Park & border; views Mount Triglav; warm welcome;
ltd san facs stretched high ssn; hiking; friendly helpful
staff; gd cycling along old rlwy track; steep site; some
pitches sm, some with good views; tap for filling
aquarolls at bottom of site."* €31.00   2019

KRANJSKA GORA *B1* (4km E Rural) *46.484438,
13.837885* **Camping Spik,** Jezerci 21, 4282 Godz
Martuljek **(51) 634466;** info@camp-spik.si;
www.camp-spik.si

Fr Ratece foll rd past Kranjska Gora to Gozd. Thro
vill, bear L over rv bdge, site ent immed on L adj
hotel. 3*, Lge, mkd, shd, EHU (10A); bbq (charcoal,
elec, gas); red long stay; twin axles; 40% statics;
phone; adv bkg acc; ccard acc; bike hire; fitness rm;
tennis adj; sauna; climbing wall. *"Conv Kranska Gora
National Park; max 2 dogs; vg rests in KG; gd walking
& cycling; LS check in at hotel; gd facs; next to Spa
Hotel."* €33.70   2019

LJUBLJANA *C2* (5km N Urban) *46.09752, 14.51870*
Ljubljana Resort, Dunajska Cesta 270, 1000 Ljubljana
(01) 5890130; ljubljana.resort@gpl.si;
www.ljubljanaresort.si

Fr Maribor take A1 twd Ljubljana, at junc Zadobrova
take Ljubljana ring rd twd Kranj & exit junc 3 sp Lj -
Ježica, Bežigrad. At x-rds turn R twd Črnuče along
Dunajska Cesta, turn R 100m bef rlwy x-ing. Fr N
(Jesenica/Karawanken tunnel) exit A2/E66 at junc
13 sp Ljubljana Črnuče & foll rd for 3.5km; at rndabt
junc with Dunajska Cesta rd turn R (1st exit); site on
L in 200m. 4*, Lge, mkd, hdg, pt shd, EHU (10A) €4.50;
bbq (elec, gas, sep area); 10% statics; phone; bus to
city at site ent (tickets at recep); Eng spkn; ccard acc;
horseriding 500m; rv fishing; tennis; bike hire; games
rm; CKE. *"Busy site by rv; gd rest; naturist sunbathing
adj pool; dishwash area; red facs LS; archery; fitness
club; pitches nr hotel poss noisy due late-night
functions; whirlpools; htd pool complex adj; some
pitches muddy when wet, conv for city; cycle & walking
path along Rv Sava; friendly, helpful staff."* €33.00,
X04.   2018

MARIBOR *B3* (5km SW Urban) *46.5355, 15.60508*
Camping Centre Kekec, Pohorska ulica 35c, 2000
Maribor 040 665 732; info@cck.si or bernard@cck.si;
www.cck.si

Fr S on A1 exit Maribor Jug; foll rd until you see
Bauhaus shopping cent on the R, turn L at this x-rd;
turn R after approx 400m; turn L after approx 100m;
site on L after approx 3km opp the Terano Hotel.
Sm, mkd, hdstg, unshd, pt sl, terr, EHU (25A) €3; bbq;
Eng spkn; adv bkg acc; ccard acc; CKE. *"Rec for larger
o'fits as lge pitches avail but care with narr ent rd; v
nice site."* €23.00   2017

NAZARJE *B2* (7km W Rural) *46.31166, 14.90916*
Camping Menina, Varpolje 105, 3332 Rečica ob
Savinji **(0)** 40525266; info@campingmenina.com

12 🐕 €3 ⛺ ♿ 🚿 🔌 MSP 🦋 📶 ▼ ⑪ ♨ ⛰

**Fr rte E57 bet Ljubljana & Celje, turn N twd Nazarje,
then dir Ljubno for 3km. Site sp.** 4*, Med, hdstg, mkd,
shd, EHU (6-16A) €3; sw nr; 10% statics; Eng spkn; adv
bkg acc; bike hire; CKE. *"Helpful owners; delightful site
in woodland; very ltd facs in winter."* **€26.00**   2016

> ## "We must tell the Club about that great site we found"
>
> Get your site reports in by mid-August and we'll
> do our best to get your updates into the next
> edition.

NOVO MESTO *C3* (11km SW Rural) *45.76735,
15.05150* **Campsite Polje,** Meniška vas 47, 8350
Dolenjske Toplice **(0)** 40466589; info@kamp-polje.si;
kamp-polje.si

🐕 ♿ (htd) ⛺ 🚿 🔌 MSP 🦋 📶 ▛nr

**W fr Novo Mesto on 419 to Dolenjske Toplice. Foll
sp.** Hdstg, mkd, pt shd, EHU (16A); bbq (charcoal, elec,
gas); sw nr; twin axles; Eng spkn; adv bkg rec; ccard
acc; canoe, canoe and scooter hire; fishing. *"Ideal NH or
longer; forest on one side, fields other; ACSI discount."*
€18.00, 1 Apr-5 Nov.   2019

PIVKA *D2* (3km S Rural) *45.708997, 14.192552*
Camp Plana, Selce 66, 6257 Pivka **(07) 0668668;**
camp.plana@gmail.com; camping-plana.com

🐕 ♿ (htd) 🍴 ♿ 🔌 🚿 MSP 📶 ▼ ⑪ ⛰

**Fr the border with Croatia at the end of E61/A7
foll rte 6 to Pivka. Site sp on R off rte 6.** Sm, hdstg,
pt shd, EHU (10A); cooking facs; sw nr; twin axles;
TV; Eng spkn; adv bkg acc; games area. *"Excel."*
€25.00, 1 Apr-31 Oct.   2018

PORTOROZ *D1* (3km S Coastal) *45.50138, 13.59388*
Camping Lucija, Obala 77, 6320 Portorož **(05)**
6906000; camp.lucija@bernardingroup.si;
www.camp-lucija.si

🐕 €5 ♿ ⛺ ♿ 🔌 MSP ▼ ⑪ ▛ 🏊adj

**Fr Koper (N) on rd 111, turn R at traff lts in Lucija.
Take next L, then 2nd L into site. Nr Metropol Hotel,
site sp.** 3*, Lge, pt shd, serviced pitches; EHU (6-10A)
€4.50; 60% statics; Eng spkn; ccard acc; bike hire; CKE.
*"Conv Piran old town by bike or bus; sea views; sep area
for tourers, extra for beach pitch; sm pitches; vg facs;
busy site; gd public beach; noise fr disco opp till 4am."*
€37.00, 11 Mar-2 Nov.   2016

POSTOJNA *C2* (5km NW Rural) *45.80551, 14.20470*
Camping Pivka Jama, Veliki Otok 50, 6230 Postojna
(05) 7203993; avtokamp.pivka.jama@siol.net;
www.camping-postojna.com

🐕 ♿ (htd) ♿ ⛺ 🚿 🔌 🦋 ▼ ⑪ ♨ ▛ ⛰ 🚣 ⛵

**Fr N or S Exit A1/E61 strt over traff lts, R at
rdbt then bear L at next, foll sp to caves grotto
(Postojnska Jama). Pass caves on R & then foll signs
for Predjama Castle. 3km after caves site sp. Narr,
winding app rd.** 3*, Lge, hdstg, shd, pt sl, terr, EHU
(6A) €3.70 (rev pol); cooking facs; 50% statics; Eng
spkn; adv bkg acc; ccard acc; tennis; CKE. *"Gd forest
site; gd rest with live Tirolean music; gd san facs, needs
updating (2017); used as transit to Croatia, open 24
hrs; caves 4km a must visit (take warm clothing!)."*
€29.00, 1 Apr-31 Oct, X09.   2018

PREBOLD *B3* (0.2km N Rural) *46.24027, 15.08790*
Camping Dolina, Dolenja Vas 147, 3312 Prebold
(03) 5724378; camp@dolina.si; www.dolina.si

12 🐕 €2 ♿ ♿ ⛺ 🚿 🔌 🦋 📶 ⑪ ▛nr 🚣(htd)

**On A1/E57 turn R 16km fr Celje sp Prebold & foll
sp, site on N edge of vill.** 3*, Sm, unshd, EHU (6-10A)
€3.30; gas; red long stay; bike hire; CKE. *"Gd clean facs
but no changing area in shwrs; helpful, friendly owner;
conv Savinja valley; gd walking."* **€20.00**   2016

PREBOLD *B3* (0.4km N Rural) *46.23832, 15.09266*
Camping Park, Latkova Vas 227, 3312 Prebold
38641472496; info@campingpark.si; www.camping
park.si

🐕 (on lead) ♿ (htd) ♿ ⛺ 🚿 🔌 🦋 ▼ ⑪ ▛nr

**Fr A1/E57 or rd 5 exit at Prebold. Foll site sp for
400m, cross Rv Savinja & site on L.** 2*, Sm, shd, EHU
(6A) inc; bbq; Eng spkn; adv bkg acc; games area;
CKE. *"V pleasant, well-kept site but ltd facs; pleasant
walks by rv; helpful owners own adj hotel; gd walking &
cycling."* **€20.00, 1 Apr-31 Oct.**   2020

> ## "I need an on-site restaurant"
>
> We do our best to make sure site information
> is correct, but it is always best to check any
> must-have facilities are still available or will
> be open during your visit.

PREBOLD *B3* (15km W Rural) *46.24458, 14.943502*
Camping Podgrad Vransko, Praprece 30, 3305
Vransko **(386)** 51229155; www.camp-vransko.com

12 🐕 ♿ (htd) ⛺ 🚿 🔌 🦋 📶 ⛰

**Foll sp off A1 at Vransko. Site 0.5km NW of town.
Well sp.** Sm, hdstg, mkd, pt shd, EHU (16A); bbq
(charcoal, elec, gas); Eng spkn; ccard acc; games rm;
games rm. *" New site (2018); v friendly, helpful owners;
MH disposal; panaramic views."* **€23.00**   2019

ROGASKA SLATINA *B3* (12km S Rural) *46.16499, 15.60495* **Camping Natura Terme Olimia,** Zdraviliška Cesta 24, 3254 Podčetrtek **(03) 8297000; info@ terme-olimia.com; www.terme-olimia.com**

†‖(htd) [wD] ♨ ⅋ 🖥 ∥ [MsP] ♈ ♈ (Ⅱ) nr ♨ 🏔 ⅌ (covrd, htd) 🛁

Fr Celje take rte E dir Rogaška Slatina. Turn S sp Podčetrtek just bef Rogaška. Site on L (waterchutes) alongside Rv Solta on Croatian border in approx 10km. 5*, Sm, unshd, EHU (10-16A) €3.20; TV; phone; adv bkg acc; ccard acc; bike hire; waterslide; golf 4km; tennis; horseriding 2km; sauna; fitness rm; CKE. *"Aqualuna Thermal Pk adj; vg walking country with wooded hillsides."* **€32.00, 15 Apr-15 Oct.** 2016

VELENJE *B3* (2km NW Rural) *46.36832, 15.08864* **Autocamp Jezero,** Cesta Simona Blatnika 26, 3320 Velenje **(03) 5866466; mastodontbar@gmail.com**

🐂 €1.50 †‖ [wD] ♨ ⅋ 🖥 ∥ [MsP] ♈ ♈ (Ⅱ) nr ♨ 🏔 nr /🏔

Exit A1/E57 at Velenje & cont to 2nd traff lts, then turn R. Turn L at 3rd traff lts & foll site sp. Site on lakeside. Med, mkd, pt shd, EHU (10A) inc; sw; 10% statics; fitness rm; tennis; games area; watersports. *"Lovely location but nr coal-powered power stn; poss unkempt LS; Velenje coal mining museum worth visit 1km; san facs need refurb (2015); poor."* **€22.00, 1 May-30 Sep.** 2015

VIPAVA *C1* (2km S Rural) *45.832168, 13.971053* **Kamp Tura,** Gradišče pri Vipavi 14a, 5271 Vipava **(08563) 96320; info@kamp-tura.si; www.kamp-tura.si**

12 🐂 †‖ [wD] ♨ ⅋ 🖥 ♈ (Ⅱ) 🏔 /🏔

Foll sp fr Vipava. Steep, narr approach, not suitable for units over 5m. TV; Eng spkn; Ccard acc. *"Gd facs; helpful owner; gd walks/climbing."* **€32.00** 2019

> ## "Satellite navigation makes touring much easier"
>
> Remember most sat navs don't know if you're towing or in a larger vehicle – always use yours alongside maps and site directions.

Legend

- France and Andorra
- Central and South East Europe, Benelux and Scandinavia
- Spain and Portugal

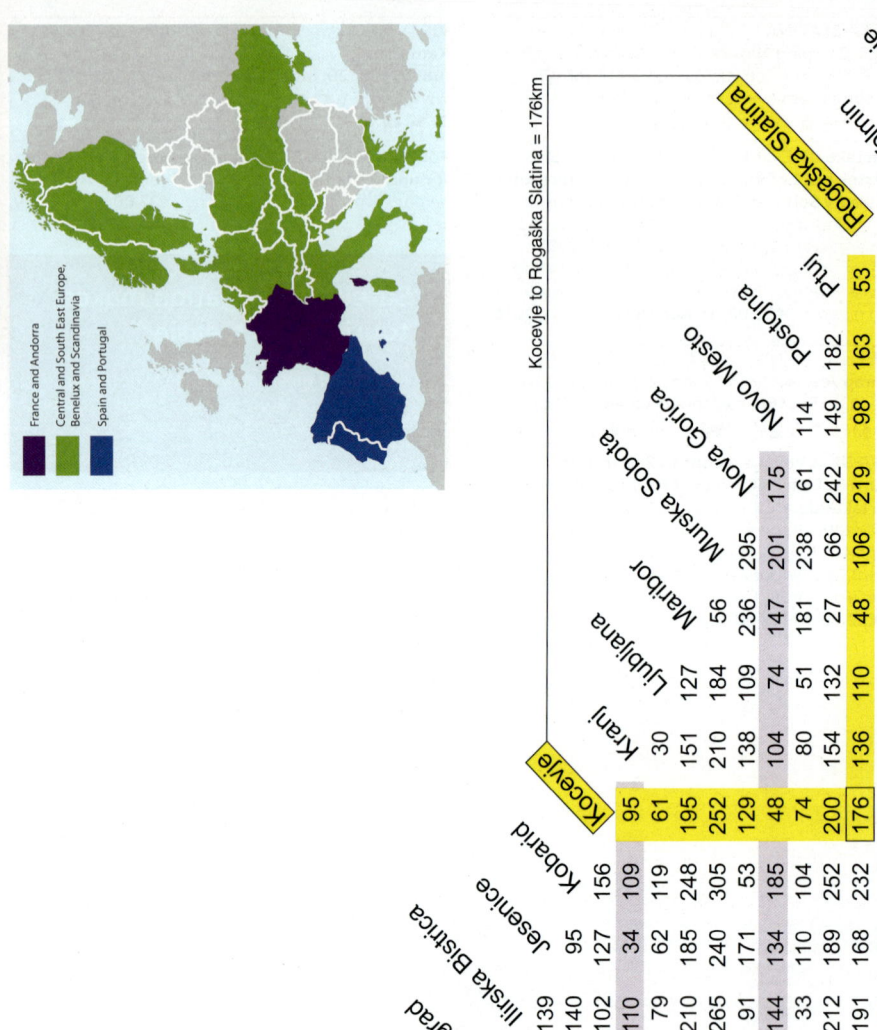

Road distance chart (distances in km) between Slovenian towns:

Bled, Bohinj Bistrica, Brežice, Celje, Dravograd, Ilirska Bistrica, Jesenice, Kobarid, Kočevje, Kranj, Ljubljana, Maribor, Murska Sobota, Nova Gorica, Novo Mesto, Postojna, Ptuj, Rogaška Slatina, Tolmin, Velenje

Kočevje to Rogaška Slatina = 176km

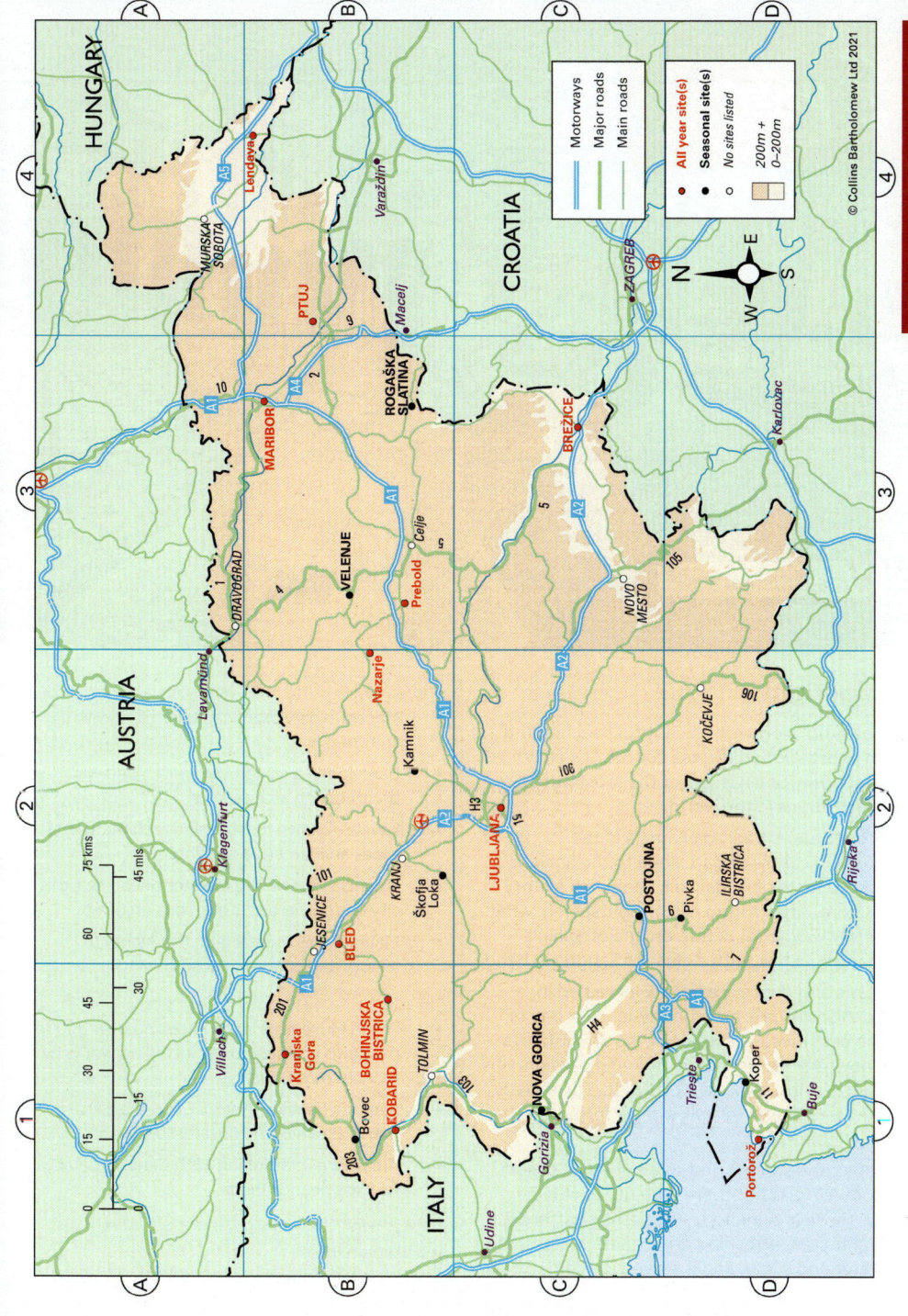

SLOVENIA

HUNGARY

AUSTRIA

ITALY

CROATIA

Motorways
Major roads
Main roads

All year site(s)
Seasonal site(s)
No sites listed

200m +
0–200m

© Collins Bartholomew Ltd 2021

N
W E
S

Lendava
MURSKA SOBOTA
PTUJ
Varaždin
MARIBOR
Macelj
ROGAŠKA SLATINA
ZAGREB
Karlovac
DRAVOGRAD
VELENJE
Celje
Prebold
BREŽICE
NOVO MESTO
Lavamünd
Nazarje
Kamnik
Klagenfurt
KOČEVJE
Villach
JESENICE
BLED
KRANJ
Škofja Loka
LJUBLJANA
H3
POSTOJNA
Pivka
ILIRSKA BISTRICA
Rijeka
Kranjska Gora
BOHINJSKA BISTRICA
KOBARID
Bovec
TOLMIN
NOVA GORICA
Gorizia
Koper
Trieste
Buje
Portorož
Udine

75 Kms
45 mls
60
45
30
30
15
15
0
0

A5
A4
A1
A2
A1
A1
A3

10
2
1
4
5
105
901
106
101
201
203
103
H4
H3
6
7
5

741

Spain

Plaza Espana, Seville

Shutterstock/May_Lana

Highlights

Boasting lively cities, beautiful beaches and an energetic and diverse culture, it's easy to see why Spain is one of the most popular destinations in the world.

From Gaudi's Sagrada Familia in the bustling centre of Barcelona to the ancient monuments of Andalusia, Spain rich history explore. After a long day of sightseeing, what better way to relax that on one of Spain's many beaches, with a glass of Sangria in hand.

Music and dance are deeply ingrained in Spanish culture, and the flamenco is one of the best loved examples of the Spanish arts. Known for its distinctive flair and passion, this dance is now popular worldwide, but there is nowhere better to soak in a performance than in its homeland.

Tapas and sangria and some of Spain's most popular fare, but there is plenty of choice for those looking to try something different. Orxata is a refreshing drink made of tigernuts, water and sugar, and is served ice-cold.

Major towns and cities

- Madrid – this vibrant capital is filled with culture.
- Barcelona – a city on the coast, filled with breathtaking architecture.
- Seville – known for stunning architecture, tapas an Flamenco dancing.
- Valencia – set on the Mediterranean sea, this city has numerous attractions on offer.
- Malaga - this coastal gem has plenty of history and culture to absorb.

Attractions

- Prado Museum, Madrid - housing over 8000 paintings and sculptures including works by Francisco de Goya.
- Sagrada Familia – Antoni Gaudí's basilica is one of Barcelona's most famous sights.
- Alhambra – a stunning 13th Century palace fortress near Granada.

Find out more

www.spain.info
E: infosmile@tourspain.es T: (0)9 13 43 35 00

Country Information

Population (approx): 46.5 million

Capital: Madrid

Area: 506,000 sq km (inc Balearic & Canary Islands)

Bordered by: Andorra, France, Portugal

Terrain: High, rugged central plateau, mountains to north and south

Climate: Temperate climate; hot summers, cold winters in the interior; more moderate summers and cool winters along the northern and eastern coasts; very hot summers and mild/warm winters along the southern coast

Coastline: 4,964km

Highest Point (mainland Spain): Mulhacén (Granada) 3,478m

Languages: Castilian Spanish, Catalan, Galician, Basque

Local Time: GMT or BST + 1, i.e. 1 hour ahead of the UK all year

Currency: Euros divided into 100 cents; £1 = €1.14, €1 = £0.88 (Feb 2021)

Emergency numbers: Police 092; Fire brigade 080; Ambulance (SAMUR) 061. Operators speak English. Civil Guard 062. All services can be reached on 112.

Public Holidays 2021: Jan 1, 6; Apr 2; May 1; Aug 15; Oct 12; Nov 1; Dec 6 (Constitution Day), 8, 25.

Several other dates are celebrated for fiestas according to region. School summer holidays stretch from mid June to mid September.

Entry Formalities

British and Irish passport holders may stay for up to 90 days in any 180 day period without a visa. Following Brexit you may be asked to show a return or onward ticket at the border to confirm your length of stay, or to prove that you have enough money for your stay.

Your passport will need to have a minimum of 6 months' validity remaining, and be less than 10 years old (even if it has over 6 months left).

Visitors arriving at a campsite or hotel must complete a registration form.

Medical Services

Basic emergency health care is available free from practitioners in the Spanish National Health Service on production of a European Health Insurance Card (EHIC). Some health centres offer both private and state provided health care and you should ensure that staff are aware which service you require. In some parts of the country you may have to travel some distance to attend a surgery or health clinic operating within the state health service. It is probably quicker and more convenient to use a private clinic, but the Spanish health service will not refund any private health care charges.

In an emergency go to the casualty department (urgencias) of any major public hospital. Urgent treatment is free in a public ward on production of an EHIC; for other treatment you will have to pay a proportion of the cost.

Medicines prescribed by health service practitioners can be obtained from a pharmacy (farmacia) and there will be a charge unless you are an EU pensioner. In all major towns there is a 24 hour pharmacy.

Dental treatment is not generally provided under the state system and you will have to pay for treatment.

The Department of Health has two offices in Spain to deal with health care enquiries from British nationals visiting or residing in Spain. These are at the British Consultate offices in Alicante and Madrid, Tel: 965-21 60 22 or 917-14 63 00.

Opening Hours

Banks : Mon-Fri 8.30am/9am-2pm/2.30pm, Sat 9am-1pm (many banks are close Sat during summer).

Museums: Tue-Sat 9am/10am-1pm/2pm & 3pm/4pm-6pm/8pm. Sun 9am/10am-2pm; most close Mon.

Post Offices: Mon-Fri 8.30am-2.30pm & 5pm-8pm/8.30pm, Sat 9am/9.30am-1pm/1.30pm.

Shops: Mon-Sat 9am/10am-1.30pm/2pm & 4pm/4.30pm-8pm/8.30pm; department stores and shopping centres don't close for lunch.

Regulations for pets

Dogs must be kept on a lead in public places and in a car they should be isolated from the driver by means of bars, netting or kept in a transport carrier.

Safety and Security

Street crime exists in many Spanish towns and holiday resorts. Keep all valuable personal items such as cameras or jewellery out of sight. The authorities have stepped up the police presence in tourist areas but nevertheless, you should remain alert at all times (including at airports, train and bus stations, and even in supermarkets and their car parks).

In Madrid particular care should be taken in the Puerto de Sol and surrounding streets, including the Plaza Mayor, Retiro Park and Lavapies, and on the metro. In Barcelona this advice also applies to the Ramblas, Monjuic, Plaza Catalunya, Port Vell and Olympic Port areas. Be wary of approaches by strangers either asking directions or offering help, especially around cash machines or at tills, as they may be trying to distract attention.

A few incidents have been reported of visitors being approached by a bogus police officer asking to inspect wallets for fake euro notes, or to check their identity by keying their credit card PIN into an official looking piece of equipment carried by the officer. If in doubt ask to see a police officer's official identification, refuse to comply with the request and offer instead to go to the nearest police station.

Spanish police have set up an emergency number for holidaymakers with English speaking staff and offering round the clock assistance - call 902 10 2 112. An English speaking operator will take a statement about the incident, translate it into Spanish and fax or email it to the nearest police station. You still have to report in person to a police station if you have an accident, or have been robbed or swindled, and the helpline operator will advise you where to find the nearest one.

Motorists travelling on motorways – particularly those north and south of Barcelona, in the Alicante region, on the M30, M40 and M50 Madrid ring roads and on the A4 and A5 – should be wary of approaches by bogus policemen in plain clothes travelling in unmarked cars. In all traffic related matters police officers will be in uniform. Unmarked vehicles will have a flashing electronic sign in the rear window reading 'Policía' or 'Guardia Civil' and will normally have blue flashing lights incorporated into their headlights, which are activated when the police stop you.

In non-traffic related matters police officers may be in plain clothes but you have the right to ask to see identification. Genuine officers may ask you to show them your documents but would not request that you hand over your bag or wallet. If in any doubt, converse through the car window and telephone the police on 112 or the Guardia Civil on 062 and ask them for confirmation that the registration number of the vehicle corresponds to an official police vehicle.

On the A7 motorway between the La Junquera and Tarragona toll stations be alert for 'highway pirates' who flag down foreign registered and hire cars (the latter have a distinctive number plate), especially those towing caravans. Motorists are sometimes targeted in service areas, followed and subsequently tricked into stopping on the hard shoulder of the motorway. The usual ploy is for the driver or passenger in a passing vehicle, which may be 'official-looking', to suggest by gesture that there is something seriously wrong with a rear wheel or exhaust pipe. If flagged down by other motorists or a motorcyclist in this way, be extremely wary. Within the Barcelona urban area thieves may also employ the 'punctured tyre' tactic at traffic lights.

In instances such as this, the Spanish Tourist Office advises you not to pull over but to wait until you reach a service area or toll station. If you do get out of your car when flagged down take care it is locked while you check outside, even if someone is left inside. Car keys should never be left in the ignition.

Spain shares with the rest of Europe an underlying threat from terrorism. Attacks could be indiscriminate and against civilian targets in public places including tourist areas.

The Basque terrorist organisation, ETA, has been less active in recent years and on 20 October 2011 announced a "definitive cessation of armed activity." However you should always be vigilant and follow the instructions of local police and other authorities.

Coast guards operate a beach flag system to indicate the general safety of beaches for swimming: red – danger / do not enter the water; yellow – take precautions; green – all clear. Coast guards operate on most of the popular beaches, so if in doubt, always ask. During the summer months stinging jellyfish frequent Mediterranean coastal waters.

There is a risk of forest fires during the hottest months and you should avoid camping in areas with limited escape routes. Take care to avoid actions that could cause a fire, e.g. disposal of cigarette ends.

Respect Spanish laws and customs. Parents should be aware that Spanish law defines anyone under the age of 18 as a minor, subject to parental control or adult supervision. Any unaccompanied minor coming to the attention of the local authorities for whatever reason is deemed to be vulnerable under the law and faces being taken into a minors centre for protection until a parent or suitable guardian can be found.

British Embassy & Consulate-General

TORRE ESPACIO, PASEO DE LA CASTELLANA 259D
28046 MADRID
Tel: 917 14 63 00
www.ukinspain.fco.gov.uk/en/

British Consulate-General

AVDA DIAGONAL 477-13, 08036 BARCELONA
Tel: 933 66 02 00

There are also British Consulates in Alicante and Málaga.

Irish Embassy

IRELAND HOUSE, PASEO DE LA CASTELLANA 46-4
28046 MADRID
Tel: 914 36 40 93
www.embassyofireland.es

There are also Irish Honorary Consulates in Alicante, Barcelona, Bilbao, El Ferrol, Málaga and Seville.

Customs Regulations

Under Spanish law the number of cigarettes which may be exported is set at eight hundred. Anything above this amount is regarded as a trade transaction which must be accompanied by the required documentation. Travellers caught with more than 800 cigarettes face seizure of the cigarettes and a large fine.

Documents

Driving Licence

The British EU format pink driving licence is recognised in Spain. Holders of the old style all green driving licence are advised to replace it with a photocard version. Alternatively, the old style licence may be accompanied by an International Driving Permit available from the AA, the RAC or selected Post Offices.

Passport

Visitors must be able to show some form of identity document if requested to do so by the police and you should carry your passport or photocard licence at all times.

Vehicle(s)

When driving in Spain it is compulsory at all times to carry your driving licence, vehicle registration certificate (V5C), insurance certificate and MOT certificate (if applicable). Vehicles imported by a person other than the owner must have a letter of authority from the owner.

Money

All bank branches offer foreign currency exchange, as do many hotels and travel agents.

The major credit cards are widely accepted as a means of payment in shops, restaurants and petrol stations. Smaller retail outlets in non commercial areas may not accept payments by credit card – check before buying. When shopping carry your passport or photocard driving licence if paying with a credit card as you will almost certainly be asked for photographic proof of identity.

Keep a supply of loose change as you could be asked for it frequently in shops and at kiosks.

Driving

Drivers should take particular care as driving standards can be erratic, e.g. excessive speed and dangerous overtaking, and the accident rate is higher than in the UK. Pedestrians should take particular care when crossing roads (even at zebra crossings) or walking along unlit roads at night.

Accidents

The Central Traffic Department runs an assistance service for victims of traffic accidents linked to an emergency telephone network along motorways and some roads. Motorists in need of help should ask for 'auxilio en carretera' (road assistance). The special ambulances used are connected by radio to hospitals participating in the scheme.

It is not necessary to call the emergency services in case of light injuries. A European Accident Statement should be completed and signed by both parties and, if conditions allow, photos of the vehicles and the location should be taken. If one of the drivers involved does not want to give his/her details, the other should call the police or Guardia Civil.

Alcohol

The maximum permitted level of alcohol is 50 milligrams in 100 millilitres of blood, i.e. less than in the UK (80 milligrams) and it reduces to 30 milligrams for drivers with less than two years experience, drivers of vehicles with more than 8 passenger seats and for drivers of vehicles over 3,500kg. After a traffic accident all road users involved have to undergo a breath test. Penalties for refusing a test or exceeding the legal limit are severe and may include immobilisation of vehicles, a large fine and suspension of your driving licence. This limit applies to cyclists as well as drivers of private vehicles.

Breakdown Service

The motoring organisation, Real Automóvil Club de España (RACE), operates a breakdown service and assistance may be obtained 24 hours a day by telephoning the national centre in Madrid on 915 93 33 33. After hearing a message in Spanish press the number 1 to access the control room where English is spoken.

RACE's breakdown vehicles are blue and yellow and display the words 'RACE Asistencia' on the sides. This service provides on the spot minor repairs and towing to the nearest garage. Charges vary according to type of vehicle and time of day, but payment for road assistance must be made in cash.

Child Restraint System

Children under the age of 12 years old and under the height of 1.35m must use a suitable child restraint system adapted for their size and weight (this does not apply in taxis in urban areas). Children measuring more than 1.35m in height may use an adult seatbelt.

Fuel

Credit cards are accepted at most petrol stations, but you should be prepared to pay cash if necessary in remote areas.

LPG (Autogas) can be purchased from some Repsol filling stations. Details of sales outlets throughout mainland Spain can be found on www.mylpg.eu

Lights

Dipped headlights is now compulsory for all vehicles on all roads at night and in tunnels. Bulbs are more likely to fail with constant use and you are recommended to carry spares.

Dipped headlights must be used at all times on 'special' roads, e.g. temporary routes created at the time of road works such as the hard shoulder, or in a contra-flow lane.

Headlight flashing is only allowed to warn other road users about an accident or a road hazard, or to let the vehicle in front know that you intend to overtake.

Motorways

The Spanish motorway system has been subject to considerable expansion in recent years with more motorways under construction or planned. The main sections are along the Mediterranean coast, across the north of the country and around Madrid. Tolls are charged on most autopistas but many sections are toll-free, as are autovias. Exits on autopistas are numbered consecutively from Madrid. Exits on autovias are numbered according to the kilometre point from Madrid.

Many different companies operate within the motorway network, each setting their own tolls which may vary according to the time of day and classification of vehicles.

Avoid signposted 'Via T' lanes showing a circular sign with a white capital T on a blue background where toll collection is by electronic device only. Square 'Via T' signs are displayed above mixed lanes where other forms of payment are also accepted.

Rest areas with parking facilities, petrol stations and restaurants or cafés are strategically placed and are well signposted. Emergency telephones are located at 2km intervals.

Motorway signs near Barcelona are confusing. To avoid the city traffic when heading south, follow signs for Barcelona, but once signs for Tarragona appear follow these and ignore Barcelona signs.

Mountain Passes and Tunnels

Some passes are occasionally blocked in winter following heavy falls of snow. Check locally for information on road conditions.

Parking

Parking regulations vary depending on the area of a city or town, the time of day, the day of the week, and whether the date is odd or even. In many towns parking is permitted on one side of the street for the first half of the month and on the other side for the second half of the month. Signs marked '1-15' or '16-31' indicate these restrictions.

Yellow road markings indicate parking restrictions. Parking should be in the same direction as the traffic flow in one way streets or on the right hand side on two way streets. Illegally parked vehicles may be towed or clamped but, despite this, you will frequently encounter double and triple parking.

In large cities parking meters have been largely replaced by ticket machines and these are often located in areas known as 'zona azul', i.e. blue zones. The maximum period of parking is usually one and a half hours between 8am and 9pm. In the centre of some towns there is a 'zona O.R.A.' where parking is permitted for up to 90 minutes against tickets bought in tobacconists and other retail outlets.

In many small towns and villages it is advisable to park on the edge of town and walk to the centre, as many towns can be difficult to navigate due to narrow, congested streets.

Madrid

In Madrid, there is a regulated parking zone where parking spaces are shown by blue or green lines (called SER). Parking is limited to 1 or 2 hours in these areas for visitors and can be paid by means of ticket machines of by mobile phone.

Pedestrians

Jaywalking is not permitted. Pedestrians may not cross a road unless a traffic light is at red against the traffic, or a policeman gives permission. Offenders may be fined.

Priority and Overtaking

As a general rule traffic coming from the right has priority at intersections. When entering a main road from a secondary road drivers must give way to traffic from both directions. Traffic already on a roundabout (i.e. from the left) has priority over traffic joining it. Trams and emergency vehicles have priority at all times over other road users and you must not pass trams that are stationary while letting passengers on or off.

Motorists must give way to cyclists on a cycle lane, cycle crossing or other specially designated cycle track. They must also give way to cyclists when turning left or right.

You must use your indicators when overtaking. If a vehicle comes up behind you signalling that it wants to overtake and if the road ahead is clear, you must use your right indicator to acknowledge the situation.

Roads

There are approximately 16,200km of highways and dual carriageways. Roads marked AP (autopista) are generally toll roads and roads marked A (autovía) or N (nacional) are dual carriageways with motorway characteristics – but not necessarily with a central reservation – and are toll-free. In recent years some major national roads have been upgraded to Autovías and have two identifying codes or have changed codes, e.g. the N-I from Madrid to Irún near the French border is now known as the A1 or Autovía del Norte. Autovías are often as fast as autopistas and are generally more scenic.

Roads managed by regional or local authorities are prefixed with the various identification letters such as C, CV, GR, L or T.

All national roads and roads of interest to tourists are generally in good condition, are well signposted, and driving is normally straightforward. Hills often tend to be longer and steeper than in parts of the UK and some of the coastal roads are very winding, so traffic flows at the speed of the slowest lorry.

As far as accidents are concerned the N340 coast road, especially between Málaga and Fuengirola, is notorious, as are the Madrid ring roads, and special vigilance is necessary.

Road humps are making an appearance on Spanish roads and recent visitors report that they may be high, putting low stabilisers at risk.

Andorra

The main road to Barcelona from Andorra is the C14/C1412/N141b via Ponts and Calaf. It has a good surface and avoids any high passes. The N260 along the south side of Andorra via Puigcerda and La Seo de Urgel also has a good surface.

Road Signs and Markings

Road signs conform to international standards. Lines and markings are white. Place names may appear both in standard (Castilian) Spanish and in a local form, e.g. Gerona/Girona, San Sebastián/Donostia, Jávea/Xàbio, and road atlases and maps usually show both.

You may encounter the following signs:

Spanish	English Translation
Carretera de peaje	Toll road
Ceda el paso	Give way
Cuidado	Caution
Curva peligrosa	Dangerous bend
Despacio	Slow
Desviación	Detour
Dirección única	One-way street
Embotellamiento	Traffic jam

Spanish	English Translation
Estacionamiento prohibido	No parking
Estrechamiento	Narrow lane
Gravillas	Loose chippings/gravel
Inicio	Start
Obras	Roadworks
Paso prohibido	No entry
Peligro	Danger
Prioridad	Right of way
Salida	Exit
Todas direcciones	All directions

Many non motorway roads have a continuous white line on the near (verge) side of the carriageway. Any narrow lane between this line and the side of the carriageway is intended primarily for pedestrians and cyclists and not for use as a hard shoulder.

A continuous line also indicates 'no stopping' even if it is possible to park entirely off the road and it should be treated as a double white line and not crossed except in a serious emergency. If your vehicle breaks down on a road where there is a continuous white line along the verge, it should not be left unattended as this is illegal and an on the spot fine may be levied.

Many road junctions have a continuous white centre line along the main road. This line must not be crossed to execute a left turn, despite the lack of any other 'no left turn' signs. If necessary, drive on to a 'cambio de sentido' (change of direction) sign to turn.

Traffic police are keen to enforce both the above regulations.

Watch out for traffic lights which may be mounted high above the road and hard to spot. The international three colour traffic light system is used in Spain. Green, amber and red arrows are used on traffic lights at some intersections.

Speed Limits

	Open Road (km/h)	Motorway (km/h)
Car Solo	90-100	120
Car towing caravan/trailer	70-80	80
Motorhome under 3500kg	80-90	100
Motorhome 3500-7500kg	80	90

In built-up areas speed is limited to 50km/h (31mph) except where signs indicate a lower limit. Reduce your speed to 20km/h (13mph) in residential areas. On motorways and dual carriageways in built-up areas, speed is limited to 80km/h (50mph) except where indicated by signs.

Outside built-up areas motorhomes under 3500kg are limited to 100km/h (62mph) and those over 3500kg are limited to 90km/h (56 mph) on motorways and dual carriageways. On other main roads motorhomes under 3500kg are limited to 80-90km/h (50-56mph) and those over 3500kg are limited to 80km/h (50mph)

It is prohibited to own, transport or use radar detectors.

Foreign Registered Vehicles

When a radar camera detects a foreign registered vehicle exceeding the speed limit, a picture of the vehicle and its number plate will be sent not only to the relevant traffic department, but also to the nearest Guardia Civil mobile patrol. The patrol will then stop the speeding vehicle and impose an on the spot fine which non-residents must pay immediately, otherwise the vehicle will be confiscated until the fine is paid.

This is to prevent offenders flouting the law and avoiding paying their fines, as pursuing them is proving costly and complicated for the Spanish authorities.

Towing

Motorhomes are prohibited from towing a car unless the car is on a special towing trailer with all four wheels of the car off the ground.

Any towing combination in excess of 10 metres in length must keep at least 50 metres from the vehicle in front except in built-up areas, on roads where overtaking is prohibited, or where there are several lanes in the same direction.

Traffic Jams

Roads around the large cities such as Madrid, Barcelona, Zaragoza, Valencia and Seville are extremely busy on Friday afternoons when residents leave for the mountains or coast, and again on Sunday evenings when they return. The coastal roads along the Costa Brava and the Costa Dorada may also be congested. The coast road south of Torrevieja is frequently heavily congested as a result of extensive holiday home construction.

Summer holidays extend from mid June to mid September and the busiest periods are the last weekend in July, the first weekend in August and the period around the Assumption holiday in mid August.

Traffic jams occur on the busy AP7 from the French border to Barcelona during the peak summer holiday period. An alternative route now exists from Malgrat de Mar along the coast to Barcelona using the C32 where tolls are lower than on the AP7.

The Autovía de la Cataluña Central (C25) provides a rapid east-west link between Gerona and Lleida via Vic, Manresa and Tàrrega. There is fast access from Madrid to La Coruña in the far north-west via the A6/AP6.

Information on road conditions, traffic delays, etc can be found on http://infocar.dgt.es/etraffic.

Violation of Traffic Regulations

The police are empowered to impose on the spot fines. Visiting motorists must pay immediately otherwise a vehicle will be confiscated until the fine is paid. An official receipt should be obtained. An appeal may be made within 15 days and there are instructions on the back of the receipt in English. RACE can provide legal advice - tel: 900 100 901.

Essential Equipment

Reflective Jacket/Waistcoat

If your vehicle is immobilised on the carriageway outside a built-up area you must wear a reflective jacket or waistcoat when getting out of your vehicle. This also applies to passengers who may leave the vehicle

Reflectors/Marker Boards for Caravans

Any vehicle or vehicle combination, i.e. car plus caravan over 12 metres in length, must display reflector marker boards at the rear of the towed vehicle. These aluminium boards must have a yellow centre with a red outline, be reflective and comply with ECE70 standards. They must be positioned between 50cm and 150cm off the ground and must be 500mm x 250mm or 565mm x 200mm in size. Alternatively a single horizontal reflector may be used measuring 1300mm x 250mm or 1130mm x 200mm.

To buy these aluminium marker boards contact www.hgvdirect.co.uk, tel: 0845 6860008. Contact your local dealer or caravan manufacturer for advice on fitting them to your caravan.

Warning Triangles

All vehicles must carry warning triangles. They should be placed 50 metres behind and in front of broken down vehicles.

Touring

A fixed price menu or 'menú del dia' offers good value. Service is generally included in restaurant bills but a tip of approximately €1 per person up to 10% of the bill is appropriate if you have received good service. Smoking is not allowed in indoor public places, including bars, restaurants and cafés.

Spain is one of the world's top wine producers, enjoying a great variety of high quality wines of which cava, rioja and sherry are probably the best known. Local beer is generally drunk as an aperitif to accompany tapas.

Spaniards tend to get up later and stay out later at night than their European neighbours. Out of the main tourist season and in non-tourist areas it may be difficult to find a restaurant open in the evening before 9pm.

Taking a siesta is still common practice, although it is now usual for businesses to stay open during the traditional siesta hours.

Spain's many different cultural and regional influences are responsible for the variety and originality of fiestas held each year. Over 200 have been classified as 'of interest to tourists' while others have gained international fame, such as La Tomatina mass tomato throwing battle held each year in August in Buñol near Valencia. Find a full list of fiestas at www.spain.info/uk or from tourist offices. Each town will also celebrate its local Saint's Day which is always a very happy and colourful occasion.

The Madrid Card, valid for one, two or three days, gives free use of public transport, free entry to various attractions and museums, as well as free tours and discounts at restaurants and shows. You can buy the card from www.madridcard.com or by visiting the City Tourist Office in Plaza Mayor, or on Madrid Visión tour buses. Similar generous discounts can be obtained with the Barcelona Card, valid from two to five days, which can be purchased from tourist offices or online at www.barcelonacard.org. Other tourist cards are available in Burgos, Córdoba, Seville and Zaragoza.

The region of Valencia and the Balearic Islands are prone to severe storms and torrential rainfall between September and November and are probably best avoided at that time. Monitor national and regional weather on www.wmo.int.

Gibraltar

For information on Gibraltar contact:

GIBRALTAR GOVERNMENT TOURIST OFFICE
150 STRAND, LONDON WC2R 1JA
Tel: 020 7836 0777
www.gibraltar.gov.gi
info@gibraltar.gov.uk

There are no campsites on the Rock, the nearest being at San Roque and La Línea de la Concepción in Spain. The only direct access to Gibraltar from Spain is via the border at La Línea which is open 24 hours a day. You may cross on foot and it is also possible to take cars or motorhomes to Gibraltar.

A valid British passport is required for all British nationals visiting Gibraltar. Nationals of other countries should check entry requirements with the Gibraltar Government Tourist Office.

There is currently no charge for visitors to enter Gibraltar but Spanish border checks can cause delays and you should be prepared for long queues. As roads in the town are extremely narrow and bridges low, it is advisable to park on the outskirts. Visitors advise against leaving vehicles on the Spanish side of the border owing to the high risk of break-ins.

An attraction to taking the car into Gibraltar includes English style supermarkets and a wide variety of competitively priced goods free of VAT. The currency is sterling and British notes and coins circulate alongside Gibraltar pounds and pence, but note that Gibraltar notes and coins are not accepted in the UK. Scottish and Northern Irish notes are not generally accepted in Gibraltar. Euros are accepted but the exchange rate may not be favourable.

Disabled visitors to Gibraltar may obtain a temporary parking permit from the police station on production of evidence confirming their disability. This permit allows parking for up to two hours (between 8am and 10pm) in parking places reserved for disabled people.

Violence or street crime is rare but there have been reports of people walking from La Línea to Gibraltar at night being attacked and robbed.

If you need emergency medical attention while on a visit to Gibraltar, treatment at primary healthcare centres is free to UK passport holders under the local medical scheme. Non UK nationals need a European Health Insurance Card (EHIC). You are not eligible for free treatment if you go to Gibraltar specifically to be treated for a condition which arose elsewhere, e.g in Spain.

Camping and Caravanning

There are more than 1,200 campsites in Spain with something to suit all tastes – from some of the best and biggest holiday parks in Europe, to a wealth of attractive small sites offering a personal, friendly welcome. Most campsites are located near the Mediterranean, especially on the Costa Brava and Costa del Sol, as well as in the Pyrenees and other areas of tourist interest. Campsites are indicated by blue road signs. In general pitch sizes are small at about 80 square metres.

Many popular coastal sites favoured for long winter stays may contain tightly packed pitches with long-term residents putting up large awnings, umbrellas and other structures. Many sites allow pitches to be reserved from year to year, which can result in a tight knit community of visitors who return every year.

If you're planning to stay on sites in the popular coastal areas between late spring and October, or in January and February, it is advisable to arrive early in the afternoon or to book in advance.

Although many sites claim to be open all year, if you're planning a visit out of season, always check first. It is common for many 'all year' sites to open only at weekends during the winter and facilities may be very limited.

Motorhomes

A number of local authorities now provide dedicated or short stay areas for motorhomes called 'Áreas de Servicio'.

For details see the websites www.lapaca.org or www.viajarenautocaravana.com for a list of regions and towns in Spain and Andorra which have at least one of these areas.

It is rare that yours will be the only motorhome staying on such areas, but take sensible precautions and avoid any that are isolated.

Some motorhome service points are situated in motorway service areas. Use these only as a last resort and do not be tempted to park overnight. The risk of a break-in is high.

Recent visitors to tourist areas on Spain's Mediterranean coast report that the parking of motorhomes on public roads and, in some instances, in public parking areas, may be prohibited in an effort to discourage 'wild camping'. Specific areas where visitors have encountered this problem include Alicante, Dénia, Palamós and the Murcian coast. Police are frequently in evidence moving parked motorhomes on and it is understood that a number of owners of motorhomes have been fined for parking on sections of the beach belonging to the local authority.

Cycling

There are around 2,200km of dedicated cycle paths in Spain, many of which follow disused railway tracks. Known as 'Vias Verdes' (Green Ways), they can be found mainly in northern Spain, in Andalucia, around Madrid and inland from the Costa Blanca. For more information see the website www.viasverdes.com or contact the Spanish Tourist Office.

There are cycle lanes in major cities and towns such as Barcelona, Bilbao, Córdoba, Madrid, Seville and Valencia. Madrid alone has over 100km of cycle lanes.

It is compulsory for all cyclists, regardless of age, to wear a safety helmet on all roads outside built-up areas. At night, in tunnels or in bad weather, bicycles must have front and rear lights and reflectors. Cyclists must also wear a reflective waistcoat or jacket while riding at night on roads outside built-up areas (to be visible from a distance of 150 metres) or when visibility is bad.

Strictly speaking, cyclists have right of way when motor vehicles wish to cross their path to turn left or right, but great care should always be taken. Do not proceed unless you are sure that a motorist is giving way.

Spanish regulations stipulate that motor cycles or bicycles may be carried on the rear of a vehicle providing the rack to which the motorcycle or bicycle is fastened has been designed for the purpose. Lights, indicators, number plate and any signals made by the driver must not be obscured and the rack should not compromise the carrying vehicle's stability.

An overhanging load, such as bicycles, should not extend beyond the width of the vehicle but may exceed the length of the vehicle by up to 10% (up to 15% in the case of indivisible items). The load must be indicated by a 50cm x 50cm square panel with reflective red and white diagonal stripes. These panels may be purchased in the UK from motorhome or caravan dealers/accessory shops. There is currently no requirement for bicycle racks to be certified or pass a technical inspection.

If you are planning to travel from Spain to Portugal please note that slightly different official regulations apply. These are set out in the Portugal Country Introduction.

Electricity and Gas

The current on campsites should be a minimum of 4 amps but is usually more. Plugs have two round pins. Some campsites do not yet have CEE connections.

Campingaz is widely available in 901 and 907 cylinders. The Cepsa Company sells butane gas cylinders and regulators, which are available in large stores and petrol stations, and the Repsol Company sells butane cylinders at their petrol stations throughout the country.

French and Spanish butane and propane gas cylinders are understood to be widely available in Andorra.

Public Transport

Madrid boasts an extensive and efficient public transport network including a metro system, suburban railways and bus routes. You can purchase a pack of ten tickets which offer better value than single tickets. In addition, tourist travel passes for use on all public transport are available from metro stations, tourist offices and travel agencies and are valid for one to seven days – you will need to present your passport when buying them. Single tickets must be validated before travel. For more information see www.ctm-madrid.es

Metro systems also operate in Barcelona, Bilbao, Seville and Valencia and a few cities operate tram services including La Coruña, Valencia, Barcelona and Bilbao. The Valencia service links Alicante, Benidorm and Dénia.

Various operators run year round ferry services from Spain to North Africa, the Balearic Islands and the Canary Islands. All enquiries should be made through their UK agent:

SOUTHERN FERRIES
22 SUSSEX STREET, LONDON SW1V 4RW
www.southernferries.co.uk
mail@southernferries.co.uk

Cover from **£60***

Red Pennant Overseas Holiday, Breakdown and Emergency Insurance

- Roadside assistance & Recovery including repatriation.

- Travel Insurance including cancellation and medical emergencies.

- Cover is available for multiple trips in a year, or for single trips up to 365 days**

- Friendly emergency services team
  Based at our Head Office, our multi-lingual team are ready to help when you need us.

For full details of cover offered, including limitations and exclusions that apply, a sample of the policy wording is available upon request.

Caravan and Motorhome Club is a trading name of The Caravan Club Limited which is authorised and regulated by the Financial Conduct Authority for general insurance and credit activities.

Call 01342 336 633 or visit camc.com/redpennant

Terms and conditions:
*Price is based on two travellers under the age of 50 on a 5 day single trip policy with motoring and personal cover. Additional premiums may apply on larger and/or vehicles over 15 years old.
** Age limits apply

AGUILAR DE CAMPOO *1B4* (3km W Rural) *42.78694, -4.30222* **Monte Royal Camping,** Carretera Virgen del Llano 34800 Aguilar de Campóo (Palencia) **979-18 10 07; info@campingmonteroyal.com; www.campingmonteroyal.com**

App site fr S on N611 fr Palencia. At Aguilar de Campóo turn W at S end of rv bdge at S end of town. Site on L in 3km; sp at edge of reservoir. Fr N take 3rd exit fr rndabt on N611. Do not tow thro town. 2*, Med, mkd, shd, pt sl, EHU (6A) inc; sw; twin axles; 50% statics; ccard acc; horseriding; watersports; fishing; lake 400yds; CKE. *"Useful, peaceful NH 2 hrs fr Santander; ltd/basic facs LS & poss stretched high ssn; barking dogs poss problem; friendly staff; gd walking, cycling & birdwatching in National Park; unrel opening dates LS; facs and site run down (2019); poor."* **€22.00** **2019**

AGUILAS *4G1* (2km SW Coastal) *37.3925, -1.61111* **Camping Bellavista,** Ctra de Vera, Km 3, 30880 Águilas (Murcia) **968-44 91 51; info@campingbellavista.com; www.campingbellavista.com**

Site on N332 Águilas to Vera rd on R at top of sh, steep hill, 100m after R turn to El Cocon. Well mkd by flags. Fr S by N332 on L 400m after fuel stn, after v sharp corner. Sm, hdg, hdstg, pt shd, pt sl, EHU (10A) €5.20 or metered; gas; bbq; red long stay; 10% statics; Eng spkn; adv bkg acc; ccard acc; bike hire; CKE. *"Gd autumn/winter stay; clean, tidy site with excel facs; ltd pitches for lge o'fits; helpful owner; fine views; rd noise at 1 end; excel town & vg beaches; v secure site."* **€34.20** **2019**

AGUILAS *4G1* (11km NW Rural) *37.45387, -1.64488* **Camping La Quinta Bella,** Finca El Charcon 31, 30889 Aguilas **968 43 85 35; info@quintabella.com; www.quintabella.com**

Fr AP7 exit at junc 878 onto RM11. Foll sp to Los Arejos. In 2km turn R foll sp to site. Med, mkd, hdstg, EHU; gas; bbq; twin axles; 30% statics; Eng spkn; adv bkg acc; ccard acc; CKE. *"V lge pitches; ideal for carnival & Easter parades; v friendly English owners; boules; m'homes should have other transport; excel."* **€20.00** **2016**

AINSA *3B2* (2.5km N Rural) *42.43555, 0.13583* **Camping Peña Montañesa,** Ctra Ainsa-Bielsa, Km 2.3, 22360 Labuerda (Huesca) **974-50 00 32; info@penamontanesa.com; www.penamontanesa.com**

E fr Huesca on N240 for approx 50km, turn N onto N123 just after Barbastro twd Ainsa. In 8km turn onto A138 N for Ainsa & Bielsa. Or fr Bielsa Tunnel to A138 S to Ainsa & Bielsa, site sp. NB: Bielsa Tunnel sometimes clsd bet Oct & Easter due to weather. 4*, Lge, mkd, shd, EHU (6A) inc; gas (elec, gas); sw nr; TV; 30% statics; phone; adv bkg acc; ccard acc; tennis; games rm; bike hire; sauna; fishing; canoeing; games area; horseriding; CKE. *"Situated by fast-flowing rv; v friendly staff; Eng spkn; gd, clean san facs; pitching poss diff due trees; no o'fits over 10m; nr beautiful medieval town of Ainsa & Ordesa National Park; excel."* **€27.90, E12.** **2019**

AINSA *3B2* (6km NW Rural) *42.43004, 0.07881* **Camping Boltaña,** Ctra N260, Km 442, Ctra Margudgued, 22340 Boltaña (Huesca) **974-50 23 47; info@campingboltana.com; www.campingboltana.com**

Follow N260 NW for 5km. After petrol stn turn L sp Barcabo. Cross bdge and keep L. Site ent on R in 1km. 1*, Lge, hdstg, mkd, hdg, shd, pt sl, terr, EHU (4-10A) €6.50; gas; twin axles; red long stay; 30% statics; phone; Eng spkn; adv bkg acc; ccard acc; horseriding 500m; fishing 600m; clsd 15 Dec-15 Jan; bike hire; games area; tennis 1km; games rm. *"Conv Ordesa National Park; adventure sports; san facs stretched high ssn; friendly, helpful staff; Ainsa old town worth visit; excel."* **€35.00** **2019**

ALBARRACIN *3D1* (2km E Rural) *40.41228, -1.42788* **Camp Municipal Ciudad de Albarracín,** Camino de Gea s/n, 44100 Albarracín (Teruel) **978-71 01 97 or 657-49 84 33 (mob); campingalbarracin5@hotmail.com; www.campingalbarracin.com**

Fr Teruel take A1512 to Albarracín. Go thro vill, foll camping sps. 2*, Lge, pt shd, pt sl, EHU (16A) €3.85; gas; bbq; 10% statics; phone; adv bkg acc; ccard acc; CKE. *"Gd site; immac san facs; pool adj in ssn; sports cent adj; gd touring base & gd walking fr site; rec; friendly staff; gd rest & shop; views striking, gd Sierras; site extended to nearly dbl; Albaraccin beautiful ancient town."* **€20.00, 4 Mar-27 Nov.** **2019**

ALBERCA, LA *1D3* (6km N Rural) *40.52181, -6.13762*
Camping Sierra de Francia, Ctra Salamanca-La
Alberca, Km 73, 37623 El Caserito (Salamanca) 923-
45 40 81; info@campingsierradefrancia.com;
www.campingsierradefrancia.com

Fr Cuidad Rodrigo take C515. Turn R at El Cabaco,
site on L in approx 2km. Med, hdg, mkd, shd, EHU
(3-6A) €3.75; gas; bbq; 10% statics; ccard acc;
horseriding; bike hire. *"Conv 'living history' vill of La
Alberca & Monasterio San Juan de la Peña; dogs free;
excel views."* **€23.50, 1 Apr-15 Sep.**   2017

ALCARAZ *4F1* (6km E Rural) *38.67301, -2.40462*
Camping Sierra de Peñascosa, Ctra Peñascosa-
Bogarra, Km 1, 02313 Peñascosa (Albacete)
967-38 25 21; informacion@campingpenascosa.com;
www.campingsierrapenascosa.com

Fr N322 turn E bet km posts 279 & 280 sp
Peñascosa. In vill foll site sp for 1km beyond vill.
Gravel access track & narr ent. 2*, Sm, mkd, hdstg,
shd, terr, EHU (6A) €4; gas; ccard acc; bike hire;
CKE. *"Not suitable lge o'fits or faint-hearted; pitches
sm, uneven & amongst trees - care needed when
manoeuvring; open w/end in winter; historical sites nr."*
€21.00   2016

> ## "There aren't many sites open at this time of year"
>
> If you're travelling outside peak season
> remember to call ahead to check site opening
> dates - even if the entry says 'open all year'.

ALCOSSEBRE *3D2* (2.5km NE Rural/Coastal) *40.27016,
0.30646* Camping Ribamar, Partida Ribamar s/n,
12579 Alcossebre (Castellón) 964 76 1601; info@
campingribamar.com; www.campingribamar.com

Exit AP7 at junc 44 into N340 & foll sp to
Alcossebre, then dir Sierra de Irta & Las Fuentes.
Turn in dir of sea & foll sp to site in 2km - pt rough
rd. Med, hdstg, mkd, hdg, pt shd, pt sl, terr, EHU
(6/10A) €4.50-6.50 (metered for long stay); gas; red
long stay; TV; 25% statics; Eng spkn; adv bkg acc;
tennis; games area; games rm; CKE. *"Excel, refurbished
tidy site in 'natural park'; warm welcome; realistic pitch
sizes; variable prices; excel san facs; beware caterpillars
in spring - poss dangerous for dogs."* **€47.00,
W04.**   2017

ALGAMITAS *2G3* (3km SW Rural) *37.01934, -5.17440*
Camping El Peñon, Ctra Algámitas-Pruna, Km 3,
41661 Algámitas (Sevilla) 955-85 53 00; info@
algamitasaventura.es; www.algamitasaventura.es

Fr A92 turn S at junc 41 (Arahal) to Morón de la
Frontera on A8125. Fr Morón take A406 & A363
dir Pruna. At 1st rndabt at ent Pruna turn L onto
SE9225 to Algámitas. Site on L in approx 10km -
steep app rd. Sm, hdg, mkd, hdstg, pt shd, EHU (16A)
€3.32; gas; bbq; 50% statics; adv bkg acc; ccard acc;
site clsd 13-24 Nov; games area; CKE. *"Conv Seville,
Ronda & white vills; walking, hiking & horseriding fr site;
excel rest; excel, clean san facs; vg site - worth effort to
find."* **€15.00**   2016

ALHAURIN DE LA TORRE *2H4* (4km W Rural)
36.65174, -4.61064 Camping Malaga Monte Parc,
29130 Alhaurín de la Torre (Málaga) 951-29 60 28;
info@malagamonteparc.com; www.malagamonte
parc.com

W fr Málaga on AP7 or N340 take exit for Churriana/
Alhaurín de la Torre. Thro Alhaurín de la Torre take
A404 W sp Alhaurín el Grande, site on R, sp. Sm,
hdg, mkd, hdstg, shd, pt sl, EHU (6A) inc; bbq; TV;
10% statics; bus 200m; Eng spkn; adv bkg acc; ccard
acc; golf nr; CKE. *"Vg site; well-appointed, clean san
facs; friendly Welsh owner; all facs open all year; sm
pitches; gd position to tour Costa Del Sol."* **€25.00**
        2019

ALICANTE *4F2* (12.5km NE Coastal) *38.41333,
-0.40556* Camping Bon Sol, Camino Real de
Villajoyosa 35, Playa Muchavista, 03560 El Campello
(Alicante) 965-94 13 83; info@campingbonsol.es,
www.campingbonsol.es

Exit AP7 N of Alicante at junc 67 onto N332 sp
Playa San Juan; on reaching coast rd turn N twds El
Campello; site sp. 2*, Sm, hdstg, mkd, pt shd, serviced
pitches; EHU (10A); red long stay; adv bkg acc; ccard
acc; CKE. *"Diff ent for long o'fits; helpful friendly staff;
poss cold shwrs; vg."* **€20.00**   2016

ALLARIZ *1B2* (1.5km W Rural) *42.18443, -7.81811*
Camping Os Invernadeiros, Ctra Allariz-Celanova,
Km 3, 32660 Allariz (Ourense) 988-44 20 06; reatur@
allariz.gal; www.allariz.gal/reatur/camping

Well sp off N525 Orense-Xinzo rd & fr A52. Steep
descent to site off rd OU300. Height limit 2.85m adj
recep - use gate to R. 3*, Sm, pt shd, EHU (6A) €4.50;
gas; red long stay; 10% statics; Eng spkn; adv bkg req;
ccard acc; horseriding; bike hire. *"Vg; steep slope
into site, level exit is avail; pool 1.5km; site combined
with horseriding stable; rv walk adj; facs v clean; hot
water; short rv side walk to interesting town; site sp in
town as Camping Hippe."* **€28.00**   2019

ALMERIA *4G1* (18km W Coastal) *36.79738, -2.59128*
Camping Roquetas, Ctra Los Parrales s/n, 04740
Roquetas de Mar (Almería) **950-34 90 85 or 950-34
38 09; info@campingroquetas.com; www.camping
roquetas.com**

🔢12 🐎 €2.25 👫 WD ♨ ♿ 🚿 ∿ MSP 🦋 ♈ 🍽 🎣 🛒 🚣 🏊
🏕 shgl 400m

Fr A7 take exit 429; ahead at rndabt A391 sp
Roquetas. Turn L at rndabt sp camping & foll sp
to site. V lge, pt shd, EHU (10-16A) €6.35-7.45; gas;
red long stay; TV; 10% statics; phone; bus 1km; Eng
spkn; adv bkg rec; ccard acc; tennis; CKE. *"Double-size
pitches in winter; helpful staff; gd clean facs; tidy site
but poss dusty; artificial shd; many long term visitors
in winter; gd dedicated cycle path along sea front."*
€24.00, E30. **2017**

ALQUEZAR *3B2* (1.5km SW Rural) *42.16454, 0.01527*
Camping Alquézar, Ctra. Barbastro s/n. 22145
Alquézar, Huesca **34 974 318 300;
camping@alquezar.com; campingalquezar.com**

🔢12 🐎 🐕 👫 WD ♨ ♿ 🚿 ∿ MSP 🦋 ♈ 🍽 ⓦ 🛒 🚣 🏔

A22 Huesca - Barbastro. Take N240 W of Barbastro,
dir Barbastro. Then A1232 & A1233 to Alquezar,
foll camping sp. Med, mkd, hdstg, pt shd, terr, EHU
(10A) inc; bbq; twin axles; Eng spkn; adv bkg acc;
ccard acc. *"Tricky access; hard 2km walk up hill to old
town; interesting town & selection of walking rtes; gd."*
€28.00 **2016**

ALTEA *4F2* (4km S Coastal) *38.57751, -0.06440*
Camping Cap-Blanch, Playa de Albir, 03530 Altea
(Alicante) **965-84 59 46; info@camping-capblanch.
com; www.camping-capblanch.com**

🔢12 👫 WD ♨ ♿ 🚿 ∿ MSP 🦋 ♈ 🍽 ⓦ 🛒 🚣 nr 🏔 🏕 shgl adj

Exit AP7/E15 junc 64 Altea-Collosa onto N332,
site bet Altea & Benidorm, dir Albir. 'No entry' sps
on prom rd do not apply to access to site. 1*, Lge,
hdstg, pt shd, EHU (5-10A) €3.50; gas; red long stay;
TV; 10% statics; Eng spkn; ccard acc; car wash; golf
5km; watersports; tennis. *"V cr in winter with long
stay campers; lge pitches; Altea mkt Tues; buses to
Benidorm & Altea; handy for lovely beach; most pitches
hdstg on pebbles; excel loc; excel walking/cycling."*
€38.00 **2019**

AMETLLA DE MAR, L' *3C2* (3km S Coastal) *40.86493,
0.77860* **Camping L'Ametlla Village Platja,** Paratge
de Santes Creus s/n, 43860 L'Ametlla de Mar
(Tarragona) **977-26 77 84; info@campingametlla.com;
www.campingametlla.com**

🔢12 🐎 👫 (htd) WD ♨ ♿ 🚿 ∿ MSP 🦋 ♈ 🍽 ⓦ 🛒 🚣 🏔 ✒ 🚣 🏊
🏕 shgl 400m

Exit AP7 junc 39, fork R as soon as cross m'way. Foll
site sp for 3km - 1 v sharp, steep bend. Lge, hdstg,
mkd, hdg, pt shd, terr, EHU (5-10A) inc; gas; bbq; red
long stay; TV; 10% statics; phone; Eng spkn; adv bkg
acc; ccard acc; games rm; bike hire; fitness rm; games
area; CKE. *"Conv Port Aventura & Ebro Delta National
Park; excel site & facs; can cycle into vill with mkt; dogs
free; diving cent; delightful site."* **€41.50** **2016**

AMPOLLA, L' *3C2* (2km SW Coastal) *40.79940,
0.69974* **Camping L'Ampolla Playa,** Playa Arenal s/n,
43895 L'Ampolla **977-46 05 35; reservas@
campingampolla.es; reservas@campingampolla.es**

🐎 🐕 👫 WD ♨ ♿ 🚿 ∿ MSP 🍽 ⓦ 🛒 🚣 🏔 🏕 50m

Exit AP7 at junc 39A twds S on N340 to km 1098.
Turn L onto TV3401 sp L'Ampolla. At rndabt after1
km go L twds L'Ampolla and at next rndabt take 1st
exit alongside campsite to ent. Med, hdg, mkd, hdstg,
shd, EHU (5-10A); bbq; twin axles; train/bus 1km;
Eng spkn; adv bkg acc; games area; CCI. *"Kite surfing;
natural park of Ebro Delta; cycling; historic ctrs; vg."*
€34.00, 4 Mar-1 Nov. **2016**

ARANDA DE DUERO *1C4* (3km N Rural) *41.70138,
-3.68666* **Camping Costajan,** Ctra A1/E5, Km 164-
165, 09400 Aranda de Duero (Burgos) **947-50 20 70;
campingcostajan@camping-costajan.com; https://
guiacampingfecc.com/campings/costajan/**

🔢12 🐎 €2 👫 (htd) WD ♨ ♿ 🚿 ∿ MSP 🦋 ♈ 🍽 ⓦ 🛒 🚣 🏔 🚣

Sp on A1/E5 Madrid-Burgos rd, N'bound exit km
164 Aranda Norte, S'bound exit km 165 & foll sp
to Aranda & site 500m on R. 3*, Med, shd, pt sl,
EHU (10A) €5 (poss rev pol &/or no earth); gas; bbq;
10% statics; phone; Eng spkn; adv bkg acc; tennis;
games area; CKE. *"Lovely site under pine trees; poultry
farm adj; diff pitch access due trees & sandy soil;
friendly, helpful owner; site poss clsd LS - phone ahead
to check; many facs clsd LS & gate clsd o'night until
0800; recep poss open evening only LS; poss cold/tepid
shwrs LS; gd winter NH; vg site for dogs."* **€20.00**
2019

ARANJUEZ *1D4* (2.5km NE Rural) *40.04222, -3.59944*
Camping International Aranjuez, Calle Soto del
Rebollo s/n, 28300 Aranjuez (Madrid) **918-91 13 95;
info@campingaranjuez.com; www.camping
aranjuez.com**

🔢12 🐎 🐕 👫 (htd) WD ♨ ♿ 🚿 ∿ MSP 🦋 ♈ 🍽 ⓦ 🛒 🚣 🏔 ✒
🚣 🏊

Fr N (Madrid) turn off A4 exit 37 onto M305. After
ent town turn L bef rv, after petrol stn on R. Take
L lane & watch for site sp on L, also mkd M305
Madrid. Site in 500m on R. (If missed cont around
cobbled rndabt & back twd Madrid.) Fr S turn off
A4 for Aranjuez & foll Palacio Real sp. Join M305 &
foll sp for Madrid & camping site. Site on Rv Tajo.
Warning: rd surface rolls, take it slowly on app to
site & ent gate tight. 3*, Lge, hdg, mkd, unshd, pt sl,
serviced pitches; EHU (16A) €4 (poss no earth, rev
pol); gas; red long stay; 10% statics; phone; ccard
acc; rv fishing; bike hire; games area; canoe hire; CKE.
*"Well-maintained site; gd san facs; rest vg value; some
lge pitches - access poss diff due trees; hypmkt 3km;
some uneven pitches - care req when pitching; pleasant
town - World Heritage site; conv Madrid by train; excel
site; free train to Royal Palace each morning; shop &
rest clsd Tuesdays."* **€35.00** **2016**

ARBIZU *3B1* (2km S Rural) *42.89860, -2.03444*
Camping Arbizu eko, NA 7100 km 5, 31839 Arbizu
**848-47 09 22; info@campingarbizu.com;
www.campingarbizu.com**

🐕 👬 wc ⚒ ♿ 🚿 ⁄ 💺 🏊 ⛱ 🍴 ⑪ 🛒 🎣 Ⓜ 🎿 ⛵ 🌳 sand

Fr A10 Irurtzun to Altsasu exit 17 onto NA-7100.
Site on R in 1km. Med, EHU (16A) inc; bbq; twin
axles; TV; Eng spkn; adv bkg acc; ccard acc; fishing;
games rm. *"Stunning views of mountains fr site; excel,
clean shwr block; v helpful, friendly staff; lots to do in
area; gd size pitches; best site; lge open camping area;
popular sw."* **€28.00, 7 Jan-23 Dec.** **2019**

ARENAS, LAS *1A4* (1km E Rural) *43.29973, -4.80321*
Camping Naranjo de Bulnes, Ctra Cangas de Onís-
Panes, Km 32.5, 33554 Arenas de Cabrales (Asturias)
**985-84 65 78; info@campingnaranjodebulnes.com;
www.campingnaranjodebulnes.com**

👬 wc ⚒ ♿ 🚿 ⁄ ⑪ 🍴 ⑪ 🛒 Ⓜ

Fr Unquera on N634, take N621 S to Panes, AS114
23km to Las Arenas. Site E of vill of Las Arenas de
Cabrales, both sides of rd. 2*, V lge, mkd, pt shd,
pt sl, terr, EHU (10A) €3.50 (poss rev pol); gas; TV;
bus 100m; ccard acc. *"Beautifully-situated site by rv;
delightful vill; attractive, rustic-style, clean san facs;
wcs up steps; poss poor security; conv Picos de Europa;
mountain-climbing school; excursions; walking; excel
cheese festival last Sun in Aug; excel rest, bars in vill;
lovely."* **€32.00, 2 Apr-9 Oct.** **2017**

ARNES *3C2* (1km NE Rural) *40.91860, 0.26780*
Camping Els Ports, Ctra Tortosa T330, Km 2, 43597
Arnes (Tarragona) **977-43 55 60; info@camping-
elsports.com; www.camping-elsports.com**

12 🐕 👬 (htd) ⚒ ♿ 🚿 ⁄ 💺 🍴 🎣 ⚡ 🎿 🛒

Exit AP7 at junc Tortosa onto C12 sp Gandesa. Turn
W onto T333 at El Pinell de Brai, then T330 to site. 2*,
Med, pt shd, EHU (6A) €5.20; TV; 10% statics; phone;
bus 1km; ccard acc; bike hire; games area; horseriding
3km. *"Nr nature reserve & many sports activities; excel
walking/mountain cycling; rock pegs req; nice site; great
views; elc kept tripping fuses so low amps; excel san
facs, poss stretched in hg ssn."* **€30.00** **2019**

AURITZ *3A1* (3km SW Rural) *42.97302, -1.35248*
Camping Urrobi, Ctra Pamplona-Valcarlos, Km 42,
31694 Espinal-Aurizberri (Navarra) **948-76 02 00;
info@campingurrobi.com; www.campingurrobi.com**

👬 wc ⚒ ♿ 🚿 ⁄ 💺 💺 🍴 ⑪ 🛒 Ⓜ 🎿

NE fr Pamplona on N135 twd Valcarlos thro Erro;
1.5km after Auritzberri (Espinal) turn R on N172.
Site on N172 at junc with N135 opp picnic area. Med,
pt shd, EHU (5A) €4.90; gas; bbq; 20% statics; phone;
Eng spkn; ccard acc; horseriding; tennis; bike hire; CKE.
*"Excel, busy site & facs; solar htd water - hot water to
shwrs only; walks in surrounding hills; ltd facs LS; poss
youth groups; overprices; poor wifi; clean; gd local
walks."* **€29.00, 1 Apr-1 Nov.** **2017**

AYERBE *3B2* (10km NE Rural) *42.31989, -0.61848*
Camping Castillo de Loarre, Ctra del Castillo s/n,
22809 Loarre (Huesca) **974-38 27 22; info@camping
loarre.com; www.campingloarre.com**

12 🐕 👬 wc ⚒ ♿ 🚿 ⁄ 💺 🍴 ⑪ 🛒 Ⓜ 🎿

NW on A132 fr Huesca, turn R at ent to Ayerbe to
Loare sp Castillo de Loarre. Pass 1st site on R (La
Banera) & foll sp to castle past Loarre vill on L; site on
L. App rd steep & twisting. Med, pt shd, pt sl, EHU (6A)
€4.50; gas; 10% statics; phone; Eng spkn; ccard acc; bike
hire; CKE. *"Elevated site in almond grove; superb scenery
& views, esp fr pitches on far L of site; excel birdwatching
- many vultures/eagles; site open w/end in winter; busy
high ssn & w/ends; pitching poss diff lge o'fits due low
trees; worth the journey; site clsd Feb; v pleasant, well
maint site; san facs clean but dated."* **€16.00** **2015**

"That's changed – Should I let the Club know?"

If you find something on site that's different
from the site entry, fill in a report and let us
know. See camc.com/europereport.

BAIONA *1B2* (1km E Coastal) *42.11416, -8.82611*
Camping Bayona Playa, Ctra Vigo-Baiona, Km 19,
Sabarís, 36393 Baiona (Pontevedra) **986-35 00 35;
campingbayona@campingbayona.com;
www.campingbayona.com**

12 🐕 👬 wc ⚒ ♿ 🚿 ⁄ 💺 🍴 ⑪ 🛒 Ⓜ 🎿 🌳 sand adj

Fr Vigo on PO552 sp Baiona. Or fr A57 exit Baiona &
foll sp Vigo & site sp. Lge, mkd, pt shd, EHU (3A) €4.80;
gas; red long stay; 50% statics; phone; adv bkg req;
waterslide; CKE. *"Area of outstanding natural beauty with
sea on 3 sides; well-organised site; excel, clean san facs;
avoid access w/end as v busy; ltd facs LS; tight access to
sm pitches high ssn; gd cycle track to town; replica of ship
'La Pinta' in harbour."* **€33.00, E49.** **2017**

BAIONA *1B2* (8km SW Coastal) *42.08642, -8.89129*
Camping Mougás (Naturist), As Mariñas 20B, Ctra
Baiona-A Guarda, Km 156, 36309 Mougás
(Pontevedra) **986-38 50 11; info@camping
muino.com**

👬 wc ⚒ ♿ 🚿 ⁄ 💺 🍴 ⑪ 🛒 Ⓜ 🎣 🎿

Fr Baiona take coastal rd PO552 S; site sp. Med,
mkd, pt shd, EHU €4.65; bbq; 80% statics; phone;
Eng spkn; ccard acc; fishing; games area; tennis;
CKE. *"Excel staff; lovely site on rocky coast; gd
for watching sunsets; gd NH; o'looks beach; vg."*
€29.00, 18 Mar-27 Mar & 15 May-15 Sep. **2016**

SPAIN

BALAGUER *3C2* (8km N Rural) *41.86030, 0.83250*
Camping La Noguera, Partida de la Solana s/n,
25615 Sant Llorenç de Montgai (Lleida) **973-42 03 34;
info@campinglanoguera.com; www.campingla
noguera.com**

12 🐕 €3.50 | 👫 🚿 🔥 ♿ 🚐 💧 / MSP 🦋 🍽 🕒 ⓗ 🏋 🏊 ⛱ ⚓

Fr Lleida, take N11 ring rd & exit at km 467 onto C13
NE dir Andorra & Balaguer. Head for Balaguer town
cent, cross rv & turn R onto LV9047 dir Gerb. Site on
L in 8km thro Gerb. App fr Camarasa not rec. Lge,
hdstg, mkd, pt shd, terr, EHU (6A) €5.15; gas; bbq; red
long stay; TV; 80% statics; phone; Eng spkn; adv bkg
acc; ccard acc; games area; CKE. *"Next to lake & nature
reserve; gd cycling; poss diff lge o'fits; friendly warden;
gd facs."* **€35.50** **2017**

BALERMA *2H4* (1km S Coastal) *36.72202, -2.87838*
Camping Mar Azul, Ctra de Guardias Viejas,
S/N 04712 Balerma **950-93 76 37; info@camping
balerma.com; www.campingbalerma.com**

12 🐕 €2.60 | 👫 🚿 🔥 ♿ 🚐 💧 / MSP 🍽 🏋 🏊 ⛱ ⚓ 🛶 100m

Exit junc 403 off A7/E15 for Balerma. Site in 6 km.
Lge, hdg, mkd, hdstg, shd, EHU (16A) €0.35 per kw;
bbq; twin axles; red long stay; TV; 4% statics; bus 1km;
Eng spkn; adv bkg acc; games area. *"Lge car park;
excel."* **€28.60** **2016**

BANYOLES *3B3* (2km W Rural) *42.12071, 2.74690*
Camping Caravaning El Llac, Ctra Circumvallació de
l'Estany s/n, 17834 Porqueres (Gerona) **972-57 03 05;
info@campingllac.com; www.campingllac.com**

12 🐕 €2.30 | (htd) 🚿 🔥 ♿ 🚐 / 🍽 🏋 🏊 ⚓

Exit AP7 junc 6 to Banyoles. Go strt thro town (do
not use by-pass) & exit town at end of lake in 1.6km.
Use R-hand layby to turn L sp Porqueres. Site on
R in 2.5km. Lge, mkd, pt shd, EHU €4.60; sw; red
long stay; 80% statics; bus 1km; site clsd mid-Dec to
mid-Jan. *"Immac, ltd facs LS & stretched high ssn; sm
pitches bet trees; pleasant walk around lake to town;
site muddy when wet."* **€30.00** **2016**

BEAS DE GRANADA *2G4* (0.8km N Rural) *37.22416,
-3.48805* **Camping Alto de Viñuelas,** Ctra de Beas de
Granada s/n, 18184 Beas de Granada (Granada)
**958-54 60 23; info@campingaltodevinuelas.com;
www.campingaltodevinuelas.com**

12 🐕 👫 (htd) 🚿 🔥 🚐 💧 / MSP 🍽 🏋 🕒 ⓗ 🏊 ⛱

E fr Granada on A92, exit junc 256 & foll sp to Beas
de Granada. Site well sp on L in 1.5km. Sm, mkd,
pt shd, terr, EHU (5A) €3.50; bbq; red long stay;
10% statics; bus to Granada at gate; Eng spkn; CKE.
*"In beautiful area; views fr all pitches; 4X4 trip to adj
natural park; gd; conv for night halt."* **€26.00** **2019**

BECERREA *1B2* (16km E Rural) *42.83315, -7.06112*
Camping Os Ancares, Ctra NV1, Liber, 27664
Mosteiro-Cervantes (Lugo) **982-36 45 56**

12 🐕 €1 | 👫 🔥 🚐 / 🦋 🍽 🕒 ⓗ 🏋 ⛱ 🛶

Fr A6 exit Becerreá S onto LU722 sp Navia de
Suarna. After 10km in Liber turn R onto LU723 sp
Doiras, site in 7km just beyond Mosteiro hamlet; site
sp. Site ent steep & narr - diff lge o'fits & lge m'vans.
2*, Med, shd, terr, EHU (6A) €3; gas; 10% statics;
fishing; horseriding; CKE. *"Isolated, scenic site; gd
rest & san facs; ltd facs LS; low trees some pitches;
gd walking; friendly owner; 17km fr nearest town."*
€21.00 **2015**

BEJAR *1D3* (15km SW Rural) *40.28560, -5.88182*
Camping Las Cañadas, Ctra N630, Km 432, 10750
Baños de Montemayor (Cáceres) **927-48 11 26;
info@campinglascanadas.com; www.campinglas
canadas.com**

12 🐕 👫 (htd) 🚿 🔥 ♿ 🚐 💧 / MSP 🦋 🍽 🕒 ⓗ 🏋 ⛱ 🛶 🛶

Fr S turn off A630 m'way at 437km stone to Heruns
then take old N630 twd Béjar. Site at 432km stone,
behind 'Hervas Peil' (leather goods shop). Fr N exit
A66 junc 427 thro Baños for 3km to site at km432 on
R. 3*, Lge, mkd, shd, pt sl, EHU (5A) €4; gas; red long
stay; TV; 60% statics; Eng spkn; ccard acc; fishing; bike
hire; games area; tennis; CKE. *"Gd san facs but poss
cold shwrs; high vehicles take care o'hanging trees; gd
walking country; NH/sh stay."* **€25.00** **2016**

BENAJARAFE *2H4* (3km E Coastal) *36.71962,
-4.16467* **Camping Valle Niza Playa,** Ctra N340, km
264,1 ES-29792 Benajarafe **952-51 31 81; info@
campingvalleniza.es; www.campingvalleniza.es**

12 👫 🔥 ♿ 🚐 💧 / MSP 🍽 🕒 ⓗ 🏋 ⛱ 🛶 (htd) 🛶 50 mtrs

On N340 (old coast rd), bet Torre Del Mar and
Benajarafe. Lge, hdg, mkd, hdstg, pt shd, EHU (10-
16A); bbq; twin axles; red long stay; TV; 20% statics;
phone; bus 100m; Eng spkn; adv bkg acc; bike hire;
games rm. *"Gd site; gymnasium; free yoga twice a
week."* **€33.00** **2017**

BENICARLO *3D2* (2.6km NE Urban/Coastal)
40.42611, 0.43777 **Camping La Alegría del
Mar,** Ctra N340, Km 1046, Calle Playa Norte,
12580 Benicarló (Castellón) **964-47 08 71; info@
campingalegria.com; www.campingalegria.com**

12 🐕 👫 (htd) 🚿 🔥 ♿ 🚐 💧 / MSP 🦋 🕒 ⓗ 🏋 ⛱ 🛶 🛶
🛶 adj

Sp off main N340 app Benicarló. Take slip rd mkd
Service, go under underpass, turn R on exit & cont
twd town, then turn at camp sp by Peugeot dealers.
Sm, hdstg, mkd, hdg, pt shd, EHU (16A) €4.90; gas; bbq;
red long stay; twin axles; 40% statics; phone; bus 800m;
Eng spkn; ccard acc; games rm; CKE. *"Friendly British
owners; access to pitches variable, poss diff in ssn; vg,
clean san facs; Xmas & New Year packages; phone ahead
to reserve pitch; excel; well run site."* **€30.00** **2016**

BENICASSIM *3D2* (0.9km E Coastal) *40.05709, 0.07429* **Camping Bonterra Park,** Avda de Barcelona 47, 12560 Benicàssim (Castellón) **964 30 00 07; info@bonterrapark.com; www.bonterrapark.com**

[12] 🐕 €2.20 🚻 (htd) [WD] 🚿 🚸 ♿ 🧺 ⚡ [MSP] 📶 🍸 🍴 🥡 🏪 ⛺ ✏ 🏊 (covrd, htd) ♨ 🏖 sand 300m

Fr N exit AP7 junc 45 onto N340 dir Benicàssim. In approx 7km turn R to Benicàssim/Centro Urba; strt ahead to traff lts, then turn L, site on L 500m after going under rlwy bdge. 4*, Lge, hdstg, mkd, shd, pt sl, serviced pitches; EHU (6-10) inc; gas; bbq; red long stay; TV; 15% statics; phone; train; Eng spkn; adv bkg acc; ccard acc; gym; games rm; tennis; bike hire; games area; CKE. *"Fabulous, excel site in gd location; excel cycle tracks & public trans; lovely beach; reasonable sized pitches; no o'fits over 10m; no dogs Jul/Aug; well-kept & well-run; clean modern san facs; access to some pitches poss diff due to trees; sun shades some pitches; winter festival 3rd wk Jan; Harley Davidson rallies Jan & Sep, check in adv; highly rec; flat rd to town; excel facs; sep car park; ACSI card acc; site organises trips out; gd rest; excel."* **€60.00, E19.** **2018**

BENICASSIM *3D2* (4.5km NW Coastal) *40.05908, 0.08515* **Camping Azahar,** Ptda Villaroig s/n, 12560 Benicàssim (Castellón) **964-30 35 51 or 964-30 31 96; campingazahar.benicasim@gmail.com; www.campingazahar.es**

[12] 🐕 €4.07 🚻 (htd) [WD] 🚿 🚸 ♿ 🧺 ⚡ [MSP] 🍸 🍴 🥡 ⛺ 🏊 🏖 sand 300m

Fr AP7 junc 45 take N340 twd València; in 5km L at top of hill (do not turn R to go-karting); foll sp. Turn R under rlwy bdge opp Hotel Voramar. Lge, mkd, unshd, pt sl, terr, EHU (4-6A) €2.90 (long leads poss req); gas; red long stay; 25% statics; phone; bus adj; Eng spkn; adv bkg acc; ccard acc; bike hire; CKE. *"Popular site, esp in winter; access poss diff for m'vans & lge o'fits; poss uneven pitches; organised events, tennis at hotel; gd walking & cycling; gd touring base."* **€38.00** **2017**

BENIDORM *4F2* (5.6km N Coastal) *38.56926, -0.09328* **Camping Almafrá,** Partida de Cabut 25, 03503 Benidorm (Alicante) **965-88 90 75; info@campingalmafra.es; www.campingalmafra.es**

[12] 🐕 🚻 (htd) [WD] 🚿 🚸 ♿ 🧺 ⚡ [MSP] 📶 🍸 🍴 🥡 🏪 ⛺ ✏ 🏊 (covrd, htd) ♨

Exit AP7/E15 junc 65 onto N332 N. Foll sp Alfaz del Pi, site sp. 5*, V lge, mkd, hdstg, hdg, pt shd, EHU (16A); bbq; twin axles; red long stay; TV (pitch); 20% statics; bus; Eng spkn; adv bkg acc; games rm; jacuzzi; sauna; gym; games area; tennis; CKE. *"Tennis, Alfaz del Pi a sh walk away; private san facs avail; wellness/fitness cent; reg bus into Benidorm; excel."* **€15.00** **2016**

BENIDORM *4F2* (3.6km NE Urban) *38.55564, -0.09754* **Camping Villamar,** Ctra del Albir, Km 0.300, 03503 Benidorm (Alicante) **966-81 12 55; camping@campingvillamar.com; www.campingvillamar.com**

[12] 🚻 [WD] 🚿 ♿ 🧺 ⚡ 🦋 🍸 🍴 🏪 ⛺ ✏ 🏊 (covrd, htd) 🏖 sand 2km

Exit AP7 junc 65. Down hill twd town, turn L at traff lts into Ctra Valenciana, turn R where 2 petrol stns either side of rd, site on L. V lge, mkd, pt shd, terr, serviced pitches; EHU (16A) €3.50; gas; red long stay; TV (pitch); 60% statics; phone; adv bkg acc; games rm. *"Excel site, esp winter; gd security; v welcoming; gd walking area; excel food; spotless san facs; great value; excel food; bus to town."* **€28.00** **2019**

BENIDORM *4F2* (1km E Coastal) *38.5449, -0.10696* **Camping Villasol,** Avda Bernat de Sarriá 13, 03500 Benidorm (Alicante) **965-85 04 22; info@camping-villasol.com; www.camping-villasol.com**

[12] 🚻 (htd) [WD] 🚿 🚸 ♿ 🧺 ⚡ 🦋 📶 🍸 🍴 🥡 🏪 ⛺ 🏊 (covrd, htd, indoor) ♨ 🏖 sand 300m

Leave AP7 at junc 65 onto N332 dir Alicante; take exit into Benidorm sp Levante. Turn L at traff lts just past Camping Titus, then in 200m R at lts into Avda Albir. Site on R in 1km. Care - dip at ent, poss grounding. 3*, V lge, hdstg, mkd, shd, EHU (5A) €4.28; red long stay; TV (pitch); 5% statics; phone; Eng spkn; adv bkg acc; ccard acc; games area; laundromat; basketball court; petanque pitches. *"Excel, well-kept site espec in winter; medical service; currency exchange; some sm pitches; friendly staff."* **€32.00** **2019**

BENQUERENCIA *2E3* (2km SW Rural) *39.29626, -06.10109* **Camping Las Grullas (Naturist),** Camino Valdefuentes 4, 10185 Benquerencia **34 631 264 504; info@lasgrullas.es; www.campinglasgrullas.es**

🚻 [WD] 🚿 ⚡ 🦋 📶 🏊 (htd)

Take EX-206 to Miajadas. After 30km take 2nd turning to Benquerencia (close to Valdefuentes vill). Site on R after 2.5 km. 1*, Sm, hdg, mkd, pt shd, EHU (4-6A) inc; twin axles; Eng spkn; adv bkg acc. *"Over 16's only; close historic town; no childrens facs; v helpful owners; gd walks fr site; vg."* **€25.00, 1 Apr-16 Oct.** **2016**

BIELSA *3B2* (8km W Rural) *42.65176, 0.14076* **Camping Pineta,** Ctra del Parador, Km 7, 22350 Bielsa (Huesca) **974-50 10 89; info@campingpineta.com; www.campingpineta.com**

🐕 €2.50 🚻 [WD] 🚿 🚸 🧺 ⚡ [MSP] 🍸 🍴 🥡 🏪 ⛺ 🏊

Fr A138 in Beilsa turn W & foll sp for Parador Monte Perdido & Valle de Pineta. Site on L after 8km (ignore previous campsite off rd). 2*, Lge, pt shd, pt sl, terr, EHU (6A) €5 (poss rev pol); gas; bbq; 10% statics; phone; ccard acc; bike hire; games area; CKE. *"Well-maintained site; clean facs; glorious location in National Park."* **€27.00, 25 Mar-2 Oct.** **2016**

BIESCAS *3B2* (3km SE Rural) *42.61944, -0.30416*
Camping Gavín, Ctra N260, Km 502.5, 22639 Gavín (Huesca) **974-48 50 90 or 659-47 95 51; info@ campinggavin.com; www.campinggavin.com**

Take N330/A23/E7 N fr Huesca twd Sabiñánigo then N260 twd Biescas & Valle de Tena. Ignore all sp to Biescas on N260 until R turn at g'ge. Drive over blue bdge & foll sp Gavin & site. Site is at km 502.5 fr Huesca, bet Biescas & Gavín. Lge, mkd, pt shd, terr, EHU (10A) inc; gas; TV; phone; bus 1km; Eng spkn; adv bkg acc; tennis; CKE. *"Wonderful, scenic site nr Ordesa National Park; poss diff access to pitches for lge o'fits & m'vans; superb htd san facs; bike hire in National Park; immac kept, excel, superb site; pitches with views, gd for walking."* **€37.00** **2016**

BILBAO *1A4* (18km N Coastal) *43.38916, -2.98444*
Camping Sopelana, Ctra Bilbao-Plentzia, Km 18, Playa Atxabiribil 30, 48600 Sopelana (Vizcaya) **946-76 19 81 or 649-11 57 51; recepcion@ campingsopelana.com; www.campingsopelana.com**

In Bilbao cross rv by m'way bdge sp to airport, foll 637/634 N twd & Plentzia. Cont thro Sopelana & foll sp on L. 1*, Med, hdg, sl, EHU (10A) €4.50; own san req; gas; red long stay; 70% statics; Eng spkn; adv bkg req; CKE. *"Poss strong sea winds; ltd space for tourers; pitches sm, poss flooded after heavy rain & poss diff due narr, steep site rds; ltd facs LS; helpful manager; site used by local workers; poss clsd LS - phone ahead to check; gd NH/sh stay only."* **€36.00** **2016**

BILBAO *1A4* (2.5km W Urban) *43.25960, -2.96351*
Motorhome Parking Bilbao, Monte Kobeta 31, 48001 Bilbao **688 809 399 or 944 655 789; kobetamendi@ suspertu.net; Bilbao.net**

A8 m'way, Balmaseda exit, dir Altamira - Alto de Kastrexana. Med, unshd, terr, EHU inc; bus adj; ccard acc. *"MH's only; on hill o'looking Bilbao; ehu & water to each pitch; v conv for visiting city by bus (every 1/2 hr); max stay 2 days; clsd 1st week of Jul; vg; full security."* **€15.00, 17 Mar-9 Jan.** **2017**

BLANES *3C3* (1km S Coastal) *41.65933, 2.77000*
Camping Blanes, Avda Vila de Madrid 33, 17300 Blanes (Gerona) **972-33 15 91; info@campingblanes. com; www.campingblanes.com**

Fr N on AP7/E15 exit junc 9 onto NII dir Barcelona & foll sp Blanes. Fr S to end of C32, then NII dir Blanes. On app Blanes, foll camping sps & Playa S'Abanell - all campsites are sp at rndabts; all sites along same rd. Site adj Hotel Blau-Mar. Lge, mkd, shd, EHU (5A) inc; gas; phone; bus; Eng spkn; ccard acc; solarium; bike hire; watersports; games rm. *"Excel site, espec LS; helpful owner; narr site rds; easy walk to town cent; dir access to beach; trains to Barcelona & Gerona."* **€37.00** **2017**

BLANES *3C3* (1.5km SW Coastal) *41.66206, 2.78046*
Camping Solmar, Calle Cristòfor Colom 48, 17300 Blanes (Gerona) **972-34 80 34; campingsolmar@ campingsolmar.com; www.campingsolmar.com**

Fr N on AP7/E15 exit junc 9 onto NII dir Barcelona & foll sp Blanes. Fr S to end of C32, then NII dir Blanes. On app Blanes, foll camping sps. Lge, mkd, hdg, shd, EHU (6A) inc; bbq; red long stay; 10% statics; bus 100m; adv bkg acc; ccard acc; games area; games rm; tennis; CKE. *"Excel site & facs; dogs free."* **€39.40, 2 Apr-12 Oct.** **2017**

See advertisement

BOSSOST *3B2* (3km SE Rural) *42.74921, 0.70071*
Camping Prado Verde, Ctra de Lleida a Francia, N230, Km 173, 25551 Era Bordeta/La Bordeta de Vilamòs (Lleida) **973-64 71 72; info@campingpradoverde.es; www.campingpradoverde.es**

On N230 at km 173 on banks of Rv Garona. Med, shd, EHU (6A) €5.50; TV; 10% statics; bus; ccard acc; bike hire; fishing; CKE. *"V pleasant NH."* **€22.00** **2016**

BROTO *3B2* (7km W Rural) *42.61576, -0.15432*
Camping Viu, Ctra N260, Biescas-Ordesa, Km
484.2, 22378 Viu de Linás (Huesca) **974-48 63 01;**
info@campingviu.com; www.campingviu.com

🔢 ♦♦(htd) 🆆🅾 ⚓♨♿🖊🅼🆂🅿 🦋 ⑪ 🚲 ⚒ ⚠

Lies on N260, 4km W of Broto. Fr Broto, N for 2km
on rd 135; turn W twd Biesca at junc with Torla rd;
site approx 4km on R. Med, pt shd, sl, EHU (5-8A)
€4.20; gas; bbq; phone; adv bkg acc; ccard acc; games
rm; bike hire; horseriding; CKE. *"Friendly owners; gd
home cooking; walking adj; skiing adj; car wash; fine
views; highly rec; climbing adj; clean, modern san facs;
poss not suitable for lge o'fits."* **€17.40**   **2016**

BURGOS *1B4* (4km E Rural) *42.34111, -3.65777*
Camp Fuentes Blancas, Ctra Cartuja Miraflores,
Km 3.5, 09193 Burgos **947-48 60 16; info@**
campingburgos.com; www.campingburgos.com

🔢 🐕€2.47 ♦♦(htd) 🆆🅾 ⚓♨♿🖊🅼🆂🅿 🦋 ⑪ 🍴🚲⚒ ⚠
🖊 ⛵

E or W on A1 exit junc 238 & cont twd Burgos. Strt
over 1st rndabt, turn R sp Cortes & then L. Look for
yellow sps to site. Fr N (N627 or N623) on entering
Burgos keep in R hand lane. Foll signs **Cartuja
miraflores & yellow camp signs.** 3*, Lge, mkd, shd,
EHU (6A) inc; gas; TV; 10% statics; phone; bus at gate;
Eng spkn; ccard acc; games area. *"Neat, roomy, adj
woodland; some sm pitches; ltd facs LS; poss v muddy
in wet; easy access town car parks or cycle/rv walk;
Burgos lovely town; gd NH to Portugal or France; San
Rafael dated; gd bus to town; excel, well maintained
busy site; gd shd; gd facs; helpful staff; gd mv service
pt; gd rest."* **€30.00**   **2019**

> ## "I like to fill in the reports as I travel from site to site"
>
> You'll find report forms at the back of this guide, or you can fill them in online at camc.com/europereport.

CABRERA, LA *1D4* (1km SW Rural) *40.85797,
-3.61580* **Camping Pico de la Miel,** Ctra A-1 Salida 57,
28751 La Cabrera (Madrid) **918-68 80 82 or 918-68 95
07; info@picodelamiel.com; www.picodelamiel.com**

🔢 🐕 ♦♦(htd) 🆆🅾 ⚓♨♿🖊 🦋 🍴 ⑪🚲 ⚠ ⛵🖊

Fr Madrid on A1/E5, exit junc 57 sp La Cabrera. Turn
L at rndabt, site sp. Lge, mkd, pt shd, pt sl, EHU (10A)
€4.45; gas; red long stay; 75% statics; phone; Eng spkn;
adv bkg acc; ccard acc; tennis; games area; sailing;
windsurfing; squash; fishing; CKE. *"Attractive walking
country; conv Madrid; mountain-climbing; car wash; ltd
touring area not v attractive; some pitches have low sun
shades; excel san facs; ltd facs LS."* **€33.50**   **2017**

CACERES *2E3* (6km NW Urban) *39.48861, -6.41277*
Camp Municipal Ciudad de Cáceres, Ctra N630,
Km 549.5, 10005 Cáceres **927-23 31 00; reservas@**
campingcaceres.com; www.campingcaceres.com

🔢 🐕 ♦♦(htd) 🆆🅾 ⚓♨♿🖊🅼🆂🅿 🍴 ⑪🚲⚒ ⚠ ⛵🖊

Fr Cáceres ring rd take N630 dir Salamanca. At
1st rndbt turn R sp Via de Servicio with camping
symbol. Foll sp 500m to site. Or fr N exit A66 junc
545 onto N630 twd Cáceres. At 2nd rndabt turn L sp
Via de Servicio, site on L adj football stadium. Med,
mkd, hdstg, unshd, terr, EHU (10A) €4.50; gas; bbq;
TV; 15% statics; bus 500m over footbdge; Eng spkn;
adv bkg acc; ccard acc; games area; CKE. *"Vg, well-run
site; excel facs; ACSI acc; vg value rest; gd bus service
to and fr interesting old town with many historical
bldgs; excel site with ensuite facs at each pitch;
individual san facs each pitch; location not pretty adj
to football stadium & indus est; town too far to walk; v
lush, free use of spa; Lydl 1.6km."* **€26.00**   **2019**

> ## "We must tell the Club about that great site we found"
>
> Get your site reports in by mid-August and we'll do our best to get your updates into the next edition.

CALATAYUD *3C1* (15km N Rural) *41.44666, -1.55805*
Camping Saviñan Parc, Ctra El Frasno-Mores, Km
7, 50299 Saviñan (Zaragoza) **976-82 54 23; info@**
campingsavinan.com; www.campingsavinan.com

🔢 🐕€2.70 ♦♦ 🆆🅾 ⚓♨♿🖊🅼🆂🅿 🦋 ⚒ ⚠ ⛵

Exit A2/E90 (Zaragoza-Madrid) at km 255 to T-junc.
Turn R to Saviñan for 6km, foll sps to site 1km S.
2*, Lge, hdstg, pt shd, terr, EHU (6-10A) €4.60; gas;
15% statics; phone; ccard acc; site clsd Jan; tennis;
horseriding; CKE. *"Beautiful scenery & views; some
sm narr pitches; rec identify pitch location to avoid
stop/start on hill; terr pitches have steep, unfenced
edges; many pitches with sunscreen frames & diff to
manoeuvre long o'fits; modern facs block but cold in
winter & poss stretched high ssn; hot water to some
shwrs only; gates poss clsd LS - use intercom; site poss
clsd Feb."* **€20.00**   **2017**

CALIG *3D2* (1km NW Rural) *40.45183, 0.35211*
Camping L'Orangeraie, Camino Peniscola-Calig,
12589 Càlig **34 964 765 059; info@camping-**
lorangeraie.es

🐕€2.50 ♦♦ 🆆🅾 ♨♿🖊🅼🆂🅿 🦋 🍴🚲⚒ ⚠ 🖊 ⛵🖊

On AP7 exit 43 Benicarlo-Peniscola. 1st R at rndabt
to Calig then foll sp to campsite. Fr N340 exit N232
to Morella, then after 1.5km turn L to Calig CV135,
foll sp to campsite. 5*, Med, mkd, hdg, pt shd, terr,
EHU (10A); bbq; twin axles; 15% statics; bus 1km; Eng
spkn; adv bkg acc; waterslide; games area. *"Excel site."*
€33.00, 1 Apr-31 Dec, E43.   **2019**

SPAIN

CALPE *4F2* (0.3km NE Urban/Coastal) *38.64488, 0.05604* **Camping Calpe Mar,** Calle Eslovenia 3, 03710 Calpe (Alicante) **965-87 55 76; info@campingcalpemar.com; www.camping calpemar.com**

12 ⛺ ⚥ (htd) WD ♨ ♿ ⚒ ✎ 🦋 ♈ ▼ ⊞ ⚓ ☕ nr ⛰ ✖
🏊 ⛱ sand 300m

Exit AP7/E15 junc 63 onto N332 & foll sp, take slip rd sp Calpe Norte & foll dual c'way CV746 round Calpe twd Peñón d'Ifach. At rndabt nr police stn with metal statues turn L, then L at next rndabt, over next rndabt, site 200m on R. Med, hdstg, mkd, hdg, unshd, serviced pitches; EHU (10A) inc (metered for long stay); bbq; red long stay; TV; 3% statics; phone; bus adj; Eng spkn; adv bkg acc; ccard acc; ice; games area; games rm; dog wash; CKE. *"High standard site; well-kept & laid out; Spanish lessons; gd security; excel; extra lge pitches avail at additional charge; car wash; gd for long stay, friendly staff; sep car park; close to beach and Lidl."*
€34.00 **2018**

See advertisement

CAMBRILS *3C2* (1.5km N Urban/Coastal) *41.06500, 1.08361* **Camping Playa Cambrils Don Camilo,** Carrer Oleastrum 2, Ctra Cambrils-Salou, Km 1.5, 43850 Cambrils (Tarragona) **977-36 14 90; camping@ playacambrils.com; www.playacambrils.com**

⛺ €4.35 ⚥ WD ♨ ♿ ⚒ ✎ ♈ ▼ ⊞ ⚓ ☕ ⛰ ✖ ≈ (htd)
⛴ ⛱ sand adj

Exit A7 junc 37 dir Cambrils & N340. Turn L onto N340 then R dir port then L onto coast rd. Site sp on L at rndabt after rv bdge 100m bef watch tower on R, approx 2km fr port. V lge, mkd, shd, EHU (6A) inc; gas; red long stay; TV; 25% statics; bus 200m; Eng spkn; adv bkg req; ccard acc; tennis; watersports; games rm; bike hire; boat hire; CKE. *"Helpful, friendly staff; children's club; cash machine; doctor; cinema; sports activities avail; Port Aventura 5km; 24-hr security; vg site."* **€46.00,** 15 Mar-16 Oct. **2018**

CAMBRILS *3C2* (11km SW Coastal) *41.02512, 0.95906* **Camping Miramar,** Ctra N340, km 1134 43892 Mont-roig del Camp **977-81 12 03; recepcio@ camping-miramar.com; www.camping-miramar.es**

⛺ ⚥ ⚥ WD ♨ ♿ ⚒ ✎ ♈ ▼ ⊞ ⚓ ⛰ ✖

Fr the AP7 take exit 37 to the N340. Turn L at KM134 to campsite. Sm, pt shd, EHU (6A) €5.20; bbq; twin axles; red long stay; 75% statics; bus; Eng spkn; adv bkg acc. *"Site on beach, walking, sw, snorkelling; vg."* **€35.00,** 1 Jan-30 Nov. **2017**

CAMBRILS *3C2* (8km SW Coastal) *41.03333, 0.96777* **Playa Montroig Camping Resort,** N340, Km1.136, 43300 Montroig (Tarragona) **977 810 637; info@ playamontroig.com; www.playamontroig.com**

⚥ (htd) WD ♨ ♿ ⚒ ✎ 🚐 ♈ ▼ ⊞ ⚓ ☕ ⛰ ✖ ≈ (htd)
⛱ sand adj

Exit AP7 junc 37, W onto N340. Site has own dir access onto N340 bet Cambrils & L'Hospitalet de L'Infant, well sp fr Cambrils. 5★, V lge, mkd, shd, pt sl, serviced pitches; EHU (10A) inc; gas; 30% statics; phone; Eng spkn; adv bkg acc; ccard acc; games rm; games area; golf 3km; tennis; bike hire; CKE. *"Magnificent, clean, secure site; private, swept beach; skateboard track; some sm pitches & low branches; cash machine; doctor; 4 grades pitch/price; highly rec."* **€53.00,** 1 Apr-30 Oct. **2017**

CAMBRILS *3C2* (8km W Coastal) *41.03717, 0.97622*
Camping La Torre del Sol, Ctra N340, Km 1.136,
Miami-Playa, 43300 Montroig Del Camp (Tarragona)
977 810 486; info@latorredelsol.com; www.latorre
delsol.com

†¦† wc ⟲ ♿ ☐ ✎ /mp ⊕ ⏀ ☗ ☖ ⟶ ▥ ☂ (htd) ⛴ ☂ sand

Leave A7 València/Barcelona m'way at junc 37 &
foll sp Cambrils. After 1.5km join N340 coast rd S
for 6km. Watch for site sp 4km bef Miami Playa. Fr S
exit AP7 junc 38, foll sp Cambrils on N340. Site on
R 4km after Miami Playa. Site ent narr, alt ent avail
for lge o'fits. 4*, V lge, mkd, hdg, shd, EHU (6A) inc
(10A avail); gas; bbq; TV; 40% statics; Eng spkn; adv
bkg acc; ccard acc; squash; games rm; gym; tennis;
sauna; bike hire; golf 4km. "Attractive well-guarded
site for all ages; sandy pitches; gd, clean san facs;
steps to facs for disabled; whirlpool; jacuzzi; access
to pitches poss diff lge o'fits due trees & narr site rds;
skateboard zone; radios/TVs to be used inside vans
only; conv Port Aventura, Aquaparc, Aquopolis; cinema;
disco; highly rec, can't praise site enough; excel."
€52.00, 15 Mar-30 Oct, E14.   2017

CANGAS DE ONIS *1A3* (16km E Rural) *43.33527,*
-4.94777 **Camping Picos de Europa,** Avin-Onís, 33556
Avín, **985-84 40 70; info@picos-europa.com;**
www.picos-europa.com

12 †¦† wc ⟲ ♿ ☐ ✎ / ⊕ ⏀ ☗ ☖ ⟶

E80, exit 307. Dir Posada A5-115. Loc on the rd
Onis-Carrena, 15 km fr Cangas de Onis and 10 km
fr Carrena, foll sps. 2*, Med, hdg, mkd, pt shd, terr,
EHU (6A) €3.80; gas; 10% statics; phone; Eng spkn;
adv bkg acc; horseriding; CKE. "Owners v helpful;
beautiful, busy, well-run site; vg value rest; modern san
facs; poss diff access due narr site rds & cr; some sm
pitches, lge o'fits may need 2; canoeing on local rvs;
conv local caves, mountains, National Park, beaches;
highly rec." **€27.00**   2019

CANGAS DE ONIS *1A3* (3km SE Rural) *43.34715,*
-5.08362 **Camping Covadonga,** 33589 Soto de Cangas
(Asturias) **985-94 00 97; campingcovadonga@**
hotmail.es; www.camping-covadonga.com

†¦† wc ⟲ ☐ ✎ / ☗ ⏀ ⊺ ⊕ ☖ ☗

N625 fr Arriondas to Cangas de Onis, then AS114
twds Covadonga & Panes, cont thro town sp
Covadonga. At rndabt take 2nd exit sp Cabrales,
site on R in 100m. Access tight. 1*, Med, mkd, pt shd,
EHU (10A) €3.50 (no earth); red long stay; bus adj; adv
bkg acc; CKE. "Sm pitches; take care with access; site
rds narr; 17 uneven steps to san facs; conv for Picos de
Europa." **€21.00, Holy Week & 15 Jun-30 Sep.**   2017

CARBALLO *1A2* (15km N Coastal) *43.29556, -8.65528*
Camping Baldayo, San Salvador de Rebordelos,
15105 Carballo **981-73 95 29; campingbaldayo@**
yahoo.es; www.campingbaldayo.com

12 ⟶ ☗ wc ⟲ ☐ ✎ / ☗ ⏀ ⊺ ☗ ☖ ▥ ☂ sand 200m

Access via DP-1916 fr Carballo. Turn L in vill and
foll sp. App rds are unmade. On site access rds
are narr with sharp corners, diff for long o'fits. 2*,
Med, hdg, mkd, hdstg, pt shd, pt sl, terr, EHU (3A)
€1.50; bbq; twin axles; 75% statics; phone; adv bkg
acc. "Sm pitches & narr camp rds poss diff lge o'fits;
poss unkempt LS; nrby lagoon with boardwalk and
bird hides; beach popular for surfing & watersports."
€15.00   2017

CARRION DE LOS CONDES *1B4* (0.4km W Rural)
42.33506, -04.60447 **Camping El Edén,** Ctra Vigo-
Logroño, Km 200, 34120 Carrión de los Condes
(Palencia) **979-88 07 14**

☗ †¦† ☗ ♿ ✎ /mp ☗ ⏀ ⊺ ⊕ ▥

Fr N231 take junc 85, go S then L at 3rd rndabt
to ctr. Site sp on L. 2*, Med, mkd, pt shd, EHU (6A)
€3.50; gas; bus 500m; Eng spkn. "Pleasant walk to
town; basic rvside site; recep in bar/rest; site open w/
ends only LS; fair NH; quite lively in high ssn; nice site
in interesting town on pilgrim rte; no lts in san block."
€19.80, 1 Apr-30 Oct.   2017

CASTELLO D'EMPURIES *3B3* (4km NE Rural)
42.26460, 3.10160 **Camping Mas Nou,** Ctra Mas Nou
7, Km 38, 17486 Castelló d'Empúries (Gerona)
972-45 41 75; info@campingmasnou.com;
www.campingmasnou.com

☗ ☗ €2.35 †¦† (htd) wc ⟲ ☗ ♿ ☐ ✎ / ☗ ⏀ ⊺ ⊕ ☖ ☗ nr ▥ ✎
☗ ☂ 2.5km

On m'way A7 exit 3 if coming fr France & exit 4
fr Barcelona dir Roses (E) C260. Site on L at ent to
Empuriabrava - use rndabt to turn. 3*, Lge, mkd, shd,
EHU (10A) €4.90; bbq; red long stay; TV; 5% statics;
phone; Eng spkn; ccard acc; tennis; games area; CKE.
"Aqua Park 4km, Dali Museum 10km; gd touring base;
helpful staff; well-run site; excel, clean san facs; sports
activities & children's club; gd cycling; excel; vg rest."
€47.50, 8 Apr-24 Sep.   2017

CASTELLO D'EMPURIES *3B3* (4km SE Coastal)
42.20725, 3.10026 **Camping Nautic Almatá,**
Aiguamolls de l'Empordà, 17486 Castelló d'Empúries
(Gerona) **972-45 44 77; info@almata.com;**
www.almata.com

☗ €6.40 †¦† wc ⟲ ♿ ☐ ✎ / ▥ ⊕ ☖ ▥ ✎ ☗ ☂ sand adj

Fr A7 m'way exit 3; foll sp to Roses. After 12km
turn S for Sant Pere Pescador & site on L in 5km.
Site clearly sp on rd Castelló d'Empúries-Sant Pere
Pescador. Lge, pt shd, EHU (10A) inc; gas; TV; adv
bkg acc; sailing school; tennis; bike hire; horseriding;
games area. "Excel, clean facs; ample pitches; sports
facs inc in price; disco bar on beach; helpful staff;
direct access to nature reserve; waterside pitches rec."
€59.00, 16 May-20 Sep.   2016

SPAIN

CASTRO URDIALES *1A4* (1km N Coastal) *43.39000, -3.24194* **Camping de Castro,** Barrio Campijo, 39700 Castro Urdiales (Cantabria) **942-94 48 97; info@ campingdecastro.com; http://campingdecastro.es/en/**

🏕🏕🏕🛒♿🚿💧♨🚻🎣 sand 1km

Fr Bilbao turn off A8 at 2nd Castro Urdiales sp, km 151. Camp sp on R by bullring. V narr, steep lanes to site - no passing places, great care req. 2*, Lge, unshd, pt sl, terr, EHU (6A) €3; 90% statics; phone; bus; Eng spkn; adv bkg acc; CKE. *"Gd, clean facs; conv NH for ferries; ltd touring pitches; narr, long, steep single track ent; great views over Bilbao bay."* **€27.00, 13 Feb-10 Dec.** **2019**

> ## "Satellite navigation makes touring much easier"
>
> Remember most sat navs don't know if you're towing or in a larger vehicle – always use yours alongside maps and site directions.

CASTROJERIZ *1B4* (1km NE Rural) *42.29102, -4.13165* **Camping Camino de Santiago,** Calle Virgen del Manzano s/n, 09110 Castrojeriz (Burgos) **947-37 72 55 or 658-96 67 43 (mob); info@campingcamino. com; www.campingcamino.com**

🏕€2🏕🏕🛒♿🚿💧♨🚻🦋🍽🎡🍺 nr

Fr N A62/E80 junc 40 dir Los Balbases, Vallunquera & Castrojeriz - narr, uneven rd. In 16 km ent Castrojeriz, sp fr BU400 where you turn onto BU404. Once on BU404 proceed for approx 500yds to next rndabt, take 2nd exit. Site 1m on the L. Fr S A62, exit 68 twds Torquemada, then take P412, then BU4085 to Castrojeriz. Do not go thro town, as rd are narr. Med, mkd, hdg, shd, pt sl, EHU (5-10A) €4 (poss no earth); TV; bus 200m; Eng spkn; games area; games rm; CKE. *"Lovely site; helpful owner; pilgrims' refuge on site; some diff sm pitches; vg; site ent narr; excel bird watching tours on req; san facs dated."* **€32.00, 15 Mar-15 Nov.** **2019**

CERVERA DE PISUERGA *1B4* (0.5km W Rural) *42.87135, -4.50332* **Camping Fuentes Carrionas,** La Bárcena s/n, 34840 Cervera de Pisuerga (Palencia) **979-87 04 24; campingfuentescarrionas@ hotmail.com; campingfuentescarrionas.com**

🏕🏕🛒♿🚿💧♨🚻🦋🍽🍺 nr 🎣 nr

Fr Aguilar de Campóo on CL626 pass thro Cervera foll sp CL627 Potes. Site sp on L bef rv bdge. Med, mkd, pt shd, EHU €3.50; 80% statics; bus 100m; games area; tennis; CKE. *"Gd walking in nature reserve; conv Casa del Osos bear info cent; rest/bar area busy at wkend; new gd clean san facs; site busy with wkenders in statics or cabins; owners v helpful and pleasant; well maintained."* **€21.00, Holy Week-30 Sep.** **2017**

CIUDAD RODRIGO *1D3* (1.5km S Rural) *40.59206, -6.53445* **Camping La Pesquera,** Ctra Cáceres-Arrabal, Km 424, Huerta La Toma, 37500 Ciudad Rodrigo (Salamanca) **923-48 13 48; campinglapesquera@ hotmail.com; www.campinglapesquera.es**

12 🐕🏕🏕🛒♿🚿💧♨🦋

Fr Salamanca on A62/E80 exit junc 332. Look for tent sp on R & turn R, then 1st L & foll round until site on rvside. 2*, Med, mkd, pt shd, EHU (6A) inc; sw nr; TV; phone; ccard acc; fishing adj; CKE. *"Medieval walled city worth visit - easy walk over Roman bdge; gd san facs; vg; improved site; friendly nice sm site next to rv, gd for NH; lovely town; v helpful staff."* **€17.00** **2017**

CLARIANA *3B3* (6km NE Rural) *41.95900, 1.60384* **Camping La Ribera,** Pantà de Sant Ponç, 25290 Clariana de Cardener (Lleida) **973-48 25 52 or 973-48 15 57; info@campinglaribera.com; www.camping laribera.com**

12 🏕🏕🏕 wc 🛒♿🚿💧♨🚻🦋🍽🎡🍺⛴🏊🚣

Fr Solsona S on C55, turn L onto C26 at km 71. Go 2.7km, site sp immed bef Sant Ponç Dam. 2*, Lge, mkd, hdstg, pt shd, EHU (4-10A) €4.60-8.45; sw nr; TV; 95% statics; phone; games area; tennis. *"Excel facs; gd site; narr pitches, can be diff to site o'fit."* **€38.00** **2016**

COLOMBRES *1A4* (3km SW Rural) *43.37074, -4.56799* **Camping Colombres,** Ctra El Peral A Noriega Kml - 33590 Colombres (Ribadedeva) **985 412 244; campingcolombres@hotmail.com; www.camping colombres.com**

12 🐕🏕🏕 (htd) wc 🛒♿🚿💧♨🚻 MSP 🦋🍽🎡🍺⛴🏊🚣
🏖 sand 3km

Turn off A8/E70 at J277. 3rd exit then 2nd exit fr rndabts. East on N634 then R opp petrol stn. Site to L 1km. Med, mkd, pt shd, terr, EHU (6A) €4.20; bbq (sep area); twin axles; 10% statics; Eng spkn; ccard acc; games area; CKE. *"Quiet, peaceful site in rural setting with fine mountain views; v helpful owners; nice pool; excel san facs; well kept & clean; immac, modern san facs; dogs free; gd walking."* **€31.50** **2017**

COLUNGA *1A3* (12km E Coastal) *43.47160, -5.18434* **Camping Arenal de Moris,** Ctra de la Playa s/n, 33344 Caravia Alta (Asturias) **985-85 30 97; camoris@des deasturias.com; www.arenaldemoris.com**

🏕🏕 wc 🛒♿💧♨🦋🍽🎡🍺⛴🏊🚣 sand 500m

Fr E70/A8 exit junc 337 onto N632 to Caravia Alta, site clearly sp. Lge, mkd, pt shd, terr, EHU (5A) €4.50; 10% statics; adv bkg acc; ccard acc; tennis; CKE. *"Lovely views to mountains & sea; well-kept, well-run site; excel, clean san facs."* **€35.00, 23 Mar-15 Sep.** **2015**

COMILLAS *1A4* (1km E Coastal) *43.38583, -4.28444*
Camping de Comillas, 39520 Comillas (Cantabria)
**942-72 00 74; info@campingcomillas.com;
www.campingcomillas.com**

🐕 👫 wc 🚿 ♨ ⚡ 🍴 ▼ ⑪ nr 🛒 🏊 ⛰ ⚓ sand 800m

Site on coast rd CA131 at E end of Comillas by-pass.
App fr Santillana or San Vicente avoids town cent &
narr rds. Lge, hdg, mkd, pt shd, pt sl, EHU (5A) €3.85;
TV; phone; adv bkg acc; CKE. *"Clean, ltd facs LS (hot
water to shwrs only); vg site in gd position on coast
with views; easy walk to interesting town; gd but rocky
beach across rd; helpful owner; pitches inbetween 2
rds."* **€29.50, Holy Week & 1 Jun-30 Sep.** **2017**

COMILLAS *1A4* (5km E Rural) *43.38328, -4.24689*
Camping El Helguero, 39527 Ruiloba (Cantabria)
**942-72 21 24; reservas@campingelhelguero.com;
www.campingelhelguero.com**

🐕 👫 (htd) wc ♨ ⚡ 🍴 ▼ 🍴 ⑪ 🛒 🏊 ⛰ ⚓ 🛶

⚓ sand 3km

Exit A8 junc 249 dir Comillas onto CA135 to km 7.
Turn dir Ruiloba onto CA359 & thro Ruiloba & La
Iglesia, fork R uphill. Site sp. Lge, mkd, pt shd, pt
sl, EHU (6A) €4.35; 80% statics; Eng spkn; ccard acc;
tennis 300m; bike hire; CKE. *"Attractive site, gd touring
cent; clean facs but some in need of refurb; helpful
staff; night security; sm pitches poss muddy in wet; v
gd."* **€30.00, 1 Apr-30 Sep.** **2016**

"There aren't many sites open at this time of year"

If you're travelling outside peak season
remember to call ahead to check site opening
dates – even if the entry says 'open all year'.

CONIL DE LA FRONTERA *2H3* (3km NE Rural)
36.31061, -6.11276 **Camping Roche,** Carril de
Pilahito s/n, N340 Km 19.2, 11149 Conil de la Frontera
(Cádiz) **956-44 22 16; info@campingroche.com;
www.campingroche.com**

12 🐕 €3.75 👫 wc ⚡ 🍴 ▼ ▼ 🍴 ⑪ 🛒 🏊 ⛰ ⚓ 🛶

⚓ sand 2.5km

Exit A48 junc 15 Conil Norte. Site sp on N340 dir
Algeciras. Lge, mkd, hdstg, pt shd, EHU (10A) €5;
red long stay; TV; 20% statics; Eng spkn; adv bkg acc;
ccard acc; games area; games rm; tennis. *"V pleasant,
peaceful site in pine woods; all-weather pitches;
friendly, helpful staff; special monthly rates; clean san
facs; superb beaches nr; excl facs; lack of adequate
management."* **€30.00, W02.** **2019**

CORDOBA *2F3* (2km NW Urban) *37.89977, -04.78725*
Camp Municipal El Brillante, Avda del Brillante 50,
14012 Córdoba **957-40 38 36; elbrillante@campings.
net; www.campingelbrillante.com**

12 🐕 👫 wc ♨ ⚡ 🍴 ▼ 🍴 ⑪ 🛒 🏊 ⛰

Fr N1V take Badejoz turning N432. Take rd
Córdoba N & foll sp to Parador. Turn R into Paseo
del Brilliante which leads into Avda del Brilliante;
white grilleblock wall surrounds site. Alt, foll sp
for 'Macdonalds Brilliante.' Site on R 400m beyond
Macdonalds on main rd going uphill away fr town
cent. Site poorly sp. 3*, Med, hdg, mkd, hdstg, pt shd,
serviced pitches; EHU (6-10A) €5.50 (poss no earth);
gas; bbq; phone; bus adj; Eng spkn; CKE. *"Well-run,
busy, clean site; rec arr bef 1500; friendly staff; easy
walk/gd bus to town; quiet but traff noise & barking
dogs off site; poss cramped pitches - diff lge o'fits; poss
travellers LS (noisy); pool adj in ssn; gd for wheelchair
users; highly rec; easy walk to beautiful city; pitches
easier to access with motor mover; Aldi & McDonald's
nrby."* **€32.50** **2019**

CORTEGANA *2 F2* (1.2km NW Rural) *37.91348,
-6.82820* **Camping Ribera Del Chanza,** Avenida de las
Norias, 21230 Cortegana **959-50 79 65 or 601 22 24
34 (mob); info@campingdecortegana.es;
campingdecortegana.com**

12 🐕 €1.50 👫 wc ♨ ⚡ 🍴 ▼ 🍴 ▼ ⑪ nr 🛒 🏊 🛶

Fr N435 dir Portugal at top of hill 2nd L sp Camping.
After 200m cross rndabt into Av de las Norias. Site
at end of road in 500m. Sm, mkd, pt shd, pt sl, EHU
€5; bbq (sep area); TV; 500m; Eng spkn; adv bkg acc;
ccard acc. *"Site in easy walking distance to Cortegana;
town has gd supermkts and shops; restored medieval
castle; walking/mountain biking trails in surrounding
hills; site closed Christmas week; excel."* **€15.50**
2019

CORUNA, LA *1A2* (11km E Rural) *43.348194,
-8.335745* **Camping Los Manzanos,** Olieiros, 15179
Santa Cruz (La Coruña) **981-61 48 25; informacion@
campinglosmanzanos.com; www.campinglos
manzanos.com**

🐕 👫 wc ♨ ⚡ 🍴 🍴 ▼ ⑪ 🛒 🏊 ⛰ 🛶

App La Coruña fr E on NVI, bef bdge take AC173 sp
Santa Cruz. Turn R at 2nd traff lts in Santa Cruz cent
(by petrol stn), foll sp, site on L. Fr AP9/E1 exit junc
3, turn R onto NVI dir Lugo. Take L fork dir Santa
Cruz/La Coruña, then foll sp Meiras. Site sp. 3*, Lge,
pt shd, EHU (6A) €4.80; gas; TV; 10% statics; phone;
Eng spkn; adv bkg req; ccard acc; CKE. *"Lovely site;
steep slope into site, level exit is avail; helpful owners;
hilly 1km walk to Santa Cruz for bus to La Coruña;
gd rest; conv for Santiago de Compostela; excel."*
€32.00, 22 Mar-30 Sep. **2018**

SPAIN

COTORIOS 4F1 (2km E Rural) 38.05255, -2.83996
Camping Llanos de Arance, Ctra Sierra de Cazorla/
Beas de Segura, Km 22, 23478 Cotoríos (Jaén) **953-71
31 39; arancell@inicia.es; www.llanosdearance.com**

12 ♦⊩⇞ & ⟋ ⊞ ⍨ Ⓗ ⊕ ⌑ ≋ nr ⟋⊼ ⛺

Fr Jaén-Albecete rd N322 turn E onto A1305 N of
Villanueva del Arzobispo sp El Tranco. In 26km to
El Tranco lake, turn R & cross over embankment.
Cotoríos at km stone 53, approx 25km on shore of
lake & Río Guadalaquivir. App fr Cazorla or Beas
definitely not rec if towing. Lge, shd, EHU (5A) €3.21;
gas; bbq; 2% statics; phone; ccard acc; CKE. "*Lovely
site; excel walks & bird life, boar & wild life in Cazorla
National Park.*" **€18.50**   **2019**

CREIXELL 3C3 (3km E Coastal) 41.16512, 1.45800
Camping La Plana, Ctra N340, Km 1182, 43839
Creixell (Tarragona) **977-80 03 04; info@campingla
plana.com; www.campinglaplana.com**

⫟ €1.10 ♦⊩⇞ ⍩ ♨ & ⟋ ⊞ ⍨ Ⓗ ⊕ ⌑ ≋ ⛱ sand adj

Site sp at Creixell off N340. Med, hdstg, shd, EHU €6;
gas; Eng spkn; adv bkg acc. "*Vg, v clean site; v helpful &
pleasant owners.*" **€23.25, 3 Mar-30 Sep.**   **2017**

CREIXELL 3C3 (3km SW Coastal) 41.14851, 1.41821
Camping La Noria, Passeig Miramar 278, 43830
Torredembarra **977-64 04 53; info@camping-lanoria.
com; www.camping-lanoria.com**

⫟ ♦⊩⇞ ⍩ ♨ & ⟋ ⍨Ⓜ ⍨ Ⓗ ⊕ ⌑ ≋ ⛺ ⛱ adj

Just outside Torredembara, going N on the old
coastal N340 rd. Lge, hdg, mkd, hdstg, pt shd, EHU
(6A) €5; bbq; twin axles; red long stay; TV; 60% statics;
bus adj; Eng spkn; adv bkg rec; games area; games rm.
"*Adj to Els Muntanyans Nature reserve, with walks &
birdwatching; rail 1.6km; beach has naturist area; some
noise fr train line bet beach & site; vg; conv for town;
sep beach area for naturist.*" **€41.00, 1 Apr-1 Oct.**
                                                              2018

CREVILLENT 4F2 (8km S Rural) 38.17770, -0.80876
Marjal Costa Blanca Eco Camping Resort, AP-7
Salida 730, 03330 Crevillent (Comunidad Valenciana)
**965-48 49 45; camping@marjalcostablanca.com;
www.marjalcostablanca.com**

12 ⫟ €2.20 ♦⊩⇞ ⍩ ♨ & ⟋ ⍨ ⍨ Ⓗ ⊕ ⌑ ≋ ⟋⊼ ⚓ ≋ (htd)

Fr A7/E15 merge onto AP7 (sp Murcia), take exit
730; site sp fr exit. 4*, V lge, hdstg, mkd, hdg, pt
shd, serviced pitches; EHU (16A) inc; gas; bbq; sw;
twin axles; TV; 30% statics; phone; Eng spkn; adv bkg
acc; ccard acc; tennis; bike hire; games area; games
rm; CCI. "*Superb site; car wash; hairdresser; doctor's
surgery; gd security; excel facs; wellness cent with
fitness studio, htd pools, saunas, physiotherapy & spa;
tour ops; new site, trees and hedges need time to
grow; lge pitches extra charge; excel, immac san facs;
nr to Elfondo birdwatching; v helpful staff.*" **€47.50,
W05.**   **2016**

CUBILLAS DE SANTA MARTA 1C4 (4km S Rural)
41.80511, -4.58776 **Camping Cubillas,** Ctra N620,
Km 102, 47290 Cubillas de Santa Marta (Valladolid)
**983-58 50 02 or 983-58 51 74; info@camping
cubillas.com; www.campingcubillas.com**

12 ⫟ €2 ♦⊩⇞ ⍩ & ⟋ ⊞ ⍨Ⓜ ⍨ nr Ⓗ ⊕ ⌑ ⟋⊼ ≋

A-62 Exit 102 Cubillas de Santa Marta. Fr N foll slip
rd and cross rd to Cubillas de Santa Marta the site is
on the R in 200m. Fr S take exit 102 take 5th exit off
rndabt, cross over m'way and then 1st L. Site on R
in 200m. Lge, hdg, mkd, unshd, pt sl, EHU (6-10A) inc;
gas; bbq; red long stay; 50% statics; phone; ccard acc;
site clsd 18 Dec-10 Jan; CKE. "*Ltd space for tourers;
conv visit Palencia & Valladolid; rd & m'way, rlwy &
disco noise at w/end until v late; v ltd facs LS; NH only;
2.5h fr Santander; adequate o'night stop.*" **€26.00**
                                                              2019

CUDILLERO 1A3 (2.7km SE Rural) 43.55416, -6.12944
Camping Cudillero, Ctra Playa de Aguilar, Aronces,
33150 El Pito (Asturias) **985-59 06 63; info@
campingcudillero.com; www.campingcudillero.com**

⫟ €2.15 ♦⊩⇞ ⍩ ♨ & ⟋ ⍨ 🦋 ⍨ ⌑ ≋ ⟋⊼ ⛺ ⚓ (htd)
⛱ sand 1.2km

Exit N632 (E70) sp El Pito. Turn L at rndabt sp
Cudillero & in 300m at end of wall turn R at site sp,
cont for 1km, site on L. Do not app thro Cudillero;
rds v narr & steep; much traff. Med, mkd, hdg, pt
shd, EHU (6A) €4.50; gas; TV; phone; bus 1km; adv
bkg acc; games area; CKE. "*Excel, well-maintained,
well laid-out site; some generous pitches; gd san
facs; steep walk to beach & vill; v helpful staff; excel
facs; vill worth a visit, parking on quay but narr rds;
diff to get to vill, very steep; sm crowded pitches.*"
€18.00, 18 Mar-27 Mar & 30 Apr-15 Sep.   **2016**

CUDILLERO 1A3 (2km S Rural) 43.55555, -6.13777
Camping L'Amuravela, El Pito, 33150 Cudillero
(Asturias) **985-59 09 95; camping@lamuravela.com;
www.lamuravela.com**

⫟ €1 ♦⊩⇞ ⍩ ⟋ ⍨Ⓜ ⍨ ⌑ ⚓ ≋ 🔥 ⛱ sand 2km

Exit N632 (E70) sp El Pito. Turn L at rndabt sp
Cudillero & in approx 1km turn R at site sp. Do not
app thro Cudillero; rds v narr & steep; much traff.
Med, mkd, unshd, pt sl, EHU €4.10; gas; 50% statics;
ccard acc. "*Pleasant, well-maintained site; gd clean facs;
hillside walks into Cudillero, attractive fishing vill with gd
fish rests; red facs LS & poss only open w/ends,
surroundings excel.*" **€22.00, Holy Week & 1 Jun-30 Sep.**
                                                              2017

DEBA *3A1* (5.7km W Coastal) *43.30577, -2.37789*
Camping Aitzeta, Ctra Deba-Guernica, Km. 3.5, C6212,
20930 Mutriku (Guipúzcoa) **943-60 33 56; aitzeta@
hotmail.com; www.campingseuskadi.com/aitzeta**

🐕 🏕 �🅦🅓 🛁 ᴒ 🖥 ✗ ❄ ⑪ nr ⏚ 🏊 ♨ ⛱ sand 1km

On N634 San Sebastián-Bilbao rd thro Deba & on
o'skts turn R over rv sp Mutriku. Site on L after 3km
on narr & winding rd up sh steep climb. Med, mkd,
pt shd, terr, EHU (4A) €3; gas; phone; bus 500m; CKE.
*"Easy reach of Bilbao ferry; sea views; gd, well-run,
clean site; not suitable lge o'fits; ltd pitches for tourers;
helpful staff; walk to town; basic facs but gd NH."*
€20.00, 1 May-31 Oct.   **2016**

DELTEBRE *3D2* (8km E Coastal) *40.72041, 0.84849*
Camping L'Aube, Afores s/n, 43580 Deltebre
(Tarragona) **977-26 70 66; campinglaube@hotmail.
com; www.campinglaube.com**

🏕 �🅦🅓 🛁 ᴒ 🖥 ✗ ❄ 🅼🅢🅟 🍽 ⑪ ⏚ 🏊 ♨ ⛱ sand adj

Exit AP7 junc 40 or 41 onto N340 dir Deltebre.
Fr Deltebre foll T340 sp Riumar for 8km. At info
kiosk branch R, site sp 1km on R. 2*, Lge, hdstg, mkd,
pt shd, EHU (3-10A) €2.80-5; red long stay; 40% statics;
phone; CKE. *"At edge of Ebro Delta National Park; excel
birdwatching; ltd facs in winter; sm pitches; pricey;
interesting local rest."* **€26.00, 1 Mar-31 Oct.**   **2018**

DENIA *4E2* (3.5km SE Coastal) *38.82968, 0.14767*
Camping Los Pinos, Ctra Dénia-Les Rotes, Km 3,
Les Rotes, 03700 Dénia (Alicante) **965-78 26 98;
lospinosdenia@gmail.com; www.lospinosdenia.com**

12 🐕 €3 🏕 ⅙ ⅙ ⍽ ⅙ ⏚ ⛱ shgl adj

Fr N332 foll sp to Dénia in dir of coast. Turn R sp
Les Rotes/Jávea, then L twrds Les Rotes. Foll site
sp turn L into narr access rd poss diff lge o'fits.
2*, Med, mkd, pt shd, EHU (6-10A) €3.20; gas; bbq;
cooking facs; red long stay; TV; 25% statics; phone;
bus 100m; Eng spkn; adv bkg acc; ccard acc; CKE.
*"Friendly, well-run, clean, tidy site but san facs tired
(Mar 09); excel value; access some pitches poss diff due
trees - not suitable lge o'fits or m'vans; many long-stay
winter residents; cycle path into Dénia; social rm with
log fire; naturist beach 1km, private but rocky shore."*
€26.40   **2019**

DENIA *4E2* (7km W Coastal) *38.87264, -0.02031*
Camping Los Patos, Playa de Les Deveses, Vergel,
03700 Dénia (Alicante) **965-75 52 93; info@camping-
lospatos.com; www.camping-lospatos.com**

12 🐕 🏕 (htd) ⅙ ⅙ 🏕 ⅙ 🅼🅢🅟 🍽 ⑪ ⏚ 🏊 ♨ ⛱ sand adj

Exit A7/E15 junc 61 onto N332. Foll site sp. Med,
hdg, mkd, pt shd, EHU (6A); gas; bbq; twin axles; red
long stay; Eng spkn; adv bkg acc; golf 1km. *"Gd site."*
€14.50   **2015**

DOS HERMANAS *2G3* (3km SW Urban) *37.27731,
-5.93722* **Camping Villsom,** Ctra Sevilla/Cádiz A4,
Km 554.8, 41700 Dos Hermanas (Sevilla) **954-72 08 28;
campingvillsom@hotmail.com; campingvillsom.
blogspot.co.uk**

🐕 🏕 ⅙ ⅙ 🏕 ⅙ ⅙ 🍽 ⑪ ⏚ 🏊 ♨ ⛱

On main Seville-Cádiz NIV rd travelling fr Seville
take exit at km. 555 sp Dos Hermanos-Isla Menor.
At the rndabt turn R (SE-3205 Isla Menor) to site
80 m. on R. 3*, Lge, hdg, mkd, hdstg, pt shd, pt sl,
EHU (8A) inc (poss no earth); gas; bus to Seville 300m
(over bdge & rndabt); Eng spkn; adv bkg acc; ccard
acc; CKE. *"Adv bkg rec Holy Week; helpful staff; clean,
tidy, well-run site; vg, san facs, ltd LS; height barrier
at Carrefour hypmkt - ent via deliveries; no twin axles;
wifi only in office & bar area; pitches long but narr, no
rm for awnings; dusty, rough, tight turns; c'vans parked
too cls."* **€29.00, 10 Jan-23 Dec.**   **2018**

EL BARRACO *1D4* (6.6km SW Rural) *40.428630,
-4.616408* **Camping Pantano del Burguillo,** AV-902
Km 16 400, El Barraco **678-48 20 69; info@pantano
delburguillo.com; www.pantanodelburguillo.com**

🐕 €2 🏕 ⅙ ⅙ 🏕 ⅙ ✗ ❄ 🍽 ⅙

31km S of Avila on N403, take AV902 W for 5km.
Site on L beside reservoir. Sm, hdstg, mkd, pt shd,
EHU inc; bbq (sep area); ccard acc. *"Mainly residential
c'vans, but staff very welcoming; a bit scruffy; open hg
ssn & w'ends only; fair."* **€27.00, 22 Jun-10 Sep.**   **2018**

"I like to fill in the reports as I travel from site to site"

You'll find report forms at the back of this
guide, or you can fill them in online at
camc.com/europereport.

ELCHE *4F2* (10km SW Urban) *38.24055, -0.81194*
Camping Las Palmeras, Partida Deula 75, 03330
Crevillent (Alicante) **966-68 06 30; laspalmeras@
laspalmeras-sl.com; www.laspalmeras-sl.com**

12 🐕 🏕 ⅙ ⅙ 🏕 ⅙ ✗ 🍽 ⑪ ⏚ 🏊 nr ♨ ⛱

Exit A7 junc 726/77 onto N340 to Crevillent. Immed
bef traff lts take slip rd into rest parking/service
area. Site on R, access rd down side of rest. Med,
mkd, hdstg, pt shd, EHU (6A) inc; 10% statics; ccard
acc; CKE. *"Useful NH; report to recep in hotel; helpful
staff; gd cent for touring Murcia; dogs free; gd rest in
hotel; gd, modern san facs; excel."* **€28.00**   **2019**

SPAIN

ESCALA, L' *3B3* (3km S Coastal) *42.10512, 3.15843*
Camping Neus, Cala Montgó, 17130 L'Escala (Gerona)
638-65 27 12; info@campingneus.com;
www.campingneus.com

🏕 €2 ⚡ 🚿 ♿ ⛽ 🚐 🦋 💧 🍴 🛒 ⚓ 🏔 🎿 ♨

⛱ sand 850m

**Exit AP7 junc 5 twd L'Escala then turn R twd Cala
Montgó & foll sp.** Med, mkd, shd, pt sl, terr, EHU (6A)
€4; gas; red long stay; TV; 15% statics; phone; bus
500m; Eng spkn; adv bkg acc; ccard acc; fishing; tennis;
car wash; CKE. *"Pleasant, clean site in pine forest; gd
san facs; lge pitches; vg."* **€48.00, 14 May-18 Sep.**
2016

ESCORIAL, EL *1D4* (6km NE Rural) *40.62630,
-4.09970* **Camping-Caravaning El Escorial,** Ctra
Guadarrama a El Escorial, Km 3.5, 28280 El Escorial
(Madrid) **918 90 24 12 or 02 01 49 00; info@camping
elescorial.com; www.campingelescorial.com**

12 🐎 ⚡(htd) 🚿 ⛽ ♿ 🚐 💧 🍴 ♨ 🛒 🏔 🎿

**Exit AP6 NW of Madrid junc 47 El Escorial/
Guadarrama, onto M505 & foll sp to El Escorial,
site on L at km stone 3,500 - long o'fits rec cont to
rndabt (1km) to turn & app site on R.** V lge, hdstg,
mkd, pt shd, EHU (5A) inc (long cable rec); gas; bbq;
TV; 80% statics; Eng spkn; adv bkg acc; ccard acc;
tennis; games rm; horseriding 7km. *"Excel, busy site;
mountain views; o'fits over 8m must reserve lge pitch
with elec, water & drainage; helpful staff; clean facs;
gd security; sm pitches poss diff due trees; o'head
canopies poss diff for tall o'fits; facs ltd LS; trains &
buses to Madrid nr; Valle de Los Caídos & Palace at El
Escorial well worth visit; cash machine; easy parking
in town for m'vans if go in early; mkt Wed; stunning
scenery, nesting storks; well stocked shop; v well run;
20min walk to bus stop for El Escorial or Madrid; rec; gd
for families; gd pool."* **€39.00** 2017

ESPOT *3B2* (0.9km SE Rural) *42.57223, 1.09677*
Camping Sol I Neu, Ctra Sant Maurici s/n, 25597
Espot (Lleida) **973-62 40 01; camping@solineu.com;
www.solineu.com**

🏕 ⚡ 🚿 ⛽ 🚐 🦋 🍴 ♨ 🏔 🎿 ♨

**N fr Sort on C13 turn L to Espot on rd LV5004, site
on L in approx 6.5km by rvside.** 2*, Med, mkd, pt shd,
EHU (6-10A) €5.80; gas; TV; ccard acc; CKE. *"Excel
facs; beautiful site nr National Park (Landrover taxis
avail - no private vehicles allowed in Park); suitable sm
o'fits only; poss unrel opening dates; 10 mins walk to
vill, many bars & rest."* **€25.60, 1 Jul-31 Aug.** 2015

ESTARTIT, L' *3B3* (1km S Coastal) *42.04972, 3.18416*
Camping El Molino, Camino del Ter, 17258 L'Estartit
(Gerona) **972-75 06 29**

⚡ ⛽ 🚐 🎿 🛒 🍴 ♨ 🏔 ⛱ sand 1km

**Fr N11 junc 5, take rd to L'Escala. Foll sp to
Torroella de Montgri, then L'Estartit. Ent town
& foll sp, site on rd GI 641.** V lge, hdg, pt shd, pt
sl, EHU (6A) €3.60; gas; bus 1km; adv bkg rec;
games rm. *"Site in 2 parts - 1 in shd, 1 at beach
unshd; gd facs; quiet location outside busy town."*
€28.00, 1 Apr-30 Sep. 2018

> ## "We must tell the Club about that great site we found"
>
> Get your site reports in by mid-August and we'll
> do our best to get your updates into the next
> edition.

ESTARTIT, L' *3B3* (2km S Coastal) *42.04250, 3.18333*
Camping Les Medes, Paratge Camp de l'Arbre s/n,
17258 L'Estartit (Gerona) **972-75 18 05; info@
campinglesmedes.com; www.campingles
medes.com**

12 🏕 €2.60 ⚡(htd) 🚿 ⛽ ♿ 🚐 🦋 💧 🍴 ♨ 🛒
🏔 🎿 (htd, indoor) ⛱ sand 800m

**Fr Torroella foll sp to L'Estartit. In vill turn R at
town name sp (sp Urb Estartit Oeste), foll rd for
1.5km, turn R, site well sp.** Lge, mkd, shd, serviced
pitches; EHU (6A) €4.60; gas; red long stay; TV;
7% statics; phone; Eng spkn; adv bkg acc; sauna;
games area; tennis; horseriding 400m; car wash;
games rm; watersports; solarium; bike hire; CKE.
*"Excel, popular, family-run & well organised site;
helpful, friendly staff; gd clean facs & constant hot
water; gd for children; no dogs high ssn; no twin axle
vans high ssn - by arrangement LS; conv National Park;
well mkd foot & cycle paths; ACSI acc."* **€47.00** 2017

ESTEPAR *1B4* (2km NE Rural) *42.29233, -3.85097*
Quinta de cavia, A62, km 17, 09196 Cavia, Burgos
947-41 20 78; reservas@quintadecavia.es

12 🏕 ⚡ 🚿 ⛽ 🍴 ♨

**Site 15km SW of Burgos on N side of A62/E80,
adj Hotel Rio Cabia. Ent via Campsa petrol stn,
W'bound exit 17, E'bound exit 16, cross over &
re-join m'way. Ignore camp sp at exit 18 (1-way).
Site at 17km stone.** 2*, Med, pt shd, EHU (6A) inc;
10% statics; ccard acc; CKE. *"Friendly, helpful owner;
gd rest; conv for m'way for Portugal but poorly sp fr
W; poss v muddy in winter; NH only; food in rest vg and
cheap; can get to Bilbao ferry in morn if ferry is mid-aft;
elec security gate; lit at night; gd NH; new san facs
(2018); site 2723 feet abv sea level, cold at night; gem
of a site; site being improved (2019)."* **€20.00** 2019

ESTEPONA *2H3* (7km E Coastal) *36.45436, -5.08105*
Camping Parque Tropical, Ctra N340, Km 162, 29680
Estepona (Málaga) **952-79 36 18; parquetropical
camping@hotmail.com; www.campingparque
tropical.com**

12 🐕 €2 ♦♦♦ wo 🛁 ♿ 🖥 🗑 ⧫ 🍽 🛒 Ⓗ 🍴 🛒 ⚲ 🏊 (covrd, htd)
🐾 shgl 1km

On N side of N340 at km 162, 200m off main rd.
2*, Med, mkd, hdg, pt shd, terr, serviced pitches; EHU
(10A) €4; gas; red long stay; 10% statics; phone; bus
400m; Eng spkn; adv bkg acc; golf nr; horseriding nr;
CKE. *"Tropical plants thro out; clean facs; tropical
paradise swimming pool; wildlife park 1km; helpful
owners."* **€27.00**   **2017**

ETXARRI ARANATZ *3B1* (2km N Rural) *42.91255,
-2.07919* **Camping Etxarri,** Parase Dambolintxulo,
31820 Etxarri-Aranatz (Navarra) **948-46 05 37; info@
campingetxarri.com; www.campingetxarri.com**
🐕 €2.15 ♦♦♦ wo 🛁 ♿ 🗑 ⧫ 🍸 🍽 Ⓗ 🍴 🛒 ⚲ ✎

Fr N exit A15 at junc 112 to join A10 W dir Vitoria/
Gasteiz. Exit at junc 19 onto NA120; go thro Etxarri
vill, turn L & cross bdge, then take rd over rlwy. Turn
L, site sp. Med, hdg, pt shd, EHU (6A) €5.50; gas; bbq;
90% statics; phone; Eng spkn; ccard acc; games area;
archery; cycling; horseriding; CKE. *"Gd, wooded site;
gd walks; interesting area; helpful owner; conv NH to/
fr Pyrenees; youth hostel & resident workers on site;
san facs gd; various pitch sizes & shapes, some diff lge
o'fits; NH only."* **€32.00, 1 Mar-1 Nov.**   **2019**

"I need an on-site restaurant"

We do our best to make sure site information
is correct, but it is always best to check any
must-have facilities are still available or will
be open during your visit.

FIGUERES *3B3* (8km NE Rural) *42.33902, 3.06758*
Camping Vell Empordà, Ctra Roses-La Jonquera s/n,
17780 Garriguella (Gerona) **972-53 02 00 or 972-57
06 31 (LS); vellemporda@vellemporda.com;
www.vellemporda.com**
🐕 €4.50 ♦♦♦ (htd) wo 🛁 ♨ ♿ 🗑 ⧫ 🦋 ⧫ 🍸 Ⓗ 🍴 🛒 ⚲ ✎
🏊 🖼

On A7/E11 exit junc 3 onto N260 NE dir Llançà. Nr
km 26 marker, turn R sp Garriguella, then L at T-junc
N twd Garriguella. Site on R shortly bef vill. Lge,
hdstg, mkd, hdg, shd, terr, EHU (6-10A) inc; gas; bbq;
red long stay; TV; 20% statics; phone; Eng spkn; adv
bkg acc; ccard acc; games rm; games area; CKE. *"Conv
N Costa Brava away fr cr beaches & sites; 20 mins to
sea at Llança; o'hanging trees poss diff high vehicles;
excel."* **€40.00, 1 Feb-15 Dec.**   **2018**

FIGUERUELA DE ARRIBA *1B3* (2km E Rural)
41.86563, -6.41937 **Camping Sierra de la Culebra,**
Carretera Riomanzanas, S/N 49520 Figueruela de
Arriba **980-68 30 20 or 630-66 13 29 (mob); info@
campingsierradelaculebra.com; www.camping
sierradelaculebra.com**
🐕 ♦♦♦ wo 🛁 ♿ 🗑 ⧫ 🦋 ♈ 🍸 Ⓗ 🍴 🛒 ⚲ 🏊 🖼

Fr S: At Alcanices on the N122 (E82) Zamora-
Braganca rd, turn N onto ZA9112. In 21km at
Mahide turn L. Site sp on L in 3km. Fr N: Exit A52
at junc 49 onto N631 dir Zamora. In 4km turn R
onto ZA912. In 28km at Mahide turn R. Site sp.
Med, pt shd, EHU (6A) €4.10; bbq; twin axles; TV;
10% statics; Eng spkn; adv bkg acc; games area. *"Fam
owned; many interesting old vill; gd bird-watching;
tennis; gd walking; gd for Braganca in Portugal; excel."*
€26.60, 5 Mar-2 Nov.   **2016**

FORTUNA *4F1* (3km N Rural) *38.20562, -1.10712*
Camping Fuente, Camino de la Bocamina s/n, 30709
Baños de Fortuna (Murcia) **968-68 50 17; info@
campingfuente.com; www.campingfuente.com**
12 🐕 €1.10 ♦♦♦ (htd) wo 🛁 ♿ 🗑 ⧫ 🍸 Ⓗ 🍴 🛒 ⚲ 🏊 (htd)

Fr Murcia on A7/E15 turn L onto C3223 sp Fortuna.
After 19km turn onto A21 & foll sp Baños de
Fortuna, then sp 'Complejo Hotelero La Fuente'.
Avoid towing thro vill, if poss. Med, mkd, hdstg,
unshd, pt sl, EHU (10-16A) €2.20 or metered; poss rev
pol; gas; bbq; red long stay; 10% statics; phone; bus
200m; adv bkg acc; ccard acc; CKE. *"Gd san facs; excel
pool & rest; secure o'flow parking area; many long-stay
winter visitors - adv bkg rec; private san facs some
pitches; ltd recep hrs LS; spa; jacuzzi; poss sulphurous
smell fr thermal baths."* **€19.00**   **2015**

FOZ *1A2* (11km E Coastal) *43.56236, -7.20761*
Camping Poblado Gaivota, Playa de Barreiros,
27790 Barreiros Lugo **982-12 44 51; www.camping
pobladogaivota.com**
♦♦♦ wo 🛁 ♨ ⧫ 🍽 🍸 Ⓗ 🍴 🛒 ⚲ ✎ 🐾 opp

Junc 516 on A8, on to N634 to Barreiros. Foll sp to
the R in Barreiros. Rd winds down to coast for 2km.
Site on L, parallel with sea. Sm, hdg, shd, EHU (6A);
bbq; Eng spkn. *"Excel."* **€30.00, 21 Mar-15 Oct.**
2016

FRANCA, LA *1A4* (1km NW Coastal) *43.39250,
-4.57722* **Camping Las Hortensias,** Ctra N634, Km
286, 33590 Colombres/Ribadedeva (Asturias) **985-41
24 42; lashortensias@campinglashortensias.com;
www.campinglashortensias.com**
🐕 €6 ♦♦♦ wo 🛁 ♨ 🗑 ⧫ 🍸 nr Ⓗ nr 🛒 ⚲ 🐾 sand adj

Fr N634 on leaving vill of La Franca, at km286 foll
sp 'Playa de la Franca' & cont past 1st site & thro
car park to end of rd. Med, mkd, pt shd, pt sl, terr,
EHU (6-10A) €5; gas; phone; bus 800m; Eng spkn; adv
bkg acc; ccard acc; bike hire; tennis; CKE. *"Beautiful
location nr scenic beach; sea views fr top terr pitches;
vg."* **€28.50, 5 Jun-30 Sep.**   **2017**

FUENTE DE PIEDRA *2G4* (0.7km S Rural) *37.12905,* *-4.73315* **Camping Fuente de Pedra,** Calle Campillos 88-90, 29520 Fuente de Piedra (Málaga) **952-73 52 94; info@campingfuentedepiedra.com; www.camping-rural.com**

Turn off A92 at km 132 sp Fuente de Piedra. Sp fr vill cent. Or to avoid town turn N fr A384 just W of turn for Bobadilla Estación, sp Sierra de Yeguas. In 2km turn R into nature reserve, cont for approx 3km, site on L at end of town. 2*, Sm, mkd, hdstg, pt shd, pt sl, terr, EHU (10A) €5; gas; bbq; red long stay; 25% statics; phone; Eng spkn; ccard acc; CKE. "Mostly sm, narr pitches, but some avail for o'fits up to 7m; gd rest; san facs dated & poss stretched; poss noise fr adj public pool; adj lge lake with flamingoes (visible but access is 4.8km away); gd." **€26.00** **2017**

FUENTEHERIDOS *2F3* (0.6km SW Rural) *37.9050,* *-6.6742* **Camping El Madroñal,** Ctra Fuenteheridos-Castaño del Robledo, Km 0.6, 21292 Fuenteheridos (Huelva) **959-50 12 01; castillo@campingel madronal.com; www.campingelmadronal.com**

Fr Zafra S on N435n turn L onto N433 sp Aracena, ignore first R to Fuenteheridos vill, camp sp R at next x-rd 500m on R. At rndabt take 2nd exit. Avoid Fuenteheridos vill - narr rds. 2*, Med, mkd, pt shd, pt sl, EHU €3.20; gas; bbq; 80% statics; phone; bus 1km; horseriding; car wash; bike hire; CKE. "Tranquil site in National Park of Sierra de Aracena; pitches among chestnut trees - poss diff lge o'fits or m'vans & poss sl & uneven; o'hanging trees on site rds; scruffy, pitches not clearly mkd; beautiful vill 1km away, worth a visit." **€13.00** **2019**

GALLARDOS, LOS *4G1* (4km N Rural) *37.18448,* *-1.92408* **Camping Los Gallardos,** 04280 Los Gallardos (Almería) **950-52 83 24; reception@ campinglosgallardos.com; www.campinglos gallardos.com**

Fr N leave A7/E15 at junc 525; foll sp to Los Gallardos; take 1st R after approx 800m pass under a'route; turn L into site ent. Med, mkd, hdstg, pt shd, serviced pitches; EHU (10A) €3; gas; red long stay; 40% statics; adv bkg acc; ccard acc; tennis adj; golf; CKE. "British owned; 90% British clientele LS; gd social atmosphere; sep drinking water supply nr recep; prone to flooding wet weather; 2 grass bowling greens; facs tired; poss cr in winter; friendly staff." **€23.50** **2017**

GANDIA *4E2* (4km NE Coastal) *38.98613, -0.16352* **Camping L'Alqueria,** Avda del Grau s/n; 46730 Grao de Gandía (València) **962-84 04 70; lalqueria@ lalqueria.com; www.lalqueria.com**

Fr N on A7/AP7 exit 60 onto N332 dir Grao de Gandía. Site sp on rd bet Gandía & seafront. Fr S exit junc 61 & foll sp to beaches. 3*, Lge, hdstg, mkd, pt shd, EHU (10A) €5.94; gas; red long stay; 30% statics; phone; bus; adv bkg acc; ccard acc; games area; jacuzzi; bike hire; CKE. "Pleasant site; helpful, friendly family owners; lovely pool; easy walk to town & stn; excel beach nrby; bus & train to Valencia; shop & snacks not avail in Jul; gd biking; no dogs over 10kg; m'van friendly; site scruffy but san facs gd; gd location; rec; gd location bet old town & beach; gd cycling & walking." **€42.00** **2019**

GARGANTILLA DEL LOZOYA *1C4* (2km SW Rural) *40.9503, -3.7294* **Camping Monte Holiday,** Ctra C604, Km 8.8, 28739 Gargantilla del Lozoya (Madrid) **918-69 52 78; monteholiday@monteholiday.com; www.monteholiday.com**

Fr N on A1/E5 Burgos-Madrid rd turn R on M604 at km stone 69 sp Rascafría; in 8km turn R immed after rlwy bdge & then L up track in 300m, foll site sp. Do not ent vill. Lge, pt shd, pt sl, terr, EHU (7A) €4.30 (poss rev pol); 80% statics; phone; bus 500m; Eng spkn; adv bkg acc; ccard acc; CKE. "Interesting, friendly site; vg san facs; gd views; easy to find; some facs clsd LS; lovely area but site isolated in winter & poss heavy snow; conv NH fr m'way & for Madrid & Segovia; excel wooded site; v rural but well worth the sh drive fr the N1 E5; clean; lovely surroundings." **€35.40, E04.** **2019**

GIJON *1A3* (9.5km NW Coastal) *43.58343, -5.75713* **Camping Perlora,** Ctra Candás, Km 12, Perán, 33491 Candás (Asturias) **985-87 00 48; recepcion@ campingperlora.com; www.campingperlora.com**

Exit A8 dir Candás; in 9km at rndabt turn R sp Perlora (AS118). At sea turn L sp Candás, site on R. Avoid Sat mkt day. 2*, Med, mkd, unshd, pt sl, terr, serviced pitches; EHU (10A) €3.50; gas; red long stay; 80% statics; phone; bus adj; Eng spkn; ccard acc; watersports; fishing; tennis. "Excel; helpful staff; attractive, well-kept site on dramatic headland o'looking Candas Bay; ltd space for tourers; easy walk to Candás; gem of a site; train (5 mins); excel fish rests; no mob signal; facs gd & clean, ltd LS; rec." **€27.50, 18 Jan-10 Dec.** **2019**

GORLIZ *1A4* (1km N Coastal) *43.41782, -2.93626*
Camping Arrien, Uresarantze Bidea, 48630 Gorliz
(Bizkaia) **946-77 19 11; recepcion@campinggorliz.
com or campingarrien@gmail.com; www.camping
gorliz.com**

🏕 €1 ♿ ⓌⒸ ♨ ♿ 🍴 / ⓙ 🍺 🏳 🍹 sand 700m

Fr Bilbao foll m'way to Getxo, then 637/634 thro
Sopelana & Plentzia to Gorliz. In Gorliz turn L at
1st rndabt, foll sps for site, pass TO on R, then R at
next rndabt, strt over next, site on L adj sports cent/
running track. Not sp locally. Lge, pt shd, pt sl, EHU
(6A) inc; gas; bbq; red long stay; 60% statics; phone;
bus 150m; Eng spkn; ccard acc; CKE. *"Useful base for
Bilbao & ferry (approx 1hr); bus to Plentzia every 20
mins, fr there can get metro to Bilbao; friendly, helpful
staff; poss shortage of hot water; very cramped; no
mkd pitches."* **€36.00, 1 Mar-31 Oct.** 2016

GRANADA *2G4* (15.3km NE Rural) *37.22657, -3.49151*
Alto de Vinuelas, Ctra Beas de Granada s/n, Beas de
Granada 18184, Granada. **958-54 60 23 or 647-30 78 12;
info@campingaltodevinuelas.com; www.campingalto
devinuelas.com**

12 🐕 ♿ ♨ ♿ / 🍴 Y ⓙ 🍺 🛶

Fr A92 take exit 256 twds Beas de Granada and
then foll signs to campsite 1.5km fr junc. 1*, Mkd,
EHU (10A) inc; gas; twin axles; TV; bus; ccard acc;
horseriding. *"Wonderful views of Sierra Nevada
fr campsite; biking; adventure sports; gd site for a
long peaceful stay or v conv for a NH; ACSI red."*
€28.00 2019

> ## "Satellite navigation makes touring much easier"
>
> Remember most sat navs don't know if you're
> towing or in a larger vehicle – always use yours
> alongside maps and site directions.

GRANADA *2G4* (13km E Rural) *37.16085, -3.45388*
Camping Las Lomas, 11 Ctra de Güejar-Sierra, Km 6,
18160 Güejar-Sierra (Granada) **958-48 47 42; info@
campinglaslomas.com; www.campinglaslomas.com**

12 🐕 ♿ (htd) ⓌⒸ ♨ ♿ 🍴 / ⭐ 🦋 ♿ Y ⓙ 🍺 🏳 🛶 ⛸

Fr A44 exit onto by-pass 'Ronda Sur', then exit onto
A395 sp Sierra Nevada. In approx 4km exit sp Cenes,
turn under A395 to T-junc & turn R sp Güejar-Sierra,
Embalse de Canales. After approx 3km turn L at
sp Güejar-Sierra & site. Site on R 6.5km up winding
mountain rd. 3*, Med, mkd, hdg, pt shd, terr, serviced
pitches; EHU (10A) €5 (poss no earth/rev pol); gas; red
long stay; bus adj; Eng spkn; adv bkg req; ccard acc;
sports area; kids entertainment; minigolf; playground;
hiking and cycling areas; CKE. *"Helpful, friendly
owners; well-run site; conv Granada (bus at gate);
waterskiing nr; access poss diff for lge o'fits; excel san
facs; gd shop & rest; beautiful mountain scenery; excel
site."* **€40.00** 2019

GRANADA *2G4* (10km SE Urban) *37.12444, -3.58611*
Camping Reina Isabel, Calle de Laurel de la Reina,
18140 La Zubia (Granada) **958-59 00 41; info@camping
reinaisabel.com; www.campingreinaisabel.es**

12 🐕 ♿ (htd) ⓌⒸ ♨ ♿ 🍴 / MSP 🦋 ♿ Y 🍺 🛶

Exit A44 nr Granada at junc sp Ronda Sur, dir Sierra
Nevada, Alhambra, then exit 2 sp La Zubia. Foll site
sp approx 1.2km on R; narr ent set back fr rd.
2*, Med, hdstg, hdg, pt shd, EHU (6A) poss rev pol
€4.20; gas; red long stay; TV; phone; bus; Eng spkn;
adv bkg rec; ccard acc; CKE. *"Well-run, busy site; poss
shwrs v hot/cold - warn children; ltd touring pitches &
sm; poss student groups; conv Alhambra (order tickets
at site), shwr block not htd; tight site; elec unrel."*
€29.00 2017

GUARDAMAR DEL SEGURA *4F2* (4km N Rural/
Coastal) *38.10916, -0.65472* **Camping Marjal,** Ctra
N332, Km 73.4, 03140 Guardamar del Segura
(Alicante) **965-48 49 45; camping@marjal.com;
www.campingmarjal.com**

12 🐕 €2.20 ♿ ⓌⒸ ♨ ♿ 🍴 / 🦋 ♿ Y ⓙ 🍺 🏳 🖊
🛶 (covrd, htd) 🍹 sand 1km

Fr N exit A7 junc 72 sp Aeropuerto/Santa Pola; in
5km turn R onto N332 sp Santa Pola/Cartagena,
U-turn at km 73.4, site sp on R at km 73.5. Fr S exit
AP7 at junc 740 onto CV91 twd Guardamar. In 9km
join N332 twd Alicante, site on R at next rndabt. 5*,
Lge, hdstg, mkd, hdg, pt shd, serviced pitches; EHU
(16A) €3 or metered; gas; bbq; red long stay; TV;
50% statics; phone; Eng spkn; adv bkg rec; ccard acc;
bike hire; tennis; sauna; CKE. *"Fantastic facs; friendly,
helpful staff; excel family entmnt & activities; recep
0800-2300; sports cent; tropical waterpark; excel; well
sign-posted; lge shwr cubicles; highly rec."* **€67.00**
2018

HARO *1B4* (0.5km N Urban) *42.57824, -2.85421*
Camping de Haro, Avda Miranda 1, 26200 Haro
(La Rioja) **941-31 27 37; campingdeharo@fer.es;
www.campingdeharo.com**

🏕 €3 ♿ (htd) ⓌⒸ ♨ ♿ 🍴 / MSP ♿ Y 🍺 🏳 🛶 (htd)

Fr N or S on N124 take exit sp A68 Vitoria/Logrono
& Haro. In 500m at rndabt take 1st exit, under rlwy
bdge, cont to site on R immed bef rv bdge. Fr AP68
exit junc 9 to town; at 2nd rndabt turn L onto LR111
(sp Logroño). Immed after rv bdge turn sharp L
& foll site sp. Avoid cont into town cent. 2*, Med,
hdg, mkd, pt shd, EHU (6A) inc; gas; bbq; 70% statics;
phone; bus 800m; Eng spkn; adv bkg acc; ccard acc;
site clsd 9 Dec-13 Jan; car wash; CKE. *"Clean, tidy,
well run, lovely site - peaceful LS; friendly owner;
some sm pitches & diff turns; excel facs; statics busy
at w/ends; conv Rioja 'bodegas' & Bilbao & Santander
ferries; recep clsd 1300-1500 no entry then due to
security barrier; excel & conv NH for Santander/Bilbao;
lge o'night area with electric; big, busy, vg site; easy
walk to lovely town; san facs constantly cleaned!"*
€30.00, 27 Jan-10 Dec, E02. 2017

HARO *1B4* (10km SW Rural) *42.53017, -2.92173*
Camping De La Rioja, Ctra de Haro/Santo Domingo
de la Calzada, Km 8.5, 26240 Castañares de la Rioja
(La Rioja) **941-30 01 74; info@campingdelarioja.com**

🏠 🐕 👫 (htd) 🚾 🔌 🛒 🍴 🍽 ⓗ ♿ 🅿 ♨ 🛶

Exit AP68 junc 9, take rd twd Santo Domingo de la
Calzada. Foll by-pass round Casalarreina, site on R
nr rvside just past vill on rd LR111. 3*, Lge, hdg, pt
shd, EHU (4A) €3.90 (poss rev pol); gas; 90% statics;
bus adj; adv bkg acc; ccard acc; bike hire; tennis; clsd
10 Dec-8 Jan; site clsd 9 Dec-11 Jan. *"Fair site but
fairly isolated; basic san facs but clean; ltd facs in
winter; sm pitches; conv for Rioja wine cents; Bilbao
ferry."* **€36.00, 10 Jan-10 Dec.**   2016

HECHO *3B1* (1km S Rural) *42.73222, -0.75305*
Camping Valle de Hecho, Ctra Puente La Reina-
Hecho s/n, 22720 Hecho (Huesca) **974-37 53 61;
campinghecho@campinghecho.com; www.camping
hecho.com**

12 🐕 👫 (htd) 🚾 🔌 🛒 🍴 ⓗ 🐟 🛶

Leave Jaca W on N240. After 25km turn N on A176
at Puente La Reina de Jaca. Site on W of rd, o'skts
of Hecho/Echo. 1*, Med, mkd, pt shd, pt sl, EHU
(5-15A) €4.20; gas; 40% statics; phone; bus 200m;
ccard acc; games area; CKE. *"Pleasant site in foothills
of Pyrenees; excel, clean facs but poss inadequate hot
water; gd birdwatching area; Hecho fascinating vill;
shop & bar poss clsd LS except w/end; v ltd facs LS; not
suitable lge o'fits; gd rest in vill."* **€27.00**   2016

HORCAJO DE LOS MONTES *2E4* (0.2km E Rural)
39.32440, -4.6358 **Camping Mirador de Cabañeros,**
Calle Cañada Real Segoviana s/n, 13110 Horcajo de
los Montes (Ciudad Real) **926 77 54 39; info@camping
cabaneros.com; www.campingcabaneros.com**

12 🏠 🐕 €2 👫 (htd) 🚾 🔌 🛒 🍴 🍽 ⓗ 🐟 nr 🛶
🛶 (indoor)

At km 53 off CM4103 Horcajo-Alcoba rd, 200m
fr vill. CM4106 to Horcajo fr NW poor in parts. Med,
hdstg, mkd, pt shd, terr, serviced pitches; EHU (6A)
€4.50; gas; bbq; red long stay; TV; 10% statics; phone;
adv bkg rec; ccard acc; tennis 500m; games area; bike
hire; games rm; laundry facilities; lounge; playground;
free Wi-Fi zone; bio park area; CKE. *"Beside Cabañeros
National Park; beautiful views; rd fr S much better."*
€30.00, E38.   2019

HOSPITAL DE ORBIGO *1B3* (1.3km N Urban)
42.4664, -5.8836 **Camp Municipal Don Suero,** 24286
Hospital de Órbigo (León) **987-36 10 18; camping@
hospitaldeorbigo.com; www.hospitaldeorbigo.com**

🏠 👫 🛒 ♿ 🍴 ⓗ nr 🛶

N120 rd fr León to Astorga, km 30. Site well sp
fr N120. Narr rds in Hospital. Med, hdg, pt shd, EHU
(6A) €1.90; bbq; 50% statics; phone; bus to León 1km;
Eng spkn; ccard acc; poss open w/end only mid Apr-
May; CKE. *"Statics v busy w/ends, facs stretched; pool
adj; phone ahead to check site open if travelling close
to opening/closing dates."* **€15.00, Easter-1 Oct.**
                                                        2016

HOSPITALET DE L'INFANT, L' *3C2* (2km S Coastal)
40.97722, 0.90083 **Camping El Templo del Sol
(Naturist),** Polígon 14-15, Playa del Torn, 43890
L'Hospitalet de l'Infant (Tarragona) **977-82 34 34;
info@eltemplodelsol.com; www.eltemplodelsol.com**

👫 🚾 🛒 🍴 ⓗ ♿ 🅿 🛶

Leave A7 at exit 38 or N340 twds town cent. Turn
R (S) along coast rd for 2km. Ignore 1st camp sp
on L, site 200m further on L. Lge, hdg, mkd, pt shd,
pt sl, serviced pitches; EHU (6A) inc; gas; red long
stay; TV; 5% statics; Eng spkn; adv bkg req; ccard
acc; INF card. *"Excel naturist site; no dogs, radios or
TV on pitches; cinema/theatre; solar-energy park;
jacuzzi; official naturist sand/shgl beach adj; lge
private wash/shwr rms; pitches v tight - take care
o'hanging branches; conv Port Aventura; mosquito
problem; poss strong winds - take care with awnings."*
€43.00, 1 Apr-22 Oct.   2016

HUMILLADERO *2G4* (0.5km S Rural) *37.10750,
-4.69611* **Camping La Sierrecilla,** Avda de Clara
Campoamor s/n, 29531 Humilladero (Málaga)
**951-19 90 90; info@lasierrecilla.com; www.camping
lasierrecilla.com**

12 🏠 €1.50 👫 (htd) 🚾 🛒 ♿ 🔌 🍴 🍽 ⓗ ♿ 🐟 nr
🅿 ♨ 🛶 (htd) 🏊

Exit A92 junc 138 onto A7280 twd Humilladero.
At vill ent turn L at 1st rndabt, site visible. Med,
hdstg, mkd, pt shd, pt sl, terr, serviced pitches;
EHU (10A) €3.50; bbq; 10% statics; Eng spkn; adv
bkg acc; CKE. *"Excel new site; gd modern, san facs; vg
touring base; gd walking; horseriding, caving, archery
high ssn; Fuentepiedra lagoon nrby; lots of facs clsd
until Jun/Jul."* **€24.00**   2019

IRUN *3A1* (2km N Rural) *43.36638, -1.80436*
Camping Jaizkibel, Ctra Guadalupe Km 22, 20280
Hondarribia (Guipúzcoa) **943-64 16 79; recepcion@
campingjaizkibel.com; www.campingjaizkibel.com**

👫 🛒 ♿ 🔌 🍴 🍽 ⓗ 🅿 🛶 sand 1.5km

Fr Hondarribia/Fuenterrabia inner ring rd foll sp to
site below old town wall. Do not ent town. Med,
hdg, hdstg, pt shd, terr, EHU (6A) €4.35 (check
earth); bbq; 90% statics; phone; bus 1km; Eng spkn;
adv bkg acc; ccard acc; tennis; CKE. *"Easy 20 mins
walk to historic town; scenic area; gd walking; gd
touring base but ltd turning space for tourers; clean
facs; gd rest & bar; helpful staff; gd lndry facs."*
€34.00, 28 Mar-15 Nov.   2017

IRUN *3A1* (6km W Coastal) *43.37629, -1.79939*
Camping Faro de Higuer, Ctra. Del Faro, 58, 20280 Hondarribia **943 64 10 08; faro@campingseuskadi.com; www.campingseuskadi.com**

⊞12 🅃 €1.20 ⍾ 🆆 ♨ ♿ ▣ ✎ 🖭 ⬦ 🍴 ⑪ ☕ ⚓ 🅼 ✏ 🏊 🖫 🏖 adj

Fr AP8 exit at junc 2 Irun. Foll signs for airport. At rndabt after airport take 2nd exit, cross two more rndabts. 2nd exit at next 2 rndabts. Cont uphill to lighthouse & foll signs for Faro. Med, mkd, hdg, unshd, pt sl, terr, EHU (10A) €5.20; bbq; cooking facs; TV; 50% statics; phone; Eng spkn; adv bkg acc; bike hire; games rm; waterslide; games area. *"Vg site on top of winding rd, is v busy outside; sep ent & exit; exit has low stone arch, be careful when leaving."* **€23.00**   2019

"There aren't many sites open at this time of year"

If you're travelling outside peak season remember to call ahead to check site opening dates – even if the entry says 'open all year'.

ISABA *3B1* (13km E Rural) *42.86618, -0.81247*
Camping Zuriza, Ctra Anso-Zuriza, Km 14, 22728 Ansó (Huesca) **974-37 01 96; contacto@camping zuriza.es; www.campingzuriza.es**

⍾ ♨ ▣ ✎ 🖭 🍴 ⑪ ⚓ 🅼

On NA1370 N fr Isaba, turn R in 4km onto NA2000 to Zuriza. Foll sp to site. Fr Ansó, take HUV2024 N to Zuriza. Foll sp to site, narr, rough rd not rec for underpowered o'fits. 1*, Lge, pt shd, pt sl, serviced pitches; EHU €6; 50% statics; phone; ccard acc; CKE. *"Beautiful, remote valley; no vill at Zuriza, nearest vills Isaba & Ansó; no direct rte to France; superb location for walking; best to call prior to journey to check opening dates."* **€18.00, 1 Jul-31 Oct.**   2018

ISLA CRISTINA *2G2* (4km E Coastal) *37.20555, -7.26722* **Camping Playa Taray,** Ctra La Antilla-Isla Cristina, Km 9, 21430 La Redondela (Huelva) **959-34 11 02; info@campingplayataray.es; www.camping taray.com**

⊞12 🅃 ⍾ ♨ ♿ ▣ ✎ 🖭 🍴 ⑪ ⚓ 🅼 🏖 sand adj

Fr W exit A49 sp Isla Cristina & go thro town heading E. Fr E exit A49 at km 117 sp Lepe. In Lepe turn S on H4116 to La Antilla, then R on coast rd to Isla Cristina & site. 2*, Lge, pt shd, EHU (10) €4.28; gas; red long stay; 10% statics; phone; bus; ccard acc; CKE. *"Gd birdwatching, cycling; less cr than other sites in area in winter; poss untidy LS & ltd facs; poss diff for lge o'fits; friendly, helpful owner; san facs basic, poor; not rec."* **€30.00**   2019

ISLARES *1A4* (1km W Coastal) *43.40361, -3.31027*
Camping Playa Arenillas, Ctra Santander-Bilbao, Km 64, 39798 Islares (Cantabria) **942-86 31 52 or 609-44-21-67 (mob); cueva@mundivia.es; www.campingplayaarenillas.com**

⍾ 🆆 ♨ ▣ ✎ 🖭 🍴 ⑪ nr ⚓ 🅼 🏖 sand 100m

Exit A8 at km 156 Islares. Turn W on N634. Site on R at W end of Islares. Steep ent & sharp turn into site, exit less steep. 1*, Lge, mkd, pt shd, EHU (5A) €4.63 (poss no earth); gas; bbq; TV; 40% statics; phone; bus 500m; adv bkg rec; ccard acc; bike hire; horseriding; games area; CKE. *"Facs ltd LS & stretched in ssn; facs constantly cleaned; hot water to shwrs and washing up; rec arr early for choice of own pitch, and avoid Sat & Sun due to parked traff; conv Guggenheim Museum; excel NH for Bilbao ferry; beautiful setting."* **€30.60, 24 Mar-30 Sep.**   2016

JACA *3B2* (10km N Rural) *42.624191, -0.543496*
Solopuent Camping, Ctra Bescos de la Garcipollera s/n 22710, Castiello de Jaca **974 35 00 46 or 644 54 51 38; info@solopuent.com; www.solopuent.com**

🅃 ⍾ (htd) 🆆 ♨ ♿ ✎ 🖭 🦋 ⑪ 🍴 ⑪ nr ☕ ⚓ nr 🅼 🏊 (htd) 🖫 🏖 shgl

Fr N240 take N330A/N330 to Castiello de Jaca. Turn R and cross bdge over rv and take rd to site 450m on R. Sm, mkd, pt shd, EHU (10A) inc; gas; bbq (charcoal, elec, gas, sep area); cooking facs; twin axles; TV; 50% statics; phone; bus/train; Eng spkn; adv bkg acc; ccard acc; games area & rm. *"Excel loc beside rv & vill; clean facs; flat pitches; min 10A supply for aldi heating, c'van shwr & cooking; wonderful mountain views, rv walks, wildlife; gd cycle rtes; excel."* **€35.00, 1 Jan-5 Nov, 4 Dec-31 Dec.**   2019

"That's changed – Should I let the Club know?"

If you find something on site that's different from the site entry, fill in a report and let us know. See camc.com/europereport.

JACA *3B2* (2km W Urban) *42.56416, -0.57027*
Camping Victoria, Avda de la Victoria 34, 22700 Jaca (Huesca) **974-35 70 08; campingvictoria@ eresmas.com; www.campingvictoria.es**

⊞12 🅃 ⍾ 🆆 ♨ ▣ ✎ 🖭 🦋 🍴 ☕ 🅼 🏊 (htd)

Fr Jaca cent take N240 dir Pamplona, site on R. Med, mkd, pt shd, EHU (10A) €5; bbq; 80% statics; bus adj. *"Basic facs, but clean & well-maintained; friendly staff; conv NH/sh stay Somport Pass."* **€18.50**   2017

JAVEA/XABIA 4E2 (1km S Rural) 38.78333, 0.17294 **Camping Jávea,** Camí de la Fontana 10, 03730 Jávea (Alicante) **965-79 10 70; info@camping javea.es; www.campingjavea.es**

Exit N332 for Jávea on A132, cont in dir Port on CV734. At rndabt & Lidl supmkt, take slip rd to R immed after rv bdge sp Arenal Platjas & Cap de la Nau. Strt on at next rndabt to site sp & slip rd 100m sp Autocine. If you miss slip rd go back fr next rndabt. Lge, mkd, pt shd, EHU (8A) €4.56 (long lead rec); gas; bbq; red long stay; 15% statics; adv bkg acc; ccard acc; games area; tennis; CKE. *"Excel site & rest; variable pitch sizes/prices; some lge pitches - lge o'fits rec phone ahead; gd, clean san facs; mountain views; helpful staff; m'vans beware low trees; gd cycling; site a bit tired but gd."* **€35.00** 2017

See advertisement

JAVEA/XABIA 4E2 (3km S Coastal) 38.77058, 0.18207 **Camping El Naranjal,** Cami dels Morers 15, 03730 Jávea (Alicante) **965-79 29 89; info@campingel naranjal.com; www.campingelnaranjal.com**

Exit A7 junc 62 or 63 onto N332 València/Alicante rd. Exit at Gata de Gorgos to Jávea. Foll sp Camping Jávea/Camping El Naranjal. Access rd by tennis club, foll sp. Med, hdstg, mkd, pt shd, EHU (10A) inc (poss rev pol); gas; bbq; red long stay; TV; 35% statics; phone; bus 500m; Eng spkn; adv bkg acc; ccard acc; bike hire; tennis 300m; games rm; golf 3km; CKE. *"Gd scenery & beach; pitches poss tight lge o'fits; dogs free; excel rest; immac facs; tourist info - tickets sold; rec; ACSI rate."* **€33.50** 2017

LAREDO 1A4 (3km W Coastal) 43.41176, -3.45329 **Camping Playa del Regatón,** El Sable 8, 39770 Laredo (Cantabria) **942-60 69 95; info@camping playaregaton.com; www.campingplayaregaton.com**

Fr W leave A8 junc 172, under m'way to rndabt & take exit sp Calle Rep Colombia. In 800m turn L at traff lts, in further 800m turn L onto tarmac rd to end, passing other sites. Fr E leave at junc 172, at 1st rndabt take 2nd exit sp Centro Comercial N634 Colindres. At next rndabt take exit Calle Rep Colombia, then as above. 2*, Lge, mkd, pt shd, EHU (6-10A) €4.30; gas; red long stay; 75% statics; bus 600m; Eng spkn; adv bkg acc; ccard acc; horseriding nr; CKE. *"Clean site; sep area for tourers; wash up facs (cold water) every pitch; gd, modern facs; gd NH/sh stay (check opening times of office for EHU release); gd bird watching."* **€26.70,** 18 Mar-25 Sep. 2016

LEKEITIO 3A1 (3km S Coastal) 43.35071, -2.49260 **Camping Leagi,** Calle Barrio Leagi s/n, 48289 Mendexa (Vizcaya) **946-84 23 52; leagi@camping leagi.com; www.campingleagi.com**

Fr San Sebastian leave A8/N634 at Deba twd Ondarroa. At Ondarroa do not turn into town, but cont on BI633 beyond Berriatua, then turn R onto BI3405 to Lekeitio. Fr Bilbao leave A8/N634 at Durango & foll B1633 twd Ondarroa. Turn L after Markina onto BI3405 to Lekeitio - do not go via Ondarroa, foll sp to Mendexa & site. Steep climb to site & v steep tarmac ent to site. Only suitable for o'fits with v high power/weight ratio. Med, mkd, unshd, pt sl, serviced pitches; EHU (5A) €3.90 (rev pol); 80% statics; ccard acc; CKE. *"Ltd facs LS; tractor tow avail up to site ent; beautiful scenery; excel local beach; lovely town; gd views; gd walking; san facs under pressure due to many tents; bus to Bilbao & Gurnika."* **€39.00,** 1 Mar-1 Nov. 2019

LEON *1B3* (7km SE Urban) *42.5900, -5.5331* **Camping Ciudad de León**, Ctra N601, 24195 Golpejar de la Sobarriba 987-26 90 86; campingleon@yahoo.es; sites.google.com/site/campingleon/

🐕 €1.50 ♦♦ WD ▲ ⅃ & ⬚ ✎ / 🦋 ♈ ▼ ⑪ ⓐ ⬚ 🏛 ⚓ 📖

SE fr León on N601 twds Valladolid, L at top of hill at rndabt & Opel g'ge & foll site sp Golpejar de la Sobarriba; 500m after radio masts turn R at site sp. Narr track to site ent. Sm, shd, pt sl, EHU inc (6A) €3.60; gas; bus 200m; Eng spkn; adv bkg acc; bike hire; tennis; CKE. *"Clean, pleasant site; helpful, welcoming staff; access some sm pitches poss diff; easy access to León; shwrs need refurb (2015); ltd public trans to and fr town."* **€19.00, 1 Jun-20 Sep.** 2019

LINEA DE LA CONCEPCION, LA *2H3* (3.6km N Urban/ Coastal) *36.19167, -5.3350* **Camping Sureuropa**, Camino de Sobrevela s/n, 11300 La Línea de la Concepción (Cádiz) 956-64 35 87; info@ campingsureuropa.es; www.campingsureuropa.es

12 ♦♦ WD ▲ ⅃ ⬚ ✎ / ♈ 🌴 sand 500m

Fr AP7, ext junc 124. Use junc124 fr both dirs. Just bef Gibraltar turn R up lane, in 200m turn L into site. Fr N on AP7, exit junc 124 onto A383 dir La Línea; foll sp Santa Margarita thro to beach. Foll rd to R along sea front, site in approx 1km - no advance sp. App rd to site off coast rd poss floods after heavy rain. Med, hdg, mkd, hdstg, pt shd, EHU €4.30; phone; Eng spkn; adv bkg acc; site clsd 20 Dec-7 Jan; CKE. *"Clean, flat, pretty site; vg, modern san facs; sm pitches & tight site rds poss diff twin axles & l'ge o'fits; sports club adj; quiet but noise fr adj sports club; ideal for Gibraltar 4km; stay ltd to 4 days; wifi in recep only; sh stay only."* **€20.00** 2016

LLANES *1A4* (8km E Coastal) *43.39948, -4.65350* **Camping La Paz**, Ctra N634, Km 292, 33597 Playa de Vidiago (Asturias) 985-41 12 35; delfin@ campinglapaz.com; www.campinglapaz.eu

🐕 €2.50 ♦♦ WD ▲ ⅃ & ⬚ ✎ / MSP 🦋 ♈ ▼ ⑪ ⓐ 🏛 🌴 sand adj

Take Fr A8/N634/E70 turn R at sp to site bet km stone 292 & 293 bef Vidiago.Site access via narr 1km lane. Stop bef bdge & park on R, staff will tow to pitch. Narr site ent & steep access to pitches. Lge, mkd, shd, terr, EHU (9A) €4.82 (poss rev pol); gas; bbq; TV; phone; Eng spkn; adv bkg acc; ccard acc; fishing; golf 4km; watersports; games rm; horseriding; CKE. *"Exceptionally helpful owner & staff; sm pitches; gd, modern san facs; mountain sports; excel views; cliff top rest; superb beaches in area."* **€42.00, Easter-30 Sep.** 2017

LLANES *1A4* (3km W Coastal) *43.42500, -4.78944* **Camping Las Conchas de Póo**, Ctra General, 33509 Póo de Llanes (Asturias) 985-40 22 90 or 674-16 58 79 (mob); campinglasconchas@gmail.com; www.camping lasconchas.com

🐕 ♦♦ WD ▲ ⅃ ⬚ ✎ / 🦋 ♈ ⑪ ⬚ 🏛 🌴 sand adj

Exit A8/E70 at Llanes West junc 307 & foll sp. Site on rd AS263. 2*, Med, pt shd, sl, terr, EHU (6A) €3.20; 50% statics; phone; bus adj. *"Pleasant site; footpath to lovely beach; lovely coastal walk to Celorio; stn in Póo vill; gd pitches for tourers; gd clean san facs; gd WiFi at recep."* **€20.00, 1 Jun-15 Sep.** 2019

LLORET DE MAR *3B3* (1km SW Coastal) *41.6984, 2.8265* **Camping Santa Elena-Ciutat**, Ctra Blanes/ Lloret, 17310 Lloret de Mar (Gerona) 972-36 40 09; santaelana@betsa.es; www.betsa.es

12 ♦♦ ▲ ⅃ & ⬚ ✎ / 🦋 ♈ ▼ ⑪ ⓐ ⬚ 🏛 ⚓ 📖 shgl 600m

Exit A7 junc 9 dir Lloret. In Lloret take Blanes rd, site sp at km 10.5 on rd GI 682. V lge, pt sl, EHU (5A) €3.90; gas; phone; Eng spkn; games area; CKE. *"Ideal for teenagers; cash machine."* **€34.60** 2016

LOGRONO *3B1* (2km N Urban) *42.47122, -2.45493* **Camping La Playa**, Avda de la Playa 6, 26006 Logroño (La Rioja) 941-25 22 53; info@campinglaplaya.com; www.campinglaplaya.com

12 🐕 €2 ♦♦ ▲ ⅃ & ⬚ ✎ / MSP ▼ ⓐ ⬚ 🏛 ⚓

Leave Logroño by bdge 'Puente de Piedra' on N111, then turn L at rndabt into Camino de las Norias. Site well sp in town & fr N111, adj sports cent Las Norias, on N side of Rv Ebro. 1*, Med, hdg, shd, EHU (5A) €4.80; gas; sw nr; 80% statics; tennis; CKE. *"Sh walk to town cent; ltd facs LS & site poss clsd; vg; nr rest."* **€25.00** 2016

LUARCA *1A3* (1km NE Coastal) *43.54914, -6.52426* **Camping Los Cantiles**, Ctra N634, Km 502.7, 33700 Luarca (Asturias) 985-64 09 38; cantiles@camping loscantiles.com; www.campingloscantiles.com

12 🐕 €1 ♦♦ WD ▲ ⅃ & ⬚ ✎ / MSP 🦋 ♈ ▼ ⑪ ⓐ 🏛 🌴 shgl

On A8 exit junc 467 (sp Luarca/Barcia/Almuña), At rndabt foll sp to Luarca, after petrol stn turn R, foll sp to site. Not rec to ent town fr W. Not rec to foll sat nav as may take you up v steep & narr rd. On leaving site, retrace to main rd - do not tow thro **Luarca**. 3*, Med, hdg, pt shd, EHU inc (3-6A) €2-2.50; gas; red long stay; phone; Eng spkn; adv bkg acc; CKE. *"Site on cliff top; some narr site rds; pitches soft after rain; steep climb down to beach; 30 min walk to interesting town & port; pool 300m; wonderful setting; san fac's OK, water in shwrs v hot."* **€23.00** 2017

SPAIN

LUMBIER *3B1* (1.3km S Rural) *42.65111, -1.30222*
Camping Iturbero, Ctra N240 Pamplona-Huesca, 31440 Lumbier (Navarra) **948-88 04 05; iturbero@campingiturbero.com; www.campingiturbero.com**

SE fr Pamplona on N240 twds Yesa Reservoir. In 30km L on NA150 twds Lumbier. In 3.5km immed bef Lumbier turn R at rndabt then over bdge, 1st L to site, adj sw pool. Well sp fr N240. 2*, Med, hdg, mkd, hdstg, pt shd, EHU (5A) €4.95; gas; bbq; 25% statics; bus 1km; tennis; CKE. *"Beautiful, well-kept site; clean, basic facs; pool 100m; excel touring base; open w/end only Dec-Easter (poss fr Sep) but clsd 19 Dec-19 Feb; eagles & vultures in gorge & seen fr site; hang-gliding; helpful staff; Lumbier lovely sm town."* €27.40, 15 Mar-15 Dec. 2019

MADRID *1D4* (13km NE Urban) *40.45361, -3.60333*
Camping Osuna, Jardines de Aranjuez 1, 28042 Madrid **917-41 05 10; camping.osuna.madrid@microgest.es**

Fr M40, travelling S clockwise (anti-clockwise fr N or E) exit junc 8 at Canillejas sp 'Avda de Logroño'. Turn L under m'way, then R under rlwy, immed after turn R at traff lts. Site on L corner - white painted wall. Travelling N, leave M40 at junc 7 (no turn off at junc 8) sp Avda 25 Sep, U-turn at km 7, head S to junc 8, then as above. 2*, Med, hdg, mkd, pt shd, pt sl, EHU (6A) €4.85 (long lead rec); 10% statics; phone; Eng spkn; CKE. *"Sm pitches poss diff lge o'fits; poss neglected LS & facs tired (June 2010); poss travellers; conv city cent; busy; gd basic facs; metro to town 600m; easy walk to metro with frequent svr into Madrid."* €33.00 2015

MADRID *1D4* (13km S Urban) *40.31805, -3.68888*
Camping Alpha, Ctra de Andalucía N-IV, Km 12.4, 28906 Getafe (Madrid) **916-95 80 69; info@campingalpha.com; www.campingalpha.com**

Fr S on A4/E5 twd Madrid, leave at km 12B to W dir Ocaña & foll sp. Fr N on A4/E5 at km 13B to change dir back onto A4; then exit 12B sp 'Polígono Industrial Los Olivos' to site. 2*, Lge, hdstg, hdg, pt shd, EHU (15A) €5.90 (poss no earth); 20% statics; phone; Eng spkn; adv bkg acc; ccard acc; games area; tennis; CKE. *"Lorry depot adj; poss vehicle movements 24 hrs but minimal noise; bus & metro to Madrid 30-40 mins; sm pitches poss tight for space; vg, clean facs; helpful staff; NH or sh stay."* €28.00 2016

MANGA DEL MAR MENOR, LA *4G2* (3.5km W Urban) *37.6244, -0.7447* **Caravaning La Manga,** Autovia Cartagena - La Manga, exit 11, E-30370 La Manga del Mar Menor **968-56 30 19; lamanga@caravaning.es; www.caravaning.es**

Take Autovia CT-32 fr Cartagena to La Manga; take exit 800B twds El Algar/Murcia; keep L, merge onto Autovia MU312; cont to foll MU-312; cont onto Ctra a La Manga & cont onto Av Gran Via; site clearly sp. Lge, hdg, hdstg, pt shd, serviced pitches; EHU (10A) inc; bbq; 10% statics; bus to Murcia and Cartagena; Eng spkn; adv bkg acc; ccard acc; watersports; tennis; games rm. *"Immac, busy, popular site; Mar Menor shallow & warm lagoon; open air cinema & children's programme high ssn; lovely location & gd for golfers; horseridng nrby; recep open 24 hrs; Mar Menor well worth visiting; vg rest; gd for families; outdoor fitness; some narr site rds & trees - rec park in car park on arr & walk to find pitch; gd walking; gym; sauna; jacuzzi; mountain biking; bird sanctuary; poss lge rallies on site Dec-Mar; excel; friendly, helpful staff; immac facs."* €38.00 2016

See advertisement

MARBELLA *2H3* (14km E Coastal) *36.48881, -4.74294*
Kawan Village Cabopino, Ctra N340/A7, Km 194.7, 29600 Marbella (Málaga) **952-83 43 73; info@ campingcabopino.com; www.campingcabopino.com**

🏠12 🐕 €2 ♿ WC 🚿 ♿ 🔥 🚮 🛗 MSP 🍴 🍸 🕪 🦽 📶 🚵 ⛵ (covrd)

🏖 sand 200m

Fr E site is on N side of N340/A7; turn R at km 195 'Salida Cabopino' past petrol stn, site on R at rndabt. Fr W on A7 turn R at 'Salida Cabopino' km 194.7, go over bdge to rndabt, site strt over. NB Do not take sm exit fr A7 immed at 1st Cabopino sp. Lge, mkd, pt shd, pt sl, EHU (6-10A) inc (poss long lead req); bbq (elec, gas); TV; 50% statics; bus 100m; Eng spkn; ccard acc; golf driving range; archery; games area; games rm; watersports; CKE. *"V pleasant site set in pine woodland; rd noise & lge groups w/enders; marina 300m; busy, particularly w/end; varied pitch size, poss diff access lge o'fits, no o'fits over 11m high ssn; blocks req some pitches; gd, clean san facs; feral cats on site (2009)."* **€36.00, E21.**   **2016**

MARBELLA *2H3* (7km E Coastal) *36.50259, -4.80413*
Camping La Buganvilla, Ctra N340, Km 188.8, 29600 Marbella (Málaga) **952-83 56 21 or 952-83 19 73; info@campingbuganvilla.com; www.campingbuganvilla.com**

🏠12 🐕 €4 ♿ WC 🚿 ♿ 🔥 📶 🍴 🍸 🚵 ⛵ 🏖 sand 350m

E fr Marbella for 6km on N340/E15 twds Málaga. Pass site & cross over m'way at Elviria & foll site sp. Fr Málaga exit R off autovia immed after 189km marker. Lge, shd, pt sl, terr, EHU (16A) inc; gas; bbq; red long stay; TV; 40% statics; phone; Eng spkn; adv bkg acc; ccard acc; fishing; tennis; games rm; CKE. *"Relaxed, conv site; helpful staff; excel beach; no dogs Jul/Aug; bus stop to Marbella at ent; 20min walk to nice beach; bigger & more shaded pitches at top of site."* **€25.00**   **2016**

MARIA *4G1* (8km W Rural) *37.70823, -2.23609*
Camping Sierra de María, Ctra María a Orce, Km 7, Paraje La Piza, 04838 María (Málaga) **620-23 22 23; info@campingsierrademaria.com; www.campingsierrademaria.es**

🏠12 🐕 ♿ WC 🔥 ♿ 📶 🦋 🍸 🕪 🚵

Exit A92 at junc 408 to Vélez Rubio, Vélez Blanco & María. Foll A317 to María & cont dir Huéscar & Orce. Site on R. Med, mkd, pt shd, pt sl, EHU (16A) €3.75; 10% statics; adv bkg acc; ccard acc; bike hire; horseriding; CKE. *"Lovely, peaceful, ecological site in mountains; much wildlife; variable pitch sizes; facs poss stretched high ssn; v cold in winter; v helpful mgrs, gd food in rest."* **€23.00**   **2016**

MARINA, LA *4F2* (1.5km S Coastal) *38.12972, -0.65000* **Camping Internacional La Marina,** Ctra N332a, Km 76, 03194 La Marina (Alicante) **965-41 92 00; info@campinglamarina.com; www.lamarinaresort.com**

🏠12 🐕 €2.14 👫 (htd) WC 🚿 ♿ 🔥 🚮 📶 MSP 🍴 🍸 🕪 🦽 📶 🚵 🏊 (covrd, htd) 🏖 sand 500m

Fr N332 S of La Marina turn E twd sea at rndabt onto Camino del Cementerio. At next rndabt turn S onto N332a & foll site sp along Avda de l'Alegría. 5*, V lge, hdstg, mkd, hdg, shd, terr, serviced pitches; EHU (10A) €3.21; gas; red long stay; TV; 10% statics; phone; bus 50m; Eng spkn; adv bkg acc; ccard acc; watersports; games rm; solarium; fishing; sauna; tennis; games area; waterslide; CKE. *"Popular winter site - almost full late Feb; v busy w/end; disco; clean, high quality facs; various pitch sizes/prices; fitness cent; bus fr gate; gd security; car wash; security; excel rest; gd site; v helpful; hire cars avail; fantastic site."* **€65.00**   **2017**

MASNOU, EL *3C3* (0.8km W Coastal) *41.4753, 2.3033* **Camping Masnou,** Ctra NII, Km 633, Carrer de Camil Fabra 33, 08320 El Masnou (Barcelona) **935-55 15 03; masnou@campingsonline.es; www.campingmasnoubarcelona.com**

🏠12 🐕 👫 🔥 ♿ 📶 MSP 🍴 🦽 🚵 🚵 ⛵ 🏖 sand adj

App site fr N on N11. Pass El Masnou rlwy stn on L & go strt on at traff lts. Site on R on N11 after km 633. Not clearly sp. 2*, Med, shd, pt sl, EHU €5.88; bbq; phone; bus 300m, train to Barcelona nr; Eng spkn; ccard acc; CKE. *"Gd pitches, no awnings; some sm pitches, poss shared; facs vg, though poss stretched when site busy; no restriction on NH vehicle movements; well-run, friendly site but v tired; gd service LS; rlwy line bet site & excel beach - subway avail; excel train service to Barcelona; excel pool."* **€35.00**   **2017**

MAZAGON *2G2* (10km E Coastal) *37.09855, -6.72650* **Camping Doñana Playa,** Ctra San Juan del Puerto-Matalascañas, Km 34.6, 21130 Mazagón (Huelva) **959-53 62 81; info@campingdonana.com; www.campingdonana.com**

🏠12 🐕 €4.10 👫 WC 🔥 ♿ 📶 🍴 🕪 🚵 🦽 🚵 🏊 🏖 sand 300m

Fr A49 exit junc 48 at Bullullos del Condado onto A483 sp El Rocio, Matalascañas. At coast turn R sp Mazagón, site on L in 16km. V lge, mkd, hdstg, pt shd, EHU (6A) €5.20; 10% statics; bus 500m; adv bkg acc; games area; site clsd 14 Dec-14 Jan; watersports; bike hire; tennis; CKE. *"Pleasant site amongst pine trees but lack of site care LS; ltd LS; lge pitches but poss soft sand; quiet but v noisy Fri/Sat nights; new (2014) lge shwr block on lower pt of site."* **€35.00**   **2019**

MENDIGORRIA 3B1 (0.5km SW Rural) 42.62416, -1.84277 **Camping El Molino,** Ctra Larraga, 31150 Mendigorría (Navarra) **948-34 06 04; info@ campingelmolino.com; www.campingelmolino.com**

🏕🐕🟥 WD ♿ ⚓ ⚑ 🚿 ♨ 🅿 🍴 🛈 🎯 🛒 🚮 🎣 ⛵ 🛶

Fr Pamplona on N111 turn L at 25km in Puente la Reina onto NA601 sp Mendigorría. Site sp thro vill dir Larraga. 1*, Med, mkd, pt shd, serviced pitches; EHU (6A) inc; gas; bbq; TV; phone; adv bkg acc; ccard acc; games area; canoe hire; waterslide; tennis; clsd 23 Dec-14 Jan & poss Mon-Thurs fr Nov to Feb, phone ahead to check; CKE. *"Gd clean san facs; solar water heating - water poss only warm; vg leisure facs; v ltd facs LS; for early am dep LS, pay night bef & obtain barrier key; friendly, helpful staff; statics (sep area); lovely medieval vill."* €29.60, 1 Feb-15 Dec.   2018

MERIDA 2E3 (4km NE Urban) 38.93558, -6.30426 **Camping Mérida,** Avda de la Reina Sofia s/n, 06800 Mérida (Badajoz) **924-30 34 53; camping-merida. negocio.site**

12 🐕 €1.65 🏕 WD ♿ ⚓ 🚿 ♨ 🚿 🦋 🍴 🛈 🎯 🛒 🚮 🎣

Fr E on A5/E90 exit junc 333/334 to Mérida, site on L in 2km. Fr W on A5/E90 exit junc 346, site sp. Fr N exit A66/E803 at junc 617 onto A5 E. Leave at junc 334, site on L in 1km twd Mérida. Fr S on A66-E803 app Mérida, foll Cáceres sp onto bypass to E; at lge rndabt turn R sp Madrid; site on R after 2km. 2*, Med, mkd, pt shd, pt sl, EHU (6A) €3.30 (long lead poss req & poss rev pol); gas; TV; 10% statics; phone; CKE. *"Roman remains & National Museum of Roman Art worth visit; poss diff lge o'fits manoeuvring onto pitch due trees & soft grnd after rain; ltd facs & run down in LS; conv NH; taxi to town costs 5-9 euros; grass pitches; bread can be ordered fr rest; poss nightclub noise at w/end."* €21.00   2019

MIAJADAS 2E3 (14km SW Rural) 39.09599, -6.01333 **Camping-Restaurant El 301,** Ctra Madrid-Lisbon, Km 301, 10100 Miajadas (Cáceres) **927-34 79 14; camping301@hotmail.com; www.camping301.com**

12 🏕 WD ⚓ 🚿 ♨ 🚿 🍴 🛈 🎯 🛒 🚮 ⛵

Leave A5/E90 just bef km stone 301 & foll sp 'Via de Servicio' with rest & camping symbols; site in 500m. Med, pt shd, EHU (8A) €5.50 (poss no earth); gas; TV; phone; ccard acc; CKE. *"Well-maintained, clean site; grass pitches; OK wheelchair users but steps to pool; gd NH; gd bird life."* €24.00   2016

MOJACAR 4G1 (9km S Rural) 37.06536, -1.86864 **Camping Sopalmo,** Sopalmo, 04638 Mojácar (Almería) **950-47 84 13; 660-73 53 68; camping sopalmo@gmail.com; campingsopalmo.com**

12 🐕 €1 🏕 WD ♿ ⚓ 🚿 ♨ 🚿 🍴 🛈 🎯 🚮 ⛵ shgl 1.7km

Exit A7/E15 at junc 520 onto AL6111 sp Mojácar. Fr Mojácar turn S onto A1203/AL5105 dir Carboneras, site sp on W of rd about 1km S of El Agua del Medio. Sm, mkd, hdstg, pt shd, terr, EHU (6A); gas; bbq; twin axles; 10% statics; Eng spkn; adv bkg acc; CKE. *"Clean, pleasant, popular site; remote & peaceful; friendly owner; gd walking in National Park; lovely san facs; gd."* €31.00   2019

MONCOFA 3D2 (2km E Urban/Coastal) 39.80861, -0.12805 **Camping Mon Mar,** Camino Serratelles s/n, 12593 Platja de Moncófa (Castellón) **964-58 85 92; campingmonmar@hotmail.com**

12 🐕 (htd) WD ⚓ 🚿 ♿ ♨ 🚿 🦋 🍴 🛈 🎯 🛒 🚮 🎣 ⛵ 🛶

☂ shgl 200m

Exit 49 fr A7 or N340, foll sp Moncófa Platja passing thro Moncófa & foll sp beach & tourist info thro 1-way system. Site sp, adj Aqua Park. 2*, Lge, hdstg, hdg, pt shd, serviced pitches; EHU (6A) inc; gas; bbq; red long stay; 80% statics; phone; bus 300m; Eng spkn; adv bkg acc; ccard acc; CKE. *"Helpful owner & staff; rallies on site Dec-Apr; mini-bus to stn & excursions; sunshades over pitches poss diff high o'fits; excel clean, tidy site."* €32.00   2019

MONTBLANC 3C2 (1.5km NE Rural) 41.37743, 1.18511 **Camping Montblanc Park,** Ctra Prenafeta, Km 1.8, 43400 Montblanc **977-86 25 44 or 492 28 38 48; montblancpark@capfun.com; www.montblancpark. com**

12 🐕 €4.50 🏕 (htd) WD ♿ ⚓ 🚿 ♨ 🚿 MSP 🍴 🛈 🎯 🛒 🚮 🎣 ⛵ 🛶

Exit AP2 junc 9 sp Montblanc; foll sp Montblanc/ Prenafeta/TV2421; site on L on TV2421. 4*, Med, hdg, pt shd, pt sl, terr, EHU (10A) inc; bbq; red long stay; 50% statics; phone; Eng spkn; adv bkg acc; ccard acc; CKE. *"Excel site; excel facs; lovely area; many static pitches only suitable for o'fits up to 7m; Cistercian monestaries nrby; conv NH Andorra."* €39.50   2019

MONTERROSO 1B2 (1km S Rural) 42.78720, -7.84414 **Camp Municipal de Monterroso,** A Peneda, 27560 Monterroso (Lugo) **982-37 75 01; campingmonterroso@aged-sl.com; www.camping monterroso.com**

🏕🐕 WD ⚓ 🚿 ♨ 🚿 🦋 🍴 🛈 🛒

Fr N540 turn W onto N640 to Monterroso. Fr town cent turn S on LU212. In 100m turn sharp R then downhill for 1km; 2 sharp bends to site. Sm, hdg, mkd, pt shd, pt sl, EHU (10A) €3.50; Eng spkn; games area; CKE. *"Helpful staff; v quiet & ltd facs LS; pool adj; vg."* €21.00, 30 Mar-24 Sep.   2017

MOTILLA DEL PALANCAR 4E1 (10km NW Rural) 39.61241, -2.10185 **Camping Pantapino,** Paraje de Hontanar, s/n, 16115 Olmedilla de Alarcón (Cuenca) **969-33 92 33 or 676-47 85 40 (mob); pantapina@ hotmail.com; www.campingpantapino.eu**

12 🐕 €1.50 🏕 WD ♿ ⚓ 🚿 ♨ 🚿 MSP 🦋 🍴 🛈 🎯 🛒 🛶

Fr cent of Motilla foll NIII; turn NW onto rd CM2100 at sp for Valverde de Júcar; site on L just bef 12km marker. 2*, Med, mkd, pt shd, pt sl, serviced pitches; EHU (6A) €4; gas; bbq; 40% statics; adv bkg acc; ccard acc; tennis; bike hire; horseriding; games area; CKE. *"Clean, attractive site but tatty statics; poor facs; gd size pitches; resident owners hospitable; poss clsd in winter - phone ahead to check; vg; san facs old but clean; ltd facs LS; gd NH; poss problem with earth on elec."* €18.00   2019

MOTRIL *2H4* (3km SW Urban/Coastal) *36.71833, -3.54616* **Camping Playa de Poniente de Motril,** 18600 Motril (Granada) **958-82 03 03; info@camping playadeponiente.com; www.campingplayade poniente.com**

12 ⊞ €1.50 ♚♟(htd) �ⓦⅅ ⛺ ♨ ♿ 🗑 ⊘ �🅟 🍽 ⓗ♨ 🏊 ⏏ 🔥 ♒ 🚣adj

Turn off coast rd N340 to port bef flyover; at rndabt take rd for Motril. Turn R in town, site sp. Lge, hdstg, mkd, pt shd, EHU (6-10) €3.35; gas; bbq (elec, gas); red long stay; 40% statics; bus; Eng spkn; adv bkg acc; ccard acc; bike hire; games rm; horseriding; tennis; golf; games area. *"Well-appointed site but surrounded by blocks of flats; gd, clean facs; helpful recep; gd shop; access diff for lge o'fits; poss lge flying beetles; excel long stay winter; lovely promenade with dedicated cycle track."* **€31.70**   2017

MUNDAKA *3A1* (1km S Coastal) *43.39915, -2.69620* **Camping Portuondo,** Ctra Amorebieta-Bermeo, Km 43, 48360 Mundaka (Bilbao) **946-87 77 01; recepcion@campingportuondo.com; www.camping portuondo.com**

12 ♚ ♚♟ ⛺ ♨ ⊘ 🍽 ⓗ♨ 🏊 ⏏ 🔥 ♒ 🚣500m

Fr Bermeo pass Mundaka staying on main rd, do not enter Mundaka. Stay on Bl-2235 sp Gernika. After approx 1km site on L down steep slip rd. Med, pt shd, terr, EHU (6A) €4.20; 30% statics; train 800m; adv bkg rec; ccard acc; site clsd end Jan-mid Feb. *"Excel clean, modern facs; pitches tight not suitable for lge o'fits; popular with surfers; conv Bilbao by train; site suitable sm m'vans only; v ltd touring space; ent is very steep single track."* **€35.00**   2016

MUROS *1B1* (7km W Coastal) *42.78100, 9.11100* **Camping Ancoradoiro,** Ctra Corcubión Muros, Km 7.2, 15250 Louro (La Coruña) **981 87 88 97; wolfgangh@ hotmail.es or campingancora@outlook.es; www.campingancoradoiro.com**

♚♟ ⓦⅅ ⛺ ♨ ⊘ 🦋 🍽 nr ⓗ♨ 🔥 🔥 🚣sand 500m

Foll AC550 W fr Muros. Site on L (S), well sp. Immed inside ent arch, to thro gate on L. 1*, Med, hdg, mkd, pt shd, terr, EHU (6-15A) €3.50; phone; bus 500m; adv bkg acc; watersports; CKE. *"Excel, lovely, well-run, well-kept site; superb friendly site on headland bet 2 sandy beaches; welcoming owner; excel rest; excel san facs; poss diff for lge o'fits; beautiful beaches; scenic area."* **€24.00, 25 Apr-16 Sep.**   2019

NAJERA *3B1* (0.6km S Urban) *42.41310, -2.73145* **Camping El Ruedo,** San Julián 24, 26300 Nájera (La Rioja) **941-36 01 02; www.campingslarioja.es**

♚♟(htd) ⓦⅅ ⛺ ♨ ⊘ 🦋 🍽 ⓗ♨ 🔥 🔥 ✎

Take Nájera town dirs off N120. In town turn L bef x-ing bdge. Site sp. Sm, pt shd, EHU (10-16A) €3 (rev pol & poss no earth); gas; TV; phone; bus 200m; adv bkg acc; ccard acc; CKE. *"Pleasant site in quiet location, don't be put off by 1st impression of town; monastery worth visit, some pitches in former bullring; san facs tired; many trees, could be diff for lge o'fits."* **€26.00, 1 Apr-10 Sep.**   2016

NAVAJAS *3D2* (1km W Rural) *39.87489, -0.51034* **Camping Altomira,** Carretera, CV-213 Navajas Km. 1, E-12470 Navajas (Castellón) **964-71 32 11; reservas@ campingaltomira.com; www.campingaltomira.com**

12 ♚ ♚♟(htd) ⓦⅅ ⛺ ♨ ♿ 🗑 ⊘ 🅟 🍽 ⓗ♨ 🔥 🔥 🔥 ♒(htd) 🚣

Exit A23/N234 at junc 33 to rndabt & take CV214 dir Navajas. In approx 2km turn L onto CV213, site on L just past R turn into vill, sp. 4*, Med, hdstg, pt shd, terr, serviced pitches; EHU (6A) inc; gas; bbq; red long stay; TV; 70% statics; phone; bus 500m; Eng spkn; adv bkg acc; ccard acc; games rm; tennis; bike hire; fishing; CKE. *"Friendly welcome; panoramic views fr upper level (steep app) but not rec for lge o'fits due tight bends & ramped access/kerb to some pitches; gd birdwatching, walking, cycling; vg, useful NH & longer; excel; stunnng waterfall with sw nrby; site renovated; excel pitches, fully serviced, new excel san facs (2019); gd loc."* **€32.50, E18.**   2019

NERJA *2H4* (4km E Rural) *36.76035, -3.83490* **Nerja Camping,** Ctra Vieja Almeria, Km 296.5, Camp de Maro, 29787 Nerja (Málaga) **952-52 97 14; info@ nerjacamping.com; www.nerjacamping.com**

12 ♚♟ ⓦⅅ ⛺ ♨ 🗑 ⊘ 🍽 ⓗ♨ 🔥 🔥 🏊 🚣sand 2km

On N340, cont past sp on L for 200m around RH corner, bef turning round over broken white line. Foll partly surfaced rd to site on hillside. Fr Almuñécar on N340, site on R approx 20km. Med, pt shd, pt sl, terr, EHU (5A) €3.75 (check earth); gas; red long stay; Eng spkn; adv bkg rec; site clsd Oct; bike hire; CKE. *"5 mins to Nerja caves; mkt Tue; annual carnival 15 May; diff access lge o'fits; gd horseriding; site rds steep but gd surface; gd views; friendly owners."* **€24.00**   2016

NOJA *1A4* (20km W Coastal) *43.46306, -3.72379* **Camping Derby Loredo,** Calle Bajada a lay Playa, 19 39160 Loredo **942 504106; info@camping loredo.com; campingloredo.com**

12 ♚ €2 ♚♟ ⓦⅅ ⛺ ♨ 🗑 ⊘ 🅟 🍽 🔥 🔥nr 🔥 🚣sand adj

Fr Santander on S10 twrd Bilbao. L at J12, foll CA141 to Pedrena/Somo. After Somo L onto CA440 Loredo. On ent Loredo L sp @400m Playa Deloredo.' Med, mkd, pt shd, EHU; gas; twin axles; 70% statics; Eng spkn; ccard acc. *"Gd loc by beach; watersports; not suitable for lge o'fits; surf board hire; busy; friendly site with fams and surfers; gd."* **€27.00**   2017

NOJA 1A4 (1km NW Coastal) 43.49011, -3.53636
Camping Playa Joyel, Playa del Ris, 39180 Noja (Cantabria) **942-63 00 81; info@playajoyel.com; www.playajoyel.com**

🚻 ⬚ ⬚ ♨ ⬚ ⬚ ♿ ⬚ ⬚ ⬚ ⓘ ⬚ ⬚ ⬚ ⬚ ⬚ ⬚ sand adj

Fr Santander or Bilbao foll sp A8/E70 (toll-free). Approx 15km E of Solares exit m'way junc 184 at Beranga onto CA147 N twd Noja & coast. On o'skirts of Noja turn L sp Playa del Ris, (sm brown sp) foll rd approx 1.5km to rndabt, site sp to L, 500m fr rndabt. Fr Santander take S10 for approx 8km, then join A8/E70. 4*, V lge, mkd, pt shd, pt sl, EHU (6A) €6.30; gas; bbq; TV; 40% statics; phone; Eng spkn; adv bkg acc; ccard acc; sailing; windsurfing; jacuzzi; tennis; games rm; CKE. *"Well-organised site on sheltered bay; cash dispenser; very busy high ssn; pleasant staff; hairdresser; car wash; no o'fits over 8m high ssn; gd, clean facs; superb pool & beach; recep 0800-2200; some narr site rds with kerbs; midnight silence enforced; highly rec."* €48.30, 3 Apr-27 Sep, E05.
2019

NUEVALOS 3C1 (1km N Rural) 41.21846, -1.79211
Camping Lago Park, Ctra De Alhama de Aragón a Cillas, Km 39, 50210 Nuévalos (Zaragoza) **976-84 90 38; lagoresort@gmail.com; www.lagoresort.com**

12 🐕 🚻 ⬚ ⬚ ♨ ⬚ ⬚ Ⴤ nr ⓘ ⬚ ⬚ nr ⬚ ⬚

Fr E on A2/E90 exit junc 231 to Nuévalos, turn R sp Madrid. Site 1.5km on L when ent Nuévalos. Fr W exit junc 204, site well sp. Steep ent fr rd. 3*, V lge, hdg, mkd, pt shd, terr, EHU (10A) €5.40; gas; bbq; red long stay; 10% statics; bus 500m; adv bkg acc; fishing; games area; boating; CKE. *"Nr Monasterio de Piedra & Tranquera Lake; excel facs on top terr, but stretched high ssn & poss long, steepish walk; lake nrby; ltd facs LS; gd birdwatching; bar 500m; only site in area; gd; very friendly owner; an oasis en rte to Madrid in picturesque setting; vg rest; gd welcome; pool not open yet (2016); rec."* €19.00
2016

OCHAGAVIA 3A1 (0.5km S Rural) 42.90777, -1.08750
Camping Osate, Ctra Salazar s/n, 31680 Ochagavia (Navarra) **948-89 01 84; info@campingosate.net; www.campingosate.net**

12 🐕 ⬚ €2 🚻 ⬚ ⬚ ⬚ ♨ ⬚ ⬚ Ⴤ ⓘ ⬚ ⬚

On N135 SE fr Auritz, turn L onto NA140 & cont for 24km bef turning L twd Ochagavia on NA140. Site sp in 2km on R, 500m bef vill. Med, mkd, pt shd, serviced pitches; EHU (4A) €5.50; gas; bbq; 50% statics; Eng spkn. *"Attractive, remote vill; gd, well-maintained site; touring pitches under trees, sep fr statics; facs ltd & poss stretched high ssn; site clsd 3 Nov-15 Dec & rec phone ahead LS; facs require maintenance (2018); TO v helpful; gd walks fr site."* €22.00
2018

OCHAGAVIA 3A1 (7km S Rural) 42.85486, -1.09766
Camping Murkuzuria, 31453 Esparza de Salazar **948-89 01 90 or 661-08 87 35; campingesparza@gmail.com; www.campingmurkuzuria.com**

🚻 ⬚ ⬚ ♨ ⬚ ⬚ Ⴤ ⬚ Ⴤ ⓘ ⬚ ⬚

Fr N or S on Pic d'Orhy rte thro Pyrenees, NA178 (Spain)/D26(France). Situated in vill. Pamplona approx 80km. Med, mkd, pt shd, EHU; bbq; twin axles; TV; phone; bus adj; Eng spkn; adv bkg acc. *"Discounted forest passes avail for Foret d'Iraty; excel."* €19.00, 15 May-30 Oct.
2015

OLIVA 4E2 (2km E Coastal) 38.93278, -0.09778
Camping Kiko Park, Calle Assagador de Carro 2, 46780 Playa de Oliva (València) **962-85 09 05; info@kikopark.com; www.kikopark.com**

12 🐕 €3.10 🚻 (htd) ⬚ ⬚ ⬚ ♨ ⬚ ⬚ ⬚ Ⴤ ⬚ ⬚ ⓘ ⬚ ⬚ ⬚ ⬚ (covrd) ⬚ ⬚ sand adj

Exit AP7/E15 junc 61; fr toll turn R at T-junc onto N332.At rndabt turn L foll sp Platjas; next rdbt take 1st exit sp Platja; next rndabt foll sp Kiko Park. **Do not drive thro Oliva. Access poss diff on app rds due humps.** Lge, hdstg, mkd, hdg, shd, serviced pitches; EHU (16A) inc; gas; bbq; red long stay; phone; Eng spkn; adv bkg acc; ccard acc; horseriding nr; watersports; games rm; bike hire; fishing; games area; tennis; windsurfing school; golf nr; CKE. *"Gd, family-run site; whirlpool; spa; very helpful staff; vg, clean san facs; excel rest in Michelin Guide; pitch price variable (lge pitches avail); cash machine; beauty cent; access tight to some pitches."* €66.00, E20.
2019

OROPESA 3D2 (4.2km N Coastal) 40.12125, 0.15848
Camping Didota, Avenida de la Didota s/n, 12594 Oropesa del Mar (Castellón) **964 31 95 51; info@campingdidota.es; www.campingdidota.es**

12 🐕 🚻 ⬚ ⬚ ♨ ⬚ ♿ ⬚ ⬚ ⓘ ⬚ ⬚ ⬚ ⬚ ⬚ sand

N on rd E-15 fr València to Barcelona, bear L at exit 45 sp Oropesa del Mar. Turn L onto N-340. Turn R at next exit, then cont strt at rndabt onto on Avenida La Ratlla. Foll camping sp. Med, pt shd, EHU (6-10A) €4.30; gas; 10% statics; adv bkg acc; ccard acc. *"Gd site, helpful friendly staff; excel pool."* €45.00
2019

OROPESA 3D2 (3km NE Coastal) 40.12786, 0.16088
Camping Torre La Sal, Camí L'Atall s/n, 12595 Ribera de Cabanes (Castellón) **964-31 95 96; info@campingtorrelasal.com; www.campingtorrelasal.com**

12 🐕 (except Jul/Aug) 🚻 (htd) ⬚ ⬚ ⬚ ♨ ⬚ ♿ ⬚ ⬚ ⬚ Ⴤ ⬚ ⬚ ⓘ ⬚ ⬚ Ⴤ nr ⬚ ⬚ (covrd, htd) ⬚ ⬚ shgl adj

Leave AP7 at exit 44 or 45 & take N340 twd Tarragona. Foll camp sp fr km 1000.1 stone. **Do not confuse with Torre La Sal 2 or Torre Maria.** 1*, Lge, hdstg, mkd, hdg, pt shd, EHU (10A) €4.20; gas; bbq; red long stay; TV; 10% statics; bus 200m; Eng spkn; adv bkg acc; ccard acc; tennis; games area; CKE. *"Clean, well-maintained, peaceful site; elec metered for long stays; night security guard."* €28.90
2019

OROPESA *3D2* (3.5km NE Coastal) *40.1275, 0.15972*
Bravo Playa Camping Resort, Cami L'Atall s/n,
12595 Ribera de Cabanes (Castellón) **964-31 95 67;
camping@bravoplaya.com; www.bravoplaya.com**

[symbols] **12** [symbols] (htd) [symbols]

[symbols] (covrd, htd) [symbol] shgl adj

**Leave AP7 at exit 45 & take N340 twd Tarragona. Foll
camp sp fr km 1000 stone. Site adj Torre La Sal 1.**
1*, Lge, hdstg, mkd, hdg, pt shd, serviced pitches; EHU
(10A) inc; gas; red long stay; TV; 10% statics; Eng spkn;
adv bkg acc; games area; tennis; sauna; CKE. *"Vg, clean,
peaceful, well-run site; lger pitches nr pool; library; more
mature c'vanners very welcome; many dogs; poss diff for
lge o'fits & m'vans; excel rest; excel beach with dunes;
excel site, spotless facs, highly rec."* **€60.00**   **2019**

PALAFRUGELL *3B3* (5km E Coastal) *41.9005, 3.1893*
Kim's Camping, Calle Font d'en Xeco s/n, 17211
Llafranc (Gerona) **972-30 11 56; info@campingkims.
com; www.campingkims.com**

[symbols]

[symbol] sand 500m

**Exit AP7 at junc 6 Gerona Nord if coming fr France,
or junc 9 fr S dir Palamós. Foll sp for Palafrugell,
Playa Llafranc. Site is 500m N of Llafranc.** 3*, Lge,
hdg, mkd, hdstg, shd, sl, terr, EHU (5A) inc; gas; bbq
(gas); red long stay; TV; 10% statics; phone; Eng spkn;
adv bkg acc; ccard acc; watersports; golf 10km; games
area; excursions; tennis 500m; games rm; CKE. *"Excel,
well-organised, friendly, fam run site; steep site rds,
new 2nd ent fr dual c'way fr Palafrugell to llafranc
for lge o'fits & steps to rd to beach; bike hire 500m;
guarded; discount in high ssn for stays over 1 wk; excel,
modern san facs; beautiful coastal area; mostly gd size
pitches."* **€51.00, 14 Apr-24 Sep.**   **2017**

PALAFRUGELL *3B3* (5km S Coastal) *41.88879,
3.17928* **Camping Moby Dick,** Carrer de la Costa
Verda 16-28, 17210 Calella de Palafrugell (Gerona)
**972-61 43 07; info@campingmobydick.com;
www.campingmobydick.com**

[symbols] €3.30 [symbols]

[symbol] shgl 100m

**Fr Palafrugell foll sps to Calella. At rndabt just bef
Calella turn R, then 4th L, site clearly sp on R.** Med,
hdstg, pt shd, sl, terr, EHU (10A); TV; 15% statics;
phone; bus 100m; Eng spkn; adv bkg acc; ccard
acc; CKE. *"Nice views fr upper terraces; gd rest;
very friendly; very pretty sm resort; lovely coastal
walks; gd value; excel; lovely sea views; great site."*
€35.00, 25 Mar-30 Sep.   **2016**

PALAMOS *3B3* (2km NE Coastal) *41.87277, 3.15055*
Camping Benelux, Paratge Torre Mirona s/n, 17230
Palamós (Gerona) **972-31 55 75; www.cbenelux.com**

[symbols] sand 1km

**Turn E off Palamós-La Bisbal rd (C66/C31) at junc
328. Site in 800m on minor metalled rd, twd sea at
Playa del Castell.** Lge, hdstg, mkd, pt shd, terr, EHU
(10A) €6.90; gas; bbq; red long stay; TV; 30% statics;
phone; Eng spkn; adv bkg acc; ccard acc; CKE. *"In pine
woods; many long stay British/Dutch; friendly owner;
safe dep; clean facs poss ltd LS; car wash; currency
exchange; poss flooding in heavy rain; rough grnd;
marvellous walking/cycling area; many little coves."*
€36.70, 24 Mar-25 Sep.   **2016**

PALAMOS *3B3* (3km W Coastal) *41.84700, 3.09861*
Eurocamping, Avda de Catalunya 15, 17252 Sant
Antoni de Calonge (Gerona) **972-65 08 79; info@
euro-camping.com; www.euro-camping.com**

[symbols] €4 [symbols]

[symbol] sand 300m

**Exit A7 junc 6 dir Palamós on C66 & Sant Feliu C31.
Take exit Sant Antoni; on ent Sant Antoni turn R at
1st rndabt. Visible fr main rd at cent of Sant Antoni.**
1*, V lge, mkd, hdg, shd, serviced pitches; EHU (6A)
inc; bbq; red long stay; TV; 15% statics; phone; Eng
spkn; adv bkg acc; ccard acc; games area; games rm;
tennis; golf 7km; waterpark. *"Excel facs for families;
fitness rm; doctor Jul & Aug; car wash; lots to do in
area; excel; lots of ssnal pitches; immac san facs;
generous flat pitches; waterpark 5km; helpful, friendly
staff."* **€54.00, 28 Apr-17 Sep.**   **2017**

PALS *3B3* (6km NE Coastal) *42.00120, 3.19388*
Camping Playa Brava, Playa Pals, 17256 Pals
(Gerona) **972-63 68 94; info@playabrava.com;
www.playabrava.com**

[symbols] sand adj

**App Pals on rd 650 fr N or S. Avoid Pals cent. Fr by-
pass take rd E sp Playa de Pals at rndabt. In 4km
turn L opp shops, in 400m turn L past golf course,
site on L bef beach. Avoid Begur & coast rd.**
3*, Lge, shd, EHU inc; gas; adv bkg acc; tennis; car
wash; bike hire. *"Guarded; gd facs for children &
families."* **€34.00, 15 May-12 Sep, E35.**   **2016**

PALS *3B3* (1km E Rural) *41.95541, 3.15780* **Camping
Resort Mas Patoxas,** Ctra Torroella-Palafrugell, Km 339,
17256 Pals (Gerona) **972-63 69 28; info@camping
maspatoxas.com; www.campingmaspatoxas.com**

[symbols] **12** [symbols] €3.60 [symbols] (htd) [symbols]

[symbols] sand 4km

**AP7 exit 6 onto C66 Palamós/La Bisbal, turn L via
Torrent to Pals. Turn R & site on R almost opp old
town of Pals on rd to Torroella de Montgri. Or fr
Palafrugell on C31 turn at km 339.** 3*, Lge, mkd,
shd, terr, serviced pitches; EHU (5A) inc; gas; red long
stay; TV; phone; Eng spkn; adv bkg req; ccard acc; bike
hire; games area; tennis; site clsd 14 Dec-16 Jan; golf
4km; CKE. *"Excel; recep clsd Monday LS; gd security."*
€47.00, E45.   **2015**

"I need an on-site restaurant"

We do our best to make sure site information is correct, but it is always best to check any must-have facilities are still available or will be open during your visit.

PALS *3B3* (4km E Rural) *41.98555, 3.18194* **Camping Cypsela**, Rodors 7, 17256 Playa de Pals (Gerona) **972-66 76 96; info@cypsela.com; www.cypsela.com**

♦♦♦ WD ♣♣♣🛠🅿/MRP🕴️♀️⛺ฅ♨️🚐🏊🏄 sand 1.5km

Exit AP7 junc 6, rd C66 dir Palamós. 7km fr La Bisbal take dir Pals & foll sp Playa/Platja de Pals, site sp. 5*, V lge, hdstg, mkd, hdg, shd, serviced pitches; EHU (6-10A) inc; gas; bbq; red long stay; TV; 60% statics; Eng spkn; adv bkg acc; ccard acc; tennis; golf 1km; games rm; bike hire; CKE. "Noise levels controlled after midnight; excel san facs; mini golf & other sports; free bus to beach; private bthrms avail; 4 grades of pitch/price (highest price shown); vg site." €56.00, 4 May-10 Sep, E36. 2016

PAMPLONA *3B1* (7km N Rural) *42.85776, -1.62250* **Camping Ezcaba**, Ctra a Francia, km 2,5, 31194 Eusa-Oricain (Navarre) **948-33 03 15; info@campingezcaba.com; www.campingezcaba.com**

12 🔥€2.95 ♦♦♦♣♣🛠⛱/♀️⛺ฅ♨️🚐🏊🏄

Fr N leave AP15 onto NA30 (N ring rd) to N121A sp Francia/Iruña. Pass Arre & Oricáin, turn L foll site sp 500m on R dir Berriosuso. Site on R in 500m - fairly steep ent. Or fr S leave AP15 onto NA32 (E by-pass) to N121A sp Francia/Iruña, then as above. Med, mkd, pt shd, pt sl, EHU (10A) €5.50; gas; phone; bus 1km; adv bkg acc; horseriding; tennis. "Helpful, friendly staff; sm pitches unsuitable lge o'fits & poss diff due trees, esp when site full; attractive setting; gd pool, bar & rest; ltd facs LS & poss long walk to san facs; in winter use as NH only; phone to check open LS; excel cycle track to Pamplona; quiet rural site; gd facs not htd." €30.00 2018

PARADA DE SIL *1B2* (3km NW Rural) *42.38941, -7.58885* **Camping Cañón do Sil**, Lugar de Castro s/n, 32740 Parada de Sil **608 537 017; info@canondosilcamping.com; www.canondosilcamping.com**

12 ♦♦♦ WD ⛱/♀️⛺🛒nr

OU-0604 to Ctra De Castro, turn R on OU-0605. Turn L to Ctra da Castro, site on L. Med, pt shd, terr, EHU €4. "Amazing location on the edge of Rv Sil Gorge; gd walks fr site; vg." €23.00 2016

PENAFIEL *1C4* (1km SW Rural) *41.59538, -4.12811*
Camping Riberduero, Avda Polideportivo 51,
47300 Peñafiel **983-88 16 37; camping@camping
penafiel.com; www.campingpenafiel.com**

Fr Valladolid 56km or Aranda de Duero 38km on
N122. In Peñafiel take VA223 dir Cuéllar, foll sp
to sports cent/camping. Med, mkd, hdstg, shd,
EHU (5A) €5; gas; red long stay; TV; 20% statics;
phone; bus 1km; Eng spkn; adv bkg acc; ccard acc;
site open w/end only LS; bike hire. *"Excel, well-kept
site; interesting, historical area; ideal for wheelchair
users; sm pitches and access diff due to trees."*
€16.50, Holy Week & 1 Apr-30 Sep. **2016**

PENISCOLA *3D2* (2km N Coastal) *40.37916, 0.38833*
Camping Los Pinos, Calle Abellars s/n, 12598
Peñíscola (Castellón) **964-48 03 79; info@
campinglospinos.com; www.campinglospinos.com**

Exit A7 junc 43 or N340 sp Peñíscola. Site sp on L.
1*, Med, mkd, hdg, pt shd, EHU (10A) €5.95; gas; bbq;
TV; 10% statics; phone; bus fr site; Eng spkn; adv bkg
acc; games rm. *"Narr site rds, lots of trees; poss diff
access some pitches; vg."* **€30.00** **2016**

PENISCOLA *3D2* (3km NE Coastal) *40.37152, 0.40269*
Camping El Edén, Ctra CS501 Benicarló-Peñíscola Km 6,
12598 Peñíscola (Castellón) **964-48 05 62; camping@
camping-eden.com; www.camping-eden.com**

Exit AP7 junc 43 onto N340 then CV141 to Peñíscola
ctr. Take 3rd exit off rndabt at seafront, after 1km
turn L after Hotel del Mar. Rec avoid sat nav rte
across marshes fr Peñíscola. 1*, Lge, hdg, mkd, pt shd,
EHU (10A) inc; gas; red long stay; 40% statics; bus adj;
ccard acc; ACSI acc. *"San facs refurbished & v clean;
beach adj cleaned daily; gd security; excel pool; easy
access to sandy/gravel pitches but many sm trees poss
diff for awnings or high m'vans; cash dispenser; poss
vicious mosquitoes at dusk; easy walk/cycle to town;
4 diff sizes of pitch (some with tap, sink & drain) with
different prices; ltd facs LS; excel."* **€53.00** **2015**

PILAR DE LA HORADADA *4F2* (4km NE Coastal)
37.87916, -0.76555 **Lo Monte Camping & Caravaning,**
Avenida Comunidada Valenciana No 157 CP 03190
**00 34 966 766 782; info@campinglomonte-
alicante.es; www.campinglomonte-alicante.es**

Exit 770 of AP7 dir Pilar de la Horadada; take the
1st L. 4*, Med, hdg, mkd, serviced pitches; EHU (16A)
€0.40; bbq; Eng spkn; adv bkg acc; ccard acc; bike hire;
games rm; CKE. *"New site; superb facs, exceptionally
clean; great location, lots of golf & gd for walks &
cycling; rec; excel; gym/wellness cent; beautifully laid
out; neat; gd pool; v gd rest; isolated, nothing around
site."* **€36.00** **2018**

PINEDA DE MAR *3C3* (1km SW Coastal) *41.61827,
2.67891* **Camping Bellsol,** Passeig Maritim 46,
08397 Pineda de Mar **937-67 17 78; info@
campingbellsol.com; www.campingbellsol.com**

Fr N, take exit AP7 Junc 9 & immed turn R onto
N11 dir Barcelona. Foll sp Pineda de Mar and turn
L twd Paseo Maritim at exit at rv x-ing. Fr S on C32,
exit 122 dir Pineda de Mar & foll dir Paseo Maritim
& Campings fr same rndabt. Beware narr rds at
other turnings. Lge, hdstg, shd, EHU (4A); red long
stay; twin axles; 15% statics; bus nrby, train 800m;
Eng spkn; adv bkg acc; CKE. *"V friendly & helpful
staff; walking; bike & moped hire; sea fishing trips; vg."*
€34.60, 19 Mar-31 Dec. **2016**

"Satellite navigation makes touring much easier"

Remember most sat navs don't know if you're
towing or in a larger vehicle – always use yours
alongside maps and site directions.

PLASENCIA *1D3* (4km NE Urban) *40.04348, -6.05751*
Camping La Chopera, Ctra N110, Km 401.3, Valle
del Jerte, 10600 Plasencia (Caceres) **927-41 66 60;
lachopera@campinglachopera.com; www.camping
lachopera.com**

In Plasencia on N630 turn E on N110 sp Ávila & foll
sp indus est & sp to site. 3*, Med, shd, serviced pitches;
EHU (6A) inc; gas; bbq; ccard acc; tennis; hike hire; CKE.
*"Peaceful & spacious; much birdsong; conv Manfrague
National Park (breeding of black/Egyptian vultures,
black storks, imperial eagles); excel pool & modern facs;
helpful owners; shop (Jul & Aug); Carrefour in town; 35
min walk to town."* **€22.00** **2016**

PLASENCIA *1D3* (14km S Rural) *39.94361, -6.08444*
Camping Parque Natural Monfragüe, Ctra Plasencia-
Trujillo, Km 10, 10680 Malpartida de Plasencia
(Cáceres) **927- 45 92 33 or 605 94 08 78 (mob);
campingmonfrague@hotmail.com; www.camping
monfrague.com**

Fr N on A66/N630 by-pass town, 5km S of town at
flyover junc take EXA1 (EX108) sp Navalmoral de la
Mata. In 6km turn R onto EX208 dir Trujillo, site on
L in 5km. 3*, Med, hdg, pt shd, pt sl, terr, EHU (10A)
€4; gas; bbq; TV; 10% statics; phone; Eng spkn; ccard
acc; tennis; archery; bike hire; horseriding; games area.
*"Friendly, helpful staff; red ACSI; vg gd rest; clean, tidy,
busy site but poss dusty, hoses avail; 10km to National
Park (birdwatching trips); rambling; 4x4 off-rd; many
birds on site; excel year round base; new excel san facs;
discounted fees must be paid in cash; pitches muddy
after heavy rain; peaceful; interesting over Halloween."*
€20.40 **2019**

Cāmping TREUMAL Costa Brava

YOU WILL FIND US ON THE BEACH ...

Apdo. Correos nº 348 17250 PLATJA D'ARO (GIRONA)
TLF. (0034) 972 65 10 95   FAX. (0034) 972 65 16 71   E mail: Info@campingtreumal.com

www.campingtreumal.com

PLAYA DE ARO *3B3* (2km N Coastal) *41.83116, 3.08366* **Camping Cala Gogo,** Avda Andorra 13, 17251 Calonge (Gerona) **972-65 15 64; calagogo@ calagogo.es; www.calagogo.es**

(htd) sand adj

Exit AP7 junc 6 dir Palamós/Sant Feliu. Fr Palamós take C253 coast rd S twd Sant Antoni, site on R 2km fr Playa de Aro, sp. 3*, Lge, pt shd, pt sl, terr, serviced pitches; EHU (10A) inc; gas; bbq; red long stay; TV; Eng spkn; adv bkg acc; boat hire; tennis; games area; golf 4km; bike hire; games rm. *"Clean & recently upgraded san facs; rest/bar with terr; no dogs Jul/Aug; diving school; site terraced into pinewood on steep hillside; excel family site."* **€52.00, 16 Apr-18 Sep.**   **2016**

"There aren't many sites open at this time of year"

If you're travelling outside peak season remember to call ahead to check site opening dates – even if the entry says 'open all year'.

PLAYA DE ARO *3B3* (2km N Coastal) *41.83666, 3.08722* **Camping Treumal,** Ctra Playa de Aro/ Palamós, C253, Km 47.5, 17250 Playa de Arro (Gerona) **972-65 10 95; info@campingtreumal.com; www.campingtreumal.com**

sand adj

Exit m'way at junc 6, 7 or 9 dir Sant Feliu de Guixols to Playa de Aro; site is sp at km 47.5 fr C253 coast rd SW of Palamós. 1*, Lge, mkd, shd, terr, EHU (10A) inc; gas; 25% statics; phone; Eng spkn; adv bkg acc; ccard acc; car wash; sports facs; games rm; tennis 1km; bike hire; golf 5km; fishing; CKE. *"Peaceful site in pine trees; excel san facs; manhandling poss req onto terr pitches; gd beach."* **€49.00, 31 Mar-30 Sep.**   **2016**

See advertisement

POLA DE SOMIEDO *1A3* (0.3km E Rural) *43.09222, -6.25222* **Camping La Pomerada de Somiedo,** 33840 Pola de Somiedo (Asturias) **985-76 34 04; csomiedo@ infonegocio.com**

nr   nr

W fr Oviedo on A63, turn S onto AS15/AS227 to Augasmestas & Pola de Somiedo. Site adj Hotel Alba, sp fr vill. Route on steep, winding, mountain rd - suitable sm, powerful o'fits only. Sm, mkd, pt shd, EHU €4.20. *"Mountain views; nr national park."* **€19.00, 1 Apr-31 Dec.**   **2016**

PONFERRADA *1B3* (16km W Rural) *42.56160, -6.74590* **Camping El Bierzo,** 24550 Villamartín de la Abadia (León) **987-56 25 15; info@campingbierzo.com; www.campingbierzo.com**

[symbols]

Exit A6 junc 399 dir Carracedelo; after rndabt turn onto NV1 & foll sp Villamartín. Bef ent Villamartín turn L & foll site sp. 2*, Med, pt shd, EHU (3-5A) €5; phone; bus 1km; adv bkg acc; CKE. *"Attractive, rvside site in pleasant, lge, level grassed area with mature trees; gd, clean facs; friendly, helpful owner takes pride in his site; Roman & medieval attractions nr; sm rv beach adj; no bus svrs into Ponferrada."* **€22.00** **2019**

PONT DE SUERT *3B2* (3km N Rural) *42.43083, 0.73861* **Camping Can Roig,** Ctra Boí, Km 0.5, 25520 El Pont de Suert (Lleida) **973-69 05 02; info@ campingcanroig.com; www.campingcanroig.com**

[symbols] €3.60

N of Pont de Suert on N230 turn NE onto L500 dir Caldes de Boí. Site in 1km. App narr for 100m. Med, mkd, hdstg, pt shd, pt sl, EHU (5A) €5.15; gas; 5% statics; adv bkg acc; ccard acc. *"NH en rte S; beautiful valley; informal, friendly, quirky site (free range poultry); v relaxed atmosphere; helpful owner; fabulous valley & national park with thermal springs; poss scruffy (2015)."* **€27.00, 1 Mar-31 Oct.** **2015**

PORT DE LA SELVA, EL *3B3* (3km W Coastal) *42.34222, 3.18333* **Camping Port de la Vall,** Ctra Port de Llançà, 17489 El Port de la Selva (Gerona) **972-38 71 86; portdelavall@terra.es**

[symbols] €2.95 shgl adj

On coast rd fr French border at Llançà take GI612 twd El Port de la Selva. Site on L, easily seen. Lge, pt shd, EHU (3-5A) €6; gas; 10% statics; phone; adv bkg acc; ccard acc. *"Easy 1/2 hr walk to harbour; gd site; sm pitches & low branches poss diff - check bef siting; san facs v clean."* **€29.00, 1 Mar-15 Oct.** **2016**

POTES *1A4* (1km W Rural) *43.15527, -4.63694* **Camping La Viorna,** Ctra Santo Toribio, Km 1, Mieses, 39570 Potes (Cantabria) **942-73 20 21; info@ campinglaviorna.com; www.campinglaviorna.com**

[symbols] (htd)

Exit N634 at junc 272 onto N621 dir Panes & Potes - narr, winding rd (passable for c'vans). Fr Potes take rd to Fuente Dé sp Espinama; in 1km turn L sp Toribio. Site on R in 1km, sp fr Potes. Do not use Sat Nav. Med, mkd, pt shd, terr, EHU (6A) €3.40 (poss rev pol); bbq; bus 1km; Eng spkn; adv bkg acc; ccard acc; bike hire; CKE. *"Lovely views; gd walks; friendly, family-run, clean, tidy site; gd pool; ideal Picos de Europa; conv cable car, 4x4 tours, trekking; mkt on Mon; festival mid-Sep v noisy; some pitches diff in wet & diff lge o'fits; excel san facs; voted 8th best camp in Spain; excel."* **€27.70, 1 Apr-1 Nov.** **2017**

POTES *1A4* (3km W Rural) *43.15742, -4.65617* **Camping La Isla-Picos de Europa,** Ctra Potes-Fuente Dé, 39586 Turieno (Cantabria) **942-73 08 96; camping laislapicosdeeuropa@gmail.com; www.campinglais lapicosdeeuropa.com**

[symbols]

Take N521 W fr Potes twd Espinama, site on R in 3km thro vill of Turieno (app Potes fr N). 2*, Med, mkd, shd, pt sl, EHU (6A) €4 (poss rev pol); gas; red long stay; 10% statics; phone; Eng spkn; adv bkg acc; ccard acc; horseriding; cycling; CKE. *"Delightful, family-run site; friendly, helpful owners; gd san facs; conv cable car & mountain walks (map fr recep); many trees & low branches; 4x4 touring; walking; mountain treks in area; hang-gliding; rec early am dep to avoid coaches on gorge rd; highly rec; lovely loc, gd facs."* **€25.00, 1 Apr-15 Oct.** **2017**

PUERTO DE MAZARRON *4G1* (5km NE Coastal) *37.5800, -1.1950* **Camping Los Madriles,** Ctra a la Azohía 60, Km 4.5, 30868 Isla Plana (Murcia) **968-15 21 51; info@campinglosmadriles.com; www.camping losmadriles.com**

[symbols] (htd) shgl 500m

Fr Cartegena on N332 dir Puerto de Mazarrón. Turn L at rd junc sp La Azohía (32km). Site in 4km sp. Fr Murcia on E15/N340 dir Lorca exit junc 627 onto MU603 to Mazarrón, then foll sp. (Do not use rd fr Cartegena unless powerful tow vehicle/gd weight differential - use rte fr m'way thro Mazarrón). Lge, hdg, mkd, hdstg, pt shd, pt sl, serviced pitches; EHU (10A) €5; gas; red long stay; bus; Eng spkn; adv bkg req; ccard acc; games area; jacuzzi; CKE. *"Clean, well-run, v popular winter site; adv bkg req; some sm pitches, some with sea views; sl bet terrs; 3 days min stay high ssn; v helpful staff, excel."* **€38.40** **2019**

PUERTO DE SANTA MARIA, EL *2H3* (2km SW Coastal) *36.58768, -6.24092* **Camping Playa Las Dunas de San Antón,** Paseo Maritimo La Puntilla s/n, 11500 El Puerto de Santa María (Cádiz) **956-87 22 10; info@lasdunascamping.com; www.lasdunas camping.com**

[symbols] sand 50m

Fr N or S exit A4 at El Puerto de Sta María. Foll site sp carefully to avoid narr rds of town cent. Site 2-3km S of marina & leisure complex of Puerto Sherry. Alt, fr A4 take Rota rd & look for sp to site & Hotel Playa Las Dunas. Site better sp fr this dir & avoids town. 3*, Lge, pt shd, pt sl, EHU (10A) inc; gas; 30% statics; phone; Eng spkn; adv bkg rec; ccard acc; sports facs; CKE. *"Friendly staff; conv Cádiz & Jerez sherry region, birdwatching areas & beaches; conv ferry or catamaran to Cádiz; facs poss stretched high ssn; pitches quiet away fr rd; take care caterpillars in spring, poss dangerous to dogs; dusty site but staff water rds; gd; excel facs; busy; guarded; excel new shwr block (2016); pool adj; old elec conns."* **€26.00** **2019**

RIAZA *1C4* (1.5km W Rural) *41.26995, -3.49750*
Camping Riaza, Ctra de la Estación s/n, 40500 Riaza
(Segovia) **921-55 05 80; info@camping-riaza.com;
www.camping-riaza.com**

12 🐕 👫👫 (htd) [wc] 🏕 🚿 🚻 🛒 💧 🦋 ♈ 🍴 Ⓗ 🛒 🛒 🗻 ⚓ 🛶

Fr N exit A1/E5 junc 104, fr S exit 103 onto N110
N. In 12km turn R at rndabt on ent to town, site on
L. Lge, hdg, unshd, EHU (10A) €4.70 (rev pol); bbq;
30% statics; phone; bus 900m; Eng spkn; adv bkg acc;
games rm; games area. *"Vg site; various pitch sizes -
some lge; excel san facs; easy access to/fr Santander or
Bilbao; dogs free; beautiful little town."* **€31.00**   **2017**

RIBADEO *1A2* (12km N Rural/Coastal) *43.554004,
-7.111085* **Rinlo Costa Camping,** Rua Campo Maria
Mendez, s/n 27715 Rinlo **679-25 52 81; info@rinlo
costa.es; www.rinlocosta.es**

12 🏕 💧 🛒 🗻 ⚓ 🛶

Fr N634 take LU141 twrds Rinlo. Over rly bdge
(0.5km) take 1st L and foll rd round for another
0.5km. Turn L and site ahead on R. Sm, EHU (6A)
€4.50; bbq; cooking facs; bike hire. **€24.00**   **2018**

RIBADEO *1A2* (18km W Coastal) *43.56237, -7.20762*
Camping Gaivota, Playa de Barreiros, 27792 Barreiros
982 12 44 51; campinggaivota@gmail.com;
www.campingpobladogaivota.com

🐕 👫👫 [wc] 🏕 🚿 🚻 🛒 💧 🦋 ♈ 🍴 Ⓗ 🛒 🗻 🛶 adj

Fr Berreiros take N634, turn L at KM 567,
betRibadeo & Foz. Foll camping sp. Med, hdg, pt shd,
EHU (6A); gas; bbq; twin axles; TV; 5% statics; phone.
*"V well cared for; superb beaches; family run; pleasant
bar & rest; excel."* **€30.00, 28 Mar-15 Oct.**   **2015**

RIBADESELLA *1A3* (3km W Rural) *43.46258, -5.08725*
Camping Ribadesella, Sebreño s/n, 33560 Ribadesella
(Asturias) **985 858293 or 985 857721; info@camping-
ribadesella.com; www.camping-ribadesella.com**

🐕 €2.50 👫👫 [wc] 🏕 🚿 🚻 🛒 💧 🦋 🍴 ⒽⒶ 🛒 🛒 🗻 (covrd, htd)
🛶 sand 4km

W fr Ribadesella take N632. After 2km fork L up
hill. Site on L after 2km. Poss diff for lge o'fits & alt
rte fr Ribadesella vill to site to avoid steep uphill
turn can be used. Lge, mkd, pt shd, pt sl, terr, EHU
(10A) €5; gas; bbq; red long stay; Eng spkn; adv bkg
acc; ccard acc; tennis; games area; games rm; CKE.
*"Clean san facs; some sm pitches; attractive fishing vill;
prehistoric cave paintings nrby; excel; not much shd;
steps or slopes to walk to top rate facs; 35min easy
downhill walk to town, shorter walk down steep lane
to beach; rec; terr site; rest has cvrd terrace and lovely
views."* **€36.00, 12 Apr-22 Sep.**   **2019**

RIBADESELLA *1A3* (8km W Rural/Coastal) *43.47472,
-5.13416* **Camping Playa de Vega,** Vega, 33345
Ribadesella (Asturias) **985-86 04 06; info@camping
playadevega.com; www.campingplayadevega.com**

🐕 👫👫 [wc] 🏕 🚿 🚻 🛒 💧 🦋 ♈ 🍴 Ⓗ 🛒 🛒 🗻 sand 400m

Fr A8 exit junc 336 sp Ribadesella W, thro Bones.
At rndabt cont W dir Caravia, turn R opp quarry
sp Playa de Vega. Fr cent of Ribadesella (poss
congestion) W on N632. Cont for 5km past turning
to autovia. Turn R at sp Vega & site. 3*, Med, hdg,
pt shd, terr, serviced pitches; EHU €4.15; bbq; TV;
phone; bus 700m; ccard acc; CKE. *"Sh walk to vg
beach thro orchards; beach rest; sm pitches not
suitable lge o'fits; poss overgrown LS; immac san facs;
a gem of a site; beware very narr bdge on ent rd."*
€24.50, 15 Jun-15 Sep.   **2017**

**"That's changed – Should I let
the Club know?"**

If you find something on site that's different
from the site entry, fill in a report and let us
know. See camc.com/europereport.

RIBEIRA *1B2* (10km N Rural) *42.62100, -8.98600*
Camping Ría de Arosa II, Oleiros, 15993 Santa
Eugenia (Uxía) de Ribeira (La Coruña) **981- 86 59 11;
rural@campingriadearosa.com; www.campingriade
arosa.com**

12 🐕 €2.50 👫👫 (htd) [wc] 🏕 🚿 🚻 🛒 💧 🦋 ♈ 🍴 Ⓗ 🛒 🛒 🗻 🛶

Exit AP9 junc 93 Padrón & take N550 then AC305/
VG11 to Ribeira. Then take AC550 to Oleiros to
site, well sp. V lge, mkd, hdg, shd, EHU (6A) inc; gas;
bbq; TV; 10% statics; phone; Eng spkn; adv bkg acc;
ccard acc; fishing; tennis; games area; games rm; CKE.
*"Beautiful area; helpful, friendly staff; excel; lots to do;
excel pool; great facs."* **€28.50**   **2015**

ROCIO, EL *2G3* (2km N Rural) *37.14194, -6.49250*
Camping La Aldea, Ctra del Rocío, Km 25, 21750
El Rocío,Almonte (Huelva) **959-44 26 77; info@
campinglaaldea.com; www.campinglaaldea.com**

12 🐕 €3 👫👫 (htd) [wc] 🏕 🚿 🚻 🛒 💧 🦋 ♈ 🍴 Ⓗ 🛒 🛒 🗻 🛶 (htd)

Fr A49 turn S at junc 48 onto A483 by-passing
Almonte, site sp just bef El Rocío rndabt. Fr W
(Portugal) turn off at junc 60 to A484 to Almonte,
then A483. 3*, Lge, hdstg, mkd, hdg, pt shd, EHU
(10A) €6.50; gas; bbq; red long stay; 30% statics;
phone; bus 500m; Eng spkn; adv bkg acc; ccard acc;
horseriding nr; CKE. *"Well-appointed & maintained
site; winter rallies; excel san facs; friendly, helpful staff;
tight turns on site; most pitches have kerb or gully; van
washing facs; pitches soft after rain; rd noise; easy walk
to interesting town; avoid festival (in May-7 weeks after
Easter) when town cr & site charges higher; poss windy;
excel birdwatching nrby (lagoon 1km); beautiul site; gd
pool & rest."* **€30.00, E24.**   **2019**

RONDA *2H3* (1km S Rural) *36.72111, –5.17166*
Camping El Sur, Ctra Ronda-Algeciras Km 1.5, 29400
Ronda (Málaga) **952-87 59 39; info@campingelsur.**
com; www.campingelsur.com

🔢 🐕 €1.70 🚻(htd) 🚾 ⚁ ⚄ ♿ 🖥 ⁄ 🅿 🦋 ♨ ⟟ ⑪ nr ⛽ 🛒
🏛 🏊

Site on W side of A369 dir Algeciras. Do not tow
thro Ronda. Med, mkd, hdstg, pt shd, sl, terr, EHU
(5-10A) €4.30-5.35 (poss rev pol &/or no earth); red
long stay; phone; Eng spkn; adv bkg acc; CKE. *"Gd rd
fr coast with spectacular views; long haul for lge o'fits;
busy family-run site in lovely setting; conv National
Parks & Pileta Caves; poss diff access some pitches
due trees & high kerbs; hard, rocky grnd; san facs poss
stretched high ssn; easy walk to town; friendly staff; vg
rest; excel."* **€27.00**   **2019**

ROSES *3B3* (1km W Urban/Coastal) *42.26638,*
3.16305 **Camping Joncar Mar,** Ctra Figueres s/n,
17480 Roses (Gerona) **972-25 67 02; info@camping**
joncarmar.com; www.campingjoncarmar.com

🔢 🐕 €2.40 🚻(htd) 🚾 ⚁ ⚄ ♿ 🖥 ⁄ ♨ ⟟ ⑪ 🛒 🏛 ✎ 🏊
🏖 sand 150m

At Figueres take C260 W for Roses. On ent Roses
turn sharp R at last rndabt at end of dual c'way.
Site on both sides or rd - go to R (better) side, park
& report to recep on L. 2*, Lge, pt shd, pt sl, EHU
(6-10A) poss no earth; gas; red long stay; 15% statics;
phone; bus 500m; Eng spkn; adv bkg acc; ccard acc;
golf 15km; games rm. *"Conv walk into Roses; hotels
& apartment blocks bet site & beach; poss cramped/
tight pitches; narr rds; vg value LS; new san facs 2015."*
€32.00   **2015**

ROSES *3B3* (2.5km W Coastal) *42.26638, 3.15611*
Camping Salatà, Port Reig s/n, 17480 Roses (Gerona)
972-25 60 86; info@campingsalata.com;
www.campingsalata.com

🐕 €2.80 🚻(htd) 🚾 ⚁ ⚄ ♿ 🖥 ⁄ ♨ ⟟ ⑪ ⛽ 🛒 🏛 🏊(htd)
🏖 sand 200m

App Roses on rd C260. On ent Roses take 1st R after
Roses sp & Caprabo supmkt. Lge, mkd, hdstg, pt
shd, EHU (6-10A) inc; gas; red long stay; 10% statics;
phone; Eng spkn; adv bkg acc; ccard acc; CKE. *"Vg area
for sub-aqua sports; vg clean facs, but not enough;
dogs not acc Jul/Aug; red facs LS; pleasant walk/cycle
to town; overpriced."* **€50.70, 12 Mar-31 Oct.**   **2016**

SAHAGUN *1B3* (1km W Rural) *42.37188, -5.04280*
Camping Pedro Ponce, Avda Tineo, s/n 24326
Sahagun **987 78 04 15; campingsahagun@hotmail.**
com; www.villadesahagun.es

🐕 🚻 🚾 ⚁ ⚄ ♿ 🖥 ⁄ ♨ ⟟ ⑪ 🛒 nr 🏛 ✎ 🏊

Leave A231 at junc 46 onto N120. Foll sp Shagun.
Site on in 1km. Lge, unshd, EHU (6A); twin axles;
60% statics; phone; bus adj; Eng spkn; ccard acc.
*"Excel municipal site; modern facs; sep area for tourers;
interesting town; vg."* **€17.00, 1 Mar-31 Oct.**   **2015**

SALAMANCA *1C3* (17km NE Rural) *41.05805,*
-5.54611 **Camping Olimpia,** Ctra de Gomecello, Km
3.150, 37427 Pedrosillo el Ralo (Salamanca) **923-08**
08 54 or 620-46 12 07; info@campingolimpia.com;
www.campingolimpia.com

🔢 🐕 €1 🚻(htd) 🚾 ⚁ 🖥 ⁄ ⟟ ⑪ ♿

Exit A62 junc 225 dir Pedrosillo el Ralo & La Vellés,
strt over rndabt, site sp. Sm, hdg, pt shd, EHU €3;
phone; bus 300m; Eng spkn; adv bkg acc; site clsd 8-16
Sep; CKE. *"Helpful, friendly & pleasant owner; really
gd 2 course meal for €10 (2014); handy fr rd with little
noise & easy to park; poss open w/ends only LS; excel;
grass pitches; clean facs; perfect; some pitches tight."*
€20.00   **2018**

SALAMANCA *1C3* (5km E Rural) *40.97611, -5.60472*
Camping Don Quijote, Ctra Aldealengua, Km 1930,
37193 Cabrerizos (Salamanca) **923-20 90 52; info@**
campingdonquijote.com; www.campingdon
quijote.com

🐕 🚻 🚾 ⚁ ⚄ ♿ 🖥 ⁄ 🅿 🦋 ♨ ⟟ ⑪ ⛽ 🛒 🏛 🏊 🖐
🏖 sand 200m

Fr Madrid or fr S cross Rv Tormes by most easterly
bdge to join inner ring rd. Foll Paseo de Canalejas
for 800m to Plaza España. Turn R onto SA804 Avda
de los Comuneros & strt on for 5km. Site ent 2km
after town boundary sp. Fr other dirs, head into city
& foll inner ring rd to Plaza España. Site well sp fr rv
& ring rd. 3*, Med, hdstg, mkd, hdg, pt shd, EHU (10A)
inc; bbq; twin axles; 10% statics; phone; bus; Eng spkn;
adv bkg acc; ccard acc; rv fishing; CKE. *"Gd rv walks;
conv city cent; 45 mins easy cycle ride 6km to town
along rv; rv Tormes flows alongside site with pleasant
walks; friendly owner; highly rec; new excel san facs
(2016); v friendly; 12 min walk to bus stop; may not be
suited for lge units; some late-night functions on w/
ends."* **€23.60, 1 Mar-3 Nov.**   **2019**

SALAMANCA *1C3* (7km E Urban) *40.94722, -5.6150*
Camping Regio, Ctra Ávila-Madrid, Km 4, 37900 Santa
Marta de Tormes (Salamanca) **923-13 88 88;**
recepcion@campingregio.com; www.camping
regio.com

🔢 🐕 🚻 🚾 ⚁ ⚄ ♿ 🖥 ⁄ 🅿 🦋 ♨ ⟟ ⑪ ⛽ 🛒 🏛

Fr E on SA20/N501 outer ring rd, pass hotel/
camping sp visible on L & exit Sta Marta de Tormes,
site directly behind Hotel Regio. Foll sp to hotel.
3*, Lge, mkd, pt shd, pt sl, EHU (10A) €3.95 (no earth);
gas; TV; 5% statics; phone; bus to Salamanca; Eng
spkn; ccard acc; car wash; bike hire; CKE. *"In LS stop at
24hr hotel recep; poss no hdstg in wet conditions; conv
en rte Portugal; refurbished facs to excel standard; site
poss untidy, & ltd security in LS; hotel pool high ssn;
hypmkt 3km; spacious pitches but some poss tight for
lge o'fits; take care lge brick markers when reversing;
hourly bus in and out of city; excel pool; vg; facs up to
gd standard & htd; highly rec."* **€23.00, E26.**   **2019**

SALOU *3C2* (1km S Urban/Coastal) *41.0752, 1.1176* **Camping Sanguli,** Paseo Miramar-Plaza Venus, 43840 Salou (Tarragona) **977-38 16 41; mail@sanguli.es; www.sanguli.es**

🐕 🚻 (htd) [WD] 🚿 👶 ♿ 🧺 🔌 [MSP] 📶 🍸 🍴 🛒 🎠 ⛺ 🚲 🏊 ♨

🏖 sand 50m

Exit AP7/E15 junc 35. At 1st rndbt take dir to Salou (Plaça Europa), at 2nd rndabt foll site sp. 5*, V lge, hdstg, mkd, shd, pt sl, serviced pitches; EHU (10A) inc; gas; bbq; red long stay; TV; 35% statics; phone; bus; Eng spkn; adv bkg rec; ccard acc; games area; waterslide; games rm; jacuzzi; car wash; tennis; CKE. *"Quiet end of Salou nr Cambrils & 3km Port Aventura; site facs recently updated/upgraded; fitness rm; excursions; cinema; youth club; mini club; amphitheatre; excel, well-maintained site."* **€75.00, 5 Apr-3 Nov. 2019**

SAN ROQUE *2H3* (7km NE Rural) *36.25031, -5.33808* **Camping La Casita,** Ctra N340, Km 126.2, 11360 San Roque (Cádiz) **956-78 00 31**

[12] 🐕 €2.67 🚻 [WD] 🚿 ♿ 🔌 [MSP] 🍴 🛒 ⛺ 🚲 🏊 🏖 sand 3km

Site sp 'Via de Servicio' parallel to AP7/E15. Access at km 119 fr S, km 127 fr N. Site visible fr rd. Lge, pt shd, pt sl, terr, EHU (10A) €4.54; red long stay; 90% statics; phone; bus 100m; Eng spkn; adv bkg req; ccard acc; horseriding; CKE. *"Shwrs solar htd - water temp depends on weather (poss cold); san facs poss unclean; friendly staff; conv Gibraltar & Morocco; daily buses to La Línea & Algeciras; ferries to N Africa (secure parking at port); golf course next to site; great rest; poor site."* **€39.50** **2016**

SAN SEBASTIAN/DONOSTIA *3A1* (7km W Rural) *43.30458, -2.04588* **Camping Igueldo,** Paseo Padre Orkolaga 69, 20008 San Sebastián (Guipúzkoa) **943-21 45 02; info@campingigueldo.com; www.campingigueldo.com**

[12] 🚻 [WD] 🚿 👶 ♿ 🧺 🔌 📶 🍸 🍴 🛒 ⛺ 🏖 sand 5km

Fr W on A8, leave m'way at junc 9 twd city cent, take 1st R & R at rndabt onto Avda de Tolosa sp Ondarreta. At sea front turn hard L at rndabt sp to site (Avda Satrústegui) & foll sp up steep hill 4km to site. Fr E exit junc 8 then as above. Site sp as Garoa Camping Bungalows. Steep app poss diff for lge o'fits. Lge, hdg, mkd, pt shd, terr, serviced pitches; EHU (10A) inc; gas; red long stay; TV; phone; bus to city adj; Eng spkn; CKE. *"Vg, clean facs; sm pitches poss diff; spectacular views; pitches muddy when wet; excel rest 1km (open in winter); pool 5km; frequent bus to beautiful, interesting town; new pool (2017)."* **€37.00** **2017**

SAN TIRSO DE ABRES *1A2* (0.5km N Rural) *43.41352, -7.14141* **Amaido,** El Llano, 33774 San Tirso de Abres **616-78 11 55; amaido@amaido.com; www.amaido.com**

🐕 🚻 [WD] 🚿 👶 ♿ 🧺 🔌 [MSP] 📶 🛒 ⛺

Head N on A6 twds Lugo & exit 497 for N-640 twds Oviedo/Lugo Centro cidade. At rndabt take 4th exit onto N-640, turn R at LU-P-6104, turn R onto Vegas, then take 2nd L. Site at end of rd. Med, hdg, pt shd, terr, EHU (6A); bbq; twin axles; TV; adv bkg acc; bike hire; games area. *"Lovely wooded site set in a circle around facs; farm animals; vg site."* **€20.00, 10 Apr-15 Sep.** **2019**

"I like to fill in the reports as I travel from site to site"

You'll find report forms at the back of this guide, or you can fill them in online at camc.com/europereport.

SAN VICENTE DE LA BARQUERA *1A4* (1km E Coastal) *43.38901, -4.3853* **Camping El Rosal,** Ctra de la Playa s/n, 39540 San Vicente de la Barquera (Cantabria) **942-71 01 65; info@campingelrosal.com; www.campingelrosal.com**

🚻 [WD] 🚿 ♿ 🧺 🔌 🦋 📶 🍸 🍴 🛒 🏖 sand adj

Fr A8 km 264, foll sp San Vicente. Turn R over bdge then 1st L (site sp) immed at end of bdge; keep L & foll sp to site. Barier height 3.1m. Med, mkd, pt shd, pt sl, terr, EHU (6A) €4.80; gas; phone; Eng spkn; adv bkg acc; ccard acc; CKE. *"Lovely site in pine wood o'looking bay; surfing beach; some modern, clean facs; helpful staff; vg rest; easy walk or cycle ride to interesting town; Sat mkt; no hot water at sinks."* **€27.00, 1 Apr-30 Sep.** **2019**

SAN VICENTE DE LA BARQUERA *1A4* (6km E Coastal) *43.38529, -4.33831* **Camping Playa de Oyambre,** Finca Peña Gerra, 39540 San Vicente de la Barquera (Cantabria) **942-71 14 61; camping@oyambre.com; www.oyambre.com**

🐕 🚻 [WD] 🚿 🧺 🔌 [MSP] 📶 🍸 🍴 🛒 ⛺ 🏊 (covrd, indoor) ♨

🏖 800m

E70/A8 Santander-Oviedo, exit sp 264 S. Vicente de la Barquera, then N634 for 3 km to Comillas exit on the Ctra La Revilla-Comillas (CA 131) bet km posts 27 and 28. 3*, Lge, hdg, mkd, pt shd, terr, EHU (10A) €6; gas; 40% statics; bus 300m; Eng spkn; adv bkg acc; ccard acc; gym, two pools, playground, laundry service, horseback riding, biking, hiking, golf; CKE. *"V well-kept site; clean, helpful owner; quiet week days LS; gd base for N coast & Picos de Europa; 4x4 avail to tow to pitch if wet; some sm pitches & rd noise some pitches; conv Santander ferry; immac san facs; excel site; staff speak gd english; rest rec; gd base to tour N coast & Picos de Europa."* **€32.30, 4 Mar-30 Oct.**

2019

 Tell us about the sites you visit – submit your reports by mid-August for them to be in the next guide

Sunêlia
àmfora
★★★★

Av. Josep Tarradellas, 2
17470 St. Pere Pescador COSTA BRAVA (SPAIN)
T. +34 972 52 05 40
info@campingamfora.com
www.campingamfora.com

SANT JORDI *3D2* (2km SW Rural) *40.49318, 0.31806*
Camping Maestrat Park, 12320 Sant Jordi (Castellón)
**964-86 08 89 or 679-29 87 95 (mob); info@maestrat
park.es; www.maestratpark.es**

[icons]

Exit AP7 junc 42 onto CV11 to Sant Rafel del Riu. At
rndabt with fuel stn take CV11 to Traiguera; then at
rndabt take 1st exit onto N232 dir Vinarós & at next
rndabt take 2nd exit sp Calig. Site 2km on L.
Sm, hdstg, mkd, hdg, pt shd, pt sl, EHU (10-16A)
€4.50; bbq; red long stay; twin axles; TV; 25% statics;
phone; bus; Eng spkn; adv bkg acc; games rm; bike
hire; CKE. *"Excel; club memb owner; excel for v lge
o'fits."* €25.00   2015

SANT PERE PESCADOR *3B3* (1km SE Coastal)
42.18180, 3.10403 **Camping L'Àmfora,** Avda Josep
Tarradellas 2, 17470 Sant Pere Pescador (Gerona)
**972-52 05 40; info@campingamfora.com;
www.campingamfora.com**

[icons] sand adj

Fr N exit junc 3 fr AP7 onto N11 fro Figueres/
Roses. At junc with C260 foll sp Castelló
d'Empúries & Roses. At Castelló turn R at rndabt
sp Sant Pere Pescador then foll sp to L'Amfora.
Fr S exit junc 5 fr AP7 onto GI 623/GI 624 to Sant
Pere Pescador. 4*, V lge, mkd, hdg, pt shd, serviced
pitches; EHU (10A) inc; gas; bbq (charcoal, elec);
red long stay; TV; 15% statics; phone; Eng spkn; adv
bkg acc; fishing; horseriding 5km; bike hire; games
rm; windsurfing school; tennis; waterslide; ice; CKE.
*"Excel, well-run, clean site; no o'fits over 10m Apr-
Sep; helpful staff; immac san facs; gd rest; private
san facs avail; poss flooding on some pitches when
wet; Parque Acuatico 18km."* €60.40, 14 Apr-27 Sep,
E22.   2019

See advertisement on previous page

SANT PERE PESCADOR *3B3* (2km SE Coastal)
42.16194, 3.10888 **Camping Las Dunas,** 17470
Sant Pere Pescador (Gerona) (Postal Address:
Aptdo Correos 23, 17130 L'Escala) **972-52 17 17
or 01205 366856 (UK); info@campinglasdunas.
com; www.campinglasdunas.com**

[icons] sand adj

Exit AP7 junc 5 dir Viladamat & L'Escala; 2km bef
L'Escala turn L for Sant Martí d'Empúries, turn L
bef ent vill for 2km, camp sp. V lge, mkd, pt shd,
pt sl, serviced pitches; EHU (6A) inc; gas; bbq; TV;
5% statics; phone; Eng spkn; adv bkg req; games
area; games rm; tennis; watersports; CKE. *"Greco-
Roman ruins in Empúries; gd sized pitches - extra for
serviced; busy, popular site; souvenir shop; money
exchange; cash machine; doctor; excel, clean facs; vg
site."* €72.50, 15 May-15 Sep.   2019

See advertisement opposite

SANT PERE PESCADOR *3B3* (1.3km S Coastal)
42.18816, 3.10265 **Camping Las Palmeras,** Ctra de
la Platja 9, 17470 Sant Pere Pescador (Gerona) **972-52
05 06; info@campinglaspalmeras.com; www.camping
laspalmeras.com**

[icons] (htd) sand 200m

Exit AP7 junc 3 or 4 at Figueras onto C260 dir Roses/
Cadaqués rd. After 8km at Castelló d'Empúries
turn S for Sant Pere Pescador & cont twd beach.
Site on R of rd. 1*, Lge, mkd, shd, serviced pitches;
EHU (5-16A) €3.90; gas; TV; phone; Eng spkn; adv
bkg acc; games area; bike hire; games rm; tennis; CKE.
*"Pleasant site; helpful, friendly staff; superb, clean san
facs; cash point; gd cycle tracks; nature reserve nrby;
excel."* €47.70, 15 Apr-5 Nov.   2016

SANTA ELENA *2F4* (0.4km E Rural) *38.34305,
-3.53611* **Camping Despeñaperros,** Calle Infanta
Elena s/n, Junto a Autovia de Andalucia, Km 257,
23213 Santa Elena (Jaén) **953-66 41 92; info@
campingdespenaperros.com; www.campingdes
penaperros.com**

[icons]

Leave A4/E5 at junc 257 or 259, site well sp to N
side of vill nr municipal leisure complex. 3*, Med,
hdstg, mkd, pt shd, serviced pitches; EHU (10A)
€4.25 (poss rev pol); gas; red long stay; TV (pitch);
80% statics; phone; bus 500m; adv bkg acc; ccard acc;
CKE. *"Gd winter NH in wooded location; gd size pitches
but muddy if wet; gd walking area, perfect for dogs;
friendly, helpful staff; clean san facs; disabled facs wc
only; conv national park & m'way; gd rest; sh walk to vill
& shops; site v rural; beautiful area."* €24.00   2017

SANTA MARINA DE VALDEON *1A3* (0.6km N Rural)
43.13638, -4.89472 **Camping El Cares,** El Cardo,
24915 Santa Marina de Valdeón (León) **987-74 26 76;
campingelcares@hotmail.com**

[icons]

Fr S take N621 to Portilla de la Reina. Turn L onto
LE243 to Santa Marina. Avoid vill (narr rd), go to
Northern end of vill bypass. Site is sp on L. 2*, Med,
pt shd, terr, EHU (5A) €3.20; 10% statics; phone;
bus 1km; ccard acc; CKE. *"Lovely, scenic site high in
mountains; gd base for Cares Gorge; friendly, helpful
staff; gd views; tight access - not rec if towing or lge
m'van."* €26.50, 1 Jun-15 Oct.   2016

SANTA POLA *4F2* (1km NW Urban/Coastal) *38.20105, -0.56983* **Camping Bahía de Santa Pola,** Ctra de Elche s/n, Km. 11, 03130 Santa Pola (Alicante) **965-41 10 12; campingbahia@gmail.com; www.campingbahia.com**

🔟 🐕 👬 (htd) 🚿 ♿ 🚽 ✉ MSP 🎏 ⚓ 🏔 🏖 🏄 sand 1km

Exit A7 junc 72 dir airport, cont to N332 & turn R dir Cartagena. At rndabt take exit sp Elx/Elche onto CV865, site 100m on R. Lge, mkd, hdstg, pt shd, EHU (10A) €3; gas; red long stay; TV (pitch); 50% statics; phone; bus adj; Eng spkn; adv bkg acc; ccard acc; CKE. *"Helpful, friendly manager; well-organised site; sm pitches; recep in red building facing ent; excel san facs; site rds steep; attractive coastal cycle path."* **€25.00**   **2019**

SANTAELLA *2G3* (5km N Rural) *37.62263, -4.85950* **Camping La Campiña,** La Guijarrosa-Santaella, 14547 Santaella (Córdoba) **957-31 53 03; info@campinglacampina.com; www.campingla campina.com**

🔟 🐕 €2 👬 WD 🚿 ♿ 🚽 ✉ 🍴 🍺 ⚓ 🏔 🏄

Fr A4/E5 leave at km 441 onto A386 rd dir La Rambla to Santaella for 11km, turn L onto A379 for 5km & foll sp. 2*, Sm, mkd, hdstg, pt shd, pt sl, EHU (10A) €4; gas; bbq; red long stay; TV; bus at gate to Córdoba; Eng spkn; adv bkg acc; ccard acc; CKE. *"Fine views; friendly, warm welcome; popular, family-run site; many pitches sm for lge o'fits; guided walks; poss clsd winter - phone to check; helpful & knowledgable owner; great site."* **€29.00, E25.**   **2017**

SANTANDER *1A4* (5km NE Coastal) *43.48916, -3.79361* **Camping Cabo Mayor,** Avda. del Faro s/n, 39012 Santander (Cantabria) **942-39 15 42; info@cabomayor.com; www.cabomayor.com**

👬 WD 🐕 🚿 ♿ 🚽 ✉ 🦋 🍦 🍴 🍺 🍺 ⚓ 🏔 🏄 🏖 adj

Sp thro town but not v clearly. On waterfront (turn R if arr by ferry). At lge junc do not foll quayside, take uphill rd (resort type prom) & foll sp for Faro de Cabo Mayor. Site 200m bef lighthouse on L. Lge, mkd, unshd, terr, EHU (10A) inc; gas; TV; 10% statics; phone; bus to Santander nrby; Eng spkn; CKE. *"Med to lge pitches; site popular with lge youth groups hg ssn; shwrs clsd 2230-0800; conv ferry; pitches priced by size, pleasant coastal walk to Sardinero beachs; gd NH; well organised & clean; gd facs but dated; no hot water for washing up; excel; gd welcome."* **€20.00, 27 Mar-12 Oct.**   **2018**

SANTANDER *1A4* (8km W Coastal) *43.47678, -3.87303* **Camping Virgen del Mar,** Ctra Santander-Liencres, San Román-Corbán s/n, 39000 Santander (Cantabria) **942-34 24 25; cvirdmar@ceoecant.es; www.campingvirgendelmar.com**

⊞ 🛉🛉 WD 🔥 🗓 & 🖪 🖉 MAP 🦋 ❟ 🍴 ⊕ 🚲 🝊 🏛 🛶 🐚 sand 300m

Fr ferry turn R, then L up to football stadium, L again leads strt into San Román. If app fr W, take A67 (El Sardinero) then S20, leave at junc 2 dir Liencres, strt on. Site well sp. 2*, Lge, mkd, pt shd, EHU (4-10A) €4; red long stay; bus 500m; adv bkg acc; CKE. *"Basic facs, poss ltd hot water; some sm pitches not suitable lge o'fits; site adj cemetary; phone in LS to check site open; expensive LS; gd for ferry; recep not v friendly."* **€27.00** **2019**

SANTIAGO DE COMPOSTELA *1A2* (3.5km NE Urban) *42.88972, -8.52444* **Camping As Cancelas,** Rua do Xullo 25, 35, 15704 Santiago de Compostela (La Coruña) **981-58 02 66 or 981-58 04 76; info@campingascancelas.com; www.campingascancelas.com**

⊞ 🐎 🛉🛉 WD 🔥 🗓 & 🖪 🖉 🦋 ❟ 🍴 ⊕ 🚲 🝊 🏛 🛶 🐚

Exit AP9 junc 67 & foll sp Santiago. At rndabt with lge service stn turn L sp 'camping' & foll sp to site turning L at McDonalds. Site adj Guardia Civil barracks. NB-Do not use sat nav if app fr Lugo on N547. 2*, Lge, mkd, shd, pt sl, terr, EHU (5A) inc; gas; bbq; TV; phone; bus 100m; Eng spkn; CKE. *"Busy site-conv for pilgrims; rec arr early high ssn; some sm pitches poss diff c'vans & steep ascent; gd clean san facs, stretched when busy; gd rest; bus to city 100m fr gate avoids steep 15 min walk back fr town (LS adequate car parks in town); poss interference with car/ c'van electrics fr local transmitter, if problems report to site recep; LS recep in bar; arr in sq by Cathedral at 1100 for Thanksgiving service at 1200; helpful owner; excel site; facs v clean; wifi vg."* **€33.60** **2017**

SANTILLANA DEL MAR *1A4* (2.5km E Rural) *43.38222, -4.08305* **Camping Altamira,** Barrio Las Quintas s/n, 39330 Queveda (Cantabria) **942-84 01 81; nfo@campingaltamira.es; www.campingaltamira.es**

🛉🛉 🔥 🗓 & 🖉 ❟ 🍴 ⊕ 🝊 🛶

Clear sp to Santillana fr A67; site on R 3km bef vill. 2*, Med, mkd, pt shd, pt sl, terr, EHU (3A)- (5A) €2 (poss rev pol); gas; TV; 30% statics; bus 100m; Eng spkn; adv bkg req; ccard acc; horseriding; CKE. *"Pleasant site; ltd facs LS; nr Altimira cave paintings; easy access Santander ferry on m'way; gd coastal walks; open w/end only Nov-Mar - rec phone ahead; excel; san facs v clean & modern; local rests nrby."* **€22.00, 10 Mar-7 Dec.** **2019**

SANTILLANA DEL MAR *1A4* (1km NW Rural) *43.39333, -4.11222* **Camping Santillana del Mar,** Ctra de Comillas s/n, 39330 Santillana del Mar (Cantabria) **942-81 82 50; www.campingsantillana.com**

⊞ 🐎 🛉🛉 WD 🔥 🗓 & 🖪 🖉 ❟ 🍴 ⊕ 🚲 🝊 🏛 🛶 🐚 🐚 5km

Fr W exit A8 junc 230 Santillana-Comillas, then foll sp Santillana & site on rd CA131. Fr E exit A67 junc 187 & foll sp Santillana. Turn R onto CA131, site on R up hill after vill. 3*, Lge, pt shd, sl, terr, EHU (6A) inc (poss rev pol); gas; 20% statics; phone; bus 300m; Eng spkn; horseriding; bike hire; tennis; golf 15km; CKE. *"Useful site in beautiful historic vill; hot water only in shwrs; diff access to fresh water & to mv disposal point; narr, winding access rds, projecting trees & kerbs to some pitches - not rec lge o'fits or twin axles; car wash; cash machine; poss muddy LS & pitches rutted; poss travellers; gd views; lovely walk to town; poor facs (2014); NH."* **€24.00** **2017**

SANTO DOMINGO DE LA CALZADA *1B4* (3.6km E Rural) *42.44083, -2.91506* **Camping Banares,** Ctra N120, Km 42.2, 26250 Santo Domingo de la Calzada **941-34 01 31; info@campingbanares.es; www.campingbanares.es**

⊞ 🛉🛉 WD 🔥 🗓 & 🖉 MAP ❟ ⊕ 🝊 🏛 🛶 🐚

Fr N120 Burgos-Logroño rd, turn N at Santo Domingo, foll sp Banares & site. 4*, Sm, unshd, pt sl, EHU (5-10A) €5.50; gas; 90% statics; Eng spkn; adv bkg acc; ccard acc; games area; tennis; CKE. *"Interesting, historic town; shops, bars, rests 3km; NH only."* **€32.60** **2016**

SANXENXO *1B2* (4.5km SW Coastal) *42.39254, -8.84517* **Camping Playa Paxariñas,** Ctra C550, Km 2.3 Lanzada-Portonovo, 36960 Sanxenxo (Pontevedra) **986-72 30 55; info@campingpaxarinas.com; www.campingpaxarinas.com**

🛉🛉 WD 🔥 🗓 & 🖉 ❟ 🌊 ❟ 🍴 🝊 🏛 🛶 sand adj

Fr Pontevedra W on P0308 coast rd; 3km after Sanxenxo. Site thro hotel on L at bend. Site poorly sp. Fr AP9 fr N exit junc 119 onto VRG41 & exit for Sanxenxo. Turn R at 3rd rndabt for Portonovo to site in dir O Grove. Do not turn L to port area on ent Portonovo. Lge, mkd, shd, pt sl, terr, EHU (5A) €4.75; gas; bbq; red long stay; TV; 75% statics; phone; bus adj; Eng spkn; adv bkg acc; ccard acc; CKE. *"Site in gd position; secluded beaches; views over estuary; take care high kerbs on pitches; excel san facs - ltd facs LS & poss clsd; lovely unspoilt site; plenty of shd."* **€32.00, 17 Mar-15 Oct.** **2016**

SANXENXO *1B2* (3km NW Coastal) *42.41777, -8.87555* **Camping Monte Cabo,** Soutullo 174, 36990 Noalla (Pontevedra) **986-74 41 41; info@ montecabo.com; www.montecabo.com**

🏕12 ⛺ WD 🚿 ⚐ 🚽 MSP 🦋 ⛱ 🍽 🄍 ♿ 🅿 ♨ 🛝 sand 250m

Fr AP9 exit junc 119 onto upgraded VRG4.1 dir Sanxenxo. Ignore sp for Sanxenxo until rndabt sp A Toxa/La Toja, where turn L onto P308. Cont to Fontenla supmkt on R - minor rd to site just bef supmkt. Rd P308 fr AP9 junc 129 best avoided. Sm, mkd, pt shd, terr, EHU €4.25; red long stay; TV; 10% statics; phone; bus 600m; Eng spkn; adv bkg acc; ccard acc; CKE. *"Peaceful, friendly site set above sm beach (access via steep path) with views; sm pitches; beautiful coastline & interesting historical sites; vg."* **€30.00** 2017

SARRIA *1B2* (2km E Rural) *42.77625, -7.39552* **Camping Vila de Sarria,** Ctra. De Pintín, Km 1 Sarria 27600 **982 53 54 67; info@campingviladesarria. com; www.campingviladesarria.com**

🐕 ⛺ WD 🚿 ♿ 🚽 MSP 🍽 ♨ 🅿 nr

Leave Sarria on LU5602 twds Pintin. Site on L in 1km. Med, pt shd, pt sl, EHU; twin axles; Eng spkn; adv bkg acc; ccard acc. *"Quiet site on Camino de Santiago Rte; excel rest; v pleasant, welcoming staff; busy w/ ends; vg."* **€22.50, Easter-30 Sep.** 2015

SAX *4F2* (6km NW Rural) *38.56875, -0.84913* **Camping Gwen & Michael,** Colonia de Santa Eulalia 1, 03630 Sax (Alicante) **965-47 44 19 or 7718 18 58 05(UK)**

🐕 ⛺ WD 🚿 ♿ 🚽 MSP 🦋 ♨ 🅿 nr

Exit A31 at junc km 191 & foll sp for Santa Eulalia, site on R just bef vill sq. Rec phone prior to arr. Sm, hdg, hdstg, unshd, EHU (3A) €1. *"Vg CL-type site; friendly British owners; beautiful area; gd NH & touring base; c'van storage avail; 3 rest nrby."* **€15.00, 15 Mar-30 Nov.** 2016

SEGOVIA *1C4* (2km SE Urban) *40.93138, -4.09250* **Camping El Acueducto,** Ctra la Granja, 40004 Segovia **921-42 50 00; informacion@camping acueducto.com; www.campingacueducto.com**

🐕 ⛺ WD 🚿 ♿ 🚽 MSP 🍽 ♨ 🅿 nr 🅿 🄍 🛝 ♿

Turn off Segovia by-pass N110/SG20 at La Granja exit, but head twd Segovia on DL601. Site in approx 500m off dual c'way just bef Restaurante Lago. Lge, mkd, pt shd, pt sl, EHU (6-10A) €5; gas; bbq; 10% statics; phone; bus 150m; bike hire; CKE. *"Excel; helpful staff; lovely views; clean facs; gates locked 0000-0800; gd bus service; some pitches sm & diff for lge o'fits; city a 'must' to visit; bus stop and gd spmkt 10min walk; site muddy after rain; unfriendly new owner (2018); cycle path to city; gd hot shwrs."* **€34.00, 15 Mar-15 Oct.** 2019

SENA DE LUNA *1A3* (1km S Rural) *42.92181, -5.96153* **Camping Río Luna,** Ctra de Abelgas s/n, 24145 Sena de Luna (León) **987-59 77 14; info@ campingrioluna.com; www.campingrioluna.com**

🐕 ⛺ (htd) WD 🚿 ♿ 🚽 MSP 🦋 ♨ 🍽 ♿

S fr Oviedo on AP66, at junc 93 turn W onto CL626 to Sena de Luna in approx 5km. Site on L, sp. 1*, Med, pt shd, EHU (5A) €3.80; bbq; sw nr; TV; phone; adv bkg acc; ccard acc. *"Vg, scenic site; walking, climbing; cent for wild boar & wolves; rural, rustic site; hot shwrs."* **€18.00, Easter & 1 May-30 Sep.** 2019

SITGES *3C3* (2km SW Urban/Coastal) *41.23351, 1.78111* **Camping Bungalow Park El Garrofer,** Ctra C246A, Km 39, 08870 Sitges (Barcelona) **93 894 17 80; info@garroferpark.com; www.garroferpark.com**

🐕 €2.65 ⛺ (htd) WD 🚿 ♿ 🚽 MSP 🍽 ♨ 🄍 ♿ 🅿 🖊 ♿ 🛝 shgl 900m

Exit 26 on the C-32 dir St. Pere de Ribes, at 1st rndabt take 1st exit, at 2nd rndabt take 2nd exit, foll rd C-31 to campsite. V lge, hdstg, mkd, hdg, pt shd, serviced pitches; EHU (5-10A) €4.10 (poss rev pol); gas; TV; 80% statics; phone; bus adj; Eng spkn; adv bkg acc; ccard acc; games rm; tennis 800m; car wash; site clsd 19 Dec-27 Jan to tourers; windsurfing; games area; horseriding; bike hire; CKE. *"Great location, conv Barcelona, bus adj; sep area for m'vans; pleasant staff; recep open 0800-2100; gd level site; quiet; gd old & new facs."* **€40.00, 22 Feb-15 Dec.** 2019

SORIA *3C1* (2km SW Rural) *41.74588, -2.48456* **Camping Fuente de la Teja,** Ctra Madrid-Soria, Km 223, 42004 Soria **975-22 29 67; camping@ fuentedelateja.com; www.fuentedelateja.com**

🐕 ⛺ WD 🚿 ♿ 🚽 MSP 🍽 ♨ 🅿 nr 🄍 ♿

Fr new ring road SO-20 follow Madrid to S edge of town. Take exit 8 sp Redonda then R at rndabt. 2*, Med, mkd, pt shd, pt sl, EHU (6A) €3 (poss no earth); gas; bbq; TV; 10% statics; phone; Eng spkn; adv bkg acc; ccard acc; CKE. *"Vg site; excel, gd for NH; vg san facs; interesting town; phone ahead to check site poss open bet Oct & Easter; hypmkt 3km; easy access to site; pitches around 100sqm, suits o'fits upto 10m; friendly staff; access fr 9am."* **€23.30, 1 Mar-31 Oct.** 2019

SUECA *4E2* (5km NE Coastal) *39.30354, -0.29270* **Camping Les Barraquetes,** Playa de Sueca, Mareny Barraquetes, 46410 Sueca (València) **961-76 07 23; info@barraquetes.com; www.barraquetes.com**

🐕 ⛺ WD 🚿 ♿ 🚽 MSP 🍽 🍽 🄍 🖊 ♿ 🛝 🛝 sand 350m

Exit AP7 junc 58 dir Sueca onto N332. In Sueca take CV500 to Mareny Barraquetes. Or S fr València on CV500 coast rd. Foll sp for Cullera & Sueca. Site on L. Med, mkd, pt shd, EHU (10A) €5.88; gas; bbq; red long stay; twin axles; TV; 70% statics; phone; bus 500m; Eng spkn; ccard acc; games area; waterslide; tennis; windsurfing school; CKE. *"Quiet, family atmosphere; conv touring base & València; quiet beach 8 min walk; helpful staff; gd."* **€33.00, 16 Jan-14 Dec.** 2017

TAPIA DE CASARIEGO *1A3* (2km SW Coastal) *43.56394, -6.95247* **Camping Playa de Tapia,** La Reburdia, 33740 Tapia de Casariego (Asturias) **985-47 27 21**

🏠 👫 🚻 🚾 🏕 ♿ 🚿 📶 🦋 💧 ▽ 🅗 🛒 ⛱sand 1m

Fr Ribadeo pass thro vill of Serentes on N634 past 1st camping sp. Site on L at 546km post, foll sp to site. 2*, Med, mkd, hdg, pt shd, pt sl, EHU (16A) €4.06; gas; phone; bus 800m; Eng spkn; adv bkg acc; CKE. *"Gd access; busy, well-maintained, friendly site; o'looking coast & harbour; poss ltd hot water; walking dist to delightful town."* **€23.00, Holy Week & 1 Jun-15 Sep.** 2015

TARAZONA *3B1* (8km SE Rural) *41.81890, -1.69230* **Camping Veruela Moncayo,** Ctra Vera-Veruela, 50580 Vera de Moncayo (Zaragoza) **976 64 90 34; antoniogp@able.es**

12 🏠 👫 🚻 🚾 🏕 ♿ 🚿 ▽ 🅗 💧 🛒 nr 🅣

Fr Zaragoza, take AP68 or N232 twd Tudela/ Logroño; after approx. 50km, turn L to join N122 (km stone 75) twd Tarazona; cont 30km & turn L twd Vera de Moncayo; go thro town cent; site on R; well sp. Med, hdg, mkd, pt shd, pt sl, EHU; gas; adv bkg acc; bike hire; CKE. *"Quiet site adj monastery; friendly owner; gd."* **€26.00** 2017

"Satellite navigation makes touring much easier"

Remember most sat navs don't know if you're towing or in a larger vehicle – always use yours alongside maps and site directions.

TARIFA *2H3* (10km NW Coastal) *36.06908, 5.68036* **Camping Valdevaqueros,** Ctra N340 km 75,5 11380 Tarifa **34 956 684 174; info@campingvaldevaqueros. com; www.campingvaldevaqueros.com**

12 🏠 👫 🚾 🏕 ▽ 🅗 💧 🛒 🅣 🍴 🅗 📶 🅣 🔺 ⛱ sandy 1km

Campsite is sp 9km fr Tarifa on the N340 twds Cadiz. Lge, pt shd, pt sl, EHU (6A); TV; 50% statics; phone; Eng spkn; adv bkg rec; games area; bike hire. *"Excel site; watersports nrby."* **€34.00** 2019

TARRAGONA *3C3* (0.6km NE Urban/Coastal) *40.88707, 0.80630* **Camping Nautic,** Calle Libertat s/n, 43860 L'Ametlla de Mar Tarragona **34 977 456 110; info@campingnautic.com; www.campingnautic.com**

🏠 👫 🚾 🏕 🚿 ♿ 🚿 ▽ 📶 🅗 🍴 🅗 📶 🅣 🔺 ⛱

Fr N340 exit at km 1113 sp L'Ametlla de Mar (or A7 exit 39). Over rlwy bdge, foll rd to L. Turn R after park and TO on R, foll signs to campsite. Lge, hdstg, pt shd, terr, EHU; TV; 25% statics; phone; bus 500m, train 700m; Eng spkn; adv bkg acc; games area; CCI. *"Vg site; tennis court; 5 mins to attractive town with rest & sm supmkt; lge Mercadona outsite town; site on different levels."* **€40.00, 6 Apr-3 Nov.** 2019

TARRAGONA *3C3* (5km NE Coastal) *41.13019, 1.31170* **Camping Las Palmeras,** N340, Km 1168, 43080 Tarragona **977-20 80 81; laspalmeras@ laspalmeras.com; www.laspalmeras.com**

🏠 €5 🚾 🏕 🚿 ♿ 🚿 ▽ 🍴 🅗 💧 🅣 🔺 🔺 🔺 🔺 ⛱sand adj

Exit AP7 at junc 32 (sp Altafulla). After about 5km on N340 twd Tarragona take sp L turn at crest of hill. Site sp. 1*, V lge, mkd, pt shd, EHU (6A) inc; gas; red long stay; 10% statics; phone; ccard acc; games rm; tennis; games area; CKE. *"Gd beach; ideal for families; poss mosquito prob; many sporting facs; gd, clean san facs; friendly, helpful staff; naturist beach 1km; supmkt 5km; excel site."* **€45.00, 2 Apr-12 Oct.** 2019

TARRAGONA *3C3* (12km E Coastal) *41.1324, 1.3604* **Camping-Caravaning Tamarit Park,** Playa Tamarit, Ctra N340, Km 1172, 43008 Playa Tamarit (Tarragona) **977-65 01 28; tamaritpark@tamarit.com; www.tamarit.com**

🏠 €4 👫(htd) 🚾 🏕 🚿 ♿ 🚿 ▽ 📶 🍴 🅗 🅗 🔺 🔺 🔺 🔺 (htd) 📶 ⛱ shgl adj

Fr A7/E15 exit junc 32 sp Altafulla/Torredembarra, at rndabt join N340 by-pass sp Tarragona. At rndabt foll sp Altafulla, turn sharp R to cross rlwy bdge to site in 1.2km, sp. V lge, hdstg, hdg, shd, pt sl, serviced pitches; EHU (10A) inc; gas; bbq; red long stay; TV; 30% statics; phone; Eng spkn; adv bkg rec; ccard acc; games area; watersports; tennis; CKE. *"Well-maintained, secure site with family atmosphere; excel beach; superb pool; private bthrms avail; best site in area but poss noisy at night & w/end; variable pitch prices; beachside pitches avail; cash machine; car wash; take care overhanging trees; Altafulla sh walk along beach worth visit; excel."* **€65.00, 14 Mar-16 Oct.** 2016

TOLEDO *1D4* (3.5km W Rural) *39.86530, -4.04714* **Camping El Greco,** Ctra Pueblo Montalban, Km.0,7, 45004 Toledo **925-22 00 90; info@campingelgreco.es; www.campingelgreco.es**

12 🏠 👫(htd) 🚾 🏕 🚿 ♿ 🚿 ▽ 📶 🍴 🅗 🅗 📶 🔺 🔺 🔺 🔺

Site on CM4000 between CM40 ring road & Puenta de la Cava bridge. Fr E foll yellow sp. Fr W look for 5 flagpoles on L next to Cirgarral Del Santoangel Custodio. 3*, Med, hdg, mkd, hdstg, pt shd, pt sl, EHU (6-10A) inc (poss rev pol); gas; bbq; phone; bus to town, train to Madrid fr town; Eng spkn; ccard acc; games area; CKE. *"Clean, tidy, well-maintained; all pitches on gravel; easy parking on o'skts - adj Puerta de San Martín rec - or bus; some pitches poss tight; san facs clean; lovely, scenic situation; excel rest (expensive); friendly, helpful owners; vg; dusty; gd rest; site poss neglected during LS; gd pool, closes fr 15 Sept; cheap bar; nice, neat site; mv service pnt basic; sh walk to city."* **€32.30** 2019

TORDESILLAS *1C3 (2km SSW Urban) 41.49584, -5.00494* **Kawan Village El Astral,** Camino de Pollos 8, 47100 Tordesillas (Valladolid) **983-77 09 53; info@ campingelastral.es; www.campingelastral.com**

12 🐕 €2.35 👫(htd) ⬜ ♨ ♿ 🚽 ♨ 🔥 MP
🦋 ⛲ 🍽 ⓗ🍺 🛒 🏛 ⛵

Fr NE on A62/E80 thro town turn L at rndabt over rv & immed after bdge turn R dir Salamanca & almost immed R again into narr gravel track (bef Parador) & foll rd to site; foll camping sp & Parador. Poorly sp. Fr A6 exit sp Tordesillas & take A62. Cross bdge out of town & foll site sp. Med, hdg, mkd, hdstg, pt shd, EHU (5A-10A) €3.60-5 (rev pol); gas; TV; 10% statics; phone; Eng spkn; ccard acc; tennis; bike hire; rv fishing; site open w/end Mar & Oct; CKE. "V helpful owners & staff; easy walk to interesting town; pleasant site by rv; vg, modern, clean san facs & excel facs; popular NH; excel site in every way, facs superb; various size pitches; worth a visit; conv o'night on rte to S of Spain/Portugal; pull thro pitches avail; excel." **€26.00, E03.** **2019**

TORLA *3B2 (1.5km N Rural) 42.63948, -0.10948* **Camping Ordesa,** Ctra de Ordesa s/n, 22376 Torla (Huesca) **974-11 77 21; camping@campingordesa.es; www.campingordesa.es**

🐕 €3 👫 ⬜ ♨ ♿ 🚽 ♨ 🦋 🍽 ⓗ 🛒 nr 🏛 ⛵

Fr Ainsa on N260 twd Torla. Pass Torla turn R onto A135 (Valle de Ordesa twd Ordesa National Park). Site 2km N of Torla, adj Hotel Ordesa. Med, pt shd, serviced pitches; EHU (6A) €5.50; 10% statics; phone; bus 1km; Eng spkn; adv bkg rec; ccard acc; tennis; CKE. "V scenic; recep in adj Hotel Ordesa; excel rest; helpful staff; facs poss stretched w/end; long, narr pitches & lge trees on access rd poss diff lge o'fits; ltd facs LS; no access to National Park by car Jul/Aug, shuttlebus fr Torla." **€22.60, 28 Mar-30 Sep.** **2016**

TORLA *3B2 (1km NE Rural) 42.63181, -0.10685* **Camping Rió Ara,** Ctra Ordesa s/n, 22376 Torla (Huesca) **974-48 62 48; campingrioara@ordesa.net; www.campingrioara.com**

🐕 👫 ⬜ ♨ ♿ 🚽 ♨ MP 🍽 ⓗ nr 🛒

Leave N260/A135 on bend approx 2km N of Broto sp Torla & Ordesa National Park. Drive thro Torla; as leaving vill turn R sp Rió Ara. Steep, narr rd down to & across narr bdge (worth it). Sm, pt shd, pt sl, EHU (6A) €4.25; bbq; TV; bus 500m; adv bkg acc; CKE. "Attractive, well-kept, family-run site; mainly tents; conv for Torla; bus to Ordesa National Park (high ssn); not rec for lge o'fits due to steep app; gd walking & birdwatching; excel; fantastic views; wonderful area." "Facs dated but functional and clean; 20m walk to Torla." **€24.00, 1 Apr-30 Sep.** **2015**

TORRE DEL MAR *2H4 (1.6km S Coastal) 36.7342, -4.1003* **Camping Torre del Mar,** Paseo Maritimo s/n, 29740 Torre del Mar (Málaga) **952-54 02 24; info@ campingtorredelmar.com; www.campingtorredelmar.com**

12 👫 ⬜ ♨ ♿ 🚽 ♨ MP 🦋 🍽 nr ⓗ nr 🛒 🏛 ⛵ 🛒
⛱ shgl 50m

Fr N340 coast rd, at rndabt at W end of town with 'correos' on corner turn twds sea sp Faro, Torre del Mar. At rndabt with lighthouse adj turn R, then 2nd R, site adj big hotel, ent bet lge stone pillars (no name sp). 2*, Lge, hdg, hdstg, mkd, shd, serviced pitches; EHU (16A) €4.00 (long lead req); gas; red long stay; TV (pitch); 39% statics; phone; tennis; CKE. "Tidy, clean, friendly, well-run site; some sm pitches; site rds tight; gd, clean san facs; popular LS; constant hot water; poorly laid out; poss flooding in parts of site; conv for town." **€39.00** **2016**

TORRE DEL MAR *2H4 (7km W Coastal) 36.71967, -4.16471* **Camping Valle Niza Playa,** Ctra N340, km 264, 1 29792 Valle Niza/Malaga **952-51 31 81; info@ campingvalleniza.es; www.campingvalleniza.es**

12 🐕 👫 ⬜ ♨ ♿ 🚽 ♨ 🍽 ⓗ 🛒 ⛵ ⛱ shgl

A7 Malaga-Motril exit 265 Cajiz Costa; at T-junc L onto N340 Coast rd twd Torre Del Mar. Site in 1km. 1*, Med, mkd, pt shd, EHU (6-10A); bbq; twin axles; TV; 50% statics; bus 0.3km; adv bkg acc; ccard acc; games area. "Gdn ctr adj; poor beach across rd; gd." **€33.00** **2017**

TORREVIEJA *4F2 (7km SW Rural) 37.97500, -0.75111* **Camping Florantilles,** Ctra San Miguel de Salinas-Torrevieja, 03193 San Miguel de Salinas (Alicante) **965-72 04 56; camping@campingflorantilles.com; www.campingflorantilles.com**

12 👫 ⬜ ♨ ♿ 🚽 ♨ MP 🍽 🛒 ⓗ 🏛 ⛵ 🛒 ⛱ sand 5km

Exit AP7 junc 758 onto CV95, sp Orihuela, Torrevieja Sud. Turn R at rndabt & after 300m turn R again, site immed on L. Or if travelling on N332 S past Alicante airport twd Torrevieja. Leave Torrevieja by-pass sp Torrevieja, San Miguel. Turn R onto CV95 & foll for 3km thro urbanisation 'Los Balcones', then cont for 500m, under by-pass, round rndabt & up hill, site sp on R. Lge, hdg, mkd, hdstg, pt shd, terr, EHU (10A) inc; gas; bbq; TV; 20% statics; adv bkg acc; ccard acc; golf nr; horseriding 10km; games rm; CKE. "Popular, British owned site; fitness studio/keep fit classes; workshops: calligraphy, card making, drawing/painting, reiki, sound therapy etc; basic Spanish classes; 3 golf courses nrby; no o'fits over 10m; recep clsd 1330-1630; walking club; friendly staff; many long-stay visitors & all year c'vans; suitable mature couples; own transport ess; gd cyling, both flat & hilly; conv hot spa baths at Fortuna & salt lakes." **€30.00, E11.** **2017**

TORROELLA DE MONTGRI *3B3* (6km SE Coastal) *42.01111, 3.18833* **Camping El Delfin Verde,** Ctra Torroella de Montgrí-Palafrugell, Km 4, 17257 Torroella de Montgrí (Gerona) **972-75 84 54; info@ eldelfinverde.com; www.eldelfinverde.com**

⛺ €4 👪 WC ♨ ♿ 🚿 🚮 ⊘ MSP 🦋 ♈ ♔ ⊺ ♨ 🛒 🎿 🏕 ⚓

🏖 sand adj

Fr N leave A7 at junc 5 dir L'Escala. At Viladamat turn R onto C31 sp La Bisbal. After a few km turn L twd Torroella de Montgrí. At rndabt foll sp for Pals (also sp El Delfin Verde). At the flags turn L sp Els Mas Pinell. Foll site sp for 5km. 4*, V lge, mkd, pt shd, pt sl, EHU (6A) inc; bbq; TV; 40% statics; ccard acc; games rm; horseriding 4km; windsurfing; fishing; tennis; bike hire; CKE. "Superb, gd value site; winter storage; excel pool; wide range of facs; sportsgrnd; hairdresser; disco; no o'fits over 8m high ssn; dogs not acc high ssn; money exchange; clean, modern san facs; all water de-salinated fr fresh water production plant; bottled water rec for drinking & cooking; mkt Mon." **€58.00, 17 May-20 Sep.** **2017**

TORROX COSTA *2H4* (2km NNW Urban) *36.73944, -3.94972* **Camping El Pino,** Urbanización Torrox Park s/n, 29793 Torrox Costa (Málaga) **952-53 00 06; info@campingelpino.com; www.campingelpino.com**

12 ⛺ €2.50 👪 WC ♨ ♿ 🚿 ⊘ ♈ ⊺ ♨ nr 🛒 🏕 🎿 🏖 sand 800m

Exit A7 at km 285, turn S at 1st rndabt, turn L at 2nd rndabt & foll sp Torrox Costa N340; in 1.5km at rndabt turn R to Torrox Costa, then L onto rndabt sp Nerja, site well sp in 4km. App rd steep with S bends. Fr N340 fr Torrox Costa foll sp Torrox Park, site sp. Lge, mkd, shd, terr, EHU €3.80 (long lead req); gas; bbq; red long stay; 35% statics; phone; Eng spkn; games area; golf 8km; car wash; CKE. "Gd size pitches but high kerbs; narr ent/exit; gd hill walks; conv Malaga; Nerja caves, Ronda; gd touring base; noise fr rd and bar; san facs adequate." **€18.00** **2019**

TOSSA DE MAR *3B3* (3km SW Coastal) *41.71509, 2.90672* **Camping Cala Llevado,** Ctra Tossa-Lloret, Km 3, 17320 Tossa de Mar (Gerona) **972-34 03 14; info@calallevado.com; www.calallevado.com**

👪 WC ♨ ♿ 🚿 🚮 ⊘ MSP 🦋 ♈ ♔ ⊺ ♨ 🛒 🏕 🎿 🚣

🏖 shgl adj

Exit AP7 junc 9 dir Lloret. In Lloret take GI 682 dir Tossa de Mar. Site well sp. 4*, V lge, mkd, shd, terr, EHU (5-10A) €3.50; gas; TV; 10% statics; phone; Eng spkn; adv bkg acc; waterskiing; tennis; windsurfing; games area; boat trips; sports facs; fishing; CKE. **€29.00, Holy Week & 1 May-30 Sep.** **2016**

UNQUERA *1A4* (5km W Rural) *43.3750, -4.56416* **Camping Colombres (formerly El Mirador de Llavandes),** Vegas Grandes, 33590 Colombres (Asturias) **985-41 22 44; info@campingcolombres. com; www.campingcolombres.com**

⛺ 👪 ♿ 🚿 ⊘ ♈ ♔ ⊺ ♨ 🛒 🏕 🎿 🏕 sand 2km

Fr N634 12km W of San Vicente de la Barquera turn at km 283/284 dir Noriega, site in 1.3km. Med, mkd, pt shd, terr, EHU (6A); gas; bbq; twin axles; TV; Eng spkn; adv bkg rec; ccard acc; games area. "Peaceful setting; excel for touring Picos; new owners, new amenities, new pool(2015); vg site; mkd cycle rtes; patrolled grnds." **€30.00, 23 Mar-20 Sep.** **2015**

VALENCIA *4E2* (16km S Rural) *39.32302, -0.30940* **Camping Devesa Gardens,** Ctra El Saler, Km 13, 46012 València **961-61 11 36; contacto@devesa gardens.com; www.devesagardens.com**

12 👪 (htd) WC ♨ ♿ 🚿 ⊘ 🦋 ⊺ ♨ 🏕 🎿 🏖 700m

S fr València on CV500, site well sp on R 4km S of El Saler. Med, hdstg, mkd, pt shd, EHU (7-15A) €5; gas; bbq; 70% statics; phone; bus to València; adv bkg acc; ccard acc; horseriding; tennis. "Friendly, helpful staff; site has own zoo (clsd LS); lake canoeing; excel; san facs being refurb (2017); lovely pool area; easy access to tourist areas." **€35.00** **2017**

VALLE DE CABUERNIGA *1A4* (1km E Rural) *43.22800, -4.28900* **Camping El Molino de Cabuérniga,** Sopeña, 39510 Cabuérniga (Cantabria) **942-70 62 59; info@ campingcabuerniga.com; www.campingcabuerniga. com**

12 🐕 €1.50 👪 ♨ ♿ ⊘ 🦋 ♈ ⊺ ♨ 🛒 🏕

Sopeña is 55 km. SW of Santander. Fr A8 (Santander - Oviedo) take 249 exit and join N634 to Cabezón de la Sal. Turn SW on CA180 twds Reinosa for 11 km. to Sopeña (site sp to L). Turn into vill (car req - low bldgs), cont bearing R foll sp to site. Med, shd, EHU (6A) check earth; gas; phone; bus 500m; adv bkg acc; ccard acc; tennis; fishing; CKE. "Excel site & facs on edge of vill; no shops in vicinity, but gd location, rds to site narr in places; lovely; open, level site with trees & well mkd pitches; lovely stone bldgs; mkd walks to nrby vill." **€29.00, E29.** **2019**

VEJER DE LA FRONTERA *2H3* (10km S Coastal) *36.20084, -6.03506* **Camping Pinar San José,** Ctra de Vejer-Caños de Meca, Km 10.2, Zahora 17, 11159 Barbate (Cadiz) **956-43 70 30; info@campingpinar sanjose.com; www.campingpinarsanjose.com**

12 🐕 €2 👪 WC ♨ ♿ 🚿 ⊘ MSP 🦋 ♈ ♨ 🛒 🏕 🎿 🚣

🏖 sand 700m

Fr A48/N340 exit junc 36 onto A314 to Barbate, then foll dir Los Caños de Meca. Turn R at seashore rd dir Zahora. Site on L, 2km beyond town. Med, mkd, shd, EHU inc; TV (pitch); 10% statics; adv bkg acc; games area; tennis. "Excel, modern facs." **€64.00** **2019**

SPAIN

VELEZ MALAGA *2G4* (16km NNW Rural) *36.87383, -4.18527* **Camping Rural Presa la Vinuela,** Carretera A-356, Km 30, 29712 La Viñuela Málaga 952-55 45 62; campingpresalavinuela@hotmail.com; www.campinglavinuela.es

⊞ 🐕 €1.10 ♯♯ wo ▲ ▤ 🗲 ⛲ 🍴 ⊛ 🅿 🛒 ⛵

Site is on A356 N of Velez Malaga adjoining the W shore of la Vinuela lake. Fr junc with A402, foll sp to Colmenar/Los Romanes. Stay on A356(don't turn off into Los Romanes). Site is on R approx 2.5km after turn for Los Romanes, next to rest El Pantano. Sm, mkd, hdstg, hdg, pt shd, terr, EHU (5A); TV; 20% statics; Eng spkn; adv bkg acc; games area; games rm. *"Excel site."* **€26.00** 2019

VILANOVA I LA GELTRU *3C3* (3km NW Urban) *41.23190, 1.69075* **Camping Vilanova Park,** Ctra Arboç, Km 2.5, 08800 Vilanova i la Geltru (Barcelona) 938-93 34 02; info@vilanovapark.com or reservas@vilanovapark.com; www.vilanovapark.com

⊞ 🐕 €12.50 ♯♯(htd) wo ▲ ☕ ♿ ▤ 🗲 📶 🍴 ⊛ 🅿 🛒 🎢
🗲 ⛵ (covrd, htd) 🚲 ⛱ sand 3km

Fr N on AP7 exit junc 29 onto C15 dir Vilanova; then take C31 dir Cubelles. Leave at 153km exit dir Vilanova Oeste/L'Arboç to site. Fr W on C32/A16 take Vilanova-Sant Pere de Ribes exit. Take C31 & at 153km exit take BV2115 dir L'Arboc to site. Fr AP7 W leave at exit 31 onto the C32 (A16); take exit 16 (Vilanova-L'Arboc exit) onto BV2115 to site. Parked cars may block loop & obscure site sp. V lge, hdstg, mkd, hdg, pt shd, terr, serviced pitches; EHU (10A) inc (poss rev pol); gas; bbq (elec, gas); sw nr; red long stay; TV; 50% statics; phone; bus directly fr campsite to Barcelona; Eng spkn; adv bkg req; ccard acc; horseriding 500m; games rm; bike hire; sauna; fishing; tennis; golf 1km; CKE. *"Gd for children; excel san facs; gd rest & bar; gd winter facs; jacuzzi; spa; fitness cent; helpful staff; gd security; some sm pitches with diff access due trees or ramps; conv bus/train Barcelona, Tarragona, Port Aventura & coast; mkt Sat; excel site; superb."* **€63.00, E08.** 2019

See advertisement

VILLAFRANCA *3B1* (1.5km S Rural) *42.26333, -1.73861* **Camping Bardenas,** Ctra NA-660 PK 13.4, 31330 Villafranca **34 94 88 46 191; info@ campingbardenas.com; www.campingbardenas.com**

12 (htd) WD ♿ 🚿 🍴 ⓗ 🛒 🏊

Fr N leave AP15 at Junc 29 onto NA660 sp Villafranca. Site on R 1.5km S of town. Med, hdstg, unshd, bbq; 30% statics; ccard acc; games rm; CCI. "Gd site for winter stopover en rte to S Spain; facs ltd in severe weather; excel rest." **€27.00** 2019

VILLAFRANCA DE CORDOBA *2F4* (1km W Rural) *37.95333, -4.54710* **Camping La Albolafia,** Camino de la Vega s/n, 14420 Villafranca de Córdoba (Córdoba) **957-19 08 35; informacion@camping albolafia.com; www.campingalbolafia.com**

🐎 €2.80 ♟ WD ♿ 🚿 🛒 / MSP 🦋 ⓨ 🍴 ⓗ 🛒 🏛 🏊

Exit A4/E5 junc 377, cross rv & at rndabt turn L & foll sp to site in 2km. Beware humps in app rd. Med, hdg, mkd, hdstg, pt shd, EHU (10A) inc (long lead poss req); bbq; twin axles; TV; 10% statics; phone; bus to Córdoba 500m; Eng spkn; CKE. "V pleasant, well-run, friendly, clean site; watersports park nrby; bar and rest clsd end May; ok for stopover."
€27.00, 15 Feb-9 Dec. 2017

VILLAMANAN *1B3* (6km SE Rural) *42.29527, -5.53777* **Camping Pico Verde,** Ctra Mayorga-Astorga, Km 27.6, 24200 Valencia de Don Juan (León) **987-75 05 25; campingpicoverde@gmail.com; http://www.verial.es/campingpicoverde/**

🐎 ♟ 🚿 ♿ 🛒 / 🦋 ⓗ 🏛 🏊 (covrd) 🛁

Fr N630 S, turn E at km 32.2 onto C621 sp Valencia de Don Juan. Site in 4km on R. 3*, Med, mkd, EHU (6A) inc; 25% statics; tennis; CKE. "Friendly, helpful staff; conv León; picturesque vill; sw caps to be worn in pool; phone ahead to check site open if travelling close to opening/closing dates." **€20.00, 15 Jun-8 Sep.** 2019

VILLARGORDO DEL CABRIEL *4E1* (3km NW Rural) *39.5525, -1.47444* **Kiko Park Rural,** Ctra Embalse de Contreras, Km 3, 46317 Villargordo del Cabriel (València) **962-13 90 82; kikoparkrural@kikopark.com; www.kikopark.com/rural**

12 WD €0.80 ♟ WD 🚿 ♿ 🛒 / MSP 🍴 ⓗ 🛒 🏊

A3/E901 València-Madrid, exit junc 255 to Villargordo del Cabriel, foll sp to site. Med, mkd, hdstg, pt shd, terr, serviced pitches; EHU (6A) €3.70; gas; sw nr; red long stay; TV; 10% statics; Eng spkn; adv bkg rec; ccard acc; canoeing; horseriding; white water rafting; fishing; bike hire; watersports; CKE. "Beautiful location; superb, well-run, peaceful site; lge pitches; gd walking; vg rest; many activities; helpful, v friendly family run site; gd hdstg; excel." **€33.00** 2015

VINAROS *3D2* (5km N Coastal) *40.49363, 0.48504* **Camping Vinarós,** Ctra N340, Km 1054, 12500 Vinarós (Castellón) **964-40 24 24; info@ campingvinaros.com; www.campingvinaros.com**

12 €3 ♟ (htd) WD 🚿 ♿ 🛒 / 🦋 ⓨ 🍴 ⓗ nr 🛒 🛒 nr 🏛 🏊 🛒 shgl 1km

Fr N exit AP7 junc 42 onto N238 dir Vinarós. Straight on at first 2 rndabt, at 3rd rndabt turn L (3rd exit) dir Tarragona. Site on R at Km1054. Lge, hdstg, mkd, hdg, pt shd, serviced pitches; EHU (6A) inc; gas; red long stay; 15% statics; phone; bus adj; Eng spkn; adv bkg rec; ccard acc; CKE. "Excel gd value, busy, well-run site; many long-stay winter residents; spacious pitches; vg clean, modern san facs; elec volts poss v low in evening; gd rest; friendly, helpful staff; rec use bottled water; currency exchange; Peñíscola Castle & Morello worth a visit; easy cycle to town; ok stopover." **€13.00** 2017

"That's changed – Should I let the Club know?"

If you find something on site that's different from the site entry, fill in a report and let us know. See camc.com/europereport.

VINUELA *2G4* (7.5km NW Rural) *36.87383, -4.18527* **Camping Presa La Viñuela,** Ctra A356, km 30 29712 Viñuela **952-55 45 62; campingpresalavinuela@ hotmail.com; www.campinglavinuela.es**

🐎 €1.10 ♟ WD 🚿 ♿ 🛒 / ⓗ 🍴 ⓗ 🛒 🏛 🏊

Site on A356 N of Velez Malaga adjoining the W shore of la Vinuela lake. Fr junc with A402, foll sp to Colmenar & Los Romanes. Stay on A356 (don't turn off into Los Romanes). Site is on R approx 2.5km after the turn for Los Romanes, next to El Pantano rest. Sm, mkd, hdstg, shd, terr, EHU (5A); TV; 20% statics; Eng spkn; adv bkg acc; games rm; games area. "Excel site; fab views." **€21.00, 1 Jan-30 Sep.** 2019

VINUESA *3B1* (2km N Rural) *41.92647, -2.76285* **Camping Cobijo,** Ctra Laguna Negra, Km 2, 42150 Vinuesa (Soria) **975-37 83 31; recepcion@ campingcobijo.com; www.campingcobijo.com**

🐎 ♟ WD 🚿 ♿ 🛒 / 🦋 ⓨ 🍴 ⓗ 🛒 🏛 🏊

Travelling W fr Soria to Burgos, at Abejar R on SO840. by-pass Abejar cont to Vinuesa. Well sp fr there. Lge, pt shd, pt sl, EHU (3-6A) €4-5.70 (long lead poss req); gas; bbq; 10% statics; phone; Eng spkn; ccard acc; bike hire; CKE. "Friendly staff; clean, attractive site; some pitches in wooded area poss diff lge o'fits; special elec connector supplied (deposit); ltd bar & rest LS, excel rests in town; gd walks." **€28.00, 1 Apr-1 Nov.** 2017

VITORIA/GASTEIZ *3B1* (5.5km SW Rural) *42.83114, -2.72248* **Camping Ibaya,** Nacional 102, Km 346.5, Zuazo de Vitoria 01195 Vitoria/Gasteiz (Alava) **945-14 76 20; info@campingibaia.com; www.campingibaia.com**

🔢 🐕 €2.20 👫 ⬚ 🏕 🛒 🍴 ⏱ 🍽 Ⓦ 🎮 🛒 ⛺

Fr A1 take exit 343 sp N102/A3302. At rndabt foll sp N102 Vitoria/Gasteiz. At next rndabt take 3rd exit & immed turn L twd filling stn. Site ent on R in 100m, sp. Sm, mkd, hdstg, pt shd, pt sl, EHU (6A) inc; gas; bbq; phone; Eng spkn; CKE. "NH only; gd, modern san facs; phone ahead to check open LS; fair site; sometimes noisy; close grouped sites." **€29.50**   **2019**

> ## "I like to fill in the reports as I travel from site to site"
>
> You'll find report forms at the back of this guide, or you can fill them in online at camc.com/europereport.

ZARAGOZA *3C1* (6km W Urban) *41.63766, -0.94227* **Camping Ciudad de Zaragoza,** Calle San Juan Bautista de la Salle s/n, 50012 Zaragoza **876-24 14 95; info@campingzaragoza.com; www.campingzaragoza.com**

🔢 🐕 €3.75 👫 (htd) Ⓦ 🏕 🛒 ♿ 🛒 🍴 ⏱ 🍽 Ⓦ 🎮 🛒 ⛺ 🏊

Fr western ring rd Z40 go E on N11A Av Manuel Rodriguez Ayuso. Pass one rndabt then R onto C San Juan Batista de la Salle to 2nd rndabt, u-turn to find site ent on R in 150m. 4*, Lge, hdstg, mkd, pt shd, pt sl, EHU (10A) €5.75; bbq; twin axles; TV; 50% statics; Eng spkn; adv bkg acc; games area; tennis. "Modern san facs; poss travellers; unattractive and tired, but conv site in suburbs; gd sh stay; poss noisy (campers & daytime aircraft); gd food at bar; helpful staff; gd NH from Bilbao ferry." **€35.00**   **2019**

ZARAUTZ *3A1* (3km NE Coastal) *43.28958, -2.14603* **Gran Camping Zarautz,** Monte Talaimendi s/n, 20800 Zarautz (Guipúzkoa) **943-83 12 38; info@grancamping zarautz.com; www.grancampingzarautz.com**

🔢 🐕 👫 (htd) Ⓦ 🏕 🛒 ♿ 🛒 🍴 ⏱ 🍽 Ⓦ 🎮 🛒 ⛺ 🏊 1km

Exit A8 junc 11 Zarautz, strt on at 1st & 2nd rndabt after toll & foll site sp. On N634 fr San Sebastián to Zarautz, R at rndabt. On N634 fr Bilbao to Zarautz L at rndabt. Lge, hdstg, mkd, hdg, pt shd, pt sl, terr, EHU (6-10A) inc; gas; bbq; TV; 50% statics; phone; train/bus to Bilbao & San Sebastian; Eng spkn; adv bkg acc; ccard acc; golf 1km; games rm; CKE. "Site on cliff o'looking bay; excel beach, gd base for coast & mountains; helpful, friendly staff; some pitches sm with steep access & o'looked fr terr above; sans facs upgraded but poor standard and insufficient when cr; excel rest; pitches poss muddy; NH for Bilbao ferry; rec arr early to secure pitch; v steep walk to beach (part naturist); gd for NH; excel train service to San Sebastian; gd shop on site; ACSI discount." **€31.00**   **2017**

ZARAUTZ *3A1* (8km E Coastal) *43.27777, -2.12305* **Camping Orio Kanpina,** 20810 Orio (Guipúzkoa) **943-83 48 01; info@oriokanpina.com; www.oriokanpina.com**

👫 Ⓦ 🏕 🛒 ♿ 🛒 🍴 ⏱ 🍽 Ⓦ nr 🎮 🛒 ⛺ 🏄 🎣
🏖 sand adj

Fr E on A8 exit junc 33 & at rndabt foll sp Orio, Kanpin & Playa. Site on R. Or to avoid town cent (rec) cross bdge & foll N634 for 1km, turn L at sp Orio & camping, turn R at rndabt to site. Lge, mkd, pt shd, pt sl, EHU (5A) inc; gas; 50% statics; phone; Eng spkn; adv bkg acc; ccard acc; car wash; tennis; CKE. "Busy, well maintained site; flats now built bet site & beach & new marina adj - now no sea views; walks; gd facs; friendly staff, useful NH bef leaving Spain; interesting sm town." **€36.00, 1 Mar-12 Nov.**   **2017**

SPAIN

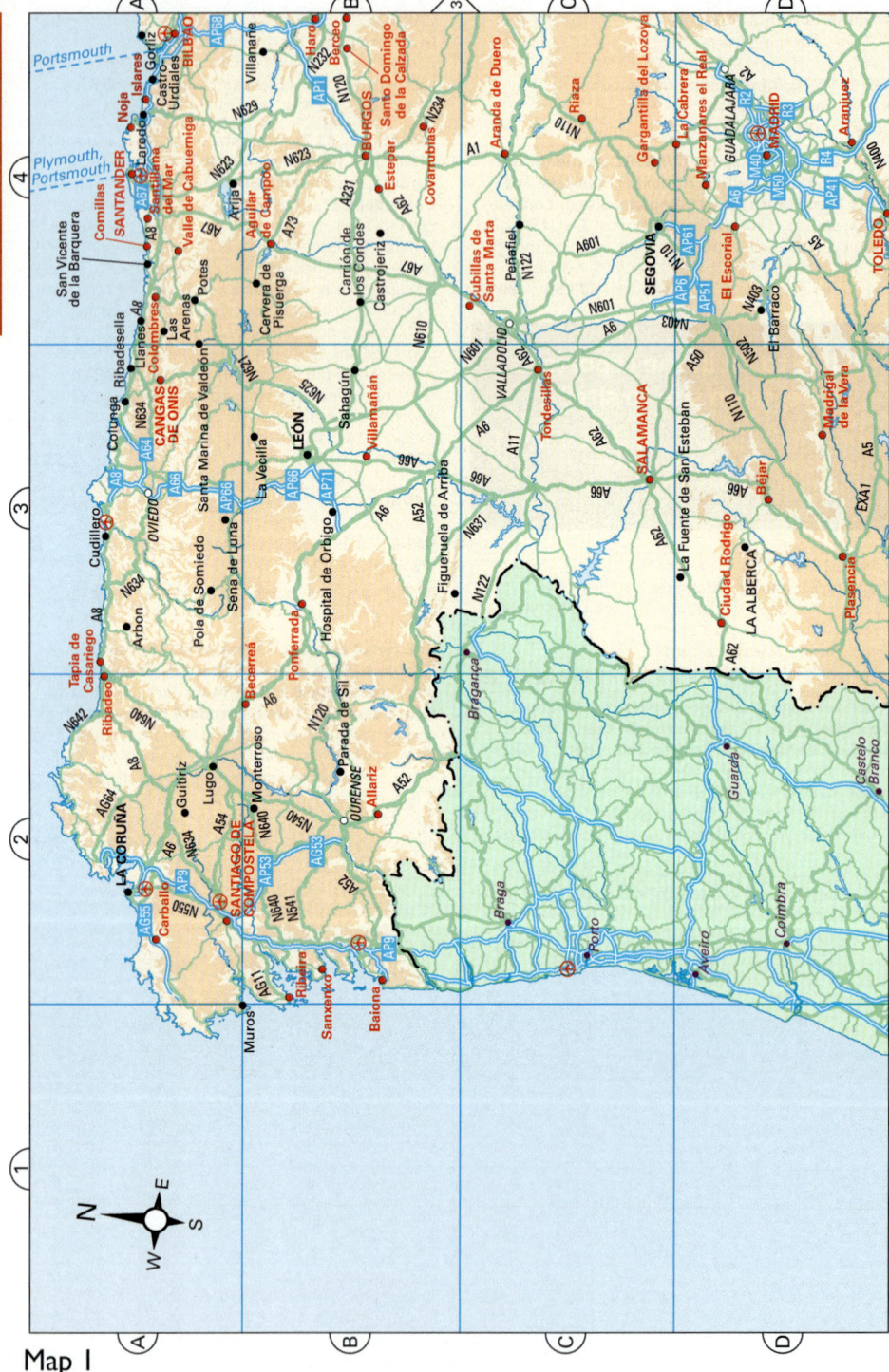

SPAIN

Map I

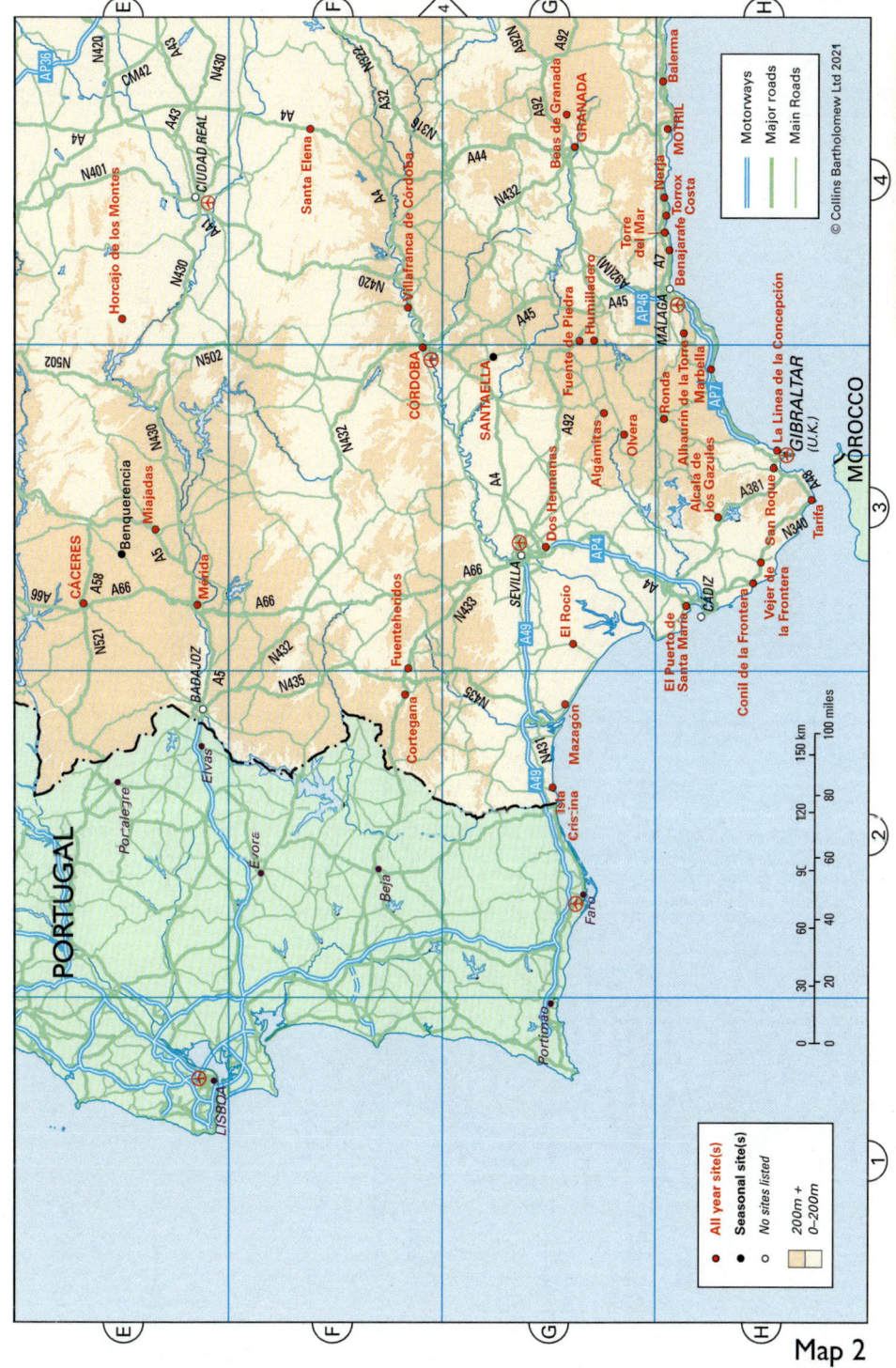

Map 2

Map 3

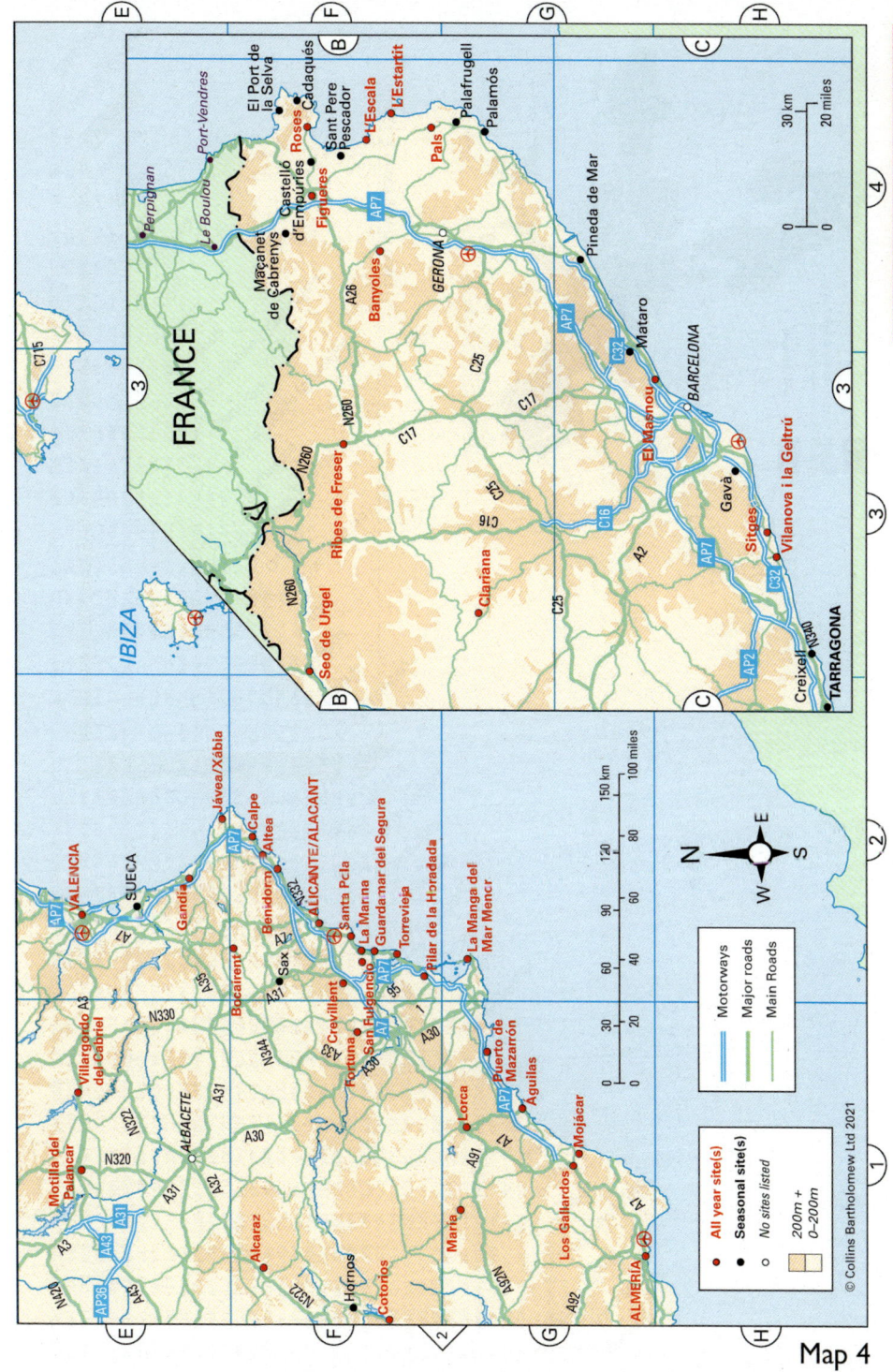

SPAIN

Map 4

803

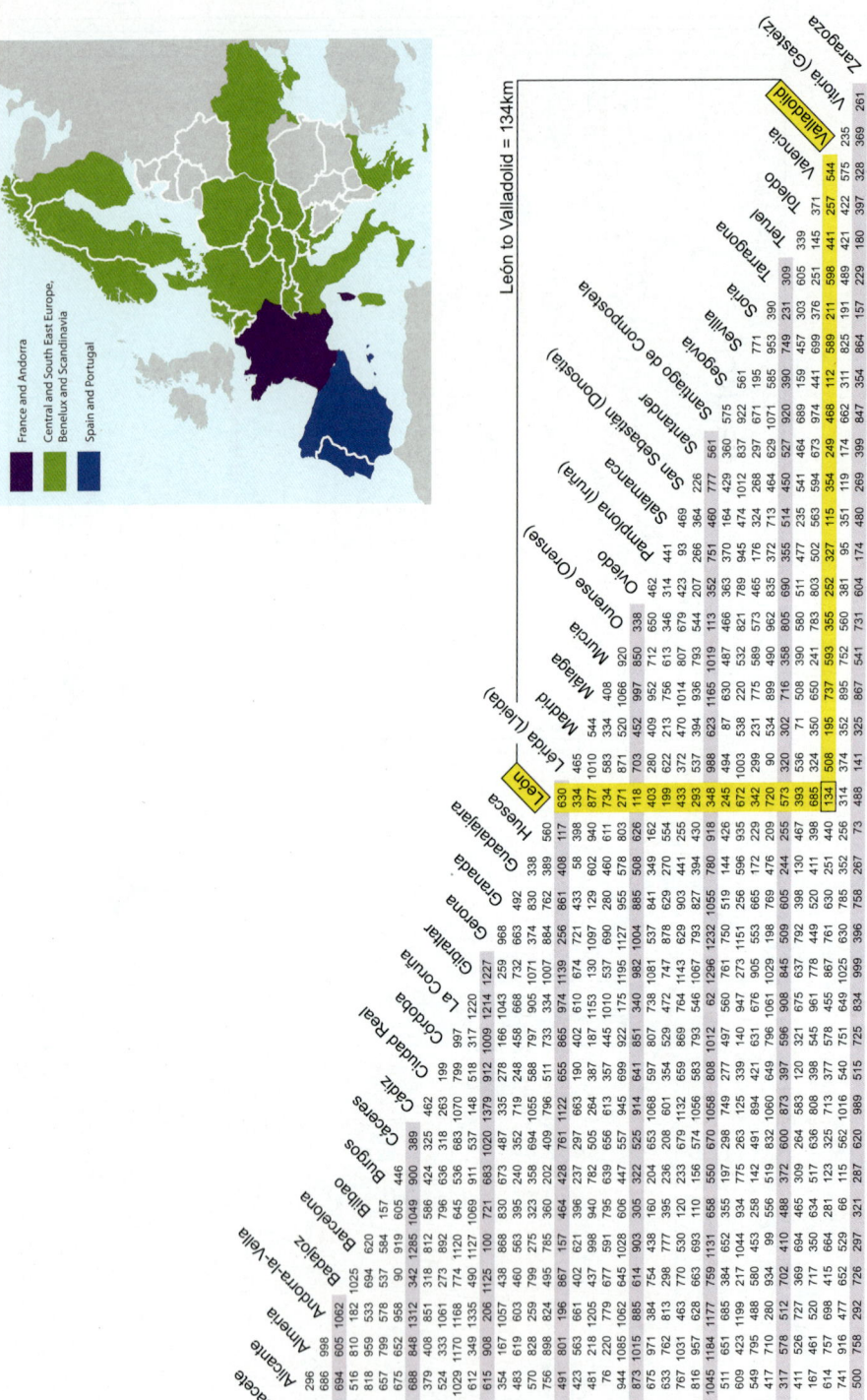

France and Andorra

Central and South East Europe, Benelux and Scandinavia

Spain and Portugal

León to Valladolid = 134km

Sweden

Gothenburg

Shutterstock/Leonid Andronov

Highlights

Renowned for combining simple beauty with functionality, Sweden is one of the design capitals of the world. This is shown in everything from gothic cathedrals and baroque palaces to its more modern creations.

As one of Europe's largest, least populated countries Sweden has a lot of green space to enjoy. An extensive network of national parks and trails mean even the most remote parts of the country are easily accessible.

Due to its shorter summers, Sweden makes the most of the long days by packing as many events into them as possible. One of these is a crayfish party, which is a traditional summertime eating and drinking celebration.

Sweden is also celebrated for its rich variety of children's literature, with Astrid Lindgren's Pippi Longstocking, or Pippi Långstrump, one of the most well-known creations.

Major towns and cities

- Stockholm – a dynamic capital city which is the home of the Nobel Prize.
- Gothenburg – this port city has plenty of history on show.
- Malmö – a green city with plenty of beautiful parks.
- Uppsala – this city has ancient roots and boast a dominating cathedral and castle.

Attractions

- Vasa Museum, Stockholm – This fascinating museum features a fantastically preserved shipwreck from the 17th century
- Sigtuna – the oldest town in Sweden, boasting a picturesque medieval centre filled with restaurants, shops and cafés.
- Drottningholm Palace – A residence of the Swedish royal family, this stunning palace has beautiful gardens.

Find out more

www.visitsweden.com
E: info@visitsweden.com T: 0046 (0) 87 89 10 00

Country Information

Population (approx): 9.9 million

Capital: Stockholm

Area: 450,000 sqkm

Bordered by: Finland, Norway

Terrain: Mostly flat or gently rolling lowlands; mountains in the west

Climate: Cold, cloudy winters, sub-arctic in the north; cool/warm summers. The best time to visit is between May and September; August can be hot and wet. Be prepared for occasional sub-zero temperatures and snowfalls, even in summer months

Coastline: 3,218km

Highest Point: Kebnekaise 2,104m

Language: Swedish

Local Time: GMT or BST + 1, i.e. 1 hour ahead of the UK all year

Currency: Krona (SEK) divided into 100 öre; £1 = SEK 11.69, SEK 100 = £8.56 (Feb 2021)

Emergency Numbers: Police 112 (or 11414 for non-emergency calls); Fire Brigade 112; Ambulance 112. Operators speak English

Public Holidays 2021: Jan 1, 6; Apr 2, 4, 5; May 1, 13, 23; Jun 6, 25, 26; Nov 6; Dec 24, 25, 26, 31.

School summer holidays are from early June to the second or third week of August

Border Posts

There are approximately 40 Customs posts along the Swedish/Norwegian border. They are situated on all main roads and are normally open Mon to Fri from 8.30am - 4pm/5pm.

Travellers with dutiable goods must cross the land borders during hours when the Customs posts are open. However, travellers without dutiable goods may cross the border outside Customs post opening hours.

The main border posts with Finland are at Haparanda, Övertornea, Pajala and Karesuando.

Customs Regulations

Visitors arriving from an EU country via a non-EU country (e.g. Norway) may bring quantities of tobacco and alcohol obtained in EU countries, plus the amounts allowed duty-free from non-EU countries. However, you must be able to produce proof of purchase for goods from EU countries and goods must be for your personal use.

Entry Formalities

British and Irish passport holders may stay for up to 90 days in any 180 day period without a visa. Following Brexit you may be asked to show a return or onward ticket at the border to confirm your length of stay, or to prove that you have enough money for your stay.

Your passport will need to have a minimum of 6 months' validity remaining, and be less than 10 years old (even if it has over 6 months left).

Medical Services

Health care facilities are generally very good and most medical staff speak English. Thre is no GP system; instead visit the nearest hospital clinic (Akutmottagning or Värdcentral) and present your passport and European Health Insurance Card (EHIC). You will be charged a fee for the clinic visit (free for anyone under 20) plus a daily standard charge if it is necessary to stay in hospital.

Prescriptions are dispensed at pharmacies (apotek) which are open during normal shopping hours. Emergency prescriptions can be obtained at hospitals. Dentists (tandläkare or folktandvård) offer emergency out-of-hours services in major cities but you may have to pay the full cost of treatment.

The use of mosquito repellent is recommended, particularly from mid June to September when mosquitos are most common. Mosquitos are generally more often encountered in the north of Sweden rather than the south.

Visitors to remote areas should consider the relative inaccessibility of the emergency services. In northern Sweden mobile phone coverage does not generally extend beyond main roads and the coast.

Opening Hours

Banks: Mon-Fri 9.30am-3pm or 5pm and until 5.30pm one day a week in larger towns. Many banks do not handle cash after 3pm and some banks will not handle cash at all.

Museums: Check locally, opening hours vary.

Post Offices: Post offices no longer exist. Mail is dealt with at local shops, kiosks and petrol stations; opening hours vary.

Shops: 8am-8pm every day. Shops generally close early the day before a public holiday.

Regulations for Pets

In order to protect the countryside and wildlife, dogs are not allowed to run off the lead from 1 March to 20 August and at other times in certain areas.

Dogs travelling directly from the UK and Ireland must be microchipped and have an EU pet passport. For more information please visit www.jordbruksverket.se (english option) and go to the 'Animals' section.

Safety and Security

Petty crime levels are much lower than in most other European countries but you should take the usual commonsense precautions. Pickpocketing is common in the summer months in major cities where tourists may be targeted for their passports and cash.

In recent years there have been incidents of 'highway robbery' from motorhomes parked on the roadside, especially on the west coast between Malmö and Gothenburg.

Sweden shares with the rest of Europe an underlying threat from terrorism. Attacks could be indiscriminate and against civilian targets in public places, including tourist sites.

British Embassy

SKARPÖGATAN 6-8,115 93 STOCKHOLM
Tel: (08) 6713000
www.ukinsweden.fco.gov.uk/en/

Irish Embassy

Hovslagargatan 5, 111 48 STOCKHOLM
Tel: (08) 54504040
www.dfa.ie/sweden

Documents

Driving Licence

A UK driving licence is only valid when it bears a photograph of the holder, i.e. a photocard licence, or when it is carried together with photographic proof of identity, such as a passport.

Money

Foreign currency may be exchanged in banks and bureaux de change.

Major credit cards are widely used both for major and minor transactions and cash machines (Bankomat or Minuten) are widespread. It is advisable to carry your passport or photocard driving licence if paying with a credit card as you may be asked for photographic proof of identity.

Driving

Accidents

In the case of an accident it is not necessary to call the police unless there are injuries to drivers or passengers and/or vehicles are badly damaged, but drivers are required to give their details to the other persons involved before leaving the accident scene. A driver leaving the scene of an accident without following this procedure may be fined.

If you are involved in an accident with a possible third party claim, you are strongly recommended to report the accident to the national Swedish insurance bureau which will act as claims agent. Contact Trafikförsäkringsforeningen in Stockholm, tel: 08 522 78100, info@ tff.se, www.tff.se.

Accidents involving wild animals (e.g. elk, reindeer, bear, wolf, etc) must be reported to the police immediately by calling 112 or 11414 and the spot where the accident took place must be marked by putting up reflective tape or anything clearly noticeable so that the police can find it easily. Collisions must be reported even if the animal involved is not injured. After reporting the accident and marking out the place, a driver may leave. Accidents involving smaller animals (badgers, foxes, etc) need not be reported.

Alcohol

Penalties for driving a motor vehicle under the influence of alcohol are extremely severe. The police carry out random breath tests. If the level of alcohol exceeds 20 milligrams in 100 millilitres of blood a fine will be imposed and driving licence withdrawn. This level is considerably lower than that permitted in the UK (80 milligrams) and equates to virtually zero. A level exceeding 100 milligrams is considered to be severe drink driving for which a jail sentence of up to two years may be imposed and licence withdrawn.

Breakdown Service

The motoring organisation, Motormännens Riksförbund (known as the 'M'), does not operate a breakdown service. It does, however, have an agreement with 'AssistanceKåren' (a nationwide road service company) which operates a 24-hour, all-year service and can be contacted free on (020) 912912 or 08 6275757 from a foreign-registered mobile phone. Phone boxes are becoming quite scarce and it is advisable to carry a mobile phone. There are normally no emergency telephones along motorways or dual carriageways. Charges for assistance and towing vary according to day and time and payment by credit card is accepted.

Child Restraint System

Children under the height of 135cm must be seated in a child restraint or child seat. A child aged 15 or over, or 135cm in height or taller, can use normal seat belts in the car.

Children under the height of 140cm are only allowed in the front seat if the passenger seat airbag has been deactivated.

Fuel

Petrol stations are usually open from 7am to 9pm. Near motorways and main roads and in most cities they may remain open until 10pm or even for 24 hours. Outside large towns garages seldom stay open all night but most have self-service pumps (possibly not for diesel) which accept credit cards. In the far north filling stations may be few and far between so keep your tank topped up. Credit cards are accepted.

LPG (known as gasol) is sold at a very limited number of petrol stations mainly located in central and southern Sweden.

Lights

Dipped headlights are compulsory at all times, regardless of weather conditions. Bulbs are more likely to fail with constant use and you are recommended to carry spares. Fog lights may be used when visibility is poor but they must not be used together with dipped headlights.

Vehicles parked or stopped on a poorly lit road at night, including dawn, dusk and bad weather, must have their parking lights switched on.

Low Emission Zones

There are Low Emission Zones (Miljözen) in Sweden. Please see www.lowemissionzones.eu for the most up-to-date information.

Motorways

There are approximately 1,900 kms of motorway and 560 kms of semi-motorway or dual carriageway, all confined to the south of the country and relatively free of heavy traffic by UK standards. There are no service areas or petrol stations on motorways; these are situated near the exits and are indicated on motorway exit signs. Please note that there are no petrol stations close to the 110km long Uppsala to Gälve motorway.

Overtaking

Take care when overtaking long vehicles. A typical long-distance Swedish truck is a six-wheeled unit towing a huge articulated trailer, i.e. a very long load.

Many roads in Sweden have wide shoulders or a climbing lane to the right of the regular lane and these permit drivers of slow moving vehicles or wide vehicles to pull over to allow other traffic to pass. These climbing lanes and shoulders should not be used as another traffic lane.

Parking

Parking meters and other parking restrictions are in use in several large towns. Vehicles must be parked facing the direction of the flow of traffic. Wheel clamps are not in use but illegally parked vehicles may be towed away and, in addition to a parking fine, a release fee will be charged.

In an area signposted 'P' parking is permitted for a maximum of 24 hours, unless otherwise stated.

Priority

Vehicles driving on roads designated and signposted (with a yellow diamond on a black background) as primary roads always have priority. On all other roads, as a general rule, vehicles coming from the right have priority, unless signs indicate otherwise. This rule is sometimes ignored however, especially by vehicles on roads regarded as major roads but not signposted as such.

At most roundabouts signs indicate that traffic already on the roundabout has priority, i.e. from the left.

Give trams priority at all times. Where there is no refuge at a tram stop, you must stop to allow passengers to board and alight from the tram.

Roads

The condition of national and country roads is good although some minor roads may be covered with oil-gravel only. Road surfaces may be damaged following the spring thaw, and some may be closed or have weight restrictions imposed during that period. Gradients are generally slight and there are no roads that need to be avoided for vehicles towing a caravan.

Road repairs tend to be intensive during the short summer season. Information on major roadworks and road conditions on E roads and major national roads can be obtained from www.trafikverket.se

There is a good road link with Norway in the far north of Sweden. The Kiruna-Narvik road is open all year from Kiruna to the border. It is a wide road with no steep gradients.

There is generally little or no heavy goods traffic on roads during the Christmas, Easter and midsummer holidays or on the days preceding these holidays so good progress can be made.

Road Signs and Markings

Road signs and markings conform to international standards. Warning lines (usually on narrow roads) are broken lines with short intervals which indicate that visibility is limited in one or both directions; they may be crossed when overtaking. Unbroken lines should not be crossed at any time.

National roads (riksvägar) have two-digit numbers and country roads (länsvägar) have three-digit numbers. Roads which have been incorporated into the European road network – E roads – generally have no other national number.

Direction and information signs for motorways and roads which form part of the European road network are green. Signs for national roads and the more important

country roads are blue. Signs for local roads are white with black numerals.

The following are some other signs that you may see:

 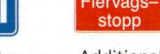

| Passing place | Additional stop sign | Accident |

Swedish	English Tanslation
Enkelriktat	One way
Farlig kurva	Dangerous bend
Grusad väg	Loose chippings
Höger	Right
Ingen infart	No entrance
Parkering förbjuden	No parking
Vänster	Left

Speed Limits

	Open Road (km/h)	Motorway (km/h)
Car Solo	60-100	90-120
Car towing caravan/trailer	70-80	80
Motorhome under 3500kg	60-100	90-120
Motorhome 3500-7500kg	70-100	90-120

Speed limits are no longer based on the category of road but on the quality and safety level of the roads themselves. As a result limits may vary from one town to another and along stretches of the same road. It is advisable, therefore, to pay close attention to road signs as speed limits are strictly enforced. If in doubt, or if no speed limit is indicated, you are advised to keep to 70 km/h (44 mph) until you see a speed limit sign.

Outside built-up areas, including expressways, speeds up to 100 km/h (62 mph) may be permitted according to road signs, providing a lower maximum speed is not applicable for certain vehicle categories. Vehicles with trailers must never exceed 80 km/h (49mph).

On motorways the maximum permitted speed is 110 or 120 km/h (68 or 74 mph). During the winter a speed limit of 90 km/h (56 mph) is in force on some motorways and dual carriageways. This limit is signposted.

In most residential areas and during certain periods in areas near schools, speed is limited to 30 km/h (18 mph) according to road signs. Periods indicated in black mean Monday to Friday, those in black in brackets mean Saturday and the eves of public holidays, and those indicated in red mean Sunday and public holidays.

Speed limits for motorhomes under 3,500kg and privately registered motorhomes over 3,500kg are the same as for solo cars. Speed cameras are in use on many roads. The use of radar detectors is not permitted.

Tolls

Tolls for private vehicles have now been introduced. The Motala by-pass (on road 50m in central Sweden) the toll will be 5 SEK and for the Sundsvall by-pass (on E4 in northern Sweden) the toll will be 9 SEK. Göteborg(E6) 9-22 SEK.

Toll Bridges

The Øresund Bridge links Malmö in Sweden with Copenhagen in Denmark and means that it is possible to drive all the way from mainland Europe by motorway. The crossing is via a 7.8 km bridge to the artificial island of Peberholm and a 4 km tunnel. Tolls (payable in cash, including EUR, SEK or DKK or by credit card) are levied on the Swedish side and are as follows for single journeys (2018 prices subject to change)

Vehicle(s)	Price
Solo car or motorhome up to 6 metres	€55 online €59 at toll
Car + caravan/trailer or motorhome over 6 metres	€110 online €118 at toll

Vehicle length is measured electronically and even a slight overhang over six metres will result in payment of the higher tariff.

Speed limits apply in the tunnel and on the bridge, and during periods of high wind the bridge is closed to caravans. Bicycles are not allowed. Information on the Øresund Bridge can be found on www.oeresundsbron.com.

Svinesund Bridge

There is a 700 metre long bridge linking Sweden and Norway on the E6, at Svinesund. Tolls are SEK24 (NOK20) for light vehicles and SEK120 (NOK100) for vehicles over 3,500kgs (2018).

Traffic Lights

A green arrow indicates that traffic may proceed with caution in the direction of the arrow but pedestrians must be given priority. A flashing amber light indicates that a crossing/turning must be made with caution.

Violation of Traffic Regulations

Police are authorised to impose and collect fines for violation of minor traffic offences which must be paid at a bank, normally within two to three weeks. Offences, which may qualify for a fine include driving without lights in daylight, speeding, lack of a warning triangle or nationality plate (GB or IRL) or a dirty or missing number plate.

If a fine is not paid and the driver is a resident of another EU country, notice of the fine will be forwarded to the authorities in the driver's country of residence. Jaywalking is not permitted; pedestrians must use official crossings.

Winter Driving

The winter months are periods of severe cold and you should be prepared for harsh conditions. The fitting of winter tyres is compulsory for vehicles from 1st December to 31st March in the event of severe winter road conditions, i.e. the road is covered with ice or snow, or if the road is wet and the temperature is around freezing point. Trailers towed by these vehicles must also be equipped with winter tyres. These regulations apply to foreign registered vehicles.

Essential Equipment

Warning Triangle

It is compulsory for foreign registered vehicles to carry a warning triangle. They should be placed as a distance of 50 meters behind the vehicle on ordinary roads and 100 meters on motorways.

Touring

Ferry services connect Sweden with Denmark, Estonia, Finland, Germany, Latvia, Lithuania, Norway and Poland; some services only operate in the summer. Full details are available from Visit Sweden, www.visitsweden.com. Scheduled car ferry services also operate between the mainland and the island of Gotland during the summer season.

In the south and centre the touring season lasts from May to September. In the north it is a little shorter, the countryside being particularly beautiful at each end of the season. Campsites are most crowded over the midsummer holiday period and during the Swedish industrial holidays in the last two weeks of July and first week of August. Tourist attractions may close before the end of August or operate on reduced opening hours.

Sweden has 15 UNESCO World Heritage sites and 29 national parks which, together with nature reserves, cover eight percent of the country. Information on national parks and nature reserves is available on www.naturvardsverket.se

Inland, particularly near lakes, visitors should be armed with spray on, rub on and electric plug-in insect repellent devices as mosquitoes and midges are a problem.

Discount cards are available in Stockholm and Gothenburg offering free public transport and free admission to many museums and other attractions, plus free boat and canal sightseeing trips. Buy the cards at tourist information offices, hotels, kiosks, some campsites and online – visit www.stockholmtown.com or www.goteborg.com.

Local tourist offices are excellent sources of information and advice; look for the blue and yellow 'i' signs. Information points at lay-bys at the entrance to many towns are good sources of street maps.

A good-value 'dagens rätt' (dish of the day) is available in most restaurants at lunchtime. A service charge is usually included in restaurant bills but an additional small tip is normal if you have received good service.

The most popular alcoholic drink is lager, available in five strengths. Wines, spirits and strong beer are sold only through the state-owned 'Systembolaget' shops, open from Monday to Friday and on Saturday morning, with branches all over the country. Light beer can be bought from grocery shops and supermarkets. The minimum age for buying alcoholic drinks is 20 years at Systembolaget and 18 years in pubs, bars and licensed restaurants.

It is not permitted to smoke in restaurants, pubs or bars or in any place where food and drinks are served.

Camping and Caravanning

Camping and caravanning are very popular, but because summer is short the season is brief - from May to early September, although winter caravanning is increasing in popularity. High season on most sites ends around the middle of August when prices and site office opening hours are reduced or sites close altogether. There are more than 1,000 campsites, about 350 of which remain open during the winter particularly in mountainous regions near to ski resorts. Those that are open all year may offer fewer or no facilities from mid-September to April and advance booking may be required.

In late June and July advance booking is recommended, especially at campsites along the west coast (north and south of Göteborg), on the islands of Öland and Gotland and near other popular tourist areas.

Approximately 500 campsites are members of the SCR (Svenska Campingvärdars Riksförbund – Swedish Campsite Owners' Association), which are classified from 1 to 5 stars. Visitors wishing to use these sites must have a Camping Key Europe card. You can buy the Camping Key Europe at campsites and you will be given a temporary card, or you can order it in advance from www.camping.se/en for 150 SEK (2018 prices). If ordering in advance you should allow at least 3 weeks for delivery.

Also aim to arrive by mid afternoon to get a better pitch, since many Swedes arrive late. It is reported that hand basins on sites often do not have plugs so it is advisable to carry a flat universal plug when touring.

Many sites have a 'Quick Stop' amenity which provides safe, secure overnight facilities on, or adjacent to, a site. This normally includes the use of sanitary facilities. 'Quick Stop' rates are about two thirds of the regular camping rate if you arrive after 9pm and leave before 9am.

Casual/wild camping is normally permitted (except in National Parks and recreational areas), however for security reasons it is not recommended to spend the night in a vehicle on the roadside or in a public car park. Instead use the 'Quick Stop' amenity at campsites. In any event local parking rules and signposting should always be observed.

Alternatively there are around 150 organised 'ställplatser' mainly intended for motorhomes but generally car and caravan outfits may also use them for an overnight stay at the discretion of the site's manager. For a list of 'ställplatser' see www.campingglädje.se/resa.

Most designated rest areas along highways are owned and managed by the Vågverket (Swedish Roads Administration) which, although not officially ranked as 'ställplatser', offer adequate parking space and various facilities for motorhomes staying overnight. A map showing these rest areas is available at local tourist offices.

Cycling

The network of cycle lanes in Sweden is growing rapidly and many cycle routes are named and signposted. In some cases cycle lanes are combined with foot paths. See www.svenska-cykelsallskapet.se.

The 'Sverigeleden' cycle trail covers the whole country and connects all major ports and cities. The 190km cycle route along the Göta Canal from Sjötorp on Lake Vänern to Mem on the Baltic coast is relatively flat and hence a very popular route.

The wearing of a safety helmet is compulsory for children up to the age of 15 and is recommended for everyone.

Electricity and Gas

On campsites the current is usually 10 amps or more and round two-pin plugs are used. CEE connections are becoming standard.

Propane (gasol) is the gas most widely obtainable at more than 2,000 Primus dealers; you will need to buy an appropriate adaptor.

It is understood that it is possible to sell back your propane cylinder at the end of your holiday and outlets will also exchange the corresponding Norwegian Progas cylinders. Recent visitors report that major distributors will refill cylinders but they must be of a recognised make/type and in perfect condition.

Butane gas is available from a number of outlets including some petrol stations. It is understood that Campingaz 904 and 907 cylinders are available but recent visitors report that they may be difficult to find, and virtually impossible in the north of the country. For more information on butane suppliers contact the Swedish Campsite Owners' Association (SCR) by email: info@scr.se

Ensure that you are well-equipped with gas if venturing north of central Sweden as it may be difficult to find an exchange point. Many sites have communal kitchen facilities which enable visitors to make great savings on their own gas supply.

The Midnight Sun and Northern Lights

The Midnight Sun is visible north of the Arctic Circle from about the end of May until the middle of July.

The Northern Lights (Aurora Borealis) are often visible during the winter from early evening until midnight. They are seen more frequently the further north you travel. The best viewing areas in Sweden are north of the Arctic Circle between September and March.

The Order of Bluenosed Caravanners

Visitors to the Arctic Circle from anywhere in the world may apply for membership of the Order of Bluenosed Caravanners which will be recognised by the issue of a certificate by the International Caravanning Association (ICA).

For more information contact bluenosed@icacaravanning.org and attach a photograph of yourselves and your outfit under any Arctic Circle signpost, together with the date and country of crossing and the names of those who made the crossing.

This service is free to members of the ICA (annual membership £20); the fee for non-members is £5. Coloured plastic decals for your outfit, indicating membership of the

Order, are also available at a cost of £4. Cheques should be payable to the ICA. For more information visit www.icacaravanning.org

Public Transport & Local Travel

Stockholm has an extensive network of underground trains (T-bana), commuter trains, buses and trams. Underground station entrances are marked with a blue 'T' on a white background. You can buy single tickets for one of three zones at the time of your journey, or save money by buying tickets in advance. A discount applies if you are aged 65 or over. Single tickets and prepaid tickets are valid for one hour after beginning your journey. Travel cards offer reduced price public transport in Stockholm for periods of 1, 3, 7 or 30 days – see www.sl.se (click on 'Visitor') for details of routes, fares and tickets.

For information on public transport systems in Göteborg and Malmö, see www.vasttrafik.se and www.skanetrafiken.se.

Stockholm is built on an archipelago of islands and island hopping ferries operate all year. You can buy single tickets or an island hopping pass for use on the Waxholmsbolaget and Cinderella fleet of ferries.

Confirm your taxi fare before setting off in the vehicle. Some companies have fixed fares which vary according to the day of the week and time of day. A full price list must be on display. Payment by credit card is generally accepted. It is usual to round up the fare shown on the meter by way of a tip.

Sweden is a country of lakes, rivers and archipelagos and, as a result, there are over 12,000 bridges. Road ferries, which form part of the national road network, make up the majority of other crossings. Most ferries are free of charge and services are frequent and crossings very short.

A congestion charge was introduced in Stockholm in 2007. Drivers of foreign-registered vehicles are exempt from the charge. For more information go to www.visitstockholm.com. In some other towns traffic restrictions may apply during certain periods and these are signposted.

When giving directions Swedes will often refer to distances in 'miles'. A Swedish 'mile' is, in fact, approximately ten kilometres. All road signs are in kilometres so if a Swede tells you it is 3 miles to a town, expect the journey to be around 30km.

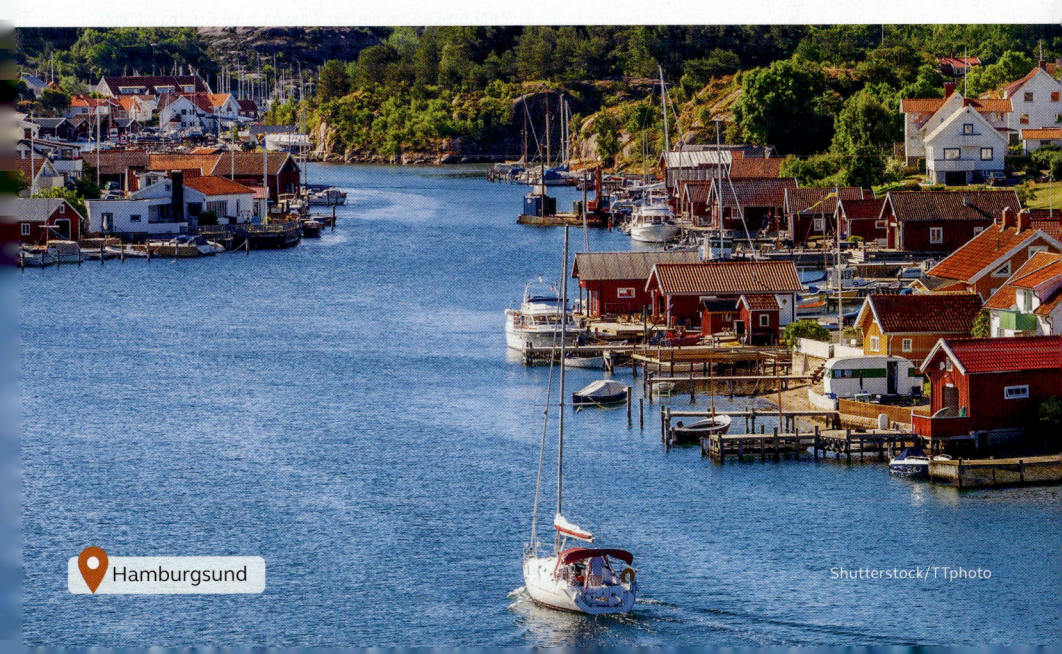

Hamburgsund

Shutterstock/TTphoto

AHUS *2F4* (1km NE Urban/Coastal) *55.94118, 14.31286* **First Camp Ahus (formerly Regenbogen),** Kolonivägen 59, 29633 Åhus **(044) 248969; ahus@firstcamp.se; firstcamp.se**

⊞12 🐕 ♟(htd) wc ☼ ♿ 🚽 🗑 ✉ MSP 🦋 ⊤ nr ⊕ nr 🏊 ⚠

♨ sand 150m

Take rd 118 fr Kristianstad SE twd Åhus. Site well sp fr ent to town. 3*, Lge, mkd, hdstg, pt shd, EHU (10A) SEK29; bbq; 10% statics; Eng spkn; ccard acc; sauna; site clsd 3 Nov-16 Dec; CKE. *"Gd base for walking, cycling, watersports; htd pool 300m; excel fishing; famous area for artists."* **SEK 260**   **2016**

ALMHULT *2F3* (2km N Rural) *56.56818, 14.13217* **Sjöstugans Camping (G5),** Campingvägen, Bökhult, 34394 Almhult **(0476) 71600; info@sjostugan.com; www.sjostugan.com**

🐕 ♟(htd) wc ☼ ♿ 🚽 🗑 ✉ MSP 🦋 ♈ ⊤ ⊕ 🏊 nr ⚠

♨ sand adj

Fr Växjö SW on rd 23, at rndabt turn W to Älmhult. Fr town cent turn N on Ljungbyvägen, site in 1.5km on lakeside, well sp. 3*, Med, pt shd, pt sl, EHU (16A) SEK45; bbq; cooking facs; twin axles; 25% statics; bus 500m; Eng spkn; adv bkg acc; ccard acc; canoe hire; sauna; games area; CKE. *"Some lakeside pitches; well-kept site; lake adj; 1st Ikea store opened here in 1958; v helpful staff; excel."* **SEK 283, 1 May-30 Sep.**   **2017**

AMAL *2E2* (1km SE Urban) *59.0465, 12.7236* **Örnäs Camping (P2),** Gamla Örnäsgatan, 66222 Åmål **(0532) 17097; ornascamping@amal.se; www.amal.se**

⊞12 🐕 ♟(htd) wc ☼ ♿ 🚽 ✉ MSP ♈ ⊤ ⊕ nr ♿ 🏊 nr ⚠

Leave rd 45 to Åmål, site sp. 4*, Sm, hdstg, pt shd, pt sl, terr, EHU (10A) inc; red long stay; 10% statics; Eng spkn; ccard acc; boat hire; fishing; bike hire; tennis; CCS; sauna. *"Gd views Lake Vänern; lake adj."* **SEK 275**   **2017**

ARBOGA *2G1* (13km S Rural) *59.28134, 15.90509* **Herrfallets Camping (U14),** 73293 Arboga **(0589) 40110; reception@herrfallet.se; www.herrfallet.se**

⊞12 🐕 ♟(htd) wc ☼ ♿ 🚽 🗑 ✉ MSP 🦋 ♈ ⊤ ⊕ 🏊 ⚠ ♒

Foll sp fr E20/E18, turn off at Sätra junc twd Arboga, cross rv. Foll sp to Herrfallet/Västermo. 4*, Med, mkd, pt shd, serviced pitches; EHU (10A) SEK40; bbq; sw; phone; ccard acc; boating; bike hire; sauna; CKE. *"Lovely spot on edge Lake Hjälmaren."* **SEK 270**   **2016**

ARJANG *2E1* (26km SE Rural) *59.30399, 12.44662* **Camping Grinsby,** Grindsbyn 100, Sillerud, 67295 Årjäng **(0573) 42022; campgrinsby@telia.com; www.campgrinsby.se**

🐕 ♟(htd) wc ☼ ♿ 🚽 🗑 ✉ MSP 🦋 🏊 ⚠

On E18 SE fr Årjäng & Sillerud, turn L at site sp. Site in 2km on Stora Bör lake. Med, hdstg, pt shd, terr, EHU (10A) SEK40; bbq; cooking facs; sw nr; 10% statics; phone; Eng spkn; adv bkg acc; ccard acc; games rm; bike hire; boat hire; CKE. *"A 'wilderness' site in beautiful setting; many walking paths; friendly, helpful staff; vg san facs."* **SEK 231, 1 May-3 Sep.**   **2017**

ARJEPLOG *1C2* (1.5km W Rural) *66.05007, 17.86298* **Kraja Camping (BD1),** Krajaudden, 93090 Arjeplog **(0961) 31500; kraja@silverresort.se; www.kraja.se**

⊞12 🐕 ♟(htd) wc ☼ ♿ 🚽 🗑 ✉ MSP 🦋 ♈ ⊤ ⊕ 🏊 🚣 (htd)

♨ sand

NW fr Arvidsjaur thro Arjeplog vill to site on R. 3*, Lge, unshd, EHU (16A) SEK40; bbq; cooking facs; sw nr; twin axles; TV; 90% statics; phone; bus 500m; Eng spkn; adv bkg acc; sauna; boating; fishing; CKE. *"Gd cent for local Lapp area; hotel on site with full facs; 20 touring pitches; v pleasant & helpful staff; keypad security at night; excel Sami silver museum in town."* **SEK 235**   **2017**

ASARNA *1B3* (9km S Rural) *62.56340, 14.38786* **Kvarnsjö Camp,** Kvarnsjö 696, 84031 Åsarna **(0682) 22016; info@kvarnsjocamp.com; www.kvarnsjocamp.com**

⊞12 🐕 ♟ wc ☼ 🗑 ✉ MSP 🦋

Fr N on E45 3km after Åsarna turn R onto rd 316 dir Klövsjo. In 8km turn L sp Cmp Kvarnsjö. In 8km cross rlwy, thro vill, site on L in 1km. Fr S 9km after Rätan turn L dir Klövsjo. In 1.5km bear R at Y-junc site in 4km. 3*, Sm, hdstg, unshd, terr, EHU (10A) SEK40; Eng spkn; adv bkg acc; sauna; CKE. *"CL-type family-run site o'looking woods & mountains; excel walking, fishing; boating, fresh bread/breakfast in high ssn."* **SEK 200**   **2017**

BOCKSJO *2F2* (5km NW Rural) *58.68058, 14.59911* **Stenkällegårdens Camping i Tiveden,** 54695 Stenkällegården **(0505) 60015; stenkallegarden@swipnet.se; www.stenkallegarden.se**

⊞12 🐕 ♟(htd) wc ☼ ♿ 🚽 🗑 ✉ MSP 🦋 ♈ ⊕ 🏊 ⚠

N on rd 49 fr Karlsborg, turn L at Bocksjö, site sp on L in 2km. Pt of rte single track with passing places. 4*, Med, mkd, pt shd, pt sl, terr, EHU (10A) SEK40; bbq; cooking facs; sw; TV; 30% statics; Eng spkn; ccard acc; fishing; boat hire; sauna; site clsd last 2 weeks Apr & 1st 2 weeks Oct; CKE. *"Gd cycling; mkd walking trails; spacious, sheltered site; clean san facs; skiing on site in winter; Tiveden National Park 5km."* **SEK 250**   **2016**

BORAS *2E3* (2.5km N Urban) 57.73885, 12.93608
Caming Borås Salteman (P11), Campinggatan 25, 50602 Borås **(033) 353280; info@ borascamping.com; www.borascamping.com**

Exit N40 fr Göteborg for Borås Centrum; foll sps to Djur Park R42 to Trollhätten thro town; well sp. 4*, Med, mkd, pt shd, pt sl, EHU (10A) SEK30; cooking facs; twin axles; TV; 10% statics; bus 350m; Eng spkn; adv bkg acc; boating; CKE. *"Gd pitches adj rv with paths; quickstop o'night facs; gd zoo 500m; pool 500m; gd, clean facs; nr sports stadium/tennis courts."* **SEK 270** 2017

BORENSBERG *2G2* (1.5km S Rural) 58.55663, 15.27911 **Strandbadets Camping,** 59030 Borensberg **(0141) 40385; info@strandbadetscamping.se; www.strandbadetscamping.se**

Foll sp for Camping Gota Canal fr Rd 34 thro town & across canal. Site 2nd site on R. 3*, Med, pt shd, EHU (10A) SEK50; cooking facs; sw; 10% statics; fishing. *"Gd base for Östergötland & Lake Vättern area; cycle rte along Göta Canal."* **SEK 190, 22 Apr-11 Sep.** 2018

DOROTEA *1C3* (0.5km SW Rural) 64.25850, 16.38833 **Doro Camping,** Storgatan 1A, 91731 Dorotea **(0942) 10238; reception@docamp.com; www.docamping.com**

Site on E side of E45. 3*, Med, pt shd, pt sl, EHU (10A) SEK50; cooking facs; sw; 10% statics; Eng spkn; sauna; site clsd Nov; golf; fishing. *"Site being extensively redeveloped (2019); most impressive rest."* **SEK 218** 2019

ED *2E2* (2km E Rural) 58.89931, 11.93486 **Gröne Backe Camping (P8),** Södra Moränvägen 64, 66832 Ed **(0534) 10144; gronebackecamping@telia.com**

App Ed on rd 164/166, site sp on Lake Lilla Le. 3*, Med, shd, pt sl, EHU (10A) SEK40; sw; ccard acc; sauna; bike hire; CKE. *"Excel for boating."* **SEK 291** 2016

EKSJO *2F3* (1km E Rural) 57.66766, 14.98923 **Eksjö Camping (F13),** Prästängsvägen 5, 57536 Eksjö **(0381) 39500; info@eksjocamping.se; www.eksjocamping.se**

Site sp fr town cent on rd 33 twd Västervik, on lakeside. 3*, Med, shd, EHU (10A) SEK45; sw nr; 10% statics; phone; ccard acc; boating; fishing; bike hire; CKE. *"Gd cent glass region; attractive countryside & old town."* **SEK 250** 2016

ENKOPING *2H1* (6km S Rural) 59.59334, 17.07146 **Bredsand Camping & Stugby,** Bredsandsvägen 22, 74948 Enköping **(0171) 80011; bredsand@nordic camping.se; www.nordiccamping.se**

Fr E18 or rd 55 foll sp to site, well sp on Lake Mälaren. 3*, Med, mkd, pt shd, pt sl, EHU (10A) SEK50; sw nr; 50% statics; CKE. *"Vg site."* **SEK 287** 2015

FALKOPING *2F2* (2km W Rural) 58.17595, 13.52726 **Mössebergs Camping & Stugby (R7),** Scheelegatan, 52130 Falkoping **(0515) 17349 or 07072 56493; mossebergscamping@telia.com; www.mossebergs camping.se**

Exit rd 184 at Falköping; foll Int'l Camping sps or sps to Mösseberg; site also sp fr rds 46 & 47 & in town. Site on plateau overlkg town. 3*, Med, mkd, pt shd, EHU SEK40; cooking facs; sw nr; 10% statics; phone; ccard acc; sauna; CKE. *"Pool 400m; site has barrier."* **SEK 230** 2018

FILIPSTAD *2F1* (1km N Rural) 59.72035, 14.15899 **Munkeberg Camping (S5),** Skillervägen, 68233 Filipstad **(0590) 50100; alterschwede@telia.com; www.munkeberg.com**

Fr Karlstad take rd 63 to Filipstad. In town foll sp for rd 246 twd Hagfors, site sp in town. 3*, Med, pt shd, pt sl, EHU (10A) SEK30; sw; 10% statics; adv bkg acc; fishing; boating; CKE. *"Beautiful lakeside site; gd for touring old mining district."* **SEK 208** 2016

GADDEDE *1B2* (0.4km NE Rural) 64.50400, 14.14900 **Gäddede Camping & Stugby,** Sagavägen 9, 83090 Gäddede **(0672) 10035; info@gaddedecamping.com; www.gaddedecamping.se**

On ent Gäddede cent on rd 342, turn R & site in 500m on R, sp. 3*, Med, mkd, pt shd, EHU (10A) SEK50; TV; 40% statics; Eng spkn; adv bkg acc; ccard acc; games area; canoe hire; games rm; sauna; fishing; CKE. *"Gd touring base 'Wilderness Way'."* **SEK 198** 2016

GALLIVARE *1C2* (1km S Urban) 67.1290, 20.6776 **Gällivare Campingplats (BD5),** Kvarnbacksvägen 2, 98231 Gällivare **(0970) 10010; info@gellivare camping.com; www.gellivarecamping.com**

On E45 app fr SW on R immed after bdge. 3*, Sm, hdstg, mkd, unshd, EHU (10A) SEK30; bbq; cooking facs; sw nr; twin axles; TV; 50% statics; phone; Eng spkn; ccard acc; bike hire; sauna; games area; CKE. *"Helpful, friendly owners; pleasant pitches on rvside; gd facs; daytime cafe opp; rest & shops 1km; sep car pk."* **SEK 160, 13 May-27 Sep.** 2018

GAMLEBY *2G2* (1km SE Coastal) *57.88475, 16.41373*
KustCamp Gamleby (formerly Hammarsbadets),
Hammarsvägen 10, 59432 Gamleby **(0493) 10221;**
info@campa.se; www.campa.se

🐕 👫 ⓌⒹ ⚒ ♨ ⓰ ♿ 🍳 ⊘ 🅼🆂🅿 🦋 ⛴ 🍽 ⓗ 🎣 🛝 🚣 ⛵ sand adj

On E22 Kalmar-Norrköping, foll sp to site 2km off
main rd. 4*, Med, mkd, pt shd, terr, EHU (10A) SEK45;
sw; 10% statics; phone; ccard acc; boat hire; tennis;
Quickstop o'night facs; sauna; bike hire; CKE. *"Clean,
well-kept, relaxing site."* **SEK 312, 1 May-15 Sep.**
2016

GESUNDA *1B4* (2km N Rural) *60.90100, 14.58500*
Sollerö Camping (W60), Levsnäs, 79290 Sollerön
(0250) 22230; info@sollerocamping.se;
www.sollerocamping.se

🕛 👫 ⓌⒹ ⚒ ♨ ⓰ ♿ 🅼🆂🅿 🦋 ⛴ 🍽 🎣 🛝

Fr Gesunda take bdge to Sollerön Island in Lake
Siljan. Site immed on R on reaching island; clearly
visible fr bdge. 3*, Lge, pt shd, pt sl, EHU (16A); sw nr;
adv bkg acc; ccard acc; tennis; boat hire; sauna; canoe
hire; CKE. *"Beautiful outlook to S across lake; gd base
for Dalarna folklore area; gd site & facs; every 7th day
is free."* **SEK 260**
2019

GOTEBORG *2E3* (22km ENE Rural) *57.758329,
12.252601* **Aspen Camping,** Seglarvagen 25, 443 30
Lerum **(0302) 71166;** info@aspencamping.se;
www.aspencamping.se

🐕 ⓌⒹ ⚒ ♨ ⓰ ♿ ⊘ 🅼🆂🅿 🍽 🛝

E20 exit 84. Foll sp to Lerum Centrum. At next
rndabt turn L under rly, then L at next rndabt. Site
on R after 600m. Med, hdstg, mkd, pt shd, pt sl, EHU
(10-16A) inc; bbq; cooking facs; sw nr; twin axles;
50% statics; train 600m; Eng spkn; games area; CCI.
*"Vg site; fishing & boat hire; mini golf on site; some
pitches clse to rlwy."* **SEK 230, 1 May-30 Sep.**   **2018**

GOTEBORG *2E3* (4km E Rural) *57.7053, 12.0286*
Lisebergsbyn Camping Kärralund (O39), Olbersgatan
1, 41655 Göteborg **(031) 840200;**
lisebergsbyn@liseberg.se; www.liseberg.se

🕛 🐕 👫 ⓌⒹ ⚒ ♨ ⓰ ♿ ⊘ 🅼🆂🅿 🍽 ⓗ 🎣 🛝

Exit E6/E20 junc 71 onto rd 40 E & foll sp
Lisebergsbyn, site well sp. Lge, unshd, pt sl, terr,
EHU (16A) inc; gas; bbq; cooking facs; twin axles;
TV; 25% statics; phone; tram 400m; Eng spkn; adv
bkg rec; ccard acc; games area; CKE. *"Boat trips
arranged; vg, well-run site; LS arr early to obtain barrier
key; poss travellers on site; cycle path to Liseberg
amusement park & town cent; impressive, organised &
professional staff; red LS & Sun-Fri; lovely site; san facs
outstanding."* **SEK 450**
2017

GOTEBORG *2E3* (7km W Urban) *57.70413, 12.02989*
Lisebergs Ställplats, Olbersgatan 9, 416 55 Göteborg
031 840 200; lisebergsbyn@liseberg.se;
www.liseberg.se

🕛 🐕 ⓌⒹ ⊘ 🅼🆂🅿 ⓗ 🛝

Take Backebogatan to Litteraturgatan. Then E6
and Delsjövägen to Olbersgatan. At rndabt take 1st
exit to Olbersgatan, Turn R & R again, site on L. Sm,
mkd, hdstg, pt shd, EHU (10A) inc; own san rec; bbq;
Eng spkn; adv bkg acc; ccard acc. *"Tram at bottom of
hill past main site ent, main site off will help with travel
info etc; excel."* **SEK 240**
2016

GRANNA *2F2* (0.5km NW Rural) *58.02783, 14.45821*
Grännastrandens Familjecamping (F3), Hamnen,
56300 Gränna **(0390) 10706;** info@grannacamping.se;
www.grannacamping.se

🐕 👫 ⓌⒹ ⚒ ♨ ⓰ ♿ ⊘ 🅼🆂🅿 🍽 ⓗ nr 🛝

In cent of Gränna down rd twd Lake Vättern, sp
Visingsö Island. 3*, Lge, unshd, EHU (10A) metered +
conn fee; sw; TV (pitch); CKE. *"Ballooning cent of
Sweden; Visingsö Island, Brahehus ruined castle,
glass-blowing 3km; vg site; gd location; some
cottages; excel, clean san facs, excel camp kitchen."*
SEK 300, 30 Apr-3 Oct.
2016

HALMSTAD *2E3* (10km S Coastal) *56.59033, 12.94430*
Gullbrannagården Camping (N27), 31031 Eldsberga
(035) 42180; mail@gullbrannagarden.se;
www.gullbrannagarden.se

🕛 🐕 👫 ⓌⒹ ⚒ ♨ ⓰ ♿ ⊘ 🅼🆂🅿 🍽 ⓗ 🎣 🛝 🏊 🎿 sand 500m

Fr S site sp on E6. Lge, pt shd, pt sl, EHU SEK45;
cooking facs; 60% statics; Eng spkn; adv bkg acc;
games rm. *"Christian-run site; church & bible classes;
alcohol discouraged; OK for those of like mind."*
SEK 290
2016

HAMBURGSUND *2E2* (1km S Coastal) *58.54075,
11.28240* **Rorviks Camping,** Rorviksangen 15 45747
Hamburgsund **05 25 33 573;** info@rorvikscamping.se;
www.rorvikscamping.se

🐕 👫 ⓌⒹ ⚒ ♨ ⓰ ⊘ 🅼🆂🅿 🛝 🏊

Take exit 103 on the E6 (bet Tatum V-Munkedal).
Foll 163 W to Kville. Turn L to Hamburgsund, cont
S 1km. Campsite on R. Lge, hdstg, mkd, pt shd, EHU
(10A) inc; bbq; cooking facs; twin axles; 10% statics;
bus 1km; Eng spkn; adv bkg acc; games area; CCI.
"Quiet, low key site in a great area; vg."
SEK 350, 1 May-31 Aug.
2019

HAMMERDAL *1 B3* (2km S Rural) *63.57513, 15.34286*
Camp Route 45, Fyran 210, 83341 Hammerdal
**(070) 6076892; info@camproute45.com;
camproute45.com**

12 🐕 ♦♦♦ WD 🔥 ♿ 🗑 ⚊ MSP 🦋 Ⓗ 🍴 🛒 nr 🏔

0.5km off E45 outside Hammerdal, 65km N
Ostersund. 3*, Sm, hdstg, unshd, EHU 10A (SEK40);
cooking facs; sw nr; twin axles; Eng spkn; adv bkg
acc; ccard acc; sauna. "Canoes for hire; English run;
comfortable kitchen/diner; elk hunting in season; cafe
with burgers; english breakfast; poss mosquitoes;
pleasant, well kept site; excel." **SEK 232**   **2018**

HAPARANDA *1D2* (15km N Rural) *65.9620, 24.0378*
Kukkolaforsen Camping (BD27), Kukkolaforsen
184, 95391 Haparanda **(0922) 31000; info@
kukkolaforsen.se; www.kukkolaforsen.se**

12 ♦♦♦ (htd) WD 🔥 ♿ 🗑 ⚊ 🍴 Ⓗ 🛒 🏔

On rd 99 on banks of Rv Torninojoki. 3*, Med, pt shd,
EHU (10A) SEK40; TV; phone; adv bkg acc; ccard acc;
sauna; bike hire; fishing; CKE. "Friendly staff; rv rapids."
SEK 280   **2016**

HARNOSAND *1C3* (2.5km NE Coastal) *62.64451,
17.97123* **Sälstens Camping (Y21),** Sälsten 22,
87133 Härnösand **(0611) 18150; salsten.camping@
telia.com**

♦♦♦ (htd) WD 🔥 ♿ 🗑 ⚊ 🦋 🍴 🛒 🏔 ⚓

On Gulf of Bothnia, E of town & on S side of inlet;
exit off E4; foll sp for Härnösand town cent, then
intn'l camping sp; then site. 3*, Sm, mkd, pt shd, terr,
EHU (10A); TV; Eng spkn; CKE. "Folk museum in town;
excel site." **SEK 250, 15 May-31 Aug.**   **2016**

HEDESUNDA *2G1* (5km SE Rural) *60.35000,
17.02100* **Hedesunda Camping (formerly Sandsnäs),**
Qvägen 68, 81040 Hedesunda **(0291) 44123; info@
hedesundacamping.se; www.hedesundacamping.se**

♦♦♦ (htd) WD 🔥 ♿ 🗑 ⚊ 🍴 Ⓗ 🛒 nr 🏔

Exit rd 67 L at sp Hedesunda. Foll camp sp thro
Hedesunda; past church, cont about 4km to
Hedesunda Island. 3*, Sm, pt shd, EHU (6A) SEK30;
gas; cooking facs; sw nr; red long stay; TV; Eng
spkn; fishing; boat hire; CKE. "Peaceful, lakeside
site; organised activities in ssn; helpful staff."
SEK 260, 1 May-31 Oct.   **2016**

HELSINGBORG *2E4* (5km S Coastal) *56.0034, 12.7300*
Campingplatsen Råå Vallar (M3), Kustgatan, 25270
Råå **(042) 182600; raavallar@nordiccamping.se;
www.nordiccamping.se**

12 ♦♦♦ (htd) 🔥 ♿ 🗑 ⚊ 🍴 Ⓗ 🛒 🏔 ⚓ 🏖 ⚓ sand

Exit E6 into Helsingborg onto rd 111 to Råå, foll
sp to camp. 3*, Lge, pt shd, EHU (10A) SEK50; gas;
10% statics; phone; ccard acc; Quickstop o'night
facs; golf 5km; fishing; sauna; CKE. "Excel, secure site
with gd facs; sports cent 2km; friendly, helpful staff;
excursions to Copenhagen via Helsingør or Landskrona;
town bus excursions to King's Summer Palace daily;
boat trips to glass works at Hyllinge." **SEK 410**   **2016**

HOGANAS *2E4* (8km N Rural) *56.27061, 12.52981*
FirstCamp Mölle (M1), Kullabergsvägen, 26042
Mölle **(042) 347384; molle@firstcamp.se;
www.firstcamp.se**

🐕 ♦♦♦ (htd) WD 🔥 ♿ 🗑 ⚊ MSP 🦋 🍴 🍷 Ⓗ 🛒 🏔 ⚓ 1.5km

Site is S of Mölle at junc of rds 11 & 111, at foot
of Kullaberg. 5*, Lge, unshd, pt sl, EHU (10A) inc;
cooking facs; 10% statics; Eng spkn; ccard acc;
games area; golf; Quickstop o'night facs; sauna;
fishing. "Steep slope to san facs; walking; Krapperups
Castle & park sh walk fr site; excel outdoor activities."
SEK 417, 1 Apr-30 Sep.   **2016**

HOVA *2F2* (8.7km NE Coastal) *58.90998, 14.28995*
Otterbergets Bad & Camping, 54891 Hova **050633
127 or 0738064 935; info@otterbergetscamping.
com; www.otterbergetscamping.com**

🐕 ♦♦♦ WD 🔥 ♿ 🗑 ⚊ MSP 🦋 🍴 🛒 ⚓ adj

Fr Laxa take E20 rd; site sp approx 4km fr Hova;
drive 2 km thro woods to site. Med, mkd, pt shd,
EHU (16A) SEK 40; bbq; cooking facs; 10% statics;
Eng spkn; adv bkg rec; sauna; CCI. "Attractive site
with private access to lake; events held such as fishing
competition & trade fairs (when site may be busy); v
helpful Dutch owners; recep 0800-2200; san facs vg;
excel." **SEK 253, 15 Apr-1 Nov.**   **2017**

JOKKMOKK *1C2* (3km SE Rural) *66.59453, 19.89145*
Arctic Camp Jokkmokk, Notudden, 96222 Jokkmokk
**(0971) 12370; arcticcamp@jokkmokk.com;
arcticcampjokkmokk.se/en/**

12 🐕 ♦♦♦ (htd) WD 🔥 ♿ 🗑 ⚊ MSP 🦋 🍴 🍷 Ⓗ 🛒 🏔 ⚓ (htd)

Sp fr rd 45. In Jokkmokk take rd 97 E, site in 3km on
N side of rd situated bet rv & rd. 4*, Lge, mkd, pt shd,
EHU (10A) SEK40 (poss rev pol); sw nr; 10% statics;
Eng spkn; adv bkg acc; ccard acc; bike hire; waterslide;
fishing; sauna; CKE. "Friendly, clean, well-maintained
site 5km inside Arctic Circle; gd area for Sami culture;
excel playgrnd; lakeside setting, gd pool; late arrival
area." **SEK 290**   **2018**

JOKKMOKK *1C2* (3km W Rural) *66.60500, 19.76200*
Skabram Stugby & Camping, Skabram 206, 96299
Jokkmokk **(0971) 10752; info@skabram.se;
www.skabram.se**

12 🐕 ♦♦♦ (htd) WD 🔥 ♿ 🗑 ⚊ MSP 🦋 🍴

Site sp fr E45 along rd 97, Storgatan. Sm, hdstg,
pt shd, EHU (16A) SEK25; bbq; cooking facs; sw nr;
twin axles; 10% statics; Eng spkn; adv bkg acc; sauna;
fishing; boating. "Vg; canoe & dog sleigh trips; relaxing
site; lovely sm fm type site; v quiet location; gd san
facs." **SEK 185**   **2017**

SWEDEN

JONKOPING *2F3* (15km S Rural) *57.66245, 14.18407* **Lovsjöbadens Camping (F7),** Hyltena, 55592 Jönköping **(036)** 182010; info@lovsjocamping.se; www.lovsjocamping.se

🐕 🚷 wc ♨ ♿ ⚡ 🌀 ✿ ☂️

Exit E4 at Hyltena, site sp on lakeside. 3*, Sm, mkd, pt sl, terr, EHU (10-16A) SEK30; bbq; cooking facs; sw; TV; 10% statics; Eng spkn; adv bkg acc; ccard acc; bike hire; boat hire; games rm; CKE. *"V friendly owners; vg site by sm lake; busy in high ssn; sm sw beach; rowing boats for hire."* **SEK 260, 15 May-15 Sep.** **2015**

KALMAR *2G3* (2km S Coastal) *56.64975, 16.32705* **Stensö Camping (H12),** Stensövägen, 39247 Kalmar **(0480)** 88803; info@stensocamping.se; www.stensocamping.se

♀♂ wc ♨ ♿ ⚡ 🌀 ✿ ☂️ sand adj

Fr E22 foll sp Sjukhus (hosp) then camping sp - this avoids town cent. Fr town cent, site sp. 4*, Lge, mkd, shd, pt sl, EHU (10A) SEK40 (check pol); cooking facs; 10% statics; phone; Eng spkn; ccard acc; boating; fishing; Quickstop o'night facs; cycling; CKE. *"Conv Öland Island (over bdge); glass factories in vicinity; walking dist to town; helpful, friendly staff; new clean san facs (2014); excel."* **SEK 276, 27 Mar-30 Sep.** **2016**

KAPPELLSKAR *2H1* (0.5km W Rural) *59.72046, 19.05045* **Camping Kapellskär (B9),** Riddersholm 985, 76015 Gräddö **(0176)** 44233

🐕 ♀♂ (htd) wc ♨ ⚡ 🌀 ✿ ☂️

Fr Norrtälje take E18 E sp Kapellskär. At ferry sp turn R, site in 1km, sp. Last 700m on unmade rd. 3*, Med, mkd, hdstg, pt shd, terr, EHU (10A) SEK40; 60% statics; Eng spkn; adv bkg acc; ccard acc; games area; bike hire; CKE. *"Conv for ferry terminal; fair site."* **SEK 272, 1 May-29 Sep.** **2015**

KARESUANDO *1D1* (2km SE Rural) *68.43396, 22.51577* **Karesuando Camping,** Laestadiusvagen 185, 98016 Karesuando **(0981)** 20139; karesuando. camping@hotmail.com; www.karesuando.se/ foretag/camping/camping.htm

🐕 ♀♂ wc ♨ ⚡ 🌀 ✿ ☂️

Travelling N on E45, in town cont past bdge to Finland onto rd 99 for approx 2km; site on L. App fr Finland, turn L after x-ing bdge; cont on 99 for 2km. Sm, unshd, EHU (10A) inc; bbq; twin axles; 50% statics; Eng spkn; adv bkg acc; sauna; games area; CKE. *"Model Sami vill on site; cash point in PO; poss mosquito prob; canoe hire avail; gd view of midnight sun on rv; unmkd pitches, fills up quickly."* **SEK 230, 18 May-18 Sep.** **2018**

KARLSHAMN *2F4* (3km SE Coastal) *56.15953, 14.89085* **Kolleviks Camping (K7),** Rådhusgatan 10, 374 81 Karlshamn **(0454)** 810 00; info@ karlshamn.se; www.karlshamn.se

🐕 ♀♂ (htd) wc ♨ ♿ ⚡ 🌀 ✿ ☂️ sand adj

Fr E22 dir Karlshamn & Hamnar (harbour), then site well sp. 3*, Med, mkd, pt shd, pt sl, EHU (10A) SEK45; red long stay; 25% statics; Eng spkn; adv bkg acc; ccard acc; canoeing; Quickstop o'night facs; CKE. *"Helpful owner; attractive location inc harbour; gd base for area; ltd facs LS; well-kept site; facs tired, poss stretched when busy."* **SEK 155, 26 Apr-14 Sep.** **2020**

KATRINEHOLM *2G2* (2km S Rural) *58.9696, 16.21035* **Djulö Camping (D6),** Djulögatan 51, 64192 Katrineholm **(0150)** 57242; info@djulocamping.se; www.djulocamping.se

12 ♀♂ ♨ ♿ ⚡ 🌀 ✿ ☂️ nr ☂️ nr /\

At Norrköping on E4 cont twd Stockholm for about 3km, turn L onto rd 55 N twd Katrineholm. Camping site sp in 2km. 3*, Lge, hdstg, pt sl, EHU (10A) SEK35; gas; sw; adv bkg acc; ccard acc; games area; bike hire; fishing; boating; CKE. *"On lakeside in lge park; well-run, friendly site."* **SEK 291** **2016**

KIL *2F1* (7km N Rural) *59.54603, 13.34145* **Frykenbadens Camping (S17),** Stubberud, 66591 Kil **(0554)** 40940; info@frykenbaden.se; www.frykenbaden.se

12 ♀♂ ♨ ♿ ⚡ 🌀 ✿ ☂️ ☂️ /\

Fr Karlstad take rd 61 to Kil, site clearly sp on lakeside. 4*, Lge, pt shd, pt sl, EHU (10A) SEK40; sw; TV; phone; adv bkg acc; fishing; Quickstop o'night facs; boat launch; bike hire; CKE. *"Very clean, spacious waterfront site; sauna SEK5; barrier key."* **SEK 376** **2018**

KIRUNA *1C1* (1.6km NE Urban) *67.8604, 20.2405* **Ripan Hotel & Camping,** Campingvägen 5, 98135 Kiruna **(0980)** 63000; info@ripan.se; www.ripan.se

12 ♀♂ (htd) wc ♿ ⚡ 🌀 ✿ ☂️ nr /\ ☂️ (htd)

Site sp fr town cent. 3*, Med, hdstg, mkd, unshd, EHU (10A) inc; TV (pitch); Eng spkn; ccard acc; sauna. *"No privacy in shwrs; easy walk to town; public footpath thro site (top end) - poss v noisy & disruptive; trips to Kirunavaara Deep Mine fr tourist info office; no security fence."* **SEK 323** **2016**

KIVIK *2F4* (1.6km N Rural/Coastal) *55.69135, 14.21373* **Kiviks Familjecamping (L35),** Väg 9, 27732 Kivik **(0414)** 70930; info@kivikscamping.se; www.kivikscamping.se

🐕 ♀♂ wc ♨ ♿ ⚡ 🌀 ✿ ☂️ shgl 1km

On rd 9 o'looking sea, sp. 3*, Med, mkd, unshd, EHU SEK35; bbq; cooking facs; TV; 20% statics; phone; Eng spkn; ccard acc; CKE. *"Steam rlwy w/end in summer at Brösarp; cider/apple area; easy walk to town; rev pol certain pitches."* **SEK 230, 16 Apr-9 Oct.** **2016**

SWEDEN

KOLMÅRDEN *2G2* (2km SE Coastal) *58.6597, 16.4006*
First Camp Kolmården (E3), 61834 Kolmården
(011) 398250; kolmarden@firstcamp.se;
www.firstcamp.se

🐕 ♟(htd) ⓦ ⛺ 🚿 ♿ 🍽 🧺 MSP 🎱 🍴 🅗 🛒 🎿 ⛰ 🏊 🛶 adj

Fr E4 NE fr Norrköping take 1st Kolmården exit
sp Kolmården Djur & Naturpark. Site on sea 2km
bef Naturpark. 4*, Lge, pt shd, terr, EHU (10A);
cooking facs; TV; 10% statics; phone; ccard acc;
waterslide; sauna; bike hire; boat hire; CKE. *"Gd site;
nr to Kilmarden zoo & aquarium; well mkd pitches."*
SEK 457, 1 Apr-30 Sep.   **2019**

KUNGÄLV *2E2* (1km SE Rural) *57.86211, 11.99613*
Kungälvs Vandrarhem & Camping (O37), Färjevägen
2, 44231 Kungälv **(0303)** 18900; info@kungalvs
vandrarhem.se; **www.kungalvsvandrarhem.se**

🐕 ♟(htd) ⓦ ⛺ 🚿 ♿ 🍽 🧺 MSP 🦋 🎱 🍴 🅗 🛒 ⛰

Exit E6 junc 85 or 86 & foll sp Kungälv cent, then sp
'Bohus Fästning'. Site sp. 3*, Sm, mkd, hdstg,
shd, EHU (12A) SEK40; bbq (gas); red long stay;
10% statics; bus adj; Eng spkn; ccard acc; CCI. *"Site
adj Bonus Fästning (fort) & Kungälv Church (17th C)
on rv bank; find pitch & check in at recep 0800-1000
& 1700-1900; door code fr recep for san facs; gd NH."*
SEK 250, 15 Apr-30 Sep.   **2019**

KUNGSBACKA *2E3* (5km SE Rural) *57.42492,
12.15860* **Silverlyckans Camping**, Varbergsvägen 875,
43433 Fjärås **(0300)** 541349; **www.silverlyckan.eu**

🐕 ♟(htd) ⓦ ⛺ 🦋 🅗 nr 🛒 nr ⛰ 🏊 sand 4km

Exit E6/E20 junc 58 dir Åsa. Site in 400m on L.
Med, unshd, pt sl, EHU (10A) SEK30; cooking facs;
10% statics; bus adj; Eng spkn; adv bkg acc. *"Vg site;
htd pool 3km; mv service pnt (refill only); rec visit
Tjolöholms Slott (castle)."*
SEK 180, 1 May-15 Sep.   **2019**

KUNGSHAMN *2E2* (2km NE Coastal) *58.36569,
11.28077* **Swecamp Johannesvik**, Wagga Nordgard 1,
45634 Kungshamn **(0523)** 32387; info@johannesvik.
nu; **www.johannesvik.nu**

12 🐕 ♟(htd) ⓦ ⛺ 🚿 ♿ 🍽 🧺 MSP 🦋 🍴 🅗 🛒 ⛰ 🏊 shgl adj

Fr E6 rte 171 to Askum, dir Kungshamn, thro
Hovenaset, over bdge. Ent to site on R (sp). 4*, Lge,
mkd, unshd, terr, EHU inc; gas; bbq; cooking facs; red
long stay; TV; Eng spkn; adv bkg acc; CKE. *"Barrier card
SEK150 dep; dep rèq; shwr card SEK6 (3mins); gd."*
SEK 381   **2017**

LANDSKRONA *2E4* (4km N Rural) *55.90098, 12.8042*
Borstahusens Camping (M5), Campingvägen, 26161
Landskrona **(0418)** 10837; bokning@motesplats
borstahusen.se; **www.motesplatsborstahusen.se**

♟(htd) ⓦ ⛺ 🚿 ♿ 🍽 🧺 MSP 🦋 🎱 🍴 🅗 🛒 ⛰ 🏊 adj

Exit E6/E20 at 'Landskrona N' & foll sp for
Borstahusen 4.5km fr E6/D20. 3*, Lge, unshd, EHU
(10A) SEK40; TV; 50% statics; phone; Eng spkn;
ccard acc; tennis; golf; bike hire; CKE. *"Gd, pleasant,
well run site on edge of Kattegat; htd pool 2km; sm
pitches; game reserve; boat to Ven Island fr town;
adj sea but no views; chalets & holiday packages."*
SEK 320, 21 Apr-11 Sep.   **2019**

LEKSAND *2G1* (4km SW Rural) *60.73061, 14.95221*
Västanviksbadets Camping (W12), Siljansnäsvägen
130, 79392 Leksand **(0768)** 128510; info@vbcl.se;
www.vbcl.se

🐕 ♟(htd) ⓦ ⛺ 🚿 ♿ 🍽 🧺 MSP 🦋 🎱 🛒

L off Borlänge to Leksand rd at Leksand S, dir
Siljansnäs. Site ent clearly visible on R in 3km at W
end Lake Siljan at Västanvik. 4*, Med, mkd, unshd,
pt sl, terr, EHU (10A) SEK45; bbq (sep area); cooking
facs; sw; TV; 10% statics; Eng spkn; adv bkg acc;
ccard acc; Quickstop o'night facs; boating; bike hire;
fishing. *"Attractive site on lakeside; friendly welcome;
ltd facs LS; lakeside pitches avail; keycard for all facs;
Dalarna/Lake Siljan traditional heart of Sweden; excel."*
SEK 292, 30 Apr-6 Sep.   **2019**

LIDKOPING *2 F2* (24.4km N Rural) *58.67381,
13.21283* **Lacko Slott Camping**, Läcko Slott
Kållandsö, 53199 Otterstad **(5104)** 84668;
info@lackoslott.se; **www.lackoslott.se**

🐕 ♟(htd) ⓦ ⛺ 🚿 ♿ 🍽 🧺 MSP 🍴 nr 🅗 nr 🏊 lake 50m

On Lake Vanern, 25km N of Lidkoping, sp fr Lacko.
Sm, mkd, hdg, shd, EHU 10A (SEK30); cooking
facs; sw nr; bus; Eng spkn; adv bkg acc; ccard acc.
*"Medieval Lacko Castle 100m; Naturum nature and
visitor ctr with rest 150m; mostly individual pitches
hidden in woods (no lake views) on promontory
opp castle; barrier key; bkg rec; lovely site; excel."*
SEK 174, 1 May-30 Sep.   **2018**

LIDKOPING *2F2* (3km N Rural) *58.51375, 13.14008*
Krono Camping (R3), Läckögaten, 53154 Lidköping
(0510) 26804; info@kronocamping.com;
www.kronocamping.com

12 ♟(htd) ⓦ ⛺ 🚿 ♿ 🍽 🧺 MSP 🦋 🎱 🅗 nr 🛒 ⛰

On Lake Vänern nr Folkparken, on rd to Läckö; at
Lidköping ring rd foll int'l camping sp. 5*, Lge, pt
shd, serviced pitches; EHU (10A) inc; gas; sw nr; TV
(pitch); ccard acc; watersports; CKE. *"V clean, friendly,
well-run site; open pinewoods on lakeside; htd pool
300m; interesting area."* **SEK 412**   **2015**

LIDKOPING *2F2 (32km NE Rural) 58.624003, 13.383631* **Kinnekulle Camping & Stugby,** Strandvägen, 53394 Hällekis **(0510) 544102; info@ kinnekullecamping.se; www.kinnekullecamping.se**

🚹♿ (htd) 🆆🅳 🚿 ♨ MᴼP 🦋 ⚓ adj, sand

Turn off E20 at Gotene for Hallekis. Outskirts of Hallekis foll sp (ignore MH NH sp) rd passes factory & heads into woods. Site in 3km. 4*, Lge, mkd, pt shd, pt sl, terr, EHU (10A) inc; 30% statics; Eng spkn; ccard acc; CKE. *"Vg; local walks in woods & hillside; barrier key card."* SEK 298, 13 Apr-9 Sep.   **2018**

LJUNGBY *2F3 (1km N Urban) 56.84228, 13.95251* **Ljungby Camping Park,** Campingvägen 1, 34122 Ljungby **(0372) 10350; reservation@ljungby- semesterby.se; www.ljungby-semesterby.se**

🚹♿ (htd) 🆆🅳 ♨ ♿ ⊿ ⚓ 🏞 🛶

Exit E4 at Ljungby N, site sp. 3*, Med, shd, EHU (10A) SEK35; ccard acc; cycling; CKE. *"Adv bkg ess high ssn; htd pool adj."* SEK 256, 1 May-31 Aug.   **2016**

LJUSDAL *1B3 (3km W Rural) 61.83894, 16.04059* **Ljusdals Camping (X21),** Ramsjövägen 56, 82730 Ljusdal **(0651) 12958; info@ljusdalscamping.se; www.ljusdalscamping.se**

12 🚹♿ (htd) 🆆🅳 ♨ ♿ ⊿ MᴼP 🍴 ♿ ⚓ 🏞 ⚓

Leave Ljusdal on Rv83 dir Ånge, site on R in 3km. 3*, Med, pt shd, EHU (10A) SEK40; cooking facs; sw nr; 10% statics; Eng spkn; adv bkg acc; ccard acc; bike hire; games area; sauna; CKE. SEK 295   **2019**

LULEA *1D2 (8km W Coastal) 65.59565, 22.07221* **First Camp Luleå (BD18),** Arcusvägen 110, 97594 Luleå **(0920) 60300; lulea@firstcamp.se; www.firstcamp.se/lulea**

12 🐕 🚹♿ (htd) 🆆🅳 ♨ ♿ ⊿ ♿ 🍴 ♿ ⚓ 🏞

⚓ sand adj

Exit E4 on R 500m N of Luleälv Rv bdge. Foll sp 'Arcus' (recreation complex). 3*, V lge, mkd, pt shd, EHU (10A) inc; cooking facs; TV; phone; Eng spkn; adv bkg acc; ccard acc; tennis 300m; car wash; sauna; bike hire; CKE. *"Excel family site; many sports facs; san facs poss stretched high ssn; htd pool complex 700m; suitable RVs & twin axles; adj rlwy museum."* SEK 365   **2019**

MALMO *2E4 (11km N Coastal) 55.68873, 13.05756* **Habo-Ljung Camping (M23),** Södra Västkustvägen 12, 23434 Lomma **(040) 411210; info@ haboljungcamping.se; www.haboljungcamping.se**

🚹♿ (htd) 🆆🅳 ♨ ♿ ⊿ ♿ MᴼP ⚓ 🏞 ⚓ sand adj

Turn off E6 dir Lomma, head N for Bjärred, site on L. 3*, Lge, pt shd, EHU (10A) SEK40; bbq; cooking facs; 5% statics; phone; Eng spkn; ccard acc; CKE. *"Conv NH; vg; location for wind & kite surfing; 20 min walk along beach to town."* SEK 396, 15 Apr-15 Sep.   **2019**

MALMO *2E4 (7km SW Urban) 55.5722, 12.90686* **Malmö Camping & Feriesenter (M8),** Strandgatan 101, Sibbarp, 21611 Limhamn **(040) 155165; malmocamping@malmo.se; www.firstcamp.se**

12 🐕 🚹♿ (htd) 🆆🅳 ♨ ♿ ⊿ ♿ MᴼP 🍴 ♿ ⚓ 🏞 ⚓

⚓ sand 250m

Fr Öresund Bdge take 1st exit & foll sp Limhamn & Sibbarp, then int'l campsite sp. Fr N on E6 round Malmö until last exit bef bdge (sp), then as above. Fr Dragør-Limnhamn ferry turn R on exit dock. Site in 1km on R, nr sea, in park-like setting. 4*, V lge, hdg, mkd, pt shd, pt sl, EHU (16A) inc (poss rev pol); gas; cooking facs; twin axles; TV; 20% statics; phone; bus to Malmo; Eng spkn; ccard acc; games rm; windsurfing; games area; bike hire; CKE. *"Easy cycle to town cent; facs poss stretched high ssn; v busy city site; well-laid out; pool 400m; conv Öresund Bdge; lovely site; v friendly, helpful staff; gd clean new (2016) san facs blocks."* **SEK 395**   **2017**

MALUNG *2F1 (1km W Rural) 60.68296, 13.70243* **Malungs Camping (W22),** Bullsjövägen, 78235 Malung **(0280) 18650; info@malungscamping.se; www.malungscamping.se**

12 🚹♿ (htd) 🆆🅳 ♨ ♿ ⊿ ♿ 🦋 ♿ ⚓ 🏞 ⚓

Fr Stöllet take rd 45 to Malung, site sp. 3*, Lge, pt shd, EHU (10A) SEK40; TV; ccard acc; car wash; fishing; Quickstop o'night facs; bike hire; boating; CKE. SEK 260   **2016**

MARIESTAD *2F2 (2km NW Rural) 58.7154, 13.79516* **Ekuddens Camping (R2),** 54245 Mariestad **(0771) 101200; www.ekuddenscamping.se**

12 🐕 🚹♿ ♿ ⊿ ♿ MᴼP 🍴 ♿ ⚓ 🏞 ⚓ (htd) ⚓

Fr E20 take turn off twd Mariestad. At 1st rndabt foll ring rd clockwise until site sp on Lake Vänern. 4*, Lge, shd, EHU (10A) SEK40; gas; phone; ccard acc; bike hire; golf 2km; sauna; Quickstop o'night facs; CKE. *"Gd views fr lakeside pitches; friendly, helpful staff; gd san facs."* SEK 294   **2019**

MARKARYD *2F3 (0.5km N Urban) 56.46475, 13.60066* **Camping Park Sjötorpet (G4),** Strandvägen 4, 28531 Markaryd **(0433) 10316; info@ markarydscamping.se; www.markarydscamping.se**

🐕 🚹♿ (htd) 🆆🅳 ♨ ♿ ⊿ ♿ MᴼP 🦋 ♿ 🍴 ♿ ⚓ 🏞

E4 fr Helsingborg (ferry) site is bet E4 N turn to Markaryd & rd 117, sp. Narr app. 3*, Sm, pt shd, pt sl, EHU (10A) inc; cooking facs; sw; 10% statics; phone; Eng spkn; ccard acc; boating; fishing; bike hire; CKE. *"Excel san & cooking facs; well-run site; new owners (2017), helpful; barrier may clse 7pm."* SEK 325, 12 Apr-29 Sept.   **2018**

MARSTRAND *2E2* (1.4km NE Coastal) *57.89380, 11.60510* **Marstrands Camping (036),** Långedalsvägen 16, 44030 Marstrand **(0303) 60584; info@marstrand camping.se; www.marstrandscamping.se**

🐕 👫(htd) 🚿 ♿ 🅿️ 🧺 MSP 🦋 🍴 🛒 🏛 🔆 shgl

Exit A6 dir Kungsälv/Marstrand & foll rd 168 to Marstrand. Site sp on Koön Island. App rd to site v narr. 4*, Med, pt shd, pt sl, EHU (10A) SEK45; cooking facs; TV; 50% statics; adv bkg acc; ccard acc; CKE. *"Ferry to Marstrand Island; recep not staffed in LS."* **SEK 350, 12 Apr-2 Oct.** 2017

MELLERUD *2E2* (15km N Rural) *58.81968, 12.41519* **Haverud Camping,** Kanalvagen 4, 464 72 Haverud **(0530) 30770; hafrestromsif@telia.com; www.hafrestromsif.se**

👫 🚿 ♿ 🅿️ 🧺 🦋 🔌 nr 🏛

Signposted in Haverund. Sm, mkd, hdstg, unshd, terr, EHU; sw nr; Eng spkn; CKE. *"Self pitch on arr, fees collected am or pay at visitors ctr at canal; gd."* **SEK 220, 25 Apr-14 Sep.** 2017

MELLERUD *2E2* (2km W Rural) *58.71288, 12.43231* **Kerstins Camping (P21),** Hålsungebyn 1, 46494 Mellerud **(0530) 12715; epost@kerstinscamping.se; www.kerstinscamping.se**

🐕 👫(htd) 🚿 ♿ 🅿️ 🧺 MSP 🦋 🛒 🏛

Fr Mellerud on rd 166 dir Bäckefors & Ed, site sp. 3*, Sm, hdg, mkd, pt shd, EHU (10A) SEK45; bbq (sep area); cooking facs; TV; 15% statics; phone; Eng spkn; adv bkg acc; games rm; CKE. *"Pleasant area; excel; sm site with open outlook to fmland on 1 side; vg site."* **SEK 282, 14 May-9 Sep.** 2018

MORA *1B4* (0.5km N Urban) *61.00853, 14.53178* **Mora Parkens Camping,** Parkvägen 1, 79237 Mora **(0250) 27600; info@moraparken.se; www.moraparken.se**

12 👫(htd) 🚿 ♿ 🅿️ 🧺 🦋 🍴 🔌 nr 🛒 nr 🏊(covrd, htd) 🔆

Fr SW site sp on rd 45. Or foll sp in town cent; site in 400m. Recep in adj hotel. 4*, Lge, mkd, pt shd, pt sl, EHU (10A) inc; TV; 10% statics; Eng spkn; ccard acc; sports facs; Quickstop o'night facs; fishing; waterslide; games rm; CKE. *"Excel site; ltd facs LS & poss unclean; suitable RVs & twin axles; conv for bear sanctuary at Orsa."* **SEK 433** 2018

NYNASHAMN *2H2* (1km NW Coastal) *58.90717, 17.93805* **Nicksta Camping (B8),** Nickstabadsvägen 17, 14943 Nynäshamn **(08) 52012780; info@nicksta camping.se; www.nickstacamping.se**

12 🐕 👫(htd) 🚿 ♿ 🅿️ 🧺 MSP 🍴 🔌 nr 🏛 🐾 adj

Fr Stockholm on Rv 73 to Nynäshamn. Foll site sp, turning R at ICA supmkt, then immed L (sp poss cov'rd by hedge.) 4*, Med, pt shd, pt sl, EHU (10A) SEK50; cooking facs; 10% statics; train 600m; Eng spkn; games area; site clsd mid-Dec to mid-Jan; Quickstop o'night facs; waterslide; bike hire; CKE. *"Gd site; ferries to Gotland & Poland."* **SEK 343** 2016

OREBRO *2G2* (3km S Rural) *59.2554, 15.18955* **Gustavsviks Camping (T2),** Sommarrovägen, 70229 Örebro **(019) 196950; camping@gustavsvik.com; www.gustavsvik.com**

🐕 👫(htd) 🚿 ♿ 🅿️ 🧺 MSP 🦋 🍴 🍽 🔌 🛒 🏛 🔆 🏊(covrd, htd) 🔆

Foll sp fr E18/E20 & rd 51 to site. 5*, V lge, mkd, pt shd, pt sl, serviced pitches; EHU (10A) SEK80 (poss rev pol); gas; bbq; cooking facs; sw nr; TV (pitch); 10% statics; phone; bus; Eng spkn; ccard acc; waterslide; solarium; gym; golf nr; CKE. *"Excel family site; excel facs; gentle stroll to town; very highly rec; beautiful site."* **SEK 240, 15 Apr-6 Nov.** 2016

ORSA *1B4* (1km W Rural) *61.12090, 14.59890* **Orsa Camping (W3),** Timmervägen 1, 79421 Orsa **(0250) 46200; info@orsacamping.se; www.orsacamping.se**

12 👫(htd) 🚿 ♿ 🅿️ 🧺 🦋 🍴 🍽 🔌 🛒 nr 🏛 🔆 🏊(htd)

Sp fr town cent & fr rd 45. 4*, V lge, pt shd, EHU (10A) SEK50; cooking facs; sw; TV (pitch); 5% statics; phone; tennis; canoe hire; fishing; waterslide; bike hire; sauna; CKE. *"Excel countryside; bear reserve 15km; gd general facs but ltd LS."* **SEK 375** 2016

OSKARSHAMN *2G3* (3km SE Coastal) *57.2517, 16.49206* **Gunnarsö Camping (H7),** Östersjövägen 103, 57263 Oskarshamn **(0491) 77220; gunnarso@ oskarshamn.se; www.oskarshamn.se**

🐕 👫(htd) 🚿 ♿ 🅿️ 🧺 🦋 🍴 🛒 🏛 🔆

Fr E22 dir Oskarshamn, site sp on Kalmar Sound. 4*, Med, pt shd, EHU (10A) SEK35; TV; 40% statics; phone; adv bkg acc; ccard acc; watersports; sauna; CKE. *"Beautiful location; many pitches with gd views; gd walking/cycling."* **SEK 332, 1 May-15 Sep.** 2016

OSTERSUND *1B3* (3km SE Rural) *63.15955, 14.6731* **Östersunds Camping (Z11),** Krondikesvägen 95, 83146 Östersund **(063) 144615; ostersundscamping@ ostersund.se; www.ostersundscamping.se**

12 🐕 👫(htd) 🚿 ♿ 🅿️ 🧺 🦋 🍴 🍽 🔌 🛒 nr 🏛 🔆 🏊

At Odensala on lakeside, well sp fr E14. 4*, Lge, mkd, hdstg, pt shd, pt sl, EHU (10A) SEK60 (poss rev pol); cooking facs; TV (pitch); 80% statics; phone; bus; ccard acc; sauna; tennis; CKE. *"Gd NH; very helpful staff."* **SEK 200** 2019

PAJALA *1D1* (1.5km SE Rural) *67.20381, 23.4084* **Pajala Camping (BD8),** Tannavägen 65, 98431 Pajala **(0978) 74180 or (0702) 107448; pajalacamping@ gmail.com; www.pajalacamping.se**

12 🐕 👫(htd) 🚿 ♿ 🅿️ 🧺 MSP 🦋 🍴 🛒 🏛

Site sp fr rd 99. 2*, Med, mkd, hdstg, pt shd, EHU (10A) SEK30; cooking facs; red long stay; TV; Eng spkn; adv bkg acc; ccard acc; sauna; tennis; bike hire; CKE. *"Clean, well-presented site; delightful owner; salmon-fishing in rv in ssn (mid-Jun approx)."* **SEK 190** 2016

RATTVIK *1B4* (1km W Rural) *60.88891, 15.10881* **Siljansbadets Camping (W8),** Långbryggevägen 4, 79532 Rättvik **(0248) 56118; camp@siljansbadet.com; www.siljansbadet.com**

🐕🐴 ⅢD 🚿 ♿ 🅿 MSP 🦋 ⚲ 🍴 Ⓗ nr 🔌 nr ⛺

Fr S on rd 70 thro Rättvik. Immed outside town turn L at rndabt, site sp on Lake Siljan. Height restriction **3.5m.** 4*, V lge, mkd, pt shd, EHU (16A) SEK50; bbq; cooking facs; sw; twin axles; TV; 15% statics; bus/train; Eng spkn; ccard acc; games area; boat hire. *"Lovely scenic lakeside location; conv town cent; excel san facs; excel site."* **SEK 355, 26 Apr-6 Oct.** **2017**

SAFFLE *2F2* (6km S Rural) *59.08326, 12.88616* **Duse Udde Camping (S11),** 66180 Säffle **(0533) 42000; duseudde@krokstad.se; www.duseudde.se**

12 🐕 🏃 🚿 ♿ 🅿 MSP ⚲ 🍴 Ⓗ 🛒 ⛺ 🎣 🏄

Site sp fr rd 45. 4*, Med, shd, pt sl, EHU (10A) SEK50; sw; red long stay; 20% statics; phone; bus; ccard acc; watersports; sauna; bike hire; Quickstop o'night facs; CKE. *"Place to relax; pool 6km; useful base for Värmland area with nature walks."* **SEK 180** **2016**

SARNA *1B3* (1km S Rural) *61.69281, 13.14696* **Särna Camping (W32),** Särnavägen 6, 79090 Särna **(0253) 10851; camping@sarnacamping.se; www.sarna camping.se**

🏃 ⅢD 🚿 ♿ 🅿 MSP 🦋 ⚲ Ⓗ nr 🔌 nr ⛺ 🏄 shgl

Turn R off rd 70 opp fire stn. 3*, Med, pt shd, terr, EHU (10A) SEK35; adv bkg acc; sauna; bike hire. *"Beautiful setting o'looking lake; pleasant town."* **SEK 245, 19 May-30 Sep.** **2016**

SIMRISHAMN *2F4* (2km N Coastal) *55.57021, 14.33611* **Tobisviks Camping (L14),** Tobisvägen, 27294 Simrishamn **(0414) 412778; info@tobisviks camping.se; http://tobisvikscamping.se**

12 🏃 🚿 🅿 MSP Ⓗ nr 🔌 nr 🏄 (htd)

By sea at N app to town. 4*, Lge, pt shd, EHU (10A) SEK50; TV; phone; ccard acc; watersports; CKE. **SEK 210** **2016**

SKANOR *2E4* (2km SE Coastal) *55.39750, 12.86555* **Calsterbo Camping & Resort (formerly Ljungens Camping),** Strandbadsvägen, 23942 Falsterbo **(040) 6024020 or (414) 401180; info@falsterboresort.se; falsterboresort.se**

🐴 🏃 (htd) ⅢD 🚿 ♿ 🅿 MSP ⚲ 🛒 🔌 ⛺ 🏄 sand 200m

Fr E6/E22 exit to W sp Höllviken onto rd 100. Foll sp Skanör/Falsterbo. Site sp on L at rndabt at ent to town, dir Falsterbo. 4*, Lge, mkd, hdstg, pt shd, EHU (10A) SEK40; bbq; cooking facs; TV; 50% statics; bus; Eng spkn; ccard acc; CKE. *"Conv Viking Vill museum; nature reserve adj; gd birdwatching, cycling; vg; aircraft noise (under flight path Copenhagen airport); new management, new recep & ongoing work on facs (2017)."* **SEK 290, 29 Apr-28 Sep.** **2017**

SKELLEFTEA *1C2* (1.5km N Rural) *64.76156, 20.97513* **Skellefteå Camping (AC18),** Mossgaten, 93170 Skellefteå **(0910) 735500; skellefteacamping@ skelleftea.se; www.skelleftea.se/skellefteacamping**

12 🐴 🏃 (htd) ⅢD 🚿 ♿ 🅿 MSP 🦋 ⚲ 🍴 Ⓗ nr 🔌 ⛺ 🏄
🏊 (htd) 🏖 sand 5km

Turn W off E4; well sp behind g'ge. Also sp as Camping Stugby. 4*, Lge, mkd, unshd, pt sl, EHU (10A) SEK60; bbq; cooking facs; TV; 10% statics; phone; Eng spkn; ccard acc; waterslide; tennis 150m; sauna; fishing; bike hire; games area; CKE. *"Friendly, clean site in pine trees on sheltered inlet; lge pitches suitable RVs & twin axles; Nordanå Cultural Cent & Bonnstan Church Vill in walking dist; if site clsd book in at Statoil stn 500m S on E4 at rndabt; excel san facs, lgr camp kitchen, helpful staff, lge supmkt nrby."* **SEK 330** **2017**

SODERHAMN *1C4* (10km SE Coastal) *61.24843, 17.19506* **Stenö Havsbad Camping (X9),** Stenövägen, 82022 Sandarne **(0270) 60000; steno@ nordiccamping.se; www.nordiccamping.se**

12 ⅢD 🚿 ♿ 🅿 MSP 🦋 ⚲ 🍴 Ⓗ 🛒 ⛺ 🏖 sand

Exit E4 at sp Bollnäs-Sandarne (S of Söderhamn turn), foll sp Sandarne at Östansjö, turn L at camping sp. 4*, Lge, shd, EHU (10A) SEK50; cooking facs; TV; 10% statics; phone; bus; adv bkg acc; ccard acc; games area; CKE. *"Adj nature reserve."* **SEK 307** **2016**

SODERKOPING *2G2* (1km N Rural) *58.49163, 16.30618* **Skeppsdockans Camping (E34),** Dockan 1, 61421 Söderköping **(0121) 21630; korskullenscamp@ hotmail.com; www.soderkopingscamping.se**

🏃 (htd) ⅢD 🚿 🅿 🅿 🔌 Ⓗ nr 🔌 nr

On E22 immed N of canal bdge. 2*, Sm, mkd, unshd, EHU SEK40; cooking facs; sw; TV; Eng spkn; ccard acc; bike hire; CKE. *"On side of Gota Canal; peaceful."* **SEK 220, 30 Apr-2 Oct.** **2016**

SORSELE *1C2* (0.4km W Rural) *65.53428, 17.52663* **Sorsele Camping (AC21),** Fritidsvägen, Näset, 92070 Sorsele **(0952) 10124; info@lapplandskatan.nu; www.lapplandskatan.nu**

12 🐴 🏃 (htd) ⅢD 🚿 ♿ 🅿 MSP 🦋 ⚲ 🔌 nr ⛺ 🏄 🏖

N on rd 45/363 fr Storuman to Arvidsjaur. In Sorsele vill turn W for 500m; site sp. 2*, Med, unshd, EHU (16A) SEK35; TV; 10% statics; phone; ccard acc; bike hire; canoeing; fishing; CKE. *"Nature reserve; hiking; interesting ancient Lapp vill; friendly, welcoming; attractive site."* **SEK 249** **2019**

STOCKHOLM *2H2* (15km N Rural) *59.43821, 17.99223*
Rösjöbadens Camping (B1), Lomvägen 100, 19256
Sollentuna **(08) 962184; info@rosjobaden.se;
www.rosjobaden.se**

12 ♠ ♦♦ ⊞ ▲ ♁ ♿ ⬛ ✎ /🚻 🦋 🐕 🛒 ⛺

Take E18 m'way N fr Stockholm, sp Norrtälje. Pass
Morby Centrum on L after 7km. Take Sollentuna
exit, turn L & foll Sollentuna rd 265/262 for approx
5km. At 2nd set of traff lts with pylons adj, turn
R on sm rd, clear sp to site. 3*, Lge, pt shd, pt sl,
EHU (16A); bbq; cooking facs; twin axles; TV (pitch);
90% statics; bus 150m; Eng spkn; adv bkg acc;
Quickstop o'night facs; boating; fishing; CKE. *"Conv
Morby Centrum, lge shopping cent, petrol, metro to
city; pleasant walks in woods & lakeside; lake sw fr
pontoons; san facs adequate; staff uninterested; site
run as a residential site; fair."* **SEK 330**   **2017**

STOCKHOLM *2H2* (12km SW Urban) *59.29558,
17.92300* **Bredäng Camping (A4),** Stora
Sällskapsväg, 12731 Skärholmen **(08) 977071;
bredangcamping@telia.com; www.bredangcamping.se**

♠ ♦♦(htd) ⊞ ▲ ♁ ♿ ⬛ ✎ /🚻 🦋 ♈ 🍴 🐕 🛒 ⛺ 🌊(htd)
🏊adj

Exit E4/E20 to Bredäng junc 152 & foll sp to site.
3*, Lge, hdstg, mkd, pt shd, serviced pitches; EHU
(16A) SEK40; cooking facs; TV; 30% statics; Eng
spkn; adv bkg acc; ccard acc; Quickstop o'night facs;
bike hire; sauna. *"Facs ltd LS & poss stretched in
ssn; v helpful staff; overspill 3km at Sätra Camping;
battery-charging; conv for Stockholm; shopping cent &
metro with free car park about 700m; lake adj; access
to Stockholm also poss by lake steamer fr pier (high
ssn) - 10 min walk; well-run site; metro 700m; vg forest
walks."* **SEK 358, 18 Apr-9 Oct.**   **2016**

STOCKHOLM *2H2* (10km W Rural) *59.33731, 17.90105*
Ängby Campingplats (A3), Blackebergsvägen 25,
16850 Bromma **(08) 370420; reservation@angby
camping.se; www.angbycamping.se**

12 ♠ ♦♦ ⊞ ▲ ♁ ♿ ⬛ ✎ /🚻 ♈ 🍴 🐕 🛒

On E4 fr Stockholm take rd 275 W twd Vällingby.
At rndabt turn L for rd 261 dir Ekerö, then R sp
Sodra Ängby, site sp. 3*, Med, mkd, pt shd, pt sl, EHU
SEK35; sw nr; TV (pitch); 10% statics; phone; train;
Eng spkn; ccard acc; waterslide; tennis; sauna; CKE.
*"Sh walk to metro stn, 20 mins to city; gd situation;
walk/cycle to Drottningsholm Palace; some sm pitches;
poss diff pitching for lge o'fits; lack of privacy in shwrs;
san facs stretched high ssn & need update; ltd facs
LS; workers living on site; site poss muddy after rain;
helpful staff."* **SEK 333**   **2016**

STROMSTAD *2E2* (3km S Coastal) *58.91350,
11.20531* **Lagunen Camping & Stugor,**
Skärsbygdsvägen 40, 45297 Strömstad **(0526)
755000; info@lagunen.se; www.lagunen.se**

12 ♠ ♦♦ ⊞ ▲ ♁ ♿ ⬛ ✎ /🚻 🦋 ♈ 🍴 🎡 🐕 🛒 ⛺ 🏊adj

On Uddevalla rd 176 out of Strömstad. Site on L.
4*, Lge, pt shd, pt sl, EHU inc; cooking facs; TV;
10% statics; adv bkg acc; ccard acc; bike hire; boat
hire. *"By lakeside (long stay); barrier card preloaded
with shwr money."* **SEK 490**   **2017**

STROMSUND *1B3* (1km SW Rural) *63.84651,
15.53378* **Strömsunds Camping (Z3),** Näsviken,
83324 Strömsund **(0670) 16410; turism@stromsund.
se or stromsunds.turistbyra@stromsund.se;
www.stromsund.se/stromsundscamping**

12 ♠ ♦♦(htd) ⊞ ▲ ♁ ♿ ⬛ ✎ /🚻 🦋 ♈ 🎡 🐕 nr ⛺ 🛶 🚣

W of rd 45, over bdge S of main town on lakeside.
4*, Lge, pt shd, pt sl, EHU (10A) SEK30; cooking
facs; 10% statics; phone; ccard acc; bike hire; fishing;
boat hire; CKE. *"In 2 parts: W side has main facs
but E quieter; go to g'ge adj when site office clsd."*
SEK 274   **2018**

"I like to fill in the reports as I travel from site to site"

You'll find report forms at the back of this
guide, or you can fill them in online at
camc.com/europereport.

SUNDSVALL *1C3* (4km SE Urban/Coastal) *62.3585,
17.37016* **Fläsians Camping & Stugor (Y26),**
Norrstigen 15, 85468 Sundsvall **(060) 554475;
bernt.ostling@gmail.com**

12 ♦♦(htd) ⊞ ▲ ♁ ♿ ⬛ ✎ /🚻 🦋 🎡 🐕 ⛺ 🏊sand adj

Clear sps on E4 in both dirs; site on E coast side
of rd. 3*, Med, mkd, pt shd, terr, EHU (10A) SEK35;
cooking facs; Eng spkn; adv bkg acc; ccard acc; fishing;
CKE. *"Sea view all pitches; gd access even in wet;
suitable RVs & twin axles; if recep clsd, site yourself &
pay later; helpful staff; some traff noise; sw pools in
Sundsvall; clean san facs."* **SEK 300**   **2017**

SVEG *1B3* (0.6km S Rural) *62.03241, 14.36496*
Svegs Camping (Z32), Kyrkogränd 1, 84232 Sveg
**(0680) 13025; info@svegscamping.se; www.svegs
camping.se**

12 ♠ ♦♦(htd) ⊞ ▲ ♁ ♿ ⬛ ✎ /🚻 ♈ 🍴 nr 🎡 🐕 ⛺

Just S of traff lts at junc rds 45 & 84. Opp Statoil at
rear of rest, well sp. 2*, Med, mkd, pt shd, EHU (16A)
SEK50; bbq; cooking facs; twin axles; TV; 15% statics;
phone; bus 300m; Eng spkn; adv bkg acc; ccard acc;
games area; bike hire; CKE. *"Gd for sh stay/NH; htd
pool 500m; many cabins used as long stay family units;
san facs excel; well organised & run."* **SEK 285**   **2017**

SWEDEN

TIMMERNABBEN *2G3* (1.5km S Rural/Coastal)
56.94405, 16.46708 **Camping Timmernabben,**
Varvsvägen 29, 38052 Timmernabben
(0499) 23861; timmernabben-camp@telia.com
🔢12 ♦♦(htd) ⬜ ⛱ ♨ ♿ ⬛ ⁄ 🦋 ♈ 🏠 ⚓shgl adj

Turn off E22, site sp. Med, mkd, shd, pt sl, EHU (10A)
inc; bbq; Eng spkn; games area; tennis; CKE. *"Tranquil
site; delightful views; gd walking & windsurfing; paths
on site not wheelchair-friendly."* **SEK 271**　　**2016**

TORSBY *2F1* (16km N Rural) *60.275763, 13.029961*
Camping 45, Overbyn 53, 68594 Torsby **(560) 31169;**
kontakt01@camping45.com; www.camping45.com
🔢12 🐕 ♦♦(htd) ⬜ ⬛ ⁄ ⚓ (htd)

18km N fr Torsby on L of E45 immed after g'ge.
Sm, pt shd, EHU (10A) inc; bbq; cooking facs; sw nr;
twin axles; TV; 30% statics; bus 100m; Eng spkn; adv
bkg acc; sauna; games rm; bike hire. *"Vg site; green
key eco award site; guided walks; canoe hire; friendly,
helpful staff."* **SEK 240**　　**2018**

TRANAS *2F2* (3km E Rural) *58.03548, 15.0309*
Hättebadens Camping (F1), Hätte, 57393 Tranås
(0140) 17482; info@hattecamping.se; www.hatte
camping.se
🔢12 🐕 ♦♦ ⛱ ♨ ♿ ⬛ ⁄ [MsP] ♈ 🍽 ⑪nr ⚓nr ⁄ 🏠

On W edge Lake Sommen on rd 131, sp. 4*, Med, mkd,
~pt shd, EHU (10A) SEK40; sw; 20% statics; phone;
Eng spkn; ccard acc; boating; fishing; Quickstop o'night
facs; bike hire; CKE. *"Generous pitches; spacious site; gd,
clean facs."* **SEK 220**　　**2016**

TRELLEBORG *2E4* (4km E Coastal) *55.3638, 13.20933*
Camping Dalabadet, Dalköpingestrandväg 2, 23132
Trelleborg **(0410) 14905; www.dalabadetscamping.se**
🐕 ♦♦(htd) ⬜ ⛱ ♨ ♿ ⬛ ⁄ [MsP] ⑪nr ⚓nr 🏠 ♈

Bet sea shore & rd 9 (Trelleborg-Ystad), E of town.
Foll sp fr town. 4*, Med, pt shd, EHU (10A) SEK30;
cooking facs; TV; 20% statics; phone; ccard acc;
tennis; sauna. *"Conv for ferries; gd; helpful recep; ltd
fac LS."* **SEK 290, 27 Apr-30 Sep.**　　**2017**

TROLLHATTAN *2E2* (1km N Urban) *58.29206,*
12.29848 **Trollhättans Camping Hjulkvarnelund (P7),**
Kungsportsvägen 7, 46139 Trollhättan **(0520) 30613**
🐕 ♦♦ ⬜ ⛱ ♨ ♿ ⬛ ⁄ [MsP] ⚓nr 🏠

Foll rd 45, site sp adj rv/canal. 3*, Med, pt shd, pt
sl, EHU (10A) SEK40; Eng spkn; tennis; CKE. *"Access
to Trollhätte Canal; beautiful, spacious wooded site;
cycles; easy walk to town & impressive gorge/waterfall;
htd pool 300m; modern, clean san facs poss stretched
high ssn."* **SEK 246, 1 May-6 Sep.**　　**2017**

UDDEVALLA *2E2* (9.5km W Rural) *58.3306, 11.8222*
Unda Camping (O30), Unda 149, 45194 Uddevalla
(0522) 86347; info@undacamping.se; www.unda
camping.se
🔢12 ♦♦(htd) ⬜ ⛱ ♨ ♿ ⬛ ⁄ [MsP] ♈ 🍽 ⑪ ⚓ 🏠 ⚓ ♈

Exit E6 junc 96 Uddevalla N onto rte 44 twd
Uddevalla Centrum. Site sp in 1km on R. 4*, Lge,
pt shd, pt sl, EHU (10A) SEK50; cooking facs; TV;
80% statics; phone; adv bkg acc; ccard acc; boat hire;
fishing; sauna; bike hire; CKE. *"Lovely situation in
nature reserve; o'flow area when full; Quickstop o'night
facs; recep hrs erratic LS; cr in high ssn."* **SEK 310**
　　2015

ULRICEHAMN *2F3* (3km S Rural) *57.77055, 13.40173*
Camping Skotteksgården (P34), Gamla
Marbäcksvägen, 52390 Ulricehamn **(0321) 13184 or**
(0705) 613184; skotteksgarden@telia.com;
www.skottek.cc
🐕 ♦♦(htd) ⛱ ♨ ♿ ⬛ ⁄ 🦋 ⑪ ⚓ 🏠

On rd 40 take dir Centrum. Foll sp Skotteksgården
to Tranemo. 4*, Sm, mkd, hdstg, unshd, serviced
pitches; EHU SEK70; cooking facs; sw nr; 10% statics;
phone; ccard acc; boat hire; sauna; fishing; bike hire;
CKE. *"Friendly, helpful owner; cycle path adj; OAY,
winter on req."* **SEK 302, 1 May-30 Sep.**　　**2018**

UMEA *1C3* (6km NE Coastal) *63.84210, 20.33815*
FirstCamp Umeå (AC12), Nydalasjön 2, 90654
Umeå **(090) 702600; umea@firstcamp.se;**
www.firstcamp.se
🔢12 ♦♦ ⬜ ⛱ ♨ ⬛ ⁄ [MsP] ♈ ⚓ 🏠 ⚓ (htd)

Sp fr E4 to N of town on lakeside. 5*, Lge, mkd, pt shd,
serviced pitches; EHU (10A) inc; sw nr; 10% statics; bus;
ccard acc; tennis; games rm; waterslide; games area;
CKE. *"Attractive site; lge pitches suitable RVs & twin
axles; excel service block; conv E4; pitches muddy in wet
weather; shop, rest & pool clsd in LS."* **SEK 299**　　**2016**

UNDERSAKER *1B3* (22km SW Rural) *63.1660,
13.0590* **Camping Vålågården,** Östra Vålådalen 120,
83012 Vålådalen **(0647) 35173; marie@valagarden.se;**
www.valagarden.se
🔢12 🐕 ♦♦(htd) ⬜ ♨ ♿ ⬛ ⁄ 🦋 ⚓ 🏠

E14 to Undersåker, turn S at hotel sp Vålådalen.
Site on L. Sm, pt shd, EHU (10A); cooking facs; TV;
20% statics; Eng spkn; ccard acc; sauna; CKE. *"Hiking
in surrounding nature reserve; magnificent mountain
scenery; friendly owners."* **SEK 210**　　**2016**

UPPSALA *2H1* (2km N Urban) *59.87133, 17.61923*
Fyrishov Camping (C12), Idrottsgatan 2, 75333
Uppsala **(018) 7274950; info@fyrishov.se;
www.fyrishov.se**

Exit E4 Uppsala N; in 300m at rndabt foll sp
Strangnas, Sala. In 2.25km exit via slip rd sp
Bjorklinge, Fyrishov. At rndabt foll sp Fyrishov, in
1.6km at traff lts turn R & immed R. Site in Fyrishov
Park adj sw & sports complex. 3*, Med, unshd, EHU
(10A) SEK45; bus; ccard acc; CKE. "Within easy access
of city cent; pool adj (sports complex behind pool); fair
NH." SEK 225   **2016**

URSHULT *2F3* (1km N Rural) *56.54476, 14.80703*
Urshults Camping (G7), Sirkövägen 19, 36013
Urshult **(0477) 20243; info@urshult-camping.com;
www.urshult-camping.com**

Rd 30 S fr Växjö, turn W onto rd 120 at Tingsryd.
In 10km at Urshult turn R, site sp on lakeside. 3*,
Med, pt shd, EHU (10A) SEK45; cooking facs; sw nr;
10% statics; Eng spkn; CKE. "Well-run site; nr Kurrebo
gardens & museum; vg." SEK 245, 27 Apr-15 Oct.
                                                    2018

URSHULT *2F3* (10km NW Rural) *56.58466, 14.69491*
Getnö Gård Naturcamping (G24), Lake Åsnen Resort,
36010 Ryd **(0477) 24011; info@getnogard.se;
www.getnogard.se**

W fr Urshult on rte 120 to junc with rte 126; turn
NW onto rte 126, site in 7km via Ålshult to Getnö
Gård. Site on shore Lake Åsnen. 4*, Med, mkd, pt shd,
pt sl, EHU (10A) SEK45; cooking facs; red long stay;
10% statics; phone; Eng spkn; adv bkg acc; fishing;
canoe hire; CKE. "Beautiful location in private nature
reserve; lake adj; needs care & attention; facs dated."
SEK 245, 1 May-10 Oct.   **2017**

VADSTENA *2F2* (4km NE Rural) *58.46448, 14.9334*
Vadstena Camping (E9), Vätterviksbadets, 59230
Vadstena **(0143) 12730; info@vadstenacamping.se;
www.vadstenacamping.se**

On rd 50, 3km N of Vadstena by Lake Vattern.
4*, Lge, mkd, pt shd, EHU (10A) SEK50; cooking
facs; 20% statics; Eng spkn; adv bkg acc; ccard acc;
sauna; fishing; tennis; waterslide; CKE. "Many local
attractions; lake adj; vg family site; htd pool 3km; cycle
path to town; gd birdwatching nrby; lakeside site with
beach." SEK 346, 1 May-12 Sep.   **2015**

VARBERG *2E3* (5km NW Coastal) *57.1165, 12.21426*
Getteröns Camping (N6), Valvikavägen 1-3, 43293
Varberg **(0340) 16885; info@getteronscamping.se;
www.getteronscamping.se**

Exit E6/E20 junc 54 Varberg Centrum, then W dir
Getterön, site sp. 3*, V lge, mkd, unshd, EHU (6A)
SEK45; 50% statics; phone; ccard acc; sauna; bike hire;
fishing; CKE. "Conv ferry to Denmark; Varberg pleasant
town; lge nature reserve nr; gd beach walk; clean san
facs; well laid-out site." SEK 290, 25 Apr-14 Sep.
                                                    2015

VASTERVIK *2G3* (3km SE Coastal) *57.73823, 16.66846*
Camping Lysingsbadets (H3), Lysingsvägen, 593 53
Västervik **(0490) 258000; lysingsbadet@vastervik.se;
www.lysingsbadet.se**

On coast 3km SE of town. Fr E22 foll sp around
S ring rd; on app to Västervik. Site well sp fr E22.
5*, V lge, pt shd, serviced pitches; EHU (10A) inc;
cooking facs; 10% statics; ccard acc; tennis; bike hire;
sauna; boat hire; waterslide; golf. "Lovely, family
site in landscaped, coastal woodland; easy access to
islands by wooden footbdge fr site; o'night m'vans
area; adj to bay; in HS EHU's taken by late afternoon."
SEK 450   **2016**

**"We must tell the Club about
that great site we found"**

Get your site reports in by mid-August and we'll
do our best to get your updates into the next
edition.

VAXHOLM *2H1* (2km W Coastal) *59.40508,
18.3047* **Waxholm Strand & Camping (B6),**
Eriksövägen, 18521 Vaxholm **(08) 54130101; info@
waxholmstrand.com; www.vaxholmstrand.com**

On rd 274 turn R immed after x-ing bdge to
Vaxholm Island, foll sp 'Eriksö Camping'. 3*, Med,
mkd, unshd, pt sl, EHU SEK40; 10% statics; phone; adv
bkg acc; ccard acc; CKE. "35 mins drive fr Stockholm;
boat trips, bike hire, ferry terminal Vaxholm-Stockholm
3.3km." SEK 210, 30 Apr-25 Sep.   **2015**

VILHELMINA *1C2* (1.5km SE Rural) *64.62131,
16.67846* **Saiva Camping (AC4),** Baksjön 1, 91231
Vilhelmina **(0940) 10760; info@saiva.se; www.saiva.se**

Sp on E site of rd 45. 3*, Med, pt shd, EHU (10A)
SEK30; TV; 10% statics; phone; ccard acc; tennis;
bike hire; CKE. "Gd; excel san facs in log style cabins,
v helpful staff; lovely lakeside setting; lake beach."
SEK 180, 20 May-1 Oct.   **2016**

VILHELMINA *1C2* (5km NW Rural) *64.64998, 16.59240* **Kolgärdens Camping,** Lövliden 16, 91292 Vilhelmina **(0940) 10304; kolgarden@vilhelmina.ac; www.kolgarden.se**

🅓 🐕 ♿(htd) 🆆 ⛽ ♿ 🚻 ∅ 🦋 💈 ☕ 🏕nr

Site sp fr E45 N of Vilhelmina. Sm, pt shd, EHU (10A) SEK35; cooking facs; TV; 50% statics; Eng spkn; sauna; fishing. *"Wonderful lakeside location; clean san facs; helpful, pleasant owner; highly rec."* **SEK 240**   **2017**

"I need an on-site restaurant"

We do our best to make sure site information is correct, but it is always best to check any must-have facilities are still available or will be open during your visit.

VINSLOV *2F4* (0.5km N Rural) *56.10988, 13.91245* **Vinslövs Camping (L2),** Troed Nelsongatan 18, 28834 Vinslöv **(070) 2077679; info@vinslovscamping.se; vinslovscamping.se**

🅓 🐕 ♿ 🆆 ⛽ ♿ 🚻 ∅ 🦋 🍴nr ⏱nr 🏕nr ⛲

Site sp of rte 21. 2*, Sm, mkd, pt shd, EHU (6A) SEK40; cooking facs; 20% statics; bus 500m; CKE. *"Htd pool adj."* **SEK 120**   **2016**

YSTAD *2F4* (3km E Coastal) *55.43286, 13.8650* **Camping Sandskogens (M15),** Österleden, 27160 Ystad **(0411) 19270; info@sandskogenscamping.se; www.sandskogenscamping.se**

🐕 ♿ 🆆 ⛽ ♿ 🚻 ∅ 💈 ☕ ⏱nr 🏕 🛶 🏖 ☀sand 100m

On N side of rd 9. 4*, Lge, mkd, shd, EHU (10A) SEK40; TV; 10% statics; phone; ccard acc; CKE. *"On Baltic coast; cycle path to beautiful town; mkd walks nrby; gd site, well-managed site; extremely helpful Eng spkn staff; high ssn expect queues checking in; CKE card req; metered shwrs; Wallander TV series studios site nr site, tours avail; cramped pitches; san facs stretched when busy."* **SEK 350, 17 Apr-21 Sep.**
2017

OLAND ISLAND

BYXELKROK *2G3* (1km N Coastal) *57.33013, 17.01211* **Neptuni Camping (H41),** Småskogsvägen 2, 38075 Byxelkrok **(0485) 28495 or 070 5428495 (mob); info@neptunicamping.se; www.neptunicamping.se**

🐕 🚻(htd) 🆆 ⛽ ♿ 🚻 ∅ 💈 🦋 🏕 ☀adj

Fr S on rd 136 thro Böda, at Byxelkrok turn R past harbour for 200m. Site on R. 4*, Med, pt shd, EHU (16A) SEK40; phone; Eng spkn; ccard acc; games area; CKE. *"Conv touring base N Öland, sh walk to harbour, rest & supmkt."* **SEK 230, 29 Apr-2 Oct.**   **2017**

DEGERHAMN *2G4* (12km S Rural) *56.23778, 16.4530* **Ottenby Vandrarhem & Camping (H57),** Ottenby 106, 38065 Degerhamn **(0485) 662062; info@ottenby vandrarhem.se; www.ottenbyvandrarhem.se**

🅓 🐕 🚻(htd) 🆆 ⛽ ♿ 🚻 ∅ 💈 🦋 🏕nr 🏊(htd) 🚤

Rd 36 S to Ottenby, bear R for 4km, site on R at youth hostel. Sm, unshd, EHU (10A) SEK40; cooking facs; 10% statics; phone; ccard acc; *"On edge Ottenby nature reserve; excel walks & birdwatching - ssn geared to bird migration; poss noise fr late arr & early risers as no barrier; dogs free; World Heritage Site on S pt of island."* **SEK 220**   **2017**

LOTTORP *2G3* (3km N Coastal) *57.17876, 17.03746* **Sonjas Camping (H39),** John Emils Gata 43, 38074 Löttorp **(0485) 23212; info@sonjascamping.se; www.sonjascamping.oland.com**

🚻(htd) 🆆 ⛽ ♿ 🚻 ∅ 💈 🦋 ☕ 🍴 ⏱ 🏕 ⛲ 🛶 ☀ 🏖(htd) 🚤 sand adj

Fr Kalmar over bdge to Öland Island, take rd 136 N thro Borgholm. Cont to Löttorp, site sp. 5*, Lge, mkd, pt shd, EHU (10A) SEK45; cooking facs; 10% statics; adv bkg acc; bike hire; sauna; tennis; fishing; CKE. *"Vg beach; excel family site; vg touring base."* **SEK 364, 1 May-4 Oct.**   **2016**

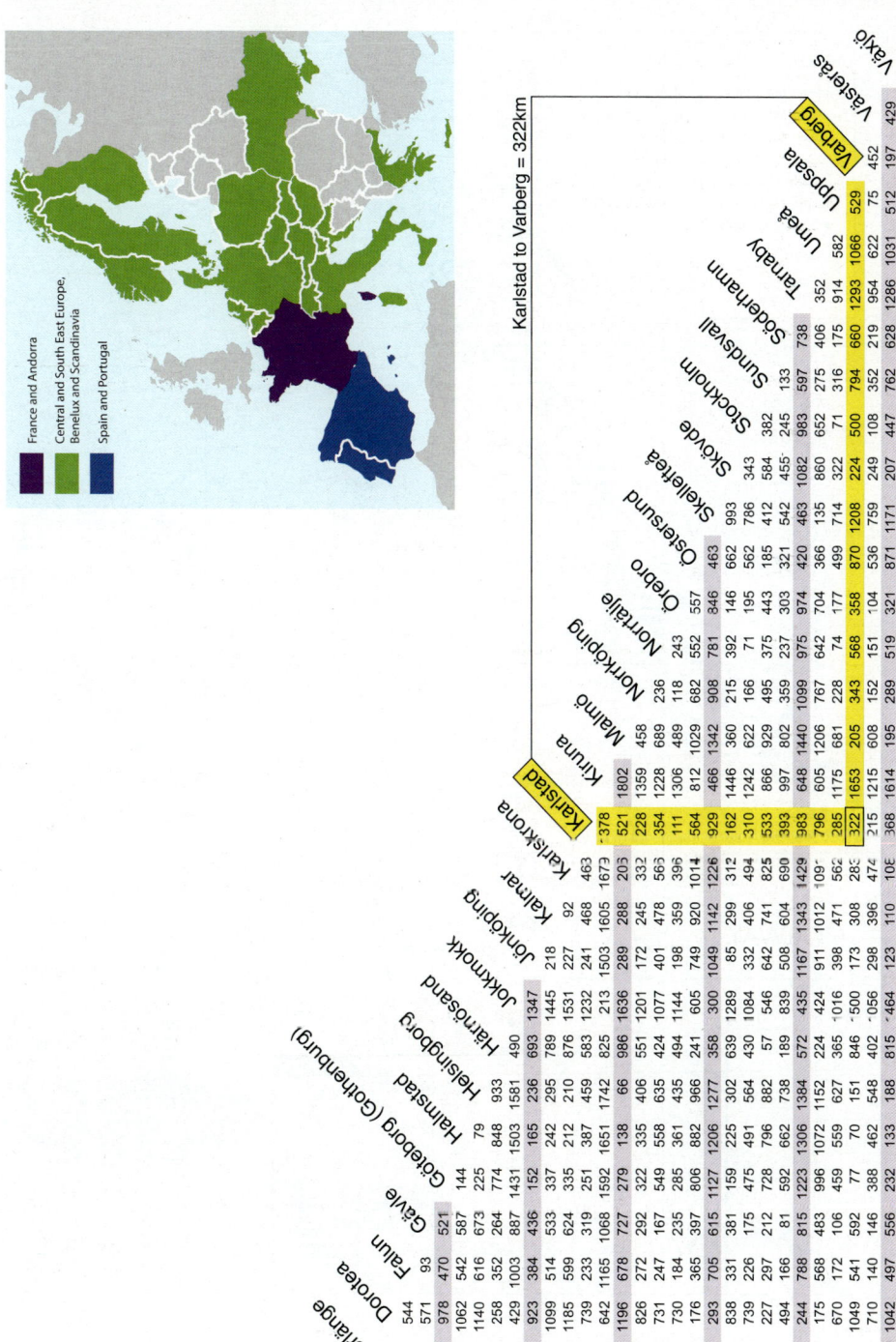

France and Andorra
Central and South East Europe, Benelux and Scandinavia
Spain and Portugal

Karlstad to Varberg = 322km

SWEDEN

Legend

▬▬	Motorways
▬▬	Major roads
▬▬	Main roads

●	All year site(s)
●	Seasonal site(s)
○	No sites listed
	200m +
	0–200m

Scale: 0 — 50 — 100 — 150 kms / 0 — 50 — 100 mls

NORWEGIAN SEA

Arctic Circle

N / W · E / S

NORWAY

FINLAND

GULF OF BOTHNIA

Tromsø
Skibotn
Trædal
Narvik
Karesuando
Muonio
KIRUNA
Pajala
Gallivare
JOKKMOKK
Rovaniemi
Størjord
Mo i Rana
Arjeplog
Haparanda
TÄRNABY
Luleå
Sorsele
Oulu
SKELLEFTEA
Gäddede
Vilhelmina
DOROTEA
Strömsund
UMEÅ
Hammerdal
Undersäker
ÖSTERSUND
Trondheim
Åsama
Ramvik
HÄRNÖSAND
Tynset
SUNDSVALL
Njurundabommen
Sveg
Drevsjø
Särna
Ljusdal
Orsa
SÖDERHAMN
Gesunda
Rättvik
GÄVLE

▼ see map 2

© Collins Bartholomew Ltd 2021

Map I

Map 2

Switzerland

Oeschinnensee

Shutterstock/Eva Bocek

Highlights

A country of mountains, lakes and natural beauty, Switzerland's high alpine peaks make it one of the world's top destinations for winter sports.

Inside the cities, you will find a world that compliments the outstanding landscape while providing a modern and vibrant outlook on life.

There is an endless supply of places to visit and experience, with mouth-watering chocolates and cuckoo clocks just the tip of the cultural iceberg.

Switzerland is renowned for being a hub for winter sports enthusiasts, but there are also a variety of traditional competitions such as Schwingen, a type of Swiss wrestling and Hornussen, a strange mixture of golf and baseball, which are still practiced today.

Switzerland also produces a delicious variety of food, with cheese being one of its specialities. Types such as Emmental and Gruyère are used to make fondue, which is often associated with the skiing culture of the Alps.

Major towns and cities

- Zürich – there are tons of museums and cultural sites in this metropolitan capital.
- Geneva – this breathtaking city is one of the world's most diverse.
- Basel – a world-leading city of culture and arts.
- Lausanne – this city has a stunning view of Lake Geneva and the Alps.

Attractions

- Jungfraujoch – admire unrivalled views from the highest railway station in Europe.
- Château de Chillon, Veytaux – an island castle on Lake Geneva.
- Kapellbrücke, Lucerne – Europe's oldest wooden covered bridge.
- Rhine Falls, Shaffhausen – discover Europe's largest waterfall.

Find out more

www.myswitzerland.com
E: info@myswitzerland.com
T: 0041 (0) 80 01 00 20 029

Country Information

Population: 8.2 million

Capital: Bern

Area: 41,285 sq km

Bordered by: Austria, France, Germany, Italy, Liechtenstein

Terrain: Mostly mountainous; Alps in the south, Jura in the north-west; central plateau of rolling hills, plains and large lakes

Climate: Temperate climate varying with altitude; cold, cloudy, rainy or snowy winters; cool to warm summers with occasional showers

Highest Point: Dufourspitze 4,634m

Languages: French, German, Italian, Romansch

Local Time: GMT or BST + 1, i.e. 1 hour ahead of the UK all year

Currency: Swiss Franc (CHF) divided into 100 centimes; £1 = CHF 1.27, CHF 10 = £7.86 (Feb 2021)

Emergency numbers: Police 117; Fire brigade 118; Ambulance 144 or 112 for any service

Public Holidays 2021: Jan 1, 2; Apr 2, 4, 5; May 13, 24; June 1; Aug 1 (National Day), 15; Nov 1; Dec 8, 25, 26.

School summer holidays vary by canton but are approximately from early July to mid/end August.

Entry Formalities

Holders of valid British or Irish passports may enter without a visa for up to 3 months.

Medical Services

There are reciprocal emergency health care arrangements with Switzerland for EU citizens.
A European Health Insurance Card (EHIC) will enable you to get reduced cost for emergency treatment in a public hospital but you will be required to pay the full cost of treatment and apply afterwards for a refund from the Department for Work & Pensions on your return to the UK. Ensure that any doctor you visit is registered with the national Swiss Health Insurance Scheme. Dental treatment is not covered.

You will have to pay 50% of the costs of any medically-required ambulance transport within Switzerland and/or Liechtenstein, including air ambulance.

If you are planning sports activities, such as skiing and mountaineering, your holiday insurance should be extended to cover these activities and should also include cover for mountain rescue and helicopter rescue costs.

Opening Hours

Banks: Mon-Fri 8.30am-4.30pm (some close for lunch; late opening once a week to 5.30pm/6pm in some towns).

Museums: Check locally as times vary.

Post Offices: Mon-Fri 7.30am-6pm (smaller branches may close for lunch); Sat 7.30am-11am.

Shops: Mon-Fri 8am/8.30am-6.30pm/7pm (closed lunch time) & Sat 8am-4pm/7pm; shops close early on the eve of a public holiday.

Safety and Security

Most visits to Switzerland and Liechtenstein are trouble-free and the crime rate is low. However, petty theft is on the increase and you should be alert to pickpockets and thieves in city centres, railway stations and public places.

You should be aware of the risks involved in the more hazardous sports activities and take note of weather forecasts and conditions, which can change rapidly in the mountains. You should be well-equipped; do not undertake the activity alone, study the itinerary and inform someone of your plans. Off-piste skiers should follow the advice given by local authorities and guides; to ignore such advice could put yourselves and other mountain users in danger.

Switzerland and Liechtenstein share with the rest of Europe an underlying threat from terrorism. Attacks could be indiscriminate and against civilian targets in public places.

British Embassy

THUNSTRASSE 50, CH-3005 BERN
Tel: 031 3597700
www.ukinswitzerland.fco.gov.uk/en

Irish Embassy

KIRCHENFELDSTRASSE 68, CH-3000 BERN 6
Tel: 031 3521442
www.embassyofireland.ch

Customs

Alcohol and Tobacco

Switzerland is not a member of the EU and visitors aged 17 years and over may import the following items duty-free:

200 cigarettes or 50 cigars or
250 g tobacco

2 litres of alcoholic drink up to 15% proof
1 litre of alcoholic drink over 15% proof

All goods are duty free up to a total combined value of CHF300, including alcohol and tobacco products.

Caravans and Motorhomes

Caravans registered outside Switzerland may be imported without formality up to a height of 4 metres, width of 2.55 metres and length of 12 metres (including towbar). The total length of car + caravan/trailer must not exceed 18.75 metres.

Food

From EU countries you may import per person 1 kg of meat and/or meat products (excluding game).

Refund of VAT on Export

A foreign visitor who buys goods in Switzerland in a 'Tax-Back SA' or 'Global Refund Schweiz AG' shop may obtain a VAT refund (7.6%) on condition that the value of the goods is at least CHF 300 including VAT. Visitors should complete a form in the shop and produce it, together with the goods purchased, at Customs on leaving Switzerland. See www.globalrefund.com for more information.

Documents

Vehicle(s)

Carry your original vehicle registration certificate (V5C), MOT certificate (if applicable) and insurance documentation at all times. Recent visitors report that drivers may be asked to produce proof of vehicle ownership at the border and failure to do so may mean that entry into Switzerland is refused. If you are driving a vehicle which does not belong to you, you should be in possession of a letter of authorisation from the owner.

Money

Prices in shops are often displayed in both Swiss francs and euros. Major credit cards are widely accepted, although you may find small supermarkets and restaurants do not accept them. Recent visitors report that some retail outlets may accept only one kind of credit card (MasterCard or VISA), not both, and it may be advisable to carry one of each. You may occasionally find that a surcharge is imposed for the use of credit cards.

Carry your credit card issuers'/banks' 24-hour UK contact numbers in case of loss or theft of your cards.

Driving

Accidents

In the case of accidents involving property damage only, when drivers decide not to call the police, a European Accident Statement must be completed.

In the case of injury or of damage to the road, road signs, lights etc, the police must be called.

Alcohol

The maximum permitted level of alcohol is 50 milligrams in 100 millilitres of blood, i.e. lower than that permitted in the UK (80 milligrams). A lower limit of 10 milligrams in 100 millilitres applies for new drivers of up to three years. A blood test may be required after an accident, and if found positive, the penalty is either a fine or a prison sentence, plus withdrawal of permission to drive in Switzerland for at least two months. Police carry out random breath tests.

Breakdown Service

The motoring and leisure organisation Touring Club Suisse (TCS) operates a 24-hour breakdown service, 'Patrouille TCS'. To call for help throughout Switzerland and Liechtenstein,
dial 140. On motorways use emergency phones and ask for TCS.

Members of clubs affiliated to the AIT, such as Tthe Caravan and Motorhome Club, who can show a current membership card will be charged reduced rates for breakdown assistance and towing, according to the time of day and/or the distance towed. Payment by credit card is accepted.

Child Restraint System

Vehicles registered outside of Switzerland that are temporarily imported into the country, have to comply with the country of registration with regards to safety belt equipment and child restraint regulations. All children up to 12 years of age must be placed in an approved UN ECE 44.03 regulation child restraint, unless they measure more than 150cm and are over seven years old.

Fuel

Prices of petrol vary according to the brand and region, being slightly cheaper in self-service stations. Credit cards are generally accepted.

On motorways, where prices are slightly higher, some service stations are open 24 hours and others are open from 6am to 10pm or 11pm only, but petrol is available outside these hours from automatic pumps where payment can be made by means of bank notes or credit cards.

There are 44 outlets (August 2015) selling LPG (GPL) – see www.jaquet-ge.ch for a list of outlets and a map showing their location.

Lights

Dipped headlights are compulsory at all times, even during the day. Bulbs are more likely to fail with constant use and you are recommended to carry spares.

Motorways

There are 1,700 km of motorways and dual carriageways. To use these roads motor vehicles and trailers up to a total weight of 3,500kg must display a vignette. Motorists using roads to avoid motorways and dual carriageways may find it necessary to detour through small villages, often with poor signposting. In addition, due to a diversion, you may be re-routed onto roads where the motorway vignette is required.

If you have visited Switzerland before, make sure you remove your old sticker from your windscreen.

There are emergency telephones along the motorways.

Mountain Roads and Tunnels

One of the most attractive features of Switzerland for motorists is the network of finely engineered mountain passes, ranging from easy main road routes to high passes that may be open only from June to October. In the Alps most roads over passes have been modernised; only the Umbrail Pass, which is not recommended for caravans, is not completely tarred. Passes have a good roadside telephone service for calling aid quickly in the event of trouble.

A blue rectangular sign depicting a yellow horn indicates a mountain postal road and the same sign with a red diagonal stripe indicates the end of the postal road. On such roads, vehicles belonging to the postal services have priority.

During certain hours, one-way traffic only is permitted on certain mountain roads. The hours during which traffic may proceed in either or both directions are posted at each end of the road. The TCS road map of Switzerland, scale 1:300,000, indicates this type of road.

Speed must always be moderate on mountain passes, very steep roads and roads with numerous bends. Drivers must not travel at a speed which would prevent them from stopping within the distance they can see ahead.

When it is difficult to pass oncoming vehicles, the heavier vehicle has priority.

Slow-moving vehicles are required by law to use the lay-bys provided on alpine roads to allow the free flow of faster traffic. This is the case where a car towing a caravan causes a queue of vehicles capable of a higher speed.

Parking

Parking in cities is difficult and it is worth using the numerous Park & Ride schemes which operate around major towns and cities. Illegal parking of any kind is much less tolerated in Switzerland than in any of its neighbours and fines are common for even minor violations.

Pay and display car parks and parking meters are used throughout the country and permitted parking time varies from 15 minutes to 2 hours. Feeding meters is not allowed. Wheel clamps are not used, but vehicles causing an obstruction may be removed to a car pound.

You may park in a 'blue zone' for limited periods free of charge providing you display a parking disc in your vehicle. These are available from petrol stations, kiosks, restaurants and police stations. Parking in a red zone is free for up to 15 hours with a red parking disc available from police stations, tourist offices, etc.

Parking on pavements is not allowed. Do not park where there is a sign 'Stationierungsverbot' or 'Interdiction de Stationner'. Continuous or broken yellow lines and crosses at the side of the road and any other yellow markings also indicate that parking is prohibited.

Priority

In general, traffic (including bicycles) coming from the right has priority at intersections but drivers approaching a roundabout must give way to all traffic already on the roundabout, i.e. from the left, unless otherwise indicated by signs. However, vehicles on main roads – indicated by a yellow diamond with a white border or a white triangle with a red border and an arrow pointing upwards – have priority over traffic entering from secondary roads.

Please be aware sometimes pedestrians have right of way and will expect vehicles to stop for them.

Roads

Switzerland has some 72,000 kilometres of well-surfaced roads, from motorways to local municipal roads, all well-signposted. Four-wheel drive vehicles must not be driven off road local authority permission.

During daylight hours outside built-up areas you must sound your horn before sharp bends where visibility is limited. After dark this warning must be given by flashing your headlights.

Dial the following numbers for information:

162: Weather information

163: Road conditions, mountain passes, access to tunnels and traffic news

187: In winter, avalanche bulletins; in summer, wind forecasts for Swiss lakes

It is also possible to obtain updated information on road conditions via teletext in larger motorway service areas.

Motorway Tax

To be able to use national roads (motorways and semi-motorways) in Switzerland, motor vehicles and trailers up to a total weight of 3,500kg must have a vehicle sticker (vignette). The ticket is valid for 14 months from 1st December every year and costs CHF40 (2015). An additional fee is charged for caravans and trailers. The sticker allows multiple re-entry into Switzerland during the period of validity.

If you enter a motorway or semi-motorway without a sticker you will be fined CHF200 and also the cost of the sticker. The stickers can be bought from custom offices, petrol stations or TCS offices in Switzerland or alternatively they can be purchased from the UK before travelling by calling the Swiss Travel Centre on 0207 420 4934.

Heavy Vehicle Tax

Vehicles (including motorhomes) over 3,500kg must pay a heavy vehicle tax on entry into Switzerland which is applicable for all roads. This charge applies for every day you are in Switzerland and your vehicle is on the road. For a 10-day pass (valid for a year) you self-select the days that your vehicle is on the road and, therefore, you are not penalised if your motorhome is parked at a campsite and not driven on a public road. This heavy vehicle tax applies to any Swiss road and replaces the need for a motorway vignette.

This particular tax is only payable at the border on entry into Switzerland and if there is any doubt about the exact weight of your vehicle it will be weighed. An inspection may be carried out at any time and is likely at the exit border. Failure to pay the tax can result in an immediate fine.

Road Signs and Markings

Road signs and markings conform to international standards.

White lettering on a green background indicates motorways, whereas state and provincial main roads outside built-up areas have white lettering on a blue background. This is the reverse of the colouring used in France and Germany and may initially cause confusion when driving from one country to the other. Road signs on secondary roads are white with black lettering.

The following are some road signs which you may encounter:

Postal vehicles have priority

Parking disc compulsory

Slow lane

One-way street with a two-way cycle lane

Speed Limits

	Open Road (km/h)	Motorway (km/h)
Car Solo	80-100	120
Car towing caravan/trailer	80	80
Motorhome under 3500kg	80-100	120
Motorhome 3500-7500kg	80	80

The fundamental rule, which applies to all motor vehicles and bicycles, is that you must always have the speed of your vehicle under control and must adapt your speed to the conditions of the road, traffic and visibility. On minor secondary roads without speed limit signs speed should be reduced to 50 km/h (31 mph) where the road enters a built-up area. The speed limit in residential areas is 30 km/h (18 mph). Speeding fines are severe.

When travelling solo the speed limit on dual carriageways is 100 km/h (62 mph) and on motorways, 120 km/h (74 mph) unless otherwise indicated by signs. On motorways with at least three lanes in the same direction, the left outside lane may only be used by vehicles which can exceed 80 km/h (50 mph).

Motorhomes with a laden weight of under 3,500 kg are not subject to any special regulations. Those over 3,500 kg may not exceed 80 km/h (50 mph) on motorways.

In dual carriageway road tunnels, speed is limited to 100 km/h (62 mph); in the St Gotthard tunnel and San Bernardino tunnels the limit is 80 km/h (50 mph).

It is illegal to transport or use radar detection devices. If your GPS navigation system has a function to identify the location of fixed speed cameras, this must be deactivated.

Traffic Jams

Traffic congestion occurs near tunnels in particular, during the busy summer months, at the St Gotthard tunnel on Friday afternoons and Saturday mornings. When congestion is severe and in order to prevent motorists coming to a standstill in the tunnel, traffic police stop vehicles before the tunnel entrance and direct them through in groups.

Other bottlenecks occur on the roads around Luzern (A2) and Bern (A1, A6 and A12), the border crossing at Chiasso (A2), the A9 around Lausanne and between Vevey and Chexbres, and the A13 BellinzonaSargans, mainly before the San Bernardino tunnel.

Traffic Lights

Outside peak rush hours traffic lights flashing amber mean proceed with caution.

Violation of Traffic Regulations

The police may impose and collect on-the-spot fines for minor infringements. In the case of more serious violations, they may require a deposit equal to the estimated amount of the fine. Fines for serious offences are set according to the income of the offender. Drivers of foreign-registered vehicles may be asked for a cash deposit against the value of the fine.

Winter Driving

Alpine winters often make driving more difficult. You should equip your vehicle(s) with winter tyres and snow chains and check road conditions prior to departure. A sign depicting a wheel and chains indicates where snow chains are required for the mountain road ahead. Snow chains are compulsory in areas where indicated by the appropriate road sign. They must be fitted on at least two drive wheels.

Essential Equipment

Nationality Plate (GB or IRL Stickers)

Strictly-speaking, it is necessary to display a conventional nationality plate or sticker when driving outside EU member states, even when vehicle number plates incorporate the GB or IRL Euro-symbol. However, the Swiss authorities have adopted a commonsense approach and confirm that it is not necessary to display a separate GB or IRL sticker if your number plates display the GB or IRL Euro-symbol. If your number plates do not incorporate this symbol then you will need a separate sticker.

Warning Triangles

All vehicles must be equipped with a warning triangle which has to be within easy reach and not in the boot.

Touring

The peak season for winter sports is from December to the end of April in all major resorts. February and March are the months with the most hours of winter sunshine and good snow for skiing. Summer skiing is also possible in a few resorts. Information on snow conditions, including avalanche bulletins, is available in English from www.slf.ch.

Besides being famous for watches, chocolate and cheese, the Swiss have a fine reputation as restaurateurs, but eating out can be expensive. Local beers are light but pleasant and some very drinkable wines are produced.

There are a number of UNESCO World Heritage Sites in Switzerland including the three castles of Bellinzona, Bern Old Town, the Monastery of St John at Müstair, the Jungfrau, the Aletsch Glacier and the Bietschhoorn region.

Liechtenstein is a principality of 160 sq km sharing borders with Switzerland and Austria. The capital, Vaduz, has a population of approximately 5,500 and German is the official language. The official currency is the Swiss franc. There are no passport or Customs controls on the border between Switzerland and Liechtenstein.

Camping and Caravanning

There are approximately 340 campsites available to touring caravanners, with around 100 sites remaining open in winter. Some sites may be nearly full with statics, with only a small area for tourers.

There are 27 Touring Club Suisse (TCS) sites and affiliated sites classified into five categories according to amenities available. All TCS campsites have a service station with facilities for emptying sanitary tanks. For further information and current rates see www.reise-tcs ch. The Swiss Camp Sites Association (VSC/ACS) produces a camping and road map covering approximately 180 sites, including charges and classification. See www.swisscamps.ch.

To download a guide to more than 40 campsites, including those open in winter, in the Bernese Oberland region of Switzerland see www.camping-bo.ch.

The Swiss are environmentally conscious with only limited scope for removing waste. Recycling is vigorously promoted and it is normal to have to put rubbish in special plastic bags obtainable from campsites. A 'rubbish charge' or 'entsorgungstaxe' of approximately CHF 3 per person per day is commonly charged.

A visitors' tax, varying according to the area, is levied in addition to the site charges.

The rules on casual/wild camping differ from canton to canton. It may be tolerated in some areas with the permission of the landowner or local police, or in motorway service areas, but local laws – particularly on hygiene – must not be contravened. For reasons of security the Caravan and Motorhome Club recommends that overnight stops should always be at recognised campsites.

Cycling

Switzerland has 9,000 km of cycle trails, including nine national cycle routes, which have been planned to suit all categories of cyclist from families to sports cyclists. Maps of cycle routes are available from www.schweizmobil.ch. Routes are marked by red and white signs. The problem of strenuous uphill gradients can be overcome by using trails routed near railway lines. Most trains will transport bicycles and often bicycles are available for hire at stations. Switzerland Tourism can provide more information.

Children under the age of 6 may only cycle on the road if accompanied by a person over 16 years of age.

Bikes may be carried on the roof of a car providing they are attached to an adequate roof rack and providing the total height does not exceed 4 metres. Bicycles carried on special carriers at the rear of a vehicle can exceed the width of the vehicle by 20 cm on each side, but the total width must not exceed 2 metres. The rear lights and number plate must remain visible and the driver's view must not be obstructed.

Electricity and Gas

Usually current on campsites varies between 4 and 16 amps. Plugs have two or, more usually, three round pins. Some campsites have CEE connections. Some may lend or hire out adaptors – but do not rely on it – and it may be advisable to purchase an appropriate adaptor cable with a Swiss 3-pin plug. Adaptors are readily available in local supermarkets.

The full range of Campingaz cylinders is available from large supermarkets.

Public Transport & Local Travel

Some towns are inaccessible by road, e g Zermatt and Wengen, and can only be reached by train or tram.

The Swiss integrated transport system is well known for its efficiency, convenience and punctuality. Co-ordinated timetables ensure fast, trouble-free interchange from one means of transport to another. Yellow post buses take travellers off the beaten track to the remotest regions. As far as railways are concerned, in addition to efficient inter-city travel, there is an extensive network of mountain railways, including aerial cableways, funiculars and ski-lifts.

Half-fare tickets are available for attractions such as cable cars, railways and lake steamers. In addition, Switzerland Tourism offers a public transport map and a number of other useful publications.

See www.swisstravelsystem.com

All visitors to campsites and hotels in Interlaken are issued with a pass allowing free bus and train travel in the area.

A ferry operates on Lake Constance (Bodensee) between Romanshorn and Friedrichshafen (Germany) saving a 70km drive. The crossing takes 40 minutes. Telephone 071 4667888 for more information; www.bodensee-schiffe.ch. A frequent ferry service also operates between Konstanz and Meersburg on the main route between Zürich, Ulm, Augsburg and Munich (Germany); information is available on a German telephone number, 0049 7531 8030; www.stadtwerke.konstanz.de. The crossing takes 20 minutes. Principal internal ferry services are on Lake Lucerne between Beckenried and Gersau, www.autofaehre.ch, and on Lake Zürich between Horgen and Meilen, www.faehre.ch. All these services transport cars and caravans.

AARBURG *A2* (1km SW Rural) *47.31601, 7.89488*
Camping Wiggerspitz, Hofmattstrasse 40, 4663
Aarburg **062 7915810; info@camping-aarburg.ch;**
www.camping-aarburg.ch

🐕 CHF1 ⚦ (htd) 🆆 ⛺ ⊟ ⚕ MP ⛲ 🛉 ⓘ nr ♨ 🛒

Exit A1/A2/E35 junc 46 sp Rothrist/Olten, foll sp to
site. 3*, Med, mkd, pt shd, EHU (6A) CHF3 (rev pol),
long lead req; gas; bbq; 25% statics; phone; CKE.
*"Conv Luzern, Zürich, Bern; picturesque, walled town;
excel, clean site; htd pool adj; friendly warden; excel
san facs; site is popular so rec adv bkg."*
CHF 29, 1 May-15 Sep.   2015

ALTDORF *B3* (2km N Rural) *46.89256, 8.62800*
Remo-Camp Moosbad, Flüelerstrsse 122, 6460
Altdorf **041 8708541**

12 🐕 ⚦ 🆆 ⛺ ⊟ ⚕ MP ⛲ ⓘ 🛒

Exit A2 at Altdorf junc 36. Foll sp Altdorf to rndabt
& turn R. Site 200m on L adj cable car & sports cent.
2*, Sm, pt shd, EHU (10A) CHF3 (adaptor loan); bbq;
80% statics; phone; Eng spkn; CKE. *"Ideal windsurfing;
useful NH en rte Italy; friendly welcome; excel san facs;
excel rest; superb views; gd base for train trip over St
Gotthard pass; plenty to see & do in Altdorf; public
pool & waterslide adj; bus & cable car combos avail."*
CHF 35   2016

BASEL *A2* (18km S Rural) *47.45806, 7.63545* **TCS**
Camping Uf der Hollen, Auf der Hollen, 4146
Hochwald **061 7120240; buero@tcscampingbasel.ch;**
www.tcscampingbasel.ch

12 ⚦ (htd) 🆆 ⛺ ♿ ⚕ 🦋 ⛰

Exit A18 at Reinach-Sud dir Dornach, S thro Dornach
dir Hochwald, uphill thro forest to site. 2*, Med, mkd,
pt shd, EHU CHF3; 90% statics; adv bkg acc; games
area; CKE. *"Gd views; peaceful, pleasant site; buy day
pass on bus."* **CHF 35**   2016

BERN *B2* (8km NW Rural) *46.96375, 7.38420*
TCS Camping Bern-Eymatt, Wohlenstrasse 62C,
3032 Hinterkappelen **031 9011007; camping.
bern@tcs.ch; www.campingtcs.ch/bern**

🐕 CHF5 ⚦ (htd) 🆆 ⛺ ♿ ⚕ MP ⛲ 🛉 ⓘ ♨ 🛒 ⛰ ✎
🏊 (htd) 🍴

Fr E on A1 exit junc 33 sp Bern-Bethlehem; foll sp
for Wohlen & site. In 200m turn R at bottom of hill
into site on shores Wohlensee. Fr W take Brunnen-
Bern exit, then sp to Wohlen. Access for lge o'fits
poss diff. 4*, Lge, hdstg, pt shd, EHU (6A) inc; gas;
bbq (charcoal, gas); TV; 80% statics; bus to Bern nrby;
ccard acc; sep car park; games area; games rm; bike
hire; fishing; CKE. *"Recep 0830-1100 & 1700-2000 high
ssn, but site yourself; various pitch sizes; clean facs; no
o'fits over 8m high ssn; helpful staff; daily mkt in Bern;
2 supmkt nrby; excel."* **CHF 56, 1 Mar-10 Nov.**   2018

BOURG ST PIERRE *D2* (0.5km N Rural) *45.95265,
7.20740* **Camping du Grand St Bernard,** 1946
Bourg-St Pierre **0 79 370 98 22; reservation@
campinggrand-st-bernard.ch; www.campinggrand-
st-bernard.ch**

🐕 ⚦ 🆆 ⛺ ⊟ ⚕ 🦋 🛉 ⛲ nr ⓘ nr 🛒 nr

Fr Martigny S to Grand St Bernard Tunnel. Site well
sp in cent of vill. 1*, Med, unshd, EHU (4A) CHF3.50;
gas; Eng spkn; ccard acc; CKE. *"Conv St Bernard
Tunnel; htd pool adj; gd views."*
CHF 32, 1 Jun-30 Sep.   2016

BRIENZ *B2* (2km SE Rural) *46.75069, 8.04838*
Camping Seegartli, 3855 Brienz **033 9511351;**
www.camping-seegaertli.ch

⚦ 🆆 ⛺ ⊟ ⚕ 🦋 🛉 🛒

Fr Interlaken take N8 sp Luzern/Brienz. Take
Brienz exit, ignore sp to site to R & take L in 1km
bef Esso stn, sp Axalp. Site in 500m on R immed
after passing under rlwy. Site on E shore of lake,
next to sawmill. 2*, Sm, pt shd, pt sl, EHU (10A)
CHF3; sw; Eng spkn; fishing; watersports; tennis; CKE.
*"Beautiful lakeside situation; well-kept site; friendly
owner; lakeside pitches boggy in wet weather; long
hose req for m'van fill-up; arr bef noon in ssn; no dogs."*
CHF 33, 1 Apr-31 Oct.   2016

BRIENZ *B2* (3km SE Urban) *46.74811, 8.04769*
Camping Aaregg, Seestrasse 22, 3855 Brienz **033
9511843; mail@aaregg.ch; www.aaregg.ch**

🐕 CHF5 ⚦ (htd) 🆆 ⛺ ⊟ ⚕ MP 🦋 🛉 ⛲ ⓘ 🛒

Fr Interlaken take N8 sp Luzern/Brienz. Take Brienz
exit, ignore sp to site to R & take L in 1km bef Esso
stn, sp Axalp. Site in 500m on R after passing under
rlwy. Site on E shore of lake, next to sawmill. 5*,
Med, mkd, hdstg, pt shd, serviced pitches; EHU (10A)
CHF5; sw nr; red long stay; train nr; Eng spkn; adv
bkg rec; ccard acc; CKE. *"Excel, busy site on lakeside;
lakeside pitches sm; pool 500m; ideal touring base;
excel, modern san facs; many attractions nrby."*
CHF 55, 1 Apr-31 Oct, S02.   2017

BRIG *C2* (3km E Rural) *46.31500, 8.01369* **Camping
Tropic,** Camping TROPIC Vandyck-Gasser family
3911 Ried-Brig **027 9232537**

⚦ ⛺ ⊟ ⚕ 🛒 ⛰

On Brig-Domodossola rd on Swiss side of Simplon
Pass. Fr Brig, exit Simplon rd at sp Ried-Brig
Termen. Site on L in 500m. Fr Simplon foll sp to
Ried-Brig, site in vill. 1*, Med, pt shd, sl, EHU CHF3;
gas; TV; Eng spkn. *"Useful CL-type NH to/fr Italy;
welcoming & helpful owners; superb scenery; san facs
adequate."* **CHF 24, 1 Jun-15 Sep.**   2020

BRIG *C2* (1km S Rural) *46.30838, 7.99338* **Camping Geschina,** Geschinastrasse 41, 3900 Brig **027 9230688; www.geschina.ch**

🐕 CHF2 🚻 [WD] 🚿 🧺 ⚡ 🦋 🍸 🛒 🍔 🛝

Foll sps twd Simplon Pass, site on R at 700m, behind pool at rv bdge. Best app fr Glis. 4*, Med, pt shd, pt sl, EHU (10A) CHF2.50; gas; red long stay; Eng spkn; adv bkg acc; fishing; CKE. *"Friendly, well-kept, family-run site; vg san facs; superb mountain & glacier views; ideal for Rhône Valley & Simplon Pass; pool adj; sh walk to town."* **CHF 29, 1 Apr-15 Oct.** **2016**

"Satellite navigation makes touring much easier"

Remember most sat navs don't know if you're towing or in a larger vehicle – always use yours alongside maps and site directions.

BRIG *C2* (6km SW Rural) *46.30177, 7.93010* **Camping Thermal Brigerbad,** Thermalbad 1, 3900 Brigerbad **027 9484837; camping@brigerbad.ch; www.thermalbad-wallis.ch**

🚻 [WD] 🚿 🧺 ⚡ 📶 🍴 🛒 🍔 🛝 ✏ 🏊 (covrd, htd) ♨

To ent Brigerbad, access the "Kantonsstrasse", which is the main rd bet Visp and Brig. Once on this rd look out for blue bdge which leads directly to the Brigerbad. Lge, pt shd, EHU €3.60; bbq; twin axles; Eng spkn; adv bkg rec; waterslide; games area; bike hire. *"Sauna landscape; fitness rm; vg."* **CHF 40, 1 May-31 Oct.** **2017**

BUCHS *B4* (0.5km W Rural) *47.16663, 9.46524* **Camping Werdenberg,** Camping Werdenberg Marktplatz 9470 Buchs **081 7561507; info@verkehrsverein-buchs.ch; https://www.verkehrsverein-buchs.ch/camping**

🐕 CHF2 🚻 [WD] 🚿 ♿ 🧺 ⚡ 🍔 nr

Fr bdge over Rv Rhine at Buchs on rd 16 dir Werdenberg & Grabs. Turn L at parking/camping sp, thro car park to site. 3*, Sm, unshd, EHU (16A) CHF4; gas; sw nr; adv bkg acc. *"Vg, attractive setting by lake with views of old town & castle; friendly owners; gd base for Liechtenstein, Appenzell & Vorarlberg; walking; plenty of activities mini golf etc; htd pool 2km; extra charge for vans over 5m; gd for families."* **CHF 34, 1 Apr-31 Oct.** **2020**

BUOCHS *B3* (1km N Rural) *46.97950, 8.41860* **TCS Camping Buochs Vierwaldstattersee (formerly Sportzentrum),** Seefeldstrasse, 6374 Buochs-Ennetbürgen **041 6203474; camping.buochs@tcs.ch; www.campingtcs.ch**

🐕 CHF4 🚻 [WD] 🚿 🧺 ⚡ [MSP] 🦋 📶 🍸 🛒 🍔 nr 🛝

Fr W on N2 m'way, exit junc 33 Stans-Süd & bear L. Foll sp Buochs. At 1st x-rds in Buochs, turn L to Ennetbürgen, in approx 1km R twd lake, sp. Fr E exit junc 34 for Buochs, turn L onto Beckenriederstrasse; at x-rds in cent of town turn R dir Ennetbürgen & foll sp as above. 3*, Med, mkd, pt shd, EHU (10A) CHF3.50 (adaptor avail); gas; sw nr; TV; 50% statics; Eng spkn; ccard acc; tennis; games rm; bike hire; fishing; CKE. *"Gd NH twd Italy; helpful staff; well-maintained facs; fine views; boat trip tickets sold on site; ferry close by; if recep clsd find own pitch & sign in later; pitches not draining well after heavy rains; v friendly staff; picturesque site; pool adj; site being redeveloped winter 2016-17."* **CHF 50, 4 Apr-4 Oct.** **2016**

BURGDORF *B2* (1.4km SE Rural) *47.05241, 7.63350* **TCS Camping Waldegg,** Waldeggweg, 3400 Burgdorf **344 222460; www.campingtcs.ch**

🐕 🚻 [WD] 🚿 🧺 ⚡ [MSP] 🦋 📶 🍴 nr 🍔 nr 🛝

Exit Bern-Basel N1 m'way at sp Kirchberg. Site in Burgdorf clearly sp. App over narr (2.7m) humpback bdge. 3*, Med, pt shd, EHU (10A) CHF4; adv bkg acc; golf; tennis; fishing. *"Conv Bern; old town of Burgdorf v interesting; pool 200m; friendly staff; clean san facs; gd NH."* **CHF 35, 1 Apr-30 Oct.** **2016**

CHAUX DE FONDS, LA *B1* (15km SW Rural) *47.06568, 6.69856* **Camping Lac des Brenets,** 2416 Les Brenets **032 9321618; campinglesbrenets@kfnmail.ch; www.camping-brenets.ch**

[12] 🐕 CHF3 🚻 (htd) [WD] 🚿 👪 ♿ 🧺 ⚡ [MSP] 🦋 🍸 🍴 🛒 🍔 🏊

Take rd 20 fr La Chaux-de-Fonds to Le Locle, foll sp Les Brenets. Foll twisting rd downhill to lake, turn & ascend to ent site on R. NB Diff L turn on descent. 5*, Med, hdstg, unshd, terr, EHU (12A) CHF4; gas; sw nr; red long stay; 80% statics; Eng spkn; adv bkg acc; ccard acc; tennis; CKE. *"Gd site o'looking Lac des Brenets & Rv Doubs; beautiful views; watch/clock museum 3km; friendly owner; ltd recep hrs, site yourself; sm pitches; excel rest; scenic touring & walking area."* **CHF 34** **2015**

CHUR *B4* (2.6km W Rural) *46.85605, 9.50435* **Camping Au Chur,** Felsenaustrasse 61, Obere Au, 7000 Chur **081 2842283; info@camping-chur.ch; www.camping-chur.ch**

[12] 🐕 CHF3 🚻 (htd) [WD] 🚿 👪 ♿ 🧺 ⚡ [MSP] 📶 🍸 🍴 nr 🛒 🍔 🛝

Site sp fr Chur Süd a'bahn exit, foll sp with tent pictogram (easily missed). 3*, Lge, pt shd, EHU (10A) CHF3.50; gas; TV; 65% statics; bus nr; Eng spkn; ccard acc; tennis; games area; CKE. *"Well-ordered, clean site; sm area for tourers; htd pool 200m; sm pitches; gd, modern facs; v soft when wet; helpful, friendly owners; interesting, old town."* **CHF 16** **2016**

SWITZERLAND

DISENTIS MUSTER *C3* (1.6km S Rural) *46.69620, 8.85270* **TCS Camping Fontanivas,** Via Fontanivas 9, 7180 Disentis-Mustèr **081 9474422; camping. disentis@tcs.ch; www.campingtcs.ch**

🐕 CHF6 ♟(htd) ⬚ ⛺ 🚿 ♿ 🚻 ✉ MSP 🦋 ☂ 🍴 ⑪ 🐶 🏪 🏔 🏕

Fr Disentis S twd Lukmanier Pass for 2.5km. Site on L. 3*, Lge, pt shd, EHU (6-10A) CHF4; gas; bbq; cooking facs; sw; TV; 25% statics; Eng spkn; adv bkg acc; ccard acc; tennis; bike hire; CKE. "Excel san facs; pool 2.5km; historic old town; gd walks." **CHF 56, 26 Apr-29 Sep.** 2016

ERLACH *B2* (0.5km N Rural) *47.04649, 7.09812* **Camping Erlach,** Stadtgraben 23, 3235 Erlach **032 3381646; camping@erlach.ch; www.erlach.ch**

🐕 CHF3 ♟ ⬚ ⛺ 🚿 ♿ ✉ MSP 🦋 🍴 ⑪ 🏪 🏔 ✏

Fr any dir foll sp for sm town of Ins; fr there foll sp Erlach. In Erlach turn L dir Le Landeron, then R twd Hotel du Port; turn L at hotel, site 200m on L by pier. 4*, Med, mkd, shd, EHU inc; gas; sw; TV; 60% statics; Eng spkn; adv bkg rec; ccard acc; games area; tennis; bike hire; CKE. "Scenic area; gd for walking & sightseeing; pleasure steamers on lake; gd, superb modern san facs; charming site; sep car park - no cars on pitch; busy, friendly; pool 3km; rec." **CHF 55, 31 Mar-15 Oct.** 2015

> ## "There aren't many sites open at this time of year"
> If you're travelling outside peak season remember to call ahead to check site opening dates – even if the entry says 'open all year'.

EVOLENE *C2* (0.8km S Rural) *46.11080, 7.49656* **Camping Evolène,** Route de Lannaz 1983 Evolène / Valais **027 2831144; info@camping-evolene.ch; www.camping-evolene.ch**

🐕 CHF3 ♟(htd) ⬚ ⛺ 🚿 ♿ ✉ MSP 🍴 ⑪ nr 🏔 🛷

Fr Sion take rd to Val d'Hérens. As app Evolène take L fork to avoid vill cent. Proceed to Co-op on L, turn sharp R & 1st L to site. Site sp. 3*, Sm, unshd, EHU (10A) CHF4; gas; 5% statics; Eng spkn; adv bkg acc; ccard acc; bike hire; CKE. "Mountain scenery; ACSI; well-kept site; snowboard hire; vg san facs; attentive owners; x-country ski hire; sh walk to vill cent, poss cr." **CHF 43, 15 May-15 Oct.** 2020

FAIDO *C3* (2.4km SE Rural) *46.47134, 8.81771* **Camping Gottardo,** 6764 Chiggiogna **091 8661562; schroeder.camp@vtxmail.ch; www.campinggottardo.ch**

🐕 CHF2 ♟(htd) ⬚ ⛺ 🚿 ♿ 🍴 ⑪ 🐶 🏪 🏔 🏊

Exit A2/E35 at Faido, site on R in 500m, sp immed bef Faido. 3*, Med, pt shd, terr, EHU (6A) CHF4; gas; red long stay; 10% statics; phone; bus 400m; Eng spkn. "On main rd fr Italian lakes to St Gotthard Pass; interesting vill; poss diff for lge o'fits, espec upper terrs (rec pitch bef white building); excel facs; gd bar & rest - home cooking inc bread, pastries; friendly, helpful staff; access to pitches v ltd in snowy conditions; excel NH." **CHF 33.7, 1 Mar-1 Nov.** 2019

FLEURIER *B1* (1.4km NW Rural) *46.90643, 6.57508* **Camping Val de Travers,** Belle Roche 15, 2114 Fleurier **032 8614262; camping.fleurier@tcs.ch; www.camping-val-de-travers.ch**

🐕 CHF3 ♟ ⬚ ⛺ 🚿 ♿ ✉ MSP 🦋 🍴 ⑪ 🏪 🏔

On Pontarlier (France) to Neuchâtel rd, site sp in Fleurier to L at start of vill. 2*, Med, pt shd, EHU (4A) CHF3; gas; 15% statics; Eng spkn; adv bkg acc; ccard acc; rv fishing; tennis; games area; bike hire. "Helpful owners; htd pool 2km; wild chamois on rocks behind site visible early morning; vg." **CHF 22, 17 Apr-26 Sep.** 2016

FRIBOURG *B2* (13km N Rural) *46.87827, 7.19121* **Camping Schiffenensee,** Schiffenen 15, 3186 Düdingen **026 4933486; info@camping-schiffenen.ch; www.camping-schiffenen.ch**

🐕 CHF3 ♟ ⬚ ⛺ 🚿 ♿ ✉ MSP 🦋 🍴 ⑪ 🐶 🏪 🛷 🎣

Exit A12 Bern-Fribourg at Düdingen & foll rd for Murten (sp). Ent poss tight lge o'fits. 4*, Lge, mkd, pt shd, EHU (10A) CHF3; 80% statics; bus; Eng spkn; adv bkg acc; tennis; CKE. **CHF 27, 1 Apr-31 Oct.** 2016

GENEVE *C1* (8km NE Urban) *46.24465, 6.19433* **TCS Camping Pointe à la Bise,** Chemin de la Bise, 1222 Vésenaz **022 7521296; camping.geneve@tcs.ch; www.campingtcs.ch**

🐕 CHF5 ♟ ⬚ ⛺ 🚿 ♿ ✉ MSP 🍴 ⑪ 🐶 🏪 🏔 🎣

Fr Geneva take S lakeside rd N5 sp Evian to Vésanez 4km. Turn L on Rte d'Hermance (D25) at traff lts & foll sp to site in 1km. 4*, Med, pt shd, EHU (4-10A) CHF4.50 (adaptor on loan, rev pol); gas; sw; TV; 60% statics; bus to Geneva; Eng spkn; ccard acc; bike hire; fishing; CKE. "Pleasant, lovely site; excel lake & mountain excursions; helpful staff; muddy when wet; bus & boat pass fr recep; some early morning aircraft noise." **CHF 80, 28 Mar-6 Oct.** 2018

GENEVE *C1 (9km W Rural) 46.20111, 6.06621*
Geneva City Camping (previously Camping du Bois de Bay), Geneva City Camping Bois de Bay Route de Bois – de – Bay 19 CH-1247 SATIGNY 022 3410505; contact@geneva-camping.ch; www.geneva-camping.ch

🐎 CHF3.50 ♦♦(htd) ᵂᴰ ⛺ ♿ 🚽 🖭 ∕ 🖭 ♈ 🍴 🛒 🎿 🅿️

Fr A1 exit sp Bernex, then foll sp to Vernier, site sp. 4*, Lge, hdg, pt shd, EHU (6A) CHF4.50; gas; bbq; 40% statics; Eng spkn; ccard acc; tennis 2km; CKE. *"V friendly; modern san facs; park & ride bus to city; don't be put off by indus site outside site."* **CHF 43, 1 Mar-31 Dec.** 2020

"That's changed – Should I let the Club know?"

If you find something on site that's different from the site entry, fill in a report and let us know. See camc.com/europereport.

GRUYERES *C2 (2km N Rural) 46.59515, 7.08069*
Camping Les Sapins, 1664 Epagny-Gruyères 026 9129575; info@gruyeres-camping.ch; www.gruyeres-camping.ch

♦♦(htd) ᵂᴰ ⛺ ♿ 🖭 ∕ 🖭 🦋 🍴 ⓝ 🛒 🅿️

Foll rd S fr Bulle sp Châteaux d'Oex. Site on L of rd sp Gruyères-Moléson. 3*, Med, pt shd, EHU (10A) CHF3; gas; 60% statics; phone; adv bkg acc; tennis. *"Neat, tidy site; Gruyères lovely medieval town; visits to cheese factory; lovely countryside; easy reach E end Lake Geneva; supmkt & fuel 2km."* **CHF 38, 1 Apr-30 Sep.** 2017

GRUYERES *C2 (6km S Rural) 46.56080, 7.08740*
Camping Haute Gruyère, Chemin du Camping 18, 1667 Enney 026 9212260; camping.enney@bluewin.ch; www.camping-gruyere.ch

12 🐎 CHF4 ♦♦(htd) ᵂᴰ ⛺ ♿ 🚽 🖭 ∕ 🖭 🦋 🍴 ⓝ 🛒 nr 🅿️ ✎

Well sp fr N (Gruyères) but not by name - foll TCS sp, not well sp fr S. Site E of rd fr Bulle to Château d'Oex, 1km S of Enney vill. Beware trains on x-ing at turn in. Diff final app, single track around blind bend. 3*, Med, hdstg, unshd, EHU (6-10A) CHF4.50 (adaptor on loan); gas; red long stay; TV; 95% statics; adv bkg acc; ccard acc; fishing; bike hire. *"Vg, modern san facs; minimal area for tourers; bread to order; mainly level cycle rte to Gruyeres; new management (2016); not rec, NH only."* **CHF 45** 2017

GSTAAD *C2 (2km NW Rural) 46.48119, 7.27269*
Camping Bellerive, Bellerivestrasse 38, 3780 Gstaad 033 7446330; bellerive.camping@bluewin.ch; www.bellerivecamping.ch

12 🐎 CHF2.70 ♦♦(htd) ᵂᴰ ⛺ 🖭 ∕ 🖭 ♈ 🅿️

App fr Saanen turn R bef Gstaad, sp. 3*, Sm, hdstg, mkd, pt shd, EHU (12A) CHF2.70; gas; TV; 60% statics; Eng spkn; adv bkg acc; tennis; fishing. *"Gd touring, walking, winter sports; rvside site; sm pitches; pool 700m; skiing; buy Gstaad Card for rd, rail & mountain transport."* **CHF 29** 2016

HAUDERES, LES *D2 (2km N Rural) 46.09303, 7.50560* **Camping Molignon,** Route de Molignon 183, 1984 Les Haudères 027 2831240; info@molignon.ch; www.molignon.ch

12 🐎 CHF3.20 ♦♦(htd) ᵂᴰ ⛺ ♿ 🚽 🖭 ∕ 🖭 🦋 🍴 ⓝ 🛒 🅿️ 🏊 (htd)

Fr Sion take rd to Val d'Hérens, turn R 2.5km after Evolène. Site sp. Rd fr Sion steep, twisting & narr in places. 4*, Med, mkd, pt shd, terr, EHU (10A) CHF3.80; gas; TV; 15% statics; phone; Eng spkn; adv bkg acc; ccard acc; CKE. *"V friendly owner; ski lift 3km; ideal for mountain climbing & walking; beautiful location."* **CHF 35** 2019

"I like to fill in the reports as I travel from site to site"

You'll find report forms at the back of this guide, or you can fill them in online at camc.com/europereport.

INNERTKIRCHEN *C3 (1.5km NW Rural) 46.70938, 8.21519* **Camping Aareschlucht,** Hauptstrasse 34, 3862 Innertkirchen 033 9712714; campaareschlucht@bluewin.ch; www.camping-aareschlucht.ch

🐎 CHF2 ♦♦(htd) ᵂᴰ ⛺ ∕ 🦋 ⓝ 🛒 nr 🅿️

On Meiringen rd out of town on R. 3*, Sm, pt shd, EHU (6-10A) CHF3; gas; bbq; 30% statics; Eng spkn; adv bkg acc; ccard acc; games rm; sep car park; CKE. *"Excel site; clean facs; gd walking; gd touring base Interlaken, Jungfrau region; pool 5km; conv Grimsel & Susten passes; rv walk to town."* **CHF 24, 1 May-31 Oct.** 2016

INTERLAKEN *C2 (5km NE Rural) 46.70761, 7.91330* **Camp au Lac,** 3852 Ringgenberg 033 8222616; camping@au-lac.ch

12 🐎 CHF2 ♦♦ ᵂᴰ ⛺ 🚽 🖭 ∕ 🖭 🦋 🍴 ⓝ 🛒

Fr Ringgenberg to Brienz, site sp on R when exit Ringgenberg. Cont under rlwy viaduct to site. 3*, Med, pt shd, pt sl, EHU (6A) CHF3 (long cable poss req); 25% statics; bus; Eng spkn; adv bkg acc; ccard acc; CKE. *"Excel site; private access to lake; magnificent setting."* **CHF 36** 2016

SWITZERLAND

INTERLAKEN (NO. 01) *C2* (8km W Rural) *46.68004, 7.81669* **Camping Manor Farm,** Seestrasse 201, 3800 Interlaken-Thunersee **033 8222264; info@manorfarm.ch; www.manorfarm.ch**

12 🐕 CHF5 ♦♦ wo ♨ ♨ ♿ ♫ ✎ MSP ¶ ▽ ⑪ nr ♨ ⅄ ⚑ ✐ ⛱

Fr W on A8 exit junc 24 Interlaken West & foll sp Thun & Gunten. At rndabt take 2nd exit twd Thun, sp Gunten; pass Camping Alpenblick on R, then site on L after bdge. 5*, V lge, mkd, pt shd, serviced pitches; EHU (6A) inc (adaptor avail); gas; bbq (charcoal, gas); sw nr; TV; 25% statics; Eng spkn; adv bkg req; ccard acc; watersports; boat hire; golf 300m; fishing; games rm; horseriding 3km; bike hire; CKE. *"Site on banks of Lake Thun; excel views; gd sized pitches; helpful staff; immac san facs; o'fits over 8m by request; money exchange; variable pitch price; excel facs for children; steamer boat trips; excursions; bkg fee; cable car & chairlift nrby; local bus pass provided free; gd walking; if staying on Super pitch, water hose with pressurised valve fitting req; site v easy to find; v pleasant and well looked after; if taking an awning a storm strap req."* **CHF 66**   2019

See advertisement

INTERLAKEN (NO. 02) *C2* (5km W Rural) *46.67969, 7.81764* **Camping Alpenblick,** Seestrasse 130, 3800 Unterseen-Interlaken **033 8227757 or 8231470; info@camping-alpenblick.ch; www.camping-alpenblick.ch**

12 🐕 CHF3 ♦♦ (htd) wo ♨ ♨ ♿ ♫ ✎ MSP ¶ ⑪ ♨ ⅄ ⚑

Fr W on A8 exit junc 24 Interlaken West & foll sp Thun & Gunten. At rndabt take 2nd exit twd Thun, sp Gunten. Site adj Motel Neuhaus & Rest Strandbad on Gunten-Thun rd. 4*, Lge, mkd, pt shd, EHU (10A) CHF4.50 (rev pol); gas; bbq; sw nr; 30% statics; phone; bus fr site ent; Eng spkn; ccard acc; watersports; fishing; golf adj; CKE. *"In beautiful situation; mountain views; excel, modern facs; bread baked on site; lake steamers fr hotel opp; gd walks nr; free bus pass to town; cycle rte to Interlaken; CHF1 to fill m'van water tank; adv bkg attracts surcharge; pool 3km; site next to shooting club, poss noisy."* **CHF 55**   2018

INTERLAKEN (NO. 04) *C2* (4.2km W Rural) *46.68555, 7.83083* **Camping Lazy Rancho,** Lehnweg 6, 3800 Unterseen-Interlaken **033 8228716; info@lazyrancho.ch; www.lazyrancho.ch**

🐕 CHF3 ♦♦ (htd) wo ♨ ♨ ♿ ♫ ✎ MSP ¶ ▽ ⑪ ♨ ⅄ ⚑ ⛱

Fr W on app to Interlaken, exit A8/A6 junc 24 sp Interlaken West. Turn L at slip rd rndabt then at rndabt take a sharp R turn (foll camping sp Nos. 3-5); at Migrol petrol stn foll sp for Lazy Rancho 4 (narr rd on L just bef Landhotel Golf); it is 2nd site. Cent of Interlaken best avoided with c'vans or lge m'vans. Rec arr bef 1900 hrs. 4*, Med, hdg, mkd, hdstg, pt shd, serviced pitches; EHU (10A) inc (adaptors provided); gas; bbq; cooking facs; TV (pitch); 30% statics; phone; Eng spkn; ccard acc; bike hire; horseriding 500m; fishing nr; tennis 2.5km; games rm; watersports nr; CKE. *"Superb views Eiger, Monch & Jungfrau; no o'fits over 7.5m high ssn; ideal for touring Interlaken, Bernese Oberland; fitness cent/spa; friendly, caring, helpful owners; sm pitches; recep 0900-1200 & 1330-2100 high ssn; 5 mins to bus stop nr Cmp Jungfrau; ask about Swiss red fare rlwy services - excel value; immac, outstanding, well-maintained site & facs; brilliant site."* **CHF 54, 18 Apr-15 Oct, S01.**   2019

INTERLAKEN (NO. 05) *C2* (2km W Rural) *46.68688, 7.83411* **Jungfrau Camp,** Steindlerstrasse 60, 3800 Unterseen-Interlaken **033 8225730; info@jungfraucamp.ch; www.campinginterlaken.ch or www.jungfraucamp.ch**

🐕 CHF4 ♦♦ (htd) wo ♨ ♨ ♿ ♫ ✎ MSP 🦋 ▽ ⑪ ♨ ⅄ ⚑ ⛱

Leave N8 at exit Unterseen. In approx 600m turn R at rndabt & foll sp to site. 4*, Med, pt shd, EHU (10A) CHF4; gas; sw nr; 40% statics; bus adj; Eng spkn; adv bkg acc; tennis. *"Visits to all Bernese Oberland vills; views of Jungfrau, Mönch & Eiger; some noise fr shooting range at w/end; town in walking dist; excel, relaxing, well-run site; high standard san facs; poss ssn workers in summer."* **CHF 50, 15 Jun-20 Sep.**   2016

INTERLAKEN (NO. 08) *C2 (3km S Rural) 46.66111, 7.86453* **Camping Oberei,** Obereigasse 9, 3812 Wilderswil-Interlaken **033 8221335; info@ campingwilderswil.ch; www.campinginterlaken.ch or www.campingwilderswil.ch**

🐾 CHF2 ⇌ (htd) 🆗 ⚒ ♨ ⚿ 🚿 🦋 ⊕nr 🛶

Fr Interlaken by-pass take rd sp Grindelwald & Lauterbrunnen to Wilderswil. Site sp 800m past stn on R in vill. Narr ent. 3*, Med, mkd, pt shd, pt sl, EHU (6A) CHF3; gas; TV; bus adj, bus/train nr; Eng spkn; adv bkg acc; CKE. *"Well-managed, relaxing, family-run site in superb scenic location; helpful owners; grnd sheets supplied if wet/muddy; blocks provided; gd, clean facs; gd touring cent; easy walk to rlwy stn; guest card gives free local train & bus travel; pool 3km; excel rec high ssn."* **CHF 41.6, 1 May-15 Oct.** **2016**

KANDERSTEG *C2 (15km N Rural) 46.58188, 7.64150* **Camping Grassi,** 3714 Frutigen **033 6711149; campinggrassi@bluewin.ch; www.camping-grassi.ch**

12 🐾 CHF1.50 ⇌ (htd) 🆗 ⚒ ♨ ⚿ 🚿 MSP 🛖 ⊕nr 🛶 ⚠

Exit rd to Kandersteg at Frutigen Dorf & in 400m L to site in 500m. 4*, Med, pt shd, EHU (10A) CHF3; gas; red long stay; TV; 50% statics; phone; Eng spkn; adv bkg acc; tennis; bike hire; fishing. *"Walking rte dir fr site to spectacular pedestrian suspension bdge; htd covrd pool 1km; 10 min walk to town."* **CHF 34** **2019**

KANDERSTEG *C2 (1.3km NE Rural) 46.49800, 7.68519* **Camping Rendez-Vous,** 3718 Kandersteg **033 6751534; rendez-vous.camping@bluewin.ch; www.camping-kandersteg.ch**

12 🐾 CHF3 ⇌ (htd) 🆗 ⚒ ♨ ⚿ 🚿 🦋 🛖 🍽 ⊕ ♨ 🛶

In middle of Kandersteg turn E dir Sesselbahn Öschinensee; site sp. 3*, Med, hdstg, pt shd, pt sl, terr, EHU (10A) (adaptors avail); gas; bbq; Eng spkn; adv bkg acc; ccard acc; games rm; bike hire; CKE. *"Excel, well-supervised site; htd pool 800m; chair-lift adj; excel walking."* **CHF 41** **2019**

KREUZLINGEN *A3 (0km E Rural) 47.64676, 9.19810* **Camping Fischerhaus,** Promenadenstrasse 52, 8280 Kreuzlingen **071 6884903; info@camping-fischerhaus.ch; www.camping-fischerhaus.ch**

⇌ 🆗 ⚒ ♨ ⚿ 🚿 MSP 🦋 🛖 🍽 ⊕ ♨ 🛶 ⚠ 🛶 (htd) 🛟

Fr Konstanz take rd 13 dir Romanshorn. Turn L at sp 'Hafen/Indus Est' off main lakeside rd, Kreuzlingen-Arbon. Camping sps fr 5km SE at Customs in Konstanz. 4*, Med, unshd, EHU (10A) inc; gas; bbq; twin axles; 60% statics; phone; bus 100m; train 1km; Eng spkn; adv bkg acc; fishing; tennis; games area. *"Facs for statics excel, but for tourers v basic; gates clsd 1200-1400 & 2200-0700; gd cycle paths."* **CHF 44, 28 Mar-21 Oct.** **2018**

LANDERON, LE *B2 (0.3km S Rural) 47.05216, 7.06975* **Camping des Pêches,** Route du Port, 2525 Le Landeron **032 7512900; info@camping-lelanderon.ch; www.camping-lelanderon.ch**

⇌ 🆗 ⚒ ♨ ⚿ 🚿 ⚿ MSP 🍽 ⊕ 🛶 ⚠

A5 fr Neuchâtel, exit Le Landeron or La Neuveville; foll site sp. 4*, Med, mkd, pt shd, serviced pitches; EHU (15A) CHF3.50; gas; TV; 60% statics; Eng spkn; adv bkg acc; ccard acc; sep car park; bike hire; tennis; fishing; CKE. *"Sep touring section on busy site; htd pool 100m; walks by lake & rv; interesting old town."* **CHF 32, 1 Apr-15 Oct.** **2016**

See advertisement

LANDQUART *B4 (3km E Rural) 46.97040, 9.59620* **TCS Camping Neue Ganda,** Ganda 21, 7302 Landquart **081 3223955; camping.landquart@tcs.ch; www.campingtcs.ch**

🐾 CHF4 ⇌ (htd) 🆗 ⚒ ♨ ⚿ 🚿 ⚿ MSP 🛖 🍽 🛶 🛶 ⚠ ✏

Exit A13/E43 dir Landquart, site sp on rd to Davos. 3*, Lge, pt shd, pt sl, EHU (6-10A) CHF4; gas; bbq; cooking facs; 60% statics; ccard acc; rv fishing; bike hire; canoeing; tennis 300m; games rm; CKE. *"Immac san facs; excel site; v helpful owner & staff; poss uneven pitches, mainly grass; if recep clsd find pitch & sign in later; many mkd walks fr site."* **CHF 46, 10 Dec-28 Feb & 19 Mar-17 Oct.** **2015**

LAUSANNE *C1* (9km E Rural) *46.48973, 6.73786*
Camping de Moratel, Route de Moratel 2, 1096
Cully 021 7991914; camping.moratel@bluewin.ch

Fr Lausanne-Vevey lakeside rd (not m/way), turn R
to Cully; sp thro town; site on R on lake shore. Ent
not sp. 3*, Sm, mkd, hdstg, hdg, pt shd, EHU (3-5A)
metered (adaptor provided); gas; sw; 80% statics; bus,
train, ferry; adv bkg acc; boating; fishing. "Vg value;
attractive, clean site with beautiful views; rec adv bkg
for lakeside pitch; friendly staff; siting poss diff for lge
o'fits; pool 3km; gd location for best pt Lake Geneva; vg
value." **CHF 26, 20 Mar-20 Oct.**   **2018**

LAUSANNE *C1* (3km W Rural) *46.51769, 6.59766*
Camping de Vidy, Chemin du Camping 3, 1007
Lausanne (Genferseegebiet) 021 6225000; info@clv.ch;
www.clv.ch

Leave A1 at Lausanne Süd/Ouchy exit; take 4th
exit at rndabt (Rte de Chavannes); in 100m filter L
at traff lts & foll site sp to L. Site adj to HQ of Int'l
Olympic Organisation, well sp all over Lausanne.
4*, Lge, mkd, pt shd, EHU (10A) inc; gas; bbq; TV;
80% statics; bus to Lausanne 400m; Eng spkn; adv
bkg acc; ccard acc; watersports; bike hire; games rm;
tennis 1km; CKE. "Excel lakeside site in attractive park;
friendly staff; sm pitches; gd train service to Geneva;
sports & recreation area adj; conv m'way; recep 0800-
2100 high ssn; no o'fits over 8m high ssn; free bus
passes for unltd bus & Metro tavel in Lausanne; gd san
facs (updated 2018); gd cycling." **CHF 42**   **2018**

> ## "We must tell the Club about that great site we found"
>
> Get your site reports in by mid-August and we'll
> do our best to get your updates into the next
> edition.

LAUTERBRUNNEN *C2* (1km S Rural) *46.58788,
7.91030* **Camping Jungfrau**, Weid 406, 3822
Lauterbrunnen 033 8562010; info@camping-
jungfrau.ch; www.camping-jungfrau.ch

S o'skirts of Lauterbrunnen sp at R fork, site in
500m. 5*, Lge, hdstg, pt shd, terr, serviced pitches;
EHU (16A) CHF2.5 (metered in winter, poss rev pol);
gas; red long stay; TV; 30% statics; phone; Eng spkn;
adv bkg rec; ccard acc; tennis; bike hire; CKE. "Friendly,
helpful welcome; fine scenery, superb situation in
vertical walled valley; rlwy tickets sold; sep car park
when site full; ski bus; ATM; close to town & rlwy stn to
high alpine resorts; ski & boot rm; superb facs; clean;
shop gd; pool 600m; excel site." **CHF 45.6, S15.**
                                                2018

LAUTERBRUNNEN *C2* (3.6km S Rural) *46.56838,
7.90869* **Camping Breithorn**, Sandbach, 3824
Stechelberg 033 8551225; breithorn@stechelberg.ch;
www.campingbreithorn.ch

Up valley thro Lauterbrunnen, 300m past
Trümmelbach Falls to ent on R. 3*, Med, unshd, EHU
(10A); gas; bbq; 60% statics; phone; Eng spkn; adv bkg
acc; tennis; fishing; CKE. "Quiet site in lovely area; arr
early high ssn; fine scenery & gd touring base; friendly
helpful owners; frequent trains, funiculars & cable cars
fr Lauterbrunnen stn (4km); Schilthorn cable car 1.5km;
excel cent for mountain walking & cycling; pool 3km;
excel, clean facs; cash only." **CHF 29**   **2018**

LEUK *C2* (15km N Rural) *46.38119, 7.62361* **Camping
Sportarena**, 3954 Leukerbad 027 4701037; info@
leukerbad.ch; https://www.sportarenaleukerbad.ch

Exit A9 at Susten & foll sp N to Leukerbad, site sp.
3*, Med, hdstg, pt shd, pt sl, terr, EHU (10A) CHF5;
bbq; TV; 20% statics; Eng spkn; adv bkg acc; games
area. "Beautiful situation; sports cent adj; pleasant,
helpful staff; htd covrd pool 200m; attractive little
town; cable cars; thermal pools nr; walks; vg."
CHF 30, 1 May-31 Oct.   **2020**

LEUK *C2* (12km E Rural) *46.30667, 7.74117*
Camping Rhône, 3945 Gampel 027 9322041; info@
campingrhone.ch; www.campingrhone.ch

Fr rd A9/E62 exit dir Gampel, site well sp on R bank
of Rv Rhône. 3*, Lge, pt shd, EHU CHF3.20; gas;
30% statics; adv bkg acc; tennis; golf; fishing. "Superb
location & touring base; gd walking, cycling; driest pt of
Switzerland; modern, clean san facs; friendly owners;
well maintained; gd pool; beautiful views; supmkt 1km."
CHF 31, 25 Mar-31 Oct.   **2016**

LEUK *C2* (4km SE Rural) *46.29780, 7.65936* **Camping
Gemmi**, Briannenstrasse 4, 3952 Susten 027 4731154
or 4734295; info@campgemmi.ch;
www.campgemmi.ch

Foll A9/E27 SE; then nr Martigny take A9/E62
to Sierre; then take E62 thro Susten. After 2km,
by Hotel Relais Bayard, take R lane (Agarn,
Feithieren), ignoring sp Camping Torrent, & foll
Alte Kantonstrasse sp Agarn. Turn R at site sp into
Briannenstrasse; site in 200m. 4*, Med, mkd, pt
shd, pt sl, serviced pitches; EHU (16A) inc; gas; bbq
(elec, gas); TV (pitch); 5% statics; Eng spkn; adv bkg
acc; ccard acc; tennis; golf; bike hire; horseriding nr;
CKE. "Outstanding site; friendly, helpful, hardworking
owners; indiv san facs some pitches; no o'fits over 9m
high ssn; private bthrms avail; gd stop on way Simplon
Pass; various pitch prices; barrier clsd 2200-0800; pool
600m; excel walking; conv A9." **CHF 41, 30 Mar-7 Oct,
S12.**   **2017**

LOCARNO *C3* (14km E Rural) *46.16978, 8.91396*
Park-Camping Riarena, Via Campeggio, 6516
Cugnasco **091 8591688; info@campingriarena.ch;**
www.campingriarena.ch

♦CHF4 [symbols]

**Exit A2/E35 Bellinzona-Süd & foll sp dir airport.
Bear R at rndabt & foll site sp to Gudo, site on R in
2km.** 4*, Med, mkd, shd, EHU (10A) CHF5 (adaptor
avail); gas; red long stay; twin axles; bus 0.5km;
Eng spkn; adv bkg acc; ccard acc; bike hire; games
area. *"Friendly, family-run site; excursions arranged;
gd cycle rtes; gate shut 1300-1500; clean san facs;
dusty site; beware acorn drop September; vg."*
CHF 53, 21 Mar-17 Oct. 2019

LOCARNO *C3* (9km NW Rural) *46.22436, 8.74395* **TCS
Camping Bella Riva,** 6672 Gordévio **091 7531444;
camping.gordevio@tcs.ch; www.campingtcs.ch**

♦CHF5 [symbols]

**Fr W end of A13 tunnel under Locarno foll sp
Centovalle & Valle Maggia. In 3km turn R to Valle
Maggia. Stay on rd which bypasses Gordévio
(approx 5km), site on L.** 4*, Lge, pt shd, EHU inc (10A)
CHF4.50; gas; sw; TV; 30% statics; Eng spkn; adv bkg
acc; ccard acc; tennis; fishing; sep car park; bike hire;
CKE. *"Attractive region; well-run site; lge tent area adj;
bus to vill nr site."* **CHF 54, 1 Apr-15 Oct.** 2020

LUGANO *D3* (7km W Rural) *45.99534, 8.90845*
Lugano, Via alla Force 14, 6933 Muzzano-Lugano
**091 9947788 or 091 9858070 LS; camping.
muzzano@tcs.ch; www.campingtcs.ch/muzzano**

12 ♦CHF5.50 [symbols] (htd) [symbol]

**Leave A2 at Lugano Nord & foll sp Ponte Tresa &
airport. In Agno turn L at traff island; foll camping
sp. In 800m, just after La Piodella town sp, look for
sm sp at rd junc with tent symbol & TCS sticker.
NB This may appear to direct you to your R but
you must make a 180° turn & take slip rd along
R-hand side of rd you have just come along - app
rd to site.** 4*, Lge, mkd, pt shd, serviced pitches; EHU
(10A) inc (long lead poss req, avail fr recep); gas; bbq;
TV; 10% statics; Eng spkn; adv bkg acc; ccard acc;
watersports; games area; horseriding 6km; tennis;
games rm; fishing; CKE. *"Idyllic location; pitches nr lake
higher price; o'fits over 7.5m HS; sep car park; modern
san facs; no cats; access to pitches poss diff lge o'fits;
boating 6km; train to Lugano 1km, or easy drive; ideal
for Ticino Lakes; day/eve aircraft noise; barrier clsd
1200-1400."* **CHF 49, S10.** 2016

LUZERN *B3* (3km E Rural) *47.0500, 8.33833*
Camping International Lido, Lidostrasse 19,
6006 Luzern **041 3702146; luzern@camping-
international.ch; www.camping-international.ch**

12 ♦CHF4 (htd) [symbols]

**Fr bdge on lake edge in city cent foll sp Küssnacht &
Verkehrshaus. Turn R off Küssnacht rd at traff lts by
transport museum (sp Lido), site 50m on L beyond
lido parking. Fr A2/E35 exit Luzern Centrum.** 4*, Lge,
mkd, hdstg, pt shd, EHU (16A) CHF4.60; gas; bbq;
sw nr; 10% statics; phone; bus, 200mtrs; Eng spkn;
adv bkg rec; ccard acc; boat trips; boat launch; CKE.
*"Ltd touring pitches cr in peak ssn, early arr rec; pool
adj (May-Sep); recep open 0830-1200 & 1400-1800
high ssn; money exchange; recep in bar LS; clean, well-
maintained facs stretched high ssn; lake ferry 200m;
helpful staff; pleasant lakeside walk to Luzern; conv
location; excel rest in Wurzenbach; transport museum
worth a visit; well-run site; free local bus tickets avail."*
CHF 50 2018

MADULAIN *C4* (0.3km N Rural) *46.58764, 9.94004*
Camping Madulain, Via Vallatscha, 7523 Madulain
**081 8540161; mail@campingmadulain.ch;
www.campingmadulain.ch**

[symbols] (htd) [symbols] nr [symbol] nr [symbol] nr

Sp fr N27 at foot of Albula Pass. 3*, Sm, pt shd,
pt sl, terr, EHU (10A) CHF2; 70% statics; Eng spkn.
"Simple CL-type site; excel san facs; helpful owner."
CHF 35, 19 Dec-10 Apr & 27 May-18 Oct. 2015

MEIERSKAPPEL *B3* (1km S Rural) *47.12175, 8.44670*
Campingplatz Gerbe, Landiswilerstrasse, 6344
Meierskappel **041 7904534; info@swiss-bauernhof.ch;
www.swiss-bauernhof.ch**

♦CHF2.50 [symbols] (htd) [symbols] (covrd, htd)

**Exit A4/E41 at Küssnacht & foll sp N to
Meierskappel. Bef ent Meierskappel turn L into
farm ent for site (sp.)** Med, pt shd, pt sl, EHU (10A)
CHF3.50 (poss rev pol); bbq; 5% statics; CKE. *"Vg,
basic farm site, poor facs (unisex), in need of refurb;
lge field - choose own pitch; conv Luzerne & Zurich."*
CHF 25, 1 Mar-1 Nov. 2015

MEIRINGEN *C3* (1.5km NW Rural) *46.73431, 8.17139*
Alpencamping, Brünigstrasse 47, 3860 Meiringen
**033 9713676; info@alpencamping.ch;
www.alpencamping.ch**

♦CHF3 [symbols] (htd) [symbols] nr [symbol] [symbol]

**Leave A8, then take rd11/6 twd Brünig Pass.
On entering Meiringen, at 1st rndabt foll camp sp
L to site.** 4*, Med, unshd, EHU (10A) CHF5.50; gas;
bbq; cooking facs; 70% statics; bus 200m, train 1.3km;
Eng spkn; adv bkg acc; site clsd Nov; CKE. *"Meeting
point of alpine passes; friendly, family-run site; excel,
modern san facs; vg walking/cycling; beautiful site with
gd views; fair."*
CHF 47, 1 Jan-31 Oct & 1 Dec-31 Dec. 2018

MENDRISIO *D3* (8km NW Rural) *45.88921, 8.94841*
Camping TCS Meride-Mendrisio (formerly Parco al Sole), Via Ala Caraa 2, 6866 Meride **091 6464330; camping.meride@tcs.ch; www.campingtcs.ch**

🅿 CHF5 ♀♂ 🆆 🛁 ⚲ ♿ ☕ ⚡ 🍽 🦋 🍴 ⊕ 🐕 🛒 nr ⛺ ✂ ⛷ (htd) 🛝

Fr A2/E35 exit Mendrisio, then foll sp Rancate & Serpiano. Steep climb. Site on L to S of vill. 4*, Med, hdstg, pt shd, pt sl, EHU (4A) CHF4.50; gas; TV; 20% statics; Eng spkn; adv bkg acc; ccard acc; lake fishing; sep car park. *"Attractive, peaceful setting away fr traff; Unesco World Heritage vill; pitches uneven in parts & v sm, some surrounded by other pitches - make sure you can get off with o'fit; site clsd to arr 1100-1700; conv Milan by train."* CHF 49, 1 May-26 Sep.   2016

MORGES *C1* (2km S Rural) *46.50360, 6.48760* **Morges,** Promenade du Petit-Bois 15, 1110 Morges **021 8011270 or 091 9858070 LS; camping.morges@tcs.ch; www.campingtcs.ch/morges**

🅿 CHF5 ♀♂ 🆆 🛁 ⚲ ♿ ☕ ⚲ 🍽 🍴 ⊕ 🛒 ⛺ ✂

Exit A1/E25 at Morges Ouest, then foll sp to lake. Site well sp on Lake Léman N shore adj pool. 3*, Lge, hdg, mkd, pt shd, EHU (6A) inc (adaptor/long lead avail); gas; bbq; sw nr; TV; 50% statics; Eng spkn; adv bkg acc; games rm; bike hire; watersports; tennis 500m; boating. *"Pleasant site but sm pitches; htd pool in complex 200m (high ssn) inc; helpful staff; clean san facs; conv Lausanne, Geneva & some Alpine passes; o'fits over 8m on req; m'van o'night/late arr area; easy walk to town & stn; cycle path around lake; vg."* CHF 60, 29 Mar-9 Oct, S14.   2017

MURG *B3* (0.5km N Rural) *47.11543, 9.21445* **Camping Murg am Walensee,** 8877 Murg **081 7381530; info@camping-murg.ch; www.murg-camping.ch**

🅿 CHF4.50 ♀♂ 🆆 ⚲ 🍽 🦋 ⊕ nr 🛒

Exit A3 junc 47 dir Murg, site sp on lake. Med, pt shd, EHU (10A) CHF3.70; sw nr; 30% statics; phone; adv bkg req. *"Spectacular outlook at water's edge; sm pitches; beautiful setting; boat trips adj; cable car 4km; vg."* CHF 49, 1 Apr-15 Oct.   2019

MUSTAIR *B4* (0.5km E Rural) *46.62405, 10.44933* **Camping Muglin,** Via Muglin 223, 7537 Mustair **081 8585990; info@campingmuglin.ch; www.campingmuglin.ch**

♀♂ 🆆 🛁 ☕ ⚲ 🍽 🦋 🍴 🍴 ⊕ ⛺

On rd 28 to Mustair. Foll sp. Med, mkd, unshd, EHU (13A); bbq; TV; adv bkg acc; games rm. *"Beautiful views; serviced pithces; walking rte fr site; lge sauna."* CHF 42, 22 Apr-29 Oct.   2017

NEUCHATEL *B1* (13km NE Rural) *47.00198, 7.04145* **TCS Camping Gampelen (formerly Camp Fanel),** Seestrasse 50, 3236 Gampelen **032 3132333; camping.gampelen@tcs.ch; www.campingtcs.ch**

🅿 CHF4 ♀♂ 🆆 🛁 ⚲ ♿ ☕ ⚲ 🍽 🍴 🍴 ⊕ ⛺ ✂ ⛷ ⛵ (htd)

Foll TCS camping sp fr turning off N5 in Gampelen - approx 4km fr vill, on lakeside. 3*, V lge, mkd, pt shd, serviced pitches; EHU (4-6A) CHF 3.50-4.50 (adaptor on loan, rev pol); gas; bbq; sw; red long stay; 80% statics; Eng spkn; adv bkg acc; ccard acc; tennis; archery; golf; fishing; watersports; CKE. *"In nature reserve; office/barrier clsd 1200-1400; office & shop hrs vary with ssn; gd, modern facs; helpful staff; Euros also acc; vg cycling around lakes."* CHF 55, 10 Apr-13 Oct.   2018

PRESE, LE *C4* (0.5km N Rural) *46.29490, 10.08010* **Camping Cavresc,** 7746 Le Prese **081 8440259; camping.cavresc@bluewin.ch; www.campingsertori.ch**

🅙12 🅿 CHF2 ♀♂ (htd) 🆆 🛁 ☕ ⚲ 🍽 🦋 🍴 ⊕ 🐕 🛒 nr ⛺ ⛵

S fr Pontresina on N29 site sp on L 5km S of Poschiavo adj Lake Poschiavo. 4*, Med, shd, EHU (10A) CHF4; gas; bbq; red long stay; TV; bus/train adj; adv bkg acc; ccard acc; games area; CKE. *"Stunning scenery; htd covrd pool 5km; walking/cycling rtes; excel; friendly owners."* CHF 36   2015

ROMANSHORN *A4* (5km SE Rural) *47.53620, 9.39885* **Camping Seehorn (formerly Wiedehorn),** Wiedehorn, 9322 Egnach **071 4771006; info@seehorn.ch; www.seehorn.ch**

🅿 CHF4 ♀♂ 🆆 🛁 ⚲ 🍽 🦋 🍴 ⊕ 🛒 ⛺

Site is 2km E of Egnach, dir Arbon. 4*, Med, mkd, pt shd, pt sl, serviced pitches; EHU (16A) CHF2.50; gas; TV; 60% statics; phone; adv bkg acc; fishing. *"Direct access Lake Constance; sep car park high ssn; statics sep; excel facs; great loc; cycle paths around lake; friendly recep; ACSI acc."* CHF 50, 1 Mar-31 Oct.   2018

SAAS FEE *D2* (4.6km NE Rural) *46.11588, 7.93819* **Camping am Kapellenweg,** 3910 Saas-Grund **027 9574997; camping@kapellenweg.ch; www.kapellenweg.ch**

🅿 CHF2.50 ♀♂ 🆆 🛁 ♿ ☕ ⚲ 🐕 🛒

Fr Visp, take Saas Fee rd to Saas Grund, cont twd Saas Almagell, site on R after 1km. 3*, Sm, pt shd, pt sl, EHU CHF3; gas; Eng spkn; fishing; golf. *"Ideal for walking; family-run site; clean san facs; beautiful scenery; if recep clsd, site yourself; bus or walk (50 mins) into town; excel site."* CHF 49, 10 May-13 Oct.   2019

ST GALLEN *A4* (9km N Rural) *47.46191, 9.36371*
Camping St Gallen-Wittenbach, Leebrücke, 9304
Bernhardzell **071 2984969; campingplatz.stgallen@
ccc-stgallen.ch; www.ccc-stgallen.ch**

🐕 👫 WD ⚓ 🛁 ⚡ / 🦋 ☂ 🍴 🐟 🛒 ⚠

Exit A1/E60 St Fiden. L in Wittenbach cent at site sp.
Cross Rv Sitter on sharp R bend, turn sharp R at sp.
3*, Med, hdstg, pt shd, EHU (6A) CHF4 (adaptor loan);
gas; bbq; TV; 30% statics; bus; Eng spkn; adv bkg acc;
ccard acc; canoeing; golf 10km; bike hire; CKE. "Gd
base for S shore of Bodensee; pleasant rvside setting;
friendly staff." CHF 32, 12 Apr-4 Oct.   **2016**

ST MARGRETHEN *A4* (3km E Rural) *47.45114,
9.65650* **Strandbad Camping Bruggerhorn,** 9430
St Margrethen **071 7442201**

👫 WD 🛁 ⚡ / 🦋 ⑪ nr 🛒 ⚠ 🏊

Exit N1/E60 dir St Margrethen, site well sp. 3*, Med,
pt shd, EHU (10A) CHF2.50 (adaptor avail); gas; sw;
Eng spkn; adv bkg acc; tennis; CKE. "Picturesque,
clean site; vg shwrs; sports cent adj; helpful staff."
CHF 36, 1 Apr-31 Oct.   **2016**

ST MORITZ *C4* (1km S Rural) *46.47843, 9.82511*
TCS Camping Olympiaschanze, 7500 St Moritz
**081 8334090; camping.stmoritz@tcs.ch;
www.campingtcs.ch**

🐕 CHF4 👫 (htd) WD 🛁 ⚡ / MSP 🦋 🍴 ⑪ nr 🛒 ⚠ 🎣

Turn S off rd N27 immed after park & ride car park.
Site 1km fr vill of Champfer. 3*, Med, mkd, pt sl, EHU
(6A) CHF4 (adaptor on loan); gas; sw nr; Eng spkn;
ccard acc; bike hire; tennis; CKE. "Gd walking area, nr
St Moritz & Maloja & Julier passes; site v high & cold
(poss snow in Aug); san facs stretched when site full; sh
walk town cent." CHF 52, 20 May-28 Sep.   **2016**

SEMPACH *B3* (1.5km S Rural) *47.12447, 8.18924* **TCS
Camping Sempach,** Seelandstrasse, 6204 Sempach
Stadt **041 4601466 or 091 9858070; camping.
sempach@tcs.ch; www.campingtcs.ch/sempach**

🐕 CHF5 👫 (htd) WD 🛁 ⚓ 👿 ⚡ / MSP 🦋 ⑪ 🐟 🛒 ⚠ 🎣 🚣

Fr Luzern on A2 take exit sp Emmen N, Basel, Bern.
Join E35 & cont on this rd to exit at Sempach sp.
Site well sp. 4*, Lge, mkd, unshd, EHU (13A) inc
(adaptor avail); gas; bbq (charcoal, gas); sw nr; TV;
60% statics; Eng spkn; adv bkg acc; ccard acc; bike
hire; watersports; fishing; golf 5km; tennis; games
rm; CKE. "Excel location on Sempacher See, 10 mins
drive fr m'way & attractive town; no o'fits over 9m high
ssn; sep car parks high ssn; sm pitches; helpful staff;
rest & beach open to public; water & bins far fr many
pitches; poss tight parking; ltd facs LS; private san facs
avail; lakeside walk to Sempach." CHF 56, 4 Apr-7 Oct,
S08.   **2016**

SIERRE *C2* (3km NE Rural) *46.30215, 7.56420*
Camping Swiss Plage, Campingweg 3, 3970
Salgesch **027 4556608; info@swissplage.ch;
www.swissplage.ch**

🐕 CHF3.50 👫 WD 🛁 ⚡ / MSP 🦋 🍴 ⑪ 🛒 ⚠

Fr A9/E62 exit at Sierre, turn L & go over bdge, Foll
sp Salgesch & Site. Fr town site well sp. 4*, Lge, shd,
EHU (10A) CHF3.60; gas; sw; Eng spkn; adv bkg req;
ccard acc; tennis. "Pleasant site in lovely location."
CHF 39, Easter-15 Oct.   **2016**

SION *C2* (9km SW Rural) *46.20578, 7.27855* **Camping
du Botza,** Route du Camping 1, 1963 Vétroz **027
3461940 or 079 2203575 (mob); info@botza.ch;
www.botza.ch**

12 🐕 CHF3.50 👫 WD 🛁 ⚓ 👿 ⚡ / MSP 🦋 ⑪ 🍴 ⑪ 🐟 🛒 ⚠
🎣 🏊 (htd) 🚣

Exit A9/E62 junc 25 S'wards over a'bahn. Site adj
Vétroz indus est, foll sp 'CP Nr.33'. 5*, Lge, mkd,
pt shd, serviced pitches; EHU (10A) CHF3.70; gas;
30% statics; adv bkg acc; ccard acc; fishing; squash;
tennis; golf 8km. "Superb site conv m'way & ski resorts;
excel facs; gd security; organised excursions; vg rest;
fine mountain views; cycle track along Rhone nrby;
some noise fr nrby airport." CHF 34.3   **2019**

SOLOTHURN *B2* (2km SW Rural) *47.19883, 7.52288*
TCS Camping Lido Solothurn, Glutzenhofstrasse 5,
4500 Solothurn **032 6218935 or 091 9858070 LS;
camping.solothurn@tcs.ch; www.campingtcs.ch/
solothurn**

🐕 CHF5 👫 (htd) WD 🛁 ⚓ 👿 ⚡ / MSP 🦋 🍴 ⑪ 🐟 🛒 ⚠ 🎣 🚣

Exit A5 dir Solothurn W, cross rv bdge. At traff lts
turn L & foll sp to site (new rd 2009). 4*, Lge, mkd, pt
shd, serviced pitches; EHU (16A) inc; gas; bbq; cooking
facs; TV; 20% statics; bus 200m; Eng spkn; adv bkg
acc; ccard acc; games rm; bike hire; tennis 200m;
fishing; boat hire; golf 100m; games area; CKE. "Gd
touring base by Rv Aare; no o'fits over 12m high ssn;
lge pitches; htd pool adj; excel facs; helpful staff; 20
mins walk to picturesque town; excel cycling paths."
CHF 58, 28 Feb-29 Nov, S13.   **2019**

SPIEZ C2 (6km SE Rural) 46.65880, 7.71688
Camping Stuhlegg, Stueleggstrasse 7, 3704 Krattigen
**033 6542723; campstuhlegg@bluewin.ch;
www.camping-stuhlegg.ch**

12 ⌂ CHF3 ᛭(htd) WD ♨ ⚑ 🖾 ✎ MSP 🦋 ☂ Ⓗⁿʳ ♨ 🛝 ⛱
✎ 🚣(htd)

13km fr Interlaken on hillside on S side of Lake Thun. Advise app fr Spiez. Fr Spiez rlwy stn heading SE turn R over rlwy bdge; foll sp Leissigen & Krattigen for 5km. In Krattigen after modern church turn R (low gear), site 500m on R. To avoid going thro Spiez town, leave Bern-Interlaken m'way at junc 19. Foll dir to Aeschi. At rndabt in Aeschi turn L to Krattigen. Turn L after 1m opp wood yard into Stuhleggstrasse. Site in 300 yds. 4*, Lge, pt shd, pt sl, terr, EHU (10A) CHF4 (some rev pol); gas; 60% statics; phone; adv bkg acc; ccard acc; site clsd last week Oct to end Nov; CKE. *"Excel well-kept, well run site; immac facs; helpful friendly staff; recep clsd 1300-1500; mountain views; gd dog-walking in area; scenic rtes fr site; ski bus; free bus service with Guest Card; gd rest; bread can be ordered."* **CHF 40**   **2019**

> ## "Satellite navigation makes touring much easier"
>
> Remember most sat navs don't know if you're towing or in a larger vehicle – always use yours alongside maps and site directions.

SUMVITG C3 (0.9km SW Rural) 46.72439, 8.92968
Camping Garvera, Campadi alla Staziun, 7175
Sumvitg **081 9431922; info@garvera.ch;
www.garvera.ch**

⌂ CHF4 ᛭(htd) WD ♨ ⚑ 🖾 ✎ ☂ Ⓗⁿʳ 🛝 nr

Fr Chur on rd 19, site well sp in Sumvitg. 2*, Sm, pt shd, terr, EHU (10A) CHF4; bus/train adj; Eng spkn. *"Excel, clean, well cared for site; friendly, helpful owners, who run nrby rest; beautiful area; gd walking; excel facs, inc a natural spring water pond; highly rec."* **CHF 34, 1 May-1 Oct.**   **2015**

SURCUOLM B3 (0.7km N Rural) 46.76053, 9.14324
Panorama Camping Surcuolm, Via Principala,
7138 Surcuolm, Switzerland **081 9333223; info@
camping-surcuolm.ch; www.camping-surcuolm.ch**

12 ⌂ CHF3 ᛭(htd) WD ♨ 🖾 ✎ MSP ♨ ☂ Ⓗⁿʳ 🛝 ⛱

Fr N19 to Ilanz & in Ilanz foll sp Valata & Obersaxen. In Valata turn L to Surcuolm, site on L. This is only rec rte - steep climbs. 4*, Med, unshd, pt sl, EHU (16A) metered; 10% statics; bus 500m; adv bkg acc. *"Mountain views; ski lift nr; popular winter site; quiet in summer; excel facs."* **CHF 41**   **2020**

SURSEE B2 (3km W Rural) 47.17505, 8.08685
Camping Sursee Waldheim, Baslerstrasse, 6210
Sursee **041 9211161; info@camping-sursee.ch;
www.camping-sursee.ch**

⌂ CHF1 ᛭ WD ♨ ⚑ 🖾 ✎ MSP 🦋 ♨ ☂ Ⓗⁿʳ 🛝 ⛱

Exit A2 at junc 20 & take L lane onto rd 24 dir Basel/ Luzern. Turn R at traff lts, foll rd 2 turn R at 2nd rndabt dir Basel to site. 3*, Sm, hdstg, pt shd, pt sl, EHU (10A); gas; bbq; sw nr; TV; 60% statics; Eng spkn; adv bkg acc; games rm; bike hire; CKE. *"Pretty site; excel san facs; gd train service to Luzern; sh walk to town cent; popular NH; gd touring base; v helpful owner; acc Euros."* **CHF 30, 1 Apr-29 Oct.**   **2017**

TENERO C3 (1.5km E Rural) 46.16890, 8.85561
Camping Campofelice, Via alle Brere, 6598 Tenero
**091 7451417; camping@campofelice.ch;
www.campofelice.ch**

᛭ WD ♨ ⚑ 🖾 ✎ MSP ♨ ☂ Ⓗⁿʳ 🛝 ⛱ ✎

Fr A2 take Bellinzona S exit & foll sp Locarno on A13. In about 12km take Tenero exit, at end slip rd foll sp to site. V lge, mkd, pt shd, serviced pitches; EHU (10A) inc; gas; red long stay; 10% statics; Eng spkn; ccard acc; tennis; CKE. *"Expensive but superb, attractive & well-equipped, v clean facs; boat moorings; pool 8km; min stay 3+ nights high ssn."* **CHF 55, 14 Mar-27 Oct.**   **2017**

See advertisement

TENERO *C3* (1km SW Urban) *46.17292, 8.84808*
Camping Miralago, Via Roncaccio 20, 6598 Tenero
091 7451255; info@camping-miralago.ch;
www.camping-miralago.ch

🗓12 🐕 CHF3 ♟(htd) ⓌⒹ ♨ ⚿ 🍽 ✉ 🦋 ⚑ 🍴 🔆 ⓗnr 🔌 🏊 ⛺

🏊(htd) 🛶

Turn L off A13 Bellinzona/Locarno rd at Tenero &
foll camping sps. 5*, Med, mkd, unshd, EHU (10A)
inc; bbq; sw nr; bus adj; Eng spkn; adv bkg acc; ccard
acc; games area; CKE. *"Beautiful area; ltd facs LS; lake
steamer pier lakefront camping; sm pitches with no
privacy hdgs; fairly new san facs; beautiful location, no
rd noise."* **CHF 93** **2019**

ULRICHEN *C3* (1km SE Rural) *46.50369, 8.30969*
Camping Nufenen, 3988 Ulrichen **027 9731437; info@**
camping-nufenen.ch; www.camping-nufenen.ch

🐕 CHF2 ♟ ⓌⒹ ♨ ⚿ ✉ 🦋 ✈ ⓗnr 🔌

On NE end of Ulrichen turn R on Nufenen pass rd.
After rlwy & rv x-ing (1km), site on R. 3*, Med, pt shd,
EHU (8A) CHF3.50; red long stay; 50% statics; phone;
adv bkg acc; tennis 2km; CKE. *"Pleasantly situated,
mountainous site with gd local facs; gd walking; san
facs basic but clean; pool 6km; recep open 0800-2100,
clsd 1230-1400; gd NH."* **CHF 35, 1 Jun-30 Sep.**
2018

ULRICHEN *C3* (8km SW Rural) *46.46480, 8.24469*
Camping Augenstern, 3988 Reckingen **027**
9731395; info@campingaugenstern.ch;
www.campingaugenstern.ch

🐕 CHF2 ♟ ⓌⒹ ♨ ✉ ✈ 🦋 ⚑ 🍴 ⓗ 🔌

On Brig-Gletsch rd turn R in Reckingen over rlwy &
rv, site sp. 3*, Med, unshd, EHU (10A) CHF4.50;
20% statics; golf; fishing; CKE. *"Nr Rv Rhône &
mountains; htd pool adj."* **CHF 37, 1 Jan-15 Mar,
11 May-16 Oct & 14 Dec-31 Dec.** **2016**

VADUZ (LIECHTENSTEIN) *B4* (7km S Rural)
47.0866, 9.52666 **Camping Mittagspitze,**
Saga 29, 9495 Triesen **3923677; info@**
campingtriesen.li; www.campingtriesen.li

🐕 CHF4 ♟ ⓌⒹ ♨ ✉ 🦋 ⚑ ⓗ 🔌 ⛺ 🏊

On rd 28 bet Vaduz & Balzers, sp. Poss diff for
lge o'fits. 4*, Med, hdstg, pt shd, terr, EHU (6A)
CHF5; gas; bbq; 80% statics; Eng spkn; ccard
acc; fishing. *"Pretty site in lovely location; excel
touring base; site yourself, recep open 0800-0830
& 1900-1930 only; fitness trail; steep, diff access to
pitches & slippery when wet; beer garden; gd rest."*
CHF 42, 1 Mar-31 Dec. **2016**

VALLORBE *B1* (0.7km SW Urban) *46.71055, 6.37472*
Camping Pré Sous Ville, 10 Rue des Fontaines, 1337
Vallorbe **021 8432309; yvan.favre@vallorbe.com**

🐕 ♟ ⓌⒹ ♨ ⚿ ✉ ✈ 🦋 🍽 ⓗnr 🔌

Foll camping sp in town. 3*, Med, mkd, pt shd, EHU
(10A) CHF5; gas; 20% statics; Eng spkn; fishing; games
area; tennis; CKE. *"Gd, clean facs; gd size pitches; site
yourself if warden absent; htd pool adj; conv for Vallée
de Joux, Lake Geneva & Jura; views down valley."*
CHF 37, 15 Apr-15 Oct. **2016**

VILLENEUVE *C1* (12km W Rural) *46.38666,
6.86055* **Camping Rive-Bleue,** Case postale 68,
1897 Le Bouveret **024 4812161; info@camping-**
rive-bleue.ch; www.camping-rive-bleue.ch

🐕 CHF3.20 ♟ ⓌⒹ ♨ ✈ 🦋 🍽 ⓗnr 🔌 ⛺

Fr Montreux foll sp to Evian to S side of Lake
Geneva. Turn R after sp 'Bienvenue Bouveret'. Foll
camp sp to Aqua Park. Site on R approx 1km fr main
rd. 4*, Lge, mkd, pt shd, EHU (10A) CHF4.20 (adaptor
avail - check earth); gas; sw; 20% statics; Eng spkn; adv
bkg acc; watersports; tennis; waterslide; sep car park;
CKE. *"Well-maintained, well-ordered, completely flat
site in lovely setting on lake; friendly staff; water/waste
pnts scarce; vg facs but red LS; 15 mins walk to vill with
supmkt; conv ferries around Lake Geneva; cars must
be parked in sep public car park; gd cyling area; free
bicycles for 4 hrs fr vill; pool adj; 1st class san block."*
CHF 43, 1 Apr-12 Oct. **2018**

VILLENEUVE *C1* (5km W Rural) *46.39333,
6.89527* **Camping Les Grangettes,** Rue des
Grangettes, 1845 Noville **021 9601503; noville@**
treyvaud.com; www.les-grangettes.ch

🗓12 🐕 CHF3 ♟(htd) ⓌⒹ ♨ ⚿ ✉ 🦋 🍽 ⓗ 🔌

Fr N9 Montreux-Aigle rd, take Villeneuve exit, at
end slip rd turn N twds Villeneuve. At 1st traff
lts turn L to Noville, turn R by PO, site sp. Narr
app rd. 4*, Med, mkd, unshd, EHU (10A) CHF4; sw;
80% statics; phone; Eng spkn; sep car park; fishing;
boating. *"Beautifully situated on SE corner Lake
Geneva o'looking Montreux; sep tourer area; pool 3km;
poss noisy in high ssn."* **CHF 39** **2019**

VISP *C2* (1.6km NW Rural) *46.29730,
7.87269* **Camping Schwimmbad Mühleye,**
3930 Visp **027 9462084; info@camping-**
visp.ch; www.camping-visp.ch

🐕 CHF2 ♟ ⓌⒹ ♨ ✉ 🍽 🔆 🔌nr ⛺

Exit main rd E2 at W end of town bet Esso petrol
stn & rv bdge at Camping sp. Site nr pool. 3*, Lge,
pt shd, EHU (13A) CHF3.50; gas; red long stay;
20% statics; Eng spkn; fishing; tennis; CKE. *"Gd
for Zermatt & Matterhorn; lge pool adj; recep at
sw pool ent; gd value espec LS; suitable lge o'fits."*
CHF 35, 10 Mar-31 Oct. **2015**

VITZNAU *B3* (0.5km SE Rural) *47.00683, 8.48621* **Camping Vitznau,** Altdorfstrasse, 6354 Vitznau **041 3971280; info@camping-vitznau.ch; www.camping-vitznau.ch**

⛺ CHF5 ♦♦ WC ♨ ♿ ⛽ ⏸ ✉ MSP 🦋 ▾ 🛶 ☇

On E edge of Vitznau, sp. Fr Küssnacht twd Brunnen turn L at RC church with tall clock tower. 4*, Lge, hdstg, pt shd, terr, EHU (16A) CHF4 (adaptors on loan); gas; sw nr; red long stay; 40% statics; Eng spkn; adv bkg rec; ccard acc; tennis; CKE. *"Excel, v clean, family-run site; friendly owner will help with pitching; max c'van length 7m high ssn; sm pitches; some site rds tight & steep; recep closes 1830 hrs; fine views lakes & mountains; Quickstop o'night facs CHF20; many activities inc walking; gd dog-walking; conv ferry terminal, cable cars & mountain rlwy (tickets avail on site); gd saving by using 'tell-pass'; lake steamer to Luzern 500m; gd pool, sm shop."* CHF 53, 30 Mar-7 Oct, S05.   2018

WINTERTHUR *A3* (3km N Rural) *47.51965, 8.71655* **Camping am Schützenweiher,** Eichliwaldstrasse 4, 8400 Winterthur **052 2125260; campingplatz@win.ch; www.camping-winterthur.info**

12 ⛺ CHF4 ♦♦ (htd) WC ♨ ⏸ ✉ MSP 🍴 ① 🛒 nr ⚡

Fr A1/E60 exit Winterthur-Ohringen dir Winterthur, turn R & foll site sp, site adj police stn in about 200m. 2*, Sm, shd, EHU CHF3; gas; 8% statics; phone; bus 250m, train; Eng spkn; CKE. *"Helpful owner; office open 0900-1100 & 1830-1930 to register & pay; find own pitch outside these hrs; sm pitches; pool 3km; gd NH; fairly gd site."* CHF 39   2018

"There aren't many sites open at this time of year"

If you're travelling outside peak season remember to call ahead to check site opening dates – even if the entry says 'open all year'.

ZUG *B3* (2km E Rural) *47.17806, 8.49438* **TCS Camping Zug,** Chamer Fussweg 36, 6300 Zug **041 7418422; camping.zug@tcs.ch; www.campingtcs.ch**

⛺ CHF5 ♦♦ (htd) WC ♨ ⏸ ✉ 🍴 ① 🛒 ⚡

Fr A4/E41 take A4a Zug-West, site sp on R in 3km on lakeside. Fr Zug take Luzern rd for 2km. Site on L under rlwy. 3*, Med, mkd, pt shd, EHU (6A) CHF4; gas; sw; 40% statics; phone; Eng spkn; ccard acc; tennis; fishing; games area; bike hire; CKE. *"Easy walk to town; pool 3km; new (2018) young owners; v clean & tidy; lovely location."* CHF 36, 29 Mar-14 Oct.   2018

ZUG *B3* (11km SE Rural) *47.127781, 8.591945* **Campsite Unterägeri,** Wilbrunnenstraße 81, 6314 Unterägeri **041 7503928; info@campingunteraegeri.ch; www.campingunteraegeri.ch**

12 ♦♦ (htd) WC ♨ ♿ ⏸ ✉ MSP 🦋 🍴 ① 🛒 ⚡ ☇ pebble lake adj

Fr Zug take rd to Unterageri. Site sp fr vill. 4*, Lge, hdstg, mkd, pt shd, EHU (rev pol); gas; sw; 40% statics; Eng spkn; adv bkg acc; ccard acc. *"Excellent sw in lake; cycling/walking; recep clsd 1200-1400; vg."* CHF 46   2018

"That's changed – Should I let the Club know?"

If you find something on site that's different from the site entry, fill in a report and let us know. See camc.com/europereport.

ZURICH *A3* (4km S Rural) *47.33633, 8.54167* **Camping Zurich Fischers Fritz (formerly Camp Seebucht),** Seestrasse 559, 8038 Zürich-Wollishofen **044 4821612; camping@fischers-fritz.ch; www.fischers-fritz.ch**

⛺ CHF3 ♦♦ WC ♨ ♿ ⏸ ✉ MSP 🍴 ① 🛒 ⚡

Fr city foll rd 3 (twd Chur) on S side of lake; foll camping sp. 1*, Lge, hdstg, pt shd, EHU (6A) CHF5; gas; bbq; sw; 80% statics; bus; Eng spkn; ccard acc; tennis; fishing; watersports. *"Parking in Zürich v diff, use bus; sm area for tourers; pool 3km; conv NH, v sm pitches; cycling into Zurich poss; only 52 plots; tent spaces."* CHF 39, 1 May-30 Sep.   2018

ZWEISIMMEN *C2* (1km N Rural) *46.56338, 7.37691* **Camping Fankhauser,** Ey Gässli 2, 3770 Zweisimmen **033 7221356; info@camping-fankhauser.ch; www.camping-fankhauser.ch**

12 ⛺ ♦♦ (htd) WC ♨ ⏸ ✉ MSP 🍴 nr ① nr 🛒 nr ⚡

N6 exit Spiez, then foll sp Zweisimmen. On o'skts of town turn L at camping sp immed bef Agip petrol stn, site on L immed after rlwy x-ing. 4*, Med, pt sl, EHU (10A) CHF3.50 or metered; bbq; 90% statics; phone; Eng spkn; adv bkg acc; fishing; golf; CKE. *"Gd NH; pool 800m."* CHF 28   2016

This is a Swiss road distance chart. Cities listed diagonally (read top-left to bottom-right):
Altdorf, Basel, Bellinzona, Bern, Brig, Chur, Delémont, Disentis, Fribourg, Genève (Geneva), Gstaad, Innertkirchen, Interlaken, La Chaux-de-Fonds, Lausanne, Lugano, Luzern, Martigny, Neuchâtel, Olten, St. Gallen, St. Moritz, Schaffhausen, Scuol/Schuls, Sion, Vaduz (Liechtenstein), Winterthur, Zermatt, Zug, Zürich

Altdorf	Basel	Bellinzona	Bern	Brig	Chur	Delémont	Disentis	Fribourg	Genève (Geneva)	Gstaad	Innertkirchen	Interlaken	La Chaux-de-Fonds	Lausanne	Lugano	Luzern	Martigny	Neuchâtel	Olten	St. Gallen	St. Moritz	Schaffhausen	Scuol/Schuls	Sion	Vaduz (Liechtenstein)	Winterthur	Zermatt	Zug	Zürich
144																													
110	244																												
155	98	255																											
118	192	161	166																										
181	230	115	243	175																									
151	44	292	93	182	239																								
62	204	80	177	108	66	268																							
188	132	286	35	178	275	124	211																						
319	268	420	172	216	410	261	324	141																					
159	204	223	81	91	272	183	66	145																					
68	187	126	91	77	153	178	88	126	263	97																			
99	155	195	59	75	210	144	120	93	230	63	34																		
189	103	291	68	164	274	61	245	66	145	149	160	126																	
257	205	358	107	152	348	201	262	73	62	83	201	166	96																
132	264	29	281	189	142	275	108	312	449	284	154	220	315	382															
42	102	142	116	151	141	109	103	149	280	134	46	74	145	219	166														
281	231	240	136	82	371	225	188	101	136	74	156	192	159	73	267	250													
196	142	295	47	142	285	81	223	44	122	149	138	104	23	74	320	155	146												
96	53	197	69	159	181	64	160	99	235	156	103	122	102	172	220	57	201	111											
179	191	218	205	289	105	201	156	236	371	318	210	256	237	310	244	139	336	245	145										
201	313	152	327	242	86	323	145	360	459	406	199	298	362	432	177	218	332	369	268	188									
147	159	246	173	262	182	109	209	206	340	291	215	229	208	279	275	110	305	216	115	82	269								
253	305	186	319	279	105	315	169	348	485	375	256	284	352	425	214	215	337	362	260	181	62	252							
170	253	215	162	53	401	250	161	129	161	120	115	88	190	99	241	273	27	166	225	356	296	326	317						
110	206	147	203	206	32	213	98	237	371	304	186	241	271	310	184	115	262	249	160	58	117	136	99	221					
119	133	219	145	232	158	141	180	177	311	216	125	188	179	249	243	81	279	188	89	59	245	29	233	299	84				
245	212	185	202	28	199	206	140	204	239	194	114	161	188	170	224	174	99	164	186	325	278	296	313	72	243	267			
67	125	166	137	181	115	135	130	169	305	164	75	103	172	241	193	28	265	182	79	112	197	82	189	293	86	51	219		
65	112	196	123	211	117	122	127	158	292	191	105	128	156	228	223	59	258	165	66	83	201	51	194	280	92	22	245	30	

Map legend:
- France and Andorra
- Central and South East Europe, Benelux and Scandinavia
- Spain and Portugal

Lausanne to Zermatt = 170km

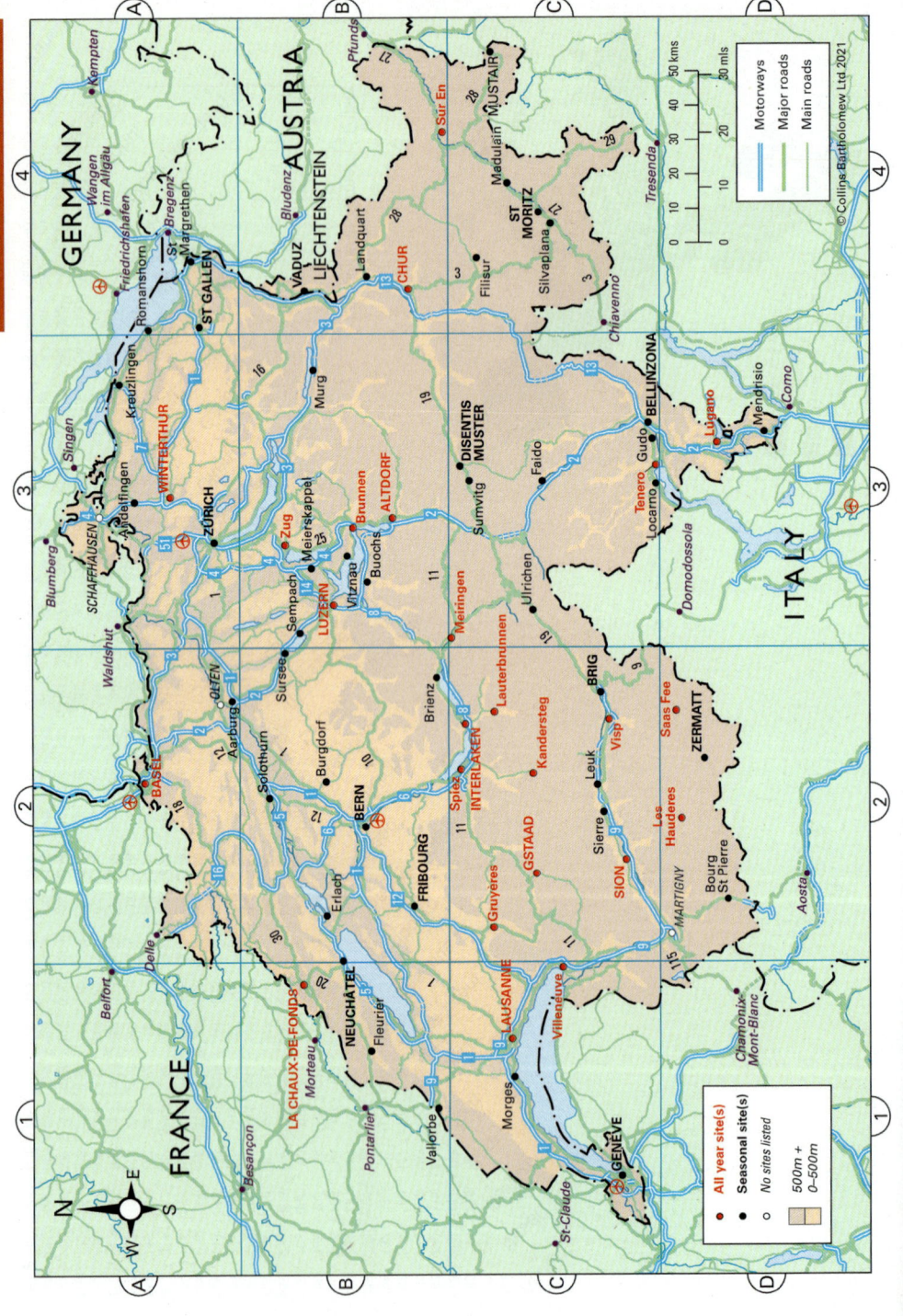

Site Report Form

If campsite is already listed, complete only those sections of the form where changes apply
or alternatively use the Abbreviated Site Report form on the following pages.

Sites not reported on for 5 years may be deleted from the guide

Year of guide used	20..........	Is site listed?	Listed on page no............	Unlisted	Date of visit	......../......../.........

A – CAMPSITE NAME AND LOCATION

Country		Name of town/village site listed under *(see Sites Location Maps)*					
Distance & direction from centre of town site is listed under *(in a straight line)*		.....................km	eg N, NE, S, SW		Urban	Rural	Coastal
Site open all year?	Y / N	Period site is open *(if not all year)*	.................../................... to ..../...................				
Site name					Naturist site		Y / N
Site address							
Telephone				Fax			
E-mail				Website			

B – CAMPSITE CHARGES

Charge for outfit + 2 adults in local currency	PRICE	

C – DIRECTIONS

Brief, specific directions to site (in km) *To convert miles to kilometres multiply by 8 and divide by 5 or use Conversion Table in guide*	
GPS	Latitude..(eg 12.34567) Longitude..(eg 1.23456 or -1.23456)

D – SITE INFORMATION

Dogs allowed	DOGS	Y / N	Price per night .... *(if allowed)*	
Facilities for disabled				
Public Transport within 5km	BUS / TRAM / TRAIN		Adj	Nearby
Reduction long stay	RED LONG STAY	Credit Card accepted		CCARD ACC
Advance bookings accepted/recommended/required		ADV BKG ACC / REC / REQ		
Camping Key Europe or Camping Card International accepted in lieu of passport			CKE/CCI	

E – SITE DESCRIPTION

SITE size ie number of pitches	Small Max 50	SM	Medium 51-150	MED	Large 151-500	LGE	Very large 500+	V LGE	Unchanged
Pitch features if NOT open-plan/grassy		HDG PITCH	Hedged	HDG PITCH	Marked or numbered	MKD PITCH	Hardstanding or gravel	HDSTG	Unchanged
If site is NOT level, is it		PT SL	Part sloping	PT SL	Sloping	SL	Terraced	TERR	Unchanged
Is site shaded?		SHD	Shaded	SHD	Part shaded	PT SHD	Unshaded	UNSHD	Unchanged
ELECTRIC HOOK UP *if not included in price above*	EL PNTS			Price.................................			Amps......................		
% Static caravans / mobile homes / chalets / cottages / fixed tents on site							.................% STATICS		
Serviced Pitched		Y / N		Twin axles caravans allowed?			TWIN AXLES Y / N		

CUT ALONG DOTTED LINE

You can also complete forms online: camc.com/europereport

E – SITE DESCRIPTION CONTINUED...

Phone on site	PHONE	Wifi Internet	WIFI
Television	TV RM	TV CAB / SAT	Playground	PLAYGRND
Entertainment in high season	ENTMNT	English spoken	ENG SPKN
Motorhome Service Point	Y / N		

F – CATERING

Bar	BAR	On site	or		Within 2km
Restaurant	REST	On site	or		Within 2km
Shop(s)	SHOP(S)	On site	or		Within 2km
Snack bar / take-away	SNACKS	On site	Y / N		
Cooking facilities	COOKING FACS	On site	Y / N		
Supplies of bottled gas on site	GAS	Y / N			
Barbecue allowed	BBQ	Charcoal	Gas	Elec	Sep area

G – SANITARY FACILITIES

WC	Heated	HTD WC	Continental	CONT	Own San recommended	OWN SAN REC
Chemical disposal point		CHEM DISP				
Hot shower(s)	SHWR(S)	Inc in site fee?	Y / N			
Child / baby facilities (bathroom)		FAM BTHRM		Launderette / Washing Machine	LNDRY	

H – OTHER INFORMATION

Swimming pool	POOL	HEATED	COVERED	INDOOR	PADDLING POOL	
Beach	BEACH	Adj	or ....km	Sand	Shingle	
Alternative swimming (lake)	SW	Adj	or ....km	Sand	Shingle	
Games /sports area / Games room	GAMES AREA		GAMES ROOM			

I – ADDITIONAL REMARKS AND/OR ITEMS OF INTEREST

Tourist attractions, unusual features or other facilities, eg waterslide, tennis, cycle hire, watersports, horseriding, separate car park, walking distance to shops etc	YOUR OPINION OF THE SITE:
	EXCEL
	VERY GOOD
	GOOD
	FAIR / POOR
	NIGHT HALT ONLY

Your comments & opinions may be used in future editions of the guide, if you do not wish them to be used please tick ....

J – MEMBER DETAILS

ARE YOU A:	Caravanner		Motorhomer		Trailer-tenter?	
NAME:			MEMBERSHIP NO:			
			POST CODE:			
DO YOU NEED MORE BLANK SITE REPORT FORMS?		YES			NO	

Please use a separate form for each campsite and do not send receipts. Owing to the large number of site reports received, it is not possible to enter into correspondence. Please return completed form to:

**The Editor, Overseas Touring Guides, East Grinstead House
East Grinstead, West Sussex RH19 1UA**

Please note that due to changes in the rules regarding freepost we are no longer able to provide a freepost address for the return of Site Report Forms. You can still supply your site reports free online by visiting camc.com/europereport. We apologise for any inconvenience this may cause.

Site Report Form

If campsite is already listed, complete only those sections of the form where changes apply
or alternatively use the Abbreviated Site Report form on the following pages.

Sites not reported on for 5 years may be deleted from the guide

Year of guide used	20..........	Is site listed?	Listed on page no.	Unlisted	Date of visit	......../........./.........

A – CAMPSITE NAME AND LOCATION

Country		Name of town/village site listed under *(see Sites Location Maps)*					
Distance & direction from centre of town site is listed under *(in a straight line)*		..................km	eg N, NE, S, SW		Urban	Rural	Coastal
Site open all year?	Y / N	Period site is open *(if not all year)*	.................../.................. to ..../..................				
Site name						Naturist site	Y / N
Site address							
Telephone			Fax				
E-mail			Website				

B – CAMPSITE CHARGES

Charge for outfit + 2 adults in local currency	PRICE		

C – DIRECTIONS

Brief, specific directions to site (in km) *To convert miles to kilometres multiply by 8 and divide by 5 or use Conversion Table in guide*	
GPS	Latitude...*(eg 12.34567)* Longitude...*(eg 1.23456 or -1.23456)*

D – SITE INFORMATION

Dogs allowed	DOGS	Y / N	Price per night .... *(if allowed)*	
Facilities for disabled				
Public Transport within 5km	BUS / TRAM / TRAIN	Adj		Nearby
Reduction long stay	RED LONG STAY	Credit Card accepted		CCARD ACC
Advance bookings accepted/recommended/required		ADV BKG ACC / REC / REQ		
Camping Key Europe or Camping Card International accepted in lieu of passport				CKE/CCI

E – SITE DESCRIPTION

SITE size ie number of pitches	Small Max 50	SM	Medium 51-150	MED	Large 151-500	LGE	Very large 500+	V LGE	Unchanged
Pitch features if NOT open-plan/grassy	HDG PITCH	Hedged	HDG PITCH	Marked or numbered	MKD PITCH	Hardstanding or gravel		HDSTG	Unchanged
If site is NOT level, is it	PT SL	Part sloping	PT SL	Sloping	SL	Terraced		TERR	Unchanged
Is site shaded?		SHD	Shaded	SHD	Part shaded	PT SHD	Unshaded	UNSHD	Unchanged
ELECTRIC HOOK UP *if not included in price above*	EL PNTS			Price..		Amps......................			
% Static caravans / mobile homes / chalets / cottages / fixed tents on site						................% STATICS			
Serviced Pitched	Y / N			Twin axles caravans allowed?		TWIN AXLES Y / N			

You can also complete forms online: camc.com/europereport

E – SITE DESCRIPTION CONTINUED...

Phone on site	PHONE			Wifi Internet	WIFI
Television	TV RM		TV CAB / SAT	Playground	PLAYGRND
Entertainment in high season	ENTMNT			English spoken	ENG SPKN
Motorhome Service Point	Y / N				

F – CATERING

Bar	BAR	On site	or	Within 2km
Restaurant	REST	On site	or	Within 2km
Shop(s)	SHOP(S)	On site	or	Within 2km
Snack bar / take-away	SNACKS	On site	Y / N	
Cooking facilities	COOKING FACS	On site	Y / N	
Supplies of bottled gas on site	GAS	Y / N		
Barbecue allowed	BBQ	Charcoal	Gas	Elec	Sep area

G – SANITARY FACILITIES

WC		Heated	HTD WC	Continental	CONT	Own San recommended	OWN SAN REC
Chemical disposal point			CHEM DISP			
Hot shower(s)		SHWR(S)	Inc in site fee?		Y / N	
Child / baby facilities *(bathroom)*			FAM BTHRM		Launderette / Washing Machine	LNDRY

H – OTHER INFORMATION

Swimming pool	POOL	HEATED	COVERED	INDOOR	PADDLING POOL	
Beach	BEACH	Adj	or ....km	Sand	Shingle	
Alternative swimming *(lake)*	SW	Adj	or ....km	Sand	Shingle	
Games /sports area / Games room	GAMES AREA		GAMES ROOM			

I – ADDITIONAL REMARKS AND/OR ITEMS OF INTEREST

Tourist attractions, unusual features or other facilities, eg waterslide, tennis, cycle hire, watersports, horseriding, separate car park, walking distance to shops etc	YOUR OPINION OF THE SITE:
	EXCEL
	VERY GOOD
	GOOD
	FAIR | POOR
	NIGHT HALT ONLY

Your comments & opinions may be used in future editions of the guide, if you do not wish them to be used please tick ....

J – MEMBER DETAILS

ARE YOU A:	Caravanner	Motorhomer	Trailer-tenter?
NAME:		MEMBERSHIP NO:	
		POST CODE:	
DO YOU NEED MORE BLANK SITE REPORT FORMS?		YES	NO

Please use a separate form for each campsite and do not send receipts. Owing to the large number of site reports received, it is not possible to enter into correspondence. Please return completed form to:

The Editor, Overseas Touring Guides, East Grinstead House
East Grinstead, West Sussex RH19 1UA

Please note that due to changes in the rules regarding freepost we are no longer able to provide a freepost address for the return of Site Report Forms. You can still supply your site reports free online by visiting camc.com/europereport. We apologise for any inconvenience this may cause.

Site Report Form

If campsite is already listed, complete only those sections of the form where changes apply
or alternatively use the Abbreviated Site Report form on the following pages.

Sites not reported on for 5 years may be deleted from the guide

Year of guide used	20..........	Is site listed?	Listed on page no............	Unlisted	Date of visit	........./........./.........

A – CAMPSITE NAME AND LOCATION

Country		Name of town/village site listed under *(see Sites Location Maps)*				
Distance & direction from centre of town site is listed under *(in a straight line)*		....................km	eg N, NE, S, SW		Urban	Rural	Coastal

Site open all year?	Y / N	Period site is open *(if not all year)*	................../.................. to ..../..................		Naturist site	Y / N

Site name					Naturist site	Y / N
Site address						
Telephone		Fax				
E-mail		Website				

B – CAMPSITE CHARGES

Charge for outfit + 2 adults in local currency	PRICE		

C – DIRECTIONS

Brief, specific directions to site (in km) *To convert miles to kilometres multiply by 8 and divide by 5 or use Conversion Table in guide*	
GPS	Latitude...(eg 12.34567) Longitude...(eg 1.23456 or -1.23456)

D – SITE INFORMATION

Dogs allowed	DOGS	Y / N	Price per night .... *(if allowed)*
Facilities for disabled			
Public Transport within 5km	BUS / TRAM / TRAIN	Adj	Nearby
Reduction long stay	RED LONG STAY	Credit Card accepted	CCARD ACC
Advance bookings accepted/recommended/required		ADV BKG ACC / REC / REQ	
Camping Key Europe or Camping Card International accepted in lieu of passport			CKE/CCI

E – SITE DESCRIPTION

SITE size ie number of pitches	Small Max 50	SM	Medium 51-150	MED	Large 151-500	LGE	Very large 500+	V LGE	Unchanged
Pitch features if NOT open-plan/grassy		HDG PITCH	Hedged	HDG PITCH	Marked or numbered	MKD PITCH	Hardstanding or gravel	HDSTG	Unchanged
If site is NOT level, is it		PT SL	Part sloping	PT SL	Sloping	SL	Terraced	TERR	Unchanged
Is site shaded?		SHD	Shaded	SHD	Part shaded	PT SHD	Unshaded	UNSHD	Unchanged
ELECTRIC HOOK UP *if not included in price above*	EL PNTS		Price................................			Amps......................			
% Static caravans / mobile homes / chalets / cottages / fixed tents on site							.................% STATICS		
Serviced Pitched		Y / N		Twin axles caravans allowed?			TWIN AXLES Y / N		

E – SITE DESCRIPTION CONTINUED...

Phone on site	PHONE		Wifi Internet		WIFI
Television	TV RM	TV CAB / SAT	Playground		PLAYGRND
Entertainment in high season	ENTMNT		English spoken		ENG SPKN
Motorhome Service Point	Y / N				

F – CATERING

Bar	BAR	On site	or	Within 2km
Restaurant	REST	On site	or	Within 2km
Shop(s)	SHOP(S)	On site	or	Within 2km
Snack bar / take-away	SNACKS	On site	Y / N	
Cooking facilities	COOKING FACS	On site	Y / N	
Supplies of bottled gas on site	GAS	Y / N		
Barbecue allowed	BBQ	Charcoal	Gas	Elec	Sep area

G – SANITARY FACILITIES

WC	Heated	HTD WC	Continental	CONT	Own San recommended	OWN SAN REC
Chemical disposal point		CHEM DISP				
Hot shower(s)	SHWR(S)	Inc in site fee?	Y / N			
Child / baby facilities (bathroom)		FAM BTHRM		Launderette / Washing Machine		LNDRY

H – OTHER INFORMATION

Swimming pool	POOL	HEATED	COVERED	INDOOR	PADDLING POOL
Beach	BEACH	Adj	or ....km	Sand	Shingle
Alternative swimming (lake)	SW	Adj	or ....km	Sand	Shingle
Games /sports area / Games room	GAMES AREA		GAMES ROOM		

I – ADDITIONAL REMARKS AND/OR ITEMS OF INTEREST

Tourist attractions, unusual features or other facilities, eg waterslide, tennis, cycle hire, watersports, horseriding, separate car park, walking distance to shops etc	YOUR OPINION OF THE SITE:	
	EXCEL	
	VERY GOOD	
	GOOD	
	FAIR	POOR
	NIGHT HALT ONLY	

Your comments & opinions may be used in future editions of the guide, if you do not wish them to be used please tick ....

J – MEMBER DETAILS

ARE YOU A:	Caravanner		Motorhomer		Trailer-tenter?	
NAME:			MEMBERSHIP NO:			
			POST CODE:			
DO YOU NEED MORE BLANK SITE REPORT FORMS?		YES			NO	

Please use a separate form for each campsite and do not send receipts. Owing to the large number of site reports received, it is not possible to enter into correspondence. Please return completed form to:

The Editor, Overseas Touring Guides, East Grinstead House
East Grinstead, West Sussex RH19 1UA

Please note that due to changes in the rules regarding freepost we are no longer able to provide a freepost address for the return of Site Report Forms. You can still supply your site reports free online by visiting camc.com/europereport. We apologise for any inconvenience this may cause.

Abbreviated Site Report Form

Use this abbreviated Site Report Form if you have visited a number of sites and there are no changes (or only small changes) to their entries in the guide. If reporting on a new site, or reporting several changes, please use the full version of the report form. **If advising prices,** these should be for an outfit, and 2 adults for one night's stay. **Please indicate high or low season prices and whether electricity is included.**

Remember, if you don't tell us about sites you have visited, they may eventually be deleted from the guide.

Year of guide used	20..........	Page No.	....	Name of town/village site listed under	
Site Name				Date of visit	.... /....... /........
GPS	Latitude...(eg 12.34567) Longitude..(eg 1.23456 or -1.23456)				

Site is in: Andorra / Austria / Belgium / Croatia / Czech Republic / Denmark / Finland / France / Germany / Greece / Hungary / Italy / Luxembourg / Netherlands / Norway / Poland / Portugal / Slovakia / Slovenia / Spain / Sweden / Switzerland

Comments:

Charge for outfit + 2 adults in local currency	High Season	Low Season	Elec inc in price?	Y / N	.............amps
			Price of elec (if not inc)		.............amps

Year of guide used	20..........	Page No.	....	Name of town/village site listed under	
Site Name				Date of visit	.... /....... /........
GPS	Latitude...(eg 12.34567) Longitude..(eg 1.23456 or -1.23456)				

Site is in: Andorra / Austria / Belgium / Croatia / Czech Republic / Denmark / Finland / France / Germany / Greece / Hungary / Italy / Luxembourg / Netherlands / Norway / Poland / Portugal / Slovakia / Slovenia / Spain / Sweden / Switzerland

Comments:

Charge for outfit + 2 adults in local currency	High Season	Low Season	Elec inc in price?	Y / N	.............amps
			Price of elec (if not inc)		.............amps

Year of guide used	20..........	Page No.	....	Name of town/village site listed under	
Site Name				Date of visit	.... /....... /........
GPS	Latitude...(eg 12.34567) Longitude..(eg 1.23456 or -1.23456)				

Site is in: Andorra / Austria / Belgium / Croatia / Czech Republic / Denmark / Finland / France / Germany / Greece / Hungary / Italy / Luxembourg / Netherlands / Norway / Poland / Portugal / Slovakia / Slovenia / Spain / Sweden / Switzerland

Comments:

Charge for car, caravan & 2 adults in local currency	High Season	Low Season	Elec inc in price?	Y / N	.............amps
			Price of elec (if not inc)		.............amps

Please fill in your details and send to the address on the reverse of this form.
You can also complete forms online: camc.com/europereport

CUT ALONG DOTTED LINE

Year of guide used	20.........	Page No.	....	Name of town/village site listed under	
Site Name				Date of visit	......./......./........
GPS	Latitude...(eg 12.34567) Longitude...(eg 1.23456 or -1.23456)				

Site is in: Andorra / Austria / Belgium / Croatia / Czech Republic / Denmark / Finland / France / Germany / Greece / Hungary / Italy / Luxembourg / Netherlands / Norway / Poland / Portugal / Slovakia / Slovenia / Spain / Sweden / Switzerland

Comments:

Charge for outfit + 2 adults in local currency	High Season	Low Season	Elec inc in price?	Y / N	............amps
			Price of elec (if not inc)		............amps

Year of guide used	20.........	Page No.	....	Name of town/village site listed under	
Site Name				Date of visit	......./......./........
GPS	Latitude...(eg 12.34567) Longitude...(eg 1.23456 or -1.23456)				

Site is in: Andorra / Austria / Belgium / Croatia / Czech Republic / Denmark / Finland / France / Germany / Greece / Hungary / Italy / Luxembourg / Netherlands / Norway / Poland / Portugal / Slovakia / Slovenia / Spain / Sweden / Switzerland

Comments:

Charge for outfit + 2 adults in local currency	High Season	Low Season	Elec inc in price?	Y / N	............amps
			Price of elec (if not inc)		............amps

Year of guide used	20.........	Page No.	....	Name of town/village site listed under	
Site Name				Date of visit	......./......./........
GPS	Latitude...(eg 12.34567) Longitude...(eg 1.23456 or -1.23456)				

Site is in: Andorra / Austria / Belgium / Croatia / Czech Republic / Denmark / Finland / France / Germany / Greece / Hungary / Italy / Luxembourg / Netherlands / Norway / Poland / Portugal / Slovakia / Slovenia / Spain / Sweden / Switzerland

Comments:

Charge for outfit + 2 adults in local currency	High Season	Low Season	Elec inc in price?	Y / N	............amps
			Price of elec (if not inc)		............amps

Your comments & opinions may be used in future editions of the guide, if you do not wish them to be used please tick ....

Name ....

Membership No. ....

Post Code ....

Are you a Caravanner / Motorhomer / Trailer-Tenter?

Do you need more blank Site Report forms? YES / NO

Please return completed forms to:

The Editor – Overseas Touring Guides
East Grinstead House
East Grinstead
West Sussex
RH19 1FH
Please note that due to changes in the rules regarding freepost we are no longer able to provide a freepost address for the return of Site Report Forms. You can still supply your site reports free online by visiting camc.com/europereport. We apologise for any inconvenience this may cause.

You can also complete forms online: camc.com/europereport

Abbreviated Site Report Form

Use this abbreviated Site Report Form if you have visited a number of sites and there are no changes (or only small changes) to their entries in the guide. If reporting on a new site, or reporting several changes, please use the full version of the report form. **If advising prices,** these should be for an outfit, and 2 adults for one night's stay. **Please indicate high or low season prices and whether electricity is included.**

Remember, if you don't tell us about sites you have visited, they may eventually be deleted from the guide.

Year of guide used 20..........		Page No.		Name of town/village site listed under			
Site Name						Date of visit	......./......./........
GPS	Latitude...(eg 12.34567) Longitude..(eg 1.23456 or -1.23456)						
Site is in: Andorra / Austria / Belgium / Croatia / Czech Republic / Denmark / Finland / France / Germany / Greece / Hungary / Italy / Luxembourg / Netherlands / Norway / Poland / Portugal / Slovakia / Slovenia / Spain / Sweden / Switzerland							
Comments:							
Charge for outfit + 2 adults in local currency		High Season	Low Season	Elec inc in price?		Y / N	............amps
				Price of elec (if not inc)			............amps

Year of guide used 20..........		Page No.		Name of town/village site listed under			
Site Name						Date of visit	......./......./........
GPS	Latitude...(eg 12.34567) Longitude..(eg 1.23456 or -1.23456)						
Site is in: Andorra / Austria / Belgium / Croatia / Czech Republic / Denmark / Finland / France / Germany / Greece / Hungary / Italy / Luxembourg / Netherlands / Norway / Poland / Portugal / Slovakia / Slovenia / Spain / Sweden / Switzerland							
Comments:							
Charge for outfit + 2 adults In local currency		High Season	Low Season	Elec inc in price?		Y / N	............amps
				Price of elec (if not inc)			............amps

Year of guide used 20..........		Page No.		Name of town/village site listed under			
Site Name						Date of visit	......./......./........
GPS	Latitude...(eg 12.34567) Longitude..(eg 1.23456 or -1.23456)						
Site is in: Andorra / Austria / Belgium / Croatia / Czech Republic / Denmark / Finland / France / Germany / Greece / Hungary / Italy / Luxembourg / Netherlands / Norway / Poland / Portugal / Slovakia / Slovenia / Spain / Sweden / Switzerland							
Comments:							
Charge for car, caravan & 2 adults in local currency		High Season	Low Season	Elec inc in price?		Y / N	............amps
				Price of elec (if not inc)			............amps

Please fill in your details and send to the address on the reverse of this form.
You can also complete forms online: camc.com/europereport

CUT ALONG DOTTED LINE

Year of guide used	20..........	Page No.	....	Name of town/village site listed under	

Site Name				Date of visit	.... /....... /........

GPS Latitude...(eg 12.34567) Longitude...(eg 1.23456 or -1.23456)

Site is in: Andorra / Austria / Belgium / Croatia / Czech Republic / Denmark / Finland / France / Germany / Greece / Hungary / Italy / Luxembourg / Netherlands / Norway / Poland / Portugal / Slovakia / Slovenia / Spain / Sweden / Switzerland

Comments:

Charge for outfit + 2 adults in local currency	High Season	Low Season	Elec inc in price?	Y / N	.............amps
			Price of elec (if not inc)		.............amps

Year of guide used	20..........	Page No.	....	Name of town/village site listed under	

Site Name				Date of visit	.... /....... /........

GPS Latitude...(eg 12.34567) Longitude...(eg 1.23456 or -1.23456)

Site is in: Andorra / Austria / Belgium / Croatia / Czech Republic / Denmark / Finland / France / Germany / Greece / Hungary / Italy / Luxembourg / Netherlands / Norway / Poland / Portugal / Slovakia / Slovenia / Spain / Sweden / Switzerland

Comments:

Charge for outfit + 2 adults in local currency	High Season	Low Season	Elec inc in price?	Y / N	.............amps
			Price of elec (if not inc)		.............amps

Year of guide used	20..........	Page No.	....	Name of town/village site listed under	

Site Name				Date of visit	.... /....... /........

GPS Latitude...(eg 12.34567) Longitude...(eg 1.23456 or -1.23456)

Site is in: Andorra / Austria / Belgium / Croatia / Czech Republic / Denmark / Finland / France / Germany / Greece / Hungary / Italy / Luxembourg / Netherlands / Norway / Poland / Portugal / Slovakia / Slovenia / Spain / Sweden / Switzerland

Comments:

Charge for outfit + 2 adults in local currency	High Season	Low Season	Elec inc in price?	Y / N	.............amps
			Price of elec (if not inc)		.............amps

Your comments & opinions may be used in future editions of the guide, if you do not wish them to be used please tick ....

Name ....

Membership No. ....

Post Code ....

Are you a Caravanner / Motorhomer / Trailer-Tenter?

Do you need more blank Site Report forms?   YES / NO

Please return completed forms to:

The Editor – Overseas Touring Guides
East Grinstead House
East Grinstead
West Sussex
RH19 1FH
Please note that due to changes in the rules regarding freepost we are no longer able to provide a freepost address for the return of Site Report Forms. You can still supply your site reports free online by visiting camc.com/europereport. We apologise for any inconvenience this may cause.

You can also complete forms online: camc.com/europereport

Index

Index

PEFC Certified

This product is
from sustainably
managed forests and
controlled sources

PEFC/16-33-254   www.pefc.org